THE WORLD OF...

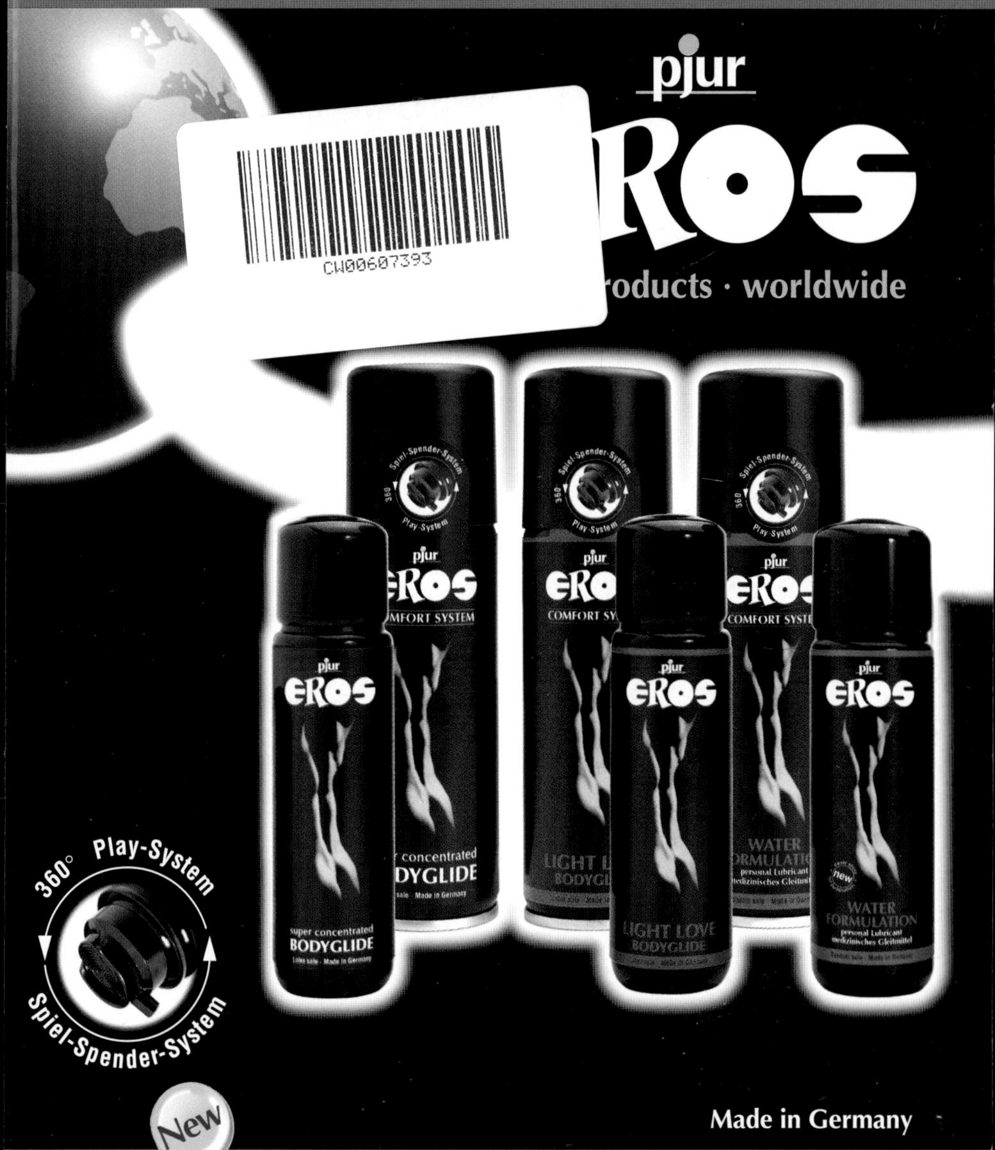

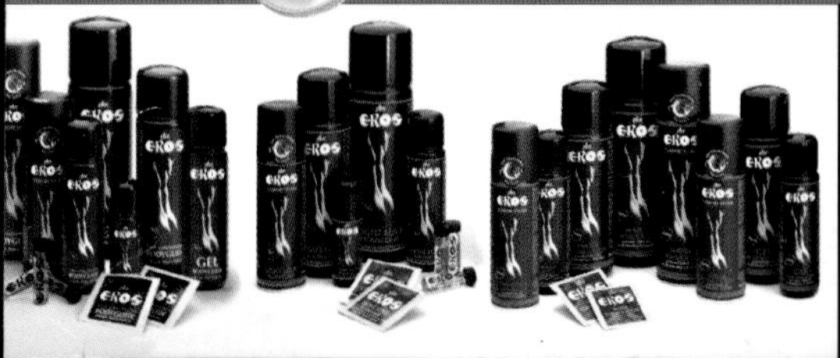

pjur group: www.pjur.com

Luxembourg:	Phone (++352) 748 989 Fax (++352) 748 990
Germany:	Phone ++49(0)6 51/ 99 10 250 Fax ++49(0)6 51/ 99 10 251
USA (NYC):	Phone (++1) 212-337-3767 Fax (++1) 212-367-9389

World-wide reliable
male escorts
Our boys fly anywhere!
Is your favourite escortboy
living in Amsterdam?
Visit our renewed internet
site & browse our database
(pictures available) at
www.peoplemale.com
• home/ hotel
visiting service
reliable and discreet
• the leading
gay escortservice
TM
PEOPLE
Male Escorts
AMSTERDAM
020-
662 999 0
24 hours a day, cards welcome
from outside the Netherlands, please
dial +31 20 662 999 0
or email info@peoplemale.com

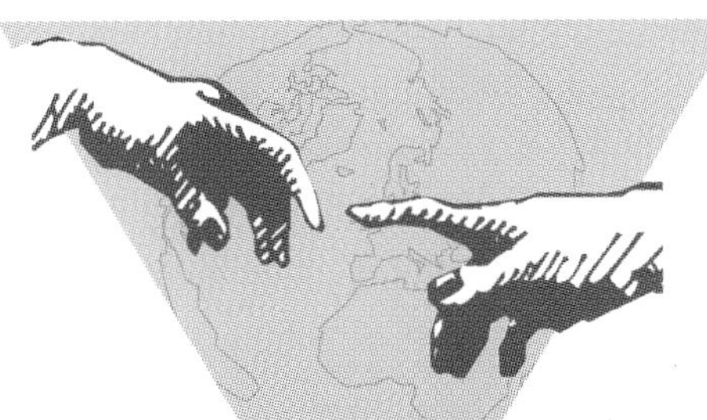

WORLD PRIDE ROMA 2000

gay • lesbian • bisexual • transgender

IN PRIDE WE TRUST!

www.worldpride2000.com

SATURDAY JULY 1ST
> DRAG KING CONTEST

SUNDAY JULY 2
> FASHION SHOW
UNO SPECCHIO PER NARCISO
> MUCCASSASSINA SPECIAL COCKTAIL PARTY

MONDAY JULY 3
> CLASSICAL MUSIC CONCERT

TUESDAY JULY 4
> DANCE PERFORMANCES
> "CALIGOLA" PARTY

WEDNESDAY JULY 5
> CONFERENCE ON HOMOSEXUALITY AND RELIGION
> THEATRE PERFORMANCES

THURSDAY JULY 6
> CINEMA PREVIEW
> WORLD PRIDE LEATHER PARTY

FRIDAY JULY 7
> YOUNG ARTISTS ROCK CONCERT

SATURDAY JULY 8
> THE WORLD PRIDE PARADE
> MEGA-CONCERT
> THE WORLD PRIDE PARTY

SUNDAY JULY 9
> ICE CREAM PARTY

DURING THE WEEK THE INTERNATIONAL ILGA CONFERENCE

1 • 9 • JULY 2000
ROME

ENERGIE JEANS X-PERIENCE

PNO PLANETOUT
AOL Keyword: PlanetOut
www.planetout.com

"MARIO MIELI" • CIRCOLO DI CULTURA OMOSESSUALE

FOR FURTHER INFORMATION
PLEASE CONTACT THE MARIO MIELI SECRETARY
OPEN FROM 9 am TO 7 pm
Tel. ++39065413985 Fax ++39065413971
E-mail: info@mariomieli.it > http://www.mariomieli.it

What is the purpose of this advertisement ?
Naturally, to draw more people to The Boots nightclub in Antwerpen.

Well, what kind of nightclub is The Boots ?
The Boots has a slogan "where your fantasies become reality". It is one of the very few places in Europe where people can live out their wildest dreams.

How can you reach the clients of The Boots ?
You *could* tell them that there is easy parking, that the building is very fine, that the decoration is tasteful, and that the drinks are reasonably priced.

But that won't be a reason for them to go to The Boots, right ?
Correct. People don't go to The Boots for these reasons. If they are looking for these things, they can just go to their local gay bar - and save a 300 km drive into the bargain.

So why *do* people go to The Boots ?
Because The Boots offers them a space in which they can live out their fantasies.

In other words, it's not the "concrete" facilities of The Boots that are important, but rather the "abstract" fantasy ?
Absolutely. In the past, The Boots has concentrated on selling its concrete assets : large, friendly, well-run, SM room, golden shower room, fine building, not expensive.

Well, what effect does that have on the marketing of The Boots ?
We need to sell the **essence** of The Boots. Guys don't come here for cheap drinks, great decor, or easy parking. They come here for fantasy, freedom, and sex.
That's what we must sell.

So, instead of selling the idea of what you can see in The Boots, you're going to sell the idea of what you can *do* in The Boots ?
Precisely. By booking through the eyes of an imaginary person who has never been to The Boots before, we can empathise with the feelings of people all over the world who have never been to The Boots - but really want to go there !

P.S. Valid identification papers must be shown on entry !!!

The Boots

Van Aerdtstraat 22 - B-2060 Antwerpen
http://www.supergids.be/theboots
e-mail:gi31685@glo.be
Tel.& Fax Weekdays: (+32) 3 231 34 83
Tel. Club: (+32) 3 233 21 36

v.z.w. The Boots - Private Bar :
Leather - Rubber - Uniform - Denim - Skins
OPEN : fridays & saturdays 22h30 - 05h00

Need the best in queer culture;
arts and news, on the Web?
Want great, live, interactive shows,
video clips and streaming?
Got the hottest, wildest,
gay photo galleries in cyberspace?
No sweat! No equal!
WWW.CHISEL.COM
Adult Video News [AVN] 1998
Winner of Best Overall Gay Site
chisel
SURF THIS MAN
SURF THIS MAN
GLOBAL GAY WEBSITE
Braucht Ihr das Beste in der
Schwulen- und Lesbenkultur;
Kunst und Nachrichten aus dem Web?
Wollt Ihr großartige, interaktive Live-Shows,
Videoclips und Streaming? Habt Ihr die heißesten,
wildesten Schwulenfoto Fotogalerien im Cyberspace?
Kein Problem! Wir sind die Besten!

KEY WEST

SPARTACUS

INTERNATIONAL GAY GUIDE

2000/2001

BRUNO GMÜNDER

Imprint

PUBLISHER BRUNO GMÜNDER VERLAG GMBH
Leuschnerdamm 31 · D-10999 Berlin · GERMANY
Tel +49 / (0)30 / 615 00 30
Fax +49 / (0)30 / 615 90 07
E-mail: info@spartacus.de

EDITOR IN CHIEF Briand Bedford · Robin Rauch

EDITORIAL TEAM Stefan Santoprete · Yvan Ladurner · Karl Echler · Oliver Ambach
Chris Nicholas · Dr. med. Martin W. Eichenlaub

TRANSLATION Oliver Ambach · Yvan Ladurner · Carsten Sinner · Antonio Plaza · Helmut Splinter

ADVERTISING SALES BRUNO GMÜNDER VERLAG GMBH
Leuschnerdamm 31 · D-10999 Berlin · GERMANY
Tel +49 / (0)30 / 615 00 3-42
Fax +49 / (0)30 / 615 91 34

COVER PHOTOGRAPHY Raymond Vino

COVER DESIGN Rudolph Haas

LAYOUT & MAPS Print Eisenherz, Berlin

PRINTING Clausen & Bosse, Leck, Germany

Please note that ***SPARTACUS***® published by BRUNO GMÜNDER VERLAG has no connection with any other business with the name of „SPARTACUS", even if advertised in this book.

Please note that the inclusion of any establishment, business or organisation in this book or the appearance on the cover or on advertisements in ***SPARTACUS***® does not necessarily reflect the sexual orientation of owners, staff or models.

ISBN 3-86187-162-9

Member of International Gay & Lesbian Travel Association IGLTA

Distribution

WORLDWIDE DISTRIBUTION
BRUNO GMÜNDER VERTRIEB
Wrangelstr. 100 · D-10997 Berlin
Tel. (+49) (30) 610 01 120
Fax (+49) (30) 615 90 08

VERTRIEB FÜR DEUTSCHLAND, ÖSTERREICH UND DIE SCHWEIZ
BRUNO GMÜNDER VERTRIEB
Wrangelstr. 100 · D-10997 Berlin
Tel. (030) 610 01 100
Fax (030) 615 90 08

DISTRIBUTION FOR AUSTRALIA & NEW ZEALAND
BULLDOG BOOKS
Unit 1, 147 Queen Street
AUS – Alexandria, NSW 2015
Tel. +61 (02) 9699 3507
Fax +61 (02) 9699 3527

DISTRIBUTION FOR BENELUX
SCALA AGENTUREN B.V.
Contactweg 28 · 1014 AN Amsterdam · Netherlands
Tel. +31 (0)20 682 89 00
Fax +31 (0)20 682 89 43

DISTRIBUTION POUR LA FRANCE
I.E.M.
208, rue St, Maur · 75010 Paris
Tel. (1) 42.41.21.41
Fax (1) 42.41.86.80

CONCESSIONARIO PER L'ITALIA
LESLIE DURHAM
Cascina Antonietta · 27050 Bagnaria (PV)
Tel. (0383) 542 104
Fax (0383) 542 105

TRIANGULO DISTRIBUCIONES
Calle Gravina, 11 · 28004 Madrid
Tel+Fax (91) 532 13 93

DISTRIBUTION PARA ESPAÑA
HARMONY LOVE
Calle Caballero, 79 · 08014 Barcelona
Tel. (93) 405 33 00
Fax (93) 405 11 48

DISTRIBUTION FOR HONG KONG AND TAIWAN
ASIA 2000 LTD.
Seabird House, unit 1101-02
22-28 Wyndham Street · Hong Kong
Tel. (852) 2530-1409
Fax (852) 2526 1107

DISTRIBUTION FOR U.K. AND IRELAND
TURNAROUND
Unit 3, Olympia Trading Estate
Coburg Road
GB – London N22 6TZ
Tel. +44 (20) 8829 3009
Fax +44 (20) 8881 5088

DISTRIBUTION FOR USA AND CANADA
BOOKAZINE COMPANY, INC.
75 Hook Road
Bayonne, N. J. 07002
Tel. (201) 339-7777
Fax (201) 339-7778

KOEN BOOK DISTRIBUTORS
10 Twosome Drive
Moorestown, N. J. 08057
Tel. (800) 257-8481
Fax (800) 225-3840

PDC
6922 Hollywood Blvd., 10th Floor
Los Angeles, CA 90028
Tel. +1 (323) 860 60 70
Fax +1 (323) 467 01 73

Single copies and our free mail order brochure may be ordered by mail from:
BRUNO GMÜNDER · Mail Order · Zeughofstraße 1 · D-10997 Berlin · GERMANY

A cooperative action of the BZgA Bundeszentrale für gesundheitliche Aufklärung
and BRUNO GMÜNDER VERLAG

Welcome to the new SPARTACUS

Preface

The new year started with spectacular parties world wide. The gay world continues to celebrate this year. Some of the major highlights this year include :

- The Mardi Gras from the 11th February to the 04th March in Sydney. Further information can be found under www.mardigras.com.au
- The EUROGAMES 2000 take place in Zurich this year from the 01st to the 04th June.
- What a coincidence that the Catholic Church is celebrating the year 2000 as a holy year and that WORLD PRIDE will take place in Rome from the 01st to the 09th July.
- Not to be forgotten are the over 50 GAY PRIDE parties taking place world wide from as early as February to November this year.

Ahead of us is an interesting and eventful year of travel and we hope that SPARTACUS will continue to supply you with the relevant information.

In putting together this latest edition, the many tips and comments proved to be very helpful. In this way you too can help in keeping future editions of SPARTACUS accurate and the most up to date gay travel guide in the world !

Briand Bedford
EDITOR IN CHIEF

How to use SPARTACUS

Spartacus is divided into sections headed by country names which appear in alphabetical order. The only exceptions to this rule are the countries and places found in the Caribbean, all of which are listed in alphabetical order under the main heading 'C' for Caribbean. Each section is further sub-divided according to city name which also appear in alphabetical order. For the USA, Canada and Australia however it has been deemed more straight forward to sub-divide the sections according to the names of states or counties. If you still have problems locating the destination of your choice, simply look it up in the index (see page 1298), where all cities are alphabetically listed in German, English, French , and Spanish.
Every country in the world has its own entry. Additionally there are entries for all independent states where information regarding the legal status of gay men, and /or scene information is available.
Directly under each main heading you will find the following information about the country:

Geographical location	➔	Western Europe
Initials by which the country is internationally recognised.	➔	Initials: UK / GB
Time - this refers to the time zone in which the country is located.	➔	Time: GMT
International Access and Country Code - these are the telephone digits required to get an international line from the country in question and to call the country in question.	➔	☎ Country Code / Access Code: 44 / 00
Language - refers to the most commonly used language spoken here.	➔	Language: English
Area - this refers to the size of the country.	➔	Area: 242,100 km^2 / 93,451 sq mi.
Currency - this refers to the currency of money used here.	➔	Currency: 1 Pound Sterling (= 100 Pence)
Population - this refers to the number of inhabitants.	➔	Population: 58,249,000
Capital - the capital city	➔	Capital: London
Religion - this refers to the most common religions practised here.	➔	Religions: 57% Anglicans, 15% other Protestants, 13% Catholics
Climate - a brief summary of climatic conditions throughout the year.	➔	Climate: Moderate climate that is moderated by prevailing southwest winds over the North Atlantic Current. More than half of the days are overcast.
Important Gay Cities - cities which are of particular interest for the gay visitor.	➔	Important Gay Cities: London, Manchester, Brighton, Edinburgh

The concluding part of each introduction gives details of the legal constitution and its relevance to gay visitors. In the same way, Spartacus gives a brief outline of each country and its people, and their attitude towards homosexuality.
Furthermore we strongly recommend that you pay close attention to the opening text for each country, where important information regarding national companies and organisations is given.
Following country information, are the city, state or county city names. Where a city has a single postal code and/or a single telephone code, this will be included with the city heading. Otherwise this information can be found for each individual listing.
The listings are grouped under individual headings. Each listing is made up of a name ❶, the relevant Spartacus codes ❷, the opening times ❸, the address ❹, the telephone number ❺, and a brief description.

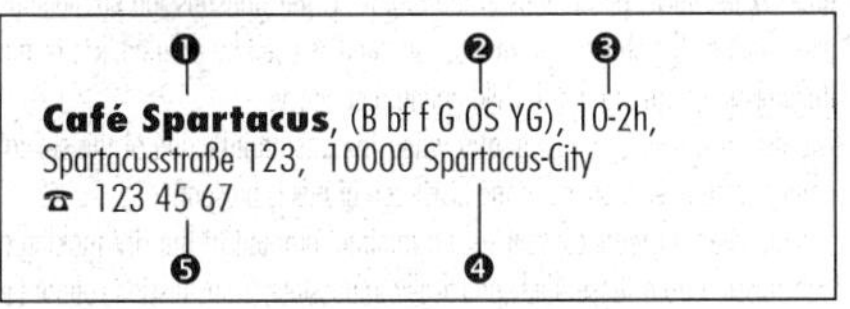

Your help and contribution in compiling this guide is much appreciated. In order to provide the most up to date information, your personal experiences and discoveries are very important to us. Please send us any new information or comments using the freepost User's Information Cards found at the back of this edition.
When sending us information about venues which may be of interest to the gay community, please be as detailed as possible. We need at least the name of the establishment, the name of a proprietor/ manager, the address (including city and country!), and telephone/fax number; a business card would be a great advantage. The more information you can send us, the better.
When informing us about a company or a non-commercial establishment, please make this clear in your description. Furthermore, we would also be happy to receive descriptions about individual countries, cities and states.

Please write to:
BRUNO GMÜNDER VERLAG GmbH – SPARTACUS-Redaktion
Postfach 61 01 04 • D-10921 Berlin • GERMANY

CODES

The Spartacus codes are:

!	A must for the international tourist
A	Art exhibits
AC	Air conditioning
AYOR	At your own risk. Dangerous place with risk of personal attack or police activity
B	Bar
bf	breakfast
CC	Major credit cards are accepted
D	Discotheque
DR	Darkroom
E	Elegant. Appropriate dress advisable
F	Food. Full meals available.
G	Gay. Exclusively or mostly male homosexuals
g	Gay and straight mixed crowd
GLM	Gay and lesbian mixed crowd
glm	Gay and lesbian and heterosexual mixed crowd
H	Hotel or pension welcoming gay guests
LJ	Leather and jeans
MA	Mixed ages
MG	Middle-aged gays
msg	Massage offered
N	Mostly of local interest and with local patrons
NG	Not exclusively gay, but interesting for gays
NU	Nudist area
OG	Mostly older gays
OS	Terrace or garden
P	Private club or strict door control
p	You must ring to enter.
pi	Swimming pool
R	Frequented by hustlers.
S	Shows or other special events
SNU	Strip shows
STV	Dragshow
sa	sauna
sb	steam bath
sol	Solarium
TV	Transvestite and / or transsexual clientele
VS	Video shows
WE	More popular on weekends
wh	Whirlpool / jacuzzi
WO	Work-out equipment available
YG	Younger gays (18-28)

Codes in lower-case letters can mean a limitation.

Health Information

1. INTRODUCTION

The first known cases of AIDS were in 1981. Since then AIDS has become one of the most significant sexually transmittable diseases that despite the effective treatment possibilities, remains to this day non-curable. Imperative is therefore is to prevent the spread of this disease. This is however, only possible when the general public has been informed and made aware of the means of transmission. It is also of great importance to have a better understanding of the disease AIDS, in order to erase the preconceptions and controversy in relation to people with AIDS and to break down the resulting prejudice. It has been estimated that in 2000 approximately 30-40 million people world wide are living and carrying the AIDS causing virus.

2. What is AIDS?

AIDS is an infectious disease which is brought about by a virus, the so-called HIV. The HIV damages the human immune system and as a result weakens the resistance. In this way the body is susceptible to harmful organisms which would normally not be a problem for a healthy body. The virus can also cause other disruptions in the body and may induce skin and nervous disorders. Even the growth of tumours can be caused by the virus.

Once the virus has landed in the body, it attacks the cells of the human immune system and adapts the metabolism to its own advantage. The virus can therefore multiply inside the cells leading to their destruction. Non-infected HIV cells of the immune system try to destroy the virus. It is however impossible for the immune system to destroy the virus completely.

7 out of 8 people who have been infected with HIV notice after a couple of days non specific type of flu like side effects, such as high temperature, sore throat, skin rash and swollen glands. These symptoms disappear after between a few days and two weeks. The HIV-infected person has thereafter no further symptoms for a while. This "non-symptomatic" phase can vary in duration but is generally a period of a few years. When the virus takes over in the body the immune system breaks down . The AIDS phase of the disease has been reached and is marked by severe illnesses such as inflammation of the eyes, lungs or brain as well as skin sarcomas. The illness is terminal.

A blood test in a laboratory can determine whether one is infected with the HIV virus. The current test can only determine this after an "incubation period" of three months. Those who carry the virus are HIV-positive otherwise one is HIV-negative.

3. Transmission of HIV

As a rule, the virus is transmitted via body secretions such as blood and sperm from someone who is HIV-positive. If blood or sperm containing the virus lands on an open wound or on the mucous membrane this could result in a HIV-infection. This means one should avoid contact with the body fluids. The most common route of transmission is sex. Risky sexual practises are anal intercourse without using a condom, (for both partners) as well as oral sex in which sperm lands in the mouth. Other transmission possibilities exist such as the shared use of infusion needles used by drug addicts or the transmission from mother to child during pregnancy.

The risk of transmission is greater when there is an infection of the sexual organs, with open wounds or the discharge of pus is present.

Saliva, sweat or tears contain such a minimal amount of the HIV making a transmission from these fluids practically impossible. Transmission cannot be caused by kissing, by using the same drinking glass or cutlery, clothing, swimming pools saunas or toilets. Even so is touching door handles, telephones etc. or contact such as handshaking or hugging as well as transmission by air or insects without risk. In all the above the HIV cannot be transmitted.

4. Safer Sex

To protect oneself when having sex from HIV transmission, one should note a few safer-sex "rules", the aim of which is to avoid the admittance of infectious body fluids. This means the following :

- The correct use of condoms by anal and oral sex
- No sperm in the mouth of your partner
- Anal sex with the use of your hand only when the finger nails are short and with rubber gloves
- Contact with sperm or blood when open wounds are present must be avoided.

Use only tested condoms which are "extra strong" and will not tear. Protect then from high and low temperatures and sunlight and only use water based lubricants in combination with condoms. Creams or lubricants which are oil based tend to weaken the condom and make it

porous. Should you suffer from a latex allergy, condoms made from polyurethane are also available. These are sadly far more expensive.

Outside the human body the HIV can survive only a short period of time. Despite this fact, it is important that dildos are thoroughly cleaned before use by a second person.

By following these rules, one can significantly reduce the risk of an HIV transmission.

A risk however is ever present.

Most people do not display the effects of an HIV infection. For this reason one should automatically assume that with unknown sexual partners an HIV infection is possible and protect oneself when having sex. This is also the case for people who are HIV-positive as an additional infection with other HIV-strains can negatively influence the development of the disease.

5. Treatment possibilities of HIV and AIDS

At present there are various medications (called anti-virus medications) which can be used in the fight against an HIV-infection. These reduce the proliferation of the virus. These medications are used in combination to increase their efficiency and to prevent the virus becoming resistant to a medication. It is not possible to completely avoid this however.

These anti-virus medications need to be taken on a regular basis. A break or delay in treatment can reduce the possible success of the therapy. It is therefore necessary to plan the consumption according to the daily program. When a therapy should start is a decision which only a doctor can make.

Medications used to fight the HIV cannot destroy the virus but help the immune system to recover and thereby extend life expectancy. Even when after therapy the HIV is no longer detectable in the blood, there is still a risk of transmission.

The scope of medical treatment for HIV infected persons is extremely varied. At the first sign of physical complaints one should seek medical advice.

In many countries self-help organisations and advice centres exist, which offer physiological social and financial support in relation to HIV and AIDS.

6. Travel and AIDS

Due to the fact that the virus which causes AIDS can be found on a global basis, one should adhere to the "safe-sex" rules in foreign countries too. Due to the fact that in some countries the correct quality condoms are difficult to obtain, one is advised to take these with you when travelling.

People who are HIV-positive or have AIDS should ensure that they take an adequate supply of anti-virus medications with them and be aware that some medications are effected by temperature or light and that they should be stored in a dry container to ensure that they remain effective. Due to the fact that they need to be taken according to a rigid time plan, it is advisable to arrange a time plan for the entire trip taking consideration of the different time zones world wide.

Especially in tropical areas one can come into contact with a multitude of pathogenic agents which are not found at home. Particularly care is advised for people who are HIV-positive where the immune system is under attack and the risk of a serious illness is increased. How one can be protected and whether inoculations are recommended can only be advised on an individual basis. Protection against attack from insects can be obtained from medications which can be applied to the skin. Clothing which covers the arms and legs is also advised. When travelling one should not forget certain medications treating for example nausea, diarrhoea, and headache as well as sun cream all of which should be compatible with the medications prescribed from your doctor. Advisable is therefore to seek the professional advise of a specialist before travelling.

Before a trip one should ensure that medical insurance is applicable in the country which one is visiting. Some insurance policies apply only when no illness was present before the trip or when no treatment during the trip was to expected.

In some countries there are entry restriction for people with HIV. It is therefore important when planning a trip to determine whether any restrictions exist. A list of the relative embassies and doctors able to speak your language in the country to be visited can be a big help in an emergency.

7. Other

A further series of sexually transferred diseases such as Hepatitis, Gonorrhoea, Syphilis as well as others can be avoided with the implementation of "safe-sex." Inoculations against Hepatitis A and B are available. An inoculation against AIDS does not exist.

Dr. med. Martin W. Eichenlaub

Willkommen im neuen SPARTACUS

Vorwort

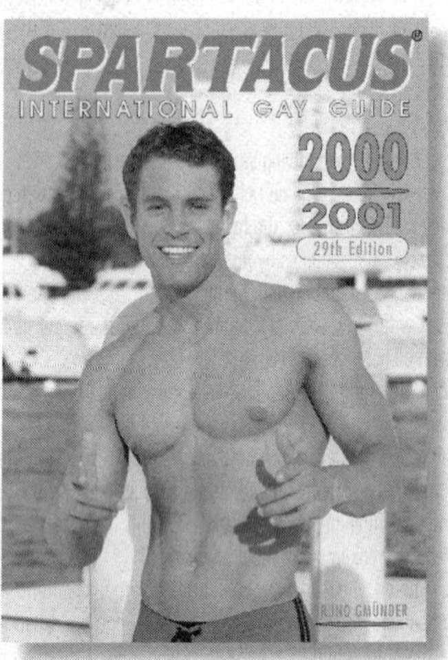

Mit spektakulären Parties weltweit begann das Jahr 2000. Die schwule Welt feiert selbstverständlich weiter. Zu den Highlights in diesem Jahr zählen unter anderem:

- Der Mardi Gras vom 11. Februar bis 04. März in Sydney. Weitere Informationen unter www.mardigras.com.au
- Die Eurogames 2000 finden vom 01. bis 04. Juni in Zürich statt

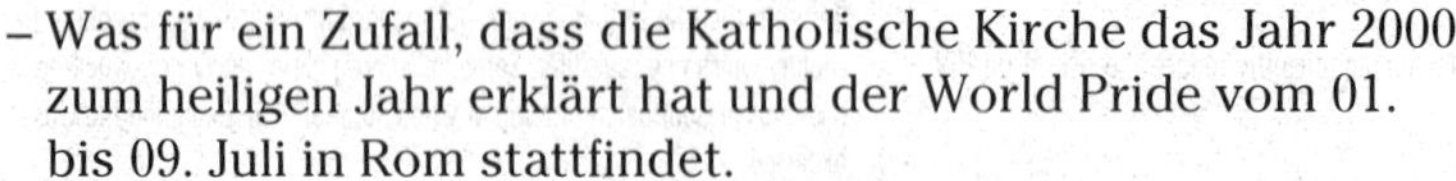

- Was für ein Zufall, dass die Katholische Kirche das Jahr 2000 zum heiligen Jahr erklärt hat und der World Pride vom 01. bis 09. Juli in Rom stattfindet.

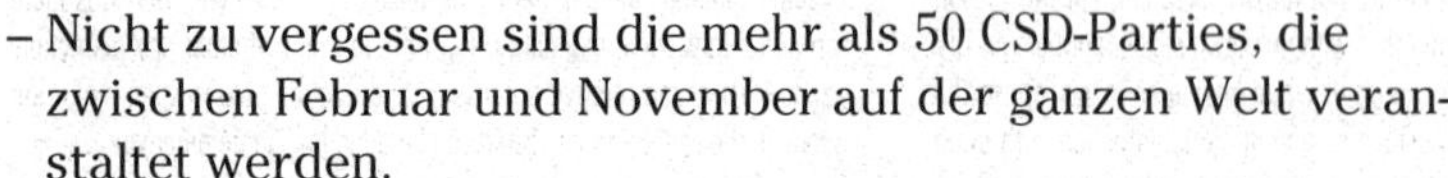

- Nicht zu vergessen sind die mehr als 50 CSD-Parties, die zwischen Februar und November auf der ganzen Welt veranstaltet werden.

Vor uns liegt also ein überaus interessantes und ereignisreiches Reisejahr und wir hoffen, dass Euch der Spartacus stets die passende Information liefert.

Bei der Erstellung der aktuellen Ausgabe waren uns die zahlreichen Rückmeldungen und Anregungen sehr hilfreich. Somit tragt auch Ihr dazu bei, dass der Spartacus auch in Zukunft der aktuellste Reiseführer der schwulen Welt bleibt!

Briand Bedford
EDITOR IN CHIEF

Wie man den SPARTACUS benutzt

Der SPARTACUS ist nach den englischen Ländernamen sortiert. Ausnahme von dieser Regel sind die Staaten und Territorien der Karibik, die wir für Sie unter „C" wie „Caribbean" alphabetisch zusammengestellt haben. Innerhalb der Länder erfolgt die Sortierung alphabetisch nach Städtenamen. BESONDERHEIT: Australien, Canada, USA. Damit Sie sich in diesen Ländern besser zurechtfinden, sind diese jeweils noch in Bundesstaaten/Territorien/Provinzen eingeteilt und erst innerhalb dieser Listung alphabetisch nach den Städtenamen sortiert.
Sollten Sie trotzdem unsicher sein, dann schauen Sie einfach im Index (siehe Seite 1298) nach. Die Namen aller Staaten sind dort in Deutsch, Englisch, Französisch und Spanisch alphabetisch einsortiert.
Für jeden souveränen Staat der Welt hat der SPARTACUS einen Eintrag vorgesehen. Zusätzlich gibt es Einträge für alle abhängigen Territorien, soweit es Informationen über die dortige gesetzliche Lage von schwulen und/oder die schwule Szene gibt.
Unter dem Länderhaupteintrag finden Sie:

die geographische Lage	➔	Western Europe
Initials sind die üblich gebrauchten Abkürzungen des Landes.	➔	Initials: UK / GB
Time gibt Ihnen die Zeitzone an.	➔	Time: GMT
Country und Access Code: Country Code ist die Vorwahlnummer des Staates aus dem Ausland. Mit dem Access Code erreichen Sie aus dem Land das internationale Telefonnetz.	➔	☎ Country Code / Access Code: 44 / 00
Language gibt Ihnen die meistverbreiteiten Sprachen an.	➔	Language: English
Area (qkm/sqm) ist die Gebietsgröße des Landes.	➔	Area: 242,100 km² / 93,451 sq mi.
Currency ist die offizielle Währung des Landes.	➔	Currency: 1 Pound Sterling (= 100 Pence)
Population gibt Ihnen die Einwohnerzahl an.	➔	Population: 58,249,000
Capital ist die Hauptstadt oder der Regierungssitz.	➔	Capital: London
Religions sind die im Land verbreiteten Religionen.	➔	Religions: 57% Anglicans, 15% other Protestants, 13% Catholics
Climate erläutert Ihnen das Klima in groben Zügen.	➔	Climate: Moderate climate that is moderated by prevailing southwest winds over the North Atlantic Current. More than half of the days are overcast.
Important Gay Cities - Städte in diesem Land, die für Schwule von besonderer Bedeutung sind..	➔	Important Gay Cities: London, Manchester, Brighton, Edinburgh

Der anschließende Vortext zeigt die rechtlichen Bestimmungen in dem Land auf, soweit sie für Schwule von Bedeutung sind.
SPARTACUS gibt auch kurze Abrisse zu Land und Leute.
Wir empfehlen Ihnen unbedingt, auch den nationalen Vorspann zu beachten. Dort finden Sie Organisationen oder Firmen von nationaler Bedeutung.
Im Anschluß folgt die Sortierung nach Städten.
Die Vorwahl/Postleitzahl einer Stadt entnehmen Sie bitte dem Stadtkopf bzw. Den Einzellistungen. Die Adresseinträge sind nach Rubriken unterteilt.
Der einzelne Eintrag enthält den Namen ❶,
die SPARTACUS-Codes ❷, die Öffnungszeiten ❸,
Adresse/Postadresse ❹, Telefonnummern ❺
und Erläuterungstexte.

❶ ❷ ❸

Café Spartacus, (B bf f G OS YG), 10-2h,
Spartacusstraße 123, 10000 Spartacus-City
☎ 123 45 67

❺ ❹

Ihre Mithilfe ist uns wichtig. Damit wir unsere Einträge auf dem möglichst aktuellen Stand halten können, sind Ihre persönlichen Erfahrungen für uns von Bedeutung. Bitte benutzen Sie für Ihre Info-Post an uns die User's Information Cards am Ende des SPARTACUS. Die Zusendung ist für Sie selbstverständlich portofrei.
Wenn Sie uns Infos über eine für Schwule interessante Einrichtung geben, dann achten Sie bitte auf jedes Detail. Wir brauchen mindestens Name, Ansprechpartner, Adresse (inkl. Stadt und Land!), Telefon/FAX. Visitenkarten sind empfehlenswert. Je mehr Informationen Sie uns liefern, desto besser.
Sollten Sie eine Firma oder nicht-kommerzielle Einrichtung leiten, dann bitten wir Sie, uns in regelmäßigen Abständen zu informieren.
Wir freuen uns übrigens auch, wenn Sie uns allgemeine Angaben über ein Land, eine Region oder eine Stadt machen.

Ihre Infos bitte an:
BRUNO GMÜNDER VERLAG GmbH – SPARTACUS-Redaktion
Postfach 61 01 04 • D-10921 Berlin • GERMANY

CODES

Die SPARTACUS-Codes sind:

!	Ein Muß für den internationalen Touristen
A	Kunstausstellungen
AC	Klimaanlage
AYOR	Auf eigenes Risiko, möglicherweise gefährlich
B	Bar
bf	Frühstück
CC	Wichtigste Kreditkarten akzeptiert
D	Disco
DR	Darkroom
E	Elegantes Publikum
F	Restaurant
G	Ausschließlich schwule Männer
g	Teilweise schwules Publikum
GLM	Ausschließlich schwul-lesbisches Publikum
glm	Teilweise schwul-lesbisches Publikum
H	Unterkunft
LJ	Fetisch-Publikum
MA	Gemischte Altersklassen
MG	Schwule mittleren Alters
msg	Massage möglich
N	Nachbarschaftsbar; Gäste vom Ort
NG	Nicht schwul, aber interessant
NU	FKK/Nacktbademöglichkeit
OG	Eher ältere Schwule
OS	Aussenplätze; Straßencafé, Terrasse, Garten
P	Privatclub/Strenge Kontrollen
p	Sie müssen klingeln
pi	Swimmingpool
R	Stricher im Publikum
S	Shows/Veranstaltungen
SNU	Stripshows
STV	Travestieshows
sa	Finnische Sauna
sb	Dampfsauna
sol	Solarium
TV	Transvestiten im Publikum
VS	Videovorführungen
WE	Betrieb vor allem am Wochenende
wh	Whirlpool/Jacuzzi
WO	Bodybuilding möglich
YG	Junge Schwule (18-28 J.)

Codes in Kleinbuchstaben bedeuten im allgemeinen eine Einschränkung.

Gesundheitsinfos

1. Vorwort

Die ersten AIDS-Fälle wurden 1981 bekannt. Seither zählt AIDS zu einer der bedeutendsten sexuell übertragbaren Krankheiten, die trotz wirksamer Behandlungsmöglichkeiten bis heute nicht geheilt werden kann. Um so wichtiger ist es, der Ausbreitung der Erkrankung vorzubeugen. Dies gelingt aber nur, wenn die Bevölkerung über die Übertragungswege aufgeklärt ist. Auch ist es von großer Bedeutung, einiges über die Krankheit AIDS zu wissen, um unbegründete Ängste und Vorurteile im Umgang mit AIDS-Erkrankten abzubauen. Im Jahr 2000 werden weltweit schätzungsweise 30-40 Millionen Menschen den AIDS verursachenden Erreger in sich tragen.

2. Was ist AIDS?

AIDS ist eine Infektionskrankheit und wird durch ein Virus ausgelöst, dem sogenannten HIV. Das HIV schädigt das Immunsystem des Menschen und schwächt dadurch die Abwehrkräfte. So wird der Körper anfällig für Erreger, die einem Gesunden normalerweise keine Probleme bereiten. Das Virus kann jedoch auch andere Störungen im Körper verursachen und beispielsweise Haut- und Nervenerkrankungen hervorrufen. Sogar Tumorerkrankungen können durch das Virus ausgelöst werden.

Gelangt das Virus in den Körper, so befällt es Zellen des menschlichen Abwehrsystems und programmiert den Zellstoffwechsel zu seinen Gunsten um. Das Virus kann sich darauf hin in den Zellen vermehren und zerstört sie schließlich. Nicht HIV-infizierte Abwehrzellen des menschlichen Immunsystems versuchen, das Virus zu besiegen. Es ist aber für das Immunsystem unmöglich, alle Viren zu vernichten.

7 von 8 Personen, die sich mit dem HIV angesteckt haben, bemerken nach einigen Tagen unspezifische grippeartige Krankheitszeichen, so zum Beispiel Fieber, Halsentzündung, Hautausschlag und Lymphknotenschwellung. Diese halten wenige Tage bis 2 Wochen an und verschwinden wieder. Dann hat der HIV-Infizierte zunächst keine Beschwerden mehr. Diese "asymptomatische Phase " kann unterschiedlich lang anhalten, in der Regel mehrere Jahre. Wenn die Viren im Körper überhand nehmen, bricht das Abwehrsystem des Menschen zusammen. Schließlich entsteht das Krankheitsstadium AIDS, das durch eine Reihe schwerer Erkrankungen gekennzeichnet ist, wie dem Kaposi-Sarkom der Haut, einer Augen-, Lungen- oder Gehirnentzündung. Schließlich verläuft die Erkrankung tödlich.

Ob man sich mit dem Virus HIV infiziert hat, kann durch Labortests im Blut nachgewiesen werden. Die gängigen Nachweisverfahren liefern erst drei Monate nach dem Infektionszeitpunkt aussagekräftige Ergebnisse. Trägt man das Virus in sich, so ist man "HIV-positiv", andernfalls "HIV-negativ".

3. Übertragungswege von HIV

Grundsätzlich gilt, daß das Virus durch Körperflüssigkeiten (Blut, Sperma, Vaginalsekret und Muttermilch) eines HIV-positiven Menschen übertragen werden kann. Gelangt zum Beispiel virushaltiges Blut oder Sperma auf offene Wunden oder Schleimhäute, so kann das Virus in den Körper gelangen und zu einer HIV-Infektion führen. Es gilt also, den Kontakt mit diesen Körperflüssigkeiten zu vermeiden.

Der sicherlich häufigste Übertragungsweg ist Sex. Riskante Sexualpraktiken sind Vaginal- und Analverkehr ohne Kondom (für beide Partner), aber auch Oralverkehr, bei dem Sperma oder Vaginalflüssigkeit in den Mund gelangt. Auch andere Übertragungswege sind möglich, wie beim Austausch blutiger Spritzenutensilien bei Drogenabhängigen oder die Übertragung in der

Schwangerschaft, bei der Geburt und durch Muttermilch auf das Kind.
Das Übertragungsrisiko erhöht sich, wenn eine Entzündung der Geschlechtsorgane vorliegt, die mit offenen Wunden, Ausfluß oder Eiterabsonderung einhergehen.
Speichel, Schweiß und Tränen enthalten HIV in so geringer Menge, daß eine Ansteckung hierdurch nicht möglich ist. Kein Übertragungsrisiko besteht beim Küssen, durch gemeinsame Benutzung von Trinkgläsern und Eßbestecken, Kleidung, Schwimmbädern, Saunen oder Toiletten. Durch Anfassen von Türgriffen, Telefonhörern u.ä., ebenso durch soziale Kontakte wie Händeschütteln und Umarmen sowie durch die Atemluft und Insekten, kann HIV ebenfalls nicht übertragen werden.

4. Safer Sex

Um sich beim Sex vor einer Ansteckung mit dem HIV zu schützen, sollten ein paar Verhaltensregeln beachtet werden (Safer Sex-Regeln), deren Ziel es ist, die Aufnahme infektiöser Körperflüssigkeiten zu vermeiden. Dies bedeutet konkret:

- Sachgemäßer Gebrauch von Kondomen beim Anal- und Oralverkehr.
- Kein Sperma in den Mund des Partners kommen lassen.
- Gebrauch einer Latexvorlage (sog. Dental Dam) beim Oralsex bei der Frau.
- Analsex mit der Hand nur mit kurzen Fingernägeln und mit Gummihandschuhen.
- Kontakt von Sperma, Blut oder Vaginalflüssigkeit mit offenen Wunden vermeiden.

Kondome sollten qualitätsgeprüft und ausreichend reißfest ("extra strong") sein. Sie sind vor Hitze, Kälte und Sonnenbestrahlung zu schützen und nur mit wasserlöslichen Gleitgels zu verwenden, da sie mit fettlöslichen Gleitmitteln (auch Cremes oder Fetten) undicht werden können. Besteht eine Latexallergie, können auch Kondome aus Polyurethan verwendet werden, die allerdings häufig teurer sind.
Außerhalb des menschlichen Körpers hat das HIV nur eine kurze Überlebenszeit. Dennoch gilt, daß z.B. Dildos vor einer Verwendung durch eine andere Person gut gereinigt werden müssen.
Durch Beachten dieser Safer Sex-Regeln wird die Risiko einer HIV-Übertragung deutlich herabgesetzt - ein Restrisiko bleibt.
Den meisten sieht man eine HIV-Infektion nicht an. Daher sollte man bei fremden Sexualpartnern grundsätzlich von der Möglichkeit einer HIV-Infektion ausgehen und sich beim Sex vor einer Übertragung schützen. Das gilt übrigens auch für bereits HIV-Positive, da eine zusätzliche Infektion mit anderen HIV-Stämmen den Krankheitsverlauf ungünstig beeinflussen kann.

5. Behandlungsmöglichkeiten von HIV und AIDS

Zur Behandlung einer HIV-Infektion gibt es unterschiedliche Medikamente (sog. antiretrovirale Medikamente), welche die Vermehrung der Viren hemmen. Diese werden allgemein miteinander kombiniert, um ihre Wirkung zu verstärken und um zu verhindern, daß die Viren auf ein Medikament unempfindlich werden. Ganz vermeiden läßt sich letzteres jedoch nicht. Diese antiretroviralen Medikamente müssen dauerhaft und regelmäßig eingenommen werden. Jede Verzögerung oder Pause kann den Therapieerfolg verringern. Die Anwendung der Medikamente muß daher dem Tagesablauf angepaßt werden. Wann mit einer entsprechenden Therapie begonnen werden sollte, kann nur ein Arzt entscheiden.
Medikamente gegen das HIV führen zwar nicht zur Virusfreiheit, können aber eine Erholung des Immunsystems bewirken und die Überlebenszeit deutlich verlängern. Selbst wenn HIV durch die Therapie im Blut nicht mehr nachweisbar ist, besteht die Möglichkeit zur Übertragung der Infektion.
Behandlungsmöglichkeiten von Erkrankungen, die mit der HIV-Infektion einhergehen, sind vielfältig. Bei Auftreten von Beschwerden sollte man rechtzeitig einen Arzt aufsuchen. In vielen Ländern gibt es bereits Selbsthilfeorganisationen und Beratungszentren, die Unterstützung bei psychologischen, sozialen und finanziellen Problemen in Zusammenhang mit einer HIV-Infektion oder der AIDS-Erkrankung geben.

6. Reisen und AIDS

Da das AIDS verursachende Virus weltweit verbreitet ist, sollten die Safer Sex-Regeln auch im Ausland beachtet werden. Da in manchen Ländern die richtigen Kondome nur schwer erhältlich sind und deren Qualität zum Teil mangelhaft ist, empfiehlt es sich, diese aus der Heimat mitzuführen.
HIV-Positive oder an AIDS Erkrankte sollten einen ausreichenden Vorrat an antiretroviralen Medikamenten mitnehmen und beachten, daß manche Medikamente hitze-, kälte- und lichtempfindlich sind und trocken gelagert werden sollten, damit sie ihre Wirkung behalten. Da sie nach einem strengen Zeitplan eingenommen werden müssen, ist der richtige Einnahmezeitpunkt bei Reisen in andere Zeitzonen zu berücksichtigen.
Vor allem in tropischen Ländern gibt es eine Vielzahl von hierzulande unbekannten Erregern. Gerade bei HIV-Positiven, deren Immunsystem angegriffen ist, können diese ernsthafte Erkrankungen verursachen. Wie man sich vor diesen schützt und ob Impfungen sinnvoll sind, kann nur für den Einzelfall beantwortet werden. Gegen Insektenstiche gibt es wirksame Medikamente zum Auftragen auf die Haut; Kleidung, welche Arme und Beine bedeckt, wird zudem angeraten. Auf Reisen sollte man auch Medikamente z.B. gegen Übelkeit, Durchfall und Kopfschmerzen sowie Sonnenschutzmittel mitnehmen, die in Kombination mit den bereits einzunehmenden Medikamenten verträglich sind. Es empfiehlt sich daher in jedem Fall, vor einer Reise einen fachkundigen Arzt zu befragen.
Vor einer Reise sollte geprüft werden, ob die bestehende Krankenversicherung auch Leistungen im Ausland übernimmt. Eigens abgeschlossene Reiseversicherungen zahlen oft nur, wenn eine Erkrankung nicht schon vor Reiseantritt bestand oder eine Behandlung während der Reise nicht zu erwarten war.
In einigen Ländern bestehen Einreisebeschränkungen für HIV-Infizierte. Daher ist anzuraten, sich bereits bei der Reiseplanung über den aktuellen Stand der Einreisebestimmungen zu erkundigen. Eine Adresse der zuständigen Botschaft und eines deiner Sprache mächtigen Arztes im Reiseland kann in Notlagen hilfreich sein.

7. Übrigens

Es gibt noch eine Reihe weiterer sexuell übertragbarer Erkrankungen, wie Hepatitis (=Leberentzündung), Tripper (=Gonorrhoe), Syphilis (=harter Schanker), Feigwarzen und andere, die sich auch durch Safer Sex weitgehend vermeiden lassen. Gegen Hepatitis A und B kann man sich impfen. Eine Schutzimpfung gegen AIDS gibt es nicht.

Dr. med. Martin W. Eichenlaub

Avant-propos

L'an 2000 a débuté par de grandioses fêtes. Mais le monde gay n'a pas fini de célébrer cette année. Parmi les musts à ne pas manquer, nous avons sélectionné :

- La fête du Mardi Gras qui se déroulera à Sydney du 11 février au 4 mars. Pour plus d'information, veuillez visiter le site: www.mardigras.com.au
- les Eurogames 2000, qui auront lieu cette année à Zurich du 1er au 4 juin,
- la première WORLD PRIDE. Le hasard du calendrier a voulu qu'en cette année, déclarée sainte par l'Eglise catholique, elle se déroule à Rome du 1er au 9 juillet,
- et enfin, plus de 50 Christopher Street Day parades qui seront célébrées à travers le monde entre les mois de février et de novembre.

Nous espérons que SPARTACUS saura vous fournir les informations nécessaires pour passer avec brio cette année intéressante et particulièrement riche en événements.

Pendant l'élaboration de cette dernière édition, les nombreux conseils et remarques que vous nous avez envoyés se sont avérés très utiles. C'est donc aussi grâce à votre contribution, que nous pouvons vous proposer cette année encore et à l'avenir le guide du voyageur gay le plus actuel au monde !

Briand Bedford
EDITEUR EN CHEF

Comment utiliser votre SPARTACUS

Le SPARTACUS est classé pays par pays. Les noms des pays sont donnés en anglais, à l'exception des états et territoires des Caraïbes, que nous avons rangés, comme „caribbean", par ordre alphabétique. Pour chaque pays, les villes sont classées par ordre alphabétique.
PARTICULARITÉS: Australie, Canada, États-Unis. Pour que vous y retrouviez mieux, ceux-çi sont rangés par états fédéraux/ territoires/ provinces , et ensuite sous-ordonnés par villes et par ordre alphabétique.Si vous avez malgré tout des difficultés à trouver un nom, vous pouvez vous reporter à l'index (voir page1298). Les noms des villes y sont classés par ordre alphabétique en allemand, anglais, français, et espagnol.
Chaque état souverain au monde a une place dans le SPARTACUS. Nous avons prévu également des informations conçernant les territoires indépendants ainsi que sur la situation juridique des homosexuels, ou la scène gay.
Pour chaque pays, vous trouverez:

sa situation géographique	➔	Western Europe
Initials correspondent à l'abréviation générale du pays	➔	Initials: UK / GB
Time vous indique sa zone horaire	➔	Time: GMT
Country et Access Code: Country code est l'indicatif à composer pour joindre ce pays depuis l'étranger. Access code vous permet d'accéder depuis le pays en question au réseau téléphonique international	➔	☎ Country Code / Access Code: 44 / 00
Language correspond à la langue officielle du pays	➔	Language: English
Area Area vous donne la superficie du pays en km²	➔	Area: 242,100 km² / 93,451 sq mi.
Currency vous indique la monnaie du pays	➔	Currency: 1 Pound Sterling (= 100 Pence)
Population: la population du pays	➔	Population: 58,249,000
Capital: la capitale ou le siège du pays	➔	Capital: London
Religions: la ou les religions du pays	➔	Religions: 57% Anglicans, 15% other Protestants, 13% Catholics
Climate: les caractéristiques climatiques générales	➔	Climate: Moderate climate that is moderated by prevailing southwest winds over the North Atlantic Current. More than half of the days are overcast.
Important Gay Cities vous indiquent le nom des principalesvilles gay	➔	Important Gay Cities: London, Manchester, Brighton, Edinburgh

Un texte d'introduction vous renseigne ensuite sur la situation des homosexuels face à la loi dans le pays en question, ainsi qu'une courte présentation du pays et de ses habitants.
Nous vous recommandons particulièrement de lire les informations concernant chaque pays, car vous y trouverez également le nom d'organisations et de de sociétés gay du pays. Vous trouverez ensuite le classement par villes. les codes postaux et indicatifs des villes seront comprises dans les différentes adresses indiquées. Les différentes adresses sont classées par catégories.
Chaque entrée comprend le nom de l'endroit en question ❶,
le code SPARTACUS ❷, les heures d'ouverture ❸, l'adresse ❹,
le numéro de téléphone ❺ et un texte d'explications.

❶ ❷ ❸
Café Spartacus, (B bf f G OS YG), 10-2h,
Spartacusstraße 123, 10000 Spartacus-City
☎ 123 45 67
❺ ❹

Votre aide nous est précieuse. Pour que nous puissions rester d'actualité, nous comptons sur vous pour partager vos expériences avec nous. Pour nous contacter, vous pouvez utiliser les cartes postales d'informations qui se trouvent à la fin de votre SPARTACUS. Bien entendu, les frais de port sont gratuits. Lorsque vous nous envoyez des renseignements sur un endroit interessant pour les homosexuels, nous vous prions d'être attentif au moindre détail. Nous avons besoin du nom de l'endroit, de la personne que nous pouvons contacter, de l'adresse (y compris la ville et le pays!), du numéro de tél. ou fax. Les cartes de visites sont les bienvenues. Au plus vous pouvez nous livrer d'informations, au mieux cela est.
Si vous êtes à la tête d'une societé ou association non commerciale, nous vous prions de nous informer régulièrement. Nous nous réjouissons également si vous nous livrez des informations générales sur un pays, une région ou une ville.

Merci d'envoyer vos informations à l'adresse suivante:
BRUNO GMÜNDER VERLAG GmbH – SPARTACUS-Redaktion
Postfach 61 01 04 • D-10921 Berlin • GERMANY

CODES

!	un must pour le touriste international
A	exposition d'art
AC	climatisation
AYOR	à vos risques et périls!
B	bar avec boissons alcoolisées
bf	petit déjeuner
CC	cartes de crédits courantes acceptées
D	boite de nuit
DR	dark room
E	tenue correcte exigée
F	restaurant
G	clientèle exclusivement gay
g	clientèle mixte: gay et hétéros
GLM	fréquenté uniquement par les gay et lesbiennes
H	hôtel ou pension où les gay sont volontiers reçus
LJ	cuir et jeans
MA	tous âges
MG	homosexuels d'âge moyen
msg	possibilité de massage
N	bar de quartier, clientèle du coin
NG	pas forcément gay, mais intéressant
NU	possibilité de nudisme
OG	homosexuels plutôt âgés
OS	plein air: cafés, terrasses, jardins
P	club privé ou contrôle strict à l'entrée
p	il faut sonner
pi	piscine
R	fréquenté aussi par des gigolos
S	spectacle ou autre manifestation
SNU	strip-shows
STV	spectacle de travestis
sa	sauna finlandais
sb	bains turcs
sol	solarium
TV	fréquenté aussi par travestis et transexuels
VS	présentation de vidéos
WE	ouvert plutôt le week-end
wh	whirlpool, jacuzzi
WO	possibilité de faire de la musculation
YG	jeunes homosexuels (18 à 28 ans)

Un code en minuscule implique en général une restriction

Informations

1. Introduction

Les premiers cas de SIDA sont apparus en 1981. Depuis lors, et en dépit des progrès thérapeutiques, le SIDA est devenue une des maladies sexuellement transmissible (MST) incurables les plus répandues au monde. L'accent doit donc être mis sur la prévention afin de ralentir la propagation de la maladie. Pour ce faire, la population doit être informée sur la maladie et ses moyens de transmission. Cette politique d'information doit aussi aider à combattre les peurs infondées et les préjugés que subissent les personnes porteuses du virus. Une estimation chiffre leur nombre entre 30 et 40 millions pour l'an 2000.

2. Qu'est-ce qu'est le SIDA?

Le SIDA est une maladie infectieuse causée par un virus dénommé VIH. Le VIH affaibli le système immunitaire et diminue ainsi la force de résistance. Le corps humain devient vulnérable face à des organismes inoffensifs pour un corps sain. Le virus peut aussi provoquer certaines maladies, par exemple cutanées ou nerveuses, mais aussi l'apparition de tumeurs.
Une fois que le virus se trouve dans le corps humain, il attaque les cellules du système immunitaire et programme leur métabolisme à son avantage. Le virus peut alors se développer dans ces cellules jusqu'à provoquer leur destruction. Les cellules du système immunitaire qui ne sont pas infectées par le VIH tentent de combattre le virus. Le système immunitaire ne peut cependant se débarrasser complètement du virus.
7 personnes infectées par le VIH sur 8 remarquent après quelques jours les symptômes d'une grippe non identifiée, tels que fièvre, angine, éruption cutanée ou inflammation des ganglions lymphatiques. Ces symptômes durent de quelques jours à deux semaines pour disparaître après. La personne infectée par le virus VIH ne ressent alors plus de symptômes. Cette phase « non symptomatique » est de durée variable, mais perdure en règle générale plusieurs années. Mais le virus peut proliférer de manière excessive et faire faillir le système immunitaire. C'est ce qu'on appelle alors le stade du SIDA déclaré. Il se marque par une série de maladies graves, telles que le sarcome de Kaposi, l'ophtalmie, la pneumonie ou l'encéphalite. En phase terminale, la maladie est mortelle.
Un test sanguin en laboratoire peut déterminer si une personne est infectée par le virus VIH. Les tests disponibles ne permettent de délivrer un résultat fiable que trois mois après avoir été en contact avec le virus. Les porteurs du virus sont appelés séropositifs, les non-porteurs séronégatifs.

3. Transmission du VIH

Le virus se transmet à travers les fluides corporels (sang, sperme) d'une personne séropositive. Une infection par le VIH peut par exemple se produire si du sang ou du sperme porteur de virus se trouve en contact avec une plaie ouverte ou des muqueuses. Il est donc nécessaire d'éviter tout contact avec ces fluides corporels.
Le moyen le plus courant de transmission est par voie sexuelle. Les pratiques sexuelles à risque sont la pénétration anale sans préservatif (pour les deux partenaires), mais aussi la fellation si du sperme se trouve dans la bouche. D'autres moyens de transmission existent, comme l'échange de seringues usagées par les toxicomanes ou la transmission de mère à enfant pendant la grossesse, à l'accouchement ou pendant l'allaitement.
Les risques de transmissions sont plus grands si les organes sexuels souffrent au préalable d'une inflammation avec plaies ouvertes ou purulentes.

Informations sur la santé

La salive, la sueur et les larmes contiennent si peu de VIH qu'une transmission à travers ces fluides est impossible. Un baiser ou l'utilisation partagée d'un verre, de services de table, l'échange d'habits ou de maillots de bain, la fréquentation de saunas ou de toilettes publiques ne présentent aucun risque de contamination. Toucher une poignée de porte ou un appareil téléphonique, serrer une main ou étreindre une personne, être en contact avec l'air ou se faire piquer par un insecte ne présentent également aucun danger.

4. Safer Sex

Afin de se protéger d'une transmission du VIH lors de rapports sexuels, il est impératif d'observer certaines règles de comportement (les règles du« safer sex ») dont le but est d'éviter de se mettre en contact avec des fluides corporels potentiellement infectés. Concrètement, cela signifie :

- Une utilisation appropriée de préservatif lors de rapports oraux et anaux
- Pas de sperme dans la bouche
- Pénétration anale avec la main uniquement avec des ongles bien coupés et des gants en latex
- Pas de sperme ou du sang sur une plaie ouverte

Les préservatifs doivent être qualitativement testés et indéchirables (« extra strong »). Protégez-les des températures extrêmes et des rayons directs du soleil et ne les utilisez qu'avec des lubrifiants solubles à l'eau. Les crèmes et lubrifiants à base de graisse ont en effet tendance à rendre les préservatifs plus poreux. En cas d'allergie au latex, il existe également des préservatifs en polyuréthane, malheureusement plus coûteux.

En dehors du corps humain, le VIH ne peut survivre que peu de temps. Malgré cela, il est important de bien nettoyer les godemichés et autres accessoires avant leur emploi par une deuxième personne.

En suivant ces quelques règles, vous pouvez réduire de manière significative les risques de transmission du VIH. Un risque infime reste cependant.

La plupart des personnes infectées par le VIH n'ont pas de symptômes apparents. Pour cette raison, il faut automatiquement considérer toute relation avec un partenaire occasionnel comme à risque et se protéger en conséquence. Cette règle est aussi valable pour les personnes séropositives, un deuxième contact avec le virus pouvant influencer négativement le cours de leur maladie.

5. Les possibilités de traitement du VIH et du SIDA

Il existe différentes sorte de médicaments (appelés médicaments antiviraux) qui permettent de ralentir la prolifération des virus. Ces médicaments sont combinés entre eux pour accroître leur efficacité et pour éviter que le virus devienne résistant à l'un d'eux. Malgré ces précautions, il peut arriver que le virus développe une résistance à un médicament. Les médicaments antiviraux doivent être pris régulièrement et à des intervalles déterminés. Un retard ou une interruption dans la prise de médicaments peut en effet amoindrir les chances de succès de la thérapie. Il est donc nécessaire de la planifier au quotidien. La décision de commencer une telle thérapie ne peut être prise que par un médecin.

Les médicaments utilisés pour la lutte contre le VIH ne peuvent détruire complètement le virus mais aident le système immunitaire à se renforcer et prolongent ainsi de manière significative l'espérance de vie des patients. Même si la présence du virus n'est plus détectable dans le sang après une telle thérapie, le risque de transmission reste néanmoins présent.

Les possibilités de traitement des maladies liées à l'infection par le VIH sont elles nombreuses. Un médecin devrait être consulté dès l'apparition des premiers symptômes.

Il existe dans de nombreux pays des organisations d'entraide et des services de consultation qui peuvent apporter un soutien psychologique, social ou financier aux personnes séropositives et aux malades du SIDA.

6. Voyages et SIDA

Puisque le virus du SIDA est répandu dans le monde entier, il est important d'observer les règles du « safer sex » aussi à l'étranger. Il est également avisé d'emporter avec soi des préservatifs de qualité, la fiabilité des produits sur le marché de certains pays étrangers n'étant pas assurée.

Les personnes séropositives ou malades du SIDA doivent emporter suffisamment de médicaments antiviraux avec eux et faire attention qu'ils ne soient pas exposés à la chaleur, au froid et à la lumière. Il est important de les conserver dans un endroit sec pour qu'ils conservent toute leur efficacité. Comme il est nécessaire de les prendre à des heures bien précises, il est conseillé de préparer un planning qui tienne compte des changements de fuseaux horaires à l'avance.

Dans les pays tropicaux, il existe des agents pathogènes inconnus sous nos propres cieux. Les séropositifs, dont le système immunitaire est déjà affaibli, risquent de s'exposer à des maladies graves. Les mesures de protection et vaccins nécessaires ne peuvent être recommandés que de manière individuelle. Cependant, on peut emporter avec soi des baumes à appliquer directement sur la peau pour se protéger des piqûres d'insectes, des médicaments contre par exemple la nausée, la diarrhée ou les maux de tête (pour autant qu'il soient compatibles avec les autres médicaments antiviraux) et on peut se couvrir entièrement les bras et jambes en guise de première protection. Il est néanmoins recommandé de consulter de toute manière un médecin spécialiste avant chaque voyage.

On devrait toujours vérifier que son assurance maladie garantit une couverture dans le pays de destination. Beaucoup de polices d'assurance ne couvrent les frais que si l'on est en bonne santé avant de partir ou que si un traitement pendant le voyage n'était pas prévisible.

Il existe dans certains pays des restrictions d'entrée pour les séropositifs. Il est donc conseillé de se renseigner à l'avance sur les politiques d'accueil touristiques des pays où l'on compte séjourner. L'adresse de l'ambassade et celle d'un médecin spécialiste dans les pays de destination peuvent être utiles en cas d'urgence.

7. Mais encore

Il existe une série de maladies sexuellement transmissible comme l'hépatite, la blennorragie, la syphilis et bien d'autres qui peuvent être en partie évitées si l'on pratique les règles du « safer sex ». Il existe des vaccins contre l'hépatite A et B. Il n'en existe pas contre le SIDA.

Dr. med. Martin W. Eichenlaub

¡Bienvenidos al nuevo SPARTACUS!

Prologo

El año 2000 empezó con fiestas espectaculares en todo el mundo. El mundo gay, naturalmente, sigue celebrando...
Las fiestas más magníficas serán entre otras:

- El MARDI GRAS en Sydney del 11 de febrero al 4 de marzo. Podéis encontrar más información en www.mardigras.com.au
- Los EUROGAMES en Zúrich del 1 al 4 de junio
- Fijáos que coincidencia, la Iglesia católica declaró el año 2000 como Año Santo, y el WORLD PRIDE (Fiesta Mundial del Orgullo Gay) tendrá lugar en Roma del 1 al 9 de julio...
- Para no olvidar las más de 50 fiestas del Día del Orgullo Gay (Christopher Street Day) que se festejarán en todo el mundo entre febrero y noviembre.

Nos espera un año de viajes muy interesante y lleno de actividades, así que esperamos que la guía Spartacus contenga todas las informaciones que os hagan falta.

Al preparar esta edición actual que tenéis entre manos, las numerosas informaciones y sugerencias de nuestros lectores nos han sido de gran ayuda. De esta forma, podéis contribuir a que Spartacus siga siendo la guía de viajes más actual del mundo gay.

Briand Bedford
REDACTOR JEFE

Como usar el SPARTACUS

El SPARTACUS ha sido ordenado según los nombres de los paises en el idioma inglés. Las únicas excepciones son los estados y territorios del Caribe, que hemos acomodados bajo „C" como „Caribbean" por estados y ciudades respectivas. PARTICULARIDAD: Australia, Canada y Estados Unidos. Para su mejor orientación están divididos en estados federales/territorios/provincias y dentro de este listín aparecen las ciudades por orden alfabetico.En caso de duda, sírvase de consultar el índice (a partir de la página1298). Allí encontrará los nombres de todo los paises ordenados alfabeticamente en alemán, inglés, francés y castellano.

El SPARTACUS ha acreditado a cada estado soberano del mundo una entrada. Además aparecen todos los territorios que no son independientes, en cuanto hay informaciones disponibles sobre la situación legal de los homosexuales y/ó el ambiente gay. Bajo la entrada principal de cada país se encuentran las siguientes informaciones:

la situación geográfica.	➔	Western Europe
Initials indican la abreviatura usual del país.	➔	Initials: UK / GB
Time informa sobre el huso horario.	➔	Time: GMT
Country y Access Code: Country Code es el préfijo del estado desde el extranjero, mientras el Access Code indica el numero que hay que marcar dentro el país para tener acceso a la red	➔	☎ Country Code / Access Code: 44 / 00
Language indica los idiomas más comunes del país..	➔	Language: English
Area (qkm/sqm) informa sobre la extensión territorial.	➔	Area: 242,100 km^2 / 93,451 sq mi.
Currency es la moneda oficial del país	➔	Currency: 1 Pound Sterling (= 100 Pence)
Population indica el número de habitantes.	➔	Population: 58,249,000
Capital es la capital o la sede del gobierno.	➔	Capital: London
Religion indica las religiones más comunes.	➔	Religions: 57% Anglicans, 15% other Protestants, 13% Catholics
Climate resume el clima en grandes rasgos.	➔	Climate: Moderate climate that is moderated by prevailing southwest winds over the North Atlantic Current. More than half of the days are overcast.
Important Gay Cities son las ciudades del país de mayor interés para el turista homosexual.	➔	Important Gay Cities: London, Manchester, Brighton, Edinburgh

La siguiente introducción explica la situación legal del país respectivo, en cuanto concierne a homosexuales. Además SPARTACUS da una corta descripción del país y de sus habitantes. También recomendamos de leer detenidamente la introducción nacional. Allí indicamos organizaciones y empresas de importancia a nivel nacional.

A continuación sigue el listín de las ciudades.El préfijo/codigo postal de cada ciudad lo encontrará junto al enunciado de la ciudad, de lo contrario lo hallará junto a la dirección en cuestión. Las entradas de direcciones están acomodados según rúbricas.

Cada entrada contiene el nombre ❶, los códigos del SPARTACUS ❷, horarios ❸, la dirección postal ❹, número de telefóno ❺ y comentarios.

❶ ❷ ❸

Café Spartacus, (B bf f G OS YG), 10-2h,
Spartacusstraße 123, 10000 Spartacus-City
☎ 123 45 67

❺ ❹

Su colaboración nos es muy importante. Para tener las entradas al día, nos interesan sus experiencias personales. Sírvase usar las User's Information Card al final del SPARTACUS para enviarnos sus informaciones y sugerencias. Se sobre entiende que cargamos con los costes de franqueo.

Si desea proporcionarnos informaciones sobre establecimientos interesantes para homosexuales, le rogamos fijarse en cada detalle. Por lo menos necesitamos nombre, persona de contacto, dirección (inclusive ciudad y país!), telefóno/fax. Tarjetas de visita son recomendables. Agradecemos las informaciones lo más detalladas posibles.

Si Vd. dirige una empresa o una institución no comercial, por favor, mandenos regularmente informaciones. También agradecemos si nos proporcionan informaciones generales sobre un país, una religión o una ciudad.

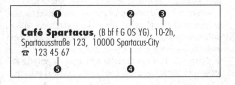

Escribanos a la siguiente dirección:
BRUNO GMÜNDER VERLAG GmbH – SPARTACUS-Redaktion
Postfach 61 01 04 • D-10921 Berlin • GERMANY

CODES

Los códigos del SPARTACUS:

!	Un deber para el turista internacional
A	Exposicionen de arte
AC	Aire acondicionado
AYOR	A riesgo própio, a lo mejor peligroso
B	Bar
bf	Desayuno
CC	Se acceptan los más importantes cartas de crédito
D	Discoteca
DR	Darkroom/sala oscura
E	Publico elegante
F	Restaurante
G	Exclusivamente público gay
GLM	Exclusivamente público gay-lesbiano
H	Hotel
LJ	Público de fetiche
MA	Edades mixtas
MG	Gays de edades medias
msg	Posibilidad de masaje
N	De interés principalmente local/clientes del sitio
NG	No es gay, pero interesante para ellos
NU	Playa nudista/posibilidad de bañarse desnudo
OG	Sobre todo gays mayores
OS	Sitios al aire libre, terraza, jardín
P	Club privado/severos controles
p	Hay que tocar el timbre
pi	Piscina
R	Prostitutos entre el público
S	Espectáculos/eventos
SNU	Shows de estriptease
STV	Shows de travestis
sa	Sauna finlandesa
sb	Sauna de vapor
sol	Solarium
TV	Travestis entre el publico
VS	Sesiones de videos
WE	Animado sobre todo los fines de semana
wh	Whirlpool/jacuzzi
WO	Posibilidad de culturismo
YG	Gays jóvenes (18-28 años)

Códigos en letras minúsculas significan en general una restrinción.

Informaciones

1. Introducción

Los primeros casos de SIDA se conocieron en 1981. Desde entonces, el SIDA se ha convertido en una de las enfermedades de transmisión sexual más importantes, que hasta hoy día, y a pesar de tratamientos eficaces, sigue siendo incurable. Por eso es tan importante prevenir la propagación de la enfermedad, pero esto sólo es viable si la población está informada sobre las vías de contagio. También es de gran importancia saber lo suficiente sobre el SIDA para poder reducir los prejuicios existentes en el trato con personas afectadas por el SIDA. En el año 2000, en todo el mundo habrá aproximadamente de treinta a cuarenta millones de personas portadoras del virus.

2. ¿Qué es el SIDA?

El SIDA es una enfermedad infecciosa causada por un virus, el llamado HIV. El virus HIV daña el sistema inmunológico y de esta forma debilita las defensas del cuerpo. El cuerpo es cada vez menos resistente a agentes patógenos que a una persona sana normalmente no le causarían ningún problema. Sin embargo, el virus puede causar otros trastornos y provocar, por ejemplo, enfermedades de la piel o del sistema nervioso e incluso puede llegar a provocar tumores.

Si el virus penetra en el cuerpo, afecta a las células del sistema inmunológico humano y manipula el metabolismo celular de tal manera que puede multiplicarse en las células hasta destruirlas. Las células del sistema inmunológico humano no infectadas por el HIV intentan vencer al virus, pero el sistema inmunológico jamás es capaz de destruir todos los virus existentes en el cuerpo.

Siete de ocho personas que se han infectado con el virus del HIV, pocos días después de la infección notan síntomas gripales no específicos (como pueden ser fiebre, infecciones de la garganta, erupciones de la piel e hinchazones de las glándulas linfáticas) que pueden tardar entre pocos días y dos semanas en desaparecer. Después, el infectado por el virus HIV por de pronto no tiene problemas de salud. Esta 'fase asintomática' según el caso puede llegar a durar hasta varios años. Una vez que la carga viral en el cuerpo se hace demasiado grande, el sistema inmunológico del infectado colapsa. Después, el infectado entra en el estadio de la enfermedad del SIDA, caracterizado por una serie de enfermedades graves como el sarcoma de Kaposi de la piel, oftalmía, pulmonía o encefalitis, y finalmente muere por causa de la enfermedad. Por medio de unos análisis de sangre es posible determinar si uno se ha infectado con el virus del HIV. Los métodos corrientes sólo permiten resultados significativos a partir de los tres meses después del momento de la infección. Un portador del virus del HIV es 'HIV-positivo', en el caso contrario se habla de 'HIV-negativo'.

3. Vías de contagio de HIV

El virus se puede contagiar a través de fluidos corporales (sangre, esperma, segregación vaginal y leche materna) de una persona HIV-positiva. Si, por ejemplo, la sangre o el esperma de una persona portadora del virus llega a entrar en contacto con heridas o mucosas, el virus puede entrar en el cuerpo y provocar la infección, por lo que hay que evitar que estos contactos ocurran.

La vía de contagio seguramente más frecuente es el sexo. Prácticas sexuales de riesgo elevado para ambos implicados son las penetraciones a„nales y vaginales sin condón, como también lo es el sexo oral, siempre que lleguen a entrar esperma o segregaciones vaginales en la boca.

Otras posibles vías de contagio son también el intercambio de jeringuillas utilizadas entre toxicómanos o la infección del hijo durante el embarazo,

durante el parto o la lactancia.
El riesgo de contagio es más elevado en casos de infecciones de los órganos sexuales acompañadas de heridas abiertas, flujos o supuración.
La saliva, el sudor y las lágrimas contienen HIV en muy bajas cantidades, de manera que no constituyen posibles vías de contagio. El besarse, beber de un mismo vaso, utilizar los mismos cubiertos o la misma ropa, ir a piscinas, saunas o lavabos tampoco implican riesgo de contagio. El virus tampoco se contagia por tocar los pomos de las puertas, auriculares de teléfonos, etc., ni por contactos sociales tan cotidianos como apretar las manos o abrazarse. Tampoco puede contagiarse el virus del HIV por el aire que respiramos o por picaduras de insectos.

4. Sexo seguro

Para protegerse de la infección del virus del HIV durante el sexo deberían tenerse en mente algunas reglas de comportamiento ('reglas de sexo seguro') cuyo objetivo es evitar que fluidos infecciosos puedan penetrar en el cuerpo. En concreto, esto implica:

- emplear correctamente condones durante el sexo anal y oral
- no correrse en la boca del otro ni permitir que le entre esperma en la boca
- empleo de protectores de látex (el llamado Dental Dam) durante el sexo oral con mujeres
- practicar el sexo anal con la mano sólo con uñas cortadas y limadas y con guantes de látex
- evitar el contacto de esperma, sangre o segregación vaginal con heridas abiertas.

Los condones deberían ser de calidad comprobada y especialmente resistentes ('extra strong'). Hay que mantenerlos alejados del calor, del frío y del sol. Es importante emplearlos únicamente con lubricantes solubles en agua, ya que lubrificantes a base de grasas (como también cremas, untos o grasas) pueden dañar los condones y dejarlos permeables. Personas con alergias al látex pueden emplear condones de poliuretano (que por cierto suelen ser más caros). Fuera del cuerpo humano, el virus del HIV no puede sobrevivir durante mucho tiempo. No obstante, antes de que los utilice otra persona, hay que limpiar siempre bien los accesorios empleados (como por ejemplo consoladores, etc.). Teniendo siempre presente estas 'reglas de sexo seguro', el riesgo de una infección con el virus del HIV se puede reducir considerablemente. Sin embargo, cierto riesgo nunca se puede descartar del todo. A la mayoría de las personas no se les nota la infección exteriormente. Por ello, en caso de actividades sexuales con personas no conocidas, siempre hay que contar con la posibilidad de que sean portadoras del virus y protegerse de un posible contagio. Esto también concierne a personas HIV-positivas, ya que una infección adicional con virus HIV de diferentes cepas puede influir de forma negativa en el desarrollo de la enfermedad.

5. Posibles terapias de HIV y SIDA

Para el tratamiento de una infección del virus HIV existen varios medicamentos (los llamados medicamentos antiretrovirales) que cohiben la multiplicación de los virus. Generalmente se combinan varios de estos medicamentos para hacerlos más eficaces y para evitar que los virus se vuelvan inmunes a un medicamento, lo cual sin embargo no se puede imposibilitar del todo. Los medicamentos antiretrovirales tienen que tomarse continua y regularmente, ya que retardar o pausar las tomas puede restringir considerablemente los posibles efectos de la terapia. Por ello, la toma de los medicamentos tiene que adaptarse perfectamente al transcurso normal del día a día de cada paciente. Sólo el médico debe decidir cuándo iniciar dichas terapias.
Los medicamentos para el HIV no pueden liberar al paciente del virus, pero pueden permitir que el sistema inmunológico se mejore, alargando de esta forma considerablemente la esperanza de vida del paciente. Incluso si, gracias a la terapia, el virus ya no se puede detectar en la sangre del paciente, continúa habiendo riesgo de contagio de la infección.
Son múltiples las posibles terapias para las enfermedades que suelen acompañar la infección del virus del HIV. En caso de problemas o enfermedades es aconsejable consultar a un médico a tiempo. En muchos países ya existen organizaciones de autoayuda y centros de información y asesoramiento que dan apoyo a personas con problemas psicológicos, sociales o financieros a causa de su infección del virus del HIV o la enfermedad del SIDA.

6. Viajar y SIDA

Ya que el virus que provoca el SIDA está extendido por todo el mundo, las 'reglas de sexo seguro' también deben seguirse en el extranjero. Como en algunos países es relativamente difícil adquirir los condones adecuados y de una calidad aceptable, es aconsejable llevarlos desde el país de partida.
Personas HIV-positivas o enfermas del SIDA deberían llevar consigo una provisión lo suficientemente grande de medicamentos antiretrovirales. Es menester considerar que algunos medicamentos no deben exponerse al calor, al frío o a la luz solar y que han de mantenerse en un lugar seco para que no caduquen antes de tiempo. Como tienen que tomarse siguiendo un horario estricto, es necesario considerar posibles diferencias horarias al programar las diferentes tomas. Sobre todo en los países del trópico, hay una gran cantidad de agentes patógenos prácticamente desconocidos en otros países. Debido a ello, especialmente las personas HIV-positivas cuyo sistema inmunológico está dañado, pueden contraer enfermedades graves. Hay que consultar al médico sobre las medidas de protección aconsejables y la conveniencia de vacunas, ya que pueden variar según el caso. Existen eficaces medicamentos que se aplican sobre la piel para protegerse de las picaduras de insectos. Además, es aconsejable llevar ropa que cubra los brazos y las piernas. En los viajes deberían llevarse medicamentos para, por ejemplo, náuseas, diarrea y dolor de cabeza, así como protección solar, que sean compatibles con la medicación que se esté tomando. Por ello es recomendable consultar a un médico competente antes del viaje. Debe comprobarse antes del viaje si el seguro de enfermedad existente cubre asistencia médica, etc. en el extranjero. Seguros de viaje contratados para este fin, muchas veces no cubren los gastos en caso de enfermedades ya diagnosticadas antes del viaje, o si la necesidad de asistencia médica durante el viaje era previsible. Algunos países niegan la entrada al país a personas infectadas con el virus HIV. Por ello, es aconsejable informarse sobre los actuales reglamentos de inmigración durante los preparativos del viaje. La dirección de la embajada competente y la de un médico que hable tu lengua pueden ser de gran ayuda en casos de emergencia.

7. Por cierto...

Hay una serie de otras enfermedades de transmisión sexual, como por ejemplo la hepatitis, la gonorrea, la sífilis, condilomas, etc., que generalmente se pueden evitar con las mencionadas prácticas de 'sexo seguro'. Hay vacunas para las formas A y B de la hepatitis. Una vacuna para el SIDA todavía no existe.

Dr. med. Martin W. Eichenlaub

Benvenuti alla nuove SPARTACUS

Premessa

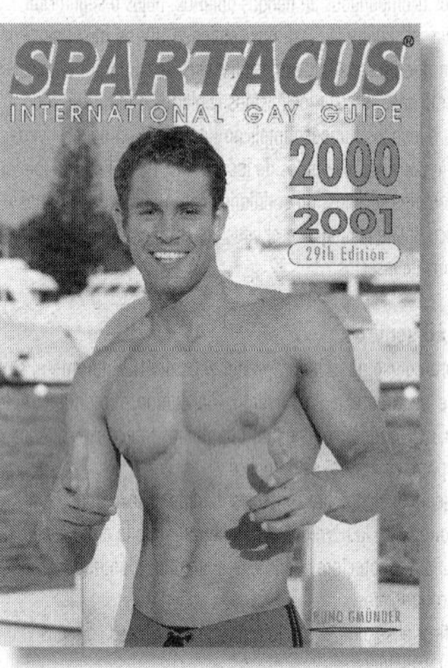

L'anno 2000 è cominciato con feste spettacolari in tutto il mondo. Il mondo gay certamente continuerà a festeggiare. Tra gli eventi più importanti di quest'anno ci sono

- Il "Mardi Gras" dal 11 febbraio al 4 marzo a Sydney. Ulteriori informazioni nel website www.mardigras.com.au
- Gli "Eurogames" saranno a Zurigo dal 1 al 4 giugno
- Che coincidenza che, oltre il Giubileo della chiesa cattolica, il primo Gay World Pride avrà luogo a Roma dal 1 al 9 Luglio!
- E non dimentichiamo che più di 50 feste per il Gay Pride saranno organizzate tra febbraio e novembre in tutto il mondo.

Allora, ci troviamo di fronte a un anno di vacanze molto interessante e pieno di eventi e speriamo che SPARTACUS vi fornisca sempre le informazioni necessarie.
Per l'aggiornamento di questa edizione ci hanno aiutato le numerose reazioni e proposte da parte dei lettori. Così, date anche voi il vostro contributo affinché SPARTACUS resti anche in futuro il guida più attuale del mondo gay!

Briand Bedford
REDATTORE CAPO

Come utilizzare lo SPARTACUS

Lo SPARTACUS è ordinato secondo i nomi inglesi dei paesi. Fanno eccezione gli stati e territori dei Caraibi, che abbiamo raggruppato in ordine alfabetico sotto la „C" come „Caribbean". Sotto il nome di un paese sono elencate le città in ordine alfabetico. ECCEZIONE: l'Australia, il Canada e gli USA. Per un migliore orientamento questi ultimi vengono suddivisi secondo gli stati federali, i territori e le province a cui corrispondono le città in ordine alfabetico.

Per ulteriori chiarimenti è utile usare l'indice a pagina 1298, dove i nomi di tutti i paesi sono elencati in lingua tedesca, inglese, francese e spagnolo in ordine alfabetico.

Abbiamo previsto un' inserzione per ogni stato sovrano. In aggiunta ci sono inserzioni per tutti i territori dipendenti nel caso in cui esistino informazioni sulla situazione legale dei gay e/o dell'ambiente gay.

Sotto l' inserzione di un paese si trova il seguente schema:

la posizione geografica	➔	Western Europe
Initials indica l'abbreviazione comune del nome del paese	➔	Initials: UK / GB
Time indica il fuso orario	➔	Time: GMT
Country e Access Code: Il Country Code è il prefisso per telefonare dall'estero in questo stato. Con l'Access Code si raggiunge la rete internazionale da questo paese.	➔	☎ Country Code / Access Code: 44 / 00
Language indica le principali lingue	➔	Language: English
Area (qkm/sqm) è l'estensione territoriale del paese	➔	Area: 242,100 km² / 93,451 sq mi.
Currency è la moneta ufficiale del Paese	➔	Currency: 1 Pound Sterling (= 100 Pence)
Population indica il numero degli abitanti	➔	Population: 58,249,000
Capital è la capitale o la sede del governo	➔	Capital: London
Religions sono le religioni più diffuse	➔	Religions: 57% Anglicans, 15% other Protestants, 13% Catholics
Climate dà conguagli approssimativi sul clima.	➔	Climate: Moderate climate that is moderated by prevailing southwest winds over the North Atlantic Current. More than half of the days are overcast.
Important Gay Cities sono le città importanti per i gay	➔	Important Gay Cities: London, Manchester, Brighton, Edinburgh

Nel prologo successivo facciamo cenno alle norme legali, se sono significative per i gay. Lo SPARTACUS fornisce anche brevi informazioni sul paese e la sua gente.

Raccomandiamo assolutamente di osservare anche il testo nazionale. Là si trovano tutte le organizzazioni o ditte di importanza nazionale.

La selezione seguente avviene a seconda delle città.

Per favore trarre il prefisso / CAP di una città dall'intestazione della città, altrimenti dai singoli elenchi. Gli elenchi sono suddivisi in rubriche.

Ogni singolo elenco contiene il nome ❶, i codici SPARTACUS ❷, orari di apertura ❸, l'indirizzo / l'indirizzo postale ❹, i numeri telefonici ❺ e ulteriori spiegazioni.

❶ ❷ ❸

Café Spartacus, (B bf f G OS YG), 10-2h,
Spartacusstraße 123, 10000 Spartacus-City
☎ 123 45 67

❺ ❹

Abbiamo bisogno del Suo aiuto. Per poter tenere le nostre segnalazioni allo stato più attuale possibile, sono per noi importanti le Sue esperienze personali. Per favore utilizzi per la Sua posta informativa la User's Information Card che si trova alla fine di questo fascicolo dello SPARTACUS. Naturalmente le spese di spedizione vanno a carico del destinatario.

In caso vengano fornite informazioni su di un locale interessante per gay, fate attenzione per favore ad ogni dettaglio. Come minimo abbiamo bisogno di: nome, persona da contattare, indirizzo (incl. città e pease!) e telefono/fax. A questo scopo sono idonei biglietti da visita. Quante più informazioni ci fornite, tanto meglio.

Se fosse dirigente di una ditta o di un'istituzione non commerciale, allora non dimentichi di informarci regolarmente. Ci rallegriamo se ci potesse fornire anche delle informazioni generali su di un paese, una regione o una città.

Vi preghiamo di inviare le Vostre informazioni al seguente indirizzo:
BRUNO GMÜNDER VERLAG GmbH – SPARTACUS-Redaktion
Postfach 61 01 04 • D-10921 Berlin • GERMANY

CODES

!	un dovere per il visitatore internazionale
A	esposizione d'arte
AC	aria condizionata
AYOR	a vostro rischio e pericolo
B	bar
bf	colazione
CC	vengono accettate le principali carte di credito
D	discoteca
DR	darkroom
E	pubblico elegante
F	ristorante
G	esclusivamente gay
GLM	exclusivamente gay e lesbiche
H	alloggio
LJ	per amanti del feticcio
MA	tutte le età
MG	gay di media età
msg	possibilità di massaggi
N	località con gente del quartiere
NG	non per forza gay, ma interessante
NU	possibilità di nudismo
OG	gay piuttosto anziani
OS	posti all'aperto; caffé lungo la strada, terrazza, giardino
P	club privato / controlli severi
p	bisogna suonare
pi	piscina
R	frequentato anche da gigolò
S	shows/spettacoli
SNU	stripshows
STV	travestie show
sa	sauna finlandese
sb	bagni a vapore
sol	solario
TV	frequentato anche da travestiti
VS	video
WE	aperto soprattutto a fine settimana
wh	whirlpool/jacuzzi
WO	possibilità di fare body-building
YG	gay giovani (18-28)

Codici in lettere minuscole significano in generale una limitazione.

Informazioni

1. Prefazione

I primi casi di AIDS (Sindrome da Immunodeficienza Acquisita, dall'inglese "Acquired Immunodeficiency Syndrome") sono stati resi noti nel 1981. Da allora l'AIDS è una delle malattie a trasmissione sessuale più frequenti che fin'ora, nonostante ci siano terapie efficaci, non si può guarire. Quindi, è ancora più importante la prevenzione contro la diffusione della malattia. Per una prevenzione coronata da successo la gente dev'essere informata bene su come si trasmette il virus. Inoltre ci vogliono informazioni sulla malattia "AIDS" per poter diminuire le paure ingiustificate ed i pregiudizi nei rapporti con i malati. Nel 2000 ci saranno approssimativamente tra 30 e 40 millioni di persone in tutto il mondo contagiate dal virus che causa l'AIDS.

2. Cos'è l'AIDS?

AIDS è una malattia infettiva e viene causata da un virus chiamato HIV. Il virus HIV attacca il sistema immunitario indebolendo le difese immunitarie contro virus, batteri, protozoi e funghi. Una persona affetta dall'AIDS è - rispetto a una persona sana - maggiormente esposta alle infezioni. Il virus può però causare anche altri disturbi nel corpo quali p.e. dermatosi e nevrosi. Un'infezione da HIV può perfino causare tumori.

Dopo esser entrato nel corpo, il virus attacca alcune cellule del sistema immunitario causando un mutamento del ricambio del tessuto cellulare a suo favore. Così il virus si moltiplica dentro le cellule fino a distruggerle. Le cellule difensive del sistema immunitario che non sono contagiate da HIV tentano di vincere il virus. Però, è impossibile per il sistema immunitario distruggere i virus completamente.

7 su 8 persone che risultano contagiate da HIV si accorgono di sintomi non-specifici di malattie influenzali, come p.e. la febbre, l'infiammazione della gola, l'eruzione cutanea e il rigonfiamento delle ghiandole linfatiche. Questi sintomi durano da pochi giorni a due settimane prima di scomparire. Poi la persona contagiata da HIV non ha più disturbi per il momento. Questa "fase asintomatica" può durare per periodi di tempo diversi, al solito per alcuni anni. Nel caso che i virus prendano il sopravvento nel corpo, il sistema immunitario dell'uomo crolla. Nasce poi la fase in cui si diagnostica l'AIDS, la fase che è caratterizzata da infezioni gravi come la Sarcoma di Kaposi o la Toxoplasmos, un protozoo che colpisce il cervello, l'occhio e il polmone. Alla fine la malattia ha esito letale.

L'infezione da HIV può essere individuata con il test di sieroposività, quindi attraverso un semplice esame del sangue. Il test, però, è significativo solo se effettuato a distanza di tre mesi dal momento del contagio (il cosìdetto "periodo finestra"). Chi è contagiato, risulta positivo al test diagnostico, altrimenti negativo.

3. Le vie di trasmissione di HIV

Di principio è valido che il virus può essere trasmesso tramite il sangue, lo sperma, il secreto vaginale e il latte materno. Se p.e. una piccola ferita o una mucosa vengono a contatto con il sangue o con lo sperma contagiati, il virus potrebbe entrare nel sangue e causare l'infezione da HIV. Dunque, è importante evitare il contatto con questi liquidi biologici.

La via più diffusa di trasmissione è sicuramente quella attraverso i rapporti sessuali. I rapporti sessuali a rischio sono la penetrazione vaginale e anale senza preservativo (rischiosi per tutti e due i partner), ma anche la stimolazione orale del pene (pompino) e quella dell'organo genitale femminile sono a rischio se lo sperma o le secrezioni vaginali entrano nella bocca. Ci

sono tuttavia altri modi di trasmissione, sia per "via ematica" (scambio di aghi e siringhe infette tra tossicodipendenti) sia per "via verticale" (dalla madre al figlio durante la gravidanza, al momento del parto o durante l'allattamento).
Il rischio è ancora più alto quando esiste un'infiammazione degli organi genitali con piccole ferite, essudazione o secrezione di pus.
Non è possibile la trasmissione attraverso la saliva, le lacrime o il sudore a causa della scarsa quantità del virus HIV che si trova in essi. Tale infezione non si può contrarre nemmeno attraverso baci, nell'uso in comune di bicchieri, stoviglie o di vestiti, in piscina, nelle saune o nei bagni né attraverso insetti. Senza correre alcun rischio è possibile toccare la maniglia della porta, la cornetta del telefono etc. e - nel vivere insieme - abbracciarsi e darsi la mano.

4. Safer sex

Per poter proteggersi da un'infezione nei rapporti sessuali, è necessario prendere in considerazione alcune regole di comportamento (le regole di "safer sex") per evitare l'assorbimento di liquido biologico contagiato. Concretamente ci vuole:

- l'uso appropriato di preservativi nei rapporti anali e orali
- non lasciar entrare sperma nella bocca del partner
- l'uso di anticoncezionali in lattice (cosidetto Dental Dam) per le donne nel rapporto orale
- il rapporto anale eseguito con la mano richiede le unghia corte e i guanti di gomma
- evitare il contatto di sperma, di sangue e di secrezione vaginale con le piccole ferite

Il preservativo dev'essere di buona qualità e abbastanza resistente ("extra strong"). È bene conservarlo in un "luogo adatto" e proteggerlo dal calore, dal freddo e dai raggi solari. Si deve usare solo con gel a base d'acqua (lubrificanti idrosolubili), visto che con gel a base di grasso (anche creme e grassi vari) possono danneggiare il preservativo. Se si è allergici al lattice si possono usare preservativi di poliuretano che però spesso sono più cari.
Al di fuori del corpo umano l'HIV ha vita breve. Tuttavia prima di usare un vibratore altrui, questi deve essere ben pulito.
Se si rispettano queste regole del "safer sex" il rischio di trasmissione dell'HIV si riduce considerevolmente, sebbene un margine di rischio resta comunque.
Nella maggior parte dei casi, un'infezione da HIV non si nota. Per questo si dovrebbe partire dal presupposto che il partner occasionale potrebbe essere sieropositivo e quindi proteggersi da un'eventuale infezione. Questo vale anche per le persone già sieropositive, visto che un'ulteriore infezione potrebbe peggiorare il corso della malattia.

5. Possibilità di trattamento dell'HIV e dell'AIDS

Per il trattamento dell'HIV ci sono diversi medicinali (cosidetti antiretrovirali) che inibiscono l'estensione del virus. In genere questi medicinali vengono combinati insieme nella terapia e così facendo si rafforza la loro efficacia e si cerca di impedire che i virus si riproducano. Inoltre con la combinazione di vari medicinali si evita che i virus possano eventualmente diventare insensibili a un certo medicinale. Questi medicinali antiretrovirali devono essere presi a lungo termine, regolarmente e con costanza. Una eventuale interruzione potrebbe influire negativamente sul successo della terapia. La somministrazione dei medicinali deve quindi essere ben scandita e adattata nel corso della giornata. Solo un medico può decidere quando bisogna che si cominci con una simile terapia.
I medicinali contro l'HIV non eliminano del tutto il virus, tuttavia possono procurare una distinzione del sistema immunitario e possono allungare il periodo di vita. Anche nel caso in cui, grazie alla terapia, l'HIV non dovesse più essere riscontrato nel sangue, resta sempre e comunque il rischio di contagiare l'infezione. Le possibilità di trattamento per le malattie correlate all'HIV sono molteplici. Nel caso di comparsa di disturbi si deve contattare in tempo un medico.
In molti paesi ci sono già organizzazioni di solidarietà e di consulenza che danno un supporto psicologico, sociale e finanziario, qualora questi ultimi abbiano un rapporto più o meno diretto con l'infezione da HIV o l'AIDS.

6. Viaggiare con l'AIDS

Poiché l'AIDS è diffusa in tutto il mondo, le regole del "safer sex" dovrebbero essere rispettate anche all'estero. Visto che in alcuni paesi i preservativi sono difficili da reperire e qualora reperibili di scarsa qualità, si consiglia di portarseli dal proprio paese.
Le persone infette da HIV e i malati di AIDS dovrebbero stare attenti anche a portare con sé una sufficiente scorta di medicinali antiretrovirali. È anche utile sapere che alcuni medicinali sono sensibili al calore, al freddo e alla luce e devono essere tenuti in posti asciutti e quindi non umidi, affinché mantengano la loro efficacia. Tenuto in considerazione il fatto che questi medicinali vanno presi secondo fisse e costanti scadenze di tempo, bisogna tener conto delle differenze di fasce d'orario nei vari paesi e conseguentemente adeguarsici e rispettare quindi l'orario di somministrazione.
Specialmente nei paesi tropicali c'è una cernita di fattori a rischio. E particolarmente per i sieropositivi, il quale sistema immunitario è già danneggiato, questi possono procurare gravi malattie. Come ci si può proteggere o se è ragionevole vaccinarsi va valutato singolarmente da caso a caso. Contro le punture di insetti ci sono efficaci medicinali che si possono spalmare sulla pelle; si consiglia quindi di indossare vestiti che coprono braccia e gambe. In viaggio è anche consigliabile portare medicinali contro p.e. nausea, diarrea e mal di testa, così come creme solari, e il tutto che sia compatibile con i medicinali che già si assumono. Si consiglia, quindi, in ogni caso di consultare uno specialista prima del viaggio.
Prima di qualsiasi viaggio bisogna anche assicurarsi se l'assicurazione offra le sue prestazioni anche all'estero. Alcune assicurazioni di viaggio spesso pagano solo se la malattia si è manifestata in viaggio e non prima e quindi anche quando non fosse necessario un trattamento durante il viaggio.
In alcuni paesi ci sono limitazioni di viaggio per persone sieropositive. Per questo si consiglia di informarsi in tempo circa l'attuale situazione delle limitazioni in questi paesi. Un indirizzo di un'ambasciata o di un dottore che parli la nostra lingua nel paese di destinazione può essere molto utile.

7. Inoltre ...

C'è una profusione di altre malattie trasmissibili sessualmente come l'epatite, la gonorrea, la sifilide, la condiloma acuminato e altre, che si possono prevenire con le regole del "safer sex". Contro l'epatite A e B ci si può fare vaccinare. Contro l'AIDS purtroppo ancora non esiste un vaccino.

Dr. med. Martin W. Eichenlaub

日本語

●はじめに

スパルタクスは、ブルーノ・グミュンダー社がお届けする、ゲイのための旅行ガイドです。世界中のゲイ・シーン最新情報（バー、クラブ、宿泊所、援助団体、グループなどが 25,000 以上、その上、各国のインフォメーションやゲイに関する法律、便利なマップ）を満載し、ますます内容が充実したスパルタクス第 28 版を、ぜひ皆さんの旅にお役立てください。

編集部長　Robin Rauch

●本誌の使い方

スパルタクスは国ごとに構成されています。それぞれの国もしくは独立した地域は英語名称で書かれ、アルファベット順に並んでいます。各国の欄は、さらにアルファベット順にそれぞれの都市に分類されますが、オーストラリア、カナダ、アメリカ合衆国の場合は、まず地域や州に分かれ、その後に都市が続きます。後ろの Index には、検索のために、国や都市の名前が英語、ドイツ語、フランス語、スペイン語で表記してあります。

●国のインフォメーション

・地理的位置

・Initials	国の略称
・Time	世界標準時
・Access Code	国際電話認識番号
・Country Code*	国番号
・Language	主要言語
・Area (qkm/sqm)	国土面積
・Currency	通貨
・Population	人口
・Capital	首都
・Religions	主な宗教
・Climate	気候
・Important gay cities	重要都市

国について、ゲイに関する法律、ゲイ運動やライフスタイル、ゲイ・シーンなどを前書きで簡単に説明してあります。グループ、組織、企業、雑誌は、その国のゲイ・カルチャーにとって重要な機関や刊行物です。ご一読下さい。

●店名欄・データ欄の読み方

各都市の市外局番と郵便番号は、都市名の隣もしくは店名欄・データ欄の中に載っています。店名欄には　①名前　②スパルタクス・コード　③住所　④電話　⑤営業時間、コメントが次のように記されています。

①　②　⑤
Cafe Spartacus (B bf f g S YG) 10-12
Spartacusstrasse123 00000 Spartacus-City ③
123 45 67 ④

●スパルタクス・コード

!	旅行者必見
A	展覧会
AC	エアコン付き
AYOR	各自のリスクを伴う、場合によっては危険
B	バー
bf	朝食
CC	主なクレジット・カード使用可
D	ディスコ
DR	ダークルーム
E	エレガントな客層
F	レストラン
G	ゲイだけ
g	一部ゲイ
GLM	ゲイ＆レズビアンだけ
glm	一部ゲイ＆レズビアン
H	宿泊所
LJ	フェチむけ
MA	幅広い年齢層
MG	30 代、40 代のゲイ
msg	マッサージ有り
N	ネーバーフッド・バー、地元の客
NG	ゲイ専門ではないが、興味深いところ
NU	ヌード・ビーチ / 全裸で水泳可
OG	比較的年輩のゲイ
OS	屋外、ストリート・カフェ、テラス、庭
P	プライベート・クラブ / 厳しいチェック
pl	プール
R	ウリ専も
S	ショー / イベント
SNU	ストリップ・ショー
STV	ドラッグ・クイーン・ショー
sa	フィンランド・サウナ
sb	スチーム・サウナ
sol	ソラリアム / 日焼けサロン
TV	女装者も
VS	ビデオ上映
W	車椅子での入場可
WE	主に週末営業の店
wh	ジェット・バス / ジャクージ

WO ボディビルディング可
YG ヤング・ゲイ (18〜28歳)
小文字のコードは、制限があることを示します。

●ご意見、情報をお寄せ下さい。
巻末のカード User's Information をお使いになれば、切手は必要ありません。

送り先 BRUNO GMUENDER VERLAG
SPARTACUS-Redaktion
Postfach 61 01 04
D-10921 Berlin
Germany
Tel: +49/(0)30/615 00 3-42
Fax: +49/(0)30/615 91 34

●エイズについて
エイズは、HIV というウイルスに感染して起きる病気です。エイズウイルスとも呼ばれている HIV は、体を病気から守っている免疫システムを破壊し、生命を脅かす危険なウイルスです。エイズウイルスは精液、血液、膣分泌液、母乳を通して感染しますが、男性同性愛者においては、コンドームなしのアナルセックスが主要感染ルートとなっています。HIV 感染からエイズが発病するまでの期間は、個人によって差があり、必ず全てのキャリアが発病するかどうかは、まだわかっていません。ただし、二次感染したり、性感染症など別の感染症にかかると、発病が早まります。人間の体には、外から入ってきたウイルスや細菌などの病原体と戦い、病気から体を守る免疫システムがあります。免疫細胞群の本体はさまざまな種類の白血球で、中でも T4 リンパ球（ヘルパー T 細胞とも呼ばれます）は、司令官といえる細胞ですが、HIV はまさにこの T4 リンパ球に巣くって破壊します。その結果、体はあらゆる病原体の侵入に対して全く無抵抗な状態になってしまいます。一般に、T4 リンパ球が減り続け、免疫システムが壊れてしまうと、エイズを発病します。エイズになると、肺、皮膚、胃腸、口の中、肝臓、神経など、体中のあらゆる場所が病原体に侵され、「日和見感染」と呼ばれるさまざまな重い感染症や悪性腫瘍を起こします。通常、T4 リンパ球は、1mm^3 の血液中に 700 個〜1000 個ありますが、エイズを発病する頃にはそれが 200 個以下に減り、最後にはほとんど姿を消してしまいます。現在有効なエイズの治療薬は非常に高価です。最近開発された 3 種類の治療薬を併用するセラピー「3 剤併用療法」は、アメリカ合衆国において薬代のみで年間 10,000 ドルもの費用がかかります。しかし、実際にはほとんどの国で、エイズ・キャリア (HIV 感染者) 一人当たりの治療費は、年間 100 ドル以下でしかありません。全エイズ患者の半数は、発病以前に HIV 抗体検査（エイズ・テスト）を受けるお金もない状態です。先進国では、3 剤併用療法のお陰で、昨年エイズで亡くなった人の数が減少しています。現在使われている治療薬は、ウイルスの増加を抑えエイズ発病を遅らせたり、エイズ患者の症状を軽くしたりすることで、大きな効果を発揮していますが、HIV 自体を殺す作用はありません。HIV の抑制には薬を常用しなければならず、キャリアが旅行をする際に、薬の効力が温度差によって失われるなど、さまざまな問題が生じてきます。詳細については「HIV 感染者へのトラベル・ヒント」をご参照ください。多くの国で、エイズに関しての相談は、公共団体、自治体、民間ボランティア団体などによって行われています。ほとんどのエイズ団体が、寄付から成り立っていることをご理解いただき、ご協力いただけると幸いです。

●セーフ・セックス
全世界の HIV 感染者数は、2300 万人以上にのぼり、100 万もの人が毎年エイズで死んでいます。エイズについて正しい知識を持ち、特に感染経路を見極めることは、全ての人にとって必要不可欠です。エイズは①誰もがかかる可能性のある病気で、特定のハイリスク・グループはありません。②エイズウイルスは、人から人へ、血液や性分泌液を通じて、直接体の中へ入ったときにうつります。③エイズの最大の感染ルートは不特定多数の相手との無防備なセックスです。特に第③のポイントはエイズがリスクのある「行為」によって感染する病気であることを示します。つまり、正しい知識に基づく行動や性行為によって、100% 予防することが出来るのです。セックスによる HIV の感染を防ぐには、コンドームは非常に有効な手段です。コンドームは HIV がパートナーの体内へ入るのを防ぎますが、最初の挿入の前に着用しないければ、効果がありません。コンドームのすべりを良くしたり、粘膜に擦り傷をつくったりするのを防ぐために、ワセリンやオイルは絶対に使わないでください。こうした油性のものは、ラテックス（コンドームの素材）の浸透性を高め、ウイルスがコンドームの膜を通り抜けてしまう恐れがあります。潤滑剤は必ず水溶性のものを使うようにしましょう。アナル・セックスの時に、必ずコンドームを使う習慣をつけましょう。コンドームは、傷つけないよう注意深く、正しく使い、パッケージの製造年月日にも注意しましょう。信頼できるパートナーを捜す、このことはあなたや相手にとって最大の予防につながります。相手とエイズやそのリスクについて話し合ったり、検査を受けたりすることは、2 人が安心してセックスを楽しむために何よりも大切な手続きです。コンドームなしのオーラルセックスは、射精しない限り、感染の危険はほとんどありません。精液が口の中に入った場合には、感染する可能性がありますので、注意してください。セックスを通じて感染する性感染症の予防には、HIV の予防と同じように、コンドームの使用が最も有効です。性感染症にかかると、性器や尿道や肛門にただれや炎症が起き、その部分の粘膜が充血して、ちょっとした刺激で破れやすくなります。そして、そういう傷口から、HIV が侵入し易くなります。男性の場合少量の膿がでて、パンツにシミがつくため、おかしいと感じたらパートナーと一緒に病院へ。性感染症は 2 人同時に治療しないと、なかなか退治できません。

● HIV 感染者へのトラベル・ヒント

HIV 感染者とエイズ発病者は、多くの国で法的にも社会的にも差別されています。ですから、旅行前に十分に下調べをするのが大切です。アメリカ合衆国のような国でも、感染者の入国を禁止していますし、無防備な性交渉をしたという理由で留置された例は、スエーデン以外の国にも見られます。不法移民者にも施療の権利を与えているフランスは例外です。ほとんどの旅行傷害保険は、HIV 感染に関し適用されません。

医療設備の充実していない場所への旅行は、抵抗力がとみに低下したエイズ・キャリアにとってリスクを伴います。現在、薬による治療を受けている人は、事前に主治医や専門家と以下の注意事項について、話し合いましょう。治療薬が飛行機の貨物室などで低温（あるいは高温）にさらされると効力を失う危険は？予防接種は？薬は、旅行に必要な分より、多めに処方してもらいましょう。主治医に治療薬の処方薬や緊急時の対応の仕方を書いてもらったり、現地の病院や医師の住所を聞くのも一考です。。スパルタクスの“Health Group”と“Help with Problems”のエイズ団体に連絡してインフォメーションを得るのもいいでしょう。入国時に問題が生じた場合に備え、エイズ団体の電話番号は常備しましょう。旅行中に病気になった時、直ちに帰国するのが最適の処置であるケースも少なくありません。格安チケットは予定変更の際に、高額のキャンセル料を要求される場合が多々あります。事前に旅行代理店で、追加料金や旅行損害保険の適応について確認しましょう。入国審査時に、エイズ治療薬が発見されにくいように、荷造りしましょう。アメリカを初め、エイズ・キャリアや患者の入国を規制する国に行くときは、薬をビタミン剤の瓶に詰め替えるなどなんらかの対処をした方が無難です。盗難や紛失の場合に備えて、全薬品を 1 つの鞄に入れるのは避けて下さい。治療薬が、現地で手に入る場合も、薬のクオリティーは国によって違います。安売り薬品や医薬品許可のない抗生物質などは、有効期限を過ぎていたり、薬効の疑わしいものが多いので、特に注意しましょう。これはコンドームと潤滑剤に関しても同じことが言えます。旅行先で感染するほとんどの病気は、飲料水や食べ物が原因です。現地人が口にする食べ物も、人により下痢、嘔吐、熱を引き起しかねません。飲料水は、市販のミネラル・ウオーターか、一度沸騰したものしか口にしないようにしましょう。食事は、生ものを避け、熱を通してあるか、作ってから時間が経ちすぎていないか確認してください。現地の伝染病は予防接種で防げます。医者や保健所で相談を受けましょう。外国には自国では非常に珍しい病気が存在するこもありますが、一般には、肝炎、小児麻痺、ジフテリアの予防で十分です。

Dr. Matthias Wienold

前言

一流的旅遊指南

SPARTACUS 男同性戀旅遊指南是由居世界領先地位的男同性戀「Bruno Gmünder」出版社出版。本旅遊指南可為您提供所需信息資料以計劃完善的旅遊行程；全球廣大同性戀界不斷走向新發展趨勢，您如果使用本旅遊指南，便可瞭解各種相關情況。

SPARTACUS 男同性戀旅遊指南可隨時提供最新動向，本書使用方法簡便，內容包括有兩萬五千餘行號地址，諸如酒吧、夜總會、酒店、支持同性戀者的組織和團體。在介紹各個國家情況時，本旅遊指南附有城市街道圖，一覽表，簡明説明資料，同時還解説同性戀者在各個國家中的法律地位。

SPARTACUS 男同性戀旅遊指南早已成為同性戀者旅遊和生活方式的代名詞了。

請諸位朋友們充分享用本書第二十八版！

Robin Rauch （羅賓・勞希）
總編輯

請各位朋友給我們大力支持！我們期望能夠隨時提供最新資訊，所以希望您們告訴我們您個人的相關經驗。請利用本旅遊指南後頁的使用者資訊卡，以與SPARTACUS編輯部聯係，不需張貼郵票。

郵寄此種資訊時，請務必註明相關細節。我們至少需要知道行號名稱、聯係人姓名、場所地址（包括國家名稱和城市）及電話和傳真號碼，寄該場所的名片當然最好，提供越多資訊資料越好。

您如果是某行號或其它機構的主管人，則請提供定期資訊資料。如果能提供關於某國家、地區或城市的一般性介紹，對我們也非常有用。

您可以來函到下列地址：

Bruno Gmünder Verlag GmbH
Spartacus-Redaktion
PO 61 01 04
D-10921 Berlin
Germany 德國
Tel: +49/(0)30/615 00 3-42
Fax: +49/(0)30/615 91 34

SPARTACUS 男同性戀旅遊指南使用方法

本書的基本編排是以國家的英文名稱來編輯，只有一個例外情況：加勒比海地區的國家和地區在「C」部分下按英文ABC一順序集中在一起（如英文之「Caribbean」），在每個國家的項目下再以城市名稱的 ABC 一順序排列。在澳洲、加拿大和美國各項目下，先按州、地區或省份排列再按城市名排列。
您如果不確定查閱方法，也可查本書索引中所有國家的英文、德文、法文和西班牙文的國家名稱，均以ABC一順序排列。
在本書中每一個主權國家有自己的編排項目，另外附上其它地區的同性戀者法律地位和同性戀界生活相關的資訊。

在每個國家主項目下，您可查詢下列資訊：
- 地理位置，
- Initials: 此為該國家的國際通用縮寫，
- Time: 時區，
- Country Code 和 Access Code: Country Code 是從國外打往該國家的國際電話區號，Access Code 是從該國家接入國際電話網的號碼，
- Language: 在該國家較通用的語言，
- Area: 國家的面積（平方公里／英、美里），
- Currency: 國家的正式貨幣，
- Population: 國家的人口數，
- Capital: 首都或政府所在地，
- Religions: 較普遍的宗教，
- Climate: 氣候情況簡介，
- Important gay cities: 對同性戀者較重要的城市。

接下來還有涉及同性戀生活的法律規定，本書也包括對各國家人民和風俗習慣的簡短解説。
請您務必注意各國家的開頭簡介，此處可瞭解到該國家中重要組織和行號情況。

其它更詳細解説再按城市順序排列：
每個城市的電話區號和郵編，請查詢該城市的標題行或各行號組織的單獨項目，地址按性質類別編排。
每個單獨項目包括下列資料：行號組織名稱、SPARTACUS代碼、地址（通信地址）、電話號碼、營業時間及其它解説。

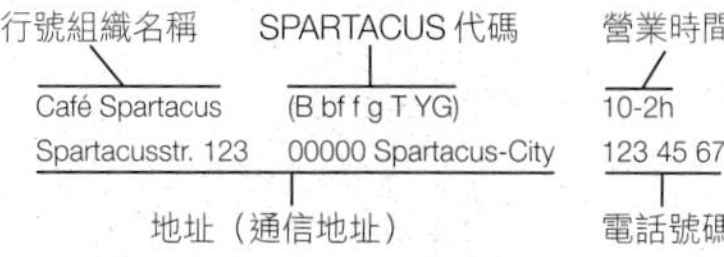

International

INTERNATIONAL ORGANISATIONS

Amnesty International
Homepage: www.amnestyinternational.com
This international organisation was launched in 1961. Strictly impartial and independant, the organisation lays emphasis on the protection of human rights. Amnesty International has further information on the world-wide legislation in respect to homosexuals. See their website for the address and telephone number of your local office of ai.

European Pride Organizers Association
c/o Hartmut Schönknecht, Elberfelder Straße 23 ✉10555 Berlin,Germany ☎ +49(0)30-392 53 11
Fax: +49(0)30-392 43 19
Voluntarily working European network of Lesbian & Gay Pride Organizations and licenser of the Europride title.

Eurpean Gay and Lesbian Sports Federation (EGLSF)
Den Haag, Netherland Breedstraat 28 ✉2513 TT
☎ +31 (70) 364 24 42

International Association of Gay Men and Lesbian Women (ILGA Administrative Office)
81 Rue du Marché au Charbon, ✉1000 Brussles Belgium
☎ +32 (2) 502 24 71. Fax: +32 (2) 502 24 71.
E-Mail: ilga@ilga.org
Homepage: www.ilga.org

International Association of Lesbian/Gay Pride Coordinators
USA 7985 Santa Monica Blvd, West Hollywood ✉CA 90046 ☎ +1-310-854-0271

International Gay & Lesbian Travel Association (IGLTA)
4331 North Federal Highway, Suite 304 ✉FL 33308 ☎ +1-954-776-2626 ☎ +1(800) 448-8550.
Fax: +1-954-776-3303 E-Mail: iglta@iglta.org
Homepage: www.iglta.org
IGLTA is an international network of travel industry business and professionals dedicated to the support of its members who have joined together to encourage gay travel throughout the world. IGLTA is committed to the welfare of gay and lesbian travelers, and to »shrinking the gay globe«. SPARTACUS is member of IGLTA.

PRIVATE ACCOMODATION

Lesbian & Gay Hospitality Exchange International,
PO Box 612, Station C ✉QC H2L 4K5 Montreal Canada
☎ +1-514-523 15 59 Fax: +1-514-523 15 59
E-Mail: lghei@odyssee.net Homepage: www.lghei.org
Non-profit home stay network, with 500 listings in 40 different countries.

Mi casa su casa (GLM)
PO Box 10327 ✉CA 94610 ☎ +1-510-531-4511 ☎ +1-800-215-2272 Fax: +1-510-531-4517 E-Mail: homeswap@aol.com
Homepage: www.well.com/user/homeswap
International home exchange and hospitality network.

SPORT GROUPS

Federation of Gay Games
584 Castro Street, Suite 343 ✉CA 94114
USA ☎ +1-415-6950-222

International Gay Bowling Organization
c/o Bill Harrison, 1284 West Jackson, ✉OH 44077 USA ☎ +1-216-357-5670

Albania

Southeast Europe
Initials: AL
Time: GMT +1
☎ Country Code / Access Code: 355 / 00
Language: Albanian, Greek
Area: 28,750 km² / 11,100 sq mi.
Currency: 1 Lek = 100 Qindarka
Population: 3.445.000
Capital: Tiranë
Religions: 70% Muslim, 30% Christians
Climate: Mild and moderate. Winters are cool, cloudy and wet, summers hot, clear and dry. The interior is cooler and wetter.

● In Albania homsexual acts are no longer punishable. Thanks to the work of the „Shoquata Gay Albania" group and also the ILGA which has it's offices in Brussels. The discussion surrounding the legal changes also helped increase awareness of homosexuality among the general public. Nevertheless, homophobia and ignorance are widespread among Albanians in general.

✱ In Albanien stehen homosexuelle Handlungen nicht mehr unter Strafe, was dem Einsatz der Gruppe „Shoqata Gay Albania" und der ILGA mit Sitz in Brüssel zu verdanken ist. Durch die Änderung des Sexualstrafrechts wurde das Thema Homosexualität in die Öffentlichkeit gerückt, jedoch begegnet ein Großteil der Bevölkerung diesem Thema noch immer mit Ablehnung und Ignoranz.

▲ En Albanie, les actes impudiques ne sont plus considérés comme un délit, ce qui est redevable à l'engagement du groupe „Snoqsta Gay Albania" et à l'ILGA siégeant à Bruxelles. Grâce à la modification du droit pénal relatif aux infractions contre les moeurs, le sujet de l'homosexualité est paru en public, mais ce sujet est encore tabou pour une grande partie de la population.

☆ Los actos homosexuales ya no están penados en Albania, gracias a los esfuerzos de la asociación „Shoqata Gay Albania" y de la ILGA con sede en Bruselas. Aunque este cambio legislativo despertó el interés público, la mayoría de los albanos sigue teniendo una actitud homófoba e ignorante acerca de los homosexuales.

❖ In Albania gli atti tra omosessuali non sono più considerati reato, grazie agli sforzi del gruppo „Shoqata Gay Albania" e dell'

ILGA di Bruxelles. Attraverso il cambiamento del diritto penale sessuale il dell'omosessualità è diventato di domonio pubblico,la popolazione in gran parte però si dimostra pur sempre sfavorevole ed ignorante verso questo tema.

NATIONAL GAY INFO

Gay Albania Foundation (A GLM MA p S)
P.O. Box 8299 Tirana ☎ +355 38 202 29 70 Fax: +355 42 305 06
Email: Gay_Albania@hotmail.com

Tiranë

HEALTH GROUPS

Action Plus
Spitali ☎ 355 53
AIDS information group affiliated with a Tirana hospital.

CRUISING

-Rruga „Deshmorët e 4 Shkurtit" (AYOR) (between Rruga „Myslym Shyri" and the River Lana)
-Park across from Hotel Dajiti (ayour) (evenings best)

Argentina

South America
Initials: ARG
Time: GMT -3
☎ Country Code / Access Code: 54 / 00
Language: Spanish (Castellano)
Area: 2,766,890 km² / 1,068,298 sq mi.
Currency: 1 Peso (arg$) = 100 Centavos.
Population: 36,265,463 (1998 est.)
Capital: Buenos Aires
Religions: 91 % Roman Catholic
Climate: Mostly moderate climate. The southeast is very dry, the southwest subantarctic.

● In Argentina homosexual acts are not in principle forebidden. Homosexual acts in public deemed to be against public morality may lead to arrest.
Under most circustances are the Argentinians liberally minded in the major cities with regard to gays. Buenos Aires has a many sides gay scene and is seen as the gay metropolis of South America. In other major cities, such as Rosario or Cordoba there continues to be a positive development of the gay movement. As in many other countries in rural districts the acceptance of homosexuality continues to be restrictive. Especially in rural areas of Argentina the Catholic Church has a major influence on the non-acceptance of homosexuality.

✸ In Argentinien sind homosexuelle Handlungen grundsätzlich nicht verboten. Vor allzu freizügigem Verhalten in der Öffentlichkeit sei jedoch gewarnt, da dies unter Umständen eine Verhaftung wegen „Verstoßes gegen die öffentliche Moral" zur Folge haben kann.
Im allegemeinen verhalten sich die Argentinier in den Großstädten Schwulen gegenüber recht liberal. Buenos Aires hat eine vielfältige schwule Szene, aber auch andere Großstädte wie Rosario oder Cordoba entwickeln sich zunehmend positiv. Wie in vielen Ländern ist auch in Argentinien die Akzeptanz von Homosexualität auf dem Lande bei weitem geringer. Gerade in ländlichen Gebieten hat die katholische Kirche starken Einfluß.

▲ En Argentine, les actes impudiques ne sont en principe pas interdits. Mais on doit toutefois vous avertir d'un comportement trop libre en public, étant donné que cela peut avoir éventuellement pour conséquence une arrestation pour cause de „dérogation aux lois qui intéressent les bonnes moeurs". Dans les grandes villes, les argentins se comportent généralement très libéralement envers les homosexuels. Buenos Aires a une scène homosexuelle variée, mais aussi d'autres grandes villes comme Rosario ou Cordoba se développent de plus en plus positivement. Comme dans de nombreux pays, l'homosexualité à la campagne et aussi en Argentine est loin d'être acceptée. N'oublions pas que l'église catholique a une forte influence, précisément dans les régions rurales.

☆ En Argentina no existe ninguna ley que prohibe las relaciones homosexuales. Sin embargo, no se recomienda un comportamiento demasiado abierto en público, ya que este podría causar una detención por „ofensa a la moral pública" En general los argentinos de las ciudades grandes se muestran relativamente liberales con los homosexuales. Buenos Aires ofrece un variado ambiente gay, pero también ciudades como Rosario y Cordoba se desarollan en este sentido muy positivamente. Como en la mayoría de los paises, la acceptación de los homosexuales entre la población rural es mucho más reducida. Argentina no es ninguna excepción, ya que en los pueblos la iglesia católica sigue teniendo una fuerte influencia.

❖ Generalmente gli atti tra omosessuali in Argentina non sono proibiti, è meglio però evitare un comportamento troppo libero in pubblico, perché ciò potrebbe portare all'arresto per „lesione della pubblica morale". Generalmente gli argentini nelle grande città si dimostrano abbastanza liberali verso i gay. Per i gay, Buenos Aires offre varie possibilità, ma anche altre città come Rosario o Cordoba stanno sviluppandosi in modo positivo. Come in altri paesi, in posti di campagna l'omosessualità è meno accettata. Soprattutto nelle zone rurali la chiesa cattolica esercita un forte influsso.

Buenos Aires - Capital Federal
☎ 011

● Buenos Aires is developing itself into the gay metropolis of South America. Compared with other cities in South America, Buenos Aires seems to be traditionally much more European and the people are open minded and tolerant. The gay tourist has a wide choice of bars and discos and something to suit every taste. Night life begins late; hardly anybody goes out before 2 am and the discos tend to close around 7 am. Buenos Aires will, however set you back a bit. A visit to a disco will cost around $ 15.

✱ Buenos Aires ist im Begriff, sich zu der schwulen Metropole Südamerikas zu entwickeln. Im Vergleich zu anderen Städten des Kontinents gibt sich Buenos Aires traditionell sehr europäisch, die Menschen gelten als weltoffen und tolerant.
Der schwule Tourist hat hier die Qual der Wahl, unter einer Vielzahl von Bars und Discos auszuwählen. Die Szene wird kaum einen Wunsch unerfüllt lassen. Das Nachtleben beginnt spät: Vor 1 Uhr ist es in den meisten Bars noch ruhig, die Discotheken füllen sich nicht vor 2 Uhr und schließen in der Regel erst um 7 Uhr früh. Allerdings ist Buenos Aires auch ein teures Pflaster, der Eintritt in die Disco kann durchaus $ 15 kosten.

▲ Buenos Aires est en train de se développer comme la métropole des homosexuels de l'Amérique du Sud. Comparée aux autres villes du continent, Buenos Aires ressemble beaucoup à une ville traditionnelle européenne, les gens passent pour être compréhensifs et tolérants. Le touriste homosexuel a ici l'embarras du choix : il est, en effet, pas facile de choisir parmi la multiplicité des bars et discothèques. La scène est à même de satisfaire tous les désirs. La vie nocturne commence tard: jusqu'à 1 heure du matin, tous est encore tranquille dans la plupart des bars, les discothèques ne se remplissent pas avant 2 heures et ferment en général seulement vers 7 heure du matin. A Buenos Aires, il est vrai, la vie est chère, l'entrée dans une discothèque peut facilement coûter $ 15.

❖ Buenos Aires está a punto de convertirse en la indiscutible capital gay de Sudamérica. En comparación con otras ciudades del continente, Buenos Aires se mostró tradicionalmente muy europeo y sus habitantes tienen fama de ser abiertos y tolerantes. El turista gay tiene aqui la dificultad de elegir entre los innumerables bares y discotecas que ofrecen un ambiente que satisface cualquier típo de deseo. La vida nocturna empieza muy tarde: la mayoría de los bares no se animan antes de la 1 de la madrugada, las discoteca no empiezan ha llenarse antes de las 2 y no suelen cerrar sus puertas antes de las 7 de la mañana. Pero Buenos Aires también es una ciudad bastante cara, donde nadie se extraña en pagar $15 por la entrada en una discoteca.

☆ Buenos Aires sta sviluppandosi alla metropoli gay dell'America meridionale. Rispetto ad altre città di questo continente la tradizione di Buenos Aires assomiglia più a quella europea, la gente viene considerata cosmopolita e aperta. Il turista gay soffre dell'imbarazzo della scelta tra una grande varietà di bar e discoteche che soddisfanno quasi tutti i gusti. La vita notturna comincia tardi: Prima dell'una nei bar è ancora abbastanza tranquillo, e nelle discoteche, che chiudono alle sette, ci si va solo dopo le due. Buenos Aires è comunque molto cara, l'entrata in discoteca costa circa 15 dollari.

NATIONAL GAY INFO

La Otra Guia
PO Box 78 Suc. Olivos ✉1636
Free gay monthly agenda Email: loguia@satlink.com

NX
Av. Callao 339, Pisos 4 y 5 ✉1022 ☎ 437 303 66
Argentinas gay monthly magazine with agenda map.
Fax: 4375 0399 Email: nexo@nexo.org
Homepage: www.nexo.org

GAY INFO

Centro de documentación gay-lesbico
Paraná 157, F ✉1017 ☎ 437 389 55 Fax: 437 389 55
La Hora
PO Box 12, suc 27 B ✉1427

TOURIST INFO

Oficina Central de Información Turística
Avenida Santa Fe 883 ✉1059 ☎ 431 222 32

BARS

Bach Bar (B d GLM s WE YG) Tue-Sun 22- ?
José A. Cabrena 4390 ✉1414 *(Between Julián Alvarez & Lavallevja)* ☎ 438 828 75
Shows at Firday nights, Karaoke at Sunday nights.
Downtown Cafe (AC B CC d F G MA s snu) Thu & Fri 22-03:00h, Sat -07:00h, Sun 20 23:00h
Alsina 975 *(Metro. Av. de Mayo)* ☎ 433 461 10
Gasoil New Generation (AC B Glm MG S snu)
Mon-Sun 23-? h Wed closed. Shows 01:30h
Bulnes 1250/Avenida Córdoba ✉ 1035 ☎ 486 440 56
Hall Cine Café (B G VS) Mon-Thu 10-04:00h, Fri & Sat 10-06:00h, Sun 13-04:00h
Av. Roque Saénz Pena 1150 ☎ 4382 7934
Café-bar in the hall of a xxx-cinema
In Vitro (B G MG S YG) Mon-Sun 23-? h.
Shows 24h and 01:30h
Azcuénaga 1007/Av. M. T. de Alvear ✉10115 ☎ 482 409 32
Incognito (B glm MA R TV) 22-06:00h
Av. Scalabrini Ortiz 1721 / Costa Rica ☎ 4833 3543
Judas (AC B CC F G MA OS S) 18-4 h, Restaurant 22-1 h
Anchorena 1158 ✉1425 *(Metro Puerreyolon)* ☎ 496 407 79
Dinner 22-01:00h. Show every night from 01:00 h .
The New Manhattan (B G S MG) Mon-Sun 22-? h. Shows 01:00h
Anchorena 1347 *(between Avenida Santa Fé and Charcas)*
☎ 482 485 50
Sagas (AC B GLM MA MG S SNU) 23-?, closed Thu.
Anchorena 1169 ✉1425 *Show: 1.30 h*
Scream (B G MA)
Cerrito 306 ☎ 4382 5253
Sitges (B d GLM MG s YG) Wed-Sun 22.30-? h
Av. Córdoba 4119 ☎ 486 137 63
Table telephones for quick contacts
Tacla (AC B bf CC DR F G MA S SNU VS)
Avenida de Mayo 1114 ✉1085 *Subway A: Lima Sation, Bus: 86, 105,*
☎ 438 187 64

DANCECLUBS

Angel's (B D G MA r snu WE) Thu-Sun 0.30-? h
Viamonte 2168 ✉1056
Contramano (AC B D G li MA OG r) Wed-Fri 0-5 h, Sat-Sun 0-7 h
Rodriguez Peña 1082/Avenida Santa Fé ✉1020
CONTRAMANO is the oldest gay bar in Buenos Aires, opened in 1984. Traditional place to meet men
Enigma (B D GLM MA) Fri-Sat 1-08:00h
Suipacha 927, local 4
Experiment (B D GLM MA r) Wed-Sun 1-? h
Carlos Pellegrini 1085
IV Milenio (! AC B D dr GLM MA s) Fri 1-? h
Alsina 934 ☎ 480 660 11

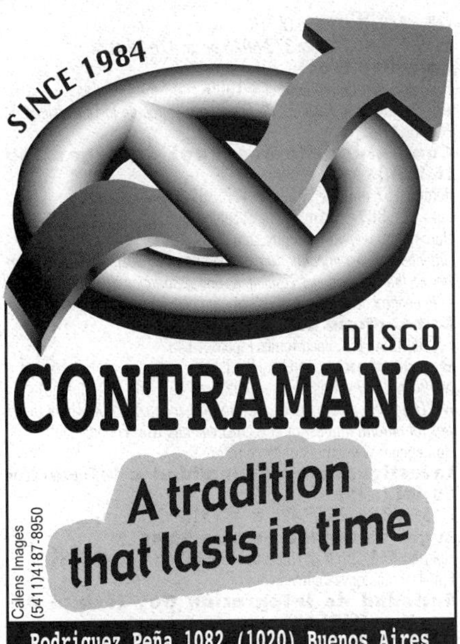

OXEN Disco (B D G MA s) Fri-Sa 0-? h
Sarmiento 1662
NEXO group disco

RESTAURANTS

Downtown Café (AC B CC d F G MA s snu)
Thu & Fri 22-03:00h, Sat -07:00h, Sun 20-23:00h
Alsina 975 ☎ 4334 6110

Enriqueta (F g)
Bulnes 1730 ☎ 482 362 09
Restaurante del pasta

Tacla (! A B CC DR F Glm OS S snu) 17-03:00h, WE -06:00h
Av. de Mayo 1114 / Av. 9 de Julio ☎ 4384 8764
Restaurant with downstairs bar and darkroom. Show Fri & Sat nights 01:00h. Good for gay information.

CAFES

Elegant (B f g OS)
Av. Santa Fe / Equador
A typical café bar during the day, but in the evening / night the terrace is a well known gay meeting place, This is true for a few Cafés in Buenos Aires

SEX SHOPS/BLUE MOVIES

Once Plus (g) Mo-Sa 10-6 h, Sun 14-2 h
Av. Ecuador 54

CINEMAS

ABC (g) Mon-Fri 9-18:00h, Sat 12-06:00h, Sun 14-06:00h
Esmeralda 506
4 cinemas. Mondays gay leather night 24-06:00h

Box Cinema (G) Mo-Sa 14.00-6.00 h, Sun 16.00-4.00 h
Laprida 1423/Av. Santa Fé

City (G) daily 8.00-6.00 h
Libertad 429/Av. Corrientes ☎ 384 90 83

Edén (G) daily 24 h
Av. Santa Fé 1833 *(Galeria Bozzini)*

Equix (G) Mon-Thu 8-2 h, Fri-Sat 8-6 h, Sun 12-2 h
Hipólito Yrigoyen 945

Ideal (G) Mon-Sat 10-6 h, Sun 14-6 h
Suipacha 378/Av. Corrientes

Multicine: Sala Oscar Wilde (G)
Lavalle 750 *(between Maipú and Esmeralda)*

Nuevo Victoria (b G MA) Mon-Sat 8-2 h, Sun 10-24 h
Hipólito Yrigoyen 965 *(Metro Av. de Mayo, Piedras)*
☎ 433 146 86

SAUNAS/BATHS

A FULL (B bf CC DR f G MA msg sa sb VS wh) Mon-Thu 12-3 h, Fri-Sun 24 h
Viamonte 1770 / Av. Callao ✉1055 *Near by subway station Callao, Subway lines: B and D* ☎ 437 172 63
Well designed sauna in an old colonial building

Unikus (B f G sa sb MA msg VS) 13-24:00h
Pueyredón 1180 ✉1118

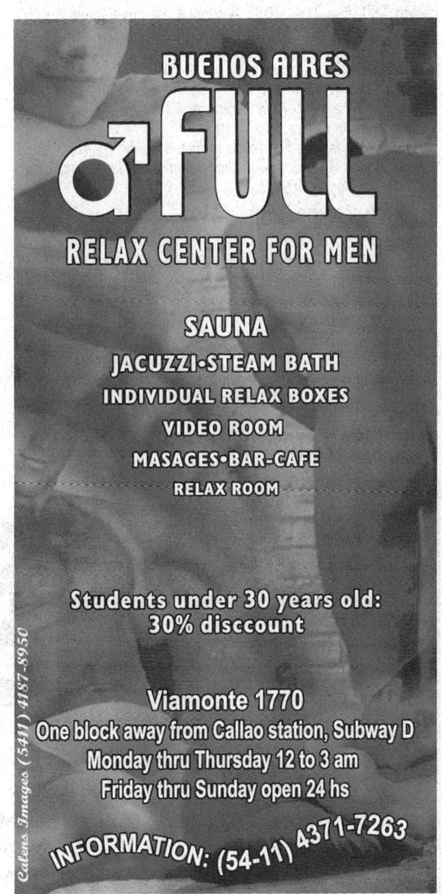

FITNESSTUDIOS

American Hot Gym (CC g VS) Mon-Fri 8-24 h, Sat 9-21h, Sun closed
Ayacucho 449 ✉1026 *(Metro Callao, Linea B)* ☎ 495 176 79
US$ 8,- per day, US$ 15,- per week, US$ 25,- for two weeks and a monthly card costs US$ 40,.

TRAVEL & TRANSPORT

Arcadia (GLM)
Florida 142, 6°N ✉1337 *(Metro Plaza de Mayo)*
☎ 432 649 10 Fax: 432 684 49
Email: info@arcadiatur.com.ar *Travel Agency.*

VIDEO SHOPS

Adult Video News
Maipú 484, 3er Piso ☎ 439 386 95

HOTELS

Lourdes (H NG)
Callao 44 ☎ 952 30 87

Hosteria Tacla (AC bf CC H NG)
Piedras 180, Piso 3 ✉ 1085 *Subway A: Piedras Station, Bus 10, 17, 59* ☎ 433 160 88

GUEST HOUSES

First. The (bf CC G H sa sol)
Defensa 1120 ✉1065 *(San Telmo)* ☎ 43 00 47 47 Email: thefirstgay@infovía.com.ar.
Located in the historic San Telmo district, 6 double rooms, 2 single rooms, all with WC, partly with shared bathroom. Rates single from US$ 40/45, double 60/70.

PRIVATE ACCOMODATION

Faraon (AC b bf CC E H VS) 24 h
Gallardo 340 ✉1408 ☎ 464 236 43 Fax: 464 242 93
Email: info@faraon.com.ar Homepage: www.faraon.com.ar
Rooms by the hour with high standards. Also all night possible.

O´tello (AC b bf CC E g H)
Arregni 4241 ✉1417
☎ 456 820 56 Fax: 456 888 29 Homepage: www.otello.com.ar
Rooms by the hour, luxuriouy thematic rooms. All night also possible.

GENERAL GROUPS

Asamblea Permanente por los Derechos Humanos (APDH)
Callao 569, 3er Cuerpo Of. 15
☎ 437 304 03 *or* ☎ *373-6073 or* ☎ *476-2061.*

Colectivo Eros
PO Box 3904 Correo Central ✉1000
Estudiantes de la Facultad de Filosofia y Letras de la Universidad de Buenos Aires.

Comunidad Homosexual de Argentina (C.H.A.)
Paraná 157 dto:F ✉1017 ☎ 437 389 55
Fax: 437 389 55 Email: cha@cuidad.com.ar
Homepage: www.mundogay.com/ar
Argentina's most important organization for gay liberation and a member of the International Lesbian & Gay Association (ILGA). They deal with political activities, legal advice, and give general information.

Convocatoria Gay
Edificio H26, PB B, Bario Tomás Espora ✉1437

Grupo Nexo Mon-Fri 13-21 h
Av. Callao 339, Pisos 4 y 5 ✉1022 ☎ 437 444 84 (Hotline)
NEXO are the publishers of the monthly magazine NX. Many activities for differnt interest groups. Just call and ask. Friendly staff.
Homepage: www.mundogay.com/ar

Investigación en Sexualidad e Interacción Social (ISIS)
PO Box 78, suc 25 ✉1425 ☎ 455 118 19

Lugar de Gay de Buenos Aires
Libertad 443, 3ro A ✉1012 ☎ 438 485 55 Fax: 438 485 55
Email: thefirstgay@infovia.com.ar

Sociedad de Integración Gay-Lésbica Argentina (SIGLA)
Paraná 122, 2do Piso ✉1017
☎ 438 245 40 Fax: 436 282 61.

HEALTH GROUPS

ACT UP Buenos Aires PO Box 143, Suc. 2B ✉1402
☎ 437 427 53 Fax: 437 427 53

Fundación HUESPED
Gascón 79 ✉1181 ☎ 498 118 28

Proyecto SINSIDA
Paraná 122 2so Piso ✉1017
☎ 438 245 40

Sida Vision Alternativa
Warnes 829 1er Piso ✉1414 ☎ 485 567 53 Fax: 477 419 21

RELIGIOUS GROUPS

Iglesia de la Communidad Metropolitana (I.C.M.) Estados Unidos 1437 dto 1 ✉1043 ☎ 438 115 59
Movimiento Ecuménico por los Derechos Humanos
Av. José María Morena 873 PB ✉1424
☎ 492 251 01

SPECIAL INTEREST GROUPS
Grupo de Jovenes „Construyendo nuestra Sexualidad"
PO Box 117, suc 2B ✉1402

SWIMMING
-Outdoor pool »Balneario Norte«

CRUISING
-Avenida Santa Fé (between Av Coronel Diaz and Rodriguez Peña, best 23-2 h)
-Avenida Santa Fé (between Av Juan B. Justo and Coronel Diaz and between Rodriguez Peña and Florida)
-Avenida Corrientes (between Av Callao and Av 9 de Julio)
-Avenida Cabildo (between Virrey del Pino and Av Monroe)
-Marcelo T. de Alvear (between Av Callao and Ecuador and on Ecuador/Santa Fé, at night)
-Lavalle (between Carlos Pelegrini and Florida, at nights)
-Plaza Dorego y Feria de antigüedades de San Telmo (11-20 h, only sundays
-Ciudad Universitaria: Dehind Universities in Nuñez by the river, in the bushes on the left hand side on the road. (Saturday, Sunday afternoon, Bus 37, 45, 160)
-Reserva Ecológica Av. Belgrano and Av. Costanera, Viamonte and Av. Costanera

Córdoba - Córdoba ✉5000

BARS
Beep! Pub (B D glm MA S) 23-? h
Sucre 173 ✉5000

DANCECLUBS
Hangar 18 Disco/Pub (A AC B CC D glm MA snu VS W WE YG) Fri-Sun 0.30-? h
Boulevard Las Heras 118 ☎ 423 89 15
La Piaf Disco (B D GLM MA STV tv W WE) Fri, Sat and before holidays 23.30-6 h
Obispo Ceballos 45 ✉5000 *(San Martín)* ☎ 471 79 14
Planta Baja (B D G) Tue-Sun 0-? h
San Martín 666 ☎ 421 47 04
Universo Pub (B D glm MA) Fri-Sat 0-? h
Boulevard Las Heras 118

GENERAL GROUPS
A.Co.D.Ho. (Ascociación contra la discriminación homosexual)
San Martin 666 PB ✉5000
☎ 421 47 04 Fax: 421 97 28

CRUISING
-Plaza San Martin
-Plaza Vélez-Sarsfield
-Avenida Argentina to Plaza Centenario on to Parque Sarmiento
-Rio Primero (along the bank)
-Pedestrian mall of Streets 9 de Julio, San Martín, Rivadavia, Ituzaingó, San Jerónimo and Rosario de Santa Fé
-Galería 9 de Julio (which is also known as „Pasaje Central", located at 9 de Julio 55 pedestrian mall)
-Calle Alvear up to Boulevard Illia
-Calle Buenos Aires (between Boulevard Illia and 27 de Abril)
-Calle Rivadavia (between 27 de Abril and 25 de Mayo)
-25 de Mayo (between Alvear and San Martín)
-9 de Julio (between San Martín and La Cañada)

Corrientes - Corrientes ✉3400 ☎0783

DANCECLUBS
Contramarcha (B D G)
Piambre 5000/Cazadores Correntinos ✉3400

La Plata - Buenos Aires ✉1900 ☎ 021

DANCECLUBS
Back Disco (B D G S) Fri Sat 1.30-5.30 h
Calle 53/Calle 5 ✉1900

HEALTH GROUPS
Campaña Stop Sida
Calle 69, 683 ✉1900
Communidad de Vida
Calle 54, 712 ✉1900

Lobos ✉7240 ☎ 0227

GENERAL GROUPS
Grupo Bain Ben
Olaverrieta 1080 ✉7240

Mar del Plata - Buenos Aires ✉7600 ☎ 023

BARS
Dicroica Bar (B G MA S)
Bolivar 2152 ✉7600

DANCECLUBS
Extasis Disco (B D G MA S) Fri Sat 23-? h
Corrientes 2044 ☎ 492 03 38

HEALTH GROUPS
Fundación Un Lugar Falucho 2576, 1° Piso, Of. 5
☎ 492 07 77
Homo Sapiens
Av. Independencia 1101 4to A
☎ 494 70 25 Fax: 494 70 25

CRUISING
-La Rambla (between Punta Iglesia and Playa Chica, at night)
-Peatonal San Martin (between Buenos Aires and San Luis, at night)
-Playa Chica (Dec-Mar, during the day)

Mendoza - Mendoza ✉5500 ☎ 061

DANCECLUBS
Queen Disco (B D GLM S TV)
Ejército de Los Andos 656 5519 ✉5500 *(Dorrego, Guayamallén)*
☎ 431 69 90

CAFES
La jungla (B f g) Salta 1843 ✉5500

SEX SHOPS/BLUE MOVIES
Sex Shop
c/o Galería Tonsa, Avenida San Martín/Catamarca ✉5500
(1° piso/1st floor)

CINEMAS
Adán xxx (g)
c/o Galería Tonsa, Avenida San Martín 1173 ✉5500
(1° piso/1st floor)
Cabinas individuales
c/o Galería Tonsa, Avenida San Martín 1173 ✉5500
(1° piso / 1st floor)

SAUNAS/BATHS
Sauna of Hotel Aconcagua (g sa)
Calle San Lorenzo 545 ✉5500 *(seven blocks from downtown)*
☎ 424 38 33
Sauna of Hotel Huentala (g sa)
Primitivo de la Reta/Amigorena ✉5500

APARTMENTS
Home (AC CC NG pi sa)
Colón/Lem ✉ 5500 ☎ 425 43 84 Fax: 425 43 89
15 studios and 18 apartments. All with phone, TV, kitchen.

CRUISING
-Avenida San Martín (between Rivadavia and Las Heras)
-Avenida Las Heras (between Avenida San Martín and Avenida Mitre)
-Avenida Mitre (between Avenida Las Heras and Espejo)
-

DANCECLUBS
S.O.S. (B glm)
Rivadavia/Mendoza ✉8300

Paraná - Entre Ríos ✉ 3100 ☎ 043

CRUISING
-Plaza 9 de Julio
-Along the Rio Arias

Pergamino - Buenos Aires ✉ 2700 ☎ 0477

BARS
GNC (B D G s)
Route 178/Ameghino ✉2700

Rosario - Santa Fé ✉ 2000 ☎ 041

BARS
Contrato Bar (B G) Thu-Sun 23-? h
Alvear 40bis ✉2000
Inizio (B G) Mon-Sun 23-? h
Mitre 1880
Ruido Blanco (B G MA) 20-? h
Weelright 1739

DANCECLUBS
Station G (B D G)
Avenida Rivadaria 2481

GENERAL GROUPS
Colectivo ARCO IRIS
Pte Roca 663, Of. 5, PO Box 208 Correo Central ✉2000 ☎ 447 02 68 Fax: 449-90 98

HEALTH GROUPS
Voluntario contra el SIDA
Pasco 1840 ✉2000 ☎ 485 03 08

Salta - Salta ✉ 4400 ☎ 087

BARS
Estacion Tequila (B G MA) 23-? h
San Luis 348
Nosotros (B D glm MA)
Juan M. Guermes 11 *(Don Emilio)*

DANCECLUBS
O'Clock Disco (B D GLM MA P s W WE) Fri Sat & before public holidays 1-5 h
La Rioja 111 ✉4400

CRUISING
-Peatonal Alberti (G) (at night)
-Parque San Martin (tv) (at night)

San Carlos de Bariloche - Río Negro ✉ 8400

BOOK SHOPS
Uppsala Libros (g)
Rolando 265 ✉8400

San Salvador de Jujuy ✉ 4600 ☎ 088

GENERAL GROUPS
Comunidad Homosexual de Jujuy
18 de Noviembre 230, Barrio Alte Brown ✉4600 ☎ 423 66 45

Santa Fé - Santa Fé ✉ 3000 ☎ 042

DANCECLUBS
Tudor Taberna Pub (B D G YG) Sat (D)
Javier de la Rosa 325 ✉3000 *(Barrio de Guadalupe)*

GENERAL GROUPS
Puente-Asociación por la Defensa de Personas Discriminados
Javier de Rosa 325 ✉3000 ☎ 460 32 38

CRUISING
-Plaza Mayo
-Plaza San Martín
-on Boats twice a week to Rio (active and busy)

Santiago del Estero - Santiago d. Estero ✉ 4200

CRUISING
-Plaza Libertad
-Along the Rio Arias

Tucumán - Tucumán ✉ 4000 ☎ 081

DANCECLUBS
Enigma para Vos (B D G MA) Fri Sat 2-? h
Monteagudo 428

CRUISING
-Plaza Independencia
-Plaza Belgrano
-Parque 9 de Julio
-Parque Avellaneda
-Around Government Palace

Viedma - Rio Negro ✉ 8500☎ 0920

GENERAL GROUPS
Colectivo Amancay
PO Box 86 ✉8500

Australia

Oceania

Initials: AUS

Time: GMT +8/+9.5/+10

☎ Country Code / Access Code: 61 (leave away the first 0 of area codes) / 0011

Language: English

Area: 7,686,850 km² / 2,967,897 sq mi.

Currency: 1 Australian Dollar (A$) = 100 Cents

Population: 18,710,000

Capital: Canberra

Religions: 71% Christians, 26% Catholics, 24% Anglicans

Climate: Generally the climate is dry. The south and east are moderate, the north is tropical.

Important gay cities: Sydney, Melbourne, Brisbane, Perth and Adelaide

● Australia consists of six federal states and two territories that are listed. The cities are alphabetically filed.
Each Australian state and territory has different legislation with respect to homosexuality. This accounts for there being no agreement on the age of sexual consent and also no agreement on anti-discrimination laws. For more exact details on a federal state refer to the corresponding capital.
There's a strong gay movement in Australia with the most recent success in Tasmania of legalising homosexuality. The gay scene of this continent is professionally organised. There are many local newspapers and regional magazines, including „Campaign" and „Outrage", allowing the gay community to consciously express itself.
Cairns in the federal state of Queensland has developed into a much beloved international holiday destination. Sydney in New South Wales is seen by many as the most important Gay Metropolis outside of course Europe and North America. Moreover, one of the most important gay events the Mardi Gras takes place in Sydney each February.

✱ Australien besteht aus 6 Bundesstaaten und 2 Territorien, die der Reihe nach aufgeführt sind. Die Städte des jeweiligen Bundesstaates bzw. Territoriums sind alphabetisch aufgeführt.
Die Verfassung Australiens gewährt den Bundesstaaten und Territorien weitgehende Selbständigkeit. Aus diesem Grunde gibt es in Australien kein einheitliches Schutzalter und keine einheitlichen Antidiskriminierungsgesetze. Die genauen Angaben für die einzelnen Bundesstaaten und Territorien finden Sie in den entsprechenden Kapiteln.
Die Schwulenbewegung Australiens ist stark. Als jüngster Erfolg ist die Legalisierung homosexueller Handlungen im Bundesstaat Tasmanien zu nennen. Die schwule Szene des Kontinents ist sehr professionell organisiert. Neben zahlreichen Lokalzeitungen geben die überregionalen Magazine „Campaign" und „Outrage" ein interessantes Bild des gestiegenen Selbstbewußtseins.
Im Bundesstaat Queensland entwickelt sich Cairns zu einem schwulen Urlaubsziel von internationaler Bedeutung. Außerhalb Europas und Nordamerikas gilt Sydney in Neusüdwales als die bedeutenste schwule Metropole. Entsprechend großartig fällt auch eines der weltweit wichtigsten schwulen Ereignisse aus, der Mardi Gras von Sydney (jeweils im Februar).

▲ L'Australie se compose de 6 Etats fédéraux et de 2 territoires énumérés l'un après l'autre. Les villes de l'Etat fédéral ou du territoire en cause sont énumérées alphabétiquement. La Constitution australienne accorde aux Etats fédéraux et territoires une large indépendance. Pour cette raison, un âge de protection uniforme et des lois antidiscriminatoires uniformes n'existent pas en Australie. Vous trouverez les données exactes des Etats fédéraux et territoires individuels aux chapitres correspondants. Le mouvement homosexuel d'Australie est puissant. Notons le succès récent de la légalisation des actes impudiques dans l'Etat fédéral de Tasmanie. La scène homosexuelle du continent est organisée de manière professionnelle. A part les nombreux journaux locaux, les magazines nationaux „Campaign" et „Outrage" donnent une image intéressante du sentiment accru de sa propre valeur. Dans l'Etat fédéral du Queensland, Cairns est en train de devenir un lieu de vacances pour homosexuels d'une importance internationale. En dehors de l'Europe et de l'Amérique du Nord, Sydney, de la Nouvelle-Galles du Sud, est considérée comme la métropole homosexuelle la plus importante. Un événement homosexuel le plus important à l'échelle planétaire est le Mardi gras de Sydney (qui a lieu régulièrement au mois de février).

☆ Australia se compone de 6 estados federales y 2 territorios. Para su mejor orientación hemos ordenado el listado por estados federales, indicando las ciudades correspondientes por orden alfabético. La constitución australiana garantiza en gran medida la autonomía de sus estados federales y territorios. Por esta razón no existe una sola edad de protección o leyes de antidiscriminación aplicables para toda Australia. Para informaciones más detalladas respecto a cada estado federal o territorio sírvanse tomar nota del capítulo correspondiente. El movimiento gay en Australia es muy fuerte. Uno de los últimos éxitos alcanzados es sin duda la legalización de relaciones homosexuales en el estado federal de Tasmania. La comunidad gay en Australia está organizada muy profesionalmente. A parte de sus numerosos periodicos locales, las revistas „Campaign" y „Outrage", de publicación nacional, reflejan la creciente autoconfianza de los gays australianos. Cairns, en el estado federal de Queensland, se está desarollando como un lugar vacacional gay con prestigio internacional. Sydney en New South Wales está considerada hoy en día la metrópoli gay más importante a nivel mundial fuera de Europa y Norteamérica. Así que uno de los eventos más espectaculares en el mundo gay tiene lugar aqui: La Mardi Gras que se celebra cada año en febrero.

❖ L'Australia comprende 6 Stati e 2 Territori, che sono elencati qui sotto. Le città del rispettivo stato / territorio sono elencate in ordine alfabetico. Secondo la costituzione dell'Australia gli Stati ed i Territori godono di un'ampia indipendenza. Per questo motivo non esistono su scala nazionale né un'età legale né una legge contro la discriminazione. Le indicazioni esatte per i singoli Stati e Territori si trovano nei rispettivi capitoli. C'è un forte movimento gay, il cui successo più recente è stato, nello stato federale di Tasmania, la legalizzazione di atti omosessuali. In tutto il continente la vita gay è organizzata in modo molto professionale. A parte i numerosi giornali locali le riviste su livello nazionale „Campaign" e „Outrage" danno un'imagine interessante dell'aumentato orgoglio dei gay. Nello stato di Queensland la città di Cairns sta sviluppandosi come luogo di vacanze su livello internazionale. Al di fuori dell'Europa e dell'America del Nord, Sydney in New South Wales viene considerata la metropoli gay più importante. In corrispondenza a questo fatto uno degli avvenimenti più famosi, il Mardi Gras di Sydney (sempre in febbraio) risulta essere una delle feste più grandi.

NATIONAL GAY INFO

Australian Gay and Lesbian Travel Association
PO Box 2174, Fitzroy ✉VIC 3065 ☎ (1902)9419-5230
Fax: (03) 9419-5230 Email: peterkj@ozemail.com.au
Homepage: www.aglta.asn.au.

Australian Lesbian & Gay Archives
PO Box 124, Parkville ✉VIC 065 ☎ (03) 9499-6334
Collects and preserves any material (magazines, press clippings, newsletters, badges, etc.) relating to lesbian/gay male life.

Campaign
1st floor, Suite 6, 66 Oxford Street, Darlinghurst ✉NSW 2010
☎ (02) 9332-3666 Fax: (02) 9361-5962
Australia's longest running gay magazine. Published monthly and containing classifieds, news, arts, entertainment and community listings. A$ 6.50.

Gay Maps Australia
PO Box 1401, Bondi Junction, ✉NSW 2022 ☎ (02) 9369 2738
Fax: (02) 9389 5450
Email: gaymaps@tma.com.au.

National Network
247-251 Flinders Lane, Melbourne ✉VIC 2000
☎ (03) 9650-5103
A political activist and social support group for lesbian, gay and bisexual people under 26 years of age.

OutRage
85 King William Street, Fitzroy ✉VIC 065 ☎ (03) 9926-1122
Fax: (03) 9926-1199
Monthly publication dates. A$ 5.00. Provides a coverage of events, news, reviews, and issues of interest to the gay community. Also containing male photography and classifieds.

NATIONAL COMPANIES

Edition Habit Press
72-80 Bourke Road, Alexandria, ✉NSW 015
☎ (02) 9310-2098 Fax: (02) 9389-2966.

AUS-Australian Capital Territory

Southeast AUS
Initials: ACT
Time: GMT +10
Area: 2,400 km² / 926 sq mi.
Population: 309,000
Capital: Canberra

In the A.C.T. the age of consent is fixed at 18 years.

Im A.C.T. liegt das Schutzalter bei 18 Jahren.

Dans l'A.C.T, la majorité sexuelle est fixée à 18 ans.

En el A.C.T., la edad de consentimiento está estipulado en 18 años.

Nell'A.C.T. l'età legale per rapporti sessuali è di 18 anni.

Canberra ☎ 02

BARS

Heaven (B F GLM) Sun, Tue-Thu 20-1 h, Fri-Sat 20-4 h.
Grema Place Civic Centre, City ✉ACT 2600 *(off Bunda Street Civic Center)* ☎ 6257-6180

Meridian Club (AC B d GLM lj MA s) Tue Wed 18-1, Thu -2, Fri 17-3, Sat 20-3 h, closed Sun Mon
34 Mort Street, Braddon ✉ACT 2614 ☎ 6248-9966
Admission A$ 5. Hellfire club on various nights.

Republic. The (B F g)
Allara Street ✉ACT 2601 *Civic Center*

Tilley's (B F glm OS s) 9-24 h
13 Wattle Street/Brigalow Street, Lyneham ✉ACT 2602 *4 kms from city centre on bus route. Close to youth hostel.* ☎ 6249-1543
Mixed bar and restaurant.

CAFES

Da Cesare (B F g)
Lonsdale Street/Eloura Street, Braddon ✉ACT 2601
☎ 6247-2946

MEN'S CLUBS

John's JO-Club (g MA NU P VS) 3rd Thu / month
PO Box 44 33, Kingston ✉ACT 2604 ☎ 6297 9967
Social relaxing evenings for like minded men. Safer sex only.

SEX SHOPS/BLUE MOVIES

Adam & Eve (A AC CC g S VS W) 9-24 h
125 Gladstone Street, Fyshwick ✉ACT 2609 ☎ 6239-1121
Sex shop with video arcade.

Champions Headquarters (AC CC DR G MA msg r s VS) 9-24 h
83 Woolongong Street, Fyshwick ✉ACT 2609 ☎ 6280-8881
Sex shop, back room, cinema.

Ram Lounges and Video
Unit 6, 83 Wollongong Street, Fyshwick ✉ACT 2601
(Next to Club X) ☎ 6280-4568

HOUSE OF BOYS

Male Company 10-4 h
161 Newcastle Street, Fyshwick ✉ACT 2601
☎ 6280-7642
Studio, outcalls, appointments.

SAUNAS/BATHS

Canberra City Steam (AC CC DR G MA sa VS) Sun-Thu 12-1, Fri-Sat 12-3 h
1 Sargood Street ✉ACT 2602 *(at O'Connor shopping center)*
☎ 6248-9785
Entrance fee from A$ 6 - 14.

GUEST HOUSES

Northbourne Lodge (AC bf CC glm H MA OS) 5
22 Northbourne Avenue, Downer ✉ACT 2602 *(Next to Dickson Shopping Centre)* ☎ 6257-2599 Fax: 6257-2599
Rates from A$ 75.

GENERAL GROUPS

Club 19 (G MA) 2nd Sat & 4th Wed
PO Box 4703 Kingston ✉ACT 2604 ☎ 6297 9967
Friendship club for male gays. Can arrange accomodation for overseas visitors. Email: googong@interact.au

FETISH GROUPS

Griffin Motor Club. The
GPO Box 10 48 ✉ACT 2601 ☎ 6258-8716

HEALTH GROUPS

AIDS Action Council of the A.C.T. Mon-Fri 9-17 h
13 Lonsdale Street, PO Box 229, Braddon ✉ACT 2601 ☎ 6257-2855 Fax: 6257-4839
. Office and Healthline.

Peer Support Network (PSN) Mo-Fr 10:00-16:00h
Westlund House, 16 Gordon Street ✉ACT 2601 ☎ 6257 4985 Fax: 6257 4838 Email: plwhaact@hotmail.com
Support for posive people, friends and family

RELIGIOUS GROUPS

Acceptance Canberra
✉ACT 2601 ☎ 6281-3977
Catholic group.

SWIMMING

-Kambah Pool (A »free beach« on the Murrumbidgee River. West of Canberra. Walk downstream from the last car park for about 1 km to a large sandy beach. Cruising very active downstream on both sides.)

CRUISING

-Museum site (off Lady Denman Drive on shores of Lake Burley Griffin)

Deakin ☎ 02

TRAVEL & TRANSPORT

Just Travel
Suite 4, 42 Ceils Court ✉ACT 2600 ☎ 6285-2644
Gay and lesbian travel services.

AUS-New South Wales

Southeast AUS
Initials: NSW
Time: GMT +10
Area: 801,600 km² / 309,498 sq mi.
Population: 6,330,000
Capital: Sydney

● In New South Wales the age of consent is fixed at 16 years of age for heterosexuals and 18 for homosexuals. There's also an anti-discrimination-law protecting homosexuals in the fields of housing and supplies.

✱ In Neu-Südwales liegt das Schutzalter bei 16 Jahren für Heterosexuelle und bei 18 Jahren für Homosexuelle. Es gibt zudem ein Antidiskriminierungsgesetz, das Homosexuelle in den Bereichen Wohnen und Versorgung schützt.

▲ Dans le New-Southwales, la majorité sexuelle est fixée à 16 ans pour les hétérosexuels et à 18 ans pour les homosexuels. Une loi anti-discriminatoire garantit aux homosexuels les mêmes droits qu'aux autres citoyens dans le domaine du logement et de l'approvisionnement.

☆ En New South Wales la edad de consentimiento es de 16 años para heterosexuales y de 18 años para homosexuales. Existe además una ley de antidiscriminación que protege la igualdad de los gays en areas como vivienda y empleo.

❖ In New South Wales l'età legale per rapporti eterosessuali è di 16 anni, per quelli omosessuali di 18 anni. Esiste una legge contro la discriminazione per la tutela degli omosessuali negli ambiti del domicilio e dell'assistenza sociale.

NATIONAL GROUPS

Boys will be boys
PO Box 1349, Strawberry Hills NSW 2012 ☎ 02/(02) 9319-2034
National support group for female to male transsexuals. Newsletter and counselling.

Adelong ☎ 02

HOTELS

Adelong's Beaufort House
77 Tumut Street ✉2729 ☎ 6946 2273 Fax: 6946 2553 Email: Beaufort@dragnet.com.au Homepage: Beaufort.dragnet.com.au
Rates A$ 45-75 .

Albury ☎ 02

HEALTH GROUPS

AIDS Task Group
PO Box 10 76 ✉NSW 2640 ☎ 6023 0340
Information, resources, seminars, community education, support and counselling on AIDS issues.

CRUISING

-Botanical gardens
-Car park (near SS&A Club, Olive Street; daytime)
-Billson Park (AYOR) (David Street; daytime)

Blackheath ☎ 02

HOTELS

Cleopatra Guest House (g H) 4
Cleopatra Street ✉2785 ☎ 4787-8456 Fax: 876-092

Kanangra Lodge (g H)
9 Belvidere Avenue ✉278 ☎ 4787-8715

Byron Bay ☎ 02

GAY INFO

Gaywaves Mon 22-24 h 2NCR FM 92.9 MHz

GENERAL GROUPS

Tropical Fruits
PO Box 771, Lismore ✉2480 ☎ 6622-4353
Gay & lesbian social group.

HEALTH GROUPS

Aids Council of New South Wales (ACON) Northern Rivers Branch
147 Laurel Avenue, Lismore ✉2480 ☎ 6622-1555.Fax: 6622-1520

SWIMMING

-Kingshead Beach (NU) (7 km south of Byron on Brokenhead Road. Make a left to Seven Miles Beach Road, drive to first park south of Broken Head Beach, walk down to Kingshead Beach through rainforest.)

Coffs Harbour ☎ 02

HOTELS

Santa Fe Luxury Bed & Breakfast (f g H pi)
Gaudrons Road, The Mountain Way, PO Box 17 63 ✉2450
☎ 6653-7700 Fax: 6653-7050
Rates from A$ 45 (bf incl.) 10 km north of Coffs Harbour. Located on 5 acres. En suite rooms with TV & VCR

GENERAL GROUPS

Four Seasons Social Group
PO Box 16 54 ✉2450 ☎ 6652-7643
Provides social activities, dances, barbeques, bush walks, etc..

HEALTH GROUPS

AIDS Council of NSW
c/o 93 High Street, PO Box 990 ✉2450 ☎ 6651-4056

SWIMMING

-Little Diggers (g NU) (5 km north of Coffs Harbour. Opposite the Big Banana. On the beach facing the sea to the left .

Corowa ☎ 02

HOTELS

Motor Inn (AC b bf f G H pi sa)
PO Box 122 ✉2646 ☎ 6033-1255

Dargan ☎ 02

HOTELS

Gays Lodge (GLM)
57 Valley View Road ✉2786 ☎ 957-3811 Fax: 957-138

Hurstville ☎ 02

TRAVEL & TRANSPORT

Breakout Tours
PO Box 504 ✉2220 ☎ 9570-5900
Fax: 9570-9200 *Gay and lesbian travel services.*

Katoomba ☎ 02

HOTELS

Tilcott (bf G H)
210 Bathurst Road ✉2780 ☎ 4782-2264
Fax: 4782-6008 *seperate gay guesthouse linked to a gay run mixed guesthouse and restaurant. Rates single A$ 55.*

Leura ☎ 02

GUEST HOUSES

Leura House (AC b bf CC E f g H) 7
Britain Street ✉2780 ☎ 4784-2035 Fax: 4784-3329
Homepage: www.bluemts.com.au/leurahouse
Beautiful historic guest houses. 11 rooms with bath/WC and balcony/terrace. 2 cottages. Rates per person - double A$ 49-69, single A$60-101, cottage A$79 (breakfast incl.)

Lismore ☎ 02

GAY INFO

Northern Rivers Gaywaves Mon 22 h (2NCR-FM 92.9 MHz)
c/o 2NCR-FM, PO Box 157 ✉2480 ☎ 6623-0888

GENERAL GROUPS

Lismore AIDS Council of NSW
113 Dawson Street,/ PO Box 60 63 ✉2480 ☎ 6622-1555
Fun and Esteem Lismore - 1st/3rd Sat

TRAVEL & TRANSPORT

North American Travel Specialists
145 Swan Street ✉2321 ☎ 4934-2088 Fax: 4934-7522
Gay and lesbian travel services.

Mudgee ☎ 02

HOTELS

Parkview Guest House (f g H MA) 99
Market Street ✉2850 ☎ 6372-4477
Rates A$ 60-90 (breakfast incl.)

Newcastle ☎ 02

GAY INFO

Newcastle 2NUR Thu 22-23 h (103.7 FM)

BARS

Islington Barracks (B D GLM S STV W YG) 18-? h, closed Mon
139 Maitland Road, Islington ✉2300 ☎ 4969-1848
Wickham Park Hotel (b D f GLM STV WE) Mon-Sat 12-3, Sun 12-22 h
61 Maitland Road, Islington ✉2296 ☎ 4969-2017

RESTAURANTS

Barry & Paul's »Little Swallows Cafe« (F GLM)
Cleary Street/Beaumont Street ✉2300 ☎ 4969-2135
Germania Club (b F g)
Hillsborough Road, Warners Bay ✉2282 ☎ 4954-6136
Gina's on Beaumont (AC b CC F glm MA OS W WE)
Lunch: Wed-Fri 11.30-14.30, Diner: Tue-Sun 18-? h
47 Beaumont Street, Haminton ✉2303 ☎ 4961-6844
Northern Italian style food.

GENERAL GROUPS

Anti-Discrimination Board
GIO Building,
400 Hunter Street ✉2300 *(1st floor)* ☎ 4926-4300
Newcastle Gay Friendship Network
c/o ACON, Hunter Branch ☎ 4929-3464 Fax: 4968-3559
Email: smusa@alinga.newcastle.edu.au *For gays under 26.*
Newcastle University Students Association (NUSA)
Shortland Union Bdg., University of Newcastle ✉2308
☎ 4968-1281

HEALTH GROUPS

AIDS Council of NSW (ACON)
Hunter Branch, PO Box 1081 ✉2300 ☎ 4929-3464
Karumah Day Centre Thu 11-15 h at Sorrento Building, 101 Scott Street (1st floor)
PO Box 1049 ✉2300 ☎ 4929-6367
Drop in centre for PWA, their relatives and friends. Free meals.

CRUISING

-Dangar Park, Maitland Road, Mayfield
-Gregson Park, Hamilton
-Islington Park, Maitland Road (exit to Criterion Hotel)
-Rocks at Susan Gilmore Beach, Memorial Drive

Penrith ☎ 02

BOOK SHOPS

Way Out West Bookshop (g) Shop 2,
Carmina Arcade ✉2750 ☎ 4731-3094
General bookstore with gay section.

GENERAL GROUPS

Penrith Area Gay Group
Box 610 ✉2750 ☎ 4731-3922
Or call Vicke ☎ 560-6148. Social group catering for men and women in the outer western suburbs. Organizes discos, barbeques and other social activities.

Pokolbin ☎ 02

HOTELS

Pokolbin Village Resort & Conference Center (AC bf CC F glm H)
188 Broke Road ✉2320 ☎ 4998-7670 Fax: 4998-7377
Gay owned resort in one of the main vineyard districts 2 hours north of Sydney. Horse riding. 12 doubles, 1 single, 3 studios and 4 apartments with bath or shower/WC, balcony, telephone, Fax, TV/video, radio, safe, kitchenette (studios) or kitchen (apartments). Rates from A$ 65.

Port Kembla ☎ 02

BOOK SHOPS

Venus Adult Book Shop
121 Wentworth Road ✉2505 ☎ 4275-2121

HEALTH GROUPS

AIDS Council of New South Wales
✉2505 ☎ 4276-2399

Robertson ☎ 02

HOTELS

Ranelagh House (f g H pi sa wh)
Illawarra Highway ✉2577 ☎ 4885-1111
Historic guest house for a quiet romantic weekend located in the suburbs. Single A$ 35-40, double 70-80 (bf incl.).

Rylestone ☎ 02

HOTELS

High Tweeters (bf glm H MA NU)
Nullo Mountain Road NSW 2849 ✉2849 ☎ 6379-6253
Farmstay accomodation in beautiful landscape, close to Wollemi National Park. Rates A$ 50,- double incl. continental bf (full bf $ 7,50 extra), minimum of 2 nights. Guided trekking tours. 270 km from Sydney.

Sydney ☎ 02

● The capital of New South Wales is Sydney. It is the oldest and largest city in Australia and probably the most well known. The hustle and bustle of the metropolis with it's sub-tropical climate and it's spectacular Sydney Harbour, Harbour Bridge and the well known Opera House. Sydney has a large gay and lesbian community which celebrates every year at the end of February the world famous Gay Parade, the Sydney Gay and Lesbian Mardi Gras. Hundreds of thousands gather on the streets to watch the spectacular costume parade and or to party to dawn.
The „Sleeze Ball" at the end of September or another Mardi-Gras event attract up to 20,000 gays, lesbians and their friends. The gay scene has established itself around the Golden Mile of Oxford Street in the suburb of Darlinghurst. Another gay centre has emmerged around King Street (New Town) the gay and lesbian presence is clearly seen. The city beaches of Manly and Bondi are also attractive meeting points for gays. The cafés and restaurants offer an interesting range of Pacific Rim- Cuisine in which Sydney's young chefs ara at the forefront.
Sydney is ideally located for the tourist to get to the Blue Mountains (a couple of hours away from the city). Newcastle and Wollongong, the Southern Highlands, Canberralm are only a short trip away from Sydney. Further North of New South Wales is the liberal district of the Northern Rivers located on Byron Bay which has a small but lively gay community.
Sydney will also maintain it's reputation as a gay metropolis in the future with the taking place of the Gay Games in the year 2002.

✱ Sydney, Hauptstadt von Neusüdwales, ist die älteste und größte Stadt Australiens. Die geschäftige Metropole mit ihrem subtropischen Klima erstreckt sich um den spektakulären Hafen mit der Harbour Bridge und dem berühmten Opera House. Sydney hat eine große schwul-lesbische Gemeinde, die sich jedes Jahr Ende Februar mit der weltweit größten Schwulenparade, der „Sydney Gay and Lesbian Mardi Gras" feiert. Hunderttausende drängen sich in den Straßen, um die kostümierte Parade an sich vorbeiziehen zu lassen oder um bis zum Morgengrauen mitzufeiern.
Der »Sleaze Ball« Ende September bzw. Anfang Oktober ist ein weiteres Mardi-Gras-Event, zu dem mehr als 20 000 Schwule, Lesben und ihre Freunde zusammenkommen. Die schwule Szene hat sich rings um die „Goldene Meile" Oxford Street in der Vorstadt Darlinghurst etabliert. Neben einem weiteren schwulen Zentrum um die King Street (Newtown) wird praktisch der ganze zentrale Stadtbereich von Schwulen und Lesben in Beschlag genommen, deren Präsenz auch dem ungeübten Auge kaum entgeht. Nicht weniger interessant für Schwule sind die Stadtstrände von Manly und natürlich der berühmte Bondi-Strand.
Die Cafés und Restaurants der Stadt bieten die interessante und abwechslungsreiche Küche des Pazifischen Raumes, in der Sydneys junge Chefs kräftig mitmischen.
Schwule Bars, schwule Hotels, schwule Saunas, schwule Fitneßstudios, schwule Strände, schwule Organisationen - selbst nüchtern betrachtet genügt es nicht, Sydney als schwules Dienstleistungszentrum zu beschreiben, es ist die schwule Hauptstadt des südpazifischen Raums.
Für den Touristen ist Sydney äußerst günstig gelegen. Die Blue Mountains sind nur einige Stunden entfernt, weitere interessante Tagesausflüge sind die benachbarten Städte Newcastle und Wollongong, die Southern Highlands bei Berri, das Weinanbaugebiet Hunter Valley oder die Hauptstadt Australiens, Canberra. Im äußersten Norden von Neusüdwales liegt der liberale Bezirk Northern Rivers um Byron Bay, das eine kleine aber lebhafte schwule Gemeinde hat.
Auch in Zukunft wird Sydney seinem Ruf als schwule Metropole gerecht, wenn sich im August 2002 schwule und lesbische SportlerInnen aus aller Welt hier zu den Gay Games 2002 treffen.

▲ Sydney, capitale de la Nouvelle-Galles du Sud, est la ville la plus ancienne et la plus grande d'Australie et probablement aussi la plus connue. La métropole commerciale avec son climat subtropical s'étend autour du port spectaculaire avec le Harbourg Bridge et le célèbre Opera House. Sydney a une grande communauté homosexuelle-lesbienne qui fête chaque année, à la fin de février, avec la plus grande parade homosexuelle mondiale, la „Sydney Gay and Lesbian Mardi Gras". Des centaines de milliers se poussent dans la rue pour laisser défiler devant eux la parade costumée ou pour fêter avec eux jusqu'à la pointe du jour. Le „Sleaze Ball" vers la fin de septembre ou le début d'octobre est un autre événement de Mardi gras, où se rencontrent plus de 20.000 homosexuels, lesbiennes et leurs amis. La scène homosexuelle s'est établie tout autour de l'Oxford Street au faubourg de Darlinghurst. A côté d'un autre centre homosexuel aux environs de la King Street (Newtown), la zone centrale de la ville est pratiquement accaparée par les homosexuels et les lesbiennes. Leur présence n'échappe à personne. Les plages de la ville de Manly et, bien sûr, la fameuse plage de Bondi sont tout aussi intéressantes pour les homosexuels. Les cafés et restaurants de la ville offrent une cuisine variée et intéressante de la région du Pacifique dans laquelle les jeunes chefs y contribuent fortement. Les bars, hôtels, saunas, centres de fitness, plages, organisations fréquentés par les homosexuels ne suffisent pas à décrire Sydney comme centre de services pour homosexuels, même considéré objectivement, c'est la capitale des homosexuels de la région du Pacifique Sud. Pour les touristes, Sydney est très bien située. Les Blue Mountains ne se trouvent qu'à quelques heures de la capitale, d'autres excursions journalières intéressantes sont les villes voisines Newcastle et Wollongong, les Southern Highlands près de Berri, la région viticole de Hunter Valley ou la capitale d'Australie Canberra. A l'extrême nord de la Nouvelle-Galles du Sud se trouve le district libéral de Northern Rivers autour de Byron Bay qui possède une petite communauté, mais très animée. Sydney satisfera également à l'avenir à sa réputation de métropole homosexuels quand au mois d'août 2002 se rencontrerons ici les sportifs homosexuels et lesbiens du monde entier pour les Gay Games 2002.

❖ Sydney, la capital de New South Wales, es la ciudad más antigua y más grande de Australia y con toda seguridad la más famosa. La vivaz metrópoli con su clima subtropical se caracteriza por su puerto espectacular con la *Harbour Bridge* y su famoso *Opera House*. Sydney cuenta con una extensa comunidad gay, que se reune cada año a finales de febrero para celebrar la fiesta más grande de homosexuales en el mundo, la *Sydney Gay and Lesbian Mardi Gras*. Miles de personas llenan las calles para ver el desfile con sus impresionantes disfraces o para participar en las fiestas que duran hasta la madrugada. El *Sleaze Ball* que se celebra a finales de septiembre o a principios de octubre es otro evento de Mardi Gras, donde se reunen más que 20.000 homosexuales, lesbianas y sus simpatizantes. El ambiente gay surgió en la „Golden Mile" de Oxford Street y sus alrededores, en los surburbios de Darlinghurst. A parte del otro centro gay que se encuentra en los alrededores de la King Street (Newton), los homosexuales y lesbianas se han apoderado casi de todo el centro de la ciudad, donde su fuerte presencia es notable hasta para los ojos nada experimentados. De especial interés para el turista gay son las playas de Manly y por supuesto la famosa Bondi playa. Los locales y restaurantes ofrecen una interesante y variada cocina de la región del Pacífico, preparados por los innovativos cocineros de la ciudad. Bares gay, hoteles gay, saunas gay, gimnasios gay, playas gay, organizaciones gay, hasta considerándolo friamente destaca el hecho que Sydney no se puede describir como centro de servicios gay, sino que es la metrópoli homosexual en la región del Pacífico. Para el turista, Sydney está situado perfectamente. Los Blue Mountains están a unas horas de distancias y otros excursiones interesantes se pueden hacer a las ciudades cercanas de Newcastle y Wollongong, a los Southern Highlands cerca de Berri, a la región vinícola Hunter Valley o a la capital australiana Canberra. En el extremo norte de New South Wales se encuentra el barrio liberal de Northern Rivers en los alrededores de Byron Bay, que cuenta con una pequeña, pero extremadamente vivaz comunidad gay. Sydney se consagrará también en el futuro como metrópoli gay, cuando en el mes de agosto en el año 2002 se reuneran aquí deportistas homosexuales y lesbianas de todo el mundo para los Gay Games 2002.

☆ Sydney, capitale del New South Wales, è la più vecchia e più grande città dell'Australia, e magari anche quella più conosciuta. La metropoli vivace con il suo clima subtropicale si estende attorno allo spettacolare porto con l'Harbour Bridge e la famosa Opera House. Sydney ha una grande comunità gay e lesbica che ha ottenuto fama internazionale grazie alla „Sydney Gay and Lesbian Mardi Gras", la più grande sfilata gay del mondo che si svolge sempre verso la fine di febbraio. Centinaia di migliaia di persone assistono alla manifestazione e festeggiano fino all'alba. A „Sleaze Ball", a fine settembre, all'inizio dell'ottobre, c'è un'altro avvenimento „Mardi Gras" che attira più di 20.000 gay e lesbiche e i loro amici. La vita gay è sorta intorno al „Golden Mile" nella Oxford Street nel distretto di Darlinghorst. Oltre a un'altro centro gay attorno alla King Street quasi tutta la città in quei giorni viene occupata dai gay e dalle lesbiche. La loro presenza dà nell'occhio anche a quelli meno „esperti". Altrettanto interessante per i gay sono le spiaggie di Manly e di Bondi. I locali e ristoranti offrono le diverse cucine tipiche del pacifico, dove i giovani chef contribuiscono al loro successo. Bar gay, alberghi gay, saune gay, palestre gay, spiaggie gay, organizzazioni gay: dal punto di vista obiettivo non basta descrivere Sydney come centro gay nel settore dei servizi, ma bensí come capitale gay del Pacifico Meridionale. Per il turista Sydney è una comoda base per escursioni. Alle Blue Mountains si arriva entro poche ore, altri posti interessanti sono le città vicine di Newcastle e Wollongong, le Southern Highlands presso Berri, le Vigne della Hunter Valley, o la capitale australiana Canberra. Nella parte più a nord del New South Wales si trova il distretto di Northern Rivers attorno alla Byron Bay con una piccola ma vivace comunità gay. Anche nel futuro Sydney soddisferà le aspettative che vengono poste ad una metropoli gay, perché nell'agosto del 2002 si incontreranno sportive/i lesbiche e gay in occasione delle Gay Games 2002.

GAY INFO

Capital Q
263 Liverpool Street, Darlinghurst ✉ NSW 2010
☎ 9332-4988 Fax: 9380-5104 Email: capq@ipacific.net.au
Homepage: www.capitalq.com.au*Published weekly. Free at gay venues.*

Gay and Lesbian WotsOn
✉2000 ☎ 9361-0655
24 hours recorded information.

Gaywaves Thu 20-22.30 h (2 SER FM 107.3 Mhz)
PO Box 473, Broadway ✉2000 ☎ 9514 9514 Fax: 9514 9599
Gay and lesbian radio program .

Sydney Gay and Lesbian Mardi Gras Association
PO Box 557 Newtown ✉NSW 2042 ☎ 9557-4332
Fax: 9516-4446 *Association organizes the annual Sydney Gay and lesbian Mardi Gras Party, Parade, Festival, and Sleaze Ball.*

Sydney Star Observer
PO Box 939, Darlinghurst ✉1300 ☎ 9380-5577 Fax: 9331 2118Email: mail@ssonet.com.au
Homepage: sso.rainbow.net.au *Sydney's weekly published gay community newspaper. One of Australia's leading gay newspapers. Very professional. Free at gay venues.*

TOURIST INFO

Sydney Visitors Information Kiosk
Mon-Fri 9-17 h
Martin Plaza, ✉NSW 2000 ☎ 9235 2424

BARS

Albury Hotel (! B F G MA STV YG) Sun-Thu 12-24, Fri-Sat 12-1 h
6 Oxford Street, Paddington ✉NSW 2021 ☎ 9361-6555
Popular bar, with body-builder barmen, drag shows.

SYDNEY

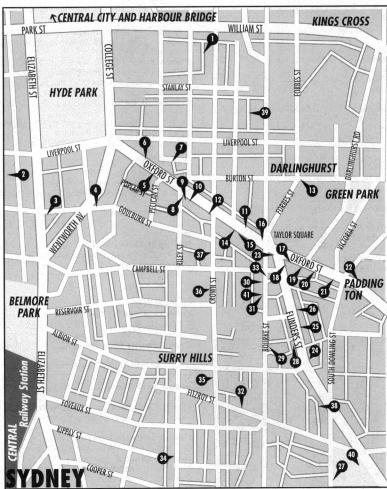

1. City Gym Fitness
2. Ram Lounge and Video Adult Entertainment
3. Southern Cross Hotel
4. Macquarie Hotel
5. DCM-Sydney Night Club Disco
6. Exchange Hotel Bar Phoenix Bar
7. King Steam Sauna
8. Signal Men's Club
9. FOD Travel Service Midnight Shift Hotel Disco
10. Numbers Bar
11. Mephisto Leather Shop
12. The Den Men's Club
13. Dov Café
14. The Probe Adult Entertainment
15. Byblos Disco
16. Oxford Hotel Bar
17. 191 Café
18. Taylor Square Restaurant
19. Bookshop Darlinghurst
20. Green Park Diner Restaurant
21. Beauchamp Hotel Bar
22. Albury Hotel Bar
23. Bananas Bar
24. Manor House Hotel
25. Bodyline Spa & Sauna
26. Taxi Club Bar
27. Park Lode Hotel
28. Flinders Hotel Bar
29. Beresford Hotel/Bar
30. Pelican Hotel
31. 415 on Bourke Hotel
32. Governors on Fitzroy Guest House
33. The Piercing Urge Shop
34. Brickfield Hill B&B Inn Hotel
35. Medina on Crown Hotel
36. City Crown Lodge International Hotel
37. Headquarters Men's Club
38. Radical Leather Shop
39. Barracks Guest House
40. Ken's at Kensington
41. The Villa Private Hotel

Banana Bar (A AC B CC d F GLM S W YG) Mon-Sat 15-3, Sun 15-24 h
1-5 Flinders Street, Darlinghurst ✉NSW 2010 *(Taylor Square)* ☎ 9360-6373
Cocktail bar and restaurant.
Beauchamp Hotel. The (AC B cc d G LJ MA N VS) Mon- Wed & Sun 12-24, Thu -1, Fri & Sat -2 h
267 Oxford Street, Darlinghurst ✉NSW 2010 *Oposite St. Vincents Hospital. Courner of Oxford and South Downing Street.* ☎ 9331-2575
Beresford Hotel (B f GLM MA N) Mon Tue 17.30-3, Wed Thu 12-3, Fri Sat 17.30-3, Sun 17.30-24 h
354 Bourke Street, Darlinghurst ✉NSW 2010 ☎ 9331-1045
Pub offering food and drink
Caesar's Bar (B G MA)
Petersham Inn Hotel, 388 Parramatta Road, Petersham ✉NSW 2049 ☎ 9569-4448
Cleveland (AC B CC d F glm MA N OS) Mon-Sat 11-4, Sun 12-24 h
433 Cleveland Street, Redfern ☎ 9698-1908
Flinders Hotel (AC B d G S SNU YG) Mon-Thu 20-3, Fri-Sat 22-7, Sun 20-24 h; shows Thu-Sun; strippers Sat 23 h
63 Flinders Street, Darlinghurst ✉NSW 2010 ☎ 9360-4929
Imperial Hotel (B D GLM s) Sun-Thu 10-?, Fri Sat -8 h
35 Erskineville Road ✉NSW 2000 ☎ 9519-9899
Thu-Sun drag shows. Fri Sat Theatre Restaurant.
Newtown Hotel (AC B D F G S VS YG) Mon-Sat 10-24, Sun 12-22 h
174 King Street, Newtown ✉NSW 2042 ☎ 9557-1329 *2 bars.*
Numbers (B D G) 10-? h
95 Oxford Street, Darlinghurst ✉NSW 2010 *(1st floor)* ☎ 9331-6099

Oxford Hotel (! B G lj YG) Mon-Thu 17-2, Fri Sat -3, Sun -24 h
134 Oxford Street, Darlinghurst ✉NSW 2010 ☎ 9331-3467
Cocktail bar „Gilligans" on the 1st floor. One of the most popular bars in Sydney.
Phoenix Bar (AC B CC D DR GLM lj MA r VS) We & Th 22:00-05:00h, Fr, Sa & Su 22:00-07:00h
c/o Exchange Hotel, 34 Oxford Street, Darlinghurst ✉2010 *200m from Hyde Park on Oxford St.* ☎ 9331 1936
Stonewall Hotel (A AC B bf CC D F GLM MA OS S WE) Mon-Fri 12-3, Sat Sun -5 h
173-175 Oxford Street, Darlinghurst ✉NSW 2010 ☎ 9360-1963
Taxi Club (B D F glm STV) 0-24 h
40 Flinders Street, Darlinghurst ✉NSW 2010 ☎ 9331-4256

DANCECLUBS

Byblos (B D G) Thu-Sat 22-? h
169 Oxford Street, Darlinghurst ✉NSW 2010
DCM-Sydney Night Club (AC B D glm MA S STV) Thu-Sun 23-? h
33 Oxford Street, Darlinghurst ✉NSW 2000 ☎ 9267-7036
Popular disco with mixed nights and gay nights. Check gay newspapers.
Midnight Shift Hotel (A AC B D GLM MA S STV VS) Bars downstairs: Mon-Sun 12-5, nightclub upstairs: Fri-Sun 23-? h
85 Oxford Street, Darlinghurst ✉NSW 2010 ☎ 9360-4319
Upstairs: Midnight Shift Nightclub, downstairs: The Shift Video Bar and the Locker Room.

RESTAURANTS

Californian Cafe. The (F GLM MA) 0-24 h
177 Oxford Street, Darlinghurst ✉NSW 2010 ☎ 9331-5587
All meals under A$ 10.
Grand Pacific Blue Room (AC B CC F g) Mon-Sat 18-3, closed Sun
Oxford Street/South Dowling Street, Paddington NSW 2021 ☎ 9331-7108
Green Park Diner (B bf F GLM) 11-23, Fri Sat -24, Sun 11-22 h
219 Oxford Street, Darlinghurst ✉NSW 2010 ☎ 9361-6171
Burgers and fresh simple food. Sydney's oldest gay restaurant. Very popular.
Side door Restaurant (B F G MA s)
283 Australia Street ✉NSW 2000 ☎ 9516-3691
Taylor Square (B F g) Mon-Sat 18.00-23, Sun 18-23 h
2 A Flinders Street, Darlinghurst ✉NSW 2010 ☎ 9360-5828
Great views of Oxford Street.
Thai Panic (F GLM OS YG) Mon-Thu 11-23, Fri-Sun 11-3 h
80 Oxford Street, Darlinghurst ☎ 9361-6406
Fresh food and funky atmosphere.
Thai Pothong (AC b CC F glm MA) 12-15, 18-23 h
294 King Street, Newtown ✉2042 ☎ 9550-6277
One of Sydney's best Thai restaurants
Yipiyiyo (AC CC F GLM MA) Mon-Thu 18.30-22, Fri Sat -23 h, closed Sun
290 Crown Street, Darlinghurst ✉NSW 2010 *(100 m south of Oxford Street)* ☎ 9332-3114

CAFES

Dov (F glm YG)
Burton/Forbes Street, Darlinghurst ✉NSW 2010
X-Core Cafe (bf F glm OS)
191 King Street, Newtown ✉NSW 2042
Unique atmosphere with pleasant cuisine.

191 Café (A bf CC F GLM MA OS YG) Mon-Fri 7-24, WE 8-1 h
191 Oxford Street, Darlinghurst ✉NSW 2010 ☎ 9360-4295
Popular café in the heart of gay Sydney, Taylor Square.

MEN'S CLUBS

Den. The (CC DR G lj VS) Mon-Thu 20-5, Fri 20-Mon 5 h
97 Oxford Street, Darlinghurst ✉NSW 2010 *(1st floor)* ☎ 9332-3402
Sexclub with coffee bar, TV & video lounge. Entry A$ 10.

Headquarters (b G MA VS) Mon-Thu 12-7, Fri 12-Mon 7 h
273 Crown Street, Darlinghurst ☎ 9331 6217

Mens Erotic Network
☎ 9212-7920 *(Craig)*

Signal (AC DR G LJ MA s VS WE) Sun-Thu 11-3, Fr-Sat 11-6
Riley Street/Arnold Square ✉NSW 2010 *(above 81, Oxford Street)* ☎ 9331-8830
A range of toys, magazines, books, underwear, leather clothing, etc. Men's sex club.

SEX SHOPS/BLUE MOVIES

Adultworld (CC g VS) 0-24 h
124 A Oxford Street, Darlinghurst ✉NSW 2010 ☎ 9360-8527

Body Play
(g) 159 Oxford Street, Darlinghurst ✉NSW 2010 *(level 2)*
Only all male peep show in Australia.

Club X (G)
429 Pitt Street ☎ 9211 5435

Club X (G VS)
26 Bayswater Road, Kings Cross ✉NSW 2011 ☎ 9357-1902

Club X (G)
711 George Street ☎ 9211 4398

Club X (G)
2G Roslyn Street, Kings Cross ☎ 9357 3152

Club X (G)
78 Darlinghurst Road, Kings Cross ☎ 9358 1812

Love Art (G VS)
779 Geroge Street ☎ 9221 1330

Numbers (G VS) 0-24 h
95 Oxford Street, Darlinghurst ✉NSW 2010 *(1st floor)*
☎ 9331-6099
Gay magazines, novels etc. Action area. Entry A$ 5.

Probe. The (CC DR G MA SNU VS) 11-1, Fri-Sun 0-24 h
159 Oxford Street, Darlinghurst ✉NSW 2010 *(level 1)*
☎ 9361-5924

Ram Lounge and Video (G VS) 9-1 h
380 Pitt Street ✉NSW 2000 *(Club X entrance. 1st floor)*
☎ 9264-3249
All day membership pass A$ 10.

Tool Shed. The (G VS) 11-1.30, Fri Sat 11-?,
Sun 13.30-23 h
198 King Street, Newtown ✉NSW 2042 ☎ 9565-1599
Adult boutique.

Toolshed (B G)
81 Oxford Street, Darlinghurst ✉NSW 2010

ESCORTS & STUDIOS

Bell Boys ☎ (0500) 55 44 60

HOUSE OF BOYS

Knightcall Male Escorts (AC CC G MG R) 11:00-late, every day.
P.O. Box 812, Kingscross ✉2011 ☎ 9368-0511

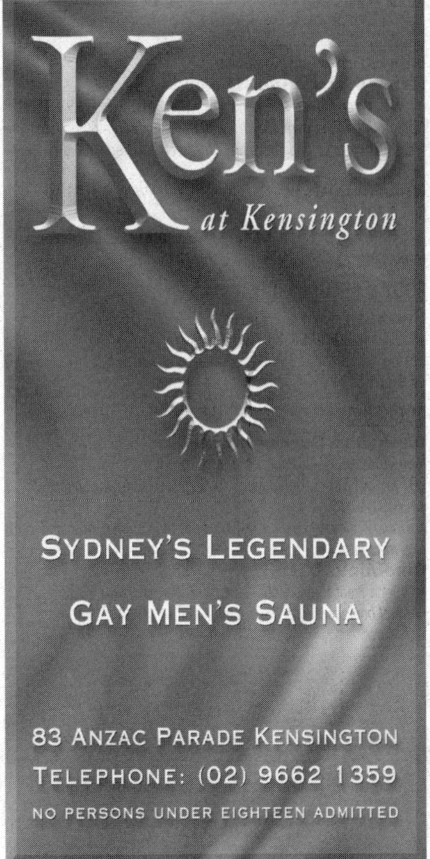

SAUNAS/BATHS

Bodyline (AC bf CC DR f G MA OS P sa sb wh YG) Mon-Thu 12-7, Fri-Sun 0-24 h
10 Taylor Street, Darlinghurst ✉NSW 2010 *(near Oxford Street)*
☎ 9360-1006

Ken's at Kensington (AC DR f G MA msg pi sa sb VS wh WO) Mon-Thu 12:00-06:00, Fri 12:00-Mon 06:00 h
83 Anzac Parade, Kensington ✉2033 *Buses from city (Taylor Square) 390, 392, 394. Railway 391* ☎ 9662-1359.

King Steam Sauna (DR f G OG P sa sb VS WE wh WO) Mon 10-1, Tue-Thu -6, Fri-Sun 0-24 h
38-42 Oxford Street Darlinghurst ✉NSW 2010 *(1st floor)* ☎ 9360-3431
Entry A$ 15, students 10.

FITNESSTUDIOS

Bayswater Fitness (g sol WO) Mon-Fri 6.30-22, Sat Sun 8-20 h
33 Bayswater Road, Kings Cross ✉NSW 2011 ☎ 9356-2555

City Gym (AC CC sb msg sa) Mo-Fr 0-24 h, Su 08:00-22:00h
107- 113 Crown Street ✉NSW 2010 *(East Sydney)* ☎ 9360-6247
Sydney's premier gay gymnasium.

Fitness Exchange. The (G) 17-? h
33 Wellington Street, Chippendale ✉NSW 2008 ☎ 9699-6514
Non-profit making gymnasium owned and run by gay members. Has weight-lifting and body-building, fitness classes, and tuition in karate.

Newtown Gym (AC CC G msg sa sol WO) Mon-Fri 6-22, Sat Sun 8-20 h
328-338 King Street, Newtown ✉NSW 2042 *(Newtown Plaza level 2)* ☎ 9557-2219

BODY & BEAUTY SHOPS

Piercing Urge. The (AC CC) Mo, Tu We & Fr 11:00-19:00h, Th-20:00h & Sa 10:00-1800h
Shop 3, 322 Bourke Street, Darlinghurst ✉2010 ☎ 9360 3179

BOOK SHOPS

Bookshop Darlinghurst. The (AC CC GLM)
Mon-Wed 10-23, Thu-Sat -24, Sun 11-24 h
207 Oxford Street, Darlinghurst ✉NSW 2010 *Taylor Square* ☎ 9331-1103
Australia's oldest gay and lesbian bookshop, magazines and cards plus local info.

Gleebooks 8-21 h
49 Glebe Point Road, Glebe ✉NSW 2037 ☎ 9660-2333
General bookstore with gay section.

EDUCATION SERVICES

Australian College of English
500 Oxford Street, Bondi Junction ✉NSW 2022 *(20th floor, Plaza Building)* ☎ 9389-0133
Intensive English courses for adults. Accommodation can be arranged.

LEATHER & FETISH SHOPS

Mephisto Leather
112 Oxford Street, Darlinghurst ✉NSW 2010 *(1st floor)* ☎ 9332 3218

Radical Leather (CC GLM) Tue-Fri 11-18, Sat -16 h
20 Hutchinson Street, Surry Hills ✉2010 ☎ 9331-7544
S&M leathergoods and made to measure apparel.

TRAVEL & TRANSPORT

Beyond the Blue
685 South Dowling Street, Surrey Hills ✉NSW 2010 ☎ 8399 0070 Fax: 8399 0073
Homepage: www.beyondthe blue.net *Gay and lesbian travel service*

Creative Tours
3/55 Grafton Street, Bondi Junction ✉NSW 2022 ☎ 9386-2111 Fax: 9386-2199
Gay and lesbian travel services and products.

Destination Downunder Mon-Fr 8.30-18 h
130 Elizabeth St. Sydney ✉NSW 2000 ☎ 9268-2111 Fax: 9267-9733 *Gay and lesbian travel agents.*

Friends of Dorothy • FOD Travel 9-17.30, Sat 9-13 h
77 Oxford Street, Darlinghurst ✉NSW 1300 *(2nd floor)* ☎ 9360-3616 Fax: 9332-3326

HHK Travel
50 Oxford Street, Paddington ✉NSW 2021 ☎ 9332-4299 Fax: 9360-2164
Travel agency for gays.

Rosemary Hopkins-In Any Event
2 Isabella Street, Balmain ✉NSW 2041 ☎ 9810-2439 Fax: 9810-3420
Project management in tourism and hospitality for the gay and lesbian community.

Silke's Travel
263 Oxford Street ✉NSW 2010 ☎ 9380-6244
FAX 9361-3729. Travel agent. Member of IGLTA and AGLTA, Mardi Gras Tour Operator.

VIDEO SHOPS

Videodrama Sun-Thu 10-22, Fri Sat 10-24 h
135 Oxford Street, Darlinghurst ✉NSW 2010
Gay owned video hire. Not x-rated but gay relevant films.

HOTELS

Aaron's Hotel (AC bf CC F glm MA W)
37 Ultimo Road ✉NSW 2000 ☎ 9281-5555 Fax: 9281-0666
Central location in theatre and entertainment disctrict. 91 double rooms, 3 single rooms with shower/WC, phone, radio, heating. Hotel provides own key, room service. Rates standard room A$ 125, deluxe 145, courtyard 185, add. bed 10, bf 9.50.

Altamont Hotel (B CC d g) 207
Darlinghurst Road, Darlinghurst ✉NSW 2010 ☎ 9360-6000 Fax: 9360-7096
14 double rooms with WC, shower or bath, balcony or terrace, TV, telephone and safe. Rates A$ 130-400. Luxury shop in the hotel.

SYDNEY's Premier Gay Boutique Hotel

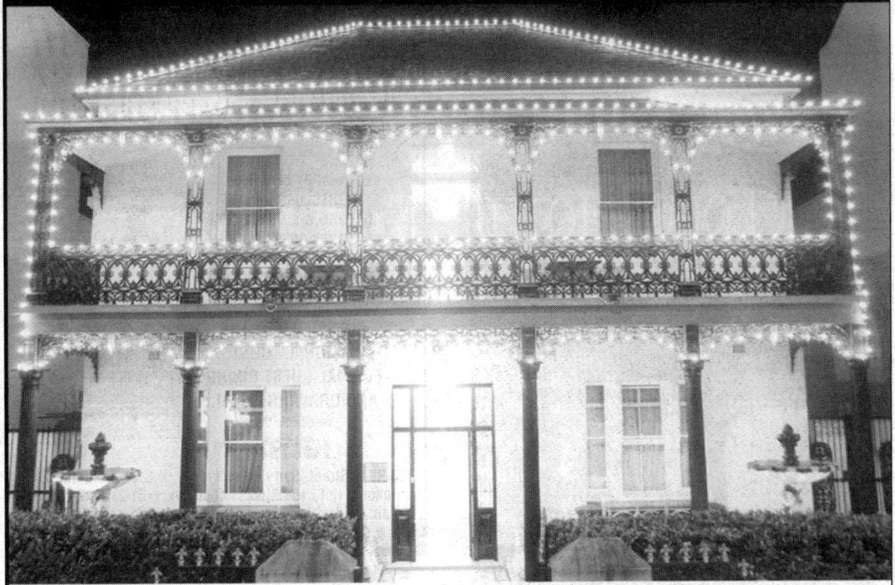

Incorporating Lush restaurant and bar *300m from Oxford St*

Featuring 20 elegantly appointed rooms and 5 serviced apartments

- Continental breakfast included
- King size beds
- Air conditining
- Mini bar
- Electronic safe
- TV video

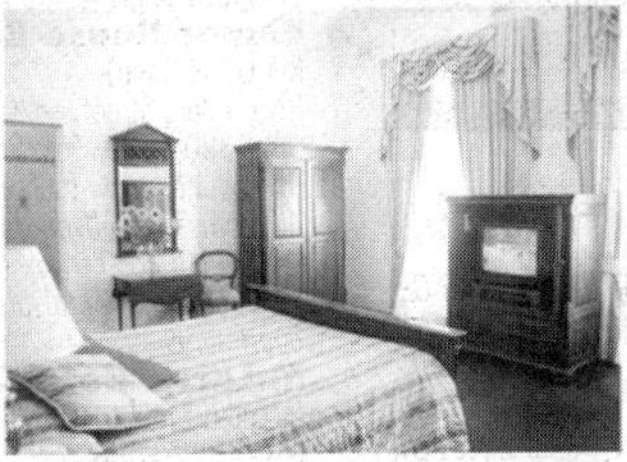

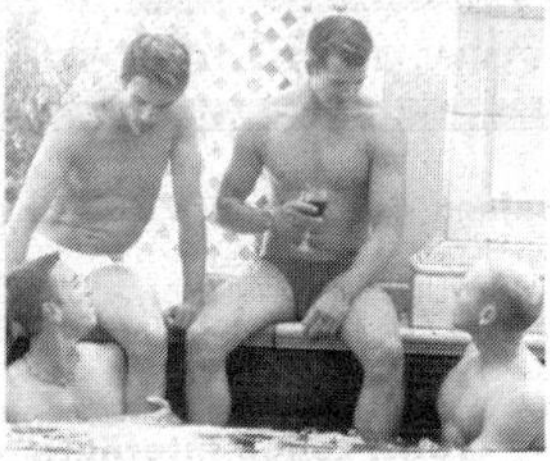

Telephone: 612 9380 6633
Facsimile: 612 9380 5016
Email: info@manorhouse.com.au
Website: www.manorhouse.com.au

MANOR HOUSE
Boutique Hotel

86 Flinders St Darlinghurst SYDNEY NSW 2010 Australia

Chelsea Guest House (AC bf CC glm H OS WO) 24h, 7 days a week.
49 Womerah Avenue, Darlinghurst ✉NSW 2010 *5 minutes to Oxford Street 7 Kings Cross.* ☎ 9380-5994 Fax: 9332 2491 Email: xchelsea@ozemail.com.au
Single A$ 70, double 110 incl. breakfast

City Crown Lodge International (AC bf CC E GLM H MA OS p VS) 8-23 h
289 Crown Street, Surry Hills, ✉NSW 2010 *(One minute walk to Oxford Street/Gay scene)* ☎ 9331-2433 Fax: 9360-7760
Email: citycrown@bigpond.co
Homepage: wheretostay.com.au/citycrownlodge
19 double rooms with shower/WC, balcony or terrace, telephone. Own key. Rates A$ 90 + tax. Elegant atmosphere. Breakfast A$ 6.

Furama Hotel Central (AC B CC glm H OS pi sa wh WO)
28 Albion Street, Surry Hills ✉NSW 2010 *(Near Central station)* ☎ 9281-0333
Located minutes walk from Oxford Street. It's a four-star gay-friendly hotel.

Hughenden. The (bf g H)
14 Queen Street, Woollahra ✉NSW 2025 ☎ 9363-4863
Fax: 9362-0398.

Macquarie Hotel (B F G H)
42 Wentworth Avenue ✉2000 ☎ 9264-9888
FAX 9267-5037 · Email hotel@cafelink.net
Centrally located near the gay scene. All rooms with bathroom and TV. Rates single A$ 60-70, double/twin 80-90.

Manor House Boutique Hotel (AC B bf CC F GLM H MA OS pi S wh)
86 Flinders Street, ✉2010 *(300m from Oxford Street)*
☎ 9380 6633 Fax: 9380 5016 Email: info@manorhouse.com.au
Homepage: www.manorhouse.com.au
All rooms with private facilities, TV/Video, radio, safe, own key. Rates A$ 100-200 + tax (low season), 165-275 + tax (high season) includes continental breakfast. 24 elegant rooms and 6 service apartments

McLaren Hotel (bf g H)
McLaren Street, North Sydney ✉NSW 2060 ☎ 9954-4622
Fax: 9922-1868
Rate A$ 140, incl. bf. For Spartacus readers 99.

Medina on Crown (AC F g H) 359
Crown Street, Surry Hills ✉NSW 2010 ☎ 9360-6666
Fax: 9267-1716
Executive apartments.

Park Lodge Hotel (AC bf CC F glm H OS W)
747 South Dowling Street/Thurlow Street ✉NSW 2016
(Moore Park)
☎ 9318-2393 Fax: 9318-2513
Email: glodge@parklodgehotel.com
Homepage: www.parklodgesydney.com
Ten minutes to the airport. Five minutes to gay venues. Restored Victorian Hotel. Rates A$ 45-60.

Pelican. The (bf G H OS) 411
Bourke Street, Darlinghurst ✉NSW 2010 *(near Taylor Square)*
☎ 9331-5344 /Fax: 9331-3150 *In the heart of the gay scene. From A$ 50-70, plus 10 for extra person.*

Ravesi's of Bondi Beach (B F g H)
Bondi Beach ✉NSW 2026 *(near Campbell Parade/Hall Street)*
☎ 9365-4422 Fax: 9365-1481 *Rates A$ 88-165.*

Rooftop Motel (AC bf CC glm NG pi)
146-148 Glebe Point Road ☎ *9660-7777 FAX 9660 7155. E-Mail: rooftop@ral.net.au*
Homepage: www.budget-motel.com.nf Located 2 km from central Sydney. 39 Rooms with shower/WC, phone, TV, radio, AC, own key. Rates double A$ 80, additional bed 10, bf 2,50-15.

Simpsons of Potts Point (AC bf CC H p)
8 Challis Avenue, Potts Point ✉NSW 2011 ☎ 9356-2199
Fax: 9356-4476
Restored boutique hotel. Rates single A$ 160, double 175, add. bed 25 (incl. bf). Open all year.

Southern Cross Hotel. The (B F g H)
Elizabeth Street/Goulburn Street ✉NSW 2000 ☎ 9282-0987
FAX 9211-1806. Close to Oxford Street.

Sullivans Hotel (AC bf CC glm H MA OS pi)
21 Oxford Street, Paddington ✉2021 ☎ 9361-0211 Fax: 936 3735
Email: sydney@sullivans.com.au Homepage: www.sullivans.com.au
Located in cosmopolitan Paddington near nightlife, art galleries, shopping. 11 km to airports, 6 km to beach. 62 rooms with shower/WC, TV and phone. Rates A$ 116-122. Bicycle hire.

Tilbury Hotel. The (B bf E H NG)
Nicholson/Forbes Streets, Woolloomooloo NSW 2011 ☎ 9358-1925
or ☎ 9357-1428. Rate A$ 45/night, 180/week, incl. bf.

Victoria Court Sydney (AC bf CC g H)
122 Victoria Street, Potts Point ✉2011 ☎ 9357 3200
Fax: 9357 7606
Email: info@VictoriaCourt.com.au Homepage: www.VictoriaCourt.com.au
Historic boutique Hotel. Close to Opera House, Oxford Street and beaches. All rooms with bath/WC, TV and phone. Rates A$ 125-250. 10% discount for SPARTACUS readers.

415 on Bourke (G H)
415 Bourke Street, Darlinghurst ✉NSW 2010 ☎ 9360-9443
Fax: 9331-3150
Close to gay venues. 4 rooms with antique furniture. Rates from A$ 55-75 per night.

GUEST HOUSES

Barracks. The (CC G H lj)
19 Palmer Lane, Darlinghurst ✉NSW 2010 *(5 minutes walk to Oxford Street/Gay scene)*
☎ 9360-5823 Fax: 9358-4996
Email: barracks@chilli.net.au Homepage: www.chilli.net.au/~barracks.
Rates for one person/night A$ 75 up to 3 days. For two people add A$ 10 to the daily rate. All 6 rooms with queen size bed and TV. Shared bathroom and kitchen. Free bf.

Brickfield Hill-Bed and Breakfast Inn (AC bf CC f GLM H MA OS P)
403 Riley Street, Surry Hills ✉NSW 2010 ☎ 9211 4886
Fax: 9212 2556 Email: fields@zip.com.au
Homepage: www.zip.com.au/~fields
An elegant four-storey Victorian terrace house in the gay district close to the city. 5 double and 5 single rooms, partly with shared bath/WC. Rates from A$ 95 to A$ 150

Darley Bed & Breakfast (bf cc glm H)
160 Darley Street, Newtown ✉NSW 2042 ☎ 9550-6625
Fax: 9550-6625
Located in the middle of Newtown. 3 double rooms, 1 single room All rooms with bath/shower/WC, balcony or terrace, TV. Hotel provides own key, car park, TV room, bicycle hire, tennis. Rates double A$ 80-90, single 65 (bf incl.)

Governors on Fitzroy (bf CC G H wh)
64 Fitzroy Street, Surry Hills ✉2010 ☎ 9331-4652
Fax: 9361-5094
Email: governor@zip.com.au Homepage: www.zip.com.au
In the heart of gay Sydney, 3 blocks from Oxford Street. 6 rooms. Rates single A$ 80, double A$ 100 inc. Breakfast. Open all year.

Villa Private Hotel. The (GLM H) 413
Bourke Street, Darlinghurst ✉2010 ☎ 9331-3602
FAX 9331-2101. Centrally located. 6 rooms with shared bath, TV, radio, kitchenette. Rates one person A$ 70, two persons 80.

APARTMENTS

Addison's on Anzac (AC B CC E F g H)
147 Anzac Parade, Kensington ✉NSW 2033 ☎ 9663 0600
Fax: 9313 621
42 apartments, rates double A$ 105, single 95. Fully furnished and serviced apartments, conveniently located.

Seventeen Elizabeth Bay Road
17 Elizabeth Bay Road ✉2011 ☎ 9358 8999

PRIVATE ACCOMODATION

Share Accommodation for Travellers (GLM)
Mo-Fr 09:30-19:00h, Sa 10:00-16:00h
Level 1, 263 Oxford Street ✉2010 ☎ 9360 7744 Fax: 9361 3729
Email: share@alpha.net.au Homepage: www.sharespace.com.au
Share accommodation from 1 week to 1 year at prices to meet all budgets.

GENERAL GROUPS

Cronulla Gay Group every 2nd Wed 20 h
PO Box 195, Cronulla ✉NSW 2230 ☎ 9521-7914
(Brian) Exists to provide both friendship and support for gay women and men.

Gay & Lesbian Family Association (GALFA)
PO Box 251, Vaucluse ✉NSW 2030 ☎ 9388-7222
Call Derek or write for information and membership.

Gay & Lesbian Rights Lobby
74-78 Oxford Street, Darlinghurst ✉NSW 2010 ☎ 9360-6650
Postal Address: PO Box 9, Darlinghurst 2010 Anti-violence project, advice on legal, custody and educational problems.

Gay Fathers
103/412 Oxford Street, Paddington ✉NSW 2021 ☎ 9360-3063

Icebreakers Tue 20-22 h
197 Albion Street, Surry Hills ✉NSW 2010 ☎ 9360-2211
Gay social group for people of any age looking for new friends. Counselling Service.

Lesbian & Gay Anti-Violence Project (GLM)
PO Box 1178, Darlinghurst ✉NSW 2010
☎ 9360-6687 Fax: 9380-5848

MAG Mature Age Gays Meets 19h 2nd and last Sa. each month.
c/o ACON, 9 Commonwealth Street, Darlinghurst ✉2010 ☎ 9206-2072

North Shore Voltairians 1st Tue 20.30 h at Victoria Cross Tavern,
Mount St./Miller St., North Sydney ☎ 9955-3542
(John) Social dinners, outings and more.

Parents-FLAG
PO Box 1152, Castle Hill ✉NSW 2154 ☎ 9899-1101
(Heather) or ☎ 9630-5681 (Mollie) Parents and friends of gays and lesbians.

Social Group for gays under 26 Meets Mon
☎ 9206-2077 *(Brent or Tim)*

FETISH GROUPS

Dolphin Motor Club (LJ) Meets 2nd Fri at „The Keep"
PO Box E362, St. James ✉NSW 2000 ☎ 9699-6588

Sydney Roadrunners Motorcycle Club
Meeting 1st Mon at „Newtown Hotel"
PO Box 405 ✉NSW 2015 ☎ 9699-9386
Meet every 3rd Sun. Phone Ian for information.

HEALTH GROUPS

AIDS Council of NSW (ACON) Mon-Fri 10-18 h
9 Commonwealth Street, Surry Hill ✉NSW 2010 ☎ 9206-2000
Bobby Goldsmith Foundation
376 Victoria Street, PO Box 97, Darlinghurst ✉NSW 2010 *(Suite 10, 4th floor)* ☎ 9360-9755
Provides financial support and accommodation in two houses for PWA and ARC. Registered Trust under the NSW Trustees Act.
Community Support Network, Inc. (CSN)
9 Commonwealth Street, Surry Hills ✉NSW 2010 ☎ 9206-2000
Discovery
☎ 9371-9868
(Kim) Support group for people with HIV/AIDS.
Gay and Lesbian line 16-24 h
☎ 9360-2211
Or call toll-free ☎ 008-80-5379
Gay Men Fighting AIDS ☎ 9519-5202
Social support group, health education, fundraising.
Kendall Centre. The
26 Kendall Centre, Harris Park ✉NSW 2150 ☎ 9893-9522
AIDS information and support, condoms, needle exchange and counselling.
Order of Perpetual Indulgence
PO Box 426, Grosvenor Place, ✉NSW 2000
Part of the international Order.

HELP WITH PROBLEMS

Twenty Ten Youth Refuge (GLM p YG) Mo-Fr 10:00-18:30h
PO Box 213, Glebe ✉2037 ☎ 9660-0539 Fax: 9552 6324
Youth refuge and support services for young gays and lesbians.

RELIGIOUS GROUPS

Acceptance Service Fri 20 h at St. Candice's Church
28 Roslyn Street, Elizabeth Streets ✉NSW 2011 ☎ 9361-5290
Social group for homosexual catholics.
Aleph
PO Box 120, 60 Blair Street, Bondi North ✉NSW 2026 ☎ 9300-9700
(Michael) Social group for gay & lesbian Jews.
Metropolitan Community Church of the Good Shepherd Sun 19 h
15 Francis Street, Darlinghurst ✉NSW 2011 ☎ 9638-3885
Fax: 9387-8371

SPECIAL INTEREST GROUPS

Asian & Friends Fri 19.30-22 h
PO Box 238, Darlinghurst ✉NSW 2010 ☎ 9558-0061
(Gus or Jim) Social group.
Choir Sydney Gay and Lesbian
PO Box
649, Darlinghurst ✉NSW 2010 ☎ 9698-2151
(Stephen) or ☎ 9361-6980 (Rob)
Queer Screen Limited (CC GLM MA)
PO Box 1081, Darlington ✉2010 ☎ 9332-4150
Fax: 9331 2988
Email: richard@queerscreen.com. *Group which organises the Sydney International Mardi Gras Film Festival*
Silk Road
c/o Acon, 9 Commonwealth Street ✉2010
☎ 9206-2000 Fax: 9206 2069
Asian gay and bisexual men. Free membership.

Sydney Bisexual Support Network
2nd/4th Mon
66 Albion Street, Surry Hills ✉NSW 2010 ☎ 9698-1207
Sydney Gay and Lesbian Business Association
PO Box 394, Darlinghurst ✉NSW 2010 ☎ 9264-6233
Monthly meetings.

SPORT GROUPS

Southern Cross Outdoor Group
PO Box 411, Dee Why ✉NSW 2099 ☎ 9907-9144
Email: scog@pinkboard.com.au
Homepage: /www.pinkboard.com.au/~scog
Walking & social group for gay men in Greater Sydney.
Team Sydney
PO Box 1037, Darlinghurst ✉NSW 2010 ☎ 9427-7729
Call Brian or Wayne ☎ 9311-3062 Sports group, regular newsletter.

SWIMMING

-Lady Jane Beach (g NU) (near South Head. Official nude beach. Lady Jane is very small and picturesque and is reached by taking the bush walk from Camp Cove.)
-Tamarama and nearby Bondi Beach (The rock area between the two beaches is the site of much heavy cruising)
-Obelisk Beach (g NU) (at Mosman, opposite side of the Harbour (from Lady Jane Bay) and next to Naval base)

CRUISING

-Rocks at Balmoral (daytime)
-Centennial Park (AYOR)
-Lady Jane Beach (amongst the rocks, but be discreet)
-Grant's Park (south side of Coogee Beach from Surf Club to Sunstrip Pool; 11-2 h)
-Cremorne Wharf (north side of harbor; 10-1 h)
-Obelisk Beach, Mosman
-Reef Beach (NU) (Seaforth)
-South Dowling Street; very cruisy but watch for bashers and police)
-Rifle Range at Maroubra
-Red Leaf Pool (Woollahra on harbor)
-Rushcutters Bay Park (AYOR at night) (all day long)
-Green Park (AYOR) (Darlinghurst)
-Rocks between Bondi Beach and Tamarama
-Alamein Fountain (AYOR R)(Fitzroy Park, Kings Cross)
All AYOR

BOOK SHOPS

Borderline Books (g)
28 Bay Street ✉2485 ☎ 5536-4275
Keyhole Bookshop (g)
9 Bay Street ✉2485 ☎ 7536-3197

Wollongong ☎ 02

DANCECLUBS

Castaways (AC b D f GLM MA OS S STV W WE) 2nd & 4th Sa/ month 20:00-02:30h
17 Chopin Street, ✉2147 *At Parramatta Golf Club. 10 min walk from Westmead & Parramatta stations.* ☎ 9674 5903
Entry A$ 5.00 - supporting people with HIV/AIDS
Chequers (A AC B CC D f GLM MA S STV YG)) Wed-Sat 20-3 h
341 Crown Street ✉2500 *(on the rooftop of Piccadilly Shopping Centre)* ☎ 4226-3788
Bar and dance club with pool tables and pin ball machines. No entrance-fee on Thu and before 22 h on Wed Fri Sat.

GENERAL GROUPS

Men's Gay & Bisexual Coming Out Group
PO Box 1144 ✉2500 ☎ 4221-4012
Advice and help.

Wollongong Out Now
☎ 4226-1163
Social group for gays & bis under 26.

HEALTH GROUPS

AIDS Council of NSW
129 Kembla Street, PO Box 1073 ✉2500 ☎ 4226-1163

SWIMMING

-Windang Beach (NU)

CRUISING

-Fairy Meadow Surf Club (at night)
-McCabe Park (AYOR-Police) (Fri and Sat night)

AUS-Northern Territory

North AUS
Initials: NT
Time: GMT +9.5
Area: 1,346,200 km² / 519,768 sq mi.
Population: 191,000
Capital: Darwin

Alice Springs ☎ 08

BARS

Oasis Motel (B F g h MA) gayish Fri 17-19 h
Gap Road ✉NT 0870 ☎ 8952 1444

Simpsons Gap Bar in Alice Springs (B g) 18-2 h
Sheraton, Barrett Drive ✉NT 0870 ☎ 8952 8000

RESTAURANTS

Casa Nostra (B F g)
Undoolya Road ✉NT 0870 ☎ 8952 6749

Swingers Café (A F glm OS S W) Mon-Tue 7.30-18, Wed-Sat -23 h, closed Sun
off Todd Mall ✉NT 0870 ☎ 8952 9291
Mainly vegetarian.

HEALTH GROUPS

AIDS Council of Central Australia Mon-Fri 9-17 h
19 Todd Street, PO Box 910 ✉NT 0871 ☎ 8953 1118
Fax: 8953 4584.

Alice Springs Hospital STD Unit Mon-Fri 8-16 h
Gap Road/Steward Terrace ✉NT 0870 ☎ 8950 2638

Darwin ☎ 08

RESTAURANTS

Genghis Khan (F g)
44 East Point Road ✉NT 0800 ☎ 8981 3883

Mississippi Queen Restaurant-Rail Car Bar
(AC B f g MA N OS s) Bar 19-2 h, reservation for restaurant
6 Gardiner Street ✉NT 0800 ☎ 8981 3358

SEX SHOPS/BLUE MOVIES

Fantasy Lane/Champions Two (AC DR g MA P VS W) 9-24 h
4 Charles Street, Stuart Park ✉NT 0820 ☎ 8941-2441
Sex shop with gay back room.

TRAVEL & TRANSPORT

Gray Link Tour Operators
PO Box 3826 ✉NT 0801 ☎ 8948-1777 Fax: 8948-1777

HOTELS

Mirambeena Resort (AC b CC F H MA pi W WO)
64 Cavenagh Street ✉NT 0800 ☎ 8946-0111 Fax: 8981-5116
Single from A$ 114, double 124. Rates per room per night plus 6% NT bed tax.

HEALTH GROUPS

Communicable Diseases Centre
Block 4, Royal Darwin Hospital, Rocklands Drive ☎ 8920 8007
Antibody testing, inpatient and outpatient services.

Northern Territory AIDS Council Inc.
Mon-Fri 10-17
GPO Box 2826 NT 0801, 1/1 Carey Street ✉NT 0800
☎ 8941 1711 Fax: 8941 2590

CRUISING

-Vesty's Beach (between Sailing Club and Ski Club showers, good at night; fairly safe, take insect repellent)
-Mindil Beach (either side of the casino)
-Lameroo Beach (NU) (below the Darwin Hotel)
-Casarina Free Beach (NU) (turn right towards the gun turret)

AUS-Queensland

Northeast AUS
Initials: QLD
Time: GMT +10
Area: 1,727,200 km² / 666,872 sq mi.
Population: 3,451,000
Capital: Brisbane

Brisbane ☎ 07

● The capital of Queensland also known as the Sunshine State. After much needed legal reform the somewhat conservative city has become a popular holiday destination for gays. Although Brisbane is an important economic centre it has not developed as rapidly as Melbourne or Sydney. Brisbane is close to the beaches and to the Gold Coast (fourty minutes to the South) and the Sunshine State is only an hour and a half to the North. There have emmerged in the past few years a vast number of gay BARS; restaurants and guest houses. Even the far North of Queensland is interesting for the gay tourist.
The Queensland style is a simple one, friendly and proud of their state with it's sub-tropical climate. A major attraction is the Mr. Gay Queensland competition held in July. The competition involves contestants from throughout the state and has been a major contribution to the development of the gay movement in Queensland.

✱ Brisbane ist die Hauptstadt des Bundesstaates Queensland, der auch den Namen „Sunshine-State" trägt. Nach einigen Gesetzesreformen ist die traditionell eher konservative Stadt heute ein sehr angenehmes Reiseziel für Schwule. Obwohl Brisbane ein wichtiges wirtschaftliches Zentrum ist, entwickelt es sich nicht so rasant wie etwa Melbourne oder Sydney. Von hier aus ist es nicht weit zu den Stränden und der Gold Coast (vierzig Minuten nach Süden) oder der Sunshine Coast (eineinhalb Stunden nach Norden). Dort und natürlich in Brisbane selbst sind in den letzten Jahren eine ganze Reihe von schwulen Bars, Restaurants und Pensionen entstanden. Selbst der äußerste Norden von Queensland ist heute für den schwulen Touristen interessant.

Den Menschen hier wird nachgesagt, sie seien einfach und freundlich und sehr stolz auf ihren Bundesstaat mit seinem subtropischen Klima. Eine große Attraktion ist der Mr.-Gay-Queensland-Wettbewerb im Juli. Er zieht Schwule aus dem ganzen Land an und stellt einen wesentlichen Beitrag zur Entwicklung des schwulen Selbstbewußtseins in Queensland dar.

▲Brisbane, la capitale du Queensland („l'état du soleil") a 1,350 millions d'habitants. Brisbane s'est débarrassée de son esprit rétrograde depuis que le Queensland a commencé à attirer les touristes. La législation concernant l'homosexualité en fait aujourd'hui un des hauts lieux du tourisme gay. Brisbane est une ville très active et un centre économique important, sans avoir toutefois le côté tentaculaire de Melbourne ou Sydney.
De Brisbane, il faut 40 minutes pour atteindre les plages et les sîtes touristiques de Gold Coast (au sud) et une heure et demie pour aller à Sunshine Coast (au nord). Comme à Brisbane, vous y trouverez toute une série d'établissements gays (bars, restaurants, pensions et, dans le nord du Queensland, centres de vacances gays) tous assez récents. Les habitants du Queensland ont la réputation d'être simples, décontractés, sympathiques, très fiers de leur état et de son climat tropical. Depuis quelques années, on procède en juillet à l'élection de M. Gay-Queesnland. Les candidats affluent des quatre coins de l'état. C'est un évènement important qui renforce la „gay pride".

❖Brisbane es la capital del estado federal Queensland, que se conoce también como „Sunshine- State". En esta ciudad, tradicionalmente muy conservadora, se han llevado a cabo algunas reformas legislativas en los últimos año y como consecuencia Brisbane se ha convertido en un destino vacacional muy agradable para homosexuales. Aunque la ciudad es un importante centro económico, no se está desarollando con la misma velocidad como por ejemplo Melbourne or Sydney. Brisbane está situada cerca de la las playas como la de Gold Coast (a 40 minutos dirección sur) o de Sunshine Coast (a hora y media hacia el norte). En estos lugares, así como en la misma ciudad de Brisbane se establecieron en el transcurso de los últimos años bares, restaurantes y hoteles gay. Incluso el extrémo norte de Queensland es hoy en día interesante para el turista homosexual. La gente de Queensland tienen fama de ser sencillos y amables, así como muy orgullosos de su estado federal con su clima subtropical. Una de las mayores atracciones es la elección de „Mr.-Gay-Queensland" que tiene lugar cada año en el mes de julio. Este evento atrae homosexuales de todo el mundo y es una de las mayores contribuciones al desarollo de la autoconfianza gay en Queensland.

☆Brisbane è la capitale dello stato federale di Queensland che viene chiamato anche „Sunshine State". Dopo alcune riforme di legge la città tradizionalmente più conservativa si presenta oggi come piacevole posto per i turisti gay. Sebbene Brisbane sia un'importante centro economico, non sta sviluppandosi altrettanto veloce come Melbourne e Sydney. Da qui non è lontano arrivare alle spiaggie ed alla Gold Coast (a 40 minuti verso sud) o alla Sunshine Coast (a un'ora e mezzo verso nord). In questi posti ed anche a Brisbane stessa hanno aperto vari bar, ristoranti e pensioni gay. Perfino l'estremo nord di Queensland risulta interessante per il turista gay. Si dice, che gli abitanti di Queensland siano cordiali, rilassati e molto orgogliosi del loro clima tropicale. Una grande attrazione nel luglio è il concorso del Mr.-Gay- Queensland, che attira i gay di tutto il paese e rappresenta un'importante contributo allo sviluppo dell'orgoglio gay.

GAY INFO

Gayline 19-22 h
✉4000 ☎ 3839-3277
Information and counselling.
Gaywaves Wed 18-21 h (FM 102.1 MHz)
✉4000 ☎ 3252-1555
Queensland Pride
PO Box 591, Mount Gravatt ✉4000 ☎ 3392-2922 Fax: 3392-2923
Free monthly publication.
Queer Radio every 2nd Wed 19-21 h
on 4ZZZ fm, 102.1
☎ 3252-1555 Email: john@4zzz.org.au

TOURIST INFO

Brisbane Visitors & Convention Bureau
PO Box 12260, Elizabeth Street ✉4002 ☎ 3221-8411 Fax: 322 95 126

BARS

Beat Nightclub (AC B D f glm MA s SNU STV) 20-5 h
677 Ann Street, Fortitude Valley ✉4006 *Brunswick train station, in Mall.* ☎ 3252-2543
Also Cockatoo Club
Hotel Wickham (B CC D F glm H MA S VS W YG) Mon-Sun 10-? h
308 Wickham Street, Fortitude Valley ✉4006 ☎ 3852-1301
Popular Sun, live music.
Options Niteclub & Cafe (B D F GLM S STV)
Café 17-?, Club 20-? h, shows Fri-Sat
18 Little Edward Street, Spring Hill ✉ 4000 ☎ 3831-4214
Raptors (B G MA) Tue-Sat 17-?, Sun 16-? h
c/o The Brunswick Hotel, Brunswick Street, New Farm ☎ (015) 72-5004
Russel's Longbar (B G MA)
Shamrock Hotel, 186 Brunswick Street, Fortitude Valley ☎ 3252 2421

RESTAURANTS

Boticelli's (B F glm)
The Broadwalk, Breakfast Creek Wharf, Newstead ☎ 3257 1501
Francesca's Restaurant
195 Wickham Terrace, Spring Hill ✉4000 ☎ 3831-4125

CAFES

Moray Café (B F g SWC) 9-22, Sun 10-15.30 h, closed Mon
Moray Street/Merthyr Road, New Farm ✉4000 ☎ 3254-1342
Ric's Café
Brunswick Street Mall, Fortitude Valley ✉4006 ☎ 3854-1772
Three Monkees Coffee & Tea House
58 Mollison Street, South Brisbane ✉4101 ☎ 3844-6045

MEN'S CLUBS

Den. The (B CC G) Mon-Thu 20-?, Fri 20-Mon ? h
187 Brunswick Street, Fortitude Valley ✉4006 *courner of Brunswick St.& Barry Drive* ☎ 3854-1981
Gay men's club and bookshop. Large range of toys, books, leather.

ESCORTS & STUDIOS

Male Order ☎ (0500) 55 66 40

SAUNAS/BATHS

Bodyline Spa & Sauna (AC b bf G MA msg P sa sb VS wh) Sun-Thu 12-3, Fri Sat 12-7 h
43 Ipswich Road, Woollongabba ✉4000 ☎ 3391-4285
Free breakfast weekends.
Wet Spa & Sauna (AC CC f G MA NU P sa sb VS wh YG) Mon-Thu 11-?, Fri Sat -3 h, Sun wet day.
22 Jeays Street, Bowen Hills ✉4006 *5 mins walk from Bowen Hills railways station* ☎ 3854-1383

BOOK SHOPS

Signal Bookshop (g) Mon-Thu 10-24, Fri-Sun 0-24 h
191 Brunswick Street, Fortitude Valley ✉4006 ☎ 3252-7191

HOTELS

Sportsman Hotel (AC B CC f GLM H MA STV) 13-? h
130 Leichardt Street, Spring Hill ✉4000 ☎ 3831-2892
Fax: 3839-2106
Rates from A$ 25-40 (bf incl.) Gay hotel and 3 bars.

GENERAL GROUPS

Foothold ☎ 3349-0897
Social and contact group for gay and bisexual men over 26.
G&L Welfare Association GLWA PO Box 1078, Fortitude Valley ✉4006 Email: glwa@queer.org.au
GLADS
☎ 3844-9599
Gay and lesbian alcohol and drug support group. Meets Wed 20 h, Gladstone Road Medical.
Jumbucks
PO Box 205, Red Hill ✉4000
Club for men over 21.
QUT Campus Queers
PO Box 511, Bulimba ✉4171
☎ 3844-4565 *or* ☎ *3255 0215 (Damien) or* ☎ *3399 5471 (Lorelle). Gay & Lesbian student group.*

FETISH GROUPS

Brisbane Boot Co
PO Box 187, Red Hill ✉4059
Meeting 1st Sat 21 h at Russels Longbar, Shamrock Hotel, Brunswick Street, Fortitude Valley.
Brisbears 3rd Sat 21 h
PO Box 6, Nundah ✉4012 ☎ 3266 8847
Email: brisbears@geocities.com *Social Club for men who like hairy men. Meets at Sportsman Hotel, downstairs bar.*

HEALTH GROUPS

Brisbane Gay & Lesbian Health Service
38 Gladstone Road, Highgate Hill ✉4101 ☎ 3844-6806
Gay male doctor, comprehensive medical service.
Gay & Lesbian Welfare Association
Helpline 19-22 h
PO Box 1078, Fortitude Valley ✉4006 ☎ 3839-3277
Queensland AIDS Council Mon-Fri 9-17 h
32 Peel Street, /PO Box 3142, South Brisbane QLD 4101 ✉4000
☎ 3444-1990 Fax: 844-4206
HIV/AIDS information and support.
Queensland Positive People
PO Box 3142, South Brisbane ✉4000 ☎ 3846-3939
HIV+ support group, Tue social day, Fri night open social support, counselling, workshops and more.
QUIVAA
93 Brunswick Street, Fortitude Valley ✉4006
☎ 3252-5390
Advice and help for injecting drug users. Needle exchange

HELP WITH PROBLEMS

Brisbane AA-Gay & Lesbian Alcoholics Anonymous Sat at RBH
☎ 3844-7840
(Matt) or ☎ *3359-0035 (Janice).*

SPECIAL INTEREST GROUPS

Australian Bisexual Network
PO Box 490,
Lutwyche ✉4030 ☎ 3857-2500
Rangers ☎ 3349-0897
☎ *Allan evenings only. Camping, adventure and social club for gay men.*
Sunboys
☎ 3848-5268
Nudist club for men. Swim nights 3rd Sun each month.

SPORT GROUPS

AFAA-Australian Free Athletic Association
PO Box 428, Spring Hill ✉4000
Queensland gay sports group.

Bundaberg ☎ 07

GENERAL GROUPS

Bundaberg Gay & Lesbian Support
PO Box 2695 ✉4670 ☎ 4152-9999
Social/support group.

SWIMMING

-Mon Repos (G NU) (All year round. Go north, past first set of rocks only)

CRUISING

-Corner of Quay and Targo Streets (in toilets or in park during the day and early evening - be discreet)

Cairns ☎ 07

TOURIST INFO

Far North Queensland Promotion Bureau Ltd.
Grafton Street/Hartley Street ✉4870 ☎ 4051-3588

BARS

Chapel Café (AC B CC F NG s) 12-2 h
91 Esplanade, Level 1 ✉4870 ☎ 4041-4222
Great ocean views and the best bar in Cairns. Best after 22 h.
Club Trix (B G MA) Tue-Sun 21-? h
53 Spence Street ✉4870 *(upstairs)* ☎ 4051-8223
John Henrys Bar and Café (A AC B F MA NG OS WE)
Thu-Tue 17-1 h, closed Wed
92 Abbott Street ✉4870 *(upstairs)* ☎ 4031-4849

RESTAURANTS

Red Ochre Grill (AC B CC F g) Mon-Fri lunch & dinner, Sat Sun dinner
43 Shields Street ✉4870 ☎ 4051-0100
Cairns premier restaurant. Seafood and Australien specialities.

TRAVEL & TRANSPORT

Ocean Spirit Cruises (B CC glm)
143 Lake Street
☎ 4031-2920 Fax: 4031-4344
Cruises, also gay-lesbian only.
Out Touring Australia (CC GLM) 0-24 h
PO Box 12 14 ☎ 4051-1485 Fax: 4052-1478
Tour and accomodation booking service.
Sugarland Car Rental (CC) 7.30-18 h
252 Sheridan Street ✉4870 ☎ 4052-1300 Fax: 4051-7154
Rent-a-car. Also two other locations at Palm Cove, Novotel Resort and Mission Beach, 30 Wonmaling Road for pick up and drop offs.

HOTELS

Lugger Bay Beach Resort (A AC B bf CC F GLM H lj MA msg NU P pi wh WO)
PO Box 18, Mission Beach ✉4852
☎ 4068-8400 Fax: 4068-8586
Beachfront luxury private resort. Room rates from A$ 45 pp/pn to 650 pn (penthouse)

Marlin Cove Quest Resort (AC CC H MA msg OS pi W wh)
2 Keem Street, PO Box 365, Trinity Beach ✉4079
☎ 4057-8299 Fax: 4057-8909
Email: regency@cairns.net.au Homepage: quest-inns.com.au
Located 15 minutes drive north of Cairns. 100 apartments with bath/shower/WC, balcony/patio, radio, kitchenette, phone. Hotel provides own key, car park, bicycle hire and tennis lawn. Rates A$ 120-190, add. bed 15.

Tentative Nests (bf F CC g H)
26 Barron Falls Road, Kuranda QLD ✉4872 ☎ 4093-9555 Fax: 4093-9053
Email: tentnests@internetnorth.com.au
Homepage: cairns.aust.com/tentnests *Open all year. 8 cabine style tents on platforms. Located deep in the rainforest. Rates from A$ 55 per person, half-board A$ 88. Car park.*

Turtle Cove Resort (! AC b bf CC f GLM H MA msg NU OS pi VS W wh WO) All year, 24h
PO Box 158 Smithfield, ✉4878 *(Captain Cook Highway near Cairns. Between Cairns and Port Douglas)* ☎ 4059-1800 Fax: 4059-1969
Email: gay@turtlecove.com.au
Homepage: www.turtlecove.com.au
Turtle Cove with 31 first class rooms, all with private facilities and ocean views as well as a private beach. Rates A$ 110-220 per room. Airport pick-up possible. If you arrive by car, call for discription how to get there

18-24 James (AC b bf CC F G H MA N OS pi sa W wh WO)
Bar/restaurant 10-24, reception 7-21 h
18-24 James Street, ✉4870 ☎ 4051-4644 Fax: 4051-0103
Email: 18_24james@internetnorth.com.au
Homepage: www.eagles.bbs.net.au/james
Free airport pickup. All rooms with TV, radio, phone, tea & coffee makers, refrigerator, shower/WC, king-size beds. Rates include free tropical breakfast. Single from A$ 95, double or twin A$ 120 per room. Additional person A$ 25 and shared rooms (max. 4) A$ 55 per person. Car hire and tours can be arranged by hotel.

APARTMENTS

Champions
☎ 4031-3004
Bed & Breakfast guesthouses offering apartements situated in or near Cairns. Reservations through QAGLR.

HELP WITH PROBLEMS

Gayline Wed-Sun 19-23 h
☎ 4051-0279

SWIMMING

-Bucchans Point/Ellis Beach (25 km north of Cairns. Take bus 2xx or 1A from city. Unofficial nude beach)
-Yorkey's Knob (20 km north of Cairns)

Noosa ☎ 07

TRAVEL & TRANSPORT

Australian Gay Travel Service
PO Box 302 ✉4567 ☎ 5447 3135 Fax: 5447 3343
Over 20 years experience in the gay travel industry.
Email: rods@ozemail.com.au

HOTELS

Bateau Ivre. Le (bf g H)
Boreen Point on Lake Cootharaba ✉4566 ☎ 4185-3164
25 km north of Noosa. Self-contained units and historical house. Gateway to Coolbola National Park. Rate A$ 52.50-65.

GUEST HOUSES

Falcons (bf CC G msg lj MA msg NU OS pi WO)
✉4573 *Please call for further details* ☎ 5448 9710 Fax: 5448 3712
Homepage: www.linstar.com.au/falcons
Located in the „sunshine coast" region of Queensland, 100 km north of Brisbane. 6 rooms with bath/WC, own key. Rates single from A$ 60, double from 70. Free continental bf.

APARTMENTS

Hideaway. The (AC bf CC f glm H NU OS pi) Open all year 24h
386 David Low Way ✉4573 ☎ 5448-1006 Fax: (014) 06 87 38
Fully self-contained holiday apartments near Noosa. Rates from A$ 55,- to A$ 110,-, close to gay bars / beach

Noosa Cove (CC GLM H MA NU OS pi WO) 82
Upper Hastings Street ✉4567 *5 mins walk from Noosa bus transit terminal* ☎ 5449 2668 Fax: 5447 5373 Email: noosacove@bigpond.com.
Homepage: www.users.bigpond.com/noosacove
Luxury studio, 1 and 2 bedroom holiday apartments- self contained- in tropical garden setting. Only 3 mins walk to beach, pool

HEALTH GROUPS

AIDS Council
Suite 7, 80 6th Avenue, PO Box 11 91, Maroochiydore ✉4558
☎ 4143-7702 Fax: 4143-3743

SWIMMING

-Alexandria Beach (45 minutes through National Park from Noosa Heads. Nude beach. Popular with gays.)
-The Spit (end of Hastings street)
-Noosa wods (mouth of Noosa river)

Peregian Beach ☎ 07

APARTMENTS

Horizons at Peregian (AC CC g H MA NU OS pi wh)
PO Box 302 ✉4567 ☎ 290 291 Fax: 5448 3711
Email: rods@ozemail.com.au *Rooms from A$ per night. All rooms with 2 bathrooms! Suites with private roof garden and spa.*

Rockhampton ☎ 07

BARS

Rocky Road Society (B G MA) Fri Sat 21-3, Sun 18-?, Wed 19-? h
Grosvenor Hotel, Alma Street/Derby Street ✉4700 ☎ 4927-4464

GENERAL GROUPS

Cruising Rockhampton/CQ Sat 21 h at Club Venus, Winsalls Hotel
PO Box 4050 ✉4700 ☎ 4934-2772
Gay social club, dinners, dance parties and more. Call Trevor for information.
Mackay M.A.G.S. PO Box 1145, Mackay ✉4740
☎ 4953-0888 *Support and social group.*

Surfer's Paradise ☎ 07

BARS

Meeting Place Bar & Club Tu-Sa 20-5 h, Su 17:00-?
26 Orchard Avenue ✉4217 ☎ 5526 2337
R.U.1.2. (B G MA) 16-? h
Paradise Center ✉4217 *(1st floor, enter from beach and upstairs)* ☎ 015) 59-0867

SEX SHOPS/BLUE MOVIES

Club R 18+ (AC b CC DR G LJ MA msg P SNU VS YG) 16-24 h
1/3 Allsion Street ✉4217 *(in basement car park at Parkrise building Look for big number ONE on front door)* ☎ 5539-0955

TRAVEL & TRANSPORT

Surfers Paradise Gay Vacations (CC G)
PO Box 7260, G.C.M.C. ✉ 4217 ☎ 5592-2223 Fax: 5592-2209
This gay-run agency specializes in finding gay friendly accommodation at discount rates from budget (from A$55 per night) to 5 star. Also multi-share at A$30 per night. Call or write for free brochure. It has its own all male gay guesthouse at A$ 50 per night.

HOTELS

Islander Resort. The (g H)
Gold Coast Highway/Beach Road ✉4217 ☎ 5592-2223

Sleeping Inn Surfers (bf G H pi) 8-22 h
26 Whelan Street ✉4217 ☎ 5592-4455 Fax: 5592-5266
Email: sleep@link.com.au
Homepage: www.worldlink.com.au/webs/sleeps/
8 double, 8 single rooms, 5 apartments, also shared rooms and dorms backpacker style. Rates - double from A$ 40, single A$ 30, additional bed A$ 15. Apartment A$ 60. Shared room or dormatory A$15 per person.

GUEST HOUSES

Paradise Retreat (AC bf G MA msg NU OS pi VS wh)
24 hours a day, 7 days a week
102 Admiralty Drive ✉4217 ☎ 5571 1414 Fax: 5531 0614
Email: staygay@ion.com.au *The only exclusively Gay accomodation in Surfers Paradise. Central Dress Circle Location, Stunning Water Views. All Amenities including Pool, Sundeck, and Video Lounge Relaxed and friendly gay environment. Comprehensive knowledge of Gay venues and activiteies on the Gold Coast.*

APARTMENTS

Stay Gay Apartments (CC G H msg)
PO Box 7260, Gold Coast Mail Centre ✉4217 ☎ 5592-2223
Fax: 5592-2209
Rates studio A$ 70, one bedroom apartments 85 per day.

GENERAL GROUPS

Gold Coast Gay Info-Line ☎ 5592-2377

HEALTH GROUPS

Gold Coast Branch, Queensland AIDS Commitee Wed 19-22 h
PO Box 13 30 ✉4217 ☎ 5538-4611
Queensland AIDS Council
105 Frank Street, Labrador ✉4215 *Runaway Bay* ☎ 5538-8922

SWIMMING

-Broadbeach (AYOR) (Opposite Broadbeach International Hotel & Oasis Shopping Complex. Be a little bit more discreet, as it is usually mixed and touristy)
-Southport Spit (AYOR) (Opposite Seaworld Dolphin and Whale Arena, very popular on Sat and Sun)

CRUISING

-The spit (dunes oposite Seaworld)

GENERAL GROUPS

Toowoomba Silver Wheat Society
PO Box 7485, Toowoomba Mail Centre ✉4350 ☎ 4639-4199
Gay & lesbian social/support group. Regular activities. Call for dates.

HEALTH GROUPS

Queensland AIDS Council 0-24 h
8 Anzac Avenue, PO Box 24 69 ✉4352 ☎ 4639-1820

CRUISING

-Margaret Street, near Queens Park
-Queens Park

Townsville ☎ 07

BARS

Sovereign Hotel (B GLM MA) Wed-Sun
807 Flinders Street ✉4810 ☎ 4771 2909

SEX SHOPS/BLUE MOVIES

Sweethearts Adult Bookshop
206a Charters Towers Road, Hermit Park ✉4810 ☎ 4725-1431

GUEST HOUSES

Sandy`s on the Strand (AC bf E G msg OS pi)
PO Box 193 ✉4810 ☎ 4772-1193
Situated on the beach front. Facilities of the room incl.shower/WC, telephone and balcony. Rates from A$ 55-65 (breakfast inc.)

SWIMMING

-Balding Bay/Rocky Bay (AYOR) (on Magnetic Island. Popular with gays who tend to congregate at the far end.)
-Beyond Pallaranda (g NU)

CRUISING

-Flinders Mall (in centre of city; daytime on week days)
-Beach and park (after dark)
-Park between Rower's Bay and Pallaranda
-Strand Park
-Queen Park

Whitsunday Island ☎ 07

HOTELS

Holiday Village (b H MA NG) Bar 11-23 h
Whitsunday Village ✉4802
This is the main rendezvous for the Whitsunday Island area of the Great Barrier Reef. Has excellent food, charming bar. An invitation to swim in the upper pool when the bar closes can have interesting results. Cool is the word here. If staying here, an end cabin has advantages.

AUS-South Australia

South AUS
Initials: SA
Time: GMT +9.5
Area: 984,000 km^2 / 379,922 sq mi.
Population: 1,485,000
Capital: Adelaide

Adelaide ☎ 08

GAY INFO

Adelaide Gay Times
PO Box 10141 Gouger Street, 55 Halifax Street ✉5000 ☎ 8232-1544 Fax: 8232 1560
Email: gt@box.net.au *Fortnightly publication. Free at gay venues.*
Gay Radio Sun 12-14 h (3 D Radio 93.7 FM)
☎ 8410-0937

TOURIST INFO

South Australian Travel Centre
1 King William Street ☎ 8212-1505 Fax: 8303-2231.

BARS

Beans Bar (B d F GLM MA S) Mon-Thu 21-3, Fri -5, Sat -3.30, Sun 19-2, women only Fri 17-21 h
258 Hindley Street ✉5000 ☎ 8231-9614
Edinburgh Castle Hotel (B D F g STV) -24, Sun -20 h
Gray Street/Currie Street ✉5000 ☎ 8410-1211

DANCECLUBS

Mars Bar (B D g MA S) 21-? h
122 Gouger Street ✉5000 ☎ 8231-9639
Popular Fri. Fri-Sun entry A$ 5.

RESTAURANTS

Magic Flute (B F g)
109 Melbourne Street ✉5000
☎ 8267-3172

CAFES

Queen of Tarts (g)
178 Hutt Street ✉5000
☎ 8223-1529
Universal Wine Bar (B g)
258 Rundle Street ✉5000 ☎ 8232-5000

SEX SHOPS/BLUE MOVIES

Pink Pussy (g)
135 b Goodwood Road, Goodwood ✉5034 ☎ 8271-5975
Full range of adult books, toys and novelties.
Ram Lounge and Video (G VS) 11-2 h
71 Hindley Street ✉5000 *(Nightlife Centre. Via Club X)*
☎ 8410-0444
Windsor Adult Bookshop (g) 364
North East Road ✉5000 *(Shop 1)* ☎ 8369-0088

SAUNAS/BATHS

Phoenix Sauna (AC b DR F G lj MA S sb sol VS wh WO YG) Mo-Th 12:00-03:00h, Fri-Sat 12:00-07:00h
147 Waymouth Street, Light Square ✉5000 *(near main train station and main bus terminal). One the first floor.* ☎ 8221 7002
Sling rooms, maze area, internet cafe. Entrance fee A$ 18, members A$ 10, membership per year A$ 5 .
Pulteney 431 (AC b DR f G MA p pi sa sb W WE wh) Mon Tue 19-1, Wed Thu Sun 12-1, Fri Sat 12-3 h
431 Pulteney Street ✉5000 *(Next to Astor Hotel)* ☎ 8223-7506
Entrance fee: casual visitor A$ 15, member A$ 12.

BOOK SHOPS

Imprints Booksellers (CC glm) Mon-Thu, Sat 9-18, Fri -21, Sun 12-18 h
80 Hindley Street ✉5000 ☎ 8231-4454

TRAVEL & TRANSPORT

Parkside Travel Mo-Fri 8.30-17.30, Sat 9-12 h
70 Glen Osmond Road ✉5063 *(Parkside)Bus stop 2*
☎ 8274-1222

HOTELS

Rochdale Bed & Breakfast (AC bf CC F glm H OS p pi) 24h
349 Glen Osmond Road, Glen Osmond ✉5064 ☎ 8379-7498
Fax: 8379-2483 Email: rochdale@camtech.net.au
All ensuite traditional B&B with fully enclosed solar heated pool. Close to city center. Easy access to beach
West End All Suite Hotel (AC B bf CC f H MA NG sa sb)
255 Hindley Street ✉5000 ☎ 8231-8333
FAX 8231-4741. Near central Business District and next to gay venues. Discounts available to SPARTACUS-readers.

PRIVATE ACCOMODATION

City Apartments (g H) Reservations: 8.30-17.30 h, Sat 8.30-12 h 70
Glen Osmond Road, Parkside ✉5063
☎ 8274-1222 Fax: 8272-7371
Centrally located 1-3 bedroom apartments. Economy, Executive, and Superior in different locations in the city. Rates from A$ 50-105.

GENERAL GROUPS

Gay and Lesbian Immigration Task Force
PO Box 110, Woodville ✉5011
Immigration Advice.

Inside Out/Work It Out
c/o The Second Story Youth Health Service, 57 Hyde St.
☎ 8232-0233
Workshops and educational programms for gays and bis under 26.

Thursday Night Drop-in Centre (b f G MA W) Thu 19.30-22.30 h
Box Factory Community Centre, 59 Regent Street South ✉5000
(between Carrington and Halifax Street, side entrance)
Social group.

HEALTH GROUPS

AIDS Council of South Australia
PO Box 907, Kent Town ✉5000 ☎ 8362-1611
Services for people living with HIV/AIDS and their lovers, families and carers, including counselling advocacy, treatments info, referrals, housing and financial assistance.

Clinic 275 Mon Thu Fri 10-16, Tue Wed 12-19.30 h
275 North Terrace ✉5000 *(1st floor)* ☎ 8226-6025
HIV-testing.

Flinders Medical Centre
Flinders Drive, Bedford Park ✉5042 ☎ 8204-5192
HIV testing. HIV clinic. Wed mornings by appointment only.

South Australian Bobby Goldsmith Foundation
PO Box 247, Kent Town ✉5000 ☎ 8362-1611
or ☎ *8212-2382 (Chris). Organization which provides living expenses for PWA in financial difficulty.*

HELP WITH PROBLEMS

Gay & Lesbian Counselling Service of South Australia 19-22, Sat Sun 14-17 h
PO Box 2011 Kent Town ✉5063 ☎ 8362-3223

People living with HIV/AIDS (MA s)
PO Box 2603 Kenttown ✉5031 ☎ 8231-0300
Fax: 8231-9989
Antibody positive support group.

RELIGIOUS GROUPS

Metropolitan Community Church Sun service 19-? h at Quaker Meeting Hall
40 A Pennington Terrace, GPO Box 10 06, ✉5000 ☎ 8298-4374

Mitrasasana
PO Box 39, Woodville ✉5011
Gay group inspired by the teachings of Buddha.

SPECIAL INTEREST GROUPS

Rainbow Connection ☎ 8268-9266 (Bob)
Gay & lesbian business group.

Young Asians
c/o The Second Story Youth Health Centre, 57 Hyde St.
☎ 8232-0233
Social/support group for gay and bisexual Asians. Asians and their friends meet 4th Sun and Asians only 2nd Sun.

SPORT GROUPS

Adelaide Happy Wanderers
☎ 8267-5112 Fax: 8267-5112
(Bart) or ☎ *(08) 8333 0667 (Jeff). Bushwalking (backpacking), camping, canoeing and bicycling for gay men. Day walks every 1st Sun.*

Team Adelaide Incorporated
GPO Box 271 ✉5001 ☎ 8264-2584
Email:mang01@senet.com.au
Bush walking, cycling, golf, netball, squash, swimming, Ten Pin Bowling, tennis, triathlon & volleyball

SWIMMING

-The Broadway (South from Glenelg near kiosk and toilet block)
-Maslin's Beach (about 50 minutes drive from Adelaide. Or take train from North Terrace, Adelaide to Noarlunga Centre and transfer to bus 741 or 742. Best on south end .
-Tennyson Beach (tram from North Terrace to Port Adelaide then bus 340 or 115 to West Lakes, some police surveillance)

CRUISING

-Unley Road Park (between Greenhill Road and South Terrace, days only)
-Glen Osmond Road (AYOR) (night and day)
All Cruising Areas are AYOR!

Barossa Valley ☎ 08

HOTELS

Lodge. The (AC B bf CC F g H MA pi) 0-24 h
RSD 120, Seppeltsfield ✉5355 ☎ 8562-8277 Fax: 8562-8344
Email: thelodge@dove.net.au *Private Georgian style homestead with en suites. Rates single A$ 265, double 365 (bf incl.)*

Top of the Valley (g H pi) 49
Murray Street, Nuiootpa ✉5355 ☎ 8562-2111 *Tourist Motel.*

Burra ☎ 08

HOTELS

Wildildie Homestead (AC bf CC F g MA)
PO Box 135, Burra ✉5417 ☎ 8892-2394
Located in typical Australian setting with kangaroos and emus. Close to Barossa Valley and Clare wine regions. Rates on request.

Clare Valley ☎ 08

HOTELS

Oldfields (glm H)
Young Street, Mintaro, PO Box 544, ✉5453 ☎ 8843-9038

Thorn Park Country House (AC B bf CC F H MA OS)
College Road, Sevenhill ✉5453 ☎ 8843-4304 Fax: 8843-4296
Email: thornpk@capri.net.au
Country house suites with en suites. Rates single A$ 175, double 260 (bf incl.). Apartment 260. Open all year.

Elizabeth ☎ 08

CRUISING

-Town Centre
-The Park
-Grove Shopping Centre

AUS-Tasmania

South AUS

Initials: TAS

Time: GMT +10

Area: 67,800 km² / 26,177 sq mi.

Population: 471,000

Capital: Hobart

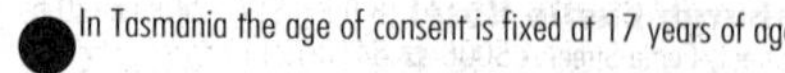
● In Tasmania the age of consent is fixed at 17 years of age.

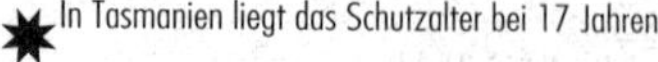
✸ In Tasmanien liegt das Schutzalter bei 17 Jahren.

▲ En Tasmanie, la majorité sexuelle est fixée à 17 ans.

☆ En Tasmania, la edad de consentimiento está estipulado en 17 años.

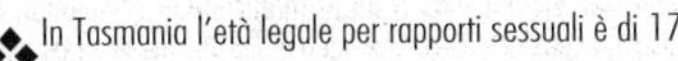

❖ In Tasmania l'età legale per rapporti sessuali è di 17 anni.

Hobart ☎ 03

GAY INFO

Gay Information Line
✉7000 ☎ 6234 8179
(24 hours recorded information)

BARS

Good Woman Inn (B F glm H) Mon-Thu 12-23, Fri-Sun 19-23. Sun 20.30 h
186 Argyle Street/Worwick, North Hobart ✉7000 ☎ 6234 4796
Front bar every evening, also budget accommodation.

RESTAURANTS

Indiscretions Restaurant (F glm) open every day for dinner, lunch Mon-Fri
186 Argyle Street ✉7000 *(upstairs at the Good Woman Inn)*
☎ 6234 4796

Rockerfellas Restaurant and Cocktail Bar
(B F G) 11 Morrison Street ✉7000 *(on Water Front)*

SEX SHOPS/BLUE MOVIES

Black Rose. The (g)
108 Harrington Street ✉7000

BOOK SHOPS

Akashic Bookshop (g)
Cat and Fiddle Arcade ✉7000

HOTELS

Lodge on Elizabeth. The (bf CC g H)
249 Elizabeth Street ✉7000 ☎ 6231 3830 Fax: 6234 2566
Email: lodgeoneliz@tassie.net.au
Rooms with phone. Rates from -single A$ 95, double 115, add. bed 25. 4 star RACT rating

Wellington Lodge (bf CC E glm H OS)
7 Scott Street, Glebe ✉7000 ☎ 6231 0614 Fax: 6234 1551
No smoking house. Rates single without shower A$ 65, with 75, double without 75, with 95 (bf incl.)

GUEST HOUSES

Corinda's Cottages (bf CC GLM H MA) All year, 24h
17 Glebe Street, Glebe ✉7000 ☎ 6234 1590 Fax: 6234 2744
Email: info@corindascottages.com.au
Homepage: www.corindascottages.com.au
Fully self-contained, 2 bedrooms with antique furnishings, coulour TV. Beautiful setting, 1 km to city centre, 15 km to airport. Prices from A$ 160-175 .

GENERAL GROUPS

Tasmanian Gay and Lesbian Rights Group
G.P.O Box 1773 ✉7000 ☎ 6224 3556 *FAX 6223 6136.*

HEALTH GROUPS

Free Sexual Health Service ☎ 6233 3557
HIV testing, support and counselling.

Positive People Tasmania Tue 13-17 h
✉7000 ☎ 6224 1034 *(David)*

SWIMMING

-Seven Mile Beach (Situated about 7 km out of Hobart, the southern end of the beach attracts a large gay attendance. No nudity, but cruisy)

Launceston ☎ 03

GAY INFO

Gay Information Line
✉7250 ☎ 6234 3254

BARS

Tramshed Bar in Great Northern Hotel
(B g h) 10-1 h
3 Earl Street ✉7250 ☎ 6231-9999

HOTELS

Brickfield Terrace (bf CC F H NG)
64 Margaret Street ✉7250 ☎ 6331 0963 Fax: 6331 7778
2 self-contained colonial cottages. Rates A$ 140 for double, each add. person 35. Each cottage sleeps 4 persons.

1A Accommodation (bf G)
1A Canning Street ✉7250
☎ 6234 1170 Fax: 6331 3454
Single studio available for gay travelers for A$60-80 incl. bf.

GENERAL GROUPS

Free Sexual Health Service
☎ 6236 22116 *HIV testing, support and counselling.*

BARS

Furners Hotel (B g H) Mon-Sat 11-23 h
42 Reiby Street ✉7315 ☎ 6225 1488
Gay group meets 2nd and 4th Fri.

AUS-Victoria

Southeast AUS
Initials: VIC
Time: GMT +10
Area: 227,600 km² / 87,876 sq mi.
Population: 4,648,000
Capital: Melbourne

● In Victoria the age of consent is fixed at 16 years of age.

✸ In Victoria liegt das Schutzalter bei 16 Jahren.

▲ Dans l'Etat de Victoria, la majorité sexuelle est fixée à 16 ans.

☆ En Victoria, la edad de consentimiento es de 16 años.

❖ In Victoria l'età legale per rapporti sessuali è di 17 anni.

Ballarat ☎ 03

GENERAL GROUPS

Ballarat Gays (BGS)
PO Box 369 ✉3350

CRUISING

-Lake Wendouree Drive

Bendigo ☎ 03

GENERAL GROUPS

Bendigo Gay Society
PO Box 1123 ☎ 5427-0312
Social and supporting group.

Cape Schanck ☎ 03

HOTELS

Cape Lodge (bf CC glm msg OS P pi sa)
134 Cape Schanck Road ✉3939 ☎ 5988-6395 *FAX 5988-6395.*
Rates double A$ 110 per night. Dinner by arrangement 30.

Daylesford ☎ 03

RESTAURANTS

Double Nut Of Switzerland (B bf CC E F glm OS wh)
Fri-Mon 10-23 h
5 Howe Street ✉3460 ☎ 5348-3981

CAFES

Boathouse (AC bf CC F glm MA OS W) 9-24 h
Lake Daylesford Foreshore, Leggat Street ✉3460 ☎ 5348-1387
Julie & Jacquis Café (bf CC F glm) Fri-Mon
5 Howe Street ☎ 5348-3981
A great meeting place for gay visitors & locals.

GUEST HOUSES

Balconies of Daylesford (bf CC f GLM lj MA msg N NU OS pi W wh)
35 Perrins Street ✉3460 ☎ 5348-1322
Email: balconys@netconnect.com.au
Gay owned on 3 acres of garden and overlooks Lake Daylesford. 2 rooms with shower/WC, 2 rooms without.
Daniels B & B (bf CC F GLM H)
27 Vanina Street, Hepburn Springs ☎ 5348 1138
Holly Lodge (bf CC glm H MA msg OS p W VS)
15 Grenville Street ✉3460 ☎ 5348-3670
Victorian home in large garden. 4 rooms. Gay owned.
Illoura Cottage (bf cc G OS)
Main Road, Hepburn Springs ☎ 5348 3151
Gay owned.
James Booth's Linton House (bf CC GLM H OS)
0-24 h
Central Springs Road ☎ 5348-2331
Rates studio/apartment A$ 145 per night.
Villa Vita (bf CC F GLM H)
Main Road, Kingston
☎ 5345 6448

Geelong ☎ 03

SWIMMING

-Point Impossible (take beach road out of Torquay to Breamlea)
-Point Addis (Situated off the Geelong road to Angleseo. Turn off 2 km past Bell's Beach. Popular.)

CRUISING

-King's Park, King's Wharf
-behind Newton Library

Hepburn Springs ☎ 03

GUEST HOUSES

Daniel's B & B (bf CC f G MA N OS p VS WE YG) 0-24 h
27 Vanina Street ✉3461 ☎ 5348 1138
Close to tourist attractions and springs complex with spas.

Melbourne ☎ 03

●The capital of Victoria has a large multicultural population of 3,200,000. Ever since it was founded in 1835, the city has exercised a big political and cultural influence on the history of Australia. Melbourne has a very European feel, and is famous for its restaurants, wine bars, cafés, as well as its parks and gardens. In the central city suburbs of Carlton, South Yarra and South Melbourne beautiful examples of Victorian terrace house archtecture can be seen. The bohemian quarters of Fitzroy and St. Kilda, the clothes shops of Prahran and Toorak are of interest to the gay visitor and here most of the gay venues are located. Melbourne has a relatively cold climate, which results in a more „indoors" and sophisticated lifestyle. In Sidney, the only fashion accessory you need is a worked-out body, whereas in Melbourne clothing and grooming are highly estimated. The gay calendar starts with the Mid-Summa Festival in late January with the popular Red Raw Gay Dance Party taking pluce on the weekend nearest Australia Day (January 26th). Other dance parties are held on major public holidays. Also of interest to gays is the Melbourne International Arts Festival, which is held annually in September. Melbourne is a good base if you want to visit the local vineyards of the Yarra Valley, the penguins on Phillip Island or the scenic beauty of the Grampians or Wilson's Promontory. An especially worthwhile destination is Daylesford, a country town and former spa (around 1900), which today is a popular resort for country-loving lesbians and gays.

✱Seit der Gründung 1835 hat die Hauptstadt des Bundesstaates Victoria einen enormen politischen und kulturellen Einfluß auf die Geschichte Australiens ausgeübt. Melbourne wirkt sehr europäisch und ist berühmt für seine Restaurants, Weinlokale, Kaffeehäuser und ebenso für seine Parks und Gärten. In den Vorstädten Carlton, South Yarra und South Melbourne finden sich schöne Beispiele viktorianischer Terrassenhaus-Architektur. Die Bohème-Viertel Fitzroy und St. Kilda, die Bekleidungsgeschäfte von Prahran und Toorak sind für den schwulen Besucher von Interesse. In diesen Vierteln findet man auch die meisten schwulen Einrichtungen. Melbourne hat subtropisch-gemäßigt Klima und so spielt sich die Kultur eher „innen" und damit „gepflegt" ab. Während in Sydney der Körper das einzige Modezubehör ist, sind in Melbourne Bekleidung und Pflege hoch geschätzt. Der schwule Kalender beginnt mit dem „Mid-Summa-Festival" im späten Januar und der populären „Red Raw Gay Dance Party", die an dem Wochenende stattfindet, das dem „Australia Day" (26. Januar) am nächsten ist. Andere Parties werden an wichtigen Feiertagen abgehalten. Das „Melbourne International Arts Festival" im September jeden Jahres ist für Schwule von Interesse. Melbourne ist ein guter Ausgangspunkt, um die Weingärten des Yarra Valley, die Pinguine auf Phillip Island oder die malerische Schönheit der Grampians sowie des Wilson's Promontory zu besuchen. Ein besonders lohnenswertes Ziel ist Daylesford, ein ländlicher Ort, der um 1900 Kurort war und heute ein beliebter Erholungsort für landliebende Lesben und Schwule ist.

▲Avec ses 3.200.000 habitants, Melbourne est le modèle-même d'une ville multiculturelle. Depuis sa fondation en 1835, Melbourne joue un rôle décisif tant sur le plan politique que culturel. L'atmosphère de Melbourne est très européenne. On y trouve d'excellents restaurants, tavernes et cafés et de splendides parcs et jardins. A Carlton, South Yarra et South Melbourne, vous admirerez les joyaux de l'architecture victorienne que sont les maisons à terrasses. Vous vous promènerez dans les quartiers artistes de Fitzroy et St Kilda et pourrez aussi faire du lèche-vitrines à Prahan et Toorak (boutiques de mode) qui sont les quartiers gays de la ville.
Le climat de Melbourne est relativement rude. La vie culturelle a lieu surtout en intérieur et est assez guindée. Alors qu'à Sydney c'est le corps qui est au centre des préoccupations de la mode, on préfère de loin à Melbourne le style et les vêtements de marque. Calendrier des mani-

festations gays: Mid-Summa Festival fin janvier, puis »Red Raw Gay Dance Party« qui a lieu le week-end le plus proche du Australia Day (26 janvier). On organise d'autres soirées à l'occasion des jours fériés importants. Le Melbourne International Arts Festival (tous les ans en septembre) attire de nombreux gays. Melbourne est le point de départ idéal pour visiter les vignobles de Yarra Valley, aller admirer les sites des Grampians et de Wilsons Promontory ou bien encore aller dire bonjour aux pingouins de Phillip Island. Daylesford, autrefois petite ville, est depuis 1990 une station balnéaire aujourd'hui très prisée par les gays et les les lesbiennes recherchant le calme et la détente. C'est une destination gay qu'il faut avoir vue!

Desde su fundación en 1835, no se convertió solamente en la capital de Victoría, sino también en eje pólitico y cultural del continente australiano. Melbourne es una ciudad conocida por su ambiente europeo, que no es famosa solamente por sus restaurantes, tabernas y cafeterías, sino también por sus parques y jardines. En las afueras de la ciudad, en Carlton, South Yarra y South Melbourne, se encuentran ejemplos de la arquitectura victoriana, unas impresionantes casas con terrazas. Los barrios de Fitzroy y St. Kild, así como las tiendas de ropa de Prahran y Toorak son de especial interés para el turista gay. En estas zonas están situados también la mayoría de los locales con clientela homosexual. Melbourne tiene un clima moderado. Por esta razón la vida no se concentra en las calles, como por ejemplo en Sydney, donde la gente lleva debido al clima poca ropa y el culto al cuerpo está siempre presente. En Melbourne se cuida mucho más la manera de vestir. El calendario gay comienza a finales de enero con el Mid-Summa-Festival y la pópular „Red Raw Gay Dance Party" que tiene lugar el fin de semana que más se acerque al Australia Day (26. de enero). Otras fiestas se llevan también a cabo durante festivos importantes. De gran atracción para gays es también el Melbourne Internacional Arts Festival, que se celebra cada año en septiembre. Melbourne es un punto de partida ideal para visitar las regiones vinícolas de Yarra Valley, los pingüinos en la Phillip Island o la pintoresca belleza de Grampians o de Wilson's Promotory. Si se quiere disfrutar de la tranquilidad rural, es digno de mención el balneario Daylesford, fundado alrededor de 1900, que se ha convertido hoy en día en un atractivo lugar para homosexuales y lesbianas.

I 3.200.000 di abitanti della capitale dello stato di Victoria sono un esempio di una particolare multiculturalità. Dalla sua fondazione,nel 1835, a oggi la città ha avuto una grande influenza politico-culturale sulla storia dell'Australia. Melbourne è molto europea ed è famosa per i suoi ristoranti, le sue enoteche, i suoi bar e altrettanto per i suoi parchi e giardini. Nei distretti periferici di Carlton, South Yarra e South Melbourne si trovano esempi molto belli di case a schiera. Per i visitatori gay i quartieri boemi di Fitzroy e St.Kilda e i negozi di abbigliamento di Prahran e Toorak sono di particolare interesse. In questi quartieri si trova la maggior parte dei locali d'ambiente. Il clima piuttosto freddo di Melbourne fa sí che la vita sociale e culturale urbana sia più raffinata che in altre città. Se a Sidney si sfoggiano bellezza e muscoli, a Melbourne contano invece abbigliamento e maniere. Il calendario gay inizia con il „Mid-Summa Festival" alla fine di gennaio durante il quale ha luogo il „Red Raw Gay Dance Party" durante il fine settimana più prossimo all'Australia Day (26 gennaio). Altri party hanno luogo in importanti giorni festivi. Il Melbourne International Arts Festival, che si svolge annualmente in settembre, è di interesse per i gay. Melbourne è un buon punto di partenza per visitare i vigneti di Yarra Valley, la stazione balneare di Daylesford, i pinguini di Phillip Island, le pittoresche bellezze di Grampians o il promontorio di Wilson. Una meta particolarmente interessante è Daylesford, stazione termale in campagna intorno al 1900, divenuta ora un luogo di villeggiatura per gay e lesbiche amanti della vita bucolica.

GAY INFO

Brother Sister 9.30-17.30 h
Suite 33a, 1st fl, 261 Bridge Road, Richmond ✉VIC 3121
☎ 9429 8844 Fax: 9429 8966

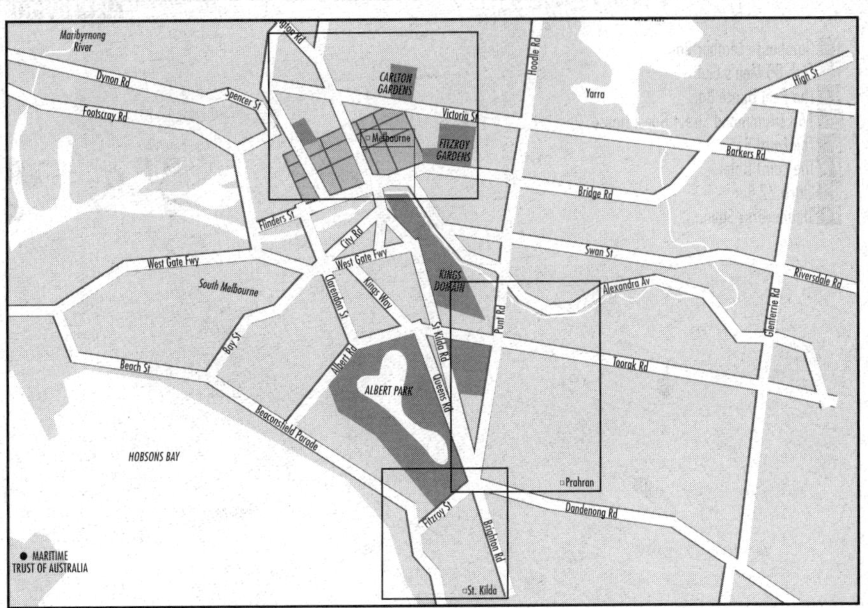

Email: brosisv@webtime.com.au.
Homepage: www.brothersister.com.au
Biweekly gay and lesbian paper. Free of charge.

Melbourne Star Observer
PO Box 205, Fitzroy ✉3065 ☎ 9419 9877 Fax: 9419 0827
Popular publication containing news, information about Melbourne's gay and lesbian scene. Published every Fri.

TOURIST INFO

Melbourne Tourist Information
City Square, Swanstan Walk/Collins Street ☎ 9790-3333

BARS

Catch 22 Bar Café (B F g)
12-14 McKillop Street
✉VIC 3000 ☎ 9670 3638

Diva Bar (B F G) 12-1 h
153 Commercial Road, Prahran ✉3181 ☎ 9826 5500

DT's (AC B CC F GLM MA S STV VS) 11.30-1 , Sun -23 h
164 Church Strret, Richmond ✉3121 ☎ 9428-5724

Jock's (AC B bf CC f G H MA S) Mon-Sat 16-1, Sun -23.30 h
9 Peel Street Collingwood ✉3066 ☎ 9417 6700
Popular, close to gay scene.

Mulcahy's Hotel (B glm) Wed-Sat 18-1, Sun 14-23 h, Fri-Sat Bootscout
700 Victoria Street, North Melbourne ✉3051 ☎ 9329 0699

Peel Dance Bar. The (AC B D G lj MA s) 22-? h
Peel Street/Wellington Street, Collingwood ✉3066
☎ 9419 4762

Prince of Wales (B g) 29
Fitzroy Street ✉3000

Three Faces (AC B D G MA S) Thu-Sun 19-? h
143 Commercial Road, South Yarra VIC 3141 ✉3000
☎ 9826 0933
Modern exclusivly gay venue. 3 bars, disco, pool table. Show at 22.30 h.

Xchange Hotel (B G N S STV VS YG) Mon-Thu 14-?, Fri -3, Sat 12-3, Sun -? h
119 Commercial Road, South Yarra ✉VIC 3141 ☎ 9867 5144
Bistro open Tue-Sat

DANCECLUBS

Hellfire Club (B D glm) Sun 22-? h
c/o Dream, 229 Queensberry Street, Carlton ✉3053
☎ 9349 1924

Party events: Enquiries to ALSO foundation ☎ 9510 5569
-Red Raw (on Australia Day, January)
-WInter Daze (Queens Birthday, early June)
-World AIDS day (late November)
-Midsumma Carnival (mid February)
-Midsumma Street Party (late January)
-Easter Party

Savage (B D G) Fri 24-9 h
629 Bourke Street ✉3000 ☎ 9419 4110

RESTAURANTS

Col's Café (A AC B CC F glm MA N OS WE) 12-1 h
20 Smith Street, Collingwood ✉3066 ☎ 9486 9433

Ninety Seven (B bf CC F glm MA OS W WE)
97 Fitzroy Street, St. Kilda ✉3182 ☎ 9525 5922

Ramjets (B F G) Tue 18-1, Wed-Sun 12-1 h, closed Mon
147 Commercial Road, South Yarra ✉VIC 3141 ☎ 9827 6260

Street Café. The (B F g)
23 Fitzroy Street, St. Kilda ✉VIC 3182 ☎ 9525 4655

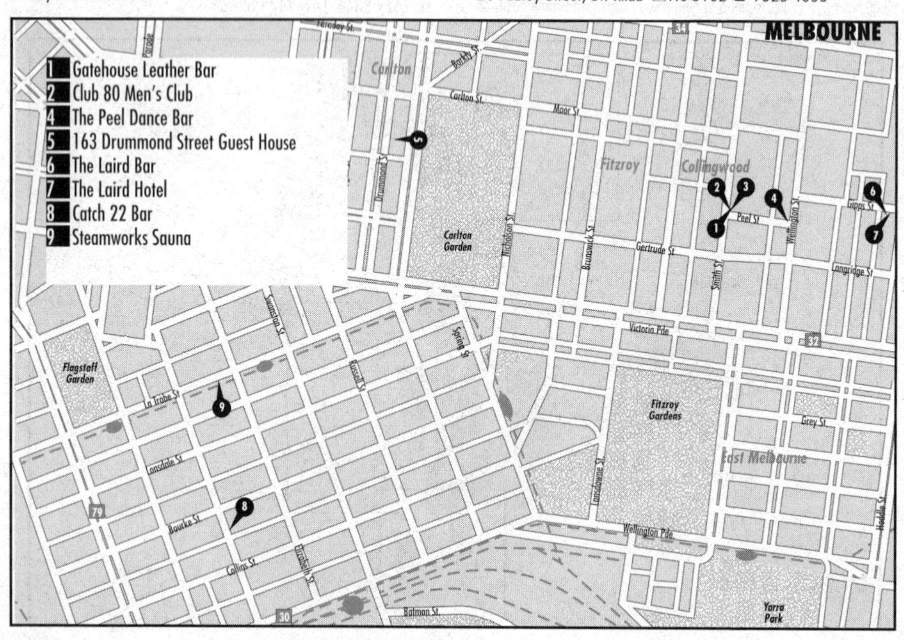

MELBOURNE - PRAHRAN

Prahran

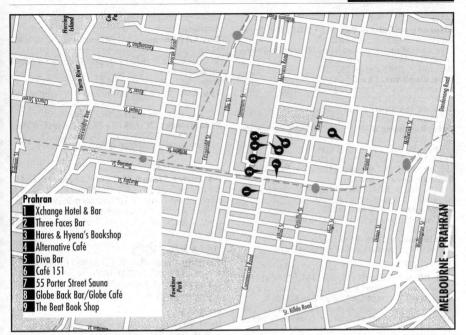

1 Xchange Hotel & Bar
2 Three Faces Bar
3 Hares & Hyena's Bookshop
4 Alternative Café
5 Diva Bar
6 Café 151
7 55 Porter Street Sauna
8 Globe Back Bar/Globe Café
9 The Beat Book Shop

MELBOURNE - ST. KILDA

St. Kilda

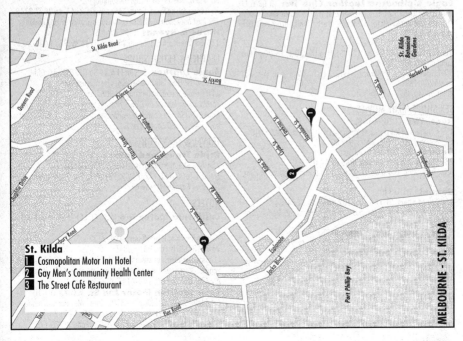

1 Cosmopolitan Motor Inn Hotel
2 Gay Men's Community Health Center
3 The Street Café Restaurant

CAFES

Alternative Cafe & Bar (B CC F GLM MA N OS TV YG) Tue 18-?, Wed-Sun 12-? h, closed Mon
149 Commercial Road, South Yarra ✉VIC 3141 *(near Prahran Market)* ☎ 9827 5997
Meals A$ 5.50-8.90 Snacks A$ 2.50-7.00
Blue Elephant. The (B F G)
194 Commercial Road, Prahran ✉VIC 3181 *(opposite Prahran market)* ☎ 9510 3654
Café de los Santos (B F g) Tue-Sun 11-1
175 Brunswick Street ✉VIC 3000 ☎ 9417 1567
Café Rumours (F GLM) Tue-Fri 11-23.30, Sat Sun 10-23.30 h
199 Brunswick Street ✉VIC 3000 ☎ 9419 5219
Café 151 (AC b bf CC F GLM OS) 12-24 h
151 Commercial Road, South Yarra ✉VIC 3141 ☎ 9826 5336
Galleon Café (b F glm) 10-24 h
9 Carlisle Street, St. Kilda ✉3182 ☎ 9534 8934
Bohemian café with good food, not expensive.
Globe Café (b f GLM) Mon-Sun 10-23 h
218 Chapel Street, Prahran ✉3181 ☎ 9510 8693
50's style café.
Kaleidoscope Café (B F g) 10-17 h
295 Sydney Road, Brunswick ✉3056 ☎ 9380 9894

MEN'S CLUBS

Club 80 (AC b DR f G lj MA p VS) Mon-Fri 17-8, Sat-Sun 14-8 h
10 Peel Street, Collingwood ✉3066 *2km NE of Melbourne city center. 300m from tram stopSmithSt/Peel St* ☎ 9417 2182
Three floors of cruising, video lounge with the latest movies, cyber lounge with internet access and coffee bar. Private rooms, pool table.
Eagle Melbourne Leather Club Bar (B DR G LJ MA P s VS) (G) Fri 21-1, (glm) Sat 21-1 h, Sun-Thu closed
Munster Terrace/Victoria Street, North Melbourne ✉3051 ☎ 9417-2100
Strict dress code, membership necessary.
Ten Plus (DR G msg sa OS VS) Mon-Thu 20-4, Fri 20-6, Sat Sun public holidays 14-6 h
59 Porter Street, Prahran ✉VIC 3181 *(Near gay venues)* ☎ 9525 0469
Male cruise club.

SEX SHOPS/BLUE MOVIES

Beat. The (CC DR Glm VS)
157 Commercial Road, South Yarra ✉VIC 3141 ☎ 9827 8748
International magazines, books, sex toys etc.
Gemini (G) 10-24 h, closed Sun
235a Smith Street, Fitzroy ✉3065 ☎ 9419 6270
Adult book shop: Gay magazines, sex aids, underwear, leather gear, cards,...
Gemini (G) 10-3 h
164 Acland Street, St. Kilda ✉3182 ☎ 9534 6074
Adult book shop: gay magazines, sex aids, underwear, leather gear, cards,...
Ram Lounge and Video (G VS)
216 Swanston Street ✉VIC 3000 *(Via Club X)* ☎ 9663 8094
Ram Lounge and Video (G VS)
74 Acland Street, St. Kilda ✉VIC 3182 *(Via Club X. 1st floor)* ☎ 9534 5835

SAUNAS/BATHS

Bay City Sauna (AC b CC DR f msg NU sa sb sol VS W WO) 12-3 h
482 D Glen Huntly Road, Elsternwick ✉VIC 3185 *(Tram 67, Stop No. 47)* ☎ 9528 2381
Admission A$ 12.
Bay City Sauna (AC b CC DR f msg NU sa sb sol VS W WO) 12-3 h
16 Cumberland Drive, Seaford ✉VIC 3198 *(south west of Melbourne)* ☎ 9776 9279
Entrance fee A$ 12.
Spa Guy (f G OG P sa wh VS) Mon-Thu 17-1, Fri-Sat 17-3, Sun 16-3 h
553 Victoria Street, Abbotsford ✉3067 ☎ 9428 5494
Steamworks (AC CC DR f G lj MA msg P pi sa sb sol VS wh WO YG) Mon-Thu 12-17, Wed-Thu 12-19, Fri 11-Mon 5 h
279 La Trobe Street ✉VIC 3000 ☎ 9602 4493

Tue students night A$ 7, from 18-3 h
55 Porter Street (AC CC DR f G MA msg P sa sb sol VS WO YG) Mon-Thu 18-7, Fri 14-7, Sat 14-Mon 7 h
55 Porter Street, Prahran VIC 3181 ✉3000 ☎ 9529 5166
Large cruising maze. Pass outs available. Popular with young disco crowd. Admission before 21 h A$ 12, after 15, low season all times 10.

BODY & BEAUTY SHOPS

Piercing Urge. The (AC CC) Mo-We 11:00-19:00h, Th & Fr 11:00-20:00h, Sa 10:00-18:00h
206 Commercial Road, Prahran ✉3141 ☎ 9530 2244
Body Jewellery shop.

BOOK SHOPS

Beat Books (AC CC MA) Mon-Thu 10-20 h, Fri 10-2 h, Sat 9-2 h, Sun 12-20 h (call for summer h)
157 Commercial Road, South Yarra, ✉VIC 3141 ☎ 9827-8748
The best bookshop in Melborne. A wide selection of gay literature.
Hares & Hyenas (GLM) 10-? h
135 Commercial Road, South Yarra ✉3141 ☎ 9824 0110

LEATHER & FETISH SHOPS

Eagle Leather (CC glm LJ MA) Su-Th 12:00-18:00h, Fr & Sa 12:00-21:00h other times by appointment
118 Hoddle Street, Abbotsford ✉3067 ☎ 9417-2100
Locally made leather and latex clothing, toys & accessories. Imports from UK, USA and Canada. Co-ordinates Melbournes Leather Festival each year (1-20 September)

TRAVEL & TRANSPORT

Pride Travel and Tours
254 Bay Street, Brighton ✉3186 ☎ 9596 7100
Freecall 1800 061 427. FAX 9596-7761. Gay Travel agency service (Anne Fitzgerald). Friendly.

HOTELS

California Motor Inn (AC B CC bf F H MA msg N NG OS pi) 0-24 h
138 Barkers Road, Hawthorn ✉VIC 3122
☎ 9818 0281 Fax: 9819 6845
Situated in pleasant suburb 1/2 h from city center. Close to gay venues. Restaurant, bar, free parking, guest laundry. Rates single A$ 110, double 130, studio 145. Open all year.
Cosmopolitan Motor Inn St. Kilda (F g H)
6 Carlisle Street, St. Kilda ✉3182 *(near Melbourne bayside cosmopolitan suburb)* ☎ 9534 0781 Fax: 9534 8262
FAX 9534 8262. All rooms with facilities. Rates A$ 70-110.

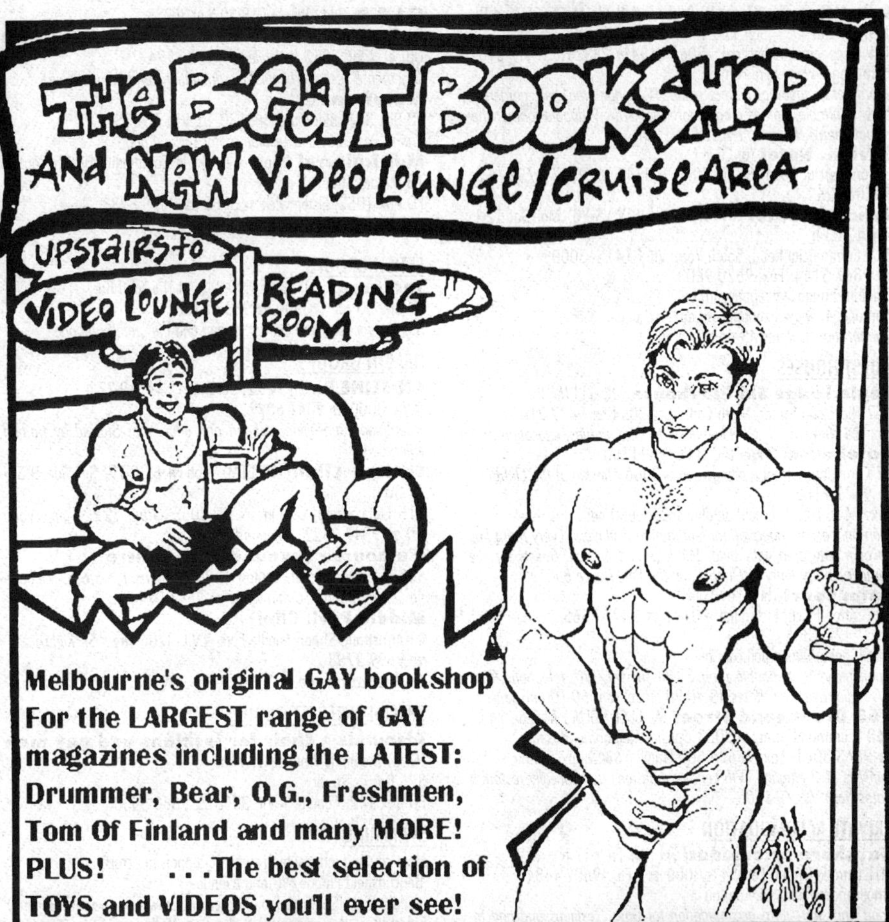
THE Beat BOOKSHOP
AND NEW VIDEO LOUNGE/CRUISE AREA
UPSTAIRS to
VIDEO LOUNGE
READING ROOM
Melbourne's original GAY bookshop
For the LARGEST range of GAY magazines including the LATEST:
Drummer, Bear, O.G., Freshmen, Tom Of Finland and many MORE!
PLUS! ...The best selection of TOYS and VIDEOS you'll ever see!

Laird Hotel. The (AC B bf CC G H LJ MA OS S) Mon-Thu 17-2, Fri-Sat 17-3, Sun 17-24 h
149 Gipps Street, Abbotsford ✉3067 ☎ 9417 2832 Fax: 9417 2109
Homepage: www.laird.com.au
Home of Melbournes leather scene. TV lounge area, beer garden, 2 bars, pooltable, games area. Boot scoot SUN. 9 double rooms, share bathrooms. Room rate A$ 55.
Saville. Hotel (bf CC H F g)
5 Commercial Road, South Yarra ✉3141 ☎ 9867 2755 Fax: 9020-9726
Xchange Hotel (B G H MA N S STV VS YG) Mon-Sat 12-1, Sun 12-23 h
119 Commercial Road, South Yarra VIC 3141 ✉3000
☎ 9867 5144 Fax: 9820 9603
Email: xchange@ozemail.com.au
Homepage: www.ozemail.com.au/~xchange
Budget rooms. Rates A$ 45-60 (bf incl.)

GUEST HOUSES

Eagle Lodge SM Playhouse (DR G LJ MA P)
647 Nicholson Street, North Carlton, ✉3054 ☎ 9417-2100
Fax: 9416-4235 *SM-Playhouse, for hire, parties, education.*
Gatehouse. The (AC bf CC G H LJ MA)
97 Cambridge Street, Collingwood ✉3066 *Checkin at the Club80*
☎ 9471 2182
Fax: 9416 0474 Email: gatehouse@club80.net
Men only accommodation for leathermen / players. Every room has its own play area with sling, bondage bed & wall. Guests receive complimentary entry to Club80 and the Peel Dance Bar.
Palm Court (bf CC e GLM H)
22 Grattan Place, Richmond ✉3121 ☎ 9427 7365
Fax: 9427 7365
Email: palmc@ozemail.com.au
Open all year. 8 double rooms with shower/WC, telephone/fax, TV/radio, own key. Rates A$ 40-90 off season, 50-100 on season
163 Drummond Street (AC bf CC f GLM) All year, 24 h
163 Drummond Street ✉3053 *Oposite Melbourne Museum*
☎ 9663 3081 Fax: 9663 6500 Email: 163@maxi.net.au
Consists of 2 elegant 19th century mansions authentically restored. Rates from A$ 70-150.

PRIVATE ACCOMODATION

Gayshare Accomodation Mon-Fri 9-17 h
501 Latrobe Street, Level 4 ✉3000 ☎ . Fax: 9602-4484
Email: mckenzie@wire.net.au
Long and short term accomodation for Gays, Lesbians and gay friendly people.
Holly Lodge Bed & Breakfast (bf CC glm MA msg OS)
19 Grenville Street, Daylesford ✉3460 ☎ 5348 3670
Fax: 5348 3670 Email: hollylodgeings@hotmail.com

GENERAL GROUPS

ALSO Foundation
35 Cato Street, Pahran ✉VIC 3182
☎ 9510 5569
Supports all manner of Lesbian and Gay community initiatives.
Gay and Lesbian Immigration Task Force
PO Box 2387, Richmond South ✉3121 ☎ 9822-0794
or ☎ 9523-7864. Help and support for immigration equality as well as gays and lesbians with overseas partners.
Gay and Lesbian Organisation of Business and Enterprise (GLOBE) (CC E f GLM MA S)
PO Box 20 63, Albert Park ✉3206 ☎ 9686 2499
Email: GLOBE@hotmail.com
Dinner -1st Mo in month, „fruits in suits" -3rd Th in month
G.L.A.D. 2nd/4th Mon 18.30 h at 3CR,
21 Smith Street, Fitzroy PO Box 4215, Melbourne University Post Office, ✉VIC 3052 *Parkville* ☎ 9576 1994
Gay men & lesbians against discrimination (and homophobia).
Motafrenz (GLM)
PO Box 351, Blackburn ✉3130 ☎ 9557 9635
Phone Ross. Gay and Lesbian motor social group.
Multicultural Meets at St. Kilda Community Health Centre, 18 Milford Street
PO Box 1052, Elsternwick ✉3185 ☎ 9525 6233
Call for information and dates.

FETISH GROUPS

Jackaroos (LJ) Tue 21.30-24 h at The Laird Bar
PO Box 50 64 ✉3000 ☎ 9663 8168
A group for gays into leather, denim and the great outdoors.

HEALTH GROUPS

AIDSLINE Mon-Fri 11-22, Sat Sun 11-14, 19-22 h
✉VIC 3000 ☎ 9347 6099
Telephone counselling, support and education. Staffed by trained volunteers.
Carlton Clinic (CC GLM) Mon-Fri 8.30-19, Sat Sun 9.30-12.30 h
115 Elgin Street, Carlton ✉VIC 3053 *(Tram 1/22-Elgin/Lygon St)* ☎ 9347 9422 *Gay and lesbian clinic.*
Melbourne Sexual Health Centre
580 Swanston Street, Carlton ✉3053 *Trams 1,3,5,6,8, Melbourne Central station 10 min walk.* ☎ 9347 0244
Middle Park Clinic
41 Armstrong Street, Middle Park ✉VIC 3206 *(near St. Kilda)*
☎ 9699 3758
Gay medical practice.

SPECIAL INTEREST GROUPS

Alsounds • Choir for lesbians and gay men (GLM) Meetings Wed 19.30 h at
325 Dorcas Street
PO Box 142, Coburg ✉VIC 3058 ☎ 9380 5538

SWIMMING

Most city and inner suburb swimming pools are cruisy.
-Beaconsfield Parade/Victoria Avenue.
-Middle Park/South Melbourne Beach (known as „Screech Beach") Situated at the end towards the Port Melbourne Lifesaving Club. Most popular gay beach in Melbourne)
-Somers Beach (NU) (Two-hour drive from Melbourne on the Merrington Peninsula)
-St. Kilda Beach (on the lawn outside Jean Jacques restaurant)
-Prahran swimming pool. 41 Essex Street, Prahran, ☎ 522-3248. (Open Oct-May. Outdoors heated public swimming. Popular with gays.)

CRUISING

Victorian police have regular plain clothes surveillance, so all areas are AYOR.
-Princes Park
-Footscray Park
-Ashburton shopping centre
-Canterbury Park, Canterbury
-Albert Park (AYOR) (along Aughtie Drive and bushy areas at night)
-Point Ormond Beach (AYOR) (end of Glenhuntly Road. Occasional bashers)

-Eildon Park, off Ackland Street next to the church.
Most beats around the city are busy (be guided by the graffiti) as are those on Bayside beaches and the Yarra river bank for 4-5 km out of the city up the river. In the suburbs most shopping complexes are busy but patrolled by in house security.)
-Flinders Street Station (AYOR) (several facilities including entrance from Elizabeth Street and at nearby Princes Bridge.)
-Spencer Street station (AYOR) (on platforms 11 and 12, very busy)
-

SWIMMING
-Sunnyside Beach (between Mornington and Mount Eliza on the Peninsula. Although this is a family beach gays tend to congregate at the far end of this scenic beach. 50 minutes drive from central city.)

Olinda ☎ 03

HOTELS
Delvin Country House (bf GLM)
25 Monash Avenue ✉3788 ☎ 9751-1800 *Fax: (03) 9751 1829. Rates from A$ 60 (single) to A$ 90 (double). Special theme dinners (e.g. murder mysteries).*

Phillip Island ☎ 03

HOTELS
Genesta House (bf CC glm H MA msg WE)
3 Genesta Street, Cowes ✉3922 ☎ 5952-3616
100 year old house with 3 guest rooms.

Stanley ☎ 03

GUEST HOUSES
Stanley Croft (AC bf CC GLM H MA NU OS P WE)
Masons Road, PO Box 332, Beechworth ✉3747 *Located between* ☎ 5728 6626 Fax: 5728 6626 Email: scroft@netc.net.au. Homepage: home.netc.net.au/scroft.
One double room with shower/WC, radio, kitchenette, own key. Rates from A$ 100 (single usage 65). Additional bed 50

Warrnambool ☎ 03

GUEST HOUSES
Kings Head (AC CC GLM H MA p)
PO Box 658 VIC 3280 ✉3280 *(Opposite Logans Beach Whale Nursery)* ☎ 5561-4569
FAX 5562-4085. E-Mail Kinghead@ansanic.com.au. Homepage http://www.ansonic.com.au.kingshead. Very quiet and secluded location. Rates from A$ 85-115.

Werribee

SWIMMING
-Campbell's Cove (NU) (at Werribee)

AUS-Western Australia

West AUS

Initials: WA

Time: GMT +8

Area: 2,525,500 km² / 975,096 sq mi.

Population: 1,822,000

Capital: Perth

● In Western Australia the age of consent is fixed at 16 years for lesbians and heterosexuals and 21 for gays.

✱ In Westaustralien liegt das Schutzalter bei 16 Jahren für Lesben und Heterosexuelle und bei 21 Jahren für Homosexuelle.

▲ En Australie occidentale, la majorité sexuelle est fixée à 16 ans pour les lesbiennes et les hétérosexuels et à 21 ans pour les homosexuels.

☆ La edad de consentimiento en Australia Occiental es de 16 años para lesbianas y heterosexuales, para homosexuales está estipulada en los 21 años.

❖ In Western Australia l'età legale per rapporti sessuali tra eterosessuali e tra donne è di 16 anni, quello tra uomini di 21 anni.

Perth ☎ 08

● The capital of Western Australia was founded in 1829 and has a population of 1,200,000. Perth is beautifully located on the Swan River and is not too far away from the harbour city of Fremantle. Perth looks out on the Indian Ocean and has many airlince connections with Africa and Asia. It has become the first Australian city that many Europeans have contact with.
It has developed into an interesting and lively gay scene with many different things on offer for the gay tourist. Perth has many wonderful shops and diverse architecture (e.g. London Court in the Tudor look).
There is plenty of attractive natural beauty. In the centrally situated Kings Park are prime examples of Australian bush flora and the wild flowers that that bloom in November are beautiful. A beloved holiday destination is Rottnest Island with a huge beach and home to the perculiar animal the Quokka. Further afield is the Darling Ranges and the wine district of the Margaret River.
Every year in October takes place for five weeks the Gay Pride Festival.

✱ Die Hauptstadt des Bundesstaates Western Australia wurde 1829 gegründet und zählt heute 1 200 000 Einwohner. Perth ist malerisch am Swan River gelegen und nicht weit von der Hafenstadt Fremantle entfernt. Im Westen Australiens gelegen blickt Perth auf den Indischen Ozean. Die Stadt hat viele direkte Flugverbindungen mit Afrika und Asien und ist oft für viele europäische Besucher die erste australische Stadt, mit der sie Kontakt haben.
In der Stadt hat sich eine interessante und lebhafte Szene entwickelt, aber auch Perth selbst hat sehr viel abwechslungsreiches zu bieten. Central Perth ist eine tolle Einkaufsgegend, die Architektur ist vielfältig (z.B. London Court im Tudor-Look).
Die Natur hat ihren besonderen Reiz: Im zentral gelegenen Kings Park ist die australische Buschflora vertreten und die Blüte der Wildblumen im November ist fantastisch. Ein beliebtes Reiseziel ist Rottnest Island mit seinem großen Strand, wo ein eigentümliches Tier, der Quokka beheimatet ist. Etwas weiter entfernt liegen die Darling Ranges und das Weinanbaugebiet Margaret River.
Jährlich im Oktober findet für fünf Wochen das Gay Pride Festival statt.

▲ La capitale de l'Australie-Occidentale a été fondée en 1829 et compte aujourd'hui 1.200.000 habitants. La ville pittoresque de Perth est située au bord du Swan River et pas très éloignée de la ville portuaire de Fremantle. A l'ouest de l'Australie, Perth regarde sur l'océan Indien. La ville comporte de nombreuses correspondances aériennes directes avec l'Afrique et l'Asie et est souvent la première ville australienne pour nombre de visiteurs européens avec laquelle ils sont en contact. En ville, il s'est développé une scène intéressante et animée, mais Perth elle-même offre également de nombreuses distractions variées. Perth est aussi un centre commercial, son architecture est multiple (p.ex. London Court dans le style du temps de Tudor). La nature a son charme tout particulier: le Kings Park situé au centre offre une flore de la brousse australienne et la floraison des fleurs sauvages au mois de novembre est fantastique.

Une destination en vogue est Rottnest Island avec sa grande plage où réside un animal singulier: le quokka. Un peu plus loin se trouve les Darling Ranges et la région viticole Margaret River. Chaque année au mois d'octobre a lieu le festival „Gay Pride" qui dure cinq semaines.

❖ La capital del estado federal de Australia Occidental se fundó en 1829 y cuenta hoy en día con 1.200.000 habitantes. Perth está situado a orillas del río Swan y muy cerca de la ciudad portuária de Freemantle. Situado en la parte occidental de Australia, Perth tiene vistas al Océano ¥ndico. La ciudad dispone de muchas conexiones aereas directas con Africa y Asia, así que para muchos visitantes europeos es la primera ciudad que conocen de Australia. En Perth no solo se ha desarollado un ambiente gay interesante y vivaz, sino también la ciudad misma tiene mucho que ofrecer. Central Perth es una zona de compras estupenda y los diferentes estilos de arquitectura son dignos de ver (como por ejemplo London Court). La naturaleza tiene un encanto especial. Es increíble el poder contemplar en el mismo centro de la ciudad (Kings Park) ejemplos de la flora salvaje australiana, que en el mes de noviembre, cuando todas las plantas están en plena floración, alcanza su mayor esplendor. De los destinos de especial interés se podrían citar Rottnest Island, no solamente por sus extensas playas, sino por el curiosísimo animal, que exclusivamente en esta región habita, el Quokka. Alejándonos un poco, encontramos Darling Ranges y la región vinícola Margaret River. Anualmente, en el mes de octubre se celebra durante cinco semanas el Gay Pride Festival.

☆ La capitale dello stato federale fu fondata nel 1829. Oggi ha 1.200.000 abitanti. Situato pittorescamente sulle rive del Swan River, all'ovest del continente sull'oceano indiano, non dista molto dal porto di Fremantle. La città possiede collegamenti aerei diretti con l'Africa e l'Asia, e spesso è la prima città australiana con cui molti turisti europei vengono in contatto. A parte la vita gay interessante e vivace, la città offre varie attrazioni. Central Perth è pieno di bellissimi negozi, l'architettura è svariata (p.es. London Court nel Tudor-Look). La natura ha il suo fascino: il Kings Park ospita molte specie della flora australiana, ed i fiori selvaggi in novembre sono spettacolari. Rottnest Island vicino a Perth è una meta turistica interessante per la sua grande spiaggia ed una suo caratteristica specie animale: il Quokka. Un po' più lontano si trovano I Darling Ranges ed i vigneti di Margaret River. Ogni anno in ottobre ha luogo per cinque settimane il Gay Pride Festival.

GAY INFO

B.P.M. Thu/Fri night RTR 92.1 FM
PO Box 298, Belmont ✉WA 6984 Fax: 9277-4268.

Gay and Lesbian Counselling Service Mon-Fr 19.30-22.30, Mo, Tu & Th 13:00-16:00h
City West Lotteries House, 2 Delhi Street ✉WA 6005 ☎ 9420 7201 Fax: 9486 9855
Information on the gay and lesbian scene. Telephone counselling. Groups such as Breakaway, 26up, galen, groovygirls and wow.

Westside Observer
PO Box 131, 541 Fitzgerald Street, North Perth ✉WA 6006 ☎ 9242-2146 Fax: 9242 2209
Email: editor@wso.com.au *Monthly publication, free at gay venues.*

TOURIST INFO

Western Australian Tourism Commission
6th Floor, 16 St. Georges Terrace, ✉WA 6000 ☎ 9220-1700
FAX 220 17 02.

BARS

Connections Night Club (AC B D GLM MA S SNU STV YG) Tue (G) 22-4, Wed Fri 22-6, Sat 21-6, Sun 20-1 h, Mon Thu closed
81 James Street, Northbridge ✉WA 6003 *(above Plaka Café)* ☎ 9328-1870
First hour every night - free entry and „nice price" drinks. Gay owned and managed.

Court Hotel. The (B F glm H S) Mon-Sat 11-23, Sun 15-21 h
50 Beaufort Street/James Street, Northbridge ✉WA 6003 ☎ 9328-5292 Fax: 9227-1570

DANCECLUBS

Dive Bar (B D G MA) Thu-Sun 18-? h
232 William Street, Northbridge ✉WA 6003 ☎ 9328-1822

SEX SHOPS/BLUE MOVIES

Ram Lounge and Video (G VS) Mon-Wed 9-23, Thu-Sat 9-24, Sun 11-24 h
114 Barrack Street ✉WA 6000 *(via Club X)* ☎ 9325-3815

Vibrations Adult Shop (AC CC G YG SNU VS YG) 354 A Charles Street, North Perth ✉WA 6006 *(opposite McDonald's)* ☎ 9242-4501

SAUNAS/BATHS

Beaufort 565 (AC CC f G lj MA msg sa sb sol wh) 12-? h
565 Beaufort Street/Vincent St., Mount Lawley ✉WA 6050 ☎ 9328-7703

Perth Steam Works (AC CC DR f G msg sa sb wh) Mon-Thu 12-1, Fri-Sat 12-3, Sun 12-2 h
369 William Street, Northbridge ✉WA 6003 *(Entry Forbes Road)* ☎ 9328-2930
Mondays A$ 10,- all day !

BOOK SHOPS

Arcane Bookshop. The (CC GLM) Mon-Thu 10-17.30, Fri 10-20, Sat 10-17, Sun 12-17 h
212 William Street, Northbridge ✉WA 6000 ☎ 9328-5073
FAX 9228-0410. Largest range of gay/lesbian books in Perth and ticket seller for gay lesbian events.

HOTELS

Court Hotel (B bf CC D F GLM H MA N OS S W) Also Bar
50 Beaufort Street ✉WA 6000 ☎ 9328-5292
Central location. Rates from A$ 35.

Criterion Hotel (B bf CC D E F glm H MA SWC W) 560 Hay Street ✉WA 6000 ☎ 9325-5155 Fax: 9325-4176
Comfortable hotel directly in the heart of the city. Rooms with bath or shower/WC, telephone, TV, radio, minibar, room service, own key. Rates (excl. tax) for single AUS$ 95, double AUS$ 112 and triple AUS$ 130 incl. full bf. Car park.

Metro Inn Apartment Hotel (AC B bf CC F H pi) 7-23 h
22 Nile Street, East Perth ✉WA 6004 ☎ 9325-1866
Fax: 9325-5374
Rates from A$ 86 (one bedroom apartment) to 144 (interconnecting apartments).

Sullivans Hotel (AC B bf CC F MA NG OS pi W)
166 Mounts Bay Road ✉WA 6000 ☎ 9321-8022 Fax: 9481-6762Email: perth@sullivans.com.au
Homepage: www.sullivans.com.au
Near Kings Park, free bus to city centre. 70 rooms AND 2 apartments with TV, shower/WC, phone. radio. Partly with balcony and safe. Rates from A$ 98,—

GUEST HOUSES

Abaca Palms (AC bf CC F G lj MA NU OS sa W wh WO)
34 Whatley Crescent, Mount Lawley ✉WA 6050 ☎ 9271-2117
Fax: 9371-5370 Email: abacpalm@multiline.com.au
Guest house close to city and venues. 8 rooms and one apartment

with bath/WC, telephone, TV/video, radio, own key. Rates single A$ 50, double 65, apartment 130.

Lawley on Guildford. The (AC bf CC GLM H OS wh)
72 Guildford Road, Mount Lawley ✉WA 6065 ☎ 9272 5501
Fax: 9272 5501
Large double rooms, private and shared bath, guest lounge, Spa, gym, grass tennis court, close to all amenities. Rates from A$ 55.

Swanbourne Guest House (AC b bf CC f g H lj MA msg N NU p pi OS VS WO) closed Jul/Aug
5 Myera Street, Swanbourne ✉WA 6010 *(Bus 36-Beach/Perth City)* ☎ 9383-1981 Fax: 9383-1981
Email: ralphk@wantree.com.au
Homepage: www.ozemail.com.au/~ksetra/sgh.html
5 min outside of Perth, 2 km to gay nude beach. All rooms with cable television. Guest House provides room service. Rates A$ 55-95 per night.

GENERAL GROUPS

Breakaway Gay Youth Group (G YG) Every 2nd Sa 12:00-17:00h
c/o GLCS, 2 Delhi Street ✉WA 6005 ☎ 9420 7201
Fax: 9486 9855
Support group via the CLCS

Breakaway-Gay Youth Group
PO Box 406 ✉WA 6001
A social and support group for people under 26. For details Gayline ☎ 9328 9044. Email: clubwest@merriweb,com.au
Homepage: www.merriweb,com.au/clubwest

Club West Social Group
PO Box 283 ✉WA 6006 ☎ 9307-5740

Country Network
GPO Box 1031 ✉WA 6001
For details Gayline ☎ 9328-9044.

Friends Perth
☎ 9227-6115
Meetings at members homes for guys 21-30. Call for information.

GAGS-Gays Activities Group Services
PO Box 8234, Stirling Street ✉WA 6000

GALE-Coalition for Gay and Lesbian Equality
PO Box 912, West Perth ✉WA 6005

Gay Outdoors Group
PO Box 263, Cottesloe ✉WA 6011

MUGALS-Murdoch Uni Gay and Lesbian Society
Student Guild, Murdoch Uni, South St., Murdoch ✉WA 6150 ☎ 9332-6335

Pride Collective
PO Box 156, Northbridge ✉WA 6003
☎ 9227 1767 Homepage: www.pridewa.asn.au
Organizers of gay pride.

Stonewall Union of Students
c/o The Secretary, PO Box 156, Northbridge ✉WA 6003
Social and support group for gay, lesbian and bisexual students.

HEALTH GROUPS

Act Up Perth
PO Box 231, Northbridge ✉WA 6003 ☎ 9227-6706

AIDS Youthline
☎ 9227-9644

Gay Men`s Health Centre by appointment
664 Murray Street, ✉WA 6005 ☎ 9429-9902

Mount Lawley Medical Centre 9-18 h
689 Beaufort Street, Mount Lawley ✉WA 6050 ☎ 9227-2455

Murray St STD Clinic
70 Murray Street ✉WA 6000 ☎ 9270-1122

People Living with AIDS
U10/105 Lord Street ✉WA 6000 ☎ 9221-3002
FAX 9221-3035

Sida Centre Mo 12-20, Tue-Fr 9-7
Unit 10, 105 Lord Street, East Perth ✉WA 6004 ☎ 9221-3002
Fax: 9221-9035
Centre for people with HIV and Aids

Western Australian AIDS Council Mon-Fri 8.30-17 h, closed Sat Sun
664 Murray Street, West Perth ✉WA 6005 ☎ 9429-9900
Fax: 9221-9035

WA AIDS Council
664 Murray Street, West Perth
☎ 9429 9900
Support, information, education.

RELIGIOUS GROUPS

Acceptance West
PO Box 83 30, Stirling Street Private Boxes ✉WA 6849
☎ 9383-3188
Catholic group.

Aleph
c/o Gay and Lesbian Counselling Service, PO Box 405, *Mt. Lawley WA 6050* ☎ 9328-9044
Social group for gay & lesbian Jews.

Resurrection Community Church Worship Sun 19.30 h
317 Bagot Road, Subiaco ✉WA 6008 ☎ 9478-3657

SPECIAL INTEREST GROUPS

Parents, Families & Friends of Lesbians & Gays Mondays 09:00-12:00h
PO Box 354, Northbridge ✉WA 6865 ☎ 9228 1005
Email: plagperth@telstra.easymail.com.au
Homepage: www.gfd.net.au/p-flag

SPORT GROUPS

Loton Park Tennis Club (GLM) Oct-May: Sat Sun 13-17 h
PO Box 8330, Bulwer Street/Lord Street ✉WA 6000 ☎ 9328-5065
Gay and lesbian tennis club.

SWIMMING

-Floriat Beach (AYOR) (Not a nude beach but attract quite a few gay people, particularly at the northern end.)
-South City Beach/Swanbourne (AYOR) (Nude beaches. Gays congregate at the southern end of South City Beach and North Swanbourne.)
-Warnbro Beach (Rockingham)
-Whitford's Beach

CRUISING

All AYOR
-Fremantle (under bridges)
-Swanbourne Beach (at night, but helicopter surveillance).
-Fawkner Park (South Perth)
-Mosman Park (south end of Mosman Bay)
-Kings Park (near barbeque area; entrance from Thomas Street)

Scarborough ☎ 08

HOTELS

Scarborough's By The Sea (g H)
96a Stanley Street ✉WA 6019 ☎ 9341 1411

Austria

Österreich

Central Europe

Initials: A

Time: GMT +1

☎ Country Code / Access Code: 43 / 00

Language: German

Area: 83,857 km² / 34,307 sq mi.

Currency: Austrian Schilling (öS). 1 EURO = 100 EuroCents; the Euro can only be used in the clearance system.

Population: 8,030,000

Capital: Wien

Religions: 78% Catholic

Climate: Alpine climate with hot summers and cold, snowy winters.

● Austria remains in terms of it's laws in Europe outdated. Homosexual acts are still punishable and the age of sexual consent still varies. Homosexual acts between men are permissible at 18. Sexual acts between straights and lesbians is set at 14. Violation of these laws can lead to a stint behind bars for upto five years. The Austrians are seen to be stock conservative. However, there has been over the last few years a loosening of the application of the laws governing homosexual acts. The gay community has concentrated itself in Vienna adding colour and liveliness to the city. Sanctions on homosexual acts up to five years behind bars.

✱ Weiterhin bleibt Österreich in seiner Gesetzgebung einer der rückständigen Staaten Europas. Noch immer gibt es im Strafrecht Bestimmungen, die ein unterschiedliches Schutzalter für Homosexuelle (18) und Heterosexuelle bzw. Lesben (14) vorsehen. Der Verstoß wird mit Haftstrafen bis zu fünf Jahren bedroht. Die Anwendung dieser Bestimmungen erfolgt jedoch uneinheitlich. Eine Liberalisierung wurde vom Parlament im Juli 1998 abgelehnt. Den Österreichern wird eine gewisse Konservativität nachgesagt. Was sicherlich nicht übertrieben ist. In den letzten Jahren jedoch hat sich viel getan, die strafrechtlichen Bestimmungen wurden gelockert. Besonders nachhaltig wirkt sich diese Klimaveränderung in Wien, der (schwulen) Hauptstadt Österreichs aus. Mit ihrer bunten und lebendigen Szene nimmt sie heute einen Spitzenplatz im deutschsprachigen Raum ein.

▲ En ce qui concerne l'homosexualité et la loi, l'Autriche reste l'un des pays les plus rétrogrades d'Europe. Selon le code pénal, la la majorité sexuelle pour les homosexuels est fixée à 18 ans et à 14 pour les hétérosexuels et les lesbiennes. Les contrevenants s'exposent à des peines de prison pouvant aller jusqu'à 5 ans. Et sachez qu'en Autriche on ne badine pas avec la loi!
On prête aux Autrichiens un certain conservatisme, ce qui n'est pas tout à fait faux. Pourtant, les choses ont commencé à bouger ces dernières années. Le code pénal est par exemple beaucoup moins restrictif que dans le passé.
Bien sûr, c'est à Vienne, la capitale gay du pays, que ces changements se font le plus sentir. Au niveau gay, c'est aujourd'hui l'une des villes les plus intéressantes des pays d'expression allemande.

☆ Debido a su legislación en cuestión homosexual, Austria sigue siendo uno de los paises más atrasados en toda Europa. Las leyes del Código Penal establecen todavía diferentes edades de consentimiento para homosexuales (18 años) y heterosexuales y lesbianas (14 años). La contravención puede conllevar una pena de hasta cinco años de cárcel. Estas determinaciones se aplican consecuentemente. Los austriacos tienen cierta fama de conservadores y esto seguramente no es ninguna exageración. Sin embargo, en los últimos años han mejorado en algunos aspectos, sobre todo, las dictaminaciones ya no se aplican con el mismo rigor. Este cambio de clima se nota sobre todo en Viena, la capital (gay) de Austria. Con su colorido y vivaz ambiente ocupa hoy en día una de las posiciones líderes entre los paises de lengua alemana.

❖ Riguardo alla liberalizzazione dell'omosessualità la legislazione austriaca è una delle più reazionarie d'Europa. Esistono ancora leggi che vietano le organizzazioni gay e lesbiche e che stabiliscono un'età legale differente per i rapporti gay (18) e eterosessuali e lesbici (14). I trasgressori possono essere condannati alla reclusione per una durata fino a cinque anni. Questa norma viene adottata conseguentemente. Si dice che l'austriaco sia in un certo senso conservativo, questo sicuramente non è esagerato. Negli ultimi anni però è cambiato molto, il rigore delle leggi penali è stato mitigato. Questo cambiamento del clima si sente soprattutto a Vienna, la metropoli (gay) dell'Austria. Con il suo ambiente vivace e svariato è una delle città più importanti per la vita gay nei paesi di lingua tedesca.

NATIONAL GAY INFO

Homosexuelle Initiative (HOSI) Wien-1. Lesben und Schwulenverband Österreichs
Tue 17-22 h
Novaragasse 40, ✉1020 Wien *(U1-Praterstern/Nestroyplatz)* ☎ (01) 216 66 04

Lambda-Nachrichten
c/o HOSI Wien, Novaragasse 40, ✉1020 Wien ☎ (01) 216 66 04 Email: hosiwien@via.at.
Homepage: www.hosiwien.gay.at
Published four times a year. öS 60 per issue. Approximately 88 pages. Austria's oldest and leading news magazine for gays and lesbians, published by HOSI. Features national and international reports. Feuilleton. Some commercial and classified advertisements.

Österreichisches Lesben- und Schwulenforum
Berggasse 7 ✉1090 Wien ☎ 01/218 56 10 Fax: 01/533 31 92
Email: oelsf@usa.net

Rosa Lila Tip Mon - Fri 17-20:00h
in der Rosa Villa, Linke Wienzeile 102 ✉1060 Wien *(U4 Pilgramgasse)* ☎ 01/ 585 43 43 Fax: 01/ 587 17 78
Email: info@villa.at Homepage: www.villa.at
Betreuung, Infos, Schwulen-, Lesben und Elterngruppen. Bibliothek, Kondome, Gleithmittel./ Gay-lesbian switchboard : Counselling, infos, glb-groups, library, condoms, lubricants

XTRA!
PO Box 77, ✉1043 Wien ☎ 01/333 10 73.
Fax: 01/333 10 73. Email: xtra@magnet.at
Monthly magazine with calendar of events, listing of Vienna's bars and organisations and other information about Vienna's gay scene. Free at gay venues. Official magazine of Safe Way.

NATIONAL COMPANIES

American Discount ☎ (02236) 22 5 96
Comics, magazines and books / Comics, Magazine und Bücher.

NATIONAL GROUPS

AGPRO - Austrian Gay Professionals
Postfach 113 ✉1050 Wien Email: info@appor.at Homepage: www.appro.at

Baden ✉ 2500 ☎ 02252

HELP WITH PROBLEMS

Power Life/Life Power
Christalnigg-Gasse 1 ✉2500
Prevention, Information.

Bregenz ✉ 6900 ☎ 05574

BARS

Wunderbar (! B bf glm MA YG) 9-1 h
Bahnhofstraße 4 ✉6900 *(near pedestrian zone)* ☎ 477 58

HEALTH GROUPS

AIDS-Hilfe Vorarlberg Counselling: Tue Thu 17-19, Wed Fri 10-13. Test: 17-19 h
Neugasse 5 ✉6900 ☎ 465 26 Fax: 469 04 14

Dornbirn ☎ 05574

SEX SHOPS/BLUE MOVIES

Blue Box Discount Erotik Videothek (CC GLM LJ VS) Mon-Sun 11-22 h
Bahnhofstraße 26 ✉6850 *(near main station)* ☎ 05572/555 30
Video rental and purchase, toys and tools, magaines, CD-roms, books.

GENERAL GROUPS

Homosexuelle Initiative (HOSI) Vorarlberg
Counselling Thu 18-20 h
PO Box 841 ✉6854 ☎ 469 04 14

Feldkirch ✉ 6803

RELIGIOUS GROUPS

Homosexualität und Glaube (HuG)
Postfach 522 ✉6803

Fügen-Zillertal ✉ 6263 ☎ 05288

HOTELS

Hotel-Garni Alpenhof (B bf g H lj MA msg OS sa sb sol WO) Mid Dec-Mid Apr, Mid May-Mid Oct
Sängerweg 490 ✉6263 ☎ 62 05 0 Fax: 620 50 50
Hotel in a romantic setting, ideal for summer and winter holidays. 50 km to Innsbruck airport. 20 rooms with bath/shower, balcony, phone, TV, safe, heating, own key. Rates single öS 430-560, double 330-520 depending on season.

Gmunden ✉ 4810

CRUISING

-Traunbrücke (YG) (below the bridge/unter der Brücke -18 h)

Graz ☎ 0316

GAY INFO

Schwulen- und Lesbenzentrum „feel free"
Rapoldgasse 24 8010 ✉8000 ☎ 32 80 80
Information, counselling, bibliotheque, café and events.

BARS

Bang (B D DR GLM OS s VS YG) Bar: Wed Thu Sun 21-2, Disco: Fri Sat -4 h
Dreihackengasse 4-10 ✉8020 ☎ 71 95 49
BARcelona (B f GLM MA r og P) 20-4 h
Reitschulgasse 20 ✉8010 ☎ 84 52 48

CAFES

Café Na Und (B f glm)
Bahnhofsgürtel 85 ✉8020
☎ 72 38 32

SEX SHOPS/BLUE MOVIES

Erotic Bazar (CC g) Mo-Sat 10-19
Bindergasse 8 ✉8010 ☎ 83 17 65
Sexworld Gayshop Austria (DR G r VS) Mon-Fri 10-13 h 14-19 h, Sat 10-17 h
Quergasse 1 ✉8020 *(near main station)*
Videos, magazines, PP, toys.

ESCORTS & STUDIOS

Amsterdam-Club (B CC DR G p R VS) 22-2 h, closed Sun
Quergasse 1/Annenstraße 53 ✉8020 ☎ 76 54 59
Gay Swinger Club

BOOK SHOPS

American Discount Mon-Fri 9-13 14-18, Sat 9-12 h
Jakoministraße 12 ✉8020 ☎ 83 23 24
International magazines, comics, books-including a gay section/ Zeitungs- und Buchladen mit schwuler Abteilung.

TRAVEL & TRANSPORT

G.B.L. Tours (CC) Mo-Fr 9-17.30
Schörgelgasse 8 ✉8010 ☎ 82 63 20 Fax: 823 066
Travel agency.

GENERAL GROUPS

Hochschülerschaft an der TU Graz Schwulenreferat
Rechbauerstraße 12 ✉8010 ☎ 873 51 22
Rosalila Panther-Schwul-Lesbische Aktionsgemeinschaft Steiermark Mon, Thu, Fri 19-22 h
c/o feel free, Rapoldgasse 24 ✉8010 ☎ 32 80 80 Fax: 31 85 40.

HEALTH GROUPS

Steirische AIDS-Hilfe Mon Wed 11-13, Fri 17-19 conselling, Tue Thu 16.30-19.30 h HIV-test
Schmiedgasse 38/I ✉8010 ☎ 81 50 50 *Fax: 81 50 50-6.*
Stop AIDS Verein zur Förderung von sicherem Sex
Rapoldgasse 24 ✉8010 ☎ 36 66 00 *Fax: 31 85 40.*

RELIGIOUS GROUPS

Homosexuelle und Glaube (HuG) 1st and 3rd Fri/month 19.30 h
c/o feel free, Rapoldgasse 24 ✉8010 ☎ 32 80 80
Fax: 31 85 40. Email: hug-steiermark@gmx.at

CRUISING

-municipal park (fountain)
-Schlammteich
-Hauptplatz
-Hauptbahnhof
-Annenpassage
-University: Vorklinisches Institutsgebäude, Parterre
-Hauptplatz
-Jakominiplatz

Innsbruck ☎ 0512

GAY INFO

Homosexuelle Initiative (HOSI) Tirol (b G MA s)
Thu 20.30-23.30 h
Innrain 100 / 1. Stock ✉6020 *(1st floor)* ☎ 56 24 03
Email: hosi-tirol@tirol.com
Different events. Call for details.

BARS

Bacchus (CC D G MA S WE) Sun-Thu 21-04:00h, Fri & Sat - 06:00h
Salurner Straße 18 ✉6020 ☎ 57 08 94
Bar / Disco with a DJ every day. New chatroom

Piccolo Bar (B d f GLM MA p YG) Mon-Sat 21-4, Sun & public holidays 18-1 h
Seilergasse 2 ✉6020 ☎ 58 21 63

Savoy-Stüberl (B d f g MA os s) Mon-Thu 10-1, Sat 13-1 h
Höttinger Au 26 ✉6020 ☎ 28 78 32

CAFES

Café im Hotel Central (B glm) 11-23 h
Erlerstraße 11 6020 ✉6020 ☎ 59 20
Piano music.

DANCECLUBS

Utopia Kulturverein (B C glm lj MA S WE) Café Utopia: Mon-Fri 18-3, Basement: Thu-Sat 21-4 h
Tschamlerstraße 3 ✉6020 ☎ 53 35 37

RESTAURANTS

Emil & Christian's Bistro Café (bf F g OS) Mon-Fri 7.30-21 h
Anichstraße 29 ✉6020 ☎ 582-780

HEALTH GROUPS

AIDS-Hilfe Tirol Tue Fri 12-15, Wed 16-19 h counselling
Bruneckerstraße 8 ✉6020 ☎ 56 36 21 Fax: 563 62 19
Additional counselling in Wörgl: ☎ (05332) 746 72.

SPECIAL INTEREST GROUPS

Libertine
PO Box 5 ✉6027
S/M Initiative.

SWIMMING

-Kranebitter Au (G MA NU) (Leave motorway A 12 Innsbruck to Bregenz at Innsbruck-Kranebitten, take road 171 to Zirl. (P) at „St. Schüt. Kasern" and get to the left bank of the river Inn. Summer only)

CRUISING

-Hofgarten (Rennweg)
-Boznerplatz

Klagenfurt ☎ 0463

BARS

Absolut (B d f GLM lj MA OS s TV WE) Mon-Fri 10-04:00h, Sat, Sun & holidays 19-04:00h
St. Veiter Straße 3 ✉9020 *(Near Stadtpfarrkirche)* ☎ 59 99 99

GENERAL GROUPS

Queer Klagenfurt (GLM)
PO Box 146 ✉9010
Hotline ☎ 50 46 90 Wed 19-21 h

HEALTH GROUPS

AIDS-Hilfe Kärnten Mon Tue Thu 17-19 counselling, Tue 17-19 h HIV-test
8.-Mai-Straße 19. 4. Etage ✉9020 *(4th Floor)* ☎ 551 28
Fax: 51 64 92 Email: kaernten@aidshilfe.or.at
Homepage: www.aidshilfe.or.at/adishilfe.

SWIMMING

-Keutschacher See (NU) (camping)
-Forstsee

CRUISING

-Schubert Park (hinter dem Theater, abends/behind theatre, evenings)
Zwischen/between Bahnhofstraße & Bushaltestelle/bus station (abends/ evenings)
-Bahnhof/railway station

Kolbnitz ✉9815 ☎ 04783

GUEST HOUSES

Gasthof Herkuleshof (H OS) 8-24 h, closed mid-January to mid-March.
Am Danielsberg 9815 ✉9815 ☎ 22 88 Fax: 22 88
Rates double from 300 öS per person (bf incl.), 430 half-board.

Krems ✉3057 ☎ 02734

GENERAL GROUPS

Schwuler Stammtisch Krems-Waldviertel
PO Box 2 3057 ✉3057 ☎ 36 36
Email: stammtisch-krems@aon.at

Leoben ✉8700 ☎ 03842

CRUISING

-Bahnhof/station

Linz ✉4020 ☎ 0732

GAY INFO

Pride
c/o Hosi Linz, Schubertstraße 36 ✉4020 ☎ 60 98 98
Homepage: www.hosi-linz.gay.at.
Email: hosi-linz@netway.at.*Regional gay paper.*

Queery Box Linz
PO Box 53 ✉4030 ☎ 30 38 89 Fax: 31 48 77
YoungsterNet, InterGay, HIVNet, GayComNet, FidoNet.

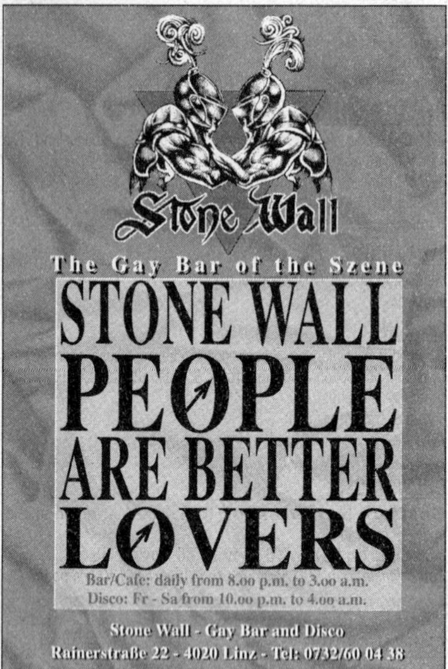

Stone Wall
The Gay Bar of the Szene
STONE WALL
PEOPLE
ARE BETTER
LOVERS
Bar/Cafe: daily from 8.oo p.m. to 3.oo a.m.
Disco: Fr - Sa from 10.oo p.m. to 4.oo a.m.
Stone Wall - Gay Bar and Disco
Rainerstraße 22 - 4020 Linz - Tel: 0732/60 04 38

BARS

Blue Heaven (AC B D DR f G MA s WE YG) Sun-Thu 20-2, Fri & Sat -4 h. Mon closed
Starhembergstrasse 11 ✉4020 *(Neustadtviertel / Bus 21)* ☎ 77 43 67
2 darkrooms and a disco.

My Way (B) Daily 19:00- ?
Goetherstrasse 51 ✉4020 ☎ 652760

SonderBar (B CC f glm s YG) Tue-Sat 19-2, Sun 17-24 h, closed Mon
Waltherstraße 11 ✉4020 ☎ 79 55 09

Stone Wall (AC B CC D f G MA r S WE) Bar/Café: daily from20-03:00h, Disco: Fri-Sat 22-4 h
Rainerstraße 22 ✉4020 ☎ 60 04 38

CAFÉS

Coffee Corner (B f GLM MA YG) 18-2, closed Sun
Betlehemstraße 30 ✉4020 ☎ 77 08 62

Cooper (B F glm) Mon-Fri 11-02:00h, Sat & holidays 15-03:00h, Sun 17-02:00h
Rainerstrasse 20 ✉4020 ☎ 65 27 14
Early breakfasts at the weekend from 03:00h

Gösser Stub'n (B F glm MA) 11-1 h, Sat & Sun 17-1 h
Starhembergstraße 11 ✉4020 *(Bus 21)* ☎ 79 70 95

SEX SHOPS/BLUE MOVIES

Erotic Center Linz (CC g) Mo-Sat 9-23
Goethe Straße 41 ✉4020

GENERAL GROUPS

HOSI Linz (GLM MA) Counselling Mon 20-22; Thu 18:30-22 h
Schubertsraße 36 ✉4020 *(Ecke Gothestr.)* ☎ 60 98 98-1/-4
Email: hosi-linz@netway.at.
Homepage: www.hosi-linz.gay.at.
Publisher of Pride-magazine.

HEALTH GROUPS

AIDS-Hilfe Oberösterreich Mon 14-18, Wed 16-20, Fri 10-14 h counselling
Langgasse 12 ✉4020 ☎ 21 70

HELP WITH PROBLEMS

Rosa Telefon Mon 20-22, Thu 18.30-22 h
☎ 60 98 98

SWIMMING

-Weikerlsee (NU YG) (south of Linz in Pichling)
-Pleschingersee (G NU YG) (Linz-Urfahn, southeastern corner of lake)

CRUISING

-Hinsenkampplatz (AYOR) (subway)
-Wiener Straße (OG) (near tram-stop »Unionkreuzung«)
-Hauptbahnhof/Main rail station (r)
-Lokalbahnhof (YG)
-Hessenplatz (WE YG)
-Volksgarten (ayor R) (am Bahnhof/near railway station)
-Kraftwerk Wilmering (YG)

Mondsee ✉ 5310

CRUISING

-Rathaus/Town hall (evenings/abends)

Salzburg ✉ 5020 ☎ 0662

GAY INFO

HOSI Salzburg (B GLM lj MA) Wed from 19:00h, Fri & Sat from 20:00h
Müllner Hauptstraße 11 ✉5020 ☎ 43 59 27
Email: hosi.salzburg@gmx.at

BARS

Kupferpfandl (B glm lj MA p YG) 17-4 h
Paracelsusstraße 14 ✉5020 *(near station)* ☎ 87 57 60

Saphir (AC B GLM)
Imbergstraße 11 ✉5020 ☎ 87 05 46

Vis a Vis (B CC d glm MA s WE) Sun-Wed 20-4, Thu-Sat -5 h
Rudolfskai 27 ✉5020 ☎ 84 12 90

2-Stein (A AC B CC D f GLM MA OS p s SNU STV W YG) Sun-Thu 18-4, Fri Sat -5 h
Giselakai 9 ✉5020 *(near Staatsbrücke)* ☎ 662/88 02 01
Disco from 22 h.

RESTAURANTS

Daimler's (AC CC F glm lj MA N YG) Bar 18-04:00 (Thu, Fri, Sat -05:00h) Restaurant 18-02:00h
Mondays closed.
Gieselakai 17 ✉5020 ☎ 87 39 67

SEX SHOPS/BLUE MOVIES

Erotic Center Salzburg (CC g) Mo-Sat 9-23
Ferd. Porsche-Str. 7 ✉5020

BOOK SHOPS

American Discount (g) Mon-Fri 9-13 14-18, Sat 9-12 h
Waggplatz ✉5020 ☎ 84 56 40

HOTELS

Hotel-Pension Fuggerhof (bf glm H MA OS sa W)
Eberhard-Fugger-Straße 9 ✉5020 *(Bus 6 / South of Kapuzinerberg)* ☎ 64 12 90-0 *Fax: 64 12 90-04.*

E-Mail hotel.fuggerhof@magnet.at.
http://www.members.magnet.at/hotel.fuggerhof
Rates single from 950 öS-1.800, double from 1.200-2.800

Pension Chiemsee (B CC H lj)
Chiemseegasse 5 ✉5020 ☎ 84 42 08
FAX 84 42 08 70. Centrally located 1000 year old house. 6 rooms with shower. Shared WC. Rates single from öS 420-480, double 860-900

Pension Lechner (bf CC H)
Rainerstraße 11 ✉5020
☎ 87 27 40 *FAX 87 93 80*

GUEST HOUSES

Frühstückspension Kammerhofer (bf glm H MA OS W)
Eberhard-Fugger-Straße 9 ✉5020 ☎ 641 29 00
FAX 641 29 04. Email: hotel.fuggerhof@magnet.at. Homepage: http://members.magnet.at/hotel.fuggerhof. Rates single ÖS 950-1800, double 1200-2800.

HEALTH GROUPS

AIDS-Hilfe Salzburg Counselling: Mon Wed Thu 17-19, HIV-test: Mon Thu 17-19 h
Gabelsbergerstraße 20 ✉5020 ☎ 88 14 88 Fax: 881 94 43
Email: salzburg@aidshilfe.or.at

HELP WITH PROBLEMS

Rosa Telefon
Fri 19-21 h ☎ 43 59 27

RELIGIOUS GROUPS

Homosexuelle und Kirche (HuK) Salzburg
Meetings 1st and 3rd Wed 20 h
c/o KHG, Philharmonikergasse 2 ✉5020 ☎ 84 13 27

CRUISING

-Staatsbrücke (daytime only/nur tagsüber between/zwischen »Café Bazar« & »Staatsbrücke«. Condom vending machine)
–Hauptbahnhof (r)

Seefeld ✉ 6100 ☎ 05212

HOTELS

Veronika. Hotel (B bf CC glm H pi sa) Open Jan-Mar, Mai-Oct and Dec.
Riehlweg 161 ✉6100 ☎ 2105
34 rooms, 11 studios and 4 apartments in a quiet location. Rates/person summer: single ÖS 850-1050, double 800-1130, studio or apartment 980-1480. Winter: single ÖS 990-1370, double 1130-1520, studio or apartment 1480-1870. Sport facilities. Garden. Bf ÖS 12.

Sölden ✉ 6450 ☎ 05254

GUEST HOUSES

Frühstückspension Herrmann Fiegl (bf glm H OS)
Schmiedhof 35 ✉6450 ☎ 26 36 Fax: 26 36
Homepage: www.members.aon.at/schmiedhof35
Nice rooms with a view. All rooms with shower/WC, balcony and bf incl. Rates/person single ÖS 350, double 320. Apartment 90 sqm with kitchen, tiled stove and sat-TV ÖS 300/person up to 6/8 persons. Pool and sauna within 10 minutes walk. Newly renovated.

St. Pölten ✉ 3100

CRUISING

-hinter der Sparkasse am Domplatz/behind the bank at Domplatz
-Ende der/End of Julius-Raab-Promenade (YG)

Steyr ✉ 4400

SEX SHOPS/BLUE MOVIES

Sex-Shop Steyr (CC g) Mo-Sat 9-19
Damberggasse 19 ✉4400

CRUISING

-Main station (YG) (15-22 h)

Thalgau ✉ 5303 ☎ 06235

GUEST HOUSES

Jausenstation Barham (b bf f H MA NG WE) 12-24 h, closed Wed & in Nov
Berg 11 5303 ✉5303 *(3 km from Thalgau)* ☎ 56 22 Fax: 56 22
Romantic guest house on a hill above the little village of Thalgau. Near the well-known Fuschl- and Wolfgangssee. All rooms with shower/WC and TV.

Velden am Wörther See ✉ 9220

SWIMMING

-Fortsee (NU) (between Velden and Pörtschach)

CRUISING

-Park gegenüber/opposite Hotel Corinthia

Villach ✉ 9500

SWIMMING

-Erlebnistherme Warmbad (g sa) (11-20 h)

Wels ✉ 4600

CRUISING

-Volksgarten (near/Nahe Messegelände, summer/Sommer)
-Busbahnhof (YG)
(12-15 h, near the SAB-IN-Buffet, popular)
-Hauptbahnhof (16-22 h)

Wien ☎ 01

● The Rainbow Parade is a distinct signal, that, from a gay viewpoint, Vienna is beginning to take its place in the rank and file of the ascending central-european metropolises. Tens of thousands of gays, lesbians and their friends have shown, that public presence is important, makes a difference an can manifest a vital beginning. The Vienese gay scene has for long been a good example. It is astonishing how many cafés, bars, discos, shops and saunas exist in this allegedly conservative city. Most of these original and charming venues are found southwest of the city center near the remarkable „Naschmarkt" (market for the sweet tooth). More shops and saunas are situated within the ringroads, on which also the town hall is found. Here the annual Vienna mega-spectacle, the Life Ball, takes place. It's only a few steps from here to the „Stephansdom" or the „Hofburg" (court castle), where -like in Schönbrunn- the gays most beloved empress Sissy resided.

✸ Die Regenbogen-Parade ist ein deutliches Signal dafür, daß sich Wien nun anschickt, aus schwuler Sicht in die Reihe der aufstrebenden zentraleuropäischen Metropolen aufzurücken. Zehntausende von Schwulen, Lesben und ihren Freunden haben gezeigt, daß öffentliche Präsenz doch sehr viel ausmacht und in dieser Form auch einen Aufbruch markieren kann.

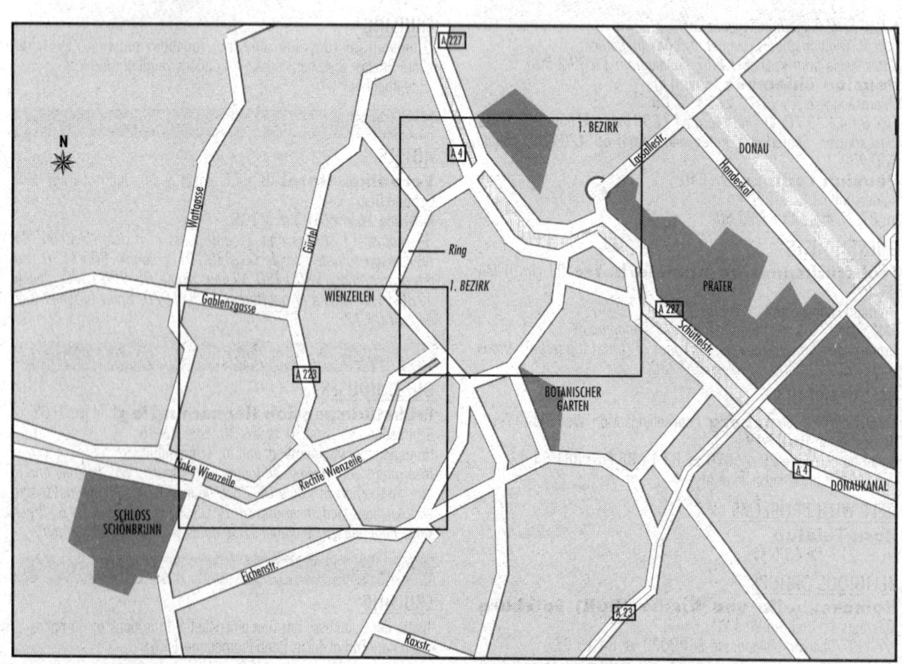

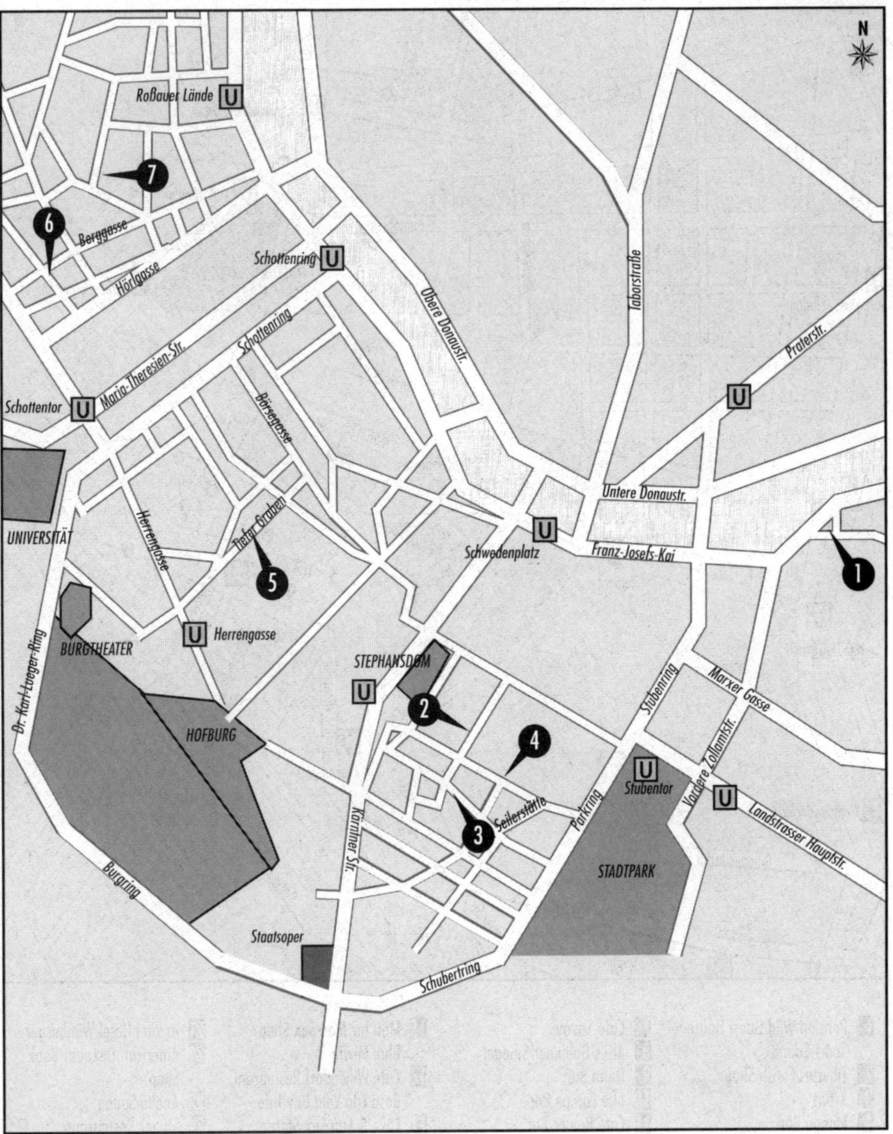

1 Urania Hotel
2 Das Versteck Bar
3 Kaiserbründl Sauna
5 Why Not Danceclub
6 Café Berg
Löwenherz Book Shop
7 Amigos Sauna

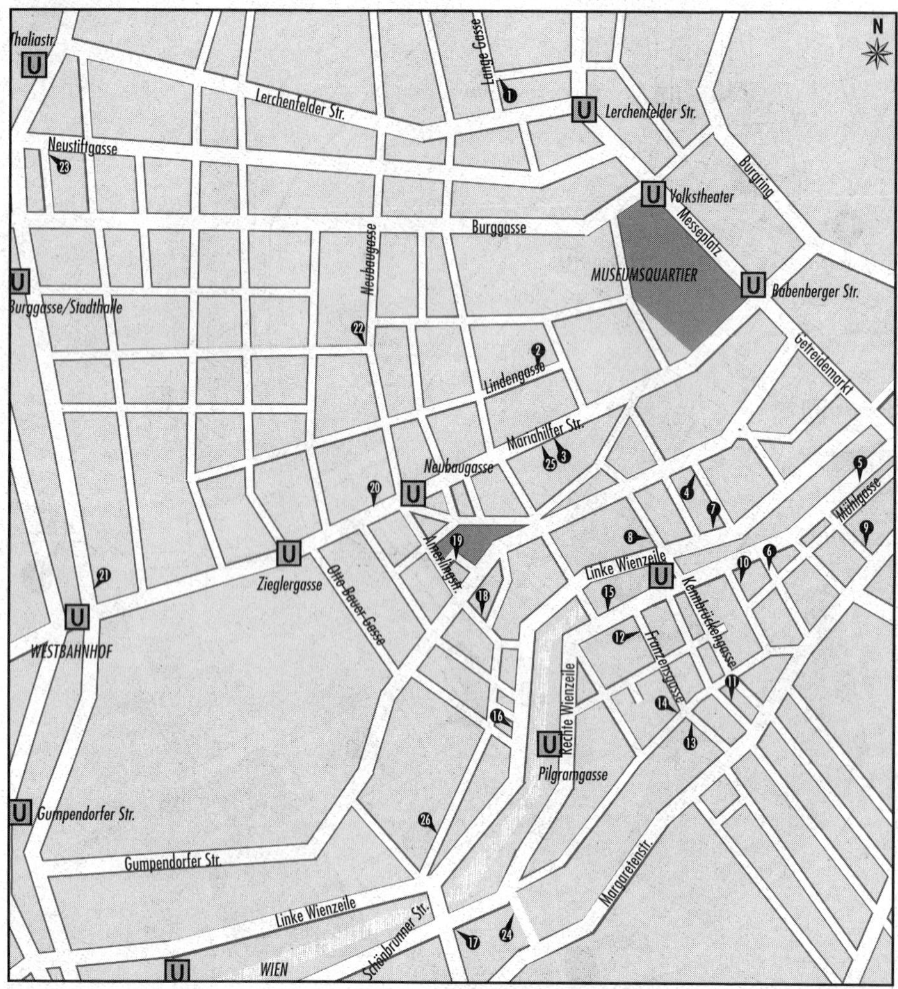

1 Pension Wild Guest House Sport-Sauna
2 Tiberius Fetish Shop
3 X-Bar
4 Mango Bar
5 American Discount Book Shop
6 Willi's Lounge Bar
7 Café Savoy
8 Alfi's Goldener Spiegel
9 Nanu Bar
10 Alte Lampe Bar
11 Café Reiner Bar
12 Living Room Bar
13 Café Joy Bar
14 Wiener Freiheit Bar
15 Man for Man Sex Shop/ Blue Movie
16 Café Willendorf Restaurant Rosa Lila Villa Gay Info
17 Love & Fun Sex Store
18 Nightshift Bar
19 Eagle Bar
20 Skyline Sex Shop
21 Arcotel Hotel Wimberger
22 American Discount Book Shop
23 Apollo Sauna
24 Stöger Restaurant
25 Sexworld International Sex Shop/Blue Movie
26 Orlando Restaurant

Die Wiener Szene hat dies schon lange deutlich gemacht. Es ist doch erstaunlich, wieviele Cafés, Bars, Discos, Läden, Saunen es gibt in dieser als konservativ verschrienen Stadt. Die meisten dieser Einrichtungen mit ihrem eigenen Charme finden sich südwestlich an den Stadtkern angrenzend um den sehenswerten *Naschmarkt*.
Weitere Lokale und Saunen finden sich innerhalb der Ringstraße, an denen übrigens auch das Wiener Rathaus liegt, das das jährliche Wiener Mega-Spektakel *LifeBall* beherbergt. Von hier aus sind es nur wenige Schritte zum Stephansdom oder zur Hofburg, in der -wie in Schönbrunn- unser aller Sissy (die Kaiserin) wohnte.

▲ La parade Arc-en-ciel est la preuve que Vienne est en passe de devenir une des métropoles gays de l'Europe centrale. Des milliers de gays et de lesbiennes -et leurs amis- ont montré que descendre dans la rue et sortir du placard permet de faire avancer les choses dans le bon sens. C'est aussi le résultat de l'action menée ces dernières années par les gays de la ville. Quand on connaît la mentalité hyperconser vatrice de la capitale autrichienne, on s'étonne de voir tant de bars, de cafés, de boîtes, de magasins et de saunas gays. La plupart des établissements gays se trouve dans le quartier au sud-ouest du centre de la ville, tout près du très joli marché „Naschmarkt". Les autres établissements sont situés dans la vieille ville, à l'intérieur du Ring le long duquel se trouve l'hôtel de Ville. C'est ici, d'ailleurs, qu'a lieu chaque année le méga spectacle du Lifeball. Du Ring, il n'y a que quelques pas pour aller à la Cathédrale St Etienne ou au Château de la Hofburg qui, avec Schönbrunn, était la résidence de la fameuse Sissi, impératrice d'Autriche.

❖ La „Fiesta del Arcoiris" (Regenbogen-Parade) es una señal clara, que Viena, desde el punto de vista gay, empieza a ponerse al mismo nivel que otras importantes ciudades centroeuropeas. Decenas de miles de gays, lesbianas y simpatizantes, han demostrado que la presencia pública juega un papel muy importante y establece al mismo tiempo una buena base de partida. El ambiente vienés lleva mostrando este hecho desde hace años. Es sorprendente que en una ciudad que se tilda de extremadamente conservadora, existan tantos bares, cafeterías, discotecas, tiendas y saunas gays. La mayoría de estos establecimientos con un encanto muy especial se encuentran al sur-oeste del centro de la ciudad, cerca del notable „Naschmarkt". Otros locales y saunas están situados en alrededores de la circular (Ringstraße) donde por cierto también se encuentra el ayuntamiento vienés (Wiener Rathaus). Aquí se celebra cada año el mega-espectáculo de Viena el LifeBall. Desde aqui se llega con pocos pasos al „Stephansdom" a la „Hofburg", -a parte de Schönbrunn- la residencia preferida de la emperatriz Sissy, tan adorada por los gays.

☆ La sfilata dell'arcobaleno è stata un chiaro segnale che Vienna, limitatamente alla vita gay, si appresta ad inserirsi nel gruppo delle più importanti metropoli dell'Europa continentale. Migliaia di gay e lesbiche ed i loro amici hanno provato che mostrandosi apertamente nella vita pubblica è possibile ottenere cambiamenti sociali. L'ambiente gay di Vienna si sta imponendo da tempo; è sorprendente vedere quanti bar, discoteche, negozi, saune ci sono in questa città reputata conservatrice. La maggior parte di questi locali, caratterizzati da un proprio fascino, si trova a sud ovest del centro storico, al limite dell'interessante Naschmarkt. Altri locali e saune si trovano all'interno del Ring, dove vi è anche il municipio di Vienna, ospite ogni anno del grande spettacolo Lifeball. A pochi passi si trovano il duomo di S.Sefano e Hofburg, antica residenza, insieme a Schönbrunn, della nostra amata imperatrice Sissy.

GAY INFO

Bussi
Life Vest Unlimited, Graf-Starhemberg-Gasse 9/4 ✉1040
☎ 505 07 42 Fax: 505 49 41-5
City-magazine with lots of stories, gossip, events, listings and a city-map.

Rosa Lila Tip Mon-Fri 17-20:00h
Linke Wienzeile 102 ✉1060 *(U-Pilgramgasse)* ☎ 585 4343
Fax: 587 1778 Email: info@villa.at Homepage: www.villa.at
Betreuung, Infos, Schwulen-, Lesben und Elterngruppen. Bibliothek, Kondome, Gleithmittel./ Gay-lesbian switchboard : Counselling, infos, glb-groups, library, condoms, lubricants

Vienna Gay Guide
c/o Pink Advertising, Wurmsergasse 35/17 ✉1150 ☎ 789 97 37 Fax: 789 97 37 Email: office@gayguide.at
Homepage: www.gayguide.at

TOURIST INFO

Wiener Tourismus Verband
Oberer Augartenstraße 40 ✉1025 ☎ 21 11 40 Fax: 216 84 92

BARS

Alfi's Goldener Spiegel (! B F G MA MG p) daily 19-2 h, Tue closed
Linke Wienzeile 46 ✉1060 *(U4 Kettenbrückengasse. Entrance/Eingang Stiegengasse)* ☎ 586 66 08
Popular bar and restaurant. Excellent Viennese cuisine.

Alte Lampe (! B f G MA OG S WE) Sun Wed Thu 18-1, Fri Sat 20-3.30 h, piano show WE 22.30-3.30 h
Heumühlgasse 13 ✉1040 *(U4 Kettenbrückengasse)* ☎ 587 34 54
Vienna's oldest gay bar. Piano show WE 22:30-03:00h. Happy hour 18-20:00h

Blue Banana Bar (B DR G MA) 15-04:00h
Praterstern /Viadukt 33 ✉1020

Café Reiner (B DR G MA p r) 21-04:00h
Kettenbrückengasse 4 ✉1040 *(U4 Kettenbrückengasse)*
☎ 586 23 62
Darkroom with cubicals

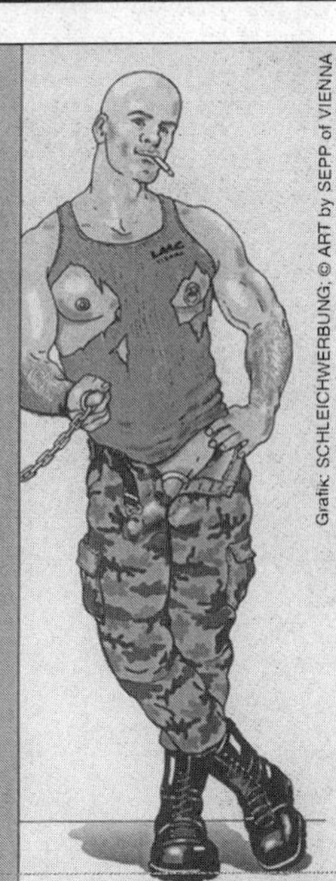

Grafik: SCHLEICHWERBUNG; © ART by SEPP of VIENNA

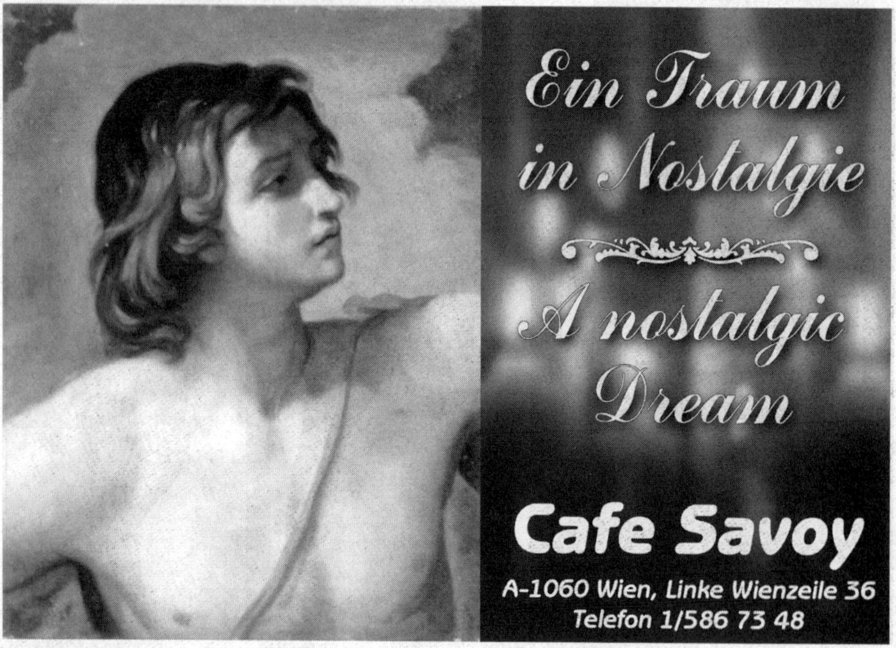

Castro (AC B d f NG MA OS s) Mon-Sat 17-03:00h, Sun & holidays 10-03:00h
Schlösselgasse 24 ✉1080 *(U-Rathaus/Schottentor-Universität)* ☎ 409 18 23
Friendly small pub.

Eagle-Bar (! AC B DR G lj MA p VS) 21-4 h
Blümelgasse 1/Amerlingstrasse ✉1060 *(U3 Neubaugasse/Amerlinggasse)* ☎ 587 26 61
Sex shop integrated: leather, rubber, videos and magazines. Friendly and popular.

Joy. Café (B f G MA) 20-4 h, Sun closed
Franzengasse 2 ✉1050 *(U4 Kettenbrückengasse)*
☎ 0222/586 59 38

[lo:sch] (B DR G LJ MA P WE) Fri & Sat 22-02:00h, Sun 18-22:00h
Fünfhausgasse 1 ✉1150 *(Ecke / on the courner of Sechshauer Str)* ☎ 895 99 79
Home of the LMC Vienna. Ask for dates and parties. Dresscode. 2 floors with darkroom, sling, changing room & shower available.

Mango Bar (AC B G p s YG) 21-4 h, Mon closed
Laimgrubengasse 3 ✉1060 *(U4 Kettenbrückengasse)* ☎ 587 44 48
Best 23-1 h. Popular and trendy.

Motto Bar-Restaurant (A AC B F g MA OS) Mon-Sun 18-4 h
Schönbrunnerstraße 30 ✉1050 *(Eingang / Entrance Rüdigergasse)* ☎ 587 06 72

Nanu Bar (AC B f G MA OS) 18-2 h daily
Schleifmühlgasse 11 ✉1040 *(U-Kettenbrückengasse)* ☎ 587 29 87
Internet-café.

Nightshift (AC B DR G lj MA VS) 22-4, Fri Sat-5 h
Corneliusgasse 8/Kopernikusgasse ✉1060 *(U4 Kettenbrückengasse)* ☎ 586 23 37
Billards. A late night bar.

Old Inn (B d f g MA OS s STV WE) 17-04:00h (kitchen - 03:00h)
Schönbrunnerstrasse 4 ✉1040 *(Near Naschmarkt)* ☎ 586 1787

Stiefelknecht (B DR f G LJ MA p s VS) 22-2, Fri Sat -4 h
Wimmergasse 20 ✉1050 *(Tram 62/65-Kliebergasse. Entrance/Eingang Stolberggasse)* ☎ 545 23 01

Versteck. Das (B glm N YG) Mon-Fri 18-24, Sat 19-24 h, closed Sun
Grünangergasse 10 1010 (*(U1 Stephansplatz - entrance downstairs)* ☎ 513 40 53
Vienna's smallest bar.

Wiener Freiheit (B f G MA N OS p s VS WE) Mon-Sat 18-4 h, Sun closed
Schönbrunner Straße 25 ✉1050 *(U4 Kettenbrückengasse)* ☎ 0222/581 58 90
no entrance-fee. Bar and disco.

X Bar. Café (B CC f G MA) Mon-Sat 14-2, Fri Sun 17-2 h
Mariahilfer Straße 45 ✉1060 *(Raimundhofpassage. U3-Neubaugasse)* ☎ 585 24 37

CAFÉS

Berg, das Café (! A AC B bf F G MA YG) 10-1 h
Berggasse 8/Wasagasse ✉1090 *(near/Nähe Universität, U2 Schottentor)* ☎ 319 57 20
Next to Löwenherz bookshop.

Savoy. Café (! B f GLM MA OS YG) Mon-Fri 17-2, Sat 9-2 h, closed Sun
Linke Wienzeile 36 ✉1060 *(U4 Kettenbrückengasse)* ☎ 586 73 48
Popular. Century old traditional café. Enjoy the 6 m high ceiling and the possibly largest mirrors in Europe.

DANCECLUBS

Liquid Gay Club Night (D G) Fri 23:00- ?
Rotgasse 9 ✉1010
Gay club night every Friday, crusing area, game & porno rooms.

U4 Heaven Gay Night (AC B D DR GLM lj OS s TV YG) Thu 23-5 h
Schönbrunnerstraße 222 ✉1120 *(U4 Meidlinger Hauptstraße)*
3 Bars, 2 Discos.

Why Not (AC B CC D f GLM p s WE YG) Fri-Sat 22- ?, Sun 21-2 h
Tiefer Graben 22 ✉1010 ☎ 535 11 58

RESTAURANTS

Café Willendorf (! B F GLM MA OS) 18-2 (meals -24 h)
Linke Wienzeile 102 ✉1060 *(U4-Pilgramgasse)* ☎ 587 17 89
Many vegetarian dishes. Near to the city center.

Café-Restaurant im Kunsthaus Wien (A b CC F MA NG OS) 10-24 h
Weissgerberlände 14 ✉1030 *(U3, U4, Schnellbahn Landstraße/ Wien Mitte)* ☎ 712 04 97

Living Room (! A B bf CC F G MA) Mon-Fri 18-2:00h
Franzensgasse 18/Grüngasse ✉1050 *(U-Kettenbrückengasse)* ☎ 585 37 07
Good Austrian wines and Austrian as well as international cuisine. WE reservations are recommended..

Orlando (A b F GLM MA OS s YG) 17-2 (meals 18-1), Sun brunch 10-14:00h
Mollardgasse 3 ✉1060 *(U Pilgramgasse)* ☎ 586 23 27
Lesbian run. Very small but fine daily menue. Brunch is popular.

Santo Spirito (B bf CC F glm OS) Lunch 11-15 Dinner - 23.30h
Kumpfgasse 7 ✉1010 *(U-Stefansplatz)*
☎ 512 99 98
Classical music and bohemian atmosphere. Best after 21:00h. Trendy

Stöger (AC B F glm MA) Mon 17-24, Tue-Sat 11-24 h, Sun closed
Ramperstorffergasse 63 ✉1050 *(U - Pilgramgasse)* ☎ 544 75 96
Rustic restaurant with excellent Austrian and international cuisine

Willi's Lounge (AC B CC F G MA N s WE) Sun-Thu 18-2, Fri Sat -4 h
Preßgasse 30 ✉1040 *(U4 Kettenbrückengasse)* ☎ 585 41 27

SEX SHOPS/BLUE MOVIES

Erotic Center Naschmarkt (CC g VS) Mon-Sat 9-23 h
Rechte Wienzeile 21 ✉1040
Big gay courner selection. Individual cubicals

Erotica (CC glm lj MA VS W) Mon-Fri 9-18, Sat -13 h
Märzstraße 1 ✉1150 ☎ 982 56 84

Sexworld Gay Shop Austria (AC CC G MA VS) Mon-Sat 10-19 h
Kettenbrückengasse 2 *(U-Bhf Kettenbrückengasse)*
☎ (0)676325 28 66

Love & Fun Store (CC glm VS) Mon- Sat 9-22:00h
Schönbrunnerstraße 95 ✉1050 ☎ 544 71 64

Love & Fun Store (CC glm VS) Mon-Sat 9-22:00h
Lerchenfelderstraße 59 ✉1070 ☎ 523 17 20

Man for Man (AC CC DR G MA VS) Mon-Sat 11-22 h, closed Sun & public holidays
Hamburgerstraße 8 ✉1050 *(U-Kettenbrückengasse)* ☎ 585 20 64
Only gay sex shop in town. Cabins, toys, books, videos.

Sex-Shop im Huma (CC g) Mon-Sat 9-18 h
Landwehrgasse 6 ✉1110

Sex-Shop Lugner City (CC glm VS) Mon-Thu 9-19:00h, Fri 9-19:30h, Sat 9-17:00h
Gablenzgasse 3-15 ✉1150 *(first floor near the lifts)* ☎ 983 67 85

Sexworld International (AC b CC g MA VS W) Mon-Fri 10-20, Sat -17 h, closed Sun & public holidays
Mariahilfer Straße 49 ✉1060 *(U-Neubaugasse)* ☎ 587 66 56
Large gay selection. Video cabins.

Sexy-Land (CC glm VS) Mon-Sat 9-22:00h
Gudrunstraße 134 ✉1100 ☎ 603 19 97

saunaguide
gay bathhouses
international
BRUNO GMÜNDER

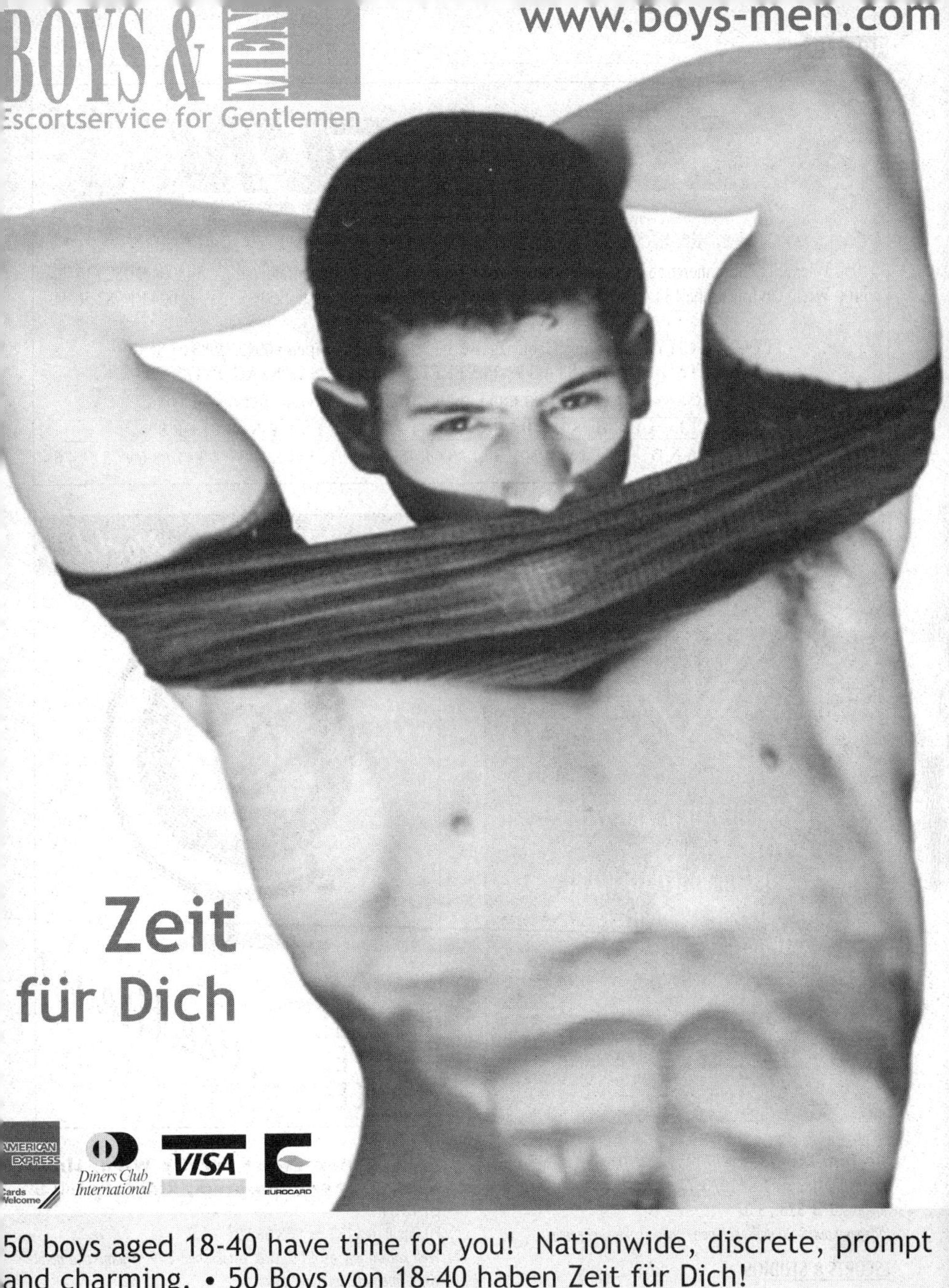

50 boys aged 18-40 have time for you! Nationwide, discrete, prompt and charming. • 50 Boys von 18-40 haben Zeit für Dich! Österreichweit, diskret, prompt und niveauvoll.

CALL (+ 43 1) 982 06 22

Skyline-Movie (g p VS) Mon-Fri 9-20 h
Mariahilferstraße 72 ✉1070 *(1. Stock/upstairs, U-Bahn Neubaugasse)* ☎ 523 75 07
Videoverkauf & -Verleih, Kabinen/ video sales and cabins.

ESCORTS & STUDIOS

Agentur CD (G msg)
Herrengasse 6-8 ✉1010 *(in center near Hofburg)* ☎ 535 8539

Boys & Men Escort Service Wien, Linz, Graz, Salzburg, Innsbruck, Klagenfurt (CC G LJ) 13-3 h
PO Box 8 ✉1131 ☎ 982 06 22
Well known gay escort service, established 1999. Home and hotel visits, international travel escorts

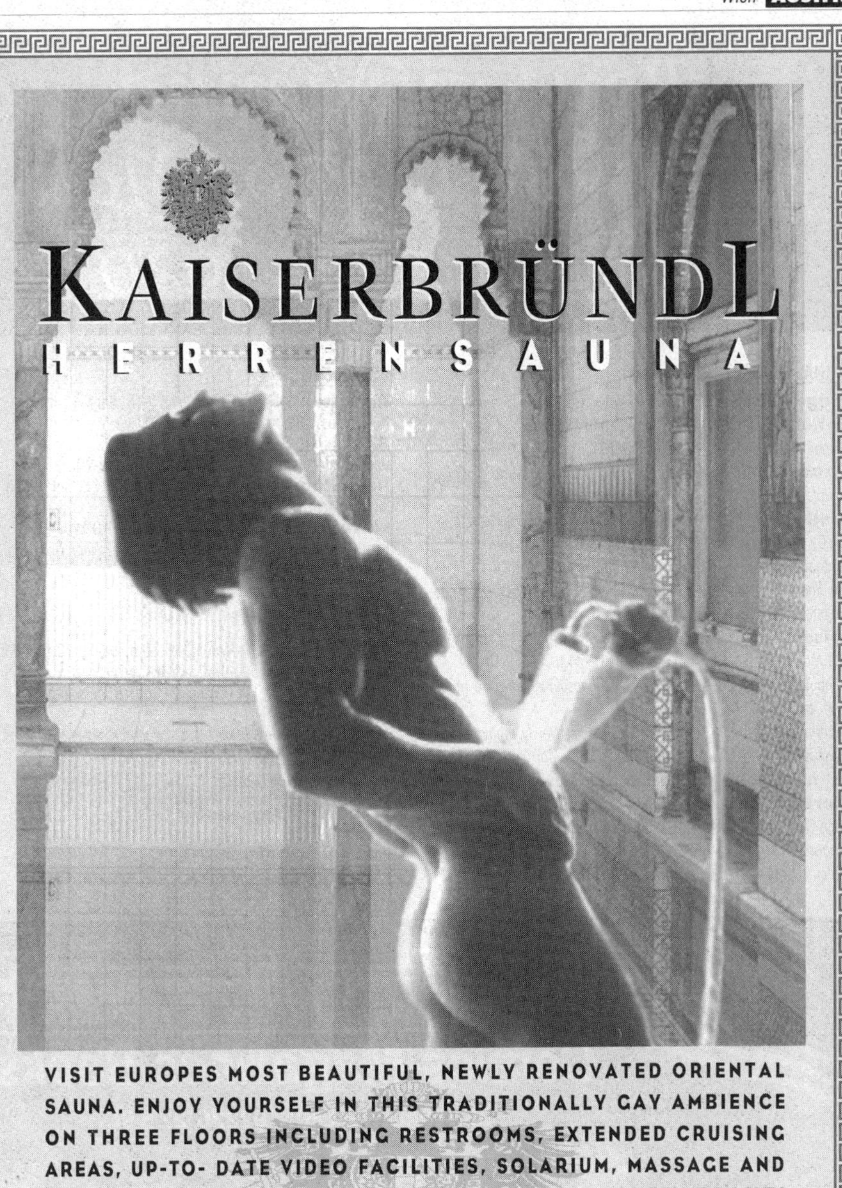
KAISERBRÜNDL
HERRENSAUNA
VISIT EUROPES MOST BEAUTIFUL, NEWLY RENOVATED ORIENTAL SAUNA. ENJOY YOURSELF IN THIS TRADITIONALLY GAY AMBIENCE ON THREE FLOORS INCLUDING RESTROOMS, EXTENDED CRUISING AREAS, UP-TO- DATE VIDEO FACILITIES, SOLARIUM, MASSAGE AND A RESTAURANT!
A-1010 VIENNA, WEIHBURGGASSE 18-20 TEL: 01/5133293
MO - TH 14-24H, FR - SA 14-02H, SU 12-24H

SAUNAS/BATHS

Amigos Sauna (B CC DR F G MA msg OS p s sa sb sol VS) Mon-Wed 20-6, Fri 20-Mo 2 h, Jack-off party Wed
Müllnergasse 5 ✉1090 *(U4 Rossauer Lände)* ☎ 319 05 14
Admission öS 200, jack-off party 100. Bohemian cuisine. Lodging possible on WE.

Apollo City Sauna (B CC DR f G MA msg OS P sa sb sol VS YG) 14-2 h
Wimbergergasse 34 ✉1070 *(U - Burggasse)* ☎ 523 08 14/13
Two floors. Own parking place. Student reduction 150, ÖS, normal price 180 ÖS

Kaiserbründl (! AC B CC DR F G MA msg pi s sa sb sol VS WO) Mon-Thu 14-24, Fri-Sat 14-2, Sun 12-24 h
Weihburggasse 18-20 ✉1010 *(U1 Stephansplatz, entrance green door)* ☎ 513 32 93
Beautiful interior: Built 1887 in moorish style. Newly renovated on 1200 m², 3 floors, 2 bars, darkroom-maze. Mon coffee & cake free. Tue partner day , Thu under 25 1/2 price.

Sport-Sauna (AC B CC f G p sa sb VS WO YG) 15-01:00h
Lange Gasse 10 ✉1080 *(U2-Lerchenfelder Strasse / Bus 13A Piaristengasse)* ☎ 406 71 56
Students reduction 95,ÖS, normal price 158, ÖS.

BOOK SHOPS

American Discount Mon-Fri 9-18, Sat 9-12 h
Neubaugasse 39 ✉1070 ☎ 523 37 07

American Discount
Donaustadtstrasse 1 1220 (Donauzentrum) ☎ 203 95 18

American Discount Mon-Fri 9.30-18.30, Sat 9-13 h
Rechte Wienzeile 5 ✉1040 ☎ 587 57 72

Löwenherz (CC G) Mon-Fri 10-19, Sat 10-17 h
Berggasse 8 ✉1090 *(Entrance Wasagasse. Near Universität. U2 Schottentor)* ☎ 317 29 82
Next to BERG, das Café.

CONDOM SHOPS

Condomi (glm MA) Mon 12-18.30 h, Tue-Fri 10-18.30 h, Sat 10-16 h
Otto-Bauer-Gasse 24 1060 Wien ✉1060 *(U3- Zieglergasse)* ☎ 581 20 60
International condoms in all forms, colors and sizes as well as lubricants, vibrators and gifts .

FASHION SHOPS

Schuh und Dessous Mon 12-18, Tue-Fri 9.30-18, Sat -13 h
Burggasse 130 ✉1070 ☎ 523 08 57
Shoes and dessous in larger sizes.

LEATHER & FETISH SHOPS

Tailors Unlimited Lederschneider (CC g) by appointment only
Graf Starhemberg-Gasse 9/4 ✉1040 *(U1-Taubstummengasse)*
☎ 505 49 41
Leather clothing made to measure./Lederbekleidung nach Maß.

Tiberius Leather Latex & Tools (A GLM LJ S)
Mon-Fri 15-18.30, Sat 11-15 h and by appointment
Lindengasse 2a ✉1070 *(U3-Neubaugasse)* ☎ 522 04 74
E-mail leather@tiberius.at
Fetish store, leather, latex, toys etc.

TRAVEL & TRANSPORT

Cosmos (glm)
Kärntner Ring 15 ✉1015 ☎ 515 33-238
FAX 515 33-139. E-mail Rainbow@cosmostravel.at. Travel agency.

Mentours-Prestige Reisen (CC) Mon-Fri 9-18 h
Passauer Platz 6 ✉1010 *(U-Nestroyplatz)* ☎ 533 06 60
FAX 533 06 50. Gay travel service./Anbieter schwuler Reisen.

HOTELS

Arcotel Hotel Wimberger (B bf CC F g H sa sb sol wh WO) Neubaugürtel 34-36 ✉1070 *(Am Europaplatz)* ☎ 521 65-0
Fax: 521 65-810 Email: wimberger@arcotel.co.at
Homepage: www.arcotel.co.at *Four star hotel in convenient location. 72 double and 37 single rooms, all with AC, phone, radio, minibar, TV, safe. Rates double from öS 2600, single 2000.*

Hotel Urania (B bf CC F G H)
Obere Weißgerberstraße 7 ✉1030 *(U-Schwedenplatz, Tram N, O)* ☎ 713 17 11 Fax: 713 56 94
All rooms with shower, WC, telefone & cable TV. Rates from EZ 650, ÖS, DZ 890, ÖS, triple 1290, ÖS, for 4 pax 1550, ÖS. Rooms per hour 380-480, ÖS for four hours.

Hotel Wien West (B E g H)
Bahnhofstraße 2 ✉3002 *(Purkersdorf)* ☎ 406 51 74 Fax: 402 21 68
65 rooms with bath/WC, balcony, phone, TV, radio, safe, own key, room service. Rates single from 450-650 öS, double 650-890, additional bed 280, apartment 1.090. Half-board +150, full-board +300.

GUEST HOUSES

Pension Wild (bf CC G H msg sa sb sol WO)
Lange Gasse 10 ✉1080 *(U 2-Lerchenfelder Strasse)*
☎ 406 51 74
Fax: 402 21 68 Email: info@pension-wild.com
Homepage: www.pension-wild.com
Centrally located. 3 single rooms, rates öS 490 (\ shower), 590 (shower), 11 double rooms, öS 690 (\ shower), 790 (shower). 2 Appartments. Bf. incl. Newly renovated.

PRIVATE ACCOMODATION

Enjoy Bed & Breakfast (bf G H MA YG) 16:30-21:00h ☎ +49 (30) 215 1666 Fax: +49 830) 217 52219
Email: Info@ebab.com Homepage: www.ebab.com
Price 25 Euro. Accommodation sharing agency. All with shower & bf.

GENERAL GROUPS

Act Up Wien Tue 20 h
c/o HOSI, Novaragasse 40 ✉1020 ☎ 216 66 04

AHOG Arbeitsgruppe der homosexuellen Männer und Frauen in der GPA Tue 16:30-18:30h Deutschmeisterplatz 2, ✉1013 ☎ 313 93-216
Email: manfred.wol@gpa.at

HOSI Wien-1. Lesben und Schwulenverband Österreichs/ HOSI-Zentrum Tue 20-?, Tue 17-22 Café Positiv, Thu 19-? h
Novaragasse 40 ✉1020 *(U-Praterstern/Nestroyplatz)*
☎ 216 66 04

Mitarbeiter für LesBiSchwule Angelegenheiten Zentralaussch. d. Österr. Hochschülerschaft Counselling Mon 12-16, Fri 13-15 h
c/o Sozialreferat im ZA/ÖH, Liechtensteinstr. 131090 ☎ 310 88 80

FETISH GROUPS

LMC Vienna Leather & Motorbike Community (G LJ MA) irregulary events Fri-Sun
PO Box 34 ✉1011 ☎ 895 9979 Email: lmcvienna@tiberius.at
Member of ECMC.Weekly events in leather bar „Lo:sch" on Sun

HEALTH GROUPS

AIDS-Hilfe Wien (A bf glm F S) Mon Wed 16-20, Thu 9-13, Fri 14-18 h
Mariahilfer Gürtel 4 ✉1060 *(U6-Gumpendorfer Str.)* ☎ 599 37 16
Fax: 599 37 16. Email: wien@aidshilfe.or.at.
Kostenlose HIV Antikörpertests / Free HIV testing. Connselling Mon, Tue & Fri 09-14:00h, Wed -13:00h, Thu 16-20:00h.

Aids-Informationszentrale Austria Die Servicestelle Tue 9-14 h, Thu 12-14 h
Fechtergasse 19/20 ✉1090 *(near Franz Josefs station)*
☎ 315 42 04 Fax: 31 54 20 46 Email: aidsinfo@aidshilfe.or.at.
No counselling.

HELP WITH PROBLEMS

Anonyme-Alkoholiker-Gruppe für homosexuelle Männer und lesbische Frauen Sat 19 h
c/o Zentrale Kontaktstelle, Geblergasse 45/III ✉1170 ☎ 408 53 77

Rosa Telefon
Tue 18-20 h ☎ 216 66 04

Schwulenberatung-Rosa Lila Tip Mon-Fri 17-20 h
Linke Wienzeile 102/3 ✉1060 *(U-Pilgramgasse)* ☎ 585 43 43

RELIGIOUS GROUPS

Homosexuelle und Kirche (HuK)
PO Box 513 ✉1011 ☎ 405 87 78
(Johannes) or ☎ (02732) 85 403 (Wolfgang).

Re'uth-Vereinigung Jüdischer Homosexueller in Österreich
Scheugasse 12/18 ✉1100 ☎ 602 40 56 *(John)*

SPECIAL INTEREST GROUPS

Libertine Meeting Fri 19 h
at Stiftgasse 8, 1070 Wien (Amerlinghaus)
PO Box 63 ✉1011 ☎ 9220333
Internet: http://info.fuwien.ac.at/HEPHY/ASE/libertine/ S/M-initiative. Publishes newsletter „Unter Druck".

SPORT GROUPS

Volleyballverein Aufschlag Mon-Fri 10-18 h
c/o Rosa Lila Villa, Linke Wienzeile 102 ✉1060 ☎ 587 17 78
E-mail Aufschlag@blackbox.at

SWIMMING

-Dechantlacke in der Lobau (NU) (Bus 91 A vom Vienna International Center zum Restaurant Roter Hiasl, dann 10 Minuten Fußweg/ take Bus 91 A from Vienna International Center to Restaurant Roter Hiasl, then 10 minutes walk)
-Donauinsel (NU) (vis-à-vis Leopoldsberg; Bus 33 B vom Franz-Jonas- Platz bis Überfuhrstrasse, dann über die »Jedleseer Fußgängerbrücke« 500 m rechts/take Bus 33 B from Franz-Jonas-Platz to Überfuhrstrasse, cross the »Jedleseer Bridge«, then 500 m to the right)
-Donauinsel »Toter Grund« (! NU) (Bus 91 A bis Steinspornbrücke. Über die Brücke, dann ca 500 m nach links. Populär./take bus 91 A to Steinspornbrücke. After crossing the bridge 500 m to the left.

Very popular)
-Wienerberg 1010 (Tram 65 →„Raxstraße", go to Sickingengasse via Raxstraße. There's a small lake, gay in the nude area)

CRUISING

-U-Bahn-Stationen/subway stations: Vorgartenstraße, Donauinsel, Keplerplatz, Lerchenfelderstraße (afternoons/nachmittags)
–Florianigasse/Langegasse (AYOR) (nachmittags/afternoons)
-Thaliastraße/Richard Wagner Platz (AYOR)
-Anfang der/Beginning of Prater Hauptallee (ayor)
-Türkenschanzpark (Hasenauerstraße / Litrowgasse & Hasenauerstraße / Gregor-Mendel-Straße, nachts/at night)
-Währingerstraße/Spitalgasse (AYOR) (mittags bis in die Nacht/noon till night)
-Babenberger Passage/Burgring
-Rathauspark (von Sonnenuntergang bis Sonnenaufgang, populär/after sunset till dawn, very popular)
-Schweizer Garten (AYOR r) (am/next to Südbahnhof; Turks, Arabs)

Wiener Neustadt ✉ 2700 ☎ 02622

SEX SHOPS/BLUE MOVIES

Art-X (AC CC glm MA) Mon-Fri 10-20 h, Sat 10-17 h
Stadionstraße 38 ✉2700 *(at FMZ)* ☎ 895 55
One of Austria's biggest erotic shops.

Erotic-Center Wr. Neustadt (CC g) Mo-Sat 9-20
Grazer Straße 81 ✉2700

GENERAL GROUPS

Mattersburger Gay-Clique
PO Box 219 ✉2700

Belarus

Eastern Europe
Initials: BY
Time: GMT +2
☎ Country Code / Access Code: 375 / 8 (wait for tone) 10
Language: Bielorussian. Russian
Area: 207,600 km² / 80,154 sq mi.
Currency: 1 Belarus-Ruble (BYR) = 100 Kopecks
Population: 10,410,000
Capital: Minsk
Religions: Russian Orthodox, Greek Catholic
Climate: Winters are generally cold, summers are cool and moist. Belarus is in between continental and maritime climates.

● Homosexuality between consenting adults is legal. The age of consent is set at 18 years for both gays and straights.

✱ Einvernehmliche Homosexualität zwischen Erwachsenen ist legal. Das Schutzalter liegt für Hetero- wie Homosexuelle bei 18 Jahren.

▲ L'homosexualité entre adultes consentants n'est pas un délit.La majorité sexuelle est fixée à 18 ans pour tous (homos et héteros).

☆ La homosexualidad por acuerdo entre dultos es legal. La edad de consentimiento es de 18 años, independientemente de la orientación sexual.

❖ L'omosessualità tra adulti consenzienti è legale. La maturità sessuale è di 18 anni per tutti.

NATIONAL GAY INFO

Belarus Lambda League for Freedom of Sexual Minorities (BLL)
PO Box 23 ✉220 006 Minsk
Email: gayforum@irex.minsk.by
Homepage: www.irex.minsk.by/~gayforum
Founded in 1998. ILGA member. AIDS prevention.

Gay.ru PO Box 1 ✉109 457 Moskva
Homepage: www.gay.ru
Russian National Websit of Gays, Lesbians, Bi- and Transseuals. The most comprehensive web-site covering all aspects of gay life in all repbulics of the former USSR, including Belarus. Reliable, exhaustive and up-to-date information. Englisch version available.

NATIONAL PUBLISHERS

Forum Lambda
PO Box 23 ✉220 006 Minsk
☎ 213 26 93
Email: gayforum@irex.minsk.by
Homepage: www.irex.minsk.by/~gayforum
Monthly gay, lesbian and transsexual magazine. Published since June 1998.

Minsk

DANCECLUBS

Oscar (Gayzer) (B D f G R S STV WE) Thu-Sat 24-6 h
43 Platonova vulitsa *(Metro Ploschad Yakuba Kolasa)*

SAUNAS/BATHS

Bathhouse (glm NG sa sb) 9-22 h
Moskovskaya vulitsa *(Metro-Institue of Culture)*

CRUISING

- „Panikovka" (YG, OG) (Metro Oktyabryaskaya, behind Yanka Kupala Theater)
- Railway station (area behind the WC on bobruyskaya vulitsa)
- Park Cheluskintsev (AYOR) (WC with interesing graffiti)

Belgium

Belgique/België

West Europe

Initials: B

Time: GMT +1

☎ Country Code / Access Code: 32 / 00

Area: 30,518 km² / 11,787 sq mi.

Currency: Belgian Franc (bfr) 1 EURO = 100 EURO Cents (The Euro can only be used in the clearance system)

Population: 10,213,000

Capital: Bruxelles/Brussel

Religions: 88% Roman Catholic

Climate: Moderate climate with mild winters and cool summers. It's rainy, humid and cloudy.

Important gay cities: Bruxelles/Brussel, Antwerpen, Gent/Gand

● The most remarkable thing in Belgium is the language battle which has been going on for several decades. Flemish (a Dutch dialect) is spoken in the Northern part of Belgium (Flanders), French is spoken in the Southern part of Belgium (Wallony). The capital Brussel is entirely bilingual. Even street signs in Brussel are written in both Flemish and French! Of course, this influences gay life in Belgium, too. There isn't a national gay organisation. However, there are separate gay organisations for either Flanders (FWH) or Wallony (Tels Quels). Homosexual acts between men over 16 are legal. The general attitude towards gays has a bit of luck, you can even see a rainbow banner. However, in a country with strong Catholic roots it is still difficult to lead an openly gay life. A recent report about suicide amongst young people (16-25) showed a high percentage of gay suicides. The report drew huge attention from media and politics. Despite these blemishes Belgium people are widely known for their hospitality. Perhaps even more famous are the excellent Belgium cuisine and chocolate delicatessens.

✱ Das Bemerkenswerteste in Belgien ist wohl der Sprachenkonflikt, der jetzt schon seit mehreren Jahrzehnten tobt.Flämisch (ein holländischer Dialekt) wird im nördlichen Teil Belgiens (Flandern) und Französisch im südlichen Teil Belgiens (Wallonien) gesprochen. Ganz Brüssel ist zweisprachig. Sogar Straßenschilder in Brüssel sind in Französisch und Flämisch geschrieben. Natürlich beeinflußt dies auch das schwule Leben in Belgien. Landesweit gibt es keine Schwulen-Organisation. Es gibt allerdings gesonderte schwule Organisationen in Flandern (FWH) und in Wallonien (Tels Quels). Homosexuelle Handlungen zwischen Männern über 16 Jahren sind legal. Die allgemeine Einstellung gegenüber Schwulen ist offen; hin und wieder kann man sogar eine Regenbogenflagge sehen. Jedoch ist es noch immer sehr schwierig, in einem streng katholischen Land offen schwul zu leben. Ein vor kurzem veröffentlichter Bericht über die Selbstmordrate Jugendlicher (16-25 J.) zeigte einen hohen Prozentsatz an schwulen Selbstmördern. Natürlich erweckte dieser Bericht großes Interesse bei den Medien und Politikern. Trotz dieser Makel sind die Belgier für ihre Gastfreundschaft bekannt. Vielleicht noch berühmter sind die belgische Küche und die belgische Schokolade.

▲ La chose la plus frappante en Belgique est certainement le conflit linguistique qui date maintenant depuis plusieurs décennies. Le flamand (un dialecte hollandais) est parlé dans la partie nord du pays (Flandre) et le français dans sa partie sud (Wallonie). La ville de Bruxelles est bilingue. Même les noms de rue sont indiqués en français et en flamand. Cela influence, bien sûr, la vie homosexuelle belge. Il n'existe aucune organisation d'homosexuels nationale. Il existe par contre organisations distinctes en Flandre (FWH) et en Wallonie (Tels Quels). Les relations sexuelles entre hommes de plus de 16 ans sont légales. L'attitude générale envers les homosexuels est ouverte, on peut même voir de temps à autre un drapeau aux couleurs arc-en-ciel. Il reste cependant très difficile, dans ce pays très catholique, de vivre ouvertement en tant que gay. Un rapport publié récemment sur le taux de suicide des jeunes (16 à 25 ans) a montré un pourcentage élevé de suicides chez les homosexuels. Ce rapport a naturellement suscité un grand intérêt auprès des médias et des hommes politiques. Malgré cette ombre au tableau, les Belges sont connu pour leur sens de l'hospitalité et bien sûr pour leur cuisine et chocolat qui ont acquis une renommée internationale.

☆ Una de las cosas que más destacan en Belgica es el conflicto entre los idiomas flamenco y francés, existente desde hace décadas. El flamenco, que es un díalecto belga, se habla en el norte (Flandes), mientras el francés se habla en el sur de Belgica, en la región de valón. La capital Bruselas es completamente bilingüe, aqui hasta los señales de tráfico están escritas tanto en flamenco como francés. Por supuesto, esta situación influye también en la vida de los homosexuales en Belgica, ya que no existe una sola organización para todo el país, sino una para cada región. En Flandes es la FWH, en la región de valón la Tels Quels. Respecto a la situación legal, la homosexualidad entre hombres majores de 18 años está permitida. En general, la actitud hacía la homosexualidad no es negativa, hasta se pueden ver banderas de arcoiris. Sin embargo, es un país tan arraigado en el Catolícismo, que sigue siendo difícil vivir abiertamente la homosexualidad. Hace poco se publicó un informe sobre suicidos de jóvenes (16-25) que reveló que un gran porcentaje eran homosexuales. Este informe llamó mucho la atención tanto por parte de los medios de communicación como por parte de los políticos. A parte de estos hechos alarmantes, los belgas son famosos por su hospitalidad. Aunque en el mundo se les conoce sobre todo por su excelente cocina y sus deliciosas chocolatinas.

❖ In Belgio il conflitto tra diverse lingue, che si manifesta già da molti anni, sembra essere di notevole importanza. Al nord (Fiammingo) si parla il fiammingo, un dialetto olandese, e al sud (vallonia) il francese. A Bruxelles vengono parlate tutte e due le lingue, ed anche le indicazioni stradali sono in francese e in fiammingo. Certamente ciò esercita un'influenza sulla vita gay. Non esiste un'organizzazione gay a livello nazionale, ma una in Fiammingo (FHW) ed una in Vallonia (Tels Quels). Sono legalmente permessi atti omosessuali tra uomini maggiori a 16 ani. L'opinione pubblica verso i gay è aperta, qua e là si vede pertanto un bandiera con i colori dell'arcobaleno. Però è sempre difficile vivere apertamente una vita gay in un paese cattolico. Un rapporto pubblicato poco tempo fa sulla quota dei suicidi in età giovanile (16-25 anni) ha dimostrato un'alta percentuale di gay. Naturalmente i media e politici si sono mostrati interessati a questo rapporto. Malgrado ciò, i Belgi sono conosciuti per la loro ospitalità, ma forse anche di più per la loro cucina e cioccolata.

NATIONAL GAY INFO

Amigo/CPC
Lambermontlaan 102 ✉1030 Bruxelles
☎ 02/242 67 40

Antenne-Rose Wed 20-23 h (Air Libre FM 107.6 MHz)
Rue du Marché au Charbon 81 ✉1000 Bruxelles ☎ 02/512 45 87

ASBL Gai Info 11-20 h, closed Sun Mon
✉1392 Hoves/Hainaut ☎ 068/28 05 52

De Gay Krant ☎ 014/37 24 40
Contact phone-number for the Dutch gay magazine.

Gay Info Line 9-17 h
☎ 09/223 69 29 Fax: 09/223 58 21

Gay Kiss Kontaktmagazine
PO Box 76 ✉2018 Antwerpen ☎ 03/666 69 89
Fax: 03/75 25 44 37
Monthly magazine with classifieds and ads of gay venues.

Gay Mag 14-19.30 h
Rue des Teitureiers 18/7 ✉1000 Bruxelles ☎ 02/512 31 08
Fax: 02/511 93 96

Queensize
Rue de Verrewinkel 5a ✉1180 Bruxelles
☎ 02/375 93 96 Fax: 02/375 36 59
Email: queensize@place.to.be
Gay monthly magazine available for free in gay venues.

Regard (GLM)
PO Box 215 ✉1040 Bruxelles
☎ 02/733 10 24 Fax: 02/732 10 81
Email: regard@euronet.be
Bi-monthly news magazine for the French speaking gay community.

Secret Magazine
PO Box 1400 ✉1000 Bruxelles
☎ 02/223 10 09 Fax: 02/223 10 09
SM-magazine with gay and non-gay ads .

Tels Quels
Rue du Marché au Charbon 81 ✉1000 Bruxelles
☎ 02/512 45 87
Cultural and political reports and comments. Interviews. List of events. International and national ads. Photos. Monthly magazine for the French speaking gay community. Cultural and political reports and comments, interviews, list of events, international and national ads, photos. For BF 100 at numerous points of sale.

Uitkomst
c/o Gespreks- en Onthaal Centrum, Dambruggestraat 204, ✉2060 Antwerpen ☎ 03/233 10 71 Fax: 03/234 33 39
Articles of general interest, gay liberation, book and film reviews, political commentary. Free copy on request.

Zizo
Vlaanderenstraat 22 ✉9000 Gent/Gand ☎ 09/223 69 29
Fax: 09/223 58 21 Email: fwh@innet.be
News, politics, culture, interviews, short stories, list of events and classifieds in Dutch.

NATIONAL HELPLINES

AIDS-Telephone /StAG
PO Box 169 ✉2060 Antwerpen ☎ 078/15 15 15

NATIONAL COMPANIES

GAY Planet-Fiesta reizen
nv. Leopoldstraat 3 ✉2000 Antverpen ☎ (3)231 0581

G Mail
PO Box 5 ✉9000 Gent/Gand
☎ 077/35 02 55 (Dutch) Email: g-mail@skynet.be
Homepage: http://www.g-mail.com

NATIONAL GROUPS

BGMC-Knalpijp
Vlaanderenstraat 22 9000 Gent/Gand
☎ 09/221 60 56 Fax: 02/270 14 91
Belgian Gay Motor Club.

De Witte Raven vzw 9-12 13-17 h closed Sat-Sun
Schijfwerperstraat 145 2020 Antwerpen ☎ 03/828 69 00
Fax: 03/825 40 13
For HIV-positive people.

Federatie Werkgroepen Homoseksualiteit (FWH) Mon-Tri 9-12.30, 13-17.15, Fri until 16.30 h
Vlaanderenstraat 22 9000 Gent/Gand ☎ 09/223 69 29
Email: fwh@innet.be
Homepage: http://www.innet.be/fwh

Liga van Gespreks- en Onthaalcentra voor Homo`s Mon-Fri 12-18
Dambruggestraat 204 2060 Antwerpen
☎ 03/233 10 71 Fax: 03/234 33 39

MSC Belgium Meeting: 1st. Fri 22-? h
at the Duquesnoy
PO Box 699 1000 Bruxelles ☎ 02/293 08 48
Email: mscbelgium@compuserve.com
National fetish group. Member of ECMC.

Werkgroep Ouders van Homofielen (W.O.H.) Ullenshofstraat 5 2170 Merksemem ☎ 03/647 18 58

Aalst/Alost 9300 ☎ 053

GAY INFO

Advies Kontakt Centrum 't Koerken (HAK)
10.30-13.30, 15.30-24 h, closed Sat Sun
St. Martensplein 2 9300 ☎ 70 38 88

BARS

Poeskaffee (AC B G MA s) Wed-Fri 15-?, Sat 10-4
Sun 16-4 h, closed on Mon Tue
Gentsestraat 14 9300 *(centre)* ☎ 77 46 79

CAFES

Allegro ma non troppo (B CC F glm MA) Tue-Thu Sun 12-24, Fri -1, Sat 10-1 h, closed on Mon
Gentsestraat 16 9300 *(centre)* ☎ 78 44 46

RESTAURANTS

Da Galeria (A B CC F glm MA s) 12-15, 17-1 h, closed on Tue
Gentesestraat 6 9300 *(5min from centre)* ☎ 77 40 63
Café Bar Restaurant with Bazilian music and exhibitions.

GENERAL GROUPS

Homo- en Lesbiennegroep Vice Versa (GLM)
PO Box 67 9300

Antwerpen/Anvers 2000 ☎ 03

● Diamonds are a girl's best friend! With no doubt Antwerpen is the headquarter of the national diamond market. You will find innumerable diamond shops along the „Lange Herentaalsc Straat". However, Antwerpen has more to offer than diamonds: the old city centre has an enormous variety of well-preserved old buildings, museums and markets. The flee-market („Vlooienmarkt") is especially famous. The lively gay scene has three major districts: the „Van Schoonhovenstraat" is the place for a drink and a flirt with the good-looking Belgium locals. You will find many bars and discos in this street. In the old city centre towards the Schelde bars and restaurants are located in historical buildings. If you would like to try an authentic Flemish dish, ask for „waterzooi", a kind of tasty thick soup. If leather is your party then you have to go to the „Van Aerdtstraat". Several leather bars and clubs are located here with exciting darkrooms and an international ambiance. For information about current gay events and parties have a look at the newspaper „De Uitkomst" which is published by the Antwerp Gay Centre GOC.

✱ Diamonds are a girl's best friend! Ohne Zweifel ist Antwerpen der Hauptsitz des nationalen Diamanten- Marktes. Man findet unzählige Juweliere auf der „Lange Herentalse straat". Allerdings hat Antwerpen mehr zu bieten als Diamanten: Im alten Stadtzentrum steht eine enorme Vielfalt an guterhaltenen alten Gebäuden, Museen und Märkten. Besonders der Flohmarkt („Vlooienmarkt") ist berühmt. Die lebhafte schwule Szene teilt sich in drei Hauptdistrikte auf: Die „Van Schoonhovenstraat" ist der richtige Ort, um bei einem Drink mit den gutaussehenden Belgiern zu flirten. Hier gibt es auch viele Bars und Discos. Im alten Stadtzentrum in Richtung Schelde befinden sich Bars und Restaurants in historischen Gebäuden. Sucht man nach authentischen flämischen Spezialitäten, sollte man „Waterzooi" probieren, eine schmackhafte dicke Suppe. Sucht man nach Leder, muß man in die „Van Aerdtstraat" gehen. Mehrere Lederbars und -clubs findet man hier mit aufregenden Darkrooms und internationaler Atmosphäre. Für Informationen über aktuelle schwule Veranstaltungen schaut man am besten in „De Uitkomst", einer Zeitung, die vom Schwulenzentrum Antwerpens GOC herausgebracht wird.

▲ Diamonds are a girl's best friend! Anvers est incontestablement le siège principal du marché national des diamants. On trouve d'innombrables joailliers dans la „Lange Herentalsestraat". Mais Anvers offre davantage que des diamants: au centre de l'ancienne ville se trouvent nombre d'édifices anciens bien conservés, des musées et marchés. Le marché aux puces („Vlooienmarkt") est particulièrement renommé. La scène homosexuelle animée se réparti en trois districts principaux: La „Van Schoonhovenstraat" est le véritable lieu pour flirter, lors d'un drink, avec des belges sympathiques. Il y a ici également beaucoup de bars et de discothèques. Au centre de la vieille ville en direction de Schelde se trouvent des bars et restaurants dans des bâtiments historiques. Si l'on recherche des spécialités flamandes authentiques, on devrait essayer „Waterzooi", un potage velouté succulent. Si l'on recherche du cuir, il faut se rendre à la „Van Aerdtstraat". On y trouve plusieurs bars et clubs de cuir avec des „darkrooms" émouvants et une ambiance internationale. Pour obtenir des informations sur les manifestations actuelles homosexuels, le mieux est de consulter le „De Uitkomst", un journal publié par le centre homosexuels d'Anvers GOC.

❖ Como ya cantaba Marilyn Monroe, los diamantes son los mejores amigos de una chica. Sin duda alguna, Antwerpen es el centro mundial del mercado de los diamantes. En la *Language Herentaalse Straat* se encuentran innumerables tiendas dedicadas a este mercado. Pero a parte de las piedras preciosas, Antwerpen ofrece mucho más: el casco viejo de la ciudad está lleno de edificios antiguos muy bien conservados, de museos y de mercadillos. Entre ellos el rastro (Vlooienmarkt) es el más famoso. El vivo ambiente gay se concentra en tres barrios distintos. La *Van Schoonhovenstraat*, una calle llena de bares y discotecas, es el sitio perfecto para tomar una copa y ligar con los guapos belgas. En el casco viejo de la ciudad dirección Schelde hay muchos edificos antiguos donde se encuentran instalados ahora bares y restaurantes. Se quieres probar un típico plato belga, pide un *waterzooi*, una sopa espesa muy rica. Si lo tuyo es el cuero, te deberías dirigir hacía la *Van Aerdtstraat*, donde se encuentran muchos bares de cuero con excitantes salas oscuras y un ambiente internacional. Para informaciones acerca de acontecimientos y fiestas gay se puede echar un vistazo al periodico *De Uitkomst*, que es editado por el centro homosexual GOC.

☆ Diamonds are a girl's best friend! Senza dubbio Anversa è il centro del mercato nazionale dei diamanti. Sulla Lange Heren-

talse Straat una gioielleria segue l'altra. Ma Anversa offre altro, all'infuori dei diamanti. Nel centro storico troverete innumerevoli case vecchie in buono stato di conservazione, musei e mercati. Molto famoso è il mercato delle pulci (Vlooienmarkt). L'ambiente gay si divide in tre settori: Nella Van Schoonhovenstraat si può benissimo flirtare con i bei belgi in uno dei bar o discoteche. Nel centro vecchio della città verso Schelde esistono molti bar e ristoranti in case storiche. Cercando specialità autentiche fiamminghe si dovrebbe provare la „Waterzooi", una delicata minestra spessa. Gli amanti del cuoio devono visitare la Van Aerdtstraat, dove si trovano alcuni bar e club con eccitanti darkrooms e un'atmosfera internazionale. Chi cerca informazioni su eventi gay attuali, li trova nel Uitkomst, un giornale pubblicato dal centro gay GOC

GAY INFO

Antwerpen Homo Gids 2000
Tolstraat 13 ✉2000
Gay map of the city published by the health group Aidstcam.

G.O.C. Antwerpen (B D G) 20-24, Fri -2,
Sat sun 22-4.30, closed Mon
Dambruggestraat 204 ✉2060 ☎ 233 10 71 Fax: 234 33 39
Also Parties. Call for info.

Radio Centraal: „Chocopot" Tue 21-22 h
(FM 101,6 MHz)
PO Box 554 ☎ 236 50 76

Uitkomst
Dambruggestraat 204 ✉2060 ☎ 233 10 17
Fax: 234 33 39 *Local gay newspaper.*

TOURIST INFO

Dienst voor Toerisme Mon-Fri 9-18, Sat Sun 9-17 h
Grote Markt 15 ✉2000 ☎ 232 01 03 Fax: 231 19 37

BARS

Bacchus (B G LJ MA) Mon-Thu 17-?, Fri-Sun 16-? h
Van Schoonhovenstraat 28 ✉2060 ☎ 233 96 66

Den Bazaar (AC B D GLM MA) Mon-Thu 12-24, Fri-Sun -5 h
Van Schoonhovenstraat 22 ✉2060 ☎ 232 91 20

Body Boys (B GLM) 14-5 h
Van Schoonhovenstraat 30 ✉2060 ☎ 203 05 43

Boots. The (! AC B DR G LJ MA P VS WE) Fri Sat 22.30-5 h
Van Aerdtstraat 22 ✉2060 *(near St. Jansplein)* ☎ 233 21 36
Fetish sex club, skinhead hangout.

Borsalino (! AC B D f G MA) 21-? h, closed on Wed
Van Schoonhovenstraat 48 ✉2060 ☎ 226 91 62

Cafe de Fiets (A B f GLM MA W) 17-?, fri 8.30-?, closed on Wed
Vrijdagmarkt 5 ✉2000 *(near Vrijdagmarkt)* ☎ 231 45 99

Cafe Hessenhuis (B f GLM MA) 10-? h
Falconrui 53 ✉2000 ☎ 231 13 56

Cafe Strange (B D G T) 21-5, Sun 16-5 h
Dambruggestraat 161 ✉2060 ☎ 226 00 72
Summertime barbecue parties.

Den Beiaard (B F g OS) 9-? h closed on Thu
Handschoenmarkt 21 ✉2000 ☎ 232 40 14

Envers d'Anvers. L' (B f G s)
Pacificatiestraat 97 ✉2000 ☎ 237 33 36
Opened October 1999

Fifty-Fifty (AC B D f GLM p) 21-?, Sun 16-? h
Van Schoonhovenstraat 40 ✉2060 ☎ 225 11 73
Very popular bar with upstairs quiet area for snacks and conversation.

Funnies (g MA tv) 21-6 h, closed Mon
Lange Beeldekenstraat 10 ✉2060 ☎ 232 12 35

Hanky Code Bar (B f G LJ MA NU OS) Mon-Thu 20-6 h
Van de Wervestraat 69 ✉2060 *(Bus 81-86-St. Jansplein)*
☎ 226 81 72

Hanky Code's Cellar (B D DR G LJ MA WE) Fri-Sun 20-9 h
Van de Wervestraat 69 ✉2060 *(Bus 81-86-St. Jansplein)*
☎ 226 81 72

Den Houten Kop (B f GLM MA tv) 19-8 h closed Tue
St. Lambertusstraat 73 ✉2600 ☎ 218 91 79

In de Roskam (B GLM MA) 17-?, WE 15-? h
Vrijdagmarkt 12 ✉2000 ☎ 226 24 10

Katshuis. 'T (B G MA W) 20-?, Fri-Sun 16-? h
Grote Pieter Potstraat 18 ✉2000 ☎ 234 03 69

New Queens (B CC G MA R) 12-5 h
Van Schoonhovenstraat 4 ✉2000 *(near central station)*
☎ 213 32 03

Playboy (AC B D GLM MA p s tv) 17-3, Sat Sun -8 h
Van Schoonhovenstraat 42 ✉2060 ☎ 231 60 06

Popi Café (B F GLM) 12-? h
Riemstraat 22-24 ✉2000 ☎ 238 15 30

Rimbaud (B GLM MA) 20-?, Sun 17-? h, closed Mon Tue
Hessenbrug 5 ✉2000 ☎ 232 79 18

Rubbzz (B G LJ MA) 22-? h
Geulincxstraat 28 ✉2000 *(15 min from the railway station)*
☎ 0495/52 03 57
Clubhouse of the Fenix skinhead movement of Antwerpen with its own skingear shop.

Twilight (AC B CC G MA OS) 16-? h
Van Schoonhovenstraat 54 ✉2060 *(near central station)*
☎ 232 67 04 *Cosy bar with garden terrace.*

CAFES

Het Gebaar (bf glm) 10.30-18 h, closed on Mon
Schuttershofstraat 14 ✉2000 ☎ 232 37 10

Overkant. D'n/The Otherside (B f G LJ MA OS)
Mon-Thu 11-23, Fri Sat -4, Sun -24 h
Van de Wervestraat/Geulincxstraat ✉2060 ☎ 226 14 97

DANCECLUBS

Havanna Beach (B D GLM) Fri-Sun 22-? h
Van Schoonhovenstraat 24 ✉2060 ☎ 232 01 43

Boots. The (B D GLM)
Van Aerdtstraat 22 ✉2060 ☎ 231 34 88
Fri-Sun 22:30-5h

Red & Blue (! AC B CC D DR E G S SNU YG) Sat 23-? h
Lange Schipperskapelstraat 11-13 ✉2000 *(near the Red Light district)* ☎ 213 05 55
The biggest gay club in Benelux.

RESTAURANTS

Grote Witte Arend (B F glm) 11.30-22.30 h, closed Tue, Nov-Apr Tue & Wed
Reynderstraat 18 ✉2000 ☎ 226 31 90

In de Schaduw v.d. Kathedraal (B bf F GLM) Wed-Sat 12-15 18-20, Sun 18-22 h.
Handschoenmarkt 17 ✉2000 *(near Kathedraal)* ☎ 232 40 14

Kertosono Indonesian Restaurant (B E F glm) 18.30-23 h
Provinciestraat 118 ✉2018 ☎ 225 02 14 *FA: 231 69 24*

O' Kontreir Restaurant (F glm) Tue-Fri 12-14.30, 18-22.30, Sat Sun 18-22.30 h, closed on Tue
Isabellalei 145 ✉2018 ☎ 281 39 76
Gay-friendly restaurant.

Kule (B F g) Tue-Sun 12-1 h
Cuylitsstraat 1 ✉2018 ☎ 237 17 95
Turkish cuisine.

Ogenblick. 'T (B G MA) Wed-Sat 11-24 h
Grote Markt 10-12 ✉2000 ☎ 233 62 62

Oi! (F glm)
Kleine Kraaiwijk 10 ✉2000 ☎ 231 06 71
Together with the SM - Fetish Roxy shop.

Preud Homme (b F g)
Suikerrui 28 ✉2000 ☎ 233 42 00
High quality belgian cuisine.

Quicherie Eiland (A AC B CC F glm MA OS W) Mon-Sat 12-14, 17-21 h, closed Sun
Isabellalei 1 ✉2018 ☎ 230 16 60
Daily meal restaurant with vegetarian/fish disches. Friendly staff.

Quick (B F g) 12-6, WE 17-6 h
De Coninckplein 29 ✉2060 ☎ 225 22 16

Tafeltje Rond (AC B CC F g) 11.30-22 h, Mon Sun & holidays closed Hoge Weg 14 ✉2600 ☎ 230 99 48

Tafeltje Rond (B F g)
Gildekamerstraat 10 ✉2000
☎ 231 65 81
Tea room and restaurant.

SEX SHOPS/BLUE MOVIES

Adonis (G VS) 12-22, Sat 14-23, Sun 13-22 h
Dambruggestraat 174 ✉2060 ☎ 226 91 51

Erotheek International (g) 12-24, Sat 12-22 h
Van Schoonhovenstraat 34 ✉2060 ☎ 233 29 40

Libidos Erotheek (g) 12-22 h
Carnotstraat 35 ✉2060 *(near central station)* ☎ 226 02 45

Roxy (g lj) 12-24 h
Kleine Kraaiwijk 10 ✉2000 ☎ 227 45 57
Rubber, leather, films.

Videotheek Gay-Ron (DR G MA VS) Mon-Fri 12-23, Sat Sun 14-22 h
Van Wesenbekestraat 54 ✉2060 *(near centralstation)*
☎ 234 04 43

Walhalla (G) 12-2 h
St.-Paulusplaats 21 ✉2000 ☎ 233 62 91
Videos, magazines, rubber/leather, piercing, removable tattoos.

Warehouse. The (G LJ) Fri-Sat 22.30-5 h
Van Aerdtstraat 22 ✉2060 ☎ 225 23 76
This shop is in „Boots" bar.

SAUNAS/BATHS

City Sauna (B F DR G sa sb VS wh) 14-24 h
Olijftakstraat 35 ✉2060 ☎ 234 19 25
Entrance-fee Bfr 300-400.

Dimitry's Sauna Bath (B DR G MA sa sb VS)
Mon-Fri 14-23, Sat 14-8 h
Greinstraat 47 ✉2060 *(10 min walk from station, Metro 3-Elisabeth)* ☎ 235 00 87
Sat only group sex for nude lovers.

Herenhuis. 'T (AC B CC d DR F G MA msg pi sa sb sol VS wh) 11-24, Fri Sat 11-2 h
De Lescluzestraat 63 ✉2600 ☎ 239 51 95
Bfr 450 except Wed Thu and -25 years Bfr 300.

Kouros Sauna (AC B CC DR F G MA msg OS P pi sa sb sol VS W wh) Mon-Sat 13-1, Sun 11-1 h
Botermelkbaan 50, ✉2900 *(Bus 61)* ☎ 658 09 37
Friendly atmosphere.

Metropolitan International Sauna (B DR G sa sb VS wh) 14-23, Fri -2, Sat -20 h, closed Sun
Sint Elisabethstraat 47 ✉2060 ☎ 213 48 21
Entrance-fee Bfr 400.

Sauna Park (B F DR G pi sa sb VS wh) 15-1, Fri Sat -6 h
Florisstraat 10 ✉2018 ☎ 226 03 93
Former Macho I. Entrance-fee Bfr 300.

SPA 55 (B DR G MA msg sa sb sol T VS wh) 14-24 h
Sanderusstraat 55 ✉2018 *(Behind Justitiepaleis, Tram 12, 24 Justitie Paleis City Mansion)* ☎ 238 31 37
5 floors, friendly atmosphere, professional massage, sun terrace. Entrance Bfr 350/450.

BOOK SHOPS

De Groene Waterman (G)
Wolstraat 7 ✉2000 ☎ 232 93 94

Pourquoi Pas
Quellinstraat 51 ✉2000 ☎ 02/227 23 27

Verschil. 'T (A b bf CC GLM MA OS) Fri 12-18, Sat 12-19, Sun 12-18 bf 12-14 h
Minderbroedersrui 42 ✉2000 *(Tram 4,11, next to shopping centre Antwerp & Groenplaats)* ☎ 226 08 04
Gay and Lesbian book and coffeeshop.

LEATHER & FETISH SHOPS

Roxy Piercingstudio (g) 14-23 h
Kleine Kraaiwijk 12 ✉12000 ☎ 232 82 89

TRAVEL & TRANSPORT

Dimane (CC GLM)
Mechelsesteenweg 39 ✉2018
☎ 213 17 85 Fax: 213 17 86 Email: dimane-pr@skynet.be

Fiesta Gay Planet (Fiesta Reizen N.V.)
(CC GLM W) Mon-Fri 9.30-13, 14-18 h, closed Sat Sun
Leopoldstraat 3 ✉2000 *(next to Bourla theater)* ☎ 231 05 81
Fax: 231 05 82 *Gay travel agent and tour operator.*

HOTELS

Astrid Park Plaza (A B CC bf g H msg sa sol pi wh WO)
Koningin Astridplein 7 ✉2018 *(opposite to Central station)*
☎ 203 12 34 Fax: 203 12 75 Email: astrid.plaza@euronet.be
Homepage: http://www.parkplazaastrid.com
229 double rooms with bath/WC phone, fax, TV, radio, minibar, safe, own key. Rates double bfr 9300, single 8300 (bf excl.), WE rate 4100 (bf incl).

Hanky Code Hotel (B bf CC G H LJ NU)
Van de Wervestraat 67 ✉2060 *(Bus 81-86-St. Jansplein)*
☎ 226 81 72
Fax: 226 26 78 Homepage: http://www.hankycode.com
Own key. 20 double rooms, 4 single rooms, 1 apartment. Rates from Bfr 1.050, breakfast buffet 200. Not really clean. No hand basin in room.

t'Herenhuis (GLM H)
de Lescluzestraat 63 ✉2600 Berchem ☎ 239 51 95

PRIVATE ACCOMODATION

Sweet Ours (GLM H)
Krugerpark, Mertenstraat 31 ✉2140 *(Tram 10/24)* ☎ 236 80 23 Fax: 236 80 23
Email: stof@mail.dma.be
Bed & Breakfast within walking distance from the gay nightlife run by a gay couple. All rooms with kitchen, bathroom and room service.

GENERAL GROUPS

ANTAR (GLM) PB 215 ✉2100 ☎ 321 67 77
Social and cultural activities gays and lesbians.

GanymedeS homojongeren (YG)
Dambruggestraat 204 ✉2060 ☎ 223 10 71
Gay youth group.

HAGAR - Homolesbische Aktiegroep
Kloosterstraat 5 ✉2000 ☎ 237 66 25

Het Roze Huis
P/a Breughelstraat 31-33 ✉2018 ☎ 440 51 40

Holebi-jongeren Enig Verschil (GLM)
PO Box 22 ✉2060 ☎ 216 37 37

Holebijongeren Kast en Co (GLM)
PO Box 346 ✉2000

Kring Homoseksuele Senioren (OG)
Dambruggestraat 204 ✉2060 ☎ 223 10 71
Group for older gays

Landelijke Belangenverdediging Homoseksualiteit
Dambruggestraat 204 ✉2060 ☎ 223 10 71
Gay liberation organization.

Roze Aktie Front (RAF) (GLM)
Congresstraat 41 ✉2060 ☎ 236 50 76

Werkgroep Ouders van Homofielen
Ullenshofstraat 5 ✉2170 *(bus 11)* ☎ 647 18 58

HEALTH GROUPS

Aidsteam Mon-Fri 9-12.30, 13.30-17 h
Tolstraat 13 ✉2000 ☎ 238 61 61 Fax: 238 05 04
Email: aidsteam@village.uunet.be *Aids prevention for gay, lesbian and bisexual people. Also publishers of a gay map of the city.*

Aidstelefoon Mon-Fri 14-22, Sat -17 h
PO Box 169 ✉2060 ☎ 078/15 15 15

De Witte Raven Mon-Fri 10-17, Tue -19 h
Schijfwepersstraat 145 ✉2020 ☎ 826 69 00 Fax: 825 40 13
Email: hiv.de.witte.raven@skynet.be

HIV-Vereniging Vlaanderen Mon-Fr 10-17 h, Helpline: Mon 14-16 Wed 19-21 h
Schijferpersstraat 145 ✉2020 *(Tram 2-VII Olympiadelaan)*
☎ 828 69 00 Fax: 820 86 50
Email: hiv-vlaanderen@hiv-vlaanderen.be
Homepage: http://www.hiv-vereniging.be
Aids organisation.

Institut voor Tropische Geneeskunde Mon-Fri 9-17 h (by appointment only)
Kronenburgerstraat 43 ✉2000 ☎ 247 64 65
AIDS test & SOA consultation.

HELP WITH PROBLEMS

D.O.K. (Konsultatieburo voor Relaties en Seksualiteit) 9-12.30, 13.30-17, Tue Thu also 19-21.30 h, closed Sat Sun
Rotterdamstraat 27 ✉2000 ☎ 234 08 48

SPECIAL INTEREST GROUPS

Classico Club
Dambruggestraat 204 ✉2060 ☎ 233 10 71
Classical music lovers.

CRUISING

-Stadspark (AYOR)
-Wooded area (between Berchem station and Grote Steenweg)
-Het Rot (linker oever, drive through Waasland tunnel, ca 1 km sooded area on left-hand side)
-Conincplein (AYOR OG)

Arlon ✉ 6700

CRUISING

-Le Belvédère (across from the church St. Donant, in summer, evenings)

Assenede ✉ 9960 ☎ 09

DANCECLUBS

Passé (B D G MA) Thu Mon 17-?, Sat Sun 14-? h
Doornend 1 ✉9960

GUEST HOUSES

T' Staaksken (AC bf F Glm H lj MA NU OS W)
Staakstraat 136/138 A ✉9960 ☎ 344 09 54 Fax: 344 09 54
Email: staaksken@skynet.be
Homepage: http://www.come.to/staaksken
Non-smoking holiday cottage located in the nature between Antwerp, Ghent and Bruges. Call for rates.

Blankenberge ✉ 8370 ☎ 050

BARS

Oosterstaketsel (B bf F g MA N)
✉8370 *(on end of east pier harbour entrance)* ☎ 41 19 12
NU in dunes nearby.

HOTELS

E.T.M. Bach (E GLM H MA msg sol)
Vissersstraat 20 ✉8370 ☎ 41 97 71
Rates Single bfr 980 double 1680 triple 2280 four 2900 (incl. bf).

APARTMENTS

Johan Dockx Apartments (GLM H) 10-16.30 h (Call ahead)
Molenstraat 13 ✉8370 ☎ 075/47 66 64

CRUISING

-Dunes direction Zeebrugge

Brugge/Bruges ☎ 050

BARS

Passe-Partout (AC B CC d DR f G lj MA p s VS) 16-?, Sun 14.30-? h, closed Wed
St. Jansstraat 3 ✉8000 *(near the big market place)* ☎ 33 47 42

RESTAURANTS

Hollywood (B CC F glm H) 11-23.30 h, closed Thu
'T Zand 24 ✉8000 ☎ 33 72 52
Miramar (b CC F g OS) 11-23 h, closed on Tue
Mariastraat 13 ✉8000 ☎ 34 72 62

HOTELS

Hotel Memling (b bf f g H)
Kuiperstraat 8 ✉8000 ☎ 33 20 96
Centrally located, all rooms with telephone, priv. bath.

GUEST HOUSES

Het Wit Beertje (bf glm H)
Witte Beerstraat 4 ✉8200 *(Bus 5/15 2rd stop from the station, 10 min on foot)*
☎ 45 08 88 Fax: 45 08 80 Email: jp.defour@worldonline.be

GENERAL GROUPS

Boomerang (YG)
P/A Benedictynenstraat 64 ✉8310
Group of young gays, lesbians and bisexuals. E-mail or write for information on activities (WE).
Email: postboomerang@hotmail.com

Holebi-Jongeren
PO Box 131 ✉8000 ☎ 37 47 02
Homocentrum Brugge Idem-Dito Meeting Fri 20, Sun 15-18 h at Bar Passe-Partout
PO Box 131 ✉8000 ☎ 33 47 42

RELIGIOUS GROUPS

Effeta Brugge PO Box 136 ✉8000 ☎ 33 77 14

CRUISING

-Minnewaterpark

Brussel/Bruxelles ✉ 1000 ☎ 02

● Whoever thinks that Brussel consists solely of the EU headquarters is wrong. For the genuine gay tourist Brussel has some interesting features. First of all, there is the magnificent „Grote Markt/Grand Place" with its impressing architecture. If modern art interests you, the „Museum von Schone Kunsten/Palais des Beaux Arts" offers interesting exhibitions of contemporary artists. Smaller, but interesting too, is the statue of „Manneken Pis", a little guy who yeah, uh urinates all day. No tourist information has ever given a plausible explanation for this statue. The gay scene is located in and around „Steenstraat/Rue des Pierres". Although Brussel is supposed to be bilingual, you had better try your best French here! Most bars and discos are within walking distance. Check out big gay parties in La Demence. These parties attract gays from all over the world and truly subscribe the cosmopolitan character which Brussel has at times. The International Lesbian & Gay Association (ILGA) is located in Brussel.

✱ Wer denkt, Brüssel bestehe einzig und allein aus dem Hauptsitz der EU, der liegt völlig daneben. Für den wahren schwulen Touristen bietet Brüssel einige interessante Sehenswürdigkeiten: An erster Stelle ist der großartige „Grote Markt/Grand Place" mit seiner eindrucksvollen Architektur zu nennen. Interessieren Sie sich für die moderne Kunst, dann bietet das „Museum vor Schone Kunsten/Palais des Beaux Arts" interessante Ausstellungen zeitgenössischer Künstler. Kleiner, aber auch interessant, ist die Statur des „Manneken Pis", die von morgens bis abends pinkelt. Keine Touristeninformation hat jemals eine plausible Erklärung für diese Statur abgegeben. Die schwule Szene befindet sich auf und um „Steenstraat/Rue des Pierres". Obwohl Brüssel angeblich zweisprachig sein soll, sollte man hier von seinem Französisch Gebrauch machen. Die meisten Bars und Diskos liegen in unmittelbarer Nähe, sodaß man sie zu Fuß erreichen kann. Empfehlenswert sind die großen Gay-Partys im „La Démence". Sie ziehen Schwule aus der ganzen Welt an und berschreiben wahrhaftig den cosmopolitischen Charakter, den Brüssel hat. Die „International Lesbian & Gay Association" (ILGA) hat ihren Sitz in Brüssel.

▲ Celui qui pense que Bruxelles se compose uniquement du siège principal de l'UE, se trompe totalement. Pour le véritable touriste homosexuel, Bruxelles offre quelques curiosités intéressantes: notons en premier lieu l'imposante „Grand-Place/Grote Markt") avec son architecture impressionnante. Si l'art moderne vous intéresse, vous trouverez des expositions intéressantes d'artistes contemporains au „Palais des Beaux-Arts/Museum vor Schone Kunsten". Plus petite, mais tout aussi intéressante, est la stature du „Manneken Pis", qui pisse du matin au soir. Aucune information touristique n'a donné une explication plausible de cette stature. La scène homosexuelle se trouve dans et autour de la „Rue des Pierres/Steensstraat". Bien que l'on dise que Bruxelles est bilingue, il vaut mieux utiliser ici son français. La majorité des bars et discothèques se trouvent à proximité immédiate, il est donc facile d'y parvenir à pied. Une recommandation: les grandes „Gay-parties" à la „Démence". Elles attirent les homosexuels du monde entier et décrivent vraiment le caractère cosmopolite de Bruxelles. Bruxelles est également le siège de l'"International Lesbian & Gay Association" (ILGA).

El que piense que Bruselas no tiene más que ofrecer que las instituciones europeas está confundido. En Bruselas hay mucho que ver para el turista interesado. En primer lugar destaca la maravillosa „Grete Markt/Grand Place" con su impresionante arquitectura. Si se es un amante del arte moderno, se debería visitar el „Museum von Schone Kunsten / Palais des Beaus Arts" que ofrece interesantes exposiciones de artistas contemporaneos. Más pequeño, pero también digno de ver es la estatua de „Manneken Pis", un chico que está orinando durante todo el día. Ninguna información turística ha sido hasta ahora capaz de dar una explicación lógica sobre esta estatua. El ambiente gay se encuentra en la „Steenstraat/Rue de Pierres" y sus alrededores. Aunque se supone que Bruselas es una ciudad bilingual, es recomendable hablar francés. A la mayoría de los bares y discotecas se llega andando. Se recomienda la visita de una de la grandes fiestas gay que tienen lugar en „La Demence". Estas fiestas atraen homosexuales de todo el mundo y confirman el carácter cosmopolita que tiene Bruselas en la actualidad. La Internacional Lesbian & Gay Association (ILGA) tiene su sede en esta ciudad.

Chi crede che Bruxelles sia costituita solo dalla sede centrale della CE, ha completamente torto. Per il vero turista gay Bruxelles offre alcune bellezze interessanti: La prima cosa da nominare è l'imposante „Grote Markt/ Grand Place" con la sua impressionante architettura. Gli interessati all'arte moderna vengono soddisfatti nel „Museum vor Schone Kunsten/Palais des Beaux Arts" che offre esposizioni d'artisiti contemporanei. Più piccola però non meno interessante è una scultura del „Manneken pis", che piscia dalla mattina alla sera. Fino a oggi nessuna informazione tursistica è stata in grado di dare una spiegazione plausibile di questa opera. L'ambiente gay si trova sulla e attorno alla „Steenstraat/ Rue des Pierres". Anche se si affferma che Bruxelles sia bilingue è meglio parlare francese. La maggior parte dei bar e discoteche sono molto vicini tra di loro e quindi raggiungibili a piedi. Sono da raccomandare i grandi party gay nel „La Dénience". Attirano i gay di tutto il mondo e rappresentano veramente il carattere cosmopolitico di Bruxelles. Anche l'ILGA, la „International Lesbian & Gay Association" ha la sua sede a Bruxelles.

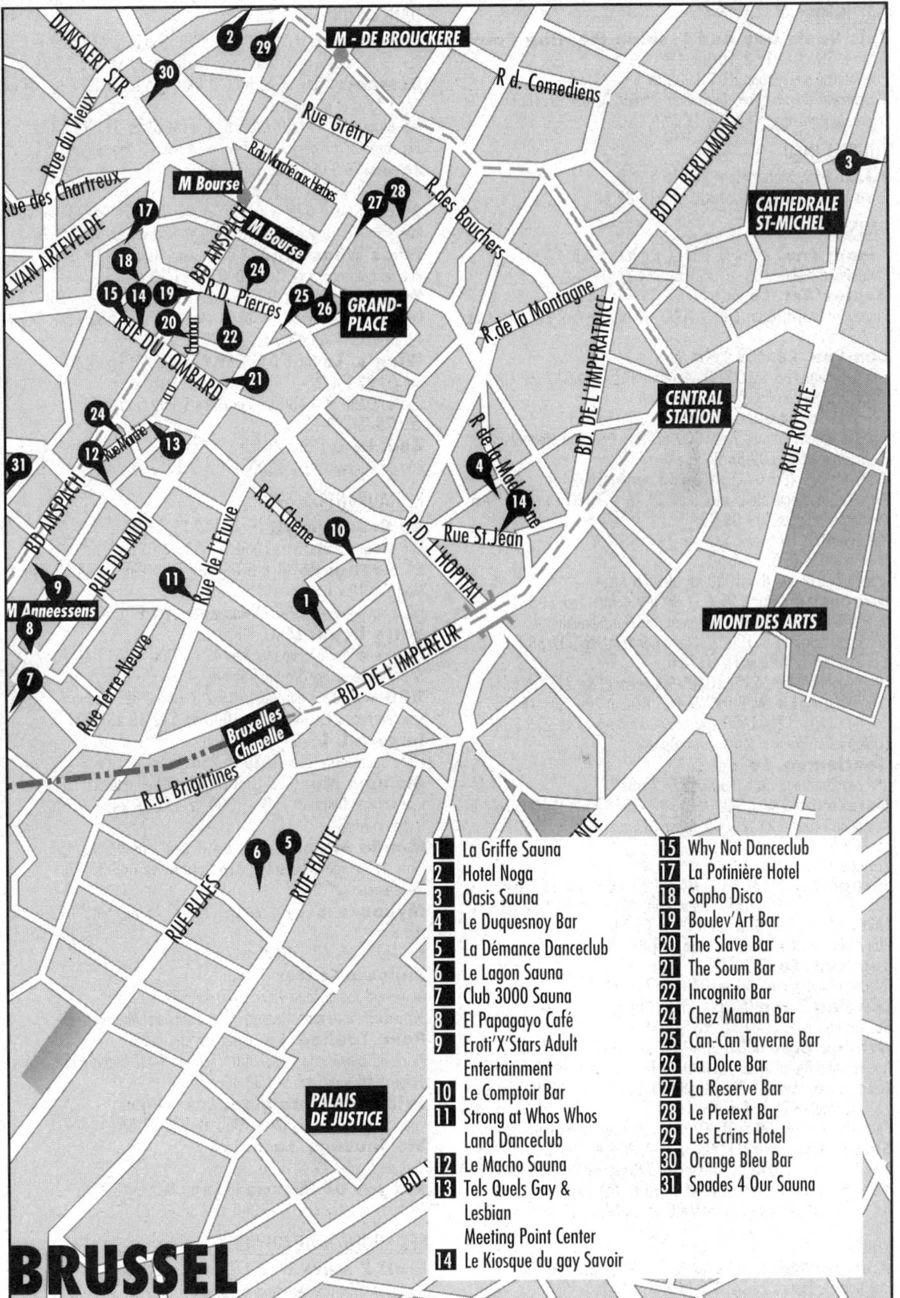
M - DE BROUCKERE
DANSAERT STR.
R d. Comediens
Rue Grétry
Rue du Vieux
Rue des Chartreux
M Bourse
M Bourse
R.des Bouchers
BD.D. BERLAMONT
CATHEDRALE ST-MICHEL
R.VAN ARTEVELDE
BD ANSPACH
R.D. Pierres
GRAND-PLACE
R.de la Montagne
BD. DE L'IMPERATRICE
RUE DU LOMBARD
CENTRAL STATION
RUE ROYALE
R.de la Madeleine
BD ANSPACH
R.d. Chêne
Rue St.Jean
R.D. L'HOPITAL
RUE DU MIDI
Rue de l'Etuve
M Anneessens
MONT DES ARTS
BD. DE L'IMPEREUR
Rue Terre-Neuve
Bruxelles Chapelle
R.d. Brigittines
RUE HAUTE
RUE BLAES
PALAIS DE JUSTICE
BRUSSEL
1 La Griffe Sauna
2 Hotel Noga
3 Oasis Sauna
4 Le Duquesnoy Bar
5 La Démance Danceclub
6 Le Lagon Sauna
7 Club 3000 Sauna
8 El Papagayo Café
9 Eroti'X'Stars Adult Entertainment
10 Le Comptoir Bar
11 Strong at Whos Whos Land Danceclub
12 Le Macho Sauna
13 Tels Quels Gay & Lesbian Meeting Point Center
14 Le Kiosque du gay Savoir
15 Why Not Danceclub
17 La Potinière Hotel
18 Sapho Disco
19 Boulev'Art Bar
20 The Slave Bar
21 The Soum Bar
22 Incognito Bar
24 Chez Maman Bar
25 Can-Can Taverne Bar
26 La Dolce Bar
27 La Reserve Bar
28 Le Pretext Bar
29 Les Ecrins Hotel
30 Orange Bleu Bar
31 Spades 4 Our Sauna

GAY INFO

Tels Quels Gay and Lesbian Meeting Point (A AC B GLM MA) 17-2, Fri Sat -4 h
Rue Marché-au-Charbon 81 ✉1000 ☎ 512 32 34
Welcoming, information, bookshop, library/Accueil, information, libraire, bibliothèque: Mon Tue 17-19 h.

TOURIST INFO

T.I.B. 9-18, winter: Mon-Sat 9-18 h
Grote Markt (Stadhuis) ✉1000 ☎ 513 89 40

BARS

Amour Fou. L' (A AC B bf CC F g MA) 9-3 h
Chaussee d'Ixelles 185 ✉1050 ☎ 514 27 09
Boulev'Art. Le (AC b f G MA OS) 10-2 h
Boulevard Anspachlaan 108 ✉1000 *(Near the stock exchange)* ☎ 512 53 62
Can-Can. Le (AC B D GLM MA p s) 16-? h
Rue des Pierres 55 ✉1000 *(near Grand Place)* ☎ 512 97 75
Karaoke nights on Fri, Shows 1x/month.
Chez Maman (AC B E G MA p S) Thu-Sun 19-?
Rue des Grands Carmes 7 ✉1000 *(100 m from the Manneken Pis, Metro-Bourse)* ☎ 502 86 96
Comptoir (B F G MA s YG) 19-3, restaurant -24 h
Place de la Vieille Halle aux Blés 24-26 ✉1000 *(près du/near Manneken Pis)* ☎ 514 05 00
Restaurant on 1st floor.
Dolce. La (B G) 15-? h
Petit-Rue-au-Beurre 8 ✉1000 ☎ 502 78 66
Duquesnoy (AC B DR G LJ MA p VS) Mon-Thu 21-3, Fri Sat -5, Sun 18-3 h, 1st Fri MSC Belgium, 3rd Sun Spanklub
Rue Duquesnoy 12 ✉1000 *(M-Gare Centrale)* ☎ 502 38 83
Eden. L' (B G) Mon-Fri 10-23 h
Place Colignonplaats 21 ✉1030 *(Schaerbeek)* ☎ 215 64 56
Gémeau. Le (AC B D G MA P s) Thu-Sat 22-? Sun 16-? h
Rue de Laeken 12 ✉1000 *(centre, Metro-Bourse)* ☎ 219 23 36
Café dansant. Typical Brussel atmosphere.
Gentleman. Le (B g) 22-? h
Rue des Chartreux 36 ✉1000 ☎ 512 6872
Horeca (B d G MA p S W) Mon 14-? Tue-Fri 11-?, Sat Sun 16-? h
Rue de la Fourche 21 ✉1000 *(close to Grand Place)*
☎ 502 50 84
Cosy bar with soft music.
Incognito. L' (AC B D G MA p S W) 16-?, Sun 15-? h
Rue des Pierres 36 ✉1000 *(Near Grand Place)* ☎ 513 37 88
Iris. L' (AC B CC GLM MG N OS s) 15-? h
Rue de la Fourche 12 ✉1000 ☎ 219 88 83
Jourdan. Le (B G MA)
Avenue d'Audergem 140 ✉1040 ☎ 724 71 90
Loading Zone (AC B CC DR G LJ P)
Rue St. Christoffe 1 ✉1000 ☎ 514 55 14
Orange Bleu (A B D GLM MA OS) Tue-Sat 16-3, Sun 19-3 h
Rue Antoine Dansaert 29 ✉1000 *(M-Bourse)* ☎ 513 98 29
Réserve. La (AC B d E G MG W) Mon Thu Fri 11-24, Sat Sun 15-24, Wed 16-22 h, Tue closed
Petit Rue-au-Beurre 2A ✉1000 *(metro Bourse)* ☎ 511 66 06
Slave. The (B DR G LJ MA p) 22-4, Fri Sat 22-6 h
Rue Plattesteen 7 ✉1000 *(Near Grand Place)* ☎ 213 47 46
Soum. The (AC B D GLM S SL SNU W YG) 12-? h
44 Rue Marché-au-Charbon ✉1000 ☎ 514 07 11

CAFES

Anatole Pub (B bf f g MA N) 11-22 h, closed Sat Sun
Rue Anatole France 73 ✉1000 ☎ 241 40 72

DANCECLUBS

Cabaret. Le (AC B D GLM WE YG) Sun only 23-7 h
Rue de l'Ecuyer 41 ✉1000 *(near La Monnaie)* ☎ 375 93 96
Démence. La (! AC B CC D DR G MA s VS) 23-7 h, Call for exact dates of gay nights
Rue Blaes 208 ✉1000 *(Near Gare du Midi)* ☎ 511 97 89
Big parties 18 times/year. 3 floors, 4 bars, 2 dancefloors,...
Sapho (B D GLM) Thu-Sat 22-? h
Rue Saint-Gery 1 ✉1000 ☎ 512 45 52
Strong (AC B D DR G lj s VS YG) Thu 22-5, Fri Sat 23-8 h
Rue Saint Christophe 1 ✉1000 *(Metro-Bourse)* ☎ 375 93 96
Whos Whos Land (B D G) Sun „Strong" 23-? h
Rue du Poincon 17 ✉1000 ☎ 075/61 13 68
Why Not (AC B CC D DR G lj MA P s VS W) 23-6, Fri Sat -7 h
Rue des Riches-Claires 7 ✉1000 *(Near stock exchange and Grande Place)* ☎ 512 63 43 *Popular.*
Wing's. Le (AC B D GLM MA P TV WE YG) Fri (GLM) Sat (L) 22-? h
Rue du Cypre 3 ✉1000 *(near Place Sainte Catherine)*
☎ 075/66 99 13
Zoo. Le (D g) Sun 21-? h
Rue du Magasin 12 ✉1000

RESTAURANTS

Au Boeuf qui rit (F glm) 12-15, 18-24 h
Rue des Bouchers 32 ✉1000 ☎ 511 96 02
El Papagayo (B F G OS YG) 12-2, Sat Sun 18-2, winter Mon-Sun 18-2 h
Place Rouppe 6 ✉1000 *(M-Anneessens)* ☎ 514 50 83
Entre Deux. L' (CC B F s)
Place de la Vieille Halle aux Blés 42 ✉1000 ☎ 511 68 73
Show-dinner every 3rd Sun/month.
H2O (A AC B E F glm MA p) 19-2 h, closed Dec 23-Jan 7.
Rue Marché-au-Charbon 27 ✉1000 ☎ 512 38 43
Imperial. L' (B F g) 8.30-0 h
Place Saint Josse 21 ✉1030 ☎ 230 35 04
Mamma Mia (CC F glm) closed on Wed and Sun noon
Rue Antoine Dansaert 158 ✉1000 ☎ 512 46 24
Italian cuisine.
Monde Allant Vert. Le (F glm) closed Sun/Mon
Chee de Vleurgatsesteenweg 316 ✉1050 ☎ 649 37 27
Vegetarian.
Mykonos (B CC F g MA OS) 12-15, 17-23, Sat 19-23 h, closed Sun
Rue Archimède 63 ✉1040 ☎ 735 17 59
Padoum Center (F msg)
Boulevard Jamar Laan 9b ✉1070 ☎ 522 10 50
Vegetarian Restaurant, Meditation hall, Californian Massage, Dietetics.
Pom' Touline. La (F g N MA s) Tue-Sat
Place du Béguinage 6 ✉1000 *(10 min from Grand Place, Metro-Sainte Catherine)* ☎ 223 33 40
Salons de l'Atalaide. Les (B F glm)
Chaussée de Charleroi 89 ✉1060 ☎ 537 21 54
Vie Sauvage. La (B F glm)
Rue de Naples 12 ✉1050
Y'a pas de Miracle (B F glm) Mon-Sat 19-1 h
Avenue Paul Dejaer 20 ✉1060 ☎ 538 48 93

SEX SHOPS/BLUE MOVIES

Erot' X Stars (G VS) 11-21 h
Boulevard Maurice Lemmonier 40 ✉1000 ☎ 513 93 44

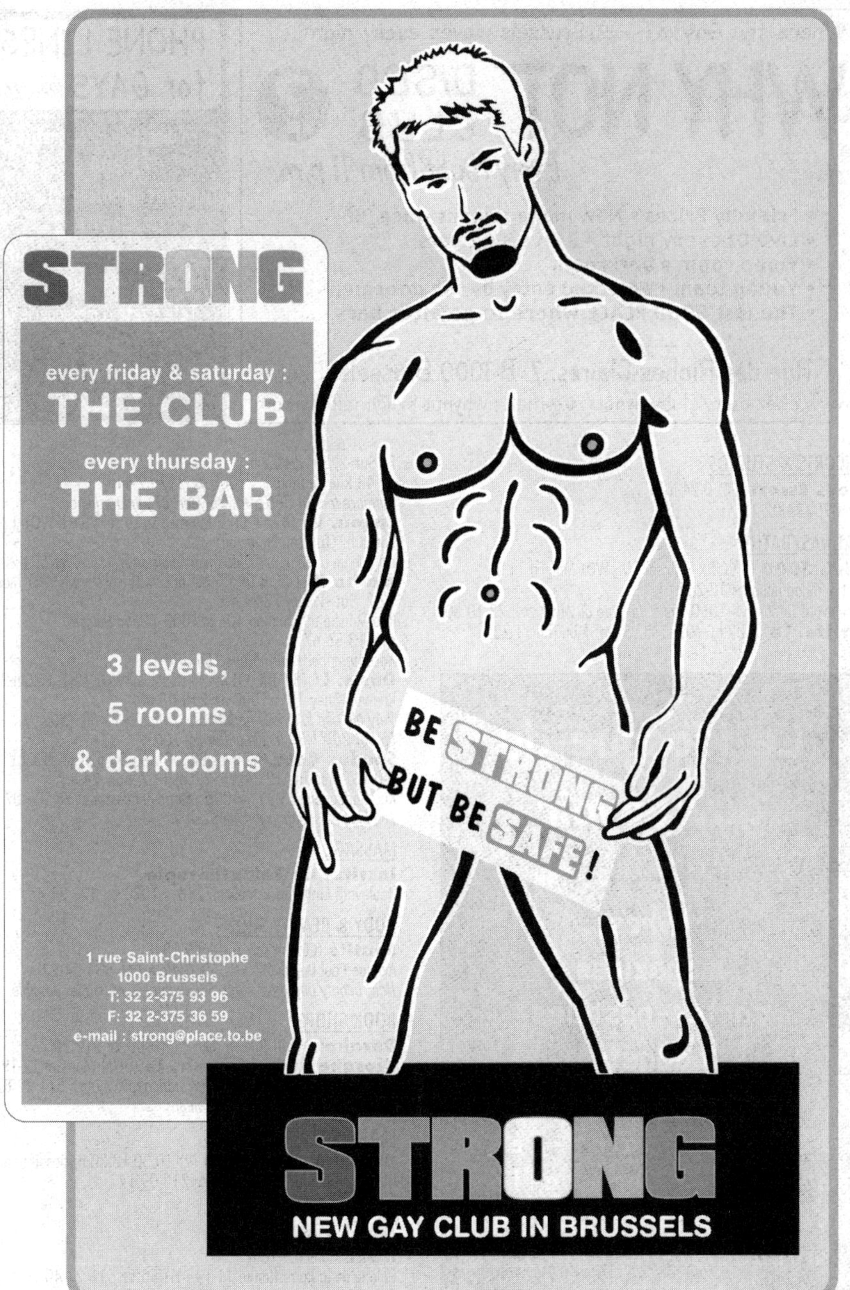
STRONG
every friday & saturday :
THE CLUB
every thursday :
THE BAR
3 levels,
5 rooms
& darkrooms
1 rue Saint-Christophe
1000 Brussels
T: 32 2-375 93 96
F: 32 2-375 36 59
e-mail : strong@place.to.be
BE STRONG
BUT BE SAFE!
STRONG
NEW GAY CLUB IN BRUSSELS

ESCORTS & STUDIOS

Boys Escort (CC) 0-24 h
☎ 095/24 02 12

SAUNAS/BATHS

Club 3000 (B CC DR G sb sol T VS WO) Mon-Fri 11-24, Sat Sun and holidays 12-24 h
Boulevard Jamar 9 ✉1060 *(near the gare du Midi)* ☎ 522 10 50

Griffe. La (B DR f G MG sa sb VS wh) Mon-Thu 11-22, Fri Sat -2, Sun 14-22 h
41-43 Rue de Dinant ✉1000 ☎ 512 62 51
Entrance-fee Bfr 300-500. 25 years of sauna tradition.

Lagon. Le (B bf F DR G MA msg sa sb sol VS wh WO) 12-24, Sat -2 h. (Tue Thu Fri mixed)
86 Rue de Livourne ✉1050 *(near Palais de la Justice)* ☎ 534 20 74

Macho 2 (! AC B DR f G MA pi s sa sb sol VS wh WO) Mon-Fri 12-2, Sat -4, Sun 12-24 h
Rue Marché au Charbon 106 ✉1000 *(Metro-Bourse)*
☎ 513 56 67
Recommended! Entrance-fee Bfr 300-450.

Oasis. L' (B F DR G H MA sa sb sol wh WO) 12-1, Fri Sat-2 h.
Rue van Orley 10 ✉1000 ☎ 218 08 00
Very big and luxurious bath house. Entrance-fee Bfr 450. Fri Sat 20-21.30 h cold buffet Bfr 100.

Spades 4our (AC b CC DR F G msg OS p pi sa sb sol VS wh WO YG) Mon-Thu 12-24, Fri -2, Sat 14-2, Sun -24 h
Rue Bodeghem 23-25 ✉1000 *(Metro-Anneessens)* ☎ 502 07 72
The biggest sauna in Belgium.

MASSAGE

Institut de Relaxtherapie
Boulevard Emile Bockstaellaan 293 ✉1020 ☎ 420 21 46

BODY & BEAUTY SHOPS

Santi's (CC glm sol) Tue-Sat 9-18 h
Avenue Paul Dejaer 22 ✉1060 *(U-Horta)* ☎ 534 64 22
Hair, beauty and dress shop. Solarium ansd massages possible.

BOOK SHOPS

Darakan (glm) Rue du Midi 9 ✉1000 ☎ 512 20 76

Kiosque du gay savoir. Le (GLM) Mon-Sat 12-19 h
Rue Saint Jean 13 ✉1000 *(near station railway)* ☎ 511 22 87
Bookshop, gadgets, postcards, videos.

LEATHER & FETISH SHOPS

Boutique Minuit (g LJ TV) 10.30-18.30 h, closed Sun
Galerie du Centre 60 ✉1000 ☎ 213 09 14
Also Mail Order.

TRAVEL & TRANSPORT

ISBEL Mon-Fri 9-18 h
Galerie de la Porte Namur 11-13 ✉1050 ☎ 511 22 40
Travel Agent.

VIDEO SHOPS

Vidéo Square at Woluwe Shopping Center (g VS)
Woluwe Saint Lambert 1200 ✉1000 ☎ 762 97 80

HOTELS

Bedford (B E F g)
Rue du Midi 135 ✉1000 ☎ 512 78 40
Downtown location/au centre, 20 km to the airport. All rooms with telephone, private bath, WC, and fridge. Fax: 514 17 59

Ecrins. Les (b bf CC G H MG)
Rue du Rouleau 15 ✉1000 *(Centrally located. 12 km to Zaventhem Airport, M-Sainte Catherine)* ☎ 219 36 57 Fax: 219 36 57
Homepage: http://www.lesécrins.com
Comfortable, hospitable 100-year old hotel. Beautiful, spacious rooms. Rates bfr 1300-2400.

Hotel Dolphy (bf CC glm H)
Boulevard Jamar 23 ✉1070 ☎ 15 20 09 39
Rates from Bfr 1300 (1 person) to 2.100 (3 persons). All rooms with shower, WC, and phone.

Hotel Noga (B bf CC f glm H)
Rue du Beguinage 38 ✉1000 *(Metro-Sainte Catherine)*
☎ 218 67 63 Fax: 218 16 03
Email: info@nogahotel.com

Potinière. La (B g H)
Place St. Géry 29-30 ✉1000
(M-Bourse) ☎ 511 01 25 Fax: 511 01 25
Centrally located. All rooms with shower/WC. Single bfr 950, double 1500 (bf incl.)

GENERAL GROUPS

Act up Bruxelles
Impasse de la Fidélité 11 ✉1000
☎ 512 02 02 Fax: 512 00 07

CHE - Cercle Homosexuel Etudiant de l'ULB
(d GLM W YG) Tue 18-20, Thu 18.30-19.30 h
Avenue Jeanne 38 ✉1050 ☎ 650 25 40
Gay students. Call for info on activities.

English-speaking Gay Group (E.G.G.)
BP 198 ✉1060 ☎ 537 47 04

Holebi's-jongeren (HLB-Brussel) (GLM)
PO Box 32 ✉1040

Homo- en Lesbienneorganisatie Infor-Homo (GLM)
De Roodebeeklaan 57 ✉1040 ☎ 733 10 24

Werkgroep Gehuwde homo's, lesbiennes en partners (GLM)
Lindestraat 106 ✉1640 ☎ 356 86 96

FETISH GROUPS

Spanklub Meeting: 3rd. Sun 15 h at the Duquesnoy
☎ 532 68 78

HEALTH GROUPS

Aide Info Sida Mon-Fri 9-20 h
Rue Duquesnoy 45 ✉1000 ☎ 511 45 29

Ex Aequo Mon-Fri 9.30-17 h
Rue de Tervaete 89 ✉1040 *(Metro-Thieffry)* ☎ 736 38 61
Fax: 733 96 17 Homepage: http://www.exaequo.be
Gay association for Aids and other sexual diseases prevention . Also shop selling condomes & lubricants.

Foundation. The Mon-Thu 10-13 14-18, Fri -17 h, closed Sat-Sun
Diksmuidelaan 49-51 ✉1000 ☎ 219 33 51
Counselling, care and buddy system for PWAs. Testing available.

Groupe de Santé d'Antenne Rose
PO Box 888 ✉1000

Service aux Séro-Positifs
☎ 219 67 95

HELP WITH PROBLEMS

Infor Homo (AC B GLM MA) Wed Fri 20-24, Helpline: Mon-Fri 20-22 h
Avenue de l'Opale 100 ✉1030 *(near R.T.B.F, Metro-Diamant)*
☎ 733 10 24 Fax: 732 10 81 Email: regard@eurnet.be
Gay Switch Board Centre.

Telegal 20-24 h
PO Box 1969 ✉1000 ☎ 502 79 38
Anonymous chat-line.

RELIGIOUS GROUPS

Communauté du Christ Liberateur Group de Chrétiems Gays A.S.B.L. (b GLM MA P WE) 2nd 4th Sun 18.30-21 h
PO Box 104 ✉1000 ☎ 762 94 70

SPECIAL INTEREST GROUPS

Girth & Mirth - Belgium asbl (CC G lj MA)
☎ 071/56 05 80 Fax: 071/51 84 01
Email: girth&mirth@must.be
Homepage: http://www.biggerworld.com
Club for fat men, bears and their admirers. Publishes a magazine „Fat Angel Times". Organizes events and conventions mostly in Brussels. Regular meetings in Oasis Sauna. Call for information on activites.

SPORT GROUPS

Brussels Gay Sport
Rue du Midi 32 ✉1000 *(Metro-Bourse)* ☎ 514 50 88 Fax: 514 51 09 Email: bgs@bgs.org
Homepage: http://www.bgs.org
Contact them for details on activities.

Federation Arc-en-Ciel
c/o Thierry Glinne, Avenue des Saison 59 ✉1050 ☎ 646 25 83

CRUISING

-Bois de la Cambre „drève de Lorraine" (near Chaussée de La Hulpe, from noon till sunset)
-Central Station (daytime in the main hall and at the buffet. From 21-1 h facilities and areas downstairs and Jardins de l'Alberti)
-Parc du Cinquantenaire (when you come from Shuman, enter the park and turn to the right) (AYOR)
-Parc Royal/Parc Astrid (until 22 h)
-Lobby of Line 3 underground station „De Brouckere" (especially exit opposite of the movie theater Eldorado)
-Place Fernand Coq
-Place de la Vaillance (WE)

Charleroi ✉ 6000 ☎ 071

BARS

Bahamas. Le (B GLM p TV) 21-6 h
Rue Vauban 13 ✉6000 *(Ville Haute)* ☎ 32 63 15

Entre Deux. L' (B glm)
Boulevard J. Bertrand 61 ✉6000 ☎ 30 03 35

Fifty-Fifty. Le (B glm)
Boulevard J. Bertrand 62 ✉6000 ☎ 30 88 60

Provence. Le (B g) 11-3 h
Rue de la Régence 69 ✉6000 ☎ 30 17 21

SEX SHOPS/BLUE MOVIES

Cine Turenne (g VS)
Rue Turenne 54 ✉6000

Fantasme (g VS)
Rue de la Turenne 45 ✉6000
☎ 30 23 29

BOOK SHOPS

Nouvelle (g)
4-6 Passage de la Bourse ✉6000 ☎ 31 81 33

HEALTH GROUPS

Sida MST info Mon-Fri 8-16 h
13 Boulevard Joseph II ✉6000 ☎ 23 31 11

CRUISING

-Hotel de Ville (rue Turenne)
-Park near Palais de Justice (AYOR) (near lion statues)

De Panne/La Panne ☎ 058

BARS

Oasis (B G)
Duikerkelaan ✉8470 *Cocktail Bar.*

CAFES

Tearoom The Classics (B F g YG) 10-24 h
Zeedijk 1 ✉8470 ☎ 41 20 19

HOTELS

Imperial (A AC B bf CC d E F g H OS S W) 9-23 h
Lepold I Esplanade 9 ✉8660 ☎ 41 42 28
Located on the beach with conference facilities.

CRUISING

-Monument Léopold Ier (Esplanade. Evenings)
-Leffrinckouke (+1 h walk near factory hall. Very popular.)

Dendermonde/Termonde

RESTAURANTS

'T Blaffertuurken (CC B F g) 11.30-23 h
Hierbaan 27 ✉9220 ☎ 052/21 80 95
International specialities.

GENERAL GROUPS

Homo- & lesbi-jongerengroep Liever Spruitjes (GLM)
PO Box 130 ✉9200 ☎ 053/21 59 43

Genk ✉ 3600 ☎ 011

CAFES

Cheers (b glm OS) winter 11-21 summer 10-1h
Rootenstraat 19, Shopping II ✉3600 ☎ 35 49 56

Gent/Gand ☎ 09

GAY INFO

Boys Town Sun 19-21 on FM 107.7; Tue 20-21 h on 103.3 (Aalst)
Vlaanderenstraat 22 ✉9000 ☎ 233 60 09
Email: Boystown@geocities.com
Homepage: http://www.xs4all.be/superstar/boystown

Fonds Suzan Daniel (GLM)
Postbus 569 ✉9000 ☎ 223 58 79 Email: suzan.daniel@skynet.be
Gay-Lesbian archives and documentation centre.

Holebi-Foon (GLM) Mon-Sat 18-22, Wed 14-22 h
Vlaanderenstraat 22 ✉9000 ☎ 238 26 26 Fax: 225 71 77
Gay and lesbian information switchboard.

BARS

Dandy's Club (B D E G h MA os p tv) 18-? h, closed Mon
Princes Clementinalaan 195 ✉9000 ☎ 220 51 81

King Street (B G MA) 21-7 h
Kammerstraat 49 ✉9000

Krypton (B D g) Sat Sun 20-? h
Ter Kameren 2 ✉9620 ☎ 360 63 27

Oase (B g)
Botestraat 84 ✉9032 ☎ 091/53 08 08

Pablo (B CC D G MA OS p YG) 21-? h
Princes Clementinalaan 195 ✉9000 ☎ 245 02 99
New decoration every two months.

Paradox (A AC B d GLM MA) Café: Thu-Sun 20-?; Club: Wed 22-?; Café + Club Sat 21-? h
Vlaanderenstraat 22 ✉9000 ☎ 233 70 40

Por que no (B g) Thu-Mon 21-? h
St. Denijslaan 155 ✉9000 ☎ 222 53 70

Zénon (B G MA) 11-1, Fri Sat 14-2 h
St. Veerleplein 7 ✉9000

CAFES

Cocteau (F g) Tue-Sun 11-? h
Jan Palfijnstraat 19 ✉9000 ☎ 233 52 68

Grote Avond. De (F g) Wed-Sun 18-3 h
Huidevetterskaai 40 ✉9000 ☎ 224 31 21

Ludwig (glm) Tue-Sun 11-1 h
Hoogpoort 37 ✉9000 ☎ 223 71 65

Sphinx (glm) Mon-Fri 19-2, Sat Sun 14-2 h
Sint Michelshelling 3 ✉9000 ☎ 225 60 86

RESTAURANTS

Avalon (B F glm) 12-14 h, closed Sun
Geldmunt 37 ✉9000

Cassis (bf CC F g MA T OS) 10-23 h
Vrijdagmarkt 5 ✉9000 *(centre)* ☎ 233 85 46

Malcontenta. La (B F glm)
Tue-Sat 12-14, Thu-Sat 20-22 h
Haringsteeg 7 ✉9000 ☎ 224 18 01

Olivier's (AC B E F g T) 12-23 h
Vrijdagmarkt 16 ✉9000 ☎ 224 20 40
Traditional cuisine.

Oranjerie (CC F glm) 12-14, 18-22 h, closed Tue Wed
Corduwaniersstraat 8 (Patershol) ✉9000 ☎ 224 10 08

Vier Tafels. De (b F g) Mon-Sun 11.30-14.30 h
Plotersgracht 6 ✉9000 ☎ 225 05 25

Walry (B F glm) 8-18 h, closed Sun
Zwijnaarsesteenweg 6 ✉9000

SEX SHOPS/BLUE MOVIES

Libidos-Erotheek (g MA VS) Mon-Sat 12-22 h
Kuiperskaai 4 ✉9000 ☎ 223 93 88

SAUNAS/BATHS

Boys Avenue (B F DR G MA sa sb VS) 12-24, Fri -1, Sun 15-24 h
Oude Schaapsmark 1A ✉9000 ☎ 225 40 78
Entrance-fee Bfr 500.

BOOK SHOPS

De Brug (glm) 6.30-22, Sun 9-21 h
Phoenixstraat 1 ✉9000 ☎ 226 38 69

Walry (g)
Zwijnaardsesteenweg 6 ✉9000 ☎ 221 85 08

HOTELS

Hotel Erasmus (bf CC g H OS) closed from 15th Dec to 15th Jan
Poel 25 ✉9000 *(central)* ☎ 225 75 91
Fax: 233 42 41 Email: jan.de.baets@pandora.be
Small friendly hotel in a 16th century house. All rooms with bath ,

GUEST HOUSES

Chambres d'amis (bf H glm OS)
Schoolstraat 14 ✉9040 *(2 km from the city centre, near Campo Santo and Sint-Amandsberg)* ☎ 238 43 47
Recently renovated and redecorated „gentleman's house".

GENERAL GROUPS

Federatie Werkgroepen Homoseksualiteit (FWH) Mon-Thu 9-17, Fri -16.30 h
Vlaanderenstraat 22 ✉9000 ☎ 223 69 29
-Werkgroep Biseksualiteit

Het Gehoor (GLM)
Sint-Niklaasstraat 7 ✉9000
☎ 225 75 99 Email: hetgehoor@skynet.be Homepage: http://users.skynet.be/hetgehoor
Gent gay and lesbian group.

Verkeerd Geparkeerd (GLM YG)
PO Box 535 ✉9000
Young gay and lesbian group. Write for info.
Email: vege@student.rug.ac.be

Werkgroep Gehuwde Homo's, Lesbiennes en Partners Gent (GLM)
Kalkoenlaan 37 ✉9032
☎ 253 80 65

Werkgroep Ouders van Homo's en Lesbiennes
Coupure 604 ✉9000 ☎ 223 58 79

RELIGIOUS GROUPS

Werkgroep Homo en Geloof Gent (GLM)
PO Box 8640 ✉9030 ☎ 226 78 01

SPORT GROUPS

Sportclub Auricula (GLM)
Korenveldstraat 17 ✉9032 ☎ 236 53 39

CRUISING

-Blaarmeersen (Watersportbaan, at foot of hill)
-Station (M. Hendrikaplein)

Hasselt ✉ 3500 ☎ 011

BARS

Renegade (AC B d f glm MA s) 20-? h closed Sun
Fonteinstraat 2 ✉3500 ☎ 28 10 28

GENERAL GROUPS

Holebi-Jongeren Nota Bene (GLM YG)
PO Box 137 ✉3500 ☎ (089) 85 65 06

Limburgs Actie Centrum Homofilie (LACH) (GLM MA W) Tue Fri 20-22
c/o C.G.S.O., Wijngaardstraat 1 ✉3500 ☎ 21 20 20

Werkgroep Gehuwde Homo's, Lesbiennes & Partners Hasselt (GLM)
Wijngaardstraat 1 ✉3500

Werkgroep Ouders van Holebi's
✉3500 ☎ 23 26 05

RELIGIOUS GROUPS

Cristen Gewoon Anders (H & G Limburg)
p/a Wijngaardstraat 1 ✉3500 ☎ 28 47 62

Herentals ☎ 014

LEATHER & FETISH SHOPS

Philippe Moda Pelle (CC GLM LJ) Mon-Fri 8-16.30, Sat 11-16.30 h
Bovenrij 25 ✉2200 *(20 min from Antwerpen, next to the Townhall)* ☎ 21 91 03
Hand made top quality leather clothing.

Herzele ☎ 053

GENERAL GROUPS

Anders (GLM)
Groenlaan 39 ✉9550 ☎ 62 64 36

Knokke-Heist ☎ 050

BARS

Apero. L' (AC B CC f g OS s) 21-6 h
Zoutelaan 3 ✉8300 *(near Lippenslaan)* ☎ 62 75 40

Night Flash Bistro (B F g MA) 19-7 h, closed Tue
Lippenslaan 48 ✉8300 ☎ 61 23 50

RESTAURANTS

De Bolle (B bf CC F GLM H MA) 11.30-14.30, 18-24 h
Vlamingstraat 62 ✉8301 *(Heist)* ☎ 51 43 04 Fax: 51 43 04
Restaurant bar with rooms to rent.

Koekelaere ☎ 051

CAFES

'T Vosmotje (B F GLM)
Marktplein ✉8280 ☎ 58 97 48

Kortrijk/Courtrai ☎ 056

GAY INFO

G.O.C. Kortrijk Wed, Thu, Sun 20-24, Fri -2, Sat -? h
Papenstraat 9 ✉8500 ☎ 21 75 42

BARS

Bronx. The (A AC B CC D E GLM MA P) Mon, Wed, Thu 22-?, Fri-Sun 21-? h, closed Tue
Kasteelkaai 5 ✉8500 ☎ 21 96 74

Burning Love (B G MA)
Doorniksewijk 113 ✉8500

Pink Panther. The (B G MA) Fri-Sun 20-2 h
Papenstraat 9 ✉8500

Vagabond (AC B CC D E f GLM lj MA p VS W) 22-? h
Meensesteenweg 80 ✉8500 ☎ 35 41 13

RESTAURANTS

'T Kopje (b F g) 13-1 h
Grote Markt ✉8500

SAUNAS/BATHS

Sauna Aquarius (B CC DR f G MA OS p pi sa sb VS wh) 13-24 h
Moeskroensesteenweg 1 ✉8501 *(between Mouscron and Kortrijk, highway N43)* ☎ 20 25 33 Fax: 25 34 58
Entrance-fee Bfr 500.

GENERAL GROUPS

Detrain Homojongeren (GLM YG)
Papenstraat 9 ✉8500 ☎ 21 75 42
Gay youth group.

Korthom / Kortrijkse Homowerking (G)
Minister Tacklaan 99 ✉8500 ☎ 22 60 71

Werkgroep gehuwde homo`s en partners (GLM)
Papenstraat 9 ✉8500 ☎ 21 75 42

mardi au dimanche 10 h - 2 h du mat
The sound music café from Paris in Liège
31, place du Marché 4000 Liège Belgique
Le petit Paris
Open Tue - Sun from 10 h AM to 2 h AM

RELIGIOUS GROUPS

Homo & Geloof Kortrijk (GLM)
Beekstraat 38 ✉8500 ☎ 22 12 61

CRUISING

-Kasteelkaai-Rooseveltplein

Kuurne ✉ 8520 ☎ 056

DANCECLUBS

After Nine (AC B D E GLM MA p s) 21-? h, closed Tue
Brugsesteenweg 102 ✉8520 ☎ 35 76 18

La Louvière ✉ 7100 ☎ 064

BARS

Pub. The (B d GLM MA) 11-?, Sat 15-?, Sun 18-? h
Rue Kerasmis 31 ✉7100 ☎ 28 00 80

Leuven/Louvain ✉ 3000 ☎ 016

BARS

Exkeet (B glm) 21-? h, closed on Sun
Nerviersstraat ✉3000 ☎ 22 30 42
Frenkies. The (A AC B d G lj MA TV W) 21-? h, closed Wed-Thu
Schapenstraat 105 ✉3000 *(near Begijnhof)* ☎ 22 77 66

CAFES

Couperus en Cocteau (b GLM MA OS) 20-1.30 h, closedon Tue & Sat
Diestsestraat 245 ✉3000 *(near station)*
On Thu host of the local gay organisation.

GENERAL GROUPS

Holebi-Jongeren Het Goede Spoor (GLM YG)
PO Box 113 ✉3000 ☎ 20 06 06

HEALTH GROUPS

De Witte Raven HIV-café Fri 20 h
St.-Michielscentrum, Naamsestraat 57a ✉3000 ☎ 20 09 06

Liège/Luik/Luttich ☎ 04

GAY INFO

Gay-Center 10-2 h
Rue de Cathédrale 9 ✉4000

BARS

Jungle. La (B G MA) 22-? h, closed Tue
20 Rue Léon Mignon ✉4000 ☎ 222 07 75
Petit Paris. Le (B bf glm MA OS) Tue-Sun 10-2 h
Place du Marché 31 ✉4000 ☎ 223 54 96
Relax Café. Le (B d f GLM MA OS S TV YG) Mon-Sat 11-?, Sun 14-? h
Rue Pont d'Avroy 22 ✉4000 *(in front of the cinema „Palace")*
☎ 223 16 46 *Drag queen shows every 3rd week.*
Rio. Le (B g) 11-23 h
Gallerie Opéra ✉4000 *(first floor)* ☎ 223 19 28
Scène. La (B g) 11-?, Sun 15-? h
Rue de la Casquette 1 ✉4000 ☎ 223 11 43
Spartacus (AC B CC d DR G LJ MA P VS WE) 22-6 h
12 Rue Saint-Jean en Isle ✉4000 *(centre)* ☎ 223 12 59

DANCECLUBS

Mama Roma (AC B D GLM MA stv) 22-? h, closed Mon Tue
16 Rue des Célestines ✉4000 ☎ 223 47 69

RESTAURANTS

Bruit qui court. Le (CC B F g) 11-24, Fri Sat -2 h, closed Sun noon
Boulevard de la Sauvenière 142 ✉4000 ☎ 232 18 18
Colombier. Le (AC B E F glm MA) 19-? h, closed Thu
En Roture 58 ✉4000 ☎ 342 27 57
Italien. L' (B g F) En Bergerue 16 ✉4000 ☎ 223 15 69

SEX SHOPS/BLUE MOVIES

Majestix (g VS)
Rue de la Cathédrale 9 ✉4000 ☎ 232 10 51

SAUNAS/BATHS

Espace Man (B f G MA sa sb sol VS wh) 14-23, Fri-Sun -3.30 h, Sat (glm)
Rue des Célestines 9 ✉4000 ☎ 222 47 41
Sauna 2000 (b F DR G sa sol VS wh WO) Mon-Thu 15-24, Fri Sat 15-6, Sun 14-23 h
Rue des Français 139 ✉4430 ☎ 246 32 54

HOTELS

Must. Le (g H) 9-24 h, Sun closed
9 Rue Henri de Dinant ✉4000 ☎ 243 35 63
Room with bath bfr 980, bf 75.

GENERAL GROUPS

Association gay et lesbiennes à Liège (GLM)
PO Box 15 ✉4000

HEALTH GROUPS

Centre d'Aide pour le SIDA (U.L.G.) Mon-Fri 8.30-12, 13.30-17 h
95 Boulevard de la Constitution ✉4000 ☎ 243 41 75

SPECIAL INTEREST GROUPS

Parents d'enfant homosexuel
Mme F. Lambert, 30 Monfort ✉4050 ☎ 380 34 91

CRUISING

-Canal Albert, Ile-de-Monsin (near Albert I Monument)
-Parc d'Avroy
-

Lommel ✉ 3920 ☎ 011

BARS

Patho (B glm)
Dorp 63 ✉3920

RESTAURANTS

Lommelshuisje (F glm H) 16-? h closed Thu
Adelberg 51 ✉3920 ☎ 55 13 04

Mechelen/Malines ✉ 2800 ☎ 015

BARS

Bonaparte (B glm) 12-? h
Veemarkt 17 ✉2800 ☎ 21 85 46
Sebastiaan (AC bf B d GLM H MA OS) 12-?, Sat 14-?, Sun 16-? h, closed Thu
Brusselsesteenweg 203-205 ✉2800 ☎ 43 00 10
Provides bed & breakfast.

GENERAL GROUPS

Homo- en Lesbiennewerking Mechelen (HL-WM) (GLM)
PO Box 4 ✉2800 ☎ 43 21 20

CRUISING

-Railway station (especially near north entrance)

Menen ✉ 8930

BARS

Lagoen (B g MA)
Wervikstraat ✉8930

Mol ✉ 2400 ☎ 014

CAFES

Cher (AC B glm MA) 16-03, Tue & Sun 9-3 h
St.-Pieterstraat 5 ✉2400 ☎ 31 95 83

Mons/Bergen ✉ 7000

BARS

Half and Half Bar (B g) 20-? h
Rue de la Coupe 36 ✉7000

SEX SHOPS/BLUE MOVIES

New Sexy World (g) 10-23 h
Rue Léopold II 17 ✉7000 ☎ 35 16 61

CRUISING

-Around church gardens
-P Heppignies near Fleurus (highway from Mons to Namur, 10 km from Charleroi; both sides, day and night)

Namur/Namen ☎ 081

DANCECLUBS

Caves d'Apollon. Les (B D G) Wed 19-? h, Fri Sat 22-? h
Rue des Tanneures 13 B ✉5000 ☎ 075/68 00 77

HOTELS

New Hotel de Lives (B bf CC F glm H MA OS W)
Chaussée de Liege 1178 ✉5101 *(6 km from centre of Namur, Bus 12 / bus stop in front of the hotel)* ☎ 58 05 13
Hotel, restaurant, pub completely renovated. Ancient style.

HEALTH GROUPS

Namur Entraide Sida
3bis Château-des-Balances ✉5000 ☎ 22 24 22

Nieuwpoort ✉ 8620 ☎ 058

BARS

Boat. De (B D F glm YG) 18-2 h closed Mon
Watersportlaan ✉8620 ☎ 23 80 56

Oostende ✉ 8400 ☎ 059

GAY INFO

GOW Oostende
PO Box 131 ✉8400 ☎ 50 25 58

BARS

Art Gallery Bistro Mercurius (A B F g MA) 10-? h
Van Iseghemlaan 28 ✉8400 ☎ 80 67 44
Azo (B G MA)
Ooststraat 57 ✉8400 ☎ 51 18 92
Calypso (AC B f GLM MA OS) 16-?, Jul-Sep 10.30-? h
Groentenmarkt 15 ✉8400 ☎ 80 15 69
Rapsody (AC B D G MA YG) 21-? h, closed Tue
St. Franciscusstraat 29 ✉8400 ☎ 80 84 73
Taverne Ushuaia (B d Glm) 16-? h
Kleine Weststraat 13 ✉8400 *(near Wapenplein/Casino)* ☎ 075/27 43 18
Valentino (B D G MA) 22-? h
Schipperstraat 50 ✉8400 ☎ 50 29 26

CAFES

Café de Flore. Le (B F GLM M) 10-5 h, closed Tue
Kursaal (Oosthelling) ✉8400
Caruso (B bf f) bf from 6 h
Nieuwstraat ✉8400
Croisette. La (B F GLM) 11-? h, off-season closed Thu
Promenade Albert I 50 a ✉8400 ☎ 70 91 65
Dewulf (A B bf f glm) 7.30-19.30 h
Kapellestraat 32-34 ✉8400 ☎ 70 05 69
Gay bf place.
Mercurius (! A B bf CC E f g h MA OS) 10-? h, closed Tue
Van Iseghemlaan 28 ✉8400 ☎ 80 67 44
Provides rooms & apartments.
Piaf's. Le (B F GLM) closed Tue
Langestraat 90 ✉8400 ☎ 70 57 65

DANCECLUBS

Men 4 Men (AC B D DR G MA P S TV VS) 21.30-? h
Sint- Franciscusstraat 22 ✉8400 ☎ 70 30 67

RESTAURANTS

Cormoran. Le (B F GLM)
Langestraat 63 ✉8400 ☎ 70 11 60
Komedie. De (B F glm) 10-? h
Louisastraat 5 ✉8400 ☎ 51 27 98
Snacks and indian specialties.
New Sint James (AC B bf F g MA OS) 7.30-22 h, closed Mon
Canadaplein 2 ✉8400 ☎ 51 18 36
Van Eyck (B F glm) 19-?, closed Thu, meals -2 h
Hertstraat 10 ✉8400 ☎ 70 35 81

SEX SHOPS/BLUE MOVIES

Adonis (G MA VS) 12-22 h
Dwarsstraat 1B ✉8400 ☎ 51 43 01

Paradise (CC g VS) 11-23 h
Madridstraat 15 ✉8400 *(80 m from the casino)* ☎ 51 36 72
Books and magazines, rubber/leather and SM toys.

SAUNAS/BATHS

Kouros II (B f DR G msg sa sb sol VS wh WO) 15-24, Sat 14-4 h
Peter Benoitstraat 77 ✉8400 *(10 min from station)* ☎ 51 34 55
Entrance-fee Bfr 500.

Thermos (B G F sa sb sol VS WO) 14-24 h
Kaaistraat 34 ✉8400 ☎ 51 59 23 *Admission Bfr 500.*

HEALTH GROUPS

De Witte Raven HIV-café
Nieuwpoortsteenweg 85 ✉8400 ☎ 50 28 82

CRUISING

-Bredene (at the beginning of the dunes near the Military Hospital on the Blankenberghe side of Oostende in afternoons)
–By pier -

Pipaix ✉ 7904 ☎ 069

DANCECLUBS

Escargot. L' (B D glm MA) Sat 21-? h
13 Chaussée de Mons ✉7904 ☎ 66 36 50

Pittem ✉ 8740 ☎ 051

BARS

Retro (B d f G MA p) Wed Thu 20-5, Fri-Sun 21.30-6 h
Tieltstraat 38 ✉8740 *(between Brugge and Kortrijk)* ☎ 46 74 47

Rekkem ✉ 8930 ☎ 056

BARS

Blue Night (AC B d E f GLM p s) Thu-Mon 20-? h, Sun gay, closed Tue Wed
Vagevuurstraat 67 ✉8930 ☎ 40 16 55

Rillaar ✉ 3202 ☎ 016

DANCECLUBS

Viertap (B D g OS TV YG) Fri-Sun & holidays 20-8 h
Molenstraat 1 ✉3202 ☎ 50 08 63

Roeselare/Roulers ✉ 8800

BARS

Patrick's Pub (AC B d G OS P YG) Fri-Tue 18-?, every 3rd Wed 19-? h (DR NU)
St. Jorisstraat 25 ✉8800 *(5 min from station)* ☎ 075/46 42 34

GENERAL GROUPS

Werkgroep Ouders van Holebis
Spechtenwegel 8 ✉8800 ☎ 051/22 32 68

St. Niklaas ✉ 9100

GENERAL GROUPS

Homo- en Lesbiennegroep De Roze Waas
Truweelstraat 85 ✉9100

Tielt ✉ 8700

BARS

Barneyz (AC B D DR G MA OS P S SNU VS W) 21-? h
Brugstokwegel 2-4 ✉8700

Tienen/Tirlemont ✉ 3300 ☎ 016

RESTAURANTS

Verleiding. De (F glm) Minderbroederstraat 16 ✉3300 ☎ 81 32 80

Tournai/Doornik ✉ 7500 ☎ 069

BARS

Byblos (B g) Rue
St. Piat 51 ✉7500 ☎ 84 35 40

George Sant (B g)
Rue de Maux 21 ✉7500 ☎ 21 10 10

Petit Pelican (B G MA) 19-6 h
Brusselsesteenweg 1 ✉7500

Rêve d'O. Le (B E g)
Rue Point de L'Europe ✉7500

RESTAURANTS

Roi de Rome (b F g) Rue des Maux ✉7500

Turnhout ☎ 014

GAY INFO

Kempische Werkgroep Homofielie (B GLM)
Wed, Fri-Sun 21-3
Driezenstraat 25 ✉2300 ☎ 42 35 83
Contact Enter Plus (G MA), Exit (YG) and Werkgroep ouders van homo's at this address.

BARS

'T Kasteeltje (B d glm) Tue-Sat 11-?, Sun 14-? h
Kateelplein 8 ✉2300

RELIGIOUS GROUPS

Homoseksualiteit en Geloof (GLM)
Polderstraat 33 ✉2360 *(Oud-Turnhout)* ☎ 41 24 25

CRUISING

-P between Exit 24 and 25(A 34)

Veerle-Laakdal ✉ 2431 ☎ 014

MASSAGE

M & B's
Vorstsebaan 38 ✉2431 ☎ 84 04 55
By appointment during the week from 16-24, WE 12-20 h

Veurne/Furnes ✉ 8630 ☎ 058

CAFES

Fortuintje (B f glm MA N) 11-?, closed on Thu
Appelmarkt 1 ✉8630 ☎ 31 14 21

RESTAURANTS

Oude Vesten. D' (AC B CC F glm MA) 10.30-1 h
Oude Vestingstraat 69 ✉8630 ☎ 31 40 74
FAX 31 44 46. Email: geert.denorme@advaluas.be.

Waasmunster ✉ 9250 ☎ 052

GENERAL GROUPS

Werkgroep Ouders van Holebis
Rhodendries 53 ✉9250 ☎ 47 90 37

Wichelen ✉ 9260 ☎ 09

BARS

Cadillac (B D GLM YG) Sat 22-6 h
Watermolenweg 100 ✉9260 ☎ 369 53 60

Belize

Central America

Initials: BZ

Time: GMT -6

☎ Country Code / Access Code: 501 / 00

Language: English. Spanish, Creole, Carib, Mayan

Area: 22,965 km² / 8,867 sq mi.

Currency: 1 Belize Dollar (Bz$) = 100 Cents.

Population: 230,000

Capital: Belmopan

Religions: 58% Roman Catholic, 28% Protestant

Climate: Tropical climate, very hot and humid. The rainy season lasts from May to February.

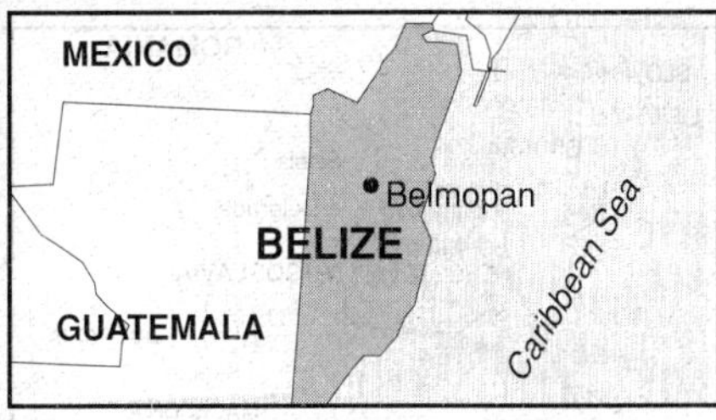

● Homosexuality is legal in Belize. However, it is worth keeping in mind that tolerance of gays among the general populace is limited.

✱ Die Ausübung homosexueller Handlungen ist in Belize legal. Allerdings sollte man beachten, daß sich die Toleranz der Bevölkerung gegenüber Schwulen in Grenzen hält.

▲ L'homosexualité n'est pas un délit à Belize. Notons cependant que, là-bas, les gens tolerent les gays, mais sans plus!

☆ En Belize la práctica del comportamiento homosexual es legal. De todas formas se debería tener en cuenta, que la tolerancia hacia los homosexuales es bastante limitada.

❖ In Belize l'omosessualità è legale, senonchè conviene tener presente che la tolleranza della popolazione è limitata.

Belize City

BARS

Bellevue Hotel (B CC D G WE YG) 22-? h
Southern Foreshore *(upstairs bar/main floor disco)*

Red Roof Lounge (B F g MA OS) Tue-Fri 17-24, Sat-3 h
3580 Sittee Street ☎ .

ESCORTS & STUDIOS

C & C Services
PO Box 22 31 ☎ 353 08

FITNESSTUDIOS

Body 2000 Carribbean Shores *(1 mile from Save U Supermarket towards Airport) $5 Daypass.*

HOTELS

Bakadeer Inn (AC bf)
Gleghorn Street *(5 min. from downtown in quiet side street)*
☎ 314 00
8 rooms with bath. Single $45 Double 55.

SPECIAL INTEREST GROUPS

For Us Club (g)
PO Box 2270

SWIMMING

-San Pedro/Ambergris Caye (Beach/Strand near/bei Ramons Village g NG YG)
-Punta Gorda (G MA) (beach at the mouth of the Moho River, only reachable by boat, boat reservations at Tourism Centre in Punta Gorda, 11 Front Street. ☎ (07) 2 834)

CRUISING

-Lindsbergs Landing (from Ramad to Pub Amnesia, Thu-Sat ca.3-2 h)

Bolivia

South America

Initials: BOL

Time: GMT -4

☎ Country Code / Access Code: 591 / 00

Language: Spanish

Area: 1,098,581 km² / 424,162 sq mi.

Currency: 1 Boliviano (Bs) = 100 Centavos

Population: 7,958,000

Capital: La Paz

Religions: 95% Roman Catholic

Climate: The climate varies with the altitude from humid and tropical to cold and dry.

● Homosexuality is not mentioned in the Bolivian law books. According to our information, the age of consent is 21. Violations may be punished with up to 5 years' imprisonment.

✱ Das bolivianische Strafgesetzbuch erwähnt Homosexualität nicht. Die Schutzaltersgrenze liegt nach unseren Informationen bei 21 Jahren. Auf Zuwiderhandlung stehen ein bis fünf Jahre Gefängnis.

▲ En Bolivie, l'homosexualité n'est pas un délit. D'après ce que nous savons, la majorité sexuelle est fixée à 21 ans. Les contrevenants risquent 5 ans de prison.

☆ El Código Penal boliviano no menciona la homosexualidad. Según nuestras informaciones, la edad de consentimiento es de 21 años. La contravención de esta disposición supone una pena que va desde uno hasta cinco años de cárcel.

❖ Il Codice Penale boliviano non nomina l'omosessualità. Secondo le nostre informazioni l'età minima per i rapporti è di 21 anni. I trasgressori possono essere condannati alla reclusione per una durata da uno a cinque anni.

Cochabamba

CRUISING

-La Plaza(dia o noche/day or night)
-El Prado (AYOR) (by night)

BARS

Bronx Bar (B D G MA p) 22-6 h, Sun-Tue closed
Pasaje Andrés Muñoz N° 2-Sopocachi *(Near Parque del Montículo)*
A little bit difficult to find but recommended.

CINEMAS

Microcine (NG)
Calle de Comercio

HOTELS

Panamericano (B F H NG)
Avenida Manco Kapac 454 ☎ 34 08 10
Downtown location. 7 km from the airport. All rooms with telephone, private bath. Single US$ 6.50, double 12.
Residencial Rosario (b F H M NG OS sa sb wh)
Calle Illampu 704
All rooms with shower, WC, heating. Rate double US$ 27. Booking essential.

CRUISING

-Plaza P. Velasco
-Plaza Mendoza
-Plaza San Francisco
-El Prado/Plaza de Estudieantes(mediodia y noche/midday and night)

Santa Cruz

BARS

Las Brujas (AYOR B glm R) -6 h
Avenida Cañoto/Avenida Landivar
Line (B D GLM r) 19-? h
Avenida 26 de Febrero, 1005

CRUISING

-Plaza 24 de septiembre
-Parque del Arenal (AYOR)
-Avenida Coñoto
-El Christo

Sucre

CAFES

Biblio Café (B NG)
Calle Nicolas Ortiz
En frente de la catedral/across from the cathedral.

CRUISING

-La Plaza(noche/night)

Bosnia-Herzegovina

Bosna i Hercegovina
Initials: BIH
Time: GMT +1
☎ Country Code / Access Code: 387 / 00
Language: Serbocroatian
Area: 51,129 km^2 / 19,741 sq mi.
Currency: Bosnian Dinar
Population: 3,365,000
Capital: Sarajevo
Religions: 44% Muslim 31% Serbian-Orthodox 17% Catholics
Climate: Summers are hot, winters cold. Areas of high elevation have short, cool summers and long, severe winters. Along the coast winters are mild and rainy.

● According to our information, homosexual acts between men in Bosnia-Hercegovina are not illegal.

✸ Nach unseren Informationen sind homosexuelle Handlungen zwischen Männern in Bosnien-Herzegowina nicht verboten.

▲ D'après ce que nous savons, l'homosexualité masculine n'est pas un délit en Bosnie-Herzégovine.

☆ Según nuestras informaciones la homosexualidad (entre hombres) en Bosnia-Herzegovina no está prohibida.

❖ Secondo le nostre informazioni l'omosessualità non è vietata in Bosnia-Erzegovina. Ciò vale però solo per l'omosessualità tra uomini.

Modriça ✉ 72400

CRUISING

-Park in Oktombarska Revulucija (day and night)

Mostar ✉ 88000

CRUISING

-Main Station

Sarajevo ✉ 71000

CRUISING

-Main Station
-Bus Station
-(P) Holiday Inn (in rear)

Zeucla ✉ 72000

CRUISING

-Park in front of Main Post Office (all night)

Brazil

Brasil

Central & northeastern South America

Initials: BR

Time: GMT -3/-4

☎ Country Code / Access Code: 55 / 00

Language: Portuguese

Area: 8,511,996 km² / 3,285,632 sq mi.

Currency: 1 Real (R$) = 100 Centavos.

Population: 169,806,557

Capital: Brasilia

Religions: 70% Roman Catholic

Climate: Mostly tropical climate, but the south is moderate.

Important gay cities: Rio de Janeiro, São Paulo, Salvador, Belo Horizonte, Recife

●The legal age of consent in Brazil is 18. A law has even been passed here to prevent the discrimination of sexual minorities. However, we have no information as to whether the police is continuing to arrest gays under the precept of »safeguarding morality and public decency«. However, there are large and colourful gay scenes in the big cities like Rio, Sao Paulo or Salvador.

✱Das Schutzalter liegt in Brasilien bei 18 Jahren. Es existiert ein Gesetz gegen die Diskriminierung sexueller Minderheiten. Allerdings wird von häufigen Übergriffen der Sicherheitskräfte vor allem auf Transvestiten und Transsexuelle berichtet. In den großen Städten aber, wie Rio, Sao Paulo oder Salvador, gibt es große und sehr bunte schwule Szenen.

▲Au Brésil, la majorité sexuelle est fixée à 18 ans pour tous. La loi protège les gays de toute discrimination liée à leur sexualité. Nous ne pouvons pas dire avec exactitude si la police continue à vouloir „protéger la morale et les bonnes moeurs" à sa façon. Dans les grandes villes comme Rio, Sao Paolo ou Salvador, ça bouge beaucoup au niveau gay.

☆La edad de consentimiento es de 18 años. Existe una ley contra la discriminación de las minorías sexuales. No nos es conocido si las fuerzas de seguridad continuan «protejiendo las costumbres y la moral pública». Pero en las grandes ciudades como Río, Sao Paulo o Salvador hay un ambiente gay muy colorido.

❖In Brasile l'etá legale per avere rapporti omosessuali é di 18 anni. Esiste una legge contro la discriminazione di minoranze sessuali. Non sappiamo se le forze dell'ordine proteggono ancora la „morale pubblica". Tuttavia nelle grandi città come Rio, San Paolo e Salvador esiste un'effervescente e variopinta vita gay.

NATIONAL GAY INFO

Grito De Alerta
Avenida Amaral Peixoto, 36 sala 1209, Niterói-RJ ☎ +55-21-722 14 58 Fax: +55-21-625 45 90

Nós por Exemplo
Rua da Glória, 30-Glória, Rio de Janeiro ☎ +55-21-252 47 57

OK Magazine c/o Trama Editorial Ltda.
PO Box 19113 ✉04.505-970 Rio de Janeiro

Angra dos Reis - Rio de Janeiro

CRUISING

-Beach in front of the town

Aracaju - Sergipe

GAY INFO

O Capital
Avenida Ivo Prado, 948 *(Centro)* ☎ 222 48 68

BARS

Aldo's Drink Bar
Rua Mal. Deodoro, 1185 *(Bairro Getúlio Vargas)*

Bug House
Rua Mariano Salmeron, 283 *(Bairro Siqueira Campos)*

Caras e Caras
Rua Napoleão Dórea, 355 *(Bairro Ataláia)*

Chico's Bar
Rua do Rosário, 555 *(Bairro Santo Antônio)*

Cine Ria Branco
Calçadão da Rua São João

Tenda do Moisés
Avenida Ivo Prado, 106 *(Centro)*

GENERAL GROUPS

Dialogay
PO Box 298 ☎ 235 81 69

Núcleo Homossexual
Caixa Postal 24, ✉49001-970

CRUISING

-O Calçadão (Rua João Pessôa; 18-24 h)
-Rua 24 horas (praia de Atalaia)

Belem - Parâ

BARS

Bar do Parque (AYOR b f G OS R) 0-24 h
Praça da República *(near Hilton)*

DANCECLUBS

Boite Luau Sexta (B D GLM OS) 22-4 h
Travessa Rui Barbosa, 729 ☎ 223 76 29

SAUNAS/BATHS

Gymnasium Apollo
Avenida Senenador Lemos

GENERAL GROUPS

Movimento Homossexual de Belém
PO Box 15 59, ✉66017-970

CRUISING

-Bar do Parque
-Bosque de Rodrigues
-Praça da Republica (YG) (Rua St. Antonio and J. Alfredo)
-Pierside and Market (day and early evenin

Belo Horizonte - Minas Gerais

BARS

Bar do Fernando (B g) closed Mon
Rua Sergipe/Avenida Brasil ✉30130 *(Savassi-suburb)*
Blue Way (B g) closed Mon
Rua Sergipe/Avenida Brasil *(Savassi-suburb)*
Caminho de Casa (B g)
Rua Barão de Macaúbas, 212 A *(Santo Antonio)*
Cantina Do Lucas (B F GLM YG)
Avenida de Lima 223, Loja 18 ✉30660 ☎ 226 71 53
POINT (B d f glm) Tue-Sat 19-? h Sun 16-? h
Rua Rio de Janeiro 1562
SO-HO (B G)
Rua Santa Rita Durão, 432 ☎ 221 77 43

DANCECLUBS

Fashion (B D G)
Rua Cláudio Manoel, 240 ☎ 223 71 71
Opera 60 (A AC B D E G SL VS YG)
Avenida Prudente de Morais, 921 ✉30380 *(Telemig Cid. Jadin)*
The Biggof's (B D G)
Rua São Paulo, 1245 Galpão Centro *(Gãlpao)*

CINEMAS

Cine Brasil
Praça Sete de Setembro
Cine Candelária
Praça Raul Soares s/n

SAUNAS/BATHS

Day Off (b f G sa sb VS WO) 13-24 h
Avenida do Contorno 4451, ✉30140 *(Funcionários)*
☎ 223 17 00
Hot House (b f g MA N sa sb)
Rua Guajajaras 1097 *(Centro)* ☎ 335 94 00
Sauna Off - 2000 (AC B CC DR f G MA msg pi sa sb VS wh WO) all time 24 h
Av. Diapoque 85 ✉30.111-070 ☎ 224 79 04
Sauna Vapore (AC B CC DR f G MA msg pi sa sb VS wh WO) all time 24 h
Rua Timbiras, 2523 ✉30.140-061 *(Centro)* ☎ 275 20 01

HOTELS

Papillon
Rua Rio de Janeiro, 639 Praça Sete *(Centro)* ☎ 212 38 11

CRUISING

-Avenida Alfonso Pena (from Rodoviaria to the town hall)
-Praca Raul Soares (R)

Brasilia - Distrito Federal

BARS

Beirute 109 W 3 Sul
Boite Aquarius (B D G WE)
Edificio Acropol, loja 12
☎ 225 99 28
Next to Cinema Superama Karim; go down the stairs at the side.
Karekas (B f g)
C-08 lote 18, loja 02, Taguatinga
Lobo Mau
W 3 Norte

CAFES

Café Savana (B F glm MA OS) 11.30-01.00 h, closed Sun
SCLN 116 Bloco A Loja 4 ✉70.773-510 ☎ 347 94 03

CINEMAS

Cine Bristol
Ed. Konic Seto de Divers°es Sul
Cine Karin
W 3 Sul

SAUNAS/BATHS

New Aquárius
Setor de Divers°es Sul *(Ed. Acropol-Subsolo)* ☎ 321 42 23
Sauna Hotel Nacional at Hotel Nacional (g)
SHS,Lote 1
Sauna Palladium (G r)
Near Praça do D.I.
Take the bus from Brasilia to Taguatinga, then a taxi to the sauna.
Thermas Calígola
Setor de Divers°es Sul *(Ed. Venâncio Junior-Subsolo)* ☎ 321 423

HOTELS

Byblos (H NG)
SHN 3, Lote E ☎ 223 25 70
If travelling alone, there is no problem taking someone home with you for the night if you have reserved a room for two.
Nacional Brasilia (H NG)
SHS, Lote 1 ☎ 226 81 81
Still one of the best hotels in town, but very expensive. If there is no official guest of the government while staying there, you can take a well dressed visitor to your room during the day. There is also a sauna where things can happen, but don't be too optimistic. 10 km to the airport. Single US$ 62, double 69 (bf incl.).

GENERAL GROUPS

Estruturação
PO Box 3636 ✉70084-970

CRUISING

-Avenida W-3 (after 24 h)
-Parque Nacional (swimming pools with warm mineral water; anywhere near the pool or the waterfall. Avoid toilets: military police!)

Curitiba - Paraná

BARS

Blue Jeans Bar (B g)
Alameda Dom Pedro II, 448
Classic Bar (B g)
Avenida Iguaçu, 550
Memories Bar (B g)
Avenida Visconte de Guarapuava, 3602

DANCECLUBS

Insanus
Rua Fernando Moreira, 185 ☎ 223 18 38

SAUNAS/BATHS

Sauna Caracalla (G sa VS) Rua Alferos Poli, 1039 ☎ 232 77 07
Sauna E Thermas 520 LTDA (AC B G MA msg N pi sa sb VS wh WO YG) 16-1 h
Avenida Souza Naves, 520/Cristo Rei ☎ 262 45 82
Therma for friends (g sa sb)
Alameda Dr. Muricy, 334 ☎ 223 67 65

CRUISING

-Rua XV de Novembre (park at the end of Rua das Flores)

Diamantina - Minas Gerais

BARS

Bar (B g)
Beco Alegrim, 39

Divinopolis - Minas Gerais

BARS

Chez Salim (B F g NG)
Avenida Primeiro de Junho/Rua Rio de Janeiro

Fortaleza - Ceará

BARS

Barraca A Pin E A Tosa (B d F glm MA N OS s WE YG) 0-24 h
Avenida Beira Mar 3101 23b-24a, Meireles ✉60.165-000 ☎ 242 49 62
Barraca do Joca (B bf F g N) 0-24 h
Avenida Presidente Kennedy, 3101, barraca 25-a *(on the Iracema Beach, across from Hotel Beira-Mar)* ☎ 261 46 03
Navy (B G) Avenida da Abolicao, 3303 c ☎ 263 31 22

DANCECLUBS

Kinze Trinta (AC B D G MA S WE) 23-6 h
Rua General Sampaio, 1530 *(Faculdade de Direito)* ☎ 252 15 49
Periferia (AC B D GLM S WE YG) 23-6 h
Rua Dragão do Mar, 260 *(near Cappitania dos Portos)* ☎ 252 32 08
Tabu Bar (B D GLM MA OS S WE) 23-6, Sun 15-6 h
Av. Santos Dumont, 1673 *(near Centro de Fisioterapia)* ☎ 261 51 23

SAUNAS/BATHS

Apollo Sauna (AC B DR f G msg p pi sa sb VS WO) daily 14-24 h
Rua Rodrigues Junior 1425 ✉60.060-001 ☎ 221 66 67
Thermus
Avenida Antônio Sales *(Aldeota)*

HOTELS

Hotel Passeio (AC bf g H MA)
Rua Dr. João Moreira 221 ✉60.030-000 *Centro, nearby Mercado Central* ☎ 226 96 40

GENERAL GROUPS

GRAB • Grupo de resistência asa branca
PO Box 421, ✉60001-970
Grupo Canto Livre
Rua Erico Mota, 1029, Parquelândia, ✉60540-170

SWIMMING

-Praia de Iracema
-Praia Canoa Quebrada (NU) (several hours from the city)
-Praia do Cumbuco (nu) (in the dunes at the far western end, 1 hour from the city, near Icarai)
-Praia Jericoacoara (several hours to the west of the city)

CRUISING

-Southwest corner of the Praça do Ferreira
-Praça do Carmo (behind the church)
-Along the downtown section of Duque de Caixas Avenue
-Downtown cinemas (by the entryways and in the restrooms)

Goiãnia - Goiás

HEALTH GROUPS

Grupo pela Vida
Rua 19, 35-Edificio Dom Abel (Centro) ✉74036-901 ☎ 225 86 39

CRUISING

-Near Teatro Goiãania (Centro)

Guarujá - São Paulo

BARS

Boate Aquarius (B g)
Avenida Floriano Peixoto, 913 *(Morro do Maluf)* ☎ 86 41 48

RESTAURANTS

Avelino's (B F g) P
raia do Pereque
Faro. II (B F g)
Rua Tracema, 38 *(Praia da Enseada)* ☎ 53 31 17

HOTELS

Casa Grande (H NG)
Avenida Miguel Stefano, 999 *(Enseada)* ☎ 86 22 23
Single US$ 57, double US$ 129.
Ferrareto (H NG)
Rua Mario Ribeiro, 564 *(Praia das Pitangueiras)* ☎ 86 11 12
Single US$ 23, double US$ 38.
Gávea (H NG)
Avenida Marechal Floriano Peixoto, 311 *(Praia das Pitangueiras)* ☎ 86 22 12 *Single US$ 52, double US$ 81.*
Guarujá Inn (H NG)
Ave da Inn Hotel ☎ 87 23 32 *Single US$ 81, double US$ 110.*

CRUISING

-Seashore Promenade around the facilities in City center
-Beach 30 km west of the city

Iguaçu, Fozdo - Paraná

HOTELS

Das Cataratas (AC B F H NG pi) Rod. BR 469 km 28 ☎ 74 26 66
Single US$ 77-107, double US$ 85-128.

Ilhéus - Bahia

HOTELS

Motel Barravento (B H NG R) Rua N. S. des Gracas *situated on Malhado beach*
Get a room in the annex with a refrigerator and priv. bath.

João Pessoa - Paraíba

RESTAURANTS

Peixada do João (F g) Rua Coração de Jesus (*Tambaú)*
Simple atmosphere but very good food.

HOTELS

Sol-Mar (H NG pi)
Avenida Rui Carneiro, 500 ☎ 226 13 50
Near airport. Single 22, double US$ 27.

GENERAL GROUPS

All-Ação Pela Liberdade Licás
Rua Abel Silva, 532, Cruz das Alomas ✉58.000-000
Movimento do Espírito Lilás
PO Box 224 ✉58001-970

SWIMMING

-Praia da Tambaba (first »official« nude beach in the northeast; about 30miles south of the town)

Macapá - Amapá

CRUISING

-The Jetty (active promenade)
-Zoological Gardens and steps to the cathedral on a small hill, downtown
-Sea Front
-Avenida Ribeiros

Maceió - Alagoas

BARS

LLe (B GLM YG)
Avenida Duque de Caxias

CINEMAS

Ideal
Avenida Dezesseis de Septiembro *(Levada)*

HOTELS

Hotel Praia Bonita (H NG)
Avenida Antonio Gouveia, 943 *(Pajuçara)*
Hotel Velamar (H NG)
Rua Antonio Gouveia, 1359 *(Pajuçara)*
Pousada Cavalo Marinho (bf F glm H)
Rua da Praia 55, Riacho Doce ✉57039.280 ☎ 355 12 47 Fax: 355 12 65 Email: cavmar@dialnet.com.br
Praia Hotel das Alagoas (H pi)
Rua Mario de Gusmão, 1300 *(Ponta Verde)*

SWIMMING

-Praia de Ponta Verde (YG) (popular)
–Jatiúca (in front of Praia Verde Hotel)
-Ilha do Croa (NU) (across the river at Barra de Santo Antonio)

CRUISING

-Praça Sinimbú (Avenida Duque de Caxias, 19-23 h)
-Praia de Jatiúca
-Praia do Francês
–Praia do Sabral

Maricá - Rio de Janeiro

HOTELS

Hotel Solar Tabauna (B bf glm H MA OS pi)
Rua Caxambú - Alto do Farol ✉249.000 *Nearby the beaches*
☎ 648 16 26

Natal - Rio Grande do Norte

HOTELS

Oasis Swiss Hotel (H)
Rua Joaquim Fabricio 291 ✉59.012-340 *between centre and beach* ☎ 202 27 66
Fax: 202 27 66

GENERAL GROUPS

GOLH (Grupo Oxente de Libertação Homossexual)
Rua Câmara Cascudo, 123 Sala 102 ✉59012-390
Grupo Habeus Corpus Potigúa
PO Box 576 ✉59022-970
SINTA
Rua Doctor José Neves, 25

RELIGIOUS GROUPS

Comunidade Fratriarcal
PO Box 346, RN 59001-970

CRUISING

-Along Potengi River

Niterói - Rio de Janeiro ☎ 24

DANCECLUBS

Disco Clube Imperial (B D F G pi S sb VS) 21-4 h. Fri & Sat shows.
Rua 2, No.20 *Recanto de Itaipuaçu. Last bus stop on the route Niterói-Itaipuaçu.* ☎ 709 22 42
Vollupya (B D G S VS)
Rua Coronel Tamarindo, 35 *(São Domingos)*

CINEMAS

Cine Central
Avenida Visconde do Rio Branco

HOTELS

Icarai Palace Hotel (AC B F NG sa)
Belisário Augusto, 21 ☎ 714 14 14
Hotel Pousada & Club Imperale (B D DR G H pi VS S)
Rua 2 n. 20 Recanto ✉24.900-000 *(Itaipuacu)* ☎ 638 15 81

SWIMMING

-Itaipu
-Recanto de Itaipuaçu

CRUISING

-São Francisco Beach and Ica Beach (from ferry take bus »Canto de Rio«)

Nova Iguaçu - Rio de Janeiro

BARS

Encantus
Rua Coronel Francisco Soares, 268 *(Centro)*
Nevada
Santa Luzia, 180 *Centro*
Rosa Choque
Avenida Governador Portela, 775 *(Centro)*

GENERAL GROUPS

28 de Junho
Rua Ataíde Pimenta de Moraes, 37 ✉26.210-210

Olinda - Pernambuco

BARS

Frutapão (B F glm OS) 17-24, Sun 16-22 h (GLM YG)
Rua do Sol 349 *(Sea Front near Busstop Olinda Carmo)*

Itapoã (! B GLM OS) 16-24 h
Avenida Markus Freire 897 *(Sea Front)*

Pool Bar at Hotel Pousada D'Olinda (B glm pi T)
Praça João Alfredo, 178 *(opposite San Pedro Church-Busstop Olina Carmo)* ☎ 439 11 63
During Carneval the intersections of Rua Prud. de Morais / Rua 13 de Maio / Rua Amparo (Quatro Cantos) !

RESTAURANTS

Atelier. l' (E F glm MA OS)
Rua San Bento 91 *(Quatro Cantos)*

Mourisco (A E F glm MA)
Praça João Alfredo 1st floor *(opposite Hotel Pousada D'Olinda-Busstop Olinda Carmo)*

Oficina do Sabor (E F glm MA OS)
Rua do Amparo 335 *(near Busstop Amparo)*

HOTELS

Hotel Pousada D'Olinda (AC B bf F glm H OS pi sol)
Praça João Alfredo 178 ✉53110 *(Olindo Historico-opposite Igreja San Pedro)* ☎ 439 11 63 Fax: 439 11 63

Pusada Peter (A AC b bf CC f H NG pi)
✉53.020-170 ☎ 439 31 71 Email: 439 31 71

GENERAL GROUPS

Grupo de Atuação Homossexual (GATHO)
Centro Luiz Freire, Rua 27 de Janeiro ✉53110 *(Carmo)* ☎ 429 34 45 Fax: 429 34 45

SWIMMING

-Olinda Casa Caiada
-Janga
-Pau Amarelo
-Maria Farinha (beach)
-Itamaraca Island (beach) (a few miles from Olind, easily accessible by bus, action possible at far end of the beach.)

CRUISING

-Beach at Praia da Enseada (15-? h, opposite Rio Doce)

Ouro Preto - Minas Gerais

BARS

Beco de Sata (B G S) 93 Rua San Jose

Porto Alegre - Rio Grande Do Sul

BARS

Bahamas (B G MA S TV VS YG) 23-? h
Avenida Farrapos, 2025 ✉90220-006

Cabaret Voltaire (B g)
Avenida Independencia, 590/Rua Garibaldi

Claudio's
Avenida João Pessoa *(near Avenida Venâncio Aires)*

Doce Vicio (B G pi) 18 h-? Closed Mon
Rua Vieira Castro, 32 *(between Jose Bonifacio & Avenida Venâncio Aires)*
Three floors with pool. Very popular befor clubs.

Fim de Seculo (B G) Thu Sun
Avenida Plinio Brasil Milano, 427 *(Auxiliadora)*

Fly Bar (B GLM) Fri-Sun 21 h-?
Rua Conçalo de Carvalho, 189

General de Gaulle (B G)
Rua Getulio Vargas *(around number 572)*
Male and female strip shows.

Ghetto (B g) Thu-Sun 23 h-?
Rua Independencia, 1004

DANCECLUBS

Enigma/Pandora Privé (! B D E GLM OS WE YG) Fri-Sat 23-? h
Rua Pinto Bandeira, 485 *(Downtown)*

Local Hero (B D G MA S)
Rua Venâncio Aires, 59 *(next to ABC Theatre)*

CINEMAS

Aurea
Avenida Julio de Castilhos

Capitólio
Avenida Borges de Medeiros

Carlos Gomes (g R)
Rua Vig. José Inacio, 335

Imperial
Rua dos Andradas, 1015

Lido (G)
Avenida Borges de Medeiros

São João
Rua Salgado Filho

ESCORTS & STUDIOS

Cowboys
☎ 331 85 74

Goodmen
☎ 228 71 60

SAUNAS/BATHS

Alternativa Tue-Sun 15-23 h
Rua Augusto Severo, 296

Hero Sauna (G B sa sb msg MA R VS) Mon-Sat 15-23 h closed Sun
Rua Visconde do Rio Branco, 390 *(Floreste. Between Travessa Azevedo & Rua Santa Rita)* ☎ 222 18 82
Young men in undershorts are hustlers (michés).

Hotel Plaza São Rafael (g sa sb msg)
Avenida Alberto Bins, 514 ☎ 221 61 00

Sauna Lucas de Oliveira (G sa pi VS) 15-23 h, Sat Sun and holidays 13-23 h
Rua Cel. Lucas de Oliveira, 24 *(between Rua 24 de Outubro and Rua Felipe Nera)*

MASSAGE

American Boys
☎ 225 55 61

Lima Rapazes
☎ 330 16 94

Rocky's
☎ 225 04 69

TRAVEL & TRANSPORT

Pink Side Travel Agency 9-? h
St. Mostardeiro, 157/CJS. 907/908 ✉90430-001
☎ 222 21 44 *or 222-304 or 222-2653 FAX 346-2650.*

GENERAL GROUPS

Nuances
PO Box 1747 ✉90.001-970 ☎ 221 63 63

HEALTH GROUPS

G.A.P.A. (HIV Positive Advice and AIDS)
Rua Luiz Alfonso, 234 *(Disque:Soliedariedade)* ☎ 221 63 67

CRUISING

-Praça Da Alfandega (toilets)
-Rua dos Andradas
-Avenida Borges de Medeiros
-Avenida Independencia
-Ipanema Bathing Resort (close to town)
-Belem Novo Bathing Resort
–Parque Farroupilha (Park-dangerous at night.)
-Rua da Praia Shopping

Porto de Galinhas - Pernambuco

HOTELS

Pousada Arco Iris (B bf F H pi sol WO) *(On the beach)*
☎ 552 14 46

SWIMMING

-Beach on seaside

Porto Seguro - Bahia

HOTELS

Pousada Cheiro Verde (b bf g H NG pi)
Estrada do Mucuge, 45820 *(near arrial d'Ajuda)* ☎ 875 12 05

Recife - Pernambuco

BARS

Bangue (B g OS YG) 17-22 h
Pátio de São Pedro *(Santo Antonio)*
Bar Savoy (B g MA OS R)
Avenida Guararapes,
147 *(Santo Antonio)* ☎ 224 22 91
Kibe (g MA OS R) Sat G R S 24-2 h
Avenida Herculano Bandeira (Pina)
Mustang (B F g MA OS)
Avenida Conde da Boa Vista *(near Mesbla)*
The gayest hours are 20-1 h.
Pit House (g MA OS)
Rua do Progresso *(Boa Vista-near Mustang)*
Porção Magica (g MA OS)
Rua do Progresso (Boa Vista-near Mustang)
Sete Cores (B D GLM MA OS R S)
Rua do Progreso, (Boa Visto-near Mustang)

CINEMAS

Ritz
Parque Treze de Maio (corner) *(Boa Vista)*

SAUNAS/BATHS

Clube Spartacus (AC B CC f G MA msg OS p R s sa sb VS WO) Sun-Thu 15.00-23.00 h Fri-Sun 15.00-5.00 h
Rua João Ivo da Silva, 95 ✉50.720-100 *(Madalena)* ☎ 228 68 28
Termas Center (B G MA msg os VS)
Rua do Sossego 62 (Boa Vista) ☎ 222 49 20
Thermas Athenas (A AC B bf CC DR f G MA msg p s sa sb VS WE YG) Sun-Thu 10.00-23.00 h Fri-Sat 10.00-9.00 h
Avenida Conselheiro Aguiar, 4790, 2nd Floor ✉51021 *(Boa Viagem)* ☎ 326 50 10

TRAVEL & TRANSPORT

Personalité Tour-Impresarial João Roma
Avenida Conselheiro Aguiar 2333 *(Boa Viagem)* ☎ 465 63 36
Travel Agent.

HOTELS

☛ see Olinda

SWIMMING

-also see Olinda
-Calhetas (near Gaibu, Cabo)
-Porto das Galinhas (40 miles from Recife)
-Gaibu- Beach (by bus from airport to Cabo and transfer)

CRUISING

-Avenida Conde de Boa Vista (AYOR r) (day and evening)
-Casa de Cultura (AYOR, TV) (shopping center on Avenida Beberibe)

Rio de Janeiro

● Rio is one of the largest and most cosmopolitan cities in the world. Including the suburbs, the city now numbers almost 16 million people. Rio has something to offer for everyone's taste. If you want to spend your days sunning on the beach and watching the masses of gorgeous gods of all races go by, and then in the evening throw yourself into the malestream of bars and discos, then the Copacabana district is the place for you. If all this commotion is too much, try the Ipanema section of town, where the pace is slower and there are fewer crowds. If you're more of a daytime person and want see what Rio's shops and markets have to offer, you will find what you are looking for in the Rio Branco district downtown. The bus service between Copacabana and the center of town is cheap and also runs regularly at night. The ride takes about ½ hour.
The Carnival, which has made Rio de Janeiro famous throughout the world, takes place every year, some time between the end of February and the beginning of March. You would be well advised to protect yourself against the high rate of criminal activity during this period.

✱ Rio gehört zu den aufregendsten Mammutstädten der Erde. Die Außenbezirke eingerechnet, zählt sie mittlerweile fast 16 Millionen Einwohner. Unterschiedlichste Bedürfnisse kommen hier zu ihrem Recht. Falls Sie gern tagsüber am weißen Strand schmoren (wo es von Schönheiten aller Rassen nur so wimmelt), um sich anschließend abends und nachts in das wilde Getümmel der Bars und Discos zu stürzen, so finden Sie Ihr Paradies vermutlich in Copacabana. Ein wenig gesetzter geht es in Ipanema zu, hier sind auch nicht ganz so viele Menschen. Wenn Sie jedoch eher ein Tagmensch sind und erleben möchten, was Rios Märkte und Läden Ihnen so alles zu bieten haben, dann sind Sie am besten in der Zentrumsgegend des Rio Branco aufgehoben. Die Busverbindungen zwischen Copacabana und der Innenstadt sind billig und werden auch nachts aufrechterhalten. Die Fahrzeit beträgt, je nach Uhrzeit, eine halbe bis eine Stunde. Der legendäre »Carneval«, der die Stadt Rio de Janeiro auf der ganzen Welt berühmt gemacht hat, findet, je nach Jahr, zwischen Ende Februar und Anfang März statt. Hierzu gehört allerdings auch das Einstellen auf eine sehr hohe Kriminalitätsrate.

▲ Rio est une des plus excitantes mégapoles du monde. 16 millions de personnes vivent dans son agglomération. Ici, tous vos souhaits seront exaucés! A Copacabana, vous pouvez vous faire dorer sur la plage au milieu de beautés de toutes races pour, le soir venu, vous plonger dans l'animation des nombreux bars et night clubs. Le paradis! A Ipanema, c'est un peu plus calme et beaucoup moins agité. Si vous êtes plutôt „du jour" et que vous voulez faire du lèche-vitrines, vous traînerez sûrement du côté de Rio Branco, dans le centre. Les bus entre Copacabana et le centre de la ville sont bon marché et circulent aussi la nuit. La durée du trajet varie d'une demi-heure à une heure.
Rio est connue dans le monde entier pour son carnaval qui a lieu chaque année vers la fin février et le début mars. Soyez sur vos gardes: recrudescence de la délinquance à cette époque-là!

☆ Río es una de las mega-ciudades más excitantes de nuestro planeta, incluiendo los barrios circundantes, cuenta actualmente con un total de casi 16 millones de habitantes. Aqui realmente es posible encontrar satisfacción para los deseos más dispares. Así sea dejarse tostar por el sol sobre las blancas arenas de la playa, donde se pueden observar bellezas de todas razas o por las noches dejarse precipitar en el tumulto incesante de bares y discotecas, si esto es lo que se busca, el paraíso está en Copacabana. En Ipanema el ritmo no es tan acelerado, y además todo está un poco menos abarrotado. En caso que usted sea un pájaro del día y desee contemplar todo lo que pueden llegar a ofrecer los comercios y mercados de Río, su lugar ideal de residencia encontraría en el centro, en los alrededores de Río Branco. Las líneas de autobúses entre Copacabana y el centro urbano son baratas y funcionan también de noche. El trayecto suele durar de 30 minutos a una hora. El carnaval, que tan famoso ha hecho a Río de Janeiro en el mundo entero, tiene lugar entre finales de febrero y principios de marzo, dependiendo del año. Lamentablemente, estos dias conllevan una alta criminalidad.

❖ Rio è una della città più cosmopolite del mondo. La popolazione, periferie incluse, ha raggiunto approssivamente i 16 milioni. Questa città offre qualcosa per i gusti di ognuno. Se volete abbronzarvi sulla spiaggia e guardare splendide bellezze di ogni razza e durante la sera tuffarvi nel tumulto di discoteche e bar, allora Copacabana è il posto che fa per voi. Ipanema al contrario è una parte della città un po' più quieta e meno affollata. Se invece preferite vivere di „giorno", visitate i mercati e i negozi che Rio ha da offrirvi, il quartiere di Rio Branco saprà prendersi cura di voi. Il servizio di autobus che collega Copacabana al centro della città è conveniente e funziona anche la notte. La durata degli spostamenti varia da mezz'ora a un'ora. Il leggendario carnevale che ha reso Rio famosa in tutto il mondo ha luogo, secondo l'anno, tra la fine di febbraio e l'inizio di marzo. In questo periodo aumenta anche il tasso di criminalitá.

TOURIST INFO

Companhia de Turismo da Cidade do Rio de Janeiro (Riotur)
Rua da Assembléia, 10 / 7. e 8. andares ✉20011-000
☎ 531 15 75 Fax: 531 25 06

BARS

Casa Grande
Rua Coronel Tamarindo, 2552 *(Bangu)* ☎ 331 21 71
Guetto (B D G MA)
Rua Muniz Barreto 448 *(Botafogo)*
Jumpin Jack (AC B d E F G N YG)
Rua Visconde Silva N° 13 *(Botafogo)*

DANCECLUBS

Boemio (B D G S) Disco Fri-Sun 23-?, show 2 h
Rua Santa Luzia, 760 *(Centro)* ☎ 240 72 59
Boite 1140 (AC B D G S YG) Fri Sat 22-?, Sun 19-? h
Rua Captião Menezes, 1140 *(Praça Seca)* ☎ 390 76 90
Popular on WE.
Boy Disco. Le (! AC B D e G P S YG) Tue-Sun 21-3 h, closed Mon
Rua Raul Pompéia, 94 *(Copacabana)* ☎ 521 03 67
Show at 1.30 h. Popular on Tue, Sat and Sun.
Cabaré Casa Nova (B D G MA S) 23-?, show 1.30 h
Avenida Mém de Sá, 25 *(Lapa)*
Cueva. La (B D G OG R) 23-? h, closed Mon
Rua Miguel Lemos, 51 *(Copacabana)* ☎ 23767 57
Gaivota (B D G) Tue-Sun 23-? h, closed Mon
Avenida Rodolfo de Amoedo, 347 *(Barra da Tijuca)*
Popular on Sun
Incontru's Disco (B D E G S) 21-3 h, WE longer
Praça Serzedelo Correia, 15A *(between Avenues Copacabana and Atlantica) (Copacabana)* ☎ 257 64 98 *Popular on Mon.*
Every Saturday there are several parties such as trippy, Welcome Project, X Party and Demente are popular with gays. Check locations.

RESTAURANTS

Amarelinho/Verdinho (B F g)
Praça de Cinelandia/Rua Alvaro Alvim, 52 *(Centro)*
Cantina Donanna (B g F)
Rua Domingos Ferreira, 63 B, RJ 22050 ☎ 255 88 41
Italian cuisine
Tamino (B F G OS) 19-4 h
Rua Arnaldo Quintela 26 *(Botafogo)* ☎ 295 18 49

SHOWS

Teatro Brigitte Blair I (B g S TV)
Senador Dantas ☎ 220 50 33
Teatro Brigitte Blair II (B g S TV)
Rua Miguel Lemos 51 H ☎ 220 50 33

CINEMAS

Astor (G)
Avenida Ministro Edgar Romeiro, 236 *(Madureira)*
Botafogo (g)
Rua Voluntários da Pátria, 35 *(Metro Botafogo)*
Bruni-Meyer (G)
Rua Amaro Cavalcante, 1 ☎ 591 27 46
Bruni-Tijuca (G)
Rua Conde de Bonfim, 370 *(Saens Pena)*
Iris (g)
Rua da Carioca, 49/51 *(Centro. Metro Carioca)*
Odeon (G)
Mahatma Gandi, 2 *(Cinelândia)*
Orly (G)
Rua Alcindo Guanabara, 17 *(Metro Cinelandia)*
Palácio I e II (G)
Rua do Passeio, 40 *(Passeio)*
Scala/Coral (G)
Praia de Botafogo, 316 C-B *(Botafogo)*
Tijuca II (G)
Rua Conde de Bonfim, 422 *(Saens Pena)*
☎ 264-5246

SAUNAS/BATHS

Bonsucesso (B g sa sb)
Rua Bonsucesso, 252B ☎ 260 93 85
Flamengo (B g sa sb)
Rua Corrêo Dutra
Nova Termas Leblon (b f g MA msg sa sb OG R VS)
15.30-6, Sat Sun 9-6 (Men), Mon Fri 9-3 h (Women)
Rua Barao da Torre, 522 *(Ipanema-off Rua Garcia D'Avila)*
☎ 287 88 99 *No private cabins.*
Roger's Thermas (b f g R sa) 16-3 h
Rua Ministro Alfredo Valadão 36, Copacabana *(between Rua Figueiredo de Magalhaes & Rua Siqueira Campos)*
Studio 64 (b f G msg sa sb WO) 15-3 h
Rua Redentor, 64 *(Ipanema, entre Joana Angélica e Maria Quitéria)*
☎ 267 11 38
Termas Catete (B G sa sb) Mon-Thu 14-1, Fri-Sun 14-6 h
Rua Correia Dutra, 34 *(Catete-Subway Catete)* ☎ 265 54 78
Termas Club 29 (G sa sb vs)
Rua Prof. Alfredo Gomes 29 *(Botafogo)* ☎ 286 63 80
Very small, no facilities, cruisy atmosphere.
Termas Ibiza (AC B f G MA sa sb VS yg) 14-6, Sat Sun 9-6 h
Rua Siqueira Campos, 202 *(Copacabana)* ☎ 235 41 77
Small but popular. Limited facilities for sex.

HOTELS

Agres (G H)
Rua Farme de Amoedo 135, Ipanema

Caprice Hotel (G H)
Avenida Nossa Sra. de Copacabana, 1079 ☎ 28758 41

Gomes Freire (G H)
Avenida Gomes Freire, 343 *(centro)*

Lips (AC B d glm H)
Rua Senador Dantas, 46 *(Centro)* ☎ 210 32 35
All rooms with TV and minibar.

GENERAL GROUPS

ARCO-IRIS
Rua do Bispo, 316/805 *(Tijuca)* ☎ 254 65 46

ASTRAL
☎ 265 57 47

ATOBA
Rua Professor Carvalho de Melo, 471, RJ 21735-110 *(Megalhães Bastos)* ☎ 331 15 27 Fax: FAX 331 1527
Email: atobamehomos@ax.ibase.org.br

CARAS E COROAS
PO Box 43.113

Triangulo Rosa
PO Box 14.601 ✉22412-970

Turma OK
Rua do Resende, 43 *(Centro)*

HEALTH GROUPS

ABIA-Associaçåo Brasileira Interdisciplinar de AIDS
Rua sete de Setembro, 48/12 ☎ 224 16 54
Fax: 224 34 14.

AIDS Hotline-AIDS Pela Vida
☎ 518 22 21

NOSS-Núcleo de Orientação em Saúde Social
☎ 242 47 57
Publishes »Nós por Exemplo«.

HELP WITH PROBLEMS

Disque Aids-Atobá
☎ 332 07 87

SWIMMING

-The beach at the end of the Rua Fame de Amvedo in Ipanema is popular with gays (on the left side, mailnly on WE).

CRUISING

-Ipanema Beach (in front of Rua Farme de Amoedo)
-Copacabana Beach (just above Copacabana Palace Hotel called »Stock Market« / bolsa de Copacabana)
-Botafogo Beach (on weekdays until midnight and on Saturdays until 2 h, very dangerous)
-Avenida Atlantica-Av. Copacabana
-Avenida Rio Branco in Cinelandia
-Praça Floriano (R) (there are small hotels in this area called »Somente Cavalheiros«, which means »men only«; you will have no problem bringing someone home with you whenever you want)
-Quinta da Boa Vista (AYOR) (closes at night)
-Parque do Flamengo (AYOR) (between Hotel Gloria and Botafogo, day and night)
-Between Santos Dumont airport and Praça XV (AYOR) (at night)
-Praia do Arpoador
-Baixo Leblon (around Pizzaria Guanabara)
-Corner Ataulfo de Paiva/Aristides Espinola
-Praça da Bandeira (closes at night)
-Via Apia (AYOR R) (Rua 1° de Marçc/Pres. Antonio Carlos, Santa Luzia. Dangerous. Police.)

Rio Verde - Goiás ☎ 75

RELIGIOUS GROUPS

Comunidade Pacifista TUNKER
PO Box 214 ✉75.901-970

Salvador - Bahia ☎ 71

Salvador was formerly the capital of Brazil and is still the cultural centre of the nation. Its culture was strongly influenced by black people brought over from Africa as slaves in colonial times. Salvador is considered the most African city in Brazil. Brazil's gays hold their own Carnival here in February on the »Praça Castro Alves«.

Salvador ist die ehemalige Hauptstadt Brasiliens und auch heute noch das kulturelle Zentrum. Die Stadt ist stark geprägt von den Nachfahren der früher von den Kolonialisten aus Afrika deportierten schwarzen Zwangsarbeitern. Man nennt Salvador die afrikanischste Stadt Brasiliens. In dieser Stadt feiern Brasiliens Schwule im Februar ihren Carnaval: sie treffen sich auf dem Platz »Praça Castro Alves«.

Salvador est l'ancienne capitale du Brésil. Elle en est restée la capitale culturelle. Fortement marquée par les descendants des esclaves noirs africains d'autrefois, on dit que c'est la ville la plus africaine du pays. C'est ici que les gays, chaque année en février, organisent leur propre carnaval. On s'y rencontre sur la place Praça Castro Alves.

Salvador es la antigua capital del Brasil y sigue siendo el centro cultural del país. Se hace notar la fuerte influencia de los descendientes de los esclavos, traidos desde el continente africano. Salvador se considera la ciudad más africana del Brasil. En esta ciudad los gays celebran anualmente en el mes de febrero su carnaval en la plaza „Castro Alves".

Salvador era in origine la capitale del Brasile è ancora adesso il centro culturale della nazione. La sua cultura è stata fortemente influenzata dagli schiavi neri portati dall'Africa. Salvador è nominata la città più africana del Brasile. Qui festeggiano gli omosessuali brasiliani il loro carnevale; il luogo d'incontro è la piazza Castro Alves.

TOURIST INFO

Empresa de Turismo da Bahia-Bahiatursa
Ed. Sede do Centro de Convençes da Bahia, Praia da Armação ✉41750-270 ☎ 370 84 01

BARS

Adé Aló (B g S)
Rua Pedro Autran, 71, 1st floor
Cantina da Lua (B g)
Terreiro de Jesus
Charles Chaplin (B g)
Rua Carlos Gomes/Rua Pedro Autran
Empório (B f G) 19-? h
Avenida Sete Setembro,✉3089/Farol da Barra
Espaço Alternativo
Rua Carlos Gomes, 141
Holmes New Look Bar (AC B D G MA WE) 22-6 h
Rua Newton Prado, 24 *(Gamboa de Cime)* ☎ 245 24 93
Minos Bar (B g)
Rua Carlos Gomes 15
Stylus (B g)
Rua Carlos Gomes, 102

DANCECLUBS

Banana República (B D g)
Rua Braulio Xavier *(Vitoria)*
Caverna (B D g)
Rua Carlos Gomes, 133
Close up (B D GLM) 22-6 h, Sat Gay
Avenida Oceânica *(Ondina)*
Sometimes gay parties.
Queens (B D DR SNU STV) Wed-Sat 0.00-5.00 h Sun 17.00-22.00 h
Teodoro Sampaio Str.160, Barris ✉40 070 150 ☎ 328 62 20
It´s also a Sex Shop with cruising area and video cabins
Tropical (AYOR B D G r stv)
Rua do Pau da Bandeira, Sé *(cross street from Rua de Chile)*

RESTAURANTS

Extudo (B F g)
Rio Vermelho
Felipe Camarão (B F g)
Rio Vermelho
Ibiza (B F g) 11-24 h
Rua Alfredo Brito, 11 *(Pelourinho)*

CINEMAS

Astor
Rua da Ajuda, 5 *(Centro Histórico)*
Cine Bahia
Rua Carlos Gomes 21 *(Centro)*
Cine Tamoio
Rua Rui Barbosa *(Centro)*
Jandaia
Baixa do Sapateiro
Liceu
Rua do Saldanha, 16 *(Centro Histórico)*
Pax
Rua J.J. Seabra, 116 *(Baixa do Sapateiro)*
Tupi
Rua J.J. Seabra, 347 *(Baixa do Sapateiro)*

SAUNAS/BATHS

Olympus (B G MA msg sa sb VS wh) 15-23 h
Rua Tuiuti, 183 ✉40060-020 *(off Carlos Gomes/Ladeira dos Alfitos, near post office)* ☎ 321 25 74
English, French, Spanish & Italian spoken. Small but friendly atosphere.
Therma Campus
Rua Dias D'ávila, 25 *(Farol da Barra)* ☎ 235 22 47
Thermas Phoenix
Rua Prado Valadares, 16 *(Nazaré)* ☎ 243 54 95

HOTELS

Barra Praia Hotel (AC bf H NG)
Rua Almirante Marquês de Leão, 172 ☎ 254 34 37
Beach location. All rooms have AC, telephone, refrigerator, priv. bath.
Costa de Marfim Guesthouse (AC bf GLM OS wh)
Rua Felipe Camarao, 442 *(Saude)* ☎ 242 40 62
All rooms with TV, bath, WC.
Enseada Porto da Barra (H NG)
Rua Barão de Itapuã *(Porto da Barra)*
Grande Hotel Da Barra (H NG)
Avenida Sete de Septembro 3564 *(Barra)* ☎ 247 60 11
Hotel Angelo-Americano (H NG)
Avenida Sete de Septembro *(Barra)*

Hotel Caramuru (H NG)
Avenida Sete de Setembro *(Barra)*
Hotel Porto da Barra (H NG)
Porto da Barra
Pensão Gloria (H NG)
Rua do Bispo 9 *(Sé)* ☎ 242 19 41

GENERAL GROUPS

Grupo Gay da Bahia / Centro Baiano Anti-Aids Meetings Wed-Fri 20 h.
Rua do Sodré, 45, PO Box 2552 ✉40.022-260 *(Bairro Dois de Julho-near Museu de Arte Sacra)* ☎ 243 49 02 Fax: 322 37 82
Publications: Boletim Do GGB „Candreno De Textos Do GGB" „AIDS E Candomble" „Guia Gay Do Cidade Do Salvador" „O Que Todo Munde Deve Saber Sobre A Homossexualidade"

HEALTH GROUPS

Disk-AIDS
☎ 245 85 00
Gapa
Rua Manoel Dias Morais, 25 *(Jardim Apipema)*
☎ 245 17 41

SWIMMING

-Porto da Barra (main gay beach, mostly on weekends)
-Farol da Barra (especially at the rocks)
-Stella Maris
-Rua J, K-itapoa

CRUISING

-Small park behind Governor's Palace (near Hotel Plaza)
-Mercado Modelo (market Sat 8-18 h)
-Shopping Iguatemi
-Shopping Piedade

Santa Maria - Rio Grande do Sul

BARS

Bus Club
Rua Andradas, 1900
Panacéia Bar
Rua Angelo Uglione ✉1697
Skato Bar
Avenida Presidente Vargas
Yellow House
Rua Riachuelo

SAUNAS/BATHS

Center Tue-Sat 14-23 h
Rua Vale Machado, 950 *(Subsolo)* ☎ 221 41 86

HOTELS

Hotel Moratim
Rua Angelo Uglione, 1629 ☎ 222 44 53
Hotel Rio
Avenida Rio Branco, 126 ☎ 221 17 01

Santos - São Paulo

BARS

Number One (B G MA S)
Av. Conselheiro Nébias, 243
☎ 233 56 67 *or* ☎ *235-6977*
Verandah Café (b g)
Avenida Conselheiro Nébias

RESTAURANTS

Churrascaria Tertulia (B F g)
Avenida Bartolomeu de Gusmao 187 *(Ponta da Praia)* ☎ 36 16 41
Gug's (B F g)
Avenida Bartolomeu de Gusmao 131 *(near Canal 6, Embaré)*
☎ 36 05 80

CINEMAS

Fugitive (g)
Rua Da. Adelina 31 *(Paquetá)* ☎ 32 36 79
Guarany Theater
Praça dos Andradas *(Centro)*
Praia Palace (g)
Avenida Da. Ana Costa 410 *(Vila Matias)* ☎ 40 97 97

HOTELS

Hotel Parque Balneario (H NG)
Avenida Ana Costa 555 *(Vila Matias)* ☎ 34 72 11
Karibe (H NG)
Rua Sao Francisco 322 *(Paquetá)* ☎ 32 92 00
Mendes Plaza Hotel (H NG)
Avenida Marechal Floriano Peixoto 42 *(Gonzaga)* ☎ 37 42 43
Scala Santos-Motel (H NG)
Avenida João Pessoa 212 *(Centro)* ☎ 32 20 88
Status-Motel (H NG)
Avenida Presidente Wilson 1375 *(José Menino)*

CRUISING

-Bars and Cafés in Plaza St. Vincente and Avenida Ana Costa
-Near Oslo Bar and Rua General Camara
-Itararé Beach
-Praça Independéncia (in the evening)
-Praça Maua (at bus stop and in the post office)

São João Del Rei - Minas Gerais

RESTAURANTS

Cantinho da Canja (B F g)
Rua Balbino da Cunha 168

São Luiz - Maranhão

GENERAL GROUPS

Grupo Gay e Lésbico do Maranhão-TIBRO
Rua do Sol, 472 ✉MA 65010-950 *(Altos São Luis)*

CRUISING

-Praia do Olho D'água (beach)
-Praça Central. (near Postoffice)

São Paulo - São Paulo ☎ 11

TOURIST INFO

Embratur-São Paulo
Rua São Bento, 380, 7. andar ✉01.011-000 ☎ 347 381

BARS

Bunker (B G S YG) Thu-Sun 21-4 h
Rua Brigadeiro Galvão, 723/Barra Funda
Caneca de Prata (B G OG R)
Avenida Vieira de Carvalho, 55 *(Santa Ifigênia)* ☎ 223-6420
Corsários (B f G)
Praça Roosevelt, 252 *(Vila Buarque)*
Mix House
Rua dos Ingleses, 357
Panif. Primavera
Rua da Consolação, 3366 *(Jardins)*

Paparazzi (AC B E F GLM MA WE VS) Daily 21.00-? h
Rua da Consolaçao, 3050 *(next to Disco Galpao-Jardins)*
☎ 881 66 65
Italian food.
Tlitz (B f g)
Rua Marques de Itu 181

CAFES

Baguette (B F glm MA) Mon-Thu 20-2, Fri Sat -6, Sun 14-2 h
Rua da Consolação 2426 *(Consolação)* ☎ 258 93 27
Best on WE.
Cachação (b F g) 18-? h
Rua Martinho Prado 25 *(Bela Vista)*
Café do Bexiga (B F g) 20-5 h, closed Mon
Rua Treze de Maio 76 *(Bela Vista)* ☎ 259 60 59
Café Soçaite (B f g) 20-5 h, closed Mon
Rua Treze de Maio 46 *(Bela Vista)* ☎ 259 65 62
Chefão (b F G)
Largo do Arouche 66 *(Vila Buarque)* ☎ 223 60 19
Cheguey Bar (B f GLM)
Rua Marques de Itu 155 *(Vila Buarque)*
Duzentos e Oito (b F)
Rua Major Sertório 208 *(Vila Buarque)*
Jeca (b F g)
Avenida São João/Avenida Ipiranga *(Centro)* ☎ 223 51 06
Jotas Hamburger (! B f g MA) 11-1 h
Rua da Consolação 2526 *(Consolação)* ☎ 257 04 09
Pixiguinha (b F)
Rua Santo Antonio 931 *(Bela Vista)*

DANCECLUBS

Anjo Azul
Rua Brigadeiro Galvão, 723 ☎ 677 924
Galpao (B D G ma s) Fri-Sat 24-5 h
Rua Concolaçao 3046 *(located in the quarter Jardins)*
☎ 881 66 65
Gent's Theater House (AC B D E f G MA S T VS) 23-4, closed Mon Tue, shows 1.30 h
Avenida Ibirapuera, 1911, (Moema) *(Indianópolis)* ☎ 572 82 27
Massivo. Clube (B D e g MA S SL YG) Thu-Sat 23-5 h
Alameda Itú, 1548 *(Jardins)* ☎ 883 75 05 *Gay on Thu.*
Nostro Mundo (B D G MA RT STV TV) 23-4, Sun 19-1 h, closed Mon Tue
Rua da Consolação, 2554 *(M° Consolação)* ☎ 257 44 81
Oldest gay disco in town: For 22 years!
Proibidu's (AYOR B D GLM TV STV) 24-6 h, closed Mon-Wed
Rua Amaral Gurgel, 253 *(Vila Buarque. M° República)* ☎ 572 37 15
Segredu's (AYOR B D GLM) 22-4 h, closed Mon-Thu
Rua Santo Antonio, 922 *(Bela Vista. M° Anhangabaú)* ☎ 259 24 92
Shelter (B D g MA YG) 23-4 h, closed Mon-Wed
Rua da Consolação 3032 *(Jardim Paulista. M° Consolação)*
☎ 852 01 02
Shock House (B D G S YG) 23-4, Sun 20-24 h, closed Mon Tue
Rua Rui Barbosa 201 *(Bela Vista. M° São Joaquim)* ☎ 285 00 16
Sky Perepepê (B D gLM MA S) 22-4 h
Rua Santo Antonio, 570 *(Bela Vista. M° Anhangabaú)*
SoGo (AC CC B D DR G VS) Thu-Sat 23.00-11.00 h, Sun 10-1.00 h
Al. Franca 1368 ☎ 306 155 13
Tunnel (AC B D f GLM MA s STV) Thu 21.00-? h, Fri & Sat 23.00-? h, Sun 19.00-? h
Rua Dos Ingleses 355 *Nearby subway station Bribadeiro, Green Line*

Volúpia (AC B D F gLm MA OS P S) 22-4, Sun 21-3 h, closed Mon-Wed
Rua dos Pinheiros 688 ☎ 852 38 77

RESTAURANTS

Arroz de Ouro (F g)
Largo do Arouche 46-1° *(Vila Buarque)* ☎ 223 02 19
Boi Na Brasa (B F g)
Rua Marquês de Itu 139 *(Vila Buarque)* ☎ 223 61 62
Chopp Escuro (b F g)
Rua Marquês de Itu 252 *(Vila Buarque)* ☎ 221 08 72
Farina. La (F g)
Rua Aurora 610 *(Santa Ifigênia)* ☎ 222 08 93
Farina. La (F g) Avenida Ipiranga, 924 *(Centro)*
☎ 223 14 45
Galeto's (F g)
Alameda Santos, 1112 *(Cerqueira César)*
Brasilian food.
Gato Que Ri. O (F g)
Largo do Arouche, 47-41 *(Vila Buarque)* ☎ 221 26 99
Italian food.
Gigetto (F g)
Rua Avanhandava, 63 *(Bela Vista)*
☎ 256 98 04
Italian food.
Montechiaro (F g)
Rua Santo Antonio 844 *(Bela Vista)*
☎ 257 40 32
Os Monges (F g) closed Mon
Rua Tuim, 1041 *(Vila Uberabinha)*
Brasilian food. Expensive.

SEX SHOPS/BLUE MOVIES

Ponto G (g)
Rua Amaral Gurgel 206 ☎ 223 30 11
Sex Shop (g)
Rua 7 de Abril 125, loja 18 *(Galeria 7 de Abril, Centro)*
Sex Shop (g)
Avenida Francisco Matarazzo, 778 *(Agua Branca)* ☎ 864 53 44

CINEMAS

América (g)
Avenida Rio Branco, 49
Art Palácio (g)
Avenida São João, 419 *(Centro)*
Avenida (g)
Avenida São João, 335 *(Centro)* ☎ 223 79 91
Central (g)
Avenida Ipiranga, 752
Cine Ipiranga I and II (g)
Avenida Ipiranga, 786 *(Centro)* ☎ 222 06 32
Dom José (G)
Rua Dom Jose de Barros, 306
Marrocos 1, 2 (G)
Rua Conselheiro Crispiano, 352
Metro I and II (g)
Avenida São João, 791 *(Centro)*
☎ 223 24 92
Olido (g)
Avenida São João, 473 *(cinemas I,II,III, Centro)*
☎ 223 32 80
Windsor (g)
Avenida Ipiranga, 974 *(Centro)* ☎ 222 25 53

ESCORTS & STUDIOS

Scort Man
☎ 259 72 02

SAUNAS/BATHS

Balneário Alterosas (B G R sa sb pi wh) 12.30-22 h
Avenida das Alterosas, 40A *(M° Vila Esperanca, Vila Guilhermina)* ☎ 958 17 12

Champion Club Termas (B G sa)
Largo do Arouche, 336 *(opposite flower market, Vila Buarque)* ☎ 222-4973

Termas Danny's (B f G MA sa sb VS) 12-24 h
Rua Jaguaribe, 484 *(Vila Buarque. M° Santa Cecilia)*

Termas For Friends (! B CC d DR f G MA msg OS pi s sa sb VS wh) 14-24 h
Rua Borges Lagoa, 287 ✉04015-050 *(Vila Mariana. M° Santa Cruz)* ☎ 571 11 51

Termas Four Seasons (G) 15-23, Fri Sat -2 h
Rua Marques de Itu, 665 *(M° Santa Cecilia)* ☎ 222 01 12

Termas Fragata (B G R sa sb SNU VS WO) 14-24 h
Rua Francisco Leitão, 71 *(Jardim América)* ☎ 853 70 61

Termas Le Rouge 80 (B G MA pi sa sb VS) 14-1, Fri Sat -5
Rua Arruda Alvim, 175 *(Pinheiros. M° Clinicas)* ☎ 852 30 43

Thermas Holiday (B f G MA sa sb VS wh) 14-24, Fri Sat -5 h
Rua Martins Fontes, 295 *(Centro. M° Anhangabaú)* ☎ 256 45 32

Thermas Lagoa (AC B CC DR f G MA msg pi R S sa sb SNU sol VS WO) Sat-Thu 14.00-24.00 h Fri 14.00-5.00 h
Rua Borges Lagoa, 287 ✉040383-030 *(2 blocks from M° Santa Cruz. Vila Clementino)* ☎ 573 96 89

HOTELS

Grant's Hotel I (g H)
Rua Consolação, 767 *(Consolação)* ☎ 231 15 64

Grant's Hotel II (g H)
Avenida Amaral Gurgel, 392 *(Vila Buarque)* ☎ 259 60 06

Luver I (g H)
Rua João Guimarães Rosa, 207 *(Consolação)*

Luver II (g H)
Rua Frei Caneca, 963 *(Consolação)*
☎ 287 70 40

Terminus (g H)
Avenida Ipiranga, 741 *(Centro)*
☎ 222 22 66

GENERAL GROUPS

Rede um Outro Olhar
PO Box 65092 ✉01390-970

HEALTH GROUPS

Ambulatorio de Saude Mental • SUD Mon Wed 9-11.30, Tue Thu 13.30-16 h
Rua Carlos Comenale 35 *(Cerqueire Cesar. Near Avenida Paulista)*
☎ 283 00 05
Free mental/psychological treatment for patients with AIDS.

Centro de Saude Santa Cecilia Mon-Fri 7-17 h
Rua Vitorino Camilo, 599 *(Santa Cecilia. M° Marechal Deodoro)*
☎ 826-7970
HIV-tests and treatment (for free).

C.O.A. Centro de Orientação e Aconselhamento em AIDS e Doeças Sexualmente Transmissíveis Mon-Fri 8-14 h
Galeria Prestes Maia, Terreo *(Centro)* ☎ 239 22 24
Orientation about AIDS and free HIV-tests.

GAPA • Grupo de Apoio a Pacientes de AIDS
Rua Barão de Tatui, 375
Grupo Pela Vida
Rua General Jardim 556 *(Near Santa Casa)* ☎ 820 35 02
Psychological treatment. Appointments by phone on Mon only.
Hospital Emilio Ribas 0-24 h
165 Avenida Dr. Arnaldo *(Pacaembu)* ☎ 881 24 33
Hospital São Paulo
Rua Napoleão de Barros 715 *(Vila Clementino)* ☎ 549 87 77
Liga De Combate A Sifilis E Outras Doenças Venereas Hosp. das Clinicas da Faculdade de Medicina
Rua Dr. Ovidio Pires de Campo/Avenida Rebouças *(Cerqueira César)* ☎ 282 28 11
SAMPA • Solidariedade, Apoio Moral e Psicologico Aplicados a AIDS
Rua Manuel de Paiva 218 *(Vila Mariana)* ☎ 571 73 96
By appointment only. Psychological treatment charged according to patient possibility.

CRUISING
-Most restrooms of subway stations (AYOR)
-Republica Square
-Mappin department store (Praça Ramos Azevedo)
-Avenida Ipiranga (AYOR R RT) (intersection of São João and São Luiz and São Luiz and Praça Roosevelt) (tv)
-Avenida República de Libano (TV) (area between Parque do Ibarapuera and the residential district of Avenida Sto. Amaro)
-Galeria Califórnia (R RT) (Rua Barão de Itapetininga 255, connecting the Barão de Itapetininga with Dom José Gaspar)
-Parque do Ibirpuera (WE) (Try the cycle paths or go by car at night)
-Praça Roosevelt (at night and on weekend)
-Rua Rui Barbosa (from Zaccaro Theatre to Village Station Cabaret)
-Rua Santo Antonio (area leading from Major Quedinho á Treze de Maio)
-MASP-São Paulo Art Museum (Avenida Paulista 1578) (Sun afternoon)
-»Autorama«-area in Ibirapera park (between DETRAN & BIENAL. Where the cars park. Nights)

São Vicente - São Paulo

BARS
Pirata Drinks (B g)
Alamdea Paulo Gonçalves s/n *(Ilha Porchat)* ☎ 682 111
Terraco Chopp (B g)
Alameda Ari Barroso 79 *(Ilha Porchat)* ☎ 681 159

RESTAURANTS
Itapura (B F g)
Avenida Newton Prado 179 *(Road to Ponte Pensil, Morro dos Barbosas)* ☎ 685 143
Terraco (B F g)
Al. Almirante Barroso 77 *(Ilha Porchat)*
☎ 687 527

SWIMMING
-Praia Itararé (near Ilha Porchat)

Teresina - Piaui

BARS
Carinhoso Bar
Rua Alvaro Mendes

CRUISING
-Praça Pedro II
-Praça Saraiva (at night, action in front of the church)

Tiradentes - Minas Gerais

BARS
Aluarte (A B g) Largo do ó 1

Vitória - Espirito Santo

BARS
Beleza's Sorveteria (B f g) Avenida Florentino Avidos 532 *(in Hotel Grand Estoril, Centro)*
Bengalo Bar (B f GLM R) 12-5 h
Rua Professor Baltazar 136 *(Centro)*

SAUNAS/BATHS
Thermas 2 19-? h
Rua Benjamin Constant/7 de Setembro *(Centro)*

CRUISING
-Jardin de Penha Gamburi
-Praia Comprido
-Praia de Camburi
-Praia de Guarapari (Castanheiras Beach)
-Praia de Costa (close to Tabajara Hotel)
-Parque Moscoso
-Promenade Embarcadouro
-In front of Sao Luis Theatre (Rua 23 de Maio)
-Plaza Costa Pereira (R)

Bulgaria

Bâlgarija

Southeastern Europe

Initials: BG

Time: GMT +2

☎ Country Code / Access Code: 359 / 00

Language: Bulgarian

Area: 110,993 km^2 / 42,854 sq mi.

Currency: 1 Lew (Lw) = 100 Stótinki.

Population: 8,240,426

Capital: Sofija

Religions: 88% Orthodox Christian

Climate: Moderate climate. Winters are cold and damp, summer hot and dry.

● The age of consent for homosexual activity is 16, while for heterosexuals it is 14. There are some signs of an emerging gay movement, although this has yet to lead to any kind of a gay scene.

✱ Das Schutzalter für Schwule und Lesben liegt bei 16, ansonsten bei 14 Jahren. Es gibt erste Zeichen einer sich entwickelnden schwulen Bewegung; eine schwule Szene aber muß sich noch entwickeln.

▲ La majorité sexuelle serait fixée à 16 ans pour les homosexuels et à 14 ans pour les hétérosexuels. Malgré tout, les choses sont en train de changer et les gays commencent à s'organiser, lentement mais sûrement.

☆ La edad de consentimiento para la homosexualidad es de 16 años, para la heterosexualidad es de 14 años. A pesar de todo, ya se pueden notar los primeros indicios de una organización gay, aún cuando los gays apenas se han movilizados.

❖ L'età minima per avere dei rapporti omosessuali è di 16 anni, di 14 per rapporti eterosessuali. Tuttavia stanno apparendo i primi segni di un movimento gay.

NATIONAL GAY INFO

BULGA
PO Box 32, 1330 Sofija ☎ (02) 58 52 71
FAX 44 38 04.

Gemini
PO Box 123, 1784 Sofia ☎ (02) 943 48 58
FAX (02) 81 72 71. E-mail geonick5@cserv.mgu.bg.

Bourgas

CRUISING

-At the main railway station and in the city park

Plovdiv

BARS

Krokodil (B G)
(near Government Hospital & Central Railway Station)

CRUISING

-Behind the Radio & Television Center (near city center)

Sofija ✉ 1680 ☎ 48

BARS

Adonis (A AC B d GLM lj MA P S SNU YG) Mon-Sun 19-6 h
Kniaz Boris I 122 *(opposite Sheraton Hotel)*

Backstage (B d G MA p) Mon-Sun 20-3 h
Dondoukov Boulevard 103 *(near the building of Darik Radio)* ☎ 44 55 13
Also known as club 103.

Flamingo Center (B D DR G MA msg P S SNU VS YG) 9-2 h
Tzar Simeon 208 ☎ 92 46 47

George (AC B d GLM LJ MA N P YG) 19.30-4 h
Lavale 17 *(Center, behind the National Museum of History)* ☎ 981 71 11

Miami Club (B G d dr MA p r VS)
Pirotska 49 ☎ (0799) 603 70

Private Club-Kayo's (B GLM P) Mon-Sun 19-6 h
Yuri Venelin 27 *(opposite National Stadium)* ☎ 80 76 46

Why Not... (B GLM p) Mon-Sun 19-6 h
31 Stamboliyski Boulevard *(downstairs)* ☎ 80 61 38

DANCECLUBS

Spartacus (B D GLM P S TV WE) Tue-Sun 0-6 h
(at underground passage in front of Sofia University)

SEX SHOPS/BLUE MOVIES

Flamingo (B g VS) Mon-Sun 9-21 h
Tsar Simeon 208 *(1st floor)*
Also video rental.

MASSAGE

Agency Kiss Contact (msg)
PO Box 63 ✉1680 ☎ 924647

CRUISING

-Orlov Most
-Vazrazhdane Square (A. Stamboliysky Blvd./H. Botev Blvd.)
-Garden behind Main Library („Doctor's Garden", near University)

Varna ✉ 9000

DANCECLUBS

Spartacus (B D GLM P S TV WE) Tue-Sun 23-5 h
(in the cellar of Varna Opera House)

GENERAL GROUPS

Contact
PO Box 707, Central Post Office ✉9000

CRUISING

The WC in front of the tennis court at Sea garden (day and night)
The thermal sourec in ath the beach ner the lift, know as „BADEN BADEN", (day and night, down in front of the zoologic Garden)

Cambodia

Kâmpuchéa

Southeast Asia

Initials: K

Time: GMT +7

☎ Country Code / Access Code: 855 / 00

Language: Khmer. French

Area: 181,035 km² / 69,898 sq mi.

Currency: 1 Riel = 10 Kak = 100 Sen

Population: 11,339,562

Capital: Phnom Penh

Religions: 95% Theravada Buddhism

Climate: Tropical climate. The rainy monsoon season lasts from May to November, the dry season from December to April. There's little seasonal temperature variation.

● We have no information concerning the legal status of homosexuelles in Kampuchea. However ILGA states, that the attitude of Kampucheans should be seen as being rather hostile.

✱ Uns liegen keinerlei Informationen zur gesetzlichen Lage Homosexueller in Kambodscha vor. Die ILGA stellt allerdings fest, daß die Haltung der Kambodschaner eher als feindselig betrachtet werden kann.

▲ Nous ne disposons d'aucune information sur la situation des gays au Cambodge. L'ILGA nous a fait savoir que les gens, là-bas, ne semblent pas être particulièrement homophiles.

☆ No poseemos información alguna sobre la situación legal de los homosexuales en Camboya. La ILGA constata que el comportamiento de los camboyanos se puede calificar de agresivo.

❖ Non abbiamo alcun tipo di informazione sulla situazione giuridica degli omosessuali in Cambogia. L'ILGA ha costatato un'attitudine ostile della popolazione nei confronti dei gay.

Phnom Penh

BARS

Martini Pub (B D glm MA OS W) 20-? h
402 Keo Mony Bud *(Near Olympic Stadium)*

Heart of Darkness (B glm MA W) 19-? h
No 26 Street 51 *(Pasteur)*

Tamarind Bar (B F GLM MA OS W) 11-1 h
No. 31, Street 240 *(Near Royal Place)* ☎ 015-914743

RESTAURANTS

Athena Restaurant & Bar (AC B F glm MA OS W) 11-24 h
140 Norodom Boulevard *Nearby Independence Mounument*
☎ 802 330

HEALTH GROUPS

Tropical & Travellers Medical Clinic
No. 88, Street 108 *(Near Wat Phnom)*
Tropical medicine, sexual diseases, HIV test the Doctor sis from the UK.

CRUISING

-Olympic stadium (inside)
-Park near Independence Monument (ayor)

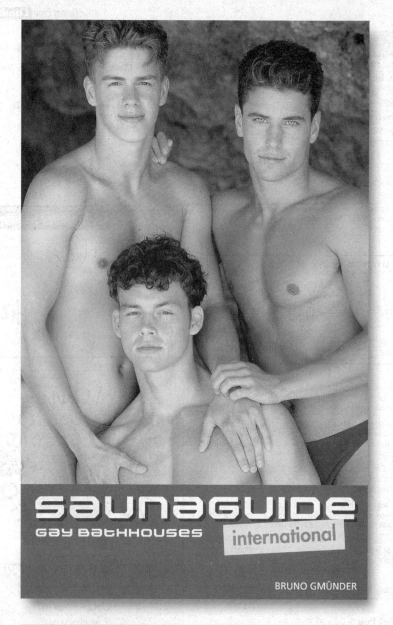

Canada

North America

Initials: CDN

Time: GMT -4/ -5/ -6/ -7/ -8

☎ Country Code / Access Code: 1 / 011

Language: English, French

Area: 9,976,319 km² / 3,844,910 sq mi.

Currency: 1 Canadian Dollar (Can$) = 100 Cents.

Population: 30,675,398

Capital: Ottawa

Religions: 87,7% Christian (46,5% Catholic, 41,2% Protestant)

Climate: Varies from Moderate in the south to subarctic and arctic in the north.

Important gay cities: Montreal, Toronto, Vancouver

● Canada is the second largest country in the world. For the convenience of the readers, listings have are organised alphabetically according to province or territory. The country is made up of 10 provinces and 3 territories, with the creation of Nunavut in April 1999.

The legal age of concent for homosexual acts in Canada is 14. . Exceptions include anal intercourse, prostitution, and sexual exploitation of relationships where the age of consent is 18 for both heterosexuals and homosexuals.

Federal legislation prohibits discrimination on the basis of sexual orientation. In British Colombia and Ontario it is possible for gay / lesbian couples to adopt children. Moreover, gays and lesbians can serve in the Canadian Army.

Canada's tends to be more liberal than its neibour the USA. Language differences (i.e. French in Quebec) is part of every day life. Canada is cultually aware and accepts different religions of its people. The population of metropolitan Toronto is already as big as that of Boston in the US. The European roots of the Southern part of Canada provide for its general tolerance of gays and lesbians.

Three very important gay cities are Montreal (Quebec), Toronto (Ontario) and Vancouver (British Columbia). The two eastern cities differ noticeably in character from Vancouver. The pace of life in Vancouver is more relaxed and the gay scene is less diverse than in Montreal or Toronto. In 1998 Glen Murray was elected mayor of Winnipeg. He is the first open gay mayor in Canada.

✱ Kanada ist das zweitgrößte Land der Erde. Damit Sie sich besser zurechtfinden, haben wir das Listing nach Provinzen bzw. Territorien neu sortiert. Darin folgen die Städte in alphabetischer Ordnung.

Das Schutzalter für homosexuelle Handlungen liegt bei 14 Jahren. Ausgenommen sind Analverkehr, Prostitution und Ausnützung eines Abhängigkeitsverhältnisses; in diesen Fällen liegt die Altersgrenze generell bei 18 Jahren, egal ob es um hetero- oder homosexuelle Handlungen geht.

Es gibt seit einigen Jahren kanadaweit gesetzlichen Schutz vor Diskrimierung aufgrund der sexuellen Identität. In British Columbia und Ontario können Schwule und Lesben problemlos Kinder adoptieren. Die kanadische Armee sieht in der Beschäftigung Homosexueller kein Problem.

Dieser relative Liberalismus liegt vor allem in einem, im Vergleich zu den benachbarten USA, wesentlich moderateren Lebensstil. Sprachdifferenzen (z.B. im frankophonen Québéc) sind Alltag, die Kultur der Inuit gehört selbstverständlich zu Kanada. Religion spielt dagegen im Alltag keine herausragende Rolle. Der Regionalismus sorgt dafür, daß die Nation nicht überhöht wird. Das Land ist zwar verstädtert, doch der größte Ballungsraum (um Toronto) ist gerade so groß wie der des US-amerikanischen Boston. Und gerade die im Osten des Landes offensichtlichen europäischen Wurzeln sorgen für ein maßvolles Klima in Kanada.

Die drei wichtigsten schwulen Städte des Landes sind Montreal (Quebec), Toronto (Ontario) und Vancouver (British Columbia). Die Unterschiede zwischen den beiden östlichen Städten und Vancouver sind allerdings beträchtlich. Während die Szene in den Städten des Westens eher beschaulich wirkt und sich Gay-Pride-Veranstaltungen noch im Wachsen befinden, sind die Großstädte des Ostens wahre Szene-Hochburgen. Entsprechend vielfältig ist die Szene, entsprechend stark ist die schwul-lesbische Bewegung.

▲ Le Canada est le deuxième plus grand pays du monde par sa superficie. Pour vous aider à mieux vous y retrouver, nous avons regroupé notre liste par provinces et territoires, puis par ordre alphabétique de ville.

La majorité pour les rapports homosexuels est fixée à 14 ans, avec cependant une exception pour les rapports anaux, la prostitution et la mise à profit d'un rapport de dépendance. Dans ces cas, la limite d'âge se situe généralement à 18 ans, qu'il s'agisse de rapports hétérosexuels ou homosexuels.

Depuis quelques années, il existe dans tout le Canada une protection contre la discrimination liée à l'identité sexuelle. En Colombie-Britannique et en Ontario, les homosexuels et lesbiennes peuvent adopter des enfants sans difficulté. L'armée canadienne est également ouverte à l'engagement d'homosexuels.

Le Canada est de manière générale plus libéral que son voisin les Etats-Unis. Les différences linguistiques (par exemple du Québec francophone) font partie de la vie quotidienne. Le pays est culturellement riche et tolérant vis-à-vis des pratiques religieuses. La plus grande agglomération urbaine (celle de Toronto) est aujourd'hui aussi grande que la ville américaine de Boston. Les racines européennes évidentes au sud du pays contribuent certainement à cette tolérance à l'égard des gays.

Les trois villes homosexuelles les plus importantes du pays sont Montréal (Québec), Toronto (Ontario) et Vancouver (Colombie-Britannique). Des différences entre l'est et l'ouest sont cependant à noter. Le mode de vie à Vancouver est plus détendu et la scène gaye moins diversifiée qu'à Montréal ou Toronto. Glen Murray, élu en 1998 à Winnipeg, a été le premier maire ouvertement homosexuel du pays.

☆ Canada es el segundo país más grande del mundo. Para su mejor orientación hemos ordenado el listado por provincias o territorios, indicando las ciudades correspondientes por orden alfabético.

La edad de consentimiento para homosexuales es de 14 años, haciendo excepción de las relaciones anales, la prostitución o el aprovechamiento de una relación de dependencia. Para estos casos la ley estipula una edad de 18 años, independientemente de la orientación sexual. Desde hace algunos años existe una ley en Canada que garantiza la igualdad de derechos para homosexuales. Por ejemplo, en British Columbia parejas gay o lesbianas pueden adoptar niños sin problema alguno y el ejército canadiense no considera problemático el reclutamiento de hombres homosexuales. Ese relativo liberalismo (en comparación con los vecinos Estados Unidos) se debe sobre todo a una postura más abierta hacía minorias. Las diferencias lingüísticas (por ejemplo en la provincia de habla francesa Québec) son rutina y la cultura de los Inuit (esquimales) forma parte de la vida canadiense. Por otro lado, la religión no juega ningún papel predominante. Debido al fuerte regionalismo, para los canadienses el concepto de la nación no tiene gran importancia. Aunque haya muchas ciudades, la mayor aglomeración urbana (Toronto y sus alrededores) es apenas tan grande como la ciudad estadounidense de Boston. En la parte oriental arraigó con más fuerza la tradición europea, garantizando de este modo un ambiente más abierto y liberal. Las tres ciudades de mayor importancia para gays son Montreal (Québec), Toronto (Ontario) y Vancouver (British Columbia), aunque las diferencias entre las dos ciudades orientales y Vancouver son enormes. Mientras el ambiente gay en las ciudades del Oeste es bastante tranquilo y fiestas como la Gay-Pride se organizan hace muy poco, las grandes ciudades del Este son verdaderas bastiones homosexuales. Estas ciudades ofrecen un ámplio ambiente y como es de esperar el movimiento gay posee gran impulso.

❖ Canada è il secondo paese più grande del mondo in superficie. Per un migliore orientamento abbiamo cambiato la lista a seconda delle province e dei territori nel cui capitolo vengono elencate le rispettive città. L'età legale per avere rapporti omosessuali è di 14 anni. Sono esclusi i rapporti anali, la prostituzione e lo sfruttamento di una relazione di dipendenza. In questi casi, l'età del consenso è di 18 anni per gli atti sia eterosessuali sia omosessuali. Da alcuni anni esistono leggi che proteggono in tutto il paese i gay e le lesbiche contro la discriminazione del loro orientamento sessuale. Nella Colombia britannica ed in Ontario gay e lesbiche possono adottare bambini. L'esercito canadese non esclude gli omosessuali dalle proprie file. Il motivo per questo liberalismo è lo stile di vita abbastanza riservato, rispetto a quello degli USA. Le difficoltà con le lingue (p.es. nel Quebec francofono) fanno parte della vita quotidiana, come anche la cultura degli Inuit è parte della Canada. Grazie al regionalismo, la religione non svolge un ruolo essenziale per tutta la nazione. Anche se il paese è urbanizzato, la zona con la più alta concentrazione di abitanti (attorno a Toronto) è grande come Boston negli USA. Sono le radici europee nella parte orientale del paese che contribuiscono a un buon clima sociale. Le tre città gay più importanti sono Montreal (Quebec), Toronto (Ontario) e Vancouver (Colombia britannica). Ci sono differenze notevoli tra le due città orientali e Vancouver. Mentre la vita gay nelle città dell'occidente è piuttosto tranquilla e gli avvenimenti di Gay Pride si stanno ancora sviluppando, e mentre le grandi città dell'oriente sono veri baluardi del movimento gay e lesbico con una grande varietà di locali e possibilità d'incontro.

NATIONAL GAY INFO

Canadian Gay, Lesbian & Bisexual Resource Directory
386 Montrose Street, Winnipeg, Manitoba ✉R3M 3M8
☎ (204) 488-1805
FAX 663-6001. Homepage: http://www.cglbrd.com.
E-Mail: cglbrd@cglbrd.com. Internet listing of gay and lesbian buisiness organization.

Fab
25 Wood Street, Suite 101, Toronto ON ✉M4Y 2P9
☎ (416) 599-9992
FAX (416) 599-9438. E-Mail: fab@myna.com. Homepage http://www.fabmag.com. Glossy national lifestyle magazine.

Footprints (GLM)
506 Church Street, Ste 200, Toronto ✉ON M4Y 2C8
☎ 416/962 8111 ☎ 1-888 962 6211 Fax: 416/962 6621
E-Mail: trips@footprintstravel.com
Homepage: www.footprintstravel.com
Tour operator specializing in the provision of worldwide adventure travel for the gay and lesbian community.

GAYroute
PO / CP 1036, Stn. „C", Montréal ✉QC H2L 4V3
For more details about all types of gay buisnesses in Canada fend for a fee of US$ 5,— or 3x IRC and a self addressed envelope. Mail order only

The Canadian Lesbian & Gay Archives Tue-Thu 19.30-22 h (and by appointment)
56 Temperance Street, Suite 201 *PO Box 639, Station A, Toronto ON, M5W 1G2* ☎ (416) 777-2755
Archives, library and research centre. Large collection of periodicals.

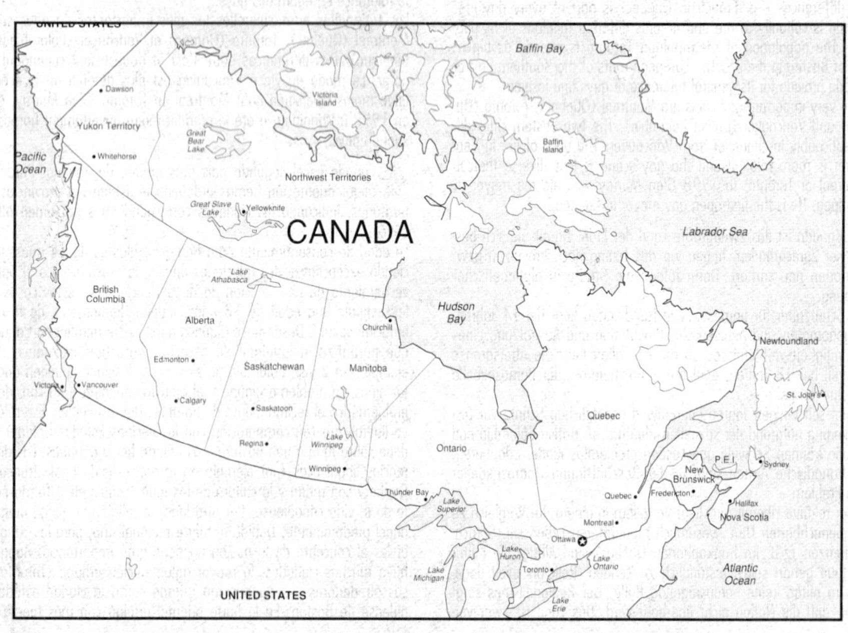

NATIONAL COMPANIES

Cachet Accommodations Network
(GLM) 10-22 h
PO Box 42, Station M, Montreal ✉QC H1V 3L6
☎ (514) 254 1250 E-Mail: be-brief@sympatico.ca
The gay and lesbian room booking service for visitors to Canada.

Glad Day Books
598 A Yonge Street, /St.Joseph, 2nd floor, Toronto ✉ON M4Y 1Z3 ☎ (416) 961-4161

Librairie L'Androgyne
3636 Boulevard St.Laurent, Montreal, Quebec H2X 2V4
☎ (514) 842-4765
Gay and lesbian books in English and French.

Little Sister's (GLM)
1238 Davie Street, Vancouver V6E 1N4 ☎ (604) 669-1753
or ☎ 1-800-567-1662 (USA and CDN). Books. Gay literature. Catalogue available.

Mack`s Leathers Inc. Mon-Wed 11-19, Thu-Fri 11-20, Sat 11-18, Sun 12-17 h
1043 Granville Street, Vancouver ☎ (604) 688-6225
Ask for brochure (videos, toys and leather articles).

Priape
1311 Ste.Catherine Est, Montreal, Quebec H2L 2H4
☎ (514) 521-8451 or toll free ☎ 800-461-6969
Books, leather, videos.

Wega Video
PO Box 366, Stn. C, Montreal H2L 4K3
☎ (514) 987 5993 *or ☎ 1-800-361-9929 (USA and CDN).*

NATIONAL GROUPS

Gay Mates-Men's national pen pal contact club
PO Box 3043, ✉SK S7K 3S9

TOURIST INFO

INFO - all about gay Canada
☎ 514/ 899 4636
Information about all services offered to visitors to Canada. FREE SERVICE

PRIVATE ACCOMODATION

Homelink International
PO Box 762, Station C, Montréal ✉QC H2L 4L6 ☎ (514) 523-4642 ☎ (800) 429-4983 (toll free) Fax: (514) 879-3299
Gay & Lesbian accomodation club. Hospitality and home exchange.

CDN-Alberta

Southwest CDN
Initials: AB
Time: GMT -7
Area: 661,000 km² / 255,212 sq mi.
Population: 2,847,000
Capital: Edmonton
Important gay cities: Calgary and Edmonton

Calgary ☎ 403

GAY INFO

Gay & Lesbian Community Services Accociation 19-22 h
206, 223 12th Avenue SW ✉T2R 0G3 ☎ 234-8973 *or ☎ 234 9752 (automated info-line).* Homepage: www.canuck.com/~glcsa
Peer support, information, library and drop-in center.

Outlooks (G) Mon-Fri 9-17:00h
Box 439, Suite 100, 1039 17th Avenue SW ✉T2T 0B2
☎ 228-1157 E-Mail: outlooks@cadvision.com
Monthly newspaper distributed nationally in Canada.

QC Magazine
PO Box 64292, 5512 4th Street NW ✉T2K 6J1 ☎ 630-2061
Fax 275 6443. Gay publication for Alberta and British Columbia.

TOURIST INFO

Calgary Convention & Visitors Bureau
Mon-Fri 8-17 h
237-8 Avenue SE ✉T2G 0K8 ☎ 263-8510
or ☎ 1-800 661-1678 (USA & CDN). FAX 262-3809.
E-Mail: destination@visitors.ab.ca

BARS

Loading Dock. The at »Detour« (B G N) 15-3 h
318 17th Avenue South West ✉T2S 0A8 ☎ 244-8537
☛»Detour« Danceclub

Money-Pennies (B F GLM) Sun-Wed 11-24:00h, Thu, Fri & Sat -03:00h
1742 10th Avenue SW ☎ 263 7411

Rekroom (B G lj MA N p) 16-3 h
213-A 10th Avenue South West ✉T2R 0A4 *(lower level)*
☎ 265-4749

CAFES

Grabbajabba (AC b CC f glm MA) Mon-Thu 7-23, Fri -24, Sun 8-23
1610-10th Street South West ✉T2R 1G1 *(Off 17th Avenue)*
☎ 244-7750

Midnight Café (B F glm MA) Mon-Fri 9-2, Sat 11-24, Sun 12-24 h
1330 8th Street SW ☎ 229-9322

DANCECLUBS

Arena (B D G MA) Thu-Sat 21-3 h
310 17th Avenue South West ✉T2S 0A8 ☎ 228-5730

Boystown (B CC D G MA P) 21-3 h
213 10th Avenue South West ✉T2R 0A4 ☎ 265-2028
Men only exept on Wed. strippers.

Detour (B D Glm MA) Wed-Sun 22-3 h. Fri men only
318 17th Avenue South West ✉T2S 0A8 ☎ 244-8537

Warehouse. The (B D GLM P YG) Tue-Sat 21-3 h
731 10th Avenue South West ☎ 264-0535

RESTAURANTS

Entre Nous (F glm) Mon-Sat 11-23, Sun 11-14 h
1800 4th Street SW ☎ 228-5525

Victoria's (AC B CC F glm SWC) 11-24, Fri-Sat -2 h
306 17th Avenue South West ✉T2S 0A8 ☎ 244-9991

SEX SHOPS/BLUE MOVIES

After Dark (g) 1314 1st Street SW ☎ 264-7399
Videos, toys, lingerie, magazines, peep shows.

Tads (g)
1506 14th Street South West ☎ 244-8239

The Erogenous Zone (G)
3812 McLoad Tr. Street
☎ 287-3100

SAUNAS/BATHS

Goliath's Saunatel (b f G MA sb wh VS) 0-24 h
308 17th Avenue South West ✉T2S 0A8 *(rear entrance)*
☎ 229-0911

BOOK SHOPS

Rainbow Pride Resource Center (A AC CC GLM MA S) Mon-Sat 12-22:00h, Sun 12-21:00h
L100 - 822 - 11th Avenue SW ☎ 266-5685
Adult videos, gifts, cards, books & magazines

LEATHER & FETISH SHOPS

B&B Leather Works (glm LJ TV) Tue-Fri 10.30-18, Sat 13-18 h. Party every 2nd/4th Fri Sat.
426 8th Avenue SE ☎ 236-7072

GUEST HOUSES

Black Orchid Manor (bf GLM H msg wh)
1401 2nd Street N.W. ✉T2M 2W2 ☎ 276 2471 Fax: 276-2470
E-Mail: lthrman@canuck.com
Homepage: www.plaza.v-wave/paladin/blackorc.html
Small B&B in Edwardian home. 3 rooms with private bath.

Foxwood B&B (bf CC GLM MA H OS wh)
1725 12th Street S.W. ✉T3T 3N1 ☎ 244-6693
E-Mail: foxwood@home.com
Homepage: www.members.home.net/foxwoodbandb
3 rooms with shared bath and one suite with private bath. TV, video. Please call for rates

Westways Guest House (bf CC G H msg wh)
216 25th Avenue South West ✉T2S 0L1 ☎ 229-1758 Fax: 228-6265 E-Mail: calgary@westways.ab.ca
Homepage: www.westways.ab.ca
All rooms with private baths.

11th Street Lodging (bf CC G H NU)
1307-11th Street S.W. ✉AB T2R 1G5 ☎ 209-0111 Fax: 209-2571 E-Mail: dulj@cadvision.com Homepage: www.11street.com
5 doubles, 4 singles with shared bath and 1 studio and 1 apartment with private bath. Rooms with balcony, radio and TV/VCR. Premium downtown location.

GENERAL GROUPS

Gay & Lesbian Academics, Students & Staff (GLASS)
29E MacEwan Hall Club, 2500 University Drive NW, *University of Calgary, T2N 1N4* ☎ 220-2872

Illusions Social Club for TV and TS Tue-Fri 10.30-18, Sat 13-16 h. Meets 2nd Sat/last Fri 19.30.
PO Box 2000, 6802 Ogden Road SE ✉T2C 1B4 ☎ 236-7072
E-mail: bnblethr@cadvision.com

Mount Royal College-Gay & Lesbian Collective
4825 Richard Road SW ☎ 686-2352

HEALTH GROUPS

AIDS Calgary Awareness Association Mon-Fri 8.30-16.30 h
Suite 200, 1509 Centre Street South ✉T2G 2E6 ☎ 508-2500
FAX 263-7358. E-mail aids_calgary@nucleus.com. Homepage http://www.nucleus.com/~aids_calgary

HELP WITH PROBLEMS

Gay Lines Calgary 19-22 h
201, 223 - 12th Avenue South west ✉T2R 0G9 ☎ 234 8973
FAX 261-9776

RELIGIOUS GROUPS

MCC Calgary
PO Box 82054,
Scarborough Post Office ✉T3C 3M5 ☎ 244-0365

SPORT GROUPS

Alberta Rockies Gay Rodeo Association (ARGRA)
#208, 223 12th Avenue South West ✉T2R 0G9
☎ 541-8140

Alpine Frontrunners Club
PO Box 22054, Bankers Hall, T2P 4J1 ☎ 244-4644

Apollo: Friends in Sports (GLM)
PO Box 22054, Bankers Hall ✉T2P 4J1 ☎ 281 3572
☎ *270-0742 (Steve). Gay, lesbian sports club.*

Camp 181
PO Box 702 Station M ✉AL T2P 2J3
Gay, lesbian outdoors group.

CRUISING

-Tennis Court on 2nd Street (between 13th & 14th Avenue South West)
-University of Calgary (Education Building, men's restroom, 2nd floor)
-13th Avenue South West (r) (between 6th & 7th Street South West)

Edmonton ☎ 403

GAY INFO

Gay and Lesbian Community Centre of Edmonton (GLCCE) Info Line: Mon-Fri 19-22, Wed 13-16 / Youth phone line: Sat 20-22 h
Box 1852 ✉T5J 2P2 E-Mail: glcce@freenet.edmonton.ab.ca Homepage: www.freenet.edmonton.ab.ca/glcce.
Info Line ☎ 488-3234. Gay events line ☎ 988-4018.
Youth phone line ☎ 488-1574.

BARS

Boots'n Saddle (B G LJ MA N P SNU STV WE) 15-2 h
10240 106th Street/103rd Avenue ✉T5J 1H7 ☎ 423-5014
Private club. Sun buffet.

Buddie's Pub (Glm)
10116 124th Street ✉T5N 1P6 *(above Jazzberry's)*
☎ 488-6636

Rebar (B CC D GLM MA N S) 19-03:00h
10551 Whyte Avenue ✉T6E 2A3 ☎ 433-3600

Secrets Bar and Grill (B F GLM)
10249 107th Street ☎ 990-1818

DANCECLUBS

Choices Nightclub (B D GLM stv) Closed Sun & Mon.
10148- 105 Street ✉T5J 1C9 ☎ 425 4591

Roost. The (AC B CC D f GLM MA OS s WE YG) Mon-Sat 16-3, Sun 20-3 h
10345-104 Street ✉T5J 1B9 ☎ 426-3150

Vicious Pink (B D GLM) Thu - Sat 21-03:00h
10149 - 105th Street

RESTAURANTS

Garage Burger Bar & Grill (AC B F G MA) 11-22 h
10242 106 Street ✉T5J 1H7 ☎ 423-5014

SEX SHOPS/BLUE MOVIES

Express Video (CC G) 13-21 h, closed Tue
202-11745 Jasper Avenue ✉T5K 0N5 ☎ 482-7480
E-mail: exec.express@v-wave.com. Adult video sales, rentals and clothing.

Pride Video (G) 10121
124 Street NW ☎ 452-7743

SAUNAS/BATHS

Down Under (AC CC DR G MA sa sb VS wh) 0-24 h
12224 Jasper Avenue/122th Street ✉T5N 3K3 ☎ 482-7960

BOOK SHOPS

Greenwood's Bookshoppe (glm) Mon-Fri 9.30-21, Sat 9.30-17.30 h
10355 Whyte Avenue ☎ 439-2005
Large independent bookstore.

TRAVEL & TRANSPORT

Canadian Arctic Expeditions Ltd. (G)
Suite 205, 10216-122 Street, ✉T5N 1L9 ☎ 482 3334
Fax: 426-2565
Offering adventure tours like 5 days polar bear observation or 6 days whale watching throughout Canada for gay and lesbian clientele.

GUEST HOUSES

Northern Lights Bed & Breakfast (G H NU pi)
8216, 151 Street ✉T5R 1H6 ☎ 483-1572
E-Mail: nlight69@hotmail.com

HEALTH GROUPS

AIDS Network of Edmonton Society Mon-Fri 9-16
201 11456 Jasper Avenue ✉T5K 0M1 ☎ 488-5816

Gay Men's Outreach Crew
c/o AIDS Network Society, 201, 11456 Jasper Avenue
☎ 988-3671
Group promoting safer sex.

RELIGIOUS GROUPS

MCC of Edmonton Meets Sun 19.15 h
10086 MacDonald Drive
Unit 151, 10342-107 Street ✉T5J 1K2 ☎ 429-2321

SPORT GROUPS

Northern Titans International Bowling Association of Alberta Meet Sat 17.15 h
at Gateway Lanes, 34 Avenue/104 Street
PO Box 1852 ✉T5J 2P2 ☎ 454-1458 *(Joe)*.

CRUISING

-Victoria Park (near the golf course)
-Hill (across from McDonald Hotel)

Lethbridge ☎ 403

GAY INFO

Gay & Lesbian Peer Support Line
Tue, Wed 19-22 h ☎ 329 4666

Red Deer ☎ 403

GAY INFO

Gay Lines of Central Alberta Wed 19-21 h
PO Box 1078 ✉T4N 6S5 ☎ 340 2198

BARS

Other Place. The (AC B CC D F GLM MA N S STV) Tue-Sun 16-3 h, SAt 20-03:00h. closed Mon
Bay 3 & 4, 5579-47 Street ✉T4N 1S1 ☎ 342-6440

CRUISING

-Canyon Park

CDN-British-Columbia

Southwest CDN
Initials: BC
Time: GMT -8
Area: 949,000 km² / 366,409 sq mi
Population: 3,933,000
Capital: Victoria

Castlegar ☎ 250

HEALTH GROUPS

AIDS Network, Outreach & Support Society (ANKORS)
903 4th Street ☎ 365-2437

Duncan ✉ V9L 3X1 ☎ 250

GENERAL GROUPS

Island Gay and Lesbian Association
PO Box 129 ✉V9L 3X1 ☎ 748-7689

Fernie ☎ 250

GUEST HOUSES

Fernie Westways Guest House (bf CC e g H msg wh)
PO Box 658, 202 4 A Avenue ✉V0B 1M0 ☎ 423-3058 Fax: 423-3059 E-Mail: fernie@westways.ab.ca Homepage: www.westways.ab.ca
Small B&B in remote but beautiful setting. All rooms with private bath, radio and TV/VCR.

Kamloops ☎ 250

GENERAL GROUPS

Gay and Lesbian Association (GLM MA) Call for details
PO Box 2071, Station A ✉V2B 7K6 ☎ 376-7311 E-Mail: galakam@yahoo.com Homepage: www.gaycanada.com/kamloops-gala

Kelowna ☎ 250

GAY INFO

Okanagan Gay / Lesbian Organization (OGLO) Infoline Mon, Thu 19-21:30h, Wed & Fri 16:30-17:30h
991 Richter Street ✉V1Y 7P4 *346 Bernard Avenue* ☎ 860-8555
E-Mail: okrainbow@hotmail.com
Support groups, social events, lending library. Dances usually held at Laurel Bldg, 1600 Ellis St.

GUEST HOUSES

The Flags Bed and Breakfast (AC bf G H NU pi sa sol wh) All year
2295 McKinley Road ✉V1V 2B6 ☎ 868-2416 Fax: 868-2416
Country setting. 3 double rooms and 1 single with bath/shower and WC on the floor. Clothing optional.

HELP WITH PROBLEMS

AA Gay/Lesbian ☎ 762-0422

Langley ☎ 604

GENERAL GROUPS

Langley Outreach 5339
207th Street ☎ 534-7921
Gay and Lesbian family service.

Nanaimo ☎ 250

GAY INFO

Gayline Mon-Fri 18-21 h
☎ 754-2585

GENERAL GROUPS

Central Island Gay & Lesbian Association
PO Box 127 ✉V9R 5K4 ☎ 741-0002

Nelson ☎ 250

PRIVATE ACCOMODATION

Dragon Fly Inn (glm)
1016 Hall Mines Road ☎ 354-1128 Fax: 354-1128
E-Mail: dragonfly@netidea.com

GENERAL GROUPS

ANKORS West Kootenay Gays and Lesbians Society
101 Baker Street ✉V1L 4H1 ☎ 354-4297
E-Mail: ankors@wkpowerlink.com
Support and advocacy services, needle exchange, community care teams.

Port Alberni

CRUISING

-Harbour Quay Promenade

Prince George ☎ 250

GUEST HOUSES

Hawthorne Bed and Breakfast (CC glm H NU WO wh)
829 PG Pulp Mill Road, RR 4, Site 7, Comp. 10 ✉V2N 2J2
☎ 563-8299 Fax: 563-0899

GENERAL GROUPS

Gay and Lesbian Association
36-1306 7th Avenue ☎ 562-6253

Prince Rupert ☎ 250

GAY INFO

Gay Info Line
PO Box 881 ☎ 627-8900

Revelstoke

GENERAL GROUPS

Lothlorien
PO Box 8557 ✉V0E 3G0
Gay & lesbian support group.

Salt Spring Island ☎ 250

GUEST HOUSES

Green Rose Bed & Breakfast (CC GLM H OS)
388 Scott Point Drive ✉V8K 2R2 ☎ 537-9927 Fax: 537-9927
Ocean-side suite with own entrance, gas fireplace, kitchenette and bath. All rooms face the sea.

Summerhill Guest House (glm H)
209 Chu-An Drive ✉V8K 1H9 ☎ 537-2727 Fax: 531 4301
E-Mail: summerhill@saltspring.com
Homepage: www.bestinns.net/canada/bc/rdsummerhill.html
3 rooms with shower/bath, balcony, own key. An island guest house overlooking magnificent Sansum Narrows

PRIVATE ACCOMODATION

Blue Ewe. The (bf CC H GLM msg NU sa wh)
1207 Beddis Road ✉V8K 2C8 ☎ 537-9344
E-Mail: blueewe@saltspring.com.
Homepage: members.ttripod.com/~blueewe.
Located on Gulf Islands. 3 double rooms with shower/bath, WC

Tofino ☎ 250

PRIVATE ACCOMODATION

West Wind (bf CC f GLM NU OS wh WO)
1321 Pacific Rim, Box 436 ✉V0R 2Z0 ☎ 725-2224 Fax: 725-2212 E-Mail: westwind@island.net Homepage: www.island.net/~westwind
Small B&B located in beautiful landscape. All rooms with private bath, balcony, Sat-TV/VCR, radio, kitchenette and hair-dryer. Free airport pick up

Vancouver ☎ 604 BC-Vancouver

● Vancouver is often compared to Hong Kong because of over a quarter million Hong Kong-Chinese people who have established themselves in this city, giving Vancouver an international flair. Investments by new immigrants have led to an economic boom, a dramatic increase in the value of properties and the construction of many new high-rise apartment and office blocks. Vancouver has a beatiful and natural setting, with the Coastal Mountains on the one side and the Pacific Ocean on the other. First class ski resorts are within easy reach. The best known ski resort „Whistler" is about 90 minutes drive from Vancouver. Whistler's Gay Ski Week attracts gay and lesbian skiers from all over the world. Stanley Park is the largest urban park in North America, with over 9 kilometers of pathways.
Vancouver is well known for its rainy weather, but it also has the mildest winters in the country. In January the average temperature is 1°C, while the rest of Canada lies under heavy blankets of snow. In the summer the average temperature from May to September is around 20°C. Popular attractions include the Capilano Suspension Bridge, Chinatown, the food market on Granville Island, the Museum of Anthropology and the shops and cafés along Robinson Street.
Many of the gay bars, cafés and guest houses are located in the West End. One would, however, expect more gay gay bars and danceclubs in a city with a population of over 2 million people. The strict regulations regarding opening and closing times effect the bar buisness. Vancouver offers the gay tourist a wide spectrum of activities from bars, clubs, saunas, gay beaches and many cruising areas. Vancouver Island is also well worth a visit.

✱ Nicht umsonst wird Vancouver immer häufiger mit Hongkong verglichen. Über eine Viertel Million Hongkong-Chinesen haben sich in den letzten Jahren hier niedergelassen und geben der Stadt, trotz Ihrer abgeschiedenen Lage, ein internationales Flair.
Die Stadt erlebt einen regelrechten Boom. Überall entstehen neue Wolkenkratzer, die Grundstückspreise schnellen in die Höhe und neue Wirtschaftszweige lassen sich in der Stadt am Pazifik nieder.
Vancouver liegt von viel Wasser umgeben eindrucksvoll am Fuße der Pacific Ranges. Erstklassige Skigebiete sind in kürzester Zeit zu erreichen. Den bekannten Skiort *Whistler* erreicht man in knapp 90 Minuten. Mit dem Stanley Park verfügt Vancouver zudem über einen der weltgrößten Stadtparks, den man auf einem 9 Kilometer langen Klippenweg umrunden kann.
Zwar ist Vancouver bekannt für seine große Anzahl an Regentagen,

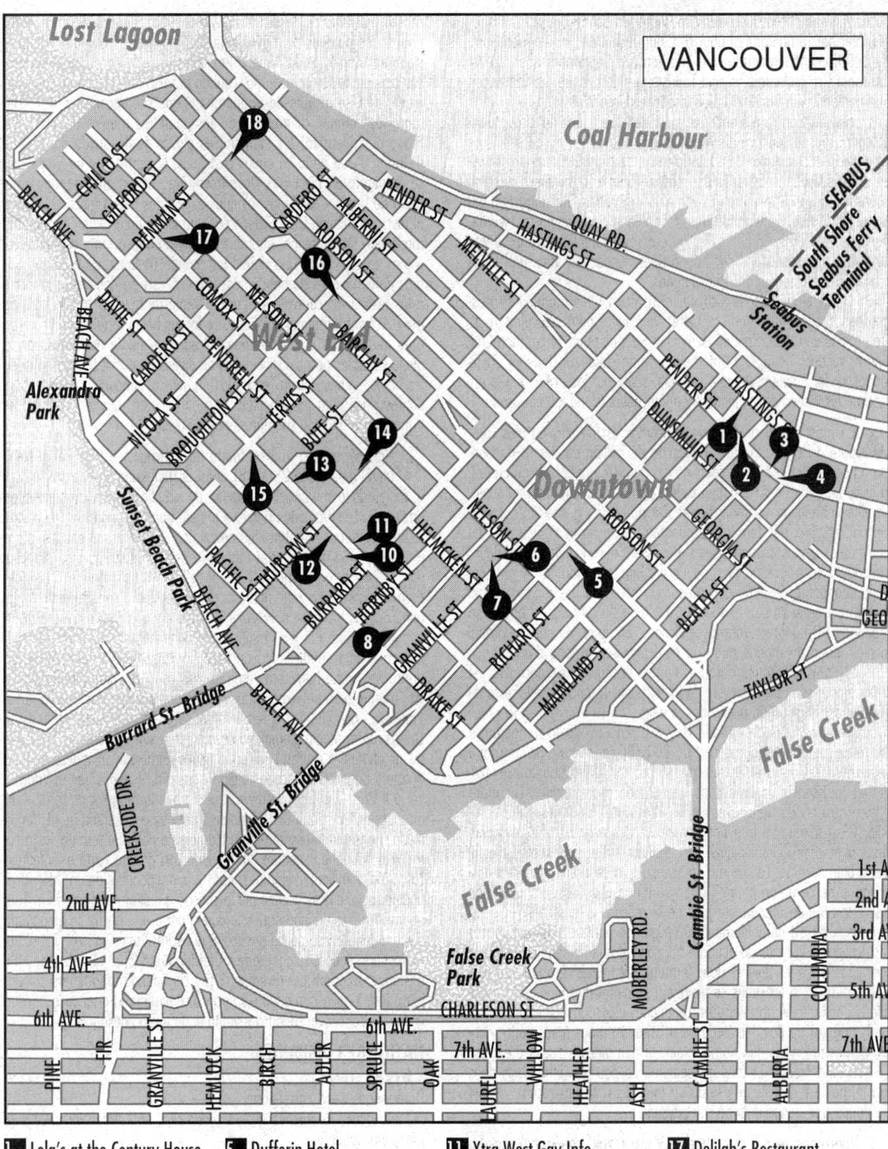

1 Lola's at the Century House Restaurant
2 Ms. T's Bar
3 Club Vancouver Sauna
4 Heritage House Hotel
Lotus Cabaret
Uncle Charlies Bar
5 Dufferin Hotel
6 Mack's Leather Inc. Leather Shop
7 Royal Hotel
8 Odyssey Disco
10 Numbers Cabaret Disco
11 Xtra West Gay Info
12 F 212 Sauna
13 Doll & Penny's Café Restaurant
14 Colibri Bed & Breakfast
15 Little Sister's Bookshop
16 West End Guest House
17 Delilah's Restaurant
18 Denman Station Bar

doch während der Rest Kanadas im Winter im Schnee versinkt, läßt es sich hier bei Temperaturen über 0°C gut aushalten. Im warmen Sommer (Durschnittstemperatur am Tag von Mai-September über 20°C) tummeln sich Einheimische und Touristen an den zahlreichen Stränden und genießen ein Bad im kühlen aber glasklaren Wasser.
Das schwule Zentrum Vancouvers ist das West End in Downtown gelegen. Hier finden sich die meisten Bars und Cafés, einige sehr gute schwule Bed&Breakfast-Unterkünfte sowie der sehr gut sortierte schwulen Buchladen Little Sister's. Die schwule Szene ist sicherlich nicht so abwechslungsreich, wie man es von einer so großen (Ballungsraum mit mehr als 2 Mio. Einwohner) und lebendigen Stadt erwarten würde. Dies liegt wohl zum größten Teil an der sehr restriktiven Vergabe von Ausschanklizensen sowie der frühen Sperrstunde. Alle Bars und Clubs schließen spätestens um 2 Uhr morgens.
Doch wenn Einheimische sich vielleicht auch über mangelnde Ausgemöglichkeiten beklagen, so bietet Vancouver dem schwulen Touristen mit seinen Bars, Saunen, schwulen Stränden und zahlreichen Cruising Areas doch genügend Unterhaltungsmöglichkeiten. Und wer etwas länger in der Pazifikmetropole verweilt, sollte auf jeden Fall einen Abstecher zur landschaftlich einmaligen Vancouver Island mit einplanen.

▲Ce n'est pas pour rien que Vancouver est de plus en plus comparé à Hongkong. Plus d'un quart de million de chinois de Hongkong se sont établis ici au cours de ces dernière années et confèrent à la ville, en dépit de sa situation isolée, une atmosphère internationale. La ville connaît un véritable boom. De nouveaux gratte-ciel naissent partout, les prix des terrains augmentent de façon vertigineuse et de nouveaux secteurs économiques s'établissent dans la ville du pacifique. Vancouver se trouve au pied du Pacific Ranges entourée de manière impressionnante de beaucoup d'eau. On accède à des régions de ski de premier ordre en peu de temps. Le lieu de ski *Whistler* est atteint en moins de 90 minutes. Vancouver dispose, en outre, du parc municipal le plus grand du monde que l'on peut parcourir le long d'un chemin d'écueil de 9 kilomètres de long. Certes, la région de Vancouver est connue pour son grand nombre de jours de pluie, tandis que le reste du Canada est englouti en hiver dans la neige, on se trouve bien ici grâce à des températures de plus de 01/2 C. En été, où la température moyenne pendant la journée est de 201/2C, et ce du mois de mai à septembre, les natifs et les touristes s'ébattent sur les nombreuses plages et jouissent d'un bain dans l'eau froide mais limpide. Le centre d'homosexuels de Vancouver est le „West End" situé au centre de la ville. C'est ici que se trouvent la majorité des bars et cafés, des pensions avec petit déjeuner ainsi que la librairie d'homosexuels Little Sister's bien assortie. La scène d'homosexuels n'est assurément pas aussi variée de ce qu'on pourrait attendre d'une ville aussi grande (zone de concentration urbaine de plus de 2 millions d'habitants) et aussi animée. Ceci est probablement dû en grande partie à l'attribution très restrictive des licences de débit de boissons et aux heures de fermeture avancées. Tous les bars et clubs ferment à 2 heures du matin au plus tard. Pourtant, si les natifs se plaignent peut-être du manque de possibilités de sortie, Vancouver offre cependant aux touristes homosexuels suffisamment de possibilités de divertissement grâce à ses bars, saunas, plages réservées aux homosexuels et nombreuses zones d'excursion (Cruising Areas). Et celui qui séjourne un peu plus longtemps dans la métropole du Pacifique devrait en tous cas faire un crochet sur l'île de Vancouver unique quant à son paysage.

☆Vancouver se compara mucho, y con razón, con Hongkong. En los últimos años más de 250.000 chinos han fijado su residencia aqui. A pesar que Vancouver se encuentre, geográficamente hablando, muy aislada, sus emigrantes le dan un carácter muy cosmopolita. La ciudad vive un auge vertiginoso, por todas partes se construyen rascacielos, los precios de vivienda suben sin parar y nuevas industrias se están estableciendo. Vancouver está situado a orillas del Pacífico al pie de las montañas Pacific Ranges. Por esta razón ofrece la zona verdaderos paraísos para la práctica del esqui, buen ejemplo es a solamente 90 minutos de distancia. Vancouver se enorgullece de tener uno de los parques de mayor extensión en todo el mundo, el impresionante Stanley Park. Aunque la ciudad tiene fama por sus numerosos dias de lluvia, en invierno, cuando el resto de Canada se cubre de nieve, aqui se disfruta de temperaturas que sobrepasan los 0°C. Durante los veranos calurosos (Con temperaturas medias de 20°C de mayo a septiembre) los inumerables playas se llenan de gente, que disfrutan de un baño en aguas cristalinas. El centro gay de Vancouver se encuentra en West End, Downtown. Aqui se concentra el mayor número de bares y cafeterias, algunos excelentes hotels gays (Bed&Breakfast), y la libería Little Sister's con una amplia oferta de literatura homosexual. Sin embargo, el ambiente gay no ofrece tanta variedad, como es de esperar de una ciudad tan grande (aglomeración úrbana con más de 2 miliones de habitantes) y vivaz. Esto se debe en gran parte a las restrictivas concesiones para la venta de bebidas alcohólicas, como a la hora temprana del cierre. Todos los bares y clubs cierran como muy tarde a las 2 de la mañana. Aunque la gente de Vancouver se queje sobre las pocas posibilidades de diversión, el turista encuentra en los bares, saunas, playas gay y las numerosas areas de cruising abundantes sitios para pasárlo bien. Uno de los sitios dignos de visitar es Vancouver Island con su impresionante paisaje.

❖Non per caso si fa il confronto tra Vancouver e Hongkong. Negli ultimi anni più di 250.000 cinesi di Hongkong si sono stabiliti qui e, malgrado la sua posizione isolata, danno alla città un carattere internazionale. La città vede un vero e proprio boom economico. Dappertutto emergono nuovi grattacieli, i prezzi degli immobili salgono alle stelle e si sviluppano nuovi settori economici nella città sul pacifico. Vancouver, situato pittorescamente ai piedi delle Pacific Ranges, è circondato da molta acqua. Le zone di prima classe per sciare sono facili da raggiungere, p.es. al famoso *Whistler* si arriva entro un'ora e mezzo. Il Stanley Park, uno dei più grandi parchi comunali, si può percorrere per mezzo di una strada sopra uno scoglio lunga 9 kilometri. Anche se Vancouver viene nominata come la città con i massimi giorni di pioggia, mentre però nel resto del paese in inverno si sprofonda nella neve, Vancouver può vantarsi di temperature sopra lo zero. Nelle calde estati (temperatura media giornaliera da maggio a settembre sopra i 20 gradi) gli abitanti e i turisti si divertono sulle numerose spiagge e godono di fare il bagno nelle acque limpide e fresche. Il centro gay di Vancouver è il West End in Downtown. Qui si trova la maggior parte dei bar, alcuni buoni soggiorni Bed&Breakfast per gay e la libreria gay Little Sister's con un buon assortimento. L'ambiente gay non è tanto vasto come ci si potrebbe aspettare da una città così grande (città e hinterland con più di 2 milioni di abitanti); questo può dipendere da una restrittiva aggiudicazione delle licenze per lo spaccio e dall'orario d'apertura. Tutti i bar e i club chiudono infatti alle due di notte. Ma anche se gli abitanti si lamentano per le poche possibilità di uscire, Vancouver con i suoi numerosi bar, saune, spiagge gay e Cruising Areas offre al turista gay abbastanza occasioni per divertirsi. E per chi intende intrattenersi un po' più a lungo nella metropoli sul pacifico, dovrebbe in ogni caso fare un salto alla Vancouver Island che vanta di un'unico paesaggio.

NATIONAL COMPANIES

Chisel (GLM)
Homepage: www.chisel.com
Art and news, interactive shows, video clips and streaming. Hot wild gay photo gallery.

GAY INFO

Gay and Lesbian Center
Business line: 10-19 / Switchboard: 19-22 h
1170 Bute Street, Suite 4 *(2nd floor)*
Houses gay/lesbian switchboard, counselling services, library, food bank and a legal clinic. Business line ☎ 684-5307 and switchboard ☎ 684-6869.

Out On The Shelves 19.30-21.30, Mon 19.30-21.30, Wen 15-18
1170 Bute Street ✉V6E 1Z6 ☎ 684-5309
Canada's largest G&L Library.
XTRA West Mon-Fri 9-17 h
501-1033 Davie St. ✉V6E 1M5 ☎ 684-9696 *Fax: 684-9697. Vancouver's gay and lesbian bi-weekly newspaper. Contains news, arts, and entertainment information.*

BARS

Club 23 West (B D GLM)
23 West Cordova Street ☎ 688-5351
Denman Station (B D G lj MA s) 19-2 h
860 Denman Street/Haro Street ☎ 669-3448
Ms T's (B G LJ) Mon-Sat 20- h
339 W Pender St ✉V6E 1T3 ☎ 682-8096
Royal Hotel Pub (B GLM S) 10-23 h
1025 Granville Street ✉V6Z 1L4 ☎ 685-5335
Live entertainment Thu-Sun
Uncle Charlies (B G MA)
c/o Heritage House Hotel, 455 Abbott Street ☎ 685-7777

CAFES

Edge Coffee Bar. The (b bf f glm) Mon-Sat 7-4, Sun -2 h
1148 Davie Street ✉V6E 1N1 ☎ 688-3395

DANCECLUBS

Celebrities (B D GLM MA) Mon-Sat 21-2, Sun 20-24 h
1022 Davie Street *(next door to Numbers)* ☎ 689-3180
Numbers (AC B D G MA VS) 20-2, Sun 20-24 h
1042 Davie Street, Burrard ☎ 685-4077 *Popular*
Odyssey. The (AC B D G s T YG) 19-2 h
1251 Howe Street ☎ 689-5256

RESTAURANTS

Delilah's (B E F glm)
1739 Comox ☎ 687-3424
Doll and Penny's (B f glm) Mon-Thu 7-4, Fri Sat 0-24 h
1167 Davie Street ☎ 685-3417
Harry's Off Commercial (B F glm)
1716 Charles Street ☎ 253-1789
Homer's Bar (b bf F glm)
1249 Howe Street ☎ 689-2444
Lola's at the Century House (B F glm)
432 Richards Street ✉V6B 2Z3 ☎ 684-5652
Award-winning cooking in elegant setting.
Mongolie Grill. The (F glm)
1108-4th Street , SW ☎ 262-7773
Taki's Taverna (B F glm)
1106 Davie Street ☎ 682-1336
Water Street Café. The (B F glm)
300 Water Street ☎ 689-2832

SHOWS

Lotus Cabaret (B GLM MA STV) 20-2 h
c/o Heritage House Hotel, 455 Abbott Street ✉V6B 2L2 ☎ 685-7777
Cabaret and bar. Popular.

SEX SHOPS/BLUE MOVIES

Willy's Books & Video (glm) 10-23 h
1109 Granville Street ☎ 685-3226

SAUNAS/BATHS

Club Vancouver (B CC DR f G MA P sa sb VS) 0-24 h
399 West Pender Street ✉V6B 1T3 ☎ 681-5719
F 212° Steam (AC CC DR f G MA P sb VS wh WO YG) Mon-Sun 0-24 h
1048 Davie Street ✉V6E 1M3 ☎ 689-9719
Membership required. There is another sauna F 212° Steam, 430 Columbia Street, New Westminster ☎877 4765
Richards Street Service Club (f G sb VS) 0-24 h
1169 Richards Street/Davie Street ☎ 684-6010

BOOK SHOPS

Little Sisters Book and Art Emporium (AC GLM MA) 10-23:00 h
1238 Davie Street ✉V6E 1N4 ☎ 669-1753 Fax: 685-0252. E-Mail: lsisters@lsisters.com Homepage: www.lsisters.com
Free maps of gay Vancouver available. Literary events.

LEATHER & FETISH SHOPS

Mack's Leathers Inc. Mon-Wed 11-19, Thu-Fri 11-20, Sat 11-18, Sun 12-17 h
1043 Granville Street ☎ 688-6225
Leather articles, body piercing.

VIDEO SHOPS

Videomatica (glm) 1855 W 4th Avenue ✉V6J 1M4 ☎ 734-0411
Good selection of gay and lesbian films.

HOTELS

Dufferin Hotel (B CC F G H lj MA OS S SNU STV)
900 Seymour Street/Smithe ✉V6B 3L9 ☎ 683-4251 Fax: 683-0611 E-Mail: indigo@direct.ca. Homepage: www.dufferinhotel.com
Hotel with restaurant and bar located in the heart of the city. Downtown Vancouver, close to the scene. Bar includes professional dancers Fri & Sat as well as nude GoGo boys every night. No coverchar-ge.
Heritage House Hotel (AC B CC d GLM H MA)
455 Abbott Street ✉V6B 2L2 ☎ 685-7777 Fax: 685-7067
Convenient location, 10 km to the airport. 110 double rooms. TV and phone (local calls free of charge) in all rooms.
Royal Hotel (GLM H)
1025 Granville Street ✉V6Z 1L4
☎ 1-877-685-5337 E-Mail: www.attheroyal.com
Newly renovated gay accommodation. Gay pub „ The Royal".

GUEST HOUSES

Albion Guest House (bf CC GLM H)
592 West 19th Avenue ✉V5Z 1W6 ☎ 873-2287
FAX 879-5682. Centrally located. Rates Can$ 50-103 (summer) and Can$ 35-65 (winter)
Colibri Bed & Breakfast (bf CC GLM H MA) All year
1101 Thurlow Street ✉V6E 1W9 ☎ 689-5100 Fax: 682 3925 E-Mail: colibri@home.com
City centre - 2 blocks to bars, clubs and restaurants.
Don's Home Away From Home Guest House (g H)
6870 MacPherson Avenue, Burnaby B.C. ☎ 435-9007
Nelson House (bf CC GLM H) closed Christmas and New Year's week
977 Broughton Street ✉V6G 2A4 ☎ 684-9793 E-Mail: bestin-van@lightspeed.bc.ca
Walking distance to downtown. 4 double rooms some with private bath and balcony, all rooms with phone and TV.
West End Guest House (bf glm H) All year
1362 Haro Street ✉V6E 1G2 ☎ 681-2889 ☎ 604/ 681-5979

E-Mail: wegh@idmail.com
Homepage: www.westendguesthouse.com
Located in the West End. Victorian style house. Rooms decorated with antiques. Reservations from 08-21:00h

GENERAL GROUPS

Gays, Lesbians and Bisexuals of UBC
SUB, PO Box 9, UBC ✉V6T 1W5 ☎ 822-4638
Lesbian and Gay Youth ☎ 684-6869
Support and activity group for teenagers.
Over 40's Group Meets last Sat
☎ 689-9219

FETISH GROUPS

Vancouver Leather Alliance (VLA)
c/o Northwind, PO Box 2253 ✉V6B 3W2
Call ☎ 88-9378 ext. 2035

HEALTH GROUPS

AIDS Vancouver 24 hours
1107 Seymour Street *(at Helmcken)* ☎ 687-5220
Houses AIDS Research Centre (switchboard, library).
Helpline ☎ 687-2437
Persons with AIDS Society
1107 Seymour Street
☎ 893-2250
Richards Street Service Club 0-24 h
1169 Richards Street/Davie Street ☎ 684-6010

SWIMMING

-Wreck Beach (G NU) (Near the University of British Columbia campus, plenty of action in the wooded area. Access by several paths with about 200 steps down from P along roadside.)

CRUISING

-Stanley Park (day and night. East of P 2nd beach)
-English Bay Bath House
-Kitsilano Park (at the pool)
-Burnette River Park (New Westminster)

Vernon ☎ 250

PRIVATE ACCOMODATION

Rainbow's End B & B (bf G wh) All year
8282 Jackpine Road ✉V1B 3M7 ☎ 542 4842
E-Mail: rainbowsend@bc.sympatico.ca

Victoria ☎ 250

BARS

BJ's Lounge (AC B CC d f GLM MA S STV VS YG)
12-02:00h, Sun 12-24:00h
642 Johnson Street / Broad ✉V8W 1M6 *(Courner of Broad and Johnson Street)* ☎ 388-0505

RESTAURANTS

Friends of Dorothy`s Café (F GLM) Mon-Wed 11.30-20, Thu-Sat 11.30-4, Sun 11-20
615 Johnson Street ☎ 381 2277
Will deliver to BJ`s Lounge.

SAUNAS/BATHS

Steamworks (CC DR f G MA msg p sa VS WO) 19-09:00h
582 Johnson Street ✉V9W 1M6 ☎ 383-6623
No membership fees

HOTELS

Camellia House (bf GLM H)
1994 Leighton Road, V8R 1N6 ☎ 370-2816

GUEST HOUSES

Weekender Bed & Breakfast (bf GLM H msg)
10 Eberts Street ✉V8S 5L6 ☎ 389-1688
Homepage: www.bctravel.com/weekender.html
Located along Victoria's scenic drive. All roomes with shower/bath/WC, telephone, heating, own key.

HEALTH GROUPS

AIDS Vancouver Island
304-733 Johnson Street, ✉V8W 3C7 ☎ 384-4554

HELP WITH PROBLEMS

AA Gay/Lesbian
☎ 381-0542

CRUISING

-Beacon Hill Park (along Dallas Road)
-The Causeway (in front of the Embassy Hotel)
-Government Street (in front of the Empress Hotel)

Whistler ☎ 604

GUEST HOUSES

Whistler Retreat. The (bf CC glm H sa wh WO)
8561 Drifter Way ✉V0N 1B8 ☎ 938-9245
E-Mail: whistler@axionet.com
Rooms with or without shower.

CDN-Manitoba

Central CDN
Initials: MB
Time: GMT -6
Area: 650,000 km² / 250,965 sq mi.
Population: 1,145,000
Capital: Winnipeg

Brandon ☎ 204

GENERAL GROUPS

Gays and Lesbians of Brandon & Elsewehre (GLOBE) Fri 19-21 h
PO Box 220 39 ✉R7A 6Y9 ☎ 727-4297

HEALTH GROUPS

AIDS Brandon
PO Box 32 ✉R7A 6Y2 ☎ 726-4020 Fax: 728-4344

Winnipeg ☎ 204

GAY INFO

Rainbow Resource Centre (GLM) Mon-Sat 19.30-22, Wed-Fri 13-16.30 h
222 Osborne Street, #1, ✉R3C 2Z6 ☎ 284-5208
Fax: 478-1160 E-Mail: wglrc@escape.ca
Phone-line, Drop-in/groups, library archive, meeting place for gay/lesbian groups. Non-profit organisation.
Swerve
200-63 Albert Street ✉R3B 1G4 ☎ 942-4599
FAX 947-0554. Email: gilmarc@escape.ca. Monthly newspaper.

BARS

Gio's (B D Glm MA p SNU W) Mon-Sat 21-2 h, Fri Sat (SNU)
272 Sherbrook Street ✉R3C 2B9 ☎ 786-1236

DANCECLUBS

Club Happenings (AC B D GLM S snu stv VS WE YG) Mon-Wed 21-2.30, Thu 20-3.45 (SNU), Fri -3 (STV), Sat -3.30 h
274 Sherbrook Street/Broadway Avenue *(upstairs)* ☎ 774-3576
Very popular on Sat nights. Gay dance bar & lounge.

Club 200 (AC B CC D F GLM MA S STV WE) Mon-Sat 16-2, Sun -22 h
190 Garry Street ✉R3C 1G6 ☎ 943-6045

RESTAURANTS

Big Ruby's (AC CC F GLM MA W) Mon-Fri 11.30-14 17-23, Sat-Sun 11-14 17-23 h
102 Sherbrook Street/Westminster Avenue ☎ 775-0188

SAUNAS/BATHS

Office Sauna Baths (AC G MA sa sb VS) 0-24 h
1060 Main Street/Burrows ☎ 589-6133
Rooms Can$ 21, lockers 16.

BOOK SHOPS

McNally Robinson (glm)
1120 Grant Avenue, Unit 4000 ☎ 475-0483

GUEST HOUSES

Winged Ox Guest House (GLM H)
82 Spence Street ✉R3C 1Y3 ☎ 783 7408 Fax: 783 7408 E-Mail: winged-ox@gaycanada.com Homepage: www.gaycanada.com/winged-ox

PRIVATE ACCOMODATION

Masson's Bed and Breakfast (glm H MA)
181 Masson Street ✉R2H 0H3 ☎ 237-9230 Fax: 237-9230 E-Mail: massbnb@home.com Homepage: www.members.home.net/massbnb

GENERAL GROUPS

Parents and Friends of Lesbians and Gays (PFLAG) Meet last Tue in Month 19:00h. Call for details
c/o 1003-100 Adamar Road ✉R3T 3X6 ☎ 275-0799

Prime Timers 2nd Wed. 19:00h
Box 260 72, 116 Sherbrook Street ✉R3K 4K9 ☎ 889-2835 ☎ 888-0451

FETISH GROUPS

C.L.U.B. Winnipeg
PO Box 16 97 ✉R3C 2Z6 ☎ 582-6331
Country, leather, uniforms, bears mixed social group.

HEALTH GROUPS

AIDS Shelter Coalition of Manitoba
202-222 Furby Street ✉R3C 2A7 ☎ 775-9173 Fax: 774-8895.

Kali Shiva
705 Broadway Avenue ☎ 477-9506 Fax: 477-9099
Volunteer care for persons living with AIDS.

Provincial AIDS/STD Line Mon-Fri 8.30-20.30 h
☎ 945-2437 ☎ 1-800-782-2437 *or* ☎ *(800) 782-2437.*

Village Clinic. The 8.30-17 h
668 Corydon ✉R3M 0X7 ☎ 453-0045
Gay/lesbian health services. Focus on AIDS related services.

RELIGIOUS GROUPS

MCC Winnipeg Tu-Thu 9-11, Tue-Wed 19-21 h. Worship Sun 19.30-? h
c/o Broadway Disciples United Church, 396 Broadway ✉RC3 4K9 ☎ 774-5354 E-Mail: mcccwpg@icenter.net
Mailing address: PO Box 26091, Winnipeg, MB R3C 4K9

SWIMMING

-Beaconia Beach (AYOR g nu) (located on Lake Winnipeg; drive on Hwy 59 about 70 km north of Winnipeg; turn west on PR 500. After you pass the gas station, continue due west on the gravel road until you reach parking lot. Walk to beach, turn left and walk about fifteen minutes to reach nudist area. Gay section is at far south end of beach.)

CRUISING

-Bonnycastle Park (ayor) (at night)
-Parking Assiniboine Avenue (between Main and Fort Street)
-TD Centre concourse (AYOR) (washrooms near the food courts)

CDN-New Brunswick

East CDN
Initials: NB
Time: GMT -4, -5
Area: 73,000 km² / 28,185 sq mi.
Population: 762,000
Capital: Fredericton

Aulac ☎ 506

PRIVATE ACCOMODATION

Georgian House (bf glm H)
E0A 3C0 ☎ 536-1481
Restored 1840 home close to Waterfowl natural park. Two rooms with shared baths. Full breakfast served. Season April to October or by appointment.. No pets.

Bathurst ☎ 506

GENERAL GROUPS

Gales nor Gays (GNG)
PO Box 983 ✉E2A 4H8
☎ 783-7440

Edmundston ☎ 418

DANCECLUBS

Arc-en-ciel (Rainbow). Disco-bar l' (B D GLM MA) Sun 22-4 h (Atlantic)
C.P. 1547, chemin de l'Arc-en-ciel, Ville Déglis, *Q.C. G5T 1B7* ☎ 853-3945
5.5 km west of the Quebec border, 25 km from Edmundston.

Fredericton ☎ 506

CAFES

Molly's Coffee House (glm)
554 Queen Street
☎ 457-9305

DANCECLUBS

G Spot (B CC D glm MA) 20-2 h, closed Mon.
377 King Street, 3rd Floor ✉E3B 1E4 ☎ 455-7768

BOOK SHOPS

Beegie's Bookstore
Fredericton Mall, Prospect Street ☎ 459-3936

Kingfisher Books (glm)
358 Queen Street ☎ 458-5531

GENERAL GROUPS

EGALE New Brunwick Chapter
785 Aberdeen Street ✉E3B 1S7 ☎ 467-2514
E-mail: righters@nbnet.nb.ca National political advocacy group.

FLAG (Fredericton Lesbians & Gays) 2nd Wed 19 h
PO Box 1556, Station A ✉E3B 5G2 ☎ 457-2156
E-Mail: U5mc@unb.ca
Homepage: www.geocities.com/WestHollywood/3074/contente.htm

Gay & Lesbian Alliance of University of New Brunswick (GALA) Meets Wed 19 h at room 19F1, Alumni Memorial Bldg. at UNB/STU
c/o Help Centre, UNB SUB, PO Box 4400 ✉E3B 5A3 ☎ 453-4955 Fax: 453-4958. E-Mail: gala@unb.ca Homepage: www.unb.ca/web/gala/webpages/gala.html

New Brunswick Coalition for Human Rights Reform
PO Box 1556, Station A ✉E3B 5G2
☎ 457-2514 E-Mail: righters@nbnet.nb.ca

Rainbow Pride (Fredericton lesbian, gay and bisxeual youth group) Meets 2nd/4th Thu 19.30
in the Senior Common Room at McConnell Hall at UNB
☎ 455-7363 E-Mail: r35s2@unb.ca

FETISH GROUPS

East Coast Bears
PO Box 1492, Station A ✉E3B 5G2
E-mail: lairbear@nbnet.nb.ca
Homepage: http://www.personal.nbnet.nb.ca/lairbear/
Group of Bears and their fans

HEALTH GROUPS

AIDS New Brunswick Mon Thu 19-22.30 h
c/o Victoria Health Centre, 65 Brunswick Street ☎ 459-7518
or ☎ (800) 561-4009. Information, referral and counselling.

RELIGIOUS GROUPS

Living Waters Community Church Sun 19 h
c/o E. Gibson, 98 Cityview Avenue ✉E3A 1S8 ☎ 472-2376
E-Mail: living_waters@hotmail.com

CRUISING

-Riverside park (AYOR) (located between the Lord Beaverbrook Hotel and the railway bridge) -YMCA swimming bath

Moncton ☎ 506

BARS

Triangles (B GLM MA)
234 St. George Street ✉E1C 1V8 ☎ 857-8779

GENERAL GROUPS

PFLAG (Parents, Family & Friends of lesbians & gays) Meets 3rd Mon 19.30-21.30 h
c/o Pierre Bourgeois, 385 rue La France, Dieppe E1A 2B8 ☎ 856-7944 E-Mail: erhay@mta.ca *(Pierre) or ☎ 536-0599 ((Eldon)*

HEALTH GROUPS

SIDA/AIDS Moncton
165-A Gordon Street ✉E1C 1N1 ☎ 859-9616 Fax: 855-4526.

Newcastle ☎ 506

PRIVATE ACCOMODATION

Fourth Generation B&B (bf glm H) PO Box 126 ✉EIV 3M3 ☎ 622-3221
3 rooms and 1 studio located in a country farm close to Strathadam. Own car recommended. English and French spoken. Nice deck overlooking Miramichi River. Open May 1 to Oct 31.

Saint John ☎ 506

DANCECLUBS

Bogarts (B D GLM) Wed-Sat 21-2 h
9 Sydney Street ✉E2L 2L1 ☎ 652-2004

GUEST HOUSES

Mahogony Manor (CC e glm H) 220 Germain Street ✉E2L 2G4 ☎ 636-8000 Fax: 636-8001 E-Mail: leavitt@nbnet.nb.ca Homepage: www.sjnow.com/mm
Victorian house with five elegant guest rooms located in the heart of uptown St. John. Rooms with private bath/WC, telephone, radio and heating. TV room with video. No pets. Smoke-free environment. Special diets may be accomodated. Open all year.

GENERAL GROUPS

PFLAG (Parents, Family & Friends of lesbians & gays) Meets 1st Fri 19 h
☎ 652-3995 *(Judith) or ☎ 648-9700 (Wayne) Location: Memorial Room, Centenary-Queen Square United Chruch, 95 Wentworth Street.*

HEALTH GROUPS

AIDS New Brunswick / SIDA Nouveau-Brunswick Mon-Fri 8-16.30 h
65 Brunswick Street ✉E3B 1G5 ☎ 459-5782
or ☎ (0800) 561-4009. E-mail: sidaids@nbnet.nb.ca

AIDS Saint John 115 Hazen Street ✉E2L 3L3
☎ 652-2437 Fax: 652-2438. E-Mail: aidssj@nbnet.nb.ca

CRUISING

-Carlton Street (r) (near Old Stone Church)
-Rockwood Park (beach and trails)

Woodstock ☎ 506

GENERAL GROUPS

PFLAG (Parents, Family & Friends of Lesbians & Gays) ☎ 328-4868 E-Mail: richardb@nbnet.nb.ca

CDN-Newfoundland

East CDN
Initials: NF
Time: GMT -4
Area: 405,000 km² / 156,370 sq mi.
Population: 564,000
Capital: St. John`s

St.John's ☎ 709

GAY INFO

Gay & Lesbian Info Line Tue Thu 19-22 h
PO Box 626, Station C ✉A1C 5K8 ☎ 753-4297
24-hour message service.

BARS

Junctions (B d glm MA)
208 Water Street ✉A1C 6E7
☎ 579 2557

Ship Inn. The (B glm MA)
265 Water Street ✉A1C 1G9 *(off Solomon's Lane)* ☎ 753 3870

Zone 2-1-6 (B CC D GLM lj MA STV VS W WE YG) Wed Sun 21-2, Fri-Sat -4.30 h
216 Water Street ✉A1C 1A9 ☎ 754-2492
The only gay bar in St. John's

RESTAURANTS

Biarritz On The Square (b F glm)
188 Duckworth Street ✉A1C 1G5 ☎ 726 3885
Seafood, lunch and dinner specials

Stella's Restaurant (b F glm)
106 Water Street ✉A1C 1A7 ☎ 753 96 25
Vegetarian dishes, seafood and delicious desserts.

BOOK SHOPS

Bennington Gate Bookstore (glm)
8-10 Rowan Street *(Lower Level, terrace on the Square, Churchill Square)*
☎ 902/576-6600
Large selection of gay and lesbian books

Wordplay Bookstore (glm)
221 Duckworth Street
☎ 726-9193 *or* ☎ *(800) 563-9100 (Toll-free).*

PRIVATE ACCOMODATION

Abba Inn (AC bf CC f glm H wh) All year
36 Queen's Road ✉A1C 2A5 *(near City Hall)* ☎ 754-0047
☎ (800)563 3959 Fax: 754-0047
E-Mail: abba@roadrunner.nf.net
Homepage: www.wordplay.com/abba_inn
Comfortable Bed and Breakfast in a refurbished Queen Anne townhouse. All rooms with en-suite bathroom, cable TV, alarm clock, radio, telephone and ceiling- fan. Non-smoking. Free bf.

Banberry House Bed & Breakfast
(bf CC glm H) 09-22:30h
116 Military Road ✉A1C 2C9 ☎ 579-8006 Fax: 579 3443
E-Mail: banberry@bigfoot.com.
Homepage: www.bbcanada.com/1780.html
Small B&B in nice Victorian home. All rooms with private bath, radio, hair-dryer and own key.

Gower House Bed & Breakfast (bf glm)
180 Gower Street ✉A1C 2A5 ☎ 754-0047
☎ (0800) 563 3959
E-Mail: abba@roadrunner.nf.net
Homepage: www.rimstarintl.com/abb00001.htm
B&B in a historic townhouse. All rooms with color cable TV and telephone, some with en-suite bathrooms

GENERAL GROUPS

NGALE (NF Gays & Lesbians for Equality)
Meets 1st/3rd at 19.30 (business)/20.30 h (support)
PO Box 6221 ✉A1C 6J9 ☎ 753-4297
E-Mail: ngale@geocities.com
Homepage: www.geocities.com/WestHollywood/4291
Location: Conference Room C, at Coroporate Office, St. John's Health Care Corporation, Waterford Bridge Road.

HEALTH GROUPS

Newfoundland and Labrador AIDS Committee
PO Box 626, Station C ✉A1C 5K8 ☎ 579-8656

CDN-Nova Scotia

East CDN
Initials: NS
Time: GMT -4
Area: 56,000 km² / 21,612 sq mi.
Population: 948,000
Capital: Halifax

Antigonish

GENERAL GROUPS

GLBX (Gays, Lesbians and Bisexuals at X)
PO Box 1842, Town Post Office ✉B2G 1F4
E-Mail: glbx@stfx.ca Homepage: www..juliet.sfx.ca/~glbx/

Halifax ☎ 902

GAY INFO

Queer News Wed 12.15 h CKDU FM 97.5 MHz

Wayves
PO Box 340 90 ✉B3J 3S1 ☎ 826-7356 E-Mail: wayves@fox.nstn.ca
Homepage: www.chebucto.ns.ca/CommunitySupport/Wayves
Free at many locations.

BARS

Club NRG (B CC D f GLM MA N OS STV YG)
2099 Gottingen Street ✉B3K 3B3

Eagle Halifax.The (B CC f G lj MA N) Mon-Sat 11.30-2. Sun 12-2 h
2104 Gottingen Street ✉B3K 3B3 *(upstairs)* ☎ 425-6976

Reflections Cabaret (AC B CC f GLM LJ MA S STV W) 16-4 h
5184 Sackville Street ✉B3S 2N1 ☎ 422-2957
Popular club. Various theme nights.

CAFES

Amadeus. Café (b glm MA OS) 5675
Spring Garden Road/South Park *(at Lord Nelson Hotel)*
☎ 423-0032

Grabbajabba (b glm MA)
5475 Spring Garden Road ✉B3J 3T2 ☎ 423-1651

Rainbow Room (B f GLM MA)
Happy hour: 16.30-19.30, 21.30-23.30 h
2104 Gottingen Street *(upstairs from Chris' Cuisine, next to Wormwoods)*
Popular for Brunch on Sun from 12-15 h

RESTAURANTS

Bistro. Le (b F glm)
1333 South Park ☎ 423-8428

SAUNAS/BATHS

Apollo Sauna Bath Club Limited (DR G MA NU p sa) 19-24 h, closed Sun
1547 Barrington Street/Blowers Street ✉B3J 1Z4 ☎ 423-6549

BOOK SHOPS

Atlantic News (CC GLM) Mon-Sat 8-22, Sun 9-22 h
5560 Morris Street ✉B3J 1C2 ☎ 429-5468
Gay magazines.

GUEST HOUSES

Bob's B&B (bf glm H wh)
2715 Windsor Street ✉B3K 5El ☎ 454-4374
Non-smoking bed and breakfast, 5 minutes drive to town center, 30 min to airport. 6 rooms with shared and private baths, balcony and radio. Rates Can$ 60-85 (bf incl.) + tax. Non-smoking establishment.

PRIVATE ACCOMODATION

Centretown B&B (AC bf CC GLM H) All year
2016 Oxford Street ✉B3L 2T2 ☎ 422-2380
E-Mail: stephenp@fox.nstn.ca
1920's style bungalow with veranda in central location. Own key. Non-smoking. Laundry facilities.

Fresh Start B&B (bf CC glm H)
2720 Gottingen Street ✉B3K 3C7 ☎ 453-6616 Fax: 453-6617

GENERAL GROUPS

BGLAD (Bisexual, Gay and Lesbian Association of Dalhousie)
c/o SUB, 6136 University Avenue ✉B3H 4J2 ☎ 494-1256
E-Mail: bglad@is2.dal.ca
Group for LGB students

Gay, Lesbian & Bisexual Youth Group at Q.E.H. ☎ 421-6797 *(Jeannie)*

Gay Men's Gathering
PO Box 36054
Social group

Humans against Homophobia (HAH) Meets Mon 18 h at room 302, Dal SUB, University Avenue
☎ 494-6662 E-Mail: nspirg@is2.dal.ca

JUKA (Black, Gay, Lesbian, Bisexuals & Friends) 2nd Sat 16 h at ACNS Offices,
5675 Spring Garden Rd., Suite 600
☎ 454-5884

Lesbian, Gay, Bisexual Youth Groups
Gay&Bisexual group meets 1st/3rd Tue 19 h at ACNS, 600-5675 Spring Garden Rd.
☎ 492-0444

PFLAG (Parents, Family & Friends of Lesbians & Gays) 3rd Mon 14 h
☎ 443-3747 E-Mail: ab274@chebucto.na.ca.

FETISH GROUPS

Tightrope 18-24 h
PO Box 33067 ✉B3L 4T6 ☎ 423-6127
Men's leather, denim, uniform group.

HEALTH GROUPS

AIDS Coalition of Nova Scotia Mon-Fri 10-16:00h
5675 Spring Garden Road, Suite 600 ✉B3J 1H1 ☎ 425-4882
☎ 902/425-7922 Fax: 422-6200 E-Mail: acns@kayhay.com
Homepage: www.nsnet/org/acns/

Anonymous HIV/AIDS Testing ☎ 455-9656

HELP WITH PROBLEMS

Gay Men and Alcohol Project (GMAP) Mon-Fri 9-17 h
c/o AIDS Coalition of Nova Scotia ☎ 425-4882
E-Mail: acns@kayhay.com

RELIGIOUS GROUPS

Affirm United
PO Box 33067 ✉B3H 4T6

Assembly of Rainbow Christians (ARC) Meets Sun 19.30 at 5-3741 Kencrest Avenue
☎ 453-5393

Safe Harbour MCC Sun 19.30 h at Universalist Unitarian Church, 5500 Inglis Street ☎ 453-9249

SWIMMING

-Crystal Crescent (g NU) (25 km from Halifax. 15 min walk from Parking. Best on the rocks.)

CRUISING

-Public Gardens

Lunenburg ☎ 902

GUEST HOUSES

Brook House (bf CC glm H)
3 Old Blue Rocks Road ✉B0J 2C0 ☎ 634-3826 Fax: 634-9426 E-Mail: awilneff@atcon.com
Two double rooms in an old country house (built around 1863) close to the historical German town of Lunenburg. Rooms with shower/WC, radio and own key. No pets. Open June 1 to Sep 30.

New Glasgow ☎ 902

HEALTH GROUPS

Pictou County AIDS Coalition
c/o PO Box 964 ✉B2H 5K7 ☎ 752-6218

Shelbourne ☎ 902

PRIVATE ACCOMODATION

Toddle Inn (bf CC glm H)
163 Water Street ☎ 875-3229 *or* ☎ *(800) 565-0000 (toll-free). Four large and tastefully decorated rooms.10% discount on weekly reservations. Close to beaches, bird and whale watching, island tours, fishing and cruises possible.*

Sydney ☎ 902

HEALTH GROUPS

AIDS Coalition of Cape Breton (ACCB)
PO Box 177 ✉B1P 6H1 ☎ 567-1766

Truro ☎ 902

GENERAL GROUPS

Central Nova Gay Men & Lesbians
last Wed/month
☎ 893-2579

Wolfville ☎ 902

GENERAL GROUPS

Valley Pride Group Meets Tue 19 h at Coffee Merchant, 334 Main Street

HEALTH GROUPS

Valley AIDS Concern Group
201-28 Webster Court ✉B4N 1H7 ☎ 679-3515

CDN-Ontario

Central-West CDN
Initials: ON
Time: GMT -5
Area: 1,067,000 km² / 411,969 sq mi.
Population: 11,408,000
Capital: Toronto

Barrie ☎ 705

BARS

Graydons & Co. (B glm)
147 Dunlop Street East ☎ 728-3418

Cambridge ☎ 519

BARS

Robin`s Nest (B glm MA) Sat
26 Hobson ☎ 621-2688

Fort Erie ☎ 905

SAUNAS/BATHS

Fort Erie Sauna (G sa sb) 0-24 h
216 Jarvis Street ✉L2A 2S5 ☎ 871-0023

Georgetown ☎ 905

GENERAL GROUPS

Gay Friends ☎ 877-5524
Informal local group holding occasional parties.

Grand Valley ☎ 519

HOTELS

Manfred's Meadow Guest House (G H NU sa sol wh WO)
R.R. N° 1 ✉LON 1G0 ☎ 925-5306 Fax: 925 0447 E-Mail: milton@frexnet.com Homepage: www.geocities.com/WestHollywood
With a man made lake. All rooms with private bath and balcony. Full board possible

Guelph ☎ 519

GAY INFO

Gay Lesbian Bi Transgendered Outline 0-24 h
☎ 836-4550
Recorded information.

CAFES

Bookshelf Café. The (b f glm) 9-21 h
41 Quebec Street ☎ 821-3311

GENERAL GROUPS

Guelph Queer Equality
c/o CSA, UC, U. of G. ✉N1G 2W1 ☎ 824-4120
E-Mail: gqe@uoguelph.ca
Rainbow Chorus ☎ 821-2539

HEALTH GROUPS

AIDS Committee of Guelph & Wellington County Mon-Fri 8-18 h
204-85 Norfolk Street ☎ 763-2255 Fax: 763-8125
Bulletin Board Info Line ☎ 763-8265.

CRUISING

-Royal City Park (along Wellington Street)
-Exhibition Park (parking lots at night)

Hamilton ☎ 905

BARS

Amigos Bar (B glm)
121 Hughson Street ☎ 546-5258
Vortex Lounge. The (B D F GLM N YG)
121 Hughson Street North *(between Wilson & Canon Street)*
☎ 546-5258
Windsor Bar (B g)
31 John Street/King William Street ☎ 522-5990

DANCECLUBS

Embassy Club (B D Glm)
54 King Street East ✉L8N 1A6 ☎ 522-7783
Dance bar.

BOOK SHOPS

Gomorrah's Books (CC GLM) Mon-Thu 12-18, Fri -20, Sat 10-18, Sun 12-16 h
158 James Street South *(Near GO station)* ☎ 526-1074
Books, cards, gifts, magazines, adult-toys.

HEALTH GROUPS

Hamilton AIDS Network (HANDS) Mon-Fri 9-17, Tue Thu 18.30-21 h
143 James Street South, Suite 900 ✉L8P 3AL ☎ 528-0854
Mailing address: PO Box 120, Station A, Hamilton-Ontario L8N 3C8. Dialogue, support, information.

HELP WITH PROBLEMS

Hamilton Gay, Lesbian and Bisexual Youth Line ☎ (800) 268-9688

Kingston ☎ 613

GAY INFO

Kingston Lesbian, Gay, Bisexueal Association
51 Queens Cres ✉K7L 2S7 ☎ 545-2960
Info-line ☎ 531-8981 (Mon-Fri 19-21 h)

BARS

Club 477 (B glm) Mon-Thu 16-1, Fri Sat 16-3 h
477 Princess Street ✉K7L 1C3 ☎ 547-2923

HEALTH GROUPS

Kingston AIDS Project
PO Box 120 ✉K7L 4V6
☎ 545-3698 ☎ 1-800-565-2209

Kitchener ☎ 519

GAY INFO

Outlook Magazine
1109-37 Vanier Drive ✉N2C 1J4
☎ 570-3453 E-Mail: outlook@easynet.on.ca

BARS

Club Renaissance (B D F Glm YG) Wed-Sun 21-3 h
24 Charles Street West ✉N2G 1H2 *(opposite Transit Center)*
☎ 570-2406

GENERAL GROUPS

Gay & Lesbian Liberation of Waterloo (GLLOW) c/o Federation of Students Mon-Fri 19-22 h. Meets Wed 19.30 h.
Univ. of Waterloo, 200 Univ. Ave W, Waterloo,ON N2L 3G1
☎ 884-4569 E-Mail: gllow@watserv1.uwaterloo.ca

CRUISING

-Victoria Park (AYOR) (parking lots at night)
-King Street (between Frederick and Victoria Streets late at night)
-Waterloo Park (summer time)

London ☎ 519

GAY INFO

Gay Line Mon Thu 19-22 h, or tape ☎ 433-3551

BARS

Appartment. The (Partners) (B f D GLM)
186 Dundas Street ☎ 679-1255
Junction. The (AC B CC G P) 0-24 h
722 York Street ✉N5W 2S6 ☎ 438-2625
☛Sauna Club London.
Taboo Lounge (B g MA)
649 Colborne Street ☎ 673-6807

SAUNAS/BATHS

Club London (AC B bf CC DR f G lj MA P sa sb sol VS W wh WO) 0-24 h
722 York Street ✉N5W 2S6 *(rear entrance from parking lot)*
☎ 438-2625
Party every Sunday. Large gay video selection (sales/rental). No membership required

CAMPING

Enchanted Forest Resort (G nu pi sa wh)
20237 Kennedy Road ☎ (800) 477-5858

GENERAL GROUPS

HALO Club (B GLM) Fri Sat -?, Mon 19-22 h
649 Colborne Street/Pall Mall ☎ 433-3762

HEALTH GROUPS

AIDS Committee of London
200-343 Richmond Street ☎ 434-1601 Fax: 434-1843.

HELP WITH PROBLEMS

AA Gay/Lesbian ☎ 473-4738
AIDS Hotline ☎ 434-8160

CRUISING

-Victoria Park (at Wellington Street and Dufferin Avenue)
Harris Park (end of Dufferin Avenue along Thames, only in summer)

Maynooth ☎ 613

GUEST HOUSES

Wildewood Guest House (F GLM MA wh) All year 09-22:00h for reservations
970 Madawaska Road ✉KOL 2S0 ☎ 338-3134
All your meals lovingly prepared, two guest rooms with views, two washrooms, comfortable queen-size beds. Rates include full breakfast and 3 course dinner. 30 minutes from Algonquin Park. 3 hours drive from Toronto or Ottawa.

Niagara Falls ☎ 905

HOTELS

Rainbow View B & B (b bf H NG)
4407 John Street, ONT L2E IA4 *(two blocks from Falls)*
☎ 374-1845
Single US$ 35, double 50.

Oshawa ☎ 905

BARS

Club 717 (B D GLM MA TV) Thu 21-3, Sun -1 h
717 Wilson Road South ✉L1H 6E9 ☎ 434-4297

Ottawa ☎ 613

GAY INFO

Capital XTRA! Mon-Fri 9-18 h
506-177 Nepean Street ✉K2P 0B4 ☎ 237-7133 Fax: 237-6651
Ottawa's gay and lesbian monthly paper
Definitely Not Straight Radio Mon 18 h
on CHUO FM 89.1
Pink Triangle Services Gayline: 19-22 h
71 Bank Street *(2nd floor)* ☎ 238-1717
Voices out of the Closet Wed 18 h
(CKCU FM 93.1)

TOURIST INFO

Ottawa Tourism and Convention Authority
130 Albert Street, Suite 1800 ✉K1P 5G4 ☎ 237-5150
FAX 237-7339.

BARS

Cellblock (AC B d G LJ MA) Wed-Sat 21-2, Sun 18-2 h
340 Somerset Street West ✉K2P 0J9 *(upstairs)* ☎ 594-0233
Centretown Pub (AC B CC D Glm lj MA N OS VS) Wed-Sat 21-2, Sun 18-2 h
340 Somerset Street West/Bank ✉K2P 0J9 ☎ 594-0233
Franky`s (B GLM MA) Mon-Fri 16-2, Sat Sun 14-2 h
303 Frank Street ✉K2P 0X7 ☎ 233-9195
Lookout Bar and Bistro. The (B F GLM MA)
41 York Street ✉K1N 5S7 *(2nd floor)* ☎ 789-1624
Silhouette Piano Bar (AC B CC GLM MG S) Thu-Sat 21-1 h
340 Somerset Street West *(downstairs)* ☎ 594-0234
Zipper Club (B d G MA s)
340 Somerset Street/Central Park *(above Centretown Pub)*
☎ 594-3560

CAFES

Market Station (b f GLM)
15 George Street ✉K1N 8W5 ☎ 562-3540
Screaming Mimi's (GLM) 369 Bank Street ☎ 234-1880

DANCECLUBS

Icon (B D G YG) Thu-Sat 20-3, Sun 23-2 h
366 Lisgar Street ✉K2P 2J3 ☎ 235-4005

RESTAURANTS

News. The (B F GLM)
284 Elgin Street ☎ 567-6397
Popular.
William Street Café (AC B F GLM)
47 William Street
☎ 241-4254
Very popular.

SEX SHOPS/BLUE MOVIES

Videó 2000 Plus (g)
691 Boulevard Saint Joseph, Hull
☎ (819) 777-3527
Good selection of gay videos.
Wilde`s (G)
367 Bank Street ☎ 234-5512
Wilde`s (G)
200 Dalhousie Street/St. Andrew ✉K1N 7C8 ☎ 562-2992
Good selection of gay videos

SAUNAS/BATHS

Club Ottawa (AC B G MA sa sb sol wh VS) 0-24 h
1069 Wellington Street/Merton ☎ 722-8978
Lockers only $6.

Steamworks (AC b G sa sb wh) 0-24 h
487 Lewis Street *(between O'Connor St. and Bank St.)*
☎ 230-8431 Fax: 231-4260.
In/out privileges on 24 hour rooms.

BOOK SHOPS

After Stonewall (CC GLM MA) Mon-Tue Wed-Thu Sat 10-18, Fri -21, Sun 12-17 h
370 Bank Street ✉K2P 1Y4 *(2nd floor opp. Wilde's)*
☎ 567-2221

GIFT & PRIDE SHOPS

One in Ten (GLM) Mon-Sat 11-23, Sun 11-20 h
216 Bank Street ☎ 563-0110
Pride accessories, videos, lingerie, t-shirts, etc.

GUEST HOUSES

Ambiance Bed & Breakfast (CC glm H)
330 Nepean Street ✉K1R 5G6 ☎ 563-0421
Email: Ambiance@istar.ca. 4 rooms with bath/shower/WC. Rates single Can$ 49-64, double 61-71.

Ottawa House (GLM H)
264 Stewart Street ☎ 233-4433

Rainbow Bed & Breakfast (GLM)
203 York Street ☎ 789-3286

Rideau View Inn (AC bf CC glm)
177 Frank Street ✉K2P 0X4 ☎ 236-9309 Fax: 237-6842
E-Mail: rideau@istar.ca
Homepage: www.home.istar.ca/~rideau
Friendly staff and atmosphere. Eight rooms, two with private bath.

GENERAL GROUPS

EGALE
306-177 Nepean Street ✉ON K2P 0B4
☎ 230-1043 Fax: 230 9395

Pink Triangle Youth Thu 15:30-17:30h
71 Bank St. *(2nd floor)* ☎ 238-1717

HEALTH GROUPS

AIDS Committee of Ottawa
111 Lisgar Street *(Council Hall)* ☎ 238-5014
Homepage: www.theaco.on.ca
Anonymous AIDS Testing at Centretown Community Health Centre Info ☎233-4443.

Living Room. The 15-21 h
207 Queen Street *(4th floor)* ☎ 563-0851 Fax: 238-3425
Toll-free 1-800-461-2182. Drop-in centre for PLWA's, people with HIV andf their friends.

RELIGIOUS GROUPS

Dignity Tue 19.30 h
at 386 Bank Street
PO Box 21 02, Station D ☎ 231-2393

SWIMMING

-Meech Lake Rapids Widerness Federal Park (! G NU WE YG) (North of Hull in Gatineau Park near Old Chelsea Park in Meech Lake Beach parking lot, then take the hiking trail at the side of the lot for about 15 min. to a small bridge, take the first path on the right and follow the edge of the lake around to the falls. Lots of winding wilderness paths to cruise.)

CRUISING

-Rockcliff Park (daytime; close to parking lots)
-Remic Rapids Park (along walking paths very busy during summer days)
-Mackenzie Street (AYOR G R RT)

Peterborough ☎ 705

GAY INFO

Rainbow Community Centre & Service Organization ☎ 876-1845
Trent Lesbian & Gay Collective ☎ 734-5414

HEALTH GROUPS

Peterborough AIDS Resource Network
PO Box 15 82, K9J 7H7 ☎ 749-9110

Port Sydney ☎ 705

HOTELS

Divine Lake Resort (b bf E F glm H MA msg pi sa wh WO)
R.R. 1, Clearwater Lake Road 848 ☎ 385-1212 Fax: 385-1283
E-Mail: divinelk@vianet.on.ca Homepage: www.divinelake.com
Located two hours from downtown Toronto. Chalets for 2 to 4 persons and cottages for 2 persons. All with facilities, balcony, TV, video, radio, kitchenette

Stratford ☎ 519

BARS

Down the Street (B glm MA)
30 Ontario Street ✉N5A 3G8 ☎ 273-5886

Old English Parlour (B g MA)
101 Wellington Street ✉N5A 2L4 ☎ 271-2772

PRIVATE ACCOMODATION

Burnside Guest Home (AC bf glm H msg NU wh) 08-22:00h.
139 William Street ✉N5A 4X9 ☎ 271-7076 Fax: 271-0265
Bed & breakfast located 80 miles west of Toronto in the festival town of Stratford. 2 rooms with shared bath/WC, phone, fax, TV, video, radio, own key.

Sudbury ☎ 705

DANCECLUBS

Zig's (AC B CC D f GLM lj MA N r S STV) Mon-Fri 20-?, Sat-Sun 14-? h
33 Elgin Street ✉P3C 5B3 ☎ 677-0614

HEALTH GROUPS

AIDS Commitee of Sudbury
23 Durham Street, ✉P3C 5E2 ☎ 688-0500

Thunder Bay ☎ 807

BARS

Backstreet Dance Klub (B GLM) Tue-Sat 16-03:00h
24 S Cumberland Street/Red River Road *(no sign)* ☎ 344-5737

GENERAL GROUPS

Lesbian Gay Bisexual Centre at Lakehead University
c/o L.U. Student Union, 955 Oliver Road ✉P7B 5E1 ☎ 343-8813

HELP WITH PROBLEMS

AIDS info line counselling Mon-Fri 8.30-17 h
☎ 345-7233
Monthly dances, socials, meetings.

1 Selby Hotel
Boots Warehouse Danceclub
2 Amacing Space B+B Guest House
3 Toolbox Bar
4 Remington's Bar
5 Club Toronto Sauna
6 Woody's and Sailor Bar
7 Priape Sex Shop
8 Black Eagle Bar
9 The Barn / Stables Bar
10 Trax V Bar
11 Sneakers Bar
12 St. Marc Spa Sauna
13 Bar 501
14 Crews Bar
15 Dundonald B&B Guest House
16 Carrington's Sports Bar
Glad Day Bookshop
Northbound Leather Shop
17 El Convente Rico Danceclub

Toronto ☎ 416

Toronto is Canada's largest city. Since the 70's it has been growing in prominence and economic prosperity. Toronto is the financial and communications centre of the nation and home to many corporate headquaters. Toronto is home to Canada's most prestigious cultural insitutions, such as the Toronto Symphony , the National Ballet and the Canadian Opera Company. Toronto has shed its boring image and has become more cosmopolitan with the influx of immigrants from all over the world. Some popular tourist attractions include the CN Tower, Casa Loma, Eaton Centre, the Ontario Science Centre and the Royal Ontario Museum.
The heart of the gay village is Church Street, between Alexander and Wellesley Streets. There are also several gay bars on the parallel strech of Yonge Street. The popularity of the Gay Pride Parade has grown considerably in the past decade, attracting more than 100,000 spectators in recent years.

Toronto umgibt der größte Ballungsraum des Landes. Seit den 70ern ist die Stadt erheblich auf Kosten Montreals gewachsen. In Toronto haben sich die großen Banken, Medienkonzerne und Firmenzentralen niedergelassen. Entsprechend prestigeträchtig sind Symphonieorchester, Ballett und Oper der Stadt. Aus der langweiligen und angestaubt wirkenden Stadt ist ein lebendiges und buntes Zentrum Kanadas geworden. Dazu tragen vor allem die vielen Einwanderer, die nach der Einreise in Toronto hängen bleiben, aber auch die Angehörigen der First Nation (der kanadischen Ureinwohner) bei.
Die *gay community* konzentriert sich um die Ecke Church Street/Wellesley Street bis hinein in die Yonge Street. Toronto ist eine durchaus sichere Stadt. Für das nächtliche Heimkommen von einer schwulen Kneipentour ist dennoch ein Taxi sehr empfehlenswert. Ob es bis dahin allerdings so spät wird, ist eher fraglich: die meisten Kneipen schließen um ein Uhr. Doch auch danach bleiben Discos, Clubs und die vielen special events, um die Nacht zum Tag zu machen.
Der Gay-Pride-Day Torontos hat sich zu einer beachtlichen Veranstaltung von enormen Ausmaßen (über 100.000 Teilnehmer) entwickelt.

Toronto est la plus grande ville du Canada. Elle a considérablement grandi en importance et s'est beaucoup enrichie depuis les années 70. Elle est devenue le centre économique et financier du pays et le siège de nombreuses entreprises nationales. Elle abrite également diverses institutions culturelles prestigieuses, telles que l'Orchestre Symphonique de Toronto ou l'Opéra et le Ballet nationaux. Toronto a réussi à se débarrasser de son image de ville ennuyeuse pour devenir un centre cosmopolite grâce, entre autres, à l'arrivée d'immigrés venus du monde entier. Ses attractions touristiques les plus cotées sont la CN Tower, la Casa Loma, l'Eaton Centre, le Ontario Science Centre et le Royal Ontario Museum.
La scène gaye se concentre aux abords de la Church Street entre Alexander Street et Wellesley Street et sur la rue parallèle, la Yonge Street. La Gay Pride de Toronto s'est développé de manière exponentielle ces dernières années pour atteindre plus de 100.000 participants lors de sa dernière édition.

Toronto es la mayor ciudad de Canadá. Desde los años 70 viene ganando en prominencia y prosperidad económica. Toronto es el centro financiero y de comunicaciones y sede de muchas grandes empresas. En Toronto se encuentran las instituciones culturales más prestigiosas de Canadá, como the Toronto Symphony, the National Ballet y the Canarian Opera Company. Toronto ha perdido su imagen de ciudad aburrida y se ha vuelto más cosmopolita por la afluencia de inmigrantes de todo el mundo. Entre las atracciones turísticas se incluyen la CN Tower, Casa Loma, Ontario Science Center y Royal Ontario Museum. El centro de la comunidad gay es Church Street, entre Alexander Street y Wellesley Street y se extiende hasta Yonge Street. La popularidad de la Gay Pride Parade ha aumentado considerablemente en la pasada década, atrayendo a más de 100.000 espectadores en los últimos años..

Toronto è circondata dalla zona più abitata del Canada. Sin dagli anni '70 la città è cresciuta a scapito di Montreal. A Toronto si sono stabilite grandi banche, l'industria delle mass-media e le centrali delle imprese. Corrispondentemente l'orchestra sinfonica, il balletto e l'opera della città sono di un'alto livello. La città noiosa e antiquata di una volta è diventata un centro canadese vivace e svariato. A ciò contribuiscono soprattutto i molti immigranti che si fermano a Toronto, ma anche gli appartenenti alla *First Nation,* cioè la popolazione originaria. Il centro della *gay comunity* si trova all'angolo della Church Street/Wellesley Street e comprende anche la Yonge Street. Anche se Toronto è una città abbastanza sicura, conviene prendere un taxì dopo un giro dei bar. Dipende però se questo giro si allunga fino a tardi, perché i bar chiudono all'una di notte. Dopo si può andare in una delle discoteche, in un club o partecipare ad uno dei numerosi eventi che fanno della notte il giorno.Il Gay Pride Day di Toronto si è sviluppato ad un avvenimento di enormi misure con più di 100.000 partecipanti.

GAY INFO

Attitude
519 Church Street, ✉M4Y 2C9 ☎ 964-1916
The official Lesbian and Gay Youth of Toronto newsletter.

Fab Magazine
25 Wood Street, Suite 104 ✉M4Y 2P9 ☎ 599-9273
Fax: 599-0964. E-Mail: fab@myna.com.

Gaywire Thu 19-20 h
(CIUT FM 89.5)

Pink Antenna Tue 11-12 h
(CKLN FM 88.1)

XTRA!
Suite 200, 491 Church Street, ✉M4Y 2C6 ☎ 925-6665
FAX 925-6674. Info ☎ 925-9872. Biweekly magazine with calendar of events, and other information about Toronto gay scene. Free at gay venues.

10 %-QTV c/o Rogers Community TV Mon 22.30, Sat 23.30 h
525 Lakeshore Boulevard West ✉M5V 1A3
Homepage: www.10percent.interlog.com

519 Church Street Community Centre Mon-Fri 9-22.30, Sat Sun 12-17.30 h
519 Church Street ✉M4Y 3C9 ☎ 392-6874
Location for numerous gay events.

TOURIST INFO

Metropolitan Toronto Convention & Visitors Association
☎ 203-2600

BARS

Bar 501 (B CC GLM MA STV W) 11-2 h
501 Church Street ✉M4Y 2C6 ☎ 944-3272

Barn. The (B CC D DR Glm LJ s VS) Mon-Thu 21-3, Fri-Sat -4, Sun 16-4 h
418 Church Street ✉M5B 2A3 ☎ 977-4702
Dance club and leather shop. Every Sun underwear party 16-21 h. Thu and Fri charity bingo nights for PWA.

Bijou. The (B DR G MA VS) 21-4 h
370 Church Street *(near Gerrard)* ☎ 960-1272
Black Eagle (! B G LJ) Mon-Fri 16-2, Sat 14-2, Sun 12-2 h
457 Church Street ✉M4Y 2C5 *(2nd Floor)* ☎ 413-1219
Leather cruise bar. Thu Bear Night and Sun Naked Night.
Byzantium (AC B CC F GLM lj MA N OS TV) 17.30-2 h
499 Church Street ✉M4Y 2C6 ☎ 922-3859
Bar and restaurant.
Carringtons Sports Bar (B glm MA)
618 Yonge Street *(2nd floor)* ☎ 944-0559
Crews (B CC G S STV) 12-2 h
508 Church Street ☎ 972-1662
Gay bar in old Victorian house. Popular. The lesbian bar Tango is in the same building.
Pegasus Billiard Lounge (B CC GLM MA) Mon-Thu 10-1, Fri -2, Sat-Sun 12-2 h
489B Church Street ✉M4Y 2C6 *(2nd floor)* ☎ 927-8832
If you prefer playing pool to dancing than this is the place for you.
Pimblett's Pub (B CC f glm MA N) 16-2 h
263 Gerrard Street East ✉M5A 2G1 ☎ 929-9525
Friendly pub
Red Spot (B F GLM)
459 Church Street ☎ 967-7768
Remington's (AC B f G MA p SNU) 11-1 h
379 Yonge Street ✉M5B 1S1 ☎ 977-2160
Male Strip club with two stages and two bars.
Sneakers (AC B CC f G MA N R W YG) 11-2 h
502A Yonge Street ✉M4Y 1X9 ☎ 961-5808
Cruisy atmosphere.
Toolbox (AC B bf DR F G H LJ MA T) Mon-Thu 17-03:00h, Fri 14-03:00h, Sat 12-03:00h, & Sun 11-03:00h
508 Eastern Avenue ✉M4M 1C5 ☎ 466-8616
Patio, leather shop, restaurant, guesthouse with priv. and shared baths. Non smoking rooms with air conditioner and cable TV
Trax V (AC B CC d f G lj MA OS STV YG) 11-2 h
529 Yonge Street ✉M4Y 1Y5 ☎ 962-5196
Fun atmosphere.
Web. The (AC B D f G MA S VS) 12-02:00h
619 Yonge Street ✉M5B 2Z5 *(2nd floor)* ☎ 922-3068
Woody's (! B CC f Glm MA STV) Mon-Fri 12-2, Sat 11-2 h
465-467 Church Street ✉M4Y 2C5 ☎ 972-0887
Popular. 5 bars. Live drag shows on Sun.
Zipperz (B D)
72 Carlton Street ☎ 921-0066

CAFES

Lucky Strike (b f glm MA) 0-24 h
473-1/2 Church Street ✉M4Y 2C5 ☎ 944-3265
Popular coffee shop serving delicious cakes, desserts and sandwiches.
Rose Cafe. The (B f glm)
547 Parliament Street ☎ 928-1495

DANCECLUBS

Bauhaus (B CC D glm MA) Mon Wed Fri-Sat 22-3 h
31 Mercer Street ✉M5V 1H2 ☎ 977-9813
Continental-style dance club, especially popular on Sat.
Boots Warehouse (! B D G MA S SL YG) 21-3 h
592 Sherbourne Street ✉M4X 1L4 ☎ 921-0665
El Convento Rico (B D glm stv)
750 College Street ☎ 588-7800
Latino Dance Club
Fly (AC B CC D f glm LJ MA p s tv) Sat 21-08:00h
8 Gloucester Street ☎ 410 5426
Guvernment (B D glm) Fri gay
132 Queens Quay E ☎ 869-9261
Industry Nightclub (AC B CC D GLM lj MA STV WE YG) Fri 22-3, Sat 23-9 h
901 King Street West, Box 20 ✉M5V 3H5 ☎ 260-2660
☎ 535-3234
Radius Night Club (D GLM)
1 Isabella Street ☎ 944-1074
Tallulah's Cabaret (B D GLM S) Fri Sat 22-3 h
12 Alexander Street ☎ 975-8555
Volcano Room (B D Glm)
650 Queen Street W/Palerston Avenue ☎ 203 3411
Warehouse. The (B D G) 22:30-04:00h
132 Queens Quay East
Home of Mr Leathermann competition.

RESTAURANTS

Alfred's Restaurant & Bar (B CC F glm MA N) Mon-Fri 11.30-22, Sat 11.30-22.30, Sun 11-22 h
634 Church Street ✉M4Y 2G3 ☎ 925-0037
Popular with business people for lunch and many gays and lesbiansin the evening. Rather expensive but delicious continental-style cuisine.
Arlequin Restaurant & Fine Foods (B CC F glm) Mon-Sat 9-24 h
134 Avenue Road ✉M5R 2H6 ☎ 928-9521
Artful Dodger (B CC F glm MA N WE) 11-2 h
10 Isabella Street ✉M4Y 1N1 ☎ 964-9511
Pub-style atmosphere. Two patios.
Charolais. Le (B F glm) Mon-Sat 17.30-22, Sun 11-14, 17.30-22 h
557 Parliament Street ✉M4X 1P7 ☎ 963-5097
French inspired cuisine, medium priced
Living Well Restaurant (A AC B CC d F glm MA N OS) Restaurant: Sun-Thu 11,30-1, Fri Sat -1.30, Bar: 18-2 h
692 Yonge Street/Isabella Street ✉M4Y 2A6 ☎ 922-6770
Mango. The (AC B CC F GLM MA N OS) 10-02:00h
580 Church Street ✉M4Y 2E5 *(Wellesly Subway Station)* ☎ 922-6525
Matignon Restaurant (B F glm)
51 St. Nicholas Street ✉M4Y 2E5 ☎ 921—9226
Sotto Voce Wine & Pasta Bar (B CC F glm OS) Mon-Wed Sun 17-1, Thu-Sat -2 h
595 College Street ✉M6G 1B2 ☎ 536-4564
Bar and restaurant painted in bright colors. Good food and wine.
Spiral Restaurant & Lounge (AC B CC E F G N OS WE) Mon-Fri 11.30-14.30, Sat-Sun 11-15, Sun-Tue 17.30-24, Wed-Sat 17.30-2 h
582 Church Street ✉M4Y 2E5 *(M° Wellesley)* ☎ 964-1102
Delicious mix of continental and Asian cuisine
Village Rainbow. The (AC B bf CC F G WE) 7-1 h
477 Church Street ✉M4Y 2C6 ☎ 0416/961-0616
Bar & Restaurant. Good breakfasts.
Wilde Oscar's (B CC F glm OS) 12-3 h
518 Church Street ✉M4Y 2C8 ☎ 921-8142
In the heart of the gay village good and hearty meals are served e.g. pizzas, steak, pastas and sea food.
Youki Asian Bar & Bistro (B CC F glm OS) Mon-Thu 17.30-23, Fri Sat -24 h
4 Dundonald Street ✉M4Y 1K2 ☎ 924-2925
Reasonably priced sushi.
Zelda's Bar, Restaurant & Lounge (B CC F GLM MA N OS s STV W WE) 11-2 h
76 Wellesley Street East ✉M4Y 1H2 *(M° Wellesley)*
☎ 922-2526

SHOWS

Buddies in Bad Times Theatre & Tallulah's Cabaret (AC B CC D GLM S W WE) Box Office: Tue-Sat 10-18, Sun 12-15 h, closed Mon. Club: Fri-Sat 22.30-3 h
12 Alexander Street ✉M4Y 1B4 *(M° College Street)*
☎ 975-8555

SEX SHOPS/BLUE MOVIES

Barbwire (DR G LJ MA VS) 10-04:00h
543 Yonge Street *(below tthe St. Marc Spa)* ☎ 934-1359

New Release Adult Video (G)
489 Church Street *(lower level)* ☎ 419/966-9815
Sales, rentals, magazines and toys.

Priape (G GLM LJ) Mon-Wec 10-19:00h, Thu-Sat 10-21h, Sun & holidays closed
465 Church Street ✉M4Y 2C5 ☎ 586-9914

SAUNAS/BATHS

Barracks. The (AC b CC G lj S sa sb) 0-24 h
56 Widmer Street/Richmond ☎ 593-0499

Cellar. The (b G MA rt sa) 0-24 h
78 Wellesley Street East *(basement-black door)* ☎ 944-3779
Entrance plain black door, very raunchy.

Central Spa (f G msg sa sb VS WO) 12-3 h
1610 Dundas Street W/Brock Avenue ☎ 588-6191

Club Toronto (AC G OS P pi r sa sb VS wh WO) 0-24 h
231 Mutual Street ✉M5B 2B4 *(one block East of Mapple Leaf Garden)*
☎ 977-4629
Popular. Four floors. Sundays complimentary buffet 16-20:00h. .

Spa on Maitland. The (AC B CC DR f G MA sa sb VS YG) 0-24 h
66 Maitland Street ✉M4Y 1C5 *(west of Church Street)*
☎ 925-1571
On the 2nd Floor. 2 saunas and 2 steam rooms.

St. Marc Spa (G f MA msg sa sb VS wh WO)
543 Yonge Street *(Between Wellesley and Maitland. Top floor. M°-Wellesley)* ☎ 927-0210 *Billards.*

BOOK SHOPS

Glad Day Books (AC CC GLM) Mon-Wed 11-18.30, Thu-Fri -21, Sat 10-18, Sun 12-18 h
598 A Yonge Street/St.Joseph ✉M4Y 1Z3 *(2nd floor)*
☎ 961-4161

This Ain't the Rosedale Library (GLM)
483 Church Street ✉M4Y 2C6 ☎ 929-9912

LEATHER & FETISH SHOPS

Doc's Leather and Latex (AC CC G GLM LJ MA r W WE) Mon-Sat 11-19, Sun 12-17 h
726 Queen Street West ✉M6J 1E8 ☎ 504-8888
New and second-hand leather/fetish wear.

Northbound Leather Ltd. (A AC CC glm LJ) Mon-Wed Sat 10-18, Thu Fri -19.30, Sun 12-17 h
7 St Nicholas Street ☎ 972-1037

TRAVEL & TRANSPORT

Mother Earth Tours
487 Dupont Street ✉M6G 1Y6
☎ 537-6691 or toll free (800) 537-2221

Talk of the Town Travel
565 Sherbourne Street ✉M4X 1W7 ☎ 960-1393

HOTELS

Selby Hotel (AC B bf CC D GLM H OS S)
592 Sherbourne Street ✉M4X 1L4 *(M°-Sherbourne)*
☎ 921-3142
or ☎ (800) 387-4788 (Toll-free in USA & CDN). FAX 923-3177. E-Mail selby@inforamp.net. Minutes from gay area and city centre. Rooms with private baths, historic rooms with fireplaces. Rates from Can$ 60/90. Recommended. Ask for the Hemingway suite.

Victoria's Mansion
68 Gloucester Street ✉M4Y 1L5
☎ 921-4625 *E-mail: victorias.mansion@sympatico.ca*
Located in the heart of the gay village. 13 double rooms, 8 single, 1 studio and 1 apartment. Rooms with facilities, TV AC, own key. Rates double Can$ 65, single 55, studio 100, apartment 125.

GUEST HOUSES

Aberdeen Guest House (AC bf CC E GLM H)
52 Aberdeen Avenue ✉M4X 1A2 ☎ 922-8697
FAX 922-5011. E-mail: aberdeengh@aol.com.
Homepage: http://www.interlog.com/~aberinn. Small B&B in Historic town centre. All rooms with shared bath and TV. Rates Can$ 80-95. Non-smoking establishment.

Acorn House B&B (bf GLM H lj)
255 Donlands Avenue ✉M4J 3R5 ☎ 463-8274 Fax: 463-9136
Small B&B. Rates for rooms with shared bath Can$ 45 (single) and 60 (double) incl. cont. bf.

Allenby Bed & Breakfast (AC bf CC g H OS pi)
223 Strathmore Boulevard ✉M4J 1P4 *(M°-Greenwood)*
☎ 461-7095
Centrally located, 9 minutes from city centre. Single Can$ 40-45, double 45-55, apartment from 100, additional bed 10.

Amazing Space B&B (AC bf CC GLM H OS)
246 Sherbourne Street ✉M5A 2S1
☎ 968-2323 or Toll free ☎ (800) 205-3694 Fax: 968-7194
E-Mail: mhughes@istar.ca
Convenient downtown location, 20 min to airport, close to gay scene

Banting House (AC bf CC e G H lj)
73 Homewood Avenue ✉M4Y 2K1 ☎ 924-1458 Fax 922-2718
Email: bantinghs@aol.com
Homepage: http://www.bbcanada.com/1960.html
Rooms with shower/WC, SAT-TV, kitchen(ette), balcony. Rates single Can$ 55-75, double 60-110, studio 90-110, apartment 140-180. Bf incl.

Catnaps Guesthouse (CC GLM H)
246 Sherbourne Street ✉M5A 2S1 ☎ 1-800-205-3694 E-Mail: catnaps@onramp.ca

DunDonald House Bed and Breakfast (AC bf CC GLM h MA msg OS sa wh WO) All year
35 Dundonald Street ✉M4Y 1K3 *(M°-Wellesley)* ☎ 961-9888
☎ (1-800) 260 7227 (toll free) Fax: 961-2120 E-Mail: dundonal@idirect.com Homepage: www.dundolnaldhouse.com
Friendly B&B in the heart of the gay village.5 double and 1 single room with TV/video and radio. Rates double/shared bath Can$ 65-135, en-suite.Sauna, hot tub, work out room free of charge. Bicycles and parking available.

House on McGill (AC bf CC glm H)
110 McGill Street ✉M5B 1H6 *(M° College Street)* ☎ 351-1503
Homepage: http://www.interlog.com/~mcgillbb/
E-mail: mcgillbb@interlog.com Small B&B. All rooms with shared bath, baclony, radio, TV/VCR. Rates double Can$ 65-85, add. bed 15, Single 50-70 incl. bf buffet.

Muther's Guest House at The Toolbox (G H lj MA)
508 Eastern Avenue ☎ 466-8616
Clean and comfortable rooms. Rates Can$ 45-60.

Ten Cawthra Square B&B & Guesthouse (AC CC E G H msg sol wh)
10 Cawthra Square ✉M4Y 1K8 ☎ 966-3074 or (800) 259-5474 (Toll-free) Fax: 966-4494.
E-mail: host@cawthra.com. Homepage: http://www.cawthra.com
Guesthouse in an elegant Victorian mansion 2 blocks from gay bars. 11 double rooms, 1 single and 3 studios, some with private bath, telephone, some with private terraces/decks, TV. Rates Can$ 79-99 (bf incl.)

PRIVATE ACCOMODATION

Two Aberdeen (AC bf CC GLM) 07-21:00h
2 Aberdeen Avenue ✉M4X 1A2 ☎ 944-1426 Fax: 944-3523
E-Mail: twoaberdeen@interlog.com
Homepage: www.twoaberdeen.com
Close to gay village & downtown. Rooms with pribate and shared bath, balcony, Sat-TV/VCR.

GENERAL GROUPS

Amnesty International Members for G&L Concerns
77 Maitland Place, Suite 820 ✉M4Y 2V6 ☎ 926-9135
Support human and gay rights worldwide by writing letters to governments urging them to respect international standards.

Gay Fathers of Toronto Mon-Thu 19-22:00h
PO Box 187, Station F, ✉M4Y 2L5 ☎ 410 0438
E-Mail: poscare@pathcom.com

Gay Lesbian and Bisexual International (GLINT) Meets Wed 18.30-20.30 h
at International Students Centre, 33A St. George St.
42A St. George Street ✉M5S 2E4 ☎ 591-7949
Support group for all those whose first language is not English.

Lesbians, Gays, Bisexuals of the University of Toronto
42A St. George Street ✉M5S 2E4 ☎ 971-7880
E-Mail: lgbout@campuslife.utoronto.ca.
Homepage: http://www.campuslife.utoronto.ca/groups/lgbout

Primetimers Toronto 3rd Sat 14-16 h
c/o Community Centre, 519 Church Street ✉M4Y 2C9
☎ 925-9872 (ext. 2970).
E-mail: cg520@torfree.net
Social group for gay and bisexual men over 40. Newsletter available.

Toronto Bisexual Network 1st Thu 18-20, 3rd Thu 20-22 h
c/o Community Centre, 519 Church Street ✉M4Y 2C9
☎ 925-9872 (ext. 2015). E-mail: steve@bi.org

Transgendered, Bisexual, Lesbian and Gay Alliance at York Mon 12-16, Wed 13-16 h
C449 Student Centre York University, 4700 Keele Street, North York M3J 1P3 ☎ 925-9872 (ext. 2116). *Student organisation.*

FETISH GROUPS

Bear Buddies Toronto
PO Box 926, Station F ✉M4Y 2N9 ☎ 925-9872 (ext. 2176) or ☎ 629-2629. *Group of hairy man and their fans*

HEALTH GROUPS

AIDS Action Now Mon-Fri 13-16.30, meets 2nd/4th Tue 20-22 h
519 Church Street ✉M6G 4A2 ☎ 928-2206
FAX 928-2185 Political group

AIDS Committee of Toronto (ACT)
399 Church Street ✉M5B 2J6 (4th floor)
☎ 340-2437 or hotline ☎ 340-8844 Fax: 340-8224.
Homepage http://www.actoronto.org.
Largest non-profit organisation in Canada. AIDS-related resource library, counselling, support groups and practical help for those affected by AIDS.

Asian Community AIDS Services (ACAS) Mon-Fri 11-19 h
107-33 Isabella Street ✉M4Y 2P7 ☎ 963-4300
FAX 963-4371 Counselling, education and support services for the East and Southeast Asian communities.
Casey House Hospice
9 Huntley Street ✉M4Y 2K8 ☎ 962-7600
The organisation wants to create a comforting environment for PWA.
Gays & Lesbians in Health Care
PO Box 78 06, Station A ☎ 366-4366
Hassle Free Clinic
556 Church Street ✉M4Y 2E3 *(2nd floor)* ☎ 922-0603
Counselling, information and support
Toronto PWA Foundation
399 Church Street ✉M5B 2J6 *(2nd floor)*
☎ 506-1400 Fax: 506-1404

HELP WITH PROBLEMS

New Start Lesbian and Gay Counselling Centre ☎ 944-3858 or ☎ (800) 363-4363 (Toll-free)
Clinical, health, social, addiction and planning services with gay doctors, counsellors and staff.

RELIGIOUS GROUPS

Integrity Toronto Meets 3rd Wed 19.30 at Holy Trinity Church (next to the Eaton Centre)
PO Box 873, Station F ✉M4Y 2N9
☎ 438-9437 or ☎ 925-9872 (ext. 2050).
E-mail: kapn@tap.net
Group of Anglican gays, lesbians and friends.

SPECIAL INTEREST GROUPS

Canadian Cross Dressers Club Tue-Fri 10-19, Sat 11-20 h
161 Gerrard Street East ✉M5A 2E4 ☎ 921-6112
E-mail: info@wildside.org
Latino Gay Group/Grupo Gay Latino (HO-LA!) Meets 1st/3rd Thu at 519 chruch Street
Xtra Box 1010, 491 Church Street, Suite 200 ☎ 928-7493

SPORT GROUPS

Frontrunners Toronto Meets Thu afternoon, Sun mornings at Church Community Centre, 519 Church St.
PO Box 892, Station F ✉M4Y 2N9 ☎ 925-9872
Running club for gay/lesbian/bisexual and transgender people.
Out & Out Club
PO Box 331, Station F ✉M4Y 2L7 ☎ 925-9872
Sports and leisure activities for gays, lesbians and friends e.g. horseback riding, cycling, skiing, canoeing, tennis, volleyball, hiking, weekend excursions and BBQs. Newsletter available.

SWIMMING

-Hanlans Point Beach (g NU) (Toronto Island; take ferry from Harbour Castle Westin Hotel) - official nude beach .
-Scarborough Beach (East of Warden Avenue; mostly gay, mostly nude, but occasional police hassle if nude)
-Kew Beach (at the footof Woodbine Avenue)

CRUISING

-Backyard (between Alexander and Maitland Streets, near Church Street)
-Church Street (between Carlton and Isabella Streets)
-Grosvenor/Bay and Yonge Streets (AYOR R)
-The steps of „Second Cup" on Church Street
-Sunnyside beach (East parking lot closest to footbridge)
-High Park (AYOR at night) (south end near Colbourne Lodge, very busy summer days too)
-Cawthra Park (behind 519 Community Centre)

Whitby ☎ 905

BARS

Bar. The (B g MA)
110 Dundas Street West ✉L1N 2L7 ☎ 666-3121

Windsor ☎ 519

GAY INFO

Gay Hotline Thu Fri 20-22 h or tape ☎ 973-4951

BARS

Club Happy Tap (AC B D GLM MA N S VS YG) Danceclub Sun 20-2, Mon 16-2, Tue-Sat 14-2, Stripclub Mon-Sat 17-2 h
1056 Wyandotte Street East ✉N9A 3K2 ☎ 256-8998
☎ 519/ 256-2737

SAUNAS/BATHS

Vesuvio Steam Bath (G sa sb T VS) 0-24 h
563 Brant Street ☎ 977-8578

GENERAL GROUPS

Gay Youth Line
1168 Drouillard ☎ 973-7671

HEALTH GROUPS

AIDS Committee of Windsor ☎ 973-0222

CDN-Prince-Edward-Island

East CDN
Initials: PE
Time: GMT -4
Area: 6,000 km² / 2,316 sq mi.
Population: 137,000
Capital: Charlottetown

Charlottetown ☎ 902

BOOK SHOPS

Reading Well Bookstore (CC W) Summer: 10-20 h, closed Sun
84 Great George Street ✉C1A 4K4 ☎ 566-2703
Gay and Lesbian section.

HEALTH GROUPS

AIDS PEI
PO Box 2762 ✉C1A 8C4 ☎ 566-2437
or ☎ 1-800 344-2437 (USA & CDN). FAX 626 3400.
E-mail: aidspei@cdngateway.pe.ca

Vernon Bridge ☎ 902

GUEST HOUSES

Blair Hall (bf glm H) COA 2E0 ☎ 651-2202
or ☎ (800) 268-7005 (Toll-free). 3-storey wooden house in nice location close to many tourist attractions like Selkirk Lobster Suppers and Orwell Corners Historic Site. Season Apr-Oct. Rates Can$ 45-50 with shared baths.
Rainbow Lodge (bf G H) June-September
Station Main ✉COA 2E0 ☎ & FAX 651-2202
or ☎ 1-800 268-7005 (USA & CDN), ☎ (905) 775-8884, FAX (905) 775-8887 (in winter). Rates Can$ 80, incl. bf..

CDN-Québec

West CDN
Initials: PQ
Time: GMT -5
Area: 1,541,000 km^2 / 594,980 sq mi.
Population: 7,419,000
Capital: Québec
Important gay cities: Montréal and Québec

Chicoutimi ☎ 418

BARS

Bistro des Anges (B GLM) 15-3 h
332 rue du Havre ✉G7N 1N4 ☎ 698-4829

Drummondville ☎ 819

BARS

Nuance. Le (B GLM MA) Wed-Sun 16-? h
336 Rue Lindsay ✉J2B 1G5 *(2nd floor)* ☎ 471-4252

HOTELS

Motel Alouette (H NG)
1975, boulevard Mercure
☎ 478-4166 *FAX 478-0090*

CRUISING

-Parc Woodyat (evenings)

Granby ☎ 450

CAMPING

Bain gai de nature (bf F G NU pi sa VS wh)
125 Rue Lussier, St-Alphonse-de-Granby ✉J0E 2A0 *(Ca. 10 mi from Granby)* ☎ 375-4765 Fax: 375-4765
E-Mail: info@editpaix.qc.ca Homepage: www.editpaix.qc.ca
Luxurious house with private lake and forest. Overnight accommodation possible as well as day visits.

Joliette ☎ 514

BARS

Flirt. Le (B G MA)
343 Rue Beaudry Sud ☎ 753-7225

Jonquière ☎ 418

BARS

Le Claire de Lune (B gLM)
2171, rue St-Dominique ✉G7X 4M9 ☎ 695-9687

GENERAL GROUPS

Association des gai-e-s du Saguenay-Lac-St. Jean (AGSL) ☎ 547-3579
(Stephane) or ☎ 693-4706 (Serge)

Magog ☎ 819

CAFES

Café Croute Ma Gogue (glm) 299, Principale Ouest
☎ 847-3925

Café sur la Table (B glm) 1117 Boulevard Bromont, local 111 *(Bromont)* ☎ 534-4244

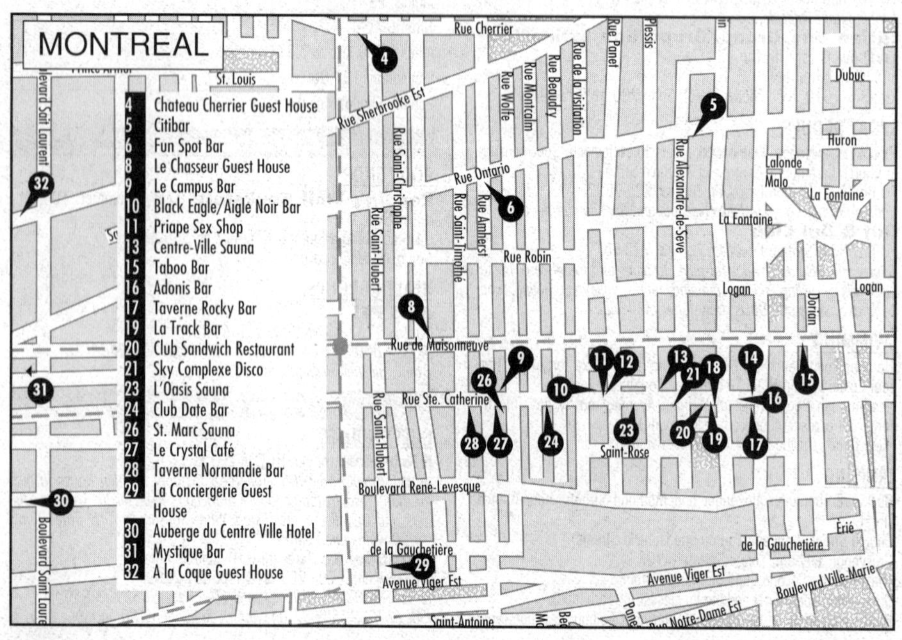

GUEST HOUSES

Potentiel. Le (Glm)
2749, chemin Fitch Bay ☎ 876-7237

Montréal ☎ 514

● Montreal is presently in a major economic revival and is in many aspects 'stronger' than Toronto. Montreal's growth is being led by its concentration of industry in the new economy (high tech sectors).The metropolitan population of Montreal is now at 3.2 million, about the same as Toronto.
Montreal is also the gay party capital of Canada with 5 annual events attracting many people from all over the world : „Black & Blue" in October, „Wild & Wet" in May, „Twist/Gay Pride" in August, „Red" in February and „Bal de Boys" for New Years Eve.
The centre of the gay village is St. Catherine Street East between Rue Amherst and Avenue Papineau. There are relatively few gay discos, but a good dozen gay saunas built up on the good custom of their customers. Those who decide to visit the city in the winter months may have to contend with extreme temperatures and heavy snowfalls (although the snow falls have been lighter in the last few years and replaced by rain). Whatever the weather, Montreal is a lively city and well worth a visit.

✱ Montreal erlebt gegenwärtig einen ökonomischen Aufschwung und ist der Toronto in vielen Aspekten überlegen. Das Wirtschaftswachstum Montreals begründet sich auf der Ansiedlung moderner Industriezweige, vor allem im Technologiebereich. Mittlerweile leben im Großraum Montreal mit ca. 3,2 Mio. Einwohnern, fast so viele Menschen wie im Ballungsraum Toronto. Montreal ist zweifellos die bedeutendste Schwulen-Metropole Kanadas und mit fünf jährlich stattfindenden Großveranstaltungen Anziehungspunkt für Menschen aus aller Welt: "Black & Blue" im Oktober, "Wild & Wet" im Mai, "Twist/Gay Pride" im August, "Red" im Februar und "Bal de Boys" an Neujahr. Das schwule Zentrum der Stadt ist die St. Cathrine Street East zwischen Rue Amherst und Avenue Papineau. Es gibt hier zwar nur relativ wenige schwule Discotheken, aber dafür ein gutes Dutzend schwule Saunen, die in der Regel auch gut besucht sind. Wer sich dafür entscheidet Montreal im Winter zu besuchen, muß mit extremen Temperaturen und heftigen Schneefällen rechnen. Aber wie das Wetter auch immer sein mag, Montreal ist eine sehr lebendige Stadt und in jedem Fall .

▲ Montréal vit actuellement un renouveau économique et dépasse sous plusieurs aspects sa rivale Toronto. Une concentration d'entreprises spécialisées en haute technologie ont contribué à cette forte croissance ces dernières années. L'agglomération de la ville compte aujourd'hui 3,2 millions d'habitants, presque autant que Toronto.
Montréal est aussi la capitale homosexuelle du Canada et organise chaque année 5 manifestations majeures qui attirent des participants du monde entier: le festival „Black & Blue" en Octobre, le „Wild & Wet" week-end en Mai, la „Twist Party/Gay Pride" en Août, la „Red Party" en Février et le „Bal de Boys" à nouvel an.
La scène homosexuelle (le Village) se concentre aux abords de la rue Sainte Catherine entre la rue Amherst et l'avenue Papineau. Il existe relativement peu de discothèques gayes mais par contre une douzaine de saunas qui se briguent la faveur de la clientèle. Celui qui compte passer un séjour à Montréal en hiver doit compter avec des températures extrêmement froides et des risques de tempêtes de neiges. Mais qu'importe le temps, Montréal est une ville chaleureuse et animée qui mérite certainement une visite.

☆ Ni la capital del país (es decir Ottawa, Ontario), ni Québec, sino Montreal es la indiscutible metrópoli gay canadiense. Despúes de París es la ciudad francófona más grande del mundo y la fuerte influencia francesa es notable en toda la provincia de Québec. Por ello, se levantan con regularidad voces pidiendo la independencia de Québec del resto de la federación. El ambiente gay se concentra en el „Village", la zona Que comprende las paradas de métro Berri-de- Montigny, Beaudry y Papineau entre Ontario y Sta-Catherine. La carencia de discotecas gay en la ciudad es compensada con la abundancia de sus estupendas saunas. Quien visite Montreal en invierno, debería estar preparado para un frío extremo, con temperaturas que bajan a menos de 15 °C, muchas veces acompañadas por fuertes nevadas. No en vano se construyeron numerosos centros comerciales subterraneos, que están conectados entre ellos: de tal modo que se pueda estar de compras, sin que molesten ni la nieve ni el frío

❖ Montreal se encuentra en pleno resurgimiento económico y es en muchos aspectos "más fuerte" que Toronto. El crecimiento de Montreal viene impulsado por su concentración industrial en la nueva economía (sector high tech). La población urbana de Montreal es de 3,2 millones de habitantes, más o menos la misma que la de Toronto.Montreal es también la capital gay de Canadá, con 5 eventos anuales que atraen a mucha gente de todo el mundo: "Black & Blue" en octubre, "Wild and Wet" en mayo, "Twist/Gay Pride" en agosto, "Red" en febrero y "Bal de Boys" en la víspera de año nuevo. El centro de la comunidad gay es St. Catherine Street, entre Rue Amherst y Avenue Papineau. Hay relativamente pocas discotecas de ambiente, pero una buena docena de saunas gay construidas conforme a las buenas usanzas de sus clientes. Los que decidan visitar la ciudad en invierno tendrán que aguantar temperaturas extremas y fuertes nevadas (aunque hay que decir que las nevadas se han ido haciendo más suaves en los últimos años y reemplazando por lluvia). Sea cual sea el tiempo, Montreal es una ciudad viva que bien merece la pena visitar.

GAY INFO

Archives Gaies Du Quebec. Les Thu 19-21 h
4067 Boulevard St.Laurent, #202 *PO Box 395, Succ. Place-du-Parc H2W 2N9* ☎ 287-9987

Centre des Gais et Lesbiennes de Montreal Mon-Fri 10-22 h
2075 Rue Plessis, PO Box 476, Suc. C ✉H2L 4K4 *(2nd floor)*
☎ 528-8424

C'est comme ca (GLM TV) Sun 23, Tue 1.30, Wed 15, Fri 22.30, Sat 19.30 h on Vidéotron Cable 9

Fugues
1212 Rue St.Hubert ✉H2L 3Y7 ☎ 848-1854 or
☎ (888) 848-1854. FAX 845-7645. E-mail: info@kiosque.com.
Homepage: http://www.kiosque.com.
Monthly magazine with calendar of events, advertising, classifieds, personal ads. Mainly French, some English. Subscription Can$ 30 per year. Free in gay venues.

Gai Ecoute 19-23 h
PO Box 384, Stn. H ✉H3G 2L1 ☎ 866-0103
French info-line.

Gay Line 19-23 h
PO Box 384, Stn H ✉H3G 2L1 ☎ 866-5090 ☎ 1-888-505-1010
Non-profit listening & referal service for the gay, lesbian and bisexual community of Quebec

Project 10 ☎ 989-4585
25 and under, English & French.

RG
c/o Editions Homeureux, PO Box 915, succ. C ✉H2L 4V2
☎ 523-9463 Fax: 523-2214.
Monthly magazine in French.

S-TEK ☎ 597-2409

TOURIST INFO

L'Office des Congrès et du Tourisme du Grand Montréal
1555 Rue Peel, Suite 600 ✉H3A 1X6 ☎ 844-5400
Fax: 844-5757

BARS

Adonis (B G SNU YG) 15-3 h
1681 Rue Sainte Catherine Est *(M°Papineau)* ☎ 521-1355
Agora (B G N) Tue - Sat 16-03:00h, Sun & Mon 16-23:00h
1160 Rue Mackay *(M°Guy-Concordia)* ☎ 934-1428
Ballroom. Le (B D GLM)
1003, rue Ste-Catherine Est, 2nd Floor ☎ 287 1360
Bar Cajun (B G)
1574, rue Ste.-Catherine Est *(M° Papineau/Beaudry)*
☎ 523-4679
Bar 889 (B GLM stv)
889, côtw Ste-Geneviève ☎ 524 5000
Black Eagle/Aigle Noir (B G LJ)
1315 Rue Ste.Catherine Est *(M° Beaudry)* ☎ 529-0040
Campus. Le (AC B G SNU) 15-3 h
1111 Rue Ste Catherine Est, ✉H2L 2G6 *(M°Beaudry)* ☎ 526-3616
Club Bolo (AC B GLM lj MA) Course: Mon Tue Thu 19-22.30, Dancing: Fri Sat 21-3, Sun 16-21 h
960 Amherst ✉H2L 3K5 *(Metro Beaudry)* ☎ 849-4777
Email: adanser@aei.ca.
Homepage: http://www.iaglcwcd.simplenet.com/bolo. Country dance club and bar. Friendly atmosphere.
Club Date (ac B G OS s) 13-3 h
1218 Rue Ste Catherine Est/Montcalm *(M°Beaudry)*
☎ 521-1242
Piano bar.
Drug Store (AC B Glm MA OS) 1
364 Rue Ste Catherine Est *(M°Beaudry/Papineau)* ☎ 524-1960
Complex of eight bars, including Le Trou (LJ).
Exotica (B GLM) Thu - Sat 22-03:00h, Sun 17-23:00h
417 rue St-Pierre *(Victoria Square)* ☎ 218 1773
Latino bar.
Fun Spot (B G MA S) 10-24 h
1151 Ontario Est/Amherst *(M°Beaudry)* ☎ 522-0416
Mystique (B G) 16-3 h
1424 Rue Stanley *(M° Peel)* ☎ 844-5711
Stereo (B D GLM) 23-11:00 h
1204 Rue Ste.Catherine Est ☎ 282 3307
Stock Bar (B G SNU) 20-03:00h
1278 St.-André ☎ 842-1336
Stud (B G LJ) 10-03:00h
1812 Rue Ste-Catherine Est *(M°Papineau)* ☎ 598-8243
Taboo (AC B G SNU) 17-03:00h
1950 Boulevard de Maisonneuve Est *(M°Papineau)* ☎ 597-0010
Taverne Normandie (AC B G MA VS) 10-24 h
1295 Rue Amherst/Rue Ste.Catherine Est *(M°Beaudry)*
☎ 522-2766
Taverne Rocky (B G lj MA) 10-24 h
1673 Rue Ste.Catherine Est *(M°Papineau)* ☎ 521-7865
Track. La (AC B G LJ MA) 21-3, Sat Sun 15-3 h
1584 Rue Ste.Catherine Est *(M°Papineau)* ☎ 521-1419
Cruisy.
West Side (B CC G SNU) 16-03:00h, Sat & Sun 19-03:00h
1071 Côte du Beaver Hall ☎ 866-4963

CAFES

Armoricain. L' (F glm)
1550, rue Fullum ☎ 523-2551
Café Clin d'Oeil (Glm) 1
429 rue Amherst *(M° Beaudry)* ☎ 528-1209

Café Deux Ciemes
1031 St. Hubert ☎ 845 33 89
Eden Café (B f GLM)
1334 Rue Ste Catherine est ☎ 524-2107
Universel (B f glm)
1030 Rue Cherrier est/Parc Lafontaine *(M° Sherbrooke)*
☎ 598-7136

DANCECLUBS

Club Unity (! AC B D Glm snu)
1400 Rue Montcalm *(M°Beaudry)* ☎ 523-4429
Larg discothèque on several levels.
Groove Society (B D Glm) Thu
1288 Rue Amherst *(M° Beaudry)* ☎ 859-9055
Mississippi Club (AC B D E GLM MA) Wed-Sun 21-3 h
1592 Rue Ste-Catherine Est ✉H2L 2J2 *(M°Beaudry)*
☎ 523-4679
Sky Complexe (B D GLM STV)
1474 Rue Ste Catherine Est *(M°Beaudry/Papineau)* ☎ 522-2475
(Sky Pub) ☎ *529-6969 (Sky Club)*

RESTAURANTS

Après Le Jour (AC B CC F GLM) 11-23 h
901 Rue Rachel Est *(M°Mont-Royal)* ☎ 527-4141
French/Italian cuisine.
Au 917 (B F GLM)
917 Rachel Est ☎ 524-0094 *French cuisine.*
Avenue. L' (B F GLM)
922 Avenue Mont-Royal *(M° Mont-Royal)* ☎ 523-8780
Bazou (AC B CC F GLM MA OS)
2004 Hôtel de Ville ✉H2X 1H5 ☎ 982-0853
Bistro L'Un et L'Autre (b F G H MA) 9-23 h
1641 Rue Amherst ✉H2L 3L4 *(M°Berri-UQAM)* ☎ 597-0878
Chablis (b CC F GLM MA OS) 11-23.20, Sat Sun 16-23.30 h
1639 Rue St.Hubert *(M°Berri)* ☎ 523-0053
French and Spanish cuisine. Brunch Sun 11 h.
Chez la Mère Berteau (B F glm) Tue-Sat
1237 de Champlain *(M° Papineau)* ☎ 524-9344
Club Sandwich (B F glm) 0-24 h
1574 rue Ste.Catherine Est *(M°Papineau)* ☎ 523-4679
Cruisy after hour bar.
Entretiens. Les (B F GLM) 10-24 h
1577 Laurier Est *(M°Laurier)* ☎ 521-2934
Vegetarian cuisine.
Exception. L' (B F GLM)
1200 Rue St-Hubert *(M° Berri-UQAM)* ☎ 282-1282
Hamburgers, fries, vegetarian dishes.
Nega Fulo (F glm)
1257 Rue Amherst ☎ 522-1554 *Brazilian cuisine.*
Ogâtô (F glm) Mon-Fri 7-24, Sat Sun 10-24 h
1301 Ste-Catherine Est ☎ 528-6222
Sandwiches, salads, desserts, cafés du monde.
Piccolo Diavolo (A AC b CC E F GLM LJ MA) Sat-Wed 17-23, Thu 11.30-14, 17-23, Fri 11.30-14, 14-24 h
1336 Ste-Catharine Est ☎ 526-1336
Italian cuisine.
Pizzedelic (F glm)
1329 Rue Ste. Catherine est ☎ 526-6011
Planète. Le (F GLM)
1451, rue Ste-Catherine Est
☎ 528-6953

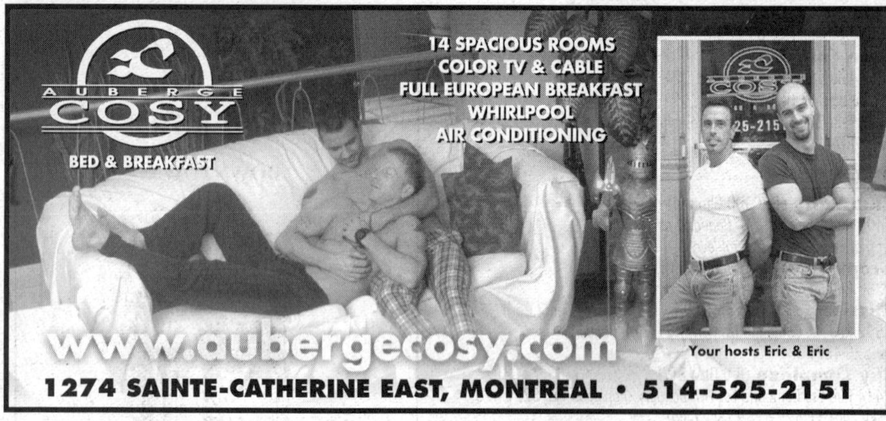

AUBERGE
COSY
BED & BREAKFAST
14 SPACIOUS ROOMS
COLOR TV & CABLE
FULL EUROPEAN BREAKFAST
WHIRLPOOL
AIR CONDITIONING
www.aubergecosy.com
Your hosts Eric & Eric
1274 SAINTE-CATHERINE EAST, MONTREAL • 514-525-2151

Saloon Café (b F g)
1333 rue Ste Catherine Est/Panet *(M°Beaudry)* ☎ 522-1333
Popular.
St-Charles. Le (B F G) 17-? h
1799 Rue Amherst H2L 3L7 *(M°Beaudry)* ☎ 526-1799
International cuisine.
Stromboli (B F Glm)
1019 Avenue Mont-Royale est ☎ 527-8500
Toasteur. Le (B F GLM)
950 Rue Roy est ☎ 527-8500

la Conciergerie
GUEST HOUSE
Your resort in the city!
EDITOR'S CHOICE AWARDS 1999 OUT & ABOUT
1019, rue Saint-Hubert, Montréal (Qc) H2L 3Y3 Canada
Tel:(514) 289-9297 Fax:(514) 289-0845
www.laconciergerie.ca info@laconciergerie.ca

SHOWS
Cabaret l'Entre-Peau (B G S TV) 21-3, Sun 15-3 h
1115 Rue Ste.Catherine Est *(M°Beaudry)* ☎ 525-7566

SEX SHOPS/BLUE MOVIES
Priape (G)
1311 Rue Ste.Catherine Est ✉H2L 2H4 ☎ 521-8451
Magazines, newspapers, leather, jeans, rubber, toys etc.

CINEMAS
Wega Video Inc. (GLM MA N VS) 10-0 h
930 Ste. Catherine Est ✉H2L 2E7 *(M° Beaudry)* ☎ 987-5993
Also mail order: PO Box 366, Station C H2L 4K3.

ESCORTS & STUDIOS
Agence Flèche (G msg) 0-24 h ☎ 254-5478

SAUNAS/BATHS
Aux Berges (B g sa sb sol) 0-24 h
1070 Rue Mackay *(M°Lucien L'Allier or Guy Concordia)*
☎ 938-9393
Centre-Ville (AC CC f G MA NU sa sb VS wh) 0-24 h
1465 Ste-Catherine Est ✉H2L 2H9 *(M°Beaudry)* ☎ 524-3486
L'Oasis (AC B f G sa sb pi VS wh) 0-24 h
1390 Rue Ste.Catherine Est *(M°Beaudry)* ☎ 521-0785
Millénium. Le (G sa sb wh VS) 0-24:00h
1166, rue Ste-Catherine Est ☎ 528 3326
Sauna Bourbon (G)
1574 Rue Ste-Catherine Est *(Métro Beaudry & Papineau)*
☎ 523-4679
Sauna du Plateau (f G OS sa sb vs wh) 0-24 h
961 Rachel est *(near Lafontaine Park)* ☎ 528-1679
Sauna St.Hubert (AC G sa VS) Mon-Thu 12-24, Fri-Sun 0-24 h
6527 St.Hubert ☎ 277-0176
Sauna Verdun (AC f G MA sa VS) Mon-Fri 11-24, Sat Sun 0-24 h
5785 Avenue Verdun, Verdun ✉H4H 1L7 *(M° Verdun)*
☎ 769-6034
Sauna 1286 (AC G sa MA wh WO VS) 0-24 h
1286 Chemin Chambly, Longueuil *(M°Longueuil. Bus8/88)*
☎ (450) 677-1286
Sauna 226 (G) 226 Boulevard des Laurentides, Laval
☎ (450) 975-4556
Sauna 456 (b f G pi sa sb VS wh) 0-24 h

456 de la Gauchetiere Ouest/St.Alexandre, ✉H2Z 1E3 ☎ 871-8341
Sauna 5018 (AC G msg OS sa sb VS wh) 0-24 h
5018 Boulevard St.Laurent H2T 1R7 *(M° Laurier)* ☎ 277-3555
St. Marc (AC B f G sa VS wh) 0-24 h
1168 Rue Ste.Cathérine Est *(M°Beaudry)* ☎ 525-8404

BOOK SHOPS

L'Androgyne Librairie (GLM) Mon-Wed 9-18, Thu Fri 9-21, Sat 9-18, Sun 11-18 h
3636 Boulevard St.Laurent/Prince Arthur ✉H2X 2V4
☎ 842-4765
Gay, lesbian books in French, English. Also by mail order.

FASHION SHOPS

Body Body (G)
1326 rue Ste Catherine Est ☎ 523-0245
Men's clothing
Joe Blo (G)
1412 rue de la Visitation/Ste-Catherine est *(M° Beaudry)*
☎ 597-2330
Men's clothing.

LEATHER & FETISH SHOPS

Bolero. II (glm)
6842/6846 Rue St.Hubert *(M° Jean Talon)* ☎ 270-6065
U-Bahn (G LJ)
1285, Amherts ✉H2L 3K9 ☎ 529 0808
Leather, Rubber and PVC clothing for men

HOTELS

Auberge du Centre-Ville (AC B bf CC f G H MA NU OS sa sb VS wh) All year
1070 Rue Mackay/René-Levesque ✉H3G 2H1 *(M°Guy-Concordia)*
☎ 938-9393 Fax: 938 -1616 Homepage: www.auxberges.ca
42 rooms, most with bath/shower/WC, all with telephone, radio, TV, AC and room service. For more details, please see website.
Hôtel Eurêka (GLM)
1553 Rue St André *(M° Berri-uqam)* ☎ 524-1355

GUEST HOUSES

Alacoque (AC bf CC F Glm H OS)
2091 St Urbain ✉H2X 2N1 *(South of Sherbrooke)* ☎ 842-0938
Fax: 842-7585 E-Mail: christian.alacoque@sympatico.ca
Homepage: www.3.sympatico.ca/christian.alacoque
An authentic town house from 1830. Well furnished. Downtown. Rates Can$ 50-100.
Angelica B & B (bf GLM H OS)
1215 Sainte Elizabeth *(Downtown)* ☎ 844-5048
Auberge Cosy (AC bf CC GLM H wh) All year
1274 rue Ste.- Catherine Est ✉H2l 2H2 *(Subway Beaudry)*
☎ 525 2151 Fax: 525 2579 E-Mail: info@aubergecosy.com
Homepage: www.aubergecosy.com
Chasseur. Le (bf CC G H MA OS) all year
1567 Rue St.André ✉H2L 3T5 *(M° Berri-Uqam)* ☎ 521-2238
Fax: 849-2051
Centrally located bed and breakfast, close to gay bars. 5 rooms with bath/WC on the corridor, 1 en-suite. Rooms with balcony, radio, heating
Château Cherrier (AC bf CC GLM H) Apr 15-Nov 15
550 Rue Cherrier, ✉H2L IH3 *(M°Sherbrooke)* ☎ 844-0055
☎ (800) 816-0055 (toll-free) Fax: 844-8438
E-Mail: chateau.cherrier@sympatico.ca
Located in the „quartier latin", close to gay village. 8 rooms in an old Tudor building, with authentic period furniture. Gay owned and operated.
Conciergerie Guest House. La (AC bf CC G LJ msg OS wh WO) All year
1019 Rue St.Hubert ✉H2L 3Y3 *(Metro Berri)* ☎ 289-9297
Fax: 289-0845 E-Mail: info@laconciergerie.ca
Homepage: www.laconciergerie.ca
Central location. 20 km to airport. 4 mins walk to the gay bars of the Village. Surrounded by a cruisy area. Sundeck. Open year round. Recommended. Rates from Can $ 80 (bath/shower/WC), 60,- (without).
Dauphins. Les (GLM H)
1281 Rue Beaudry ☎ 525-1459
Dorion Touristes (G H)
1477 Rue Dorion ☎ 523-2427
Hôtel Pierre (GLM H)
169 Rue Sherbrooke Est ✉H2X 1C7 ☎ 288-8519
Centally located. Rooms with bath or shower, WC, telephone, fax, TV, video, kitchenette, own key and room service. Rates on request.
Maison Chablis (AC CC G H MA sol OS)
1641-43 St-Hubert ✉H2L 3Z1 *(M°Berri)* ☎ 527-8346 Fax: 596-1519 E-Mail: chablis@mlink.net Homepage: www.mlink.net/~chablis/
Downtown location near gay village. 8 double rooms, 5 single rooms.
Roy d' Carreau (bf GLM OS)
1637 Amherst ✉H2L 3L4 *(M°Beaudry/Berry-UQAM)*
☎ 524-2493 Fax: 489-3148 E-Mail: kings@cam.org
Homepage: www.cam.org/~kings
St.Christophe. Le (bf CC G H NU OS sol wh) all year
1597 St.Christophe ✉H2L 3W7 *(M° Berri)* ☎ 527-7836
Fax: 526-6488 E-Mail: info@stchristophe.com.
Homepage: www.stchristophe.com
5 rooms each with a different decoration some either private or shared bath. In the gay village
Three Cats Guest House. The (bf G h LJ MA p)
c/o POB/CP 1036, Station „C" ✉H2L 4V3 ☎ 899 5582
For leather fettish guests. Close to East Village area. Call for further information and address
Traversin. Le (bf G OS)
4124 Saint-Hubert ✉H2L 4A8
☎ 597-1546 E-Mail: travrsin@homeniscience.com
Homepage: http://www.homeniscience.com/le_traversin
A nice non-smoking Bed & Breakfast in the heart of Montréal.
Turquoise (bf G H NU OS)
1576 rue Alexandre de Sève ✉H2L 2V7 *(M°Beaudry)*
☎ & FAX 523-9943
B&B in a Victorian mansion with a large and sunny garden. 4 rooms and one suite (2 queen size beds) with shared bath/WC, own key. Rates single Can$ 40-50, double 50-60 and suite 60-90, bf buffet included.

PRIVATE ACCOMODATION

Au Stade B&B (AC bf f GLM MA p sol WO)
PO Box 42 Station M, ✉H1V 3L6 ☎ 254-1250 E-Mail: bebrief@sympatico.ca
Bed and breakfast located close to Olympic Village and 20 min. to airport, 5 min. to gay area. 3 rooms with shared baths and balcony, phone, fax, TV, video, radio, own key. Call for rates.
Bed and Breakfast du Village (bf GLM H)
1279, rue Montcalm ✉H2L 3G6 ☎ 522-4771 Fax: 522-7118
E-Mail: bbv@total.net Homepage: www.gaibec.com/bbv
Dortoir. Le (bf G H MA)
2042 Rue de la Visitation ✉H2L 3C7 *(M° Beaudry or Berri/UQAM)* ☎ 597-2688 E-Mail: Rubywell@videotron.ca
Small B&B Use of kitchen and laundry. Bicycles available. Close to restaurants and bars.

Home Suite HOM
PO Box 762, Station C ✉H2L 4L6
☎ 523 46 42 ☎ 523 61 07 or ☎ 1-800-429-4983 (USA & CDN), E-Mail: homeswap@gaytrip.com
Homepage: www.gaytrip.com
Gay and lesbian accomodation club. Hospitality and home exchange, private B & B. Contact Francois Chalot for information about membership.

L'un et l'autre B&B (AC b bf CC G)
1641, Amherst ✉H2L 3L4 ☎ 597 0878 E-Mail: info@aubergell.com Homepage: www.aubergell.com
Beautifully renovated house in the heart of Montréal's gay village with outdoor terrace/Jolie maison rénovée sise au coer du Village avec terrasse-soleil.

Pain d'Epice B&B Ginger Bread House (bf CC glm)
1628 Rue St.Christophe ✉H2L 3W8 ☎ 597-2804
Fax: 273-9477 E-Mail: gingerbreadhouse@gai.com
Homepage: www.gai.com/gingerbreadhouse
2 chambres à proximit'du village/ 2 rooms near to the village

Zip Centre-Ville (AC bf G MA sa wh) 08-21:00h
1210 Dalcourt ✉H2L 2W6 *(M° Beaudry)* ☎ 524-4372
E-Mail: rbarrette@cedep.com Homepage: www.pointzip.qc.ca
Central location. 5 rooms with bath/WC, radio, kitchenette, own key.

CAMPING

Camping Plein Bois (G)
550 chemin St. Henri, Ste Marthe, Cté Vaudreuil *(located west of Montreal)* ☎ (450) 459-4646
Open April 29 to Sep 5

GENERAL GROUPS

Association des lesbiennes et gais de l'Université de Québec à Montréal (ALGUQAM)
1259, rue Berri, 9th Floor ☎ 987-3039
Publisher of monthly informational magazine »Homo sapiens«.

Aux Prismes Sat 20 h
PO Box 5514, Succ. B ✉H3B 4P1 ☎ 963-9710
Social/recreational group for gays, lesbians and their friends; events include movies, debates, tours, and picnics. Meetings at 1259 Rue Berri, 9th floor.

Jeunesse Lambda Fri 19.30 h
1301 Rue Sherbrooke ☎ 528-7535
Discussion and social group for people younger than 25.

LBGTM-Lesbian, Bisexual, Gay and Transgender Students of McGill Mon-Fri 12-15, 19-22 h
3480 McTavish, Apt. 429 *(M°Peel)* ☎ 398-6822
Student organization.

Le Triangle, Association Communautaire homosexuelle de l`Université de Montréal
C-7123, Pavillon Lionel-Groulx, 3200 Jean-Brillant ☎ 270-8856 *or* ☎ *389-1964*

Relance. La Tue 19.15 h
Room Z-3023, Pavillon Garneau, Université de Quebec à *Montreal, 1750 Rue St.André* ☎ 522-5931
Association of gay fathers in Montreal.

FETISH GROUPS

Club Baron-Montreal
PO Box 490 05, Place Versailles ✉H1N 3P6 ☎ 254 7948

Club de Cuir Prédateurs Montreal
PO Box 171, Succ. C ✉H2L 4K1
Social group for men interested in leather.

M.C.Faucon Inc.
PO Box 152, Station C, H2L 4K1

HEALTH GROUPS

ACCM Aids Community Care Montreal
2075, rue Plessis ☎ 527-0928
Support groups, counselling, legal and financial services.

Comité SIDA-Québec
1001 Rue St.Denis ☎ 285-6471
Organisme officiel du Gouvernement du Québec sur le SIDA sous la responsabilité de l'hôpital St-Luc de Montréal.

Info-SIDA ☎ 521-7432
Information about transmission, symptoms, treatment etc. in French

RELIGIOUS GROUPS

Yakhdav ☎ 933-7387
Jewish gay & lesbian support & social group.

SPECIAL INTEREST GROUPS

Association des Motocyclistes Gais du Quebec
PO Box 47618, Succ. Plateau Mont-Royal ✉H2H 2S8
Social group promoting gay presence in motorcycling world; bimonthly newsletter; garage and driving school.

Bad Boy Club Montreal
E-Mail: information@bbcm.org Homepage: www.bbcm.org
Information on the 5 annual party events in Montreal : „Black & Blue", „Wild & Wet", „Twist/Gay Pride", „Red" and „Bal de Boys" Please call, send an e-mail or visit the website for further information.

L'Association des Gais et Lesbiennes Asiatiques de Montreal 2nd Fri 19.30-21.30 h
A-1920, Pavillon Hubert Aquin , Université du Québec à *Montreal* ☎ 528-8424
Support, discussion and social group for Asian gays and lesbians.

SPORT GROUPS

Ligue Lambda
PO Box 57 01, succ. C ☎ 287-9694

CRUISING

-Rue Ste.Catherine est (St.Hubert street to Wolfe street, after 21 h)
-In front, in the little park west of Church Marie-Reine-du-Monde
-Parc Baldwin (M°Papineau)
-Rue Champlain (R) (between Ste.Catherine est and René-Lévesque est boulevard)
-

Mont-Tremblant ☎ 819

PRIVATE ACCOMODATION

Versant Ouest (bf CC GLM) all year
110 Chemin Labelle ✉J0T 1Z0 ☎ 425-6615
E-Mail: verso@cil.qc.ca. Homepage: www.versant-ouest.qc.ca
Open year round. 90 min. by car from Montreal and 5 min. from the skiing resort of Tremblant. Nice country B&B house. 4 rooms with bath/WC.

Percé ☎ 418

DANCECLUBS

Auberge de la montagne (AC B D F g MA) 0-24 h
G0C 2L0 *(le garcantua)* ☎ 782-5535

Prévost ☎ 450

BARS

Secret. Le (G) 17-3 h
3029, Boulevard Labelle ☎ 224-7350

Québec City ☎ 418

Quebec City is the capital of the same named province and is seen as the heart of the French speaking culture in Canada. The outer suburbs are very American in style and the inner part of the city is predominantly French architecture with many of the old building under historical protection. Quebec is a strange mixture of North America and France.
The gay scene is rather small but lively. The city has many first class restaurants heavily frequented by gays and lesbians. In Quebec the winter is very long and lasts from November to April. February is one of the coldest months with temperatures sinking to under minus 20° Celsius. The cold winter does not prevent the Quebecoise from celebrating their Winter Carneval. The colourful Quebec Carneval is heavily visited by tourists and it is even worth making a trip from Montreal or Toronto.

Quebec City ist die Hauptstadt der gleichnamigen Provinz und gilt als Wiege der französischsprachigen Kultur in Kanada. Während sich die Stadt in ihren Außenbezirken mit ihren Highways, Shoppingmalls und ausgedehnten Wohngebieten sehr amerikanisch gibt, strahlt die denkmalgeschützte und äußerst sehenswerte Altstadt ein geschichtsträchtiges Flair aus, das eher an Frankreich als an Nordamerika erinnert.
Die Szene ist klein aber lebendig. Die Stadt verfügt über zahlreiche erstklassige Restaurants, von denen einige fast ausschließlich von Schwulen und Lesben besucht werden.
Nicht vergessen sollten Besucher, daß Quebec auch die Kältekammer Kanadas genannt wird, und dies nicht ohne Grund. Der Winter ist lang und dauert von November bis April, wobei die Temperaturen im Februar zum Teil unter minus 20° C absinken. Dies hindert die Quebecoise aber nicht daran, jedes Jahr im Februar ausgiebig ihren Winterkarneval zu feiern. Dieses bunte Spektakel lockt auch viele Touristen an und lohnt auf jeden Fall einen Abstecher von Montreal oder Toronto aus.

La métropole du Québec est la capitale de la province de même nom et est considérée comme le berceau de la culture francophone du Canada. Bien que la ville dans ses quartiers extérieurs avec ses highways, shoppingmalls et zones résidentielles soient très américains, la remarquable vielle ville classée monuments historiques reflète une atmosphère historique rappelant plutôt la France que l'Amérique du Nord. La scène est petite, mais animée. La ville dispose d'un grand nombre de restaurants de première catégorie dont certains sont fréquentés presque exclusivement par les homosexuels et les lesbiennes. Les visiteurs ne devraient pas oublier que le Québec est également désigné „chambre froide" du Canada, et cela non sans raison. L'hiver est long et dure du mois de novembre jusqu'au mois d'avril, encore qu'il faille souligner que les températures descendent au mois de février audessous de 20° C. Cela n'empêche cependant pas les québécoises de fêter amplement leur carnaval d'hiver. Ce spectacle de variétés attire aussi de nombreux touristes et un crochet de Montréal ou de Toronto en vaut la peine.

Québec City es la capital de la provincia del mismo nombre y es considerada como la cuna de la cultura francófona en Canada. Mientras las afueras de la ciudad se semeja mucho a los Estados Unidos, con sus grandes careteras, centros comerciales y extensas zonas de viviendas, el centro de la ciudad refleja un ambiente muy especial que recuerda más a Francia con sus antiguos edificios dignos de ver. El ambiente gay es pequeño, pero muy vivaz. La ciudad cuenta con excelentes restaurantes, algunos de ellos visitados exclusivamente por clientela gay. El apodo de Québec es, y con mucha razón, „cámara frigorífica de Canada", debido a su largo invierno que dura desde noviembre hasta abril, con temperaturas que bajan frecuentemente a menos de 20°C. Pero este hecho no significa ningún obstáculo para que anualmente sus habitantes celebren apasionadamente la fiesta de carnavales en febrero. Este fantástico espectáculo atrae siempre muchos turistas, que vienen desde Montreal o Toronto para no perderse estas fiestas.

Quebec City è la capitale della provincia omonima e viene considerata la culla della cultura francofona in Canada. Mentre i quartieri periferici con gli Highways, Shoppingmalls ed estese zone residenziali sono tipici per l'America, il bel centro storico pieno di monumenti nazionali rievoca il passato e le sue radici francesi. La vita gay è piccola ma vivace. Si trovano numerosi ristoranti di prima classe, di cui alcuni vengono frequentati esclusivamente dai gay e lesbiche. Non è da dimentacare che Quebec viene nominato il „frigorifero" di Canada. C'è un motivo. L'inverno è lungo e dura da novembre fino ad aprile, e le temperature calano fino ai 20 gradi sotto zero, un fatto che non inibisce i Quebecoise a festeggiare il carnevale. Questo allegro avvenimento attrae anche molti turisti, e vale la pena fare una scappata da Montreal o Toronto.

GAY INFO

Magaizine de Québec. Le
707 Boulevard Charest Ouest, ✉G1N 4T1 ☎ 529 5892
Monthly newspaper published in French.

Relais d'espérance
617 Rue Montmartre ☎ 522-3301
Information, coffee-shop, encounters, AIDS related help and information.

BARS

Amour Sorcier (A B d f GLM MA N OS s) 14-03:00h
789 Cote Ste-Genevieve ✉G1R 3L6 ☎ 523-3395

Couronne. La (B G S) 15-3 h
310 Rue de la Couronne ☎ 525-6593

Drague. Le (B G lj N os s tv VS) 9-24 h
815 rue St. Augustine/St. Joachim ☎ 649-7212

Mâle. Bar (B G LJ MA) 770 Côte Sainte Geneviève
☎ 648-9497

CAFES

Chez Victor (b bf glm)
145 rue St. Jean ☎ 529-7702

Kookening Kafe (b bf glm)
565 rue St. Jean ☎ 521-2121

DANCECLUBS

Ballon Rouge. Le (B D G YG) 22-3 h
811 rue St. Jean ☎ 647-9227 *Dance bar.*

RESTAURANTS

Cafe Zorba (b F glm)
854 rue St. Jean ☎ 525-5509 *Greek cuisine*

Chez Garbo (B F GLM)
157 Chemin Sainte Foy ☎ 529-9958

Hobbit. Le (B bf F glm)
700 rue Saint Jean ☎ 647-2677

Manhattan. Le (B F glm)
36 Côte de la Fabrique
☎ 694-0172

Piazzetta. La (B F glm)
565 rue St. Jean ☎ 529-7489

Restaurant Diana (B F glm) 20-1 h
849 rue St. Jean ☎ 524-5794
Italian and Greek cuisine.

SEX SHOPS/BLUE MOVIES

Empire Lyon (G)
873, rue St-Jean ☎ 648 2301
Videos, magazines, clothing, leather & sex toys

Importation Delta (CC G LJ MA) Sun & Mon 12-18:00h, Tue, Wed & Sat 10-18:00h, Thu & Fri -21:00h
875 rue St. Jean ✉G1R 1R2 ☎ 647-6808
Men's underwear, leather, toys, videos, pride products & more.

Olympius Video (G) 762

rue St. Jean ☎ 523-7393 *Video sales and rentals*

SAUNAS/BATHS

Hippocampe Sauna (G sa sb sol VS) 0-24 h
31 rue McMahon ☎ 692-1521

Sauna . Le 853 (G sa sb wh)
853, rue St-Jean ☎ 522 5525

Sauna Backboys (G) 0-24:00h
264 Rue de la Couronne ✉G1K 6C8 ☎ 521 6686

Sauna Bloc 225 (B G MA sa sb) 225 rue St. Jean
☎ 523-2562
Also sale of underwear and sale/rental of videos.

GUEST HOUSES

Coureur des Bois Guest House. Le (bf GLM H MA OS)
15 rue Ste. Ursule ✉G1R 4C7 ☎ 692-1117
or ☎ (Toll-free) (800) 269-6414. Located within the walls of old Quebec City. All rooms with shared baths. Rates Can$ 30-65 incl. cont. bf. No kids, pets on request.

727 Guest House. Le (AC bf GLM H msg OS sol wh)
727 Rue d'Aiguillon ✉G1R 1M8 ☎ 648-6766 or ☎ (toll-free) (800) 652-6766. Fax: 648-1474.
European-style guest house located in the old part. Rooms with private and shared bath, color TV. Rates Can$ 30-66 incl. cont. bf.

GENERAL GROUPS

Groupe gai de l'Université Laval
PO Box 25 00, Pavillon Lemieux, Ste.Foy *(Cité universitaire)*
☎ 656-2131 ext. 8950.Information, support, gay library.

FETISH GROUPS

Cuirassés de Québec. Les
PO Box 520 64, Succ. St. Fidele ✉G1L 5A4

HEALTH GROUPS

MIELS-Quebec
175 Rue St-Jean, bur. 200, G1R 1N4
☎ 649-1720 AIDS-Hotline ☎ 649-0788.

Regroupement des personnes vivant avec le VIH/SIDA Mon-Thu 11-19, Fri 11-17 h
at Salon Hospitalite ☎ 529-1942

HELP WITH PROBLEMS

Relais de L'espérance
617 Montmarte ☎ 522-3301
Groupe d'entraide face a l'homosexualité et le SIDA.

CRUISING

-Lac Vert
-Rue St.Denis

Rimouski ☎ 418

GAY INFO

Regroupement des lesbiennes et gais de l'est du Québec Wed 19-22 h
PO Box 31 ✉G5L 7B7 ☎ 722-4012
24 hour recorded messages.

Rouyn-Noranda ☎ 819

BARS

Station D (B glm MA)
82 Perreault Ouest ☎ 797-8696

GENERAL GROUPS

AGAT
PO Box 576 ✉J9X 5C6
Gay & lesbian social and support group.

Sept-Îles ☎ 418

CAFES

Café du Port (b glm) 11-24 h
495 Avenue Brochu ✉G4R 2X2 ☎ 962-9311
Email: cafeport@bbsi.net.

Sherbrooke ☎ 819

BARS

Complexe 13-17 (B Glm D)
13-15-17 Bowen sud
Sauna ☎ 569-5580, Disco ☎ 569-2241, Pub ☎ 562-2628.

RESTAURANTS

Café Bla-Bla (B F GLM)
Rue King ☎ 565-1366

SAUNAS/BATHS

Sauna L'Équus (G sa sb wh VS)
15 Rue Bowen Sud ☎ 569-1166

GENERAL GROUPS

L'Association des gais et lesbiennes de l'Université de Sherbrooke
2500 Université, Centre social ☎ 564-5013

CRUISING

-Rue Wellington
-Carrefour de l'Estrie Centre

St.François-Du-Lac ☎ 514

CAMPING

Domaine Gay Luron (B CC D F G NU pi) May 1st-September 15th
261 Grande-Terre ✉J0G 1M0 ☎ 568-3634 *FAX 568-2055.*
Camp ground. Rates for appartments and cabins Can$ 39-59.

St.Hyacinthe ☎ 514

BARS

La Main Gauche (AC B D E GLM MA OG S SWC W YG)
15-3 h
470 rue Mondor ✉J2S 5A7 ☎ 774-5556

St.Jean sur Richelieu ☎ 450

BARS

Bar La Pompe (B GLM) Wed-Sat 20-3 h
151 Rue Champlain ✉J3B 6V5 ☎ 346-9512

Trois Rivières ☎ 819

BARS

Mirage. Le Gay on Sat. only
109 rue Laviolette / Notre Dame ✉G9A 1T7 ☎ 375-3030

L'Embuscade (A AC B d f glm MA N T s)
12-03:00h. GLM on Thu.
1571, Badeaux ✉G9A 4T4 ☎ 374 0652

Upton ☎ 450

CAMPING

Camping Plein Vent (G H) Apr-Sep only
1110 Montee de la Rivière, Upton PQ, ✉J0H 2E0 ☎ 549-5831
Country Center for men only. Gay camping ground.

CDN-Saskatchewan

Central CDN

Initials: SK

Time: GMT -6

Area: 652,000 km^2 / 251,737 sq mi.

Population: 1,024,000

Capital: Regina

Moose Jaw ☎ 306

GAY INFO

Lesbian & Gay Committee of Moose Jaw
PO Box 1802 ✉S6H 7K8 ☎ 692-2418
or ☎ 691-5187.

Ravenscrag ☎ 306

HOTELS

Spring Valley Guest Ranch (bf F g H)
Box 10, SON 2CO ☎ 295-4124

Regina ☎ 306

GAY INFO

Pink Triangle Community Services Tue Fri 20.30-23 h
PO Box 24031, Broad Street PO ✉S4P 4J8 ☎ 526-6046
Health, education and support group.

BARS

BRIXX Dance Bar (B d GLM S) 20:30-03:00h
1422 Scarth Street ☎ 522-7343 *Dance bar and gay activities center.*

CAFES

Just Bean Brewed (f glm)
2201 Broad Street ☎ 522-5535
Roca Jack's (f glm YG) 1939 Scarth Street ☎ 347-2550

BOOK SHOPS

Sutherland Books
1833 Hamilton Street ☎ 565-2808
Gay and lesbian section.
The Book End 1856 Scarth Street ☎ 757-7902
Good selection of gay magazines.

GENERAL GROUPS

EGALE Regina
PO Box 24031, Broad Street PO ✉S4P 4J8
Gay/Lesbian rights lobbying group.
Gay Community of Regina Inc. (GCR)
PO Box 34 14 ✉B4P 3J8 ☎ 522-7343 E-Mail: glcr@sk.sympatico.ca
in the BRIXX Dance bar, 2070 Broad Street.
Lesbian & Gay Pride Planning Committee of Regina
PO Box 24031, Broad Street PO ✉S4P 4J8
☎ 757-4605

HEALTH GROUPS

AIDS Regina
1852 Angus Street ✉S4T 1Z4 ☎ 525-0905
or ☎ 1-877-210-7623. 24hr tape on AIDS.
Gay roman catholics and friends.
Koinonia Services 2nd 4th Sun 19 h at Wesley United, 3913 Hillsdale Avenue
PO Box 31 81 ✉S4P 3G7 ☎ 525-8542
Interfaith group of gays & lesbians.

CRUISING

-Scarth Street (R) (2000 & 2100 blocks)
-Cornwall Centre Mall
-Wascana Park (College Avenue section)

Saskatoon ☎ 306

GAY INFO

Gay and Lesbian Line Mon-Fri 12-16.30, Tue-Sat 19.30-22.30 h ☎ 665-1224
or ☎ (800) 358-1833 (Toll-free)
Perceptions
PO Box 8581 ✉S7K 6K7 ☎ 244-1930
FAX 665-1280. E-mail perceptions@the.link.ca. Community newspaper.

BARS

Diva`s (B GLM MA P) Tue-Sat 20-2.30, Sun -0.30 h
110 220 3rd Avenue South ✉S7K 1M1 *(side alley entrance)*
☎ 665-0100

GENERAL GROUPS

Parent Support Group ☎ 664-4228
(Dennis Morrison) Support/education group for parents and families of gays.

HEALTH GROUPS

AIDS Saskatoon AIDS Hotline: Mon-Fri 9-17 h
130 Idylwyld Drive North ✉S7L 0Y7☎ 242-5005
or 1 800-667-6876. *Non-profit, gay and non-gay people welcome.*
Gay and Lesbian Health Services (GLHS)
203 220 3rd Avenue S ☎ 665-1224 E-Mail: glhs@home.com
Lesbian and gay health agency. ☎ toll free 1-800-358-1833.
Persons Living With AIDS (PLWA) Network of Saskatchewan
810 Dufferin Avenue, PO Box 71 23 ✉S7K 4J1 ☎ 373-7766
Support and services for PLWA, families, friends and partners.

SWIMMING

-Cranberry Flats

CRUISING

-Spadina Crescent (R) (between Medical Arts Building and Broadway Bridge, evening and night)

CDN-Yukon Territory

Northwest CDN

Initials: YT

Time: GMT -8

Area: 536,000 km^2 / 206,949 sq mi.

Population: 32,000

Capital: Whitehorse

Whitehorse ☎ 403

GENERAL GROUPS

Gay and Lesbian Alliance of the Yukon Territory
PO Box 56 04 ✉Y1A 5H4 ☎ 667-7857

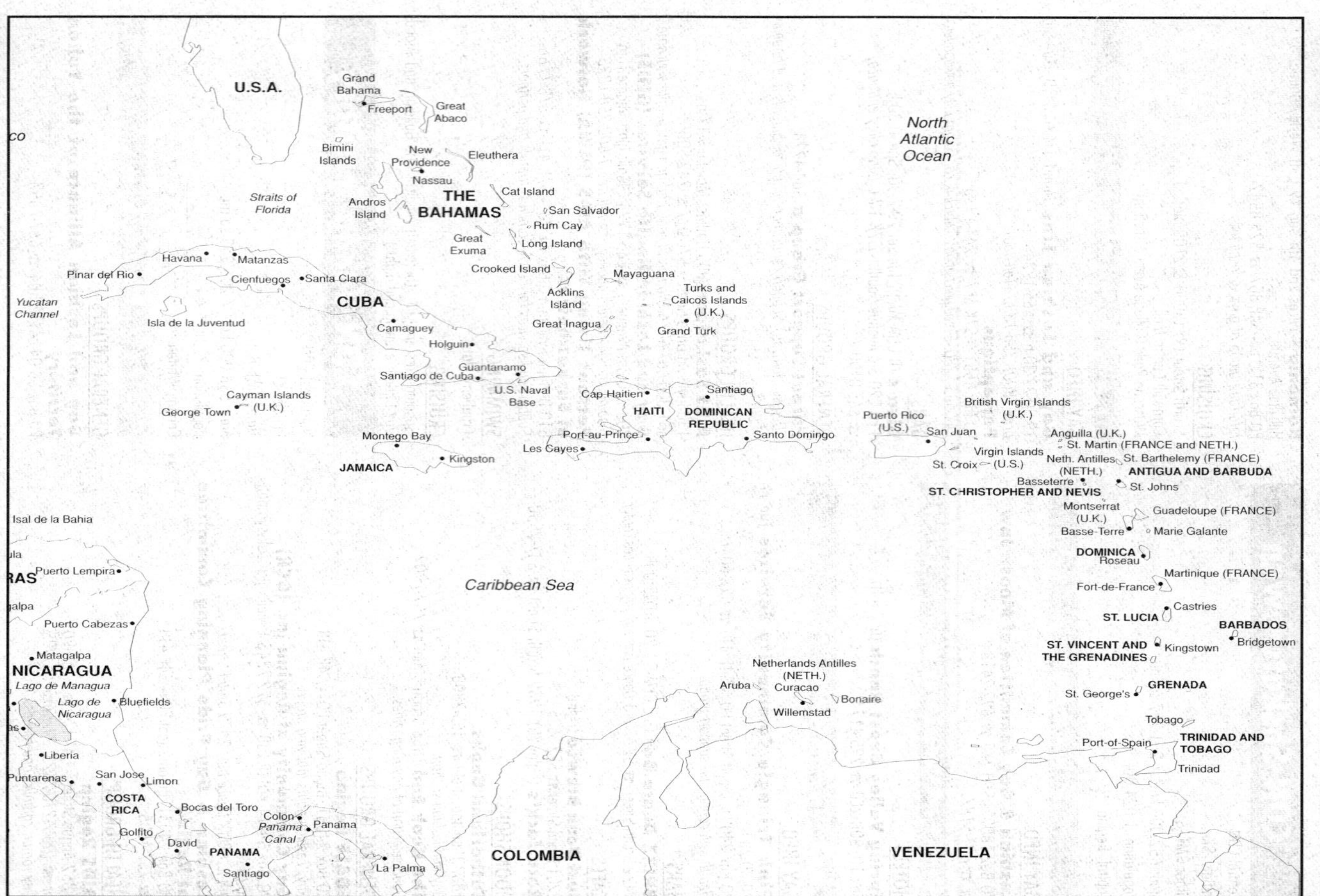
U.S.A.
Grand Bahama
Freeport
Great Abaco
North Atlantic Ocean
CO
Bimini Islands
New Providence
Nassau
Eleuthera
Straits of Florida
Andros Island
THE BAHAMAS
Cat Island
San Salvador
Rum Cay
Great Exuma
Long Island
Havana
Matanzas
Pinar del Rio
Cienfuegos
Santa Clara
Crooked Island
Mayaguana
Acklins Island
Turks and Caicos Islands (U.K.)
Yucatan Channel
CUBA
Isla de la Juventud
Great Inagua
Grand Turk
Camaguey
Holguin
Guantanamo
Santiago de Cuba
U.S. Naval Base
Cayman Islands (U.K.)
George Town
Cap-Haitien
Santiago
HAITI
DOMINICAN REPUBLIC
British Virgin Islands (U.K.)
Puerto Rico (U.S.)
San Juan
Montego Bay
Port-au-Prince
Santo Domingo
Anguilla (U.K.)
St. Martin (FRANCE and NETH.)
Les Cayes
Virgin Islands
Neth. Antilles (NETH.)
St. Barthelemy (FRANCE)
JAMAICA
Kingston
St. Croix (U.S.)
ANTIGUA AND BARBUDA
Basseterre
St. Johns
ST. CHRISTOPHER AND NEVIS
Montserrat (U.K.)
Guadeloupe (FRANCE)
Isal de la Bahia
Basse-Terre
Marie Galante
DOMINICA
Roseau
RAS
Puerto Lempira
Caribbean Sea
Martinique (FRANCE)
Fort-de-France
Puerto Cabezas
Castries
ST. LUCIA
BARBADOS
Bridgetown
ST. VINCENT AND THE GRENADINES
Kingstown
Matagalpa
Netherlands Antilles (NETH.)
NICARAGUA
Lago de Managua
Aruba
Curacao
GRENADA
St. George's
Lago de Nicaragua
Bluefields
Bonaire
Willemstad
Tobago
TRINIDAD AND TOBAGO
Liberia
Port-of-Spain
Trinidad
San Jose
Puntarenas
Limon
COSTA RICA
Bocas del Toro
Colon
Panama
Panama Canal
Golfito
David
PANAMA
COLOMBIA
VENEZUELA
Santiago
La Palma

Caribbean

Aruba

Caribbean

Initials: ARU (NL)

Time: GMT -4

☎ Country Code / Access Code: 297-8 (no area codes) / 00

Language: Dutch, Papiamento, English, Spanish

Area: 193 km² / 75 sq mi.

Currency: 1 Aruba-Florin (Afl) = 100 Cent

Population: 69,000

Capital: Oranjestad

Religions: over 80% Catholic

Climate: Tropical marine climate with little seasonal temperature variation.

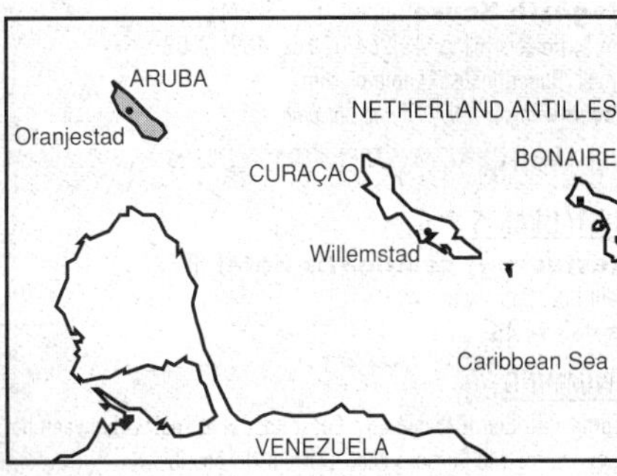

● Aruba is an autonomous territory of the Netherlands with special status. Gays lead a relatively untroubled and safe life. The age of consent is 16 and sex between men is legal.

✱ Aruba ist autonomer Teil der Niederlande mit Sonderstatus. Schwule können auf Aruba relativ unbehelligt und sicher leben. Das Schutzalter liegt bei 16 Jahren und einvernehmlicher Sex zwischen Männern ist legal.

▲ Aruba est une île autonome des Pays-Bas jouissant d'un statut particulier. Pour les gays, la vie y est relativement sûre et calme. La majorité sexuelle est fixée à 16 ans et les relations entre hommes sont tolérées si elles sont placées sous le signe du consentement mutuel.

☆ Aruba es una parte autónoma de los Países Bajos que posee un status especial. Homosexuales pueden vivir en la isla relativamente seguros y tranquilos. La edad de protección son los 16 años, y el sexo por acuerdo entre hombres es legal.

❖ Aruba è una parte autonoma dei Paesi Bassi con statuto speciale. Qui i gay possono vivere senza essere importunati. L'età legale per rapporti sessuali è di 16 anni, ed i rapporti tra uomini sono legali purchè biconsensuali.

Oranjestad

BARS

Cellar (B G MA) Wed Thu-Sat 22-4 Klipstraat 2

SEX SHOPS/BLUE MOVIES

Hot Spot Adult Entertainment (AC CC GLM MA) Mon-Sat 14-22 h
Waterweg 1 ☎ 826 932

CRUISING

-Eagle Beach 16-sunset h (between La Quinta Resort and Dutch Village Hotel)
-Malmok 14-18 h (by the beach)

Barbados

Caribbean

Initials: BDS

Time: GMT -4

☎ Country Code / Access Code: 1-246 (no area codes) / 011

Language: English, „Bajan"

Area: 430 km² / 166 sq mi.

Currency: 1 Barbados Dollar (BDS$) = 100 Cents.

Population: 263,000

Capital: Bridgetown

Religions: 70% Christian

Climate: Tropical climate. The rainy season lasts from June to October.

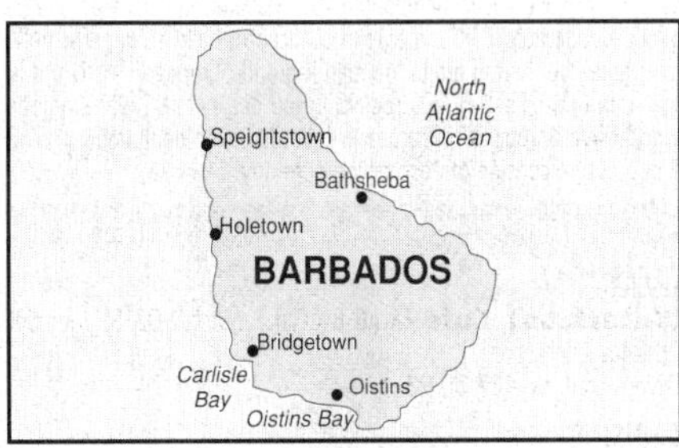

● Homosexuality is illegal in Barbados. According to reports, gays are not bothered by the police, and Barbados is said to be one of the most liberal islands of the English-speaking South Caribbean. Nonetheless, the gay scene is rather hidden from the public eye. Gay life takes place mostly on the southern coast (St. Michael, Christ Church) as well as on the west coast (St. James). Cruising is done on the beach and from cars. Especially worth mentioning are the Thanksgiving Festival that takes place in July and the Arts Festival in November. Please note that the places listed below are not exclusively gay.

✱ Homosexualität ist auf Barbados illegal. Allerdings werden Schwule nicht von der Polizei verfolgt: Barbados gilt als eine der liberalsten Inseln der anglophonen südlichen Karibik. Trotzdem ist die einheimische Schwulenszene von der Öffentlichkeit abgeschirmt. Das schwule Leben spielt sich vor allem an der Südküste (St. Michael, Christ Church) sowie an der Westküste (St. James) ab. Man cruist am Strand oder per Auto-Blickkontakt.
Erwähnenswert sind vor allem das im Juli stattfindende „Erntedank-Festival" und das sogenannte „Künstlerfest" im November.

Bitte beachten Sie, daß die aufgeführten Lokale nicht ausschließlich schwul sind.

A la Barbade, l'homosexualité est un délit. D'après ce que nous savons, la police laisse la paix aux homos. La Barbade passe pour être l'une des îles les plus tolérantes des Caraïbes. Pourtant, les gays s'y font très discrets. Les principaux lieux gays se trouvent surtout sur la côte sud (St. Michael, Christ Church) et sur la côte ouest (St. James). On drague à la plage et en voiture.
A voir: la grande fête de la Grâce (pour la récolte, en juin) et la fête des Artistes (en novembre). Aucune des adresses données ci-dessous ne peut être considérée comme exclusivement gay.

La homosexualidad es ilegal en Barbados. De acuerdo a los informes, los gays no son perseguidos por la policía. Barbados es considerada como una de las islas más liberales de los angloparlantes del Pacífico Sur. A pesar de todo, el ambiente gay de los nativos se mantiene en cubierto, la vida gay se da sobre todo en la costa sur (St. Michael, Christ Church) así como también en la costa Occidental (St. James). El „cruising" se practica en la playa o viajando en coche con contactos a primera vista.
Digno de mención es el Festival de la Cosecha (en julio de cada año), así como la llamada Fiesta de los Artistas (noviembre).
Ninguna de las direcciones que se mencionan son exclusivamente gay.

L'omosessualità è illegale nelle Barbados. Secondo i nostri dati però i gay non vengono disturbati dalla polizia; pare che le Barbados siano tra le isole Caraibiche meridionali di lingua inglese più liberali. Stranamente però la vita gay è piuttosto nascosta e ha luogo soprattutto sulla costa meridionale (St. Michael, Christ Church) e su quella occidentale (St. James). Ci si incontra sulla spiaggia e nelle macchine. Qui hanno luogo in luglio il grande Cropover Festival e in novembre l'Art Festival due ragioni in più per evitare l'alta stagione e godersi le Barbados senza grandi folle. Nessuno dei luoghi seguenti può essere considerato esclusivamente gay.

Bridgetown

CAFÉS

Waterfront Cafe (A AC B CC d F MA NG OS S) Mon-Sat 10-24 h
Cavans Lane ☎ 427 00 93

CRUISING

-Broad Street

Christ Church

BARS

Buddies (AC B CC d F GLM MA S STV YG) 18-? h
„Iriston" Worthing *(opposite to Sandy Beach Hotel)* ☎ 435 65 45

APARTMENTS

Roman Beach Apartments (glm H)
Enterprise Coast Road, Oistin Town ☎ 428 76 35
Modest, reasonably priced accomodation. Sharing possible. Self-catering rooms with electric fans. Informal and friendly.

CRUISING

-Long Bay Beach (near the airport, also called „Chancery Lane Beach", usually quiet, lots of bushes, discreet nude bathing, take no valuables!)
-Rockley Beach (also called „Accra Beach", crowded on weekends and evenings. Easy contacts)
-Saint Lawrence Gap (AYOR R) (after dark)

Lower Carlton

BARS

John Moore's Bar (B g MA)

Speightstown

BARS

Derrick's Bar (B g MA)
Fisherman's Pub (B g MA)

St. James

RESTAURANTS

Coach House (B F g) 12-15/18-2 h
Paynes Bay
☎ 432 11 63
Live music most nights.

GUEST HOUSES

Hogarth House (AC B bf CC E F G MA)
Lot 5, Holders Hill ☎ 432 64 02 Fax: 432 64 02
Email: Hogarthhouse@hotmail.com
Rooms with shower/WC and balcony.

St. Joseph

RESTAURANTS

Restaurant at Atlantis Hotel (B F g)
Tent Bay, Bathsheba
☎ 433 94 45

SWIMMING

-Cattlewash Beach (along East Coast Road, best part is between holiday houses and Barclays Park. Discreet NU possible.)
-Batts Rock Beach (popular with bushes, cliffs, etc. West Coast)

St. Michael

RESTAURANTS

Waterfront Café (B F g swc) 10-24 h, closed Sun
The Careenage, Bridgetown
☎ 427 00 93
Very popular. Live music.

CRUISING

-Baxter's Road (AYOR R RT WE) (off Broad Street, at night)

St. Peter

HOTELS

The Palace (B F g H)
Road View *Located on the oceanfront, near Mullins Beach.*
☎ +1-246-422 32 40

Worthing

DANCECLUBS

Shells 22-? h.
(off main road near Police Station)
Gay Party every two weeks on Sat. Very popular. Reasonable prices.

Cuba

Caribbean

Initials: C

Time: GMT -5

☎ Country Code / Access Code: 53 / 119

Language: Spanish

Area: 110,860 km² / 42,803 sq mi.

Currency: 1 Cuban Peso (cub$) = 100 Centavos

Population: 11,115,000

Capital: La Habana

Religions: 40% Roman Catholic

Climate: Tropical climate that is moderated by trade winds. The dry season lasts from November to April, the rainy season from May to October.

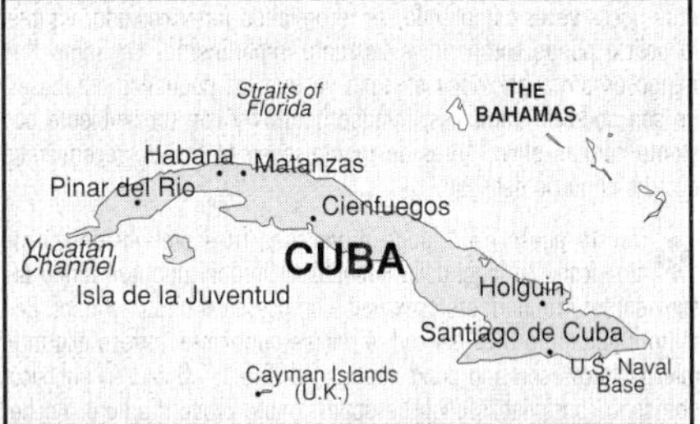

● According to Article 303 of the Cuban penal code it is illegal to display homosexuality in public. Transgressions may be punished
with prison sentences of three months up to one year. With respect to AIDS, draconic measures have been taken which are supposedly intended to stop the spread of the disease. Certain 'high-risk groups' (to which homosexuals surprisingly do not belong) are forced to
take an AIDS test. Anyone testing HIV-positive, and regardless of whether they show symptoms of AIDS, is committed to a 'sanitorium'
and isolated from society.

▲ Selon l'article 303 du code pénal cubain ("attentat à la pudeur"), il est interdit d'afficher son homosexualité en public. On risque, sinon, 3 à 12 mois de prison. Les autorités cubaines prennent des mesures extrêmement strictes pour endiguer l'épidémie du sida. On fait subir des tests de dépistage aux groupes à risques parmi lesquels on ne compte pas forcément les homosexuels. Les séropositifs, même ceux qui n'ont pas développé la maladie et ne présentent aucun symptôme, sont obligés de vivre isolés du reste de la population, dans des "sanatoriums" tout particulièrement créés à cette intention.

✱ *Gemäß Artikel 303 des StGb (Erregung öffentlichen Ärgernisses) ist es verboten, seine Homosexualität in der Öffentlichkeit zum Ausdruck zu bringen. Es drohen zwischen 3 und 12 Monaten Haft. In Bezug auf AIDS werden strenge Maßnahmen vorgenommen, die angeblich dazu dienen sollen, eine weitere Verbreitung der Krankheit einzudämmen. Aus diesem Grunde werden bestimmte Risikogruppen (überraschenderweise nicht die Schwulen) dem HIV-Test unterzogen. Wer HIV-positiv ist ohne Krankheitssymptome zu haben, wird ebenso wie AIDS-Kranke in ein eigens für sie geschaffenes »Sanatorium« zwangseingewiesen und von der Gesellschaft isoliert.*

☆ Según el articulo 303 del Código Penal cubano, está prohibido mostrarse abiertamente como homosexual en público. La contravención de esta disposición supone una pena que va desde tres meses hasta un año. Con respecto al SIDA se toman ahora medidas severas, según dicen, para parar la proliferación de la enfermedad. Por ello, personas que pertenecen a grupos de alto riesgo estan obligados a someterse a una prueba de SIDA, aunque sorprendentemente no se considera a los homosexuales como grupo de riesgo. Todas las personas que den un resultado positvo en la prueba de SIDA, demuestre o no sintomas de la enfermedad, se le interna a la fuerza en un „sanatorio" establecido para este propósito en las afueras de la Habana, aislando los enfermos de SIDA rigurosamente del resto de la sociedad.

❖ Rispetto al passato la situazione dei gay cubani sta migliorando sebbene l'articolo 303 del codice penale punisca la manifestazione pubblica dell'omosessualità. I trasgressori possono essere puniti con l'arresto da tre mesi ad un anno. Per ciò che concerne l'AIDS, sono state adottate delle misure molto drastiche per contenere l'espansione della malattia. Determinati gruppi a rischio, sorprendentemente non i gay, devono sottoporsi ad un HIV-test. Anche i sieropositivi senza sintomi della malattia, vengono rinchiusi in un apposito „sanatorium" ed isolati dalla società.

La Habana

BARS

Casa de las Infusiones (B glm) 11-22 h
Mercaderes/Obispo *(Old Town)*

Karachy Club (B D glm YG) 17 y K *(Vedado)*

CAFES

D'Giovanni (B F GLM) Empedrado/Tacón *(Old Town)*
Gay especially in the afternoon. Italian cuisine, pastries.

DANCECLUBS

Disco Jocker (AC B D GLM YG) Tue-Sun 21-4 h, closed Mon
Linea y 10 *(Vedado)*

Eco Disco (B D GLM YG) Tue-Sun 21-4 h, closed Mon
Linea y F *(Vedado)*

CINEMAS

Yara Movie (g YG) *(Vedado near Hotel Habana Libre)*

SWIMMING

-Santa Maria Beach/Mi Cayito (G) (east of Havana from Mar Azul Hotel to Itabo Hotel)
-El Chivo (AYOR g) (east of Havana)

CRUISING

All cruising areas are AYOR.
-Fraternidad Park
-Central Park
-Monte street
-Feria de la Juventud
-Teatro Nacional (especially after opera performances)
-Heladeria Copelia (WE)
-Prado Street

Dominican Republic

República Dominicana

Caribbean

Initials: DOM

Time: GMT -4

☎ Country Code / Access Code: 1-809 (no area codes) / 011

Language: Spanish. English

Area: 48,422 km² / 18,696 sq mi.

Currency: 1 Dominican Peso (dom$) = 100 Centavos.

Population: 8,232,000

Capital: Santo Domingo

Religions: 94% Roman Catholic

Climate: Tropical maritime climate with little seasonal temperature variation and variation in rainfall.

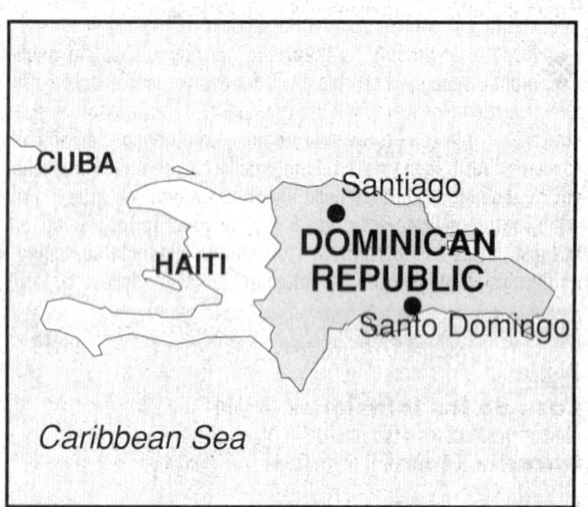

● This country is a popular vacation spot for tourists from the U.S. and Western Europe. The laws of the Dominican Republic make no distinction between gay and straight relations between adults (over 18 years). However, Article 330 of the penal code punishes »every violation of decorum and good behavior on public streets« with a penalty of up to two years in prison, so it is advisable not to display too much affection in public. Although the law is rarely applied, the police can take a very hostile attitude.

For getting around in Santo Domingo, we recommend the use of taxis, because although the bus system is cheap and communicative, it is not very effective. You should, however, agree on the cost with the taxi-driver before starting your journey.

✱ Das Land ist ein beliebter Urlaubsort US-amerikanischer und westeuropäischer Touristen. Die Gesetze der Dominikanischen Republik machen zwischen schwulen und heterosexuellen Beziehungen Erwachsener (über 18 Jahre) keinen Unterschied. Allerdings kann man nach Paragraph 330 des Strafgesetzes für „...jedes Übertreten der Schicklichkeit und des guten Betragens auf öffentlichen Straßen mit einer Haftstrafe von bis zu zwei Jahren Gefängnis..." geahndet werden. Zu intensive Liebesbekundungen sind also in der Öffentlichkeit nicht empfehlenswert. Auch wenn dieser Paragraph nicht oft angewandt wird, kann die Polizei doch sehr feindselig werden. In Santo Domingo sollten Sie lieber ein Taxi nehmen als die nicht besonders effektiven aber kommunikativen und billigen Kleinbusse. Vorher aber unbedingt den Preis aushandeln!

▲ La République Dominicaine est un lieu de villégiature très prisé par les Américains et les Européens. La législation dominicaine ne fait pas de distinction entre homosexuels et hétérosexuels, mais protège les mineurs (majorité: 18 ans). Signalons cependant que, selon l'article 330 du code pénal, on risque 2 ans de prison pour tout „débordement de décence ou de comportement dans les lieux publics". Il n'est donc pas conseillé d'afficher ses préférences au grand jour! Même si cet article n'est quasiment plus appliqué, vous risquez d'avoir des ennuis avec la police locale.

A San Diego, circulez en taxi, mais veillez bien à fixer le prix de la course auparavant. Evitez les petits bus ni bon marché, ni efficaces, mais où on peut, en revanche, faire des rencontres!

☆ Este país es uno de los lugares vacacionales más preferidos por los turistas norteamericanos y europeos. Las leyes dominicanas no hacen ninguna comparación en lo referente a actividades heterosexuales u homosexuales entre adultos mayores de 18 años. Se puede sin embargo ser penado por «cualquier incumplimiento a la descencia o al buen comportamiento en las vías públicas» con una pena máxima de 2 años de prisión. No son recomendadas intensivas demostraciones amorosas en público. Aunque este artículo muy pocas veces es aplicado, se recomienda tener cuidado, ya que la policía puede comportarse bastante impertinente. En Santo Domingo es preferible viajar en taxi, ya que los pequeños autobuses no son nada de puntuales, aunque baratos y con un ambiente bastante comunicativo. Antes de montarse en el taxi se recomienda acordar el precio del viaje.

❖ Questo paese è un luogo di vacanze fra i preferiti dai turisti americani. Le leggi della Repubblica Domenicana non fanno distinzioni tra i rapporti eterosessuali e omosessuali olte i 18 anni. Peraltro il paragrafo 330 del codice penale punisce le „offese alla morale pubblica" con una pena massima di 2 anni. Quindi in pubblico non sono consigliabili lunghe e appassionate prove d'amore. Anche se questo paragrafo viene raramente applicato, la polizia può essere molto intollerante. In Santo Domingo è meglio spostarsi in taxi che con i poco efficienti ma economici e comunicativi autobus. Cercate di trattare sempre il prezzo prima di salire!

Las Terrenas

APARTMENTS

Paraiso Suizo (bf glm H T) Playa Bonita ☎ 240 61 18
Fax 240-6118. Bungalows. On premises restaurant El Coco.

Puerto Plata

HOTELS

Hotel Barlovento (AC B bf CC D E F G H pi s W WO)
Costambar ☎ 586 44 26 Fax: 320 86 10.
Email: t.vacacional@codetel.net.do

GUEST HOUSES

Bugalows el Carite (B bf D F H pi R S YG)
Cabarete
☎ 571 04 15 Fax: 571 04 16

Laguna Bonito (B glm H pi sa wh)
Escondido Bay (Casa 73) *(Sosua)* ☎ 471 16 94 Fax: 471 16 94
Homepage: www.DomRep-Reisen.de

Samaná

HOTELS

El Paraiso (AC B bf CC F G NU OS pi S VS WO YG)
☎ +49-171-890 66 94 Fax: 368 25 45

Santiago

RESTAURANTS

Pez Dorado. El (B F glm)
C. El Sol # 43 ☎ 582 25 18

HOTELS

Mercedes Hotel (b f glm H)
C. 30 de Marzo # 18
☎ 583 11 71

CRUISING

-Parc at Calle El Sol (after 18 h)

Santo Domingo

BARS

Café Capri (B F glm MA OS s) Thu-Sun 21-3 h
Avenida Tiradentes # 20, Naco *(beside the Naco Hotel)*
Drake's Bar (B glm MA OS r)
C. La Atarazana, Colonial City *(in front of Alcazar de Colon)*
O'Hara's Place (B f GLM MA OS) Wed-Sun 19-2 h, closed Mon Tue
C. Danae # 3, Gascue. ☎ 682 84 08
Phönix (ayor B G OG R) Wed-Sun 18-23 h
Calle Polvorín 10 *(Zona Colonial)* ☎ 688 79 05
St. Michael's Grand Café & Restaurant (B e F glm ma OS s YG) Wed-Sun 18-3 h
Avenida Lope de Vega # 26, Naco. ☎ 541 66 55

CAFÉS

Yuca Cafe (B bf h F) 8.00-2.00 h
Calle Proyecto Paredes 3 *(Bocachica)*

DANCECLUBS

Disco Free (AC B D glm MA N S TV WE YG) Thu-Sun 10-5 h
Avenida Ortega y Gaset, 13 *(near Avenida John F. Kennedy)*
☎ 565 81 00
El Bochinche Bar & Disco (B D GLM MA r S WE) Sun-Thu 23-3 h, closed Mon
C. El Seybo/20, altos
Güácara Taína Disco. La (AC B D e MA NG S) Wed-Sun 20-3
Avenida Mirador de Sur *(near Parque Paseo de los Indios)*
☎ 533 10 51
Located in a natural cave.
Penthouse. El (B D GLM MA R S tv WE) 23-5 h
Calle El Seybo/20, altos.

RESTAURANTS

Cafe Cogo (b F g)
Calle Sánchez 153 ☎ 687 96 24
Pitiri (AC B E F glm MA) 12-15, 19-24, closed Sun 12-15 h
C. Nicolás de Bar # 6/Eduardo Gener, La Esperilla *(in front of the National Conservatory of Music)* ☎ 541 54 78

CINEMAS

Lido (AYOR glm r) 17-23.30 h
Avenida Mella

HOTELS

Aida Hotel (H)
C. El Conde # 464 ☎ 657 28 80
Rooms with fans or AC. Rates US$ 23 per night. Central location close to gay bars.

APARTMENTS

Laurel Apartments (AC bf F glm H)
Avenida Caonabo # 41 ☎ 530 47 24
Kitchenettes in all units. Good value but a few miles away from the centre.

GENERAL GROUPS

Colectivo Ciguay
PO Box 156-9

HEALTH GROUPS

AIDS Hotline Mon-Fri 8-18 h
☎ 541 44 00
Amigos Siempre Amigos PO Box 22231, El Huacal
☎ 759 88 32

SWIMMING

-Boca Chica Beach (50 km from the city)
-Embassy Beach (About 65 km from the city. Take Avenida Las Americas, highway to San Pedro de Macoris. Beach on the right filled with cocconut palms.)

CRUISING

-Plaza Independencia (r)
-Parque Colón (r)
-Playa Guibia (r) (Avenida Washington, El Malecon)
-Parque Mirador Sur (evenings)

Grenada

Caribbean

Initials: WG

Time: GMT -4

☎ Country Code / Access Code: 1-473 (no area codes) / 011

Language: English

Area: 344 km² / 133 sq mi.

Currency: 1 East Carribean Dollar (EC$) = 100 Cents

Population: 95,000

Capital: Saint George's

Religions: 59% Catholic, 34% Protestant

Climate: Tropical climate that is tempered by northeast trade winds.

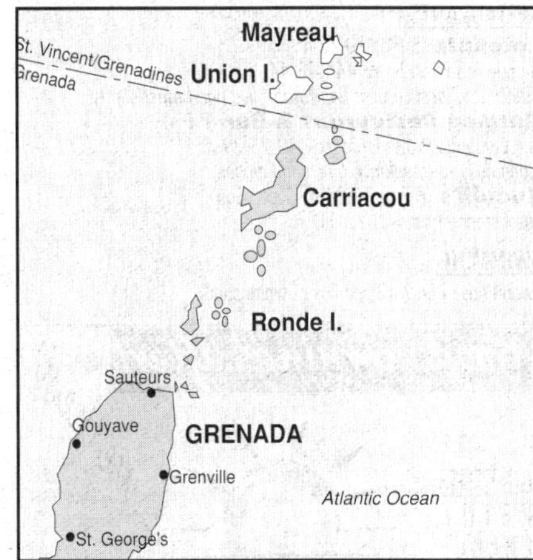

● To our knowledge, homosexuality is illegal in Grenada and the neighboring island of Carriacou to the north. The tourist industry is developing steadily, and is concentrated around St. George to the south. There is no gay scene per se; the following places should only be used as starting points.

✱ Unseres Wissens nach ist Homosexualität auf Grenada illegal, wie auch auf der nördlich gelegenen Nachbarinsel Carriacou. Die Tourismusindustrie hat sich in den letzten Jahren stark weiterentwickelt, ist aber vor allem um die Stadt St. George's im Süden konzentriert. Es gibt keine Schwulenszene; die folgenden Adressen sollten nur als Ausgangspunkte dienen.

▲ D'après ce que nous savons, l'homosexualité est un délit à Grenade et sur l'île voisine de Carriacou (au nord). L'industrie touristique est en plein essor, tout particulièrement à St George, dans le sud. Pas de vie gay à proprement parler. Les établissements mentionnés ci-dessous ne sont cités qu'à titre d'information.

❖ Por lo que sabemos la homosexualidad es ilegal en Grenada y en Carriacou, la isla vecina que queda al norte. La industria de turismo se está desarrollando y estableciendo casi exclusivamente en St. George, en el sur del país. No existe un ambiente gay propiamente dicho; las siguientes direcciones sirven sólo como punto de partida.

☆ Per quanto ne sappiamo, l'omosessualità è illegale a Grenada e su Carriacou, l'isola vicina situata al nord. L'industria del turismo si sta sviluppando quasi esclusivamente nel territorio di St. George al sud. Non c'è una vita gay vera e propria; i seguenti luoghi dovrebbero essere usati solo come punti di riferimento e di base.

St. George's

BARS

Fantasia 2001 (AC B D) 20.30-? h
Morne Rouge ☎ 444 42 24
Hillcrest Bar (B) closed Sun
Tru Blue ☎ 444 44 58
Internatinal Cubby Hole (B D F)
The Caranage
☎ 440 29 27
St. James Hotel Bar (g)
Grand Etang Road *(downtown)* ☎ 440 20 41

RESTAURANTS

Coconuts (B F g) 10-22 h
Grande Anse Beach' ☎ 444 46 44
French and local cuisine; beachfront; live band most nights.
Nutmeg Restaurant & Bar (B F g)
The Caranage Water Front ☎ 440 25 39
Open daily for breakfast, lunch and dinner.
Rudolf's (B F g) 10-24 h, closed Sun
The Carenage ☎ 440 22 41

SWIMMING

-Grand Anse Beach (3.5 miles of white sand)

Guadeloupe

Caribbean
Initials: GUA (F)
Time: GMT -4
☎ Country Code / Access Code: 590 (no area codes) / 00
Language: French; Créole
Area: 1,780 km^2 / 687 sq mi.
Currency: 1 French Franc (FF) = 100 Centimes
Population: 444,000
Capital: Basse-Terre
Religion: Roman Catholic
Climate: Subtropical climate that is tempered by trade winds. The humidity is relatively high.

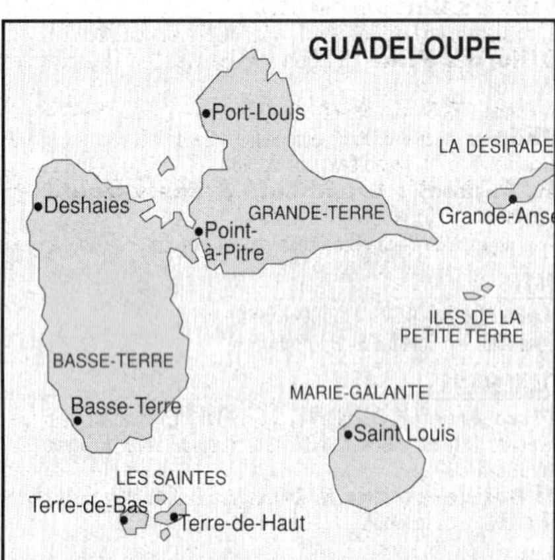

● The French penal code is in effect here (☛ France). The island is sunny and, in every sense of the word, heavenly. Most of the people are of African descent. Compared with other Caribbean countries, the cost of living is somewhat higher.

✱ Es gelten die Strafbestimmungen ☛Frankreichs. Die Insel ist sonnig und paradiesisch, die meisten Menschen sind afrikanischer Herkunft. Die Lebenshaltungskosten liegen hier, verglichen mit anderen karibischen Ländern, eher hoch.

▲ La législation française (☛France) est en vigueur à la Guadeloupe. Ile ensoleillée et paradisiaque. La population est d'origine africaine. Le coût de la vie est, comparé aux autres pays des Caraïbes, plutôt élevé.

❖ El Código Penal francés (☛Francia) es vigente en esta isla caribeña. Guadalupe disfruta de un clima soleado y es verdaderamente paradisíaca, la mayoría de los habitantes son de origen africano. El costo de la vida es aquí más bien alto si se compara con el de otros países caribeños.

☆ E'in vigore il codice penale francese (☛Francia). L'isola è soleggiata e paradisiaca. La maggior parte degli abitanti è di origine africana, il costo della vita è, in confronto agli altri paesi dei Caraibi, piuttosto elevato.

Basse Terre - Guadeloupe ✉ 97100

RESTAURANTS

L'Orangerie (b F glm)
Desmarais ✉97100 ☎ 81 01 01

Gosier - Guadeloupe ✉ 97190

DANCECLUBS

Gaypar. Le (B D GLM VS) 22.30-? h
6 Rue Simon Radegonde ✉97190 ☎ 84 38 89

Les Saintes - Guadeloupe

HOTELS

Auberge Les Petits Saints (A AC B F glm MA pi sa)
Les Anacardiers, La Savasse-Terre-de-Haut ☎ 99 50 99
An ideal island get-away. Take boat or plane from Guadeloupe.

Pointe-à-Pitre - Guadeloupe ✉ 97110

BARS

Le Pomme Cannelle (B g)
Road Pointe-à-Pitre ↔ Gosier ✉97110
(Leave the road near fort and at the 2nd circle turn right)

HEALTH GROUPS

Centre hospitalier de Pointe-à-Pitre Service de néphrologie
☎ 82 88 88
HIV testing.

Différence Positif Guadeloupe
10-23 h
☎ 26 80 88

CRUISING

-Rue Duplessis (along La Darse, the old port)
-Rue de Nozieres
-Rue Frebault
-Rue René Boisneuf

Ste.Anne - Guadeloupe ✉ 97180

BARS

Chez Elles (B F glm) Wed-Sun 19-? h
Les Galbas ✉97180 *(opposite village artisanal)* ☎ 88 92 36

SWIMMING

-Plage de la Caravelle (NU) (possible contacts with tourists and locals in the afternoon; best part of island Plage de Tarare, on road to Pointe des Châteaux)

St.François - Guadeloupe ✉ 97118

BARS

Iguane Café (b F g MA OS)
Dinner every night except Tue Sun lunch & dinner
Route de la Pointe des Chateaux ✉97118 ☎ 88 61 37
A friendly smile and great food. A must on the way back from the gay beach at Pointe Tarare.

SWIMMING

-Pointe Tarare (legal nudist beach)

St.Barthelemy ✉ 97133

SWIMMING

-Grande Saline (nude sun bathing is possible but is not officially allowed; keep your shorts handy)

St.Martin

● St. Martin's falls under the jurisdiction of faraway Guadaloupe and thus belongs to France's overseas territories. The northern part of the island is French, the south is Dutch. The island of St. Martin is the perfect place for a relaxing holiday and has wonderful beaches (also with nude sunbathing).

✱ St. Martin wird vom Regionalparlament des weit entfernten Guadeloupe regiert und ist damit Teil des französischen Überseedepartements. Der Nordteil der Insel ist französisch, der Süden niederländisch. St. Martin ist eine herrliche Insel für Urlaub und Erholung mit wundervollen Stränden (FKK ist möglich).

▲ St Martin est administrée par la lointaine Guadeloupe et fait ainsi partie de l'Union Européenne. Le nord de l'île est français, le sud est hollandais. On passe d'agréables et reposantes vacances à St Martin. On y trouve de merveilleuses plages, accessibles également aux naturistes.

☆ A pesar de que St. Martin queda bastante lejos de Guadalupe, está bajo su jurisdicción y forma parte de la colonia francesa. No obstante la isla está dividida en la parte francesa del norte y la parte holandesa del sur.
St. Martin es una hermosa isla para las vacaciones y el descanso, con playas maravillosas (también para amantes del nudismo).

❖ San Martino viene governato dal parlamento regionale della lontana Guadalupa e insieme a quest'ultima fa parte dei territori d'oltre mare francesi. La parte settentrionale dell'isola è francese, quella meridionale olandese. Quest'isola meravigliosa con le sue splendide spiaggie (anche per nudisti) è un posto ottimo per passare le vacanze e per rilassarsi.

BARS

Pink Mango (B G) 22-3 h
✉97150 *(Baie Nettlé)* ☎ 87 59 99

RESTAURANTS

Kontiki Plage (B F g)
(Orient-Bay Beach) ☎ 87 43 27

SWIMMING

-Baie Rouge
-Baie Orientale (NU) (Cruising area is between Boo Boo Sam and Coco Beach restaurants and in the far south of the beach just after the Club Orient)

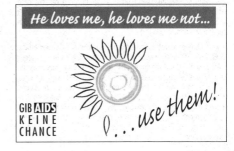

Jamaica

Caribbean
Initials: JA
Time: GMT -5
☎ Country Code / Access Code: 1-876 (no area codes) / 011
Language: English
Area: 10,990 km² / 4,243 sq mi.
Currency: 1 Jamaican Dollar (J$) = 100 Cents
Population: 2,539,000
Capital: Kingston
Religions: 48% Protestant, 5% Catholic, 26% other religions
Climate: Tropical climate, hot and humid. The interior is moderate.

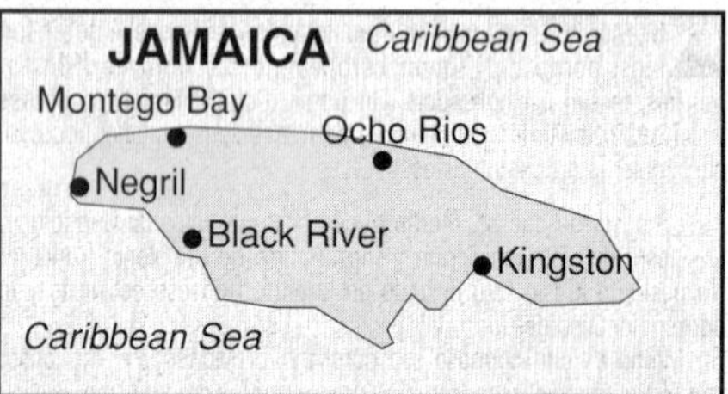

Homosexual acts are unconditionally prohibited. Paragraphs 76-79 of the Jamaican penal code prescribe imprisonment with hard labour for up to ten years. Attempted gay seduction is likewise harshly punished with up to seven years imprisonment-with or without labour, according to the judgement of the court. Fortunately, these laws are only rarely enforced, but they do have an influence on the lifestyle of gay men in Jamaica. The general population is quite homophobic, as was confirmed by the German embassy in Kingston. Not surprisingly, under these circumstances, Jamaica offers no gay scene in the western sense of the word, although Kingston is said to be relatively open-minded.

Homosexuelle Handlungen sind ohne Ausnahme verboten. Die Art. 76-79 des jamaikanischen Strafgesetzes sehen Gefängnisstrafen mit Zwangsarbeit bis zu 10 Jahren vor. Versuchte Verführung zu schwulem Sex wird ebenfalls hart bestraft, und zwar mit bis zu sieben Jahren Haft – je nach Ermessen des Gerichts mit oder ohne Zwangsarbeit. Glücklicherweise werden diese Gesetze relativ selten angewandt, aber dennoch prägen sie das Lebensgefühl schwuler Männer auf Jamaica. Die Durchschnittsbevölkerung ist entsprechend homophob. Dieser Umstand wurde auch von der deutschen Botschaft in Kingston bestätigt. Folglich gibt es keine „schwule Szene" im westlichen Sinne, auch wenn sich Kingston relativ aufgeschlossen gibt.

L'homosexualité est un délit à la Jamaïque. Selon les articles 76 à 79 du code pénal jamaïcain, on risque les travaux forcés ou la prison, 10 ans maximum. Tout rapport avec un mineur est puni de 7 ans de prison avec ou sans travaux forcés, selon les jurés. Heureusement, ces articles ne sont que très rarement appliqués, mais il n'en reste pas moins qu'ils influencent fortement le comportement des homosexuels du pays. Les Jamaïcains sont, en général, assez homophobes, ce que nous a confirmé l'ambassade d'Allemagne à Kingston. Ceci explique l'absence de vie gay à l'occidentale, même si Kingston est une ville assez ouverte et tolérante.

Las actividades homosexuales están rotundamente prohibidas. Los párrafos 76-79 del Código Penal jamaica preveen penas de encarcelamiento con trabajos forzados de hasta 10 años. Los intentos de seducción homosexual son igualmente perseguidos con dureza, incluso hasta con 7 años de prisión -dependiendo de la decisión del tribunal el que sea o no con trabajos forzados. Afortunadamente estas leyes son aplicadas muy raramente, pero determinan en gran medida la vida y la situación de los gays jamaicanos. En general la sociedad jamaicana es muy homófoba, esta situación fue confirmada por la embajada alemana en Kingston. Debido a ello, no existe un ambiente gay como el que se conoce en Europa occiendental, aunque la ciudad de Kingston se muestra relativamente liberal.

Gli atti omosessuali sono incondizionatamente proibiti. I paragrafi 76-79 del codice penale giamaicano prescrivono l'imprigionamento e i lavori forzati fino a 10 anni. Anche i tentativi di seduzione gay vengono puniti duramente, cioè con prigione fino a sette anni (secondo l'apprezzamento del giudice con o senza lavori forzati). Anche se queste leggi vengono per fortuna raramente applicate, influiscono lo stile di vita dei gay giamaicani. Dunque la popolazione è abbastanza omofoba. Questa situazione è stata confermata anche dall'ambasciata tedesca a Kingston. Quindi non esiste un ambiente gay nel senso occidentale del termine, anche se la popolazione si dimostra abbastanza aperta.

Kingston

HOTELS

Lawrence Bed & Breakfast (F H MA NG)
Easiest to reach 6-13 h.
1 Denham Avenue, Meadow Brook Estate, Kingston 19 ☎ 933 13 72

Muscle and Art-Bed and Breakfast (bf g H)
1 Denham Avenue ✉19 ☎ 933 13 72

SWIMMING

-Wyndham Rosehall Resort Beach (next to cruise ship terminal)

Negril

GUEST HOUSES

Tingalaya's
West End Road ☎ 957 01 26

Savanna la Mar

GUEST HOUSES

Moun Tambrin Resort (CC g H)
PO Box 210
☎ 997 58 95 Email: jamountambrin@toj.com
Homepage: www.jamaicaescapes.com
Located in the south-west of the island.

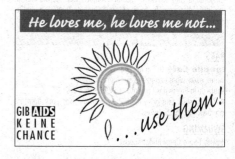

Martinique

Caribbean

Time: GMT -4

International Access Code: 00

International Country Code: 596 (No area codes)

Language: French; Créole

Area: 1,102 km² / 425 sq mi.

Currency: 1 French Franc (FF) = 100 Centimes

Population: 375,000

Capital: Fort-de-France

Religion: vast majority Roman Catholic

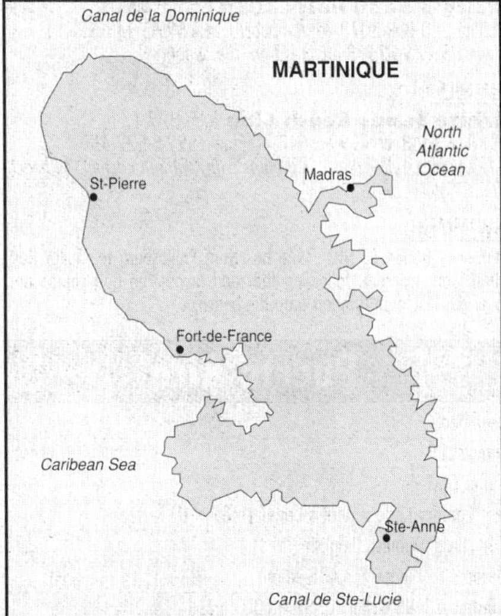

Climate: Tropical climate with warm days and ocean breezes. Heat is seldom excessive. Summers and winters are comfortable.

Martinique is a French »Departement d'Outre-Mer/D.O.M.«, i.e., it belongs to France's overseas territories. The inhabitants (and visitors) are therefore subject to the same laws as in ☛France. Martinique has become a very popular vacation island for Europeans, combining exotic tropical beauty with European and French comforts. This makes a holiday here particularly uncomplicated and enjoyable.

Martinique ist ein französisches »Département d'Outre-Mer/D.O.M.« und gilt damit als Teil des französischen Mutterlandes. Es gelten für die Bewohner (und Besucher) dieselben gesetzlichen Rechte und Pflichten wie in ☛Frankreich. Martinique ist ein beliebtes Touristenziel für Europäer geworden, verbinden sich doch auf dieser Insel tropische Schönheit und Exotik mit europäischem und französischem Komfort. Das macht den Urlaub hier natürlich besonders einfach und angenehm.

La Martinique est un département d'outre-mer français et fait donc partie intégrante de la France. Les habitants et les touristes ont les mêmes droits et les mêmes obligations qu'en ☛France métropolitaine. C'est un lieu de villégiature apprécié des Européens. La douceur tropicale, l'exotisme et le confort à la française rendront votre séjour particulièrement agréable.

Martinica es un «Dèpartement d'Outre-Mer/D.O.M» francés, y como tal es también considerada parte de la Madre Patria: Francia. Tanto para visitantes como para sus habitantes son valederas ☛las leyes francesas. Martinica es hoy en dia una atracción turística para europeos, donde se conjugan a la perfección las bellezas exóticas de una isla tropical con el confort europeo. Por esta razón el turista puede disfrutar aqui unas vacaciones agradables sin complicaciones.

La Martinica è un „département d'outre mer/D.O.M." francese, quindi una parte della Francia. Legalmente i suoi abitanti ed i suoi visitatori sono soggetti agli stessi obblighi e doveri dei francesi. La Martinica è diventata un'amata meta turistica per gli europei che trovano su quest'isola una buona fusione di bellezza esotica e confort francese, un fatto che vi permette di passare delle vacanze piacevoli senza complicazioni.

Diamant ✉ 97223

HOTELS

Palm Beach (AC B bf CC glm H pi)
Entrée du Bourg ✉97223 ☎ 76 47 84
8 single rooms and 2 triple rooms with bath or shower, WC, telephone/fax, terrace, sat-TV, kitchen, safe, own key, room service. Rates single FF 300-400, triple 380-480. Adittional bed 100. Bf incl. Half board FF 95, full board 190.

Fort-de-France ✉ 97200

HEALTH GROUPS

AIDES-Martinique Call Wed 15-18, Thu 19-21 h
PO Box 10 75, Cedex 97209 ✉97200 ☎ 63 12 36

CRUISING

-Parc de la Savanne (in front of Hotel Impératrice along the sea)

Les Trois Islets ✉ 97229

GUEST HOUSES

Carbet. Le (AC bf G MA NU OS wh) winter: 30.11-30.4; summer: 30.6-15.8
18 Rue des Alamandas, Anse Mitan ✉97229 *(20 min from the airport)* ☎ 596-66 03 31 Fax: 596-66 03 31
Email: dominique.celma@wanadoo.fr
Near the beach. 3 rooms with loggia and kitchenette. Quiet and intimate location. Rates FF 245. Ferry from airport 20 min.

Schoelcher ✉ 97233

CRUISING

-Plage Madiana

Ste.Anne ✉ 97227

SWIMMING

-Les Petites Salines (No nudism allowed)

CRUISING

-Plage des Salines (WE) (in the south of the island, near Savane des Petrifications)

Netherlands Antilles

Nederlandse Antillen

Caribbean

Initials: NA (NL)

Time: GMT -4

☎ Country Code / Access Code: 599 / 00

Language: Dutch and Papiamento; English, Spanish.

Area: 800 km^2 / 309 sq mi.

Currency: 1 Netherland Antilles Gilder (NAf) = 100 Cents

Population: 198,000

Capital: Willemstad (on Curacao)

Climate: Tropical climate that is moderated by northeast trade winds.

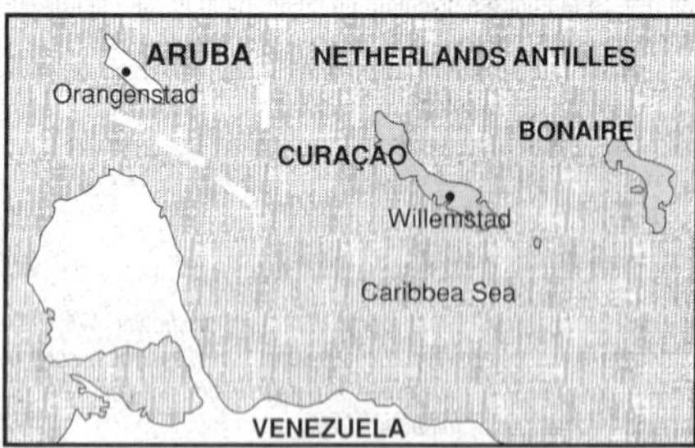

●Under Article 255 of the penal code, homosexual acts are legal between adult males, and the age of consent is set at 16. The attitude of the general public towards homosexuality, however, is somewhat less tolerant than that of the Dutch mother country.

✷Homosexuelle Handlungen werden in Artikel 255 des Strafgesetzbuches abgehandelt. Zwischen erwachsenen Männern sind sie legal, und das Schutzalter liegt bei 16 Jahren. Allerdings ist die öffentliche Meinung Homosexuellen gegenüber hierzulande etwas weniger tolerant als im niederländischen »Mutterland«.

▲L'article 255 du code pénal fait état de l'homosexualité qui, entre hommes adultes, n'est pas considérée comme un délit. La majorité sexuelle est fixée à 16 ans. D'après ce que nous savons, l'article 255 n'est pratiquement plus appliqué, mais notez bien que les gens, là-bas, sont bien moins homophiles qu'en métropole (Hollande).

☆El artículo 255 del Código Penal dictamina sobre las actividades homosexuales. Estas son declaradas legales entre hombres adultos y la edad mínima de consentimiento queda fijada en 16 años. La opinión pública de este país es menos tolerante con los gays que la de la madre patria; Holanda.

❖Gli atti omosessuali vengono trattati nel paragrafo 255 del codice penale. Sono legali tra uomini adulti, l'età del consenso è di 16 anni. Comunque, l'opinione pubblica verso l'omosessualità è meno tollerante rispetto a quella della „madrepatria" olandese.

Bonaire - Sorobon

BARS

Karels Beach Bar (B NG yg) live music on Sat evening

Bonaire - Sorobon

Kaya Kachi Craane *(opposite Zeezicht Bar)*

APARTMENTS

Ocean View Villas (AC CC GLM H NU)
Kaya Statius van Eps 6 ☎ +599-7-61 05 Fax: +599-7-43 09
Email: info@oceanviewvillas.com
3 apartments with shower/WC, terrace, TV, kitchen, own key. Rates from US$ 80 / night.

Sorobon Beach Resort (H NG NU)
PO Box 14, Island Bonair ☎ +599-7-80 80

Sunset Beach Hotel-Bonaire Sunset Villas (B F H NG OS) PO Box 333 ☎ +599-7-84 48

St. Maarten

BARS

Mary's Boon Hotel (AC B bf F glm H MA OS)
Juliana, PO Box 2078 *(at the beach)* ☎ +599-5-442 35
Twin US$ 75-125. 3 minutes from the airport.

HOTELS

White Sands Beach Club (glm H) 7-17 h
PO Box 3043 ☎ +599-5-543 70 Fax: +599-5-522 45
17 chalets, suites and 2 bedrooms with/without kitchen. All beachfront. Call for rates.

SWIMMING

-Cupecoy Beach (g NU) (take bus from Philipsberg to Mullet Bay, then walk 20 min. following the road across the golf course and over the hill, then turn left onto the beach)

Puerto Rico

Caribbean

Initials: PR

Time: GMT -5

☎ Country Code / Access Code: 1-787 / 011

Language: Spanish, English

Area: 8,897 km^2 / 3,435 sq mi.

Currency: 1 US Dollar (US$) = 100 Cents

Population: 3,806,000

Capital: San Juan

Religions: 80% Catholic

Climate: Tropical marine climate that is mild. There's little seasonal temperature variation.

Important gay city: San Juan

●Puerto Rico is neither a state of the US, nor independent, but 'freely associated' with the US. The Puertoricans are US-citizens but

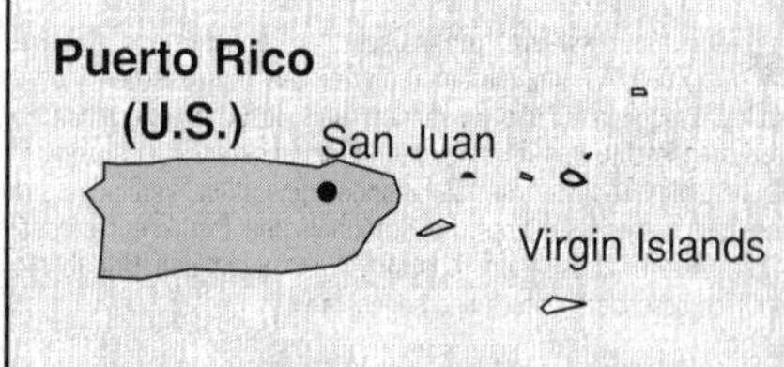

they are not entitled to vote in US-elections. This political position 'in between' and considerable customs privileges ensure economical prosperity for this Caribbean island. We do not have any information concerning the penal code, but we assume, that homosexuality is open to prosecution. Still Puerto Rico is the most liberal island in the whole of the Caribbean Sea. Gay activities take place wholly in the capital San Juan.

✱ Puerto Rico ist weder ein US-Staat, noch selbständig, sondern „frei assoziiert" mit den USA. Die Puertoricaner sind zwar Bürger der USA, besitzen aber kein Stimmrecht bei US-Wahlen. Diese politische Mittelstellung und erhebliche Zollvergünstigungen sichern dieser Karibikinsel wirtschaftliches Wohlergehen.
Zwar liegen uns keine juristischen Informationen vor, aber wir vermuten, daß Homosexualität strafbar ist. Trotzdem ist Puerto Rico die liberalste Insel in der gesamten Karibik. Schwule Aktivitäten konzentrieren sich ganz und gar auf die Hauptstadt San Juan.

▲ Porto Rico ne fait pas partie de la Confédération américaine et n'est pas non plus indépendante. L'île est „associée" aux Etats-Unis. Les gens là-bas ont la citoyenneté américaine, mais ne disposent pas du droit de vote. Grâce à son statut mixte et à une certane liberté en matière de douanes, l'île jouit d'une certaine prospérité.
Nous ne disposons d'aucune information concernant la situation des gays face à la loi. Il semblerait cependant que l'homosexualité soit passible des tribunaux. Il n'empêche que Porto Rico est une des îles les plus tolérantes des Caraïbes. La capitale gay de l'île, c'est San Juan.

☆ Puerto Rico no es ni independiente ni un estado norteamericano, sino un estado libre asociado a los Estados Unidos. Los puertorriqueños son ciudadanos norteamericanos sin tener el derecho al voto en las elecciones norteamericanas. Esta situación política asi

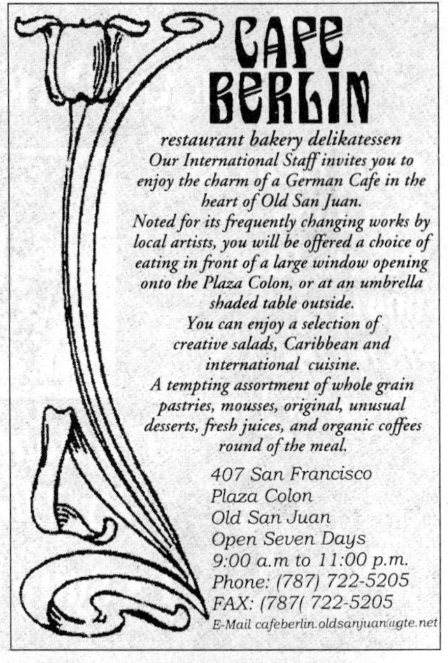

como las suntuosas ventajas aduaneras y migratorias, le brindan gran auge económico a esta isla caribeña. No poseemos informaciones judiciales respecto al trato de la homosexualidad en la isla, pero suponemos que ella es penada. A pesar de ello, Puerto Rico es una de las islas caribeñas más liberales. Las actividades homosexuales se concentran por completo en la capital San Juan.

❖ Porto Rico non è nè indipendente nè uno stato degli USA, ma „liberamente associato"agli USA. I portoricani sono cittadini degli USA, però non hanno diritto di voto nelle elezioni parlamentari degli USA. Questo compromesso politico e le agevolazioni doganali assicurano il benessere economico di quest'isola caraibica. Non abbiamo informazioni concrete ma presumiamo che qui l'omosessualità sia illegale. Nonostante ciò Porto Rico è l'isola più liberale dei Caraibi. Le attività gay sono concentrati alla capitale di San Juan.

NATIONAL GAY INFO

Caribbean Heat
1505 Loiza Street, Suite 78, Santurce, ✉00911 ☎ 726 18 07
About 32 pages, US$ 4. The only gay magazine in the Caribbean. Articles about health, entertainment, arts and travel.

Puerto Rico Breeze
100 Calaf Suite 100, San Juan,
PR 00918-1323 ☎ (787) 282 71 84

Aguada

HOTELS

San Max (H NG) closed May & Jun
PO Box 12 94 ✉00602 ☎ 868 29 31
Room with bath. Rates US$ 25. Two persons 30. Full kitchen. Minimum stay 3 days.

San Juan

● For the Caribbean, San Juan, with its highways and highrise buildings in the tourist quarter *Concado*, seems to have a very american feel to it. In this quarter (with its most beautiful bathing beach) and in Ocean View right next to it are most of the gay accomodations, venue and clubs. Approximately one kilometre distant lies the old town of San Juan, *Viejo San Juan*, which is so remarkable that its inscribed in the World Heritage List of UNESCO. Here is the right place to go shopping and there are many nightclubs and bars.

✸ Für karibische Verhältnisse wirkt das von Highways durchzogene San Juan mit den Hochhäusern im Urlauberviertel *Condado* sehr amerikanisch. In diesem Viertel (mit wunderschönem Badestrand) und nebenan in Ocean View liegen auch die meisten schwulen Unterkünfte und Ausgehmöglichkeiten. Etwa einen Kilometer entfernt liegt die Altstadt San Juans, *Viejo San Juan*, die so sehenswert ist, daß die UNESCO sie in ihrer Welterbeliste verzeichnet. Alt-San-Juan ist auch die richtige Gegend zum Shoppen und Bummeln.

▲ Les autoroutes urbaines traversent San Juan, les tours se dressent dans le quartier résidentiel de Condado: on a l'impression d'être aux Etats-Unis. C'est à Condado (plages merveilleuses) et à Ocean View que vous trouverez la plupart des pensions gays, des bars et des boîtes. A un kilomètre de là, vous avez la vieille ville de San Juan. Elle fait partie du patrimoine de l'UNESCO. Viejo San Juan est le lieu idéal pour faire du shopping et sortir le soir.

☆ San Juan, con sus Highways y sus rascacielos en la región vacacional *Condado*, se caracteriza por su aparencia norteamericana. En Condado, con sus maravillosas playas, y en el sector Ocean View se encuentran la mayoría de locales, pensiones y lugares de diversión gay. A 1 km. de distancia se encuentra la ciudad vieja San Juan, que por su belleza e importancia histórica, fue incluída dentro de la lista Patrimonio Cultural Mundial de la UNESCO. San Juan Viejo es el lugar ideal para ir de compras y disfrutar de la vida nocturna.

❖ San Juan ha un aspetto molto americano: è attraversata da autostrade, il suo orizzonte è disegnato dai grattacieli del quartiere turistico di *Condado*. In questo quartiere (con una spiaggia favolosa) ed nell'*Ocean View* si concentrano gli alberghi ed i locali gay. Ad un chilometro di distanza si trova il centro di San Juan, *viejo San Juan* , che per la sua bellezza è stato messo sotto protezione artistica dall'Unesco. Questa zona è la migliore per fare un giro dei negozi e per uscire di sera.

BARS

Barefoot Bar (B F g H MA N R) 9.00-4.00 h
2 Calle Vendig ✉PR 00907 *(Condado)* ☎ +1-809-725 20 55
or ☎ *725-2055. Meals 9-17, happy hour 17-19 h.*
Rooms & apartments available.

Juniors Bar (B D g N P SNU) 18-2, Sun 15-2 h
602 Calle Condado *(Condado)*

DANCECLUBS

Eros (B D G MA SL SNU YG) Wed-Sun 21-4 h, Mon closed
1257 Avenida Ponce de Leon, Stop 18 *Santurce (next to Metro Cinema)* ☎ 722 11 31
Extiting hightech disco. Regular parties and theme night, AIDS benefit. Shows Thu and Sun, strippers, bands.

Escape (B D G MA S) Sat 20-? h
181 O'Neill Street, Hato Rey

The Abbey in the Lazer (B D G) Sun
251 Calle Cruz

RESTAURANTS

Cafe Berlin (A AC B bf CC F GLM MA OS) 9-23 h
407 San Francisco, Plaza Colon *(Old San Juan)* ☎ 722 52 05
Restaurant, bakery, delicatessen. Mostly vegetarian cuisine.

Cafe Gambaro (B F g) 320
Calle Fortaleza ☎ 724 45 92

Condado Inn (B GLM MA) 11-? h
6 Avenida Condado *(Condado)* ☎ 724 71 45
Dinner only. Home style food.

Panaché Restaurant & Bar (AC B F G MA N OS)
11.30-15, 18-23 h
1127 Calle Seaview *Condado* ☎ 725 82 84
Excellent southern French cuisine. Overlooking beach. Inexpensive.

SEX SHOPS/BLUE MOVIES

Condom Mania (g)
353 San Francisco Street *(Old San Juan)* ☎ 722 53 48

SAUNAS/BATHS

Steamworks Bathhouse (AC CC DR f G MA P sa sb VS wh WO) 0-24 h
205 Calle Luna ✉PR 00902 *(Old San Juan)* ☎ 725 49 93
Popular. In historic old San Juan.

HOTELS

Atlantic Beach Hotel (AC B bf CC d F GLM H MA OS r S SNU STV wh YG) 1 Calle Vendig ✉PR 00907 *(Condado, Center of Hotel Area* ☎ +1-787-721 69 00 Fax 721-6917
Central location on beach. Restaurant. Deckbar and Sundeck. Jacuzzi. Rooms with direct dial telephone, cable TV, priv. bath and WC. Single US$ 60-90, double 75-105 (off-season). Single 75-110, double 90-125 (high-season). Reservation essential in high-season Dec-Apr.

Beach Buoy Inn Guest House (glm H)
1853 Mc Leary *(Ocean Park)* ☎ 728 81 19

Casa del Caribe (AC bf CC H W) ☎ 877-722-7139 (toll free)
57 Calle Caribe ✉00907

Condado Inn (B F GLM H s)
6 Avenida Condado *Condado* ☎ 724 71 45

Numero Uno On the Beach (B F glm H pi) 1 Calle Santa Ana, Ocean Park ✉PR 00911 ☎ 726 50 10 Fax: 727 54 82

GUEST HOUSES

Embassy Guest House (AC B CC F GLM H MA OS)
1126 Calle Seaview ✉PR 00907 *(Condado)* ☎ 725 82 84
All rooms with private bath and TV. Rates US$ 45-85 (low season), 65-135 (high season). All rooms have private bath, air-condition, ceiling fans, refrigerator, coffee maker and color cable TV.

LaCondessa Inn Guest House (glm H)
2071 Calle Cacique ✉PR 00912 *(Ocean Park)* ☎ 727 36 98

L'Habitation Beach (AC B bf CC F glm MA OS pr sol) 1957 Calle Italia ✉PR 00911 *(Condado)* ☎ 727 24 99
Fax: 727-2599 Email: habitationbeach@msn.com
Homepage: ww.geocities.com/TheTropics/Cabana/9206
Central location directly on the beach. All rooms have private baths. Rates US$ 66-87 (Dec 15-Apr 15) and US$ 47-69 (Apr 16-Dec 14), bf incl.

Ocean Park Beach Inn (AC B bf CC GLM H MA OS) 3 Calle Elena, ✉PR 00911 *(Ocean Park)* ☎ 728 74 18
Fax: 728 74 18
Located at the gay beach. 10 Rooms with sundecks and priv. bath. Rates from 70-115 (incl. bf) in a double room, weekly rates (incl. one free night). Also studio with kitchenette. Please see website for more details.

Ocean Walk Guest House (B bf CC f GLM H MA OS pi) 1 Calle Atlantic ✉PR 00911 *(Ocean Park)* ☎ 728 08 55
Fax: 728 64 34
Formerly Spanish style homes converted to an attractive compound of 40 rooms situated right on the beach. Close to gay venues. Rates USD 35-100, incl. bf. Studio apartments also available.

SWIMMING

-Beach between La Concha Hotel and Dupont Plaza Hotel (R) (especially next to Atlantic Beach Hotel, more tourists than locals)
-Ocean Park (more locals, busy on Sun)

CRUISING

-Plaza Rio Piedras (near University, Hato Rey)
-Calle San Francisco, Old San Juan (R)
-Plaza de Armas, Old San Juan
-Plaza de las Americas
-Plaza Colon (bus stop)

Saint Kitts & Nevis

Caribbean
Initials: KN
Time: GMT -4
Area: 261 km² / 101 sq mi.
Population: 42,000Captial: Basseterre
Religions: 87% Christian
Climate: Subtropical climate, that is tempered by constant sea breezes. Little seasonal temperature variation. The rainy season lasts from May to November.

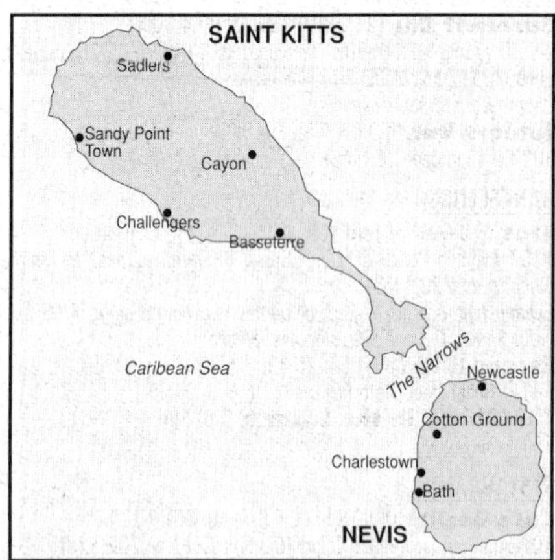

Basseterre - St. Kitts

HOTELS

Ocean Terrace Inn (B F H NG pi)
PO Box 65, W1
☎ 465 27 54

CRUISING

-Frigate-Beach (WE)
-Along seafront (dock area and particularly where local buses depart)

Charlestown - Nevis

HOTELS

Four Season Resort (AC B F H NG pi)
PO Box 565
Single/double US$ 220-385. Reservations: New York (212) 980-0101, London 834 44 22, Düsseldorf (0211) 35 41 98, Paris (01) 42.08.83.90.

Virgin Islands of the USA

Caribbean

Initials: VI

Time: GMT -4

Area: 344 km^2 / 133 sq mi.

Population: 105,000

Capital: Charlotte Amalie (on St. Thomas)

Religions: Protestant

Climate: Subtropical climate that is tempered by easterly tradewinds. There's relatively low humidity and little seasonal temperature variation. The

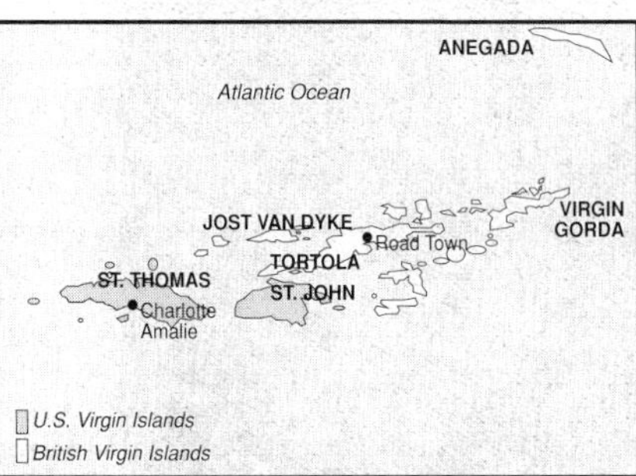

The Virgin Islands are the nearest neighbours to Puerto Rico. The northeastern part are called the *British Virgin Islands*, the southwestern part the *U.S. Virgin Islands*. For the average tourist these islands are mainly a station on their Caribbean cruise to buy duty free goods. Next to that there are gay hotels and the fundamental gay entertainment amenities in Frederiksted on *St. Croix*. And more is not needed. You don't take a gay holiday on a Caribbean island. You go here to lounge on a beautiful beach in a lovely tropical climate, to recreate and play in a sparkling ocean.

Die Jungferninseln liegen in unmittelbarer Nachbarschaft zu Puerto Rico. Der nordöstliche Teil sind die *British Virgin Islands*, der südwestliche die *U.S. Virgin Islands*.
Der Durchschnittstourist besucht diese Inseln vor allem als Station einer Karibik-Kreuzfahrt und um hier günstig zollfrei einzukaufen.
Daneben gibt es auf *St. Croix* in Frederiksted und auf *St. Thomas* schwule Hotels und eine Grundausstattung an schwulen Unterhaltungsmöglichkeiten. Mehr ist auch nicht nötig, denn auf einer Karibikinsel macht man keinen schwulen Urlaub. Hierher fährt man, um sich im angenehmen tropischen Klima an einem wunderschönen Strand im herrlichen Meer zu tummeln und zu erholen.

Les Iles Vierges sont voisines de Porto Rico. Le Nord est britannique, le Sud est américain. En général, on y vient pour faire des achats en duty free. A Frederiksted sur St Croix et sur St Thomas, il y a plusieurs hôtels gays et suffisamment de possibilités sortir et cela suffit largement, car on ne vient pas aux Caraïbes pour passer des vacances 100% gays. On y vient pour la douceur du climat et pour les plages enchanteresses.

Las Islas Virgenes se localizan en las cercanías de Puerto Rico. La parte noreste es llamada *British Virgin Islands*, y la parte suroeste *U.S.Virgen Islands*. La mayoria de los turistas que hacen un crucero por el Caribe bacen aqui una parada para aprochevar los interesantes precios de esta zona libre de impuestos. Pero en *St. Thomas* existen también unas cuantas pensiones y locales de diversión gay. Mucho más tampoco hace falta, ya que el objetivo de la mayoria de los turistas gay es disfrutar del excelente clima, las bella playas y el mar azul, y no se echa de menos una infrastructura homosexual.

Le Isole Vergini sono situate nelle immediate vicinanze di Porto Rico. A nord est vi sono le *British Virgin Islands* e a sud ovest le *US Virgin Islands*. Normalmente i turisti si fermano solo per fare scalo durante una crociera e per fare acquisti senza pagare tasse doganali. A Frederiksted, in *St. Croix* e a St. Thomas vi sono alcuni hotel e locali per gay. Non ci vuole di più, dato che ai Caraibi non si viene per il sesso, ma per godersi il clima e le spiaggie.

St. Croix

BARS

On The Beach Bar & Grill (B F glm)
PO Box 19 08, Frederiksted, VI 00841 ☎ 772 12 05

St. Tropez (B glm)
67 King Street

HOTELS

On The Beach (AC B bf F glm H MA OS pi wh)
PO Box 1908, Frederiksted, VI 00841 ☎ 772 12 05
Toll free ☎ (800) 524-2018. Beautiful beachfront hotel welcoming gays and non-gays alike. Reservation necessary. All rooms with kitchenette, priv. bath, and balcony. Rates 65-180, incl. bf.

SWIMMING

-Frederiksted, Beach of Hotel On the Beach

St. John

GUEST HOUSES

Oscar`s Guesthouse (AC CC H NU YG)
Estate Pastory #27, P.O.Box 117, Cruz Bay ✉VI 00831
☎ 776 61 93

St. Thomas

TRAVEL & TRANSPORT

Rafting Adventures (NG) Maritime Services Int'l., Inc., 82 Red Hook Center ☎ 779 20 32 *Snorkel-Sightsee-Tours.*

HOTELS

Blackbeard's Castle (AC B CC F glm MA N OS pi)
38 Dronningens Gade, ✉VI 00804 ☎ 776 12 34
Rates (single/double) US$ summer 60-95 / 75-110, winter 110-150 / 125-175 (all prices + tax, bf incl.)

Danish Chalet Guest House (AC B H NG OS pi)
Solberg Road, Charlotte Amalie ✉VI 00803 *(Gamble Norisideve's)*
☎ 774 57 64 Toll-free ☎ (800) 635-1531.
Central location, 10 min to the airport. All rooms with fridge, priv. bath. Single US$ 45-80 (bf incl.)

Harbor Lites (glm H)
Nisky Mail Box 442 ☎ 775 24 76

Hotel 1829 (AC B CC F H NG pi)
Goverment Hill, Charlotte Amalie ✉VI 00802, *(above the post office)* ☎ 776 18 29
Downtown location, 15 min to the airport. The gourmet restaurant offers French and American specialities (try the soufflés). All rooms have AC, telephone, priv. bath, frigidaire, cable TV.
Toll-free ☎ (800) 524-2002.

Secret Harbor Beach Resort (g H)
6280 Estate Nazareth ☎ 775 65 50
Toll free ☎ (800) 524-2250.

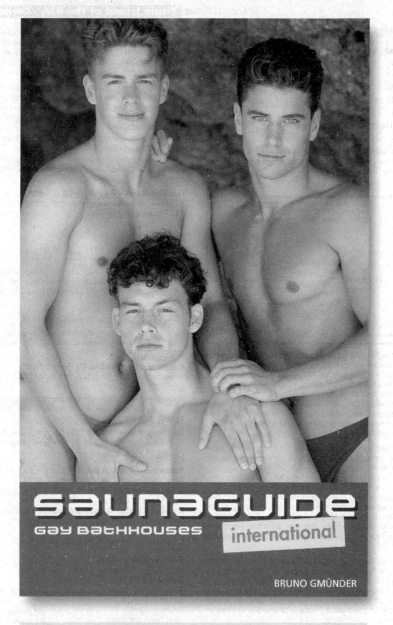

Chile

South America

Initials: RCH

Time: GMT -4

☎ Country Code / Access Code: 56 (Leave away the first 0 of area codes) / 00

Language: Spanish

Area: 756,945 km² / 292,256 sq mi.

Currency: 1 Chilean Peso (chil$) = 100 Centavos.

Population: 14,824,000

Capital: Santiago de Chile

Religions: 89% Roman Catholic

Climate: Moderate climate. Desert climate in the north, the south is cool and damp.

●According to Article 365 of the Chilean penal code, anal intercourse is illegal. Infractions are punishable with prison sentences of between 541 days and 3 years (or 5 years in so-called „serious" cases). This law is still applied, though not extensively. The end of the Pinochet regime has evidently not led to greater freedom for homosexuals. The Catholic Church, which provided refuge for many opponents of Pinochet's dictatorship, is now taking advantage of its moral position to oppose homosexuality and the development of a more liberal society.

✱Artikel 365 des chilenischen Strafgesetzbuches verbietet Analverkehr zwischen Männern. Die Zuwiderhandlung wird mit Gefängnisstrafen zwischen 541 Tagen und drei, in sogenannten schweren Fällen bis zu fünf, Jahren geahndet. Dieses Gesetz wird von den Gerichten noch immer, wenn auch nicht mehr extensiv, angewandt. Das Ende des Regime Pinochet hat offensichtlich nicht zu einer völligen Befreiung der Schwulen geführt: die katholische Kirche, die während der Pinochet-Diktatur vielen Regimegegnern Unterschlupf gewährte, versucht heute ihre moralische Position gegen die Schwulen und eine Liberalisierung der Gesellschaft zu mißbrauchen.

▲Au Chili, la pénétration anale entre hommes est un délit (article 365 du code pénal). Les contrevenants s'exposent à des peines de prison allant d'un an et demi à 3 ans, et dans certains jusqu'à 5 ans cas dits „graves". Cet article est toujours appliqué, toutefois moins rigoureusement.
La fin du régime Pinochet n'a apparemment pas amené la libéralisation que l'on attendait: l'Eglise catholique qui a pourtant protégé les opposants du temps de la dictature essaie désormais de profiter de sa position morale pour lutter contre les gays et empêcher une évolution des mentalités dans la société.

☆El artículo 365 del Código Penal chileno prohibe el coito anal entre varones. El quebrantamiento de esta ley supone una pena que va desde 541 día hasta 3 años y en los llamados casos graves de 5 años de cárcel. Esta disposición se sigue aplicando, aunque cada vez con menos rigor. El fin de la dictadura de Pinochet no supusó ningúna mejora de la situación de los homosexuales. La iglesia católica, que durante la dictadura apoyó y escondió a muchos opositores, sigue utilizando hoy en día su fuerte influencía moral en contra de la comunidad gay.

❖L'articolo 365 del codice penale cileno proibisce tutti gli atti omosessuali. Essi possono essere perseguiti con una pena che va da un anno e mezzo a tre anni di reclusione. Nei cosiddetti „casi gravi", la sentenza può raggiungere anche i cinque anni. Negli anni

passati, per quanto ne sappiamo, questa legge severa è stata sempre meno applicata.
La fine del regime di Pinochet non ha portato evidentemente alla emancipazione dei gay: la „sacra" chiesa cattolica, che durante la dittatura concedeva asilo agli oppositori del governo, cerca oggi di approfittare della propria posizione morale a detrimento dei gay e della liberalizzazione della societá.

NATIONAL GAY INFO

Centro de Estudios de la Mujer
Purísma 353, Santiago *(Barrio Bellavista, Recoleta)* ☎ (02)/ 777 1194

Colectivo Lésbico Feminista Ayuquelén
PO Box 70131, Correro 7, Santiago 7 Email: Ayuquele@netline.cl

El Otro Lado PO Box 512 64 Correo Central Santiago-1 ☎ (02) 543 27 05

Follies
PO Box 34, Santiago-35 ☎ (02)85 15 43
Fax: (02)-233 63 24

Lambda News
Augustinas 2085, PO Box 535 97, Correo Central Santiago *(esquina Avenida Brasil, Santiago Centro)*
☎ (02) 687 35 95 Fax: (02) 687 35 95
Email: lambnews@interactiva.cl Homepage: www.lambdanews.cl

MOVILH-Movimiento de Liberción Homosexual
Violler No. 87, PO Box 52834, Santiago *(Santiago Sur)*
☎ (02)-634 75 57 Fax: (0)2-635 913 Email: movilh@entelchile.net.
Gay liberation movement, active since 1991.

TOURIST INFO

Sernatur
Av. Providencia / Santa Beatriz *(Providencia)*
☎ 251 84

HEALTH GROUPS

Comisión Nacional del SIDA
Mac Iver 541
☎ 630 06 73
Also Corporación Chilena de Prevención del Sida ☎ 222 52 55 E-Mail : cilaids@cchps.mic.cl

Antofagasta ☎ 055

DANCECLUBS

Boy´s (ac B D G S MA) Fri-Sat 22-5 h
(Calama opposite of Vega Central)

Máscaras (ac B D G S MA) Fri & Sat 22-5 h
(At the corner Taltal/Calbuco)

RESTAURANTS

Bavaria (B F glm)
José Santos Ossa *(At the corner Baquedano)*
Typical cuisine

HOTELS

Antofagasta (AC bf glm F H OS pi WO)
Balmaceda s/n
☎ 26 82 59

Apart Hotel Diego de Almagro (bf F H)
Condell 2624 ☎ 26 83 31

Plaza (AC bf glm F H) Baquedano 461 ☎ 26 90 46

CRUISING

-Plaza Colòn (g MA r)

Arica ☎ 058

HOTELS

Diego de Almagro (bf F glm H)
Sotomayor 490
☎ 22 44 44

Hostería Arica (bf F glm H OS pi)
Avenida Commandante San Martín 599 ☎ 25 45 40

San Marcos Hotel (bf glm F H)
Sotomayor 367 ☎ 23 29 70
Centrally located hotel with garden. All rooms with telephone, TV, private bath, WC.

GENERAL GROUPS

Agrupación de Homosexuales Pucará
Granaderos 2077 ☎ 31 39 61

CRUISING

-Beach »El Laucho« (next to the Hotel Arica in the
-Plaza Colón (Square in front of City Hall and the Vicuña Square next to it at day-time).
-Plaza Vicuña Mackenna, (at day-time)

Calama ☎ 055

DANCECLUBS

Brocatto di Piu (ac b D GLM) Fri-Sat 0-6 ?
Antogfagasta 1462 ☎ 31 7511

RESTAURANTS

Maracuyá (B F glm)
Avenida Commandante San Martin 0321 ☎ 22 76 00

HOTELS

Alfa (bf F glm H)
Sotomayor 2016 ☎ 34 24 96

Hosteriá Calama (bf F glm H)
Latorre 1521 ☎ 34 15 11

Park Hotel Calama (bf f glm H)
Camino Aeropuerto 1392 ☎ 34 22 08

Castro - Isla de Chiloe ☎ 065

RESTAURANTS

Central (B F MA NG)
San Martin 457 ☎ 63 47 49

Sancho (b F MA NG)
Thompson 213 ☎ 63 20 79

HOTELS

Unicornio Azul (AC bf F glm H)
Avenida Pedro Montt 228 ☎ 63 23 59

GUEST HOUSES

Hospedaje Llapui (ac bf glm H)
O'Higgins 657 ☎ 63 32 17

Chillan ☎ 042

BARS

Kalhúa (B D G MA)
Panamericana Sur km 412 ☎ 23 78 74

Concepción ☎ 041

RESTAURANTS

Chateau. Le (AC B F glm)
Colo-Colo/O'Higgins

HOTELS
Alborada (AC B bf F glm H)
Barros Arana 457 ☎ 24 21 44
Araucano. El (AC B bf F glm H)
Caupolicán 521 ☎ 23 06 06

SWIMMING
-Playa Blanca (G MA) (Located south of Concepción, approximately one hour by bus/car between the cities of Coronel and Lota).

CRUISING
–Paseo Peatonal Barros Arana (g MA) (busy after 21 h).
-Paseo Peatonal Aníbal Pinto (g MA) (busy after 21 h).

Horcon ☎ 0569

HOTELS
Hosteriá Arancibia (bf F glm H)
Avenida La Playa s/n.
Residencial Juan Esteban (bf glm H)
Pasaje Miramar 2 ☎ 33 51 53
Clean, comfortable rooms with private bathroom.

SWIMMING
-Cau-Cau (G MA NU)

Iquique ☎ 057

DANCECLUBS
Escape (B D G MA) Bajo Molle, km 8

Isla de Pascua - Rapanui ☎ 039

DANCECLUBS
Tavake (D glm) 23-? h
Hanga Roa

HOTELS
Hanga Roa (bf F glm H) Avenida Pont s/n., Hanga Roa ☎ 22 32 99
Hotu Matúa (bf F glm H)
Avenida Pont s/n., Hanga Roa ☎ 22 32 42
Orongo Easter Island (bf F glm H) Avenida Policarpo Toro s/n., Hanga Roa ☎ 22 32 94 Fax: 22 32 94

La Serena ☎ 051

BARS
Best (ac B D GLM MA S) Balmaceda 3390, Paradero 6 1/2, La Pampa ☎ 24 26 07
Remaking (ac B D GLM MA)
Avenida Francisco de Aguirre 062 ☎ 21 06 32

DANCECLUBS
Diva (B D G MA) Fri Sat
Colo-Colo 4456 *(Loteo Aeroparque)*

HOTELS
Berlin (bf F glm H)
Cordovez 535 ☎ 22 29 27
Casablanca (AC bf F glm H)
Vicuña 414 ☎ 22 55 73
Francisco de Aguirre (AC bf F glm H)
Cordovez 210 ☎ 22 29 91

CRUISING
-Playa El Faro (g MA) (Dunes north of El Faro Monument).

Punta Arenas ☎ 061

BARS
Bossanova (B G MA)
Avenida España 1198 ☎ 24 19 78

Rocas de Santo Domingo ☎ 035

HOTELS
Intihuasi (bf F glm H)
Avenida Litoral 54 ☎ 28 31 04
Rocas de Santo Domingo (bf F glm H)
La Ronda 130 ☎ 44 43 56

SWIMMING
-Dunas de Rocas de Santo Domingo (G MA NU) (Dunes south of the town).

San Antonio ☎ 035

RESTAURANTS
D'Borques (b F glm MA)
Avenida Chile del Balneario Llo-Lleo
Juanita (b F glm MA)
Antofagasta 159

HOTELS
Hotel de Turismo del Jockey Club (bf F glm H)
Avenida 21 de Majo 202 ☎ 21 17 77
Imperial (bf F glm H)
Avenida Centenario 330 ☎ 21 16 76

SWIMMING
-Dunas de Llo-Lleo (G MA NU) (South towards the end of the dunes).

CRUISING
-Plaza Central de Llo-Lleo (g MA) (In the public pool/Balneario).

San Pedro de Atacama ☎ 055

RESTAURANTS
Estaka. La (b bf F glm)
Solcor s/n.
Traditional food, meat and vegetarian dishes.
Tambo Cañaveral (b bf F glm)
Caracoles *(esquina Toconao)*
Traditional food

HOTELS
San Pedro de Atacama. Hosteriá (bf F glm H)
Solcor s/n.
Takha Takha. Hosteriá (bf F glm H)
Tocopilla s/n.

GUEST HOUSES
Residencial Juanita (bf F glm H)
La Plaza s/n.

CRUISING
-Plaza de San Pedro (g)

Santiago ☎ 02

GAY INFO
Disque Amistad (g MA) 0-24 h
☎ 700 10 10

Radio Nuevo Mundo 93 AM (G) Sat 15.30 h
The program „Triángulo Abierto" is produced by the MOVILH.
Radio Tierro 130 AM Mon-Fri 19.20 h
Program „Crónicas Radiales"

BARS

Bar Willy / Bar Fox (B glm MA S) 22-04:00h, WE - 05:00h
Avenida 11 de Septiembre 2224 local 19 *(Comun Providencia, Passeo Las Palmas)* ☎ 381 18 06
During the day mixed public, in the evening turns into Bar Willy - gay with stripshow on the 1st floor.
Dionisio (B F GLM MA S) Mon-Sat 21-? h
Bombero Nuñez 111 *(esquina Dardinac, Barrio Bellavista, Recoleta)* ☎ 737 60 65
Shows Wed-Sat 0-03:00h
Tu club (B G MA)
Copiapó 685 ☎ 634 19 63

CAFÉS

Tavelli (! AC bf f glm OS)
Avenida Providencia *(between Andrés de Fuenzalida and Las Urbinas, Providencia)* ☎ 231 98 62 *Very popular.*

DANCECLUBS

Amadeus (B D G MA)
Pedro de Valdivia 1781 piso 4 *(Caracol Madrid, at the corner Av. Francisco Bilbao, Comuna Ñuñoa)*
Bokhara (B D G S YG) 20-05:00h, WE-07:00h
Pio Nono 430 *(Bellavista)* ☎ 732 10 50
Bunker Santiago (! B D G MA S STV YG) Fri, Sat & before holidays 0-06:00h. Shows 02:00h
Bombero Nuñez 159/Andrés Bello *(Barrio Bellavista, Recoleta)* ☎ 777 37 60
Cero (B D G MA) Fri & Sat 23-06:00h
Euclides 1204, Par. 2 Gr. Avenida ☎ 551 72 98
Fausto (! AC B D G MA S snu STV VS) Mon-Sat 22:30-? h, Show 02:00h
Avenida Santa María 826/San Francisco *(Providencia)* ☎ 639 96 29
Naxos (ac B D G MA S STV) Tue-Sun 24-? h
Alameda Bernardo O'Higgins 776/San Francisco *(Centro)* ☎ 639 96 29 *Popular*
Quasar (ac B D G MA S STV VS) Fri & Sat 0-06:00h
Coquimbo 1458/Aldunate *(Santiago Sur)* ☎ 671 12 67
Large, very popular disco.
Queen (B D f GLM MA STV YG) 23-? h
Coronel Santiago Bueras 128/Irene Morales *(Centro)* ☎ 639 87 03

RESTAURANTS

Capricho Español (! A AC B CC F G MA OS s) 20-03:00h
Purisima 65 ☎ 777 76 74
Spanish and international cuisine
Eneldo (B F glm)
Ernesto Pinto Lagarrigue 195 *(Bellavista)* ☎ 732 04 28
International cuisine.
Pizza Nostra. La (A B F glm MA OS)
Avenida Providencia 1975/Pedro de Valdivia *(Providencia)* ☎ 231 98 53
Italian food. Nice atmosphere.
Prosit (b f glm MA OS)
Avenida Providencia/Avenida Vicuña Mackenna *(Plaza Italia. Providencia)*
Fast food. Popular with gays later at night and on WE.

SEX SHOPS/BLUE MOVIES

Eros (g VS) Mon-Sat 11-21:00h
Caracol Madrid, Av. Pedro de Valdivia 1783 *(local 186, 4th Floor)* ☎ 251 67 29
Sex Shop Chile (g P VS)
Caracol Madrid, Av. Pedro de Valdivia 1783, local 186 *(esquina Avenida Francisco Bilbao, cuarto piso, Ñuñoa)* ☎ 251 67 29

CINEMAS

Capri (g og VS) 11-23:00h
Santo Domingo 834 ☎ 639 24 14
Cinelandia (g MA VS)
Pasaje Puente 540/Catedral, Local 1047 *(Centro)*
Please note that showing anal penetration in films is forbidden under Chilean law. Due to this reason the cinemas just screen heterosexual porn films.

SAUNAS/BATHS

Baños Chacabuco (b g MA OG r sb) 10-21, Sun 10-14 h
Chacabuco 33 *(Centro)* ☎ 681 74 62
The cabins on the first floor are for the straights, gays can rent cabins on the second floor. Be discreet.
Baños Turcos Miraflores (b g OG r sb) 7-21, Sun 7-14 h
Miraflores 353 *(Segundo Subterráneo, Centro)* ☎ 639 55 04
Relaxed atmosphere. Be discreet.
Gimnasio JR (! b G MA p sb WO) 15-21 h
Ricardo Matte Pérez 0372/Condell *(Providencia)* ☎ 225 19 70
Cabines available.

FITNESS STUDIOS

Protec (g WO)
Alonso Ovalle 1585 *(Santiago Sur)*

NEWS STANDS

Ediciones Yugoslavia (g)
Pasaje Catedral, Catedral 1063/Bandera, local 512 *(Centro)*
Free Shop Magazine (g)
Huérfanos 530/Santa Lucía, local 10 *(Centro)* ☎ 639 49 18

VIDEO SHOPS

Video's (g P VS)
Rosas 3017 *(esquina Maipú, Centro)*
☎ 681 36 62
Please note that the commercial use of pornography is forbidden under Chilean law. Magazines and videos may be bought by adults (18 years and older) for private use only.

HOTELS

Sao Paulo (bf F glm H)
San Antonio 356/Huérfanos *(Santiago Centro)* ☎ 39 80 31

GENERAL GROUPS

PAFALH (Padres, Famialares y Amigos de Lesbianas y Homosexuales)
Augustinas 2085 *(Santiago Centro)* ☎ 687 35 95

HEALTH GROUPS

Comisión Nacional del SIDA
Monjitas 689 *(6th floor, Santiago Centro)* ☎ 639 40 01

INFORMATION AND EDUCATION

EDUK ☎ 737 52 67
Education and information about AIDS.

FRENASIDA (Frente Nacional de prevención del SIDA)
Dieciocho 120 *(Santiago Sur)* ☎ 698 11 80
Library containing lots of information about HIV/AIDS.
GEAMN (Gente para un Amor Nuevo)
☎ 635 17 60
For people living with HIV/AIDS.
R.E.O.S.S. (Redes de Orientación en Salud Social)
Melipilla 3432, Avenida Independencia al 3400 *(Conchalí)*
☎ 736 55 42
HIV information, counselling and testing.

HELP WITH PROBLEMS

CAPVVIH (Centro de Apoyo a personas viviendo con VIH)
San Antonio 501, dpto. 702 *(Santiago Centro)* ☎ 633 69 66
Legal help and advice for gays and lesbians and people living with HIV/AIDS.
Cruz Roja Chilena
☎ 737 89 34 *Helpline*
Teléfono SIDA 0-24 h
☎ 800 20 21 *Helpline*

RELIGIOUS GROUPS

Movimiento Marianista
Colegio Santa María de la Cordillera *(Puente Alto)* ☎ 542 09 27

CRUISING

-Plaza de Armas (g MA R) (Ahumada esquina. Compañia, after 21 h)
-Avenida Providencia (g MA) (from 22 h)
-Parque Metropolitano (AYOR g MA) (Cerro San Cristóbalo, daytime)
-Parque Uruguay (AYOR g MA) (from Avenida Los Leones and Avenida Manuel Montt, along Mapocho river in Providencia, after 15 h)
-Parque Gran Bretaña (AYOR g MA) (Between Avenida Providencia and the River Mapocho, from Avenida Elcodoro Yáñez hasta Avenia Vicuña Mackenna in Providencia, after 21 h)
-Cerro Santa Lucia (AYOR g MA R) (daytime only)
-Plaza Indira Gandhi (AYOR g R YG) (Avenida Santa Mariá, next to the clinic INDISA and the Sheraton Hotel in Providencia, along the river and next tp Plaza Indira Gandhi, after 15 h, busy at night)
-Parque Forestal (AYOR g MA) (from Plaza Italia to Miraflores, along the river Mapocho in Santiago Centro, be very careful at night).
-Paseo Ahumada (g MA) (from the Alameda Bernardo O'Higgins to the Plaza del Armas in Santiago Centro, after 21 h)
-Paseo Huérfanos (g MA) (from calle Santa Lucía to Calle Bandera, Santiago Centro, after 21 h)
-Plaza Italia (g MA) Avenida Vicuña Mackenna esquina Avenida Providencia, next to entrance of Metro station Baquedano and the Restaurante Prosit, after 22 h, very busy on WE)

Talca ☎ 071

DANCECLUBS

Halloween (ac b D g MA TV)
Flor de llano, Parcela 1

RESTAURANTS

Alero de Gastón (F NG)
2 Norte/2 Oriente

HOTELS

Plaza (AC B bf glm H)
Poniente 1141 ☎ 22 61 50

Talcahuano ☎ 041

DANCECLUBS

Divine (B D G MA STV) Fri-Sat 0-? h
Caupolicán 52

HOTELS

De la Costa (bf glm H)
Colón 648 ☎ 54 59 30
France (bf glm H)
Aníbal Pinto 44 ☎ 54 21 30

Valparaiso ☎ 032

BARS

Foxy (B D f GLM STV) Fri-Sat 23-? h
Independencia 2446/Simón Bolivar ☎ 23 35 77
Tacones (B glm) 22-2 h
Huito 301/Brasil

DANCECLUBS

Scandal (B D G)
Yungay 2229 ☎ 59 60 83

RESTAURANTS

Bar Inglés (B F glm)
Cochrane 851 ☎ 21 46 25
Chilean cuisine
Bote Salvavidas (B F glm)
Muelle Prat s/n *(2nd floor)* ☎ 25 14 77
Specialized in seafood
Café Turri (B F glm)
Templeman 147 *(Cerro Concepción)* ☎ 25 20 91
International cuisine

HOTELS

Lancaster (bf F glm H)
Chacabuco 2362 ☎ 21 73 91
Reina Victoria (bf glm H)
Plaza Sotomayor 190 *(next to the Plaza Sotomayor)* ☎ 21 22 03

CRUISING

-Plaza Victoria (g MA r) (17-24 h)
-Avenida Pedro Montt (the two blocks leading to Plaza Victoria, late afternoon until late at night).

Viña del Mar ☎ 032

BARS

Polonius (B G MA p WE) Thu-Sat 23-3 h
Avenida Valparaíso 1131

DANCECLUBS

New Soviet (ac b D GLM STV) 23-? h
Arlegui 346 *(at the end of the alley)* ☎ 68 87 93

RESTAURANTS

Cap Ducal (B F glm MA)
Avenida Marina 51 ☎ 62 66 55
International cuisine
Chez Gerald (AC B F glm MA)
Avenida Perú 496 ☎ 68 92 43
International cuisine
Club Alemán (B F glm MA)
Salvador Donóso 1337 ☎ 23 33 50
German and Chilean food.

El Castillo (B F glm MA)
Washington 714 ☎ 28 19 74
Chilean cuisine.

GIFT & PRIDE SHOPS

Gaivota (G MA)
Galería Cristal, Local 20

HOTELS

Alcanzar (bf F glm H)
Alvarez 646 ☎ 68 32 14
Rooms with private bath, telephone and TV.
Miramar (AC bf F H NG OS WO)
Calceta Abarca s/n ☎ 62 66 77
Very luxurious hotel in beachfront location. Very expensive.
O'Higgins (AC bf F H NG OS WO)
Plaza Vergara s/n
☎ 88 20 16
San Martin (AC bf F glm H OS)
Avenida San Martín 667
☎ 68 91 91

SWIMMING

-Caleta Abarea (g MA) (next to Hotel Miramar)
-Los Marineros (g MA) (at the south end of Las Salinas, next to the Escuela Armamentos de la Marina Nacional)
-Las Salinas (g MA) (2 km north of the city, popular with marines)
-Dunas de Mantagua (G MA) (north of Viña, between the beaches playa Ritoque and playa Roca Negra. Very popular. Take the bus P to Punta Piedra and exit at the beach between Concón and Quintero).

CRUISING

-Calle Valparaíso (g MA) (main shopping area downtown, especially in the evening and late at night, near Samoiedo Cafe)
-Plaza Vergara (g MA) (busy at night)

China

Eastern Asia
Initials: TJ
Time: GMT +8
☎ Country Code / Access Code: 86 / 00
Language: Chinese (Putonghua) or Mandarin
Area: 9,560,980 km² / 3,691,494 sq mi.
Currency: 1 Renminbi ¥uan (RMB.¥) = 100 Fen
Population: 1,255,091,000
Capital: Beijing
Religions: Confucianism, northern Buddhism (Mahajana 100 Million), Taoism, Sunnite Moslem (14 Million)
Climate: The climate is extremely diverse and ranges from tropical in the south to subarctic in the north.

● There is no paragraph explicitly against homosexuality in the Chinese penal code. It is, however, considered to disrupt the „principle of harmony". The gradual process of liberalisation in China is nevertheless making itself felt for homosexuals, too. Gay scenes are beginning to emerge in Peking and Shanghai, and tolerance is increasing.
Guests have to pay for any objects which are broken in their hotel rooms during their stay (even if it is only a toothmug), so it is a good idea to check the condition of your room(s) upon arrival.
People with HIV/AIDS are not allowed to enter China. Anyone trying to do so may be turned away.

✸ Immer wieder wird deutlich, daß die chinesische Gesellschaft nicht von Toleranz gegenüber Schwulen und Lesben geprägt wird. Doch die (wirtschaftliche) Öffnung des Landes und die Angliederung Hong Kongs üben auch einen liberalisierenden Einfluß auf die Menschen und den Staat aus. Die chinesischen Gesetze gehen auf Homosexualität nicht ein. In Hong Kong sind einvernehmliche Kontakte zwischen Männern über 21 entkriminalisiert.

Die schwule Szene Hong Kongs gehört zu den sehenswertesten Asiens. Die Angliederung des Stadtstaates an das Mutterland hat nicht zu den befürchteten schweren Repressionen geführt. Die Volksrepublik hält sich an die Vereinbarung „Ein Land, zwei Systeme". In China selbst haben sich in Beijing, Guanghzou und Shanghai kleine schwule Szenen gebildet. Und man wird davon ausgehen können, daß zunehmende wirtschaftliche Prosperität diesen Trend verstärken wird.
Die Adressen Hong Kongs finden Sie aufgrund der noch immer gravierenden strukturellen Unterschiede zum Rest der Volksrepublik als Sonderkapitel am Ende des China-Teils.

▲ En Chine, l'homosexualité n'est pas un délit. Elle est, toutefois, considérée comme une atteinte au principe d'harmonie. Les homosexuels chinois commencent à sentir les effets de l'ouverture du pays sur l'Occident. A Pékin et Shangaï: premiers signes de la mise en place d'un milieu gay et d'une certaine tolérance vis-à-vis des gays.
Si vous cassez ou endommagez quoi que ce soit à l'hotel (le verre à dents par exemple), vous êtes tenu de le remplacer à vos frais. En entrant dans votre chambre, pensez bien à dresser un état des lieux et un inventaire. Les séropositifs et les sidéens n'ont pas le droit d'entrer et de séjourner en Chine. On les refoule à la frontière.

☆ En el código penal chino no existe ninguna ley en contra de la homosexualidad: se considera como contravención al principio de la armonía. La lenta apertura del país se ha dejado también sentir por los gays. Muy cuidadosamente se han ido formando en ciudades como Peking y Shanghai lo que podría llamarse el principio de la tolerancia frente a la homosexualidad. Si se rompen objetos que están en la habitación del hotel (por ejemplo el vaso para cepillarse los dientes), deben ser pagados por el huésped. Es conveniente asegurarse del estado de la habitación al llegar al hotel. Turistas infectados con HIV se les niega la entrada al país. En caso contrario podrían ser deportados.

❖ Nella legge cinese non c'è un paragrafo contro l'omosessualità, che però viene considerata contraria al principio d'armonia. Tuttavia anche i gay beneficiano della lenta riapertura del paese. A Pechino e a Shangai si stanno creando le basi per lo sviluppo della comunità gay; è consigliabile di accertarsi esattamente dello stato in cui si trovano le stanze d'albergo prima del pernottamento: ogni oggetto che viene rovinato deve essere rimborsato. Turisti infettati di HIV non possono entrare in Cina; possono essere rimandati indietro.

Anshan

CRUISING
-Square in front of Main station
-Xiaodongmen Park

Baoding

CRUISING
-Opposite Hebei Yingjuyuan/Theatre

Beijing ☎ 010

BARS
Butterfly Bar (AC B CC D G MA) Sanlitun Road 10 *(At the bginning of Sanlitun Road)* ☎ 64 15 14 13
Half & Half Café (B G N YG) 11.30-1 h
Sanlitun Nanlu 15 ☎ 641 669 19

DANCECLUBS
Nightman Disco (AC B D glm N VS WE YG)
2 Xibahenanli ☎ 64 66 25 62

CRUISING
-Quinghuachi at Zhushikou Street (after dark)
-Wangfujing Street and Bathhall (after dark)
-Tiantan Park (after dark)
-Worker's Cultural Palace (after dark)
-Dungtan Park (after dark)
-Grey brick WC in N°2 Taijichang Lane (after dark)
-Toilet at the intersection of Sidan
-Roadside WC in front of the Peking Exhibition Centre
-Youyi Shangdian (Friendship Store, WC 2nd floor)

Cangzhou

CRUISING
-Long Distance Bus Terminal
-Jiuhe Hotel (opposite the hotel)

Chengdu ☎ 028

CRUISING
-Sichuan newspaper building (in front of)
-Workers cultural palace

Chongqing ☎ 0811

HOTELS
Renmin Hotel (H NG)
175 Renmin Lu FAX ☎ 385 14 21
Fax: 385 20 76
Shaping Grand Hotel (H NG)
84 Xiaolonkan New Street, PO Box 6300030 ☎ 686 31 94
Fax: 686 32 98

Dalian ☎ 0411

CRUISING
-Jianmin Bath Hall
-Railway station (square in front of it)
-Zhongshan Park

Guangzhou

BARS
42nd Street (B F glm MA)
399 Huanshi Dong Lu

RESTAURANTS
Milano's (B F glm)
3-103 Xin Chen Bei Jie, Tianhe Dong Lu

HOTELS
Nanhu Resort Hotel (H NG)
Nanhu South Lake *(at the foot of White Cloud Mountain)*
☎ 87 77 63 67
White Swan Hotel (AC B CC F H NG pi sa sb WO)
Shaiman Island

CRUISING
-Cultural Park (after dark among the movie watching audience)
-Toilet facing Cultural Park entrance
-Beijing Road WC

Haicheng

CRUISING
-Zhongjie Bath Hall

-2 WCs near entrances of Ping'An Park (after dark)
-WC in front of Teachers' University (Shi Da) on Yu Hua road (very cruisy after dark, especially in summer).

Tianjin ☎ 025

SAUNAS/BATHS

Jinling Hotel (b H NG)
Sky Palace Bar (Jazz band) in the evenings. Lots of tourists.
Qinghuachi Bathhall
City Center

HOTELS

Nendels Victory Hotel (H NG)
11 Jin Tang Road
(Tanggu) ☎ 938 58 33 Fax: 998 44 70

Wuhan ☎ 027

HOTELS

Xuangong Hotel (H NG)
45 Jianghan Yi Road *(Wu Han)* ☎ 281 44 04
Rates RMB 24-45.

CRUISING

-Port
-Changjiang bridge

Xian ☎ 0296

HOTELS

New World Dynasty Hotel (CC H NG pi sa sb WO)
48 Lian Hu Lu ☎ 721 68 68 Fax: 721 97 54.
Renmin (People's) Mansion (H NG)
319 Dongxin Jie ☎ 222 51 11
Lots of young tourists. Twin RMB 83-140.

CRUISING

-In front of the Hotel „Dasha"
-Railway station

Hong Kong Island

Eastern Asia
Initials: HK
Time: GMT +8
☎ Country Code / Access Code: 852 (no area codes) / 001
Language: English, Chinese
Area: 1,071 km^2 / 414 sq mi.
Currency: 1 Hong Kong Dollar (HK$) = 100 Cents
Religions: Christian majority; Buddism; Confucianism
Climate: Tropical monsoon climate. Winters are cool and humid. Spring through summer is hot and rainy, fall warm and sunny.

GAY INFO

Contacts (GLM)
GPO Box 13427 ☎ 2817 9447
FAX 2817 9120.Hong Kong`s only Lesbian and Gay magazine.

BARS

CE Top (AC B D F g OS S YG)
12-4, disco 21-4 h
9/F 37-43 Cochrane Street, Central *(entrance opposite of Park`n Shop)* ☎ 2544-3584
With disco
CK (B) 20-3 h
2/F 14-16 Johnson Road, Wanchai ☎ 2521-3511
Club `97 (B D g) Fri 18-22.20, Teadance 1st. Sun afternoon, Gay Fri -22 h & 1st Sun
9 Lan Kwai Fong, Central ☎ 2810-9333
Homme Base (AC B CC D G MA)
Hollywood Road, 2nd Floor, Central
H2O (B G P) 20-4 h
474-476 Lockhardt Road, Causeway Bay *(Hop Yee Building, 2nd floor)* ☎ 2834-6451
Karaoke.
Rice Bar (B G) 33
Jervois Street, Central ☎ 2851 4800
Smart's Club (B G) 8-? h
18 Shelter Street, Causeway Bay ☎ 2895-0488
Karaoke.
Why Not (B G YG) Sun-Thu 20-2, Fri Sat & before holidays 20-3 h
12/F Kyoto Plaza, 491-499 Lockhart Road, Causeway Bay ☎ 2572-7808
Karaoke lounge, café & bar.
Works (B d E GLM MA VS) Tue-Sat 19-1.30, Sun -3.30 h
1/F 30-32 Wyndham Street *(MTR Central)* ☎ 2868 6102
The largest GLM bar in Hong Kong.
ZIP (AC B CC d F G OS s YG) 17-4
Grnd.F 2 Glenealy Street, Upper Central ☎ 2533-3595

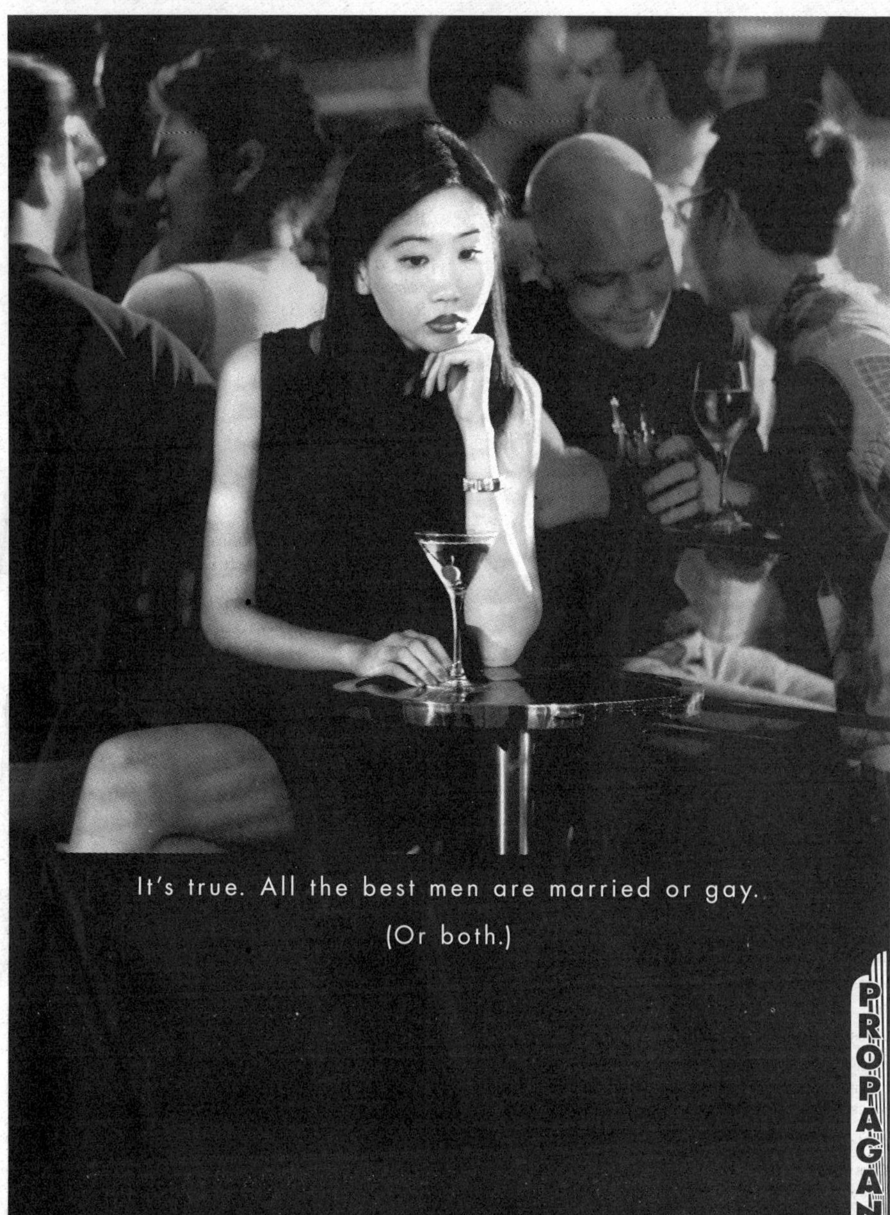
It's true. All the best men are married or gay.
(Or both.)
PROPAGANDA
PROPAGANDA, LOWER GROUND FLOOR, 1 HOLLYWOOD ROAD, CENTRAL. TELEPHONE (852) 2868 1316.

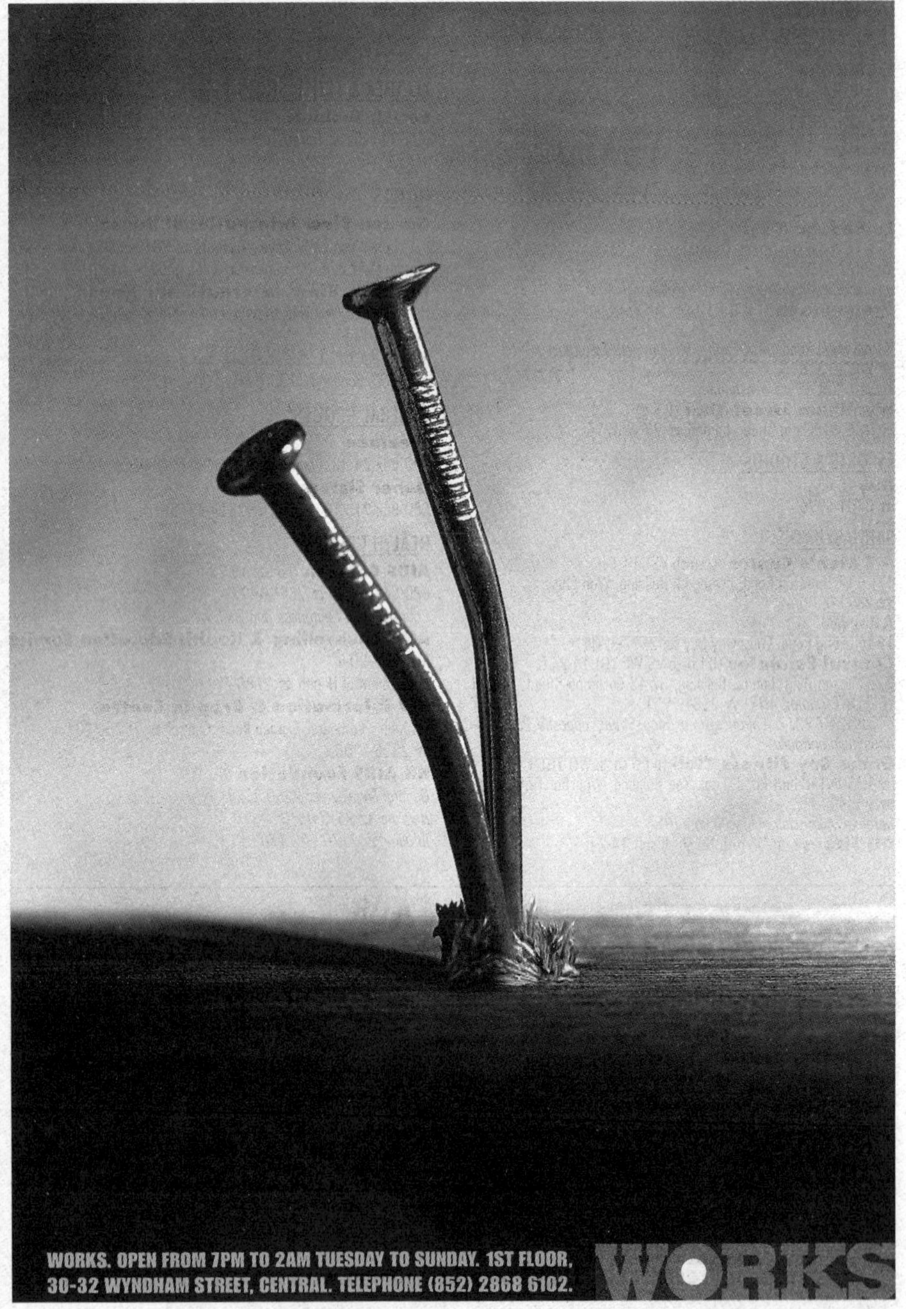
WORKS. OPEN FROM 7PM TO 2AM TUESDAY TO SUNDAY. 1ST FLOOR,
30-32 WYNDHAM STREET, CENTRAL. TELEPHONE (852) 2868 6102.
WORKS

DANCECLUBS

Propaganda (B D E GLM MA VS) Sun-Fri 21-3.30, Sat -4.30 h
1 Hollywood Road *(MTR Central Station, near Escalator)*
☎ 2868-1316
Largest GLM-Bar/Disco in Hong Kong.

RESTAURANTS

Garage (B F glm) 12-22, Sat & bank holidays 16-2, Sun closed (except before bank holidays)
G/F., 35 Peel Street, Central ☎ 2542-1488
or ☎ 2544-6432.

La Bodega (B F g)
31 C/A Wyndham Street, Central
☎ 2877 3101
up-market spanish style cuisine, excellent wine list.

Propaganda (! B D E F GLM MA VS) Sun-Fri 19-3.30, Sat - 4.30 h
1 Hollywood Road *(MTR Central Station, near Escalator)*
☎ 2868-1316
Largest GLM bar-disco-restaurant.

Wyndham Street Thai (B F g)
G/F 38 Wyndham Street, Central ☎ 2869 6216

ESCORTS & STUDIOS

Guy (G msg)
☎ 8101-6996

SAUNAS/BATHS

A E Men's Centre (G sa sb VS) 14-1 h
1/F 114 Thomson Road, Kwong Ah Building, Wan Chai,
☎ 2591-0500

AA (g MA)
19 Lan Fong Road, Causeway Bay ☎ 2577-3705

Central Escalator (B f G sb VS WE YG) 14-24 h
2/F Cheung Hing Comm. Building, 37-43 Cochrane Street, *Central (Hillside Escalator, MTR)* ☎ 2581-9951
or ☎ 2581-9961. Entrance from Gage Street, opposite Park'n'Shops main entrance.

Game Boy Fitness Club (b f G sa sb WO YG) 12-2 h
324-330A Lockhart Road, Fook Yee Building, Wanchai *(2nd floor)*
☎ 2574-3215
Karaoke. Admission only with your ID.

QQ Fitness (g MA msg NG sa sb sol) 14-2 h
14 Burrows Street, Wanchai *(King Dao Building, 3rd floor)* ☎ 2527-7073
or ☎ 2527-8276.

LEATHER & FETISH SHOPS

Fetish Fashion (CC GLM) Tue-Sun 11-19 h, closed Mon
52-60 Lyndhurst Terrace, Central *(1st floor)* ☎ 2544-1155

HOTELS

Garden View International House (H NG)
1 McDonell Road, Mid Levels *(center)* ☎ 2877-3737
Run by the YMCA. Not expensive and a good standard.

Harbour View International House (H NG) 4 Harbour Road, Wanchai *(next to Convention & Exhibition Center)*
☎ 2520-1111
Run by the YMCA. Not expensive and a good standard. Single HK$ 350-500, double 400-500, twin 500-600.

GENERAL GROUPS

Freemen
GPO Box 24 43, Central ☎ 9106-4983 *(English)*

Queer Sisters
GPO Box 913 13, Central ☎ 2314-4348 *(English)*

HEALTH GROUPS

AIDS Concern Thu Sat 19-22 h
GPO Box 33 50 ☎ 2898-4422
Counselling in Cantonese and English.

AIDS Counselling & Health Education Service
Mon-Fri 8-20 h
Department of Health ☎ 2780-2211

HIV Information & Drop-In Centre
St. John's Cathedral, Garden Road, Central ☎ 2525-7207 or
☎ 2525-7208.

HK AIDS Foundation
General Enquires ☎ 2560-8528
Helpline ☎ 2513-0513
Infoline ☎ 2170 222 170

CENTRAL ESCALATOR

SAUNA

STEAM BATH

JACUZZI

RESTROOMS

REFRESHMENTS

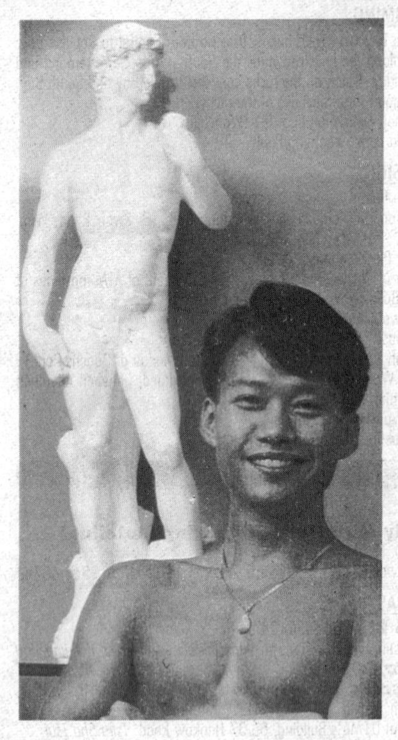

1/2 PRICE ENTRY WITH THIS AD

Tel. 9198 2836, 2581 9951 Opening Hrs. 1400-0000

2/F. 37-43 Cochrane St., Central Hong Kong.

(Taxi ask for Lyndhurst Terrace, above Dublin Jack Pub)

中環閣麟街 37-43 號祥興商業大廈電梯 2 字樓

(近中環半山電動樓梯,的士由擺花街入,在 **Dublin Jack Pub** 樓上)

QEH AIDS Hotline
☎ 2780-2211
☎ 2710-2553 or ☎ 2710-2571.

SWIMMING

-Middle Bay (G) (Take bus 320 or 6a from Central to Repulse Bay. Walk along the beach towards the South. Cruisy Sat afternoon and on Sunday. Action on the rocks between Middle Bay and South Bay. Wear good shoes because of the rocks)
-Morisson Swimming Pool (g) (Wanchai)
-Victoria Park Swimming Pool

CRUISING

-Middle Bay
-Morrison Hill Road Public Swimming Bath (Oi Kwan Road, Wanchai)
-Pacific Place Shopping Mall
-Corner of Pedder Street/Queens Road, in front of ATM machines at China Building. Very busy between 17-20 h.
-Lan Kwai Fong (AYOR-police)
-Ice House Street (near Queen Road Central)
-Gutzlaff Street (two blocks above Central Market at Queens Road)
-Shing Wong Street (stairs on Hollywood Road, between Aderdeen Street and Man Mo Temple)
-MTR-Wanchai
-Queens Road East/Queensway

Kowloon

BARS

Wally Matt (former Walzing Mathilda) (B F g) 18-3h
9 Cornwall Avenue, Tsimshatsui *(near Mody Road)* ☎ 2367-6874

SAUNAS/BATHS

Blue Blood (g MA) 14-24 h
20 Austin Avenue, Tsim Sha Tsui *(Perfect Commercial Building, 3rd floor)* ☎ 2302-0780
Bobson's Fitness Club (B G sb VS) Mon-Fri 15.30-1, Sat Sun 15-1 h
3/F Flat D, Ma`s Building, 35-37 Hankow Road, *Tsim Sha Tsui* ☎ 2376-2208
Jonathan's Fitness Club (msg NG sa sb sol) 16.30-24 h
42 Carnavon Road, Tsim Sha Tsui ☎ 2369-8174
KK 14-2 h
16/F Block A, Fuk Lok Building, 19-21 Jordan Road, ☎ 2388-6138
Rome Club (b G sa sb YG) 15-24 h
2/F Chiap Lee Building, 27 Ashley Road, Tsimshatsui ☎ 2376-0602
Karaoke.
Yuk Tak Chee Bath House (g msg OG sb) 12-24 h
123 Prince Edward Road, Mongkok ☎ 2393-9505 *or ☎ 2393-1109.*

BOOK SHOPS

Swindon's Bookstore (NG)
Ocean Terminal Shopping Mall, Tsimshatsui
General bookstore with small gay section.

HOTELS

Y.M.C.A. Hotel (AC F g H pi r sa wh)
41 Salisbury Road ☎ 2369-2211
Downtown location, 10-15 minutes to the airport. Hotel with garden. All rooms with telephone, partly kitchenette, bath/WC.
Y.M.C.A. International House (AC F H NG) 23 Waterloo Road ☎ 2771-9111
4 km from the airport. Downtown location. Single HK$ 300, double 330-400. Bf not included.

GENERAL GROUPS

10% Club
PO Box 722 07, Central post Office ☎ 2314-8726
Registered association that fights for political and social acceptance. Servicing, social and educational gatherings.

HELP WITH PROBLEMS

AIDS Couselling & Health Education Service
c/o Queen Elizabeth Hospital, Wylie Road ☎ 2710-2429

RELIGIOUS GROUPS

Isavara
PO Box 743 42, Kowloon Central Post Office ☎ 2782-0649
Fax: 2374-5948.
Gay Buddhist group.

CRUISING

-Hong Kong Hotel (near coffeeshop)
-New World Centre (main entrance, 12-20 h)
-Ocean Center
-Kowloon Park Swimming Pool
-Ocean Terminal (Ocean Center & Harbour City)
-Yau Ma Tei car park (basement and 1st floor)

Lantau Island

HOTELS

Babylon Villa (glm H) 29
Lower Cheung Sha
☎ 2980-2872

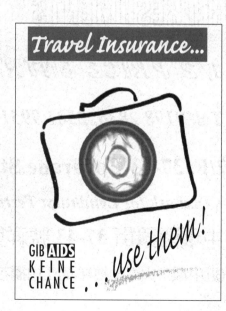

Harbin ☎ 0451

BARS

Bu Luo Bar (B glm MA) 18-2 h
257 West Da Zhi Street *(Nangang)* ☎ 632 01 10
Pop Bar (B glm MA)
47 Gexin Street *(Nangang)* ☎ 262 09 29

CRUISING

-Jiuzhan Park
-Yiman Street
-Zoological Garden

Nanjing ☎ 025

HOTELS

Shuang Men Lou Guest House (H NG)
185 North Hu Ju Road ☎ 880 59 61
40 minutes to the airport. Single US$ 30, double 36.

CRUISING

-Intersection at downtown Sinjiekuo
-Worker's Cultural Palace
-Near the Wutaishan Gymnasium and on the hills nearby

Shanghai ☎ 021

● Nowadays, the only major Chinese city with a visible gay presence is Shanghai. The harbour quarter, which dates back to colonial times, is called the „Bund" and is the most popular cruising area in Shanghai. Many gays meet there in the afternoon, and towards evening the paths are full of promenading couples. WARNING: Beware of invitations to any so-called „Gay Bar", and to avoid trouble, do not order anything until you have seen the price list.

✸ Shanghai ist heute die einzige Stadt mit einer sichtbaren schwulen Präsenz in ganz China. „Der Bund" heißt das alte Hafenviertel aus der Kolonialzeit und ist die beliebteste Cruising Area der Stadt. Schon in den frühen Nachmittagsstunden treffen sich täglich zahlreiche Schwule, abends füllen sich die Wege des Parks mit Pärchen. Eine Warnung: Vorsicht bei Einladungen in eine sogenannte „Gay Bar". Um Ärger zu vermeiden sollte man nichts bestellen, ohne vorher die Karte mit den Preisen gesehen zu haben.

▲ Shanghaï est aujourd'hui la seule ville de Chine qui peut se vanter d'avoir une infrastructure gay digne de ce nom. L'ancien quartier portuaire, „The Bund", (héritage de l'époque coloniale) est le lieu de drague le plus fréquenté de la ville. Dès les premières heures de l'après-midi, on se retrouve ici et, le soir venu, on se promène en couples dans le parc, ignorant apparemment les risques auxquels on s'expose en affichant ainsi son homosexualité.
Attention: Méfiez-vous des invitations dans un soi-disant „Gay Bar". Pour éviter les ennuis, ne commandez qu'après avoir jeté un coup d'oeil sur les prix des consommations.

☆ Shanghai es hoy en día la única ciudad en toda la China que tiene un ambiente gay. El viejo barrio portuario, que data del tiempo colonial y llamado „La alianza" es hoy en día la zona favorita para practicar el »cruising« (ligue). Ya a horas tempranas de la tarde se reunen aquí todos los días muchos gays. Por las noches, los caminos del parque se llenan con parejas. Advertencia: ten cuidado con invitaciones en el llamado „Gay Bar". Para evitar malos entendidos no pidas nada antes de mirar la lista de precios.

❖ Shanghai è l'unica città cinese con una visibile presenza gay. Il vecchio quartiere portuale *Der Bund*, il cui nome risale ai tempi coloniali, è la cruising area della città. Tutti i giorni già nel primo pomeriggio si incontrano numerosi gay, e di sera le coppiette affollano i sentieri del parco. Fate attenzione se venite invitati in un cosidetto „gay bar". Per evitare problemi controllare sempre la lista dei prezzi prima di ordinare.

BARS

Anton's Bar (B G YG)
500 Zhongshan East No. 1 Road *(Bund)*
Asia Blue (B d G)
181 Jin-xian Road ☎ 62 17 60 65
Eddy's Bar (AC B D G MA STV S) 18-4 h
No. 1 Lane 860, Nanjing Xi Lu Road ☎ 62 71 90 57
Feeling Bar (B G MA)
Ruijin Road 207 ☎ 64 73 60 97
Hawallan Bar (B G MA N)
Wei Hai Road *(Near Nanjing Road 904)* ☎ 62 47 78 68
Judy's Too (B F glm)
176 Mao Ling Lu ☎ 64 73 14 17
K.M. Bar (AC B G MA N) 18-4 h
o. 513 Hai Fang Road ☎ 62 56 42 09

DANCECLUBS

Xiang-yin (Eddy's) (! AC B D G MA N S WE) 14-4 h
1, Lane 860 Nanjing West Road ☎ 62 71 90 57

RESTAURANTS

Frankie's Place (B F glm)
81 Tong Ren Road ☎ 62 47 08 86

HOTELS

Jinjiang Hotel (H NG)
59 Maoming Nanlu ☎ 62 53 42 42
One of the largest and best equipped hotels in Shanghai; very convenient for exhibition hall, Jing Jiang Club and the Jin An Park. Rates RMB 136-195. Fax: 62 58 25 82-45 67
Peace Hotel (B D H NG)
20 Nanjingdonglu *(downtown)* ☎ 63 21 12 44
Bar, disco and hotel near the cruising area; has replaced the former disco of the Jing Jiang Hotel. The lobby and the café are also very cruisy. RMB 85-171.

SWIMMING

-Jin Jiang Club (the indoor swimming pool of the hotel is opened in winter)
-Guoji Julebu (International) Club (a favorite summertime watering spot for foreign residents)

CRUISING

-Waitan (near Huangpu Park on The Bund, downstream from the Peace Hotel and Nanjing Road; area below the sightseeing boat dock and the bus loop)
-Jin An Park (not far from the Exhibition Hall and Jin Jiang Hotel)
–at the intersection near Qingan Temple

Shijiazhuang ☎ 0311

CRUISING

-WC to the right of the Norman Bethune Memorial entrance (very cruisy, even during daytime).

Colombia

Northwest coast of South America

Initials: CO

Time: GMT -5

☎ Country Code / Access Code: 57 (leave away the first 9 of area codes) / 009

Language: Spanish; Indian languages

Area: 1,138,914 km^2 / 439,735 sq mi.

Currency: 1 Columbian Peso (col$) = 100 Centavos

Population: 38,580,949

Capital: Santafé de Bogotá

Religions: over 95% Roman Catholic

Climate: Tropical climate along the coast and eastern plains. Highlands are cooler.

●Although homosexuality is not mentioned in the law and the age of consent is 18 years, Columbian society in general has a negative attitude towards homosexuality. The police are known to harass gay men. Contact with male prostitutes can sometimes be dangerous. Also, we strongly recommend that you leave valuables in your hotel safe, as the crime rate is very high. Tourists generally do not need an HIV test. A test may be required, however, from citizens of the USA, Haiti and African nationals. For visas other than tourist visas, one must be free of infectious diseases.

✱Obwohl Homosexualität im Gesetz nicht erwähnt wird, und das Schutzalter bei 18 Jahren liegt, hat die Gesellschaft eine überwiegend negative Einstellung zu Schwulen. Es ist bekannt, daß die Polizei schwule Männer verfolgt.
Das Land leidet unter einen hoher Kriminalitätsrate. Zudem haben die gewalttätigen Auseinandersetzungen zwischen der Drogenmafia und dem Staat, denen auch zahlreiche Zivilisten zum Opfer gefallen sind, zu einer Verrohung der Gesellschaft geführt. Für die Schwulen und Lesben Kolumbiens bedeutet dies, daß sie häufig nicht nur verbalen Angriffen ausgesetzt sind.
Trotz dieser ungünstigen Voraussetzungen finden sich in vielen Städten, vor allem aber natürlich in der Hauptstadt Santafé de Bogota, zahlreiche schwule Lokale, die relativ sichere Orte in diesem unsicheren Land darstellen.

▲Bien que le code pénal ne fasse pas état de l'homosexualité et que la majorité sexuelle soit fixée à 18 ans, les Colombiens sont dans l'ensemble plutôt anti-homos. La police ne cesse de harceler les gays. Evitez donc les ennuis! La délinquance est un problème sérieux en Colombie. Laissez donc votre argent et vos objets de valeur à l'hôtel!
Les touristes ne sont pas obligés de se soumettre à un test de dépistage pour entrer en Colombie, à l'exception des personnes venant des Etats-Unis, de Haïti et d'Afrique. Pour obtenir un visa (à l'exception d'un visa touristique), il faut prouver que l'on n'est pas atteint d'une maladie contagieuse.

☆A pesar de que la homosexualidad no se menciona en la ley y la edad de consentimiento es de 18 años, la opinión pública es negativa ante los homosexuales. También se sabe que la policía molesta a los gays. El contacto con prostitutos es peligroso. Debido a que existe un alto porcentaje de criminalidad, es recomendable dejar los objetos de valor en el hotel. En general los turistas no necesitan someterse a una prueba de SIDA. Sin embargo, esta puede ser exigida a visitantes provenientes de los EEUU, Haiti y Africa. De igual forma todas las personas que solicitan un visado (excepto el visado de turista) tienen que demostrar que no non portadores de enfermedades contagiosas.

❖Sebbene l'omosessualità non sia menzionata dalla legge e l'età del consenso sia di 18 anni, la società in generale ha un atteggiamento negativo verso il problema. La polizia è conosciuta per la sua durezza verso i gay. I contatti con i prostituti maschi possono essere piuttosto pericolosi a causa dei furti. Vi raccomandiamo di lasciare i vostri soldi e gli oggetti di valore in albergo. Turisti non devono presentare il risultato di un HIV-test. Però è possibile che venga richiesto dai turisti proveniente dagli USA, da Haiti o dall'Africa. Chi richiede un visto (se non si tratta di un visto per turismo) deve provare di non soffrire di una malattia contagiosa.

Armenia ☎ 967

BARS

Amemonos Amor (B D GLM MA) 20-3 h
Carrera 18

Copa (B GLM MA)
Pasaje Comercial, Carrera 14

HOTELS

Maitamá (B F glm H NG)
Carrera 17, N°21-29 ☎ 44 34 00
Central location, 20 min to the airport. All rooms have telephone, frigde, priv. bath, color TV.

Zuldemayda (B glm H NG)
Calle 20, N° 15-38 ☎ 44 42 00

Barranquilla ☎ 958

BARS

Baco Bar (B d G)
Carrera 44 B, N°70-46

Del Prado Bar (AC B E g MA R)
Carrera 54, N°70-10 *(in Hotel Del Prado)*

CINEMAS

Cine Rex (r)
Carrera 45, N° 37-20 Centro ☎ 370 43

CRUISING

-Plaza Colón
-Plaza Bolivar and Paseo Bolivar

Cali ☎ 92

BARS

Bonston (B G MA)
Avenida Colombia, 8-58
Chapien (B G MA)
Avenida Colombia, 6-28
Charles (B G MA)
Carrera 3, 10-55
Golden (B G MA)
Calle 9, 3-36
Mandonna (B G MA)
Avenida Colombia, 8-74
Manhattan (B G S TV)
Calle 16, N°4-25
Pine Manor (B D g)
Calle 17 N, N°6-23
Tropical Video Bar (B G MA VS)
Avenida 8a Norte,
10-118 ☎ 661 00 58
Unicornio Club Campestre (B D G)
Avenida 4 A Oeste, N°6-30

DANCECLUBS

Ulises Club Discotec (B D g)
Avenida Colombia 8-47 ☎ 881 64 69

SHOWS

Romanos Club Discotec (B D g STV) Show Tue Thu-Sun
Carrera 3, N° 9-47 ☎ 880 40 65

SAUNAS/BATHS

Cali Club (G sa)
Avenida Colombia, 7-18
Romanos (B G sa)
Carrera 3a, 9-47 ☎ 880 40 65
Spartacus (G sa)
Carrera 23a, 8A-15

Cartagena ☎ 95

DANCECLUBS

Saffari's Club (B D G)
Calle del Quartel con Estanco del Aguardiente
Via Libre (B D G)
Calle de la Soledad 9-52

HOTELS

Montecarlo (B F H NG)
La Matuna, Centro ☎ 664 50 13

CRUISING

-Beach »Playa Boca Granda« (AYOR) (all day long)
-Carrera 2 (AYOR) (known as »Avenida San Martin«, Boca Grande)
-Beach close to Hotel Capilla del Mar, Boca Grande (AYOR)
-Beach in front of Hotel Don Blas, Boca Grande (AYOR)
-La boca Chica (AYOR) (1 hour boat ride from pier in centre of town)

Cúcuta ☎ 975

BARS

Baru (B g)
Avenida la 6-95
Cervezeria (B G)
Avenida 4, N°6-72

HOTELS

Amaruc (AC B F H NG)
Avenida 5, N°9-73 ☎ 72 76 25
Centrally located, 15min to the airport. All rooms with telephone, priv. bath and balcony.
Casablanca (AC B F H NG pi)
Avenida 6, N°14-55 ☎ 72 29 93
Centrally located, all rooms with telephone, priv. bath and balcony.

Medellin ☎ 94

BARS

Baru Bar (AC B D G R WE)
Carrera 50, N° 55A-05 *(Downtown, 2nd floor)* ☎ 512 15 10
Be careful. Surrounding area is unsafe at night.
Camerata. La (B E glm N)
Calle 51, N° 64C-27 ☎ 230 22 97
Contauros (B G YG)
Carrera 47 #54-27 *(2nd floor)*
Ceres (B G OG)
Calle 56, N° 49-69 *(Downtown)* ☎ 512 16 46
Be careful, surrounding area is unsafe at night.
Ebano & Marfil (! AC B CC E F GLM YG)
Calle 56, N°45-73 *(Downtown)* ☎ 254 50 74
Big old house turned into big bar.
Luchos II (B CC D G YG)
Calle 58, N° 47-18 *(Downtown)* ☎ 284 52 20
Mision. La (! B E G MA WE YG)
Calle 44, N° 73-53 ☎ 270 57 22
Tebes (AYOR B D G MA WE)
Calle 58, N° 53-101 *(Downtown, second floor)* ☎ 251 48 57
Be careful, surrounding are is unsafe at night, no sign at the door.

DANCECLUBS

Labias (B D G YG)
Cra. 52, N°57-55 ☎ 512 56 69
Plataforma (! AC D E G S YG) Thu-Sat
Calle 44, N°68-59 *(San Juan)*
Three floors. Popular.
Skala (B D glm MA VS WE)
Calle 44, N° 79-75 ☎ 250 48 88
Teatro (! AC B CC D E G WE)
Calle 44, N° 73-51 *3 bars, 1 disco, videos, no sign at doors.*
Toque de Queda (! AC B D E G MA VS WE YG) Tue-Sat
Calle 44, N° 73-51 ☎ 412 09 55

RESTAURANTS

La Isla (B g R)
Calle 56, N°49-101

SAUNAS/BATHS

Barbacoas (B G msg NU P sb sol VS)
Calle 57A, N° 46-47
Club Casa Loma (B E G msg NU P pi sa sb sol VS) Tue-Sun 13-22 h
Calle 50, N° 38-25 *(Downtown)* ☎ 217 24 51
Tabomar (b g sa sb sol VS) Tue-Sun 10-20 h
Carrera 45, 46-27 ☎ 251 54 32

GENERAL GROUPS

Movimento de Liberación Sexual
c/o León Zuleta, PO Box 65 25 ☎ 238 26 91
Publisher of »El Otro«.

CRUISING

-Carrera Junin between Calles 56 and 47

Neiva ☎ 988

BARS

Marion (B D g)
Calle 25, N°4-88

CRUISING

-Carrera 4 (between calles 8 and 9)

Pasto ☎ 927

DANCECLUBS

Peko's (B D G) 16-62,
Carrera 27

San Andrés ☎ 9811

HOTELS

Casablanca (glm h NG pi)
Avenida Costa Rica, N°1-40 ☎ 233 30
Isleño (gLM H)
Avenida Colombia, N°5-11 ☎ 239 90

CRUISING

-Along Avenida Colombia(from Hotel Isleño to Hotel Aquarium; (in the evening on the beach opposite Avenida Colombia)

Santa Marta ☎ 95

DANCECLUBS

40 Disco Bar (B D G)
Carrera 2a, 19-49

CRUISING

-Avenida Rodrigo Carrera 1C

Santafé de Bogotá ☎ 91

BARS

Anónimos (B G MA) Tue-Sun 18-1, Fri Sat -3 h
Avenida Caracas, 52-77
Bar Frances (B G MA)
Calle 86, 13 A 28 ☎ 217 52 89
Blues Bar (B G MA)
Calle 86, 13 A 30
Cabo'e (B G MA)
Carrera 7/Calle 49
Calles de San Francisco (B D g MA S) Mon-Sat 9-3 h
Carrera 10, 24-42
C.D. Bar (B G MA)
Avenida Caracas, 56-13
Figaro (B G MA) Calle 23, 6-07, int. 6
Muy Personal (B G MA)
Calle 58, 10-07
Paco's Club (B G MA)
Calle 57, 8-69, Local 114
Pantera Roja (B D GLM MA S) 18-? h
Calle 32, N°14-14 ☎ 288 51 40
Dance club, local music, reservation necessary.
Secretos y Compañia (B G MA)
Avenida Caracas 51-85
Te Odio Bar (B G) Wed-Sat 22-3 h
Calle 80, N° 13A-28 ☎ 618 33 37

DANCECLUBS

Babilonia Club (B D G)
Carrera 15, 72-48
Bianca (B D G)
Carrera 22, 67-27 ☎ 255 47 94
Boys Club (B D G MA S) Wed-Sat 22-4 h
Avenida Caracas N°37-68 *(Barrio Teusaquillo)* ☎ 28724 42
Champang Club (B D G)
Carrera 13, 33-82
Cruising Bar (B D G)
Carrera 7, 48-93 ☎ 245 53 37
Doble Via (B D G)
Carrera 9, 61-84
Enjalma y Loma (B D G) Fri-Sat 19-1, Sun 12-1 h
Via La Calera, km 4.5 ☎ 632 08 80
Estudio Uno (B D G)
Calle 100, 17-55, Sotano
Extaxis (B D G)
Calle 66, 13-41
Flag (B D G) Carrera 18/
Calle 82 ☎ 616 73 56
Giros Club (B D G)
Carrera 13, 35-31
Lujuria (B D G S VS) Thu-Sat 20.30-3 h
Transversal 18, N° 79-59 *(Centro Comercial »Los Heroes«, 1st floor)* ☎ 257 32 70
Playa Blanca (B D G)
Calle 57, 9-27 ☎ 235 72 25
Punto 59 (B D G MA) Tue-Sat 20-2, Sun 15-23 h
Carrera 13, N° 59-24, Interior 6 *(Centro Comercial »Acuario«)*
Saffari's Club (! B D G MA S) Thu-Sat 22-3 h
Avenidas Caracas N° 73-26 ☎ 217 82 62
Septima Estacion (B D F G) Fri-Sun
Via La Calera, km 7 ☎ 860 89 18
Seven (B D G)
Calle 66, 13-50, int 101
Tasca Santamaria (B D G)
Calle 23, 6-7, int. 101
Zona Franca (! AC B CC D E G MG S W WE YG) Fri Sat 20-0.30 h
Calle 74, 15-51 ☎ 235 31 48

RESTAURANTS

San Antonio (AC B CC F G MG OS s WE YG) Restaurant 12-18, Disco 19-0.30 h
Via La Calera, km 6 *(Near Peaje de Patios)*

SEX SHOPS/BLUE MOVIES

Centro Eros Videos (glm VS)
Carrera 9, N° 18-51, Local 113-114 ☎ 281 88 11
Mixed sex shop with gay/bi/hetero and tanssexual videos!
Chapinero Eros Videos (glm VS)
Carrera 13, N° 64-67, Local 204 ☎ 217 28 45
Mixed sex shop with gay/bi/hetero and transsexual videos!
Ibiza Club (G VS) 12-23 h
Calle 66, 15-50 ☎ 255 38 38
Monte Carlo Club (G VS)
Calle 66, 10-81
Unicentro Sex Video (glm VS)
Avenida 15, N° 119A-03, Local 230 ☎ 215 53 57
Mixed sex shop with gay/bi/hetero and transsexual videos!
Vea Videos (G VS)
Carrera 13, 64-67 ☎ 217 27 40

CINEMAS

Dorado. El 13-21 h
Calle 17, N°4-60
Teatro Esmeralda 11-21 h
Carrera 7, N°22-20

SAUNAS/BATHS

Baltimore (b CC f g msg sa sb sol VS wh WO) 0-24 h
Calle 33/Carrera 15-17 *In Hotel Maria Isabel* ☎ 245 26 50
Reduced student rates. Recommended!

Monroe's Club (B G sa sb VS wh WO) Sun-Tue 14-22, Wed Thu -24, Fri Sat -1 h
Carrera 16A No. 79-24, El Lago ☎ 318 07 31
30% reduction for students.

Turcos 82 (G sa sb)
Carrera 13, 24-70

Turcos 82 (B f G sa sb) 0-24 h
Calle 82, N°15-73 ☎ 256 6136

Ulises (B DR f G MA sa sb VS WO) 0-24 h
Carrera 15, N°32-26 ☎ 232 58 09

HOTELS

Spartacus (B G H)
Avenida Caracas 44-34 ☎ 232 27 95

GENERAL GROUPS

Proyecto Lambda
☎ 287 05 01
Gay group

HEALTH GROUPS

Fundacion Eudes
Casa »El Tonel«, Calle 85, N° 35-28 ☎ 256 56 29
Information about AIDS, and help for HIV+ and People With AIDS (PWA).

Servicio de Salud de Bogotá 7-12 h
Carrera 23, N° 22A-26 ☎ 268 10 64
V.D. treatment.

Costa Rica

Central America

Initials: CR

Time: GMT -6

☎ Country Code / Access Code: 506 (no area codes) / 00

Language: Spanish

Area: 51,100 km² / 19,730 sq mi.

Currency: 1 Costa-Rica-Colón (¢) =100 Céntimos

Population: 3,604,642

Capital: San José

Religions: 89% Roman Catholic

Climate: Tropical climate. The dry season lasts from December to April, the rainy season from May to November.

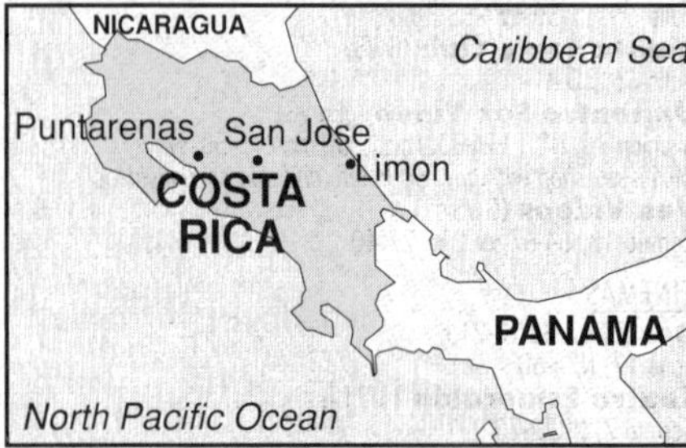

Homosexuality is legal from the age of 18. Despite the strong influence of the Catholic church, society largely tolerates gays.

Das schwule Schutzalter liegt bei 18 Jahren. Trotz des nicht geringen Einflusses der katholischen Kirche toleriert die Gesellschaft Homosexualität weitestgehend.

Au Costa Rica, la majorité sexuelle est fixée à 18 ans pour les homosexuels. Malgré le poids de l'Eglise catholique dans le pays, les gens sont, généralement, plutôt tolérants envers les homosexuels.

La edad de consentimiento homosexual es de 18 años. A pesar de la fuerte influencia de la religión católica, la población tolera de una u otra forma la homosexualidad.

L'età legale è di 18 anni. Malgrado il forte influsso della chiesa cattolica la società tollera ampiamente l'omosessualità.

NATIONAL GAY INFO

Asociación de Lucha por el Respecto a la Diversidad Sexual
PO Box 1766-2050, San Jose ☎ 250 94 81

Fundación Vida
Calle 1 y 3, Avenida 1, San José
☎ 221 58 19

Gente 10
PO Box 1910-2100, San Jose
Bimonthly magazine.

Triangulo Rosa
PO Box 366-2200, Coronado
☎ 234 24 11

Limon

SWIMMING

-Playa Bonita (4 km north of Limon. Take bus from Calle 4, Avenida 4 in Limon)
-Playa Cahuita (a national park 43 km south of Limon, reached by bus or taxi. Limited accomodations in Cahuita. Beach has one of the finest coral reefs outside of Australia.)

CRUISING

-Vargas Park
-Avenida 2 and Calle 1 (facing the sea)

Nosara

GUEST HOUSES

Roger Harrison (G H)
PO Box 9-5233 *(Nicoya, Guanacaste)* ☎ 680 07 49

Puntarenas

CRUISING

-Paseo de Los Turistas (next to the beach)

Quepos ✉ 6350

BARS

Cockatoo (B GLM MA)
Carretera al Parcque Nacional *(on rooftop of a restaurant)*

DANCECLUBS

Maracas Disco (B D glm)
(aside of the former harbour)
☎ 777 07 07

RESTAURANTS

Barba Roja (B F glm) *(besides Hotel Casa Blanca)*
American style, steaks and seafood.
Café Milagro (B f glm)
Downtown Quepos *(across from Hotel Casa Blanca)* ☎ 777 17 07
Dulú (B F GLM)
Carretera al Parque Nacional ☎ 777 12 97 *Costarican cuisine.*
El Gran Escape (B G glm)
Downtown Quepos ☎ 777 03 95
Costarican cuisine, fresh seafood, tex-mex.

HOTELS

El Colibri Aparthotel (glm H)
Carretera al Parque Nacional ☎ 777 04 32 Fax: 777 04 32
Hotel California (glm H) Carretera al Parque Nacional, Entrada „El Salto" ☎ 777 12 34 Fax: 777 10 62
Email: hotelcal@sol.racsa.co.cr Homepage: www.icr.co.cr/hcalifornia
Hotel Casa Blanca (bf CC GLM H OS pi)
Carretera Manuel Antonio, Apartado 194 ✉6350 *(Manuel Antonio)* ☎ 777 02 53
Guest house overlooking the pacific ocean near Manuel Antonia National Park. 4 rooms with bath, 2 suites and 2 apartments (4-5 persons). 20 minutes walking distance to nude/gay beach. Rates rooms US$ 65, suites 90, apartments 140,
Hotel Restaurant Plinio (F glm H)
Carretera al Parque Nacional ☎ 777 00 55 Fax: 777 05 58
Hotel and restaurant.
Makanda By The Sea (glm H)
Carretera al Parque Nacional, entrada „La Mariposa" ☎ 777 04 42 Fax: 777 10 32
Email: makanda@sol.racsa.co.cr Homepage: www.makanda.com
Plantación. La (bf CC G H NU pi)
PO Box 94-6350 (Manuel Antonio) ☎ 777 13 32 Fax: 777 04 32
Email: quepos@bigrubys.com. Homepage: www.bigrubys.com
Please call or see our website for details on special prices. Restaurant on site. Nude sunbathing.

San José ✉ 2050

BARS

Bambu (B GLM MA)
Avenida Central *(San Pedro; next to the bank on the left side from San José) Good on Thu.*
Cantábrico. El (B f GLM MA)
Avenida 6 *(between Calle Central and 2)* ☎ 233 57 97
Best early evening.
Cuartel de la Boca del Monte (B F glm WE YG)
Avenida 1 *(between Calle 21 & Calle 23)*
Bar and restaurant. Very popular.
El Pucho (B g) daily 18-? h
Avenida 8, calle 11 ☎ 223 53 43
Unicornio (B GLM MA)
Avenida 8 *(between Calle 3 & 5)* ☎ 221 55 52

CAFES

Monte Carlo (B F g r) 0-24 h
Avenida 4/Calle 2 *Gay especially late on WE.*

DANCECLUBS

Amnesia (B D G) Fri-Sat 21.30-3 h, shows 22.30 h
Avenida 2/Calle 8 ☎ 256 66 49
Avispa. La (B D GLM MA YG) 20-2/?, Sun 17-? h, Mon closed
Calle 1 *(between Avenida 8 and Avenida 10)* ☎ 223 53 43
No sign. Downhill from Cucharones on left side of the street. Best on Sun (18- h) and Tue (21- h).

BoysBar (B D G SNU) Fri Sat 22-? h
Complejo Convoy *(Antiguo Kilates, Tibás)*
Cucharones. Los (B D Glm MA YG) Wed-Sun 19-? h
Avenida 6 *(between Calle Central and Calle 1, Across the street from the Chinese restaurant).* ☎ 233 57 97
Déjà-Vu (! AC B D GLM MA S YG) Wed-Sat 21-?, Sun 18-24 h, Mon Tue closed.
Calle 2 *(between Avenida 14 and 16)* ☎ 223 37 58
Best on Fri, Sat (22- h)

RESTAURANTS

Bchinche (B f glm) Mon-Sat -24 h, closed Sun
Avenida 10/Calle 11 *(south of Teatro Lucho Barahona)*
Snackbar, popular Thu-Sat.
Café Mundo (! A AC B CC F g MA OS YG) Mon-Fri 11.00 to 23.00 h, Sat 5.00-24.00 h, Sun closed
Avenida 9, Calle 15, Casa1372 *Locatot in the historic district of Amón-Otoyu* ☎ 222 61 90

SAUNAS/BATHS

Decameron (b G MA sa) 12-24 h
Avenida 10 *(between Calle 5 and 7)*
Exóticas (AC b DR f G OS sa VS WO) Mon-Thu 14-22, Fri Sat - 23, Sun 13-21 h
Avenida Segunda, 1762 *(between Calles 17 and 19)*
Jano (G MA sa)
Calle 1 *(between Avenida 4 and 6)*
Paris Sauna (b DR G msg sa sb VS WO) Tu.- Th. 12:00 - 02:00 h, Fr & Sa. 12:00 -04:00h
Calle 7, Avenida 7 *100 north of the park Morazano, 100 from Holiday Inn.* ☎ 222 2737
Entrance fee from 1.200.-1.600,

EDUCATION SERVICES

ILISA Instituto de Idiomas (CC f glm MA NG OS) Mon-Fri 7.30-16.30 h
☎ 225 24 95 Fax: 225 46 65
Spanish language school located in San Pedroin the suburb of San José. Call for exact location.

TRAVEL & TRANSPORT

Tiquicia Travel (glm)
200 oeste y 100 sur de La Controlaria General *Sabana Sur* ☎ 296 35 78 Fax: 196 35 78
E-mail tiquicia@sol.racsa.co.cr.
Homepage http://www.internetcr.com/tiquica

HOTELS

Ambiance. L' (F g H)
Calle 13 BO Box 1040 ✉2050 *(San Pedro)* ☎ 222 67 02 Fax: 223 04 81
Small hotel in renovated house. Gays are welcome. Also Restaurant.
Colours Costa Rica (b bf CC d F GLM H N MA pi wh)
8-21 h Fax: 296 15 97 Email: colours@sol.racsa.co.cr
Homepage: www.colours.ne
Boulevard Rohmoser *(Northwest corner of the triangle)* ☎ 232 35 04
10 minutes from downtown. English speaking staff. Rates US$ 59-109 (bf incl.) It´s also a bar & reestaurant (La Esquina) as well as a tour service for entire country.
Hotel Kekoldi (bf CC glm H)
Avenida 9, Calle 3 Bis, PO Box 12150-1000 ☎ 223 32 44
Fax: 257 54 76
Email: kekoldi@sol.vacsa.co.cr. Homepage: http://www.kekoldi.com.
14 rooms with shower/WC, telephone, safe. Rates single US$ 30-32, double 42-45, triple 55-59 plus tax 16,39%. Breakfast incl.

Villa El Palmito (G H)
Apto 1288-1250 Escazù *(near San Josè)* ☎ 289 53 12
10 minutes from downtown San José and 20 min from the airport.

GUEST HOUSES

Joluva Guest House (bf CC GLM H MA)
Calle 3bis, 936 *(beetween Avenida 9 and 11)* ☎ 223 79 61
Fax: 257 76 68 Email: joluva@sol.racsa.co.cr
Homepage: www.hotels.co.dr/joluva.htm
Close to gay scene. 3 double, 5 single rooms, with satellite TV and partly shower/WC.

CRUISING

The police regularly carry out raids at the following cruising areas!
-Parque Central, Calle Central and Avenida Segunda (especially at the Café Soda Palace and Porla Café)
-Park La Sabana (ayor) (popular) (between airport and city; in the southwest, next to Municipal Stadium)
-Plaza de la Cultura (popular) (in front of the National Theater and at the Plaza and also in the basement; between Calle 3 and 5; busy in the late afternoon and evening, late hours can be dangerous)
-El Pueblo (day and night)
-Parque Nacional (Avenidas 1 and 3, Calles 15 and 19; (AYOR) - at night
-Central Avenue (between Calle 3rd and 11th)

San Ramón ✉ 4250

GUEST HOUSES

Hacienda Los Alpes (AC bf G H MG NU OG OS) Nov-Aug
PO Box 231 ✉4250 *(17 km from San Ramón, to reach by taxi or own 4-wheel)* ☎ 284 62 91 Fax: 445 57 18 (post office)
Minimum stay 1 week, reservation needed. Rates per person DM 100, 3rd person DM 50.

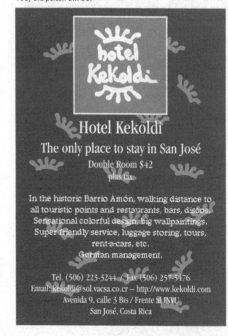

Croatia

Hrvatska

Southeastern Europe

Initials: HR

Time: GMT +1

☎ Country Code / Access Code: 385 / 00

Language: Serbo-Croatian

Area: 56,538 km² / 21,829 sq mi.

Currency: 1 Kuna (HRK) = 100 Lipa

Population: 4,4671,584

Capital: Zagreb

Religions: 76% Catholic, 11% Orthodox, 1% Slavic Muslim

Climate: Mediterranean and continental climate. The continental climate is predominant with hot summers and cold winters. Along the coast, winters are mild and summers dry.

● The age of consent in Croatia is 14 for heterosexual and 18 for homosexual activity.

✱ In Kroatien liegt das Schutzalter für Sex zwischen Mann und Frau bei 14, für gleichgeschlechtlichen Sex bei 18 Jahren.

▲ En Croatie, la majorité sexuelle est fixée à 14 ans pour les hétérosexuels et à 18 ans pour les homosexuels.

☆ La edad de consentimiento para heterosexuales es de 14 años, para el sexo entre homosexuales es de 18 años.

❖ In Croazia l'età legale per avere rapporti eterosessuali è di 14 anni mentre per rapporti omosessuali bisogna aver compiuto 18 anni.

SWIMMING

-Lokrum Island (MA NU) (Boat from the old harbour of Dubrovnik. At the end of nudist beach and the rocks on the south side. Action in woods behind.)

Hvar ☎ 021

SWIMMING

-190Sveti Jerolim (Island-MA NU) Boat from the harbour of Hvar (city). South side of the island. Action in the bushes.

Kanegra ☎ 052

SWIMMING

-Beach near the Slovenian border on the southern coast of the Bay of Piran (MA NU WE) (Roads from Umag or Savudrija HR or Prtoroz in Slovenia. Action in the woods behind the nudist beach.

Krk ☎ 051

SWIMMING

-Njivice (MA NU) (trough village and auto-camp, enter forest by doors in fence, gay area 10-15 min walk along sea shore)
-Near camping sites in Baška (Bunculuka) and Krk (Politin)

Osijek ☎ 033

BARS

Copacabana On the bank of the Drava River
Well-known and busy.

CRUISING

-Behind the Hotel Osijek
-City Park on the Drava.

Porec ☎ 052

SWIMMING

-Cervar (G NU) (along the coast in the direction of Autocamp Ulika)
-Bijela uvala (G NU) (4 km south of Porec, direction of Funtana, between Autocamp Bijela Uvala and Funtana)

CRUISING

-Park Naftaplin (evenings)

Rab ☎ 051

CAFÉS

Sandra (B g YG)
(centre of town)

SWIMMING

-Nudist beach of the city of Rab (G MA NU) (by boat from the harbour. At the end of the nudist beach. Action in the woods.

Rijeka ☎ 051

CAFÉS

Kvorum (B g S YG) 20-4 h
(Bus 32 to Voloske)
Python (B g MA) 18-2 h
Fiorello la Guardia *(at Guvernerova palača)*

SWIMMING

-Bunker (NU) (take bus 32 to Preluka, then walk back through the big curve, turn down to sea-shore)
-Medveja (NU YG) (25 km from Rijeka by bus 32, nude section outside the village)

CRUISING

-Zabica (near main bus terminal and Kapucinska church)

Rovinj ☎ 052

SWIMMING

-Monsena (G NU) (at the end of autocamp, direction of Lim fjord)
-Crveni otok (NU) MA (In the center, near the temple)
-Polari Camping (g NU YG)

CRUISING

-near Hotel Park (evenings)

Split ☎ 021

HEALTH GROUPS

Teleapel Split 19-7 h
☎ 36 56 66

SWIMMING

-Šetalište Bačvice (city center, late evening and night)
-Duilovo (take bus going there, then walk by the sea to the rocky end)
-Medena (G NU) (30 km north of Split, rocky beach under pine forest in the northern part of Medena hotel complex)

CRUISING

-Main railway station
-City Park (near monument)
-Main Railway Station
-Main Bus Station
-Park & coast behind the Main Bus Station (active)

Umag ☎ 052

SWIMMING

-Crveni vrh (G NU) (direction of Autocamp Kanegra)

Vrsar ☎ 052

SWIMMING

-Beach between Belvedere and Autocamp Petalon

Zagreb ☎ 01

BARS

Bad Boy Club (A AC B CC D DR G MA JSNU VS YG) 17-4 h
Ksaver 210 ✉10 000 *(Center)* ☎ 467 75 01

CAFÉS

KIC (A B f glm MA NG YG)
Preradoviceva *(Café on 1st floor)*
Teatar (B f glm MA NG OS) 10-23
Nikole Tesle *(in passage across from Croatia Airlines)*

DANCECLUBS

Aquarius (AC B D glm NG YG) Gayest on Sat 22-? h
(Recreational center Jarun)

SEX SHOPS/BLUE MOVIES

Eros (g)
Obrtnički prolaz 1a
Pigalle (g)
Gajeva 21

SAUNAS/BATHS

Kupališta Diana (B g MA msg NG NU pi sa sb) Gayest Tue Fri 12-19, Sat 10-15 h
Ilica 8 *(In the passage, last building)*
Ask for sauna. Action possible.

HEALTH GROUPS

Referalni centar za AIDS 12-15 h
Mirogojska 8 ☎ 42 56 31

SWIMMING

-Jarun lake (G MA NU) (Southern part of the eastern peninsula. Otok mladosti. From noon on)

CRUISING

-Trg bana Jelacica (underpass near Preska Street, exit Trg Republike)
-Glavni kolodvor (Main Railway Station)
-Zapadni kolodvor (West Railway Station late in afternoon)
-Glavni kolodvor (shopping center Importanne Maksimir, evenings)
-Branimirova (OG) (near main bus terminal)
-Studentski centar (YG) (Savska 25. Building inside courtyard, restaurant and cinema, afternoon and early evening)
-Botanicki vrt (g MA R) (-20 h at Mihanoviceva) Mihanoviceva Street. Mostly in the afternoon.
-Maksimir Park (g MA) (entrance from Bukovacka/Petrova Street. Western edge of the woods, late afternoon & evening)
-Trg kralja Kresimira IV (G) (south-western part of the park at night)
-Tomisbrov trg (in front of station)
-Ribnjak Park

Cyprus

Kypros • Kibris

Eastern Mediterranean Sea

Initials: CY

Time: GMT +2

☎ Country Code / Access Code: 357 (south) and 90 (north) / 00

Language: Greek, Turkish, English

Area: 9,251 km² / 3,572 sq mi.

Currency: 1 Cypriot Pound (Z =100 Cents (south part). 1 Turkish Lira (TL) =100 Kurus

Population: 748,982

Capital: Nicosia (south part), Lefkosa (north part)

Religions: 78% Greek Orthodox, 18% Muslim

Climate: Moderate, mediterranean climate with hot, dry summers and cool, wet winters.

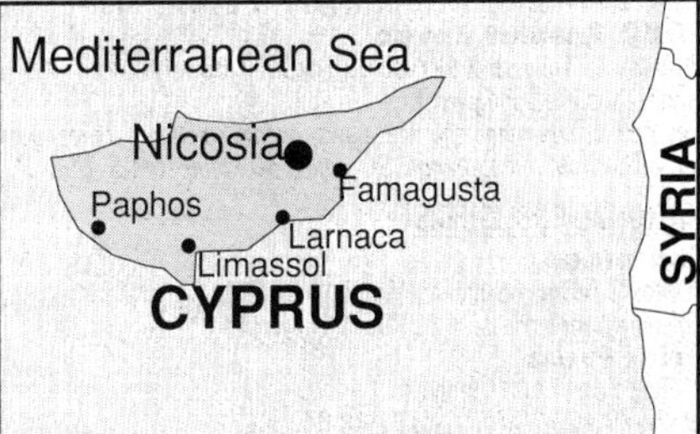

● From international pressure in May 1998 the notorious paragraph 171 has been abolished, which totally forbid homosexual acts. Although the old paragraph has been barely applied over the past few years it is to be feared with new regulations or agreements that there will be a worsening of the situation for homosexuals in Cyprus including the setting the age of sexual consent for homosexuals at 18 and the forbidding of personal classified ads for homosexuals.

✱ Zwar wurde auf internationalen Druck im Mai 1998 der berüchtigte Paragraph 171 abgeschafft, welcher ein Totalverbot homosexueller Handlungen beinhaltet hatte. Während der alte Paragraph in den letzten Jahren kaum noch angewandt wurde, ist zu befürchten, daß neue Bestimmungen eine Verschlechterung der Lage der Homosexuellen auf Zypern mit sich bringen könnte. Dazu gehört die Erhöhung des Schutzalters für Homosexuelle auf 18 Jahre sowie die Einführung eines sogenannten Werbeverbots für Homosexualität, welches unter anderem auch die Schaltung von Kontaktanzeigen verbietet.

▲ Sous la pression internationale, Chypre a aboli en mai 1998 son célèbre paragraphe 171 qui interdisait les rapports homosexuels. Même si ce paragraphe n'avait été appliqué que rarement ces dernières années, il est à craindre que de nouvelles législations (par exemple une loi fixant l'âge de la majorité sexuelle des gays à 18 ans ou l'interdiction pour les homosexuels de faire paraître des annonces de rencontre) détériorent le statut des homosexuels dans l'île.

☆ El artículo 171 que prohiba terminantemente las relaciones homosexuales, fue abolido en mayo de 1998 por presión internacional. Sin embargo, con las nuevas regulaciones legislativas no se espera ninguna mejora para los gays del país. Esto se hace notar por la edad de consentimiento que está estipulada ahora en 18 años y la llamada „prohibición de publicidad homosexual", que por ejemplo no permite poner anuncios de contacto.

❖ Dopo la pressione internazionale nel maggio 1998 è stato abilito il famigerato paragrafo 171 che vietatava tutti gli atti omosessuali. Mentre negli ultimi anni questo vecchio paragrafo era stato applicato solo raramente, si può aspettare che nuovi regolamenti peggioreranno la situazione dei gay del Cipro. A ciò appartiene l'aumento dell'età legale per atti omosessualità, qui incluso tra l'altro il divieto di mettere inserzioni d'annunci d'incontro.

BARS

Alaloum Disco Bar (AC B D glm) 21-03:00h
Loutron No. 1, Old Port *(in old town)* ☎ 05/369 726

Famagusta (north part) ☎ 392

SWIMMING

-Bedis Beach (between town and ruins; behind the bushes)

CRUISING

-City Walls (on top of main entrance to city. Climb up through the ramp way)
-Road from Port Gate toward Petek Pastanesi

Kyrenia (north part) ☎ 392

SWIMMING

-Kale arkasi (swimming behind the castle)

CRUISING

-Old Harbour Pier (Towards lighthouse. Pick up along the pier)

Larnaca (south part) ☎ 04

CRUISING

-Phinikoudes Beach (day and night)

Limassol (south part) ☎ 05

BARS

J & A-Jacarè Bar (B MA NG STV) 21-1 h
Popiland, 67, Georgiou A'Yermasoyia *(opposite Park Beach Hotel. Entrance at rear)* ☎ 32 06 35
Recommended.

SAUNAS/BATHS

Spartacus Steam Bath (G MA msg sa sb) 14-20 h
Lountrou Street 3 *(near Old Port)* ☎ 35 33 85

SWIMMING

-Dhassoudi Beach (through main entrance, then to the far end)
-Pissouri Beach (NU) (5 km west of Evdimou)
-White Rocks (between »Govenor's Beach« and »Ayios Georgios Alamanos«- monastery)
-Beach at Amathous hotel (500m from the hotel behind a stone wall, for 200 m)

CRUISING

-Anexartisias Street (at night)
-Hagios Andreas Street (only during hours when shops are open)
-Makarios Avenue (SWC g)
-Municipal gardens (all day until sunset)
-Sea front-Molos (next to the Old Port; at night)
-Dhassoudi Beach (at day)
-Behind the Central Bus Station (daytime)

Nicosia/Lefkosa ☎ 02/392

BARS

Bastione (B F NG s)
6 Athina Avenue *(near „green line" in old town)* ☎ 43 31 01
Busy late.

Edvokia Bar (B f MA NG) 30,
Athena Avenue *(Old town near Famagusta gate)*
Best place to start.

GENERAL GROUPS

Gay Liberation Movement of Cyprus
☎ 44 33 46

CRUISING

South part:
-Eleftherias Square and Park bolow, also toilets
-Garden Café (opposite museum)
-Constantinos Palelogos Avenue (from Eleftheria Square to Ochi Square)
-Municipal parking place and toilets (close to the Central Post Office 16-19, 22-? h)
North part:
-Kugulu Park (next to Kyrenia Gate)
-Arasta (Shopping Centre towards the cathedral and market place, late at night)

Paphos (south part) ☎ 06

CRUISING

-Apostolus Pavlos Avenue(between „day and night newspaper shop" and castle.)

Czech Republic

Česká republika

Central Europe

Initials: CZE

Time: GMT +1

☎ Country Code / Access Code: 420 / 00

Language: Czech

Area: 78,864 km² / 30,449 sq mi.

Currency: 1 koruna (Kč) = 100 Haléřu

Population: 10,286,470

Capital: Praha

Religions: 30% Catholic; 8% Protestant

Climate: Moderate climate. Summers are cool, winters cold, cloudy and humid.

● Homosexuality is legal. The age of consent is fifteen.

✱ Homosexualität ist legal. Die gesetzliche Schutzaltersgrenze liegt bei 15 Jahren.

▲ En République Tchèque, l'homosexualité n'est pas un délit. La majorité sexuelle y est fixée à 15 ans.

☆ La homosexualidad es legal. La edad de consentimiento es de quince años.

❖ L'omosessualità è legale. L'età del consenso è di 15 anni.

NATIONAL GAY INFO

Amigo
PO Box 60 ✉18021 Praha 0 ☎ & Fax: (02) 684 65 48.
E-mail amigo@czn.cz
Homepage http://www.amigo.cz
Gay contact magazine and gay guide to the Czech republic. Some information in German and English. Mail order.

Sdruzení organizací homosexuálních obcanú v ČR (SOHO)
Senovážné námestí 2 ✉110 00 Praha 1 ☎ 2-242 57 133

SOHO Absolut Revue
Husitská 7, Praha ☎ 2-627 83 48 Fax: 627 83 49
Email: chodora@pha.pvtnet.cz
Gay and lesbian magazine with news, events calendar, stories, poetry, AIDS-information, photos. 50 pages, 40 korun (DM 5, US$ 3).

NATIONAL PUBLISHERS

Fox press
PO Box 3 ✉360 05 Karlovy Vary 5
Calendars, magazines.

Princ Press
PO Box 73 ✉14801 Praha 414
☎ 2-679 107 70 Fax: 2-679 118 04
Publisher of Princ, Princ Kontakt and Hard Boy. Also videos.

NATIONAL COMPANIES

GIC Distribuce
Krakovská 3, Praha 3
☎ 2-264 408 Fax: 2-264 408
Distribution company. Publications, magazines, calenders, videotapes, posters, post cards, photos, toys etc.

Brno ☎ 05

BARS

H 46 (B GLM) daily 18-5 h
Hybeova 46

Barclub „H46" (B f GLM MA N p r) 18-4 h daily
Hybesova 46 ✉602 00 *Tram No. 1, 2 Station „Hybešovc" 10 min form main railway station in direction fair area* ☎ 412 110 51
friendly, reasonable prices

Marcus Bar (AC B CC GLM MA p VS) daily 15-24 h
Uvoz 24 ✉602 00 *(in the city centre)* ☎ 432 454 04
it´s also a gay sex shop with darkroom and video shows

Philadelphia Club (B G MA) 16-1h daily
Milady Horákové 1a ☎ 257 77 30

DANCECLUBS

Diskotéka u Richarda (AC B D F GLM MA VS) Fri, Sat 20-10 h
Luzpbs 30 ✉613 00 ☎ 572 937

Gibon Club (B D DR G) Mon-Sat 17-1/? h
Pekaska 38
also Bar

Kings (B D DR G S) Wed-Sat 21-? h
PekaRská 7
Sklípek u Richarda (B D GLM MA p) Fri, Sat 20-6 h
Lužova 29 ✉613 00 ☎ 57 29 37

GENERAL GROUPS

Lambda-men
PO Box 18 ✉602 00 ☎ 57 29 37
Stud
Roubalova 5 ✉60200 ☎ 43 21 58 45

HEALTH GROUPS

Mestská hygienická stanice Mon 16-18 h
Sypka 25 ☎ 45 21 21 74

CRUISING

-Ceská ulice
-Park in front of New Opera House

Cheb ☎ 0166

BARS

Gay Bar Bert (B G) Thu-Sun 18 h - open end
Evropská 30 ✉35002 ☎ 336 88

Chomutov ☎ 0396

GENERAL GROUPS

Gay Klub „Adam"
c/o Nadace Sokrates Most, Budovatelu 1988 434 11 Most ✉43000

České Budějovice

GENERAL GROUPS

Jivak (B D GLM) 2nd & 4th Sat 20.30-4 h
Boženy Nemcové 2 ✉37000
Lambda České Budějovice
PO Box 33, 389 01 Vodňany ✉37000 ☎ 382 057

HEALTH GROUPS

Stop AIDS Mon-Fri 7-8, Thu 16-18 h
☎ 323 08

CRUISING

-Main railway station

Hoštka ☎ 0411

GUEST HOUSES

Penzion U Vikomta/Jaroslav Pilnaj - Gay Club (B d F G H LJ NU P sa SNU)
Pod nádražím 281 ✉41172 ☎ 814 171 Fax: 814 171
Accomodations, restaurant, café, sauna, pool, disco, drag shows on Sat. Recommended for WE & holidays. 50 km north-west of Prague.

Liberec ☎ 048

HEALTH GROUPS

AIDS Stop
✉46000 ☎ 327 223

Litvínov ☎ 035

GENERAL GROUPS

Gay Klub »4« Litvínov
Meziborská 856 ✉43600 ☎ 530 07

Most ☎ 035

GENERAL GROUPS

Nadace Sokrates 434 11 ☎ 243 31

Olomouc ☎ 068

BARS

Retrobar Diva (B glm) Mon-Fri 18-?, Sat Sun 19-? h
Pavelčákova 17 ✉77100

SEX SHOPS/BLUE MOVIES

City Fox (b G) Mon-Sat 10-20 h
Sokolská ☎ 523 39 75

GENERAL GROUPS

Ucho Olomouc
PO Box 54, 772 54 ✉77100 ☎ 641-20 22 59

Ostrava ☎ 069

BARS

G-Centrum (B F G H sa) daily 16-? h
Frdecká 62
Snackbar Fiesta (B d f g) 13-?, Sun closed
Tr. 28 Ríjna 59 ✉70200 *near Hotel Palace* ☎ 615 86 59

GENERAL GROUPS

Klub Lambda
PO Box 377 ✉730 77 ☎ 662 61 18 (men)

HEALTH GROUPS

Linka duvěry zdraaví Nonstop.
☎ 23 43 59

SWIMMING

-Lazne Hulvaky (Wed, Fri, take tram 4, 8, or 9 from the city) 681 79 81

CRUISING

-In front of Hotel Ostrava (Imperial) (at New Church, námesti Národni)

Pardubice ☎ 040

GENERAL GROUPS

Lega Pardubice
PO Box D 6 530 02 Pardubice 1 ✉53000 ☎ 516 052
Publisher of Gay press.

Plzeň ☎ 019

BARS

U Mušketyru (B g) Tue-Thu 12-24, Fri -3, Sat 17-3, Sun -24 h
Havlíčkova 26 ✉30000

GENERAL GROUPS

Patrick Club PlzeňP
olitickych vězňu 31, 320 02 ✉30100 ☎ 27 12 97
(evenings)

HEALTH GROUPS

Help Line Tue 14-16 h
☎ 22 43 25

CRUISING

-Main railway station

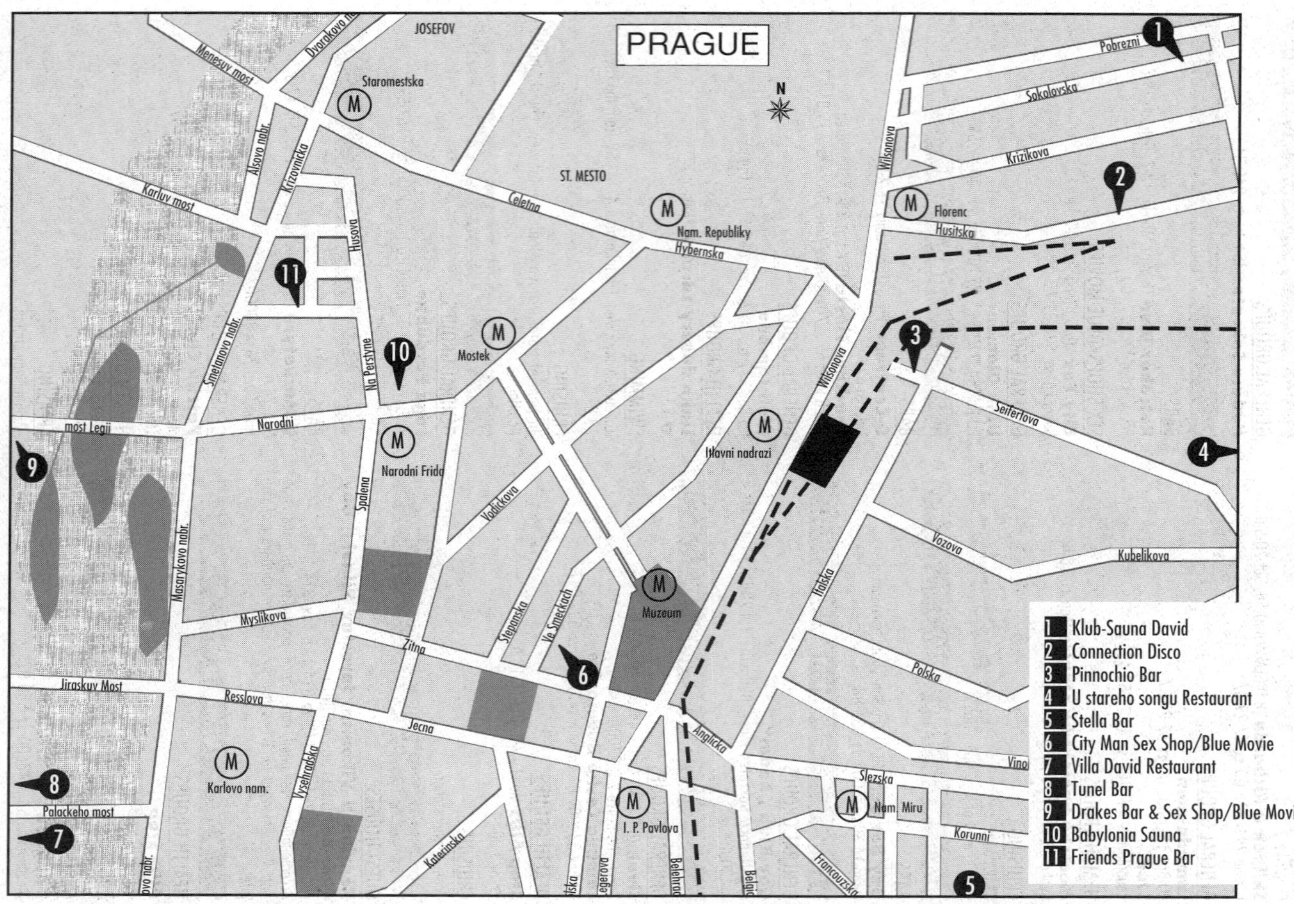
PRAGUE
N
1 Klub-Sauna David
2 Connection Disco
3 Pinnochio Bar
4 U stareho songu Restaurant
5 Stella Bar
6 City Man Sex Shop/Blue Movie
7 Villa David Restaurant
8 Tunel Bar
9 Drakes Bar & Sex Shop/Blue Movie
10 Babylonia Sauna
11 Friends Prague Bar
JOSEFOV
Staromestska
Menesuv most
Dvorakovo n
Alsovo nabr.
Krizovnicka
Karluv most
Husova
ST. MESTO
Celetna
Nam. Republiky
Hybernska
Pobrezni
Sokolovska
Krizikova
Wilsonova
Florenc
Husitska
Smetanovo nabr.
Na Perstyne
Mostek
most Legii
Narodni
Narodni Frida
Hlavni nadrazi
Seifertova
Spalena
Vodickova
Vozova
Kubelikova
Masarykovo nabr.
Myslikova
Stepanska
Ve Smeckach
Muzeum
Italska
Zitna
Polska
Jiraskuv Most
Resslova
Jecna
Anglicka
Vino
Slezska
Karlovo nam.
Palackeho most
Vysehradska
I. P. Pavlova
Nam. Miru
Korunni
Katerinska
Legerova
Belehrad
Belgic
Francouzska

Praha ☎ 02

● Prague castle Hradcany, seen from Charles' Bridge at night, is an unforgettable sight. But with the Town Hall in the old part of the city, and the National Gallery and Hotel Europa on Wenceslas Square (the latter being a perfect example of Art Nouveau), Prague offers one breathtaking sight after another. Here you will find one of the most unspoilt historic city centers in Central Europe. While other eastern and central European cities are finding the new economic climate difficult, Prague is booming. This, coupled with the liberal attitude of the Czech people and Prague's central location, have helped encourage the development of a considerable gay scene. The best way to get around Prague is by metro (fast, cheap and reliable), with trams and buses completing the public transport system. In light of the hordes of tourists who visit Prague, spring or fall are probably better times to travel than summer.

✱ Der Hradčany bei Nacht von der Karlsbrücke aus gesehen: ein Anblick, den kaum ein Tourist so schnell vergißt. Neben dem Altstädter Rathaus, der Nationalgalerie und der Jugendstil-Perle Hotel Europa am Wenzelsplatz bietet die Innenstadt geradezu einen atemberaubenden Anblick nach dem anderen: Prag ist sicherlich eines der schönsten historischen Stadtensembles Mitteleuropas.
Während in anderen Großstädten des östlichen Mitteleuropas die Entwicklung nur schwer vorankommt, »boomt« Prag. Dies und die relativ liberale Einstellung der Tschechen, wie auch die günstige Lage im Herzen Europas haben sich hier eine beachtliche schwule Szene entwickeln lassen.
Für's Vorankommen in der Stadt ist die Metro (schnell, billig und zuverlässig) zu empfehlen, Strassenbahn und Bus ergänzen das Netz. Angesichts der Touristenmassen in der Stadt sind sicherlich eher Frühjahr und Herbst gute Reisezeiten.

▲ Le Château de Prague, la nuit depuis le Pont-Charles: inoubliable! L'ancien hôtel de Ville sur la splendide place du Marché, la Galerie Nationale et l'hôtel Europa (joyau du style art déco) sur la place Wenceslas: la vieille ville de Prague regorge de curiosités et de bâtiments magnifiques. Prague est sans conteste une des plus belles villes d'Europe centrale.
Alors que les autres villes d'Europe centrale ont du mal à „décoller", Prague est, elle, en plein essor, en plein changement. Le milieu gay en profite. Il est, lui aussi, en pleine évolution, ce que favorisent la situation géographique avantageuse du pays et l'esprit ouvert et tolérant des Tchèques.
Pour les transports en commun, utilisez le métro (rapide, bon marché et ponctuel) et le réseau complémentaire de tramways et de bus. La meilleure époque pour visiter Prague est sans aucun doute le printemps ou l'automne, vu les hordes de touristes qui encombrent les ruelles de la vieille ville de mai à septembre.

☆ El centro de la ciudad ofrece edificios tan encantadores, que algunas veces se hace dificil centrar la vista, entre ellos el Viejo Ayuntamiento, la Galería Nacional y el Hotel Europa en la Plaza Wenzel (un ejemplo perfecto del Arte Nuevo). Indudablemente el centro histórico de Praga es uno de los más bellos en Europa Central. Mientras las otras ciudades orientales se desarollan muy lentamente, Praga está en pleno auge.

❖ La vista del *Hradcany* di notte dal ponte Carlo è una sensazione che nessun turista può dimenticare facilmente. Il centro della cittá offre oltre al *vecchio municipio* la *Galleria Nazionale* e, in piazza Vinceslao, il magnifico *Hotel Europa*, perla dell'art nouveau. Praga è sicuramente una delle città storiche più belle d'Europa. Mentre nelle altre grandi città dell'Europa centrale lo sviluppo procede lentamente, Praga sta vivendo un boom. Questo, la liberale attitudine dei cechi e la favorevole posizione al centro dell'Europa hanno favorito lo sviluppo di un considerevole ambiente gay. Per gli spostamenti urbani vi consigliamo la metropolitana:veloce, economica e puntuale; autobus e tram completano la rete. Considerate le orde di turisti che invadono Praga a Natale e in estate, vi consigliamo di visitarla o in autunno o in primavera.

GAY INFO

Gay Information Centre
Kakovská 3, Praha 1 ☎ 26 44 08 Fax: 26 44 08

Gay Internet Site
Email: gayprague@usa.net
Homepage: www.gayprague.com.

Mr. Fetish - gay internet magazine
Homepage: www.mrfetisch.cz

BARS

A-Club (B G MA) 18-6 h, Fri Sat disco
Milíčova 25, Praha 3

Club Angel (AC B CC D DR f G MA S SNU STV VS W) 17-5/? h
Kmochova 8, Praha 5, Smichov ✉150 00 *(M-Andél)*
☎ 57 31 61 27

Drake's (B CC DR G MA msg r S VS) 0-24, SNU 21 h, Sun free buffet
Petrinska/Zborovská, 150 00 Praha 5 *(Smíchov. M-Andel, Tram 6,9,12)* ☎ 53 49 09
Friends Prague (AC B GLM VS) 14-3 h
Náprstkova 1 ✉110 00 ☎ 21 63 54 08
Gay L-Club (B D f G MA pr S SNU) 21-? h
Lublaňská 48 ✉120 00 *(Tram 4, 16, 22, 34 Vinohrady Disco Metro C: I.P. Pavlova)* ☎ 90 00 11 89 536
Also a restaurant.
La Provence/Banana Café/Tapas Bar (A AC CC D E F g MA s snu) Restaurant 12-24 h
Tapas Bar 11-01 h
Banana Café 20-01 h
Štupartska 9 ✉110 00 *near Oldtownplace* ☎ 232 48 01
Happy Hour 12-17 h, Live piano 18.30-21.30 h, every weekend - programm
Piano Bar (B f G MA) 17-22 h
Milešovská 10, Praha 3
Pinocchio (B D DR f G H MA r s SNU STV) 0-24 h
Seifertova 3 ✉130 00 *(nearby Metro C „Hlavni Nádraží or tram 5, 9, 26 night troam 55, 58 stop olzanova)* ☎ (0)603-77 81 27
Also disco, erotic centre, sex-shop and accomodation.
SAM (AC B DR G LJ p) 21-4/? h, Fri parties
Cajkovského 34 *(Tram-Lipanska)* ☎ 24 23 96 57
It is possible here to change clothes and rent leather gear. Hard to find. Red light by the door.
Stella (B F GLM OS) 20-5 h
Lužická 10 ☎ 24 25 78 69
Tom's Bar (B D DR F G MA p s VS WE YG) Fri Sat 21-4 h
Pernerova 4 ✉180 00 *(Karlín. M-Križíkova/Florenc, Tram 8, 24)* ☎ 232 11 70
Tunel (AC B DR G LJ VS) 21-? h
Plenská 41, Praha 5, Smichov ✉150 00 *(Metro B Sation Anděl)*
U Dubu (B F G) Mon-Sun 10-15, 18-24 h
Záhrebská 14, *(Metro B Station Palackého náměsti)*
U Střelce (B G stv) 18-4, Fri Sat -6 h, Fri Sat STV
Karoliny Světlé 12 *(M-Národni třída)* ☎ 24 23 82 78

CAFÉS

Café Relax (AC B G) Mon-Sat 9-? h Sun 13-? h
Soukenická 7 ☎ 248 188 92
Érra Cafe (AC B bf f GLM OS) 9-23 h
Konviktská 11 11000 Praha 1 *(M-Márodmí)* ☎ 24 23 34 27
Centrally located.
Kafírna u Českého Pána (B G) Mon-Fri 11-22 h, Sat, Sun 14-22 h
Kozi 13 ✉110 00 *(Near Metro Staroměstská)* ☎ 232 82 83
Small cosy café-bar near the Jewish quarter.
U Českého Pána (B f glm) Mon-Sun 18-24 h
Tynska 7 ☎ 232 82 83

DANCECLUBS

New Ater Dark Connection (B D DR GLM MA r S SNU STV VS) 21-6 h
Rokycanova 29 ✉130 00 *Bus 136 bus stop: „Ulice Rokycanovca" Bus 133, 204 bus stop: „Ulice Husitská"*
Escape (AC B D F G MA SNU) 19-5 h, daily
V jáme 8 ✉110 00 *(Near Vaclavské námesti, Metro Můstek or Muzeum)* ☎ (0)602-403 744
Bar, restaurant and Danceclub, after 22 h disco, shows with admission.
GEJZEE..R (AC B D DR GLM MA VS YG) 17-04 h daily
Bompjtsfdl's 5ß *(Near Metro Náměsti Miru)* ☎ 225 160 36
Biggest gay danceclub in Prague with 2 bars.

U Petra Voka (B D DR F GLM s YG) 20-? h, Thu (S)
Na Bělidle 40 *(Smíchov, M-Anděl)* ☎ 53 06 94

RESTAURANTS

ARCO (B F G H MA) daily 17-3 h
Voroněžská 24/172 *(Near Metro NámÆstí míru)* ☎ 717 429 08
Also bar and guesthouse, rooms with breakfast
Bazaar Mediteranée (bf glm S T) 11-1 h
Nerudova 40 *Near castle and Charles bridge* ☎ 90 05 45 10
Coq Noir open daily 11-3 h
Karlova 25 ☎ 24 23 89 29
Steak House, Café Club, Bar
U Kapra (B F MA NG OS) 11-1 h
Eatecká 7 ✉110 00 *(M-Staroméstská)* ☎ 24 81 36 35
Czech and international cuisine.
U starého songu (B F glm) Sun-Thu 18-24/?, Fri Sat - 2/? h
Štítného 27 ✉1f30 00 ☎ 22 78 20 47
Villa David (B F GLM MA) 11-23 h
Holubova 5 ✉150 00 *(Radlice. M-Radlicka, Tram 14-Laurova)* ☎ 90 01 12 93
European cuisine.

SEX SHOPS/BLUE MOVIES

City Man (G) 14-20 h
Krakovská 2 ✉110 00 *(Nové Mesto)*
Videos, magazines, calendars, guides, post cards, posters, original photos, rubber, lubricants, vibrators etc.
Drake's (B CC DR G MA msg r S VS) 0-24, SNU 21 h, Sun free buffet
Petrinska/Zborovská, 150 00 Praha 5 *(Smíchov. M-Andel, Tram 6,9,12)* ☎ 53 49 09
Heaven (b DR G VS) Mon-Sat 11-24, Sun 14-24 h
Gorazdova 11, 120 00 Praha 2 *(M-Karlovo nam.)* ☎ 24 92 12 82
Video Center (g) Mon-Sat 9-21, Sun 14-21 h
Veletržní 41 ✉120 00 *(Tram 5, 17, 24 or 26 or 14)*
Video Center (g) Mon-Sat 9-20, Sun 14-20 h
Žitná 28 ✉120 00 *(Tram 4, 6, 16, 22)*
Video Center (g) Mon-Sat 9-20, Sun 14-29
Americká 14 ✉120 00 *(M-Náměsti Míru. Tram 4, 22)* ☎ 25 36 56
Video Erotic Center (g) Mon-Fri 9-20 h
Bořivojova 105 ✉130 00 *(Tram 9)* ☎ 27 56 10
Leather articles on sale.
Video Erotic Studio (g) Mon-Fri 9-20, Sat 10-20, Sun 14-20 h
Jana Zajíce 4 ✉170 00 *(Tram 1, 8, 25, 26)* ☎ 37 77 16

ESCORTS & STUDIOS

Callboy Robin (G msg P S SNU) 0-24 h
☎ 0602/33 25 71
☛Budapest, Hungary.

HOUSE OF BOYS

Czech Mate (CC G H MA msg R S VS) 0-24 h, Sun buffet 20 h
Petrinska 5, 150 00 Praha 5 *(Smichov; M-Andel, Tram 6,9,12)* ☎ 53 49 09

SAUNAS/BATHS

Aqua Club 2000 (B D G msg sa) 12-4 h (disco 21-4 h)
Husitská 7, Praha 3 *(Žižkov)* ☎ 627 89 71
Babylonia (B G MA msg sa sb sol VS wh WO) 14-3 h
Martinská 6 ✉110 00 *(near Metro Karlovo námÆstí or Metro Můstek)* ☎ 24 23 23 04
very popular

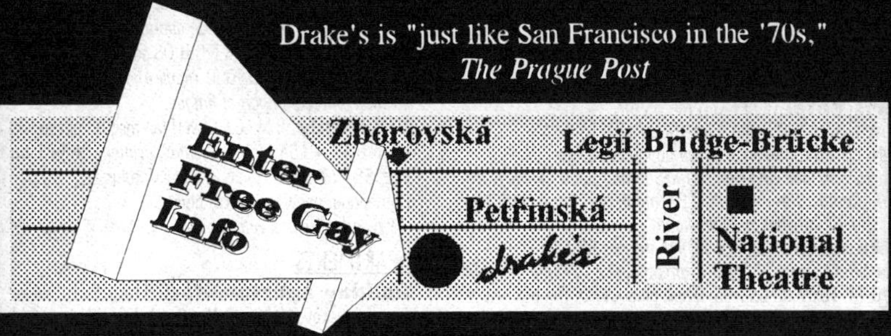
Enter
Free Gay
Info
Zborovská
Legií Bridge-Brücke
Petřínská
drake's
River
National
Theatre

David Club Sauna (AC B CC DR f G MA msg N P sa sb sol VS wh) 12-24/? h daily
Sokolouská 44 ✉186 00 *(Karlín)* ☎ 231 67 68
This was the first gay sauna of Prague. Cosy and intim.

Gay Sauna Chaos (B G sa sb VS) 17-2 h
Dušni (mezi c 13-15) ☎ 24 23 85 10

Klub-Sauna David (B CC f G MA msg sa sb VS wo) 14-2 h
Sokolovská 44, ✉180 00 *(Tram 24, 8. M-Krizikova)* ☎ 231 78 69
Last admission two hours before closing time.

Sauna Marco (B DR G MA msg sa sb VS wh) 14-3 h
Lublanská 17 12000 Praha 2 *(Metro I.P.Pavlova*
☎ 29 23 07
Small but pupular.

MASSAGE

Gay Relax 17-24 h
(M°-Strašnická) ☎ (0603) 45 22 02
By appointment only. German and English spoken.

HOTELS

Holger's Hotel (B bf F G H MA OS p)
Nad Privozem 3 14700 Praha 4 ☎ (0602) 31 15 16
Fax: 44 46 03 60 Homepage: www.amigo.cz/holger
Also bar (9-22 h) and restaurant (Thu-Sun and public holidays 17-21.30 h). Room rates from Kc 72 /night. All rooms with shower/WC, SAT-TV, minibar and telephone.

Villa Mansland (B bf CC f G MA msg r s SNU)
Stepnicna Street 9 ✉182 00 *Trams 10, 17, 24 nightline 54*
☎ 683 10 24 Fax: 900 051 55 Email: pragconnect @mbox. vol.cz
Homepage: www.pragconnect.com
Gay hotel and holiday apartments, gay information and booking service

GUEST HOUSES

Pension Haus Holger (b bf G H OS)
Pod Sychrovem II/47 101 00 Praha 10 *(Tram11-Chodovská)*
☎ 76 40 42 Fax: 76 40 42
Reservation ☎ (0)602-311 516. 5 double rooms with bath/WC on the corridor, 2 apartments with bath/WC. Rooms with balcony, satellite-TV, radio, minibar, heating. Guest house provides room-service. Very busy, very friendly, good breakfast. Rates double DM 71, apartment (2 persons) 102, add. bed 22.

Pension Tusculum (B bf G H OS)
Vodňanského 1, Břevnov ✉169 00 (Tram22-Orinopol)
☎ 20 51 02 77 Reservation ☎ (0)602-31 15 16.
Fax: 44 46 03 60 Homepage: www.amigo.cz/holger
7 double rooms, partly with bath/WC, 1 apartment. All rooms with phone, TV, radio and minibar. Guest house provides room service and parking. Rates DM 74-85, apartment 115, add. bed 22.

Penzion David (B F G H OS sa)
2525/5 Holubova ✉15000 *(Radlice)* ☎ 54 98 20 Fax: 54 98 20
Located in a restful part of Prague.

Villa Andy (B bf CC F GLM H MA msg OS pi r sa wh)
U Šipku 10 ✉154 00 *(non-central location)* ☎ 581 66 81
Fax: 581 668 12 Email: villaandy@atlas.cz
Homepage: www.amigo.cz/andy
16 twin bed rooms with shower/WC, SAT-TV, direct-dial telephone.

APARTMENTS

Holiday Apartments (G H msg)
Chocholouskova 4/III ✉180 00 *(M-Palmovka)* ☎ 561 16 33
Central location, with kitchen, bath, WC, phone, satelite-TV, safe, heating. Rates Kc 1000-1500 per day. Discount for longer stays.

PRIVATE ACCOMODATION

Holiday Apartments (GLM) 9-17 h
c/o Pragocongress, Opatovická 14 ✉110 00 *(M-Národni)*
☎ 24 91 11 04 Fax: 24 91 33 33
Flats in the center of town: 1 pers. Kc 1260, 2 pers. 720, 3 pers. 630, 4 pers. and more 540. (Prices for each pers.)

J + J (G)
Hlavní 85 ✉141 00 ☎ 727 680 15
Email: james_prague@hotmail.com Homepage: htttp//come.to/J+J

Prague Home Stay (GLM H)
J. M. Lány, Pod Kotlářkou 14 ✉159 00 *(Tram 4, 7, 9 Korlářka)*
☎ 52 73 88 Fax: 52 73 88
Agency offering private accomodations.K

Ron´s Rainbow Guesthouse (G) Bulharská 4 ✉101 00 *(near centre, net traom stop „ Ruska")*
☎ 717 315 17 Fax: 717 315 17
Email: ronprague@hotmail.com
Homepage: http://www.travel.to/gay-prague

GENERAL GROUPS

SOHO-Sdružení organizací homosexuálních občanu v ČR
Senovážné námestí 2 11000 Praha 1 ☎ 24 22 38 11 or
☎ (0601) 213 840

HEALTH GROUPS

Aids Helpline Krajská hygienická stanice Mon-Thu 13-16 h
Dittrichova 17, 120 00 Praha 2 ☎ 29 17 73

Aids Prevence Mon-Fri 8-12 h
☎ 29 16 51-4/284

Institute of Sexuology Mon-Fri 8-12 h
Karlovo námestí 32, ✉120 00 ☎ 249 043 79 Fax: 249 046 09

Lighthouse - Cech AIDS Help Society daily 9-18 h
Malého 3 ✉180 00 ☎ 248 142 84 Fax: 248 103 45

SAP-Česká společnost AIDS pomoc Helpline 18-20 h
☎ 02/21 21 09 56

RELIGIOUS GROUPS

LOGOS Fara církve českobratrské evangelické Helpline: Wed 19-22 h
U školské zahrady 1, 182 00 Praha 8 *(Kobylisy)* ☎ 24 22 03 27

SWIMMING

Plavecky stadion Podolí (B g NG pi sa sb) Mon-Fri 9-21, Sat Sun 9-20 h
Podolská 74, ✉140 00 ☎ 439 15 13
Best after 18 h.

CRUISING

-Kinsleho Namestí
All cruisings are very AYOR!
-Main railway station (Hlavní nádraží) (R)
-Letná Park

Prostějov ☎ 0508

GENERAL GROUPS

PV Klub Prostějov
Dolní 43 ✉796 01

Slany

GENERAL GROUPS

G & L klub
PO Box 32, 274 01 ✉27401

Sokolov ☎ 0168

GENERAL GROUPS

Gay Klub Sokolov
Slavíckova 1691 ✉36505 ☎ 62 42 54

Teplice ☎ 0417

GENERAL GROUPS

Gay klub
PO Box 17, ✉415 03 ☎ 410 58

Šumperk

GENERAL GROUPS

Junior
PO Box 15 ✉27401

Usti nad Labem ☎ 047

BARS

Eurobar (B D glm) Mon-Fri 17-1, Sat, Sun -3 h
Velká hradebni ✉40000

GENERAL GROUPS

Spolek Mykonos Wed 15-16 h
PO Box 218 ✉40001 ☎ 520 04 72

HEALTH GROUPS

Help Line
✉40000 ☎ 406 38

CRUISING

-Západni nádrazi (West Railway Station)

Denmark

Danmark

Northern Europe

Initials: DK

Time: GMT +1

☎ Country Code / Access Code: 45 (no area codes) / 00

Language: Danish, Faroese, Greenlandic

Area: 43,093 km^2 / 16,634 sq mi.

Currency: 1 Danish Krone (dkr) = 100 Öre

Population: 5,333,617

Capital: København

Religions: 91% Evangelical Lutheran

Climate: Moderate climate, humid and overcast. Winters are mild and windy, summers cool.

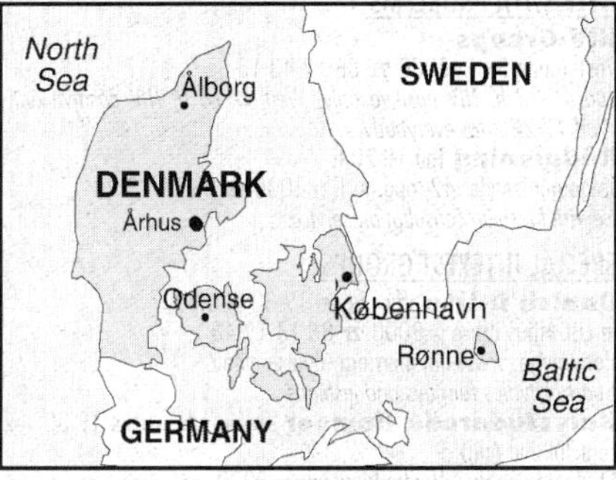

● Denmark, along with Norway, Sweden and the Netherlands, is one of the most liberal and gay-friendly countries in Europe. The age of consent is 15. Anti-discrimination laws have been in effect since 1987, homosexual couples enjoy the same inheritance rights as heterosexuals (since 1986), and from 1989 onwards homosexual couples have been able to marry at registry offices. One of the partners does have to be a Danish citizen and homosexual couples cannot adopt children. Since 1994, such registered partnerships also exist in Greenland. Gay visitors will find that Danes are exceptionally friendly and tolerant.

✱ Dänemark ist, zusammen mit Norwegen, Schweden und den Niederlanden, eines der liberalsten und schwulenfreundlichsten Länder des europäischen Kontinents. Das Schutzalter liegt bei 15 Jahren. In Dänemark gibt es seit 1987 Anti-Diskriminierungs-Regelungen. Homosexuelle Paare sind heterosexuellen im Erbrecht gleichgestellt (seit 1986), seit 1989 können homosexuelle Paare ihre Partnerschaft registrieren lassen. Ein Partner muß allerdings dänischer Staatsbürger sein; Adoptionen sind homosexuellen Paaren nicht möglich. Seit 1994 gibt es die eingetragene Partnerschaft auch in Grönland. Die dänische Bevölkerung steht Schwulen und Lesben ausgesprochen tolerant und freundlich gegenüber.

▲ En ce qui concerne l'homosexualité, le Danemark est un des pays les plus progressistes d'Europe. La majorité sexuelle y est fixée à 15 ans. Depuis 1986, les couples homosexuels jouissent des mêmes droits que les hétérosexuels pour les questions d'héritage. Depuis 1987, une loi anti-discriminatoire protège les gays et les lesbiennes et depuis 1989, le „concubinage enregistré" (équivalent du PACS) garantit aux homosexuels les mêmes droits qu'à un couple hétérosexuel. Attention: au moins l'un des partenaires doit avoir la nationalité danoise! Les couples homosexuels ont également le droit d'adopter des enfants. Depuis 1994, le „concubinage enregistré" est légal au Groenland.
Les Danois sont ouverts et tolérants envers les gays et les lesbiennes.

☆ Dinamarca es junto con Noruega, Suecia y Los Paises Bajos, uno de los paises europeos más liberales en cuestiones homosexuales. La edad de consentimiento es de 15 años. Desde 1987 hay una reglamentación de antidiscriminación, desde 1986 las parejas homosexuales son tratadas de igual manera que las heterosexuales, sobre todo en cuestiones de leyes sucesorias (herencia). Desde 1989 las parejas gay pueden registrar su relación, aunque sea requisito que uno de ellos posea la nacionalidad danesa. Hasta ahora a las parejas gay no se permite la adopción de niños.
Desde 1994 existe también un registro de parejas en Groenlandia.
La población danesa se muestra frente a la homosexualidad muy tolerante y amigable.

❖ La Danimarca, insieme alla Norvegia e ai Paesi Bassi, è uno dei paesi europei più liberali e più aperti alla causa omosessuale. L'età legale per avere dei rapporti sessuali è di 15 anni. In Danimarca esistono leggi contro la discriminazione (dal 1987) che garantiscono agli omosessuali il diritto di registrare ufficialmente le loro relazioni e il diritto all'eredità. Tuttavia le registrazioni sono possibili solo se almeno uno dei partner è danese e il diritto di adozione viene ancora negato. Dal 1994 la registrazione è possibile anche in Groenlandia. La popolazione è tollerante e aperta verso i gay.

NATIONAL GAY INFO

Landsforeningen for Bøsser og Lesbiske, Århus-afd Thu 18-19 h
Jægergårdsgade 42 ✉8100 Århus *(stair A, 1st floor, same building as PAN Disco/Club)* ☎ 86/13 19 48
Denmarks national organization for gay men and lesbian women, founded in 1948. Local groups in all areas.

PAN Bladet & X-Pansion
Teglgårdstræde 13, PO Box 10 23 København ☎ 33/11 19 61
Fax: 33/39 00 83 Email lbl-panblad@lbl.dk
Magazine for the members of LBL. National gay and lesbian list of events. Also lists, addresses etc. of non-LBL-groups. Founded in 1954. Approximately 28 pages. Monthly publication including personal ads, news, AIDS info, book, film and theater reviews. Free to members, institutions, libraries, etc. Dkr 150 per year.

PAN-Info Thu, Sun & Mon 20-22 h
☎ 33 36 00 86
Information on what's going on in gay and lesbian Denmark

NATIONAL COMPANIES

Danske Bjørne Video ApS (CC G)
Risbrigvej 10 -Industri III, PO Box 162 ✉6330 Padborg
☎ 73/67 47 20 Fax: 73/67 47 37
Videos, toys, magazines, CDs etc.

Euro Shop APS
Stationsvej, PO Box 57 ✉6360 Tingler ☎ 73/67 00 77
Fax: 73 67 00 80

Aabenraa ✉6200

BARS

Pan Café (B d f GLM MA WE) Fri-Sat 20-24/2 h
Nygade 55 A ✉6200 ☎ 74 62 11 48

GENERAL GROUPS

LBL Sønderjyllandsafdelingen Tue 19-21 h
PO Box 282, Nygade 55A ✉6200 ☎ 74 62 11 48
Discussions, social activities. Pan Café Fri-Sat 20-24 h

Aalborg

BARS

PAN Aalborg (B D GLM MA s WE) Thu 21-2 h, Fri, Sat 22-5 h
Danmarksgade 27 A ✉9000 *(Main railway station)* ☎ 981 222 45
Bar and night club.

GENERAL GROUPS

Landsforeningen for Bøsser og Lesbiske, Ålborg-afdeling (b GLM S) Wed 17-19 h, Thu 19-23 h
PO Box 12 44, Tolbodgade 27 ✉9100 *(Near habour)*
☎ 98 16 45 07

CRUISING

-Kildeparken (entrance from Vesterbro near toilets and Gammel Kaervej)
-Area of bushes and trees near race course (entrance up the slope from Skydebanevej just after the race course entrance; daytime, summer only)

Århus

GAY INFO

Biblioteket Mon 19-22 h
Jægergårdsgade 42 a/l, PO Box 362 ✉8000 ☎ 86 13 19 48
Lends books (gay literature) to members.
Radio Hiv, Håb og Kærlighed Thursday evening in even weeks (2nd & 4th), 19-20 h.
Jægergårdsgade 42 ✉8000
Århus center 98.7, West 92.2, South 89.5, North 107,6, STOFA 100.75, JTAS 100.2 MHz.

BARS

Mens Club Århus/SLM Denmark (B DR G LJ MA P VS) Fri-Sat 21-2 h,
Østbanetorvet 8 st.th., PO Box 370 ✉8100 ☎ 86 19 10 89
Leather bar for gay men only

CAFÉS

Pan Club (B D F GLM OS) Mon-Thu 18-01 h , Fri 18-06, Sat 20-06, Sun 20-01
Jægergårdsgade 42 ✉8000 ☎ 86 13 43 80

DANCECLUBS

Pan Club (B D F GLM OS p) Wed-Thu 23-3, Fri-Sat -5, Sun 22-2 h, 2nd Fri/month (L)
Jægergårdsgade 42 ✉8000 ☎ 86 13 43 80

SEX SHOPS/BLUE MOVIES

A Center Video (AC DR g MA VS) 12-24 h
Rosenkrantzgade 16 ✉8000 *(near railway station)* ☎ 86 13 01 13
Gay Club Århus
Paradisgade 11 ✉8000
Gay sex-cinema, videos, magazines etc.

GENERAL GROUPS

Landsforeningen af Bøsser og Lesbiske, Ungdomsgruppen Youth Group of Gays and Lesbian Tue 20-22 h
Jægergårdsgade 42, PO Box 362 ✉8100 *(door A, 1st floor)*
☎ 86 13 19 48 Fax: 86 13 25 48
Youth group for gays and lesbian under age 28. New ones are introduced TUE 19.30 h.
☎ during the meeting.
Youth Group Tue 19 h
c/o Pan Club, Jægergårdsgade 42 ✉8000 ☎ 86 13 43 8

FETISH GROUPS

SMil S/M Club Tue 20-22 h
PO Box 198 ✉8100 ☎ 86 13 70 23
Leather/SM group for heteros and gays.

HEALTH GROUPS

Aids-Info Århus 19-23 h
Vestergade 5B ✉8000 ☎ 86 13 65 13
AktHIV-Huset 9-16 h
Vestergade 5B ✉8000 ☎ 86 18 16 46 Fax 86 19 11 56
Information about HIV and AIDS. Help for HIV+ and PWA. Café for HIV+ Wed 12-18, Thu 19-22 h.
Marselisborg Hospital Medicinsk Ambulatorium Tue 10-11 & 16-18 h, Thu 8-10 h, Fri 8-9 h.
✉8000 ☎ 86 14 27 77
HIV tests and counselling. Dial the number and ask for extension 235.
STOP AIDS-Kampagnen Mon-Fri 10-16 h
Frederiksgade 20, 3.sal, Postboks 362 ✉8100 ☎ 86 12 88 00

HELP WITH PROBLEMS

HIV-Groups
Vestergade 5 B ✉8000 ☎ 86 12 43 13
Tue 19-22 h, HIV positive only, Wed 12-16 h, HIV positive only, Wed 19-22 h for everybody.
Rådgivning Thu 18-20 h
Jægergårdsgade 42, opg. A, l. ✉8000 ☎ 86 13 19 48
Gay and lesbian consultation service.

SPECIAL INTEREST GROUPS

Danish D-Lite office hours 19.30 - 20.30
at LBL-Århus'office ✉8000 ☎ 86 13 19 48
Homepage: www.gaysport.org/danish dlite/
Sport acitvities for gays and lesbians
Halvstuderede Homoer Thu in odd weeks 19.30 (except Jul and Aug)
Studenternes Hus, Nordre Ringgade ✉8000
Activities for gay and lesbian students in Århus

SWIMMING

-Den Permanente (NU) (at Risskov)
-Mariendal Havbakker (NU)
-Ballehage (nu) (near Højbjerg, afternoon)
-Fløjstrup Stand (NU)

CRUISING

-Central Station
-Botanisk Have (main entrance to Den Gamle By at Eugen Warmings Vej)
-Mindeparken (Near Oddervej).
-Havnen Pier 3
-Tangkrogen (near Chr. Filtenborgs Plads, along the beach, summer after dark)

Års ✉ 9600

HOTELS

Haus Branabur (bf G H)
Svoldruprej 101, Vognsild ✉9600 ☎ 98 65 86 75

Ballerup ✉ 2750

GENERAL GROUPS

Bisværmen (G)
✉2750 ☎ 33 25 60 65
Gay and Lesbian Group

HELP WITH PROBLEMS

Lokalforening for bøsser og lesbiske i Ballerup og omegn ✉2750 ☎ 33 25 60 65

Esbjerg

CAFÉS

Tulipan (B GLM) Thu 19.30-22.30, Sat 20-24 (even weeks only), Sun 14-17 h (1 Oct-1 Apr only)
Nørrebrogade 102 ✉6700 ☎ 75 45 19 48
Café Thu 19.30-22.30 h. Parties 2nd Sat/month 21-?

SEX SHOPS/BLUE MOVIES

Week-End Sex (g)
Torvegade 11 ✉6700

GENERAL GROUPS

LBL Thu 19.30-22.30
Nørrebrogade 102, PO Box 10 33 ✉6701 ☎ 75 45 19 48

SWIMMING

-Houstrup Strand (G NU) (near Lønne. From the P walk 500m in direction of the nude beach. Very popular.)

CRUISING

-City park/byparken (cruising near the water tower and the art museum)
-Banegaarden/Central station
-Vestkraftvej (at toilet and phone booth, best late evening and night)
-Molevej (at toilet)

Fano Sonderho ✉ 6720

HOTELS

Kromann's Hotel Fisherestaurant (B bf F glm H MA OS) Eastern-OCT, christmas/sylvester
Sønderland 7 ✉6720 ☎ 75 16 44 45 Fax: 75 16 43 26
Single room from Dkr 390, double from 490.

Faxe Ladeplads ✉ 4654

SWIMMING

-Beach on the „Feddet" (by the inlet of Præsto Fjord; after the P there is a nudist beach, and further on the beach will become more and more gay)

Fredericia ✉ 7000

BARS

Club 77 (B D GLM h MA) Thu 22-2, Fri-Sat 23-5 h
Dalegade 77 ✉7000 *(ground floor)* ☎ 75 93 12 28

SWIMMING

-Trelde Næs

CRUISING

-Stationen/railway station
-The battlement »Volden«
-Norgesgade (toilet)

Frederikshavn

GENERAL GROUPS

Get-Together Group ☎ 98 42 81 74
Homepage: www.gaynord.dk/bliv.htm

Grenaa ✉ 8500

SWIMMING

-The island of »Anholt« (g) (very long and wonderful beach)

Haderslev ✉ 6100

GENERAL GROUPS

Profil (GLM) 2nd Fri
PO Box 112 ☎ 74 54 31 94

CRUISING

-Toilets on the »Jomfrustien«

Helsingor ✉ 3000

GENERAL GROUPS

B.I.H. (G) Thu 18-20 h
☎ 49 20 23 03
Gay and Bisexual men in Helsingør. Café meetings 1st and 3rd Sat 20 h

CRUISING

-railway station

Herning ✉ 7400

GENERAL GROUPS

Club Fristedet (GLM)
PO Box 48, Nørregade 7 ✉7400 ☎ 97 12 12 42
Café in room 7-06, Kulturellen, Nørregade 7 on Thu 19.30-22 h. Parties 1st Sat in Feb, Apr, Jun, Aug, Oct and Dec.

CRUISING

-Parking in Danmarksgade
-Toilets at the parking behind supermarket Føtex on Bredgade.

Hillerød ✉ 3400

GENERAL GROUPS

S.L.O.T.S.B.I.O. (GLM) Last Sat in Butikken
Møllestrade 3 ✉3400 ☎ 42 26 17 41

Hjørring ✉ 9800

GENERAL GROUPS

GayNordDK
Postboks 243 ✉9800
Email: Redaktion@gaynord.dk Homepage: www.gaynord.dk/
Infos on gay and lesbian activities in the north of Jutland.

Holbæk ✉ 4300

BARS

Café Oasen (B GLM) Fri 19.30-24; lesbian night 2nd Fri 19-23 h
Foreninghuset, Jernbanevej 16 ✉4300 *(entrance in courtyard, 1st floor)*

GENERAL GROUPS

Landsforeningen for Bøsser of Lesbiske
✉4300 ☎ 53 63 45 09
LBL Sjælland ✉4300 ☎ 59 43 19 95

Karrebæksminde

SWIMMING

Beach on the Vesterhave side (just before the bridge turn to the right, after the [P] walk about 500 m to the north-west)

København

● Denmark's capital city is an economical, commercial and transportation center, in addition to being the undisputed fun-metropolis in Scandinavia with a relatively large gay scene. Copenhagen is a cheerful, colourful and open-minded city where the people are very friendly and the gay scene is very non-pretentious.
Our tips:
-A day trip per boat to swedish Malmö (45 min journey)
-A beach outing to „Nordseeland" (☛ Swimming), which is easy to reach with public transport.
-The Erotic Museum in Kobmagergade, a history of sexual pleasure.

✱ Dänemarks Hauptstadt ist Wirtschafts- und Handelszentrum, Verkehrsknotenpunkt und die unumstrittene Fun-Metropole in Skandinavien mit einer beachtlichen schwulen Szene. Kopenhagen zeichnet sich durch eine besonders heitere, bunte und aufgeschlossene Atmosphäre aus, die auch manchen Regentag erträglich macht.
Unsere Tips:
-Tagesausflug (45 min Fahrzeit) mit dem Boot ins schwedische Malmö
-Strandausflug nach Nordseeland (☛ Swimming), gut mit öffentlichen Verkehrsmitteln zu erreichen
-Erotikmuseum in der Købmagergade (unverkrampfte historische Darstellung aller sexuellen Spielarten)

▲ Copenhague est le centre économique et commercial de la Scandanavie. C'est aussi la capitale fun du nord de l'Europe. La vie gay y est trépidante. L'atmosphère de Copenhague est détendue, sympathique et vivante, ce qui rend les jours de mauvais temps plus supportables. Nous vous conseillons: une excursion d'une journée en bateau (45 minutes) à Malmö, en Suède; un tour (transports en commun!) à la plage de Nordseeland (☛Swimming); une visite au Musée de l'érotisme dans la Købmagergade (historique de toutes les pratiques sexuelles possibles et imaginables).

☆ La capital danesa no es solo un centro económico y comercial y un nudo de transporte internacional, sino la indiscutible metrópolis de diversión escandinava con una abierta y fuerte comunidad gay. Copenague se caracteriza por su ambiente especial, colorido y abierto, un hecho que recompensa hasta los dias de lluvia.
Nuestros consejos:
-Excursión (45 min. de viaje) en barco a Malmö (Suecia).
-Excursión a la playa de Nordseeland (☛Swimming), donde se puede llega con medios de transporte público.
-Museo erótico en la Købmagergade (presentación histórica de todos los prácticas sexuales sin tabus).

❖ La capitale della Danimarca è un centro economico e commerciale, un crocevia di traffici internazionali e, con la sua considerevole vita gay, l'indiscussa metropoli del divertimento dell'Europa scandinava. Copenhaghen si contraddistingue per la sua atmosfera serena, colorata ed aperta che rende sopportabili anche i giorni di pioggia. I nostri consigli:
-escursione in spiaggia al Nordseeland (☛Swimming) raggiungibili facilmente con mezzi pubblici;
-museo erotico a Købmagergade (mostra storica e disinibita di tutti i giochi erotici).

NATIONAL GROUPS

Copenhagen Gay Life
☎ 3314 7676
Homepage: www.copenhagen-gay-life.dk
Copenhagen's own network for gay buisnesses and organisations
LBL - National Association for Gays and Lesbians Mon-Fri 10-16:00h
Teglgårdstræde 13 ✉1452 ☎ 3313 1948

GAY INFO

Bøssehuset
Fristaden Christiania *(Entrance Refshalevej 2)* ☎ 32 95 98 72
Call for info.
Landsforeningen for Bøsser og Lesbiske/ LBL Mon - Fri 10-16 h
Teglgårdstræde 13 ☎ 33 13 19 48 Email: lbl@lbl.dk
Homepage: www.lbl.dk
-Københavnsafdelingen (=local section of the LBL)
-Aftenskolen for bøsser og lesbiske / night school for gays and lesbians with lectures of interest to students
-LBL library
-Pan-Bladet & X-Pansion (☛National Gay Info)
-Pan Idræt (athletic association within LBL; ☎ 33 13 19 48 Mon 19-21 h)
-Lærergruppen (gay teachers'group; ☎ 33 13 19 48)
-Rådgivningen (personal consultation Thu 18-20 h, ☎ 33 13 19 48)
-Ungdomsgruppen (group for young gays and lesbians)
-Samværsgruppen (group of gays of all ages meets Wed, ☎ 33 11 19 61 20-22 h
-Youth hotline ☎ 33 36 00 80 Tue 19-21 h
LBL Library Mon-Fri 17-19, Sat 13-15 h
Teglgårdstræde 13 ✉1007 ☎ 33 36 00 85
The only gay/lesbian archives in Denmark (photos, posters, pamplets, press cuttings, tape records and documents).
Radio Rosa
Teglgårdstræde 13, baghuset ✉1452 ☎ 33 33 04 04
Fax: 33 36 00 83 Email: lbl-radiorosa@lbl.dk
FM 91.4 and cable FM 91.4. Broadcast in English on Thu. twice/month.

TOURIST INFO

Københavns Turistinformation
Bernstorffsgade 1 ✉1577 ☎ 33 11 13 15 Fax: 33 93 49 69

BARS

Amigo Bar (B g) 22-?
Schønbergsgade 4 ✉1906 Frederiksberg ☎ 31 21 49 15
Café Intime (B d g) 17-02 h, Sat 20-02 h
Allegade 25, ✉2000 Frederiksberg ☎ 38 34 19 58
Slightly old fashioned but very friendly.
Can Can (AC CC GLM MA TV) Mon-Sun 14-2 h
Mikkel Bryggers Gade 11/Lavendel Strade ✉1342 *(50 m to Town Hall)* ☎ 33 11 50 10
Friendly gay bar in the center of the city
Centralhjørnet (B G MA) Mo - Fri 11-01 h, Sat - Sun 05-10 h, 15-01 h
Kattesundet 18/Lavendelstræde ✉1458 ☎ 33 11 85 49
Cosy Bar (B G MA) Sun-Wed 23-6, Thu-Sat 23-7 h
Studiestræde 24 ✉1455 ☎ 33 12 74 27
Popular and cruisy. One of the oldest bars in Copenhagen. Best in the early hours of the morning .Great music and interesting atmosphere.
Masken Bar (B GLM MA) 16-2, Sat-Sun 15-02 h, Thur 20-2h „Girls' night"
Studiestræde 33 ✉1455 ☎ 33 91 67 80

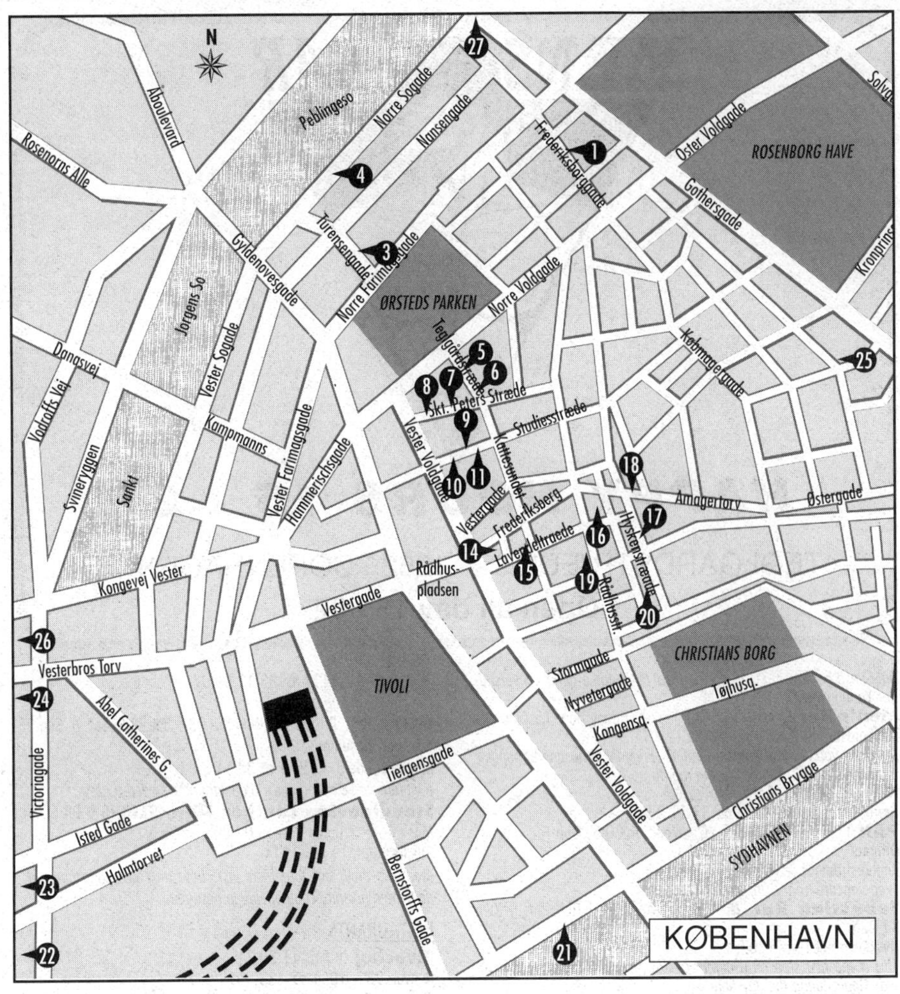

1 Hotel Windsor
2 SLM-Scandinavian Leather Men
3 Babooshka Café
4 Loke Cinema
5 LBL
6 Men's Bar
7 Soho Kitchen Restaurant
8 Never Mind Bar
9 Cosy Bar
10 Masken Bar
11 Amigo Sauna
14 can-can Bar
15 Centralhjørnet Bar
16 PAN Danceclub
17 Sebastian Bar & Café
18 Size Bar
19 Company 37 Body and Beauty Shop
20 Queen Victoria Restaurant
21 At Carsten's Guesthouse
22 Klub Kino Sex Shop
23 Men's Shop Sex Shop
24 Body Bio Sauna
25 Mauritsen Dance Bar
26 Amigo Bar
27 Looky Looky Sex Shop

Sat-Sun breakfast 5-10 h. The perfect place for a quiet conversation. Young crowd.

Men's Bar (! AC B G LJ MA) 15-2 h, Happy Hour 15-21 h
Teglgardstræde 3 ✉1452 ☎ 33 12 73 03
A must if you are into jeans or leather, Friendly atmosphere, popular brunch on the first Sunday in the month

Never Mind (B d G MA) 22-6 h
Nørre Voldgade 2 ✉1358 ☎ 33 11 33 08

PAN (! B CC f GLM OS YG) Wed-Sat 20-5, Sun-Tue only in summer
Knabrostræde 3 ✉1210 ☎ 33 11 37 8
Wed-Sat café from 20h, disco from 23h.

Sebastian Bar & Café (AC B CC f GLM MA N YG) 12-02h
Hyskenstræde10 ✉1207
This is the first stop on a night out. Very popular and a young crowd. Meals during the day only.

Size Video & Dance bar (AC B CC GLM MA VS YG) Thu 20-3, Fri Sat -5 h
Vimmelskaftet 41 F ✉1161 K *(on Strøget, in a narrow passage between Jack & Jones and Pizzabar)* ☎ 33 25 75 95
Look for the rainbow flag on the main pedestrian street. International atmosphere.

CAFÉS

Babooshka (A B F gLM MA YG) 16-1, Sun 14-23 h
Turesensgade 6 ✉1368 ☎ 33 15 05 36

Kafe Knud/HIV Huset (B G MA) Wed-Thu 16-22 h
Skindergade 26
Café for HIV+ and PWA.

DANCECLUBS

Mouritsen Dance Bar (AC B D GLM S YG) Wed & Sun 20-03h, Thu, Fri & Sat 20-06h
Gl. Mønt 17 ✉1117 ☎ 33 12 66 02
New in Copenhagen. Popular.

PAN (! B CC D GLM YG) Wed-Thu 23-5, Fri 23-5, Sat -6, Sun 23-4 h (only in summer)
Knabrostræde 3 ✉1210 ☎ 33 11 37 84
A vibrant and exciting place. Popular and crowded. Cruisy.

Scandinavian Leather Men/SLM (B D DR GLM LJ MA) Fri 22- ? Doors close at 02:00h
Studiestræde 14 A ✉1544
Members only, but foreigners just show their passports and get a daily membership. Leather club in basement.

RESTAURANTS

Elverhøj (B F g) 11:30-24h
Nyhvan 23 ✉1051 ☎ 3332 0999
Gay friendly hotel situated along the canal in the historical part of the city.

Queen Victoria (B bf CC e F glm) 17-24 h
Snaregade 4 ✉1205 ☎ 33 91 01 91
Popular restaurant owned by a well known drag queen. Good Danish cuisine. Rather expensive, but here you dine with the local celebrities. Reservations recommended for dinner.

SoHo Kitchen Restaurant (AC B bf CC E F glm) Sun-Thu 17-22 h, Fri-Sat 17-24 h
Sankt Pedersstræde 34 ✉1753 ☎ 33 63 99 04
Urban american cuisine, fine seafood steaks and more. Vegetarian available on request.

Teglkroen (B CC F glm) Mon-Fri 11-23 h
Teglgårdstrade 17 ✉1452 K ☎ 33 12 84 08
Recommended. Danish (Smørebrod) and French cuisine.

SEX SHOPS/BLUE MOVIES

Body Bio (b DR G MA sa VS) 12-01 h
Kingosgade 7, ✉1623 *(Take Bus No. 6 to Kingosgade)*
Popular cruising place. Some straight guys looking for fun and don't be afraid, sometimes some straight couples.

Copenhagen Gay Center (B DR f G sa sol VS) 10-05:00h
Istedgade 36 ✉1650 ☎ 33 22 23 00
Also rents porno videos. Free coffee.

ep-production (g) Mon-Sat 11-19:00h
Kattesundet 10 ✉1458 ☎ 3311 6406
Shop for gay and straight clientele. Publisher of the Danish gay magazine "Cock".

Klub Kino (g) Mon-Thu 10-02:00h, Fri -Sun 24h
Sommerstedgade 23 ✉1718

Looky Look (b g MA VS) Sun - Fri 12-01 h, Sat 20-02 (NG)
Randersgade 49 ✉2100
Small sex club with a mixed gay and bisexual clientele. Sat. night 20-02:00h straight couples

Men's Shop (CC G MA s VS) 10-02.00h
Viktoriagade 24/Istedgade, ✉1655 V ☎ 33 25 44 75
Copenhagen's largest and best equipped pornoshop for gay men with magazines, books, toys, leather and rubber items. Three video rooms behind the shop.

CINEMAS

Loke (DR G MA p) 15-01 h. Closed on Saterdays.
Nørre Søgade 23 ✉1370 ☎ 33 32 19 73
Biggest gay cinema in town with cubicals and small dark zone area. Three video rooms. Shop with magazines, toys and videos. Cover charge 40DKr.

SAUNAS/BATHS

Amigo Sauna (B f G MA sa sb sol VS YG) 12-7, Fri-Sat -8 h
Studiestræde 31 A ✉1455
Copenhagen's only real gay sauna. Recently renovated. Three floors with lots of cubicals, dark rooms, several video rooms as well as sling rooms and mazes. Busy at WE.

BODY & BEAUTY SHOPS

Company 37 (g)
Rådhusstræde 5 ✉1466 ☎ 33 14 76 76
Haircuts. Studentdiscount Mon-Wed 250DKr

BOOK SHOPS

Bookshop Café (b f GLM) Mon-Fri 17-19 h
Teglgårdstræde 13 ✉1452 ☎ 33 36 00 81
Non-commercial bookshop run by LBL with internet café.

DECORATION

van Rosen (g) Mon-Fri 12-18 h Sat 10-14
Rosengården 10 ✉1174 ☎ 33 13 81 38
Asian furniture.

FASHION SHOPS

Underwear for Gentlemen (g)
Gothersgade 27 ✉1123 ☎ 33 14 04 84
Special shop for sexy and trendy underwear.

LEATHER & FETISH SHOPS

Cruz Leather Works (G LJ MA) 11-17.30, Sat -14 h
Studiestræde 29, ✉1455 ☎ 33 14 90 17
Call for appointment outside store hours. Everything made to measure within a few days.

complete offer
see page Germany/Berlin
KØBNHAVN
- from DKK 180 -
overnight accomodation service
· about 600 beds · more than 20 cities ·
enjoy
bed &
breakfast
central booking office Berlin +49-30-21 51 666 4:30-9:00 pm local time
Fax +49-30-21752219 · info@ebab.com · www.ebab.com

SM-Bladet/SM-Shop 11-18, Fri -19, Sat 10-14 h, closed Sun
Studiestrade 27, ✉1455 København K ☎ 33 32 33 03

TRAVEL & TRANSPORT

Inter-Travel ApS 10-17.30 h
Frederiksholms Kanal 2 ✉1220 ☎ 33 15 00 77

HOTELS

Hotel Jørgensen (g H)
Rømersgade 11 ✉1362 ☎ 33 13 81 86

Hotel Windsor (bf CC G H MA) Check in 8-23 h
Frederiksborggade 30 ✉1360 *(2nd floor. S-Tog Nørreport)*
☎ 33 11 08 30 Fax: 33 11 63 87
Email: hotelwindsor@inet.uni-2.dk
Homepage: www.hotelwindsor.dk
The only gay hotel in Copenhagen. Traditional and unpretentious tourist class hotel. Within walking distance to all gay locations. Single rooms from 400 DKK, Double rooms from 500 DKK, breakfast included.

APARTMENTS

Holiday Apartment (H g p) Office hours 09-23 h
Sankt Gertruds Stræde 6A, 2.th ✉1129 ☎ 26 20 35 20
Email: tonny@email.dk
Holiday apartment for 1,2 or 3 persons. Hotel-like bedroom, big frunished kitchen, nice bathroom, cable tv. DKr 500 per night.

PRIVATE ACCOMODATION

At Carsten's (B&B) (GLM H OS YG) Reservation 11-21 h
Christians Brygge 28 ✉1559 V *(5th floor)* ☎ 33 14 91 07
Email: Carstens@vip.cybercity.dk
Homepage: www.copenhagen-gay-life.dk/atcarstens
Centrally located, 5 min. walk to gay scene. Own key, shared bath, kitchen and laundry. Rates double Dkr. 450. Extra persons Dkr. 125. Also shared dormitory for back packers-bring own bedding/sleeping bag. Rates Dkr. 125. Wonderful location, good views. Now with even more rooms available. Rooftop parties in summer.

Enjoy Bed & Breakfast (bf G H MA YG) 16:30-21:00 h
☎ +49 (30) 215 1666 Fax: +49 (30) 217 52219
Email: Info@ebab.com Homepage: www.ebab.com
Price 20 Euro. Accommodation sharing agency. All with shower & bf

GENERAL GROUPS

Bøssernes Befrielsesfront/BBF Meetings Mon 20 h
1407 København, Christiania, Bøssehuset ☎ 31 95 98 72
Anarchist gay group, bøssehuset (=gay house) is situated in the free state of Christiania, in the same house as Karlsvognen. Parties on Saturdays, theater, cabaret, various „competitions". Call Pan information ☎ 33 13 01 12.

HOVSA Club for Gay Hikers
☎ 38 87 80 71

FETISH GROUPS

SLM-København
Studiestræde 14 ✉1455 ☎ 33 32 06 01
Email: slm-cph@email.dk or ecmc-slm@post3.tele.dk.
Homepage: www.slm-cph.dk
Member of ECMC.

HEALTH GROUPS

Positivgruppen Mon-Thu 10-16, Fri 12-14 h
PO Box 159 ✉2000 Frederiksberg ☎ 31 86 32 33
Group of gays or bisexual men who are HIV-positive and live in Copenhagen or Sjælland (Sealand). Organized in small groups.

STOP AIDS Mon-Fri 10-16:00h
Amagertorv 33 ✉1160 ☎ 33 11 29 11
A non profit organisation, supported by the government promoting AIDS awareness

HELP WITH PROBLEMS

AIDS Hotline 9-23:00h every day.
☎ 3391 1119
„Kafe Knud" - Skindergade 26 is the meeting place for PWA

RELIGIOUS GROUPS

Markens Liljer/Metropolitan Community Church
Teglgårdstræde 13 ☎ 31 83 32 86
Service Sun 17 h, Reverend: Mia Andersen.

SPECIAL INTEREST GROUPS

Gay Summer Camp
Vendersgade 8, ✉1363 ☎ 33 11 55 81

SMil S&M Club (g LJ) Mon 18-21 h.
Sorgenfrigade 8 A *(2nd floor)* ☎ 31 81 05 50
Association for S/M; gay and straight persons can become members. SMil is for all ages. Publishes an own SM magazine. Gay-Together party last Sun 20h (Dress-code).

SWIMMING

-Bellevue Strand (Public beach 8 km north of Copenhagen city. Used by many gay men; especially the northern part of the beach against the wall)
-Charlottenlund (8 km from København)
-Frederiksberg Svømmehal (g MA pi sa sol) (8-20, Sat 7-13 h, closed Sun. Helgesvej 29, 2000 Frederiksberg; take bus N°2 or train F and get off at Frederiksborg station)
-Tisvilde Strand (Public beach in North Sjælland (Sealand). Go by train E to Hillerød, then change to private railroad for Tisvildeleje. The beach is about 2 km from the station; pass the P and go 1-2 km further west: The beach will gradually get more and more nude and gay. Some action in the dunes and in the wood behind the beach)

CRUISING

-Amor parken (Tagemsvej-Blegdamsvej)
-Charlottenlund Skov (Take the S-train to Charlottenlund Station and pass under the railway into the wood in direction of the castle; the action is usually between the castle and the Danmarks Akvarium in the evenings and at night.)
-Ørstedsparken Centrally located between Nørre Voldgade and Nørre Farimagsgade. Action during the day but mostly nights
-Utterslev Mose (Follow the motorway to Hillerød. About 8-9 km from the city you will find a P with a public convenience building on your right. Round this building and in the bushes 100 m away you will find the action. Take bus 63 from Rådhuspladsen. Daytime and evenings, summernights.)

Koge ✉ 4600

SWIMMING

-Ølsemagle Revle (about 4 km north of Køge)

CRUISING

-At the harbor/ved havnen

Kolding ✉ 6000

BARS

Lobito (B D G MA) Wed 19-23, Sat 21-2 h
Dyrehavegårdsvej 38 ✉6000 *(1st floor)* ☎ 75 54 10 23

Næstved ✉ 4700

GENERAL GROUPS

LBL Næstved (GLM)
Café Rosa at Agora, Glentevej 23 every 2nd/4th Fri 19-24 h
Glentevej 23 ✉4700

Nykobing F ✉ 4800

GAY INFO

Hotline every 2nd Thu 20-22 h
Vendersgade 8 ☎ 55 85 55 19

GENERAL GROUPS

Klubben for bosser og lesbiske i Nykøbing F
Ejegodskolen, Fjordvej 46 ✉4800 ☎ 53 88 00 70 or ☎ 53 87 34 78 or 54 94 33 26

SWIMMING

-Marielyst Strand (near the nude area)

Nykobing M ✉ 7900

GENERAL GROUPS

B.L.I.S. (Bøsser og lesbiske i Skive)
Box 285 ✉7900 ☎ 97 71 08 09
Parties: 1st Saturday in February, April, June, August, October, and December.

Odense ✉ 5000

DANCECLUBS

Lambda Disco and Café (B CC D GLM lj MA s WE)
Disco: 1st Sat 22-4; cafe: Wed 20-24, Sat 22-4 h
Vindegade 100 KLD ✉5000 ☎ 66 17 76 92

SEX SHOPS/BLUE MOVIES

Antikvaren (g)
Dronningegade 24 ✉5000 ☎ 66 12 86 08
Pornocentrum (g) 10-22 h
St. Gråbrødrestræde 7 b, Odense C ✉5000
Also sex shop. 4 film rooms, 1 with gay-porno films. Video rentals.
Sexshop (glm VS)
Vindegade 110 ✉5000 ☎ 66 19 05 33
3 film rooms, one with gay film. Video rental.

GENERAL GROUPS

Lambda • Bøsser og Lesbiske på Fyn Wed 18-20 h
PO Box 11 92, Vindegade 100 ✉5000
☎ 66 17 76 92

HEALTH GROUPS

AIDS-Info (døgnvagt) Mon-Fri 08-23 h, Sat, Sun 14-23 h
Sankt Anne Plads 2 ✉5000 ☎ 65 91 11 19
Information and help with questions about AIDS and HIV-antibodies.

SWIMMING

-Hverringe Strand (Nude bathing near Kerteminde. About 2 km on the road along the »Nordstranden« in direction of Hverringe Slot. The entrance to the beach is at the [P] in the »Hverringe-skoven«)

CRUISING

-Park „Munke Mose" (along the brook, evening and night)
-Square Albani Torv (underground)

Roskilde ✉ 4000

GENERAL GROUPS

Trianglen (GLM) Tue 19, 2n/4th Fri 19 h, party 1st Fri
Køgevej 44 ✉4000 ☎ 42 38 23 02

CRUISING

-Railway station

Skagen ✉ 9990

HOTELS

Finns Hotel Pension (bf CC F glm H MA NG OS)
Østre Strandvej 63 ✉9990 ☎ 98 45 01 55
Homepage: www.skaw.dk/finnshotelpension
Old woodhouse with a private atmosphere. Own key, car park. Rates single Dkr 275-325, double 525-725.

SWIMMING

-Beautiful long beach on the west coast (g NU)

Slagelse ✉ 4200

GENERAL GROUPS

Lesbiske og Bøssere i Slagelse (LOBS) 1st & 3rd Fri 19-23 h (GLM)
Slotsgade 6 ✉4200 ☎ 58 50 61 12

Sønderborg ✉ 6400

GENERAL GROUPS

Sønderbrog-gruppen (G) 20-23 h
PO Box 102 6400 ✉6400 ☎ 74 42 02 18
Young Gay and Lesbian Group (G)
Postboks 102 ✉6400 ☎ 74 42 24 49
1'eren ✉6400 ☎ 74 43 05 14

CRUISING

-At [P] behind supermarket »Kvickly«
-Esplanade (Strandpromenaden) (between castle and yacht-harbor)

Sorø ✉ 4180

GENERAL GROUPS

LBL Sjælland
Rylevænget 18 ✉4180 ☎ 53 63 01 64

Svendborg ✉ 5700

SWIMMING

-Beach on the south-eastern part of the small island of »Thurø«.

CRUISING

-Railway station (in front of Hotel Svendborg)

Tisvilde ✉ 3220

SWIMMING

-Tisvilde strand (NU)

Tonder ✉ 6270

GENERAL GROUPS

BITO
✉6270 ☎ 74 78 32 72
Coffee club for gay men.

Vanloese ✉ 2720

FETISH GROUPS

ECMC Secretariat
Clausholmvej 3 A ✉2720 Email: ecmc-slm@post3.tele.dk
ECMC's European Club's secretariat.

Vejle ✉ 7100

CRUISING

-Railway station

Viborg ✉ 8800

GENERAL GROUPS

Ny Manton (G)
☎ 20 95 95 14
Gay Group meetings every 1st and 3rd Wed 19-22 at Medborgerhuset (Blue Room), Vesterbrogade

CRUISING

-[P] behind the supermarket »Schou-Epa«
-Around the cathedral
-[P] A13

Ecuador

Northwestern South America

Initials: EC

Time: GMT -5

☎ Country Code / Access Code: 593 / 00

Language: Spanish, Quechua

Area: 283,561 km² / 109,483 sq mi.

Currency: 1 Sucre (S/.) = 100 Centavos

Population: 12,336,572

Capital: Quito

Religions: 95% Roman Catholic

Climate: Tropical climate along the coast that becomes cooler towards the inland.

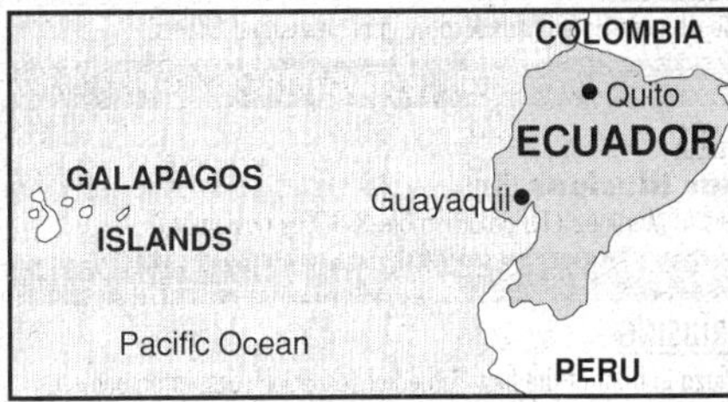

● Article 516 of the penal code punishes homosexual acts with up to 8 months imprisonment. This term may even be increased if a dependent relationship exists .
Bars and meeting points tend to be hidden and are subject to frequent arbitary police raids.

✸ Gemäß Paragraph 516 des Strafgesetzes werden homosexuelle Handlungen mit bis zu acht Monaten Haft geahndet. Diese Strafe kann bei einem Abhängigkeitsverhältnis noch erhöht werden. Bars und Treffpunkte sind schwer zu finden und werden oft von der Polizei durchsucht.

▲ En République des Equateur, l'homosexualité est un délit (article 516 du code pénal). On risque des peines de prison allant jusqu' à 8 mois et plus même, si une relation d'indépendance entre les partenaires peut être prouvée.
Bars et lieux de rencontre discrets et secrets, mais régulièrement „visités" par la police.

☆ Según el artículo 516 del Código Penal, actividades homosexuales son castigadas hasta con 8 meses de prisión. La pena es mayor en caso de que exista una relación de dependencia.
Bares y puntos de encuentro existen solamente a escondidas y son frecuentemente controlados por redadas policiales.

❖ Con l'articolo 516 del codice penale l'omosessualità viene punita con la reclusione fino a 8 mesi. La pena verrà aumentata quando sussiste un rapporto di dipendenza. I bar e i luoghi d'incontro sono piuttosto nascosti e spesso vengono controllati dalla polizia.

NATIONAL GAY INFO

G&L Guia Ecuador
PO Box 1717-1002 Quito ☎ (09) 477 776
Email: giguia@hotmail.com

Atacames

SWIMMING

-Beach near Hotel Villas Arco Iris and newsstand Cheers.

Baños

BARS

Bar Illusions (B g)
Luis A. Martínez (16 de diciembre & 12 de noviembre)

Cuenca ☎ 07

CRUISING

-Plaza in front of the hew cathedral (especially Sun afternoon)

Guayaquil ☎ 04

BARS

Club. El (B GLM s) Mon-Thu 19-24 h, Fri, Sat 19-2 h
Luis Urdaneta y Ximena 608 ☎ 302 113
Marco´s (B D GLM) Wed-Sat 22-3 h
V. E. Estrada 1310 A

DANCECLUBS

JUDA (B D GLM) Wed-Sat 22-3 h
10 de Agoste & Los Rios

HOTELS

Hotel Velez (H)
Velez 1021 y Quito *(1 1/2 blocks from Parque del Centenario)*
☎ 52 54 30

CRUISING

-Promenade, Avenida 9 de Octubre
-Parque Centenario (ayor)

Quito ☎ 02

BARS

Bar-ril (Ana Maria) (B G) Wed-Sat 17-24 h
L. García & 6 de Diciembre
Dionisios (B Glm s) Wed-Sat 10-2 h
Manuel Larrea 550 y Riofrío *(Manuel Larrea between the streets Checa and Riofrío in the Mariscal area in the modern center, near Parque Ejido)* ☎ 557 759
Friendly and popular, access through outside stairs. Thu-Sat cultural events.
Habana Café (B GLM) 17-2 h
Juan Leon Mera 134 ES y Calama *(Mariscal, located at the corner.)*
☎ (0)9-590 911
Alternative bar

CAFÉS

El Cafecito (B F glm) 17-24 h
Cordero 1124 *(Mariscal)*
Café Alternativo, with a mixture of guests. Very good meals - mainly vegetarian although rather too expensive.
El Pobre Diablo (B f glm) Mon-Sat 17- ? h
Santa Maria y J. L. Mera
Gay owned mixed alternative café. Small snacks. Periodical exhibitions such as photographical expositions.
El Portón Azul (B glm) 17-24 h
Rábida y Colón *(in the North of Mariscal*
New and not well known as yet. In the lively northern part of the city (La Mariscal) where the Yuppie scene from Quito is to be found every Friday night.

DANCECLUBS

Footloose (Victor´s) (B D G TV P) Fri, Sat 22-5 h
General Bassano ES & Av. 6 de Diciembre *(Right on the corner of both streets, Mariscal)*
Has a bad reputation but is, as always, a good meeting place. Ring the door bell.

Lunatika (B D glm) Mon-Sat 21:30-2 h
Orellana 899 & Yánes Pinzón *(In the new city center)*

Matrioshka (B D G) Thu-Sat 17-2 h
Pinto 376 & Juan Leon Mera *(In the new city center)*

Seseribó (B D glm YG) Fri Sat 21-4 h
Veintimilla 325 & Av. 12 de Octobre *(In the Basement)*
Mostly Salsa music. Gays and lesbians dance as mixed couples. The majority of the guests are heterosexual.

Spartakus (B D GLM TV p) Thu-Sun 22-2/? h
UNP e Iñaquito *(In the north at the coren of UNP and Iñaquito)*
Very popular

CINEMAS

Hollywood (NG)
Av. Venezuela
No gay videos, but very cruisy.

GUEST HOUSES

El Ciprés (H G)
Lérida 381 & Pontevedra *(In the La Flresta area)*
☎ 549 561 Fax: 549 558
Not the most attractive guesthouse, but exclusively gay and inexpensive.

PRIVATE ACCOMODATION

Cumbre Andina (bf f g H)
Av. 18 de Septiembre 368 & Av. Amazonas 2nd Floor
☎ +49-7851-480 345 Fax: +49-7851-480 562
Email: info@ecuatour.com Homepage: www.ecuatour.com
It´s also a language school and a gay info center for Ecuador. Call for further information.

HELP WITH PROBLEMS

La Linea ☎ 526 527

CRUISING

-Parque El Ejido (by daytime, in the new city center, at night AYOR beware of the police!)
-Avenida Rio Amazonas (R) (after sunset, near Hotel Hilton-colón)
-La Moriscal (AYOR)

Egypt

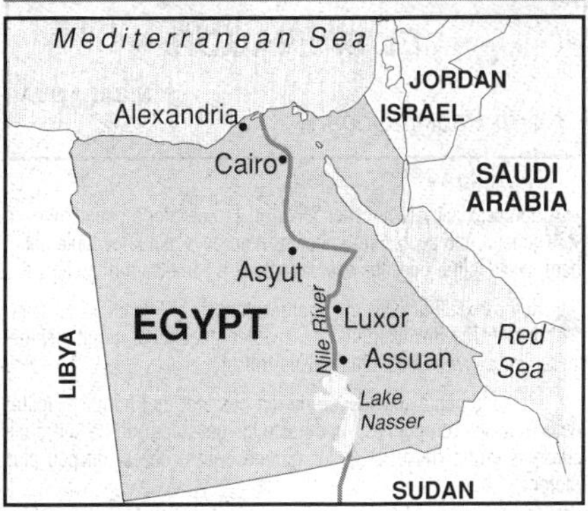

Misr
Northeastern Africa
Initials: ET
Time: GMT +2
☎ Country Code / Access Code: 20 / 00
Language: Arabic. French and English as languages of commerce
Area: 997,739 km² / 385,227 sq mi.
Currency: 1 Egyptian Pound (E) = 100 Piasters (PT)
Population: 66,050,004
Capital: Cairo (Al-Qâhirah)
Religions: 94% Moslem (almost all Sunni)
Climate: Desert climate. Summers are hot and dry, winters moderate.

● Homosexuality is not illegal in Egypt. Caution should however be taken, as Egypt also has regulations on „offences against public morals and sensitivities" which are vague enough that they could be used against you. Men are not openly gay in Egypt, so as not to be outcast by their families and society. The police cannot be considered gay-friendly. In light of recent attacks against tourists by militants Muslims, we strongly recommend you not to openly display homosexuality; this opinion was confirmed by the German embassy in Cairo. When entering the country, it is important to demand that your currency declaration be stamped and signed. It is also advisable to declare all valuables before entering, as they could otherwise be confiscated upon departure.

✸ Homosexualität ist in Ägypten nicht verboten. Allerdings gilt auch für Ägypten, daß ein „Verstoß gegen die öffentliche Moral oder die allgemeinen Empfindungen" nicht näher definiert wird. Schwule treten in Ägypten nicht öffentlich in Erscheinung, um nicht von Familie und Gesellschaft geächtet zu werden. Die Polizei kann nicht als schwulenfreundlich bezeichnet werden. Angesichts der Angriffe auf Touristen von seiten radikaler Moslems kann nur empfohlen werden, sein Schwulsein nicht „zu demonstrieren", wie die deutsche Botschaft in Kairo meint. Bei der Einreise ist es nicht ganz unwichtig, darauf zu bestehen, daß die Währungsdeklaration abgestempelt und unterschrieben wird. Man sollte auch die mitgeführten Wertsachen deklarieren, da sie sonst bei der Ausreise konfisziert werden können.

▲ L'homosexualité n'est pas un délit en Egypte. Signalons cependant que personne ne définit de façon précise ce qu'est une enfreinte à „la morale publique et au bon ordre". Les gays n'affichent pas leur homosexualité en public pour ne pas s'exposer au mépris des leurs ou de la société. La police est plutôt homophobe. Compte tenu des attentats perpétrés par les extrémistes contre des touristes, l'ambassade d'Allemagne au Caire recommande de ne pas trop faire état de son homosexualité.
A votre arrivée en Egypte, n'oubliez pas de bien faire tamponner et signer votre déclaration de devises. Déclarez aussi les objets de valeur que vous possédez. Ils pourraient vous être confisqués lors de votre sortie du pays.

☆ En Egipto la homosexualidad no está prohibida, no obstante aquí tampoco se define claramente la famosa claúsula «incumplimiento contra la moral pública o sentimientos generales». Para no ser discriminados por la familia y la sociedad, los gay no se muestran en público. La policia no es precisamente conocida por su amabilidad con los homosexuales. Debido a los ataques de musulmanes radicales contra turistas se recomienda no „demostrar abiertamente" la homosexualidad, como lo formula la embajada alemana en el Cairo. A la hora de entrar al país es importante insistir en que la declaración de divisas sea sellada y firmada. Se debería también declarar los objetos de valor, ya que a la hora de salir del país podrían ser confiscados.

L'omosessualità non è illegale in Egitto, tuttavia vengono punite le „offese alla morale pubblica". I gay egiziani non manifestano la loro condizione per non sconvolgere la famiglia e la società. La polizia non può essere definita tollerante nei confronti dei gay. L'ambasciata tedesca in Kairo consiglia, dopo l'esperienza dei passati attacchi ai turisti da parte di estremisti musulmani, di non ostentare la propria omosessualità in pubblico. Entrando nel paese è importante farsi timbrare e firmare la dichiarazione della valuta. Vi consigliamo inoltre di dichiarare i vostri oggetti di valore all'arrivo nel paese, per evitare che alla partenza vi possano essere confiscati.

Alexandria/El Iskandarya ☎ 03

HOTELS

Cecil (AC B F H NG OS)
16 Saad Zaghoul Square ☎ 480 70 55
Downtown location, 10 min to the airport. All rooms have AC, telephone, fridge, private bath, balcony, TV and radio. US$ 26-30.

Crillon (g H)
5 Adib Street

CRUISING

-Stanley Bay
-Montuzah Park
-Squares and gardens in the city center
-Tram endstation at Gare Ramleh (evening)
-Ramleh Square
-Saad Zaghloul Square and around telephone kiosk

Assuan/Aswan ☎ 097

CRUISING

-Boat landing and garden in front of Oberoi Hotel on Elephantine Island
-Landing stage near Kalabsha Hotel (close to the Cataract Gardens)
-Around Railway station

Cairo/El Qâhira ☎ 02

BARS

Al American (B NG)
Tal'at Harb/Sitta W-'Asshrin Julyu

Harry's Bar (B NG)
Cairo Marriott Hotel ☎ 340 88 88

Heliopolis Sheraton Hotel (B NG)
Uruba Street, Horreya ☎ 266 55 00
The Swan Bar & The Lobby Bar.

CAFÉS

Amphitrion Café (B F NG)
Al-Ahram Street, Nozha, Heliopolis
3 min. walk from Roxy Square. Open-air and indoor bar, café and restaurant.

DANCECLUBS

Amonn Disco (B D NG)
Sphinx Square

Disco at Borg Hotel (B D NG)

ESCORTS & STUDIOS

ARABESCORT (g msg)
A descreet male escort service from/within Egypt. A small number of hand-picked, sexy, hairy, clean and well-hung real Arab men, English and French speaking, Masseurs available.

Qualaqua Best 9-19 h
Khan Al-Khalyly

CRUISING

-Talaat Harb-Street/Tahrir Square
-Tahrir Square (little garden in the middle, at night, best Wed, Thu)
-Café Fishaawi, Khan El Khalili, El Hussein quarter
-Café Umm Kulthuum (downtown near Tawfikia square, best Thu)

Luxor/Al-Uqsur ☎ 095

BARS

Etap Hotel Bar (B G H r)
Nile Corniche
Also try the Dakka Bar and the swimming pool (8-20 h).

CRUISING

-The Corniche (from the Museum to the winter Palace Hotel)
-Park between Temple of Amon and Luxor Hotel
-Landing place for Nile river-boats (near Winter Palace Hotel)
-Banana Island (at night)

El Salvador

Pacific coast of Central America

Initials: ES

Time: GMT -6

☎ Country Code / Access Code: 503 (no area codes) / 0

Language: Spanish; regional Nahuatl, Maya

Area: 21,041 km² / 8,124 sq mi.

Currency: 1 El-Salvador-Colon (¢) = 100 Centavos

Population: 5,752,067

Capital: San Salvador

Religions: 92% Roman Catholic

Climate: Tropicalclimate. The rainy season lasts from May to October, the dry season from November to April.

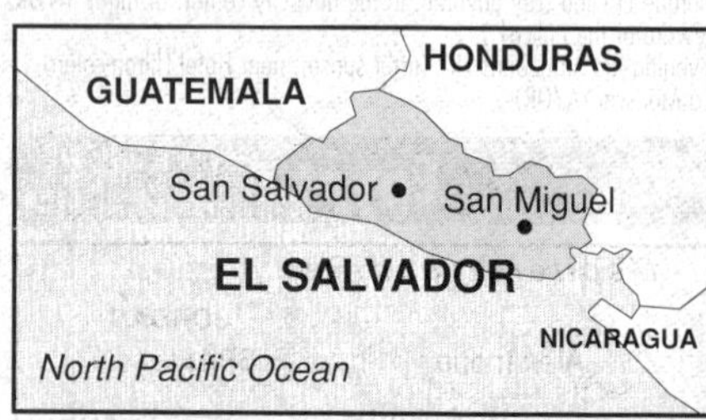

Homosexuality is not mentioned in El Salvador's penal code. In general, the people in rural areas hate gays and know little about them, while in the cities the overall attitude is somewhat more liberal.

Homosexualität wird im Strafgesetzbuch El Salvadors nicht erwähnt. Die Bevölkerung ist Schwulen gegenüber negativ eingestellt. Eine schwule Subkultur existiert nicht.

Le code pénal salvadorien ne fait pas état de l'homosexualité. Dans les campagnes, on déteste les gays dont on ne sait d'ailleurs pas grand chose. Dans les grandes villes, on est un peu plus tolérant.

En el Código Penal de El Salvador no se menciona la homosexualidad. La población rural odia a los gays aunque casi no sabe nada de ellos. Sin embargo, en las ciudades más grandes el ambiente es algo más liberal.

Il codice penale di El Salvador non fa menzione dell'omosessualità. In generale però, la gente in campagna odia i gay o non ha nessun interesse nei loro confronti, mentre nelle città il clima è di solito più liberale.

San Salvador

BARS

Arpa. El (B g)
Boulevard San Antonio Abad *(near San Luis Mall)* ☎ 225 04 29
Luna. La (A B g)
2289 Calle Berlin *(north of Boulevard Los Heroes)* ☎ 225 49 87
Milenium (B G MA WE) Cond. Juan Pablo II

DANCECLUBS

Escape (AC B D GLM)
(near Col. escalón)
Kairos (B D g YG)
(in front of Bloom Hospital)
Marios (B D NG YG)
Zona Rosa
Olimpo (B D G) Wed-Sat 22-?, Sun 17-24 h, closed Mon Tue
Alameda Juan Pablo II/Condominio Juan Pablo II No.315 *(600m west of Boulevard de Los Héroes)*
Oráculos (B D G YG) Wed-Sat 21-4 h
Condominio 2000/Boulevard de los Héroes *(1st floor)* ☎ 225 04 27
Padrisimo (B D g YG)
Zona Rosa
Silvercup (AC B D G S WE)
Condominio Juan Pablo II

RESTAURANTS

Ventana. La (B bf F NG)
(in front of San Luis Mall)

CINEMAS

Dario (AYOR NG)
Calle Ruben Darío
Majestic (AYOR NG)
Avenida España

EDUCATION SERVICES

Spanish Language Center (G)
Col. Lourder 6G, Planes de Rend ☎ 280 52 85

GENERAL GROUPS

Entre Amigos
☎ 225 42 13
Mano Amigo ☎ 260 72 49

HEALTH GROUPS

Fundasida ☎ 225 42 13

SWIMMING

-Majagual Beach
-La Libertad Beach

CRUISING

-Morazan Park/2nd Avenue (AYOR R)
-Metrocentro Mall(Centro Comervial, Boulevard de los Heroes)
-Zona Rosa (Boulevard Hipodromo)
-Acajutla Port (R)

Estonia

Eestsi

Northeastern Europe

Initials: EST

Time: GMT +2

☎ Country Code / Access Code: 372 / 8 (wait for tone) 00

Language: Estonian, Russian, Ukrainian

Area: 45,100 km² / 17,413 sq mi.

Currency: 1 Estonian Crown (ekr) = 100 Senti

Population: 1,421,335

Capital: Tallinn

Religions: Evangelical Lutheran, Russian Orthodox

Climate: Maritime climate. Winters are wet and moderate, summers cool.

Homosexuality between consenting adults is leagal. The age of consent is 14 for girls and 16 for boys, regardless of sexual orientation.

Einvernehmliche Homosexualität zwischen Erwachsenen ist legal. Das Schutzalter liegt, ungeachtet der sexuellen Orientierung, für Mädchen bei 14, für Jungen bei 16 Jahren.

L' homosexualité entre adultes consentants n'est pas un délit. En Estonie, la majorité sexuelle est fixée à 14 ans pour les filles et à 16 ans pour les garçons et ce, quelle que soit leur orientation sexuelle.

La homosexualidad por acuerdo entre dultos es legal. La edad de consentimiento, sin importar la orientación sexual, es de 16 años para varones; para mujeres es de 14 años.

L'omosessualità tra adulti consenzienti è legale. L'età legale per avere rapporti sessuali è, indipendentemente dall'orientamento, di 14 anni per le ragazze e di 16 per i ragazzi.

NATIONAL GAY INFO

Gay.Ru
PO Box 1 ✉109 457 Moskva Homepage: www.gay.ru
Russian National Website of Gays, Lesbians, Bi- and Transsexuals. This web-site covering all aspects of gay life in all republics of the former USSR, including Estonia, Reliable, exhaustive and up-to-date information. English version available.

Pärnu

CRUISING

- Beach of Pärnu

Tallinn

BARS

Mercator (AC B D f GLM) 17-2 h
7 Toompuiestee

X Baar (AC B DR F GLM) 13-24 h, Sat-Sun 15-24 h
Sauna 1 ☎ 620 92 66

DANCECLUBS

Nightman (AC B D f glm MA S) Wed Thu 18-2, Fri Sat 21-6 h
Vineeri 4 *(Bus 5/18/36-Vineeri)* ☎ 551 11 32
Karaoke on 2nd Wed. Shows 3 times a month on Sat. Entrance-fee ekr 50 on Fri Sat, ekr 25 on Wed-Thu.

GENERAL GROUPS

Eesti Gayliit
PO Box 142 ✉EE0090 ☎ 506 32 52 (GSM)
Estonian gay union.

Eesti Lesbide Ja Binaiste Ühing (Eesti Lesbiühing)
PO Box 3245 ✉EE0090 ☎ 551 11 32
Email: eluell@saturn.zzz.ee
Estonian union of lesbians and bisexual women.

FETISH GROUPS

Eesti Nahkmeste Klubi
Po Box 5705 ✉EE0003 Email: wassar@hotmail.com
Estonian leather club.

HEALTH GROUPS

AIDS Prevention Centre
Narva Street 48 ✉EE10150 ☎ 641 08 08

Espo Ühistu
48 Narva mnt. ✉EE0010 ☎ 641 08 08
HIV+ organization. Email: aids@anet.ee

SPECIAL INTEREST GROUPS

Gendy
PO Box 5759 ✉EE11202 ☎ 528 23 68
Email: gendy.estonia@mail.ee Homepage: www.hot.ee/gendy
Organization for transsexual people.

SWIMMING

- Pirita Rand. Beach on the right side from beach station to the end of the beach (area befor the stones and in forest)
- Klooga Rand. in the dunes (40 minutes by train from Tallinn)
- Stromi Rand. On the left side form beach station cruising in forest

CRUISING

- Harju Mägi-Park (entrance from Vabaduse Väljak, the best is Linda Monument)
- Toompea

Tartu

CRUISING

-Banks of Emajõgi River
-Laululava (the song festival field. Wed to Sat from April to October from 19-22 h)

Fiji

Viti

South Pacific Ocean

Initials: FJI

Time: GMT +12

☎ Country Code / Access Code: 679 (no area codes) / 05

Language: English and Fijian, Hindi

Area: 18,274 km² / 7,056 sq mi.

Currency: 1 Fiji-Dollar ($F) = 100 Cents

Population: 822,000

Capital: Suva

Religions: 53% various Christian denominations, 38% Hindu, 8% Moslem

Climate: Tropical marine climate. There's only slight seasonal temperature variation.

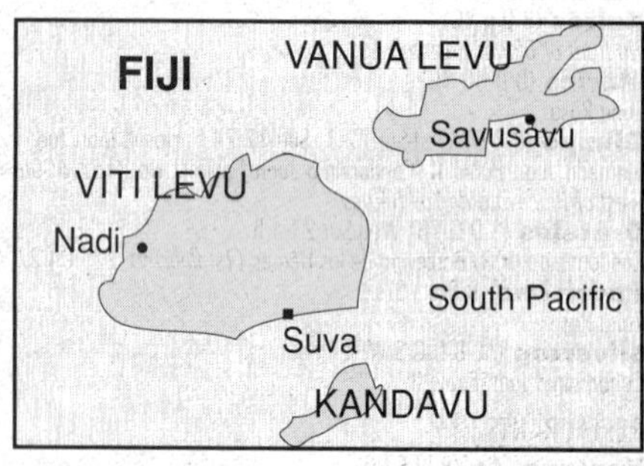

● Paragraphs 168-170 of the Fiji penal code make homosexuality completely illegal. Even an »attempt« is punishable. The maximum penalty for gay sex is 14 years imprisonment and for »attempted gay sex« seven years.

✸ Gemäß den Artikeln 168-170 des Strafgesetzbuches der Fidschi-Inseln sind homosexuelle Handlungen verboten, selbst der »Versuch« ist strafbar. Die Höchststrafe für vollzogenen schwulen Sex ist 14 Jahre, die für »versuchten« schwulen Sex sieben Jahre Haft.

▲ Aux Iles Fidji, toute forme d'homosexualité est un délit (articles 168 à 170 du code pénal), même les „tentatives". On risque 14 ans de prison maximum. Pour une „tentative", on risque 7 ans.

☆ Según establecen los artículos 168-170 del Código Penal de estas islas,todo tipo de actividad homosexual queda terminantemente prohibida, incluso el intento está penalizado. La pena más alta por actos sexuales de tipo homosexual son 14 años de cárcel, por un «intento» de acto sexual pueden caer siete años de condena.

❖ I paragrafi 168-170 del codice penale delle isole Figi vietano ogni atto omosessuale e lo puniscono con la reclusione fino a 14 anni. Anche i tentativi di seduzione omosessuale sono punibili, la pena massima è di sette anni.

Korolevu

HOTELS

Man Friday Resort (B F GLM H)
PO Box 20 *(Coral Coast)* ☎ 500 185

Nadi

HOTELS

The West's Motor Inn (AC B F CC NG pi)
Queens Road ☎ 72 00 44 Fax: 72 00 71
Email: westsmotelinn@is.com.fj
Located near international airport. 62 rooms with bath/shower/WC. All rooms with phone, balcony/terrace, radio. Hotel provides own key, car park and room service Rates $f 66 per room, additional bed 15, bf 11-15.

Suva

BARS

Dragon. The (B g)
Victoria Parade
O'Reilly's (B g)
5 McArthur Street ☎ 312 884

DANCECLUBS

Lucky Eddie's / Urban Jungle (B D g)
217 Victoria Parade *(Above O'Reilly's Bar)*
Sugar Shack (B D g)
54 Camavon Street ☎ 305 707
Traps (B D g) Mon-Sat
305 Victoria Parade ☎ 312 922

RESTAURANTS

Bad Dog Café (A F g)
McArthur Street/Victoria Parade *(Next to O'Reilly's)*
Leonardo's (B F g) Lunch & dinner, closed Sun
215 Victoria Parade ☎ 312 968
Scott's (B F g) Mon-Sat lunch & dinner, Sun dinner only
59 Gordon Street ☎ 305 620

APARTMENTS

Town House Apartments (AC B F g H)
3 Forster Street, Central Suva ☎ 300 055 Fax: 303 446
Rooms with private baths.

Finland

Suomi

Northern Europe

Initials: SF

Time: GMT +2

☎ Country Code / Access Code: 358 / 00 or 990 or 994 or 999

Language: Finnish, Swedish

Area: 338,145 km² / 130,558 sq mi.

Currency: 1 Finnmark (Fmk) = 100 Penniä. 1 EURO = 100 EURO Cents (The Euro can only be used in the clearance system)

Population: 5,149,242

Capital: Helsinki/Helsingfors

Religions: 90% Christian

Climate: Cold moderate climate. Its potentially subarctic, but comparatively mild because of the moderating influences of the North Atlantic Current, the Baltic Sea, and tenthousands of lakes.

● The age of consent for homosexual acts is 18 and for heterosexuals 16. A parliamentary decision about an adjustment in this respect is still overdue. But more important to the Finnish gays and lesbians is, that registered relationships are introduced in the near future, Finnland being the only country in Scandinavia without such an arrangement. One has to wait and see how Finnish society will react to these demands. Anyway, in every day life Finnland has nearly reached the standard typical for Scandinavia. Every major city has a more or less active gay organisation, of which the most active is the state-supported SETA.

✱ Das Schutzalter für sexuelle Handlungen liegt sowohl für Homo- als auch Heterosexuelle bei 16 Jahren, bei Vorhandensein eines Autoritätsverhältnisses bei 18 Jahren. Vor kurzem wurde auch das Werbeverbot für Homosexualität aufgehoben, so daß jetzt strafrechtliche Gleichheit zwischen Homo- und Heterosexualität besteht. Die finnische Gesellschaft öffnet sich zusehens, so daß zumindest im Alltag Finnland inzwischen skandinavisches Niveau erreicht hat, wenngleich es noch keine weitreichenden Rechte für schwule Partnerschaften wie in den anderen skandinavischen Ländern gibt. Jede größere Stadt hat jedoch eine mehr oder weniger aktive Schwulenorganisation. Die aktivste ist die SETA, die auch vom Staat finanziell unterstützt wird.

▲ En Finlande, la majorité sexuelle est fixée à 18 ans pour les homosexuels et à 16 ans pour les hétérosexuels. Le Parlement est en train d'étudier la possibilité de baisser l'âge de la majorité sexuelle à 16 ans pour tous. Bien plus important encore: on envisage d'instaurer bientôt un PACS. La Finlande pourrait donc rattraper son retard par rapport aux autres pays scandinaves. Attendons donc de voir comment les Finlandais vont réagir à ces changements. Autrement, pas de différence notable dans la vie de tous les jours avec les autres pays nordiques. Dans chaque grande ville, il y a un groupe gay plus ou moins actif. Le plus connu et le plus actif est le SETA. Il est subventionné par l'Etat.

☆ Las actividades homosexuales estan permitidas legalmente a partir de los 18 años de edad, las relaciones heteros son legales a partir de los 16 años. La decisión del parlamento para nivelar este „hueco" no se prevee en un futuro cercano. De cualquier forma para los gays y lesbianas finlandeses es más importante el hecho de que proximamente aqui, como en los otros países escandinavos, también será posible el registro legal de noviazgo. Queda abierta la cuestión de como reaccionará la sociedad finlandesa con respecto a estas decisiones constitucionales. Respecto al ambiente gay se puede asegurar que Finlandia ha casi alcanzado el nivel de sus países vecinos. Cada gran ciudad posee una organización gay más o menos activa. La más activa de ellas es la SETA, que es apoyada económicamente por el Estado.

La maturità sessuale è di 18 anni per gli omosessuali e di 16 per gli eterosessuali. Manca ancora una delibera parlamentare per appianare queste differenze. Senonchè per i gay e per le lesbiche finlandesi è più importante che in un futuro prossimo anche in Finlandia, come in tutti gli altri paesi scandinavi, siano possibili le relazioni registrate. Bisognerà poi vedere la reazione della società finnica riguardo a tali riforme. Nella vita quotidiana, in ogni caso, la Finlandia ha quasi raggiunto il livello scandinavo. In ogni grande città vi è un'organizzazione gay più o meno attiva. La più attiva, SETA, è finanziata dallo stato.

NATIONAL GAY INFO

Boyztown
PO Box 18 00531 Helsinki
Email: BTlenti@starmail.com
Contact magazine for gay men. Information and debates on gay life. Published quarterly.

Mensroom
PO Box 353 00151 Helsinki

SETA (Seksuaalinen Tasavertaisuus ry) Mon-Tue 12-16, Wed 12-18, Thu 12-16, Fri 12-14
Hietalahdenkatu 2 B 16 00180 Helsinki ☎ (09) 612 32 33
Fax: (09) 612 32 66 Email: nfo@seta.fi. Homepage: www.seta.fi

Z Magazine (GLM)
Hietalahdenkatu 2 B 16 00180 Helsinki ☎ (09) 612 32 33
Fax: 09) 612 32 66

NATIONAL PUBLISHERS

Ihme Oy
Suotorpantie 15 E 14, 02130 Espoo Fax: (09) 547 42 90

NATIONAL GROUPS

Finnish AIDS Council Mon-Fri 10-17 h
Hietaniemenkatu 5 00100 Helsinki ☎ (09)454 20 70
Fax: (09)454 20 70 Email: info@aidscouncil.fi
Homepage: www.aidscouncil.fi

Helsinki - Uudenmaan Lääni 01000 ☎ 09

GAY INFO

Helsingin seudun SETA ry (GLM) Mon Tue 10-16, Wed-Thu 12-18, Fri 10-14 h
Hietalahdenkatu 2 B 16 00180 ☎ 612 32 33
Fax: 612 32 66 Email: info@seta.fi
Very active gay and lesbian rights organization. Ask for their services.

Radio SETA Thu 18-18.30 h (FM 100,3 MHz)
(capital area only)

SETA-Library (GLM) Mon Tue 10-16, Wed Thu 12-18, Fri 10-14 h
Hietalahdenkatu 2 B 16 00180 ☎ 135 83 02

TOURIST INFO

Helsinki City Tourist Office May-Sep: Mon-Fri 8.30-18, Sat Sun 10-15; Oct-Apr: Mon-Fri 8.30-16 h
Pohjoisesplanadi 19 00100 ☎ 169 37 57

BARS

Con Hombres (AC B CC dr G LJ MA N OS) Mon-Fri 16-2, Sat Sun 14-2 h
Eerikinkatu 14 00100 ☎ 60 88 26

Escale (A AC B CC d G MA s) 15-2 h
Kansakoulukatu 1 00100 ☎ 693 15 33

Lost & Found (! AC B CC D F GLM MA s) 17-4, Sat Sun 15-4, Hideaway Bar: 22-4 h
Annankatu 6 ☎ 680 10 10
Very popular.

Mann's Street (AC B cc d f GLM lj MA S STV) 15-3 h daily
Mannerheimintie 12 A1 00100 ☎ 612 11 03

Nalle Pub (B GLM OS W) 15-2 h
Kaarlenkatu 3-5 ☎ 701 55 43

Terrace Bar (B F NG YG) Mon-Sat 9-22 h
Pohjois-Esplanadi 41 *(6th floor at the Stockmann department store)* ☎ 66 55 66
Popular „post-shopping" refreshment oasis.

Tom's Club (B G LJ) Sat 22-2 h
☎ 680 29 48

DANCECLUBS

Dare to be (B D YG) Mon 22-4 h
at Nylon, Kaivokatu 12

DTM (! B D GLM WE YG) 21-4 h
Annankatu 32/Kansakoulukatu *(Near bus station)* ☎ 694 11 22
THE disco in Helsinki.

RESTAURANTS

Goa House (B F glm) Mon-Fri 11-23, Sat Sun 12-23 h
Viides Linja 16 ☎ 73 50 11
Indian cuisine.

3. Linja (B F glm) 18-2 h
Kolmas Linja 6 ☎ 753 31 00
Pasta, salads, chicken.

SEX SHOPS/BLUE MOVIES

ERIK 10 (G) Mon-Fri 9-18 h, Sat 10-14 h
Eerikinkatu 10 00100 ☎ 602 368

Keskusvideo (G) 9-21, Sun 12-21 h
Eerikinkatu 10 00010 ☎ 645 383

King's Sex Video (g) 9-22, Sat 9-16, Sun 12-16 h
Iso Roobertinkatu 38 00120

Sex Center (g) 10-18, Sat 10-15 h
5 Linja 8 ☎ 773 30 04
Also mail order.

Sex Shop Finland (g)
Pengerkatu 24 00500

Sex 42 (g) 9-18, Sat 9-14 h
Iso Robertinkatu 42 ☎ 62 60 89

SAUNAS/BATHS

Talli Baari & Sauna (AC DR G MA sa W) Wed Sun 18-2 h
Lepakko, Porkkalankatu 1 00180 ☎ 25 34 04 53

CONDOM SHOPS

Kondomeriet (g) Mon-Fri 10.30-19, Sat 10.30-16 h
Mannerheimintie 5 *(in Hansatalo-Shopping Center)*
Condoms, postcards, t-shirts and gifts.

LEATHER & FETISH SHOPS

Decadenz (g) Forum Shopping Centre
Leather, boots, jackets.

GENERAL GROUPS

OHO-Gay and Lesbian Students of Helsinki University (GLM YG) Tue 19-21 h
Mannerheimintie 5B ✉00100 *(5th floor)* Fax: 612 32 66
Email: hory@yahoo.com

FETISH GROUPS

Kinky Club
PO Box 9 ✉00521
Gay and straight S/M

HEALTH GROUPS

Helsingin Aids-tukikeskus Mon 10-20, Tue-Thu 13-17, Fri 13-16 h
Hietaniemenkatu 5 ✉00100 *(4th floor)* ☎ 454 35 36
HIV testing, information and psychosocial support.
Positiivi-yhdistys ry Mon-Wed & Fri 10-16, Thu 14-20 h
☎ 685 18 45 Fax: 694 63 87
Organization for HIV+ people.

HELP WITH PROBLEMS

Helpline (GLM TV) Wed Sun 18-21 h
☎ 612 32 33

SPECIAL INTEREST GROUPS

MSC Finland- Tom´s Club (b DR f G LJ MA P VS) Fri 1-6 h, Sat 1-7
PO Box 48 ✉00531 ☎ 680 29 48 Email: mscfin@sci.fi
Homepage: www.sci.fi/nmscfin
Association of leather, uniform, rubber, SM,B

SWIMMING

-Pihlajasaari (island 15 minutes by boat from Merisatama, the southernmost part of town)
-Tikkurilan uimahalli (in Tikkurila near youth-hostel)
-Uimastadion (g pi sa) (Outdoor pools near the Olympic stadium, open mid May to mid Sep)

CRUISING

-Stockmann department store (2nd & 5th floor)
-Main railway station (Metro-level, where the shops are)
-Mäntymäki AYOR (P and park near Olympic Stadium)
-Laakso (in the Keskuspuisto/Central park behind the race track, evenings)
-last P highway 6 from Porvoo → Helsinki

Hyvinkää - Uudenmaan Lääni ✉ 05800 ☎ 19

SAUNAS/BATHS

Hyvinkään uimala (b NG sa)
Teermäenkatu 6 ✉05800
Best on Tue.

GENERAL GROUPS

Amigo kerho 56
PO Box 27 ✉05910

Joensuu - Pohjoiskarjalan Lääni ✉ 80100 ☎ 13

BARS

Molly's Pub (AC B CC MA N NG)
Torikatu 20 ✉80100 ☎ 277 511
Wanha Jokela (A AC B bf F H MA N NG S)
Torikatu 26 ✉88100 ☎ 122 891
Old favorite of the local gays and lesbians. Also popular among intellectuals and artists.

DANCECLUBS

EastWest (AC B CC D NG YG WE)
Torikatu 20 ✉80100 ☎ 277 511
Not exclusively gay but worth a visit. Young and trendy clientele.

SEX SHOPS/BLUE MOVIES

Seksipuoti Soho (AC NG SNU VS)
Kauppakatu 17 ✉80100 ☎ 127 395
Email: joen.soho@soho.inet.fi Homepage: http://come.to/sohosex
Very gay friendly, gay videos for rental and sale, toys, magazines, private shows, etc...

SAUNAS/BATHS

Kuntohovi (AC B bf CC F H MA msg NG pi sa sol wh WO)
Nepenmaenkatu 2 ✉80100 ☎ 172 21
Luxurious sauna and swimming resort. Wide variety of services offered.
Virkistysuimala Vesikko (AC MA N NG pi sa sol)
Uimarintie 1 ✉80100 ☎ 267 53 54
Popular among locals for rcreational swimming. However there is a busy gay cruising going on weekday nights

GENERAL GROUPS

Joensuun SETA Demian Klubi ry (b d GLM MA)
Hotline 19-21 h
PO Box 188 ✉80101 ☎ 362 68 65 Email: demian.klubi@sci.fi
Homepage: www.seta.fi/demianklubi
Disco and other activities arranged regularly throughout the year at the Aavapirti. Ask or check the website for current information.

HEALTH GROUPS

Red Cross Tue 17-20 h
Kauppakatu 35 ☎ 226 336
Anonymous and free HIV-testing, support and information

SWIMMING

-Linnulahti (NG, popular beach during summertime, lots of yourng people - see cruising)
-Aavaranta (NG MA, popular beach during simmertime)

CRUISING

-Linnuanlahti (simmertime only, the rocks behind the trees to the right of the beach, very cruisy at sunny weahter)
-Virkistysuimala Vesikko (NG, MA, very cruisy weekday nights)

Jyväskylä - Keskisuomen Lääni ✉ 40100 ☎ 014

GAY INFO

Jyväskylän Seta • Pink Club ry (GLM) Thu 19-?, switchboard Wed 19-21, Youths 1st Sat 15-?, Discussions Sun 16-18 h
Yliopistonkatu 26, PO Box 410 40101 ✉40101 *(2nd floor)*
☎ 310 06 60 Email: pinkclub@seta.fi
Homepage: www.cc.jyu.fi/~tpkeskit/pink/

BARS

Hemingway's (B f g)
Kauppakatu 32 *(at pedestrian street)*

DANCECLUBS

Lillukka (GLM) For times ask at ☛ Jyväskylän Seta (Gay Info)
Taitoniekantie 9

SAUNAS/BATHS

Jyväskylän uimahalli (NG pi sa sol wh wo)
Seminaarinkatu 15

CRUISING

-Harju Park (in the center)
-Taulumäki (hill beside lake Tuamiojärvi)

Kokkola - Vaasan Lääni ✉ 67100 ☎ 06

GENERAL GROUPS

Club Sebastian ry/SETA Kokkola (GLM)
PO Box 242 67101 ✉67100

Kotka - Kymenlaakso ✉ 48000 ☎ 05

GENERAL GROUPS

Kymen SETA ry (GLM)
PO Box 134 48101 ✉48000 ☎ 125 65

Kuopio - Kuopion Lääni ✉ 70100 ☎ 17

BARS

Emigrant (B g)
Kauppakatu ✉70100
Henry's Pub (B g)
Kauppakatu ✉70100
Maxim's (B g)
Kauppakatu
Rosson Pub (B glm)
Haapaniemenkatu

GENERAL GROUPS

Kuopion seudun SETA-Hile ry (GLM) Wed Thu 18-20 h
PO Box 213 ✉70101 *(3rd floor)* ☎ 261 95 56

SWIMMING

Kuopion uimahalli (NG pi sa sol) Mon-Fri -20, Sat & Sun -16 h
Hannes Kolehmaisen katu 3
Best on weekdays.

Lahti - Hämeen Lääni ✉ 15000 ☎ 03

GENERAL GROUPS

PH Seta ry (GLM) Wed 14-21
Rauhankatu 2 15150 ✉15000 *(2nd floor)* ☎ 75 17 971

CRUISING

-Radiomäki

Mariehamn - Ahvenanmaa Åland ✉ 22100 ☎ 018

BARS

Brittany Bar (B g WE)
Norra Esplanaden 3 ✉22100
Hotel Arkipelag (B F glm H) Wed Fri disco, other days orchestra
31 Strandgaten ✉22100 ☎ 140 20
Expensive.
Medley Night Club (B glm) -3 h
Ålandsvägen 44 ✉22100
Pub Adlon (B g) Hamngatan 7

GENERAL GROUPS

Vildrosorna Tue Thu 19-21 h
PO Box 133 ✉22101 ☎ 049-90 73 64

CRUISING

-Lilla Holma Island

Oulu - Oulun lääni ✉ 90100 ☎ 08

BARS

Hilpeä Huikka & Yöhuikka (B glm) Mon-Sat 17-3 h
Mäkelininkatu 13 ✉90100
Madison (B F g) Sun-Thu 11-1 h Fri, Sat 11-2 h
Isokatu 18 ✉90100

SEX SHOPS/BLUE MOVIES

Sex-Market (g) Mon-Fri 10-18, Sat 10-14 h
Pakkahuoneenkatu 34 ☎ 375 985
Gay section with magazines, videos etc.

SAUNAS/BATHS

Oulun Uimahalli (g pi sa) Mon-Fri 7-21 h, Sat, Sun 10-17h
Pikkukankaantie 3 *(Kaksila Sports Center)*
Many gay men, bu be discreet.
Raatin Uimahalli (g pi sa) Mon-Fri 2-21 h, Sat, Sun 10-17 h
Raatinsaari
Many gay men, but be discreet

GENERAL GROUPS

Oulun Seta ry (GLM) Tue 19-21 h
PO Box 177 ✉90101 ☎ 376 932
Homepage: www.netppl.fi/~ouseta/
Disco twice a month, call for details.

HEALTH GROUPS

Oulun AIDS-Tukikeskus Mon, Wed, Fri 9-15 h; Tue, Thu 9-19 h
Kirkkokatu 16 A 8 ☎ 379 398 Fax: 379 485

CRUISING

-Oritkari park (3 km south-west of center)
-Hupisaaret (the park on the northern side of center, area behind the Summer Theater.)

Pori - Turun ja Porin lääni ✉ 28000 ☎ 02

BARS

Café Anton (B g)
Antinkatu 11 ✉28000
Green Pepper (B glm)
Herttuantori

SAUNAS/BATHS

Keskustan uimahalli (g pi sa) Mon-Fri 6-20 h, Sat 8-17 h, Sun 10-15 h, Jul-Aug: Mon-Fri 12-20 h; Wed 16-20 h women
Kuninkaanhaanaukio 3

GENERAL GROUPS

Porin Seudun SETA ry Helpline ☎ 231 03 35 Wed 18-21h
PO Box 261 ✉20101 ☎ 0600 902 61
Parties once a month.

Rovaniemi - Lapin Lääni ✉ 96100 ☎ 016

BARS

Pub Paha Kurki (B glm)
Koskikatu 5 ✉96100
Pub Tupsu (B glm)
Hallituskatu 24

Roy Club (B glm)
Korkalonkatu ✉96100

DANCECLUBS

Maxim's (B D glm)
Koskikatu 11 ✉96100

SAUNAS/BATHS

Uimahalli Vesihiisi (g pi sa) Tue evenings popular
Nuortenkatu 11

GENERAL GROUPS

Rovaniemen SETA ry Fri 20-22 h
PO Box 1216 96101, Hallituskatu 24 ✉96100 *(Entrance from the end of the house downstairs)* ☎ 31 01 41
Parties once a month.

Seinäjoki - Vaasan Lääni ✉ 60000 ☎ 06

CRUISING

-Törnävänsaari

Tampere - Hämeen Lääni ✉ 33100 ☎ 03

GAY INFO

Tampereen SETA Ry (GLM) Mon-Fri 11-15 h, Helpline ☎ 214 29 69 Tue 20-22 h
PO Box 381 33101, Hämeenpuisto 41 A 47 ✉33100
☎ 214 87 21

BARS

Hospital Bar (B GLM) Mon Tue Thu 16-24, Wed Fri-Sun -2 h, Happy Hour: Mon-Fri 17.30-19 h
Näsilinnankatu 22 ☎ 222 98 70
Mixei (B D f GLM OS S VS) Sun Wed Thu 22-3, Fri Sat 22-4 h
Otavalankatu 3 ✉33100 ☎ 222 03 64

SEX SHOPS/BLUE MOVIES

Eros (g) 10-18, Sat 10-15 h
Satamakatu 5
Mansen Video (g VS) 10-18, Sat 10-14 h
Hämeenpuisto 45
Big gay selection. Also mail order.

HEALTH GROUPS

Tamperen AIDS tukikeskus Mon-Fri 10-15 h, Hotline: Mon Wed Fri 15-18 h
Aleksanterinkatu 33A, PO Box 19 ✉33101 ☎ 213 33 07
Fax: 213 38 19 Email: Tre@aidscouncil.fi

CRUISING

-Alasenjärvi (surroundings of lake Alasenjärvi)
-Park Eteläpuisto (Park at the southern end of Hämeenpuisto and the area at the lakeside. In the evening.)

Turku - Turun ja Porin Lääni ✉ 20500 ☎ 02

BARS

Café Bar Pyramid (B GLM) 12-2 h
Kauppiaskatu 4 ✉20501
Jack's and Mike's (B d GLM lj MA s) Mon-Tue 17-2 h, Wed-Sun 18-3 h
Humanlistonkatu 17 B ✉20100 *(Next to railway station)*
☎ 251 58 07

DANCECLUBS

Speedway (B D GLM) Sat 23-3 h
Humalistonkatu 3

RESTAURANTS

Turun kasvisravintola Verso (F glm) Mon-Fri 11-17 h
Linnankatu 3 *(2nd floor)* ☎ 251 09 56

GENERAL GROUPS

Homoglobiini 1st & 3rd Mon 19-? h at ☛Jack's and Mike's (not Jun-Aug)
PO Box 288 ✉20101 Email: omoglobiini@seta.fi
Homepage: http://org.utu.fi/tyyala/homoglobiini/
Turun SETA ry (GLM) Mon-Fri 11-15, Tue-Thu 12-18 h, Helpline ☎ 231 03 35 Wed 18-21 h
PO Box 288, 20101, Rauhankatu 1 cB 22 ☎ 250 06 95
Fax: 251 29 05

HEALTH GROUPS

Turun AIDS-tukikeskus Mon Tue 13-19, Wed-Fri 9-15 h
Hotline: 233 62 79 Mon-Fri 10-15 h
Humalistonkatu 10 AS 18, PO Box 850 ✉20101 *(4th floor)*
☎ 253 47 46 Fax: 233 79 63 Email: Tku@aidscouncil.fi

SWIMMING

-Ruissalo Saaronniemi (g NU) (Nudist beach on the Island of Ruissalo behind the camping area)
-Samppalinna (g pi sa) (Outdoor swimming pool)
-Turun Ulimahalli (g NU pi sa) (Men only Tue Thu Sat 13-20, best after 17 h, Rehtorinpellontie 4, popular among gays.)

CRUISING

-Urheilupuisto (sporting park, around the ponds and cliffs near the upper sand field. From sunset till late at night.)

Vaasa - Vaasan Lääni ✉ 65000 ☎ 040

BARS

Café Ernst (B F glm)
Hietasaarenkatu 7 ✉65000
Fondis Street Bar (B glm) Mon Tue Thu 16-1, Wed Sat 16-3, Fri 16-2 h
Hovioikeudenpuistikko 15
Fontana (B D glm) 22-3, Wed Sat 21-4 h
Hovioikeudenpuistikko 15
Kleine Olga (B glm) Mon-Fri 17-2, Sat 14-2, Sun 18-24 h
Vaasanpuistikko 18 *(Hallinkuja)*
Public Corner (B glm) 12-1 h
Vaasanpuistikko 18
Voho ☎ 733 76 77

GENERAL GROUPS

Vaasan seudun SETA ry (GLM) Parties once a month
PO Box 162 ✉65101 ☎ 040-521 01 30

CRUISING

-Ahvensaari (behind the Ice Hall)
-Uimahalli (g) (swimming hall, Hietalahdenkatu 8, Tue & Thu evenings best)

France

Western Europe

Initials: F

Time: GMT +1

☎ Country Code / Access Code: 33 (Do not dial the first „0" of phone numbers) / 00

Language: French. Regional languages (Basque, Bretton, Alsacian, Catalan, Corsican, Occitanian)

Area: 543,965 km² / 209,971 sq mi.

Currency: 1 French Franc (FF) = 100 Centimes. 1 EURO = 100 EURO Cents (The Euro can only be used in the clearance system)

Population: 58, 804,900

Capital: Paris

Religions: 90% Roman Catholic

Climate: Generally summers are mild and winters cool. Along the Mediterranean winters are mild and summers hot.

Important gay cities: Lyon, Marseille, Nice, Paris, Toulouse

● France is a country rich in culture and tradition with social tolerance to life and it`s gay community. Homosexuality is not seen as a crime and the age of sexual consent is generally at 16. Despite impressions to the contrary, the French are a very open and friendly people, even when they are not always able to be perfect in foreign languages.
Establishing contact needs some effort, but once contact is made, they will be proud to show you their city and district,turning your holiday into a dream.

In the 80`s emerged many gay establishments, such as Bars, Centres, Newspapers and Radio Stations. The gay movement has increased in importance and the Euro Gay Pride took place in Paris in 1997. It is not surprising to see in many public places two women or two men holding hands. A large gay press, channels to establish contact (Minitel, Telephone Networks), Bars, Saunas, a gay film culture, books and events account for the decline in the number of those still closeted. Today major figures in the public eye and also politicians have disclosed their homosexual tendencies. Recognition of same sex relationships, despite many difficulties, has been voted by the Parlament.
France is indeed not only Paris, but also the provinces. There has been the emmergence within the provinces in the last few years of many gay establishments, such as in Lyon, Toulouse or on the Côte d'Azur. Moreover, within the provinces it is possible to get to know the typical French cuisine, bountiful offerings, and friendliness of the locals inhabitants. Even when there are no bars or saunas to be found in the locality there are widespread opportunities to get to know people on the streets, on the beaches and also at events.

✱ Frankreich ist ein Land reich an Kultur und Traditionen. Auch ein tolerantes Land, hier leben und schwul zu sein ist leicht. Homosexualität ist kein Vergehen und die sexuelle Mündigkeit liegt generell bei 16 Jahren. Auch wenn man manchmal den gegenteiligen Eindruck gewinnen könnte, sind die Franzosen charmant und offenherzig, auch wenn sie nicht immer mit Fremdsprachen glänzen können. Zur Kontaktaufnahme muß man schon einmal eine kleine Anstrengung hinnehmen. Habt Ihr aber erst einmal Anschluß gefunden, so lieben die Franzosen nichts mehr, als stolz ihre Stadt und ihre Region zu zeigen: Eure Ferien können schnell zu einem Traum werden! In den 80er Jahren entstanden viele homosexuelle Einrichtungen: Bars, Zentren, Zeitschriften und Radiosender. Die Schwulenbewegung gewann an Bedeutung und 1997 fand EuroGayPride in Paris statt. Homosexuelle verstecken sich immer weniger. An vielen Orten ist man nicht mehr erstaunt zwei Frauen oder zwei Männer Hand in Hand auf der Straße zu sehen. Eine große schwule Presse, Möglichkeiten des Kennenlernens (Minitel, Telefonnetzwerke, Bars, Saunas), eine schwule Filmkultur, Bücher und Veranstaltungen haben nicht zuletzt zu dieser Aufklärung geführt. Heutzutage stehen auch Personen des öffentlichen Lebens und aus der Politik offen zu ihrer Homosexualität. Die Anerkennung gleichgeschlechtlicher Lebensgemeinschaften, trotz zahlreicher Schwierigkeiten, tritt dieses Jahr in Kraft. Frankreich heißt aber nicht nur Paris. Denn es gibt auch die Provinz. Auch dort haben sich in den letzten Jahren viele schwule Einrichtungn etabliert, in Städten wie Lyon, Toulouse oder an der Côte d'Azur. Eher dort als in Paris könnt Ihr das typische Frankreich kennenlernen, mit seiner Reichhaltigkeit, seiner Gastronomie und der Freundlichkeit. Und, selbst wenn Ihr dort keine Bar oder Sauna vorfindet, gibt es doch überall Möglichkeiten Leute kennenzulernen, auf den Straßen, an den vielen Stränden, auf Veranstaltungen...

▲ La France est un pays riche en traditions et en culture. C'est aussi un pays de tolérance, où vivre et être gay y est facile. L'homosexualité n'est pas un délit et la majorité sexuelle est fixée à 16 ans. Attention toutefois, les autorités sont parfois pointilleuses sur la notion d'«outrage public à la pudeur». Même s'ils donnent souvent l'impression du contraire, les Français sont des gens charmants, ouverts et désireux de faire la connaissance d'étrangers. Cependant, il est vrai qu'ils ne brillent pas par leur connaissance des langues étrangères et un effort est souvent nécessaire pour un premier contact. Mais une fois ce premier pas franchi, vous découvrirez des gens chaleureux, qui adorent faire visiter leur ville, leur région, et vos vacances deviendront vite un rêve. Les années 80 ont vu la naissance de nombreux lieux où l'homosexualité s'est affichée: bars, associations, presse et radios. Avec l'organisation de la première Gay Pride puis, en 1997, de l'Euro Gay Pride, le militantisme a pris de l'importance. Des moyens de rencontre diversifiés (Minitel, réseaux téléphoniques, internet, bars et saunas), une riche culture cinématographique et littéraire gaye, et de nombreuses manifestations ont contribué à cet essor. On voit aujourd'hui des personnalités publiques revendiquer ouvertement leur homosexualité et il n'est plus rare de croiser dans la rue deux hommes ou deux femmes se tenant par la main. La reconnaissance juridique du couple gay (le PACS) a, malgré de nombreuses difficultés, été enfin voté par l'Assemblée Nationale en 1999. Mais la France, c'est aussi la province, plus discrète. De nombreux pôles gays s'y sont développés ces dernières années dans des villes comme Lyon, Toulouse, ou sur la Côte d'Azur. C'est là, bien plus qu'à Paris, que vous découvrirez la France typique, généreuse, avec sa gastronomie et la gentillesse naturelle de ses habitants. Vous constaterez d'ailleurs que même s'il n'y a pas de bar, de sauna, ou de clubs, les contacts se lient facilement, que ce soit dans la rue, sur les nombreuses plages naturistes, ou au cours de manifestations locales.

☆ Francia es un país rico en cultura y tradiciones. Sin embargo es un país tolerante, dónde es fácil vivir abiertamente la homosexualidad. Aquí la homosexualidad no es ningún delito y la edad de consentimiento está estipulado en 16 años para ambas orientaciones sexuales. Aunque a veces a uno le podría dar la impression contraria, los franceses son encantadores y abiertos, pero hablar otros idiomas no es precisamente uno de sus méritos más fuertes. Así que para entablar conversacion uno se tiene que esforzar al principio. Pero una vez que se ha establecido contacto, el francés se desvive para enseñaros orgullosamente su ciudad y su región, ¡así que vuestras vacaciones se pueden volver en nada de tiempo en un verdadero sueño! En los años 80 se fundaron innumerables establecimientos gay, entre ellos bares, centros, revistas y emisoras de radio. El movimiento gay ganó importancia y en año 1997 tuvo lugar la primera EuroGayPride en Paris. Las parejas homosexuales se esconden cada vez menos. En muchos sitios ya no se sorprende nadie, cuando dos mujeres o dos hombres pasean cogidos de la mano por las calles. Una amplia prensa gay, posibilidades de encuentro (Minitél, lineas telefónicas, bares, saunas), una cultura cineasta gay, libros y organizaciones han contribuido en gran parte a la acceptación social de la homosexualidad. Hoy en día, hasta famososos y póliticos no tienen problemas en reconocer públicamente su homosexualidad. La acceptación legal de parejas homosexuales està entrará en vigor en 1999. Pero Paris no es toda Francia, están también las provincias. Aquí también se establecieron en el curso de los últimos años muchas instituciones gay, sobre todo en ciudades como Lyon, Toulouse o por la Costa Azul. Son sitios mucho más adecuados que Paris para conocer la Francia típica, con su variedad, su cultura gastronómica y amabilidad. Y, aúnque a lo mejor allí no encontreís ningún bar o una sauna, existen múltiples posibilidades de conocer a gente, ya bien en las calles o en una de sus numerosas playas o fiestas.

❖ La Francia è un paese ricco di cultura e tradizioni, ma anche un paese tollerante: come gay si può viverci facilmente. L'omosessualità non viene considerata reato, e l'età legale per rapporti sessuali è generalmente di 16 anni. A volte però si può avere l'impressione opposta, perché i francesi non possono brillare sempre con le lingue straniere, ma a parte questo sono affascinanti ed aperti. Per mettersi in contatto bisogna fare qualche sforzo con la lingua francese. Una volta fatte delle conoscenze, la cosa che i francesi amano di più è far vedere la loro città e la loro regione. E così le vostre vacanze possono diventare un sogno. Negli anni ottanta sono emerse molte istituzioni gay: bar, centri di comunicazione, riviste e stazioni radio. Il movimento gay è diventato sempre più importante, e nel 1997 a Parigi si è svolta l'EuroGayPride. Gli omosessuali si nascondono sempre di meno. In molti posti non c'è più nulla di speciale vedere due donne o uomini caminare tenendosi per mano. La stampa, le possibilità di conoscersi (Minitel, reti telefoniche, bar, saune), una cultura di film gay, librerie e diversi eventi hanno, tra l'altro, favorito a quest'apertura. Oggi anche persone della vita pubblica si dichiarono omosessuali. La legge per il convivenze tra omosessuali, malgrado alcune difficoltà, è entrata in vigore nel 1999.
Ma con la Francia non si intende solo Parigi: c'é anche la provincia. Anche lì, per esempio a Lyon, a Toulouse o alla Costa Azzurra, si sono aperti molti posti gay. In tali luoghi è più facile conoscere la Francia tipica nella sua ricchezza, gastronomia e gentilezza. Anche se in alcuni luoghi non trovete un bar o una sauna, ci sono dappertutto delle opportunità di conoscere della gente, per esempio per la stra-

da, sulle numerose spiaggie, durante una delle tante manifestazioni o in occasione di spettacoli...

NATIONAL GAY INFO

Agenda Projet X & Projet X Magazine
Immeuble Métropole 19, 134/140 Rue d'Aubervilliers ✉75019 Paris ☎ 01.53.35.98.50 Homepage: http://www.rezo.fr
Gay SM monthly featuring the European and North American gay SM and fetish establishments, meetings points and parties. Publisher of the Guide Hard (every two years).

Guide Gai Pied
LFM, Immeuble Métropole 19, 134/140 Rue d'Aubervilliers ✉75019 Paris ☎ 01.53.35.98.50
Fax: 01.43.57.80.40 Homepage: http://www.gaipied.fr
Gay and lesbian guide for France and the French speaking parts of Belgium and Switzerland. On sale at newstands and bookshops.

Illico, Double Face, Idol, Ex Aequo
99 Rue de la Verrerie ✉75004 Paris ☎ 01.48.04.58.00
☛ *National Publishers - Illico Groupe*

LSG-Ligue Esperantiste Gay Internationale
c/o J.E.F.O., 4bis Rue de la Cerisaie ✉75004 Paris
Minitél: 3614 CNX, b.a.l. LSG. Gay association communicating in Esperanto (further addresses in Austria, Germany, UK and USA).

Syndicat National des Entreprises Gaies
44 Rue du Temple ✉75004 Paris ☎ 01.44.59.81.01
Fax: 01.44.59.81.03 Homepage: http://www.sneg.com
Minitel 3615 SNEG. Also coordinates Aids prevention in the Gay and Lesbian community.

Têtu
2 Boulevard de Magenta ✉75010 Paris ☎ 01.48.03.84.30
Fax: 01.48.03.29.00 Email: tetu@tetu.com
Homepage: http://www.tetu.com
Glossy, stylish gay newsmagazine.

3. Keller
3 Rue Keller ✉75011 Paris ☎ 01.43.57.21.47 Fax: 01.43.57.27.93
Monthly magazine of the Paris Gay & Lesbian Centre. ☛ Introduction Paris.

NATIONAL HELPLINES

Sida Info Droit
☎ 0 800 636 636 (toll-free)

Sida Info Service
☎ 0 800 840 800 (toll-free)

NATIONAL PUBLISHERS

Cahiers Gai-Kitsch Camp
G.K.C., B.P. 36 ✉59009 Lille ☎ 03.20.06.33.91
Rare editions of gay texts. Ask for the catalogue. Also organises the Gay Film Festival in Lille.

Collection „Un sur Dix"
D.L.M. Editions, 3 Rue de Castelnau ✉34090 Montpellier
☎ 04.67.72.18.18
Literature et essais gay, catalogue disponible.

Groupe David Gerard
115 Rue du Temple ✉75003 Paris ☎ 01.42.71.73.73
Supplier of services télématiques like 3615 GAY, BRONX, TBM, TORSO...

Groupe Gai Pied
Immeuble Métropole 19, 134/140 Rue d'Aubervilliers ✉75019 Paris ☎ 01.53.35.98.50
Publisher of L.F.M., Gai Pied Guide, E.T.R., Projet X and electronic networks.

Illico Groupe
99 Rue de la Verrerie ✉75004 Paris
☎ 01.48.04.58.00 Fax: 01.48.04.05.92
Publishes Illico, Double Face (these two for free at gay venues in Paris) and Idol, Trixx, Fresh and Ex Aequo.

NATIONAL COMPANIES

Comme des Anges Productions (G VS)
B.P. 30 ✉75680 Paris ☎ 01.42.26.10.15 Fax: 01.42.63.45.10
Homepage: http://commedesanges.com
Producer of gay erocitc videos. Mail-order.

Editions gaies et lesbiennes
15 Rue d'Estrées ✉75007 Paris ☎ 01.46.33.35.31

Gay Pied Boutik
Immeuble Métropole 19, 134/140 Rue d'Aubervilliers ✉75019 Paris ☎ 01.53.35.98.50
Minitél 3615 Gayboutik. Gay fiction, videos, erotic books and videos, fashion, gadgets.

IEM Mail Order
PO Box 276 ✉75464 Paris ☎ 01.42.41.21.41
Write for free catalogue. Selection of videos, photobooks, CDRoms, leather and latex clothing and accessories, underwear, condoms etc.

Men Store • Groupe Illico
99 Rue de la Verrerie ✉75004 Paris ☎ 01.48.04.58.00
Catalogue in Illico magazine.

New Millenium Production
5 Rue Frédéric Loliée ✉75020 Paris ☎ 01.43.73.23.05
Fax: 01.43.73.23.05 Email: new.millenium.jrod@mageos.com
Film production company.

Opale
199bis Bld Beaurepaire, B.P. 527 ✉59059 Wasquehal Cedex
☎ 03.20.99.94.00
Mail order.

Queerbox.com
129 Rue du Faubourg St. Antoine ✉75011 Paris ☎ 06.09.37.21.23 01.42.46.60.83
E-business, shopping and services, books, travel, art, sex-shop, etc.

Riviera Gay Travel
3 rue des Mimosas ✉06400 Cannes ☎ 04.92.98.32.20 Email: contact@rivieragaytravel.com
National gay travel agency.

SR Films (JNRC) (G VS)
PO Box 119 ✉13443 Marseilles ☎ 06.07.54.99.55
Office and casting: 1, rue Pytheas, 13001 Marseille. The films of Jean-Noël René Clair. Gay erotic videos.

Tom's Boutic 8 Allée des Tulistes ✉69130

NATIONAL GROUPS

Girth & Mirth France
P.B. 972 ✉25022 Besançon Cedex ☎ 03.81.47.01.41
Association for „Bears Daddy's" and other large gays and their friends. Organises meetings and parties in Lyon, Marseille and Nice.

Rando's
B.P. 419 ✉75870 Paris
Walking and hiking group.

Achères ✉ 78260

CRUISING

-Saint-Germain (forest/forêt)

Agde ✉ 34300

BARS

☛ Cap d'Agde

Agen ✉ 47000

HEALTH GROUPS

Dispensaire antivénérien
26 Rue Louis-Vivent ✉47000 ☎ 05.53.96.50.50
HIV testing.

CRUISING
-Quais de la Garonne
-Jardin Jayan
-Bords de la Garonne (after pont du canal)

Aigues-Mortes ✉ 30220

RESTAURANTS
Café de Bouzigues (AC b CC F glm OS)
7 Rue Pasteur ✉30220 ☎ 04.66.53.93.95
Camargue. La (A AC B CC E F MA N NG OS S TV W) Tue-Sun lunch and dinner
19 Rue de la République ✉30220 ☎ 04.66.53.86.88
Cuisine Camargue style.
Goulue. La (AC b F glm OS) 12-14.30, 19-23 h, closed Oct-Mar
2 Ter, Denfert Rochereau ✉30220 ☎ 04.66.53.69.45
Local, international and fish specialties.
Incognito. L' (CC glm F MA OS WE) 12-14.30, 18.30-22.30 h, Closed Dec-Feb
Place de la Viguerie ✉30220 ☎ 04.66.53.94.91
Minos. Le (b CC e F g OS)
7 Place St. Louis ✉30220 ☎ 04.66.53.83.24

HOTELS
Royal Hotel (AC bf F H MA NG OS pi)
Route de Nimes ✉30220 ☎ 04.66.53.66.40

SWIMMING
-Plage de l'Espiguette (tale Road D255 to the Phare de L'Espiguette, P on the big chargeable at the extreme end, on the beach go to the left, gay after 1.5 km)

Aiguines ✉ 83600

HOTELS
Vieux Château (B F glm H)
✉83600 ☎ 04.94.70.22.95 Fax: 04.94.70.22.95

Aix-en-Provence ✉ 13100

BARS
L'Arène (AC B CC d DR G p s VS YG) 12-2 h
38 Rue des Bernardines ✉13100 ☎ 04.42.27.66.90
The gay meeting-place of Aix.

SAUNAS/BATHS
Aix Sauna Club (AC b DR G MA sa sb sol VS) 12-20.30, Wed Fri 12-24 h
8bis Rue Annonerie Vieille ✉13100 *(entre la Rue Aude et la Rue Bedarrides)* ☎ 04.42.27.21.49
Admission FF 76.

TRAVEL & TRANSPORT
Council Travel Services
12 Rue Victor-Leydet ✉13100 ☎ 04.42.38.58.82

HEALTH GROUPS
Centre de santé
3 Avenue Paul Cézanne ✉13100 ☎ 04.42.23.35.19
Dispensaire d'hygiène sociale
✉13100 ☎ 04.42.21.50.44
Avant le vieux hôpital.

CRUISING
-Cours Mirabeau
-Parc Jourdan (AYOR) (jour et nuit/day and night)

Aix-les-Bains ✉ 73100

CRUISING
-Plage/beach de Brison-St-Innocent
-Parc des Thermes
-Petit-Port
-Esplanade du lac (Avenue du Grand Port)
-Cours Mirabeau
-Parc Jourdan (jour et nuit/day and night)

Albertville ✉ 73200

CRUISING
-Les Trois Etoiles (Avenue des Chasseurs-Alpins, garden)
-P at the swimming pool

Albi ✉ 81000

HEALTH GROUPS
Hôspital d'Albi Dispensaire antivénérien
Boulevard Sibille ✉81000 ☎ 05.63.54.08.75

CRUISING
-Place de la Cathédrale (passage)
-Monument aux Morts

Alençon ✉ 61000

HEALTH GROUPS
Centre hospitalier d'Alençon, service de médecine II
25 Rue Fresnaiz ✉61000 ☎ 02.33.32.30.49
HIV-testing.
Dispensaire
56 Rue du Jeudi ✉61000 ☎ 02.33.26.04.23

Alfortville ✉ 94140

CRUISING
-Quai Blanqui (swimming-pool)

Allauch ✉ 13190

DANCECLUBS
Mare aux Diables. La (B D G OS s) Fri Sat & evenings before holidays
Chemin de Bon-Rencontre ✉13190 ☎ 04.91.68.24.10
Car or taxi necessary.

Alpe D'Huez ✉ 38750

RESTAURANTS
Petite Taverne. La (b F glm OS) 1 Dec-30 Apr & 1 Jul-31 Aug 8-2 h
Galerie des 4 soleils, Hameau de l'Eclose ✉38750
☎ 04.76.80.32.25

Ambilly ✉ 74100

SAUNAS/BATHS
King Sauna (B CC DR f G sa sb sol VS wh) 14-23, Sun -20 h, Tue Fri mixed
39 Avenue Jean-Jaurès, Immeuble l'Imperial ✉74100
☎ 04.50.38.68.12

Amiens ✉ 80000

GAY INFO
Homophonies Wed 20.05 (FM 94,1 MHz)
R. Amiens ✉80000

GENERAL GROUPS

GLH d'Amiens ✉80000 ☎ 03.22.91.24.49

HEALTH GROUPS

Centre médico-social
16bis Rue Fernel ✉80000 ☎ 03.22.91.07.70
Service départemental de vénérologie
3 Boulevard Guyencourt ✉80000 ☎ 03.22.89.46.30

CRUISING

-P Montjoie (between Amiens & St-Fuscien)
-The garden at the circus
-Behind Hatoie-Tivoli
-Railway Station

Angers

GAY INFO

Radio Gribouille Mon 22-24 h (99.7 MHz)
160 Avenue Pasteur ✉49100

BARS

Cordonnerie (a AC B G MA VS) 14-2 h
6 Rue Boisnet ✉49100 *(Place St. Serge)* ☎ 02.41.24.07.07
Dupont T & D (B f G T) 11-2 h
43 Rue Toussaint ✉49100 ☎ 02.41.88.15.64
Variétés. Les (B G YG) 9-2 h
33 Boulevard Foch ✉49100 ☎ 02.41.88.46.62

SAUNAS/BATHS

Maine. Le (b DR G sa sb VS wh) 14-21, Fri Sat -24 h
6 Rue Valdemaine ✉49100 ☎ 02.41.20.30.16
144. Le (DR G sa sb VS wh) 13-1 h, Mon and Thu mixed.
144,146 rue Larevellière ✉49100 *Direction St. Barthélémy.*
☎ 01.41.60.39.74

HEALTH GROUPS

Centre hospitalier d'Angers, Service consultations externes
1 Avenue de l'Hôtel-Dieu ✉49033 ☎ 02.41.35.34.19
HIV-testing.
Dispensaire Gougerot
Avenue de l'Hôtel-Dieu ✉49100 ☎ 02.41.88.69.51

HELP WITH PROBLEMS

Chiron J.P.
36 Rue Florent-Cornilleau ✉49100 ☎ 02.41.60.38.76
Psychotherapies.

RELIGIOUS GROUPS

David et Jonathan
B.P. 5101 ✉49051

CRUISING

-Railway station
-Jardin des Plantes (day)
-Jardin du Mail
-Place de La-Rochefoucault
-Place du Maréchal-Leclerc
-Place du Tertre
-Château (Esplanades du Pont-Ligny)
-Montée Saint-Maurice (in front of the fountain)

Anglet ✉ 64600

BARS

Saint Georges (B CC DR F g H sa sb VS)
96 Avenue de Biarritz ✉64600 ☎ 05.59.41.21.58

SWIMMING

-Plage de Chiberta (be discreet)

Angoulême ✉ 16000

DANCECLUBS

George Sand Club (AC B D DR Glm MA p S SNU VS W YG) 23-5 h, closed Mon Tue
92 Rue de Limoges ✉16000 ☎ 05.45.68.46.15

SAUNAS/BATHS

Sauna Bleu Marine (b DR G MA P sa sb VS wh) 14-24 h, in summer closed Sun, in winter closed Tue
10 Rue Nesmond ✉16000 ☎ 05.45.94.43.11
Newly renovated.

HEALTH GROUPS

Dispensaire d'hygiène sociale
20 Rue Léonard-Jarraud ✉16000 ☎ 05.45.92.03.77

CRUISING

-Jardin vert (at daytime)
-Place Pablo Cassals (near the barracks, night)
-Place de New York
-Around the theatre
-Les Ramparts
-Forêt de la Braconne(6 km north of Angoulême. Take road 141 to Limoges, turn to the right at second road after passing »Les Rassats«. Very busy at daytime)

Annecy ✉ 74000

BARS

Comédy Café (AC B CC d G MG) 17-1 h in winter, 17-2 h in summer.
Passage des Sorbiers - 13 Rue Royale ✉74000 *Near the Post office.* ☎ 04.50.52.82.83
X.DR. Bar (AC B dr f G OS P YG) Winter 14-1, Summer -2 h, Closed on Tue
13 Avenue du Rhône ✉74000 ☎ 04.05.51.04.20

DANCECLUBS

Stud'. Le (B D GLM MA P) 23-5 h
9 Avenue du Rhône ✉74000 ☎ 04.50.45.01.04

SAUNAS/BATHS

Oxygène (b DR sa sb wh VS) Mon-Thu (G) 13-20, Fri (g) 13-24, Sat Sun (g) 13-20 h
12 Avenue Mandallaz ✉74000 *(Near Banque de France)*
☎ 04.50.51.16.05
Sauna des Romains (b DR G MA sa sb VS) 14-23, Fri Sat -2 h
15 Rue de Narvik ✉74000 ☎ 04.50.57.89.52

BODY & BEAUTY SHOPS

Salon sur Cours Tue-Sat 9-18 h
18 Rue Sainte-Claire, Cours Bagnorea ✉7400 ☎ 04.50.45.32.11
Hairdresser's and beauty shop.

SWIMMING

-Pont d'Onnex sur le Fier, Annecy-le-Vieux

CRUISING

-Place des Romains
-Place Tochon
-Place de la Mairie
-Place Stalingrad
-Place de la Visitation
-P at the SNCF station

Annemasse ✉ 74100

SEX SHOPS/BLUE MOVIES

King Video Club & Boutique (DR G MG VS) 14-23, Sun 14-20 h
39 Avenue Jean Jaurès ✉74100 *(opposite Ambilly town hall)*
☎ 04.50.38.68.12

SAUNAS/BATHS

King Sauna (AC B CC DR f G MA p sa sb sol VS wh) 14-23, Sun 14-20 h
39 Avenue Jean-Jaurès ✉74100 *(opposite town-hall of Ambilly)*
☎ 04.50.38.68.12
Finnish sauna, steam bath, cabins, video.

BODY & BEAUTY SHOPS

Salon Liberty (AC CC GLM p TV YG) 10-19 h, closed on Sun
16 rue du Commerce ✉74100 ☎ 04.50.84.27.27

HEALTH GROUPS

Dispensaire d'hygiène sociale
25 Rue du Chablais ✉74100 ☎ 04.50.37.05.70

CRUISING

-P in front of cemetery (under Place André)
-Clairière de l'ancien Ball Trap

Annonay ✉ 07100

CRUISING

-Place du Champ-de-Mars
-Post office/La poste

Anse ✉ 69480

CRUISING

-Ancien Aérodrome

Antibes ✉ 06600

BARS

Rendez-Vous. Le (B f glm MA) Tue-Sat 18-0.30 (Oct-Apr), Tue-Sun 18-2.30 h (May-Sep)
5 Cours Massena ✉06600 ☎ 04.93.34.17.77

SEX SHOPS/BLUE MOVIES

Eroshop (AC CC g lj VS) Mon-Sat 10-23 h
6 Rue Vauban ✉06600 *(2 minutes from the port, near Placo de Gaulle)* ☎ 04.93.34.09.04
The only daytime cruising place. Big screen room and DVDs.

HOTELS

Garoupe. La (b F g H) 19.45-23 h, 15 Jun-30 Sep
81 Boulevard Francis-Meillant ✉06600 ☎ 04.93.61.54.97
Hôtel Méditerranée (b bf H MA NG OS)
6 Avenue Maréchal Reille ✉06600 ☎ 04.93.34.14.84
Fax: 04.93.34.43.31
Centrally located. 5 minutes to the beach. Rooms with TV, telephone, bath/WC.
Relais du Postillon. Le (A B bf CC F glm H MA OS) Restaurant: 8-23 h, closed Sun evening
8 Rue Championnet ✉06600 *(In old town, close to post office)*
☎ 04.93.34.20.77 Fax: 04.93.34.61.24
Email: postillon@riviera
Restaurant and hotel.

HEALTH GROUPS

Dispensaire d'Hygiène sociale
6 Rue de l'Isle ✉06600 ☎ 04.93.34.32.33

CRUISING

-The garden of the railway station
-Phare de la Garoupe
-Fort Carré
-Remparts du Port-Vauban (evenings)

Arcueil ✉ 94110

HEALTH GROUPS

Dispensaire municipal
3 Rue du 8-Mai-1945 ✉94110 ☎ 05.45.47.10.33

CRUISING

-Quai Gambetta
-Parc Public

Argeles-sur-Mer ✉ 66700

BARS

Pot-Chic. Le (AC B CC D DR GLM MA OS p S SNU TV VS W)
Fri-Sun and before public holidays 23-? h, Jul-Aug: Mon-Sun
Boulevard de la Mer ✉66700 *(Centre Commercial Costa Blanca)*
☎ 04.68.81.08.86

RESTAURANTS

Crêperie Alexandre (b CC F glm OS TV W YG) 01 Apr-30 Sep 12-1 h
Rue des Roses ✉66700 ☎ 04.68.81.41.08

SWIMMING

-Tancande (NU) (between Cap Rederis & Abeille near Banyuls, summer only)
-River Tech (on the street from Argeles Plage Nord to St. Cyprien, [P] before and after the brigde over the river Tech)

CRUISING

-La Pinède

Argenton-sur-Creuse

RESTAURANTS

Rive Droite Pizzeria (AC b CC F glm OS) 19-21.30, closed Sun, Restaurant 12-13.30, 19-21.30 h
8 Rue Ledru-Rollin ✉36200
Italian food.

GUEST HOUSES

Manoir des Remparts. Le (A AC bf CC F glm H lj MA OS s) 14 Rue des Remparts ✉36800 ☎ 02.54.47.94.87
Email: willem.prinsloo@wanadoo.fr

Arles

RESTAURANTS

Tropical (B bf f glm OS) 10-1 h, closed 15.Nov to 15.Feb
28 Rue Porte de Laure ✉13200 ☎ 04.90.96.94.16

APARTMENTS

Camargue Passion (glm H MA)
B.P. 7 ✉13129 ☎ 04.42.48.80.40 Fax: 04.42.86.89.10
Email: camarguepassion@compuserve.com
Homepage: http://www.provenceweb.fr/13/camargue-passion
Located 10 mins from gay nudist beach Piémanson. Apartments and studios in the village. Guest house in Domaine de l'Amérique.

SWIMMING

-Salin de Giraud (NU) (beach of Piémanson, at Rhône mouth)

CRUISING

-Jardin public
-Cimetière
-Quai du Rhône
-Avenue de la gare

Arpajon ✉ 91290

HEALTH GROUPS

Dispensaire d'hygiène sociale
25bis Route d'Egly ✉91290 ☎ 01.64.90.14.54

CRUISING

-Forest de la-Roche-Turpin (6 km west of Arpajon)

Arras ✉ 62000

HEALTH GROUPS

Dispensaire prophylactique
30 Rue de Turenne ✉62000 ☎ 03.21.71.14.04

CRUISING

-Le Jardin Minelle (Rue R. Salengrò)
-Le Jardin du Gouverneur (Boulevard Crespel)

Arzon ✉ 56640

CRUISING

-Plage naturiste

Asnelles ✉ 14960

SWIMMING

-Les Meuvaines (G) (between Vers-sur-Mer & Asnelles)

Asnières sur Seine ✉ 92600

CRUISING

-Swimming Pool
-Quai du Dr-Dervaux
-Métro Station

Aubenas ✉ 07200

CRUISING

-Château

Aubervilliers ✉ 93300

CRUISING

-Quai Gambetta

Auch ✉ 32000

HEALTH GROUPS

Centre hospitalier, Service consultations
Route de Tarbes, 32011 Cedex ✉32000 ☎ 05.62.61.32.32
HIV-testing.

Dispensaire d'hygiène sociale
Rue Irénée David ✉32000 ☎ 05.62.05.22.75

CRUISING

-Jardin Ortholan (WC by day/de jour; P by night/la nuit)
-P RN 124
-Place Denfert-Rochereau

Aups ✉ 83630

SWIMMING

-Plage Naturiste (NU) (Les Salles sur Verdon)

Aurillac ✉ 15000

HEALTH GROUPS

Centre hospitalier
Service de médecine A ✉15000 ☎ 04.71.46.56.10
HIV-testing.

SWIMMING

-Plage Naturiste (NU) (Use the motorways N 120, D 61, D 18, D 207 direction St-Gérons. At the dam turn the first street left to Rénac-Plage. In front of P follow the right bank)

CRUISING

-Place du Gravier

Auxerre ✉ 89000

HEALTH GROUPS

Centre hospitalier d'Auxerre
Résidence Saint Germain, PO Box 51 64 ✉89000
☎ 03.86.48.47.18
HIV-testing.

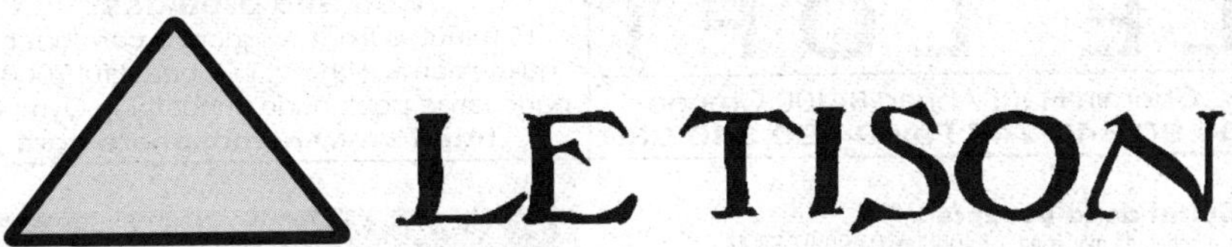

RELIGIOUS GROUPS

David et Jonathan
B.P. 394 ✉89000
Gay christians; monthly meetings

CRUISING

-Passage Soufflot (very busy when it gets dark)
-Near the church St-Pierre (at the little dark place in thecentre of town)
-La Passerelle (At the quays of the river Yonne)

Avignon ✉ 84000

BARS

Cid Café. Le (AC B f glm MA OS s) 7-1.30 h
11 Place de l'Horloge ✉84000 ☎ 04.90.82.30.38
Esclave Bar. L' (AC B D G S VS) 22.30-5 h
12 Rue du Limas ✉84000 ☎ 04.90.85.14.91
1st floor. Gay videos. Still THE gay place in Avignon.
L et M (B f glm MA OS s) summer 10-3, winter 7-1 h
40 Rue des Lices ✉84000 ☎ 04.90.86.19.67

DANCECLUBS

Cage. The (AC B D DR GLM MA P S VS) Fri-Mon 23-5 h
Gare Routière ✉84000 *(1st floor of the Bus station/1er étage de la Gare routière)* ☎ 04.90.27.00.84
Kiproko (AC B CC D GLM p S SNU) Fri Sat Mon 23-? h
22 Boulevard Limbert ✉84000 ☎ 04.90.82.68.69
Tison. Le (AC B CC D DR GLM LJ MA os p pi S SNU TV VS wh)
Fri-Mon 22.30-5.30, cabaret at 2 h
Quartier de la Gare ✉13570 Barbentane *(5 km from Avignon)*
☎ 04.90.94.94.46
Disco club with garden and pool.

RESTAURANTS

Au Petit Bedon Rose (A AC CC F g) 12-13.45, 19.30-0 h, closed Sun, Mon/lunch
70 Rue Joseph-Vernet ✉84000 ☎ 04.90.82.33.98
Croisière s'amuse. La (F glm)
Centre Commercial Le Galaxie, Route de Montfaret ✉84000
☎ 04.90.87.67.67

SAUNAS/BATHS

Sauna H Club (AC b DR f G MA sa sb sol VS) 12-22, Sat -24 h
20 Rue Paul Manivet ✉84000 ☎ 04.90.85.00.39
Popular afternoons.

HOTELS

Loft. Le (bf G H MA NU OS pi sol WO)
Chemin Haut Abrian ✉84100 Orange ☎ 04.90.34.07.47
Fax: 04.90.34.09.80
Email: hotel@homophere.com Homepage: www.homosphere.com
In the countryside, easy access to highway,station and historic town of Orange. Large park and pool.
Mas La Bonoty (b CC F glm MA OS pi)
Chemin de la Bonioty ✉84210 Pernes Les Fontaines
☎ 04.90.61.61.09 Fax: 04.90.61.35.14
20 km from Avignon.

GENERAL GROUPS

Club La Licorne (A B DR G p VS YG)
B.P. 272 ✉84011 ☎ 06.62.49.99.93
Homepage: http://pero.wanadoo.fr/clublalicorne
Leisure club for the Provence. Call for dates.

HEALTH GROUPS

Centre hospitalier
19 Rue Brossolette ✉84000 ☎ 04.90.82.28.00

Hôpital de la Durance
Consultation de médecine ✉84000 ☎ 04.90.87.38.44
HIV testing.

RELIGIOUS GROUPS

David et Jonathan
B.P. 181 ✉84009

SWIMMING

-Piscine de la Barthelasse (on the island of Barthelasse, very popular)

CRUISING

-Between the bridges/entre les ponts de Bompas et de Taracon
-City-wall (between Gate St. Michel and rue de la République)
-La Durance (30 mins drive from Avignon)

Bagnolet ✉ 93170

HEALTH GROUPS

Dispensaire LPV
4 Rue du Lieutenant-Thomas ✉93170 ☎ 02.43.64.03.21

CRUISING

-Passerelle sur le périphérique (Rue Lucien-Lambeau)

Bains-les-Bains ✉ 88240

HOTELS

Auberge Chez Dino (B CC F H OS) closed in Jan, Restaurant 10-2, Mon 10-18 h
Hautemogey ✉88240 ☎ 03.29.30.41.87
Rooms with fridge, bathroom, WC, balcony, garden. 30 km from airport, suburb location. Rates FF 250/night, 1500/week.

Bandol ✉ 83150

HOTELS

Auberge des Pins. L' (b bf CC F glm H MA OS pi) Mon Tue evening closed (low season)
2249 Route du Beausset ✉83150 ☎ 04.94.29.59.10
Fax: 04.94.32.43.46
Suburb location, 45 min from airport, 5 km from beaches and city centre. You'll get a free apéritif on quoting SPARTACUS as your source of accomodation. Private pool reserved for gays,

Hotel Ile Rousse (AC B CC F E glm MA pi)
17 Boulevard Louis Lumière ✉83150 ☎ 04.94.29.33.00 Fax: 04.94.29.49.49
Luxury establishment with 2 restaurants, private beaches and salt-water pool.

CRUISING

-Aire d'autoroute entre Bandol et Toulon

Barbentane ✉ 13570

RESTAURANTS

Moulin à Huile. Le (b F g)
Avenue Bertherigue ✉13570 ☎ 04.90.95.57.76

Bar-le-Duc ✉ 55000

CRUISING

-Parc (between/entre Rue de la Maréchal-Rue Mgr-Aimond)
-Place des Basques

Barneville-Carteret ✉ 50270

SWIMMING

-Les Moitiers-d'Allonne (NU)

Bayonne ✉ 64100

BARS

Ostadar (B CC f glm MA OS S) 9-2 h, closed in winter
Avenue Léon Bonnat ✉64100 *(opposite public garden)*
☎ 05.59.25.76.22

SAUNAS/BATHS

Sauna San Marco (b CC g sa sol vs) Sun-Thu 14-22 Fri-Sat 14-0 h
20 Rue des Faures ✉64100 ☎ 05.59.59.46.17

CRUISING

-P St-Léon (also the gardens on the parking/aussi les jardins au-dessus)
-Gare SNCF/railway station
-Château Vieux/old castle
-Sur les remparts et place des Basques

Beaucaire ✉ 30300

DANCECLUBS

Coquemar. Le (B D g) Fri Sat Sun 22-? h
Château de Beaucaire, 2 Rue Camille-Desmoulins ✉30300
☎ 04.66.59.17.76

Beaulieu-sur-Mer ✉ 06310

RESTAURANTS

African Queen (b CC E F glm MA OS) 12-24 h
Port de plaisance ✉06310 ☎ 04.93.01.14.60
Popular with gays from Monaco and abroad.

CRUISING

-P at the bridge/au pont (direction Monaco)

Beaumont-Hague ✉ 50440

SWIMMING

-Dunes (NU) (D118 towards Biville to Vasteville)
-Plage de la Vieille-Eglise

Beauvais ✉ 60000

CRUISING

-RN 17 (direction de Senlis)
-Table Ronde

Belfort ✉ 90000

HEALTH GROUPS

Centre hospitalier de Belfort
28 Avenue Jean-Jaurès ✉90000 ☎ 03.84.28.17.12
HIV-testing.

CRUISING

-P A 36 Séveans → Belfort

Beniers/Pasquet ✉ 34500

CRUISING

-Parc des Poètes
-Place de la Victoire

Benodet ✉ 29118

SWIMMING

-Beach of/Plage de Mousterlin (third entry on the right side/troisième entrée à droite)
-Plage de la Table d'Orientation

Berck ✉ 62600

GAY INFO

Radio Style FM FM 90.9/102.9 MHz
173 Rue de l'Impératrice ✉62600 ☎ 03.21.84.82.82
Regional radio with some gay content and AIDS-info.

BARS

Welcome Bar (B bf glm MA OS)
6 Avenue du General de Gaulle ✉62600 ☎ 03.21.0931.00

SWIMMING

-Beach in the north of the town/plage au nord de la ville (G NU)

Bergerac ✉ 24100

RESTAURANTS

Enfance de Lard. L' (A CC F glm) Lunch & dinner; closed Tue
Place Pélissière ✉24100 ☎ 05.53.57.52.88
French cuisine in 12th century house, on 1st floor, view of 12th century church. Large fireplace and opera music.

CRUISING

-Parc Jean-Jaurès (night)
-Eglise Notre-Dame (WC)
-Rives de la Dordogne (behind the dam, in summer)

Besançon ✉ 25000

DANCECLUBS

Privé. Le (B CC D DR GLM MA P S TV VS) 23-4 h, closed Mon
1 Rue Antide-Janvier ✉25000 ☎ 03.81.81.48.57

GENERAL GROUPS

Choc. Le (Collectif homo de Franche-Comté)
B.P. 63 ✉25013 ☎ 03.81.83.58.05
Meetings/réunions Centre Pierre Bayle, 27 Rue de la République. Wed 18-20 h. Contact Rosa Hilfe (RFA).
Girth & Mirth Alpes Jura Hotline 10-22 h
B.P. 972 ✉25022 ☎ 03.81.88.06.18
Email: g.m-alpjura@wanadoo.fr
Club for big gay man and their admirers. Monthly events (please call for information).

HEALTH GROUPS

Dispensaire antivénérien
15 Avenue Denfert-Rochereau ✉25000 ☎ 03.81.80.80.88

CRUISING

-Le Parc Micaud (night, at the border of Doubs river/au bord du Doubs)
-Square Elisée-Cusenier
-Parc du centre-ville
-P St.Paul (Night)
-Jardin des Senteurs
-P Pont de la République (Corner of bridge and avenue Gaulard. Night and day)

Béthune ✉ 62400

HEALTH GROUPS

Centre médico-social
Rue du Banquet Réformiste ✉62400 ☎ 03.21.57.66.35

CRUISING

-Jardin public (behind la place du Jeu de Paume)
-Parc de Beuvry (Boulevard Poincaré)
-Parc de la Gare-d'Eau

Béziers ✉ 34500

GAY INFO

Tendances gaies 24 h (FM 96 MHz)
✉34500

BARS

Bar Kephren (AC B CC DR G lj MA p s VS) 21.30-2.30 h, closed Mon
5 Rue Nougaret ✉34500 ☎ 04.67.49.02.20
Rotonde. La (B g) Allée Paul Riquet ✉34500
☎ 04.67.76.35.32

RESTAURANTS

Crèmerie. La (b CC F glm MA OS s) closed Sun and Mon lunch
1 Place de la Madeleine ✉34500 ☎ 04.67.28.54.26
Cheese specialities. Tea shop afternoons.
Madison. Le (b F g) 20-24 h, closed 1.-8.Jul
5 Rue Louis-Blanc ✉34500 ☎ 04.67.31.60.08
Scaramouche. Le (b F g)
23 Rue Tourventouse ✉34500 ☎ 04.67.28.55.39
Storia. La (b F glm) closed Sun
Rue de l'Argenterie ✉34500 ☎ 04.67.28.18.11

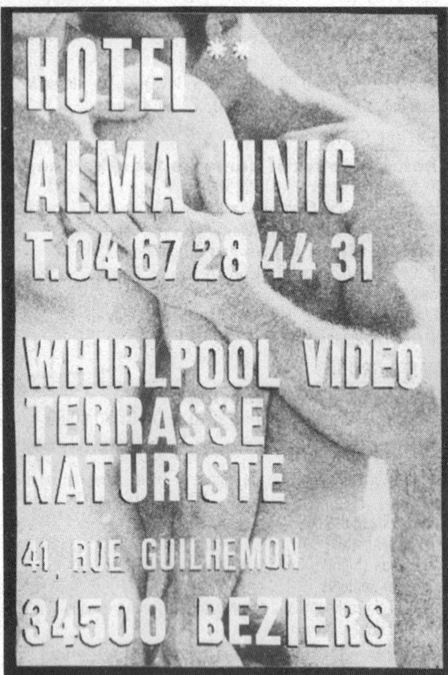

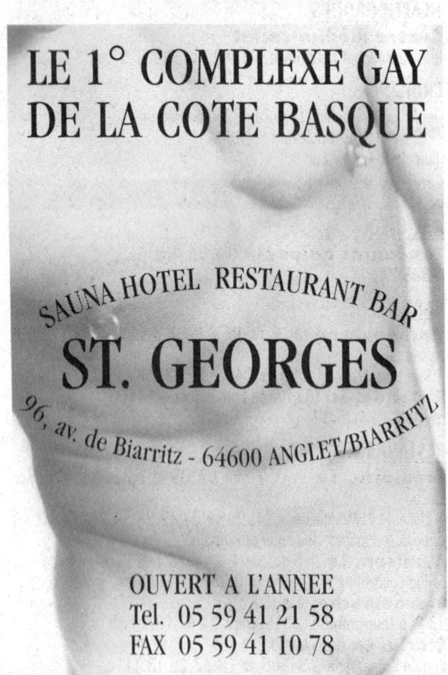

SEX SHOPS/BLUE MOVIES

Video Show (g VS) 11-24 h
5 Rue Victor Hugo ✉34500 ☎ 04.67.62.37.16
Large sex shop and cinema. Underwear, leather, latex and S/M accessories and more. 10% for Spartacus readers.

SAUNAS/BATHS

Kheops. Le (AC B DR f G MA p sa sb VS) 12-20.30 h
5 Rue Berlioz ✉34500 ☎ 67.49.31.37

HOTELS

Hôtel Alma Unic (bf CC glm H MA NU OS VS wh) reception -24 h
41 Rue Guilhemon ✉34500 ☎ 04.67.28.44.31
Fax: 04.67.28.79.44
Friendly. Rooms with private bath & WC. Ask for Christian. Free breakfast with SPARTACUS. Nude sunbathing on the terrace.

Revélois. Le (B bf CC F g H MA) Restaurant closed on Sun
60 Avenue Gambetta ✉34500 *(near park Plateau des Poètes)*
☎ 04.67.49.20.78 Fax: 04.67.28.92.28

APARTMENTS

Chambres d'Hôte du Moulin (bf Glm H NU OS pi)
6 Chemin du Moulin, 34310 Poilhes La Romaine ✉34500
☎ 04.67.93.46.22
Located 16 km from Béziers, near „le canal du midi", 20 km from the sea. Private naturist pool.

HEALTH GROUPS

Dispensaire anti-vénérien
2 Boulevard Pérréal ✉34500 ☎ 04.67.76.90.80

CRUISING

-Gare SNCF
-Jardin des Bassins réservoirs
-Plateau des Poètes (day/jour)
-Plage à Serigrau (dunes entre camping naturiste et l'arbre)
-Plage à Fleury d'Aude

Biarritz ✉ 64200

GAY INFO

Triangle Rose Tue Sat 20 h (FM 96,8 MHz)
✉64200

BARS

Bakara (B CC g OS S) 9-3, Jan/Feb Mon-Wed 9-20 Thu-Sun 9-2 h
Place Sainte-Eugénie ✉64200 ☎ 05.59.24.05.34
Sea views. Intimate salon.

Caveau. Le (B D G S) bar 17-5, disco 23-6 h
4 Rue Gambetta ✉64200 ☎ 05.59.24.16.17
Also danceclub.

Opera Café (AC B bf CC d GLM H MA OS p s) Bar 12-5, disco 22-5 h
31 Avenue de Verdun ☎ 05.59.24.27.85

DANCECLUBS

City's Bar. Le (AC B CC D GLM OS S YG) 8-5 h
31 Avenue de Verdun ✉64200 ☎ 05.59.24.27.85

RESTAURANTS

Pitchino (F glm) 19-23 h closed Mon
49 Rue d'Espagne ✉64200 ☎ 05.59 41 15 30
Pizzeria/Italian food.

SAUNAS/BATHS

St. Georges. Le (B bf CC F glm H MA OS s sa sb) 14.30-2 h
96 Avenue de Biarritz ✉64600 Anglet *(RN 10 Biarritz → Bayonne)* ☎ 05.59.41.21.58
Also hotel and restaurant. Special weekend rates. Quote SPARTACUS when reserving.

HOTELS

Opera (AC B bf CC d GLM H MA OS p s)
31 Avenue de Verdun ✉64200 ☎ 05.59.24.27.85
Fax: 05.59.22.21.55
Gay hotel above private gay bar.

SWIMMING

-Plage du Miramar (towards lighthouse, under cliffs)
-Plage du Port-Vieux

CRUISING

-Chémin du Pavillon chinois
-Phare de Biarritz
-Last bus stop ligne 1 Hôtel de Ville
-Place Bellevue

Bidart ✉ 64210

SWIMMING

-Place des 200 marches (D 911)

Biscarosse ✉ 40600

BARS

Bar'Ils (B D glm) 22-2 h
46 Rue du Grand Vivier ✉40600 ☎ 05.58.78.36.30

SWIMMING

-Route d'Arcachon (G NU)

Blagnac ✉ 31700

CRUISING

-Vieux-Pont

Blois ✉ 41000

BARS

Petit Amiral. Le (AC B CC GLM lj MA OS) 14-3 h
12 Rue du Puit Châtel ✉41000 ☎ 02.54.78.81.83

HEALTH GROUPS

Centre hospitalier de Blois
1B Mail Pierre Charlot ✉41016 ☎ 02.54.78.00.82
HIV-testing.
Dispensaire
10 Rue de la Garenne ✉41000 ☎ 02.54.78.03.09

CRUISING

-Jardin des Lices
-Foret de Russy (route de Vierzon)

Bonnieux ✉ 84480

RESTAURANTS

Fournil. Le (b F g) 12-14.30, 19-22 h, Oct-Feb closed Sun & 5.Jan-15.Feb
5 Place Carnot ✉84480 ☎ 90.75.83.62

PRIVATE ACCOMODATION

Bed & Breakfeast J. C. (bf G pi)
Route Pont Julien ✉84480 *3 km from the village.*
☎ 90.75.86.52

Bordeaux ✉ 33000

GAY INFO

Minitel: 3615 ALLOGAY

BARS

Moyen Age. Le (B G MA) 22-2 h, closed Tue
8 Rue des Remparts ✉33000 *(next to Place Gambetta near Hôtel de Ville)* ☎ 05.56.44.12.87
The oldest gay bar in France. And still popular and gay...
TH. Le (AC B CC DR G LJ MA s VS) 22-2 h, closed Mon
15 Rue Montbazon ✉33000 ☎ 05.56.81.38.16
Theme nights.

MEN'S CLUBS

Traxx (B DR G LJ MA p VS WE) 14.3, Fri Sat -7 h
38 Rue Arnaud Miqueu ✉33000 ☎ 05.56.44.03.41
Large fantasy complex with gay shop.

DANCECLUBS

Key West (B D GLM MA p YG) 22-4
32/34 Rue Cornac ✉33000 ☎ 05.56.48.22.13
Bar-Discotheque.
Yellow Moon. Le (B D DR G MA s VS) 23-4 h
6 Rue Louis Combes ✉33000 ☎ 05.56.51.00.79
Two bars, videoroom, three floors.
18. Le (! AC B CC D G p) 23-4 h
18 Rue Louis de Foix ✉33000 ☎ 05.56.52.82.98

RESTAURANTS

Bistrot M.A.P. (b F glm MA OS) 19.30-2 h, closed on Mon
62 Rue de la Devise ✉33000 ☎ 05.56.48.19.92
Cafetière. La (B F Glm)
14 Rue des Faussetts ✉33000 ☎ 05.56.51.66.55
Cave à Jules. La (AC CC E F g MA) Mon-Sun 12-14 19.30-22.30 h, closed Sat lunch
56 Rue du Mirail ✉33000 ☎ 05.56.91.44.69
Cuisine régionale.
Pizza Jacono (b CC F g) Mon Wed-Sat 12-14, 19.30-23, Sun 19.30-23 h
19 Rue de la Devise ✉33000 ☎ 05.56.51.01.48
Credit cards accepted.

SEX SHOPS/BLUE MOVIES

Boîte à Films. La (glm VS) 10-2 h
26 Rue Rolland ✉33000 ☎ 05.56.01.14.26
Videos, magazines, etc.
Love Vidéo (AC DR CC g VS) 10-1 h
221 Rue Cours de la Marne ✉33000 ☎ 05.56.91.68.55
Clothes and accessories.
Love Vidéo (AC DR CC g VS)
20 Rue G. Bonnac ✉33000 ☎ 05.56.44.74.25
Star'x (CC g MA VS) Special gay movies Tue Fri 11-1 h
46 Cours Alsace Lorraine ✉33000 ☎ 56.81.81.55

SAUNAS/BATHS

Sauna Club 137 (AC b f G sa sb sol VS wh) 13.30-1 h, Tue Fri late nights
137 Quai des Chartrons ✉33000 ☎ 05.56.43.18.49
Bordeaux's all gay sauna. Theme nights.

Sauna Ferrere (b f glm sa sb sol VS wh) 12-20, Sat Sun 13-20 h
18 Rue Ferrère ✉33000 ☎ 05.56.44.53.01
Newly renovated.

Sauna Thiers (AC b CC DR f G MA pi sa sb sol VS wh) 13-1, Tue Fri Sat -4 h
329 Avenue Thiers ✉33100 *(Bus 2, 4, Pont Saint Emilion)* ☎ 05.56.32.00.63

HELP WITH PROBLEMS

SOS Homo Tue 20-1 h
✉33000 ☎ 05.56.81.51.66

CRUISING

-Aire de Sestas (Autoroute)
-Bois de Bordeaux (de Bruges) (AYOR) (along the lake/vers le lac)
-Les jardins de Mériadeck (night/nuit)
-Ecole de la Santé Navale (park in front of the school/parc face à l'Ecole, Place Renaudel)
-Place d'Arlac (AYOR)
-Parc Bordelais (Cauderan, jour)

Bouc-Bel-Air ✉ 13320

CRUISING

-Cimetière/cemetery (in the evening towards the industrial area of Milles)

Boulogne Billancourt ✉ 92100

HEALTH GROUPS

Dispensaire
13 Rue Rieux ✉92100 ☎ 05.46.05.03.02

CRUISING

-Métro station Billancourt (in front of brasserie Rex)
-Quai Quatre-Septembre

Boulogne-sur-Mer ✉ 62200

BARS

Horloge. L' (B G f) 9-22 h
5 Rue Monsigny ✉62200 ☎ 03.21.31.47.29

CAFES

Bistroquet. Le (B f g) open all day
46 Place Dalton ✉62200 ☎ 03.21.30.57.69

DANCECLUBS

Pharaon. Le (B D CC E glm MA p WE) Thu-Sat 21-6 h
27 Rue du Vivier ✉62200 ☎ 03.21.30.03.89

GENERAL GROUPS

Arc-en-Ciel Côte d'Opale
B.P. 271 ✉62204 ☎ 03.21.33.82.95

CRUISING

-Porte Neuve
-Remparts (Ville haute)

Bourg-en-Bresse ✉ 01000

GIFT & PRIDE SHOPS

Coutellerie Sannajust Tue-Sat 9-12, 14-19 h
20 Rue Victor-Basch ✉01000 ☎ 04.74.23.61.21
Jewellery and other gifts to make gay hearts beat faster.

HEALTH GROUPS

Test HIV anonym et gratuit-C.H. de Fleyriat
01000 *(Consultations externes)* ☎ 04.74.45.41.89

CRUISING

-Champs de Foire
-P de la Basilique (behind l'église du Sacre-Coeur)
-La Plaine du Bastion
-Le square Bel-Air
-Parc de la Visitation
-Square Joubert
-Square des Quiconces

Bourges 18000

HEALTH GROUPS

Centre hospitalier de Bourges Service de biologie
4 Rue Sulton 18000 ☎ 02.48.24.09.46
HIV-testing.

RELIGIOUS GROUPS

David et Jonathan
B.P. 3013 18027

CRUISING

-RN 76 (20 km-Bourges, direction Moulins)
-P Palais des Congrès (le soir/in the evening)
-Parking du Lac d'Oreon
-Place Séracourt

Bray-Dunes 59123

CRUISING

-In the dunes/dans les dunes (in the summertime/l'été)

Brehal 50290

SWIMMING

-Bréville-sur-Mer(beach near the shooting- ground/plage près du champ de tir)
-nudist beach (along golf-course/longer le terrain de golf)

Bressuire 79300

CRUISING

-Mairie (arcades, evening/le soir)
-Place de la Libération
-Place St.Jacques
-Place St.Jean
-Place de la Brèche
-Rue Gambetta
-Jardin des Plantes

Brest 29200

BARS

Lak-Atao (B glm MA) 21-1 h, closed Tue
63 Rue Louis Pasteur 29200 ☎ 02.99.44.49.84
Only frequented by gays in the evening.
Village Café. Le (AC B G MA snu VS) Winter 17-1, summer 18-1, before public holidays -2 h
2 Rue Duquesne 29200 ☎ 02.98.80.05.22

RESTAURANTS

Marina (b F g) 12-14, 19-23 h
16 Rue de Siam 29200 ☎ 02.98.80.09.61
Menus FF 48. Also Italian food.
Vitavi (B F g) 12-14, 19-23 h, closed Thu
109 Rue Jean-Jaurés 29200 ☎ 02.98.43.30.70
Pizzeria.

HEALTH GROUPS

AIDES-Armor Call Mon 19.30-22.30 h
1 Rue de l'Harteloire 29200 ☎ 02.98.43.18.72

SWIMMING

-Plage de Corsen (25 km de Brest)
-Dunes de Keremna (2 km de Treflez)
-Plage de Trezien

CRUISING

-Jardins Kennedy (AYOR) (day and night)
-Quais du port
-Cours d'Ajot
-Aire du Pont-de-Buis
-Bois de Keroual
-Jardin Beaupré

Briançon 05100

CAFES

Crêperie Hélène Chaix (AC b CC F glm lj MA) 12-22 h, closed Mon
40 Grande Rue 05100 ☎ 04.92.21.11.81
Restaurant, crêperie, salon de thé.

CRUISING

-P Avenue Vauran
-P du Général Blanchard
-P Place de l'Europe
-Les Bois des Genès
-Parc de la Schappe
-P de la Schappe

Brive-la-Gaillarde 19100

BARS

Nuage. Le (B CC F g OS P) 18-2, closed Mon
2 Avenue Jean-Charles Rivet 19100 ☎ 05.55.87.36.79
Bar-restaurant.

DANCECLUBS

Crazy Boy (B D G) Fri-Sun 23-6 h
Chateau de la Rage Noailles 19100 ☎ 05.55.85.84.19
Take motorway/autoroute south of Brive exit Noailles.

SEX SHOPS/BLUE MOVIES

Ciné Vidéo Shop (CC g VS) Mon-Thu 14-19.30, 21-23, Fri 10-23, Sat 10-12.30 14-18 h
44 Avenue Jean-Jaurès 19100 ☎ 05.55.23.19.49

HEALTH GROUPS

Centre hospitalier de Brive
Service des urgences 19100 ☎ 05.55.92.60.00
HIV testing.

CRUISING

-Jardins de la Guierle (late afternoon and evening)
-Place Thiers (evening)

Cabourg 14390

HOTELS

Hôtel du Golf (CC F g H OS pi) Restaurant 12-14, 19.30-24 h
Avenue de l'Hippodrome 14390 ☎ 02.31.24.12.34
Room with WC FF 310/435, bf 45. Menues 98-230.

1 EURO =

40,3399	BEF	40,3399	LUF
1,95583	DEM	2,20371	NLG
166,386	ESP	13,7603	ATS
6,55957	FRF	200,482	PTE
0,787564	IEP	5,94573	FIM
1936,27	ITL		

Caen ✉ 14000

BARS

Zinc. Le (B G MA) 8-2, Fri Sat -4 h, closed on Sun
12 Rue du Vaugeux ✉14000 ☎ 02.31.93.20.30

DANCECLUBS

Joy's. Le (B CC D g MA S) 23-5 h
12 Passage du Bief ✉14000 *(a côte de la FNAC)* ☎ 02.31.85.40.40

Phil and Bea (B D G MA) -3 h
189 Rue St. Jean ✉14000 ☎ 02.31.86.60.05

SAUNAS/BATHS

Arc-En-Ciel Sauna Club (b CC d DR G p sa sb wh WO YG) Men only: 13-22 h, except Fri Sun
17 rue de Varignon, Impasse Dumont ✉14000 ☎ 02 31 93 19 00

HEALTH GROUPS

Aides Basse-Normandie Mon-Fri 14-17 h
2 Rue du Marais ✉14007 ☎ 02.31.84.36.63

Centre de Prophylaxie et MST
3 Rue des Cultures ✉14000 ☎ 02.31.94.84.22
HIV-testing.

Dispensaire d'Hygiène sociale 9-12, 14-17 h
Place Félix-Eboué ✉14000 ☎ 02.31.84.81.70
Poste 13 24.

CRUISING

-P of the castle/du château
-Place Royale (garden/le jardin)
-Plage de Franceville (à 15 min de Caen, par la route direction Cabourg /15 min from Caen, motorway direction Cabourg)
-Promenade Fossé St-Julien
-Promenade du Long du Cours
-Quartier du Vaugeux

Cagnes-sur-Mer ✉ 06800

RESTAURANTS

Entre Cour et Jardin (b e F glm MA) 19.30-24 h
102 Montée de la Bourgade ✉06800 *(Haut de Cagnes)* ☎ 04.93.20.72.27
An excellent gastronomic halt in the historic old town of Haut de Cagnes.

HEALTH GROUPS

Centre Médical
Rue du Chevalier-Martin ✉06800 ☎ 04.93.20.64.73

CRUISING

-Next to castle museum

Cahors ✉ 46000

HEALTH GROUPS

Centre hospitalier de Cahors Sce. de médecine interne
Rue Président-Wilson ✉46000 ☎ 05.65.20.50.50
HIV-testing.

Dispensaire 92 Rue Joachim Murat ✉46000 ☎ 05.65.35.27.98

CRUISING

-Salle des fêtes
-P Gambetta

Caissargues ✉ 30132

CRUISING

-Canal du Bas-Rhône (Route de Saint-Gilles)

Calais ✉ 62100

BARS

London Bridge (B F GLM MA) Bar 12-2, restaurant -23 h
12 Place d'Armes ✉62100 ☎ 03.21.85.85.79

CRUISING

-Citadelle (Boulevard Esplanade, de jour/by day)
-Dunes de Blériot
-Parc Richelieu

Camaret-Sur-Mer ✉ 29129

SWIMMING

-Plage de Losmarch

Cannes ✉ 06400

GAY INFO

Minitel: 3615 ALLOGAY
✉06400

TOURIST INFO

Tourist Info
Esplanade Président Georges Pompidou 06403 ✉06400
☎ 04.93.39.24.53
FAX 04.93.99.37.06.

BARS

Vogue Bar (AC B CC glm MA p) 19-2.30 h, closed Mon
20 Rue du Suquet ✉06400 ☎ 04.93.39.99.18
Zanzibar (AC B CC G MA OS) 18.30-5 h
85 Rue Félix-Faure ✉06400 ☎ 04.93.39.30.75

RESTAURANTS

Barbarella (b F glm YG) every evening
14-16 Rue St. Dizier ✉06400 ☎ 04.92.99.17.33
Bistro de la Galerie. Le (A b CC F g) 19.30-23 h, closed Mon
4 Rue Saint Antoine ✉06400 ☎ 04.93.39.99.38
French cuisine.
Croisette. La (b F g) Tue-Sat 12-14.30, 19-22.30, Sun Mon 12.-14.30 h
15 Rue Commandant-André ✉06400 ☎ 04.93.39.86.06
Italian cuisine.
Dauphin. Le (AC F glm MA) 12-14, 19-22.30 h, closed Sun except during Festival
1 Rue Bivonac Napoléon ✉06400 *(Near Palais des Festivals)*
☎ 04.93.39.22.73
Popular with gays.

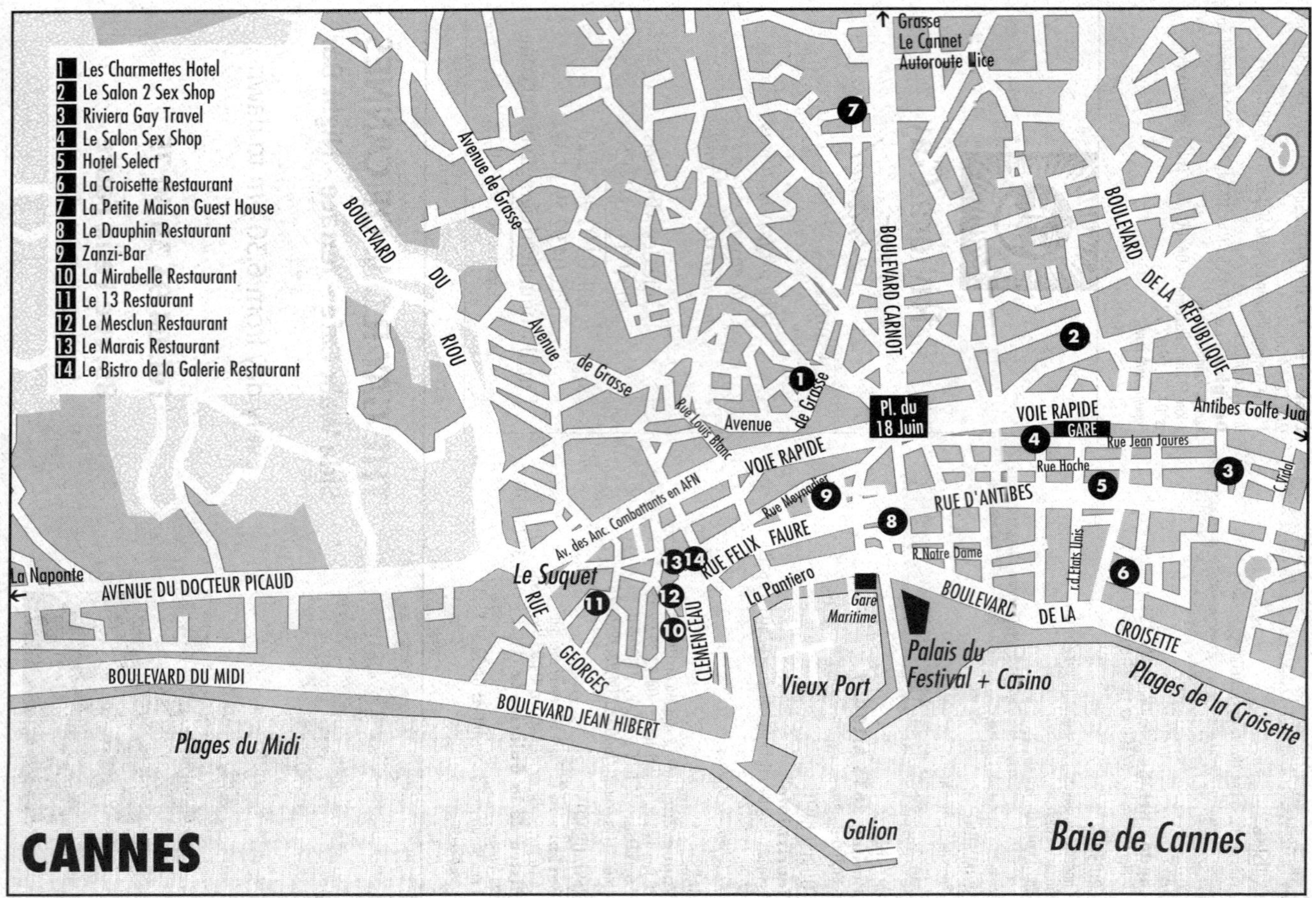
1 Les Charmettes Hotel
2 Le Salon 2 Sex Shop
3 Riviera Gay Travel
4 Le Salon Sex Shop
5 Hotel Select
6 La Croisette Restaurant
7 La Petite Maison Guest House
8 Le Dauphin Restaurant
9 Zanzi-Bar
10 La Mirabelle Restaurant
11 Le 13 Restaurant
12 Le Mesclun Restaurant
13 Le Marais Restaurant
14 Le Bistro de la Galerie Restaurant
Grasse
Le Cannet
Autoroute Nice
BOULEVARD CARNOT
BOULEVARD DE LA RÉPUBLIQUE
Avenue de Grasse
BOULEVARD DU RIOU
Avenue de Grasse
Avenue de Grasse
Pl. du 18 Juin
VOIE RAPIDE
GARE
Antibes Golfe Juan
Rue Jean Jaures
Rue Hoche
C. Vidal
Rue Louis Blanc
VOIE RAPIDE
Rue Meynadier
RUE D'ANTIBES
Av. des Anc. Combattants en AFN
RUE FELIX FAURE
R. Notre Dame
r. d. Etats Unis
La Naponte
AVENUE DU DOCTEUR PICAUD
Le Suquet
RUE GEORGES
CLEMENCEAU
La Pantiero
Gare Maritime
BOULEVARD DE LA CROISETTE
Palais du Festival + Casino
Vieux Port
BOULEVARD DU MIDI
BOULEVARD JEAN HIBERT
Plages du Midi
Plages de la Croisette
Galion
Baie de Cannes
CANNES

Marais. Le (AC b CC E F glm MA OS W) 19.30-23 h, closed Mon
9 Rue du Suquet ✉06400 ☎ 04.93.38.39.19

Max (A AC F glm MA) 12-13.30 h, 19-22.30 h, closed Mon except Jul. Aug. & holidays.
11 Rue Louis Perissol ✉06400 ☎ 04.93.39.97.06

Mirabelle. La (b E F g MA) 20-23 h, closed Tue & 1.-15.Dec
24 Rue Saint Antoine/2 Rue du Suquet ✉06400
☎ 04.93.38.72.75
Reservation necessary.

13. Le (A CC F glm OS) 19-24.30 h
13 Rue C. Perrissol le Suquet ✉06400 ☎ 04.93.39.85.19

SEX SHOPS/BLUE MOVIES

Salon. Le (g VS) 9.30-12.30, 14.30-19.30 h, closed Sun
13 Rue de Mimont ✉06400 ☎ 04.93.68.16.36

Salon. Le (AC CC G MA VS) 8.30-24 h, Sun 14-24 h
32 Rue Jean Jaurès ✉06400 ☎ 04.93.68.91.82

Video Sex (AC CC g VS) 10-24 h
6 Rue Jean Jaures ✉06400 ☎ 04.93.68.91.82

TRAVEL & TRANSPORT

Riviera Gay Travel 9.30-12.30, 14-18.30 h, closed Sat Sun
15 rue du Cdt. André ✉06400 *(1st floor, close to centre)*
☎ 04.92.98.32.20 Fax: 04.92.59.14.37
Email: Contact@rivieragaytravel.com
Homepage: http://www.rivieragaytravel.com

HOTELS

Charmettes. Les (AC bf G H MA OS)
47 Avenue de Grasse ✉06400 ☎ 04.93.39.17.13
Fax: 04.93.68.08.41 Email: hotelcharmcannes@aol.com
All rooms with shower or bath, mini-bar, phone, air condition, sat-TV.

Hotel des Allées (CC g H)
6 Rue Emile-Negrin ✉06400 *(central location)* ☎ 04.93.39.53.90
Fax: 04.93.99.43.25
Email: des-allees@infonie.fr
Select (AC bf glm H MA)
16 Rue Hélène Vagliano ✉06400
(Town center) ☎ 04.93.99.51.00 Fax: 04.92.98.03.12

GUEST HOUSES

Petite Maison. La (bf G H msg NU OS sol VS)
22/4 Rue Maurice Derché ✉06400 ☎ 06.60.98.16.12
Fax: 04.93.45.07.95
Nice hotel 5 min from the beach.

GENERAL GROUPS

Fierte Gay et Lesbien Côte d'Azur
11/11bis Rue Hélène Vagliano ✉06400 ☎ 04.93.45.06.97
Fax: 04.93.45.07.95

HEALTH GROUPS

Centre médical
74 Avenue Clémenceau ✉06400 ☎ 04.93.39.06.36

CRUISING

-Beach/plage de La Batterie (AYOR at night)
-Beach/plage Ile Ste-Marguerite
-Square Carnot
-Square Frédéric-Mistral (beach)
-Boulevard de la Croisette

Cap-d'Agde ✉ 34300

BARS

Casa Nueva (B F glm MA OS TV) 15 Mar-15 Oct: Mon-Sun, winter: WE 17-3 h
Colline 5, Port Nature ✉34300 *(Quartier Naturiste)*
☎ 04.67.26.08.15
Bar and restaurant.
Look. Le (B CC glm OS s) Easter-December: 17-2; low season: WE 17-1 h
Village Naturiste ✉34300 *(opposite port)* ☎ 04.67.26.30.42
Winch. Le (b bf CC F glm MA) Apr-Sep 9-3 h
Plage de la Roquille ✉34300 ☎ 04.67.01.28.60

SWIMMING

-Marseillan plage (G NU) (Between Sète and Cap d'Adge, to be reached via N112. Pass junction Cap d'Agde and follow next junction to the right, direction Marseillan plage. When at the beach walk to the right, direction Cap d'Adge, and you will find yourself at the enormous gay nude beach. The access to the dunes is strictly forbidden, frequent police controls)

CRUISING

-Bois-Joli (camping)
-Plage de Roche Pongue (at night)
-Place du Barbecue (late, summer)
-P au bord de l'Herault

Cap-d'Ail ✉ 06320

CRUISING

-Beach/Plage des Pissarelles (500 m-Cap-d'Ail)

Carcassonne ✉ 11000

BARS

BAR. Le (B glm) 17-2 h

31 Boulevard Omer Sarrault ✉11000 ☎ 05.68..25.90.26

RESTAURANTS

Ecu d'Or. L' (b CC F g) 12-14, 19-22, closed Tue, Jul-Sept 12-14, 19-22 h, closed 15.Nov-15.Dec
7 Rue Porte-d'Aude, cité Médiévale ✉11000 ☎ 04.68.25.88.64
French cuisine à la carte.

Ecurie. L' (AC b CC E F glm OS W) 12-14, 20-22 h, closed Sun
43 Boulevard Barbès ✉11000 *(Near Place General de Gaule)* ☎ 04.68.72.04.04
18th century stable/garden setting.

Saladou. Le (b CC F glm OS)
5 Place du Petits Puits ✉11000 ☎ 04.68.71.23.56
Lunch and dinner everyday in summer. In winter closed Sun evening & Mon.

GUEST HOUSES

Aux Deux Colonnes (bf glm H MA OS)
3 Avenue de Limoux ✉11250 ☎ 04.68.69.41.21
Fax: 04.68.69.69.02
Outside Carcassonne, direction Limoux. Open all year.

HEALTH GROUPS

Hôpital
57 Rue d'Alsace ✉11000 ☎ 04.68.25.79.76

CRUISING

-Boulevard Marcou (in the evening/le soir)
-Boulevard de Varsovie (in the evening/le soir)

Carcés ✉ 83570

RESTAURANTS

Mas de Canta-Dié (A bf F g H OS) 11.30-14, 19.30-22 h, closed Tue
Route de Carcès Cotignac ✉83570 *(2,8 km from Cotignac direction Carcés)* ☎ 04.94.77.72.46

Carentan ✉ 50500

CRUISING

-Place Valnoble

Carnac ✉ 56340

DANCECLUBS

Appalooza. L' (B D DR GLM s) Jul-Aug 23-?, Sep-Jun Fri-Sun & before public holidays 23-? h
Route de Auray-Quiberon, Carnac, Bretagne Sud ✉56340 ☎ 02.97.52.16.17
Liveliest gay spot in the south of Brittany. Club on two levels, 2 types of music.

Carnon ✉ 34250

CRUISING

-Plage du grand travers

Carolles ✉ 50740

SWIMMING

-Plage de Carolles (10 km to the south of Granville)

Carqueiranne ✉ 83320

SWIMMING

-Plage du Bau-Rouge (NU) (on the rocks/sur des rochers)
-Plage du Bau-Rouge (within reach D 86)

Cassis ✉ 13260

SAUNAS/BATHS

Aqua Douches (AC B CC f G MA p sa sb VS wh WO) Open everyday.
34 Rue de l'Arène ✉13260 *(30 min from Marseille and 1 h. from St. Tropez. Towmn centre Cassis)* ☎ 06.14.63.28.19

SWIMMING

-Calanque de Port-Pin (NU)
-La pointe Cacau
-Cap Canaille (NU) (go east from the town, direction Route des Crêtes, there's a non marked steep way to a [P]. On the beach turn east. Gay at the end of the nude beach)

CRUISING

-Autoroute Marseille-La Ciotat

Casteljaloux ✉ 47700

SWIMMING

-Etang de la Laguë (nude bathing AYOR)

Castillon ✉ 06500

HOTELS

Bergerie. La (A B d F g H NU OS pi W) closed Nov-Mar except for groups
✉06500 *(10 km-Menton, Route de Sospel)* ☎ 04.93.04.00.39
About 40km from Airport Nice. Rooms with telephone, batthroom, WC and balcony./Distance à l'aéroport de Nice: 40 km. Téléphone à la chambre, salle de bain, WC et balcon.

CRUISING

-At the old harbour/Au Vieux Port (in the evening/le soir)

Castres ✉ 81100

FASHION SHOPS

Just for Men Mon 14-19, Tue-Sat 9.30-12, 14-19 h
4 Place Pélisson ✉81100 *Near Jean Jaurès Museum.* ☎ 63.59.74.99
Fashion, gadgets, decorations, jewelry.

HEALTH GROUPS

Centre hospitalier Jean-Pierre-Cabarrou/ Service de médecine
✉81100 ☎ 05.63.71.63.71
HIV-testing

CRUISING

-Centre culturel
-Jardins de l'Evêché

Cauterets ✉ 65110

HOTELS

Aladin Hotel Club (B g H pi WE)
Avenue Général Leclerc ✉65110 *(Centre)* ☎ 05.62.92.60.00

Cavalaire-sur-Mer ✉ 83240

SWIMMING

-beach in front of/plage en face de »Camping Bon Porteau« (NU)

Cerbère ✉ 66290

SWIMMING

-Criques et Calanques (NU)

Ceret ✉ 66400

CRUISING

-Le Bourdigou (behind the blockhouse)

Cergy ✉ 95000

CRUISING

-First [P] after you left Paris

Châlons-sur-Marne ✉ 51000

CRUISING

-Grand Jard (in winter/en hiver)
-Petit Jard (in summer; in the surroundings/aux alentours, en été)

Chalon-sur-Saone ✉ 71100

HEALTH GROUPS

Centre hospitalier
Quai de l'Hôpital ✉71100 ☎ 03.85.48.06.65

CRUISING

-A6, exit/sortie Chalons, direction Montceau-les-Mines (in the forest/ dans le bois)

Chambéry ✉ 73000

DANCECLUBS

Quartier Général (B D DR GLM LJ MA p S VS) Fri Sat 23-4 h
RN6 St. Cassin ✉73000 ☎ 79.69.11.22
Sex Club Dance.

GENERAL GROUPS

G.A.I.C.H.A - Groupe d'Actions, d'Information et de Contacts Homosexuels Alpins
1st. Fri each month 20.30-23
Rue Saint-Francois ✉73000 ☎ 79.28.37.54

HEALTH GROUPS

Centre hospitalier de Chambéry Service de dermatologie
✉73000 ☎ 04.79.96.50.50
HIV testing.
Dispensai
321 Chemin des Moulins ✉73000 ☎ 04.79.33.20.81

CRUISING

-Railway station/gare SNCF
-Lycée
-Parc Clos Savoiroux
-Parc du Verney
-[P] of the castle
-Place de Genève

Chamonix-Mont-Blanc ✉ 74400

CRUISING

-Bords de l'Arve
-Hameau Les Bois (à 3,5 km de Chamonix)
-Hôtel de Ville

Charleville-Mézières ✉ 08000

HEALTH GROUPS

Centre de médecine préventive
3 Rue Gervaise ✉08000 ☎ 03.24.56.13.23

Centre hospitalier de Charleville Sérvice de médicine interne
✉08000 ☎ 03.24.56.70.70
HIV-testing.

CRUISING

-Pond of Bairon/Étang de Bairon (at the beach/ face à la plage)
-Square Bayard
-Square du Mont-Olympe

Chartres ✉ 28000

DANCECLUBS

Privilège. Le (B D g) Fri Sat 22.30-? h
1-3 Place Saint Pierre ✉28000 ☎ 02.37.35.52.02

GUEST HOUSES

Grange du Bois. La (bf glm OS)
34 La Grange du Bois ✉28190 *(30 km west of Chartres, RN 23 direction Le Mans)* ☎ 02.37.37.44.00 Fax: 02.37.37.44.00

HEALTH GROUPS

Dispensaire
1 Rue G. Lelong ✉28000 ☎ 02.37.35.61.71

CRUISING

-Cathedra (in the evening/le soir)

Château Thierry ✉ 02400

CRUISING

-Château
-Place de l'Hôtel-de-Ville

Châteaudun ✉ 28200

CRUISING

-Parc du Château
-Promenade du Mail

Châteaurenard ✉ 13160

RESTAURANTS

Wagon. Le (b F g) 20-6 h
Grand Quartier, Parking du Stax ✉13160 ☎ 04.90.94.43.24

Châtel-Censoir ✉ 89660

CRUISING

-Bois d'Arcy

Châtellerault ✉ 86100

RESTAURANTS

Écurie. L' (B CC F GLM OS) 12-14, 19-24, Sun 12-14 h
141 Avenue Louis-Ripault ✉86100 ☎ 05.49.21.24.82
French cuisine.

HEALTH GROUPS

Dispensaire de prophylaxie
Rue Rabelais ✉86100 ☎ 05.49.54.41.86

CRUISING

-Railway station/Gare SNCF

Châtillon-sur-Loire ✉ 45360

BARS

Clin d'Oeil (B glm MA) Tue-Fri 10.30-24, Sat 13-24 h, closed Sun evening & Mon
17 Grande-Rue ✉45360 ☎ 02.38.31.45.86

Chaumont ✉ 52000

HEALTH GROUPS

Centre hospitalier de Chaumont Consultations externes
2 Rue Jeanne-d'Arc ✉52014 ☎ 03.25.30.70.30
HIV-testing.

CRUISING

-Square Philippe-Le Bon (in front of the SNCF railway station)

Chauvry ✉ 95560

RESTAURANTS

Trèfle à Quatre-Feuilles. Le (b F glm OS) 12.30-14, 20-22 h, closed Tue Wed
19 Grande Rue ✉95560 ☎ 02.39.69.26.00
20 km north of Paris in direction of Enghien.

Cherbourg ✉ 50100

BARS

Freedom Café. Le (AC B CC d g MA OS) 9-11
Rue Blondeau ✉50100 ☎ 02.33.94.08.88
Bar-café.

RESTAURANTS

Stone Wall. Le (b CC F glm) closed Sun lunch
18-20 Rue des Fossés ✉50100 ☎ 02.33.93.37.37

HEALTH GROUPS

Centre hospitalier Louis-Pasteur Sce de dermatologie
46 Rue du Val-de-Seine ✉50100 ☎ 02.33.20.70.00
HIV-testing.

CRUISING

-Place Napoléon
-Port du Roule

Chinon ✉ 37220

HOTELS

Relais de la Poste (B F glm H OS)
Place de l'Eglise ✉37190 *(16km from Chinon, direction Azay le Rideau)* ☎ 02.47.95.51.16
Hotel and restaurant. Quote SPARTACUS for free breakfast.

Cholet ✉ 49300

CRUISING

-Railway station/Gare SNCF
-Jardin du Mail

Chorges ✉ 05230

CRUISING

-Lac de Serre-Ponçon

Clamart ✉ 92140

HEALTH GROUPS

S.O.S. SIDA
Hôpital Antoine-Béclère, 157 Rue de la Porte-de-Trivaux ✉92140 ☎ 05.45.37.44.44

CRUISING

-Place du Garde (rencontres parfois dans le bois/in the forest)

Clermont-Ferrand ✉ 63000

BARS

Viennois. Le (B GLM) 8-1, Fri-Sat -2 h
3 Rue Barrière-de-Jaude ✉63000 ☎ 04.73.34.12.74

SEX SHOPS/BLUE MOVIES

Erotic Vidéo (CC g VS W) 10-23 h, closed Sun
10-12 Rue Saint Dominique ✉63000 ☎ 04.73.37.65.48
Kama Sutra Video (GLM MA VS)
17 Rue des Tanneries ✉63000 ☎ 04.73.77.74.19
Sexy Night (CC DR glm lj MA msg S VS) 18-? h
6 Rue Sainte Geneviève ✉63000 ☎ 04.73.34.25.40

SAUNAS/BATHS

Eden Sex Bud (CC DR glm MA pi sa sol VS WO)
16 Rue Ramond ✉63000 ☎ 04.73.93.84.15
Sex shop and sauna. Video screen and large fantasy area.
Salins. Les (AC B DR f G MA sa sb sol VS wh WO) 14-0 h
5 Avenue Marx Dornoy ✉63000 *(close to Place des Salins & bus station)* ☎ 04.73.29.26.10
Discrete private male club. Clean & friendly.
Thermos. Le (DR G MA OS sa VS) 13-20 h
77bis Avenue Edouard-Michelin ✉63000 *(Gare SNCF)* ☎ 04.73.92.93.25

HEALTH GROUPS

Dispensaire Emile-Roux
32 Avenue Vercingétorix ✉63000 ☎ 04.73.35.12.16
HIV testing.

CRUISING

-Jardin Lecoq
-Place de la Poterne
-Nouvelles Galleries
-Place des Bughes
-Square Blaise-Pascal

Clermont-l'Hérault ✉ 34800

CRUISING

-Lac de Salagou

Clichy ✉ 92110

HEALTH GROUPS

Hôpital Beaujon
100 Boulevard du Général-Leclerc ✉92110 ☎ 02.47.39.33.40

CRUISING

-Parc Roger-Salengro
-Quai de Clichy

Cluses ✉ 74300

CRUISING

-Place Claude Anthoine
-Place des Allobroges

Colmar ✉ 68000

CRUISING

-Parc Rapp (fountain/fontaine)
-Parc du Château d'eau

Colombes ✉ 92700

CRUISING

-Parc de l'île Marante (AYOR)

Compiègne

DANCECLUBS

Phuture (B CC D DR G P s SNU VS YG) 23.30-? h
10-14 Rue des Boucheries ✉60200 ☎ 03.44.86.14.14
In 13th century vaulted crypt. Theme evenings.

HEALTH GROUPS

Centre hospitalier Médecine interne
42 Rue de Paris ✉60208 ☎ 03.44.20.99.20
HIV-testing.

CRUISING

-La Faisanderie
-Le Quai Fleurant-Agricola (at the autobahn exit Ressons)
-Place du Château
-Ressons-sur-Matz (at the motorway exit in direction of Amiens in the bushes)
-Carrefour du Puits-du-Roy

Concarneau ✉ 29110

CRUISING

-Jardins du Porzou
-Toilettes/facilities of gare routière (at the harbor/sur le port)

Corbeil-Essonnes ✉ 91100

HEALTH GROUPS

Dispensaire d'hygiène sociale
1 Rue Pierre-Sémard ✉91100 ☎ 01.64.96.02.49
HIV testing.

Corrençon-en-Vercors ✉ 38250

HOTELS

Caribou. Le (B CC d F glm H OS pi sa sol) Disco Fri 22-2, Sat -3, restaurant 12-14.30, 19-22 h
Le Clos de la Balme ✉38250 ☎ 04.76.95.82.82
Fax: 04.76.95.83.17
Suburb location. All rooms have private bath. Horse riding in summer, skiing in winter.

Corse

Ajaccio ✉ 20000

HEALTH GROUPS

Centre hospitalier Notre-Dame-de-la Miséricorde
27 Avenue de l'Impératrice-Eugénie ✉20000 ☎ 04.95.29.90.90
Anonymous HIV testing.

SWIMMING

-Beach next to the airport (Especially in and around the small tower at the end)

CRUISING

-Terre plein de l'aéroport (last parking lot on the right, summer)

Algajola ✉ 20220

SWIMMING

-Gay part on the rocks at the end of the beach

Bastia ✉ 20200

SEX SHOPS/BLUE MOVIES

Extrem' Vidéo (AC CC g VS) 11-1 h
1 Boulevard Auguste Gaudin ✉20200 ☎ 04.95.31.91.44

HEALTH GROUPS

Centre Hospitalier Général Faconaja
Route Impériale ✉20200 ☎ 04.95.55.11.11
HIV-testing.

SWIMMING

-Barcaggio (before villiage, leave D 253 and walk 2 km east)
-Villages naturistes (50 km sur la côte est)

CRUISING

-Café des Platanes
-Jardin Romieux
-Place De-Gaulle
-Place Saint-Nicolas (after 21h, AYOR)

Belgodere ✉ 20226

SWIMMING

-Palasca (plage/beach)

Bonifacio ✉ 20169

SWIMMING

-Beach/plage »Baie de Stagnolo« (south of/au sud de la plage de Tonara)

Calvi ✉ 20260

SWIMMING

-Plage de Calvi

Corbara ✉ 20256

SWIMMING

-Baie de Gienchetu

Galeria ✉ 20245

SWIMMING

-Caillouteuse (direction Calvi, D 351)

L'Ile-Rousse ✉ 20220

SWIMMING

-Algajola (north of the beach many gays/beaucoup des gais au nord)

Propriano ✉ 20110

SWIMMING

-Beach/plage (NU) (between/entre plage du Capu Laurosu & plage de Porto Glio)

Saint-Florent ✉ 20217

SWIMMING

-Beach at the rocks/plage aux rochers (NU)

Santo-Pietro-di-Tenda ✉ 20246

SWIMMING

-Anse de Faggiola

Cosne-Cours-sur-Loire ✉ 58200

CRUISING

-Banks of the Loire/Bords de Loire
-Jardins Sévigné (AYOR)
-Jardins du Pont de Loire (AYOR)

Cotignac ✉ 83570

RESTAURANTS

Mas Canta-Dié. Le (CC F glm OS pi)
Route de Carces ✉83570 ☎ 04.94.04.66.57

Creil ✉ 60100

CRUISING

-Park/Parc (after 21 h; stay in your car or walk/A partir de 21 h, à pied ou en voiture)

Creully ✉ 14480

CRUISING

-Jardin public (behind post office)

Criel-sur-Mer ✉ 76910

SWIMMING

-Beach/Plage (NU) (under the steep coast between Mesnil-Val-Beach and Criel; be careful at flood-tide/Sous la falaise entre Mesnil-Val-Plage et Criel; dangereux à marée haute)

Crozon ✉ 29160

SWIMMING

-Plage du Lost-March (between Cap de la Chevre and Pointe des Dinan. Taking the D255 turn right ca. 3 km behind Morgat, direction La Palue. Near the small village there's a [P], 1 km to the beach, gay area on the left.)

Dax ✉ 40100

CRUISING

-Allée du Bois du Boulogne (AYOR) (la nuit/at night)
-Cathédrale
-Ancienne Gendarmerie
-Parc des Arènes

Deauville ✉ 14800

BARS

Club 94 (B G) 22-? h
94 Avenue de la République ✉14800 ☎ 02.31.98.16.16

CRUISING

-Beach/Plage (3 km-Caen)
-Behind/Derrière le Casino

Dieppe ✉ 76200

SWIMMING

-Plage du Petit-Ailly/Beach (NU)
-Piscine/Swimming Pool(sur la plage le soir/at the beach in the evening)

Dijon ✉ 21000

RESTAURANTS

Concorde. La (B F g OS) 7-2 h
2 Place d'Arcy ✉21000 ☎ 03.80.30.69.43
French cuisine from FF 35-65.

SEX SHOPS/BLUE MOVIES

Librairie Érotique (CC G VS) 10-24, Sat 10-20 h, closed Sun
64 Rue Berbisey ✉21000 ☎ 03.80.30.74.09

SAUNAS/BATHS

Sauna Bossuet (AC B DR GLM MA sa sb VS) 14-0.30 h
25 Place Bossuet ✉21000 ☎ 03.80.49.97.45
Sauna Relaxe (b DR G MA sa sb VS) 14-20 h
97 Rue Berbisey ✉21000 *(Bus 5/7/16/19-Hôpital general)*
☎ 03.80.30.14.40

HEALTH GROUPS

Dispensaire antivénérien
1 Rue Nicolas-Berthot ✉21035 ☎ 03.80.63.66.00
HIV testing.

CRUISING

-Parc de l'Arquebuse
-Les Allées du parc (Cours du Général-De-Gaulle)
-[P] du Lac Kir

Dinan ✉ 22100

SWIMMING

-Plorien/Vieux Bourg (NU) (in the little bay between the coast and Sables d'Or/criques entre la côte et Sables d'Or)

CRUISING

-Promenade des Douves (below the ramparts/au pied des remparts)
-Cours du Général-De Gaulle
-Parc l'Arquebuse (only in the afternoon)

Dinard ✉ 35800

CRUISING

-Promenade de la pointe du Moulinet
-Promenade du Clair-de-lune

Diou ✉ 03490

DANCECLUBS

Bataclan. Le (B CC D glm p S SNU TV VS) Fri-Sun 23-4 h
Ecluse de Putay ✉03490 ☎ 04.70.42.90.03

Divonne-les-Bains ✉ 01220

CRUISING

-Square municipal
-Route de Crassier

Dole ✉ 39100

CRUISING

-Parcey (8 km south of Dole at a gravel-pit near river Loue)

Dompierre-sur-Mer ✉ 17139

CRUISING

-Bois de Dompierre (3 km behind la Rochelle at Pont de Chagnolet)

Douai ✉ 59500

CRUISING

-Parc Charles-Bertin

Douarnenez ✉ 29100

SWIMMING

-Le Rheum (between/entre la plage de St.Jean & Sables-Blancs; late at night/drague tardive)
-Les/The Dunes (12 km from Douarnenez; during the summer season cruising day and night without interruption; beyond season only from 12 to 14 h /à 12 km de Douarnenez entre 12 et 14 h hors saison, à n'importe quelle heure tout l'été)
-Les Roches blanches (at the edge of the bay, pass along the path of the customs officials; by day also cruising in the wooden huts/Au bord de la baie, le long du sentier des Douaniers; la journée drague dans les blockhaus)

Draguignan ✉ 83300

CRUISING

-Jardin de la Sous-Préfecture (during the day; be discreet)
-Jardin de la gare (day and night)
-Route de Montferrat (sometimes AYOR) (a la sortie du camp militaire de Canjuers (21km) le vendredi soir, soldiers auto stop, be discreet)

Ducey ✉ 50220

RESTAURANTS

Au Rocher de Tombelaine (B CC F g) 8.30-24 h, closed Oct-Mar
Le Bourg Courtils ✉50220 ☎ 02.33.70.96.65

Duclair ✉ 76480

RESTAURANTS

Auberge du Bac. L' (B CC F g) 12-15, 19-22 h, closed Mon morning
2 Rue Alphonse-Calais, Bac de Jumièges ✉76480
☎ 02.35.37.24.16
Menu FF 95-215.

Dunkerque ✉ 59240

HEALTH GROUPS

Centre de prophylaxie des MST
4 Rue Monseigneur-Marquis ✉59240 ☎ 03.28.24.04.00
HIV-testing.
Tandem c/o ADIS, 6 Rue Marengo ✉59140
☎ 03.28.59.19.19
FAX 03.28.63.71.14.

CRUISING

-behind church/derrière l'église St.Martin
-Passerelle de la Douane (le soir/in the evening)

Durfort ✉ 30170

PRIVATE ACCOMODATION

Vieille Maison. La (A bf CC GLM H msg OS)
✉30170 ☎ 66.77.06.46 Fax: 66.77.55.14
Email: vieillemaison@turqoise.fr
Homepage: http://www.turquoise.fr/vieillemaison
Beautiful old house with 4 rooms to rent dedicated to creatifity and art.

Eauze ✉ 32800

CRUISING

-Marché aux Légumes
-Parc Beaulieu

Embrun ✉ 05200

CRUISING

-Garden at the railway station/jardin de la gare
-Postoffice/la poste
-Jardin de l'Archevêché

Epernay ✉ 51200

CRUISING

-Le Jard (in front of the palace of justice/face au palais de justice)
-Covered market/Marché couvert

Epinal ✉ 88000

HEALTH GROUPS

Centre hospitalier d'Epinal Consultations de médecine interne
P.B. 3353 ✉88000 ☎ 03.29.31.31.31
HIV-testing.

CRUISING

-Petit Parc (right border between préfecture and Champ de Mars/Rive droite de la «Moselle», entre la préfecture et le Champ de Mars)

Epone ✉ 78680

CRUISING

-P d'Epone (sur l'autoroute de Rouen entre les sorties Flins et Epone, dans le 2 sens, jour et nuit/on motorway between exits Flins and Epone on both sides, day and night)

Etampes ✉ 91150

CRUISING

-P de Guillervalle

Etel ✉ 56410

CRUISING

-Erdeven (beach/plage)

Etretat ✉ 76790

SWIMMING

-Plage du Tilleul (NU) (south of the beach/au sud de la plage)

Evreux ✉ 27000

HEALTH GROUPS

Centre hospitalier d'Evreux Service dermato-vénérologie
✉27000 ☎ 02.32.31.49.49
HIV-testing.

CRUISING

-Jardin de l'Evéché

Eymoutiers ✉ 87120

RESTAURANTS

Moulin de l'Enfant. Le (b F g) 12-14.30, 19-? h, closed Mon
✉87120 ☎ 05.55.69.24.03

Eze-sur-Mer ✉ 06360

SWIMMING

-Beach/plage de St.Laurent-d'Eze

Fayence ✉ 83440

RESTAURANTS

Pressoir. Le (b F g s) 12-?, 19.30-? h, Nov-May closed Mon
5 Grande Rue Seillans ✉83440 ☎ 04.94.76.85.85
Style of the Fifties.

Figeac ✉ 46100

CRUISING

-Le Celle (facilities and the gardens, in the evening/les toilettes et les jardins, le soir)

Fleury-d'Aude ✉ 11560

RESTAURANTS

Pili Pili. Le (CC F glm MA OS) 1 Jul-15 Sep every evening, 16 Sep-30 Jun Fri-Sun evening
1 bis Avenue de Beziers ✉11560 ☎ 04.68.33.51.30
8 km from Pisse-Vache naturist beach, 16 km from Beziers.

SWIMMING

-Pisse-Vache (NU) (beach between St. Pierre and Les Cabanes de Fleury, 1 km-camping municipal)

Foix ✉ 09000

HEALTH GROUPS

Centre hospitalier de Foix Service de médecine interne
18 Allée de Villote ✉09000 ☎ 05.61.05.41.30
HIV-testing.

CRUISING

-behind the postoffice/derrière la poste.

Fontainebleau ✉ 77300

CRUISING

-Croix du Grand-Maître (in the forest and in the surroundings of the bridge/En fôret et vers l'aqueduc)

Fontenay-le-Comte ✉ 85200

CRUISING

-Place du Champ-de-Foire

Fos-sur-Mer ✉ 13270

CRUISING

-the dunes/les dunes (entre/between la pointe St.Gervais et/and la Centrale EDF)

Fougères ✉ 35300

CRUISING

-Aire de repos (RN 2, exit/sortie Rennes, direction Fougères)
-Place de la Douve

Fouras ✉ 17450

SWIMMING

-Beach/plage de l'Espérance

Frehel ✉ 22240

SWIMMING

-Plorien (Vieux-Bourg)

Fréjus ✉ 83600

RESTAURANTS

Auberge des Adrets (bf F g H) Restaurant: 12-14, 19-22.30 h, closed Mon & 11.Nov-14.Dec & 1.-15.Mar
Lieu dit Auberge-des-Adrets, RN7 ✉83600 ☎ 04.94.40.36.24

SWIMMING

-Dunes de St-Aygule

Freyming-Merlebach ✉ 57900

CRUISING

-Around the church (but not inside!)/autour de l'église (mais pas à l'intérieur!)
-Frontière luxembourgeoise (45 min from Metz)

Gaillard ✉ 74240

SEX SHOPS/BLUE MOVIES

Vidéo Club franco-suisse (g VS) 10-24 h
1 Rue de la Libération ✉74240 ☎ 04.50.38.14.30

Gallargues-le-Montueux ✉ 30660

PROPERTY SERVICES

Agence Yves Lozé Mon-Fri 9-12, 15-19, Sat 9-12 h
33 Rue de Vergeze ✉30660 ☎ 04.66.35.38.56
Property agency.

Gap ✉ 05000

HEALTH GROUPS

Aides Provence Antenne de Gap 1st Tue 14-16 h
24 Rue Saint-Arey ✉05000 ☎ 04.92.53.43.93
Centre hospitalier de Gap. Service de médecine
1 Place Auguste-Muret, PO Box 62 84 ✉05000 ☎ 04.92.40.61.61
HIV-testing.

CRUISING

-Jardin de la Pépinière
-La patinoire

Gardanne ✉ 13120

CRUISING

-Place de la République

Gennevilliers ✉ 92230

HEALTH GROUPS

Centre médico-social municipal
3 Rue de la Paix ✉92230 ☎ 02.47.94.33.71

CRUISING

-Gare de Grésillons

Gien ✉ 45500

CRUISING

-Place du Château

Gigny-sur-Saone ✉ 71240

DANCECLUBS

Why Not. Le (AC B CC D GLM OS p pi SNU WE YG) Fri-Sun & before public holidays 23-5 h
Chateau de la colonne ✉71240 ☎ 03.85.44.81.71
Garden & swimming pool in summer.

Golf Juan ✉ 06100

SWIMMING

-Plage de la Batterie (near service station between Cannes and Golf Juan, popular nudist beach)

Gourin ✉ 56110

DANCECLUBS

Starman. Le (B D DR GLM H lj M p s TV) Sat gay 23-5 h
4 Rue de la Gare ✉56110 ☎ 02.97.23.66.78
Disco and private hotel.

HOTELS

Calèche. La (B F g H) Restaurant Thu-Tue 12-14, 19-22 h
4 Rue de la Gare ✉56110 ☎ 02.97.23.40.35
Rooms with bath, some with WC. Rates FF 100-150, bf 26.

Grenoble ✉ 38000

GAY INFO

Minitel: 3615 ALLOGAY
✉38000

BARS

George V (AC CC D G MA p W)
124 Cours Berriat ✉38000 ☎ 04.76.84.16.20
Queen's. Le (B TV VS) 10-1, Sun 18-1 h
62 Cours Jean-Jaurès ✉38000 ☎ 04.76.54.13.70
Rutli. The (AC B CC G MA p W) 17-1 h, Sun 18-1, summer 19-1 h, closed Mon
9 Rue Etienne Marcel ✉38000 ☎ 04.76.43.21.16
2nd bar upstairs at WE.

SEX SHOPS/BLUE MOVIES

Sexashop (G VS) 9-22, Sun 15-22 h
2 Rue de Miribel ✉38000 ☎ 04.76.46.70.86

SAUNAS/BATHS

Saint-Ferjus. Le (b G sa sol VS) 14-21, Fri 14-24 h
22 Rue Saint Ferjus ✉38000 ☎ 04.76.54.13.70

HOTELS

Hôtel Rochambeau (g H) 8-24 h, closed Sun
13 Avenue Rochambeau ✉38000 ☎ 04.76.96.05.34
Pets welcome.

HEALTH GROUPS

AIDES, Dauphiné-Savoie Mon Wed 19.30-22 h
PO Box 381 ✉38015 ☎ 04.76.46.07.58
Help and information about Aids/Entraide et information sur le Sida.
Centre dép. de santé
23 Avenue Albert-1er-de-Belgique ✉38000 ☎ 04.76.87.62.40
HIV testing.

RELIGIOUS GROUPS

David et Jonathan B.P. 792 ✉38035

CRUISING

-Piscine Bemat
-Monument des Diables bleus
-Hôtel-de-Ville (night/nuit)
-Parc de l'Ile-Verte
-Rue Malherbe (garden/jardin)
-Champs-sur-Drac (summer)
-Etangs de St-Egrève (summer)
-Monument des Diables bleus
-Parc Paul-Mistral
-Parc Foch
-Place Victor-Hugo

Grignan ✉ 26230

BARS

Greco. Le (CC D DR GLM MA OS p pi s VS)
Le Fraysse (Hamlet) on the D4 ✉26230 ☎ 04.75.46.51.66
Fax: 04.75.91.10.38
Discotheque, bar, restaurant everyday. Bar & restaurant open only in summer with pool, rooms available. Disco: Fri Sat 23-5, in summer + Sun.

Gruissan ✉ 11430

RESTAURANTS

Brin de Folie. Le (CC F G OS) Thu-Mon 12-14, 19-22.30, Apr-Sep Mon-Sun 12-14, 19-23.30 h
Place du Cadran-Solaire ✉11430 *(At Grazel beach)*
☎ 04.68.49.14.08
Thierry and Christian welcome you.

SWIMMING

-Beach/plage (NU) (between/entre Plage de Narbonne & Plage de Gruissan)

CRUISING

-Etang de Mateil

Guérande ✉ 44350

DANCECLUBS

Villa la Grange (B CC D g MA) Jul-Aug: 23-6, Apr-Sep: Fri Sat 23-6 h
Ch. de la Nantaise ✉44350 ☎ 40.60.00.58
Most famous danceclub of La Baune.

Guéret ✉ 23011

HEALTH GROUPS

Centre hospitalier de Guéret. Service de médecine
39 Avenue de la Sénatorerie ✉23011 ☎ 05.55.51.70.00
HIV testing.

CRUISING

-Place Bonhyaud (gare SNCF/railway station)

Guillaumes ✉ 06470

CRUISING

-Lac de Serre

Hendaye ✉ 64700

SWIMMING

-Plage d`Abbadia (NU)

CRUISING

-Parc du Château d'Abbadia

Herbignac ✉ 44410

RESTAURANTS

Eau-de-Mer. L' (B F g) 12-15, 19-22 h, closed 1.Oct-1.Mar
Kermoureau-Pompas ✉44410 ☎ 02.40.91.32.36

Honfleur ✉ 14600

BARS

Charles V. Le (B G MA p s SNU VS W) May-Sep: 12-3, Oct-Apr: 16-3 h closed Tue, some Fri theme parties
25 Boulevard Charles VF ✉14600 ☎ 02.31.89.96.70
Bar and small video room.

RESTAURANTS

Au Gai Luron (CC F glm OS s) closed Wed evening, Thu lunch and dinner, Jul-Aug open every day
20 Place Sainte Catherine ✉14600 ☎ 02.31.89.99.90

CRUISING

-Marché aux poissons (behind the fish market, summer only 17-19 h)

Hossegor ✉ 40150

BARS

Tilt. Le (AC B CC GLM N S YG) 19-3 h
366 Avenue du Touring Club ✉40150 ☎ 05.58.41.71.34

RESTAURANTS

Pizzaiol. Le (AC B CC F glm MA OS) Summer: 12-1, winter: 12-15 19-24 h
376 Avenue du Touring Club ✉40150 *(town center next to Hotel Key West)* ☎ 05.58.43.57.04

HOTELS

Key West (bf CC glm H MA) open all year
366 Avenue du Touring Club ✉40150 ☎ 05.58.43.57.04
Fax: 05.58.43.65.74 Email: pizzaiol@wanadoo.fr
Motel style hotel. Reception at restaurant Pizzaiol next-door and bar Le Tilt.

SWIMMING

-Nudist beach/plage naturiste

Houplines ✉ 59116

BARS

Café Brasserie la Nouvelle France (B g) 7.30-21, Sun 7.30-14 h
84 Rue Carnot ✉59116 ☎ 03.20.77.46.82

Hourtin ✉ 33990

SWIMMING

-Hourtin-plage (au sud/in the south)
-Plage du Pin sec (Naujac-sur-Mer. Au nord/in the north)

Hyères ✉ 83400

SWIMMING

-Rochers de Gien (NU) (Côte sud-ouest)
-Plage des Salins (last beach; the restaurant »Chez Pimpin« marks the entrance to the nude section)

Ile du Levant ✉ 83400

HOTELS

Chez Valery (B F glm H NU)
✉83400 ☎ 04.94.05.90.83 Fax: 04.94.05.92.95
Restaurant and hotel with 8 rooms and 4 bungalows.
Eglantine. L' (GLM H NU) 1 May-30 Sep
Corniche l'arbousier ✉83400 ☎ 04.94.05.92.50
Fax: 04.94.05.92.50
Located in the naturist island in the mediteranean. Rooms & apartments to rent. Simple accomodation in large villa.

CRUISING

-Ile-du-Levant (behind the castle, evening/ derrière le château, le soir)
-Jardin Denis
-Bus station/gare des bus

Ile sur la Sorgue ✉ 84800

RESTAURANTS

Petit Jardin. Le (F b glm)
19 Place Rose Gouclard ✉84800 ☎ 04.90.20.87.67

Issy-les-Moulineaux ✉ 92130

HEALTH GROUPS

Hôpital Corantins-Celton
37 Boulevard Gambetta ✉92130 ☎ 05.45.54.95.33

CRUISING

-Pont et Ile de Billancourt
-Parc Henri-Barbusse

Ivry-sur-Seine ✉ 94200

HEALTH GROUPS

Dispensaire municipal
64 Avenue G. Gosnat ✉94200 ☎ 05.46.72.38.38

CRUISING

-Parc J.-Coutant
-Piscine municipale (avec sauna ouvert jusqu'à 21 h)

Jargeau ✉ 45150

CRUISING

-Pier of the Loire/Jetée de la Loire (go 10 kms in direction to Jargeau, you find it close by the training route of the driving school; in summer, the gays are busy and in great number/A 10 km vers Jageau, à la hauteur de la piste d'auto-école; plage bien frequentée en été)

Joue-les-Tours ✉ 37300

DANCECLUBS

Cage. La (B D g S) 22-4 h
1 Avenue de Bordeaux ✉37300 ☎ 02.47.28.81.81
Entrance during shows: FF 50-100.

Juan Les Pins ✉ 06160

SAUNAS/BATHS

Amadeus Club (b G sa sb sol) Winter: 14-22, summer 14-24 h
67 Boulevard Raymond Poincaré ✉06160 ☎ 04.93.61.03.31
Fun relaxed atmosphere in kitch decor.

La Barre-de-Monts ✉ 85550

SWIMMING

-Plage des Lays (NU)

La Chaise Dieu ✉ 43160

RESTAURANTS

Grange. La (b F glm OS) Jul-Sep 12-24; winter 12-14 19-21 h
Rue St. Martin ✉43160 ☎ 04.71.00.02.00

La Ciotat ✉ 13600

SWIMMING

-Rocher du Liouquet (to the left behind Cap Saint-Louis)

La Croix-Valmer ✉ 83420

SWIMMING

-Beach/Plage du Brouis

La Faute-sur-Mer ✉ 85460

SWIMMING

-Pointe d'Arcais (beach/plage)

La Ferté Gaucher ✉ 77320

GUEST HOUSES

Fontaine aux Loups. La (bf F glm H pi)
✉77320 *(9 km from La Ferté Gaucher by D215 direction Montmirail)* ☎ 01.64.03.76.76 Fax: 01.64.03.76.77
Email: ceranrs@club.internet.fr
Country retreat 1 hour from Paris.

La Grande-Motte ✉ 34280

RESTAURANTS

Brasserie de la Mer/Chez Fabrice (b CC F g) 12-15, 19-24 h
Quai d'Honneur ✉34280 ☎ 04.67.56.75.93
French cuisine. Glossy atmosphere on the harbour. Lunch and dinner.

FASHION SHOPS

Boutique Fabrice Soliveres (CC G) 11-19, closed Tue, Jul-Aug 10-23 h
Quai d'Honneur ✉34280 ☎ 04.67.56.75.93

HOTELS

Hôtel Azur (H GLM pi) closed 1.Dec-6.Jan
Presqu'île du Port ✉34280 ☎ 04.67.56.56.00
Fax: 04.67.29.81.26
Beach location. Small bedrooms equipped with AC, mini-bar, telephone, colour TV. Room with shower/WC FF 495, with bath/WC 595, bf 42.

CRUISING

-Le Grand Travers (between Carnon and la Grande Motte)
-Point Zéro

La Plaine-sur-Mer ✉ 44770

SWIMMING

-Criques de Prefailles (beach in front of/ plage en face de camping municipal)

La Rochelle ✉ 17000

BARS

Insolite. L' (B G MA) 14-2, Sun 17-2 h
12 Rue Bletterie ✉17000 *300 m. from the harbour.* ☎ 05.46.41.90.51

DANCECLUBS

Tuxedo Café (B D G) 21-5 h
Place de la Préfecture ✉17000 ☎ 05.46.50.01.22
Bar disco.

SAUNAS/BATHS

Atlantis. L' (b CC DR f G MA sa sb VS WO) 13-21, Sat 15-24, Sun 14-21 h, Fri mixed
12 Rue de l'Arsenal ✉17000 *(Centre ville, Vieux Port)* ☎ 05.46.41.15.89
Hot and cold drinks free.

FASHION SHOPS

X'trem Mod' (CC glm YG) 10.30-19 h, closed Sun Mon morning
26 Rue Bletterie ✉17000 ☎ 05.46.28.10.00
Underwear, fashion, shoes and accessories. 5% discount for Spartacus readers.

HEALTH GROUPS

Centre hospitalier de la Rochelle, Service médecine interne
Rue Albert-Schweitzer, PO Box 38 49, 17019 Cedex ✉17000
☎ 05.46.27.33.33
HIV-testing.

SWIMMING

-Le Marouillet (à 12 km de La Rochelle)
-Plage de St-Jean-des-Sables (NU) (à 8 km de La Rochelle)

CRUISING

-Casino (public garden, evening/jardin public, le soir)
-Rue Thiers (afternoon and evening/l'après-midi et le soir)
-Bridge/pont de Chagnolet
-Le Marché couvert (Rue Thiers)
-Parc d'Orbigny (derrière le casino)
-P de la Tour carrée (a proximité de lar mer/close to the ocean)

La Roche-sur-Yon ✉ 85000

GENERAL GROUPS

Association Aides Vendée lutte contre le Sida Mon-Fri 16-19 h
✉85000 *Porte 106* ☎ 02.51.46.20.62

HEALTH GROUPS

Centre hospitalier de la Roche-sur-Yon
Les Oudairies, 85024 Cedex ✉85000 ☎ 02.51.44.61.73
HIV-testing.

SWIMMING

-Beach/plage (NU)

CRUISING

-Cours Bayard
-Railway station/gare SNCF
-Place de la Vendée

La Seyne-sur-Mer ✉ 83500

SWIMMING

-Plage de Fabregas (at night/la nuit)
-Beach/plage du Jonquet (G NU)

La Teste ✉ 33260

SWIMMING

-Nudist beach/plage naturiste

La Tranche-sur-Mer ✉ 85360

SWIMMING

-Conches (beach between/plage entre Longeville & La Tranche)

Labastide-Saint-Pierre ✉ 82370

CRUISING

-Aire de repos de Campsas

Labenne ✉ 40530

SWIMMING

-Labenne-Cap-Breton (plage près de la chapelle/beach near the little church)

Lacanau ✉ 33680

SWIMMING
-Wood house of Lion/Maison forestière du Lion
-Le Porge-Océan (Best Jul-Sep)

Lagny-sur-Marne ✉ 77400

CRUISING
-Base de loisirs de Jabline (on the southwest side of the lake, at the border of the „Marne"/côté sud-ouest du lac, au bord de la Marne)

L'Aiguillon-sur-Mer ✉ 85460

SWIMMING
-Beach/Plage de la Pointe d'Arcais

Lamure sur Azergues ✉ 69870

GUEST HOUSES
Château de Pramenoux (bf glm F H OS s)
✉69870 ☎ 04.74.03.16.43 Fax: 04.74.03.16.28
10th-12th century Château in the mountains of Beaujolais. Comfortable rooms and table d'hôtes. Large room for receptions.

Landeronde ✉ 85150

BARS
Damier. Le (B CC D G) Fri-Sun 22.30-5 h, Jul-Aug Wed-Sun 23.30-5 h
RN 260 → La Roche sur Yon ✉85150 *(between La Roche sur Yon and Sables d'Olonne)* ☎ 02.51.34.29.09

Langres ✉ 52200

CRUISING
-Place Bel-Air (at night/la nuit)

Lannion ✉ 22300

SWIMMING
-Beach of/Plage de Beg-Leguer (NU) (between Lannion and Trebeurden; difficult access/entre Lannion et Trebeurden; accès escarpé)

CRUISING
-[P] at the cemetery (in the afternoon)

Lauzerte ✉ 82110

GUEST HOUSES
Jardin Secret. Le (bf f glm H OS pi sa sb wh)
c/o Maison Tournesol, Rue de la Garrigue ✉82110
☎ 05.63.95.72.88
Small guest house with a garden, pool, sauna and steam room in a medieval town between Montaubon & Cahors. 90 km to Toulouse airport.

Laval ✉ 53000

BARS
Vulcain. Le (B glm) Mon-Sat 18-2 h
32 Grande Rue ✉53000 ☎ 02.43.56.09.86

GENERAL GROUPS
WATT!! Les Courants Homosexuels Wed 20-22 h
13 Rue des Béliers ✉53000 ☎ 02.43.69.35.08
Gay and lesbian association. Welcoming and information.

HEALTH GROUPS
Centre hospitalier de Laval, Service de médecine interne 7
37 Rue du Haut-Rocher, B.P. 4280 ✉53024 ☎ 02.43.66.50.00
HIV-testing.

RELIGIOUS GROUPS
David et Jonathan
B.P. 462 ✉53008

CRUISING
-Bois de l'Huisserie
-Basilique d'Avesnières

Lavaur ✉ 81500

BARS
Taverne de la Dame du Plô. La (AC B CC d f glm H MA OS p s) 18-4 h, Sun afternoon only, closed Mon
5 Rue Père Colin ✉81500 ☎ 05.63.41.38.77
Piano Bar and art gallery with accomodation available. In 16th century building. In the middle of the triangle Toulouse-Albi-Castre.

Le Cannet ✉ 06110

CRUISING
-Jardin du Tivoli
-Place Bellevue
-Le Lavoir
-[P] St-Sauveur
-Terminus des bus

Le Château-d'Oléron ✉ 17480

CRUISING
-Public garden/jardin public

Le Cheylard ✉ 07160

CRUISING
-Pont Pierre

Le Conquet ✉ 29217

SWIMMING
-Plage du nord de Lanse des Sablons (take the road D28 direction Ploumguer, then left to Porz Illien)

CRUISING
-Halles St-Louis

Le Coudray ✉ 28630

HEALTH GROUPS
Hôspital Fontenoy-Le-Coudray Service de pneumologie
Rue Claude-Bernard ✉28630 *PO Box 18 10* ☎ 02.37.30.30.30
HIV-testing.

CRUISING
-In front of the cathedral/Devant la cathédrale

Le Croisic ✉ 44490

SWIMMING
-La Turballe (Pen-Bron, beach behind the pyramid/plage après la pyramide)

Le Grau-du-Roi ✉ 30240

SWIMMING

-Plage Port-Camargues
-Plage de l'Espiguette (G NU) (for explanation ☛ Aigues-Mortes)

CRUISING

-Quai Laperouse

Le Havre ✉ 76600

BARS

Bar du Bassin (B CC GLM s) 15-2, Sat Sun 18-2 h
79-81 Quai George V ✉76600 ☎ 02.35.41.28.82
Once a month theme night.
Etage Bar. L' (B CC G) 19.2 h, closed on Thu
137 Rue d'Etretat ✉76600 ☎ 02.35.48.50.59
Village. Le (B GLM) 18-2 h
74-76 Rue Voltaire ✉76600

RESTAURANTS

Grignot. Le (F glm) 12-1 h
53 Rue Racoye ✉76600

SAUNAS/BATHS

Hot Way (b g p sa VS wh YG) 14-22, Sun 15-22 h
60 Rue Dauphine ✉76600 ☎ 02.35.22.58.52

SWIMMING

-Beach/Plage du Ste.Adresse (NU) (at the end near airport/au bout près de l'aéroport)
-Beach/Plage du Tilleul (23 km from Le Havre towards Etretat, after the rocks/23 km du Havre en direction de Etretat, après les rochers)

CRUISING

-Forest of/Forêt de Montgeon (AYOR) (in the surroundings of/aux alentours du Château d'Eau)
-Place Danton

Le Lavandou ✉ 83980

SWIMMING

-Nudist beach/plage naturiste

Le Lude ✉ 72800

CRUISING

-In the gardens of the castle/les jardins du château

Le Mans ✉ 72000

BARS

Arc-En-Ciel Bar. L' (A B CC GLM MA TV)
2 Rue Dorée ✉72000 ☎ 02.43.23.80.16

DANCECLUBS

Limite. La (B CC D GLM MA p s) 23.30-5 h, closed Mon Tue
7 Rue Saint-Honoré ✉72000 ☎ 02.43.24.85.54

SEX SHOPS/BLUE MOVIES

Sex Shop 72 (AC CC DR GLM MA TV VS YG) 10-22, Sun & public holidays 15-20 h
72 Rue Bourg Belé ✉72000 ☎ 02.43.28.51.39

SAUNAS/BATHS

Nil. Le (AC b CC G MA sa sb VS wh) 15-22.30, Mon Wed 15-21 h, closed Tue
36 Rue de Fleurus ✉72000 *(close to the train station)*
☎ 02.43.23.26.81

HEALTH GROUPS

Centre Hospitalier Général Service de dermatologie
194 Avenue Rubillard, 72037 Cedex ✉72000 *(Pavillon Duperrat)*
☎ 02.43.43.43.43
HIV-testing.

RELIGIOUS GROUPS

David et Jonathan Helpline/Ligne Homofil: Wed-Thu 20-23 h
B.P. 28004 ✉72008 ☎ 02.43.28.25.63

CRUISING

-Esplanade des Jacobins (night/nuit)
-Jardin de Tesse(avenue de Paderborn)
-Place de Pontlieue (WC)
-P Tertre
-P Cormier

Le Palais ✉ 56360

BARS

Frégate. La (B g) 8-2 h, closed Oct-Mar
Quai de l'Acadie ✉56360 ☎ 02.97.31.43.76

SWIMMING

-Beach/plage du Dotchau (NU)

Le Pouliguen ✉ 44510

BARS

Petit Navire. Le (B CC d GLM MA OS P) Jun-Sep 9-3 & Fri Sat Sun in winter; other days 9-1, closed Tue (not Jul Aug)
7 Rue du Gal. Leclerc ✉44510 ☎ 02.40.42.41.59

Le Puy-en-Velay ✉ 43000

HEALTH GROUPS

Centre hospitalier E.-Roux Service de médecine interne
Boulevard du Dr Andrichantemesse ✉43000 ☎ 04.71.05.66.77
HIV testing.

CRUISING

-Jardin Henry-Vinay
-Place Michelet
-Place du Breuil

Le Touquet ✉ 62520

CRUISING

-In the dunes

Lege-Cap-Ferret ✉ 33950

SWIMMING

-Lege (nu) (Nudists in the north/naturistes au nord)

Lens ✉ 62300

GENERAL GROUPS

Paragays Tue Fri 21-23 h
✉62300 ☎ 03.21.28.32.89

HEALTH GROUPS

Centre hospitaler de Lens Centre de Pneumologie
B.P. 2562 ✉62300 ☎ 03.21.70.04.90
HIV-testing.

CRUISING

-Public garden/jardin public
-Parc de Glissaies (behind the railway station/derrière la gare)

Les Rousses ✉ 39400

CRUISING

-Lake of/Lac des Rousses (behind the rocks in the little wood. Pretty hot in summer/derrière le rocher dans le petit bois. L'été, assez chaud)
-Around the Tourism House, close to the telephone booth/autour de la maison du Tourisme vers la cabine teléphonique

Lesconil ✉ 29138

SWIMMING

-Beach/Plage (NU) (leave at Lesconil and go in direction of Lechiagat, take the country-lane to the left/A la sortie de Lesconil en direction de Lechiagat, chemin de terre à gauche)

Leucate ✉ 11370

RESTAURANTS

Restaurant Le Clos de Ninon (A B F glm) 12-15, 19-1, meals -23 h
12 Avenue Francis Vals, Leucate-Village ✉11370
☎ 04.68.40.18.16

SWIMMING

-Beach of Leucate/Leucate-Plage (NU) (north of the straight-families' beach/au nord de la plage familiale)
-Northern beach of the villages Ulysse and Aphrodite/Plage du nord commune aux villages naturistes

Levallois-Perret ✉ 92300

CRUISING

-Parc Louis-Rouquier

Lille ✉ 59000

GAY INFO

Lesbian & Gay Pride Lille
15 Rue Malpart, B.P. 222 ✉59002 Email: LGPLille@apg-tm.com
Organises the city's gay pride.
Minitel 3615 ALLOGAY
Minitel 3615 BOB

BARS

Activy. L' (B GLM MA)
6 Rue Anatole France ✉59000
Mam'zelle Fifi (B GLM MA OS) 11-2 h
59 Jacques Louchard, Les Terrasses Ste Catherine ✉59000
Ramponneau. Le (AC B E glm lj MA N p W) Tue-Fri 8-1, Sat-Sun 16-1, Mon 8-20 h
22 Square du Ramponneau ✉59800 *(M° Rihour), Façade de l'Esplanade* ☎ 03.20.74.49.80
The Mum's Bar (AC B CC G p s SNU YG) 21-2, Sun 16-2 h
4 Rue Doudin ✉59000 *(M° Rihour. In the old town)* ☎ 03.20.06.32.22
Look for the gay flag.

DANCECLUBS

Zenith. Le (B D GLM P) Thu-Sun 23-? h
74 Avenue de Flandre ✉59650 *(surbub of Lille)* ☎ 03.20.89.92.29

RESTAURANTS

P'tits Lous. Les (B F g) Tue-Fri 12-14.30, 19-23.30, Sat 19-.23.30, Sun 12-15 h, 12-25 Aug and 23 Dez-5 Jan closed
4 Place de la Nouvelle Aventure ✉59000 ☎ 03.20.57.15.05

SEX SHOPS/BLUE MOVIES

Boîte à Films. La (DR g MA VS) 10-1 h
39 Rue de Roubaix ✉59800 ☎ 03.20.51.29.51
Cinesex (AC CC glm VS) 10-23, Sun 12-23 h
41 Rue des Ponts-de-Comines ✉59000 ☎ 03.20.06.25.83
Golden Boy (AC CC glm s VS) 10-23 h
14 Rue de la Quenette ✉59800 *(M° Gare)* ☎ 03.20.06.34.26
Sex shop and video projection room/Sex shop et salle de projection vidéos.
Sex Center (AC CC g s VS) 10-24 h
41 Rue des Ponts de Comines ✉59800 *(M° Rihour)* ☎ 03.20.06.25.83
Erotics products, videos and DVD's.

SAUNAS/BATHS

Bains. Les (AC B DR F G sa sb sol wh VS WO YG) 12-23, Fri -24, Sat 14-24, Sun -23 h
52 Rue de Cambrai ✉59000 *(M°-Porte de Valenciennes)* ☎ 03.20.53.02.02
The gay meeting place of the North.

GENERAL GROUPS

Abou-Nawas Project
La Bassée 33 ✉59480
Support and contact for muslim and arab gays and lesbians. Only by post.
Andromède
B.P. 1016 ✉59011 ☎ 03.20.30.65.54
Email: andromede@minitel.net
Youth group.
Comité pour la Reconnaissance Sociale des Homosexuels (CRSH)
B.P. 51 ✉59008 ☎ 03.20.31.90.67
Email: sladent@worldnet.fr
Group acting for the recognition of gay rights.
Gai-Kitsch Camp
B.P. 36 ✉59009 ☎ 03.20.06.33.91 Email: GKC@worldnet.fr
Homepage: http://fglb.qrd.ord:8080/fgrd
Minitel 3615 GKC Organizer of a gay flim festival. Also books publishers.
J'en suis - J'y reste (B d GLM) Tue 18-23, Wed 16-20, Fri 20-23 h
19 Rue de Condé ✉59000 ☎ 03.20.52.28.68
Fax: 03.20.52.28.68
Call for more details on activities. Friday girls only.

HEALTH GROUPS

Association Aides
209 Boulevard de la Liberté ✉59800 ☎ 03.28.52.05.10
FAX 03.28.52.05.11. Minitel 36 15 AIDES.
Centre de Prévention Santé
8 Rue de Valmy ✉59000 ☎ 03.20.54.57.73

HELP WITH PROBLEMS

SOS Solitude gaie 0-24 h
✉59000 ☎ 03.20.04.24.17

RELIGIOUS GROUPS

David et Jonathan
B.P. 332 ✉59026
Gay christians/homos chrétiens.

SPORT GROUPS

Ch'ti Randos B.P. 18 ✉59008
Organises walking tours and hiking/Gays randonneurs.

CRUISING

-University campus/Campus Universitaire (in the surroundings of the library/Autour de la bibliothèque)
-Belgian border/Frontière belge (see/voir Courtrai, Kuurne, Mouscron, Pipaix, Tournai, Bonsecours and/et Willaupuis)
-Bois de Boulogne (ayor) (Forest of Boulogne; at the north end, behind the stad. along the canal and in the groves; at night also on the [P] of the avenue Mathias-Delobel/A l'extrémité nord, derrière le stade, le long du canal, dans les bosquets; la nuit sur le [P] de l'avenue Mathias-Delobel)
-Bois de Phalempin (Forest of Phalempin, south of Lille, go 15 km on the A1 highway, leave it at exit Seclin and then take the road D8./Au sud de Lille, 15 km par autoroute A1, sortie Seclin, puis route D8)
-Groves in the northern part of town/Bosquets du péripherique nord Boulevard Robert-Schumann (go by car direction St.André; esplanade/en voiture, direction St.André; esplanade)
-Railway station/gare SNCF
-Square de la Porte-de-Roubaix (AYOR)
-Place de la République

Limoges ✉ 87000

BARS

Café Traxx (b d glm MG OS) Mon-Fri 12-2, Sat 15-12 h
Place Fontaine des Barres 12 ✉87000 ☎ 05.55.32.07.55
Volcanique. Le (B g) 7.30-2, Sat Sun 5-2 h
51 Ave du Général Leclerc ✉87000 ☎ 55.77.41.13
Mixed bar. Mainly gay after 21 h.

DANCECLUBS

Club Boy (B D G MA OS p S TV VS YG) 23-5 h, show Sun
Rue Solignac ✉87000 ☎ 05.55.31.19.41
Weekly theme parties.
Panthère Rose. La (B D DR G) Thu-Sun 23-6 h
56 Rte du Pont St. Marial ✉8700 ☎ 55.32.27.14

SAUNAS/BATHS

Sauna Eros (AC b CC DR G p sa sb sol VS wh YG) 14-2, Fri Sat -4 h
8 Rue Jean Jaurès ✉87000 ☎ 05.55.32.74.48
Two establishments at the same address, one gay, one mixed.

HEALTH GROUPS

Centre hospitalier R.U. Dupuytren Service de médecine A
2 Avenue Alexis-Carel ✉87000 ☎ 05.55.05.66.52
HIV testing.

CRUISING

-Bois de la Bastide (AYOR)
-Garden of/Jardin de l'ancien Palais de l'Évéché
-Champ de Juillet (AYOR R TV)
-[P] Cora (Route de Paris)
-Place de la Cathédrale (AYOR)

Limoges-Branchard ✉ 870280

HOTELS

Auberge de l'Etape (F H s)
RN 20 ✉870280 ☎ 55.37.14.33 Fax: 55.37.24.80

Limoux ✉ 11300

HOTELS

Hotel Moderne et Pigeon (B bf F H OS) Restaurant closed Sat lunch and Mon
1 Place General Leclerc ✉11300
☎ 04.68.31.00.25 Fax: 04.68.31.12.43
Renovated 18th century mansion. Quote SPARTACUS.

GENERAL GROUPS

Homosexualités Audoises
B.P. 27 ✉11303

Lisieux ✉ 14100

CRUISING

-Public garden/jardin public
-Hôtel-de-Ville
-Railway station/Gare SNCF
-Rue du Char

L'Isle-Adam ✉ 59290

CRUISING

-Rond Point de Paris (in the forest at route D64E, watch out for official guardians on horseback)

Loison-sous-Lens ✉ 62218

BARS

Club 175. Le (AC B CC D G MA p s YG) Bar: Mon-Thu 21-?, Disco: Fri-Sun 22-? h
175 Route de Lens à Lille ✉62218 ☎ 03.21.28.05.30

Lons-le-Saunier ✉ 39000

HEALTH GROUPS

Centre hospitalier Service consultations externes
110 Rue du Regard ✉39000 *PO Box 50 21* ☎ 03.84.47.29.00
HIV testing.

CRUISING

-Public garden/Jardin Public

Lorient ✉ 56100

BARS

Bar Drôles de... (B GLM MA) Jun-Sep 18-1, Oct-May Mon-Sat 15-1, Sun 18-1 h
26 Rue Jules Legrand ✉56100 ☎ 02.97.21.08.73

SEX SHOPS/BLUE MOVIES

Espace Broadway (AC glm VS) 11-20, Mon 13-23, Fri 11-23 h, closed Sun & Aug
15 Rue Poissionière ✉56100 ☎ 02.97.21.81.64
Local gay information available. 10% reduction for Spartacus readers.
Love Love (g VS) 10-12, 14-23 h, closed Sun
44 Rue Maréchal-Foch ✉56100 ☎ 02.97.21.29.75

SAUNAS/BATHS

Koros-ko. Le (CC DR G MA sa sb sol VS wh) Mon-Sun 14-22 h, Wed and Sat 14-24 h, mixed on Fri
18 Rue Lazare Carnot ✉56100 ☎ 02.97.35.07.50
Mixed on Fridays.

CRUISING

-Jardin Le Faoudic (Place Anatole-le-Braz, harbour/port)
-Ile de Groix (beach on the west coast/ plage sur la côte ouest)
-Kaolins (nudist beach/plage naturiste)

Luchon ✉ 31100

HOTELS

Hôtel Panoramic (b bf CC E F g H MA)
6 Avenue Carnot ✉31100 ☎ 05.61.79.30.90
Fax: 05.61.79.32.84 Email. hotel.panoramic@wanadoo.fr

Lunay ✉ 4136

PRIVATE ACCOMODATION

Château de la Vaudourière (bf CC g H MA)
✉4136 ☎ 02.54.72.19.46
Antique shop and Bed & Breakfast.

Lunel ✉ 34400

BARS

Zeeboys. Le (B D GLM OS S YG) 23-?, closed Mon Tue Wed, Show: Fri-Sun 2.30 h
Route de Nîmes ✉34400 *(RN 113)* ☎ 04.67.71.02.01
Disco between Nimes and Montpellier.

Lunéville ✉ 54300

CRUISING

-Parc du Château

Lyon ✉ 69000

GAY INFO

Lésgayt'on (GLM) Wed 23-? h on FM 91.5 MHz
✉69000 ☎ 04.78.21.05.94 Email: lesgaysbb@multimania.com
Homepage: http://www.multimania.com/lesgaysbb
Minitel 3615 ALLOGAY
Minitel 3615 BOB

TOURIST INFO

Tourist Info
Place Bellecour, PO Box 22 54 ✉69214 ☎ 04.78.42.25.75
FAX 04.78.42.04.32.

BARS

Bar du Centre (AC B CC G MA p) 8-3, Sun 17-3 h
3 Rue Simon Maupin ✉69002 *(M° Bellecour. Opposite Sauna Bellecour)* ☎ 04.78.37.40.18
Broadway. Le (AC B CC DR GLM MA p s VS) 21-? h, closed Tue
9 Rue Terraille ✉69001 ☎ 04.78.39.50.54
Cocktail bar
Forum Bar (AC B CC DR GLM lj MA OS p VS) 17-2, Fri Sat -3 h
15 Rue des Quatre Chapeaux ✉69002 ☎ 04.78.37.19.74
Motor Men Bar (AC B DR G lj MA OS) 19-2, Fri Sat 3 h
2 Rue Bellecordière ✉69000 ☎ 04.72.56.06.06
Ruche Café. La (AC B glm MA)
22 Rue Gentil ✉69002 ☎ 04.78.37.42.26
Spartac Café (AC B F GLM MA) 10-1 h
3 Place St. Paul ✉69000 ☎ 04.78.28.03.32
Verre à Soi. Le (AC B CC d f GLM p TV YG) 11-3, Sat 19-3 h, closed Sun
25 Rue des Capucins ✉69001 *(M° Croix Paquet)*
☎ 04.78.28.92.44
Many theme parties. Happy hour 11-20 h + promotions.

MEN'S CLUBS

Backstage (AC CC DR G MA P VS) 14-24 h
1 Rue des Capucins ✉69001 *(M° Hotel de Ville)*
☎ 04.78.30.60.44
Sex shop with cruising and video cabin area on 3 floors. Theme nights.
Brick System Video (bf DR G p VS) 13-3, WE -5 h
1 Grande Rue de Feuillants ✉69001 *(Metro Croix Paquet)*
☎ 04.72.00.29.57
Trou. Le (AC b CC DR G lj MA p VS) Mon-Thu 19-5, Fri Sat -7, Sun 14-5 h
6 Rue Romarin ✉69001 *(M° Hôtel de Ville)* ☎ 04.78.39.98.69
Video labyrinth and sling. Spartacus readers ask for special rates.
1er Sous-Sol (CC G p VS) 14-3, Fri Sat -7 h
7 Rue du Puits-Guillot ✉69001 *(M° Hôtel de Ville)*
☎ 04.78.29.28.87
500 sq.m. of cruising/drague.

DANCECLUBS

Divine Comédie. La (AC B D glm s) 23-6 h, closed Mon Tue
30 Montée St.Sébastien ✉69001 *(M° Parquet)* ☎ 04.78.30.15.12
Echiquier. L' (AC B D GLM MA P S SNU) 22-? h, closed Tue
38 Rue de l'Arbre Sec ✉69008 *(near Hotel de Ville)*
☎ 04.78.29.18.19
Karaoké on Mon and Wed. Theme parties.

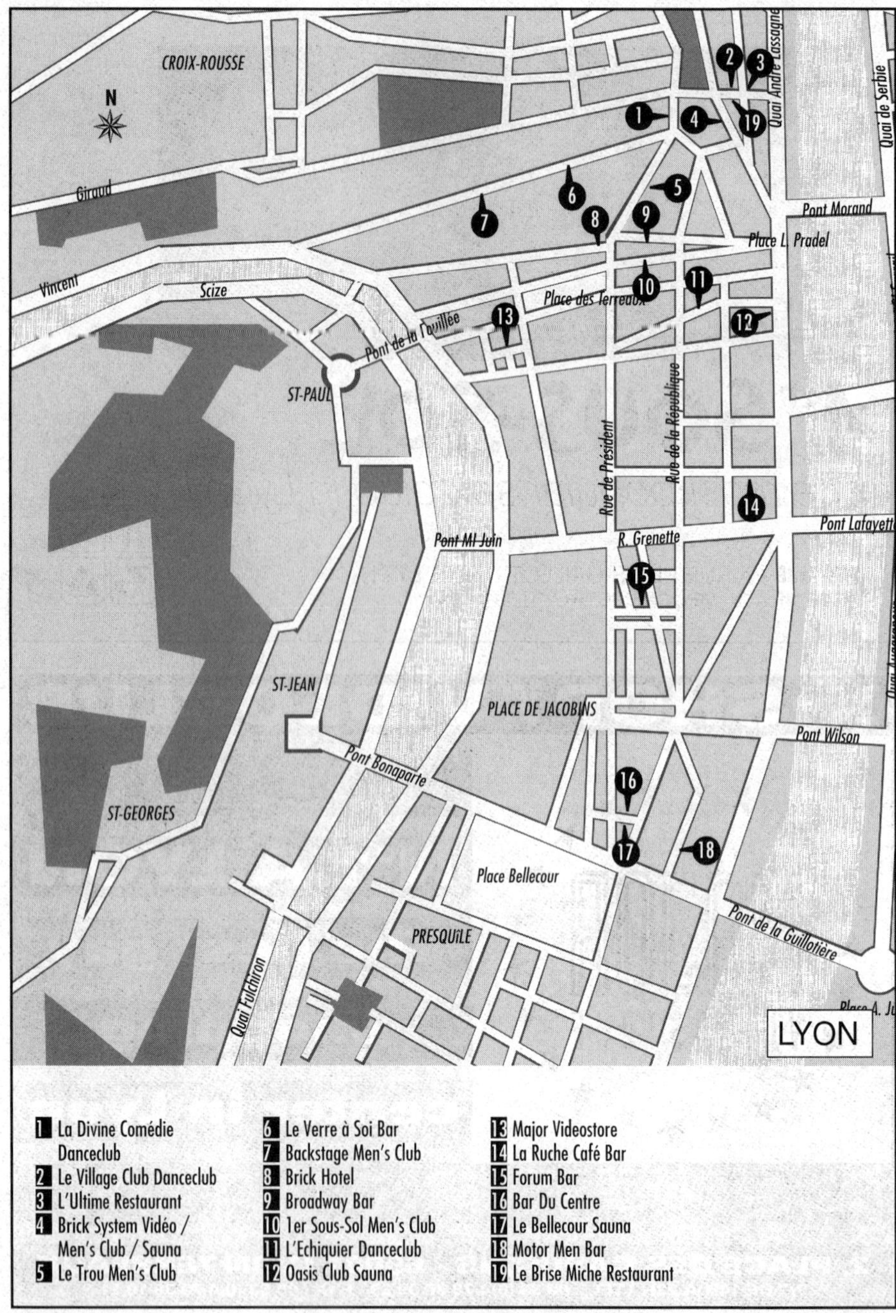
CROIX-ROUSSE
N
Giraud
Vincent
Scize
Quai André Lassagne
Quai de Serbie
Pont Morand
Place L. Pradel
Place des Terreaux
Pont de la Feuillée
ST-PAUL
Rue de Président
Rue de la République
Pont Lafayette
Pont MI Juin
R. Grenette
ST-JEAN
PLACE DE JACOBINS
Pont Wilson
Pont Bonaparte
ST-GEORGES
Place Bellecour
Pont de la Guillotière
PRESQUILE
Quai Fulchiron
LYON
1 La Divine Comédie Danceclub
2 Le Village Club Danceclub
3 L'Ultime Restaurant
4 Brick System Vidéo / Men's Club / Sauna
5 Le Trou Men's Club
6 Le Verre à Soi Bar
7 Backstage Men's Club
8 Brick Hotel
9 Broadway Bar
10 1er Sous-Sol Men's Club
11 L'Echiquier Danceclub
12 Oasis Club Sauna
13 Major Videostore
14 La Ruche Café Bar
15 Forum Bar
16 Bar Du Centre
17 Le Bellecour Sauna
18 Motor Men Bar
19 Le Brise Miche Restaurant

Bar-Cyber-Vidéo-Musik-Cruising-Bar
LAX
WELCOME TO THE FUTURE
www.brick-system.com
2 rue coysevox Lyon 1er

Village Club. Le (AC B D GLM YG) 21-3 h
6 Rue Violi ✉69001 ☎ 04.72.07.72.62
Popular bar and disco.

RESTAURANTS

Brise Miche. Le (A b CC F GLM MA) Closed on Tue
15 Rue Royale ✉69001 ☎ 04.72.07.88.14
Lunch and dinner.

Chez les Garçons (b F glm)
5 Rue Cuviers ✉69005 ☎ 04.78.24.51.07

Feuillants. Les (b CC F glm N YG) 12-13.30 & 19.30-23 h, closed Sun & Mon midday
5 Petite rue des Feuillants ✉69001 *(M° Hotel de Ville)*
☎ 04.78.28.20.50
French cuisine. Popular since 1970.

Gargotte. La (b F glm)
2 Rue Royale ✉69001 ☎ 04.78.28.79.20

Goulue des Pentes. La (b F glm)
37 Rue Imbert Colomes ✉69000 ☎ 04.78.29.41.80

Grain de Sel. Le (b F glm)
2 Rue David Girin ✉69002 ☎ 04.78.42.77.19

Totila (F GLM MA)
10 Rue du Pr Weill ✉69006 ☎ 04.78.52.95.74
Restaurant Bar Pizzeria. Fun place.

Ultime. L' (B F GLM MA)
23 Tue Royale ☎ 04.78.27.23.37
Lunch and dinner except Sat Sun dinner only.

Un sans l'Autre. L' (b F G) Closed Wed and lunchtime on Sat Sun
20 Rue Royale ✉69001 ☎ 04.78.30.43.29

SEX SHOPS/BLUE MOVIES

Boîte à Films. La (AC CC g MA p VS) 10-1 h
24 Rue Lanterne ✉69000 ☎ 04.72.00.83.36

Brick System Shop (CC G p VS) 12-0.30, WE -5 h
1 Grande Rue des Feuillants ✉69001 ☎ 04.72.00.29.57
Sexy clothes, leather & latex, gadgets, magazines etc. Rent and sale of videos. A new shop is opening in March. Call for details.

Major Videostore (CC G VS) 14-22 h
2 Place des Capucins ✉69001 *(Metro Hôtel de Ville. Near Place des Terreaux)* ☎ 04.78.39.09.28
Large selection of videos. Sale and rental. Also accessories and gadgets.

SAUNAS/BATHS

Bellecour. Le (AC B F G lj MG p sa sb VS) 12-22, Fri-Sun 12-24 h
4 Rue Simon-Maupin ✉69002 *(M° Bellecour, opposite Bar du Centre, 1st floor)* ☎ 04.78.38.19.27
Reduced entrance-fee after 20 h on week days. Special price for age under 26 y/o.

Brick System Sauna (AC b CC f G p sa sb sol VS wh WO) 12-3, Fri Sat 12-5 h
1 Grande Rue des Feuillants/Rue Violi ✉69001 *(M° Croix Paquet)*
☎ 04.72.00.29.57
Sauna complex with separate shop & video club.

Mandala. Le (B f G sa sb pi VS wh WO) 12-24 Fri Sat -6 h
9 Rue Boissac ✉69002 *(near Place Bellecour)*
☎ 04.78.42.74.28

Oasis. L' (B f G sa sb sol VS wh WO) 13-24 h
10 Quai Jean Moulin ✉69001 *(M° Hotel de Ville)*
☎ 04.78.39.03.82

BODY & BEAUTY SHOPS

Gentlemen
28 Rue Paul Chenavard ✉69001 ☎ 04.78.27.96.38

BOOK SHOPS

Etat d'esprit (A GLM) Mon-Thu 13-20, Fri 13-21 Sat 11-21 h
19 Rue Royale ✉69001 ☎ 04.78.27.76.53
Gay and lesbian community bookshop. Exhibitions of art, discussions, debates. Open to all.

FASHION SHOPS

Be Boy. The (CC glm) 10-19, Mon 13-19 h, closed Sun
9 Rue Gentil ✉69002 *(M° Cordeliers)* ☎ 04.78.39.81.42
Fashion, underwear & gadgets.

GIFT & PRIDE SHOPS

Kiosque Fleuri. Au 7.30-20.30 h, closed Mon
Place Maréchal-Lyautey ✉69006 *(M° Foch)* ☎ 04.78.89.57.86
Small gifts.

Veyret
2 Grande Rue de la Guillotère ✉69007 ☎ 04.78.72.23.84

LEATHER & FETISH SHOPS

Tom's Boutic Mon-Fri 10-12, 14.30-19 h, Sat by appointment only
41 Quai Pierre Size ✉69000 ☎ 04.72.00.05.35

MAIL ORDER

Comme Des Anges (G VS)
1 Rue des Capucins ✉69000 ☎ 04.72.00.86.87

HOTELS

Brick Hotel (B bf CC GLM H)
9 Rue Ste Catherine ✉69001 ☎ 04.78.28.11.01
Fax: 04.78.28.05.34 Homepage: http://www.brick-system.com
Located in the centre of the gay area. Call for rates. Quote Spartacus.

GENERAL GROUPS

Accueil Rencontres Informations Loisirs (ARIS) Mon Fri 19-22 h
16 Rue St. Polycarpe, B.P. 1125 ✉69203 ☎ 04.78.27.10.10
Information on the gay life and problems. Meetings of different gay associations.

Forum Gai & Lesbien
17 Rue Romarin ☎ 04.78.39.97.72
Cercle de Bacchus.

Rando's Rhône-Alpes
B.P. 173 ✉69406
Organises walking tours and hiking/Organise des randonnées pédestres dans la nature.

FETISH GROUPS

MCRA Lyon
B.P. 3010 ✉69394 ☎ 04.72.33.03.39 Email: yhuneau@imaginet.fr Homepage: http://www.imaginet.fr/~yhuneau/mcra.html
Member of ECMC.

HEALTH GROUPS

Association de Lutte contre le Sida (A.L.S.)
Mon-Fri 10-18 h
24 Impasse de la Gerbe ✉69400 ☎ 04.74.65.92.54

Association de Lutte contre le Sida (A.L.S.)
Mon-Fri 10-18 h
16 Rue Pizay, B.P. 1208 ✉69209 ☎ 04.78.27.80.80

Hôpital Edouard-Herriot Pavillon P
5 Place d'Arsonval, ✉69008 ☎ 04.72.34.46.89
Free HIV-testing.

Hôtel Dieu
71 Quai Jules Courmont ✉69002 ☎ 04.78.42.29.26
Free HIV-testing.

RELIGIOUS GROUPS

David et Jonathan
B.P. 2055 ✉69603

SWIMMING

-Port Gallaud (left bank, north of the bridge)

CRUISING

-Parc de Parilluy (WE)
-Parc de la Tête d'Or
-Tennis courts in Gerland (22-4 h summers; from avenue Leclerc, drive south, past Mercure Hotel, then straight (3km) to Port Edouard Heriot, park on the left, crawl through holes in fence onto the sports grounds)
-Quais du Rhône (r) (especially in front of sauna on quai Jean Moulin)
-Gare SNCF Pont Dieu
-Parc de Gerland (car park and football field)
-Quai du Rhône (under the bridges)

Mâcon

GUEST HOUSES

Salamandre. La (bf CC glm H OS) closed in Feb
Grand Rue ✉71250 *(30 km from Mâcon TGV station)*
☎ 03.85.59.91.56 Fax: 03.85.59.91.67
Email: info@la.salamandre.fr
Dinner possible on reservation.

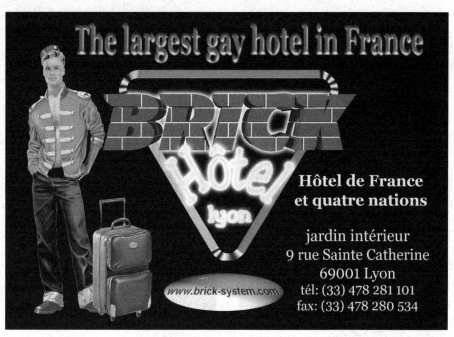

GAY MARSEILLE
THE NEW
CANCAN
Discothèque
3, 5, 7 rue Sénac
13001 Marseille
Tél.: 04 91 48 59 76

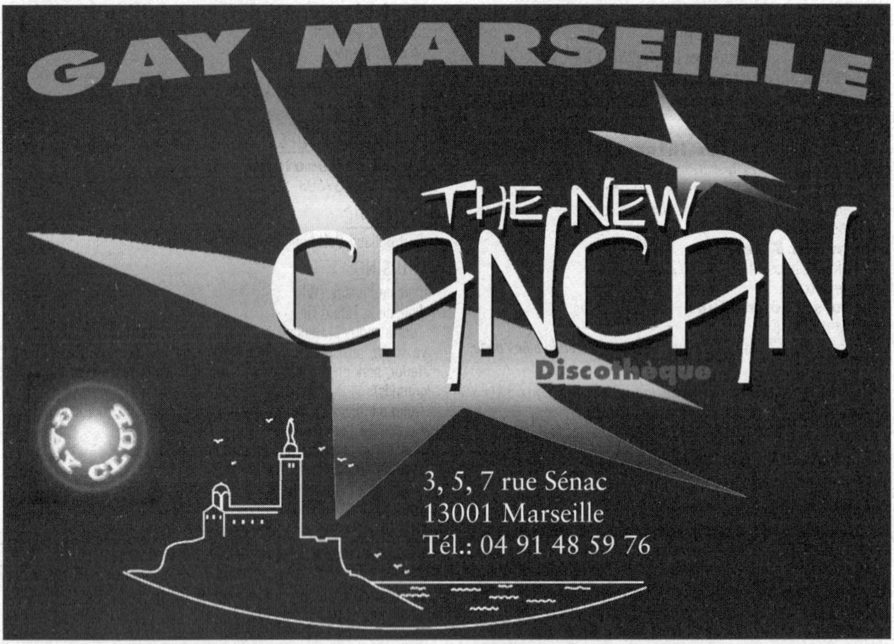

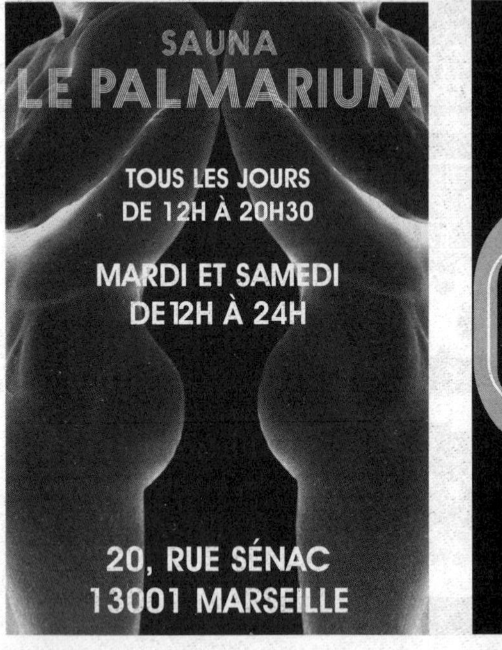

SAUNA
LE PALMARIUM
TOUS LES JOURS
DE 12H À 20H30
MARDI ET SAMEDI
DE 12H À 24H
20, RUE SÉNAC
13001 MARSEILLE

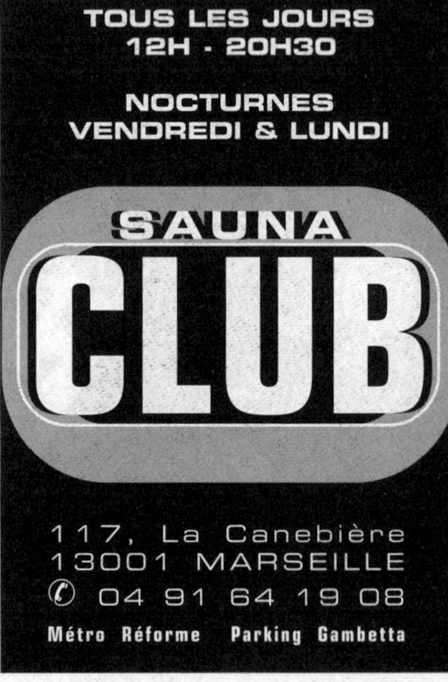

TOUS LES JOURS
12H - 20H30
NOCTURNES
VENDREDI & LUNDI
SAUNA
CLUB
117, La Canebière
13001 MARSEILLE
04 91 64 19 08
Métro Réforme Parking Gambetta

HEALTH GROUPS

Centre médico-social
268 Rue des Epinoches ✉71000 ☎ 03.85.38.79.55
HIV testing.

CRUISING

-Quai Lamartine (above the Saône-river/sur la Saône)

Mandelieu ✉ 06210

CRUISING

-La Napoule (beach/plage)

Marmande ✉ 47200

RESTAURANTS

Auberge du Moulin d'Ané (CC F g OS) Tue-Sat 12-13.45 18.30-0, Sun 12-16 h
D933 Route de Périgeux/Virazeil ✉47200 ☎ 05.53.20.18.25

CRUISING

-Place Fiolhe (la nuit/at night)
-Plaine de Loisirs

Marseille ✉ 13000

GAY INFO

Association pour la création du Centre G&L Méditerranén
1, Rue Chateauredon ✉13000 *(Métro Noailles)*
☎ 04.91.33.72.65 Fax: 04.91.54.00.20
Information about Gay scene, groups and HIV.

IBIZA News gay information
c/o Association Gay Information sur le SIDA, 27 Rue ✉13006
☎ 04.91.33.24.33 Fax: 04.91.33.29.60
Available at gay venues. Eight editions a year.

Minitel
✉13000
-3615 ALLOGAY -3615 GPH -3615 MALCOLM

TOURIST INFO

Tourist Info
4 La Canebière ✉13000 ☎ 04.91.54.91.11 Fax: 04.91.33.05.03

BARS

Eden. L' (B G) 16-2 h, closed Mon
7 Rue Curiol ✉13000 *(M° Le Vieux Port)* ☎ 04.91.47.30.06

Enigme Bar. L' (AC B CC DR G lj MA p s) 18-3 h
22 Rue Beauvau ✉13001 *(M° Vieux Port)* ☎ 04.91.33.79.20
Private gay bar. All associations welcome.

MP Bar (AC B CC GLM p VS WE) 18-2 h
10 Rue Beauvau ✉13001 *(M° Vieux Port)* ☎ 04.91.33.64.79

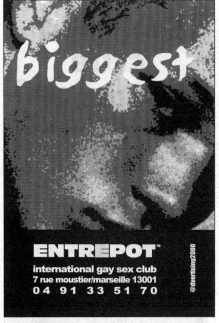

New York (AC B bf F g MA OS) 9-? h
33 Quai des Belges ✉13000 *(vieux port)* ☎ 04.91.33.91.79

MEN'S CLUBS

Entrepôt (AC DR G MA p VS) 14-2, Fri Sat -6 h
7 Rue Moustier ✉13001 *(M° Noailles. Parking Julien)*
☎ 04.91.33.51.70
Huge complex. Fantasies for everyone.

F.S.M.C./Le Meine Shaft (B DR G LJ MG P VS) Fri Sat 23-? h
28 Rue Mazagrin, B.P. 70 ✉13244 ☎ 04.91.48.49.34
Club with strict dress code.

CAFÉS

Arcenaulx. Les (A AC B bf CC F g)
25, Cours d'Estienne-d'Orves ✉13000 ☎ 91.54.77.06
Also bookshop.

DANCECLUBS

Mare au Diable. La (B CC D G OS p s VS WE YG) Fri-Sat and eve of holidays 23-? h
Chemin de Bon Rencontre ✉13190 ☎ 04.91.68.24.10
In a suburb of Marseille. Car or taxi required.

New Can Can. The (AC B CC D DR GLM p VS s WE) Thu-Mon 23-6
3-7 Rue Senac ✉13001 ☎ 04.91.48.59.76
The gay disco of Marseille.

RESTAURANTS

Bessonière. La (B F GLM) 19-24 h
40 Rue Sénac *(M° Noailles, Headquarters of Act up Marseille)* ☎ 04.91.94.08.43

Bistro Venitien After show service-2h
29, cours Julien ☎ 04.91.47.34.34
Italian food.

Chez Alex (AC b CC F GLM MG OS stv) 12-14, 18-24 h, closed Sun
43 Rue Curiol ✉13000 ☎ 04.91.47.80.12

Pizzeria Phyteas (b F g) 12-14, 19-23 h, closed Wed, 1.Jun-15.Sep 12-14, 19-23 h
12 Rue Phyteas ✉13001 *(M° Vieoux-Port)* ☎ 04.91.33.11.92

Scalino (b F glm MA OS W) 12-15, 19-? h, closed Sun Mon lunch
78 Cours Julien ✉13006 *(Centre Ville, Quartier des Artistes)* ☎ 04.91.42.79.69

SEX SHOPS/BLUE MOVIES

Eros Center (AC CC DR glm MA N VS) 9.30-24 h
5 Boulevard Garibaldi ✉13001 *(M° Noailles)* ☎ 04.91.92.72.30

Sexashop (g VS) 9.30-24, Sat -20 h, closed Sun
6 Rue Corneille ✉13000 *(M° Le Vieux Port)* ☎ 04.91.33.71.91
Revues, accessoires, magazines, videos.

SAUNAS/BATHS

Aqua Douches (AC B CC f G MA p sa sb VS wh WO) Open everyday
34 Rue de l'Arène ✉13260 Cassis *(30 min from Marseille and 1 h. from St. Tropez. Town centre Cassis)* ☎ 04.42.01.79.78

MP Sauna (bf CC DR f G sa sb sol VS wh) Mon-Fri 8-24, Sat Sun 12-24 h
82 La Canebière ✉13001 ☎ 04.91.48.72.51

Olympic J.L. (B CC G MA sa sb VS) 12-20.30, Tue Fri Sat 12-24 h
28 Rue Jean Roque ✉13006 *(M° Noailles)* ☎ 04.91.47.35.61

Palmarium. Le (B G sa sb VS) 12-20.30, Tue Sat 12-24 h
20 Rue Sénac ✉13001 *(M° Réformés)* ☎ 04.91.47.43.93

Sauna Club (b G sa sb VS) 12-20.30, Mon Fri 12-24 h
117 La Canebière ✉13001 *(M° Les Réformés. Parking Gambetta)* ☎ 04.91.64.19.08

Sauna Club Salvator (b DR G sa sb VS wh) 12-21 h
20 Boulevard Salvator ✉13006 ☎ 04.91.42.99.31

HOTELS

Hôtel du Prado (B g H) 7-1 h
80 Avenue du Prado ✉13000 ☎ 04.91.37.55.34
Centrally located, 12 km from the airport. Rooms without bath and tel. Single FF 118-181, double 240. (bf incl.). No bath or telephone in room.

New Hotel Astoria (AC bf CC g H)
10 Boulevard Garibaldi ✉13000 *(Métro Noailles)* ☎ 04.91.33.33.50 Fax: 04.91.54.80.75

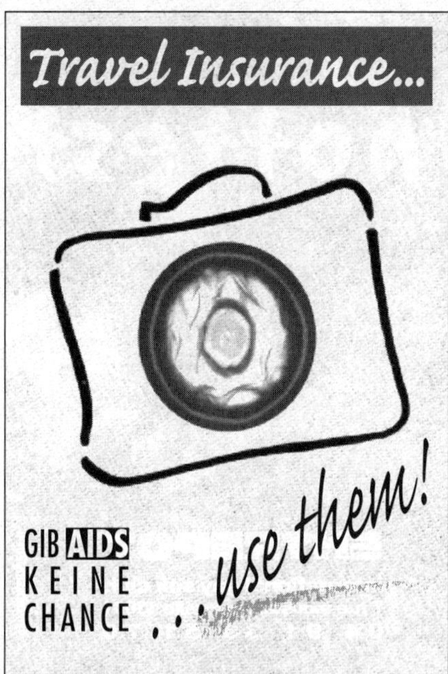
Travel Insurance...
GIB AIDS
KEINE
CHANCE
...use them!

Saint Ferréol's Hotel (AC bf CC glm H wh) Closed August 1st.-21st.
19, Rue Pisancon ✉13000 *(M° Vieux Port)* ☎ 04.91.33.12.21
Fax: 04.91.54.29.97
All rooms with telephone, satTV and jacuzzi. Helpful staff. Special rates for SPARTACUS readers.

Sphinx (bf g H)
16 Rue Sénac ✉13001 *(M°Noaille)* ☎ 04.91.48.70.59
Central to gay places. Ideal for small budget.

GENERAL GROUPS

Collectif Gai & Lesbien Marseille & Provence Mon Wed Fri 16-19 h
1 Rue Ferrari ✉13005 ☎ 04.91.42.07.48
Organises gay parties from time to time/Organise les Bals Gays de temps au temps.

HEALTH GROUPS

Dispensaire Central
39 Rue Francis-de-Pressenssé ✉13001 ☎ 04.91.90.11.24
HIV testing.

HELP WITH PROBLEMS

Association des Médecins gais Tue 20-22 h
✉13000 ☎ 04.91.94.19.91

SOS Amitiés
✉13000 ☎ 04.91.76.10.10

SPECIAL INTEREST GROUPS

Association Motocycliste Alternative (A.M.A.)
B.P. 212 ✉13178 ☎ 04.91.94.18.07
Gay and lesbian bikers of southern France.

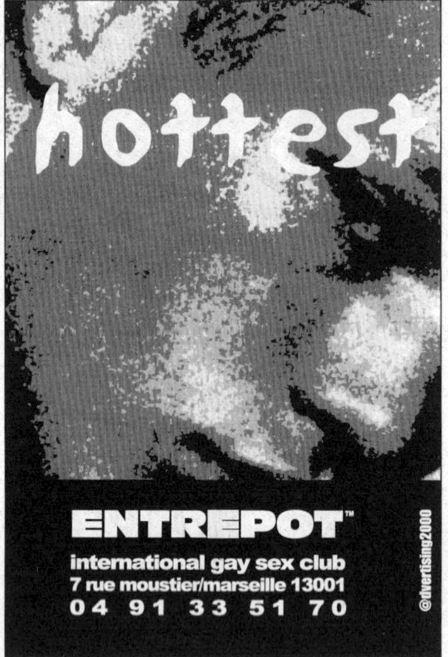

SWIMMING

-Le Montrose (direction Ponte Rouge, after Prado beach; follow Avenue Montredon, turn to the right at the chapel to get to the [P] in front of the beach; to get there by bus, take N° 19)
-Les Gaudes (east of Marseille)
-Le Mont-Rose (gay beach/plage gaie, terminus bus 19)
-Madrague de Montredon (NU) (beach/plage)
-Callelongues (NU) (beach/plage)

CRUISING

-Rue George, Square Sidi-Brahim, bd Sakakini, bd Chave
-Rue Maurice-Bourdet
-Boulevard Voltaire
-Canebière (sex-shop-galerie)
-Railway station/gare SNCF (AYOR)
-Métro Vieux-Port
-Parc Borely ([P] IBM)

Martigues ✉ 13500

CRUISING

-Quai du Général-Leclerc
-[P] Avenue Salvador-Allende (swimming-bath/piscine)
-Rue Verdun(near garden and beach/près du jardin et plage)
-Beach/plage du Ponthau (NU)

Meaux ✉ 77100

HEALTH G2ROUPS

Centre hospitalier Général
6/8 Rue Saint-Pierre ✉77100 ☎ 01.64.33.49.35
HIV testing.

CRUISING

-Les quais (at night)

Mende ✉ 48000

CRUISING

-Palais de justice (in the evening/le soir)
-P Stade du Chapitre (day and night)
-P Stade de Mirandol (evenings only)

Mennessis ✉ 02700

BARS

Parilla Club. La (B D F g) Bar: 16-22, Disco 22- 5h, closed Mon
38 Rue Demosthène-Gauthier ✉02700 ☎ 03.23.57.25.08
Bar, restaurant, disco (camping possible).

Menton ✉ 06500

CRUISING

-The high Jetty along the old harbour (especially at night in summer)
-Avenue Winston Churchill (especially at night in summer)

Merville/Franceville ✉ 14810

SWIMMING

-La Redoute (beach near/plage près de Franceville)

Metz ✉ 57000

BARS

Privilège. Le (AC B CC D Glm p S SNU TV) 22-5 h, theme nights and shows: Fri Sat, closed Mon
20 Rue aux Ours ✉57000 *(near Tribunal)* ☎ 03.87.36.29.29
Disco bar.

RESTAURANTS

Bagatelle. Le (AC g F) 12-? h
29 Rue du Pont des Morts ✉57000 ☎ 87.32.49.08

SAUNAS/BATHS

Blue Club Sauna (B G sa sb VS) 14-22 h
8 Rue Sebastien Leclerc ✉57000 ☎ 87.18.09.40

HEALTH GROUPS

Centre hospitalier Beausecours. Service de dermatologie
1 Place Philippe-de-Vigneulles ✉57038 ☎ 03.87.63.13.13
HIV-testing.

CRUISING

-Bon secours (close to the hospital/près de l'hôpital)
-Ile de Saulcy
-Passage du Sablon
-Square de Luxembourg
-Gare SNCF/railway station
-Ile-aux-Moines
-Rest area „La Croue" (motorway Strasbourg-Paris)

Meudon ✉ 92190

CRUISING

-Bois de Meudon (at the park borderline/aux abords du parc)

Meximieux ✉ 01800

CRUISING

-Port Galland

Meyzieu ✉ 69330

CRUISING

-Parc de Jonage

Millau ✉ 12100

CRUISING

-At the old bridge of Tarn/Au vieux pont du Tarn
-Jardin de la Gare (Avenue de la République towards Cahors)
-Quai de la Tonnerie (banks of Tarn)

Mimizan ✉ 40200

SWIMMING

-Les dunes Remembert (north side, near the military area)

CRUISING

-Public garden behind the church/Jardin public derrière l'église de Mimizan Bourg (summer only)
-P Remembert (beach, summer only)

Moissac ✉ 82200

BODY & BEAUTY SHOPS

Arnaud Maurel Coiffure 9-12, 14-19. Fri Sat 9-19 h, closed on Sun
11 Boulevard Camille Delthil 82200 ✉82200 *(20 kms from Montauban)* ☎ 05.63.04.93.95
Hair-dresser. 10% reduction for 1st customer with Spartacus.

Montargis ✉ 45200

CRUISING

-Forest of Montargis/Forêt de Montargis (go in the direction of Nemours; the action is in front of the Château d'Eau)

Montauban ✉ 82000

HEALTH GROUPS

Centre hospitalier de Montauban Service de médecine interne
✉82000 ☎ 05.63.03.51.01
HIV-testing.

CRUISING

-Cours Foucault
-Espace Mendès-France
-Gare routière
-Jardin Montauriol
-Place de la Cathédrale
-Jardin des Plantes

Montbéliard ✉ 25200

HEALTH GROUPS

Dispensaire
40 Faubourg de Besançon ✉25200 ☎ 03.81.91.12.35

CRUISING

-Pool of Brognard/étang de Brognard (in the summertime, along the highway on the right side in direction Montbéliard/l'été, le long de l'autoroute, à droite dans le sens Montbeliard)
-P at the city market/parc du champ de foire (facilities/toilettes)
-P at the castle/parking du château (facilities; at night/toilettes; la nuit)

Montceau-les-Mines ✉ 71300

CRUISING

-Banks of the canal (facilities in front of the church square, right at the beginning of the forest/toilettes sur les quais, face à la place de l'église, juste à l'entrée du bois)
-Rive du lac du Plessis (au fond à gauche/in the rear, left hand)

Montcombroux-Les-Mines ✉ 03130

HEALTH GROUPS

Gaillards. Les
✉03130 ☎ 70.99.64.54 Fax: 70.99.62.89
Email: aristos@cs3i.fr
Homepage: http://www.cs3ifr/abonnes/aristos/index.html
Quiet house that offers palliative care for people with AIDS.

Mont-de-Marsan ✉ 40000

HEALTH GROUPS

Dispensaire
1 Avenue Aristide Briand ✉40000 ☎ 05.58.46.27.27
HIV testing.

CRUISING

-Rocade Saint-Justin
-P Donjon Lacataye (all night long)

Montélimar ✉ 26200

CRUISING

-Railway station/gare SNCF
-Champ-de-Mars
-Boulevard Marredesmares

Montluçon ✉ 03100

CRUISING

-Avenue Marx-Dormoy (gas station Mobil)
-Avenue de la Gare
-Esplanade du Vieux Château
-Jardin Wilson
-Parking du quai Louis-Blanc
-Bords du Cher/Parc des Expositions

Montpellier ✉ 34000

GAY INFO

Minitel: 3615 ALLOGAY
Minitel: 3615 BOB

BARS

Café de la Mer (B glm MA OS W) 8-1, Sun 15-1, Jul Aug -2 h
5 Place du Marché-aux-Fleurs ✉34000 ☎ 04.67.60.79.65

MEN'S CLUBS

Chantier. Le (AC CC DR G lj MA VS) 15-3 h
25-27 Rue J.-J. Rousseau ✉34000 ☎ 04.67.60.91.98

DANCECLUBS

T H T (AC B D DR GLM MA p VS W) 22-? h
29 Avenue de Castelnau ✉34000 ☎ 04.67.79.96.17
Villa Rouge (AC B D G p s) Fri-Sun 22-? h
Route de Palavas ✉34970 ☎ 04.67.06.52.15

RESTAURANTS

Pomme d'Or. La (CC F GLM lj MA OS s) 12-14 19-23.30 h, Sun evening only
23 Rue du Palais-Guilhem ✉34000 ☎ 04.67.52.82.62

SEX SHOPS/BLUE MOVIES

L'Exotique (AC g MA VS) 10-22 h
6bis Rue Cope-Combes ✉34000 ☎ 04.67.60.64.61

SAUNAS/BATHS

Brick Sauna (AC CC DR f G MA sa sb VS wh WO) 12-? h
10 Avenue de Lodève ✉34000 ☎ 04.67.58.25.27
New and biggest sauna in the region.

Hammam Club (B g MA msg OS sa sb sol VS WO) 14-19 h
2 Rue de la Merci ✉34000 ☎ 04.67.58.22.06
Nude sunbathing on the terrace in summer.
Sauna de la Gare (b CC f G sa sb sol VS YG) 12-1 h
8 Rue Levat ✉34000 *(near the railway station)*
☎ 04.67.58.61.42

HOTELS

Guilhem. Le (AC bf CC g H OS)
18 Rue Jean-Jacques Rousseau ✉34000 *(bus 2/3/5 /7 stop Henri IV)* ☎ 04.67.52.90.90 Fax: 04.67.60.67.67
Hotel Ulysse (bf glm H)
338 Avenue de Saint Maur ✉34000 *(near/près du Palais des Congrès)* ☎ 04.67.02.02.30 Fax: 04.67.02.16.50
Centrally located with underground parking. Shady garden.

GUEST HOUSES

Amairadou. L' (bf F g H MA OS pi sa sol wh WO)
620 Chemin de Montpellier ✉34400 *(between Nîmes and Montpellier)* ☎ 04.67.86.80.65
Luxury rooms, restaurant, park and pool.

HEALTH GROUPS

Centre hospitalier R. de Montpellier
555 Route de Ganges ✉34000 ☎ 04.67.33.93.02
Hôpital St-Charles Consultations des MST
Rue Auguste-Broussonet ✉34000 ☎ 04.67.33.64.90
HIV-testing.

SWIMMING

-Beach/Plage (between Théâtre de la Mer and La Corniche)
-Beach/Plage de Grand Travers (between/entre la Grande Motte & Carnou)
-Beach/Plage des Aresquiers/Frontignan (NU) (after parking lot ca. 2km towards Palavas)

CRUISING

-Place des Arceaux (Car cruising)34059 Cedex
-Promenade du Peyrou
-Autoroute A9 (between Nîmes and Montpellier, aire de Saint-Aunès, km 91.5, direction Nîmes/Montpellier, day and night) 34059 Cedex
-Garden/Jardin des Beaux-Arts
-Le Polygone
-Forest/Forêt des Aresquiers, Vic la Gardiole, Frontignan

Morlaix ✉ 29210

RESTAURANTS

Brocéliande. Le (b CC F glm MA) 20-23 h, closed Tue
5 Rue des Bouchers ✉29210 ☎ 02.98.88.73.78
Mention that you choose the restaurant from SPARTACUS: Get's you a free aperitif.

HEALTH GROUPS

Centre de médecine préventive
Rue de Kersaint-Gilly ✉29210 ☎ 02.98.88.50.56

CRUISING

-Viaduc (in the evening/le soir)
-Aire Saint-Servais

Mougins ✉ 06250

CRUISING

-Next to car museum (highway A8, exit Bréguières, on the other side of the highway after passing the bridge which leads to the highway)

Moulins ✉ 03000

HEALTH GROUPS

Centre hospitalier de Moulins Consultations dépistage
65 Rue de Paris ✉03000 ☎ 04.70.20.88.00
HIV testing.

CRUISING

-Bords de l'Allier
-Square

Moustiers-Sainte-Marie ✉ 04360

HOTELS

Hôtel de la Ferme Rose (bf CC g H OS) 8-24 h, closed 15 Nov-15 Mar
✉04360 ☎ 04.92.74.69.47 Fax: 04.92.74.60.76
1 km from Moustiers-Ste Marie. Piano bar in the evening. Superb location.

Mulhouse ✉ 68100

BARS

Latino Cafe (B CC G MA OS YG) 15-1.30 h
16 Passage du Théâtre ✉68100 ☎ 03.89.66.56.52
Latest music in the evening.

DANCECLUBS

Caesar Palace. Le (AC B CC D DR f glm MA s SNU VS W) Thu-Mon 22-4 h
192 Rue de la Banlieue ✉68110 *(Illzach)* ☎ 03.89.46.27.88
Late night restaurant and mixed disco complex with several different styles.
Discothèque le „JH" (AC B CC D Glm MA p s snu VS YG) Thu-Mon 22.30-4 h
32 Quai du Forst ✉68100 ☎ 03.89.32.00.08
The biggest gay disco in the heart of France.
Gémeaux. Le (AC B CC D DR Glm MA p SNU) 23-? h, closed Tue
3 Rue J. Ehrmann ✉68100 ☎ 03.89.66.19.60
Centrally located disco bar on two levels.

SAUNAS/BATHS

Sauna Club LG (B DR G MA sa sb VS) Mon Wed Sun 14-21, Tue Thu Sat 14-23, mixed on Tue Thu 20-23 h
69 Rue de Bâle ✉68100 ☎ 89.36.01.02

HEALTH GROUPS

Centre de Dépistage Mon 10-13, Tue 16-19, Wed 15-18 h
Hôpital de Moenchsberg, Rue du Dr. R. Laennée ✉68100 ☎ 03.89.54.90.33
Gratis and anonymous HIV testing.
Centre hospitalier E. Muller Service de dermatologie
✉68100 ☎ 03.89.64.64.64
HIV testing.

RELIGIOUS GROUPS

David et Jonathan B.P. 2014 ✉68058

CRUISING

-Parc Salvatore (AYOR r)

Nancy ✉ 54000

GAY INFO

Minitel: 3615 ALLOGAY
Minitel: 3615 BOB

RESTAURANTS

Autre Jour. L' (B F g OS)
159bis Rue Saint-Dizier ✉54000 ☎ 03.83.30.42.96
Traditional french cuisine.

Bistrot de Gilles. Le (CC F g OS) 12-14.30 19-23.30 h
31 Rue des Maréchaux ✉54000 *(near Place Stanislas)* ☎ 03.83.35.43.73
French cuisine.

SAUNAS/BATHS

Sauna Club LG (B DR G MA sa sb VS) 14-23 h, mixed on Tue 20-23 h.
5 Rue Alfred Mezières ✉54000 ☎ 04.83.36.65.59

GENERAL GROUPS

Association Homonyme Mon 18-20 h
✉54000 ☎ 03.83.27.91.71
Youth group.

HEALTH GROUPS

Centre hospitalier R. de Nancy
29 Rue du Maréchal de Lattre de Tassigny ✉54037 ☎ 03.83.57.61.61

CRUISING

-Aire de Villers-Clairleu (en voiture sur l'autoroute A 33, direction Strasbourg; été/by car on highway A 33, in direction Strasbourg; summer)

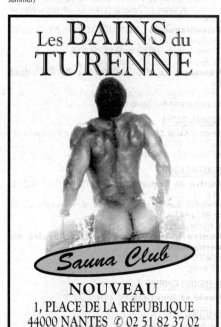

Nantes ✉ 44000

GAY INFO

Minitel: 3615 ALLOGAY
Minitel: 3615 BOB

BARS

Amazone. L' (B TV) 18-2, Jun-Aug 14-2 h
4 Rue des Chapeliers ✉44000 ☎ 40.36.61.88

Arche. L' (B G) 17-2 h
8 Boulevard Lelasseur ✉44000 ☎ 40.40.79.31

Ferry. Le (B G F) 10-15, 17.30-2 h
15 Rue du Bâtonnier Guinaudeau ✉44000 *In front of/En face du Pont Anne de Bretagne* ☎ 02.40.73.59.79
Also restaurant.

Petit Marais. Le (B G MA s) 17-2 h
15 Rue Kervegan ✉44000 ☎ 02.40.20.15.25

Plein Sud. Le (a AC B CC G OS) 17-2 h, closed Mon
2 Rue Premion ✉44000 ☎ 40.47.06.03

Second Souffle. Le (B GLM MA) 18-2 h
1 Rue Kervegan ✉44000 ☎ 02.40.20.14.20

DANCECLUBS

Temps d'Aimer. Le (B CC D G) 23-5 h, closed Mon
14 Rue Alexandre-Fourny ✉44000 ☎ 40.89.48.60

SEX SHOPS/BLUE MOVIES

Boîte à Films. La (G VS) 9-2, Sun 12-1 h
16bis Allée du Commandant-Charcot ✉44000 ☎ 40.37.03.03

SAUNAS/BATHS

Bains du Turenne. Les (AC b CC DR G sa sb sol VS wh YG) Mon Tue Thu 12-22, Wed Fri -24, Sat 14-2, Sun -22 h
1 Place de la République ✉44000 ☎ 02.51.82.37.02
Gay sauna on several floors.

Spartacus Club (AC B DR MA G sa sb VS wh) 14-21, Fri -23, Sat -24 h
16 Rue Fouré ✉44000 ☎ 51.82.43.70

FITNESSTUDIOS

Gymn'axe (g sa WO) For men only: Mon 13-21.30, Wed 8.30-21.30, Fri 8.30-22 h
3bis Rue Louis Blanc ✉44200 ☎ 40.47.74.17

GENERAL GROUPS

Soeurs de la Perpétuelle Indulgence. Les
117 Bd Ernest Dalby ✉44000 ☎ 51.81.03.53

HEALTH GROUPS

Amitié-Sida
21 Rue Dufour ✉44000 ☎ 02.40.29.12.28
Help for people with HIV or AIDS.

Centre hospitalier universitaire de Nantes
Place Alexi-Ricordeau ✉44035 ☎ 02.40.08.31.34
HIV-testing.

Dispensaire Jean V
Rue Durant-Gasselin ✉44000 ☎ 02.40.73.18.62

RELIGIOUS GROUPS

David et Jonathan
B.P. 12521 ✉44325
Gay chrétiens/Christian gays.

SPECIAL INTEREST GROUPS

Gay Randonneurs Nantais
42 Rue des Hauts-Pavés ✉44000 ☎ 02.40.75.25.65
Publishes monthly bulletin. Organises, walks, foreign trips and evenings.

CRUISING

-Place Louis-XVI. (Cours St.Pierre, St.André)
-Parc de Procès (night/la nuit)
-Square Elisa-Mercoeur (Allée Baco)
-Beaulieu
-Bords de l'Erdre

Narbonne ✉ 11100

HEALTH GROUPS

Centre de diagnostic des maladies dysimmunitaires
5 Avenue du Bois-Roland ✉11100 ☎ 04.68.90.68.90
HIV-testing.

CRUISING

-Pont de l'Avenir
-Jardin du palais du travail
-Cours Mirabeau

Neris-les-Bains ✉ 03310

CRUISING

-Syndicat d'initiative (in front of the building/en face du bâtiment)

Neufchatel-en-Bray ✉ 76270

RESTAURANTS

Auberge du Bec Fin. L' (B CC F g MA OS) 12-15, 19-22 h, closed Mon evening
Megnières en Bray ✉76270 ☎ 02.35.94.15.15

Neuilly-en-Thelle ✉ 60530

BARS

Corps de Garde. Le (B D DR F g p s W) Fri Sat 20-5 h
4 Rue Driard ✉60530 ☎ 03.44.26.72.26

Neuilly-sur-Seine ✉ 92200

HEALTH GROUPS

Hôpital communal 9-19 h
36 Avenue du Général-Leclerc ✉92200 ☎ 02.47.47.11.44

CRUISING

-Porte de Bagatelle (vers le bois/near the woods)

Nevers ✉ 58000

HOTELS

Château Quentin. Le (bf F glm H OS W) open Apr-Oct
Route du Pont ✉58110 ☎ 03.86.84.08.95
Located between Nevers and Château Chinon. Country retreat. Pick-up at Nevers railway station possible. Special rate for SPARTACUS readers.

HEALTH GROUPS

Centre hospitalier Service de médecine B
1 Avenue Colbert ✉58000 ☎ 03.86.68.30.30
HIV testing.

CRUISING

-Park in the centre of town/parc du centre-ville
–Porte du Croux

Nice ✉ 06000

GAY INFO

Minitel: 3615 ALLOGAY

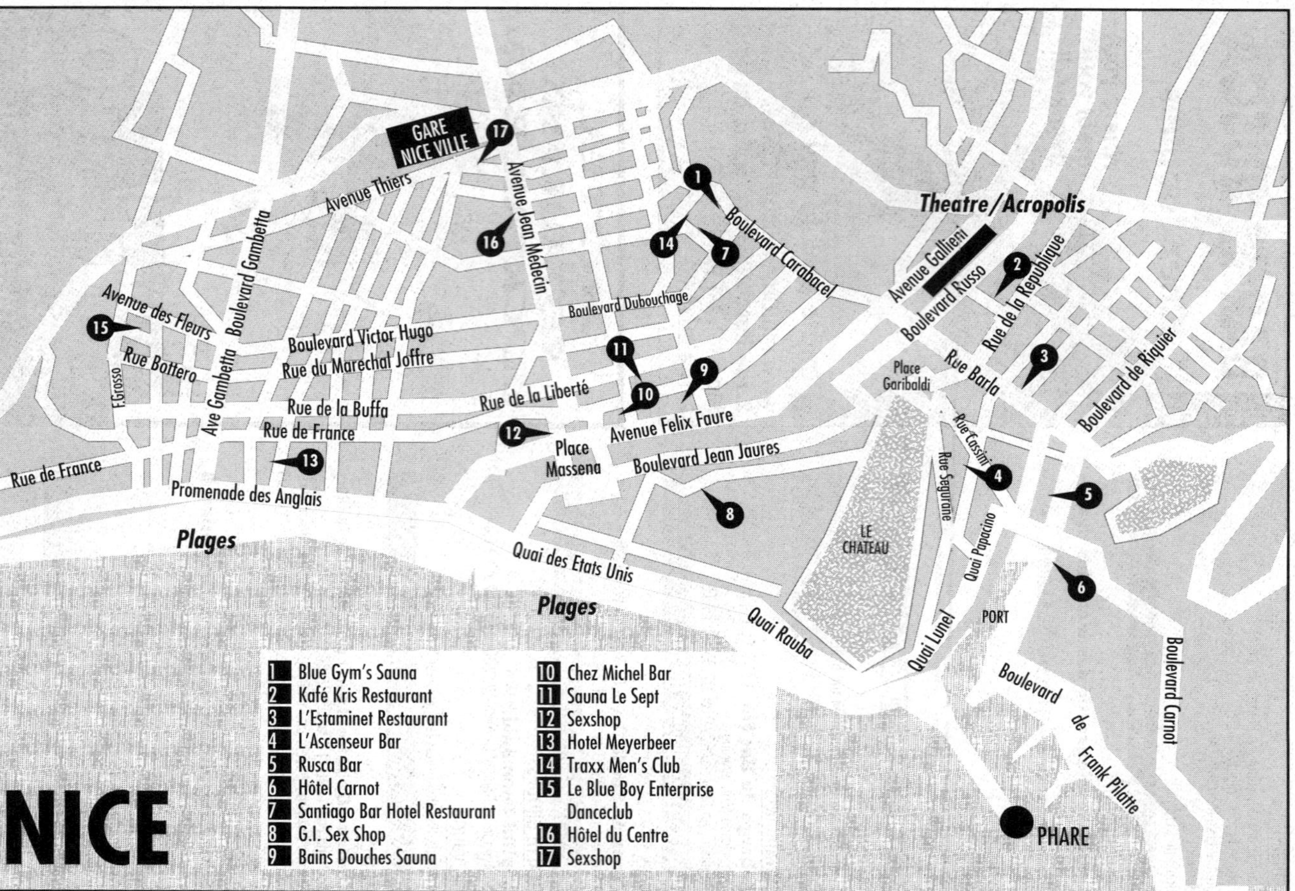
NICE
1 Blue Gym's Sauna
2 Kafé Kris Restaurant
3 L'Estaminet Restaurant
4 L'Ascenseur Bar
5 Rusca Bar
6 Hôtel Carnot
7 Santiago Bar Hotel Restaurant
8 G.I. Sex Shop
9 Bains Douches Sauna
10 Chez Michel Bar
11 Sauna Le Sept
12 Sexshop
13 Hotel Meyerbeer
14 Traxx Men's Club
15 Le Blue Boy Enterprise Danceclub
16 Hôtel du Centre
17 Sexshop
GARE NICE VILLE
Avenue Thiers
Avenue Jean Médecin
Theatre/Acropolis
Avenue Gallieni
Boulevard Russo
Rue de la Republique
Boulevard Carabacel
Boulevard Dubouchage
Avenue des Fleurs
Boulevard Gambetta
Boulevard Victor Hugo
Rue du Marechal Joffre
Rue Bottero
F.Grosso
Ave Gambetta
Rue de la Buffa
Rue de France
Rue de la Liberté
Avenue Felix Faure
Place Massena
Boulevard Jean Jaures
Place Garibaldi
Rue Barla
Boulevard de Riquier
Rue Cassini
Rue Segurane
Quai Papacino
Rue de France
Promenade des Anglais
Plages
Quai des Etats Unis
Plages
Quai Rauba
LE CHATEAU
Quai Lunel
PORT
Boulevard de Frank Pilatte
Boulevard Carnot
PHARE

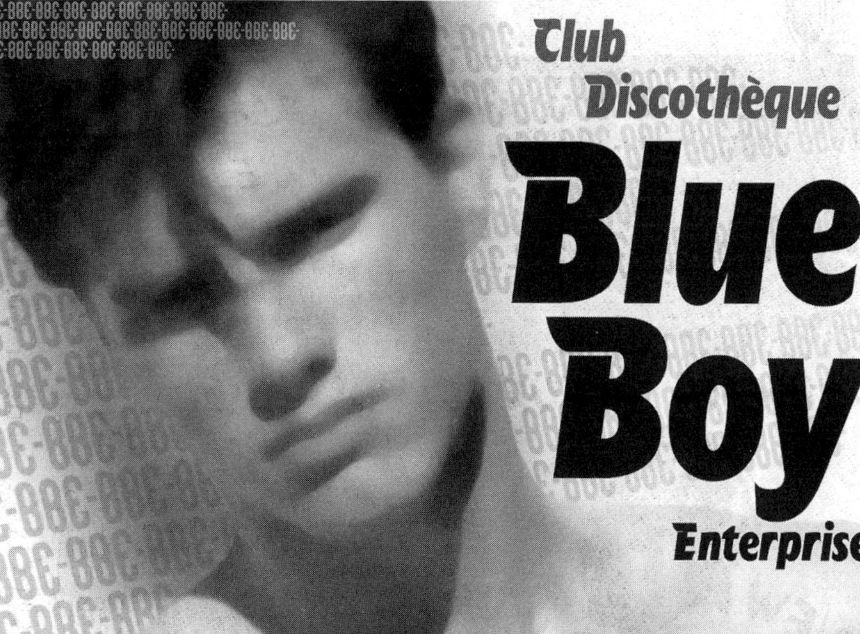

9, rue Spinetta - 06000 Nice - France - 04 93 44 68 24

SEX SHOP
G.I
MEN FOR MEN
4 FLOORS OF CRUISING
CINEMA 4 EUROS
& STIMULATION
NEW D.V.Ds.
• LABYRINTH
• PRIVATE CABIN PROJECTIONS
• BIG SCREEN CINEMA
• LARGE COLLECTION OF VIDEOS
& GADGETS
8, DESCENTE CROTTI - VIEUX NICE - 04 93 80 29 49
THE HIPEST GAY PLACE IN TOWN...
near the Massena place

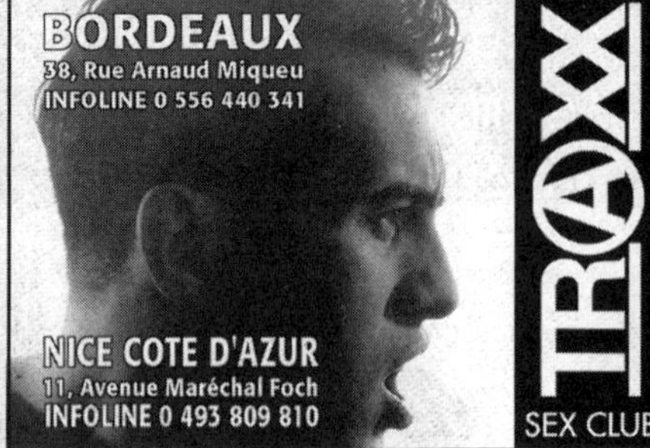

TOURIST INFO

Tourist Info
Acropolis Esplanade Kennedy, B.P. 79 ✉06000
☎ 04.93.87.07.07 Fax: 04.93.92.82.98

BARS

Ascenseur. L' (AC B CC d f G MA p) 21-2.30 h
18bis Rue Emmanuel Philibert ✉06300 ☎ 04.93.26.35.30
American style bar with pool.

Cherry's Café (AC B CC d F glm OS s) Fri-Sun private night bar from 20 h
35 Quai des Etats-Unis ✉06300 ☎ 04.93.18.85.45
3 floors with sea view.

Chez Michel (AC B g) 12-1 h
1 Rue Alberti ✉06000 ☎ 04.93.85.43.90
Bar-tabac for an early drink.

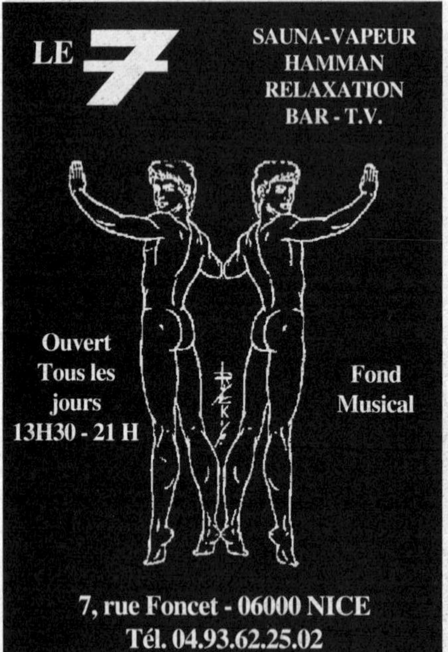

Rusca Bar (AC B CC GLM MG OS p s) 21-2.30 h
2 Rue Rusca ✉06000 *(next to the church on the port)*
☎ 04.93.89.46.25

Santiago. Le (AC B CC F H GLM) 18-2.30 h, closed on Mon
28 Rue Lépante ✉06000 ☎ 04.93.13.83.01
Centrally located cocktail bar, restaurant and hotel. French cuisine until 22.30 h.

MEN'S CLUBS

Traxx (AC b CC DR G lj MA p VS) 14-2, Fri Sat -4, Sun 15-2 h
11 Avenue Maréchal Foch ✉06000 ☎ 04.93.80.98.10

CAFÉS

CD. Le (b F glm) 11-0.30 h
22 Rue Benoit Burico ☎ 04.93.92.47.65

DANCECLUBS

Blue Boy Enterprise. Le (B.B.E) (AC B CC D G MA p S YG) 23-5 h
9 Rue Spinetta ✉06000 *(Rue Spinetta is a side street off the Boulevard François Grosso between the Avenue des Orangers and the Rue Bottero)* ☎ 04.93.44.68.24
2 floors, 2 bars.

RESTAURANTS

Arbalete. L' (F glm MA) 19-0.30 h
8, Rue Jules-Gilly, Vieux Nice ✉06300 *(behind „Cours Saleya")*
☎ 04.93.80.58.28

Cave. La (AC CC F g OS) 12-14, 19-22.30 h
Rue Francis Gallo ☎ 04.93.62.48.46
Good for low prices.

Chez Cyriaque (b F glm MA) 19-0.30 h
12 Rue Rosetti *(Vieux Nice)* ☎ 04.93.92.68.47
Mediteranian cuisine.

Goutte de Pluie. La (F GLM) every evening except Mon
5 Rue Jules-Gilly ✉06300 *(Vieux Nice, close to Cours Saleya)*
☎ 04.93.85.85.44
Traditional cooking.

Kafe Kris (b F glm OS) 9.15-18 h, closed Sun
3 Rue Smolette ☎ 04.93.26.75.85

Latinos. Le (AC b F GLM MA)
6 Rue Chauvain ✉06000 ☎ 04.93.85.01.10
Tapas specialties.

L'Estaminet (b CC F glm MA) 12-14.15, 19-22.30 h, closed Sat lunch, Sun
21 Rue Barla ☎ 04.93.55.41.55

Table Coquine. La (AC CC F GLM MA OS) closed Mon, Sat (lunch)
44 Avenue de la République ✉06000 *(near Palais des Congrès)*
☎ 04.93.55.39.99

SEX SHOPS/BLUE MOVIES

G.I. Sex Shop (AC CC DR G lj MA VS YG) 10-24, Sun and public holidays 14-20 h
8 Rue Descente Crotti ✉06000 *(Place Massena/Vieille Ville/near Palais de Justice)* ☎ 04.93.80.29.49
Videos, gadgets and cruising on 4 floors. Big screen cinema and latest DVDs.
Sex-Shop (g VS) 9-23 h, Sun closed
7 Rue Masséna ✉06000
Sex-Shop (g VS) 9-23 h, Sun closed
23 Rue Belgique ✉06000

SAUNAS/BATHS

Bains Douches (AC B DR f G p sa sb VS wh YG) 13-22 h
7 Rue Gubernatis ✉06000 *(Close to Place Massena sun bus station Félix Faure)* ☎ 04.93.80.28.26
Three floors of fun created by Nice's professional gay team (25 years of experience). And now even more...
Blue Gym's (AC b f G sa sb sol VS wh WO) 12-0.30, tea parties Tue Thu 17-18 h
7 Avenue Désambrois ☎ 04.93.80.71.11
Cruisy place.
Sept. Le (b G sa sb sol wh YG) 13.30-21 h
7 Rue Foncet ✉06000 ☎ 04.93.62.25.02

HOTELS

Hôtel Ascain San Pedro (bf g H) 8-12, 15-19 h
28 Rue Meyerbeer ✉06000 ☎ 04.93.88.95.65
Fax: 04.93.82.09.25 Email: hotel-france@geocities.com Homepage: http://www.geocities.com/WestHollywood/Heights/4059
All rooms with kitchenette. Special rates for Spartacus readers on reservation. Free gay map available.
Hôtel Bahia Vista (B F GLM MA VS pi)
Bd Napoleon III, Pont St. Jean ✉06230 Villefranches-sur-Mer
☎ 04.93.76.21.50 Fax: 04.93.01.29.77
Panoramic bar and restaurant with swimming-pool on the roof. Quote SPARTACUS for discount rates (-20%).
Hôtel Carnot (AC bf CC f glm H MA) 7-23 h
8 Boulevard Carnot ✉06300 *(Nice harbour/Port de Nice)*
☎ 04.93.89.56.54 Fax: 04.93.55.48.18
Mixed, but gays are welcome. All rooms with telephone, kitchenette, priv. bath, TV, balcony.

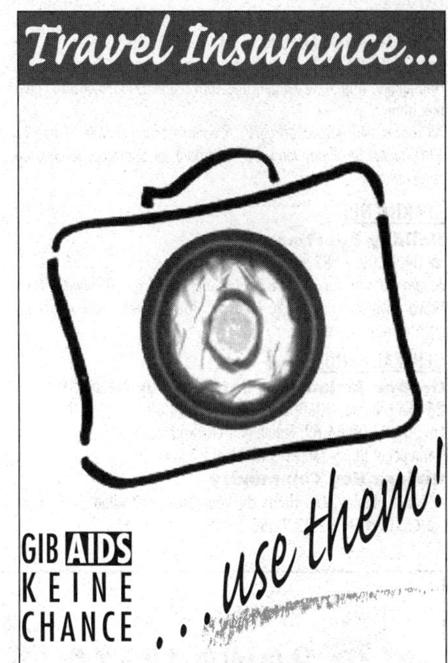
Travel Insurance...
GIB AIDS
KEINE
CHANCE
...use them!

Hôtel du Centre (bf H MA NG OS)
2 Rue de Suisse ✉06000 ☎ 04.93.88.83.85 Fax: 04.93.82.29.80
Email: hotel-centre@webstore.fr
Homepage: http://www.webstore.fr/hotel-centre
Near railway station. 10 minutes from the beach. Gay welcome. Quote Spartacus for a discount.
Hôtel le Santiago (A B CC F GLM H)
28 Rue Lépante ✉06000 ☎ 04.93.13.83.01
Rooms with kitchenette and bath above gay bar and restaurant.
Hôtel Lyonnais (bf glm H MA) Réception: 8-22.30
20 Rue de Russie ✉06000 ☎ 04.93.88.70.74
Fax: 04.93.16.25.56
Budget hotel in the centre of Nice.

Hôtel Meyerbeer Beach (bf F GLM H MA p) 8-12, 15-19h
15 Rue Meyerbeer ✉06000 ☎ 04.93.88.95.65
Fax: 04.93.82.09.25 Email: hotel.meyerbeer.beach@wanadoo.fr
Homepage: http://www.geocities.com/Eureka/Plaza/8506/gay-prix.html
All rooms with kitchenette, TV, telephone, shower, WC. Rates FF 280/night. Bf all day long. 10% discount for Spartacus readers on reservation.

APARTMENTS

Holiday Apartments
☎ 04.92.09.13.82
Studio 43 sqm for rent on the hills behind Nice, 10 minutes from down town and the beach. Rates FF 3500/week, 700 weekend. 20% discount off-season.

GENERAL GROUPS

Groupe Action Gay Côte-d'Azur (G.A.G)
28 Rue Leponte ✉06000 ☎ 04.93.92.34.32
Fax: 04.93.08.84.69 Email: gagca@worldnet.net
Homepage: http://services.worldnet.fr/gagca
Riviera Gay Community
c/o Bill Shipley, Les Hauts de Vaugrenier, 10 Allée du Ponson ✉06570 ☎ 04.92.02.92.55

HEALTH GROUPS

Accueil Aide aux Malades Information Sida AAMIS „Le Phoenix"
10 Rue de Maeyer ✉06300 ☎ 04.93.55.90.35
Fax: 04.93.55.87.24
Help for HIV+ and their friends and families.
Dispensaire antivénérien
2 Rue Edouard Berri ✉06000 ☎ 04.93.85.12.62
HIV-testing.

RELIGIOUS GROUPS

David et Jonathan
B.P. 4221 ✉06304

SWIMMING

-Jetée du port (NU)
-Coco Beach/Cap Nice (NU) (Bus at harbour to Coco Beach, small staircase down, climb rocky beach to the lett)

CRUISING

-Rue Masséna, avenue Jean-Médecin (afternoon/l'après-midi)
-Around the lighthouse day and evening all year round/Autour du Phare jour et soir toute l'année
-Parc Ferber (R)/Promenade des Anglais
-Parc du Château
-Square Alsace-Lorraine (R)

Nîmes ✉ 30000

DANCECLUBS

Gate Dance Club (AC D DR G lj MA OS p s VS W) Fri Sat 23-6, Sun 18-4 (gay tea dance), open Jul-Aug Wed-Sun
Route de Sauvre ✉30900 *(Km 7, Exit Nimes-Ouest from Autoroute)* ☎ 04.66.23.36.08

Lulu Club (AC B CC D DR G lj MA P S VS YG) Bar 18-23, disco 23-? h, closed Sun-Mon
10 Impasse Curaterie ✉30000 *(5 mins walk from the station)* ☎ 04.66.36.28.20

RESTAURANTS

Ophélie (AC CC F glm MA OS w) 20-23 h, closed Sun Mon
35 Rue Fresque ✉30000 *(Near Romain Arena)*
☎ 04.66.21.00.19

SEX SHOPS/BLUE MOVIES

DIPA Sex Shop (AC CC g VS) 10-20 h, closed Sun
Impasse de la Curaterie ✉30000 ☎ 04.66.21.33.33

Hall du K7 (CC G VS) 10-19.30 h, closed Sun
24 Boulevard Courbet ✉30000 ☎ 04.66.36.08.12

SAUNAS/BATHS

Nîmes Club Sauna (AC B CC DR f G MA pi sa sb sol VS wh) 12-24 h, Sat irregularly theme nights
7/9 Rue Fernand-Pelloutier ✉30900 ☎ 04.66.67.65.18

HEALTH GROUPS

AIDES-Languedoc-Nord Mon 18-20, Wed 18-22 h
B.P. 183 ✉30012 ☎ 04.66.76.26.07

Centre hospitalier régional
Centre Gaston-Doumergues ✉30000 ☎ 04.66.27.41.11
HIV-testing.

CHRU de Nîmes
✉30000 ☎ 04.66.27.31.75
AIDS councelling and treatment/Dépistage et tratement Sida et MST.

CRUISING

-St.Aunes (clearing/aire A9, direction Montpellier, 40 km-Nîmes)
-Boulevard Jean-Jaurès
-Behind the railway station/derrière la gare SNCF
-Jardin La Fontaine (afternoon, evening/après-midi, soir)
-Gorges du Gardon, via motorway Nîmes-Uzès (at [P] Gardon, Pont St. Nicolas then walk about 1-2 km in direction to the river, also nude bathing)

Niort ✉ 79000

BARS

Flamand. Le (AC B CC E glm MA p s) 22-4 h, closed Sun Mon
12 Rue Baugier ✉79000 ☎ 05.49.73.12.69

HEALTH GROUPS

Centre hospitalier de Niort. Service de réanimation
35 Avenue Saint-Jean-d'Angély ✉79021 ☎ 05.49.32.79.79
HIV-testing.

Dispensaire
28 Rue Paul-Bert ✉79000 ☎ 05.49.24.46.51

CRUISING

-Railway station/gare SNCF (WC)
-Halles ([P] du Moulin du Milieu)
-Garden/Jardin des Plantes
-Petit bois de la Tranchée (2 km from Niort, take road N 10 direction Bordeaux/2 km de Niort, direction Bordeaux par la route N 10)
-Place St-Jean
-Place de la Brèche

Noirmoutier-en-L'Ile ✉ 85330

RESTAURANTS

Blé Noir. Le (b F g) 11-3 h
14 Place Saint Louis ✉85330 ☎ 02.51.39.18.17
Crêperie-saladerie.

Offranville ✉ 76550

CRUISING

-[P] at RN 27, Grande Côte

Olonne-sur-Mer ✉ 85340

SWIMMING

-Sauveterre (beach, the gay nude area is 1 km north of [P])

CRUISING

-Casino des Sports (in front and in the garden at night)
-Lac du Tauchet
-Square du Jet d'Eau

Orange ✉ 84100

RESTAURANTS

Roselière. La (F glm)
4 Rue Renoyer ✉84100 ☎ 04.90.34.50.42

HOTELS

Loft. Le (bf G MA NU OS pi sol WO)
Chemin Haut Abrian ✉84100 ☎ 04.90.34.07.47
Fax: 04.90.34.09.80 Email: hotel@homophere.com
On the countryside, easy access to highway, train and historic town of Organge. A short drive from Avignon. Large pool and park.

Orchamps ✉ 39700

DANCECLUBS

Espace 39 (B D g s) 22-5 h, closed Mon
Nenon ✉39700 ☎ 03.84.70.60.71

Orléans ✉ 45000

BARS

Petit Amiral. Le (A B CC d G MA OS p) 11-3, Sat 14-3, Sun 18-3 h
205 Rue de Bourgogne ✉45000 ☎ 02.38.81.00.11

RESTAURANTS

Arrozoir. L' (E F glm MA OS) 12-14, 19-22.30, Sat 19-23 h, closed Sun
224 Rue de Bourgogne ✉45000 *(opposite bar „Le Petit Amiral")*
☎ 02.38.81.01.08

GENERAL GROUPS

Groupe Action Gai 4th Fri 18.30-20 h
46ter Rue Sainte-Catherine ✉45000 *(Maisons des associations)*

HEALTH GROUPS

Centre hospitalier Orléans-la-Source (Service maladies infectieuses)
Avenue de l'Hôpital ✉45000 ☎ 02.38.51.43.61
HIV-testing.

SWIMMING

-Ile Arrault

CRUISING

-Quai St-Laurent
-La Source (take the road RN 20, you find it on the right side behind the hospital; crossing in front of the Novotel/Sur la RN 20, après la sortie de l'hôpital sur la droite; carrefour face au Novotel)
-Bois de Semoy

Pacy-sur-Eure ✉ 27120

RESTAURANTS

Auberge du Saint-Aquilin (B F g) 12-15, 19-22 h
42 Rue Charles-Ledoux ✉27120 ☎ 02.32.36.01.40

Paimpol ✉ 22500

SWIMMING

-Beach of/Plage de Notorat (go from Plauzec 6 km direction Notorat, go down to the right side/à 6 km de Plauezek à Notorat, à droite en bas)

CRUISING

-Harbour/port

Pamiers ✉ 09100

CRUISING

-Esplanade de Millane

Paray-le-Monial ✉ 71600

CRUISING

-Parc „Moulin Liron" (behind/derrière le camping)
-Promenade de la Rivière (behind/derrière „Hotel Prieuré")

Paris ✉ 75000

● Paris is Paris! The perfect start for a journey of discovery of the fascinating continents of Europe and of course the gay metropolis of the world. In the past few years there has developed a host of restaurants, shops and enterprises serving the gay community and being provided by gays themselves. There`s always something interesting going on day and night in the bars, in the main streets, and in the clubs.The historical district Maraus,from the rue Vielle du- Temple to the rue des Archives over the rue Saint-Croix-de- la-Bretonnerie is the heart of the gay scene, that extends from the Halls to the Bastille. Paris offers a huge cultural programme: Exibitions, Concerts, Cinemas, Theatres -more current information is available in the Pariscope, or for all gay events and parties refer to the many free gay publications available in nearly all bars. Don't forget that the Metro is closed from 1am til 5:30am. When you leave a club in the early hours it's best to take a taxi or night bus. France still falls somewhat behind, when it comes to gay hotels. So remember to reserve your hotel room in advance. After all, it's always peak season no matter what time of the year.

✸ Paris, ist eben Paris! Der ideale Start für eine Entdeckungsreise des faszinierenden Kontinents Europa und eine der Schwulenmetropolen der Welt. In den letzten Jahren hat sich hier ein schwules Leben mit viel Gastronomie, Geschäften und Unternehmen für Schwule von Schwulen entwickelt. Ein schillerndes Treiben in den Bars, den Straßen im Zentrum, in den Diskotheken, Tag und Nacht. Der historische Stadtteil Marais, von der rue Vieille-du-Temple bis zur rue des Archives über die rue Saint-Croix-de-la-Bretonnerie ist das Zentrum des schwulen Viertels, das sich von den Hallen bis zur Bastille erstreckt. Paris bietet aber auch ein großes kulturelles Programm: Ausstellungen, Konzerte, Kinos, Theater: mehr Informationen in Pariscope, oder für alle schwulen Veranstaltungen und Parties -schaut in den zahlreichen kostenlosen Zeitschriften nach, die fast in allen Bars ausliegen. Achtung: die Métro fährt nicht zwischen 1 Uhr nachts und 5.30 Uhr morgens. Wenn Ihr aus einer Diskothek kommt, nehmt ein Taxi oder den Nachtbus. Was schwule

Hotels betrifft, ist Frankreich etwas im Rückstand. Man muß lange Zeit im voraus reservieren, was nicht zuletzt daran liegt, daß in Paris das ganze Jahr Hochsaison ist!

▲ Paris, c'est Paris! Tout simplement. C'est le point de départ idéal pour une découverte du fascinant continent européen et une des premières villes gayes du monde. En plus d'un réseau important de lieux de rencontres, de nombreuses boutiques et entreprises de services pour les gays, tenues par des gays, ont vu le jour ces dernières années. Paris-lumière, Paris la nuit, c'est aussi pour eux. Une vie trépidante anime les bars, les boutiques, les rues du centre, les discothèques, 24 heures sur 24. Le quartier historique du Marais, de la rue Vieille-du-Temple à la rue des Archives en passant par la rue Sainte-Croix-de-la-Bretonnerie, est le centre d'un axe qui va des Halles à Bastille et qui regroupe l'essentiel de la vie gaye. Paris, c'est aussi une vie culturelle intense: expositions, concerts, cinémas, théâtres; consultez le *Pariscope* ou, pour les événements gays et les sorties, les nombreux journaux gratuits disponibles dans presque tous les bars. Attention, les métros ne circulent pas entre une heure et cinq heures trente. En sortant de boîte, il faudra prendre un taxi ou un bus de nuit. En ce qui concerne les hôtels gays, la France est vraiment en retard, il faut réserver longtemps à l'avance quelle que soit la période, car à Paris, la saison dure toute l'année.

☆ Se sabe de sobra que Paris es un encanto. Es la ciudad ideal como punto de partida para descubir el fascinante continente europeo y se ha vuelto una verdadera metrópoli gay. En los últimos años se ha desarollado aqui una vida con muchos bares, restaurantes y tiendas para la clientela homosexual. En los bares, en las calles del centro y en las discotecas se encuentra un ambiente animadísimo tanto de día como de noche. El barrio histórico de Marais, que se extiende de la rue Vielle-du-Temple, sobre rue des Archives hasta la rue Saint-Croix-de-la-Bretonnerie es el centro de la zona gay, que abarca Les Halles y la Bastilla. Paris ofrece además una extensa vida cultural, con exposiciones, conciertos, cine y teatro. Informaciones más detalladas se encuentran en la guía de ocio llamado Pariscope o para actividades o fiestas gay se recomienda echar un vistazo a las númerosas revistas gratuitas, que se pueden consultar en casi todos los bares de la ciudad. Cuidado: Entre la 1 y las 5:30 de la mañana no funciona el métro, así que se tiene que coger un taxi o un autobus nocturno. Paris no se caracteriza precisamente por su gran oferta de hoteles gay. En la mayoría de los casos hay que hacer las reservas con mucho adelanto, ¡entre otras cosas porque Paris está siempre en temporada alta!

❖ Parigi è sempre Parigi! Come una delle metropoli gay si offre come base ideale per l'esplorazione del continente europeo. Negli ultimi anni si è sviluppata una vita gay con gastronomia, negozi di gay per gay. Un incessante giro pulsante e brillante nei bar, sulle strade e nelle discoteche, tutta la giornata fino all'alba seguente. Il quartiere storico di Marais, tra la Rue Vieille-du-Temple, la Rue des Archives e la Rue Saint-Croix-de-la- Bretonnerie, è anche il centro del quartiere gay, che si estende fino a Les Halles e alla Bastille. Parigi però offre anche un vasto programma culturale: mostre, concerti, cinema, teatro. Più informazioni si trovano nel „Pariscope" o nei numerosi giornali distribuiti gratuitamente nei bar. Attenzione: La Métro è chiusa tra le 1 e le 5.30 del mattino. Uscendo dalla discoteca conviene prendere un taxi o i bus notturni. Per quanto riguarda gli alberghi gay, la Francia è ancora un po' indietro. Bisogna prenotare molto tempo in anticipo, perché a Parigi è sempre alta stagione!

DATING AGENCIES

Freedhom (GLM MA) 10-19 h
3 Rue Saint Honoré ✉75008 ☎ 01.44.94.90.46
Fax: 01.44.94.90.48 Homepage: http://www.fredhom.fr
The only gay dating agency in Paris.

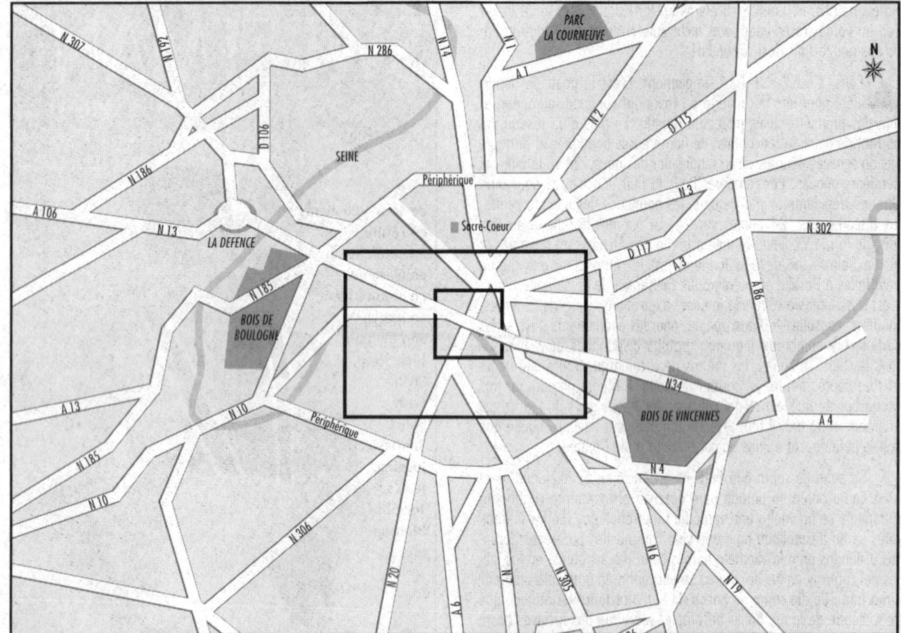

GAY INFO

Centre Gay & Lesbien (CGL) (GLM) Mon-Sat 12-20 h, Café Positif: Sun 14-19 h
3 Rue Keller ✉75011 *(M° Bastille/Voltaire/Ledru-Rollin)*
☎ 01.43.57.21.47 Fax: 01.43.57.27.93 Email: cglparis@cglparis.org
Contact for many gay and gay-lesbian groups. Shop, café, library. Information about HIV and Aids.

e.m@le
Immeuble Metropole 19, 134-140 Rue Aubervilliers ✉75019
☎ 01.53.35.98.54 Fax: 01.53.35.98.80
Magazine published by Groupe Gai Pied. Every Thu. Available for free in gay establishments.

Garcons
8 Rue du Faubourg Poissonière ✉75010 ☎ 01.56.56.01.12
Fax: 01.48.24.95.80 Email: garcons@wanadoo.fr
Gay magazine for Paris published 11/year. 10 F.

GPH Le Guide Gai Pied sur Minitel
Pour consultation: 36 15 G.P.H.

Illico - Double Face
99 Rue de la Verrerie ✉75004 ☎ 01.48.04.58.00
Fax: 01.48.04.05.92 Email: groupeillico@mail2.imaginet.fr
Monthly free news magazine and its supplement. Available in gay establisments.

Out Hebdo
65 Rue du Faubourg Saint-Denis ✉7519 ☎ 01.53.24.62.02
Fax: 01.53.24.16.22
Homepage: http://www.outhebdo.com
News weekly leaflet in French available for free at gay venues.

Radio FG 98.2 0-24 h (FM 98,2 MHz)
57 Rue de Rivoli ✉75001 ☎ 01.40.13.88.28
Fax: 01.40.13.88.07

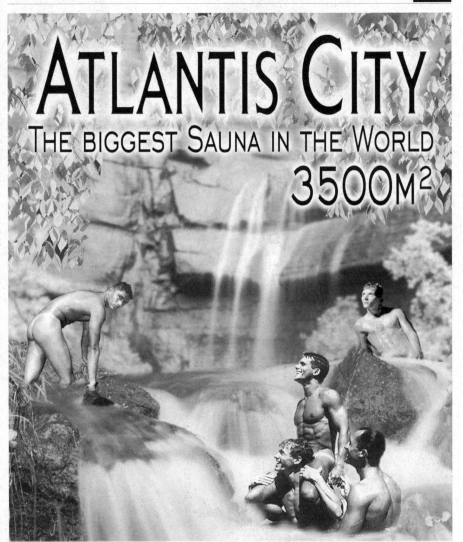

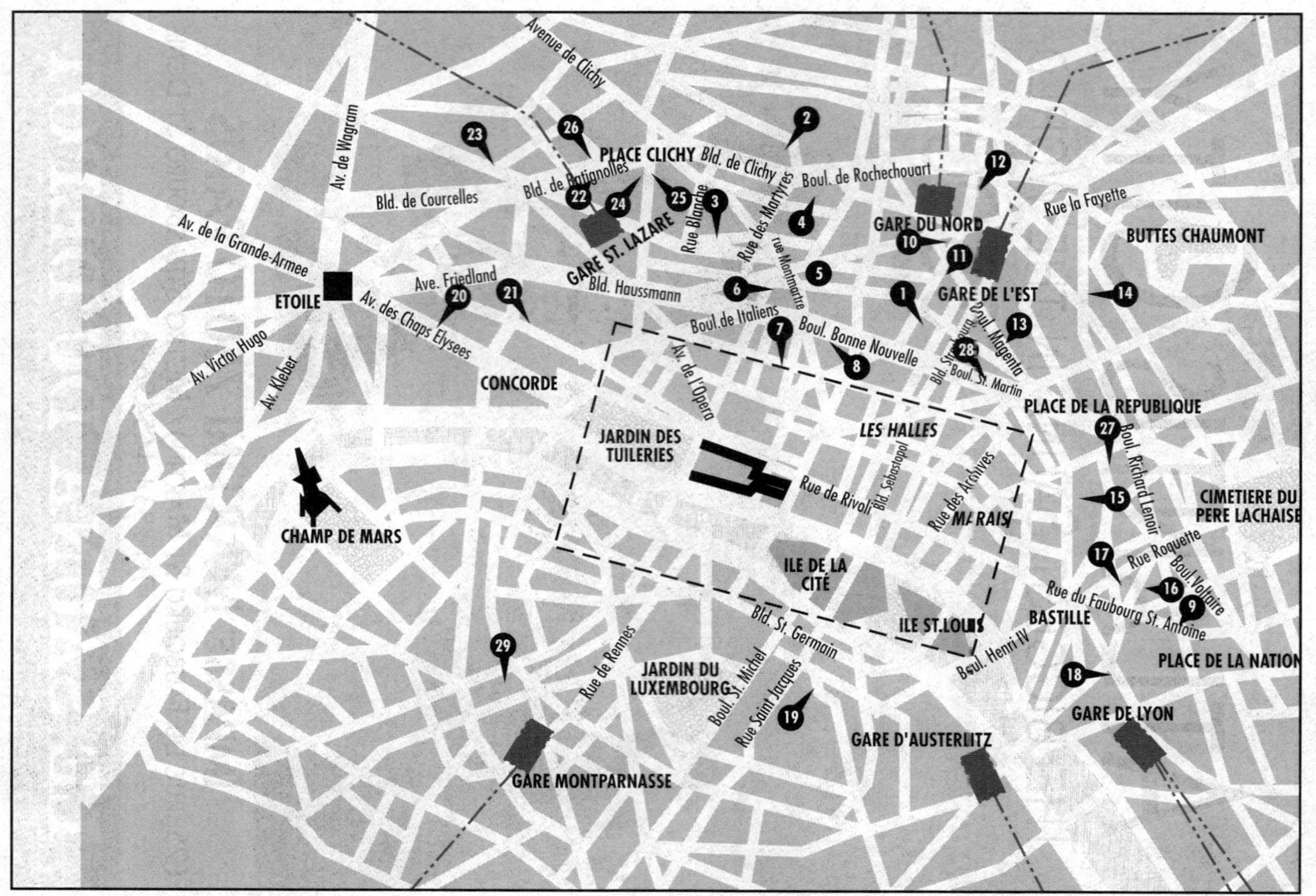
Avenue de Clichy
Av. de Wagram
PLACE CLICHY Bld. de Clichy
Bld. de Batignolles
Bld. de Courcelles
Boul. de Rochechouart
Rue la Fayette
BUTTES CHAUMONT
GARE DU NORD
GARE ST. LAZARE
Rue Blanche
Rue des Martyres
rue Montmartre
Av. de la Grande-Armee
ETOILE
Ave. Friedland
Bld. Haussmann
GARE DE L'EST
Av. des Chaps Elysees
Boul.de Italiens
Boul. Bonne Nouvelle
Bld. Strasbourg
Boul. Magenta
Boul. St. Martin
Av. Victor Hugo
Av. Kleber
CONCORDE
Av. de l'Opera
PLACE DE LA REPUBLIQUE
JARDIN DES TUILERIES
LES HALLES
Boul. Richard Lenoir
Rue de Rivoli
Bld. Sebastopol
Rue des Archives
MARAIS
CIMETIERE DU PERE LACHAISE
CHAMP DE MARS
ILE DE LA CITÉ
Rue Roquette
Boul. Voltaire
Rue du Faubourg St. Antoine
BASTILLE
ILE ST.LOUIS
Bld. St. Germain
Boul. Henri IV
PLACE DE LA NATION
Rue de Rennes
JARDIN DU LUXEMBOURG
Boul. St. Michel
Rue Saint Jacques
GARE DE LYON
GARE D'AUSTERLITZ
GARE MONTPARNASSE
1
2
3
4
5
6
7
8
9
10
11
12
13
14
15
16
17
18
19
20
21
22
23
24
25
26
27
28
29

1 Atlantis City Sauna
2 Mykonos Sauna
3 Espace Vidéo
4 Mec Zone
5 IDM
6 Le Mandala
7 Euro Men's Club
8 Scorpion
9 Caviar & Co. Restaurant
10 Key West
11 Chalet Maya
12 Talisman
13 Station Video
14 IEM
15 La Station Sex Shop
16 La Luna
17 Le Keller
18 Le Saint Hubert
19 Le Petit Prince
20 Queen
21 Banque Club
22 French Art Vidéovision
23 Hôtel des Batignolles
24 IEM
35 Yanko
26 King Sauna
27 Hotel Beaumarchais
28 Louxor Hotel
29 L'Hemis

Reseaux télématiques
-3615 GAY
-3615 BRONX
-3615 TORSO
-3615 ESPACE MAN
-3615 MANVPC
-3615 NOX
-3615 BOB
-3615 ALLOGAY
-3615 GPH
☛ also introduction France

TOURIST INFO

Tourist Info 127 avenue des Champs-Elysées ✉75008 ☎ 01.49.52.53.54 Fax: 01.49.52.53.00

BARS

Acces Soir Café (A B CC GLM MG s) 18-2 h
41 Rue des Blancs Manteaux ✉75004 ☎ 01.42.72.12.89

Akhénaton Café (A AC B glm MA) 14-2 h
12 Rue du Plâtre ✉75004 *(M° Hôtel-de-Ville/Rambuteau)* ☎ 01.48.87.02.59

Amnesia Café (AC B CC f G MA) 10-2 h
42 Rue Vieille-du-Temple ✉75004 *(M° Hôtel-de-Ville)* ☎ 01.42.72.16.94

Arambar. L' (b f CC glm MA s) 12-2 h
7 rue de la Folie Mericourt ✉75011 ☎ 01.48.05.57.79

Au Gobelet d'Argent (B G lj s TV) 17-? h
11 Rue du Cygne ✉75001 *(M° Etienne Marcel)* ☎ 01.42.33.29.82

Banana. Le (AC B glm MA OS S SNU TV YG) 16-? h
13-15 Rue de la Ferronnerie ✉75001 *(M° Châtelet/Les Halles)* ☎ 01.42.33.35.31

Bar du Palmier. Le (AC B F g OS) 17 h-dawn
16 Rue des Lombards ✉75004 *(M° Chatelet/Les Halles)* ☎ 01.42.78.53.53
Good atmosphere, bar cocktails.

Bar Hôtel Central (AC B G H MA) 16-2, Sat Sun 14-2 h
33 Rue Vieille-du-Temple ✉75004 *(M° Hôtel-de-Ville)* ☎ 01.48.87.99.33
Friendly, international gay rendez-vous and the only Gay Hotel in Paris!

Bears' Den (AC B CC G MG lj VS) 16-2 h
6 Rue des Lombards ✉75004 ☎ 01.42.71.08.20
Bears, daddies and friends.

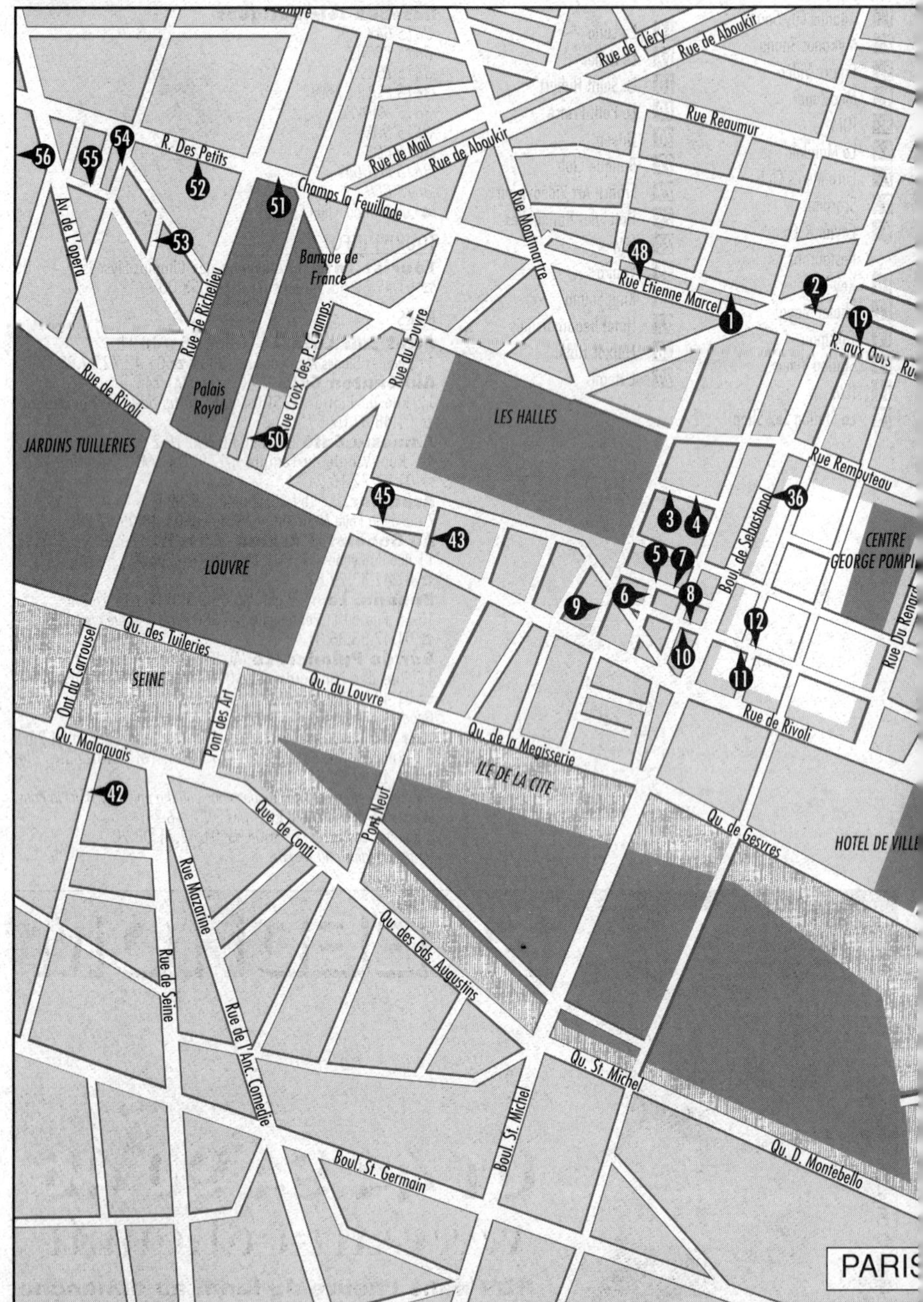

Rue de Cléry
Rue de Aboukir
Rue Reaumur
R. Des Petits
Rue de Mail
Rue de Aboukir
Champs la Feuillade
Av. de L'opera
Rue Montmartre
Banque de France
Rue Etienne Marcel
R. aux Ours
Rue de Richelieu
Rue Croix des P. Champs.
Rue du Louvre
Rue de Rivoli
Palais Royal
LES HALLES
JARDINS TUILLERIES
Rue Rambuteau
Boul. de Sebastopol
CENTRE GEORGE POMPI
LOUVRE
Rue Du Renard
Qu. des Tuileries
Ont du Carrousel
SEINE
Qu. du Louvre
Pont des Art
Rue de Rivoli
Qu. Malaquais
Qu. de la Megisserie
ILE DE LA CITE
Que. de Conti
Pont Neuf
Qu. de Gesvres
HOTEL DE VILLE
Rue Mazarine
Qu. des Gds. Augustins
Rue de Seine
Rue de l'Anc. Comedie
Qu. St. Michel
Boul. St. Michel
Boul. St. Germain
Qu. D. Montebello
PARIS

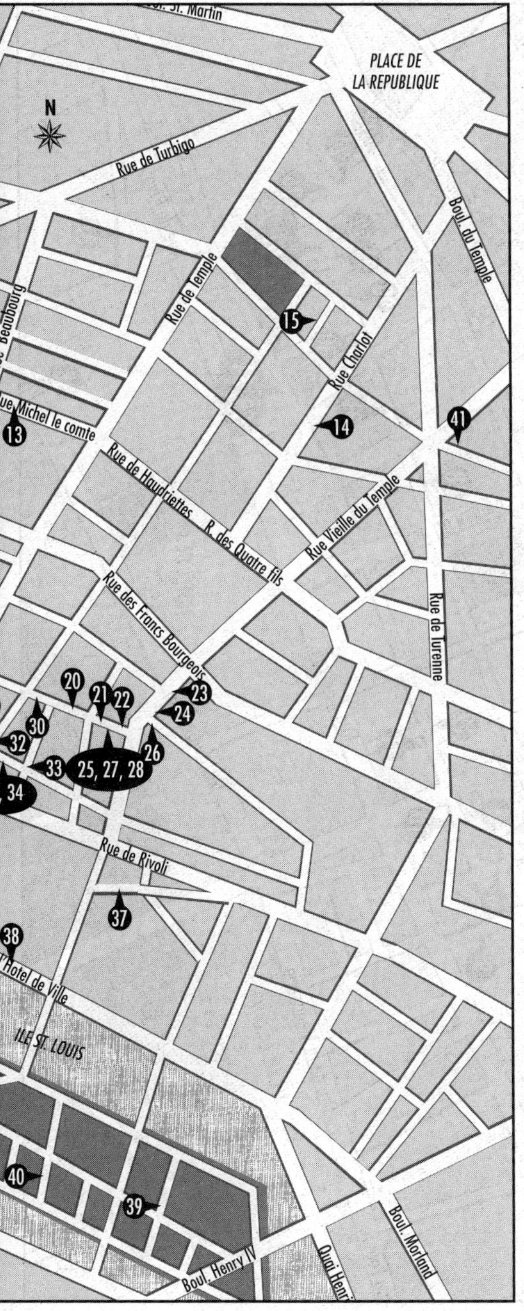

1 Le Monde à l'Envers
2 Le Denicheur
3 Kiosque Forum
4 Agora Hotel
5 Le Banana
6 L'Amazonial / Le Tropic
7 Le Cirque
8 Au Diable des Lombards
9 Chez Max
10 Le Club
11 Sex Shop Ets Cochon
12 Le Bar du Palmier
13 Le Duplex
14 One Way
15 Madame Sans Gêne
16 Le Mic-Man
17 QG
18 Le Gai Moulin Restaurant
19 Le Depot Bar
20 TTBM
21 Les Mots à la Bouche
22 Bar/Hotel Central
23 Le Colimaçon
24 Amnesia Café
25 Boy'z Bazaar
26 Okawa Bar
27 Fond de Cour
28 Factory's Fashion Shop - Coffee Shop Café
29 L'Eglantine
30 Mixer Bar
31 Le Divin
32 Chez Tsou
33 Le Quetzal
34 Thermik Bar
36 Sweetman Fashion Shop
37 Amadéo
38 L'Arene
39 Auberge de la Reine Blanche
40 Chaumiere en l'Isle
41 Hôtel Beaumarchais
42 Le Vieux Casque
43 Yanko
44 Le Petit Goulot
45 IEM
48 Matinée Soirée
50 Univers Gym
51 Club 18
52 L'Insolite
53 La Champmeslé
54 Le Til't Sauna
55 Le Vagabond
56 Le Transfert

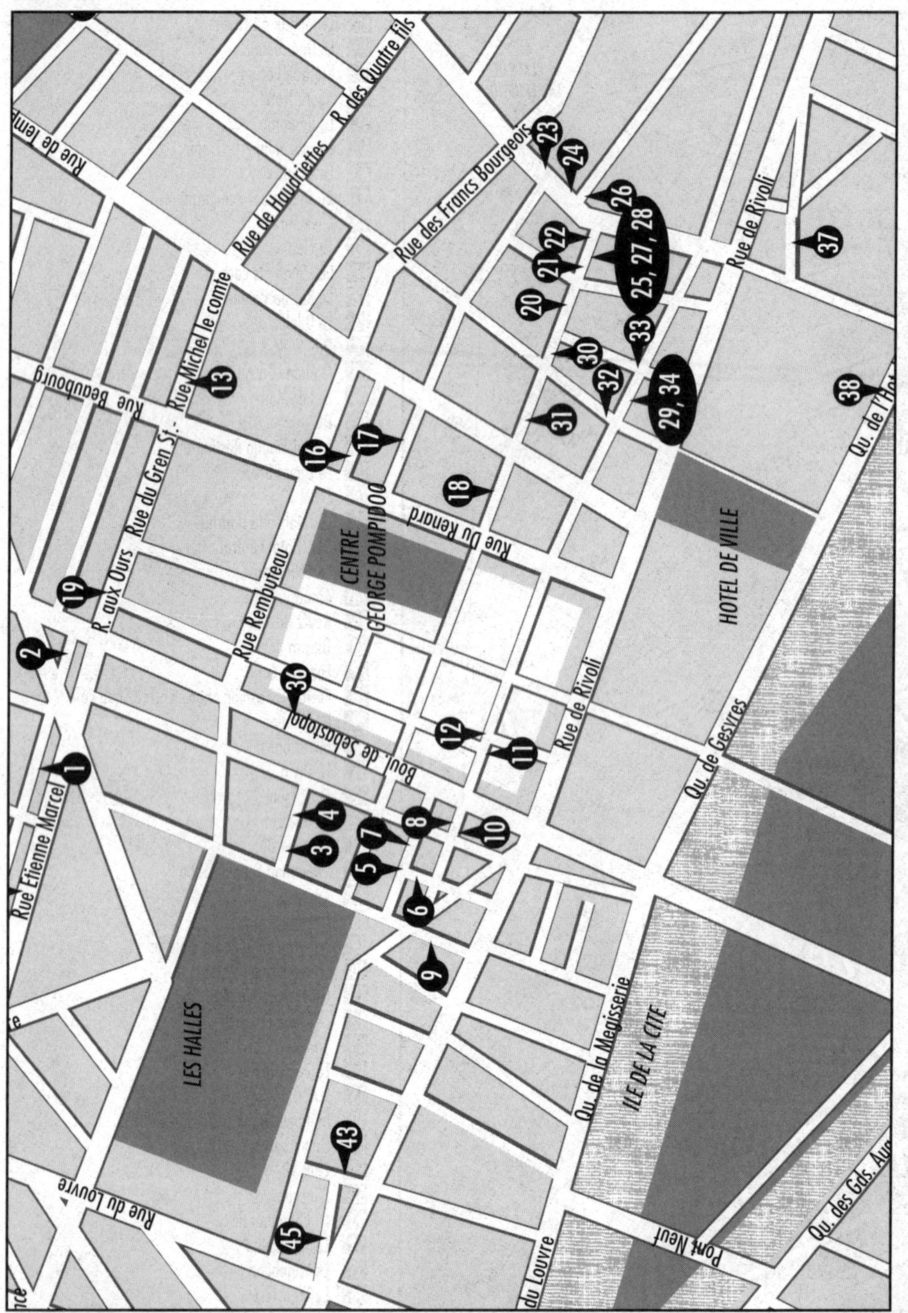
Rue de Temp
R. des Quatre fils
Rue de Haudriettes
Rue des Francs Bourgeois
Rue de Rivoli
Rue Beaubourg
Rue Michel le comte
Rue du Gren St.
R. aux Ours
Rue Rambuteau
CENTRE
GEORGE POMPIDOO
Rue Du Renard
HOTEL DE VILLE
Rue de Rivoli
Boul. de Sebastopol
Qu. de Gesvres
Rue Etienne Marcel
LES HALLES
Qu. de la Megisserie
ILE DE LA CITE
Rue du Louvre
du Louvre
Pont Neuf
Qu. des Gds. Au
Qu. de l'Hot
1
2
3
4
5
6
7
8
9
10
11
12
13
16
17
18
19
20
21
22
23
24
26
25, 27, 28
29, 34
30
31
32
33
36
37
38
43
45

Bunker. Le (AC B G LJ VS) 21-2 h
23 rue du Temple ✉75003 ☎ 01.42.74.05.15
Basement bar under Café Rude.
Café Cox (AC B G MA OS) 13-2 h
15 Rue des Archives ✉75004 ☎ 01.42.72.08.00
Café Rude (B glm F) 12-2 h
23 rue du Temple ✉75004 ☎ 01.42.74.05.15
Cap Horn Bar. Le (AC B D G WE YG) 16-2 h
37 Rue des Lombards ✉75001 *M° Châtelet-Les Halles*
☎ 40.28.03.08
Champmeslé. La (B gLM S) 18-6 h
4 Rue Chabannais ✉75002 *(M° Quatre-Septembre)*
☎ 01.42.96.85.20
Shows Thu.
Cirque. Le (AC B DR glm MA VS) Thu-Sat 22-5, Sun 17-5 h
5/7 Rue de la Ferronnerie ✉75001 *(M° Chatelet/Les Halles)*
☎ 01.40.41.00.10
Three bars, including the Underbar.
Dépôt. Le (AC B CC D DR G S SNU VS W) 12-7 h
10 Rue aux Ours ✉75003 *(M° Etienne Marcel/Rambuteau)*
☎ 01.44.54.96.96
Large disco bar and sex-club on three floors, with videos and laser shows.
Duplex. Le (A B GLM MA) 20-2 h
25 Rue Michel-le-Comte ✉75003 *(M° Rambuteau)*
☎ 01.42.72.80.86
Feeling. Le (B glm MA) 15-2 h
43 Rue Ste.Croix de la Bretonnerie ✉75004 ☎ 01.48.04.70.03

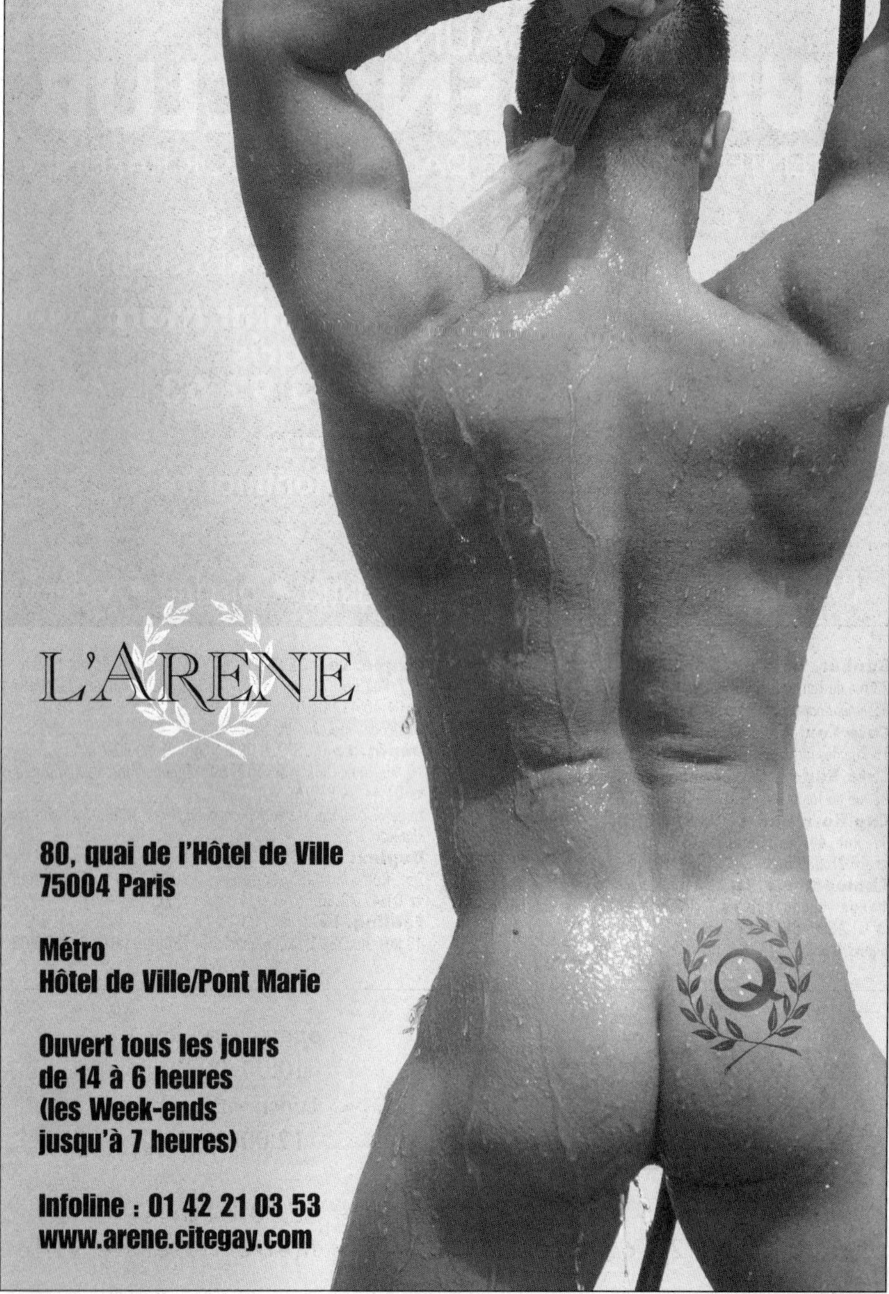
L'ARENE
80, quai de l'Hôtel de Ville
75004 Paris
Métro
Hôtel de Ville/Pont Marie
Ouvert tous les jours
de 14 à 6 heures
(les Week-ends
jusqu'à 7 heures)
Infoline : 01 42 21 03 53
www.arene.citegay.com

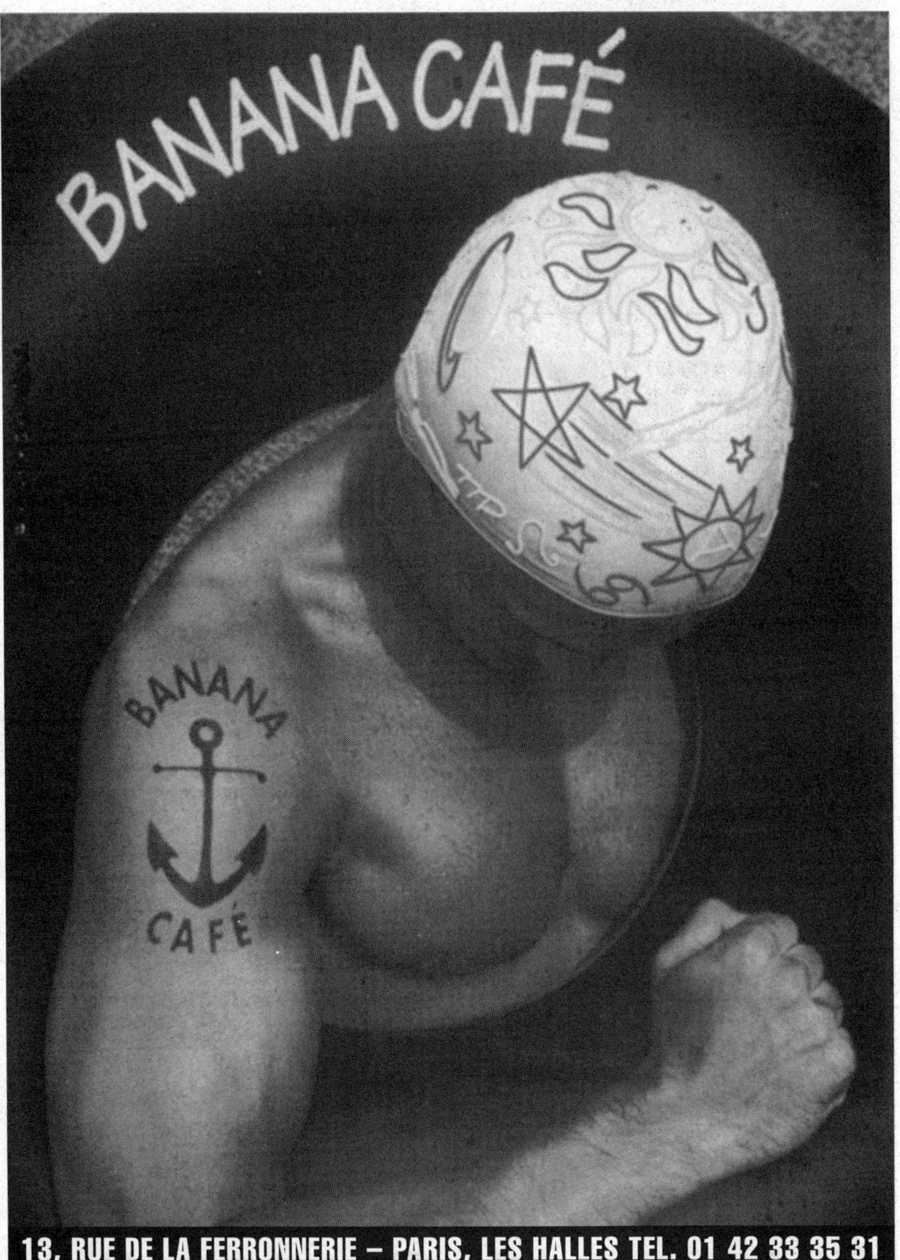
BANANA CAFÉ
BANANA
CAFÉ

Impact Bar. L' (B G)
18 rue Grenéta ✉75002 ☎ 01 42 21 94 24
Interface Bar (A B CC G MA) 15-2 h
34 Rue Keller ✉75011 ☎ 01.47.00.67.15
Keller's (AC B CC DR G LJ MG p) 22-2 h
14 Rue Keller ✉75011 *(M° Bastille)* ☎ 01.47.00.05.39
Pool table. Locker-room and showers. Strict dress-code: Leather or jeans and t-shirt.
Mathis Bar (B GLM) 21-? h, closed on Sun
3 Rue Ponthieu ✉75008 *(M° Franklin-Roosevelt)*
☎ 01.53.76.01.62
Mec Zone (AC B G LJ VS) 21-6, Sun 18-6 h
27 Rue Turgot ✉75009 *(M° Anvers)* ☎ 01.40.82.94.18
Mic-Man. Le (AC B DR G MA VS) 12-2 WE and bank holidays -4 h
24 Rue Geoffroy-l'Angevin ✉75004 *(M° Rambuteau)*
☎ 01.42.74.39.80
Friendly atmosphere. Happero 19-21 h: 30% reduction on all consumations.
Mixer Bar (AC B CC d glm VS YG) 16-2 h
23 Rue Sainte Croix de la Bretonnerie ✉75004
☎ 01.48.87.55.44
Oiseau Bariolé. L' (AC B GLM) 16-2 h
16 Rue St.Croix de la Bretonnerie ✉75004 ☎ 01.42.72.37.12
Okawa (A AC B CC F GLM MA S) 9-2 h
40 Rue Vieille du Temple ✉75004 ☎ 01.48.04.30.69
One Way (AC B G lj MA VS) 17-2 h
28 Rue Charlot ✉75003 *(M° République)* ☎ 01.48.87.46.10
Friendly atmosphere, cruising bar.
Onix. L' (B glm OS)
15 Rue des Lombards ✉75004

LE DEPOT

KELLER'S
www.kellers.fr
Raunchy Cruise Bar
14, RUE KELLER 75011 PARIS. METRO BASTILLE TEL : 01 47 00 05 39 - INTERN. 33(1) 47 00 05 39
Tenue HARD éxigée.
(Jean's, tee-shirt, débardeur tolérés)
RCS 76 B 1792
PARIS
La direction se reserve le droit d'admission - Dessin : Xavier GICQUEL - Créa : Blue Box 01 40 26 76 67

Open Café (B CC f glm MA OS) 10.30-2 h, brunch 12-17 h
17 Rue des Archives ✉75004 ☎ 01.48.87.80.25

Piano Zinc (AC B CC G MA S) 18-2 h
49 Rue des Blancs Manteaux ✉75004 ☎ 01.40.27.97.42
Piano Bar.

Piétons. Les (B F glm) 11-2 h
8 Rue des Lombards ✉75004 ☎ 01.48.87.82.87

Quetzal. Le (AC B G MA OS) 17-5 h
10 Rue de la Verrerie ✉75004 *(M° Hôtel-de-Ville)*
☎ 01.48.87.99.07
Very popular! Two bars. Games room on the 1st floor.

Skeud (AC B glm) 12.30-2 h
35 Rue Sainte Croix de la Bretonnerie ✉75004 *(M° Hotel de Ville)*
☎ 01.40.29.44.40 *Bar with dj, techno and house.*

Slider's Bar (B DR f G lj MA OS) 17-2 h
138 Rue du Faubourg Saint Martin ✉75010 *(M° Gare de l'Est)*
☎ 01.43.55.18.34

Thermik Bar (AC B G MA) 16-2 h
7 Rue de la Verrerie ✉75004 ☎ 01.44.78.08.18
Theme parties.

Tropic Café. Le (B CC d GLM MA OS TV W YG) 16-4 h
66 Rue des Lombards ✉75001 ☎ 01.40.13.92.62
Opposite Amazonial.

Unity Bar (B gLM MA) 12-1 h
176-178 Rue Saint Martin ✉75003 ☎ 01.42.72.70.59
Mostly women, party atmosphere.

Vagabond Bar. Le (AC B G F lj MA p) 18-4 h, closed Mon
14 Rue Thérèse ✉75001 *(M° Pyramides)* ☎ 01.42.96.27.23
Intimate cocktails, elegant dining and a great bar until late. French cuisine. Oldest gay bar/restaurant in Paris.

MEN'S CLUBS

Arène. L' (AC B CC DR G lj P S VS YG) 14-6, WE -7 h
80 Quai de l'Hôtel de Ville ✉75004 *(M° Hôtel de Ville/Pont Marie)* ☎ 1.42.21.03.53
Three floors of fantasy and films. Popular.
Banque Club (AC B CC DR G lj NU P VS) 16-2, Sun 14-2 h
23 Rue de Penthièvre ✉75008 *(M° Miromesnil)*
☎ 01.42.56.49.26
Three floors. Porno and music videos. Bar and big screen video.
Docks (AC b G DR LJ MG P VS) 16-2 h
150 Rue St. Maur ✉75010 *(M°Goncourt)* ☎ 01.43.57.33.82
Glove. The (B DR G lj) 22-2, Fri Sat -7, Sun 16-2 h
34 Rue Charlot ✉75003 ☎ 01.48.87.31.36
Men's Club (G P) 17-06:00h
34 Boulevard de Clichy ✉75018 ☎ 1.42 59 52 24
QG (AC B CC DR G LJ MG P VS) 17-8 h
12 Rue Simon le Franc ✉75004 ☎ 01.48.87.74.18
Dress code leather, jeans, uniform, latex.
Rangers. The (AC b DR G LJ MA VS) 13-24 h
6 Boulevard St.Denis ✉75010 *(M° Strasbourg St.Denis)*
☎ 01.42.39.83.30
Transfert. Le (AC B DR G LJ MA p VS) 24-? h
3 Rue de la Sourdière ✉75001 *(M° Tuileries)*
☎ 01.42.60.48.42
Hard cruising bar. Strict dress code leather, uniform, jeans, latex.
Trap. The (AC B DR G lj MA p SNU VS) 23-4 h
10 Rue Jacob ✉75006 *(M° Odéon)* ☎ 01.43.54.53.53
Good videos. No entry for older people.

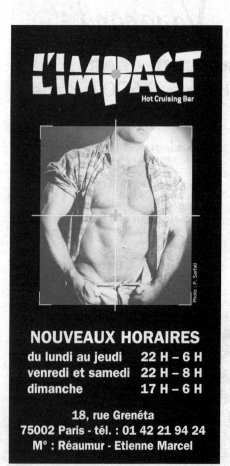

CAFÉS

Coffee de l'Open Café (CC F GLM OS YG) 12-24 h
15 Rue des Archives ✉75004 ☎ 01.48.87.80.25
Coffee-Shop. Le (b F G VS YG) 12-2 h
3 Rue Sainte Croix de la Bretonnerie ✉75004 ☎ 01.42.74.24.21
Tropic Café (G) 16-? h
66 Rue des Lombardes ✉75001 ☎ 01.40.13.92.62

DANCECLUBS

Bains. Les (AC B F D glm MA s) Gay Sun Mon and certain theme nights
7 Rue de Bourg l'Abbé ✉75003 ☎ 01.48.87.01.80
Boîte à Frissons au Tango (D GLM MA s TV WE) Fri Sat 22.30-5 h
13 Rue au Maire ✉75003 ☎ 01.42.72.17.78
Rétro style dance evening for gays, lesbians and non-homophobic straights.

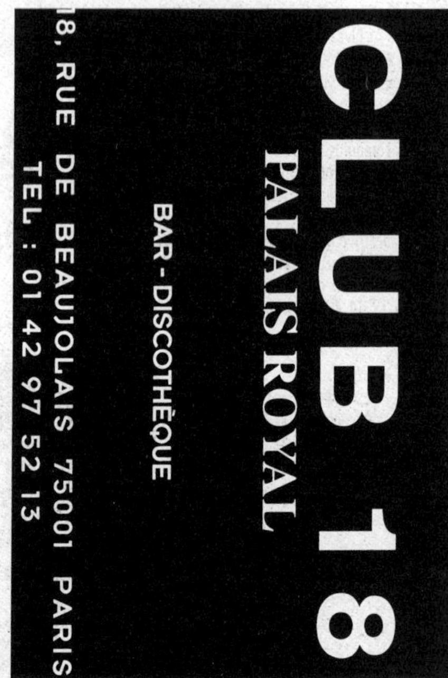

CLUB 18
PALAIS ROYAL
BAR - DISCOTHÈQUE
18, RUE DE BEAUJOLAIS 75001 PARIS
TEL : 01 42 97 52 13

Club. Le (AC B D G YG) 23.30-? h
14 Rue Saint-Denis ✉75001 *(M° Châtelet/Les Halles)* ☎ 01.45.08.96.25
International, very friendly.

Club 18 (AC CC D DR G MA P) 23-6 h, closed Mon-Wed
18 Rue de Beaujolais ✉75001 *(M° Palais-Royal)* ☎ 01.42.97.52.13
Shows Wed Fri and Sun.

Dépôt. Le (AC B CC D DR G S SNU VS W) 12-7 h
10 Rue aux Ours ✉75003 *(M° Etienne Marcel/Rambuteau)* ☎ 01.44.54.96.96
Large disco and sex-club on three floors, with videos and laser shows.

Divan Du Monde. Le (B D GLM S) 23-? h
75 Rue des Martyres ✉75018 *(M° Pigalle)* ☎ 01.44.92.77.66

Folies Pigalle (B D GLM s) Black-Blanc-Beur Tea Dance: Sun 17.30-23.30 h (☎ 01.42.80.12.03)
11 Rue Place Pigalle ✉75009 *(M° Pigalle)* ☎ 01.48.78.25.56
Black-Blanc-Beur: Infoline ☎ 01.42.80.12.03.

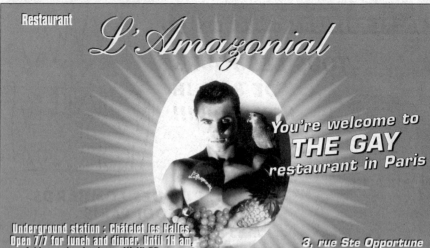

Gibus. Le (D G GLM MA P s W YG) Wed-Sat 24-7 h
18 Rue du Faubourg du Temple ✉75011 *(M° République)*
☎ 01.47.00.78.88

Insolite. L' (B D G) 23-5 h
33 Rue des Petits-Champs ✉75001 *(M° Pyramides)*
☎ 01.42.61.99.22
Good atmosphere.

London. Le (AC B CC D DR G MA p VS) 22-7 h
33bis Rue des Lombards ✉75001 *(M° Châtelet)*
☎ 01.42.33.41.45

Luna. La (AC B DR G VS) 23-6 h Mon Tue video bar 22.30-4 h
28 Rue Keller ✉75011 *(M° Bastille)* ☎ 01.40.21.09.91

Queen (B D G lj P S YG) 24-6 h
102 Avenue des Champs Elysées ✉75008 *(M° Georges V)*
☎ 01.53.89.08.90
Theme nights and visiting international djs.

Scorp. Le (B D DR glm lj STV YG)
25 Boulevard Poissonière ✉75002 ☎ 01.40.26.01.30

RESTAURANTS

Alivi (F glm OS) closed Sat Sun noon
27 Rue du Roi de Sicile ✉75004 ☎ 01.48.87.90.20
Corsican specialties.

Amadéo (CC F glm MA S) 12-14, 20-23 h, closed Sat lunch & Sun all day
19 Rue Françis Miron ✉75004 ☎ 01.48.87.01.02
Music classic and lyric.

Amazonial. L' (AC b CC F glm MA OS s SNU TV W) Sun-Thu 12-15 19-1, Fri Sat -1.30 h
3 Rue Sainte Opportune ✉75001 *(M° Châtelet/Les Halles)* ☎ 01.42.33.53.13
International cuisine, Sun brunch. Soirée cabaret.

Au Bistrot de la Place (AC CC b F GLM OS)
2 Place du Marché Sainte Catherine ✉75004 *(M°St.Paul)* ☎ 01.42.78.21.32

Au Diable des Lombards (AC B bf CC F GLM MA) 8-1, brunch daily 10-17 h
64 Rue des Lombards ✉75001 *(M° Châtelet Les Halles)* ☎ 01.42.33.81.84
American restaurant and bar.

Auberge de la Reine Blanche (AC b CC F glm MA) Mon-Tue 12-15 18-24, Thu 18-24, Fri-Sun 12-24 h, closed Wed, Thu lunch
30 Rue Saint-Louis en l'Ile ✉75004 ☎ 01.46.33.07.87

Aux Trois Petits Cochons (b F GLM) closed Mon
31 Rue Tiquetonne ✉75002 ☎ 01.42.33.39.69

Baptiste. Le (A CC F glm MA) closed Sat lunch and Sun
11 Rue des Boulangers ✉75005 *(Near Université Jussieu)* ☎ 01.43.25.57.24

Bûcheron. Le (B F glm) 12-15 & 18.30-22.30, Sun brunch 11-16, bar 7-22 h
9 Rue du Roi de Sicile *(M° St. Paul)* ☎ 01.48.87.71.31

Canaille. La (AC B CC F glm MA s) Mon-Fri 11.45-14.15, Mon-Sun 19.30-24 h
4 Rue Crillon ✉75004 *(M° Quai-de-la-Rapée)* ☎ 01.42.78.04.71

Caviar & Co. (AC CC F glm MA) Tue-Fri 12-14, Tue-Fri 19.30-24 h, closed Sun Mon
5 Rue de Reuilly ✉75012 *(M° Faidherbe-Chaligny)* ☎ 01.43.56.13.98
Excellent fish restaurant.

Chalet Maya (A AC b E F glm MA OS) 11.30-14.30, 18.30-24, closed Sun
5 Rue des Petits-Hôtels ✉75010 *(M° Gare de l'Est)* ☎ 01.47.70.52.78
French cuisine.

Chaumière en l'Ile. La (b F glm MA OS) 12-24 h
4 Rue Jean du Bellay ✉75004 ☎ 01.43.54.27.34
Weekend service no stop. Free drink with SPARTACUS guide. Sunny terrace with view of Notre Dame.

Chez Max (CC F g) 12-14, 20-24 h
47 Rue Saint Honoré ✉75001 ☎ 01.45.08.80.13
Specialités landaises. Beaucoup d'artistes.

Chez Raymonde (AC CC d F GLM MA TV) 19.30-? h, closed Mon Tue
119 Avenue Parmentier ✉75011 ☎ 01.43.55.26.27
Dinner dance, popular French retro style./ Ambiance ginguette.

Chez Tsou (F g MA OS)
16 Rue des Archives ✉75004 *(M° Hôtel de Ville)* ☎ 01.42.78.11.47
Chinese restaurant.

Colimaçon. Le (F g)
44 Rue Vieille du Temple ✉75004 ☎ 01.48.87.12.01

Croc Man (F glm) closed Sat and Sun midday
6 Rue Geoffroy L'Angevin ✉75004 ☎ 01.42.77.60.02

Divin. Le (AC CC F G MA W) 12-14, 19.30-23.30, Sat 19.30-23.30 h
41 Rue Sainte-Croix-de-la-Bretonnerie ✉75004 *(M° Hotel de Ville)* ☎ 01.42.77.10.20
Charming and intimate. Traditional french and provençal cuisine. Quote Spartacus for a free aperitif.

Eclache & Cie (AC bf cc F GLM MA) 8.30-2 h
10 Rue Saint Merri ✉75004 ☎ 01.42.74.62.62
Sociable place.
Eglantine. L' (b F G) 11.30-14.30 19.30-23 h closed Sun Mon
9 Rue de la Verrerie ✉75004 *(M° Hôtel-de-Ville)*
☎ 01.48.04.75.58
Traditional cuisine, you'll get a warm welcome from Danielle.
Equinox (A AC CC F glm MA s) 11.30-14.30, 19.30-2 h, closed Mon
33-35 Rue des Rosiers ✉75004 ☎ 01.42.71.92.41
Cuisine Québecoise.
Fond de Cour (AC CC F GLM MA OS W) 12.30-14, 19.30-24 h
3 Rue Sainte-Croix-de-la-Bretonnerie ✉75004 *(M° Hôtel-de-Ville)*
☎ 01.42.74.71.52
Gai Moulin. Le (CC F GLM) 19-0.30 h
4 Rue Saint-Merri ✉75004 ☎ 01.48.87.47.59
Hémis. L' (A B F glm MA S) 9-15, 18-22.30, WE -23.30 h, closed Sun Mon
21 Rue Mademoiselle ✉75015 ☎ 01.48.56.80.32
Homo Sapiens. L' (AC B CC F GLM MG) 19.30-24 h, closed Sun
29 Rue Tiquetonne ✉75002 *(M° Etienne Marcel)*
☎ 01.40.26.94.85
K. Le (F GLM)
20 Rue Keller ✉75011 ☎ 01.53.36.03.96
Krokodil (B F G) 17-2 h
20 Rue de la Reynie ✉75004 ☎ 01.48.87.55.67
Lanterne. La (CC F g MA OS W)
9 Rue du Tunnel ✉75019 ☎ 01.43.39.15.98
Loup Blanc. Le (A CC F glm) 20-0.30, Sun brunch 12-17 h
42, Rue Tiquetonne ✉75002 ☎ 01.40.13.08.35
Madame sans gêne (AC CC F G MA) 12-14, 19.30-23.30, Fri-Sat -24 h, closed Sat Sun lunch
19 Rue de Picardie ✉75003 ☎ 01.42.71.31.21
Matinée Soirée (CC F glm MA OS) Mon-Thu 12-14.30, 19.30-22.30, Fri Sat 19.30-23 h, closed three weeks in Aug & Sun
5 Rue Marie-Stuart ✉75002 *(M° Châtelet/Les Halles)*
☎ 01.42.21.18.00
Traditional cuisine.
Monde à l'Envers. Le (F G MA) 12-14 20-23.30, Sat Sun 20-23.30 h, closed Mon
35 Rue Tiquetonne ✉75002 *(M° Etienne Marcel)*
☎ 01.40.26.13.91
Traditional cuisine. Good atmosphere.
O'2 F (CC F glm MA) Tue-Thu 20-23.30, Fri-Sun -0.30 h
4 Rue de Roi de Sicile ✉75004 ☎ 01.42.72.75.75
Petit Bonheur. Au (F GLM)
9 Rue St.German L'Auxerrois ✉75001 *(M° Châtelet)*
☎ 01.42.21.17.12
Petit Picard. Le (F glm)
42 Rue St. Croix de la Bretonnerie ✉75004 ☎ 01.42.78.54.03
Petit Prince. Le (AC b F glm MA) 19.30-0.30 h
12 Rue du Lanneau ✉75005 *(M° Maubert-Mutualité)*
☎ 01.43.54.77.26
Reservation! Very popular, nice atmosphere.
Petite Chaumière. La (CC F glm MG) 19.30-24 h
41 Rue des Blancs Manteaux ✉75004 ☎ 01.42.72.13.90
Piano Show (B F g S) 20.30-21 h closed Mon
20 Rue de la Verrerie ✉75004 *(M° Hôtel-de-Ville)*
☎ 01.42.72.23.81
„Diner Spectacle," be sure to get there before 21h when the show starts.
Plateau 26 (AC B d F glm MA S) 19-2, Sat Sun -3.30 h
26 Rue des Lombards ✉75004 ☎ 01.48.87.10.75
Rude. Le (B F GLM) 19.30-24, Sat -1, Sun brunch 11-16.30 h
23 Rue du Temple ✉75004 ☎ 01.42.74.05.15
Temps au Temps. Le (F g) 12-14 20-22.15 h, closed Sat midday and Sun
13 Rue Paul Biert ✉75011 ☎ 01.43.79.63.40
Tibourg. Le (AC CC F glm) 12-14, 19-23.30 h
29 rue du Bourg-Tibourg ✉75004 ☎ 01.42.74.45.25
Vieux Casque (CC F glm MA) 19-23 h, closed Sun
19 Rue Bonaparte ✉75006 *(M° Saint-Germain-des-Prés)*
☎ 01.43.54.99.46
Wagon 7 (AC B F glm MA OS s) 20-24 h, closed Sat midday and Sun
7 Rue Boursault ✉75017 *(M° Rome)* ☎ 01.42.93.41.57
Real railway carriage of the famous Orient Express with old furniture. A piano bar Fri and Sat evenings.

SEX SHOPS/BLUE MOVIES

Big Shop (CC GLM VS YG) 10-24 h
2 Rue de la Cossonnerie ✉75001 *(M° Chatelet-Les Halles)*
☎ 01.42.21.47.02
Sex shop, accessories and gadgets. Latex section. Rental and sale of videos. Cinema and cabins.
ETS Cochon - Sex-Shop 21 (AC CC glm MA VS) 10-2 h
21 Rue des Lombards ✉75004 *(M° Chatelet/Les Halles)*
☎ 01.40.27.98.09
IEM (G LJ VS) 10-19.30 h, closed Sun
208 Rue Saint-Maur ✉75010 *(M° Goncourt)* ☎ 01.40-18.51.51
The biggest gay sex shop in Europe. Sometimes gay art exhibits.
IEM Les Halles (G VS) 12-22, Sun 14-22 h
43 Rue de l'Arbre Sec ✉75001 *(M° Louvre-Rivoli)*
☎ 01.42.96.05.74

IEM
Shopping On Line
Visit our web site :
www.iem.fr
XXX VIDEOS
LEATHER
RUBBER
SEX-TOYS
ACCESSORIES
DVD...
Premier Gay Store in France !
MAGAZINES
BOOKS
UNDERWEAR
CD ROMS
LUBRICANTS
CONDOMS...
IEM SAINT-MAUR
208, rue Saint-Maur 75010 Paris
Métro GONCOURT - Tél : 01 40 18 51 51
Ouvert de 10h à 19h30 • Fermé le dimanche
Open 10 am to 7.30 pm • Closed on sunday
e-mail : iem-paris@easynet.fr
CATALOGUE DE VENTE PAR CORRESPONDANCE GRATUIT SUR DEMANDE ÉCRITE ET SIGNÉE
ATTESTANT VOTRE MAJORITÉ / ASK FOR OUR FREE MAIL ORDER CATALOG.
CERTIFY THAT YOU ARE 18 YEARS OF AGE OR OLDER. DATE AND SIGNATURE REQUIERED TO :
IEM - B.P. 276 - 75464 PARIS CEDEX 10 - FRANCE
© PHOTOS : DR / HERVÉ BODILIS / IEM

IEM Liège (G VS) 11.30-19.30 h, closed Sun
33 Rue de Liège ✉75008 *(M° Liège)* ☎ 01.45.22.69.01

Kingdom Gay Men's Shop (CC GLM VS) 14-23, Sun 15-20 h
19 Rue Keller ✉75011 *(M° Bastille)* ☎ 01.48.07.07.08
Gay men's shop with video room in the basement. Near The Bastille.

La Station (AC CC G MA VS) 11-20 h, closed Sun
37 Rue Amelot ✉75011 ☎ 01.43.55.50.55
Vidéos , magazines, gadgets and sex toys. 5% reduction with SPARTACUS guide.

Menstore (CC G) Mon-Fri 9.30-18, Sat 12-18 h
99, Rue de la Verrerie ✉75004 *(5th. floor)* ☎ 01.48.04.57.11
Also mail order.

Rexx (A G lj MA VS) 13-20 h, closed Sun
42 Rue de Poitou ✉75003 *(M° Saint-Sebastien-Froissart)* ☎ 01.42.77.58.57
Leather and latex clothes to measure.

Sex-Shop du Dépôt. Le (AC CC G MA VS) 12-8 h
Impasse Martini, 25 Rue Faubourg Saint Martin ✉75010 *(M° Etienne Marcel/Rambuteau)* ☎ 01.44.54.96.96
Part of the Atlantis City Sauna complex.

TTBM (AC CC GLM) 12-22, Sun 15-22 h
16 Rue St.Croix de la Bretonnerie, ✉75004 *(M° Hotel de Ville)* ☎ 01.48.04.80.88
Leather/Cuir, Latex, Accesoires. Mail order 3615 TTBM.

Vidéovision (AC CC G VS) Mon-Sat 11-19 h, closed Sun
62 Rue de Rome ✉75008 *(M° Europe)* ☎ 01.42.93.66.04

Yanko (G VS) Mon-Sat 10-0.30, Sun 14-24 h
10 Place de Clichy ✉75009 *(M° Place de Clichy)*
☎ 01.45.26.71.19
Cinemas and cabins.

Yanko (G LJ) 12-20, Sun & public holidays 14-20 h
54 Rue de l'Arbre Sec ✉75001 *(M° Chatelet/Louvre-Rivoli)*
☎ 01.42.60.55.28

SAUNAS/BATHS

Athletic World (bf f G sa sb VS WO) 12-1, WE 16-1 h
20 rue du Bourg-Tibourg ✉75004 *(M° Hotel de Ville/St. Paul)*
☎ 01.42.77.19.78
Gym, sauna and breakfast rendez-vous in the heart of the Marais.

Atlantis City Sauna (A AC B F G s sa sb sol VS wh WO W) 12-2 h
Impasse Martini, 25 Faubourg Saint Martin ✉75000
☎ 01.44.54.96.96
To feed all your senses in one gigantic complex. Very big place.

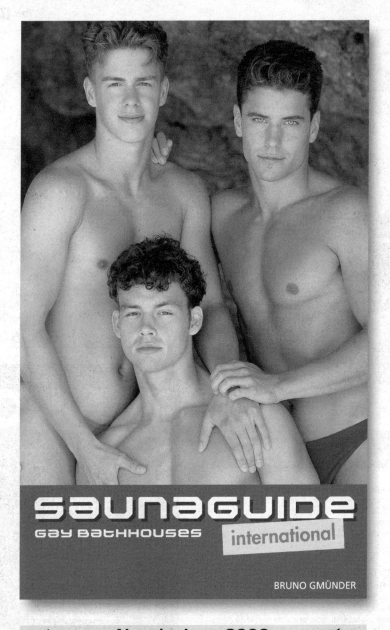

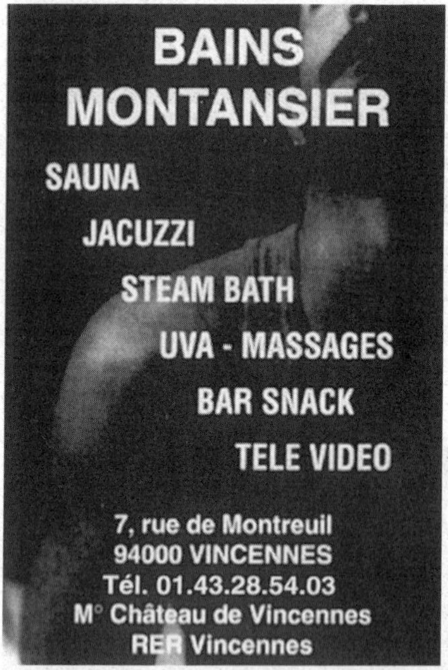

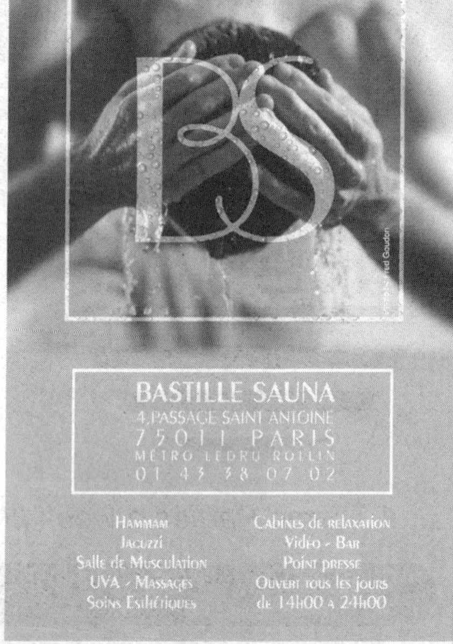

BAINS
MONTANSIER
SAUNA
JACUZZI
STEAM BATH
UVA - MASSAGES
BAR SNACK
TELE VIDEO
7, rue de Montreuil
94000 VINCENNES
Tél. 01.43.28.54.03
M° Château de Vincennes
RER Vincennes

BS
BASTILLE SAUNA
4, PASSAGE SAINT ANTOINE
75011 PARIS
MÉTRO LEDRU ROLLIN
01 43 38 07 02
Hammam
Jacuzzi
Salle de Musculation
UVA - Massages
Soins Esthétiques
Cabines de relaxation
Vidéo - Bar
Point presse
Ouvert tous les jours
de 14h00 à 24h00

PRÉNOM : MARC
AGE : 24 ANS
PROFESSION : MAÎTRE NAGEUR
LOISIRS : PLANCHE À VOILE, VOLLEY BALL
SAUNA PRÉFÉRÉ : IDM
DE PLUS EN PLUS
HOT...
DE PLUS EN PLUS
SEX
SAUNAS - HAMMAM - U.V.A. GRATUITS
VIDEOS - SALLE DE MUSCULATION
SALON TV - BAR - CABINES
OUVERT TOUS LES JOURS DE 12H À 1H
SAUF VSD DE 12H À 2H
IDM
for us !
4, RUE DU FAUBOURG MONTMARTRE 75009 PARIS
M° GRANDS BOULEVARDS
photo : François Rousseau

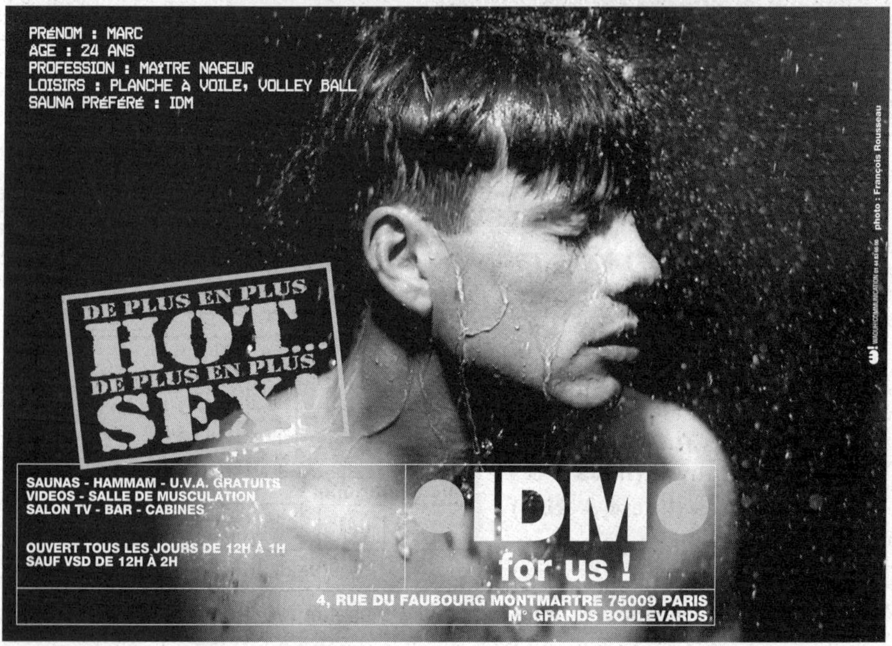

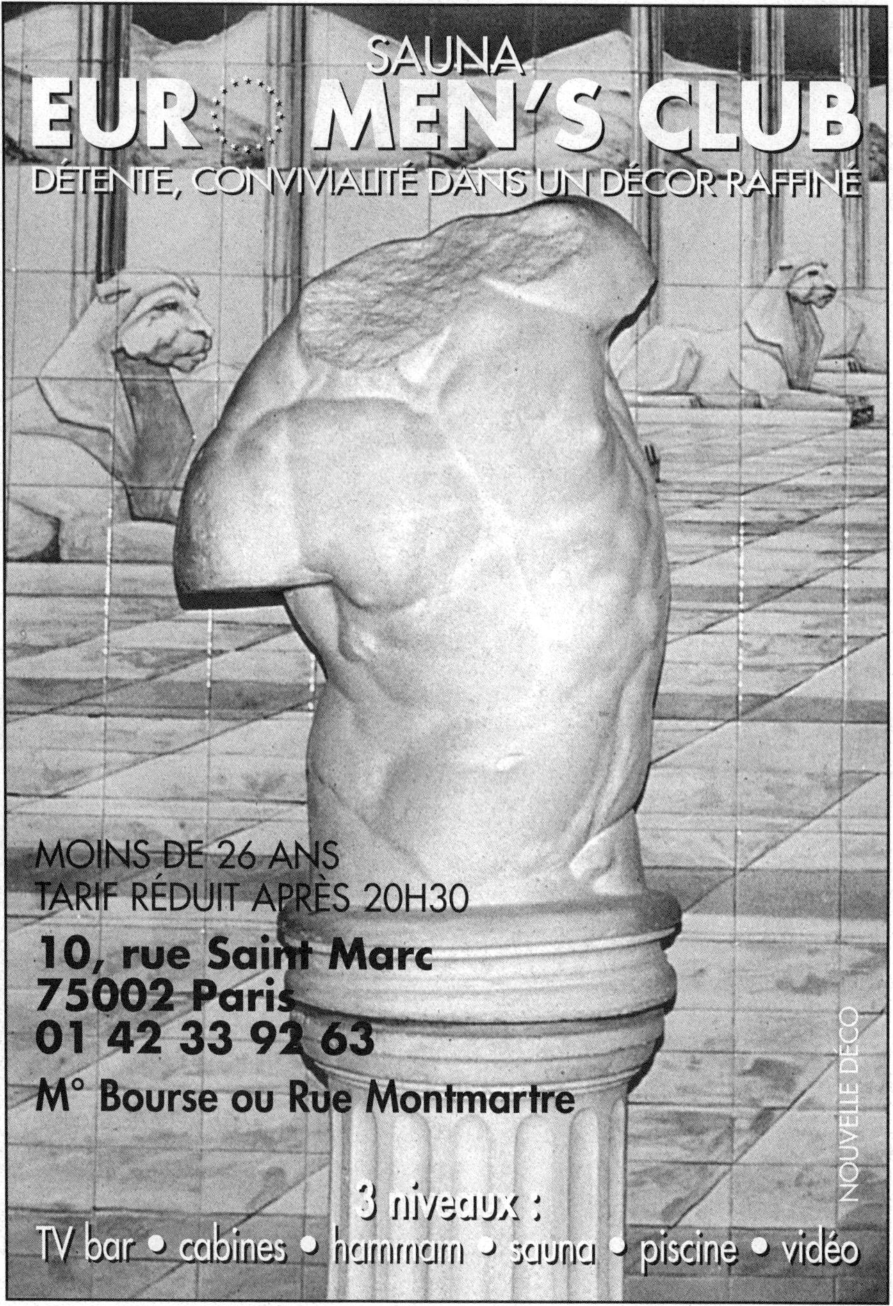
SAUNA
EURO MEN'S CLUB
DÉTENTE, CONVIVIALITÉ DANS UN DÉCOR RAFFINÉ
MOINS DE 26 ANS
TARIF RÉDUIT APRÈS 20H30
10, rue Saint Marc
75002 Paris
01 42 33 92 63
M° Bourse ou Rue Montmartre
NOUVELLE DECO
3 niveaux :
TV bar • cabines • hammam • sauna • piscine • vidéo

KEY WEST

Bains Montansier ☛ Vincennes
Bastille Sauna (AC B g MA msg sa sb sol VS wh WO) 14-24 h
4 Passage Saint Antoine ✉75011 *(M° Ledru-Rollin)*
☎ 01.43.38.07.02
Sign at the entrance door is „BS".
Club Univers Gym (AC b CC DR f G msg p s sa sb sol VS wh WO YG) 12-1, Fri Sat -2 h
20-22 Rue des Bons Enfants ✉75001 *(M° Palais Royal)*
☎ 01.42.61.24.83
Close to the Louvre. 4 theme parties a week. Very popular, young fun crowd.
Euro Men's Club (AC B DR f G lj MA pi sa sb sol VS wh) Mon-Sun 12-23 h
10 Rue Saint-Marc ✉75002 *(M° Bourse/Rue Montmartre)*
☎ 01.42.33.92.63
IDM Sauna (b G sa sb vs
4 Rue du Faubooourg ✉75009 ☎ 01.45.23.10.03
Key West (b f G P sa sb sol VS WO) 12-1, Fri Sat -2 h
141 Rue Lafayette ✉75010 *(M° Gare du Nord)*
☎ 01.45.26.31.74
Giant jacuzzi gym. CYBEX equipment. Big, beautiful and popular. New aquarium and giant TV screen. For members only.
King Sauna Night & Day (AC b DR f G MG P sa sb VS) 13-7 h
21 Rue Bridaine ✉75017 *(M° Rome)* ☎ 01.42.94.19.10
Mandala. Le (B f G sa sb sol VS wh WO) 12-1, Fri and Sat -6 h
2 Rue Drouot ✉75009 *(M° Richelieu Drouot)* ☎ 01.42.46.60.14
Sauna Mykonos (G MA P sa sol sb VS wh) 12.30-24 h
71 Rue des Martyrs ✉75018 *(M° Pigalle)* ☎ 01.42.52.15.46
For members only.

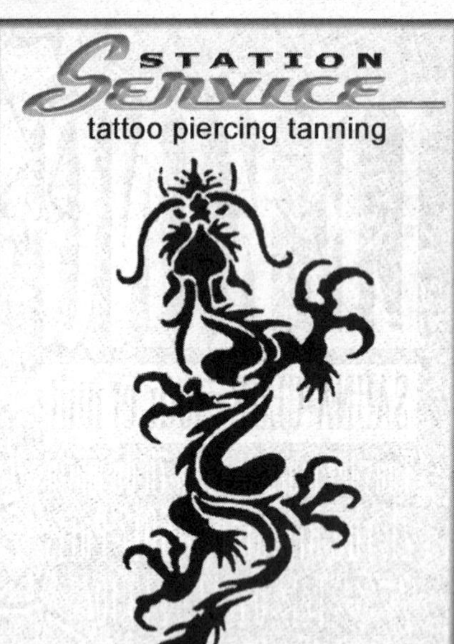

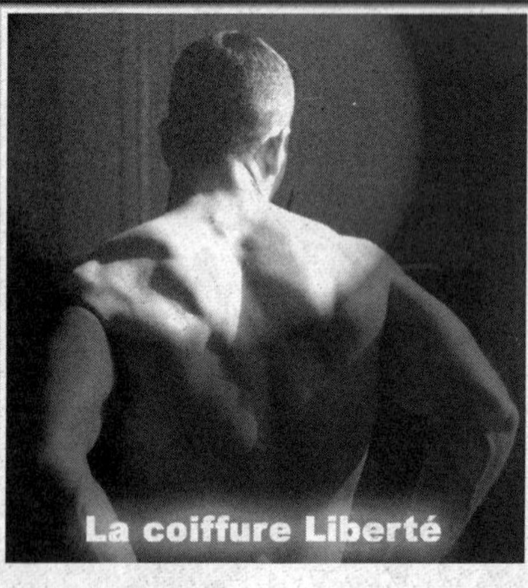

Tilt Institut (AC B f g MA sa VS) 16-7 h
41 Rue Sainte Anne ✉75001 *(M° Pyramides)*
☎ 01.42.96.07.43
Top Sauna (G MA sa VS) 11-2, Sun 12-0 h
117 Rue Saint Denis ✉75001 ☎ 01.40.13.09.26
Sauna and sex shop.

FITNESSTUDIOS

Body-Gym (g WO) 8-21.30, Sat 9-19, Sun 10-14 h
157 Faubourg Saint-Antoine ✉75012 *(M° Faidherbe-Chaligny)*
☎ 01.43.73.77.88
Body-building, aerobic, stretching etc.
Club Auteuil (B f g sa WO) 8-22 h
11 Rue Chanez ✉75016 ☎ 01.46.51.88.18
IDM (B DR f G P sa sb sol VS WO YG) 12-1, Fri Sat -2 h
4 Rue du Faubourg Montmartre ✉75009 ☎ 01.45.23.10.03
Body building studio. Membrers only.
Ken Club (B F g sa sb wh WO) Mon, Wed, Fri 9.30-21, Tue Thu 7.30-23, WE 9.30-18 h
100 Avenue du Président Kennedy ✉75016 ☎ 01.46.47.41.41

BODY & BEAUTY SHOPS

Abraxas (AC CC glm MA) 12-22 h
Rue Saint Merri ✉75009 ☎ 01.48.04.33.55
Tatoos and piercing.

Body MEN Village (G) 12-22 h
25 Rue du Temple ✉75004 *(M° Hôtel de Ville)*
☎ 01.42.72.17.16
Esthetique.

City looks salon (CC g)
23 Rue aux Ours ☎ 01.42.72.29.24

Rock-Hair 10-19 h, closed Sun
7 Boulevard Beaumarchais ✉75004 *(M° Bastille)*
☎ 01.42.77.01.97
Beauty and barber shop.

Space Hair Coiffure
10 Rue Rambuteau ✉75004 ☎ 01.48.87.28.51

Station Service pour la Peau (AC glm MA sol) 10-21, Sat 11-20 h, closed on Sun
60 Rue Quincampoix ✉75004 ☎ 01.48.04.35.34
Solarium, tatoos, piercing.

BOOK SHOPS

Funambule. Le 16-19 h, closed Sun Mon
48 Rue Jean-Pierre Timbaud ✉75011 *(M° Parmentier)*
☎ 01.48.06.74.94
Gay books and publications.

Mots à la Bouche. Les (A CC GLM) Mon-Sat 11-23, Sun 14-20 h
6 Rue Sainte-Croix-de-la-Bretonnerie ✉75004 *(M° Hôtel-de-Ville)*
☎ 01.42.78.88.30 Fax: 01.42.78.36.41
Paris' famous gay bookshop with the largest stock of gay literature. Ask for catalogue./Librairie gaie réputée de Paris où l'on trouve le plus grand choix de livres gais.

Pause Lecture (A CC GLM) Mon-Sat 11-24, Sun 13-24 h
61 Rue Quincampoix ✉75004 *(near Les Halles)*
☎ 01.44.61.95.06 Fax: 01.44.61.95.05
New gay bookshop and gallery.

DECORATION

Persona Grata (glm) 11-20 h
21 Rue Bourg-Tibourg ✉75004 *(M° Hotel de Ville)*
☎ 01.42.72.97.77
Home decoration & cadeaux.

FASHION SHOPS

Aux Nuits de Salem (CC g)
13 Rue Commines ✉75003 *(M° Filles du Calvaire)*
☎ 01.42.78.12.01 Fax: 01.42.78.20.24
Farces et Attrapes./Costume and disguise rental.

Boutique et les Hommes. La (CC glm) 11-14.30, 16-20 h, closed Sun
88 Rue des Dames ✉75017 *(M° Rome)* ☎ 01.42.93.10.21
Clothes and gifts.

Boys' Zone (glm MA) 12-20 h
25 Rue Vieille du Temple ✉75004 *(M° Hôtel de Ville)*
☎ 01.48.87.52.54
Men's fashion.

Boy'z Bazaar (CC G) 12-24 h
5 Rue Sainte Croix de la Bretonnerie ✉75004 *(M° Hotel de Ville)*
☎ 01.42.71.94.00
Clothes, leather and accessories for men.

Boy'z Bazaar N°2 Videostore (CC G VS) 14-22, Fri Sat 13-23 h
38 Rue Sainte Croix de la Bretonnerie ✉75004
☎ 01.42.71.80.34

Eric Filliat (glm) closed Sun
24 Rue Vieille du Temple ✉75004 *(M° Hotel de Ville)*
☎ 01.42.74.72.79
Men's fashion.

Eric Filliat 11-19.30 h, closed Sun
39 Rue des Lombards ✉75001 ☎ 01.42.33.72.43
Men's fashion.

Factory's (CC G) 12-20, Fri Sat -22 h
3 Rue Sainte Croix de la Bretonnerie ✉75004 *(M° Hotel de Ville)*
☎ 01.48.87.29.10
Fashion and accessories for gay men.

Free Lance Homme 11-19, Sun 14-19 h
16 Rue Bourg-Tibourg ✉75004 *(M° Hotel de Ville)*
☎ 01.42.77.01.55
Shoes.

Phylea (g lj) 10.30-20 h, closed Sun
61 Rue Quincampoix ✉75004 *(M° Rambuteau)*
☎ 01.42.76.01.80
Fantasy fashion and lingerie for shows and parties. Plastic, leather, latex and metal.

Sweetman (AC glm MA) 11-19.30 h, closed Sun
36 Boulevard Sébastopol ✉75004 ☎ 01.42.77.55.00

GALLERIES

Stéphane Plassier (glm) 12-20, Sat 14-22 h
8 rue du Trésor ✉75004 *(M° Hotel de Ville)* ☎ 01.40.29.10.22

GIFT & PRIDE SHOPS

Bô (g) 11-20.30, Sun 14-20 h
8 rue St. Merri ✉75004 ☎ 01.42.72.84.64
Gifts and decoration for table and home.

Dom (Glm)
21 rue Sainte Croix de la Bretonnerie ✉75004 *(M° Hotel de Ville)*
☎ 01.42.71.08.00
Cadeaux and decoration.

NEWS STANDS

Kiosque Colisée (g)
44 Avenue des Champs-Elysées ✉75008 *(M° Franklin-Roosevelt)*

Kiosque des Amis (g MA) 10-22.30 h
29 Boulevard des Italiens ✉75009 *(M° Opéra)*
Big selection of gay magazines plus the usual newspapers, including those in foreign languages. Friendly owner gives latest information about bars and restaurants to clients.

Kiosque des Deux-Magots (g)
170 Boulevard Saint-Germain ✉75006 *(M° Saint-Germain-des-Près)*

Kiosque Forum (CC glm) Sun-Thu 7-22, Fri Sat -24 h
10 Rue Pierre Lescot ✉75001 *(M° Châtelet/Les Halles)*
☎ 01.40.26.37.04
International press news stand and a veritable window on the world of gay magazines & newspapers both French and foreign. In the heart of gay Paris. Opposite the Metro/RER.

Kiosque Hippopotamus (g)
1 Boulevard des Capucines ✉75002 *(M° Opéra)*

Kiosque Rennes Montparnasse (G) 7-22 h
6 Place du 18-Juin-1940 ✉75006

Kiosque Saint-Michel (g)
21 Boulevard Saint-Michel ✉75006 *(M° Cluny/La Sorbonne)*

Kiosque 21 (g)
21 Boulevard Montmartre ✉75002 *(M° Rue Montmartre)*

PHARMACIES

Pharmacie du Village (CC GLM) 8.30-20.30 h, closed Sun
26 Rue du Temple ✉75004 ☎ 01.42.72.60.72

PR & PHOTOGRAPHY SERVICES

Comme des Anges Agency
B.P. 30 ✉75860 ☎ 01.42.26.10.15
The only French gay publicity and model agency.

Ory's Image (CC g)
23 Boulevard Poissonière ✉75002 ☎ 01.42.33.05.30
Photographic laboratory.

TRAVEL & TRANSPORT

Euro Gays Travel (CC GLM MA) Mon-Fri 10-13.30 14.30-19, Sat 11-17 h
23 Rue Bourg Tibourg ✉75004 *(2nd floor)* ☎ 01.48.87.37.77
Fax: 01.48.87.39.99 Email: eurogays@aol.com
The biggest gay travel agent in France. Write for brochure.

Voyages de Martine. Les (glm)
247 Avenue Daumesnil ✉75012 ☎ 01.43.45.75.54
Fax: 01.43.40.45.24

VIDEO SHOPS

Boutique Man (G) 11-19 h, closed Mon Sun
41 Rue Volta ✉75003 *(M° Arts & Metiers)* ☎ 01.42.78.59.29

Boy'z Bazaar (CC Glm VS) 15-24 h
38 Rue Sainte Croix de la Bretonnerie ✉75004 *(M° Hotel de Ville)*
☎ 01.42.71.80.34
Videostore. The best gay videos to rent, in the Marais.

French Art (AC CC G VS) 9.30-19 h, closed Sun
64 Rue de Rome ✉75008 *(M° Rome)* ☎ 01.45.22.57.35
Cadinot's famous shop!

Station Vidéo (g VS) 10-19.30 h
56 Boulevard Magenta ✉75010 *(M° Gare de l'Est)*
☎ 01.43.79.82.82

Talisman (G VS) 10-19 h, closed Sun
1 Rue de l'Aqueduc ✉75010 *(M° Gare-du-Nord)*
☎ 01.40.36.19.18

HOTELS

Agora (bf glm H)
7 Rue de la Cossonnerie ✉75001 *(M° Châtelet/Les Halles)*
☎ 01.42.33.46.02
Centrally located. 40 min to the airport. Rooms with priv. bath and tel.

Hôtel Acacias (g H)
20 Rue du Temple ✉75004 ☎ 01.48.87.07.70

Hôtel Beaumarchais (AC bf CC glm H)
3 Rue Oberkampf ✉75011 *(M° Filles du Calvaire/Oberkampf)*
☎ 01.53.36.86.86 Fax: 01.43.38.32.86
Close to the Marais and the Bastille. All rooms with bath/shower and WC, satellite TV.

Hôtel Central Marais (B G H)
33 Rue Vieille-du-Temple ✉75004 *(M° Hôtel-de-Ville)*
☎ 01.48.87.56.08 Fax: 01.42.77.06.27
The only gay hotel in Paris.

Hôtel des Batignolles (bf glm H)
26-28 Rue des Batignolles ✉75017 *(M° Rome)*
☎ 01.43.87.70.40
Bath and WC on each floor.

Hôtel des Nations (bf CC glm H MA)
54 Rue Monge ✉75005 *(M° Place Monge)* ☎ 01.43.26.45.24
Fax: 01.46.34.00.13 Email: hoteldesnations@compuserve.com
Homepage: http://www.hoteldesnations.com
Quote Spartacus for special reduced rates.

Hôtel d'Estrées (B bf CC glm H MA OS)
2bis Cité Pigalle ✉75009 ☎ 01.48.74.39.22
Fax: 01.45.96.04.09

Hôtel Louvre-Richelieu (bf CC glm H)
51 Rue de Richelieu ✉75001 ☎ 01.42.97.46.20
Fax: 01.47.03.94.13 Email: joelg111@club.internet.fr

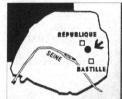

RÉPUBLIQUE
SEINE
BASTILLE

Au cœur de Paris, à deux pas du Marais et de la place de la Bastille, un tout nouvel hôtel.

In the very heart of Paris, close to the Marais and Bastille Square, a brand new hotel.

HÔTEL BEAUMARCHAIS

3 rue Oberkampf 75011 Paris
Tél : 01 53 36 86 86
Fax : 01 43 38 32 86

Métro : Filles du Calvaire ou/or Oberkampf Bus : n° 96 • 20 • 63

Hôtel Moderne du Temple (bf CC glm H)
3 Rue d'Aix ✉75010 *(M° Goncourt/Republique)*
☎ 01.42.08.09.04 FAX 01.42.41.72.17
Email: vlado-flundarek@libertysurf.fr

Hôtel Mondia (bf CC glm H MA)
22 Rue du Grand Prieuré ✉75011 ☎ 01.47.00.93.44
Fax: 01.43.38.66.14 Email: hotel.mondia@wanadoo.fr

Louxor (bf CC g H)
4 Rue Taylor, ✉75010 *(M° République)* ☎ 01.42.08.23.91
Fax: 01.42.08.03.30 Email: hotel.louxor@wanadoo.fr
All rooms with bath/shower and WC, satellite TV and phone.

Royal Aboukir (bf CC g H)
106 Rue d'Aboukir ✉75002 *(M° Sentier)* ☎ 01.42.33.95.04
Fax: 01.42.33.05.79
Rooms with bath/WC, phone, mini-bar, and TV.

Saint-Hubert. Le (B bf CC glm H)
27 Rue Traversière ✉75012 ☎ 01.43.43.39.16
Fax: 01.43.43.35.32
Rooms with phone, bathroom, WC and TV.

55 Guest House. Le (bf g H)
55 Avenue Reille ✉75014 ☎ 01.45.89.91.82
Fax: 01.45.89.91.83
Very exclusive apartments in art déco style.

APARTMENTS

Paris Marais Studio Guesthouse (GLM H)
☎ 01.42.77.62.40 Email: parismarais@hotmail.com
A large choice of studios in the centre of Paris to rent for a stay of three days or more. Call for more information.

PRIVATE ACCOMODATION

Enjoy Bed & Breakfast (bf G H MA YG) 16:30-21 h
☎ +49 (30) 215 1666 Fax: +49 (30) 217 52219
Email: Info@ebab.com Homepage: www.ebab.com
Price 25 Euro. Accommodation sharing agency. All with shower & bf.

Vacational Rental
☎ 01.45.59.07.93 USA ☎ +1.41.52.55.82.70

GENERAL GROUPS

Act Up Paris 12-17 h
45 Rue de Sedaine ☎ 01.49.29.44.75 Fax: 01.48.06.16.74
Email: actup@actup.org
Activist Association fighting AIDS and discrimination. Call for more info.

Atitud-inn (G H NU OS sa)
129 Rue Faubourg St.Antoine ✉75011 ☎ 01.43.46.60.83
Homepage: http://www.atitud-inn.com
Association for weekends and holidays in the country.

GBH (b f glm MA N p s sa VS WO YG) 17-24 h
20 bis Rue Henri Martin, Ivry-sur-Seine ✉94200 *(M° Léo Lagrange-Ligne 7)* ☎ 01.46.70.28.28 Fax: 01.46.70.08.29
Email: centreGBH@aol.com
Centre de convivialité.

Juristes gais. Les
B.P. 240 ✉75765 ☎ 01.46.31.24.06

Lumière et Justice
32 Rue Berzélius ✉75017 ☎ 01.42.26.70.48

MAG-Jeunes Gais et Lesbiennes
B.P. 48 ✉75521 ☎ 01.49.29.15.91 Fax: 01.43.14.03.18
Homepage: http://www.starnet.fr/homepages/iria/mag
Meeting „accueil" Thu 18-20 h at CGL, 3 rue Keller.

Mâles Fêteurs. Les (G)
P.B. 234 ✉75524 Paris Cedex 11 Email: jeans501@muenster.de
Homepage: http://www.muenster.de/homepages/Male.html

Santé et Plaisir Gai
B.P. 234 ✉75865 Paris Cedex 19 ☎ 01.42.72.81.82
Organises jack off parties every 3rd Sun 14.45-17 h at „London", 33 Rue des Lombards, 75001 Paris.

SOS-Homophobie Mon-Fri 20-22 h
B.P. 117 ✉75523 ☎ 01.48.06.42.41 Fax: 01.43.47.09.69
Association for the fight against homophobia.

FETISH GROUPS

ASMF Paris
B.P. 2 ✉75965 Paris Cedex 20
Member of ECMC.

M.E.C. - Mecs en caoutchouc
B.P. 19 ✉77191 ☎ 01.64.87.07.92
Association Gay Latex. 15 meetings/year. Publishes a magazine „Plank".

HEALTH GROUPS

Aides Mon-Fri 14-17.30 h
247 rue de Belleville ✉75019 *(Metro Telegraphe)*
☎ 01.44.52.00.00 Fax: 01.44.52.02.01
Homepage: http://home.worldnet.fr/aidesidf/
Help for HIV-positive people.

ARCAT-SIDA
94 Rue Buzenval ✉75020 ☎ 01.44.93.29.29

Association des Artistes contre le SIDA
5 Rue du Bois-de-Boulogne ✉75116 ☎ 01.45.00.53.53

Association des Médecins Gais (AMG) We 18-20, Sat 14-16 h
B.P. 433 ✉7552 ☎ 01.48.05.81.71
Contact for many gay and gay-lesbian health or medical groups. Contact also possible through C.G.L.
Centre de dépistage anonyme et gratuit Mon-Fri 17-18, Sat 9.30-12 h
218 Rue de Belleville ✉75020 ☎ 01.47.97.40.49
CRIPS-Centre Régional d'Information et de Prévention du SIDA Tue-Fri 13-20, Sat 10-17 h
B.P. 53 ✉75755 *(Tour Montparnasse, 12th floor, 33 Avenue du Maine)* ☎ 01.53.80.33.33 Fax: 01.56.80.33.00
CRIPS offers documentation, training and consultation, information, evaluation/assessment, meetings and a newsletter.
Kiosque Info Sida & Toxicomanie
36 Rue Geoffrey l'Asnier ✉75004 *(Also: 6 Rue Dante, 75005 Paris)* ☎ 01.44.78.00.00 Fax: 01.48.04.95.20
Information on AIDS and drug addiction and prevention. Documents, condoms and lubricants free.
Sida Info Droit (SID)
190 Boulevard de Charonne ✉75020 ☎ 01.80.16.36.36
Sida Info Service (SIS)
190 Boulevard de Charonne ✉75020 ☎ 08.00.84.08.00
(Toll-free in France)
Soeurs de la Pérpetuelle Indulgence. Les
3 Rue Saint Jérôme ✉75018 ☎ 01.44.92.06.12
Email: spi.paname@voila.fr
Homepage: http://perso.wanadoo.fr/spi.paname/

RELIGIOUS GROUPS

Beit Haverim Wed 20-22 h
B.P. 375 ✉75526 ☎ 01.40.40.00.71 Fax: 01.42.40.53.11
Email: beit-haverim@yahoo.com
Gay and lesbian jewish group, advice, cultural and social activities organised.
David et Jonathan
92bis Rue de Picpus ✉75012 ☎ 01.43.42.09.49
Mémorial de la Déportation Homosexuelle.
Eglise MCC (CET et CCL)
23 Rue Berzelius ✉75017 ☎ 01.48.05.24.48

SPECIAL INTEREST GROUPS

Choeur Gai International de Paris C.I.G.A.P.
c/o C.G.L., 3, Rue Keller ✉75011
Auditions every Wen. at 19.30 h, Cathédrale Américaine, ave. George V.
Homo Sweet Home - Association des étudiants gays d'Ile de France (YG)
29 Blvd Magenta ✉75010 ☎ 40400030
Gay student association organising different activities. Call for more information.

SPORT GROUPS

Fédération Sportive Gaie et Lesbienne (CGPIF) Fri 17-19 h
B.P. 120 ✉75623 ☎ 01.48.05.55.17 Fax: 01.48.05.55.95
Email: cgpif@cgpif.org
Federation of Paris sports groups.

CRUISING

-Jardin des Tuileries/Quai des Tuileries 75001
-Square de la Tour Saint-Jacques 75004
-Square Sully Morland 75004
-Champs de Mars 75007 (Near the/vers l'Ecole militaire, nights/la nuit)
-Canal Saint-Martin 75010 (M° Jean Jaurès, on the banks/sur les quais)
-Terre-Plein/Parking 75011 (across from/face 44 Boulevard Richard Lenoir. Nights/La nuit)
-Bois de Vincennes 75012 (Sud Rte de la Tourelle autour de parking)
-Nation 75012 (in the centre/sur le terre-plein central)
-Quai 75013 (On the TGB level/Au niveau de la TGB)
-Trocadéro 75016
-Porte Dauphine 75016 (on the side of the Russian embassy/du côté de l'Ambassade de Russie)
-Square des Batignolles 75017
-Parc des Buttes-Chaumont (AYOR) 75019 (roundabout, nights/aux alentours, la nuit)
-Cimetière di Père Lachaise (southern side/côté sud. Tombe Anna de Noailles)
-Place d'Anvers (ayor R) (at night)
-Place du Paraguay/Place du Maréchal de Tassigny (R) (M° Porte Dauphine. At night)
Quai du Canal Saint-Martin (promenade downstairs Quai de Valmy, unter the bridge. M° Jaures)
-Bois de la Verrière (NU) Sunbathing and cruising. 30 minutes south of Paris (M° Massy-Verrières)
-Porte de Maillot (near the monument of De Lattre)
-Gare de l'Est 75010 (near Café Taverne)
-Gare du Nord (in front of platform N° 10)
-Gare Saint-Lazare (level -1, besides Metro exit)

Pau ✉ 64000

BARS

Gowest. Le (A AC B CC G MA p s) 16-2, Sun 18-2 h, closed Tue, Jul-Sep 16-3 h
6 Rue René Fournets ✉64000 ☎ 05.59.27.71.45
Also men's fashion shop.

RESTAURANTS

Aragon. L' (B F NG OS)
18 Boulevard dés Pyrénées ✉64000 ☎ 05.59.27.12.43
French cuisine, nice view.
Etna. L' (b CC F g) 12-14.30, 19-0 h
16 Rue du Château ✉64000 ☎ 05,59.27.77.94
Mermoz. Le (b F g OS) 11-14.30, 18-1, closed Tue & Aug
39 Avenue Jean-Mermoz ✉64000 ☎ 05.59.32.54.19
Menu FF 70-220. French cuisine.

SEX SHOPS/BLUE MOVIES

Kitsch (CC G VS) 14-20 h, closed Sun
13 Cours Bosquet ✉64000 ☎ 05.59.27.68.67

SAUNAS/BATHS

Sauna Eros (AC B DR f G MA P sa sb VS wh) 14-2, Fri Sat -4 h
8 Rue René Fournets ✉64000 *Quartier Hedas* ☎ 05.59.27.48.80
Also a boutique for accessories. Theme evenings.
Sauna le Centaure (B DR G lj MA N p sa sb VS) 13.30-20 h
15 Rue d'Orléans ✉64000 ☎ 05.59.27.30.41
Friendly welcome with free snack./Accueil convivial petit buffet gratuit. Intimate sauna.

HOTELS

Hôtel Restaurant Hervé Garrapit (bf CC F glm H MA OS pi)
Place de la Boiterie ✉40190 *(65 km to the North of Pau, 100 km from Biarritz)* ☎ 05.58.45.20.08
Fax: 05.58.45.34.14 Email: hotelrestauranthervégarrapit@wanadoo.fr Homepage: http://www.ch-demeures.com/garrapit
„Hôtel de charme" and gastronomic restaurant. Luxury rooms. Garden and pool.

HEALTH GROUPS

Centre hospitalier de Pau

17bis Rue E. Guichenne ✉64000 ☎ 05.59.84.13.50
Dispensaire Antivénérien. Centre Haute Rive
145 Avenue Buros ✉64011 ☎ 05.59.92.48.12
HIV testing.

HELP WITH PROBLEMS

Solidarité Positive Meetings: Tue 14.30-16.30, Thu 19-21 h
9 Rue Louis-Barthou ✉6400 ☎ 05,59.27.63.88
Self-help association for people with HIV and AIDS.

CRUISING

-Boulevard Barbanègre
-Cour de la Gare de Marchandises (soldiers!)
-Parc Beaumont
-Parc Nitot
-Place de Verdun
-(P) Souterrain des Halles
-Place Marguerite-Caborde

Périgueux ✉ 24000

DANCECLUBS

An des Roys. L' (AC B CC D GLM lj MA p s TV) Fri, Sat and Holiday Eves 23-5 h
51 Rue Aubarède ✉24000 ☎ 05.53.53.01.58
Sauna under construction.

HEALTH GROUPS

Centre hospitalier Dujaric-de-la-Rivière (Consultations MST)
B.P. 12010 ✉24019 ☎ 05.53.07.70.00
HIV-testing.

CRUISING

-Garden/Jardin de la Tour de Vesone (daytime only/de jour uniquement)
-Garden/Jardin des Arènes (daytime only/de jour uniquement)
-Parc Aristide-Briand (evening/soir)

Pernes Les Fontaines ✉ 84210

HOTELS

Mas La Bonoty (B CC F glm H pi OS)
Chemin de la Boniots ✉84210 ☎ 04.90.61.61.09

Perpignan ✉ 66000

RESTAURANTS

Doña Maria (b F glm MA)
23 Rue Jean Payra ✉66000 ☎ 04.68.35.00.90
French and Catalane cuisine.

SEX SHOPS/BLUE MOVIES

Défi (G lj VS) 9-24 h
10 Avenue Leclerc ✉66000 ☎ 04.68.52.44.25
Also mail order/également vente par correspondance: B.P. 4051, 66000 Cedex.

SAUNAS/BATHS

Aquatic Club. L' (AC CC G MA pi sa sb VS wh) 15-22 h
13 Rue Rouget de l'Isle ✉66000 ☎ 04.68.34.48.50
B H (DR G sa sb VS wh WO) 12-24 h
1 Quater Rue G. Buffon ✉66000 *Near the station.*
☎ 68.55.10.11

BOOK SHOPS

Futur Antérieur. Le (CC G) 9-12, 14-19 h, closed Sun Mon
8 Rue du Théatre ✉66000 ☎ 04.68.34.20.45
Gay bookshop/librairie gaie.

HEALTH GROUPS

Dispensaire antivénérien
25 Rue de la Petite-Monnaie ✉66000 ☎ 04.68.66.46.89
HIV-testing.

CRUISING

-Passage Rive-Gauche
-Place Bistan
-Route de Canet (dangerous in the evening!/dangeureux le soir!)

Perrignier ✉ 74550

BARS

Ram Dam. Le (AC B CC D E glm MA OS p WE) Fri Sat 22-5 h
Route des Bons-Saint-Didier ✉74550 ☎ 04.50.72.40.43

Perros-Guirec ✉ 22700

SWIMMING

-Beach of/Plage de Testraou (on summernights/les soirs d'été)

CRUISING

-Town hall/Hôtel de ville (by day/de jour)

Pinet ✉ 34850

BARS

Echiquier. L' (AC B D G p) Fri Sat
Domaine de Saint-Jean des Sources ✉34850 ☎ 04.67.77.17.51

Plan-de-la Tour ✉ 83120

SWIMMING

-The beach/La plage

Plouarzel ✉ 29229

SWIMMING

-Plage/beach Trezien

Plouescat ✉ 29221

SWIMMING

-Plage/beach Keremna (2 km → Treflez)

Plouharnel ✉ 56640

SWIMMING

-Plage/beach d'Erdeven

Poissy ✉ 78300

HEALTH GROUPS

CP de médecine préventive
13 Rue Jacob-Courant ✉78300 ☎ 01.30.74.15.38

CRUISING

-Parc Messonier

Poitiers ✉ 86000

BARS

George Sand Club (AC B D DR Glm MA P S SNU VS YG) 22-4, Fri- Sat -5 h
25 Rue Saint-Pierre-le-Puellier ✉86000 *(behind the Town Hall)*
☎ 05.49.55.91.58

SAUNAS/BATHS

George Sand Sauna (AC b G OS pi sa sb sol VS wh WO) 14-24 h
56 Boulevard Pont Achard ☎ 05.49.41.77.67
Sauna with pool and garden.

HEALTH GROUPS

Aides Poiteau-Charentes B.P. 467 ✉86012 ☎ 05.49.42.45.45

Centre hospitalier Service des maladies infectieuses ✉86000 ☎ 05.49.44.39.05
HIV-testing.

CRUISING

-Avenue du Recteur-Pineau (campus Rabelais)
-Garden/Jardin de la Villette (evening/le soir)
-Garden/Jardin des Coloniaux (evening/le soir)
-Parc de Blossac

Pont-Audemer ✉ 27500

HOTELS

Cloches de Corneville. Les (B bf CC F glm H lj MA OS) closed Mon lunch & Nov-Mar
Route de Rouens ✉27500 *(Corneville-sur-Risle)* ☎ 02.32.57.01.04
Fax: 02.32.57.10.96
Located 35 km from Honfleur, Rouen and Le Havre.

Pontcarre ✉ 77135

CRUISING

-P Forêt d'Armainvilliers

Pont-Croix ✉ 29122

SWIMMING

-Beuzec-Cap-Sizun (NU) (on the other side of the great beach which is a bit difficult to reach, go across the rocks or look for the little hidden path and find the cosy nudist beach in one of the bights/de l'autre côté de la grande plage; accès dificile par les rochers ou par un passage sur une route de terre; superbe petite plage naturiste dans une crique)

CRUISING

-Beside the road to Audierne/Chemin d'Audierne (on the seaside; in summer the main gay orgy centre of the whole region, sometimes even in winter/bord de mer; haut lieu d'orgie en été et parfois même en hiver)

Pont-d'Ain ✉ 01160

CRUISING

-Place des Marronniers
-Market Place/Place du marché
-Along the riverside/Le long des quais (in the evening)

Pont-de-Fillinges ✉ 74250

DANCECLUBS

Athénée. L' (B D G STV) Fri-Sat 23-5, Sun 19-1.30 h
Route de Boëge ✉74250 *(à 15 km de Genève)*
☎ 04.50.36.42.87

Pont-L'Abbé ✉ 29120

BARS

Bar Gavroche (B g) 17-24 h, closed Mon
46 Rue Victor-Hugo ✉29120 ☎ 02.98.82.32.74

SWIMMING

-Beach of/plage de Tréguennec (NU) (between/entre Tronoen et Tréguennec)

Port-la-Nouvelle ✉ 11210

SWIMMING

-Beach/Plage des Montilles (NU) (take road D 709, turn left and follow the rails for 1 km)

Port-Vendres ✉ 66660

SWIMMING

-Beach of l'Ollioulle (B)

Privas ✉ 07000

HEALTH GROUPS

Centre hospitalier des Privas. Service de médécine
Avenue Pasteur, B.P. 1623 ✉07000 ☎ 04.75.64.11.77
HIV testing.

Puteaux ✉ 92800

CRUISING

-La Défense (shopping mall/centre commercial and (P))

Quend-Plage ✉ 80120

CRUISING

-In the dunes of the beach/dans les dunes de la plage

Quimper ✉ 29000

BARS

Carpe Diem (A B glm) Tue-Sun 18-1 h, closed Mon
54bis Avenue de la Libération ✉29000 ☎ 02.98.90.00.21

CAFÉS

Coffee Shop (AC B CC DR GLM MA OS p VS) 17-1 h
26 Rue du Frout ✉29000 ☎ 02.98.95.43.30
Theme evenings.

SEX SHOPS/BLUE MOVIES

Duo Shop (AC CC g MA VS) Mon-Sat 10-1 h
14 Rue de Concarneau ✉29000 *(Near the station)*

HEALTH GROUPS

Centre hospitalier Laennec
Avenue Y.-Theopot ✉29000 ☎ 02.98.90.30.30

CRUISING

-Keradennec (forest/bois)
-Public garden of the theatre/Jardin public du théâtre
-Kermoysan (shopping centre in the city/allée du centre commercial)
-(P) at the Glacière (close to the footbridge/ près de la passerelle)
-Place de La-Tour-d'Auvergne
-Place de la Tourbie (place de l'Ancien-Champ-de-Foire)
-Place de la gare/Station square
-Place du Guéodet

Ramatuelle ✉ 83350

BARS

CoCo Beach
Route de l'Epi ✉83350 ☎ 04.94.79.83.25
Beach bar in summer/Bar du plage en été.

RESTAURANTS

Aqua Club (B F g) 10-20.30, Oct-Apr Sat-Mon 10-17 h
Pampelonne Ramatuelle ✉83350 ☎ 04.94.79.84.35

SWIMMING

-La Bastide Blanche (G NU) (between/entre Escalet & Pointe de la Douane)
-Baie de Pampelone

Rambouillet ✉ 78120

CRUISING

-Etang de coupe-garage (Route de Saint-Léger, afternoons)

Reims ✉ 51100

DANCECLUBS

Lilas Club. Les (B D G MA p s VS W) 23-4 h, closed 15 days in August
75 Rue de Courcelles ✉51100 ☎ 03.26.47.02.81
A video bar and a discotheque.

HEALTH GROUPS

Hôpital Sébastopol Service de dermatologie
48 Rue de Sébastopol ✉51100 ☎ 03.26.40.79.97
HIV-testing.

CRUISING

-Low promenades/Basses Promenades (in front of the railway station/face à la gare)
-Place Drouet-d'Erlons
-Railway station/Gare SNCF (opposite facilities/tasses en face)
-Parc Léo-Lagrange (in front of the stadium; all day, esp. sat sun morning/face au stade; la journée surtout; samedi et dimanche matin)
-Place du Boulingrin (facilities close to the monument tributing to deads/tasses près du monument aux morts)

Remiremont ✉ 88200

CRUISING

-Promenade du calvaire

Remoulins ✉ 30210

SWIMMING

-Gorges du Gardon
-Beach of Collias

Rennes ✉ 35000

GAY INFO

Minitel: 3615 BOB
Minitel: 3615 ALLOGAY

BARS

Bernique Hurlante. La (B CC glm MA) 16-1 h, closed Sun & 14 Jul-10 Aug
40 Rue de St.Malo ✉35000 *(Near Place St. Anne)*
☎ 02.99.38.70.09
Library next to the bar where you can buy, borrow or consult over 1500 gay books.
Bon Accord. Le (B CC f GLM MA S) 16-1 h
45 Rue Duhamel ✉35000
Carpe Diem. Le (B f glm YG) 11-1 h, closed Mon
21 Boulevard de Chezy ✉35000
Chat Bleu. Le (B DR glm MA VS) 17-1 h
36 bis Rue du Pont-des-Loges ✉35000 ☎ 02.99.31.86.47
Underground with darkroom and videos/Sous-sol salon avec darkroom, vidéos.

DANCECLUBS

Batchi. Le (B D GLM) 23-5 h, closed Mon
35 Rue Vasselot ✉35000 ☎ 02.99.79.62.27

SAUNAS/BATHS

Sauna California (AC b CC DR G MA sa sb sol VS wh WO) 13-22.30, Wed Sat -1h
7 Rue de Léon ✉35000 ☎ 02.99.31.59.81

HEALTH GROUPS

Centre hospitalier R. Pontchaillou Bloc de urgences
2 Rue Henri-Le-Guilloux ☎ 02.99.28.43.02
HIV testing.

RELIGIOUS GROUPS

David et Jonathan
B.P. 3905 ✉35039
Gay Christians/homosexuels chrétiens.

CRUISING

-Le Champ de Mars (roundabout/autour de la Salle omnisports)
-Place des Lices (WC des Halles)
-A Mi-Forêt
-Le Contour de la Motte (square et WC)
-Boulevard Magenta (square and WC near the ex police station/près de l'ex-commissariat)
-Place Le Bastard
-Boulevard Magenta
-Le Thabor (jardin botanique/botanic garden)
-Sauna municipal de la piscine
-Place du Marché/Market Place
-Rue Toullier

Riec-sur-Belon ✉ 29340

GUEST HOUSES

Ferme de Pen-Prat - Gîte d'étape (bf g lj H MA OS)
✉29340 *15 km from Quimperlé. Bus: Quimperlé-Quimper.*
☎ 98.06.46.89
Typical farm, bring your own sleeping bag. Leather appreciated (ask Jean-Bernard for more information).

Rochefort ✉ 17300

DANCECLUBS

Cage. La (B D GLM MA p TV) Fri-Sun 23.30-5 h
34 Rue Denfert Rochereau ✉17300 *(Opposite to/En face du Parking du Cour Roy-Bry)* ☎ 05.46.87.01.30

SEX SHOPS/BLUE MOVIES

Sex-Shop (AC glm VS) 9.30-12, 14.30-20 h, closed Sun, Mon morning
13 Rue Cochon du Vivier ✉17300 ☎ 05.46.99.93.63

CRUISING

-Monument Pierre-Loti
-L'ex-Jardin de la Marine (after/après 22 h, stop between/entre Rochefort-BA 721)

Rodez ✉ 12000

HEALTH GROUPS

Dispensaire
Rue de Paraire ✉12000 *PO Box 12 16* ☎ 05.65.68.60.83
HIV-testing.

CRUISING

-Bus station/station de bus (by day/le jour)
-Place Foch

Romans-sur-Isère ✉ 26100

RESTAURANTS

Charrette. La (B F g s) 11-2 h, closed Sun
Route de Grenoble ✉26100 ☎ 04.75.02.04.25

CRUISING

-Square Marcel-Carné
-Place du Champ-de-Mars
-Place Jules-Nadi
-Quais de l'Isère

Romilly-sur-Seine ✉ 10100

CRUISING

-Parc de la Berchère

Romorantin-Lanthenay ✉ 41200

CRUISING

-Square Ferdinand-Buisson

Roquebrune-Cap-Martin ✉ 61907

SWIMMING

-Beach at the old castle ruin/plage près de la ruine du vieux château (near railway station, take Rue de la Gare)
-Rocks/rochers de Cap-Martin (behind the big wall/derrière la grande bâtisse)

Roscoff ✉ 29211

SWIMMING

-Tourelle Marie-Stuart (at the harbour, in the evening/au port, le soir)
-Plage de Sainte-Anne-la-Palue (in the/dans les dunes)

Roubaix ✉ 59100

CRUISING

-Avenue Le-Nôtre (behind the Barbieux park in the groves/derrière le parc Barbieux, dans les bosquets)

Rouen ✉ 76000

GAY INFO

Minitel:
-3615 BOB
-3615 ALLOGAY
-3615 GPH

BARS

Bloc House (A B CC GLM MA p s VS) 19-2 h, closed on Sun
138 Rue Beauvoisine ✉76000 *(M° Beauvoisine)*
☎ 02.35.07.71.97
Theme parties with DJ.
XXL Bar (B CC d DR G MA p SNU VS YG) 22-4 h, closed Sun Mon
25-27 Rue de la Savonnerie ✉76000 *(Near the cathedral)*
☎ 02.35.88.84.00
Monthly theme parties.

DANCECLUBS

Opium (AC B CC D Glm LJ p S SNU STV W YG) Fri-Sun 23-5 h
2 Rue Malherbe ✉76100 *(south bank of the river)*
☎ 02.35.03.29.36
Sun transvestite show, Fri male striptease.

RESTAURANTS

Bougainvillier. Le (CC F MA) 12-14.30, 19-22.30 h, Sun afternoon closed
35 Rue Percière ✉76000 *(M° Palais de Justice)*
☎ 02.35.07.73.32
Gourmandine (b F g) 11-18, Fri Sat Sun 11-23 h
236 Rue Martainville ✉76000 ☎ 02.35.71.95.13
Closed at Christmas.
Molière. Le (B bf F glm) 7.30-20 h, closed Sun
30 Rue des Augustins ✉76000 ☎ 02.35.70.76.11

SAUNAS/BATHS

Square. Le (A B DR g MA p sa VS) 13-20, closed Sun
39 Rue St.Nicolas ✉76000 *(Beetween town hall and cathedral)*
☎ 02.35.15.58.05
Sauna and videos.

Trois Colonnes. Les (B DR f MA sa sb VS WO) 14-22, Tue Fri Sat -24 h
4 Impasse des Hauts Mariages ✉76000 *(M° Hôtel de Ville, Quartier St. Maclou)* ☎ 02.32.08.40.66
Sauna on two levels.
8. Le (B G sa sol VS) 14-23 h
8 Place Saint-Amant ✉76000 ☎ 16/02.35.15.06.29

CONDOM SHOPS

Halloween (CC G MA)
10 Rue St. Nicolas ✉76000
Boutique specialising in condoms and men's underwear. Also clothes and accessories. Quote SPARTACUS for a discount.

HOTELS

Hôtel des Carmes (bf CC g H)
33 Place des Carmes ✉76000 *(between cathedral and town hall)* ☎ 02.35.71.92.31 Fax: 02.35.71.76.96
Quote SPARTACUS for special rates.

HEALTH GROUPS

Hôpital Charles-Nicole Service de vénérologie
✉76000 ☎ 02.35.08.80.40
HIV-testing.

RELIGIOUS GROUPS

David et Jonathan
B.P. 561 ✉76006
Gay christians/homos chrétiens.

CRUISING

-Woods nearby Novotel (next to Faculté de Médicine, at the southern exit of the city in direction Paris)
-Square Verdrel and rue du Baillage (right in the middle of the city, near rue Jeanne d'Arc)
-Left side of the Seine river/Rive gauche de la Seine (near Jeanne d'Arc bridge/près du Pont Jeaanne d'Arc)
-[P] Aire parking de Bord
-[P] Robert-le-Diable
-Forêt de la Londe
-Forêt-Verte
-Port maritime
-Stade Saint-Exupéry
-Rue Henri-Dumont

Royan ✉ 17200

RESTAURANTS

Anjou Restaurant. L' (B CC F g) 9-24 h, closed Wed
19 Rue Font de Chevre ✉17200 ☎ 05.46.05.09.49

SWIMMING

-La Côte sauvage/Plage de la Bouverie
-Plage de la Palmyre
-Plage de la Grande Côte
-At the beach/à la plage Royan
-At the beach/à la plage de la Cèpe

Rue ✉ 80120

SWIMMING

-Dunes (1 km south of Quend-Plage)

Saintes ✉ 17100

BARS

Salamandre. La (B CC g MA) 18-2 h
11 Quai de la République ✉17100 ☎ 05.46.74.20.33

DANCECLUBS

Grillon. Le (AC CC D E GLM lj MG P W WE) Thu-Sun 23-5, summer: Tue-Sun 23-5 h
12 Rue Pierre Schoeffer, Coucoury ✉17100 ☎ 05.46.74.66.98

RESTAURANTS

Borsalino. Le (b F g) 11.45-15, 18.45-23 h
12 Cours National ✉17100 ☎ 05.46.74.31.78

SEX SHOPS/BLUE MOVIES

Sex-Shop (AC CC glm MA VS) 10-12 14-19.15 h, closed Sun & holidays
9-10 Quai de la République ✉17100 ☎ 05.46.74.51.72
Latest gay videos.

HOTELS

Hôtel Climat de France (bf CC F glm H OS pi)
Route de Royan ✉17100 *(35 km from the beach, 5 min from the center of town)* ☎ 05.46.97.20.40 Fax: 05.46.92.22.54
Hotel-restaurant with an open-air pool in summer, heated and covered in winter.

CRUISING

-Arc de Triomphe
-Palais de Justice
-Charente (at the border/au bord)

Salin de Giraud ✉ 13129

SWIMMING

- Beach (G NU)

Sallanches ✉ 74700

CRUISING

-Place Grenelle

Salon-de-Provence ✉ 13300

CRUISING

-Place Morgan (market-place/place du marché)
-Monument Jean-Moulin (RN 113, direction Avignon)
-Aire de Senas (on the highway/sur l'autoroute)

Sandillon ✉ 45640

SWIMMING

-Beach (very popular in summer)

Sartilly ✉ 50530

SWIMMING

-Genets-Dragery

Saumur ✉ 49400

CRUISING

-Square Verdun (behind the public library/derrière la bibliothèque municipale)

Saverne ✉ 67700

CRUISING

-Château des Rohan

Savines-le-Lac ✉ 05160

CRUISING

-Round the sea/autour du lac
-Camping (forest/fôret de Boscodon)

Savonnières

GUEST HOUSES

Prieuré de Granges (bf H NG OS pi)
15 rue de Fontaine ✉37510 ☎ 02.47.50.09.67
Fax: 02.47.50.06.43 Email: salmon.eric@wanadoo.fr
Guest house with pool. Close to Tours.

Saxel ✉ 74420

RESTAURANTS

Tétras. Le (B F g)
Super-Saxel ✉74420 ☎ 04.50.39.00.70

Sazaret ✉ 03390

CAMPING

Petite Valette. La (bf DR F glm H MA msg OS) Apr-Oct
La Valette ✉03390 ☎ 04.70.07.64.57 Fax: 04 70.07.25.48
55 camping spots on 110 m2. Reasonable.

Sceaux ✉ 92330

CRUISING

-Parc de Sceaux

Sedan ✉ 08200

CRUISING

-Place du Château
-Place du Marché

Seignosse ✉ 40510

SWIMMING

-Plage des Casernes (G)

Sennecey-le-Grand ✉ 71240

DANCECLUBS

Plaka. Le (AC B CC D G YG) Fri Sat 22.30-4 h
Gigny/Saône-between Chalon sur Saône and Tommans ✉71240 *(A6/RN6)* ☎ 03.85.44.81.71
Situated in a lovely building from the 17th century.

Sens ✉ 89100

HEALTH GROUPS

Dispensaire anti-vénérien
13 Rue de Laurencin ✉89100 ☎ 03.86.65.21.34

CRUISING

-Market place/Place du marché
-Jardin du Clos le Roi

Serignan ✉ 34410

SWIMMING

-Plages naturistes

Sète ✉ 34200

CRUISING

-Quai de la Résistence-Rue F. Mistral
-Beach/plage (théâtre de la Mer-la Corniche)
-Môle Saint-Louis
-Quai du Port

Sevran ✉ 93270

SWIMMING

-Bois de Sevran

Sevres ✉ 92310

CRUISING

-Piscine/pool

Soissons ✉ 02209

HEALTH GROUPS

Centre hospitalier de Soissons. Consultations de médecine
46 Avenue Général-De-Gaulle, B.P. 404 ✉02209
☎ 03.23.59.11.02
HIV-testing.

CRUISING

-Avenue du Mail

Sotteville-les-Rouen ✉ 76300

CRUISING

-Place de la Mairie

Soulac-sur-Mer ✉ 33780

SWIMMING

-Plage de la Négade (NU)

St.Aubin-sur-Scie ✉ 76550

CRUISING

-(P) at road RN 27 (at the big coast)

St.Brieuc ✉ 22000

HEALTH GROUPS

Centre hospitalier la Beauchère Service de médecine A
10 Avenue Marcel-Proust ✉22000 ☎ 02.96.78.22.08
HIV-testing.

SWIMMING

-Beach/plage des Rosaires (nu) (at the edge of the Horaine, behind the commune of Plérin. Nudism is tolerated. When reaching the beach, go to the right/pointe de la Horaine, après la commune de Plérin. Le naturisme est toléré. A droite en arrivant sur la plage.)

CRUISING

-Jardins des Remparts/park of the ramparts (in the surroundings of ramparts and in front of the palace of justice/aux alentours des remparts et près du palais de justice)
-Jardin des Promenades
-(P) du Champs de Mars
-Yffiniac Aire-de-repos

St.Chamas ✉ 13250

RESTAURANTS

Bergerie. La (F g) 12-13.30, 20-21.30 h, closed Sun
Le Gueby Sud ✉13250 ☎ 04.90.50.82.29

CRUISING

-Route de Berre

St.Cirques-en-Montagne ✉ 07510

HOTELS

Cévènnes. Les (B F g H) 8-22.30 h
✉07510 ☎ 04.75.38.93.73

St.Clar ✉ 32380

HOTELS

Hôtel Rison (B bf F g H) Restaurant 12-13.30, 19-21 h, closed Tue
Place de la Lomagne ✉32380 ☎ 05.62.66.40.21

St.Cyprien ✉ 66750

SWIMMING

-beach/plage (NU)

CRUISING

-Toilets near the harbour/Toilettes municipales près du port

St.Denis-de-Jouhet ✉ 36230

BARS

Terre d'Ivry. La (B D glm) Thu-Mon 23-4 h
✉36230 ☎ 02.54.30.77.95
Sun Soirée gaie/Sun Gay evening.

St.Dié ✉ 88100

CRUISING

-Place du marché
-Parking de la Pêcherie
-Parc du centre-ville

St.Dizier ✉ 52100

CRUISING

-Parc Le Jard (on the (P) beside the park/sur le (P) le long du parc)

St.Etienne

BARS

Bar Le Club (B CC GLM p s) 19-1.30, Fri Sat 20-1.30 h, closed Sun
3 Place Villeboeuf ✉42000 ☎ 04.77.33.56.25

RESTAURANTS

Frascati chez Jacky (b F g)
24 Rue du Grand Gonnet *(Place Jacquard)* ☎ 04.77.32.37.27

SAUNAS/BATHS

Sauna Le 130 (AC B DR f G MA sa sb VS wh) 13-20, Sun Tue 13-22 h
3 Rue d'Arcole ☎ 04.77.32.48.04
Sauna Libération (B G MA N sa VS) 13-20 h
5 Avenue de la Libération ✉42000 ☎ 04.77.33.53.96

HEALTH GROUPS

Dispensaire d'Hygiène sociale
14 Rue de la Charité ✉42000 ☎ 04.77.32.68.17
Hôpital de Bellevue Service maladies infectieuses
Pavillon 1bis Boulevard Pasteur ✉42023 ☎ 04,77.42.77.22
HIV testing.

CRUISING

-Jardin des Plantes
-Place Anatole-France
-Place Carnot
-Place Villeboeuf

St.Florent ✉ 20217

SWIMMING

-Beach/plage Saint Florent (route Marines du Soleil)

St.Georges-d'Oléron ✉ 17190

SWIMMING

-Beach/plage des Saumonards

St.Germain-en-Laye ✉ 78100

RESTAURANTS

Crêperie de Montardat (F g) 12-23 h, closed Mon
9 Rue Anesse-de-Montardat ✉78100 ☎ 02.39.73.33.83
Crêperie Larcher (A CC F glm) 12-14.30, 19-23 h
9 Rue Saint-Pierre ✉78100 ☎ 01.30.61.51.25

St.Gilles-Croix-de-Vie ✉ 85800

SWIMMING

-Beach/plage du Petit-Pont

CRUISING

-Ramblais (close to the/près des cafés)
-Pedestrian street/Rue Piétonne
-Bridge/Pont Jaunay

St.Girons ✉ 09200

CRUISING

-Place Guynemer

St.Jean-de-Luz ✉ 64500

SWIMMING
-Beach/plage des Deux-Jumeaux

CRUISING
-Promenade Alfred-Pose

St.Jean-de-Muzols ✉ 07300

DANCECLUBS
Starnight (AC B CC D f GLM MA P pi S SNU)
1 Chemin du Passon Frais ✉07300 *(15 km from Valence on the riverside)* ☎ 04.75.08.08.62

St.Julien-en-Born ✉ 40170

SWIMMING
-Lit-et-Mixte (NU) (plage à 1 km de la plage sud/beach 1 km from south beach)

St.Laurant-Nouant ✉ 41220

BARS
Boy's Club. Le (B CC D DR GLM MA p s SNU VS) Fri-Sun & before public holidays 23-5 h
5 Mocquebaril ✉41220 *(between Blois & Orléans by autoroute, exit Beaugency)* ☎ 02.54.87.21.39
Theme nights/Soirées à thème.

HOTELS
Maison du Passant. La (bf CC glm H MA OS)
La Petite Boulaie ✉41220 *(near Château de Chambard)*
☎ 02.54.87.74.03

St.Lô ✉ 50001

HELP WITH PROBLEMS
Syndicat PTT de la Manche CFDT
75 Rue Torteron ✉50001 ☎ 02.33.57.06.97
Self-help group for people with HIV and AIDS.

CRUISING
-Les Remparts (close to the church /près de l'église Notre-Dame)

St.Louis ✉ 68300

GAY INFO
Radio Dreyekland MH2 FM/UKW 104.6: Sun 19-21 h (GLM)
B.P. 198 ✉68300 ☎ 03.89.67.65.66

St.Malo ✉ 35400

SEX SHOPS/BLUE MOVIES
Sex Shop St. Malo (AC CC glm MA VS YG) 11-20 h
4 Rue du Puits aux Braies ✉35400 ☎ 02.99.56.01.51

CRUISING
-Parc Bel-Air
-Jardin du Cavalier
-Les Remparts
-Place Vauban
-Square Canada
-Hôtel des Finances (rue Toullier)
-SNCF/Railway station
-Square de la Briantais

St.Martin-d'Auxigny ✉ 18100

DANCECLUBS
Mandragore. La (B CC D G) Fri Sat 22.30-4 h
Vignoux-sous-les-Aix ✉18100 ☎ 02.48.64.55.76
Entrance FF 60.

St.Martin-de-Jussac ✉ 87200

BARS
Fiacre. Le (B D g) Fri Sat 22-? h
✉87200

St.Maur ✉ 36250

CAFÉS
Terres Noires. Les (b bf CC g MA N OS) 7-22, Sat -19 h, closed Sun
Route Nationale 20, Exit 14 from A20 ✉36250 *(Zone Commerciale CAP SUD)* ☎ 02.54.27.00.64
Cruisy at lunch. Truckers.

St.Meloir-des-Ondes ✉ 35350

SWIMMING
-Saint-Coulomb (beach to the east of Chevrets beach/plage à l'est de la plage des Chevrets)

St.Meme-les-Carrières ✉ 16720

RESTAURANTS
Villageois. Le (b F g) Wed-Sun 12-14, 19.30-21.30 h
✉16720 ☎ 05.45.81.93.03

St.Michel ✉ 16470

HEALTH GROUPS
Centre hospitalier de Saint Michel Consultations de médecine
✉16470 ☎ 05.45.24.40.40
HIV-testing.

CRUISING
-Le Jardin vert
-Place Victor-Hugo
-Place de New York
-Place du Théâtre

St.Nazaire ✉ 46000

SEX SHOPS/BLUE MOVIES
Exhibi. L' (AC CC g lj MA TV VS)
19 Bis Rue Cardurand ✉46000 *(Near the station)*
☎ 02.40.22.15.62
Quote Spartacus for special services.

HEALTH GROUPS
Centre hospitalier Service de dermatologie
✉44600 ☎ 02.40.90.60.60
HIV-testing.

SWIMMING
-Crique de Chemoulin (NU)

CRUISING
-Hôtel de ville (WC)
-Cirque de Chemoulin (beach between/plage entre St.Marc and Ste.Marguerite)
-Tharon-Plage (beach/plage des Sables d'Or)

-Parcours Vitta Vittel (especially in the evening/particulièrement le soir)
-P Parc Paysager
-Avenue de Plaisance (in the evening)

St.Paul de Vence ✉ 06570

CAFES

Cocarde. La (AC CC E F glm MA) 10-22 h
23 Rue Grande ✉06570 ☎ 04.93.32.86.17
Culinary innovations. Andreas and Stephan are at your service and will also be delighted to help you organize all your parties.

St.Pol-de-Leon ✉ 29250

SWIMMING

-Lieu-dit Le Dossen (behind the forest of/derrière la forêt de Santec)

St.Quai-Portrieux ✉ 22410

BARS

Davy's Bar (B g) Fri-Sun 15-1 h
3bis Place de la Plage ✉22410 ☎ 02.96.70.56.91

DANCECLUBS

Étrier-Club. L' (B D g) Fri Sat 23-5 h
3bis Place de la Plage ✉22410 ☎ 02. 96.70.53.42
Open every day in summer/En saison, ouvert tous les soirs.

SWIMMING

-Au Vieux-Bourg (NU) (nudism in a few smaller bays; take the exit to the small village of Pourry/quelques criques naturistes; accès à partir du lieu-dit Pourry)
-Le Val-André (NU) (vast beaches which also welcome nudists; between Pleneuf-Val-André and Ville-Berneuf/vastes plages qui accueillent quelques naturistes; entre Pleneuf-Val-André et Ville-Berneuf)
-Beach/plage de Lortuais (north of the village, behind the cape of Erquy; wonderful landscape/au nord du village, après le cap d'Erquy; plage magnifique)

St.Raphael ✉ 83700

BARS

Pipe-Line (AC B CC d f glm MA p s TV VS W) 22-5 h, Winter: closed Mon
16 Rue Charabois ✉83700 *(behind Townhall)*
☎ 04.94.95.93.98

CRUISING

-Place Lamartine

Strasbourg ✉ 67000

RESTAURANTS

Au Coin du Feu (B CC F glm OS) Tue-Sun 10-14.30 19-23.30 h
10 Rue de la Rape ✉67000 *(in front of the cathedral/au pied de la cathédrale)* ☎ 03.88.35.44.85
French cuisine.

Horloge Astronomique (b F glm OS) 12-14.30, 19-23 h
2 Rue de la Rape ✉67000 *(au pied de la cathédrale/at the cathedral)* ☎ 03.88.35.46.37
Next to Hôtel Suisse.

Petit Ours (F GLM) 12-14.30, 19-23.30 h
3 Rue de l'Ecurie ✉67000 *(300 m. from the cathedral)* ☎ 03.80.43.25.31
French cuisine with natural flavours.
Petit Tonnelier. Le (A AC b CC E F glm MA N OS TV YG) 12-14, 19-23 h, closed Sun lunch
16 Rue des Tonneliers ✉67000 *(near the Cathedral)* ☎ 03.88.32.53.54
Pleasant gay welcome. Fresh market products. Last order 23 h.

SAUNAS/BATHS

Equateur (B CC DR f G MA p sa sb VS) 14-24, Sat -1.30 h
5 Rue de Rosheim ✉67000 *(Bus CT9 10/20 Ste. Aurelie, Tram A Gare Centrale)* ☎ 03.88.22.25.22
Reduced entrance-fee after 21 h.
Oasis Club Sauna (b f G sa sb sol VS WO YG) 14-24 h
22 Rue de Bouxwillor ✉67000 ☎ 03.88.23.03.19
☛Kehl, Germany

FASHION SHOPS

Algorithme (g) 10-12 14-19 h, closed Mon
3 Rue Brulé ✉67000 ☎ 03.88.75.94.76
Men's fashion. Another shop is also open 3 Rue l'Epine.
Fisherman 10-19, Mon 14-19 h, closed Sun
7 Rue du Chaudron ✉67000 ☎ 03.88.32.62.18
Men's sportswear.

HOTELS

Hôtel Suisse (CC F glm H MA OS)
4 Rue de la Rape ✉67000 *(Close to the cathedral/près de la cathédrale)* ☎ 03.88.35.22.11 Fax: 03.88.25.74.23
Centrally located. Nice hotel with 2 stars. Rooms with private bath, SAT-TV, phone.

HEALTH GROUPS

Hospices Civils de Strasbourg
1 Place de l'Hôpital ✉67000 ☎ 03.88.16.17.18
Cliniques de Dermatologie et de Vénérologie. HIV-testing.

RELIGIOUS GROUPS

Association des Étudiant(e)s GAys et Lesbiennes de Strasbourg E.GA.L.E.S.
21 Rue Brulé ✉67000 ☎ 03.88.24.59.78 Fax: 03.88.24.59.78

CRUISING

-Les Gravières
-Parc de la Citadelle (AYOR)
-Quai Finkmatt
-Rue Saint-Arbogast
-Rue Saint-Léon
-Bathing lake in Roppenheim (beside the highway Strassbourg → Lauterbourg, WE and evenings)
-Centre Administratif (behind the Centre, in the Parc Place de l'Etoile, summer only)
-Schiltigheim (behind the supermarket Prisunic)

St.Rémy-de-Provence ✉ 13120

CRUISING

-Place de la République

St.Romain en Viennois ✉ 84110

GUEST HOUSES

Calade. La (bf H OS)
Rue Calade ✉84110 *2 km from the historical village Vaison-la-Romaine.* ☎ 90.46.71.79 Fax: 90.46.51.82
Charmant house with four bedrooms and a tower with a terrace that overlooks the village, the church and the surrounding hills.

St.Sebastien ✉ 23160

BARS

Bastien. Le (B CC g) 8-1 h, closed Tue
La Goutte-Jean ✉23160 ☎ 05.55.63.40.65

St.Trojan-les-Bains ✉ 17370

SWIMMING

-beach/plage (NU) (on the street going to the forest/sur la route d'accès à la forêt)

St.Tropez ✉ 83990

DANCECLUBS

Esquinade. L' (AC D GLM MA P SNU YG) 23.30-6 h, summer Mon-Sun, winter Fri Sat
2 Rue du Four ✉83990 ☎ 04.94.98.87.45
Pigeonnier. Le (B D glm MA p tv) 23-? h, closed 20 Jan-15 Mar
13 Rue de la Ponche ✉83990 ☎ 04.94.97.36.85

RESTAURANTS

Chez Maggy (AC B CC F glm MG TV) Pentecote-end Oct 19-? h
7 Rue Sybille ✉83990 *(Near town hall)* ☎ 04.94.97.16.12
Chez Nano (b F g)
Place de l'Hôtel de Ville ✉83990 ☎ 04 94.97.01.66
Entrecôte 21. L' (b F g) 19.30-1 h
21 Rue du Portail-Neuf ✉83990 ☎ 04.94.97.40.02
Swing . Le (b F g TV) Till dawn.
Quai Jean-Jaures
Sumptuous Empire decor, theme evenings, gogo dancers.

GUEST HOUSES

Cigognes. Les (AC bf G H lj MA NU pi)
803 Chemin du Carry ✉83310 ☎ 04.94.54.04.14
Fax: 04.94.54.04.14
2 double rooms with bath/WC, radio, own key, room service. Open all year.

HEALTH GROUPS

Dispensaire d'hygiène sociale
✉83990 ☎ 04.94.97.03.01

SWIMMING

-L'Escalet
-Tour des Muscadins et citadelle

CRUISING

-Le Port (L'Escalet, near the maritime cemetery/près du cimetière marin)

St.Vivien-de-Médoc ✉ 33590

HOTELS

Résidence les Fougères (g H) 12-21 h, closed Oct-Feb
Grayan-l'Hôpital ✉33590 ☎ 05.56.09.56.38

SWIMMING

-Grayan-et-l'Hôpital (beach/plage)

Suresnes ✉ 92150

CRUISING

-Railway station/Gare de Longchamp (square attenant/at the park beside)
-Railway station/Gare du Mont-Velérien (derrière la gare/behind the railway station)

Talence ✉ 33400

CRUISING

-Bois de Thouars

Talmont-Saint-Hilaire ✉ 85440

RESTAURANTS

Saint-Hubert. Le (B F g H) 12-14, 19-21, Tue 12-14 h, closed Wed
Avenue de la Plage-le-Veillon ✉85440 ☎ 02.51.22.24.04

Tarare ✉ 69170

CRUISING

-P Viaduc
-Railway station/gare SNCF

Tarascon-sur-Ariège ✉ 09400

CRUISING

-At the border of Ariège/au bord de l'Ariège

Tarbes ✉ 65000

RESTAURANTS

Braisière. La (b F g) 19.30-0.30 h, closed Mon
22 Avenue Bertrand-Barere ✉65000 ☎ 05.62.34.10.00

HEALTH GROUPS

Aides Hautes-Pyrénées Mon-Fri 9-12, 14-19 h
4 Place Brau Hauban ✉65000 ☎ 05.62.34.95.14
Fax: 05.62.51.31.98 Email: aides.aides@libertysurf.fr
Centre hospitalier de Tarbes
Boulevard Maréchal de-Lattre-de-Tassigny ✉65013
☎ 05.62.51.51.51
HIV-testing.

CRUISING

-Massay (le jardin près du musée, le your/the garden at the museum, daytime)
-Place du Foirail (AYOR) (le soir/by night)

Tarnos ✉ 40220

SWIMMING

-Nudiste beach/plage naturiste

Tergnier ✉ 02700

BARS

Parilla Club. La (B CC D F g) 15-24, Restaurant 16-22, closed Mon, Disco Fri Sat 22-4 h
38 Rue Demosthène-Gauthier Mennessis ✉02700
☎ 03.23.57.25.08

Theoule-sur-Mer ✉ 06590

SWIMMING

-La Napoule

Thonon les Bains ✉ 74200

BARS

Tiffany's. Le (B CC glm MA OS p) 18-3 h
6 Place du 8 Mai 1945 ✉74200 ☎ 04.50.71.88.91

DANCECLUBS

Must. Le (AC B CC D g MA N P W) 23-5, closed Mon-Wed except Jul & Aug; closed 2-26 January
119 Avenue St.Disdille ✉74200 ☎ 04.50.71.98.98

RESTAURANTS

Resaurant La Tour (AC B CC F glm MA OS)
Avenue du Général Leclerc, Port de Rives ✉74200
☎ 04.50.71.13.87

SWIMMING

-Geneva Lake/Lac Leman (G NU) (beach 15 min on the pathway after the pool of Thonon-les-Bains, below Château Pipaille/plage à 15 min de distance de la piscine de Thonon-les-Bains, en dessous du château Pipaille)

CRUISING

-Promenade du Belvédère (night/nuit)

Tignes ✉ 73320

RESTAURANTS

Bouf Mich. Le (b F glm)
✉73320 ☎ 04.79.06.51.80

Toulon ✉ 83000

BARS

Aqua Bar (B F glm)
3 Boulevard Pierre-Toesca ✉83000 ☎ 04.94.92.01.23
Bar restaurant.
Arlequeen (AC B bf CC GLM p VS) Winter: 15-1, summer 17-4 h
1 Rue Etienne Dauphin ✉83000 *(center of town)*
☎ 04.94.94.95.50
Bar Côté Jardin (B bf CC E f glm MA OS) 8-2 h
437 Littoral Frédéric-Mistral le Mourillon ✉83000
☎ 04.94.41.38.33
Terrace overlooking the sea. Popular with Navy Officers.
Texas (B G) 16-1, May-Sep -3 h
377 Avenue République ✉83000 *(next to the Mairie)*
☎ 04.94.89.14.10

DANCECLUBS

Boy's Paradise (B D G)
1 Boulevard Pierre-Toesca ✉83000 ☎ 04.94.09.35.90
Pussy Cat. Le (B D gLM) Thu-Sun 23-4 h
655 Avenue de Claret ✉83000 ☎ 04.94.92.76.91

SEX SHOPS/BLUE MOVIES

Box Vidéo (g VS)
4 Place Armand Valée ✉83000 ☎ 04.94.91.40.25
XXL (g VS)
3 Avenue de Besagne ✉83000 ☎ 04.94.93.11.91

SAUNAS/BATHS

AGS- Les Mouettes (b G sa OS pi sol VS WO) 14-21 h
87 Chemin de la Pinède ✉83000 *(Villa les Mouettes près de/near Tour Royale)* ☎ 04.94.42.38.73
Blue Hot (b G sa sb MA) 13-21, Fri -1 h
16 Place Vincent Raspail ✉83000 ☎ 04.94.91.49.55

HEALTH GROUPS

Cité sanitaire
132 Avenue Lazare-Carnot ✉83076 ☎ 04.94.89.90.20
Dispensaire antivénérien
Avenue Lazarre-Carnot ✉83000 ☎ 04.94.89.90.42
HIV testing.

RELIGIOUS GROUPS

David et Jonathan
B.P. 5135 ✉83093

SWIMMING
-Beach/plage de Fabregas
-Beach/plage du Mourillon

CRUISING
-Avenue Auguste-Berthon
-Railway station/gare SNCF
-Jardin du Mourillon
-Place de la Porte-d'Italie
-Port de Bandol
-La Bedoule (highway/autoroute Toulon-Marseille)
-Square Alexandre-III (garden/jardin centre ville)
-Fort du Cap Brun
-Place du Théâtre

Toulouse ✉ 31000

TOURIST INFO
Tourist Info
Donjon du Capitol ✉31000 ☎ 05.61.11.02.22

BARS
Aphrodisiaque. L' (B glm)
1 Rue des Chalets ✉31000 ☎ 05.61.63.81.82
B Machine. Le (B glm)
37 Place des Carmes ✉31000 ☎ 05.61.55.57.59
Bar La Ciguë (AC B CC D G YG) 18-2, Sat -5 h
6 Rue de la Colombette ✉31000 ☎ 05.61.99.61.87
Deux G. Les (AC B glm) 15-2 h
5 Rue Baronie ✉31000 ☎ 05.61.23.16.10
Quinquina. Le (B CC G) 8-22, Sun 18-22 h
26 Rue Peyras ✉31000 ☎ 05.61.21.90.73

LA CIGUË
bar à musique
ouvert tous les jours
à partir de 18h
6, rue de la colombette
31000 toulouse
info : 05 61 99 61 87

PHySiC CLub
BAR
VIDEO
ONLY FOR
MEN
14, rue D'AUBUISSON
TOULOUSE
Tél. 05 61 62 81 29

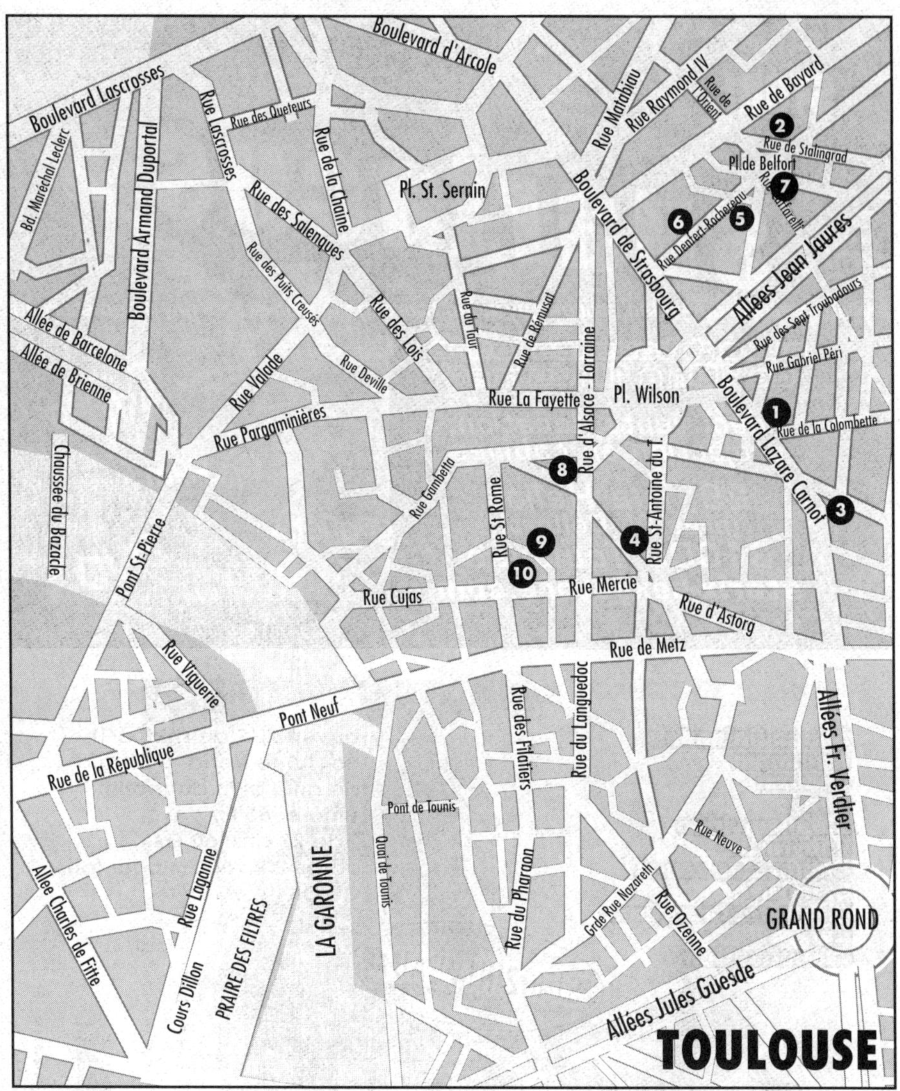

1 Bar La Ciguë
2 Le Sand's Bar
3 Le Physic Club Men's Club
4 Le Président Sauna
5 Spartacus Gay Video Shop/ Blue Movie
6 Eros Sex Shop Blue Movie
7 Colonial Sauna
8 Le Shanghai Danceclub
9 Les Deux G Bar
10 Le Quinquina Bar

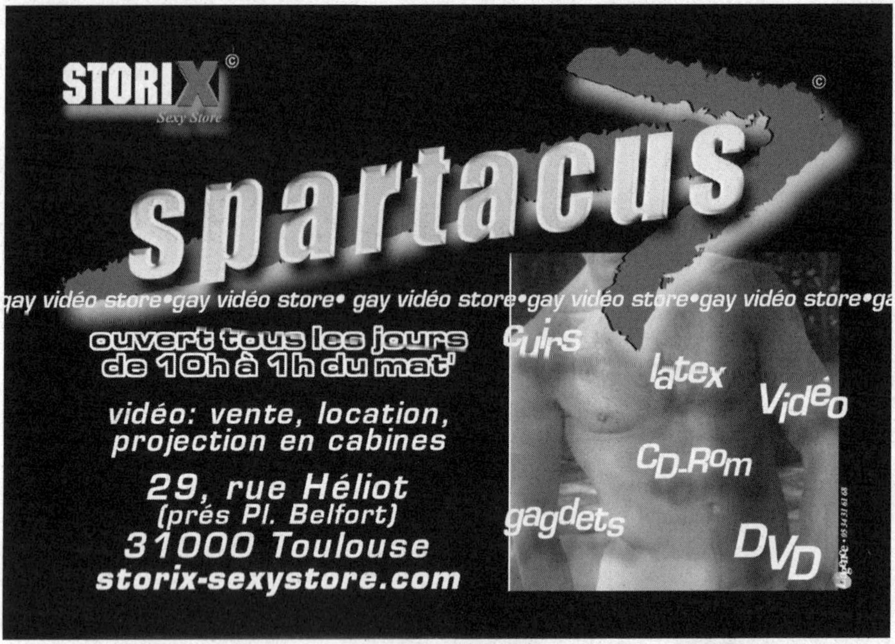
STORIX ©
Sexy Store
spartacus ©
gay vidéo store•gay vidéo store• gay vidéo store•gay vidéo store•gay vidéo store•ga
ouvert tous les jours
de 10h à 1h du mat'
vidéo: vente, location,
projection en cabines
29, rue Héliot
(prés Pl. Belfort)
31000 Toulouse
storix-sexystore.com
cuirs
latex
Vidéo
CD-Rom
gadgets
DVD

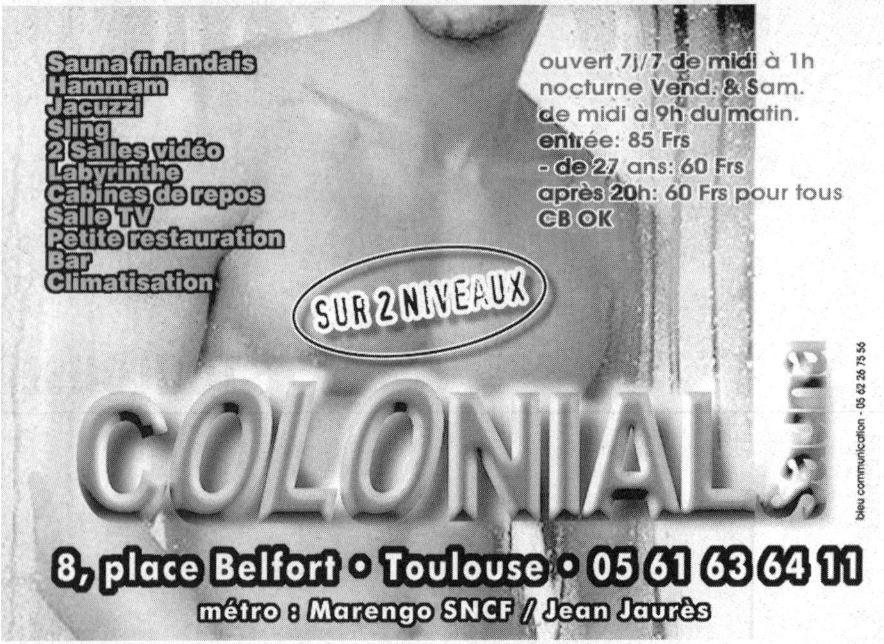
Sauna finlandais
Hammam
Jacuzzi
Sling
2 Salles vidéo
Labyrinthe
Cabines de repos
Salle TV
Petite restauration
Bar
Climatisation
ouvert 7j/7 de midi à 1h
nocturne Vend. & Sam.
de midi à 9h du matin.
entrée: 85 Frs
- de 27 ans: 60 Frs
après 20h: 60 Frs pour tous
CB OK
SUR 2 NIVEAUX
COLONIAL sauna
8, place Belfort • Toulouse • 05 61 63 64 11
métro : Marengo SNCF / Jean Jaurès
bleu communication - 05 62 26 75 56

Sand's. Le (A AC B CC GLM MA p W YG) 18-2, Sat -4 h, closed Mon
31 Rue de Stalingrad ✉31000 ☎ 05.61.63.03.05
Scot Tea. Le (B glm)
35 Rue du Taur ✉31000 ☎ 05.61.12.38.48

MEN'S CLUBS

Physic Club (AC B DR f G lj MA VS) 16-2, Sat -4 h
14 Rue d'Aubuisson ✉31000 ☎ 05.61.62.81.29

DANCECLUBS

Shanghai. Le (B D g VS) 23-? h, gay Tea Dance Sun 16-22 h
12 Rue de la Pomme ✉31000 ☎ 05.61.23.37.80
Backroom, video.

RESTAURANTS

Bistrot d'Eugène (B F glm)
3 Rue Delacroix ✉31000 ☎ 05.61.62.28.27
Copains d'abord. Les (B F glm)
38 Rue du Pont de Guilheméry ✉31500 ☎ 05.61.20.41.50
Diables. Les (b F glm MA) closed Sun and Mon evening
45 Rue des Tourneurs ✉31000 ☎ 05.61.22.11.63
Rose Bonbon. Le (B F glm)
Imp. de la Colombette ✉31000 ☎ 05.61.63.48.46
Table d'Aline. La (B F glm)
7 Quai St.Pierre ✉31000 ☎ 05.61.23.24.07

SEX SHOPS/BLUE MOVIES

Boîte à Films. La (g VS) 10-2 h
23 Rue Denfert-Rochereau ✉31000 ☎ 05.61.62.76.75
Eros (g VS) 13-2 h
22 Rue Denfert-Rochereau ✉31000 ☎ 05.61.63.44.72
Spartacus Gay Vidéo Shop (CC G MA VS) 10-1 h
29 Rue Héliot ✉31000 ☎ 05.61.63.63.59

SAUNAS/BATHS

Colonial Sauna (AC B CC DR f G MA p sa sb sol wh VS) Fri Sat -9 h
8 Place Belfort ✉31000 *(M° Marengo SNCF/Jean-Jaurès)* ☎ 05.61.63.64.11
Reduced entrance-fee after 20 h and for under 27 years.
Président. Le (AC b G sa sb VS) 11-21.30, Sun 12-21.30 h
38 Rue d'Alsace-Lorraine ✉31000 ☎ 05.61.21.52.18

TRAVEL & TRANSPORT

Rainbow Horizon
15 Grande Rue St. Nicolas ✉31300 ☎ 05.61.42.70.75
Gay cultural guides and interpreters for Toulouse and its region.

GENERAL GROUPS

Extra Muros
B.P. 439 ✉31009 ☎ 05.61.33.09.47
Homepage: http://www.infonie.fr/public_html/bodoc
Gais et Lesbiennes en Marche (GELEM)
66 Boulevard Maurens, App. 88 ✉31270 ☎ 06.11.87.38.81
Fax: 05.61.62.29.49 Email: gelem@altern.org
Organizers of the Gay and Lesbian March of Toulouse.

HEALTH GROUPS

Aides Pôle de Toulouse Mon-Fri 9-12, 14-18 h
122 Avenue du Général Bourbaki ✉31200 ☎ 05.34.40.22.60
Fax: 05.34.40.22.61
Centre hospitalier la Grave. Dispensaire antivénérien
Place Lange ✉31000 ☎ 05.61.77.78.59
HIV-testing.

SPECIAL INTEREST GROUPS

Jules et Julies
Comité des Étudiants, Université du Mirail, 5 Allée Machado ✉31058
Gay and lesbian student group.
Rando's Pyrénées B.P. 1332 ✉31160
Gay walking and hiking group/gays randonneurs.

CRUISING

-Cours Dillon (AYOR) (very popular; day & night, but especially between 18-23 h/populair; toute la journée, mais surtout de 18 à 23 h)
-Géant Casino Mirail (all day action in the bushes, very mixed/dans les bois, toute la journée; très mélangé)
-Garden of Plants/Jardin des Plantes (in the afternoon/l'après-midi)
-Les Quais (AYOR) (Port de la Daurade, Beaux-Arts)
-Gare SNCF/railway station (rue Compans)
-Place Wilson et Place Roosevelt, Square de Gaulle (AYOR) (at night/la nuit)
-Saint Aubin (21-2 h)
-Ile du Ramier
-Behind Théâtre Garonne (Digne de la Garonne, Rue du Château d'Eau)

Tours ✉37000

GAY INFO

Maison des Homosexualités de Touraine (M.H.T.) 18-22, Fri Sat special parties, disco
1ter Rue des Balais ✉37000 *(Vieux Tours, near Place du Grand Marché)* ☎ 02.47.20.55.30 Fax: 02.47.20.55.30
Association Bar.
Point Gay Thu 18-20 h
c/o MHT, 1ter Rue de Balais ✉37000

BARS

Hélios. L' (B G) ?-2 h
16 Rue Docteur Fournier ✉37000 ☎ 02.47.44.14.14
Lionceau. Le (B DR g lj OS s) 17-2 h, Sun in summer -21 h
55 Rue de Commerce ✉37000 ☎ 02.47.61.17.13
Open Bar (AC b CC f glm MA p s YG) Mon-Fri 17-2, Sat 18-2 h, closed Sun
128 Boulevard Béranger ✉37000 *(near the Saint-Elois church)* ☎ 02.47.37.67.60
Theme nights/Soirées thématiques.

DANCECLUBS

Gamme au Club 71. La (AC B D GLM MA s) 22.30-5 h, closed Mon
71 Rue Georges Courteline ✉37000 ☎ 02.47.37.01.54
☛ Joue-le-Tours

RESTAURANTS

Chez Nello (B F glm S) 17-2 h
8 Rue Auguste Chevallier ✉37000 ☎ 02.47.39.12.11
Cabaret/Shows.

SEX SHOPS/BLUE MOVIES

Miroir des Hommes (AC DR GLM MA VS W) 9-2
34 Rue Michelet ✉37000 ☎ 02.47.61.13.18
Videos and individual cabins. 8 projection rooms.

SAUNAS/BATHS

Thermes Grammont. Les (AC b DR G lj MA N sa sb VS) 14-21 h, Jul Aug 16-22 h
22bis Avenue Grammont ✉37000 *(near Town Hall and railway station)* ☎ 02.47.05.49.24

HOTELS

Château des Ormeaux (bf g H pi OS)
Route de Noizay, Nazelles ✉37530 ☎ 02.47.23.26.51 Fax: 02.47.23.19.31
Email: chateauxdesormeaux@wanadoo.fr
Homepage: http://perso.wanadoo.fr/chateauxdesormeaux
Luxury rooms in a private chateau located 20 minutes from Tours. Swimming pool, large park. Horse riding.

GENERAL GROUPS

Jeunes et étudiant(e)s homosexuel(le)s de Tours Tue 20-22 h
c/o MHT, 1ter Rue de Balais ✉37000
Youth and student gay and lesbian group.

HEALTH GROUPS

Centre hospitalier R. de Tours
2 Boulevard Tonnelé ✉37044 ☎ 02.47.34.81.11
Dispensaire polyvalent
5 Rue Jehan-Fouquet ✉37000 *PO Box 44 26* ☎ 02.47.66.88.41
HIV-testing.

CRUISING

-Quai d'Orléans (AYOR) (around the Library, at night/autour de la Bibliothèque, la nuit)
-Jardin du Musée
-Jardin des Prébendes d'Oé
-Bois de la Ville-aux-Dames (5 km west of Tours direction Montlouis)

Trappes ✉ 78190

HEALTH GROUPS

CP de médecine preventive
Rue Hector-Berlioz ✉78190 ☎ 01.30.62.88.27

Tregunc ✉ 29128

SWIMMING

-Beach/plage de Trez-Belleg-Hivan.

Trouville-sur-Mer ✉ 14360

RESTAURANTS

Vallée d'Auge. La (B CC F g OS) Wed-Sun 12-24 h
3-5 Boulevard d'Hautpoul ✉14360 ☎ 02.31.88.07.98
French specialities.

Troyes ✉ 10006

HEALTH GROUPS

Centre de prévention dermatologie et vénérologie
1 Avenue des Lombards ✉10006 ☎ 03.25.49.00.27
HIV-testing.

CRUISING

-Behind the hospital/Derrière l'hôpital
-La Vallée Suisse/"The Swiss Valley" (the park beside the boulevard Gambetta, close to the railway station; in the afternoon and at night/ Jardin le long du Blvd Gambetta, près de la gare l'après-midi et le soir)
-Beach of Villepart/Plage de Villepart (On the bank of the river Seine; take road RN 71 in direction to Dijon, exit Bréviande, left hand; wait until the hour when the white collar clerks leave their offices/Bord de Seine, prendre la RN 71, direction Dijon; à la sortie de Bréviande, sur la gauche; heure de sortie des bureaux)
-Tourist office/Syndicat d'Initiative

Tulle ✉ 19000

CRUISING

-au pied de la Cathédrale Notre-Dame

Uzes ✉ 30700

GUEST HOUSES

Marronniers. Les (b bf glm MA OD pi)
Place de la Mairie ✉30580 *(12 km from the historic town of Uzes, North-West of Avignon)* ☎ 04.66.72.84.77
Fax: 04.66.72.85.78 Email: lesmarronniers@hello.to
Homepage: http://www.hello.to/lesmarronniers
Possibility of evening meals.

Valence ✉ 26000

BARS

Ambigu Bar (AC B D GLM MA) 17-4 h
13 Avenue Gambetta ✉26000 ☎ 04.75.56.95.04

SAUNAS/BATHS

Hylas Club Sauna (AC b DR G MA p sa sb VS wh YG) 11-21 h, closed Tue and May 1st-8th
40 Avenue de Verdun ✉26000 *(Bus 8-stop Sully, in the Polygone commercial centre)* ☎ 04.75.56.03.62

HEALTH GROUPS

Dispensaire du Polygone
Rue Maryse-Bastié ✉26000 ☎ 04.75.43.75.59
HIV testing.

CRUISING

-Parc Jouvet
-Rue des Musiques
-Rue G.Rey, Jardin de l'Ancienne-Préfecture
-Barrage de Charmes-sur-Rhône

Valenciennes ✉ 59322

HEALTH GROUPS

Centre hospitalier de Valenciennes Consultations externes
Avenue Monaco ✉59322 ☎ 03.27.14.33.33
HIV-testing.

CRUISING

-Aire d'Hordan (both sides of the motorway Valenciennes-Paris/sur l'autoroute Valanciennes- Paris, de chaque côté)
-Parc de la Rhonelle
-Parc Froissart (close to P Charles de Gaulle (22-2 h)
-Soccer field/Terrain de foot de Vauban (22-2 h)
-Aire de Millonfosse

Vallon-pont-d'Arc ✉ 07150

CRUISING

-Beach/Plage des Templiers

Vals-les-Bains ✉ 07600

CRUISING

-Parc du Casino (very popular in summer/très fréquenté en été)

Vandoeuvre-les-Nancy ✉ 54511

HEALTH GROUPS

Centre hospitalier de Brabois. Service maladies infectieuses
Tour Drouet, Rue de Morvan, B.P. 4013 ✉54511 ☎ 03.83.55.81.20 *HIV-testing.*

Vannes ✉ 56000

BARS

Menphis Bar (B G MA) 18-2 h, closed on Mon in winter
33 rue Maréchal Leclerc ✉56000 ☎ 02.97.47.00.06

CRUISING

-Le Port (P) Maison des familles

Vaucresson ✉ 92420

BODY & BEAUTY SHOPS

Institut Anne Vromet
24 Avenue du Bois de la Marche ✉92420 ☎ 02.47.41.09.79
Beauty service per correspondence.

Vendays-Montalivet ✉ 33930

SWIMMING

-Beach/plage de Montalivet

Vendome ✉ 41100

BARS

Saint Martin (B G MA) 12-0-30 h
24 Place St.Martin ✉41100 ☎ 02.54.77.23.63

Verdun ✉ 55100

HEALTH GROUPS

Centre hospitalier de Verdun Service de médecine B
2 Rue d'Antouard ✉55100 ☎ 03.29.83.84.85
HIV-testing.

CRUISING

-Rue du Général-Leclerc, Cours Clouet

Verrières ✉ 63320

RESTAURANTS

Restaurant-Snack le Collier de la Reine Closed Mon.
✉63320 ☎ 04.73.88.53.48
☞Paris: hotel listings.

Verrières-le-Buisson ✉ 91370

GUEST HOUSES

Alain's Bed & Breakfast (bf glm H MA sa)
4 Sentier des Gatines ✉91370 *(M° Massy-Verrières)*
☎ 01.69.20.67.69
Booking necessary. Owner picks you up at the Métro Station.

CRUISING

-Bois de Verrières (Route A86 Clamart to Créteil; nude sunbathing in summer)

Versailles ✉ 78000

RESTAURANTS

Terrasse. La (b F glm) 19-2 h
11 Rue Saint Honoré ✉78000 *(next to the cathedral, close to RER and chateau)* ☎ 01.39.50.76.00
South-East specialities. Open late but reservation advised.

CRUISING

-Avenue St. Claud (Beginning of the street opposite the Chateau foot paths/au début de la rue en face des sentiers pédestres du château)

Verteuil-sur-Charente ✉ 16510

HOTELS

Relais de Verteuil. Le (AC B D F glm H s VS WE) Disco Thu-Sun 20-5 h
RN 10, Les Nègres ✉16510 ☎ 05.45.31.41.14
Fax: 05.45.31.40.71

Vesoul ✉ 70014

HEALTH GROUPS

Centre hospitalier Paul-Morel Service de dialyse
41 Avenue Aristide-Briand ✉70014 ☎ 03.84.75.26.00
HIV testing.

Vichy ✉ 03200

SAUNAS/BATHS

Anthares Sauna Club (AC b DR f G MA p sa sb VS wh YG) 14-24 h, by theme nights -4 h
164 Avenue des Graviers ✉03200 ☎ 04.70.32.89.38

HEALTH GROUPS

Dispensaire municipal
21 Rue d'Alsace ✉03200 ☎ 04.70.98.61.89

CRUISING

-Parcs d'Allier
-Pont-Barrage
-Wood/Bois de Serbannes
-Les Iles
-Place de la Poste (Boulevard des Etats-Unis/rue d'Italie)
-Quatre-Chemins (au centre du quartier des cafés/right in the middle of the cafes' area)

Vieille-St-Girons ✉ 40560

SWIMMING

-St.Girons (beach in the south/plage au sud)

Vierzon ✉ 18100

CRUISING

-Abords du Canal
-Jardin de la Mairie
-(P) Bricolage Service

Vieux-Boucau-les-Bains ✉ 40480

HOTELS

Hôtel d'Alvret (B F g H) Jun-Nov 9-1 h
Avenue de la Plage ✉40480 *(Port d'Albret)* ☎ 05.58.48.14.09

SWIMMING

-Nudist beach in the north/plage naturiste au nord

Villard-de-Lans ✉ 38250

RESTAURANTS

Caribou. Le (B D F g H) closed Oct & Nov
Le Clos-de-la-Balme ✉38250 *(Correncon-en-Vercors)*
☎ 04.76.95.82.82
Restaurant 12-14.30 19-22 h. Disco Fri 22-2 Sat -3 h.

Villefranche-sur-Mer ✉ 06230

CRUISING

-Syndicat d'Initiative

Villeneuve de Marsan ✉ 40190

HOTELS

Hervé Garrapit Hotel Restaurant (CC F glm H OS)
4Place de la Boiterie ✉40190 ☎ 05.58.45.20.08
Fax: 05.58.45.34.14
Email: hotelrestauranthervegarrapit@wanadoo.fr
Homepage: www.ch-demeures.com/garrapit
Hotel with gastonomic restaurant.

Villeneuve-les-Avignon ✉ 30400

RESTAURANTS

Saint André. Restaurant le (CC F glm OS) Tue-Sun 12-14 19.30-22 h
4 bis, Montée du Fort ✉30400 ☎ 04.90.25.63.23
Trendy crowd. Gastonomic restaurant.

Villeneuve-Saint-Georges ✉ 94190

HEALTH GROUPS

Centre hospitalier intercommunal. Service maladies infectieuses
✉94190 ☎ 05.46.86.20.00
HIV testing.

Dispensaire
8 Rue des Vignes ✉94190 ☎ 02.43.89.00.69

Villers-sur-Mer ✉ 14640

SWIMMING

-Auberville (G NU)

Villiers-les-Ormes ✉ 36250

BARS

Nicolas II. Le (B D F G) 22-4 h
✉36250 *(6 km from/de Châteauroux)* ☎ 02.54.36.68.68
Bar-disco 22-4, restaurant Wed-Sun 20-5 h.

Vincennes ✉ 94300

SAUNAS/BATHS

Bains Montansier (AC b DR f G MA msg sa sb VS wh) 12-20, Sat Sun 9.30-20 h
7 Rue de Montreuil ✉94300 *(M° Château de Vincennes/RER Vincennes)* ☎ 01.43.28.54.03
Entrance-fee FF 100.

HEALTH GROUPS

Dispensaire municipal
6 Rue Pierre Brossolette ✉94300 ☎ 02.43.28.33.20

CRUISING

-Château (alleys, east side/allées, côté est)

Vitrolles ✉ 13140

CRUISING

-Route de Marignane

Vitry-sur-Seine ✉ 94400

CRUISING

-Quai du Port-à-L'Anglais

Vouziers ✉ 08400

HEALTH GROUPS

Dispensaire
Rue Henrionnet ✉08400 ☎ 03.24.30.83.66

Wissant ✉ 62179

SWIMMING

-Beach/plage de Wissant (NU) (in the dunes/dans les dunes)

French Polynesia

Polynésie française

South Pacific

Initials: TAH

Time: GMT -10

☎ Country Code / Access Code: 689 (no area codes) / 00

Language: French, Tahitian

Area: 3,521 km² / 1,359 sq mi.

Currency: 1 CFP Franc = 100 Centimes

Population: 232,000

Capital: Papéete (Tahiti)

Religions: About 55% Protestants, 24% Roman Catholic

Climate: Tropical, but moderate climate.

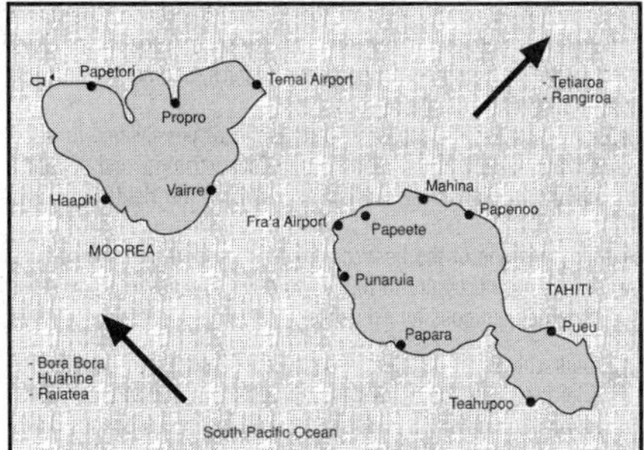

● Tahiti is the largest of the ca. 115 Polynesian islands. The capital city of Papéete has a population of 30,000. Most tourists come to the island during the Bastille Celebrations, which begin each year on July 14 and last for three weeks. French laws concerning homosexuality aapply here.

✱ Die größte der ca. 115 Inseln Polynesiens ist Tahiti. Die Hauptstadt Papéete hat 30.000 Einwohner. Die meisten Touristen kommen während der »Bastille«-Feiern auf die Insel, die jeweils am 14. Juli beginnen und drei Wochen andauern. Es gelten die französischen Gesetze zur Homosexualität.

▲ Tahiti est la plus grande des 115 îles de la Polynésie Française. Papeete, la capitale, compte 30.000 habitants. Les touristes y affluent tous les ans, au 14 juillet, pour célébrer pendant 3 semaines la commémoration de la Prise de la Bastille. Même législation qu'en France métropolitaine.

☆ Tahiti es la más grande de las 115 islas de la Polinesia Francesa. La capital Papéete tiene 30,000 habitantes. La mayor parte de los turistas visitan esta isla para fiestas como la de la Bastilla que comienza el 14 de julio y dura tres semanas. Aquí rigen las leyes francesas con respecto a la homosexualidad.

❖ Tahiti è la più grande delle 115 isole della Polinesia Francese. La capitale è Papéete (30.000 ab.). Molti turisti arrivano sull'isola durante le celebrazioni per la presa della Bastiglia, che cominciano ogni anno il 14 luglio e durano tre settimane. Anche per quanto riguarda l'omosessualità, qui sono in vigore le leggi francesi.

NATIONAL GAY INFO

Te Anuanua o te Fenua
PO Box 369, Papeete, Tahiti ☎ 77.31.11 *or* ☎ *& FAX 45.30.77.*

Manihi - Kaina

HOTELS

Climat de France Kaina Village (B F H NG) PO Box 24 60, Papéete, Tahiti ☎ 42 75 53
Holiday complex-resort. Approximately 90 minutes by air from Tahiti-Faaa. Comprises 16 Polynesian style bungalows. „Fare" of six rooms. All watersports, including scuba diving, deep sea fishing, water skiing, and a visit to pearl oyster beds. Local arrangements can be made in Papeete with most travel agencies. Single CPF 12.345-18.350, double 19.040-29.200 (either with half or full board).

Moorea - Haapiti

HOTELS

Club Med (B F NG pi)
PO Box 10 10 ☎ 56 15 00 Fax: 56 19 51

Moorea - Papetoai

HOTELS

Refuge du Lézard. La (AC B bf CC F Glm NU OS pi W wh)
PO Box 13 03 22, Punaauia Fax: 58 25 74
First and only gay resort in romantic French Polynesia. Opening fall 1999.

Tahiti - Mahina

SWIMMING

-Pointe Vénus (WE) (From the harbour take Le Truck N° 60 to Mahina.)

Tahiti - Papéete

BARS

Cave. La / Royal Papeete (B D NG WE)
Boulevard Pomare ☎ 42 01 29
106. Le (B D NG WE)
Boulevard Pomare ☎ 42 72 92

RESTAURANTS

Corbeille d'Eau. La (B F g)
Front de Mer Paofai ☎ 43.77.14
French cuisine.

HOTELS

Beachcomber Parkroyal (AC B F H NG OS pi)
PO Box 60 14, Faa'a ☎ 42 51 10 Fax: 43 61 06
Beach location. All rooms have AC, telephone, fridge, priv. bath, balcony, mini bar, TV. Single US$ 170-200, double 200-230.
Bel Air
Lagoon Shore, PO Box 354 ☎ 42 82 24
3.5 miles from town.
Hyatt Regency (AC B F NG OS pi wh)
PO Box 10 15, Matavi Bay ☎ 48 11 22
Expensive and luxurious: US$ 195-500.
Maeva Beach Hotel (B F H NG)
PO Box 60 08, FAAA ☎ 42 80 42 Fax: 43 84 70
Matavai (AC B F H NG OS pi)
Valle Tipaerui, PO Box 32 ☎ 42 67 67 Fax: 42 36 90
Rooms with AC, telephone, priv. bath, balcony, radio. Single FCP 8.800, double 11.700.
Tahiti Budget Lodge (b f glm H)
Rue de Frere Alain ☎ 42 66 82
Central location. Rates US$ 43 (1 or 2 persons), 48 with shower/WC.

CRUISING

-Beach south of Maeva Beach Hotel (Lots of Mahoos and Raerae)
-The way from the main road to the Bel Air Hotel (bushes on the left)
-Park Bougainville near post-office (MA) (locals in their cars about 21 h)

Tahiti - Papenoo

SWIMMING

-Surf Beach (WE YG)

Tahiti - Punaauia / Paea

SWIMMING

-White sand beaches

Germany

Deutschland

Central Europe

Initials: D

Time: GMT +1

☎ Country Code / Access Code: 49 (leave away the first 0 of area codes) / 00

Language: German

Area: 356,945 km² / 138,975 sq mi.

Currency: 1 Deutsche Mark (DM) = 100 Pfennige. 1 EURO = 100 EURO Cents; The Euro can only be used in the clearance system.

Population: 82,401,000

Capital: Berlin

Religions: 41% Roman Catholic, 41% Protestant

Climate: Moderate and marine climate. Winters and summers are cool, cloudy and wet. In the Alps occasional warm Föhn-winds. The relative humidity is high.

Important gay cities: Berlin, Frankfurt/Main, Hamburg, Köln, München.

● The political climate in Germany in the 90's has opened further the discussion of homosexuality and the law. It is strongly foreseeable that the loop holes in the legal constitution of Germany, particulary with regard to equality and anti-discrimination, are likely to become legally enforced. Political support for gay partnerships has been given by four of the five parties in the Houses of Parliament. It's probable that gay partnerships will be enacted into law.

Germany is a federation of 16 states, each having considerable autonomy in internal decision making. This autonomy has lead to registration of gay and lesbian partnerships in Hamburg, anti-discrimination policy within certain lands, such as Berlin, Brandenburg and Thüringen. Additionally, there are also similiar policies in effect in other lands.

Despite legal and political acceptance of homosexuality, discrimination continues in certain parts of the Federal Republic of Germany. Although it is possible to lead an open life style in the major cities, such as Berlin, Hamburg, Cologne and Munich, stigmatisation continues in rural and Catholic regions.

Germany provides the tourist with a wealth of possibilities to discover the long history of the country, traditions, customs and of course it's many attractions besides the Berlin Wall or the Heidelberg Castle.

Germany has one of the best constructed transport systems of Europe, so it is not necessary to be tied to a car to enjoy the gay scene and also the numerous tourist sights.

✱ Deutschland ist auf dem Weg zu einer gesetzlich verankerten Gleichstellung von Schwulen und Lesben in den letzten Jahren gut vorangekommen. Ein in der Verfassung festgeschriebenes Diskriminierungsverbot für Homosexuelle gibt es zwar noch nicht, aber durch die Veränderung der politischen Verhältnisse in der Bundesrepublik ist mit einem solchen Schritt zu rechnen. Die Vorbereitungen zu einer zumindest partiellen Gleichstellung homosexueller Lebensgemeinschaften zur heterosexuellen Ehe laufen bereits: vier der fünf im Bundestag vertretenen Parteien haben sich für eine mehr oder weniger weitgehende Gleichstellung ausgesprochen. Wahrscheinlich wird die Rechtsform einer „eingetragenen Partnerschaft" für nichteheliche Gemeinschaften eingeführt. Deutschland ist eine Föderation aus 16 Bundesländern, die bei der Innenpolitik eine gewisse Autonomie besitzen. Dies zeigt sich auch in verschiedenen Gesetzen zur Gleichstellung von Homosexuellen. In Hamburg gibt es bereits die eingetragene Partnerschaft für Schwule und Lesben gibt, andere Bundesländer, wie Berlin, Brandenburg und Thüringen, haben ein ausdrückliches Diskriminierungsverbot von Homosexuellen in ihren Länderverfassungen festgeschrieben. In anderen Bundesländern gibt es ähnliche Regelungen unterhalb der Verfassungsebene.Doch trotz der rechtlichen verankerten Gleichstellung gibt es in der deutschen Bevölkerung noch immer ein starkes Toleranzgefälle. Während es in den großen Städten möglich ist, die eigene Homosexualität offen auszuleben, gilt sie besonders in ländlichen und katholisch geprägten Gebieten nach wie vor oft als Makel. Viele Schwule und Lesben ziehen deshalb in eine Großstadt, vor allem in die schwulen Hochburgen, wie Berlin, Hamburg, Köln und München. Hier unterscheidet sich Deutschland also wenig von seinen europäischen Nachbarn. Touristisch gesehen ist Deutschland ein Land der tausend Möglichkeiten: Die mehr als tausendjährige Geschichte hinterließ überall im Land ihre sehenswerten Spuren jenseits von Berliner Mauer und Heidelberger Schloß. Deutschland verfügt über eines der am besten ausgebauten öffenltichen Verkehrsnetze Europas. Deshalb kann man die Szene und die Sehenswürdigkeiten der großen Städte auch ohne Auto problemlos erkunden.

▲ L'Allemagne est sur la voie d'une reconnaissance légale des droits des gays et lesbiennes. Il est vrai qu'il n'existe pas encore une interdiction de la discrimination des homosexuels fixée dans la constitution, mais on peut s'attendre à une telle avancée grâce à la modification de l'échiquier politique allemand. Les préparatifs à l'adoption d'une loi entérinant la reconnaissance des couples homosexuels sont en cours: quatre des cinq partis représentés au parlement fédéral ont donné leur consentement à une reconnaissance plus ou moins étendue. Il est probable que ce sera sous la forme juridique d'une „union enregistrée". L'Allemagne est une fédération se composant de 16 Etats fédérés qui ont une certaine autonomie dans la politique intérieure. Ceci se manifeste également dans les diverses lois concernant les homosexuels. A Hambourg, il existe déjà une union enregistrée pour homosexuels et lesbiennes, d'autres Etats fédérés comme Berlin, Brandenbourg et Thuringe ont entériné une interdiction formelle de la discrimination homosexuelle dans leur constitution de Land. Il existe encore des réglementations similaires dans d'autres Lands. Mais malgré cette reconnaissance lé-

EXTRASTARK
The original
LONDON
the condom.

galement entérinée, il subsiste une forte disparité de tolérance parmi la population allemande. Alors que dans les grandes villes il est possible de vivre ouvertement son homosexualité, la stigmatisation persiste dans les régions rurales et catholiques. C'est pourquoi beaucoup de gays et lesbiennes s'installent dans une grande ville, en particulier dans les fiefs homosexuels comme Berlin, Hambourg, Cologne et Munich. Ici, l'Allemagne se différencie donc peu de ses voisins européens. Au point de vue touristique, l'Allemagne est un pays qui offre de nombreuses curiosités: l'histoire millénaire a laissé partout dans le pays des vestiges moins connus peut-être que le mur de Berlin ou le château d'Heidelberg mais tout aussi intéressants. L'Allemagne dispose du réseau de transport public le mieux structuré d'Europe. On peut donc apprécier la scène et les curiosités des grandes villes même sans voiture.

☆ En los últimos años la situación legal de gays y lesbianas ha progresado notablemente en Alemania. Todavía no se ha incorporado una ley de antidiscriminación en la constitución, pero con el reciente cambio político parece cada vez más probable. La igualación de parejas homosexuales, aunque sea sólo parcialmente, está en camino. Cuatro de los cinco partidos políticos representados en el parlamento se han declarado a favor de esta cuestión en mayor o menor medida. Por ello es de esperar que se introduzca una forma legal de „relación registrada" para parejas de hecho. Alemania es una federación formada por 16 *laender,* que poseen en gran medida autonomía en cuestiones de política interior. Este hecho se refleja en los diferentes leyes que existen respecto a la igualdad de derechos para homosexuales. En Hamburgo las parejas gay y lesbianas se pueden registrar, otros estados federales como Berlín, Brandenburgo y Turinga prohiben expresamente la discriminación en sus constituciones regionales. En otras partes de Alemania existen leyes parecidas. Pero a pesar de la situación legislativa, la realidad en la sociedad alemana se presenta de manera distinta. Mientras en las ciudades grandes se puede vivir abiertamente la homosexualidad, la situación sigue siendo muy dificil en zonas rurales o con fuerte influencia católica. Por ello, muchos gays y lesbianas fijan su residencia en sitios como Berlín, Hamburgo, Colonia o Munich, que son bastiones homosexuales. En este aspecto Alemania no se diferencia mucho de sus vecinos europeos. Desde el punto de vista turistico, Alemania es un país de múltiples posibilidades: Ejemplos de su larga história dignos de ver no se reducen a la Puerta de Brandenburgo o al castillo de Heidelberg. Alemania dispone de una de las mejores redes de transporte público en toda Europa. Debido a ello, se puede precindir sin problema del coche para visitar los lugares de interés o los sitios de ambiente.

❖ La Germania ha fatto molti progressi negli ultimi anni sulla strada verso una equiparazione dei diritti dei gay e delle lesbiche. Non esiste però ancora una legge contro la discriminazione di omosessuali, ma grazie al cambiamento politico un tale passo è da aspettarsi. Sono già in corso le preparazioni per una equiparazione legale, almeno parziale, delle convivenze omosessuali con i matrimoni eterosessuali: quattro dei cinque partiti rappresentati nel Bundestag si sono espressi per una equiparazione più o meno ampia; è probabile che venga introdotta la forma giuridica da una „convivenza registrata" per coppie di fatto. La Germania è uno stato federale composto di 16 Bundesländer (stati federali) che godono di una certa autonomia nella politica interna. Ciò si può vedere nelle diverse leggi che riguardano l'equiparazione dei diritti degli omosessuali. Ad Amburgo esiste già una convivenza registrata per coppie omosessuali. Nelle costituzioni di Berlino, Brandeburgo e la Turingia esiste un espolicito divieto per quanto riguarda la discriminazione di omosessuali. In altri Länder esistono regolamenti simili su un livello inferiore alla costituzione. Malgrado quest'equiparazione legale esiste ancora un dislivello per quanto riguarda la tolleranza in generale. Mentre nelle grandi città è possibile vivere apertamente una vita gay, nei posti di campagna o dominati dal cattolicesimo l'omosessualità vie-

TREFFE HEISSE JUNGS
AUS DEINER GEGEND
LIVE
EGAL WOHER DU KOMMST!
18+ Phonevision 2,77 DM/min.
005 996 4831

ne ancora visto come una macchia; è per questo motivo che molti gay e lesbiche vanno nelle città, soprattutto nei baluardi gay come Berlino, Amburgo, Colonia e Monaco di Baviera. In questo senso la Germania non si distingue dai suoi vicini europei. Dal punto di vista turistico, la Germania è un paese dalle mille possibilità. La storia di un millennario del paese ha lasciato, oltre il muro di Berlino e il castello di Heidelberg, la sue traccie. La Germania dispone di una delle migliori reti di comunicazione d'Europa. Così è possibile esplorare l'ambiente gay e le altre bellezze delle grandi città anche senza macchina.

NATIONAL GAY INFO

Adam
c/o Foerster Verlag, Sprendlinger Landstraße 120, ✉63069 Offenbach ☎ (069) 831022/3 Fax: (069) 84 75 17

Box
PO Box 29 03 41 ✉ 50525 Köln ☎ 0221/9541312
Fax: 0221/954 13 11 E-Mail: boxcentral@netcologne.de
Homepage: www.box-online.de
Monthly publication (middle of each month) with regional editions. Featuring news, comments, reports, satire, erotics, scene-gossip, classifieds and dates. For free at gay venues.

Downtown
c/o Michael Sürth Verlag, Homburger Straße 22, ✉50969 Köln ☎ (0221) 3603025 Fax: (0221) 360 30 25
Monthly, published last Fri in month. News from the gay scene and classifieds. Free at gay venues.

Du & Ich
c/o Leine-Verlag, Herrenstraße 15, ✉30159 Hannover
☎ (0511) 130 51 Fax: (0511) 17 357
Most traditional of the German gay magazines. Reports on German and international gay scene, entertainment and politics. Lots of personals; is published monthly, DM 15.

Forum Homosexualität und Literatur
Thu 12-16 h c/o Uni-GH Siegen, FB 3, ✉57068 Siegen
☎ (0271) 740-4588
Research on the aspects of homosexuality and literature.

Freies Tagungshaus Waldschlößchen
Mon-Fri 8.30-12.30, Wed 15-18 h 37130
Reinhausen ☎ (05592) 382 Fax: 05592-17 92
Email waldschloesschen@t-online.de
Homepage http://www.waldschloesschen.org

Freshmen
c/o Bruno Gmünder Verlag, PO Box 610104 ✉10921 Berlin
☎ (030) 615 00 30 Fax: (030) 615 90 07
Bimonthly publication. Introducing erotic photography and stories. DM 19.95.

Gay Express
c/o Verlag W.-D. Fritsch Verlag, Einemstraße 6, ✉10787 Berlin ☎ 030/261 97 01 Fax: 030/261 97 02
Monthly publication. Regional reports about the gay scene and diary of events of Hamburg, Berlin and Frankfurt. Engaged political reports. Commercial and classified ads. Free at gay venues.

Gay-Privat
c/o Der heiße Draht, PO Box 6163 ✉30061 Hannover
☎ (0511) 3809552

MacMan Cologne
http://macman.org
MacMan Cologne-The German Queer Resources Directory.

MÄNNERaktuell
c/o Bruno Gmünder Verlag, PO Box 61 01 04 ✉10921 Berlin
☎ 030/615 00 30 Fax: 030/615 91 10.
E-Mail: MAENNERakt@aol.com
Monthly publication with news, articles, reviews, gay guide, photographs and personal ads on about 120 pages. DM 14.80.

Manbase Deutschland
http://www.manbase.com/de
The gay magazine in the internet.
Events: http://www.manbase.com/termine

Outline
c/o Krämer Medien Verlags GmbH, Lützowerstr.89-90 ✉10785 Berlin ☎ 030/23 00 56 42 Fax: 030/23 00 56 43
E-Mail: info@outline-magazin.de
Homepage: www.outline-magazin.de
A monthly magazine focusing on society, culture and lifestyle with events and happenings in the gay and lesbian scene. DM 6.80.

QUEER Mon-Fri 10-18 h
Pipinstraße 7 ✉50667 Köln ☎ (0221) 57 97 60
Fax: (0221) 579 76 66 E-Mail: queer@pride.de
Homepage: http:/ www.queer.de
National monthly newspaper. Four regional editions. Contains political news, arts & culture, lifestyle, events, address-listings, classifieds etc. For free at gay venues.

RIK
c/o First medien GmbH, Kamekestraße 14 ✉50672 Köln

☎ 0221/9521133 Fax: 0221/ 510 72 24
E-Mail: first01@aol.com
Monthly magazine. Featuring comments, satire, gossip, classifieds, dates. For free at gay venues.

ScOUT!
http://www.myscout.com
Internet database, gay internet search engine.

Stiefel. Der
c/o Venker, Palmstraße 39 ✉ 50672 Köln
Publication of the clubs united in the SKVdC. Four times a year for free for members.

SubMission
Welserstraße 24 ✉ 10777 Berlin
Homepage: www.sub-mission.com
Gay fetish magazine featuring stories and classifieds.

Vary
Mainzer Landstraße 109 ✉ 60329 Frankfurt/M
☎ 069/ 25 00 43 Fax: 069/70 76 01 86
Monthly magazine for Germany.

NATIONAL PUBLISHERS

Albino Verlag
Leuschnerdamm 31 ✉ 10999 Berlin ☎ 030/615 00 30
Fax: 030/615 90 07
Gay fiction./Schwule Literatur.

Bruno Gmünder Verlag
Leuschnerdamm 31 ✉ 10999 Berlin ☎ (030) 615 00 30
Fax: 030/615 03 37 E-Mail: Spaberlin@aol.com
Publisher of SPARTACUS International Gay Guide, National Editions, ...von hinten series, SCHWULE MÄNNER pocket almanac/gay guide, MÄNNERaktuell-magazine, FRESHMEN-magazine, fiction, non-fiction and photo books.

Foerster Verlag
Sprendlinger Landstraße 120 ✉63069 Frankfurt/M
☎ (069) 297 86 81 Fax: (069) 84 75 17.
Publisher of gay magazines (ADAM), gay erotic magazines (Boy oh Boy, HOMOH, Gay Guys) and fiction.

Janssen Verlag
PO Box 15 07 01 ✉10669 Berlin
☎ 030/881 15 90 Fax: 030/ 881 59 80
E-Mail: ayart@galerie-janssen.de
Homepage: www.galerie-janssen.de
Photo-books, comics and videos.

MännerschwarmSkript
Neuer Pferdermarkt 32 ✉20359 Hamburg ☎ 040/430 26 50
Fax: 040/430 29 32
Publisher of books and mail order of books, videos, and CDs.

Pink Rose Press Verlag
Lerchenstraße 100 ✉22767 Hamburg ☎ 040/43188170
Fax: 040/43 18 81 72 E-Mail: piropr@aol.com
Publisher of Gay German Guide and different CDRoms.

Quer Verlag
Akazienstraße 25 ✉10823 Berlin
☎ (030) 78702339 Fax: (030) 788 49 50
E-Mail: querverlag@aol.com
Publisher of gay and lesbian fiction and non-fiction.

Verlag rosa Winkel
PO Box 62 06 04 ✉10796 Berlin
☎ (030) 85729295 Fax: 030/ 85 72 92 96
E-Mail: osawinkel@t-online.de
Publisher of bibliophile gay reprints and general gay literature.

NATIONAL COMPANIES

Adonis Gay Versand (G)
Bornstraße 14 ✉44135 Dortmund ☎ (0231) 57 36 19
Fax: (0231) 83 72 23
Leather, toys and accessories. Catalogue for free.

Black Jump
PO Box 80 02 46 ✉ 81602 München
☎ 089/48004333 Fax: 089/48 00 43 32.
Toys, condoms, lubricants, leather, rubber, slings, S/M and fetish accessories. Also rental service. Create their own collection of slings. Large showroom.

Bruno Gmünder Versand 0-24 h
Zeughofstraße 1 ✉10997 Berlin ☎ 030/610 01 200
Fax: 030/610 01 222 E-Mail: bgvmail@aol.com
Fiction, non-fiction, photo-books, videos, calendars, CDs, etc. Catalogue for free.

DE AH'A-Vertrieb
PO Box 61 01 49, Dieffenbachstraße 33, ✉10921 Berlin
☎ 030/69008713 Fax: 030/69 00 87 42
Sales department of Deutsche AIDS-Hilfe.

Edition Manfred Salzgeber
Schloßstraße 29, ✉ 12163 Berlin ☎ 030/793 41 81
Fax: 030/93 38 88.
Gay film distributor.

Hellas Medien International Hotline 9-20 h
Am Webermoor 6 ✉19395 Karow ☎ (038738) 700 22
E-Mail: Hellas_Medien@t-online.de
Books, videos, toys, underwear. Catalogue for free.

HRS Versand
PO Box 70 05 03 ✉60555 Frankfurt/M ☎ (069) 68 27 98
Sex aids and toys. Catalogue for free.

Janssen Versand
PO Box 15 07 01 ✉10669 Berlin
☎ 030/881 74 69 Fax: 030/881 59 80
E-Mail: gayart@galerie-janssen.de
Homepage: www.galerie-janssen.de

K.A.B.- Kühn/Clabes Versandhandel GbR
PO Box 10 08 40 ✉47008 Duisburg ☎ (0203) 33 44 82
Fax: (0203) 33 44 82
Toys, leather, piercing, motorbike-fashion, etc.

Lambda-Soft Michael Nithammer
PO Box 15 09 ✉58745 Altena Fax: 02352) 232 34
Gay software.

Lifestyle Versand (CC) 10-20 h
PO Box 21 07 42 ✉50532 Köln ☎ (0221) 81 03 27
Fax: (0221) 81 06 30
Toys, leather, cock rings, lubricants, underwear, books, piercing jewelry.

London Condom
Am Waltershof 46 ✉41066 Monchengladbach

Männer natürlich (G MA)
Im Mühlenbach 81 ✉ 53127 Bonn ☎ 0228/25 44 34
Fax: 0228/ 25 42 19
Tour operator for group-travelling.

MEC MAIL ORDER (CC) Mon-Fri 10-22, Sat 10-18 h
Rathenauplatz 24 ✉50674 Köln ☎ (0221) 94070333
☎ (0800) 863 37 93 (toll free)
Underwear, swimwear and clubwear.

OBoy!
Stöckigstraße 2 ✉95463 Bindlach ☎ (09208) 658 00
Fax: (09208) 65 80 81 E-Mail: info@oboy.de
Homepage: www.oboy.de
Underwear, beachwear and nightwear.

Passepartout
PO Box 10 32 03, ✉20022 Hamburg
☎ 040/28 05 32 55 Fax: 040/ 28 05 30 03
E-Mail: info@passepartout-vakuumpumpen.de
Homepage: www.passepartout-vakuumpumpen.de
Vacuum pumps, SM and metal toys. New in January 2000 - Dildos. See website www.dildo-toys.de

Pride Company (GLM MA) Mon-Fri 10-16:00h
Höninger Weg 100 A ✉50869 Köln ☎ 0221/3680 100
Fax: 0221/3860 111 E-Mail: company@pride.de
Homepage: www.pride.de
A national company catering for the gay and lesbian community. The Pride Company has many small branch companies. These include : (with e-mail address)
-Pride Assekuranz - Insurance : assekuranz@pride.de
-Pride Collections - Fashion mail order : collections@pride.de
-Pride Consulting - company consultation : consulting@pride.de
-Pride Entertainment - Casting agency, Production : entertainment@pride.de
-Pride Finance - Finance department : finance@pride.de
-Pride Online - internet provider : online@pride.de
-Pride Telecom - telecommunications : telecom@pride.de

PRO-FUN media GmbH (CC GLM)
Rödelheimer Landstraße 13a ✉60487 Frankfurt/M
☎ 069)/707677-0 Fax: 069/ 70 76 77 11
E-Mail: service@pro-fun.de Homepage: www.pro-fun.de
Toys, books, videos, CDs, posters, piercings. Free catalogue under ☎ 0800-776 38 61

Topversand
PO Box 11 29, ✉85749 Karlsfeld ☎ (08131) 910 50
Fax: (08131) 926 69 *Clothes, accessories, videos, books, etc.*

Union Versand
PO Box 2718-5 ✉55516 Bad Kreuznach ☎ (0671) 324 73
Books, magazines, videos, toys, leather, rubber, piercing.

Vimpex GmbH
PO Box 14 04 ✉24572 Bad Bramstedt ☎ (04192) 810 00
Toys and leather articles.

www.homo.de
Alte Gasse 51 ✉60313 Frankfurt/M ☎ 069/28 12 60
Fax: 069/297 75 42 E-Mail: shop@homo.de
Gay internet book shop.

NATIONAL GROUPS

Bisexuelles Netzwerk BINE e.V. Tel: Mon, Wed 17-18 h
PO Box 61 02 14, ✉10923 Berlin ☎ 030/211 74 05
National association of bisexual groups and organizations.

Bund Lesbischer und Schwuler JournalistInnen e.V.
PO Box 30 42 04 ✉ 10724 Berlin
Homepage: www.gaymedia.de
Federation of gay and lesbian journalists.

Bundesarbeitsgemeinschaft Schwule im Gesundheitswesen
Warthestraße 70 ✉12051 Berlin ☎ 030/628 37 05
Fax: 030/62 80 44 89
National interest group of gays working in the health system.

Bundesverband der gehörlosen Lesben und Schwulen e.V.
Meeting every 2nd & 4th Fri / Month from 19:00h Zirkusweg 11 ✉ 20359 Hamburg
Fax: (040) 31 79 22 43 E-Mail: bgls_gehoerlos@hotmail.com
Homepage: www.home.t-online.de/home/bgls-/index.htm

Bundesweiter Arbeitskreis schwuler Soldaten (BASS)
c/o LSVD Berlin-Brandenburg, PO Box 59 01 13, ✉10419 Berlin ☎ (040) 61 04 97 Fax: (040) 61 04 97
E-Mail: info@BASSoldaten.de Homepage: www.BASSodaten.de
National working group of gay soldiers.

Cutting Club
PO Box 10 04 05 ✉46524 Dinslaken
E-Mail: cuttingclub@eurocirc.org
Organization for cut gays and those who want to be circumcised.

Deutsche AIDS-Hilfe e.V.
Dieffenbachstraße 33, ✉10967 Berlin *(U-Schönleinstraße)*
☎ 030/690087-0 Fax: 030/69 00 87-42
E-Mail: dah@aidshife.de
Homepage: www.aidshilfe.de

Deutscher Beirat für homosexuelle Frauen und Männer bei den AA
Postfach 42 08 21 ✉12068 Berlin
You can ask for the meetings-list of the gay and lesbian AA groups in Europe in writing.

Feet Back
Postfach 21 34 ✉65770 Kelkheim
Group for foot-fetish people.

GA-Gay Architects
PO Box 61 03 53 ✉10926 Berlin

Gay Skinhead Movement
Postfach 10 02 53 ✉10562 Berlin
E-Mail: gsmgermany@geocities.com
Homepage: www.geocities.com/WestHollywood/Heights/2618
Union of gay skinheads (non racist), no fetish-club.

Green Berets International e.V. (GBI)
PO Box 10 20 17 ✉45020 Essen ☎ 0201/891 44 31
Fax: 0201/891 44 12 E-Mail: gbi_ev@gmx.de
Homepage: www.green-berets.de
Pacifist and unpolitical group of uniform lovers. Regional groups in different cities in Germany and the Netherlands.

Homosexuelle Adventisten in Deutschland e.V.
PO Box 10 07 23 ✉64207 Darmstadt ☎ (06151) 537612
E-Mail: HADInfo@aol.com
Homepage: www.sdakinship.org
National organization of gay and lesbian adventists in Germany.

Homosexuelle Selbsthilfe e.V.
Löwengasse 27, ✉60385 Frankfurt/M Fax: (069) 46 50 68.

Homosexuelle und Kirche (HuK)
PO Box 11 02 01 ✉37047 Göttingen ☎ 0241/123 46
Fax: 0241/42 85 01 28 Homepage: www.huk.org
Geschäftsstelle Mainz (Johannes) ☎ (06131) 88 31 31

International Support Group for Information Transfer and Networking
Elberfelder Straße 23 ✉10555 Berlin ☎ 030/392 53 11
☎ 030/812 22 52 Fax: 030/392 43 19

LSG-Gay Esperantist League
c/o Schwule Eintracht, PO Box 60 01 ✉76040 Karlsruhe
International Gay Association communicating in Esperanto/Internationale schwule Organisation, die in Esperanto kommuniziert.

LSVD Berlin-Brandenburg / Bundesgeschäftsstelle
Katzbachstraße 5, ✉10965 Berlin
☎ 030/44008240 Fax: 030/ 44 00 82 41
E-Mail: berlin@lsvd.de Homepage: www.lsvd.de
Information, counselling, addresses, events, programs.

Positiv e.V. Mon-Fri 8.30-12.30 h
Waldschlößchen ✉37130 Reinhausen ☎ (05592) 1792 Fax: (05592) 1792 E-Mail: waldschloesschen@t-online.de
Organiser of nationwide get-togethers for people with HIV and AIDS.

Sozialdemokratischer Arbeitskreis gegen die Diskriminierung Homosexueller
PO Box 22 80 ✉53012 Bonn

Völklinger Kreis e.V.-Bundesverband Gay Manager
Leyendeckerstraße 1 ✉50825 ☎ (0221) 546 19 79
Association of gay managers.

Zentrale Erfassung: Homosexuellendiskriminierung (ZEH)
c/o HSH, PO Box 47 22 ✉30047 Hannover

Aachen ☎ 0241

GAY INFO

Stonewall
Postfach 12 88 ✉52013 ☎ 54 37 36
Homepage http://macman.org/stonewalltac For free at gay venues.

BARS

Gentlemen (B D f GLM lj MA OS p s) 20-6 h, Sun Mon closed
Promenadenstraße 31 ✉52062 ☎ 401 57 96

RESTAURANTS

P33 (B F g MA N WE) 17-2, Fri-Sat -3 (meals -24 h)
Promenadenstraße 33 ✉52062 ☎ 40 37 33

SEX SHOPS/BLUE MOVIES

Filme Video Magazine
Adalbertsteinweg 1 B ✉52070 ☎ 54 19 03
Fax: (0 22 38) 84 05 03
Heterosexual sex shop with a separate gay section.

Orion (g) Mon-Fri 10-20, Sat -20 h
Roermonder Straße 60 ✉52072 *(across/gegenüber Arbeitsamt)* ☎ 15 91 17

Sexy Villa Nova (g VS) Mon-Sat 10-22 h
Heinrichsallee 2, ✉52062 ☎ 90 199 12/11

Super Sex Basar (AC g MA VS) Mon-Fri 10-18.30, Thu -20.30, Sat -14 h
Gasborn 17 ✉52062 ☎ 20635 Fax: 20635

BOOK SHOPS

Backhaus Buchhandlung (CC g) Mon-Wed 9-18.30, Thu-Fri -20, Sat -16 h
Trichtergasse 14 ✉52064 ☎ 212 14

Mayersche Buchhandlung (g)
Ursulinerstraße 17-19 ✉52062 ☎ 477 70

TRAVEL & TRANSPORT

Horizon Reisen (glm) Mon-Wed 10-13, 14.30-18.30, Thu-Fri 10-13, 14.30-20, Sat 10-13 h
Stau 35-37 ✉26122 ☎ 0441/261 33 Fax: 0441/264 66

GENERAL GROUPS

Knutschfleck. Jugendgruppe
Kasinostraße 37 ✉52066 ☎ 281 64
E-Mail: Knutschflk@aol.com
Gay youth group age 15-27.

LSVD Aachen Euregio
PO Box 42 49, 52134 Herzogenrath ☎ (02406) 969080

Rainbow e.V.
Kasinostraße 37 ✉52066 ☎ 401 97 00
E-Mail: Rainbow@gmx.de

Schwulenreferat an den Aachener Hochschulen Mon 20 Coming Out Gruppe, Tue 18 Café, Wed 20 Plenum, Thu 19-21 h Beratung
Königstraße 14-16 ✉52064 ☎ 346 32
Also gay library/auch schwule Bibliothek.

Selbsthilfegruppe für Eltern homosexueller Jugendlicher
c/o AKIS, Lagerhausstraße 23-25 ☎ 490 09
S.i.d.A.H. Schwule in der AIDS-Hilfe
Zollernstraße 1, ✉52070 ☎ 53 25 58

HEALTH GROUPS

AIDS-Hilfe Aachen e.V.
Counselling ☎ 194 11 Mon, Tue, Thu 10-16 h, Wed/Fri 10-12 h
Zollernstraße 1 ✉52070 ☎ 53 25 58 Fax: 90 22 32
Jeder 1. Montag im Monat Frauentelefon

HELP WITH PROBLEMS

Rosa Telefon Tue 19-21 h
☎ 346 33
Schwules Überfalltelefon
☎ 192 28

RELIGIOUS GROUPS

Homosexuelle und Kirche (HuK), Regionalgruppe Aachen
Meeting every other Mon 19 h at Clubraum KHG, Pontstraße 72a
c/o Bernd Schulte, Friedrichstraße 95 ✉52070 ☎ 90 24 01

CRUISING

-Saarstraße/"Ehrenmal" (ayor r) Popular.
-Universität, Hauptmensa, Keller/University, Hauptmensa, basement.
-Kármán-Auditorium, unterhalb/below Fo 1
-Bushof und/and Volkshochschule, Petersstraße
-Hauptbahnhof/Main rail station

Ahaus ☎ 02561

GENERAL GROUPS

Euregio-Gays Wed 20-22 h
c/o AIDS-Hilfe, Marktstraße 16 ✉48683 ☎ 96 20 10

HEALTH GROUPS

AIDS-Hilfe Westmünsterland (GLM MA lj OS p)
Marktstraße 16 ✉46325 *(100m from town hall)* ☎ 19 411
Fax: 96 20 1 E-Mail: jul-hotline.ahwm@tobit.net
Homepage: www.tobit.net/aidshilfe

Ahlen ☎ 02382

HEALTH GROUPS

AIDS-Hilfe Ahlen e.V. Mon 9-12 17-19, Tue Thu 9-12 15-17, Wed Fri 15-17 h
Königstraße 9 ✉59227 ☎ 194 11

Albstadt ☎ 07431

CRUISING

-Across from Ebingen town hall.

Altenau ☎ 05328

HOTELS

Haus Waldfrieden (b bf g H MA sa) Sauna-Club 20-? h (WE)
Bürgermeister-Breyel-Weg 1-3 ✉38707 ☎ 14 50 / 252
Hotel with club-bar and sauna. Rooms with balcony. Rates Single DM 45, double 35-55/person (bf incl.)

Altenkirchen ☎ 02681

GENERAL GROUPS

SIW-Schwule im Westerwald every other week Wed 20-?
c/o Haus Felsenkeller, Heimstraße 4, ✉57610 ☎ 709 86

Amberg ☎ 09621

CAFES

Wiener Café (AC F glm MA) 09-18:00h
Vilstalstrasse 84 ✉92245 ☎ 775135

GENERAL GROUPS

Lederclub Burgfalken Oberpfalz 1st Fri 20 h
PO Box 17 21 ✉92207 ☎ 648 81 Fax: 648 81
E-Mail: burgfalken@amberg.gay-web.de

HEALTH GROUPS

AIDS-Hilfe Amberg-Sulzbach Mon Thu 19-21 h.
Meets 3rd Sun 11-14 h at Café Kontakt
Münzgässchen 3 ✉92224, PO Box 11 02 ✉92201 ☎ 49 69 29
E-Mail: aidshilfe@gay-web.de
Homepage: www.amberg.gay-web.de/ah

CRUISING

-Herrenstraße

Arnstadt ✉ 99310

GENERAL GROUPS

Homosexuelle Aktion Arnstadt e.V.
c/o Mike Böhm, Auf dem Anger 8, ✉99310

Aschaffenburg ☎ 06021

BARS

Uwe's Bistro (B G) 16-01:00h, Tue closed.
Strickergasse 19 ✉63739 ☎ 21 95 93

CAFES

Café ABdaten (f GLM YG) Thu 20:00h
Kirchhofweg 2 *(In youth center / Jugendkulturezentrum)*

SEX SHOPS/BLUE MOVIES

Orion (g) Mon-Fri 10-19, Sat 9-16 h
Ludwigstraße 7 ✉63739 *(Across from Main station)* ☎ 254 35

Ascha/Straubing ☎ 09961

GUEST HOUSES

Froschauer Hof „Bei Manfred und Werner" (B d G H MA msg N NU OS S SNU STV VS) Mon-Fri 18-24 h, Sat 15-2 h, Sun 15-23 h
Froschauer Straße 2 ✉94347 *(near Shell gas station)*
☎ & Fax: 91 04 77 Email: frosch.ascha@t-online.de
Homepage: http://home.t-online.de/home/frosch.ascha
Rates from 40-80 DM. Transfer to station 30 DM.

Augsburg ☎ 0821

BARS

Bistro Giorgio (B F GLM MA) 15-1 h
Georgenstraße 33 ✉86152 ☎ 508 43 14

DANCECLUBS

David's (D glm) Thu-Sat 17-04:00h, Sun 15-03:00h
Prinzregentenstrasse 1 ✉86150 ☎ 518718

SEX SHOPS/BLUE MOVIES

Inkognito (g) 9-24:00h
Theaterstrasse 6 ✉86152 ☎ 153652
Erotic shop with gay cinema and cubicals

Orion (g) Mon-Fri 10-20, Sat 9.30-16 h
Leonhardsberg 17/Mittlerer Graben ✉86150 ☎ 15 16 39

GENERAL GROUPS

Schwulen- und Lesbengruppe Augsburg (SCHAU) Fri 20-22 h
c/o ESG Zentrum, Völkstraße 27 ✉86150 ☎ 15 92 42

Schwulenreferat im AStA der Uni Augsburg Wed 16-17.30 h
Universitätsstraße 2 ✉86159 *(Room 2080)* ☎ 598 51 68/69

HEALTH GROUPS

AIDS-Hilfe Augsburg e.V. Wed 17-19 h
Morellstraße 24 ✉86159 ☎ 194 11

CRUISING

-Park »Rotes Tor« 0-24 h
-Wertachbrücke/Wertachstraße (AYOR) 0-24 h
-Meringer Au (lake on the right hand side)

Backnang ✉ 71522

CAFES

Tante Emma (AC B CC f GLM MA OS) Mon-Thu 11-24:00h, Fri & Sat 11-01:00h, Sun 14:30-24:00h
Willy-Brandt-Platz 3 ✉71522 ☎ 954844

Bad Bergzabern ☎ 06343

CRUISING

-Fussgängerzone/Pedestrian zone
-P bei/at Sparkasse

Bad Homburg ☎ 06172

SEX SHOPS/BLUE MOVIES

Erotik Oase (glm VS) Mon-Fri 11-19, Sat 11-14.30 h, Sun closed
Louisenstraße 32 ✉61348 *(In pedestrian zone)*

CRUISING

-Old railway station/Alter Bahnhof
-U-Gonzenheim

Bad Kreuznach ☎ 0671

BARS

BaLoo (B CC D G MA s) 20-1, Fri Sat -2 h
Bosenheimer Straße 158 ✉55543 ☎ 726 26

Spartacus (B f GLM lj MA OG s) 20-1, Fri Sat -2 h
Rüsselsheimer Straße 50 ✉55545 ☎ 415 35

DANCECLUBS

Hexenkeller (B D GLM) Wed-Sat 20- ?
Schloßgartenstraße 29 ✉55583 ☎ 06708/66 15 04

SEX SHOPS/BLUE MOVIES

Orion (g) Mon-Fri 10-20, Sat 9.30-16 h
Mannheimer Straße 206 ✉55543 *(At Schaadt'scher Platz)*
☎ 628 80

CRUISING

-P Konrad-Frey-Straße (at night, near railway station/nachts, nahe Bahnhof)

Bad Salzuflen ☎ 052 22

SEX SHOPS/BLUE MOVIES

Novum BBZ Erotik Markt (g vs) Mon-Sat 9.30-21.30 h
Neue Straße 8, ✉ 32108 ☎ 856 66

Bad Tölz ☎ 08041

GENERAL GROUPS

SchuTz-Schwule in Tölz und im Oberland e.V. (GLM) 1st/3rd Fri 20 h
Benediktbeurer Strasse 2 ✉83646 ☎ 96 12

HELP WITH PROBLEMS

Rosa Telefon 1st/3rd Fri 20-21.30 h
Benediktbeuer Strasse 2 ☎ 96 12

Bad Urach ☎ 07125

VIDEO SHOPS

Videoland (g vs) Mon-Fri 9.30-12.30, 15-19.30, Sat 9-20, Sun 9.30-12 h
In der Musel 32/Stuttgarter Straße ✉72574 ☎ 71 11
Bücher, Videos. Verleih und Verkauf./Books, videos, also for rent.

Bad Wörishofen ☎ 08247

HOTELS

Hotel Reblaus (AC bf F g H MA NG OS) Restaurant 11.30-24 h, closed Tue
Hans-Holzmann-Straße 1 ✉86825 ☎ 10 31 Fax: 340 50
Small, centrally located hotel. Rooms with all facilities, Radio/TV, Minibar, partly with balcony. Rates Single DM 90-155, double 180-310 (bf incl.).

Baden-Baden ☎ 07221

BARS

Odeon (AC B CC f G MA s) Thu-Tue 20-1 h
Balzenbergstraße 41 ✉76530 ☎ 280 28

HOTELS

Hotel Regent (A B bf CC F glm H MA s)
Eichstraße 2 ✉76530 *(central location)* ☎ 90 75-0 Fax: 256 61
Email: info@regent-hotel-bad-bad-com
Homepage: www.regent-hotel-bad-bad.com
22 rooms with shower/WC, TV, telephone. Rates DM 120-220.

CRUISING

-Lichentaler Allee (between Kunsthalle and tennis lawn, best 22-1 h)

Bamberg ☎ 0951

BARS

Pausen-Stübla. Zum (B d F glm MA) 11-14, 18-1, Sat 19-2, Sun 19-1 h, closed Wed
Martin-Luther-Straße 4/Dr.-von-Schmitt-Straße ✉96050
☎ 234 68

SEX SHOPS/BLUE MOVIES

Orion (g) Mon-Fri 9.30-20, Sat 9.30-16 h
Luitpoldstraße 16 ✉96052 ☎ 218 59

GENERAL GROUPS

Uferlos-Schwule und Lesben in Bamberg e.V. Meetings Thu 19.30 h
at Pro familia, Kunigundenruhstraße 24 PO Box 17 42 ✉96008
☎ 247 29 E-Mail: uferlos@bamberg.gay-web.de
Homepage: www.bamberg.gay-web.de

HEALTH GROUPS

AIDS-Beratung Oberfranken Mon-Fri 9-12 h
Kunigundenstraße 24 ✉96050 ☎ 279 98 Fax 279 98

CRUISING

-Hauptbahnhof/main station
-Am Kranen (unter den Brücken/under the bridges)
-Tiefgarage/underground garage
-Obstmarkt
-Kaufhaus Hertie/Hertie department store

Bansin ☎ 038378

GUEST HOUSES

Villa von Desny (CC bf g H MA NU OS wh) All year
Strandpromenade 4 ✉17429 *(The island Usedom)*
☎ 2430 Fax: 24324
Beach location. Guest house and Café.

Barby ☎ 039298

GUEST HOUSES

Colphus. Am (B bf CC d F glm H OS) 8-24 h
Otto-Beckmann-Straße 14 ✉39249 ☎ 73 17 Fax: 73 17
Café, restaurant and guest house.

Bayreuth ☎ 0921

GENERAL GROUPS

Vereinigung Homosexualität und Gesellschaft e.V. (VHG) Meetings Mon 20 h at Underground, von-Römer-Straße 15
PO Box 10 12 45 ✉95412 ☎ 85 29 28

HEALTH GROUPS

AIDS-Beratungsstelle Oberfranken Mon-Fri 8.30-13.30, Thu 8.30-17 h
Schulstraße 15 ✉95444 ☎ 825 00

HELP WITH PROBLEMS

Rosa Telefon Mon 18.30-20 h
☎ 85 29 28

CRUISING

-Festspielpark (summer)
-Main rail station/Hauptbahnhof
-Festspielpark
-[P] Albrecht-Dürer-Straße
-near/nahe Hallenbad

Bergisch Gladbach ☎ 0172

GENERAL GROUPS

GayL Bergisch-Gladbacher Gruppe für Schwule, Lesben und Bisexuelle
PO Box 10 02 48 ✉51402 ☎ 4873085
E-Mail: GayL@eurogay.net
Homepage: http//www.gayl.notrix.de, e-mail:GayL@eurogay.net
Infos, Termine und Beratung per Telefon. Information by telephone

Berlin ☎ 030

● Berlin is a city with many different places of interest for it's gay visitors and also it's gay community. There are a variety of clubs from the West to the East and of course many good-looking men. Many rainbow coloured flags of the gay community are proudly hung in the gay triangle: Wittenbergplatz, Nollendorfplatz and Victoria-Luise-Platz, located in the heart of Schöneberg. In Kreuzberg, and in the whole of Prenzlauer Berg exist a wide range of things to do from sitting in a street cafe to sweating it out in a sauna. The scene in Berlin is much more clear cut than in other cities. The SNAXX Club has etablished itself in Europe as venue for „Hardtrance" and fetish parties. Evening entertainment is well taken care of around the construction sites of the Hackeschen Höfe with numerous assortments of clubs, bars, coffee shops and tea dances. A trend magazine from Japan has given the Sunday parties at the WMF a place in the top ten of things to do in the city.

✸ Berlin ist eine Stadt ohne Zentrum. Und das ist gut so: An den unterschiedlichsten Orten öffnen sich hier die Geheimtüren zu angesagten Clubs und schönen Männern. Im Schöneberger Dreieck zwischen Wittenbergplatz, Nollendorfplatz und Viktoria-Luise-Platz wehen dem Besucher stolz die Regenbogenfahnen ins Gesicht. Auch in Kreuzberg und im ganzen Prenzlauer Berg ist schwules Leben vom Straßencafé bis zur Sauna gut etabliert. Die Szene steht im Ruf, etwas markiger zu sein als die anderer deutscher Städte. Kein Wunder, daß sich hier mit dem SNAXX Club das Venue aus Hardtrance und Fetischparty Europas überhaupt herausbilden konnte. Doch auch für den Freund gut swingender Abendunterhaltung wird gesorgt. Rund um die Hackeschen Höfe entwickelt sich entlang der vielen Baustellen eine edle, durchaus schwule Clubkultur aus weißweinsüchtigen Modenschauen und silbrig dekadenten Teadances. So wählte jüngst ein bedeutendes japanisches Trendmagazin die Sonntagsparties im WMF in die Ewigkeits-Top Ten der glamourösesten Dinge der Welt. An der Garderobe dort stehen, wie überall in der Stadt, viele berühmte Koffer herum. Und das hat seinen Grund.

▲ Berlin est une ville qui n'a pas de centre. Et c'est tant mieux: aux endroits les plus divers s'ouvrent des portes secrètes menant aux soirées et aux mâles sexy. A l'intérieur du triangle du „Schöneberg", entre la „Wittenbergplatz", la „Nollendorfplatz" et la „Viktoria-Luise-Platz", des drapeaux aux couleurs de l'arc-en-ciel flottent fièrement au

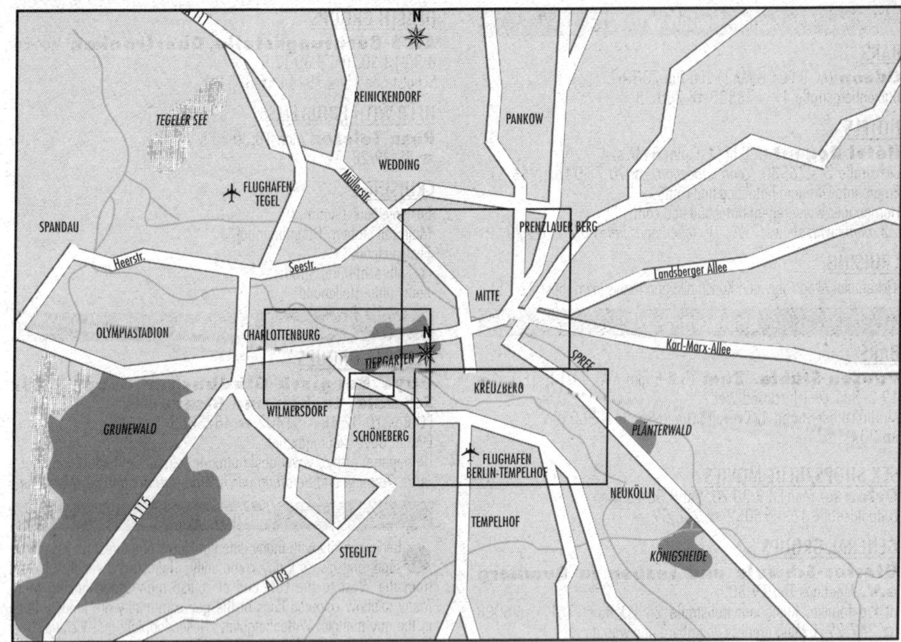

nez du quidam. Dans le „Kreuzberg" également et dans tout le „Prenzlauer Berg", la vie gaye est bien établie, depuis les cafés de rue jusqu'aux saunas. Le milieu a la renommée d'être le plus animé d'Allemagne. Ce n'est donc pas étonnant que l'arrivée en Europe de la hardtrance et de soirées fétichistes ait pu se faire ici avec le „SNAXX Club". Cependant, les adeptes de soirées étincelantes qui où l'on danse ne sont pas en reste. Tout autour des „Hackeschen Höfe" se développe, le long des nombreux chantiers, une vie nocturne gaye prisée des amateurs de mode qui féquentent, un verre de vin blanc à la main, un des thés dansants décadents du „Mitte". Récemment, un important magazine en vogue du Japon a élu les soirées dominicales du WMF parmi les 10 choses éternelles les plus séduisantes au monde.

☆ De hecho en la actualidad Berlín no dispone de un solo centro. Pero esto no significa un inconveniente, al contrario, en sitios muy diferentes se abren ahora las puertas secretas de clubs de moda y hombres guapos. En el triangulo del barrio de *Schöneberg*, que abarca *Wittenbergplatz*, *Nollendorfplatz* y *Victoria Luise Platz* el visitante puede contemplar innumerables banderas de arcoiris. Pero también en los barrios de *Kreuzberg* y de *Prenzlauer Berg* la vida gay con sus bares y saunas está bien establecido. El ambiente berlinés tiene fama de ser más duro en comparación con otras ciudades alemanas. Por ello no es de extrañar que precisamente aquí se encuentra el SNAXX Club, el sitio de hardtrance y fetichismo más famoso en toda Europa. Pero también para el amante de la diversión nocturna más moderada Berlín tiene mucho que ofrecer: En los alrededores de los *Hackesche Höfe*, al lado de innumerables obras, sumergen nuevos clubs gay. Aquí se organizan pasarelas de moda y bailes de té decadentes visitados por gente muyarreglada que degustan un vaso de buen vino blanco. Recientemente una importante revista japonesa de nuevas tendencias tituló las fiestas del domingo en el WMF como una de las cosas más glamorosas de todos los tiempos. Es uno de los sitios predilectos por famosos y famosillos quienes disfrutaron y siguen disfrutando la buena marcha berlinesa.

❖ Berlin è una città senza centro. Questo comporta anche dei vantaggi: Nei posti più svariati si aprono le porte segrete per entrare nei club *en vogue* o per godersi i begl'uomini. Nel triangolo di *Schöneberg* tra il *Wittenbergplatz*, *Nollendorfplatz* e *Viktoria-Luise-Platz* le bandiere con i colori dell'arcobaleno sventolano esprimendo l'orgoglio degli abitanti. Anche a Kreuzberg e nell'intero quartiere del Prenzlauer Berg la vita gay si è ben stabilita includendo i bar con terrazze sulle strade e le saune. Si dice che l'ambiente gay sia un po' più estrema rispetto a quello delle altre città tedesche. Non è da stupirsi che quì si è stablilito lo SNAXX Club, *il* posto in Europa per gli amanti di Hardtrance e party di feticcio. Ma anche per coloro che preferiscono una sera più leggera trovano il loro modo di divertimento. Attorno alle Hackesche Höfe lungo i numerosi cantieri si sta sviluppando una cultura di club gay con sfilate di moda e vino bianco e di té danzanti brillanti e decadenti. Recentemente un'importante rivista trendy giapponese ha eletto le feste della domenica nel WMF come le cose più glamour del mondo, così che si sono annoverate per eterno nei luoghi Top Ten.

GAY INFO

Aha-Lesben- und Schwulen-Zentrum Sun 17-22 h (Café)
Mehringdamm 61, ✉10961 *(2nd floor. U-Mehringdamm)*
☎ 692 36 00 E-mail: aha@eurogay.net
Homepage: http://eurogay.net/mitglieder/aha
Different events each month, call for informations

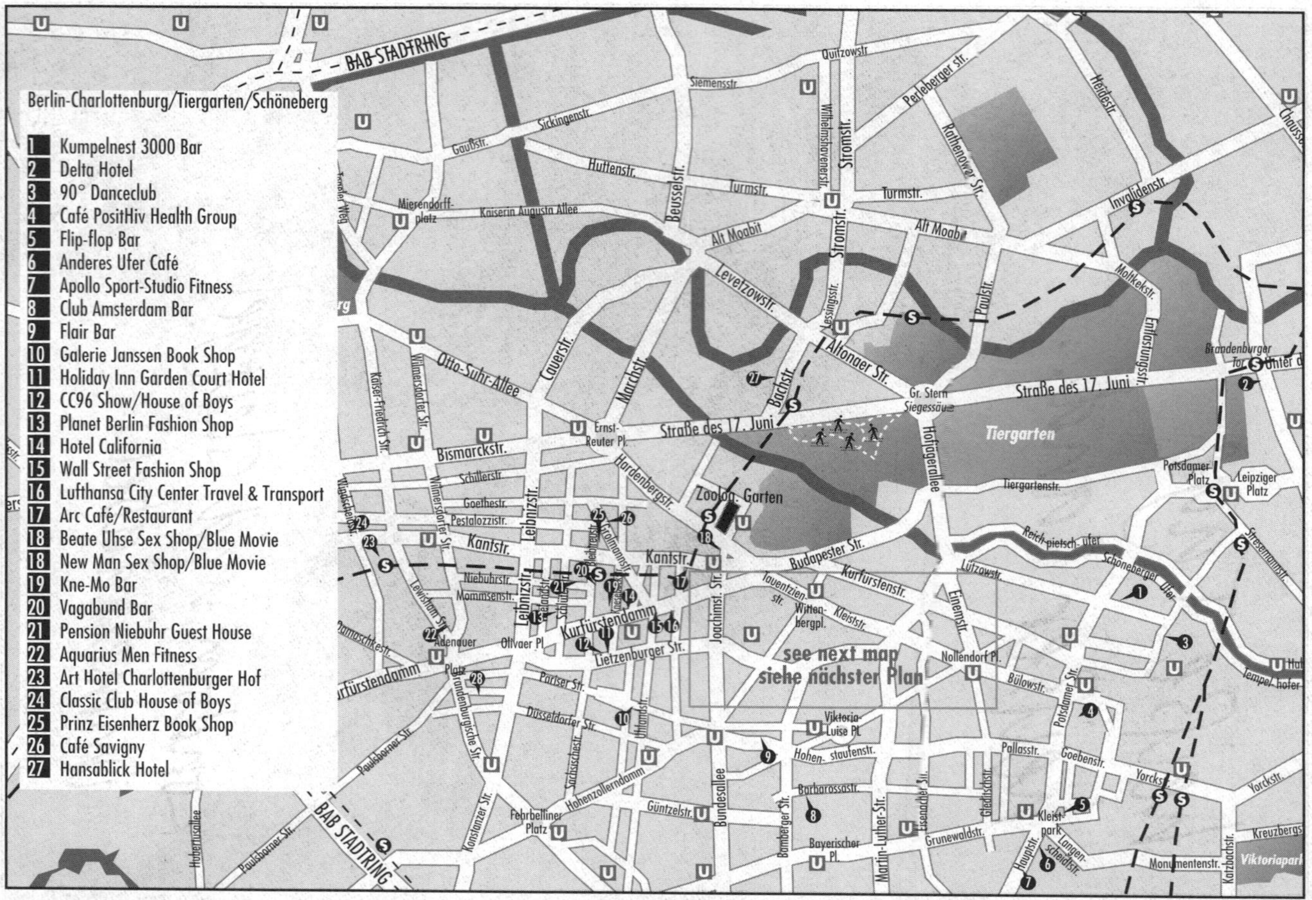
Berlin-Charlottenburg/Tiergarten/Schöneberg
1 Kumpelnest 3000 Bar
2 Delta Hotel
3 90° Danceclub
4 Café PositHiv Health Group
5 Flip-flop Bar
6 Anderes Ufer Café
7 Apollo Sport-Studio Fitness
8 Club Amsterdam Bar
9 Flair Bar
10 Galerie Janssen Book Shop
11 Holiday Inn Garden Court Hotel
12 CC96 Show/House of Boys
13 Planet Berlin Fashion Shop
14 Hotel California
15 Wall Street Fashion Shop
16 Lufthansa City Center Travel & Transport
17 Arc Café/Restaurant
18 Beate Uhse Sex Shop/Blue Movie
18 New Man Sex Shop/Blue Movie
19 Kne-Mo Bar
20 Vagabund Bar
21 Pension Niebuhr Guest House
22 Aquarius Men Fitness
23 Art Hotel Charlottenburger Hof
24 Classic Club House of Boys
25 Prinz Eisenherz Book Shop
26 Café Savigny
27 Hansablick Hotel
see next map
siehe nächster Plan
Tiergarten
Straße des 17. Juni
Zoolog. Garten
Hofjägerallee
Gr. Stern Siegessäule
Brandenburger Tor
Potsdamer Platz
Leipziger Platz
Kurfürstendamm
Kantstr.
Hardenbergstr.
Ernst-Reuter Pl.
Budapester Str.
Kurfürstenstr.
Nollendorf Pl.
Viktoria-Luise Pl.
Bundesallee
Fehrbelliner Platz
Adenauer Platz
Bismarckstr.
Otto-Suhr-Allee
Alt Moabit
Stromstr.
Levetzowstr.
Altonaer Str.
Heidestr.
Invalidenstr.
Rathenower Str.
Potsdamer Str.
Schöneberger Ufer
Reichpietsch-ufer
Lützowstr.
Einemstr.
Martin-Luther-Str.
Hauptstr.
Kleistpark
Yorckstr.
Viktoriapark
BAB STADTRING

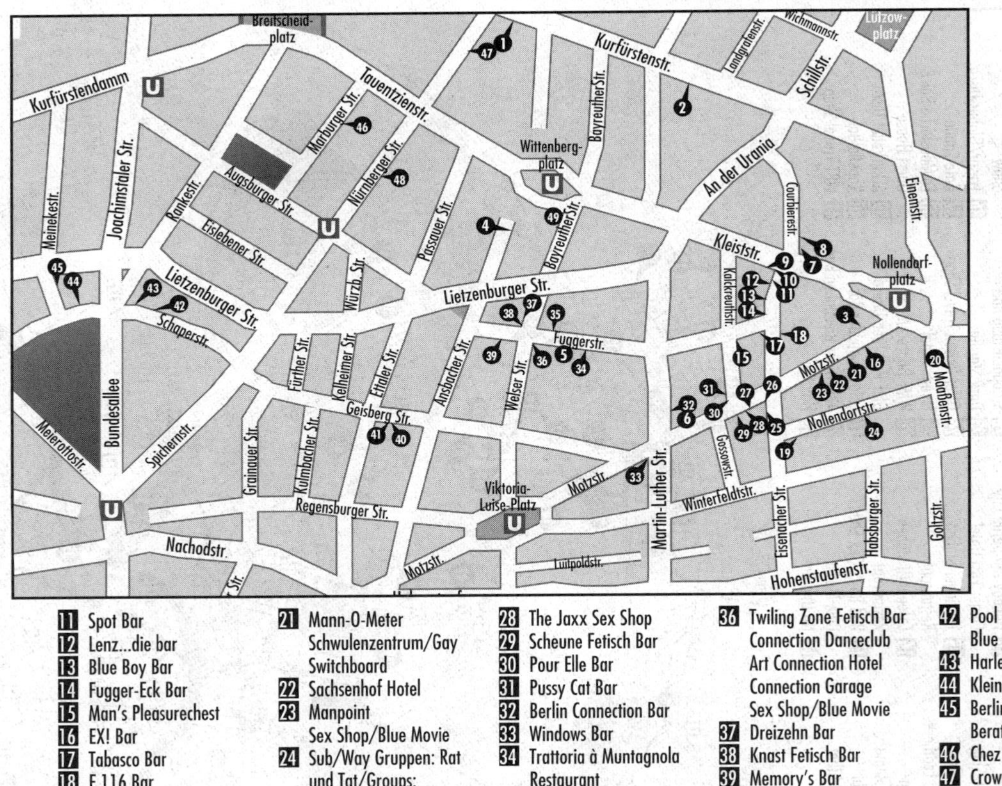

Berlin-Schönerberg Nord

1 Apollo Sauna
2 Steam Sauna
3 Omnes Restaurant
4 Andreas Kneipe Bar
5 Prinzknecht Bar
6 Lukiluki Restaurant
7 Movie Bar
8 Playground Sex Shop
9 Kleist Casino Danceclub
10 New Action Fetisch Bar
11 Spot Bar
12 Lenz...die bar
13 Blue Boy Bar
14 Fugger-Eck Bar
15 Man's Pleasurechest
16 EX! Bar
17 Tabasco Bar
18 E 116 Bar
19 Good Vibration/Mister B Store
20 Café Berio
21 Mann-O-Meter Schwulenzentrum/Gay Switchboard
22 Sachsenhof Hotel
23 Manpoint Sex Shop/Blue Movie
24 Sub/Way Gruppen: Rat und Tat/Groups: Counselling
25 Tom's House Guest House
26 Tom's Bar
27 Hafen Bar
28 The Jaxx Sex Shop
29 Scheune Fetisch Bar
30 Pour Elle Bar
31 Pussy Cat Bar
32 Berlin Connection Bar
33 Windows Bar
34 Trattoria à Muntagnola Restaurant
35 City Men Sex Shop Blue Movie
36 Twiling Zone Fetisch Bar Connection Danceclub Art Connection Hotel Connection Garage Sex Shop/Blue Movie
37 Dreizehn Bar
38 Knast Fetisch Bar
39 Memory's Bar
40 Arco Hotel
41 Bavaria Apotheke Pharmacy
42 Pool Berlin Sex Shop Blue Movie
43 Harlekin Bar
44 Kleine Philharmonie Bar
45 Berliner AIDS-Hilfe Beratung/Counselling
46 Chez Nous Show
47 Crowne Plaza Berlin City Center Hotel
48 Bruno's Bücher/Books
49 Comfort Hotel Auberge

BERLIN-MITTE/
PRENZLAUER BERG

1 Sonntagsclub Gay Info
2 Schall & Rauch Bar & Guest House
3 Adam Book Shop
4 Amsterdam Bar
5 Black Style Leather & Fetish Shop
6 Treibhaus Sauna
7 Pick Ab! Bar
8 Romeo Nachtbar
9 Greifbar
10 Zum Burgfrieden Bar
11 Darkroom Bar
12 Geierwally's... Bar
13 Stiller Don Bar
14 Holiday Inn Berlin City Center East Hotel
15 Thüringer Stuben Restaurant
16 Offenbach Stuben Restaurant
17 Bad Boy'z Sex Shop/ Blue Movie
18 Na Und Bar
19 Enzmann Travel & Transport
20 Jim's Bar
21 Café November
22 Schoppenstube Bar
23 Dark Star Bar
24 Offer Reisen Travel Shop
25 Myer's Hotel
26 WMF Danceclub GMF Gay Teea Dance
27 Café Senefelder Bar
28 Altberliner Bierstuben Bar
30 Flax Bar
31 Sonderbar
33 Besenkammer Bar
34 Oh-ase Bar
35 BKA-Zelte Schloßplatz Show
36 Tresor/Globus Disco
37 Gate Sauna
38 Le Moustache Bar & Guest House
39 Ackerkeller Disco
40 Kapelle Bar
41 WBT Travel Shop

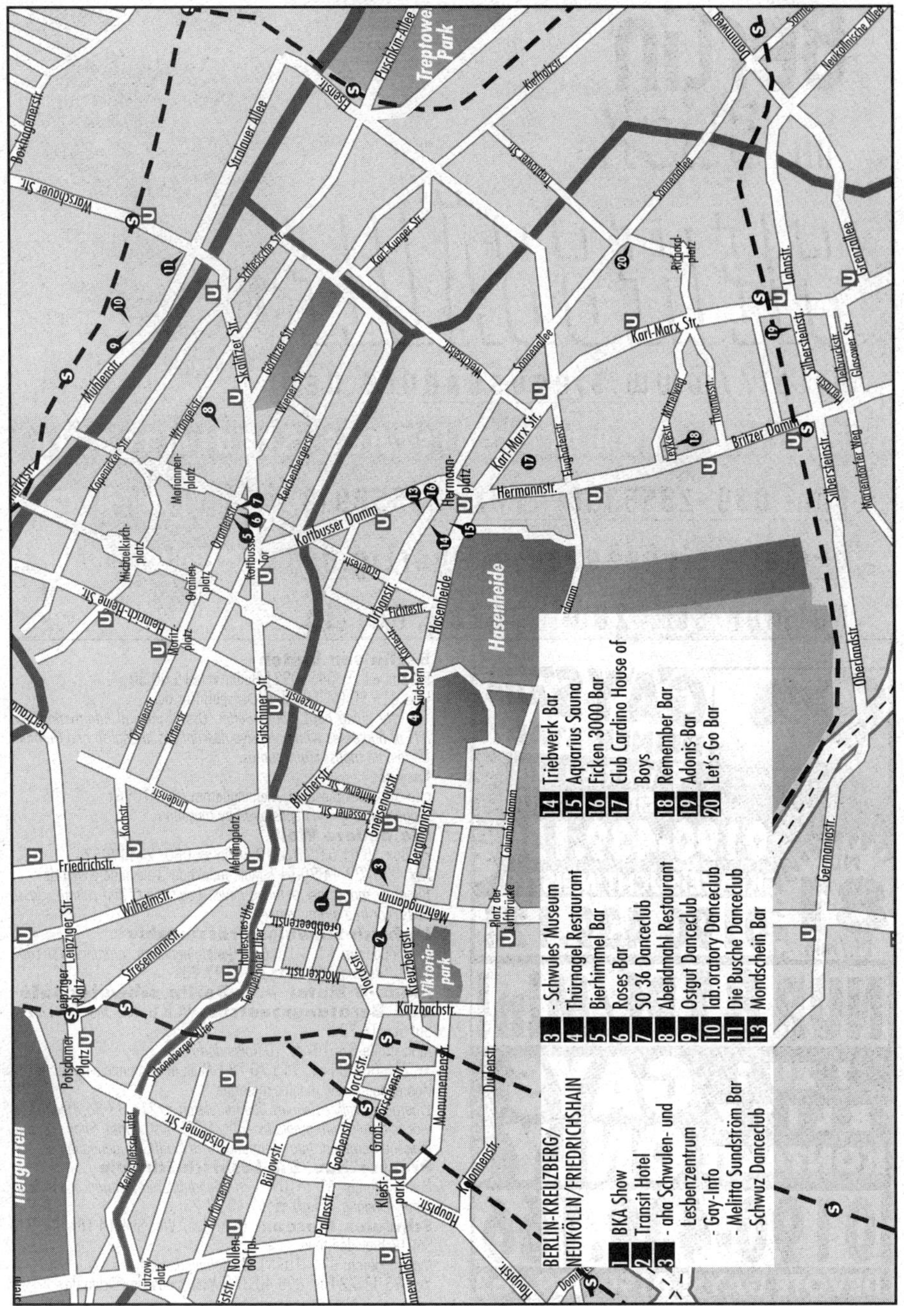
BERLIN-KREUZBERG/
NEUKÖLLN/FRIEDRICHSHAIN
1 BKA Show
2 Transit Hotel
3 - aha Schwulen- und Lesbenzentrum
- Gay-Info
- Melitta Sundström Bar
- Schwuz Danceclub
3 - Schwules Museum
4 Thürnagel Restaurant
5 Bierhimmel Bar
6 Roses Bar
7 SO 36 Danceclub
8 Abendmahl Restaurant
9 Ostgut Danceclub
10 lab.oratory Danceclub
11 Die Busche Danceclub
13 Mondschein Bar
14 Triebwerk Bar
15 Aquarius Sauna
16 Ficken 3000 Bar
17 Club Cardino House of Boys
18 Remember Bar
19 Adonis Bar
20 Let's Go Bar
Treptower Park
Hasenheide
Viktoria-park

Berlin von hinten
PO Box 61 01 04, 10921 Berlin ☎ 615 00 30
Fax: 615 90 07. E-Mail: info@spartacus.de
The city guide book about Berlin. Useful general information and lots of addresses with extensive descriptions in English and German. Up-to-date maps. Erotic photos.

Capri
c/o Schwules Museum, Mehringdamm 61 ✉10961
Magazine of the »Friends of a gay museum«.

Die andere Welt
PO Box 35 01 51 ✉10210 Berlin ☎ 030/29449052
Fax: 030/29 44 90 51 E-Mail: redaktion@die-andere-welt.de
Bimontly magazine featuring news, health, arts and culture, classifieds. For free at gay venues.

Lesbisch-Schwules Pressearchiv
Mehringdamm 61 ✉10961 *(U-Mehringdamm, entrance 1st courtyard/Eingang 1. Hof)* ☎ 69 40 17 23

Mann-O-Meter e.V. Berlin schwules Info- und Beratungszentrum (A b G MA) Mon-Fri 17-22, Sat Sun 16-22 h
Motzstraße 5 ✉10777 *(U-Nollendorfplatz)*
☎ 216 80 08 Fax: 215 70 78 E-Mail: info@mann-o-meter.de
Homepage: www.mann-o-meter.de
Emergency call/Schwules Überfalltelefon ☎216 33 36. Health service and help with problems (HIV/AIDS). Also Coffee Shop. Psychologische Beratung, Info+Beratung zu HIV/AIDS. Jugendgruppe.

Presseschau. Die Lesbisch-Schwule
Mehringdamm 61 ✉10961 *(U-Mehringdamm, entrance 1st courtyard/Eingang 1. Hof)* ☎ 69 40 17 23

Schwules Museum (! A GLM) Wed-Sun 14-18, Thu -21, Sat 17 h guided tour
Mehringdamm 61 ✉10961 *(U-Mehringdamm)*
☎ 693 11 72 Fax: 693 40 37 E-Mail: smuseum@clan.de

Sergej
Sergej Medien- und Verlags-GmbH, Kopenhagener Straße 14 ✉10437 ☎ 44 34 07 86 Fax: 44 34 07 88
Email: sergej@pride.de *Gay-lesbian monthly free at gay venues.*

Siegessäule Mon-Fri 10-17 h
c/o Jackwerth Verlag, Kulmerstraße 20a ✉10783 *(U7-Kleistpark)* ☎ 23 55 39-0 Fax: 23 55 39-19 E-Mail: siegessaeule@berlin.de
Homepage: www.siegessaeule.de
Free gay-lesbian monthly for Berlin featuring news and events.

TOURIST INFO

Berlin Tourismus Marketing GmbH
Am Karlsbad 11 ✉10785 ☎ 25 00 25 Fax: 25 00 24 24

BARS

Aah-Haa (B bf f GLM s OS YG) 17-2 h
Donaustraße 112 ✉12043 *(U-Rathaus Neukölln/Hermannplatz)* ☎ 61 30 44 93

Ad Libitum (B GLM MA OS) 16-5 h
Simon-Dach-Straße 36 ✉10245 *(U-Samariterstraße)* ☎ 29 00 08 72 *16-20h:"two for one"*

Adonis (B bf d f DR G N OS P S VS YG) 0-24 h
Pappelallee 32a ✉10437 *(S/U-Schönhauser Allee)* ☎ 447 98 88

Albrecht-Klause (B G MA) Mon-Fri 16- ? Sat 14-?, Sun 18-?
Albrechtstraße 125 ✉12165 *(U-Steglitz)* ☎ 791 56 21

Altberliner Bierstuben (B F G lj MA N OS) 12-2 h
Saarbrücker Straße 17 ✉10405 *(U8-Senefelder Platz)* ☎ 442 61 30

Amsterdam (AC B f glm H OS TV YG) Mon-Sat 16-6, Sun 14-6 h
Gleimstraße 24 ✉10437 *(U/S-Schönhauser Allee)* ☎ 448 07 92
Café with accommodation available.

Andreas' Kneipe (! B G lj MA MG) Sun-Thu 11-3, Fri/Sat 11-4 h
Ansbacher Straße 29 ✉10789 *(U-Wittenbergplatz)* ☎ 218 32 57
Popular pub.

Besenkammer (B f G MA) 0-24 h
Rathausstraße 1, ✉10178 *(U/S-Alexanderplatz under the S-Bahn bridge)* ☎ 242 40 83
Small beer bar.

Bierhimmel (B f g YG) 14-3 h
Oranienstraße 183 ✉10999 *(U-Kottbusser Tor)* ☎ 615 31 22

Blue Boy Bar (B bf f Glm MA p r VS) 0-24 h
Eisenacher Straße 3a ✉10777 *(U-Nollendorfplatz, Bus119/N19)* ☎ 218 74 98

Blühende Landschaften (B GLM)
Samarrterstraße 29 ☎ 42 01 37 83

Burgfrieden. Zum (B DR f G lj MA s) 19-6, 2nd bar „Gruft" Fri-Mon 22-5 h
Wichertstraße 69 ✉10439 *(S/U-Schönhauser Allee, northern exit)*
Traditional pub-style. Popular Mon Happy Hour 20-22 h.

Club Amsterdam (B G MA og) 19-3 h, Sun closed
Barbarossastraße 38, ✉10779 *(U-Güntzelstraße)* ☎ 213 32 32
Club Culture Houze (AC B d f G lj MA msg p S VS)
Görlitzer Straße 71 ✉10997 *(at Görlitzer Park)* ☎ 61 70 96 69
Bar on 2 floors with video-room, playground and shower. Special event partys: -Mon 19-4 h Naked Sex Party (Gay) -Wed 20-4 h Gay SM Party (Gay) -Thu 19-4 h SM + Fetish Club (mixed) -Fri 20-5 h SM + Fetish Club (mixed) -Sat 22-8 h Gay Party -Sun 17-4 h Couple Club (mixed)
Club Trommel (AC B D G GLM lj MA N p s TV WE) 21-? h, closed Tue
Thomasstraße 53 ✉12055 *(U-Leinestraße)* ☎ 686 73 45
Around for over 26 years - the oldest gay bar in Neuköln
Dandy Club (B DR G lj MA N p VS W WE) 22-? h, 1st & 3rd Fri „Underwear Safer Sex Party"
Urbanstraße 64 ✉10967 *(U-Hermannplatz)* ☎ 691 90 13
Dark Star (B DR G lj MA N p s VS) 22-6/?, Naked Safer Sex Party 1st & 3rd Sat 18-20 (-24 h)
Schönhauser Allee 39a ✉10435 *(U-Eberswalder Straße)*
☎ 442 42 13
Darkroom (B DR G LJ MA) 22-6 h
Rodenbergstraße 23 ✉10439 *(U/S-Schönhauser Allee)*
☎ 444 93 21
Dreizehn (B G N OS) 17-5 h
Welserstraße 27 ✉10777 *(U-Wittenbergplatz)* ☎ 218 23 63
Eulenspiegel (B d G MA p s) 19-3 h
Ebersstraße 58 ✉10827 *(U-Innsbrucker Platz)* ☎ 782 38 89
E116 (AC B G MA N OS r) 20-02:00h
Eisenacher Straße 116 ✉10777 *(U1/2-Nollendorfplatz)*
☎ 217 05 18
Ficken 3000 (d DR G LJ MA p VS YG) Mon-Sun 22-? h
Urbanstraße 70 ✉10967 *(U-Hermannplatz)* ☎ 69 50 73 35
Flair (B f g MA N OS) 6-5 h
Nachodstraße 5, ✉10779 *(Eingang/entrance Grainauer Straße)*
Flax (AC f B bf GLM OS s) Mon-Fri 17-03:00h, Sat 15-05:00h, Sun 10-03:00h
Chodwieckistraße 41 ✉10405 *(Tram-Winsstraße)*
☎ 44 04 69 88
Fledermaus (B d G MA N s vs) 12-4, Fri Sat -6 h
Joachimsthaler Straße 14-19 ✉10719 *(U-Kurfürstendamm)*
292 11 36
Flip-Flop (B f G MA N) 19-?, Sun 11-?, Brunch: Sun 11-16 h
Kulmer Straße 20a ✉10783 *(U-Kleistpark/S/U-Yorckstraße)*
☎ 216 28 25
Fugger-Eck (AC B d f GLM lj MA N OS s) 13-05:00h
Eisenacher Straße 3a ✉10777 *(U1/15/12/2/4-Nollendorfplatz)*
☎ 218 35 06
Geierwally's Stieftochter im Ausland- Das Café an der Spitze (B f glm N OS YG) 18-open end
Prenzlauer Promenade 3 ✉13086 *(S-Prenzlauer Allee)*
☎ 471 30 17
Greifbar (AC B DR G MA p VS) 22-6 h
Wichertstraße 10/Ecke Greifenhagener ✉10439 *(S/U-Schönhauser Allee)* ☎ 444 08 28
Hafen (! B G MA s TV YG) 21-?, winter 20- h
Motzstraße 19 ✉10777 *(U-Nollendorfplatz)* ☎ 211 41 18
Trendy and popular.
Harlekin (B f G MA N OS) 16-?, Sun 14-? h
Schaperstraße 12-13 ✉10719 *(U9-Spichernstraße)*
☎ 218 25 79
Irrtum (B G)
Gabelsbergerstraße 6 ☎ 42 01 80 00
Jim's (B bf GLM MA N s) Mon-Thu 10-3, Fri Sat Sun 14-3 h
Eberswalder Straße 32 ✉10437 ☎ 440 63 79
Kapelle (B bf glm MA YG) 10-3, WE 10-3/? h
Zionskirchplatz 22-24 ✉10119
Kleine Philarmonie (B G MA N) 18 -?
Schaperstraße 14 ✉10719 *(U-Spicherstraße)* ☎ 883 11 02
Knast (AC B DR G LJ MG VS WE) 21-5 h
Fuggerstraße 34/Welserstraße ✉10777 *(U-Wittenbergplatz)*
☎ 218 10 26
Jail decore.
Kne-Mo (B d E f g MA N OS) 16-4 h, in winter 18-4 h, Sun closed
Knesebeckstraße 35, ✉10623 *(S-Savignyplatz)* ☎ 883 45 47
Kumpelnest 3000 (B d glm MA TV) 17-5 h, weekend open end
Lützowstraße 23/Potsdamer Straße ✉10785 *(U-Kurfürstenstraße)*
☎ 261 69 18
Very popular on WE, not very gay then.
Cocktail bar.

lab.oratory (B DR G)
Mühlerstraße 26-30 ✉10243 *(S/U-Warschauer Straße)*

Lenz... die Bar (AC B CC G MA OS) 19-? h
Eisenacher Straße 3 ✉10777 ☎ 217 78 20
Cocktail bar.

Let's go (B f G MA N R) 18-1, Fri Sat -3 h
Hertzbergstraße 22 ✉12055 *(U-Karl-Marx-Strasse)* ☎ 687 09 34

Memory (B d F g lj MA OS) 16-? h
Fuggerstraße 37 ✉10777 *(U1/15/12/2-Wittenbergplatz)*
☎ 213 52 71

Mondschein (B f G MA N) 20-3, Fri Sat -5; Safer Sex Party 2nd & 4th Sun admission 20-22 h
Urbanstraße 101, ✉10967 *(U-Hermannplatz)* ☎ 693 23 55

Moustache. Le (B d DR F G lj MA s) 20-3/? h, Mon closed
Gartenstraße 4 ✉10115 *(U-Oranienburger Tor/Rosenthaler Platz, S-Nordbahnhof)* ☎ 281 72 77

Movie (B f GLM lj MA OS W) Mon-Fri from 16- ? Sat & Sun from 18 - ?
Kleiststraße 7/Courbièrestraße ✉10787 *(U-Nollendorfplatz)*
☎ 211 77 02

Na Und (B f glm MA N OS) 0-24 h
Prenzlauer Allee 193/Dimitroffstraße ✉10405 *(S-Prenzlauer Allee)*
☎ 442 89 48
Neuer Oldtimer (B G MA) 14-3 h
Lietzenburger Straße 12 ✉10789 *(U-Wittenbergplatz)*
☎ 23 62 03 54
New Action (! B DR G LJ MA p VS) Mon-Sat 20-? Sun 13-? h
Kleiststraße 35/Eisenacherstraße, ✉10787 *(U-Nollendorfplatz)*
☎ 211 82 56 *Very cruisy, best daily after 1 h.*
Offenbar (B bf G MA) 10-2, bf -16 h
Schreinerstraße 5 ✉10247 *(U-Samariterstraße)* ☎ 426 09 30
Oh-ase (B f Glm MA N OS) Mon-Sat 10-2/?, Sun 14-2/? h
Rathausstraße 5, ✉10178 *(U/S-Alexanderplatz)* ☎ 242 30 30
Pick ab! (! B DR G p VS) 22-6 h
Greifenhagener Straße 16 ✉10437 *(S/U-Schönhauser Allee)*
☎ 445 85 23
Pour Elle (B d gLM p OS YG) 19-5, Fri Sat 21-5 h
Kalckreuthstraße 10, ✉10777 *(U1/15/12/2/4-Nollendorfplatz)*
☎ 218 75 33
Prinz Knecht (B d DR f GLM lj MA OS VS) 15-3 h
Fuggerstraße 33 ✉10777 *(U-Wittenbergplatz)* ☎ 218 14 32
Pussy-Cat (B d f GLM N OS p TV) 18-6 h, Tue closed
Kalckreuthstraße 7, ✉10777 *(U-Nollendorfplatz)* ☎ 213 35 86
Remember (B G MA N) 14-1 h
Leykestrasse 18 ✉12053 *(U-Leinestrasse)* ☎ 62 70 51 83
Riviera (B G MA N)
Glasower Straße 51 ✉12051
Romeo Nachtbar (B f G MA) 23-8/? h
Greifenhagener Straße 16 ✉10437 *(S/U-Schönhauser Allee)*
☎ 447 67 89

Roses (! B GLM MA TV YG) 21.30-5/? h
Oranienstraße 187 ✉10999 *(U-Kottbusser Tor)* ☎ 615 65 70
Popular and trashy, best after midnight.
Schall & Rauch-Bar, Restaurant + Pension (! AC B bf F GLM H MA OS YG) 9-3 h
Gleimstraße 23 ✉10437 *(U/S-Schönhauser Allee)* ☎ 44 33 97-0
Popular.
Scheune (! B DR G LJ MA p VS) 21-7, Fri Sat -9, Naked Sex Party Sun 17.30-21, Rubber Party last Fri 21-2 h
Motzstraße 25 ✉10777 *(U-Nollendorfplatz)* ☎ 213 85 80
Best after midnight.
Schoppenstube (B D DR f G MA OS p s) 22-7 h
Schönhauser Allee 44 ✉10435 *(U-Eberswalder Straße)*
☎ 442 82 04
The oldest gay bar in the east part of Berlin
Senefelder. Café (B d F Glm MA) Sun-Thu 19-3, Fri Sat Disco 20-5 h
Schonhauser Allee 173, ✉10119 *(U-Senefelder Platz)*
☎ 449 66 05
Shambala (B f glm N) 18-3 h, Mon women only 21 h
Greifenhagener Straße 12 ✉10437 *(S/U-Schönhauser Allee)*
☎ 447 62 26
Jungle atmosphere!
Sonderbar (A B d f GLM MA OS) 20-8 h (in Summer from 18:00h)
Käthe-Niederkirchner-Straße 34, ✉10407 *(Near/Nähe »Märchenbrunnen«)* ☎ 425 84 94
Spot (B CC f GLM MA OS s) Mon-Fri 16-4, Sat Sun -? h, winter 18-open end
Eisenacher Straße 2 ✉10777 *(U-Nollendorfplatz)* ☎ 213 22 67
Stahlrohr (B DR G lj MA p VS W) 20-06:00h
Greifenhagener Straße 54 ✉10437 *(U- Schönhauserallee)*
☎ 447 327 47
Stiller Don (! A B f GLM lj MA OS) 19-? h
Erich-Weinert-Straße 67, ✉10439 *(S/U-Schönhauser Allee)*
☎ 445 59 57
Popular and friendly.
Tabasco (B f G MA p R) 18-6/?, Fri 18-Mon 6 h
Fuggerstraße 3 ✉10777 *(U-Nollendorfplatz)* ☎ 214 26 36
Tom's Bar (! B DR G lj MA) 22-6, Fri Sat -? h
Motzstraße 19 ✉10777 *(U-Nollendorfplatz)* ☎ 213 45 70
Very cruisy. Popular Mon (2-4-1).
Toni's (AC B d f GLM MA N OS) 16-1, Fri Sat -? h, closed Tue
Mecklenburgische Straße 20 ✉10713 *(U-Heidelberger Platz)*
☎ 824 25 45
Twilight Zone (B DR G LJ MA VS) Fri Sat 0-?, Wed Sun 1-? h
Welserstraße 24, ✉10777 *(U-Nollendorfplatz)* ☎ 218 14 32
☛ *also Disco Connection.*
Vagabund (B d G MA OS p) 17-? h
Knesebeckstraße 77, ✉10623 *(U-Uhlandstraße)* ☎ 881 15 06
Very late bar.
Windows Café-Bar-Bistro (B F GLM MA OS) 14-4 h
Martin-Luther-Straße 22 ✉10777 ☎ 214 23 94
Good and low priced meals.
Zandvoort (B D G N p s) Mon-Sat 20-? h, closed Sun
Friedrich-Karl-Straße 15 ✉12103 *(U-Ullsteinstraße)* ☎ 752 20 77

CAFES

Anderes Ufer (B f GLM MA OS W) 11-2 h
Hauptstraße 157 ✉10827 *(U-Kleistpark)* ☎ 784 15 78
First openly gay café in Europe, best in the afternoon and 22-24.
Arc (AC B bf CC F GLM MA OS W YG) Summer 8-2, Winter 11-2 h
Fasanenstraße 81a ✉10623 *(U/S-Zoologischer Garten/Bus149)*
☎ 313 26 25
Café-bar-restaurant in S-Bahn arches.

Aztek (AC B CC F glm) Mon-Fri 16-1, Sat & Sun 12-? h
Danziger Straße 47, Prenzlauer Berg ☎ 44 04 52 52
Latin american cuisine. Café and Cocktail bar. Daily from 20:00h all cocktails DM 7.

Berlin Connection Café & Bistro (! B F G lj MA OS) 14-2 h
Martin-Luther-Straße 19 ✉10777 *(U-Wittenberplatz/Nollendorfplatz)* ☎ 213 11 16
Tue from 20 h Beck's Beer Bust!

Café Aedes (AC bf CC)
Rosenthalerstrasse 40/41 ✉10178 *(In Hackeschen Höfen)*
☎ 282 2103

Café Berio (bf f glm MA OS TV W WE) 8-1 h
Maaßenstraße 7 ✉10777 *(U-Nollendorfplatz)* ☎ 216 19 46
Popular. Amazing 24h breakfast available

Café Doppelfenster (B D G YG) Tue 16-2, Wed Thu -21, Fri -4/? h
Ackerstraße 12 ✉10115 *(U-Rosenthaler Platz/Oranienburger Tor)*
☎ 280 72 16

Cafe November (bf CC F GLM) Sun-Thu 10-2, Fri Sat -3 h
Husemannstrasse 15 ✉10435 (U-Senefelder Platz/Eberswalder Straße) ☎ 442 8425

Café Resto Jung (bf F glm)
Stuttgarter Platz 21 ✉10627 ☎ 32 702 446

Café Rix 10-1 h
Karl-Marx-Strasse 141 ✉12043 ☎ 686 9020

Café Savigny (B bf f g OS) 9-2 h
Grolmanstraße 53/54, ✉10623 *(S-Savignyplatz)* ☎ 312 81 95
Trendy and popular.

Da Neben (A AC B bf f GLM MA s WE) Mon-Fri 8-2, Sat Sun 10-2 h
Motzstraße 5 ✉10777 *(U-Nollendorfplatz)* ☎ 21 75 38 27

Melitta Sundström (A B bf f D GLM MA OS TV W) 10-4, Sat 10-Sun 4h
Mehringdamm 61 ✉10961 *(U-Mehringdamm)* ☎ 692 44 14
Best on Sat. Also a gay bookstore.
Oxonmagenta (AC bf CC F glm) 19-23:00h
Greifenhagener Strasse 48 ✉10437 ☎ 4473 6482

DANCECLUBS

Ackerkeller (B D G YG) Tue 21-2, Fri 22-4/?, 3rd Sat Party
Ackerstraße 12, Hinterhaus, ✉10115 *(U-Rosenthaler Platz/U-Oranienburger Tor)* ☎ 280 72 16
Popular. Entrance Ackerstraße 13.
Amaris (AC b D) Thu, Fri & Sat 22-06:00h
Warschauer Platz 18 *(U / S- Warschauerstrasse)* ☎ 29 007 029

MULTISEXUAL • MULTICULTURAL • MULTICONCEPTIONAL
SO36
www.so36.de
ORANIENSTR. 190 • 10999 BERLIN-KREUZBERG
U-BHF KOTTBUSSER TOR, BUS 128, N 29
WEEKLY
MONDAYS : 11:00 pm
ELECTRIC BALLROOM
GAY-STRAIGHT MIXED TECHNOPARTY
WEDNESDAYS : 11:00 pm
HUNGRIGE HERZEN
GAY-LESBIAN HOUSEPARTY
SUNDAYS : WINTER 5:00 pm SUMMER 7:00 pm
CAFE FATAL
LESBIAN-GAY STANDARD DANCING
MONTHLY
EVERY 2nd TUESDAY : 7:00 pm
BINGO BAR
GAMBLING FOR CHARITY
EVERY 3rd FRIDAY : 10:00 pm
JANE BOND
WOMEN, LESBIANS, DRAGS AND OTHER FEMALES. HOUSEPARTY
4th SATURDAY BIMONTHLY : 8:00 pm
SALON ORIENTAL
TURKISH/GERMAN BELLYDANCE DRAGSHOW
EVERY 4th SATURDAY : 11:00 pm
GAYHANE
HOMORIENTAL DANCEFLOOR
...AND CONCERTS, SPECIAL EVENTS AND PARTYS WATCH OUT FOR FLYERS!

Busche. Die (D GLM MA OS s) Wed Sun 21.30-5, Fri Sat 22-6 h, closed Mon Tue Thu
Mühlenstraße 11-12, ✉10243 *(S/U-Warschauer Straße. Opp. Berlin Wall/East Side Gallery)* ☎ 296 08 00
The most extra ordinary gay disco of Berlin.

Connection (! AC B D DR GLM lj MA S SNu STV VS WE YG) Fri Sat 22-? h
Fuggerstraße 33 ✉10777 *(U-Wittenbergplatz)* ☎ 218 14 32
Admission DM 10. Huge cruising area on three floors. ☛ Sex Shop/Blue Movie Connection Garage.

GMF-Gay Tea Dance (B D G OS p S TV) Sun 21-3 h
at WMF, Johannisstraße 19 ✉10117 *(S/U-Friedrichstraße)*
☎ 21 47 41 00 *Popular*

KC Kleist-Casino Berlin International (D f G MA s OS W) Wed-Sat 20-?, disco Thu-Sat 22-? h
Kleiststraße 35 ✉10787 *(U-Wittenbergplatz/Nollendorfplatz)*
☎ 23621976

Kit Kat @ Metropol (b G)
Nollendorf Platz *(U-Nollendorfplatz)*

Kleine Busche (b D GLM)
Warschauer Platz *(S/U-Warschauer Straße)* ☎ 29 60 800

Kleist-Casino-Berlin (D f G MA OS s) Wed-Sun 21:00h-? Fri, Sat & Sun disco from 22:00-?
Kleststrasse 35 ✉10787 *(U-Wittenbergplatz)* ☎ 236 219 76

Ost-Gut (B D DR G)
Mühlenstraße 26-30 ✉10243 *(S/U-Warschauer Straße)*

SchwuZ (! AC B D GLM MA S STV TV WE) Fri & Sat 23-?.
Mehringdamm 61 ✉10961 *(U-Mehringdamm)* ☎ 6950 7892
☎ 693 70 25
Newly renovated. Reasonable prices. Mixed crowd. See press for program details

SO 36 (! AC D GLM lj MA S TV W YG) Mon 23-?, Wed 22-?, Sun 17-? (summer 19-? h)
Oranienstraße 190 ✉10999 *(U-Kottbusser Tor/Görlitzer Bahnhof)*
☎ 61 40 13 06
Weekly parties: „Electric Ballroom" on Mon, „Hungrige Herzen" on Wed, „Café Fatal" on Sun. Also monthly parties. Please call or see add for details.

Tresor/Globus (B D g OS YG) Tresor: Fri Sat 24-?, Globus: Wed Fri Sat 24-?, Sun 23-6 h, best Sun
Leipziger Straße 126a, ✉10117 *(U/S-Potsdamer Platz)*
Techno and house in the building of the former Reichsbank.

90° (B D G p S OS TV) Thu 23-5 h
Dennewitzstraße 37 ✉10785 *(U-Kurfürstenstraße)*
☎ 21 47 41 00
Check the local gay papers for up-to-date parties and dance events.

RESTAURANTS

Abendmahl (B F glm OS) 18-1, meals -23.30 h
Muskauer Straße 9 ✉10997 *(U-Görlitzer Bahnhof)* ☎ 612 51 70
Vegetarian and fish meals. Reservation recommended.

Arc (AC B bf CC F GLM MA OS W YG) summer 10-2, winter 11-2
Fasanenstraße 81a ✉10623 *(U/S-Zoologischer Garten)*
☎ 313 26 25

Biberbau Restaurant (b F g) 18-1 h, closed Tue
Durlacher Straße 15 ✉10715 *(U/S-Bundesplatz)* ☎ 853 23 90
International cuisine.

Kern (b bf CC F GLM N) Daily from 10- ? h
Fuggerstrasse 18 ✉10777 *(U - Wittenbergplatz)* ☎ 21 96 86 06

Lukiluki (AC CC F GLM TV) 19-2, Sun 10-2, kitchen -1 h
Motzstraße 28 ☎ 23 62 20 79

Offenbach-Stuben (AC CC F glm) 18-? h
Stubbenkammerstraße 8 ✉10437 *(S-Prenzlauer Allee/U2-Eberswalder Straße)* ☎ 445 85 02

Thüringer Stuben (B F g MA) Mon-Fri 16-1, Sat/Sun 12-1 h
Stargarder Straße 28 ✉10437 *(S/U-Schönhauser Allee)*
☎ 44 63 33 91

Thürnagel (AC B F g MA) 18-0.30, meals -23.30 h, Summer: Mon closed
Gneisenaustraße 57 ✉10961 *(U-Südstern)* ☎ 691 48 00
Vegetarian cuisine.

Trattoria á Muntagnola (F g OS) 12-24 h
Fuggerstraße 27, ✉10777 *(U-Wittenbergplatz)* ☎ 211 66 42
Southern Italian cuisine.

SHOWS

BKA-Berliner Kabarett Anstalt (glm MA S)
Mehringdamm 32-34 ✉10961 *(S-Yorckstraße/U-Mehringdamm)*
☎ 251 01 12
Entrance-fee show: DM 22-36, parties: DM 10-15. beginning depends on the event

BKA-Zelte (bf d F glm MA OS S W) Show: Wed-Sun 20-24, Parties: 23-5 h
Schloßplatz ✉10178 *(S/U-Alexanderplatz. Near Palast der Republik)* ☎ 251 01 12
Entrance-fee show: DM 20-35, parties: 10-15.

CC 96 Men Strip Show (AC B CC d f G MA msg P S SNU STV TV VS W wh) 12-4 h
Lietzenburger Straße 96 ✉10719 *(U-Uhlandstrasse. Bus 119, 129, 229, 209)* ☎ 883 26 50

Chez Nous (CC STV) Shows 20.30 and 23 h
Marburger Straße 14 ✉10789 ☎ 213 18 10
Entrance fee DM 15.

Lützower Lampe (d E glm MA p S STV TV W) 20.30-? h
Witzlebenstraße 38, ✉14057 *(U2-Sophie-Charlotte-Platz)*
☎ 321 20 97
Cabaret/Piano Bar.

Luftschloß (B d f MA OS)
Schloßplatz ✉10178 ☎ 20 16 62 60

SEX SHOPS/BLUE MOVIES

Bad Boy'z (CC G VS YG) Mon-Sat 13-1, Sun & public holidays 15-1 h
Schliemannstraße 38 ✉10437 *(U-Eberswalder Straße)*
☎ 440 81 65
3rd Sat Safer Sex Party „Youngster's Gay Spartaciade" (check the press for dress code!) Well worth a visit !

MAN's
pleasurechest
Shop & Blue Movies
10777 Berlin • Kalckreuthstr. 15 / Fuggerstr.
10 - 01 Uhr • So + Feiertags 13 - 01 Uhr

Beate Uhse (b f g VS) 19-24 h
Joachimsthaler Straße 4 ✉10623

City Men Shop & Video (G MA VS) Mon-Thu 11-1, Fri Sat -2, Sun 14-1 h
Fuggerstraße 26 ✉10777 ☎ 218 29 59

Connection Garage (CC G lj MA VS W) Mon-Sat 10-1, Sun & public holidays 14-1 h
Fuggerstraße 33 ✉10777 *(U-Wittenberplatz)* ☎ 218 14 32
E-Mail: order@connection.berlin.com (for orders)

Good Vibration Store/Mr B (GLM) Mon-Fri 12-20, Sat 10-16 h
Nollendorfstraße 23 ✉10777 *(U-Nollendorfplatz)* ☎ 21 75 28 38
Fax: 21 75 28 27 Email: goodvibration@t-online.de
Homepage: www.goodvibrations.de *Also mail order.*

Jaxx Club. The (AC CC DR G VS YG) Mon-Sat 12-3, Sun 13-3 h
Motzstraße 19 ✉10777 *(U-Nollendorfplatz)* ☎ 213 81 03
Popular, especially Tue & WE.

Man's pleasure chest (G lj VS) 10-1, Sun & public holidays 13-1 h
Kalckreuthstraße 15/Fuggerstraße 5 ✉10777 *(U-Nollendorfplatz)* ☎ 211 20 25

New Man (AC CC DR G MA r VS) Mon-Sat 10-0.30, Sun 12-0.30 h
Joachimstaler Straße 1-3 ✉10623 *(U-Zoologischer Garten)* ☎ 88 68 32 89

Playground (CC G lj VS W) Mon-Sat 12-24 h, closed Sun & public holidays
Courbièrestraße 9 ✉10787 ☎ 218 21 64
Tailor-made leather and rubber. Also piercing.

Gay-Kino und
Video-Kabinen

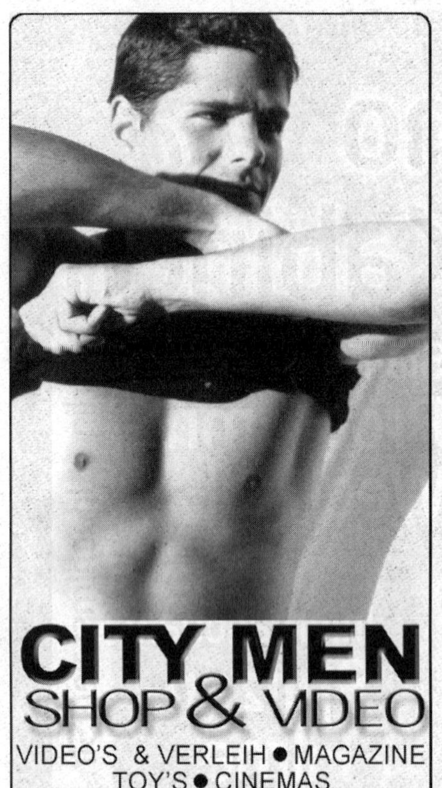

Pool Berlin (DR G MA r VS) Mon-Sat 10-22, Sun & public holidays 16-22 h
Schaperstraße 11/Joachimsthaler Straße ✉10719 *(U-Kurfürstendamm/Spichernstraße)* ☎ 214 19 89

ESCORTS & STUDIOS

Classic Agency (CC G msg)
☎ 324 44 54 ☎ (0172) 394 41 39
20-30 international men (18-35 years old) of all types.

HOUSE OF BOYS

Classic Club (B CC G MA R s VS wh) Mon-Sat 20-5 h, closed Sun
Windscheidstraße 16/Kantstraße ✉10627 *(U-Wilmersdorfer Straße)* ☎ 324 44 54

Club Cardino (CC f G MA R VS) 15-4, Sun & public holidays 17-4 h
Mainzer Straße 4 ✉12053 *(U-Herrmannplatz)* ☎ 622 46 22

SAUNAS/BATHS

Apollo Sauna (AC B CC DR f G MA msg p sa sb sol VS WO) 13-7 h
Kurfürstenstraße 101 ✉10787 *(U-Wittenbergplatz)* ☎ 213 24 24
Mon Thu reduced admission. Entrance-fee DM 19-22.

Aquarius Sauna (A AC B bf d DR f G MA msg OS pi sa sb sol VS W wh) 0-24 h
Hasenheide 13 ✉10967 *(U-Hermannplatz)* ☎ 691 39 20
Germany's biggest sauna opening soon.

Gate Sauna (AC B bf CC DR f G MA msg p sa sb sol VS wh) 11-7, Fri 11-Mon 7 h
Wilhelmstraße 80/81 ✉10117 *(U-Mohrenstraße/S-Unter den Linden)* ☎ 229 94 30
Mon Fri admission DM 18, Wed admission for guys -25 10, Sat Sun 7-12 h 2-4-1.

Steam Sauna Club (B bf F G lj MA msg p sa sb sol VS wh) 11-7, Fri 11-Mon 7 h
Kurfürstenstraße 113 ✉10787 *(U-Wittenbergplatz)* ☎ 218 40 60

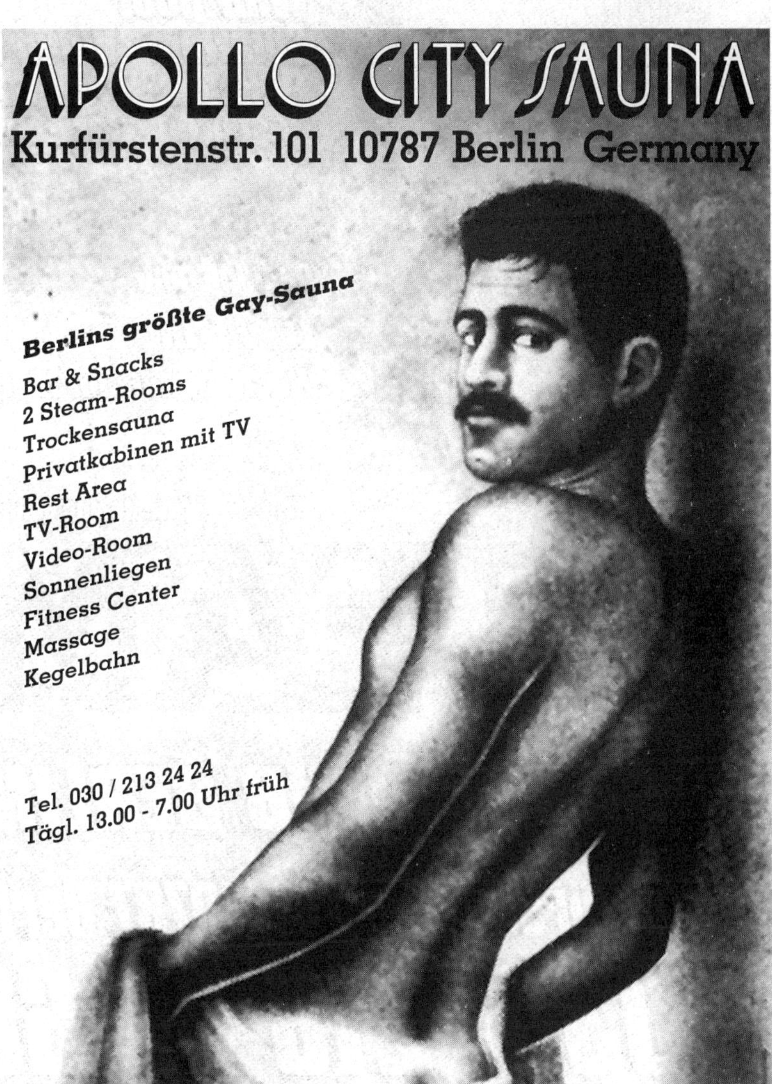
APOLLO CITY SAUNA
Kurfürstenstr. 101 10787 Berlin Germany
Berlins größte Gay-Sauna
Bar & Snacks
2 Steam-Rooms
Trockensauna
Privatkabinen mit TV
Rest Area
TV-Room
Video-Room
Sonnenliegen
Fitness Center
Massage
Kegelbahn
Tel. 030 / 213 24 24
Tägl. 13.00 - 7.00 Uhr früh

Treibhaus Sauna (AC B bf DR f G MA p sa sb sol VS wh YG) Mon-Thu 15-7, Fri 15-Mon 7 h
Schönhauser Allee 132 ✉10437 *(S/U-Schönhauser Allee. Tram 50, 52, 53)* ☎ 448 45 03
Special rates for students, reduced rates Tue Thu.

FITNESSTUDIOS

Apollo Fitness-World (g sa sb sol WO)
Borodinstraße 16 ✉13088 ☎ 927 42 31
Apollo Sport-Studio (AC G sa sb sol WE wh WO YG) Mon-Fri 10-22 h, Sat 13-19 h, Sun 13-18 h
Hauptstraße 150 ✉10827 *(U-Kleistpark)* ☎ 784 82 03
Aquarius Men Fitness (AC glm MA WO) Mon, Wed & Fri 10-23, Tue & Thu 07-23, Sat & Sun 10-22:00h
Wilmersdorfer Strasse 82-83 ✉10629 *(Adenauerplatz)*
☎ 324 10 25
Swiss Training (g WO)
Immanuelkirchstraße 14 ✉10405 ☎ 44 35 83 44
Swiss Training (glm MA sa sol) Mon-Fri 10-22, Sat 10-17h, closed Sun
Alboinstraße 36-42 ✉12103 ☎ 754 15 91

MASSAGE

Centro Delfino (G msg) 16-22:00h
Wilmersdorfer Strasse 82/83 ☎ 342 45 88 ☎ 324 10 25 (appointments)
Short massage from 22 DM, including use of sauna.

BODY & BEAUTY SHOPS

Brillant (CC) Mon-Wed 10-19, Thu Fri -20, Sat 10-16 h
Schlüterstraße 53 ✉10627 *(S-Savignyplatz)* ☎ 324 19 91
Optician.

STEELWARE-Professional Piercing Mon-Fri 10-10 h (by appointment)
☎ 785 19 08 or ☎ 789 90 365

BOOK SHOPS

Adam Buchladen (CC) Mon-Fri 10-20 h, Sat 10-16 h
Gleimstraße 27 ✉10437 *(U/S-Schönhauser Allee)* ☎ 448 07 67

Bruno`s (! A CC G) Mon-Sat 10-22 h
Nürnberger Straße 53 ✉10789 *(U-Wittenbergplatz)* ☎ 21 47 32 93
Also video rental.

Galerie Janssen (A AC CC) Mon-Sat 11-20 h
Pariser Straße 45 ✉10719 *(U1/9-Spichernstraße)* ☎ 881 15 90
Online shopping: www.bodies.de

Prinz Eisenherz Buchladen (! CC GLM) 10-19, Sat -16 h, closed Sun
Bleibtreustraße 52 ✉10623 *(S-Savignyplatz)* ☎ 313 99 36
Homepage: www.prinz-eisenherz.com *Also mail order.*

EDUCATION SERVICES

Neuhaus
Erich-Weinert-Straße 6 ✉10439 *(S/U-Schönhauser Allee)*
☎ 44 73 39 66 Homepage: www.neuhaus-institut.de
Gay-lesbian language school

FASHION SHOPS

Planet Berlin Mon-Fri 11-20, Sat 11-16 h
Schlüterstrasse 35 ✉10629 *(S-Savignyplatz)* ☎ 885 2717

Wall Street-Men's Fashion (AC CC g lj MA s) Mon-Sat 10-20 h, closed Sun
Uhlandstraße 175 ✉10719 *(U-Uhlandstraße)* ☎ 881 16 83
Fashion shop, international designers.

LEATHER & FETISH SHOPS

Black Style (CC G) Mon-Fri 13-18.30, Thu -20, Sat 10-14 h
Seelower Straße 5 ✉10439 *(S/U-Schönhauser Allee)*
☎ 44 68 85 95 *Latex wear creation and mail-order.*

Leathers-Lederwerkstatt Berlin (G) Tue-Fri 12-19.30, Sat 12-16 h
Schliemannstraße 38 ✉10473 ☎ 442 77 86

PHARMACIES

Bavaria Apotheke (CC glm)
Geisbergstrasse 29 ✉10777 ☎ 23621225

Löwen Apotheke
Mainzer Straße 3 ✉10247 ☎ 294 22 07

Regenbogen Apotheke (CC glm W) Mon Tue Thu 8-20, Wed Fri 8-18.30, Sat 9.30-14 h
Welserstraße 24 ✉10777 *(U-Wittenbergplatz/Viktoria-Luise-Platz)*
☎ 235 04 50 Fax: 21 47 98 82

TELECOMMUNICATION

Pride Online Mon-Fri 10-19, Sat -14h
Kalckreuthstraße 7 ✉10777 ☎ 21 45 87 12 Fax: 21 45 87 11
E-Mail: online@pride.de
Communication products and services.

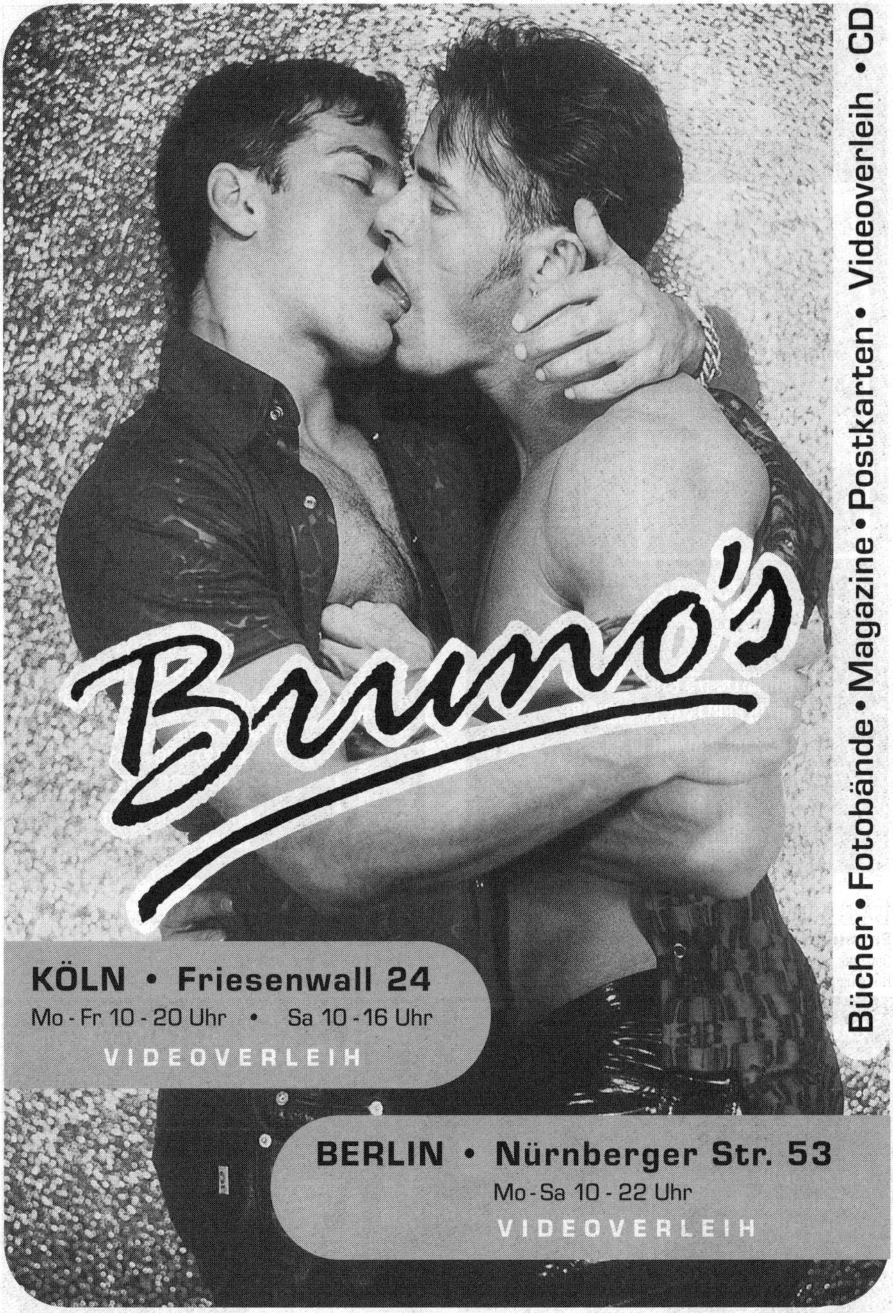

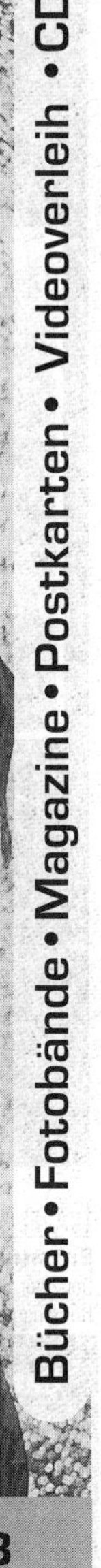

Bruno's
Bücher • Fotobände • Magazine • Postkarten • Videoverleih • CD
KÖLN • Friesenwall 24
Mo - Fr 10 - 20 Uhr • Sa 10 - 16 Uhr
VIDEOVERLEIH
BERLIN • Nürnberger Str. 53
Mo - Sa 10 - 22 Uhr
VIDEOVERLEIH

TRAVEL & TRANSPORT

Enzmann GmbH Touristik Servive
Danziger Straße 12 ✉ 10453 ☎ 44 34 08 70 Fax: 442 44 70
Homepage: http://www.Enzmann.com

ES Autovermietung Mon-Sat 8-18.30 h
Florastraße 67 ✉ 13187 *(near S-Bahnhof Pankow)*
☎ 48 63 82 95 Fax: 485 10 95
Low rates for gays.

Lufthansa City Center Mo-Fr 10-20, Sat -15h
Kurfürstendamm 220 ✉10719 ☎ 88 75 38 00
Fax: 88 75 38 01 E-Mail: info@lccberlin.de
Homepage: www.lhcc.de/lcc-berlin

MILU Reisen & EVENT INCENTIVE GbR Mon-Fri 10-19, Sat 11-14 h
Motzstraße 23, ✉10777 (U-Nollendorfplatz) ☎ 217 64 88
Fax: 214 33 74. Email: milu-reisen@t-online.de

Offer Reisen Mon-Fri 10-18.30h
Husemannstraße 5 ✉10435 *(U-Senefelder Platz)* ☎ 44 34 18 75

Over the rainbow Mo-Fr 10-21h
Flughafen Tempelhof, Haupthalle d ✉12101 *(Main hall)*
☎ 69 51-26 52 Fax: 69 51-26 55
E-Mail: : over the rainbow travel@compuserve.com
Homepage: www.overtherainbow.de
Travel agent in Tempelhof airport, hall d.

Reisebüro Creativ Mon-Fri 10-18 h, Sat 9-14 h
Hohenzollerndamm 11 ✉ 10717 ☎ 881 40 01
Fax: 885 49 56

Reisecounter Mon-Fri 9.30-19 h, Sat 9.30-13 h
Karl-Liebknecht-Straße 21 ✉10178 ☎ 247 35 84
Travel agent.

Schwule Mitfahrzentrale Mon-Fri 9-20 h, Sat 10-14 h
Yorckstraße 52 ✉10965 ☎ 216 40 20 Fax: 215 20 67
Gay give-a-lift centre.

Travel X (glm) Mon-Fri 10-18.30 h, closed Sat Sun
Pestalozzistraße 72 ✉10627 *(U-Wilmersdorferstraße/S-Charlottenburg)* ☎ 324 95 92 Fax: 324 09 66. Email: travel-x@t-online.de
Located in the traffic-free zone Wilmersdorfer Straße.

Vedema Reisen (g) Mon-Fri 10-19, Sat 10-13 h
Prenzlauer Allee 61, ✉10405 ☎ 421 00 60
Travel agency.

World Business Travel
Anklamer Straße 38 ✉10115 ☎ 448 38 45 Fax: 449 00 67.
Email: wbt.berlin@t-online.de

HOTELS

Arco Hotel (bf CC glm H MA OS)
Geisbergstraße 30 ✉10777 *(U-Wittenbergplatz)* ☎ 23 51 480
Fax: 21 47 51 78 E-Mail: arco-hotel@t-online.de
All rooms with shower/WC, SAT-TV, phone and safe. Own key. Very central location, right in the gay scene. Rates single DM 110-140, double 140-175 (bf incl.)

Art Connection Cityhotel Berlin (bf CC GLM H LJ MA msg W WO) Reception: 8-22 h
Fuggerstraße 33 ✉10777 (U-Wittenbergplatz) ☎ 217 70 28
Fax: 217 70 30. E-mail Hotel@sub-mission.com
Homepage: www.sub-mission.com or www.arthotel-connection.de
Located near gay bars. 8 double rooms, 8 single rooms, 1 suite. All rooms with shower/bath, partly WC. TV, phone, radio, minibar, safe, own key. Rates double from DM 170, single from 110. Add. bed DM 60. VCR for rent. Hotel features a leather darkroom.

Art-Hotel Charlottenburger Hof (A B bf CC F H MA NG OS) 0-24 h
Stuttgarter Platz 14 ✉10627 *(U-Wilmersdorfer Straße/S-Charlottenburg)* ☎ 32 90 70 Fax: 323 37 23
E-Mail: charlottenburger.hof@t-online.de
Homepage: www.charlottenburger-hof.de
Central location, close to gay scene. Rooms with shower/WC, cable TV, phone and safe, some with whirpool. Rates single from DM 110-140, double 120-200..

Atrium Hotel Helle Mitte (H NG) 0-24:00h
Kurt-Weil-Gasse 7 ✉12627 ☎ 9922 2300 Fax: 9922 2310
E-Mail: Atrium-Hotel-Helle-Mitte@t-online.de
Homepage: www.atrium-hotelhellemitte.de

California. Hotel (B bf CC H NG sa sol WO)
Kurfürstendamm 35 ✉10719 *(U-Uhlandstraße/S-Savigny Platz)*
☎ 880 12-0 Fax: 88 01 21 11 Email info@hotel-california.de
Homepage http://www.hotel-california.de
50 rooms with bath/WC, telephone/fax, TV/video, safe, some with balcony. Sauna and fitness-room. Rates single DM 155-205, double 185-235 incl. bf.

Comfort Hotel Auberge (bf CC g H)
Bayreuther Straße 10 ✉10789 *(U-Wittenbergplatz)* ☎ 235 00 20
Fax: 23 50 02 99
Located in the heart of the City, near the reputated ware house KaDeWe and at walking distance to the nearby gay venues. All rooms with shower/WC, telephone, TV, radio, safe and own key. Rates single DM 160, double 210. Additional bed 40. Buffet bf incl.

Crowne Plaza Berlin City Center (H NG)
Nürnberger Strasse 65 ✉10787 *(U-Wittenbergplatz)* ☎ 210 070
Fax: 213 2009 E-Mail: hicpberlin@aol.com
Homepage: crowneplaza.com
4 Star superior first class hotel (NG). Double room from 225,- to 254, DM

Hansablick (b bf CC f g H)
Flotowstraße 6 ✉10555 *(S-Tiergarten/U-Hansaplatz)* ☎ 390 48 00 Fax: 392 69 37 E-Mail: reserv@hotel-hansablick.de Homepage: www.hotel-hansablick.de
Comfortable hotel near the river Spree in central location. All rooms with shower/WC, hair-dryer, cable-TV, radio and minibar, some with balcony. Rates single DM 135 and double 155-215 bf buffet incl.

Holiday Inn Berlin City Center East (H NG)
Prenzlauer Allee 169 ✉10409 *(S-Bahn Prenzlauer Allee)* ☎ 446 610 Fax: 446 61661 E-Mail: HolidayInn@Circle-Hotels.com
3 Star hotel . Double rooms from 195-224, DM

Holiday inn Garden Court Berlin (H NG)
Bleibtreustrasse 25 ✉10707 *(U-Uhlandstrasse)* ☎ 880930 Fax: 88093939 E-Mail: BERLINHIGC@aol.com
3 Star hotel. Double rooms from DM 195 to 224.

Hotel California (bf CC f H NG)
Kurfürstendamm 35 ✉10719 ☎ 880120 Fax: 8801211 E-Mail: info@hotel-california.de

Hotel-Pension Zum Schild (bf CC glm H lj MA)
Lietzenburger Straße 62/Marheinekestraße ✉10719 (S/U-Zoologischer Garten, U-Spichernstraße) ☎ 88 59 250 Fax: 885 92 588
14 double rooms and 10 single rooms. Most rooms with shower/WC, balcony, telephone, safe, heating, own key, laundry service, TV on request. Double from DM 98, single from DM 59 bf incl. TV-room, parking no problem.

Myer's Hotel (AC bf CC glm H)
Metzer Straße 26 ✉10405 ☎ 44 01 40 Fax: 44 01 41 04
Rooms with bath/WC, telephone, Fax, radio, hair-dryer. Opening rates from 89 DM (single) or 129 DM (double).

Park Hotel ☛ Wittenberg/Bad Schmiedeberg

Sachsenhof. Hotel (bf CC lj NG) 0-24 h
Motzstraße 7 ✉10777 *(U-Nollendorfplatz)* ☎ 216 20 74 Fax: 215 82 20 *Central location in gay area. 48 double rooms, 19 single rooms, partly with bath/shower/WC. All rooms with TV, phone and heating. Hotel provides own key. Rates double DM 99-156. single DM 57-120. Add. bed 30, bf 10.*

Transit (bf CC H) 0-24 h
Hagelberger Straße 53-54 ✉10965 *(U-Mehringdamm)*
☎ 789 04 70 Fax: 789 04 777 Email: welcome@hotel-transit.de
Homepage: www.hotel-transit.de *49 rooms with 1-6 beds, all with shower. DM 35, single 90, double 105 (bf incl.)*

GUEST HOUSES

Eulenspiegel Pension (G H) 0-24h
Ebersstraße 58 ✉10827 *(S/U-Innsbrucker Platz)* ☎ 782 38 89 Fax: 782 38 89

Hotel-Pension Gunia (bf CC glm H) 8-23 h
Eisenacher Straße 10/Motzstraße ✉10777 *(U-Nollendorfplatz)*
☎ 218 59 40 Fax: 218 59 44 E-Mail: hotelgunia@t-online.de
Spacious rooms, with shower/WC, cable-TV. Rates for a single DM 80-150, double DM 130-180 extra bed DM 50.

Le Moustache (B CC G H lj)
Gartenstraße 4 ✉10115 *(U-Oranienburger Tor/Rosenthaler Platz, S-Nordbahnhof)* ☎ 81 72 77 Fax: 81 72 77
Central location in the east of Berlin. Rooms with fridge and coffee-maker, partly with TV. Rates single from DM 50 double from DM 80.

Pension Niebuhr (bf CC glm H MA) 9-21 h
Niebuhrstraße 74 ✉10629 *(S-Savignyplatz)* ☎ 324 95 95
☎ 324 95 96 Fax: 324 80 21 Email: info@pension-niebuhr.de
Centrally located. Rooms with shower/WC, cable tv, phone, radio or bathroom on corridor. Bf will be served in the room from 7 h. Rates single DM 95-140, double 120-170.

Schall & Rauch-Bar, Restaurant & Pension (B bf F GLM H OS) 9-3 h
Gleimstraße 23 ✉10437 *(S/U-Schönhauser Allee)*
☎ 448 07 70 Fax: 443 39 722
All rooms with shower/WC, TV and phone.

Tom's House (bf CC G H)
Eisenacher Straße 10 ✉10777 *(U-Nollendorfplatz)* ☎ 218 55 44
Fax: 213 44 64 *All rooms with shower, WC and TV.*

APARTMENTS

Schneider Appartment (glm H LJ MA)
c/o Hennes Fink, Pariser Straße 63 ✉10719 *(U-Spichernstraße)*
☎ 881 18 28 Fax: 881 18 28
Near Ku'damm and many gay bars. Apartment DM 80-150. Furnished with kitchen, cable TV, shower/WC and seperate entrance.

Villa von Desny Appartment
Fuggerstraße 24 *(near Wittenbergplatz)* ☎ (038378) 24 30
Fax: 243 24
1 bedroom apartment, pantry kitchen, shower & WC. Rates from DM 70 (singles) to DM 100 (double). Booking is made through „Villa von Desny" in Bansin (Germany).

PRIVATE ACCOMODATION

Enjoy Bed & Breakfast (bf G H MA YG) 16.30-21 h
Motzstraße 5 ✉10777 *(U-Nollendorfplatz)* ☎ 215 16 66
Fax: 217 52219 E-Mail: Info@ebab.com
Homepage: www.ebab.com
Price 40 DM Accommodation sharing agency. All with shower and bf.

Mitwohnzentrale (g)
Yorckstraße 52 ✉10965 *(S-Yorckstraße)* ☎ 194 30

GENERAL GROUPS

ACT UP Berlin/Feuer unterm Hintern 2nd & 4th Thu 20 h at Berliner AIDS-Hilfe ☛ Health & AIDS Service
c/o Mann-O-Meter, Motzstraße 5, ✉10777 ☎ 216 80 08

Amnesty international-Aktionsgruppe Homosexualität Mon 17-19 h
c/o Stephan Cooper, Karl-Stieler-Straße 2 ✉12167 ☎ 796 28 74
Fax: 796 53 40, E-mail: h0444zyu@rz.hu-berlin.de

Arbeitsgemeinschaft homosexueller Lehrer in der GEW
Ahornstraße 5 ✉10787 ☎ 883 23 01
Fax: 21 99 93 50

Arbeitskreis Homosexueller Frauen und Männer in der Gewerkschaft HBV
Am Köllnischen Park 2 ✉10179 ☎ 27 87 73 25

Arbeitskreis Lesben und Schwule in der ÖTV
Engeldamm 70 ✉10179 ☎ 86 52 12 46
Fax: 86 52 75 91

Autonomes Schwulenreferat im AStA der FU
Kiebitzweg 23 ✉14195 ☎ 83 90 91-18
Plenum Wed 18 h, ASTA-Haus.

Berliner Bären Bartmänner
c/o Mann-o-Meter, Motzstraße 5 ✉10777 ☎ 216 80 08

EPOA-European Pride Organizers Association 18-? h
c/o Hartmut Schönknecht, Elberfelder Straße 23 ✉10555
☎ 392 53 11 Fax: 392 43 19
Email: hartmut.schoenknecht@t-online.de

Feet Back e.V. Meeting: 3rd Fri 21 h
at Flip Flop, Kulmer Straße.Postfach 21 34 ✉65770
☎ 69 40 10 63 or ☎ (0177) 654 40 00

Fraktion Bündnis 90/Die Grünen-Schwulenbereich
Oranienstraße 25 ✉ 10999 ☎ 615 00 50

Gemeinschaft der „verkehrten" Gehörlosen Berlin'85 e.V. Wed 18-20 h (Schreibtelefon)
Schönhauser Allee 36-39 ✉10435 ☎ 440 85 69
Fax: 440 85 69

HAPol Homosexueller Arbeitskreis Polizei e.V. Berlin-Brandenburg
Postfach 35 04 12 ✉10213 ☎ 0177/337 80 72
E-Mail: hapol@berlin.gay-web.de
Homepage: www.berlin.gay-web.de/hapol

Heavy Teddies Girth & Mirth Nord-Ost e.V.
PF 440 110 ✉12001 ☎ 70 78 33 36 Fax: 70 78 33 38.
Email HvyTeddies@aol.com *Meetings every 2nd Saturday/month, 20 h at Jim's, Eberswalder Straße. Every 4th Saturday/month, 15 h at Gate Sauna, Wilhelmstraße 81. Every 4th Sunday/month, 16 h at Memory's, Fuggerstraße 37*

ILGA Informationsbüro Berlin 18-? h
c/o Hartmut Schönknecht, Elberfelder Straße 23 ✉10555
☎ 392 53 11 Fax: 392 43 19
Email: hartmut.schoenknecht@t-online.de

Initiative HomoMonument
c/o Albert Eckert, Fehrbelliner Straße 87 ✉10119 ☎ 285 34-201
Fax: 44 34 10 71 Email eckert@boell.de

Jugendnetzwerk Lambda e.V. Counselling
☎ 29 66 85 88 Mon Wed Fri 17-20 h
Kopernikusstraße 23 ✉10245 ☎ 282 79 90 Fax: 28 59 89 89
E-Mail lambda-berlin@JPBerlin.de

KomBi Kommunikation und Bildung vom anderen Ufer Mon-Thu 10-16 h
Kulmer Straße 11 ✉10785 ☎ 215 37 42 Fax: 215 37 42

Lesbisches und Schwules Büro Film e.V.
P.O. Box 817 ✉10047 ☎ 859 34 23 Fax: 859 34 23

Lila Archiv e.V. Mon-Thu 8-15 h, Fri 8-14 h
Choriner Straße 9 ✉10119 ☎ 448 57 13

LSVD-Landesverband Berlin-Brandenburg
Katzbachstraße 5 ✉10965 ☎ 44 00 82 40 Fax: 44 00 82 41.
Email: berlin@lsvd.de. Homepage: http://www.lsvd.de

MännerMinne Schwuler Männerchor Berlin
c/o Olaf Müller, Zillestraße 72 ✉10585 ☎ 342 29 73
Gay choir.

Magnus-Hirschfeld-Gesellschaft e.V. Forschungsstelle zur Geschichte der Sexualwissenschaft
Chodowieckistraße 41 ✉10405
☎ 441 39 73 Fax: 441 39 73 E-Mail: mhg@magnus.in-berlin.de
Homepage: www.magnus.in-berlin.de

MannsBilder Schwuler Foto-Club e.V. (G) Tue 20-23h
c/o Mann-O-Meter, Motzstraße 5 ✉10777 ☎ 745 17 26 E-Mail: MBilderSFC@aol.com Homepage: www.members.aol/mBilderSFC

MILES and more & Bi-Nats Mon-Fri 10-18 h
Katzbachstraße 5 ✉10965 (U-Yorckstraße) ☎ 44 00 82 40
Fax: 44 00 82 41 Email berlin@lsvd.de

Mutvilla-Lesbisch-schwule Interessenvertretung an der Humboldt-Universität Berlin
Unter den Linden 6-8 ✉10099 ☎ 20 93 26 03
Fax: 20 96 23 96

Pride Collection. The
c/o ISGITN, Elberfelder Straße 23 ✉10555 ☎ 392 53 11
The Pride Collection collects any material concerning the history of the Christopher Street Day, especially posters, media coverage, merchandising- articles and more.

Queerstudien
c/o Institut Kultur- und Kunstwissenschaften der *Humboldt-Uni*
☎ 308 82-246 Fax: 308 82-258 E-mail: thinius@rz.hu-berlin.de

Referat für Lesben, Schwule und Bisexuelle an der ev. FH Berlin
Reichensteiner Weg 24 ✉14195

Referat für Lesben und Schwule im AStA der TFH
Luxemburger Straße 10 ✉13353

Romeo und Julius Meeting: Thu 18.30-20 h, Kalkreuthstraße 7
c/o Mann-O-Meter, Motzstraße 5 ✉10777 ☎ 216 80 08
Gay youth group.

Rosa Cavaliere e.V. Meeting/Treffen Mon 19 h at Gemeindesaal Alt-Schöneberg, Hauptstraße 48
c/o Dieter Kremer, Ramlerstraße 21 ✉13355 ☎ 464 17 67
Gay Choir/Schwuler Chor.

Schlips e.V.
PO Box 08 02 25 ✉10002 ☎ 651 52 13 Fax: 651 52 13
E-Mail: eike.stedefeldt@topwave.de
Gay and lesbian information and press service.

Schwestern der Perpetuellen Indulgenz Priorei Berlin 20-23 h
Mehringdamm 65 ✉10961 *(Hinterhaus/backyard)*
☎ 788 44 18 E-Mail: gabi@dieschwestern.org
Homepage: www.dieschwestern.org/termine.htm

Schwule Internationale Berlin e.V. Meeting 1st & 3rd Sat 19.30 h
c/o Mann-O-Meter, Motzstraße 5 ✉10777 ☎ 216 80 08

Schwule und Lesbische Paare Regionalgruppe Berlin (SLP e.V.)
Tegeler Weg 105 ✉10589 ☎ (0511) 13 17 219
Homepage: http://www.macman.org./slp

Schwulenreferat im AStA der TU Café Tue Wed 12-17 h
Marchstraße 6 ✉10587 *(3rd floor)* ☎ 314 27 701
Plenum Tue 18 h.

Sonntags-Club e.V. (A d GLM MA OS S TV VS) 17-24 h
Greifenhagener Straße 28 ✉10437 *(U-Shönhauserallee)*
☎ 449 75 90 E-Mail: info@sonntags-club.de
Counselling and information center where parties and exhibitions are held on a regular basis.

Two-In-One -AG Lesben- und Schwulenpolitik in der PDS Hotline Mon-Fri 14-17 h
Kleine Alexanderstraße 28 ✉10178 Fax: 44 05 23 13
Email: AGuenther1@compuserve.de
Please call for detailed information.

Verliebte Jungs
c/o aha, Mehringdamm 61 ✉10961 ☎ 692 36 00
Gay youth group.

FETISH GROUPS

Berlin Leder und Fetisch
Nollendorfstraße 28 ✉10777 ☎ 215 00 99 Fax: 216 10 60
E-Mail: info@blf.de

Motorradclub Lederbären Berlin (MCLB)
c/o Mann-O-Meter, Motzstraße 5 ✉10777 ☎ 215 14 58 *(Wolfgang) Treffen/meetings 1st Sun 11 h, 3rd Sat 13 h at parking Hohenzollerndamm/Emserstraße. Bikers only.*

MSC Berlin e.V.
c/o Hartmut Wokatsch, Eilerstraße 20 ✉14165
Member of ECMC.

Quälgeist Berlin e.V. call Fri & Sat evening
Merseburgerstraße 3, 2. Hof ✉10823 ☎ 788 57 99 *SM-group.*

HEALTH GROUPS

Berliner AIDS-Hilfe e. V. (GLM MA) Mon-Thu 12-18, Fri 12-15 h
Meinekestraße 12 ✉10719 *(U-Spichernstrasse)* ☎ 88 56 400
Fax: 88 56 40-25 E-Mail: info@Berlin.Aidshilfe.de

Café PositHiv Sun-Fri 15-? h, Sat 18-? h
Alvenslebenstraße 26 ✉10783 (U-Bülowstraße) ☎ 216 86 54
Fax: 216 86 55

Felix Pflegeteam Mon-Thu 9-17, Fri -16 h
Meinekestraße 12 ✉10719 ☎ 887 111-80 Fax: 887 111-88

H.I.V. (Hilfe, Information, Vermittlung) e.V. Mon-Fri 9-15 h
Lilienthalstraße 28, ✉10965 ☎ 691 80 33
Society for home care and home-nursing, financial help for AIDS-patients and HIV-positives.

Lighthouse
c/o Berliner AIDS-Hilfe, Meinekestraße 12 ✉10719
☎ 88 56 400 or ☎ 624 98 52

Pluspunkt Berlin e.V. Mon-Fri 11-17 h, Mon 15-17 h counselling
Ueckermünder Straße 1a ✉10439 *(U/S-Schönhauser Allee)*
☎ 446 68 80 or ☎ 44 66 88 11 (Detlef) or ☎ 44 66 88 99 (Andreas)

Prenzelberger AIDS-Projekt-"jederMann e.V." Mon-Thu 15-20, Fri 13-18 h
Greifenhagener Straße 6 ✉10437 ☎ 444 17 64 Fax: 445 60 00
Counselling ☎ 444 65 55.

Sub/Way Berlin e.V. Mon 11-18, Tue Thu Fri 14-18 h
Nollendorfstraße 31 ✉10777 *(U-Nollendorfplatz)* ☎ 215 57 59
Fax: 217 56 049
Help and counselling for hustlers and callboys.

ZiK GmbH-Zuhause im Kiez
Perleberger Straße 27 ✉10559 ☎ 398 96 00
Living and Nursing projekt for people with HIV and AIDS.

zukunft positiv
Mommsenstrasse 45 ✉10629
☎ 32 70 70 70 Homepage: www.zukunftpositiv.de

HELP WITH PROBLEMS

Infoladen Berlin Thu 19-21, Wed 19-? h
Kopenhagener Straße 14 ✉10437 ☎ 448 21 84

Pluspunkt Berlin e.V. (Hilfe für Positive)
Mon-Fri 11-17 h, Mon 15-17 h counselling
Ückermünder Straße 1a, ✉10439 *(S/Tram-Bornholmer Straße)*
☎ 448 62 19 Fax 448 67 20

Schwule Hilfe und Beratung
Mommsenstraße 45 ✉10629 ☎ 194 46

Schwulenberatung & Kursiv e.V. Mon-Fri 11-19h
Mommsenstraße 45 ✉10629 ☎ 194 46 (counselling)
☎ 32 70 3040 Fax: 32 70 30 41
E-Mail: schwulenberatung@bln.de
Homepage: www.beratung.das-berlin.de
Schwules Überfalltelefon 18-21 h
c/o Mann-O-Meter, Motzstraße 5 ✉10777 ☎ 216 33 36
Fax: 215 70 78
Help for gay-bashed.
SUB/WAY-Querstrich Tue 14-16 h
☎ 217 56 048
Help for hustlers.

RELIGIOUS GROUPS

Gesprächskreis Homosexualität in der Evangelischen Advent Gemeinde Mon Thu Fri 9-12, Tue 15-18, Meeting: 2nd & 4th Tue 19.30 h
Danziger Straße 201/203 ✉10407 ☎ 423 34 56
Fax: 423 34 56
Yachad-Verein jüdischer Lesben und Schwuler
c/o Mann-O-Meter, Motzstraße 5 ☎ 216 80 08

SPORT GROUPS

Berliner Regenbogenforellen e.V.
Pflügerstraße 68 ✉12047 ☎ 624 23 94
Gay and lesbian swimming.
Gaysha-Karate für Schwule und ihre FreundInnen (MA)
c/o Stephan Bauchwitz, Kaiserdamm 35 ✉14057 ☎ 302 85 78
Kung-Fu-Gruppe
Kontakt über Dietmar ☎ 611 47 63
Pink-Pong e.V.
☎ 621 69 94 or ☎ 838 57 16 Fax: 838 66 25
Homepage http://www.tu-berlin.de/~insi/gol/pinkpong.html
Taktlos Mann Tanzt
☎ 393 83 34 *Ballroom Dancing.*
Vorspiel-Sportverein für Schwule und Lesben Berlin e.V. Mon 17-20, Thu 10-13 h
Friedr.-Ludw.-Jahn Sportpark, Cantianstraße 24 ✉10437
☎ 440 57740 Fax: 440 57741 E-Mail: vorspiel@t-online.de
Breites Sportangebot, auch Gruppen für HIV-Positive und ältere Menschen. Ausführliches Programm jeden Monat neu im Szenemagazin „Sergej".

SWIMMING

-Strandbad Müggelsee (S-Friedrichshagen, Tram-Fürstenwalder Damm/ Müggelseedamm)
-Halensee (S-Halensee; Bus-Rathenauplatz. Not the lido but the lawn beside Halenseestraße at Rathenauplatz)
-Teufelssee (S-Grunewald, than a 15 minutes walk)
-Grunewaldsee (Bus 119 to »Hagenplatz« then take Königsallee to the the lake)
-Tiergarten (»Tuntenwiese«) (U-Hansaplatz; Bus 100/187. For tanning only.)
-Strandbad Wannsee (S-Nikolassee, than take bus-shuttle to Strandbad, right behind the nude section)

CRUISING

-Siegessäule/Großer Stern (between »Hofjägerallee« and »Straße des 17. Juni«)
-Grunewald (LJ) (at P Pappelplatz/Auerbachtunnel)
-Volkspark Wilmersdorf
-Körnerpark (near S/U-Neukölln)
-Preußenpark (U-Fehrbelliner Platz)
-Park U-Turmstraße
-Volkspark Friedrichshain (at »Märchenbrunnen«)
-Viktoriapark
-Wittenbergplatz (AYOR) (popular)

Biberach ☎ 07351

GENERAL GROUPS

Homosexuellen Emanzipationsgruppe Landkreis Biberach (HELB) (MA)
PO Box 18 10 ✉88388 ☎ 803 84
Meeting Thu 20-23 h, Ehinger Straße 19 in Jugendhaus Abseits.

Bielefeld ☎ 0521

GAY INFO

Autonomes Schwulenreferat der Uni Bielefeld Mon-Fri 12-14 h, Sun/Mon closed
c/o AStA, PO Box 110 01 31 ✉33501 ☎ 106 34 24
Fax: 106 30 32.
What's up
c/o Aids-Hilfe, Artur-Ladebeck-Straße 26 ✉33602
Small leaflet-like newsletter for the area.

BARS

Muttis Bierstube (B d G MA p) 21-? h Tue closed (Summer)
Friedrich-Verleger-Straße 20, ✉33602 *(Busstation Kesselbrink)*
☎ 618 16
Roland's Eck (B d F g MA p) 23-5 h
Heeper Straße 28, ✉33607 ☎ 622 36

CAFES

Café Flutsch (B G) Mon-Fri 12-14 h
Universitätsstraße 25, ✉33615 *(in der Uni)* ☎ 106 34 24
Gallery on 1st floor/Galerie im 1. Stock.
Café im Autonomen Schwulenreferat der Uni Berlin (AC G) Mon-Fri 12-14 h, Sat/Sun closed
Universitätsstraße 25 ✉33615 ☎ 106 34 24
Magnus (B F GLM MA OS s VS YG) 18-?
August-Bebel-Straße 126 ✉33602 *(Tram 3)* ☎ 629 53
Fax: 14 35 51.
Schäfers Café in der Kunsthalle (A bf F glm MA OS WE) Tue-Sun 9.30-24 h, Mon closed
Artur-Ladebeck-Straße 5, ✉33602 *(Tram 1-Adenauer Platz)*
☎ 17 40 77

DANCECLUBS

Alte Hechelei (B D GLM YG) 2nd Sat 21-4 h
Heeperstraße 37 ✉33607 *(Ravensberger Park)* ☎ 625 58
Bitches Brew (AC B D GLM YG) Fri 22-? h
Feilenstraße 31 ✉33602 ☎ 63059
Far Out (AC B D g YG) 22-3 h
Niederwall 12 ✉33602 *(Near town hall/Nähe Rathaus)* ☎ 17 59 58
Fax: 766 57
Take Off (B D GLM) GLM Wed 22-? Sat 23-?, G Fri 23-? h
Detmolder Straße 241 ✉33605

SEX SHOPS/BLUE MOVIES

SexPoint (g VS) Mon-Fri 10-21, Sat 12-21 h
Detmolder Straße 77 ✉33604 ☎ 679 78
Shop Intim (g) 9-24, Sun 13-24 h
Bahnhofstraße 47, ✉33602 ☎ 17 95 50

SAUNAS/BATHS

Sauna 65 (B DR f G MA OS sa sb sol VS WO) Sun-Thu 14-24 h, Fri Sat -? h
Niedermühlenkamp 65 ✉33604 ☎ 656 59
Mon-Fri reduced rates between 14-17:00h

BOOK SHOPS

Buchladen Eulenspiegel Mon-Fri 9-18.30 h, Sat 10-15 h
Hagenbruchstraße 7 ✉33602 ☎ 17 50 49 *Fax: 13 35 10.*

GENERAL GROUPS

AStA der KiHo Bethel
Remterweg 47 ✉33617

Schwusos Bielefeld 1st Wed 19 at SPD, 3rd Wed 19 h at Magnus
c/o Jusos, Arndtstraße 8/Karl-Eilers-Straße ✉33602
Gay social democrats.

HEALTH GROUPS

AIDS-Hilfe Bielefeld e.V. Tue- Fri 10-14, Wed 10-16, Thu 10-20 h
Artur-Ladebeck-Straße 26 ✉33602 *(Adenauerplatz)*
☎ 194 11 Fax: 133369 E-Mail: aids-bielefeld@pride.de
Homepage: www.bielefeld.aidshilfe.de

HELP WITH PROBLEMS

HomoPhon Tue 18-20 h
c/o Autonomes Schwulenreferat der Uni Bielefeld ☎ 106 34 24

Schwules Überfalltelefon
☎ 19 228

RELIGIOUS GROUPS

Ökumenische Arbeitsgruppe Homosexuelle und Kirche HuK e.V. Thu 20-22.30 h
Ralf Sauk, Waldstraße 78 ✉33739 ☎ 14 34 60 *(Hannes)*

SPORT GROUPS

Sportverein Warminia Bielefeld
c/o Kesselbrinkbad, August-Bebel-Straße 91 ✉33602 ☎ 669 69
Email warminia@gmx.net
Badminton, Fitness, Volleyball, Schwimmen, Kraftsport, Tischtennis.

CRUISING

-Hauptbahnhof (r)
-University Bielefeld (EG, gegenüber/across Caféteria)
-Park hinter/behind Ravensburger Spinnerei (AYOR)

Bingen

CRUISING

-Rheinanlagen (between Disco Palazzo and KD Schiffahrtsgesellschaft)

Bitterfeld ☎ 0177

GENERAL GROUPS

SchwulLesBische Initiative Bitterfeld-Wolfen Thu 18.30-?
Hahnstückenweg 4a ✉06749 ☎ 03493/(0177) 3359032 or ☎ (0172) 944 49 50 E-mail bbz@gux.net

Böblingen ☎ 07031

SEX SHOPS/BLUE MOVIES

Erotic Video Shop (g VS) Mon-Sat 9-1, Sun 13-1 h
Klaffensteinstraße 10 ✉71032 ☎ 22 74 73

Multi-Video-Show (g VS) Mon-Sat 9-24, Sun 16-24 h
Wilhelmstraße 27 ✉71034 ☎ 22 16 47

Sexshop (g VS) Wilhelmstraße 27 ✉71034

GENERAL GROUPS

Schwulengruppe
c/o Alfred Mayer, Parkstraße 4 ✉71034

CRUISING

-Kongreßzentrum
-Busbahnhof/bus station
-Postplatz 16 (unterirdisch/underground Stuttgarter Straße/Sindelfinger Straße

Bocholt ☎ 02871

BARS

Old Paddy (B f g MA) Tue-Sun 21-4 h, closed Mon
Franzstraße 21 ✉46395 *(Nähe Bahnhof/near railway station)*
☎ 160 60

SEX SHOPS/BLUE MOVIES

Erotik-World (g VS) Mon-Sat 10-23 h
Münsterstraße 63 ✉46395 *(Close to Stadtring/Nähe Stadtring)*
10 cabins, 2 with gay porns, popular/10 Kabinen, davon 2 mit schwulen Pornos, populär.

GENERAL GROUPS

Homosexuelle Initiativgruppe und Freunde Meetings 2nd 4th Fri 20 h
c/o Familienbildungsstätte, Ostwall 39 ✉46397 ☎ 36 41

CRUISING

-Langenbergpark
-(P) Aasee

Bochum ☎ 0234

GAY INFO

Radioprojekt DIN 4 1/2
Ruhrwelle Bochum 105,0 MHz FM/UKW
Radioproject from and for people that »don't serve as standard«.

BARS

Coxx (B G MA) 20-3 h
Ehrenfeldstraße 2 ✉44789 ☎ 33 72 96
Freibad (A B F glm MA N OS) 18-3 h
Clemensstraße 2 ✉44789 *(U-Schauspielhaus)* ☎ 31 21 35
Orlando (A AC bf CC F GLM MA OS TV W YG) Sun-Thu 10-1, Fri Sat -3 h
Alte Hattinger Straße 31 ✉44789 *(Schauspielhaus)* ☎ 342 42

CAFES

Café Zauberhaft (AC B bf f G lj MA YG) Sun 15-20 h
Kulturzentrum Bhf Langendreer, Wallbaumweg 108 ✉44892 *(S-Bochum-Langendreer)* ☎ 28 08 22

DANCECLUBS

After Eight (B D G) Sat 20-1 h
c/o Zwischenfall, Alte Bahnhofstraße 214 ✉44892 ☎ 28 76 50
BO-YS (AC B D F G lj MA OS W WE YG) 1st Sat 22-4 h
Kulturzentrum Bhf Langendreer, Wallbaumweg 108 ✉44892 *(S-Bochum-Langendreer)* ☎ 280 822
Very popular. Entrance-fee DM 12.
Stargate (AC D DR G lj S SNU VS WE YG) Fri Sat and before holidays 23-5 h
Hans-Böckler Straße 10-12 ✉44787 *(„City-Passage")* ☎ 138 88
Entrance fee DM 9.
Zarah und Leander (AC B D F GLM lj MA OS WE YG) every 5th Saturday/month, 22-4 h
c/o Kulturzentrum Bahnhof Langendreer, Wallbaumweg 108 ✉44892 *(S-Bahn station Bochum-Langendreer Line 1)* ☎ 28 08 22 *Entrance fee DM 10/12.*
Zwischenfall (A D glm lj S WE) We 22-4, Fr-Sun 22-?
Alte Bahnhofstraße 214 ✉44892 ☎ 287 650

SEX SHOPS/BLUE MOVIES

Sexyland (g) 9-18.30, Sat -14 h, closed Sun
Humboldstraße 34/Südring ✉44787
Show Center (DR g lj MA s SNU STV TV VS) 10-24, Wed Fri Sat Sun 10-1
Rottstraße 16, ✉44793 ☎ 162 71

BOOK SHOPS

Belle et Triste (GLM s W) Tue-Fri 10-20, Sat -16 h, closed Sun Mon
Humboldtstraße 36 ✉44787 *(S-Hauptbahnhof/U-Engelbertbrunnen)* ☎ 68 86 88 Fax: 68 86 99
Homepage: http://www.belle-et-triste.de

GENERAL GROUPS

Autonomes Schwulenreferat der Bochumer Ruhr-Universität Mon 10-16 h, Thu 12-17 h
AStA der Universität, Universitätsstraße 150, ✉44801 ☎ 700 22 26

HEALTH GROUPS

AIDS-Hilfe Bochum e.V. Mon & Tue 10-12:00h, Tue & Thu 18-20:00h
Bergstraße 115 ✉44791 ☎ 519 10 or ☎ 519 19

HELP WITH PROBLEMS

Rosa Strippe Bochum e.V. Counselling: Mon 19-21, Wed Thu 18-20, Fri 14-16 h
Eislebener Straße 14 ✉44892 ☎ 194 46
Open counselling Wed 16-18 h.

CRUISING

-Main railway station (ayor R)
-Railway station Präsident (Dorstener Straße)
-Ruhruniversität (Building GA 03 Süd)
-Freiligrathstraße/Bergstraße

Bonn ☎ 0228

GAY INFO

Bunte Welt Mon 19-19.30 on FM 98.9/cable 94.55
Outcome
c/o Schwulenreferat, AStA Uni Bonn, Nassestraße 11 *53113*
Schwulen und Lesben Zentrum Bonn e.V.
(AC B D GLM s YG)
Am Frankenbad 5 ✉53111 *(Altstadt)* ☎ 63 00 39 or ☎ 19446
Fax: 65 00 50.
Homepage http://home.t-online.de/home/ZentrumBonn

BARS

Boba's Bar (AC B d G MG p YG) Tue-Sun 21-3 h, Mon closed
Josefstraße 17 ✉53111 *(near/nähe Kennedybrücke)*
☎ 65 06 85
Le Copain (B Glm MA MG) Sun-Thu 17-1, Fri Sat -2 h
Thomas-Mann-Straße 3a ✉53111
Sharlie (AC B CC DR G lj MA p VS YG) 21-5 h
Theaterstraße 2/Kölnstraße ✉53111 *(Tram: Bertha-von-Suttner-Platz)* ☎ 766 78 68
Zarah L. (B glm MA S) 18-1 h. Mon women only. Wed, Fri, Sat 21.30 & 23 h Show.
Maxstraße 22 ✉53111 ☎ 63 46 35

CAFES

Café Z (AC d GLM MA s) Mon (G), Tue (L), Thu 20-24, closed Wed Fri Sun
Schwulen- u. Lesbenzentrum Bonn, Am Frankenbad 5 ✉53111
☎ 63 00 39 Fax: 65 00 50 *1st Sat (G) 2nd Sat (L) party 21-? h*

DANCECLUBS

Ysabeau (AC B D glm MA P s W) Café Tue-Thu 22-5, Dance Fri-Sat 22-5, Sun -4 h
Kaiserpassagen, Martinsplatz 2a ✉53113 ☎ 65 16 15
Disco with ballroom-dancing.

RESTAURANTS

La Vita (F g) 12-14.30/18-23.30 h Mon closed
Kessenicher Straße 165 ✉53129 *(Tram Dottendorf)* ☎ 23 50 45
Italian Cuisine/Italienische Küche.

SEX SHOPS/BLUE MOVIES

Erotik-Shop (g VS) 10-20, Sat -14, Sun closed
Berliner Freiheit 18, ✉53111 ☎ 65 50 41

HOUSE OF BOYS

Gesellschafter-Team Latour (G msg P VS) 11-23 h
(Troisdorf) ☎ (0171) 8020860

BOOK SHOPS

Buchladen 46 (GLM) Mon-Wed 10-19, Thu Fri -20, Sat -16 h
Kaiserstraße 46, ✉53113 ☎ 22 36 08 Fax: 21 74 67

PR & PHOTOGRAPHY SERVICES

Michael Gehrke Public Relations
Rudolf-Hahn-Straße 20 ✉53225 ☎ 46 61 41 Fax: 47 88 42
E-Mail mgpr.bonn@t-online
Homepage http://www/webmagazin.com
Advertising agency, PR, web services.

TRAVEL & TRANSPORT

Bon(n) Voyage Touristik (GLM MG) Mon-Fri 10-13 14-18.30, Sat 10-13 h
Thomas-Mann-Straße 56 ✉53111 *(near Main station)* ☎ 631595
Fax: 9851818

GENERAL GROUPS

Autonomes Schwulenreferat im AStA der Uni Bonn (G W) 12-14 h, Sat-Sun closed
Nassestraße 11, Raum 2, ✉53113 *(1st floor)* ☎ 73 70 41
Fax: 26 22 10
Freie Konferenz der StudentInnenschaften an Fachhochschulen e.V.
Reuterstraße 44 ✉53113

HEALTH GROUPS

AIDS-Hilfe Bonn e.V. Mon, Wed & Thu 10-13, 14-17, Tue 10-17, Fri 10-13, 14-15 h
Weberstraße 52 ✉53113 ☎ 94 90 90 Fax: 949030
E-Mail: ahb@aids-hilfe-bonn.de
Homepage: www.aids-hilfe-bonn.de
Counselling ☎ 194 11. "Die Gummibärchen" in Café „Queerbeet".

HELP WITH PROBLEMS

Schwules Beratungstelefon Mon Wed 19-21 h
☎ 194 46

Schwules Überfalltelefon Mon 18-21, Wed 8-14 19-21 h
☎ 0221/192 28
Help in case of gay-bashing.

SPORT GROUPS

Bonner Hupfdohlen-schwuler und lesbischer Sportverein e.V.
PO Box 27 34 ✉53017 ☎ 65 57 94
E-Mail: hupfdohlen@aol.com

CRUISING

-Hofgarten (ayor) (Hinter der Universität am Rheinufer/behind the university at river Rhine; Straße/street »Am Alten Zoll«)
-Dornheckensee (Bonn-Ramersdorf, summer only)
-Universität (1.Etage/1st floor)

Borken ☎ 02861

GENERAL GROUPS

SchiBo-Schwule in Borken Tue 20-22 h (ungerade Wochen/uneven weeks)
c/o DRK-Bildungshaus BUG, Burloer Straße 148 ✉46325
☎ 633 43 & 652 60

Bottrop ☎ 02041

CRUISING

-Stadtgarten (am Quadrat)

Bovenden ☎ 0551

GENERAL GROUPS

Schwule*Hilfe*Göttingen
P.O. Box 11 51 ✉37116 ☎ 8 33 55 Fax: 8 33 55
Including prison counselling. Winner of the Cup International for the best gay counselling group 1998

Brandenburg ☎ 03381

CRUISING

-Park Humboldt-Hain (AYOR) (an der Jahrtausendbrücke/at the bridge)

Braunschweig ☎ 0531

GAY INFO

Schwulenzentrum für BS Mon-Wed
c/o Queer, Bohlweg 25 c ✉38100 ☎ 240 89 99
-Games 1st Tue 20 h
-Videos and slide-shows 2nd Tue 20 h
-Readings 3rd Tue 20 h
-Classical music 4th Tue 20 h
-Coming-out youth group 1st Wed 18 h
Further information via internet, Homepage: http://www.braunscheig.lanobis.de/vereine/aids.hilfe/

BARS

Atelier (B d f GLM MA) 19 h - open end
Leonhardstraße 7 ✉38102 *(near/Nähe Stadthalle)* ☎ 767 07
Why Not (B d f GLM lj MA p s STV WE) 20-2, Fri Sat 20-5 h, Sun 15-2 h
Echternstraße 9 ✉38102 ☎ 441 66

DANCECLUBS

Queer! (CC D GLM lj s WE) Thu 20-2, Fri Sat 22-5, Sun 17-2 h, closed Mon-Wed
Bohlweg 25c ✉38100 ☎ 120 35 12/11 Fax: 120 35 10
Email: queer_bs@hotmail.com

SEX SHOPS/BLUE MOVIES

Boutique intim (g) Mon-Fri 9-20, Sat -16 h
Friedrich-Wilhelm-Straße 31, ✉38100 *(opposite/gegenüber Post)*
☎ 449 22
Frankies Erotik-Shop (G) Mon-Fri 14-20.30, Sat 10-17 h, closed Sun
Fallersleber Straße 27 ✉38100 *(Tram-Fallersleber Tor)*
☎ 147 74
Orion (g) Mon-Fri 9.30-20 h, Sat 9.30-16 h, Videoshop: Mon-Sat 9-23 h
Ägidienmarkt 9/Auguststraße ✉38100 ☎ 432 83
Sex Bazar (g) Mon-Wed, Fri 9-18.30, Thu -20.30, Sat -14, Videoshop: Mon-Sat 9-23 h
Wendenstraße 51, ✉38100 ☎ 404 40
Sex intim (g) Mon-Fri 9-22, Sat -20 h
Malertwete 3/Güldenstraße, ✉38100 ☎ 435 41

BOOK SHOPS

Buchhandlung Roters (g) Mon-Fri 10-13, 15-18, Sat 10-13 h
Wendenstraße 51 ✉38100 ☎ 496 00

GENERAL GROUPS

ComeOut Gruppe 2nd & 4th Thu 20 h
c/o AstA-TU, Katharinenstraße 1 ✉38106
Homosexuelle Unigruppe Braunschweig (HUBS) Schwulenreferat beim AStA der TU
Wed 10-12 h (bf) at AStA-Café
Katharinenstraße 1, ✉38106 ☎ 391 45 55/56
-Come Out Jugendgruppe (2. & 4. Thu 20 h)
Jugendnetzwerk Lambda Niedersachsen e.V. Mon-Fri 11-16 h
Karlstraße 97, ✉38106 ☎ 34 48 83
VSE-Verein für Sexuelle Emanzipation e.V.
Tue 20-? h, Sun 15-18 h
c/o Andreas Paruszewski, Virchowstraße 5 ✉38118
☎ & Fax: 280 96 36

HEALTH GROUPS

Braunschweiger AIDS-Hilfe e.V. Mon Tue Thu 10-16, Wed-Fri 10-13 h
Eulenstraße 5 ✉38114 ☎ 580030 ☎ 0531/ 58 00 30
Fax: 58 00 330
Homepage: www.braunschweig.lanobis.de/vereine/aids.hilfe/
-(last Wed of quarter) Gay men, 40 of age and up.
-Gay Outdoor Club ☎ 33 58 50 (Michael).
-Bisexual group.
-Gay and lesbian café Sun 15-18 h

HELP WITH PROBLEMS

Rosa Telefon Thu 20-22 h
☎ 194 46

RELIGIOUS GROUPS

Homosexuelle und Kirche (HuK)
Wolfgang Buchmeier, Ilsenburger Stieg 9, 38667 Bad *Harzburg*
☎ 525 45

SPORT GROUPS

Schwimmgruppe WARMBADEN Thu shortly before closing time at
Badezentrum Gliesmarode, Sammelumkleide II
☎ 34 03 64 *(Thomas)*
Schwul-lesbischer Sportverein Braunschweig e.V.
☎ *742 77 (Carsten) -Fitness*
☎ *89 65 40 (Holger) -Volleyball*
☎ *82 666 (Mark) -Badminton*
☎ *790558 (Norbert)*

SWIMMING

-Island in Salzgittersee (Lawn on the hill, summer only).
-Kennelbad (summer only).
-Bienroder See (nude bathing area).

CRUISING

-Am Rathaus
-Kohlmarkt
-Wolfenbütteler Straße (near Bürgerpark)
-Kennedyplatz
-Museumspark
-Museumspark (next to the theatre, evenings)
-P Kennel

Bremen ☎ 0421

GAY INFO

Rat & Tat Zentrum für Schwule + Lesben e.V. (GLM MA s YG) Mon, Wed & Fri 11-13, Tue 15-18 h (counselling)
Theodor-Körner-Straße 1 ✉28203 ☎ 70 41 70
Cafe KWEER Tue Wed Fri 20-1, Sun 15-19 h
☛Hamburg

BARS

Bienenkorb (B F g MA r) 16-6, Sat Sun 19-6 h
Rembertistraße 32 ✉28203 ☎ 32 72 29
Bronx (CC DR G LJ MA p VS) 22-? h
Bohnenstraße 1b/Gertrudenstraße ✉28203 ☎ 70 24 04
Confession (B d f GLM LJ MA SWC) Tue-Thu 19-2, Fri Sat 21-? h, Sat lesbian and gay only
Humboldtstraße 156 ✉28203 ☎ 738 22
David (B bf F g MA p) Mon-Fri 21-3 h, Sat 21-6 h, Sun 15-? h
Rembertistraße 33 ✉28203 ☎ 339 84 18
Leinen los (B G MA) Tue-Sun 17-? h, closed Mon
An der Weide 24 ✉28195 ☎ 32 77 23
Queens (B G MA YG) 21-5, Fri Sat -? h
Außer der Schleifmühle 10 ✉28203 ☎ 32 59 12
Rendezvous. Zum (B f glm MA) Mon-Sun 17-2 h
Elisabethstraße 34, ✉28217 ☎ 38 31 59

CAFES

Kweer (A B f Glm MA YG s) Tue Wed Fri 20-1, Sat 17.30-19.30 (YG), Sun 15-19 h
Theodor-Körner-Straße 1 ✉28203 ☎ 70 00 08

DANCECLUBS

Monopol (B D G MA)
Ostertorswallstraße 95 ✉28195 ☎ 32 19 40
Check the local gay papers for up-to-date parties and dance events.

SHOWS

Madame Lothar/Travestietheater im Schnoor (CC d f p S STV) Wed-Sat and before holidays 20-? h
Kolpingstraße 9, ✉28195 ☎ 337 91 91

SEX SHOPS/BLUE MOVIES

Gay Movie (G r VS) 10-24, Sun 12-24 h
An der Weide 22, ✉28195 *(Near/Nähe Hauptbahnhof, across/gegenüber Post)* ☎ 337 81 79
Men's Seven (AC b DR G lj MA r VS) Mon-Sat 11-23.30, Sun and public holidays 15-23.30 h
Am Dobben 7 ✉28203 *(Tram 1/4/10-Rembertistraße)*
☎ 32 36 87
Blue movie entrance fee DM 14, student 10.
Video-World (G VS) 9-24, Sun 13-23 h
Rembertistrasse 56, ✉28195 ☎ 32 58 98
Video-World (g VS) 8-23, Sun 13-23 h
Pieperstraße 7/Martinistraße, ✉28195 ☎ 122 85

SAUNAS/BATHS

City Club Sauna (B f g MA sa sol VS) 17-1 h, (G) Tue Sat, closed Sun
Humboldtstraße 144, ✉28203 *(Bus10-Humboldtstraße)*
☎ 70 14 65
Straight videos.
Perseus Club-Sauna (B G sa sb VS WO) 16-24, Sat 16-Sun 24 h
Waller Heerstraße 126 ✉28219 ☎ 38 51 00
Thu 2-4-1.
Steam Sauna-Walle (B bf DR F G MA msg OS s sa sb sol VS) Summer: Tue-Fri 18-1, Sat Sun 16-1, Winter:16-1, Tue 12-1, Sat Sun 0-24 h
Steffensweg 157/Karl-Peter-Straße, ✉28217 *(Tram10-Wartburgstraße)* ☎ 396 60 97
Entrance fee DM 23, student 18, only 16 on Sun.

BOOK SHOPS

Humboldt-Buchhandlung (g) Mon 13-19 h, Tue-Fri 10-19 h, Sat 10-16 h
Ostertorsteinweg 76, ✉28203 ☎ 777 21
With gay selection.

Phönix (g) Mon-Fri 9-20, Sat -16 h
Sögestraße 46, ✉28195 ☎ 17 10 77
General bookstore with gay section.

Wohlthat'sche Buchhandlung (g) Mon-Wed 9.30-19, Thu Fri -20, Sat -16 h
Wenkenstraße 2/Am Brill ✉28195 ☎ 143 20

LEATHER & FETISH SHOPS

H M Leder (CC G LJ MA p s) Tue-Fri 12-20, Sat -16 h, Sun & Mon closed
Neukirchstraße 18 ✉28215 ☎ 37 14 30
Homepage: www.hm-leder.com (online mailorder)

GENERAL GROUPS

Samstagsschwestern Sat 15-17.30 h
c/o Rat & Tat Zentrum, Theodor-Körner-Straße 1 ✉28203 ☎ 70 41 70

S.A.M.T. -radikale Schwulengruppe
c/o Sielwallhaus, Sielwallstraße 38 ✉28203

FETISH GROUPS

Green Berets International e.V. RV Nord/Bremen Hansekompanie
PO Box 10 60 02 ☎ (0172) 5844171
Fax: (040) 36 03 22 70 66 or (089) 66 61 73 22 50
Email gbi96@aol.com
Homepage: http://www.planet-interkom.de/baum1/gbi.html

LC Nordwest e. V. 4. Fri
Zone 283, Kornstraße 283
c/o Rat & Tat Zentrum, Theodor-Körner-Straße 1 ✉28203 ☎ 70 41 70

HEALTH GROUPS

AIDS-Hilfe Bremen e.V. Hotline Mon-Fri 10-17 h
Am Dobben 66 ✉28203 ☎ 719 25 Counselling ☎ 70 13 13
Fax: 70 20 12 Email: AIDS-HilfeBremen@t-online.de

HELP WITH PROBLEMS

Schwule Beratung Mon Wed Fri 11-13, Tue 15-18, lesbian Wed 11-13 h
c/o Rat und Tat Zentrum, Theodor-Körner-Straße 1 ✉28203 ☎ 70 41 70
Gay counselling.

RELIGIOUS GROUPS

Homosexuelle und Kirche (HuK) Bremen & umzu
Thorsten Tonne, Hinter dem Amtshof 16, 27356 *Rotenburg* ☎ (04261) 24 21

SPORT GROUPS

Club der Rosa Tanzenden Bremen e.V. (GLM MA)
PO Box 10 64 21 ✉28064 ☎ 21 55 04 Fax: 21 55 20
Ballroom dancing.

Wärmer Bremen
(GLM MA) c/o Rat & Tat Zentrum, Theodor-Körner-Straße 1 ✉28203 ☎ 70 41 70 E-Mail: rattathb@gmx.de
Gay sports group.

SWIMMING

-Unisee (southeast the beach, facility, dunes. Evenings: in the northeast bushes/Südöstlich der Strand, Klappe, Dünen. Abends: im Nordosten ein Wäldchen)

CRUISING

-Bürgerpark (ayor) (Entrance/Eingang »Stern«, from dusk on/ab Dämmerung, by car enter at/mit dem Auto Einfahrt bei »Parkhotel«)
Raststätte Mahndorf
-[P] Oldenburger Straße (ayor r) (under the fly over Hochstraße, across/ unter der Hochstraße, gegenüber Arbeitsamt)
Wallanlagen (Diagonally across from Na-Und-sauna, near the pedestrian tunnel/Beim Fußgängertunnel gegenüber Sauna Na Und)

Bremerhaven ☎ 0471

BARS

Why Not (B d GLM lj MA S STV WE YG) 20-? h, closed Mon
Körnerstraße 33 ✉27576 *(Bus-Körner-/Goethestraße)*
☎ 50 15 25

SEX SHOPS/BLUE MOVIES

Erotic Kino & Shop 14-23, Sat 15-23, Sun 17-23, cinema: 15-23 h
Körnerstraße 4 ✉27576 ☎ 41 22 26

HELP WITH PROBLEMS

Rosa Telefon Sun 18-20 h
☎ 440 10

CRUISING

-Weserdeich am alten Leuchtturm(Nähe/near Zoo)

Bruchsal ☎ 07251

SEX SHOPS/BLUE MOVIES

Sex Shop (g) Mon-Sat 10.30-19.30 h
Bahnhofsplatz 10 ✉76646 ☎ 85 69 99

Bühl ☎ 07223

GENERAL GROUPS

Schwubis - Gruppe für junge und erwachsene Schwule (G MA YG) according to agreement
PO Box 16 14 ✉77806 ☎ 88 66 Fax: 88 76
Meetings, counselling, coming-out, help, info-pool

Calw ☎ 07051

GENERAL GROUPS

Schwalw e.V. Mon-Fri 18-20 h
☎ 35 32

Celle ☎ 05141

SEX SHOPS/BLUE MOVIES

MMV-Erotic Shop (g VS) Mon-Fri 10-18.30, Sat -13 h, closed Sun
Hannoversche Straße 41, ✉29221

GENERAL GROUPS

SCHWINC
c/o PO Box 15 25 ✉29205 ☎ 285 77
Meeting every Monday at 8 pm at Celleschen AIDS-Hilfe, Großer Plan 12

HEALTH GROUPS

Cellesche AIDS-Hilfe e.V.
Großer Plan 12 ✉29221 ☎ 236 46
Counselling ☎ 194 11, Thu 14.30-18 h.

HELP WITH PROBLEMS

Schwules Beratungstelefon der SchINK e.V. Thu 17-19 h
☎ 194 46

CRUISING

-Schloßpark
-Mühlenmasch
-Französicher Garten (nights)
-Schloßpark (western part)

Chemnitz ☎ 0371

GAY INFO

CheLSI e.V. (B D DR G lj MA) Tue Thu Fri 15-22, Sat 18-23, Sun 15-23 h
Hainstraße 109 ✉09130 *(Bus-Lessingstraße)* ☎ 500 94
Fax: 558 67

BARS

Barbarossa Clubkeller (B g YG) Tue-Sun 19-? h
Barbarossastraße 88 ✉09112 ☎ 30 64 34
Blue Sky (B DR f GLM p r STV SNU VS) Sun-Thu 17-1, Fri & Sat 20-4 h
Lessingstrasse 10 ✉09130 *(behing the central station)*
☎ 0172/3447451
Casablanca (B D S SNU STV) Mon-Thur Bar from 20, Fri & Sat dico from 21h
Jägerstrasse 5-7 ✉09111 ☎ 64 46 201
Man's Point (CC DR G lj MA p VS YG) 20-? h
Lessingstr. 10 ✉09130 *(Bus 21/22-Lessingstraße)*
☎ 0172/351 94 05
Marleen (B d G MG p r TV) Tue-Sun 20:30-?
Hainstraße 89, Sonnenberg ✉09130 *(near main station)*
☎ 402 85 76
Seventy-four (AC B CC D F GLM lj MA s WE) Bar: Thu Sun Mon 20-?, Sat Sun 21-?; Disco Fri Sat 23-? h
Blankenauer Straße 74 ✉09113 *(Bus 26-Hochhaus Furth)*
☎ 450 31 85
Fri Sat dance-club.

DANCECLUBS

Lait Solair (B D GLM) Sat 21-? h
Schulstraße 38 ✉09125 ☎ 522 82 80

RESTAURANTS

Brosius (B F glm)
Yorckstraße 9 ✉09130 *(Tram-Gablenzplatz)* ☎ 404 06 38

BOOK SHOPS

Wittwer Bahnhofsbuchhandlung (g)
Bahnhofstraße 1 ✉09111 ☎ 42 98 65

HEALTH GROUPS

AIDS-Hilfe Chemnitz e.V. Tue & Thu 15-20, Fri 9-14 h
Hauboldstraße 6 ✉09111 ☎ 194 11 ☎ 0371/41 52 23.
Fax: 41 52 23

SPORT GROUPS

Sportverein QUEERSCHLÄGER Chemnitz e.V.
PO Box 825 ✉09008 E-Mail: queerschlaeger@hotmail.com
Homepage: members.tripod.de/Queerschlaeger/
Volleyball, Swimming, cycling, skiing

CRUISING

-Straße der Nationen/Rathausstraße (At tourist information. Popular)
-Kaßbergauffahrt (tunnel at Fabrikstraße)
-Central tram stop (Tunnel, 8-18 h)
-Schloßteichpark (Promenadenstraße between Kurt-Fischer-Straße and Müllerstraße. Popular.)
-Main rail station (from 20 h)

Clausthal-Zellerfeld ☎ 05323

GENERAL GROUPS

Rosa Harz Wed 19-21
Hotline ☎ 05323-39 25
c/o AStA, Silberstraße 1 ✉38678 ☎ 72-22 56

Coburg ☎ 09561

GENERAL GROUPS

COlibri Meeting Tue 19.30 h
at Spittelleite 40
PO Box 26 19 ✉96415 ☎ 55 01 20
E-Mail: COlibri@coburg.gay-web.de
Homepage: www.coburg.gay-web.de

HEALTH GROUPS

Aids-Hilfe Coburg/Landkreis e.V. Tue 10-12, Wed Thu 19-22 h
Neustadter Straße 3 ✉96450 ☎ 63 07 40

CRUISING

-Public toilet at Angerparkplatz

Coppenbrügge ☎ 05156

GUEST HOUSES

Berggaststätte Felsenkeller (A B bf CC F glm lj s OS WE) Thu 17-?, Fri Sat (reservation), Sun 11.30-22 h
Felsenkellerweg 11 ✉31863 ☎ 234

Cottbus ☎ 0355

BARS

Café Marie 23 (A B f glm MA OS) 20-? h
Marienstraße 23 ✉03046 *(At/am Busbahnhof)* ☎ 79 19 75

Resi - Musikbar (B d GLM) Tue-Fri 20-? h, Sat 21-? h, Sun + Mon closed
An der Werkstatt 9 a ✉03046 *(close to Stadttheater - direction Ströbitz)* ☎ 70 21 25
Disco every Friday and Saturday.

CAFES

Cubana (B F g MA OS) Mon-Sat 10-24, Sun 14-24 h
Stadtpromenade ✉03046

SEX SHOPS/BLUE MOVIES

Orion Erotikshop (g) Mon-Wed, Fri 9-18.30, Thu -20.30, Sat -14 h
Friedrich-Ebert-Straße 15 ✉03044 *(Near Lausitzer Hof)* ☎ 79 63 48

GENERAL GROUPS

Lebensart e.V. Tue 16-20 h
Straße der Jugend 100, PO Box 10 05 17 ✉03046 ☎ 232 73
Disco on Fri Sat 21-5 h in „Resi", An der Werkstatt 9 A, Cottbus-Ströbitz

SWIMMING

-Kiesgrube Sachsendorf (g NU) (the side of the forest)
-Badesee Branitz (g NU) (the big lawn. May-Sep)

CRUISING

-Spremberger Straße (21-? h)

Cuxhaven ☎ 04721

GENERAL GROUPS

Cux-Treff (G MA) 2nd & 4th Tue 20-22 h
c/o Aktions- und Kommunikationszentrum, Bernhardstr. 48 ✉27472 *48 27472* ☎ 329 48

Damp

CRUISING

-beach in front of Wellenbad (in the evening)
-nude beach (by day)

Darmstadt ☎ 06151

BARS

Harlekin (A B bf d f Glm MA OS) Mon-Sun 19-3 h
Heinheimer Straße 18 ✉64289 ☎ 71 28 81

CAFES

Café Hans (B f glm) Mon-Sat 9-1, Sun 10-1 h
Dieburger Strasse 19 ✉64287 ☎ 42 53 16

SEX SHOPS/BLUE MOVIES

Boy-Shop (G VS) 8.30-1 h
c/o Dolly Buster Center, Elisabethenstraße 44a ✉64283 ☎ 224 30

Heguwa Mon-Fri 9-20 h, Sat 9-16 h
Ludwigstraße 8 ✉64283 ☎ 2 42 33
Video cabins, video rental.

Orion (g) Mon-Fri 9-20, Sat -16 h
Heidelberger Straße 36 ✉64285 ☎ 29 19 18

Video World (AC CC DR MA VS) Mon-Sat 9-01, Sun 13-01 h
Elisabethenstraße 40 ✉64283 ☎ 251 33

GENERAL GROUPS

Louisetta Schwul-lesbisches Kulturzentrum (A GLM MA s) look for city magazines
c/o SchwuF e.V., Mauerstraße 4 ✉64289 *(bus stop Alexanderstraße)* ☎ 78 35 15 Fax: 78 35 15
Café and communication centre for events, culture and meetings.

Pink and Purple Meeting Tue 20-22 h at „Louisetta"
c/o Louisetta, Mauerstraße 4 ✉64289

HEALTH GROUPS

AIDS-Hilfe Darmstadt e.V. Mon-Fri 9-12 h, Mon-Thu 13-17 h
Saalbaustraße 27 ✉64283 ☎ 280 73
Counselling ☎ 2 80 73, Fax: 280 76.

CRUISING

-Main station/Hauptbahnhof
-Park Herrengarten (around WC)

Deggendorf ☎ 0991

CRUISING

-Busbahnhof (during the day WC, at nights P)

Deißlingen ☎ 07420

HOTELS

Die Krone (bf F g H) 12-13.30, 18-22 h, closed Mon
Hauptstraße 38 ✉78652 ☎ 529 Fax: 23 03
Nouvelle-German and French cuisine. Hotel-rates single DM 55-65, double 106-120.

Detmold ☎ 05231

GENERAL GROUPS

Schwulenreferat AStA der Musikhochschule Detmold (GLM s YG)
Neustadt 22 ✉32756 ☎ 97 59 00
Email: SchwuLesDT@gmx.de

CRUISING

-Kaiser-Wilhelm-Platz
-Kronenplatz (behind railway station)
-parking garage (near Hospital)

Diessen am Ammersee ☎ 08807

SHOWS

Grüne Mambar (B g MA N NG S STV) Thu-Sun 20-1 h
Johannisstraße 7 ✉86911 *(in Hotel-Restaurant „Mauerhansl")*
☎ 94 88 31
Shows on Thu Fri Sat. No entrance-fee.

Dillenburg ☎ 02771

HEALTH GROUPS

AIDS-Hilfe Gießen e.V.-Zweigstelle Dillenburg Wed 12-13 h
Bismarckstraße 30 ✉35683 ☎ 194 11

Dippoldiswalde ☎ 03504

SEX SHOPS/BLUE MOVIES

Gundis Erotik Paradies (AC g MA VS W) 10-20 h, Sun, holidays closed
Industriering 11 ✉01744 ☎ 61 26 71

Donaueschingen ☎ 0771

SEX SHOPS/BLUE MOVIES

Intim-Shop (g) Mon-Fri 10-18.30, Sat -13 h, Sun closed
Josefstraße 27 ✉78166 ☎ 31 14

SWIMMING

-Kleiner Riedsee (NU) B 33 Donaueschingen → Tuttlingen. In Pfohren → Camping »Riedsee«. P am Camping. 10 min by foot along the wood.

CRUISING

-Schloßpark (at the source of th river Donau on the right side of the castle)
-Station (in the park on the opposite)

Donauwörth ☎ 0906

GENERAL GROUPS

Aids-Hilfe Nordschwaben e.V. Fri 15-21 h
c/o Peter Wimmer, Stadtmühlenfeld 32 ✉86609 ☎ 216 01

Dortmund ☎ 0231

GAY INFO

KCR-Kommunikations-Centrum Ruhr e.V. (bd GLM MA s W) Please call for details
Braunschweiger Straße 22 ✉44145 *(U-Münsterstraße/Lortzingsstraße/Brunnenstraße)* ☎ 83 22 63
Homepage: www.dortmund.gay-web.de/kcr

BARS

Blue Magic (B G MA) Wed-Sun 16-?, Mon Tue 18-? h
Olpe 41 ✉44135 ☎ 57 42 34
Burgtor Club (B d G MA s VS) 14-1, Fri Sat -3, Sun 19-1; Show: Sat 22 h
Burgwall 17, ✉44135 ☎ 57 17 48
Café Blu (B bf F glm MA OS W) Mon-Sun 18-1 h
Ruhrallee 69, ✉44139 *(U-Landgrafenstraße/Stadthaus)*
☎ 12 61 77
Club 64 (AC B D DR f G lj MA p) 21-? h, Mon closed (open on/before public holidays)
Rheinische Straße 64 ✉44137 *(Bus/Tram-Heinrichstraße)*
☎ 14 32 30
Dito Club (B G MA) Mon-Sat 9-3, Sun 17-3 h
Bornstraße 14 ✉44135 ☎ 586 41 44
Don-Club (B d G lj MA) Sun-Thu 21-4 h, Fri-Sat 21-open end
Johannisborn 6, ✉44135 ☎ 55 32 21
Fledermaus (B G OS R) Mon-Fri 10-1 Sat-Sun 11-1 h
U-Bahnpassage Hauptbahnhof ✉44137 ☎ 14 97 85
Luzifer (B G MA) 19-2 h
Märkische Straße 46 ✉44141 ☎ 575 90 91
Nouvelle (B G MA OS R) Mon-Sun 0-24 h
Ludwigstraße 9, ✉44135 *(At/am Burgwallplatz)* ☎ 57 45 40
Rote Marlene (AC B d DR G lj MA p) Tue-Sun 21-? h, closed Mon
Humboldtstraße 1-3 ✉44137 ☎ 14 95 20
Sidi Club (B D glm MA) Mon-Thu 20-5, Fri -?, Sat-Sun 20-? h
Burgwall 5 ✉44135 ☎ 52 55 59
The Boots Club (B DR G LJ p VS) Fri-Sat 20-3, Sun 20-2 h, Mon-Thu closed
Bornstraße 14 ✉44135 *(close to main station)* ☎ 557 20 10

RESTAURANTS

Kittchen (AC B bf F g lj MA N s W) 11-1 h
Gerichtsstraße 19 ✉44135 ☎ 52 44 42
German food/Deutsche Küche.

SEX SHOPS/BLUE MOVIES

Adonis Center (G) 12-18.30, Sat 10-14 h
Bornstraße 14, ✉44135 *(Near/Nähe Hauptbahnhof)*
☎ 57 36 19
Orion (g) Mon-Fri 10-20, Sat 9-16 h
Rheinische Straße 85 ✉44137 ☎ 721 40 31
Studio X Kino Center (g LJ MA VS) Mon-Sat 9-23, Sun 14-23 h
Münsterstraße 12 ✉44145 *(500 m away from railway station)*
☎ 81 46 39

SAUNAS/BATHS

Fontäne (A AC B CC f G lj MG p sa sb sol VS) 15-22 h, closed Thu
Gutenbergstraße 50 ✉44139 ☎ 52 39 99
Sauna am Burgwall (A AC B CC f G lj MA sa sb sol VS wh) 15-23, Sat -2 h
Leuthardstraße 9, ✉44135 ☎ 57 46 00
Also gay magazines and books for sale. Entrance-fee DM 17-27.

BOOK SHOPS

Litfass Der Buchladen (glm) Mon-Fri 10-20, Sat -14 h
Münsterstraße 107 ✉44145 *(U-Münsterstraße)* ☎ 83 47 24
General bookshop with gay section.

GENERAL GROUPS

Freundeskreis für Hörgeschädigte Dortmund-Mengede Meeting 1st Sat 16 h
Ammerstraße 44 ✉44359 ☎ 359 31
LSVD Ortsverband Dortmund e.V. Mon 15-17 h, Wed 18-20 h
Braunschweiger Straße 22 ✉44145 *(near Nordmarkt)*
☎ 16 48 66 or ☎192 28 Fax: 863 09 80
E-mail dortmund@lsvd.de
Schwul-lesbischer Arbeitskreis Dortmund e.V. (SLADO)
c/o AIDS-Hilfe Dortmund e.V., Möllerstraße 15 ✉44137
Fax: 168 65 E-mail 101731.777@compuserve.com
SchwuSos und Andere-Schwule in der SPD
c/o SPD Dortmund, Brüderweg 12 ✉44135 ☎ 58 56 17
Fax: 52 46 79.
Meeting/Treffen 2nd Wed 18-? h in KCR, near Nordmarkt, Braunschweiger Straße 22, 44145 Dortmund.
SODOM Schwuleninitiative der Uni Dortmund Thu 16-h (Room # 418)
c/o AStA der Universität, Emil-Figge-Straße 50, ✉44227
☎ 755 25 84

FETISH GROUPS

MSC Rote Erde Dortmund e.V. 3rd Fri 20 h at ☛Café Blu, 22 h at ☛Rote Marlene
PO Box 10 27 39 ✉44027 Email: RoteErde@aol.com
Member of ECMC.

HEALTH GROUPS

AIDS-Hilfe Dortmund e.V. Mon Tue Fri 10-15, Wed 14-19, Thu 10-15 h
Möllerstraße 15 ✉44137 ☎ 194 11 or ☎ 168 64 Fax: 168 65
All around Aids e.V.
Reichenberger Straße 40 ✉44225 ☎ & Fax: 77 96 26
E-mail aids@ms-net.de

HELP WITH PROBLEMS

Schwules Überfalltelefon
☎ 192 28
19446 - Dortums Schwule Infoline Wed 20-22 h
c/o KCR, Braunschweiger Straße 22 ✉44145 ☎ 194 46

CRUISING

-Westpark (Entrance Ritterhaustr., popular)
-Main Station (ayor)
-Kaufhof, Westenhellweg

Dresden ☎ 0351

GAY INFO

Gegenpol
PO Box 10 04 08 ✉01074 ☎ 803 33 64
Fax: 80 33 400 E-Mail: redaktion@gegenpol.net
Homepage: www.intercomm.de/gegenpol
The gay/lesbian magazine for Sachsen/Das SchwuLesbische Mazagine für Sachsen
Gerede Dresdner Lesben, Schwule und alle Anderen e.V. (GLM MA OS s VS) Mon 10-12, Tue 10-18, Thu 10-12 h
Prießnitzstraße 18 ✉01099 ☎ 802 22 50 Fax: 802 22 60
E-Mail: gerede@gmx.net Homepage: www.bigfoot.com/~gerede
24 h-Serviceline ☎ 802 22 70
Pink Pages Dresden
http://www.aolmembers/aol.com/DresdenGay/

BARS

Bunker (b DR G LJ MA p) Fri & Sat 22-? h (Sat Dresscode)
Prießnitzstraße 51 ✉01099 *(Tram-Schauburg)* ☎ 441 23 45
Lederclub/Leather club.
Club Inteam (B d E F GLM MA s WE) Tue-Thu 20-2, Fri Sat -4, Sun 15-2, closed Mon
Franz-Liszt-Straße 13 ✉01219 *(Tram-Julius Otto Straße)*
☎ 470 01 48
Denkbar (B F glm MA) Mon-Fri 11-1 h, Sat-Sun 18-1 h
Tieckstraße 9 ✉01099 ☎ 804 39 57
Down Town (AC B D G YG) G Mon 21-? h
Katharinenstraße 11-13 ✉01099 ☎ 803 64 14
Queens (AC B d DR GLM MA S SNU STV) 20-? h
Görlitzer Straße 3 ✉01099 ☎ 803 16 50
Scheune (B glm) 17-02:00h, WE 10-02:00h
Alaunstrasse 36/40 ✉01099 ☎ 804 55 32
Zeitgeist (B GLM) Mon-Thu 11-01:00h, Fri & Sat -03:00h, Sun 18-03:00h
Großenhainer Straße 93 ✉01127 ☎ 8400510
Art-Bar. Sundays from 18:00h gay lesbian night café.

CAFES

Café Flo (B f glm) Mon-Sat 19:00 - ?
Louisenstrasse 77 ✉01099 ☎ 801 54 55
Face (b f glm MA) 12.30-2 h
Görlitzer Straße 35 ✉01099
Miguel's (A AC B F GLM MA OS s) 18-24 h
Louisenstraße 11 ✉01099 *(Dresden-Neustadt)* ☎ 804 60 72

DANCECLUBS

Gay Dance by Onkel Ralf (B G s SNU STV VS W YG)
Monthly gay dance. Please call for details.
Bischofsplatz 6 ✉01097 ☎ 804 29 57
Riesa efau (B D GLM YG) 1st Fri & 3rd Sat 21-? h
Adlergasse 14 ✉01067 ☎ 866 02 11

RESTAURANTS

Der Rudi (B F glm MA) 11-2 h
Fechnerstraße 2a ✉01139 ☎ 858 79 90
La Vie en Rose (B CC F glm MA OS) Sun-Thu 12-24, Fri Sat -2 h
Alaunstraße 64 ✉01099 *(Tram-Albertplatz/Alaunplatz)*
☎ 803 61 61 Fax: 829 47 19
Walters Café und vegetarisches Restaurant (CC g) 11-24 h
Königsbrückerstraße 58 ✉01099 *(near Albertplatz)* ☎ 826 39 95
Excellent vegetarian cuisine at reasonable prices.

SEX SHOPS/BLUE MOVIES

Gundis Erotik Paradies (AC g MA VS W) 10-20 h, closed Sun
Rudolf-Leonhard-Straße 11 ✉01097 ☎ 804 13 97

Orion (g) Mon-Fri 9-20, Sat -16 h
Großenhainer Straße 82 ✉01127 ☎ 858 47 27

SAUNAS/BATHS

Antinoos (b G MA p sa sb sol VS) Winter: Tue-Thu 17-2, Fri-Sat -3, Sun -24, closed Mon, Summer: open from 18 h
Reisewitzer Straße 28 ✉01159 ☎ 421 40 03

Man's Paradise (AC CC DR G MA p pi sa sb sol VS wh) Every day 13-05:00h
Friedensstraße 45 ✉01099 ☎ 802 25 66

BOOK SHOPS

Das internationale Buch (g) Mon-Fri 9-19, Sat 9-14, 1st Sat -16 h
Kreuzstraße 4 ✉01067 ☎ 495 41 90

CONDOM SHOPS

Condomi Mon-Fri 11-20, Sat 10-16 h
Katharinenstraße 11-13 ✉01099

TRAVEL & TRANSPORT

Flamingo Reisen Mon-Fri 10-18 h
Leipziger Straße 139 ✉01139 ☎ 849 68 68 Fax: 849 68 69

HOTELS

Holiday Inn Dresden (AC bf CC H NG)
Stauffenbergallee 25a ✉01099 ☎ 81 510 Fax: 81 51 333
Homepage: www.holiday-inn-dresden.de

GENERAL GROUPS

Young GAYneration Dresden 1st/3rd Sat 16 h at Saftladen, Wiener Straße 41
PO Box 16 02 49 ✉01288 ☎ 803 33 64
(Jens) Gay youth group.

HEALTH GROUPS

AIDS-Hilfe Dresden e.V. Office : Mon, Wed, Fri 9-14, Tue &,Thu 9-18:00h
Bischofsweg 46 ✉01099 ☎ 441 61 41 ☎ 0351/441 61 42
Counselling ☎ 194 11. Mon 9-13+17-19, Tue 9-13, Thu 15-18 h

HELP WITH PROBLEMS

Schwules Überfalltelefon Tue 19-22 h
☎ 0341/192 28

Streetworker der AIDS-Hilfe Dresden e.V. Thu 14-17 h
Florian-Geyer-Straße 3 ✉01307 ☎ 441 61 43

SWIMMING

-Kiesgrube Dresden-Leuben (NU MA) (Tram2/12-Lasallestraße) Walk the Salzburger Straße up to the [P], through the gate, after the second gate to the right. Cruising/Tanning only.
-Auensee (NU MA) (near Moritzburg)

CRUISING

- Altmarkt/Webergasse/Wallstraße(*small wood*)

Duisburg ☎ 0203

GAY INFO

Pink Channel 2nd + 4th Wed 20.04-20.56 h
(FM 92,2 MHz Kabel/cable FM 101,75 MHz)

BARS

Café Berlin (B f GLM MA OS p s) 16-2?, Fri-Sat -5? h
An der Bleek 40-42 ✉47051 *(U-Steinsche Gasse, exit Sonnewall)*
☎ 242 73

Harlekin (B f G h MA p s) Mon-Sat 11.50-? Sun 9.50-? h
Realschulstrasse 16, ✉47051 ☎ 262 44
You can rent two rooms for DM 35 each here.

Pilsstübchen (f G H MA MG YG) Mon-Sun 12-1 h
Hohe Straße 24, ✉47051 ☎ 28 71 62

SHOWS

Kleinkunstbühne Senftöpfchen (A AC B d F GLM MA OS S STV WE YG) Tue-Fri 17-24, Sat Sun 12-24 h, closed Mon
Ziegelhorststraße ✉47169 *(Corner of Röttgersbachstraße)*
☎ 50 12 45

SEX SHOPS/BLUE MOVIES

Gay Sex Shop (g VS) 10-18.30, Sat 10-14 h
Beekstraße 82, ✉47051 ☎ 274 40

World of Erotic (G VS) 9-24, Sun 12-23 h
Kasinostraße 4a ✉47051

SAUNAS/BATHS

Gay Sauna Duisburg (b DR MA p sa sb sol VS) 15-23, Sat -24 h
Krummacher Straße 49 ✉47051 ☎ 244 10
Oasis die Sauna (B CC DR f G OS p sa sb VS) Mon-Thu & Sun 15-01:00h, Fri & Sat 15-03:00h.
Hamborner Straße 33 ✉47179 ☎ 495408

MEN'S CLUBS

M + M Club (B G P MA) Thu & Fri 20:00- ?
Wagnerstrasse 14 ✉76448 *(South of the Maischer Strasse)*
☎ 536 1414
Between Karlsruhe and Baden Baden. The first gay-swinger-club in Germany. Various activities. Call for details

BOOK SHOPS

Mayersche Buchhandlung (g)
Kuhstraße 33 ✉47051 ☎ 929 64 16
Mayersche Buchhandlung
Galeria, Kuhstraße 33 ✉47051 ☎ 92 96 40

GENERAL GROUPS

Der „Neue Vv'74-Ein schwuler Freundeskreis"
PO Box 11 01 12 ✉47141
Homosexuelle Kultur Duisburg (HoKuDu e.V.) 2nd Mon 20-22 h at AIDS-Hilfe, Friedenstraße 100
PO Box 10 07 09 ✉47007 ☎ 66 66 33 Fax: 37 69 35
E-mail W-Thomas@t-online.de
Pink Power Meets Wed 20 h, Counselling ☎ Tue 20-22 h.
Musfeldstraße 161-163 ✉47053 ☎ 66 33 83
SchwuBiLe-Referat Thu 13-17 h (Café) Room F030
c/o AStA GH Duisburg, Lotharstraße 65, ✉47048 *(Room/Raum LF 022)* ☎ 37 00 47

HEALTH GROUPS

AIDS-Hilfe Duisburg/Kreis Wesel e.V. Mon 19-21, Tue 11-14, Wed-Fri -16 h
Friedenstraße 100 ✉47053 ☎ 66 66 33 or ☎ 1 94 11
Fax: 699 84 E-Mail: ahdukw@metronet.de
HoKuDu meets here every 2nd Mon, Email: monthwulf@hokudu.de

HELP WITH PROBLEMS

Pro Familia Homosexuellenberatung
Tue 19-21 h
Oststraße 172, ✉47198 *(Neudorf)* ☎ 35 07 00
(Kontaktmöglichkeit zur Eltern- und Verheiratetengruppe)
Rosa Telefon Tue 20-22 h
☎ 66 33 83

RELIGIOUS GROUPS

HuK Regionalgruppe Ruhrgebiet
PO Box 10 07 15 ✉47007 ☎ (02932) 701337 (Thomas)

CRUISING

-Rathaus Hamborn (Town Hall Hamborn)
-Ruhrorter Friedhof (Ruhrorter Cemetary)
-main railway station (R)
-Kantpark (behind museum → Realschulstraße)
-Kleiner Park (Mercatorstraße/Hauptbahnhof)

CRUISING

-Town Hall

Düsseldorf ☎ 0211

GAY INFO

Café Rosa Mond e.V. (A B d GLM MA OS s W) Mon 18-?, Tue-Sun 20-? h
Oberbilker Allee 310 ✉40227 *(S-Oberbilk-Philipshalle)*
☎ 99 23 77 Fax: 99 23 76
Homepage http://www.ruhr-online.de
Gay Hotline ☎ 77 52 42. Gay Counselling ☎ 77 52 12
Gay and lesbian center.
Köln/Düsseldorf von hinten
c/o Bruno Gmünder Verlag, PO Box 61 01 04, 10921 Berlin
☎ (030) 615 00 30 Fax: 615 90 07
E-Mail: info@spartacus.de
The city guide book about Düsseldorf and Cologne. Useful general information and lots of addresses with extensive descriptions in English and German. Up-to-date maps. Erotic photos.
Lesben- und Schwulenzentrum Düsseldorf e.V.
Lierenfelder Straße 39 ✉40231 ☎ 737 00 30 Fax: 737 00 34

BARS

Bel Air (B f G MA R) 12-5 h
Oststraße 116 ✉40210 *(Nähe HBF /near central station)*
☎ 16 19 78

Club Flair (B G MA) Daily from 18:00h
Charlottenstraße 62, ✉40210 ☎ 164 6086

Comeback (AC B f G MA R s) 13-5 h
Charlottenstraße 60, ✉40210 *(Entrance/Eingang Bismarckstraße)* ☎ 164 09 78

Five Club (B d f GLM MA) 17-2 h, Fri-Sat 15-3 h, Sun 15-3 h
Grupellostraße 5, ✉40210 ☎ 369 48 16

Harlekin (B G MA) Mon-Fri 17-5, Sat Sun 20-? h
Corneliusstraße 1 ✉40215 *(Tram Luisenstraße)* ☎ 37 46 28

Insider (AC B f G MA N STV) 11-05:00h
Gupellostraße 32 ✉40210 *(U-Oststraße)* ☎ 36 42 18
Thu and Sun - drag show from 22:00h.

Le Clou (AC B f G MA R) Sun-Thu 12-2, Fri Sat -3 h
Grupellostraße 7, ✉40210 ☎ 36 43 65

Mailbox (A AC B F g MA OS) 10-1 h
Konrad-Adenauer-Platz 1 ✉40210 ☎ 164 05 53
Terrace very popular in summer.

Murphy's Bar-Café (AC B DR G LJ MA p s) Mon-Thu 20-3, Fri & Sat 20-5, Sun 15-3 h
Bismarkstrasse 93 ✉40210 *(entrance Karlstrasse)* ☎ 171 0381
Sundays from 15-18 h - Murphy's pastry party- coffee and cake - DM 8,50 eat as much as you can !

Musk (! B DR G LJ MA) Thu-Sat 21-5, Sun-Wed 21-3 h
Charlottenstraße 47, ✉40210 ☎ 35 21 54
Thu and WE popular.

Nähkörbchen (B GLM MA) Tue-Fri Sun 18-1 h, Sat -3 h, closed Mon, Sun 15 h coffee and cake
Hafenstraße 11 ✉40213 *(Tram Benrather Straße)* ☎ 323 02 65

Studio 1 (B f G MG) 17-5 h
Jahnstraße 2 a ✉40215 *(S-Bilk)* ☎ 37 87 43

Theater-Stube (B Glm MA) 13-2, Fri-Sat 13-3 h
Luisenstaße 33, ✉40215 ☎ 37 22 44

Twist (B f glm MG) 16-03:00h, Thu & Sat reduced prices.
Grupellostraße 32 ✉40210 *(near the central station)* ☎ 36 95 48

Wespennest (B f g MA) 11-1, WE -3 h
Bergerstraße 24 ✉40213 *(U-Heinrich-Heine-Allee)* ☎ 32 83 26

Wilma (B G MA p r) 13-5 h
Charlottenstraße 60, ✉40210 ☎ 35 17 37

ZAKK (A B glm MA OS S WE YG) Mon-Sat 18-23 h, Disco Fri 21-6 h & Sat 22-4 h
Fichtenstraße 40 ✉40233 *(U-Kettwiger Straße)* ☎ 973 00 80

MEN'S CLUBS

C.O.K. (B G LJ MA OS P S sa sb VS WE) Fri, Sat ,Sun & holidays from 16 h
Ackerstrasse 137 *2 Floors with steam and dry saunas. Special parties at WE - leather, rubber, or NU. Parties from 20:00h. Cubicals, slings, Video room and cinema, golden shower room, showers and lockers.*

CAFES

Bernstein. Café (B F g OS YG) 9-1 h
Oststraße 158 ✉40472 ☎ 35 65 20

Extra Dry. Café (B F g OS YG) Mon-Sun 17-1 h
Friedrichstraße 125, ✉40217 *(S-Bilk)* ☎ 34 47 01

Spitz. Café (AC B bf F g MA OS YG) Mon-Sun 9-1 h
Hunsrückenstraße/Bolkerstraße, ✉40213 *(U-Heinrich-Heine-Allee)* ☎ 32 27 70

Strada. La (A AC f G MA OS YG) daily 11-3 h
Immermannstraße 32 ✉40210 *(U-HBF)* *Popular.*

Tom Thomas in der Mata Hari Passage (B bf f g MA OS YG) 7.30-1 h
Hunsrückenstraße 33, ✉40213 *(U-Heinrich-Heine-Allee)* ☎ 13 19 71

1 Sex Messe Sex Shop
2 Murphy's Bar
4 City Appartement
6 Ramrod Danceclub
7 Mailbox Bar
8 Gay Sex Messe Sex Shop/ Blue Movie
9 Gerothek Sex Shop
11 Bel Air Bar
12 Erotik 63 Sex Shop/ Blue Movie
13 Musk Bar
14 Comeback Bar - Wilma Bar
15 Phoenix Sauna
16 Five Club Bar
17 Le Clou Bar
19 Valentino Danceclub
20 Bhaggy Danceclub
22 City Sauna
23 Harlekin Bar
24 Theater-Stube Bar
25 Nähkörbchen Bar
26 Wespennest Bar
27 Café Tom Thomas in der Mata Hari Passage
28 Ratinger Hof Danceclub
29 Motivation-Team

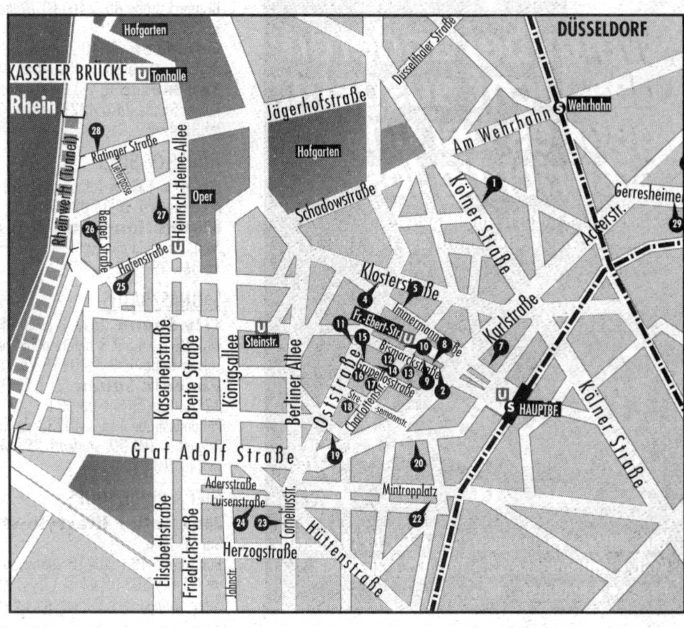

DANCECLUBS

Bhaggy (B D g MA WE YG) Thu 22-5 h, Fri Sat 22 h
Graf-Adolf-Straße 87 ✉40210 ☎ 37 90 55
Popular on WE. Entry DM 10-15.

Königsburg (! B D GLM lj MA S TV YG) 21-05:00h (Irregular)
Königsstraße 8 ✉47798 *(Krefeld)* ☎ 85 06 50
Entrance DM 20 including cover charge

La Rocca (B D GLM MA S TV WE YG) Sat 22- ?
Grünstraße 8 ✉40210 *(U- Hauptbahnhof)* ☎ 83 67 10
Admission DM 18. Very gay.

Moondance Schwoof für Schwule (B D G MA OS s VS W)
Oberbilker Allee 310 ✉40227 ☎ 99 23 77 ☎ 77 52 12 (Infos)
Locations for SCHWOOF parties vary. Please call for the latest infos.

Ratinger Hof (B D g MA tv) Fri-Sun 23-5 h
Ratinger Straße 10 ✉40213 *(U-Tonhalle)* ☎ 32 87 77
House music.

Valentino (B D gLM YG) Mon-Sun 20-5 h
Bahnstraße 63, ✉40210 ☎ 36 29 59

RESTAURANTS

Colopic (AC CC F g MA W) 11.30-24 h
Mertensgasse 5-9 ✉40213 ☎ 13 47 40
Italian cuisine.

Tannenbaum (a F g OS) 17-1 h
Tannenstraße 3/Herrmannplatz ✉40476 *(U-Frankenplatz)*
☎ 454 10 92

Ziegelstübchen (B F g MA) 17-1, Sun 11-? h
Ziegelstraße 31 ✉40468 ☎ 42 72 31

SEX SHOPS/BLUE MOVIES

Erotic 63 (CC g VS) 10-23, Sun 10.30-23.30 h
Bismarckstraße 63 ✉40210 ☎ 35 46 01

Gay Sex Messe (CC G MA VS) Mon-Sat 9-1, Sun 12-1
Bismarckstraße 88 ✉40210 *(Nähe/near Hauptbahnhof)*
☎ 35 25 86

Gerothek (G) 10-24 h, Sat -21, closed Sun
Bismarckstraße 86, ✉40210 ☎ 35 67 50

Sex Messe (g VS) 9-24 h, closed Sun
Kölner Straße 24 ✉40211 *(Near/Nähe Hauptbahnhof)*
☎ 35 47 89

HOUSE OF BOYS

Men's Eden (CC G msg p sa) 14-23 h, closed Sun
Ackerstraße 1 ☎ 36 02 03

Motivation-Team (AC CC msg p R VS W) 13-24 h, closed Mon, closed in august
☎ 361 39 93

SAUNAS/BATHS

City Sauna (A AC B bf CC DR F G MA msg N p s sa sb sol VS wh) 12-1, Fri Sat & before public holidays 12-6 h
Luisenstraße 129 ✉40215 *(near Hauptbahnhof)* ☎ 37 39 73

Phoenix Sauna (! b CC DR G MA msg p sa sb sol VS wh) 12-06:00h, Fri-Sat -08:00 h
Platanenstraße 11a ✉40233 ☎ 66 36 38
Admission DM 30, students 25.-, Mon-Fri -13 h DM 18.-, Tue Happy Day DM 25.-

GIFT & PRIDE SHOPS

Max Seller lifestyle-store (b CC G) Tue-Fri 11-19 h, Sat 10-16 h
Bahnstraße 48 ✉40210 *(between Oststraße & Berliner Allee)*
☎ 02 11/323 08 41
Sexy clothes, toys & tools, books etc.

VIDEO SHOPS

Videothek Tümmers (g) 0-24 h, closed Sun
Konrad-Adenauer Platz 12 ✉40210 ☎ 36 32 29
Angebot an schwulen Filmen/selection of gay films.

HOTELS

City Appartement Hotel (bf CC glm H) Reservation 6.30-19 h
Klosterstraße 53 ✉40211 (S-Oststraße) ☎ 93 60 20
Fax: 35 84 75 *Apartments with kitchen, cable TV, minibar and telephone. Single from DEM 109-255 and double DEM 130-275 incl. breakfast. Special rates on demand.*

PRIVATE ACCOMODATION

Enjoy Bed & Breakfast (bf G H MA YG) 16:30-21:00h ☎ 030/215 1666 Fax: 030/217 52219
E-Mail: Info@ebab.com Homepage: www.ebab.com
Price 40 DM. Accommodation sharing agency. All with shower & bf.nd double DEM 130-275 incl. breakfast. Special rates on demand.

GENERAL GROUPS

AStA-Schwulenreferat der HHU/FHD Mon-Thu 13.15-14, cozy get-together: Wed 19-? h
Universitätsstraße 1 ✉40225 *(Gebäude 24.21, Raum 00.27)*
☎ 0221/811 52 83 Fax: 811 46 12
E-Mail: schwule@uni-duesseldorf.de
Homepage: http://www.schwulenreferat.de

Elternselbsthilfe Meeting Sat 18 h
☎ 27 84 99 (Herr Wiedemann)

Kuckucksei-Schwule Jungendgruppe Düsseldorf Tue 18-22 h
at Loft-Café/AIDS-Hilfe, Oberbilker Allee 310
Oberbilker Allee 310 ✉40227 *(courtyard/Hinterhof)* ☎ 770 950
Fax: 770 95-27 E-Mail: 100712.2641@compuserve.com
Homepage: http://eurogay.net/mitglieder/kuckucksei

Lesben- und Schwulenzentrum Düsseldorf e.V. (A AC B bf D GLM MA S WE)
Lierenfelder Straße 39 ✉40231 ☎ 737 00 30 Fax: 737 00 34
Mon from 20:00h - choir „LuSZD-Schrei", Tue from 19:00h Ladies-café, Wed from 19:00h Café Total, Thu from 20:00h Dance course, Fri from 20:00h JuLe, every 2nd Fri/month from 22:00h - „Friday Nite Club" - men only . Every 1st 6 & 3rd Sat/month „Crusing" in Schwoof.

Schwusos Düsseldorf
c/o SPD, Kavalleriestraße 22 ✉40213 ☎ 32 92 41
Fax: 32 80 89

FETISH GROUPS

LM Düsseldorf Meeting: last/letzten Fri
at Club „Musk" 21 h. P.O. Box 10 20 05 ✉40011
Member of ECMC.

SMart
☎ (0234) 43 55 88 *SM-Gruppe.*

HEALTH GROUPS

AHD gem. GmbH. Ambulanter Pflegedienst
Mon-Fri 10-13, 14-16 h
Borsigstraße 34 ✉40227 ☎ 72 01 86

AIDS-Hilfe Düsseldorf e.V. Mon-Fri 10-13, 14-16 h
Oberbilker Allee 310 ✉40227 ☎ 194 11 Fax 77 09 527
Counselling ☎ 77 09 50, Sun-Fri 20-22 h. -Tue 18-22 h, coming-out group. -Fri 18-22 h, group for hiv-positiv men. -Wed 19-21.30, addiction-help.

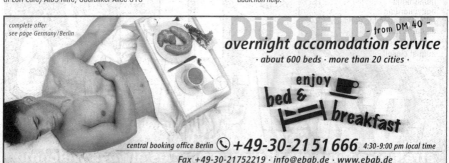

HELP WITH PROBLEMS

DGSS-Institut 9-22 h also at the weekend.
Gerresheimer Straße 20 ✉40211 ☎ 35 45 91 Fax: 35 45 77 E-Mail: schwulenberatung@sexologir.org Homepage: www.sexologie.org
Counselling. HIV-testing. Gay Switchboard.

Schwules Überfalltelefon
☎ 0221/192 28

RELIGIOUS GROUPS

Ökumenische Arbeitsgruppe Homosexuelle und Kirche HuK e.V. Regionalgruppe Düsseldorf
Franz Frenger, Feldstraße 17 ✉40479 ☎ 492 03 77

SPORT GROUPS

Düsseldorf Dolphins e.V.
c/o Hans Georg Saur, Lassallesstraße 9 ✉40627 ☎ 27 33 87
Swimming, horseback-riding, fitness/workout, hiking, bicycling, table-tennis, American football.

SWIMMING

-Rheinstadion (stairs)
-Angermunder Baggersee = Kalkumer Baggerloch
-Düsseldorf-Himmelgeist (South of the city), P near church, from there 20 minutes walk south to the river Rhine, popular.

CRUISING

-Hofgarten, Area Rhein/Inselstraße and Oper (best 22-1 h,popular)
-Schwanenspiegel Elisabethstraße/Haroldstraße (paths around the pond -23 h)
-Graf-Adolf-Platz
-Schadowplatz
-Kirchplatz
-Nordpark (until 21 h)
-South cemetery
-Northern cemetery (main entrance)
-Hanielpark (until 16 h)

Egestorf ☎ 04175

BARS

Papperla-Pub (B g) 18-? h
Ahornweg 7, ✉21272 ☎ 10 73

Eisenach ☎ 03691

GENERAL GROUPS

AIDS-Hilfe Wartburgkreis Tue 10-15, Thu 14-19
Marienstraße 57 ✉99817 ☎ & Fax: 21 40 38

Elmshorn ☎ 04121

HEALTH GROUPS

AIDS-Hilfe für die Kreise Pinneberg und Steinburg e.V. Office open Mon-Fri 8.30-11.30 h
Königstraße 34 ✉25335 ☎ 31 02

Emden ✉ ☎ 04921

CAFES

Alte Post 1st Sat in month 20-24:00h
Cirksenastrasse 2a ✉26721 ☎ 872108

GENERAL GROUPS

Schwulen- und Lesbengruppe Emden Hotline: Mon-Fri from 16 h
c/o Aids- und Drogenberatung, Am alten Binnenhafen 2, ✉26721 ☎ 87 16 65

CRUISING

-park in front of main railway station
-Hesel carpark on the old B75 in the direction Remels - in the woods on both sides of the road.

Erfurt ☎ 0361

GAY INFO

SwiB-Zentrum (A d f GLM MA s VS YG)
Windthorststraße 43 a ✉99096 *(near main station)*
☎ 346 22 90 Fax: 346 22 98. *Gay-info-center, switchboard.*

BARS

Columbus-Klatsch (B G MA) Mon-Sun 20-? h
Blumenstraße 78 ✉99092 ☎ 260 35 14

Das OX's Clubkeller des Thüringer Lederclub e.V. (b DR f G LJ MA s VS) Sat 21-4 h
Windthorststraße 43 a ✉99096 *(near Hauptbahnhof)* ☎ 346 22 90

Uferbar (b CC d DR f GLM H MG msg NU OS p TV VS YG) 19-? h
Boyneburgufer 3 ✉99089 ☎ 643 14 03 or ☎ 566 83 23. *Room to let: single DM 60, double 80. Bf DM 10.*

CAFES

SwiB-Café (A GLM MA VS YG) Wed, Fri, Sun 19-24 h
c/o SwiB Zentrum, Windthorststraße 43 a ✉99096 *(near main station)* ☎ 346 22 90 Fax: 346 22 98
Please call for further information regarding general, fettish and health groups & private accommodation

SEX SHOPS/BLUE MOVIES

Beate Uhse international (g) Mon-Sat 9-22 h, closed Sun
Johannesstraße

Beate Uhse international (g) Mon-Sat 9-22 h, closed Sun Magdeburger Allee 60-62 ✉99086

Starlet Erotik (DR g MG VS) Mon-Fri 9.30-20, Sat -16 h, closed Sun Thomasstraße 4 ✉99084 *(Tram-Hauptbahnhof)*
☎ 540 39 24

Videoworld (g VS) Mon-Sat 10-23, Sun 14-22 h
Schillerstraße 55 ✉99096 *(near/Nähe Eisenbahnbrücke)*
☎ 643 21 36

BOOK SHOPS

Haus des Buches-Carl Habel GmbH (g) Mon-Fri 9-20, Sat -16 h
Juri-Gagarin-Ring 35 ✉99084 ☎ 59 85 80
General book shop with gay section.

GUEST HOUSES

Pension Uferbar (B bf CC G H lj msg)
Boyneburgufer 3 ✉99089 ☎ 566 83 23 or ☎ 643 14 03
All rooms with shower/WC, phone, minibar, room service, own key. Rates single/double DM 80 (bf incl.)

GENERAL GROUPS

HAE e.V.
PO Box 20 02 30 ✉99041 ☎ 225 25 56

FETISH GROUPS

Thüringer Lederclub e.V. (TLC)
PO Box 124 ✉99003 ☎ 731 22 33 Fax: 731 24 58

HEALTH GROUPS

AIDS-Hilfe Thüringen e.V. Tue Wed 10-15, Thu 14-19 h
Windthorststraße 43 a ✉99096 ☎ 731 22 33
Fax: 346 22 98 Homepage: http://www.aidshilfe.de

HELP WITH PROBLEMS

Rosa Telefon / Anti-Gewalt-Telefon
Wed 18-23 h
c/o AIDS-Hilfe Thüringen e.V., Filßstraße 8 ✉99089 .☎ 346 22 90

SWIMMING

- Baggersee (quarry) / Stotternheim between Stotternheim and Schwerborn

CRUISING

-Johannesstraße (Kaufmannskirche to Alhambrakino via Hertie)
-Main station hall/Hauptbahnhofshalle
-Parking place Radisson hotel / Juri-Gagarin-Ring near Signalpassage - back exit
-City park (behing the central railway station)

Erlangen ☎ 09131

GAY INFO

Fliederfunk-Das schwule Magazin Thu 21-22 h (FM 95,8 MHz on air, 93,6 MHz Erlangen;97,65 MHz cable Erlangen)
c/o Radio „Z", Kopernikusplatz 12, 90459 Nürnberg
☎ (0911) 45 00 60

DANCECLUBS

Männerdisco E-Werk (AC B D G lj MA) 2nd Wed 20.30-1 h; every 1st Fri Frauendisco (only women) 20-2 h
Fuchsenwiese ✉91054 *(Near Main station)* ☎ 09131/800 50

GUEST HOUSES

Haus Hubertus (bf H OS) Tue-Sun 11-1 h
54668 ☎ 06525/828
Fax: 93 61 71. Email: HBe4007203@aol.com. Appartments in quiet area with shower/bath, kitchen, TV, balcony. Rates/person DM 45-85.

CRUISING

-Gerberei (Parking garage)
-Bibliotheque of University (Ground floor)
-Friedrich-List-Straße (Underpass)
-Hugenottenplatz (5-22 h)
-[P] at Friedrich-List-Straße/Haus des Handwerks

Eschwege ☎ 06692

GENERAL GROUPS

Max & Moritz Tue 20-? h
Wierastraße 13 ☎ 70 85

Essen ☎ 0201

BARS

Café Dax (AC B bf CC glm MA) 10-1 h
Viehofer Strasse 49 ✉45127 ☎ 24 88 404
CARO Sonderbar (AC B f G MA OS YG) Sun-Thu 14-1 h, Fri-Sat 14-? h
Vereinstraße 16 ✉45127 *(near Kennedyplatz)*
Im Büro (B f G MA R) Mon-Thu 16-4, Fri 16-4, Sat 18-4, Sun 18-? h
Rellinghauser Straße 6, ✉45128 ☎ 22 61 51
Number Two. Club (A AC B CC f G lj MA p r W YG) 20-? h
Kleine-Stoppenberger-Straße 17 ✉45171 ☎ 831 55 11
Quarterback (A B CC F glm MA s) Sun-Thu 11-1, Fri-Sat 19-4 h
Alfredistraße 33-35 ✉45127 *(near town hall)* ☎ 22 61 04
Musicvideos.
Tiffany (! AC B f G lj MA p) Tue-Sun 20-5 h
Steeler Straße 83 ✉45127 ☎ 23 61 61

DANCECLUBS

Number One (AC B CC D DR G lj N p s SNU STV WE) Mon-Fri Sat and before public holidays 22-05:00 h
Lindenallee 71 ✉45127 ☎ 23 66 82
Power + Glory (B D G YG) Every 2nd Sat
c/o Jugend & Kulturzentrum Zeche Karl, Hömannstraße 10 *45128 (Altenessen)* ☎ 73 39 20

SEX SHOPS/BLUE MOVIES

Eros-Boutique (AC DR G MA VS) Mon-Sat 10-22, Sun 16-22 h
Klarastraße 19 ✉45130 *(Essen-Rüttenscheid)* ☎ 78 83 21
Man Moviethek (G VS YG) Mon-Thu 12-1, Fri Sat 12-4, Sun 14-1 h
Vereinstraße 22/Lindenallee ✉45127
Entry DM 13,- (4 drinks incl.)/Eintritt DM 13,- (4 Freigetränke inkl.)
Orion (g) Mon-Fri 9.30-20, Sat 9.30-16 h
Lindenallee 80, ✉45127 *(Near Stadtsparkasse)* ☎ 22 63 02
Wiscot The World of Him (G VS) Mon-Sat 10-24 h, Sun 12-24 h
Friedrich-Ebert-Straße 70-72 ✉45127 ☎ 208 90

HOUSE OF BOYS

K.V. Essen 14-23 h
☎ 22 81 19

SAUNAS/BATHS

Phoenix Sauna (AC b CC DR f G MA msg p pi sa sb sol VS wh) Mon-Fri 12-6, Sat Sun -8 h
Viehoferstraße 49 ✉45127 *(U-Viehoferplatz)* ☎ 248 41 66
Ruhrtalsauna (B F OS pi sa sb VS wh WO) 14-? h
Ruhrtalstraße 221 ✉45219 *(Kettwig)* ☎ 49 46 22
St.Tropez-Sauna (A B CC DR F G lj MA msg p s sa sb sol VS YG) 12-23:00h
Am Freistein 54 ✉45141 *(U-Am Freistein)* ☎ 32 25 41

BOOK SHOPS

Stirnberg Bahnhofsbuchhandlung (g)
Hauptbahnhof/U-Bahn Passage ✉45127 ☎ 22 30 74

GIFT & PRIDE SHOPS

MAX SELLER lifestyle-store (CC G) Tue-Fri 12-20 h, Sat 10-16 h
Vereinstraße 18 ✉45127 *(near Kennedyplatz)* ☎ 23 60 10
Fax: 203 01. *Clothes, toys, tools, books, magazines, videos.*

HOTELS

Frohnhauser Hof (g H)
Lise-Meitner-Straße 28 ✉45144 ☎ 73 40 61
Single DM 65-75, double 85-120.

GENERAL GROUPS

Fun Project (G lj) Mon-Thu 17-21, Fri 11-14 h
Borbeckerstraße 4 ✉45355 ☎ 68 43 79

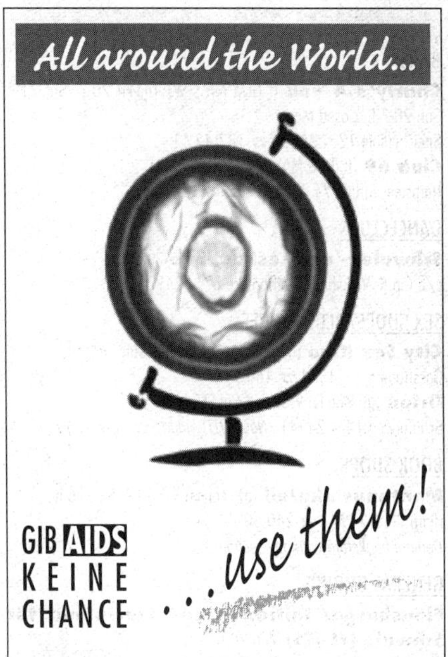

Viehofer Straße 49
Tel.: 24 88 404
daily 10.00 a.m. – 01.00 a.m.

BADESLUST
auf 1500 qm

SAUNA
Viehoferstr. 49 • 45127 Essen
U Viehofer Platz Direkt in der Fußgängerzone 10 Min. Hbf
ab 12 Uhr • täglich Nachtsauna • werktags bis 13 Uhr Eintritt DM 18.-

Phoenix Köln • Kettengasse 22 • Tel: 0221-2573381
Phoenix Düsseldorf • Platanenstr. 11a • Tel: 0211-663638

Homosexuelle Initiative Essen (HIE) 1.Fri 20-22 h at Wiese, Pferdemarkt 7 45127
PO Box 10 15 30, ✉45015 ☎ 20 76 77
Schwul AG der Uni Essen Wed 14-17, Fri 13-16 h
Universitätsstraße 2 ✉45141 ☎ 183 23 48
Fax: 183 33 96 E-mail niedermeier@uni-duisburg.de

FETISH GROUPS

LFRR Essen
Meetings in Tiffany, Steeler Straße 83
PO Box 10 21 04 ✉45021 ☎ 23 61 61
Email: volkerr@toshiba-teg.com. *Member of ECMC.*
SKVdC-Sekretariat PO Box 10 03 24 ✉45003
Email: skvdc@aol.com.
ECMC's German speaking Club's secretariat.

HEALTH GROUPS

AIDS-Hilfe Essen e. V. (g MA W) Mon 9-12, Tue 9-12 18-20, Thu Fri 9-12 h
Varnhorststraße 17 ✉45127 ☎ 23 60 96, 19411
Fax: 20 02 35. Counselling ☎19 411.
Prävention Projekt Inform e.V. Mon-Fri 11-16 h, 1st Sat Jack-Off Party at ☛ Sauna St. Tropez (22-23 h)
PO Box 29 03 41, 50525 Köln ☎ (0221) 954 13 3
Fax: (0221) 954 13 11
AIDS prevention.

SPORT GROUPS

Pott-Pritschen Wed 18 h
at Burghof-Gymnasium, City Centre ☎ 23 97 36 (Rainer)
Gay sports group.

CRUISING

-Helbingstraße/Frau-Bertha-Krupp-Straße (2 parking lots)
-Hauptbahnhof/Main station (R)
-Uni Essen (Bibliothek, Foyer, Toiletten/library, foyer, toilets)

Esslingen ☎ 0711

GENERAL GROUPS

Rosa zwiebel (roz) (d GLM lj MA s W) Wed 20.30 h
c/o Jugendzentrum Komma, Maillestraße 5-9 ✉73728
☎ 31 49 77 *(Markus)*

CRUISING

-Promenadenweg (Near/Nähe Hauptbahnhof)
-Plienhausbrücke/Neckarstraße (-20 h)
-Kleiner Markt (behind Neues Rathaus. -20 h)
-Marktplatz → Untere Beutau/Geiselbachstraße (underpass -20 h).

Euskirchen ☎ 02251

SEX SHOPS/BLUE MOVIES

Erotik-Shop (g VS) 10-19, Sat -14 h
Kölner Straße 64, ✉53879 ☎ 524 72

Fernwald ☎ 06404

SEX SHOPS/BLUE MOVIES

Orion (g) Mon-Fri 9-18.30, Sat 9-13 h
Hauptstraße 52 ✉35463 *(A5 Frankfurt → Kassel, Exit 10 »Fernwald«)* ☎ 74 00

Flensburg ☎ 0461

BARS

Charly's 4 you (f GLM MA s W) Tue-Fri 20-?, Sat 21-?, Sun 20-? h, closed Mon
Speicherlinie 12 ✉24937 ☎ 182 42 11
Club 69 (B d f G MA) 21-? h, closed Sun
Harrisleer Straße 71 ✉24939 ☎ 473 79

DANCECLUBS

Schwulen- und Lesbendisco 2nd Sat 22-4 h
c/o C.u.K. Volksbad, Schiffbrücke 67 ✉24939

SEX SHOPS/BLUE MOVIES

City Sex Kino (g VS) Mon-Sat 10-24, Sun 16-23 h
Gasstraße 5 ✉24534 ☎ 466 99
Orion (g) Mon Fri 9.30-19, Sat -15 h
Schäferweg 14 ✉24941 *(Near CITTI-Markt)* ☎ 504 01 77

BOOK SHOPS

Montanus akutell (g) Mon-Fri 9.30-19, Sat -16 h
Holm 20 ✉24937 ☎ 240 50
General bookstore with gay section.

GENERAL GROUPS

Flensburger Initiative und Treffpunkt für Schwule (FL-ITS) Mon 20 h
at ADS-Speicher, Segelmacher Straße 15
Postlagernd ✉24901 ☎ 122 64 Fax: 121 85
FL-ITS-Café »MÄNNERTrauma« Sat 20 h at ADS-Speicher, Segelmacherstraße 15

HEALTH GROUPS

AIDS-Hilfe Flensburg e.V. Mon-Fri 9-17 h
Südergraben 53 ✉24937 ☎ 255 99
Care counselling ☎ 177 11.
Counselling ☎ 194 11 Wed 18-21, Thu 16-19 h.
Fax: 124 50 Email: AIDSFlbg@aol.com

HELP WITH PROBLEMS

Rosa Telefon Flensburg Tue 18-19 h
☎ 213 47

SWIMMING

-Holnis near Glücksburg (NU) (past Glücksburg 3 km further, then follow the signs to the »Strand«.)

CRUISING

-Municipal park (at night, popular)
-WC at Nordtor

Frankenthal ☎ 0172

HOTELS

Merkur Post Hotel (bf glm H) Eisenbahnstraße 2 ✉67227 ☎ 06233/(0172) 6241217 Fax: 270 26
Single room 40-70 DM, double room 70-160 DM.

Frankfurt ☎ 069

● Jim Henson, the creator of the Muppet Show on his visit to Frankfurt, was reported to of said: „Frankfurt is the Athens of Germany." That is naturally not true. Certainly the beloved colour of the 200-Mark note (light red) passes hands frequently at he announced Loft-House-Parties or at the C5-Industry at it's latest Club 78. Frankfurt is the city for „Applewoi" and „Handkas with Music" and also the Financial Capital of Germany. The Bergerstraße and the Elefantengasse are the main areas for those addicted to shopping; along with the Central Bar and has become known as Mainhattan. The scene is charmingly smart and the party crowd is not that of Berlin and Cologne, according to the gay magazine GAB. High earnings and a majestic gay life style are typical in the city made of money.

✸ Als Jim Henson, der Erfinder der Muppet-Show, einmal in Frankfurt war, soll er gesagt haben: Frankfurt ist das Athen Deutschlands. Das stimmt selbstverständlich nicht. Doch die Lieblingsfarbe aller Frankfurter ist hellrot: Die Farbe der 200-Mark-Scheine. Die gehen hier, in den angesagten Lofthaus-Parties oder dem C5 Industry mit seinem frischen Club 78, en passant über den Ladentisch. Denn Frankfurt ist nicht nur die Hauptstadt von „Äppelwoi" und „Handkäs mit Musik". Frankfurt ist auch die Hauptstadt des Geldes. Die Parkettgeschäfte an der Börse. Die einzigartige Skyline am wolkenlosen Himmel. Das Kaufrauscheldorado Zeil, die Berger Straße und die Bar Central in der Elefantengasse: daraus wurde Mainhattan gemacht. Und deshalb ist die Szene hier auch so smart. Denn das schwule Stadtmagazin GAB beweist: Die Partycrowd hält zusammen, ist nicht so stark zerklüftet wie in den deutschen Mekkas schwulen Lebens Berlin und Köln. Hochfinanz und edles schwules Leben passen eben doch zusammen wie Ernie und Bert. Und die, das ist mittlerweile sogar bewiesen, sind schwul.

▲ Lorsque Jim Henson, l'inventeur du „Muppet show", est venu un jour à Francfort, il paraît qu'il a dit: Francfort est l'Athènes allemand. Cela n'est pas vrai bien sûr. Cependant, la couleur préférée des Francfortois est le rouge clair. La couleur du billet de 200 marks. Ici, ils circulent en passant sur les comptoirs au cours des fêtes renommées ayant lieu sous les lofts, ou au „C5 industry" avec son Club 78. En effet, Francfort n'est pas seulement la capitale du vin de pomme (Äppelwoi) et du petit fromage au cumin arrosé de marinade (Handkäs mit Musik). Francfort est aussi la capitale de l'argent. L'eldorado d'amateurs de shopping se situe sur le „Zeil", la „Berger Straße" et le „Bar Central" dans „l'Elefantengasse", qui forment ensemble le „Mainhattan". Et c'est pourquoi le milieu est si smart ici. Le magazine gaye de la ville GAB l'atteste: la foule des fêtes se serre les coudes, n'est pas aussi fissurée que dans les paradis allemands de la vie pédé que sont Berlin ou Cologne. Les finances de haut niveau et la vie gaye haut de gamme sont ici indissociables.

☆ Dicen que cuando Jim Henson, el padre de la Muppet Show, llegó la primera vez a Francfort, la denominó como Atenas de Alemania. Por supuesto esto no es verdad, aunque el color preferido de sus habitantes es el rojo claro de los billetes de 200 marcos, que cambian de mano a un ritmo vertiginoso, ya sea en las pópulares fiestas de Lofthouse o en el C5 Industry con su nuevo Club 78. Francfort no se caracteriza solo por su típica bebida el „Äppelwoi" (una especie de sidra) o la música folklorica, sino es indudablemente la capital del dinero. Esto se hace notar por las agitadas actividades en la bolsa y los impresionantes rascacielos que provocan la comparación con Manhattan. Templos del consumo son *Zeil*, la *Berger Straße* y el Bar Central en la *Elefantengasse*. Todo esto contribuye a ese ambiente tan especial de la ciudad. La revista de ocio gay GAB refleja que aquí la comunidad homosexual está mucho más unida que por ejemplo en Berlín o Colonia. Con esto se demuestra que el mundo financiero y la elegante vida gay pegan muy bien juntos, como Epi y Blas. Y estos dos heróes del Barrio Sésamo son comprobadamente homosexuales, ya que tienen un dormitorio común.

❖ Si dice che, quando Jim Henson, l'ideatore della Muppet-Show, si trovava in visita a Francoforte, abbia detto: Francoforte è l'Atene della Germania. Sicuramente non è vero. Ma il colore preferito di tutti gli abitanti di Francoforte è il rosso chiaro, cioè il colore dei biglietti da 200 marchi, che vanno en passant sul bancone in occasione delle feste nel Lofthaus o nel C5 Industry con il suo Club 78. Dunque Francoforte non è solo la capitale del „Äppelwoi" (un tipo di mosto di mela fermentato) e „Handkäs mit Musik" (un formaggio con un forte odore), ma anche del denaro. La Zeil ossia l'Eldorado per gli appassionati dello shopping, la Berger Straße, il Bar Central nella Elefantengasse: da tutto ciò deriva il soprannome Mainhattan (dal fiume Meno) per Francoforte. E per questo anche l'ambiente gay è abbastanza smart, e la rivista gay locale GAB ne dà la prova: la „partycrowd" forma un gruppo più unito in rispetto ai gruppi delle due altre due mecche tedesche della vita gay: Berlino e Colonia. I due mondi dei soldi e della vita gay di alta classe vanno bene insieme come Ernie e Bert (due figure bambole di una serie televisiva per bambini). E questi due sono gay, come è stato provato, perché dormono insieme in un letto.

GAY INFO

Frankfurt von hinten
c/o Bruno Gmünder Verlag, PO Box 61 01 04, 10921 Berlin
☎ (030) 615 00 30 Fax: 615 90 07.E-Mail: info@spartacus.de
The regional guide book about Frankfurt am Main and the federal states of Hesse, Rhineland-Palatine, Saar and Thuringia. Useful general information and lots of addresses with extensive descriptions in English and German.

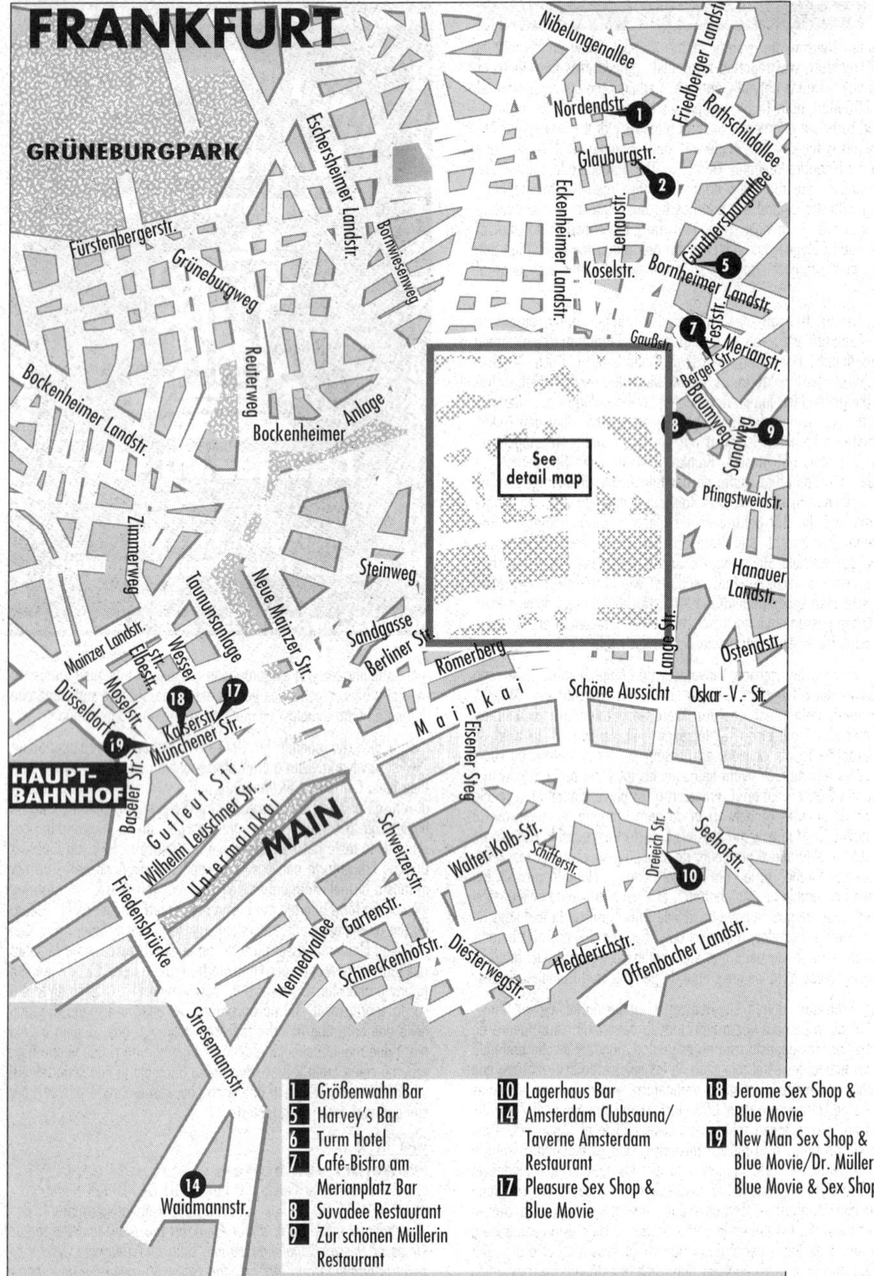
FRANKFURT
GRÜNEBURGPARK
Nibelungenallee
Friedberger Landstr.
Rothschildallee
Nordendstr.
Glauburgstr.
Eschersheimer Landstr.
Eckenheimer Landstr.
Lenaustr.
Günthersburgallee
Fürstenbergerstr.
Grüneburgweg
Bornwiesenweg
Koselstr.
Bornheimer Landstr.
Gaußstr.
Feststr.
Merianstr.
Berger Str.
Reuterweg
Bockenheimer Landstr.
Bockenheimer Anlage
Baumweg
Sandweg
See detail map
Pfingstweidstr.
Zimmerweg
Steinweg
Hanauer Landstr.
Taunusanlage
Neue Mainzer Str.
Mainzer Landstr.
Wesser str.
Elbestr.
Sandgasse
Berliner Str.
Römerberg
Lange Str.
Ostendstr.
Düsseldorfer Str.
Moselstr.
Kaiserstr.
Münchener Str.
Mainkai
Schöne Aussicht
Oskar-V.-Str.
Eisener Steg
HAUPT-BAHNHOF
Baseler Str.
Gutleut Str.
Wilhelm Leuschner Str.
Untermainkai
MAIN
Schweizerstr.
Walter-Kolb-Str.
Schifferstr.
Dreieich Str.
Seehofstr.
Friedensbrücke
Gartenstr.
Kennedyallee
Schneckenhofstr.
Diesterwegstr.
Heddrichstr.
Offenbacher Landstr.
Stresemannstr.
Waidmannstr.
1 Größenwahn Bar
5 Harvey's Bar
6 Turm Hotel
7 Café-Bistro am Merianplatz Bar
8 Suvadee Restaurant
9 Zur schönen Müllerin Restaurant
10 Lagerhaus Bar
14 Amsterdam Clubsauna/ Taverne Amsterdam Restaurant
17 Pleasure Sex Shop & Blue Movie
18 Jerome Sex Shop & Blue Movie
19 New Man Sex Shop & Blue Movie/Dr. Müller's Blue Movie & Sex Shop

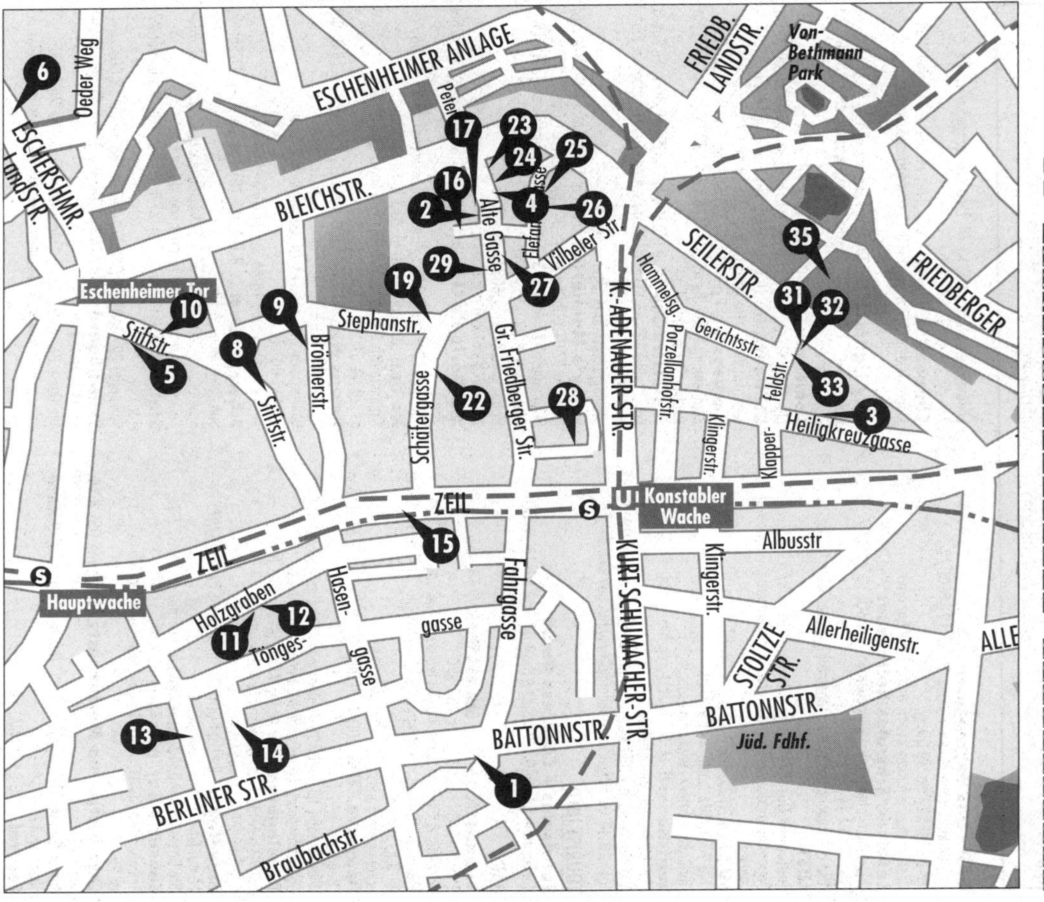

FRANKFURT AM MAIN
Innenstadt / City Center

1 Golden Gate Sauna
2 KISS Help with Problems
3 Why Not Bar
4 Pro Fun Media Store Pride Shop
5 Tangerine Bar
6 Turm Hotel
8 Stall Bar
9 Blue Angel Danceclub
10 Bannas Bar
11 City Lights Bar
12 Heaven Sex Shop & Blue Movie
13 Liliput Café
14 Sunset Restaurant
15 Birmingham Pub Bar
16 Comeback Bar
17 Oscar Wilde Buchhandlung
19 Lucky's Manhattan Bar
Lucky's Store Sex Shop
20 Hotel Scala
22 Zum Schweijk Bar
23 Switchboard Gay Info
24 Mr Dorian's Club Bar
25 Central Bar
26 Treibhaus Bar
28 Caesar's Bar
29 Continental Bathhouse Sauna
31 Bau Bar
32 Chapeau Bar
33 Na Und Bar

GAB - Das Gaymagazin
c/o Verlag Tycoon Media, PO Box 10 22 19 ✉60022
☎ 29 00 52 Fax: 29 60 97.
Best magazine for gay events in the Frankfurt area.

Lesbisch/Schwules Kulturhaus Wed 18-20 h
c/o Emanziptaion e.V., Klingerstraße 6 ✉60313 ☎ 297 72 96
Fax: 29 30 44
Also c/o Lebendiges Lesben Leben e.V.. Office: Wed 16.30-20 h.

LUST
Postfach 54 06, 65044 Wiesbaden ☎ (0611) 37 77 65
Bimonthly magazine for the Greater Frankfurt area. For free at gay venues.

SUB Mon 20-22, Tue 8-10 h
(FM 97.1 MHz, cable 99.85 MHz)
Homepage: http://www.radiosub.de.

Switchboard (A B f G MA) Tue-Thu 19-24, Fri & Sat -01, Sun 15-24:00h, closed Mon
Alte Gasse 36 ✉60313 *(U / S- Konstablerwache)* ☎ 28 35 35
Fax: 28 44 01 E-Mail: switchboard@frankfurt.gay-web.de

TOURIST INFO

Tourismus + Congress GmbH
Kaiserstraße 56 ✉60329 ☎ 21 23 88 00 Fax: 21 23 78 80

BARS

Bannas (AC B bf CC e f GLM MA s SNU STV) 18-10 h
Stiftstrasse 34 ✉60313 ☎ 288 990
Cocktails & Cigarre club, exclusive Whiskeys and Cognacs

Bau (AC B G glm LJ MA p s VS WE) Mon-Thu 21-2 h, Fri & Sat 21-3 h, Sun 6- ?
Eckenheimer Landstrasse 136 ✉60318

Bearcave. The (B) Mon-Thu 20-2 h, Fri Sat 20-3 h, Sun (Beerbust) 17-2 h
Wiesenstraße 13 ✉60385 *(U-Bornheim Mitte)* ☎ 469 30 45
Gaybar for bears, bikers, uniform and leather friends.

Birmingham Pub (B f g MA OS p) 21.30-6 h
Zeil 92 ✉60313 *(S/U-Konstablerwache)* ☎ 28 74 71
Gay from 21.30 h and later

Blue Key (AC B CC d f GLM MA P r S SNU STV TV VS WE) 16-4 h Fri, Sat, Sun open end
Alte Gasse 26 ✉60313 *(S/U-Konstablerwache)* ☎ 28 37 53

Caesar's Bar (B Glm MA p) 20-? h
Gelbehirschstraße 10 ✉60313 *(S/U-Konstablerwache)*
☎ 29 34 72

Café-Bistro am Merianplatz (B bf g MA OS) 8-24, Sun 10-24 h
Berger Straße 31-33 ✉60316 *(S/U-Konstablerwache, U-Merianplatz)* ☎ 49 38 66

Central (! AC B GLM MA) Sun-Thu 20-2, Fri Sat -3 h
Elefantengasse 13 ✉60313 *(S/U-Konstablerwache)* ☎ 29 29 26
Trendy „in" bar for students.

Chapeau (AC B f G MG N OG) 16-1 Fri Sat -2 h, closed Wed
Klapperfeldstraße 16 ✉60313 *(S/U-Konstablerwache)*
☎ 28 52 23

City Lights (AC B bf GMA) 6-1, Fri Sat -2 h
Holzgraben 11 ✉60313 *(S/U-Konstablerwache)* ☎ 92 87 08 13
Late night bar.

Comeback (AC B f G MA R) 13-2, Fri Sat -4 h
Alte Gasse 33-35 ✉60313 *(S/U-Konstablerwache)* ☎ 29 33 45

Größenwahn (B F glm N OS YG) Mon-Sun 16-2 h
Lenaustraße 97/Nordendstraße ✉60318 ☎ 59 93 56

Harveys (B bf F glm MA OS YG) Sun-Thu 9-1, Fri & Sat -2 h
Bornheimer Landstraße 64 ✉60316 ☎ 49 73 03
Popular. mixed crowd

Iks-Bistro-Bar (AC B f GLM lj MA N OS) 19.30-2, Fri Sat -3
Koselstraße 42 ✉60318 *(U-Musterschule, Tram-Friedberger Platz)*
☎ 596 23 89
Meeting placet for deaf gay group.

Lucky's Manhattan (AC B bf CC f GLM lj MG OS W YG) Mon-Thu 12-01:00h, Fri & Sat -02:00h, Sun -01:00h
Schäfergasse 27 ✉60313 *(S/U-Konstablerwache)* ☎ 28 49 19

Maybe (B DR G VS) Mon-Thu 20-02:00h, Fri & Sat 21-3 h
Elefantengasse 11 ✉60313 ☎ 29 29 50
Bar with dark room and cruising area

Mr. Dorian's Club (B f G MA p s) Sun-Thu 18-2, Fri & Sat -3 h.
Alte Gasse 34, ✉60313 *(S/U-Konstablerwache)* ☎ 29 45 06

Na Und (B f Glm MG OG p) 20-2 h, Fri Sat -3 h
Klapperfeldstraße 16, ✉60313 *(S/U-Konstablerwache)*
☎ 29 44 61

Petras Naomi (AC bf F G lj MA OS P s) Mon-Fri 19-3, Sat 11-15 and 19-3, Sun 11-15 and 16-24 h.
Bleichstrasse 38 ✉60313 *(U -Eschersheimer Turm)*
☎ 498 00 16
Kitchen is open until 1:00h. WE bf buffet 11-15 h

Schwejk. Zum (! B G lj MA YG) Tue-Thu 11-1, Fri-Sat -2, Sun 15-1, Mon 16-1 h
Schäfergasse 20 ✉60313 *(S/U-Konstablerwache)* ☎ 29 31 66
Popular and friendly. The number one in Frankfurt.

Stall (! B DR G LJ MA VS YG) 21-4, Fri Sat -? h, in summer 22-4 h
Stiftstraße 22 ✉60313 *(U-Eschenheimer Tor)* ☎ 29 18 80

Switchboard (A B f G MA s) Tue-Thu 19-24, Fri-Sat -1, Sun 15-24 h, closed Mon
Alte Gasse 36 ✉60313 *(U/S-Konstablerwache)* ☎ 28 35 35
Info-Café for the AIDS helpgroup. Ask for the dates of different activities.

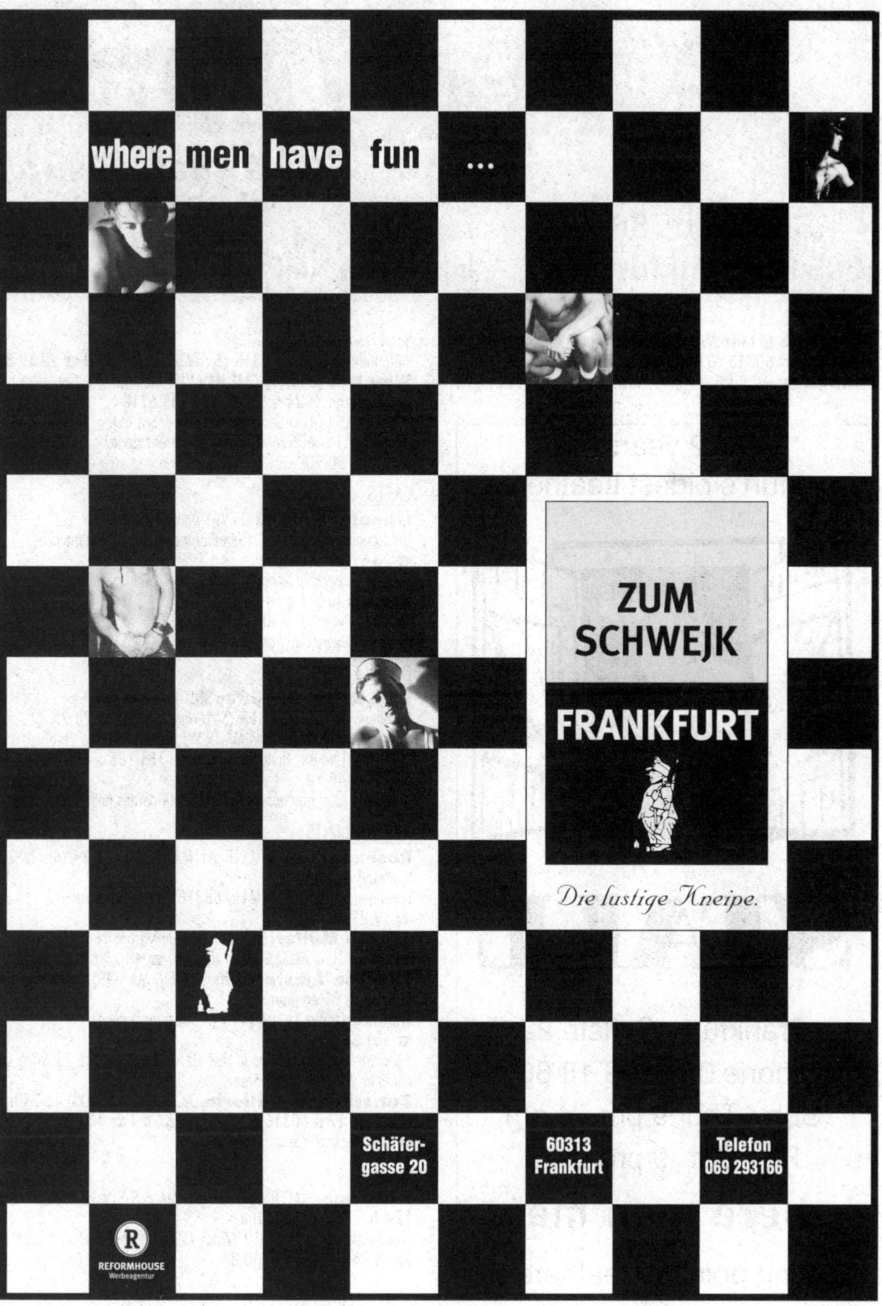
where men have fun ...
ZUM
SCHWEJK
FRANKFURT
Die lustige Kneipe.
Schäfer-
gasse 20
60313
Frankfurt
Telefon
069 293166
REFORMHOUSE
Werbeagentur

Tangerine (B f Glm MA N p) 11-4, Fri-Sat -5/?, Sun 16-4 h
Stiftstraße 39 ✉60313 *(U-Eschenheimer Tor)* ☎ 28 48 79
Treibhaus (AC B f G MA R VS) Mon Tue Thu Sun 17-2 h, Fri Sat 17-3 h, Wed closed
Elefantengasse 11 ✉60313 *(S/U-Konstablerwache)* ☎ 29 12 01
Why Not (B bf CC f GLM MA r WE) Mon-Sat 9-4, Sun 17-4 h
Heiligkreuzgasse 24 ✉60313 ☎ 9139 6918
Zippo (B f GLM) Sun-Thu 17-1, Fri & Sat -2 h
Cranachstr.1 ✉60596 *(Courner of Gartenstrasse)*
☎ 61 99 30 90

CAFES

Liliput (! B bf f G MA OS YG) Daily 9-22 h
Liebfrauenberg ✉60311 *(Sandhofpassage. S/U-Hauptwache)*
☎ 28 57 27
Popular, especially at noon, huge garden area in summer.
Sunset (B bf F glm) Daily 10-2 h
Liebfrauenberg 37 ✉60313 ☎ 20 23 0
Breakfast every day from 10:00h

DANCECLUBS

Blue Angel (AC B D G lj p SNU TV VS YG) 23-? h
Brönnerstraße 17 ✉60313 *(S/U-Hauptwache)* ☎ 28 27 72
Love Ball (D DR GLM MA TV W) Sat 22-? h
c/o L.O.F.T-house, Hanauer Landstraße 181-185 ✉60314
☎ 94 34 48 14
Check the local gay papers for up-to-date parties and dance events.

RESTAURANTS

Rosengärtchen (CC F glm MA MG OS) 18-24 (meals -23) h, closed Mon
Eckenheimer Landstraße 71 ✉68318 *(U-Glauburgstraße)*
☎ 59 21 74
Schöne Müllerin (glm F OS) Daily from 16-24 h
Baumweg 12 ✉60316 *(Near the zoo)* ☎ 43 20 69
Taverne Amsterdam (! B F G MA s VS) Tue-Sat 14-24, Sun -23 h, closed Mon
Waidmannstraße 31 ✉60596 *(S-Stresemannallee)*
☎ 631 33 89
Excellent traditional German and Hessian cuisine until 21.30 h. Located in the Amsterdam Sauna.
Zur schönen Müllerin (AC CC F glm MA OS) 16-24 h
Baumweg 12 ✉60316 *(U-Merianplatz/Zoo)* ☎ 43 20 69
Frankfurter and Hessean cuisine.

SHOWS

Flamingo (AC B CC d E f glm MA p S STV TV WE) Mon-Sat 17-4 h, 17-21 h Happy Hour
Glauburgstraße 1 ✉60318 *(Tram 12-Rohrbachgasse)*
☎ 55 75 44 Fax: 498 08 84

Gerdas Kleine Weltbühne (AC glm STV)
Offenbacherstrasse 11 ✉63165 ☎ 06108/75491
E-Mail: post@gerdas.de *Please call for details and prices.*

SEX SHOPS/BLUE MOVIES

Beate Uhse International (g) Mon-Fri 9-20, Sat -16 h
Kaiserstraße 53 ✉60329 *(S/U-Hauptbahnhof)* ☎ 23 62 80

Beate Uhse International (g VS) Mon-Fri 9-20, Sat - 16 h
Stiftstraße 4 ✉60313 *(S/U-Hauptbahnhof)*

Beate Uhse International (g) Mon-Fri 9-20 h, Sat 9-16 h
Kaiserstraße 64 ✉60329 *(S/U-Hauptbahnhof)*

Beate Uhse International (g) Mon-Fri 9-20, Sat -16 h
Kaiserstraße 79 ✉60329 *(S/U-Hauptbahnhof)*

Dr. Müller's Blue Movie & Sex Shop (g VS)
Mon-Fri 9-20, Sat -16 h; cinema 12-24 h
Kaiserstraße 66/Moselstraße, ✉60329 *(S/U-Hauptbahnhof)*
☎ 25 27 17

Heaven (! CC G lj VS) Mon-Sat 11-24, Sun & holidays 13-23h
Holzgraben 9 ✉60313 *(S/U-Konstablerwache. Near Zeil)*
☎ 29 46 55
Huge selection (5.000) of videos. Europes largest movie all male shop.

Jerome (AC DR G MA VS) Mon-Thu 12-23, Fri Sat -24, Sun 15-23
Elbestraße 17 ✉60329 *(S/U-Hauptbahnhof)*
☎ 25 39 79

Lucky's Store (g) 10-20 h
Schäfergasse 27 ✉60313 *(1st floor, above Lucky's Manhattan)*
☎ 91 39 97 54
Video and book store.

New Man (CC DR G LJ MA VS YG) Mon-Sat 9-24 h, Sun & holidays 12-24 h
Kaiserstraße 66 ✉60329 *(S/U-Hauptbahnhof. 1st floor)*
☎ 25 36 97

Orion (g) Mon-Fri 9-20, Sat -16 h
Friedberger Landstraße 126/Rohrbachstraße ✉60316 *(at Nibelungenplatz)* ☎ 43 11 26

Pleasure Sexshop (AC CC DR g MG OG VS) Mon-Sat 9-24, Sun 12-23 h
Kaiserstraße 51 ✉60329 *(S/U-Hauptbahnhof)* ☎ 23 37 72
4 films in a row in a large cinema

ESCORTS & STUDIOS

Boy's Zone 11-1 h
☎ 96 20 04 54

Playground (AC CC G msg P wh) 14-23 h
(U-Musterschule) ☎ 59 39 06
SM studio on 1st floor. Please call after 11:00h for further details.

HOUSE OF BOYS

City Boy's (CC G msg p) Tue-Sun 12-24 h
(U-Eschersheimer Tor/S-Konstabler Wache) ☎ 91 39 95 16

Men's World (AC CC G msg OS) 14-23:00h
(U - Höhenstrasse) ☎ 59 12 82

SAUNAS/BATHS

Club Sauna Amsterdam (B DR F G MG s sa sb sol wh VS) Tue-Sat 14-23, Sun -22 h, closed Mon
Waidmannstraße 31/Kennedyallee ✉60596 *(S/Tram-Stresemannallee)* ☎ 631 33 71
Popular and friendly. Very good food. 4 floors.

Continental Bath House (AC B CC DR F G msg p s sa sb sol VS WE WO YG) Sun-Thu 14-4, Fri Sat and before holidays -8 h
Alte Gasse 5 ✉60313 *(S/U-Konstablerwache)* ☎ 28 27 57
Entrance-fee DM 19-25. Tue singles DM 19, Wed 2 for DM 30. Popular later.

Golden Gate (AC B CC f G msg p sa sb sol VS WO YG) 14-1, Fri Sat 14-3 h
Braubachstraße 1/Fahrgasse ✉60311 *(S/U-Konstablerwache)*
☎ 28 28 52
Modern with a large fitness area.

BOOK SHOPS

Montanus Aktuell (g)
Hauptwache Passage ✉60313
☎ 92 91 92 62

Oscar Wilde Buchhandlung & Mail Order (A AC CC GLM MA) Mon-Fri 11-20, Sat 10-18 h, closed Sun
Alte Gasse 51 ✉60313 *(S/U-Konstabler Wache)* ☎ 28 12 60
Books, CDs, CD-ROMs, videos and accessoires.

Wohlthat'sche Buchhandlung (CC glm) Mon-Fri 9-20 h, Sat 9-16 h
Neue Kräme 14-16 ✉60311 *(U-Römer)* ☎ 28 00 64

FASHION SHOPS

Manstore Mon-Fri 12-20 h, Sat 10-16 h
Schäfergasse 20-22 ✉60313 *(near Zeil)* ☎ 28 32 42
Since 1989. Underwear for men. 25 different labels from all over the world.

Modeshop für Dich (LJ MA msg STV VS) Mon-Fri 10-20 h, Sat 10-16 h
Bolongardstraße 175 ☎ 308 93 08
Erotic shop, videos, magazines, toys, tools, leather, latex, rubber.

GIFT & PRIDE SHOPS

PRO-FUN media STORE (CC GLM VS YG) Mon-Fri 11-20, Sat 10-16 h
Alte Gasse 32 ✉60313 ☎ 13 37 70-47 ☎ 069/70 76 77-0.
Fax: 13 37 70-48 E-Mail: service@pro-fun.de
Homepage: www.pro-fun.de

LEATHER & FETISH SHOPS

Fetische-Leder, Latex und Lack Mon 14-18, Tue-Fri 10-18, Sat 10-13 h
Rotlintstraße 11 ✉60316 ☎ 43 91 87

TRAVEL & TRANSPORT

Good Buy Flugreisen
Egenolffstraße 38 ✉60316
☎ 94 41 45 04/5/6
Fax: 43 98 97 *Travel Agency.*

Reisebüro Schott
Zeilgalerie, Zeil 112-114 ✉60313 *(5th floor)* ☎ 204 33
Fax: 286 71 *Travel agency.*

HOTELS

Alexander am Zoo (bf CC MA NG sa sb)
Waldschmidtstraße 59-61 ✉60316 *(U-Habsburgerallee/Zoo)*
☎ 94 96 00 Fax: 94 96 07 20. Homepage bestwestern.com
Central location. 45 double rooms, 5 single rooms and 9 apartments with bath/WC, phone, satellite TV, radio, minibar, kitchenette, safe, heating. Hotel provides own key and parking. Rates double DM 182-322, single 147-322, apartment 259-452, Sauna included in rate, add. bed DM 50, breakfast DM 23.

Best Western Hotel Scala (CC bf glm H) 0-24 h
Schäfergasse 31 ✉60313 *(S/U-Konstablerwache)* ☎ 13 81 11-0
Fax: 28 42 34 E-Mail: info@scala.bestwestern.de
Centrally located near the gay scene. 32 double rooms and 8 singles. All rooms with bath/WC, phone, TV, radio, minibar. Rates single from DM 120-245, double from DM 160-295 (incl. breakfast) Weekend Rates single DM 120, double DM 160. Rates are subject to change.

Hotel Breesen
Varrentrappstraße 73 ✉60486 *(U-Bockenheimer Warte)*
☎ 97 06 16-0 Fax: 97 06 16 10.
Very close to university and exhibition grounds. 12 rooms with shower/WC, TV, phone. Own key. Rates single DM 115-165, double 160-260 (suite) (bf incl.)

Hotel West (bf g H)
Gräfstraße 81 ✉60486 *(U-Bockenheimer Warte)* ☎ 247 90 20
18 rooms with shower/WC, TV and minibar. Reception 6.30-22 h. Rates single DM 92-110, double 170 (bf incl.)

Turm Hotel (bf CC f glm H MA) 0-24 h
Eschersheimer Landstraße 20 ✉60322 *(U-Eschersheimer Tor)*
☎ 15 40 50 Fax: 55 35 78 E-Mail: turmhotel@aol.com
Homepage: http://members.aol.com/turmhotel
Central location in a safe area, 5 min from gay scene. 32 single rooms (DM 129-175), 18 twin, 25 double rooms (190-270). Bf incl. All rooms with minibar, cable-TV, telephone, modem connection, radio. Gay information available at the reception. No higher rates during fairs. For more information call us or see our web site.

PRIVATE ACCOMODATION

bed & breakfast
P.O. Box 10 05 22 ✉60005 ☎ (0177) 2206200
Fax: 069-945 90 00 6. Email bedandbreakfast@gmx.de
Homepage http://www.bedandbreakfast-ffm.de

Bettenbörse Tue-Fri 19-21 h
c/o Switchboard, Alte Gasse 36 ✉60313 *(S/U-Konstablerwache)*
☎ 28 35 35
The gay switchboard offers private accomodations.

Enjoy Bed & Breakfast (bf G H MA YG) 16:30-21:00h
☎ 030/215 1666 Fax: 030/217 52219
E-Mail: Info@ebab.com Homepage: www.ebab.com
Price 40 DM. Accommodation sharing agency. All with shower & bf.

GENERAL GROUPS

Arbeitskreis Homosexualität der ÖTV Frankfurt
☎ 25 69-258
(Erich Mentropp). Group for homosexual unionists.

Bartmänner Frankfurt 1st Sat 20 h
c/o Switchboard, Alte Gasse 36 ✉60313
Group for bearded men and their admirers.

Frankfurt Community e.V.
PO Box 17 02 33 ✉60076 ☎ 59 79 05 75 Fax: 59 79 05 75
Organizer of charities and the Frankfurt CSD.

Frankfurter Schwule, AStA-Schwulenreferat (G s YG) Office: Wed 13-15, Thu 12-13 h, hang-out: daily 13-14 h at Gelbe Mensa
StudentInnenhaus, R. 135 Mertonstraße 26-28 ✉60054
☎ 79 82 30 52 Fax: 70 20 39
E-Mail: schwule@stud.uni-frankfurt.de
Homepage: www.rz.uni-frankfurt.de/stud/schwulenreferat
Rosa Bibliothek Wed 13-16, Rosa Café Wed 13-16, Rosa Sprechstunde Thu 12-13 h.

Gay Net Stammtisch Wed 20 h
c/o Switchboard, Alte Gasse 36

Gruppe 30 plus Thu 18-20 h
c/o AIDS-Hilfe, Friedberger Anlage 24 ✉60316 ☎ 46 99 08 00
Fax: 46 99 94 95. E-mail rosahilfe@rhein-main.net

Hannchen-Mehrzweck-Stiftung
Löwengasse 27 ✉60385 ☎ 55 10 31 Fax: 55 10 31
Foundation to support gay self-help groups.

LSVD Hessen (GLM MA) Meet 1st Wed/month at 20:00h
PO Box 17 03 41 ✉60077 ☎ 0173/ 437 9809
Homepage: www.lsvd.de
The group BINATS - gays living in a binational partnerschaft meets here every 3rd Sat / month. 20 h

Mainsirenen Meeting Tue 20 h at Markusgemeinde, Falkstraße 55
Schwalbacher Str. 72 ✉60326 ☎ 75 00 85 50
E-Mail: mainsirenen@frankfurt.gay-web.de
Homepage: www.frankfurt.gay-web.de/mainsirenen
Gay choir group .

Rund & froh Sat 17 h at IKS Bar
☛ Switchboard Gay Center

Schwule Väter 3rd Fri 20 h
c/o Switchboard, Alte Gasse 36 ✉60313 ☎ 28 35 35

Schwusos
c/o SPD, Fischerfeldstraße 7 11 ✉60311
☎ 495 05 80 Fax: 495 05 80

Tolleranzen
c/o Stephan Grütering, Kettenhofenweg 113 ✉60325
☎ 74 65 16 Fax: 74 65 17.

Unschlagbar-Das schwule Anti-Gewalt-Projekt 2nd & 4th Thu 19.30 h
c/o Switchboard, Alte Gasse 36 ✉60313 ☎ 28 35 35
Fax: 28 44 01.
Project against gay bashing.

FETISH GROUPS

FLC Frankfurt e.V.
PO Box 11 13 23 ✉60048
☎ 596 82 06 E-Mail: flc.frankfurt@pride.de

MSC Rhein-Main, Frankfurt
☛ *Wiesbaden*

HEALTH GROUPS

AIDS-Hilfe Frankfurt e.V. Tue-Thu 19-24, Fri-Sat -1, Sun 15-24 h
Friedberger Anlage 24 ✉60316 ☎ 405 86 80
Fax: 40 58 68 40.

Regenbogendienst 10-13 h, Sat-Sun closed
Eiserne Hand 12 ✉60318 ☎ 59 13 93 Fax: 59 76 056
Ambulatory nursing care/domestic helps.

HELP WITH PROBLEMS

Informationszentrum für Männerfragen
Mon Thu 17-20 h
Sandweg 49 ✉60316 ☎ 495 04 46 Fax: 495 04 46
E-Mail: infozentrum@maennerfragen.de
Support and counselling for coming-out, bisexuality, transsexuality, identity problems and partnership problems.

KISS Mon Wed 14-19, Thu 16-20 h
Alte Gasse 37 ✉60313 *(S/U-Konstablerwache)* ☎ 29 36 71
Fax: 29 36 71
Counselling for hustlers.

Rosa Hilfe Frankfurt Sun 18-21 h
c/o V.S.B.N., PO Box 11 19 03 ✉60054 ☎ 194 46
Fax: 469 99 495 E-Mail: rosahilfe@rhein-main.net

Schwule Abstinente Alkoholiker Gruppe SAAG Wed 20-22 h
c/o Evangelischer Regionalverband, Hospitalstraße 42 ✉65929 *(Johannes Busch Haus)* ☎ (06192) 70 62

RELIGIOUS GROUPS

Homosexuelle und Kirche (HuK)
Markus Buchmann, PO Box 17 01 28 ✉60675 ☎ 800 49 44
(Thomas) Meeting: First Sunday Switchboard, Alte Gasse 36, 17 h Third Sunday Evangelische Friedensgemeinde, Frankenallee 150, 17 h.

SPORT GROUPS

Frankfurter Volleyball Verein e.V. (FVV)
☎ 70 79 31 33 E-Mail: 069441173@t-online.de
Homepage: members.aol.com/fvvev/welcome.html
The gay sports club of Frankfurt.

SWIMMING

-Langener Waldsee (G) (Take B44 to Mörfelden-Walldorf. Then look carefully for the signs to »Sering-Werk/Regatta/Badesee« and turn left there. Go to the nude area.

CRUISING

-Main railway station (ayor R)
-University (1st floor above Cafeteria)
-Airport (Section C, next to Disco Dorian Gray & behind Dr.Müllers Sex Shop)
-U-Konstablerwache (MA) (B-level, near Entrance U6/U7 direction Heerstraße. 12-21 h)
-U-Nordwestzentrum (MA) (12-16 h)
-U-Alte Oper (by day only)
-Paulsplatz (Paulskirche/Römerberg)
-Friedberger Anlage 8ayor)
-Grüneburgpark (at end of August-Siebert-Straße)

Freiberg ☎ 03731

GENERAL GROUPS

G.A.Y.-Schwulesibische Jugendgruppe Freiberg Meets 2nd/4th Sun 16 h
at Begegnungsstätte des DHB e.V., Fischerstraße 38
c/o Andreas Möckel, PO Box 1630 ✉09586

Freiburg ☎ 0761

GAY INFO

Schwule Welle im Radio Dreyeckland Thu 19.30-21, Fri 13.30-15 (FM 102.3 MHz / cable 93.6 MHz)
Adlerstraße 12 ✉79098 ☎ 310 28 Fax: 318 68

BARS

Belle Epoque (B F G MA) Mon-Thu 16-2, Fri 16-3, Sat 14-3, Sun 19-21 h
Grünwälderstraße 21 ✉79098 ☎ 372 00

Garçons. Les (B bf f glm MA OS) Mon-Sat 6:30-24, Sun 9-24 h
Bismarckallee 4-9 ✉79098 *(in the Freiburg central train station)* ☎ 2927220

Sonder Bar (AC B G MA) Mon-Thu 13-1, Fri 13-2, Sun 16-1h
Salzstraße 13 ✉79098 *(ca. 50 m vom/from Berthold's Brunnen Richtung/direction Schwaben Tor, versteckter Eingang/hidden Entrance)* ☎ 339 30

CAFES

Café Légère (B F g YG) Mon-Sat 10-1, Sun 15-1 h.
Niemenstraße 8 ✉79098 *(Near Martins Tor & »McDonalds«)* ☎ 328 00 *Popular on Sun.*

DANCECLUBS

Divino (AC B D g MA P S WE YG) Wed & Fri 23-4, Sat 23-5, Sun 20-2 h
Humboldtstraße 3 ✉79089 *(In der Nähe vom/Near by Martinstor)* ☎ 345 85

Mr Specktakel (B D G YG WE) Sun 21-2 h
Grünwälderstraße 16-18 ✉79098 *(Entrance cinema „Harmonie" in the basement)* ☎ 202 19 20

SAUNAS/BATHS

Thermos Club Sauna (B F G MA sa sb VS) 16-23, Sat Sun 14-23 h, closed Mon
Lehener Straße 21 ✉79106 ☎ 27 52 39
Friendly stuff, small but good, popular

BOOK SHOPS

Jos Fritz (g) Mon-Fri 9-19 h, Sat 10-16 h
Wilhelmstraße 15 ✉79098 ☎ 268 77

VIDEO SHOPS

Manhattan No. 1 (g) 8-24 h
Christaweg 54 ✉79114 ☎ 45 68 90 Fax: 456 89 28

Manhattan No. 1 (g) Mon-Sat 10-22 h
Haslacher Straße 78 ✉79115 ☎ 49 92 21

HOTELS

Hotel am Rathaus (AC bf CC g H) Reception 7-24 h
Rathausgasse 4-8 ✉79098 *(In pedestrian zone)* ☎ 296 160
Fax: 296 1666 E-Mail: am-rathhaus.freiburg@eurohotel-online.com
Homepage: www.eurohotel.de/am-rathaus.freiburg.html
Nice hotel with comfortable rooms, all with bath or shower/WC, TV, telephone, minibar, own keys. Single DM 110-125, double DM 185, additional bed DM 40, bf buffet incl. Domestic animals allowed. Own garage (DM 15 per day).

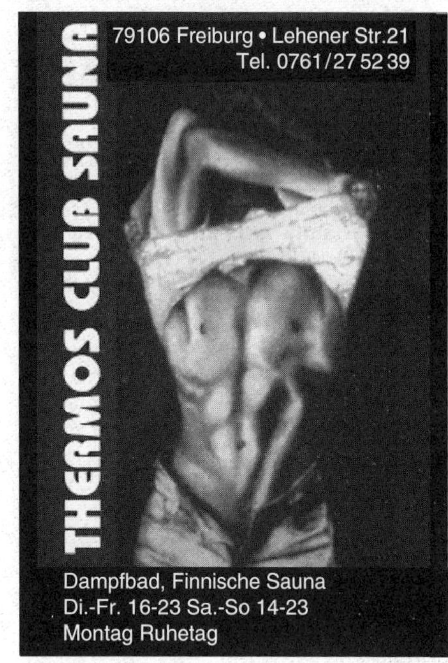

GENERAL GROUPS

AK Schwule, Lesben und Transsexuelle im DGB Freiburg
Rohrgraben 5 ✉79115 ☎ 386 76-0
Fax: 27 47 32 E-Mail: dgb@freiburg.gay-web.de
Homepage: www.freiburg.gay-web.de/dgb
Gay and lesbian unionists.

Rosekids e.V.-schwul-lesbische Jugendgruppe Freiburgs Wed (G) 19.30-? h
Engelbergerstraße 3 ✉79106 ☎ 28 18 74
Telephone during the meetings./Telefon während der Treffen.

IM ZENTRUM VON FREIBURG ERWARTET SIE EIN MODERNES HOTEL - GARNI MIT ALLEM KOMFORT.
FÜHLEN SIE SICH WOHL!

EZ AB DM 130,-, DZ AB DM 195,-
NICHTRAUCHERZIMMER VERFÜGBAR

RATHAUSGASSE 4-8
79098 FREIBURG TEL: 0761 - 29 61 60 FAX: 0761 - 29 61 666
E-MAIL: HOTEL@AM-RATHAUS.DE

Schwusos-Arbeitskreis Meeting 1st Mon 19 h
at Café Rheinfall, Rheinstraße/Katharinenstraße
c/o SPD, Habsburgerstraße 85 ✉79104 ☎ 50 08 79
Fax: 50 08 79 E-Mail: schwusos@jusosfreiburg.de

HEALTH GROUPS

AIDS Selbsthilfe HIV Positiv e.V. 18-18.30 h
PO Box 12 27 ✉79012 ☎ 231 31
Call for dates of meetings

Beratungsstelle AIDS-Hilfe Freiburg e.V.
Mon-Fri 10-13, Mon Tue Thu 15-17, Wed 17-19 h
Habsburgerstraße 79 ✉79104 ☎ 27 69 24 ☎ 19 411 (Hotline)
Fax: 28 81 12

HELP WITH PROBLEMS

Rosa Hilfe e.V. 19-20 h, meetings Fri 20-? h
Eschholzstraße 19 ✉79106 ☎ 251 61 Fax: 6 03 56.

RELIGIOUS GROUPS

Homosexuelle und Kirche
Andreas Schuhmann, Hartkirchweg 17 ✉79111
☎ 433 37 *(Andreas).*

SPECIAL INTEREST GROUPS

Breisgau-Bären Freiburg 4th Sun 16 h at
☛Sonderbar
☎ (0781) 227 14 (Jürgen).

SWIMMING

-Baggersee Niederrimsingen (g, NU) (B 31 exit Gündlingen) or Bus-Gündlingen, cruising/action in the wood behind the nude beach)
-Opfinger Baggersee (NU) (in the wood behind the nude area)
-Nimburger Baggersee (NU) (BAB 5 approach Freiburg Nord. The whole lenght of south and west side.)
(all only in summer)

CRUISING

-Colombi Park (opposite of Colombihotel, at night, popular)
-Turmstraße (r) (next to Colombihotel)

Freital ☎ 0351

SEX SHOPS/BLUE MOVIES

Erotik Shop Freital (g) Mon-Fri 9-18.30, Sat 9-13 h
Lutherstraße 27, ✉01705 ☎ 64 40 72

Fremdingen ☎ 09086

HEALTH GROUPS

AIDS-Hilfe Ansbach/Dinkelsbühl e.V.
c/o Georg Großeibel, Raustetten 9, ✉86742

Friedberg ☎ 06131

HEALTH GROUPS

AIDS-Hilfe Gießen, Zweigstelle Friedberg
Mon 18-20 h, Wed 20-21 h
Gesundheitsamt, Europaplatz ✉61169 ☎ 194 11

Friedrichshafen ☎ 07541

GENERAL GROUPS

LesGays
c/o Jugendhaus Molke, Meisterhofener Straße 11 ✉88045
☎ 38 67-25

CRUISING

-Bundesbahnhafen at Seeparkplatz (Ruderclubhaus)

Fulda ☎ 0661

GAY INFO

Gayzette c/o Regenbogentreff, Künzeller Straße 15 ✉36043
☎ & Fax: 901 44 47

Regenbogentreff Wed 20-22 h
Künzeller Straße 15 ✉36043 ☎ & Fax: 901 44 47
Information and counselling center.

BARS

Fleckviehalle (AC B d f GLM lj MA OS W WE YG) Disco: Mon-Thu 22-1 (Thu G), Fri Sat -3, Sun closed, Beer garden: 15-? h
Ruhrstraße 3 ✉36043 ☎ 942 89 21

GENERAL GROUPS

AStA-Schwulenreferat der Fachhochschule Fulda Tue 11-14; Meeting: Wed 20-? h
at Ludwig-Beck-Straße 11-13, Room 16
Ludwig-Beck-Straße 7 ✉36037 ☎ 962 91 40 Fax 662 51

SchwuLesBische Organisation Fulda e.V.
PO Box 204 ✉36002

HEALTH GROUPS

AIDS-Hilfe Fulda e.V. Mon 11-13, Tue Thu 14-16
Friedrichstraße 4 ✉36037 ☎ 770 11
Fax: 24 10 11 ☎*-Counselling Tue 11-13 h, Mon 14-16 h (☎ 1 94 11). Private counselling Mon 14-16 h, Thu 11-13 h*

HELP WITH PROBLEMS

Informations- und Beratungstelefon
Wed 20-22 h ☎ 194 46

CRUISING

-Frauenberg [P]

Garmisch-Partenkirchen ☎ 08821

CRUISING

-Kurpavillon

Geislingen ☎ 07331

CAFES

Connexion (bf d DR F G lj r WE YG) Sun-Thu 6-1, Fri Sat -3,
Steingrubestraße 7 ✉73312 ☎ 94 40 42

Geldern ☎ 02833

GENERAL GROUPS

Schwuler Stammtisch
c/o Zum Schwarzbrenner, Kapuzinerstraße 4, ✉47608
☎ 87 70 50

Gelsenkirchen ☎ 0209

BARS

Club »La Mirage« (B d f G MA s) 21-5 h
Selhorststraße 6-10, ✉45879 *(Near/Nähe Hauptbahnhof; Fina Parkhaus)* ☎ 20 11 06

RESTAURANTS

Schwarze Schaf. Das (B F g) 17-? h, closed Sat
Florastraße 24/Hansemannstraße ✉45879 ☎ 261 01

SEX SHOPS/BLUE MOVIES

Höhepunkt Medienvertrieb GmbH (G LJ MA VS)
Mon-Fri 10-22:00h, Sat 10-16:00h, Sun - closed
Wanner Straße 133 ✉45888 ☎ 255 80

L.G.S. (CC glm lj MA) Mon-Fri 9-18.30, Sat -14, 1st Sat -16 h
Bochumer Straße 76 ✉45886 ☎ 222 14
Leather, rubber, sexshop. Medical piercing on 1st Sat.

Live Erotika (g VS) Mon-Sat 9-24, Sun 12-24 h
Augustastraße 11 ✉45879

TRAVEL & TRANSPORT

Ticket Point 8-18.30 h
De-la-Chevallerie-Straße 22 ✉45894 ☎ 38 63 86
Fax: 38 63 888.

GENERAL GROUPS

Bigruppe Fri 15-17 h
c/o AIDS-Hilfe, Husemannstraße 39-41 ✉45879 ☎ 194 46

Gehörlosen-Club für Schwule & Lesben 1991 e.V.
PO Box 10 04 29, ✉45804 ☎ 20 05 41 (Schreibtelefon)
Fax: 20 16 45.

Jugendnetzwerk Lambda NRW e.V. Landesbüro Westfalen
Wanner Straße 6 ✉45879
E-mail: Jugendnetzwerk.lambda@t-online.de

RUBI Ruhrgebiets Bi-Gruppe (MA p) Every 2nd Wed 20 h
c/o AIDS-Hilfe Gelsenkirchen e.V., Husemannstraße 39-41 ✉45879 ☎ 39 97 89 ☎ 0209/2 55 26 Fax: 20 91 66
E-Mail: XUferlos@aol.com

Schwule Jugendgruppe Young Connections Mon 19-21 h
c/o AIDS-Hilfe, Husemannstraße 39-41 ✉45879

HEALTH GROUPS

AIDS-Hilfe Gelsenkirchen e.V. Mon Wed Fri 12-17, Thu 15-17 h
Husemannstraße 39-41, ✉45879 ☎ 194 11
Email: aidshilfege@cww.de Homepage:
www.geocities.com/WestHollywood/Heights/1547/index.html

CRUISING

-Gardens at bus station
-Schloß Berge

Gemünden am Main ☎ 09351

SWIMMING

-Badesee/Lake »Sindersbach« (g WE YG) (→ Ruppertshütten)

Gera ☎ 0365

CRUISING

-Park der Jugend (called »Knochenpark«, Talstraße)

Gerolzhofen ☎ 09382

GENERAL GROUPS

Rosa Rebe Counselling Mon 20-22 h
☎ & Fax: 46 68

Gießen ☎ 0641

BARS

Anders als (B D GLM MA OS S STV) 20-1, Thu-Sat -3 h
Schanzenstraße 9 ✉35390 ☎ 781 64

Bonaparte (B G MA s) Mon-Sun 20-1 h
Liebigstraße 66 ✉35390 ☎ 756 49
The oldest gay bar in Gießen

Select (B D f glm MA)
Fasanenweg 28 b ✉35390

CAFES

Café Einstein (A B F glm MA OS) 9-1, Sun 10-1, meals -23 h
Mühlstraße 10 ✉35390 ☎ 757 53

SEX SHOPS/BLUE MOVIES

Orion (g)
Gottlieb-Daimler-Straße 3, 35440 Linden

Orion (g) Mon-Fri 9-18.30, Sat 9-13/14 h
Schulgasse 9/Markttraße, 35452 Heuchelheim

GENERAL GROUPS

Autonomes Schwulenreferat im AStA der Justus-Liebig-Universität Gießen
Otto-Behagel-Straße 25 D ✉35394

Die Schwestern der Perpetuellen Indulgenz Priorei Gießen
c/o Jan-Steve von Janicki, Hindemithstraße 13/22 ✉35392 ☎ 920 39 74
Organization for AIDS prevention.

HOMO e.V. Meeting: 2nd Wed 19-24 h
Diezstraße 8 ✉35390 ☎ 194 46 Fax: 394476

Schwules Infocafé (G MA) Wed 21-? h
Südanlage 20 HH ✉35390 ☎ 75112

HEALTH GROUPS

AIDS-Hilfe Gießen e.V. Mon Wed Fri 10-14, Thu 14-18 h, closed Tue
Diezstraße 8 ✉35390 ☎ 194 11 Fax: 39 44 76
E-Mail: ah-gi@t-online.de

HELP WITH PROBLEMS

Rosa Telefon Wed 19-21 h
☎ 194 46

CRUISING

-Park an der Ostanlage (opposite Behördenzentrum)

Gladbeck ☎ 02043

GENERAL GROUPS

Schwule Initiative Gladbeck
Rosa Telefon Tue 19-22 h
c/o Bündnis 90/Grüne, Friedenstraße 5, ✉45964 ☎ 254 12

CRUISING

-Karstadt department store
-P (opposite post office 1, Bahnhofstr. 82-86, late evenings 22-? h)
-Liebigstraße (opposite Hauptzollamt, late evenings 22-? h)
-Park near Ostanlage (opposite Behördenzentrum (Bus stop Behörden- zentrum), late evenings 22-? h)

Gleichen-Reinhausen ☎ 05592

GAY INFO

Waldschlößchen/Freies Tagungshaus Mon-Fri 8.30-12.30, Wed 15-18 h
✉37130 ☎ 382 Fax: 17 92.
Rooms for seminars and guest-groops. Please ask for for the program.

HEALTH GROUPS

Positiv e.V. c/o Waldschlößchen, ✉37130 ☎ 17 38
Fax 17 92.

Gnandstein ☎ 034344

CAFES

Burg Gnandstein (B F g H NG T WE) Mon Tue closed ✉04655 *(B95 between Chemnitz and Leipzig, exit Dolzenheim)*
☎ 612 20 Fax 614 10.
12th Century Castle, now hotel, restaurant and café.

Goch ☎ 0209

GENERAL GROUPS

Lesbisch-Schwuler-Stammtisch Goch
Meets 1st/3rd Tue 20 h at Bistro Esprit
Herzogenstr. 6

Göppingen

CRUISING

-Marktplatz
-Hohenstaufenhalle (behind)
-Alter Friedhof

Görlitz ☎ 03581

SEX SHOPS/BLUE MOVIES

Orion (g) Mon-Fri 9-19, Sat -14 h
Landeskronstraße 4 ✉02826 ☎ 40 65 25

HELP WITH PROBLEMS

schwubs Wed 18-21 h
PO Box 300 533 ✉02810 ☎ 30 69 96 Fax: 30 69 97

Göttingen ☎ 0551

CAFES

Café Chups (g) Sun-Thu 10-2, Fri Sat -3 h
Kornmarkt 9 ✉37073 *(Next to Altes Rathaus)*
☎ 48 79 29

DANCECLUBS

Faces (B D f GLM) 15-? h
Nikolaistraße 22 ✉37073 ☎ 531 49 49
ManDance (AC B D DR GLM lj s VS YG) 2nd Sat 22-4 h
musa, Hagenweg 2 ✉37079 *behind the „Zollamt"*
☎ 0173/95 15 870

SEX SHOPS/BLUE MOVIES

Orion (g) Mon-Fri 9.30-20, Sat -16 h
Jüdenstraße 13a, ✉37073 ☎ 443 26

BOOK SHOPS

Montanus aktuell (g) Mon-Fri 9.30-20, Sat -16 h
Kornmarkt 7 ✉37073 ☎ 446 43

VIDEO SHOPS

Videothek Globus (g) 10-20 h, closed Sun
Geismarlandstraße 25a ✉37083 ☎ 476 57

HEALTH GROUPS

Göttinger AIDS-Hilfe e.V. Mon-Fri 10-13 h
Obere Karspüle 14, ✉37073 ☎ 437 35 Fax: 41027
E-Mail: aids-hilfe.goettingen@t-online.de

HELP WITH PROBLEMS

Rosa Telefon Mon 20-22 h ☎ 194 46
Schwulen Hilfe Göttingen S.H.G.
PO Box 11 51, ✉37116 Bovenden ☎ & Fax: 833 55

CRUISING
-Jacobi Kirchhof / church yard (between Weender-Jüdenstraße)
-Herkulus Einkaufszentrum (shopping center, popular)
-Careé Einkaufszentrum (shopping center, popular)
-University

Goslar ☎ 05321

HOTELS
Haus Waldfrieden
☛ Altenau

SAUNAS/BATHS
Zum Radeberger (B f) 17-? h
Große Fahnenstraße 10 ✉99867 *(near Altem Strandbad)*
☎ 70 77 71

Greifswald ☎ 03834

GENERAL GROUPS
Rosa Greif-schwul-lesbischer AK in Vorpommern e.V. Thu 19.30 (Café), last Fri 21 h (Rosa Schwoof) at St. Spiritus, Lange Str. 49
PO Box 12 03, ✉17489 ☎ & Fax: 89 70 34
Tue 15-17 h, Wed 18-22 h Coming-out group.

CRUISING
-Wallanlagen (between Mühlentor and Fleischerstraße)

Grewesmühlen ☎ 03881

HEALTH GROUPS
Aidshilfe c/o AWO Thu 12-16 h
Rudolf-Breitscheidt-Straße 27 23936 ☎ 71 00 51 + Fax:

Gummersbach ☎ 02261

GENERAL GROUPS
Schwule Gruppe Oberberg (GLM MA) Meets every 2nd Wed 20 h
PO Box 31 01 75 ✉51616 ☎ 2 54 49
Contact ☎ (02265) 91 52 Joachim

Gütersloh ☎ 0 52 41

GENERAL GROUPS
Coming-Out-Gruppe Gütersloh Meeting Wed 20 h
c/o Kulturzentrum Alte Weberei, Bogenstraße 1-8 ✉33330

Hagen ☎ 02331

BARS
Krönchen (B f glm MA) Mon-Thu 19-1 h, Fri-Sat 19-3 h, Sun closed
Körnerstraße 47, ✉58095 *(Near/Nähe Volkspark)* ☎ 324 26
Regenbogen (B f GLM s) Tue-Fri 17-24 h, Sat 17-3 h, Sun 15-3 h, Mon closed
Graf-von-Galen-Ring 13 ✉58095 ☎ 18 38 43
or ☎ 0177/346 69 22

SEX SHOPS/BLUE MOVIES
Cine Bar (b DR G MA p VS W) Mon-Sat 11-24, Sun 12-24 h
Hindenburgstraße 22 ✉58095 ☎ 18 40 56
Entrance-fee DM 15 incl. 2 drinks.
Homo-Kino im Sex Shop (g VS) Mon-Sat 9-24, Sun 13-24 h
Kampstraße 21, ✉58095
Orion (g) Mon-Fri 9.30-20, Sat 9-16 h
Frankfurter Straße 62-64 ✉58095 ☎ 023 31/325 34

GENERAL GROUPS
„aMANNda" Wed 20.30 h
Kulturzentrum, Pelmkestraße 14, ✉58089 ☎ 33 69 67
Boy Dreams Wed 18-20 h
c/o AIDS-Hilfe Hagen e.V., Körnerstraße 82 ✉58095
☎ & Fax: 33 88 33
Coming Out/AIDS-Beratung für Jugendliche.
Elterngruppe homosexueller Söhne und Töchter every other Tue 19.30 h
c/o VHS-Villa Post, Wehringhauser Straße 38 ✉58089
☎ 207 35 89

HEALTH GROUPS
AIDS-Hilfe Hagen e.V. Mon 20-22 h, Tue 19-21 h, Wed 9-12 h
Körnerstraße 82 ✉58095 *(Entrance/Eingang C)* ☎ 19 411

HELP WITH PROBLEMS
Gay Line Hagen Mon 20-22 h
c/o AIDS-Hilfe, Körnerstraße 82 ✉58095 ☎ 33 88 33

SPORT GROUPS
SC Moving Man e.V. Tue 21 (Badminton), Thu 20.30 (Volleyball), every 2nd Fri 20 h (Bowling)
c/o Volker Haeske, Unternahmerstr. 47 ✉58119 ☎ 33 88 33
Badminton at WOS-Eilpe (World of Sports), Eilper Straße. - Volleyball at Käthe-Kollwitz-Sporthalle - Bowling at Kegel- & Bowlingcenter Dortmund, Marlinkrodtstraße 212-214.

CRUISING
-Main rail station
-Volkspark
-Johanniskirchplatz

Halberstadt ☎ 03941

HEALTH GROUPS
AIDS-Hilfe Halberstadt e.V. Mon Tue 20-22 h
Finckestraße 7, ✉38820 ☎ 60 16 66

Halle Saale ☎ 0345

GAY INFO
Begegnungs- & Beratungs-Zentrum (BBZ) »lebensart« e.V. schwul-lesbische Interessengemeinschaft (GLM MA p)
Schmeerstraße 22 ✉06108 *(Tram-Marktplatz)* ☎ 202 33 85
Fax: 202 33 85 E-Mail: BBZ-Lebensart@TOP.east.de
Call for opening hours and details.
Homo sum Wed 17-22 h
c/o BBZ „lebensart" e.V., Schmeerstraße 22 ✉06108
☎ 202 33 85 Fax: 202 33 85.
Monthly gay-lesbian newsletter from and about Halle. For free.

BARS
Blue Velvet (B CC d DR f G MA r s STV TV) Mon-Sun 12-1 h, lunch
Alter Markt 29-30 ✉06108 ☎ 517 03 59

DANCECLUBS

Easy Schorre (AC B D f GLM lj s SL VS WE YG) every other Sun 21-4.30 h
Philipp-Müller-Straße 77-78 ✉06110 *(Tram-Rannischer Platz)*
☎ 21 22 40
Gay disco every 2nd Sun.

Pierrot (AC b D DR f GLM lj MA s SNU STV WE) Mon-Thu 18:00-?, Fri & Sat 20:00-?
Großer Sandberg 10 ✉06108 ☎ 290 3231

Thalia-Gewölbe (B D G YG) Sat 21-4 h
Thaliapassage 1 ✉06108 ☎ 388 00 15

BOOK SHOPS

Litfass (glm) Mon-Fri 9-19, Sat 10-14 h
Rannische Straße 14/15, ✉06108 ☎ 202 42 63
General bookstore with gay section.

Sagner & Co, Proteus Buchhandel Mon-Fri 9-18 h, Sat Sun closed
Adolfstr. 10 ✉06114 ☎ 522 4994
Also safer-sex articles.

GENERAL GROUPS

Lesben- und Schwulenverband in Deutschland (LSVD) e.V. Landesverband Sachsen-Anhalt: Aussenstelle
Friedrich-Hesekiel-Straße 22 ✉06132 ☎ 775 93 83

HEALTH GROUPS

AIDS-Hilfe Halle e.V. Mon 14-18 h, Tue Thu 10-22 h, Wed Fri 10-14 h
Böllberger Weg 189 ✉06110 ☎ 230 90-0
Fax: 23 09 04, ☎ 19 411 *(couselling). Rainbow breakfast Sat 11 Counselling Mon 18-20 h, Wed 16-18 h, Thu 16-20 h*

HELP WITH PROBLEMS

Überfalltelefon Wed 18-22 h
☎ 192 28

SPORT GROUPS

Saaleperlen
☎ 521 19 30 Homepage: www.saaleperlen.de
Gay sports group/ Schwul-Lesbischer Sportverein.

CRUISING

-Stations
-Waisenhausring/Hansering (near Leipziger Turm, -24 h, popular)
-FKK-Kanal/nude swimming (obere Aue, B 80 Angersdorf → Wörmlitz, popular)

Haltern

SWIMMING

-Baggersee (Flaesheimer Straße at Flaesheim)
-Selberseen I & II (Münsterstraße at Sythen)

Hamburg ☎ 040

● The atmosphere of a harbour city is in Hamburg omnipresent. The Red Light District around the Reeperbahn in the St. Pauli offered the vast number of sailors in the past a much needed change from long journeys on the seas.

Today the Reeperbahn is a popular meeting point for the Hamburger and visitors to the city. It's the hub of sexual activity with an endless number of bars, cafés, clubs and prostitution. Certainly not to be missed by the tourist wanting to strike it lucky. It's highly recommended to take a small trip to the City Park, Elbvorte and Alster to discover exquisite restaurants serving mouth watering dishes. There are a host of cultural things to do from theatres to museums.

The gay community has rooted itself in St. Georg, the second Red Light District of Hamburg. In St. Georg gays walk hand in hand and visit the most popular gay café: Café Gnosa with it's wide selection of cakes and gateauxs. You are also able to find in this neighbourhood gay literature, rubber and leather in Mr. Chaps. And not to far from the many sides streets of the quarter, around the Pulverteich is Tom's or Rudi's Nightclub. Those who travel to Hamburg will discover many different sides of this warm, friendly city, and perhaps those with a little bit more patience an actual Hamburger. Once the heart of a northerner is captured, you will have made a friend for life.

✸ Der Flair einer Hafenstadt ist in Hamburg allgegenwärtig. Das Rotlichtviertel um die Reeperbahn in St. Pauli bot früher den zahlreichen Seemännern reichlich Abwechslung nach einer langen Reise auf hoher See. Heute vertreiben sich die Hamburger und die unzähligen Besucher der Hansestadt ihre Abendstunden in der berühmten Ausgehmeile. Egal ob man auf der Sache nach Bars, Clubs oder käuflichem Sex ist, hier wird der schwule Tourist fündig. Neben dem zweitgrößten Hafen in Europa, bietet die Handelsmetropole Hamburg aber noch mehr. Stadtpark, Elbvororte und Alster sind einen Ausflug wert, exquisite Restaurants bereiten Gaumenfreuden, Theater und Museen bieten kulturelles für jeden Geschmack und die Lange Reihe in St. Georg, Hamburgs zweitem Rotlichtviertel in unmittelbarer Nähe des Hauptbahnhofs, hat sich in den letzten Jahren zu einer lebendigen schwulen Umgebung entwickelt. Hier schlendern Schwule Hand in Hand, hier lädt das traditionelle Café Gnosa zu leckeren Torten, hier findet man schwule Literatur im Blendwerk oder Lack und Leder im Mr. Chaps. Von der Langen Reihe ist es auch nicht weit in das ebenfalls in St. Georg gelegene Ausgehviertel um den Pulverteich, wo p.i.t., Tom's oder Rudi's Nightclub ihre schwulen Gäste empfangen. Wer nach Hamburg reist wird schnell feststellen können, wie abwechslungsreich, schön und freundlich diese Stadt ist-auch wenn man vielleicht etwas länger Geduld haben muß einen echten Hamburger kennenzulernen. Wenn man erstmal das Herz eines Nordlichts gewonnen hat, hat man einen Freund fürs Leben.

▲ Partout à Hambourg, on respire l'ambiance d'une ville portuaire. Le quartier chaud autour de la „Reeperbahn" à St Pauli offrait autrefois aux nombreux marins beaucoup de distractions après un long voyage en mer. Aujourd'hui, les Hambourgeois et les innombrables visiteurs de la ville hanséatique passent leurs soirées dans la célèbre avenue des sorties. Peu importe qu'il cherche un bar, un club ou du sexe, le touriste gay trouve ce qu'il veut. En plus d'être le deuxième plus grand port d'Europe, cette métropole commerciale a bien des trésors à decouvrir. Le Parc municipal (Stadtpark), les faubourg au bord de l'Elbe et l'Alster méritent une visite, des restaurants exquis procurent les plaisirs du palais, les théâtres et les musées offrent de la culture pour tous les goûts et la „Lange Reihe" à St Georg, le deuxième quartier chaud de Hambourg tout près de la gare centrale, a évolué ces dernières années vers une ambiance gaye animée. Des homosexuels y flânent main dans la main, le traditionnel Café Gnosa invite à déguster de délicieuses tartes, on trouve de la littérature gaye à Blendwerk ou des articles en vernis ou en cuir chez „Mr Chaps". De la „Lange Reihe", il n'y a qu'un pas jusqu'à l'avenue des sorties située à St Georg autour du „Pulverteich" où p.i.t., le club de nuit de Tom ou Rudi accueillent leurs hôtes. Quiconque vient à Hambourg constatera rapidement combien cette ville est variée, belle et conviviale, même s'il faut avoir de la patience avant de rencontrer un vrai Hambourgeois. Quand on éprouve pour la première fois de la sympathie pour un Allemand du Nord, on a un ami pour la vie.

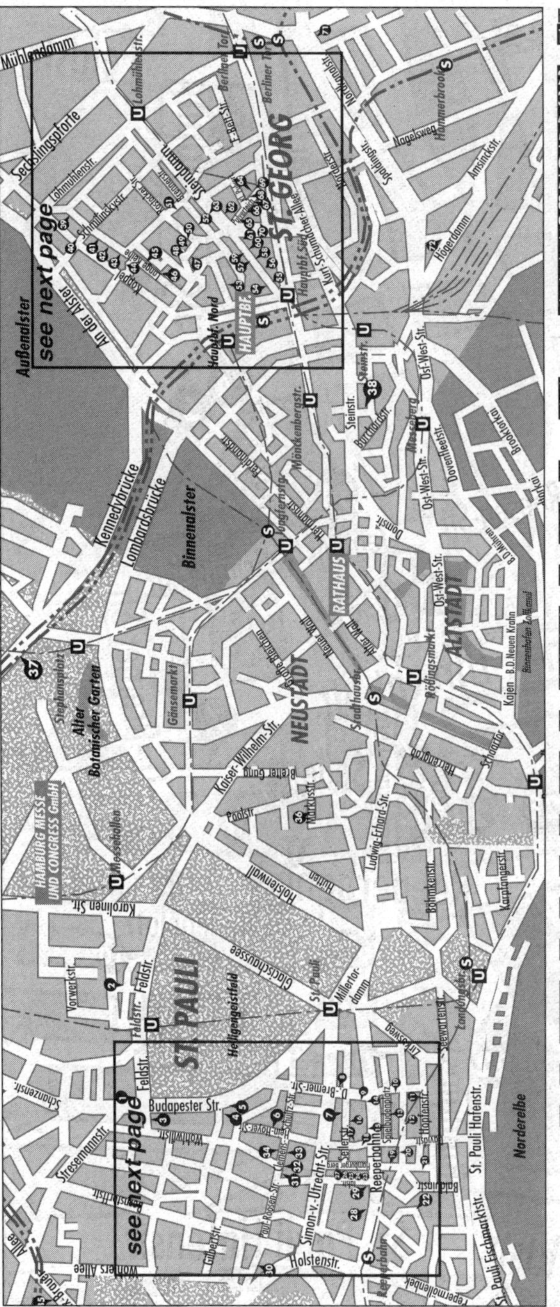

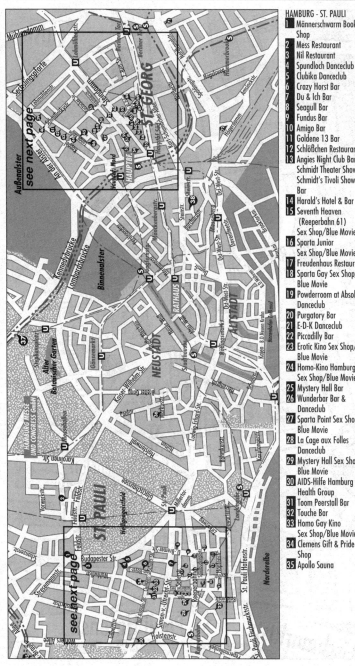

HAMBURG - ST. PAULI
1 Männerschwarm Book Shop
2 Mess Restaurant
3 Nil Restaurant
4 Spundloch Danceclub
5 Clubika Danceclub
6 Crazy Horst Bar
7 Du & Ich Bar
8 Seagull Bar
9 Fundus Bar
10 Amigo Bar
11 Goldene 13 Bar
12 Schlößchen Restaurant
13 Angies Night Club Bar
Schmidt Theater Show
Schmidt's Tivoli Show & Bar
14 Harald's Hotel & Bar
15 Seventh Heaven (Reeperbahn 61) Sex Shop/Blue Movie
16 Sparta Junior Sex Shop/Blue Movie
17 Freudenhaus Restaurant
18 Sparta Gay Sex Shop/ Blue Movie
19 Powderroom at Absolut Danceclub
20 Purgatory Bar
21 E-D-K Danceclub
22 Piccadilly Bar
23 Erotic Kino Sex Shop/ Blue Movie
24 Homo-Kino Hamburg Sex Shop/Blue Movie
25 Mystery Hall Bar
26 Wunderbar Bar & Danceclub
27 Sparta Point Sex Shop/ Blue Movie
28 La Cage aux Folles Danceclub
29 Mystery Hall Sex Shop/ Blue Movie
30 AIDS-Hilfe Hamburg Health Group
31 Toom Peerstall Bar
32 Touche Bar
33 Homo Gay Kino Sex Shop/Blue Movie
34 Clemens Gift & Pride Shop
35 Apollo Sauna

HAMBURG - CITY CENTER
36 Willy's for You Bar
37 Café Schuh
38 Cafe Spund

HAMBURG - ST. GEORG
39 Blendwerk Book Shop
40 Bistro des Artistes Café
41 Café Gnosa
42 Sparta City Sex Shop/ Blue Movie
43 Café Uhrlaub
44 Mr. Chaps Leatherworks Shop
45 Pension Sarah Petersen
46 Twist Café
47 Romeo Bar
48 Extratour Bar
49 Comeback Bar
50 Bajadere Bar
51 Black Bar
52 My Way Bar
53 Adria-Hof Hotel
54 Henry's Show Center Sex Shop/Blue Movie
55 Hotel Village
56 Seventh Heaven Erotic Discount Sex Shop
57 Hotel Schweriner Hof
58 New Man im WOS (Steindamm) Sex Shop/Blue Movie
59 New Man Plaza Sex Shop/Blue Movie
60 Seventh Heaven Sex Shop/Blue Movie
61 Mystery World Sex Shop/Blue Movie
62 Rudi's Night Club Bar
63 Bei Franz Bar
64 Hein & Fiete Gay Info
65 New Man City Sex Shop
66 Pulverfaß Cabaret Show
67 Hotel Königshof
68 Male Bar
69 Dragon Sauna
70 Tusculum Bar
71 Salvation Danceclub
72 Chaps Bar

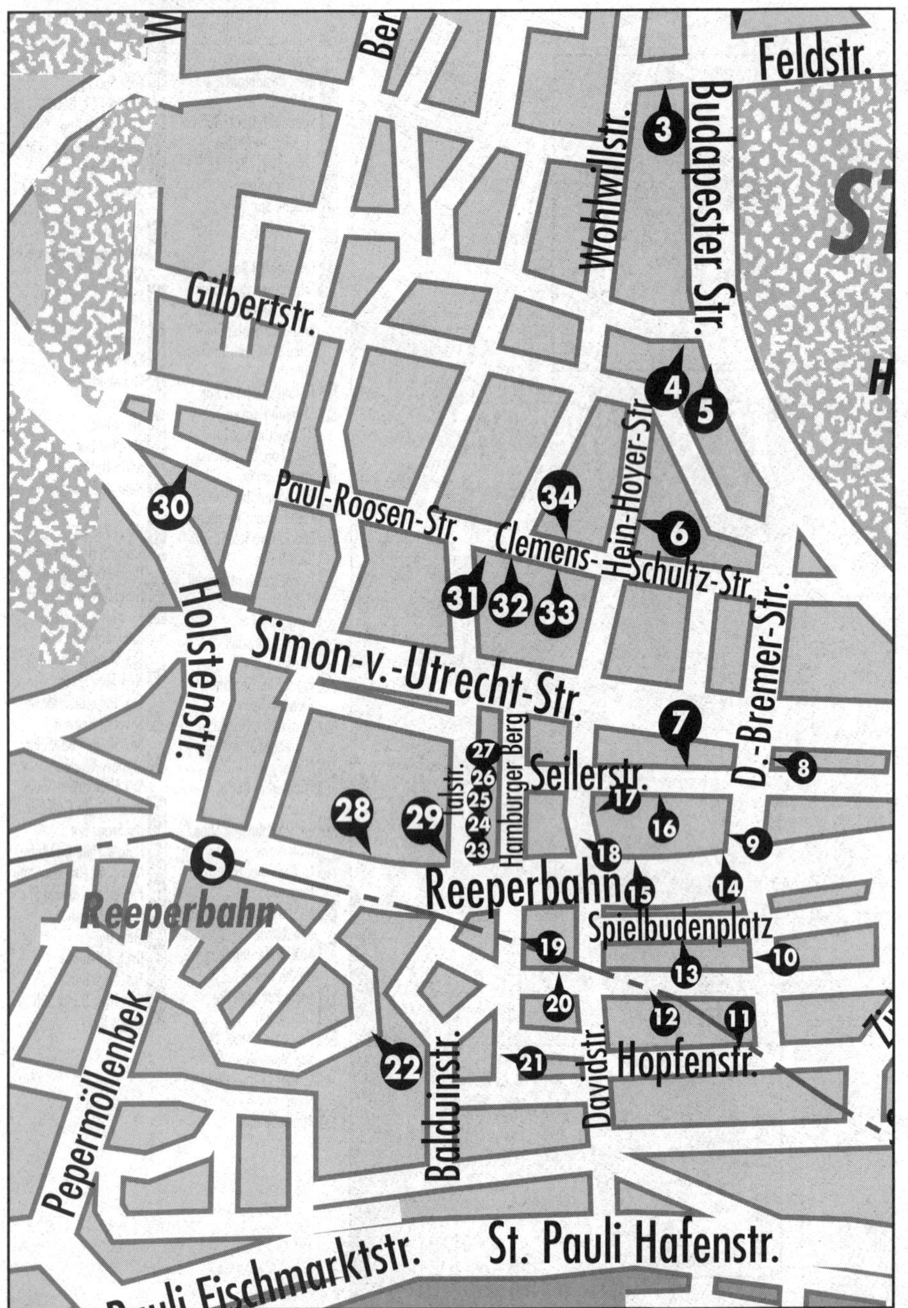
Feldstr.
Budapester Str.
Wohlwillstr.
Gilbertstr.
Paul-Roosen-Str.
Hein-Hoyer-Str.
Clemens-Schultz-Str.
Holstenstr.
Simon-v.-Utrecht-Str.
D.-Bremer-Str.
Seilerstr.
Talstr.
Hamburger Berg
Reeperbahn
S
Reeperbahn
Spielbudenplatz
Pepermöllenbek
Balduinstr.
Davidstr.
Hopfenstr.
St. Pauli Hafenstr.
Pauli Fischmarktstr.
3
4
5
6
7
8
9
10
11
12
13
14
15
16
17
18
19
20
21
22
23
24
25
26
27
28
29
30
31
32
33
34

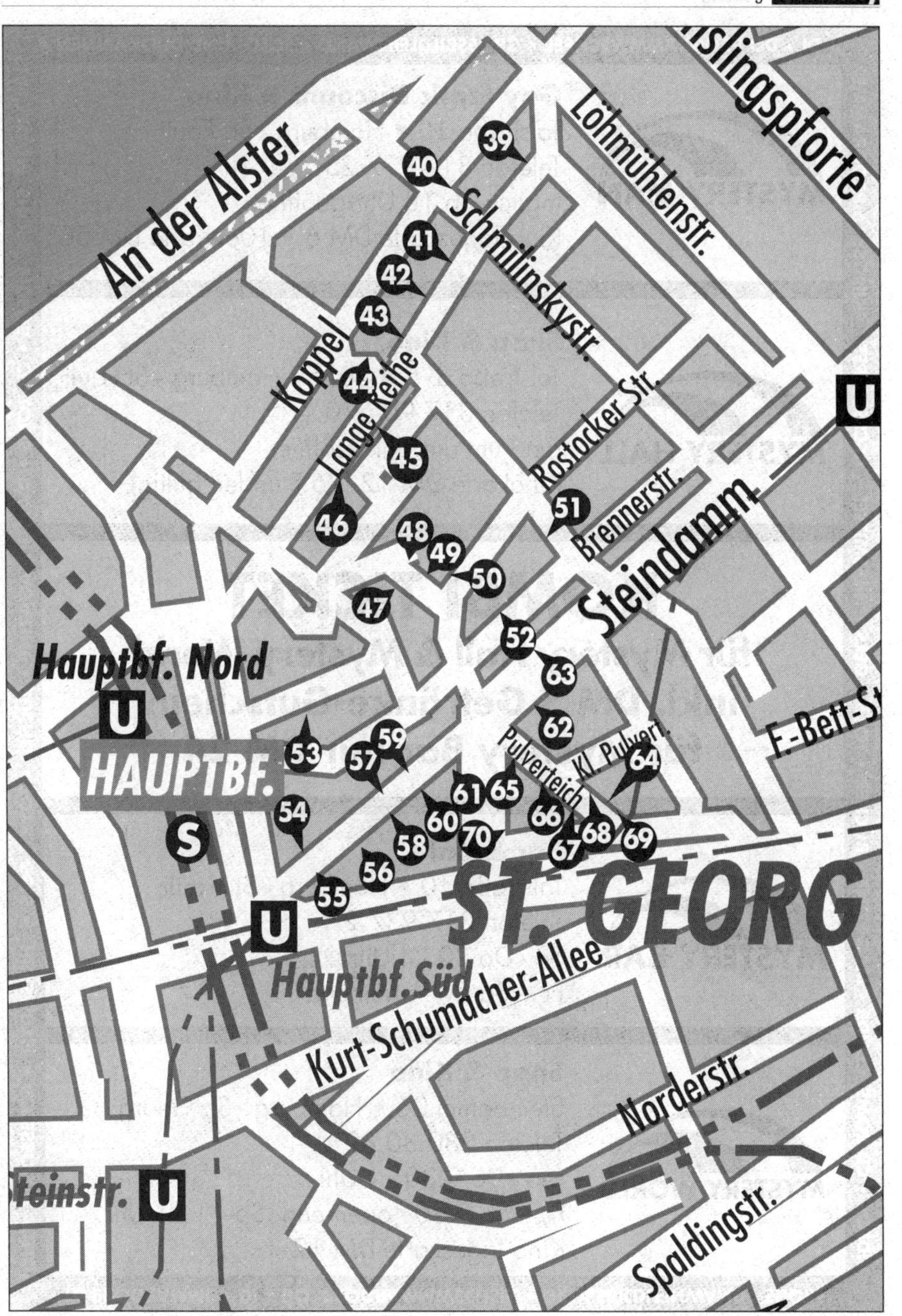
An der Alster
Löhmühlenstr.
Schmilinskystr.
Koppel
Lange Reihe
Rostocker Str.
Brennerstr.
Steindamm
Hauptbf. Nord
HAUPTBF.
Pulverteich
Kl. Pulvert.
F.-Bett-St
ST. GEORG
Hauptbf. Süd
Kurt-Schumacher-Allee
Norderstr.
Spaldingstr.
Steinstr.
39
40
41
42
43
44
45
46
47
48
49
50
51
52
53
54
55
56
57
58
59
60
61
62
63
64
65
66
67
68
69
70

☆ El ambiente caracteristico de una ciudad portuaria se hace notar en Hamburgo por todas partes. El barrio St. Pauli en las alrededores de la *Reeperbahn* ofreció en el pasado a innumerables marineros diversión variada despúes de un largo viaje en alta mar. Hoy en día este districto se ha convertido para los hamburgeses y los numerosos visitantes de la ciudad en una zona de marcha nocturna. El turista gay que busque bares, clubs o sexo pagado, encuentra aquí indudablemente de todo. Hamburgo no solamente es la segunda ciudad portuaria más grande de Europa, sino además un importantísimo centro comercial que tiene mucho más que ofrecer. El parque municipal, los elegantes barrios a orillas del río Elba, tanto como el lago Alster son dignos de ver. Pero también la gastronomia con sus exquisitos restaurantes y la amplia vida cultural con teatros y museos ofrece algo para cada gusto. En el barrio de *St. Georg*, cerca de la estación central, en la calle *Lange Reihe* se ha desarollado en los últimos años un animado ambiente gay. Aquí se pasean parejas homosexuales cogidos de la mano y el tradicional *Café Gnosa* seduce con sus buenísimas tartas. La libreria *Blendwerk* ofrece una amplia gama de literatura gay y en la tienda *Mr. Chaps* se encuentra de todo hecho de cuero o latex. La *Lange Reihe* no cae lejos de la zona de marcha en las alrededores del *Pulverteich*, también ubicado en el barrio de St. Georg, donde merecen los clubs p.i.t, Tom's o Rudi's una visita. El visitante de Hamburgo notará en seguida que esta ciudad se caracteriza por su variedad, belleza y ambiente hospitalario. Aunque el típico hamburgés tiene fama de ser introvertido, una vez que se haya conquistado el corazón de uno, será una amistad para toda la vida.

❖ L'atmosfera di una città portuale si sente dappertutto ad Amburgo. Una volta il quartiere alle luci rosse attorno alla Reeperbahn in St. Pauli offriva ai numerosi marinai diverse opportunità di svago dopo un lungo viaggio sul mare. Oggi sono gli abitanti ed i turisti della città delle repubbliche marinare tedesche, le Hanse, che passano le loro serate nella famosa strada. Qualunque cosa ci si cerchi, un bar, un club o sesso a pagamento, il turista gay trova di tutto. A parte il porto, che è il secondo in Europa come vastità, la metropoli economica Amburgo offre molto di più. Il parco comunale e i sobborghi lungo i fiumi Elba e Alster valgono la pena di una gita; ristoranti squisiti offrono cibo prelibato; teatri e musei soddisfanno ogni gusto e la via Lange Reihe in St. Georg, il secondo quartiere a luci rosse vicino alla stazione centrale, è diventato negli ultimi anni un vivace ambiente gay. Qui i gay camminano tenendosi per mano. Il tradizionale *Café Gnosa* invita a gustosissime torte, nel *Blendwerk* si trova letteratura gay, nel *Mr. Chaps* si trova lacca e cuoio. Poco distanta dalla *Lange Reihe* si trova un quartiere altrettanto situato in *St. Georg* attorno al *Pulverteich* che offre svariate occasioni per uscire di sera come il *p.i.t, Tom's* o *Rudi's Nightclub*. Il visitatore si renderà velocemente conto della varietà, bellezza e gentilezza della città, anche se ci vuole un po' di pazienza per fare la conoscenza di un vero nativo d'Amburgo. Ma quando si ha rapito il cuore di „un'aurora boreale", si ha trovato un'amico per tutta la vita.

GAY INFO

Hamburg von hinten
c/o Bruno Gmünder Verlag, PO Box 61 01 04 ✉10921 Berlin
☎ 030/615 00 30 Fax: 030/615 90 07
E-Mail: info@spartacus.de *The city guide book about Hamburg and Hanover. Useful general information and lots of addresses with extensive descriptions in English and German. Up-to-date maps. Erotic photos.*

Hamburger Gay Information 8-16 h
PO Box 60 54 20 ✉22249 ☎ 46 27 02 Fax: 460 27 69.
Homepage: www.gaycity.de/hgi
Monthly newsletter with advertising and dates of events. Free at gay venues.

Hein & Fiete (G lj MA s) Mon-Fri 18-21, Sat 16-19 h
Pulverteich 21, St Georg ✉20099 *(U/S-Hauptbahnhof)*
☎ 24 03 33 Fax: 24 06 75
The LSVD meets every 2nd Wed / month at 19:30h in the „Regenbogen Café" ☛ AIDSHILFE

Hinnerk Mon-Fri 14-18 h
Koppel 97 ✉20099 ☎ 24 06 45 Fax: 24 06 50
Email: redaktion@hinnerk.deHomepage: http://www.hinnerk.de
Monthly free fay magazine for Hamburg featuring news, reports and addresses.

Magnus Hirschfeld Centrum/Kommunikations- und Beratungszentrum für Homosexuelle Mon-Fri 16-01:00h, Fri - open end, Sat from 15:00h, Sun from 11:00h
Borgweg 8 ✉22303 *(U-Borgweg)* ☎ 27 87 78 00
Fax: 278 778 02 Homepage: www.mhc@hamburg.gay-web.de
Counselling ☎ 279 00 69. Gay center with Café and library . Ask for their programme and all the groups meeting here

Pink Channel - Radio für Schwule Sat 19-20, 1st and 3rd Sat 19-21 & 22-23h, FM 96.0 MHz
Pulverteich 23 ✉20099 ☎ 280 51 29-0 Fax: 280 51 29-1.
E-Mail: PinkCH@pso.de Homepage: www.pso.de/channel

Radio Schwarzer Adler 3rd Tue 21-22 h at
OK Hamburg, Ferdinand-Beit-Straße 9 ✉20099 ☎ 24 92 73
Gay leather- and SM-radio.

Schwulenkultur e.V. Mon Wed Thu 19-21, Sat 16-19 h
Kleiner Pulverteich 23 ✉20099 *(U/S Hauptbahnhof)*
☎ 28 05 49 13

Szene-Guide Fun World Studio, Breite Straße 60 ✉22767
☎ 38 41 94 Fax: 38 87 05. E-Mail: sgh@funworld.de
Homepage: www.funworld.de
Advertising, maps and some dates of events. Free at gay venues.

TOURIST INFO

Tourismus-Zentrale Hamburg GmbH 8-20 h
PO Box 10 22 49 ✉20015 ☎ 30 05 10
E-Mail: Info@hamburg-tourism.de
Homepage: www.hamburg-tourism.de

BARS

Amigo Bar (B G MA N) 21-? h
Taubenstraße 23 ✉20359 *(S-Reeperbahn/U-St.Pauli)*
☎ 31 64 36

Angie's NightClub (AC B CC glm S TV WE) Wed-Sat 22-? h
Spielbudenplatz 27-28 ✉20359 *(S-Reeperbahn/U-St.Pauli)*
☎ 31 77 88-0

Bajadere (B G N R s) 14-4 h
Rostocker Straße 1 ✉20099 *(S-Hauptbahnhof)* ☎ 24 01 52

Baustelle (B G YG) Thu 21-? h
Kleiner Schäferkamp ✉20357
Low priced drinks and fun atmosphere

Black (AC bf D DR G LJ MA VS) 22-4, Fri Sat -6 h
Danziger Straße 21 ✉20099 *(S-Hauptbahnhof)* ☎ 24 08 04
Dresscode

Can Can (B F G MA N) 12-4, WE 0-24 h
Danziger Straße 63 ✉20099 *(U/S-Hauptbahnhof)* ☎ 24 60 51

Central (B d F g MA OS) Mon-Thu 12-24, Fri & Sat -2, Sun 15-24 h
Lange Reihe 50 ✉20099 *(S/U-Hauptbahnhof)* ☎ 28 05 37 04
Large selection of vegetarian meals.

Chaps (B DR G LJ MG VS) Sun-Thu 20-?, Fri-Sat 22-? h
Woltmanstraße 24 ✉20097 *(S-Hauptbahnhof)* ☎ 23 06 47

Comeback (B f G N R) 12-2 h
Zimmerpforte 3 ✉20099 ☎ 28 05 38 43

Crazy Horst (B bf CC f g MA N) 21-8 h
Hein-Hoyer-Straße 62 ✉20359 *(S-Reeperbahn)* ☎ 319 26 33

Du & Ich (B f G MA N P r VS) Sun-Thu 20-4, Fri-Sat 21-? h, closed Wed
Seilerstraße 38a ✉20359 *(S-Reeperbahn/U-St.Pauli)*
☎ 31 59 69

Extratour (B f G MA OS r YG) Mon-Thu 11-3, Fri-Sun -4 h
Zimmerpforte 1 ✉20099 *(S-Hauptbahnhof)* ☎ 24 01 84

Fehmarn-Stube (B G N OG) 17-1, Sat 20-? h, closed Sun
Landwehr 35 ✉22087 *(U-Wartenau)* ☎ 254 27 54

Ferdi's (B G MA) Mon-Sat 11-2, Sun (summer closed) 15-2 h
Ferdinandstraße 2a ✉20095 ☎ 30 39 27 63

Franz. Bei (B bf f G MA OS TV) Mon-Sat 18-11, Sun closed
Steindamm 37 ✉20099 *(U/S-Hauptbahnhof)* ☎ 280 25 12

Fundus (B bf f G MA N OS R) 0-24 h
Detlef-Bremer-Straße 54 ✉20359 *(S-Reeperbahn/U-St.Pauli)*
☎ 319 17 26

Goldene 13 (B d GLM MA TV) Wed-Sun 21-? h
Hopfenstraße 28 ✉20359 *(S-Reeperbahn/U-St. Pauli)*
☎ 31 79 26 05
Nice atmosphere
Hansa Molle (B f G MA N) 0-24 h
Stralsunder Straße 4 ✉20099 *(S-Hauptbahnhof)* ☎ 24 50 05
Ika (B d gLM MA) Wed Thu 19-24, Fri Sat 21-? h
Budapester Straße 38, ✉20359 ☎ 31 09 98
Jürgens Pub & Bar (B G N R) Mon-Thu 11-3, Fri Sat 10-?, Sun 12-4 h
Hansaplatz 1 ✉20099 *(S-Hauptbahnhof)* ☎ 24 95 92
Male (B CC DR f G lj MA VS) Mon-Sun 20-? h, connected to Pit-Disco
Pulverteich 17 ✉20099 *(S-Hauptbahnhof)* ☎ 280 30 56
My Way (B G MA OS r) Sun-Thu 19-4
Brennerstraße 2 ✉20099 *(S-Hauptbahnhof)* ☎ 24 08 16
Mystery Hall (A AC B bf CC d DR f G lj MA s VS) Mon-Thu 20-?, Fri Sun 15-? h
Talstraße 10 ✉20359 *(S-Reeperbahn)* ☎ 31 79 37 27
Olli's Down Town (B d f G MA OS) daily 20-? h
Gustav-Freytag-Straße 9 ✉22085 0 *(near Alster)* ☎ 22 71 78 51
Piccadilly (B G MA og) 20-4 h, closed Thu
Silbersacktwiete 1 ✉20359 *(S-Reeperbahn)* ☎ 319 24 74
Purgatory (AC B d glm MA N WE) Sun-Thu 22-4, Fri-Sat -6 h
Friedrichstraße 8 ✉20359 *(S-Reeperbahn)* ☎ 31 58 07
Rendezvous (B bf f G MA N) Mon-Thu 19-2, Fri-Sat -4, Sun 16-24 h
Pulverteich 18 ✉20099 *(S-Hauptbahnhof)* ☎ 28 05 14 37
Romeo (B G R) 9-3, Fri-Sun 0-24 h
Zimmerpforte 2 ✉20099 *(S-Hauptbahnhof, Near/Nähe Hansaplatz)* ☎ 280 17 38
Rudi's Night Club (B CC f G lj MA R) 18-8, Fri-Sat -? h
Steindamm 58 ✉20099 *(S-Hauptbahnhof)* ☎ 24 72 74
Popular.
Schmidts Tivoli (AC B bf f glm MA OS) 10-2, Fri-Sat -4 h
Spielbudenplatz 27-28 ✉20359 *(S-Reeperbahn/U-St. Pauli)*
☎ 31 77 88-0
Theatre: beginning 20, Sun 19 h
Schmidt-Theater (B f glm OS S) 17-?, Mon closed
Spielbudenplatz 24 ✉20359 *(S-Reeperbahn/U-St.Pauli)*
☎ 31 77 88-0
Schuh. Café (AC B G lj MA OS) Mon-Thu 17-1, Fri-Sat -?, Sun 15-24/? h
im Dammtorbahnhof ✉20354 *(U/S-Dammtorbahnhof)* ☎ 44 09 58
Seagull (B f G MA N s) Mon-Fri 18-?, Sat 20-?, Sun 16-? h
Detlev-Bremer-Straße 37 ✉20359 *(S-Reeperbahn/U-St.Pauli)*
☎ 31 01 28
Seute Dern (B gLM N) 17-? h
Kohlhöfen 15 ✉20355 *(Near Großneumarkt)* ☎ 34 26 63
Tom's Saloon (! A B DR G LJ MA VS) 22-? h
Pulverteich 17 ✉20099 *(S-Hauptbahnhof)* ☎ 280 30 56
Very popular on Wed and weekends.
Toom Peerstall (B f G MA) 14-4, Fri-Sat -9 h
Clemens-Schultz-Straße 44 ✉20359 *(S-Reeperbahn/U-St. Pauli)*
☎ 319 35 23
Touche (B G MA N) Tue-Sat 18-?, bf Sun from 4 h
Clemens-Schultz-Straße 42 ✉20359
Tusculum (B F G MA N OS s) Mon-Sun 0-24 h
Kreuzweg 6 ✉20099 *(S-Hauptbahnhof)* ☎ 280 36 06
Uhlenhorster Stübchen (B f G MG N) Sun-Thu 20-4 h, Fri-Sat 20-? h
Schenkendorfstraße 3 ✉22085 ☎ 227 36 86
Popular.
Willi's For You! (B f G lj MA) 16-1?h
Markusstraße 4 ✉20355 *(S-Stadthausbrücke)* ☎ 348 03 88
WunderBar (AC B d G MA WE YG) Sun-Thu 21-4 h, Fri Sat -7 h
Talstraße 14 ✉20359 *(S-Reeperbahn)* ☎ 317 44 44
Trendy and popular. Disco at the weekend.

CAFES

Bistro des Artistes (B bf F G MA OS) 15-?, Sun 11-?, meals 17-23 h, Sun brunch from 11 h
Schmilinskystraße 19/Koppel ✉20099 *(S-Hauptbahnhof)*
☎ 24 60 83
Cosy. Café (B f g OS YG) Mon-Fri 11-2 h, Sat 19-3 h
Beim Schlump 5/Grindelallee, ✉20144 *(U-Schlump, Bus102/105)* ☎ 45 89 68
Feel Good (f GLM MA s) Mon-Thu 16-01:00h, Fri & Sat open end, Sun 11-22:00h
Borgweg 8 ✉22303 ☎ 278 77801
Breakfast only on Sun 11-15:00h
Fradkin. Café (B bf glm MA) 10-24, Sun 11-24 h
Eulenstraße 49 ✉22765 *(S-Altona)* ☎ 390 31 83
Gnosa. Café (! A bf f GLM OS YG) 11-1, Mon 18-1, Fri-Sat -2 h
Lange Reihe 93 ✉20093 *(S/U-Hauptbahnhof)* ☎ 24 30 34
Very popular, an institution.
Magnus. Café (A B D f GLM MA s W YG) 15-24
Borgweg 8 ✉22303 *(U-Borgweg)* ☎ 27 87 78 01
Mistral. Café (B F GLM MA OS) 16-1.30 h, meals 17.30-23.30 h
Lehmweg 29 ✉20251 ☎ 420 77 02
Popular.
Spund. Café (B G lj MA OS) 10-24 h, Sun 15-24 h
Mohlenhofstraße 3 ✉20095 *(U-Mönckebergstraße. Near Hauptbahnhof)* ☎ 32 65 77

enjoy
striped nights
at:
E.D.K.!
E.D.K. house-club
Gerhardstr. 3
Hamburg St. Pauli
edk@skipfuture.de
fax: (+49) 040 319 56 45

Twist. Café-Bar (b f glm OS) Mon-Sat 8-20 h, Sun closed
Carl-von-Ossietzky-Platz 1 ✉20099 *(S-Hauptbahnhof)*
☎ 280 17 39

Uferlos. Café (B bf F glm MA OS S) 11-? h
Barmbeker Straße 62 ✉22303 ☎ 279 24 55

Uhrlaub. Café (B bf F glm MA OS) 8-2 h
Lange Reihe 63 ✉20099 *(S-Hauptbahnhof)* ☎ 280 26 24

Unter den Linden (B bf f glm MA OS) 11-1 h
Juliusstraße 16 ✉22769 *(U-Feldstraße)* ☎ 43 81 40
Popular

Winterhuder Kaffeehaus (b bf f glm MA) 9-24, Sun 10-24 h
Winterhuder Marktplatz 16 ✉22299 *(U-Hudtwalckerstraße)*
☎ 47 82 00

DANCECLUBS

Camelot (B D GLM YG) Fri 22-? h
Hamburger Berg 13, ✉20359 *(S-Reeperbahn)* ☎ 317 44 89
Popular.

Clubika (B D GLM MA) Fri 22-? h
Budapester Straße 38 ✉20359 *(U-Feldstraße)* ☎ 030/31 09 98

Disco im MHC (B d f GLM MA W) last Sat/month 22-? h
Borgweg 8 ✉22303 *(U-Borgweg)* ☎ 27 87 78 00

E.D.K. (AC B D glm MA p s TV W WE) Fri Sat and before public holydays 0-?h
Gerhardstraße 3 ✉20359 *(S-Reeperbahn)* ☎ 319 56 45

Gay Factory (! B D GLM MA s) monthly Sat 22-? h
Fabrik, Barnerstraße 36 ✉22765 *(S-Altona)* ☎ 39 10 70

Gaylaxy (B D DR G) irregularly Sat 22-? h
at Pleasure Dome, Anckelmannplatz ✉20537 *(S/U-Berliner Tor)*
Check local press for dates and varying location.

La Cage aux Folles (! AC CC D G MA SNU STV) Sun 23-6 h
c/o La Cage, Reeperbahn 136 ✉20359 *(U-Reeperbahn)*
☎ 317 90 481 *Entrance-fee DM 15.*

Paola Club (B D Glm S) Fri 22 h
Lucky Strike, Nobistor 10 ✉22767

P.i.t. (! AC B D G YG) Wed-Sat 23-? h; connected to cruise bar Male
Pulverteich 17 ✉20099 *(S-Hauptbahnhof)* ☎ 280 30 56

Powderroom at Absolut (! B D GLM TV WE YG) Sat 23-5 h
Hans-Albers-Platz 15 ✉20359 *(S-Reeperbahn/U-St.Pauli)*
☎ 317 34 00
One of the best places in town.

Salvation (B D G MA) 2nd/4th Sat 22-? h
c/o Heaven, Anckelmannplatz 3 ✉20357 *(S-Berliner Tor)*
Popular

Spundloch (B CC D f G MA) Wed Thu Sun 21-4 h, Fri Sat 22-? h
Paulinenstraße 19 ✉20359 *(U-Feldstraße)* ☎ 31 07 98

Swoosh Club. The (B D glm MA) Sat 23-? h
Neuer Kamp 30 ✉20357

RESTAURANTS

Freudenhaus (CC F glm MA) Every day from 18:00- ?
Hein-Hoyer-Straße 7-9/Seilerstraße ✉20359 *(U-St. Pauli/S-Reeperbahn)* ☎ 31 46 42
The only restaurant in St. Pauli serving German cuisine. Interesting.

Mess (B F NG) Mon-Fri 12-15, Mon-Sun 18-1h
Turnerstraße 9 ✉20357 *(U-Feldstraße/Messehallen)* ☎ 43 41 23
Nil (B F glm MA OS) Mon-Fri 12-14.30, Mon-Wed 18.30-24 h
Am Pferdemarkt 5 ✉20359 *(U-Feldstraße)* ☎ 439 78 23
Very good food, reservation recommended.
Opus (B F glm MA OS) Sun, Tue-Thu 18.30-23, Fri Sat -24 h, closed Mon
Max-Brauer-Allee 80 ✉22765 *(S-Altona/Holstenstraße)*
☎ 389 28 39
Phuket (B F g MA) 18-24 h, closed Mon
Davidstraße 31 ✉20359 *(U-St. Pauli/S-Reeperbahn)* ☎ 31 58 54
Good Thai cuisine
Schlößchen (AC F g lj MA NG) 18-? h, closed Mon
Kastanienallee 28 ✉20359 *(S-Reeperbahn, U-St.Pauli)*
☎ 31 77 88-16
Schlößchen (AC B CC F glm MA) Tue-Sat 18-? h
Kastanienallee 32 ✉20359 *(U-St. Pauli/S-Reeperbahn)*
☎ 31 77 88 16
Störtebecker (B F g MA) Mon-Fri 11-22 h
Bernhard-Nocht-Straße 68 ✉20359 *(U-St. Pauli/S-Reeperbahn)*
☎ 31 54 40
Nice view on the river Elbe. Good food.
Vasco da Gama (B CC F glm MA) 12-24 h
Danziger Straße 21 ✉20099 ☎ 280 33 05
Portugese and Spanish cuisine
Weite Welt (A AC B d F g MA NG OS) Mon-Thu 18-24 h, Fri-Sat 18-1 h
Große Freiheit 70 ✉22767 *(S-Reeperbahn)* ☎ 319 12 14
Fine dining in a beautiful garden. Reservation recommended.

SHOWS

Pulverfass Cabaret (B F g STV) Shows 20.30, 23.15, 2 h; entrance 19.30 h
Pulverteich 12 ✉20099 *(U/S-Hauptbahnhof)* Fax: 280 23 47
Diner shows. Please call for details
Schmidt (Theater, Kneipe, Varieté) (AC B CC MA NG S) Tickets 12-19 h ☎ 31 77 88-99
Spielbudenplatz 27-28 ✉20359 *(U-St. Pauli/S-Reeperbahn*
☎ 31 77 88-0 Fax: 31 77 88-74.
Restaurant: Tue-Sat 18-?h; Nightclub: Wed-Sat 22-?h Also Tivoli-der Kulturpalast

SEX SHOPS/BLUE MOVIES

Erotic Kino Shop (g VS) Sun-Thu 11-4, Fri-Sat 0-24 h
Talstraße 2/Reeperbahn ✉20359 *(S-Reeperbahn)* ☎ 319 37 68
Erotica Kino-Center (g VS) 10-4, Sun 14-24 h
Hein-Hoyer-Straße 12/Reeperbahn ✉20359 *(S-Reeperbahn)*
☎ 31 28 32
Henry's Show Center (g VS) 9-2, Fri Sat -4 h
Steindamm 7 ✉20099 *(U/S-Hauptbahnhof)*
Homo Gay Kino und Shop (g VS) Mon-Sat 10-24, Sun & holidays 12-24 h
Clemens-Schultz-Straße 43 ✉20359 *(S-Reeperbahn)* ☎ 31 50 68
Homo Kino Hamburg (! AC CC DR G lj MA VS) 0-24 h
Talstraße 8 ✉20359 *(S-Reeperbahn, U-St.Pauli)* ☎ 31 24 95
Mystery Hall (G lj u VS) 0-24 h
Talstraße 3-5/Reeperbahn ✉20359 ☎ 31 79 05 70
Mystery World (glm VS)
Steindamm 26 ✉20359 ☎ 280 30 82
New Man City (! CC G VS) Mon-Thu 10-0.30, Fri Sat -5, Sun 13-0.30 h
Pulverteich 8, ✉20099 *(Near/Nähe Hauptbahnhof)* ☎ 24 01 49
Popular.
New Man im WOS (CC G VS) 9.30-0.30, Sun 11-24 h
Steindamm 16-22, ✉20999 *(U/S-Hauptbahnhof)* ☎ 24 16 95
New Man Plaza (! CC G VS) Mon-Thu 10-0.30, Fri Sat -1.30, Sun 13-0.30 h
Steindamm 21, ✉20099 *(U/S-Hauptbahnhof)* ☎ 24 52 31
Seventh Heaven (g VS) 0-24 h
Reeperbahn 61 ✉20359 ☎ 31 12 61
Seventh Heaven (g VS) 9-1 h
Steindamm 24 ✉20099 *(U/S-Hauptbahnhof)* ☎ 28 05 38 70
Seventh Heaven Erotic Discount (CC G) 0-24 h
Steindamm 14 ✉20359 ☎ 28 05 63 92
Sexshop Reeperbahn 118 (g) 0-24 h
Reeperbahn 118/Talstraße ✉20359 *(S-Reeperbahn)*
☎ 317 53 16
Sexy Heaven (AC CC DR g) 0-24 h
Spielbudenplatz 5/Reeperbahn ✉20359
Sparta City (G VS) Mon-Thu 10-24, Fri Sat -1, Sun 12-24 h
Lange Reihe 93 ✉20099 *(U/S-Hauptbahnhof/Bus108)*
☎ 280 27 41
Sparta Gay (! G VS) 0-24 h
Hein-Hoyer-Straße 5-7 ✉20359 ☎ 319 62 29
Sparta Junior (G VS) Sun-Thu 10-1, Fri-Sat -6 h
Seilerstraße 49 ✉20359 *(U-St.Pauli/S-Reeperbahn)* ☎ 31 40 95
Sparta Point (! G VS) 0-24 h
Talstraße 18 ✉20359 *(S-Reeperbahn)*
Sparta Shop (G) 9-2 h
Reeperbahn 54 ✉20359

HOUSE OF BOYS

☛Hotels with the codes „B" and „R".

SAUNAS/BATHS

Apollo Sauna (B G MA msg sa sol VS) 13-24 h
Max-Brauer-Allee 277 ✉22769 *(U/S-Sternschanze/Bus112)*
☎ 43 48 11
Admission DM 20-22.
Dragon Sauna (AC B CC DR F G MA msg sa sb sol VS wh YG) Mon-Thu 12-1, Fri 12-Mon 1 h
Pulverteich 37 ✉20099 *(U/S-Hauptbahnhof)* ☎ 24 05 14

BOOK SHOPS

Blendwerk (A CC glm) Mon-Fri 11-19, Sat -16 h
Lange Reihe 73 ✉20099 ☎ 24 00 03
Buchladen Männerschwarm (CC GLM MA) Mon-Fri 10-19, Sat -16 h, closed Sun
Neuer Pferdemarkt 32, St Pauli ✉20359 *(U-Feldstraße)*
☎ 43 60 93 ☎ 430 26 50
Stilke Aktuell (g) Bahnhof Altona UG, Paul-Nevermann-Platz ✉22765 ☎ 39 77 94

CONDOM SHOPS

Condomerie Sun-Thu 12-1, Fri Sat 11-15 h
Spielbudenplatz 18 ✉20359 *(U-St.Pauli)* ☎ 319 31 00

GIFT & PRIDE SHOPS

Clemens Gay Store (CC G) Mon-Fri 11-19, Sat -16 h, closed Sun
Clemens-Schultz-Straße 77 ✉20359 *(U-St. Pauli)* ☎ 31 79 17 63
Fax: 31 79 17 64 Homepage: www.clemensHH.de
Gay shop. Also Mail-Order and Online-Shopping.

LEATHER & FETISH SHOPS

B-Shop 10-23 h
Steindamm 4 ✉20099 ☎ 24 80 30

NEW
MAN
Shops & Kinos

Günter Skarupke by appointment
Cuxhavener Straße 266 ✉21149 ☎ 701 73 88

Mr. Chaps Leatherworks (G CC LJ) Mon-Fri 11-19, Sat 11-15 h
Gurlittstraße 47 ✉20099 *(U/S-Hauptbahnhof/Bus108)*
☎ 24 31 09
Fax: 24 60 97. Email Fairland-Group@t-online.de. Tailor made fashion in leather and latex. Sales of toys, rubber, leather, rubberboots, gloves and pants.

Used Second Hand Shop Mon-Fri 15-19, Sat 12-15 h
Koppel 107 ✉20099 *(S/U-Hauptbahnhof)* ☎ 24 59 79

TRAVEL & TRANSPORT

Reisebüro am Hellkamp (CC) Mon-Fri 10-18.30, Sat 10.30-13h
Hellkamp 17, ✉20255 *(U-Osterstraße)* ☎ 40 19 61 86 or ☎ 0800 20 255 00 (freecall) Fax: 491 91 00
E-Mail: hellkamp@aol.com Homepage: www.gaytravel.de

Reisepunkt Eppendorf Mon-Fri 9-18, Sat 10-13 h
Eppendorfer Weg 193 ✉20253 ☎ 422 22 61 *Travel agency.*

Ticket Kontor (CC glm MA) 10-18.45 h, Sat 11-15 h
Feldstraße 37 ✉20357 *(U-Feldstraße)* ☎ 430 10 76
Fax: 430 34 58

Ticket Kontor II Mon-Fri 10-19, Sat 11-15 h
Lange Reihe 91 ✉20099 *(next to Café Gnosa)* ☎ 24 50 56
Fax: 24 92 44. *Travel agency.*

HOTELS

Adria Hof (g H) 0-24 h
Ellmenreichstraße 24 ✉20099 ☎ 24 62 80 Fax: 24 62 80
Email: Hamburg@gaytel.de Homepage: www.gaytel.de
Single from DM 80, double from 100. All rooms with shower, WC, TV and safe.

Eden Hotel Garni (bf CC glm MA) 0-24 h
Ellmenreichstraße 20 ✉20099 *(near main station)* ☎ 24 84 80
Fax: 24 15 21. Rates (incl. shower/bath & WC, breakfast) -Single DM 130-170. -Double DM 190-225. Additional bed DM 50.

Florida Hotel / Bar Exquisit (B bf G H S) 0-24 h
Spielbudenplatz 22 ✉20395 ☎ 31 43 93 *Fax: 317 45 54.*

Galerie-Pension Sarah Petersen (A b bf glm H MA OS s) 8-23 h and by appointment
Lange Reihe 50 ✉20099 ☎ 24 98 26 Fax: 24 98 26
Homepage: www.galerie-hotel-sarah-petersen.de
Centrally located, very close to the gay scene. Newly restaured landmark. Prices from DM 100 to 320 (incl. bf), mini-bar, kitchenette, desks and fax. All rooms with shower and cable TV.

Harald's Hotel & Bar (B CC f G H lj MA R s SNU) 0-24 h
Reeperbahn 54 ✉20359 *(S-Reeperbahn)* ☎ 31 33 63
Fax: 31 33 60 *Also bar! Only gay hotel direct on the Reeperbahn. Comfortable rooms. Close to theatres.*

Königshof. Hotel (A bf CC GLM H LJ OS) 7-22 h
Pulverteich 18 ✉20099 *(near main station)*
☎ 28 40 74 0 Fax: 28 40 74 74
E-Mail: Hotelkhh@aol.com
Homepage: www.members.aol.com/hotelkhh.
18 double and 4 single rooms with shower/WC. All rooms have phone, cable-TV, Fax, radio, heating. Hotel provides own key and parking. Rates single from DM 80-130, double from DM 135-160 (bf incl.)

Nord. Hotel (bf CC H)
Bremer Reihe 22 ✉20099 ☎ 280 51 733 Fax: 280 51 733
Singles DM 60, Doubles DM 120 (bf incl.)

Schweriner Hof. Hotel (CC E glm H)
Steindamm 19 ✉20099 ☎ 280 4323 Fax: 280 4224
Homepage: www.funworld.de/Schweriner-Hof.
Single rooms from 60,- DM, Double rooms from 85,-

Village. Hotel (bf CC GLM H MA)
Steindamm 4, St Georg ✉20099 ☎ 24 61 37 Fax: 45 03 00 30
Homepage: www.Hotel-Village.de
17 rooms and 4 apartments. Most rooms with shower/WC, balcony, telephone, Fax, Sat-TV, radio, heating, own key. Doubles from DM 70-140, singles DM 90-145 and apartments (information upon request), bf DM 12.

GUEST HOUSES

Ars Vivendi-Gästehaus am Deich (bf CC msg pi)
Stormarnstraße 5, Glückstadt ✉25348 *(Bus-Marktplatz)*
☎ 04124/937311 Fax: 93 73 12
E-Mail: ars-vivendi-gaestehausadeich@t-online.de
Homepage: www.glorylands-palace.com/ars.vivendi.htm
3 rooms and 1 apartment. Shower/WC, phone/fax, TV/video, safe.

PRIVATE ACCOMODATION

Enjoy Bed & Breakfast (bf G H MA YG) 16:30-21 h
Motzstraße 5 ✉10777 ☎ 030/215 16 66
Fax: 030/217 52219
E-Mail: info@ebab.com Homepage: www.ebab.com
Price 40 DM. Accommodation sharing agency. All rooms with shower and bf.

Schwule Übernachtungsmöglichkeiten 19-21, Sat 16-19 h, closed Sun
c/o Hein & Fiete, Kleiner Pulverteich 17-21 ✉20099
☎ 24 03 33

GENERAL GROUPS

Arbeitskreis Homosexualität in der ÖTV Hamburg
☎ 285 81 20

Big Spender Mon-Fri 11-17 h, Sat + Sun closed
Brennerstraße 90 ✉20099 ☎ 24 00 62
Organisers of the „Walk against AIDS" and the big „Red, Hot & Dance Party" every December.

International Association for Worldwide Queenism
c/o Männerschwarm, Neuer Pferdemarkt 32 ✉20359
Magazine: Die Putte

LAG Schwulesbenpolitik im Bündnis '90/GAL/Die Grünen
c/o Thomas Mohr, Bahrenfelder Straße 244 ✉22765
☎ 280 47 17

Plenum Sexualität und Herrschaft Mon 20.30 h
Brigittenstraße 5 ✉20359

Schwule Väter und Ehemänner Meets 1st/3rd Tue in room 12 at 20 h
c/o Kulturzentrum Rieckhof, Rieckhofstraße 12 ✉21073
☎ 765 36 74 *(Bernd) or* ☎ *75 98 35 (Thomas)*

Schwulenreferat im AStA der Uni Hamburg
Tue Thu 16-18 h
Van-Melle-Park 5 ✉20146 ☎ 45 02 04 37

Schwusos Hamburg 1st Tue
c/o SPD-Haus, Kurt-Schumacher-Allee 10 ✉20097 ☎ 692 85 23

SPI-Schwestern der Perpetuellen Indulgenz
c/o Maikowski, Querstraße 5 ✉20359
Organization for AIDS prevention.

Tom & Jerry (G YG) Fri 19 h
c/o Hein & Fiete, Pulverteich 21 ✉20999 *(St. Georg)*
☎ 24 03 33 E-Mail: TomJerryHH@yahoo.com
Homepage: www.hamburg-web.de/tom+jerry
Group for young gays until 26 years. Meetings at Hein & Fiete.

Transsexuellentreff Thu 18 h
c/o Goldbekhaus, Moorfurthweg 9 ✉22301

New in Hamburg
Nord

WHERE BOYS BECOME MEN
Harald's
HOTEL
& BAR
· the only GAY Hotel in the heart of St.Pauli
· on the famous Reeperbahn
· 24 hour service and bar
· individual rooms with shower, WC, phone, TV
· daily from 7 a.m. breakfast-buffet
· parkingspace is available

FETISH GROUPS

LCH Hamburg e.V. Meets 1st Thu at Chaps, 2nd at Black, 3rd at Toms, 4th at Willi's For You
c/o Reiner Hölscher, Reineckestraße 16 ✉22761 ☎ 899 12 23
E-Mail: 100773.562@compuserve.com
Every 4th Sun the members meeting takes place at Haus der Judend, Bei der Schilleroper.

MSC Hamburg e.V. Meets 2nd/4th Fri at Chaps 22-? h
☛ Bars
PO Box 30 36 83 ✉20312 E-Mail: mschamburg@aol.com

HEALTH GROUPS

AIDS-Hilfe Hamburg e.V. Mon, Wed, Thu 9-12, 13-16, Tue, Fri 9-12 Paul-Roosen-Straße 43 ✉22767 ☎ 319 69 81
Fax: 319 69 84.Email: aidshilfe-hamburg.de
Counselling ☎ 194 11 Mon-Fri 19-21 h
Regenbogen-Café Sun 15-18, Breakfast at Regenbogen Café Wed 10-12 h. Ask for different groups and activities including the LSVD which meets every 2nd Wed/moth at 19:00h

Hamburg Leuchtfeuer AIDS-Hilfe GmbH
Mon-Fri 8.30-16 h
Unzerstraße 1-3 ✉22767 ☎ 38 73 80 Fax: 38 61 10 12
E-Mail: hospiz@hamburg-leuchtfeuer.de
Homepage: www.hamburg-leuchtfeuer.de

HELP WITH PROBLEMS

Basis Projekt e.V. Mon 15-19, Tue-Fri 12-16; Counselling Wed 11-16 h
St. Georgs Kirchhof 26 ✉20099 ☎ 280 16 07

Beratung für Schwule Mon-Fri 14-18, Tue Wed 19-22 h
c/o MHC, Borgweg 8, ✉22303 ☎ 279 00 69

Homosexuellenberatung im Beratungs- und Seelsorgezentrum St. Petri Tue 18-20, Sun 15-18 h
Kreuslerstraße 6-8, ✉20095 ☎ 33 58 45

Sexualberatungsstelle der Abteilung für Sexualforschung
c/o Universität Hamburg, Poppenhusenstrasse 12, ✉22305
☎ 47 17 22 25

RELIGIOUS GROUPS

Basisgemeinde der Metropolitan Community Church (MCC) Service Sun 18 h
at CVJM-Haus, An der Alster 40
c/o Prävention e.V., Kleiner Pulverteich 21 ✉20099 ☎ 51 56 08

HuK- Ökumenische Arbeitsgruppe Homosexuelle und Kirche e.V.
Wolfgang Finsterer, Bürgerstraße 6 ✉22081 ☎ 29 57 36

Schwule in der reformierten Kirche 1st/3rd Sun 15 h
c/o Ev. ref. Kirche, Palmaille 6 ✉22767 ☎ 639 93 39

SPECIAL INTEREST GROUPS

BGLS- Bundesverband der Gehörlosen Lesben & Schwulen e.V. Meet every Fri 19:00h
Zirkusweg 11 ✉20359 Fax: 317 927 56
E-Mail: bgls@bgls.de Homepage: www.bgls.de
A group for deaf gays and lesbiands. Signlanguage courses for gays and lesbians who can hear. Please contact the DSG. Their e-mail address : gebaerden-hh@t-online.de.

SPORT GROUPS

Hamburg Frontrunners
c/o Franz Müller, Haakestraße 33 ✉21075 ☎ 79 14 31 75
Group meets Tue and Sat. Call for further informations.

Sportgruppe für HIV-positive Männer und Frauen
c/o Aids-Beratung der BAGS, Lübeckertordamm, ✉20099
☎ 24 88-34 41

Startschuß-schwul/lesbischer Sportverein Hamburg e.V. Mon-Fri 16-21, Sat 16-19 h
c/o Hein & Fiete, Pulverteich 21 ✉20099 *(S/U-Hauptbahnhof)*
☎ 24 03 33 E-Mail: startschuss@hamburg.gay-web.de
Homepage: hamburg.gay-web.de/startschuss
Please call for details on the sports available and the times

SWIMMING

-Eichbaumsee (g NU) (Moorfleeter Deich at Allermöhle))
-Boberger See (g NU) (Bergedorfer Straße at Billstedt))

CRUISING

-Blindengarten (Stadtpark)
-U-Ritterstraße
-U-Jungfernstieg
-EKZ Poppenbüttel
-U-Saarlandstraße
-Uni (Philosophenturm, basement, popular)
-Hundsburger Brücke
-S-Schnelsen
-Stadtpark (ayor lj MA YG) (U-Borgweg)) Popular
-Planten und Blomen (Dammtordamm/Gorch-Fock-Wall))

-Jakobi-Park (Wandsbecker Chaussee, Hamburg-Eilbeck, U-Ritterstraße)
-Gustav-Mahler-Park (BAT)
-A7 Hamburg in the direction Quickborn P Bönningsteadt (both sides)

Hameln ☎ 05151

SEX SHOPS/BLUE MOVIES

Orion (g) Mon-Fri 9.30-20, Sat -16 h
Kopmanshof 8, ✉31785 *(Passage Osterstraße 32)* ☎ 246 08

GENERAL GROUPS

Homosexuelle Initiative »Rosa Hameln« every other Thu 20 h
c/o Komm'zentrum Sumpfblume, Am Stockhof 2a ✉31785
☎ 455 10

CRUISING

-Rathausplatz (on the square and in the underpass)
-Bürgerpark (on the left behind the tourist information -20 h)

Hamm ☎ 02381

BARS

Palazzo (B GLM MA OS s SNU STV TV) Mon-Wed 17-01:00h, Fri & Sat 17-04:00h. Sun - closed
Werler Straße 101 ✉59063 ☎ 95 32 32
Once a month dragshow,or strip show. Free admission.

SEX SHOPS/BLUE MOVIES

Pegasus (GLM MG VS) Mon-Fri 13-19, Sat 10-14, closed Sun
Werler Straße 95 ✉59063 ☎ 54 02 40 *Mail-order.*
Sex & Gay Shop (b g MA W) 10-15 h
Gallberger Weg 41 ✉59063 ☎ 518 57

GENERAL GROUPS

LesBiSchwules Dreamteam (GLM YG) 18.30-23 h
c/o AIDS-Hilfe, Werler Straße 105, ✉59063 ☎ 55 75
Rosa Engel / Schwulengruppe Hamm (GLM) Mon-Thu 08:30-12.30 13:30-16:00h, Fri 08:30-12:30h, Wed 19:30-22:30h.
c/o AIDS-Hilfe, Werler Straße 105 ✉59063 ☎ 55 75

HEALTH GROUPS

AIDS-Hilfe Hamm e.V. Mon-Fri 9-16 h
Werler Straße 105 ✉59063 ☎ 194 11 or ☎ 55 75. Fax: 55 76.

CRUISING

-P at Wasser- und Schiffahrtsamt
-A1 - Exit Bockum-Hövel
-Ostenallee/Exerzierplatz
-Werler Straße/Alleestraße
-Chattanmoga-Platz (across Stadtsparkasse)

Hanau ☎ 06181

BARS

Mutter Courage (B F G MA) 20-1, Sun 15.30-1 h
Glockenstraße 25 ✉63450 ☎ 280 81

HEALTH GROUPS

Aids-Hilfe Hanau e.V. Mon 9-12 h, Tue 14-20 h, Thu 14-19 h
Alfred-Delb-Straße ✉63450 ☎ 310 00 Fax: 310 01
Hanauer AIDS-Beratung und Schwulenhilfe Maintal
Johannisweg 1, 63477 Maintal-Dörnigheim
☎ 491970

CRUISING

-Hauptbahnhof

Hannover ☎ 0511

GAY INFO

Hamburg Hannover von hinten
c/o Bruno Gmünder Verlag, PO Box 61 01 04, 10921 Berlin
☎ 615 00 30 Fax: 615 90 07 Email: Spaberlin@aol.com
The city guide book about Hanover and Hamburg. Useful general information and lots of addresses with extensive descriptions in English and German. Up-to-date maps. Erotic photos.
HIP-Home Info Phone
☎ 36 33 88
Home-Centre information line
HOME-Zentrum Meets Thu 20 h
Johannssenstraße 8 ✉30159 ☎ 36 33 44 Fax: 36 33 90.
Jugendgruppe, Chor, Gehöhrlosengruppe, Transsexuellengruppe, Coming-Out Gruppen für Lesben und Schwulen, Gruppe für Eltern von Lesben/Schwulen, Suchtgruppe, Selbsterfahrungsgruppe sowie Fragen und Probleme zu Coming-Out, Partnerschaft, HIV/AIDS, Gewalt, Sucht, Rechts-, Sozial- und medizinische Fragen.
Mimikry Hotline Tue 20-22 h
c/o HOME e.V., Johannssenstraße 8 ✉30159 ☎ 36 33 44
Newspaper for Home e.V. members. Published every third month.
Radio Florian 3rd Sun 18 h at FM 106,5 Mhz. Meets Wed 20 h at Radio Flora.
Zur Bettfedernfabrik 1 ✉30451 ☎ 210 85 68
Rosa Leine TV 1st Fri 21 h at Offener Kanal Hannover
Georgsplatz 11 ✉30159 ☎ 367 01 34
Schwullesbisches Archiv Hannover (SARCH)
PO Box 47 22 ✉30047 ☎ 66 10 55
Verein zur Erforschung der Geschichte der Homosexuellen in Niedersachsen (VEHN)
PO Box 47 22 ✉30047 ☎ 66 10 55
Zentrale Erfassung Homosexuellendiskriminierung (ZEH)
c/o HSH, PO Box 47 22 ✉30047
☎ 66 10 55

TOURIST INFO

Hannover Tourist Büro Mon-Fri 9-19 h, Sat 9.30-15 h
Ernst-August-Platz 2 ✉30159 ☎ 30 14 22

BARS

Backstairs (B DR G LJ MA P VS) Wed Fri-Sat 23-? h
Lange Laube 24 ✉30159 *(Entrance/Eingang Hausmannstraße; unter/below Vulcano)*
Barkarole (B G MA OG P) Sun Wed Thu 21-1, Fri Sat -3 h, closed Mon, winter 20- h
Konkordiastraße 8 ✉30449 ☎ 44 53 08
Belvedère (A F GLM lj MA OS S SNU STV TV) Mon-Thu 15-2, Fri Sat -3, Sun 16-2 h
Gretchenstraße 16 ✉30161 *(S-Sedanstraße)* ☎ 388 33 01
Burgklause (B f G MA N OG) 18-2, Sat 13-2 h
Burgstraße 11 ✉30159 ☎ 32 11 86

Café Caldo (B f G OS YG) Mon-Fri 18-2 h, Sat 20-3 h, Sun 16-2 h
Bergmannstrasse 7 ✉30159 *(near Arbeitsamt)* ☎ 15 17 3
Cafe with cocktail bar.

Cage aux Folles. La (B f Glm N r s) 17-?, Fri-Sun 19-? h
Kronenstraße 4 ✉30161

Cup (! B f G lj MA) 20-2 h
Escherstraße 11 ✉30159 ☎ 161 02 98

Fiacre. Le (AC B CC DR F G H MA OS R s VS) 11-3, Fri Sat -5h
Weißekreuzstraße 20 ✉30161 ☎ 34 23 37
Guest house included. Rates DM 99-119 (bf and one bottle sparkling wine incl.)

Hole. The (B DR G LJ) Tue 20-?, Wed-Sat 21-? h, Sun parties
Franckestraße 5 ✉30165 *(U-Werder Straße)* ☎ 352 38 95

Kulmbacher Eck (f glm MA N W) 16-? h, closed Sun
Hallerstraße 6 ✉30161 ☎ 348 24 52

Melody (B G N) 19-5 h
Friesenstraße 67 ☎ 31 86 89

Odeon Café (B F g S) 20-5, Fri Sat -7 h
Odeonstraße 5 ✉30159 ☎ 144 27

Opus Musik-Café (B f G MA OS YG) Mon-Fri 18-?, Sat Sun 20-? h
Lange Laube 24 ✉30159 *(Entrance/Eingang Hausmannstraße)*
☎ 138 58

Oui. Club (B bf f G MA N r) 6-2 h
Hallerstraße 30 ✉30161 ☎ 388 03 33

Projekt Café in der Schwulen Sau (! B d GLM s YG) 20-2, closed Mon Thu, Sun 15-19 h Cake feast
Schaufelder Straße 30 ✉30167 *(S-Lutherkirche)* ☎ 700 05 25

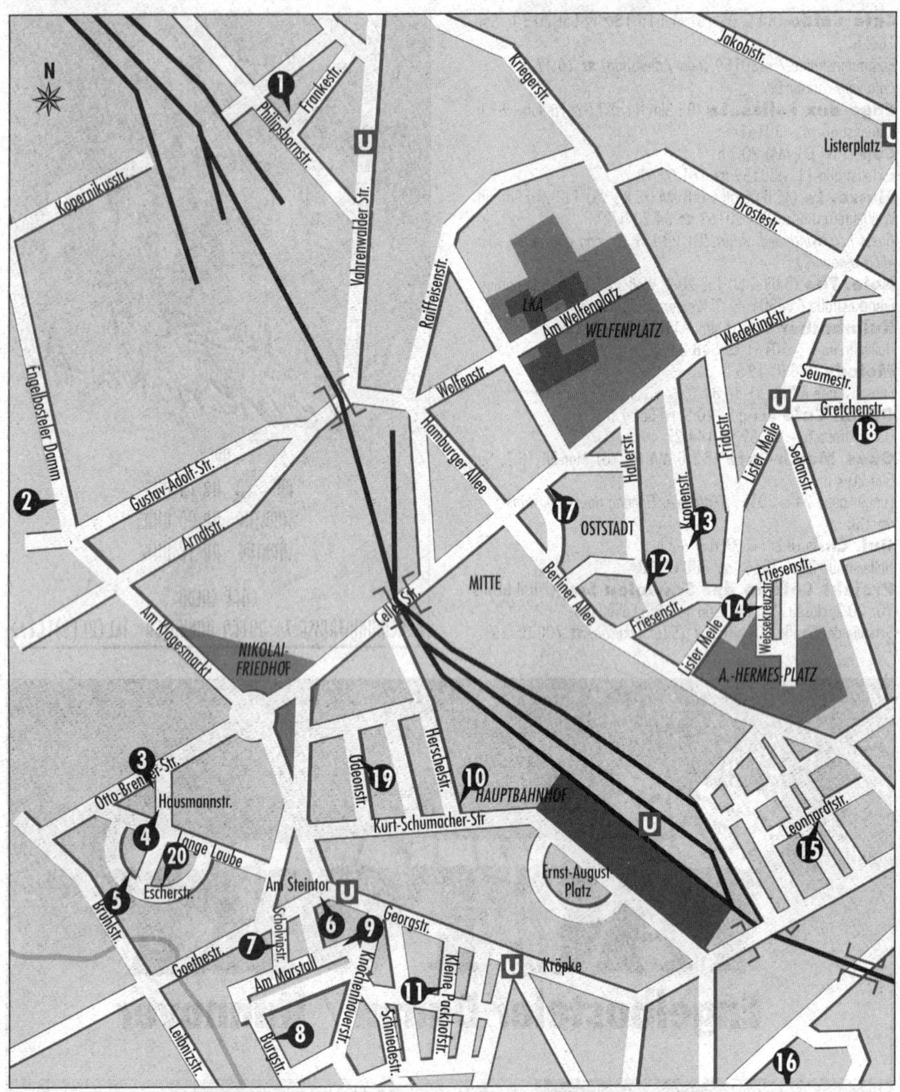

1 The Hole Leather Bar
2 Men's Factory Danceclub
3 Vulkan Sauna
4 Vulcano Danceclub
Opus Musik-Café Bar
Backstairs Bar
5 Cup Bar
6 Men's Point Sex Shop/
Blue Movie
7 Kools Sex Shop
Blue Movie
8 Burgklause Bar
9 Sexshop No. 6
10 Video-World Sex Shop
11 Beate Uhse International
Sex Shop/Blue Movie
12 Club Oui Bar
13 La Cage Aux Folles Bar
14 Le Fiacre Bar
15 Alcazar Cabaret Show
16 HOME-Zentrum Gay Info
17 Sex Point Sex Shop/
Blue Movie
18 Belvedère Bar
19 Odeon Bar
20 Caldo Bar

MAN
HANNOVER VIDEO-WORLD
Shop • Kino • Verleih
Herschelstraße 1a, nahe Hbf.
Mo-Sa 9-23 Uhr · So 13-23 Uhr

CAFES

Café Konrad (A bf F GLM MA OS) 10-24 h, Fri & Sat -1 h
Knochenhauer Straße 34 ✉30159 *(S-Markthalle)* ☎ 32 36 66

Doko's Café Deli (b F GLM) Mon-Fri 9-18.30, Sat Sun 11-18.30 h
Limmerstraße 58 ✉30451 ☎ 45 52 31
Good cakes and vegetarian dishes. More lesbian than gay.

DANCECLUBS

Konvex (B D g MA WE) Thu-Sat 22-? h
Georgstraße 26 ✉30159 *(S-Kröpcke)*
Popular techno and house club. Best on Sat.

Men's Factory (! B D DR G lj MA VS WE) Fri 22-? (g), Sat & before public holidays 22-? (G) h
Engelbosteler Damm 7 ✉30167 ☎ 70 24 87

Schwule Sau (! B d GLM YG) 3rd Fri 20-? h
Schaufelder Straße 30a ✉30167 ☎ 700 05 25
Popular gay and lesbian party

Vulcano (AC B D G MA p VS WE) Wed Fri-Sun 22-? h
Lange Laube 24 ✉30159 *(Entrance/Eingang Hausmannstraße)*
☎ 137 88

RESTAURANTS

Lister Turm (B bf F glm OS) 10-2 h
Walderseestraße 100 ✉30177 ☎ 696 56 03

SHOWS

Alcazar Cabaret (B d F g MA STV) Wed-Sun 19-5, shows 22.30 and 24, Fri Sat also 3.15 h
Leonhardstraße 11 ✉30175 ☎ 34 46 10

SEX SHOPS/BLUE MOVIES

Beate Uhse International (g VS) Mon-Fri 9-20, Sat -16 h
Kleine Packhofstraße 16 ✉30159 ☎ 36 89 70

Demand (g VS) Mon-Fri 9-21, Sat -16 h
Hamburger Allee 55 ✉30161 ☎ 34 25 26

Kool's (DR VS) Mon-Sat 9-24, Sun 13-24 h
Scholvinstraße 2 ✉30159 ☎ 363 15 40

Men's Point (AC b DR G lj MA VS) 9-2 h
Goethestraße 7 ✉30169 *(U-Steintor)* ☎ 32 47 64

Queer 32 (DR D MA TV VS YG) 11-23, Sun 15-23 h
Celler Straße 32/Sodenstraße ✉30161 ☎ 31 94 59

Reitwall Sex (g TV VS) Mon-Sat 9-24, Sun 10-23 h
Reitwallstraße 6-7 ✉30159 ☎ 32 05 41

Sexshop No. 6 (g) 9-? h
Am Marstall 4 ✉30159

Videomarkt Cinema (g VS) Mon-Fri 11-20, Sat 8-20 h
Am Klagesmarkt 9 ✉30159 ☎ 177 35

Video-World (G VS) 9-23, Sun 13-23 h
Herschelstraße 1a ✉30159 *(Near main station)* ☎ 189 73

ESCORTS & STUDIOS

Patrik
☎ (0171) 185 12 12

Jens
☎ (0171) 515 95 33

Tom
☎ (0172) 513 70 98

HOUSE OF BOYS

Royal House of Boys 12-? h
☎ 350 51 91 ☎ 0171-180 17 78

le fiacre
...wo Jungs Herren treffen!
BAR
RESTAURANT
PENSION
seperate club-room
and rooms by hour
available
weißekreuzstraße 20
30161 hannover
+49-511-342337
www.lefiacre.de

SAUNAS/BATHS

Vulkan Sauna (bf DR f G H lj MA p sb sol VS WE wh YG) 13-?, Sat Sun 0-24 h. All night sauna at weekend.
Otto-Brenner-Straße 15 ✉30159 *(Entrance Hausmannstraße)*
☎ 151 66

BOOK SHOPS

Buchhandlung Annabee (GLM MA) Mon-Fri 10-19, Sat -14 h
Gerberstraße 6 ✉30169 *(Bus-Gerberstraße/U-Königswortherplatz)*
☎ 131 81 39
Books, magazines and CDs.

FASHION SHOPS

MEC Galerie Luise (CC g) Mon-Fri 10-20, Sat 9.30-16 h
Galerie Luise ✉30159 ☎ 363 26 76

GIFT & PRIDE SHOPS

Masculinum (AC G) Wed-Fri 16-19, Sat 11-15 h
Listerstraße /Baumbachstraße 4/ ✉30163 *(near Lister Platz)*
☎ 62 10 24 Fax: 62 10 24

LEATHER & FETISH SHOPS

S.W.3 (CC glm LJ MA) Mon-Wed 10-18.30, Thu Fri -19, Sat -16 h
Herschelstraße 32 ✉30159 ☎ 131 72 29
Latex and leather.

VIDEO SHOPS

Videomarkt Cinema (g) 9-20 h, closed Sun
Am Klagesmarkt 9 ✉30159 ☎ 177 35

GUEST HOUSES

Pension Oui (G H R)
Hallerstraße 35 ✉30160 ☎ 388 03 33
Rates double DM 90-160, Relax-rooms 40-60 without/with shower).

Pensions Frisch (G H MA p)
Otto-Brenner-Straße 15 ✉30159 *(Entrance/Eingang Hausmannstraße)* ☎ 151 66
Part of the Vulkan Sauna. Central location. All rooms with shower/WC. Double DM 80 (no bf), entrance to sauna 10.

PRIVATE ACCOMODATION

Enjoy Bed & Breakfast 16.30-21 h
☎ 030/215 16 66 Fax: 030/217 52219
E-Mail: Info@ebab.com Homepage: www.ebab.com
Price DM 40 Accommodation sharing agency. All with shower & bf.

GENERAL GROUPS

Aktionsgruppe Homosexualität Hannover (HSH)
PO Box 47 22 ✉30047 ☎ 66 10 55

SchwuBiLes (Schwul-Bi-Lesbische-Selbsterfahrungsgruppe) Meets 1st Sun at Café Safran, Königsworther Straße 39 c/o UJZ Glocksee, PO Box 6065 ✉30060

Schwusos - Schwule Sozialdemokraten Niedersachsen
☎ 283 42 79 Fax: 85 82 60.
Email: niedersachsen@schwusos.de.
Homepage: http://www.schwusos.de. Gay socialist group.
Call or check homepage for further information.

SHS-Schwule Studenten Hannover term time only c/o AStA der Uni Hannover, Welfengarten 1 ✉30167 ☎ 762 50 61 *Gay student group.*

FETISH GROUPS

Leguan Meets 2nd/4th Tue 19.30 h c/o Home, Johanssenstraße 8 ✉30159 ☎ 36 33 44

MSC Hannover e.V. Meets 1st Sat 21 h at Cafe Konrad, Knochenhauerstraße 34 PO Box 41 49 ✉30041 ☎ 88 70 84
Homepage: www:hannover.gay-web.de Fax: 88 70 64
Email: mschannover@writeme.com
Homepage: http://hannover.gay-web.de/msc
Member of ECMC.

HEALTH GROUPS

Hannöversche AIDS-Hilfe e.V. Mon-Thu 9-16, Fri 9-14, Counselling: Mon Wed Fri 19-21 h Johannssenstraße 8, ✉30159 ☎ 194 11

Lazaruslegion-Christenbeistand für AIDS-Kranke und HIV-Infizierte e.V. (glm p) Mon-Thu 9-18, Fri -13h

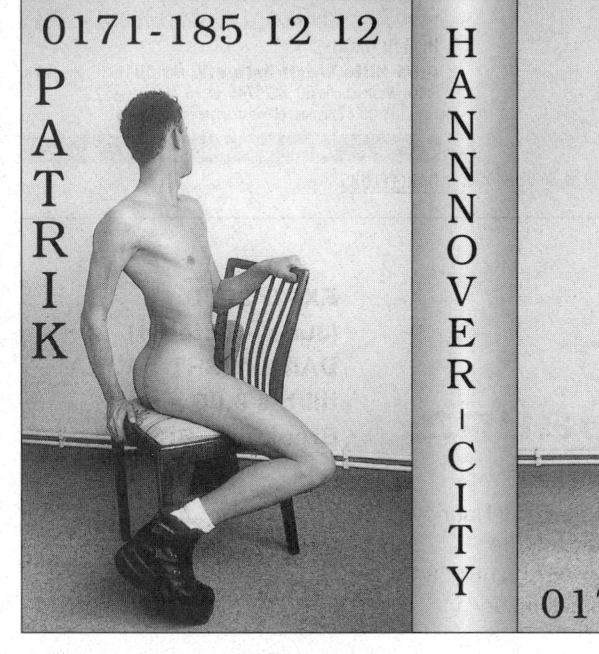

Podbielskistraße 57 ✉30177 ☎ 62 50 41 Fax: 394 14 53
E-Mail: Lazarusregion.Hannover@gmx.de
Homepage: www.nananet.de
Counselling and services for people with HIV and AIDS.

SIDA e.V.-Ambulanter Pflegedienst für AIDS-Kranke
Ferdinand-Wallbrecht-Straße 34 ✉30163
☎ 66 46 30

HELP WITH PROBLEMS

AA-Meeting für Lesben und Schwule Meets 2nd/4th Tue 19.30 h
c/o Home, Johanssenstraße 8 ✉30159
☎ 36 33 44

Beratungstelefon für Schwule und Lesben
Thu 18-20 h
c/o Home, Johannssenstraße 8 ✉30159
☎ 36 33 44 Fax: 36 33 90.

RELIGIOUS GROUPS

HuK Hannover e.V.
Schuhstraße 4 ✉30159 *(next to the Mart church)*
☎ 363 29 78 Fax: 363 29 78

SPORT GROUPS

SLS Leinebagger Hannover e.V.
c/o Home-Zentrum, Johannsesenstraße 8 ✉30159 ☎ 36 88 44
Email: leinebagger@gaysport.org
Multi-section gay and lesbian sports club.

SWIMMING

-Ricklinger Kiesteiche (MA NU) (Südlich des/south of Südschnellweg) -Freiseebad Maschsee

CRUISING

-Am Klagesmarkt (OG)
-Marktkirche (popular)
-Busumsteige Viergrenzen, Podbielskistraße
-Am Zoo (popular)
-Eilenrieder Stadtwald
-ZOB near Hauptbahnhof/main station
Schneiderberg Park (ayor) (nachts/at night)
Eilenrieder Stadtwald am Zoo/at the zoo (ayor) (nachts/at night)
-P Ricklinger Kiesteiche (Bullenwiese, after dawn)

Heide ☎ 0481

HEALTH GROUPS

AIDS-Hilfe Westküste e.V. Mon 10-13.30, Thu -16 h
Große Westerstraße 30, ✉25746 ☎ 76 76
Fax: 789 08 62. Email: alt-westkueste@t-online.de

Heidelberg ☎ 06221

DANCECLUBS

Mata Hari (B D glm p YG) 22-3 h
Oberbadgasse 10 ✉69117 *(Entrance Zwingerstraße)* ☎ 18 18 08

SEX SHOPS/BLUE MOVIES

Beate Uhse International (AC CC g VS) Mon-Sat 10-1 Sun 14-1 h
Kurfürstenanlage 53, ✉69115 *(Near/Nähe Hauptbahnhof)*

Sex-Shop (g VS) Mon-Sat 9-23 h
Merianstraße 3/Heugasse ✉69117 *(Entrance/Eingang Heugasse)* ☎ 298 99
Popular sex shop with straight blue movies, gay magazines, videos etc.

BOOK SHOPS

Buchhandlung Wohltaht (CC) Mon-Fri 9-20, Sat -16 h
Hauptstraße 156 ✉69117 ☎ 16 27 02

HOTELS

Hotel Goldener Hecht (bf g H MA) 6.30-22 h
Steingasse 2 ✉69117 ☎ 16 60 25 Fax: 16 60 25
Central location.

GENERAL GROUPS

Rosa Prinzen-Schwule Jugendgruppe Heidelberg Fri 20 h at ☛AIDS-Hilfe
PO Box 10 48 64 ✉69038 ☎ 18 13 23

Schwulenverband in Deutschland (SVD) Regionalgruppe Heidelberg/Rhein-Neckar
Meeting 3rd Tue 20 h
at Scharfes Eck, Neugasse 69117
PO Box 10 48 64 ✉69038

Schwuler und lesbischer Arbeitskreis
Wed 13-14 h
Lauerstraße 1 ✉69117
E-mail queer-hd@fsk.ini-heidelberg.de

Unsere Kasse-Verein zur Förderung schwuler Kultur, Politik und Gemeine e.V.
☎ 124 81 *(Christoph)*

HEALTH GROUPS

AIDS-Hilfe Heidelberg e.V.
Counselling ☎ 19411 Mon, Tue, Fri 11-13 h, Tue 16-19 h, Wed 16-18 h
Untere Neckarstraße 17 ✉69117 ☎ 16 17 00 Fax: 16 88 37.

CRUISING

-Kaufhof department store (Hauptstraße)
-Adenauerplatz (popular)
-Hauptbahnhof
-Universitätsbibliothek (Kellergeschoß, mittags/downstairs, noon)
-Horten department store
-Mensa Neuenheimer Feld
-Alte Brücke Nord
-Park an der/at Kurfürstenanlage (AYOR) (östlich der Stadtbücherei, nachts/east of public library, at night)

Heilbronn ☎ 07131

GENERAL GROUPS

HEH Schwule Freizeitgruppe Heilbronn Wed 20-22 h at ☛AIDS-Hilfe
PO Box 20 23 ✉74010 ☎ 890 64

HEALTH GROUPS

AIDS-Hilfe Unterland e.V. Mon/Wed 10-16, Thu 13-18, Fri 10-14 h
Wilhelmstraße 3 ✉74072 ☎ 194 11

RELIGIOUS GROUPS

HuK Regionalgruppe 1st & 3rd Sun 19 h
at Diakonische Bezirksstelle, Schellengasse 7-9
PO Box 29 01 ✉74019 ☎ 133 64

SWIMMING

-Katzenbachsee at Brackenheim

CRUISING

-Alter Friedhof/old cemetery (ayor)
-Hauptbahnhof/Main station
-Rathaus/Town Hall
-Harmonieunterführung

Herdecke ☎ 02330

HEALTH GROUPS

AIDS-Hilfe EN e.V. Mon 8-13 h
c/o Krisenladen, Hauptstraße 14, ✉58313 ☎ 31 53

Herne ☎ 02325

HEALTH GROUPS

AIDS-Hilfe Herne e.V. Mon 9-11, Thu 16-19 h
Hauptstraße 94 ✉44651 ☎ 609 90
Counselling ☎ 194 11

CRUISING

-Wanner Sportpark, Franzstraße/Rathausstraße
-Bahnhof Herne/Train station
-Saalbau Wilhelmstraße/Stadtgarten

Herten ☎ 02365

GENERAL GROUPS

Les SchwuBi Wed 19.30-21.30 h
ProFamilia, Bergstraße 11, Marl
c/o Brinkmann, PO Box 11 29 ✉45669
02366/(02365) 474 86

CRUISING

-Parking lot Main post office

Hildesheim ☎ 05121

CAFES

Café Sonderbar in der Hildesheimer AIDS-Hilfe e.V. (B GLM MA s) Sun 16-20 h
(Bus3-Moltkestraße) ☎ 51 66 12
New adress! Please ask Hildesheimer AIDS-Hilfe/ Neue Adresse! Bitte bei der Hildesheimer AIDS-Hilfe nachfragen.

SEX SHOPS/BLUE MOVIES

Beate Uhse Sex Shop (g VS)
Bahnhofsallee ✉31134

GENERAL GROUPS

Kraut und Rüben (A b d GLM lj MA)
c/o AIDS-Hilfe e.V., Zingel 14 ✉31134 ☎ (0177) 2072065
Café: Sun 16-19.30 h at FEZ, Annenstr. 23, party: 3-monthly at Kulturfabrik, Langer Garten 1, call for exact dates.

HEALTH GROUPS

Hildesheimer AIDS-Hilfe e.V. Mon, Tue, Thu 9-12, Wed 15-17 h
Zingel 14 ✉31134 ☎ 194 11 ☎ 133127
Fax: 13 08 43

SWIMMING

-Tonkuhle (g NU) (Blauer Kamp, at the university/bei der Universität. Summer only/nur im Sommer)

CRUISING

-Paul-von-Hindenburg-Platz (PVH)
-Neustädter Markt
-Bohlweg/Pfaffenstieg (am Dom/at the dome)
-Almstor
-Ehrlicherpark

Hof ☎ 09281

BARS

Schnürsenkel (B d f g MA YG) 19-2 h, closed Wed
Fabrikzeile 1 ✉95028 ☎ 446 13

DANCECLUBS

Gay-Bi-Lesbian party at Viva (AC B D GLM MA n) last Sun 21 h
Hohensass 2 ✉95030 *(Bus5-Hohensass, by car take B 15)*
☎ 645 22
Very popular with locals

SEX SHOPS/BLUE MOVIES

Beate Uhse International (g) Mon-Fri 9.30-18, Sat 9.30-13 h
Brunnenstraße 2 ✉95028 ☎ 84499
Orion (g) Mon-Wed 9.30-18, Thu Fri -20, Sat 9-14 h
Biengäßchen 12 ✉95028 ☎ 14 12 51
Sex Shop (g) Mon-Fri 9-18, Sat 9-13 h
Klosterstraße 30 ✉95028 ☎ 2931

CRUISING

-Stadtpark/Stadtbücherei

Höxter ☎ 05271

GENERAL GROUPS

Schwulesbische Initiative Höxter-Holzminden
PO Box 14 13, 33029 Brakel ☎ 92 13 32

Hoyerswerda ☎ 03571

GENERAL GROUPS

Bubenkiste Hoyerswerda
PO Box 29 21 ✉02967
Men only Schwulengruppe
PO Box 34 33 ✉02965

HELP WITH PROBLEMS

Rosa-Hilfe-Telefon Tue Thu 17-23 h
☎ 726 67

Husum ☎ 04841

CRUISING

-Schloßpark (ayor)
-Bahnhof
-Schloßgang

Ilmenau ☎ 03677

GENERAL GROUPS

LSVD Thüringen
PO Box 01 23 ✉98683

Ingolstadt ☎ 0841

BARS

Pinocchio (AC B d f GLM lj MA OS s YG) Sun, Tue & Wed 18-1, Thu 18-2, Fri Sat 20-3 h, Mon closed
Am Nordbahnhof 4 ✉85049 ☎ 91 07 10 Fax: 91 07 10

SEX SHOPS/BLUE MOVIES

Amor & Co. (g VS) 9-23 h, closed Sun
Höllbräugasse 5 ✉85049 *(Near „Quelle")* ☎ 326 24
Erotik-Super-Markt (g) Mon-Sat 10-23 h, closed Sun-
Dollstraße 17 ✉85049

GENERAL GROUPS

Romeo und Julius e.V. Thu 20-22, Counselling Wed 20-22 h
c/o Bürgertreff »Alte Post«, Kreuzstraße 12 ✉85049
☎ 30 56 08

HEALTH GROUPS

AIDS-Hilfe und Arbeiterwohlfahrt
c/o Thomas Thöne, PO Box 21 09 15 ✉85024 ☎ 93 66 33

SWIMMING

-Hirschweiher (G MA NU) (Fuchsschüttweg, only to be reached thru/zu erreichen über Sebastian-Kneipp-Straße and/und Große Zellgasse)

CRUISING
-Hindenburgpark (nach Sonnenuntergang/very busy after sunset)
-Near/Nähe Nordbahnhof
-Franziskanerstraße (OG) (behind/hinter Neues Rathaus -19 h)

Insel Juist ☎ & Fax:

GUEST HOUSES
Haus Maike + Gästehaus de Vries all seasons
Gräfin-Theda-Straße 24 ✉26571 ☎ 04935/3 53 (& Fax:)
15 double rooms, 4 single rooms, 8 apartments. All rooms with shower/bath/WC, balcony or terrace. Sauna, solarium. Rates from 55-210 DM incl. breakfast.

Iserlohn ☎ 02371

BARS
Why Not (AC D f GLM lj MA s SNU STV) Sun-Thu 18-2, Fri Sat -3 h
Viktoriastraße 1, ✉58636 ☎ 120 02

Ismaning ☎ 089

RELIGIOUS GROUPS
Homosexuelle und Kirche (HuK)
c/o L. Volleth, Taxestraße 35 ✉85737

Itzehoe ☎ 04821

GENERAL GROUPS
Schwitz-Schwuleninitiative (GLM MA) Meeting: 1st Thu 20-21.30 h
c/o AWO, Markt 7 ✉25524 ☎ 3484

Jena ☎ 03641

SEX SHOPS/BLUE MOVIES
Beate Uhse International (g) Mon-Fri 9-20 Sat -16
Saalstraße 6 ✉07743

HEALTH GROUPS
AIDS-Hilfe Weimar, Beratungsstelle Jena Mon 11-20 h
Rathenaustraße 10 ✉07745 ☎ 194 11
Office ☎ 61 89 98 (Mon, Wed-Fri 11-15.30 h)

CRUISING
-Paradiespark
-station/Bahnhof Jena-Paradies

Kaiserslautern ☎ 0631

BARS
Café Sonderbar (B glm MA) Fri, Sat & Mon 17- ?, Sun 20- ? Tue closed.
Glockenstraße/Mozartstraße ✉67655 ☎ 638 06
Kulisse (B G MA) 20-1, Fri Sat -2 h, closed Tue
Mainzer Straße 6 ✉67657 ☎ 669 31
Take-Off (B G) 20-1, Fri Sat -2 h, closed Mon
Königstraße 3 ✉67655 ☎ 180 40

DANCECLUBS
Blue Eye (D GLM MA p s WE YG) Wed-Thu 22-3 h, Fri-Sat 22-4 h
Burgstraße 21 ✉67659 *(near town hall)* ☎ 958 44
Joy II (B D f glm MA) Fri Sat 22-4 h
Burgstraße 21 ✉67659 *(near town hall/nähe Rathaus)* ☎ 958 44
Nanu (B D Glm MA VS YG) Wed-Sun 22-? h, closed Mon Tue
Rudolf-Breitscheid-Straße 58 ✉67655 *(1st floor)* ☎ 311 44 25

SEX SHOPS/BLUE MOVIES
Amor Co. (g VS) Mon-Fri 9-20, Sat -14; cinema Mon-Sat 9-24, Sun 14-22 h
Richard-Wagner-Straße 5 ✉67655
Orion (g) Mon-Fri 10-20, Sat 9.30-16 h
Burgstraße 15 ✉67659 ☎ 95 02 20
VEW Video Erotic World (g VS) Mon-Sat 9-23, shop: -20 h
Weberstraße 29 ✉67655 ☎ 686 89
Video-World (CC glm MA VS W) Mon-Sat 9-23 h
Rosenstraße 4 ✉67655 *(near Hauptbahnhof)* ☎ 89 19 75

GENERAL GROUPS
AStA-Schwulenreferat Uni Kaiserslautern
Wed 11.30-12.30 h, party last Friday of the month
Uni Kaiserslautern, Geb. 46, Erwin-Schrödinger-Straße ✉67663
☎ 205-3918 Fax: 205-3523
E-Mail: schwulenreferat.kaiserslautern@eurogay.ne
Homepage: www.kaiserslautern.gay-web.de/asta.
Lauterjungs und -mädels e.V. Wed 20-? h
c/o AIDS-Hilfe, Pariser Straße 23 ✉67655 *(Entrance yard)*
☎ 27 02 26 Fax: 311 03 43 E-Mail: lauterjungs@eurogay.net
Homepage: www.kaiserslautern.gay-web.de/lauterjungs
Gay lesbian youth group.

HEALTH GROUPS
AIDS-Hilfe Kaiserslautern e.V. Counselling Mon Thu 19-21 h
Pariser Straße 23 ✉67655 *(entrance Bleichstraße)*
☎ 194 11 ☎ 0631/180 99 Fax: 108 12
E-Mail: aidshilfe@vereine.kaiserslautern.de
Homepage: www.kaiserslautern.de/shg/aids

CRUISING
-P Frachtstraße (near station)
-WC Pfalztheater

Karbach ☎ 05631

CAFES
Das T (A AC bf F glm MA) Mon-Sat 8-18 h, Sun closed
Bahnhofstraße 14-16 ✉34497 ☎ 980 92

Karlsruhe ☎ 0721

GAY INFO
Radio Rosa Rauschen Fri 18-19, Sat 12-13 h (FM 104,8 MHz; cable: FM 100,2)
Steinstaße 23 ✉76133 ☎ 38 78 58
Fax: 38 50 20 The editors meet Tue 20 h./Die Redakteure treffen sich jeden Di um 20 h.
RoBin-Rosa Bibliothek und Infothek Mon 19.15-20 h
c/o Gewerbehof, Steinstraße 23 ✉76133

BARS
Erdbeermund (B D Glm MA) 20-1 h, closed Mon Tue
Baumeisterstraße 54 ✉76137 ☎ 37 42 42
Miró (A B bf F G MA OS TV YG) 16-1 h
Hirschstraße 3 ✉76133 *(Entrance Hirschhof. Tram/Bus-Europaplatz)* ☎ 214 32

Musikcafé Die Zwei (B glm MA) Mon-Sat 11-3, Sun 18-3 h
Douglasstraße 34 ✉76133 ☎ 20 58 75

DANCECLUBS

Care (B D GLM YG) Wed 21-3 h
Hirschstraße 18, ✉76133 ☎ 215 25
Club Tropica (AC B D G GLM MA s YG) 22-05:00 h
Bunsenstraße 9 ✉76135 *(entrance Kriegsstraße)* ☎ 85 49 80
Little Diva Tue Thu 22-3, Fri Sat 23-5, Sat Sun 6-? h
Amalienstraße 44 ✉76133 ☎ 203 03 02

SEX SHOPS/BLUE MOVIES

Blue Movie (AC g VS) 9-24, Sun 13-24 h
Kaiserstraße 33 ✉76131 *(Multi-Media-Video-Show)* ☎ 37 42 87
Erotic Point (CC g MA VS) 9-24, Sun and holidays 16-23 h
Hardtstraße 21 ✉76185 ☎ 55 35 75
Heiner's Shop (g VS) Mon-Fri 8.30-20, Sat -16 h
Mathystraße 9 ✉76133 ☎ 35 83 35
Mixed Sex Shop with selection of gay magazines, books and videos.
Orion (g) Mon-Fri 10-20, Sat -16 h
Bürgerstraße 7g ✉76133 *(Im Parkhaus/Parking garage »Ludwigsplatz«)* ☎ 298 91

ESCORTS & STUDIOS

Dieter F. (AC bf DR LJ msg OS p SNU VS W) ☎ 454 14 or ☎ (0172) 722 91 40

HOTELS

Hotel Regent ☛Baden-Baden

SAUNAS/BATHS

Adonis Sauna (B G MA og OS sa sb VS) 15-24 h
Lameystraße 12a ✉76185 ☎ 55 50 51
Gay bath with small gay shop. Entrance fee 24,- DM./Schwule Sauna mit Shop. Eintritt 25,- DM.
Aquarium Sauna (! B DR G MA p sa sb VS YG) Sat, Sun and holidays 14-24, Tue-Fri 16-24 h, Mon closed
Bachstraße 46 ✉76185 *(Tram-Philippstraße, Eingang im Hinterhof, Entrance in the backyard)* ☎ 955 35 33
The largest sauna in Karlsruhe with over 500 square meters, beautiful designed & very popular
Bernhard Sauna (AC B CC DR f G sa sb VS YG) 15-1 h
Bernhardstraße 2 ✉76131 *(Tram-Durlacher Tor)* ☎ 69 67 67
Entrance in the court-yard.

BOOK SHOPS

Buch Kaiser Ta-Bu-La (g) Mon-Fri 9.30-20, Sat -20 h
Kaiserstraße 199 ✉76133 ☎ 209 44
Montanus aktuell (AC CC g) Mon-Fri 9.30-20, Sat -16 h
Kaiserstraße 127 ✉76133 ☎ 38 04 42
general bookstore with gay section.

GENERAL GROUPS

Die Schrillmänner Meeting Wed 19 h
c/o Gewerbehof, Steinstraße 23 ✉76133
Gay chorus/Schwule Gesangsruppe
Schwule Eintracht Karlsruhe
PO Box 60 01 ✉76040
Schwule Jugendgruppe Lucky Boys
c/o AIDS-Hilfe, Stephanienstraße 84 ✉76133 ☎ 262 60
Schwule Väter Karlsruhe Meeting 1st Mon 20 h.
Gewerbehof, Steinstraße 23 ✉76133 ☎ 262 60
Call Aids-Hilfe for information.
Schwuler Stammtisch Meeting Mon 20 h
c/o Weißer Stern, Am Künstlerhaus 45
SCHWUNG-Schwule Unigruppe Meeting 2nd Mon 20 h at Gewerbehof, Steinstraße 23
c/o ASta Universität Karlsruhe, Adenauerring 7 ✉76131
Warmer Blitz-Schwule Gruppe Karlsruhe
PO Box 68 64 ✉76048

HEALTH GROUPS

AIDS-Hilfe Karlsruhe e.V. Counselling Mon Wed 15-18, Fri 10-14; Café Regenbogen Thu 16-20
Stephanienstraße 84 ✉76133 ☎ 194 11 or ☎ 26 26 0

HELP WITH PROBLEMS

Coming-Out-Gruppe
c/o AIDS-Hilfe, Stephanienstraße 84 ✉76133 ☎ 262 60
Counselling and support/Beratung und Hilfe
Rosa Telefon Mon-Fri 19-24 h
☎ 37 93 52 or ☎ 247 44

RELIGIOUS GROUPS

Homosexuelle und Kirche (HuK) Nordbaden
PO Box 21 06 38 ✉76156 ☎ 81 77 73 *(Hans & Ralph)*

SWIMMING

-Epple-See (g MA NU YG) (7 km ausserhalb nahe Rheinstetten-Forchheim/7 km from the city near Rheinstetten-Forchheim)
-Baggersee Leopoldshafen (Nähe/near Eggenstein-Leopoldshafen)

CRUISING

-Nymphengarten (AYOR) (Nähe/near Landesmuseum, Kriegsstraße, nachts/ at night)

-Rheinhafen (Action findet sich im kleinen Park auf der anderen Seite des Ⓟ/get to the small park on the other side of Ⓟ)
-Main railway station/Hauptbahnhof (R)
-Albtalbahnhof, Straßenbahnhaltestelle/Albtal railway station, tram station (r)

Kassel ☎ 0561

BARS

Bel Ami (B D G) Summer: Mon Wed-Thu 16-1, Fri Sat -3 h, Winter: 19-? h, closed Tue
Wilhelmshöher Allee 84 ✉34119 ☎ 288 80 90
Mann-O-Mann (B f G MA) Mon-Thu 19-01:00h, Fri & Sat 19-03:00h. Sun - closed
Friedrich-Ebert-Straße 118 ✉34119 *(Tram-Bebelplatz)*
☎ 188 54
No Limit (B f GLM MA OS) Sun-Thu 18-1, Fri Sat -3 h, 1st Fri party
Wilhelmshöher Allee 116 ✉34119
Suspekt Café-Bar (A B GLM MA) Tue-Thu Sun 13-1, Fri Sat -2 h, every 1st Sun Rainbow-Breakfast
Fünffensterstraße 14 ✉34117 *(Near Rathaus)*
☎ 10 45 22
Popular.

DANCECLUBS

R•U•K-Zuck (AC B D GLM MA s) Wed 21-2, Fri 22-3, Sat -5 h
Frankfurter Straße 131 ✉34121 *(Near/nahe Auestadion)*
☎ 227 29
Spot (B D GLM s YG) Sun 21-4 h
Ölmühlenweg 10-14 ✉34123
☎ 562 09

SEX SHOPS/BLUE MOVIES

Amor & Co Mon-Sat 9-24, Sun -22 h
Untere Königsstraße 74 ✉34117

City Sex Shop (g VS) 10-18.30, Sat 10-14, 1st Sat -16 h
Grüner Weg 10/Sickingenstraße ✉34117 ☎ 175 87

Orion (g) Mon-Fri 9.30-20, Sat -16 h
Friedrichsplatz 11 ✉34117 *(near/nahe Staatstheater)* ☎ 182 39

Pleasure (g) Mon-Sat 9-23, Sun 14-22 h
Kölnische Straße 7 ✉34117 ☎ 77 44 37
Special area «Gay Point»

Sex-Point (g VS) 10-24, Sun 15-23 h
Kölnische Straße 18 ✉34117 ☎ 71 18 41
Gay cinema and shop. Videos for rent, magazines, toys and leather articles for sale.

Video-World (g VS) 8.30-23.30, Sun 13-23 h
Hedwigstraße 5 ✉34117 *(Near/nahe Karstadt)* ☎ 78 04 40

BOOK SHOPS

Buch Habel (g) Mon-Fri 10-20, Sat -16 h
Obere Königstraße 39 ✉34117 *(Königs-Galerie)* ☎ 70 75 30

Montanus Aktuell im DEZ (g)
Frankfurter Straße 225 ✉34134 ☎ 941 38 94

Vaternahm Bahnhofsbuchhandlung (g)
Hauptbahnhof ✉34117 ☎ 77 40 04

HOTELS

Haus Lengen (AC B bf DR f G H MA sa sb sol VS WO) Sauna opening hours: Mon-Thu 15.30-23, Fri Sat -1 h, closed Sun
Erzbergerstraße 23-25 ✉34117 *(formally „Uwe's Pferdestall)*
☎ 168 01 Fax: 780 794
Newly renovated and enlarged sauna. Single room from DM 60 and double room DM 85.

GENERAL GROUPS

Autonomes Schwulenreferat im AStA der Uni Kassel Wed 13-16, Thu 16-18, Fri 14-18 h
Nora-Platiel-Straße 9 ✉34109 ☎ 804-38 19

Elterngruppe homosexueller Kinder Mon-Fri 9-12, Tue 13-16, Thu 14-18 h
Frau Wienold, Evangelische Bildungsstätte, Pestalozzistraße 32 ✉34119 ☎ 153 67

HEALTH GROUPS

AIDS-Hilfe Kassel e.V.
Motzstraße 4 ✉34117 ☎ 10 85 15 Fax: 10 85 69
Helpline: ☎ 194 11 Mon, Fri 11-13, Wed 18-20 h

HELP WITH PROBLEMS

Rosa Telefon Fri 18-22 h
c/o Pro Familia, Frankfurter Straße 133a ✉34121 ☎ 274 13

SWIMMING

-Bugaseen Fuldaaue (NU) (cruising, too, in worse weather/ Cruising auch bei schlechterem Wetter)

CRUISING

-Weinberg (Henschelgarten)
-P Messehallen
-Kulturbahnhof (R)
-Uni (Mensa, at „Menü 2")

Kehl ☎ 07851

SAUNAS/BATHS

Atrium (AC CC DR f G MA msg OS sa sb sol VS WO) 14-24, Sat -1 h, Tue Wed (glm)
Schulstraße 68 ✉77694 ☎ 48 27 05

CRUISING

-between town-hall and police station (zwischen Rathaus und Polizeiwache)

Kempten ☎ 0831

BARS

Le Filou. Club (B D f GLM MA OS s) 20-1, Fri Sat and before public holidays -3 h
Stuibenweg 1 ✉87435 ☎ 268 29

SEX SHOPS/BLUE MOVIES

Inkognito (AC g lj MA VS) Mon-Sat 9-23
In der Brandstatt 5 ✉87435 ☎ 16869

GENERAL GROUPS

GSC Allgäu
☎ (08321) 222 00 Email: gsc@gmx.de
Contact Wendelin and Andreas. Social activities for gays living in and around Kempten and Sonthofen./2-3 monatliche Veranstaltungen wie Wanderungen, Skifahren oder Radtouren.

CRUISING

-Hofgarten (nachts zwischen/nights between »Residenz« & »Orangerie«)
-Salzstraße

Kiel ☎ 0431

GAY INFO

HaJo 1. & 3. Tue 19 h
Westring 278, ✉24116 Fax: 170 99. E-mail HajoKiel@aol.com
Monthly publication for Schleswig-Holstein.
HUCH! Schwulen- und Lesben-Zentrum (GLM) Fri 12-14, Sun 19-21 h
Westring 278, ✉24116 ☎ 194 46 *Fax: 170 99.*
-Schwuler Männerchor Kiel (Wed 20 h)

BARS

Alhambra-Bar (AC B d f GLM MA OS p r) Mon-Sat 19-4 h, Sun closed
Herzog-Friedrich-Straße 92 ✉24103 *(near central station)* ☎ 67 64 24
Ca Va (A B f GLM MA MG OS YG) 18-3 h
Holtenauer Straße 107 ✉24105 *(Bus4/44-Düppelstraße. Near/neben Schauspielhaus)* ☎ 854 19
Coming Out (B DR G MA s VS) 18-5, Video rental: Mon-Fri 18-5, Sat -24 h
Schuhmacherstraße 28, ✉24103 ☎ 948 93
Harlekin (B Glm MA VS) 20-4 h
Kirchhofallee 38, ✉24114 ☎ 636 48
Popular.

DANCECLUBS

Pumpe (B D f GLM MA) 1st, 3rd & 5th Sat 22-3 h
Haßstraße 22, ✉24103 ☎ 961 61

RESTAURANTS

Kieler Ansichten (B F glm OS) Mon-Sat 12-23, Sun 10-23 h
Hasselfelde 20 ✉24149 ☎ 23 97 30

SEX SHOPS/BLUE MOVIES

Beate Uhse Sexshop (g) 9-23.30, Sun 14-? h
Wall 12, ✉24103 ☎ 97 08 33
Orion (g) Mon-Fri 9-20, Sat 8-16 h
Winterbeker Weg 44, ✉24114 *(At »plaza«)* ☎ 68 65 59
World of Sex-WOS (g VS) 10-24, Sun 12-24 h
Schuhmacherstraße 31, ✉24103 ☎ 932 55
WOS-Markt (g) 10-24, Sun 12-24 h
Eggerstedtstraße 11, ✉24103

BOOK SHOPS

Zapata (g) Mon-Fri 9-18, Sat -13 h
Jungfernstieg 27 ✉24103 ☎ 936 39

GENERAL GROUPS

Die andere Männergruppe 8-20 h
Königsweg 19 ✉24103 ☎ 67 69 83 or ☎ 97 97-980
HAKI e.V. Mon 9.30-15 h, Wed 15-19 h, Thu 9-12 h
Westring 278, ✉24116 ☎ 170 90
Fax: 170 99. Counselling „Rosa Telefon" ☎ 0431-19446. (Fri 12-14 h, Sun 19-21 h)
Kieler Jungs und Deerns Fri 19 h
c/o Huch, Westring 278 ✉24116
Gay youth group/Schwule Jugendgruppe.
Schwulenreferat im AStA der Christian-Albrecht- Universität Mon-Fri 10-14 h
Westring 385, ✉24118 ☎ 880-26 47

FETISH GROUPS

Kiel gibS/Mir
Meeting 4th Mon at Storchnest, Gutenbergstraße 66 ☎ 130 55
(Counselling and information) Tue 19-20 h.

HEALTH GROUPS

AIDS-Hilfe Kiel e.V. Mon-Fri 10-13 h (counselling)
Knooper Weg 120 ✉24105 ☎ 194 11

HELP WITH PROBLEMS

Rosa Telefon Fri 12-14, Sun 19-21 h
☎ 194 46

SWIMMING

-Lindhöft (NU) (Strand in der Eckernförder Bucht 22 km nordwestlich von Kiel. B 503 Ausfahrt »Camping Lindhöft«. 200 m nördlich vom Campingplatz. Action in den Büschen./Beach at Eckernförder Bucht, 22 km northwest of Kiel. Leave route B 503 at »Camping Lindhöft«, follow road up to the shore. 200 m north of camp ground is the gay area. Action in the bushes.)

CRUISING

-Dreiecksplatz
-Hertie department store (Near/Nähe Hauptbahnhof. 1. Etage)
-Schrevenpark (popular)

Kirchheim-Teck ☎ 07021

SWIMMING

-Bürgerseen (Landstraße Kirchheim-Nürtingen, der kleinste See/smallest lake)

Kitzingen ☎ 09321

FETISH GROUPS

Schwuler Lederclub Franken 20-? h
PO Box 25 ✉97302 ☎ 226 66

Kleve ☎ 02821

GENERAL GROUPS

Na und...?!-Schwule Jugendgruppe (W YG) Wed 18-? h
Teestube, Regenbogen 14 ✉47533 ☎ 231 57
PO Box 20 21 24, 47568 Goch.
Schwulengruppe (GLM W) Wed 18-20 (Young Gay`s group), Wed 20-?
c/o Teestube, Regenbogen 14 ✉47533 ☎ 231 57

HEALTH GROUPS

AIDS-Hilfe Kreis Kleve e.V. Mon Tue 9-12 13-16, Thu 20-22 h
Lindenallee 22 ✉47533 ☎ 76 81 31 Fax: 76 81 33
Tue 9-14 h im AWD-Building, Gerhard-Storm-Straße 56.

Koblenz ☎ 0261

BARS

Bistro „Der Zauberlehrling" (AC d f GLM MA R s) Mon-Thu 20-1, Fri Sat -2 h, closed Tue
Baedeckerstraße 29 ✉56073 ☎ 412 89
ChaCha (C F glm MA r S TV W) Wed Thu 21-3, Fri Sat 21-4 h, once a month gay party
Alte Heerstraße 130 ✉56076 *(Horchheim)* ☎ 973 01 16

RESTAURANTS

Rheinzoll-Stube (B F g MA)
Rheinzollstraße 16 ✉56068 ☎ 177 79

SEX SHOPS/BLUE MOVIES

Amor & Co. (g VS) Mon-Fri 9.30-21 h
Löhrstraße 8 ✉56068 ☎ 334 38
Journal (g VS) 10-21, Sat 10-14 h, closed Sun
An der Liebfrauenkirche 12 ✉56068 ☎ 30 97 68
Penny (g VS) 9.30-22, Sat -14 h, closed Sun
Löhrstraße 65 ✉56068 ☎ 366 55

FASHION SHOPS

SOX (AC CC g) Mon-Fri 9.30-20 h, Sat 9.30-16 h
Löhrcenter, EG ✉56058 ☎ 914 31 16
Men's underwear.

GENERAL GROUPS

Aids-Beratung Koblenz Mon 9.30-13, 13.30-18.30 h
Rizzastraße 14 ✉56068 ☎ 149 91
By appointment.
Elternhorizont Tue 19-21 h
c/o Helmut Tibes, Horchheimer Höhe 13 ✉56076 ☎ 973 06 59

SJK-Schwule Jugendgruppe Koblenz (GLM s YG) Counselling Thu 19.30-21, Meeting Fri 19.30 h
Rizzastraße 14 ✉56068 ☎ 149 91 E-Mail: sjk@RZ-online.de
Homepage: www.sjk-online.de

HEALTH GROUPS

AIDS-Hilfe Koblenz e.V. Wed 19-21 h
Löhrstraße 53 ✉56068 ☎ 194 11
Fax: 172 35

CRUISING

-Deutsches Eck (where Mosel and Rhein flow together; evenings)
-Hauptbahnhof/main railway station

Köln ☎ 0221

● A summer in Cologne: The smell of the expresso machines, transvestites fighting and drinks being ordered. In Cologne every waiter is a king, every rose seller a fairy tale princess. No where else are there so many warm days to lift the spirits. Moreover, Cologne is ranked after Amsterdam and Sydney as the having most gay inhabitants. And that is certainly before the much beloved city of San Francisco. There are endless trips made from the crowded train stations to numerous districts of Cologne. There`s a high concentration of cafés, clubs and places to meet in the heart of the city. The city is well known for festivals, such as CSD and Carneval. There's the Hay Market which is home to Fathers' day and warm pubs. There's also Rudolfplatz with it's trendy locations, the Transfert (where many part-time students chill out from their studies), The White Distillery known as Die Brennerei Weiß, where transvestites are found hugging each other after their bitching sessions.

✱ Ein Sommer in Köln. Das Geräusch der Espressomaschine. Zwei steinalte Transvestiten streiten sich. Jemand bestellt noch ein Getränk. In Köln ist jeder Kellner ein König, jede Rosenverkäuferin eine schöne Fee. Nirgendwo sonst baumelt die schwule Seele derart luftig in den Himmel. Das liegt am Klima. Köln hat ganz viele lässig warme Sommertage. Und daran, daß in Köln- nach den Städten Amsterdam und Sydney- die meisten Leute schwul sind. Und das noch vor, beispielsweise, San Francisco. Führen in Berlin schier endlose Reisen in bauchigen S-Bahnen von einem Stadtteil in den anderen, ist man in Köln schnell von der Altstadt ins Belgische Viertel gelupft. Die hohe Konzentration von Cafés, Clubs und Connections streichelt das Herz -und Konkurrenz belebt das Geschäft. Köln ist aber auch die Stadt der Feste, von CSD und Karneval. Da ist der Heumarkt mit seinem ewigen Vatertag, den gutmütigen Kneipiers. Da ist der Rudolfplatz mit seinen trendy locations. Im Transfert chillen sich Teilzeitstudenten ein. Die Brennerei Weiß bewirtet zwei Damen. Um genau zu sein, sind es zwei steinalte Transvestiten. Und schau mal: Jetzt geben sie sich die Hand.

▲ Un été à Cologne. Le bruit du percolateur. Deux vieux travestis se disputent. Quelqu'un commande encore un verre. A Cologne, tout garçon de café est un roi, toute vendeuse de roses une belle fée. L'ambiance gaye ne se balance nulle part ailleurs de façon aussi légère dans le ciel. Ceci est dû au climat (Cologne a beaucoup de journées d'été chaudes et détendues) et au fait qu'à Cologne la plupart des gens sont gays (après Amsterdam et Sydney). Et avant des villes comme San Francisco, par exemple. Si à Berlin des voyages pratiquement interminables dans des RER pleins à craquer conduisent d'un quartier à l'autre, à Cologne on est transporté rapidement de la vieille ville dans le quartier belge. La concentration élevée de cafés, clubs et lieux de contacts caresse le coeur, et la concurrence anime les affaires. Mais Cologne est aussi la ville des fêtes, de la CSD (Christopher Street Day) et du carnaval. On y trouve le „Heumarkt" avec son éternelle fête des réjouissances, ses bistrotiers d'un bon naturel. Voilà la „Rudolfplatz" avec ses „trendy locations". Au „Transfert" des étudiants à temps partiel se rafraîchissent. La distillerie Weiß sert deux dames. Ou plutôt deux vieux travelos, qui se tiennent par la main.

☆ Un verano en Colonia. Se oye el ruido de la máquina de café, alguien pide otra copa. Dos viejos travestis están discutiendo. En Colonia se acepta cualquier estilo de vida, aquí todo el mundo se puede realizar y por ello es el lugar ideal para muchos gays. Por una parte debido al clima, ya que Colonia cuenta con muchísimos días de verano y por otra parte es la ciudad, despúes de Amsterdam y Sydney, con el mayor número de habitantes homosexuales. Aquí la comunidad gay es más grande que por ejemplo en San Francisco. Mientras en Berlín uno está obligado a pasar horas enteras en transporte público para moverse entre los distintos barrios, en Colonia se llega comodamente andando desde el casco antiguo al *Belgisches Viertel*. En pocos metros cuadrados encontramos aquí innumerables cafeterias, bares y clubs y desde luego la competencia favorece al negocio. Colonia es también la ciudad de las fiestas, como el Christopher Street Day y carnavales. Durante todo el año merece la pena una visita del *Heumarkt* con sus encantadores bares o del *Rudolf-*

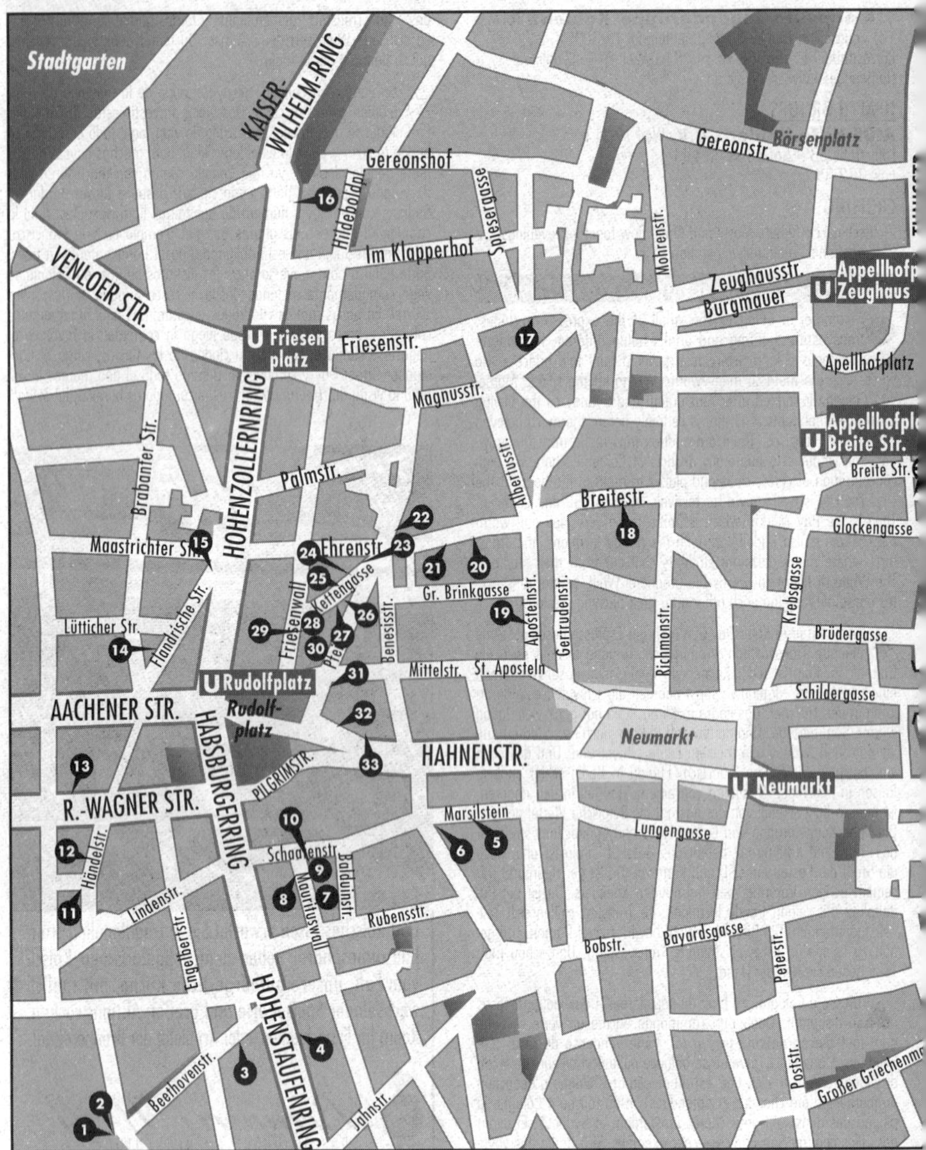

Stadtgarten
KAISER-WILHELM-RING
Gereonshof
Hildeboldpl.
Spiesergasse
Gereonstr.
Börsenplatz
Mohrenstr.
Im Klapperhof
VENLOER STR.
Zeughausstr.
Burgmauer
Appellhofplatz Zeughaus
U Friesenplatz
Friesenstr.
Apellhofplatz
Magnusstr.
HOHENZOLLERNRING
Appellhofplatz Breite Str.
Breite Str.
Albertusstr.
Palmstr.
Breitestr.
Brabanter Str.
Glockengasse
Maastrichter Str.
Ehrenstr.
Kettengasse
Friesenwall
Gr. Brinkgasse
Benesisstr.
Apostelnstr.
Gertrudenstr.
Richmonstr.
Krebsgasse
Brüdergasse
Lütticher Str.
Flandrische Str.
Mittelstr.
St. Apostein
Schildergasse
U Rudolfplatz
Rudolfplatz
AACHENER STR.
HABSBURGERRING
Neumarkt
HAHNENSTR.
PILGRIMSTR.
U Neumarkt
R.-WAGNER STR.
Marsilstein
Lungengasse
Schaafenstr.
Händelstr.
Mauritiuswall
Balduinstr.
Lindenstr.
Rubensstr.
Bayardsgasse
Bobstr.
Engelbertstr.
Peterstr.
HOHENSTAUFENRING
Beethovenstr.
Jahnstr.
Poststr.
Großer Griechenmarkt

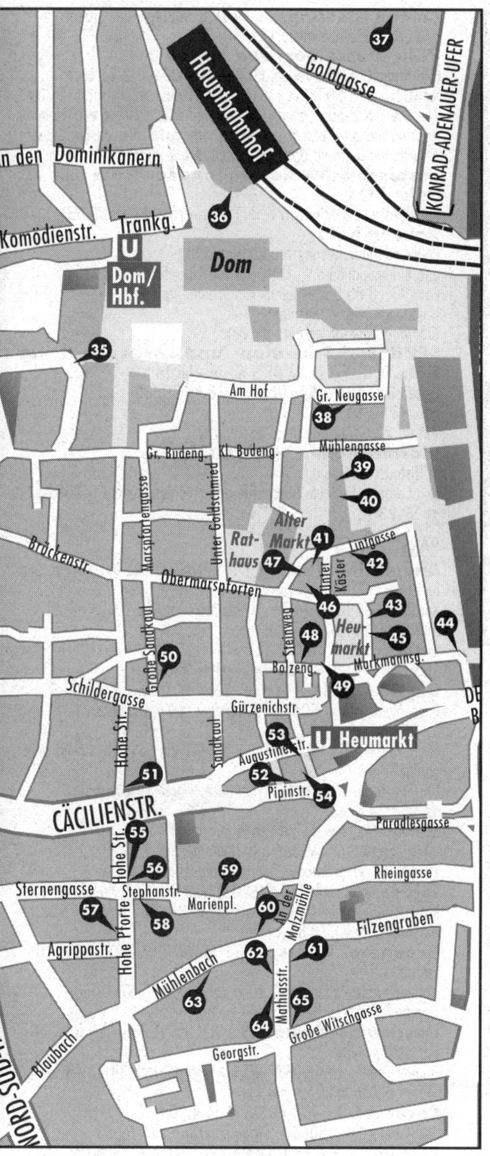

A Friesenplatz/Rudolfplatz

1 Vampire Bar
2 Fenysinn Bar
3 AIDS Hilfe Köln
4 Esplanade Hotel
5 George Sand Bar
6 Clip Café
7 Park Bar/Restaurant
8 Schampanja Bar
9 Corner Bar
10 Huber Café
11 Central Café
Chelsea Hotel
12 Der Faun Sauna
Jot Jelunge Shop
13 Gym Fitness
14 Whistle Stop Café
Restaurant
15 Tingel Tangel/
Moulin Rouge Show
16 Kaiserhof Theater
17 Badehaus am
Römerturm
18 Sex Messe Sex Shop
Blue Movie
19 Gloria Café & Danceclub
20 Mec Underwear Fashion
21 Mec Fashion Shop
22 Star Treff Show
23 Elinor's Café
24 Sex und Gay Center
(Kettengasse)
Sex Shop/Blue Movie
25 Phoenix Sauna
26 Ganymed Book Shop
27 Gästehaus Kettengasse
Guesthouse
28 Barflo Bar
29 Bruno's Bücher/ Books
30 Nana's Restaurant
31 Sex und Gay Shop
Sex Shop/Blue Movie
32 Brennerei Weiß
Bar/Restaurand
33 Transfert Bar
34 Lulu Danceclub
G-Punkt Party
35 Hotel Königshof
36 Alter Wartesaal Disco
Coconut Party
37 Valentino House of Boy

B Altstadt/Heumarkt

38 Senftöpfchen Theater
39 Beim Pitter Bar
40 Go In Café
41 Comeback Bar
42 Rembrandt's Bar
43 Verquer Bar
44 Restaurant Domerie
45 Bangkok Restaurant
46 Hühnerfranz Bar
47 Le Carussel Bar
48 Backbord Bar
49 Em Bölzje Bar
50 Monte Christo Bar
51 Royal Hotel am
Augustinerplatz
52 Bei Udo Bar
Quo Vadis Café
Zille Bar
53 Beim Sir Bar
Timp Künstlerklause
Bar/Hotel/Show
54 Stiefelknecht Fetisch Bar
55 Sex Discount Sex Shop
/Blue Movie
56 Teddy Treff Bar
57 Zipps Fetisch Bar
58 Chains Fetisch Bar
59 Vulcano Sauna
60 My Lord Bar
61 Hands Fetisch Bar
62 Sex und Gay Center
(Matthiasstraße)
Sex Shop/Blue Movie
63 Sauna 30
64 Gay Sex Messe Sex Shop
Blue Movie
65 Teddy Travel Shop

platz, que se carateriza por sus lugares de moda. En el *Transfert* se encuentran muchos estudiantes que se preparan para la marcha nocturna. En la *Brennerei Weiß* se atiende a dos señoras. Para ser más preciso son dos viejos travestis. !Y mirad! Ahora se dan la mano.

Un'estate a Colonia. Il rumore della macchina da caffè. Due travestiti vecchissimi si litigano; qualcuno ordina qualcosa da bere. A Colonia ogni cameriere è un ré, ogni venditrice di rose una fata. In nessun'altro posto l'anima gay emana la sua allegria; è così grazie al clima. Colonia è caratterizzata da molti giorni estivi abbastanza caldi. E perché Cologna, dopo Amsterdam e Sydney, presenta la più alta percentuale di abitanti gay, ancora più alta di quella di San Francisco. Se a Berlino bisogna viaggiare nelle infinite Métro da un quartiere all'altro, a Colonia si arriva con un salto dal centro storico al Belgisches Viertel. L'alta concentrazione di caffé, club e punit d'incontro è un vero piacere, e la concorrenza stimola gli affari. Ma Colonia è anche la città delle feste, del CSD e del carnevale. Ecco l'Heumarkt con la sua eterna festa del papà, ecco il Rudolfplatz con i suoi „trendy locations". Nel Transfert due studenti a tempo perso ballano in trance. Nella Brennerei Weiß vengono ospitate due signore, per essere precisi, si tratta di due vecchissimi travestiti, ma guarda: adesso si stringono le mani.

GAY INFO

Centrum Schwule Geschichte e.V. (GLM) Tue 10-16, Wed Fri 15-18 h
Vogelsanger Straße 61 ✉50823 ☎ 52 92 95 Fax: 52 92 95

Checkpoint 10-17 h
Pipinstraße 7 ✉50667 *(U-Heumarkt)* ☎ 20 20 360 / -61/-62
Fax: 92 57 68 45. E-Mail: checkup@netcologne.de
Gay and Lesbian Centre for information, health and services

Cologne feelings 1st Fri 19 h on Bürgerfunk station
c/o Schulz, Kartäuserwall 18 ✉50678

Köln/Düsseldorf von hinten
c/o Bruno Gmünder Verlag, PO Box 61 01 04, 10921 Berlin
☎ (030) 615 00 30 Fax: 615 90 34 E-Mail: info@spartacus.de
The city guide book about Cologne and Düsseldorf. Useful general information and lots of addresses with extensive descriptions in English and German. Up-to-date maps. Erotic photos.

Lesbisch-Schwules Jugendzentrum (GLM YG)
Tue-Fri 17-22 h
Kamekestraße 14 ✉50672 ☎ 194 46 *Fax: 93 18 80 83.*

Raus in Köln
Public editorial meeting Thu 20 h at SCHULZ
c/o Emanzipation e.V., Kartäuserwall 18 ✉50678
Fax: 93 18 80 85. E-Mail rik@macman.org
Homepage: www.macman.org/rik
City magazine for lesbians and gays.

SCHULZ / Schwulen- und Lesbenzentrum Köln (A B d f GLM MA OS S W) Tue Thu 14 h
Kartäuserwall 18 ✉50678 ☎ 93 18 80 80/88
Fax: 93 18 80 85.
4th Fri 22 h Türk Gay Disco.

Warme Meilen 1 Mar-14 Oct 15 h
at Historisches Rathaus
c/o Centrum Schwule Geschichte e.V., Wahlenstraße 1 ✉50823
☎ 52 92 95

BARS

Anders im Schulz (A B bf f GLM MA OS S W) 10-1 h, Sun brunch
Kartäuserwall 18 ✉50678 *(U-Chlodwigplatz)* ☎ 93 18 80 22
Sun breakfast brunch.

Backbord (B f G MA) 11-1 h
Steinweg 4 ✉50667 *(U-Heumarkt)* ☎ 258 14 79

Barflo (AC B bf CC f GLM OS YG) 10-01:00h
Friesenwall 24 d ✉50672 *(U-Rudolfplatz/Friesenplatz)*
☎ 257 32 39

Bei Udo (B g MA) Tue-Thu Sun 16-1, Fri Sat -3 h, closed Mon, winter from 17 h
Vor St. Martin 12 ✉50667 *(Entrance/Eingang Pipinstraße)*
☎ 258 23 47

Beim Pitter (AC B f GLM lj MA N OS) 11-1 h
Alter Markt 58-60 ✉50667 *(U-Heumarkt)* ☎ 258 31 22
Popular bar in downtown Cologne. Largest outdoor area.

Bilderschreck (B f g MA OS) Mon-Thu 18-2, Fri-Sun 19-3 h
Königswinterstraße 1/Gottesweg ✉50939 *(Tram 18/19-Sülzburgerstraße)* ☎ 41 78 85

Brennerei Weiss (AC B F GLM MA OS W) Sun-Thu 10-1, Fri Sat -3 h
Hahnenstraße 22 ✉50667 *(U-Rudolfplatz)* ☎ 257 46 38
Sun brunch 11-15 h.

Buschwindröschen (B d GLM MA s) Every day from 21 h
Fri. lesbians only
Bonner Straße 84 ✉50677 *(U-Severinstraße)* ☎ 34 23 43
Please call for the latest program

Carussel. Le (B d f G MA R) 19-4.30 h
Alter Markt 4-6 ✉50667 *(U-Heumarkt)* ☎ 257 69 53

Chains (AC B d DR G LJ MA VS) from 22-?. Sun from 16 h. (naked sex parties)
Stephanstraße 4 ✉50676 *(U-Heumarkt)* ☎ 23 87 30
Fri-Sun from 22 h minimum charge/Mindestverzehr DM 5. The largest leather/fettish bar in Cologne.

Clip (AC B G YG) 21-3, Fri Sat -4.30 h
Marsilstein 29 ✉50676 *(U-Heumarkt)*
☎ 240 92 92

Comeback (AC B f G MA OS STV) 15-3, Fri & Sat -4:30, Sun 13-3 h
Alter Markt 10 ✉50667 *(Opp. Town Hall/Gegenüber Rathaus)* ☎ 257 76 58

Corner (! B G lj MA) 19-? h
Schaafenstraße 57-59 ✉50676 *(Near/Nähe Rudolfplatz)* ☎ 24 90 61
Popular. Best time 20-23 h. Good music

Daddy's (B G MG) 18-02:00h, Fri & Sat -03:00h
Stephanstraße 2/Hohe Pforte ✉50676 ☎ 240 94 42

Em Bölzje (B G MG og) 11-1 h
Bolzengasse 4 ✉50667 *(U-Heumarkt)* ☎ 258 23 48

Filmdose (B g MA) Sun-Thu 19-2 h
Zülpicher Straße 39 ✉50674 *(U-Dasselstraße/Bhf. Süd)* ☎ 23 96 43

George Sand (B F gLm MA p s) 20-1, Wed Fri Sat -3, 1st Sun from 11.30 h, Mon Tue closed
Marsilstein 13 ✉50676 *(U-Heumarkt)* ☎ 21 61 62

Hands (AC B DR G LJ MA W WE) 21-2, Fri-Sat -3 h
Mathiasstraße 22 ✉50676 *(U-Heumarkt)* ☎ 24 31 45

Hohenstaufen Klause (B glm lj f OS s) Mon-Fri 11-15, Sat & Sun 18-1 h
Schaevenstrasse 5 ✉50676 *(Rudolfplatz)* ☎ 240 31 02

Hollywood (AC B f GLM MA OS) 17-4 h
Heumarkt 43 ✉50667 ☎ 257 42 19

Hühnerfranz (AC B bf f G lj MA R TV W WE YG) 7-3 h
Hühnergasse 2 ✉50667 *(U-Heumarkt)* ☎ 25 35 36
Early morning breakfast from 7 h.

Kaisergarten (B F G MA OS S) 18-1 h, closed Mon
Kaiserstraße 202 ✉51145 ☎ 02203/219 36

Kattwinkel (AC B d f GLM MG N OS s WE YG) 12-01:00h (April to October), 18-01:00h (October-March)
Greesbergstraße 2 ✉50668 *(Near/Am Eigelsteintor)* ☎ 13 22 20

Monte Christo (B d G lj MA) 23-6, Sat Sun (D), best time from 1 h
Große Sandkaul 24 ✉50667 ☎ 257 68 40

My Lord (AC B F G MG) 17-3 h, closed Thu
Mühlenbachstraße 57 ✉50676 ☎ 23 17 02

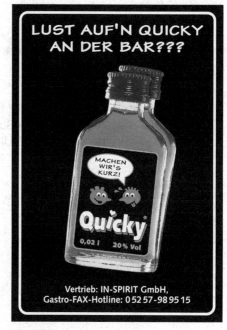

Park (B GLM MA YG) Sun-Thu 20-2, Fri Sat -3 h
Mauritiuswall 84 ✉50676 *(Near/Nähe Rudolfplatz)* ☎ 21 33 57
Popular

Rembrandt's (B d f Glm lj MA MG r s STV W WE YG) 16-2, Fri Sat -3 h
Lintgasse 4 ✉50667 ☎ 257 78 27

Schampanja (B G MA s YG) Sun-Thu 20-2, Fri Sat -3 h
Mauritiuswall 43 ✉50676 *(U-Rudolfplatz)* ☎ 240 95 44
Popular.

Sir. Beim (B f GlM MA OS) 14-1/?, Fri Sat 14-4 h
Heumarkt 27-29 ✉50557 *(U-Heumarkt)* ☎ 25 68 35
Stiefelknecht (AC B d DR G LJ MA p s VS YG) 22-04:00h
Pipinstraße 9 ✉50667 *(Heumarkt)* ☎ 258 07 72
Teddy Treff (AC B d Glm lj MA s WE) Sun-Thu 20-01:00h, Fri & Sat 20-03:00h, Mon. closed
Hohe Straße 2/Stephanstraße ✉50667 *(U-Heumarkt)* ☎ 24 83 10
Various events. Call for information.
Valentino (AC B CC G H MA msg p R S SNU VS W WE) Sun-Thu 15-1, Fri Sat -3 h
Altenberger Straße 13 ✉50668 *(2 min. from central station)* ☎ 13 70 79
Strip shows Fri Sat from 20 h.

Vampire (A d gLm MA) Tue-Thu 20-1, Fri-Sat -3 h, Sun 20-1 Mon closed
Rathenauplatz 5 ✉50674 *(U-Rudolfplatz)* ☎ 240 12 11
Verquer (AC bf f GLM lj MA OS) Mon-Fri 14-01:00 h, Sat & Sun 12-03:00 h,
Heumarkt 46 ✉50667 *(Altstadt)* ☎ 257 48 10
Sun: breakfast for night crawlers from 6-8 h..
Zicke. Zur (B G MA s STV) Tue-Sat 19-1, Sun 16-1 h, closed Mon
Rheingasse 34-36 ✉50674 ☎ 240 89 58
Zille (AC B f G lj MA N) 19-3 h
Pipinstraße 5 ✉50667 ☎ 258 17 83
Zipps (AC B f G LJ MA) Sun-Thu 20-2, Fri Sat -3 h
Hohe Pforte 15 ✉50676 *(U-Heumarkt)* ☎ 240 60 76

CAFES

Café Central (B bf F g MA OS YG) Sun-Thu 7-3, Fri Sat -4 h
Jülicher Straße 1 ✉50674 ☎ 20 71 50
Café Huber (f G N s YG) Sun-Thu 14-2, Fri Sat -3 h
Schaafenstraße 51 ✉50676 *(U-Rudolfplatz)* ☎ 240 65 30
Café Philipp's (A AC bf F glm MA OS W WE) Mon-Sat 11-1, Sun 10-1 h
Philippstraße 1 ✉50823 *(U-Körnerstraße)* ☎ 51 53 33
Elinor's (! AC B bf F G MA OS YG) Mon-Sat 10-1, Sun & holidays 11-1 h
Kettengasse 2 ✉50672 *(U-Rudolfplatz)* ☎ 257 32 66
Popular.
Feynsinn (B bf F g OS) Mon-Sat 9-1, Sun 10-1 h
Rathenauplatz 7 ✉50674 *(U-Zülpicher Platz)* ☎ 240 92 09
Gloria Café (A AC B bf D f GLM MA OS S WE) Mon-Thu 9-1h, Fri & Sat 09-03:00h, Sun 11-01:00h
Apostelnstraße 11 ✉50667 *(U-Neumarkt)* ☎ 258 36 56
Everchanging program, please call for details
Go-In (B f G MA OS) 11-3, Sun & public holidays 13-3 h
Alter Markt 36-42 ✉50667 ☎ 258 22 14
Quo Vadis (AC b bf CC F GLM LJ MA OS s YG) 12-1 h
Vor St. Martin 8-10 ✉50667 *(Entrance/Eingang Pipinstraße)* ☎ 258 14 14
Transfert (! AC B bf d f G lj MA OS YG) 11-1, Fri Sat -3
Hahnenstraße 16 ✉50667 *(U-Rudolfplatz)* ☎ 258 10 85
Music Café in the center of the Bermuda Triangle

DANCECLUBS

Coconut Gay Special Disco-Party (B D G lj MA YG) irregularly 6x/year Sun or before holidays 22-5 h
(old waiting room at main station/Alter Wartesaal Hbf.)
☎ 13 30 61
Popular. Carnaval and Pride are a must.

Flash (B D G) Wed Thu Sun 19-1, Fri Sat -3 h
Alter Markt 4-6 ✉50667 ☎ 258 45 60
Gloria Club (A AC B D glm S TV YG)
Apostelnstraße 11 ✉50667 ☎ 25 44 33 or ☎ 258 36 56
Popular. Different parties. Check local press for date of „Rosa Sitzung" (Gay and lesbian carnival).
Joystick (B D GLM STV) once a month Sun 23-? h
c/o Gloria, Apostelnstraße 11 ✉50667 ☎ 25 44 33
Lulu (! AC B D DR GLM lj MA s TV VS WE) Fri Sat & before holidays 23-4.30 h
Breite Straße 79/Schwertergasse ✉50667 *(U-Appellhofplatz)* ☎ 257 09 30
No Limit (B D GLM LJ) 1st Sat, admission from 21-23 h
Clevischer Ring 119 ✉51063 *(Mühlheim)*
Party for S/M lovers. Admission 50,- DEM, all drinks and meals included.
U 27 (b D G YG) every 2nd Fri 22.30-3 h
c/o Schulz, Kartäuserwall 18 ✉50678 *(U-Chlodwigplatz)* ☎ 93 18 80 80
For gays, lesbians and friends up to 27.

RESTAURANTS

Alcazar (B F g MA OS) Mon Tue Thu 12-2, Wed Fri -3, Sat 18-3, Sun 18-2 h
Bismarckstraße 39 a ✉50672 *(U-Friesenplatz)* ☎ 51 57 33
Meals 12-14.30, 18-23.30 h.
Anders Ehrenfeld (B bf F glm MA s) 9-1, bf 9-17, meals 12-15, 18-23 h
Klarastraße 2-4 ✉50823 *(U-Körnerstraße)* ☎ 510 14 73
French and local cuisine.
Bangkok Restaurant (F glm) Tue-Sun 17-1h, Mon closed
Heumarkt 54 ✉50667 ☎ 258 12 58
Central (bf F g) 7.30-1, Fri Sat -? h
Ehrenstraße 1-3 ✉50672 *(U-Apellhofplatz)* ☎ 25 68 34
Die Zeit der Kirschen (A AC B F glm MA OS s W) Mon-Fri 11.30-1, Sat 17-1, Sun 10-1 h
Venloer Straße 399 ✉50825 *(U-Venloer Straße)* ☎ 954 19 06
Fine international cuisine. Brunch on Sun and public holidays.
Domerie (b CC E F glm MA OS) Tue-Sun 18-24 h, Mon closed
Buttermarkt 42 ✉50667 ☎ 257 40 44
Harvey's (F glm) 18-1, Fri 16-3 h
Weißenburgsraße 58 ✉50670 *(U-Reichensperger Platz)* ☎ 72 42 27
Nana's Restaurant-Bar (B F g MA) 17-1 h, meals 18-23.15, Fri Sat -0 h
Pfeilstraße 15 ✉50672 ☎ 257 30 70
Oscar's (a B F g MA s) 12-1 h, Mon closed
Sudermannstraße 12 ✉50670 *(U-Ebertplatz)* ☎ 72 00 11
Whistle Stop Café (AC B bf F g MA OS) 9-1, Fri Sat -? h, bf 9-15, meals 11.30-23.30 h
Flandrische Straße 18 ✉50674 *(U-Rudolfplatz)* ☎ 257 07 30

SHOWS

Kaiserhof (AC B F glm MA S) Shows from Tue-Sun, Ticket Box Tue-Sat 10-20 h, Sun & holidays 16-20 h Mon. closed.
Hohenzollernring 92 ✉50672 *(U-Friesenplatz)* ☎ 139 27 72
E-Mail: info@kaiserhof-theater.de
Senftöpfchen-Theater (g STV) Tickets: Mon-Fri 16-20, Sat Sun from 18 h
Große Neugasse 2 ✉50667 ☎ 258 10 58
Star-Treff (B g STV) Wed Thu Sun 19.30-?, Fri Sat -3 h, Wed Thu dinner spectacle
Turiner Strasse 2 ✉50668 ☎ 25 50 63
Shows: Wed Thu Sun 20.15, Fri Sat 19.45 & 22.45 h. Admission DM 15.
Timp (B CC d GLM H MA p STV W) Show at 1 h
Heumarkt 25 ✉50667 ☎ 258 14 09
Tingel Tangel/Moulin Rouge (B g MA STV) 20-4.30 h
Maastrichter Straße 6-8 ✉50672 ☎ 25 26 01

SEX SHOPS/BLUE MOVIES

Erotik Shop 13 (AC CC DR LJ MA TV VS W WE) Mon-Sat 10-24, Sun and public holidays 14-24 h
Im Dau 13 ✉50678 *(Tram/Bus-Waidmarkt)* ☎ 31 71 60
Blue movie entrance-fee DM 12 without time limit.
Gay Sex Messe (CC G VS) 10-1 h
Mathiasstraße 13 ✉50676 ☎ 24 82 17
Mike Hunter Sexshop (g VS) Mon-Fri 9-22, Sat 12-1, Sun -24 h
Hohe Straße 2/Stephanstraße ✉50667 ☎ 240 20 34
Video cabins.

Orion (g) Mon-Fri 9.30-20, Sat -16 h
Blaubach 6-8/Hohe Pforte ✉50676 *(Across Polizeipräsidium)*
☎ 21 84 30

Sex & Gay Shop (g VS) 9-1, Sun 12-24 h
Pfeilstraße 10 ✉50672 *(am/at Rudolfplatz)* ☎ 25 62 78

Sex Discount (g VS) 9-24 h
Hohe Straße 8 ✉50667

Sex Messe (CC G VS) Mon-Sat 8-1, Sun 10-1 h
Breite Straße 153 ✉50667 ☎ 258 17 08

Sex und Gay Center (G VS) 10-1 h
Mathiasstraße 23 ✉50676 ☎ 23 53 01

Sex und Gay Center (G VS) 10-1 h
Kettengasse 8 ✉50672 ☎ 258 09 18

HOUSE OF BOYS

Valentino (AC B CC G H msg p R S SNU VS) Sun-Thu 15-1, Fri & Sat 15-3 h
Altenberger Straße 13 ✉50668 *(S/U-Hauptbahnhof)*
☎ 13 70 79

SAUNAS/BATHS

Badehaus am Römerturm (! AC B CC DR E F G msg NU OS p pi sa sb sol VS wh YG) Mon-Fri 13-1, Sat 12-early Sun, Sun 12-23 h
Friesenstraße 23-25 ✉50670 ☎ 257 70 06
Admission DM 35. One of the most beautiful saunas in Europe. All night sauna Sat.

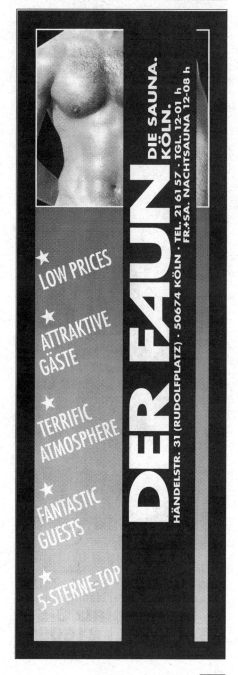

Faun. Der (! AC CC DR f G MA msg OS p sa sb sol VS YG) 12-1, Fri & Sat -8 h (all night sauna)
Händelstraße 31 ✉50674 *(near Rudolfplatz)* ☎ 21 61 57
Entrance-fee DM 20, after 19 h DM 25. Student DM 21. On Tue two for DM 30. Thu from 18 h DM 17, Fri DM 21.

Phoenix Sauna (! B CC G msg p pi sa sb sol VS YG) 12-6, Sun and public holidays 8 h
Kettengasse 22 ✉50672 *(U- Rudolfplatz)* ☎ 257 33 81
Admission DM 25, students DM 30, -13 h DM 18.

Sauna 30 (B F DR G MA sa sb sol pi wh) 14-23 h
Mühlenbach 30 ✉50676 *(Tram 1, 2 Heumarkt)* ☎ 21 73 86
Entrance-fee DM 19-24.

Vulcano (B f G msg OG p sa sb VS) 11-23, Sun -22, Sat night sauna -8 h
Marienplatz 3-5 ✉50676 ☎ 21 60 51
Admission DM 24. Since more than 25 years.

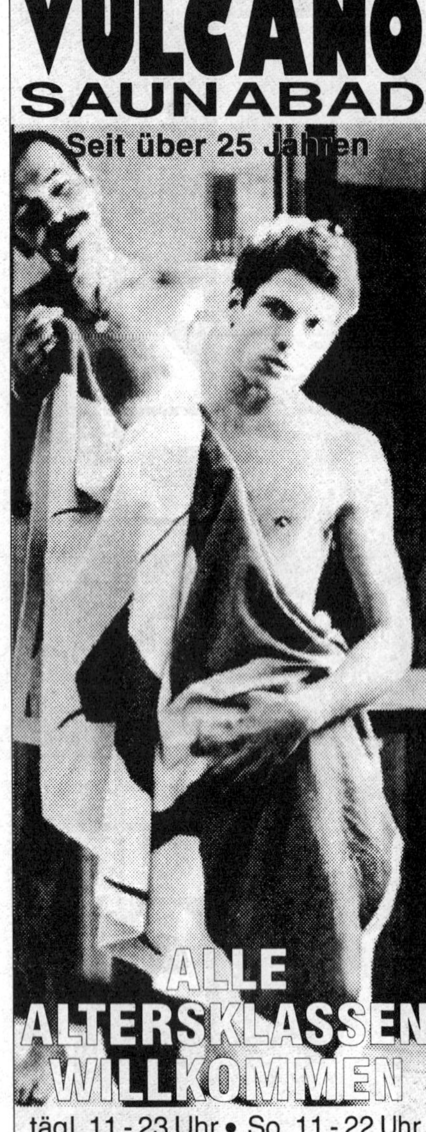

FITNESSTUDIOS

Gym Fitness (b f g msg sa WO) Mon-Fri 6-24, Sat 8-20, Sun 10-20 h
Richard-Wagner-Straße 12 ✉50674 *(U-Rudolfplatz)* ☎ 258 11 58

BOOK SHOPS

Benedikt Taschen Verlag Buchhandlung (g)
Hohenzollernring 53 ✉50672 ☎ 257 33 04

Bruno's (! A CC G) Mon-Fri 10-20, Sat 10-16 h, closed Sun
Friesenwall 24 ✉50672 *(U-Rudolfplatz)* ☎ 925 26 94
Also video rental.

Ganymed (A CC G MA WE) Mon-Fri 10-20, Sat 10-16 h
Kettengasse 3 ✉50672 *(U-Rudolfplatz, opp. Phoenix-Sauna)* ☎ 25 11 10
Books and CDs

Mayersche Buchhandlung
Neumarkt Galerie, Neumarkt 2 ✉50667 ☎ 203 070

Montanus Aktuell GmbH (g)
Rhein-Center, Aachener Straße 1253, EG 50858 K-Weiden *(Köln-Weiden)* ☎ 02234-94 61 50

CONDOM SHOPS

Condomi (glm) Mon-Fri 10.30-20 h, Sat 10-16 h
Limburger Straße 22 ✉50672 *(U-Friesenplatz)* ☎ 25 11 86
Condoms and presents.

EDUCATION SERVICES

Rosa Aquarius (bf f G H MA msg OS)
Hochstraße 63A, 50374 Erftstadt-Erp ☎ (02235) 691884
Fax: 69 18 82. Email rosaaquarius@hotmail.com. *Seminars and education for gay men. Accomodation possible.*

FASHION SHOPS

Boutique MAN (G MA) Mon-Fri 17-20, Sat 11-16 h
Mathiasstraße 9 ✉50676 ☎ 240 7408 Fax: 240 7408
Leder und Textilien, auch Maßanfertigung/ leather and clothes, also custom-made.

MEC (AC CC g) Mon-Fri 10-20, Sat -16 h
Ehrenstraße 27 ✉50672 *(U-Rudolfplatz)* ☎ 258 10 80
Designer men's wear, shoes, accessoires.

MEC underwear (AC CC G) Mon-Fri 11-20, Sat 10-16 h
Ehrenstraße 23 ✉50672 ☎ 258 05 63
Underwear, sportswear, clubwear.

Rudi's Brillenerlebnis (CC GLM MA) Tue Wed 10-14,15-19, Thu & Fri -20, Sat 10-16, closed Sun Mon
Heumarkt 55-57 ✉50667 *(U-Heumarkt)* ☎ 925 37 19
Glasses, contact lenses,souvenirs

LEATHER & FETISH SHOPS

Cosmic Ware Mon-Fri 12-18.30, Sat 11-15 h
Engelbertstraße 59-61 ✉50674 *(U-Rudolfplatz)* ☎ 240 12 01
Rubber, S/M etc.

Mode Pforte (NG) Tue Wed Fri 10-18.30, Thu -19 and by appointment, Sat -14/16/18 h
Hohe Pforte 24/Stephanstraße 2 ✉50676 ☎ 24 75 67
Modische Lederbekleidung/Fashionable leather wear.

Nima Lapelle Lederstudio Mon-Fri 10-20, Sat -14 h
Wolfsstraße 16 ✉50667 ☎ 257 83 15
Fashionable leather and erotic specials./ Ledermode und besondere Erotika.

Bruno's
Bücher • Fotobände • Magazine • Postkarten • Videoverleih • CD
KÖLN • Friesenwall 24
Mo - Fr 10 - 20 Uhr • Sa 10 - 16 Uhr
VIDEOVERLEIH
BERLIN • Nürnberger Str. 53
Mo - Sa 10 - 22 Uhr
VIDEOVERLEIH

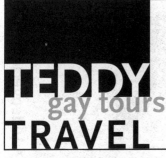

Secrets Tue Wed Fri 13.30-18.30, Thu -20.30, Sat 10-14/16 h
Marienplatz 1 ✉50676 ☎ 24 41 00
Lederbekleidung/Toys/S-M-Artikel/Piercing/Gummi/Jeans/Wet-Look/ Bücher/Postkarten/Kunstdrucke und Grafiken.

TRAVEL & TRANSPORT

G-Tours (cc G) Mon-Fri 10-18.30, Sat 10-16 h
Schwalbengasse 46 ✉50667 ☎ 925 89 10
Fax: 92 58 91 19 *Gay travel agency.*

Pride Travel Mon-Fri 10-19:00h
Höninger Weg 100A ✉50969 *(Opp. Stadion Süd)* ☎ 3680 140
Fax: 3680 111 E-Mail: travel@pride.de

Reisebüro im Bazaar de Cologne 9-18.30, Thu -20, Sat 10-14, 1st Sat -16 h
Mittelstraße 12-14 ✉50672 ☎ 257 02 21/22 Fax: 25 61 50

Teddy Travel (GLM lj) 9.30-18.30, Sat 10-13 h, Sun closed
Mathiasstraße 4-6 ✉50676 ☎ 21 98 86 Fax: 24 17 74
E-Mail: teddy-travel@t-online.de
Homepage: www.gay-cologne.de/teddy-travel
Travel agent and tour operator./ Reisebüro und -veranstalter. Own catalogue/Eigener Katalog. Also contact for Raffles Gay Sailing.

HOTELS

Ahl Meerkatzen von 1264 (B bf g H)
Mathiasstraße 21 ✉50676 *(Near/Nähe Heumarkt)*
☎ 23 48 82 Fax: 23 48 85
Central location. 15 km to the airport. Rooms with telephone, TV, priv. bath/WC. Single DM 87-145, double 110-195, bf incl. During exhibiton times from 195, double from 295.

Ascot (AC B bf CC g H MA sa sol WO) Hohenzollernring 95-97 ✉50672 *(U-Friesenplatz)* ☎ 95 29 65-0 Fax: 952 965 100
Upscale hotel with private atmosphere. Single DM 150-251, double 211-370. Bf DM 24.

Augustinerplatz. Hotel am (B bf CC E glm H)
Hohe Straße 30 ✉50667 *(Tram-Heumarkt)*
☎ 27 28 02-0 Fax: 27 28 02-77
53 rooms with bath/shower/WC, telephone/fax, TV/radio, bar, safe, room service. Rates single DM 109-139, double 159-189. Additionnal bed DM 50. Buffet bf incl. Half board DM 30.

Callas am Dom (bf CC g H msg s)
Hohe Straße 137 ✉50667 *(2 min. from Central Station)*
☎ 258 38 38 Fax: 258 38 39.
Single rooms DM 110-220/double rooms 150-350. Special weekend prices. Also Last-Minute from 19 h. Einzelzimmer DM 110-220/Doppelzimmer 150-350. Sonderpreise am Wochenende. Last-Minute ab 19 h.

Chelsea (A B bf F g H OS YG) Jülicher Straße 1 ✉50674 *(U-Rudolfplatz)* ☎ 20 71 50 Fax: 23 97 37
Centrally located. Charming. Single DM 129, double DM 179, suites DM 300 (1 person), DM 320 (2 persons), DM 350 (3 persons). Also low-budget accommodation.

★ LUXUS-ZIMMER
★ WHIRLPOOL
★ ÜBERNACHTUNGS MÖGLICHKEIT
★ LEDERSTUDIO - ALLE TOUREN
★ MASSAGEN
★ BEGLEITSERVICE
★ HAUS- u. HOTELBESUCHE
★ TÄGLICH AB 15 UHR
Kai, Dein ständiger Ansprechpartner!
Homepage: http://www.valentino.de
GAY-CLUB
Valentino
ALTENBERGER STR. 13 • KÖLN Telefon 0221 / 137079
Hinterausgang Hauptbahnhof Öffnungszeiten: So-Do 15-01 Fr+Sa 15-03

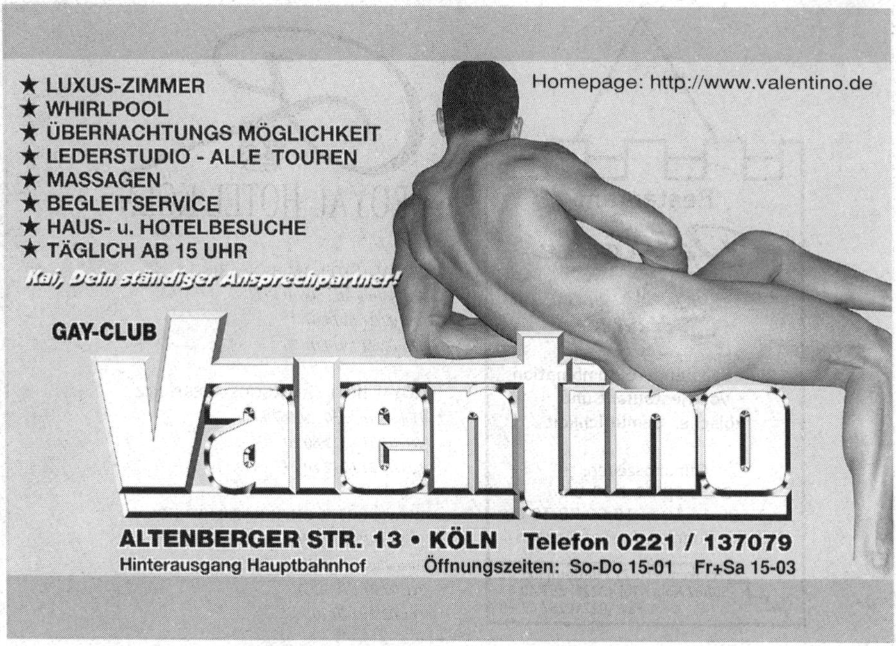

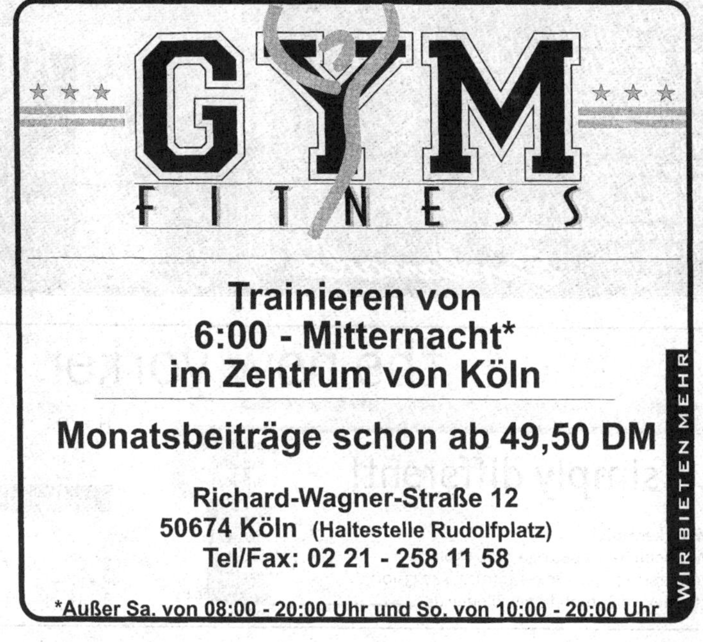

GYM
FITNESS
Trainieren von
6:00 - Mitternacht*
im Zentrum von Köln
Monatsbeiträge schon ab 49,50 DM
Richard-Wagner-Straße 12
50674 Köln (Haltestelle Rudolfplatz)
Tel/Fax: 02 21 - 258 11 58
*Außer Sa. von 08:00 - 20:00 Uhr und So. von 10:00 - 20:00 Uhr
WIR BIETEN MEHR

Restaurant

Domerie

&

Sitanis

Cocktail & Dreams

Die etwas andere Kombination von Restaurant und kölscher Gemütlichkeit

Öffnungszeiten:
Di-Sa 18.00-1.00 Uhr
So 12.00-14.30 u. 18.00-22.30 Uhr
Montag Ruhetag (außer Messen)

Frankenwerft 27 / Buttermarkt 42
50667 Köln • Tel. (0221) 257 40 44
Fax (0221) 257 42 69

ROYAL HOTEL KÖLN

ROYAL HOTEL AM HANSARING
Hansaring 96 · 50670 Köln
Tel. 02 21 / 914 01 8
Fax 02 21 / 914 01 79

ROYAL HOTEL AM AUGUSTINERPLATZ
Hohe Straße 30 · 50667 Köln
Tel. 02 21 / 272 80 20
Fax 02 21 / 272 80 277

ROYAL HOTEL RHEINKASSELER HOF
RESTAURANT WINTERGARTEN
Amandustraße 6-10 · 50769 Köln
Tel. 02 21 / 70 92 70
Fax 02 21 / 70 10 73

PRIVAT HOTEL
KÖLN · COLOGNE · COLONIA · KEULEN
★ „THE" WELL-KNOWN DESIGN HOTEL ★
NEXT TO THE BEST GAY BARS (CITY-CENTER)
CHARMING TEAM & COSY ATMOSPHERE
SINGLE DM 155,- DOUBLE DM 205,-
***WEEKEND:** SINGLE DM 135,- DOUBLE DM 175,-*
HOHENSTAUFENRING 56
• D - 50674 KÖLN
• TEL. (02 21) 921 55 70 • FAX (02 21) 21 68 22
E-mail: esplanade.hotelcologne@t-online.de

Esplanade

the new yorker.®

HOTEL

... simply different!

the new yorker Hotel
Deutz-Mülheimer-Straße 204 • 51063 Köln
Fon: +49(0)221/4733-0 • Fax: +49(0)221/4733-100
e-Mail: thenewyorkerhotel@netcologne.de

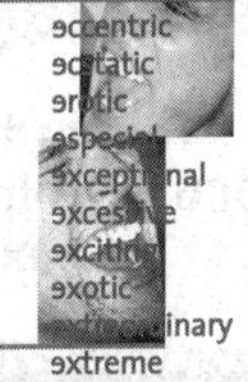

eccentric
ecstatic
erotic
especial
exceptional
excessive
exciting
exotic
extraordinary
extreme

WORLDWIDE HOSPITALITY
GOLDEN TULIP
HOTELS

COLOGNE
EUROPE

Conti Hotels Rheingold (B bf CC glm H lj MA sa)
Engelbertstraße 33-35 ✉50674 *(Tram/U-Rudolfplatz)*
☎ 92 40 90 Fax: 24 25 75.
Rates single DM 150, double 180 (incl. bf).

Conti Hotels Richard Wagner (bf CC glm H lj MA)
Brüsseler Straße 40-42 ✉50674 *(Tram-Moltkestraße)* ☎ 925 92 80
Rates single DM 150, double 180.

Conti-Hotel Rheingold (AC B bf CC glm H MA sa sol)
0-24 h
Engelbertstraße 33-35 ✉50674 *(U/Tram-Rudolfplatz)*
☎ 924 09-0 Fax: 24 25 75
Central location./Zentrale Lage. All rooms with bath/shower, WC, TV and phone./Alle Zimmer mit Bad/Dusche, WC, TV und Telefon. Single from DM 150, double from 180, suite from 260,- (bf incl.).

Cumulus (b bf CC g H MA)
Friesenstraße 33 ✉50670 *(U-Friesenplatz)* ☎ 925 98 70
Fax: 925 98 78
Central location. All rooms with shower/WC, phone, cable-TV, radio, VCR, computer/fax connection. Rates from single DM 140, double 180 (bf incl.)

Esplanade (A bf CC g H MA sa sol)
Hohenstaufenring 56 ✉50674 *(Near/Nähe Rudolfplatz)*
☎ 921 55 70 Fax: 216 822
E-Mail: esplanade.hotelcologne@t-online.de
Centrally located. Rooms with shower/bath/WC, TV, radio and minibar. Single from DM 155, double fromDM 195, Weekend rates single from 135, double from 175. Designer hotel.

Germania (G H p) Große Sandkaul 24-26, ✉50667 *(Near/Nähe Heumarkt)* ☎ 257 68 49 or ☎ 257 68 69
Centrally located. All rooms with phone, partly with shower. Rates single from DM 55 (with shower 70), double 90 (with shower 110). No breakfast.

Heinzelmännchen (bf H NG)
Hohe Pforte 5 ✉50676 *(Near/Nähe Heumarkt)* ☎ 21 12 17
Central location. 20 minutes to the airport. All rooms with telephone, partly with bath/WC and balcony. /Zentrale Lage. 20 Minuten zum Flughafen. Zimmer mit Telefon, teilweise mit Bad/WC und Balkon. Single DM 70, double 108, bf incl.

Hotel Königshof (AC bf CC H)
Richartzstraße 14-16
☎ 257 87 71 Fax: 257 87 62

Hubertushof (bf g H)
Mühlenbach 30 ✉50676 *(Near/Nähe Heumarkt)* ☎ 21 73 86
Fax: 21 89 55
Centrally located./ Zentrale Lage. Single from DM 60, double DM 80, bf. incl..

New Yorker Hotel. The (H)
Deutz-Mühlheimer-Strasse 204 ✉51063 ☎ 47 330
Fax: 47 33 100 E-Mail: thenewyorkerhotel@netcologne.de
Grand opening was on the 25.11.'99

Royal Hotel am Augustiner Platz (bf CC H NG)
Hohe Straße 30 ✉50667 ☎ 272 80 20

Royal Hotel am Hansaring (bf CC H NG)
Hansaring 69 ✉50667 ☎ 258 14 09

Royal Hotel Rheinkasseler Hof (bf CC H NG)
Amandustreaße 6-10 ✉50669 ☎ 70 92 70

Timp. Hotel (B CC d MA S STV TV W) Drag shows 1-4 h
Heumarkt 25 ✉50667 ☎ 258 14 09
Centrally located. 20 minutes to the airport. Rates single DM 60, double 120. No bf. Shower/WC on the corridor.

GUEST HOUSES

Gästehaus Kettengasse (bf CC G H)
Pfeilstrasse 43 ✉50672 ☎ 257 09 50 E-Mail: GHKoeln@aol.com

PRIVATE ACCOMODATION

Enjoy Bed & Breakfast (bf G H MA YG) 16.30-21 h
Motzstraße 5 ✉10777 ☎ (030) 215 16 66
Fax: (030) 217 52 219 E-Mail: Info@ebab.com
Homepage: www.ebab.de *Price 40 DM. Accommodation sharing agency. All with shower and bf.*

Schwule Übernachtungsmöglichkeiten
7-21 h
c/o Checkpoint, Pipinstraße 7 ✉50667 ☎ 925 76 68

GENERAL GROUPS

AK Schwule bei Bündnis 90/Die Grünen
c/o Bündnis 90/Grüne Köln, Bürgerstraße 2 ✉50667
☎ 22 12 59 19 Fax: 22 12 45 55

Arbeitskreis lesbischer & schwuler Polizeibediensteter Nordrhein-Westfalen
PO Box 30 01 69 ✉50777 ☎ 02831/946 66
Fax: 02129-588 95. Email: lanax@t-online.de
Homepage: http://home.t-online.de/home/lanax/alspol.htm

Bartmänner Köln e.V.
PO Box 29 03 41 ✉50525
Group for hairy/bearded men and their admirers./ Gruppe für haarige/bärtige Männer und ihre Liebhaber. Meetings 1st and 3rd Mo in „Quo Vadis".

Boy Trek Meeting Thu 17-22 h
Lesbisch-Schwule Jugendzentrum, Kamekestraße 14 ✉50672
☎ 194 46

Dicke Freunde Köln meets 2nd Sat 19-22 h at Beim Pitter
c/o Ullrich Naudsch, Laudahnstraße 35 ✉50937 ☎ 42 54 66
E-Mail: Dicke-Freunde-Koeln@t-online.de *Call for other dates.*

Kölner Lesben- und Schwulentag e.V. (KLUST)
c/o Hans-Jürgen Lichterfeld, Maarweg 221 ✉50823
☎ 739 01 94 or ☎ 202 03-45 Fax: 739 01 94
Organizes CSD (Gay Pride) Cologne.

Lesben- und Schwulenverband in Deutschland (LSVD) e.V. (GLM MA) Mon-Fri 9-17 h
Pipinstraße 7 ✉50667 ☎ 925 96 10 Fax: 92 59 61 11
E-Mail: NRW@lsvd.de Homepage: www.lsvd.de
Türk Gay (1st Mon 17 h) Ermis (Greek gay group)

Iglf-Lesbian & Gay Liberation Front Mon-Fri 16-18, Tue-Fri 20-22 h
Kartäuserwall 18, ✉50678 ☎ 9318 8016 Fax: 9318 8016
E-Mail: Iglf@aol.com
Contains Lglf-library with over 2000 titels on G&L issues.

Liberale Demokraten-Die Sozialliberalen
PO Box 71 05 11 ✉50745

Rosa Funken Köln von 1995
Zugweg 12 ✉50677
Gay carnival club/schwuler Carnevals Verein.

Schwule Väter Köln 1st Fri 20 h
at Moltkestraße 123, ground floor, 50674 Köln
c/o Der Andere Buchlanden, Wahlenstraße 1 ✉50823
☎ 52 05 79

Schwusos-Schwule Sozialdemokraten
c/o SCHULZ, Kartäuserwall 18 ✉50678

Triviatas-1. schwuler Männerchor Köln e.V. Mon-Fri 10-18 h
c/o Peter Junge, Venloer Straße 16 ✉50672 ☎ 202 03 20
Choir rehearsals Mon 20-22 h at SCHULZ, Karfäuserwall 18 50678 Köln.

Türk-Gay 1st Sat 17 h, Disco 4th Fri from 22 h in SchULZ
Pippinstraße 7, ✉50474 ☎ 925 96 10 Fax: 92 59 61 11
E-Mail: svd.nrw@t-online.de
Schwulengruppe für Türken. Türkische Disco im Sch.U.L.Z. jeden 3. Fri.Gay group for Turks

Völklinger Kreis e.V.
Leyendeckerstraße 1 ✉50825
☎ 546 19 79 Fax: 954 17 57.
Homepage: http://www.vk-online.de/
Headoffice of the association of gay managers.

FETISH GROUPS

Köln oliv
PO Box 29 03 41 ✉50525 ☎ (0228) 23 44 51
Offene Gruppe, für alle die auf Uniformen stehen. Unpolitisch, waffenlos, nur für den Spaß.

Leather Friends Cologne United Colours
(G LJ MA) Every 2nd and 4th Mon 20 h
at Zipps, Hohe Pforte 13-17
PO Box 451 025 ✉50885 E-Mail: leatherfriends@hotmail.com

LSMA Köln
PO Box 1457 ✉53777 Eitorf ☎ & Fax: (0228) 23 44 51
(Wolfgang) SM/Body Art. Köln Oliv . SM and fetish parties. Call for dates.

MS Panther Köln e.V. (G LJ MA) Meeting 3rd Sat 20 h
at Café Quo Vadis
PO Box 19 03 25 ✉50500
Publisher of »Panther Info«, monthly. Gay motorcyclers meet every 2nd Fri 19 h at „Quo Vadis".

HEALTH GROUPS

AIDS-Hilfe Köln e. V. Mon-Fri 10-13, 14-17 h
Beethovenstraße 1 ✉50674 *(Tram-Zülpicher Platz)* ☎ 20 20 30
Fax: 23 03 25 Email: aids-hilfekoeln@ndh.net
Rainbow cafe for PWA, HIV+ and their friends Tue-Fri 15-22, Sun - 20 h. Closed Mon.

AIDS-Hilfe NRW e.V. Landesverband Mon-Thu 9-12.30 13.30-17, Fri 9-12.30 13.30-15 h
Hohenzollernring 48 ✉50672 *(U-Friesenplatz)* ☎ 925 99 60
Fax: 925 99 69 E-Mail: landesverband@aids-hilfe-nrw.org

SchwIPS - Schwule Initiative für Plege & Soziales Mon-Fri 10-17:00h
Pipinstrasse 7 ✉50667 *(near Rudolfplatz)* ☎ 92 57 68 10 or
☎ 92 18 30 0 (positiv leben GmbH) Fax: 92 18 30 18
The ambulant nursing service „positiv leben GmbH" is based here /Pflege & Betreuungszentrum - Rubenstrasse 8-10, 50676 Köln - open from 10-17 h Mon to Fri.

Schwule Initiative für Pflege und Soziales e.V. (SchwIPS) Mon-Fri 9-17 h
Rubensstraße 8-10 ✉50676 *(Near Heumarkt)* ☎ 92 18 30-0
Fax: 92 18 30-18

HELP WITH PROBLEMS

HerzensLust-Koordination NRW Mon-Fri 8-12.30, Mon Thu 13.30-17, Fri 13.30-15 h
c/o AIDS Hilfe NRW e.V., Hohenzollernring 48 ✉50672
☎ 92 59 96-0 Fax: 92 59 969
Email Landesverband@AIDS-Hilfe-NRW.org

Schwules Überfalltelefon Köln Mon Wed Fri 19-21 h c/o LSVD, Pipinstraße 7 ✉50667 ☎ 192 28
Gay bashing: Helpline.

Sozialwerk für Lesben und Schwule e.V.
(GLM MA W YG) Mon-Fri 10-18 h
Karthäuserwall 18 ✉50678 ☎ 93 18 80-83
E-Mail: info@sozialwerk-koeln.de
Homepage: www.sozialwerk-koeln.de
Counselling Mon-Fri 16-18, Tue-Thu 20-22 h ☎ 19 446.

RELIGIOUS GROUPS

HuK Regionalgruppe Köln
c/o Michael Schnippering, Beueler Bahnhofsplatz 24, ✉53225 Bonn ☎ 2582888 *(Martin)*

MCC Köln service: 2nd & 4th Sat 15.30 h
c/o Schulz, Kartäuserwall 18 ✉50678

Yachad Mon Fri 16-18, Tue Thu 18-22 h
☎ 194 46
Jewish gays and lesbians/Jüdische Schwule und Lesben.

SPORT GROUPS

Chaos Köln
☎ 240 90 67 *Volleyball.*

Cologne Hot Balls Schwul-lesbische Squashgruppe (GLM MA) Tue 20-22 h
c/o Stephan Heller, Moltkestraße 70 ✉50674
E-Mail: toenges@netcologne.de. Every November Rainbow-Cup.

Sport Club Janus e.V. Köln „Erfrischend anders seit 1980" (GLM MA) Office Tue 16-19 h
Pipinstraße 7 ✉50667 *(Heumarkt)* Fax: 925 59 31
E-Mail: info@sc-janus.de Homepage: www.sc-janus.de
Over 53 sport possibilities and sports parties.

TGC Seitenwechsel Cologne e.V.
c/o Vayu Pogacar, Universitätsstraße 77 ✉50931
☎ & Fax: 400 96 93
Gay and lesbian ballroom dancing.

Wing-Tsung Selbstverteidigung Mon-Thu 14 h
☎ 92 59 61 18 *Gay and Lesbian.*

SWIMMING

-Bleibtreusee (g NU) (near/Nähe Euskirchen)
-Hallenfreizeitbad Bornheim (g sa) (Rilkestr. 6, 53332 Bornheim)
-Baggersee Köln-Porz/Gremberghoven (an der/on B4)
-Agrippa-Bad (Ha-:llenbad) (Agrippa Straße)
-Aqualand (Wed 18:30-23:00h MA, NU) www.aqualand.de

CRUISING

-»Park« Aachener Weiher (AYOR) (Tag und Nacht, populär/day and night, popular.)
-Brühler Landstrasse/Hitzeler Strasse (AYOR; police)
-Cranachwäldchen (nu)
-Mühlheimer Stadtgarten (ayor MG OG)
-Parkanlage Theodor-Heuss-Ring am/at Ebertplatz
-Parkplatz Phantasialand BAB 553 near Brühl (MA LJ)
-Baggersee Köln-Porz/Gremborghoven BAB 4

Königstein ☎ 06174

TRAVEL & TRANSPORT

Travelman (GLM MA) Mon-Fri 9-18 h
Im Hainchen 18 ✉61462 ☎ 93 18 73 Fax: 252 90
E-Mail: travelhouse@t-online.de
Organizer of traveling in gay groups throughout the world./Anbieter schwuler Gruppenreisen weltweit.

Konstanz ☎ 07531

BARS

Aber Hallo (B d GLM MA p r S SNU STV TV) Mon-Tue 20-1, Fri Sat 21-2, closed Sun
Kreuzlinger Straße 46 ✉78462 ☎ 258 29

DANCECLUBS

Excalibur (B G MA YG) Sun 21-1 h
Blätzleplatz ✉78462 *(Close to »Hertie« department store. Bus-Schnetztor)* ☎ 214 24

SEX SHOPS/BLUE MOVIES

Film- und Videoshop (g VS) 10-1/? h
Emmishoferstraße 4 ✉78462 ☎ 213 40
Kino und Treffpunkt/meeting place. Magazine, Videos, Vorführungen.
Sexyland (g VS) Mon-Fri 10-20, Sat -16 h, closed Sun
Kreuzlinger Straße 5 ✉78462 ☎ 220 26

SAUNAS/BATHS

Relax-Center Hyperion (AC B CC d DR f G lj MA msg OS p R sa sb sol VS WO) Mon-Sun 15-23 h, Wed closed
Gottlieb-Daimler-Straße 3 ✉78467 ☎ 610 61

GENERAL GROUPS

Boys Only Mon 19 h Schwimmen im Jacobsbad, 21 h
Schulze & Schulze Stammtisch Email: bok@konstanz.gay-web.de
Homosexuelle in Konstanz (HIK) (b G MA) Tue 20-? h, Fri 21.30-? h
Friedrichstraße 21 ✉78467 ☎ 645 35
E-Mail: hik@konstanz.gay-web.de.
Homepage: www.konstanz.gay-web.de/hik/

HEALTH GROUPS

AIDS-Hilfe Konstanz e.V. Mon-Tue Thu-Fri 10-12, Tue Thu 16-18 h
Münzgasse 29 ✉78462 ☎ 211 13
E-Mail: aidshilfe.konstanz@t-online.de
Homepage: konstanz.aidshilfe.de
Counselling/Beratung ☎ 19 411. Positiven-Café Thu 17-19 h

HELP WITH PROBLEMS

Rosa Telefon Mon 20-22 h
☎ 164 46

RELIGIOUS GROUPS

HuK Regionalgruppe Bodensee/Oberschwaben
Postfach 10 18 12 ✉78418 ☎ 290 72 *(Michael & Peter)*
E-mail Benedictus@t-online.de

SPORT GROUPS

Schwule Wandergruppe Bodensee
Postfach 10 11 18 ✉78411 ☎ 290 72
Hiking group. Call for dates and further information.

CRUISING

-Stadtpark/municipal park
-Schnetztor underpass (next to Sexyland, popular)/Unterführung am Schnetztor (neben Sexyland, popular)
-Restaurant in/im Hertie (Dept. Store)
-Laube (OG)
-Sternenplatz (selten/seldom)

Krefeld ☎ 02151

BARS

Schickeria (AC B D f G MA p s VS) 21-5 h
Westwall 33 ✉47798 ☎ 288 55
Karaoke/Show on Wed.

DANCECLUBS

Jogis Top Inn (B D g MA YG) Fri Sat & before holidays 22-5
Neue Linnerstraße 85, ✉47798 ☎ 236 24
Tollhaus (B D GLM YG) Sun 19-? h
Ostwall 4-6 *19-20 h all drinks half price.*

GENERAL GROUPS

Arbeitskreis Schwulenpolitik
c/o DIE GRÜNEN, Roßstraße 200, ✉47798 ☎ 77 73 44
Schwulenreferat im ASTA der FH Niederrhein Wed 14.30-16.30, Fri 12-14 h
Frankenring 20, ✉47798 ☎ 77 68 78

HEALTH GROUPS

AIDS-Hilfe Krefeld e.V. Mon-Fri 10-13, Wed 19.30-21.30 h
Nordwall 83, 47798, PO Box 108, ✉47701 ☎ 194 11

SWIMMING

-Elfrather See (Krefeld-Gartenstadt) am Surfsee auf dem Berg/ Elfrather Lake (in Krefeld-Gartenstadt) at surfers lake on the hill.

CRUISING

-Stadtgarten/municipal garden (AYOR)

Kronach ☎ 09261

HOTELS

Schlosshotel Fischbach (B bf F g H MA NU OS pi S sa)
Fischbach, ✉96317 ☎ 30 06 Fax: 31 51
Rooms partly with TV & phone./Zimmer teilweise mit TV und Telefon. Rates from DM 50 (bf incl.)

1 EURO =

40,3399	BEF	40,3399	LUF
1,95583	DEM	2,20371	NLG
166,386	ESP	13,7603	ATS
6,55957	FRF	200,482	PTE
0,787564	IEP	5,94573	FIM
1936,27	ITL		

Lahr ☎ 07821

GENERAL GROUPS

Homosexuelle Informationsgruppe Ortenau/Baden (HIOB) (B d GLM MA) Tue 20-?, Fri 21-?, 1st Sat 21-? h
Alte Bahnhofstraße 5 ✉77933 ☎ 383 83

Landau ☎ 06341

HEALTH GROUPS

AIDS-Hilfe Landau e.V. Tue 19-21 h
Weißenburger Straße 2b ✉76829 ☎ 194 11
or Mon Wed Fri 13-16 h ☎ 886 88. Rainbow café 1st and 3rd Sun 18 h. Frauencafé 2nd Sun 18 h.

HELP WITH PROBLEMS

Rosa Telefon Wed 20-22 h
☎ 194 46

CRUISING

-Hauptbahnhof/Main Rail Station
-Schwanenweiher im/in Ostpark (near/Nähe Hauptbahnhof)

Landshut ☎ 0871

CRUISING

-Landtorplatz
-Naherholungsgebiet Gretlmühle, 2. Baggersee
-Stadtpark Klinikum Parkhausausgang

Leipzig ☎ 0341

GAY INFO

LUST last Sun 19.30-20 h FM 97,6 MHz, cable 104,05 MHz
c/o Radio Blau, Steinstraße 18 ✉04275 ☎ 301 00 97
Querele
c/o AIDS-Hilfe, Ossietzkystraße 18 ✉04347 ☎ 2 32 31 26
RosaLinde Leipzig e.V. (A B D f GLM MA S STV VS WE) daily 20-1 h, Sat open end
Lindenauer Markt 21 ✉04177 *(Tram-Lindauer Markt)* ☎ 484 15 11
Fax: 484 15 20. Email kontakt@rosalinde.de
Disco „Rosa Libre" Sat 22 h. Café-Betrieb from 20-01:00 h. Choir „Die Kirschblüten": rehearsals Mon 20 h. Variete and show: rehearsals Tue 19 h. Dancing lessons: Wed 19 and 20.30 h.

BARS

Advokat (B G MA) 18-4 h
Brühl ✉04109 *(between Nikolaistraße and Ritterstraße)*
Black Horse (B f glm MA YG) 17-2 h
Roßstraße 12 ✉04103 *(near/nahe Hauptpost/Gewandhaus)*
☎ 960 96 05 *Irish pub*
Inside (B glm) 19-? h, Sun closed
Dölitzer Straße 28 ✉04277 ☎ 391 13 01
Löwenzwinger (G LJ MA p) 1st/3rd Sat 21-? h
Ossietzkystraße 18 ✉0437 ☎ 232 31 26
Leather & fetish party. Guests welcome

CAFES

Café Hochschwul (G YG) Thu 18 h
c/o AG Hochschwul, Uni Leipzig, Augustusplatz 11 ✉04109
☎ 973 78 54

DANCECLUBS

Anyway. Club (AC B D DR f G lj MA p s VS YG) Mon, Tue, Thu 20-4 h, Wed, Fri, Sat 22-5 h, Sun closed
Dorotheenplatz 3b ✉04109 ☎ 212 77 07
Bar and Disco. Call for details and times.
Blaue Trude (B D DR G lj MA OS s SNU WE) 20-4 h, weekends open end
Katharinenstraße 17/Am Sachsenplatz ✉04109 *(near Alter Markt)*
☎ 212 66 79
Always entrance free
Jam-Dance Hall (AC B D f G S YG)
Große Fleischergasse 12 ✉04109 *(near department store Hortenkaufhaus)* ☎ 961 74 32
Gay every 2nd Sunday.
Rosa Linde e.V. (B D GLM) Sat Sun 22-? h
Lindenauer Markt 21 ✉04177 ☎ 484 15 11
Popular.

SEX SHOPS/BLUE MOVIES

Erotik-exclusiv (g)
Kuhturmstraße 6 ✉04177
Erotik-Shop (g) Mon-Fri 10-18.30, Sat -12.30 h
Universitätsstraße 18 ✉04109
Orion (g) Mon-Fri 9-19, Sat -16 h
Bernhard-Göring-Straße 36 ✉04107 *(Nahe/Near Bayerischer Bahnhof)* ☎ 213 20 95

SAUNAS/BATHS

Clubsauna Stargayte (! AC B DR F G MA NU p sa sb sol VS WO YG) Sun-Thu 15-2, Fri Sat 15-8 h
Otto-Schill-Straße 10 ✉04109 ☎ 961 42 46
Biggest gay sauna in the area (200 sq. meters) 2 floors with 2 bars. A covered atrium and large dark room labyrinth.

Phoenix Sauna (B f DR G msg sa sb sol VS) Sun-Thu 13-1, Fri-Sat -6 h
Große Fleischergasse 12 ✉04109 ☎ 960 79 99
Fri & Sat 25 „Partner day" for gays under 25 year old.

BOOK SHOPS

Connewitzer Verlagsbuchhandlung (CC glm s) Mon-Fri 10-20, Sat -16 h
Schuhmachergäßchen 4 ✉04109 *(Speck's Hof)* ☎ 960 34 47

TRAVEL & TRANSPORT

Anders Reisen Mon-Fri 10-19, Sat -14 h
Industriestraße 43,Plagwitz ✉04229 ☎ 479 24 37
Fax: 479 24 39 E-Mail: info@anders-reisen-leipzig.de
Homepage: www.anders-reisen-leipzig.de

PRIVATE ACCOMODATION

Enjoy Bed & Breakfast (bf G H MA YG) 16.30-21 h
☎ (030) 215 16 66 Fax: (030) 21 75 22 19
E-Mail: info@ebab.com Homepage: www.ebab.de.
Price from DM 50 Accommodation sharing agency. All with shower and bf.

GENERAL GROUPS

HochschWul-die Studentengruppe Cafe Thu 18 h in main building room 2-30 (2nd floor)
c/o StuRA der Uni. Leipzig, Augustusplatz 11 ✉04109
☎ 973 78 50

J.u.n.g.S. & Jule 3rd Sat 16 h, 2nd Sat 17 h
c/o AIDS-Hilfe, Ossietzkystraße 18 ✉04347 ☎ 232 43 26
E-Mail: j.u.n.g.s.@gmx.de *Gay youth group for young gays.*

SMILE-Gesprächskreis 1st Tue 20 h
c/o Café Kleinod

FETISH GROUPS

Lederclub Leipzig 3rd Sat 18 h (downstairs at AIDS-Hilfe)
c/o AIDS-Hilfe Leipzig, Ossietzkystraße 18 ✉04347
☎ 232 31 26

HEALTH GROUPS

abc LEIPZIG e.V.-Verein für Sexualaufklärung und Prävention Mon-Fri 12-16.30, Sat 10-14 h
Ritterstraße 4 ✉04109 *(Theaterpassage)* ☎ 961 59 99
Fax: 961 59 95
Information, prevention, condoms. as well as literature.

AIDS-Beratung und Betreuung im Gesundheitsamt Mon 9-12, Tue 9-18, Thu 12-18.30, Fri 9-12 h
Gustav-Mahler-Straße 1-3 ✉04109 ☎ 123 68 91/94
Free and anonymous HIV-testing and Safer Sex counselling.

AIDS-Hilfe Leipzig e. V. (A f g MA OS) Counselling: Mon Wed 10-18, Tue Thu -21, Fri -1, Cafe: Tue Thu 15-21 h
Ossietzkystraße 18 ✉04347 *(Tram-Ossietzkystraße)*
☎ 232 31 27 Fax: 2333968 E-Mail: info@leipzig.aidshilfe.de

HELP WITH PROBLEMS

Schwules Überfalltelefon Tue 19-20 h
☎ 192 28
Help for victims and witnesses of anti-gay violence.

RELIGIOUS GROUPS
Arbeitskreis Homosexualität der ESG Leipzig Fri 18-? h
Alfred-Kästner-Straße 11 ✉04275 *(Tram10/11/24/28/58-Kurt-Eisner-Straße)* ☎ 688 85 47 *(Reinhard)*
HuK Regionalgruppe Leipzig
PO Box 10 06 31 ✉04006 E-mail GKnob@t-online.de

SPORT GROUPS
Sport-Club Rosa Löwen e.V.
PO Box 10 04 34 ✉04004
E-mail: Loewen.Leipzig@gaysport.org
Homepage: http://www.gaysport.org/rosaloewen/

SWIMMING
-Kulkwitzer See (B 87 Leipzig-Markranstädt, northern side/Nordseite)
-Ammelshainer Seen (A 14 → Dresden to »Naunhof«, cruising between the two lakes)

CRUISING
-Clara-Zetkin-Park (lj) (Klingerweg/Nonnenweg)
-Schillerpark (Schillerstraße/Moritzbastei. Popular)

Lemgo ☎ 05261

GENERAL GROUPS
Schwulenreferat/Schwulen- und Lesbengruppe
c/o AStA FH Lippe, Liebigstraße 87 ✉32657

CRUISING
-P Regenstorplatz (Regentorstraße, day and night)

Leonberg ☎ 07152

GENERAL GROUPS
SchwuBSi - Schwule Initiative Böblingen Sindelfingen
c/o Erich Lauer, Neuköllner Straße 9 ✉71229
☎ & Fax: 90 23 42 Email: schwubsi@boeblingen.gay-web.de
Homepage: http://boeblingen.gay-web.de

Leverkusen ☎ 0214

HEALTH GROUPS
AIDS-Hilfe Leverkusen e.V. Mon Wed 9-12, Tue 19-21, Thu 19-21 h
Lichstraße 36a ✉51373 ☎ 40 17 66
Betroffeneberatung: Wed 18-20 h

Limburg ☎ 06431

SEX SHOPS/BLUE MOVIES
Orion (g) Mon-Fri 9-20, Sat -16 h
Westerwaldstraße 111-113 ✉65549 *(at Lahn-Einkaufszentrum)* ☎ 221 31

CRUISING
-Bahnhof/railway station
-Stadthalle/Municipal hall (Tiefgarage und Platz davor/Parking garage and square in front of)

Lingen ☎ 0591

SEX SHOPS/BLUE MOVIES
Erotic World (AC g MA r VS) Mon-Sat 10-23 h
Tecklenburger Straße 2 ✉49809 ☎ 15 05

GENERAL GROUPS
Am anderen Ufer der Ems e.V. (GLM) Meeting 3rd Sun 16-18 h
c/o AIDS-Hilfe Emsland e.V., Mühlenstraße 3 ✉49808 *49808* ☎ 583 94 Fax: 541 21 E-Mail: AH.Emsland@t-online.de
Coming-Out-Gruppe „Einsteiger" (YG) 1st & 3rd Fri 20-22
PO Box 1165 ✉49781 ☎ 541 21

HEALTH GROUPS
AIDS-Hilfe Emsland e.V. Mon Wed Thu Fr 10-13, Mon Wed 14-17h
Mühlenstrasse 3 ✉49808 ☎ & Fax 54 121
Regenbogenfrühstück Wed 10-12 h.

Lippstadt ☎ 02941

CRUISING
-P hinter dem Bahnhof/behind Train station
-Grüner Winkel
–Bahnhof/Train station

Löbau ☎ 03585

GENERAL GROUPS
Rosa Power e.V. (b bf D DR f GLM MA s SNU STV VS WE) Mon-Fri 10-12 h
Promenadenring 12 ✉02708 *(Room 12)* ☎ 40 39 24
Monthly party. Call for details.

Lübeck ☎ 0451

BARS
CC Chapeau Claque (A B d G GLM MA N s TV WE YG) Tue-Thu 21-3, Fri Sat -4, Sun 21-2 h, closed Mon
Hartengrube 25-27 ✉23552 ☎ 773 71
Flamingo (b f G MA OS R N) Mon-Fri 17-?, Sat 20-? h, closed Sun
Marlesgrube 58 ✉23552 ☎ 70 48 36
V.I.P. Club (B G lj MA p YG) Mon Wed Thu 20-3, Fri Sat -4, Sun 18-3 h, closed Tue
Marlesgrube 61, ✉23552 ☎ 79 66 20

SEX SHOPS/BLUE MOVIES
Orion (g) Mon-Fri 9-20, Sat 9-16 h
Ziegelstraße 232 ✉23556 *(At „plaza")* ☎ 896 69 66
Orion (g) Mon-Fri 9-20, Sat 9-16 h
Kantstraße ✉23566 *(»plaza« Messenring)* ☎ 62 35 61
Seventh Heaven (AC CC DR g lj MA VS YG) 9-23, Sun 12-23 h
Lederstrasse 2-4 ✉23552 ☎ 70 69 50
Sparta Shop (G VS) 9-24, Fri-Sat -4 h
Hüxstraße 15 ✉23552 ☎ 724 53
World Of Sex-WOS (g VS) 9.30-24, Sun 12-24 h
Wahmstrasse 32, ✉23552

BOOK SHOPS
Pressezentrum (g)
Breite Straße 79 ✉23552 ☎ 799 60 70

TRAVEL & TRANSPORT
Ticketkontor Mon-Fri 10-13, 14-18 h
Fleischhauerstraße 80 ✉23552 *(near Niederegger-Marzipan Shop)* ☎ 702 07 74 Fax: 702 07 99
Travel agency with very good service, friendly staff/Reisebüro mit gutem Service

PRIVATE ACCOMODATION
Enjoy Bed & Breakfast (bf G H MA YG) 16:30-21 h

☎ 030/215 1666 Fax: 030/217 52219
E-Mail: Info@ebab.com Homepage: www.ebab.com *Price from 45 DM. Accommodation sharing agency. All with shower & bf.*

GENERAL GROUPS

Homosexuelle Initiative Lübeck (HIL)
Wed 20-22 h
PO Box 18 23 23506, c/o ESG, Königstraße 23 ✉23552
☎ 798 71 16

Schwule Aktion Lübeck e.V.-SAL
PO Box 18 23, ✉23556 ☎ & Fax: 70 58 88

HEALTH GROUPS

Hilfe für HiV-Positive e.V. Counselling Mon-Fri 10-15 h
Reiferstraße 21 ✉23554 ☎ 47 45 95

Lübecker AIDS-Hilfe e. V. Counselling: Tue Thu 18-20 h
Engelsgrube 16 ✉23552 ☎ 194 11 or Mon-Fri ☎ 725 51 or 70 41 33

HELP WITH PROBLEMS

Rosa Telefon Wed 20-22 h
☎ 798 71 16

SWIMMING

-Brodner Ufer, Travemünde (NU)

CRUISING

-Wallstraße (up to the Holstentor (r) and [P] at river Trave)
-Katzenberg (ayor r) (between Possehl and Stadtgraben)
-Mühlentorteller
-Burgtorteller (Gustav-Radbruch-Platz)

Lüdenscheid ☎ 02351

SEX SHOPS/BLUE MOVIES

Sex and Gags (g VS) 9-19, Thu -20.30, Sat 9-14 h
Lessingstraße/Knapper Straße ✉58507

HEALTH GROUPS

AIDS-Hilfe im Märkischen Kreis e.V. Mon 19-21 h
Duisbergweg 3, ✉58511 ☎ 232 02

CRUISING

-Parkpalette -18 h *Popular.*

Ludwigsburg ☎ 07141

BARS

Sonny's Club-Bar (AC B d f G lj MA P s TV WE) 19-3 h, closed Sun
Kirchstraße 30 ✉71634 ☎ 90 16 66

SEX SHOPS/BLUE MOVIES

Beate Uhse international (CC glm MA VS) Mon-Sat 9-22, cabins -23 h, Sun closed
Stuttgarter Straße 56 ✉71638 ☎ 90 18 21

VIDEO SHOPS

Erotik Markt (g) Mon-Fri 9-20, Sat -16 h
Mathildenstraße 19 ✉71638 ☎ 92 96 14
Video rental

CRUISING

-Parking lot/Parkplatz Leonberger Straße 11, corner/Ecke Bahnhofstraße
-Stadtpark/town park »Bärenwiese«, Schorndorfer Straße/Fasanenstraße

Ludwigshafen ☎ 0621

BARS

Alter Treffpunkt (AC B d g MA p STV WE) 20-1, Fri Sat -4, closed Mon
Gräfenaustraße 51 ✉67063 ☎ 51 13 92

Come Back (B G MA p) 20-1, Fri Sat -3 h
Welserstraße 10 ✉67063 ☎ 51 25 51

SEX SHOPS/BLUE MOVIES

Amor & Co. 9-23, Sat -24, Sun 14-22 h
Ludwigstraße 54-56 ✉67059 ☎ 51 99 06

Mike's (AC g MA VS) Mon-Fri 10-23, Sat -1
Amtsstraße 1 ✉67059 ☎ 51 02 12

Orion (g) Mon-Fri 9.30-20, Sat -16 h
Yorckstraße 28/Mundenheimer Straße ✉67061 ☎ 58 31 21

Sexladen (g VS) Mon-Sat 9-23 h
Bahnhofstraße 14 ✉67059 ☎ 51 72 40

Sexyland (g VS) Mon-Fri 9-20, Sat -16 h
Ludwigstraße 10 ✉67059
Mixed sexshop with gay section.

GENERAL GROUPS

Pfundskerle Girth & Mirth Südwest
c/o Frank Lohöfer, Altholzweg 25 ✉67065 ☎ 54 44 26
E-Mail: Pfundskerle@geocities.com
Homepage: www.geocities.com/WestHollywood/4795.
Special club-events: - 1st Sat/month, 17 h at New Paragon, Frankfurt/Main - 2nd Sat/month, 17 h at Butch, Mannheim Sauna-Meeting: - 1st Sat/month, 14 h at Club Amsterdam, Frankfurt/Main - 4th Sat/month, 15 h at Hot House Club, Mannheim

SWIMMING

-Baggersee »Blaue Adria« (on the island/auf der Insel)

CRUISING

-Ebertpark (Haupteingang,links, populär/main entrance, to the left, popular)
-Hauptbahnhof/main railway station

Lüneburg ☎ 04131

BARS

501 (B F GLM) 11-2 h
Bardowicker Straße 20 ✉21335

GENERAL GROUPS

AStA-Schwulenreferat der Uni Lüneburg
Mon-Fri 10-12.30 h
Scharnhorststraße 1 ✉21335 ☎ 78 15 10 Fax: 78 15 18
E-mail asta-gay@uni-lueneburg.de

Lüneburger Schwulengruppe und Rosa Telefon (Salzsäue) Fri 18 h
c/o AIDS-Hilfe, Katzenstraße 3, ✉21335 ☎ 194 46

Salzsäue Fri 19-?
c/o Aids-Hilfe Lüneburg e.V., Am Sande 50 ✉21335 ☎ 40 35 05

HEALTH GROUPS

AIDS-Hilfe Lüneburg e.V. Mon Wed 9-11.30, Tue 14-16 h
Am Sande 50 ✉21335 ☎ 194 11
or ☎ 40 35 50. By appointment.

SWIMMING

-Kalkbruchsee (NU)
-Volgershalle (hinter d. Fachhochschule f. Wirtschaft, Nordwest Ecke)

CRUISING

-Wall/Bardowicker Stadtmauer/Liebesgrund (22-? h)
-Am Werder/Lüner Straße
-Main station/Bahnhof
-Graalwall

Lützensommern ☎ 036041

GENERAL GROUPS

Jugendnetzwerk Lambda e.V. Bundesverband
Tagungshaus Rittergut ✉99955 ☎ 449 83

Magdeburg ☎ 0391

BARS

Gummibärchen (A AC B bf f GLM MA s) Mon-Fri 13-1, Sat 17-2, Sun 15-1 h
Liebigstraße 6 ✉39104 *(Tram2/3/9/10/12-Hasselbachplatz)* ☎ 543 02 99

Tiffany (B F G MA WE YG) 20-? h
Sternstraße 29 ✉39106 ☎ 543 22 09
Disco on weekend.

SEX SHOPS/BLUE MOVIES

Gay Shop (DR G MA r VS) Mon-Fri 13-20, Sat 10-16 h
Bernburger Straße 1a ✉39104 ☎ 401 52 29

Orion (g) Mon-Fri 10-20, Sat -16 h
Mittagstraße 28 ✉39124 *(Near/Nahe Arbeitsamt)* ☎ 251 55 80

BOOK SHOPS

CloneZone (CC GLM) Mon-Sat 14-22. Sat 16-22 h video rental only
Liebigstraße 6 ✉39104 *(S-Hasselbachplatz)* ☎ 543 16 77

GUEST HOUSES

☛ Barby

GENERAL GROUPS

Les-bi-schwules Referat im Studentenrat der Universität Magdeburg
Postfach 41 20 ✉39016 ☎ 671 26 30

LSVD Sachsen-Anhalt (f G p) Wed 19-22h
W.-Rathenau-Straße 31 ✉39106 *(near Universitätsplatz)*
☎ 543 25 69 Fax: 543 25 69
Tue 20-22 counselling, Wed 19-22 gay Info. Sun 16-20 h gay info. Gay victims emergency telephone ☎ 19228 (schwules Überfalltelefon)

HEALTH GROUPS

Aids-Beratung Caritasverband Thu 14-18 h
Max-Josef-Metzger-Straße 3 ✉39104 ☎ 596 12 08

AIDS-Hilfe Magdeburg e.V. Mon-Fri 9-12, Counselling Mon-Fri 12-20 h
Weidenstraße 9 ✉39114 ☎ 541 08-49 Fax: 541 08 49.
Counselling ☎ 194 11. E-mail AIDS-Magdeburg@t-online.de

HELP WITH PROBLEMS

Überfalltelefon Tue 20-22 h
c/o SVD, Postfach 1906 ✉39009 ☎ 192 28
Help in case of gay-bashing.

SWIMMING
-Neustädter See (NU) (S-Rothensee/Eichweiler)

CRUISING
-Glacis Anlagen (Sachsenring/Adelheidtring. Popular)
-Bahnhof/railway station
-Haus des Lehrers/Teacher's house

Mainz ☎ 06131

BARS
Jolifante (AC B F glm MA OS W) Sun-Thu 17-1, Fri-Sat -2 h
Leibnizstraße 55 ✉55118 ☎ 61 41 30

CAFES
Mel's Café Bistro (A B bf F GLM MA S TV) Tue-Fri 15-1, Sa 10:30-1, So 10:30-21 h. Mon closed.
Holzhofstrasse 24 ✉55116 *(near south train station)*
☎ 23 88 23

SEX SHOPS/BLUE MOVIES
Pink Movie (g vs) Mon-Sat 8-20, Sun 11-18 h
Zanggasse 17 ✉55116 ☎ 22 62 62
Stephans Sex Boutique (g VS) Mon-Wed 9-19, Thu Fri -20, Sat -14 h
Dominikanerstraße 5a ✉55116 ☎ 22 16 50

BOOK SHOPS
Carl Habel Buchhandlung (g) Mon-fri 9.15-20, Sat 9-16 h
Am Brand 33 ✉55116 ☎ 28 81 40
Wohlthat'sche Buchhandlung (glm W) Mon-Fri 8.30-20, Sat -16 h
Große Bleiche 8 ✉55116 ☎ 22 23 53

GENERAL GROUPS
Autonomes Schwulenreferat im AStA der Uni Mainz (G s) Tue & Thu 16-18, Wed 14-16, 19:30-22 h
Staudinger Weg 21 ✉55128 ☎ 39 48 03
Bündnis 90/Die Grünen im Landtag Rheinland Pfalz Arbeitsbereich Lesben- und Schwulenpolitik
Kaiser-Friedrich-Straße 3 ✉55116 ☎ 208 31 58
E-Mail: akll@landtag.rlp.de
Schwuguntia e.V. Meeting: 1st Sun 15 h
at Schwulenreferat, Staudinger Weg 15
Münsterstraße 19 ✉55116
Young Companions e.V. (G YG) Meeting: 1st & 3rd Thu 19 h
at AIDS-Hilfe Mainz, Hopfengarten 19 ☎ 23 38 72 Fax: 23 38 74
Youthgroup -26 years /Jugendgruppe -26 Jahre.
2nd and 4th Thu meeting at „Kamin" (Kapuzinerstraße)

FETISH GROUPS
MSC Rhein-Main Frankfurt
c/o Ralf Knöfler, Martin-Josef-Straße 4 ✉55129
Member of ECMC.

HEALTH GROUPS
AIDS-Hilfe Mainz e.V. Office: Mon Wed 10-17, Tue Thu -19, Fri -15 h
Hopfengarten 19 ✉55116 ☎ 22 22 75 Fax: 23 38 74
Klinikum der Johann-Gutenberg-Universität Mon Wed Thu 8-12 h
Langenbeckstraße 1, ✉55131 ☎ 17 71 97

RELIGIOUS GROUPS
HuK-Homosexuelle und Kirche e.V. Mainz
Steffen Brammer, Groß-Gerauer Weg 67, ✉64295 *Darmstadt*
☎ 31 50 50

CRUISING
-Bahnhof (r)
-Rheinhalle (Grüne Brücke/Green Bridge)

Mannheim ☎ 0621

GAY INFO
GAYSzene Mannheim
http://www.rheinneckar.de/~astro/gayszene.htlm

BARS
Butch (AC B CC F G lj MA OS W) Mon-Thu 18-1, Fri -3, Sat 16-3, Sun -1 h
S 6, 21 ✉68161 (Near Nationaltheater) ☎ 10 19 03
Fax: 156 56 45
Butch-Keller (AC B CC d DR G LJ MA WE) Thu 20-1, Fri-Sat 21-3 h, Sun -1 h
S 6, 21 ✉68161 (near Nationaltheater) ☎ 10 19 03
Fax: 156 56 45.
Café Klatsch (AC B f G lj MA OS W YG) 19-3, Sat Sun 16-3 h
Hebelstraße 3 ✉68161 *(near Nationaltheater)* ☎ 156 10 33
Very popular.
Club Ballerino (AC D f GLM MA r s TV VS W YG) 20-3 h
Friedrichs-Ring 30 ✉68161 ☎ 139 48
Cristal
E 3, 11 ✉68159 *(Near Paradeplatz)*
Heidelbeaer (B bf G lj MA) 19-1 h
Neckarauer Straße 85 ✉68199 ☎ 85 61 38
Jack-Off: every 4th Sun admission 20-21.30 h. Uniform & Leather party: every 2nd Sat admission 20.30-21.30 h.
Jail's (! B DR G LJ MA) Fri-Sun 21-? h please call for details
Angelstraße 5-9 ✉68199 *(next to M&S Connexion)*
☎ 854 41 46
300 sq.m. darkroom area.
KoKo
Tattersallstraße 24 ✉68165
Petit Paris (AC B bf d F GLM lj MA S STV WE) Mon-Thu 15-1, Fri -3, Sat 5-3, Sun 5-19 h
T3, 2-3 ✉68161 ☎ 10 16 96
XS Café Bar (A AC B bf f G YG) Mon-Sat 11-1, Sun 14.30-1
N7, 9 ✉68161 (Kunststraße) ☎ 0261/15 23 78
Zelle (A B G lj MA N) 19-1 h
Schwetzinger Straße 96 ✉68165 *(Tram-Kopernikusstraße. Near main station)* ☎ 40 96 69

DANCECLUBS
Club Action (B D GLM) Sat & Sun 20-05:00h
U5, 13 ☎ 15 34 35
M & S Connexion (! AC B D DR f G lj MA OS s VS W YG) Sat (G) 215, 2nd Sat „Gay Werk" (GLM), Sun (G only) 20-? h
Angelstraße 33 ✉68199 ☎ 854 41 44
1st Sun „Macho Time", 3rd Sun Dress Code, admission DM 20. 5 clubs, 7 bars on 3 floors. Germany's biggest disco.
T6 (AC B D DR f GLM lj MA s VS WE) Wed-Sun 21-5 h, Sun special events
T6, 14/16 ✉68161 *(Near Nationaltheater)* ☎ 10 27 79

RESTAURANTS
Spagettioper im Geheimrat (b F g MA) 17-5 h
K 2, 31 ✉68159 ☎ 15 19 64

SEX SHOPS/BLUE MOVIES

Beate Uhse Kino 4 (G VS) Mon-Sat 8-24, Sun 11-24 h
Kaiserring 26-28 ✉68161

Beate Uhse Laden (g) Mon-Fri 9.30-20, Sat -14 h
L14, 12 ✉68161

Binokel Sex Shop (G VS) Mon-Sat 13-23, Sun 16-23 h
J 2, 18 ✉68159 ☎ 221 17

Cruising Point (g VS) Mon-Sat 12-24, Sun 15-24 h
Mittelstrasse 15 ✉68169 *(Alter Meßplatz)* ☎ 364 07

Erotic Shop (g) Mon-Fri 9-19, Sat -16 h
M2, 3 ✉68161 ☎ 265 80

Studio 7 (AC DR G MA VS) 11-24, Sat 11-6h, Sun and public holidays 16-24 h
Heinrich-Lanz-Straße 32 ✉68165 *(Tram-Tattersaal)* ☎ 44 93 06

ESCORTS & STUDIOS

Mike
☎ 0172/72 46 126

SAUNAS/BATHS

Hot House Club Sauna (AC B DR F G MA msg OS sa sb sol VS WE) Wed, Sat, Sun & public holidays 14-23, Thu 16-22 h
Ladenburgerstraße 23 ✉68309 *(Käfertal)* ☎ 73 72 60

Vital Sauna (AC B f G MA msg OS p pi r s sa sb VS) Mon-Fri 16-24, Sat Sun & public holidays 14-23 h
Rheinhäuser Straße 50 ✉68165 ☎ 40 95 36

BODY & BEAUTY SHOPS

Ars Subcutan Wed Fri 13-18.30, Thu -20, Sat 10.30-14 h
Alphornstraße 41 ✉68169 *(Neckarstadt)* ☎ 318 91 83
Piercings, Brandings, Cuttings.

BOOK SHOPS

Andere Buchladen. Der (G) Mon-Fri 10-20, Sat -14 h
M 2, 1 ✉68161 *(Tram-Paradeplatz)* ☎ 217 55
Large selection of gay books, CDs and videos. Good for information about the local gay scene. Frequent readings.

FASHION SHOPS

MAN-Store (CC) Mon-Fri 11-19, Sat 10-16 h
ÖVA Passage P 7, 6-7 ✉68161 ☎ 10 37 75

LEATHER & FETISH SHOPS

ERTE-Leder Design by appointment only
Schwetzinger Straße 116 ✉68165 ☎ 40 40 89

TRAVEL & TRANSPORT

Discus Travel
Schwetzinger Strasse 93 ✉68165 ☎ 40 96 27 Fax: 44 13 40
Homepage: www.discustravel.de

GIV Reisen
Schwetzinger Strasse 93 ✉68165 ☎ 44 88 66 Fax: 44 13 40

GENERAL GROUPS

Arbeitskreis homosexueller Polizisten in BW
Postfach 102845 ✉68028 ☎ (07254) 6769

Mannheim Bären Treff Meeting last Sunday of the month at 18 h
Butch Keller, S6 21 ☎ 10 56 61
Email mannheimbears@geocities.com. Social group for bears and their admires.

Quietschboys und Girls Meeting: Fri 19-? h at Arbeitslosencafé, M 1
PO Box 10 17 11 ✉68017 ☎ 19 446
Gay and lesbian youth group of SchAM.

SchAM e.V. (Schwule Aktion Mannheim)
PO Box 12 18 41 ✉68069 ☎ 31 85 94
Counselling and Infos from gays to gays/ Beratung und Infos von Schwulen für Schwule
Tue 19-21 h ☎19 446. Group for parents of lesbian daughters and gay sons/ Elterngruppe lesbischer Töchter und schwuler Söhne ☎06322 / 98 05 92. Group for older gays/Gruppe älterer Schwule in Café Leux, Mannheim, E 3,11
every other/jeden 2. Fri 19.30-? h, ☎19 446. Aerojazz in Großer Saal (EG)/Bürgerhaus Neckarstadt-West, Lutherstraße 15-17, 68169 Mannheim ☎19 446.

Schlagseite Mannheim/Heidelberg
PO Box 10 52 03, ✉69042 ☎ (06221) 279 85
SM-group.Also c/o Aids-Hilfe Mannheim, PO Box 12 01 13. ☎ 286 00

Schwule Motorradfahrer Rhein / Main / Neckar ☎ 33 37 59
Call Klaus for information about gay motor bike group.

VLSP-Verein lesbischer Psychologinnen und schwuler Psychologen
Postfach 29 07 60 ✉68177 ☎ 44 99 35
Every 1st Thu at 20 h at Aids-Hilfe Mannheim.

Völklinger Kreis-Bundesverband Gay Manager
c/o Richard Meyer, Kopernikusstraße 63 ✉68165 ☎ 44 33 07

FETISH GROUPS

LC Mannheim e.V. Mon 19-22 h
PO Box 10 21 17 ✉68021 ☎ 339 14 47
Meetings: at „Butch" on Thu at 18 h and every 4th Sat at 18 h, at „Zelle" every 1st Sun at 11 h and every 2nd Fri at 19 h.

RUBCLUB e.V. Mannheimer Straße 45 ✉68309
☎ 0172/733 44 44
Party at „MS Connection" every 1st Sat, strictly rubber dresscode

HEALTH GROUPS

AIDS-Hilfe Mannheim-Ludwigshafen e.V.
Mon Tue Fri 10-13, Wed 15-18 h
L 10, 8 68161, PO Box 12 01 13 ✉68052 ☎ 28 600 or ☎ 293 22 49 or ☎ 19 411 (counselling)
E-Mail: aids-hilfe@mannhein-net.de
Homepage: www.contactpoint.de

Wohnprojekt Joachim Bulla e.V. Tue-Fri 10-17 h
Angelstraße 33 ✉68199 ☎ 85 61 66
Lighthouse project, counselling and support.

HELP WITH PROBLEMS

Rosa Hilfe Tue 19-21 h
☎ 194 46

Selbsthilfegruppe Für Transsexuelle Menschen Mon 18-20, Wed 17-18 h
☎ 685 86 03
By appointment.

SPORT GROUPS

Mannemer Volley Dolls e.V. 19.30-22 h
PO Box 12 12 02 ✉68063 ☎ 262 30
E-Mail: volleydolls@t-online.de
Volleyball and bowling.

CRUISING

-Schloßpark (hinter der Uni auch spät nachts/behind university, late at night too)
-Friedrich-Ebert-Brücke (along the promenade, Neckarufer and Sportplatz, even late at night)
-Friedrich-Ebert-Brücke (Tunnel)
-Hauptbahnhof
-Hauptfriedhof-Klinikum (Tunnel)

Marburg ☎ 06421

BARS

Havanna Acht (B GLM YG) 20-2, Sat 21-2 h,GLM only on Sunday
Lahntor 2 ✉35037 ☎ 234 32

KFZ (B GLM YG) Mon 21.30-1 h
Schulstraße 6 ✉35037 ☎ 68 20 53

BOOK SHOPS

Roter Stern Buchhandlung & Antiquariat
(A bf CC f glm) Mon-Fri 10-19, Sat -16 h, Café: 10-19h
Am Grün 28 ✉35037 ☎ 247 87

GENERAL GROUPS

Autonomes Schwulenreferat im AStA der Uni Marburg Meeting Wed 14-16 h
Erlenring 5 ✉35037 ☎ 17 03 15

Tuntonia e.V. Mon-Fri 10-14 h
Bahnhofstraße 27 ✉35037 ☎ 68 20 53 Fax: 624 14
Infoline ☎ 194 46 *Call for information on gay sports group, gay fathers and husbands, and group for older gays.*

HEALTH GROUPS

AIDS-Hilfe Marburg e.V. Mon-Thu 10-13, Mon 14-16, Thu 19-21 h, Café 1st Sun 15.30 h
Bahnhofstraße 27 ✉35037 ☎ 645 23 Fax: 624 14.

HELP WITH PROBLEMS

Rosa Telefon Mon 19-21 h
☎ 194 46
1st Wed 19-21 h, counselling

CRUISING

-Toilet at the central bus station (below the motorway bridge)
-Schülerpark (near railway line and river Lahn)

Memmingen ☎ 08331

GENERAL GROUPS

Homosexuelle in Memmingen (him) Mon 19.30-21 h
PO Box 11 10 87681, Hallhof 5a I ✉87700 ☎ & Fax: 484 57
E-mail aids-hilfe@t-online.de

HEALTH GROUPS

AIDS-Hilfe Memmingen-Allgäu e.V. Mon Wed Fri 10-14, Groups: (G) Mon 19.30-21.30, (L) Fri 19.30-21.30 h
Hallhof 5a ✉87700 ☎ & Fax: 484 57

Menden ☎ 02373

GENERAL GROUPS

Homosapiens-Gruppe für Schwule Thu 19.30 h
Am Vollmersbusch 43 *(in der Kindertagesstätte)* ☎ 676 50
Homepage: http://www.freeyellow.com/members/eisbrecher
Schwules Chorprojekt Thu 20-22 h
☎ 90 34 55
Gay choir

Metzingen ☎ 07123

BARS

Club Apollo e.V. (B G MA VS) Wed Fri 21-?, Sat 22-? h, Fri Videotime
Dachsweg 2/Wolfkrubstraße ✉72555 *(Neuhausen, near Hofbühlhalle)* ☎ 157 25

Minden ☎ 0571

BARS

Delfter Stuben (B d f G lj MA p s) 21-? h, Mon closed
Pionierstraße 1a, ✉32423 *(Nähe/near Hauptbahnhof)*
☎ 320 18 63

SEX SHOPS/BLUE MOVIES

Orion (g) Mon-Fri 10-20, Sat -16 h.
Bäckerstraße 68, ✉ 32423 ☎ 877 15

SAUNAS/BATHS

Viktoria Sauna (B f DR G MA sa sb sol VS wh) Wed-Sun 15-23 h, closed Mon Tue
Viktoriastraße 22-24 ✉32423 *(2 min from railway station)*
☎ 357 15
Entrance-fee DM 18-22.

GENERAL GROUPS

GAYliens Mon 20 h
at „Nähkörbchen", Ritterstraße 1
PO Box 12 22 ✉31597 Uchte
Gay youth group.
Schwarm e.V. Meets every Thu 20 h
at Kulturcafé Weingarten, Königswall, 32423 Minden
Schwule Initiative Minden (SchwIM) Meeting Wed 19 h in Stella Café
c/o BÜZ, Seidenbeutel 1 ✉32423 ☎ 88 00 38

CRUISING

-Alter Friedhof (tagsüber/daytime)
-Weserglacis

Moers ☎ 02841

GAY INFO

Pink Channel Duisburg
FM 102.4 MHz

SEX SHOPS/BLUE MOVIES

Orion (g) Mon-Fri 9.30-19, Sat -16 h.
Neu-Markt-Eck, ✉47441 *(in the mall/im Einkaufzentrum)*
☎ 211 70

BOOK SHOPS

Aragon (g) Mon-Fri 10-19, Sat -16 h
Homberger Straße 30, ✉47441 ☎ 297 72

GENERAL GROUPS

DeLSI Demokratische Lesben- u. Schwuleninitiative Meeting Fri 20.30 h
c/o Jugendzentrum, Südring 2a, ✉47441 ☎ 256 25
Fax: 160 82 *Youth centre.*

HEALTH GROUPS

AIDS-Beratung Mon 14-16, 18-19 h
c/o Gesundheitsamt, Mühlenstraße 9-11 ✉47441 *(room 32)*
☎ 20 23 32
Anonymous free HIV test and counselling.

CRUISING

-Hauptbahnhof/Main station (left across street)
-Schloßpark

Mönchengladbach ☎ 02161

BARS

C'est la vie (A AC B D f glm MA p S W) Tue Thu-Sun 20-?, showtime 24 & 2 h
Gasthausstraße 67, ✉41061 ☎ 17 57 64
Germania Stübchen (AC B Glm MA OS p) 20-2 h
Gasthausstraße 68 ✉41061 ☎ 17 66 30

SEX SHOPS/BLUE MOVIES

New Man im WOS-Markt (G VS) 10-24, Sun 12-24 h
Hindenburgstraße 201 ✉41061

BOOK SHOPS

Montanus aktuell (g NG) Mon-Fri 9-19.30, Sat -16 h
Hindenburgstraße 153, ✉41061 ☎ 207976
General bookstore with gay section.

GIFT & PRIDE SHOPS

MAN Shop (CC g MA VS YG) Mon-Sat 10-24 h, Sun & holidays 13-23 h
Hauptstraße 16 ✉41236 *(Rheydt-Zentrum)* ☎ 94 45 86

GENERAL GROUPS

Schwulenreferat im AStA der FH Niederrhein/Mönchengladbach
Webschulstraße 21 ✉41065

HEALTH GROUPS

AIDS-Hilfe Mönchengladbach/Rheydt e.V.
Mon-Fri 9-17 h by appointment
Rathausstraße 13 ✉41061 ☎ 17 60 23 or ☎ 194 11.

HELP WITH PROBLEMS

Homophone counselling Sun 18-20 h
c/o Aids-Hilfe, Rathhausstraße 13 ✉41061 ☎ 17 60 23

CRUISING

-Hauptbahnhof/Main train station

Montabaur ☎ 02602

GENERAL GROUPS

Schwuler Stammtisch 1st & 3rd Wed 20-? h
at Villa Sonnenschein, Wilhelm-Mangels-Straße 17
☎ 178 84

Morbach ☎ 06533

HOTELS

Haus Hubertus (B bf f glm H MA p) 20 h
Belgiumstraße 3, Hinzerath ✉54497 ☎ 21 83
Im Hunsrück. Single DM 45, double 90 incl. bf.

Moritzburg ☎ 035207

RESTAURANTS

Dreispitz. Zum (CC F g MA) 11-24 h (meals -23)
Schlossallee 5 ✉01468 ☎ 8 22 00
Popular restaurant located in an old house built in 1727. Traditional cuisine.

München ☎ 089

● Munich is home to the Oktober-Fest where beer is drunk in large quantities or Maß as the Germans would say. The Beer Gardens have become a popular meeting place for gays. It'sstrongly recommended to give the Beer Garden on the Flaucher a try. You will find there many handsome Bavarians sitting on one of the numerous wooden benches sipping a beer.Another must is the English Garden. The streets on the Viktualienmarkt and Glockenbach are often frequented by gays. The proud gay community in Munich strongly contradicts the opinion that this city is very conservative. Try the local specialities such as „Weißwürst" and „Brezel".

✱ München ist die Oktoberfest-Stadt. Und mittlerweile sind hier sogar die Biergärten schwul, wo zu einer verfolgten Minderheit nur gehört, wer ein 0,3-Bier bestellt oder sein Maß mit beiden Händen zum Hals führt. Wir empfehlen besonders den Biergarten am Flaucher. Schöne Bajuwaren machen es sich auf schmalen Holzbänken bequem. Später werden sie auf den taubenetzten Maiwiesen des Englischen Gartens ihr Geheimnis enthüllen. Dann zeigen sie uns das Land der Regenbögen: Es sind die schönen Straßen an Viktualienmarkt und Glockenbach, wo schwule Männer Liebe geben. Damit ist München das Filetstück Bayerns. Doch viele Menschen in Deutschland sagen: Nach Bayern fahre ich nicht, dort ist es mir zu konservativ. Das stimmt nicht. Über all die Jahre hat sich in München ein neues schwules Selbstverständnis entwickelt. Stolz präsentiert es sich der Öffentlichkeit. Und das hat eine lange Tradition: schließlich lebte schon das berühmte Münchner Kindl allein unter Männern. Es war nämlich ein Mönch.

▲ Munich est la ville de l'Oktoberfest. Et entre temps, même les brasseries en plein air sont gayes, là ou on fait partie d'une minorité poursuivie si on commande une bière de 0,30 l ou si on porte à sa bouche sa chope de bière d'un litre en la tenant à deux mains. Nous recommandons particulièrement la brasserie de plein air „am Flaucher". De beaux Bavarois sont assis confortablement sur des bancs de bois étroits. Plus tard, ils révéleront leurs secrets sur les prés recouverts de rosée du „Jardin anglais". Après ils nous montrent le pays des arcs en ciel. Il s'agit des belles rues au „Viktualienmarkt" et de „Glockenbach" ou des pédés donnent de l'amour. Munich est ainsi le meilleur morceau de la Bavière. Pourtant, beaucoup de gens en Allemagne disent: je ne vais pas en Bavière, c'est trop conservateur. C'est faux. Au cours des années, l'image gaye que Munich se fait d'elle-même a évoluée. Elle se présente fièrement au public. Et ceci est une longue histoire, le célèbre „Münchner Kindl" vivait bien avec des hommes uniquement. Il s'agissait en effet d'un moine.

☆ Una gran parte de los turistas viene a Munich para ver el Oktoberfest y probar la famosísima cerveza. Ya hay hasta terrazas gay y minorias perseguidas aquí son solo los que piden la típica cerveza en formato „pequeño" de 0,3 l o los que levanten la autentica jarra de un litro con las dos manos. Se recomienda especialmente la terraza al lado del *Flaucher*, donde guapos bavarianos se apiñan en los banquillos. Más tarde se reunen en los *Maiwiesen* del conocido *Englischer Garten*, un parque de la ciudad, donde los amantes del nudismo se exponen al sol en los dias de verano. El ambiente gay se concentra en las calles del Viktualienmarkt y Glockenbach. Allí se encuentran sitios encantadores, que distinguen Munich del resto de Bavaria. Pero muchos dicen, que no van a Bavaria, porque les parece un sitio demasiado conservador. Esto no es verdad. Durante los últimos años en Munich se ha desarollado una nueva autoconfianza gay, que es demostrada con mucho orgullo. Y esta actitud tiene una larga tradición: El famoso Münchner Kindl ya vivía solo entre hombres, porque era monje.

❖ Monaco di Baviera è la città dell'Oktoberfest. Anche le birrerie all'aperto sono gay, dove viene perseguitato come rappresentante di una minoranza quello che ordina solo una birra da 0,3 litri o leva il boccale da un litro con tutte le due mani. Consigliamo per primo la birreria al *Flaucher* sul fiume Isar, dove i bei bavaresi si accomodano su stretti banchi di legno. Più tardi riveleranno il loro segreto, stendendosi nudi sui prati dei giardini inglesi bagnati di rugiada e ci faranno vedere il paese degli arcobaleni, cioè le belle strade del mercato centrale *Viktualienmarkt* e del quartiere *Glockenbach*, dove i begl'uomini sono pronti adonare il loro cuore. Così Monaco è il posto migliore della Baviera. Ma tanti tedeschi dicono: Non vado in Baviera perché là sono troppo conservativi. Ma non è vero. A Monaco negli ultimi anni si è sviluppata un'atmosfera gay „naturale" che si presenta con orgoglio al pubblico. Ha anche una lunga tradizione, perché già il „Münchner Kindl" (stemma della città di Monaco rappresentante un bambino, il „Kindl") visse da solo tra uomini. Era un monaco.

GAY INFO

München Nürnberg von hinten
c/o Bruno Gmünder Verlag, PO Box 61 01 04, ✉10921
☎ (030) 615 00 30 Fax: 030/615 90 07
E-Mail: info@spartacus.de
The city guide book about Nurenberg and Munich. Useful general information and lots of addresses with extensive descriptions in English and German. Up-to-date maps. Erotic photos.

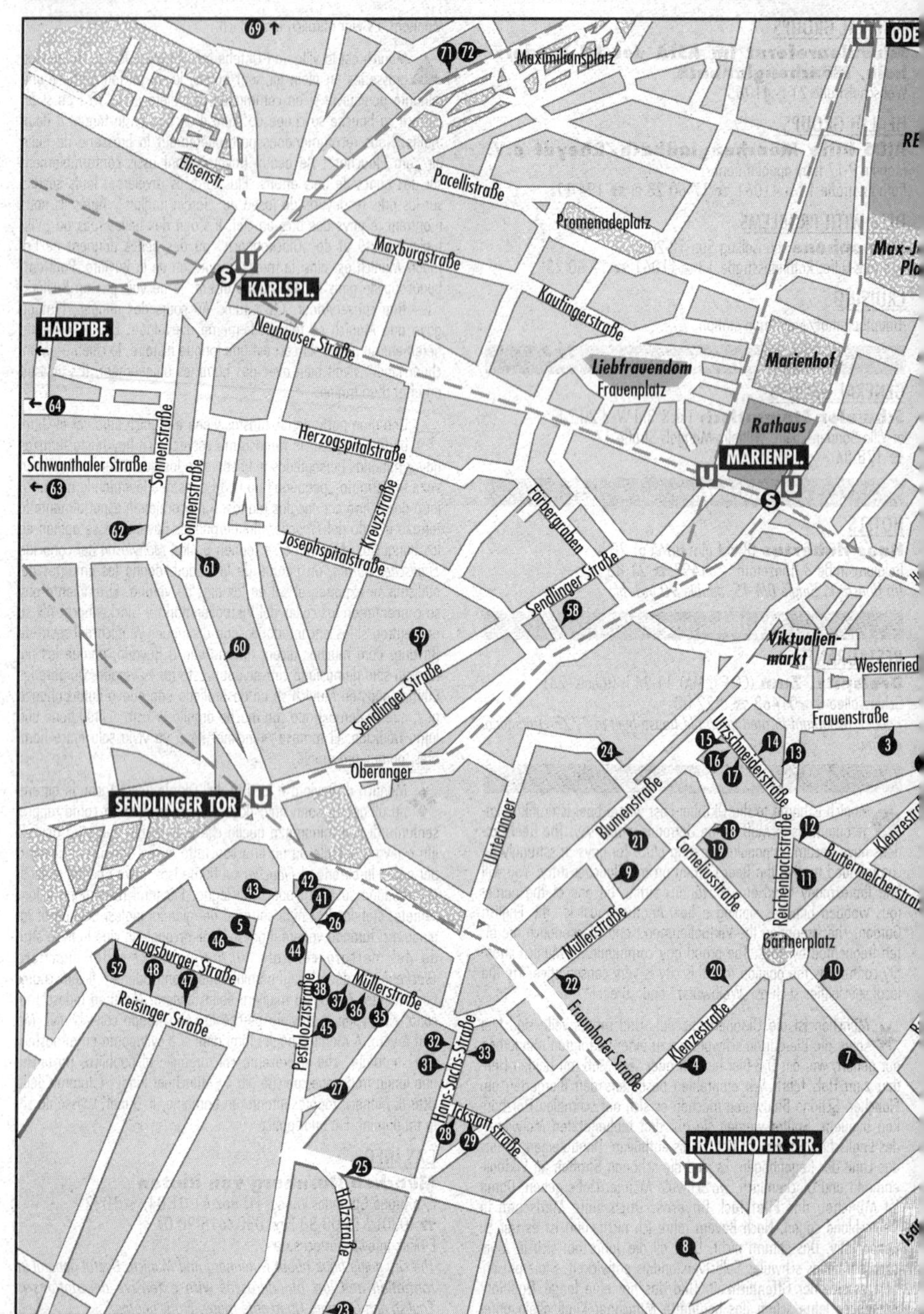
Maximiliansplatz
Elisenstr.
Pacellistraße
Promenadeplatz
Maxburgstraße
KARLSPL.
HAUPTBF.
Kaufingerstraße
Neuhauser Straße
Liebfrauendom
Frauenplatz
Marienhof
Rathaus
MARIENPL.
Herzogspitalstraße
Schwanthaler Straße
Sonnenstraße
Sonnenstraße
Kreuzstraße
Josephspitalstraße
Färbergraben
Sendlinger Straße
Sendlinger Straße
Viktualienmarkt
Westenried
Frauenstraße
Oberanger
SENDLINGER TOR
Unteranger
Utzschneiderstraße
Blumenstraße
Corneliusstraße
Reichenbachstraße
Buttermelcherstraße
Klenzestraße
Müllerstraße
Gärtnerplatz
Augsburger Straße
Reisinger Straße
Pestalozzistraße
Müllerstraße
Fraunhofer Straße
Klenzestraße
Hans-Sachs-Straße
Ickstattstraße
FRAUNHOFER STR.
Holzstraße
Max-J
Pla

1 Tattenbach Restaurant
2 Petit Café-Bar
3 Marktklause Bar
4 Morizz bar
5 Café Paris
6 Klenzestüberl - Bei Dominic Bar
7 Follow Me Sex Shop
8 Gay's Heaven Sex Shop
9 Prosecco Bar
10 Cornelius Men Sex Shop/ Blue Movie
11 Deutsche Eiche Restaurant & Hotel & Sauna
12 Juice Bar
13 Pension Seibel
14 Buddy Sex Shop/Blue Movie
15 Alexander's Bar
16 New World Café
17 Colibri Bar
18 My Life Bar
19 Old Mrs. Hendersen Danceclub
20 Theaterklause Bar
21 Zur Feuerwache Bar
23 Beim Franz Restaurant
24 Adamatschka Bar
25 Seitensprung Restaurant
26 Cutglass Piercing Shop
27 Spike Fetisch Bar
28 Max & Milian Book Shop
29 Mylord Bar
31 Drei Glöcklein Bar
32 Nil Café
33 Teddy-Bar
35 BAU Bar
36 Pension Eulenspiegel
37 SUB Café & Gay Center
38 Ochsengarten Bar
41 SpeXter Erotic Store Sex Shop Rendezvous Café
42 Pimpernel Bar
43 The Stud Danceclub
44 Edelheiss Bar
45 Atlantis Travel Shop
47 Pop AS Bar
48 Tabasco Bar
52 Cock Bar
58 Stadt München Guest House
59 Villanis Café
60 New York Danceclub
61 Iwan Bar
62 Sex-Point Sex Shop/Blue Movie
69 Schwabinger MENsauna
71 Fortuna Danceclub
72 Soul-City Danceclub

Münchner Hochschwulen Tue 20 h (term time)
Leopoldstraße 15 ✉80802 ☎ 15 98 02 57
E-Mail: hochschwul@gmx.de
Homepage: www.hochschwul.home.pages.de

Our Munich
Pestalozzistraße 10 ✉80469 ☎ 260 185 03 Fax: 26 02 50 81
E-Mail: ourmunich@pride.de Homepage: www.ourmunich.de
Gay magazine for Greater Munich. News, events, classifieds. For free at gay venues.

Rosa Seiten (GLM)
c/o PC-Print GmbH, Adalbertstraße 16 ✉80799 ☎ 380 19 10
Fax: 34 73 81 E-Mail: info.muk@rosaseiten.com
Homepage: www.rosaseiten.com
Local gay directory. Free at gay venues. Only in German.

SUB-Schwules Kommunikations- und Kulturzentrum (A B f G MA s YG) 19-22, Fri Sat 19-24, Infoservice Mon Sun 19-22 h
Müllerstraße 43 ✉80469 *(U-Sendlinger Tor)* ☎ 260 30 56
Fax: 26 02 28 19. E-Mail: sub-muenchen@t-online.de
Homepage: www.subonline.org
Kommunikationszentrum, Infothek, Beratung, Gruppen. Center for communication, information, counselling, groups.
-Café Sun-Thu 19-23, Fri-Sat -24 h
-"Raureif"-Gruppe für ältere Schwule Wed 19.30-21 h
Freizeit-Jugendgruppe „J.U.N.G.S." Fri 19.30 h
-Anonyme Alkoholiker Fri 20 h
Jugendgruppe „Tadzio" Sat 19.30 h
-Schwule/Bisexuelle Väter und Ehemänner 1st and 3rd Wed 20 h
-Projekt Prävention ☎ 26 02 28 58 Mon-Fri 13-18 h
Beratungsstelle ☎ 194 46 Mon-Fri 19-22 h
Anti-Gewalt-Projekt ☎ 192 28 Mon-Fri 13-18 h
SCHWUPOs und LESPOs (schwul-lesbische Polizisten)
Sub-Zentrum ☎ 26 02 28 19 Mon-Fri 13-18 h

Uferlos (GLM) Fri 20-21 h on FM 92.4 MHz, FM 96.75 MHz
c/o Münchner AIDS-Hilfe e.V., Lindwurmstraße 71 ✉80337
☎ 201 14 68 E-Mail: info@uferlos.muc.de
Gay radio magazine.

TOURIST INFO

Fremdenverkehrsamt
Sendlinger Straße 1 ✉80331 ☎ 233 03 00 Fax: 233-3 02 33

BARS

Adamatschka Bar (AC B CC f G MG OS R YG) Sun-Thu 6-1, Fri Sat -3 h.
Sebastiansplatz 3 ✉80331 *(U-S-Marienplatz)* ☎ 26 02 62 32

Alexander's Bar & Café (AC B CC f G MA R) 16-1, Fri & Sat -3 h
Utzschneiderstraße 4 ✉80469 *(U/S-Marienplatz, near/nahe Viktualienmarkt)* ☎ 260 54 98
The best R-coded bar in Munich.

Bau (! B d DR G lj MA YG) 20-3 h
Müllerstraße 41 ✉80469 *(U-Sendlinger Tor)* ☎ 26 92 08
Leather and rubber bar .

Bolt (B f G LJ MA) 15-3 h
Blumenstraße 15 ✉80331 ☎ 26 43 23

Bongo Bar (B CC d f glm MA OS S WE) Wed Thu 20.30-3, Fri Sat -4 h
Grafinger Straße 6 ✉81671 *(U/S-Ostbahnhof)* ☎ 49 00 12 60
In Kunstpark Ost, the mass entertainment center in the east part of the city

Café im SUB (! A B G MA s W YG) Sun-Thu 19-23, Fri Sat -24 h
Müllerstraße 43 ✉80469 ☎ 260 30 56
Cafe in the gay center.

Cock (B G lj MA N) 20-1, Sat -3 h
Augsburgerstraße 21 ✉80337 *(U-Sendlinger Tor)* ☎ 26 59 95

Colibri Bar (B f G MA N) 10-22 h
Utzschneiderstraße 8 ✉80469 *(Near/nahe Viktualienplatz)* ☎ 260 93 93

Drei Glöcklein (B G MA N) 11-22 h
Hans-Sachs-Straße 8 ✉80469 *(U-Sendlinger Tor)* ☎ 26 61 75

Edelheiß (AC B bf f G lj MA) Sun-Thu 11-1, Fri & Sat -3 h
Pestalozzistraße 6 ✉80469 *(U-Sendlinger Tor)* ☎ 26 54 53

Erdnüßchen (B f G MA N) 10-22 h
Klenzestraße 4 ✉80469 *(Tram 17/18/20)* ☎ 29 16 39 93

Evita 1 (B F glm) Daily 11-1 h
Kreittmayerstrasse 2 *(U1 Stiglmaierplatz)* ☎ 54 29 07 77

Feuerwache. Zur (B f G lj MA) 11-1, happy hour 11-17 h
Blumenstraße 21a ✉80331 *(U-Sendlinger Tor, Tram 17 +18)* ☎ 260 44 30
A friendly bar to quench your thirst with fun drinks and small snacks. Sat from 11:00h „Weißwürst-bf DM 8,—"

Fred's Pub (B G MA VS) Mon-Thu 19-01:00h, Fri & Sat 20-03:00h, Sun & holidays 20-01:00h
Reisingerstraße 15 ✉80337 *(U-Sendlinger Tor)* ☎ 26 02 28 09
Gay movie bar

Iwan (B d F g MA OS W YG) Sun-Thu 12-2, Fri-Sat 17-3 h
Sonnenstraße 19 ✉80331 ☎ 55 49 33
Bar-restaurant.

Juice (B F GLM MG N) 16-1 h
Buttermelcherstraße 2a ✉80469 *(nahe/near Viktualienmarkt, Tram 17/18/20)* ☎ 26 47 46
Popular and friendly gay bar with a small restuarant in which one can eat well at reasonable prices.

Klimperkasten (B f G MG N) 19-? h
Maistraße 28 ✉80337 *(U-Goetheplatz)* ☎ 53 76 39
Piano bar with comfortable atmosphere.

Marktklause (B f G MA N R) 14-1 h
Frauenstraße 20 ✉80469 *(Near/nahe Viktualienmarkt, S-Isartor)* ☎ 29 90 76

Morizz (! AC B E F Glm MA s YG) Sun-Thu 19-2, Fri Sat -3 h
Klenzestraße 43 ✉80469 *(Near/nahe Gärtnerplatz)* ☎ 201 67 76
Probably the most attractive bar in Germany. Also restaurant. Enjoy cocktails and Thai cuisine.

My Life (B F glm MA S W YG) Fri Sat 6-3 h, Sun-Mon 6-1 h, Tue-Thu 17-1 h
Rumfordstraße 2/Müllerstraße ✉80469 *(U/S-Marienplatz)* ☎ 260 44 19
International cuisine.

Mylord (B d f GLM MA N s TV) Sun-Thu 18-1, Fri Sat -3 h
Ickstattstraße 2a ✉80469 *(U-Sendlinger Tor/Frauenhofer Straße)* ☎ 260 44 98
Nostalgy-club. Tranvestites meeting every Fri, Oldies on Wed, Single-Party on Mon.

Nil (! B f G MA OS YG) 15-3 h
Hans-Sachs-Straße 2 ✉80469 ☎ 26 55 45
Einzig wirklich schwules Straßencafé in der Hans-Sachs-Straße/ The only real gay sidewalk cafe in Hans-Sachs-Straße.

Ochsengarten (! AC B G LJ MA) 22-3 h
Müllerstraße 47 ✉80469 *(U-Sendlinger Tor, exit Müllerstraße)* ☎ 26 64 46
Leather bar. Local club of MLC / Clublokal des MLC.

Petit Café (B G MA N) 15-22 h
Marienstraße 2 ✉80331 *(S-Isartor/Marienplatz)* ☎ 29 56 72

Pimpernel (AC B CC D F G lj MA p R TV W) 0-7 h, warm meals the whole night
Müllerstraße 56 ✉80469 *(U-Sendlinger Tor)* ☎ 26 71 76
Late night plush meeting place. Food all night.

Pop As (A B G lj MA) 20-? h
Thalkirchnerstraße 12 ✉80337 ☎ 260 91 91
Klublokal des MLC e.V. Hilfe für ECMC-Clubmitglieder/Clubhouse of MLC e.V. Any help for members of ECMC-clubs.

Prosecco (B f G MA s YG) 18-4, Sun & holidays 14-4 h, kitchen -3 h
Theklastraße 1 ✉80469 *(Tram 17/18/20)* ☎ 260 57 14

Rendezvous (B CC f GLM MA OS) 15-1 h, Fri & Sat -03:00 h
Müllerstraße 54 ✉80469 *(U-Sendlinger Tor)* ☎ 260 41 25

Spike (B f G LJ MA OS) Sun-Thu 15-1, Sun. brunch from 11 h
Holzstraße 14 ✉80469 *(U- Sendlinger-Tor)* ☎ 26 02 62 37

Sunshine Pub (B f G MA N r) 6-3 h
Müllerstraße 17 ✉80469 *(Tram 17/18/20)* ☎ 260 93 54

Tabasco (AC B DR f G LJ MA) Tue-Thu 17-01, Fri & Sat -3, Sun 15-1 h
Reisingerstraße 5 ✉80337 *(former Löwengrube)* ☎ 232 09941
Also small sex shop.

Teddy Bar (B f G lj MG OG) Daily 18-3 h. Sun & holidays - bruch from 11 h
Hans-Sachs-Straße 1 ✉80469 *(U-Sendlinger Tor)* ☎ 260 33 59
Popular.

Theaterklause (B G MG N OG) 11-1 h, closed Wed
Klenzestraße 30 ✉80469 *(Near/nahe Gärtnerplatz, U-Fraunhofer Straße)* ☎ 26 94 93 92

CAFES

Café Glück (A B F glm OS YG) Mon-Fri 16-1, Sat 14-1, Sun 10-1 h
Palmstraße 4 ✉80469 *(U-Fraunhofer Straße)* ☎ 201 16 73
Sun bf from 10-16 h

My Way (b f GLM MA s OS) Mon-Sat 9-22 h, Sun & holidays 10-22 h
Ligsalzstraße 13 ✉80339 ☎ 51 00 91 33

Petit Café (B G) 15-22 h
Marienstrasse 2 ✉80331 ☎ 29 56 72
A very small café, but interesting

Rick's Cafébar (B bf f glm) Mon-Sat 7-1, Sun 9-1 h
Augustenstraße 112 ✉80798 *(U-Josephsplatz)* ☎ 523 49 95

Villanis (bf F glm MA OS W) 10-1, Sun and public holidays 11-1 h
Kreuzstraße 3b ✉80331 *(U-Sendlinger Tor)* ☎ 260 79 72

DANCECLUBS

Boom Boom. The (! AC B CC D G S TV YG) Sun 20-2 h
c/o Park-Café, Sophienstraße 7 ✉80333 *(U/S-Karlsplatz)*
☎ 69 38 08 44
Very popular tea-dance with house music and hot go go boys

Fortuna (AC B CC D GLM MA OS WE) Fri 22:30-6, Sat 23-6 h
Maximiliansplatz 5 ✉80333 ☎ 470 76 74

New York (AC B CC D f GLM MA p) Sun-Thu 23-4 h, Fri Sat 23-open end
Sonnenstraße 25 ✉80331 *(U-Sendlinger Tor)* ☎ 59 10 56

Old. Mrs. Hendersen (AC B CC D GLM MA p S STV YG) Wed-Sun 21-4, (STV) Wed-Fri Sun 21 h
Müllerstrasse 1 ✉80469 *(U/S-Isartor)* ☎ 26 34 69
Showtimes : Wed-Sun 20:30h

OCHSEN
GARTEN
MÜNCHEN
MÜLLERSTR. 47 - 80469 MÜNCHEN
www.ochsengarten.de

Teddy-Bar
Teddy Bar
München
Hans-Sachs-Str. 1
80469 München
Tel. 260 33 59

Zur
Feuer-
wache

Soul-City (D f glm S TV WE YG) Disco: Thu Fri (g) 22-6, Sat (GLM) 22-8 h, Cabaret: Fri-Sun 20-23 h
Maximiliansplatz 5 ✉80333 ☎ 55 33 01 or ☎ 59 52 72
1st Fri lesbian night, 2nd Fri fetish night, 3rd Fri Happy Gays. Best after 02:00h. Late night meeting place.
DM 10, cover charge
Stud. The (! AC B D DR G LJ MA S SNU VS WE) Thu & Sun 23-4, Fri & Sat -5 h, Mon-Wed closed
Thalkirchner Straße 2 ✉80337 *(U-Sendlinger Tor)* ☎ 260 84 03
Bavarias largest JL club
Top Or Bottom Club in Mandarin Lounge (B D G lj YG WE) Only Fri 23-4 h
Herrogspital-Street 6, 1. Stock ✉80333 *(1st Floor)* ☎ 263720
A disco on the first floor of a former housing block../Zu einer Disco umgebaute Wohnung im 1. Stock. Eingang durchs Treppenhaus. Vocal house Music

RESTAURANTS

Beim Franz (B F G MA) 18-1 h
Holzstraße 41 ✉80469 ☎ 260 75 47
Excellent Bavarian cuisine.
Der Neue Kanzleirat (AC B bf CC F glm OS) 10-1 h, meals until 24 h
Oettingerstraße 36 ✉80538 *(Tram 17-Paradies Straße)*
☎ 22 00 84 *Traditional Bavarian cuisine.*
Deutsche Eiche (! B F G MA) 7.30-1 h
Reichenbachstraße 13 ✉80469 *(Near/nahe Gärtnerplatz, Tram 17/18/20)* ☎ 23 11 66 0
Good traditional Bavarian cuisine.
Seitensprung (bf F GLM MA OS W) Mon-Thu 12-1, Fri -2, Sat 11-2, Sun -1 h
Holzstraße 29 ✉80469 *(U-Fraunhofer Straße/Sendlinger Tor)*
☎ 26 93 77
Popular. Late breakfasts on Sat, Sun & holidays 11-16 h
Tattenbach (B CC F glm MA OS s YG) Mon-Thu 11:30-14:30, 17-1, Fri & Sat 19-2, Sun 19-1 h
Tattenbachstraße 6 ✉80538 *(U-Lehel)* ☎ 22 52 68
Bar and restaurant well known both for its interior design as for its food.
Wirtshaus am Herrgottseck (AC bf CC F glm H OS) 8-24 h
Mariahilfplatz 4 ✉81541 ☎ 688 72 35
Old Munich specials.
Wirtshaus Zum Isartal (AC b d F glm MA N OS S STV TV) Mon-Thu 11-2, Fri -3, Sat & Sun 10-3 h
Brudermühlstraße 2 ✉81371 *(U-Brudermühlstraße)* ☎ 77 21 21
Bavarian rustical cuisine with opera and drag shows. Large and popular beer garden open until 03:00h.

SHOWS

Bel Étage (CC g MA S STV) 19.30-1 h
Feilitzschstraße 12 ✉80802 *(U-Münchner Freiheit)* ☎ 33 90 13
Entrance-fee DM 24-35.

Harlekin Sisters (STV) Sun-Fri 12-18 h
Buttermelcher Straße 4 ✉80469 ☎ 26 56 44
Top-class drag shows. One to four artists available./Travestie-Show der Spitzenklasse. Allein oder bis zu vier Künstler buchbar.

SEX SHOPS/BLUE MOVIES

Black Jump (CC GLM LJ MA p) By appointment only
Orleansstraße 51 ✉81602 *(S-Ostbahnhof)* ☎ 48 00 43 33
Also mail order

Buddy Shop (G VS) Mon-Fri 10-20, Sat -16 h
Utzschneiderstraße 3 ✉80469 ☎ 26 89 38

Cornelius Men (CC G lj VS) Mon-Fri 10-20, Sat -16 h
Corneliusstraße 19 ✉80469 *(Near/nahe Gärtnerplatz)*
☎ 201 47 53
Also two gay cinemas and a large variety of books, leather & toys.

Erotic World (g) Mon-Fri 9-20, Sat -16, cinema Mon-Sat 9-1, Sun 11-1 h
Schwanthalerstraße 9/Sonnenstraße ✉81549

Follow me (CC G) Mon-Fri 10-20, Sat -16 h
Corneliusstraße 32 ✉80469 *(U-Fraunhofer Straße)* ☎ 202 12 08
Leather, rubber, toys videos to rent / buy.

Gay's Heaven (DR G MA VS) Mon-Sat 10-20 h, Son closed.
Baaderstrasse 82 ✉80469 *(U - Frauenhoferstrasse)*
☎ 20 00 98 04
Erotic store with books, magazines, toys. Videos to rent / buy, large non-stop cinema

Sex Point (AC b CC DR G MA VS) Shop: Mon-Sat 9-23 h, Cinema: Mon-Sat 11-24 h, Sun 12-24 h
Sonnenstraße 14 ✉80331
Special price on Mondays. 1 large and 5 small cinemas. Cubicals. Large selection

Sex World (g MA VS) Mon-Fri 9-22, Sun -16 h, Cinema: Mon-Sat 14-22 h
Sonnenstraße 12 ✉80331 *(U/S-Karlsplatz)* ☎ 55 47 33

Spexter Erotic Store (A CC DR G LJ MA VS YG) Mon-Fri 10-20, Sat 10-16 h
Müllerstraße 54 ✉80469 *(U-Sendlinger Tor)* ☎ 26 02 48 64
Large screen videos; sale of made to measure leather, rubber and uniform wear. Sat reduced entrance price

Weissblauer Gay Shop (AC CC G MA VS YG) Mon-Fri 9-20, Sat -18 h
Theresienstraße 130 ✉80333 *(U-Theresienstraße)* ☎ 52 23 52

CINEMAS

Atlantik Cinema (G VS)
Kino 2, Schillerstraße 3 ✉80331

ESCORTS & STUDIOS

Bad Boys
☎ 316 990 70

David
☎ (0171) 271 3283

Oliver and Tom
☎ (0171) 610 46 47

HOUSE OF BOYS

Marcel's Gesellschafterteam München MGM
☎ 39 86 39 ☎ (0171) 800 11 20
More than 30 young men available!

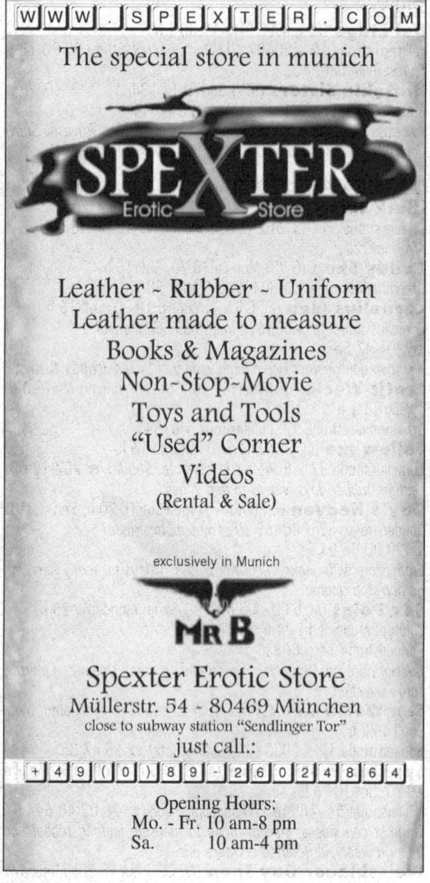

SAUNAS/BATHS

Badehaus Deutsche Eiche (! B CC DR F G MA msg OS sa sb sol WO) 14-7 h
Reichenbachstraße 13 ✉80469 *(Near/nahe Gärtnerplatz, Tram 17/18/20)* ☎ 23 11 66 0
Entrance-fee DM 15-25.

Dom Pedro Gay Club (B f G MA msg pi sa sb sol) 12-24, Mon Jack-off-party
Fasaneriestraße 18 ✉80636 *(Near/nahe Leonradplatz, Tram 20-Leonrodplatz)* ☎ 129 32 76
Small but popular sauna. Jack-Off party every Mon.

Mathilden (b g MA sa, sb) Daily 9-23 h
Mathildenstrasse 5 ✉80336 ☎ 55 45 73
Four different types of saunas as well as a turkish bath „Hamam".

Schwabinger MEN Sauna (B DR F G MA msg p S sa sb sol VS) 15-1 h
Düsseldorfer Straße 7 ✉80804 *(U2-Scheidplatz/U3-Bonner Platz)* ☎ 307 23 42
Entrance-fee DM 22. Student 18. From 22 h only 11 DM.

TS 27 (B DR f G MA msg OS p S sa sb sol WO) 24 hours
Schleissheimer Strasse 426 / Geb. 12 ✉80935 *(U2-Frankfurter Ring)* ☎ 359 70 68
Also with bar, bistro, restaurant and beer garden.

Wetterstein. Sauna (g MG NG sa sb) Mon-Fri 11-21, Sat 8-20, Sun -14 h
c/o Hotel Wetterstein, Grünwalder Straße 16 ✉81547 *(Tram15/25-Wetterstein)* ☎ 697 00 33

BODY & BEAUTY SHOPS

Cutglass Piercing Studio Mon-Fri 12-19 h, Sat by appointment only. Müllerstraße 54 ☎ 26 35 08
Body Piercing Studio

Rainbow Club Tue-Fri 16-23:00h, Sat & Sun 13-1 h, Mon closed.
Landwehrstraße 3 ✉80336 ☎ 54 83 22 61
The first Gay- Wellness-Center in Munich, Special rates for students, members etc.

BOOK SHOPS

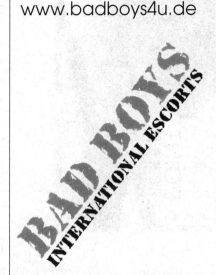

Max & Milian (CC Glm) Mon-Fri 10.30-14, 15.30-20, Sat 11-16 h
Ickstattstraße 2 ✉80469 ☎ 2260 33 20
(U-Sendlinger Tor/Fraunhoferstrasse/Tram-Müllerstraße)
Large selection of books, magazines, videos and CDs.

GIFT & PRIDE SHOPS

Our Munich Shop (CC GLM) Mon-Fri 10-20, Sat 16 h
Müllerstraße 36-38 ✉80469 *(U-Sendlinger Tor)* ☎ 601 85 03

LEATHER & FETISH SHOPS

Demask Munich (AC CC glm) Mon-Fri 10-19, Sat -16 h
Gabelsbergerstrasse 68 ✉80333 ☎ 527 475
Rubber and leather clothing & equippment. Full range - from street/club wear to heavy rubber & leather.

Hard Line (CC G LJ) Mon-Fri 11.30-19, Sat 11-15 h
Müllerstraße 33 ✉80469 ☎ 260 60 17
Professional piercing studio and large selection of rubber and leather wear.

TRAVEL & TRANSPORT

Atlantis Travel GmbH Mon-Fri 9-20, Sat 9-14 h
Pestalozzistraße 17 ✉80469 ☎ 23 66 60-0 Fax: 23 66 60 55
E-Mail: tom@atlantis-travel.de. Homepage: www.atlantis-travel.de

Gaygantic Tours Mon-Fri 9-18:30, Sat 9-14 h
Dom-Pedro-Strasse 16 ✉80637 ☎ 15 91 90 86

HOTELS

Hotel Deutsche Eiche (bf CC GLM H MA YG) 0-24 h
Reichenbachstraße 13 ✉80469 *(S/U-Marienplatz)* ☎ 23 11 660
Fax: 23 11 66-98 E-Mail: info@deutsche-eiche.com
Homepage: www.deutsche-eiche.com
Central location. All rooms with shower/WC, TV, phone. Also restaurant.

Hotel Moosbeck-Alm ☛ Rottenbuch

Hotel Seibel (AC bf H) all year, 24 h
Theresienhöhe 9 ✉80339 *(U5 Theresienwiese)* ☎ 540 14 20
Fax: 54 01 42 99. E-Mail: Hotel Seibel@t-online.de
Homepage: www.seibel-hotels-munich.de
Three star hotel. 45 rooms with shower/bath/WC, telephone and cable-TV. Own key. Fine Italian cuisine.

Seibel's Park Hotel (B bf CC F H MA OS sa) all year, 18 hours daily
Maria-Eich-Straße 32 ✉81243 ☎ 829 95 20 Fax: 82 99 52 99
E-Mail: Seibels-Park-Hotel@t-online.de
Homepage: www.seibel-hotels-munich.de
Four star hotel in city center. Please call for prices.

40,3399	BEF	40,3399	LUF
1,95583	DEM	2,20371	NLG
166,386	ESP	13,7603	ATS
6,55957	FRF	200,482	PTE
0,787564	IEP	5,94573	FIM
1936,27	ITL		

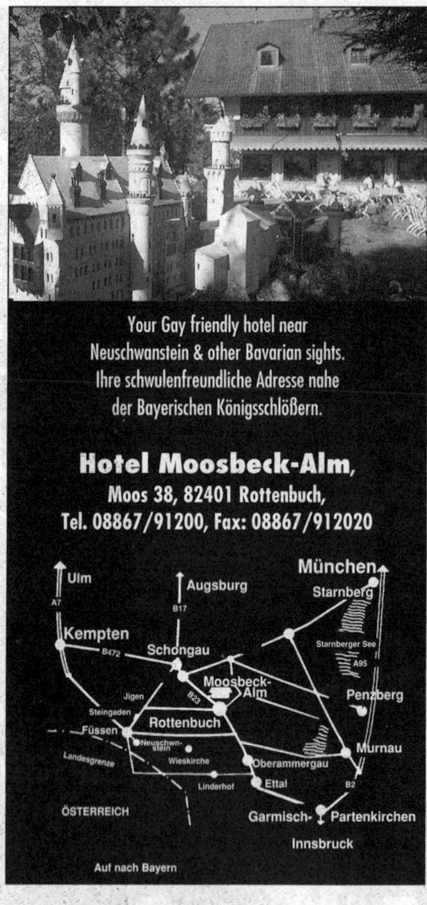

GUEST HOUSES

Eulenspiegel. Pension (bf GLM H lj MA) 8-12.30, 15.30-22 h
Müllerstraße 43a ✉80469 *(Tram-Sendlingertor-Platz)*
☎ 26 66 78 Fax: 26 66 78
Centrally located, next to the Bar Ochsengarten.

Pension Stadt München (bf CC g H) Dultstraße 1/I ✉80331 *(Near Marienplatz)* ☎ 26 34 17 Fax: 26 75 48
All rooms with shower, radio, shared WC. Own key. Rates from DM 120 in a double room and DM 80 in a single room per night, including bf.

Seibel. Pension (bf CC f glm H MA) 24h
Reichenbachstraße 8 ✉80459 *(Viktualienmarkt. U-Marienplatz)*
☎ 231 91 80 Fax: 26 78 03 E-Mail: Pension.seibel@t-online.de
Homepage: www.seibel-hotels-munich.de
Directly in the gay area.

PRIVATE ACCOMODATION

Enjoy Bed & Breakfast (bf G H MA YG) 16:30-21 h
c/o Mann-O-Meter, Motzstraße 5 ✉10777 ☎ (030) 215 16 66
Fax: 030/217 52 219 E-Mail: Info@ebab.com
Homepage: www.ebab.de
Price from 45 DM. Accommodation sharing agency. All rooms with shower and bf.

GENERAL GROUPS

Big Spender in München e.V. Mon Wed Thu 20-22 h
Rumfordstraße 32 ✉80469 *(Rückgebäude/backyard)*
☎ 29 85 26 Fax: 9 84 72
AIDS charities.

Homosexuelle Alternative (HALT) Wed 20 h
c/o ESG, Friedrichstraße 25 ✉80801 *(U-Giselastraße)*
Social activities for gays

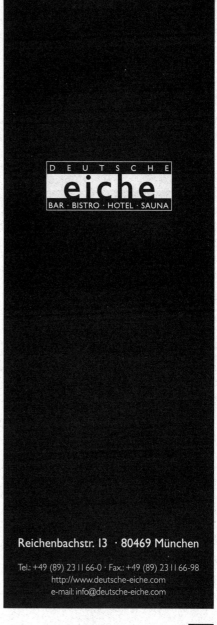

Jugendnetzwerk Gleich & Gleich
c/o Sub e.V, Müllerstraße 43 ✉80469 ☎ 260 30 56

Münchner Hochschwulen. Die-AStA Schwulenreferat Tue 20 h (during term)
Leopoldstraße 15 ✉80802 ☎ 15 98 02 57
E-Mail: Hochschwule@bigfoot.com

Münchner SchwulLesbische Gehörlose e.V.
Meets 2nd and 4th Sat 16 (winter) or 19 h (summer)
Müllerstraße 44 ✉(80469) *(Rückgebäude)* ☎ 260 67 34
Fax: 260 67 30.

rosa liste münchen e.V. schwul-lesbische WählerInneninitiative (GLM) 3rd Tue 19 h
at Sub Klenzestraße 43 ✉80469 *(U-Sendlinger Tor)*
☎ 201 65 34 Fax: 201 65 34 Homepage: www.rosa-liste.de

SCHWUNG AG
Horst Schreck c/o Café Iwan ☎ 20 23 92 85
A group in Munich who would like to open a gay center and are selling stocks in order to raise the funds.

SLAM Schwul-lesbische Akademie München
Marion Hölzl c/o Rosa Liste, Klenzestraße 43 ✉80469
☎ 201 65 34 Fax: 201 65 34

VIVA TS Selbsthilfe München e.V. Meets Fri
at SHZ München, Bayernstraße 77a/Rückgebäude
Obere Mühlstraße 22 ✉81247 ☎ 89 16 19 65
Self-help group for transsexuals.

Völklinger Kreis e.V.-Bundesverband Gay Manager ☎ 149 39 04 *(Thilo) or* ☎ *930 66 01 (Rainer) or* ☎ *436 16 03 (Walter) Association of gay managers/Verband schwuler manager*

FETISH GROUPS

Isarbären Meets 2nd Fr at/im Cock, sauna 2nd Sun
at TS 27 Sauna ☎ 54 07 07 80 E-Mail: Isarbear@aol.com
Group of heavy gay men and their fans/Gruppe bäriger Schwuler und ihrer Freunde.

MLC München e.V. 12-2 h
PO Box 33 01 63 ✉80061 ☎ 48 53 05 Fax: 48 53 05
E-Mail: MLCeV@aol.com Homepage: members.aol.com/MLCeV
Organizes the annual Oktoberfest meeting and summer-rafting on the river Isar. Phone for participation as early as possible.

HEALTH GROUPS

AIDS-Beratung des Gesundheitshauses Mon-Fri 8-11, Tue 15-18, Thu 14-15 h
Lindwurmstraße 41 ✉80337 ☎ 23 32 09 00
Counselling and anonymous free HIV-testing.

Café Regenbogen Tue 17.30-22 h
c/o Aids-Hilfe, Lindwurmstraße 41 ✉80337 ☎ 23 32 09 00
Meeting place for PWA and HIV and their friends on Wed 18-22 h

Katholische AIDS-Seelsorge Thomas Schwaiger Tue 11-12, Thu 15-16 h
Leopoldstraße 11 ✉80802 ☎ 38 10 31 42 Fax: 38 10 31 24.
(Pfarrer Ulrich Keller).

Münchner AIDS-Hilfe e.V. Mon-Thu 9.30-18, Fri -14, Counselling ☎ 194 11 Mon-Fri 19-21.30 h
Lindwurmstraße 71 ✉80337 *(U-Goetheplatz)*
☎ 54 46 47-0 Fax: 54 46 47-11
E-Mail: beratungsstelle@muenchner-aidshilfe.de
Homepage: www.muenchner-aidshilfe.de.

Psychosoziale AIDS-Beratungsstelle der Caritas Mon-Fri 9-12.30, Tue-Thu 14-17 h
Schrenkstraße 3 ✉80339 ☎ 50 03 55 20 Fax: 50 03 55 26
Free and confidential HIV-testing. Counselling.

HELP WITH PROBLEMS

Katholisch-reformierte Seelsorge
Pettenkoferstraße 8b ✉80336 ☎ 54 48 76 77
or ☎ (0172) 890 45 59.

Marikas-Innere Mission München e.V. Fri 12-17 h Mon-Thu by appointment
Dreimühlenstraße 1 ✉80469 *(Bus 58/32-Kapuzinerstraße)*
☎ 725 90 84 Fax: 74 79 39 43.
Meeting place and advice center for male prostitutes / former prostitutes. Free place to sleep and other services offered

Überfalltelefon Mon-Fri 19-22 h
☎ 192 28

RELIGIOUS GROUPS

HuK-Arbeitsgruppe Homosexuelle und Kirche e.V.
PO Box 38 01 73 ✉80614 ☎ 96 77 11 *(Leo)*

SPORT GROUPS

Front Runners München Lauftreff Sun 16 h
☎ 308 87 23 *(Patrick)* or ☎ 769 71 65 *(Ulf)*

GOC-Gay Outdoor Club
☎ 692 74 70 *(John)*. E-Mail: Munich_Hiker@compuserve
Hiking, mountain hiking, biking, ski tours/ Wandern, Bergtouren, Radwanderungen, Skitouren

L.U.S.T. Lesbischer und Schwuler Tanzclub Fri 20 h
Friedrichstraße 25 (ESG) ✉80801 ☎ 723 95 77

Racket Club München e.V.
☎ 178 46 82 *(Manfred)* or ☎ 26 58 54 *(Steve) Schwul-lesbischer Tennis-, Badminton- und Squashverein.*

Soccer Streetboys München e.V. Meets Wed 21.30 h
at Seitenspring ☎ 46 87 54 *(Christian)*

Volleyball Bavaria Rosé
☎ 78 10 69 *(Oliver)* or ☎ 76 70 02 22 *(Thomas)*

SWIMMING

-Englischer Garten (g NU) (Eierwiese at/am Eisbach)
-Großhesseloher Brücke (1 km north of the bridge between river Isar and the channel. [P] at Conwentzstaße, cross the channel on the pedestrian bridge. Cruising to the right, around sunset.)
-Pupplinger Au (WE) (Near Wolfratshausen, follow the signs to „Klärwerk Weidach", where the rivers Isar and Loisach meet)
-Wolfratshausen/Ascholding (from Wolfratshausen go to Egling, at the bridge over the river Isar turn right to Ascholding, take the first [P] and go down the paths to the river Isar)

CRUISING

-Fraunhoferstraße
-Odeonsplatz (popular)
-Scheidplatz (ayor, r)
-U-Max-Weber-Platz
-U-Holzapfelkreuth
-U-Stieglmaierplatz
-Pasinger Bahnhof
-Herkommerplatz
-U-Westendstraße
-U-Stachus/Karlsplatz (R)
-Innsbrucker Ring
-Karl-Preis-Park
-Giesinger Bahnhof
-Hauptbahnhof
-Josephsplatz
-U-Theresienwiese popular
-Messegelände
-Kolumbusplatz
-Universität
-Herkomerplatz
-Englischer Garten. (Eingang Lerchenfeldstraße/Prinzregentenstraße weiter zur Flußbrücke, ab da cruising area/ Entrance at Lerchenfeldstraße/Prinzregentenstraße proceed to the bridge, lots of action)
-Luitpoldpark (AYOR) (facility at Scheidplatz, cruising on the hill)

Mühlhausen ☎ 03601

BARS

Nische (B f g LJ) Mon-sat 17-1 h
Schaffentorstraße 26 ✉99974 ☎ 42 41 07

HEALTH GROUPS

AIDS-Hilfe Unstrut-Hainich-Kreis e.V. 9-15, Tue 9-23 h, closed Sat+Sun
Wanfrieder Straße 113 ✉99974 ☎ 44 62 18
Fax: 44 62 18. Group/Gruppe (G) Tue 19-23 h. Group/Gruppe (L) Wed 20-22 h.

Mülheim an der Ruhr ☎ 0208

GAY INFO

Blitz Tue 18.05-18.45 h (FM 92,9 via Kable/cable 106,2 MHz)
c/o Radiowerkstatt, Berthold-Brecht-Haus, ✉46045 ☎ 825 28 47

CAFES

Café Leinpfad (B f g NG T YG) 15-1 h, Oct-Apr closed Mon
Dohne 74, ✉45468 ☎ 38 08 81

DANCECLUBS

Cruise & Queer (B D GLM) 4th Sat 22.30-? h
Ringlokschuppen, Am Schloß Broich 38 ✉45479 ☎ 412 59 21

SHOWS

Travestie-Show-Theater Gerdas Kleine Weltbühne (S TV) Offenbacher Strasse 11 ✉63165
☎ 06108/75491 E-Mail: post@gerdas.de Homepage: www.gerdas.de

GENERAL GROUPS

Enterpride-Schwule Jugendgruppe Meeting Mon 18-?h at Ringlokschuppen, Am Schloß Broich 38
☎ 412 59 22
Fax: 993 16 13, E-mail: enterpride@schwule.org
Momepage: http://schwule.org/enterpride/

Sozialverein für Lesben und Schwule e.V.
c/o Ringlokschuppen, Am Schloß Broich 38 ✉45479
☎ 412 59 21
Fax: 993 16-13. E-mail svls@schwule.org. Homepage http://schwule.org/svls/

HEALTH GROUPS

Herzenslust An Schloss Broich 38 ✉45479 ☎ 412 59 20
Fax: 993 16 13. Email herzenslust@ruhr-west.de.
HIV-prevention fro gays and bisexuals.

HELP WITH PROBLEMS

Schwules Beratungstelefon Wed 19-21; Online Counselling: Mon 21-23 h

☎ 194 46 E-mail beratung@schwule.org
Homepage http://www.schwule.org/beratung/

CRUISING

-Rhein-Ruhr-Zentrum

Münster ☎ 0251

GAY INFO

KCM Schwulen- und Lesbenzentrum e.V. (b D GLM MA WE) Wed 20-24, 3rd Fri 20-23, 2nd and 4th Sat 21-?, 1st Sun 15-18h
Am Hawerkamp 31 ✉48155 ☎ 66 56 86 Fax: 66 56 61
E-Mail: KCM@muenster.de
Counselling ☎ 19446.

BARS

Maxx (B G MA) Mon-Sat 17-1, Sun 13-1 h
Maximilianstraße 2 ✉48147 ☎ 230 10 97
Na Und...? (AC B CC D f G lj MA s W) 20-? h, closed Mon
Sonnenstraße 43, ✉48143 ☎ 430 13

CAFES

Malik. Café (A B bf F glm MA) 9-1 h
Frauenstraße 7 ✉48143 ☎ 442 10

DANCECLUBS

Différent. Le (AC B CC D f GLM lj MA s W WE) Fri Sat & before holidays 22-5 h
Hörster Straße 10, ✉48143 ☎ 51 12 39

SEX SHOPS/BLUE MOVIES

Erotic World (AC CC g) 10-24, Sun 11-24 h
Wolbecker Straße 1 ✉48155 *(Near Hauptbahnhof)* ☎ 478 33
Erotikuss (AC CC G VS) Mon-Sat 10-22, Sun 17-22 h
Mauritzstraße 20 ✉48143 ☎ 51 14 61

SAUNAS/BATHS

Saunabad Insel (A DR f G MG msg OS p pi s sa sb sol VS YG) Sun-Thu 13-24, Fri Sat 13-1 h Sun 13-24:00h
Geringhoffstraße 46/48 ✉48163 ☎ 78 64 58
Stern Sauna (B f g p pi sa sb sol) Wed/Sat 14-22 h
Sternstraße 29 ✉48145 ☎ 66 24 66

BOOK SHOPS

Hippopotame. L` (g) Mon-Wed 9.30-18.30, Thu Fri -20, Sat -16 h
Ludgeristraße 55, ✉48143 ☎ 51 80 11

LEATHER & FETISH SHOPS

Serious Piercing (AC glm lj MA p)
Graelstraße 45 ✉48153 ☎ 53 11 76
Only piercings, no tattoos, appointment necessary.

GENERAL GROUPS

Autonomes Schwulenreferat der Uni Münster
Schloßplatz 1 ✉48149 ☎ 832 30 56
Fax: 51 92 89
Homophon-Erster scwuler Männerchor Münster
c/o Berthold Lensing, Siverdesstrasse 15 ✉48147 ☎ 230 30 23
Email: homophon@muenster.org
Homepage: http://www.muenster.org/homophon
Pädophilen Selbsthilfegruppe Bielefeld c/o Unterstützerkreis, Postfach 8005 ✉48043
Schwulenberband in Deutschland (SVD) Ortsgruppe Münster e.V. Tue 19-21 h
Schaumburgstraße 11 ✉48145 ☎ 648 22
E-mail svdms@muenster.net.
Schwulenreferat im AStA der FH Tue 16-18.30, Wed-Thu 11-13 h
Corrensstraße 25 ✉48149 ☎ 820 01/2
Völklinger Kreis e.V. Regionalgruppe Münster-Osnabrück PO Box 44 07 ✉48025 ☎ 52 46 45
(Michael) or ☎ 26 35 36 (Alois). Fax: 66 56 61.
Email: vk@muenster.gay-web.de.
Homepage: http://www.muenster.org/vk.

HEALTH GROUPS

AIDS-Hilfe Münster e.V. Tue-Fri 14-19 h
Schaumburgstrasse 11 ✉48145 ☎ 19 411 or ☎ 60 96 00
Fax: 635 55

HELP WITH PROBLEMS

Rosa Telefon Münster Wed 20-22, Fri 18-20 h
☎ 194 46
Schwules Überfalltelefon Tue 19-21 h
☎ 192 28
Help in case of gay-bashing.

RELIGIOUS GROUPS

Homosexuelle und Kirche (HuK)
c/o Andreas Bunge, Peterstr. 2 ✉48151 ☎ 79 87 616
E-Mail: huk@gmx.net

SPORT GROUPS

AndroGym schwul-lesbischer Sportverein Münster e.V.
PO Box 44 07 ✉48025 ☎ 609 04 98
Email: androgym@muenster.de

SWIMMING

-Gelmer (NU) (Kanalübergang, unbenutzter Arm des Dortmund-Ems-Kanals/ canalbridge, unused part of the Dortmund-Ems-canal)

CRUISING

-Park am Buddenturm (Promenade und Park um den Turm/promenade and park around the tower)
-Ludgeriplatz (AYOR)
-Domplatz

Neubrandenburg ☎ 0395

GAY INFO

Initiative Rosa-Lila
Friedrich-Engels-Ring 45, Villa Regenbogen ✉17019
☎ & Fax: 544 20 77
Homepage http://home.t-online.de *Gay and lesbian center. Ask for their different groups and activities.*
Rosalila Tue-Thu 16-20h, Sat 10-12:00h
PO Box 10 11 47 ✉17019
Every three months for free in gay venues in Mecklenburg-Vorpommern. Initiative Rosa-Lila *has the same contact telephone number. Please call for details.*

BARS

Incognito (B DG MA p s VS) Tue-sat 20-?, Sun & Mon closed
Rossower Strasse 19 ✉17034 ☎ 4228937

SEX SHOPS/BLUE MOVIES

Orion (g) Mon-Fri 10-20, Sat 9-16 h
Voßstraße 2 ✉17033 ☎ 566 72 63

GIFT & PRIDE SHOPS

buchOrt Tue-Thu 16-20, Sat 10-12 h
Friedrich-Engels-Ring 45 ✉17033 ☎ 544 14 93

GUEST HOUSES

Nobel-Hobel Pension (B bf d f g H MA N OS)
Morgenlandstraße 25 ✉17033 ☎ 566 51 57

GENERAL GROUPS

Die Wilden Engel - Theaterverein
c/o Initiative Rosa-Lila, PO BOX 10 11 47 ✉17019
☎ 582 51 34 Fax: 582 51 19

HELP WITH PROBLEMS

Schwul-lesbisches Beratungstelefon Wed 10-12 16-20 h
☎ 194 46

SWIMMING

-Buchort (NU)

CRUISING

-Wallabschnitt (Friedländer Tor → Fangturm)

Neukirchen ☎ 09947

HOTELS

Hardy's Landhaus (B bf d G H lj MA OS p sa) all year
Grauhof 33 ✉93453 ☎ 10 55
Rates per person/night: single or double with shared shower DM 55, double with shower 60. Half board. Bf.

Neumünster ☎ 04321

BARS

Everybody's (B g MA N WE YG) Sun-Thu 19-1, Fri Sat -3h
Esplanade 29 / Christianstrasse ✉24534 ☎ 447 11
Na und (B d f g MA YG) 20-5 h, closed Sun
Kieler Straße 48 ✉24534 ☎ 471 37

HEALTH GROUPS

AIDS-Hilfe Neumünster e.V.
☎Couselling 19-21:00h Mon, 16-18:00 Thu
Wasbeker Straße 93 ✉24534 ☎ 66866 Fax: 66866

Neuruppin ☎ 03391

PRIVATE ACCOMODATION

Haus Seehof (G H sa) all year
Seehof Nr. 10 ✉16818 *(at the Ruppiner-sea)* ☎ 2405
E-Mail: Haus.seehof@t-online.de

Neuss ☎ 02131

CRUISING

-Hauptbahnhof/Main train station (r OG)
-Kaufhaus Humer, Breslauer Straße

Neustadt ☎ 04561

GENERAL GROUPS

Schwulengruppe Ostholstein
c/o Kulturwerkstatt Forum, Wieksbergstraße 2-4 ✉23730
☎ 30 65

Neu-Ulm ☎ 0731

GENERAL GROUPS

Rosige Zeiten e.V.
PO Box 12 52 ✉89202 ☎ 253 60 E-Mail: rosigezeit@aol.com
Homepage: www.members.aol.com/rosigezeit

Neuwied ☎ 02631

BARS

Club-David (B d G MA p s W) 20-1, Fri Sat -2, Winter: Sun 15-1 h
Schloßstraße 26 ✉56564 ☎ 35 68 10

RESTAURANTS

Restaurant „Im Leuchtturm" (F glm) 11-1, Sun 11-14:30, 17:30-1 h, Tue closed
Schloßtraße 13 ✉56564 ☎ 23668

SEX SHOPS/BLUE MOVIES

Connection (g VS) Mon-Sat 10-22 h
Schloßpassage ✉56564 *(1st floor/1. Etage)*

Orion (g) Mon-Fri 9-19.30, Sat 9-16 h
Schloßstraße 69 ✉56564 ☎ 319 65

GENERAL GROUPS

Schwule Gruppe für Jung und Alt Meeting Fri 20 at Bar Amsterdam ☎ 35 80 76

CRUISING

-Schloßpark, Eingang Rhein, abends/Castle grounds, entrance near river, evenings.
-Baggersee, nähe Feuerwehr, nur Sommer/Small lake near fire-brigade, summer only.

Norderney ☎ 04932

CRUISING

-Nude beach near the Oase, turn right and walk along the dunes. After 500 m gays meet in the dunes (May-Sep only)

Nordhorn ☎ 05921

GENERAL GROUPS

Schwulengruppe Thu 19-20.30
c/o AIDS-Hilfe, Bentheimer Straße 35 ✉48501 ☎ 194 46
Gay group. Call Winnie for information.

HEALTH GROUPS

AIDS-Hilfe Grafschaft Bentheim e.V. (glm MA) Mon Fri 16-18, Tue-Thu 9-11 h
Bentheimer Straße 35 ✉48529 *(Europaplatz / Rathaus - Town Hall)* ☎ 194 11 Fax: 194 46 E-Mail: 1122-582@online.de
Meeting gay group Thu 19.30-20.30 h. HIV-Tests, counselling

HELP WITH PROBLEMS

Manphone-Schwulenberatung Thu 19-20.30 h
PO Box 1812 ✉48507 ☎ 194 46 ☎ 05921/194 11
E-Mail: 1122-582@online.de
Group evenings with local meetings. Gay counselling for parents. Organisation of trips to CSD venues etc

Nürnberg ☎ 0911

GAY INFO

Fliederlich e.V. (A GLM MA s WE) Tue 10-12, 13-16, Wed 16-21 h. Café Sun 14-21:00h
Gugelstraße 92 ✉90459 ☎ 42 34 57-0
E-Mail: fliederlich@nuernberg.gay-web.de
Homepage: www.nuernberg.gay-web.de/fliederlich
Gay and lesbian center. Please call for details or see our web site

Nürnberger Schwulenpost
c/o Fliederlich, Gugelstraße 92 ✉90459 ☎ 42 34 57 11
E-Mail: nst@fliederlich.com
Monthly publication, free at gay venues or by subscription.

Rosa Piste
Gugelstraße 92 ✉90459 ☎ 42 34 57 11 Fax: 42 34 57 21
Free scene and shopping guide/Kostenloses schwules Branchenbuch

BARS

Alt Prag (B G MA) Mon-Sat 11-24, Sun and public holidays 15-24 h
Hallplatz 29 ✉90402 ☎ 24 33 41

Amico Bar (B d f G MA) Sun-Wed 20-2, Fri-Sat -3 h, closed Thu
Köhnstraße 53 ✉90478 *(Bus 43/44)* ☎ 46 32 92

Entenstall. Zum (AC B G LJ MA OS WE) Mon-Thu 19-1, Fri & Sat -2, Sun 18-1 h
Entengasse 19 ✉90402 *(U-Weißer Turm/Opernhaus)*
☎ 244 84 30 *Home of the Nuremberg Leather Club NLC-Franken/Clublokal des NLC-Franken*

King's Pub (B f g OS W) Mon-Fri 11-3, Sat Sun 20-3 h, Summer: Sat 14-3 h
Dr.-Kurt-Schuhmacher-Straße 8 ✉90402 ☎ 244 77 03

La Bas (B f G MA OS R) 11-1 h
Hallplatz 31 ✉90402 ☎ 22 22 81

Little Hendersen (B D G H p R OS WE) Mon-Thu 11-4, Fri Sat -5 h
Frauengasse 10 ✉90402 ☎ 241 87 77
Overnight stays possible.

Na und (B d F GLM lj MA OS r s WE) Mon-Thu 11-14.30, 18-1, Fri 18-2, Sat 19-3, Sun 18-1 h
Marienstraße 25 ✉90402 ☎ 22 73 20

NOXX (B G) 21-4 h
Engelhandsgaße 22 ✉90402 ☎ 22 51 09

Petit Café (B bf G MA r) 15-1 (Apr-Oct), 17-1 (Nov-Mar), Sat Sun 6-1 h
Hinterm Bahnhof 24 ✉90459 ☎ 45 41 18

Savoy (B f G MA TV) Mon-Thu 18-2, Fri Sat 16-3, Sun -2 h
Bogenstraße 45 ✉90459 ☎ 45 99 45

Toy Bar (B DR G MA r VS) 20-4 h
Luitpoldstraße 14 ✉90402 ☎ 241 96 00

V 8 (B f G MA OS s YG) 18-1, Fri Sat -3 h
Moltkestraße 2 ✉90429 *(Entrance/Eingang Deutschherrnstraße)* ☎ 28 80 39

Vicking-Club/Babel Bar (B G LJ MA VS) 20-1, Fri-Sat -3 h
Kolpinggasse 42 ✉90402 *(U-Opernhaus)* ☎ 22 36 69

Willich (B bf f glm OS) 17-1, Sat Sun 10-1 h
Volprechtstraße 3 ✉90429 *(U1-Gostenhof)* ☎ 287 90 05

Zum Walfisch (! AC B bf CC f G H lj MA OS YG) Mon-Thu 11-1, Fri-Sat -2, Sun 15-1 h
Jakobstraße 19 ✉90402 *(U-Weißer Turm/Opernhaus)*
☎ 241 80 30
Sundays and holidays coffee & cake with classical music 15-18 h

CAFES

Café Max (B g MA) 17-1 h
Breitscheidstraße 18 ✉90459 ☎ 44 59 03

Cartoon (! B G MA OS YG) 11-1, Sun 14-1 h
An der Sparkasse 6 ✉90402 *(Near/nahe Lorenzkirche)*
☎ 22 71 70

Confetti (A f GLM MA s vs WE YG) Sat 16-20, Sun 14-21 h
Gugelstraße 92 ✉90459 *(Near/nahe Christuskirche, U-Maffelplatz, Tram 8)* ☎ 42 34 57-0
Cafe of Fliederlich Nuremberg's Gay-Union/Café des Nürnberger Schwulenvereins

Felix (A B f GLM OS YG) Mon-Sun 14-02:00h, Sun 6-10 h (Breakfast)
Weißgerbergasse 30 ✉90403 ☎ 224280

Lichtblick (B bf G MA) 1st and 3rd Sun 14-18 h
Bahnhofstraße 13-15 ✉90402 *(U-Hauptbahnhof)*
Cafe of the AIDS-Hilfe

Zur Quetsch'n (B d f Glm MA) Sun-Thu 17-24, Fri-Sat 15-1 h
Wiesenstraße 85 ✉90459 ☎ 450 11 38

DANCECLUBS

DESI Stadtteilzentrum (B d GLM YG) monthly Sat 21-3 h
Brückenstraße 23 ✉90419 *(Bus 34-Großweidenmühlstraße)*
☎ 33 69 43

Mach 1 (AC B D g MA S YG) Gay on 1st & 3rd Sun only 22-4 h
Kaiserstraße 1-9 ✉90403 *(U - Lorenzkirche)* ☎ 20 30 30

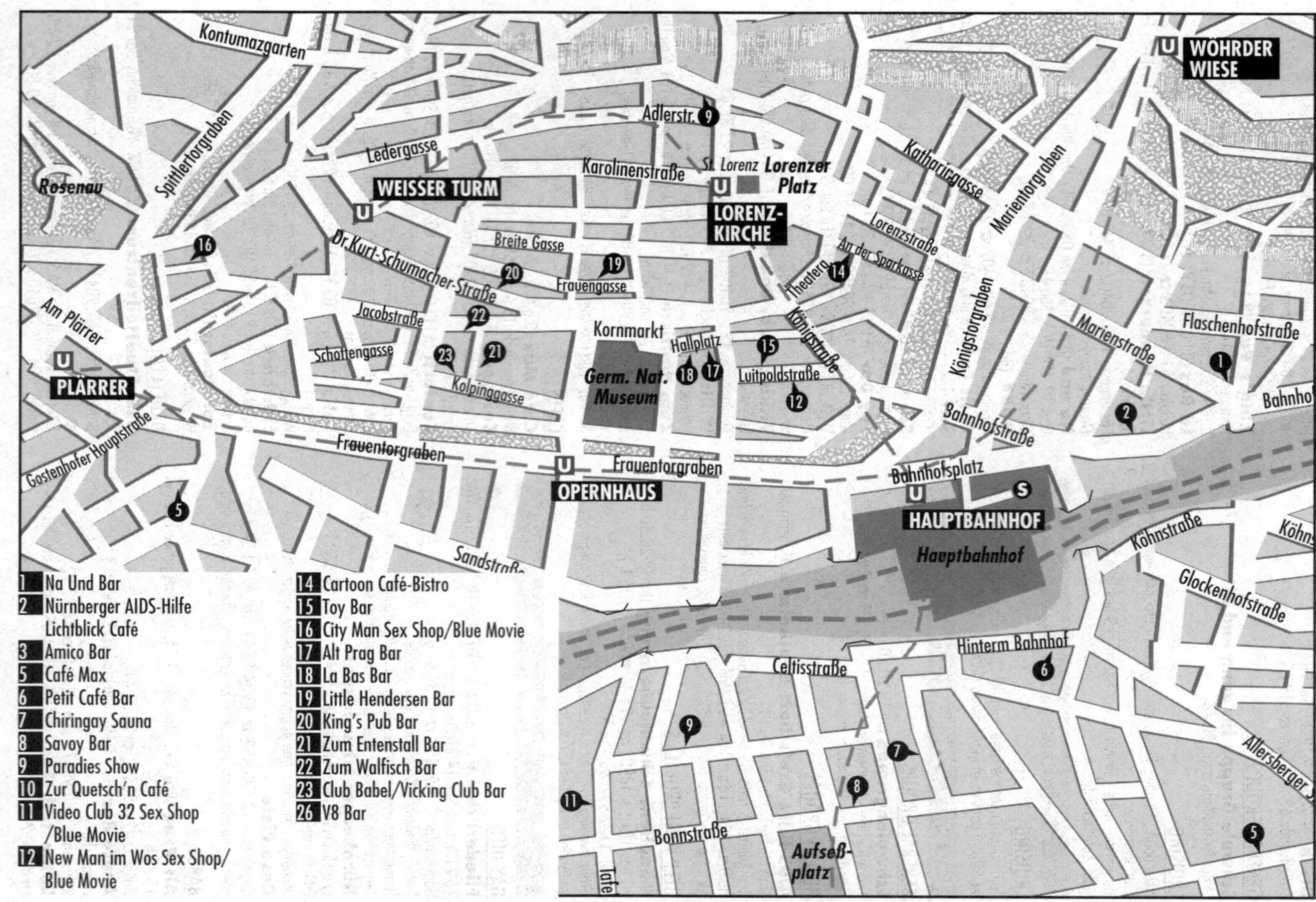
WÖHRDER WIESE
Kontumazgarten
Spittlertorgraben
Rosenau
Ledergasse
WEISSER TURM
Adlerstr.
Karolinenstraße
St. Lorenz
Lorenzer Platz
LORENZ-KIRCHE
Katharinengasse
Marientorgraben
Lorenzstraße
An der Sparkasse
Theatergasse
Breite Gasse
Dr.Kurt-Schumacher-Straße
Frauengasse
Am Plärrer
PLÄRRER
Jacobstraße
Schottengasse
Kolpinggasse
Kornmarkt
Hallplatz
Germ. Nat. Museum
Königstraße
Luitpoldstraße
Königstorgraben
Marienstraße
Flaschenhofstraße
Bahnhof
Bahnhofstraße
Gostenhofer Hauptstraße
Frauentorgraben
OPERNHAUS
Bahnhofsplatz
HAUPTBAHNHOF
Hauptbahnhof
Köhnstraße
Glockenhofstraße
Sandstraße
Hinterm Bahnhof
Celtisstraße
Allersberger
Bonnstraße
Aufseß-platz
Tafe
1 Na Und Bar
2 Nürnberger AIDS-Hilfe Lichtblick Café
3 Amico Bar
5 Café Max
6 Petit Café Bar
7 Chiringay Sauna
8 Savoy Bar
9 Paradies Show
10 Zur Quetsch'n Café
11 Video Club 32 Sex Shop /Blue Movie
12 New Man im Wos Sex Shop/ Blue Movie
14 Cartoon Café-Bistro
15 Toy Bar
16 City Man Sex Shop/Blue Movie
17 Alt Prag Bar
18 La Bas Bar
19 Little Hendersen Bar
20 King's Pub Bar
21 Zum Entenstall Bar
22 Zum Walfisch Bar
23 Club Babel/Vicking Club Bar
26 V8 Bar

Twilight (! AC B D f GLM lj MA s YG) Fri 22:-4, Sat -5, Sun -3, Mon & Tue closed
1st Wed/month & 4th Thu/month 22-2 h.
Nimrodstrasse 9 ✉90441 *(Tram stop - Dianaplatz)* ☎ 9414656

RESTAURANTS

Gasthaus im Pegnitztal (F glm OS) 11-24 h
Deutschherrnstraße 31 ✉90429 ☎ 26 44 44
Traditional and vegetarian cuisine. Party service available.
Majorka (b F g) Tue-Sun 11-14, 17-1 h, closed Mon
Hintere Ledergasse 2 ✉90403 ☎ 22 45 14
Italian cuisine
Omas Küche (B F g MA OS W) Tue-Sun 11.30-14, 17.30-22 h, closed Mon
Ostendstraße 97 ✉90482 ☎ 54 31 56

SHOWS

Paradies (B CC glm MA S TV) Shows 20.15, Fri Sat 20, 23, closed Mon
Bogenstraße 26 ✉90459 *(U-Aufseßplatz)* ☎ 44 39 91
Plushy ambience. Good shows./Plüschiges Ambiente. Gute Shows. Reservation from 18.30 h.

SEX SHOPS/BLUE MOVIES

Beate Uhse Sexshop (g) Mon-Fri 9.30-20, Sat 9-16 h
Königstraße 69 ✉90402 ☎ 241 89 15
City-Man (CC DR G MA VS) 13.30-23 h
Mostgasse 14 ✉90402 *(U-Plärrer/Weißer Turm)* ☎ 244 88 99
Combination card for here and Video Club 32 available
New Man im WOS (CC DR G MA VS) 10-24, Sun 12-24 h
Luitpoldstraße 11 ✉90402 ☎ 20 34 43
Orion (g) Mon-Fri 10-20, Sat 9.30-16 h
Landgrabenstraße 125/Alexanderstraße ✉90459 ☎ 439 78 12
Sex Intim Center (g) Mon-Fri 9-20, Sat -14 h
Hallplatz 21 ✉90402 ☎ 205 95 89
Video Club 32 (CC G MA VS) 14-22 h
Tafelfeldstraße 32 (Rückgebäude), ✉90443 *(near central station/nähe HBF)* ☎ 44 15 66

SAUNAS/BATHS

Aquaduct Club Sauna (b G p sa sb sol VS)
Reindelstraße 11 ✉90402
Chiringay Club Sauna (B bf CC DR f G MA msg p sa sb sol VS) Mon-Thu 12-3, Fri 12 through to Mon 3 h
Comeniusstraße 10 ✉90459 *(U-Hauptbahnhof)* ☎ 44 75 75
The largest sauna in Nürnberg. Three floors
Sauna-Club 67 (b DR G MA p sa sol VS) Mon-Thu 14-24, Fri 14-Sun 24 h
Pirckheimerstraße 67 ✉90408 *(In the court yard, Tram 9-Maxfeldstraße)* ☎ 35 23 46

FITNESSTUDIOS

Swiss Training Mon-Fri 10-22, Sat 10-17, Sun 13-17 h
Regensburger Straße 330 ✉90480 ☎ 401 01 80

BOOK SHOPS

Buchhaus Campe (glm) Mon-Fri 9-20, Sat 9-16 h
Karolinenstraße 13 ✉90402 ☎ 992 08 25
Bücherkiste (g) Tue-Fri 10-18, Sat -14, closed Mon
Schlehengasse 6 ✉90402 ☎ 22 24 23
Small gay section.

CONDOM SHOPS

Condomi Nürnberg (CC glm) Mon-Fri 10-19, Sat -16 h
Ludwigstraße 57 ✉90402 *(U-Plärrer/Weißer Turm)* ☎ 23 27 84
Condoms, lubricants, gifts.

LEATHER & FETISH SHOPS

Black Jump Call for appointment
Orleansstraße 51 ✉81667 ☎ 448 10 73
Sin-A-Matic Mon-Fri 12-20, Sat 10-16 h
Ludwigsplatz 1a ✉90403 *(U-Weißer Turm)* ☎ 230 59 86
Professional piercing studio

TRAVEL & TRANSPORT

Ticketours Reisebüro GmbH Der Reisemacher (CC) Mon-Fri 9-19, Sat 9-13 h
Kirchenweg 1 ✉90419 *(Near Friedrich-Ebert-Platz)* ☎ 37 86 900
Fax: 37 86 901 E-Mail: ticketours@t-online.de

HOTELS

Zum Walfisch (! B f CC G H) Jakobstraße 19 ✉90402 *(U-Opernhaus/Weißer Turm)* ☎ 241 83 35 Fax: 241 83 35
Each room is simply furnished with shared bath/WC. Clean and reasonably priced. Central location. ./Alle Zimmer sind einfach ausgestattet, Bad/WC auf dem Gang. Sauber und preisgünstig. Zentrale Lage

PRIVATE ACCOMODATION

Enjoy Bed & Breakfast (bf G H MA YG) 16:30-21:00h c/o Mann-O-Meter, Motzstraße 5 ✉10777
☎ 030/ 215 1666 Fax: 030/217 52219
E-Mail: Info@ebab.com Homepage: www.ebab.com
Price from 40 DM. Accomodation sharing agency. All rooms with shower and bf.

GENERAL GROUPS

Bine (Bisexuelles Netzwerk) 1st Wed 20 h
☎ 418 00 91 *(Christina)* or ☎ 287 63 58 *(Helmut)*
Emanzipation Nürnberg e.V. ☎ 46 39 27
(Jürgen Wolf)
Gelesch Meets at Café Real, Königsstraße 55
c/o Gehörlose e.V., Süd-Treff 44
Group for deaf gay and lesbians. Write for more information./ Gruppe gehörloser Schwulen und Lesben. Weitere Informationen bitte schriftlich anfordern.
Jugendgruppe Ganymed 2nd and 4th Mon 19 h (up to age 25)
c/o Fliederlich, Gugelstraße 92 ✉90459

FETISH GROUPS

Nürnberger Lederclub e.V. (NLC) (b DR G LJ P)
1st Sat 21 h at NLC-Keller, Schnieglingerstr. 264
Schnieglinger Strasse 264 ✉90427 *0(U-Muggenhof)*
☎ 326 20 01 Fax: 31 17 58 E-Mail: nlc@nuernberg.gay-web.de
Homepage: www.nuernberg.gay-web.de/nlc
Dress code leather, rubber, fetish, uniform. Entrance from 21-23 h.
Pegnitzbären Nürnberg
c/o Dirk Billmann, Am Ruhstein 24, 91054 Buckenhof ☎ 572 64
Fax: 572 64 E-Mail: Peter.Thung@t-online.de.
Group of heavy and hairy men and their fans. Meetings at „Cafe Cartoon" every 3rd Fri 19 h.

HEALTH GROUPS

AIDS-Beratung im Gesundheitsamt Tue 8-11, 13.30-15.30, Thu 9-11, 13.30-17 h
Burgstraße 4 ✉90403 *(Bus 36-Rathaus)* ☎ 231 27 67
Counselling and free and anonymous HIV testing/Beratung sowie kostenloser und anonymer HIV-Test.

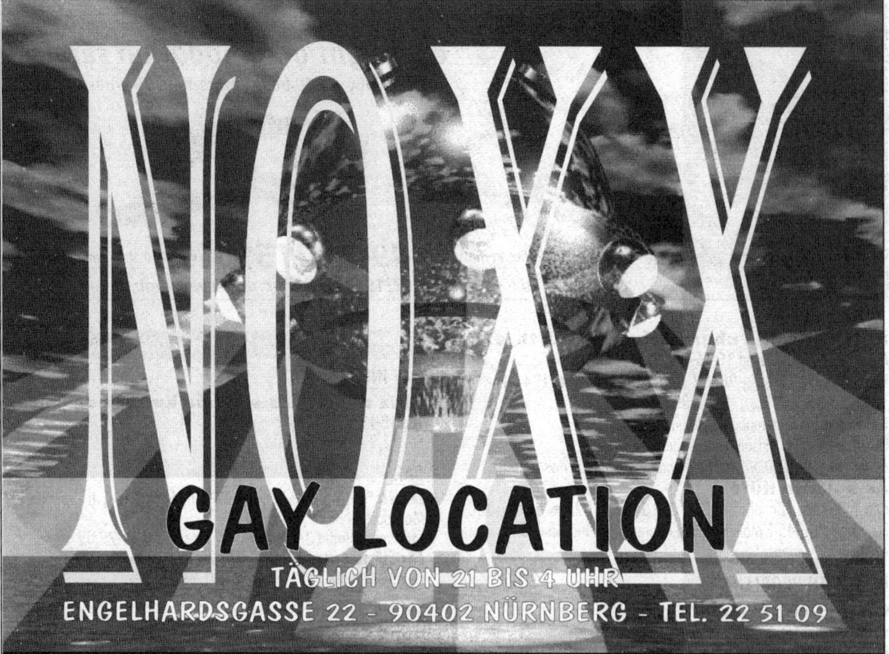
NOXX
GAY LOCATION
TÄGLICH VON 21 BIS 4 UHR
ENGELHARDSGASSE 22 - 90402 NÜRNBERG - TEL. 22 51 09

AIDS-Hilfe Nürnberg-Erlangen-Fürth e.V.
Mon 14-19, Tue & Wed 10-16, Thu 10-19, Fri -13 h
Bahnhofstraße 13-15 ✉90402 *(U-Hauptbahnhof)* ☎ 194 11
☎ 230 90 35 (Office). Fax: 230 903 46
E-Mail: aidshilfe.nuerenberg@t-online.de
Homepage: www.aidshilfe-nuerenberg.de
Counselling, prevention, self-help and community activism.

Ambulante Hilfe
c/o AIDS-Hilfe, Bahnhofstraße 13/15 ✉90402 ☎ 23 09 330
Fax: 230 90 345 E-Mail: aidshilfe.nuerenberg@t-online.de
Home-care, support.

HELP WITH PROBLEMS

Coming-out-Gruppe by appointment
☎ 42 34 57 15

Rosa Hilfe Wed 19-21 h
☎ 194 46

Schwules Überfalltelefon
c/o Fliederlich, Gugelstraße 92 ✉90459 ☎ 194 46
Counselling by appointment/Beratung nach Absprache

RELIGIOUS GROUPS

Homosexuelle und Kirche (HuK) Every 1st Sun/month, Gustav-Adolph-Kirche, Allersberger Straße 116
c/o Erich Schimpf, Mettlacher Straße 5 a ✉90469 ☎ 48 47 09 E-Mail: Judith.Hubert@t-online.de

SPORT GROUPS

Rosa Panther Schwul-Lesbischer Sportverein e.V.
c/o Fliederlich, Gugelstraße 92 ✉90459
Volleyball, jogging, table tennis, swimming, soccer and badminton.

SWIMMING

-Birkensee (NU) (along the street from Schwaig to Diepersdorf near/nahe Autobahnkreuz Nürnberg an der Straße von Schwaig nach Diepersdorf)
-Freizeitbad „Palm Beach" (NU)

CRUISING

-Stadtpark/municipal park (nur im Sommer/summer only)
-P Celtisstraße (ayor) (Near/Nähe Hauptbahnhof. Busy/Gut besucht)
-Hauptbahnhof/main railway station (ayor R)
-U-Plärrer
-Hallertor (Brücke)
-U-Frankenstraße

Oberhausen ☎ 0208

GAY INFO

Blitz at six, das schwule Kulturmagazin
Tue 18-19 h
FM 92,9 MHz or FM 104,0 MHz

BARS

Maik's (d g MG) Tue-Thu 16-2 h, Fri-Sat 16-1 h, Sun 13-19, Mon closed
Stöckmannstraße 36 ✉46045 *(near station)* ☎ 29 09 19

Montparnasse (B G MA) 20-1, 4-12 h
Helmholtzstraße 7 ✉46045 ☎ 20 43 02

SAUNAS/BATHS

Condor Sauna (AC B bf CC DR f G MA msg s sa sb sol VS wh) 12-23:00h, Fri & Sat 12-07:00h
Concordiastraße 32 ✉46049 *(at BERO-Zentrum, right hand side of Eingang Nord)* ☎ 80 44 25

GENERAL GROUPS

ISIT Meeting Tue 17-21, Sun 16-18 h
John-Lennon-Platz 1 ✉46045 ☎ 29 02 09 Fax: 20 35 84

HEALTH GROUPS

AIDS-Hilfe Oberhausen e.V. Office: Mon-Thu 10-16, Fri 10-14 h
Langemarkstraße 12, ✉46045 ☎ 80 65 18

CRUISING

-Bero-Zentrum
-Grillopark (Nähe Hauptbahnhof/near main railway station & Schwartzstraße)

Oberstdorf ☎ 08322

CRUISING

-Kurpark (near facility and Konzerthaus)

Oberursel ☎ 06171

CRUISING

-Near/nahe Stadthalle

Offenbach ☎ 069

BARS

Würtenbergische Weinstube (b F g OS) 18-01:00h, Fri & Sat -03.00h
Taunusstrasse 19 ☎ 88 95 35

DANCECLUBS

Club X (B D glm) Fri 23:00- ?
Bierberer Strasse 267 - 269

BOOK SHOPS

BAM - Buchladen Am Markt 9-19, Sat -15 h
Wilhelmsplatz 12 ✉63065 ☎ 88 33 33

APARTMENTS

Alexander's Garden Apartment
PO Box 10 19 07 ✉63019 ☎ 82 16 54
Centrally located apartment. 1 week DM 700,-.

GENERAL GROUPS

Schwule Stammtisch
☎ 82 36 31 59 *Youth group.*
Schwule Väter
c/o Wilfried Wember, Lützowstraße 4 ✉63067 ☎ 88 71 31

HEALTH GROUPS

AIDS-Hilfe Offenbach e.V. Mon Thu 10-12.30, 13.30-16 h, Tue 16-20 h
Frankfurter Straße 48 ✉63065 ☎ 88 36 88 Fax: 88 10 43
E-Mail: ahilfe2000@aol.com

CRUISING

-Busingpark
-P A661 Exit before Taunusring

Offenbach-Hundheim ☎ 06382

HOTELS

Hotel Restaurant Alte Abtei (bf F g H MA sa)
Hauptstraße 52 ✉67743 ☎ 33 25
All rooms with bath/shower/WC, TV, telephone.

Offenburg ☎ 0781

BARS

Tabu (AC B D f Glm MA YG) 20-1, Fri-Sat -4 h, closed Tue
Hauptstraße 102 ✉77652 ☎ 742 43

SEX SHOPS/BLUE MOVIES

Erotic-Kino-Center (AC CC g MA TV VS) Mon-Fri 9.30-24, Sat 9.30-16, Sun and public holidays 16-24 h.
Unionrampe 6 ✉77652 ☎ 235 53

HEALTH GROUPS

AIDS-Hilfe Offenburg e.V. (glm) Mon & Tue 10-13, Wed 16-18, Thu 17-20 h
Malergasse 1 ✉77652 *(Ecke/corner Steinstraße)* ☎ 194 11
☎ 0781/771 89 Fax: 240 63

SWIMMING

-Burgerwaldsee (g MA NU WE) (→ Schutterwald)
-Nonnenweirer Baggersee (zwischen Lahr und Rhein)

CRUISING

-Burgerwald (zwischen See und Autobahnparkplatz)

Oldenburg ☎ 0441

GAY INFO

Lesben- und Schwulenzentrum Oldenburg Na Und e.V. Wed 19-22 h
Ziegelhofstraße 83 ✉26121 ☎ 777 59 23
Fax: 764 78

Rosige Zeiten Meeting 2nd & 4th Wed 18.30 h at Na Und e.V. Gay Center
c/o Na Und Presse e.V., PO Box 38 04 ✉26028 ☎ 777 59 23
Fax: 764 78 *Zweimonatliches Regionalmagazin für Schwule und Lesben./ Bimonthly regional magazine for gays and lesbians.*

BARS

Hempels (A B GLM MA W YG) Mon (G) Thu (L) Fri (GLM) 20-24 h
Ziegelhofstraße 83 ✉26121 ☎ 777 59 90
Schwarzer Bär (AC B D DR G lj MA p WE YG) Bar: Tue-Thu 21-2, Disco: Fri Sat -5, LJ-Party (Dresscode) 1st & 3rd Mon 21 h
Donnerschweer Straße 50 ✉26123 ☎ 885 07 37
Zwitscherstübchen (B G MA OS YG) 21-2, Fri Sat -5, Sun 16-2 h
Bahnhofsplatz 5 ✉26122 ☎ 177 53

DANCECLUBS

Club Pulverfaß (AC B D g MA p) 22-2, Fri Sat -5, Summer: 16-2, Fri Sat 18-5 h
Kaiserstraße 24 ✉26121 ☎ 126 01
Männerfabrik (D DR G LJ MA) 3rd Sat 22-4/? h
c/o Kulturzentrum Alhambra, Hermannstraße 83, ✉26135
☎ 146 72
Rosa Disco (AC B D GLM MA YG) last Sat 22-5 h
c/o Kulturzentrum Alhambra, Hermannstraße 83, ✉26135 *(Bus-Nordstraße)* ☎ 777 59 23

RESTAURANTS

Elsässer Restaurant (AC E glm MA OS W) Tue-Sat 18/?, Sun and holidays 12-? h
Edewechter Landstraße 90 ✉26131 ☎ 50 24 17
Mon for groups, please request.

SEX SHOPS/BLUE MOVIES

Intimchen (g VS) 9-24 h, closed Sun
Kaiserstraße 9-11, ✉26122 ☎ 272 91

BOOK SHOPS

Carl von Ossietzky Buchhandlung (g) Mon-Wed 9.30-19, Thu Fri -20, Sat -16 h
Markt 24 ✉26122 ☎ 139 49
General bookstore with gay section.

FASHION SHOPS

Boah! Men's Underwear (GLM) Mon-Fri 11-20, Sat 10-16 h
Donnerschweerstraße 39 ✉26123 ☎ 824 37
Underwear and books.

TRAVEL & TRANSPORT

Horizont Reisen (glm) Mon-Sat 10-13, Mon-Wed 14.30-18.30, Thu Fri 14.30-20 h
Stau 35-37, Postfach 2324 ✉26013 ☎ 26 133
Fax: 26 466

GENERAL GROUPS

Come Together Foundation International
Staugraben 7 ✉26122 ☎ 277 72
Fax: 277 72. E-mail: ComeTogether@GeoCities.com
Homepage: www.geocities.com/westhollywood/heights/2319
Penpals, b&b exchange, hospitality exchange worldwide.

Lesben und Schwulentag Nordwest e.V. (LUST)
c/o Na Und e.V., Ziegelhofstraße 83 ✉26121 ☎ 777 59 23
Fax: 764 78 *Organizer of gay pride Oldenburg.*
Rosa Tanzkurs
c/o Angela Trautwein, Billungerweg 23 ✉26131
☎ 0781/560 01 60 *Dance group.*
Schwulenreferat im AStA Tue 10-12, Thu 14.30-16.30h, Café: Mon 13-15h
Uklhornsweg 49-5526129 ☎ 798-25 78
E-Mail: schwulenreferat@uni-oldenburg.de

FETISH GROUPS

SMart
PO Box 1925 ✉26009

HEALTH GROUPS

Oldenburgische AIDS-Hilfe e.V. Mon-Fri 9-12, Mon 14-16, Wed 14-18, Thu 17 h
Bahnhofstraße 23 ✉26122 ☎ 145 00 Fax: 142 22

RELIGIOUS GROUPS

HuK Regionalgruppe Oldenburg
Ben Khumalo & Ubbo Seegelken, Alte Ziegelei 4 ✉26197 *Huntlosen* ☎ 59 21 26 *(Natalie)*

CRUISING

-Park hinter den Theater/behind the theater
-Cäcilienpark
-Near/Nähe Theater

Olpe ☎ 02761

GENERAL GROUPS

Schwulen-Selbsthilfegruppe
PO Box 15 49, ✉57445

HEALTH GROUPS

AIDS-Hilfe Kreis Olpe e.V. Mon 19-21 h
Kampstraße 26, ✉57462

Olzheim ☎ 06552

HOTELS

Haus Feldmaus (A AC bf F H NG OS sa WE) Restaurant: Tue-Sat 18-22.30, Sun 12-13.30 h, closed Mon
Knaufspescher Straße 14 ✉54597 *(Near/nahe Prüm)* ☎ 78 14
Fax: 71 25. *Located 100 km from Bonn and Cologne. All rooms with phone, priv. bath and some with balcony/terrace, TV on request. All individually furnished.*

Oranienburg ☎ 03301

SWIMMING

-Bergwitzsee (6 km from Oranienburg near the Velten autobahn exit. Or take train to Borgsdorf, then 2,5 km by foot. The gay section and cruising area are at the peninsula on the smaller lake side, popular)

Osnabrück ☎ 0541

GAY INFO

GAYfm 104.8
PO Box 27 32 ✉49017 ☎ 230 39
Fax: 205 20 48, Email ThkGayfm@T-Online.de *Call for venues.*

BARS

K-G (B d G MA) Mon Wed Thu Sun 20-2, Fri Sat -3 h, closed Tue
Johannisstraße 46/47 ✉49074 ☎ 205 17 01
Theo. Bei (B G MA OS) 20-? h, closed Mon
Pottgraben 27, ✉49074 ☎ 20 15 70

CAFES

Café M. (b G MA) Mon 18-22, Fri Sat 18-23, Sun 15-20 h
Bramscher Straße 23 ✉49088 ☎ 653 37 Fax: 80 47 88
Youth group/Jugendgruppe „Verliebte Jungs" Thu 19-21 h.

DANCECLUBS

New Bivalent (AC b D f G lj MA p r s TV W WE) Sun-Thu 21-3, Fri Sat -5 h
Johannisstraße 131, ✉49074 ☎ 982 76 80
Vex (B D GLM MA) Thu-Mon 21-? h
Bohmter Straße 69 ✉17333

SEX SHOPS/BLUE MOVIES

Men's Life (AC DR G lj MA VS) Mon-Sat 10-23, Sun and public holidays 14-23 h
Möserstraße 39 ✉49074 *(100 m from railway station)*
☎ 2020 846

BOOK SHOPS

Montanus-Phoenix aktuell (g) Mon-Fri 9-20, Sat -16 h
Große Straße 15-16, ✉49074 ☎ 227 87
General bookstore with gay section.

GENERAL GROUPS

Autonomes Schwulenreferat der Uni Tue 12-15, Thu 18-20 h
Alte Münze 12 ✉49074 ☎ & Fax: 969 48 16
Schwule Coming Out Gruppe Tue 20.30 h
c/o Lagerhalle, Rolandsmauer/Heger Tor, ✉49074 ☎ 227 22
Verliebte Jungs Thu 19-21 h
c/o Café M, Bramscher Straße 23 ✉49088 ☎ 653 37
Gay youth group.

HEALTH GROUPS

AIDS-Hilfe Osnabrück e.V. Mon-Fri 10-14 h
Koksche Straße 4, ✉49080 ☎ 80 10 24
Gay counselling by appointment Mon 17-19 h

CRUISING

-Hauptbahnhof (r)
-Katharinenkirche
-Reifeisenpark (ayor) (Opposite Hauptbahnhof & P across the street. Popular)
-Gertrudenberg/Bürgerpark (near Hasetorbahnhof around Rosengarten. Popular weekend nights)

Paderborn ☎ 05251

BARS

Stadtgespräch (A B d f GLM MA s VS W WE YG) Mon Wed Thu 19-2, Fri Sat -4 h, closed Tue
Franziskanergasse 4 ✉33098 ☎ 216 16

SEX SHOPS/BLUE MOVIES

Amor & Co. (g VS) 10-20 h
Mühlenstraße ✉33098

LEATHER & FETISH SHOPS

Master & Servant (glm LJ MA) Mon Wed Fri 14-20 h, Tue Thu 16-20 h, Sat 14-18 h
Paderwall 1 ✉93102 *(next to hotel Ibis)* ☎ 266 11
Piercing and fetish studio.

GENERAL GROUPS

AK Schwip-Schwul in Paderborn Thu 20-23 h
c/o AIDS-Hilfe, Friedrichstraße 51 ✉33102 ☎ 28 02 98
Parties, coming-out group, sports group.

AStA-Referat Schwule und Lesben der Universität GH Paderborn Mon Wed 16-18 h
Warburger Straße 100 ✉33098 ☎ 60 31 74/70

Radio „Schrillkörper" Every 2nd Tue 20 h
c/o AIDS-Hilfe, Friedrichstraße 51 ✉33102 ☎ 28 02 98

Schwuler Stammtisch Meets every 1st Sun 20 h
at Acatraz, Neuhäuser Straße 1, 33102 Paderborn

HEALTH GROUPS

AIDS-Hilfe Paderborn e.V. Mon-Thu 10-16, Fri 10-13 h
Friedrichstraße 51, 33102, PO Box 11 68, ✉33041 ☎ 194 11
Café Jedermann Thu 20-23 h. Call ☎ 28 03 19 for further information.

HELP WITH PROBLEMS

Coming out Gruppe Paderborn 19-21 h
c/o Aids-Hilfe, Friedrichstraße 51 ✉33102 ☎ 28 02 98

SPORT GROUPS

Känguruh
c/o AIDS Hilfe, Friedrichstraße 51 ✉33102 ☎ 28 02 98
Volleyball.

CRUISING

-Maspernplatz (auch/also WC)

Passau ☎ 0851

BARS

Bistro 4 U (B G MA YG) 20-03:00h
Brunngasse 9 ✉94032 *(pedestrian zone)* ☎ 37419

SEX SHOPS/BLUE MOVIES

Beate Uhse (g) Mon-Fri 10-20, Sat -16 h
Bahnhofstraße 2 ✉94032 ☎ 340 70

Orion (g) Mon-Fri 9-19, Sat -16 h
Franz-Stockbauer-Weg 1 ✉94032 ☎ 75 13 13

GENERAL GROUPS

HIP e.V. Mon & Fri 20-? h, Sat 18-21:00h
Milchgasse 15 ✉94032 ☎ 325 41
E-Mail: gay_passau@eurogay.net
Homepage: www.eurogay.net/mitglieder/gay_passau
Homosexuellen Interessengemeinschaft Passau
-PLC Passauer Leder Club 2nd Sat 20 h
-Youth group 1st & 3rd Sat 20 h

L.u.S.T.-Lesben- und Schwulentreff an der Uni During term time only
Innstraße 40 ✉94032 *(Clubraum II)*

HEALTH GROUPS

AIDS-Beratungsstelle Niederbayern Mon-Fri 9-13, Thu also 14-19 h
Bahnhofstraße 16b ✉94032 ☎ 710 65

HELP WITH PROBLEMS

Rosa Telefon Fri 20-22 h
☎ 325 41

SWIMMING

-Innstufe between Neuhaus and Mittich

CRUISING

-Schanzelbrücke (below daytime/darunter tagsüber)
-Rathaus
-Nibelungenhalle (rear side)
-Innpromenade (between/zwischen Innsteg & Krankenhaus evenings/abends)

Pforzheim ☎ 07231

BARS

Shadow (B glm) Tue, Wed & Sat 19-05:00h
Westliche 3 ✉75172 *(in pedestrian zone)* ☎ 155569

SEX SHOPS/BLUE MOVIES

Multivideoshow & Sexshop (g VS) Mon-Sat 9-24, Sun 16-24 h
Am Waisenhausplatz 26 ✉75172 ☎ 35 67 39

Sex-Shop Maxima (g VS) 9-24 h
Berliner Straße 12 ✉75172 ☎ 10 25 62

GENERAL GROUPS

Schwule Initiative Pforzheim
Pfälzer Str 20 ✉75177 ☎ 343 84
Call Dominik (18-23 h) for information.

CRUISING

-Hauptbahnhof/main railway station (Bereich Gleis 1/area at platform 1)
-Stadthalle/municipal hall & Theater (Enzufer)
-Park (Landesgartenschaugelände)
-Schloßpark (across/gegenüber Hauptbahnhof)
-Marktplatz/Rathaus
-Turnplatz
-Meßplatz

Pfullingen ☎ 07121

GENERAL GROUPS

SchwuBert (Schwule Bewegung Reutlingen)
c/o Claus Gessinger, An der Echaz 13 ✉72793
☎ 0177/338 56 11

Plauen ☎ 03741

SEX SHOPS/BLUE MOVIES

Erotik-Shop (g) Mon-Fri 9-12.30 13.30-18, Sat 9-12, closed Sun
Bergstraße 30 ✉08523

GENERAL GROUPS

Schwule und Lesben in Plauen e.V. S.L.i.P. Tue 19.30 h
at Café Schwabing, Gartenstraße 41 PO Box 700 ✉08502

Potsdam ☎ 0331

BARS

La Leander (! A AC B bf F GLM MG OS) 12-02:30h
Kurfürstenstraße / Bekerstraße ✉14467 *(S- Nauener Tor)*
☎ 270 65 78
A wonderful café/bar with home made cakes and great service.

GENERAL GROUPS

Homosexuellen Integrationsprojekt Potsdam e.V.-HIP Tue 18-19, Thu 17-24, Fri 18-21 h
Berliner Straße 49, Haus der Jugend ✉14480 ☎ 29 20 65
Fax: 29 20 65
Landesverband Brandenburg Lesben und Schwule BLuS e.V.
Heinrich-Mann-Allee 103, Haus 16 ✉14473 ☎ 866 51 73
SuLUP-Schwule und Lesben an der Uni Potsdam
Hauptstraße 134, 14476 Eiche *(Room 329)*
Tabulos LesBiSchwule Initiative Potsdam e.V.
PO Box 97 04 12 ✉14443
Vier Jahreszeiten e.V.
Heinrich-Mann-Allee 103, Haus 16 ✉14473 ☎ 29 20 65

HEALTH GROUPS

AIDS-Hilfe Potsdam e.V. Mon Wed 14-20 h
Berliner Straße 49, ✉14467 ☎ 280 10 60
Fax: 280 10 70 *Counselling ☎ 194 11.*

SWIMMING

-Baggersee (Potsdam-Am Stern. Nuthestraße, exit „Am Stern". The lake is located at the end of the street Fichtenallee. Cruising near the railway line.)

CRUISING

-Colonnade at the Friedenskirche (Park Sanssouci)
-Bassinplatz (bei den Häusern/near the houses)

Rathenow ☎ 03385

SEX SHOPS/BLUE MOVIES

Orion (g) Mon-Fri 9-20, Sat 8.30-16 h
Milower Landstraße/Gustav-Freytag-Straße, ✉14712 *(at plaza, Havel Park)* ☎ 50 35 39

Ravensburg ☎ 0751

DANCECLUBS

Doala (GLM) Wed 21-4 h
Pfaumenstiel 31 ✉88212

GENERAL GROUPS

SSOS Mon 20 h in Bärengarten
PO Box 20 03 ✉88190 ☎ 168 96 or ☎ 49 042

HEALTH GROUPS

AIDS-Hilfe Ravensburg e.V. Office Tue Thu 10-14 h
Frauenstraße 1 ✉88212 ☎ 35 40 72
Fax: 35 40 77
Positif Aids-Hilfe Ravensburg e.V.
Frauenstraße 1 ✉88212 ☎ 194 11

SWIMMING

-Rössler Weiher (Weingarten near Ravensburg)

Recklinghausen ☎ 02361

BARS

Chateau (B f Glm MA) Wed-Sun 18-? h, closed Mon & Tue.
Herner Straße 8a ✉45657 ☎ 90 06 99

SEX SHOPS/BLUE MOVIES

Erotima Videothek (g VS) Mon-Sat 9-22, Sun 14-22 h
Dortmunder Straße 1-3 ✉45665 ☎ 456 01
MEO-Team (CC G P) Mon-Sat 13:-16:00h
Henrichenburger Strasse 116 ✉45665 ☎ 943298
Bondage and SM toys & fetish products

GENERAL GROUPS

GAYneration Meeting: Wed 19.30 h at „Altstadtschmiede", Kellerstraße 10
c/o Brinkmann, Lohweg 44 ✉45665 Email: eurogay.net
Homepage: http://eurogay.net/mitglied/GAYneration *Gay and Lesbian youth group.*

CRUISING

-Am Neumarkt (Recklinghausen Süd), Toiletten am Marktplatz/toilets at Marktplatz (Bus 205 vom HBF bis Neumarkt/take bus 205 from main railway station to Neumarkt)
-Rathauspark (OG)
-Erlbruckpark (at town hall/am Rathaus)

Regensburg ☎ 0941

BARS

Jeans (AC B GLM lj MA s) 20-1, Fri Sat -3 h
Glockengasse 1 ✉93047 ☎ 517 82
Na Und (AC B f GLM MA S VS WE) Mon-Thu 20-2, Fri Sat and public holidays -3 h
Jakobstraße 7 ✉93047 *(Arnulfsplatz)* ☎ 56 57 56
Pegasus (B DR G MA p VS) 21-4 h
Ladehofstraße 4 ✉93047 *(near Court of Justice)* ☎ 467 06 29

CAFES

Allegro (b bf f glm MA YG) 10-1, Fri Sat -2 h
Weiße-Lamm-Gasse 1, ✉93047 ☎ 527 14

DANCECLUBS

Sudhaus (B D Glm MA YG) Thu 23-3 h
Untere Bachgasse 8 ✉93047 ☎ 519 33

SEX SHOPS/BLUE MOVIES

Orion (g) Mon-Fri 9-20, Sat 9-16 h
Bahnhofstraße 24, ✉93047 *(Castra-Regina-Center)* ☎ 56 23 98

Videoworld (g VS) 9-23 h, closed Sun
Spiegelgasse 5 ✉93047 ☎ 541 29

HOTELS

D'Orphee (bf F g H)
Wahlenstraße 1 ✉93047 *(Reception at Untere Bachgasse 8)*
☎ 59 60 20 Fax: 59 60 20
Centrally located gay-friendly hotel. Call for rates.

GENERAL GROUPS

RESI e.V.-Regensburger Schwulen- & Lesben-Initiative (b G MA S VS) Wed Fri Sat 20-1 h
Blaue-Lilien-Gasse 1 ✉93047 ☎ 514 41
E-Mail: info@resi-online.de

HEALTH GROUPS

AIDS-Hilfe Regensburg e.V. (g p YG) Counselling Mon & Wed 18-20 h
Bruderwöhrdstraße 10 ✉93055 ☎ 79 12 66 Fax: 795 77 67
E-Mail: vorstand.ahr@gmx.de
Homepage: www.gay-in-regensburg.de/aidshilfe
☎ *Counselling 194 11*

SWIMMING

-Almer Weiher (bei/near Geisling. B8 Richtung/direction Straubing.)

CRUISING

-Der Wackel (Park at Albertstraße. Near Main railway station. 22-? h/ Park entlang der Albertstraße. Nähe Hauptbahnhof. 22-? h)
-P Neue Bahnhofsstraße/Margaretenstraße
-Vor der Grieb (gegenüber/opposite »Sudhaus«, -18 h)
-Main railway station/Hauptbahnhof (r)
-City park/Stadtpark (Prüfeningerstraße, -18 h)
-University/Universität (at/beim Audimax, entrance/Eingang K)
-Vor der Grieb (gegenüber/opposite »Sudhaus«, -18 h)
-Main railway station/Hauptbahnhof (r)
-City park/Stadtpark (Prüfeningerstraße, -18 h)
-University/Universität (at/beim Audimax, entrance/Eingang K)

Rendsburg ☎ 04331

SEX SHOPS/BLUE MOVIES

Intim-Boutique (g)
Oberreiderstraße 16, ✉24768 *(Near/Nähe Paradeplatz)*
Gegenüber/opposite Kreiskrankenhaus.

Rheine ☎ 05971

HEALTH GROUPS

AIDS-Hilfe Kreis Steinfurt e.V. Mon-Fri 9-14 h
Thiemauer 42 ✉48431 ☎ 540 23 or ☎ 194 11. Fax: 540 04
HIV/Aids counselling, prevention, youth and drug counselling.

Rosenheim ☎ 08031

BARS

Jägerstüberl (b d f GLM lj MA s) 11-2, Sun and public holydays 18-2h
Nicolaistraße 13 ✉83022 ☎ 346 65

Theaterschenke (B f g) 20-1 h, closed Mon
c/o Theater am Markt, Ludwigplatz 14 ✉83022 ☎ 379 73

SEX SHOPS/BLUE MOVIES

Orion (g) Mon-Fri 9.30-19.30, Sat -16 h
Atrium, Münchener Straße/Riederstraße ✉83022 ☎ 21 97 42

CRUISING

-Park zwischen Friedhof und Kapuzinerkloster/Park between cemetery and Kapuzinerkloster
-Hauptbahnhof/main railway station

Rösrath ☎ 02205

GENERAL GROUPS

CUF-Jugendclub
Im Pannenhack 96, PO Box 20 21 24 ✉51503 ☎ 878 33
Email cuf.marcel@t-online.de
Homepage http://pages.vossnet/marcelcgu

Rostock ☎ 0381

GAY INFO

Rat + Tat e.V. (F GLM MA OS) Mon 10-13, 15-17, Tue 14-18, Thu 14-19 h
Leonhardstraße 20 ✉18057 ☎ 45 31 56 Fax: 45 31 61

BARS

Aalglatt (f G MA) Mon 20-1, Tue-Thu 14-1, Fri-Sun 21-1 h
Kistenmacherstraße 17 ✉18055 *(Tram-Steintor)*
☎ 493 42 14

Gerd's Bierbar (A AC B CC F glm MA OS p) Mon-Thu 11-23, Fri-Sat -2 h, closed Sun
Schnickmannstraße 7 ✉18055 *(in Café/Restaurant „Windspiel")*
☎ 493 49 61

RESTAURANTS

Kaminstube (B F g MA OS) 17-24, Fri Sat 18-24, summer: Mon-Sun 18-24 h
Burgwall 16, ✉18055 ☎ 313 37
German cuisine.

SEX SHOPS/BLUE MOVIES

Orion (g) Mon-Fri 8.30-20, Sat -16 h
(at Hanse Center) ☎ 68 01 46

BOOK SHOPS

Die andere Buchhandlung (g) 9-18.30, Sat 9-13 h, closed Sun
Ulmenmarkt 1 ✉18057 ☎ 492 05 13

GUEST HOUSES

Stadtmitte. Pension (bf G H)
Augustenstraße 74 ✉18055 *(Near central station)* ☎ & Fax: 490 22 20
Single room (\bath, WC) DM 60 incl. bf. Double (\bath, WC) DM 100 incl. bf.

Unser Bauernhof (bf f G MA NU OS)
Stralsunder Chaussee 36, Wiepkenhagen ✉18320
☎ 038225/304 18
Nice farm house just 20 km from the sea and beautiful beaches. Two rooms with shared, one with private bath, minibar, telephone, heating, own key. Single DM 35-55, double DM 50-65, bf incl. Half-board DM 10 extra. Car park, TV-room./
Homepage: http://unser-bauernhpf.mysite.de

GENERAL GROUPS

Referat Schwule und Lesben (STuRa der Universität) Thu 19-23 h
August-Bebel-Straße 28, ✉18055 ☎ 498 28 63

HEALTH GROUPS

AIDS-Hilfe im Rat & Tat e.V. Mon 10-13 15-17, Tue 14-18, Thu 14-19 h
Leonhardstraße 20 ✉18057 ☎ 45 31 56 ☎ 0381/ 194 11 Fax: 45 31 61 E-Mail: info@rostock.aidshilfe.de

SWIMMING

-Markgrafenheide (! NU) (from Warnemünde take the car ferry to Hohe Düne, from there go 5 km to Markgrafenheide, there go to the camp ground [P]. Go further by foot ca. 20 minutes, on the beach go 20 min to the east.)
-Warnemünde (10 minutes west of tower 6 of the DLRG)
-Elmenhorst (road to the beach, [P] there, 10 minutes to the west, there's a rocky beach)

CRUISING

-University (in Main building, ground floor/Hauptgebäude, EG; popular)
-Kröpeliner Straße (hinter/behind Hotel Warnow; 9-18 h)
-Wall (MA) (zwischen/between Kröpeliner Tor & Rosengarten)

Rottenbuch ☎ 08867

HOTELS

Hotel Moosbeck-Alm (B bf DR E F glm H MA msg NU OS pi sol WE WO YG)
Moos 38 ✉82401 ☎ 912 00 Fax: 91 20 20

Rottweil ☎ 07420

RESTAURANTS

Die Krone (CC F H OS) Tue-Sat 17.30-24 h, Sun afternoon & evening, Mon closed
Hauptstraße 38 78652 Deißlingen-Lauffen ✉78627
☎ 529 Fax: 23 03 *Restaurant and guest-house.*

SEX SHOPS/BLUE MOVIES

Esctasy (g VS) 10-19.30, Sat -13 h, closed Sun
Friedrichsplatz 9 ✉78628 ☎ 0741/415 86
Intim-Boutique (g) 9-12.30/14-18.30, Thu -20, Sat 9-13 h, closed Sun
Königstraße 88 ✉78628 ☎ 0741/127 14

CRUISING

- On highway A81 /E41 car park Eschachtal between Rottweil and Villingenschwen on both sides of the highway.

Rüsselsheim ☎ 06142

ESCORTS & STUDIOS

John (G LJ) 10-23 h
☎ 631 00 or ☎ (0172) 610 96 10

CRUISING

-Rail station/Bahnhof
-Karstadt (1st floor)

Saarbrücken ☎ 0681

BARS

Black Hole (AC B DR f G lj MA p R s VS) 18:-01:00h
Schillerplatz 16 ✉66111 *(Entrance/Eingang Bleichstraße 4)*
☎ 39 88 57
Darkroom with sling. Leather toys etc on sale too
Bohème. La (AC B G MA OS) 18-1, May-Sep 16-1 h, closed Sun
Kronenstraße 10 ✉66111 ☎ 328 83
Boots (B d DR G LJ MA p VS) Mon, Wed, Thu 21-3, Fri Sat -5, Sun -2 h, closed Tue
Mainzer Straße 53 ✉66121 ☎ 614 95
Hufeisen (AC GLM MA p TV W) closed Tue
Mainzer Straße 27 ✉66111
Madame (B f GLM MA p) Tue-Thu 21-3, Fri & Sat -4, Sun -2 h
Mainzer Straße 4 ✉66111 ☎ 329 63
Perspektive 1 (B g MA) 19-1 h, Thu (G)
Rotenbergstraße 10 ✉66111 ☎ 390 44 02
Take Off (AC f GLM lj MG s SNU WE) 20-4 h
Mainzer Straße 8 ✉66111 ☎ 390 44 45
Teddy Treff (B G MA p r) 20-3, Fri Sat -5 h
Mainzer Straße 57 ✉66121 ☎ 656 08
Tenne (B F glm MA) Mon-Fri 10.30-24/? h, Sat Sun closed
Eisenbahnstraße 60-62 ✉66117 ☎ 563 43
Villa Kunterbunt (AC B GLM LJ MA OS S W YG) 19-1 h
Herbergsgasse 7/St. Johannes Markt ✉66111 ☎ 37 66 44

DANCECLUBS

Big Ben (AC D f GLM LJ MA p s sa STV TV WE YG) 19-? h, Mon closed
Försterstraße 17 ✉66111 ☎ 358 55
Diva (D GLM LJ MA s WE) Fri/Sat 23-5 h
Reichsstraße 10 ✉66111 *(Main station/Saargalerie)* ☎ 390 88 22
Fri Lesbian Night, Sat Night + Gay.
Warme Nächte (AC B D GLM lj MA r s TV W) 2nd Sat, 22-5h
c/o Garage, Bleichstraße 11-19 ✉66111 ☎ 39 79 91

SEX SHOPS/BLUE MOVIES

Beate Uhse Sexshop (g VS) Cinema Mon-Thu 9-24, Fri Sat -1, Sun 14-23 h
Bahnhofstraße 74 ✉66111 ☎ 354 01
City Live (g VS) 10-24, Sun 14-24, Fri-Sat cinema -1 h
Viktoriastraße 26a ✉66111 ☎ 390 81 21
Orion (g) Mon-Fri 10-20, Sat -16 h
Trierer Straße 36 ☎ 460 44
Roxy Kino 4 (g VS) 10-24, Sun 14-24 h
Bahnhofstraße 109 ✉66111 ☎ 325 44
Showcenter (g) 11-0.30 h
Kaiserstraße 46 ✉66111 ☎ 39 85 23
Video Center (CC g MA) Mon-Fri 9-19.30, Sat -14, 1st Sat -16 h
Mainzer Straße 11 ✉66111 ☎ 39 70 77
Video Dream World (g) Mon-Thu 9-24, Fri Sat -1, Sun 11-24 h
Bahnhofstraße 17/Kohlwaagstraße 5 ✉66111 ☎ 390 48 80

BOOK SHOPS

KulTour (CC glm W) Mon-Wed 9-19, Thu Fri -20, Sat -16 h
Berliner Promenade 12 ✉66111 ☎ 326 70
Large gay-lesbian department.

GENERAL GROUPS

Bündnis 90/Die Grünen-LAG Schwulenpolitik
c/o Patrick G.W. Müller, Parkstraße 1 ✉66111 ☎ 39 97 00
Lesben- und Schwulenverband Saar e.V. (LSVD Saar) Mon-Thu 10-12 h & 13-15 h, Fri 10-12 h
Blumenstrasse 24 ✉66028 ☎ 39 88 33
E-Mail: LSVDSaar@aol.com.
Saar-Rogues Fri 19 h at AIDS-Hilfe Saar
PO Box 10 17 25 ✉66017 ☎ 311 12

FETISH GROUPS

Leder Club Saar (LC-Saar) Infos at Boots 21-? h; Meeting last Sun at Boots 20 h
c/o Wachenhausen, Uhlandstraße 2 ✉66121 ☎ 68 45 66
Email: rainer.altmeyer@t-online.de *Member of ECMC.*

HEALTH GROUPS

AIDS-Hilfe Saar e. V. Mon Tue Thu 9-12, 14-17, Wed 9-12, 14-20, Fri 9-12 h
Nauwieser Straße 19 ✉66111 ☎ 194 11 ☎ 0681/31112
Fax: 342 52 *Cafe Wed 18, Sat 19, Sun 17 h.*
Überfalltelefon/gay victims emergency ☎ 192 28 on Fri 19-20 h

HELP WITH PROBLEMS

Schwul-lesbisches Überfall- und Beratungstelefon
☎ 192 28 E-mail SUT19228@aol.com

RELIGIOUS GROUPS

Homosexuelle und Kirche (HuK)
c/o Thomas Wagner, Graf-Simon-Straße 12 ✉66117 ☎ 538 60
Fax: 538 69

SPORT GROUPS

Frauen Volleyball - Die Pippies Fri 18.30 h
c/o Mugllbergschule ☎ 37 66 44
Rosa Feder - Badminton (G) Sat 17 h
c/o Hettlage Sportcenter, Auf der Bellevue

SWIMMING

-Steinbachweiher/Steinbachtal (Buss22-Rußhütte, 2nd lake/2. See)

CRUISING

-Park at Staatstheater (r) (Saaruferanlagen)
-Am Staden (near Ulanen Pavillon)
-Liegewiese Alter Flughafen (g) (Römerstraße)
-Main station/Hauptbahnhof (R)

Saarlouis ☎ 06831

SEX SHOPS/BLUE MOVIES

Video Dream World (g) Mon-Sat 9.30-23.30, Sun 14-23 h
Zeughausstraße 12 ✉66740 ☎ 401 52

Salzgitter ☎ 05341

SEX SHOPS/BLUE MOVIES

Orion (g) Mon-Fri 9.30-20, Sat 9.30-16 h
Berliner Straße 76 ✉38226 *(Lebenstedt)* ☎ 128 10

Sandförde ☎ 039741

RESTAURANTS

Restaurant Krause (B bf F CC g H MA OS)
Chausseestraße 9 ✉17309 *(on the B 109 between Pasewalk and Anklam)* ☎ 807 03
German cuisine. Also guest house. All rooms with TV and shower, shared WC. Rates: double 90, single 50 (bf incl.)

Schöfflengrund ☎ 06445

TRAVEL & TRANSPORT

Logo Projekt und Reisen
Zum Waldgraben 18 ✉35641 ☎ 92 27 77 Fax: 92 27 78
E-mail: LogoReisen@aol.com

Schöllnach ☎ 09903

HOTELS

Mühle. Die (B d F G H MA OS sa sol)
Englfing 16 ✉94508 ☎ 562 Fax: 26 14
Rooms with shared bath/WC. Rates half board DM 65/person.

Schwabach ☎ 09122

CRUISING

-Stadtpark (summer only/nur im Sommer)
-Marktplatz (Tiefgarage/underground garage)

Schwäbisch Gmünd ☎ 07171

HEALTH GROUPS

AIDS-Hilfe Schwäbisch Gmünd e.V. Tue Thu Fri 17-18.30
Bocksgasse 23 ✉73525 *(Werdich- Passage)* ☎ 19 411

Schweinfurt ☎ 09122

SEX SHOPS/BLUE MOVIES

Orion (g)
Fischerrain 27 ✉97421

Schwerin ☎ 0385

BARS

Absolut. Bierpub Mon-Sat 20-?, Sun -4 h
(Breakfast Buffet)
Münzstraße 36 ✉19055 ☎ 581 42 99
Saitensprung (AC B bf d F GLM H MA p s VS YG) 20-? h, Mon closed
Von-Thünen-Straße 45/Obotritenring ✉19053 ☎ 71 29 67

DANCECLUBS

Restaurant Casino (B D GLM YG) Sat 21-3 h
Pfaffenstraße 3 ✉19053 ☎ 56 10 43

SEX SHOPS/BLUE MOVIES

Love Line (g) 9-18 h, closed Sat Sun
Großer Moor 17 ✉19055
Orion (g) Mon-Fri 9-20, Sat -16 h
Margaretenhof *(at plaza in EKZ, Warnitz)* ☎ 486 66 85
Sex Shop Erotik-Kaufhaus (g VS) 9-22 h, closed Sun
Goethestraße 62, ✉19053

GUEST HOUSES

Saitensprung (AC B bf d F GLM H MA p s VS YG)
Von-Thünen-Straße 45/Obotritenring ✉19053 ☎ 71 29 67
Fax: 71 29 67
Single room DM 40, double 60, bf 10/ Einzelzimmer ab DM 40, Doppel ab 60.

GENERAL GROUPS

Klub Einblick e.V. (GLM MA p) Mon-Fri 17-? h
Lübecker Straße 48 ✉19053 *(near Marienplatz)* ☎ 55 55 60
Fax: 581 19 26 E-Mail: info@schwerin.gay-web.de
Homepage: www.schwerin.gay-web.de
Landesverband der Lesben und Schwulen in Mecklenburg-Vorpommern-Lambda e.V.
Wismarsche Straße 190 ✉19053 ☎ 53 75 54

HEALTH GROUPS

AIDS-Hilfe Westmecklenburg Tue 14-20, Thu 10-16 h
Wismarsche Straße 190 ✉19053 ☎ 56 86 45
Café Mon 19-? h

HELP WITH PROBLEMS

Beratung für Homo-, Bi- und Transsexualität Tue 14-20, Thu 10-16 h
☎ 581 19 27

Telefon des Vertrauens 9-16 h
☎ 518 04 09

SWIMMING

-Schweriner See (Zippendorfer Strand/beach)
-Vorbecker See (Bus 6 von/from Hermann-Duncker-Straße nach/to Vorbeck)
-Kaninchenwerder im/in the Schweriner See (NU) (mit der Fähre der »Weißen Flotte« von der Schloßbrücke oder Tippendorf/take the »Weißen Flotte« ferry from Schloßbrücke or Tippendorf.)

CRUISING

-Westuferpromenade Ziegelsee (Dr.-Hans-Wolf-Straße, evenings/abends)

Seebad Bansin ☎ 038378

HOTELS

Villa von Desny (B bf CC g lj)
Strandpromenade 4 ✉ 17429 *(near the beach)* ☎ 24 30
Fax: 243 24 *All 11 rooms and 2 appartments with bath/shower/WC, balcony or terrace, telephone, fax, TV, Video, radio, minibar. Single rooms DM 90-160, double rooms DM 100-170, apartments DM 160-320, breakfast incl.*

Siegburg ☎ 02241

BARS

La Playa (B d f GLM MA OS W) Tue-Sun 19-? h, closed Mon; winter: Tue-Fri 19-?, Sat-Sun 19-? h, closed Mon
Frankfurter Straße 85b ✉53721 ☎ 59 07 92
Homepage: http://www.LP-info.com/LaPlaya.

Siegen ☎ 0271

GAY INFO

Schwulen Begegnungs Zentrum (SBZ) Siegen (A B d G lj MA s) Mon Wed Fri Sun 20-?, Tue 18.30-?, Thu 19.30-?h, counselling Wed 9-13h
Marienborner Straße 16a ✉57074 ☎ 532 97
E-mail siseV@eurogay.net
Homepage http://eurogay.net/mitglieder/sis
Sometimes party on Sat (22-?h)

BARS

Darling (B CC D f GLM MA p s STV) Tue-Thu 21-4, Fri-Sun -5 h, closed Mon
Geisweider Straße 4 ✉57078 ☎ 834 65

Incognito (B f GLM MA p) 20-1 h, closed Mon & Sun , last Fri Lesbian
Hundgasse 12 ✉57072 ☎ 575 23

SEX SHOPS/BLUE MOVIES

Lady S (g VS) Mon-Sat 10-22 h
Effertsufer 104 ✉57072 ☎ 335 65 56

Orion (g) Mon-Fri 9.30-20, Sat 9-16 h
Hagener Straße 71 ✉57072 *(Near/Nähe Globus-Center)* ☎ 454 08

GENERAL GROUPS

Autonomes Schwulenreferat Uni-GH Siegen
Meets Tue 12-16 h
at Building AR-M, room M-002, Adolf-Reichwein-Str. 2 ✉57068

HEALTH GROUPS

AIDS-Hilfe Siegen-Wittgenstein e.V. Tue Thu 20-22 h
Sandstraße 12, ✉57072 ☎ 222 22

HELP WITH PROBLEMS

Rosa Telefon Wed 19-21, Thu 16-18 h
☎ 194 46

CRUISING

-Park & [P] at/am Oberen Schloß (popular/beliebt)
-Rathaus/Town Hall

Sigmaringen ☎ 07571

GENERAL GROUPS

Romeo & Julius
PO Box 58 ✉72485 ☎ 32 68 Fax: 3231
E-Mail: info@alb.gay-web.de Homepage: www.gay.alb.de
Organised social events (cinema, Disco etc), counselling and self-help groups and information and public awareness programs

Singen ☎ 07731

HEALTH GROUPS

AIDS-Hilfe Konstanz Außenstelle Singen
Wed 11-13 h
Mühlenstraße 17 ✉78224 ☎ 684 21

Soest ☎ 02921

GENERAL GROUPS

Schwul-lesbischer Stammtisch (B GLM) Fri 20-?
c/o Bürgerzentrum „Alter Schlachthof", Ulricher Tor 4 *59494*

HEALTH GROUPS

AIDS-Hilfe Soest e.V. Mon 16-20, Tue Wed 9-12 h
c/o Jugendcafé, Siechenstraße 9 ✉59494 *(Near/Nähe Hallenbad)* ☎ 28 88

CRUISING

-An der Reitbahn (accross from the new hall/gegenüber der neuen Stadthalle)

Solingen ☎ 0212

BARS

Café Cobra (B bf d f g OS s YG) Merscheider Straße 77-79 ✉42699 ☎ 33 25 65

Vogelsang (B F g MA) 18-2 h
Focher Straße 84 ✉42719 ☎ 531 21

GENERAL GROUPS

Gay Talk Tue 20.30-? h
c/o Café Cobra, Merscheider Straße 77-79 ✉42699 *(Bus 681-Brunnenstraße)*

Herzenslust (G MA) Tue 20-? h
c/o Schwulengruppe Solingen, Herscheider Straße 77-79 ✉42699 *(near station Solingen-Ohligs)*

HEALTH GROUPS

AIDS-Hilfe Solingen e.V. Mon-Thu 14-18, café last Sun 15 h
Ringstraße 4 ✉42719 ☎ 194 11

Sonthofen ☎ 08321

SPORT GROUPS

Gay Summit Club Allgäu (GSC Allgäu) (G MG WE YG) 18-22 h
c/o Wendelin Martin, Moltkestraße 8 ✉87527
E-Mail: GSC@gmx.de Homepage: www.GSC.home.pages.de
Outdoor activities.

Speyer ☎ 06232

CRUISING

-Dompark
-Binsfeld (between Speyer and Ludwigshafen near Waldsee)
Outdoor activities.

Stade ☎ 04141

GENERAL GROUPS

Homosexuelle in Stade (H.i.S.) Every 1st and 3rd Mon 20 h at DRK-Haus
Poststraße 21 (2nd floor)

Stendal ☎ 03931

SEX SHOPS/BLUE MOVIES

Orion (g) Mon-Fri 9-12.30, 13.30-20, Sat 9-16 h
Winckelmannstraße 4 ✉39576 *(Near Uengliger Tor)* ☎ 21 28 39

St.Ingbert ☎ 06894

BARS

Castro (B d GLM MA s) Mon-Sat 18-1, Sun and public holydays 15-1h
Ensheimer Straße 1a ✉66386 ☎ 69 09

Stralsund ☎ 03831

SEX SHOPS/BLUE MOVIES

Erotic Boutique (CC glm MA VS) Mon-Fri 10-20, Sat -16 h
Mauerstraße 9 ✉18439 ☎ 29 08 69 Fax: 49 71 15

SWIMMING

-Strand nördlich von/beach to the north of »Alte Fähr«

CRUISING

- Frankenteich (near Bahnhof)

Straubing ☎ 09421

CRUISING

-WC at railway station (day)
-Park near railway station (nights)

Stuttgart ☎ 0711

GAY INFO

Blättle
c/o LC Stuttgart e.V., PO Box 13 12 16 ✉70069
Monthly for members of LC Stuttgart.

GayConnect
☎ 901 86 68 *Mailbox.*

Rainbow
c/o AIDS-Hilfe, Hölderlinplatz 5 ✉70193 ☎ 194 11
Three times a year for free in gay venues.

Schwulst
c/o Buchladen Erlkönig, Bebelstraße 25 ✉70193
☎ & Fax: 63 91 39

Stuttgart & Zürich von hinten
c/o Bruno Gmünder Verlag, PO Box 61 01 04, 10921 Berlin
☎ (030) 615 00 30 Fax: 615 91 34 Email info@spartacus.de
The city guide about Stuttgart, the federal state of Baden-Wurttemberg and the three Swiss cities of Basel, Berne and Zurich. Useful general information and lots of addresses with extensive descriptions in English and German. Up-to-date maps. Erotic photos.

Weissenburg - Schwul/lesbisches Zentrum (A AC d f lj MA W) Mon-Fri 17-22:00h, Sun 15-22:00h, Sat - call for info.
Weißenburgstraße 28a ✉70180 *(U-Österreichischer Platz)*
☎ 640 44 92 ☎ 640 44 94 Fax: 640 44 95

BARS

Boots (AC B G lj MA VS) 20-1, Fri Sat -2 h
Bopserstraße 9/Heusteigstraße, ✉70180 ☎ 236 47 64

Eagle (AC B DR f LJ P VS) Sun-Thu 21-1, Fri Sat -2 h
Mozartstraße 51 ✉70180 *(U-Österreichischer Platz)*
☎ 640 61 83
2nd Sat „Black leather night", 3rd Sun „S/M Session" (entry 16-17 h only), 1st Fri „Hard core night" strict dress code. Every Tue Happy hour from 21 h

Finkennest (B DR F G MA R) 14-1, Fri Sat -2 h
Weberstraße 11d ✉70182 ☎ 24 11 42

Goldener Heinrich (B F g og) Sun-Thu 10-1, Fri-Sat 10-2 h
Leonhardstraße 3 ✉70182 ☎ 24 58 27

Jakobstube (B G MA) 10-1, Fri Sat -2, Sun 15-1 h
Jakobstraße 6 ✉70182 ☎ 23 54 82

Monroe's Pub (B F Glm MA OS) Mon-Sat 12-5, Sun 15-5 h
Schulstraße 3 ✉70173 *(Nähe/near Rathaus. Upper floor/Obere Etage)* ☎ 226 27 70 *Popular.*

Seven (AC B F G MA OS) Wed Thu Sun 18-3, Fri Sat -5 h, closed Mon Tue
Bolzstraße 7 ✉70173 *(Entrance Friedrichstraße 31* ☎ 226 27 54

Treffpunkt Kellergewölbe (B DR f G LJ MA P) last Sat 20.30-4 h
Blumenstraße 29 ✉70182 *(U-Olga-Eck)* ☎ 236 11 26

CAFES

Café Tocchetto (bf f glm MA OS) Mon-Fri 10-16 h, Thu 10-20 h
Büchsenstraße 34/36 ✉70174 *(c/o Aids-Beratungsstelle der ev. Gesellschaft Stuttgart)* ☎ 205 43 88
HIV & Aids information available

Flair. Café (AC B f GLM s YG) 18-4 h
Hirschstraße 2 ✉70183 *(S-Stadtmitte/U-Rathaus)* ☎ 226 14 15

Jenseitz. Café (B bf f GLM YG) 10-1, Tue 18-1 h
Bebelstraße 25, ✉70193 *(U-Schwab-/Bebelstraße)* ☎ 63 13 03

Magnus (B F GLM) 15-3, Fri 15-Mon 3 h
Rotebühlplatz 4/Kronprinzstraße ✉10173 ☎ 223 89 95

THOMAS
STUTTGART
PENTHOUSE-WOHNUNG IM ZENTRUM VORHANDEN
0172 - 711 94 86

Waschsalon (B f GLM MG W YG) 10-1, Sat 16-2 h
Charlottenstraße 27 ✉70182 *(Tram-Olgaeck)* ☎ 236 98 96
Popular.

DANCECLUBS

Kings Club (KC) (! B D Glm YG) 22-6 h, closed Mon Tue
Calwer Straße 21, ✉70173 *(Eingang/entrance Gymnasiumstraße)* ☎ 226 45 58

Laura's Club (B D GLM lj MA s YG) 22-6 h
Rotebühlplatz 4/Kronprinzenstraße ✉70173 ☎ 29 01 60

RESTAURANTS

Emilie (b F glm MA OS) 18-24 h, Sun closed
Mozartstraße 49 ✉70180 *(near Olgastraße)* ☎ 649 19 00

Johannisburg (B F g MA) 11-14.30, 18-23, Sat 18-23, Wed 11-14.30 h
Lembergstraße 19 ✉70186 ☎ 46 69 84

Tauberquelle (b F glm MA OS s) 12-24 h
Torstraße 19 ✉70173 *(U-Rathaus)* ☎ 23 56 56

Weißes Rössl (AC CC d F G lj S STV WF) Mon 12-15:00h, Tue-Fri 12-15 17-24, Sat 16-1 and Sun 12-22 h
Schwabstrasse 32 ✉70197 ☎ 6158499

SEX SHOPS/BLUE MOVIES

Beate Uhse International (g) Mon-Fri 9.30-20, Sat -16 h
Marienstraße 24/Sophienstraße ✉70178 ☎ 61 37 48

Binokel (G VS) Tue-Sat 14-23:00h, Sun 16-23 h
König Karl Strasse 85 ☎ 5490681

Blue Box (AC G MA VS) Mon-Sat 10-1, Sun & public holidays 14-1 h
Steinstraße 15 ✉70173 *(opposite Kaufhof carpark)* ☎ 2264076

City Sex Shop (g) 9-18.30, Thu -20.30, Sat 9-14/16/18, closed Sun
Bärenstraße 5 ✉70173

Da capo Sex-Laden (g VS) Mon-Fri 9-20, Sat -16 h
Blumenstraße 22/Charlottenstraße, ✉70182 ☎ 236 47 34

Dr. Müller's Sex Shop (g) Mon-Fri 9.30-20, Sat -16 h
Alte Poststraße 2 ✉70173 ☎ 29 55 61

Erotik Shop T.E. (g VS) Mon-Fri 9-20, Sat -16 h
Rotebühlplatz 1, ✉70178 ☎ 62 53 40

Insider Video (G) Mon-Sat 12-21.30 h, closed Sun
Böblingerstrasse 185 ✉70199 *(U-Bihlplatz)* ☎ 649 40 23
Over 1.900 videos for sale and to rent

New Man (g VS) Mon-Sat 9.30-21.30, Sun 14-20 h
c/o MAXX, Waiblinger Straße 7 ✉70372 *(S-Bad Cannstatt)* ☎ 509 44 00

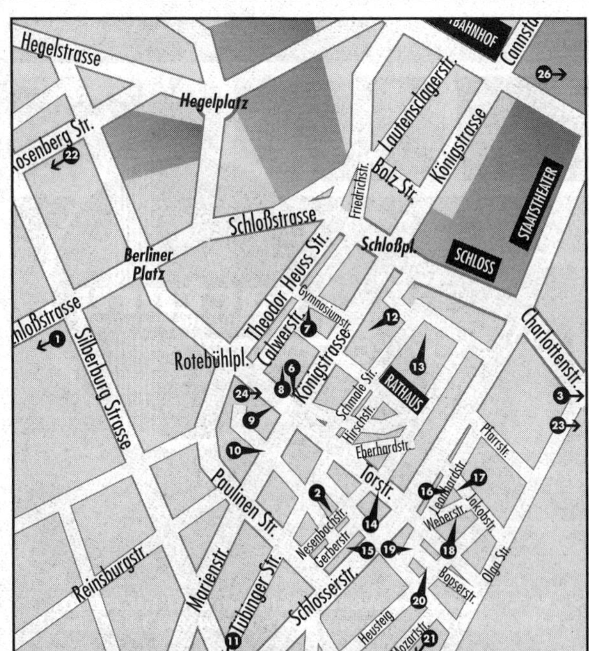

STUTTGART

1 Café Jenseitz
2 Buchladen Erlkönig
3 Viva-Sauna Relax
6 Laura's Club Danceclub
7 Kings Club (KC) Danceclub
8 Dr. Müller's Sex Shop
9 Erotik Shop T.E. Sex Shop/Blue Movie
10 Beate Uhse International Sex Shop
11 Insider Video Sex Shop/Blue Movie
12 Monroe's Pub Bar
13 City Sex Shop
14 Tauberquelle Restaurant
15 Olympus Sauna
16 Goldener Heinrich Bar
17 Jakobstube Bar
18 Finkennest Bar
19 Hotel am Wilhelmsplatz
20 Boots Bar
21 Eagle Bar
22 Factory Sauna
23 Café Waschsalon
24 Café Magnus
26 Johannisburg Restaurant

Mo+Do
Eintritt
15,DM
Dampfbad
Bistro
Sauna
Solarium
Fitnessraum
Dachterrasse
factory
the body obsession
MEN'S SAUNA&FITNESS
factory · Schwabstr. 33 · 70197 Stuttgart-West · Telefon 0711-615 4000
www.factory-sauna.de · S Schwabstraße · Open: So-Fr 14-24, Sa 14-2 Uhr

ESCORTS & STUDIOS

Thomas
☎ (0172) 711 94 86

HOUSE OF BOYS

House of Boys Stuttgart
☎ 23 67 836 ☎ (0190) 86 99 01

SAUNAS/BATHS

Factory (AC B DR f G MA OS p sa sb sol VS WE WO YG) Sun-Fri 14-24, Sat -2 h
Schwabstraße 33 ✉70197 *(S-Schwabstraße)* ☎ 615 40 00
Entrance-fee DM 23, student and age under 26 y/o only 18.

Olympus Sauna (B G MA p sa sol VS) 14-24 h
Gerberstraße 11, ✉70178 ☎ 649 89 19
Eintritt/entrance DM 20./Reduced 15.

Viva-Sauna Relax (AC B DR G MA sa sb sol VS YG) 14-24 h
Charlottenstraße 38 ✉70182 *(U-Olgaeck)* ☎ 236 84 62
Entrance-fee DM 25.-, DM 21.- for all under 21 years of age. Tue is 2 for 1.

BOOK SHOPS

Buchladen Erlkönig (CC GLM s W) Mon-Fri 10-20, Sat -16 h
Nesenbachstraße 52 ✉70178 *(S/U-Stadtmitte)* ☎ 63 91 39
E-Mail: erlkoenig@pride.de
Also mail order.

TRAVEL & TRANSPORT

Flying ticket Reisecenter (GLM)
Flamingoweg 1 ✉70378 *(Kaufzentrum Neugereut)* ☎ 953 78 20
Fax: 539 02 97 E-Mail: flying@stuttgart.netsurf.de

Gablenberger Reisebüro (glm MA) Mon-Fri 9.30-13 15-18, Wed 9.30-13, Sat 9.30-12.30 h
Gablenberger Hauptstraße 64 ✉70186 ☎ 480 05 35
Fax: 480 04 34 E-Mail: Gablenberger-Reisebuero@t-online.de

Reisebüro am Ostendplatz (glm MA) 9.30-13 15-18, Wed 9.30-13, Sat 9.30-12.30 h
Ostendstraße 69/1 ✉70188 *(Ostendpassage)* ☎ 285 90 59
Fax: 285 90 58

HOTELS

Hotel am Wilhelmplatz (B bf F g H)
Wilhelmplatz 9 ✉70182 *(U-Österreichischer Platz)* ☎ 21 02 40
Fax: 210 24 99 *Central location. All rooms with shower/WC, cable-TV, phone and minibar. Rates single DM 120, double 150. Weekend rates single 95, double 120 .*

PRIVATE ACCOMODATION

Enjoy Bed & Breakfast (bf G H MA YG) 16.30-21 h
☎ 030/215 16 66 Fax: 030/217 52219
E-Mail: Info@ebab.com Homepage: www.ebab.com
Price 40 DM. Accommodation sharing agency. All with shower & bf.

GENERAL GROUPS

Arbeitskreis Homosexualität in der ÖTV
c/o M. Pozsgai, Antoniusstraße 5, 73249 Wernau

Bisexuellen-Gruppe Stuttgart 1st Mon 19.30 h
c/o KIS-Zentrum, Marienstraße 9 ✉70178 ☎ 262 13 55

Initiativgruppe Homosexualität Stuttgart e.V. (ihs) Office Tue 19-21 h
Weißenburgstraße 28a ✉70180 ☎ 640 44 94
Fax: 640 44 95 Counselling ☎ 0711-19446 Fri 19-21 h
Email ihs@gmx.de Homepage http://eurogay.net/mitglieder/ihs

RosaLie-SchwuLesBische Unigruppe Tue 19.30 h
c/o Zentrales Fuchschaftsbüro, Keplerstraße 17 ✉70174 *(room 2.58 on 2nd floor)* ☎ 121 30 74
E-Mail: RosaLie@faveve.uni-stuttgart.de
Homepage: www.uni-stuttgart.de/rosalie

Selbsthilfegruppe für Eltern homosexueller Kinder Mon 10-12, 18-22, Tue Thu 15-18, Meeting: 4th Fri 19.30-21.30 h at room 6
c/o KISS, Marienstraße 9/Sophienstraße ✉70178 ☎ 640 61 17
Fax: 607 45 61

SVD Baden-Württemberg Störzbacher Straße 25 ✉70191 ☎ 65 93 52 Fax: 65 93 42

FETISH GROUPS

LC Stuttgart e. V.
PO Box 13 12 16 ✉70069
E-Mail: lcstgtd@aol.com or lcstuttg@aol.com
Homepage: members.aol.com/lcstgtd/index.html

HEALTH GROUPS

AIDS-Beratungsstelle der Ev. Gesellschaft Stuttgart e.V Mon-Fri 10-16 h
Büchsenstraße 34-36 ✉70174 (S-Stadtmitte) ☎ 205 43 88
Fax: 2054 312 *Cafe Tocchetto every 2nd and 4th Sun 14-18 h 1st and 3rd Thu 18-22 (not only) for people with HIV/Aids.*

AIDS-Hilfe Stuttgart e.V. Mon-Thu 10-12, 14-17, Fri 10-12 h
Hölderlinplatz 5 ✉70193 ☎ 224 69-0 or ☎ 194 11 Mon Thu Fri 18.30-21 h. Fax: 224 69 99
Positive Wed 18.30-21 h. every 1st Sun brunch 11-14h

HELP WITH PROBLEMS

Rosa Telefon Fri 19-21 h
☎ 194 46

SPORT GROUPS

Abseitz Stuttgart e.V. Mon 19-21 (office)
c/o Weißenburg, Weißenburgstraße 28 A ✉70180 ☎ 640 44 90
Badminton/volleyball.

SWIMMING

-Baggersee/Man-made lake Kirchentellinsfurt (NU) (B27 Stuttgart Richtung Tübingen, bei Abzweig Kirchentellinsfurt wenden, Ausfahrt Nürtingen. Vom Hauptsee links. Am hinteren Teil des zweiten Sees./B27 Stuttgart direction Tübingen, turn back at exit Kirchentellinsfurt and take exit Nürtingen. Go left at the first lake. It is the back of the second lake.)

CRUISING

-Kursaal-Anlagen (König-Karl-Straße 8/Wildbader Straße in Bad Cannstatt)
-[P] Planetarium (R)
-Unterer Schloßgarten (near the Rossebändiger/fountain)
-Mittlerer Schloßgarten (near Café am See, by night only)
-TV tower in Stuttgart-Degerloch
-beim Fernsehturm/at the TV-tower. Hinter dem Kiosk/behind the news stand
-Klett-Passage
-Mittlerer Schloßgarten (near Café am See)
-Bismarckplatz

Suhl ☎ 03681

SEX SHOPS/BLUE MOVIES

Orion (g) Mon-Fri 9-19.30, Sat -16 h
Oberhofer Straße 8, 98544 Zella-Mehlis ☎ 03 682 461 22

HEALTH GROUPS

AIDS-Hilfe Tue Wed 10-15, Thu 10-19, Fri 8-12 h
Am Bahnhof 15 ✉98529 ☎ 72 00 84

CRUISING

-Stadtpark (after dusk)

Timmendorfer Strand ☎ 04503

RESTAURANTS

Beiboot (B F glm s) 16-2 h, Tue closed
Strandallee 204 ✉23669 *(c/o Hotel Leuchtturm)* ☎ 88 19 96

Titisee-Neustadt ✉79822 ☎ 07651

HOTELS

Hotel Rheingold garni (b bf g H sa sol)
Jägerstraße 25 ✉79822 ☎ 84 74 Fax: 880 04
All rooms with shower/WC, TV, bf-buffet. Single DM 85 and double DM 148.

Traunstein ✉83261 ☎ 0861

GENERAL GROUPS

Chiemgay
PO Box 11 11 ✉83261

SWIMMING

-Chiemsee (g NU) (A 8 München → Salzburg, [P] 2 km after exit/nach Ausfahrt Felden. Through underpass to the lake, path to the right)

CRUISING

-Maximiliansplatz
-Main train station/Hauptbahnhof

Trier ☎ 0651

GAY INFO

Schwule Informations- und Beratungsstelle SchMITZ Thu 18-20 h
Mustorstraße 4 ✉54290 ☎ 42 514 Fax: 425 14
-LSVD Rheinland-Pfalz
-Gay and grey 3rd Sat 18-20 h
-Gayliens 2nd & 4th Sat 17-20 h (gay youth group)

BARS

Palette (B f G MA p s) 20-1, Fri Sat -2/? h
Oerenstraße 13b ✉54290 ☎ 426 09
Werner's (AC B f glm s T W WE) 21-3, summer OS 19-24 h
Jüdemerstraße 28 ✉54290 ☎ 761 08 *Popular.*
Zur Lagune (B GLM p YG) Mon-Thu 20-3, Fri & Sat -4h
Karl-Marx-Strasse 86 ✉54290 ☎ 75373

CAFES

SchMIT-Z: Café Verkehrt (A B d f G MA OS s W) Thu-Sat 20-24, Sun & public holidays 16-20 h
Mustorstraße 4 ✉54290 *(Bus-Mustorstraße)* ☎ 425 14

DANCECLUBS

HOMOsapiens (B D GLM MA)
c/o Exil, Zurmeinerstraße 114 ✉54292
Irregular, look out for flyers.
Homosphère (B D GLM MA) Last Sat 21-? h
c/o Domfreihof ✉54290
Treff 39 (B D g p vs YG) 21-3 h
Paulinstraße 39 ✉54292 ☎ 124 63

SEX SHOPS/BLUE MOVIES

Amor & Co. (g) Mon-Sat 9-22 h
Wallstraße 1 ✉54290
Erotik Markt (CC g) Mon-Sat 10-22 h, closed Sun
Karl-Marx-Straße 70a ✉54290 ☎ 423 71
Orion (g) Mon-Fri 9-20, Sat 9-16 h
Metzelstraße 27/Zuckerbergstraße ✉54290 ☎ 751 82

BOOK SHOPS

Gegenlicht (glm W) Mon-Wed 9.30-18.30, Thu Fri -20, Sat 9-16 h
Glockenstraße 10 ✉54290 ☎ 765 80

GENERAL GROUPS

Schwulenforum Trier (SchwuFo) Mon 20 h
Mustorstraße 4 ✉54290 ☎ & Fax: 425 14
Schwulenreferat im AStA der Uni Trier Mon-Fri 10.30-14.30 h
Universitätsring 12b ✉54286 *(University block B, room B15)*
☎ 201 21 16 ☎ 0651/201 21 17
E-Mail: astrarosa@uni-trier.de
Homepage: www.trier.gay-web.de/schwulenreferat

HEALTH GROUPS

AIDS-Hilfe Trier e. V. Mon Tue Thu 9-16, Wed -19, Fri -13 h
Saarstraße 48 ✉54290 ☎ 970 440
E-Mail: aidshilfe.trier@t-online.de
-Other groups such as youth counselling phoneline ☎ 970 44 22 Wed from 15-19:00h;
-Gay and Grey for gays over 40 ☎ 974 04 40 and
-Gayliens - gay youth group ☎ 970 44 22 (e-mail: gayliens@hotmail.de) are also part of the AIDS-Hilfe Trier.

HELP WITH PROBLEMS

Beratung im SchMIT-Z Thu 18-20 h
Mustorstraße 4 ✉54290 ☎ 425 14
Rosa Telefon Trier Sun 20-22 h
☎ 194 46

RELIGIOUS GROUPS

Homosexuelle und Kirche (HuK) e.V. Regionalgruppe Trier
J. Ziegler, PO Box 40 71 ✉54230 ☎ 428 94

CRUISING

-Palastgarten between Kurfürstliches Palais and Kaiserthermen (r)
-Nells Park
-Mehringer Höhe
-Uni (Zentralbibliothek)

Troisdorf ☎ 02241

HEALTH GROUPS

AIDS-Hilfe Rhein-Sieg-Kreis e.V. Mon-Fri 10-12.30 h. Meets 4th/Thu 19 h
Am Bürgerhaus 3 ✉53840 ☎ 780 18
Youth group Tue Thu 14-17 h. Counselling.

Tübingen ☎ 07071

SEX SHOPS/BLUE MOVIES

Erotik-Shop (glm VS) 10-18, Sat 10-14 h
Collegiumsgasse 4 ✉72070 *(1st floor)* ☎ 271 11

GENERAL GROUPS

Coming Out-Gruppe
☎ 194 46
GayDay e.V.
c/o Thomas Heerdt, Gertrud-Bäumer-Straße 6 ✉72074 ☎ 0177/337 34 37
Initiativgruppe Homosexualität Tübingen (IHT)
PO Box 17 72 72007, Herrenberger Str. 9 ✉72070 ☎ 448 43
Meetings Thu 20 h at AIDS Hilfe ☛ Health Service
LuSchT Lesben und Schwule Tübingen Cafe: Winter: 15-19 h, Summer: 16-20 h
PO Box 16 25 ✉72006, Herrenberger Straße 9 ✉72070 ☎ 448 43
Every Wed: Schwul/lesbische Tacko-Bar at Sudhaus, Hechinger Straße 203 72072 at 21.30. Every Thu: Schwuler Treff in movie theatre Arsenal.

HEALTH GROUPS

AIDS-Hilfe Tübingen-Reutlingen e.V. Mon Wed-Fri 10-12h, Café: Wed 16-19h, Thu 15-17h
Herrenberger Straße 9 ✉72070 ☎ 499 22
E-Mail: info@tuebingen.aidshilfe.de

HELP WITH PROBLEMS

Rosa Telefon Fri 20-22 h
PO Box 16 25 ✉72006 ☎ 194 46

RELIGIOUS GROUPS

Homosexuelle und Kirche (HuK) 2nd & 4th Wed 20 h
PO Box 16 07 72007, Herrenberger Straße 9 ✉72070 ☎ 448 43

SPORT GROUPS

Taktlos Meeting Mon 20-21.30
at Studentendorf Waldhäuser-Ost (big hall), Fichtenweg 5

SWIMMING

-Strand/beach in Kirchentellingsfurt (NU) (Zwischen/between Tübingen & Nürtingen. Schwule finden sich am kleineren der beiden Seen./There are two lakes. The smaller one is gay.)

CRUISING

-Park am Neckar (Nähe/near Alleenbrücke, nachts/at night)
-Mensaklappe der Mensa 1 (entrance Wilhelmstraße, 12-14 h)
-Stadtpark (between Derendinger Allee and Anlagensee)
-Alter Botanischer Garten/Old Botanical Garden (Wilhelmstraße)
-Busbahnhof/bus station (Unterführung/subway Europaplatz)

Tuttlingen ☎ 07461

GENERAL GROUPS

Kuckucksei
PO Box 45 22 ✉78510 E-Mail: kuckucksei@alb.gay-web.de
Homepage: http://kuckuck.home.pages.de/

HELP WITH PROBLEMS

Rosa Telefon (Glm) ☎ 16 47 55

Überlingen ☎ 07551

SWIMMING

-Bodensee (NU) (B31 Überlingen → Sipplingen)

Uelzen ☎ 0581

GENERAL GROUPS

Schwul-lesbischer Treff Meeting Wed 20 h
St.-Viti-Straße 22 ✉29525 ☎ 97 07 17

Ulm ☎ 0731

BARS

Alten Fritz. Zum (B f G MA OS YG) Mon Wed Thu 18-2, Fri -3, Sat 19-3, Sun -2 h, closed Tue
Karlstraße 9 ✉89073 ☎ 653 00
Wiblinger Eck (AC B f G MA p r) 16-1 h
Erenäcker 18 ✉89079 ☎ 48 21 51

CAFES

Café Viva (B f glm MA OS) Mon-Thu 11-24, Fri Sat -0.30, Sun 14-24 h
Herdbruckerstraße 20 ✉89073 ☎ 602 12 14

DANCECLUBS

Schwullesbische Disco (B D DR GLM YG) 2x Sat 22-?, 1x Sun 20-2 ? h
c/o Donauturm *(near Maritim Hotel/convention center)*
Watch out for dates published in gay newspapers.
Tangente (B D G YG) Sun 22.30-? h
Frauenstraße 29 ✉89073 ☎ 659 66

RESTAURANTS

Bei Erika (B G MA) Mon-Sat 17-2 h, Sun and holidays closed
Olgastraße 141 ✉89073 ☎ 253 23

SEX SHOPS/BLUE MOVIES

Amor & Co. (g VS) Mon-Sat 9-24, Sun 13-23 h
Ulmer Gasse ✉89073 ☎ 61 08 95
Orion (g) Mon-Fri 9-20, Sat -16 h
Neue Straße 22/Zinglerberg ✉89073 ☎ 61 86 86

GENERAL GROUPS

Rosige Zeiten e.V. Meeting Mon 20-22 h
at »Zum Alten Fritz«, Korbstraße 9, 89073 Ulm
PO Box 1252, ✉89202 Neu-Ulm ☎ & Fax: 253 60
Publishers of Mixx, a bi-monthly free newsletter.
SchwUlm Wed 20-22, Fri 20-22 (Coming-Out-Gruppe)
c/o AIDS-Hilfe, Furttenbachstraße 14 ✉89077 ☎ 194 46
Fax: 931 75 27 E-mail Coming1Out@aol.com

HEALTH GROUPS

AIDS-Hilfe Ulm/Neu-Ulm/Alb-Donau e.V.
Mon-Fri 9.30-12.30, Mon Fri 19.30-21 h
Furttenbachstraße 14 ✉89077 ☎ 194 11 or ☎ 373 31
Fax: 931 75 27

CRUISING

-Rosengarten (unterhalb/underneath Adlerbastei from 22 h)
-Donauhalle, Straßenbahnendhaltestelle Line 1 Friedrichsau (tagsüber/ during the day)
-Waldbaggersee Senden (Sommer, ganztags/Summer all day)
-Hauptbahnhof/main railway station
-Herdbrücke
-Donauhalle, Tramlinie/tramline 1, Friedrichsau (tagsüber/during daytime)

Unkel ☎ 02644

GENERAL GROUPS

Die Insel Meets 1st/3rd Wed 20 h
at „Fritz", Asbacher Straße 25, 53545 Linz
PO Box 02 16 ✉53569 ☎ 47 82
Homepage: http://www.lp.info.com/insel

Unna ☎ 02303

DANCECLUBS

Doppelherz 22 h every 2 months
at Kulturzentrum Lindenbrauerei. Call for dates.
Massener Straße 33-35 ✉59423 ☎ 25 11 20

GENERAL GROUPS

Rosa AufSchwUNg Tue 19.30 h
c/o Kulturzentrum „Lindenbrauerei" Massener Str. ✉59423
☎ 0231/25 11 20 *Gay group.*

Vechta ☎ 04441

CRUISING

-1st [P] B 69 Vechta → Diepholz

Viersen ☎ 02162

HEALTH GROUPS

AIDS-Hilfe Kreis Viersen e.V. Mon Wed Fri 9-13 h
Gereonstraße 75 ✉41747 ☎ 349 87

Villingen-Schwenningen ☎ 07721

BARS

Club 46 a (A B d Glm lj MA p WE) 21-24, Sat -2 h, closed Mon-Tue, Sat on on public holidays disco
Dauchinger Straße 46 a ✉78056 *(in Schwenningen, entrance from backyard nr. 46)* ☎ 639 09
Forum (B F GLM MA) 18-1, Fri Sat -2, Sun 15-1
Bärengasse 20 ✉78050 *(Villingen)* ☎ 50 43 50
Pfeffermühle. Club-Sauna (AC B d f G MA OS p S sa sb VS) 16-?, Sat Sun 15-? h, closed Tue
Alte Tuttlinger Straße 4 ✉78056 ☎ 56 69

SEX SHOPS/BLUE MOVIES

Loveland (g) 10-13, 14.30-18.30, Sat 10-13 h, closed Sun
Neckarstraße 115 ✉78056 *(in Schwenningen)*
Orion (g) Mon-Fri 9-20, Sat -16 h
Alleenstraße/Hans-Sachs-Straße 27 ✉78054 *(in Schwenningen)*
☎ 217 70

SAUNAS/BATHS

Club Sauna Pfeffermühle (B F G MA sa sb VS) 16-?, Sat-Sun 15-? h, closed Tue
Alte Tuttlinger Straße 4 ✉78056 ☎ 07720/56 69

HELP WITH PROBLEMS

Rosa Telefon
☎ 07461/16 47 55

CRUISING

-Bahnhof/main railway station Schwenningen
-Karl-Marx-Straße (ayor)

Volkenroda ☎ 036025

HOTELS

Deutsche Eiche (b bf d F glm H lj MA OS s WE)
Hauptstraße 24 ✉99998 ☎ 503 42 Fax: 503 42
Also restaurant.

Völklingen ☎ 06898

CAFES

Sissis Schlössje (AC f GLM MA s OS W) Mon-Wed 14-1, Thu-Sat -3, Sun 10-1 h
Forbacherpassage 6 ✉66333 ☎ 29 78 99

Weiden ☎ 0961

GENERAL GROUPS

HIBISSkus Schwule Initiative Weiden Thu 19.30-21 h
c/o Diakoniezentrum, Sebastianstraße 18 ✉92637 *(Rückgebäude)* ☎ 389 31 55

Weimar ☎ 03643

CAFES

L.S.D. (Lesbisch-Schwules Date) (B DR f GLM MA s) Wed Fri Sat 20-?, closed Mon Tue Thu Sun
c/o Aids-Hilfe Weimar e.V., Erfurter Str. 17 ✉99423 ☎ 85 35 35

DANCECLUBS

Felix Disco at Jugendclub Nordlicht (B D f GLM MA OS s) 1st 3rd 5th Sat 22-3 h
Stauffenbergstraße 20a ✉99423 *(Bus 1)* ☎ 42 78 03

HEALTH GROUPS

AIDS-Hilfe Weimar & Ostthüringen e.V. Mon Tue 11-15, Wed 11-20 h
Erfurter Straße 17 ✉99423 ☎ 85 35 35 Fax: 85 36 36

CRUISING

-Park an der Ilm (between Burgplatz and Platz der Demokratie)
-Wittumspalais

Wernigerode ☎ 03943

SEX SHOPS/BLUE MOVIES

Orion (g) Mon-Fri 10-20, Sat -14 h
Langer Stieg 4 ✉38855

Wesel ☎ 0281

HEALTH GROUPS

AIDS-Hilfe Duisburg/Kreis Wesel e.V. Di 14-17, Wed 19-21, Thu 9-12, Fri 19-21, Café Sun 16-? h
Herzogenring 4 ✉46483 ☎ 194 11 or office ☎ 299 80
The group „ Gay nach Wesel" has the same telephone number

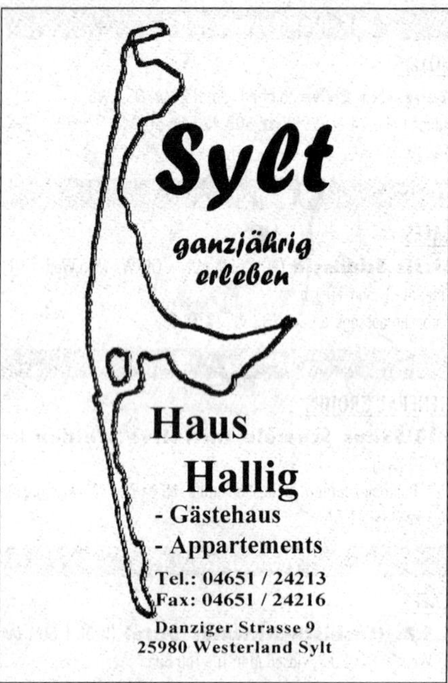

Sylt
ganzjährig
erleben
Haus
Hallig
- Gästehaus
- Appartements
Tel.: 04651 / 24213
Fax: 04651 / 24216
Danziger Strasse 9
25980 Westerland Sylt

Gesundheitsamt Wesel Fri 8-9.30 h
Jülicher Straße 6 ✉46483 *(room 201)* ☎ 207 29 81
Anonymous free HIV test and Aids counselling.

CRUISING

-Heubergpark (between Postturm und Hallenbad/between Telecom-tower and indoor-swimming pool)

Wesselburenerkoog ☎ 04833

GUEST HOUSES

Gästehaus Jüan (bf glm H MA OS) 8-23 h
Dammstraße 28 ✉25764 ☎ 41 55

Westerland - Sylt ☎ 04651

BARS

Nanu (B g MA s) 21-3 h
Strandstraße 23 ✉25980 ☎ 928 00
Ringelspiel (B G lj MA) 18-? h
Andreas-Dirks-Straße 2 ✉25980 ☎ 92 77 56

DANCECLUBS

Kleist-Casino (KC) (AC B CC D GLM lj MA p r s) 22-5/6 h
Elisabethstraße 1a ✉25980 ☎ 242 28

RESTAURANTS

Dechters Hüs (F glm N OS) 12-23 h
Gurtstig 2, 25980 Keitum *(near Sylt-Ost)* ☎ 318 84
Vegetarian and fish cuisine.
Franz Ganser (B F g OS) Tue-Sat 18-23, Sun 12-14.30 h
Bötticherstraße/Boysenstraße, ✉25980 ☎ 229 70 *French cuisine.*
Zum Lister Happen (B F glm OS stv) Wed-Wed 18-? h, closed Tue
Listlandstraße 19, 25992 List *(16 km from Westerland)* ☎ 87 08 06

SAUNAS/BATHS

Steam Beach Club (G sa sb) 14-24:00h
Bötticherstrasse 3 ✉25980 ☎ 835 249
Wed & Sat „Steam Day" 21 DM. WE special price.

HOTELS

Marin-Hotel-Sylt (g H)
Strandstraße 23 ✉25980 ☎ 928 00 Fax: 286 94
E-Mail: marin.hotel.sylt@t-online.de
Homepage: www.marinhotel.de
5km from the airport. Downtown location. Partly equipped with kitchenette, priv. bath/WC, TV and phone. Rates apartments DM 60-210, single 88-165, double 140-304 (bf incl.)
Pension Möwennest (B bf g H)
Seestrasse 8 ✉25996 Wenningstedt ☎ 413 51
Single DM 65, double 90 (bf incl.) Rooms with shower/WC.

GUEST HOUSES

Haus Hallig (bf GLM H lj MA OS) all year
Danziger Straße 9 ✉25980 ☎ 242 13 Fax: 242 16
All rooms with bath/WC. The guesthouse offers a garden. Single from DM 60-100, double from 85-160 (bf incl.)

SYLT
NEU
ERÖFFNET
STEAM
Mittwoch & Samstag
`STEAM´ Tag
21,-
Öffnungszeiten:
Tgl. ab 14 Uhr
`STEAM´
Beach Club
Bötticherstr.3 25980 Westerland (Sylt) Tel: 04651/835249
www.oops-design.de

HUSSMANN
FERIENWOHNUNGEN
FÜR IHREN
URLAUB AUF SYLT !
Wir bieten Ihnen:
in fast allen Inselorten
Appartements in versch. Größen
Ferienhäuser (teilw. unter Reet)
für 1-6 Personen
BUCHUNG & INFORMATIONEN
WILHELMSTRASSE 6
25980 WESTERLAND/SYLT
TEL. (0 46 51) 2 20 02 · FAX 2 20 74
e-mail: hussmannsylt @ t-online.de
http://www.abc-sylt.de/hussmann

APARTMENTS

Apartment Vermietung & Betreuung - Ch. Schwarzer (g MA OS)
Bundiswung 9 ✉25980 ☎ 824620 Fax: 824620
1 to 3 room apartments from 120 to 245 DM per day with telephone, cable TV, bath/shower, Quiet location please call Mr Schwarzer for further details

Haus Hallig Apartments (g H)
Böttiger Straße 3 ✉25980 ☎ 24213
Apartments with kitchen, shower/WC, TV and phone. Apartements mit Küche, Bad/WC, TV und Telephon. Rates from DM 50-150.

Haus Koralle
Nordmarkstraße 5 ✉25980 ☎ & Fax: 94 41 30
Apartments in central location with kitchen, telephone, TV, some with terrasse. Rates person/night DM 60-180.

Hussmann Ferienwohnungen (g H)
Wilhelmstraße 6 ✉25980 ☎ 220 02 Fax: 220 74
Email: hussmannsylt@t-online.de
Homepage: www.abc-sylt.de/hussmann
40 completely furnished appartments. 1 room app. (max. 2 persons) DM 55-160, 2 room app. (max. 4 persons) 120-200 (low-/high-season). Central location, close to bars.

Lönö-Apartment-Vermietung (g H OS)
Bundiswung 31 ✉25980 ☎ 273 19 Fax: 271 08
Apartments and studios for rent with kitchen, shower/WC, telephone, safe. Please call for details.

HEALTH GROUPS

AIDS-Hilfe Sylt e.V./AIDS-Projekt Sylt „Söring Soldar" Mon Tue 10-12, Thu 16-19 h
c/o Villa Nordfriesland, Bundiswung 9 ✉15980 ☎ 64 44
Meeting „Klönschnak" Thu 19-21 h.

SWIMMING

-Oase zur Sonne (15 min walk south from Westerland. This spot takes its name from the nearby café which is located in the dunes. You'll need to purchase either a day ticket or a subsription ticket before you are allowed to go on the beach./ Ca. 15 Minuten Fußweg Richtung Süden von Westerland aus. Der Strandabschnitt ist nach dem Café in den Dünen benannt. In der Saison braucht man eine Kurkarte bzw. eine Tageskarte, um an den Strand zu kommen.

CRUISING

-Kurpromenade (near Kurhaus. From dawn to 4 h/ab Dunkelheit bis 4 h)
-Stephanstraße (Alter Kursaal/Stadtcafé am/on Rathausplatz)
-Bahnhof (r)

Wetzlar ☎ 06441

DANCECLUBS

Schwulenfete Wetzlar (B D f GLM) Last Fri 21-? h
c/o Harlekin im Riesen, Gullgasse 9 ✉35578

SEX SHOPS/BLUE MOVIES

Orion (g) Mon-Fri 9.30-19, Sat -16 h
Karl-Kellner-Ring 12 ✉35576 ☎ 478 57

Wiesbaden ☎ 0611

BARS

Hauptmann von Köpenick (B f GLM MA OS r YG)
Sun-Thu 11-1, Fri Sat -2 h
Mauergasse 10 ✉65183 ☎ 37 61 02

Joy (B d GLM YG) 19.30-1, Fri Sat -2, kitchen -23, Fri Sat -24 h
Dotzheimer Straße 37 ✉65185 *(Entrance/Eingang Zimmermannstraße)* ☎ 30 75 59

Robin Hood (F GLM MA r s) 16-1, Fri Sat -3 h
Häfnergasse 3 ✉65183 ☎ 30 13 49
English style pub.

Spartakus 20-? h
Mainzer Straße 129 ✉65187 ☎ 71 84 32

Trend (AC B f Glm lj MA N OS) 14-02:00h, Fri & Sat -3, Sun 15-2 h (Winter - opening times one hour later).
Am Römertor 7 ✉65183 ☎ 37 30 40
A comfortable meeting point for locals as well as visitors of all ages.

DANCECLUBS

Pussy Cats (B D glm MA p) 22-4 h
Adlerstraße 33 ✉65183 ☎ 517 39

SEX SHOPS/BLUE MOVIES

City Video Sex Shop (g) Mon-Fri 9-20, Sat -16; Cinema Mon-Sat 9-24 h
Mauritiusplatz 1 ✉65183 ☎ 30 48 40

Orion (g) Mon-Fri 9.30-20, Sat -16 h
Bismarckring 44/Wellritzstraße ✉65183 *(At Sedanplatz)*
☎ 945 04 52

SAUNAS/BATHS

Club-Sauna (B F G MA p sa sb VS YG) 15-23, Fri Sat -24 h
Häfnergasse 3 ✉65183 *(Drei-Lilien-Platz)* ☎ 30 55 74
Entrance-fee DM 16-25.

BOOK SHOPS

Forum Medienhandel AG (g)
Mauritiusstraße 5 ✉65183 ☎ 17 35 46

CONDOM SHOPS

La Condoma Mon-Wed, Fri 9-18.30, Thu -20.30, Sat - 14/16/18 h
City Passage ✉65183 *(Exit/Ausgang Schwalbacher Straße)*
Condoms etc./Kondome und mehr.

GENERAL GROUPS

Lesbisch-Schwules Netzwerk in Hessen
c/o Rosa Lüste, PO Box 54 06 ✉65044 ☎ & Fax: 37 77 65
Rosa Lüste
PO Box 54 06 ✉65044 ☎ & Fax: 37 77 65 *Call after 18 h*
Smalltown Boys Mo 19.30 h
at Joy, Dotzheimerstraße 37/Zimmermannstraße
Schwule Jugendgruppe/Gay youth group

FETISH GROUPS

MSC Rhein-Main, Frankfurt
Eleonorenstraße 4 ✉65185 ☎ 37 69 65

HEALTH GROUPS

AIDS-Hilfe Wiesbaden e.V. Mon Tue Thu Fri 10-14 h, Counselling phone Mon Fri 19-21 h Tue Thu 10-12 h
Karl-Glässing-Straße 5 ✉65183 ☎ 194 11 Fax: 37 72 13
☎ *30 92 11 Mon, Tue, Thu, Fri 10-14 h*
Breakfast on 1st Fri/month 11-13 h.

HELP WITH PROBLEMS

Gewalt gegen Schwule
☎ 30 26 86
LUST-Lesben Und Schwulen-Telefon
Mon 18-21 h
PO Box 54 06 ✉65044 ☎ 37 77 65

CRUISING

-Main station/Hauptbahnhof (r)
-Karstadt, Kirchgasse, 2nd floor (YG)
-Hertie, Kirchgasse, 2nd floor (YG)
-Reisinger Anlagen (ayoor r) (am Bahnhof, nachts/in front of railway station, at night)

Wilhelmshaven ☎ 04421

BARS

mai pen lai (B G) Sun-Thu 20-2 h, Fri Sat 20-3 h
Ebertstraße 128 ✉26382 *(near station)* ☎ 99 54 34
Every 2nd Saturday special event.
My Way (B f GLM OS) Sun-Thu 20-2, Fri Sat -3 h
Bismarckstraße 89 ✉26382 ☎ 335 94
Sonne. Zur (B f g MA) 21-5, Sun 18.30-? h
Grenzstraße 21 ✉26382 ☎ 215 02
Zoff (B f glm MA YG) Mon-Thu Sun 21-2, Fri-Sat -3 h
Bismarkstraße 121 ✉26382 ☎ 329 78

CAFES

Heiko's Tannenhof (A AC bf f glm MA N OS WE) Tue-Sat 13-23 h, Sun 10-23 h, Mon closed
Kleiststraße 49 ✉38440 *(next to Woolworth)* ☎ 05361/175 53 or ☎0171-639 39 79 Email Tannenhof@aol.com

SEX SHOPS/BLUE MOVIES

Orion (g) Mon-Fri 10-20, Sat -16 h
Marktstraße West 117 ✉26382 ☎ 13 64 08

GALLERIES

ELCO!
Parkstraße 3 ✉26382 ☎ 994 776

GENERAL GROUPS

Schwulesbisches Referat im AstA der FH
Friedrich-Pfaffrath-Straße 101 ✉26389 ☎ 837 53 Fax: 84 666.
E-Mail: slb@asta.fh-wilhelmshaven.de
Homepage: http://www.fh-wilhelmshaven.de/asta.

HEALTH GROUPS

Wilhelmshavener AIDS-Hilfe e.V. Mon-Fri 1 0-16 h
Bremer Straße 139, ✉26382 ☎ 194 11

SWIMMING

-Hooksiel-Campingplatz (g MA NU) (left side/linke Seite, best Sat Sun)
-Klein Wangerooge/Banter See (Coming from the P, take the first path to the left. Best time 12-20 h. In sumer only)(

CRUISING

-Hertie department store
-Adalbertplatz/Köhler Park (r)

Wismar ☎ 03841

GENERAL GROUPS

Na Und e. V. Mon 19 h
Lübsche Str. 11 ✉23966 ☎ 27 43 21
Gay & lesbian group/Schwul-lesbischer Verein
Why Not e.V./AIDS-Hilfe Westmecklenburg
Mon Thu 9-11.30, Tue 18-20 h
Breite Straße 54 ✉23966 ☎ & Fax: 21 47 55
-Café Sun 15-20 h
-Library Sun 15-20 h

HELP WITH PROBLEMS

Telefon des Vertrauens Mon Thu 9-12, Tue 18-21 h
☎ 21 47 55

SWIMMING

-Wohlenberger Wieck
-Ostseebad Boltenhagen
-Insel Poel
-Zierow
-Hohenwieschendorf (Near/Nähe Grankow)

CRUISING

-Am Lindengarten (by day/tagsüber)
-Lindengarten am/at the Rostocker Tor

Witten ☎ 02302

DANCECLUBS

Werk-Stadt (B D f G s YG) Mar-Sep 3rd Sat 22-3 h
Mannesmannstraße 2 ✉58455

SEX SHOPS/BLUE MOVIES

Orion (g) Mon-Fri 10-20, Sat 10-16 h
Johannisstraße 26 ✉58452 *(Near bus station/Nähe Busbahnhof Kornmarkt)* ☎ 847 02

GENERAL GROUPS

Schwule Gruppe Witten Meets 2nd/4th Sun 15.30 h, later at Cafe Blué, Ruhrallee 69, Dortmund
c/o DPWV, Dortmunder Straße 13 ✉58455 ☎ 15 59
Mon Tue 10-12, Wed -15 h. 1st and 3rd Sun social activities, call for details.

Wittenberg ☎ 034925

HOTELS

Park Hotel
Domnitzscher Straße 3 ✉06905 Bad Schmiedeberg/Wittenberg
☎ 670 Fax: 67 16

Wolfratshausen ☎ 08171

HEALTH GROUPS

AIDS-Projekt Oberland e.V.
Gebhartstraße 2 ✉82515 ☎ & Fax: 91 00 91

Wolfsburg ☎ 05361

SEX SHOPS/BLUE MOVIES

Orion (g) Mon-Fri 9.30-20, Sat -16 h
Poststraße 1/Porschestraße ✉38440 *(Passage)* ☎ 129 18

GENERAL GROUPS

Rosa Wolf Wolfsburg e.V. Mon 17-22, Tue 20-22, Wed 19.30-22, Fri 19-22h, last Sun 15-17h
Schachtweg 5a ✉38440 ☎ & Fax: 29 29 29 or ☎ 194 46
E-mail RosaWolfeV@aol.com
Homepage www.rosawolf.wolfsburg.de

HEALTH GROUPS

AIDS-Hilfe Wolfsburg e.V. Mon-Wed 9-15, Thu 9-22, Fri 9-15 h
Schachtweg 5a ✉38440 ☎ 194 11 ☎ 133 32 (Office)

CRUISING

-Park am Großen Schillerteich am Betonspielplatz/Park at the Großen Schillerteich near playground area (abends/evenings)

Worms ☎ 0177

GENERAL GROUPS

DIe NOrmalen Schwulen (DINOS) Meeting Mon 20-?h at IKOS-Zentrum
PO Box 13 31 ✉67503 ☎ 06241/(0177) 5083461
E-mail: DINOS_WORMS@GEOCITIES.COM
Wormser Unabhängige Schwulen- und Lesbengruppe (WUSCHL) Mon 20 h
at IKOS, Ludwigstraße 31 PO Box 24 27 ✉67514 ☎ 2383684

Wuppertal ☎ 0202

BARS

Keller Club (»KC«) (B GLM MA) 19-? h, closed Wed
Schloßbleiche 32 ✉42103 *(Eingang/entrance Wirmhof)* ☎ 45 55 35
Marlene (B f glm MA WE YG) 19-1 h, gay on Wed/Sun, closed Thu
Hochstraße 81 ✉42105 ☎ 31 64 28
Schankhaus Merlin's (B f GLM MA s TV W) 19-3 h
Hochstraße 65 ✉42105 ☎ 309 79 63
Wunderbau Tue-Sun 15-1 h, Mon closed
Calvinstraße 9

CAFES

Café Crème (B bf F g MA YG) 8.30-1, Sat Sun 10-1 h
Briller Straße 3 ✉42105 ☎ 30 43 63

SEX SHOPS/BLUE MOVIES

Orion (g) Mon-Fri 10-20, Sat 10-16 h
Armin-T.-Wegner-Platz 15 ✉42103 *(Elberfeld. City-Center-Passage)*
☎ 44 63 00
Starlife Gay (G) 10-24 h, closed Sun
Höhne 4 ✉42275 *(Barmen)* ☎ 59 31 33
Starlife Gay (G VS) 10-1, Fri Sat -3, Sun 12-22 h
Neumarktstraße 14 ✉42103 *(Elberfeld)* ☎ 45 31 06
Videoland (g) Mon-Fri 6-13 h 15-20 h, Sat 7-18 h, Sun 10-12 h
Westkotter Straße 146 ✉42277 *(Bus-Germanenstraße)* ☎ 51 18 06

SAUNAS/BATHS

Theo's Sauna Club (! B F G MA msg OS sa sb sol VS wh WO) 15-23, Sat 13-2 (Night-sauna), Sun 13-23 h, closed Thu
Uellendaler Straße 410 ✉42109 *(Elberfeld)* ☎ 70 60 59

BOOK SHOPS

Adrian Buchhandlung (g) Mo-Fr 10-20, Sa 10-16 h
Klotzbahn 1 ✉42105 *(Rathausgalerie)* ☎ 244 20 60
Köndgen Buchhandlung (g) 9.30-20, Sat -16 h
Friedrichstraße 51 ✉42105 ☎ 248 000

GENERAL GROUPS

AStA-Schwulenreferat der Gesamthochschule Wuppertal Cafe Tue 12-14, meets Tue 19 in Mensagebäude, last Tue 19h Filmabend (movies)
Max-Horkheimer-Straße 15 ✉42119 ☎ 439 28 74
Bergbären-Bartmänner und -freunde Wuppertal/Solingen/ Remscheid
c/o Laaser/Mund, Ostersbaum 18 ✉42107 ☎ 45 09 41
Meetings: every 1st and 3rd Fri at „Keller Club (KC)", Schloßbleiche 32 at 21 h and every 2nd Sat at „Theo's Sauna Club", Uellendahler Straße 410 at 17 h.
Schwulengruppe Wuppertal Meeting Wed 20 h
c/o Börse, Raum 5, Viehhofstraße 125 ✉42117

HEALTH GROUPS

AIDS-Hilfe Wuppertal e.V. Mon-Fri 10-15 h
Hofaue 9 ✉42103 *(Elberfeld)* ☎ 194 11

HELP WITH PROBLEMS

Rosa Telefon Tue 20-22 h
c/o AIDS-Hilfe, Hofaue 9 ✉42107 ☎ 45 00 04

RELIGIOUS GROUPS

Ökumenische Arbeitsgruppe Homosexuelle und Kirche (HuK) e.V. Regionalgruppe Wuppertal
Peter Kemmann, Osterstraße 105, 42551 Velbert ☎ 258012
E-mail pkemmann@aol.com

SPECIÀL INTEREST GROUPS

Börse. Die (A AC d S) Wolkenburg 100 ✉42119
☎ 243 220 Fax: 243 2222 E-Mail: dieboerse@wtal.de
Local events such as gay tea dance etc . Please call for information

CRUISING

-Adlerbrücke (opposite Opernhaus)
-Neumarkt (evenings)

Wurmannsquick ☎ 08572

GUEST HOUSES

Schwuler Bauernhof (H MA NU)
Bemberg 6 ✉84329 ☎ 913 55 Fax: 913 56.
Email: guenther@t-online.de *Guests will be fetched from Mühldorf/Obb. railway station. Double rooms with shared bath/WC, balcony, telephone, fax, Sat-TV, video. Rates p.p. DM 50 incl. full-board. Own parking. Bar.*

Würzburg ☎ 0931

GAY INFO

WuF-Zentrum e.V. (d G MA OS) Thu 20-?, 4th Sat 21 h
Nigglweg 2 ✉97082 ☎ 41 26 46
E-Mail: wuf@wuerzburg.gay-web.de
Homepage: www.wuerzburg.gay-web.de/wuf
Youth Group „GayWürz" meets 1st/3rd Fri 20.30 h

BARS

Kontrast-Kneipencafé (B F GLM OS) Mon-Fri 16-1 h
Juliuspromenade 4 ✉97070 ☎ 5 55 31 Fax: 5 55 31
Sonderbar (B bf f glm MA) 11-2 h
Bronnbachergasse 1/Karmelitenstraße ✉97070 ☎ 5 43 25
Warsteiner Treff (B glm MA) 13-1, Sun 15-1 h, closed Wed
Glockengasse 15 ☎ 57 30 03

DANCECLUBS

Art (CC E glm MA p s TV WE YG) Sat 22-5 h
Beethovenstraße 1 ✉97080 *(Tram-Röntgenring)* ☎ 130 01
Gay Disco (B D Glm lj YG) 1st Sat 22-3 h at Dance Hall
c/o AKW, Frankfurter Straße 87 ✉97082

SEX SHOPS/BLUE MOVIES

Claudia-Sexshop (g) Mon-Fri 9-18, Sat 9-13 h
Bahnhofstraße 3 ✉97070 ☎ 143 61

BOOK SHOPS

Neuer Weg (glm) Mon-Fri 9-20, Sat 9-16 h
Sanderstraße 23-25 ✉97070 *(Tram-Sanderring)* ☎ 355 91-0
Gay-lesbian section

GENERAL GROUPS

GayWürz Schwule Jugendgruppe Würzburg
Every 1st and 3rd/month 20.30 h at WuF-Zentrum
PO Box 68 43 ✉97018
Email: gaywuerz@wuerzburg.gay-web.de
Homepage http://wuerzburg.gay-web.de/gaywuerz
Only for gays between 16 and 26 years.
UnArt e.V.
PO Box 67 06 ✉97017 E-mail: filmfest@wuerzburg.gay-web.de
Homepage: http://wuerzburg.gay-web.de/filmfest
Organisers of the gay filmfestival and other cultural activities.

FETISH GROUPS

LC WÜ-Lederclub Würzburg Meets 2nd/4th Fri 21 h at WuF-Zentrum, Niggelweg 2
PO Box 68 43 ✉97018 ☎ 78 46 817 Fax: 78 46 818
E-Mail: lcwue@wuerzburg.gay-web.de
Homepage: wuerzburg.gay-web.de/lcwue
Dresscode nights every 2nd Sat at WuF-Zentrum in the months of Jan, Mat, May, July, Sep and Nov (entry 21-23 h only).

HEALTH GROUPS

AIDS-Beratung der Caritas Mon-Fri 9-12, 14-17 h
Friedrich-Spee-Haus, Röntgenring 3 ✉97070 ☎ 32 22 60
AIDS-Hilfe Würzburg e.V. Counselling Tue 11-13 19-21, Thu 19-21 h
Grombühlstraße 29 ✉97080 ☎ 19 411 Fax: 2 20 20

HELP WITH PROBLEMS

Rosa Hilfe Unterfranken Wed 20-22 h, except public holydays
PO Box 68 43 ✉97018 ☎ 19 446 Fax: 41 26 47
E-Mail: rosahilfe@wuerzburg.gay-web.de/rosahilfe
Homepage: www.wuerzburg.gay-web.de/rosahilfe

SWIMMING

-Sommerhäuser Badesee (Road B 13 to Ochsenfurth/Ansbach. At Sommerhausen to [P] Wildpark. Along gardens to the lake (20 min).
- Baggerseen Dettelbach- und Hörblach- approx. 20km east of Würzburg on the B22 motorway. large flooded quarrys (Baggerseen) with nudist area (FKK-Bereich)

CRUISING

-Ringanlagen (Nähe/near Sanderring/Amtsgericht)
-Husarenpark (Ringpark zwischen/between Husarenstraße & Rennweger Ring, nach/after 21 h)
-Hauptbahnhof/Main rail station

Zittau ☎ 03583

CRUISING

-Park hinter/behind Weberkirche (from dawn to 23 h)

Zweibrücken ☎ 06332

DANCECLUBS

Rendezvous (AC B D f G lj MA OS p s WE) 21-3 h, closed Mon & Tue
Ernstweilertalstraße 150 ✉66482 ☎ 133 50
Hard to find. Call for directions.

Zwickau ☎ 0375

SAUNAS/BATHS

Thermo Club Sauna cTs (AC B DR f G MA p sa sb sol VS wh) Mon Wed Thu Sun 15-24, Fri Sat -6 h, closed Tue
Leipziger Straße 40 ✉08056 *(Near Neumarkt)* ☎ 29 60 10
Entrance-fee DM 25, students 10-20.

GENERAL GROUPS

AK Homosexualität
c/o Innere Mission, Römerstraße 11 ✉08056
ju.L.S.e.V. „junge" Lesben und Schwule e.V. (b) Mon 18-23 h
Innere Schneeberger Straße 23, 7th floor, ✉08056 ☎ 204 01 32 ☎ 0177-678 50 57.

HEALTH GROUPS

Zwickauer AIDS-Hilfe „ZASA" e.V. Wed 20 h
Hauptstraße 18-20 ✉08056 ☎ 83 53 65 Fax: 83 53 70
☎ 78 10 17 or ☎ 29 33 00

CRUISING

-Hauptbahnhof/main railway station (after 20 h)
-Kaufhaus Horten (im zentrum/in city centre)
-Schwanenteichanlagen

Gibraltar

South Europe
Initials: GBZ
Time: GMT +1
☎ Country Code / Access Code: 350 (no area codes) / 00
Language: English, Spanish
Area: 6.5 km² / 2.5 sq mi.
Currency: 1 Gibraltar Pound (Gib£) = 100 New Pence (p)
Population: 27,000
Climate: Mediterranean climate. Winters are mild, summers warm.

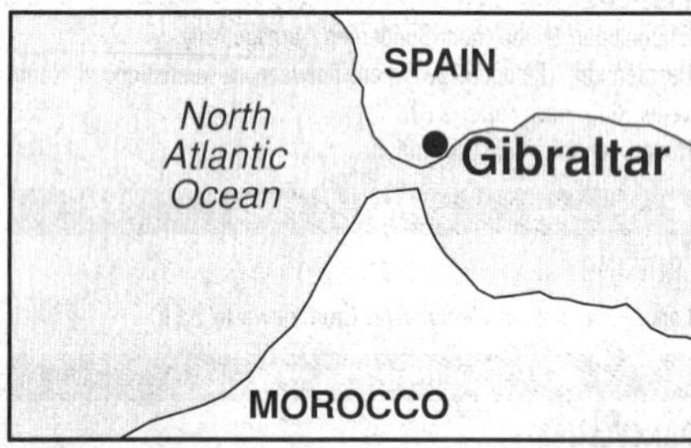

● Homosexuality is no longer forbidden in Gibraltar, and the age of consent is 18. No gay scene as such is to be found here; gays meet in each other's homes or go to the Spanish towns along the Costa del Sol. If you are spending your holidays on the Costa del Sol or just passing through, it is worth making a day-trip to Gibraltar for shopping and sightseeing.

✱ Homosexualität ist in Gibraltar nicht mehr verboten. Das Schutzalter ist auf 18 Jahre festgelegt. Eine Szene im eigentlichen Sinne gibt es nicht. Man trifft sich privat oder besucht die spanischen Städte entlang der Costa del Sol. Es lohnt sich eine Tagestour nach Gibraltar zu machen, um die Sehenswürdigkeiten zu besuchen oder einzukaufen, falls man sich an der Costa del Sol aufhält.

▲ A Gibraltar, l'homosexualité n'est plus un délit. La majorité sexuelle y est fixée à 18 ans. Pas de vie gay à proprement parler. On se retrouve en privé ou on fait un saut dans les stations balnéaires de la Costa del Sol. Gibraltar vaut le détour pour ses curiosités ou pour y faire quelques emplettes.

☆ En Gibraltar la homosexualidad no está prohibida. La edad de consentimiento ha sido fijada en 18 años. Aquí no existe un ambiente gay propiamente dicho. Los gays que viven aquí se reúnen en sus casas o van a las ciudades españolas, situadas a lo largo de la Costa del Sol. Merece la pena hacer una excursión a Gibraltar para hacer una visita túristica o para ir de compras.

❖ A Gibilterra l'omosessualità non è più proibita. L'età legale per avere rapporti sessuali è di 18 anni. Non c'è una vera vita gay in questa penisola. Gli abitanti gay si incontrano privatamente o vanno nelle città spagnole lungo la Costa del Sol. Se siete in vacanza sulla Costa del Sol o la state visitando, vale però lo stesso la pena di passare un giorno a Gibilterra per fare lo shopping o per dare un'occhiata alle sue curiosità.

Gibraltar

BARS

Charles' Hole-in-the-Wall (AC B g MA) 20-0.30 h WE-1.30
5 Castle Street ☎ 753 75
Not gay, but gay-owned and nice. Most of the clients are sailors (British Navy). Before you try to make contacts you should talk with Charles. The wrong approach could get you into trouble here!

DANCECLUBS

Casanova (B D g OS) 22.30-4.30 h. Gay on Thu Sun
9 Horse Barrack Lane *(11a Horse Barrack Court)*

Greece

Ellås
Southeastern Europe
Initials: GR
Time: GMT +2
☎ Country Code / Access Code: 30 / 00
Language: Greek
Area: 131,957 km² / 50,949 sq mi.
Currency: 1 Drachme (DR) = 100 Lepta
Population: 10,662,138
Capital: Athinai
Religions: 98% Greek Orthodox
Climate: Moderate climate. Winters are mild and wet, summers hot and dry.

● Greece, that's Athens and Mykonos. Which is true and not true. Of course, Greece is far more. The age of consent is 17 years of age for homosexuals but only 15 for heterosexuals. There is no outspoken anti-gay legislation, but some laws are open to interpretation. So, gays cruising should have their passports with them. There are very active gay groups in Athens and Thessaloniki, but their activities do not reach far beyond the city limits. The situation of gay men in everyday life is rather bleak. Compared to the other mediterranean countries they can lead a good life, but in comparison with Europe, Greek gays must still grow in their self-confidence. Gays mostly take their holidays on the Cyclades, and here mainly on the island of Mykonos, but some islands like e.g. Santorin are catching up fast. The Greek islands are a welcome change to the western mediterranean.

Griechenland, das ist Athen und Mykonos. Das stimmt und das stimmt natürlich nicht. Denn selbstverständlich ist Griechenland weit mehr.
Zwischen Männern über 17 sind homosexuelle Beziehungen legal, für heterosexuelle Beziehungen gilt allerdings ein Schutzalter von nur 15 Jahren. Eine anti-schwule Gesetzgebung gibt es zumindest nicht expressis verbis. Aber: es gibt gesetzliche Bestimmungen, die auslegbar sind. Und wer cruist, sollte immer seinen Paß dabei haben.
In Athen und Thessaloniki gibt es höchst aktive schwule Gruppen. Die Wirkung ihrer Arbeit aber reicht in diesem mediterranen Land nicht weit in die ländlichen Gegenden Griechenlands hinein. Im Alltag ist die Situation schwuler Männer eher mässig. Im Vergleich zu anderen Mittelmeer-Staaten geht es griechischen Männern sicher eher gut, doch im europäischen Vergleich müssen die griechischen Schwulen noch an Selbstbewußtsein zulegen.
Seinen Urlaub verbringt man in Griechenland natürlich auf den Kykladen, und dort eben in erster Linie auf der Insel *Mykonos*. Auch wenn inzwischen andere Inseln (z.B. Santorin) im Kommen zu sein scheinen. Die griechische Inselwelt ist eine willkommene Abwechselung zum westlichen Mittelmeer.

La Grèce? C'est Athènes et Mykonos! C'est vrai et ce n'est pas vrai à la fois, car la Grèce, c'est ça et bien plus encore! L'homosexualité masculine n'est pas un délit, à condition d'avoir plus de 17 ans. La majorité sexuelle est fixée à 15 ans pour les hétérosexuels. Pas de législation anti-homo à proprement parler, mais on peut interprêter les textes comme ci et comme ça... Ayez toujours votre passeport sur vous, même -et surtout- quand vous allez draguer. Les associations gays d'Athènes et de Thessalonique sont particulièrement actives. Malheureusement, leur action n'atteind pas les petites villes de province. En général, on peut dire que la situation des gays est plutôt moyenne. Comparés aux autres pays méditérranéns, les gays grecs ne sont pas trop mal lotis, mais comparés aux autres pays de l'Union européenne, il reste encore beaucoup à faire. Vacances en Grèce, ça veut dire les Cyclades, ça veut dire Mykonos, même si d'autres îles (comme Santorin, p. ex.) attirent depuis peu les touristes. La Grèce et ses archipels: hier comme aujourd'hui, le paradis sur terre.

¿Grecia? ¿Esto es Atenas y Mykonos? Por supuesto esto no es todo lo que Grecia tiene para ofrecer. Relaciones homosexuales son legales entre hombres mayores de 17 años, aunque la edad de consentimiento para heterosexuales está estipulada en 15 años. No existe una legislación expresamente anti- gay, pero hay muchas claúsulas que se pueden interpretar como tales. Así que cuando se va de cruising, es recomendable llevar siempre el pasaporte. En Atenas y Thessaloniki hay grupos gay muy activos, pero desgraciadamente su campo de acción no se filtra hasta las zonas rurales. En comparación con otros paises del Mediterráneo la situación en Grecia no es la peor, aunque desde el punto de vista europeo los homosexuales griegos necesitan demostrar aún más su autoconfianza. Entre los lugares vacacionales gay destacan las *Kykladen* y allí especialmente la isla de *Mykonos*. Pero también otras islas como por ejemplo *Santorini*presentan un desarollo interesante, así que Grecia se ha convertido en un destino encantador para pasar las vacaciones en el Mediterráneo.

Atene e Myconos sono la Grecia. Ciò è vero solo in parte, visto che il paese è ben di più due soli luoghi. La maturità sessuale è di 17 anni per i rapporti omosessuali e di 15 per quelli eterosessuali. Almeno expressis verbis non esiste una legislazione conro i gay, ma esistono regolamenti che possono essere interpretati ambiguamente. Chi va in cerca di compagnia dovrebbe portare il passaporto sempre con sé. Ad Atene e a Tessalonica esistono gruppi gay molto attivi. L'effetto del loro lavoro, però, non raggiunge le zone più remote di questo paese mediterraneo. Nella vita di tutti i giorni la situazione dei gay è piuttosto moderata. Rispetto ai gay di altri paesi del Mediterraneo i gay greci hanno ancora una vita facile, rispetto a quelli dell'Europa continentale invece dimostrano poca consapevolezza dei propri diritti. Le vacanze in Grecia si trascorrono naturalmente alle Cicladi ed in prima linea a Myconos, anche se ora altre isole stanno acquistando popolarità. L'arcipelago greco è un piacevole diversivo nel Mediterraneo occidentale.

Alexandroúpolis ☎ 0551

CRUISING

-Promenade and park at the sea near the Fanar Main Street (close to Hotel Alex)
-Nea Makri Beach
-Kokkina Vrahia Beach

Argos ☎ 0751

CRUISING

-Central Square
-Railway Station

Athina ☎ 01

GAY INFO

A.K.O.E Tue Fri 20-23 h
21 Patission Street *(7th floor)*
Odos Panos
39, Didotou Street
To Kraximo
PO Box 42 28 ✉10210 ☎ 365 22 49
Magazine for radical homosexual expression. Also publishes a gay guide to Greece.

TOURIST INFO

Athens Area Tourist Organisation
2, Amerikis Street ☎ 322 31 11-9

BARS

Alexander`s (AC B D Glm STV YG) 23-? h
44 Anagnostopoulou Street *(Kolonaki)* ☎ 364 66 60
Cruising bar upstairs, disco downstairs. Busy from 0 h.
Aquarius (B G)
8 Lembesi Street ☎ 923 02 64
Betty's Club (B G R TV)
32 Odyssea Androutsou Street *(Koukaki)* ☎ 922 16 22
Gaga (B G) Mon closed
58 Kimninon Street. ☎ 641 04 42
Gallery (B G SNU)
9 Simirnis Street ☎ 825 19 66
Granazi (B G)
20 Lembessi Street *(Makrigianni)*
Kirki (B F glm YG)
31 Apostoulou Pavlou Street *(at Thission Square)* ☎ 346 86 70
Very popular.
Lambda (AC B D DR G MA S VS YG) 11-? h
15 Lembesi st. *(off Sygrou Ave.)* ☎ 922 42 02
Mexico (B G)
249 Thisseos Street *(Tzizities)* ☎ 951 00 75

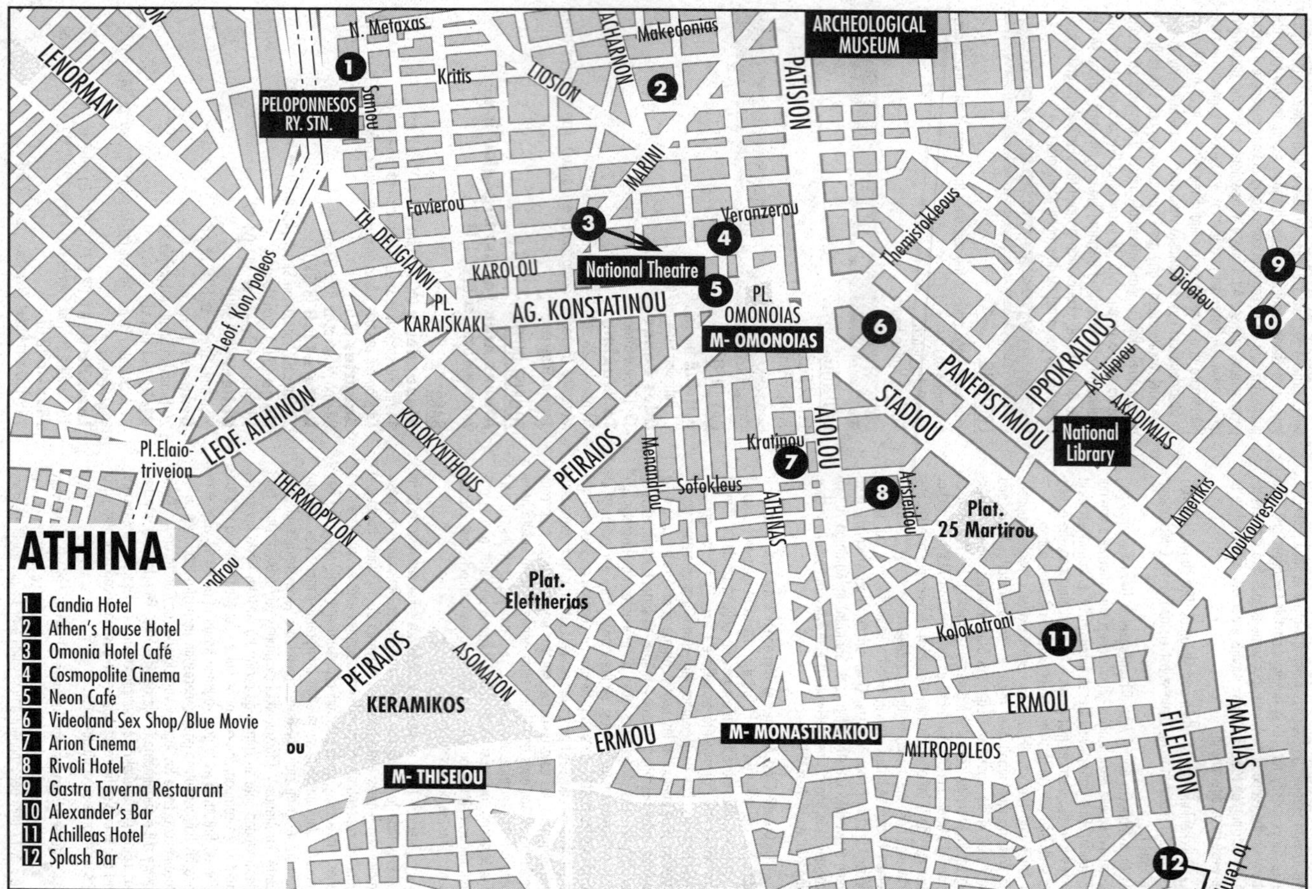
ATHINA
1 Candia Hotel
2 Athen's House Hotel
3 Omonia Hotel Café
4 Cosmopolite Cinema
5 Neon Café
6 Videoland Sex Shop/Blue Movie
7 Arion Cinema
8 Rivoli Hotel
9 Gastra Taverna Restaurant
10 Alexander's Bar
11 Achilleas Hotel
12 Splash Bar
ARCHEOLOGICAL MUSEUM
National Library
National Theatre
PELOPONNESOS RY. STN.
M- OMONOIAS
M- MONASTIRAKIOU
M- THISEIOU
PATISION
ACHARNON
Makedonias
MARINI
LIOSION
Kritis
N. Metaxas
Samou
Favierou
TH. DELIGIANNI
KAROLOU
AG. KONSTATINOU
PL. KARAISKAKI
PL. OMONOIAS
Veranzerou
Themistokleous
PANEPISTIMIOU
STADIOU
IPPOKRATOUS
AKADIMIAS
Asklipiou
Didotou
Amerikis
Voukourestiou
AMALIAS
FILELINON
to Lemp
ERMOU
MITROPOLEOS
Kolokotroni
Plat. 25 Martirou
Aristeidou
AIOLOU
Kratinou
ATHINAS
Sofokleous
Menandrou
PEIRAIOS
Plat. Eleftherias
ASOMATON
KERAMIKOS
KOLOKYNTHOUS
THERMOPYLON
LEOF. ATHINON
Leof. Kon/poleos
Pl.Elaio-triveion
LENORMAN

Mi-Ar (B G MA)
Amerikis Square
Mainly Greek music.
Odyssea (B glm)
116 Ermou Street *(Thesseion*
Picadilly (B G R)
21 Magnesias Street
Porta (AC B f GLM MA) 21-4 h
10 Phalirou Street *(Makrigianni)* ☎ 324 96 60
Smile (B f G MA R) ?-3 h
75 Agathoupoleos/Acharnon Street *(near Victoria Square)*
☎ 864 53 98
Splash (B G MA S VS)
10 Makriyanni/Chatzichristou st. ☎ 924 96 48
Ta Paidia-The Guys (B G MA YG) Sun-Thu 10-3.30, Fri Sat -? h
8 Lempesi Street ✉117 42 *(Makrigianni)* ☎ 921 4244
Greek music.

CAFÉS

Bacchanales (B F G MA)
Poulopoulou 38 ☎ 341 25 05
De Profundis (b f Glm YG) 18-2 h
1 Hajimihali Street *(Plaka)* ☎ 323 17 64
Everest (b g YG) 9-3.30 h
Tsacaloff Street *(Kolonaki)*
Minion Café (f g MA)
Omonia Square *(9th floor of a shopping mall)*
Omonia Hotel Café (H R TV)
Omonia-Square
Oval Café (b f glm)
5 Tositsa Street *(near Exarchia Square)*
Style (B GLM)
Keitis & Chiou Street *(nearby Larissis railway station)*

DANCECLUBS

City Club (B D G S TV) 23-? h
4 Korizi Street ✉11743 *(Makriyianni)* ☎ 924 07 40

RESTAURANTS

Gastra Taverna (B F G) 20.30-2 h, closed Sun & Jul Aug
1 Dimaki Street *(Kolonaki)* ☎ 360 27 57
Popular! Good food but a little expensive. Reservation requested.

SEX SHOPS/BLUE MOVIES

Emporio private cabins (G VS)
39 Sokratous Street *(1st floor)* ☎ 522 23 13
Emporio sex video (G VS) 31
Veranzerou Street *(5th floor)* ☎ 522 72 35
Redline Video Sex Shop (g VS)
Heroon Polytechniou Street 4A (4th. floor) *(Pereaus)*
☎ 411 25 08
Videoland (g VS) Mon-Fri 11-22, Sat -24, Sun 12-18 h
Panepistimiou Street 65 *(2nd Floor, Omonia)*
Videorama 11-22 h
1, Emmanouil Benaki Street/Stadiou Street *(8th floor, office 6)*
☎ 321 47 38

CINEMAS

Arion (g VS) 16-24 h
Athenas Street *(near Kotjia Square)*
Athinaikon (g VS)
Athinas Street ☎ 522 18 26
Averoff (g VS)
Eolou/Likourgou Street
Cosmopolite (g VS)
Kotopuli Street *(Omonia Square)*
Laou ?-3 h
Megalou Alexandrou Street
Omonia (g VS) ?-3 h
Santovriandou Street *(behind Omonia Square)*
Mostly gay but straight films shown.
Star (g VS)
10 Agiou Konstantinou Street *(near Omonia Square)* ☎ 522 58 01
1st and 2nd floor gay also cruising in the WC, but AYOR.

TRAVEL & TRANSPORT

Aenaon Travel (CC g) Mon-Fri 10-19 h, closed Sat Sun
56 Panepistimiou ✉106 78 *(near Omonia Square)* ☎ 330 49 73
Fax: 330 49 75 *Travel agency.*
Yorgos (G)
PO Box 30002 ✉10033 ☎ 321 03 22 Fax: 323 51 25
Travel Agency

HOTELS

Athens House (B F H NG)
4 Aristotelous Street, Athens 102 ☎ 524 05 39
12 km to the airport. Convenient location. All rooms with balcony.
Candia Hotel (AC B F g H pi)
40 Deligiani Street ☎ 524 61 12
15 km to the airport. Downtown location. All rooms with phone, bath and balcony.
Kissos Hotel (g H)
6 Maisonos Street *(Vathis Square)* ☎ 524 30 11
Rivoli Hotel (B F g H)
10 Achilleos Street *(Metaxourghion Square)* ☎ 523 97 14
Many hotels in the Plaka district are not recommended.

HEALTH GROUPS

AIDS-Hotline
☎ 722 22 22
Andreas Syngros Hospital 8-11 h
5 Ionos Dragoumi Street *(Ilissia)* ☎ 52 70 38
Hygionomiki Scholi Athinon
196 Alexandras Avenue *(Ambelokipoi)* ☎ 646 74 73
Greek center for AIDS research.

SWIMMING

-Asteria Beach (take a Voula bus from the city)
-Varkiza-Limanakia Beach (take the Varkiza bus from Zapion N° 117, 1st and 2nd station of Limankia; the rocky part of the beach is exclusively gay)

CRUISING

-Kaningos Square (YG) (bus terminus near Omonia Square, from 21 h)
-Dimachia Square (day and night)
-Small park near railway station Larissis (AYOR) (opposite Hotel Candia, late
-Kolonaki Square and surrounding cafés
–Phokinos Negri and surrounding cafés
-Pedion Areos Park (southeast section near Kolokotroni Street)
-Area accross Zappion Park (near the church of Agia Fotini)
-Syngrou Avenue (R TV)
-Athinas Street (R TV)
-Alexandras Avenue (near Katsandoni Street)
-Flower Market, Athinas Avenue (21-23 h)
-Koumoundourou Square (afternoon and night; Piraeus Avenue)
-Kaniggos Square (OG) (day)
-Zappion Park (day and night)
-Pedion Square
-Royal Gardens (near the duck pond)

Chios ☎ 0271

TRAVEL & TRANSPORT

Alfrend's
4 Voukourestion Street ☎ 360 30 03
Travel agent.

CRUISING

-Emporiou (on the beach)
-Daskalopetra (on the beach)
-Around Kara Ali's tomb

Corfu ☎ 0661

☛ Kérkyra

Crete ☎ 081

☛ Kriti

Galaxidion ☎ 0265

HOTELS

Ganimede Hotel (AC B bf F glm H MA OS) November closed
Gourgouris Street 20 ✉33052 *(in the centre)* ☎ 413 28
Fax: 42 160
From Athens by bus 4 times a day, ask at airport bus station for Delphy.

Kalamata ☎ 0721

HOTELS

Elite (B D H NG)
2 Navarinou ☎ 250 15

CRUISING

-Port Authority Park
-Railroad station

Kavalla ☎ 051

CRUISING

-Platia Fuad
-Promenade along sea front (near the harbor)

Kérkyra - Kérkyra ☎ 0661

CRUISING

-Park (uphill behind the shopping centre)
-Square at the fountain in front of Hotel Astir
-Aleko Swimming Pool

Kérkyra - Mirtiotissa ☎ 0661

BARS

Eros Bar (AC B G h NU OS S SNU YG) 17-3 h
✉49100 *(Next to Glyfada beach)* ☎ 940 25

GUEST HOUSES

Panorama (g)
✉49100 ☎ 94025

SWIMMING

-Nudist beach (near Pelekas)

Korinthos ☎ 0741

CRUISING

-Central Square
-Railroad station
-Ahilleas Place

Kos ☎ 0242

BARS

Coco Bar (B f glm OS)
4 Antimachou Str. ☎ 261 81

DANCECLUBS

Limit Bar (AC B D glm YG)
6 Al. Diakou *(in bar street)* ☎ 264 84

RESTAURANTS

Pasalimani Restaurant (B d F glm OS)
2 Sokratous *(Tarzan Beach)*

SWIMMING

-Tingaki gay beach (Take bus from Kos to Tingaki. At sea front drop off point take the left turning by restaurant „Alikes", through the bull bushes to the 1st junction. Turn right down to beach, turn left. Cruising in sand dunes.)

CRUISING

-Harbour
Toilets at steps leading to Archway
-Harbour (Archway and fortress area)
-Gardens (Taxi area)
-Old ruins behind Taxi area

Kriti - Chania ☎ 0821

BARS

Triiris (B G p)
Platia Hortson ☎ 410 36

Kriti - Iraklion ☎ 081

BARS

Tassos Place (B glm) 11-5 h
Handakos 26

DANCECLUBS

Athina Disco (B D NG)
Veniselou Square

RESTAURANTS

Kastro Restaurant (b D F MA NG YG) 21.30-2 h
Doukos Bofor
Interesting Cretan dancing by locals.

CRUISING

-Park of National Resistance (ayor) (next to old city-wall)

Kriti - Koutsouras ☎ 0843

HOTELS

Okeanis (AC B bf CC F H MA NG OS pi) April - November open, Restaurant daily 12-23 h
✉72055 ☎ 516 18 Fax: 516 18
Email: okeanis.ed@worldonline.nl
Hotel and apartments with hotel service. Very friendly and clean. Prices form 10.00 DR

Larissa ☎ 041

CRUISING

-Garden at the Main Square
-Railroad station (café)
-At the river (at night)

Lesbos - Mitilini ☎ 0251

CRUISING

-Park behind and in front of theater
-Beach

Lesbos - Molyvos ☎ 0251

BARS

Cucko's (B GLM) 12-2 h

SWIMMING

-Eftalou Beach (Bays East of Eftalou, Bus Anaxos-Molyvos-Eftalou. NU glm)

Loutrakion ☎ 0741

BARS

Jimmy's Place (B NG)
Veniselou Street

Mykonos ☎ 0289

● After a period of relative inactivity , the island of Mykonos has once again become a paradise for gay tourists from around the world. For this reason a generally young crowd is to be found here, enjoying lots of parties and action. Mykonos can be reached from Athens by boat (6-7 hours) or by plane (1/2 hour). The town of Mykonos itself is idyllic, full of winding streets and charming squares. These streets tend to be devoid of street signs, which makes it difficult to find your way around at first (and explains why the listings below contain descriptions rather than exact addresses). Once you have memorized a few landmarks, though, it becomes much easier.

✱ Nach einer Ruhephase ist diese Insel wieder zum Eldorado schwuler Touristen aus aller Welt geworden. Aus diesem Grund findet man hier auch überwiegend jüngeres Publikum, viel Trubel und Action. Von Athen aus per Flugzeug (1/2 Stunde) oder Schiff (6-7 Std.) erreichbar. Die Stadt Mykonos selbst ist eine verwinkelte, idyllische Kleinstadt. Das macht das Zurechtfinden nicht leicht, doch wenn man sich ein paar prägnante Punkte merkt, dann funktioniert auch das.

▲ Après une période creuse ces dernières années, Mykonos est de nouveau le paradis gay qu'elle était il y a 15 ans. La population estivale y est très jeune et ça bouge énormément! On y arrive par avion depuis Athènes (une heure et demie) ou par bateau (6 à 7 heures).
Mykonos elle-même est une charmante petite ville pleine de coins et de recoins sympathiques. Comme les rues n'ont généralement pas de panneaux indicateurs, nous ne pouvons pas vous donner les adresses exactes. On peut cependant s'y retrouver assez rapidement: retenez des points de repères à partir desquels vous pourrez vous orienter.

☆ Despúes de un periodo de silencio esta isla se ha convertido nuevamente en un paraíso para turistas gay de todo el mundo. Esto es en parte la razón por la que se encuentran aquí tantos jóvenes y tanta marcha. Desde Atenas se llega a la isla en avión (media hora de vuelo) o en barco (de 6 a 7 horas de travesía). La ciudad de Mykonos es muy ídilica pero por sus innumerables callecitas no es tan facil orientarse. Por ello damos a continuación más bien descripciones que direcciones exactas de los sitios. Una vez memorizado unos cuantos puntos de referencia de la ciudad, a uno no le cuesta tanto encontrar los lugares indicados.

❖ Dopo un periodo di calma Mykonos è ritornata l'Eldorado dei gay di tutto il mondo. Per questo motivo qui c'è molta azione e molta gente giovane. Mykonos può essere raggiunta da Atene in nave (6-7 ore) o in aereo (1/2 ora). Tipiche dell'isola sono le stradine tortuose, gli edifici bianchi e gli stupendi mulini a vento, il paesaggio è veramente idillico. La città è abbastanza piccola e non avrete problemi ad orientarvi dopo una breve perlustrazione.

TOURIST INFO

Municipal Information Office
☎ 222 01 Fax: 222 29

BARS

Icaros (B D G MA OS s YG) 22-3 h
Agia Kiriaki ☎ 227 18
Two bars, roof terrace; gay owned.
Kastro's (B G MA)
(besides the Paraportiani church) ☎ 230 71
Classical music, relaxed atmosphere. Go during cocktail hour to view the spectacular sunset.
Manto's (B GLM OS)
Mantoyianni Street *(near Pierro's)*
Montparnasse (B glm MA) 11-2 h
Classic music. There is also a gallery.

Thomas' Bar (B glm) Apr-Oct 20-2 h
☎ 268 66
Located near the old harbour.

DANCECLUBS

City Club (B D G MA)
2 Inglesi ✉84600 ☎ 233 50

Pierro's (B D Glm s)
Mantoyianni Street ☎ 221 77

RESTAURANTS

Caesar (F g)
Goumenio Square ☎ 231 104

Yves Klein Blue (B F glm)
Ag. Saranda ☎ 273 91

TRAVEL & TRANSPORT

Mykonos Accomodation Center Sun closed, daily 9-14 h, 17-21 h (summer months open Mon-Sun 8-22 h)
Enoplon Dynameon & Malamatenias ✉84600 *(1st floor, at the end of main street Matoyianni)* ☎ 231 60 Fax: 241 37
Email: mac@mac.myk.forthnet.gr
Homepage: www.mykonos.forthnet.gr/travel/mac/mac12.htm
Reservations for all hotels, apartments, villas on Mykonos and travel services for islands in the Cyclades & Athens

HOTELS

Carrop Tree (AC B bf cc glm H)
PO Box 110 ✉84600 ☎ 233 00 Fax: 221 62
15 double rooms, 2 single rooms, 2 triple rooms. All rooms with shower/WC, balcony/terrace, heating. Hotel provides own key and car park.

Elysium (B bf CC E f GLM msg OS pi sa wh WO) 0-24 h
Area School of Fine Arts ✉84600 *(150m from central bus station)*
☎ 239 52
The hotel is built in traditional myconian architecture. Panoramic view over Mykonos city and ocean. 42 rooms, 3 suites. All rooms with AC, phone, radio, fridge, safe, Sat-TV.

Geranium (e glm H MA OS) April-October
Ano Skoli Kalon Technon *(on top of hill of art school)* ☎ 228 67
Fax: 246 24

Mantalena (H g)
PO Box 94 ☎ 229 54 Fax: 243 02
Nice Hotel with friendly staff, overlooking Mykonos harbour. Rooms and apartments available, rates on request.

Petasos Beach Hotel (AC g H pi)
Platys Yiallos ✉84600 ☎ 226 08 Fax: 24 101
Email: petasos@myk.forthnet.gr
Homepage: www. vacations.forthnet.gr/petabeach.html
Three miles out of the town of Mykonos, located at the most characteristic seashore of the island (Platys Yalos), near bus stop. Rooms with phone, TV, minibar and balcony.

APARTMENTS

Compound. The (b G H OS pi) April-Mid of November
Matogianni 10 ✉84600 ☎ 220 98
Furnished Studios. Rooms with WC, some with kitchenette. Rates on request. Ask at Express on the harbour.

Villa Konstantin (G H OS) April-October 24 h
✉84600 ☎ 262 04 Fax: 262 05
700 m from Mykonos-City, quiet location. Studios and apartments, rates on request.

SWIMMING

-Super Paradise (G NU) (Take bus from Mykonos City to Plati Yalou. From there boats go between 9 and 19.30 h to and fro Super Paradise. You can alos take the direct bus to Paradise Beach. You have to walk 15 mins. along the cliffs.
-Elia Beach (g) It's a favorite of gay sun worshippers. It can be reached by bus or by boat from the harbor, otherwise take the bus to Plati Yalou, and from there the little fishing boat will take you.
-Agrari Beach (g)
-Paradise Beach (g)
-Paranga Beach (g) (10 mins. by foot from Plati Yialos)

CRUISING

-Panorama Beach
-Panagia Paraportiani church (ayor) (sunset till dawn. Popular. Many tourists)

Nafplion ☎ 0752

CRUISING

-Promenade along the sea (at the very end)
-Kolokotroni Park

Paros - Naousa ☎ 0284

BARS

Kavarnis Bar & Creperie (B F GLM N OS) Mon-Sun 19.30-?
(near the Post Office at the top of the Square)

Les ZinZins (A AC B bf d f GLM MA) Easter-End of october, 11-3 h
✉84401 ☎ 533 55

To Kyma (B bf F glm H ma N OS W) 9.30-1 h
Ag. Anargiri ✉84400 ☎ 520 25
Bar - restaurant - hotel.

RESTAURANTS

Le Carre (F g OS)
(Main Square)

HOTELS

Fotilia (AC B bf CC f glm H MA N OS pi R wh YG) April-October
✉84402 *150 m from centre of village* ☎ 525 81 Fax: 525 83
Prices from 16.000 GDR.

Manos (AC B bf f glm H lj MA OS pi) April-October
✉84401 *(350 m form the spuare of Naoussa)* ☎ 511 14
Fax: 517 41 Email: tzanis@par.forthnet.ger
Homepage: ww.hotelmanos.gr

SWIMMING

-Monastiri (Beach on the Bay of Naoussa. Nude sunbathing is permitted, cruising on the left-hand side, when facing the sea)

Paros - Parikia ☎ 0284

RESTAURANTS

Levantis (B F g OS YG) closed Nov 1st-Mar 31st
Castro Parikia ☎ 236 13

St. Yado's (B F glm)
(along seafront) Mostly vegetarian cuisine.

Paros - Paros ☎ 0284

DANCECLUBS

Chez Leonard (B D g MA) 23-? h
(at the harbour) ☎ 514 41
Recommended.

Pátrai ☎ 061

CRUISING

-Railway station
-Area around the lighthouse
-Park above the town (Psila Alonia)
-Olga Square (cinema)
-Kalogria Beach (NU)

Piraeus ☎ 01

BARS

Anonimous (B g)
49 Filellinon *(near Passalimani)* ☎ 452 39 77
Blow (B g)
184 Koundouriotou Street
Flying In (B G STV) Sat STV
34 Harileou Street ☎ 453 39 93
Tet-a-tet (AC B F G)
200 Praxitelous Street

HEALTH GROUPS

State General Hospital Vassilissa Frideriki
8-11 h
6 Phanariotou/Petrou Rali Street *(Nikea, Piraeus)* ☎ 491 88 40

CRUISING

-Promenade around Passaliami (YG) (19.30-? h)

Ródos ☎ 0241

BARS

Berlin. Bar (B G MA) 21-? h
Orfanidoustreet 47 *(near Alexia Hotel)* ☎ 322 50

RESTAURANTS

Rhobel (CC F glm OS) 11-13.30, 17-23 h
G. Leontos 13-15 ✉85100 ☎ 759 38
Belgian Restaurant.

GUEST HOUSES

Pink Elephant (AC bf CC g H OS)
Irodotou 420 ☎ 224 69 Fax: 224 69
Centrally located, clean, gay-friendly.

SWIMMING

-Faliraki nudist beach (15 minutes by bus from Rhodos; walk to right about 2 km along the beach to third cove)
-Beaches near Thermes Kalitheas (on the rocks near Pinewood area, right side from the small family beach)

CRUISING

-Park opposite Tourist Police
-Right side of Nevrion Café
-Aquarium
-Mandraki Place
-Near Agora
-Between Mandraki Place and post office
-Between Nevrion Café and Cathedral
-Entrance to Son et Lumière
-Park opposite Tourist Police (popular)
-Park near Copacabana Café
-Park beside St. Francis' Church and Thense Hotel

Samos ☎ 0273

BARS

Barino (B bf f g YG) 8-3 h only during summer!
Kokkari Village *(near central Square)*

RESTAURANTS

Cock's Egg. The (To Avgo tou Kokora) (b F MA NG) 13-2 h
Kokkari village *(next to Barino Bar, by the sea)*
Excellent food, not expensive.
Eros Restaurant (F g)
(located at the habour of Kokkari, nearby Bar „Barino") ☎ 926 36

CRUISING

-Tsamadou beach (g NU) (Kokkari village, bus from Samos town)

Santorini ☎ 0286

CRUISING

- Red Beach (A bay behind Red Beach)

Skiathos ☎ 0427

BARS

Adagio (B GLM MA) 22-03 h
Evagelistrias 14 *(Near to post office)* ☎ 210 52
Kalypso (AC B g) 9-? h
Filokleous Gerogiadou *(near new port)* ☎ 230 51
Pixida (B G) May-Oct
M. Annaniou 8 *(near Papadiamanti Square)* ☎ 94-16 33 09 (mobile)
Small, relaxing bar with a nice atmosphere.

APARTMENTS

Villa Elena (bf e glm H msg pi)
Agios Antonios ☎ 218 37 Fax: 212 49 236 57
Open from May-Oct/Nov, for special arrangements in winter too. 2 apartments (2 rooms) and 2 apartments (1 room) with shower or bath/WC, radio, kitchenette, balcony, own key and TV/video on request. Call/fax for price list and special offers. Panoramic views and 20 minutes by foot to the next beach (bus link as well). Rental car recommended.

SWIMMING

-Banana Beach (nudist beach next to Kokounaries Beach; buses from town; take bus to last stop, then walk right over a small hill and through an olive grove)
-Tsougias Island (take the boat from Skiathos, approximately hourly departures)

Thessaloniki ☎ 031

CAFÉS

De Facto (B glm OS YG)
19 Pavlou Mela Street ☎ 26 36 74

SEX SHOPS/BLUE MOVIES

Laïkon (g NG r) 10-2 h
Monastiriou St. 4 *(Near Vardari Square)*
Videorama (g VS) 14-22 h
Filikis Eterias Street 3 (2nd floor) ☎ 26 90 84

GENERAL GROUPS

O.P.O.T.H Wed 21-23 (English spoken)
PO Box 108 39 ✉541 10 ☎ 94-41 41 60 (Mobile) Fax: 76 39 06
Email: opoth@ilga.org
Homepage: www.geocities.com/WestHollywood/Heights/2958
Member of ILGA. Free monthly available in major bookshops and gay bars.

HEALTH GROUPS

AIDS Hotline ☎ 42 20 21

CRUISING

All are AYOR
-Park around Zoological Garden (every night from dusk on)
-Kalamaria Park
-Odos Megalou Alexandrou
-Lefkos Pirgos (White Tower)
-Plateia Aristotelou (at bus station „Vardari")
-Plateia Axios (at the end of Odos Egnatias)
-Ethniko Swimming Pool
-YMCA (XANO) (park and swimmingpool)

Thira - Firostefani ☎ 0286

RESTAURANTS

Taverna Il Cantuccio (F g MA) 20-24 h
☎ 220 82
Italian cuisine. In high season reservation recommended.

Thira - Ia ☎ 0286

HOTELS

Zoe House (g H lj MA OS)
(20 min. from airport) ☎ 714 66
Located in the old village Ia, near the volcano. All rooms with Bath, & kitchenette. Rate from DR 13.000 per house and night.

CRUISING

-Castle of Ia

Thira - Koloubos ☎ 0286

SWIMMING

-Koloubos (NU) (on the left side)

Thira - Oia ☎ 0286

APARTMENTS

Oia Mare Villas (glm H)
☎ 710 70 Fax: 710 70
Hotel apartments with TV, radio, fully equipped kitchen, private bath and WC. All rooms with private terrace and seaview. Rates from US$ 80-200 for a double (2 persons). Daily maid service.

Thira - Thira ☎ 0286

BARS

Franco's Bar (B f g MA)
Odós Marinatos ☎ 228 81
Closed in winter. Classical music.

CAFÉS

Jazz Café (B glm MA OS) 12-2 h
(near Franco's Bar) ☎ 234 27
Occasionally live Jazz music.
Meridiana Internet Cafe (AC B CC F g MA OS) 9-24 h
PO Box 52 ✉84700 *(near church)* ☎ 234 27
Papagallino (B glm) 7.30-16 h
☎ 230 11

RESTAURANTS

Barbara's Restaurant (B F glm MA OS) 12-2 h
c/o Hotel Lucas *(below Lucas Hotel)* ☎ 234 27

HOTELS

Hotel Atlas (bf H pi) May-October
Karterados ✉84700 ☎ 234 15 Fax: 234 15
Rates from DR 7.000 (single) to DR 18.000 (double).
Kavalari Hotel (bf CC glm H)
PO Box 17 ✉84700 ☎ 224 55 Fax: 226 03

Volos ☎ 0421

BARS

Sanitarium (B G) 23-3 h
Iasonos/Ag. Nicolou Street

CAFÉS

Santan (B f G YG) 23-3 h
Olgas/Alexandras Street

CRUISING

-Dimarchiou Park

Xanthi ☎ 0541

CINEMAS

Oscar (g)

CRUISING

-Main square

Guam

Oceania
Initials: GU
☎ Country Code / Access Code: 1-671 (no area codes) / 011
Language: English; Chamorro
Area: 549 km² / 212 sq mi.
Currency: 1 US Dollar (US$) = 100 Cents.
Population: 159,000
Capital: Agaña
Climate: Tropical marine climate. Warmth and humidity are moderated by northeast trade winds. The dry season lasts from January to June, the rainy season from July to December. There's little seasonal temperature variation.

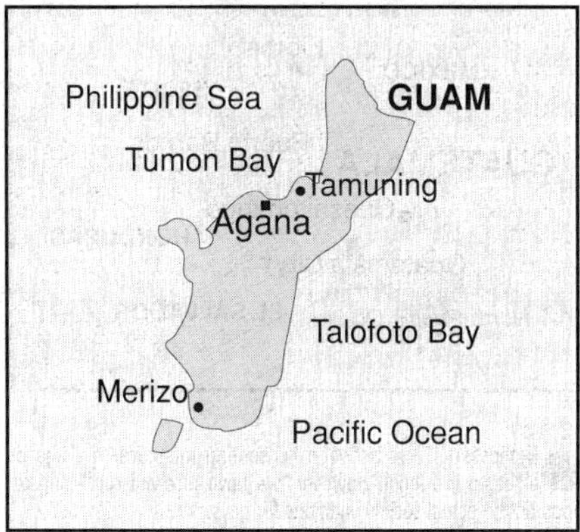

Agaña ✉ GU 96910

GENERAL GROUPS

Guam Friends
PO Box 1861 ✉GU 96910
Gay group

Tamuning

CRUISING

-Bank of Hawaii (AYOR r tv) (rear parking lot, 24-5 h)
-ITC Building (toilets)

Tamuning

DANCECLUBS

Onyx. The (AC B D E glm YG)
San Vitores Road *(at Sand Castle Complex)*

CRUISING

-Y'pao beach (ayor G) (near Hilton Hotel, 21-3 h)

Guatemala

Central America

Initials: GCA

Time: GMT -6

☎ Country Code / Access Code: 502 (no area codes) / 00

Language: Spanish; 23 Indian (Maya-Quiché) languages and dialects

Area: 108,889 km² / 42,042 sq mi.

Currency: 1 Quetzal (Q) = 100 Centavos

Population: 12,007,580

Capital: Ciudad de Guatemala/Guatemala City

Religions: 75% Roman Catholic; 25% Protestant

Climate: Tropical climate. The lowlands are hot and humid, the highlands cooler.

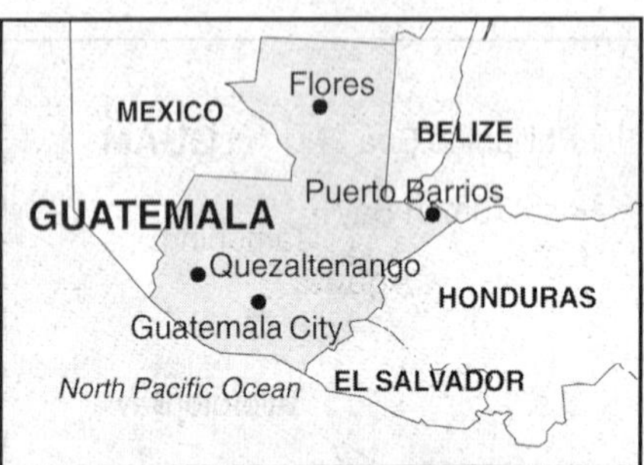

● Homosexual acts between consenting men over the age of eighteen are legal. However, we have received conflicting reports on the actual social conditions for gays.

✱ Einvernehmliche homosexuelle Handlungen zwischen Männern über 18 Jahren sind dem Gesetz nach erlaubt. Allerdings hat gerade die ländliche Bevölkerung ein negatives Bild von Schwulen.

▲ Au Guatemala, l'homosexualité n'est pas un délit, à condition que les partenaires soit tous deux majeurs et consentants. Pour le reste, nous ne disposons que d'informations contradictoires.

☆ De acuerdo a la constitución del país, el trato homosexual entre hombres majores de 18 años, si es de acuerdo mutuo, está permitido. Sobre la situación real nos han llegado sin embargo informes contradictorios.

❖ Gli atti omosessuali tra uomini maggiorenni e consenzienti sono legali. Comunque, abbiamo ricevuto delle informazioni contrastanti sulla reale condizione sociale dei gay.

NATIONAL GAY INFO

Grupo C'aslen
4a Avenida 3-39 Zona 1, Ciudad Guatemala

Antigua

CRUISING

-Main Square
-Plaza de Armas
-Earthquake ruins (guides pleasant and helpful)

Ciudad de Guatemala

GAY INFO

Support Organization for An Integral Sexuality Confronting AIDS (OASIS)
11 Calle 4-51, zone 1 ☎ 232 33 35 Fax: 232 33 35
Social centre, infos about gay scene and AIDS.

BARS

Encuentro. El (B f G) 17-23, Sun 20-22 h
Cine Los Capitos, 6 Avenida 12 *(Zona 1. 3rd floor)*
Nice and friendly.

DANCECLUBS

Pandora Box (B D G P YG) Fri 21-1.30, Sat -2.30 h
Ruta 3 No. 3-08, Zona 4

RESTAURANTS

El Buen Gusto Oriental (B F NG)
6 Avenida/Calle 15-16 *(Zona 1)*
Chinese cuisine.

CRUISING

-5th and 6th Avenue between 6th and 15th Street (these streets and intersections comprise the main „downtown" activity areas; several parks lie within these areas)
-Calle de amore (near Plaza de Armas)

Panajachel

BARS

Circus Bar (B F NG) 18-1 h
Live music.

DANCECLUBS

Circus Disco (B D g) 20-1 h
(opposite Circus Bar)

Puerto Barrios

SWIMMING

-Matias de Calvez beach

Puerto San José

BARS

Hotel Chulamar (B g WE)
On the beach, ocean front. Fancy beach resort, nice mixed crowd on weekends only.

SWIMMING

-Beaches (many of the lifeguards like action, be discreet)

Honduras

Central America

Initials: HN

Time: GMT -6

☎ Country Code / Access Code: 504 (no area codes) / 00

Language: Castillian; Spanish; English partly

Area: 112,088 km² / 43,277 sq mi.

Currency: 1 Lempira (L) = 100 Centavos

Population: 5,861,955

Capital: Tegucigalpa

Religions: 90% Catholic

Climate: The climate is subtropical in the lowlands and moderate in the mountains.

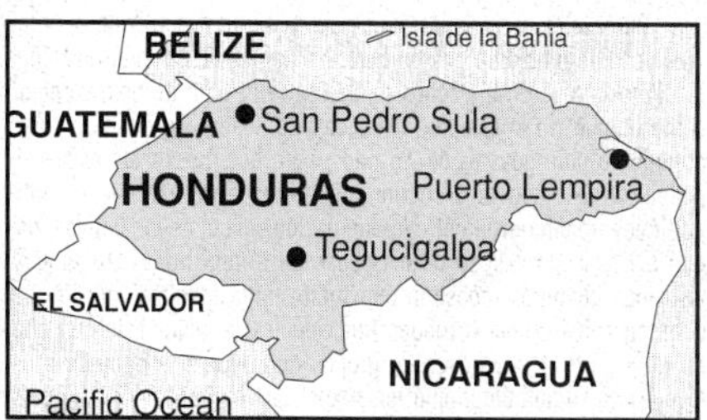

● There are no specific laws that apply to homosexuality. This does, anyway, not mean, that the situation is very favorite for gays in Honduras. There are no efforts to create any anti-discriminatory regulations, police and military raids are often told of. This situation developed since AIDS is known of.

✸ Es gibt keinerlei gesetzliche Regelungen, die sich mit Homosexuellen beschäftigen. Es gibt keinerlei Bestrebungen, Anti-Diskriminierungsregelungen zu treffen. Seit dem Bekanntwerden von AIDS sehen sich Schwule häufig verbalen und physischen Attacken von staatlicher wie auch gesellschaftlicher Seite ausgesetzt. Nach neuesten Informationen hat sich die Situation von Schwulen und Lesben in den letzten Jahren eher noch verschlechtert.

▲ Pas de législation anti-homos aux Honduras, ce qui ne veut pas dire que, là-bas, les gays ont la vie facile. Personne n'est à l'abri des discriminations et des chicanes de la police et de l'armée, par exemple, qui „visitent" régulièrement les lieux gays. Depuis l'apparition de l'épidémie du sida, la situation ne s'est pas améliorée.

☆ Aunque en Honduras no exista una legislación anti-homosexual, la situación para los gays no es nada favorable. No hay aspiraciones para reformas legislativas y se sabe que los gays son molestados por militares y policias con frecuencia. Esta situación se agravó con la problematica del SIDA.

❖ Non esistono leggi che menzionano l'omosessualità. Tuttavia ciò non significa che la situazione in Honduras sia particolarmente buona. Non esiste neppure il proposito di emanare una legge contro la discriminazione dei gay. Si parla invece di ripetute violenze contro i gay da parte della polizia e dei militari. Questa situazione esiste da quando si conosce l'AIDS.

San Pedro Sula ✉ 21105

BARS

Corcel Neuro (B G TV)
✉21105 ☎ 52 50 75 *ask for Megal for direction.*

DANCECLUBS

Terrazas Video Discoteque (AYOR B D g R tv)
15 Avenida 10 Calle S.O. *(Esquina Zona Viva)*

HEALTH GROUPS

AIDS CAPS Hombres
PO Box 43 17

Asociacion Hondureña de Homosexuales y Lesbianas Contra el SIDA
PO Box 33 49 ✉21105

CRUISING

-Park in center of city (enter from Gran Hotel Sula)

Tegucigalpa

GENERAL GROUPS

Grupo Prisma
PO Box 45 90

CRUISING

-Parque Central (AYOR) (arround the cathedral)
-Parque La Libertad (AYOR) (in the suburb Comayaguela, dangerous after dark)

Hungary

Magyar

Central Europe

Initials: H

Time: GMT +1

☎ Country Code / Access Code: 36 / 00

Language: Magyar (Hungarian)

Area: 93,033 km^2 / 35,920 sq mi.

Currency: Forint (Ft)

Population: 10,208,127

Capital: Budapest

Religions: 64% Roman Catholics; 23% Protestant

Climate: Moderate climate. Winters are cold, cloudy and humid, summers are warm.

During the past few years, an interesting and lively gay scene has emerged in Eastern Europe, especially in Hungary. Also the countryside in Hungary seems to reach a turningpoint: There are monthly gay parties in a lot of cities. There are no anti-sodomy laws as such in Hungary, but the age of consent for gay sex is 18, while for straights it is 14. Same-sex marriage is not possible, but the law makes no explicit distinction between homo- and heterosexual partnerships and gay or lesbian partnerships can get registred. Many gays in Hungary have difficulty acknowledging their gay identity, reflecting a lack of self-esteem due to their social environment. But for all that, Hungarians seem to have no trouble at all enjoying their gay lifestyle. Hungary's gay night spots are typically crowded. Visitors can even find themselves feeling somewhat irritated at Hungarians' frankness with respect to sex, because Hungarian gays are very quick to tell you their wishes and expectations.

Innerhalb der letzten paar Jahre entstand eine lebendige und interessante schwul-lesbische Szene in Osteuropa, insbesondere in Ungarn. Auch auf dem Land tut sich etwas: Monatliche Parties finden vielerorts regelmäßig statt. Schutzalter für schwulen Sex ist 18, für Heterosexuelle 14; Schwule Ehe ist nicht zugelassen, aber das Gesetz macht keinen Unterschied zwischen homo- oder heterosexuellen Lebensgemeinschaften,- eine Registrierung ist möglich. Viele Schwule und Lesben in Ungarn haben ein wenig ausgeprägtes Selbstbewußtsein. In Ermangelung von Jugend- oder Coming-Out-Gruppen übernehmen junge Schwule und Lesben viel zu oft Lebenskonzepte der Älteren. Dennoch sind sie durchaus genußfähig und Ungarns schwule Treffpunkte sind sehr belebt. Besucher sind auch oft erstaunt erstaunt über die Direktheit, mit der mit sexuellen Wünschen und Erwartungen umgegangen wird.

Au cours des dernières années, il s'est développé en Europe de l'Est un milieu pédé et lesbien animé et intéressé, particulièrement en Hongrie. Même à la campagne ça remue: des fêtes ont lieu tous les mois régulièrement dans beaucoup d'endroits. Le sexe pédé est interdit avant 18 ans, pour les hétérosexuels c'est 14 ans. Le mariage pédé est interdit, mais la loi ne fait pas de différence entre les concubinages entre homosexuels et hétérosexuels, il est possible de faire une déclaration. Beaucoup de pédés et de lesbiennes en Hongrie ont une image d'eux-mêmes peu marquée. A cause du manque de groupes de jeunes ou de groupes de sortie, beaucoup de jeunes pédés et lesbiennes adoptent trop souvent les concepts de vie des plus âgés. Cependant, ils sont parfaitement capables de jouissance et les points de rendez-vous pour pédés sont très fréquentés en Hongrie. Les visiteurs sont souvent étonnés de la franchise avec laquelle on s'occupe des désirs sexuels et des aspirations.

Durante el curso de los últimos años se ha desarollado un interesante ambiente gay en Europa Oriental, sobre todo en Hungría. Pero incluso en las zonas rurales se nota algo de este cambio, como demuestra la celebración regular de fiestas. La edad de consentimiento para gays es de 18 años, para heterosexuales está estipulada en 14. Aunque el matrimonio homosexual no está permitido, la ley no diferencia entre la orientación sexual de las parejas, así que existe la posibilidad de inscribirse en el registro. Pocos gays y lesbianas húngaros muestran una fuerte autoconfianza, por lo que adoptan con frecuencia modos tradicionales de vida. Esto se debe en gran parte a la escasez de grupos que ayuden y apoyen a los jóvenes en su autodeterminacion sexual. Sin embargo, los húngaros disfrutan el sexo y los sitios de encuentros gay son muy frecuentados. Muchas veces al visitante le sorprende la sinceridad con que se expresan los deseos y expectativas sexuales.

Durante gli ultimi anni nei paesi dell'est si è sviluppato un'ambiente lesbico-gay vivace ed interessante, sopratutto in Ungheria. Anche nei posti di campagna sta cambiandosi qualcosa: regolarmente in molti posti vengono organizzati delle feste. L'età legale per avere rapporti gay è di 18 anni, per quelli eterosessuali di 14 anni; il matrimonio gay non è permesso, ma non si fanno distinzioni tra convivenze omosessuali e eterosessuali; è possibile farsi registrare. Molti gay e lesbiche non si dimostrano orgogliosi di se stessi. Per mancanza di gruppi per giovani o di coming out i giovani gay e lesbiche adottano i concetti di vita dell'altra generazione. Nonostante ciò, sono capaci di divertirsi, e i punti d'incontro in Ungheria vengono frequentati in gran numero. Spesso i turisti si stupiscono del modo diretto con cui gli ungheresi trattano i desideri e aspettative che riguardano il sesso.

NATIONAL GAY INFO

Gay.hu
http://fules.c3.hu/gay.hu/
Hungary's gay online magazine.

Mások
PO Box 388 ✉1461 Budapest ☎ (01) 266 99 59.
Fax: (01) 266 99 59 Email: masok@masok.hu
Homepage: www.masok.hu
Monthly publication featuring news, advertising, photos and classifieds.

Szuper Erosz
PO Box 1242, 1242 Budapest
Monthly publication (64 pages) with news, ads, photos. English and German gay information. Map of Budapest.

NATIONAL COMPANIES

Connection Csomagküldö (G)
PO Box 701/1027 ✉1399 Budapest ☎ (01) 303 61 13 Fax: (01) 133 25 85
Email: Connection@mail.datanet.hu
Homepage: www.datanet.hu/connection/
Videos, magazines, vibrators, dolls, dildos, etc.

Budapest ☎ 01

● Budapest („Paris of the East") has always been known as a gay metropolis in Eastern Europe. Beside bars, dance clubs, the famous baths and the cruising spots, there are gay and lesbian groups doing political activities, counseling and socializing activities, gayorientated AIDS-prevention, publication of gay papers and broadcasting gay radio magazines. A Gay Switchboard takes care for the wellbeing of gay tourists before, during and after their stay. Since '97 there is a Gay Pride event every year and in 2001 the Budapest Gay Pride will be a official event of Europride Vienna. Just by occupying during sunset, one of the seats along the Korzo near the Erzsebet bridge and March 15th Square (the most crowded cruising area), you can get a good idea of what gay society in Budapest is like.

✷ Budapest („Paris des Ostens") war schon immer die schwule Metropole im Osten. Neben Bars, Discos, den berühmten Bädern und den Cruisingplätzen, haben Gruppen und Organisationen politische Aktivitäten und Ansätze einer schwulen Community entwickelt, beraten und machen AIDS-prävention, verlegen Zeitschriften und produzieren schwule Radiomagazine. Ein „Gay Switchboard" kümmert sich um das Wohlbefinden schwuler Touristen vor, während und nach ihrer Reise. Seit '97 findet jährlich ein Gay Pride statt, und 2001 wird der Budapest Pride offizieller Teil des Europride Wien sein. Einen Eindruck, was schwules Leben in Budapest ist, gewinnt, wer sich kurz vor Sonnenuntergang im Sommer auf einer der Bänke am „Korzo" niederlässt, nahe der Elisabeth-Brücke und dem Platz des 15. März.

▲ Budapest (le „Paris de l'Est") a toujours été la métropole pédé à l'Est. En plus des bars, discothèques, bains renommés et lieux de rencontre, des groupes et des organisations ont développé des activités politiques et les prémices d'une communauté pédé. Ils conseillent et pratiquent la prévention contre le SIDA, ils publient des revues et produisent des magazines pédés à la radio. Un „Gay Switchboard" s'occupe du bien-être des touristes pédés, pendant et après leur voyage. Depuis 1997, un „Gay Pride" a lieu une fois par an et en 2001, le „Budapest Pride" fera partie officiellement de „Europride" à Vienne. Pour se faire une idée de la vie pédé à Budapest, il faut s'asseoir sur un banc au bord du „Korzo" en été, juste avant le coucher du soleil, près du Pont Elisabeth et de la Place du 15 mars.

☆ Budapest, que se conoce también como el París del Este, siempre fue una metrópoli gay en centro Europa. A parte de bares, discotecas, los famosos baños y sitios de cruising han surgido multiples grupos y organizaciones, que defienden los intereses de la comunidad gay, desarollan actividades póliticas, aconsejan, trabajan en la prevención del SIDA, públican revistas y producen programas de radio. Para los turistas homosexuales se creó un „Gay Switchboard", que se encarga del bienestar del visitante, antes, durante y despúes de su estancia en Hungría. Desde 1997 se organiza anualmente un Gay Pride y en 2001 Budapest formará parte oficial del Europride Viena. Para hacerse una idea como es la vida gay en Budapest se recomienda pasarse en verano poco antes de la puesta del sol por los bancos del *Korzo*, cerca del puente Isabel y de la plaza del 15 de marzo.

❖ Già da sempre Budapest („Parigi dell'oriente") è la metrepoli gay dell'est. A parte i bar, le discoteche, i famosi bagni e le possibilità per il cruising, gruppi e organizzazioni hanno sviluppato

PORNVIDEO
DARK ROOM
BÁR
DARLING
Video- Drink Bar
Budapest, V., Szép utca 1.
(Our Bar situated between
ASTORIA metro station
on the red line and the
FERENCIEK TERE metro
station on the blue line.)
Phone: +36 (1) 267-3315
OPEN EVERY EVENING
19-03

delle attività politiche e iniziato a stabilire una comunità gay. Tra le diverse iniziative sono da elencare i servizi di consulenza e di prevenzione contro l'AIDS, la pubblicazione di riviste e la mandata in onda di trasmissioni gay nelle radio locali. Un „gay switchboard" si occupa del benessere dei turisti gay prima, durante e dopo il loro viaggio. Dal'97 ogni anno ha luogo un Gay Pride, e nel 2001 il Budapest Pride sarà ufficialmente una parte integrata dell'Europride di Vienna. Un'impressione della vita gay a Budapest si può ricavare sedendosi su uno dei banchi vicino al ponte Elisabeth e alla Piazza del 15 marzo in una sera d'estate poco prima del tramonto.

GAY INFO

Gay Switchboard Budapest (GLM) Hotline 16-20 h
PO Box 752 ✉1437 Budapest ☎ +36 309 32 33 34 (from abroad)
Fax: 351 20 15 Email: budapest@gayguide.net
Homepage: http://gayguide.net
Gay tourist information, gay organisation, accomodations. Information on gayowned accomodation Daily updated Gay Guide Budapest, Online Forum & Dictionary in the Internet, Hotline every day; all E-mails are eplied within 48 hours; english and german spoken.

TOURIST INFO

Tourinform Budapest
PO Box 215 ✉1364 ☎ 117 59 64 Fax: 117 59 64
Email: tourinform@hungary.com
Homepage: www.hungary.com/tourinform

BARS

Action (! AC B DR f G lj MG P VS) Every day 19-04:00h
V, Magyar utca 42 ✉1052 *(Near Hotel Korona. M°BlueLine-Kálvin tér)* ☎ 266 91 48 Email: action@mail.tvnet.hu
Homepage: www.action.bartexinfo.hu

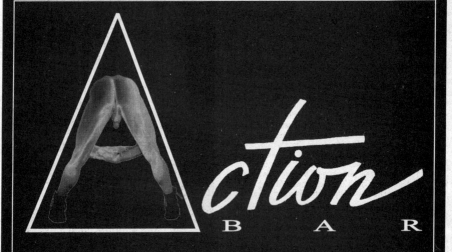

Angel Bar (! AC B D DR F GLM MA p S STV VS WE) Thu 22-24 h, Fri-Sun 22-5 h
VII, Szövetség utca 33 ✉1074 *(M° Baross tér.)* ☎ 351 64 90
Two floors, three bars, restaurant, darkroom, large disco, very popular.
Darling (AC B DR G MA P VS YG) 19-03:00h
V, Szép utca 1 *(Near Hotel Astoria. M°BlueLine-Ferenciek tere)*
☎ 267 33 15
Very small bar.
Mystery Bar (AC B E f G MA p) Mon-Sat 21-4 h
V, Nagysándor József utca 3 ✉1054 *(M°BlueLine-Arany János utca. Near US Embassy)* ☎ 312 14 36
No Limit Bar (B G MA R) 20-3 h
V, Semmelweis utca 10 ☎ 117 09 02

CAFÉS

Capella Caffe (B D f g MA) 18-4, Mon Tue -2 h
V, Belgrád rakpart 23 *(M°BlueLine-Ferenciek tere)* ☎ 267 26 16

DANCECLUBS

CHAOS (A AC B CC D f G MA) daily 21-5 h, Galeria Mon-Fri 10-18h Sat 10-13 h
Nagy Diófa utca 3 ✉1072 *(In the Centre of Pest, earby Hotel Astorie and Blaha Lujza Place. Red Metro Line: Astoria or Blaha Lujza tér)* ☎ 344 48 84
Music pub and danceclub but also art gallery
Angel Privat Club (BD F G STV) Thu 22-24, Fri-Sun 22-5 h
Bp VII, Szövetség utca 33

RESTAURANTS

Amstel River Cafe (AC B bf F g MA OS) Mon-Sat 9-23, Sun 11-23 h
Párizsi utca 6 ✉1052 *(M° Blue Line-Ferenciek tér)* ☎ 266 91 48
Exclusive restaurant. Gays are welcome.
Fenyógyöngye (B F g H) 12-24 h
II, Szépvölgyi utca 155 ✉1025 *(Bus 65/65a)* ☎ 325 97 83
Reservation recommended.
Wurlitzer Restaurant (AC B CC F G MA) Tue-Sat 18-24 h
Wesselényi u. 49 ✉1077 *(Centrally located, near EMKE)*
☎ 351 02 31
Central Budapest, close to gay area. Exclusively gay, with Hungarian cuisine.

SEX SHOPS/BLUE MOVIES

Apollo Video Shop (G VS) Mon-Fri 10-18 h
VI, Terér Körut 3 *(M° red line-EMKE)* ☎ 342 19 11
Videos, magazines, toys, gay cinema.
Erosz Sexshop (g) Mon-Fri 10-18 h
VII, Nyngati Pályaudvar, Nyugat Aruház *(M°blueline-Nyugati Pu)*
Videos, magazines, toys.

Erotic Cinema & Video (AC g MA VS) 10-2 h
Hegedus Gyula 1, XIII K ☎ 111 80 35
Intim Center (g VS) 10-20 h.
V, Károly körut 14 *(M°redline-Astoria)*
Videos, magazines, toys, video cabins.
Intim Lapüzlet és Videotéka (G) Mon-Fri 10-18, Sat 10-14 h
VII, Dob utca 17 *(M°redline-Astora)* ☎ 112 02 46
Videos, magazines, toys.
Privat Erotic Shop (g) Mon-Fri 10-18 h
XIII, Szent István körút 24 *(M°BlueLine-Nyugati Pu)*

ESCORTS & STUDIOS

Rainbow & Tailored Tours
☎ 209 380 400

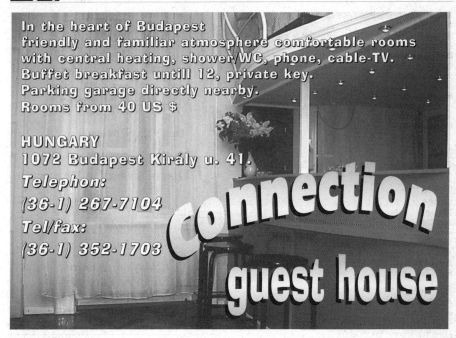

SAUNAS/BATHS

Gellért (g MA msg sa sb sol) Mon-Fri 6-18, Sat Sun -15 h
XI, Kelenhegyi utca 4 *(at Hotel Gellért, Gellért tér, Bus 7, Tram 47/49, 18/19)* ☎ 466 61 66
Best time 16-18 h

Király (G MA msg sa sb) Mon Wed Fri 7-18 h
II, Fö utca 84 *(M°RedLine-Battyhányi tér)* ☎ 202 36 88
Recommended.

Lukács Iszapfürdö (G MA pi sb) Tue Thu 6.30-19, Sat 6.30-13 h, Sun closed
II, Frankel Leo utca 26-29 *(MetroRedLine-Battyhányi tér)* ☎ 115 42 80
From M° take bus 86 or 60 two stops direction Margaret Bridge. Walk a little straight ahead to the nearest passenger/pedestrian crosswalk and go to the yellow building in front of you. Ask for a ticket for iszapfürdö. After dark, wild action in the nude pool. (autumn and winter only)

Rácz (G sa sb WO YG) Tue Thu 7-18 h
I, Hadnagy út 8-10 *(M°BlueLine-Ferenciek tere)* ☎ 356 13 22
Best Sat 15-18 h. From M° take bus 7 direction Buda one stop. Walk back a little, after the Elizabeth bridge turn left.

Széchenyi (G MA OG sa sb) Mon-Fri 7-18, Sat -13, Sun -12 h
XIV, Allatkerti utca 11 *(M°YellowLine-Széchenyi Fürdö)* ☎ 121 03 10

TRAVEL & TRANSPORT

Cruise Victory Co. Travel & Ticket Agency (AC CC GLM) Mon-Fri 9-17.30 h, Sat Sun closed
Va`ci utca 9 ✉1052 ☎ 267 38 05 Fax: 267 38 07

Toucan Tourist (glm) Mon-Thu 9.30-17.30, Fri -13.30 h, Sat Sun closed

Radnoti 7 utca 15/B 1137 ☎ 329 74 81 Fax: 357 54 23
Hotel booking, gay map, information and service.

Tpg Tavel & Air Service (CC glm) Mon-Fri 9-17.30 h
Va`ci utca 9 ✉1052 ☎ 267 38 05 Fax: 267 38 05

3H Hungarian Handling & Holiday Ltd (CC glm) Mon-Fri 9-17.30 h, Sat Sun closed
Va`ci utca 9 ✉1052 ☎ 267 38 05 Fax: 267 38 05

GUEST HOUSES

Connection Guest House (b bf CC G H)
Király utca 41 ✉1072 *(M° Red Line-Deák tér)* ☎ 267 71 04
Fax: 352 17 03 Email: connectionbt@freemail.hu
4 double rooms with shower/WC, telephone, SAT-TV, heating, own key and room service. Central location. Rates US$ 30-75. Additional bed US$ 25.

KM-Saga (bf glm H MA)
Lonyai Utca, Nr. 17, III Floor, Door Nr 1. ✉1093 ☎ 217 19 34
Gay-owned, exclusive, discreet guest-residence in 1890s environments with modern comforts. Central location near the National Museum. All rooms with cable TV own key and some with shared baths.

Pipacs Guesthouse (G)
Kossuth L. u. 12 ✉1053 *(Central located)* ☎ 317 73 34
Fax: 317 73 94 Email: poppy@mail.tvnet.hu
Homepage: www.gaybudapest.hu
Single (US$ 39), double rooms (US$ 46-49), apartments (US$65), free internet and e-mail service, city tours. For reservations contact melengay@mail.tvnet.hu.

APARTMENTS

Connection Services (G) Mon-Fri 7.30-16.30, after hours message & fax.
PO Box 701/10 27 ✉1399 ☎ 303 61 13 Fax: 133 25 85

Private flats in the city, rates from 85-150 DM/flat/day incl. free car transfer from airport or train station & back.

Daniel Zamfir (G H)
Fiumei út. 21-23, VII, Iph. II. floor 84 ✉1081 ☎ 303 20 78
3 apartments between 30 qm and 50 qm with TV, kitchen, bath and phone.

Lindemann Private Apartments (H)
Pipa utca 6/2 ✉1093 *(M° Kelety station)* ☎ 215 53 78
Fax: 215 53 78 Email: budapest@engeli.com
Homepage: www.engeli.com/lindenmann
Rates from DM 60, per person/night. Central location. Own entrance and key.

PRIVATE ACCOMODATION

Budapest's Friend's Apartments (AC bf CC GLM H)
Mon-Fri 9-17.30 h, Sat Sun closed
c/o Cruise Victory, Váci utca 9 ✉1052 ☎ 267 38 05
Fax: 267 38 05

Poppy
☎ 317 73 94 Fax: 266 57 98 Email: poppy@elender.hu
Homepage: www.poppy.bartexinfo.hu

GENERAL GROUPS

Háttér Baráti Társaság a Melegkért
PO Box 50 ✉1554 ☎ 390 96 50 Email: Hatter@c3.hu
Homepage: www.c3.hu/~hatter

Lambda Budapest
PO Box 388 ✉1461 ☎ 266 99 59
Email: masok@masok.hu Homepage: www.masok.hu

HEALTH GROUPS

Meta 17-7 h
PO Box 44 ✉1387 ☎ 247 0188

PLUSS
PO Box 29 ✉1450 ☎ +36-603 437 73
HIV positives self-help association.

RELIGIOUS GROUPS

Kesergay
Ovegylet, PO Box 50 ✉1554
Jewish gays and lesbians.

Öt Kenyér
PO Box 25 ✉1461
Gay catholics.

SPORT GROUPS

Vándor Mások
PO Box 2 ✉1360 ☎ 446 01 56
Hiking group.

SWIMMING

-Délegyhazy lakes (South of Budapest. Train from Józsefvárosi station to Délegyhaza, then ½ an hour walk.)
-Omszki Tó (From M° red line Battyhányi take Suburban train HÉV to Budakalász station. Turn right. 30 min walk.)
-Palatinusz Strandfürdo (pi NU) (May 1-Sept 1) 7-20 h. XIII Margitsziget. Huge, lavish, modern swimming pools, gardens, lawns, hot springs, maze and nude sunbathing on roof. Action under the showers and in the toilets on 1st and 2nd floor.)
-Csillaghegyi Strandfürdö (From M° red line Battyhányi tér take the Suburban train (HÉV) to Csillaghegy station. Cold water basin, nudist part on the top of the hill.)
-Széchenyi (pi sb NU) (May 1-Sept 1) 7-20 h. XIV Allatkerti utca 11. (M° yellow line end stop Széchenyi Fürdö.) Swimming pools, nude gay sunroof. Hot water basin for action. Steam room.

CRUISING

-Népliget park (AYOR)
-Duna korzo (AYOR Rumanian R)
-Feneketlen tó melleti park (Park next to the Feneketlen tó)
-Erzsébet hid melleti park (Park near Elizabeth Bridge)
-Margit hid budai hidföjénél levö park (Park at the abutment of the Margaret Bridge in Buda)
-Városliget (City park between Széchenyi baths and Museum of Fine Arts)
-Vérmezö (near the Déli railway station. Popular
-Duna Corso (AYOR R) (along the Duna from Hotel Marriot to Erszébet- Bridge. Popular)
-Népliget a Planetárium mögött (AYOR) (Népliget Park, behind planetarium. Popular)

Debrecen ☎ 052

HEALTH GROUPS

Megyei Bör-Nemibeteggondozo Intezet Mon Wed Fri 8-17.30, Tue Thu 8-15.30, Sat 8-12.30 h
Külsövásár tér 1 ☎ 31 52 69

CRUISING

-Main Railway Station
-Thermal Baths, Leninpark (mainly OG)
-Bus station
-MAV Allómas (Railway Station) (early evening; the swimming pools at the Thermal Baths in the Leninpark are cruisy)
-Petöfi tér-infront of the main railway station.
-Déry tér-in front of the Déry Museum.
-kalvin tér-behind the Nagytemplon.

Dunaujváros ☎ 025

RESTAURANTS

Restaurant & Hotel Szélkakas (B F g h MA) 0-24 h
Lokomotiv 1a *(near city center)* ☎ 31 00 32

CRUISING

Highway 6 (g LJ) (action)

Eger ☎ 036

HOTELS

Köntös Pazio (g H)
Servita utca 29 ☎ 31 57 22

CRUISING

-Érsek kert (Park between the bus station and Basilica)

Egerszalók ☎ 036

CRUISING

-Thermal bath (g NU) (outside the town with camping facilities, cruising within the little woods)
-Ersek kert-park (between bus station and basilica)

Gyöngyös ☎ 037

HEALTH GROUPS

Bugat Pal Korhaz Bör-Nemibeteggondozo Intézet Sun-Thu 8-14 h
Bartók Béla utca 24 ☎ 31 15 40
No charge for treatment or medicine.

Miskolc ☎ 046

HEALTH GROUPS

Megyei Bör-Nemibeteggondozo Intézet Mon-Fri 7.30-17, Sat 7.30-12.30 h
I. Bajcsy-Zsilinszky utca 13 ☎ 33 65 85

CRUISING

-Centrum Department Store (around bar and WC)
-Tiszai railway station (in the restaurant's WC)
-Tapolca swimming pool (in summer)

Nyiregyhaza ☎ 042

SEX SHOPS/BLUE MOVIES

Amor Sex Shop (g)
Vay Adám krt 4-6
Intim Center (g)
Deák F. utca 36 ✉4400

CRUISING

-Railway station

Pécs ☎ 072

BARS

Adonis Gay Club
Fábián Béla köz 7 ☎ 31 63 34

CRUISING

-Szent István tér (in front of Dom)

Siófok ☎ 084

HEALTH GROUPS

Bör-Nemibeteggondozo Intézet Mon Tue Thu Fri Sat 8.30-10, Wed 8.30-13 h
Uj Rendelö Intézet ☎ 31 05 12

CRUISING

-Street behind Hotel Europa (near railway station; summer only)

Sopron ☎ 099

HEALTH GROUPS

AIDS Segély
Magyar utca 14 ☎ 33 33 99
Anonymous, free HIV testing.

Szeged ☎ 062

BARS

Hagi Restaurant (F g)
Kelemen utca *(opposite Hotel Royal)*
Viràg Café (E F g) 10-24 h
Klauzal Tér 1/Kelemen Street

HEALTH GROUPS

Börklinika Mon-Sat 8-13, Mon Thu 4.30-7.30 h
Korányi rkp. 8-10 ☎ 31 13 75

CRUISING

-Main railway station (2nd floor)
-Széchényi tér (near Main Post Office)

Székesfehervár ☎ 022

CRUISING

-Main railway station

Iceland

Island

near Artic Circle in North Atlantic Ocean

Initials: IS

Time: GMT

☎ Country Code / Access Code: 354 (no area codes) / 00

Language: Icelandic

Area: 103,000 km² / 39,768 sq mi.

Currency: 1 Icelandic Crown (ikr) = 100 Aurar

Population: 276,000

Capital: Reykjavík

Religions: 93% Protestant

Climate: The climate is moderated by the North Atlantic Current. Winters are mild and windy, summers damp and cool.

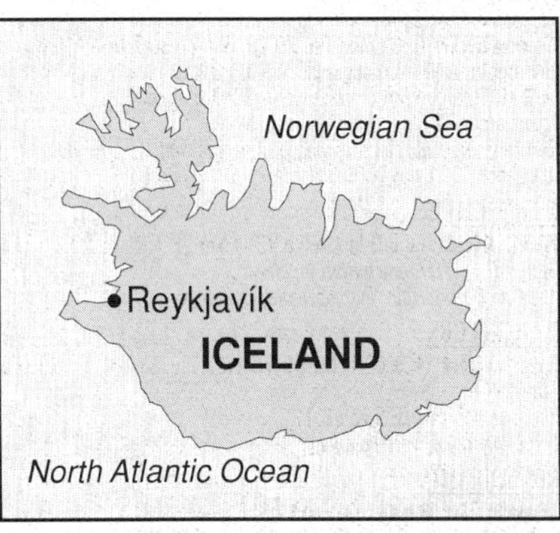

● Homosexuality between consenting adults is legal; the age of consent is 16. Meanwhile it is possible for gay couples to have their relationship registered. With this, Iceland has joined rank with the most progressive countries in Scandinavia.

✱ Einvernehmliche Homosexualität zwischen Erwachsenen ist legal, das gesetzliche Schutzalter liegt bei 16 Jahren. Inzwischen ist es homosexuellen Paaren auch in Island möglich, sich registrieren zu lassen. Damit hat das Land zu den fortschrittlichen skandinavischen Ländern aufgeholt.

▲ En Islande, l'homosexualité entre adultes consentants n'est pas un délit. La majorité sexuelle est fixée à 16 ans. Depuis peu, les couples homosexuels peuvent profiter du contrat d'union civile. L'Islande a ainsi rattrappé le retard qu'elle avait par rapport aux autres scandinaves.

☆ La homosexualidad por acuerdo entre adultos es legal, la edad de consentimiento es de 16 años. A los homosexuales islandeses les es también posible registrar legalmente su reflación. Con esto Islandia se situa al mismo nivel que sus vecinos escandinavos.

❖ L'omosessualità tra adulti consenzienti è legale. La maturità sessuale è di 16 anni. Ora anche in Islanda le coppie gay possono farsi registrare come nucleo familiare. Con questo passo l'Islanda si è allineata agli altri paesi scandinavi.

Reykjavik

GAY INFO

Reykjavik Gay Center (A b CC GLM MA YG) Office: Mon-Fri 11-12 h, Center: Mon, Thu 20-24 h, Fri 21-2 h Sat 14-18h & 21-2 h
Laugavegur 3 ✉100 *(4th floor)* ☎ 552 78 78 Fax: 552 78 20
Email: gayice@mmedia.is
Homepage: www.gayiceland.com/reykjavik
Rainbow room Café and gay library. Metting place for gay groups: AA group meets Tue 21 h, Parents' supporting group Sat 14 h, Reigious group Sun 17, Youth group Friday nights.
Samtakafréttir
PO Box 1262 ✉121
Monthly newsletter published by Samtökin '78

BARS

Næsti Bar (B CC glm MA N) 12-1 h, Fri-Sat 12-3 h
Rainbow Room (! A B CC GLM MA YG)) Mon,Thu 20-24 h, Fri 21-2 h, Sat 14-18 h & 21-2 h.
c/o Gay Center
The place to go before going to the disco
Samtökin (b G) Mon Thu 20-23, Sat 21.30-2 h
Lindargata 49/Frakkastígur ☎ 552 85 39
22 (B CC d glm MA)) 12-1, Fri-Sat 22-3 h disco
Laugavegur 22
The most popular place among gay people and the 2nd floor disco is almost 100% gay on weekends.

MEN'S CLUBS

MSC Club (CC b G LJ MA P p VS)) Sat 22-1 h
Bankastr. 11 *(Entrance from Ingólfsstr.)*
Men only, Dresscode: leather, jeans, uniforms.

DANCECLUBS

Spotlight (! B CC D GLM S YG WE) Thu 23-1 h, Fri 23-4 h, Sat 23-5 h
Hvefisgata 8-10 ☎ 562 68 12
Large gay disco, very popular.

RESTAURANTS

Jómfrúin Restaurant (CC F glm)
Lækjargata 4 ✉101 ☎ 551 01 00 Fax: 551 00 35

SAUNAS/BATHS

Sundlaug Vesturbæjar (g pi sa sb sol)
Hofsvallagata ☎ 551 50 04
Public swimming pool, but sauna frequented by gays.

GUEST HOUSES

Guesthouse Luna (CC g H)
Spitalastigur 1 ✉101 ☎ 511 25 00 Fax: 511 28 01
Email: luna@islandia.is Homepage: http://home.islandia.is/luna
Tower Guesthouse (CC g H)
Grettisgata 6 ✉101 ☎ 552 55 22 Fax: 552 55 22

APARTMENTS

Room with a View (CC g H) Laugavegur 18 ✉101 *(6th floor)* ☎ 552 72 62 Fax: 552 72 62

GENERAL GROUPS

FSS Association of Gay, Lesbian and Bisexual Students Samtökin '78
c/o Gay Center ☎ 552 78 78 Fax: 552 78 20 Email: gay@hi.is
Homepage: www.hi.is/pub/gay
Member of International Gay & Lesbian Association and of the Nordic Gay Council. Coffeeshop and gay library Mon-Thu 20-23 h, gay disco every third month. Open House also Sat 22-02 h. Foreign visitors are welcome. AA group meets Tue 21 h.

FETISH GROUPS

MSC Iceland
PO Box 53 21 ✉125 ☎ 562 12 80
Email: msc@this.is Homepage: www.this.is/msc

HEALTH GROUPS

AIDS Switchboard Wed 17-18 h
☎ 562 22 80
Health Centre
Baronsstigur 47 ☎ 552 24 00
Free treatment.
Húd og Kynsjúkdómadeild (Department of Dermatology and Veneral Diseases)
Pverholt 18 ☎ 560 23 20

CRUISING

-Oskjuhlid (hill with bushes outside the Scandic Hotel at the airport.)

India

Bhárat • Indien • Inde

Asia

Initials: IND

Time: GMT +5.5

☎ Country Code / Access Code: 91 / 00

Language: Hindi, with Devanagari script and arabic numerals; English; regional languages

Area: 3,287,590 km² / 1,269,010 sq mi.

Currency: 1 Indian Rupie (iR) = 100 Paise

Population: 984,003,683

Capital: New Dehli

Religions: 80% Hindu, 11% Moslem, various religious minorities (Sikhs, Christians, Buddhists)

Climate: Varies from tropical monsoon climate in the south to moderate in the north.

Gay sex is illegal in India. Article 377 of the Indian penal code forbids »carnal intercourse against the order of nature with man, woman or animal« . Article 294 prohibits »obscene behaviour« of any kind in public, and it seems that this law is being used by the police to arrest gays if caught cruising or having sex in public toilets. A gay movement is slowly beginning to emerge in India, as shown by the fact that gay groups are being formed and demonstrations organized.

✱ Schwule Handlungen sind in Indien illegal. Artikel 377 des indischen Strafgesetzbuches verbietet »carnal intercourse against the order of nature with man, woman or animal« (dt.: »fleischlicher Verkehr gegen die Ordnung der Natur mit Mann, Frau oder Tier«). Artikel 294 beinhaltet »obszönes Verhalten« gleich welcher Art in der Öffentlichkeit. Offensichtlich benutzt die Polizei diesen Artikel, um Schwule beim Klappensex oder Cruisen zu verhaften.
Inzwischen beginnt sich auch in Indien eine Schwulenbewegung zu bilden. Erste Demonstrationen und das Bilden schwuler Gruppen sind Anzeichen dieser Tendenz.

▲ En Inde, l'homosexualité est un délit. L'article 377 du code pénal indien condamne le «carnal intercourse against the order of nature with woman, man or animal». En français: «tout rapport charnel contre l'ordre de la nature avec une femme, un homme ou un animal». L'article 294, lui, condamne tout „comportement obscène" en public. Il semble que la police se réfère à cet article pour justifier razzias et descentes dans les toilettes publiques et les lieux de drague.
En Inde, on assiste actuellement à la naissance d'un mouvement d'émancipation homosexuelle. La création d'associations gays et de premières manifestations dans la rue en sont les premiers signes.

☆ Las relaciones sexuales entre gays son ilegales en la India. El artículo 377 del Código Penal establece que está prohibida «carnal intercourse against the order of nature with man, woman or animal» («reclación carnal con hombre, mujer o animal en contra del orden de la naturaleza»). El artículo 294 hace referencia al «comportamiento obseno» en público de cualquier tipo. Se piensa que la policia utiliza este artículo para detener a gays en los aseos públicos o cuando practican el cruising.
Entre tanto, también en la India se ha comenzado a formar un movimiento gay. Protestas y la fundación de grupos son muestras de esta tendencia.

❖ La pratica omosessuale, in India, è vietata. L'articolo 377 del codice penale indiano proibisce il „rapporto carnale contro natura con uomo, donna o animale". L'articolo 294 punisce „comportamenti osceni" di qualunque genere in pubblico. Ovviamente la polizia ne approfitta per arrestare i gay nei gabinetti e nelle altre zone d'incontro. Nel frattempo anche in India iniziano a formarsi i primi movimenti gay. Alla fine del '92 a Nuova Dehli i gay hanno manifestato, in occasione di una conferenza sull'AIDS, per i loro diritti. L'avvenimento ha ottenuto un grande spazio nella stampa nazionale

Bombay - Maharashtra

NATIONAL PUBLISHERS

Pride Publications Private Ltd
10 Riviera, 15th Road off North Avnue ✉400-054
Fax: 22 640 0128 Email: www.bombay-dost.com

GENERAL GROUPS

The Humsafar Trust
PO Box 69 13 ✉400054
☎ 618 74 76

Gulbarga - Karnataka

GAY INFO

Freedom
PO Box 80 ✉585 102

Indonesia

Southeast Asia
Initials: RI
Time: GMT +7/+8/+9
☎ Country Code / Access Code: 62 / 001 or 008
Language: Bahasa Indonesia. English as language of commerce
Area: 1,904,569 km² / 735,354 sq mi.
Currency: 1 Rupiah (Rp) = 100 Sen
Population: 212,941,810
Capital: Jakarta
Religions: 88% Moslem
Climate: Tropical climate that is hot and humid. In the highlands it's more moderate.

● Homosexual acts are legal. Homosexuality has traditionally been an integral part of Indonesian culture, and many married men also maintain sexual relations with members of the same sex. Only in the country's new, western-style middle class has homophobia taken root. There are, evidently, no laws which specifically deal with HIV or AIDS. Nevertheless, more general regulations provide for the denial of entry or even quarantine of affected persons.

✱ Homosexuelle Handlungen werden in Indonesien nicht kriminalisiert und sind traditioneller Bestandteil der indonesischen Kultur. Viele verheiratete Männer pflegen so weiterhin gleichgeschlechtliche Kontakte. Homophobie ist eher ein Kennzeichen der Mittelschicht und der Traditionalisten.
Es gibt offenbar keine indonesischen Vorschriften, die sich konkret mit HIV/AIDS befassen. Die Möglichkeit der Restriktionen gegen betroffene Personen reicht jedoch von der Einreiseverweigerung bis zur Quarantäne.

▲ En Indonésie, l'homosexualité n'est pas un délit. Elle ferait même plutôt partie de la culture indonésienne. Les hommes mariés entretiennent fréquemment des relations homosexuelles. Une certaine homophobie se fait sentir au sein de la toute nouvelle couche sociale orientée sur le mode de vie occidental. Apparemment aucune réglementation concernant le sida et la séropositivité. En revanche, restrictions concernant l'entrée ou le séjour des séropositifs et des sidéens: elles vont du refus du permis de séjour à la quarantaine.

☆ Las actividades homosexuales no están criminalizadas y forman tradicionalmente parte de la cultura indonesia. Así que muchos hombres siguen manteniendo contactos sexuales. Sin embargo, las nuevas clases medias del país, más occidentalizadas, se muestran cada vez más homófobas. Según nuestros datos no hay reglamentación que se ocupe concretamente del HIV/SIDA. Las posibilidades de restricciones contra personas afectadas van desde la prohibición de entrada al país hasta la cuarentena.

❖ Gli atti omosessuali sono legali. L'omosessualità è parte integrante delle tradizioni culturali dell'Indonesia. Anche gli uomini sposati mantengono delle relazioni sessuali con persone dello stesso sesso. Soltanto nella nuova classe media di gusti occidentali, l'omofobia sta aumentando. Non ci sono ne leggi ne regolamenti che trattano in modo concreto il problema AIDS. Persone infette si aspettino un rifiuto del permesso d'entrata nel paese o l'isolamento se già ci si trovano.

NATIONAL GAY INFO

Buku Seri IPOOS
PO Box 7631/JKBTN, ✉11470 Jakarta
Bimonthly publication of IPOOS. Approximately 52 pages, in Indonesian. Copy US$ 5, annual subscription 30. Free personal ads in Indonesian and English.

Gaya Nusantara Meeting 1st Sun 10-12.30 h
Jalan Mulyosari Timur 46, Surabaya, East Java ✉60112
☎ (0)31-593 49 24 Fax: 0)31-593 90 70
Publishes Gaya Nusantara, a monthliy publication with 60 pages, in Indonesian with English summary. Copy US$ 5, annual subscirption US$ 60- Free personal ads.

Indonesian Gay Society (IGS) Meeting 2nd Sun 10.30, Karaoke night last Sat 20, Phone hours 16-20 h
PO Box 36/YKBS, Yogyakarta 55281 ☎ *(0274) 620 17 (9-13 h)*
Publishes Jaka-Jaka.

Jaka-Jaka IGS, PO Box 36/YKBS ✉55281
Bimonthly publication of IGS. 20 pages, in Indonesian. Copy US$ 3, annual subscription 18. Free personal ads.

Amboina - Maluku ☎ 0911

GENERAL GROUPS

GAYa Intim PO Box 1102 ✉97011

Balikpapan - Kalimantan Timur

CRUISING

-Monumen, Paradise (Suprapto Street g tv 21-? h)
-Freedom Field (Lapangan Merdeka) (tv)
-TC (The Club) (Stal Kuda Street, Sat 23-? h

Bandung - Jawa Barat ☎ 022

BARS

Marabu Club
Jalan Suniaraja/Jalan Braga

Pub Papandayan Hotel (B g)
Jalan Gatot Subroto

Tropicana Night Club (B D g MA)
Jalan Eickmann/Jalan Chiampleas

DANCECLUBS

LA Dreampalace (B D g) Wed GLM
Jalan Asia-Africa (Plaza)

Lipstick (B D g)
Alun Alun

HOTELS

Istana (AC B F g H MA OS pi)
Jalan Lembong 21-44 ☎ 43 30 25
All rooms have AC, telephone, fridge, priv. bath. Rates on request.

Kumala Panghegar (AC B D F g H MA OS pi)
Jalan Asia Afrika 140 ☎ 521 41
First class hotel centrally located, 5 km from the airport.

Panghegar (AC B F H pi sa WO)
Jalan Merdeka 2 ☎ 43 07 88
Convenient location, 20 min to the airport.

Savoy Homann Panghegar Heritage (AC B F g H MA OS pi)
Jalan Asia-Afrika 112 ✉40262 ☎ 43 22 44 Fax: 43 61 87
Email: homann@panghegaronline:com
Homepage: www.asiatravel.com/savoyhoman

GENERAL GROUPS

Gaya Priangan
PO Box 1819, ✉40018 ☎ 250 43 25

HEALTH GROUPS

Sidikara Foundation
☎ 30 06 19
AIDS service.

Yayasan PRIAngan
PO Box 1819, ✉40018 ☎ 250 43 25

CRUISING

-Taman Badak Putih (G r) (Park with statue of a white rhino, near city hall, Jalan Meredeka, every night)
-Alun-alun Bandung (G r) (Town square, every night)
-Bandung Indah Plaza (G) (Third floor, late afternoon)

Banjarmasin - Kalimantan Selatan ☎ 0511

DANCECLUBS

Bobo Discotik (g tv) Tue night
Matt Discotik (g tv) Fri night
Shinta Discotik (g tv) Wed night

Batam - Riau

BARS

Club 5-0 (G)
New Holiday Hotel ✉29432
Gay meeting-place.

Golden Gate Discotik (glm)
Nagoya Plaza Hotel

Regina Palace Discotiq (B D G)
Best Sat Sun. Discreet.

Bogor - Jawa Barat

BARS

Karaoke Mulia (B glm) Sat
Entry Rp 3,500

GENERAL GROUPS

New Friendship Club
PO Box 2055 ✉16020

CRUISING

-Shopping centers and public park and garden

Denpasar - Bali ☎ 0361

GENERAL GROUPS

Gaya Dewata 9.30-15.30 h
Jalan Belimbing Gg Y N°4 ✉80231 ☎ 22 26 20

HEALTH GROUPS

Yayasan Citra Usadha Indonesia 9.30-15.30 h
Jalan Belimbing Gg Y N° 4 ✉80231 ☎ 222 620 Fax: 235 982
(ATTN: Dr. Tuti Parwati)

Gianyar - Bali

GENERAL GROUPS

Gaya Dewata-Gianyar Tromol Pos 9 ✉80502

Jakarta ☎ 021

BARS

Jalan Jalan (B d glm stv)
36/F Nenara Imperium Building, Jalan Rasuna Said, *Kuningan*
☎ 835 39 79
JJ DoIt (B F g) 11-5 h
JL. Tanah Abang Timur II No. 16 *(next door to Tanamur discotheque)*
Music Room (B glm) 21-3 h
Lapangan Banteng *(Borobudur Inter Continental Hotel)* ☎ 380 55 55

DANCECLUBS

Klimax Discotheque (B D G r) Sun 22-2 h
Jalan Gayah Mada
New Moonlight discotheque (B D glm MA)
Jalan Hayam Wuruk 120/Jalan Mangga Besar *(Barat, Kota)*
☎ 600 21 62
Sofian Hotel Diskotik (B D GLM) Night & day.
Jalan Saharjo
Stardust (B D g) night & day.
Jalan Pangeran Jayakarta/Jalan Hayam Wuruk *(Jayakarta Tower Building) Very Popular.*
Tanamur Discotheque (B D glm r) Very gay Tue Thu
Jalan Tanah Abang Timur *(Central Jakarta)*
Very popular. Gay section at rear of the dance floor.
Voilà (B D g) Gay only Sun, 21-2 h
Jalan Rasuna Said, Gedung Patra Jasa *(Patra Jasa Building 4th floor)*

RESTAURANTS

Cafe Batavia (B g MA S) 0-24 h
Taman Fatahillah ☎ 691 55 31
Seafood and Western cuisine.
Jakarta International Cafe (F g) 12-23
JL. Jaksa

MASSAGE

Julian's place (G MA msg)
Jalan Cikajong 56, Block Q *Kebayoran Baru, Jakarta Selatan 12170*

GENERAL GROUPS

Ikatan Persaudaraan Orang-orang Sehati (IPOOS)/Gaya Betawi Mon Wed-Fri 9-18 h
PO Box 7631/JKBTN ✉11470 ☎ 566 05 89
Persekutuan WGL Jakarta
c/o Menteng Beauty Salon, Jalan Gondangdia Lama 28, *Jakarta Pusat 10300*

HEALTH GROUPS

Hotline AIDS Mitra Indonesia Mon-Fri 15-20 h
Jalan Kebon Kacang 9 N°78, Jakarta Pusat ✉10240
☎ 310 08 55 Fax: 310 08 55

CRUISING

-Lapangan Banteng (g R RT) (Park across Hotel Barobudur)
-Taman Suropati (G r) (Park on Jalan Diponegoro, every night)
-Atrium Senen (Monday Atrium) Senen Triangle in front of Studio 21.
-Block M Plaza and Terminal (Kebayoran Bari district)
-Big and Beautiful Market, Block M(Pasaraya Big and Beautiful Blok M) Bathroom on the ground floor, entrance from the parking area. MA day & night)
-Sogo (Plaza Indonesia/Grand Hyatt Hotel/Hotel Indonesia circle. Day & Night)
-Ancol swimming pool (under the waterfall Sun)
-Art Market (Pasar Seni) 20-23 h
-Tugu Senen/Gelanggang (Senen Monument/Arena) R
-Grand Duta/Mulya Agung Movie Theater (Jalan Kramat Raya/Jalan Kwitang) R
-Senen Bus Terminal (R) Si Unyil WC.
-Dangdut Senen (beside the Monday arena opposite bus terminal. R
-Cililitan (outside old bus terminal. Only Sat night!)
-Cinere Movie House (Gedung Bioskop Cinere) Night.
-Ciputat-Sahara Movie House (Gedung Bioskop Sahara) (in the courtyard)
-Sarinah Shopping Centre (ground floor, at McDonalds)

Jayapura - Irian Jaya ☎ 0976

CRUISING

-Irian Street (g) (in front of shopping complex)
-A. Yani Street (g) (in front of Bintang Mas Store)
-Imbi Park (Taman Imbi) (g tv)
(town centre)
-Taman Pelabuhan Kapal (Dermagea) Park (g tv)

Jember - Jawa Timur

CRUISING

-Town Square (alun-alun) (nightime tv)
-Small restaurant (warung) (in alley in front of Station 22-? g)

Kebumen - Jawa Tengah ☎ 0287

GENERAL GROUPS

GO • Gay Organisation PO Box 109 ✉54301
☎ 611 00
(after 18 h, ATTN: Pras)

Kediri - Jawa Barat

DANCECLUBS

Sky Disc (B D g)
c/o Hotel Merdeka
Best Tue Sat.

GENERAL GROUPS

GYSKA
PO Box 202 ✉64101

CRUISING

-Town Square (alun-alun).

Kuta - Bali ☎ 0361

BARS

Black Shadow (B G MA) Mon-Sat 19-? h
Gelael Top Plaza *(Jl. Legan, near New Bounty Mall)*
Café Luna (B g OS YG)
Jalan Legian
Popular after midnight.
Goa 2001 (B d F g MA R) 20-2 h
Jalan Legian *(Seminyak)*
Very popular meeting place before going on to the disco's. Best after 23 h.

Hulu. Cafe (B G MA S STV YG) 17-1 h closed Mondays
J.L. Sahadewa 23 A *(Legian)* ☎ 75 68 48
Show nights Wed, Fri, Sat, Sun.

DANCECLUBS

Double Six 66 (B D glm pi)
(Seminyak) ☎ 73 12 66
Gado-Gado (B glm) Sun Tue Wed Fri nights.
Jalan Dhyana Pura Seminyak ☎ 73 09 55
Route 66 (B G R S YG) Sat 23-4 h
(Located directly at the beach)

RESTAURANTS

La Lucciolla Restaurant & Beach Club (B F g N OS YG) 8-19 h
Jalan Oberoi *(at Pura Petitenget Beach)* ☎ 26 10 47
Italian cuisine.

BODY & BEAUTY SHOPS

Eddy's Hair & Beauty Salon (g)
Jalan Raya Kartika Plaza ☎ 539 29
Klhan Hairdressing Salon (! AC g msg) 9-20 h
JL. Tangkuban Perahu No. Ruko 3G, Kerobokan ☎ 730 702
Complete hairstyling & Cremebath (hair/neck treatment with upper body msg) or Lulur (full-body msg) & info about gay scene.

TRAVEL & TRANSPORT

Hanafi
Poppies Lane I, 77 ✉80361 ☎ 75 64 54 Fax: 75 25 61
Pottery shop and travel services.

HOTELS

Asana Santhi (G H)
Jalan Tegalwangi 18 ✉80361 ☎ 75 12 81 Fax: 75 26 41
Rates from US$ 30.
Bunga Seminyak Cottage (AC H NG pi wh)
Jalan Camplung Tanduk, Seminyak ☎ 512 39 Fax: 529 05
20 minutes to the airport. 25 minutes to Denpasar. All rooms with bath, telephone, TV, Mini Bar. Rates on request.
C-Line Gallery and Art Café (A B F g H NG OS)
Kartika Plaza 33 ☎ 512 85
Between Santika Beach and Bali Bintang Hotel.
Resor Seminyak (bf H NG)
Jalan Lasmana, Seminyak ✉80361 ☎ 73 08 14

APARTMENTS

Villas. The (AC cc glm H msg pi)
Jalan Raya Seminyak 56 ☎ 730 840 Fax: 730 840
Rates for single $ 115-145, 3 bedroom villa $ 190-250.

SWIMMING

-Beach south of Oberoi Hotel in Legian (g R)
-Beach north of where Jalan Pantai meets the beach
-Kuta beach (NU) (Northern part, be discreet)

CRUISING

-Lapangan Puputan (G r tv) (between Surapati & Veteran Streets. 18-23 h Sat later)

Malang - Jawa Timur ☎ 0341

GENERAL GROUPS

IGAMA Meeting 3rd Sun 19 h
Jalan Raya Sumbersari 254-C ✉65145 *(c/o Yoseph Bridal Salon & Dance Group)*

CRUISING

-Town Square (alun-alun) (nest to Lippobank. G)
-Next to Station (tv G)
-Next to Brawijaya Museum (Wed night)
-Arjosari Terminal (Sat night)

Manado - Sulawesi Utara

CRUISING

-Pasar 45 (station and terminal complex) (g tv) (21-? h)
-Near Balai Wartawan & Arta Pusara Bank (nighttime)
-People's Unity Park (Taman Imbi) (g tv) (Centre of town)

Medan - Sumatera Utara ☎ 061

CAFES

TD (Tembakau Deli)
Jalan Tembakakau Deli/Balia Kota *(near Deli Plaza & Darma Deli Natour Disco-near town center)*
Lots of gay men.

DANCECLUBS

Dynasty (B D glm)
Jalan Imam Bonjol 17 *(Danau Toba International Hotel)*
Exclusive rendezvous spot for gay & hetero.
S'carpark (glm)
Istana Plaza *(main floor)*
Entry Sat Rp 10,000.

MASSAGE

Sejahtera
Jalan S Parman
(tunanetra) Many gay masseurs & meeting point.

GENERAL GROUPS

Gaya Deli
PO Box 25/Medan-Baru ✉20154

SWIMMING

-Swimming pool at the Tiara Hotel (Jalan Cut Mutia Rp 10,000)

CRUISING

-Lampangan Merdeka, Jalan Blai Kota (R) (evening only)
-Danau Toba International Hotel (lobby, coffeeshop and swimming pool)
-Olympia Plaza (top floor)

Mojokerto - Jawa Timur

CRUISING

-Town Square (alun-alun) (next to the military police building. Nighttime. G)

Padang - Sumatera Barat

CRUISING

-Jalan Samudera Beach (g)

Palembang - Sumatera Selatan ☎ 0711

CRUISING

-Five Days & Five Nights Monument (Tugu Lima Hari Lima Malam) (nights)
-Nusa Indah Park (Taman) (nights)
-(Taman) Talang Semut Park (Best Sat night)

Pasuruan - Jawa Timur

RESTAURANTS

Pasar Poncol g after 21.30 h
Nusantara Street *(beside Himalaja Cinema)*

SAUNAS/BATHS

Banyubiru baths Sun daytime.
(17 kilometers from Pasuruan)

CRUISING

-North Town Square (alun-alun) (night, tv G)

Pekanbaru - Riau ☎ 0761

GENERAL GROUPS

Gaya Siak
c/o Yayasan Utama, Jalan Diponegoro 8, ✉28111

HEALTH GROUPS

Yayasan Utama
Jalan Diponegoro 8 ✉28111 ☎ 376 45 Fax: 376 45

CRUISING

-Central Market
-Circle in front of Taman kaca Mayang
-Senapelan Plaza
-Taman Hiburan Gelora

Salatiga - Jawa Tengah

CRUISING

-Salatiga Plaza (in front of and across the street, every night, best on Sat night)
-Jalan Sudirman (Sat night)

Sanur - Bali ☎ 0361

DANCECLUBS

Number-One (B D g p S WE YG)
Jalan Batu Jimbar ☎ 880 97

Semarang - Jawa Tengah ☎ 024

HOTELS

Hotel Candi Indah (AC B f H NG)
Jalan Dr. Wahidin 112 ☎ 31 25 14 Fax: 31 25 15

GENERAL GROUPS

Gay Semarang
Jalan Ngesrep Timur V/46 ✉50000

CRUISING

-Simpang Lima (G r) (next to the Citraland building site, also generally on the square)
-Jalan Menteri Supeno (G r TV) (Along the street)
-Matahari Department Store (G R) (near the juice bar)

Sidoarjo - Jawa Timur

CRUISING

-Town Square (alun-alun) (near the public telephones beside the Mahkota cinema and the street next to it. Sat night best. G)

Surabaya - Jawa Timur

BARS

Bonog's African Jungle Bar (B glm) Sat best
Sheraton Hotel, Jalan Embong Malang

Desperado Mexican Bar (B glm) Fri Sat best
Shangri-La Hotel, Jalan Mayjen Sungkono

DANCECLUBS

Station Top Ten Fri Sat best
6/F Plaza Tunjungan, Jalan Tunjungan

SHOWS

Red Top Cabaret (B glm S) Sat best
Jalan Semut

GENERAL GROUPS

DPD Hiwaria MKGR Ja-Tim
Jalan Kenikir 7 ✉60131 ☎ 535 05 17
Gaya Baya Meeting 2nd Sun 18h
Jalan Dupak Bangunrejo I/19 ✉60179
Gaya Nusantara (GN)
Jalan Mulyosari Timur 46 ✉60112 ☎ 593 49 24
Fax: 593 90 70 Email: doetomo@server.indo.net.id
Persekutuan Hidup Damai
Jalan Ngagel Rejo Kidul 113 ✉60245 ☎ 588 418
Perwakos (Persatuan Waria Kotamadya Surabaya) (G TV)
Jalan Kanginan III/10 ✉60131 ☎ 517 068
Yayasan Kemanusiaan
Jalan Jojoran Gg 3 Perintis N° 10 ✉60285 ☎ 594 10 75

CRUISING

-Kalifornia (G r tv) (Ketabang Kali. Along the entrance bridge of the Plaza Surabaya complex, after 22 h. Best Thu Sat.)
-Taman Remaja Surabaya (G r TV) (Amusement Park next to Surabaya Mall, Jalan Kusuma Bangsa. Thu 21-22.30 open-air drag show.)
-Texas, Terminal Joyoboyo (G r RT tv) (Along the river at the public transport terminal. Best Sat.)
-Bambu Runcing or SP (espay) (g R) (Park next to Surabaya Post building, Jalan Panglima Sudirman)
-Irian Barat Street (nighttime)
-Tunjungan Plaza (shopping centre, evening)

Tanjungkarang-Telukbetung - Lampung

DANCECLUBS

Oya Discotheque Sat night
Jalan Jos Suarso, Sukaraja *(Telukbetung district)*
Rp 6,000.

CRUISING

-Around the monument in front of the Golden Movie House (Bioskop Golden) (Tanjungkarang district. Nights)
-Between Jalan Pemuda and the main crossroads (Tanjungkarang district nights.)
-Near King Supermarket (Tanjunkarung Plaza, days, YG)

Tegal - Jawah Tengah

CRUISING

-Tegal Station (Stasiun) (night, in front)
-Mosque Square (east side in front of Dewa Cinema, night)
-In front of Susana Baru Hotel (night).

Ubud - Bali ☎ 0361

CAFES

Prada-Cafe & Guest House (AC B bf CC F GLM H MA OS) JL. Kajeng 80571 Glanyar ☎ 975 122
High standard, US$ 55/night (incl. bf.).

HOTELS

Bali Spirit Hotel & Spa (B bf G H msg NU OS pi)
(At the end of the Post Office Road) ☎ 97 40 13 Fax: 97 40 12

Ujungpandang - Sulawesi Selatan ☎ 0411

BARS

Donald's Canteen (B g) 11-22 h
Karunrung
Losari beach pub & restaurant (B F g)
Makassar Golden Hotel

DANCECLUBS

Belopa disco (D g) Sat night, Sun morning
Marannu city Hotel, S. Hasunuddin Street
Jumbo Roller-Disco (g) Thu Sat night
Timor Street
Zig Zag Disco
Makassar Golden Hotel

GENERAL GROUPS

Gaya Celebes • Lembayung Celebes • Saensasi Dolls Mon 22-2 h
PO Box 1309 90013 ✉90000 ☎ 51 09 43
Various organizations including AIDS service.

HEALTH GROUPS

Hotline AIDS'PUS-Triple M' 10-16 h
PKBI, Jalan Landak Baru 55 ✉90135 ☎ 871 051

CRUISING

-Karebosi Field (g tv) (nighttime)

Yogyakarta ☎ 0274

BARS

Borobodur Bar & Restaurant (B g MA r S) 13-1 h
Jalan Passar Kembang 17 *(Near railway station)*
THR Purawisata (STV) Show Thu
Jalan Brigjen Katamso

RESTAURANTS

Legian Restaurant (b F g)
Jalan Perwakilan
Garden restaurant with nice atmosphere.
Mirota (B F g)
Jalan F.M. Noto *(Kotabaru)*
Indonesian fast food.
Panca Ria Terrace (b F g) best after 21 h
Jalan Malioboro *(in front of Mutiara Hotel)*
Pesta Perak (b F g)
Jalan Tentara Pelajar
Indonesian cuisine.

HOTELS

Dusun Jogja Village Inn (AC CC F glm H MA pi)
JL. Menukan N° 5 ✉55153 *(in front of Radio Yasika FM-bus N°2 from bus Station)* ☎ 37 30 31 Fax: 38 22 02
Email: jvigecko@indo.net.id Homepage: www.jvidusun.co.id
Stylish & full of character. Good food including vegetarian. Good selection of movies and music. Manager Paul can provide additional info.

GENERAL GROUPS

Indonesian Gay Society (IGS)
PO Box 36/YKBS ✉55281 ☎ 56 20 17

HEALTH GROUPS

Lentera
PKBI, Jalan Tentara Rakyat Mataram Gg kapas Jt. ✉*55231*
☎ 58 67 67 Fax: 58 67 67 Email: lentera@ins.healthnet.org

CRUISING

-Alun-Alun Utara (North Square, in front of Sultan Palace)
-In front of Gedong Agung, Benteng Vredeberg & Seni Sono
- Marlioboa Shopping Center

Ireland

Éire

West Europe in North Atlantic Ocean

Initials: IRL

Time: GMT

☎ Country Code / Access Code: 353 / 00

Language: Irish (Gaelic) and English

Area: 70,284 km^2 / 21,137 sq mi.

Currency: 1 Irish Pound (Ir = 100 Pence)

Population: 3,619,480

Capital: Dublin / Baile Atha Cliath

Religions: 93% Roman Catholic, 3% Anglican

Climate: Moderate maritime climate, that is modified by the North Atlantic Current. Winters are mild, summers are cool. There's a consistent humidity and it's overcast about half the time.

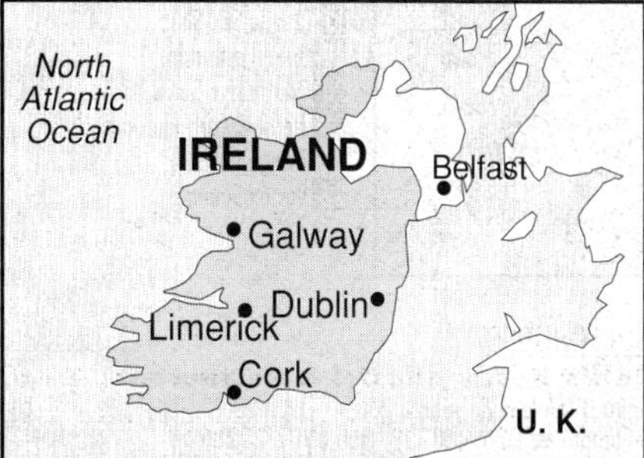

● Ireland lies on the edge of Europe, which does however not mean, that its population is especially backward. In contrast to the British mainland the conditions in Ireland are rather progressive. The age of consent is 17 for everbody; there is no special legislation for the military; anti-dicriminatory laws are in discussion. Main protagonist of these and more overall social modernisations is the president of Ireland Mary Robinson.
By the way: the gay-lesbian newspaper of Ireland, the Gay Community News, is generously supported by the Irish state.

✸ Irland liegt am Rande des europäischen Kontinents. Das bedeutet aber nicht, daß seine Bewohner besonders rückständig seien. Im Gegensatz zu den benachbarten Briten sind bei den Iren die Verhältnisse recht fortschrittlich: das Schutzalter liegt einheitlich bei 17 Jahren, für das Militär gelten keine Sondergesetze, Anti-Diskriminierungsbestimmungen sind in der Diskussion.
Gallionsfigur all dieser und weiterer allgemeingesellschaftlicher Modernisierungen war die ehemalige Präsidentin Irlands, Mary Robinson. Übrigens: Die schwul-lesbische Zeitung des Landes, die Gay Community News wird großzügigerweise vom irischen Staat unterstützt.

▲ L'Irlande est le pays le plus excentré au sein de l'Union européenne, ce qui ne veut pas dire que l'on y est en retard par rapport aux autres. En comparaison avec leurs voisins britanniques, les Irlandais sont plutôt à la page: majorité sexuelle à 16 ans pour tous (homos et hétéros), armée assez tolérante, législation anti-discriminatoire en préparation. Tous ces changements sont dûs à l'action et l'influence de Mary Robinson, la Présidente de la République. Ah oui: le Gay Community News, le seul journal gay du pays, est généreusement subventionné par l'Etat!

☆ Irlanda está situada al límite del continente europeo, pero esto no quiere decir que sus habitantes tengan una mentalidad cerrada. En comparación con su vecino Inglaterra, la situación en Irlanda es bastante progresiva. La edad de consentimiento es de 17 años, independientemente de la orientación sexual. No existen regulaciones especiales para el servicio militar y la introducción de leyes contra la discriminación gay se está discutiendo. A próposito: La revista gay-lesbiana del país, la *Gay Community News*, está subvencionada generosamente por el estado irlandés.

❖ L'Irlanda è situata ai limiti del continente europeo. Ciò non significa però che i suoi abitanti abbiano una mentalità arretrata. Contrariamente ai vicini del Regno Unito gli irlandesi sono progrediti: la maturità sessuale è di 17 anni per tutti, per il servizio militare non esistono regolamenti particolari e finalmente sono in discussione nuove leggi contro la discriminazione dei gay. Mary Robinson, il presidente irlandese, è stata la promotrice di questi ed altre modernizzazioni sociali. A proposito, il gay community news, il giornale omosessuale nazionale, viene generosamente sovvenzionato dallo stato.

NATIONAL GAY INFO

Gaeilgeori Aerach Aontaithe
c/o Roy O'Gealbhain, 10 Fownes Street, Dublin 2
Irish Speaking Gay Group.

Gay Community News
6 South William Street, Dublin 2 ☎ (01) 671 09 39 or
☎ 671 90 76. Fax: 671 35 49. E-mail gcn@tinet.ie
Irelands gay and lesbian magazine. Monthly free at gay and lesbian venues. Featuring news and events.

Irish Names Quilt
53 Parnell Sqare, Dublin 1 ☎ (01) 873 37 99

MSC Ireland Meeting: last Fri at The George, Dublin
Hirshfeld Centre, 10 Fownes Street
Leather, denim, uniform club for men who like their men to be men.

SPARTACUS Britain + Ireland
c/o Bruno Gmünder Verlag, PO Box 61 01 04, D-10921 Berlin
☎ +49/30/6150030 Fax: 615 91 34
E-mail: Spaberlin@aol.com

Baltimore ☎ 028

HOTELS

Rolf's Holiday Hostel & Restaurant „Café Art" (bf CC glm H)
☎ & Fax: 202 89
12 double rooms with shared bath and WC. Rates IR£ 12.50 per person in double room, 7-9 in dormitory.

Beara ☎ 027

PRIVATE ACCOMODATION

Island's End B&B (bf F glm H OS)
Rossmackowen, Beara *(Near Glengarriff, Bantry Bay)* ☎ 600 40
Fax: 600 40
Very friendly B&B. 5 double rooms with spectacular views over the sea and mountains. Rates Ir£ 15 p.p./night (bf incl.) Shower/bath in the hall. Dinner available.

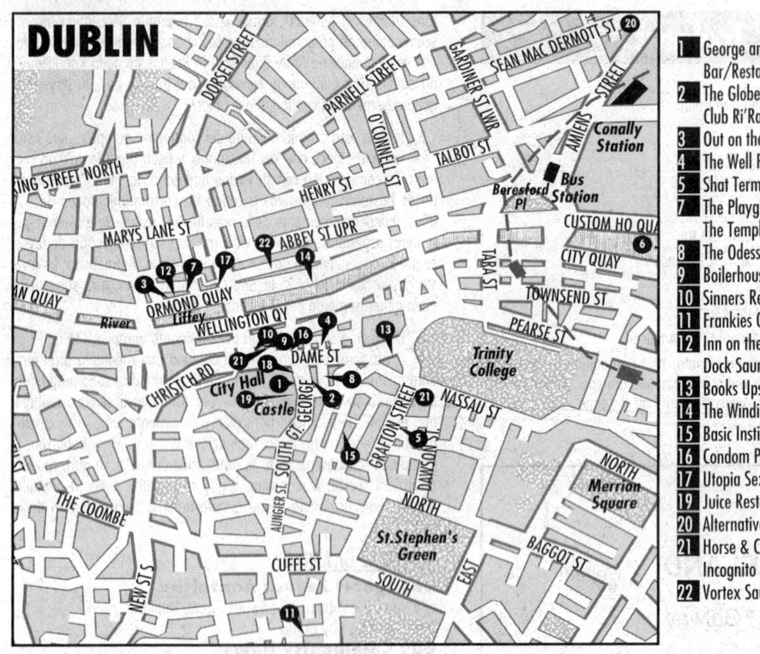

1 George and Block Nightclub Bar/Restaurant
2 The Globe Bar Club Ri'Ra Danceclub
3 Out on the Liffey Bar
4 The Well Fed Café
5 Shat Term Solutions
7 The Playground Party in The Temple of Sound Danceclub
8 The Odessa Restaurant
9 Boilerhouse Sauna
10 Sinners Restaurant
11 Frankies Guest House
12 Inn on the Liffey Guest House Dock Sauna
13 Books Upstairs Book Shop
14 The Winding Stair Book Shop
15 Basic Instincts Sex Shop
16 Condom Power Sex Shop
17 Utopia Sex Shop
19 Juice Restaurant
20 Alternative Guest House
21 Horse & Carriage Guest Hotel Incognito Sauna
22 Vortex Sauna

Cork ☎ 021

GAY INFO

Lesbian & Gay Resource Group
8 South Main Street *(at The Other Place)* ☎ 27 84 70

Other Place. The (Lesbian & Gay Community Centre)
8 South Main Street *(Entrance via Other Side Bookshop)*
☎ 27 84 70 E-mail lesgay@indigo.ie

BARS

Loafers Bar (! A B GLM MA N OS) Mon-Sun 17-23.30 h
26 Douglas Street ☎ 31 16 12 *Beer garden.*

CAFÉS

Other Side Café. The (b D F GLM MA) Café Mon-Fri 10.30-17.30, Club Fri Sat 23-2.30 h, 1st Fri women only
8 South Main Street ☎ 27 84 70

Quay Co-op Restaurant and Wholefood Shop (F glm) Mon-Sat 9-19 h
24 Sullivans Quay ☎ 31 76 60

DANCECLUBS

Other Place Club. The (B D GLM MA s) Fri-Sat 23-2.30
8 South Main Street ☎ 27 84 70

BOOK SHOPS

Other Side Bookshop. The (GLM) Mon-Sat 11-17.30
8 South Main Street ☎ 27 84 70

HOTELS

☛ also Skibbereen and Beara, West Cork

GUEST HOUSES

Rolf's Holiday Hostel & Restaurant (A B bf CC f glm H MA OS) All year
Baltimore ☎ 028/ 20289 Fax: 028/ 20289
Seaside resort with sailing, fishing, waterskiing etc.

Roman House (bf CC GLM H)
3 St. John's Terrace, Upper John Street ☎ 50 36 06
Small, comfortable guest house. Each room with TV and tea / coffee making facilities. Rates £ 18-20 (bf incl.)

HEALTH GROUPS

AIDS Helpline Cork Mon-Fri 10-17, Tue 19-21 h
☎ 27 66 76

Dublin ☎ 01

● Dublin is picturesquely situated on the side of the river Liffey. With its population of nearly 1 million, over a quarter of the whole irish population live in its borders. Around the city center, which is remarkably small, numerous suburbs are grouped, of which, roughly spoken, the southern ones are the more prosperous, the northern ones the poorer. This smallstructured community also shows in the gay scene, which can be calles very young and lively. Mixed parties are becoming more and more popular. All venues can easily be reached by foot.

✸ Dublin liegt malerisch an den Ufern des Liffey und beherbergt im Großraum mit fast 1 Million Einwohnern über ein Viertel aller Einwohner Irlands.
Die Stadt hat ein bemerkenswert kleines Zentrum, um das sich zahlreiche Vororte herum gruppieren. Dabei kann grob gesagt werden, daß die südlichen die wohlhabenderen, die nördlichen die ärmeren sind.

Irelands largest, best and most professional Sauna & Leisure Club for men

1, Great Strand Street, (at Capel St Bridge),
Dublin 1, Ph: 00-353-1-8780898.

Daily from 13.00 hrs – 0.500 am
Fri 13.00 hrs – Mon 05.00 am (64 hrs open!)

Café / Wine Bar
5 floors of cruising space

- **Sauna / Steam room**
- **Fantasy Dungeon**
- **Mirror Rooms**
- **40 private rest cubicles**
- **Maize & Pleasure Glories**

Visit our Website at
Basic-Instincts.com

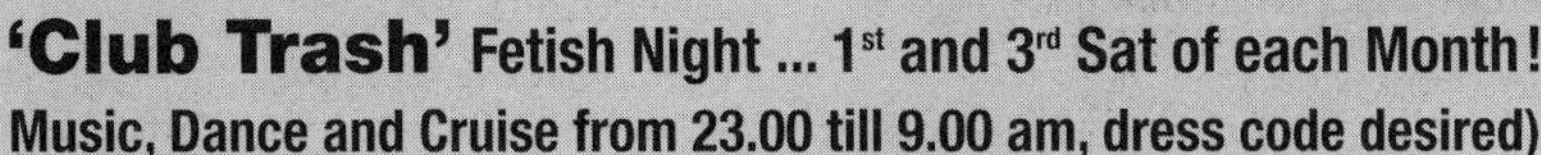

'Club Trash' Fetish Night ... 1st and 3rd Sat of each Month!
Music, Dance and Cruise from 23.00 till 9.00 am, dress code desired)

BASIC INSTINCTS LTD

56, South William Street • Dublin 2 • Tel. 00-353-1-6712223

City Centre location • Open 7 days

Irelands best adult / fetish store Leather / Rubberwear
Greeting Cards / Novelties
Huge Magazine / Video Section (mail order service)
Designer Underwear / Swimwear (serving all your needs)

Die kleinteilige Struktur setzt sich in der schwulen Szene fort, die als sehr jung und lebendig bezeichnet werden kann. Gemischte Parties werden hier immer populärer. Alle Etablissements können leicht zu Fuß erreicht werden.

▲ Dublin est située sur la Liffey. Avec son million d'habitants (un quart de la population du pays), Dublin a su conserver de son charme pittoresque. Le centre ville est assez petit: Dublin, c'est principalement des districts périphériques avec, au nord, la banlieue pauvre et, au sud, les quartiers riches. Le milieu gay est lui aussi de petite taille, bien que très jeune et très vivant. Les fêtes et soirées „mixtes" sont de plus en plus courrues. Tous les lieux gays peuvent être atteints à pied.

☆ Dublín, situada a orillas del río Liffey, cuenta junto con su periferia con casi un millon de habitantes, que supone un 1/4 del total de la población irlandesa. El centro de la ciudad es sorprendentemente pequeño y en sus alrededores se agrupan númerosos barrios. Se dice que los del sur son más ricos, mientras los norteños suelen ser más pobres. Esta estructura dispersa se refleja también en el ambiente gay, que se puede describir como joven y vivaz. Las fiestas mixtas gozan de gran pópularidad. A todos los sitios de ambiente se puede llegar andando.

❖ Dublino, situata pittorescamente sulla riva del Liffey, ospita, includendo la sua periferia, quasi un milione di abitanti, oltre un quarto degli abitanti del paese. La città possiede un piccolo ma interessante centro storico intorno al quale si raggruppano numerosi quartieri periferici. Di questi quelli meridionali sono benestanti mentre quelli settentrionali sono più poveri. Questa struttura si riflette anche nell'ambiente gay, che può essere definito giovane e spumeggiante. Le feste miste sono sempre più in voga. Tutti i locali sono situati nel centro e sono raggiungibili a piedi.

GAY INFO

Gay Switchboard Dublin Sun-Fri 20-22, Sat 15.30-18 h
Carmichael House, North Brunswick Street ✉D 7 ☎ 872 1055
Email: GSD@iol.ie Homepage: www.iol.ie/~gsd/

TOURIST INFO

Dublin Tourist Centre
Suffolk Street ✉D2 ☎ 605 77 77 Fax 605 77 87.

BARS

George and Block Nightclub (! AC B CC D F G lj S STV TV W) Wed-Mon 10.30-2.30, Tue -23.30 h
89 South Great George Street ✉D 2 ☎ 478 2983

Globe. The (AC B f glm W YG) Mon-Sat 12-23.30, Sun 16-23 h
11 South Great George Street ✉D 2 ☎ 671 1220

Out On The Liffey (AC B D G GLM MA STV) Mon-Fri 10.30-0.30, Sat Sun -1.30 h
27 Upper Ormond Quay, ✉7 *(Over Capel St. Bridge, besides Ormond Hotel)* ☎ 872 2480

CAFES

Well Fed Café. The (A AC F glm MA W) Mon-Sat 12-21 h
Resource Centre, 6 Crow Street, ✉D 2 *(Temple Bar area)* ☎ 667 2234

DANCECLUBS

Absolut Paradise (! AC B D GLM MA S WE YG) Sat 22.30-2.30 h
The Tivoli Theater, Francis Street, Christchurch ✉2
☎ 353/405 53005
Admission Ir£ 8 (members 6). National and international live entertainment.

Club Ri'ra (B D f glm YG) Mon 23.30-3 h (glm)
Dame Court ✉D 2 *(Behind The Globe bar)* ☎ 671 1220

Flirt at the Tivoli, Tivoli Theatre (AC B D GLM MA S WE YG) Sat 21:30-02:30h
Francis Street ☎ 405/53005

Kitchen. The (B D GLM)
East Sussex Street ✉D 2 ☎ 677 6178

Playground in The Temple of Sound (B D GLM MA s YG) Sun, Mon, holiday 22.30-? h
Ormond Hotel, Ormond Quay ✉D 1 ☎ 872 1811

Wonderbar (! AC B D GLM MA S WE YG) Sat 22.30-2.30 h
Temple Bar Music Centre, Curved Street, Dublin 2
☎ 353/405 53005
Admission Ir£ 8 (members 6). National and international live entertainment.

RESTAURANTS

George Bar & Bistro. The (AC B CC F glm W) Mon-Fri 12-20 h
89 South Great Georges Street ✉D 2 ☎ 478 2983

Juice (AC CC glm NG) Sun-Thu 11-22, Fri-Sat 11-24 h
South Great George Street ✉D 2 ☎ 475 7856

Mark's Bros (B F glm) 11-23 h
7 South Great Georges Street ☎ 677 10 85
Vegetarian cuisine.

Odessa. The (B F glm NG YG) Mon-Sun 12-24 h
13/14 Dame Court ✉D 2 *(Off Dame Street)* ☎ 670 7634

Sinners Restaurant (CC F glm)
12 Parliament Street ✉D 2 ☎ 671 9345

SEX SHOPS/BLUE MOVIES

Basic Insincts (CC g MA) Mon-Sat 10.30-18.30, Thu -20, Sun 12-18 h
56 South William Street ✉D 2 *(Off Grafton Street, near Powers Ct. Shopping Centre)* ☎ 671 2223
Large gay video and magazine department as well as rubberwear. Mail order service.

Condom Power (CC glm) Mon-Sat 9-18, Thu-20 h
57 Dame Street ✉D 2 *(Basement. Opposite Rehab Lottery)* ☎ 677 8963

Utopia (CC g) Mon-Sat 9.30-18, Thu -20, Sun 12-18 h
164 Capel Street ✉D 2 ☎ 872 9045

SAUNAS/BATHS

Boilerhouse. The (AC b bf CC DR F G MA sa sb sol VS wh YG) Mon-Thu 13-5, Fri 13-Mon 5 h
12 Crane Lane *(beside Olympia Theatre off Damce St.)* ☎ 677 31 30

Dock Sauna. The (AC b CC DR F G lj MA msg NU r s sa sb VS) 21 Upper Ormond Quay ✉7 *(Same entrance as guesthouse „Inn On The Liffey")* ☎ 872 41 72
Entrance fee Ir£ 7 from 6-14 h, 8 all other times.

Incognito Sauna (! f G MA sa sb VS) Mon-Thu 13-5, Fri-Sat & Bank Holiday 13-9, Sun 14-5 h
1-2 Bow Lane East ✉D 2 *(Off Aungier Street. Basement of The Horse and Carriage)* ☎ 478 3504

Vortex (DR f G LJ MA msg S sa sb sol TV VS YG) 13-5 h, Fri 13-Mon 5 h (64 hours open !)
1 Great Strand Street *(at Capel Street Bridge)* ☎ 878 08 98
Sauna and Leisure Club for men. Café/wine bar, 5 floors of cruising space, sauna/steam room.

BOOK SHOPS

Books Upstairs (CC glm) Mon-Fri 10-19, Sat -18, Sun (summer) 14-18 h
36 College Green ✉D 2 (Opposite Trinity College) ☎ 679 6687
Fax: 679 6807

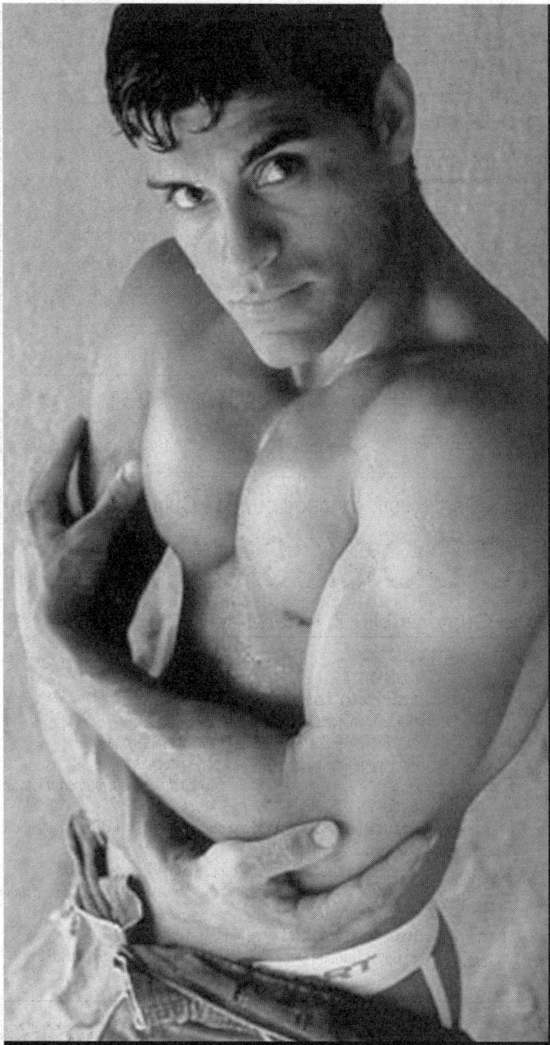

THE BOILERHOUSE

Dublin's Best & Biggest Sauna

CAFÉ

JACUZZI

SAUNA

STEAM ROOM

SOLARIUM

PRIVATE ROOMS AVAILABLE BY APPOINTMENT

Open Monday to Thursday
13.00 to 05.00

and All Weekend from
Friday 13.00 to Monday 05.00

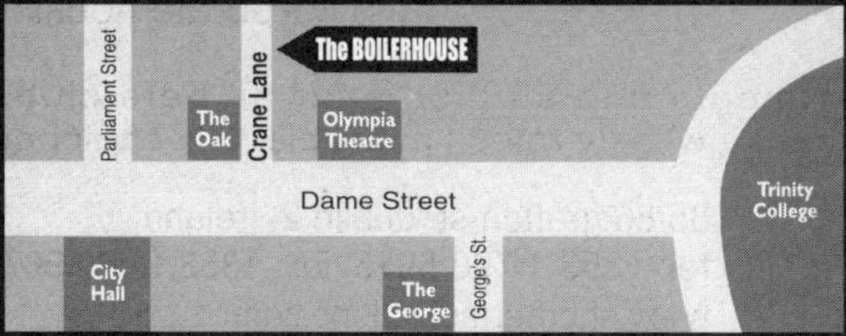

The Boilerhouse

12 Crane Lane, Dublin 2

Telephone (01) 677 3130
Web site www.the-boilerhouse.com

HOTELS

Horse & Carriage Guest Hotel. The (bf CC GLM H OS sa)
15 Aungier Street ✉D 2 ☎ 478 3537 Fax: 478 4010
Email: liamtony@indigo.ie Homepage: indigo.ie/~liamtony.h&c.html
Rates from single Ir£ 40 per personincl.bf. Free entry to sauna for hotel guests.

GUEST HOUSES

Alternative Guest House. The (AC CC GLM MA msg VS W) Reception: Mon-Sun 8-23.30 h
61 Amiens Street ✉D 1 *(Near main train / bus station)*
☎ 855 3671
Studio rooms with shower/WC, kitchenette and satellite TV. Rates double Ir£ 55.

Fairfield Lodge (CC G H OS)
Monkstown Avenue, Monkstown, Co. Dublin
☎ 280 3912 Fax: 280 3912 Email: jsb@indigo.ie
Homepage: indigo.ie/~jsb/webpage/studio.htm
Located 8 km from city centre. Self contained studio apartment. Rates Ir£ 73 p.p./night, 293 p.p./week.

Frankies Guest House (bf CC GLM H OS W) Reception: Mon-Sun 9-23.30 h
8 Camden Place ✉D 2 *(Off Camden Street)* ☎ 478 3087
☎ *475 21 82 (guestline). Rates single from Ir£ 27.50, double from 44 (bf incl.)*

Inn on the Liffey (bf CC G H MA)
21Upper Ormond Quay ✉7 *(same entrance as Dock Sauna)*

☎ 677 08 28 Fax: 872 4165 Email: innontheliffey@hotmail.com
Homepage: www.clubi.ie/guest_and_sauna
Newly refurbished and under new management. All rooms en-suite. TV in all rooms. Irish breakfast served. Free entrance to „the Dock Sauna"

APARTMENTS

Short Term Solutions (CC G H MA p WE YG) Mon-Fri 9.30-18 h, closed Sat Sun
85/86 Grafton Street ✉2 ☎ 790 59 15 Fax: 670 96 71
Email: info@shorttermsolutions.com
Homepage: www.shorttermsolutions.com
Fully equiped apartments with TV/video, phone and kitchen. Near all bars and clubs.

PRIVATE ACCOMODATION

Home Bureau *(near all bars/clubs and saunas)*
☎ 679 22 22 Fax: 670 96 71
Homepage: www.shorttermsolutions.com
Apartments & studios, 1/2 beds/studios fully equipped. Weekend rates available.

GENERAL GROUPS

Muted Cupid Theatre Group Meeting: Tue 19.30 h at 6 South William Street, Dublin 2

HEALTH GROUPS

AIDS-Helpline Dublin Mon-Fri 19-21, Sat 15-17 h
☎ 872 4277
Dublin AIDS Alliance
53 Parnell Square ✉D 1 ☎ 873 3799
Gay Men's Health Project Tue 20-21.30, Wed 18.30-20.30 h
Baggot Street Clinic, 19 Haddington Road ✉D 4 ☎ 660 2189

RELIGIOUS GROUPS

Reach
PO Box 4625 ✉D 2 *Gay Christian group.*

SWIMMING

-"Forty Foot" (g NU)
-Seapoint (g) (close to Forty Foot)
-Dollymount (G NU) (Sand dunes at the far end are quite cruisy)

CRUISING

-Palmerston Park (Best 0.30-6 h)
-Phoenix Park (Very busy at night but AYOR. This park is huge and the most popular cruising areas vary, ask locals for exact location of action.)

Galway ☎ 091

GAY INFO

Gay Help Line Tue Thu 20-22 h
PO Box 45 ☎ 56 61 34

BARS

Centurion Bistro Wine Bar (bf CC F g H MA S STV)
20 Lower Abbeygate Street
Also includes a Bed and Breakfast.

BOOK SHOPS

Pearls of Wisdom (glm)
4 Quay Street

HEALTH GROUPS

AIDS Help West Mon-Fri 10-12, Thu 20-22 h
Oznam House, Augustine Street ☎ 24 14 89

Kilkenny ☎ 056

RESTAURANTS

Motte Restaurant. The (CC F g MA p) Tue-Sat 19-21.30 h (last orders), closed Sun-Mon
Plas-Newydd Lodge, Inistioge, Co. Kilkenny *(15 miles from city)*
☎ 586 55

Limerick ☎ 061

GAY INFO

Gay Switchboard Limerick Mon-Tue 19.30-21.30 h
PO Box 151, GPO ☎ 31 01 01

Skibbereen ☎ 028

PRIVATE ACCOMODATION

Mont Bretia B&B (bf GLM MA p)
Adrigole Townland ☎ 33 663
Farmhouse in the countryside. Rates Ir£ 20 p.p. (bf incl.) Dinner available, bike hire possible.

Waterford

RESTAURANTS

Haricots (B F glm) O'Connell Street
Vegetarian and wholefood.

Israel

Yisra'él • Isra'il

Western Asia

Initials: IL

Time: GMT +2

☎ Country Code / Access Code: 972 / 00 or 012 or 013 or 014

Language: modern Hebrew (Ivrit) and Arabic

Area: 21,946 km^2 / 8,473 sq mi.

Currency: 1 New Shekel (NIS) = 100 Agorot

Population: 5,643,966

Capital: Jerusalem (Yerushalayim)

Religions: 82% Jewish, 14% Moslem

Climate: Moderate climate. Southern and eastern desert areas are hot and dry.

● Israel is characterized by a unique combination: a very tolerant society and an advanced legal system on one hand, and a very limited gay scene on the other.
Although religious parties have considerable power, recent years have seen great steps toward the full integration of gay men and lesbians into society. The SPPR (Society for the Protection of Personal Rights), the only gay and lesbian organization in the country, succeeded in pushing through the decriminalisation of anal intercourse (1988), in 1991 there followed an anti-discrimination clause in labour legislation, and in 1993 a sub-committee for homosexual rights was formed in the Knesset. In 1994 a court ruled that employers should treat the partners of gay employees the same as they do the partners of their heterosexual employees.

✷ Die Situation israelischer Schwuler ist durch eine besondere Kombination von Umständen geprägt: eine recht tolerante Gesellschaft mit einer fortschrittlichen Gesetzgebung auf der einen, eine sehr begrenzte schwule Szene auf der anderen Seite.
Anfang der 90er Jahre gab es, trotz des großen Einflusses der religiösen Parteien, große Schritte in Richtung einer vollen Integration von Schwulen und Lesben in die Gesellschaft. Die SPPR (Gesellschaft zum Schutz der persönlichen Rechte), die einzige schwul-lesbische Organisation des Landes, konnte große Erfolge erringen: 1988 die Entkriminalisierung des Analverkehrs, 1991 einen Antidiskriminierungszusatz im Arbeitsrecht, 1993 schließlich die Einrichtung eines Knesset-Unterausschusses für homosexuelle Rechte und Antidiskriminierungsrichtlinien in der Armee. 1994 schließlich entschied ein Gericht, daß ein Arbeitgeber den Lover eines schwulen Mitarbeiters genauso behandeln muß, wie den/die Lebensgefährten/in eines Hetero-Mitarbeiters.

▲ En Israël, d'énormes progrès ont été réalisés en ce qui concerne l'intégration des gays et des lesbiennes dans la société et ce, malgré l'influence encore énorme exercée par les partis religieux.
Ces dernières années, la SPPG (Société pour la protection des droits individuels), la seule association gaye du pays a remporté de substantiels succès. En 1988, elle a réussi à faire décriminaliser la pénétration anale. En 1991, elle a fait passer une loi condamnant la discrimination des homosexuels (hommes et femmes) sur leur lieu de travail. En 1993, elle a réussi à mettre en place à la Knesset un groupe de travail qui planche sur les mesures à prendre pour supprimer la discrimination des homosexuels au sein de l'armée. En 1994, finalement, un tribunal a décidé qu'un employeur devait traîter l'amant d'un de ses employés de la même façon que les femmes ou conjointes de ses collègues hétérosexuels.

☆ La situación de los homosexuales israelitas está marcada por una combinación de circunstancias especiales. Por un lado una sociedad tolerante con una legislación progresiva, por otro lado un ambiente gay muy limitado. A pesar de la fuerte influencia de los partidos religiosos, durante los últimos años se consiguieron grandes avances hacía una integración de gays y lesbianas en la sociedad júdia. La S.P.P.R. (Sociedad para la Protección de los Derechos Personales), la única organización gay y lesbiana del país, ha alcanzado grandes exitos; en 1988 la despenalización del coito anal; en 1991 una claúsula de antidiscriminación en la legislación laboral; en 1993 la formación de una comisión para derechos homosexuales en el parlamento y directivas para el ejercito. En 1994 decidó un tribunal, que un empresario está obligado a tratar el amante de un empleado gay del mismo modo que la pareja de un empleado heterosexual.

❖ La situazione dei gay israeliani è marcata da una particolare combinazione di determinanti: una società molto tollerante con una progredita legislazione da una parte, un ambiente gay molto limitato dall'altra. Malgrado la considerevole influenza dei partiti religiosi, negli ultimi anni sono stati fatti grandi passi verso una piena integrazione dei gay e delle lesbiche nella società. La SPPR (società per la protezione dei diritti della persona), l'unica organizzazione omosessuale del paese, ha raggiunto diverse mete: nel 1988 la legalizzazione dei rapporti anali, nel 1991 un paragrafo antidiscriminante nella legislazione del lavoro, infine, nel 1993 un sottocomitato del Knesset per i diritti degli omosessuali e l'antidiscriminazione nell'esercito. Nel 1994 infine un tribunale ha deciso che un datore di lavoro deve trattare il compagno di un suo dipendente gay come il compagno/a di un dipendente eterosessuale.

NATIONAL GAY INFO

Association for Lesbians, Gay Men and Bisexualsj in Israel (The AGUDA)
PO Box 376 04 ✉ 61375 Tel Aviv ☎ 3-629 36 81
Fax: 3-525 23 41 Email: sppr@netvision.net.il
Homepage: www.geocities.com/WestHollywood/hights/8917
National organization of Israel. ☛ Tel Aviv and Haifa for their community centers.

Israel Update
c/o The Agudah, PO Box 376 04, Tel Aviv
English bulletin of the Israeli group. Published every six months.

GAY INFO

Hazman Havarod
PO Box 14595 Tel Aviv
Monthly Hebrow newspaper - Inforation in English

Akko ☎ 04

CRUISING

-Old City Wall (by the lighthouse; evenings)

Beer Sheva ☎ 07

CRUISING

-Gan Ha'atsma'oot/Independence Park (north of Museum of the Negev on Derech Ha'atsma'oot; early evenings)

Eilat ☎ 07

BARS

Nisha (B glm) 23-? h
Nepton Hotel

CAFÉS

Cafe Neto (B F g) 21-24 h
(the mole in front of the sea)

SWIMMING

-Red Rock Hotel (g)

CRUISING

-Ofira Park (near Tedi's Bar)

Haifa ☎ 04

GAY INFO

Haifa Community Center (HCC)
6 Nordau Street ☎ 867 26 65
Ask for their different activities.

CAFÉS

Afuch Al Afuh (B g) 12-? h
2 Hilel ☎ 862 76 93
Cafe Beneinu (B g) 21.30-1 h, Fri 21.30-6 h
94 Hilel
Cafe Katan (B F g) Sun-Thu 10-2 h , Fri -18 h
22 Massada *(Hadar)* ☎ 846 04 99
Cafe Neto (B g) 19:30-2 h
11 Moria (Merkaz Hakarmel) ☎ 836 04 83

DANCECLUBS

Natanzon (B D GLM) Sat 22.30-? h
10 Natanzon Str. *(Near Paris Square)*
Opera (B D G) Thu 23-? h
15 Hasnamal

RESTAURANTS

Hotentot (g F) 9.30-3 h
8 Simatat Amos *(Hadar)*

SWIMMING

-Atlit (G) (summer only, 1 km north of Atlit)

CRUISING

-Gan Ha-Zicaron/Memorial Park (across the street from City Hall)

Jerusalem ☎ 02

CAFÉS

Café del Arte (B F GLM)
28 Hillel St. ☎ 623 27 58
Zig Zag (B F g) 8.30-1 h
3 HaMaalot Street ☎ 625 34 46

DANCECLUBS

Q Dance (B D glm) Daily open
1 Yoel Salomon
Vibe (B D glm STV) Thu Fri 22-? h
15 Heleny Hamalka *(Migrash HaRusim)*

BOOK SHOPS

Timol Shilshom (b f glm) 7.30-3 h
5 Yoel Salomon str.
It's also a Café

CRUISING

-Gan HaAtzmaut/Independence Park 0-24 h (near Plaza Hotel)
-King David Park (behind the hotel, active mainly at dusk)
-Central bus station (pedestrian tunnel -18 h)

Nahariyya ☎ 04

CRUISING

-Park behind the beach (beach patrols are only for security)

Natanya ☎ 09

SWIMMING

-Gaash Beach (NU) (right under the Wingate Institue, summer only)

CRUISING

-Gan Shlomo/King Solomon's Park (behind the movie theater at the sea's edge at the end of Herzl Street; day and night)

Tel-Aviv-Yafo ☎ 03

GAY INFO

Tel Aviv Community Center (TACC)
28 Nachmani Street ☎ 629 36 81 Fax: 525 23 41
Email: sppr@netvision.net.il
Ask for their different activities.

BARS

Abi's (B F G MA VS) 22-4 h
40 Geula Street *(near Allenby Street)* ☎ 510 12 19
DIVA (B F glm, STV) 12-3 h
The waiters are in drag.

He-She (B f GLM OS TV YG) Mon-Sat 20-? h
8 Hashomer Street *(2nd floor, Nahlat Binyamin area)* ☎ 510 09 14
Minerva Bar Gallery (A AC B CC d F gLm MA OS S) Mon-Sun 20-? h
98 Allenby St. *(Corner of Beit-Hshoeva Alley No. 20)* ☎ 566 60 51
Also a little book store with magzines, cards and gifts
OUT (AC B CC f G MA N WE YG) 22-? h
45 Nahalat Binyamin St.
Two floors with 2 Bars exclusively designed

CAFÉS

Bazel Cafe (B CC F g) 7-1 h
42 Bazel Street ☎ 546 18 75
Cafe Bialik (B F g OS)
1 Bialik Street
Very fashionable.
Café Nordau (B F glm) Mon-Sun 0-24 h
145 Ben Yehuda Street/Arlozerov Street ☎ 524 01 34
Israeli & International food. Pleasant atmosphere. Bar upstairs.
Pet Cafe (B F glm H) 9-2 h
34 Pinsker ☎ 546 18 75
Sandy Bar-Diner (b bf f glm) 7-4 h
56 Allenby

DANCECLUBS

Exit Parties (B D DR GLM MA s STV WE) Thu 24-5h
☎ 516 01 86
Look for information and invitation in Bars Saunas and Sex Shops. they change the location from time to time.
FFF Friendly Fredoom (! B D DR G MA) Fri 24-8 h
58 Allenby Street
In summer location will change - info in Sexy Shop.
Mix Morning Parties (B D glm) Sat 6-13 h
Ask for invitations at Sexy Shop.
Scene (B D G) Mon 22-? h
56 Allenby Street
Women Parties (D B L) Thu 10-?
☎ 50 635 604 (Ilana)
Weekly lesbian Parties. Call for more information
Please check at bars or Sexy Shops for updates on varying party locations.

SHOWS

Carrousel (AC B CC f glm MA S STV W) Mon-Sat 22-3 h, closed Sun
36 Pinsker Street *(near Dizengoff Centre)* ☎ 620 22 41

SEX SHOPS/BLUE MOVIES

Sexy Shop (CC DR G VS) Sun-Thu 11-24, Fri 11-16, Sat 18-24 h
150 Dizengoff Street/Gordon Street ☎ 523 17 96
Providing good informations for gay tourists. Wide range of magazines, videos, cabins and toys.

SAUNAS/BATHS

City Sauna (B DR F sa sb VS) Sun-Wed 12.30-24 h, Thu 12.30 -5 h, Fri 23-6 h, Sat 15-24 h
113 Hahashmonaim Street ✉62965 ☎ 624 11 48
2 floors. One of the biggest gay saunas in the middle east.

Paradise Sauna (AC B CC d DR f G MA msg p s sa sb VS wh) Sun-Thu 12-6, Fri 19-Sun 6 h (non stop)
75-Allenby Street ✉61000 ☎ 6202 188 Fax: 6202 193

TRAVEL & TRANSPORT

Gil Travel (CC) Sun-Thu 8-18 h, Fri 8-14 h
29 Hamered ☎ 514 00 40 Email: Russavi@isdn.Net.il

HOTELS

Olympia Hotel (AC B CC H F NG msg pi os wo)
164 Hayaakon St. ✉63415 ☎ 524 21 84 Fax: 524 72 78
Email: olympia@infolink.net.il

HEALTH GROUPS

Israel AIDS Task Force
PO Box 867 ✉61008 ☎ 566 16 39 Fax: 560 23 16

SWIMMING

-Hilton Beach (g) (right under the Independence Park, summer)

CRUISING

-WC Rothschild/Shenkin Streets
-WC Ben Gurion/Shlomo HaMelech Streets
-Gan HaAtzmaut/Independence Park (North of Hilton Hotel, 0-24 h)
-Gan Meir (King George Street, south of the Dizingoff Centre, after dark)
-Gan HaRakevet (pedestrian tunnel connecting bus and train stations and in the parks around, 0-24 h)
-Gan HaChashmal (R) (near the old Central Bus Station, parallel to Barzilay, Levontine and HaChashmal Streets, after dark)
-New Center Bus Station (3rd & 6th floor)
-WC Rothchilede/Shenkin Streets
-WC Ben Gurion/Shlomo HaMelech Streets

Ziqim ☎ 07

SWIMMING

-Ziqim Beach (By car go from Ashqelon 7 km southward to Ziqim, turn westward to the sea. Or take the bus from Ashqelon to the last stop and walk towards the sea. On the beach turn to the right, to the north for 500m)

Italy

Italia

Southern Europe

Initials: I

Time: GMT +1

☎ Country Code / Access Code: 39 / 00

Language: Italian

Area: 301,302 km^2 / 116,303 sq mi.

Currency: Italian Lira (Lit). 1 EURO = 100 EURO Cents (The Euro can only be used in the clearance system)

Population: 57,243,000

Capital: Roma

Religions: 98% Roman Catholic

Climate: Predominantly Mediterranean climate. Alpine climate in the far north, the south is hot and dry.

Important gay cities: Milano, Torino, Bologna, Firenze, Roma, Padova, Viareggio, Taormina

Gay life in Italy is strongly influenced by Catholicism and the Vatican. Traditional Christian morals and the „Macho" image in the Italian society make it difficult for many gays to live an open homosexual lifestyle. The family ties are so strong that even in the large cities young gays live with their parents.
Of importance is also the extreme cultural difference for gays, lesbians and transsexuals living in the north compared to those living in the south of Italy, where Rome is considered the „boarder". Gay life in the industrial north - in cities such as Turin and especially Malan is not unlike any large city in northern Europe. Exclusively gay locations, such as bars, saunas and discos as well as the increasing number of clubs and pubs in which a mixture of gays and heterosexuals are to be found.
The south - an agricultural region which tends to be poorer and has a higher unemployment rate than the north functions in many ways in a totally different principle : tradition has more weight although the people often appear to be friendlier and open. Gay life tend to take place on a „piazza" or in a cruising park. Gays tend not to display their preference in public although contact to heterosexual men is not uncommon. The difference between gay and „straight" is not as important as the difference between „active" or „passive".
There are no discrimination laws concerning homosexuality and this since 1889. The age of consent is 14 for both sexes. Caution is advised with young men between 14 and 18 where accusations of corruption of minors can be claimed. Prostitution is legal from 18. Equal rights discussions such as an anti-discrimination law are still subject to much opposition. The opposition from the church , Christian political parties as well as the fascists under Fini make the situation for gays more difficult. Several communities however offer a kind of official partnership. Pisa is one of the leading cities in this respect. This year the „Gay World Pride" takes place in Rome. Over 300 000 gays, lesbians and transsexuals are expected. A possibility to make more publicity for gay emancipation.
An active group in this field is the „Arci Gay" (head office in Bologne) who are also involved in AIDS counselling. This is a non-profit organisation, receiving no financial aid from the Italian government. The majority of Italians have their annual holiday in August. Many bars, discos and saunas are traditionally closed until the beginning of September. In the gay seaside resorts (such as Taormina, Riccione and Rimini) many of the locations have just opened at this time of the year. For gay summer tourists the new exciting place to be is the seaside resort of Viareggio and Torre del Lago. The aim is to create an Italian „Mykonos".

Schwules Leben in Italien ist eng verbunden mit dem weiterhin großen Einfluß von Katholizismus und Vatikan. Traditionelle christliche Moralvorstellungen und der ausgeprägte „Machismo" der italienischen Gesellschaft erschweren es vielen italienischen Schwulen, ihre Homosexualität offen zu leben. Zumal die Bindung an die Familie im allgemeinen sehr eng ist, daß selbst in den Großstädten junge Schwule kaum alleine, sondern in der Regel bei ihren Eltern leben.
Zu berücksichtigen für die Situation von Schwulen, Lesben und Transsexuellen und ergo schwulem Leben sind dabei gravierende kulturelle Unterschiede zwischen dem Norden und dem Süden des Landes, wobei Rom die „Grenze" darstellt. Schwules Leben in den Industriestädten des Nordens wie Turin und vor allem Mailand ist annähernd vergleichbar mit dem der Großstädte Nordeuropas. Es gibt sowohl rein schwule (bzw. lesbischwul gemischte) Einrichtungen wie Saunen, Bars und Diskotheken als auch immer mehr Clubs und Kneipen, in denen eine bunte Mischung von Heteros/as und offenen Lesben und Schwulen anzutreffen ist. Doch auch im Norden sind „Tages-Cafés" für Schwule noch eine Seltenheit.
Der vor allem agrarisch geprägte und weitaus ärmere Süden (mit einer bedeutend höheren Arbeitslosenquote) funktioniert in vielerlei Hinsicht nach vollkommen anderen Regeln: Traditionen haben hier noch mehr Gewicht, oft erscheinen einem die Leute jedoch als herzlicher und offener. Schwules Leben (wie auch das Nachtleben im allgemeinen) findet eher im Freien statt, ob auf der „Piazza" oder im Cruising-Park. Schwule leben selten offen, demgegenüber sind sexuelle Begegnungen mit heterosexuellen Männern nicht ausgeschlossen: die Unterscheidung zwischen „schwul" und „hetero" ist oft weniger wichtig als die zwischen „aktiv" und „passiv" (vielleicht in eingeschränktem Maße vergleichbar mit schwuler Realität in arabischen Ländern).
Seit 1889 gibt es keine Gesetze mehr gegen Homosexualität. Das Schutzalter liegt für beide Geschlechter bei 14 Jahren. Bei Männern zwischen 14 und 18 sollte man vorsichtig sein, da bei ihnen der Vorwurf der „Korrumpierung" zutreffen kann, falls es für jene das „erste Mal" war. Prostitution ist ab 18 Jahren legal.
Rechtliche Gleichstellungsmaßnahmen - wie z.B. ein Anti-Diskriminierungsgesetz - werden zwar diskutiert, sind aber noch

erheblichem Widerstand ausgesetzt. Allerdings bieten einige Kommunen eine Art eingetragener Partnerschaft auch für lesbische und schwule Paare an (deren Vorteile jedoch vor allem von Heteros/as genutzt werden), die mitunter die erleicherte Vergabe von Wohnberechtigungsscheinen beinhaltet. Pisa war hierbei Vorreiterin.
Dieses Jahr wird der erste „Gay World Pride" in Rom (vgl. Anzeige auf den ersten Seiten) stattfinden, zu dem bis zu 300.000 Schwule, Lesben und Transsexuelle erwartet werden. Sicherlich eine große Chance, um im Kampf für Emanzipation weiter voranzukommen.
Wichtiger Träger dieser Emanzipationsbestrebungen sind die Initiativgruppen des „Arci Gay" (mit Hauptsitz in Bologna) bzw. „Arci Lesbica" und/oder davon unabhängige Gruppen, die in allem größeren Städten eine Vielzahl an Angeboten (von Infos zu schwulem Leben über Beratung bis hin zu kulturellen Veranstaltungen) bereitstellen. Neben anderen überregionalen Anti-AIDS-Organisationen sind sie oft auch Ansprechpartner für den AIDS-Bereich. Dabei wird die Arbeit praktisch ausschließlich ehrenamtlich geleistet, da von staatlicher Seite mit wenigen Ausnahmen keine Gelder zur Verfügung gestellt werden.
Die Mehrheit der Italiener hat vor allem im August Ferien. Viele Bars, Diskotheken und Saunen sind dann bis Anfang September geschlossen. In den für schwulen interessanten Badeorten (traditionell z.B. Taormina, Riccione und Rimini) sind die Diskotheken und Bars jedoch gerade dann geöffnet. Für schwulen Sommertourismus ist seit neuestem die „Versilia", vor allem die Mittelmeerorte Viareggio und Torre del lago, interessant. Das erklärte Ziel, ein italienisches „Mykonos" zu schaffen, zeitigt schon erste Erfolge mit einigen interessanten Bars und Diskotheken.
Ausschließlich schwule Hotels/Guesthouses gibt es mit ganz wenigen Ausnahmen nicht in Italien. Die von uns empfohlenen Hotels sind „gayfriendly". Die Spartacus-Redaktion wäre von daher froh, Rückmeldungen von unseren Lesern zu erhalten, ob die gelisteten Hotels diesem Kriterium wirklich Genüge tragen.
In vielen Einrichtungen ist ein „Clubausweis" erforderlich, der meistens direkt vor Ort ausgestellt wird. Am gebräuchlichsten ist dabei die „Tessera" des Arci Gay.

▲ La vie des homosexuels en Italie est profondément influencée par le Vatican et le catholicisme. La morale traditionnelle chrétienne et le machisme inhérents à la société italienne sont des obstacles qui empêchent beaucoup de gays de vivre ouvertement leur homosexualité. A cela s'ajoute le rôle prédominant de la famille qui incite beaucoup de jeunes gays, même dans les grandes villes, à rester longtemps au bercail.
Le mode de vie des gays, lesbiennes et transsexuels diverge en fonction des fortes différences culturelles qui divisent le pays entre son nord et son sud (la frontière invisible entre ces deux mondes passe au sud de Rome). Dans les grandes villes industrielles du nord, telles que Milan ou Turin, la vie gaye s'apparente à celle d'autres grandes métropoles du nord de l'Europe. Il existe des établissements destinés uniquement aux homosexuels (hommes et femmes), tels que saunas, bars, clubs, ainsi qu'un nombre croissant d'endroits mixtes où les gays n'ont plus à se cacher. Les établissements de jour restent par contre encore rares.
Dans le sud, moins industrialisé, plus pauvre et avec un fort taux de chômage, la situation est toute autre : malgré des traditions encore bien ancrées dans la société les gens sont ici plus chaleureux et ouverts. La vie gaye (comme toute la vie nocturne d'ailleurs) se passe en plein air, sur les places ou dans les parcs. Peu de gens vivent ouvertement leur homosexualité mais cela n'empêche pas pour autant d'avoir des relations sexuelles entre personnes de même sexe. La différence entre homos et hétéros semble ici avoir moins d'importance que celle entre actif et passif (un peu comme dans le monde arabe).
L'Italie a abrogé ses lois homophobes en 1889 déjà. La majorité sexuelle est fixée à 14 ans pour les deux sexes, mais on courre le risque d'être condamné pour „corruption" en cas de rapports poussés avec un jeune de moins de 18 ans pour qui c'est la „première fois". La prostitution est légalement autorisée à partir de 18 ans.
Des mesures pour l'égalité des droits, par exemple une loi anti-discriminatoire, on été discutées mais rencontrent encore beaucoup de réticences. Certaines communes offrent cependant un contrat d'union civile aux gays et lesbiennes qui, par exemple, leur facilite l'accès à la location d'appartements subventionnés. Pise a été la première ville du pays à instaurer ce type de contrat.
Cette année aura lieu à Rome la première « Gay World Pride » (voir la publicité dans les pages qui suivent) dont on attend plus de 300.000 participants. Une occasion rêvée pour faire avancer les causes liées à l'émancipation des gays dans le pays.
Les principaux acteurs de cette émancipation sont les associations culturelles «Arci Gay»et « Arci Lesbica » (dont le siège est à Bologne) ainsi que toute une série d'associations indépendantes qui offrent une divers services (informations, consultations, manifestations culturelles, etc.) dans toutes les grandes villes. Ces organisations sont, avec l'aide d'autres groupements, également sur le front de la prévention et des services liés au Sida. Ceci de manière presque exclusivement bénévole puisque l'État, à quelques exceptions près, se refuse à financer ces associations.
La majeure partie des Italiens prennent leurs vacances au mois d'août. Beaucoup d'établissements sont donc fermés pendant cette période, à l'exception de ceux des villes touristiques balnéaires comme Taormina, Riccione ou Rimini qui ouvrent justement pendant l'été. Pour le touriste estival, nous recommandons particulièrement la Versilie et ses stations balnéaires Torre del Lago et Viareggio (regarder sous Viareggio dans le guide). Le but déclaré des ces stations est de créer un Mykonos italien et ils offrent déjà un nombre de bars et clubs très intéressants.
Des hôtels ou gîtes exclusivement gays n'existent quasiment pas en Italie. Les hébergements que nous vous proposons sont donc uniquement des lieux où les gays sont bien accueillis. L'équipe rédactionnelle de Spartacus serait d'ailleurs reconnaissante si vous pouviez nous faire part de vos expériences dans les établissements que nous mentionnons cette année.
Beaucoup d'établissements exigent à leur entrée une carte (la plus courante est celle de l'association Arci Gay) mais la plupart d'entre eux vous en fourniront une directement sur place.

☆ Para comprender la vida gay en Italia, hay que tener presente que existen dos tipos diferentes de culturas homosexual. En las grandes ciudades del Norte se parece la vida gay a la de los paises del Norte de Europa, mientras en el sur el estilo de vida es mucho más mediterráneo. Los sitios de encuentro para homosexuales son al aire libre, cines o saunas, es decir en lugares que no son exclusivamente gay. La mayoría de los bares, pubs y discotecas son „mixtos" y por ello se recomienda un comportamiento discreto. Aunque los hombres italianos se demuestren muy afectuosos entre ellos, este trato no tiene nada que ver con homosexualidad. Se hace notar que la frontera entre el norte liberal y el sur conservador es la ciudad de Roma. Desde 1889 no existen leyes que prohiben la homosexualidad y la edad de consentimiento es de 14 años, independientemente de la orientación sexual. Sin embargo, se puede ser acusado de „corrupto" si se mantiene una relacion con un jóven entre 14 y 18 años siendo esta su primera experiencia sexual. La prostitución es legal a partir de los 18 años. No existen persecuciones oficiales, excepto ocasionales controles de documentos en parques por parte de la policia. Sin embargo, los italianos menosprecian un comportamiento demasiado afeminado y la homosexualidad se tolera solamente, si no es mostrada abiertamente. El contrario provoca sobre todo en el sur reacciones violentas. Esto explica en parte la dificultad de diferenciar hombres gay en las calles y el hecho de que la mayoría de las entradas a los sitios de ambiente están escondidas. La mayoría de los grupos italianos pertenecen a la asociación nacional „ARCI GAY", que tiene sucursales en todas las grandes ciudades. La oficina principal tiene su sede en Boloña. Existen tres grupos de gays católicos, dos asociaciones de prevención e información sobre el SIDA y la revista *Babilonia* que se pública mensualmente. Candidatos, cuya homosexualidad no es un secreto, han sido votados en Mílan y Torino. Aunque se dice que Italia es el „País del Papa", la influencia católica ha disminuido de forma drástica durante los últimos años. Sin embargo, la mentalidad católica sigue siendo suficientemente fuerte para obstacular, por ejemplo, la públicidad de preservativos, que apenas se encuentran en bares o saunas. Temporada alta para sitios que son tradicionalmente interesantes para el turista gay (como Taormina, Capri, Venecia, Florencia, Roma, Ricciones etc) son los meses de verano. La mayoría de la gente en los centros industriales como Mílan o Torina se van de vacaciones en el mes de agosto. Durante esta época se cierran casi todos los bares, discotecas y asociaciones. A pesar que el ambiente gay se concentra en las grandes ciudades, existen muchas veces sitios de ambiente en las afueras que también indicamos.

❖ La vita gay in Italia è profondamente influenzata dal cattolicesimo e dal vaticano il cui ruolo continua ad essere ancora molto importante. La tradizionale morale cristiana e il „machismo" della società italiana rendono difficile per molti gay italiani di vivere la propria omosessualità apertamente. A questo si aggiunge il fatto che il legame alla famiglia è molto forte tanto che anche nelle grosse città giovani gay vivono generalmente presso le loro famiglie.
Per la situazione di vita di gay, lesbiche e transsessuali sono da tenere in considerazione importanti differenze culturali tra nord e sud dove Roma rappresenta la linea di „confine". La vita gay nelle città industrializzate del nord, come Torino e soprattutto Milano, è paragonabile con quella delle grandi città del nordeuropa. Ci sono sia locali esclusivamente gay (o gay-lesbici) tipo saune, bar, discoteche, sia un crescente numero di club e pub nei quali si può incontrare una varietà di gente con diversi orientamenti sessuali, dagli etero a lesbiche e gay che vivono la loro sessualità all'aperto. Anche se al nord stesso i bar diurni sono ancora molto rari.
Al sud, meno industrializzato, più povero e con una alta percentuale di disoccupazione, la situazione è per tanti aspetti molto diversa: le tradizioni hanno, qui, un peso molto importante nella vita di ogni giorno, anche se le persone sembrano essere più sincere e aperte. La vita gay (come anche la vita notturna in generale) si svolge all'aperto in piazza come ai „cruising parks". I gay sono raramente „dichiarati", però di contro gli „incontri" con uomini eterosessuali non sono rari: la differenza tra gay ed etero è, spesso, meno importante di quella tra attivo e passivo (forse, in certi limiti, parogonabile con la realtà gay dei paesi arabi).
Non esistono dal 1889 leggi contro l'omosessualità; l'età del consenso è di 14 anni sia per i rapporti gay che per quelli eterosessuali, anche se si può essere accusati di aver „corrotto" un ragazzo tra i 14 e i 18 anni nel caso che quest'ultimo non avesse mai avuto rapporti sessuali prima d'allora. La prostituzione dei maggiorenni è legale.
Provvedimenti sulla parità di diritti come p.e. la legge antidiscriminatoria vengono discussi, però c'è ancora molta opposizione contro di essi. Tuttavia alcuni comuni offrono anche a coppie gay e lesbiche la possibilità di iscriversi in un registro per le unioni civili che tra altri vantaggi prevede anche quello di accedere più facilmente alle graduatorie per l'assegnazione degli appartamenti. Pisa è stata la prima città che ha portato avanti un progetto di questo genere.
Quest'anno si svolgerà a Roma il primo „Gay World Pride" (vedere inserzione sulle prime pagine) dove si aspettano fino a 300.000 gay, lesbiche e transsessuali. Sicuramente una buona chance per la lotta per l'emancipazione.
Importanti sostenitori di questi sforzi sono le associazioni culturali dell' „Arci Gay" (con sede principale a Bologna) e „Arci Lesbica" e tutta una serie di associazioni indipendenti che offrono in tutte le grandi città una profusione di servizi (da informazione sulla vita gay, consulenza fino a manifestazioni di tipo culturale). Queste organizzazioni, insieme ad altre organizzazioni di prevenzione, offrono spesso consulenza e servizi nel campo dell'AIDS. In queste organizzazioni il lavoro offerto è quasi sempre di tipo volontario poichè lo stato, eccetto qualche eccezione, non mette a disposizione fondi per finanziare le suddette.
La maggior parte degli italiani vanno in ferie soprattutto ad agosto. Molti bar, discoteche e saune sono quindi chiuse fino a inizio settembre. Tuttavia nei luoghi turistici interessanti per i gay come per esempio Taormina, Riccione e Rimini, le discoteche e i bar sono aperti. Per il turismo estivo gay da segnalare è la Versilia, in particolare i luoghi balneari come Viareggio e Torre del lago (vedere solo Viareggio!). Lo scopo dichiarato di riuscire a creare una Mykonos italiana mostra già i primi risultati con alcuni bar e discoteche molto interessanti.
Infine, per quanto riguarda hotel e pensioni gay, a parte alcune eccezioni, si può ben dire che non ce ne sono in Italia. Gli hotel che vi consigliamo sono quelli cosidetti „gayfriendly". La redazione di Spartacus vi sarebbe quindi molto grata se ci possiate confermare che gli hotel elencati corrispondono veramente al criterio di „gayfriendly". In molti locali è richiesta una tessera che di solito viene emessa sul luogo. La più usuale tra le tessere è quella dell'Arci Gay.

NATIONAL GAY INFO

ANLAIDS- Associazione Nazionale per la Lotta Contro l'Aids Mon-Fri 9-18 h
Via Barberini 3 ✉00187 Roma ☎ 06 482 09 99
Fax: 06 482 10 77 Email: anlaids@anlaids.it
Homepage: http://www.anlaids.it
National coordination of ANLAIDS. Gives information about Aids Organisations in Italy.

Archivio Massimo Consoli
Via Dario Bellezza 1 ✉00040 Fratocchie (Roma)
☎ 06 93 54 75 67 Fax: 06 93 54 74 83
Available only by appointment to professionals.

Arci Gay Nazionale Mon-Fri 15-18 h
Piazza di Porta Saragozza 2 ✉40123 Bologna
☎ 051 644 70 54
Head office of Arci, the only national organization of Italy with 29 branches nationwide: Information, gay archive, videos, meetings/ ARCI-Gay centro nazionale; informazioni, documentazione, convegni, manifestazioni.

Arci Gayline 0-24 h
✉40123 Bologna ☎ 166 117 117 Fax: 051 644 67 22
Email: arcigl@iperbole.bologna.it
National infoline. Information about gay life in Italy.

Arcitrans (Onlus) Infoline Wed 20-23 h
✉20100 Milano ☎ 02 89 40 17 49 Email: arcitrans@iol.it
National association of transsexuals, transgender and drags.

Babilonia
Via Astura 8 ✉20141 Milano ☎ 02 569 64 68
Fax: 02 55 21 34 19 Email: babilonia@iol.it
Homepage: http://www.babilonia.net
The national gay magazine of Italy. Featuring news, reports, lifestyle, arts, classifieds and a gay guide. Lit 10.000 at newsstands.

Contatti
Via Aosta 37 ✉10015 Ivrea ☎ 0125 490 24 Fax: 0125 490 24
Email: contatti@contatti.it Homepage: www.contatti.it
Gay, lesbian and straight monthly printed in Italy and distributed in the news-stands all over Italy. Monthly newspaper with hundreds of classifieds and personal ads. Written in Italian. Published by A.C.R.I.

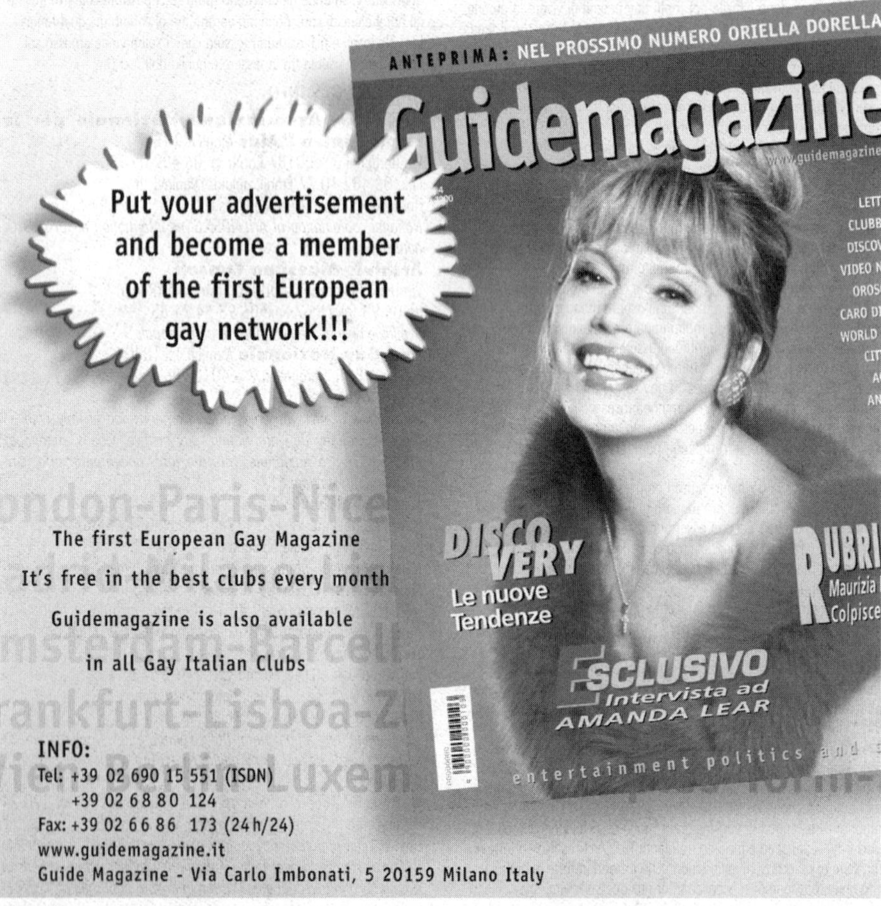
Guidemagazine
For the Best
in Gay scene, entertainment
politics & sex in Europe!!!
Put your advertisement
and become a member
of the first European
gay network!!!
ANTEPRIMA: NEL PROSSIMO NUMERO ORIELLA DORELLA
Guidemagazine
DISCO VERY
Le nuove
Tendenze
ESCLUSIVO
Intervista ad
AMANDA LEAR
entertainment politics and
The first European Gay Magazine
It's free in the best clubs every month
Guidemagazine is also available
in all Gay Italian Clubs
INFO:
Tel: +39 02 690 15 551 (ISDN)
+39 02 68 80 124
Fax: +39 02 66 86 173 (24h/24)
www.guidemagazine.it
Guide Magazine - Via Carlo Imbonati, 5 20159 Milano Italy

La nuova rivista gay italiana. Di liberazione

Pride & Guide

The new italian gay review. forfreedom

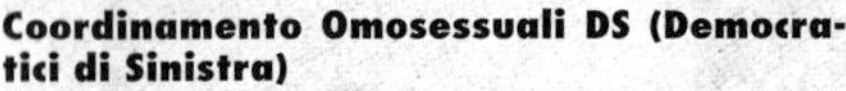

Coordinamento Omosessuali DS (Democratici di Sinistra)
c/o Federazione Romana DS, Via del Circo Massimo 7 ✉00153 Roma ☎ 06 57 30 25 71 Fax: 06 57 30 25 74

Gruppo Di Lavoro Sull'Omosessualitá (G.L.O.) Nel Partito Di Rifondazione Comunista (PRC)
c/o PRC, Via Tarabochia 3 ✉34121 Trieste ☎ 040 63 40 00

Guide Magazine
Via Carlo Imbonati 5 ✉20159 Milano ☎ 02 688 01 24
Fax: 02 668 61 73 Email: guidemagazine@guidemagazine.it
Homepage: www.guidemagazine.it
Monthly gay magazine printed in Italy and distributed in the main cities in Europe. Free magazine available in clubs, bars, saunas, restaurants, gay shops. Written in Italian. Published by A.C.R.I.-Edizioni Cassiche

LILA-Lega Italiana Lotta Contro L'Aids
☎ 02 51 00 23

Marco
c/o Edizione Moderne, PO Box 171 82 ✉20170 Milano
☎ 02 29 51 74 90 *Personal ads and Gay Guide section.*

Maschio
PO Box 171 60 ✉20170 Milano ☎ 02 29 51 74 90
Erotic publications, dedicated to the male nude. Single copy Lit 10.000.

Ministero Della Sanita-Centro Operativo AIDS
☎ 167 86 10 61 (Free call) Email: noignet@tin.it
Homepage: http://www.gay.it/noi/

Pride & Guide
Via San Nicolao 10 ✉20123 Milano ☎ 02 89 01 59 40
Fax: 02 789 01 39 90 Email: echoteam@tiscalinet.it
Free gay monthly available in all gay venues.

Sex Guide International Mon-Fri 10-20 h
Via Ferentano 48 ✉00178 Roma ☎ 06 712 89 564
Fax: 06 712 79 514 Email: info@sexy-guide.com
Homepage: www.sexy-guide.com

NATIONAL PUBLISHERS

Babilonia Edizioni Mon-Fri 9-18 h
Via Astura 8 ✉20141 Milano ☎ 02 569 64 68
Fax: 02 55 21 34 19 Email: babilonia@iol.it
Homepage: www.babilonia.net
Publisher of gay monthly „Babilonia".

Echo Communication Mon-Fri 9-12.30, 14-19 h, closed in Aug
Via San Nicolao 10 ✉20123 Milano ☎ 02 89 01 59 40
Fax: 02 89 01 39 90 Email: echoteam@tiscalinet.it
Homepage: http://www.echoteam.it
Publisher of the gay monthly „Up.City".

Edizioni Gruppo Abele (E.G.A.)
Via Giolitti 21 ✉10123 Torino ☎ 011 839 54 44
Books on gay topics. Publisher of Italian gay bibliography.

Gay.it Mon-Fri 15-19 h
Via San Lorenzo 38 ✉50127 Pisa ☎ 050 55 56 18
Fax: 050 55 56 18 Homepage: http://www.gay.it
Actual informations for gay tourists.

Omo Edizioni Mon-Fri 10-20 h
Via Ferentano 48 ✉00178 Roma ☎ 06 712 89 564
Fax: 06 712 79 514 Email: info@sexy-guide.com
Homepage: www.sexy-guide.com

NATIONAL COMPANIES

Frisco
Via F. Veracini 15 ✉50144 Firenze ☎ 055 35 73 51
Fax: 055 35 73 51 *Richiedere cataloghi/Ask for catalogue.*

Mec Mail Order Italy
PO Box 67, Frazione Lunata ✉55010 Capannori
☎ 0583 30 32 61 *Underwear and fashion bathing-suits.*

Abano Terme - Padova ✉ 35031

SWIMMING

-Piscine Termali (-23h)

CRUISING

-Gardens in front of Caffe delle Termele(Spring and summer)

Agrigento ✉ 92100

BARS

Galleria. La (B g R)
Via Atenea 123 ✉92100

RESTAURANTS

Kalos (B F g R)
Salita Filino 1 ✉92100 *(Near railway station/Stazione ferroviaria)*

HOTELS

Colleverde Park Hotel (AC B bf CC F H OS sol W)
Via Panoramica dei Templi ✉92100 *(1 km from station)*
☎ 0922 29 555 Fax: 0922 29 012
Rates single Lit. 120.000, double 200.000, incl. bf.

Foresteria Baglio della Luna (AC B bf CC E F H W)
Contradda da Maddalusa ✉92100 *(Valle dei Templi)*
☎ 0922 51 10 61 Fax: 0922 59 88 02
Upper scale rooms. Rates Lit. 390.000-850.000.

SWIMMING

-Località San Leone (NU)
-Le Dune (last bus stop/capolinea circolare)

CRUISING

-Posteggio Autobus/bus parking (behind/dietro Astor cinema)
-Railway station/Stazione FS
-Piazza Vittorio Emanuele (in front of main post office/ davanti alla posta centrale)
-Viale della Vittoria (at bus stop/fermata bus)
-Piazza Fratelli Rosselli (R)
-Villa Communale

Airole - Imperia ✉ 18030

RESTAURANTS

Nido. Il (B F g) 18-20 h
Via Roma 1 ✉18030 ☎ 0184 20 00 92
Gays are welcome.

SWIMMING

-Fiume Roya Beach (NU) (100 m from Roman bridge/dal ponte romano)

CRUISING

-Via Madonna (only during the summer/solo estate)

Alassio - Savona ✉ 17021

CRUISING

-Torre Saracena (open from/aperta April-November)
-La Capannina (in front of the building, street at the lake/davanti all'edificio, strada al lago)
-Harbor/porto

Alba - Cuneo ✉ 12051

CRUISING

-Railway station/Stazione FS
-Via Maestra
-Piazzale della S.A.U.B.
-Piazza Savona (near fountain/vicino alla fontana)
-Piazza Tanaro (NU) (on the bank of the river, spring-autumn/riva del fiume, primavera-autunno)

Alessandria ✉ 15100

BARS

Mistraal (B CC G P S) 21.30-? h
Via Mazzini 40 ✉15100 ☎ 0131 68 129

CINEMAS

Cristallo (g) 20-24 h
Piazza Ceriana 17 ✉15100 *(near/vicino Zona Cristo)*
☎ 0131 34 12 72

HEALTH GROUPS

Ospedale civile ✉15100 ☎ 0131 30 61
Test and information about AIDS/test e informazioni sull'AIDS.

CRUISING

-Railway station/stazione FS
-Lungo Tanaro Magenta (by car, at night/in auto, di sera)
-Circonvallazione (truckers/camionisti)

Altopascio ✉ 55011

CRUISING

-Parking areas (along the A11 motorway (Firenze-Mare), parking areas in both directions)(AYOR, police controls)

Ancona ✉ 60400

BARS

No Tied Club (G) Thu Sun 22-? h
Via della Brecciata 25 ✉60016 *(Marina di Montemarciano, between Ancona and Senigallia, direction Chiaravalle/tra Ancona e Senigallia direzione Chiaravalle)* ☎ 071 91 52 34

GENERAL GROUPS

Arcigay Arcilesbica Ancona (GLM lj MA) Wed 19.30-23 h
Corso Mazzini 64 ✉60121 ☎ 071 20 30 45 Fax: 071 20 30 50
Email: alfaweb@ntt.it

HEALTH GROUPS

Clinica Medica
c/o Ospedale Regionale Torretta ✉60100 ☎ 071 59 61
HIV-testing.

CRUISING

-Piazza Ciriaco (afternoon and night/pomeriggio e sera)
-Area Passetto (21-? h, panoramic view/zona panoramica)
-Railway station/Stazione FS
-Via XX Settembre, V. G. Marconi (TV) (near/vicino Banca d'Italia)
-Piazza Stamira (R TV)
-Via Panoramica (at the end of the street in direction of the forest/in fondo alla strada, direzione foresta)

Anzio - Roma ✉ 00042

CRUISING

-Riviera di Ponente (mixed, early hours, best in winter/misto, prime ore, meglio d'inverno)
-Piazzale del Porto (best in winter/meglio di inverno)
-Via Fanciulla d'Anzio

Aosta ✉ 11100

GENERAL GROUPS

Arcigay Arcilesbica Aosta
Via Martinet 4 ✉11100 ☎ 0360 48 35 37 Fax: 0165 32 034

HEALTH GROUPS

Ospedale Civile/Reparto dermatologico
Via Ginevra ✉11100 ☎ 0165 30 41

CRUISING

-Railway station/stazione FS (in the gardens in front of the building/ giardini antistanti)
-Mura Romane (also at the P on the right of the railway station/e posteggio a destra della stazione ferroviaria)
-Strada per l'autoporto valle d'Aosta (truckers, sometimes police patrols/camionisti, accertamenti Guardia di Finanza)
-Laghetti di Quart/Brissogne (you can see the lakes from the motorway, as you approach the exit (Autostrada A5 Torino-Aosta), near the camping site Du Lac, be careful/ all'uscita del Casello Autostrada A5 Torino-Aosta, si possono vedere dalla strada, vicino al camping Du Lac. Luogo appartato e discreto)

Aprica - Sondrio ✉ 23031

CRUISING

-Public swimming hall/Piscina comunale
-Pineta (behind the camping/dietro il campeggio)

Arborea - Cagliari ✉ 09021

CRUISING

-Beach/spiaggia 29 (camping „S'ena Arubia")

Arezzo ✉ 52100

GUEST HOUSES

Priello Bed & Breakfast (bf CC glm OS)
Localita Priello 244 ✉52033 ☎ 0575 79 12 18
Fax: 0575 79 21 18 Homepage: http://www.ruby.he.net/~priello
Historic mountain-top farm house.

HEALTH GROUPS

Ospedale Provinciale
Via Fonte Veneziana 1 ☎ 0575 30 52 153
Infectious diseases department.

CRUISING

-Arena Eden (at P after 20.30 h)
-Il Prato (AYOR R) (in the gardens/nei gardini)

Ascoli Piceno ✉ 63100

CRUISING

-Piazza del Popolo
-Railway station/stazione FS (in the gardens/nei giardini, close to Hotel Jolly/vicino Hotel Jolly)
-Rua dell'Industria (near/vicino Piazza S. Agostino)

Asti ✉ 14100

SEX SHOPS/BLUE MOVIES

Videoclub XXX (g VS)
Via Malta 6 ☎ 0141 30 506

GENERAL GROUPS

Simply Normal Asti Italy
✉14100 ☎ 0347 80 89 888

SWIMMING

-Lungo Tanaro (NU) (pass S. Fedele in direction of the bridge, behind the bridge there is a sign-post to the paths, which all end at the beach/oltre S. Fedele, direzione ponte; dietro questo è una freccia per i sentieri, che portano tutti alla spiaggia)

CRUISING

-Bus Station/Stazione Autobus (YG) (police checks)
-Via Artom (close to railway station and along the street, police checks/vicino stazione e lungo la strada, controlli polizia)
-Railway Station/Stazione FS (also in the gardens/anche nei giardini)
-Piazza d`Armi

Aurisina - Trieste ✉ 34011

SWIMMING

-Filtri Beach (NU) (near/vicino Bellariva Restaurant)

Avellino ✉ 83100

CRUISING

-Viale Italia (also in the bar nearby/anche nel bar vicino)
-Piazza Kennedy (at night/di notte)
-Villa Communale (Near the toilets/Vicino al WC)

Bareggio - Milano ✉ 20010

CRUISING

-Canale Villoresi (on both sides in the bushes/sui due lati, nei cespugli)

Bari ✉ 70100

SEX SHOPS/BLUE MOVIES

Europa 92 (g) 9-13, 14-19.30 h
Via Pisanelli 16/18 ✉70100 *(Stazione Centrale FS)*
☎ 080 54 25 990

CINEMAS

Salottino (g)
Via Stoppelli II 10 ✉70100 ☎ 080 55 83 427

SAUNAS/BATHS

Millennium Bath (AC B DR G P OS sa sb sol VS wh WO YG) Tue (L) 16-24, Wed-Sun 15.30-24 h
Via Adriatico 13 ✉70100 ☎ 080 53 42 530

NEWS STANDS

Kiosk/Rivendita giornali
Piazza Aldo Moro ✉70100

HEALTH GROUPS

Anlaids Medicalline: 9-12, 16-19 h
Via Osvaldo Marzano 10 ✉70124 ☎ 080 50 25 426
Fax: 080 50 22 936
Network Nazionale „Gruppo C" Progetto di Ricerca Aids
✉70100 ☎ 080 76 20 08
Helpline for people with HIV/Aids.
Policlinico di Bari 8-12 h
Piazza G. Cesare 11 ✉70100 ☎ 080 54 73 111

CRUISING

-Lungomare Nazario Saurio (R) (on the pier, in summer, mixed/sul mòlo, estate, misto)
-Piazza Umberto (AYOR)
-Piazza Aldo Moro
-North railway station/Stazione nord (in the evening/sera)
-Central station/Stazione centrale (R)
-Via Sparano and Corso Cavour (at Saicaf Bar in Corso Cavour)
-Fiera del Levante (TV) (by car only)
-Facoltà di Lettere e Filosofia (near post office, behind/dietro Piazza Re Umberto)
-Public park/giardini pubblici (between the universities/fra le università)
-Lungomare (tv) (towards/direzione San Giorgio)
-Lido Marziulli (summer spot/posto estivo)

Bassano del Grappa - Vicenza ✉ 36061

BARS

Bar Nuovo (B g) ?-1 h
Via Matteotti 42 ✉36061 ☎ 0424 32 39 17
Olimpia (B g YG) 8-22 h
Via Roma 63 ✉36061 ☎ 0424 52 40 08

RESTAURANTS

Vecchia Trattoria Gamba (AC F glm) Wed-Mon 12-15, 19.30-24 h
Strada Cartigliana 273 ☎ 0424 56 60 20
Not gay, but gays welcome, good cooking, reservation appreciated/non gay, ma gay benvenuti, buona cucina, gradita prenotazione.

CRUISING

-Railway station/Stazione FS (also nearby area, e. g. in the gardens during daytime/anche attorno, per esempio, nei giardini di giorno)
-Via Chilesotti (at night/di notte)
-Viale Venezia (barracks area/zona caserma)
-Viale Monte Grappa (R, tv)

Benevento ✉ 82100

HEALTH GROUPS

Network Nazionale „Gruppo C" Progetto di Ricerca Aids
✉82100 ☎ 0824 31 51 26
Helpline for people with HIV/Aids.

Bergamo ✉ 24100

GAY INFO

Arci Gay Tue 17-19, Thu 20-22.30, Sun 15-18 h
Via Baschenis 9/b ✉24100 *(bus 4,8; Borgo Palazzo)*
☎ 035 25 86 50

TOURIST INFO

A.P.T.
Via Vittorio Emanuele 20 24100 ✉24100
☎ 035 21 31 85 Fax: 035 23 01 84

BARS

Divina Fashion Bar (B E glm YG) Mon-Sat 19-2 h
Via Borgo S. Caterina 1 ✉24124 *(near Accademia Carrara)*
☎ 035 21 84 21

DANCECLUBS

Get Up (AC B bf d DR G lj MA OS P s VS W) Tue-Sun 22-?, Fri & Sat -7h
Via Bianzana 46 ✉24100 *(near Rondó delle Valli, bus 2/11/15)*
☎ 035 344 460
4 darkrooms. DJ on Wed and WE.
Nite Lite Club (! AC B D DR G OS P s YG) Thu 22-2, Sat -5, Sun -3 h
Via Baschenis 9 ✉24122 *(Bus 7, 5 min walk from the railway station)* ☎ 035 24 43 00
Arcigay membership required/Tessera Arcigay.

SEX SHOPS/BLUE MOVIES

Magic America (CC g p) Closed on Mon morning
Via Fantoni 30 ✉24121 ☎ 035 24 92 97

CINEMAS

Ritz (AYOR g) 14.30-24 h
Via Verdi 8 ✉24100 ☎ 035 24 21 24

SAUNAS/BATHS

City Sauna Club (! AC B CC DR f G MA msg P sa sb sol VS wh W) Sep-May 14-2, Jun-Aug 15-2 h, closed Tue
Via della Clementina 8/Via Borgo Palazzo ✉24100 *(Bus 5, 8)*
☎ 035 24 04 18
One of Europe's biggest and most comfortable gay saunas/sauna gay tra le più grandi e confortevoli d'Europa; abbonamenti. Free condoms/Preservativi gratis.

Club 63 (AC B DR G f MA sa sb VS W wh WO) Sun-Wed 15-2, Fri-Sat 15-5 h
Via San Lazzaro 63 ✉24100 *(corner Via Palma il Vecchio, 5 min from railway station)* ☎ 035 21 89 22
Arcigay membership required.

GENERAL GROUPS

Agedo Associazione Genitori Parenti E Amici Di Omosessuali after 20 h
✉24100 ☎ 035 36 16 74

Arcigay Arcilesbica Bergamo
Via Baschenis 9/b ✉24122 ☎ 035 25 86 50

HEALTH GROUPS

Anlaids
Casa Accoglienza Oasi di Gerico, Via Conventino 3 ✉24100
Fax: 59 82 71

Centro Malattie A Trasmissione Sessuale 10.30-12.30 h
Largo Barozzi 1 ✉24100 ☎ 035 26 94 47

CRUISING

-Piazzale Malpensata (TV)
-Piazzale Cimitero (di sera in macchina/in the night by car)

Bibione Pineta - Venezia ✉ 30020

SWIMMING

-Spiaggio Libera (along the dunes/lungo le dune)

Biella ✉ 13051

CRUISING

-Railway station/stazione S. Paolo
-Viale Carducci (behind the hospital/dietro l'ospedale)
-Largo Cusano (Piazza V. Veneto)

Boario Terme - Brescia ✉ 25041

CRUISING

-Railway station/Piazzale della stazione (21-24 h, summer only/solo estate)

Bologna ✉ 4100

GAY INFO

Arcigay Nazionale Mon-Fri 15-18 h, closed in Aug, Mon 12-16 Arcilesbicat
Piazza di Porta Saragozza 2 ✉40123 *(Bus 33, 32)*
☎ 051 64 47 054 Fax: 051 64 46 722
Email: arcigl@iperbole.bologna.it
National headquarters

Idea Lavoro
Via S. Stefano 57 ✉40100 ☎ 051 27 12 92
Fax: 051 27 14 06 Email: staff@idealavoro.com
Recruitment agency. Information on employment opportunities in Italy.

BARS

Cassero. Il (! B d GLM MA P s YG)
Piazza Porta Saragozza 2 ✉40100 *(in the arch in the middle of the square. Bus 20, 33)* ☎ 051 64 46 902
Bar, shows, video shows, exhibitions, debates, parties. Sun disco/Bar spettacoli, proiezioni video, mostre, dibattiti, feste. Dom discoteca. Arcigay membership required/tessera Arcigay. Call for opening hours

DANCECLUBS

Cream (AC B D G P YG) Thu 23-4 h
c/o Kinki Club, Via Zamboni 1 ✉40125 ☎ 0335 58 54 640 (Infoline)

Kinki Club (AC B D glm MA P YG) Fri Sat 23-5, Sun -4 h
Via Zamboni 1 ✉40125 ☎ 051 52 22 76
Very mixed in the weekend.

Pachito Club (! AC B D DR F G lj MA P s VS) Bar Wed-Thu 23-3.30, Fri-Sat -6, Sun 18-3.30 h
Via Polese 47/C ✉40124 ☎ 051 24 39 98
Arcigay membership required/tessera Arcigay. 3rd Sat/month LJ night with show in the „Red Zone".

RESTAURANTS

Ristorante-Pizzeria Speedy (AC B CC F glm) 12-15.30, 19-1 h, closed on Mon
Via Saragozza 65/A ✉40123 *(Bus 20,32,33,37,38)*
☎ 051 58 50 54

SEX SHOPS/BLUE MOVIES

Andromeda (g) 9.30-12, 15-19 h, closed Sun
Via San Simone 1/2 ☎ 051 22 59 76
Clothing, video, mail order/vendita corrispondenza, video, abbigliamento, novita settimanali.

Magic America (CC g p W) Closed Mon morning
Via Don Minzoni 4B ✉40100 *(corner/angolo Piazza dei Martiri)*
☎ 051 24 55 04 *Large gay section.*

CINEMAS

Continental (OG r) 15-24 h
Via Emilia Ponente 221 ✉40100 *(near „Ospedale Maggiore")*
☎ 051 38 58 71

SAUNAS/BATHS

Cosmos Club (AC b E f G MA msg p sa sb sol VS) Sun-Fri 12-1.30, Sat -3 h
Via Boldrini 22 int. 16 ✉40121 ☎ 051 25 58 90
(5 minutes from main railway station, in courtyard through iron gate, look for green light over bell)

New Vigor Sauna (B DR G MA sa sb VS wh YG) Sun-Thu 14-2, Fri Sat -5 h
Via San Felice 6 B ✉40100 ☎ 051 23 25 07
Reduced entrance-fee after midnight and for age under 25 y/o. Arcigay membership required.

BOOK SHOPS

Libreria Feltrinelli 9-19.30 h, closed Sun
Piazza di Porta Ravegnana ☎ 051 26 13 92
Gay section, Spartacus gay guide.

NEWS STANDS

Kiosk/Rivendita Giornali
Piazza Porta S. Vitale 1 ✉40100

HOTELS

Guercino. Il (AC B bf CC g H MA W)
Via Luigi Serra 7 ✉40129 *(near railway station)* ☎ 051 36 98 93
Rooms with bath. Rates single Lit 120.000, double 180.000 bf incl. English and French spoken.

GENERAL GROUPS

Agedo Associazione Genitori Parenti E Amici Di Omosessuali Sat 13-17 h
☎ 059 52 53 91

Arcigay Arcilesbica Centro di Documentazione Archivio Videoteca Mon-Thu 15-19, Mon Wed 22-0.30 h, closed Aug
Piazza di Porta Saragozza 2 ✉40123 ☎ 051 64 46 824
Fax: 051 64 46 722 Email: dor5142@iperbole.bologna.it
Books, videos, international magazines.

Arcigay Arcilesbica S.C.O.T. (Servizio Counselling Omosessuale Telefonico) Gay phone: Tue-Fri 20-23, Lesbian line: Mon 20-22 h
Piazza di Porta Saragozza 2 ✉40123 ☎ 051 64 46 820
Email: arcigl@iperbole.bologna.it

Arcigay „Circolo 28 Giugno - Il Cassero"
Piazza di Porta Saragozza ✉40123 ☎ 051 64 46 902
Cultural centre, meeting point/Centro culturale, punto d'incontro.

HEALTH GROUPS

Anlaids
Via Irnerio 53 ✉40126 ☎ 051 63 90 727

Arcigay GASP! Gay Aids Prevenzione E Salute Mon 17-20, Tue 14-18 h
c/o Il Cassero ☎ 051 64 46 820
Closed in Aug.

HELP WITH PROBLEMS

Dott. Pietrantoni Luca
☎ 0338 62 93 754
Psychologist.

Dott.ssa Casamassima Franca
☎ 051 39 72 84
Psychologist.

CRUISING

-Main Railway Station/Stazione Centrale FS (R)
-Via Bovi Campeggi (near facilities/vicino gabinetto)
-Car park Michelino (mainly by car)
-Via Michelino, Fiera Zone

Bolzano/Bozen ✉ 39100

BARS

Centaurus Bar (B G) Wed, Sat 21-24 h
Talfergasse 1 ✉39100 ☎ 0471 97 63 42

NEWS STANDS

Kiosk/Rivendita Giornale (g)
Via della Mostra (Mustergasse) *(P. Talvera/Talferbrücke Richtung Gries neben Siegesdenkmal)*
Kiosk/Rivendita Giornale (g)
Via Perathoner *(bus station/autostazione)*
Kiosk/Rivendita Giornale (g)
Via Cagliari ✉39100 *(15 min. walk from city center)*

HEALTH GROUPS

LILA (Lega Italiana Lotta contro l'Aids) Mon-Thu 8.30-12, 14-18, Fri 8.30-14 h
Via Bari 14/A ✉39100 ☎ 0471 93 22 00 Fax: 0471 93 22 00

HELP WITH PROBLEMS

Rosa Telefon/Linea Gay Tue 20-22
✉39100 ☎ 0471 97 63 42

RELIGIOUS GROUPS

Circolo Arcigay Centaurus Wed Sat 21-24 h, Tue 20-22 h
Via Talvera 1 ✉39100 ☎ 0471 97 63 42 Fax: 0471 97 63 42
Gay group, also religous group.

SWIMMING

-Stadtbad/Swimming Hall Bozen (NG pi) (just in winter 19-21 h. Via Trieste/Triester Straße)
-Freibad/Lido (g NG pi) (summer 9-19 h near Stadtbad)
-Strand am Talferfluß/beach at river Talvera (G MA NU) (take road to Sarnthein, 2 km from Bozen stop at parking place Sill, from there a short walk down the valley)
-Africa at river Talfer (G MA NU) (take road to Sarnthein/Sarentino, 4 km from Bozen turn off at sign „Bar Seeberger Jausestation" and drive to end of road. From there, walk 500 m up the river.

CRUISING

-Parco Petrarca (neben/near/vicino Piazza Victoria, AYOR)

Bormio - Sondrio ✉ 23023

CRUISING

-Piscina termale sauna
-Solarium Di Bormio 2000

Bra - Cuneo ✉ 12042

CRUISING

-Giardini della Rocca

Brescia ✉ 25100

BARS

Re Desiderio (A B f G) 15-1 h, closed Mon
Vicolo Lungo 11 ✉25121 ☎ 030 49 499

DANCECLUBS

Out Limits Disco (AC B D DR f G OS VS) Fri Sat 22-5
Via Ugo Foscolo 2, Paderno Franciacorta ✉25050 ☎ 030 65 75 36
Highway A4 MI-VE exit „Ospitaletto". 2 km from the exit. /Autostrada A4 MI-VE uscita „Ospitaletto". A 2 km dal casello. 2 dancefloors: House and commercial music.

SEX SHOPS/BLUE MOVIES

Europa 92 (g)
Via dei Mille 22 ☎ 030 37 58 459
Magic America (CC g p W) Closed on Mon morning
Oberdan/Via Scuole 20/C ✉25100 ☎ 030 39 84 53
Magic America (CC g p) Closed on Mon morning
Via Lamarmora 146A ✉25124 ☎ 030 34 93 94

NEWS STANDS

Kiosk/Rivendita Giornali (g)
Piazza Garibaldi/Via Milano
Kiosk/Rivendita Giornali (g)
Stazione FS

GENERAL GROUPS

Agedo Associazione Genitori Parenti E Amici Di Omosessuali In the evening.
☎ 030 26 91 701
Orlando - Centro culturale di iniziativa omosessuale Fri 21-24, Sun 15-20 h
Piazzale Arnaldo 21 ✉25121 ☎ 030 47 601 Fax: 030 494 65
Email: orlandoarci@yahoo.com
Homepage: http://www.geocities.com/westhollywood/park/6273

HEALTH GROUPS

Centro Dermoceltico
Via Galilei 22
Presso USSL 41.

CRUISING

-Public Garden (Via Ugoni)
-APAM Bus Satation (police)
-Railway Station FS (R TV) (also around the building
-Via Torrelunga and Via Spalto S. Marco (behind the jail)
-Via Eritrea (after 23 h)
-Via Nullo (AYOR) (behind Vantiniano cemetery)
-Giardini del Castello (AYOR) (in the parks close to S. Pietro church; evenings only)
-Lungo il Fiume Mella (only daytime in summer)
-Viale Italia (R TV)
-Zona Carmine
-Zona Industriale (MA YG) (Via Grandi/Via Perotti, by car, weekdays after 21, WE after 13 h)

Brindisi ✉ 72100

CRUISING

-Corso Umberto
-Central Station/Stazione Centrale (R) (also surrounding area/anche dintorni)
-Parco della Rimembranza

Cagliari ✉ 09100

BARS

Circolo Samba-Tessera AICD (A AC B F MA P S W YG)
Via Mameli 122 ✉09100 ☎ 070 65 13 48

SEX SHOPS/BLUE MOVIES

Sixtynine Sexy Shop (G P VS) 10-13 17-20.30, Mon 17-20.30 h
Via Bayle 69 ✉09100 ☎ 070 66 95 50
Toys, videos, clothing, rubber and leathers, gadgets, magazimes, CDs.

CINEMAS

Astoria (g MA)
Via Col del Rosso

GENERAL GROUPS

Kaleidos - Associazione di cultura omosessuale Tue 18-20, Fri Sun 20-22 h
Via Leopardi 3 ✉09100 Email: aco.kaleidos@tiscali.it

HEALTH GROUPS

Anlaids Infoline: Mon-Fri 9-13 h
Via Bembo 25 ✉09131 ☎ 070 49 70 50 Fax: 070 48 69 70
Centro Epidemiologico Sardo
Via Cadello 9/b ✉09100
Prof. Paolo Emilio Manconi.

SWIMMING

-Cala Fighera (g NU) (5 km from Cagliari, Bus N°11, under the casern, on the rocks)
-Terra Mala (G NU) (20 km from Cagliari, on the way to Villasimius, last stop of 1Q bus, turn left and walk 700 metres along the shore)
-Piscina Rei, swimmig pool, Cala Mosca, on the dunes

CRUISING

-Piazza Matteotti (in front of the railway station, all the day/fronte stazione, tutto il giorno)
-P Chiesa Bonaria (all the day/tutto il giorno)
-P Fiera, via C. Colombo (+ 22 h)
-Via Roma (under the porch, soldiers)

Caiolo - Sondrio ✉ 23010

CRUISING

-River Livrio, on Albosaggia-Caiolo road, near Caiolo signpost, follow path to river, summer afternoons on foot or bicycle

Camerino - Macerata ✉ 62032

CRUISING

-Rocca Borghese (gardens, at night/giardini, notte)
-Piazza Principale

Campobasso ✉ 86100

HEALTH GROUPS

Ospedale A. Cardanelli
Via U. Petrella 10 ✉86100 ☎ 0874 40 91
HIV testing.

CRUISING

-Railway Station/Stazione FS

Canosa di Puglia - Bari ✉ 70053

CINEMAS

D'Ambra (G)
Via Piave 9 ✉70053 ☎ 0883 96 18 97
Action in the corridor.

SWIMMING

Go to the beach through the parking lot, then walk for 10 minutes towards right. Dunes and busches. Nudity.

Capo d'Orlando ✉ 98071

BARS

Oasis Club (B g F OS VS) 21-2 h, Closed on Wed and in Aug
Via Forno 51 ✉98071 ☎ 0941 90 13 18
Typical sicilian cuisine.

Capri - Napoli ✉ 80073

BOOK SHOPS

Conchiglia. La (g)
Via le Botteghe 12 ✉80073 ☎ 081 83 76 577

SWIMMING

-L'Arsenale (NU) (occasionally/occasionalmente)

CRUISING

-Via Krupp (also nearby in the park/anche vicino nel parco)
-Piazzetta di Capri

Casale Monferrato - Alessandria ✉ 15053

CINEMAS

Poli (g)
Via Guazzo 13 ✉15053 ☎ 0142 45 20 81

Caserta ✉ 81100

TRAVEL & TRANSPORT

Di Matteo Viaggi e Turismo Mon-Fri 9-13, 16-20, Sat 9-13 h
Via Liberta 94 ✉81024 *(7 km from Caserta)* ☎ 0823 40 59 62
Fax: 0823 40 59 63 Email: pinodm@tin.it
Homepage: http://www.dimatteo.it *Specialized in gay travelling.*

HEALTH GROUPS

Network Nazionale „Gruppo C" Progetto di Ricerca Aids
✉81100 ☎ 0823 23 23 11
Helpline for people with HIV/Aids.

CRUISING

-Palazzo Reale (very AYOR) (in the gardens/nei giardini)
-Piazza Vanvitelli (in the evening; mixed, pleasant atmosphere/di sera; misto, ambiente piacevole)

Cassano d'Adda - Milano ✉ 20062

CRUISING

-River Adda beach, follow paths from Cassano-Rivolta road

Castelfranco Veneto - Treviso ✉ 31033

TRAVEL & TRANSPORT

Alex & Julian Viaggi (CC) Tue-Sat 9-13, 15-20 h
Piazza Europa Unita 24 ✉31033 ☎ 0423 72 31 78
Fax: 0423 74 44 44

PEGASO'S
CLUB
Via Canfora, 9
95128 CATANIA
Tel. 095.445438
Info line:
0347.1734371
0347.7267661
Giovedì BAR
Venerdì Discobar
Sabato Disco
Domenica Disco + Cabaret
The Trans Monsters show
D.J. Poppins
• PRIVE'
• DARK ROOM
• AMERICAN BAR
• MAXI SCHERMO
INGRESSO TESSERA
UNO CARD

Castellamare di Stabia - Napoli ✉ 80053

CRUISING

-Villa Comunale (also surrounding area/anche dintorni)
-Railway Station/Stazione Circumvesuviana

Catania ✉ 95100

GAY INFO

Centro di Iniziativa Gay-Lesbica-Trans „Open Mind" 17-20 h
Via Gargano 33 ✉95129 ☎ 095 53 26 85 Fax: 095 74 61 734
Email: openct@tin.it
Information, Counseling, Library, Cinema, Vocal box/Informazioni, Telefonico amico, Biblioteca, Rassegne cinema, Messageria vocale.

BARS

Moon Club Pub (glm) closed Mon
Via Empedocle 66 ✉95100
Mainly lesbian.
Nievski (B F glm MA s) 20-2 h, closed Mon
Scalinata Alessi 15/17 ✉95100 ☎ 095 31 37 92
Occasionally concerts and movies/Ogni tanto concerti e rassegne cinematografiche.
SottosopraPub (B glm MA) Thu-Sun
Via S. Fulci 9 ✉95100 ☎ 095 37 72 62

DANCECLUBS

Pegaso's Club (B D DR G TV VS s) Open from Oct to June only. Thu-Sun 22.30-? h
Via Canfora 9 ✉95128 ☎ 0347 72 67 661 (Infoline)
Arcigay card required. Disco on Sat and Sun. Cabaret and dragshow on Sun.
Pegaso's Estate (B bf D GLM MA OS pi s W) Open from Jun to Sep on Sat and Sun
Via Viale Kennedy 80 ✉95100 *(Entrance/Ingresso Lidi Playa)*
☎ 0347 72 67 661 (Infoline)
Shows on Sun. Call for more details.

SEX SHOPS/BLUE MOVIES

Erotica
Via Caronda 120 ☎ 095 50 50 10
Tentazione
Corso delle Province 38 ☎ 095 38 36 00

CINEMAS

Nuovo Sarah (g OG)
Via A. di Sangiuliano 124 ✉95100 ☎ 095 53 98 67

HOTELS

Hotel Moderno (bf H)
Via Alessi 9 ✉95124 *(Near the Dome)* ☎ 095 32 62 50
Fax: 095 32 66 74
Single room Lit 100.000, Double room 150.000 with bath, TV, phone and bf. Discreet gays welcome.

HEALTH GROUPS

Aids' italians fighters league (LILA)
Via G. Sanfilippo 10 ✉95100 ☎ 095 55 10 17
Ospedale Garibaldi
Piazza S. Maria di Gesù ✉95100
Public hospital. Second division of infectious diseases.
Ospedale Maurizio Ascoli
Via Passo Gravina 187 ✉95100 ☎ 095 75 11 111
Public hospital.

CRUISING
-Piazza Grenoble (only by car)
-Portorossi (touristic harbour behind Piazza Europa-nude beach also)
-Villa Bellini (townpark's toilets, only afternoon)
-Porto (harbour, near the lighthouse, by car)
-Caito (the cliff behind the railway station-nude beach alo)

HEALTH GROUPS
Ospedale Civile
Via Pio X ✉88100 ☎ 0961 88 31 11
HIV tests.

CRUISING
-Railway Station/Stazione FS (R) (also in front, afternoon and evening/anche davanti, pomeriggio e sera)

Cava dei Tirreni - Salerno ✉ 84013

CRUISING
-Municipio (square in front, cruising by car, at night/piazza davanti, in macchina, di notte)

Cefalù - Palermo ✉ 90015

CRUISING
-Beach promenade/Lungomare

Cervia Milano Marittima - Ravenna ✉ 48015

CRUISING
-Foce del Canale (day and night/giorno e notte)
-Harbour/Porto (and surrounding area/e dintórni)

Chieuti - Foggia ✉ 71010

SWIMMING
-Chieuti Beach (70 km from Foggia. Walk 2 miles along the beach to the right of the railway station. Take food and drinks with you. Action is in the pine wood)

Civitanova Marche - Macerata ✉ 62013

CRUISING
-Piazza Cristo Re (night/notte)
-Via Leonardo da Vinci

Civitavecchia - Roma ✉ 00053

CRUISING
-Terme de „la Ficoncella" (at the highway exit, about 4 km from the city/vicino all'uscita dell'autostrada, circa 4 km dal centro)

Clusone - Bergamo ✉ 24023

CRUISING
-Main Road/Strada provinciale (MA) (woods, all times/pineta, qualsiasi ora)

Cologno Monzese - Milano ✉ 20093

CRUISING
-At the Metro stations/stazioni Metro

Como ✉ 22100

BARS
Halloween (B F glm s)
Piazza S. Rocco/Via Napoleona ✉22100
Ibiza (B g)
Via Foscolo 5 ✉22100 ☎ 031 30 46 52

CINEMAS
Italia
Via Marchesi 6 *(Ponte Chiasso)* ☎ 031 53 01 35

GENERAL GROUPS
Arcigay Arcilesbica Como Circolo „Koiné"
Sun 20.30-22.30 h
c/o LILA, Via Odescalchi 19 ✉22100 ☎ 031 30 07 61
Fax: 031 26 18 08

CRUISING
-Circle around soccer stadium.(+22 h)
-Stazione centrale FS (AYOR)
-Main road between Lomazzo-Turate, wood on the right side/Strada provinciale Lomazzo-Turate, bosco a destra (day and night by car/di giorno e di sera in macchina)

Cosenza ✉ 87100

DANCECLUBS
Moana Multiclub (B D g)
Via Siriomarco, Tortora Marina ☎ 0985 72 325

BOOK SHOPS
Domus (g)
Corso d'Italia ✉87100 ☎ 0984 23 110
Seme. Il (g)
Via Nicola Serra/Via Gramsci ✉87100 ☎ 0984 36 373

NEWS STANDS
Del Guidice (g)
Viale Roma 87
Edicola di Permesso. L' (g)
Corso Mazzini 4 ✉87100

HOTELS
Grisaro (g H)
Viale Trieste 38 ✉87100 ☎ 0984 27 952 Fax: 0984 27 838

HEALTH GROUPS
Ospedale Civile dell'Annunziata
✉87100 ☎ 0984 72 91
HIV tests.

CRUISING
-Stazione FS/railway station
-Giardini pubblici/public gardens

Creazzo - Vicenza ✉ 36051

SAUNAS/BATHS
Rainbow Club (AC b f g p sa sb MA) 15-1 h
Via Valscura 2/A ✉36051 ☎ 0444 52 26 47
Clean and quiet./Locale pulito e tranquillo

Crema - Cremona ✉ 26013

BARS
Charlie Brown (AC B D G YG) 21.30-1.30 h
✉26013 *(5 km east of/est di Crema)* ☎ 0373 78 05 52
Best Thu night/meglio giovedi sera

Cremona ✉ 26100

GAY INFO
Arcigay Arcilesbica „La Rocca" Fri 21-23.30 h, closed Aug
Via Speciano 4 ✉26100 *(Bus 1, near the Dome)*
☎ 0372 20 484 Fax: 0372 20 484

SEX SHOPS/BLUE MOVIES

Adamo ed Eva (AC CC g VS) Mon 15-20, Tue-Sun 10-20 h
Via Rosario 56 ✉26100 *(near Boschetto)* ☎ 0372 23 407

Mela Proibita. La (g) Closed Mon
Galleria Kennedy 12 ☎ 0372 36 118

HEALTH GROUPS

Gruppo C ☎ 0372 45 17 55
Free HIV test.

Network Nazionale „Gruppo C" Progetto di Ricerca Aids ☎ 0372 45 17 55
Helpline for people with HIV/Aids

CRUISING

-Via Lungo Po Europa (near the camping site, day/vicino campeggio, giorno)
-Foro Boario (near Stadium, by night/vicino Stadio, di notte)

COUNTRY CRUISING

-Soncino (on the state highway from Brescia to Cremona after Soncino, a little before the bridge, turn right, two roads enter the fields and then walk along the river Oglio, day/sulla statale Brescia-Cremona dopo Soncino, poco primma del ponte, a destra, due strade entrano nei campi e poi corteggiano il fiume Oglio, di giorno)
-Rivolta d'Adda (in the province of Cremona along the Adda River/lungo il fiume Adda)

Crotone ✉ 88074

CINEMAS

Apollo (g) Via Regina Margherita ✉88074

CRUISING

-Viale Regina Margherita

Cuneo ✉ 12100

CINEMAS

Italia (g)
Via Ponza di San Martino Gustavo 2/B ✉12100 ☎ 0171 69 29 51

HEALTH GROUPS

Ospedale Infettivi S. Croce
Via Michele Coppino 26 ✉12100 ☎ 0171 44 11

CRUISING

-Railway Station/Stazione FS (facilities and gardens/stazione, e giardino)
-Viale Marconi (TV) (police)
-Corso Kennedy (R) (police)
-Corso Gesso gardens/giardini

Desenzano del Garda - Brescia ✉ 25015

BARS

Scarabeo (B g) 18-3 h, closed Tue
Vicolo Duomo 13/A ✉25015 ☎ 030 91 40 085

DANCECLUBS

Art Club-European Dance Club (AC B D GLM OS S YG) Wed Fri-Sun 3-4 h
Via Mantova 1/A ✉25015 *(Highway Milano-Venezia, exit Desenzano, turn left, 300 m)* ☎ 030 99 91 004

RESTAURANTS

Sirenetta. La (F glm) closed Mon
Lungo Lago Cesare Battisti 59 ✉25015 ☎ 030 91 40 524

SEX SHOPS/BLUE MOVIES

Tuttisensi (g) closed Mon
Via le Motta 40 ✉25015 ☎ 030 91 21 667
Write/call for free mail oder catalogue/Per ricevere i cataloghi e il listino prezzi tel. e fax

FASHION SHOPS

Lucky 49 (CC) 9.30-12.30, 16-19.30, Summer: also 21.30-23.30 h
Via Roma 18, Duomo Galleria ✉25015 *(Historical centre)*
☎ 030 91 41 789
Men's underwear & beachwear/negozio di intimo e costumi da bagno)

SWIMMING

-Punta del Vò (rocky beach on road 572, 1 km from the village, daytime only/spiaggia sassosa, SS 572, 1 km dal paese, solo di giorno)
-Rocca di Manerba (G NU) (take the road to Salò, turn off at Moniga del Garda (centro) and follow the signs)
Parco naturale to the end of the road (but don't follow the signs „Manerba del Garda"!) Then take via Marinello on foot to the beach (15 min.)

CRUISING

-Punto del Vò (afternoon above the road, night at P)

Elba, Isola d' - Livorno ✉ 57036

CRUISING

-Harbour/Porto

Empoli - Firenze ✉ 50053

CRUISING

-Viale B. Buozzi (gardens of railway station and in the handicraft laboratories area, by car in the evening)
-Zona Artigianale Carraia

Enna ✉ 94100

CRUISING

-Around the Castello Lombardo/attorno al Castello Lombardo

Eraclea Mare - Venezia ✉ 30020

CRUISING

-Isola del Morto (NU) (beach/spiaggia). Very cruisy.

Fabriano - Ancona ✉ 60044

CRUISING

-Stadium/stadio (evening, night/sul tardi)

Fano - Pesaro ✉ 61032

CRUISING

-Viale Buozzi (behind the monument/dietro al Monumento)
-Football stadium/Stadio Calcistico (near entry/presso l'entrata)
-Beach between Fano and Pesaro/spiaggia tra Fano e Pesaro (NU)

Fermo - Ascoli Piceno ✉ 63023

CRUISING

-Between the archs of Lido di Fermo and Lido Tre

Ferrara ✉ 44100

CINEMAS

Mignon (g)
Porta S. Pietro 18 ✉44100 ☎ 0532 76 01 39

CRUISING

-Wall 200 m from railway station/mura 200 m dalla stazione
-Stazione FS

Firenze ✉ 50100

GAY INFO

Giglio Fucsia. Il (GLM)
Email: pinklily@gay.it Homepage: http://www.gay.it/pinklily
Gay & Lesbian guide for Florence and Tuscany. Free copy.
Viva Piazza
c/o Demomedia, Via Nazionale 17 ✉50123 ☎ 055 28 21 62
Fax: 055 28 90 63
Culture magazine with gay news section.

TOURIST INFO

A.P.T. Mon-Sat 8.30-13.30 h
Via Manzoni 16 50121 ✉50100 ☎ 055 23 320
Fax: 055 23 46 286

BARS

Café Cabiria (B d F glm) 8.30-1, Fri Sat -2 h, closed Tue
Piazza Santo Spirito 4/R ☎ 055 21 57 32
DJ music on Thu-Sun from 22 h.
Crisco (AC B CC DR f G lj MA P s VS) 22-3.30, Fri Sat -6 h, closed Tue
Via S. Egidio 43/R ✉50100 *(behind the church)* ☎ 055 24 80 580
Shows during the week-end/Spettacoli fine settimana.
Piccolo Caffé. Il (A B GLM MA W YG) 17-2 h
Via Borgo Santa Croce 23/R ✉50122 ☎ 055 24 17 04
Very popular.
Rose's (B F glm) 8-1, Sun 17-1 h
Via del Parione 26/R *(near Piazza S. Trinità)* ☎ 055 28 70 90
Also sushi bar.

Tabasco Bar (AC B CC D E GLM MA P W) 24-6 h
Piazza S. Cecilia, 3r ✉50123 ☎ 055 21 30 00
Y.A.G. Bar (AC B CC GLM S VS YG) 17-3 h
Via de' Macci 8R ✉50122 ☎ 055 24 69 022
Video bar, cruising place.

DANCECLUBS

Flamingo Bar and Disco (A AC B CC D GLM MA P s) 20-4 h, closed in Aug
Via Pandolfini 26/R ✉50123 ☎ 055 24 33 56
Disco Thu-Sun.
Timida Gozilla at Auditorium Flog (D GLM) 2nd. or 3rd. Sat 22-3 h. Info from Azione Gaylesbica
Via M. Mercati 24 b

RESTAURANTS

Colonnine. Le (AC B bf CC F glm) Bar 7-1, Restaurant 12-14.30, 19-1 h, Mon closed
Via dei Benci 6R ✉50122 *(Near/vicino Piazza S. Croce)*
☎ 055 23 46 417 Fax: 055 23 46 417
Bar, restaurant, pizzeria.
La Vie en Rose (A CC F glm MA) 19.30-24 h, closed Tue
Borgo Allegri 68/R ✉50122 *(Near Piazza Santa Croce)*
☎ 055 24 58 60
Candle lights dinner.
Trattoria San Zanobi (F glm)
Via san Zanobi 33/a R ☎ 055 47 52 86

SEX SHOPS/BLUE MOVIES

Frisco International Import (G) 9-13, 15.30-19.30 h, closed Sat Sun
Via Veracini 15 ✉50100 *(Bus 17,29,30,35)* ☎ 055 35 73 51
Mailorder, wholesale videos, lubricants, condoms/Vendita per corrispondenza e all'ingrosso di video, lubrificanti, profilattici.
Magic America (CC g p) Closed on Mon morning
Via Guelfa 87/R ✉501 ☎ 055 21 28 40

CINEMAS

Arlecchino (OG R) 15.30-24 h
Via de' Bardi 47/R ✉50100 *(near Ponte Vecchio)*
☎ 055 28 43 32
Italia (g) Gay movies: Wed
Piazza Alinari ☎ 055 21 10 69

SAUNAS/BATHS

Florence Baths (A AC B CC DR f G MA msg P sa sb sol VS W wh WO) 14-2, Jun-Sep 15-2 h
Via Guelfa 93/R ✉50123 *(near railway station)*
☎ 055 21 60 50

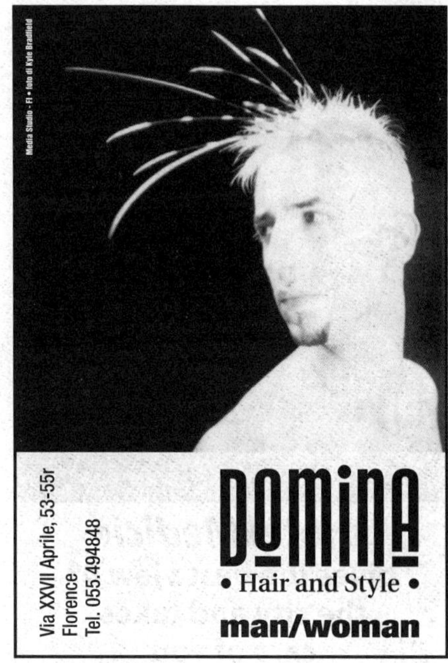

BODY & BEAUTY SHOPS

Domina
Via 27 Aprile 53-55 R
☎ 055 49 48 48 *Hair and style for men and women.*

BOOK SHOPS

City Lights 16-24 h, closed Mon
Via di S. Niccolò 23/R ☎ 055 23 47 882 Fax: 055 23 47 882
Gay section. Literature and video festival.
Libreria del Cinema Crawford (CC NG) 9.30-13, 15.30-19.30 h, closed Sun
Via Guelfa 14/R ✉50129 *(Near the Dome/Vicino al Duomo)*
☎ 055 21 64 16
Cinema specialized book-shop. Also post-cards, photos, magazines and posters.

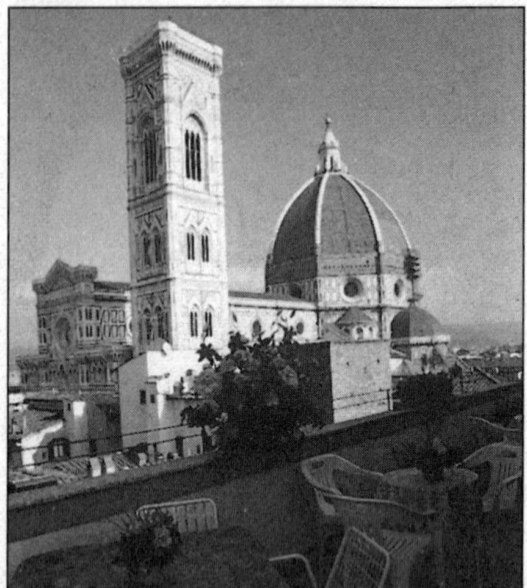

DECORATION

Mondo dell'Arte. Il (CC GLM lj YG) Tue-Sat 9.30-12.30, 15.30-19.30, closed Mon Sun
Via Ponte all'Asse 15/17/R ✉50123 ☎ 055 36 65 95

FASHION SHOPS

Giardino d'Inverno. Il (CC glm MA) 9-13, 15-19.30 h, closed Sun and Mon morning
Via del Melarancio 8/R ✉50123 *(near station FS)* ☎ 055 21 13 91
Men's & women's under- and beachwear. 10% discount for Spartacus readers.

Sandro 10-13, 15-19 h, closed Sun and Mon morning
Via Tosinghi 7/R ✉50122 ☎ 055 21 50 63
Men's and women's wear.

GIFT & PRIDE SHOPS

Cornice é... (CC glm) 9.30-19.30 h
Via del Melarancio 15/R ✉50123 *(Stazione di Santa Maria Novella)* ☎ 055 21 58 31

NEWS STANDS

Edicola Balsimelli
Piazza Santa Maria Novella
Babilonia magazines and gay books. Open till late at night.

TRAVEL & TRANSPORT

Queernation Holidays (CC GLM) Mon-Fri 9.30-19, Sat 9.30-12.30 h
Zannetti 18/R ✉50123 *(Central/Centro)* ☎ 055 28 41 83
Fax: 055 23 96 661 Email: queernation.holidays@dada.it
Homepage: http.//www.queernationholidays.com
Gay travels in Italy and all over the world, gay and gay friendly hotels, flight tickets, personal offers, information about the Florence and italian gay scene/Viaggi per gay in Italia e nel mondo, hotel gay e gay friendly, biglietteria aerea, pacchetti personalizzati, info point sulla „scena" gay de Firenze e d'Italia.

HOTELS

Hotel Cellai (AC B bf CC H OS)
Via 27 Aprile 14 ✉50129 *(Close to railway station)* ☎ 055 48 92 91
Fax: 055 47 03 87 Email: info@hotelcellai.it
Homepage: www.hotelcellai.it
Very central location. Charming, old-fashioned hotel, splendid view from the terrace. Rates Lit single 120.000-210.000, double 190.000-320.000.

Hotel Medici (B bf CC g H OS)
Via de Medici 6 ✉50123 ☎ 055 28 48 18 Fax: 055 21 62 02
Email: medici@dada.it
Located in historical center. Rooms with TV and phone, with/without bath. Rates single Lit 70.000-150.000, double 110.000-270.000. bf incl. Roof garden. Appartments on request. Information about gay scene available.

Hotel Morandi alla Crocetta (AC bf CC H)
Via Laura 50 *(near Piazza della SS. Annunziata)* ☎ 055 23 44 747
Fax: 055 24 80 954 Email: welcome@hotelmorandi.it
Homepage: http://www.hotelmorandi.it
Rates single Lit 150.000, double 260.000. Rooms with bath, TV and phone. Reservation per fax with credit-card only. Garage. Very gay friendly

Hotel Tina (CC glm H)
Via San Gallo 31 ✉50129 ☎ 055 48 35 19 Fax: 055 48 35 93
Rates single Lit 70.000-100.000, double 100.000-140.000. Own key at night. Friendly staff. Information about gay scene available.

Hotel Wanda (bf glm H)
Via Ghibellina 51 ✉50122 *(Near the cathedral/vicino dal Duomo, Bus 14)* ☎ 055 23 44 484 Fax: 055 24 21 06
Single room Lit 120.000-150.000, Double room 150.000-200.000, with/without bath, some with TV and frescoes.

Mona Lisa (H NG)
Borgo Pinti 27 ✉50100 ☎ 055 24 79 751 Fax: 055 24 79 755
Very good and well located. Rates single Lit 250.000-300.000, double 380.000-480.000. Buffet bf incl.

Palazzo Vecchio (g H)
Via Cennini 4 ✉50100 ☎ 055 21 21 82 Fax: 055 21 64 45
Rates single Lit 100.000, double 160.000-200.000. Rooms with bath and TV. Bf incl. Car park.

GUEST HOUSES

Dei Mori (AC bf glm MG)
Via Dante Alighieri 12 ✉50122 *(between the Duomo and Signoria square)* ☎ 055 21 14 38 Fax: 055 21 14 38
Email: deimori@bnb.it Homepage: www.bnb.it/deimori
Rates single Lit 90.000, double 170.000 (bf incl.). Own key. Non smoking hotel. Small and friendly/Ambiente familiare. Early booking advisable/Prenotare in anticipo.

Pensione Savonarole (bf H NG)
Viale Matteotti 27/Via Cavour ☎ 055 58 78 24
Rates single Lit 98.000, double 130.000 (bf incl.). Rooms with bath. Reduced car park fee for clients.

PLP Guest House (F glm H)
Via G. Marconi 47 ✉50131 *(near/vicino Campo di Marte)*
☎ 055 57 20 05
Rates single Lit 50.000-70.000, double 80.000-100.000. Own key at night.

GENERAL GROUPS

Azione Gay e Lesbica „Finisterrae" Mon-Fri 18-20 h
c/o SMS Andrea del Sarto, Via Manara 12 ✉50135 *(2nd floor/ 2° piano)* ☎ 055 67 12 98 Fax: 055 62 41 687
Email: Gaylesbica.Fi@agora.stm.it
Homepage: http://www.agora.stm.it/gaylesbica.fi
Gay and lesbian political association. Meeting, library. Monthly parties, shows. Health consultations, HIV test. Touristic information/Associazione politica gay e lesbica. Reunioni, Centro di documentazione. Feste mensili, spettacoli. Consulenze sulla salute, test HIV. Informazioni turistiche.

Coordinamento Queer Meetings: Wed 21-24 h
c/o Ireos, Via del Ponte all'Asse 7 *(Bus 22)* ☎ 055 35 34 62
Informal coordination of gay-lesbian-transgender working groups for social action, culture, tourism and free time, parties, gay film club./Insieme informale di gay-lesbice-transgender per iniziative sociali, culturali, turistiche e ricreative, incontri, feste, gay cineclub.

Ireos-Centro Servizi Per La Comunità Queer Mon-Fri 16-19, Wed 21-24 h
Via del Ponte all'Asse 7 *(Bus 22)* ☎ 055 35 34 62
Gay, lesbian and more association, gay tourist information desk, social action, psychological counseling, courses, workshops, meetings, message board/Associazione di volontario di e per gay lesbiche e non solo, informazioni, orientamento, messaggi, accoglienza turistica, aggregazione, ascolto psicologico, corsi, gruppi di lavoro, incontri.

HEALTH GROUPS

Ambulatorio Dell'Unità Operativa Malattie Infettive Di Careggi
Viale Morgagni ☎ 055 427 74 52
Anonymous free HIV test.

Centro AIDS
Ponte Aniccheri *(Ospedale Santa Maria Annunziata Di Ponte Aniccheri)* ☎ 055 24 96 512

Centro MTS (Malattie Trasmissione Sessuale)
Piazza Brunelleschi, Cortile Ateneo ☎ 055 27 581

Ireos Mon-Fri 16-19 h
Via del Ponte all'Asse 7 *(Bus 22)* ☎ 055 35 34 62
Free psychological and medical counseling on Mon, free and anonymous HIV test, courses, self-help groups, home-care, physical therapy./Servizi gratuiti: consulenze specialistiche e psicologiche (lun), test HIV anonimo; corsi, gruppi di autoaiuto, assistenza domiciliare, attività psicofisiche.

HELP WITH PROBLEMS

Dott.ssa Sandonini Mirella
☎ 055 47 60 22
Psychologist.

SPECIAL INTEREST GROUPS

Extramuros
c/o Ireos, Via del Ponte all'Asse 7 *(Bus 22)* ☎ 055 35 34 62
Gay-lesbian hiking, trekking, travelling group/Occasioni d'incontro tra gay e lesbiche e non solo, scoprendo tesori della natura e della cultura: visite, passeggiate, viaggi.

SWIMMING

-Piscina Costoli (swimming pool, facilities and showers/bagni e docce; best late afternoon/meglio pomeriggio tardi; be discreet/discrezione)

CRUISING

-Viale delle Cascine (AYOR R TV) (P behind disco Meccanó)
-Campo di Marte stadium/stadio
-Viale Lincoln-Washington(on the bike path from „Ponte della Vittoria" to „Ponte all'Indiano" at night on foot or by bike)
-Highway Florence-Rome A1/autostrada Firenze-Roma A1 (P between Firenze Sud/Incisa, both directions)
-Gas station Florence North-Florence South A1/aera di servizio Firenze Nord-Firenze Sud A1. „Scandicci", both directions

Foggia ✉ 71100

CINEMAS

Dante (g) 16.30-23 h
Via Duomo 7 ✉71100 ☎ 0881 77 64 39
Garibaldi (g) 16.30-23 h
Via Garibaldi 80 ✉71100 ☎ 0881 74 85 47

HEALTH GROUPS

Ospedale Riuniti
Viale Pinto ✉71100 ☎ 0881 73 11 11

CRUISING

-Porta Manfredonia (TV)
-Piazza Cavour (at night/di notte)
-Viale XXIV Maggio
-Railway Station/Stazione FS (R) (also in the gardens/anche giardini and on the square to the right of the station/e nella piazza sulla destra della stazione)

Forlì ✉ 47100

GAY INFO

Romagna Sera - Settimanale Indipendente
Casella Postale 300 ✉47100 ☎ 0335 54 57 911
Email: primamano@libero.it
Local newspaper with gay ads „Messagi e incontri".

NEWS STANDS

Kiosk/Rivendita Giornali (g)
Via Costa-Gramsci ✉47100

GENERAL GROUPS

Arcigay Arcilesbica Forlì
Via Fratelli Bandiera 3 ✉47100 ☎ 0543 45 86 66
Fax: 0543 45 86 65

HEALTH GROUPS

Ospedale Morgagni
✉47100 *(Analisi cliniche)* ☎ 0545 73 17 17
Test and information about AIDS/test e informazioni AIDS

Gaeta - Latina ✉ 04024

CRUISING

-At the harbour/al porto
-Via Sampierdarena ☛Genova (by night and by car only)

Gallipoli - Lecce ✉ 73014

SWIMMING

-Liberia beach/Spiaggia Libera (From Gallipoli go to Ugento. Action in the pine forest on the right 1 km behind the Hotel Costa Brada)

Garda - Verona ✉ 37016

SWIMMING

-Punta S. Viglio at Baia delle Sirene, at the end and on the right side of the nudist beach, action in the evening and in summer only/in località Baia delle Sirene, in fondo a destra spiaggia naturista, solo d'estate, azione di sera (take the APT Bus 62-64, stop at S. Viglio/da VR prendere il Bus APT 62-64 e scendere a S. Viglio)

Genova ✉ 16100

BARS

Aqua Club (AC B f G MA P VS YG) 21-3 h, closed Tue
Salita Salvatore Viale 15/R 16128 ✉16100 *(from Via XX Settembre)* ☎ 010 58 84 89
Arcigay membership required.
Cage. La (AC B bf D DR f G MA VS) 22-4 h, closed Mon
Via Sampierdarena 167/R ✉16131 *(Bus 20, 1)* ☎ 0347 35 75 656 (Infoline)
Drink compulsory. Completely renovated. Very busy. Arcigay Card compulsory.

DANCECLUBS

Altra Notte Extreme. L' (AC B D DR GLM MA snu WE)
Sat, Days before holidays 23-5 h
Via di Francia 28 16011 Arenzano *(Autostrada Genova → Savona, exit Arenzano, after 100 m on the right, under La Culletta Restaurant. 100 m a destra, sotto ristorante La Culletta)* ☎ 0347 35 75 656 (Infoline)

RESTAURANTS

Bruno (b F g) 12-15. 19.30-22.30 h
Vico Casana 9/1 ✉16100 *(first floor)* ☎ 010 24 76 307

SEX SHOPS/BLUE MOVIES

Magic America (CC g p) Closed on Mon morning
Via Teodosia 7/R ✉16129 ☎ 010 31 67 83
Seventeen (g) 10-13, 15.30-22, Wed -21.30 h
Piazza Verdi 1-4/R ☎ 010 57 00 451
Gay articles, condoms, videos, books & magazines.
Seventeen (g) 12-24, Wed -21.30 h
Corso Gastaldi 173 ✉16131 ☎ 010 52 20 841
Gay articles, condoms, videos, books & magazines.

CINEMAS

Centrale (g) 14.30-24 h
Via S. Vincenzo 13/R ☎ 010 58 03 80
Cristallo 14-22 h
Largo della Zecca 1/R ☎ 010 25 10 574
Gioiello (AC g MA tv W) Mon-Fri 10.30-24, Sat-Sun 14.30-24 h
Via Balbi 101/R ☎ 010 26 13 51

SAUNAS/BATHS

Aqua Club (AC f G MA P sa sb wh) 15-24 h, closed Tue
Salita Salvatore Viale 15/R ✉16128 *(from Via XX Settembre)* ☎ 010 58 84 89
Service bar.

NEWS STANDS

Kiosk/Rivendita Giornali (g) 0-24 h
Piazza de ferrari 32/R ✉16125

HOTELS

Mini Hotel (b g H)
Via Lomellini 6/1 ✉16124 ☎ 010 24 65 876
Rooms with bath, gays welcome/Gay ben accetti

GENERAL GROUPS

CGIL-Osservatorio Per I Diritti-Centro Gay Tue Thu 15-18 h
Via San Giovanni Acri 6 ✉16100 ☎ 010 60 28 213
Fax: 010 60 28 200
Isola che non c'é. L' Wed 20-23, Sun 15-17.30 h
Via San Luca 15/7 ✉16123 ☎ 010 26 75 30
Email: isola@softhome.net Homepage: http://www.go.to/isola
Gay culture club. Library with videos. Cinema, parties.
Tram Dei Devianti. Il (G) Tue 21-23 h
Via San Luca 15/7 ✉16124 ☎ 010 26 75 30

HEALTH GROUPS

Anlaids „Alberto Terragna" Wed 15-18 h
Piazza Embriaci 3/1 ✉16123 ☎ 010 25 14 242
Fax: 010 25 14 242
LILA-Lega Italiana Lotta Contro L'Aids Mon-Fri 10-12, 13-17 h
Via Milano 58/B1 ✉16126 ☎ 010 24 62 915

SWIMMING

-See Pieve Ligure.
-Spiaggia Nudista-Varigotti (near Savona: from Noli in direction of Varigotti)

CRUISING

-Mura delle Cappucine and Giardini Coco (gardens) (AYOR) (near/adiacente Galliera hospital)
-Via Moresco (on the riverbank by night)
-Punta Vagno (Giardini Govi) (near the water clearing plant Corso Italia by day)
-Via Sampierdarena, near „La Cage" (by car, at night)

Ghisalba - Bergamo ✉ 24050

CRUISING

-Road/Strada provinciale Milano-Brescia (bridge over/ponte sul Serio)

Girifalco - Catanzaro ✉ 88024

CINEMAS

Ariston (g)
Via della Repubblica ✉88024 ☎ 0968 74 90 33

Godega di Sant'Urbano - Treviso ✉ 31010

SAUNAS/BATHS

Hobby One Club (AC B DR f G MA msg P p sa sb sol VS W wh) 16-2, Summer: 19-2 h
Via Leonardo Da Vinci 4 ✉31010 *(Behind „Manhattan" discotheque)* ☎ 0438 38 82 56

Gorgonzola - Milano ✉ 20064

HEALTH GROUPS

Network Nazionale „Gruppo C" Progetto di Ricerca Aids
✉20064 ☎ 029 51 31 06
Helpline for people with HIV/Aids

Grosseto ✉ 58100

HEALTH GROUPS

Ospedale della Misericordia
Via Senese ✉58100 ☎ 0564 48 52 19
Infectious diseases department

SWIMMING

-Marina di Alberese (wonderful natural landscape, many gays, crowded)
-Marina di Grosseto (along the SS 322 „delle Collacchie", 3 miles south of Castiglione delle Pesciaia, near „Le Marse" camping)

CRUISING

-Around the city wall

Ischia - Napoli ✉ 80077

GUEST HOUSES

Sabina - Bed & Breakfast (bf H)
Via Campagnano 20 ✉80070 ☎ 081 90 11 79 Fax: 081 99 14 14
Private villa in a lovely location on the island Ischia (near Napoli). Transfer from and to the port. Rates with bf Lit 30.000-40.000/person.

CRUISING

-Harbour in Porto on the left side near lighthouse
-Maronti beach behind hotel La Jondola

Isola Capo Rizzuto ✉ 88076

CAMPING

Camping Pizzo Greco
PO Box 57 ✉88076 ☎ 0962 79 92 82

Isole Tremiti - Foggia ✉ 71040

CRUISING

-Nudist beach/spiaggia nudista (best July, September/meglio luglio/settembre)

Ispra - Varese ✉ 21027

CRUISING

-Beach: follow directions for Diva Venus disco; path on the left (NU)

Ivrea - Torino ✉ 10025

SEX SHOPS/BLUE MOVIES

Videoclub XXX (g VS)
Via Aosta 35 ☎ 0125 49 328

CRUISING

-Piazza Freguglia
-Piazza del Rondolino, close to/vicino del Cinema Sirio (by car/in macchina)
-Corso Re Umberto, Giardini Lungodora (on foot, evenings/a piedi, di sera)
-Highway A5/Autostrada A5 Scarmagno-Pietra Grossa (by car)

Jesolo - Venezia ✉ 30020

BARS

Movida (B D g) Fri-Sun 22-3 h, only in summer
Via Belgio 149 ✉30020 ☎ 0421 96 17 19

SWIMMING

-Isola del Morto • Eraclea (Punta Sabbioni, 18km from Jesolo Lido. After „Camping Marina di Venezia" or better between the camping and the lighthouse. Dunes)

CRUISING

-Via Berlino / Via Firenze

La Maddalena - Sassari ✉ 07024

BARS

Crystal Bar (B f DR GLM VS YG) 12-2 h, Thu closed
Via Amendola 8 ✉07024 *(Ferries)* ☎ 0789 73 87 06
Popular

Rolling Rock Cafè (bf G VS YG) 17-4 h
Via Luca Spano ✉07024 *(near Piazza XXIII Febb.)*

La Spezia ✉ 19100

CINEMAS

Diana (g)
Via Sapri 68 ✉19100 ☎ 0187 73 71 79

HEALTH GROUPS

Ospedale
Via Vittorio Veneto ✉19100 ☎ 0187 53 31 11
Infectious diseases department

CRUISING

-Public gardens/Giardini Pubblici (from the Garibaldi monument to the end of the harbour/dal monumento a Garibaldi fino alla capitaneria di porto)

Lanciano - Chieti ✉ 66034

SWIMMING

-Spiaggia Le Morge

L'Aquila ✉ 67100

CRUISING

-Castle/Castello

Latina ✉ 04100

GENERAL GROUPS

Collettivo Di Cultura Omosessuale
c/o PRC, Piazzale Trampolini 33 ✉04100 ☎ 0773 66 24 76
Political gay group, telephone help line

CRUISING

-Railway Station/Stazione FS (Piazzale del Palazzetto dello Sport)
-Viale Michelangelo
-Via dei Mille

Lecce ✉ 73100

BARS

Nostromo (B D G P VS) Fri Sun 21-1, Sat 21-3 h
Via Vincenzo Morelli 25 ✉73100 *(500 m from the station)*
☎ 0832 25 60 38

HEALTH GROUPS

Azienda Ospedaliera Vito Fazzi
✉73100 ☎ 0832 66 11 11
Test and information about AIDS/test e informazioni AIDS

SWIMMING

-San Cataldo (Coming from Lecce turn left to »La Darsena«)

CRUISING

-Viale Oronzo Quarta (all day)
-Camera di Commerce (Via Petraglione by night by car)

Lecco ✉ 23900

CINEMAS

Marconi (g)
Viale Dante 32 ✉23900 ☎ 0341 36 27 31

CRUISING

-Railway Station/Stazione FS
-Lungolago (only in summer)

Legnago - Verona ✉ 37045

GAY INFO

Arcigay Arcilesbica Legnago Wed 21-23 h
c/o Riccardo Facchin, Piazza della Liberttà 10 ✉37045
☎ 036 83 83 72 24
Local section of Arcigay-Arcilesbica, political and cultural activities/sezione locale dell'Arcigay-Arcilesbica, attivitá politica e culturale

Legnano - Milano ✉ 20025

CRUISING

-Via Milano and park nearby/e parco vicino

Livorno ✉ 57100

RESTAURANTS

Germoglio. Il (F g) in the evening only
Via della Campana 31 ✉57100 ☎ 0586 88 071
Vegetarian cuisine only.

CINEMAS

Jolly (g)
Via Michon ✉57100
X-rated movies.

SWIMMING

-Sassoscritto (NU) on the cliffs (9 miles south of Livorno, near restaurant Sassoscritto, at km 304 marker on the Aurelia road)

CRUISING

-Piazza Dante (r) (in front of railway station (22-2 h)
-Zona industriale Picchianti (highway exit Livorno Centro. Follow centre indications. At the Circus, drive to Picchianti Industrial Area. In the open area, at night.)

-Lungomare dell'Ardenza (on the seaside, near Bagni Fiume, south of the Naval Academy, in the afternoon and at night, on foot, on the seaside and on the steps)

Lucca ✉ 55100

CINEMAS

Mignon (g)
Piazza San Quirico ✉55100 ☎ 0583 49 65 26
X-rated movies.

Nazionale (g)
Via Vittorio Emanuele ✉55100 ☎ 0583 53 435
Sometimes interesting encounters.

CRUISING

-Hospital, Via Delano Roosevelt e strade adiacenti/and streets nearby (by car at night)
-Porta Elisa (inside of the city walls, near the ramparts, on the right side of the city gate, by foot)
-A 11, area sosta/parking di Altopascio, both directions(AYOR, police controls)
-A 11, area servizio/service area Versillia nord, direction Firenze

Macerata ✉ 62100

CRUISING

-Sferisterio (summer/estivo)
-Public gardens/giardini pubblici

Malcesine - Verona ✉ 37018

SWIMMING

-Scogli delle Gallerie (State road to Riva del Garda, park your car at the last tunnel before Torbole. Then follow the path and go to the little beaches, nudity, action on the paths, from Verona take the APT Bus 63/Statale per Riva del Garda, scendere per un sentiero all' ultima galleria prima di Torbole; spiaggette per naturisti, azione sui sentieri, da VR prendere il Bus APT 63)

Maleo - Milano ✉ 20076

CRUISING

-Ponte (bridge on the road to Cremona/sul fiume adda strada per Cremona)

Manfredonia - Foggia ✉ 71043

CRUISING

-Sea coast/Lungomare (near the castle and in the gardens; also on the beach/vicino al castello e nei giardini, anche in spiaggia)

Mantova ✉ 46100

SEX SHOPS/BLUE MOVIES

Tuttisensi (g MA VS W) closed Mon morning
Via Vivenza 70 ✉46100 ☎ 0376 26 35 02

HEALTH GROUPS

Network Nazionale „Gruppo C" Progetto di Ricerca Aids
✉46100 ☎ 0376 77 11 60
Helpline for people with HIV/Aids

CRUISING

-Piazzale Palazzo Te (at night/di notte)

Marcelli di Numana - Ancona ✉ 60026

CRUISING

-Foce del Fiume Musone (during the day at the beach and in the forest/di giorno sulla spiaggia e nella foresta)

SWIMMING

-Nudist beach (G) (2 km south of Marina di Bibbona, near the camping)

Marina di Carrara ✉ 54036

CRUISING

-Tenuta di Marinella, Piazzale Camion (Via G. da Verazzano, along the seaside)
-Pineta (pine tree woods in the docks area)
-Pineta di Villa Ceci (Villa Ceci's pinetree wood, via Marco Polo)
-Scogliera di Levante (between the end of the river Lavello and the Molo di Levante (southernmost harbour). Summer only)

Marina di Cecina - Livorno ✉ 57023

SWIMMING

-Quagliodromo (NU) (beach in the area)

Marina di Pisa ✉ 56013

SWIMMING

-Calambrone (among sand dunes of the shore, half-way between the former children health resorts and the effluent canal. Daytime only)
-Spiaggia Libera Comunale (between Tirrenia and Marina di Pisa, near the US Army beach)

CRUISING

-Pine tree wood (By day only. Get in the first pine-tree wood you find while driving along Bigattiera Road from Pisa)

Marina di Ravenna - Ravenna ✉ 48023

SWIMMING

-Tratto Costiero (between Marina di Ravenna and Punta Marina, among the dunes and in the pine forest. Be discreet!/fra Marina di Ravenna e Punta Marina, fra le dune e nella pineta. Discrezione!)

Massa ✉ 54100

HEALTH GROUPS

Ospedale Generale
Via Sottomonte 1 ✉54100 ☎ 05 85 49 31
Infectious diseases department. HIV test.

Matera ✉ 75100

CRUISING

-Railway Station/Stazione FS (occasional meetings, also in front of the station/incontri occasionali, anche davanti)

Merano/Meran - Bolzano/Bozen ✉ 39012

BARS

Ponte Romano (B YG) 18-1 h, closed Wed
Via Ponte Romano/Sommerpromenade 3 ✉39012

FASHION SHOPS

Leo's Boutique
Leonardo da Vinci Strasse 13 ✉39012 *(in courtyard/in cortile)*
☎ 0473 23 73 68

CRUISING
-Gardens and avenue around railway station/giardini di fronte alla stazione
-Path between Ponte Romano and Ponte Tappeiner/passeggiata del Passirio (R)

HOTELS
Pension Sonnenheim (bf F g H) All year
Meransen 90 ✉39037 ☎ 0472 52 01 57
Rooms with bathroom/WC, balcony, phone & fax

Messina ✉ 98100

BARS
Haiti (B G)
Via T. Cannizzaro ✉98100
Select (B g)
Via T. Cannizzaro ✉98100 *(near/vicino university)*

CINEMAS
Capitol (g)
Via N. Bixio 70 ✉98100 ☎ 090 29 35 422

HEALTH GROUPS
Anlaids
Viale Regina Elena 223 ✉98121 ☎ 090 46 138

CRUISING
-Harbor area/Zona Porto (R)
-Villetta public gardens/giardini pubblici (Via T. Cannizzaro, behind/dietro Royal Palace Hotel)
-Railway Station/Stazione FS
-Piazza Cairoli (north and south/nord e sud)
-Marittima Railway Station/Stazione
-Viale San Martino (evenings only/solo sera)

Mestre - Venezia ✉ 30170

HEALTH GROUPS
Centro Dermoceltico USL 36
Via S. Maria dei Battuti ✉30170 ☎ 041 98 78 68
HIV-test

CRUISING
-Under the overpass between Mestre and Marghera (ayor YG) (Via Electricità (off Via Fratelli Bandiera) and side streets, especially near the truck scale, also street along the canal next to the Ship Yard. Busy after dark)
-Via Ca'Marcello (occasionally at night by car)

Milano ✉ 20100

GAY INFO
Altro Martedì. L' Tue 22-23 h, FM 101,5 and 107,6 MHz
c/o Radio Popolare, Via Stradella 10 ☎ 02 29 52 41 41
Biblioteca, Videoteca, Centro Di Documentazione Wed 21-24 h
c/o C.I.G., Via Evangelista Torricelli 19 ✉20136
Centro di Iniziativa Gay-ARCIGAY (C.I.G.)
(GLM s YG) Mon-Fri 17-20, Sun 15-20 h
Helpline/telefono amico on Tue Thu Fri 20-24, Trans helpline on Wed 20-23 h
Via E. Torricelli 19 ✉20136 *(courtyard/cortile)* ☎ 02 58 10 03 99
Fax: 02 839 46 04 Email: cig.milano@tiscali.it
Political and cultural activities, conferences, 28th June Festival, international library and archive, anti-Aids programme, coordination with Milan universities gay groups./Attività politiche e culturali, conferenze, festa 28 Giugno, archivio e biblioteca internazionale, attività anti-Aids, punto di conttato per i gruppi gay delle università milanesi.
Golden BBS
PO Box 107 34 ✉20110 ☎ 02 67 07 38 28
Fax: 02 66 98 65 33
Banca dati di annunci con e senza foto. Inserzioni. Immagini e animazioni per qualsiasigusto „hard".
Pride
Internal newspaper of C.I.G.
Speed Demon Mon 21.45-22.45 h, FM 98,0 MHz (Milano), 106,5 area BR, CR, PC
c/o Radio Onda d'Urto ☎ 02 28 27 494
Up City (Gay map)
Echo Communication, via San Nicolao 10 ✉20123
☎ 02 890 159 401 Fax: 02 890 139 41
Email: echoteam@tiscalinet.it Homepage: www.upcity.com
Gay map. Available in all gay venues/Disponibile in tutti i locali gay.

TOURIST INFO
A.P.T.
Via Marconi 1 ✉20123 ☎ 02 72 52 43 00
Fax: 02 72 52 42 50

BARS
After Line (AC B f D GLM YG) 10-15, 18-02:00h.
Via G. B. Sammartini 25 ✉20100 *(Metro Stazione Centrale)*
☎ 02 66 92 130
Disco-bar.

1. Alexander's Club Sauna
2. One Way Danceclub
3. Company Club
4. Transfer Club Danceclub
5. Cocksucker Bar
6. Hotel Durante
7. Libreria Babele Bookshop
8. Afterline Bar/ Restaurant Hot Line
9. Know How Sexshop
10. Lady San Crispino Restaurant & Hotel
11. Hotel Charly
12. Next Groove Café
13. Magic Sauna
14. Il Sottomarino Giallo Danceclub
15. Erotika Video & Sex Shop
16. Plastic Danceclub
17. HD Danceclub
18. Thermas Sauna
19. Partiqular Danceclub
20. Centro d'Iniziativa Gay Switchboard
21. Teddy Sauna
22. The Base Danceclub
23. Segreta Danceclub
24. Gasoline/G.T.D. Danceclub
25. Uiti Bar
26. Zip Danceclub
27. Argos Bar
28. Due Amici Restaurant
29. Querelle Bar
30. Nuova Idea International Danceclub
31. Magazzini Generali Danceclub
32. Pape' Satan' Danceclub
33. Ricci Bar
34. L'Edicolaccia News Stand
35. Molto Bar
36. Pervert Danceclub
37. Sex Sade Sex Shop
38. Energie Fashion Shop
39. Castro Gift & Pride Shop
40. Hotel America
41. Metro Sauna
42. Cruising Canyon

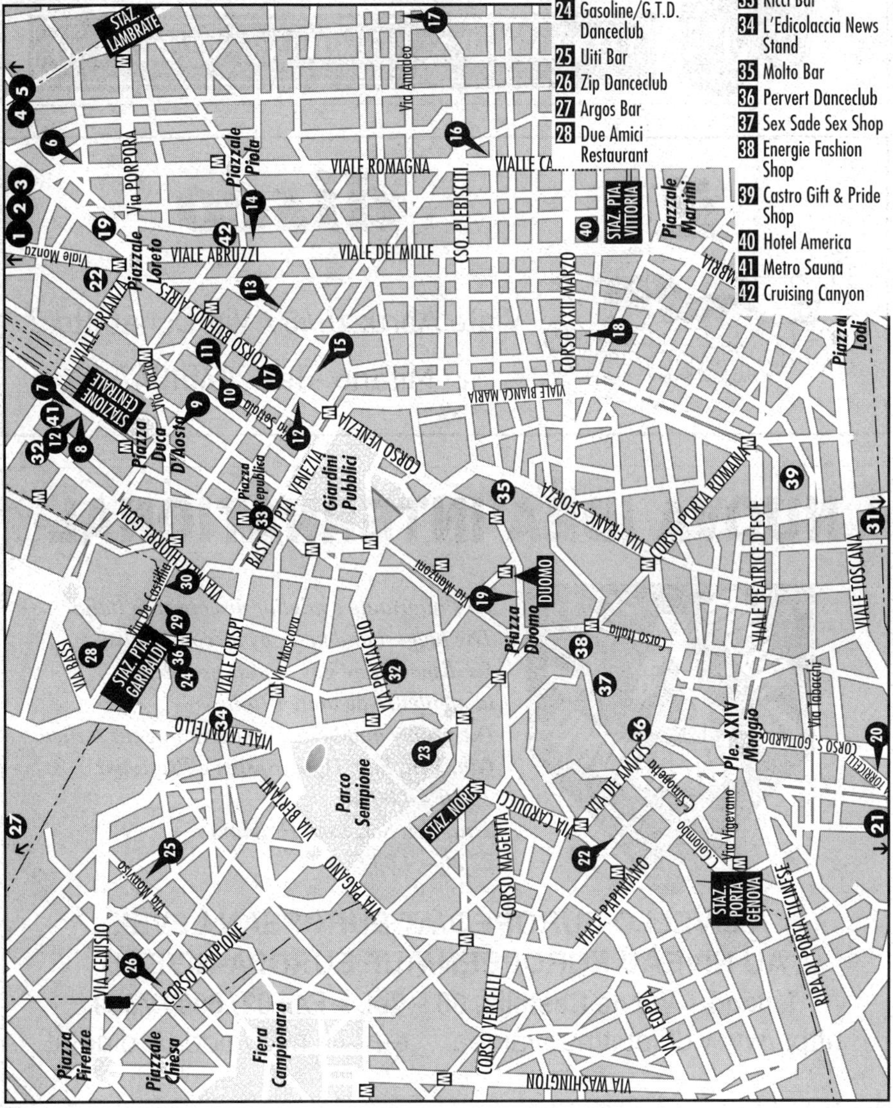

Argos Bar (AC B d DR f Glm lj MA P snu VS) 22-3, Fri-Sat-6 h
Via Resegone 1/via Lancetti ✉20158 *(Bus 90,91,92/ Tram 3/Ferrovia circolare fermata lancetti)* ☎ 02 60 72 249
Weekly parties, male striptease on Thu and Sun. Disco bar.

Birreria Uno Alternativa. La (AC B f GLM YG) 19.30-3 h
Via Borsieri 14 ✉20154 *(Metro-Garibaldi)* ☎ 02 69 00 32 71
„Alternative" pub and internet café

Cocksucker (B DR G LJ P VS) Fri & Sat 22.30-4, admission until 1 h, Sun 16:30-21:00h admission 'til 18 h. Wed & Thu 22-2 h
Via Derna 15 ☎ 02 26 82 57 12
Dress code. Also accessories retail. 1st and 3rd Sun theme parties 16.30-21 h, admission until 18 h. Accommodation on request (about Lit 50.000). Arcigay membership required.

Company Club (AC B DR G lj P VS) Sun-Thu 22-3, Fri-Sat 22-6 h, Mon closed
Via Benadir 14 ✉20132 ☎ 02 28 29 481
Three darkrooms. Arcigay membership required.

Cuore Bar (A AC B glm MA W) 18-2 h
Via Gian Giacomo Mora 3 ✉20135 *(near Colonne di S. Lorenzo/Tram 3)* ☎ 02 58 10 51 26
Very popular, but only few gays.

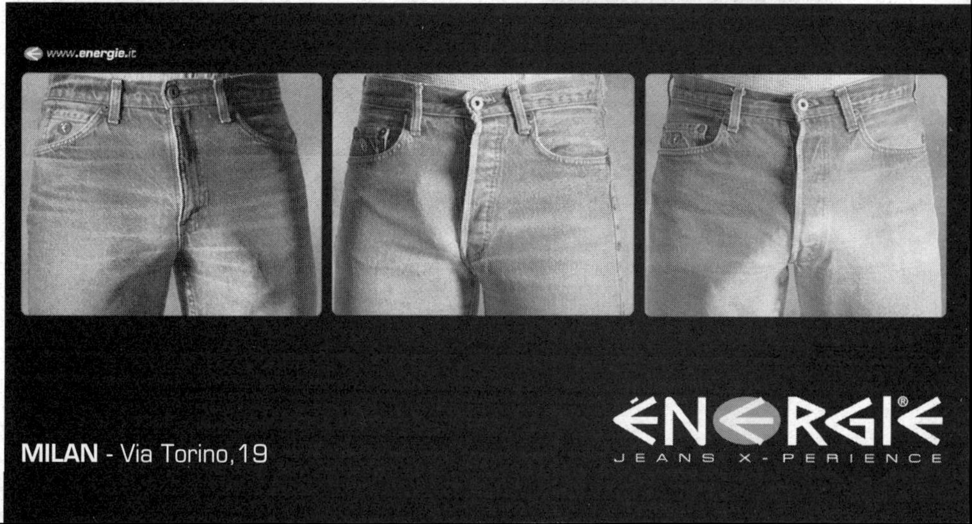

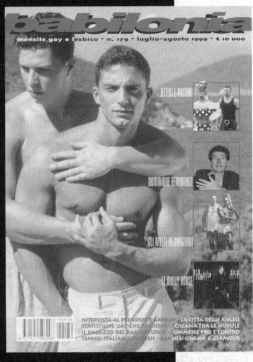

Elephante. L' (AC B f glm YG) 18.30-2 h
via Melzo 22/via Lambro ✉20129 *(Metro Porta Venezia)*
☎ 02 29 51 87 68
Oriental Happy Hour 18.30-21.30 h. Brunch on Sun 12-16 h.
Molto (A AC B CC d glm YG) 19-2 h, closed Mon
Via Borgogna 7 ✉20121 *(Metro-San Babile)* ☎ 02 76 02 45 12
Also closed in Aug. Nice bar, rather „kitsch".
Next-Groove (A AC B bf f glm YG) 10-2 h
Via Sammartini 23 ✉20125 *(metro St. Centrale)* ☎ 02 66 98 04 50
Querelle (AC B GLM lj p s) 21-1.30, Fri Sat -3 h, Mon closed
Via de Castillia 20 ✉20100 *(Metro Gioia)* ☎ 02 68 39 00
Cabaret shows on Wed. Arcigay Membership card/tessera Arcigay.
Recycle (B GLM S) Wed-Sun 21 1 h
Via Calabra 5 ✉20158 *(Bus 90/91/92/Tram 3/Ferrovia circolare Lancetti)* ☎ 02 37 61 531
Lesbian discobar, mixed on Wed and Thu. Internet access, cabaret, concert and pool.
Ricci Bar (B bf f GLM MA YG) 7-2 h, closed Mon
Piazza Della Republica 27/Via Pisani ✉20124 *(Metro-Piazza della Republica)* ☎ 02 66 98 25 36
Popular, after 22 h. DJ.
Uiti Bar (B G R) 20.30-2 h, Tue closed
Via Monviso 14 ✉20100 *(Metro Porta Garibaldi)* ☎ 02 34 51 615
Zelig Café (AC B f glm MA OS s YG) 21.30-2 h, closed Mon
Viale Monza 140 ✉20126 *(Metro-Gorla)* ☎ 02 27 00 13 93
From Oct to Mai: Dragshow on Fri with very famous comedians, Jazz music on Tue and Latin American music on Thu.

MEN'S CLUB

Cruising Canyon (DR G) 0-24 h
Via Paisiello 4 ✉20124 ☎ 0339 56 06 328 (Infoline)

DANCECLUBS

bar partiqular (a AC B CC D DR Glm s) Wed, Fri 23-4 h
c/o Q, Via Padova 21 ☎ 02 28 00 15 15
House music. Open all the week but Wed and Fri are more interesting for gays.
Base. The (AC b D glm s YG) Sat 23-5 h
Via Natale Battaglia 12 *(Metro-Loreto)* ☎ 02 58 10 27 66
„Camouflage Lab" on Sat, „Privé gay" with house music. Expensive
Gasoline (AC B CC D glm S YG) Thu 23-5 h
Via Bonnet 11a *(Metro Garibaldi)* ☎ 0335 66 94 781 (Infoline)
Rock and pop music. Nice place, nice people.
G.T.D. - Gay Tea Dance (! AC B D CC G S YG) Sun 17-22 h, Closed in Jul-Aug
c/o Gasoline, Via Bonnet 11a *(Metro Garibaldi)*
☎ 0347 22 01 024 (Infoline)
70s, 80s music. Popular.
HD (B D G MA) 23-3 h, Wed Thu Sun closed
Via Tajani 11/Via Caruso ✉20133 *(Bus 61, Entrance/entrata in Via Caruso)* ☎ 02 71 89 90
Small but nice/piccolo e carino. Men's strip on Mon, Cabaret show on Fri.
Lili La Tigresse (AC B D glm MA) 22.30-3 h
Via Broggi 1 *(Metro-Lima)* ☎ 02 29 53 03 75
Fashion bar with trendy music
Magazzini Generali (B D glm YG) Fri Sat 23-? h
Via Pietrasanta 14 ☎ 02 55 21 13 13
Lots of gays on Fri. House music and more.
Metropolis (AC B CC D DR f G MA P s VS YG) Tue, Fri, Sun 23-? h
Via Broni 10 ✉20123 *(Metro Corveto/Lodi)* ☎ 02 56 81 55 70
Gay night on Tue and Sun, Fetish night on Fri.
Nuova Idea International (AC B D glm MA OS s tv) Thu-Sun 22.30-4 h
Via de Castillia 30 ✉20124 *(Metro Gioia)* ☎ 02 6900 78 59
Two dance halls, one disco and one with band, holding 2500 people, very popular with younger and older gays, gay „rainbow" /Due piste, una disco e una di liscio con orchestra, molto frequentato sia da giovani che da non, „arcobaleno" gay. Drink included/Consumazione compresa. Cabaret, drag shows, striptease on Thu.
Oca Dipinta. L' (B D F G S) Thu
Ss. Paullese km 17.3000 ☎ 02 906 50 27
Restaurant, live music show and night dance. Outside Milan.
One Way (AC b D DR G lj MA P VS) Fri-Sat 22.30-4 h
Via Felice Cavallotti 204, Sesto S. Giovanni *(Metro Sesto-Marelli, Sesto Rondo)* ☎ 02 24 21 341
Membership or passport required/tessera Arcigay
Pape' Sata'n (! AC B D G YG) Sun 23.30-3.30 h
Via Fiori Chiari, 17/A ✉20121 ☎ 02 72 02 18 41
Very trendy house party.
Pervert (! AC B D glm MA s tv VS YG) Wed 23.30-6 h, closed Mid Jul-Mid Sept
Corso Como 15, c/o Hollywood *(Metro Garibaldi)*
☎ 0338 19 20 193 (Infoline)
House, Hardhouse. Popular.

AFTER LINE

gay disco-bar for men-women

APERTO TUTTE LE SERE

... MILANO'S FAVORITE BAR

Foto di Antonio Ambrosioni

METRO AFTER

Sala Metro Disco Dance

OASI ROSA
LESBO PARTY

via Sammartini 25 - MILANO (Metro Stazione Centrale)
Tel. 02/6692130, Fax 02/67070832, www.afterline.com

NUOVA APERTURA

via Sammartini, 23
Milano - tel. 02 67072048
OPEN **h 10 /15 - 18/02**

Plastic (B D DR glm MA s SNU TV VS YG) 23.30-4, Fri Sat 24-6 h, closed Mon Wed
Viale Umbria 120 ✉20135 *(Tram 12, 24, Bus 92)*
☎ 02 73 39 96 *Also closed in Aug. Thu is gay/lesbian night with strip and drag shows, karaoke. 3 dance floors: various music styles.*

Segreta Disco Club (AC B D DR GLM MA P s) Wed Fri-Sat 22.30-? h, closed Aug
Piazza Castello 1 ✉20123 *(Metro-Cairoli)* ☎ 02 86 03 07
Very popular on Sat, quite expensive.

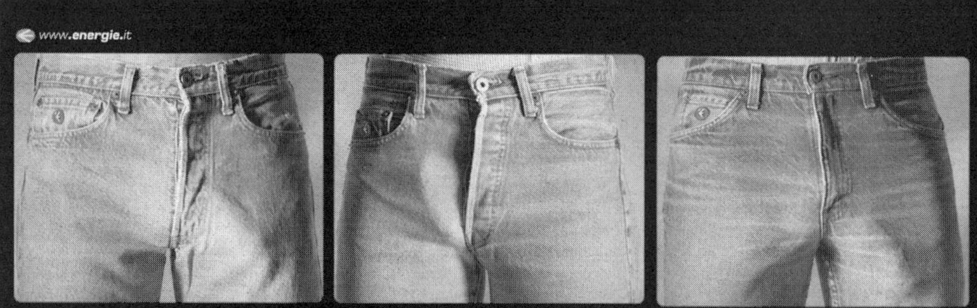

Sottomarino Giallo. Il (B D GLM p s) 22.30-? h, closed Mon Tue, Wed Thu Fri Sun (GLM), Sat Lesbian only
Via Abruzzi 48/Via Donatello 2 ✉20131 *(Metro Loreto)*
☎ 02 29 40 10 47
Special parties on Thu, shows on Fri, live music on Sun.

Transfer Club (B D DR lj MA pi VS) Fri Sat 22-6 h
Via Breda 158 ☎ 02 27 00 55 65

Zip Club (AC b D DR f glm MA p R s tv VS) from 2 h, closed Mon Tue
Corso Sempione 76/Via Salvioni ✉20154 *(Tram 1, 19, 33)*
☎ 02 33 14 904

RESTAURANTS

Due Amici (B F g OS) 8-16, 18.30-3, Sat -6 h
Via Borsieri 5 ✉20159 *(Metro Garibaldi, exit Gugliemo Pepe)*
☎ 02 66 84 696
Nice garden in summertime.

Hot Line (AC b bf CC F GLM) 10-15, 18-2 h, closed on Tue
Via Sammartini 23 ✉20125 *(100m from the railway station/della stazione centrale, Metro Stazione Centrale)* ☎ 02 67 07 20 48
Pub restaurant.

Lady Ristorante (B F glm H) Tue-Sat 20-24 h, closed Mon Sun
Via Settala 48 *(Metro Lima)* ☎ 02 29 51 06 58
Fax: 02 43 614

Risotteria. La (b CC F g) 20-23 h, closed Sun
Via Dandolo 2 ✉20122 ☎ 02 55 18 16 94

Volpe e l'Uva. La (B F g) 12.30-14.30, 19.30-22.30 h, closed Sun and Mon
Via Senaro 45 *(Metro Monte Napoleone/Turati)*
☎ 02 76 02 21 67

SHOWS

Alexander Cabaret (B glm MA S) 23-3 h, closed Tue, shows Thu-Sun
Via Ronzoni 2 *(Area Navigli)* ☎ 02 89 40 23 30

Sei Favolosa Anche Tu
Via Carlo Imbonati 5 ✉20159 ☎ 02 68 80 124
Fax: 02 66 86 173 Email: favolosa@guidemagazine.it
Arts & Show Dario Enriquez & Maurizio Conti. Nation-wide popular cabaret and theatre show with more than 30 of the best drag and theatre actors in Italy. Available every week in the best locations. See gay magazines for dates and addresses.

SEX SHOPS/BLUE MOVIES

Erotika Video Shop (g) 9-21 h, Sun closed
Via Temperanza 6 ✉20127 ☎ 02 28 98 195
Biggest sex shop in Italy./Piu' grande sexy shop d'Italia.

Erotika Video Shop (G) Mon-Sat 9-21 h
Via Sammartini 21 ✉20125 ☎ 02 67 38 04 04

Erotika Video Shop (g) Mon-Sat 9-21 h
Via Melzo 19 ✉20129 ☎ 02 29 52 18 49

Europa 92 (g) Mon-Sat 9-19.30 h
Viale G.B. Sammartini 21 *(Metro-Stazione Centrale)*
☎ 02 66 93 217
Gay articles, videos, magazines, rubber and leather articles.

Europa 92 (g) Mon-Sat 9-21 h
Viale G.B. Sammartini 25 *(Metro-Stazione Centrale)*
☎ 02 66 98 24 48 *Gay articles, videos, magazines, large offer of rubber and leather articles.*

Europa 92 (g) Mon-Sat 9-19.30 h
Viale Umbria 50 ☎ 02 54 69 582

Europa 92 (g) Mon-Sat 9-19.30 h
Via Stradella 12 ☎ 02 28 26 356

Magic America (CC g p) Closed Mon morning
Via Amadeo 46 ✉20129 *(Zona Città Studi - Bus 93/61 - Tram 5)*
☎ 02 76 10 083

Magic America (CC g p) Closed on Mon morning
Viale Umbria 50 ✉20135 *(Zona Porta Romana)*
☎ 02 54 65 679

Magic America (CC g p W) closed Sun and Mon morning
Viale Tibaldi 14 ✉20136 *(Metro-Fermata Romolo)*
☎ 02 83 76 953

Magic America (CC g p W) Closed on Mon morning
Viale Brianza 28 ✉20127 *(Metro Stazione Centrale)*
☎ 02 26 82 12 99

Magic America (CC g p) Closed Mon morning
Via Bramante 20 ✉20154 *(Zona Paolo Sarpi)* ☎ 02 34 94 118

Magic America (CC g p W) Closed Mon morning
Viale Misurata 17 ✉20146 *(Zona piazza Bolivar)*
☎ 02 42 39 980

Maxi Sexy Shop (g) Mon 14.30-19.30, Tue-Sat 9.30-19.30 h
Via Andrea Doria 48 ✉20124 ☎ 02 67 06 420

Sex Sade Mon 15-19.30, Tue-Sat 10-13, 14.30-19.30 h
Via S. Maria Valle 1/ Via Torino ✉20123 *(Metro Missori/Duomo/Tram 2/3/14)* ☎ 02 80 48 80

Studio Know How Entertainment (G)
Mon-Sat 9-12.30 13.30-19 h. Sun closed.
Via Antonio da Recanate 7 ✉20124 *(M° Centrale F. S.)*
☎ 02 67 39 12 24
Gay articles, videos; also mail order/Articoli gay, video; anche vendita per corrispondenza.

Yamato Shop (g)
Via Lecco 2 ✉20124
☎ 02 29 40 96 79 *Japanese gay videos and more.*

CINEMAS

Ambra (g) 14-24 h
Via Clitumno/Via Padova ✉20123 ☎ 02 26 82 26 10

Roxy (G r)
Corso Lodi 129 ✉20100 ☎ 02 56 92 304

Zodiaco (g) 14-23.30 h
Via Padova 179 ☎ 02 25 67 602

ESCORTS & STUDIOS

Gianluca Escort (G msg R) Mon-Fri 17-24, Sat Sun 10-24 h
☎ 0339 50 21 595

Massimo Escort (G msg R) Mon-Fri 17-24, Sat-Sun 10-24 h
☎ 0339 86 86 633

Stefano Escort (G msg R) Mon-Fri 17-24, Sat-Sun 10-24 h
☎ 0347 22 05 716

SAUNAS/BATHS

Alexander's Club (B f G sa sol wh VS) 14-1, Fri Sat -2, Fri Sat Alexander's Bar 2-5 h
Via Pindaro 23 ✉20128 *(Metro Villa S. Giovanni)*
☎ 02 25 50 220
Arcigay card required/Tessera Arcigay.

Magic Sauna (B f G msg sa sb sol VS) 11-24 h, closed Tue, Summer: 10-24 h
Via Maiocchi 8 ✉20129 *(4th floor/4° piano)*
☎ 02 29 40 61 82
Terrace with bar. In Aug also open on Tue.

Metro Sauna Club (! AC B DR f G MA P sa sb VS wh YG)
Sun-Thu 13-2, Fri Sat -3 h
Via Schiapparelli 1 ✉20100 *(Metro-Stazione Centrale)*
☎ 02 66 71 90 89

Teddy Sauna Club (AC b DR f G msg P sa sb VS wh YG)
11.30-24 h, closed Wed
Via Renzo e Lucia 3 ✉20142 *(Bus 59, 95/Metro-Famagosta)*
☎ 02 84 66 148
With cabins. English, French, German, Spanish spoken. Behind/Dietro Hotel dei Fiori. Monthly meetings of „Magnum" (4th Sat of the month). Arcigay membership required/Tessara Arcigay.

Thermas (! AC B f DR G sa sb sol VS wh WO YG) 12-24 h
Via Bezzecca 9 ✉20135 *(Tram 9, 29, bus 60, 73/Metro-Duomo)*
☎ 02 54 50 355
Friendly, hygenic, comfortable, young atmosphere. Tue and Thu after 19.30 reduced entrance fee. Low prices for young people (18-25).

13 24 (AC B DR G P pi sa sb sol VS wh WO) 13-24 h
Via Oropa 3 *(Metro Cimiano)*

MASSAGE

Massimo (GLM MA msg) 11.30-18.30 h, closed Sun and Aug
Via Carlo Goldoni 38 *(Metro Porta Venezia)* ☎ 02 70 10 52 77
15% discount for 10 massages./Sconto 15% per 10 massagi.

BODY & BEAUTY SHOPS

Body and Soul piercing studio Tue-Fri 15-20, Sat 11-18 h
Via Vigevano 11 ✉20144 ☎ 02 83 73 051

BOOK SHOPS

Libreria Babele (CC GLM) Mon-Sat 9.30-19.30, Sun closed
Via Sammartini 23 ✉20125 *(Metro 2/3 near stazione Centrale F.S.)* ☎ 02 66 92 986
Milan's only completely gay and lesbian book and video shop. English and French spoken. Also order by catalogue.

Mondadori Mon-Sat 9.30-23, Sun 10.30-23 h
Corso Vittorio Emanuele 24/26 *(Metro-San Babila)*
☎ 02 76 00 58 33
Large gay section with books and magazines.

CONDOM SHOPS

Love City Mon Tue 15.30-19.30, Wed-Sat 11-19.30 h
Corso Di Porta Ticinese 105 ☎ 02 58 10 54 72
Erotic wear, condoms.

FASHION SHOPS

Energy
Via Torrino 19

Gallery-A (CC g) Mon 15-19.30, Tue-Sat 10-13, 14.30-19.30 h. Closed in Aug
Piazza S. Giorgio/Via Torino ✉20123 *(Near the Dome, Metro Duomo/Tram 2/14/3)* ☎ 02 80 53 252

GIFT & PRIDE SHOPS

Castro Market (GLM) Tue-Sat 9.30-19.30 h
Via San Rocco 5 ✉20135 *(Metro Porta Romana)*
The only shop with gay & pride merchandise in Italy. Music, cds, videos, underwear, pridewear, guides and magazines.

NEWS STANDS

Edicolaccia Edicola e Libreria. L' 0-24 h
Piazza Baiamonti 1 ✉20154 ☎ 02 33 60 85 16
Large number of video and imported magazines.

Kiosk/Rivendita Giornali
Piazza Oberdan/Via Tadino *(Metro Porta Venezia)*
☎ 02 29 53 15 09

Kiosk/Rivendita Giornali 0-24 h
Corso Buenos Aires 4 *(Outside/davanti Farmacia, Metro Porta Venezia)* ☎ 02 29 51 65 57

Kiosk/Rivendita Giornali
Piazza Lima *(Metro Lima)* ☎ 02 29 53 14 17

TRAVEL & TRANSPORT

Ircam Viaggi Via de Amicis 44 *(Metro-S. Ambrogio)*
☎ 02 86 91 54 75 Fax: 02 86 91 19 37 *Travel agent.*

HOTELS

America (AC bf CC GLM H)
Corso XXII Marzo 32 ✉20135 ☎ 02 73 81 865
Fax: 02 73 81 490 Email: info@hotelamericamilano.com
Single room 50.000-60.000, Double room 80.000-12.000, including bf, phone, TV. Central location. The only gay hotel in Milan.

Antica Locanda Solferino (bf CC g H)
Via Castelfidardo 2 ✉20100 *(Metro Moscova)* ☎ 02 65 70 129
Fax: 02 65 71 361
Mixed, but gays welcome/Misto, gay benvenuti. Rates single Lit 150.000, double 200.000. Rooms with bath. Bf incl.

Hotel Charly (bf CC g H)
Via Settala 76 ✉20124 *(Metro Lima, Tram 1, 33, 60)*
☎ 02 20 47 190 Fax: 02 20 47 190 Email: charlyhotel@mclink.it
Homepage: www.italiaabc.it/az/charly
Rates: single Lit 70.000 to 100.000, double 120.000 to 140.000. TV/video, telephone.

Hotel Durante (CC H g OS)
Piazza Durante 30 ✉20131 *(Metro Loreto/Pasteur)*
☎ 02 26 14 50 50 Fax: 02 26 14 50 50
All rooms with WC, television and telephone. Rates on request. Gay welcome. Nice hotel with small garden.

Lady San Crispino (b bf CC F glm H OS)
Via L. Settala 48 ✉20124 *(Metro-Lima/Stazione Centrale)*
☎ 02 29 52 35 50 Fax: 02 20 53 614
Rates single Lit 110.000, double 160.000. All rooms with bath, shower, telephone, TV. Bf incl.

GENERAL GROUPS

Agedo (Associazione Genitori Parenti E Amici Di Omosessuali) Thu 14-17 h
☎ 02 89 40 17 49 Email: agedo@geocities.com
Homepage: http://www.geocities.com/WestHollywood/8748

Magnum Club
PO Box 17140 ✉20128 ☎ 0347 43 27 489 (Infoline)
Girth & Mirth/Orsi

FETISH GROUPS

Leather Club Milano (G LJ)
PO Box 3750 ✉20090 ☎ 0338 81 52 396
Email: lcmilano@leatherinitaly.com
Homepage: http://www.leatherinitaly.com
1st Sat every month in the company club. Member of ECMC.

HEALTH GROUPS

Anlaids
Via Koristka 3 ✉20154 ☎ 02 33 60 86 01 Fax: 02 33 60 86 85
Helpline on Wed 18-20 ☎33 60 86 83.

A.S.A./Associazione Solidarietà AIDS Mon-Fri 9-19, Sat -14 h
Via Arena 25 ✉20125 *(Metro S. Agostino)* ☎ 02 58 10 70 84
Fax: 02 58 10 64 90
Information, advice, psychological and legal advice, self-help groups for HIV-positives, documentation centre/Informazioni, consulenze, assistenza psicologica e legale. gruppi di auto-aiuto per sieropositivi, centro documentazione.

LILA-Lega Italiana Lotta Contro L'Aids Hotline Mon-Fri 9-13, 14-18 h
via Rogoredo 41 ✉20138 ☎ 02 51 00 23 Fax: 02 51 51 02
Email: lila@ecn.org Homepage: www.ecn.org/flash/lilamilano
Prevention, information, street work project for prostitutes. Legal and psychological counseling, self-help group.

Nucleo Operativo Prevenzione Aids
Via Fiamma 6 ☎ 02 73 83 370
HIV test by appointment, psychological support.

HELP WITH PROBLEMS

Dott. Salvi Mon-Sat 9-20 h
Via Ponte Seveso 39 ✉20125 *(Metro Centrale F. S.)*
☎ 02 25 35 385
English spoken, français parlé. Astrology, tarot, indian massage/Astrologia, tarocchi, massaggi indiani, shiatzu.

Istituto Gay Counseling Mon-Fri
☎ 02 83 23 465
Therapy and counseling for individuals, couples and groups.

RELIGIOUS GROUPS

Gruppo del Guado Wed 21-23 h
Via Pasteur 24 *(Metro Pasteur)* ☎ 02 28 40 369
Group of gay Christians/gruppo gay cristiani.

SPECIAL INTEREST GROUPS

Joy Mon 15.30-18.30, Fri 15.30-17.30 h
Università degli Studi, Via Festa del Perdono 3 *(Auletta „A")*
Gay student group.

Triangolo Silenzioso
c/o C.I.G., Via Evangelista Torricelli 19 ✉20136
Deaf gay group.

SPORT GROUPS

A.T.OMO Associazione Tennisti OMOsessuali Every 1st and 3rd Mon 21-23 h
c/o C.I.G., Via Evangelista Torricelli 19 ✉20136

Ga.Te.Volley Wed 21-24 h
c/o C.I.G., Via Evangelista Torricelli 19 ✉20136

Gruppo Pesce Milano-Milan Swimming Group
☎ 0335 83 41 956 Email: pesce@mv.itline.it
Homepage: http://www.gaysport.org

Kaos Milano
Via Sismondi 6 ☎ 02 70 12 36 07
Gay soccer team.

Ski Group Milano
c/o C.I.G., Via Evangelista Torricelli 19 ✉20136 ☎ 02 58 10 03 99
Fax: 02 83 94 604 Email: skigroup-it@geocities.com
Organization of gay people who love skiing.

SWIMMING

-Abbiategrasso-River Ticino (On Milano-Vigevano road, 30 km, P at bridge; walk for about 2 km southwards down east bank; action everywhere and NU/Sulla strada Milano-Vigevamo, 30 km, P prima del ponte. Camminare circa 2 km verso sud sulla sponda est. Azione dapertutto, NU).
-Piscina Ponzio (Via Ampere, Metro-Piola, in summer)

CRUISING

-Metro Porta Garibaldi
-Metro Lambrate, Al Bagni della Stazione FS
-Central railway station/Metro Stazione Centrale (ayor r)
-Piazza Trento (R)
-Ortomercato/Via Monte Cimone (by car, at night/sera)
-Via Novara (AYOR) (at Bosco in Città by night)
-Piazza Leonardo Da Vinci (in the garden on the square at night)
-Parco Nord (AYOR) (near Viale Fulvio Testi, by night)
-Idroscalo park (AYOR r) (east side/Lato Est. Segrate, night and day in summer)
-La Fossa (Viale Zola along the northern railway, cruisy day and night, very busy)

Mirandola - Modena ✉ 41037

CRUISING

-Piazzale G. Marconi (behind the/dietro il Teatro Nuovo)
-Via Spagnola (at night, cruising by car/di notte, in macchina)

Modena ✉ 41100

DANCECLUBS

Wovoka Club (B D G P) Wed Fri Sat 22.30-3 h
Via Canaletto 152/D ✉41100 ☎ 059 31 32 44
Lesbian night every second Sat. Gay night every Fri.

SEX SHOPS/BLUE MOVIES

Magic America (CC g p) Closed on Mon morning
Via San Giovanni Bosco 212 ✉41100 *Near/vicinanze Stabilimento Maserati)* ☎ 059 36 45 58

CINEMAS

Adriano (g)
Via Selmi/Corso Canalchiaro 57 ✉41100 ☎ 059 21 91 41

Odeon (g)
Piazza Matteotti 9 ✉41100 ☎ 059 22 51 35

CRUISING

-Railway Station/Stazione FS (also in the gardens/anche nei giardini)
-Giardino Ducale
-A1 Milano → Roma P Castelfranco at km 177
-Under Cialdino flyover (Viale Monte Kosica, Via Dogali, coach station)
-Via Minutara in front of Aeronautica Militare
-P New Palasport
-Viale dello Sport (facilities outside Iperoop)
-P at public swimming pool Pergolesi

Modica ✉ 97015

HEALTH GROUPS

Anlaids Medicalline: 9-14 h
Via Fosso Tantillo 14/A ✉97015 ☎ 093 27 61 934
Fax: 093 27 61 934

Molfetta - Bari ✉ 70056

CRUISING

-Villa Comunale (especially at night/specialmente di notte)
-Molo del Porto (R) (sometimes harbor workers/alle volte scaricatori del porto)

Monte Isola - Brescia ✉ 25050

HOTELS

Residence Vittoria (B F glm H OS)
Via Sensole ✉25050 ☎ 03 09 88 62 22 Fax: 03 09 88 62 22
Hotel located directly by the Lago d'Iseo. Nice view. All studio apartments have private bath/kitchenette and balcony overlooking the lake. Own small beach.

Montecatini Terme - Pistoia ✉ 51016

DANCECLUBS

Area Disco Club (AC B D F GLM H MA OS pi s W) Sat 23-4.30h
Via Pietre Cavate ✉51016 ☎ 0572 82 016
„Freedom" gay disco night. Week-end ticket: dinner + disco + bed + bf.

CRUISING

-Park around Terme Tettuccio
-In front of railway station

Montesilvano - Pescara ✉ 65016

DANCECLUBS

Alter Ego (AC B D G) Thu Sat 23-?, last Sun 21-? h
Via Napoli 27 ✉65016 ☎ 0854 45 50 37

Monticiano ✉ 53015

CRUISING

-Bagni di Petriolo, Terme d'acqua calda/hot spring water in river itself driving along the National Road 233 from Siena, after 25 km, follow Bagni di Petriolo headings. P near the old Thermal Building, before the bridge on the Farma river. Go down to the river, on the left side of the road (especially gay in the night but staye discreet)

Monza - Milano ✉ 20052

CRUISING

-Piazza Carducci (Centro Elettronico Comunale)
-Viale Reale (WE) (on the left side of the building/all sinistra)
-Railway Station/Stazione FS

Napoli ✉ 80100

GAY INFO

Arcigay Arcilesbica Napoli
Via San Geronimo 17-20 ✉80139 *(tram 1; bus 106,111)*
☎ 081 55 18 293 Fax: 081 26 88 08

BARS

Bar B (AC B d DR f G MA P s SNU VS) Sat 22.30-5.30 h
Via Giovanni Manna 14 ✉80133 *(near the university and railway station)* ☎ 081 28 76 81
Disco bar with a video room and a labyrinth.

Ferdinand Strasse (B f d GLM MA s) Tue-Sun 20-2 h
Piazza Portanova 8 ✉80134 ☎ 081 20 73 90
Tue Cabaret/Teatro, Fri Erotic show, Sun Dancemusic

DANCECLUBS

Exess Disco Club (AC B D GLM MA S) Sun 22-?
Via Martucci 28/30 *(Metro-Piazza Amedeo)* ☎ 0339 54 77 466 (Infoline)

Other Side Group. The (D)
☎ 0338 6175071
Discoclub on Sat from Jun till Sept. Call for Info.

Queens by Madison Street (AC B CC D F GLM MA P s SNU) Oct-May 23.30-? h
Via Sgambato 47 ✉80129 *(Metro Rione Alto)*
☎ 0338 61 75 071 (Infoline)
Restaurant on the first floor, Disco (House, Commercial, Underground) on the ground floor.

SEX SHOPS/BLUE MOVIES

Sexi Shop-C (g)
Calata San Marco 2-3 ☎ 081 55 16 353

CINEMAS

Argo (ayor tv)
Via A. Poerio 4 ☎ 081 55 44 764

Casanova (g OG tv) C
orso Garibaldi 330 ☎ 081 20 04 41

Eden (g)
Via G. Sanfelice 15 ☎ 081 55 22 764
Crowded/Frequentato.

Iride (g OG tv)
Via A. Poerio 7 ☎ 081 28 79 08

Trianon (g tv)
Piazza Calenda

SAUNAS/BATHS

Bar B (AC B DR f G MA msg P sa sb VS wh) May-Sept: 14-1, Oct-Apr: 12-1 h
Via Giovanni Manna 14 ✉80133 *(Near the university and railway station)* ☎ 081 28 76 81

Blu Angels (A AC B F G MA msg P S sa sb sol VS wh WO) 14:30-1, Sat & Mon 10-1 h
Centro Direzionale Isola A/7 ✉80133 *(Near the railway station/Vicino alla stazione centrale)* ☎ 081 56 25 298
Three floors, Labyrinth, Pizzeria service, Info HIV/Aids, Concerts, Books/Tre piani, Labirinto, Servizio pizzeria, Info Aids, Concerti, Libri.

HOTELS

Belvesuvio Inn (B bf d F glm H OS pi sol)
Via Panoramica F. 40 ✉80040 *(5 km from airport, 6 km from the station)* ☎ 081 77 11 243 Fax: 081 57 45 051
Room with bf from USD 40. Ranch with horses and other animals. Beautiful garden. Excursions organised.

GENERAL GROUPS

Agedo Associazione Genitori Parenti E Amici Di Omosessuali Mon 16-19 h
☎ 081 55 18 293

HEALTH GROUPS

Anlaids
Via Santa Maria in Portico 3 ✉80122 ☎ 081 68 07 37
Fax: 081 66 96 79

Network Nazionale „Gruppo C" Progetto di Ricerca Aids
☎ 081 76 86 300
Helpline for people with HIV/Aids.

HELP WITH PROBLEMS

Dott. Sommantico Massimiliano
☎ 0338 95 87 560
Psychologist.

RELIGIOUS GROUPS

I Tralci
PO Box 66 ✉80100

SWIMMING

-Marechiaro Rocks (!) (from via Posillipo-via Marechiaro; mixed)
-Scogliera di Mergellina (very central, chaotic, frequent contacts, mixed/molto centrale, caotica, incontri frequenti, ma mista)
-Scogliera di Santa Lucia (mixed, but many opportunities/mista, ma molte possibilità)

CRUISING

-Via Brin (by car, busy)
-Piazza Municipio (R TV) (at night, in the gardens in front of Palazzo S. Giacomo/di notte, anche nei giardini davanti)
-Railway Station/Stazione Ferroviaria (p. Garibaldi, good meeting place, hustlers, anytime)
-"Cumana" Railway Station/Stazione Ferroviara (at night)
-Piazza Carlo III (occasional meetings/incontri occasionali)
-Via Acton (R TV) (in the garden/nei giardini)
-Versuviano railway station/stazione (facilities/bagno)
-Viale Kennedy (R TV) (at night/di notte)
-Via Marina (R TV) (at night/di notte)
-Capodimonte Park (AYOR) (morning and afternoon/matina e pomeriggio)
-Adiacenze Palasport (R TV) (at night/di notte)
-Piazza Bellini (g) (meeting place in summertime at night/punto d'incontro d'estate di notte)
-Metro Mergellina, WC (AYOR)
-Metro Vanvitelli , WC (AYOR)

Nerviano - Milano ✉ 20014

DANCECLUBS

Cinema Vittoria (B D DR G VS) 17-0.30, Sun 15-0.30 h
Via Casati 5 ✉20014 ☎ 0331 58 61 00

Nettuno - Roma ✉ 00048

CRUISING

-Railway Station/Stazione FS
-Piazzale Santa Maria Goretti

Nicotera Marina - Cosenza ✉ 88034

SWIMMING

-Spiaggetta (between Sabbie d'Oro campsite and the Valtur village; very gay and nice in the summer/fra campeggio Sabbie d'Oro e villagio Valtur; molto gay e piacevole d'estate)

Nola - Napoli ✉ 80035

CRUISING

-Circumvesuviana Railway Station/Stazione FS

Novara ✉ 28100

CRUISING

-Via Raffaele Sanzio
-Gardens (in front of the police station and around the (P)/giardini davanti alla polizia e altorno (P))

Numana - Ancona ✉ 60026

BARS

Act Up-Seven Up (B d G WE) Fri-Sat
Plazza del Santuario 15 ✉60026 ☎ 071 93 11 756

Olbia

SWIMMING

-Porto Ferro (NU) near Arlghero (at the end on the right on the rocks/in fondo sulla destra nelle calette e nelle rocce)
-Maria Pia, Alghero beach/lido (in the last part on the trees side direction Fertilia/nell'ultima parte alla fine degli alberi direzione Fertilia)
-Liscia Ruja (NU) Costa Smeralda (from Olbia direction Arzachena, in a place called Cala di Volpe on the rocks/da Olbia direzione Arzachena, zona Cala di Volpe nelle calette e sulle rocce)

CRUISING

-Harbour/Porto Isola Bianca (at night, after the departure of boats/la notte dopo la partenza delle navi)

Orbetello ✉ 58015

SWIMMING

- Giannella (20 miles south of Grosseto, along the road from Albinia to Santo Stefano. Beach and busches, crowded day and night.)

Oristano ✉ 09170

SWIMMING

-Marina di Arborea (G MA NU) (Strada mare 29)
-Is Arenas beach/spiagga (take from Oristano the direction of Cuglieri, turn at the camping Nurapolis, walk around 2 km on the beach at the end of the (P) on the left side/Oristiano direzione Cuglieri, bivio camping Nurapolis, dal parcheggio alla fine della strada camminare per ca. 2 km sulla spiaga verso sinistra)

CRUISING

-Torre Grande pine trees wood, after Orbia direction Cagliari/Pineta Torre Grande, dopo Orbia dirrezion Cagliari(by car and on foot/in macchina e a piedi)

Ortona - Chieti ✉ 66026

CRUISING

-Beach/spiaggia „Lido Riccio"

Paderno Fraciacorta - Brescia ✉ 25050

DANCECLUBS

Out Limits Disco (B D GLM) Fri (women only) Sat 23-4, Sun 22-3 h
Via Ugo Foscolo 2 ✉25050 ☎ 030 65 75 36

Padova ✉ 35100

GAY INFO

Tralaltro
Publication of Circolo Tralaltro. Available in the book-shops Feltrinelli and Il Mercantino.

BARS

Brief Encounter (AC B d DR f GLM MA P s SNU VS W) 21-5 h, closed on Mon
Via Settima Strada 5 ✉35100 *(Exit Padova Est Zona Industriale Nord)* ☎ 049 77 60 73
Disco on Tue Fri-Sun.
Cafè Relax (B glm) Thu Sun 22-?h
Via Navigazione interna 38/A ✉35100 ☎ 049 776 414
Flexo Videobar (AC B DR f G MA P s VS YG) 21.30-3, Fri Sat -4h,closed Mon Tue
Via N. Tommaseo 96/B ✉35100 *(Bus 18)* ☎ 049 807 47 07
Tartan's Birreria (B f glm) 19-2 h, closed Sun
Via Cesare Battisti 177 ✉35100 ☎ 049 875 66 39
Tiratardi (AC B f glm) 18-2 h, closed Sun and Aug
Via Palermo 20 ✉35142 *(Bus 5/near Bassanello)* ☎ 049 65 20 83

DANCECLUBS

Black & White (AC B D DR G MA VS) Fri 22-5, Sat 22-6 h
Viale Navigazione Interna 38/A ✉35100 *(Zona Industriale Nord)*
☎ 049 77 64 14
CSEN card required.

So & So (AC B D DR G MA OS P S VS W) Fri Sat 22.30-6 h
Via Julia 59, Perarolo di Vigonza ✉35100 ☎ 049 893 46 11

RESTAURANTS

Taverna Nane Della Giulia (A B F glm MA) 12.30-14.30, 20-1 h, closed Mon
Via Santa Sofia 1 ✉35100 ☎ 049 66 07 42

SEX SHOPS/BLUE MOVIES

Magic Top Sex Shop (g) 9.30-12.30, 15-20, 22-1h, closed Sun; Mon morning
Via Tommaseo 96/C ✉35131 ☎ 049 807 24 14
Gay articles, S/M and leather goods, videos, underwear.

CINEMAS

Ducale (g) 18-24, Sun 16-24 h
Via Facciolati 34 ✉35100 ☎ 049 85 01 41

SAUNAS/BATHS

Metro Sauna Club (AC B DR f G MA P sa sb VS W wh) Wed 20-2, Thu Fri 14-2, Sat 20-3, Sun 15-2 h
Via Turazza 19 ✉35100 *(Bus 18)* ☎ 049 807 58 28

Miami Club (B f G MA msg s sa sb sol VS wh) 15-1 h, closed in Aug
Via Pellizzo 3 ✉35128 *(4th floor/bus 15,18)* ☎ 049 77 64 64

Olympus Club (AC B DR f G MA P sa sb VS wh) Mon Tue 14-2, Wed Sat Sun -20.30 h, Thu Fri closed
Via Nicolò Tommaseo 96/A ✉35100 *(Near central station. Bus 5, 18)* ☎ 049 807 58 43
Relax cabins. Arcigay membership required.

BOOK SHOPS

Libreria Feltrinelli
Via S. Francesco 7 ✉35100 ☎ 049 875 46 30

VIDEO SHOPS

Target (g) 9.30-12.40, 15.30-19.40, Sat -20 h, closed Sun Mon
Piazzale Mazzini 6 ✉35137 ☎ 049 876 32 32
Video rental (gay film but no sex videos).

GENERAL GROUPS

Circolo Tralaltro
Via S. Sofia 5 ✉35100
☎ 049 876 24 58 Fax: 049 875 60 05 Homepage: http://www.geocities.com/WestHollywood/2550/pd.htm
Meetings on Mon 21.30-23 h. Health counselling on Tue 21-23 h. Information on HIV, prevention, support. Anonymous free HIV test. Vaccination against hepatitis A B E. Youth group Thu 18-20 h.

HEALTH GROUPS

Ospedale Civile-Divisione Malattie Infettive 8-14 h
Via Giustiniani 2 ✉35100 ☎ 049 821 37 65
Anonymous free HIV test.

HELP WITH PROBLEMS

Dott. Pasimeni Carmelo
✉35100 ☎ 049 875 87 65
Psychologist.

RELIGIOUS GROUPS

Incontro. L' Call Tralaltro for information

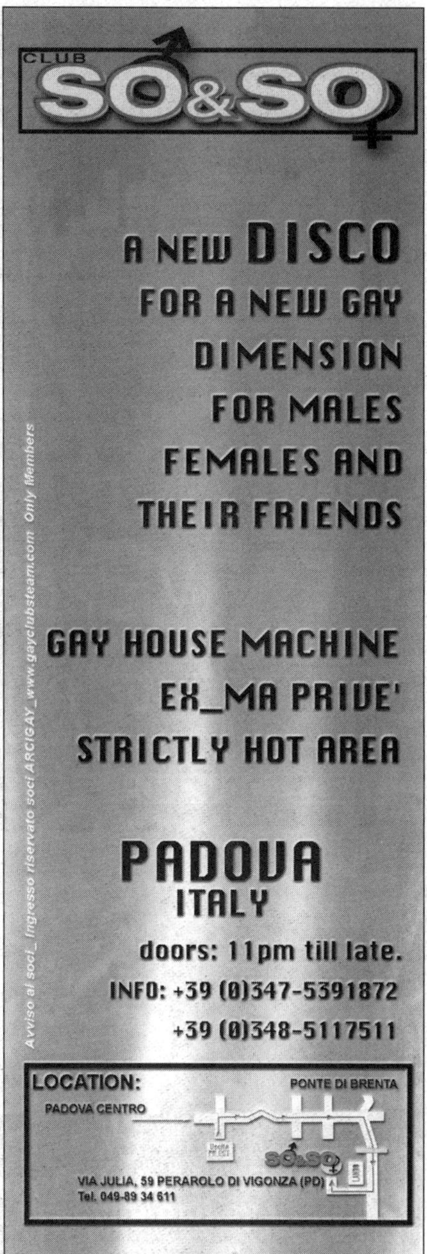

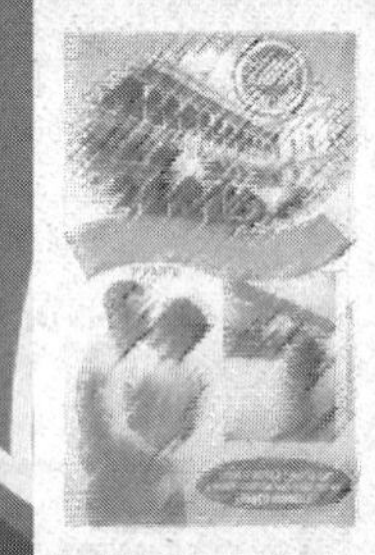

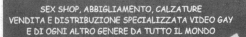

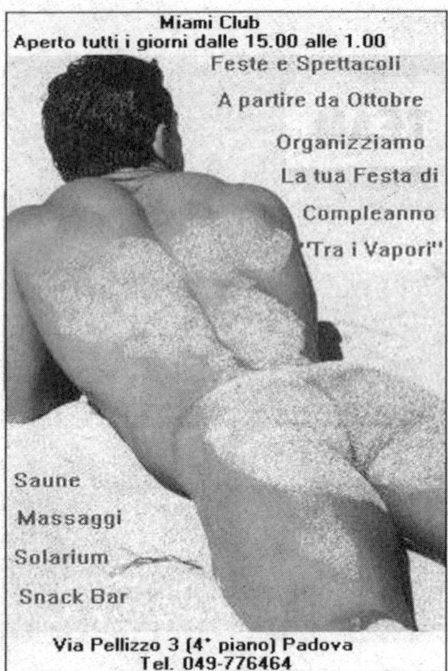
Miami Club
Aperto tutti i giorni dalle 15.00 alle 1.00
Feste e Spettacoli
A partire da Ottobre
Organizziamo
La tua Festa di
Compleanno
"Tra i Vapori"
Saune
Massaggi
Solarium
Snack Bar
Via Pellizzo 3 (4° piano) Padova
Tel. 049-776464

c/o Evangelic Church, Corso Milano 6 ✉35100

CRUISING

-Via Manzoni (AYOR) (Giardini di Pontecorvo)
-Giardinetti di Via Morgagni (AYOR)
-Via Loredan, zona universitaria (TV)
-Via Tommaso Grossi
-Highway Valdastico (A31), [P] at the exit Thiene/Autostrada Valdastico (A31) nel [P] All'uscita Thiene
-Railway Station/Stazione FS (AYOR)

Palermo ✉ 90100

GAY INFO

Arcigay Arcilesbica Palermo Meetings of Arcilesbica on Wed 21.30 h
Via Genova 7 ✉90133 ☎ 091 33 56 88 Fax: 091 61 13 245

BARS

Exit (AC B d f G MA s W) 21-3 h
Piazza S. Fransisco di Paola 39/40 ✉90141 ☎ 091 61 11 990
Disco bar.
I Grilli Giu (A B f glm MA W) Mon closed
Largo Cavalieri di Malta 11 ✉90133 *(historical centre/centro storico)* ☎ 091 58 47 47

DANCECLUBS

Feste in discoteca-itineranti „Vannigrilli - Invito a Nocce" (B D glm s YG WE)
☎ 0360 65 78 58
Call for info. House music club.

RESTAURANTS

Ristorante „I Grilli" (CC F glm) 20.30-? h, Mon and Jul-Sep closed
Largo Cavalieri di Malta 21 ✉90133 ☎ 091 33 41 30
Cosy atmosphere.

CINEMAS

Embassy
Via Mariano Stabile 223 ✉90100 ☎ 091 58 64 94
Etoile
Via Mariano Stabile 241
Orfeo (g r)
Via Maqueda 25

BOOK SHOPS

Altroquanto Mon-Sat 9-13.30, 16-19.30 h
Corso Vittorio Emanuele 145 ☎ 091 61 14 732
Library with gay and lesbian books, magazines, comics and videos (non porno).

LEATHER & FETISH SHOPS

Cuioa.Le Mon.Sat 9-13, 16-19.30 h
Via Ponticello 28 ✉90133 *(historical centre/centro storico)*
☎ 091 61 72 831
Traditional work of leather objects/Lavorazione artigianale oggetti di cuoio.

HEALTH GROUPS

Anlaids
Via Saverio Scrofani 44 ✉90143 ☎ 091 62 62 425
Fax: 091 62 62 425

SWIMMING

-Sferracavallo beach/spiaggia (very cruisy)
-Vasca delle Vergine (Barcarello) (on the rocks/rocce)

CRUISING

-Railway Station/Stazione FS (6-23.30 h)
-Foro Italico public garden/Giardino publico (days and nights)
-Via Gaetano Daita (TV) (evenings)
-Parco della Favorita, behind/dietro l'Ippodrome (days and nights)
-Giardino Inglese, WC (days)

Parma ✉ 43100

DANCECLUBS

Andromeda (b D G MA OS S) Fri Sat 22-3 h
Via Gramsci 5 ✉43019 *Soragna (Autostrada A1 Milano-Roma, exit/uscita Fidenza)* ☎ 0335 57 33 604 (Infoline)
Boy - Hippopotamus (AC B D glm s YG) Thu 23-4 h, closed from Jun to Aug
Via E. Lepido 28 ✉43100 *(Bus 3, over the/sopra il Bowling Parma)* ☎ 0521 48 38 13

SEX SHOPS/BLUE MOVIES

Magic America 9.30-12.30, 15.30-20 h, closed Sun and Mon morning
Borgo del Parmigianino 31/D ✉43100 *(zona centro vicinanze duomo)* ☎ 0521 20 62 73

CINEMAS

Ritz
Via Venezia 129 ✉43100 ☎ 0521 27 32 72

SWIMMING

-Spiaggia del Taro (after the bridge over the Taro River, walk towards Monte, where the action sometimes takes place/raggiunto il punte sul Taro, dirigerrsi verso Monte, ove c'è qualche volta attività)

CRUISING

-River/fiume Parma (right-hand side)
-Railway Station/Stazione FS (on the square/in piazza)

-Parco Ducale (in summer/d'estate)
-Mercati Generali (R TV) (after 23 h)

BARS

Jolanda (B f glm MA OS) Mon-Sat 9-24 h (some gays after 21-24 h)
Via Rismondo ✉27100

NEWS STANDS

Kiosk/Rivendita Giornali (g)
Piazza Petrarca
Kiosk/Rivendita Giornali (g)
Piazza Vittoria/Via Mascheroni

HEALTH GROUPS

Network Nazionale „Gruppo C" Progetto di Ricerca Aids
✉27100 ☎ 0382 52 70 67 *Helpline for people with HIV/Aids.*

SWIMMING

-Lido di Pavia (NU) (P Lanche)
-Pieve del Cairo (River Agogna: on the road from Pieve del Cairo to Sannazzaro de Burgondi, turn right before bridge over river, continue for 400 m. Beach by the waterfall, mixed.)

CRUISING

-Customs depot/Dogana (AYOR) (Via Donegana, truckers)
-Old railway bridge over river Ticino/Vecchio ponte della ferrovia sul Ticino (until/fino alle 3 h)
-Strada Persa (by car/in macchina until/fino alle 3 h)
-Via Rismondo (around castle at night, on foot and by car/attorno al castello, di notte, a piedi e in macchina)
-A7 Milano-Genova (Battuda-Parking lot at km 17 southbound only)

Perugia ✉ 06100

GAY INFO

Arcigay Arcilesbica „Omphalos" (B d GLM MA OS P) Wed, Fri, Sat
Via Fratti 18 ✉06123 *(near Piazza IV Novembre)* ☎ 075 57 23 175

BARS

Onphalos (B D G MA) Wed-Sat 21-? h
Via Fratti 18 ✉06100 ☎ 075 57 23 175 *Run by Arci Gay*

RESTAURANTS

Bocca Mia. La (A AC CC F NG YG) 13-14.30, 20-23 h, closed Sun and Aug
Via Rocchi 36 ✉06121 ☎ 075 57 23 873

SEX SHOPS/BLUE MOVIES

Paradise Sexy Shop (g LJ VS) 9.30-13, 15.30-20 h, closed Sun
Via Gerardo Dottori 90, San Sisto ✉06100 *(Bus 55, 57)*
☎ 075 52 70 121 *Large range of rubber, S/M video./ Vasto assortimento video, gomma, S/M videocassette.*

HEALTH GROUPS

Anlaids
Via Giacomo Matteotti 37 ✉06074 ☎ 075 51 71 189

CRUISING

-Piazzale Bellini (in front of/davanti Sant'Anna Station/stazione)

Pesaro ✉ 61100

GENERAL GROUPS

Arcigay Arcilesbica Pesaro
Via Branca 22 ✉61100 *(Libreria Lucienolo)* ☎ 0721 37 01 94

CRUISING

-Piazza Carducci (AYOR) (P at the market)

Pescara ✉ 65100

BARS

Heroes Bar (B f P)
Via E. Flaiano 21 ✉65127 ☎ 085 66 921
Arcigay membership required/tessera Arcigay.

HEALTH GROUPS

Anlaids
Via Torquato Tasso 29 ✉65121 ☎ 085 42 19 428
Fax: 085 42 20 959

CRUISING

-Porta Nouva station/stazione
-Piazza Salotto
-Piazza Maggio

Piacenza ✉ 29100

DANCECLUBS

Ice (AC B CC D DR F G OS s YG) Sat 23-5 h
Via dell'Aguzzafame ✉29100 *(In Fianco del Castello, highway exit/autostrada uscita Piacenza Ovest)* ☎ 0523 48 29 35

CINEMAS

Roma (g)
Via Capra 48 ✉29100 ☎ 0523 32 13 28

GENERAL GROUPS

Agedo Associazione Genitori Parenti E Amici Di Omosessuali Mon-Fri 9-17 h
✉29100 ☎ 0523 57 10 61
Arcigay Arcilesbica
Via G. Taverna 137 ✉29100 ☎ 0523 49 92 68

SWIMMING

-Beach by the river Po/Spiaggia sul Po (direction Piacenzo-Milano follow signs to C. San Sisto, park your car and walk to the area below the motorway bridges/direzione Piacenza-Milano, seguire frecce C. San Sisto; parcheggiare e raggiungere la zona sotto i ponti dell'autostrada.)

CRUISING

-Girone del Vescovo (under the bridges and motorway-P, also along the river/sotto i ponti e P autostrada, anche lungo il fiume)
-Railway station/Stazione FS (occasional meetings in the garden and in the building/incontri occasionali nel giardino e nell'edificio)
-Piazza della Cittadella
-Bar Bologna (in front of the bar, opposite the railway station/davanti al bar, di fronte all stazione)
-Viale S. Ambrogio
-Monumento al Pontieri (R TV) (on the square/sulla piazzo)
-P Fiorenzuola autostrada exit/uscita autostrada
-Lungo Po (meetings between Nino Bixio swimming pool and Via da Feltre/incontri fra piscina Nino Bixio e Via da Feltre)
-Lungo la Foce del Trebbia (YG)

Pinerolo - Torino ✉ 10064

DANCECLUBS

Break (B D e G MA OS S) Sat 21-3 h
Corso Torino 18 ✉10064 ☎ 0121 70 393

SEX SHOPS/BLUE MOVIES

Videoclub XXX (g VS)
V.le della Rimembranza 32 ☎ 0121 32 30 98

GENERAL GROUPS

Simply Normal Pinerolo (TO) Italy
✉10064 ☎ 0339 43 44 177

CRUISING

-Piazza Canova (MA) (di sera/evenings

Pisa

RESTAURANTS

Stazione di Ristoro „Leopolda" (B F glm) Sun closed
Piazza Guerrazzi 11 ✉56125 *(Near railway station/Vicino alla stazione)* ☎ 050 48 587
Tuscany cuisine/Cucina Toscana

SEX SHOPS/BLUE MOVIES

Tentazioni Sexy Shop 9.30-13, 16-20 h, closed Sun and Mon morning
Via Rosellini 13/E ✉56124 ☎ 050 54 00 54
Biggest gay shop in Tuscany: toys, videos, magazines, leather articles and video cabin.

SAUNAS/BATHS

Siesta Club 77 (AC B DR f G MA P sa sb VS)
Via di Porta a Mare 25/27 ✉56122 *(500 m from Station/FFSS 500 m circa)* ☎ 050 42 075
Arci membership required.

BODY & BEAUTY SHOPS

Laura Alberti Tue-Sat 9-18 h
Via Pardo Roques 4 ✉56123 *(near Porta Lucca)* ☎ 050 56 44 84

BOOK SHOPS

Libreria Tra Le Righe
Via Corsica 8 ☎ 050 83 01 77
Gay books. Bar inside the book-shop. Reductions for ArciGay members.

HOTELS

Royal Victoria Hotel (B bf CC H OS W)
Via Lungarno Pacinotti 12 ✉56126 ☎ 050 94 01 11
Fax: 050 94 01 80
Homepage: http://www.csinfo.it/royalvictoriahotel
*Single room Lit 90.000-145.000, Double room 110.000-180.000, bf incl. Historical hotel*** (1837).*

GENERAL GROUPS

ArciGay Pride Wed 21-23, Thu 17-19, 21-23 h
via San Lorenzo 38
☎ 050 55 56 18 Fax: 050 55 56 18
Homepage: www.gay.it/pride
Group for HIV and people with problems. Also infoline.

HEALTH GROUPS

Anlaids 9-11-19-22 h
Via Valtriano di Fauglia 40 ✉56043 ☎ 050 64 41 45
Fax: 050 64 40 55
Ospedale Cisanello
☎ 050 59 69 18 *Anonymous free HIV test.*

SWIMMING

-Tirrenia (g NU) (Beach to the south of Camp Darby's beach/ Spiaggia libera a sud del bagno di Camp Darby)

CRUISING

-Giardini Scotto (G OG) (afternoon)
-Lungarno Guadalongo (along Arno river, by car at night)
-Stazione FS (by day inside the station, at night in the nearby streets as well)

Pistoia ✉ 51100

CRUISING

-Zona industriale Sant'Agostino (by car at night)
-Stazione FS, toilets (AYOR, r)

Poggibonsi ✉ 53036

CRUISING

-P at Salceto Area (by night)

Pompei - Napoli ✉ 80045

CRUISING

-Circumvesuviana Railway Station/Stazione FS (R) (police/polizia)
-Villa dei Misteri

Ponsacco - Pisa ✉ 56038

DANCECLUBS

Insomnia (AC B D GLM OS S) Sat 23-4.30h
Via di Gello ✉56038 *(take motorway Firenze-Pisa-Livorno exit Pontedera-Ponsacco)* ☎ 0587 73 39 14

Ponte San Pietro - Bergamo ✉ 24036

CRUISING

-Parco del Fiume Brembo (at the beach on River Brembo/sulla riva del Brembo/last bus of Bus 5/8 from the center of Bergamo AYOR)

Pordenone ✉ 33170

GENERAL GROUPS

Arcigay Arcilesbica Pordenone Mon Tue (evening)
c/o Casa del Popolo Di Torre, Via Carnaro 10 ✉33170

CRUISING

-Garden near railway station/giardino vicino alla stazione

Porto Recanati - Macerata ✉ 62017

CRUISING

-Beach (between/fra Porto Recanati and Marcelli di Numana)

Positano - Salerno ✉ 84017

HOTELS

Hotel Poseidon (B CC F g H msg OS pi WO) closed Dec-Mar
Via Pasitea 148 ✉84017 ☎ 089 81 11 11 Fax: 089 87 58 33
Email: poseidon@starnet.it Homepage: www.starnet.it/poseidon
Rates double Lit 290.000-330.000 (low-season), 330.000-370.000 (mid-season), 370.000-410.000 (high-season), Also beauty center and gym facilities.

Villa Franca (AC B bf CC F H OS pi sol) closed Nov-Mar
Viale Pasitea 318 ✉84017 ☎ 089 87 56 55 Fax: 089 87 57 35
Email: hrf@staret.it Homepage: www.starnet.it/villa_franca
Rates Lit 300.000-380.000.

Potenza ✉ 85100

CRUISING

-Parco Montereale (gardens at the swimming pool and by the Santa Maria barracks, after 21.30 h/giardini alla piscina e alla caserma Santa Maria, da 21.30 h)

Prato ✉ 50047

SEX SHOPS/BLUE MOVIES

Moulin Rouge (g)
Piazzale Falcone e Borsellino 3 ✉50047 ☎ 0574 57 56 92
Over 4000 videos. Underwear and S/M articles.

CRUISING

-Viale Galilei (ayor) (gardens next to the playground/giardini accanto al campo giochi)
-Loc. il Cascido (daytime, between railway and the river Bisenzio/di giorno, fra la ferrovia e il fiume Bisenzio)
-Railway station/Stazione FS (also in the gardens, near Agip Motel/anche nei giardini, vicino al Motel Agip)

Ragusa ✉ 97100

CRUISING

-Kamarina beach (by/adiacente Club Med)
-Playa Grande (between village and mouth of River Irminio, left of disco La Fazenda, also on the beach below./tra villagio e foce del fiume Irminio)
-square in front of railway station and side streets/piazzale antistante stazione centrale e vie laterali)
-Sampieri beach (opposite/contrada Pisciotto)

Ranzanico - Bergamo ✉ 24060

BARS

Triangolo.Il (B D g) Fri Sat Sun 21.30-1.30 h (Fri G)
Via Nazionale 5 ✉24060 ☎ 035 82 91 87

Ravenna ✉ 48100

BARS

Chalet dei Giardini (B bf F glm OS YG) 7-2 h
Viale Santi Baldini 4 ✉48100 *(inside city garden near the station)*
☎ 0544 47 07 58

CINEMAS

Alexander (g)
Via Bassa del Pignataro 6 ✉48100 ☎ 0544 39 787

Roma (g)
Via Bixio 19 ✉48100 ☎ 0544 21 22 21

GENERAL GROUPS

Arcigay Arcilesbica „Evoluzione"
Via G. Rasponi 5 ✉48100 *(near/vicino Piazza del Popolo, Bus 4/44)* ☎ 0544 21 97 21 Fax: 0544 21 97 22
Email: arcigay@iol.it

SWIMMING

- Lido di Classe (NU) (between Ravenna and Cervia, free beach north of the kiosk bearing the same name. Large pine forest. Gay zone of the beach is near the river surrounding the beach itself, in the northern area/fra Ravenna e Cervia. Spiaggia libera al nord dell'edicola omonima. Pineta larga, zona gay vicino al fiume, verso norde)
-Lido di Dante (NU) (free beach beyond the campsites, on the right; dunes and pine trees/spiaggia libera oltre il campeggio, a destra e pineta)

CRUISING

-Railway Station/Stazione FS (late at night, also in the side streets/notte tardi, anche nelle via laterali)
-Public gardens/Giardini pubblici (ayor R) (Viale S. Baldini, till late/fino a tardi)
-Piazzale and Viale Farini (R)
-Piazza Mameli (R)
-Via Rocca ai Fossi (R)

Reggio Calabria ✉ 89100

CRUISING

-Villa Comunale (good opportunities at night/buone occasioni di notte)
-Via Marina (some meetings at night/alcune incontri di notte)
-Central Station/stazione centrale (main hall and square in front of the building/salone principale e piazzale davanti)

Reggio Emilia ✉ 42100

SEX SHOPS/BLUE MOVIES

Magic America (g) closed Sun and Mon morning
Via Fabio Filzi 7 ✉42100 *(Zona S. Stefano)* ☎ 0522 30 19 00

CRUISING

-Giardini pubblici/public gardens (AYOR OG) (near/vicino Astoria Hotel)
-Central station/stazione centrale (AYOR R) (also on the square in front of the station/anche nella piazza davanti)
-Porta Santo Stefano (day and night, by car and on foot/giorno e notte, in macchina e a piedi)

Riccione - Rimini ✉ 47838

BARS

Bombo (AC B bf f GLM MA OS s) Summer: 0-24 h, winter: 6-2 h
Viale Ceccarini 142 ✉47838 ☎ 0541 69 03 52

DANCECLUBS

Villa delle Rose. La (b D G) Fri-Sun -4 h
Villaggio Argentina, Zona Camilluccia ✉47838 *(South of Riccione/verso Misano Adriatico)* ☎ 0541 60 91 81

SEX SHOPS/BLUE MOVIES

Eros Center (g)
Viale Dante 116 ✉47838 ☎ 0541 64 86 86

HOTELS

Garni Ceccarini 140 (CC glm H MA)
Viale Ceccarini 140 ✉47838 *(near station/vicino stazione)*
☎ 0541 69 03 52 Fax: 0541 69 03 70
Email: garniceccanni@riccione
Rooms with telephone, TV, shower/WC, heating. 10% discount to Spartacus readers.

GENERAL GROUPS

Arcigay Arcilesbica Rimini A. Turing Wed 20.30-23.30 h
Viale D'Annunzio 164 ✉47838 ☎ 0541 64 86 58
Fax: 0541 64 86 58

SWIMMING

-Along the sea/Lungamore Libertà (Viale Ceccarini area)
-Among bathing cabins on the beach/fra le cabine in spiaggia (MA, foreigners/stranieri)

CRUISING

-Behind Hotel Savioli (winter)
-Della Rotonda (Near Hotel Mediterraneo, end of Viale Ceccarini/vicinio Hotel Mediterraneo, in fondo al Viale Ceccarini)

Rieti ✉ 02100

CRUISING

-Railway Station/Stazione FS
-Gardens in front of barracks, Viale dei Flavi
-Facilities under Town Hall

Rimini ✉ 47037

DANCECLUBS

Classic Club (B D DR G MA P S VS) winter only Sat 23-7 h, June and July WE only, in August every day
Via Feleto 11 ✉47037 ☎ 0541 73 11 13
Exit highway Rimini Sud, on the right direction Riccione/Ancona, Coriano, San Lorenzo. Arcigay membership required./Tessera Arcigay

SEX SHOPS/BLUE MOVIES

Eros Center (g)
Viale Vespucci 29 A ✉47037
Magic America (g) closed Thu afternoon
Viale Regina Elena 94 ✉47900 *(Lungomare)* ☎ 0541 39 19 77
Large section of gay videos.

GENERAL GROUPS

Arcigay Arcilesbica
Via Bellini 2 ✉47041 ☎ 0541 78 11 16

CRUISING

-Grand Hotel (only/solo TV) (gardens, roundabout/giardini e rondò)
-Railway Station (YG)
-South Rimini/Rimini sud (at Miramare, between Centro Talasso Terapico and Colonia Bologna)
-Seafront/Lungomare (among cabins/fra le cabins 73-85)

Riva del Garda - Trento ✉ 38066

BARS

Cascata Varone (B f g OS) 9-18 h (march-october)
Via Cascata 12 ✉38066 *(3km from Riva del Garda)*
☎ 0464 52 14 21
best on Sun.

CRUISING

-Beach between „Punta Lido" and „Sabbioni Beach" (at night)
-Cruisy beach (NU) (take road to Torbole-Malcesine. Then take small stairs just at the end of the 5th tunnel behind Torbole.)

Roma ✉ 00100

● With a history going back 3000 years Rome is not only the most important attraction in Italy, but probably in the whole world. There is hardly a tourist who could possibly overlook the fascination of this city with its countless churches, monuments and treasures. It's easy to get the impression that one is in a huge museum. Rome is also the administrative centre and seat of parliament, government and state president. Also from the gay point of view the city with its 3 million people has a lot to offer. But nevertheless one should not compare Rome with Amsterdam, Paris or London. The Vatican as centre of the Catholic Church continues to excercise a not insignificant influence on the capital's gay city life, and this manifests itself in a number of ways. Bars and discos are constantly under threat of closure which explains in part the short lifespan of many gay establishments. Practically all gay pubs and discos lie behind closed doors. Usually you have to ring before you can get in. The pub scene in Rome is not particularily well-developed, night life taking place on the numerous squares where tourists flock. But nevertheless a number of new pubs and bars are appearing and the latest development in some discos is the offer of one gay and lesbian day every week on a weekday. The monthly magazine „AUT" published by the organisation „Circolo Mario Mieli" contains articles on culture and politics as well as the latest information on gay-lesbian Rome. „Circolo Mario Mieli" will coordinate together with other organisations the first world-wide World Pride in the year 2000 which will very probably lead to controversy in the city as it prepares for it's millennium celebration. In order to further finance its honorary work every Friday „Circolo Mario Mieli" arranges the „Muccassassina", one of the most popular and interesting lesbian-gay-transsexual parties in Rome. About 18 miles (30 km) from Rome lies Ostia and souther there other sandy beaches frequented by gays.

✱ Rom ist mit seiner fast 3000jährigen Geschichte die bedeutendste Touristenattraktion nicht nur Italiens, sondern sogar im Weltmaßstab. Kaum ein Tourist wird sich der Faszination der ewigen Stadt, seiner unzähligen Kirchen, Monumente und Kunstschätze entziehen können, die den Eindruck vermitteln, sich in einem riesigen Museum zu bewegen. Rom ist zudem Verwaltungshauptstadt mit Sitz von Parlament, Regierung und Staatspräsident. Auch in schwuler Hinsicht hat die 3-Millionen-Einwohner-Metropole einiges zu bieten, doch sollte man Rom nicht mit Amsterdam, Paris oder London vergleichen. Der Vatikan als Machtzentrum der katholischen Kirche übt weiterhin einen nicht zu unterschätzenden Einfluß auf das schwule Hauptstadtleben aus, was sich in vielerlei Hinsicht bemerkbar macht. Schwule Bars und Diskotheken sind latent von Schließung bedroht, womit sich zumindest zum Teil die Kurzlebigkeit vieler schwuler Etablissements erklären läßt. So sind auch praktisch alle schwule Kneipen und Diskotheken gut von der Öffentlichkeit abgeschirmt, man muß also klingeln, um eintreten zu können. Rom hat im allgemeinen keine ausgeprägte Kneipenszene, das Nachtleben spielt sich zum großen Teil auf den zahlreichen, von Touristen bevölkerten Plätzen ab. Dennoch entsteht gerade eine Vielzahl neuer Lokale, während einige Diskotheken seit neuestem einen „schwulen Tag" in der Woche anbieten. Das Monatsmagazin „AUT", vom „Circolo Mario Mieli" herausgegeben, enthält neben Artikeln zu Kultur und Politik die neuesten Informationen über das lesbischule Rom. Der „Circolo Mario Mieli" wird neben anderen Organisationen im Jahr 2000 den weltweit ersten „World Pride" ausrichten, was wohl noch zu einigen Kontroversen in der Stadt des „2000jährigen Jubiläums" führen wird. Um seine weitgehend ehrenamtliche Arbeit zu finanzieren, gibt es mit dem „Muccassassina" jeden Freitag eine der am meist besuchten und spannendsten lesbisch-schwulen-transsexuellen Parties Roms. Von Rom aus sind es nur knapp 30 Kilometer bis nach Ostia und den auch von vielen Schwulen frequentierten Sandstränden weiter südlich am Mittelmeer.

▲ Rome, ville historique de plus de 3000 ans, est une des attractions touristiques les plus prisées non seulement d'Italie, mais aussi du monde entier. Peu de touristes peuvent résister aux charmes de la Ville éternelle, de ses églises innombrables, des ses riches trésors artistiques et magnifiques monuments. Rome est aussi, avec ses plus de trois millions d'habitants, la capitale de l'Italie, siège du président, du parlement et du gouvernement. Sa scène gaye a beaucoup à offrir pour autant que l'on ne la compare pas à des villes comme Amsterdam, Paris ou Londres. Le Vatican, siège du pouvoir de l'Eglise catholique, a en effet depuis toujours influencé la vie gaye de la cité : les établissements homosexuels sont en permanence menacés de fermeture, ce qui explique la courte longévité de la plupart d'entre eux et pourquoi il est encore fréquent de devoir sonner à leur porte. Il n'y a pas de café gay de jour mais par contre beaucoup de bars et clubs au centre ville ou près de la gare principale, la Stazione Termini. La scène s'est beaucoup développée depuis quelques années et plus en plus de soirées sont organisées durant la semaine. Le mensuel « AUT », édité par le « Circolo Mario Mieli », propose, en plus d'articles culturels et politiques, des nouvelles fraîches sur le Rome des gays, lesbiennes et transsexuels. Ce « Circolo » est d'ail-

leurs, parmi d'autres groupements, un des organisateurs de la première « World Pride » qui se tiendra au mois de juillet 2000 et dont on attend plus de 300'000 participants venus du monde entier (voir la publicité dans les pages qui suivent). C'est l'occasion pour le mouvement gay italien, en cette année sacrée pour l'Eglise, de faire avancer les causes liées à l'émancipation des gays et aux droits égaux pour tous.
A trente kilomètres seulement de Rome se trouve aussi Ostia, dont les plages de sables méritent un détour tant elles sont assidûment fréquentées par les gays romains.

☆ En los umbrales del tercer millenium de su historia, Roma es uno de los sitios predilectos para turistas de todo el mundo. Es dificil no sentirse cautivado por la fascinación de la ciudad eterna, cuya historía se hace notar por todas partes con sus innumerables museos, iglesias y tesoros de arte, dando al visitante la impresión de moverse en un gigantesco museo. Roma es además la capital administrativa y la sede del parlamento, del gobierno y del presidente del país. Pero también desde el punto de vista gay la metrópoli con su tres millones de habitantes tiene mucho que ofrecer, aunque no se puede comparar con ciudades como Amsterdam, París o Londres: El vaticano, autoridad suprema de la iglesia católica, sigue teniendo una gran influencia sobre la vida gay de esta capital, que se hace notar en varios aspectos. Bares y discotecas gay se ven siempre amenazados de cierre, que explica la corta duración de estos establecimientos y la dificultad de encontrarlos. En casi todos los sitios de ambiente es necesario llamar al timbre para poder entrar. En general, la marcha nocturna no se concentra en pubs, sino más bien en las numerosas plazas de la ciudad. Pero últimamente abren muchos nuevos locales y algunas discotecas ofrecen un „dia gay" en la semana. La revista mensual „AUT" no solo publica artículos sobre cultura y política, sino también las últimas noticias sobre la vida gay-lesbiana de Roma. La editorial de esta revista el „Circolo Mario Mieli" será uno de los organizadores del primero „World Pride", que tendrá lugar en el año 2000 y que provocará controversias en la ciudad. Para financiar el trabajo de esta organización, cuyos miembros son en su mayoría voluntarios, se celebra cada viernes la „Muccassassina", una de las fiestas gay-lesbiana-travesti más excitantes y más frecuentadas en toda Roma. Roma cae muy cerca de Ostia (a unos 30 kilometros) y de otras bellas playas mediterraneas muy frecuentadas por homosexuales.

❖ Con la sua storia di quasi 3 millenni Roma è il posto turistico più importante non solo dell'Italia, ma anche di tutto il mondo. Nessun turista potrà sottrarsi all'attrazione della città eterna con le sue innumerevoli chiese, monumenti e tesori d'arte, che danno l'impressione di muoversi in un museo immenso. Inoltre Roma è la capitale d'Italia con la sede del Parlamento, del Governo e del Presidente dello Stato. Anche per quanto riguarda la vita gay, la metropoli con oltre 3 millioni di abitanti a qualcosa da offrire. Bisogna però tenere presente che non si deve fare un confronto con Amsterdam, Parigi o Londra. Il Vaticano come centro del potere della chiesa cattolica ha sempre la sua influenza sulla vita gay nella capitale, un fatto che si fa riscontra per molti aspetti: per esempio i bar e le discoteche gay corrono il rischio di essere chiusi, cosa che può spiegare la vita breve di tanti locali gay. Così anche molti bar e discoteche si trovano nascosti, e bisogna suonare il campanello per poter entrarvi. In genere a Roma la vita notturna non si svolge nei locali, ma piuttosto nelle piazze affollate anche dai turisti. Nonostante ciò si stanno aprendo numerosi locali nuovi, e molte discoteche offrono ogni settimana una „serata gay". Il mensile „AUT" pubblicato dal „Circolo Mario Mieli" contiene, a parte gli articoli sulla cultura e la politica, le ultime informazioni sulla Roma gay e lesbica. Il „Circolo Mario Mieli" organizzerà, oltre ad altre associazioni, il primo „World Pride" nel 2000, cosa che sicuramente susciterà alcune polemiche nella città del giubileo cristiano. Per il finanziamento del lavoro quasi del tutto volontario ogni venerdì viene organizzata la „Muccassassina", la festa più grande, più frequentata e più eccitante di Roma per gay, lesbiche e transsessuali. Da Roma sono solo 30 kilometri fino al lido di Ostia e, un po' più a sud lungo il mare, alle spiaggie di sabbia molto frequentate anche dai gay.

GAY INFO

Archivio Massimo Consoli
Via Dario Bellezza 1 ✉00040 *(5 minutes from Via Appia, 20km from Roma)* ☎ 06 93 54 75 67 Fax: 06 93 54 74 83
The largest Gay and AIDS Archives in Europe. More than 5.000 books, 1.900 in English. Magazines in all languages-English, French, Spanish and Italian spoken. Admission free, by appointment for people with real interest.

Aut
Monthly gay magazine for politics, culture and roman gay scene. Available in gay bars. For further information call „Circolo Mario Mieli" ☎ 065 41 39 85.

Cronache del 2000 - Quotidiano d'informazione
Casella Postale 754 ✉00187 ☎ 0335 54 57 911
Email: primamano@libero.it
Free local newspaper with gay ads „Messagi e incontri".

Eden
☎ 06 70 30 10 20
Chat line

Radio Effetto Diversità FM 93.3 on Fri 19-20 h

Rome Gay News
Via Einaudi 33, 00040 Frattocchie RM ☎ 06 93 54 75 67
Fax: 06 93 54 74 83
Gay press agency with international news for the Italian mainstream press and national news for the International non-gay press (sent by fax). Sex yellow pages.

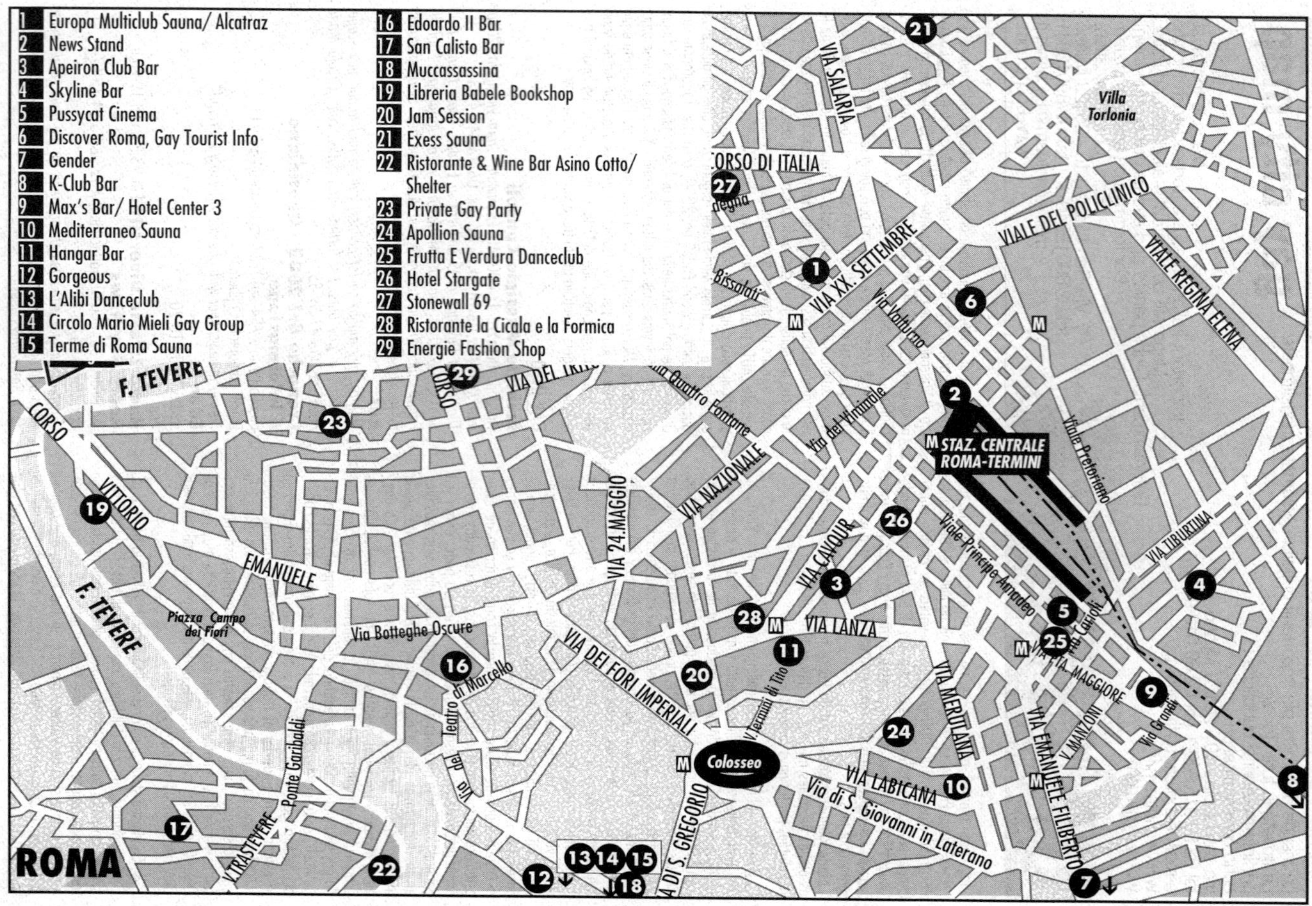
1 Europa Multiclub Sauna/ Alcatraz
2 News Stand
3 Apeiron Club Bar
4 Skyline Bar
5 Pussycat Cinema
6 Discover Roma, Gay Tourist Info
7 Gender
8 K-Club Bar
9 Max's Bar/ Hotel Center 3
10 Mediterraneo Sauna
11 Hangar Bar
12 Gorgeous
13 L'Alibi Danceclub
14 Circolo Mario Mieli Gay Group
15 Terme di Roma Sauna
16 Edoardo II Bar
17 San Calisto Bar
18 Muccassassina
19 Libreria Babele Bookshop
20 Jam Session
21 Exess Sauna
22 Ristorante & Wine Bar Asino Cotto/ Shelter
23 Private Gay Party
24 Apollion Sauna
25 Frutta E Verdura Danceclub
26 Hotel Stargate
27 Stonewall 69
28 Ristorante la Cicala e la Formica
29 Energie Fashion Shop
ROMA
Villa Torlonia
VIA SALARIA
CORSO DI ITALIA
VIALE DEL POLICLINICO
VIALE REGINA ELENA
VIA XX. SETTEMBRE
Via Volturno
STAZ. CENTRALE ROMA-TERMINI
Viale Pretoriano
VIA TIBURTINA
Via Quattro Fontane
Via del Viminale
VIA NAZIONALE
VIA CAVOUR
Viale Principe Amadeo
VIA LANZA
VIA 24.MAGGIO
VIA DEI FORI IMPERIALI
V. Termini di Tito
Colosseo
VIA MERULANA
VIA LABICANA
Via di S. Giovanni in Laterano
VIA EMANUELE FILIBERTO
V. MANZONI
Via Grandi
VIA S. MAGGIORE
Via Carioli
VIA DI S. GREGORIO
Via del Teatro di Marcello
Via Botteghe Oscure
Piazza Campo dei Fiori
CORSO VITTORIO EMANUELE
F. TEVERE
Ponte Garibaldi
V. TRASTEVERE
CORSO
Bissolati
VIA DEL TRITONE

TOURIST INFO

Discover Roma
Via Vicenza 56 ✉00185 *(2nd floor)* ☎ 06 44 70 38 87
Fax: 06 49 38 37 11 Email: discoverroma@jahoo.com
Homepage: www.discoverroma.com
Offers free services to incoming gay tourists.

E.P.T.
Via Parigi 5 ✉00185 ☎ 06 48 89 92 53 Fax: 06 48 89 92 28

BARS

Alcatraz (AC B d DR G lj MA P s SNU VS) Thu-Sun 22-3 h
Via Aureliana 38 ✉00187 *(Metro-Repubblica)* ☎ 06 42 01 32 86
One day connected with the sauna „European Multiclub"/Un giorno attaccato con la sauna „European Multiclub".

Apeiron Club (AC B DR G MA P S VS) 22-? h, closed Sun
Via dei Quattro Cantoni 5 ✉00186 *(Metro Cavour)* ☎ 06 48 28 820

Asinocotto Wine Bar (AC B CC F GLM MA s) 17-24 h, Mon closed

Via dei Vascellari 48 ✉00153 ☎ 06 58 98 985
Wide choice of Italian wines.
Bar S. Calisto (B glm YG) 5.30-1 h, closed on Sun
Piazza di S. Calisto 3-5 *(Trastevere District)*
Very crowded on summer in front of the bar. All kind of people.
Caesar Club (B f glm MA) Mon-Sun 18-3 h
Circonvallazione Gianicolense 64/B-C ✉00152 *(Travestere Railway Station)* ☎ 06 58 18 163
Friendly staff. Piano-bar on week-end.
Edoardo II (AC B G MA P S VS YG) 22.30-3 h, closed Wed
Vicolo Margana 14 ✉00186 ☎ 06 69 94 24 19
Disco bar with DJ. On Thu „secret messages"nights/"Biglietti segreti".
Gender (B DR glm MA s tv) 23-4 h, closed Mon
Via Faleria 9 *(Metro-S. Giovanni)* ☎ 06 70 49 76 38
Transgender club.
Hangar Video Bar (AC B DR G lj MA P r s SNU VS) 22.30-2 h, closed on Tue
Via in Selci 69 ✉00184 *(Metro A Via Cavour/Metro B Piazza Vittorio, vicino al Colosseo/near the Colosseum)* ☎ 06 48 81 397
Incognito 2000 (B F glm MA P R) 20-3 h
Via Casilinia Vecchia 146 ✉00167 *(near Via Casilina/going down at the Fiat shop)* ☎ 06 78 43 567
Refugium Peccatorum Café (AC B f glm MA s) 20-2 h, Mon closed
Vicolo della Penitenza 17 ✉00165 *(Trastevere district)*
☎ 06 68 77 032
Live music.
Shelter (AC B F GLM MA p YG) 21-4 h, Summer: 22-4 h, closed in Aug
Via dei Vascellari 35 ✉00153 *(Bus 75, 170, 780/Tram 8)*
Skyline (AC B DR G MA P s VS) Tue-Thu 22.30-2, Fri-Sat -3, Sun: Oct-Mai 17-2, Jun-Sep 22.30-2 h, Mon closed

Via degli Aurunci 26/28 ✉00185 *(San Lorenzo district, near Termini)* ☎ 06 44 40 817

MEN'S CLUBS

K Day and Night (AC B DR G LJ NU P VS YG) 16-4 h
Via Amato Amati 6/8 ✉00176 *(10 min from the terminal station, Bus 105/Tram Acotral)* ☎ 0347 62 20 462

DANCECLUBS

Agatha (Festa Della Radio Città Futura)
Fri 23-? h
Brancaleone, Via Levanna 11 *(Area Montesacro)* ☎ 06 49 14 37 (Infoline)
Techno, underground, drum & bass. Mixed party in an alternative cultural centre („Centro Sociale").

Alibi. L' (AC B D GLM MA OS S TV) 23.30-4.30 h, closed Mon Tue
Via di Monte Testaccio 39/44 ✉00181 *(Metro Piramide)*
☎ 06 57 43 448
In summer OS with VS and soft music/d'estate terrazza con video e musica sottofondo.

Frutta e Verdura (AC B D DR glm MA P tv) S
at-Sun 4.30-10 h
Via Principe Umberto 36 ✉00184 *(Metro-Manzoni/Vittorio Emanuele)* ☎ 0347 87 97 063
After hours place.

Gorgeous Night. The (AC B D GLM P S YG) Tue 23h, Closed in Jun
c/o Goa, Via Libetta 13 *(M Garbatella)* ☎ 0328 61 24 284 (Infoline)
Trendy party.

H@rd Core (B D DR SNU VS) Thu 23.300-? h
c/o Qube, Via di Portonaccio 212 ☎ 0339 71 04 432
Hot club for hot men.

Jam Session (AC B D DR G MA P s) Wed only 23-4 h
Via del Cardello 13/A ✉00186 ☎ 06 69 94 24 19

Max's Bar (AC B D G H YG) Wed Thu 22.30-3, Fri Sat -4.30, Sun -3.30 h
Via Achille Grandi 3/7 ✉00186 *(Portamaggiore, Metro Manzoni, Underneath/sotto Hotel Grandi)* ☎ 06 70 30 15 99

Muccassassina (B D DR GLM S YG) Fri 22.30-5 h
Alpheus, Via del Commercio 36 ✉00100 *(Metro-Piramide)*
☎ 06 54 13 985
Call for information. Very popular.

Private Gay Party (AC B d G MA P S) Thu (G) 22-? h
c/o The Gallery, Via della Maddalena 12 *(Near Pantheon)*
☎ 0328 61 24 284

Saturgay (AC B G D MA P YG) Sat only 22-? h
c/o Follia, Via Ovidio 17 *(Near Piazza Cavour)* ☎ 06 68 30 84 35
Two rooms, two atmospheres (house & commercial music)

Stonewall 69 (AC B D DR f GLM S VS YG) Thu only 23-4.30, closed in summer
c/o Discoteca Veleno, Via Sardegna 27 ✉00199 *(Metro Barberini/Bus 80)* ☎ 06 85 55 522

RESTAURANTS

Asinocotto di Giuliano Brenna. Ristorante (F glm MA) 20-23:00h Sun - lunch, Mon closed.
Via dei Vascellari 48 ✉00153 *(Tram 8 nearby Piazza Belli in Trastevere)* ☎ 06 58 98 985
Fine and creative Mediterranean cuisine.

La Cicala e la Formica (AC CC glm MA OS) 19-24 h, closed Sun and in Aug
Via Leonina 17 ✉00184 *(Metro Cavour)* ☎ 06 48 17 490

Osteria da Nerone (B F G) Sun closed
Via delle Terme di Tito 96 ☎ 06 47 45 207

SEX SHOPS/BLUE MOVIES

Cobra (g) Mon-Sat 9-20 h
Via Barletta 23 *(Metro Ottaviano)* ☎ 06 37 51 73 50

Cobra (g) Mon-Sat 9-20 h
Via G. Giolitti 307/313 *(Metro-Vittorio)* ☎ 06 44 70 06 36
Underwear, magazines, retail and rental of gay videos/Oggettistica, abbigliamento intimo, riviste, noleggio e vendita di gay video.

Europa 92 (g) Mon 15-19.30, Tue-Sat 9.30-13.30, 15-19.30 h
Via Vitelleschi 38/40 *(near Piazza Risorgimento)* ☎ 06 68 71 210
Gay articles, videos, magazines and books.

Follie d'Amore (g) Mon 16-21, Tue-Sat 10-13, 16-21 h
Via Cavour 323 ☎ 06 69 92 43 72

Sexy Moon Gay Shop (GLM) Mon-Sat 10-20 h
Via A. Nobel 38 ✉00146 *(Railway st. Trastevere)* ☎ 06 55 94 376

CINEMAS

Ambasciatori (g)
Via Montebello 101 *(Metro Termini)*
☎ 06 49 41 290

Pussycat (AC g MG VS)
Via Cairoli 96/98 ✉00185 *(Metro Vittorio, near railway station Termini)* ☎ 06 44 64 961

Tiffany (g)
Via A de Pretis 11 ☎ 06 48 82 390 *Popular.*

ESCORTS & STUDIOS

International Escort Service
☎ 0335 60 51 309
Photo models for studio sessions, shows, publicity etc.

SAUNAS/BATHS

Apollion Sauna (AC DR f G msg p sa sb VS wh YG) Sun-Thu 14.30-23, Fri Sat -3/4 h
Via Mecenate 59/a ✉00184 *(Metro-Piazza Vittorio)*
☎ 06 48 25 389

Europa Multiclub (AC B DR f G MA msg P pi sa sb sol VS wh YG) Winter: Mon-Thu 15-24, Fri Sat 14-6, Sun 14.30-24 h, Summer: Sun-Thu 15-24, Fri Sat 15-6 h
Via Aureliana 40 ✉00187 *(Metro Repubblica)* ☎ 06 48 23 650
Also beauty salon. Arcigay membership required. Access to/collegato Bar Alcatraz.

Exess (AC B CC DR f G msg P sa sb sol WE wh YG) Fr-Sat 15-22 h (G)
Via Ombrone 1 ✉00198 *(Metro-Policlinico/Tram 19/30)*
☎ 06 85 58 398

Mediterraneo Sauna (AC B DR G msg P sa sb sol VS wh YG) 14-24 h
Via Pasquale Villari 3 ✉00184 *(Metro Manzoni/Colosseo)*
☎ 06 77 20 59 34
Sauna on three floors. Arcigay membership required.

Terme di Roma Internazionale (AC B CC DR G msg sa sb sol RT VS wh WO YG) Sun-Thu 13-24, Fri & Sat -2 h
Via Persio 4 ✉00178 *(Bus 765 from Metro-Arco di Travertino)*
☎ 06 71 84 378

BODY & BEAUTY SHOPS

Gilcagne (AC CC glm MA)
Via della Croce 35 ✉00187 *(historical centre, Metro A-Spagna)*
☎ 06 67 91 124 *Beauty shop and hair dresser.*

BOOK SHOPS

Edizione E Libreria Croce
Via S. Pincherle 66/68 ✉00146 *(near Metro-Marconi)*
☎ 06 55 84 927
Gay section.

Libreria Babele (CC GLM) Mon-Sat 10-19.30 h, closed Sun
Via dei Banchi Vecchi 116 ✉00186 ☎ 06 68 76 628
Rome's only gay book and video shop. Wide range of lesbian literature./Unica libreria gay a Roma. Ampio spazio alla letteratura lesbica.

Rinascita
Via delle Botteghe Oscure 1 ☎ 06 679 71 36
Large gay section.

FASHION SHOPS

Energy
Via del Corso 486/7

NEWS STANDS

Libreria la Bancarella
Piazza Alessandria 2 *(Porta Pia)* ☎ 06 85 30 30 71

TELECOMMUNICATION

Splashnet summer: 9-1, winter 9-23 h
Via Varese 33 ✉00185 ☎ 3906 49 38 04 50 Email: splashnet@yahoo.com Homepage: www.splahnet.it
Internet and laundromat!

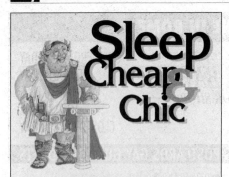

TRAVEL & TRANSPORT

Travel Job Tour Operator (g) 9-16.30 h, Sat Sun closed
Via Vittorini 103 ☎ 06 50 04 607

Travel Job Tour Operator (g) 9-16.30 h, Sat Sun closed
Via Paolo di Dono 137-139 ✉00142 ☎ 06 50 30 272
Fax: 06 50 05 603

Zipper 9.30-18.30, closed Sat Sun
Via Castelfidardo 18 ✉00185 *(2nd floor)* ☎ 06 48 82 730
Fax: 06 48 82 729 Email: zipper.travel@flashnet.it
Gay travel agency, tourist service, organization of international gay meetings.

HOTELS

Adas (AC bf H)
Via Cavour 233 ✉00184 *(Near Metro Cavour)* ☎ 06 47 41 432
Fax: 06 47 44 852
Single room 110.000, Double 160.000 with bf, bath, TV and phone.

Cambridge (AC B bf CC H)
Via Palestro 87 ✉00185 *(200 m from the terminal station)*
☎ 06 44 56 821 Fax: 06 49 38 49 17
Single room 100.000-160.000, Double room 130.000-230.000 with bf, TV, phone, minibar.

Center 3 (glm)
Via Achille Grandi 7 ✉00185 *(Metro-Manzoni)* ☎ 06 70 30 00 58
Fax: 06 70 30 00 59
Rates single Lit 80.000-250.000, double 100.000-320.000. All rooms with shower, WC, TV.

Hotel Benjamin (bf glm H)
Via Boezio 31 ✉00192 *(Metro Ottaviano-San Pietro/Bus 492/64, Near Vatican)* ☎ & Fax: 06 68 80 24 37
Nice and comfortable rooms in the centre of Rome with bath on the floor. Early booking advisable/Camere piacevoli e confortevoli al centro di Roma. I bagni sono al corridoio. Si prega di prenotare in anticipo.

Hotel Labelle (AC bf CC glm H MA) Via Cavour 310 ✉00184 *(Metro Colosseo/Cavour)* ☎ 06 67 94 750
Fax: 06 69 94 03 67
Rates single without shower Lit. 60.000-90.000, with shower 150.000, double without shower 80.000-130.000, with shower 120.000-180.000. Bf not incl.

Hotel Stargate 2 (B bf CC F H msg)
Via Farini 52 ✉00185 *(central, near Stazione Termini)*
☎ 06 47 82 48 44 ax: 06 47 88 07 49
Email: informa@stargatehotels.com
Homepage: www.stargatehotels.com *Check the web site for rates.*

Scott House Hotel (AC B bf CC H MA)
Via Gioberti 30 ✉00185 *(Stairway A, 4th, near station/Scala A 4°piano, vicino Stazione Termini)* ☎ 06 44 65 379

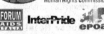

Fax: 06 44 64 986 Email: info@scotthouse.com
Homepage: http://www.italyhotel.com/roma/scotthouse
All rooms with bath, central heating, TV, telephone and safe. Elevator. Fax. 24 hour friendly service. Single room Lit 50.000-200.000, double 60.000-250.000

Tre Stelle (AC B F glm H)
Via S. M. della Battaglia 11 ✉00185 *(200 m from the terminal station)* ☎ 06 44 63 095
Single room 60.000-100.000, Double room 80.000-160.000, room sharing possible.

GUEST HOUSES

Sleep Cheap and Chic (AC bf glm H MA)
Via delle Baleniere 112 ✉00121 Ostia Lido ☎ 06 56 94 283
Fax: 06 56 94 283 Email: b.b.chic@usa.net
Homepage: www.summerweb.com/sleepcheapchic
Rates/person Lit 60.000 incl. bf.

PRIVATE ACCOMODATION

Enjoy Bed & Breakfast (bf G H MA YG)
16:30-21:00h
☎ +49 (30) 215 1666 Fax: +49 (30) 217 52219
Price 40 Euro. Accommodation sharing agency. All with shower, bf.

GENERAL GROUPS

Arcigay Roma Caravaggio
Via Lariana 8 ✉00199 ☎ 06 85 55 522 Fax: 06 86 32 81 75
Political activities, help-line, self-help groups, bar, exhibitions, film and theatre, distribution of condoms and information brochure on Aids./Attività politiche, telefono amico, gruppi di self help, bar, mostre, rassegne cinematografiche e teatrali, distribuzione preservativi e materiale informativo sull'Aids.

Circolo di Cultura Omosessuale Mario Mieli „WORLD PRIDE 2000 ORGANIZER"
Mon-Fri 9-20 h
Via Corinto 5 ✉00146 *(Metro B-San Paolo, Entrance/Entrata: Via Efeso/Via Ostiense 2a)* ☎ 06 54 13 985 Fax: 06 54 13 971
Email: mario.mielti@agora.stm.it
Homepage: http://www.mariomieli.it
Call for information on activites.

HEALTH GROUPS

Anlaids Mon-Fri 10-19 h
Via Barberini 3 ☎ 06 44 70 01 71 Fax: 06 48 21 077
Email: anlaids@anlaids.it Homepage: www.anlaids.it

Associazione Positifs Mon-Fri 9-17 h
Viale di Valle Aurelia 111 ✉00167 ☎ 06 63 80 365
Fax: 06 63 80 74 Email: ass.positifs@agora.stm.it
Information on Aids treatment available.

Clinica Dermosifilopatica del Policlinico Gemelli 8-12 h
Largo Agostino Gemelli 8 ✉00100 ☎ 06 01 30 15

Istituto Dermopatico Dell'Immacolata
Via Dei Monti di Creta 104/114 ☎ 06 66 461

Lega Italiana Lotta Contro L'Aids (LILA)
Counselling: Mon Wed 10-13, Thu 16-19 h, Legal counselling Mon Wed Fri 16-19 h.
Via Alessandria 129 ✉00198 *(near Piazza Fiume)*
☎ 06 88 48 426

Ospedale S. Giovanni Aids centre: Mon Sat 8-13 h
Via di S. Giovanni in Laterano 149 ☎ 06 77 05 53 28
HIV test by appointment: call „Circolo Mario Mieli" ☎ 065 41 39 85

Istituto Gay Counselling Mon-Fri 11-13, 16-19 h, closed in Aug
Via Saluzzo 40 ✉00182 *(Metro Ponte Lungo)* ☎ 06 70 29 037
Counselling and therapy, group therapy.

SWIMMING

-Beach south of Ostia/Spiaggia sud di Ostia (nice dunes/belle dune; by car: from Lido die Ostia in direction Anzio, after km-sign 8; by bus: Bus 07 from Ostia till last stop, then on foot for 2 km to km-sign 8, beach bar Stabilimento Balneare Settimo Cielo)

CRUISING

-Colosseo Quadrato (Metro Magliana, gardens near Palazzo Civiltà del Lavoro/ Giardini vicino al bar Palombini) (AYOR)
-P. Belle Arti »Valle Giulia« (in front of National Gallery, opposite hustlers/davanti Galleria National) (AYOR r)
-Monte Caprino (very busy/molto frequentato)
-Villa Borghese, Galoppatoio (tardo pomeriggio, sera, molto frequentato/late afternoon, evening, very busy)
-Via Montenero (20-22 h) (r)

Rovereto - Trento ✉ 38068

BARS

Chicco Bar (B g) Daily 8-1 h
Piazza Stazione ✉38068 ☎ 0464 43 49 22

Salerno ✉ 84100

SEX SHOPS/BLUE MOVIES

Mediart (g)
Viale Leucosia 91 ✉84100 *(zona Mercadello)*

GENERAL GROUPS

Arcigay Arcilesbica Salerno
Piazza Vittorio Veneto 2 ✉84100 ☎ 089 22 06 23
Fax: 089 25 32 05

CRUISING

-Railway Station/Stazione FS (occasional/occasionale, daytime)
-Seafront/Lungomare
-Square in front of/piazzo davanti Hotel Jolly (at night/di notte)
-Pineta (12 km from Salerno, summertime in the afternoon/d'estate, pomeriggio)
-Villa Communale

Salsomaggiore Terme - Parma ✉ 43039

HOTELS

Marinella (F g H OG)
Via Castllazzo 80 ✉43039 ☎ 0524 57 82 97
All rooms with phone, private baths and WC. Rates on request.

San Benedetto del Tronto - Ascoli Piceno ✉

DANCECLUBS

Censura (B D GLM)
Via Pasubio 1/F ✉63039 ☎ 0735 75 73 71
Call for info.

CRUISING

-Railway Station/Stazione FS
-Cinema delle Palme (garden behind the cinema/giardini dietro il cinema)
-Muro del Pianto (garden behind Roxy Hotel/nei giardini dietro all'Hotel Roxy)
-Pineta (woods at the seashore/sul mare)
-Punta Nina (beach between/spiaggia fra Pevaso and Benedetto, behind/dietro Pensione Il-Contadino)

San Remo - Imperia ✉ 18038

CRUISING

-Park gardens/Giardini del parco (evening/sera)
-Porto Vecchio (in summer, along the pier/in estate lungo il molo)
-Marsaglia (R)
-Railway station/stazione FS (main hall/salone principale)
-Lungo Mare delle Nazzioni

San Vincenzo - Livorno ✉ 57027

SWIMMING

-La Torraccia (NU) (near the campnig „La Torraccia")

Santa Margherita Ligure ✉ 16038

HOTELS

Hotel La Vela (bf B g H sol)
Corso Nicolò Cuneo 21 ✉16038 ☎ 0185 28 47 71
Homepage: http://www.lavela.it
Gays welcome. All rooms with bath, TV and telephone.

Sant'Ilario d'Enza - Reggio Emilia ✉ 42049

CRUISING
-Enza river/fiume

Sassari ✉ 07100

BARS
Borderline (B GLM) Fri, Sun 21-?, Sat 22-? h
circolo Arci Nuova Associazione, via Rockfeller 16/C ✉07100
☎ 079 21 90 24

GENERAL GROUPS
Arcigay Arcilesbica Infoline: Tue, Thu
Via M. Zanfarino 22 ✉07100 ☎ 079 27 55 40
Movimento Omosessuale Sardo Mon Tue Thu Fri 9.30-13.30, 17.30-20.30, Wed Sun 20.30-22.30 h
Via Rockfeller 16/c ✉07100 ☎ 079 21 90 24 Fax: 079 21 90 24
Email: movimento.omosessual@tiscalinet.it
Helpline, information on gays and Aids/Telefonico amico e informazione su omosessualità e Aids.

CRUISING
-Corso Giò Maria Angioi (r tv) (from 22 h, on foot or by car)
-Quarto pettine (zona Platamona) (winter by car, summer also by foot)
-Railway station/Stazione FS (and the place in front at night/e nella piazzetta antistanche di notte)
-Alghero (in summer on the seafront between the/d'estate sul lungomare tra il Bar Arca and the Bar de Tramonto, be discreet/discreto)

Sasso Marconi - Bologna ✉ 40037

GUEST HOUSES
Albergo Triana e Tyche (b bf CC f g H msg NU OS sol)
Viale J.F. Kennedy 9/2 ✉40037 *(700 m from station)*
☎ 0516 75 16 16 Fax: 0516 75 17 02
Single Lit. 45.000-90.000, double 880.000-180.000. Special rates for long stays and Spartacus readers.

Saturnia ✉ 58050

CRUISING
-Terme (natural hot waters bathing pools and waterfall (not in the hotel but in the fields of the countryside amidst reeds). Drive along the road from Manciano and park immediately past the bridge on the sulphureous stream, near the dilapidated mill. Mostly at night: be discreet)

Savona

GENERAL GROUPS
Arcigay Arcilesbica Savona Tue Thu 21-23h
Via Giacchero 22/2 ✉17100 ☎ 019 80 74 94 Fax: 019 82 57 44

SWIMMING
-Varigotti, castello (up the hill with the small castle besides the tunnel, on the left side to the sea/salire al castello, scendere giù con la corda; the left bay is interesting)

CRUISING
-Loano (seaside from railway station Loano in direction Borghetto, [P] ex-railway stop near Piazza del Popolo, at night/Lungomare da stazione FS Loano in direzione Borghetto, [P] ex-stazione FS vicino Piazza del Popolo, la notte)

Scandicci - Firenze ✉ 50018

CRUISING
-Outside the building of „Teatro Magazzini"
-[P] Scandicci Autostrada A1/E Milano-Roma, northbound only/solo corsia nord

Sciacca - Agrigento ✉ 92019

CRUISING
-Terme Selinuntine

Senigallia - Ancona ✉ 60019

BARS
Pensierostupendo (B D glm) Thu-Sun 21.30 h until Jun 15th, Tue-Sun 21.30 h after Jun 15th
Strada della Bruciata ✉60019 ☎ 0347 47 58 758
At residential centre „Le Piramidi" direction Monterado, after 7 km on the left./Centro Residenziale „Le Piramidi" prendere direzione per Monterado, a 7200 mt sulla sx. UNO card required./Ingresso con tessera UNO.

RESTAURANTS
Al Molo (b F g)
Via Banchina di Levante 6 ✉60019 ☎ 071 61 634

CRUISING
-Giardini Morandi (R)

Sesto Fiorentino ✉ 50019

SEX SHOPS/BLUE MOVIES
Erotica - La Cosa Sexy Shop (g) closed Sun and Mon morning
Viale Togliatti 131 ✉50019 ☎ 0554 21 64 70
Underwear, S/M articles, gay videos and magazines. Babilonia publications available.

Sibari - Cosenza ✉ 87070

CRUISING
-Beach „Pineta di Thurio" near Foggia Cantinella (best 14-18 h)

Siena ✉ 53100

BARS

Re Artu (B g) 22-2 h
Via C. Angiolieri 116 ✉53100
115 (B g) 21-1 h
Via dei Rossi 115 ✉53100

GENERAL GROUPS

Arcigay Arcilesbica Ganimède Wed 21.30-23 h
Via Roma 56 ✉53100 ☎ 0577 28 89 77 Fax: 0577 27 15 38
Email: ganimede@gay.it
Homepage: http://www.gay.it/arcigay/siena
Phone-line, counseling, weekly meetings, shows, exhibitions

CRUISING

-Railway Station/Stazione FS
-Via Roma
-Piazza del Campo
-Fortezza Medicea (at foot of the little garden and along Viale Viattorio Veneto, but only from 22-1 h, and during the day, especially in the afternoon, Viale G. Marconi/al piede del giardinetto e lungo Viale Vittorio Veneto solo 22-1 h, e durante il giorno, specialmente il pomeriggio, Viale G. Marconi)

Siracusa ✉ 96100

CINEMAS

Capitol (g)
Via Italia 32 ✉96100 ☎ 0931 75 61 11

GENERAL GROUPS

Arcigay Arcilesbica Siracusa Athena
Via F. Crispi 88 ✉96100 ☎ 0931 22 712 Fax: 0931 21 674

CRUISING

-Pantheon (gardens/giardini)
-Apollo temple/tempio
-Lido Sayonara (Località Fontane Bianche)

Sondrio ✉ 23100

SEX SHOPS/BLUE MOVIES

Magic America (g) Closed on Mon morning
Via Mazzini 46 ✉23100 ☎ 0342 56 72 92 Fax: 0342 56 72 92

CRUISING

-Via Samaden and Zona Agneda (evenings/sera by car)

Sorrento - Napoli ✉ 80067

SWIMMING

-Bagni Regina Giovanna (NU) (popular/frequentato)

CRUISING

-Villa Communale (at night; also at the end of the avenue/di notte; anche in fondo al viale)
-Piazzetta V. Veneto (in the gardens/nei giardini)

Spessa Po - Pavia ✉ 27010

SWIMMING

-Along River Po/lungo il Po (g MA NU r) (afternoons/pomeriggio)

Spresiano - Treviso ✉ 31027

SWIMMING

-Ponte della Priula (NU) (between Treviso and Conegliano, on River Piave; coming from Treviso take the path on the right after Ponte restaurant, just before Ponte della Priula; swimming, action, also in winter/fra Treviso e Conegliano, venendo da Treviso imboccare il sentiero a destra dopo il ristorante Ponte; poco prima di Ponte della Priula; nuoto, azione, anche d'inverno)

Stromboli - Messina ✉ 98050

HOTELS

Sciara. La (B F g H OS pi sol)
Via S. Barnao ✉98050 ☎ 090 98 60 04
All rooms have telephone, priv. bath and balcony.
Sirenetta (B bf F glm H OS pi sol)
Via Marina N° 33 ☎ 090 98 60 25
Beach location, all rooms have telephone, priv. bath and balcony. Recommended.

CRUISING

-Spiaggia Lunga (in fondo alla Rocca/at bottom of Rocca)

Taormina - Messina ✉ 98039

BARS

Casanova Bar (AC B CC f MA N OS) 18-3 h, closed on Wed in winter
Vico Paladini 2/4 ✉98039 ☎ 0942 23 945
Cocktail bar, crepes and sandwiches.
Re del Sole (B f g) May-Oct
Spisone Strada Statale 114 ☎ 0942 62 53 85
Beach bar near the gay beach „Rocce Bianche". Restaurant service until 16 h.
Shatulle (B f g OS) Mar-Jul: 9-?, Aug-Feb: 17-? h, closed on Mon
Piazzetta Paladini 2 ✉98039 ☎ 0942 62 61 75
Cocktail bar and creperie.

DANCECLUBS

Discoteca Marabù (B D g) 23-6 h, summer only
Via Iannuzzo *(near Taormina)* ☎ 0942 65 30 29
Techno house music, many gays on Tue.
Discoteca Taitu (B g D) 23-6 h, winter only
Via Vulcano 3 *(near Taormina)* ☎ 0942 51 407
Techno house music.
Perroquet (B D GLM S YG OS) Jul-Aug 22.30-4, winter only Sat Sun
Piazza San Domenico 2 *(opposite Hotel San Domenico)*
☎ 0329 41 28 001 (Infoline)
Dragshow on Fri and Sat in summer. Recommended.

BOOK SHOPS

Edizione Vittorio Malambri
Corso Umberto 108 ✉98039 ☎ 0942 24 621
Photos, books, videos and calendars on Wilhelm von Gloeden/Collezione fotografica, libri, videocassette, calendri su Wilhelm von Gloeden.

HOTELS

Hotel Romantik Villa Ducale (AC B bf CC E f H MA NG OS wh) Closed Jan 15-Mar 1
Via Leonardo da Vinci 60 ✉98039 ☎ 0942 28 153
Fax: 0942 28 710 Email: villaducale@tao.it
Charming hotel, excellent views, small and intimate, very discreet. Rates Lit. 180.000-380.000. Suite 600.000/Albergo di charme, panoramicissimo, piccolo e intimo, molta discrezione.
Hotel Splendid (bf B CC F g H pi OS) Closed Nov-Mar except 31st Dec and 1st Jan
Via Dietro Cappucini ✉98039 *(Centrally located)* ☎ 0942 23 500
Fax: 0942 62 52 89
Single room Lit 80.000, Double room 140.000 with phone, priv. bath, bf and balcony.

Hotel Villa Schuler (B bf CC glm H MA msg OS) closed Dec-Feb
Piazzetta Bastione/Via Roma ✉98039 ☎ 0942 23 481
Fax: 0942 23 522 Email: schuler@tao.it
All rooms have priv. bath, balcony with a great sea-view. Rates from Lit. 112.000 (single)-166.000 (double) incl. bf.

Pensione Adele (bf H g)
Via Apollo Arcageta *(near Porta Catania)* ☎ 0942 23 352
Fax: 0942 23 352
Single room Lit 70.000, Double room 136.000, bf and dinner incl. Cosy atmosphere.

GUEST HOUSES

Isoco Guest House (AC bf GLM H OS)
open only from Apr to Oct
Via Salita Branco 2 ✉98039 *(Central, near San Antonio church)*
☎ 0942 23 679 Fax: 0942 23 679
Email: isocohouse@aol.com
Beautiful view on the coast/Bellissima veduta panoramica sulla costa. Double from Lit 99.000 to 159.000 with TV, minibar.

SWIMMING

-Rocce Bianche (G MA NU) (take any beach/spiaggia bus, the gay beach is at the white rocks between Re del Sole andd Caparena)
-Fondaco Parrino (G MA NU) (Strada Statale 114, near Capo St. Alessio. Take bus direction Messina or Forza d'Argo, step out at Camping Paradise. Cruising)

CRUISING

-Parco Triangolo (in front of Hotel Excelsior)

Taranto ✉ 74100

CINEMAS

Flamma (g)
Via Gorizia ✉74100

GENERAL GROUPS

Arcigay Arcilesbica Taranto
Via Sannio 25 ✉74100 ☎ 099 732 46 97

HEALTH GROUPS

Ospedale SS. Annunziata
Via Bruno ✉74100

SWIMMING

-Scogliera delle Donne Maledette (NU) (7 km from Taranto; romantic spot; Also known as Le Conchette/7 km da Taranto, posto romantico; anche chiamato Le Conchette)

CRUISING

-Seafront/Lungomare
-Viale Virgilio (R TV) (at night/di notte)
-Railway Station/Stazione FS
-Arsenale Militare (entrance/ingresso)
-Ponte Punta Penn (TV) (near/vicino Caserma Aeronautica)

Tarquinia - Viterbo ✉ 01016

CRUISING

-Piazza Cavour (evenings/sera)
-Tarquinia Lido (near/vicino Porto Clementino, all day in the summer/tutto il giorno d'estate)

Termoli - Campobasso ✉ 86039

CRUISING

-Railway station/stazione FS
-Port, near red lamp/molo del porto, faro rosso

Terni ✉ 05100

HEALTH GROUPS

Ospedale Generale Provinciale
Viale Tristano di Ioannuccio ✉05100 ☎ 0744 57 141
HIV-test.

CRUISING

-Giardini Via Lungonera Savoia
-Viale Fonderia
-Stadium/stadio Libero Liberati
-Corso Tacito

Torino ✉ 10100

GAY INFO

Agedo Associazione Genitori Parenti E Amici Di Omosessuali
✉10100 ☎ 011 52 11 116
Call for information.
Diversamente
Monthly publication of Maurice-Circolo Culturale Gay e Lesbico.
Fondazione Sandro Penna
Via S. Chiara 1 ✉10100 ☎ 011 52 12 00 33
Library, gay press, cultural centre, archive. Call for appointment.
Informagay Tue 21-23, Sat 17-20 h
Via S. Chiara 1 ☎ 011 43 65 000 Fax: 011 43 68 638
Email: infogay@arpnet.it
Telephone help, Aids group, parties, cultural events. National secretariat of Forum Aids Italia.
Maurice-Centro di Documentazione Thu 16-19 h
Via Basilica 3/5 ✉10122 ☎ 011 52 11 116
Fax: 011 52 11 132 Email: maurice@arpnet.it
Homepage: http://www.arpnet.it/maurice/
Maurice-Circolo Culturale Gay E Lesbico Mon-Sat 15-19 h
Via della Basilica 3/5 ✉10122 ☎ 011 52 11 116
Fax: 011 52 11 132 Email: maurice@arpnet.it
Homepage: http://www.arpnet.it/maurice/
Cultural group, gayline, meetings, lectures, entertainment, lending library and archive, lesbian group/circolo culturale, linea gay, riunioni, conferenze, spettacolli, biblioteca e archivio con prestito, gruppo lesbico.

BARS

Caffè Lerì (B f g s) 21.30-3 h, closed Mon
Corso Vittorio Emanuele II, 64 ✉10100 ☎ 011 54 30 75
Concerts, piano-bar, cocktails.
Male. II (AC B F GLM MA W) 20-3, Sat Sun -4 h, closed Tue
Via Lombardore 10/Via Barbania *(Bus 57)* ☎ 011 28 46 17
Single party on Thu. Bears night on Fri. Italian and French cuisine.
On The Road Café (B F glm s tv) non-stop
Via Monginevro 5 ✉10138
Video, Internet, DJ. Theme parties, drag on Sat./Bar molto misto con video e posti internet. Serate a tema. Ogni tanto DJ. Sabato tanti travestiti.
Radio Kingston (B d F g s YG) 11-15, 19-2 h, closed Sun
Via Ormea, 78/D ☎ 011 65 02 346
Nice restaurant-Bar with ska music, DJ, theme parties. Only few gays.
Route 66 (B d glm s) Tue-Sat 21.30-2 h, closed Sun Mon
Via Silvio Pellico 4 ✉10125
Gay night dance on Fri.

CAFÉS

Les Chats (AC B bf f glm MA N) 7.30-20 h, closed Sun
Via Carlo Alberto 28 ✉10123 *(Bus 61, Tram 18)*
☎ 011 56 25 361

DANCECLUBS

Il Centralino-Dietrich (AC b D GLM MA s) Fri Sun 24-4, Sat -5 h
Via delle Rosine 16/A ☎ 0335 53 49 808 (Infoline)
Metropolis Club (AC B D G WE) Sat 0-4 h
Via Principessa Clotilde 82 *(near Piazza Statuto)* ☎ 011 48 41 16
Musica commerciale.
Must. Le (A AC B CC D DR f GLM lj MA s SNU VS W) Tue-Sun 22.30-? h, closed Mon, Disco: Thu-Sat
Via Porta Palatina 23 ✉10122 *(in front of the church)*
Closed Jul-Sep 15.
Pop Planet (D glm s) Sat 24-5 h
c/o Vertigo, Corso Massimo D'Azeglio 3 ☎ 0347 47 58 758
Garage and house music. Theme parties.

SEX SHOPS/BLUE MOVIES

Drop Out (g) Mon 13-19.30, Tue-Sat 10-19.30 h
Via Carlo Alberto 41 ✉10123 *(in the court)* ☎ 011 81 25 345
Large section with videos, underwear, magazines, accessories (also S/M).
Erotika (g) Mon-Sat 9-21
Belfiore 20 ✉10125 *(Near railway station Porta Nuova)* ☎ 011 65 79 44
O (g) Mon 14.30-19.30, Tue-Sat 9.30-12.30, 14.30-19.30 h
Via Sacchi 40 ✉10128 ☎ 011 59 15 85
Large gay section.
Temptation Sexy Shop (glm) Mon-Sat 9.30-20 h
Via San Pio V 7/c *(30 m from railway station Porta nuova)*
☎ 011 66 90 706
Videos to rent and for sale/Vendite e noleggio videocassette in italiano e in lingua originale.

Videoclub XXX (g VS)
C. so G. Cesare 21/C ☎ 0348 34 15 409
Videoclub XXX (g VS)
Via Asuncion 3A ☎ 011 61 11 64

CINEMAS

Hollywood (MA r) 10.30-1.30 h
Corso Regina Margherita 106 ☎ 011 52 12 385
Regina (g MA r) 15-24 h
Corso Regina Margherita 123 ✉10122 *(Near/vicino Porta Palazzo, Tram 3/4/16/Bus 12/50/51/77)* ☎ 011 43 62 092
Roma (g)
Via San Donato 10/bis ☎ 011 48 77 65
Busy/Frequentato.

SAUNAS/BATHS

Antares (B DR f G p sa sb VS YG) 13-24 h, Mon closed
Via Pigafetta 73/D 10129 ✉10100 *(near Largo Orbassano, Bus 64, tram 10,12)* ☎ 011 50 16 45
Blue (! f G msg P sa sb sol VS WO YG) 15-1, Sat-Sun 14-2 h, Wed closed
Corso Vigevano 41 ✉10152 *(Bus 52/46/49)* ☎ 011 24 90 004
San Martino Sauna (G MA sa sb sol) 15-20 h, closed Tue
Corso S. Martino 8/G ✉10122 *(near Porta Susa railway station)* ☎ 011 53 37 94
011 Sauna Club (! AC B DR F G MA p s sa sb VS wh) Mon-Fri 15-2, Sat -4 Sun -1 h, Tue and Aug closed
Via Messina 5/D ✉10153 *(Tram 18 - Bus 63)* ☎ 011 28 42 63
Reduction for students and soldiers/Promozione per studenti e militari

BOOK SHOPS

Libreria Luxemburg (AC CC g) Mon 15.30-19.30, Tue-Sat 9-19.30 h
Via Battisti 7 ✉10123 *(Centro storico)* ☎ 011 56 13 896
International book-shop. Friendly gay information, videos and gay literature.

DECORATION

Carta. Di (CC) 9.30-12.30, 15.30-19.30
Piazza Vittorio Veneto 1 ✉10124 ☎ 011 81 23 685
Luxury stationery, candles, interior design.

FASHION SHOPS

Non Solo Intimo (CC g) Mon 15-19.30, Tue-Sat 10-13, 15-19.30 h
Via Carlo Alberto 41 ✉10123 ☎ 011 83 73 16

NEWS STANDS

Kiosk/Rivendita Giornali
Corso Regina Margherita 143/D
Kiosk/Rivendita Giornali
Piazza Castello 163/Via Garibaldi
Kiosk/Rivendita Giornali
Corso Vittorio Emanuele II 58
Opposite railway station/di fronte Porta Nuova stazione FS.

TRAVEL & TRANSPORT

Blue (CC GLM) 15-18 h, Wed closed
Corso Vigevano 41 ✉10152 ☎ 011 24 90 004 Fax: 011 28 39 96
Tour operator.
Yag Tours (CC GLM) Mon-Sat 9.30-12.30, 15-19 h
Via S. Anselmo 2/H ✉10100 *(near railway station/vicino stazione Porta Nuova)* ☎ 011 65 87 72 Fax: 011 668 99 75
Email: yagtours@xoommail.com

HOTELS

Hotel Napoleon (B bf CC glm OS)
Via XX Settembre 5 ✉10121 ☎ 011 56 13 223 Fax: 011 54 08 20
Rates single Lit 140.000, double 190.000 (bf incl.). All rooms with bath, TV, refrigerator. Gays welcome: 30% discount for Spartacus readers.

GENERAL GROUPS

Sportello Gay presso CGIL Mon Wed 14.30-17.30 h
c/o V. Pedrotti 5 ☎ 011 24 42 435
Centro per la lotta contro le discriminazioni degli omosessuali sul posto di lavoro.
LILA-Lega Italiana Per La Lotta Contro L'Aids Mon 19-22, Wed Fri 18-20 h
Corso Regina Margherita 190/E ✉10152 ☎ 011 43 61 043
Information, psychological and legal counselling, home care.
Linea Trans (Movimento Italiano Transessuali - MIT)
☎ 011 52 11 116
Simply Normal - Nazionale E Torino
c/o Maurizio Cagliuso, Piazza Vittorio 18 ✉10123
☎ 0338 46 77 653 Fax: 011 99 88 094
Email: simply.normal@iol.it
Homepage: http://www.geocities.com/WestHollywood/9734

HEALTH GROUPS

Anlaids Mon Wed Fri 15-19 h
Via C. Botta 3 ✉10122 ☎ 011 43 65 541 Fax: 011 43 65 541
Email: p-anlaids@iol.it
Prevention and information.
Consultorio di Sessuologia, Mauriziano Hospital
Largo Turati 62 *(Tram 4, Bus 41, 63)*
☎ 011 50 80 111
Information for transsexuals, psychological support until the operation.
Gruppo Solidarietà AIDS (GSA) Mon 21-23 h
Via S. Chiara 1 ✉10122 ☎ 011 43 64 749 Fax: 011 43 68 638
Support for AIDS patients.
Istituto Malattie Infettive - Ospedale Amedeo Di Savoia
Corso Svizzera 164 ✉10149
Free anonymous HIV test.
Philadelphia Thu 21-23 h
Via Baretti 8 ✉10125 ☎ 011 65 75 82
Gay association for health and against AIDS.

RELIGIOUS GROUPS

Agape-Gruppo Gay Credenti
✉10060 *(Eucumenic centre in Val Germanasca)*
☎ 0121 80 75 14 Fax: 0121 80 76 90
Summer camp „Faith and homosexuality"/Campo estivo „Fede e omosessualità".
Davide e Gionatha Gruppo Omosessuali Credenti Tue 20.30-23 h
Via Giolitti 21/A ✉10100 ☎ 011 88 98 11
Christian meetings, lectures, entertainment.

CRUISING

-Corso Marche (near corner Regina Margherita in gardens) (police checks)
-Lumini, Cimitero Monumentale, Lungo dora colletta (by car night and day/in macchina)
-Stazione di Porta Nuova e Porta Susa (R) (police checks/controlli polizia)
-Corso Siccardi (Ai WC/at toilets)

-Valentino Park (by car, also on foot/in macchina, anche a piedi, Corso Galilei/Viale Marinai d'Italia)
-Corso Palestro (in the public toilet)
-Parco delle Vallere, Moncalieri (by car during the day only)
-Piazza d'armi (evenings/de sera)

Torre del Greco - Napoli ✉ 80059

BARS

Makumba (B D g YG) 22-? h, but gay only Sat night
Via De Gasperi 141 ✉80059
Good music/buona musica.

Trapani ✉ 91100

CINEMAS

Diana (g) Sat Sun
Via dei Mille ✉91100 *(Hall B)* ☎ 0923 21 163

CRUISING

-Beach/spiagga Scogliera delle Vergini

Trento ✉ 38100

GENERAL GROUPS

Arcigay Arcilesbica Trento
c/o Centro „B. Disertori", Piazza Mostra 19 ✉38100
☎ 0461 98 08 71 Fax: 0461 23 55 81

CRUISING

-Piazza Dante (in front of railway station)(AYOR)
-Piazza de Gaspari

Treviso ✉ 31100

SEX SHOPS/BLUE MOVIES

Magic America (CC g p) Clossed on Mon morning
Via Castello d'Amore 7/9 ✉31100 *(Zona Stadio Calcio)*
☎ 0422 30 40 99 Fax: 0422 30 40 99

CRUISING

-Little park along the old city walls facing the railway station/Giardinelli lungo le vecchie mura di fronte alla stazione FS

Trieste ✉ 34100

RESTAURANTS

Arco Di Riccardo (b F g)
Via Trionfo 3 ✉34100 ☎ 040 63 84 35

SEX SHOPS/BLUE MOVIES

Magic America (CC g p W) Closed Mon morning
Viale Miramare 11 ✉34135 *(near Stazione Centrale)*
☎ 040 41 27 35

GENERAL GROUPS

Arcigay Arcilesbica Trieste
Via Strada di Rozzol 79 ✉34100 ☎ 040 39 61 11
Fax: 040 30 12 16

SWIMMING

-Costa dei Barbari (! NU glm) Sistiana (across from the bar Costa dei Barbari. From carpark walk down hill then to the left)

CRUISING

-Railway Station/Stazione FS
-Molo Audace (pier opposite Piazza Unità-late evenings)
-Viale Romolo Gessi (nights only, from Campo Marzio up the hill on viale Romolo Gessi. All the hillside and gardens on the right)

Tropea - Cosenza ✉ 88038

SWIMMING

-Beach at Santa Damenica (rocky beach between spiaggia formicoli and spiaggia riendi)

CRUISING

-Piazza Vittorio Veneto (public gardens/giardini pubblici)
-Corso Vittorio Emanuele (till late at night/fino a tardi)

Udine ✉ 33100

BARS

Camparino. Il (B glm) until 24 h
Viale Volontari della Liberta 3A ✉33100 ☎ 0432 47 01 77

SEX SHOPS/BLUE MOVIES

Magic America (CC g p) Closed Mon morning
Via Manzini 38/A ✉33100 ☎ 0432 29 73 45

CINEMAS

Diana (g OG)
Via Cividale 81 ✉33100 ☎ 0432 28 29 79

GENERAL GROUPS

Arcigay Arcilesbica Udine (B G)
PO Box 237, Via Palmanova 10 ✉33100 *(cortile interno/interior courtyard)* ☎ 0432 52 38 38 Fax: 0432 50 55 30
Mon gay bar, gays from the whole region

CRUISING

-Piazza I Maggio and gardens/e giardini

Varazze - Savona ✉ 17019

CRUISING

-Piani d'Invrea, along the rocks/passeggiata scogliera
-Railway station, inside, outside/stazione, interno e esterno

Varese ✉ 21100

GAY INFO

Arcigay Arcilesbica Varese Wed 20.30-23, Sun 21-23 h
Via Piave 6 ✉21100 *(near station)* ☎ 0332 23 59 59

BARS

Magazzino. Il (B glm) Closed Mon
Via Armellini ✉21100

NEWS STANDS

Kiosk/Rivendita Giornali (g)
Piazza S. Guiseppe

HEALTH GROUPS

Network Nazionale „Gruppo C" Progetto di Ricerca Aids ☎ 0332 26 43 56
Helpline for people with HIV/Aids.

CRUISING

-Piazzale Kennedy (R AYOR) (police)
-North Railway Station (R AYOR) (police)
-Cimitero di Giubiano-Via Maspero (AYOR)

Varzi - Pavia ✉ 27057

CRUISING

-Piazza della Fiera (evenings/sera)

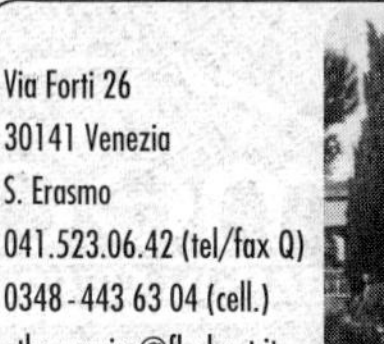

Velturno/Feldthurns - Bolzano/Bozen ✉ 39040

DANCECLUBS

Papillon (B D glm) Wed-Sun 21.30-2.30 h, Thu GLM
Schrambach 25 ✉39040 ☎ 0472 85 53 95

Venezia ✉ 30100

GAY INFO

Arcigay Arcilesbica Venezia (! B F GLM MA W) Daily 18-24 h, closed Mon
Cannaregio 883/A ✉30123 ☎ 041 72 11 97 *Gay center with bar, restaurant, lots of cultural events, sometimes shows.*

BARS

Centro Culturale „ Ai Miracoli" (A B E H MA NG) 16-24 h, closed Tue
Campiello dei Miracoli 6075 ✉30131 *(Rialto-Ca' D'Oro)*

NEWS STANDS

Kiosk/Rivendita Giornali
Rialto 10/53

TRAVEL & TRANSPORT

Venice à la Carte (CC GLM)
Dorsoduro 3167 ✉30123 *(Historical centre, next to the Grand Canal, Water bus-Ca' Rezzonico)* ☎ 041 27 70 564
Fax: 001 240 208 72 73 Email: alvise@tourvenice.org
Personalised visits of all interesting and secret aspects of Venetian life. Tailor-made and personalised holidays, adapted to ones own cultural interests (music, antiques, art, historic sites, private houses and gardens, etc.). Accompaniment with a knowledgable, mixed (Venetian & Amercian) couple. All daytime expenses included.

HOTELS

Hotel Sardegna (AC bf CC H NG)
Calle del Forno 2655 ✉30100 ☎ 041 72 22 31
Fax: 041 72 07 14
Single Lit 150.000-180.000, Double Lit 200.000-250.000 with bath, television and phone. Not gay, but discreet gays are welcome./Non gay, ma gay discreti benvenuti.

Lato Azzurro. Il (A AC bf H MA msg OS W)
Via Forti 26 ✉30141 *(near Murano)* ☎ 041 52 30 642
Fax: 041 52 30 642 Email: other.venice@flashnet.it
Rates Lit 90.000 (double) and 110.000 (triple), with bath/shower, bf at Lit. 5.000.

GENERAL GROUPS

Agedo Associazione Genitori Parenti E Amici Di Omosessuali Wed Fri 20-22 h
✉30100 ☎ 041 53 40 796

HEALTH GROUPS

Network Nazionale „Gruppo C" Progetto di Ricerca Aids
✉30100 ☎ 041 98 78 68
Helpline for people with HIV/Aids.

SWIMMING

-Lido di Sottomarina
-Chioggia (R) (in the dunes/nelle dune)
-Lido Alberoni Beach/spiaggia (MA NU) Take bus to Alberoni (southern end of the island), walk to the Adriatic Sea, turn ruight. Cruising and sunbathing in the dunes and in the woods. Very busy)
-Brussa-Portogruaro (NU)

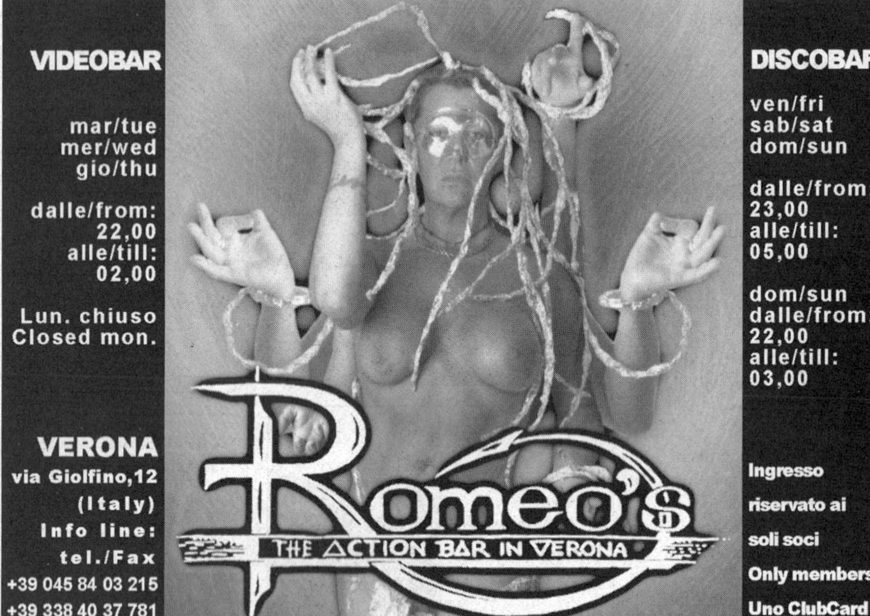

CRUISING

-San Marco (along the fence of the Royal Gardens next to the Piazza along the water front. Mostly in warm months from 22 h)

Ventimiglia - Imperia ✉ 18039

SWIMMING

-Balzi Rossi (Coming from Ventimiglia through the first tunnel, (P) before the gas station, go down, pass under the railway line, to the left)

Vercelli ✉ 13100

CRUISING

-Piazza Mazzini (occasional police patrols/occasionalmente controli di polizia)

Verona ✉ 37100

GAY INFO

PINK
✉37100
Queer magazine published by the local section of Arcigay-Arcilesbica. Available in gay bars in town. Information about political issues and the local scene./Pubblicato dall' Arcigay-Arcilesbica di Verona, é disponible nei bar gay della città. Parla della scena gay-lesbica e di diritti civili.

TOURIST INFO

A.P.T. Mon-Sat 9-19 h
Piazza Erbe 38 ✉37100 ☎ 045 80 68 680
Fax: 045 80 68 680

BARS

Bar Al Semaforo (B G MA r TV) Summer: 20-2, Winter: 19-2 h, closed Mon
Via Unitá d'Italia 100 ✉37132 *(in S. Michele)* ☎ 045 97 64 01
Campofiore (B f GLM MA) 9-15, 20-2, Mon 9-15 h, closed Sun
Via Campofiore 35 ✉37121 *(near University)* ☎ 045 80 32 534

CAFÉS

Café Bukowski (B glm YG) 19-2 h, closed Wed
Vicolo Amanti 6 ✉37100 *(near All'Arena)* ☎ 045 80 11 417
Crowded Fri-Sun, Sun mostly gay.

DANCECLUBS

Alter Ego (B D glm) Fri 23-4, Sat -5 h
Via Torricelle 9 ✉37100 *(area Torricelle)*
B Side (AC B bf D DR f G MA OS P pi s SNU W) Sat 23-4.30 h
Via Fontanelle 28, S. Bonifacio ☎ 0368 93 13 09 (Infoline)
Pool with garden Mai-Aug. A4 MI-VE, exit Soave/S. Bonifacio. Outside turn left, direction S. Bonifacio. After 2.5 km right, direction Legnago. After 3 km.
Romeo's Club (AC B CC d DR f G MA P s VS W) Videobar : Tue-Thu 22-02:00h
Discobar : Fri & Sat 23-5, Sun 22-3 h, Mon closed
Via Nicoló Giolfino 12 ✉37133 *(area Porta Vescovo-Bus 11/12/13)* ☎ 045 84 03 215
Video and disco bar. DJ at week-ends

RESTAURANTS

Antico Tripoli (AC CC F g OS) 13-14.30, 19.30-23 h
Via Spagna 2 ✉37123 *(Near Basilica S. Zeno)*
☎ 045 80 35 756
Hänsel + Gretel (B bf F glm OS) 11-15, 18-2, Sat-Sun 11-2 h
Via Corgnano 103 ✉37010 ☎ 045 77 33 994

SEX SHOPS/BLUE MOVIES

Europa 92 (g) 9.30-13, 14.30-19.30 h, closed Sun Mon
Via Scarsellini 30 ☎ 045 80 09 714

Videos, condoms, underwear, toys, magazines/Video, preservativi, biancheri intima, accessori, riviste.

Magic America (CC g p) Closed Mon morning
Via Cantarane 17/A ✉37129 *(Zona Porta Vescovo)*
☎ 045 80 05 234
Videos, magazines, toys/video, accessori, riviste.

SAUNAS/BATHS

City Sauna Club (! AC B CC DR f G MA msg sa sb VS W wh) Sep-May: 14-2, Jun-Aug: 15-2 h, closed Thu
Via Giolfino 12 ✉37131 *(Porta Vescovo. Bus 11/12/13)*
☎ 045 52 00 09
Free condoms. Internet café. One of Europes biggest and most comfortable gay-saunas/Sauna gay tra le più grandi e confortevoli d'Europa.

GENERAL GROUPS

Arcigay „Pianeta Urano" Phone: Mon-Tue 21-23 h, Meetings: Mon 21-23 h c/o PRC, Via Frangini 9/A
c/o Arci, Via N. Sauro 2 ✉37129 ☎ 0347 65 67 753
Fax: 045 65 67 753 Email: planetur@tin.it
Political and cultural activities, meetings, lectures, Aids information, youth group/Attività politiche e culturali, riunioni, conferenze, informazione Aids, gruppo giovani.

Circolo Pink-Centro Di Iniziativa E Cultura Gay E Lesbica Verona Help-line: Tue Thu 21-23, Sat 15-18 h
Via Scrimiari 7 ✉37129 ☎ 045 80 12 854 (Help-line)
Email: pinkvr@tin.it
Gay and lesbian culture centre. Mon 21-23 h: Presentation of cultural events, films, books and debates/Serate culturali „diversamente": presentazioni di film, libri, dibattiti. Tue 21-23 h: Lesbian group/Gruppo lesbiche. Thu 21-23, Sat 15-18 h: Meetings/Aggregazione.

HEALTH GROUPS

Anlaids Infoline: Mon, Wed, Fri, Sat 19-22 h
Interrato Acqua Morta 46 ✉37129
☎ 045 800 50 16 66 (Infoline) Fax: 045 59 29 99

Gruppo C Mon-Fri 8.30-12.30, Sat by appointment; Hotline 14.30-17, Sat 8.30-12.30 h
Via Germania 20 ✉37135 ☎ 045 86 22 232
Information on HIV, prevention, psychological support, anonymous free HIV test.

CRUISING

-C. O. N. I. (streets around the gyms, as far as Alfa Garage, only at night/strade altorno palestre, fino al garage Alfa, solo di notte)
-Piazzale della Stazione (In front of the railway station, the round street near the church Tempio Vorivo/di fronte alla stazione ferroviara, la rotonda davanti alla chiesa del Tempio Votivo)(R TV).
-Industrial zone/-Zona Industriale (coming from „Verona Sud" turn left behind „Metro" in direction Alpo, in the tunnel at night/proveniendo da „Verona Sud" dopo magazzini Metro girare a sinistra direzione Alpo, sotto il cavalca via, di notte).
-Lazzaretto (a little bit outside from district Porto S. Pancrazio, on the bridge over the Adige, turn left and walk along the Adige to the ruins of the old military hospital, in the afternoon/leggermente fuori città, proveniendo dal quartiere Porto S. Pancrazio si passa il ponte sull'adige e poi si gira a sinistra, proseguendo lungo l'adige; ai ruderi del vecchio lazzaretto, di pomeriggio).

Viareggio ✉ 55049

BARS

Bocachica (B F glm) 12-6 h, Mon closed
Viale Europa 1 ✉55048 ☎ 0584 35 09 76
Music bar and cocktails. Traditional fish food.

Mama Mia (B F Glm YG) Open all day until late
Viale Europa ✉55048 *(way along the sea/passeggiatta a mare)*
☎ 0584 35 11 11
Crowded bar restaurant.

Voice Music Bar (g)
Viale Margherita 61, Passeggiata a mare ✉55049 ☎ 0584 45 814
Open till late.

DANCECLUBS

Barrumba (B CC D DR F GLM OS P pi s VS W wh) 16-4 h, closed Oct-Apr
Viale Kennedy 6 ✉55049 *(near Lecciona beach)*
☎ 0584 35 17 17
Disco, bar and restaurant.

Frau Marleen (B D GLM tv) only in summer/solo estate: Sat Sun 23-? h
Lungomare ✉55049 ☎ 0584 34 22 82

Kama-Kama (B D g) Sat 23-4 h
Via per Camaiore/Capezzano Piànore ✉55049 *(8 km east of Viareggio)*
Techno, Houseclub.

RESTAURANTS

Osteria N.1 (g) closed Mon
Via Nicola Pisano 140 ✉55049 ☎ 0584 43 88 967

Ristorante Europa (B g F) Viale Europa 3 ✉55048
☎ 0584 35 02 73
Fish specialities, cosy atmosphere.

Rugantino (g) Tue closed
Via Sant' Ambrogio 8 ✉55049 ☎ 0584 53 598
Fresh fish available.

Tito del Molo (g)
Molo del Greco ✉55049 ☎ 0584 96 20 16
Fish food.

Vignaccio. Il

Via della Chiesa 26 *(15 km from Viareggio)* ☎ 0584 91 42 00
Typical Tuscany cuisine/Cucina Toscana.

CINEMAS

Supercinema (r)
Passeggiata a mare Campioni ✉55049 ☎ 0584 96 24 08

BOOK SHOPS

Libreria Babele
Viale Marconi 32 ✉55048 ☎ 0584 35 20 91
Gay and lesbian books.

DECORATION

Antichità Luigi Tommasi
Via San Martino 42 ✉55049 ☎ 0584 96 28 97
Antiques and gifts.

HOTELS

CavMare Mon-Fri 9-13, 15.30-19, Sat 9.30-12 h
Via Matteotti 3 ✉55049 ☎ 0584 49 776
Hotel reservation service. For special offers for single and groups, ask for „friendly Versilia").

APARTMENTS

Rociane. Le
Frazione Pedona 184 ✉55041 *(15 km from Viareggio)*
☎ 0584 98 43 87 Fax: 0584 98 43 87
Email: info@lerociane.it Homepage: www.lerociane.it
Hillside holiday villas and appartments for rent./Ville e appartamenti per vancaza in collina. Prices on request.

CAMPING

Camping Europa
Viale dei Tigli ✉55048 ☎ 0584 35 07 07 Fax: 0584 34 25 92
Not particularly gay but located directly behind the gay beach „Leccione".

CRUISING

-Via Zara (G R) (by car and on foot by night, also nearby areas, in the pine wood)
-Viale dei Tigli (in the pinetree wood in front of the gay beach)

Vicenza ✉ 36100

CINEMAS

Kursaal (g OG) 17-24, Sun 16-24 h
Stradella Soccorso Soccorseto ✉36100 ☎ 0444 32 49 30

SAUNAS/BATHS

Saint Vincent Club (AC b D G P sa sb sol VS) Fri 21-2, Sat 21-4, Su 15-24.30 h
Via Vecchia Ferriera 143 *(near motorway exit/vicino casello autostrada uscita Vicenza Ovest)* ☎ 0444 96 11 21

FETISH GROUPS

Moto Leather Club Veneto (G LJ)
c/o Bedin, PO Box 259 ✉36100 ☎ 0444 32 12 90
Email: mlcv@geocities.com.
Homepage: http://www.geocities.com/WestHollywood/4081/

HEALTH GROUPS

Arcigay Arcilesbica 2nd Fri 21-22.30 h
Contrà Fontanelle 5 ✉36100 ☎ 0444 50 72 30
AIDS counselling service and free HIV testing.

CRUISING

-Railway Station/Stazione FS (AYOR) (at night-also in nearby areas, e.g. in the Campo Marzio gardens/anche attorno per es. nei giardini di Campo Marzio)
-P Largo Bologna (at night ba car or on foot/di notte, in auto e a piedi) -Motorway/Autostrada A31 „Valdastico"
-P Villa Tacchi (both sides day & night/sui due lati, notte e giorno)

Viterbo ✉ 01100

BARS

X-Ciak (B glm)
Via Cairoli 24 ✉01100

SEX SHOPS/BLUE MOVIES

Cobra (g)
Via Cardarelli 59/61 ✉01100 ☎ 0761 35 37 48

GENERAL GROUPS

Circolo Di Cultura Pansessuale „Dionysios"
Via San Rocco 19 ✉01100 ☎ 0761 30 45 10

CRUISING

-Piazza Gramsci
-Bullicame Park

Vittorio Veneto - Treviso ✉ 31029

CRUISING

-Largo Foro Boario (along the river/e sul lungofiume adiacente)
-Via F. da Milano (beside the »Varietà«-cinema/nei pressi del cinema Varietà)
-Piazza del Popolo (city park, next to the railway station/giardini, davanti alla stazione FS)

Voghera - Pavia ✉ 27050

CRUISING

-Via Papa Giovanni (R YG) (at night)

Japan

Nippon

Between Sea of Japan & wesstern Pacific Ocean

Initials: J

Time: GMT +9

☎ Country Code / Access Code: 81 / 001

Language: Japanese. English as commercial language

Area: 377,801 km² / 145,831 sq mi.

Currency: Yen (¥)

Population: 125,931,533

Capital: Tokyo

Religions: 80% Buddhist or Shinto, or a mixture of the two

Climate: The climate varies from tropical in the south to cool moderate in the north.

● Homosexual acts are not illegal and also not mentioned in the law. The age of sexual consent is 18. The influence of the gay movement outside Japan has accounted for the emmergence in the 90's of the Lesbian and Gay Parade in Tokyo, the LesBiGay March in Sapporo, as well as the International Lesbian and Gay Film and Video Festival. The question remains open what other influences the emmancipation in the West will have on the development of culture and society in Japan. The older generation in Japan continues to be intolerant of gays. Coming out is difficult because of the pressure to get married imposed by family and society. Many gays are therefore forced to follow a double life style. The group „Occur" and other politically active groups are beginning to set up much more contact with other outside groups, such as prostitutes and transvestites. Unfortunately there are no gay information shops. Besides Tokyo and Osaka there are other gay localities in major cities. However, gay foreigners are often not welcomed in saunas or other establishments because of fear. Gay establishments are often difficult to find. Therefore, we would like to explain the Japanese address system to you. A normal address consists of the district name and a combination of three numbers together. For example, Shinjuku-ku 2-12-3. The first number shows the city district (here Nr. 2) in Shinjuku-ku, the second number the block in the district (here Nr. 12) and the third the house number (here Nr. 3). Street orientation is facilitated by the green signs (for the block -here 2-12) found on the lamp posts and electricity pylons, and the blue signs (for house numbers -here 12-3) on the houses.

✸ Homosexualität ist in Japan nicht illegal, sie wird in Gesetzen nicht erwähnt. Das Schutzalter liegt in Japan bei 18 Jahren. Unter dem Einfluß der im Ausland agierenden Schwulenbewegung finden seit Anfang der 90er Jahre die *Lesbian & Gay Parade* in Tokyo, der *LesBiGay March* in Sapporo sowie das *Tokyo International Lesbian & Gay Film & Video Festival* statt. Jedoch bleibt hier die Frage offen, welche Wirkung diese westlich entwickelte Form der Emanzipation auf die andere Kultur und Gesellschaft Japans hat. Die Einstellung der japanischen Bevölkerung, insbesondere der älteren Generation, gegenüber Schwulen ist intolerant. Ein Coming-out ist schwierig. Immer noch sind der familiäre und gesellschaftliche Druck so groß, daß sich Schwule zur Heirat gezwungen sehen. Sie führen ein Doppelleben. Die Gruppe *OCCUR* und andere politisch aktive Gruppen beginnen sich immer mehr zu vernetzen. Sie arbeiten of mit anderen randständigen Gruppen wie Prostituierten oder Transsexuellen zusammen. Besonders intensiv ist die Zusammenarbeit mit lesbischen Gruppen. Leider gibt es keine schwulen Info-Läden für ausländische Touristen. Neben Tokyo und Osaka findet man auch in anderen größeren Städten schwule Lokale. Jedoch sind Ausländer aus Angst vor kulturellen Unterschieden nicht überall willkommen. Der Zutritt zu den Saunen wird meistens verwehrt. Schwule Lokale sind häufig sehr schwierig für Touristen zu finden. Deshalb möchten wir Ihnen an dieser Stelle das japanische Adreßsystem erklären. Eine normale Adresse setzt sich aus dem Namen des Stadtteils und einer Kombination von drei Zahlen zusammen. Zum Beispiel: »Shinjuku-ku 2-12-3«. Dabei gibt die erste Zahl das Stadtviertel (hier Nr.2) im Stadtteil Shinjuku-ku an, die zweite Zahl den Block im Viertel -also Block 12- und die dritte Zahl bezeichnet die Hausnummer -hier Nummer 3. Als Orientierungshilfe im Straßen-Alltag gibt es an den Laternen- oder Strommasten Schilder in weiß auf grün, die die Nummer des Blocks im Viertel angeben (hier: 2-12) und an den Häusern Schilder in weiß auf blau, die die Hausnummer (hier: 12-3) im Block angeben. Oft finden sich an Kreuzungen Pläne des Stadtviertels, aus denen die Nummern der Blöcke ersichtlich sind.

▲ L'homosexualité n'est pas interdite au Japon, elle est simplement ignorée. L'âge de la majorité sexuelle est fixée au Japon à 18 ans. Sous l'influence de mouvements homosexuels venant de l'étranger, depuis le début des années 90 ont lieu la *Lesbian and Gay Paradeà* Tokyo, la *LesBiGay March* à Sapporo, et le *Tokyo International Lesbian and Gay Film and Video Festival.* Mais il reste à savoir quelle est l'influence de cette forme développée d'émancipation occidentale sur la culture et la société si différentes du Japon. L'attitude de la population japonaise, surtout de la génération plus âgée, vis-à-vis des homosexuels est intolérante. Il est difficile de faire son coming-out. La pression familiale et sociale reste si forte que les homosexuels se sentent encore obligés de se marier. Ils ménent donc une double vie. De plus en plus, le groupe *occur* ainsi que d'autres groupes politiquement actifs commencent à tisser des liens avec d'autres groupes minoritaires tels que les transsexuels ou les prostituées. Le travail avec les groupes de lesbiennes est particulièrement intensif. Mais malheureusement, il n'y a pas de magazines d'information pour les touristes gays. Dans d'autres villes que Tokyo et Osaka, on trouve aussi des endroits gays. Mais les étrangers ne sont pas toujours les bienvenus, par peur des différences culturelles. L'acces aux saunas est en général refusé. Les établissements gays sont très difficiles à trouver pour les touristes. C'est la raison pour laquelle nous voudrions vous expliquer le système d'adresses japonais. Une adresse normale est composée du nom du quartier, et d'une combinaison de trois chiffres. Par exemple: „Shinjuku-ku 2-12-3" Le premier chiffre indique le quartier (2), il s'agit en l'occurrence du quartier Shinjuku-ku, le deuxième chiffre indique le numéro du pâté de maisons (12), et le troisième chiffre indique le numéro de rue (3). Pour se retrouver dans la vie de tous les jours, des pancartes vertes sur blanc sont accrochées aux poteaux d'électricité, qui indiquent le numéro du pâté de maisons du quartier (ici 2-12), et aux maisons des signes blanc sur bleu qui indiquent le numéro de la maison dans le pâté de maisons (ici 12-3).Souvent, aux coins des rues, on trouve des plans de quartier sur lesquels figurent les numéros de pâtés de maison.

☆ En Japón la homosexualidad no es ilegal y no se menciona en la legislación. La edad de consentimiento es de 18 años. Bajo la influencia de la comunidad gay internacional se organiza desde los principios de los años 90 la *Lesbian & Gay Parade* y el *International Lesbian & Gay Film & Video Festival* en Tokio, como la *LeBi-Gay March* en Sapporo. Sin embargo, hay que preguntarse, si estas muestras de emanzipación occidentalizadas tengan el mismo efecto sobre la cultura y sociedad tan sumamente diferente en Japón. La actitud de intolerancia de los japonéses hacia los homosexuales, se nota sobre todo por parte de los mayores. Un coming-out es difícil de realizar, ya que la presión de la familia y de la sociedad siguen siendo muy fuertes. Por ello, muchos gays se ven obligados a contraer matrimonio y hacer una vida doble. El grupo *OCCUR* y otras organizaciones muy activas en el campo político estrechan cada vez más su colaboración, incluiendo grupos de marginados como prostitutas y transexuales. Especialmente fructífera es la cooperación con grupos de lesbianas. Desgraciadamente no existen para turistas sitios de información gay. Pero bares de ambiente no se encuentran solamente en Tokio y Osaka, sino también en otras ciudades grandes. Sin embargo, extranjeros no son siempre bienvenidos, tal vez por el miedo a otras culturas. Como consecuencia, escasamente se permite a turistas la entrada en saunas. Aprovechamos la ocasión para explicarle el sistema japonés de direcciones.En general una dirección se compone del nombre del barrio y una combinación de tres números. Por ejemplo: „Shinjuku-ku 2-12-3". La primera cifra indica el barrio (2) en la zona de la ciudad llamada Shinjuku-ku, la segunda determina el bloque del barrio (en este caso el bloque número 12) y el tercer número equivale al número de la calle (3). Para la mejor orientación en la ciudad, los postes de fárolas o de la red électrica están provistos con letreros blancos con fondo verde que indican el número de bloque en el barrio correspondiente (aquí: 2-12) y las casas con letreros blancos con fondo azul, que indican el número de casa en el respectivo bloque (en este caso: 12-3). A menudo se encuentran en los cruces mapas de orientación, que informan sobre los números correspondientes de los bloques.

❖ L'omosessualità in Giappone non è vietata e non viene citata nelle leggi. L'età legale in Giappone è di 18 anni. Sotto l'influenza del movimento gay all'estero dall'inizio degli anni 90 anche in Giappone hanno luogo: la *Lesbian & Gay Parade* a Tokio; la *LesBi-Gay March* a Sapporo e infine il *Tokyo International Lesbian & Gay Film & Video Festival*. Però resta ancora da chiedersi, quale effetto abbia questa forma occidentale d'emancipazione sulla cultura e società giapponese. L'atteggiamento della popolazione e soprattutto della generazione anziana si mostra intollerante verso i gay. Il coming-out diventa difficile. La pressione svolta dalla famiglia e dalla società sui gay fa sì che molti si sentono costretti a sposarsi. Coloro svolgono così una doppia vita. Il gruppo *Occur* e altre associazioni attive in politica cominciano a unificarsi sempre di più. Spesso questi gruppi gay lavorano anche insieme ad altre associazioni di emarginati come gruppi di prostitute o transessuali. La collaborazione tra gruppi di gay e di lesbiche è molto intensa. Purtroppo non esistono centri d'informazione gay per turisti stranieri. Dopo Tokio e Osaka, anche in altre città si trovano diversi locali gay. Però a volte gli stranieri non sono troppo ben venuti a causa della paura delle differenze culturali. L'ingresso alle saune viene perciò molto spesso vietato agli stranieri. I locali gay a volte sono molto difficili da trovare per i turisti, perciò spieghiamo qui il sistema indirizzario giapponese: Un'indirizzo normale consiste dal nome della circoscrizione e una combinazione di tre numeri; per es.: „Shinjuku-ku 2 12-3". La prima cifra (no. 2) indica il quartiere della circoscrizione Shinjuku-ku; la seconda l'isolato (no. 12) e infine la terza (no. 3) il numero di casa. Un'ulteriore aiuto all'orientamento stradale offrono sia i cartelli verdi con la scritta bianca, attaccati ai pali e alle lanterne dell'illuminazione (in questo caso 2-12); come i cartelli blu con la scritta bianca, attaccati ai muri delle case, che indicano il numero (in questo caso 12-3) nell'isolato. Spesso agli incroci si trovano piantine del quartiere, che indicano i numeri degli isolati.

NATIONAL GAY INFO

Barazoku/Daini Shobo Ltd.
5-2-11 Daizawa, Setagaya-ku, Tokyo
☎ (0)3-342 154 62

OCCUR (Association for the Lesbian & Gay Movement) 19-22 h
4-43-4-201, Honcho Nakao-ku, Tokyo 164 *(near Shin-Nakano Station)* ☎ 33 83 55 56 Fax: 32 29 78 80
Gay & Lesbian youth group taking a political stance.

Sabu
San Building, 26-3 Sanei-cho, Shinjuku-ku, Tokyo
☎ (0)3-335 923 41

Sampson
Kameikan, PO Box 66, Shitaya Post Office, Taito-Ku, Tokyo
☎ (0)3-384 129 01

The Gay
T.I.Y. Shuppan, PO Box 209, Shinjuku-ku, Tokyo
☎ (0)3-336 351 97

Amagasaki ☎ 06

BARS

Jun (B G R)
Kanda-Nakadori 3-77, Yamamoto Building *(3rd floor)*
☎ 413 13 81

Aomori ☎ 0177

BARS

Caravan (B G) 18-24 h
Hurukawa 1-2-16 *(near railway station)* ☎ 73 37 75

Fukuoka ☎ 092

BARS

Bros. (B f G MA N) 21-4 h, closed Mon
4-9-4 Sumiyoshi, Hakata-Ku ☎ 411 62 53

Crescent Moon (B G YG) 20-3 h, closed Mon
2-19-1-1 Haruyoshi, Chuo-ku ☎ 731 00 05

Hachibankan (B G) 19.30-3, Sat -4 h, closed Wed
Hakata-ku, Sumiyoshi 2-13-6 (Suminoe Bld. No. 2-103)
☎ 291 23 10

Plan-B (AC B G YG) 20-4 h
1-11-36 Haruyoshi, Chuo-ku *(south of Sumiyoshi bridge)*
☎ 724 90 07

Shin (B g MG) 20-3 h
4-27-18 Sumiyoshi, Hakata-ku ☎ 482 91 23

Sichimensho (B G MA YG) 20-3 h
4-13-15 Sumiyoshi, Hakata-ku ☎ 441 90 37

SEX SHOPS/BLUE MOVIES

Hakata Anzu-ya (g) 12-3 h
4-15-3 Sumiyoshi, Hakata-ku ☎ 412 39 25

Hakata Budo-ya (g) 14-24 h
3-9-23-3 Sumiyoshi, Hakata-ku ☎ 272 36 28

SAUNAS/BATHS

Hisen Kaikan (B g sa VS) 12-24 h
5-18-18 Sumiyoshi, Hakata-ku ☎ 413 70 98

GENERAL GROUPS

Gay in Fukuoka (G.I.F.)
☎ 801 14 87

CRUISING

-Higashi Koen Park
-Vivre 21 department B 1 toilet
-IMS building 6 f toilet
-IWATAYA department 3 f toilet
-Solaria Plaza 5 f toilet

Hakodate ☎ 0138

BARS

Yorozuya (B G) 19-2 h
20-9 Matsukaze-Cho ☎ 27 06 61

Hamamatsu ☎ 053

BARS

Odamari Gyalu (B G)
Hamamatsu S Building, 180-4 Kagimachi *(4th floor)* ☎ 55 03 59

SWIMMING

Nakatajima beach, take bus no. 19 from main station, get of at the terminus, walk 20 minutes down the road. At the small hotel called car road turn towards the beach (G, popular at WE in summer).

CRUISING

-Wajiyama Koen (park) after 22 h

Hiroshima ☎ 082

BARS

Nomakuen (B G) 18-? h, closed every 3rd Thu
Naka-ku, Nagaregawa-machi 5-19, Kyoei Bld. 1st Fl.
☎ 246 46 21
Only Japanese welcome.

Paul (B G)
Shintenchi Leisure Building, Shintenchi 1-9, Naka-ku *(2nd floor)*
☎ 243 40 87

26 (Niroku) (B f G) 18-3 h
Shoei Building, 1-13 Tanakamachi, Naka-ku *(3rd floor)*
☎ 249 00 13

CRUISING

-Riverside Park

Kanazawa ☎ 0762

BARS

Shinjugai (AC B G YG) 20.30-1.30 h
2F Nozaki Bldg., 1-8-23 Katamachi *(next to Saigawa bridge, walk 10 minutes)* ☎ 233 30 02

CRUISING

-Kenrokuen

Kobe ☎ 078

BARS

Taro (B f g)
Kamitani Building, 4 Kano-cho, Chuo-ku *(3rd floor)* ☎ 332 54 43

Kochi ☎ 0888

BARS

Katsukazan (AC B d f G lj MA N TV W) 19-1 h
1-3-7 Minami-Harimaya-Cho ☎ 23 77 99

Kokura ☎ 093

BARS

Hisen (B f G) 2-14
Kofunaba, Kita-ku *(Hisen Kaikan)*
☎ 551 14 14

P-Man (B G) 19-3 h, closed Tue
Kita-ku, Konya-machi 10-3, Yamazaki Building *(2nd floor)*
☎ 531 71 03

Kumamoto ☎ 096

BARS

October 86 (B G)
Isei Building, 1-36 Shinshigai *(4th floor)* ☎ 355 66 00

Power (AC B G MA) 19-4 h
1-6-5-2F Shimotori (Arcade St.) *(Line 2, Tram Stop Torichosuzi*
☎ 354 67 12

Kyoto ☎ 075

BARS

Accele (B G YG) 20-4 h
Itou Bld, 3F, Shijo-Kiyamachi Agaru, Nigashigawa *(Hankyu Railways-Kawaramachi Station, near Takashimaya departmentstore)*
☎ 212 40 50

C'est bon (! B G OG) 19-2 h
Shijo Kawara-machi-agaru, Futasujime, Higashi-iru ☎ 211 03 85

Shu's (B G MA) 20-2 h
No 13 st., Shijo-Kiyamachi Agaru *(Hankyu Railways-Kawaramachi Station, near Takashimaya departmentstore)* ☎ 251 67 92

V-Zone (B G YG) 20-4 h
Shjo-Ninshi Kiyamachi 2-suji-Agaru, Ocean Bld 5 F *(Hankyu Railways Kawaramachi St., Takashimaya departmentstore)*
☎ 212 19 33

SHOWS

Cine Friends (G MA S)
Senbon nakadachiori agaru Higashi iru, Kamigyoko *(Bus-Senbon Nakadachiuri)* ☎ 441 14 60
From Senbon Nakadachiuri crossing, go north, turn first right, the theater is about 50 m from here on the left.

Matsuyama ☎ 0899

BARS

Snack Now (B G MA) 19-1 h
1-6-7 Nibancho ☎ 45 77 32
Sometimes foreigners.

Nagasaki ☎ 095

BARS

BanBan (B g)
Kabashimamachi, Kuraoka Bldg *(2nd floor)* ☎ 822 97 03

Chiki-Chiki (B G)
6-1, Kajiya-Machi ☎ 827 29 55
Near Plaza Hotel. After leaving the hotel, take second right. The bar is at the end of the street on the left.

Nagoya ☎ 052

BARS

Camps (B G)
(near Kanaya Hotel) ☎ 951 14 45
Several blocks away from main gay bar area. Sign in English. Past Tokai TV offices and near Kanaya Hotel; Eastern Building 1st floor.
GI Club (B G)
Castle Kanko Building ☎ 264 10 24
Not military! Initials from owner and former owner. Nice crowd, mixed ages. Sign in English outside the building and by the door on 3rd floor.
Kuriko (B G) 21-4 h
Nishishin Building 2F, 4-4-9 Sakae Naka-ku ✉460-0008 *(near Tokyu Hotel, subway station Sakae)* ☎ 251 01 50
Little hard to find. Sign in English and Japanese.
Mac (B G MA)
(near Camps bar) ☎ 931 57 36
Small and friendly. Sign in Japanese.
Noburu (B G) closed Sun
Naka-ku, Sakae 4-11-10, Tokyo Building *(4th floor)* ☎ 241 28 52
Star Johne (AC B G WE YG) 19-2, Sat -5 h
Dairokuwako Bldg. Part2 3F, 4-12-24 Sakae, Naka-ku *(close to Chunichi Bldg.)* ☎ 242 57 27

SAUNAS/BATHS

Tohko Sauna (G H sa)
2-4-22, Shiragane, Showa-ku *(near Nagoya Sogo Bank)*
☎ 881 89 63
Dirty, but good action. Single foreigners might have problems with entry.

Naha ☎ 098

BARS

Akira (B G) 20-4 h, closed Wed
2F ☎ 868-7423
City Hunter (B G) 22-8 h, closed Tue
☎ 866-6189
Danke (B G) 21-4 h
2F ☎ 866-4227
Resort (B G) 20-4 h, closed 4th Sun
3F ☎ 866-8924
Sabu (B G) 20-4 h, closed Thu
1F ☎ 867-7041
Shiki (B G)
2F ☎ 867-9966
Shingo (B G) 22-4 h
(1st on the left side) ☎ 862-4031
Sunset (B G) 21-5 h, closed Mon
3F ☎ 869-9244
Tampopo (B G) 20-5 h
☎ 863-7189
Tayou No Ko (B G OG) 20-4 h
☎ 861-5570
Umi (B G) 20-2 h, closed Tue
2F ☎ 867-0433
To the gay snacks take Kokusai Dori Street, then Heiwa Dori Street. At the YanYan-Shop the Street divides in three. Take the very small left one. In the beginning there are some of the listed bar-snacks. If you go to the end of the street turn left then right and you will find the others.

SWIMMING

-Naminoue beach (near Tomari harbour, recently cruisy)

CRUISING

-Kokusai shopping center (Kokusai Dori Street)
-Yogi Park (near Naha's prefectural library, hospital and main police office)

Narita ☎ 03

CRUISING

-Natita JR Station (Go out the West Exit. This leads to New Narita-City. Go down the stairs. There are 3 curb-side bus stops. By #2 there is a WC. During the rush hour (18-20 h) a lot of cruising takes place there between train & bus. If you're in a hotel nearby, an invitation might be easily accepted. Alternately go out the east exit, turn left and 20m along the building there is another WC.

Niigata ☎ 025

BARS

New Shiro (B G)
7 Kami Okawamae Dori, Sakai Building, 2nd Fl. ☎ 224 16 96

RESTAURANTS

Ja Ja (B F G MA) 20-2 h, closed Tue.
2F Ing. Bld. 1-2-26 Benten *(Near Niigata Station)* ☎ 241 80 74

Okayama ☎ 086

BARS

Waka Taisho (B G)
Heiwa-cho 7-28, Nishigawa Family Building *(2nd floor)*
☎ 222 64 95

Osaka ☎ 06

BARS

Adonis (B G YG) 23-8
Doyama-cho, Kita-ku *(upper floor)*
☎ 312 24 29
Across the street from Christopher. Quiet.
Boys (B G OG) 16-24 h
Doyama-cho 16-19, Kita-ku ☎ 313 48 00
Butch Bar (B G MG YG) 20-2 h
13-4 Juon Doyama Building, Doyama-cho Kita-ku *(5th floor)*
☎ 636 387 31
English spoken. Foreigners welcome.
Christopher (B D G lj MA)
16-4 Doyama, Kita-ku, Pearl Leisure Building *(basement)*
☎ 315 13 80
Christopher Bar in the back. Sign out on 1st level and on bar in English. Cover charge ¥ 2.000 incl. one drink. Very friendly.
Garçon (B G R) 17-1 h
Minami-ku, Namba 4-8-12, Taiko Center B1 ☎ 643 65 39
Garcon Cerkle (B G) 19-5 h
Minami-ku, Nam-ba 4-3-16, GT Town Building *(3rd floor)*
☎ 643 05 41
Go Ban Gai (B G R) 16-11.30 h
Matunoki Building, 11-2 Doyama-cho, Kita-ku ☎ 315 19 80
H 2 (B G MA)
Chuo-Ku, Nanba 4-3-16, GT Building 5th floor ☎ 644 08 09
Homme (B G R) 16-1 h
Kita-ku, Doyama-cho 8-18, Kirishima Leisure Bld., B1
☎ 311 19 36
Hoshi (B G MA) 19-2 h
Kita-ku, 16-6 Doyama-cho ☎ 312 67 41
If (B g)
Naka-Dori Leisure Bld. 2F ☎ 312 41 48
Kids Club (B G) 16-11.30 h
Sanyo Kaikan, 8-23 Doyama-cho, Kita-ku ☎ 312 27 47

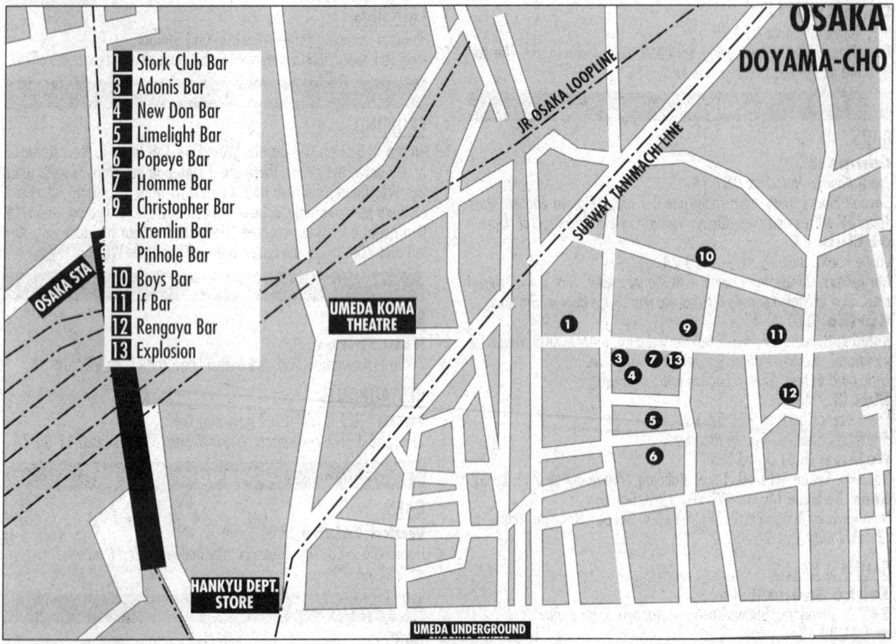

OSAKA
DOYAMA-CHO

1 Stork Club Bar
3 Adonis Bar
4 New Don Bar
5 Limelight Bar
6 Popeye Bar
7 Homme Bar
9 Christopher Bar
Kremlin Bar
Pinhole Bar
10 Boys Bar
11 If Bar
12 Rengaya Bar
13 Explosion

JR OSAKA LOOPLINE
SUBWAY TANIMACHI LINE
OSAKA STA
UMEDA KOMA THEATRE
HANKYU DEPT. STORE
UMEDA UNDERGROUND

Kremlin (B CC G MA) Sun-Thu 20-3, Fri Sat -5 h
M2F Pearl Leisure Bldg, 16-4 Doyama-Cho, Kita Ku ☎ 365 06 56
Limelight (B G)
OK Building, 16-6 Doyama-cho, Kita-ku *(2nd floor)* ☎ 361 43 36
Nagasaki (B G)
Kita-ku, Doyama-cho 6-14, Shoei Kaikan 104 ☎ 312 60 03
New Don (B G MA)
16-5 Doyama-cho, Kita-ku *(2nd floor)*
☎ 315 93 12
Around the corner from Christopher in the small alley. Call if you need help. Nice place.
Physique Pride Osaka (! B CC G MA YG) 20-? h
8-23 Doyama-Cho, Kita-ku ☎ 530 00 27
International mixed gay bar. English spoken.
Pinhole (AC B CC f G MA) 22-4 h, Tue closed
16-4, 2F, Pearl Leisure Building, Doyama-cho ☎ 314 55 86
Popeye (B G) 16-23.30 h
Kita-ku, Doyama-cho 6-15 *(3rd floor)* ☎ 315 15 02
Rengaya (B G) 19.30-3 h
Kita-ku, Doyama-cho 11-2 Matsu no ki Building *(1st floor)*
☎ 315 66 28
Roman (B G STV) 16-12, Sat 15-? h, closed Sun
Kita-ku, Chashitsu-cho 4-18, Hayashi Building *(3rd floor)*
☎ 375 14 88
Only Japanese welcome. S/M bar.
Stork Club (B d E f G MA)
Stork Building, 17-3 Doyama-cho, Kita-ku *(2nd floor)*
☎ 361 44 84
Stork South (B G)
Coq d'Or Building B 2, 5-72 Namba Shin-chi, Minami-ku
☎ 643 40 01
Yacht (B G VS) 15-18, videos 18-3 h
Minami-ku, Namba 4-7-9, Nanshin Kaikan Building *(2nd floor)*
☎ 643 67 34
Yakan-Hiko (B G) 19-2 h, closed Tue
Kita-ku, Doyama-cho 16-4, Pearl Leisure Building *(3rd floor)*
☎ 314 15 18

DANCECLUBS

Explosion (! B D G MA s YG) 19-6 h
B-1 Sanyo-Kaikan, 8-23, Doyama-cho, Kita-ku ✉530-0027 *(Hankyu Umeda Station)* ☎ 312 50 03
Largest Gay disco in Japan.

SEX SHOPS/BLUE MOVIES

Plaza Apple Inn
Moto-Machi 1-11-5, Naniwa-ku, Ishimoto Building ☎ 633 48 78

SAUNAS/BATHS

Adan (g H sa YG) 0-24 h
Naniwa-ku, Moto-machi 1-7-19 ☎ 631 23 50
Only Japanese welcome.

BOOK SHOPS

Etc Box 12-23 h
Cosmo Plaza Building, 11-2 Doyama-cho, Kita-ku *(basement)*
☎ 316 00 95

CRUISING

-Under Health Centre (near Sonezaki Police Station)
-Department Store Hankyu (underground)
-National Railway Station

Sapporo ☎ 011

BARS

Be Be Lu (B G R)
Minami 5-jo, Nishi 5-chome, Chuo-ku ☎ 512 53 92
BJ (B g YG) 20-4 h
1st floor, S.A. Building, Minami-6-jo Nishi-6-chome ☎ 512 50 13
Bonta (B g OG)
3rd floor, S.A. Building, Minami-6-jo Nishi-6-chome ☎ 531 13 33
Chaplin (B G) 20-3.30 h
5th floor, S.A. Building, Minami 6-jo, Nishi 6-chome ☎ 531 13 34
Ciao (B G MA yg)
2nd fl., 5-jo Shinmachi Bld, Minami 4-jo, Nishi 6-chome
☎ 531 93 31 *(At corner of intersection South 5/West 5. Down small street). Very nice and friendly.*
Crew (B g MA) 19-3 h
3rd floor, S.A. Building, Minami-6-jo, Nishi-6-chome ☎ 512 93 89
Friend (B g MA)
3rd floor, Chisan Hotel, Minami-7-jo, Nishi-5-chome ☎ 562 43 96
James (B G YG) 19.30-2.30 h
2nd floor, S.A. Building, Minami 6-jo, Nishi 5-chome ☎ 512 29 97
Two block from intersection South 5/West 5. Sign in Japanese. Bartender speaks some English.
La Cave (! B G MA)
S.A. Builing, Minami 6-jo, Nishi 6-chome *(9th floor)* ☎ 531 67 34
Meeya (B d G MG) 20-5 h
S-A Building, Minami: 6-jo, Nishi 6 chome *(3rd floor)*
☎ 521 06 83
Mishima (B g OG) 19-2 h
Chuo-ku, Minami-5-jo, Nishi-5-chome *(2nd floor)* ☎ 531 11 68
New Elsa (B g MA) 20.30-3 h
3rd floor, S.A. Building, Minami-6-jo, Nishi-6-chome ☎ 531 72 63
New Kabuki (B g MA) 19-2 h
1st floor, Tada Building, Minami-5-jo, Nishi-6-chome ☎ 531 23 77
Ni Zero San (203) (B g MA) 19-3 h
4th floor, New Keiwa Bld., Minami-5-jo, Nishi-6-chome
☎ 513 12 50
North Boy (B G R) 19-3 h
Susukino Minami 5, Nishi 6, New Keiwa Building *(8th floor)*
☎ 512 70 74
Only Japanese welcome.
Prism (B g YG) 20-3 h
4th floor, Dai-6(roku) Asahi Kanko Building, *Minami-6-jo, Nishi-6-chome*
☎ 512 67 90
Shigeru (B g MA) 19-2 h
New Kaiwa Building, B1, Minami-5-jo, Nishi-6-chome
☎ 531 72 78
Toi et Moi (! B MA) 19-3 h
2nd floor, 5•6 Building, Minami-5-jo, Nishi-6-chome ☎ 512 69 54

BOOK SHOPS

Shirokuma-do Shoten (g) 11-23 h
Shinwa Plaza B1, Minami-3-jo, Nishi-9-chome ☎ 261 54 06

GENERAL GROUPS

ILGA Japan, Sapporo Meeting 1st Wed 19-21 h
c/o Hirahira, N18 W5, Kita-ku, Sapporo 001 ☎ 756 05 18

CRUISING

-Odori Park (Nishi 11-chome)
-Sapporo Railroad Station
-Yuraku Cinema
-Sauna at Basment of Hotel Line

Sendai ☎ 022

BARS

Hoshi (B G) 19-2 h, closed Sun
Kokubun-cho, 2-1-13, Heimat Building *(3rd floor)* ☎ 224 54 68

Leo (B G) closed Tue
Kokubun-cho, 1-6-1, Social Sanro Building B1 *(basement)*
☎ 265 96 47
Take a taxi to Kanihachi Restaurant, small side street, downstairs under restaurant. Bar about 3rd door on the right side of hallway.

Mirai Toshi (B G) 18-2 h
Ichiban-cho, 1-chome, Tohoku Taihokumon mae ☎ 262 75 80

Taiho (B g) 2nd & 4th Sun 19-0.30 h
Daisan (No.3) Fujiwara Building, Ichiban-cho *(3rd floor)*
☎ 263 03 28

1.4 Ichi Ten Yon Bar (B G)
Kokubuncho 2-8-1, 18 Building *(5th floor)* ☎ 264 30 55
Two blocks behind Hotel Rich, 1 1/2 blocks to the left at the Noodle Shop and the Drug Store. Also other gay bars in the building. Sign says „1.4", on the 5th floor.

SAUNAS/BATHS

Sendai Business Inn (G sa) 0-24 h
Eko Building Kakyoin 1-2-19, Aoba-ku *(5th floor)* ☎ 263 02 31
Only 2 minutes from Sendai station.

Tokyo ☎ 03

●Tokyo has the largest gay scene of the country. Foreigners can orientate themselves with help of the magazines „Tokyo Classified" and „Tokyo Night Life" both written in English. Most of the gay bars are located in the district of Shinjyuku-ni-chome. The Japanese are known to be polite and friendly to foreigners. Unfortunately they speak only a little English and often dare not to begin a conversation in English. In the bars, such as „GB" or „Fuji" it's very easy to open up contact with locals.

✱Tokyo hat die größte schwule Szene des Landes. Ausländische Besucher können sich mit Hilfe der englischsprachigen Stadtmagazine *Tokyo Classified* und *Tokyo Night Life* orientieren. Im Stadtteil Shinjyuku-ni-chome konzentrieren sich die schwulen Bars. Japaner sind aus Prinzip Ausländern gegenüber höflich und freundlich. Bedauerlicherweise sprechen nur wenige Englisch bzw. trauen sich nicht, es zu tun. In Bars, wie „GB" oder „Fuji" kann man jedoch sehr leicht Kontakt mit Einheimischen aufnehmen.

▲Tokyo est la ville avec la plus grande scène gay du pays. Les visiteurs étrangers peuvenr s'orienter grâce à des magazines tels que *Tokyo Classified* et *Tokyo Night Life*. Dans le quartier de Shinjyuku-ni-chome, on trouve une forte concentration de bars gays. Les japonais sont polis et sympathiques par principe avec les étrangers. Malheureusement, beaucoup ne parlent pas l'anglais ou n'osent pas. Mais dans certains bars comme „GB" ou „Fuji", il est très facile de faire connaissance avec des japonais.

☆Tokio dispone del más amplio ambiente gay en todo el país. Para turistas las revistas de ocio *Tokyo Classified* y *Tokyo Night Life*, ambas escritas en inglés, son de gran ayuda para encontrar los lugares interesantes. Los sitios de ambiente se concentran en el barrio Shinjyuku-ni-chome. En general, los extranjeros son tratados de manera muy amable y cortés, pero desgraciadamente muy pocos japonéses saben inglés o mejor dicho se atreven a hablarlo. Sin embargo, en bares como el „GB" o „Fuji" es muy facíl entablar contactos.

❖Tokio vanta del più vasto ambiente gay del paese. I visitatori stranieri si possono orientare con l'aiuto delle due riviste *Tokyo Classified* e *Tokyo Night Life*. Nel quartiere Shinjyuku-ni-chome si concentrano i bar gay. I giapponesi sono tradizionalmente molto cordiali e amichevoli con gli stranieri. Purtroppo solo in pochi parlano l'inglese o non si azzardano a parlarlo. Però nei bar come il „GB" o il „Fuji" si può venire facilmente in contatto con la gente del posto.

GAY INFO

Gay Help Line ☎ 56 93 45 69
Answering machine. Leave message and be sure to give your room number and name, if you are staying at a hotel.

TOURIST INFO

Tourist Information Centre
Kotani Building, 1-6-6 Yurakucho, Chiyoda-ku, Tokyo 100 ☎ 35 02 14 61

GENERAL GROUPS

International Friends/Passport
CPO Box 180 ☎ 56 93 45 69
Provides information and publishes a magazine.

CRUISING

-Ginza Street around Sony Building
-Hibiya Park
-Olympic Park (between swimming pool and Akasaka side, at night)
-At Shinbashi Daiichi Building (underground)
-Shimbashi Station
-Tabata Railway Station
-Shibuya Station (south exit)
-Jingu Pool (Sendagaya)
-Komazawa Koen Park
-Toilets at Ueno station

Tokyo - Chiyoda-ku

PHARMACIES

American Pharmacy
1-1 Yurakucho *(at Nikkatsu International Building)*
☎ 32 71 40 34
Drugstore.

HOTELS

Tokyo Y.M.C.A Hotel (H MA NG yg)
7 Mitoshiro-cho, Kanda ☎ 293 19 11

Tokyo - Minato-ku

MEN'S CLUBS

Treffpunkt Akasaka (G)
Maeda Bld. 4F, Akasaka 5-4-17 ☎ 55 63 05 23
A small but clean cruising room. Admission fee.

SEX SHOPS/BLUE MOVIES

Apple Inn (g)
1-13-5 *(2nd floor)* ☎ 35 74 14 77
Near Shimbashi station. The gay books are upstairs.

Tokyo - Nakano-ku

BARS

Puchi Marco (B G) 19-2 h, closed Wed
3-41-3 *(3rd floor)* ☎ 33 89 80 33
Just out of Arai Yakushi-Mae station.

Tokyo - Ota-ku

BARS

Hachan (B G) 20-1 h
Ookayama Station, B1 *(south entrance)* ☎ 37 27 47 06

Mitaka (B G) 19-2 h
7-60-9 ☎ 37 35 67 65

Tokyo - Shibuya-ku

BARS

LAX (B G)
2-8 Fuyo Building *(3rd floor)* ☎ 34 96 41 90

Matsuri (B F G MA) 15-24 h
1-9-4 Tokan Shibuya Castle Building *Shibuya-ku* ☎ 34 09 29 93

BOOK SHOPS

Paradise Hokuo
2-13-3 ☎ 33 70 56 41

Tokyo - Shinagawa-ku

BARS

Hana (B G) 19-2 h
3-14-5 ☎ 37 85 37 92

Yuzan (B G) 19-2 h
5-4-19 ☎ 34 71 66 18

Tokyo - Shinjuku-ku

BARS

Anderson (B G R) 16-3 h
2-18-10 Anderson Building *(2nd floor)* ☎ 33 41 03 82

Arty Farty (B G)
2-17-4 Shinjuku *(basement)* ☎ 335 653 88
Popular, inexpensive with an international atmosphere.

Bakkasu (B f GLM s)
2-14-7 Watanabe Building ☎ 33 52 96 40

Billy (B G) 19.30-4 h
2-2-15 ☎ 33 50 57 59

Brutus (B G R) 17-2 h
55 Dai-Ichi Building *(2nd floor)* ☎ 33 50 52 32
Only Japanese welcome.

Capture (B CC G) 19-5 h
Watanabe Building 4th Fl., 2-14-7 Shinjuku ☎ 3357 6926

Century (B G msg R) 12-24 h
2-14-8 Daisan Tenko Building *(6th floor)* ☎ 33 56 16 28

College No Osama (B G R) 17-2 h
2-15-8 Nagira Building *(2nd floor)* ☎ 33 52 39 30
English spoken. Many host boys.

Fitness Boy (B G R)
2-7-3 Bira Heights 310 ☎ 33 41 89 94

Fuji Bar (B G) 19.30-3 h
12-16-2 *(basement No. 104)* ☎ 33 54 27 07 *Popular.*

GB Bar (! B D G VS) 20-1 h
2-12-3 Shinjuku Plaza Building *(basement)* ☎ 33 52 89 72
Around the corner from Fuji Bar. Sign „GB" on sidewalk.

Hatten-Hachi (8.8) (B G) 2-15-13
Shigemi Building *(2nd floor)* ☎ 33 54 66 95

Hoshi (B G R) 17-10 h
2-21-15 ☎ 371 88 56 *Only Japanese welcome.*

Janny Shonentai (B G R) 11-23.30 h
2-11-10 Shinjuku Center Building ☎ 33 52 67 67

Janny's (B G R) 18-3 h
2-15-10 Daiichi Tenko Building *(6th floor)* ☎ 33 56 22 02

Janny's Boys (B G R) 2-14-4
Daisan Fujiwara Building *(3rd floor)* ☎ 33 54 88 28

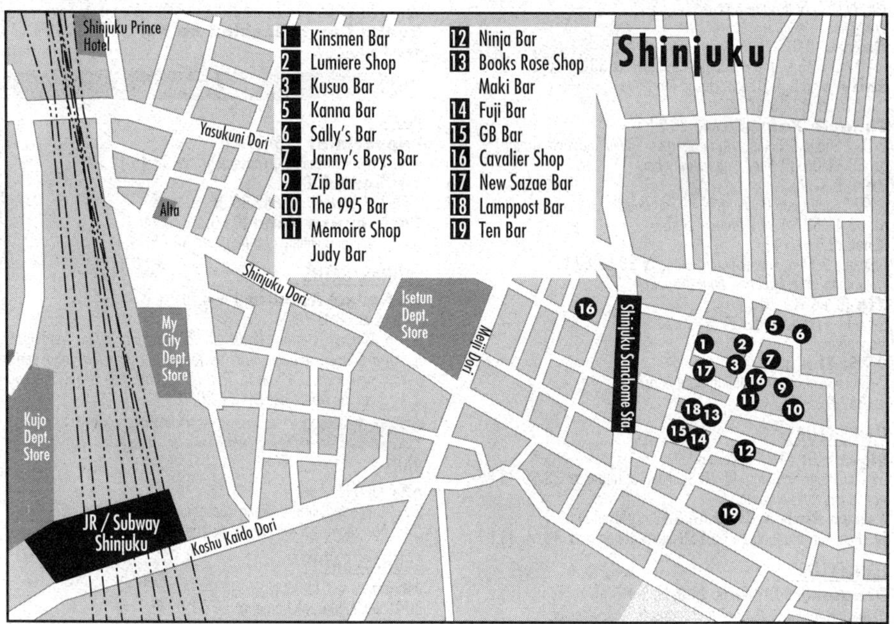

Jiyu-No-Megami (B G) 18-3 h
2-14-13 Yuni-Building *(#302)* ☎ 33 54 06 52
Judy (B G) 2-14-7
Watanabe Building ☎ 341 93 53
Kanna (B G) 20-4 h, closed Tue
2-15-13 Dai-Ni Nakae Building *B1* ☎ 33 54 68 24
Kingsmen (B GLM) Fri Sat 21-5 h, possibly open during the week
2-18-5 Oda Building *(2nd floor)* ☎ 33 54 49 49
One block from Fuji Bar on a corner. Windows overlook the street.
Kirinkan (AC B f g MA) 18-2 h
201 New White Bldg, 1-30-12 *(Metro Shinjuku-Gyoen-Mae)*
☎ 32 26 63 69
Kusuo (B G) 19-3 h
2-17-1 Sunflower Building *(3rd floor)* ☎ 33 54 50 50
Lamppost (B G) 19-3 h
2-12-15 *(2nd floor)* ☎ 33 54 04 36
Leo (B g)
2-14-36 Tsutsui Building *(2nd floor)* ☎ 33 54 76 99
Maki (B G)
2-12-15 *(4th floor)* ☎ 33 41 89 91
Menkura (B G YG)
2-14-9 Shimazaki Building *(2nd floor)*
☎ 33 56 05 89
New Sazae (B GLM) best after 24 h
2-18-5 Ishikawa Building *(2nd floor)* ☎ 33 54 17 45
Ninja (B G R) 18-4 h
2-13-7 Nakahara Building *(1st floor)* ☎ 33 52 25 25
Pierrot (B G) 18-3 h
2-7-3 *(3rd floor)* ☎ 33 52 19 39
P.O.Box • Party Office Box (AC B G N) 19.30-3 h
2-15-13 Shinjuku, Hosono Building 1F ☎ 33 54 80 03
Poplar Bar (B G) 18-2 h
2-12-16 Saint Four Building (basement 103) *(Subway Marounouchi-Shinjuku Sanchome)* ☎ 33 50 69 29
Foreigners welcome.
Ranya (B G)
3-10-7 Dai 33 Kyutei Building *(1st floor)* ☎ 33 56 60 00
Sally`s (B f g) 20-4 h, closed Mon
2-12-15 ☎ 33 56 64 09
Snuggle Bear (B G MA) 20-2 h
2-10-2 Ehana Building, 4th floor *(near Shinjuku-Gyoen Station)*
☎ 33 41 06 80 *Bear type friendly bar.*
Ten (B g MA)
2-7-2 Sunny Coop Building 204 *(2nd floor)*
☎ 33 41 50 54 *Very friendly staff.*
Zinc (B G) 18-4 h
Shinjuku 2-14-6, Hayakawaya Bldg. ☎ 33 52 62 97
New opened cocktail bar. English spoken.
Zip (B d G YG) 20-5 h
2-14-11 *(1st floor)* ☎ 33 56 50 29
Very popular.
995. The (B G)
2-chome, Sakagami Building *(3rd floor)*
☎ 352 09 95

MEN'S CLUBS

Signal (G) 14-22 h, closed Sun
5F Daini-Kunisha Bldg., 11-10 Shinjuku 3Chome ☎ 33 55 33 89
Foreigners not welcome.
Tokyo Men's Club (G) 22-5 h, closed Sun
5F Daini-Kunisha Bldg., 11-10 Shinjuku 3Chome ☎ 33 55 33 89

DANCECLUBS

Dragon (B D G) Tue-Thu 21-3, Fri Sat -5 h
In the basement of the building facing GB bar. Popular.

SEX SHOPS/BLUE MOVIES

Books Rose (G) 11-3 h
2-12-15 *(basement)* ☎ 33 41 06 00
Cavalier (G) 11-23 h
3-11-2 Muraki Building *(basement)* ☎ 33 54 79 76
Climax (g)
1-13-7 Dai 19 Tokyo Building *(1st floor)* ☎ 32 00 22 46
Lumiere (G) 12-7 h
2-17-1 Sunflower Building *(1st floor)* ☎ 33 52 33 78
Gifts, books, magazines, videos: large selection. Recommended.
Memoire (G) 12-6 h
2-14-8 Tenko Building *(1st floor)* ☎ 33 41 17 75
Gifts, postcards, magazines.

SAUNAS/BATHS

Paragon (G sa sb) 16-12 h
2-17-4 ✉160 ☎ 33 53 33 06
Sky Gym (G sa YG) 14-11 h
2-5-12 Rashington Palace *(10th floor)* ☎ 33 52 10 23
Only Japanese welcome.

HEALTH GROUPS

AIDS Action Sun 10-18 h
☎ 32 35 50 71
AIDS Care Project Thu 18-22, Sun 19-22 h
☎ 33 78 90 95
HIV to Jinken Jyoho Centre 2nd/4th Sun 19-21 h
☎ 52 59 07 50
Okubo Hospital 10-18 h, closed Sun & holidays
1-17-10 ☎ 33 61 80 47
Place Tokyo 2nd/4th Sat 19-21 h
☎ 53 86 15 75
Tokyo Eiseikyoku AIDS Taisakushitsu Mon-Fri 9-17 h
☎ 53 20 44 85
Ugoku Gay to Lesbian no Kai Tue-Thu 19-22 h
☎ 33 80 22 69

Tokyo - Taito-ku

BARS

Peppermint (B G) 19-4 h
4-20-1 Mimasu Building *(basement)* ☎ 38 45 10 93
Yuukontei (B G)
7-10-2 *(2nd floor)* ☎ 842 35 87
24 Asakusa Ueno (B f GLM) 18-2 h
7-7-11 Shinei Building *(1st floor)* ☎ 38 45 19 42

SAUNAS/BATHS

24 Kaikan Asakusa (F G sa sb)
2-29-16 ☎ 38 41 78 06
Go to Asakusa station. Walk up the shopping street leading to Asakusa Cannon temple. Past the temple on your left you'll see a yellow sign with „24" on it. That is the back-side of the building. Entry is on the front-side. Entry ¥ 2000.

Tokyo - Toshima-ku

BARS

»X« (B G LJ) 18-2 h
2-2-7 Daigo Maejima Building *(basement)* ☎ 39 82 87 47
S/M backroom; 15 minutes walk from Ikebukuro Station.

SAUNAS/BATHS

Jinya (G sa) 16-12 h
30-19 Ikebukuro Ni-Chome ☎ 59 51 09 95

Yokohama ☎ 045

BARS

Pegasus (B F G YG) 17-2 h, closed Wed
☎ 242 97 68
Arrive at Sakuragicho Station, Exit at Toyoko Line exit and head towards the Key Coffee sign. At the fourth traffic light turn left. At the third street turn right. The bar is one and a half blocks down on the left. The sign is red with white letters.
Tomo (B G)
Naka-ku, Noge-cho 1-5, Minato-Kosan-Building *(2nd floor)* ☎ 231 22 36

CRUISING

-Isezaki-cho shopping street (1st-2nd section on left; afternoon and evening)

Jordan

al-Urdunn
Middle East
Initials: JOR
Time: GMT +2
☎ Country Code / Access Code: 962 / 00
Language: Arabic
Area: 91,867 km^2 / 35,461 sq mi.
Currency: 1 Jordan-Dinar (JD) = 1,000 Fils
Population: 4,434,978
Capital: Amman
Religions: 95% Moslem
Climate: Mostly dry desert climate. The rainy season in the west lasts from November to April.

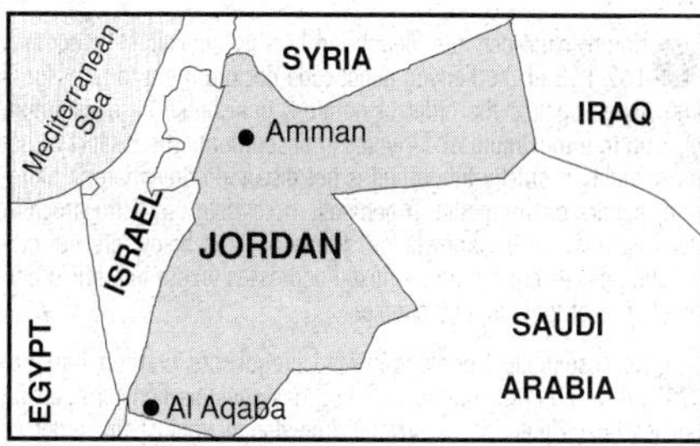

The meeting places listed below are, without exception, mixed. There is no visible gay scene in Jordan. Homosexuality is strictly prohibited and can lead to imprisonment (German embassy, Amman). Although unsusual for an Islamic country, hotels and bars in Jordan do serve alcoholic beverages. Inform yourself about the necessary vacinations before going on your trip.

Es gibt in Jordanien keine eingrenzbare schwule Szene: Homosexualität ist streng verboten und mit Gefängnisstrafe bedroht (Deutsche Botschaft, Amman). So können wir im Listing nur gemischte Treffpunkte erwähnen. Ungewöhnlicherweise wird in jordanischen Hotels übrigens Alkohol ausgeschenkt. Wir empfehlen Ihnen, sich vor einer Reise über notwendige Impfungen zu informieren.

Il n'y a pas vraiment de vie gay en Jordanie. L'homosexualité y est interdite: c'est un délit et on risque la prison. Aucun des lieux mentionnés ci-dessous n'est vraiment gay. Les bars et boîtes sont tous mixtes. En Jordanie, on sert de l'alcool dans les bars et les hôtels, ce qui est inhabituel pour un pays islamique. Avant votre départ, renseignez-vous sur les vaccinations nécessaires.

Los puntos de encuentro que damos a conocer son todos mixtos. En Jordania no hay un ambiente gay, la homosexualidad está estrictamente prohibida y es penada con cárcel. (Segun informaciones de la embajada alemana en Amman). No es costumbre que en bares y hoteles sean servidas bebidas alcohólicas. Antes de un viaje a Jordanía, se recomienda informarse sobre la vacunación necesaria.

Gli atti omosessuali sono proibiti, e puniti con la reclusione (ambasciata tedesca, Amman). Non c'è una vera vita gay e i luoghi d'incontro elencati qui sotto hanno una clientela mista. Nei bar e negli hotel giordani vengono raramente serviti alcolici. Prima di intraprendere il viaggio, informatevi sulle vaccinazioni necessarie.

Amman ☎ 06

BARS

KitKat Bar (B g MA NG) 16-23.30 h.
Basman Street *(near Hussein Mosque)*
Ask Taxi driver to take you there.
Salute Bar (AC B D F NG MA OS) Thu
Villa d'Angelo Restaurant, Circle Road *(below second circle)*

DANCECLUBS

Scandal Disco (AC B D g NG) Thu Fri 22-3 h
Circle Road
From 6 circle behind Amra Hotel in the lower level of Sand Rock Hotel.

RESTAURANTS

Zuwaddeh Restaurant (B F OS) 13-16 h, 19-24 h
Fuhais *(Fuhais Village)* ☎ 720 677
Fuhais is a small village 10 min. outside of Amman.

CRUISING

-Old Roman Amphitheatre
-On the left of Al Husyni Grand Mosque at Rasheed Al Madai Street
-Hashimiya Square (R) (in front of amphitheatre and Odeon)

Kerak ☎ 03

CRUISING

-In the ruin of the old castle

Kazakhstan

Kazakstan
Central Asia
Initials: KAZ
Time: GMT +6
☎ Country Code / Access Code: 7 / 8 (wait for tone) 10
Language: Kazak
Area: 2,717,300 km^2 / 1,049,150 sq mi.
Currency: 1 Tenge = 100 Tiin
Population: 16,854,000
Capital: Akmola
Religions: 47% Muslim, 44% Russian Orthodox, 2% Protestant
Climate: Dry continental climate. Winters are cold, summers hot.

● Kazakstan has lifted the total ban on homosexuality (Article 104.1 of the penal code).

✱ Kazakstan hat das Totalverbot homosexueller Handlungen (Artikel 104.1 StGB) aufgehoben.

▲ Le Kazakstan a supprimé l'interdiction totale des pratiques homosexuelles (Article 104. 1 StGB).

☆ En Kazajistán se abolió el artículo 104.1 del Código Penal que prohibía estrictamente las relaciones homosexuales.

❖ In Kazakistan i rapporti omosessuali non sono più illegali.

Almaty ☎ 03272

BARS

Club Rainbow (B d F glm stv)
☎ 67 99 44
Spartacus (B d F glm snu,)
51 Nurmakov Street *(at the corner of Sovetskay Street)*
☎ 68 12 10
There is a admission fee

GENERAL GROUPS

Kontrast
PO Box 108 ✉96 Fax: 33 86 10

CRUISING

- City Park, near the old Orthodox Russian Cahtedral

Kenya

Kenya
East Africa
Initials: EAK
Time: GMT +3
☎ Country Code / Access Code: 254 / 000
Language: Swahili; English
Area: 582,646 km^2 / 224,960 sq mi.
Currency: 1 Kenyan Shilling (K.Sh.) = 100 Cents
Population: 28,337,000
Capital: Nairobi
Religions: 26% Protestant, 26% Catholic, 27% African nature religions
Climate: The climate varies from tropical along coast to dry in the interior.

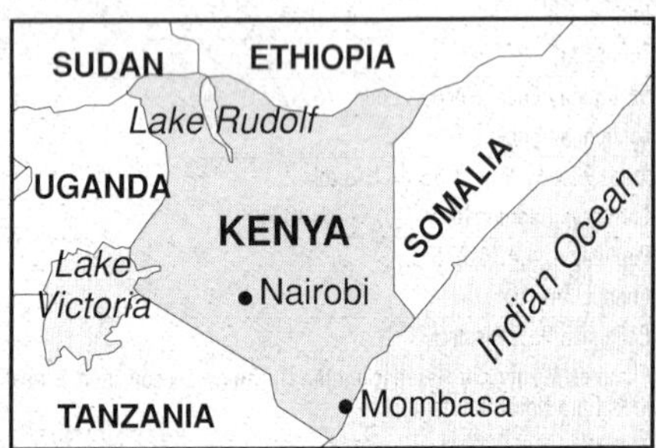

● Homosexual acts are illegal and harshly punished. Paragraphs 162-165 of the Kenyan penal code declare them to be »carnal knowledge against the order of nature«, punishable by a minimum of 5 up to a maximum of 14 years imprisonment. The subject of homosexuality is strictly taboo and is not discussed anywhere in literature, politics or the media. A generally accessible gay infra-structure does not exist to our knowledge. The bars listed below are not gay meeting places but are rather mixed addresses where one has a better chance of meeting gay people.

✱ Homosexuelle Handlungen sind illegal und werden hart bestraft. Die Paragraphen 162-165 des kenianischen Strafgesetzbuches bezeichnen sie als »carnal knowledge against the order of nature« (dt. etwa: »Widernatürlicher Geschlechtsverkehr) und ahnden sie mit Haft zwischen mindestens fünf und höchstens 14 Jahren.
Homosexualität als Thema ist in Kenya streng tabu und wird nirgends in Presse, Literatur und Politik diskutiert. Eine allgemein zugängliche schwule Infrastruktur existiert unseres Wissens nicht. Die unten angegeben Bars sind keine Schwulentreffpunkte, sondern gemischte Adressen, wo man eine etwas größere Chance hat, einen Schwulen kennenzulernen.

▲ Au Kenya, l'homosexualité est un délit qui est sévèrement puni. Conformément aux articles 162 à 165 du code pénal kényan, les „carnal knowledge against the order of nature" (en français: „actes charnels contre nature") peuvent vous coûter cher:

entre 5 ans minimum et 14 ans maximum de prison. L'homosexualité est un sujet tabou au Kenyia. On n'en parle jamais dans la presse, la littérature ou en politique. Pas vraiment d'infrastructure gaye. Les bars mentionnés ci-dessous ne sont pas vraiment des lieux gays. Ce sont plutôt des adresses mixtes où on aura un peu plus de chance qu'ailleurs de rencontrer quelqu'un.

☆ Las actividades homosexuales son ilegales y son objeto de duras sanciones. Los artículos 162-165 del código penal keniano las califican de «carnal knowledge against the order of nature» (algo así como „actos carnales contra natura") y son sancionados con penas de encarcelamiento que van desde 5 hasta 14 años.
En Kenia la homosexualidad es un tema completamente tabú y no se debate ni en la prensa ni en las obras de carácter literario, ni en la vida política. Que nosotros sepamos, tampoco existe una infraestructura gay. Los bares que citamos a continuación no son sitios de ambiente, sino direcciones mixtas, donde quizás haya posibilidad de algún tipo de contacto.

❖ Gli atti omosessuali sono illegali e duramente puniti. I paragrafi 162-165 del codice penale del Kenya, li definiscono come „conoscenza carnale contro l'ordine della natura" punibili con la prigione da cinque a quattordici anni. L'argomento dell'omosessualità costituisce un tabù mai discusso nella letteratura, dai politici e nei mass-media. Per quanto ne sappiamo, non esiste una infrastruttura gay generalmente accessibile. I bar indicati qui sotto non possono essere considerati dei punti d'incontro gay, ma dei luoghi dove si può avere almeno una piccola possibilità d'incontrare qualcuno.

Kisumu ☎ 035

DANCECLUBS

Club. The (B D g N NG P WE YG) Wed Fri Sat 21-? h
at Hotel Royal

Mombasa ☎ 011

RESTAURANTS

Fontanella Restaurant (AC B F NG OS) 8-22.30 h
Moi Avenue/Nyerere Avenue City House ☎ 237 56
International specialties.

Tamarind Restaurant (B CC F g OS) 12.15-14.30 h, 18.45-22.15 h
Sino Road near Old Nyali Bridge, PO Box 857 85 ☎ 47 17 47
Open-air restaurant serving international and African specialties, especially seafood.

Nairobi ☎ 02

RESTAURANTS

Carnivori (AC B CC F GLM OS) 12-14.30, 18.45-22.15 h
Langata Road, PO Box 566 85 ☎ 50 17 79
African specialities (roast meats with salads and sauces).

Tamarino Restaurant (AC B CC F GLM) 12-2, 18.30-22 h
Harambee Avenue, PO Box 744 93 *(National Bank Building)*
☎ 33 89 59
International and African specialties (seafood).

CRUISING

-Kenyatta Avenue
-Back of GPO, Kenyatta Avenue and around Intercontinental Hotel (especially Sun afternoon)
-Sarit Centre (lower ground floor)

Korea-South

Taehanmin`guk
Eastern Asia
Initials: ROK
Time: GMT +9
☎ Country Code / Access Code: 82 / 001
Language: Korean
Area: 99,263 km² / 38,325 sq mi.
Currency: 1 Won (W) = 100 Chon
Population: 46,416,800
Capital: Seoul
Religions: 28% Christian, 21% Buddhist, Confucians (an ethical code, not a religion)
Climate: Moderate climate with rainfall heavier in the summer than in winter.

● There are no anti-gay laws in South Korea, but there is still a stigma attached to being gay. Openly gay behaviour is therefore not advisable. Korean men are affectionate and may walk around hand in hand, but this is only a friendly gesture and should not be misunderstood.

✱ Homosexuelle Handlungen zwischen Erwachsenen sollen in Süd-Korea nicht verboten sein. Das Schwulsein aber ist stigmatisiert. Es ist ratsam, sich unauffällig zu verhalten. Koreaner sind herzlich und laufen gerne Hand in Hand mit Freunden durch die Straßen, was aber nicht als eine schwule Geste mißverstanden werden sollte.

▲ Officiellement, l'homosexualité est tolérée en Corée du Sud. Les homosexuels y sont cependant plutôt mal vus. Il est donc conseillé de se faire assez discret. Les Coréens sont chaleureux et aiment bien marcher main dans la main dans la rue. Attention: n'en tirez pas pour autant des conclusions hâtives!

☆ Las relaciones homosexuales entre adultos no están prohibidas, sin embargo el ser homosexual continua siendo un estigma. Es aconsejable no llamar la atención. Los hombres coreanos muestran su afección tomandose de la mano, esto no tiene mas significado que el de un gesto amable.

❖ In Corea del Sud i rapporti omosessuali tra adulti non dovrebbero essere illegali. L'omosessualità tuttavia non è benaccetta. è consigliabile non ostentare troppo le proprie preferenze. I coreani sono socievoli e passeggiano spesso in strada mano nella mano con i loro amici, questo, però, non deve essere frainteso come un gesto omosessuale.

Pusan

BARS
Telephone (B G MG)
(Accross from the Samsung Theatre)

CRUISING
Wharves across the bridge.

Seoul ☎ 02

GAY INFO
Chingusai
Gay magazine, available at gay bars. Published by the group of the same name.

BARS
California (B D G MA) 12-? h, disco: Fri Sat
72-32 Itaewon Yongsan ☎ 749 77 38
Trance (B G MA) Yongsan-gu, It'aewon-dong 136-42 ☎ 797 34 10
Why Not? (B G MA)
137-4 Yongsan-ku, Itaewon ☎ 795 81 93

DANCECLUBS
Spartacus (! B D G MA VS)
128-11 Itaewon-Dong, Yongsan-Ku ☎ 749 77 38

CRUISING
-Tapkol Park (popular late afternoon, on right side OG, near monument YG)

Latvia

Latvija
Northeast Europe
Initials: LR
Time: GMT +2
☎ Country Code / Access Code: 371 / 00
Language: Latvian. Russian
Area: 64,600 km^2 / 24,942 sq mi.
Currency: 1 Lat (Ls) = 100 santimi
Population: 2,448,000
Capital: Riga
Religions: Protestants
Climate: Wet maritime climate. Winters are moderate, summers cool.

● Homosexuality between consenting adults is legal in Latvia. The Latvian parliament adopted a new Criminal Code in July 1998 which makes 16 the age of consent for everyone. In 1999 a draft law on domestic partnerships was submitted to the Latvian Parliament for consideration and it is likely to be adopted.

✷ Einvernehmliche Homosexualität zwischen Erwachsenen ist in Lettland legal. Das lettische Parlament setzte im Juli 1998 das Mindestalter von 18 auf einheitlich 16 Jahre, ungeachtet der sexuellen Orientierung. 1999 wurde dem lettischen Parlament ein Gesetzentwurf zur eingetragenen Partnerschaft vorgelegt, der wahrscheinlich verabschiedet wird.

▲ L'homosexualité en Lettonie est légale. Le parlement letton a baissé l'âge de la majorité sexuelle de 18 à 16 ans, quelque soit l'inclination sexuelle des partenaires. En 1999, un projet de loi concernant l'union civile a été proposé au parlement et sera certainement adopté.

☆ La homosexualidad en Letonia es legal. El parlamento letón decidió en julio de 1998 de reducir la edad de consentimiento de 18 a 16 años, independientemente de la orientación sexual.

❖ L'omosessualità in Lettonia è legale. Nel luglio 1998 il parlamento della Lettonia ha abassato l'età legale dai 18 ai 16 anni ugualmente per etero e omosessuali.

NATIONAL GAY INFO
Homoseksualitates Informacijas Centrs HIC
PO Box 65 ✉1001 Riga ☎ 951 95 51
Homosexuality information center. AIDS information, personals, www-board, homophobia info, links. English version available. Publishes the monthly newspaper „10%".
Latvie?u Gejklubs
A/K 425 ✉1001 Riga
Latvian Gay-club/pen club.

NATIONAL HELPLINES
AIDS Hotline
☎ 522 222

NATIONAL PUBLISHERS
Elwis (G)
PO Box 117 ✉LV 5674 Dagda
National gay newsletter

Riga ☎ 02

BARS
Video Bar „XXL" (AC B CC d DR F G MA p s VS)
daily 11-6 h
Alfréda Kalhina Iela 4 ✉1050 *(Near the railway station Maritas Iela, in the center)* ☎ 728 22 76

DANCECLUBS
Purvs (B D GLM MA S) 21-6 h, closed Mon
Matisa iela 60/62 ☎ 731 17 17
808 (B D DR GLM MA) 21-6 h
8 Alfreda Kalnina iela ☎ 940 68 08

SEX SHOPS/BLUE MOVIES
Labi (g VS) 0-24, gay films Sat 9-5 h only
Elizabetes iela 22

ESCORTS & STUDIOS
Logos (G) 0-24 h
6 Veru Str., of. 5 ☎ 732 41 00
Also a video production and model agency.

HEALTH GROUPS

Agihas
PO Box 391 ✉1001
Support group of HIV+ people and people living with AIDS.

Health Center
Baznicas lela 18 ☎ 728 37 39
Medical clinic, STDs and HIV tests, health care.

Valsts Infektologijas Centra AIDS Nodala
Linezera lela 3 ☎ 252 98 95
State medical clinic, STDs and HIV tests.

HELP WITH PROBLEMS

Veselibas Centrs
Baznicas iela 18 *Health Center.*

SWIMMING

-Kalngale (NU) (Train direction Saulkrasti to Kalngale. 30 min walk north along beach)
-In?upe (NU) (Train direction Saulkrasti to In?upe. 30 min walk south along the beach)
-Lielupe (NU) (Train direction Jurmala to Lielupe. Bus 1 to last stop. 20 min walk to north)

CRUISING

-The Square (in front of the University main building across from Raina bulvaris 18)
-Arkadijas parks (AYOR) (Tram 10. Near the toilets)
-Grizinkalns (AYOR) (Park on Pernavas street/J Asara street)

Lebanon

Lubnan

Middle East

Initials: RL

Time: GMT +2

☎ Country Code / Access Code: 961 / 00

Language: Arabic

Area: 10,400 km² / 4,015 sq mi.

Currency: 1 Libanese Pound (L

Population: 3,505,794

Capital: Bayrut

Religions: 60% Moslem, 40% Christian

Climate: Mediterranean climate. Winters are mild to cool and wet, summers hot and dry. The mountains experience heavy winter snowfall.

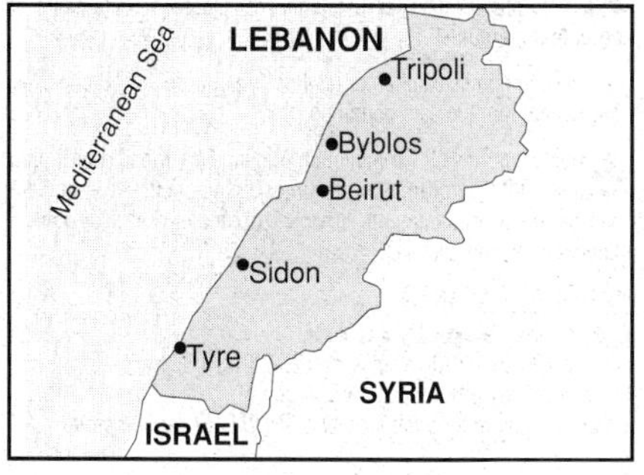

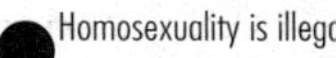

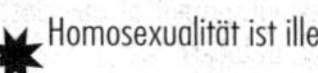

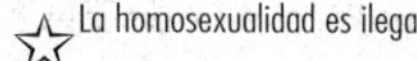

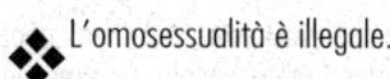

Bayrut ☎ 1

BARS

B 018 (B d g) Thu-Sat 22-6 h
Quarantina *(near Forum de Beirut)*

Orange Mecanik (B D g) Thu-Sat 22-6 h
Hirsh Tabet *(25 min from Beirut)*

SAUNAS/BATHS

Hammam Nuhza (MG NG sa sb) 0-24 h
19 Rue Kasti *(Sécteur Sérail)*
Be discreet.

SWIMMING

-Paradise Beach at Jbeil

CRUISING

-Ramel El Beida

Liechtenstein

Central Europe

Initials: FL

Time: GMT +1

☎ Country Code / Access Code: 41-75 (no area codes) / 00

Language: German

Area: 160 km² / 62 sq mi.

Currency: 1 Swiss Franc (sfr) = 100 Rappen

Population: 31,717

Capital: Vaduz

Religions: 87% Catholic, 8% Protestant

Climate: Continental climate. Winters are cold and cloudy with frequent snow or rain. Summers are cool to moderately warm, cloudy and humid.

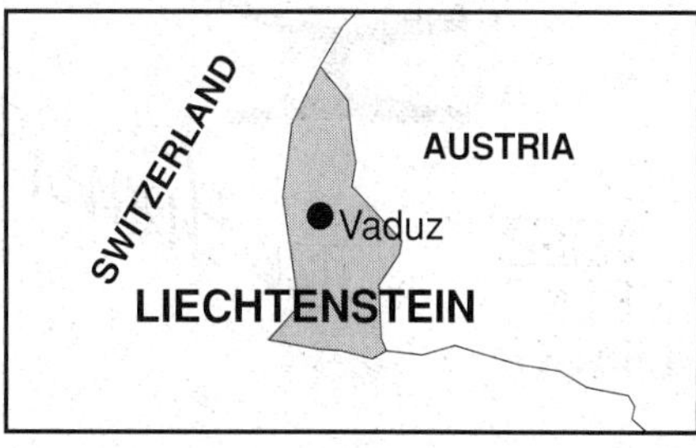

●The age of consent in Liechtenstein is 18 for homosexual acts and 14 for heterosexual activity. Here, as in Austria, »promotion of homosexuality« is forbidden. The establishment of gay/lesbian associations is also prohibited (officially, at least).

✱Das Schutzalter liegt in Liechtenstein bei 18 Jahren für homosexuelle Handlungen, jedoch bei 14 für heterosexuellen Sex. Wie in Österreich ist hier die „Werbung für Homosexualität", genauso wie die Gründung schwul-lesbischer Vereine (zumindest offiziell) verboten.

▲Au Liechtenstein, la majorité sexuelle est fixée à 18 ans pour les homosexuels et à 14 pour les hétérosexuels. Comme en Autriche, il est interdit de „promouvoir l'homosexualité".

☆La edad de consentimiento para el sexo homosexual es de 18 años, para el sexo heterosexual es de 14. Al igual que en Austria, aquí también se prohibe oficialmente la „promoción de la homosexualidad", por ejemplo anuncios de contactos, así como fundaciones o asociaciones gay-lesbianas.

❖L'età legale per i rapporti omosessuali è di 18 anni, quella per i rapporti eterosessuali è invece di 14 anni. Come in Austria anche qui sono vietate campagne a favore dell'omosessualità e organizzazioni gay.

Schaan

HEALTH GROUPS

AIDS-Hilfe Liechtenstein Mon 18-20, Thu 8-10 h
Postfach 207 ✉9494 ☎ 232 05 20

Schwule und Lesben in Liechtenstein und Umgebung (FLAY)
Postfach 207 ✉9494 ☎ 232 05 20

Lithuania

Lietuva
Northeast Europe
Initials: LT
Time: GMT +1
☎ Country Code / Access Code: 370 / 8 (wait for tone) 10
Language: Lithuanian. Russian, Polish
Area: 65,200 km² / 25,174 sq mi.
Currency: 1 Litas=100 Cent
Population: 3,710,000
Capital: Vilnius
Religions: mostly Roman Catholics
Climate: Maritime climate. Winters and summers are moderate.

●Homosexuality between consenting adultis is legal. The age of consent is set at 18 years for everyone

✱Einvernehmliche Homosexualität zwischen Erwachsenen ist erlaubt. Das Schutzalter liegt, unabhängig von der sexuellen Orientierung, bei 18 Jahren.

▲En Lituanie, l'homosexualité entre adultes (plus de 18 ans) n'est pas un délit, si la relation est placée sous le signe du consentement mutuel.

☆El sexo homosexual entre adultos (a partir de los 18 años) por acuerdo mutuo está permitido.

❖Nell'estate del '93 il parlamento lituano ha modificato il paragrafo 122: ora i rapporti tra omosessuali adulti e consenzienti sono permessi. Naturalmente la violenza carnale e la seduzione di minorenni restano punibili.

NATIONAL GAY INFO

Lietuvos Geju Lyga LGL
PO Box 28 62 ✉2000 Vilnius ☎ (2) 233 30 31
Email: lgl@gay.lt Homepage: www.gay.lt
Lithuanian gay association including SOLIDA LGL lesbian group

Lithuanian Youth Gay League LYGL
PO Box 2861 ✉2000 Vilnius
Lithuanian Movement for Sexual Equality (LSSL)
PO Box 720 ✉2038 Vilnius☎ (2) 265 59 40

Kaunas ☎ 7

DANCECLUBS

Mefistofelis (B D GLM p) Fir-Sat 21-6 h
Kalnieciai ☎ 897 64 94

CRUISING

-Laisves Aleja
-Vilniaus Gatve
-Park near bus station
-Ramybes Park
-Azuolynas Park

Klaipeda ☎ 61

BARS

Bolero (B g WE) Sat 22-? h
16 Stadiono gatve ☎ 216 018

SWIMMING

-Smiltyne (male nude beach, left side)

CRUISING

-Skulptury parkas

Palanga ☎ 36

SWIMMING

-Male nude beach (north side of city, Vanagupe area)

CRUISING

- Near Naglis cinema at night

Vilnius ☎ 2

GAY INFO

Gay Information Helpline ☎ 333 031
Naglis
Nemenčines pl. 25 ✉2016
Bimonthly

CAFES

Opera (B g) 12-22 h
Tylioji 4
Stikliai Aludé (B F g) 9-22 h
Stikliu gatve 18

DANCECLUBS

Men's Factory (B D f G WE) Fri-Sat 22-6 h
Zygimantu gatve 1 ☎ 998 50 09
Gay disco bar.

HEALTH GROUPS

Lietuvos Aids Profilaktios Centras
c/o Dr. Saulius Caplinkas, Moletu Plentas 40 ✉2021 ☎ 35 04 65
Fax: 35 02 25

CRUISING

- Pylimo Street opposite the trolleybus stop »Klaipeda«
- Gedimino prospektas
- Luki kiu Square

Luxembourg

Letzebuerg • Luxemburg
Western Europe
Initials: LUX
Time: GMT +1
☎ Country Code / Access Code: 352 (no area codes) / 00
Language: French, German, Letzebuergs
Area: 2,586 km^2 / 998 sq mi.
Currency: 1 Lux. Franc (Flux) = 100 Centimes. 1 EURO = 100 EURO Cents (The Euro can only be used in the clearance system)
Population: 425,000
Capital: Luxembourg
Religions: 95% Roman Catholic
Climate: Modified continental climate with mild winters and cool summers

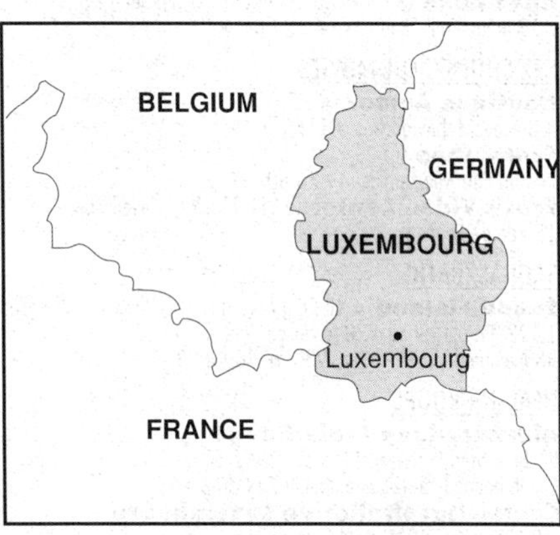

● The age of consent for both homosexual and heterosexual activity is 16 (Article 372 of the penal code). Luxembourg has a small gay scene centred around the capital.

✱ Das gesetzliche Schutzalter für hetero- wie homosexuelle Handlungen liegt generell bei 16 Jahren (Art. 372 Stgb). Seit dem vergangenen Jahr gibt es auch in Luxemburg ein Anti-Diskriminierungsgesetz, daß eine Benachteiligung aufgrund der sexuellen Orientierung unter Strafe stellt.

▲ Au Luxembourg, la majorité sexuelle est fixée à 18 ans pour les gays (article 372 bis du code pénal). Récemment, la majorité sexuelle est passée à 14 ans pour les hétérosexuels. On a vite fait le tour des bars et boîtes gays du Grand Duché.

☆ La edad de consentimiento legal para actividades tanto homo como heterosexual es de 16 años (art. 372 del Código Penal). Desde el año pasado existe una ley prohibe la discriminación de personas a causa de su orientación sexual.

❖ L'età del consenso per i gay è di 18 anni (Art. 372 bis del codice penale), di 14 per gli eterosessuali. Il Lussemburgo è un piccolo paese con una vita gay di dimensioni ridotte concentrata principalmente sulla capitale.

Bettendorf

HOTELS

Hotel Vallée de la Sûre (B bf F g H MA) 10-24 h
34 route d´Echternach ✉9355 ☎ 80 30 75 Fax: 80 37 47

Eich

BARS

Chez Gusty (B d GLM MA N S TV) Tue-Fri 6.30-1, Sat 6.30-3, Sun 17-1 h
101 Rue d'Eich ✉1461 ☎ 43 12 23

Esch-Sur-Alzette

GAY INFO

IGHL - Info
Carmen Kronsmagen, 7 Rue du Bois

Luxembourg

BARS

Chez Mike (B f GLM MA OS tv VS) 7-1, Fri-Sat 12-3 h
30 Avenue Emile Reuter ☎ 45 32 84

SEX SHOPS/BLUE MOVIES

Boutique Amour (g VS)
4 Boulevard d'Avranches ✉1160
Erotic Shop (g)
Rue Du Fort Neipperg ☎ 49 36 60
Erotic Video Center (g VS) 11-19 h, closed Sun
15 Rue de Reims

SAUNAS/BATHS

Sauna Finlandia (B CC g msg pi sa sb sol OS wh) Mon-Thu 12-22, Fri -21, Sat 14-20 h, closed Sun
58 Avenue de la Liberté ✉1930 ☎ 48 46 23

HEALTH GROUPS

Aidsberodung Croix-Rouge
94 Boulevard Patton ✉2316 ☎ 40 62 51
Email: henrigoedertz@handitel.lu *FAX 40 62 55.*
Centre Hospitalier de Luxembourg
4 Rue Barblé ✉1210 ☎ 44 11-1
Free testing.
Laboratoire National de Sante
42 Rue du Laboratoire ✉1911 ☎ 49 11 91-1
Free testing.
Onofhängeg AIDS-Hellef Lëtzebuerg Asbl
Organisation Mon 16.30-19.30 Wed Fri 15-18 h.
23 Rue des États-Unis PO Box 917, L-2219 ☎ 49 81 94
Fax: 29.16.26
Stop Aids Now asbl (A g)
94 Boulevard Patton ✉2316 ☎ 40 62 51 Fax: 40 62 55

CRUISING

-City Park/Parc Municipal (near RTL)
-Main railway station/Gare Central
-P Patinoire Kokelesheur (AYOR) (evenings, but frequent police controls)

Mondorf-Les-Bains

SWIMMING

-Domaine Thermal (B F NG msg NU MA OS pi sa sb sol wh WO)
☎ 670 11 (Best thermal bath. Many gays at the pool and in the sauna).

Petange

SWIMMING

-Parc de la mairie (around the city hall and into the park, evenings only)

Remich

HOTELS

Auberge des Cygnes (bf CC F g H s) 10-1 h
11 Esplanade ✉5533 *(In front of the river „Moselle" in the middle of the Esplanade)* ☎ 69 88 52 Fax: 69 75 29
All rooms with shower, WC and phone./Alle Zimmer mit Dusche, WC und Telefon. Rates double Flux 1.900, single 1.600. Also a restaurant.

Rosport

HOTELS

Hotel-Restaurante de la Poste (bf CC F glm H MA OS) 10-23 h
7 Route d'Echternach ✉6580 ☎ 73 50 03
Rates Single Flux 1200, double 1.800.

Rumelange

BARS

Cafe Mini's Theaterstuff (B f glm H MA OS p s)
15-1 h. Thu closed.
40, Grand Rue ✉3730 ☎ 56 48 26

Malaysia

Southeast Asia
Initials: MAL
Time: GMT +8
☎ Country Code / Access Code: 60 / 00
Language: Malay, Chinese, English
Area: 329,758 km^2 / 127,320 sq mi.
Currency: 1 Malayan Ringgit (RM) = 100 Sen
Population: 20,932,900
Capital: Kuala Lumpur
Religions: Muslim, Buddhist, Hindu
Climate: Tropical climate. There are annual southwest (April to October) and northeast (October to February) monsoons.

According to our information, homosexuality as such is no longer punishable by law. We were not able to determine the exact legal regulations, but we assume that only sex in public toilets and cruising can lead to problems. Homosexuality is never mentioned in the media (Islam being somewhat of a state religion) and is considered taboo. For this reason, one should behave with extreme caution. The country is made up mostly of mountains, rain forests and rice fields. In addition, Penang (»The Pearl of the East«), Langkawi, Pangkor, as well as the east coast of the Malayan peninsula, offer some of the most beautiful beaches in the Far East.

Nach unserem Kenntnisstand stehen homosexuelle Handlungen in Malaysia nicht mehr unter Strafandrohung. Wir konnten zwar keine genauen Rechtsvorschriften ausmachen, aber wir gehen davon aus, daß nur Klappensex und Cruising Probleme bereiten könnten.
In den Medien ist Schwul- oder Lesbischsein tabuisiert, da der Islam in etwa den Rang einer Staatsreligion einnimmt. Schon aus diesem Grund sollte man sich in diesem Land sehr vorsichtig verhalten.
Einen großen Teil des Landes machen Berge, Regenwälder und Reisfelder aus. Darüberhinaus bieten die Inseln Penang (»Perle des Ostens«), Langkawi und Pangkor sowie die Ostküste der malayischen Halbinsel einige der schönsten Strände des Fernen Ostens.

D'après ce que nous savons, l'homosexualité n'est plus un délit en Malaysie. Nous n'avons pas réussi à obtenir de plus amples informations sur la législation en vigueur, mais tout nous donne à penser que la fréquentation des parcs et des toilettes publiques peut vous causer de sérieux désagréments. L'homosexualité est un sujet tabou. Rien d'étonnant à cela, vu que l'Islam est la religion d'Etat. Donc: prudence est mère de sûreté! La majeure partie du pays est faite de montagnes, de forêts tropicales et de rizières. Sur les îles de Penang („Perle de l'Orient"), de Langkawi et de Pankor, ainsi que sur la côte Est du pays, vous trouverez quelques unes des plus belles plages de l'Extrême-Orient.

Según sabemos, la homosexualidad ya no es perseguida en Malasia. Aunque no hemos podido obtener informaciones confiables sobre leyes o reglamentaciónes en vigor, suponemos que solamente el sexo en aseos públicos y el cruising pueden traer serios problemas. En los medios de comunicación la homosexualidad es un terma tabú, debido a la fuerte influencia del islam, que se puede considerar como la religión oficial. Por ello, se recomienda un comportamiento muy cauteloso. Una gran parte del país está formado por montañas, selvas y campos arroceros. En las islas Penang („Perla del Este"), Langkai y Pangkor así como el litoral Este de la península malaya se encuentran las más lindas playas del lejano oriente.

Secondo le nostre informazioni, in Malesia l'omosessualità non è più perseguibile. Non ci sono state presentate nè leggi nè regolamenti, ma possiamo immaginare che possiate avere dei problemi solo cacciando in gabinetti pubblici o in zone simili. Per la stampa e la televisione l'omosessualità resta un tabù. L'islamismo ha quasi assunto il ruolo di religione nazionale, per questo motivo in questo paese ci si deve comportare con molta discrezione. Una larga parte del paese è montuosa con foreste piovose e risaie. Inoltre, Penang („La perla dell'Est"), Langkawi, Pangkor, così come la costa est della penisola vantano alcune fra le più belle spiagge dell'estremo oriente.

Johore Bahru ☎ 07

CRUISING

-Sungai Segget (near traffic cirlce with fountain and nearby carpark. Late night, weekends)

Kuala Lumpur ☎ 03

BARS

Blue Boy (B D G MA s) 22-4 h
54 Jalan Sultan Ismail ✉50250 *(entrance off Jalan Sultan Ismail, behind Pizza Hut)* ☎ 242 10 67
Admission M$ 11.

CAFES

Café Silhouette (B glm STV) STV 22 h
19A-LGF-12 UOA Centre, Jalan Pinang/Jalan Perak

SAUNAS/BATHS

Babylon KL (G sb WO) 1
46 Jalan Batu Estate *(off Jalan Segambut)* ☎ 621 2139
Hot Top Corner (G sa sb)
40-6A Jalan Sultan Ismail *(near Blue Boy)* ☎ 244 96 48
Otot 2 (G sa sb)
7a 2/F Jalan Ipoh Kechil *(off Jalan Raja Laut)* ☎ 444 33 69
Ryu Member's Sauna (G sb wh WO VS)
56A&B Jalan Pingai, Taman Pelangi *(behind Leisure Mall)*
☎ 607-333 32 08

HOTELS

Fortuna Hotel (AC B F H NG)
87 Jalan Berangan ☎ 241 91 11 Fax: 241 82 37
Lodge Hotel (b F H NG pi)
Jalan Sultan Ismail ☎ 242 01 22 Fax: 241 68 19
Centrally located. 50 rooms with bath/WC, AC, TV and phone.

GENERAL GROUPS

Pink Triangle Mon, Wed & Fri 19.30-21.30
7c Jalan Ipoh Kecil *(off Jalan Raja Laut, near Grand Central Hotel)*
☎ 444 46 11 Fax: 444 46 22 Email: isham@pop7.jaring.my

CRUISING

-Sungei Wang Plaza, Jalan Bukit Bintang (commercial centre between Hotel Apoll and Regent Hotel, 3rd floor)
-Kota Raya (shopping complex on Jalan Chen Lock)
-Merdeka Square (AYOR OG) (20-? h)
-Lot Ten Shopping Center (Near Regent Hotel. In front on street level and also on 2nd floor at Deli France)
-Jalan Sultan Ismail (near Regent Hotel and Blue Boy)
-Star Hill Shopping Center (Jalan Bukit Bintang, opposite Regent Hotel)
-KL Plaza (Coffee Bean and Tea Leaf at entrance)

Kuantan ☎ 09

SWIMMING

-Tekluk Cempedak Beach (G WE)

Kuching - Sarawak ☎ 082

HOTELS

Aurora Hotel (AC B F g)
McDougall Road ☎ 24 02 81
Downtown neighborhood location, all rooms with telephone, frigde, priv. bath, balcony and radio.

CRUISING

-Kuching Plaza Shopping Centre (R TV)
-Merdeka Place (tv) (next to hotel)
-Merdeka Place
-Aurora Hotel

Penang ☎ 04

CAFES

Beach Blanket Babylon (B f glm YG)
16 Jalan Bishop ☎ 263 81 01

DANCECLUBS

Party Box (B D g S TV)
Club House No.1, Mar Vista Resort, Batu Ferringghi

HOTELS

Golden Sands (AC B F H NG OS sa)
Batu Ferringhi Beach ☎ 881 19 11
Beach location, 13 km to the airport. All rooms with bath/wc, telephone, balcony, tea/coffee machine and fridge. Single M$ 140-195, double 165-225.

Lone Pine (AC B F H NG)
10th Mile, Batu Ferringhi Beach ☎ 881 15 11 Fax: 881 12 82
Suburb location, 45 min to the airport, all rooms with telephone, frigde, priv. bath and balcony

CRUISING

-Batu Feringghi Beach
-Waterfall at Botanical Garden.
-Park next to Dewan Siri Pinang

Malta

South Europe

Initials: M

Time: GMT+1

☎ Country Code / Access Code: 356 (no area codes) / 00

Language: Maltese, English

Area: 316 km² / 122 sq mi.

Currency: 1 Maltese Lira (Lm) = 100 Cents

Population: 379,563

Capital: Valletta

Religions: 97% Roman Catholic

Climate: Mediterranean climate. Winters are mild and rainy, summers hot and dry summers.

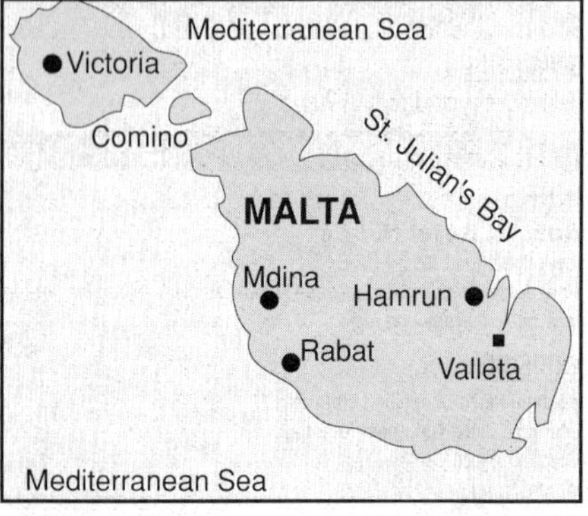

● Homosexuality between adult men is permitted by law and the age of consent is 18. The people in Malta tend to be high-spirited, and are known for their hospitality. Malta is above all a treasure-trove for those interested in archaeology and classical architecture.

✱ Homosexualität zwischen erwachsenen Männern ist dem Gesetz nach erlaubt. Die Schutzaltersgrenze liegt bei 18 Jahren. Die Malteser sind temperamentvoll und ausgesprochen gastfreundlich. Erwähnenswert ist, daß Malta eine wahre Fundgrube für die Freunde antiker Architektur und der Archäologie ist.

▲ A Malte, l'homosexualité entre hommes adultes n'est pas un délit. La majorité sexuelle y est fixée à 18 ans. Les Maltais ont du tempérament et sont très accueillants. A noter: Malte regorge de trésors d'architecture antique et de sîtes archéologiques splendides.

☆ La ley autoriza la homosexualidad entre hombres adultos. La edad mínima legal de consentimiento está fijada en 18 años. Los malteses son un pueblo temperamental y particularmente hospitalario. Es digno de mencionar que Malta es un verdadero i paraígo para los amantes de la arquitectura antigua y de la arqueología.

❖ L'omosessualità tra adulti di sesso maschile è permessa. L'età legale è di 18 anni. I maltesi sono pieni di temperamento e conosciuti per la loro ospitalità. Desideriamo sottolineare che Malta rappresenta un vero scrigno per tutti coloro che amano l'architettura antica e l'archeologia.

Gozo - Gharb

RESTAURANTS

Salvina Restaurant (B g F)
Restaurant: daily 12-14.30 h, 19-22 h Bar: 10-15 h, 19-24 h, closed Thu
21 Frenc Ta`L-Gharb Street, GRB 102 *(near Ta'Pinu-Church)*
☎ 55 25 05
Closed for a few weeks in Nov and Feb. Roof terrace. Friendly atmosphere.

Gozo - Marsalforn

BARS

Marsalforn Hotel (g H)
Rabat Road ☎ 556 147

Tritons (B F)
Rabat Road *(near Marsalforn Hotel)*

CINEMAS

Victoria
Very active in winter.

SWIMMING

-San Blas Bay (Direction of Nadur. Sometimes NU but then AYOR)
-Ramla Bay (Nadur)

Malta - Bugibba

RESTAURANTS

Da Michelle (B F g OS) 19-23 h
Triq it-Turisti ✉SPB 05 *(1st street behind Boulevard)* ☎ 58 21 31
Gay-friendly restaurant. Good food. Menu Lm 7-9. Ask for Victor.

Malta - St. Julians

BARS

Lady Godiva (AC B d GLM MA OS S STV VS YG) Sun-Thu 21-2 h, Fri-Sat 21-5 h
Wilga Street *(Paceville)* ☎ 39 10 58

Nix Bar (B gLm) daily 10-22 h
Manuel Dimeck Str.

Malta - Ta'Xbiex

CRUISING
-Yacht marina Gardens (AYOR) (After sunset)

Malta - Valletta

BARS
Tom Bar (B G) 20.30-1 h
1 Crucifix Hill *(Floriana)* ☎ 25 07 80

CRUISING
-Valletta Bus Terminal (AYOR)
-Republic Street (R)
-Garden around the Commonwealth Air Forces Memorial
-Independence Avenue (bus terminus on the right side of the Phoenicia Hotel)

Malta - Zebbug

SWIMMING
-Gnejna Bay (AYOR) (take bus 46, than walk through the the narrow passage NU on remote rock plateau)

Mauritius

Southwestern Indian Ocean

Initials: MS

Time: GMT +4

☎ Country Code / Access Code: 230 / 00

Language: English

Area: 2,040 km² / 794 sq mi.

Currency: 1 Mauritius Rupie (MR) = 100 Cents

Population: 1,168,256

Capital: Port Louis

Religions: 52% Hindu, 28% Christian

Climate: Tropical climate that is modified by southeast trade winds. Winters are warm and dry (May to November), summers anre hot, wet and humid (November to May).

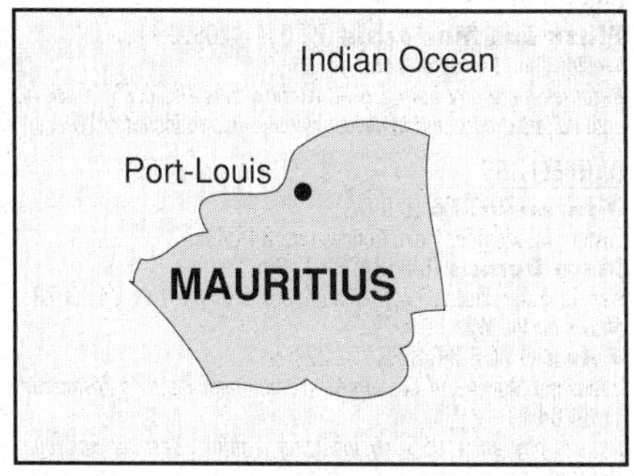

Curepipe

CRUISING
-Toilet at Jan Palach Sud Bus Station (daytime)
-Area around Jan Palach Arcade (AYOR) (evening)

Floreal

HEALTH GROUPS
Prevention Information Lutte contre le Sida (PILS) Tue-Fri 9-13 h
Impasse du Dr. Mayer, Rue Georges Guibert ☎ 697 89 09

Grand Bay

DANCECLUBS
Number One (B D g YG) 22-? h
Royal Road

Perybere

SWIMMING
-Perybere Public Beach

Trou-aux-Biches

SWIMMING
-Trou aus Biches Public Beach (next to Trou aux Biches Hotel)

Mexico

Southernmost State in North America

Initials: MEX

Time: GMT -6/ -7 /-8

☎ Country Code / Access Code: 52 /

Language: Spanish

Area: 1,958,201 km² / 756,061 sq mi.

Currency: 1 Mexican Peso (mex$) = 100 Centavos

Population: 98,552,800

Capital: Mexico City (Ciudad de México)

Religions: 89% Roman Catholic

Climate: The climate varies from tropical to desert.

Important gay cities: Acapulco, Mexico City, Monterrey, Puerto Vallarta

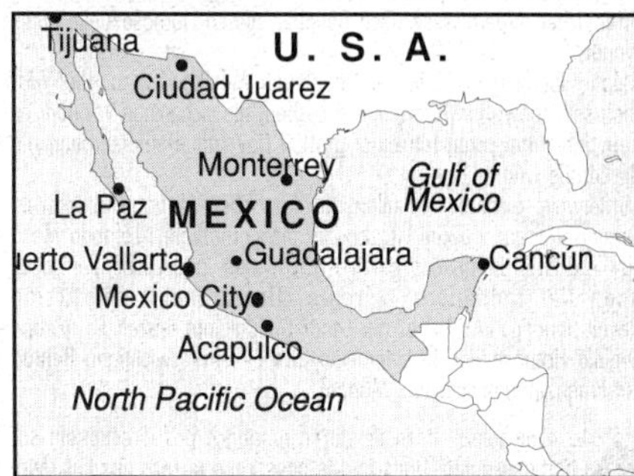

Mexican federal law does not mention homosexuality. Laws governing »public morality« are often arbitrarily enforced against homosexuals throughout Mexico. Homosexuals enjoy much more freedom in the capital, Mexico City. Here, for example, gays

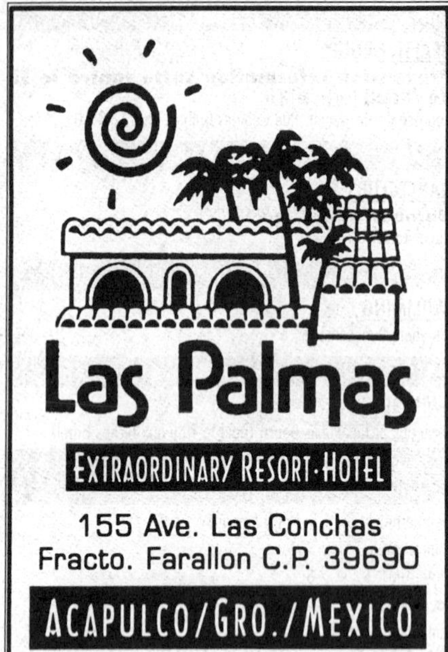

and lesbians were confident enough to hold a large Gay Pride demonstration as early as 1982. Since then, gay liberation groups have been set up in all Mexican cities, such as »Lambda Mexico«, organisers of the only gay and lesbian centre in the city, and the radical »Frente Homosexual de Acción Revolucionaria/FAHR«. The »Grupo Orgullo Homosexual de Liberación/GOHL« has done important work in the city of Guadalajara for gay rights.

Das Schutzalter liegt in Mexico bei 18 Jahren. In ganz Mexiko werden oft die gesetzlichen Bestimmungen über die »Erregung öffentlichen Ärgernisses« nach Belieben gegen Homosexuelle angewandt.
Relativ liberal geht es in der Hauptstadt Mexiko-City zu. Hier trifft man selbstbewußte Schwule und Lesben, die sich schon vor über einem Jahrzehnt offen mit einer großen Gay-Pride-Demonstration auf die Straße wagten.
Mittlerweile existieren in allen mexikanischen Metropolen schwule Organisationen: z.B. in Mexiko-City die gemäßigte »Lambda Mexico« -sie ist Trägerin des einzigen Schwulen- und Lesbenzentrums- und die radikalere »Frente Homosexual de Acción Revolucionaria/FAHR«. In der Stadt Guadalajara leistet die »Grupo Orgullo Homosexual de Liberación/GOHL« einen wichtigen Beitrag zur Emanzipation schwuler Männer.

Le code pénal mexicain ne se prononce pas directement sur l'homosexualité. Dans tout le pays, on a recours aux lois réprimant «l'offense publique à la pudeur» comme moyen d'action contre les gays qui auraient l'audace de s'afficher en plein jour.
A Mexico-City, la capitale, la situation est, en revanche, normale. Les gays y sont à l'aise. Voilà déjà 10 ans que, pour la première fois, ils sont descendus dans la rue pour fêter la Gay Pride avec leurs copines, les lesbiennes. Il y avait 4.000 personnes dans la rue. Depuis, il y a une association ou un groupe gay dans chaque grande ville mexicaine. A Mexico-City, c'est la „Lambda Mexico" qui gère le seul centre homo-lesbien du pays. Le „Frente homosexual de acción revolucionaria/FAHR" est, lui, plus engagé. A Guadalajara, le groupe „Grupo Orgullo Homosexual de Liberación/GOHL" travaille à l'émancipation des gays.

Las leyes federales mexicanas no mencionan la homosexualidad. Sin embargo, las disposiciones referente al „escandalo público" se aplican frecuentemente contra los homosexuales, sin ningún tipo de criterio. Por el contrario, en la Ciudad de México se difruta de un ambiente relativamente liberal, donde el orgullo gay se demuestra abiertamente. Aquí se organizó ya en 1982 la primera manifestación de Gay-Pride. Así mismo, han ido surgiendo en todas las metrópolis mexicanas organizaciones de liberación gay: por ejemplo la moderada »Lambda México«, en Ciudad de México, que es la iniciadora del único centro para gays y lesbianas, o la más radical »Frente Homosexual de Acción Revolucionaria/FAHR«. En la ciudad de Guadalajara, el »Grupo Orgullo Homosexual de Liberación«/GOHL« presta una importante contribución para la emancipación de los gays.

Le leggi federali del Messico non includono l'omosessualità. Le leggi che proteggono „la pubblica moralità" vengono spesso usate in maniera arbitraria contro i gay riconoscibili su tutto il territorio del paese. Nella capitale, Mexico City, l'omosessualità è vista con occhi più liberali. Per esempio, nel 1982, le lesbiche e i gay dichiarati hanno organizzato la prima Manifestazione dell'Orgoglio Omosessuale con 4.000 partecipanti. Da allora si sono formati vari gruppi di liberazione gay in tutte le città messicane, come „Lambda Mexico", una delle più attive organizzazioni a Mexico City o il più radicale „Frente Homosexual de Acción Revolucionaria/FAHR". Nella città di Guadalajara il „Grupo Orgullo Homosexual de Liberaciòn/GOHL è molto attivo nella lotta per l'emancipazione dei gay.

NATIONAL GAY INFO

Mexicanos Contra el SIDA, Confederación de Organismos no Gubernamentales, A.C.
Calzada de Tlalpan 613, Col. Alamos, Mexico City-D.F. *03400* ☎ 530 27 71

Acapulco - Guerrero ☎ 74

BARS

Plaza Las Mariachis (B f G MA N OS) 24 hours
Avenida Juan Escudero *(Zócalo)*
Becomes more gay from 1-6 h, jukebox, beer US$0.75, check out pool hall next door and taxi-washing boys in parking lot (AYOR)

DANCECLUBS

Diferencia. La (B D G S)
Costera M. Alemán, Plaza Condesa ☎ 84 04 1
Disco Demas (B D GLM S) 22-? h.
Privada Piedra Picuda 17 *(Behind Carlos & Charles)* ☎ 84 13 70
Shows on the WE.
Relax (! AC B D G S VS YG) 22-5 h
Lomas del Mar 4 *(off Costera M. Aleman near Denny's Restaurant)* ☎ 84 04 21
Tourists pay entry US$ 10 including 1 drink. Best on Sat night. Thu/Sat Strip shows.

RESTAURANTS

Le Bistroquet (b CC F g OS)
Andrea Doria 5, Costa Azul
☎ 84 68 60
International cuisine

CINEMAS
Dorado 2000 (NG)
Plan de Ayala 1-6 *(Col. Progreso)*

HOTELS
Acapulco Las Palmas (AC B bf CC F G H msg NU OS pi wh) 0-24 h
Avenida Las Conchas 155, Fracto. Farallon ✉CP39690 *(Fracto. Farallon)* ☎ 87 08 43 Fax: 87 12 82
Email: bobbyjoe@acapulco-laspalmas.com
Homepage: www.acapulco-laspalmas.com
2 minutes from Condesa Gay Beach and bars. Airport pick-up. 15 premier rooms and suites. Clothing optional. Air conditioned rooms and suites.
Luna del Mar Hotel (H NG)
Costera Miguel Aleman/de la Cosa ☎ 84 00 71
Villa Costa Azul (! AC GLM H MA OS pi) 15.Nov-15.May
Fdo. Magallanes 555, GRO 39850 ☎ 84 54 62
Villa Tiffany (CC G H MA pi)
Calle Villa Vera 120 ☎ 294 78 49
In gay area, close to bars and gay beach.

GUEST HOUSES
Villa Roqueta (AC B bf CC G H msg OS pi sa wh WO) All year / 24h
24 San Marcos, Las Playas ✉GRO 393600 ☎ 294 7849
Fax: 294 7849 Email: van4@prodigy.net
Former Gloria Gaynor Estate now a luxuary guesthouse non the cliffs. All rooms with ocean view. Pool and bar 11 double rooms with shower/WC. Rates from US$ 125. Free airport transfers.k>

CRUISING
-Beto's Beach (near Condesa, Chichifos)
-Flecha Roja (AYOR) (bus station)

Aguascalientes - Aguascalientes ☎ 49

BARS
Circulo. El (B G)
Calle del Horneado s/n

RESTAURANTS
Mitla (b F g OS)
Calle Madero 220
Wolworth (B F GLM)
5 de Mayo/Victoria *Best after 20 h.*

FITNESSTUDIOS
Ojo Caliente (g sa WO)
Carretera Aguascalientes-San Luis Potosi

Arriaga - Chiapas ☎ 966

GENERAL GROUPS
Gruppo Pisis
6a Sur/5a Avenida, Poniente 522 ✉30450

Campeche - Campeche ☎ 981

CRUISING
-Plaza Principal/Plaza de Independencia

Cancún - Quintana Roo ☎ 98

BARS
Blue City (B D G S) Tue-Sun
Avenida Yaxchilán 12 *(Centro)*
Caramba (B D G YG) Mon-Sat 22-6 h
Avenida Tulum 87 ☎ 84 00 32

Pent House (B D G)
Claveles 7
Picante Hot Bar (! B d GLM MA VS) 22-2 h
Avenida Tulum 19/20 *(Plaza Galerias)*

RESTAURANTS
Mykonos (AC B F g) 13-24 h
Party Center Shopping Mall ☎ 845 310
Seafood and Greek cuisine.

FASHION SHOPS
Pierro's Boutique (g) daily 10-14, 17-21 h, closed on Sun
Plaza Bonita 10-E *(Centre-near Market 28)*

SWIMMING
-The Mirador (across from the Ruinas del Rei)
-Beach near Club Med (AYOR)
-Beach at Sheraton
-Playa del Carmen (g) (50 min. by bus, walk left along the beach north)

CRUISING
-Avenida Tulum (late)
-Beach between hotels Camino Real & Caribe Hilton
-Palapa Park (opposite Cinema Blanquita, at night)

Chihuahua - Chihuahua ☎ 14

BARS
Bar Chindo's (B G)
Calle Sexta 300
Bar Gambrinus (B G)
Trias 300 *(around the corner from Hotel Posada Tierra Blanca)*

CRUISING
-Plaza de la Constitución
-Plaza Hidalgo

Ciudad del Carmen - Campeche ☎ 938

DANCECLUBS
Umma-Guma Palace (B D glm)
Calle 26 y 55 *(opposite Puerto Pesquero)*
Local music.

RESTAURANTS
Tropical Guacamayos (B F glm)
Calle 55 y 26 *(opposite Puerto Pesquero)* ☎ 201 02

Ciudad Juarez - Chihuahua ☎ 16

BARS
G&G (B d g)
Lincoln 1252
Madelon. La (B D GLM STV)
Santos Degollado 771 *(Centro)*
Nebraska (B F glm)
Calle Mariscal 251 *(Centro)*
Olímpico (B GLM)
Avenida Lerdo 210 Sur *(Centro)*
Quijote. El (B g TV)
Calle Mariscal 721 *(Centro)*
Rex Bar (B D glm)
Calle Mariscal 186 Norte *(Centro)*
Ritz (B GLM)
Ignacio de la Peña
Sarawak (B D g)
Avenida Juárez Norte *(Centro)*

DANCECLUBS
MN'MS (B D g STV)
Avenida Juárez Norte *(opposite X.O. Laser)*
Omare (B D G)
Ignacio de la Peña y Rámon Corona *(Centro)*
X.O.Laser (B D g)
Avenida Juárez 832 Norte *(Centro)*

RESTAURANTS
Coyote Invalido (B F g)
Avenida Lerdo, Pasaje Continental *(Centro)*
Escondida. La (B F GLM)
Calle Ignacio de la Peña 366 *(around the corner from Olímpico)*

Colima - Colima ☎ 331

BARS
Terraza Azul. La (B GLM) 20-? h
Gabino Barreda y Avenida Francisco I. Madero *(on top of Hotel Flamingo)*

CINEMAS
Micro 2001 (NG)
Maclovio 47-A/Venustiano Carranza *(Centro)*

Córdoba - Veracruz ☎ 271

CRUISING
-Mercado/Market Juarez, Calles 7 & 9 (WE YG)
-Sidewalk cafés on El Portal Zevallos

Cuernavaca - Morelos ☎ 73

BARS
Shadeé (B D G S) Fri-Sun, show Sat.
Avenida Adolfo López Matéos *(across from the DIF gas station)* ☎ 12 43 67
Terraza. La (B glm)
Calle Salazar 1, local 5

CAFES
Parroquia (b f g OG OS)
Guerrero
V.I.P.S. (B g YG)
Boulevard Juarez *(near Cuauhnahuac Museum)*

GENERAL GROUPS
Grupo Encuentro de Amigos
PO Box 1-1161 ✉6200

HEALTH GROUPS
Cadena Contra el Sida A.C.
Francisco Leyva 403, Colonia Centro ☎ 18 45 76

RELIGIOUS GROUPS
Iglesia de la Comunidad Metropolitana (ICM) Renovación Cuernavaca Wed-Sun 18-? h.
Leandro Valle 524-A

CRUISING
-Zocalo/Plaza Morelos/Jardín Juarez
-Mercado/market (Sun)

Culiacan - Sinaloa ☎ 67

BARS
Don Quijote (B g s)
Boulevard Madero 507

GENERAL GROUPS
Grupo Culiacán Gay
PO Box 884, 8000

CRUISING
-Plaza Obregon/Zocalo (AYOR YG)

Durango - Durango ☎ 181

BARS
Arthur's (B D GLM STV)
Bruno Martinez 134 Sur
Eduardo's (B F g)
20 de Noviembre 805

CRUISING
-Zocalo (20 de Noviembre & Juarez)

Ensenada - Baja California Norte ☎ 667

BARS
Coyote Club (B D GLM MA VS) Tue-Sat 21-3, Sun 18-2 h
1000 Boulevard Costero N°4 & 5/Diamante *(near Corona Hotel)*
Hola Verde (B D G YG) 16-3 h
2nd Street *(1st floor)* *Crowded Fri Sat after 23 h.*

Guadalajara - Jalisco ☎ 3

BARS
Angel. El (B F GLM MA) Chapultepec/José Guadalupe, Zuno *(Sector Juárez 3)*

Botanero. El (B G S TV) Tue-Sun 19-23 h.
Javier Mina y la 54
Wed & Sat admission fee.
Chiva's (B f G MA) 8-5 h
Calle Degollado 147/Avenida López Costilla ☎ 613 16 17
D.O.K. (B g)
Calle 66 No. 30 ☎ 643 98 12
Panchòs (B g)11-24 h.
Maestranza 179 *(Centro)*
Unicornio (B g)
Avenida López Mateos Sur Núm.

CAFES

Máscaras (! B f G MA YG) 8-5 h
Calle Maeztranza 238/Priscilliano Sánchez *(2 blocks from Degollado Theater)*
Pancho junior (B D glm MA) 8-2
Calle Galeana 180

DANCECLUBS

Angel's (AC B D E F G MA S) 0-3 h
Avenida La Paz 2030 ☎ 615 25 25
El Taller (! B D G S ma S YG) 22-12 h
Calle 66 #30, Sector Reforma
La Malinche (B D glm MA) 22-2 h Tue-Sun
Alvaro Obregon 1230 *(Sector Libertad)*
Monica's (B D f glm SNU STV) 22-12 h
Calle Medrano/Calle 68 *(Sector Libertad)*
Popular. Drag & strip shows Fri-Sun.
Noa Noa (B D glm MA)
Calle Molina
Romano's (B D G) Tue-Sun
Calle 54 *(Across from „La Comanche"-Sector Libertad)*
Sahara (B D Glm STV SNU)
Plaza del Sol
Vagoas (B D G) Wed-Sun
Avenida Circunvalación/Avenida Prolungación Alcalde *(Sector Hildalgo)*

SEX SHOPS/BLUE MOVIES

Gold Dreams
Jesús García 806 *(Sector Hildalgo)* ☎ 614 45 16

CINEMAS

Cine México (g)
Calle Enrico Días de Léon

SAUNAS/BATHS

Baños Galeana (AYOR b g sa sb) 7-20 h
Galeana 159 *(near Lopez Catilla Street)* ☎ 613 62 86
Action in steam room mostly.

HELP WITH PROBLEMS

Grupo Neuróticos Anónimos Gay
PO Box 1-4045

RELIGIOUS GROUPS

Iglesia de la Comunidad Metropolitana (ICM)
PO Box 1-4045

CRUISING

-Avenida Juarez (AYOR)
-Plaza de los Mariachis (AYOR)
-Pedro Moreno Street

Guanajuato - Guanajuato

CRUISING

-Zocalo (Jardin de la Union opposite Teatro Juarez)

Irapuato - Guanajuato ☎ 462

BARS

Los Alamos (B g)
Carretera Iratuato-Silao km. 3 1/2
Señorial (B F g)
Obregón 481 ☎ 751 52

Ixtapa Zihuatanejo - Guerrero ☎ 753

BARS

Splash (B f g MA YG VS) 12-24 h
Calle Ejido Esquina/Calle Vicente Guerrero *(in front of Comermex Bank)* ☎ 408 80

Jalapa - Veracruz ☎ 281

BARS

Mansion. La (B D G S TV) Fri Sat
Highway toward Banderillas *Drag shows.*

CRUISING

-Parque Juarez

La Paz - Baja California Sur ☎ 682

BARS

Talizman (B glm NG)
Belisario Dominguez/5 de Mayo

Leon - Guanajuato ☎ 47

BARS

Amigo, El (B g) -24 h
Belisario Dominguez 423 P.B.
Bagoas (B D g)
Alfredo Veladez/Mar Baltico

CRUISING

-Mercado/market (Mon Tue)
-Zocalo

Manzanillo - Colima ☎ 333

BARS

Osteria Bugatti (b D F GLM)
Las Brisas ☎ 215 13

CRUISING

-Plaza Santiago and Playa Santiago
-Plaza San Pedrito
-Zona Roja

Mazatlan - Sinaloa ☎ 69

BARS

Fandangos (B D g)
Avenida Camarán Sábalo *(Zona Dorada)*
Pepe Toro (AC B CC D E GLM MA N) Thu-Sat
Avenida de las Garzas 18 ✉82100 *(Zona Dorada)* ☎ 14 41 76

CRUISING

-Beach walk from Valentino's to the El Pollo Soco restaurant.

Mérida - Yucatan ☎ 99

DANCECLUBS

Kabukis (B D glm MA STV) open Thu, Fri, Sat
Calle 49 x 56-A *Drag shows*
Romanticos (B D g) 21-3 h, show Fri Sat
Calle 60 N°461 *(between 51 and 53)* ☎ 64 64 70

HOTELS

Casa San Juan (AC bf Glm H)
Calle 62 #545A, 69 x 71, Centro ✉97000 ☎ 23 68 23
Pantera Negra (bf glm H NG) 24 hours
547 B Calle 67, x 68 y 70 *(close to main bus station)* ☎ 24 02 51
Posada 49 (A AC H OS) 8-24 h
Calle 49 N°514A ✉97000 *(between 62 and 64)* ☎ 24 54 39
Centrally located. Rates US$ 15-25.

CRUISING

-Zoccalo (Parque Centrale)
-Santa Lucia Park (after 16 h)
-Calle 60 (between Zoccalo and Santa Lucia Park)
-Cinema Premiere

Mexicali - Baja California Norte ☎ 65

BARS

Expendio Marimbas (B D GLM)
Tuxtla Gutiérrez Guanajuato *(Colonia Pueblo Nuevo)*
Manolo's Bar (B G)
Prolongación Reforma *(Centro)*
Pancho's Place (B G)
Avenida Juárez 33 *(Centro)*
Roco Bar (B D GLM)
Avenida Madero *(Centro)*

CRUISING

-Chapultepec Park (downtown)

Mexico City - D.F. ☎ 5

● The gay scene in this vast city of 20 million, is concentrated in the „Zona Rosa": Paseo de la Reforma, Avenidas Insurgentes, Liverpool, Londres, Hamburgo, Florencia, Amberes and especially in the Avenidas Genova and Niza. This is also the area where most of of the prostitutes, male and female, are to be found.

✷ Die Schwulenszene dieser 20 Millionen Einwohner zählenden Großstadt ist konzentriert in der „Zona Rosa": Paseo de la Reforma, Avenidas Insurgentes, Liverpool, Londres, Hamburgo, Florencia, Amberes und ganz besonders in den Avenidas Genova und Niza. In dieser Gegend arbeitet auch das Gros der mexikanischen Prostituierten, ob männlich oder weiblich.

▲ Les quartiers gays de cette métropole de 20 millions d'habitants sont connus sous le nom de «Zona rosa»: Paseo de la reforma, Avenidas Insurgentes, Liverpool, Londres, Hamburgo, Florencia, Amberes et surtout la Avendia Genova et Niza. C'est dans ce coin que travaillent aussi la plupart des prostitués mexicains, hommes et femmes.

☆ El ambiente gay de esta gran ciudad de 20 millones de habitantes está concentrado en la „Zona Rosa":Paseo de la Reforma, Avenidas Insurgentes, Liverpool, Londres, Hamburgo, Florencia, Amberes y sobre todo en las Avenidas Génova y Niza. Es la bona clave de prostitución.

❖ La vita gay in questa grande città di 20 milioni di abitanti, è concentrata nella „Zona Rosa": Paseo de la Reforma, Avenidas Insurgentes, Liverpool, Londres, Amburgo, Florencia, Amberes e soprattutto nelle Avenidas Genova e Niza. Questa è anche la maggiore area di prostituzione maschile e femminile della città.

GAY INFO

Boys and Toys
A.P. 5-208 ✉06500

TOURIST INFO

Mexico City Tourism Office
Amberes 54 ✉06600 ☎ 525 93 81 Fax: 525 93 87

BARS

Angel Azul. El (! B D G MA S YG) A
v. Universidad 1905, Coyoacán ☎ 662 67 30
El Ansia (B D G MA SNU STV) Wed-Sat
Algéciras 26, Col. San José Insurgentes ☎ 611 61 18
Anyway, Exacto, The Door (! AC B D GLM S WE YG)
Avenida Monterrey 47, Col Roma *(near Metro Insurgentes)*
Very good, 3 floors, 3 clubs, friendly and relaxed.
Box (B D G MA S) Sat 23-? h
Versalles 64 Col. Juaréz
Butterflies (AC B D GLM MA S TV WE) Mon-Sun 21-4 h
Izazaga 9/Eje Central *(Metro Salto del Agua, right of the church)*
☎ 761 18 61
All kinds of music, mostly modern, pop & folkoric Mexican. Crowded WE. Large place.
Cantina del Vaquero (B D DR G lj SNU VS) 17-? h
Algeciras 26, Col Insurgentes Mixcoac ☎ 559 821 95
Caztzi (B D G S) Thu- Sat
Carlos Arellano 4, Cd. Satélite
El Celo 200 (B G S) Tue-Sun 18-? h
Londes 104 *(Zona Rosa)* ☎ 551 447 66
Show performance & gogo dancer.
El Punto (B G)
Insurgentes Sur 228, Col. Roma *(Between Durango & Colima)*
El Taller (B D G s) Tue-Sun
Florencia 37-A, Sótano *(Zona Rosa)* ☎ 533 49 84
Hot boys dancer.
Kim-Bar-a (B D G) Thu-Sat
José Clemente Orozco 9 & Eje 5 sur Col. Napoles
La Estación (B G LJ MA) Mon-Sun 16- ? h
Hamburgo 234 *(Zona Roas)* ☎ 520 707 27
Leather bar.
Mina 14 (B D G MA SNU) 24 h
Mina 36 atrás del Blanquita
El Numerito (B D G MA S) Wed-Sat
Av. de la Republica 9 *(Metro Jaime Vite)* ☎ 703 23 18
Penelope Mix Club (B D G MA S) Thu-Sat
Antonio Caso 60 Col. San Rafael ☎ 556 614 72

MEN'S CLUBS

La Casita I (B DR G lj p VS YG) 24 h
Viaducto M. Aleman 72, Col Algarin ☎ 519 88 42
Only men under 35.
La Nueva Casita II (B G) 24 h
Insurgentes Sur 228 ☎ 551 446 39

CAFES

Ananga Ranga (B GLM OS)
Tamaulipas 134-A Col. Condesa
Mediterraneo (b g f)
Florencia 37-A *(Zona Rosa)*

DANCECLUBS

El Andro (B D glm MA S) Wed-Sat
Londres 77 *(Zona Rosa)* ☎ 551 116 13
Enigma (B D G STV) Tue-Sun 21-5 h
Calle Morelia 111 *(Colonia Roma)* ☎ 520 773 67

Kaos (B D G STV) Wed-Sun
Querétaro 217/Medellín *(Colonia Roma)* ☎ 264 25 67
Los Rosales (B D Glm STV)
Calle Pensador Mexicano 11 *(Centro)*
Spartacùs (B D G STV) Fri-Sat 21-5 h
Avenida Cuaúhtemoc 8 *(Colonia Maravillas Ciudad Neza)*
☎ 763 80 28
Taller. El (AC B CC D f G lj MA SNU VS) 21-3 h Tue-Sun
Florencia 37A, ✉03740 *(Zona Rosa, Metro Insurgentes)*
☎ 533 49 70
Friendly staff, good music. Strip shows Wed/Thu. Admission
Tom`s (B D g lj) Tue-Sun.
Insurgentes sur 357, esq. Hermosillo
68 Versalles (B D G MA) Sun 20-? h
Versalles 68, Col. Juárez ☎ 566 74 81

RESTAURANTS

Vips del Angel (B F glm NG)
Reforma/Florencia *(Zona Rosa, Metro Insurgentes or Sevilla)*
☎ 546-1567

CINEMAS

28 de Marzo (g)
República de Colombia 88 *(Centro)*

SAUNAS/BATHS

Baños Finesterre (glm MA msg sb W) 6-21, Sun 6-16 h
Manuel Maria Contreras 11, Col. San Rafael ✉06140 *(Metro San Cosme)* ☎ 535 35 43
Recommended.
Baños Señorial (b G msg sa sb) Mon-Sat 6-20 h, Sun 6-15 h
Isabel la Católica 92/Calle Regina *(Centro-Metro Isabel la Católica)*
☎ 709 07 32
Baños Torrenueva (G MA msg sa sb) 6-21 h
Alvaro obregón No. 42, Col Roma ✉1500 *(Condesa. Metro Cuauhtémoc) Not very clean.*

FITNESSTUDIOS

Club San Francisco (g sa sol wh WO) 6.30-22, Sat 9-16 h
Rio Panuco 207, Colonia Cuauhtémoc *(Metro Chapultepec)*
☎ 511 47 06

GIFT & PRIDE SHOPS

Vaquero. El (Querelle) Tue-Sat 15-1 h
Insurgentes Sur 1231 *(Local Isla) Mags, videos, etc.*

TRAVEL & TRANSPORT

Viajes Bru 10-19 h
Kepler 92, D.F. 11590 *(near Anzures)* ☎ 545 25 76
Travel agent.

HOTELS

New Hotel Ambar (H)
San Jeronimo 105, Esq. Pino Suarez, Centro ✉06090 ☎ 522 01 05
Gay-friendly hotel.

GENERAL GROUPS

Alianza-Gay and Lesbian entrepreneurs
PO Box 6-962 ✉06602 Email: 74563.2046@compuserve.com.
Circulo Cultural Gay
AP 75-237, CP ✉06760
Colectivo Sol
Avenida Universidad 1900, Edificio 2, Departmento 402 *(PO Box 13-320, 03500)* ☎ 666 68 49 Fax: 606 72 16
Operates a non-profit gay archive.

HEALTH GROUPS

AMAC Bolivia 5, Centro ☎ 772 07 78 *or* ☎*639 9195.*
Ser Humano AC
Claveria 75

HELP WITH PROBLEMS

Alcohólicos Anónimos Gay
Culiacán apt. 122-Altos, Colonia Hipódromo, Condesa

RELIGIOUS GROUPS

MCC-ICM
PO Box 7-1423, 06700

CRUISING

-Alameda Parque (ayor), Avenida Juarez
-Chapultepec Bosque (Park), Castle Hill
-Zona Rosa (best at: Calle Genova, Calle Londres, Calle Niza, Avenida Insurgentes, Pasaje Jacaranda and Pasaje Toulouse)
-Metro Insurgentes
-Metro Chapultepec
-Metro Universidad
-Metro Sevilla
-Metro Balderas Hidalogo (near Alameda Park)
-Parque Hundido (ayor)

Monterrey - Nuevo Leon ☎ 8

BARS

Bongole (! AC B D GLM MA N S WE) Wed Fri Sat 22-3 h
Avenida Constitucion *(Down „Cenno de las Mitnas" mountain)*
Best in Northern Mexico, modern music, excellent environment.
Casablanca (B d g N OS TV) Fri Sat 20-2, Sun 19-1 h
Villa de Santiago N.L.
Charaos (B D G S) Mon-Sat
Zaragoza/Isaac Garza *(Centro)*
Wed strippers.
Suarez (AYOR B G STV) 0-24 h
Guerrero Nte. near Marco Polo Corner

CAFES

Cabaña. La (AC B F g) Mon-Sun 12-1 h
Matamoros *(between Cuauthemoc y Pino Suárez Ave.)*

DANCECLUBS

Vongole Disco (AC B CC D E G S YG) Wen, Fri, Sat 21-4 h.
Blvd. Pedreras #300 ☎ 336 03 35

NEWS STANDS

Revistería Johnny
Aramberri 807

GENERAL GROUPS

Abrazo
México 224, Colonia Azteca, San Nicolas de los Garza *44100*

SWIMMING

-Baños Del Norte (Mercado del Norte)

CRUISING

-Zona Rosa-Plaza Hidalgo (from 17-21 h)
-Sanborns Zona Rosa News Stand
-Galerias Monterrey Shopping Mall (Public Bath)
-Padre Mier Street/Juarez Ave
-Padre Mier Street/Cuauthemoc Ave
-Villa de Santiago (WE) (La Boca Lake area)
-Morales Street

Morelia - Michoacan ☎ 43

BARS

Canarios. Los (B D F s)
Prolongación de Avenida Madero

Eloines. Los (B D G STV SNU) Thu-Sun
Avenida Madero Ote. 5030

Jaula. La (B D G)
Ricon de los Compadres 90 *Drag shows.*

No Que No (B D G S TV) Thu-Sun
Avenida Campestre, en Rincon de los compadres ☎ 15 18 11

CRUISING

-Bus station
-Plaza de los Martires/Zocalo (AYOR YG)

Naucalpan de Juarez

CRUISING

-Plaza Satelite

Nuevo Laredo - Tamaulipas

BARS

Gambrinus (B g)
Avenida Ocampo y González

Gusano (B g)
Avenida Matamoros y Dr. Mier

Oaxaca - Oaxaca ☎ 951

BARS

Arcos. Los (B D GLM)
20 de Noviembre

Kaftan's (B d g)
c/o Hotel Misión de Los Angeles, Calzada Porfirio Diaz

DANCECLUBS

502 (B D g TV YG) 23-? h
Portirio Diaz 502

RESTAURANTS

Jardin. Del (B CC F glm OS) 7.30-0.30 h
Portal de Flores 10 *(on the Zocalo)* ☎ 620 92
Mexican specialties.

GENERAL GROUPS

Grupo Renacimiento
Victoria 504 Altos, Colonia Centro, CP 68000

CRUISING

-Alameda (across from cathedral)
-Zocalo (with its arcade)
-Mercado (AYOR) (Sat is market day)

Orizaba - Veracruz ☎ 272

BARS

Sky Drink (B D g) Wed-Sat
Madero Norte 1280

DANCECLUBS

Tukanes Bar (B D G S) 21-?
Madero Norte 1280
Wed/Fri no admission. Sat strippers.

CRUISING

-Plaza Principal

Patzcuaro - Michoacan ☎ 454

CAFES

Escudos. Los (b g OS)
Portal Hidalgo 73

CRUISING

-Mercado/market (Fri)
-Plaza Principal/Plaza Grande

Playa del Carmen ☎ 954

HOTELS

Aventura Mexicana Resort (AC B bf CC F H MA pi s wh) Ave 10y Calle 22, Playa del Carmen ☎ 318 76 Fax: 318 76
Comfortable gay-friendly resort.
Email: Hotelaventura@playadelcarmen.com

Global Cooling (AC B CC GLM H pi)
C/10 Norte bis # 20 Y 25 AV. ✉77710 ☎ 305 37

Puebla de Zaragoza - Puebla ☎ 22

BARS

Jaleo's (B D GLM S WE) Thu-Sat 23-5 h
Reforma Sur 3121

Keops (B D GLM SNU STV) Fri-Sun 22-05 h
14 Poniente No. 101 San Andreas Cholula *(12 km from Puebla)* ☎ 47 03 68

SAUNAS/BATHS

Club Las Termas (G msg sa sb sol wh) 7-19 h, closed Mon
Calle 5 de Mayo 2810 ✉72260 ☎ 32 95 62

CRUISING

-Zocalo/Plaza de la Constitution

Puerto Vallarta - Jalisco ☎ 322

BARS

Club Paco-Paco (B D G SNU VS) Tue-Sun 12-6, disco from 22, SNU 0.30 h
Ignacio L. Vallarta, 278-3 ✉48380 *(Col. Emiliano Zapata)*
☎ 218 99 *Drag and strip shows Fri/Sat.*
Lio's (B F glm) 10-2 h
264 Ignacio L. Vallarta/Lázaro Cárdenas ☎ 240 60
Paco's Ranch (B G S MA)
Calle Venustiana Carranza 239 *(Entrance through Paco Paco)*

CAFES

Marilyn's (B F GLM MA OS) 8.30-23 h
Isla Rio Cuale ☎ 221 48 Fax:221 48
Tito's (Blue Chairs) (B F G MA)
Los Muertos beach (south) *(At the gay beach)*

DANCECLUBS

Balcones. Los (! B D GLM) 21-3 h
Juárez 182/Libertad ☎ 246 71
Porqué No (AC B D glm) 17-4 h
Morelos 101 Plaza Rio ☎ 303 03
Bar upstairs, disco in the basement.

RESTAURANTS

Adobe Café (CC F glm) 18-23 h, closed Tue
Basilio Badillo 252 ☎ 267 20 or ☎ 319 25.
Mexican food.
Choco Banana (b F glm) 9-20 h
147 Calle Amapas
Fonda Viejo Vallarta (B F glm) 11-24 h
Morelos 484 *(upstairs)*
Mexican food, steaks, seafood.
Lunatics (B F glm) 18-23 h
Ignacio L. Vallarta 179 *(Col. Emiliano)* ☎ 261 42
Restaurant and bar.
Ristorante Romano (B CC F glm) 13-23 h, sat dinner only
☎ 207 25 or ☎ 204 94. *Italian food.*
Santos (B F glm MA) Mon closed
Francisco Rodriguez 136
International cuisine.

FITNESSTUDIOS

Gym-Spa 465 (b g msg sa wh WO)
Olas Altas 465 ☎ 256 32
Tito's Gym (b g sb WO) Mon-Fri 6-23, Sat 8-20, Sun 10-14 h
(Near flea market, at Cuale river) ☎ 222 77

TRAVEL & TRANSPORT

Amadeus Tour's Tours on Thu & Sun
Olas Altas 449 ✉48380 *(Col. Emiliano Zapata)* ☎ 328 15
Fax: 235 20 *Organizes gay excursions.*
P.V. Journeys Tours on Wed & Fri
☎ 476 27 *Organizes horseback rides.*
Rainbow Cruise Tours on Sat
☎ 260 59 *Organizes gay tours.*

HOTELS

Casa Dos Comales (g H)
Calle Aldama 274 ☎ 320 42
Gay-friendly B&B.
Casa Panoramica (bf G H pi)
Crratera a`Mismaloya ☎ 236 56
Paco Paco-Descanso del Sol (AC G H pi)
583 Pino Suarez ☎ 302 77 Fax: 267 67
All rooms with TV and phone.
Quinta Maria Cortez
132 Calle Sagitario ☎ 153 17
Rates US$ 75-240 (depending on room and season).
Vallarta Cora (AC B GLM H MA msg NU OS pi R)
Calle Pilitas 174 ☎ 328 15 Email: coragay@pvnet.mx
Villa Blanca (g H)
Amapas 349 *(Col. Emiliano Zapata)* ☎ 261 90
Near the gay beach. Rates on request.

SWIMMING

-Playa Los Muertos

CRUISING

-Beach opposite Océano Hotel
-Dorado Beach

Queretaro - Queretaro ☎ 42

CRUISING

-Alameda (AYOR)
-Zocalo/Plaza Obregon/Plaza de la Constitución (AYOR)

Reynosa - Tamaulipas ☎ 89

CRUISING

-Plaza opposite America Hotel (19-22 h)

Saltillo - Coahuila ☎ 84

CRUISING

-Parque Alameda
-Plaza de Armes
-Transportes del Norte (bus depot)

San Luis Potosi - San Luis Potosi ☎ 48

BARS

Sheik (B D G STV) Fri-Sun. Show Fri/Sat.
Prolongación Zacatecas 347 *(Fracc. San Juan)* ☎ 12 74 57

Tampico - Tamaulipas ☎ 12

BARS

Astorga (B G)
Plaza *(near post-office)*
Black Noire (B d g)
Madero *20 minutes from Tampico by taxi.*
Clandestin (B D G SNU) Thu-Sat 21-? h.
Avenida Hildalgo y Violetas 3400 *(Colonia Las Flores)*
Queens (B D G STV)
(from the harbor the first street to the right after 100 m)

CRUISING

-Liberty Plaza -Plaza de Armas

Tijuana - Baja California Norte ☎ 66

GAY INFO

Gay & Lesbian Info Line
☎ 88 02 67

BARS

Bar D.F. (B GLM)
Plaza Santa Cecilia *(near Calle Tercera)*
Not especially recommended.

Noa Noa (B D GLM STV) 22-? h
Calle 1/Avenida D 150 *(2 blocks east of avenida Revolución)* ☎ 86 22 07
Ranchero Bar (! B G YG) 13-3 h
Plaza Santa Cecilia *(Near Calle Primera)*
Taurino. El (B G MA) 0-24 h
189 Avenida Niños Heroes *(Zona Norte between 1st Street and Coahuila)* ☎ 85 24 78
Terraza 9 (B G S TV) Thu-Sun
Calle 5a *(West of Revolución)*

DANCECLUBS

Equipales. Los (B D g S TV) Mon-Sun
Calle 7 2024/Avenida Revolución *(Zona Centro)* ☎ 88 30 06
Mike's Disco (B D G S TV)
Avenida Revolución/Calle 6 *Drag and strip shows.*

GENERAL GROUPS

Y Que!
PO Box 904 ☎ 80 99 63

RELIGIOUS GROUPS

ICM Tijuana
MCC of Tijuana services Sun 17 h at Calle Tercera 1810-11 (P America).

SWIMMING

-Rosarita Beach, B.C.N. (half an hour south of Tijuana)
-along the coast from Playas Tijuana to Punta Bandera

CRUISING

-Near Noa Noa & El Taurino
-Park at Amerika parking (in heart of Zona Norte at 1981 Calle 3a, 3rd Street)
-Revolución (from 2nd to 8th Street)
-4th Street (from Constitución across Revolución to Maderos)
-7th Street (from Revolución to Maderos)
-Zona del Rio
-Plaza Santa Cecilia (AYOR) (by night)
-Plaza Rio Shopping Centre (WE YG) (area near central arcade cafeteria)

Tlaquepaque - Jalisco ☎ 3

HOTELS

Casa Domingo (B bf E F H MA NG OS)
Calle Morelos 288 ☎ 657 38 46 Fax: 657 38 46
Tlaquepaque is an „outskirt" of Guadalajara.

BARS

Bar El Conde (B F g)
Pasaje Curi Norte 201 E
Bar El Jardín (B GLM)
Avenida Hidalgo Oeste 100 D
Cafe del Rey (B F NG)
Portal 20 de Noviembre

CRUISING

-Mercado (Fri)
-Zocalo/Plaza de Los Martires

Tonalá - Chiapas

GENERAL GROUPS

Grupo Arcoiris
Calle 16 de Septiembre/Joaquin M. Gutierrez 157

Torreón - Coahuila ☎ 17

BARS

Balmori Club (B g)
Valdéz Carrillo/Allende
Bobby Bar (B GLM)
Ramos Arispe 76 Sur
El Z 8 (B f G)
Corona Norte 28/Allende

Tuxpan - Veracruz ☎ 783

CRUISING

-Avenida Juárez (near hotels)

Tuxtla Guiterrez - Chiapas ☎ 961

BARS

Latin Lover (B D GLM)
Oriente 541B *(4a Norte)*
Sandy's Bar (B GLM TV)
9a Avenida Sur/Periférico

CRUISING

-Plaza Belisario Dominguez

Veracruz - Veracruz ☎ 29

BARS

Acuario's (B F GLM)
Canales/Revolución
Cid. El (B F GLM S)
Américo Vespucio 178 *(opposite Estadio Pirata Fuente)*
Hip-Pop-Potamus (B GLM STV WE)
Fracc. Costa Verde *(Centro)*

DANCECLUBS

Club Mediterraneo (B D) Thu-Sat
Avenida Veracruz 927 ☎ 24 01 47
Deeper (B D G SNU) Thu-Sat
Idaza 1005 *(between Victoria and Revillagigedo)* ☎ 35 02 65

Villahermosa - Tabasco ☎ 93

CRUISING

-Central Camionera de Primera (A.D.O. Bus Station)
-Plaza Hidalgo (opposite cathedral)
-Plaza de Armas

Zacatecas - Zacatecas ☎ 492

BARS

El Elefante (B D G)
Calle Parra 255

CRUISING

-Plaza Hidalgo
-Plaza de las Armas

Zihuatanejo/Ixtapa - Guerrero ☎ 753

HOTELS

Casita. La (B CC G H MG msg OS sol) Bar 18-24 h
Paseo Escenica ✉40880 *(Camino a playa La Ropa S/N-in front of rest. Kontiki)* ☎ 445 10 Fax: 445 10
All rooms with terrace and sea view. Room US$ 45 (low-season), US$ 55 (high-season).

Monaco

Western Europe

Initials: MC

Time: GMT +1

☎ Country Code / Access Code: 377 (no area codes) / 00

Language: French; „Monegasco"

Area: 1.95 km^2 / 0.75 sq mi.

Currency: 1 French Franc (FF) = 100 Centimes

Population: 32,000

Religions: 95% Roman Catholic

Climate: Mediterranean climate. Winters are mild and wet, summers hot and dry.

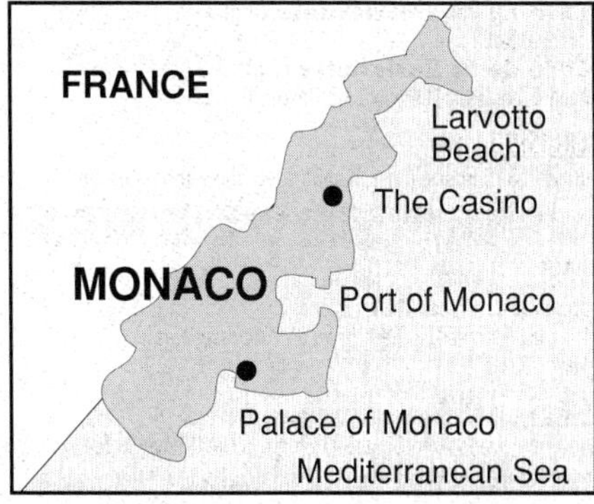

Monte Carlo

CRUISING

Monte Carlo Country Club (at end of parking lot under tennis courts, take path down the stairs, when going upstairs on the other side bushes on right)

Morocco

Al-Magreb

Northwestern Africa

Initials: MA

Time: GMT

☎ Country Code / Access Code: 212 / 00 (wait for tone)

Language: Arabic, Berber Dialects,French

Area: 446,550 km^2 / 172,413 sq mi.

Currency: 1 Dirham (DH) = 100 Centimes

Population: 29,114,500

Capital: Rabat

Religions: 98% Sunnite Moslem (state religion)

Climate: Mediterranean climate, becoming more extreme in the interior.

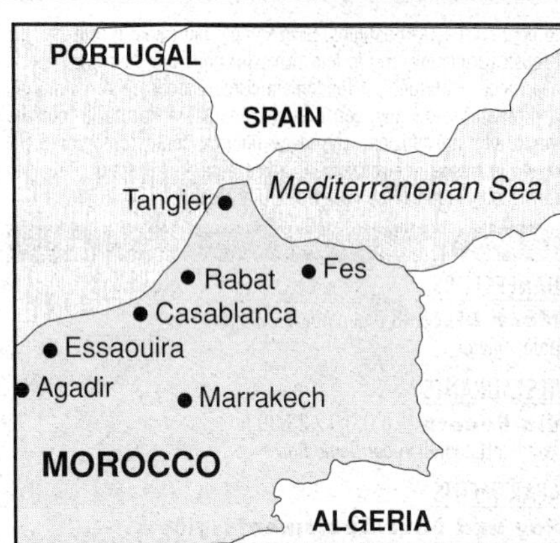

● Homosexual acts are reportedly illegal and punishable under Article 489 of the penal code with a penalty of 6 months to 3 years imprisonment and a fine of 120 to 1,200 dirhams. It is becoming increasingly apparent that affluent Western tourists and their demands are not always welcome. Islamic fundamentalists have also become noticeably more aggressive towards gays in recent years; no doubt due in some degree to prostitution, which is rigorously combatted. According to our information, Agadir and Marrakech are (especially for gays after nightfall) downright dangerous!

✱ Homosexualität ist dem Vernehmen nach illegal und wird gemäß Artikel 489 des Strafgesetzes mit 6 Monaten bis 3 Jahren Haft und einer Geldbuße von 120 bis 1200 Dirhams bestraft. Die Abneigung gegen den westlichen Wohlstandstourismus und seine manchmal peinlichen Auswüchse vergrößert sich zunehmend. Auch ist der fundamentalistische Islam in den vergangenen Jahren immer feindseliger gegen Schwule vorgegangen. Dazu trug offensichtlich auch die enorme Prostitution bei.
In Agadir am Atlantik kann man allerdings zu jeder Jahreszeit einen ruhigen Erholungsurlaub verbringen.

▲ Au Maroc, l'homosexualité est un délit (article 489 du code pénal). On s'expose à des peines de prison allant de 6 mois à 3 ans maximum et à des amendes de 120 à 1.200 dirhams. Le tourisme à l'occidentale (et ses conséquences souvent fâcheuses) est de plus en plus décrié. Ces derniers temps, les fondamentalistes de l'Islam prennent position de plus en plus durement contre les homosexuels et utilisent les méfaits de la prostitution que l'on combat, par ailleurs, assez vigoureusement, pour discréditer l'homosexualité. On nous a rapporté qu'à Agadir et Marrakech, les touristes gays, surtout, feraient mieux de ne pas sortir après la tombée de la nuit.

☆ La homosexualidad es ilegal y es perseguida según el artículo 489 del Código Penal con una sentencia a prisión desde 6 meses hasta 3 años y una multa de 120 a 1200 dinares. Se nota cada vez más, que los turistas de los paises ricos de Occidente y sus demandas no son siempre bienvenidas. En los últimos años ha incrementado la agresión de los fundamentalistas islámicos contra los gays, sobre todo a causa de la prostitución proliferante, que está perseguida rigurosamente. Segun nuestras informaciones las ciudades de Agadir y Marrakesch son para turistas (especialmente en la oscuridad y en solitario) no son recomendables, en absoluto.

❖ L'omosessualità è illegale ed è punita dal paragrafo 489 del codice penale con la prigione da sei mesi a tre anni e una multa da 120 a 1,000 dirhams. Si fa sempre più chiaro il concetto che i turisti occidentali, con le loro richieste, non sono benvenuti. Si sa che, negli ultimi anni, il fondamentalismo islamico è diventato più aggressivo verso i gay; senza dubbio, questo è dovuto, in qualche modo, alla prostituzione che viene rigorosamente combattuta. Secondo le nostre informazioni Agadir e Marrakesch sono città poco consigliabili ai turisti (soprattutto se gay e soli).

Agadir ☎ 08

DANCECLUBS

Moon Disco (B D glm MA r) 22-5 h
Hotel Agador

RESTAURANTS

Via Veneta (F g OS) 12-23.30 h
Avenida Hassan II *(near Dome Bar)*

APARTMENTS

Ray and Dave Apartments (g H)
PO Box 12 95, Tamraght
18 km from Agadir. Car rental adviced. Superb location. Gay owned.

SWIMMING

-Inezgane (8 km from Agadir; beach at mouth of River Sousse; main beach between P.L.M. Hotel Dunes d'Or and la Douche; municipal showers)
-Tarhazoute (NG) (go with the green busses 12 or 14 from Avenue Mohammed to the north. You will reach a quiet beach with camping area)

CRUISING

-in front of all the cinemas (afternoons are best)
-along Avenue Hassan II (late evening)

Asilah ☎ 09

CRUISING

-There is a well-known market every Sunday in a village about 3 km from the coast where many of the young men will make it very clear that they are ready, willing and able.

Casablanca ☎ 02

BARS

Café de France (B g) Rue P.
Sorbier *(across the square from Hotel Casablanca)* ☎ 236 79

SWIMMING

-Plage Ain Diab

CRUISING

-Souterrain/Subway (YG) (Place Mohamed V)

El Jadida ☎ 03

HEALTH GROUPS

Centre de Santé mornings

CRUISING

-The three principal cafés facing the Municipal Theatre in Place Mohamed V
-Beach 2 km north of the Hotel Maharba
-Street from Place Mohammed V to Hotel Bruxelles
-Beach road to Houzia Beach (about 3 to 4 km north from El Jadida)

Essaouira ☎ 04

RESTAURANTS

Minzah. El (A B F NG) 8-23 h
3 Avenue Oqba Ibn Nafia *(near Jardins du Mechouar)* ☎ 47 23 08
Fish specialities.

HEALTH GROUPS

Centre de Sante mornings

CRUISING

-Bus Station, Place Hassan II
-The Beach (dunes to the south of the bay)

Fes ☎ 06

BARS

Café de Florence (B F g)
Avenue Hassan II
Café de la Renaissance (B g)
Avenue Mohamed V
Café de la Resistance (B g)
Avenue des Etats-Unis/Avenue Hassan II

CRUISING

-Boulevard Gardens in the Medina (near the Bartha Museum)

Marrakech ☎ 04

BARS

Renaissance Bar (B g)
Avenue Mohamed V *(near Hotel les Ambassadeurs)*
Very cruisy.

CAFES

Any cafe overlooking Square El F'naa. Sit and have coffee, you will soon be approached.

RESTAURANTS

Poële d'or. La (B F NG) 12-15, 19.30-23.30 h
Rue Allal Ben Ahmed *(Centre Ville Europeenne)* ☎ 44 81 20
French cuisine.

SWIMMING

-Douche Medina (200 meters from Grand Place)

CRUISING

-Avenue Mohamed V
-Place Jemma El Fnaa
-Piscine Municipale (behind Hotel Palais Badia)
-Piscine de la Koutoubia

Rabat ☎ 01

BARS

Florida Bar (B g)
Avenue Al'lal ben Abdul'lah

CRUISING

-Sidi Moussa Beach (by day)

Tangier/Tanger ☎ 09

BARS

Balima Hotel Bar (B g H r)
12 Rue Magellan ☎ 393 46
Best between 21-1 h. Rooms by the hour in the same house.

BBC (B F GLM)
On the beach.
Café Pilo (B NG) Rue de Fés
Crowded around dawn.

SWIMMING

-Atlas Beach
-Coco Beach
-Mustapha Beach Club
-Neptuno
-In front of Café Sherazade
-In front of Soleil Lounge

CRUISING

-All the cafés in the Petit Socco, a small, lopsided square in the Medina, particularly the Café Central. The whole length of the sea front (Avenue d'Espagne and Avenue des F.A.R.). Safe enough by day but has become a very dangerous area by night and should be avoided (muggings). It is also advisable not to visit the Medina area unaccompanied at night.
-Bazaar Kinitra
-Rue du Mexique (especially the bottom part, 19-? h)

Tetouan ☎ 09

CRUISING

-Place Hassan II (in front of Palace of the Khalifa)

Tiznit ☎ 08

CRUISING

-Main Square (in the evening)

Zagora

CRUISING

-Around Grand Hotel (in the evening)

Namibia

Southwest Africa
Initials: NAM
Time: GMT +2
☎ Country Code / Access Code: 264 / 09
Language: English. Afrikaans, German
Area: 823,144 km² / 317,816 sq mi.
Currency: 1 Namibia-Dollar (N$) = 100 Cents
Population: 1,653,000
Capital: Windhoek
Religions: 90% Christian
Climate: Desert climate that is hot and dry. Rainfall is sparse and erratic.

● Under South African »Common Law«, homosexuality was considered a crime. This law has not been brought to bear since the 1960's, however, and no more recent prosecutions are known of, particularly since independence. Nevertheless, homosexuality in general is probably considered a punishable offence according to the »Sexual Offences Act«. (German Embassy, Windhuk)

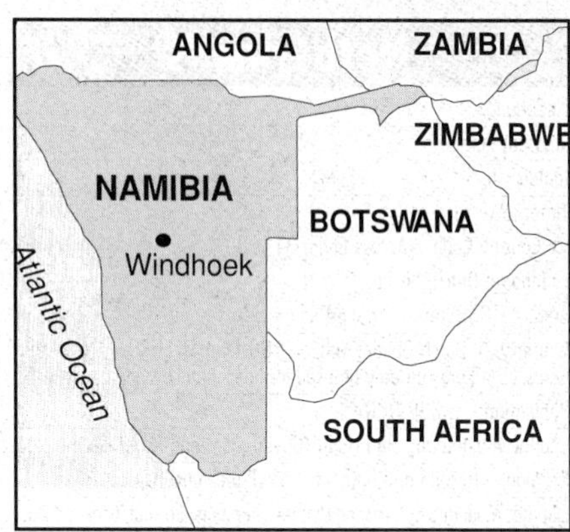

✱ Momentan liegen uns keine genauen Informationen vor, inwiefern sich die Liberlisierung der südafrikanischen Gesetzgebung bezüglich Homosexualität auch positiv auf Namibia auswirkt. Das gesellschaftliche Klima ist in Namibia für Schwule auf jeden Fall nicht so liberal wie im Nachbarland. So ließ es sich der Präsident Namibias Sam Nujoma nicht nehmen, Homosexuelle als „weiße Perverse" zu beschimpfen.

▲ Selon la Common Law sud-africaine, l'homosexualité est considérée comme un délit. Les derniers procès antihomos remontent aux années 60. Depuis l'indépendance du pays, on fiche la paix aux homosexuels, mais, d'un autre côté, l'homosexualité relève toujours des dispositions du „Sexual Offences Act" et est donc réprimée. (Ambassade d'Allemagne, Windhuk).

☆ En la Common Law sudafricana la homosexualidad ha sido tratada como un delito. Sin embargo las últimas penas datan de los años 60, en la joven historia de esta nación (sobre todo desde su independencia) no son conocidas sentencias por comportamiento homosexual. La homosexualidad es tratada bajo las determinaciones del Sexual Offences Act y por ende también penada, (Embajada Alemana, Windhuk).

❖ Secondo le *Common Law* sudafricane l'omosessualità è un crimine. Le ultime condanne però risalgono agli anni '60, e non ne sono conosciut alcune negli ultimi anni. In ogni caso l'omosessualità è punibile dal „Sexual Offences Act". (Ambasciata tedesca, Windhuk).

NATIONAL GROUPS

Rainbow Project (TRP) 1st Wed 18 h
at 84, Burg Street, Windhoek, PO Box 26 122,
Email: trp@iafrica.com.na

Windhoek ☎ 61

BARS

Casablanca Bar (B D F Glm OS YG) 22-4 h
Nelson Mandela Drive/Sam Nujoma Drive

CRUISING

-in front of Kalahari Sands Hotel (bus station)

Netherlands

Nederland

Western Europe

Initials: NL

Time: GMT +1

☎ Country Code / Access Code: 31 / 00

Language: Dutch, Frisian

Area: 41,864 km² / 16,164 sq mi.

Currency: 1 Dutch Guilder (hfl) = 100 Cent. 1 EURO = 100 EURO Cents (The Euro can only be used in the clearance system)

Population: 15,739,000

Capital: Amsterdam, Den Haag (Government and Royal Residence)

Religions: 36% Roman Catholic, 26% Protestant

Climate: Moderate and marine climate. Summers are cool, winters mild.

Important gay cities: Amsterdam, Rotterdam, Den Haag

● The Netherlands is one of the most liberal countries in the world regarding equal rights for homosexuals and lesbians. The age of consent is 16. There are strict rules regarding younger men, especially if a dependant relationship is exploited by an older man. Although the Netherlands does not recognise „gay marriages", „registered partnerships" (which are legally binding) do exist. Currently, ways are being considered in introducing 'alternative lifestyles'. New anti-discrimination laws were passed in 1992. If violated, the offenders are subject to fines or imprisonment.

Liberality and respect for human rights are traditional in the Netherlands. A situation to which Amsterdam's COC has also contributed. It has built up a network of groups and meeting points in all Dutch cities and in may smaller towns. But the COC is just one part of the influential and well-developed gay and lesbian movement. There are many gay associations representing particular religious, ethnic, professional, project-oriented and party-political interests. These range from conservative to communist groups, but all come together once a year to form the „Roze Front" and celebrate Gay and Lesbian Pride Week. There is often nevertheless an enormous difference between urban and rural attitudes and gay men living in the Dutch countryside have to cope with the same problems as their counterparts throughout Europe.

✱ Die Niederlande sind heute eines der fortschrittlichsten Länder, was die Gleichstellung von Schwulen und Lesben in der Gesellschaft angeht. Für jüngere Männer gelten strikte Schutzbestimmungen, vor allem wenn ein Älterer eine Abhängigkeitssituation ausnutzt. Zwar kennen die Niederlande noch keine „schwule Ehe", doch es gibt „registrierte Partnerschaften" (ein rechtsverbindlicher Vertrag). Zur Zeit wird geprüft, generell alternative Lebensformen zur Ehe zu registrieren. Seit 1992 bestehen zusätzlich Antidiskriminierungsbestimmungen, die bei Zuwiderhandlung zu empfindlichen Gefängnisstrafen oder Geldbußen führen können.

Liberalität und Achtung der Menschenrechte haben in den Niederlanden Tradition. Einer der Pfeiler ist das Amsterdamer COC. Es unterhält heute Arbeitsgruppen und Geselligkeitszentren in allen größeren und vielen kleineren Städten des Landes. Doch nicht nur das COC macht die entfaltete und einflußreiche Schwulen- und Lesbenbewegung aus; daneben existieren viele religiöse, ethnische, berufsbezogene, projektorientierte und parteipolitische Homosexuellengruppen: von konservativ bis kommunistisch. Sie alle schließen sich einmal jährlich in der „2Roze Front" zusammen, um die „Gay and Lesbian Pride Week" zu feiern. Doch auch in den Niederlande sollte man nicht vergessen, daß es ein zum Teil enormes Gefälle zwischen den Großstädten und dem Land gibt. Die schwulen Holländer auf dem Land plagen die gleichen Probleme wie ihre Geschlechtsgenossen in ganz Europa.

▲ Les Pays-Bas sont aujourd'hui un des pays les plus homophiles du monde. L'égalité des droits des gays et des lesbiennes dans la société n'est pas un mythe. En Hollande, la majorité sexuelle est fixée à 16 ans, et les jeunes garçons sont protégés par la loi, tout particulièrement si un homme plus âgé fait jouer sa situation d'adulte pour créer une situation de dépendance. Les gays hollandais ne peuvent, certes, pas encore se marier, mais vivre en „concubinage enregistré", une sorte de contrat d'union civile. Actuellement, on est en train d'étudier la possibilité de traiter les „formes de vie alternatives" de la même façon que le mariage. Depuis 1992, toute personne dont le comportement porte atteinte à la sexualité d'autrui peut être traduite en justice. Les contrevenants se voient infligés de lourdes amendes ou peines de prison.

Aux Pays-Bas, la liberté et les droits de l'Homme sont bien ancrés dans la société. Le COC d'Amsterdam en est un des piliers. Il est présent dans tout le pays, jusque dans les petites villes de province. Le COC n'est pas le seul à propager la bonne parole. Il y a en Hollande un large éventail de groupes gays religieux, ethniques, professionnels ou encore affiliés aux divers partis politiques, des conservateurs aux communistes. Une fois par an, tout ce petit monde se retrouve sous la bannière du „Roze Front", pour descendre dans la rue à l'occasion de la „Gay and Lesbian Pride Week". Cependant, il existe aussi en Hollande une différence de taille entre les attitudes urbaines et rurales, et les homosexuels vivant dans les régions plus reculées du pays sont confrontés aux mêmes problèmes discriminatoires que l'on trouve dans d'autres pays d'Europe.

☆ Los Países Bajos son considerados hoy en día uno de los países más avanzados en materia de igualdad de derechos para gays y lesbianas. La edad de consentimiento es de 16 años. Existen reglamentaciones especiales para proteger a jovenes, sobre todo en el caso de que una persona mayor se aproveche de una situación de dependencia. Los Países Bajos aún no conocen el matrimonio entre homosexuales, pero existe un «registro de noviazgo» (un contrato legal). Por el momento se está probando una alternativa general a la forma de vida en matrimonio. Desde 1992 existen leyes de antidiscriminación que en caso de contravención podrían ser penadas con cárcel o multas.

La libertad y el respeto a los derechos humanos tienen gran tradición en los Paises Bajos. Una de las columnas principales lo es la

Amsterdamer COC. Esta organización tiene grupos de trabajo y centros sociales en las ciudades grandes y pequeñas del país. Pero no solamente la COC influye en el movimiento lesbiano y gay del país; existen también gran cantidad de grupos religiosos étnicos, profesionales, orientados a determinados proyectos así como grupos políticos, que se mueven desde el campo conservativo hasta el comunista. Todos estos grupos se reunen una vez por año en el llamado «Frente Rosa» para celebrar el «Gay and Lesbian Pride Week». No se debe olvidar que también en Los Países Bajos hay una gran diferencia entre las grandes ciudades y las zonas rurales. Los homosexuales holandeses de las zonas rurales tienen por lo general los mismos problemas que sus semejantes en el resto de Europa.

I Paesi Bassi sono oggi uno dei paesi più progrediti circa l'uguaglianza dei gay e delle lesbiche nella società. L'età legale per dei rapporti sessuali è di 16 anni. Per i ragazzi più giovani sono in vigore delle leggi più rigorose, soprattutto quando un uomo più anziano approfitta di un rapporto di dipendenza per ottenere dei favori sessuali. A dire il vero neppure i Paesi Bassi conoscono „il matrimonio gay" benché esistano delle „relazioni registrate" con un contratto giuridico. Attualmente vengono esaminati dei contratti alternativi al matrimonio. Dal 1992 esistono ulteriori leggi antidiscriminatorie la cui trasgressione può condurre a pene carcerarie o ad ammende.
La liberalità e l'osservanza dei diritti dell'uomo sono in Olanda una tradizione: uno dei pilastri è il COC di Amsterdam, che sovvenziona gruppi di lavoro e centri d'incontro in tutte le grandi e in molte piccole città del paese. Tuttavia il COC non è il solo organo di coordinamento dello sviluppato ed influente movimento gay: parallelamente esistono numerosi gruppi omosessuali saldati da interessi di matrice religiosa, etnica, professionale e politica (dai conservatori ai comunisti). Tutti questi gruppi si uniscono una volta all'anno nel „fronte rosa", per festeggiare la „gay and lesbian week". Purtroppo non bisogna dimenticare che anche nei Paesi Bassi esiste un divario, talvolta enorme, tra metropoli e campagna. I gay olandesi di provincia vivono sotto la stessa pressione che opprime tutta Europa.

NATIONAL GAY INFO

Ami en Marcel
PB 427 ✉3300 AK Dordrecht
Gay porno magazine.

Binky
Herengracht 24a ✉2511 EJ Den Haag
Bi-monthly publication with 60 pages, hfl. 6.95. Macho magazine with photographies, stories and personal ads.

Centurion
PB 93506 ✉2509 AM Den Haag
S/M magazine; 4 times a year. 100 pages with photographies and personal ads. hfl 9.95.

Circuit (G. Leather)
Diepenbrockstraat 14 ✉6044 SH Roermond
Monthly magazine of Rurals Motorclub. Some English texts.

COC Headoffice 9-16 h
PB 3836 ✉1001 AP Amsterdam *(Visiting address: Rozenstraat 8, Tram 13/17/14/20-Westermarkt)* ☎ 020/623 45 96
☎ 020/620 75 41 (deaf people) Fax: 020/626 77 95
Homepage: http://www.coc.nl
Largest gay and lesbian organisation in the Netherlands „for the integration of homosexuality". Founded in 1946, publisher of XL, Expreszo, head office of local COC organisations around the country. Tries to influence the political debate in the Netherlands. Wide range of activities including help for HIV+, mentally retarded, young, deaf and old gays among others.

Culture and Camp
Gerard Doustraat 160 F ✉1073 VZAmsterdam
☎ 020/679 91 88
Lifestyle magazine for free on 30 pages.

David Boy (voor de leerboys) en Boy Smile
PB 3061 ✉3003 AB Rotterdam
Lots of information about the Rotterdam scene.

Drummer
RoB, Weteringschans 253 ✉1017 XJ Amsterdam
☎ 020/625 46 86 Fax: 020/627 32 20
The world's leading fetish magazine for gay males.

Expreszo 9-16 h
c/o COC Headoffice, PO Box 3836 ✉1001 AP Amsterdam
☎ 020/623 45 96 Fax: 020/626 77 95
Homepage: http://www.expreszo.nl
Bimonthly 30 pages magazine aimed at young gays and lesbians (Hfl 7,50).

Freshmen (G) Mon-Thu 8.30-17, Fri -12.30 h
Hoofdstraat 64-66 ✉5683 AB Amsterdam ☎ 499/39 10 00
Fax: 499/39 06 06
Bimonthly gay erotic magazine published in co-operation with Bruno Gmünder Verlag. 68 pages in full color.

Gay Garden Club
PB 15672 ✉1001 ND Amsterdam ☎ 020/688 12 43
Fax: 020/688 12 43
Homepage: http://www.gayplanet.nl/gaygardenclub

Gay Krant. De
c/o Best Publishing Group, PB 10 ✉5680 AA Best
☎ 0499/39 10 00 Fax: 37 26 38 E-Mail: gaykrant@gayworld.nl
Homepage: http://www.gayworld.nl./gaykrant
Biweekly publication; price: hfl 4.95. Approx. 40 pages, gay information newspaper with reports about all areas of gay life: society, politics, arts, culture, entertainment. Also with an small English summary. Focuses on gay life in the Netherlands.

Gay News
PB 76609 ✉1070 HE Amsterdam ☎ 020/679 15 56
Fax: 020/675 38 61
Completely English-Dutch newspaper with reports and reviews from all aspects of gay life. Large cultural section. Free publication, complete listing of gay places in the Netherlands.

Homodok/Lesbisch Archief Amsterdam
(GLM) Mon-Fri 10-16 h
Nieuwpoortkade 2a ✉1055 RX *(Near Sloterdijk sation, Bus 15/18/21, Tram 10/12/14)* ☎ 020/606 07 12
Fax: 020/606 07 13 E-Mail: info@homodok-laa.nl Homepage: http://www.homodok-laa.nl

HOMologie PB 16584 ✉1001 RB Amsterdam
Bimonthly publication. hfl 6.95. Cultural magazine for emancipation of lesbians and gays.

Landelijk Netwerk voor Biseksualiteit LN-Bi
PB 75087 ✉1070 AB Amsterdam ☎ 077/354 97 76

MaGAYzine
c/o Best Publishing Group, PB 10 ✉5680 AA Best
☎ 0499/39 10 00 Fax: 0499/39 06 03
Bimonthly publication with pin up models for Hfl 15.

Regenbooggids (GLM) Mon-Thu 8.30-17, Fri -12.30 h
Hoofdstraat 64-66 ✉5683 AG Best ☎ 0499/39 10 00
Fax: 0499/39 06 03
Annual gay yellow pages for the Netherlands and Belgium.

Roze Gebaar
PB 15511 ✉1001 NA Amsterdam Fax: 020/470 56 31
Gay and lesbian deaf group.

Sjalhomo
PB 2536 ✉1000 CM Amsterdam ☎ 020/683 50 73
☎ 020/690 09 79
Jewish gay organization with some local branches.

Squeeze
PB 8671 ✉3009 AR Rotterdam ☎ 010/452 50 82
Fax: 010/452 47 86
Bimonthly gay glossy with lots of fashion, interviews, beauty and gay items.

Stichting Homo-Monument
Westerstraat 16 ✉1015 MJ Amsterdam *(Monument location: On Westermarkt, near Anne Frank House and Western Church, Tram 1/2/5/13/17/20)* ☎ 020/626 71 65
The monument for gays and lesbians was erected in 1987 by the whole Dutch gay community. Originally aimed to be a place for remembrance and for warning, it is also nowadays a place for mourning about deceased friends, a place to meet, and a symbolic place for tourists to express their belonging to the gay community.

XL 9-16 h
PB 3836 ✉1001 AP Amsterdam *(Visiting address: Rozenstraat 8, Tram 13/17/14/20-Westermarkt)* ☎ 020/623 45 96
Fax: 020/626 77 95
Bimonthly magazine featuring reports and reviews about all relevant topics of gay and lesbian life. Very interesting international reports. Informations about all COC activities (member groups are listed). Approx. 48 pages (Hfl 6,95).

NATIONAL HELPLINES

Gay and Lesbian Switchboard (GLM) 10-22 h
PB 11573 ✉1001 GN Amsterdam ☎ 020/623 65 65
☎ 020/422 65 65 (deaf people)
Homepage: http://www.switchboard.nl
Information and Helpline. Teletext page 447.

NATIONAL PUBLISHERS

Desmodus International BV
(LJ) Weteringschans 253 ✉1017 XJ Amsterdam
☎ 020/639 30 23 Fax: 020/627 32 20
Write to PO Box 16602, 1001 RC Amsterdam. Publishes Drummer Magazine and Drummer Tough Customers. Own videolabel, wholesale of RoB products and other US magazines.

NATIONAL COMPANIES

Delta Boek
PB 92 ✉2980 AB Ridderkerk
Books.

Easy Mail (CC G)
PB 76613 ✉1070 HE Amsterdam

Europost (G)
PB 1019 ✉1000 BA Amsterdam

Expectations Warmoesstraat 32 ✉1012 JE Amsterdam
Leather and rubber.

Gay Safe c/o Central Middelen Depot
PB 64 ✉2501 CB Den Haag ☎ 070/346 56 00
Condoms.

Gayway.nl Mail Order
PB 11186 ✉2301 ED Leiden ☎ 071/576 92 23
Fax: 071/572 19 03 Homepage: http://www.gayway.nl
Mail order company for gays. Sell almost anything from underwear to poppers.

Intermale
Spuistraat 251 ✉1012 VR Amsterdam
☛ *Bookshops (A'dam).*

P+E Postorders (G)
PB 6102 ✉3002 AC Rotterdam ☎ 010/474 83 60
Leather, rubber and films.

SandMark (G LJ)
PB 76561 ✉1070 HD Amsterdam ☎ 020/777 81 44
S/M articles and publications. Mail order from Netherlands.

Stichting Safe Service
PB 3836 ✉1001 AP Amsterdam ☎ 020/623 37 94
Fax: 020/624 96 91 Homepage: www.coc.nl/safeservice.htm
Condoms and lubricants.

Video Post Service (VIPS)
PB 583 ✉2700 AN Apeldoorn ☎ 079/342 62 16
Mail order.

Video 63 (G VS) 11-21 Sat -18 Sun 13-15 h
PB 3204 ✉7345 ZG Amsterdam ☎ 055/312 19 48
Video Mail-order.

Vrolijk Paleisstraat 135 ✉1012 ZL Amsterdam
☎ 020/623 51 42 Fax: 020/638 38 07

NATIONAL GROUPS

Castigatio (GLM LJ)
Oude Holterweg 18 ✉7416 WG Deventer ☎ 0570/62 93 81
Spanking Club.

Empowerment Lifestyle Services
Vinkenstraat 166a ✉1013 JV Amsterdam ☎ 653/862 958
Fax: 020/421 32 06 E-Mail: empower@xs4all.nl
Homepage: http://www.xs4all.nl/~empower
Advisors and consultants for gay and lesbian emancipation on Dutch and European levels.

Stichting De Kringen Kanaalweg 21 ✉3526 KL Utrecht
☎ 030/288 86 36
Organises conversation groups for gays and lesbians.

Stichting Landelijk Overleg Wergroepen Ouders van Homoseksuele Kinderen (SLOW) (GLM)
PB 152 ✉6970 AD Brummen ☎ 0575/56 48 58
Group dealing with the question of gays/lesbians and children.

VSSM-Vereniging Studiegroep Sado-Masochisme (g LJ)
PB 3570 ✉1001 AJ Amsterdam ☎ 592/40 71 63
E-Mail: info@vssm.nl Homepage: http://www.vssm.nl
S/M group and S/M-party organizer in all the country. Also publishes a magazine „Kerfstok" in Dutch on themes relative to S/M practices, as well as some brochures and books. Call or visit the website for details.

HEALTH GROUPS

SAD-Schorerstichting Mon-Fri 9-17 h
P.C. Hooftstraat 5 ✉1071 BL Amsterdam *(tram 2/5)*
☎ 020/662 42 06 Fax: 020/664 60 69
E-Mail: info@sadschorer.nl Homepage: http://www.sadschorer.nl
Counselling (HIV), prevention and education for gays and lesbians.

COUNTRY CRUISING

Route A1 (E8)
-Hengelo-Amersfoort-Amsterdam 28.9 km (Section betweeen Baarn and Huizen. De Witte Bergen. Take the exit for Soest at 28.9 km, but continue on the parallel road towards Amsterdam, until you see the sign for the motel-restaurant, turn left at top of exit road, park at the end of the short road. Walk through the area of trees and sand on the left at the end of the road.)
-21.6 km (Section near Naarden. [P] without name. In cars and adjacent bushes, mainly at night, but some daytime possibilities.)
-Amsterdam-Amersfoort-Hengelo 20.6 km ([P] without name. Section near Naarden. In cars and bushes, day and evening. Not very busy.)
-27.8 km (Section between Huizen and Baarn. De Witte Bergen. Take the exit for the motel-restaurant, turn left of top of exit road, drive over the bridge crossing the motorway, park at the end of the short road. Walk through the area of trees and sand on the left at the end of the road.)

Route N2 (E9)
-Liege-Utrecht (De Baan behind Makro, Gagel, in section Eindhoven-Best) Route A4 (E10)
-Amsterdam-Den Haag (at Amsterdam end of motorway, Nieuwe Meer, beach behind Eurohotel, days and evenings)
Route A27 (E37)
-Breda-Almere, [P] Bosberg, 90.2 km (Section near Hilversum. In cars, and in adjacent forest. Main area is in the trees ahead of [P]-area, turn left after you climb through hole in fence.)
-96.8 km (De Witte Bergen. Section Hilversum-Almere. Take exit onto A1, direction Amsterdam. Take next exit from A1 (restaurant). Turn left at stop of exit road, park at the end of the short road. Walk through the area of trees and sand on the left at the end of the road.)
Route A28 (E35)
-Amersfoort-Zwolle-Groningen, Laakse Strand (Take exit Nijkerk and follow direction Lelystad-Almere. Over the bridge, and turn into loop road which takes you under the same bridge. 2.5 km further turn left at sign Laakse Strand. At end of road you will find cruising in the big [P]; evenings. Same [P] is also good for nude beach (NG) in the daytime.)
-Strand Horst (Follow »Strand« direction. At several [P]s, left or right, is cruising. Evenings best)
-[P] Section Zwolle-Harderwijk (near Zwolle)
-[P] Glimmermade (Section Assen-Groningen, 7 km south of Groningen, off northbound carriageway) Route A58
-Breda-Tilburg [P] Leikant (near Gilze, follow pathway to wooded area, very popular)
Route A67 (E34)
-Antwerpen-Duisburg, Section in the Netherlands. Formerly E3, now with new number E34, 46.2 km, [P] Leysing (Parked cars, and a hole in the fence leading to forest area, day and night)
-[P] Oeienbosch, 15.2 km (Parked cars, and adjacent forest area, day and night)
-9.5 km, E3 Strand (Leave motorway and follow sign-boards either E3 Strand or E3 Plas. You have to pay to go in. Sunbathing, swimming, cruising. Mixed. Sunny days only.)
-[P] Beerze, 0.2 km (Parked cars, and adjacent forest. This is the last [P] in the Netherlands before the Belgian frontier. Day and night)
Route A79
-Maastricht-Aachen, [P] Keelbos
-Aachen-Maastricht, [P] Ravenbos
Route N228 (E37)
-Amersfoort-Maarn (Section to south of Amersfoort, near Leusden. Den Treek recration area, by Trekerpunt, day and evening, before dark. Leave N228 at 4.9 km and follow the [P] signs. Use either [P] or explore woodland area.) Route A12 (E35)
-Arnheim → Utrecht, [P] 't Ginkelse Sand
-117.2 [P] Grysoord (between Arnhem and Ede, northside)
Route A1
-81.3 [P] (Southside)
-N345 [P] Bussloo (turn left at km 7.7, 9km east of Apeldoorn)
-48.4 on N31 (Southside, between Appelscha and Smilde, 15-20 h)
Route A29 Rotterdam ↔ Bergen op Zoom
-[P] between exits Numansdorp and Oud-Beyerland
A 28 (E232) Zwolle ↔ Meppel
-[P] between exists Ommen and Nieuwleusen

Alkmaar ☎ 072

BARS

Shippertje. 'T (B glm) Thu-Sun 21-2, Wed 22-2 h
Kanaalkade 77 ☎ 515 02 92

DANCECLUBS

De Kleine Unie (B D glm) Sun 17-2 h
Koorstraat 12

SEX SHOPS/BLUE MOVIES

Eros (CC glm W) Mon 13-18, Tue Wed Fri 10-18, Thu 10-21, Sat 10-17 h, closed Sun
Luttik Oudorp 112 ✉1811 MZ *(near Chees Market)*
☎ 512 15 51

Erotheek (g VS) 11-22 h, closed Sun
Koningsweg 17 ✉1811 LK ☎ 515 77 15

H. T. (G VS lj) 11-23 h
De Laat 6 ✉1811 EJ ☎ 515 66 17

GENERAL GROUPS

COC-Alkmaar (glm) Bar: 1st Fri (YG) 15-18, 1st Sat (D) & 4th Sat (D YG) 22-2.30 h
PB 1040 ✉1801 KA *(Bierkade 14 A)* ☎ 511 16 50

CRUISING

-Molen van Piet
-[P] „Geestmerambacht" (Alkmaar-Schagen, southern parking, take paths to nudist beach area, sunset and after dark, be discreet)

Almere ☎ 036

GENERAL GROUPS

COC-Flevoland (GLM)
Salviapad
14 ✉1338 XC ☎ 536 40 61
Call for info on activities.

CRUISING

-Zilverstrand (NU) (at Hollandse Brug, take exit Muiderzand direction Zilverstrand from Route A6. Last part of nudist area is gay)

Alphen aan de Rijn ☎ 0172

BARS

Luzern (B glm) 12-18, Thu 12-21, Fri Sat 12-?, Sun 12-17 h.
Hooftstraat 102

Ameland ☎ 0519

HOTELS

Hotel 't Honk (H glm)
J.W. Burgerstr. 4 ☎ 55 42 56

Amersfoort ☎ 033

BARS

WHAM (B d GLM MA s) Wed 21-24, Sat 22-2 h
Hendrik van Viandenstraat 13ab ✉3811 CB ☎ 461 26 54

GENERAL GROUPS

Anti-discriminatie meldp.
Zuidsingel 45 ☎ 472 87 28

CRUISING

-Den Treek recreation area (road Amersfoort-Maarn, near Trekerpunt)
-Plantsoen-West (between Koppelpoort and Stadthuis)
-Birkhoven (at the sand pits)

Amsterdam ☎ 020

● Amsterdam has, without a doubt, earned the title of the gay capital of Europe, leaving the other metropoles far behind. In no other city has the gay scene been so actively involved in combatting AIDS and its consequences. No other town has so prominently honoured its gay citizens victims of the nazis (*Gay monument*, Westermarkt/ Keizersgracht). No other city has such a liberal attitude towards prostitution and drug-consumption. So it is no wonder that Amsterdam has formed such an intensive and compact gay scene. You will find 3 gay centres on a stretch of 1.5 kilometres: *Warmoesstraat, Rembrandtplein* and *Kerkstraat.* Just a walk along the canals *Grachten* will give you insights into the sizzling gay life . The Dutch sociability *gezelligheid* is a guarantee for a worthwhile and friendly stay. Also one date not to forget: on April 30th the Dutch celebrate their queens birthday in the streets and thousands of gays take part in the festivities, celebrating their own personal *Koninginnedag.*

✱ Ohne Zweifel: Amsterdam verdient vor allen anderen Metropolen den Titel der schwulsten Hauptstadt Europas. Keine andere Stadt war in der schwulen Szene so aktiv, um die Krankheit AIDS und ihre Folgen bekämpfen zu können. Keine andere Stadt hat ihre von den Nazis ermordeten schwulen Mitbürger so prominent geehrt (*Homomonument*, Westermarkt/Keizersgracht). Und kaum eine andere Stadt Europas sieht Prostitution und Drogengebrauch so liberal wie Amsterdam.
Kein Wunder also, daß sich in Amsterdam eine derart intensive und dichte Szene gebildet hat. Auf einer Laufstrecke von eineinhalb Kilometern liegen gleich drei schwule Zentren: *Warmoesstraat, Rembrandtplein* und *Kerkstraat.* Schon ein solcher Spaziergang sagt sehr viel über das brodelnde schwule Leben zwischen den *Grachten.* Dabei sorgt die niederländische *gezelligheid* dafür, daß ein Besuch in Amsterdam immer sehr übersichtlich und menschlich bleibt.
Einen Tag, den man im internationalen schwulen Jahresablauf nicht vergessen sollte: Am 30. April eines jeden Jahres feiern die Niederländer auf den Straßen des Landes den Geburtstag ihrer Königin. Und in Amsterdam feiern dann Tausende von Schwulen ihren ganz persönlichen *Koninginnedag.*

▲ Pas l'ombre d'un doute: Amsterdam est LA capitale gay de l'Europe! Aucune autre ville n'a su combattre aussi activement et efficacement le sida. Aucune autre ville n'a su rendre hommage aussi sincèrement aux homosexuels victimes de la discrimination et de la barbarie nazies („Homomonument", Westermarkt/Keizergracht). Aucune autre ville d'Europe ne règle les problèmes liés à la drogue et la prostitution d'une façon si libérale. Tout ça, c'est Amsterdam! Rien d'étonnant à ce qu'Amsterdam soit la Mecque gay d'Europe. Les hauts-lieux gays sont dans la „Warmoestraat", la „Keerkstraat" et sur le „Rembrandtplein". On peut tout faire à pied: c'est une jolie promenade le long des canaux („Grachten"). L'hospitalité et la gentillesse des Hollandais rendront votre séjour à Amsterdam encore plus agréable. Le 30 avril est un jour important dans le calendrier gay hollandais: c'est l'anniversaire de la reine Béatrix. Tout le monde est dans la rue pour faire la fête. Les gays sont de la partie et ne sont pas en reste: eux aussi fêtent leur „Koninginnedag".

☆ No hay duda: Amsterdam se ha guanado, delante de las otras ciudades europeas, el título de capital gays europea. Ninguna otra comunidad gay fué y sigue siendo tan comprometida en la activa lucha contra el SIDA. Además es una de las pocas ciudades que recuerda sus victimas homosexuales durante la dictadura nazi en un sitio tan importante (*Homomonument, Westermarkt/Keizersgracht*) Amsterdam mantiene una postura muy liberal hacia la prostitución y el consumo de drogas y se ha desarollado un intenso y compacto

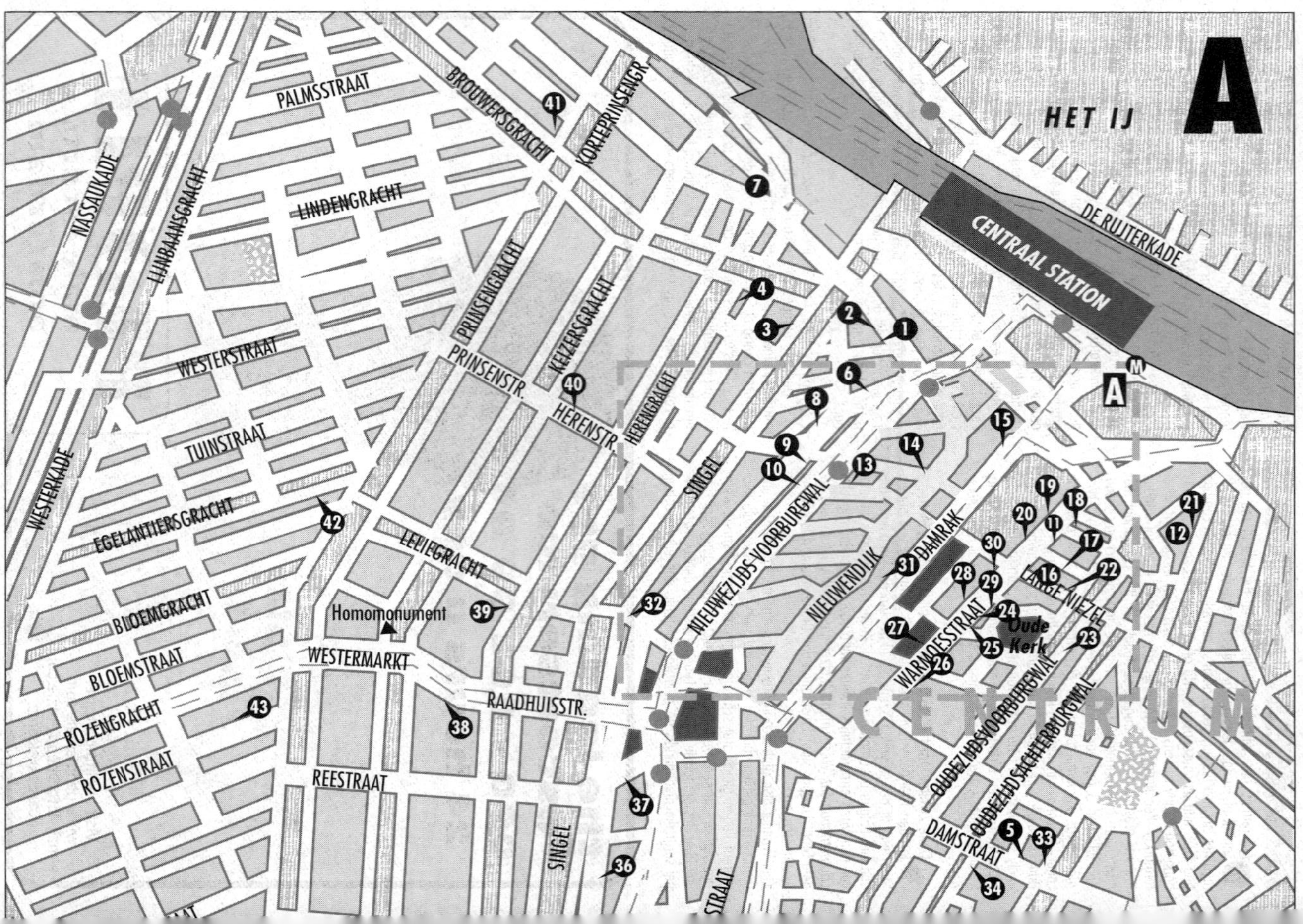
A
HET IJ
DE RUIJTERKADE
CENTRAAL STATION
CENTRUM
LANGE NIEZEL
Oude Kerk
OUDEZIJDSACHTERBURGWAL
OUDEZIJDSVOORBURGWAL
WARMOESSTRAAT
DAMRAK
DAMSTRAAT
NIEUWENDIJK
NIEUWEZIJDS VOORBURGWAL
SINGEL
HERENGRACHT
KEIZERSGRACHT
PRINSENGRACHT
HERENSTR.
PRINSENSTR.
KORTEPRINSENGR.
BROUWERSGRACHT
RAADHUISSTR.
LELIEGRACHT
Homomonument
WESTERMARKT
REESTRAAT
PALMSSTRAAT
LINDENGRACHT
WESTERSTRAAT
TUINSTRAAT
EGELANTIERSGRACHT
BLOEMGRACHT
BLOEMSTRAAT
ROZENGRACHT
ROZENSTRAAT
LIJNBAANSGRACHT
NASSAUKADE
WESTERKADE
STRAAT

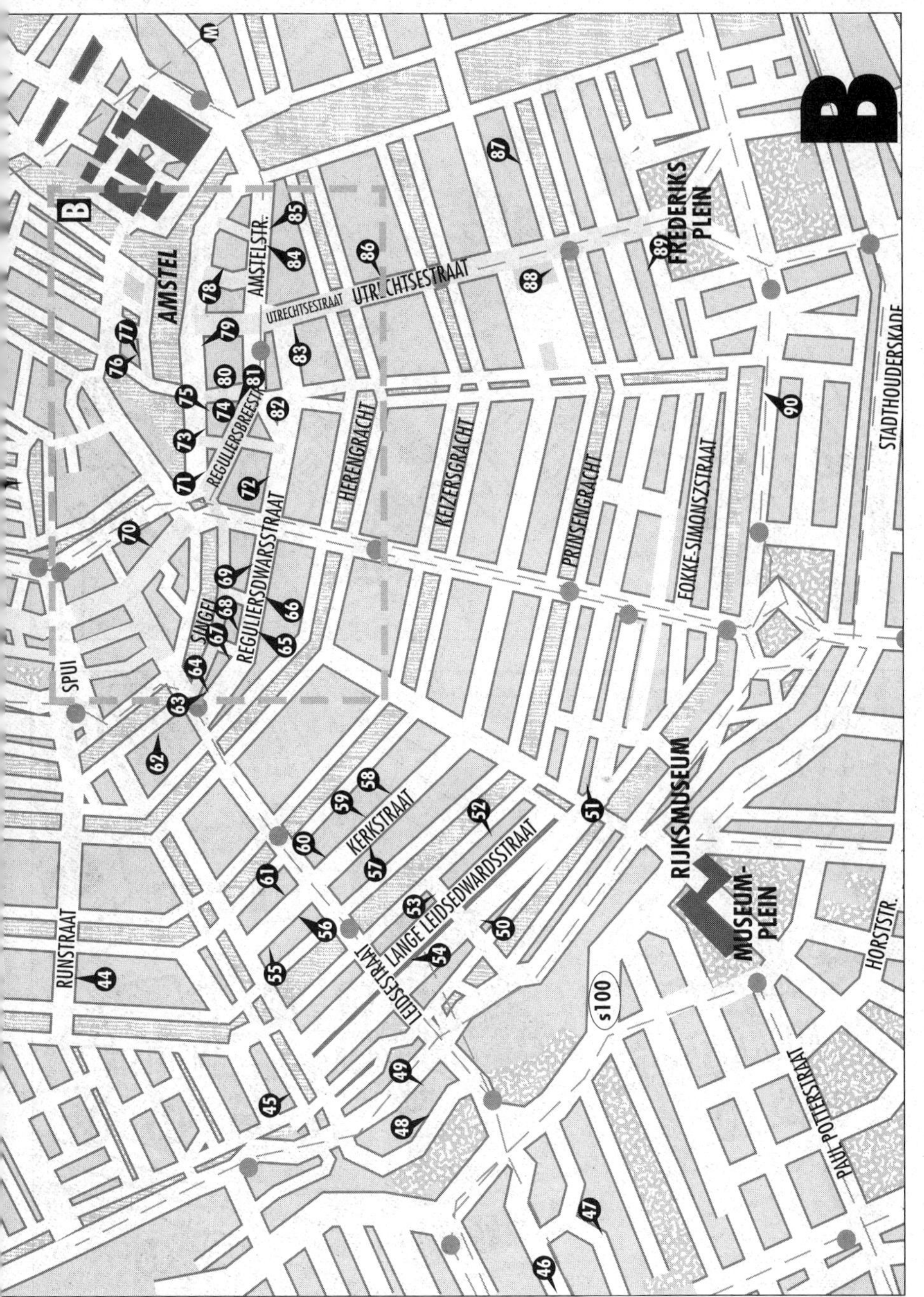
B
AMSTEL
AMSTELSTR.
UTRECHTSESTRAAT
HERENGRACHT
KEIZERSGRACHT
PRINSENGRACHT
FOKKE-SIMONSZSTRAAT
FREDERIKS PLEIN
STADTHOUDERSKADE
REGULIERSBREESTR.
REGULIERSDWARSSTRAAT
SINGEL
SPUI
RUNSTRAAT
KERKSTRAAT
LANGE LEIDSEDWARSSTRAAT
LEIDSESTRAAT
RIJKSMUSEUM
MUSEUM-PLEIN
HORSTSTR.
PAUL-POTTERSTRAAT
s100
44 45 46 47 48 49 50 51 52 53 54 55 56 57 58 59 60 61 62 63 64 65 66 67 68 69 70 71 72 73 74 75 76 77 78 79 80 81 82 83 84 85 86 87 88 89 90

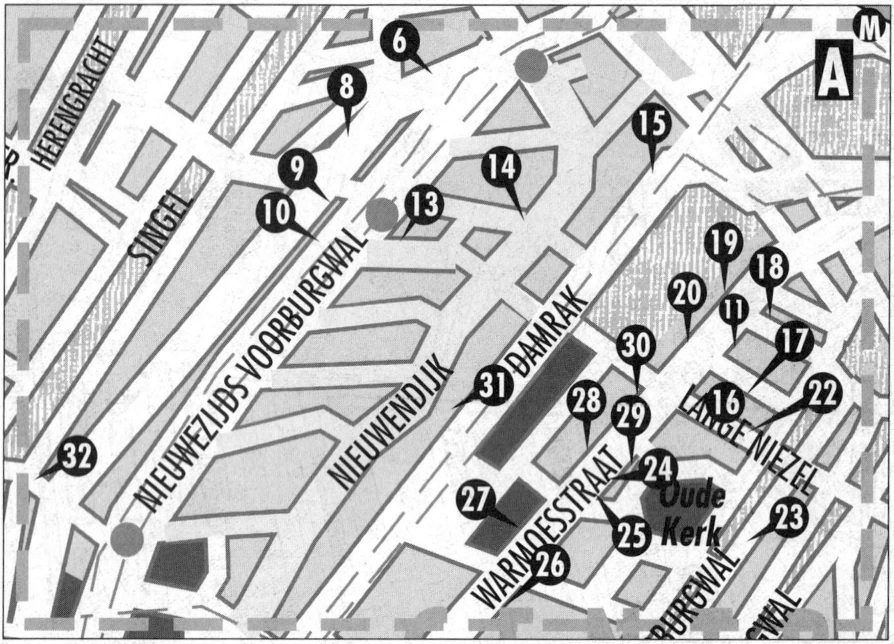

A

HERENGRACHT
SINGEL
NIEUWEZIJDS VOORBURGWAL
NIEUWENDIJK
DAMRAK
WARMOESSTRAAT
LANGE NIEZEL
Oude Kerk
BURGWAL
GWAL

6 8 9 10 11 13 14 15 16 17 18 19 20 22 23 24 25 26 27 28 29 30 31 32

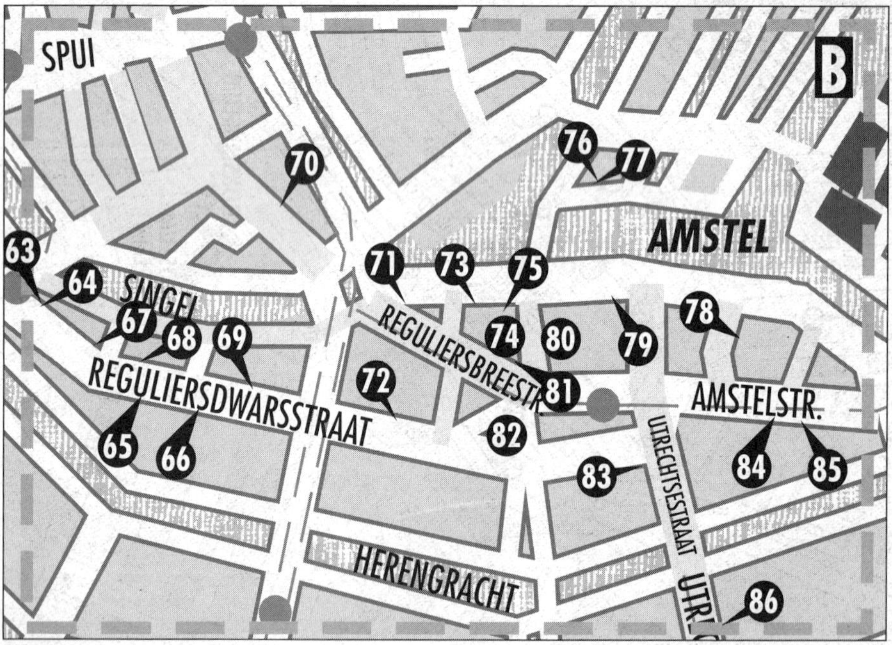

B

SPUI
AMSTEL
SINGEL
REGULIERSDWARSSTRAAT
REGULIERSBREESTR.
AMSTELSTR.
UTRECHTSESTRAAT
HERENGRACHT
UTR.

63 64 65 66 67 68 69 70 71 72 73 74 75 76 77 78 79 80 81 82 83 84 85 86

A

1 Alfa-Blue Sex Shop
2 Le Salon Sex Shop
3 E & D City Amsterdam Apartments
4 New York Hotel
5 Body Manipulations
6 Boys for Men House of Boys
7 Barangây Guest House
8 Krua Thai Restaurant
9 Man to Man Sex Shop
Boysclub 21 House of Boys
10 Why Not House of Boys
Blue Boy Bar
11 Getto Café
12 Queens Head Bar
13 Cuckoo's Nest Bar
14 The Web Bar
15 Museum of Sex
16 Boomerang Sauna
17 Centre Apartments Amsterdam
18 Stable Master Bar / Hotel
19 Mister B Leather & Fetish Shop
20 Café Maria Bar
21 Black Tulip Hotel
22 Monico Bar
23 Anco Bar / Hotel
24 Club Jacques Bar
25 Argos Bar
26 Condomerie Het Gulden Vlies
Condom Shop
27 Cockring Danceclub
28 The Eagle Bar
29 Mister B Leather & Fetish Shop
30 Dirty Dicks Bar
31 Drake's of LA Sex Shop
32 't Sluisje Restaurant
33 Gay Krant Reisservice Travel Shop
34 Homodok Documentation Center
35 Upstairs Pancake House Restaurant
36 Intermale Book Shop
37 Vrolijk Book Shop
38 Rainbow Palace Hotel
39 Sunhead of 1617 Guest House
40 Maes B&B Guest House
41 Doll's Place Bar
42 Jordan Canal House Hotel
43 COC Café, Danceclub, Information
Center & COC Netherlands

B

44 Robin and Rik Leather & Fetish Shop
45 Thermos Day Sauna
46 Prinsen Hotel
47 Quentin Engeland Hotel
48 Hotel Quentin
49 Freeland Hotel
50 Cuts and Curts Body & Beauty Shop
51 Black Body Leather & Fetish Shop
52 Mandate Fitness
53 Orfeo Hotel
54 Flightbrookers Private Accomodation
55 De Spijker Bar
56 Cosmo Bar
57 Thermos Night Sauna
58 Meia Meia 66 Bar
59 The Bronx Sex Shop
60 Camp Café
61 Golden Bear Hotel
62 D.O.K. Danceclub
63 Saturnino Restaurant
64 Havana Bar
65 Havana Club Danceclub
66 Exit Danceclub
67 Downtowne Café
68 April Bar
69 Mantalk Fashion Shop
70 American Book Center
Book Shop
71 Gaiety Bar
72 Reality Bar
73 Mix Bar
74 Café de Steeg
75 Amstel Taveerne Bar
76 Amsterdam House Hotel
77 Le Shako Bar
78 The Music Box Bar
79 Milord Bar
80 Le Montmartre
de Paris Bar
81 Entre Nous Bar
82 Le Monde Café/
Restaurant
83 Lellebel Bar
84 IT Danceclub
85 De Krokodil Bar
86 Sluizer Restaurant
87 Orlando Hotel
88 ITC Hotel
89 Frederik Park House
Hotel
90 RoB Leather &
Fetish Shop

ambiente gay. En un trayecto de 1,5 kilometros se encuentran tres centros gays: *Warmoesstraat, Amstelstraat/Halvemaansteeg* y *Regulierschwarsstraat.* Un paseo por esta zona da una buena impresión de la marcha de ambiente entre los *Grachten* (canales). Los holandeses son famosos por su *gezelligheit* (sociabilidad) que junto con su musica popular garantizan una estancia agradable. Hay dos fechas claves para la comunidad gay de esta ciudad: El 30 de abril se celebra el cumpleaños de la reina Beatrice, en este día la ciudad entera se convierte en una gran fiesta, con innumerables puestos en la calle, espectáculos, grupos de musica y muchisimos gays que celebran su *Koninginnedad* (día de la reina) de manera muy particular. En agosto tiene lugar anualmente la Amsterdam Pride. Uno no debería perderse la impresionante Canal Parade, donde docenas de barcos decorados fantasticamente pasan por los *Grachten.*

❖ Amsterdam merita senza dubbi il titolo di capitale gay europea. Nessun'altra *gay comunity* fa tanti sforzi nella lotta contro l'AIDS e le sue conseguenze. Inoltre non c'è un'altra città che abbia eretto un monumento per le vittime del nazismo (l'*Homo monument al Westermarkt/Keizersgracht*). E nessun'altra città è così aperta verso la prostiuzione e l'uso di droghe leggere. Quindi non c'è da stupirsi che ad Amsterdam è sorto un grande ambiente gay. In un distretto lungo 3 kilometri si trovano tre centri gay: la *Warmoesstraat*, l'*Amstel/Halvemaansteeg* e la *Reguliersdwarsstraat.* E la *gezelligheid* (cordialità/accoglienza) olandese con la tipica musica vi dà la garanzia di un bellissimo soggiorno. Ci sono due date che bisogna segnarsi nel calendario gay: il 30 aprile quando gli olandesi festeggiano il compleanno della regina Beatrice, e la città diventa un crogiolo di mercati giganteschi, di navi, di shows spettacolari e di tanti gay che festeggiano il loro proprio *Koninginnendag* (giorno della regina). Ogni anno in agosto ha luogo l'Amsterdam Pride. Un dovere assoluto è il *Canal Parade,* una sfilata di dozzine di navi decorate in modo bello ed elegante che si svolge per i tanti canali.

GAY INFO

Amsterdam City Guide
c/o Bruno Gmünder Verlag PO Box 610104
✉10921 Berlin ☎ 030/615 00 30 Fax: 030/615 90 07
E-Mail: info@spartacus.de
The city guide book about Amsterdam

COC Amsterdam Information Center
Wed-Sat 13-17 h
Rozenstraat 14 ✉1016 NX ☎ 623 40 79 Fax: 626 83 00

Culture and Camp
Gerard Doustraat 160 F ✉1073 VZ ☎ 679 91 88
Monthly gay art and literature magazine.

Gay & Lesbian Switchboard Mon-Sun 10-22 h
☎ 623 65 65 ☎ 422 65 65
(deaf and hard hearing people) *General information concerning pubs and clubs, legal and medical problems, etc.*

Gay & Night
PO Box 10757 ✉1001 ET ☎ 427 48 11 Fax: 624 65 97
E-Mail: welcome@gay-night.nl Homepage: www.gay-night.nl
Monthly free newspaper focusing on entertainment, travel, film, interviews, music and sex. Bilingual (English/Dutch) with a complete listing of gay activities. Also publisher of Gay Map G.B.A.

Gay News Amsterdam
PO Box 76609 ✉1070 HE ☎ 679 15 56 Fax: 675 38 61
Homepage: www.gayamsterdam.com
Popular free gay publication with monthly listing of events, parties, and activities. Bilingual (English and Dutch).

Homodok/Documentatiecentrum Homostudies (GLM) Wed-Fri 10.30-16.30 h
Oudezijds Achterburgwal 185 ✉1012 DK ☎ 525 26 01
Fax: 525 30 10 E-Mail: homodok@sara.nl Homepage:
http://www.dds.nl/~gldocu/homodok.htm
Gay and lebian information centre and archive.

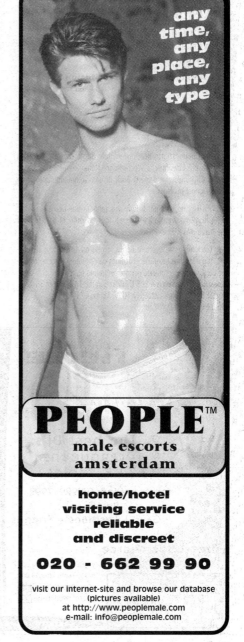

MVS-Radio 18-21 h on FM 106.8, on cable 103.8
PB 11100 ✉1001 GC ☎ 620 02 47
Pink Television Mon 21-22 h
on local Amsterdam TV
Wilma TV (Glm) Mon 20-21 h
on local Amsterdam TV

TOURIST INFO

VVV Amsterdam Centraal Station 9-17 h
Stationsplein 10 ✉1012 AB ☎ 06 340 340 66 Fax: 625 28 69

BARS

● The Amsterdam Bars often close one hour later during the summer months and on Fri/Sat night.

✱ Die Öffnungszeiten der Amsterdamer Bars, Cafés etc. beziehen sich auf gewöhnliche Wochentage. Normalerweise sind sie an den Wochenenden, und meist auch in den Sommermonaten, eine Stunde länger geöffnet.

▲ En été, les bars amstellodamois ferment une heure plus tard; de même, vendredi et samedi tous les clubs et bars ferment une heure plus tard.

❖ Los horarios de apertura de los locales en Amsterdam se refieren a los días laboriales. Los fines de semana y durante los meses de verano están abierto normalmente una hora mas.

Amstel Taveerne (! B G OS S) Sun-Thu 16-1, Fri Sat 15-2 h
Amstel 54/Halvemaansteeg ✉1017 AB ☎ 623 42 54
One of the oldest Dutch bars.

Anco Bar (B bf f G H LJ MA) 9-22, happy hours 16-18 h
Oudezijds Voorburgwal 55 ✉1012 EJ ☎ 624 11 26
April (! A B GLM MA VS) Sun-Thu 14-1, Fri Sat 14-3 h
Reguliersdwarsstraat 37 ✉1017 BK ☎ 625 95 72
Modern, trendy. Live TV-Connection with „Exit". Renovated, with spinning bar.
Argos (! AC B DR G LJ) Sun-Thu 22-3, Fri Sat -4 h
Warmoesstraat 95 ✉1012 HZ *(Near central station)*
☎ 622 65 95 *Oldest leather bar in Europe and the only one with a host. Very friendly staff, check for special events.*
Biecht. De (B G MA TV S) Sun-Thu 20-2, Fri Sat -3 h
Kerkstraat 346 ✉1017 JA ☎ 420 80 74
Café de Huyschkaemer (AC B CC d F GLM MA) 15-1, 15-3 h weekend
Utrechtsestraat 137 ✉1017 VM ☎ 627 05 75
International cuisine, not expensive.
Café de Steeg (! AC B G S) Sun-Thu 17-1, Fri Sat 16-3 h
Halvemaansteeg 10 ✉1017 CR ☎ 620 01 71
Café Lellebel (AC B glm OG R STV TV) Mon-Thu 21-03, Fri Sat 20-04, Sun 20-03 h
Ultrechtsestraat 4 ✉1017 VN *(tram 4, 9 and 14 stop Rembrandt-Square)* ☎ 427 51 39
Drag-Travestie Café with shows, karaoké and other in-house specialities
Camp Café (B bf CC F G MA N OS W) 17-1, (kitchen -22.30) h
Kerkstraat 45 ✉1017 GB ☎ 622 15 06
Daily menu, Dutch cuisine, more popular in the evenings.
Casa Maria (B G lj MA OS tv) 12-1, Fri Sat -3 h
Warmoesstraat 60 ✉1012 JG ☎ 627 68 48
This bar - where drinks are cheap - is popular with the Gay community. Snacks on Sun from 15 h.
Club Jacques (AC B DR LJ MA W) Sun-Thu 20-3, Fri Sat 21-4 h
Warmoesstraat 93 ✉1012 HZ ☎ 622 03 23
Best after 24 h.

COC-Amsterdam (AC B GLM MA) Mon 13-17, Tue-Thu 20-24
Rozenstraat 14 ✉1016 NX ☎ 626 30 87 ☎ 020/623 40 79

Cosmo Bar (AC B CC G MA N) 24-3, Fri Sat -4 h
Kerkstraat 42 ✉1017 GM *(Irame 1/2)* ☎ 624 80 74

Cuckoo's Nest (AC B DR G lj MA OS VS) Sun-Thu 13-1, Fri Sat 13-2 h
Nieuwezijds Kolk 6 ✉1012 PV ☎ 627 17 52

Dirty Dicks (B DR G LJ p) Fri/Sat 0-? h
Warmoesstraat 86 ✉1012 JH ☎ 627 86 34

Doll's Place (B glm MA N) 21-3, Fri Sat 21-4 h
Vinkenstraat 57 ✉1013 JM ☎ 627 07 90

Eagle. The (B G LJ MA) 22-4, Fri Sat 22-5 h
Warmoesstraat 90 ✉1012 JH ☎ 626 86 34
Staff well known as the most unpleasant in Europe. Skip it.

Entre Nous (B G MA WE) 20-3, Fri Sat -4 h
Halve Maansteeg 14 ✉1017 CR ☎ 623 17 00

Gaiety (B G MA YG) 16-1, Fri-Sat -2 h
Amstel 14 ✉1017 AA ☎ 624 42 71
Nice atmosphere. Popular with young people.

Getto (A AC B CC F GLM lj MA VS) Tue 19-1, Wed-Sat 16-1, Sun -24 h, closed Mon
Warmoesstraat 51 ✉1012 HW ☎ 421 51 51
Tue women only, Thu bingo, Fri-Sun DJs, Happy hours 17-19 h. 1st Mon/month Karaoke night (5 Hfl.). International cuisine, also vegetarian dishes. Prices from Hfl 18.50.

Havana (! AC B D GLM s YG) 16-1, Fri 16-3, Sat 14-3, Sun 14-1 h
Reguliersdwarsstraat 17 ✉1017 BJ ☎ 626 01 58
Elegant.

Krokodil Bar. De (B G OG s) 16-2 h
Amstelstraat 34 ✉1017 DA ☎ 626 22 43
Oldest bar in Amsterdam. Sun afternoon very popular (!). Pub atmosphere.

Meia Meia 66 (AC B G MA N OS s) 14-1, Fri Sat -3 h
Kerkstraat 63 ✉1017 GC ☎ 623 41 29

Milord (B G MA) 18-1, Fri Sat -3 h
Amstel 102 ✉1017 DA ☎ 622 83 35

Mix (AC B GLM MA) Sun-Thu 20-3, Fri Sat -4 h
Amstel 50 ✉1017 AB ☎ 622 52 02

Monico Bar (B glm MA N r) 12-2 h
Lange Niezel 15 ✉1012 GS ☎ 623 74 41

Montmartre (! B GLM lj s YG) 17-1, Fri Sat 16-3 h
Halvemaansteeg 17 ✉1017 CR ☎ 620 76 22
Beautiful wallpaintings by Eppo Doeve.

Music Box. The (AC B CC G MA R) 21-3, Fri-Sat -4 h, Mon closed
Paardenstraat 9 ✉1017 CX *(Near Rembrandtplein)* ☎ 620 41 10
Hustler bar.

Night Life (B G R) 20-3, Fri Sat -4 Sun 17-3 h
Paardenstraat 7 ✉1017 CX ☎ 420 92 46
Hustler Bar.

Queens Head. The (B G lj MA tv s) 17-1, Fri Sat 16-3 h
Zeedijk 20 ✉1012 AL ☎ 420 24 75
Bingo night on Tue hosted by Dusty, Plush/kitsch decoration.

Reality (B G MA) Sun-Thu 20-3, Fri Sat -4 h
Regulierdwarsstraat 129 ✉1017 BL ☎ 639 30 12
Popular meeting place for black men and their friends.

Shako. Le (AC B G MA N OS) 22-3, Fri Sat -4 h
's Gravelandseveer 2 ✉1011 KM *(opposite Amstel Taveerne)*
☎ 624 02 09
Very social talkcafé, friendly owner. Popular on Tue.

Soho (AC B d GLM s YG) Mon-Thu 20-3, Fri Sat -4, Sun 16-3 h
Reguliersdwarsstraat 36 ✉1017 BM *(near the flower market)*
☎ 330 44 00
Classy bar on two floors. 1st floor: British pub, 2nd floor American style.

Spijker. De (B DR f G lj MA vs) 13-2, Fri Sat -3 h
Kerkstraat 4 ✉1017 GL ☎ 620 59 19
Western and leather bar.

Stable Master Bar (B G lj) 20-1, Fri Sat 20-2 h, closed Tue Wed
Warmoesstraat 23 ✉1012 HT ☎ 624 55 73
Jack-off parties, admission hfl 10.

Vandenberg (B F g) 16-1 h
Lindengracht 95 ✉1017 BM ☎ 622 27 16
Kitchen opens at 17.30 h.

Vivelavie (B gLm) Sun-Thu 12-1, Fri Sat -2 h
Amstelstraat 7 ✉1017 DA ☎ 624 01 14

Web. The (! AC B DR F G LJ VS) 14-1, Fri Sat -3 h
St. Jacobusstraat 4 & 6 ✉1012 NC ☎ 623 67 58
Action starts in this horny bar in the afternoon. Sunday busiest day. DJs on WE, Lottery on Wed.

Why Not (B CC G MA S) 16-1 h
Nieuwezijds Voorburgwal 28 ✉1012 RZ ☎ 627 43 74
Shows at weekends.

MEN'S CLUBS

Trash (B D G LJ) 3rd Sat 22-? h
K.N.S.M. Laan 13 *(shuttle bus from Barbizon Palace Hotel at Centraal Station)*
Strict dresscode, hot and horny atmosphere.

CAFÉS

Downtown (! A bf G MA OS) 10-19 h
Reguliersdwarsstraat 31 ✉1017 BJ ☎ 622 99 58
The world's best apple pie.

Mankind (B F glm MA OS) 11-1 h
Weteringstraat 60 ✉1017 SP ☎ 638 47 55

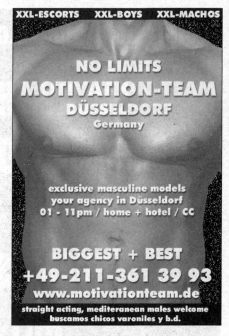

Friendly gay bar/café with canal view in museum quarter. Small meals served.
Otherside. The (b f G) 10-1 h
Reguliersdwarsstraat 6 ✉1017 BM ☎ 625 51 41
Non-alcoholic coffee shop.

DANCECLUBS

COC-Amsterdam (AC B D GLM WE YG) Fri-Sat 23-4 h, Sat women only
Rozenstraat 14 ✉1016 NX ☎ 623 40 79
Cockring (! AC B D DR G MA snu VS) Sun-Thu 23-4, Fri-Sat -5 h
Warmoesstraat 96 ✉1012 JH *(Near central station)* ☎ 623 96 04
A bit of leather. Two floors. Very popular. Strip shows on Thu and Sun.
D.O.K. (! AC B D dr GLM MA S snu stv) Wed 23-4 h
Singel 460 *(next to gay area, Tram 1/2/5)* ☎ 06/22 91 79 92
Trendy crowd.
Exit (! AC B D DR G MA OS) Sun-Thu 23-4, Fri Sat 23-5 h
Reguliersdwarsstraat 42 ✉1017 BM ☎ 625 87 88
On two floors. Popular.
IT (! AC B D G S YG) Thu Fri Sun 23-4, Sat (G) -5 h
Amstelstraat 24 ✉1017 DA ☎ 625 01 11
Very big gay disco in former flora palace.
Meat Factory (AC B D G lj P S TV VS YG) 1st & 3rd Fri
c/o The Industry, Paardenstraat 17 ✉1017 CX
Trut (B D GLM YG) Sun 23-4, doors open 23-24 h
Bilderdijkstraat 165 ✉1053 KP

RESTAURANTS

De Jaren Restaurant (B F g MA OS) 10-1, Fri Sat -2 h
Nieuwe Doelenstraat 20-22 ✉1012 CP ☎ 625 57 71
Fax: 624 08 01
Garage. Le (AC CC F glm) 12-14, 18-23 h
Ruysdaelstraat 54-56 ✉1071 XE ☎ 697 71 76
Trendy place with excellent wines and meals from Hfl 40.- upwards.
Gerard (AC B CC F g glm lj MA) 17.30-23 h, closed Tue
Geldersekade 23 ✉1011 EJ ☎ 638 43 38
Daily, fresh products and specials. French cuisine.
Getto (A AC B CC F GLM lj MA VS) Tue 19- 01h (women only) Wed-Sat 16-1, Sun -24 h, closed Mon.
Warmoesstraat 51 ✉1012 HW ☎ 421 51 51
Tue women only, Thu bingo, Fri-Sun DJs, Happy hours 17-19 h. 1st Mon/month Karaoke night (5 Hfl.). International cuisine, also vegetarian dishes. Prices from Hfl 18.50.
Hemelse Modder (AC B CC F glm MA) 18-1,
Last order 22 h, closed Mon
Oude Waal 9 ✉1011 BZ ☎ 624 32 03
French Italian cuisine, nice atmosphere. Popular.
Kooning van Siam. De (B F g) 17.30-23 h, closed Tue
Oudezijds Voorburgwal 42 ✉1012 GE ☎ 623 72 93
Intimate restaurant on two floors with authentic Thai food. Take a water taxi to arrive here!
Kort (B CC F g YG) 11.30-23 (kitchen -22 h), Tue closed
Amstelveld 12 ✉1017 DJ ☎ 626 11 99
French/Mediterranean cuisine.
Krua Thai (B F g) 17-22.30 h
Spuistraat 90A ✉1012 TZ ☎ 620 06 23
Moeders Pot (B F glm) 17-22 h
Vinkenstraat 119 ✉1013 JN ☎ 623 76 43
Monde. Le (B bf F glm MA OS) 8-23; Nov-Feb: Mon-Fri 16-22, Sat-Sun 8-23 h
Rembrandtsquare 6 ✉1017 CV ☎ 626 99 22
Typical Dutch meals at moderate prices.
Pancakes Upstairs (F GLM MA) 12-19, Sat -18, Sun -17

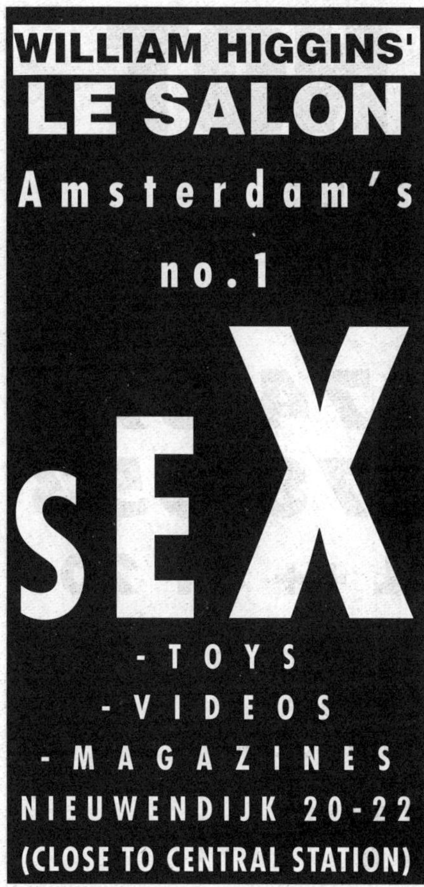

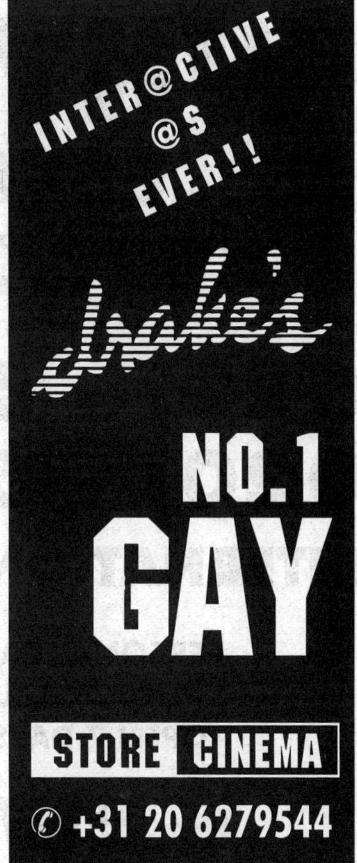

h, Mon closed
Grimburgwal 2 ✉1012 GA *(Central, between Damsquare and the flower market, Tram 4/9/14/16/20/24/25-Rokin/Spui)*
☎ 626 56 03
The smallest restaurant in Europe with typical dutch staircase and canal house.
Saturnino (B F glm) 12-24 h
Reguliersdwarsstraat 5H ✉1017 BJ *(Tram 1/2/5/11)*
☎ 639 01 02
Sluisje. 'T (B F glm MA STV) 16-1 h, closed Wed, STV Thu-Sun
Torensteeg 1 ✉1012 TH ☎ 624 08 13
Popular grillbar-steakhouse.
Sluizer (b F g) 12-24, Sat Sun 17-24 h
Utrechtsestraat 41-45 ✉1017 VP ☎ 622 63 76
French cuisine, not very expensive. Reservation adviced.
Walem (B F bf glm) 10-1, Fri Sat -3 (lunch -16.30, dinner -22.30 h)
Keizergracht 449 ✉1017 DK ☎ 625 35 44
International and French cuisine. Huge menu in the evenings. Recommended, reservations for dinner advised.

SEX SHOPS/BLUE MOVIES

Adonis (DR G VS) Mon-Fri 10-1, Fri Sat -3 h
Warmoesstraat 92 ✉1012 JH ☎ 627 29 59
Cinema, darkroom, bookshop, erotic toys.
Alfa-Blue (CC g) 9-2 h
Nieuwendijk 26 ✉1012 ML ☎ 627 16 64
Bronx. The (CC G VS) 12-24 h
Kerkstraat 53-55 ✉1017 GC ☎ 623 15 48
Sale, hire, wholesale. Very big selection. Excellent videotheque. Also gay mail order.
Drake's of LA (AC CC G VS YG) 9-2 h
Damrak 61 ✉1012 LM *(200 m walking South of Central Station)*
☎ 627 95 44
Gay movies and video cabins, many with added ventilation.

WHY NOT

ESCORTS

OUR NAME SPEAKS FOR ITSELF
ASK ANYONE

(020) - 6274 374
(020) - 6278 653

INTERNATIONAL ++ 31 20

PERSONAL CALLERS WELCOME
PHOTO ALBUMS AVAILABLE
OPEN 7 DAYS 12.00 - 02.00

TAKE ANY CHANCES
YOUR SATISFACTION IS GUARANTEED WITH A

WHY NOT BOY

ALL BOYS OVER 18
NEW GUYS ALWAYS WELCOME

N.Z. VOORBURGWAL 28 • 1012 RZ AMSTERDAM
opposite Holiday Inn Crown Plaza Hotel

A Great Time
Guaranteed by the Very Best Boys in Amsterdam

Home & Hotel visits
Dinner dates and attractive rates for the entire night

020 - 675 57 50
24 hours a day,
cards accepted

Call now! You'll come back to us.

Black & White

body builders, leather, sm-masters, spanking, students and much, much more...

020 - 679 50 98

24 hrs, all cards acc.

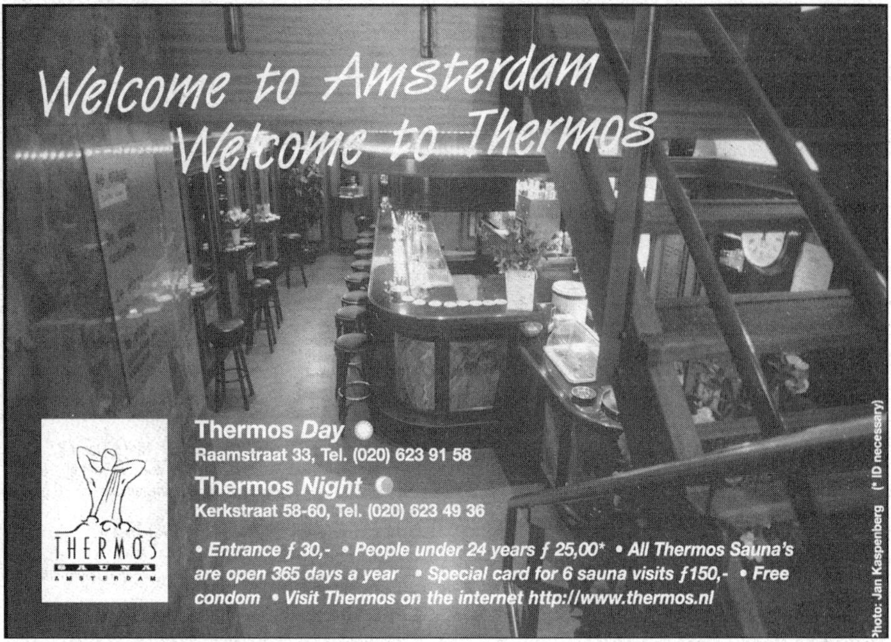

Man-to-Man (CC DR G MA VS) 11-1 h
Spuistraat 21 ✉1012 SR *(near Central Station)* ☎ 625 87 97

William Higgins Le Salon (AC CC G VS YG) 9-24h, Sun 12-24h
Nieuwendijk 20-22 ✉1012 ML ☎ 622 65 65
Over 16 years in the William Higgins tradition. Store with books, magazines, videos, cinema, peep shows, etc. Gay and leather movies as well as video cabins, many with added ventilation.

CINEMAS

Filmtheater Desmet (B GLM MA WE)
Plantage Middenlaan 4A ✉1010 DD ☎ 627 34 34
Call for dates of Gay art films at WE.

ESCORTS & STUDIOS

Aa Boys (G) 0-24 h
☎ 675 57 50 *24 hour service.*

Amsterdam Boys Escort (CC) 0-24 h
☎ 389 29 82 Homepage: www.amsterdamboysescort.com
European boys, student types.
Call Boys (CC G lj)
☎ 679 50 98
City Boys (G)
☎ 400 44 55
Homo Escorts (G)
☎ 662 31 42
Michael's Boys Escort (CC G) 0-24 h
☎ 618 18 24 Homepage: www.michaelsboysescorts.com
High quality long established escort service.
People male escorts (CC G LJ) 0-24 h
☎ 662 99 90 E-Mail: info@peoplemale.com Homepage: www.peoplemale.com
Very well-known, long established gay escort service. Home and hotel visits.

HOUSE OF BOYS

Blue Boy/Why Not (AC B CC G msg R SNU VS W) 12-2 h
N.Z. Voorburgwal 28 ✉1012 RZ ☎ 627 43 74 Fax: 627 86 53 E-Mail: welcome@whynot.nl Homepage: www.whynot.nl
The oldest and largest house of boys in Amsterdam. 15-20 boys on premises, more available on portfolio.
Boys for Men (AC B CC G R SNU VS) 15-2 h
Spuistraat 44b ☎ 638 15 12
Nice, polite student types, relaxed atmosphere in a bright and clean place.
Boys. The (G STV) Sun-Thu 17-3, Fri Sat -4 h
Amstel 140 ✉1017 AE ☎ 622 80 36 Fax: 624 73 90
Boysclub 21 (AC B CC G SNU VS wh) 12-2, Fri Sat -3 h
Spuistraat 21 ✉1012 SB *(above Man to Man)* ☎ 622 88 28
International boys, 4 standard rooms, 1 VIP room with spa.
Try It (B CC G msg N p R VS) 13-24 h
Kuiperstraat 86 ✉1074 EN ☎ 662 70 91
Small establishment in cellar out of the city centre.

SAUNAS/BATHS

Boomerang (B CC f G MA sa sb wh) 9-23 h
Heintje Hoeksteeg 8 ✉1012 GR *(alley opposite to police station, just off Warmoestraat)* ☎ 622 61 62
New sauna opened in summer 99. Hfl 25.

Modern (b G OG) 12-18 h, closed Sun & holidays
Jacop van Lennepstraat 311 ✉1053 JJ ☎ 612 17 12
Especially for older gays. Entrance-fee Hfl 25.

Thermos Day (! A AC B CC DR F G MA msg pi s sa sb sol VS wh YG) 12-23, Sat Sun & holidays 12-22 h
Raamstraat 33 ✉1016 XL *(Tram 5/2/1-Leidseplein)*
☎ 623 91 58
Huge sauna on 5 floors with bar, restaurant, roof terrace, sun beds, beauty salon, hair dresser. very clean and friendly. Entrance-fee Hfl 30. (-25 years Hfl 25).

Thermos Night (AC b CC DR f G MA sa sb VS wh YG) 23-8 h
Kerkstraat 58-60 ✉1017 GM *(Tram 5/2/1-Leidseplein)*
☎ 623 49 36
Entrance-fee Hfl 22.50-30.

FITNESSTUDIOS

Mandate Gay Gym (AC b G sa sol WO) 11-22, Sat 12-18, Sun 14-18 h
Prinsengracht 715 ✉1017 JW *(Trams 1/2/3)* ☎ 625 41 00
Day ticket Hfl 20.

BODY & BEAUTY SHOPS

Body Manipulation (CC glm MA) Mon- Wed 12-18, Thu -21, Fri Sat -19, Sun 17 h
Oude Hoogstraat 31 ✉1012 CD *(near Nieuwmarkt)*
☎ 420 80 85
Piercing studio. Many languages spoken.

Cuts and Curls Hairstyling (A CC GLM LJ MA W) Mon Fri 10-19, Tue -20, Wed -18, Thu 10-21,Sat 9-17 h
Korte Leidsedwarsstraat 74 ✉1017 RD *(near Ryksmuseum)* ☎ 624 68 81
Hairstylist and barber for rough types.

Thermos Beautysalon (CC glm msg) 12-20 h
Raamwarstraat 5 ✉1016 XN *(entrance trough Thermos sauna day or from the street)* ☎ 623 91 58
Hairstyling, body and facial cosmetics, waxing, massage.

BOOK SHOPS

American Book Center. The (CC g) Mon-Fri 10-20, Thu -22, Sun 11-18 h
Kalverstraat 185 ✉1012 XC *(Near Muntplein)* ☎ 625 55 37
English language gay section downstairs, literature, magazines, travel books.

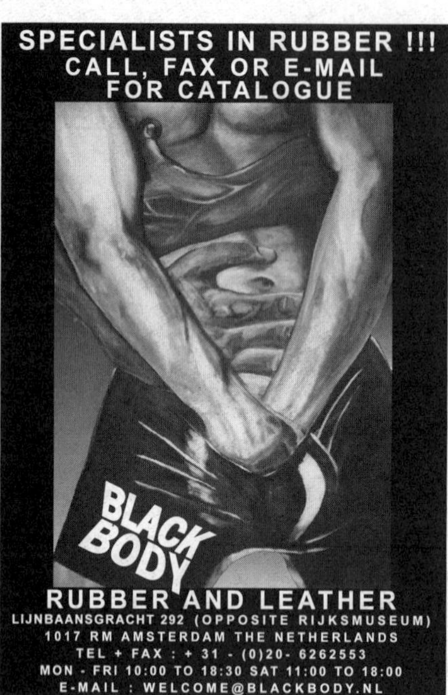

Intermale (G) 10-18, Thu -21 h, closed Sun
Spuistraat 251 ✉1012 VR ☎ 625 00 09 Fax: 620 31 63
Wide selection of gay literature, magazines and non-porn videos.

Vrolijk Boekhandel (GLM) Mon-Fri 10-18, Thu -21, Sat 10-17 h
Paleisstraat 135 ✉1012 ZL *(near the Royal Palace)* ☎ 623 51 42
Gay books in many languages, soft porn magazines, art films. Also mail order.

Zwart Op Wit (glm) 9.30-19, Sat -18, Sun 12-18 h
Utrechtsestraat 149 ✉1017 VM ☎ 622 81 74
Small gay section (Dutch and English).

CONDOM SHOPS

Condomerie Het Gulden Vlies 10-18 h
Warmoesstraat 141 ✉1012 JB
For all sorts, colors, tastes and sizes of condoms.

FASHION SHOPS

Man Talk (G) 10-18, Thu -21 h, closed Sun
Reguliersdwarsstraat 39 ✉1017 BK ☎ 627 25 25
Big selection of underwear, swimwear, perfumes for men.

LEATHER & FETISH SHOPS

Black Body (AC CC G LJ W) Mon-Fri 10-18.30, Sat 11-18 h, closed Sun
Lijnbaansgracht 292 ✉1017 RM *(Tram 6/7/10 stop Ryksmuseum/Spregelstraat)* ☎ 626 25 53 E-Mail: welcome@blackbody.nl
Specialized in rubber. More than 500 rubber clothing models in stock. Also large leather collection. Call for catalogue. Also mail order.

Demask (A g LJ TV) 10-19, Thu -21, Sun 12-17 h
Zeedijk 64 ✉1012 MB ☎ 620 56 03
Rubber and leather shop with gallery.

Mister B (CC G LJ W) Mon-Wed Fri 10-18.30, Thu -21, Sat 11-18, Sun 13-18 h
Warmoesstraat 89 ✉1012 HZ ☎ 422 00 03
E-Mail: misterb@mrb.nl Homepage: www.mrb.nl
Leather and rubber wear, toys, tattos and piercings. Magazines and cards.

RoB (CC G LJ) Mon-Fri 11-18.30, Sat -17 h, closed Sun
Weteringsschans 253 ✉1017 XJ ☎ 625 46 86 Fax: 627 32 20

E-Mail: info@rob.nl Homepage: http://www.rob.nl
Handmade leather and rubber clothing. Very good reputation. Toys, videos, cards. Also mail order. Catalogue for hfl 25.

RoB (CC G LJ) 13-19, Sat -20, Sun 14-18 h
Warmoesstraat 32 ✉1012 JE *(2 min from station)* ☎ 420 85 48 Fax: 420 85 48 E-Mail: info@rob.nl Homepage: http://www.rob.nl
2nd RoB shop in Amsterdam.

Robin and Rik Leermakers (CC G) Mon 13-18.30 Tue-Sat 11-18.30 h
Runstraat 30 ✉1016 GK ☎ 627 89 24
Hand-made own leather collection.

TRAVEL & TRANSPORT

Flightbrokers (CC GLM) Mon-Fri 9-20, Sat 10-17 h
Lange Leidsedwarsstraat 96 ✉1017 NM *(near Leidseplein, Tram 1/2/5)* ☎ 420 28 14 Fax: 420 28 17
E-Mail: info@flightbrokers.nl Homepage: www.flightbrokers.com
Travel agent and internet place.

HOTEL SANDER

10 minutes from Kerkstraat

- ★ All rooms with en-suite bathroom
- ★ Colour Cable T.V.
- ★ Direct dial telephone
- ★ F.M. Radio
- ★ Personal safe

- Elevator ★
- 24 hr bar & coffee lounge ★
- Laundry & dry cleaning ★
- Garden & terrace ★
- Rates include breakfast ★
- Credit cards accepted ★

Jacob Obrechtstraat 69
1071 KJ Amsterdam

Tel: 020 - 662 75 74
Fax: 020 - 679 60 67

htlsandr@xs4all.nl

www.xs4all.nl/~htlsandr/

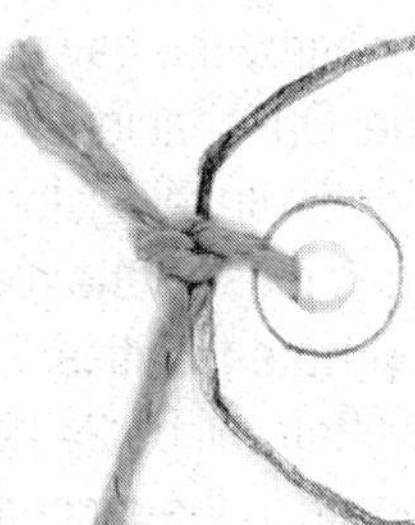

Frederik Park House
S. Hotel, XXL. Rooms
Frederiksplein 22 Amsterdam
Tel:+31 629060460 Fax:+31 206207879
E mail: frederik.park.house@wxs.nl

HOTEL ORLANDO

A ROOM OF ONE'S OWN

DESIGNHOTEL IN 17TH CENTURY CANAL HOUSE IN THE HEART OF AMSTERDAM. 5 ROOMS EACH TASTEFULLY APPOINTED. PRINSENGRACHT 1099
1017 JH AMSTERDAM - TEL. (020) 638 69 15

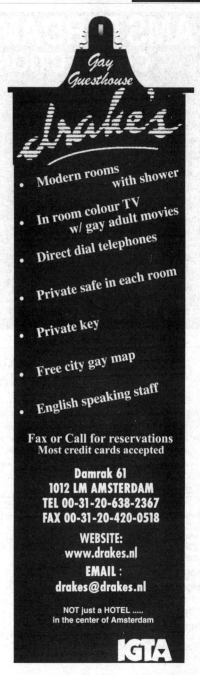

Gay Krant Reisservice Mon 14-18, Tue-Fri 10-18, Sat 10-16 h
Kloveniersburgwal 40 ✉1012 CW ☎ 421 00 00 Fax: 620 62 17
E-Mail: travel@gayworld.nl Homepage: http://www.gayworld.nl
Travel agent and De Gay Krant shop.

VIDEO SHOPS

Gay Rental Video 13-1 h
N. Z. Voorburgwal 51 ✉1012 RD ☎ 622 52 20

HOTELS

Amsterdam House Hotel (b bf CC glm H MA)
's Gravelandveer 3-4 ✉1011 KM ☎ 624 66 07 Fax: 624 13 46
E-Mail:amshouse@euronet.nl
Homepage: www.amsterdamhouse.com
Central location near Rembrandt plein. All rooms en-suite, with TV, phone, safe, VCR. Hotel provides own key. Rates per room from hfl 175 (bf incl.).

Black Tulip (bf CC G H LJ MA W)
Geldersekade 16 ✉1012 BH *(close to Central Station)*
☎ 427 09 33 Fax: 624 42 81 Homepage: www.blacktulip.nl
All rooms with private bath, phone, minibar/fridge, safe. All rooms with sling and bondage hooks. Hotel provides additinal leather and S/M equipment, own key. Rates from hfl 190 (bf incl.) Recommended.

Freeland Hotel (bf CC G H)
Marnixstraat 386 ✉1017 PL ☎ 622 75 11 (reservations)
☎ 627 75 78 (for guests) Fax: 626 77 44
Most rooms en-suite, all with color TV, telephone, full bf.

HOTEL
THE
GOLDEN
BEAR

Golden Bear. The (A b bf CC GLM li H MA N)
Reception: 8-23 h
Kerkstraat 37 ✉1017 GB *(central, Line 1/2/5-Pinsengracht)*
☎ 624 47 85 Fax: 627 01 64 E-Mail: hotel@goldenbear.nl
Homepage: www.goldenbear.nl
Comfortable. Friendly staff. Rates hfl 100-210 incl bf. All rooms with tel, tv, video with/without shower/WC. Recommended.

Hotel Anco (B bf CC f G H lj MA) Bar 9-22 h
Oudezijds Voorburgwal 55 ✉1012 EJ ☎ 624 11 26
Fax: 620 52 75 E-Mail: info@ancohotel.nl
Homepage: www.ancohotel.nl
Very near leather bars. All rooms with shared shower/WC.

Hotel Orlando (bf CC g H)
Prinsengracht 1099 ✉1017 JH *(near Rembrandtplein / tram 4 stop Utrechtsestraat)* ☎ 638 69 15 Fax: 625 21 23
Luxury hotel in a 17th century canal house. Centrally located (near the Amstel river). 5 beautifully decorated rooms with bath/shower, tv, minibar and tel. Friendly staff. Own key for guests. Single hfl. 130-200, double 150-250 incl. bf.

ENJOY THESE GREAT BED & BREAKFAST IN AMSTERDAM

Maes B&B

Relax in a cosy home ambience in residential townhouse. In historical city centre, a short walk from the Central Station, Museums and shops. Near all Gay nightlife and sauna's.

Ken Harrison and Vladimir Melnikov
Herenstraat 26 Amsterdam
Tel:+31 20 427 5165/ Fax:+31 20 427 5166

Email:maesbb94@xs4all.nl
http://www.xs4all.nl/~maesbb94

SUNHEAD OF 1617

Canal House, most rooms with toilet, shower , tv-vcr, fridge, tea/coffee facilities. Own keys, quiet yet central location.
Tel: +31 20 626 1809 / Fax: +31 20 626 1823
Carlos Cecilio
Herengracht 152
Email: carlos@sunhead.com
http://www.sunhead.com

BED & BREAKFAST barangây

Quiet rooms in colonial style, coffee/tea making facilities. TV, fridge, radio alarmclock. We serve a wonderful breakfast in your room.

Right in the old centre, you'll find shops, bars, canals and more just around the corner. Only 5 min. walk from the nearest gay scene.

WIMMO & GODWIN
DROOGBAK 15
TEL. +31 20 777 99 15
FAX +31 20 770 62 99

http://travel.to/barangay
barangay@hot.a2000.nl

Your tropical hide-away just 3 min. from Central Station

Hotel Prinsen (B bf glm H OS)
Vondelstraat 36-38 ✉1054 GE ☎ 616 23 23 Fax: 616 61 12
E-Mail: manager@prinsenhotel.demon.nl
Homepage: www.prinsenhotel.demon.nl
Central location. All rooms with phone, shower, WC, TV, some with bath, balcony. Rates single hfl 185-225, double 250 275.

Hotel Quentin (B bf CC glm H MA OS)
Leidsekade 89 ✉1017 PN *(Tram 1/2/5/11-Leidseplein)*
☎ 626 21 87 Fax: 622 01 21
Centrally located, 30 mins. by bus to the airport. All rooms with TV and phone, some with bath. Hotel provides own key. Rates from single hfl 67.50-110, double 110-240, triple 165-260. Recommended.

Hotel Quentin Engeland (b bf CC g H MA OS)
Roemer Visscherstraat 30 ✉1054 EZ ☎ 689 23 23 Fax: 685 31 48
Downtown location, 15 km to the airport. Hotel with garden. Rooms en suite/shared facilities. Single hfl 85-145, double 110-175, triple 170-240.

Hotel Sander (B bf CC glm H MA OS WO)
Jacob Obrechtstraat 69 ✉1071 KJ ☎ 662 75 74 Fax: 679 60 67
E-Mail: htlsandr@xs4all.nl Homepage: www.xs4all.nl/~htlsandr/
All rooms en-suite, with TV, phone, radio, safe. Rates single hfl 145-185, double 185-225, triple 260-320.

ITC Hotel (B bf CC GLM H MA)
Prinsengracht 1051 ✉1017 JE ☎ 623 02 30 Fax: 624 58 46
E-Mail: office@itc-hotel.com Homepage: www.itc-hotel.com
Nice hotel centrally located. Late bf, personal attention and own front door keys. Single Hfl 80-95, Double 145-175, Triple 225 with/without WC/shower.

New York Hotel (B bf CC GLM H)
Herengracht 13 ✉1015 BA ☎ 624 30 66 Fax: 620 32 30
16 min. by train from the airport. Quiet downtown location, 10-20 min from local gay bars. All rooms with priv. bath, TV and phone. Rates single hfl 150, double 200-250 (bf incl.)

Orfeo (B bf CC G H)
Leidsekruisstraat 14 ✉1017 RH ☎ 623 13 47
Rooms with telephone (direct calls). Single Hfl 75-165, double 115-185 (incl. bf). Weekly rate incl. 1 night free. Special off season rates. Running for 30 years now. Recommended.

Rainbow Palace Hotel (bf g H MA)
Raadhuisstraat 33 B ✉1016 DC ☎ 626 70 86 ☎ 625 43 17
Fax: 420 54 28
Centrally located. All rooms with TV, radio, phone, minibar, partly with shower. Hotel provides own key. Rates from hfl 90. Recommended.

Stable Master Hotel (B f G H LJ MA VS) Bar 20-1, Fri-Sat 20-2 h, closed Tue-Wed
Warmoesstraat 23 ✉1012 HT ☎ 625 01 48 Fax: 624 87 47
Double (Hfl 175) and single rooms with colour TV, fridge, own key. Apartments available from Hfl 200.

GUEST HOUSES

Drake's Guest House (CC G H VS)
Damrak 61 ✉1012 LM ☎ 638 23 67 Fax: 420 05 18
E-Mail: drakes@xs4all.nl Homepage: www.xs4all.nl/~drakes/

Frederik Park House (A bf CC glm H OS)
Frederiksplein 22 ✉1017 XM *(central, Tran 4-Frederiksplein)*
☎ 420 77 26 ☎ 06/29 06 04 60 Fax: 620 78 79
E-Mail: frederik.park.house@wxs.nl
Hotel guesthouse with rooms 40 m² from Hfl 200 incl. bf. Different decorations. Quiet, next to a park with bars and restaurants at the corner. Personal attention and insight guide to Amsterdam.

Jordaan Canal House (bf CC G H MA OS)
Eglantiersgracht 23 ✉1015 RC ☎ 620 15 45 Fax: 638 50 56
E-Mail: Hanspluygers@csi.com
Canal side quiet and cosy hotel in the old city centre. All rooms with bathrooms, tv and hifi. Advance booking advised. Rates from hfl 195 per room per night. Recommended.

Sunhead of 1617 (bf CC GLM H MA)
Herengracht 152 ✉1016 BN ☎ 626 18 09 Fax: 626 18 23
E-Mail: info@sunhead.com Homepage: www.sunhead.com
Central, but quiet location. Mostrooms with shower/WC, all with tv, fridge, coffee/tea facilities and microwave. Own key. Rates hfl 185-195, with canal view 195-215.

APARTMENTS

Amsterdam Connection (G)
☎ 625 74 12
Comfortable apartments all with shower, TV, radio, kitchenette and own key. Rates start at hfl 110.

Amsterdam House (AC CC glm H MA)
Amstel 176a ✉1017 AE ☎ 626 25 77 Fax: 626 29 87
Self catering apartments and house boats. Rates from Hfl 125 one person, double 225, triple 295.
US Reservations: ☎ (904) 677-5370 or ☎ (800) 618-1008 (toll-free), Fax (904) 672-6659.

Centre Apartments Amsterdam (G H LJ MA)
Heintje Hoekssteeg ✉1012 GR ☎ 627 25 03 Fax: 625 11 08
E-Mail: caa-gd@wxs.nl
Homepage: www.gay-apartments-amsterdam.nl
Fully furnished self catering apartments with tv, hifi, video (to rent) and safe. Rates: 1-3 people Hfl 295, studios 245, extra bed 50.

E&D City Apartments Amsterdam (G H LJ)
Single 34 ✉1015 AA ☎ 624 73 35 Fax: 428 48 30
E-Mail: nicenew@worldonline.nl
Centrally located in the Jordaan quarter. 2 people apartments for the leather man and his friend. Minimum stay 3 nights.

PRIVATE ACCOMODATION

Barangây (bf G) Droogbak 15 *(3 min from Central Station)*
☎ 777 99 15 ☎ 62/ 504 54 32 Fax: 770 62 99
E-Mail: barangay@hot.a2000.nl Homepage: www.travel.to/barangay
Bed and Breakfast

Enjoy Bed & Breakfast (bf G H MA YG) 16:30-21:00h
☎ +49 (30) 215 1666 Fax: +49 (30) 217 52219
E-Mail: Info@ebab.com Homepage: www.ebab.com
Price 20 Euro. Accommodation sharing agency. All with shower & bf.

Flightbrokers (GLM H) Mon-Fri 9-20, Sat 10-17
Lange Leidsedwarsstraat 96 ✉1017 NM ☎ 420 28 14
Fax: 420 28 17 E-Mail: info@flightbrokers.nl
Homepage: http://www.flightbrokers.com

Maes Bed & Breakfast (bf CC GLM MA)
Herenstraat 26 ✉1015 CB ☎ 427 51 65 Fax: 427 51 66
E-Mail: maesbb94@xsall.nl Homepage: www.xs4all.nl/~maesbb94
In the Jordaan area. All rooms are nicely decorated and en suite. Non-smoking establishment. Rates hfl 125-175.

GENERAL GROUPS

Act Up
PO Box 15452 ✉1001 ML ☎ 639 25 22

Amsterdam Stetsons. The (GLM) Mon 19.30-22.30, Tue 20-23 h at The Cruise Inn, Zeeburgerdijk 271, Amsterdam-Oost
☎ 419 98 51 ☎ 693 57 54
Country and western line dancing and instruction.

Gay and Lesbian Association (GALA) (GLM)
PO Box 158 15 ✉1001 NH ☎ 616 19 79
Organises factory parties and other gay festivals.

Gay and Lesbian Studies (GLM)
Oude Achterburgwal 185 ✉1012 DK *(Dam Square)* ☎ 525 22 26
Fax: 525 26 14 E-Mail: hekma@pscw.uva.nl
Homepage: http://www.pscw.uva.nl/internationalschool

Homogroep VSSM
PB 3570 ✉1001 AJ ☎ 420 21 78

Stichting IHTA (A GLM S STV) Tue Thu Fri 14-17 h
1e Helmershaat 17BG ✉1054 CX ☎ 676 36 26 Fax: 676 36 26
E-Mail: ihta@wxs.nl Homepage: http://home.wxl.nl
International gay and lesbian art projects.

FETISH GROUPS

Master Terry's SM Society & School
Pienemanstraat 46 ✉1072 KV *(Tram 25)* ☎ 671 06 82
S&M instruction for gay & bisexual males only.

MS Amsterdam
PO Box 35 40 ✉1001 AH
☎ & Fax: 620 35 83
Member of ECMC.

HEALTH GROUPS

Aids Fonds
Keizersgracht 390-392 ✉1016 GB ☎ 626 26 68
Fax: 627 52 21
A.I.D.S.-Infolijn Mon-Fri 14-22 h
☎ 06/022 22 20
Fight for Life Foundation
Keizersgracht 670 ✉1017 ET ☎ 627 50 93
HIV-Café 4 US
Rozenstraat 14 ✉1016 NX ☎ 623 40 79
HIVnet Computernetwork for HIV and Aids
Van Limburg Stirumstraat 22A ✉1051 BB ☎ 684 19 69
Fax: 681 15 04
HIV-Vereniging Nederland Mon, Wen, Fri 13-16, Tue, Thu 20-22.30, Sat 20-0.30
1e Helmersstraat 17 ✉1054 CX ☎ 616 01 60 Fax: 681 15 04
Homepage: http://www.hivnet.org
Association that safeguards the interests of people who are carriers of hiv (medical, welfare, juridical, social, assistential, representational). Saturday HIV-Café.
Stichting Duc d'Alf
PB 1331 ✉1000 BH ☎ 618 25 95
Stichting No Time
PB 93006 ✉1090 BA ☎ 689 08 97
Venereal disease Clinic GG & GD Mon-Fri 8-10.30, 13.30-15.30 h
Groenburgwal 44 ☎ 555 58 22 ☎ 555 52 70
Fax: 555 57 51
Free testing for EC citizens. AIDS testing anonymous if wanted NOT free of charge: Nieuwe Achtergracht 100

HELP WITH PROBLEMS

HIV-Plusline Mon Wed Fri 13-16, Tue Thu 20-22.30 h
☎ 685 00 55
Assistance service.
Project Jongens Prostitutie (G YG)
N. Z. Voorburgwal 38 ☎ 555 54 62 ☎ 555 52 90

RELIGIOUS GROUPS

Christelijk Homo Jongeren (GLM)
PO Box 14722 ✉1001 LE ☎ 023/539 11 87
Stichting Sjalhomo (G)
PB 2636 ✉1000 CM ☎ 023/531 23 18

SPECIAL INTEREST GROUPS

Gay Bridge Club
Lijnbaansgracht 185 ✉1016 XA ☎ 627 93 80
Gay Garden Club. The (G)
PB 15672 ✉1001 ND ☎ 688 12 43 Fax: 688 12 43
E-Mail: ancion@wol.nl Homepage: http://www.gaygardenclub.nl
Europe's only pink club for green fingers. Monthly meeting in Holland, trips abroad, lectures....

SPORT GROUPS

Gay Swim Amsterdam (GLM)
☎ 625 20 85
Tijgertje (glm)
PB 10521 ✉1001 EM
☎ 673 24 58
Sports organization including self defense, (karate), basketball, wrestling, joga, fitness-training, aerobics, badminton, volleyball and swimming.

SWIMMING

☛ Zandvoort

CRUISING

-Vliegenbos, Meeuwenlaan (AYOR) (Amsterdam Noord)
-Vondelpark (very popular at night)
-Oosterpark
-Sarfatipark (busy at night)
-Nieuwe Meer. Take tram 2 and stop before the last stop then walk direction north. popular in summer, daytime
-Oosterdok (next to main post office by C.S.)
-Bilderdijkpark (busy at night)

Apeldoorn ☎ 055

BARS

Schouw. De (AC B d DR GLM MA OS W WE) Fri 22-2, Sat 23-4, Sun 14-19, Mon 20-23 (door closed at 21.30) h
Spadelaan 8 ✉7331 AL ☎ 541 70 35 ☎ 33 32 49
Special sex parties. Call for dates.

SEX SHOPS/BLUE MOVIES

Christine Le Duc (CC g VS) Mon-Fri 10-22, Sat -17.30 h
Asselsestraat 131 ✉7311 EJ ☎ 522 51 04
Cinema Shop Station (DR g MA VS) Mon-Fri 11-23, Sat Sun 11-19 h
Stationsdwarsstraat 20 ✉7311 NW *(near station)* ☎ 522 11 81
Station (DR g MA r VS) 10.30-18 h
Stationsdwarsstraat 20 ✉7311 NW ☎ 522 11 81
Tutti Frutti (B DR f G MA sa VS) 10-24, Sun 13-24 h
Marktstraat 15 ✉7511 LH *(near market place)* ☎ 522 42 73
Shop, sauna, movie place.

GENERAL GROUPS

COC-Apeldoorn (GLM)
PB 15 ✉7300 AA ☎ 533 22 32
Call for info on activities.

GALLERIES

Galerie Ho-EenSeven (A G MA) Thu-Sun 13-17 h or by appointment
Schoolstraat 17 ✉4241 XA ☎ 56 42 86 Fax: 56 41 90
E-Mail: info@ho-eenseven.nl
Specialises in male nudes.

Arnhem ☎ 026

BARS

Brazzon (B GLM YG) 17-1 Thu-Sun -2 h
Nieuwstraat 66 ✉6811 HX ☎ 370 34 60
Café Noir (B GLM) Coehoornstraat 8 ✉6811 LA
☎ 442 80 72
HIV+ café on Wed.
Diva (B GLM) Mon Wed 17-1 Thu Sun -2 h. closed on Tue
Rodenburghstraat 63 ✉6811 HX ☎ 370 34 84
Entre Nous (B D f GLM) Fri Sat 22-4 Sun 20-3 h
Sweerts de Landastraat 65 ✉6814 DB ☎ 445 06 52
Yentl (A B d GLM MA S) Tue-Sun 17-1, Thu-Sat -2 h, closed Mon
Nieuwe Keyebergseweg 158 ✉6811 BV *(Next to theatre)*
☎ 370 42 03
Bar and art gallery.

CAFÉS

Café Spring (B f GLM MA OS) Wed-Sat 16-2, Sun-Tue 16-1 h
Bovenbeekstraat 5 ✉6811 CV *(near central station)*
☎ 442 50 36

Keldercafé Dwars (B GLM MA) Wed-Sat 22-4 h
Sweerts de Landasstraat 65 ✉6814 DB ☎ 445 06 52

SEX SHOPS/BLUE MOVIES

Christine Le Duc (CC g VS) Mon-Fri 10-22, Sat 10-17.30 closed Sun
Walstraat 55 ✉6811 BD ☎ 445 65 77

GENERAL GROUPS

COC-Midden Gelderland (GLM) Wed Fri 13-18, Thu 13-18, 19-21 Sat 13-17 h
PB 359 ✉6800 AJ *(Nieuwstad 50)* ☎ 442 31 61
E-Mail: mail@cocmg.demon.nl
Advice, information and shop for gays and lesbians. Call for info on activities.

HEALTH GROUPS

Aidsoverleggroep
c/o GG & GD, Broerenstraat 55 ✉6811 EB

CRUISING

-Park Sonsbeekpark (near westside entrance at Zijpendaalseweg, evenings and nights)
-Rozendaalsebos
-Railway station

Assen ☎ 0592

CRUISING

-Asserbos 15-20 (city park, directly behind ice stadium)
-Parking space Snelweg (Assen-Noord/Assen-West, by small petrol station off Assen-West)
-A28 (E35) Assen-Groningen (parking space Glimmenade, 7km south of Groningen, off north-bound carriageway)
-De Moere (NU) (12 km southeast of Assen, lake on west-side, 14-20 h)

Baarle Nassau ☎ 013

SEX SHOPS/BLUE MOVIES

Fun House (g VS) 10-22 h
Nieuwstraat 22 ✉5111 CW ☎ 507 91 62

Bergen ☎ 072

HOTELS

Vie en Rose. La (bf glm H MA OS)
15 Mar-31 Dec
Ruinelaan 34 ✉1861 LL ☎ 589 50 23 Fax: 589 50 23
E-Mail: lavieenrosebergennl@xahoo.com
Downtown location. 3 km to sea. 7 double (Hfl 90), 3 single (45) with shared WC.

Bergen aan Zee ☎ 072

CRUISING

-Beach near Pile 36 and nude area between piles 31 and 32

Bergen op Zoom ☎ 0164

BARS

Café Dwars (B GLM MA s) Mon-Thu 20-2, Fri 17-2.30, Sat 20-2.30, Sun 16-2 h
Engelsestraat 14 ✉4611 RR ☎ 23 08 16

COC-Café (B D GLM MA) Fri-Sat 22-2.30, Last Sun/month 16-22 h
Blokstallen 4 ✉4611 WB *(close to Gevangenpoort)* ☎ 25 42 35
Bar Disco. Special parties are organised on a regular basis.

GENERAL GROUPS

COC-Bergen op Zoom (GLM) PB 590 ✉4600 AN
☎ 25 42 35
Call for info on activities.

Best ☎ 0499

BARS

Manus (B G MA) 11.30-2 h
Nieuwstraat 92

CRUISING

-De Baan (behind Makro, Gagel)
-Route E9 (Eindhoven/Best)

Boekel ☎ 0492

BARS

Sam Sam (AC B CC f GLM MA OS S) Wed-Sat 19-?, Sun 15-?
Volkelseweg 7 ✉5427 RA ☎ 32 43 25 Fax: 32 10 98.

RESTAURANTS

Restaurant 't Swaenlje (AC B CC F glm MA OS) 16-23 h
Volkelsweg 7 ✉5427 RA ☎ 32 43 25

Bourtange ☎ 0599

CAMPING

Boerderij „La Cagnotte" (b bf GLM MA) Apr 1st-Sep 30th
1e Pallertweg 5 ✉9545 TV *(near German border, old fortress)*
☎ 35 42 74
Camping spots and 1 log cabin. Reservations necessary. From F8.60. No pets.

Breda ☎ 076

BARS

Café Romeo (B GLM MA s) 19-2, Sat Sun 17-2 h, closed on Tue
Nieuwstraat 19 ✉4811 WV ☎ 521 80 31
Sun evening shows.

First floor (B G LJ) Fri-Mon 21-2, Tue 21-1 h
Molenstraat 5 ☎ 521 50 05 *Dresscode on Mon.*

Now en ?! (B GLM) 20-1, Thu-Sat 20-2, Sun 16-2 h
Molenstraat 5 ☎ 521 50 05
Venise (AC B D GLM MA OS s TV) Mon-Wed 20.30-2, Thu-Sun 16-2 h
Halsstraat 30 ✉4811 HX ☎ 521 67 02

SEX SHOPS/BLUE MOVIES

Christine Le Duc (CC g VS) Mon-Fri 10-22, Sat 10-17.30 h, closed Sun
Haagdijk 14 ✉4811 TT ☎ 522 57 77
Also blue movies.

SAUNAS/BATHS

Sauna Liberty (B DR f G MA sa sb VS) 14-24, Sun 14-22 h
Chassésingel 1 ✉4811 HA *(Bus 3/7)* ☎ 522 09 76
Sauna with friendly bar.

BOOK SHOPS

Vrije Boekhandel. De (g) 9-18 h
Veemarkt 40 ✉4811 ZG ☎ 514 54 91

GENERAL GROUPS

COC-Breda (GLM) Danscafé: (B D G MA W WE) Fri Sat 0-4 h
PB 1420 ✉4800 GG *(Sint Annastraat 10)* ☎ 522 66 62

CRUISING

-Valkenberg (Citypark opposite Central Station)
-liesbos (near E10)
-Kalix Berna (A27 direction Utrecht)
-Galgewaard (A27 direction Breda, popular)
-Lage Aard (A58 direction Tilburg-Breda, unofficial nude area)
-Galderse Meren (NU) (recreation area 7km south of Breda. Northern lake)

Bussum ☎ 035

GENERAL GROUPS

HoLé (AC B GLM YG) Thu 21-24 h youth Café „Opsessie"
Brediusweg 1 ✉1401 AA *(2nd floor)* ☎ 694 88 99
Fax: 694 77 91 E-Mail: reloos@worldonline.nl
Homepage: http://www.huisen.dds.nl/~relo/index.html
For youngsters under 30.

Callantsoog ☎ 0224

CRUISING

-Sand dunes near nudist beach (direction Petten; also Pile 16)

Capelle a.d. Ijssel ☎ 010

GENERAL GROUPS

Stichting Reborn (b f glm MA p TV) Mon-Fri 10-17 2nd Fri 21-2 h
Maria Danneelserf 10 ✉2907 BD ☎ 458 34 69

Delft ☎ 015

BARS

D.W.H. (Delftse Werkgroep Homoseksualiteit) (AC B d DR GLM MA) Mon (safe sex) 22-24, Wed Sun 21-0.30, Fri -2, Sat/once a month (D) 22-3.30 h
Lange Geer 22 ✉2611 AN *(near station, opposite to the het Leger-museum)* ☎ 214 68 93
Kijlekit. De (B G MA)
Phoenixstraat 96 ☎ 214 10 96

RESTAURANTS

Bodega „De Kejser" (B F g OS) 12-24, meals served -22.30 h
Markt 17 a ✉2611 GP ☎ 213 49 96
International cuisine. Try the fondue. Menu available from hfl 25-40, à la carte 25-50.

Delfzijl ☎ 0596

CRUISING

-Zoo Promenade (harbor area)

Den Haag ☎ 070

BARS

Boko Bar (A AC B d F Glm MA W) Thu-Mon 21-2 h
Nieuwe Schoolstraat 1 ✉2514 HT ☎ 427 35 97
Café de Landman (B g) 16-1 h
Denneweg 48 ✉2514 CH ☎ 346 77 27
Popular.
Frenz (AC B d G MA s snu stv) Thu-Sun 20-3 h, closed Mon-Wed
Kazernestraat 106 ✉2514 CW *(Near Central Station, behind Hotel des Indes)* ☎ 363 66 57
Stairs (AC B D G lj MA) 22-2, Sun 17-2 h, closed Mon
Nieuwe Schoolstraat 11a ✉2514 HT ☎ 364 81 91
Triumpf (B GLM) 16-1 h
Kettingstraat 4-6 ✉2511 AN ☎ 346 71 07
Vink (AC B f G MA r s) 16-1 h
Schoolstraat 30 ✉2511 AX ☎ 365 03 57

CAFES

Internetcafé Den Haag (B F glm MA W) 17-1 h, closed on Sun
Elandstraat 48 ✉2513 GT *(Tram 3-Elandstraat)* ☎ 363 62 86

DANCECLUBS

Strass (AC B D GLM tv) Fri-Sat 22-5 h
Balistraat 1/Javastraat ✉2585 XK ☎ 363 65 22
The only after hours place in Den Haag.

RESTAURANTS

B'engel - Eet & Drinkgelegenheid (B CC F glm MA OS s) 17-1 (kitchen 10.15-22.30 h)
Hooikade 2 ✉2514 BH *(central, Tram 1/9/7- Dr. Kuyperst)* ☎ 364 28 98
Bar restaurant located in the Hague's canal environment.

SEX SHOPS/BLUE MOVIES

Christine Le Duc (CC g VS) Mon-Fri 10-22, Sat -17.30 h
Piet Heinplein 1 ✉2518 CA ☎ 362 52 95
Hotlips (G VS) 12-24 h
Herengracht 50A ✉2511 EJ ☎ 345 05 10
Also gay cinema.
Mulder (g VS) 10-24, Sat 10-18 h, closed Sun
Herengracht 24a ✉2511 EJ ☎ 346 27 27

HOUSE OF BOYS

Ted Jacobs (B G) 13-24, Sat 13-18 h, closed Sun
Hoge Zand 92a ✉2512 EN ☎ 346 00 37

SAUNAS/BATHS

Eldorado (AC B G msg R sa sol VS) Mon-Fri 13-24, Sat -18 h, Sun closed
Hogezand 90 ✉2512 EN *(Tram 6, 2, 10)* ☎ 020/346 00 37
Entrance-fee Hfl 29,50. Part of Ted Jacobs House of Boys.

Fides (B f DR G MA sa sb sol VS) 14-24 h
Veenkade 20 ✉2513 EG ☎ 346 39 03
Clean and friendly sauna. Entrance-fee Hfl 25.

BOOK SHOPS

American Book Center. The (CC g) Mon-Sat 10-18, Thu -21 h, closed Sun
Lange Poten 23 ✉2511 CM ☎ 364 27 42
General bookstore with gay section (English language)
Ruward (g)
Spui 231 ✉2511 BP ☎ 363 08 79

TRAVEL & TRANSPORT

Gay and Lesbian Travel List
Weimarstraat 412 ✉2562 HX ☎ 363 65 63
Short term housing in private homes in different countries.

HOTELS

Astoria (b bf glm H MA) 7-23 h
Stationsweg 139 ✉2515 BM ☎ 384 04 01 Fax: 380 78 91
Shower and WC in all rooms.
Bellevue (g H)
Stationsweg 80 ✉2515 BP ☎ 380 17 51 *Rooms per hour.*

GENERAL GROUPS

COC-Haaglanden (GLM) Bar: (B d GLM MA) Wed 17-24, Thu 21-2, Fri Sat -1.30 h, Sat: women only
Scheveninseveer 7 ✉2514 HB *(next to the Queen's palace „Noordeine")* ☎ 365 90 90 E-Mail: coc@dehaag.demon.nl

HEALTH GROUPS

AIDS Spreekuur Tue Thu 19-21 h
Van Beverningkstraat 134 ✉2582 VL ☎ 354 16 10

CRUISING

-Het Haagsebos-Leidsestraatweg (AYOR R) (near station)
-De Scheveningsebosjes-Jacobsweg (safe, between the trees, very busy)

Den Helder ☎ 0223

BARS

Chez Nous (B D G) 22-2 Fri Sat -4 h closed Mon Tue
Emmastraat 105 ✉1782 PC ☎ 61 44 45

GENERAL GROUPS

COC-Kop von Noord-Holland (GLM)
Vismarkt 5 ✉1781 DA ☎ 61 87 38 *Cal for info on activities.*

SWIMMING

-Strandslag Droogeweert (G NU) (by the small firewatch tower in the dunes)

CRUISING

-Kennedypark

Deventer ☎ 0570

GENERAL GROUPS

COC-Ijsselstreek (GLM)
Assenstraat 151 ✉7411 JZ ☎ 61 91 49
Call for info on activities.

Doetinchem ☎ 0314

BARS

Mi Ami (B D glm) Thu-Sat 20-2, Sun 16-2 h
Dr Hubernoodtstraat 50 ✉7001 DX ☎ 32 68 78

GENERAL GROUPS

Stichting Homoseksualiteit Achterhoek
PO Box 8031 ✉7000 DE ☎ 36 08 11

Domburg ☎ 0118

APARTMENTS

Jonathan Appartments (H)
Domburgseweg 30 ✉4357 NH *(500 m from village/200 m from beach)* ☎ 58 37 10 Fax: 58 37 10

Dordrecht ☎ 078

CAFES

Nickolson (B g) Sun 21-1 h
Voorstraat 426 ✉3311 CX ☎ 613 37 88

GENERAL GROUPS

COC-Dordrecht (GLM)
PB 934 ✉3300AX *(Dolhuisstraat 4)* ☎ 613 17 17
Call for info on activities.

CRUISING

-De Merwelanden (near Spaarbekken)
-Weizigtpark (close to central station)

Ede ☎ 0318

BARS

Feestje. 'T (B D G) Thu Sun 21-2, Fri Sat 21-3 h
De Halte 7A ✉6711 NZ *(centre)* ☎ 69 44 51

Eindhoven ☎ 040

BARS

Charlies Pub (AC B d F g MA OS) Wed-Sun 17-2 h
Dommelstraat 36 ✉5611 CL *(round the corner from De DansSalon)* ☎ 243 88 04
Club Funki Bizniz (B G MA) 19-2, Fri-Sat 14-2, Sun 16-2 h, Mon closed.
Stratumsedijk 35
Nephews (AC B d f glm MA OS p s) 21-4 h
Stratumsedijk 14 ✉5611 ND *(Bus 6/7/8 Stratumsedijk)*
☎ 211 80 13 Homepage: http://www.lichtstad.com/nephews/
Micky Mouse decoration.
Pêcheur. Le (AC B D f GLM YG) 21-2 h Fri Sat -4 h closed Tue
Stratumsedijk 37A ✉5611 NB ☎ 211 91 03
Queen's Pub (B GLM MA) 20-2, Sun 16-2 h, closed Thu
Lambertusstraat 42 ✉5615 PH ☎ 244 25 06
Shakespeare (B G MA) 20-2 h
Kloosterdreef 108
Vagevuur (B DR G LJ MA P s WE) Call for programme
Kanaaldijk Noord 11 ☎ 244 27 44

CAFES

Café Boschdijk (B GLM MA) Tue-Sun 12-2 h
Boschdijk 229 ☎ 243 91 42

DANCECLUBS

Danssalon. De (AC B D E f GLM MA S WE) Sun gay night 21-2 h
Stationsplein 4 ✉5600 AP *(Near central station)* ☎ 245 63 77
Last Sun/month black dresscode.

SEX SHOPS/BLUE MOVIES

Christine Le Duc (CC g VS) Mon-Fri 10-22, Sat 10-17.30 h, closed Sun
Willemstraat 33 ✉5611 HB ☎ 243 90 81

SAUNAS/BATHS

Jaguar (B f DR G NU OS sa sb sol VS) 12-24, Sun 13-20, Sat 12-2 h free soup
Ledeganckstraat 1 ✉5615 KC ☎ 251 12 38
Entrance-fee Hfl 22,50.

Royal (B F DR G H pi sa sb sol VS wh WO) Mon-Thu 12-24, Fri-Sun 12-8 h
Stratumsedijk 23f ✉5611 NA *(8 min from station)* ☎ 211 08 40
Renovated and clean. Recommended. Also hotel. Entrance-fee Hfl 25.

HOTELS

Hotel Royal (bf CC G H)
Stratumsedijk 23F ✉5611 NA ☎ 212 13 30 Fax: 211 65 93
Single Hfl 112.50, double room Hfl 125 incl. bf and parking place. All room with shower/WC, tel, TV.

GENERAL GROUPS

COC-Eindhoven (GLM) Café (B f GLM MA OS): Mon-Fr 10-16, Tue Thu Fr 21-1, Sun 15-22 h
PB 206 ✉5600 AE *(Prins Hendrikstraat 54)* ☎ 245 57 00
Lesbian 1st & 3rd Wed 21-? h.

De Kringen (B GLM MA) 2nd 4th Sat 20.30-1 h
PO Box 6323 ✉5600 HH
at Studentenbunker, room Eskafé, Kennedylaan/v.d. Heuvellaan.

CRUISING

-Dommelplantsoen (Elzentlaan/Jan Smitzslaan/Anna Frank Plantsoen)
-"E3 plas" (NU) (between Eersel and Vessem)
-De Hut van Mie Pils, Waalre (moors between Eindhoven & Leende)
-De Baan (behind Makro; Gagel, E9 Eindhoven)

Emmen ☎ 0591

GENERAL GROUPS

COC-Drenthe (GLM)
PB 2242 ✉7801 CE ☎ 62 03 13 *Call for info on activities.*

SWIMMING

-De Kleine Rietplas (g NU) (in summer on WE or week days late)

CRUISING

-Marktplein (near Stadthuis)
-Bargeresbos (right and left side)

Enschede ☎ 053

GAY INFO

COC Mediatheek Thu 19-21 h
Walstraat 12-14 ✉7511 GH

BARS

For You (B G MA) 21-4, Sun 16-4 h.
Molenstraat 22 *(near station)* ☎ 432 03 01

Poort van Kleef (B f glm OS) 10-2 h
Oude Markt 19 ☎ 432 37 02

CAFÉS

Café Stonewall (AC B d g GLM MA OS S) Thu 19.30-23.30 (YG) Fri -2, Sat 15.30-2, Sun -20.30 h
Walstraat 12-14 ✉X ☎ 431 70 14

RESTAURANTS

Hans & Heinz Bistro (B F NG) 17-1 h closed Wed
Walstraat 5 ☎ 432 52 62

Petite Bouffe. La (A AC CC E glm MA OS) 17.30-22 h, closed Mon Tue
Deurningerstraat 11 ✉7514 BC ☎ 435 85 91
French cuisine.

SEX SHOPS/BLUE MOVIES

Amsterdam (G VS) 12-23, Sat -18, Sun 14-18 h
Molenstraat 14-16 ✉7514 DK ☎ 433 74 01

SAUNAS/BATHS

Bölke. 't (AC B DR F G MA msg pi sa sb VS wh WO) Sun-Thu 14-24, Fri Sat 14-2 h
Molenstraat 6-8 ✉7514 DK *(Near railway station)* ☎ 434 13 41

GENERAL GROUPS

COC-Twente/Achterhoek (GLM) Mon 14-14 (L) Wed 10-11.30 Fri 13-14 h
PB 444 ✉7500 AK *(Walstraat 12-14)* ☎ 430 51 77
Call for info on activities.

CRUISING

-Volkspark
-Vliegveld, Veldschoterweg
-Het Rutbeek (5 km southwest of Enschede, follow cycle-path east side, 15-20 h)

Epen ☎ 043

HOTELS

Vier Jaargetijden. De (B bf F g H MA OS)
Wilhelminastraat 43 ✉6285 ☎ 455 21 77
Downtown neighborhood location, 20 min from Maastricht airport. All rooms with priv. bath. Single hfl 45-50, double 90-100 (bf incl.).

Gemert ☎ 0492

GENERAL GROUPS

Stichting Homo Groep Gemert (B GLM MA YG) Mon 20-24, last Sun 15-18 h
Ruyschenberghstraat 3, PO Box 167 ✉5420 AD ☎ 36 68 94

Goes ☎ 0113

BARS

Kelderbar (B g) Tue-Wed 20-2, Thu-Sat -4 h
Blauwe Steen 5

CRUISING

-Poelbos
-Oostendestraat

Gouda ☎ 0182

SEX SHOPS/BLUE MOVIES

Bureau 700 (g VS) 13-18 h, closed Sun
Raam 66 ✉2801 VM ☎ 51 43 81

Erotheek (g VS) 10.30-22.30, Sat -21 h
Waluisstraat 9 ✉2802 SB ☎ 58 23 02

VIDEO SHOPS

Liberty (g) 10-22 h
Vredebest 22 ✉2801 AS ☎ 58 53 90

GENERAL GROUPS

COC-Gouda (GLM)
PB 3026 ✉2800 CC *(Spieringstraat 113 A)* ☎ 52 46 34
Call for info on activities.

CRUISING

-Bus station
-Railway station
-Houtmansplantsoen, near band stand
-Ysselpark

Groningen ☎ 050

BARS

Café Leto (A B f G OS s) 15-2 h, closed Tue
A-Kerkstraat 20 ☎ 313 59 60
El Rubio (B GLM MA OS s TV) Sun-Fri 16-?, Sat 15-? h
Zwanestraat 26 ✉9700 ☎ 314 00 39
Koningin. De (B gLm MA)
Boteringstraat 60
For lesbians and their friends.
Mac. The (AC B D DR F Glm lj MA SNU VS YG) 23-?, Sun 17-? closed Mon-Wed
Hoge der A 3 ☎ 312 71 88
Rits. De (B G) 16-1, Fri Sar -2 h
Pottenbakkersrijge 2 ☎ 318 01 66
Small coffee bar.

DANCECLUBS

Golden Arm. De (B D DR GLM P) Thu-Sun 23-6 h
Hardewikerstraat 7 ✉9712 GR ☎ 313 16 76

RESTAURANTS

Twee Dames. De (F glm MA p S) 18-23 h, closed Sun and Mon
Ged. Zuiderdiep 64 ✉9711 HK *(next to Pathé Cinema)*
☎ 314 20 52
Cabaret/piano/entertainment every evening. Show starts at 21 h.

SEX SHOPS/BLUE MOVIES

Christine Le Duc (CC g VS) Mon-Fri 10-22, Sat -17.30 h, closed Sun
Zuiderdiep 88 ✉9711 HL ☎ 318 26 30
Videotheek 3000 (G VS) 11-23, Sat 13-19, Sun 17-22.30 h
Ged. Zuiderdiep 130 ✉9711 HM ☎ 314 42 21

SAUNAS/BATHS

Sauna t' Pakhuisje (B f DR G ma sa sb sol VS wh) Mon-Thu 14-24, Fri 14-Sun 20 h
Schuitemakerstraat 17 ✉9711 HW ☎ 312 92 88

HOTELS

Friesland (g H)
Kleine Pelsterstraat 4 ☎ 312 13 07

GENERAL GROUPS

COC-Groningen (GLM)
PB 144 ✉9700 AC *(Kraneweg 56)* ☎ 313 26 20
Call for info on activities.

CRUISING

-Behind Main Post Office
-Noorderplantsoen
-P „Glimmermade" E35 (A28) Assen (Groningen, north-bound)
-Hoornseplas (south, near road Haren, Groningen)
-Nude beach (action until late)
-Stadspark

Haarlem ☎ 023

BARS

Gay Café Wilsons (B d f G MA s) Wed Thu Sun 20-2, Fri Sat 22-4, closed Mon Tue
Gedempte Raamgracht 78 ✉2011 WK ☎ 532 58 54
Jeltes (B glm) 16-2, Fri Sat 16-4, Sun 17-2 h
Schagelstraat 15
Justesse. La (B G MA) 20-2, Fri Sat 17-4 h, closed on Mon & Tue
Ged. Oudegracht 127 ☎ 532 40 52

DANCECLUBS

Lounge Stalker (B D GLM MA) last Sat
Kromme Elleboogsteeg 20
Hosted by famous Dutch transvestite Dolly Bellefleur.

SEX SHOPS/BLUE MOVIES

Christine Le Duc (CC g VS) Mon-Fri 10-22, SSat -17.30 h, closed Sun
Generaal Cronjéstraat 77 ✉2021 JC ☎ 525 97 35

CINEMAS

Gay-Sex Cinema (DR G VS) 12-24 h
Turfsteeg 2 ☎ 531 11 00
Roxy Sex Theater (DR G VS) 12-24 h
Kleine Houtstraat 77 ☎ 532 51 39

BOOK SHOPS

Agora (glm) Mon 13-18, Tue Wed Fr 10-18, Thu -21, Sat -17 h
Zijlstraat 100 ✉2011 TR ☎ 531 31 82

GENERAL GROUPS

COC-Kennemerland (GLM) Mon-Fri 10-16 h
PB 342 ✉2011 GR *(Gedempte Oudegracht 24)* ☎ 532 54 53
Call for info on activities.

CRUISING

-Haarlemmerhout (park, Hertenkamp) after dark
-Bolwerk (behind the station) after dark

Heerlen ☎ 045

BARS

Bodytalk (AC B d G LJ MA s) Tue-Thu 21-2, Fri-Sun -3 h, closed on Mon
Gringelstraat 3 ✉6412 AK *(near railway station)* ☎ 572 74 63
Gay Cocktail (B D GLM MA) 21-3 h Fri Sat (G DR VS)
Oude Kerkstraat 7 ✉6412 XD ☎ 522 69 53
Splash N.Y Café (AC D G MA N p S YG) Tue-Thu 21-2, Fri Sat -3, Sun 15-3 h, Mon closed
Kemkensweg 7 ✉6412 AV ☎ 572 83 26

DANCECLUBS

Splash N.Y. (AC D GLM S TV YG) Sun 21-3 h
Pancratiusstraat 44 ✉6411 KC ☎ 571 12 66

SEX SHOPS/BLUE MOVIES

Christine Le Duc (CC g VS) Mon 13-18.30, Tue-Sat 9-18.30 h, closed on Sun
Dautzenbergstraat 5 ✉6411 LA ☎ 571 75 53

GENERAL GROUPS

COC-Heerlen (GLM)
Honigmanstraat 2 ✉6411 LL ☎ 571 73 87
Call for info for activities.

Hengelo ☎ 074

PR & PHOTOGRAPHY SERVICES

Vakfotografie Ulrich (A p YG)
Breemarsweg 396 ✉7553 JC ☎ 290 96 76 Fax: 290 96 76
E-Mail: vfulrich@introweb.nl Homepage: http://www.vfulrich.nl

'S Hertogenbosch/Den Bosch ☎ 073

BARS

Club Chez Nous (AC B D GLM MA s) 22-4 h
Vughterstraat 158 ✉5211 GH ☎ 614 25 92
COC-Café The Cockpitt (B D GLM MA) Thu 20-1, Fri-Sat -2, Sun 15-1 h
Vughterstraat 277 ☎ 614 16 75
Kings (B glm) Fri Sat 22-4 h
Vughterstraat 99A ☎ 613 44 79

CAFES

Stamineeke. 'T (B f g MA) Tue Wed 12-1, Thu Fri -2, Sat Sun 14-2 h
Ie Korenstraatje 16 ✉5211 EJ ☎ 614 36 46

SEX SHOPS/BLUE MOVIES

Christine Le Duc (CC g VS) Mon-Fri 10-22, Sat -17.30 h, closed Sun
Vughterstraat 62-64 ✉5211 GK ☎ 612 31 76

VIDEO SHOPS

Cinetex Video Verhuur BV (CC g MA VS) Mon-Sat 11-22 h
Vughterstraat 111 ☎ 614 34 86

GENERAL GROUPS

COC-Den Bosch (GLM)
PB 1420 ✉5200 BL *(Vughterstraat 277)* ☎ 614 16 75 E-Mail: denbosch@coc.nl Homepage: http://www.coc.nl/denbosch/
Call for info on activities.

HEALTH GROUPS

Buddyproject
☎ 642 12 21
Help for people with AIDS.

CRUISING

-Tennisbaan-Heekellaan (evening)
-Railway station (r)

Hilversum ☎ 035

BARS

COC-Café Happe Tappe (AC B d F GLM lj MA s snu) 22-1 h
Naarerstraat 43 *(15 min from station)* ☎ 697 03 70
So What (AC B GLM MA OS) 16-1, Fri-Sat -2 h
Noorderweg 72 ✉1221 AB ☎ 683 10 03

SEX SHOPS/BLUE MOVIES

Black & White Sexshop (g MA VS) 10-23 h
Vaartweg 24c ☎ 621 97 85
Gay film video cabines

GENERAL GROUPS

COC't Gooi en omstreken (GLM)
PB 1631 ✉1200 BP *(Tagrijn, Koninginnewg 44)* ☎ 697 03 70
Call for info on activities.

CRUISING

-Route A27 (E37) Breda (Almere, at km 90.2)
-P Bosberg (near Hilversum)

Hoek van Holland ☎ 01747

CRUISING

-Nudist beach between piles 116110 and 116360 (Rechtzeestraat, between two camping areas opposite 's Gravenzande)
-Maasvlakte (opposite road to first Overslag service)

Hoogeveen ☎ 0528

CRUISING

-N37 → Emmen (1st P after Hoogeveen)

Hoorn ☎ 0229

CRUISING

-P De Koggen (A7 from Purmerend to Hoorn)
-P ABC (after 16 h)
-Westerdijk (near De Hulk; summer only)

Hulst ☎ 0114

GENERAL GROUPS

Stichting Tent
Wilhelminastraat 1 ✉4564 AC ☎ 31 59 20
Help with coming out problems.

Ijzendijke ☎ 0117

BARS

Homotel Queen (A CC f G H MA OS p sa wh) 19-5 h
Landpoortstraat 10 ✉4515 CB ☎ 30 23 27
Mercury Gay Bar (B CC D p S VS YG) 19-5 h
Landpoortstraat 10 ✉4515 CB ☎ 30 23 27

Klazienaveen ☎ 0591

SEX SHOPS/BLUE MOVIES

Lektuurhal Candy (g VS W) Tue-Fri 13-18 h
Langestraat 168 ✉7890 AC ☎ 39 02 22 Fax: 39 02 23

Leeuwarden ☎ 058

GAY INFO

AnnA Blaman Huis (AC GLM p W) Mo Fr 13-17, Tue-Thu 14-18, Thu -21
PO Box 40 62, Zuidvliet 118 ✉8901 EB ☎ 212 18 29
Fax: 213 91 31 E-Mail: 101560.2554@compuserve.com
Intercultural information-place.
COC Friesland Gay Switchborad / Service Center (GLM) Mon-Fri 13-17 h
Noordvliet 11 ✉8921 GD *(10 min from the station)*
☎ 212 49 08 Fax: 212 49 08 E-Mail: info@friesland.coc.nl
Homepage: http://www.friesland.coc.nl

BARS

COC Friesland Café (B d GLM MA s) Sat 21-1 h
Maria Annastraatje 5-7 ✉8911 HP *(5 min from station)*
☎ 212 49 08
2nd Sat/month: women only; 4th Sat/month (YG) -30 years.
Incognito (B D GLM) 22.30-3 h
Noordvliet 13 ☎ 212 60 82
Koningin. De (B GLM MA) Sun-Thu 20-2, Fri Sat 16-4 h
Tuinen 3 ✉8911 KB ☎ 213 74 87

CRUISING

-Ringerspark
-[P] Groningsestraatweg
-Citypark (near museum Prinsentuin, evenings and nights)

Leiden ☎ 071

GAY INFO

Holland Centraal (GLM MA p) 24 hour broadcasts, Office 9-21 h
Oude Rün 57 ✉2301 CA *(old town centre, within close range of everything)* ☎ 512 75 15 Fax: 512 75 83
Local Radio Station incl. TV Newletter, Teletekst.

BARS

Odessa (B F GLM OS YG) Thu 22-1 h
Hogewoerd 18 ☎ 512 33 11

RESTAURANTS

Koekop. De (b CC F glm) 18-24 h, closed Mon
Lange Mare 60 ☎ 514 19 37
Medium sized restaurant with international cuisine and famous for its desserts.

BOOK SHOPS

Manifest (glm) Mon 13-18, Tue Wed Fr 9-18, Thu -21, Sat -17 h, closed Sun
Hooglandse Kerkgracht 4 ✉2312 HT ☎ 512 56 91
General bookstore with gay section.

GENERAL GROUPS

COC-Leiden (GLM) PB 11101 ✉2301 EC *(Langegracht 65)*
☎ 522 06 40
Call for info on activities.

CRUISING

-Plantsoen
-Vlietlanden (NU)

Maastricht ☎ 043

BARS

COC-Café Rose (B d GLM MA s) Fri 14-17, Fri-Sat 21-2, Thu Sun 20-2 h
Bogardenstraat 43 ☎ 321 83 37
Falstaff (B G MA) 10-2 h
Amersplein 6
Ferme. La (B d f G MA p) Mon Wed Thu 20-2, Fri Sat 21-3, Sun 16-2 h, closed onTue
Rechtstraat 29 ✉6221 EG ☎ 321 89 28 Fax: 343 15 27
Gare. La (AC B D E GLM MA p s W) 22-5 h, closed on Mon
Spoorweglaan 6 ✉6221 BS ☎ 325 90 90
Rembrandt (B G MA) 20-2 h
Markt 32

DANCECLUBS

Kadans. De (AC B D g OS s YG) Sun-Tue 10-2, Wen-Sat 10-5
Kesselskade 62 ✉6211 EN ☎ 326 17 00

RESTAURANTS

Pieterspoort. De (b F g) 12-22 h, closed Tue
Sint Pieterstraat 8a ☎ 325 00 74
Suhnothai Restaurant (! CC F g MA OS) 17-? h Mon closed
Tongersestraat 54 ✉6211 LP *(across the university)*
☎ 321 79 46

SEX SHOPS/BLUE MOVIES

B-1 (g) 10-24 h
Kommel 3 ☎ 314 56 41
Also sexshop.

BOOK SHOPS

Tribune (g) 9-18 h, closed Sun Mon
Kapoenstraat 8 ☎ 325 19 78

GENERAL GROUPS

COC-Maastricht (GLM)
Bogaardenstraat 43 ✉6211 SN ☎ 321 83 37
Call for info on activities.

CRUISING

-Mgr. Molenpark (at St. Lambertuslaan in Villapark)
-Oudenhof

Middelburg ☎ 0118

GENERAL GROUPS

COC-Midden-Zeeland (GLM)
Lange Noordstraat 52 ✉4331 CE ☎ 61 22 80

CRUISING
-Park Molenwater

Naarden ☎ 035

DANCECLUBS
Club Kogh (AC B d DR GLM lj MA msg P S sa sol VS)
Binnenhof 327 ✉1412 LA *(3 min from station)* ☎ 678 12 79
Entertainment house parties, Playroom, Video shows. Different locations.

GENERAL GROUPS
Homo Ontmoetingen/Homo Initiatieven Nederland/Homo 2000 (GLM)
Binnenhof 327 ✉1412 *(3 min from station)* ☎ 678 12 79
Group, contacts, meeting point.

Niekerk ☎ 0594

CAMPING
Heerenborgh. De (G MA NU pi) April-September
Niekerkerdiep 1 ✉9822 AH *(between Grootegast and Zuidhorn, end of Havenstraat)* ☎ 50 34 46 Fax: 50 34 46
E-Mail: heeren.borgh@worldonline.nl
Homepage: http://callisto.worldonline.nl/~301161
Caravan and camping place for gay men only.

Nieuwegein ☎ 030

CRUISING
-Park Oudegin (near tramstop Merwestein)
-P 300m to Plofsluis

Nijmegen ☎ 024

BARS
Bakkertje. 'T (AC B D GLM MA P s) Wed-Sat 20-?, Sun 19-? h, closed Mon Tue
Van Welderenstraat 65 ✉6511 MD ☎ 080/323 13 48
Café de Plak (A B D F g MA OS YG) 11-1, Thu 22.30-? h
Bloemerstraat 90 ☎ 322 27 57
Eend. d' (B G MA) 12-2, Sun 14-2 h
Van Welderenstraat 87
Mets (B d GLM MA N) 12-2, Sun 14-2 h
Grotestraat 7 ✉6511 VB *(centre)* ☎ 323 95 49
Revolutie. De (B G MA) Sat 23-5, Sun 5-10 h
Parkweg 98
Late night café.
Verjaardag. De (B g) 20-2 h
Van Welderenstraat 77 ☎ 360 61 66

DANCECLUBS
Gay Club Nijmegen (B D GLM) Fri Sat 23-5 h
Graafseweg 32-34
Mythe. De (B D f GLM MA s) Bar Thu 20-4, Fri 21-4, Sat -5, Sun 16-2; Disco Thu Fri 23-4, Sat -5 h
Platenmakersstraat 3 ✉6511 TZ *(centre)* ☎ 322 01 55
Popular mixed male/female bar & disco.
My-Way (B D G) Mon-Thu 20-2, Fri Sat -4, Sun 18-3 h
2e Walstraat 96 ☎ 360 42 72

RESTAURANTS
Steiger. De (A b E F glm MA) 17-24 h, closed Mon Tue
Reguliersstraat 59 ✉6511 DP ☎ 322 90 77

SEX SHOPS/BLUE MOVIES
B-1 (g) 9.30-24, Sun 14-23 h
Bloemenstraat 37 ☎ 323 74 53
Christine Le Duc (CC g VS) Mon-Fri 10-22, Sat -17.30 h
Bloemerstraat 78 ✉6511 EM ☎ 360 56 14

SAUNAS/BATHS
Azzura (AC B DR F G MA s sa sb snu sol VS wh YG) Mon Tue Thu 14-24, Fri-Sat 12-2 Sun 12-22 h, closed on Wed
Kerkberg 22 ✉6573 DN *(Near Nijmegen, Bus 6, behind the church)* ☎ 684 18 08
Gay sauna with bar and eating area. Entrance-fee Hfl 29,50.

BOOK SHOPS
De Feeks-Boekhandel (GLM W) Mon 13-18, Tue Wed Fri 10-18, Thu 10-21, Sat 10-17 h
Van Welderenstraat 34 ✉6511 ML *(accross Het Bakkertje)*
☎ 323 93 81
Gay and lesbian bookshop. Free catalogue on request.

FASHION SHOPS
Bofkont! (CC g sol) Mon-Sat 9.30-18, Thu -21.30 h
Bloemerstraat 39 ✉6511 EC ☎ 360 45 25
Male underwear and gay solarium.

GENERAL GROUPS
COC-Nijmeren (GLM)
PB 552 ✉6500 AN *(Villa Lila, In de Betouwstr. 9)* ☎ 323 42 37
Call for info on activities.

HEALTH GROUPS
SVG
☎ 322 61 41

CRUISING
-Hunerpark
-Kelfkenbosch (near Traianusplein)
-Goffertpark (only evenings)
-De Elsthof-forest along grootstalseweg (only daytime)

Noordwijk ☎ 071

CRUISING
-NU beach north of Langevelderslag near Zandvoort
-N 206 near Rijnsburg

Numansdorp ☎ 0186

SWIMMING
Haringvlietbrug (parallel road to A 29, beach near Haringvlietsluijses)

Ommen ☎ 0529

CRUISING
-N48 Ommen → Raalte (1st P after Ommen)

Oostkapelle ☎ 0118

SWIMMING
-Beach (The beach to the right of the path is frequently visited by gays)

Oss ☎ 0412

GENERAL GROUPS
COC-Brabant-Noordoost (GLM)
PO Box 551 ✉5340 AN *(Sint Barbaraplein 6)* ☎ 62 66 66
Call for info on activities.

Prinsenbeek ☎ 076

LEATHER & FETISH SHOPS

Rimba. Factory of leather SM articles
PO Box 33 ✉4840 AA ☎ 541 44 84 Fax: 42 07 03

Purmerend ☎ 0299

GENERAL GROUPS

COC-Purmerend (GLM)
PB 786 ✉1440 AT *(Wijkcentr. „Vooruit", Wilhelminalaan 1 A)*
☎ 42 03 70
Call for info on activities.

Raalte ☎ 0572

GENERAL GROUPS

COC-Raalte (GLM)
PB 250 ✉8100 AG ☎ 35 67 16
Call for info on activities.

Roden

CRUISING

-Cruising forest Menshinebos (lj MA) (near P Menshingeweg)

Roermond ☎ 0475

BARS

Mix. De (A B CC E f G MA OS S W) 16-2, Fri-Sat -3 h
Venlosepoort 3 ✉6041 CG ☎ 31 58 50
Sjinderhannes (A AC B G LJ MA s) 21-2 Fri Sat -3 h closed Tue
Swalmerstraat 42 ☎ 33 31 19
-1st Sat Rubbermens-club, 2nd & last Sat MSC Limburg, 3rd Sat Black Angels Köln, last Sun 15 h VSSM.

SEX SHOPS/BLUE MOVIES

B-1 (G VS) 10-24 h
Kraanpoort 6 ☎ 0457/32 97 10
Also blue movies.
Climax (g VS) 10-18 h
Willem II Singel 22a
Also blue movies.

SAUNAS/BATHS

Dingeman Sauna (! B G MA OS sa sb sol VS wh) 13-24 h
Willem II Singel 14 ✉6041 GH *(near railway station)*
☎ 33 62 36
Entrance-fee Hfl 25.

Roosendaal ☎ 0165

BARS

Déjà-Vu (AC B D E GLM MA P S SNU TV) Mon Thu 19-1 Fri Sat 19-2 Sun 16-2 h closed Tue Wed..
Damstraat 101-103 ✉4701 GM *(near railway station and inner city)* ☎ 54 86 78
Bar, café and disco.

CRUISING

-Emile van Loonpark (near city-center, 16-23 h)

Rotterdam ☎ 010

GAY INFO

Apollo (B GLM s YG) Fri 18-2 h
PO Box 1490 ✉3014 TP *(Josefstraat 32)* ☎ 436 14 44

BARS

Bak. De (A f G lj MA OS s) 16-2 h
Schiedamse Vest 146 ✉3011 BG *(U-Churchill plein)*
☎ 433 47 83
Showtime (STV) Thu 22, Happy Hour Sun 17-18 h, then free food.
Bonaparte (B GLM d) 14-4, Fri Sat 14-5 h
Nieuwe Binnenweg 117 ☎ 436 74 33
Cosmo Bar (B G lj) 20-2 h
Schiedamsesingel 133 ☎ 412 36 68
Gossip (! AC B CC G S YG) Summer: 11-1, Fri Sat -2; Winter: 14-1, Fri Sat -2; Happy hour 17.30-18.30 h
Van Oldenbarneveltstraat 88 ✉3012 GV *(M-Beurs)* ☎ 412 19 44
Thu showtime 22 h.
Keerweer (AC B f GLM) Mon- Thu 17-4, Fri Sun 16-5, Sat -6
Keerweer 14 ☎ 413 12 17
Sociable drinking place located in a small alley around the corner of Binnenwegplein. Best after 1 h.
Loge'90 (AC B G) 12-4, Fri Sat -5 h
Schiedamsedijk 4 ☎ 414 97 45
Marietjes Minibar Tue-Thu 15-1, Fri Sat 15-2 h
Noordplein 119 ☎ 265 38 36
Shaft (B G LJ) 21-2, Fri Sat 23-5 h, closed on Wed
Schiedamsesingel 137 ☎ 414 14 86
Strano (B GLM) Mon-Thu 15-2, Fri -3, Sat 14-3, Sun -2, happy hour Mon-Sun 18-19 h
Van Oldebarneveldtstraat 154 ✉3012 GX ☎ 412 58 11

DANCECLUBS

Gay Palace (B D GLM) 23-4, Fri Sat -5 h
Schiedamsesingel 139 ☎ 414 14 86
Nighttown 22-5 h, ask for special gay events
Gouvernestraat 4C ☎ 436 40 54
Vibes 1st Sun 22-? h
Westersingel 50 ☎ 436 63 89

SEX SHOPS/BLUE MOVIES

Cano (A AC B DR f glm LJ MA VS) 12-24 Sun 12-18 h
Provenierssingel 30 ✉3033 EL *(near Central Station and centre)*
☎ 467 6348
Christine Le Duc (CC g VS) Mon-Fri 10-22, Sat -17.30 h, closed Sun
Schieweg 108 ✉3038 BC ☎ 467 95 27

ESCORTS & STUDIOS

Escort service 0-24 h
☎ 213 01 60
24 hours a day, 7 days a week.

HOUSE OF BOYS

Boys Factory. The (CC G msg) 14-1, Fri Sat 14-2 h
'S Gravendijkwal 92 ✉3014 EH ☎ 225 17 25
Also Escort service.

SAUNAS/BATHS

Cosmo Sauna (B F DR G msg OS sa sb sol VS wh) 13-23, Fri Sat nightsauna -8, Sun 14-22 h
Schiedamse Singel 133 ✉3012 BA ☎ 412 36 68
Entrance-fee Hfl 12,50-25.
Finland (B DR G MA msg sa sb sol) 13-23.30, Fri Sat 13-2 h
Grondherendijk 7 ✉3082 DD ☎ 429 70 29
Entrance-fee Hfl 22,50.
Spartacus (B f DR G sa sb sol VS wh) 13-6, Sat Sun 14-6 h
'S Gravensdijkwal 130 ✉3015 CC ☎ 436 62 85
Nice, intimate, recommended. Entrance-fee Hfl 25, after 22 h 15.

LEATHER & FETISH SHOPS

Massadshop (g LJ MA TV) 9-18, Fri -21, Sat -17 h, closed Sun-Mon
Zaagmolendrift 35-41 *(Tram6/9)* ☎ 466 43 68
Leather and rubber equipments, magazines.

HOTELS

Bagatelle (g H MG p) 8-23 h
Proveniersingle 26 ✉3033 EL ☎ 467 63 48 Fax: 467 63 48
Single Hfl 45, double 68-88 (bf incl.)

GENERAL GROUPS

COC-Rotterdam (GLM) Tue Thu 20-22 h
PB 768 ✉3000 AT *(Schiedamsesingel 175)* ☎ 414 15 55

FETISH GROUPS

MS Rotterdam
PO BOX 221 84 ✉3003 DD
Member of ECME.

CRUISING

-Kralingsebos
-Rozenpark, Kralingen
-Museum Boymanspark (AYOR)
-Behind railway station, Statenpad (R RT)
-under Willemsbrug

Schagen ☎ 0224

GENERAL GROUPS

Pink Café
PB 106 ✉1740 AC ☎ 21 31 99

Scheveningen ☎ 070

DANCECLUBS

Glitz Gay-Nite (Club Exposure Danceclub) (B D DR G SNU VS) Every 3rd Fri of the month 22.30-? h
Westduinweg 232 ✉2583 AK ☎ 354 33 56

HOTELS

Hotel Seabreeze (bf glm H NU)
Gevers Deynootweg 23 ✉2586 BB ☎ 352 41 45 Fax: 351 48 30
One hour from the airport. Two minutes to the beach. Apartment for 5 persons available.

Schiedam ☎ 010

BARS

Mallemolen. De (B f g OS) 17-1, Fri-Sat 16-4.30, sun 16-1, closed Mon
Vlaardingerstraat 17 ☎ 426 34 47
Melody (AC B G s) Tue-Thu 19-1, Fri -2 Sat 16-2, Sun -1 h
Singel 230 ☎ 427 07 65

CRUISING

-P & Sportspark Harga near Novotel Schiedam

Sneek ☎ 0515

RESTAURANTS

Stoofje. 'T (B CC F g MA) 17-24 h, Mon closed
Oude Koemarkt 9-11 ✉8601 EH ☎ 41 74 38

St. Anthonis ☎ 0485

RESTAURANTS

Heksenboom. De (AC B CC F glm MA OS) Fri/Sat 11-? Sun 10-?,Apr-Sept Tue-Thu 11-?,Oct-Mar Wed 12-18 Jul/Aug 10-?
Bosweg 40 ✉5845 EB ☎ 38 28 03 Fax: 38 28 03
Also possible to make reservations on closed days with minimum of 15 guests.

Terneuzen ☎ 0115

CAFES

Uientuin. De (B G MA)
Nieuwstraat 6

GENERAL GROUPS

COC-Zeeuws-Vlaanderen (GLM)
Dijkstraat 3 ✉4531 CM ☎ 630 654
Call for info on activities.

Terschelling - West Terschelling ☎ 0562

HOTELS

Spitsbergen Pension (bf glm H MA msg NU)
Burg. Reedekerstraat 50 ✉8881 CB *(next to the post office)*
☎ 44 31 62 Fax: 44 31 62
Rates single Hfl 50, double 75/day, 750/week. Near the beach, harbour and woods.

CRUISING

-Beach West Terschelling (NU)(between Paal 7 & 8)

Texel - De Koog ☎ 0222

RESTAURANTS

Taveerne. De (AC B D E F GLM MA) 16.30-2 h
Dorpstraat 119 ☎ 31 75 85

CRUISING

-Beach (NU)(between pile 26.4 and 27.4)

Tiel ☎ 0344

GAY INFO

COC-Tiel/Rivierenland (GLM)
PB 223 ✉4000 AE ☎ 61 63 73
Call for info on activities.

Tilburg ☎ 013

BARS

Dynasty. Le (B GLM) Mon-Fri 21-24, Sat 16-3, Sun -24 h
Stadthuisstraat 17 ✉5038 XZ ☎ 467 22 57
My Way (B D GLM) 21-3 h, closed Tue-Wed
Leon van Vechtstraat 1 ☎ 536 78 27
Popcorn (B D GLM lj MA OS p S tv) 18-?, Sat 14-? h
Paleisring 19 ✉5038 WD ☎ 543 32 18

SEX SHOPS/BLUE MOVIES

Candy Shop (g) 10-23, Sat 10-18 h
Korvelseweg 215 ☎ 543 23 94
Also house with boys; S/M.
Gay Cinema Candy (G VS) 10-1, Sun 13-1 h
Korvelseweg 217 ☎ 543 23 94
Also house with boys.

GENERAL GROUPS

COC-Tilburg (GLM)
Stadshuisplein 344 ✉5038 TH ☎ 535 90 50
Call for info on activities.

CRUISING

-Wilhelminakanaal Biest-Houtakker
-A58 Breda-Tilburg, P Leikant (near Gilze)

Utrecht ☎ 030

GAY INFO

COC-Utrecht (B D GLM) Disco: 20-1, Fri-Sat 21-2, Sun 20.30-2 h
PB 117 ✉3500 AC *(Oude Gracht 221)* ☎ 020/231 88 41

BARS

Bodytalk (! AC B D DR f G lj MA OS p s VS W) Mon-Thu 20-3, Fri Sat 16-5, Sun 16-4 h
Oudegracht 64 ✉3511 AS *(Centre, near main railway station)*
☎ 231 57 47 *Regular special events. Terrace at water front in summer. Monthly booklet.*
Pann Café (B d f GLM YG) Thu 22-3 h
Oudegracht 221 ✉3511 NH *(water level)* ☎ 293 37 22
Wolkenkrabber (A B f GLM OS) 16-2 h
Oudegracht 47 ☎ 231 97 68
Popular bar, friendly atmosphere.

DANCECLUBS

PANN Fest (B D f GLM YG) 3rd Sat 22-4 h. (except Jul, Aug)
Bemuurde Weerd W.Z. 3 ✉3513 BH ☎ 293 37 22
Roze Wolk. De (AC B D GLM p s YG) 22-4, Fri Sat -5 h, closed on Mon
Oudegracht 45 *(Water Level)* ☎ 232 20 66
Very popular.

RESTAURANTS

River Kwai (B g F) 17-22, Fri Sat -22.30 h
Oudegracht 184 ✉3511 NP ☎ 232 18 51

SEX SHOPS/BLUE MOVIES

Dali's Erotheek (AC CC DR GLM LJ MA VS) Mon-Fri 10-23, Sat 11-20 h, closed on Sun
Amsterdamsestraat 197 ✉3351 CB ☎ 244 09 75
Davy's Erotheek (AC CC DR glm MA VS) Mon-Fri 10-23, Sat 12-20
Amsterdamsestraatweg 197 ✉3551 CB ☎ 243 68 15

BOOK SHOPS

Rooie Rat. De (g) 9-18, Thu -21, Sat -17
Oudegracht 65 ✉3511 AD ☎ 231 789
Leftist bookshop with gay/lesbian department.

HOTELS

Bed & Breakfast Memory (bf CC H)
Prinses Markgrietstraat 5 ✉3554 GA ☎ 242 07 37
Fax: 242 07 37
Friendly hotel with good bf and low prices.

GENERAL GROUPS

ILGA Support Group Utrecht
Herenweg 93 ✉3513 CD ☎ 234 09 12
Orpheus (GLM)
PB 14121 ✉3508 Se ☎ 020/639 07 65
Homepage: http://www.xsall.nl/~orpheus
Stichting de Kringen (GLM)
Kanaalweg 21 ✉3526 KL ☎ 288 86 36
Provincial organisation for gay men, women and youngs.

CRUISING

-Museumbrug, Prinsesselaan
-Sterrenwacht (at the end of Nieuwegracht)
-Hogelandse Park (near Museumlaan, 19-24 h)

Veghel ☎ 04130

HEALTH GROUPS

SVG Mon-Fri 9-17 h
☎ 679 15

Velp

SAUNAS/BATHS

Odyssee (B F DR G pi sa sb sol VS) Sun-Fri 13-23 h
Frederikstraat 5

Venlo ☎ 077

SEX SHOPS/BLUE MOVIES

B-1 (g VS) 10-23 h
Havenkade 12 ☎ 334 83 38
Also blue movies.

GENERAL GROUPS

COC-Noord-en-Midden-Limburg (GLM)
PB 611 ✉5900 AP ☎ 351 84 12 *Call for info on activities.*

CRUISING

-Park opposite railway station (northern part, evenings and nights)

Vlaardingen ☎ 010

CRUISING

-Likkebaardboss (NU) (first [P] from Vlaardingen)

Vlissingen ☎ 0118

HOTELS

Admiraal Logies (bf g H NU OS)
Badhuisstraat 201 ✉4382 AM ☎ 41 37 52 Fax: 41 37 52
All rooms with shower, WC and TV. Rates Hfl 50 per person (bf incl.)

CRUISING

-Nollebos

Vrouwenpolder ☎ 0118

SWIMMING

-Beach (Path at campingsite Oranjezon to the beach. Some gays on the right)

Waalre ☎ 040

BARS

Hut van Mie Pils. De (B g) 11-18, Fri-Sun -23 h
Leenderweg 1

Wageningen ☎ 0317

GENERAL GROUPS

Homogroep Wageningen (B D GLM S YG) Fri 21.30-3 h at De Wilde Wereld, Burgstraat 1, disco 1st & 3rd Fri
Burgtstraat 1 ✉6701 DA ☎ 42 28 35 E-Mail: hgw@freemail.nl
Homepage: http://huizen.ddsw.nl/bewoners/hgw

Winschoten ☎ 0597

SEX SHOPS/BLUE MOVIES

De Pottekijker (CC g VS W YG) Mon-Fri 15-21, Sat 12-17
Pottebakkerstraat 27 ✉9671 LD ☎ 41 24 85 Fax: 42 04 33
Homepage: http://www.taboe.com *Sex shop + mail orders.*

Zandhuisen ☎ 0561

CAMPING

Vlegel. De (G MA NU OS pi) Apr 1-Okt 1
Oldeberkoperweg 23 ✉8389 TE ☎ 43 31 13
Homo-camping.

Zandvoort ☎ 023

BARS

Adonis (B G MA OS) 20-3 h, closed Mon Wed
20 'tjerk Hiddestraat ☎ 571 31 10
Mix. The (B G MA) 21-3 h
Stationstraat 17 ✉2042 LD ☎ 573 10 09

CAFES

Eldorado (B glm) 8-24 h (summer only)
Zuidstarnd 6 ☎ 571 82 29 *Little bar on the beach.*

HOTELS

Astoria (B bf F g H OS)
Dr. C. A. Gerkestraat 155-157 ✉2042 ER ☎ 571 45 50
All rooms with shower or bath and WC. Rates from hfl 105-160 per person.
Hotel Hoogland (AC B bf CC F g OS sol W)
Westerparkstraat 5 ✉2042 AV ☎ 571 55 41 Fax: 571 42 00
All rooms with shower/WC, TV and phone. Rates single Hfl 60-100, double 120-160 (bf incl.)

SWIMMING
-Zuidstrand (go by bike or 40 min by foot along the beach. The gay beach is near the nude beach. Cruising in the dunes behind the beach)

Zeist ☎ 030

SEX SHOPS/BLUE MOVIES
Dali's Erotheek (AC CC DR GLM LJ MA VS) Mon-Fri 10-23, Sat 11-20 h, closed on Sun
J. v. Oldenbarneveltlaan 82 ✉3705 HG ☎ 699 23 32

Zoetermeer ☎ 079

GENERAL GROUPS
COC-Zoetermeer (GLM)
Frankrijklaan 35 ✉2711 CV *(Van't Hoffplein 1)* ☎ 343 33 36
Call for info on activities.

Zwolle ☎ 038

GAY INFO
COC-Zwolle (B GLM) Tue 20-24, Fri 21-1 h
Kamperstraat 17 ✉8011 LJ ☎ 421 00 65

HEALTH GROUPS
HIV Vereniging
☎ 455 16 03

CRUISING
-Rode Toren Plein
-Railway station
-Potgietersingel (evenings and nights)

New Caledonia

Nouvelle-Calédonie

Initials: NC

Time: GMT +11

☎ Country Code / Access Code: 687 (no area codes) / 00

Language: French

Area: 19,058 km^2 / 7,358 sq mi.

Currency: 1 CFP Franc = 100 Centimes

Population: 189,000

Capital: Nouméa

Religions: Christian

Climate: Tropical climate that is hot and humid. It's modified by southeast trade winds.

● In 1998 a referendum is due to be held in this French 'Territoire d'outre Mer". (Overseas Territory) to decide on independence. Currently, as far as homosexuality is concerned, the same laws apply here as in ☛ France.

✸ Neu-Kaledonien ist ein Überseeterritorium mit eingeschränkter Abhängigkeit in dem die gleichen Gesetze wie in ☛ Frankreich gelten.

▲ En 1998 aura lieu un référendum sur l'indépendance dans ce territoire d'outre-mer français. Actuellement, même législation qu'en ☛ France.

☆ En el año 1998 se llevará a cabo en este «Territoire d`Outre-Mer» francés (territorio de ultramar con independencia limitada) un referendum para decidir sobre su independencia. Por el momento continuan siendo validas las leyes ☛ francesas.

❖ Nel 1998 in questo „territoire d'outre-mer" avrà luogo un referendum per o contro l'indipendenza. Attualmente sono ancora in vigore le leggi ☛francesi.

Nouméa

BARS
Bilboquet Village (B F g)
(city center near Berheim Library) ☎ 28 43 30
Byblos. Le (B D g YG)
44 Rue Anatole France ☎ 28 14 36
Café de Paris (B D E F g YG) 22-4 h
Rue de Sébastopol/Rue de la Somme
Barman speaks English. Meeting place for tourists, airline personnel etc., who can give leads to local scene, parties, etc..
Metropolis (B D g S YG) 22-4 h
Rue Surleau, Immeuble „Le Surcouf" *(opposite cathedral)*
☎ 27 17 77
Paris Club. Le (B D g YG)
45-47 Avenue de Sebastopole ☎ 28 28 29
St.Hubert (B F r)
Place des Cocotiers/Sébastopol ☎ 27 21 40 *Cruisy.*
421 New Center Club (B D g YG)
c/o New Center, Route 1, 7km ☎ 28 57 00

DANCECLUBS
Star Struck (B D g YG)
Anse Vata

HOTELS
Nouméa Village Hotel (AC B F H NG OS pi)
1 Rue Sébastopol *(downtown)* ☎ 28 30 06
Centrally located. All rooms with telephoe, kitchenette, priv. bath, and WC. Single CFP 5.380-6.980, double 6.180-8.080.

SWIMMING
-Plage de Nouville (G NU) (between Cimetiere de Nouville and Kuendu Hotel)

CRUISING
-Baie des Citrons
-Around Brandshell (late evenings)
-Quartier Latin (AYOR R TV)

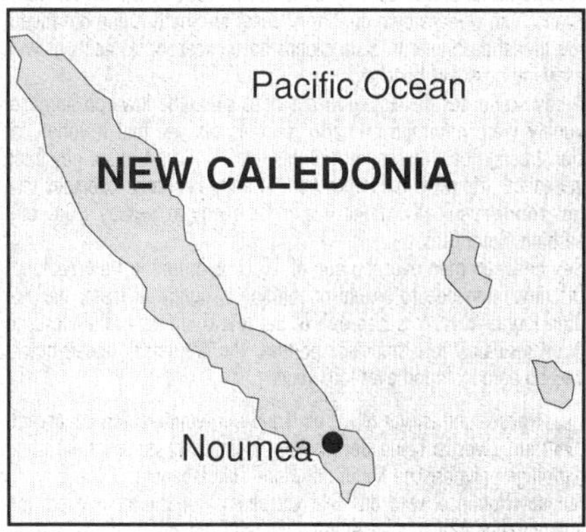

New Zealand

Oceania

Initials: NZ

Time: GMT +12

☎ Country Code / Access Code: 64 / 00

Language: English, Maori

Area: 270.986 km² / 104,628 sq mi.

Currency: 1 New Zealand Dollar (NZ$) = 100 Cents

Population: 3,625,400

Capital: Wellington

Religions: 50% Protestant, 15% Catholic

Climate: Moderate climate with sharp regional contrasts.

Important gay cities: Auckland, Christchurch, Wellington.

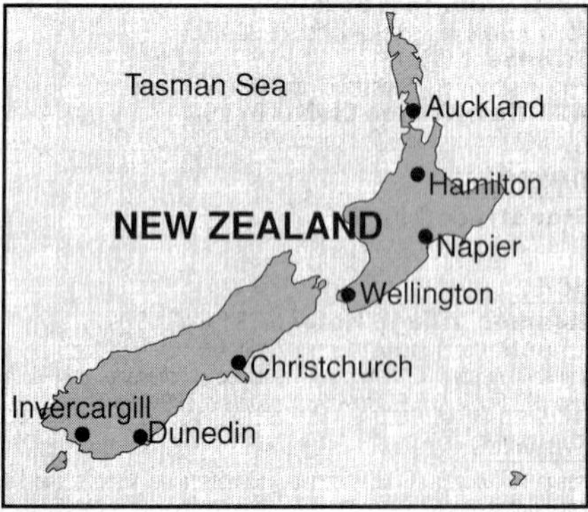

● New Zealand is a highly scenic country with a small friendly population and a rich Polynesian culture among its indigenous Maori people. Volcanic and thermal activity offers spectaclar sights on the North Island, while the South Island boasts beautiful mountains, glaciers and forests. Rotorua and the Bay of Islands on North Island, and Queenstown and Franz Josef on South Island are favourite tourist destinations. Both islands have excellent ski fields as well as world-class surf beaches.

A gay scene has developed in the cities since the laws on homosexuality were reformed in 1986, and visitors will find a variety of clubs, bars, guesthouses, restaurants, and saunas. A major gay festival called „Hero" is held each year in early February: overseas visitors can conveniently attend this on their way to Sydney's Gay and Lesbian Mardi Gras.

Sex between men over the age of 16 is permitted in New Zealand. Discrimination due to sexual orientation is outlawed under the Human Rights laws. It is also one of the few countries in the world to grant residency to a same-sex partner. The partnership must, however, be demonstrated over four years.

✱ Neuseeland ist vor allem ein Land mit wunderbaren Landschaften. Zwar ist seine Bevölkerung klein, doch dafür ist die mannigfaltige polynesische Kultur der Maori sehr lebendig.

Auf der Nordinsel wird das Bild vor allem von Thermalquellen und vulkanischer Aktivität bestimmt, während auf der Südinsel Berge, Gletscher und Wälder vorherrschen. Beliebte Touristenziele sind Roturua und die „Bay of Islands" auf der Nordinsel, Franz Josef und Queenstown auf der Südinsel.

Seit 1986 (damals wurden die gesetzlichen Bestimmungen zur Homosexualität reformiert) hat sich in den Städten eine ansehnliche schwule Szene entwickelt. Eine ganze Reihe von Clubs, Bars, Unterkünften, Restaurants und Saunen bietet sich dem Touristen an. Besonders günstig ist die Gelegenheit zum Besuch im frühen Februar. Auf dem Weg zum „Sydney Gay and Lesbian Mardi Gras" läßt sich ein Abstecher zum größten schwulen Fest Neuseelands „Hero" machen.

Sex ist in Neuseeland zwischen Männern über 16 Jahren erlaubt. Dem gleichgeschlechtlichen Partner wird hier das Aufenthaltsrecht gewährt. Damit ist Neuseeland eines der wenigen Länder mit solcher Rechtspraxis, auch wenn die Partnerschaft bereits vier Jahre bestehen muß.

▲ La Nouvelle Zélande est un pays splendide, très peu peuplé et de culture polynésienne. Les indigènes s'appellent les Maoris. Dans le nord de l'île, on trouve des volcans et des sources thermales. Le sud, lui, est fait de montagnes, de forêts et de glaciers. Les hauts-lieux touristiques sont, dans le nord, Rotorua et Bay of Islands et Queenstown et Franz Josef, dans le sud.

Depuis la réforme du code pénal en 1986, les choses ont commencé à bouger pour les homosexuels, dans les grandes villes surtout où on trouve maintenant de nombreux clubs, bars, pensions, restaurants et saunas gays. Tous les ans, début février, a lieu le „Hero", un festival gay qui attire les foules. Les touristes européens peuvent combiner cet évènement avec le Gay and Lesbian Mardi Gras de Sydney, en Australie.

L'homosexualité entre hommes adultes (plus de 16 ans) n'est pas un délit en Nouvelle Zélande. C'est un des rares pays au monde qui reconnaît les relations entre personnes du même sexe. Pour cela, il faut prouver que la relation tient depuis au moins 4 ans.

☆ Nueva Zelanda es sobre toto un país con paisajes maravillosos. La afable población es poca númerosa y sigue manteniendo viva la rica cultura de sus indígenos, los Maori. El país está formado por dos islas: la norteña está caracterizada por sus fuentes termales y vólcanes, mientras en la sureña predominan montañas, glaciares y bosques. Roturua y los „Bay of Islands" son los sitios más frecuendados por turistas en la isla del Norte, mientras en el sur Franz Josef y Queenstown atraen a muchos visitantes. Desde 1986 (el año cuando se llevaron a cabo las reformas legislativas referente a la homosexualidad) se ha desarrollado en las ciudades un ambiente gay muy considerable. El turista puede elegir entre varios clubs, bares, hoteles, restaurantes y saunas. Al principios de Febrero es muy buena fecha para hacer una visita: Quien participe en el „Sydney Gay and Lesbian Mardi Gras" debería aprovechar la oportunidad para hacer una pequeña excursión a la fiesta gay más grande de Nueva Zelanda, llamada „Hero". Aquí el sexo entre hombres mayores de 16 años está permitido. Nueva Zelanda es uno de los pocos paises que concede a la pareja de un homosexual el permiso de residencia, siempre y cuando la relación tenga más de cuatro años de antigüedada.

❖ La bellezza della Nuova Zelanda è in rapporto diretto con la cordialità della sua popolazione e con la ricchezza della cultura polinesiana, tenuta viva dagli indigeni Maori. Sulla North Island Vulcani e getti termali offrono una vista spettacolare mentre montagne, foreste e ghiacciai sono le particolarità della South Island. Le destinazioni favorite dai turisti sono: Roturua e Bay of Islands sulla North Island e Queenstown e Franz Josef sulla South Island. Da quando, nel 1986, sono state modificate le leggi contro l'omosessualità, nelle varie città sono sorti locali di ogni tipo, come bar, discoteche, ristoranti e saune. Ogni anno all'inizio di febbraio ha luogo un festival chiamato „Hero": i visitatori d'oltre oceano possono assistere a questa manifestazione facendo scalo durante il loro viaggio verso il Mardi Gras di Sydney. In Nuova Zelanda sono permessi i rapporti omosessuali tra maggiori di 16 anni. Inoltre questo paese è uno dei pochi al mondo a concedere il permesso di residenza a compagni stranieri dello stesso sesso: tuttavia bisogna dimostrare che la relazione esiste da almeno quattro anni.

NATIONAL GAY INFO

Express-New Zealand's newspaper of gay expression
56 Brown Street, PO Box 47-514, Ponsonby, Auckland 2
☎ (0)9-361 01 90 Fax: 376 20 19 E-Mail: express@outnet.co.nz
New Zealands bi-weekly read gay and lesbian publication. Free at gay venues. NZ$ 2 from newsagents.

HERO Project Trust Board (GLM)
PO Box 184 Auckland ☎ (0)9 630 91 94 Fax: (0)9 375 37 91
E-Mail: seanlofts@metrocity.co.nz
Homepage: http://nz.com/Queer/HERO/
HERO is the major G&L event in NZ. It is comprised of a three-week arts, cultural and sporting festival, culminating in the HERO parade and dance party in mid-February. This is Aukland's equivalent of Sydney's Gay and Lesbian Mardi-Gras.

Lesbian & Gay Archives of New Zealand (LAGANZ)
Manners Street, Wellington ☎ (04) 474 30 00
Research library and national lesbian/gay archives.

NZ Gay & Lesbian Managed Accomodation Guide
c/o R. Harris, N° 2 R.D., Palmerston Otago ☎ (03) 465 1742

NZ Gay & Lesbian Tourism Association Inc.
Private Bay MBEP 255 ✉6001 Auckland ☎ (0)9-303 42 62
Fax: (0)9-303 42 62 E-Mail: info@nzglta.org.nz
Homepage: http://nz.com/aglb/nzglta

NZ Gay Hospitality Exchange
PO Box 25-165 ✉8030 Christchurch ☎ (0)3-379 94 93
Hosting of gay overseas visitors.

NZ Quilt Project. The
PO Box 7024, Wellesley St, Auckland ☎ (0)9-358 32 45
Fax: (0)9-302 23 38
Promoting AIDS awareness and remembrance through memorial quilts.

OUT! Magazine (CC G) Mon-Fri 9-18 h
45 Anzac Avenue, Private Bag 92126 Auckland *(2nd floor)*
☎ (0)9-377 90 31 Fax: (0)9-377 77 67
E-Mail: out@nz.com Homepage: www.outnz.net.nz
New Zealand's national gay magazine with news, features, personals, mailorder and venue information, NZ$ 5.

PUMP-Pride & Unity for Male Prostitutes
PO Box 11-412, Manners Street, Wellington
Support & information for male prostitutes.

NATIONAL HELPLINES

AIDS National Hotline 0-24 h
☎ (0)800-802-437
AIDS counselling & information

NATIONAL PUBLISHERS

Express-New Zealand's newspaper of gay expression Mon-Fri 9-17 h
PO Box 47514, 56 Brown Street, Ponsonby *(ground floor)*
☎ (0)9-376 20 18 *FAX 376-2019.*

Lawrence Publishing Co. (NZ) Ltd.
Private Bag 921 26, 45 Anzac Avenue, Auckland 1 *2nd floor*
☎ (0)9-377 90 31 Fax: (0)9-377 77 67 E-Mail: out@nz.com
Publisher and distributors.

NATIONAL GROUPS

Deaf Gays & Lesbians in New Zealand
PO Box 15 07 69 New Lynn, Auckland ☎ (0)9-827 05 42

Gay Sport New Zealand
PO Box 90778, Auckland ☎ (0)9-625 75 97
E-Mail: tquayle@outnet.co.nz
National umbrella group for gay and lesbian sports groups and clubs.

NZ AIDS Foundation (National Office)
31-35 Hargrave Street, Ponsonby, Auckland ☎ (09) 303-3124
Fax: 309-3149. E-Mail: nzaf@iconz.co.
Prevention/education, anonymous, confidential, free HIV testing and counselling, support services for people living with HIV/AIDS.

Akaroa ☎ 03

GUEST HOUSES

Totara Vale Retreat (bf CC GLM MA NU OS p wh)
Dawbers Road, Le Bons Bay ☎ 304 71 72 Fax: 304 71 82
E-Mail: Erik.Lussell@xtra.co.nz
Located 90 min. from Christchurch 15 min from Akaroa by car.

Auckland ☎ 09

● Auckland is the largest city in New Zealand and has a large Polynesian population. It is a clean, modern city with excellent restaurants, hotels and tourist services. Auckland is built around two harbours and a number of extinct volcanic hills with lush greenery and fine beaches. The inner city suburbs of Ponsonby, Grey Lynn, Mt. Eden and Parnell have significant gay populations. Ponsonby is well known for its restaurants and wine bars.

✱ Auckland ist die größte Stadt Neuseelands. Das Straßenbild wird auch durch den hohen polynesischen Bevölkerungsanteil geprägt. Sauber und modern ist diese Stadt, die exzellente Restaurants, Hotels und touristische Dienstleistungen bietet. Mehrere erloschene Vulkane und erstklassige Strände umgeben Auckland, daß an zwei Buchten entstand. Die Vororte Ponsonby, Grey Lynn, Mt. Eden und Parnell haben einen beachtlichen Anteil an schwuler Bevölkerung. Ponsonby selbst ist sehr bekannt für seine Restaurants und Weinstuben.

▲ Auckland est la plus grande ville de Nouvelle Zélande. La majorité des Aucklandais est d'origine polynésienne. La ville est moderne, propre et jouit d'une excellente infrastructure touristique (hôtels, restaurants, services...). Auckland a été construite sur d'anciennes collines volcaniques, au bord de deux baies. Les arrondissements du centre-ville Ponsoby, Grey Lynn, Mont Eden et Parnell revêtent un intérêt particulier pour le touriste gay. Ponsoby est réputé pour ses excellents restaurants et ses nombreux bars à vin.

☆ Auckland es la ciudad más grande de Nueva Zelanda. Lo primero que llama la atención es la gran concentración de población polinesia. La ciudad es limpia y moderna y ofrece excelentes restaurantes, hoteles y servicious turísticos. Auckland se encuentra entre encantadoras playas y varios vólcanes, que ya no son activos. Los barrios del cinturón de la ciudad como Ponsonby, Grey Lynn, Mt. Eden y Parnell poseen un considerable número de habitantes gay. Ponsonby mismo es famoso por sus restaurantes y tabernas.

❖ Aukland, la più grande città della Nuova Zelanda, ha una grande comunità polinesiana. è una città moderna e pulita con eccellenti ristoranti, hotel e servizi turistici; è costruita intorno a due porti ed a numerose colline vulcaniche, in mezzo ad una vegetazione lussureggiante ed a spiagge incantevoli. I distretti centrali Ponsonby, Grey Lynn, Mt.Eden e Parnell hanno una rilevante comunità gay. Ponsonby è conosciuta per i suoi ristoranti e per le sue enoteche.

GAY INFO

Gayline/Lesbianline Mon-Fri 10-22 Sat Sun 17-22 h
☎ 303 35 84
Information, support, counselling, referral.

In The Pink Sun 20-21 h (95 BFM)
c/o AUSA, Private Bag Ak ☎ (025) 749 549

QYC-Queer Youth Chronicle
Wellesley St, Auckland 1
Bimonthly youth update.

Rainbow Youth Hotline 0-24 h
☎ 376 41 55
Information line for gay and lesbian youth.

The G & T Breakfast Show (Gays on Thursdays) Thu 7 h (AM 810 kHz)
PO Box 6551, Wellesley Station, Auckland 1 ☎ 302 02 38
Fax: 302 02 37
Gay & lesbian radio show.

The Pride Centre 10-16.30 h
33 Wyndham Street ☎ 302 05 90 Fax: 378 98 08
Gay, lesbian, bisexual, transpeople centre for social contact and information.

This Way Out-Gay & Lesbian Radio Magazine Sat 11.40-12.25 h (AM 810 kHz)
PO Box 6551, Wellesley Street ☎ 523 11 93 Fax: 302 02 37

Triangle Community Television Ltd.
PO Box 78034, Grey Lynn ☎ 376 73 85
Community Access TV.

Triangle Productions (Gays & Lesbian TV)
☎ 377 4142 E-Mail: Q@triangle.org.nz
Homepage: www.triangle.org.nz
Producers of gay and lesbian programmes for broadcast on Triangle TV.

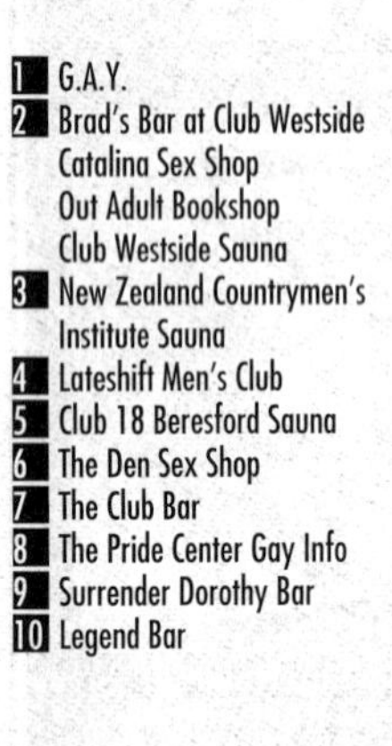

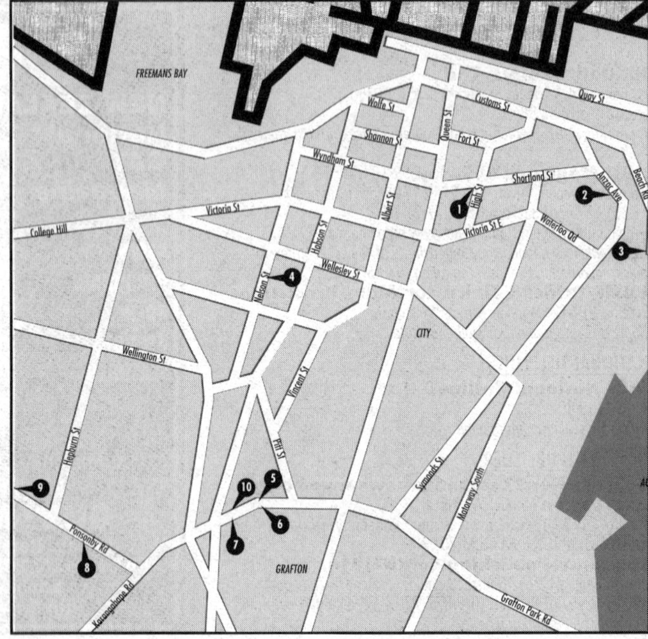

TOURIST INFO

Auckland Visitor Center
Wellesley St. *(behind Civic Theatre)* ☎ 366 68 88 Fax: 358 46 84

BARS

Brad's Bar at Club Westside (B f G MA NU sa sb W wh) 12-2, Fri Sat 0-24 h
45 Anzac Avenue *(above OUT! Bookshop)* ☎ 377 77 71
Bar Accompanying gay sauna.

Divas Bar & Café (! B G d STV)
1 Anzac Avenue ☎ 357 09 64
Downstairs is the new MOJO's club.

Karacters (B d G MA s) Thu-Sat 19-? h
ST George Tavern, Wallace Road, Papatoetoe ☎ 277 99 55
South Auckland's only gay bar.

Legend Bar (B D GLM S STV W) Mon-Sun 16-? h
335 Karangahape Road ☎ 377 60 62
Featuring drag shows Fri Sat nights.

Shooters Bar & Café (B CC F glm) 12-? h
5 Mercury Lane *(off K'Road)*
Venue for VOLT leather club every 2nd Sat.

Sinners (B D glm s WE) Wed-Sun 20-? h
373 Karangahape Road, Newton ☎ 308 99 85
Late night dance club and bar.

Surrender Dorothy (B f glm) Mon-Sat 17-0.30 Sun 17-23.30 h
Shop 3, 175 Ponsonby Road, Ponsonby ☎ 376 44 60
Under new management! Popular neighbourhood gay and lesbian bar with an emphasis on camp and kitsch. Free taxis to G.A.Y. midnights on Thu, Fri & Sat.

Urge (! B CC d G lj MA N VS) Thu - Sat 20-3 h, Sun 18-24 h
490 Karangahape Road ☎ 307 21 55

MEN'S CLUBS

Lateshift Safe Sex Men's Cruise Club (AC CC DR f G LJ MA VS WE) Fri Sat and public holidays 20-6, Sun-Thu -3 h
25 Dundonald Sreet, Newton ☎ 373 26 57
Safe Sex Cruise Club, fetish playrooms, extensive maze, pool table, pinball, cable TV, drinks and snacks.

Volt (G LJ MA P) From 22:00h-?
PO Box 6841, Newton
Leathermen's club. Meets at Shooters Bar on 1st, 3rd and 5th Sat in month. Theme nights.

CAFÉS

Kamo Bar & Café (B F glm) Sun-Wed 11-20, Thu-Sat -2 h
382 Karangahape Road ☎ 377 23 13

Quasar Café (g) 7-16 h
3 O'Connel Street ☎ 309 01 51

Salsa Bar & Café (B CC E F glm MA) 15-23.30 h
137A Richmond Road, Ponsomby ☎ 378 81 58
Popular local bar & café.

DANCECLUBS

G.A.Y. Club & Bar (B D G OS p) Wed - Sat 21-4 h
5 High Street *(Entrance - High St)*
Opened in December 1999 !

Hero (B CC D GLM)
PO Box 184 *(4th floor)* ☎ 307 10 57
Major Gay & Lesbian Festival, dance party and parade held February each year.

Mojo's Club (B D SNU)
1 Anzac Aveune *(Downstairs at DIVAS)* ☎ 357-0964
Private wine bar with dance floor and pool table. Fri and Sat SNU.

RESTAURANTS

Bayou Cafe (B F glm) 17.30-? h
422 Richmond Road *(Greylynn)* ☎ 376 70 55
Bring your own alcohol. Best on Sun.

Wagamamas (B F glm) 12-15 h, 18-?
173 Karangahape Road, Newton ☎ 373 32 99 Fax: 529 92 86

SEX SHOPS/BLUE MOVIES

Catalina Video Distributors (NZ)
The OUT! Centre, 45 Anzac Avenue, Bag, 921 26 Auckland 1
☎ 377 90 31
Retailer/distributor of gay videos.

Den. The (DR G VS) Mon-Sun 11-? h
348 Karangahape Road ☎ 307 91 91
Gay magazines, videos, leather, adult toys and more.

OUT! Adult Bookshop (G) Mon-Sat 11-22, Sun 13-22 h
The OUT! Centre, 45 Anzac Avenue, City (ground floor)
☎ 377 77 70 Fax: 377 77 67
Full range of adult gay products: videos, toys, lubes, sex magazines & books and more. Inner city location.

SAUNAS/BATHS

Club Westside (B CC DR f G MA sa sb VS W wh WO)
Mon-Thu 12-2, Fri-Sat 0-24 h (non-stop)
45 Anzac Avenue, City *(1st floor, above OUT! bookshop)* ☎ 377 77 71
Popular inner-city sauna, cruise club and Brad's licensed bar. Gym, maze, bunkrooms. Sun features „Jocks & G Strings". Student discounts.

Club 18 Beresford (G sa sb VS wh) Sun-Thu 15-2, Fri Sat -6 h
18 Beresford Street *(Off Pitt Street)* ☎ 377 55 71
Near gay clubs and bars.

New Zealand Countrymen's Institute (G sa sb VS wh WO) Sun-Thu 12-1, Fri Sat 12-5 h
151 Beach Road, Parnell *(opposite Shell service station)* ☎ 366 17 81
Men's sauna. Gym.

Wingate Club (CC DR f G MA NU pi sa sb VS wh WO) 12-? h
80 Wingate Street, Avondale ☎ 828 09 10 *Suburban Country club atmosphere. Off street parking. Heated outdoor pool und secluded outdoor sun bathing.*

BOOK SHOPS

Onehunga Book Exchange (g)
163 The Mall, Onehunga *(opposite ASB)* ☎ 622 17 66
Buy, sell and exchange gay books and magazines.

OUT! Bookshop (! CC G) 11-23 h
The OUT! Centre, 45 Anzac Avenue *(ground floor)* ☎ 377 77 70
Fax: 377 77 67 E-Mail: out@nz.com Homepage: www.outnz.net.nz
Gay books, magazines, cards, videos, adult toys, video hire. Community notice board. Auckland's only fully exclusively gay bookshop.

TRAVEL & TRANSPORT

Dolphin Travel (CC GLM) 8.30-17 h, 24-hour phone service
20 Georgina Street, Freemans Bay *(Bus-College Hill)* ☎ 376 66 11
Fax: 376 66 16 E-Mail: inbound@dolphin-travel.co.nz

Grey Lynn Travel Mon-Fri 9-18, Sat 10-16 h, closed Sun
555 Great North Road, Grey Lynn ✉1002 *(Western Springs Bus-Surrey Crescent Shops)* ☎ 376 35 56 Fax: 376 63 63
E-Mail: glt@greylynntravel.co.nz *Toll free* ☎ *(508) 842-538*
Travel agency.

Travel Desk New Zealand (GLM W) Mon-Fri 9-17 h
c/o The OUT! Centre, 45 Anzac Avenue ✉92126 *(2nd floor above OUT! Bookshop)* ☎ 377 90 31 Fax: 377 77 67
E-Mail: traveldk@ihug.co.nz *Gay owned and operated.*

HOTELS

Darlinghurst Quest Inn (bf CC glm H)
52 Eden Crescent ✉1001 ☎ 366 32 60 Fax: 366 32 69
E-Mail: qrc@questapartments.com.au
Homepage: www.questapartments.com.au.
Rates studio NZ$ 144, apartments 175-210. All rooms with shower/WC, balcony, telephone, SAT-TV, minibar, kitchen, own key and room service. Continental bf NZ$ 11-81.

Dryden Lodge (GLM H)
27-31 Dryden Street, Grey Lynn ☎ 378 08 92 Fax: 378 12 82

GUEST HOUSES

Awatea (Glm H)
☎ 378 63 95 *B & B homestay in Ponsonby.*

The Brown Kivi Travellers Hostel (B CC glm MA OS YG) Office: 8-20 h
7 Prosford Street, Ponsoby *(Link Bus-Redmonds Street)*
☎ 378 01 91 Fax: 378 01 91 E-Mail: enquiries@brownkivi.co.nz
Cosy travelers hostel in renovated two-stokey colonial home located 5 minutes from the beach. Accommodation in 4 to 6 beds dormitories with lockers or two double rooms. Shared bath. Kitchen with cooking and eating utensils. Coin operated laundry. Rates dormitory NZ$ 17-18 a night per person, double NZ$ 40.

Herne Bay B&B & Serviced Apartments (GLM H)
4 Shelley Beach Road, Herne Bay ☎ 360 03 09 Fax: 360 03 89
5 rooms and 4 apartments with shower/WC, fax, minibar and kitchenette. Own key. Rates single NZ$ 65-85, double NZ$ 75-95, apartment NZ$130. Additional bed $20. Bf incl. Weekly and winter rates by negociation.

APARTMENTS

Pacific Westmount Serviced Apartments (AC bf CC F glm H MA OS)
23 Upper Queen Street ☎ 356 7211 Fax: 356 7116
Email: andreas@dynpac.co.nz. *Rates from NZ$ 135.*

GENERAL GROUPS

Auckland Gay & Lesbian Welfare Group
Office hours: Thu-Fri 9-17 h
45 Anzac Avenue *(3rd floor)* ☎ 303 35 84 E-Mail: aglw@xtra.co.nz
Counselling and support.

Auckland Lesbian & Gay Lawyers Group
Wellesley Street
Support & networking for lawyers and law students.

Auckland University Gay Students Association Fri 17-19 h
c/o Student Union Auckland University, Room 114 *(Exec. lounge, 1st floor) Social group for gay & bisexual students & friends, on & off campus.*

Bears
c/o KUBS Wellesley St.
Support and social group for hairy men, friends and admirers.

Couples (Auckland) NZ
PO Box 6251, Wellesley St. ☎ 627 23 38
For gay couples in relationships. Friendship/support/social activities.

Gay Auckland Business Association (GABA)
(GLM) PO Box 30 92 ☎ 378 90 30 Fax: 520 40 92
E-Mail: dbgrove@hug.co.nz
Association of gay and lesbian business people.

Gay Diners (G)
☎ (021) 613 136
Wine and dine and meet new people. Gay Matchmaking Club.

Mercury Motorcycle Club Meets 3rd Fri of month.
PO Box 26-335, Epsom ☎ 479 79 20

Parents of Lesbian & Gays Support Group
☎ 846 78 89
Contact/support group for parents of gays & lesbians.

Rainbow Youth Trust Mon-Fri 10-16 h
Wellesly Street ☎ 376 41 55 ☎ 376 66 50 (24-hour info line)
Fax: 376 66 50 E-Mail: aniwa@outnet.co.nz
Meetings held every 2nd Sun at Kamo Café, 382 Karangahape Road for queer youth under 26.

The Fifth Season -Gay Garden Group-
☎ 827 30 36
Gay & Lesbian garden group. Monthly garden visits, social activities, quarterly newsletter.

Transexual Outreach (TOPS) Mon-Fri 9-16 h
c/o PO Box 68 501 ☎ 09/366-6106
Education, health, referral service.

Whakapuakitanga
☎ 309 45 72 *For young Maori Men.*

HEALTH GROUPS

A.D.I.O.-Needle Exchange
227a Symonds Street ☎ 309 85 19

AIDS-Hotline 0-24 h
☎ 358 00 99
Information and counselling.

Auckland Sexual Health Service
Building 16, Auckland Hospital ☎ 307 28 85
Free and confidential testing.

Body Positive / 12 on 12 Group Mon Tue 14-16 Wed 17-19 Thu Fri 14-16 h
3 Poynton Terrace, Newton ☎ 309 39 89 E-Mail: bp_nz@ihug.co.nz
HIV positive men's support group, drop-in centre, 12-on-12 peer support groups.

Cairnhill Health Centre
95 Mountain Road, Epsom ☎ 630 95 07
(Dr. Chris Thomas or Dr. Mike Pohl) after hours ☎ 630-5332 Fax: 630-9515

Community AIDS Resource Team (CART)
76 Grafton Road ☎ 367 74 36
Health support for those living with AIDS/HIV at home. Education and counselling.

Dr. Michael Pohl-Cairnhill Health Centre (g p)
Mon-Fri 8.30-17.30 h
95 Mountain Road, Epsom ✉1003 *(near Mercy Hospital)*
☎ 630 95 07 Fax: 630 95 15
Specialized in gay men's health including HIV/AIDS issues. Consulting fee NZ$ 38 per 15 minutes.

Herne Bay House
☎ 376 11 92 *Long and short term accommodation for people with AIDS/HIV. 24 hr cover by registered nurses.*

NZ AIDS Foundation Burnett Ctr/Auckland Support Service Mon-Thu 8.30-17 Fri 8.30-15.30 h
3 Poynton Terrace, Burnet Centre, Newton ☎ 309 55 60
Fax: 302 23 38 E-Mail: nzaf@iconz.co.nz
Free confidential HIV testing. Gay related counselling & practical support for people living with HIV/AIDS.

HELP WITH PROBLEMS

Aquarius Gay & Lesbian Alcoholics Anonymus Meeting: Tue 19.30-20.30 h at
The Pride Centre, 33 Wyndham Street ☎ 815 24 66

Icebreakers for Men (YG)
☎ 376 66 33 ☎ 303-3584 (Gayline), ☎ 376-4155
(Rainbow Youth) Social Support for men under 26 who are gay or bisexual.
Lesbian & Gay Narcotics Anonymous Mon 19-? h
All Saints Church Hall, Ponsonby Road ☎ 303 14 49

RELIGIOUS GROUPS

Ascent Mass 1st Wed 19.30 h, gathering 3rd Wed
PO Box 47465, Ponsonby *(at St Benedicts, Newton)* ☎ 849 78 09
Catholic group.
Auckland Community Church Service Sun 19.30 h
St.Matthews in the City, Hobson Street *Wellesley Street*
☎ 638 77 96
A Christian service of worship particularly serving those who are gay.
Evangelical Gay/Lesbian Network
Wellesley Street
Universal Fellowship of Metropolitan Churches Meets Sun 19.30 at
Methodist Church, Pitt St/Group discussion Tue 19.30 h
PO Box 3964 ✉1001 ☎ 629 09 27 ☎ 636 80 86
Homepage: http://nz.com/nz/queer/mccauckland/index.html
Serving the spiritual needs of the gay, lesbian, bisexual and transgender community.
Zen 2000 Buddhist Association
PO Box 6132, Wellesley Street ☎ 373 45 28

SPORT GROUPS

Auckland Gay Bowling Organization
PO Box 90-779, Auckland Mail Centre ☎ 849 36 53
Auckland Gay Tramping Club
Wellesley St ☎ 480 73 43
Monthly tramping trips for varying degrees of fitness.
Gay Sport New Zealand / Team Auckland
PO Box 90778 ☎ 625 75 97
Multi sports group.
Team Auckland
☎ 378 13 33 E-Mail: maiden@ihug.co.nz
Auckland Mulit Sports organization

SWIMMING

-St. Leonard's Beach (Catch bus to Takapuna, e.g. Long Bay Bus 839, and walk south; walk down the steps at the end of St. Leonard's Road; left is the predominately gay swimming area)
-Long Bay (30 km north of the city, reached by Long Bay Bus 839; gay area is 5 min. walk around rocks at the northern end, labelled Pohutakawa Bay)
-Ladies Bay (Catch 769 Glendowie bus along waterfront to St Heliers, ladies Bay is next beach to South. Follow road along cliff until you reach path heading down to beach)

CRUISING

all AYOR
-Albert Park
-Domain (around Winter Gardens area)
-Ladies Bay (in bushes behind the beach)
-Long Bay/Pohutakawa Bay (most cruising in bushes around cliff at north end of the beach)
-Student Union Building (basement)
-Customs Street West (outside Customs House on street)
-Avondale (Roxbard Road-extreme caution suggested)
-Newton Road (New North Road at shopping centre)
-Kingsland (New North Road at shopping centre)
-Parnell Rose Gardens
-Cheltenham Beach
-High Street (below car park)

Bay of Islands/Northland ☎ 09

HOTELS

Kaitia Hotel (H NG)
☎ 408 03 60 Fax: 408 03 61
Gateway to Northland/Cape Reinga, large

GUEST HOUSES

Orongo Bay Homestead (F g H)
Aucks Road, RD 1, Russell ☎ 403 75 27 Fax: 403 76 75
E-Mail: orongo.bay@clear.net.nz
Luxury accomodation in historic house with fine dining. 4 rooms with bath/WC en suite, fax, hair-dryer and heating.

Blenheim ☎ 03

PRIVATE ACCOMODATION

Blenheim Gay Homestay (bf GLM OS p)
PO Box 62 ☎ 578 22 59 E-Mail: ewood@mlb.planet.gen.nz
One double room NZ$ 40-60.

GENERAL GROUPS

Blenheim Lesbian/Gay Contact
PO Box 62 ☎ 578 22 59

CRUISING

-Alfred Street
-Scott Street (by Olympic Pool)
-All AYOR

Charleston ☎ 03

HOTELS

Pyramid Farm (bf F G H OS)
Highway 6, Westport
Situated on the coastal road between Westport and Greymouth, set in picturesque native forest. Activities: bush walks, surfing, fishing. Single NZ$ 15-25, double 25-38 (bf incl.).

Christchurch ☎ 03

GAY INFO

Dextours (AC bf GLM MA)
c/o Rainbow House, 9 The Crescent, St Martins ✉8002
☎ 337 14 38 E-Mail: mfraser.rainbowhouse@clear.net.nz
Ettie Rout News
PO Box 21-285, Edgeware ☎ 379 19 53 Fax: 365 24 77
Monthly local gay info.
Gayline Christchurch Mon 20-21, Sat 19.30-22 h
PO Box 25-165 ☎ 379 39 90 (24 h)
Info about local places and events for lesbians and gays. Also contact for:
-Futures Forum (LGB activist group)
-Icebreakers (Support group for young gays & lesbians)
-Men loving men-Oral history project
Loud & Queer Wed 18-19 h (RDU 98.3 FM-student radio)
c/o Canterbury Students Association, Private Bag

BARS

UBQ Southern Boys (AC B CC D f G MA N S W) 19-? h
88 Lichfield Street ✉8001 *(opposite „Dick Smith Electronics" store)*
☎ (0)21-379 29 10
Special Feature & drag show nights.

MEN'S CLUBS

Menfriends (b CC DR f G lj MA P RT sa sb VS sh YG) Mon-Fri 12-? h, Sat 10.30-? h, Sun 13-? h
83 Lichfield Street *(upstairs)* ☎ 377 17 01
Sauna, cruise club and shop. Special feature nights - Tue „Young 'n Hung" if you are under 23 and have more than 7"in your pants - entrance $8 .

DANCECLUBS

Platinium (B D GLM)
78 Lichfield St. ☎ 377 78 91

SAUNAS/BATHS

Colombo Sauna (b CC DR f G MA MG P sa sb VS wh)
Mon-Fri 11-? h, Sat-Sun 13-? h
661 Colombo Street *(upstairs)* ☎ 366 73 52
Incudes a OUT! Bookshop. Sun strip - every Sun 13-18:00h. Spice nites every Tue.

BOOK SHOPS

Davids Book Exchange (g VS)
181 High Street ☎ 366 20 57 *Gay magazines, books and videos.*
Kate Sheppard Bookshop (glm)
145 Manchester Street ☎ 379 07 84
OUT! Bookshop (G) Open until 23:00h
c/o Colombo Healthclub, 661 Colombo Street ☎ 366 73 52
Huge selection of reading material and full range of American WET lube as well as videos, adult toys, poppers.
Scorpio Books (AC CC glm) Mon-Thu 8.30-17.30, Fri -21, Sat 9.30-16, Sun 12-16 h
79 Hereford Street/Oxford Terrace ✉8015 ☎ 379 28 82

TRAVEL & TRANSPORT

Settlers Travel Ltd. (CC) Mon-Fri 8.30-17.30 h
26 New Regent Street ☎ 379 51 87 Fax: 379 86 29

GUEST HOUSES

Rainbow House Bed & Breakfast (bf GLM H)
9 The Crescent ✉8002 *(off the ends of Hillsborough Terrace)*
☎ 337 14 38 Fax: 337 14 96
E-Mail: mfraser.rainbowhouse@clear.net.nz Homepage:
http://members.tripod.com/~martin_fraser/index.htm
Located 8 minutes from downdown Christchurch. Rates NZ$ 30-40. Additional bed 15. Bf incl.
Rehua Mews Homestay (bf CC F GLM H MA msg OS wh)
PO Box 2155 ☎ 355 78 20 Fax: 379 30 87
E-Mail: homestay@rehuamews.co.nz
Located in the upmarket area of Merivale, Rates NZ$ 60 (single), NZ$ 90 (double).
Victorian Bed & Breakfast (f g MA)
16 Godley Quay, Lyttleton ☎ 328 74 74

PRIVATE ACCOMODATION

Glendurgan Homestay (bf G) ☎ 329 41 04
Private home with great views 30 mins. from city.
NZ Gay Hospitality Exchange 386 Oxford Terrace
☎ 379 94 93 E-Mail: df@burnside.school.nz (Feb-Nov)

GENERAL GROUPS

Boy's Own (G YG) Sun 16-19 h at
☛UBQ Bar/Club ☎ 379 18 21
Gay youth group.
Campus Queers
c/o University of Canterbury Students' Association *Ilam Road*
☎ 348 70 69
Gay Information Line 24 h
PO Box 25-165 ☎ 379 39 90 E-Mail: df@burnside.school.nz (Feb-Nov)
Gays & Lesbian Everywhere in Education (GLEE)
PO Box 25-165 ☎ 379 94 93 ☎ 313 44 95 Fax: 379 94 93
E-Mail: df@burnside.school.nz
Supports students and teachers. Monthly meetings.
Gays & lesbians in business (GLIB)
PO Box 22-099 ☎ 366 33 12 Fax: 381 01 73 E-Mail: glib@xtra.co.nz

HEALTH GROUPS

HIV Support Group
☎ 379 19 53 *(Contact Terry, NZ AIDS Foundation, Ettie Rout Centre)*
NZ AIDS Foundation
Ettie Rout Clinic, 31 Asaph St. ☎ 379 19 53 Fax: 365 24 77
Homepage: ettie@ihug.co.nz *Information and support.*

HELP WITH PROBLEMS

Gayline Mon 20-21, Sat 19.30-22 h
PO Box 25-165 ✉8002
☎ 379 47 96 *Phone counselling and information.*
Gaylink
PO Box 25-165 ☎ 379 94 93
Anti Violence Project; Police Liaison. Contact Robin.

RELIGIOUS GROUPS

All Saints Metropolitan Community Church
Sun 11 h
PO Box 13 468 ☎ 389 32 35
Ascent Meetings 3rd Thu of month
PO Box 22-718 ☎ 355 85 76 *Support group for gay Catholics.*

SPORT GROUPS

Avon Mens' Netball Club
☎ 338 11 03
Gay Sport New Zealand Team Christchurch
c/o Dan Knowles, PO Box 212 85 ☎ 385 10 01
E-Mail: ettie@ihug.co.nz.
Lambda Walkers
PO Box 21-285 ☎ 366 09 62 *Walks every 2nd Sun.*

CRUISING

-North Hagley Park (next to Rolleston Avenue)
-Waimairi Beach (1km north of the Surf Club in dunes)
-Spencer Park (along the sand dunes)
-All AYOR
-Arts Centre (Relleston Avenue)
-Brighton Pier (New Brighton Beach)
-Denton Park (Sports Pavillion)
-Hagley Park (Armagh Street Entrance of changing shed)
-Jellie Park (Greers Road)
-Malvern Park (Innes Road)
-Manchester Street Car Park (Manchester Street)
-North Beach Surf Pavillion (in changing shed)
-St. Albans Park (Madras street around changing shed)
-Wordsworth Street (next Colombo Street Corner)

Dunedin ☎ 03

GAY INFO

Dunedin Gay Radio•One Tue Thu 18-19 h (FM 91 MHz)
☎ 477 19 69
Thu »Tea with the Boys«, Tue »Lesbian show«
Gayline 0-24 h Answering machine.Wed 17.30-19-30 Fri 19.30-22.30 h
PO Box 1382 ☎ 477 20 77
Info & support for gays, friends and family.
Otago Gaily Times
Private Bag 6171 ☎ 474 77 32
Monthly local gay info.

CAFES

Tangenté Café (A AC bf CC F glm MA W WE) 8-15.30 h
111 Moray Place ☎ 477 02 32
Zambesi (b f g MA) 2nd & 4th Fri
Moray Plaace *(next to Fortune Cafe)* ☎ 477 20 77

SAUNAS/BATHS

Body Works (DR G MA P sa VS wh YG) Mon Tue Thu 17-24, Wed 12-24, Fri 12-2, Sat 14-2, Sun 14-23 h
284 Princes Street ☎ 477 82 28
Private mens club, spa cruise area and sauna.

BOOK SHOPS

Modernway Books (g)
331 George Street ☎ 477 66 36
Southern Books (g)
225 King Edward Street

TRAVEL & TRANSPORT

Otago Campervans (G) 0-24 h
40 Franklin Street ☎ 473 09 36 Fax: 473 09 46
Fully self-contained 2-berth campervans.

GENERAL GROUPS

Gay/Bi Boys On Campus Meets every 2nd week Wed 13-14 h in Otago Room.
c/o OUSA, PO Box 1436 ☎ 477 20 77
Clubs and socials organized.
Icebreakers
c/o Gayline, PO Box 1382 ☎ 477 20 77
Social group for gays under 25 years.
Queerspace Thu 19.30-23 h
Tangente Café, Upper Money Race
Queer social space / companionship.
Tuatua
PO Box 1382 ☎ 477 20 77
Social group for men over 30.
Youth Esteem Services (YES)
☎ 473 97 20 *Youth Group for those under 25. Contact Gayline.*

HEALTH GROUPS

NZ AIDS Foundation Otago
154 Hanover Street ☎ 474 02 21 Fax: 474 76 31
Sexual Health Clinic
☎ 474 95 65 *Free STD info and treatment.*

HELP WITH PROBLEMS

Gayline Wed 17.30-19.30 Fri 19.30-22.30 h
PO Box 13 82 ☎ 477 20 77
For information and help.

RELIGIOUS GROUPS

Ascent Dunedin
PO Box 5328, Moray Place ☎ 477 20 77
Catholic-based gay and lesbian group. Others with different religious interests welcome.

SPORT GROUPS

Gay Sports New Zealand Team Dunedin
Libby Knight, 30 Chambers Street ☎ 472 55 99
Multi sports group.

CRUISING

-Jubilee Park (Queens Avenue)
-Smailles Beach
-St. Clair Beach (at sand dunes and by Barnes Memorial Lookout)
-All AYOR
-Dowling Street (opposite Queens Gardens)
-Upper Botanic Gardens
-Albany Street (near George Street)

Fielding ☎ 04

GUEST HOUSES

Bed & Breakfast (g H)
☎ 323 93 77
Homestay accomodation.

Gisborne ☎ 06

PRIVATE ACCOMODATION

Gisborne - Gay Villa -Bed & Breakfast- (GLM)
☎ 863 04 13

GENERAL GROUPS

Gisborne Gay Support Wed 19.30-21.30 h
PO Box 929 ☎ 863 04 13
Contact and support group.

Hamilton ☎ 07

GAY INFO

Different Strokes Sun 20-22 h (89 FM)
Private Bag 3059 ☎ 838 44 40
Social Tendencies BBS 0-24 h
☎ 846 26 03

BARS

Next Door Bar (B GLM) Wed-Sun 17.30-3 h
10 High Street, Frankton ☎ 847 86 35

SAUNAS/BATHS

10 High (b f G sa sb VS) 17.30-1.30 h
10 High Street, Frankton ☎ 847 86 35

GENERAL GROUPS

Gaylink Drop-in Centre Wed 20-22 h
☎ 855-54 29 (24 h)
Parents of Gay Waikato
☎ 827 49 35
Supportive parents group.

HEALTH GROUPS

NZ AIDS Foundation (Waikato)
3/17 Ohaupo Road ☎ 838 35 57 ☎ 838 35 11
Fax: 838 35 14

HELP WITH PROBLEMS

Waikato Gay and Lesbian Support and Information Service (GLM MA) Wed 20-22 h (drop-in centre)
4 Te Aroha St. (Link House) ☎ 855 54 29
24 h telephone answer phone, message regulary updated.

RELIGIOUS GROUPS

MCC Waikato (GLM) Sun 17 h
PO Box 52 17, Frankton ☎ 855 06 51

SPORT GROUPS

Team Hamilton/Cambridge
☎ 827 58 67

CRUISING

All are AYOR
-Garden Place
-City Square
-Memorial Park (also known as Parana Park)
-Victoria Lake (near miniature railway)
-Towpath near Waikato River

Hastings ☎ 06

MEN'S CLUBS

Embassy Cruise Club (G b f MA VS) Tue 11-14 h, Wed-Thu 16-1 h, Sat, 16-3 h, Sun 17-21 h
King St/Heretauna St. ☎ 870 71 11

BOOK SHOPS

Stortford Lodge Bookshop (g)
1102 Heretaunga Street

GUEST HOUSES

Providencia Country House (AC bf CC glm H msg)
225 Middle Road, R.D. 2, Hawkes Bay ☎ 877 23 00
Homepage: http://nz.comwebnz/tpac/gaynz/Prov.dencia.html
Beautiful historical house in the middle of a prosperous wine region. Three rooms with bath/WC.

CRUISING

-Cornwell Park

Hokitika ☎ 03

PRIVATE ACCOMODATION

Beache House (B CC F H NG OS)
139 Rovell Strett ✉7900 *(Main street on seafrontage)*
☎ 755 63 349 Fax: 755 63 49
E-Mail: beachhouse1999@hotmail.com
Accommodation for backpackers, Cafe & Bar, gay friendly. Double NZJ$ 40.

GENERAL GROUPS

Wild Wild West Gay Club
☎ 768 03 66

Invercargill ☎ 03

GAY INFO

Gayline (GLM) Gayline: Wed 17.30-19.30 Fri 19.30-22.30 h
☎ 477 20 77

CRUISING

All AYOR
-Town Hall (back of Tay Street)

Kaitaia ☎ 09

HOTELS

Kaitaia Hotel (B g H)
☎ 408 03 60 Fax: 408 03 61
Historic Hotel near 90 mile beach at Bay of Plenty.

PRIVATE ACCOMODATION

Awanui Homestay (G)
☎ 406 77 70 *Retreat for men, NZ$20 per night.*

Levin ☎ 04

GENERAL GROUPS

Rainbow Club Meetings last Sat of month.
Po Box 134, Otaki Railway ☎ 293 71 77
Friendship & social contact group for Kapiti/Harawhenuc area.

Masterton ☎ 06

GUEST HOUSES

Koeke Lodge (E G H)
„Koeke" Upper Plain Road
☎ 377 24 14 E-Mail: koekelodge@ytra.co.nz
4 rooms with shower/WC, radio. Rates single NZ$ 75, double 95-120. Additional bed 30. Half-board.

Mount Maunganui ☎ 07

CAFES

Muffin Boutique (bf F glm)
195 Mt. Maunganui Road ☎ 575 8674

FASHION SHOPS

Bad Boys (CC) 9-17, Sat Sun 10-16 h
150 Maunganui Road *(at Phoenix Shopping Centre)* ☎ 575 80 87
Fax: 575 80 87 *Menswear, shoes, hire Suits, dry cleaning agents.*

GENERAL GROUPS

Fabulous Group (Social Men Grop)
☎ 599 04 33

CRUISING

-Papamoa Beach (nude bathing in the sand dunes)
-Soundshell (Marine Parade/Grace Avenue)
-The Mall (Harbourside-Changing Sheds)

Napier ☎ 06

GUEST HOUSES

Cornucopia Lodge (AC B bf CC F GLM pi)
361-367 State Highway 5 R.D. 2 Eskdale ✉4021 ☎ 836 65 08
Fax: 836 65 18 E-Mail: info@cornucopia-Lodge.com
Homepage: www.cornucopia-Lodge.com

Decor City Motor Lodge (CC g H)
308 Kennedy Rd. ☎ 843 43 42 Fax: 423 75 65
E-Mail: decocity@xtra.co.nz

GENERAL GROUPS

Regal Meeting 3rd Sat at
Baycity Club, Milton Road
☎ 835 74 82

HEALTH GROUPS

Luft MD. Dr. Alex J. Westshore Medical Centre, 138 Charles Street ☎ 835 94 16 Fax: 835 08 55
E-Mail: alex@ramhb.co.nz

HELP WITH PROBLEMS

Gayline/Icebreakers Mon-Sun 17-20 h
☎ 835 74 82

CRUISING

-Soundshell
–Anderson Park (Auckland Road-Greenmeadows)
-Spriggs Park (Hardinge Road)

Nelson ☎ 03

RESTAURANTS

Ribbetts Restaurant (F g)
20 Tahunanvi Drive ☎ 548 69 11

HOTELS

Te Puna Wai Lodge (bf CC f GLM LJ MA OS)
24 Richardson Street, Port Hills ✉7001 ☎ 548 76 21
Fax: 546 76 21 E-Mail: richardhewetson@clear.net.nz
Restored historic colonial villa, sea & mountain views. Languages: english, german, spanish, french, danish, polish, portuguese, russian. From NZ$ 115.

GUEST HOUSES

Palmgrove Guest House (bf g H)
PO Box 4022, Nelson South ☎ 547 28 27 ☎ 545 07 97
E-Mail: kevin@ts.co.nz or ntilly@xtra.co.nz
Homepage: www.ts.co.nz/kevin
Central location. 2 double rooms, 4 single rooms, partly with WC/bath. All rooms with balcony, telephone, TV, radio, heating, own key. Rates single NZ$ 35-45, double 70-85. Additional bed 15. Bf incl.

PRIVATE ACCOMODATION

Golden Bay Homestay (bf G H)
C/- H Harries NZ Post, Takata ☎ 525 97 81
Homestay accomodation.
Henry's
Burnside Road, R.D.1, Takaka PO Box 209 ☎ 525 97 81
Homestay acommodations at Golden Bay National Park.
Nelson Famestay (bf D G H)
☎ 522 44 84 *Short or long country farm stays.*

CAMPING

Autumn Farm (NU)
R.D. 1 ✉7172 *(Golden Bay at the top of the South Island)*
☎ 525 9013 E-Mail: stay@autumnfarm.com
Homepage: www.autumnfarm.com
Set in 15 acres of secluded woodlands. Communal bathhouse, kitchen and laundry plus comfortable guest house.

GENERAL GROUPS

Nelson Countrymens Group (over 30's Social Group)
☎ 548 64 70
Spectrum (G MA) Thu 19.30-22.30 h
PO Box 40 22, Nelson South *(Meets at 42 Franklyn Street)*
☎ 545 07 97 E-Mail: kevin@ts.co.nz
Homepage: www.ts.co.nz/~kevin/
Social and support group.
Spectrum Drop-In Centre Thu 19.30-22.30 h
42 Frankly Street

RELIGIOUS GROUPS

Ascent
138 Vanguard Street ☎ 355 85 76
Catholic gay support group.

CRUISING

-At the Cathedral
-Tahuna Beach
-Rabbit Island (Beach)

New Plymouth ☎ 06

GENERAL GROUPS

Taranaki Pride Alliance
PO Box 6074, Moturoa
Gay, lesbian, bi and transperson contact and publishers of the Rainbow Times.

SWIMMING

-Black Beach (near New Plymouth during summer)

CRUISING

-By the State Hotel

Palmerston North ☎ 06

BARS

Club Q (Manawatu Lesbian & Gay Rights Association) (B D f GLM MA S) Fri, Sat 20-? h
PO Box 14 91 ☎ 358 53 78
Contact Gayline for address and schedule of events.

GUEST HOUSES

Bed and Breakfast (g H)
☎ 323 93 77

GENERAL GROUPS

Manawatu Chapter Gay Couples
☎ 323 93 77
Manawatu Lesbian and Gay Rights Association Fri 20 Sat 21.30 h
PO Box 14 91 ☎ 358 53 78
Social/Welfare group for gay men, lesbians and bisexuals. Club Q (behind Square Edge shopping complex, upstairs) opens Fri 20-?, Sat 21-? h.

HELP WITH PROBLEMS

Gayline/Lesbianline 0-24 information, Wed Fri 19-22 counselling
☎ 358 53 78
Also contact for Icebreakers (Support group for gays under 26)

SPECIAL INTEREST GROUPS

Club Farout Thu, Fri & Sat from 20 h

CRUISING

-City Square
-Milverton Park

Queenstown ☎ 03

GUEST HOUSES

Coneburn (bf CC G NU sa wh)
PO Box 274 ☎ 442 23 81
Guest house in rural setting. Single NZ$ 55, double/twin 75.

GENERAL GROUPS

Queer Queenstown
PO Box 1215 ☎ 441 81 83

CRUISING

-Waterfront Jetty (city center)

Rotorua ☎ 07

GAY INFO

Gayline Information & Support Tue 19-21 h
☎ 348 35 98
Confidential support, friendship and info for gays & bisexuals.

Rotorua Gay Information/What's On
☎ 348 01 93

GUEST HOUSES

Troutbeck-Homestay and Bed & Breakfast
(bf CC F GLM H MA)
PO Box 242, 16 Egmont Road, Ngongotaha ☎ 357 47 95
Fax: 357 47 80 E-Mail: trouthbeck@troutbeck.co.nz
Homepage: http://nz.com/webzn/troutbeck
Homestay (bf incl.) accomodations. Rates NZ$ 50 for a single, NZ$ 70 for a kingsize double. Dinner NZ$15 p.p.

PRIVATE ACCOMODATION

Ascott Villa - Rotarua (H)
7 Meade St. ☎ 348 48 95 ☎ 348 83 84
Homepage: www.ascottvilla.co.nz

CRUISING

-The Domain (Lakeside Park)
-Kerosene creek (natural hot water stream and swimming pool)
Kuirau Park, lake front.

Takaka - Golden Bay ☎ 03

GUEST HOUSES

Autumn Farm (bf F G H NU OS p)
Central Takaka Road ✉7172 ☎ 525 90 13
E-Mail: stay@autumnfarm.com Homepage: www.autumnfarm.com

Taupo ☎ 07

PRIVATE ACCOMODATION

Boulevard Spa Motel (H NG)
261 Waihi Rd. ☎ 800-369 000 Fax: 578 32 68
Gay owned accommodation

CRUISING

-Small public garden near new library (SH1, central Taupo)
-Waterfront (public toilets)

Tauranga ☎ 07

GAY INFO

Tauranga Gayline 2nd & 4th Wed in Month 14-20:00h
all other Wed. nights 18-22:00h
☎ 577 0481 *New information and helpline.*

SEX SHOPS/BLUE MOVIES

Nauti Nik Naks (g)
41 B The Strand

SPORT GROUPS

Bay of Plenty Tramping Club Meets last Sun in month.
☎ 544 21 15

CRUISING

-Memorial Park
-Tauranga Domain (Hamilton/Cameron Road)

Timaru ☎ 03

CRUISING

-Central Stafford Street (underground)
-Caroline Bay (near rail viaduct and Loop Road)

Waikanae

SWIMMING

-Peka Peka (NU OG) (5 km North of Waikanae. Turn left off SH1 into Peka Peka Road. The gay area is about 200 m north along beach)

Wanganui ☎ 06

HEALTH GROUPS

Wanganui HIV/AIDS Co-Ordinator
c/o Youth Advice Centre, 58 Dublin St. ☎ 347 13 83

CRUISING

-P-area of the Olympic Swimming Pool (by the yacht harbor)
-Uretiti Beach (NU) (go onto the beach from the car P and turn right, keep walking until you are out of the mixed area)

Wellington ☎ 04

● The capital of New Zealand is located at the southern tip of the North Island and because of the fresh breezes is called „Windy City". Wellington is not surprisingly a bit conservative owing to it being the centre for government administration with many governmental authorities located there. Wellington is worth visiting because of it's mild climate and wonderful position between ocean and mountains and not forgetting it's small lively gay scene.

✱ Die Hauptstadt Neuseelands liegt am Südzipfel der Nordinsel und wird nicht zu Unrecht „windy city" genannt, weht hier doch eigentlich immer eine frische Brise.
Wellington ist das Verwaltungszentrum des Landes und Sitz diverser Behörden und so wundert es nicht, daß man sich hier etwas konservativer als im legeren Auckland gibt. Doch das ausgeglichene und milde Klima, die wunderschöne Lage zwischen Ozean und Bergen, sowie eine kleine aber lebendige Szene, machen einen Stop auf jeden Fall lohnenswert.

▲ La capitale de la Nouvelle Zélande se trouve à la pointe sud de l'île du nord, et n'est pas nommée pour rien „windy city", même si c'est toujours une brise fraiche qui souffle ici. Wellington est le centre administratif du pays et le siège de nombreuses administrations, et il n'est donc pas surprenant que les gens soient un peu plus conservateurs qu'à Auckland. Mais le climat doux et équilibré, la situation géographique magnifique, entre l'océan et les montagnes, et un milieu gay petit mais vivant font qu'un arrêt dans cette ville en vaut la peine.

☆ La capital de Nueva Zelanda se encuentra en el más extremo sur de la isla norteña y su apodo es, y con mucha razón „windy city", ya que aquí siempre corre una suave brisa. Wellington es el centro administrativo del país y la sede de varios ministerios y oficinas estateles. Por ello, no es de extrañar que la gente de aquí se muestra más conservadora en comparación con el liberal Auckland. Pero un visita merecerá sin duda la pena, no solo por el agradable clima, sino tambíen por la situación impresionante de Wellington entre oceano y montañas y su pequeño, pero muy animado ambiente.

❖ La capitale della Nuova Zelanda è situata sul punto meridionale dell'isola settentrionale, e a causa della permanente brezza è comprensibile che la città venga nominata la „windy city". Wellington è il centro amministrativo e la sede di diverse istituzioni. Quindi non c'è da stupirsi che quì l'atmosfera è un po' più conservativa in rispetto ad Auckland, dove la vita è più facile. Però il clima mite ed equilibrato, la posizione meravigliosa tra oceano e montagna, e un'ambiente gay piccolo ma vivace, valgono la pena di fermarvisi.

GAY INFO

Awhina Newsletter
PO Box 7287, Wellington South ☎ 389 31 69
Information about Aids. Publishers of Q Community Events Calender.
Gay Broadcasting Collective Sat 11.15-12.15 h (AM 783 kHz)
PO Box 24-165 Manners St ☎ 385 87 83
Gay Switchboard 19.30-22 h
PO Box 11-372 ☎ 385-0674
To contact GAYZE in Action, mens social sports group (rugby, indoor-cricket, soccer etc.) phone switchboard. To contact Pentagon Group, social group for gays 20-35 age, call switchboard. To contact Hutt Valley Gay Group, local neighbourly fellowship, phone switchboard or write to PO Box 44 138 VIC, Lower Hutt. Meets 2n Wed each mon. To contact Boy Zone, fortnightly Group for young gay & bisexual men (16-30) call switchboard.

BARS

Bojangles (B D F GLM MA S)
60 Dixon St. ☎ 384 84 45
Chad's Bar @ Club Wakefield (B F G) 12-? h
15 Tory St. *Bar is part of Club Wakefield Sauna & Cruise Club.*
The Dome (A AC B bf CC D F Glm MA N OS S WE YG)
Tue-Sun 11-3 h, Mon closed
0 Kent and Cambridge Terraces *(Middle of the road)* ☎ 385 65 66

MEN'S CLUBS

Sanctuary (CC DR G LJ MA P) Tue Sun 20-24, Wed Thu -2, Fri Sat -6 h, Mon closed
39 Dixon Street ✉6001 *(3rd floor)* ☎ 384 15 65
Cruise Club, $ 8 before 20 h and $ 12 after 20 h. Tue/Wed 2 for 1 night, Sunday free for students with I.D.
Valve Wed 20- ?
154 Vivian Street ☎ (0800) 4 BADBOYZ
For bisexual and gay men. Also skinheads, evis, uniforms, leathers bears and kubs.

CAFES

Eva Dixons Place (F g)
35A Dixon Street ☎ 384 10 00
Madison Café (F g)
106 Oriental Parade, Oriental Bay ☎ 384 48 11
Popular café for gay men to see and be seen.

RESTAURANTS

Brasserie Flipp (B F g)
103 Ghusnee Street ☎ 385 94 93

SEX SHOPS/BLUE MOVIES

Out! Bookshop (G) Mon-Sat 11-23 h
15 Tory Street *(same building as Wakefield Sauna)* ☎ 385 44 00
Gay magazines, books, videos, adult supplies. Wellington's only gay adult shop. Also Wellington office of OUT! Magazine.

ESCORTS & STUDIOS

Adam Male Escorts
☎ 384 85 15 *Incalls and outcalls available.*
Imaginations
☎ 387 73 40
Wellington Gay Escorts
☎ 386 22 29

SAUNAS/BATHS

Club Wakefield (B DR f G MA sa sb sol VS W wh WO) 12-2, Thu- 3, Fri & Sat -6 h
15 Tory Street *(in the centre)* ☎ 385 44 00
Popular men's sauna, incorporates „Chad's „ licensed bar.

FITNESSTUDIOS

Les Mills World of Fitness (NG WO)
1st Floor 74 Cuba Mall ☎ 384 88 98
Inner city gym popular with gay men.

BOOK SHOPS

Unity Books (GLM)
57 Willis Street ☎ 499 42 45 Fax: 499 42 46
E-Mail: unity.books@clear.net.nz

TRAVEL & TRANSPORT

Gaylink Reservataion Centre (CC GLM)
PO Box 11-462 ✉6001 ☎ 384 18 65 Fax: 384 18 35
E-Mail: reznz@gaylink.co.nz
Homepage: http://webnz.com/tpac/gay
For online reservations and vacation planning on Internet for New Zealand, Australia and Soutz Pacific.
Gaylink Tours Ltd. (CC GLM)
P.O.Box 11-462 ✉6001 ☎ 384 18 87 Fax: 384 58 20
E-Mail: reznz@gaylinktours.co.nz
Homepage: www.gaylinktours.co.nz
Providing semi-structured independent, small group and chauffeur tours for New Zealand, Australia and South Pacific.
Rainbow Rentals (CC G)
PO Box 11-462 ✉6001 ☎ 384 18 65 Fax: 384 18 35
E-Mail: reznz@rainbowrentals.co.nz
Homepage: http://webnz.com/tpac/gaynz/Rainbow
Providing rental car and campervan hirer throughout New Zealand.

HOTELS

Trekkers. Hotel/Motel (B bf F g H MA sa wh YG)
213 Cuba Street/Dunlop Terrace ☎ 385 21 53 *Single from NZ$*

PRIVATE ACCOMODATION

Wellington Homestay (G H)
☎ 387 30 49 *Private homestay in central Wellington.*

GENERAL GROUPS

Gay Task Force Meets 1st Mon in month.
☎ 479-6310 *(Des Smith) Activist organization.*
Gays and Lesbians Everywhere in Education-GLEE (GLM) Meets 2nd Tue in month
☎ 568 24 92
Gays of the Hutt
☎ 385 06 74 *Local neighbourhood fellowship.*
Icebreakers
☎ 385 06 74 E-Mail: ice-breakers@geocities.com
For young people who think they might be gay.

HEALTH GROUPS

AIDS/HIV Hotline 24 hrs
☎ 0800 802 437 *Counselling and information service.*
Area Health Board Aids Programme Co-Ordinator
☎ 472 56 79
Body Positive
PO Box 7287, Wellington South ☎ 389 31 69 Fax: 389 42 07
HIV Support Group Meets fortnightly
☎ 389 31 69 *Group support and information sharing.*

NZ AIDS Foundation Wellington (Awhina Centre)
45 Tory St, PO Box 9247 ☎ 381 66 40 Fax: 381 66 41
Confidential HIV testing and counselling.

HELP WITH PROBLEMS

Counselling Services
☎ 384 55 49 *(John Mayesm) private counsellor.*

Narcotics Anonymous Lesbian & Gay Group
Mon 18 h
St Andrews on the Terrace, 30 The Terrace

RELIGIOUS GROUPS

Ascent (GLM MA)
PO Box 276 ☎ 387 32 05 *Support group for gay lesbian catholics, monthly mass and social activities.*

„Galaxies" - Lesbian, Gay & Bisexual Christian Group »Galaxies« Meets 1st Sun 19.30 h each month at St. Andrews-on-the-terrace
PO Box 5203 Wellington ☎ 379 56 90 E-Mail: edginter@actrix.gen.nz
Homepage: http://nz.com/NZQueer/Galaxies

SPORT GROUPS

Capital Walking Group 1st Sun each month
☎ 473 10 19

Gay Sports New Zealand Team Wellington
Kerri Swinn, 14 Akatea Street, Berhanpore *South* ☎ 389 38 30

Wellington Gay Cycling Group
☎ 389 49 41

SWIMMING

-Breaker Bay (at Wellington Harbor entrance; catch bus 3 to last stop and walk either up through Pass of Branda or take coast trail around Point Dorset)
-Paekakariki Beach (20 min out of Wellington North (State Highway 1). entrance to QEII park opposite railway crossing. Drive down to beach-P 6)

CRUISING

–Thorndon Road

West Coast ☎ 03

GAY INFO

Gayline Westport Wed Fri 19-20.30 h
PO Box 185 ☎ 789 60 27
Information and help

Whangarei ☎ 09

GAY INFO

Gay Help Tue Thu 19-21.30 h
PO Box 7 ☎ 37 76 20
Support, counselling & information.

GENERAL GROUPS

Gay Noth Social Group
PO Box 1081 ☎ 21-864 E-Mail: john@merlin.ne.nz
Homepage: http://nzco.co.nz/NZ/Queer/GayNorth/

HEALTH GROUPS

Northland Health HIV/AIDS Network
PO Box 10173, Te Mai ☎ 430 41 01

SWIMMING

-Uretit Beach (MA NU) (Travel 30 km south from Whangerei. Uretiti is well signposted on the East Coast. Gay section is at south end of beach)

Nicaragua

Central America
Initials: NIC
Time: GMT -6
☎ Country Code / Access Code: 505 / 00
Language: Spanish; English
Area: 130,682 km² / 50,456 sq mi.
Currency: 1 Gold-Córdoba (C$) = 100 Centavos
Population: 4,583,380
Capital: Managua
Religions: 90% Roman Catholic
Climate: Tropical climate in the lowlands, cooler in the highlands.

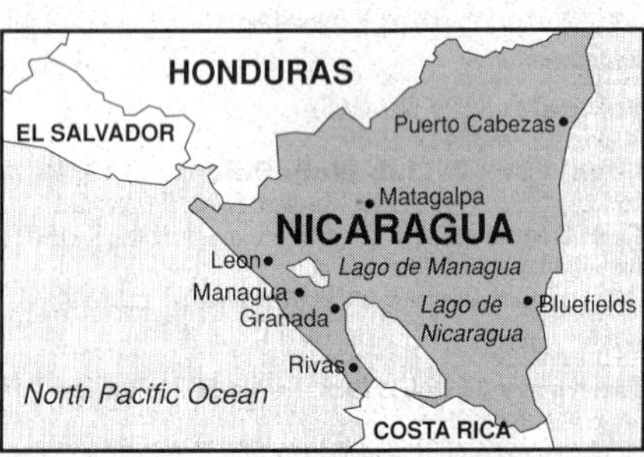

● The Nicaraguan president Violeta Chamorro signed a law in the summer of 1992 by which anyone convicted of „committing" anal intercourse can be sentenced to up to 8 years in prison. Those who work with children or young adults, such as teachers, can be sentenced to as much as 20 years' imprisonment. Gay and lesbian activists fear that this law might be used against the gay and lesbian movement.

✱ Im Sommer 1992 hat die nicaraguanische Präsidentin Violeta Chamorro ein Gesetz unterzeichnet, nach dem des Analverkehrs „Überführte" zu Haftstrafen von bis zu acht Jahren verurteilt werden können. Personen, die Kinder und Jugendliche beaufsichtigen, können in solch einer Situation zu bis zu zwanzig Jahren Haft verurteilt werden. Nach Ansicht von schwulen und lesbischen Aktivisten kann dieses Gesetz auch gegen die Schwulen- und Lesbenbewegung gerichtet werden.
In letzter Zeit kommt es immer häufiger zu Übergriffen auf Schwule. Erst im Frühjahr 1998 wurde zwei Schwule von Anwohnern ermordet.

▲ En 1992, la présidente du Nicaragua, Violeta Chamorro, a fait passer une loi „anti-pénétration-anale". Les homosexuels risquent jusqu'à 8 ans de prison et les personnes qui travaillent le domaine socio-éducatif, 20 ans. Les associations gays nous ont fait savoir que cette loi peut également être appliquée contre tout ce qui peut ressembler de près ou de loin à de l'homosexualité.

☆ En verano de 1992, la presidenta nicaragüense Violeta Chamorro firmó una ley, según la cual culpables de coito anal pueden ser condenados a penas de cárcel de hasta ocho años. Personas que cuidan de niños y adolescentes, como por ejemplo profesores, pueden ser condenadas a penas de prisión de hasta veinte años.

Según la opinión de activistas gays y lésbianas, esta ley también puede ser utilizada contra el movimiento homosexual.

Nell'estate 1992 il Presidente del Nicaragua, Violeta Chamorro, ha firmato una legge secondo la quale il rapporto anale è punibile con la reclusione fino a otto anni. Persone come gli insegnanti, che sorvegliano bambini e ragazzi, possono essere condannati fino a vent'anni di prigione. Secondo l'opinione di militanti gay e lesbiche questa legge può essere applicata anche contro il movimento omosessuale.

Managua

BARS

Pacu's (B D f GLM MA) 19-? h
1 Cuadro a Lago, 1/2 cuadro Arriba *(Puente el Eden)*
Somos (B D GLM S) Sat
Gonzalez Paso-1 „a lago" *(in front of Parque de las Palmas)*

DANCECLUBS

Discotecha Medianoche (! AC B D f G S YG) Fri-Sun 19-6 h
35 Avenida Linda Vista ☎ 266 34 43

CRUISING

-Cinema Gonzalez
-Park near A.C. Sandino Stadium (sidewalks around Laguna di Tiscapa)
-Plaza de la Revolucion
-Inside the ruins of the cathedral Las Ruinas de la Cathedral (ayor)
-Near mausoleum of Carlos Fouseca (AYOR)
-Gardens near Ruben Dario Teatro
-Camino de Oriente (Fri-Sun between Lobo's Jack and Infinito)
-Parque de las Piedrecitas (AYOR) (at night)

Norway

Norge
Northern Europe
Initials: N
Time: GMT +1
☎ Country Code / Access Code: 47 (no area codes) / 00
Language: Norwegian
Area: 323,878 km² / 125,049 sq mi.
Currency: 1 Norwegian Kroner (nkr) = 100 ¢re
Population: 4,420,000
Capital: Oslo
Religions: 88% Lutheran Protestant
Climate: Moderate climate along the coast, modified by North Atlantic Current. The interior is colder. The west coast is rainy all year round.

The age of consent in Norway is 16 years of age. Legislation was passed in 1981 which protects gays and lesbians from discrimination, and in 1993 a law was passed recognizing the partnerships of homosexual couples. The legal situation resembles that in Denmark, giving gays and lesbians exactly the same status as heterosexuals (with the exception of adoption rights).
The Norwegian scene is concentrated in the cities of Oslo, Bergen and Trondheim, and here you will find exclusively gay bars. In smaller towns it is common for the discos to hold a gay and lesbian night once a week. The atmosphere here is, however, so gay-friendly that gays and lesbians are socializing more and more with straight people, to the point that mixed meeting places are gradually becoming the norm.
Norway has two decidedly interesting and professional gay publications: »Løvetann« (= 'dandelion') dealing with sexual politics, and the news & entertainment magazine »Blikk«.

In Norwegen liegt das Schutzalter bei 16 Jahren. Für Schwule und Lesben gibt es gesetzlichen Schutz vor Diskriminierung (seit 1981) und ein Gesetz zur registrierten Partnerschaft für homosexuelle Paare (1993). Das Gesetz ist dem dänischen sehr ähnlich und stellt Hetero- und Homopaare -bis auf die Adoption- gleich.
Die Szene des Königreiches konzentriert sich auf die Städte Oslo, Bergen und Trondheim. Hier gibt es reine Schwulenkneipen. Ansonsten, in den kleineren Städten, ist es nicht unüblich, daß allgemeine Discos einen wöchentlichen »Schwulen- und Lesbentag« pflegen. Da jedoch das gesellschaftliche Klima so schwulenfreundlich ist, vermischen sich die Schwulen und Lesben immer mehr und immer unverkrampfter mit den Heteros, und allmählich werden gemischte Treffpunkte die Regel.
Norwegen hat zwei außerordentlich interessante und professionelle Zeitschriften für Schwule: Das sexualpolitische Fachblatt »Løvetann« (dt.: »Löwenzahn«) und das populäre Nachrichten- und Freizeitmagazin »Blikk«.

En Norvège, la majorité sexuelle est fixée à 16 ans. Les gays et les lesbiennes norvégiens ont la loi de leur côté: loi antidiscriminatoire (1991) et loi sur le „concubinage enregistré" (1993), l'équivalent du PACS. La législation norvégienne sur les droits des homosexuels s'inspire largement de la législation danoise: les couples homosexuels jouissent des mêmes droits que les couples hétéros, sauf en ce qui concerne l'adoption d'enfants.
Oslo, Bergen et Trondheim sont les principales villes gays du pays. On y trouve des bars exclusivement gays. Sinon, dans les petites villes, les boîtes de nuit organisent une fois par semaine une „soirée gay et lesbienne". La Norvège est un pays homophile où on peut vivre vivre sa différence au grand jour. Résultat: les gays et les les-

biennes sont de plus en plus intégrés au reste de la population. Les lieux de rencontre mixtes sont devenus la règle. En Norvège, il y a 2 excellentes revues gays: le „Løvetann" („Dent de lion") (sexe et politique) et le magazine d'information et de divertissement „Blikk".

Homosexuales y heterosexuales son iguales ante la ley. Desde 1981 existe una ley contra la discriminación que protege esta igualdad de derechos. Existe también desde 1993 un registro de noviazgo homosexual, esta ley es muy parecida a la danesa, situa a parejas homosexuales al mismo nivel de las heterosexuales incluso en cuestiones de adopción.
El «ambiente» gay del reinado noruego se concentra en las ciudades de Oslo, Bergen y Trondheim-en estas ciudades hay bares gay «puros». Por lo demás, es bastante habitual que discotecas de ciudades pequeñas organicen un «Día de los gays y lesbianas» una vez por semana. Por otro lado el clima social noruego es de lo más afable para con los homosexuales. Los gays y las lesbianas suelen mezclarse cada vez más con los heterosexuales y lentamente sitios de reunión mixtos son los más habituales.
Noruega tiene dos revistas para gays extraordinariamente bien hechas e interesantes: La revista especializada en temas de contenido político sexual «Løvetann» (en español: «diente de león») y la revista de actualidades y entretenimiento „Blikk".

L'età legale per avere rapporti omosessuali è di 16 anni. Dal 1991 le leggi norvegesi proteggono i gay e le lesbiche da discriminazioni legate alla sessualità. Dal 1993 le coppie omosessuali possono registrare legalmente le loro relazioni. Questa legislazione, molto simile a quella danese, uguaglia gli omosessuali agli eterosessuali anche nel diritto di adozione. La vita gay norvegese si concentra nelle città di Oslo, Bergen e Trondheim, dove troverete dei locali esclusivamente gay. Altrimenti, nelle piccole città, è spesso abitudine, per le discoteche, di avere una notte alla settimana per gay e lesbiche. Da quando l'atmosfera generale in Norvegia è così favorevole ai gay e pochi di essi nascondono la loro omosessualità, i gay e le lesbiche si uniscono sempre di più e con sempre meno difficoltà agli eterosessuali e i luoghi d'incontro misti stanno diventando sempre più comuni. La Norvegia vanta due riviste gay molto interessanti e valide: la pubblicazione politico/sessuale „Løvetann" (Bocca di Leone) e la rivista di notizie e intrattenimento „Blikk".

NATIONAL GAY INFO

Blikk (! GLM)
St. Olavsplass 2 ✉0130 Oslo ☎ 22 99 22 80 Fax: 22 99 22 99
E-Mail: post@blikk.no Homepage: www.glnetwork.no/blikk
Monthly newpaper, approx. 48 pages, Reports on Norwegian and international topics, cultural reports, guide. Some personal ads.

Exit
Osterhaus'gate 5 ✉0183 Oslo ☎ 22 20 80 16
Fax: 22 20 82 28 E-Mail: exit@image.no
High profile, glossy gay magazine for Norway.

FPE-NE (Forening for transvesitter)
PO Box 1968, Vika ✉0125 Oslo

Killkontakt (! G)
PO Box 96 56, Grønland ✉0133 Oslo ☎ 22 20 37 36
Fax: 22 49 15 24 *Norwegian/Swedish sex & contact magazine with a lot of personal ads/phone ads.*

LEK (glm)
PO Box 7123, Homansbyen ✉0307 Oslo ☎ 22 56 55 10
Monthly sex/contact magazin. (Some personal ads)

LLH•Landsforeningen for lesbisk og homofil frigjøring Mon-Fri 9-16 h
St.Olavsplass 2, PO Box 68 38, 0130 Oslo ☎ 22 36 19 48
Fax: 22 11 47 45. *The national gay/lesbian rights organization. Local groups spread nationwide.*

Løvetann (GLM)
PO Box 6745, St. Olavsplass ✉0130 Oslo ☎ 22 36 00 78
Fax: 22 20 61 75
Bimonthly publication. Six copies 165 kroner. About 60 pages. Political and cultural reports, reviews and essays of a high standard.

SMIL-Sadomasochitisk Forening
PO Box 3456 ✉0406 Oslo ☎ 22 17 05 01

Ungdomstelefonen
☎ 90 10 02 77 *Help line for young gays.*

Ålesund - Møre og Romsdal

BARS

Sjøhuset (B D g)
Notengsgt 1

Studenten (B g)
Keiser wilhelms g 2b ☎ 70 15 25 22

GENERAL GROUPS

LLH Nordvestlandet
PO Box 665, Sentrum ✉6001 ☎ 94 40 50 62

CRUISING

-Borgernes vei (tour path behind the town mountain Aksla)
-Byparken (Town park)
-Kaiområdene (Harbor areas)
-Bus station/Rutebilsentralen
-Town hall square/Rådhusplassen

Alta - Finnmark

GENERAL GROUPS

Landsforeningen for Lesbisk og Homofil frigjøring (LLH), Finnmark lag
PO Box 12 07 ✉9501 ☎ 78 43 08 05

Åndalsnes - Møre og Romsdal

CRUISING

-Gatekjøkkenet (during the day at the harbor)
-Railway station/Jernbanestasjonen

Bergen - Hordaland

BARS

Fincken. Café (A B f glm MA) Mon Tue 12-23, Wed-Thu -2, Fri Sat -3, Sun 18-23 h
Nygårdsgate 2a ☎ 55 32 13 16 *In the afternoon more a café.*

CAFES

Kafé Permanenten (B f glm) Tue-Fri 11-17, Sat Sun 12-17
Nordahl Bruns gatan 9 ☎ 55 31 05 02

Opera. Café (b f glm)
Engen 24 ☎ 55 23 03 15

SAUNAS/BATHS

Tropic Sauna (f g MA msg sa sol VS) Wed (G) 16-21 h (not G: Mon-Fri 11-21, Sat-Sun 12-18 h)
Nye Sandviksvei 48 A ✉5035 ☎ 55 32 65 33 *VS only Wed (when G).*

GENERAL GROUPS

Landsforeningen for Lesbisk og Homofil Frigjøring (LLH) Wed 19-21 h
Nygårdsgaat 2a, PO Box 312, ✉5001 *(2nd floor)* ☎ 55 31 21 39 Fax: 55 96 12 10

Støttegruppa for homofile og deres familier
☎ 55 12 25 81

Uglesett-Gay and Lesbian Student Group
PO Box 11 16 ✉5001
Student group. Phone HBB for info.

FETISH GROUPS

LMC Bergen
PO Box 44 18 ✉5028 ☎ 91 14 18 32

HEALTH GROUPS

Helseutvalget for Homofile
PO Box 318, Nygårdsgaat 2a, ✉5001
☎ 55 32 16 20 Fax: 55 96 12 10

HIV/AIDS Info
☎ 55 20 00 88

RELIGIOUS GROUPS

Guds Løvetenner
c/o Kvarteret, Olav Kyrres gatan 53 ✉5015
Open church group for lesbians and gays.

SPORT GROUPS

Bardots/LLH (GLM)
PO Box 312 ✉5001
Volleyball.

CRUISING

-Rasmus Meyers Allé
-Skoltegrunnskaien (near ships)

Bodo - Nordland

BARS

Piccadilly Pub (B glm)
Storgata 4B *(At Norrøna Hotel)* ☎ 75 52 55 50

GENERAL GROUPS

Landsforeningen for Lesbisk og Homofil frigjøring (LLH) (GLM)
Café Tue 21-23 Hålogalandsgate 7 ✉8001 ☎ 75 52 27 75

HEALTH GROUPS

Rådgivningskontoret for HIV/AIDS
Biskop Kroghs gt. 15, ✉8017 ☎ 75 53 43 58

Drammen - Buskerud

BARS

Børsen Musikkbar (B g)
Bragernes Torg 13 ☎ 32 89 41 15

CAFES

Kafé Unique (B g)
Bragernes Torg 5 ☎ 32 83 17 00

HEALTH GROUPS

Smittevernkontoret Mon-Sat 8-15 h
Gamle Kirkeplass 2 ✉3019 ☎ 32 80 63 73

CRUISING

-Spiraltoppen (by WC and the old cannons)
-P by Damtjern.

Follo

DANCECLUBS

Reenskaug disko (B D glm)
Storgate 3, Drøbak ✉1440
(In Reenskaug Hotel)

GENERAL GROUPS

As homofile og lesbiske studentforening
PO Box 12 48, 1432 Ås-NLH

LLH Folloavdelinga
PO Box 48, Hebekk ✉1406

SPORT GROUPS

LLH-Follos Volleyball
☎ 64 93 95 38

Førde - Sogn og Fjordane

DANCECLUBS

Treskeverket (B D E F g H MA)
c/o Sunnfjord Hotel, Storehagen 2, ✉6800 ☎ 57 82 16 22

GENERAL GROUPS

LLH Nordvestlandet
PO Box 367 ✉6801 ☎ 90 68 06 67

Frederikstad - Østfold

BARS

Punktum (B glm MA)
Nygaardsgatan

GENERAL GROUPS

LLH østfold
PO Box 1119, Gamle ✉1631 ☎ 69 32 44 69 Fax: 69 32 44 69.

HEALTH GROUPS

Rågivningskontoet mot aids 18-20 h
Hassinveien 34 ✉1604 ☎ 69 39 46 69

CRUISING

-Tollbodbrygga (by the river from the library to the Ferra to Gamblebyfergen)

Gjovik - Oppland

GENERAL GROUPS

Ungdomsgr i Oppland
☎ 61 13 22 26 E-Mail: uioppland@usa.net

CRUISING

-Resting place at the Biri-side of the Mjøs-bridge (Mjøsbrua)
-Roof of the Domus-toilets

Grimstad - Aust-Agder

BARS

Skyline (B glm MA)
Jyskestredet

Hamar

GENERAL GROUPS

Åpen Kirkegr/LLH
☎ 61 19 51 52

Harstad - Nordland

GENERAL GROUPS

LLH Sør-Troms og Ofoten-lag
PO Box 20 97, Kanebogen ✉9405 ☎ 77 06 59 48

Haugesund - Rogaland

BARS

Flytten Pub (B g)
Smedasundet 87 ☎ 52 71 73 03

HELP WITH PROBLEMS

Opplysningstelefon Mon-Fri 17-22 h
☎ 90 93 21 17

Helegeland - Nordland

GENERAL GROUPS

LLH Nordland lag, avdeling Helgeland
PO Box 439, Sandnessjøen ✉8801 ☎ 75 04 36 98

Indre Troms

GENERAL GROUPS

Aktivitetsgr for homser
☎ 77 83 33 37
Støttetelefon for homofile og lesbiske
☎ 77 83 86 37

Kongsvinger

GENERAL GROUPS

Stjerneskudd, gr. for bifile, lesber og homser
PO Box 537 St.sida ✉2201 ☎ 91 15 11 50
Villskudd-Kongsvinger, ungdomsgr.
PO Box 282 ✉2201 ☎ 92 80 95 28
E-Mail: Villskudd@hotmail.com
Homepage: www.geocities.com/WestHollywood/Village/2103/

Kristiansand - Vest-Agder

BARS

Kafe Kilden (B glm MA)
Rådhugate 11 ☎ 38 02 96 20
Markens (B d glm MA) Disco Fri Sat
Markengate 13

GENERAL GROUPS

LLH Kristiansand lag Tue 11-13, Thu 16-18 h
PO Box 45 98 Grim ✉4602 ☎ 38 02 00 48

HEALTH GROUPS

PLUSS Sørlandet
PO Box 239, Sentrum ✉4604 ☎ 38 02 84 08

Kristiansund - Møre og Romsdal

BARS

Endestasjonen (B e f g H MA)
Storgate 41-43 ☎ 71 67 64 11
Pontongen (B f g H MA)
Berndorffstr. 1 ☎ 71 67 30 11
Tordenskiold (B e f g H MA)
Hauggaten 16 ☎ 71 67 40 11

Lillehammer - Oppland ✉ 2601

BARS

Ludvig ølstue (B glm MA)
Wiesesg 2 ☎ 61 25 89 60

GENERAL GROUPS

LLH Hedmark og Oppland lag
PO Box 423 ✉2601 ☎ 61 19 51 52

Molde - Møre og Romsdal

BARS

Alexis (B D E f g H MA)
Storgate 1-7 ☎ 71 25 11 33
Dockside (B f g MA)
Torget 1 ☎ 71 21 50 33

GENERAL GROUPS

Guds Anemoner
PO Box 71 ✉6400
LLH Nordvestlandet
PO Box 71 ✉6400

Oslo ☎ 30

● Norways capital city is the starting point to a spectacular landscape. The train ride from Oslo to Bergen is reputed to be of special scenic beauty. But even from the city of Oslo you can reach untouched nature (Oslofjord, Sognsvann, Holmenkollen a.s.f.) in the shortest of time by public transport. Oslo is a very modern city, surprisingly multicultural, and it offers everything you expect from a modern metropolis. In the short months of the summer, life is enjoyed to the maximum. On weekends the whole of Oslo seems to be up and about. The gay scene is small but very friendly and, contrary to other european metropolises, very unpretentious.
Our tips:
- Vigelandpark, with its expressive granite- and bronce-sculptures depicting lifes cycle.
- Vikings ships on the peninsula Bygdøy (boats ride!)

✱ Norwegens Hauptstadt ist der Ausgangspunkt in eine spektakuläre Landschaft. Die Eisenbahnfahrt von Oslo nach Bergen gilt dabei als landschaftlich besonders reizvoll. Aber selbst von Oslo aus ist man innerhalb kürzester Zeit per öffentlichem Verkehrsmittel in unberührter Natur (Oslofjord, Sognsvann, Holmenkollen etc.) Oslo ist sehr modern, überraschend multikulturell, und hat alles, was man von einer modernen Großstadt erwartet. In den kurzen Sommermonaten wird das Leben in vollen Zügen genossen, und ganz Oslo scheint am Wochenende unterwegs zu sein.
Die Schwulenszene ist zwar klein, aber ausgesprochen freundlich und im Gegensatz zu anderen europäischen Großstädten sehr unprätentiös.
Unsere Tips:
-Vigelandpark mit ausdrucksstarken Granit- und Bronzeskulpturen, die den Lebenskreislauf darstellen
-Wikingerschiffe auf der Halbinsel Bygdøy (Bootsfahrt!)

▲ Un paysage spectaculaire vous attend aux portes d'Oslo! Prenez le train d'Oslo à Bergen, vous découvrirez les splendeurs du paysage norvégien, au chaud depuis votre compartiment. Depuis Oslo, on est vite en plein coeur de la nature, une nature sauvage accessible par les transports en commun: Oslofjord, Sognsvann, Holmemkollen... La capitale norvégienne est moderne et étonnement multiculturelle. Elle a tous les avantages d'une grande ville. Les Norvégiens profitent au maximum des quelques beaux mois d'été qui leurs sont donnés et, les week-ends, on a l'impression que tout Oslo est dans la rue. L'infrastructure gay d'Oslo peut sembler assez peu développée, mais notez bien que les gens y sont bien plus souriants et ouverts que dans certaines autres grandes villes d'Europe. A voir absolument: 1. le Vigelandpark et ses impressionnantes sculptures de bronze et de granit représentent les différentes étapes de la vie et 2. les drakkars des Vikings sur la presqu'île de Bygdøy (prenez le bâteau!).

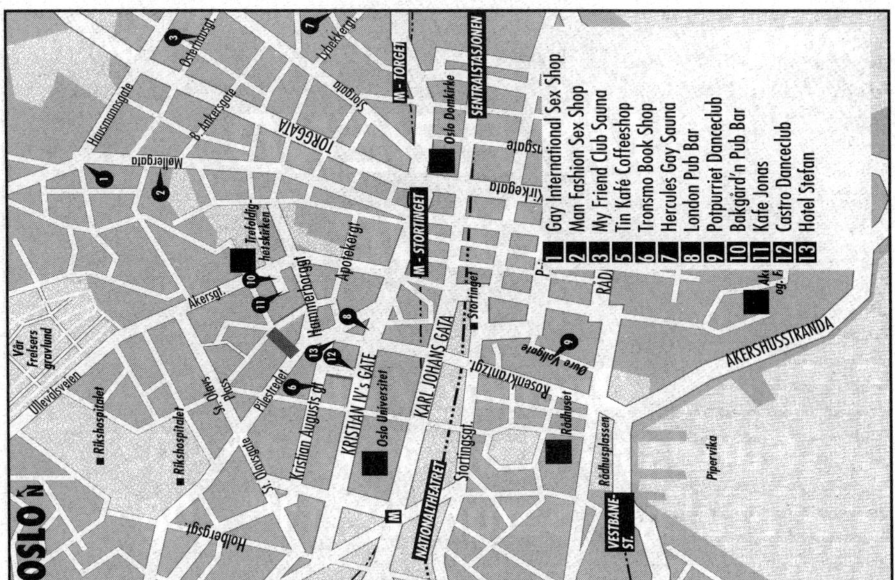

La capital noruega es el punto ideal de partida para visitar paisajes espectaculares. El trayecto en tren entre Oslo y Bergen está considerado una maravilla. Desde Oslo con transporte público y sin necesidad de recorrer grandes distancias podemos visitar parques naturales intactos como Oslofjord, Sognsvann, Holmenkollen etc. Oslo es moderna, sorprendentemente multicultural y cuenta con todo lo que se espera de una gran ciudad. En los meses de verano la vida se disfruta al máximo, los fines de semana da la impresión de que toda la ciudad se encuentra de paseo. El ambiente gay es pequeño pero muy afable y al contrario que en a otras ciudades europeas muy poco pretencioso. Nuestros consejos:
- El parque Vigeland, muestra esculturas de granito y bronce que representan el ciclo de la vida.
- Barcos vikingos en la península Bydoy (viaje en barco).

La capitale della Norvegia è un punto di partenza per raggiungere una campagna spettacolare. Il percorso ferroviario da Oslo a Bergen è particolarmente stimolante. Da Oslo con i mezzi pubblici si arriva in poco tempo a luoghi in cui la natura è ancora intatta (Oslofjord, Sognsvann, Holmenkoller etc.). Oslo è molto moderna, sorprendentemente multiculturale e offre tutto ciò che ci si aspetta da una grande città. Durante i corti mesi estivi le giornate vengono vissute intensamente, e la fine settimana tutta Oslo esce a passeggio. L'ambiente gay è piccolo ma molto cordiale. Al contrario delle altre città europee Oslo è naturale e sincero. I nostri consigli:
- Vigelandpark con espressive sculture in granito e in bronzo che rappresentano il ciclo della vita;
- Navi vichinghe sulla penisola Bygdoy (viaggio in traghetto).

TOURIST INFO

Oslo Promotion A/S
Grev Wedels plass 4 ✉0151 ☎ 22 33 43 86

BARS

Bakgård'n Pub (AC B CC DR G MA OS) Sun-Thu 14-2, Fri-Sat 14-4 h
Teatergt 3 ✉0158 *behind the courthouse* ☎ 22 20 62 99
Lowest beer prices in town.

London Pub (! B d GLM MA) 18-4, Sat-Sun 15-4 h
C.J. Hambros Plass 5 ✉0164 ☎ 22 70 87 00
Popular, best after 23 h. Billard. Pub-style atmosphere. Choose your favourite tunes from the juke box. Piano Bar.

Naboens Mat & Vinhus (B F glm MA OS) 11-1, Sun 12-1 h
Smalgangen 31 *(Grønlands torg)* ☎ 22 17 50 53

CAFES

Coco Chalet (b f g)
Prinsensg 21 ☎ 22 33 32 66
Charming café.

Habibi Café (b f g)
Storgt 14 *(Grønland square)* ☎ 22 17 98 31
Middle-eastern cuisine. Inexpensive.

Kafe Jonas (AC B CC d F GLM MA OS) Sun-Thu 15-0, Fri 15-2, Sat 11-2 h
Teatergt 3 ✉0158 *Behind the courthouse* ☎ 22 20 62 99
Dinner is also served. Homemade cakes.

Tin Kafé (B f GLM MA) Sun 18-21, Wed 19-22 h
Olavs plass 2 ☎ 22 11 33 60

DANCECLUBS

Castro (! B D G s YC) Tue-Sun 21-4 h
Kristian IV gate 7-9 ☎ 22 41 51 08
1st floor Disco (70's/80's), 2nd floor Club mix, 3rd floor chill-out lounge. Occasional drag shows and go-go boys. Very popular.

Potpurriet (B F gLM D MA OS s) Sun-Thu 16-2, Fri-Sat 16-6 h
øvre Vollgate 13 ☎ 22 41 14 40

SEX SHOPS/BLUE MOVIES

Gay International (G) 10-19, Sat -15 h
Rostedsgate 2, Grønland ✉0133 ☎ 22 20 37 36
Man Fashion (G) Mon-Fri 12-19, Sat 11-16 h
Möllergt. 47, ✉0179 ☎ 22 36 06 03
A lot of leather and toys.

SAUNAS/BATHS

Boy's Club (DR G sa sol Vs WO)
Parkveien 62 ✉0254 *(near Royal Castle)* ☎ 22 35 50 51
Hercules Gay Sauna (AC b CC DR f G MA msg pi sa sb sol VS wh) Sun-Thu 12-2 h, Fri-Sat 12-8 h
Stenersgate 22A ✉0184 *(4th floor, opposite Oslo Spectrum/Plaza Hotel)* ☎ 22 17 17 35
Free condoms and lube.
My Friend Club (AC DR G MA sa sol VS) Sun-Thu 15-2, Fri-Sat 15-8
Calmeyers Gate 15 B ✉0183 ☎ 22 20 36 67

BOOK SHOPS

Tronsmo Bøker & Tegneserier (GLM) 10-17, Thu -18, Sat -15 h, closed Sun
Kristian Augustsgate 19 ✉0130 ☎ 22 20 25 09
Wide range of gay and lesbian books.

HOTELS

Hotel Stefan (b bf CC F H NG)
Rosenkrantz gate 1 ✉0159 *(Opposite London Pub)*
☎ 22 42 92 50 Fax: 22 33 70 22
Comfortable hotel close to the gay scene. All rooms with shower/WC, TV and telephone. Special weekend rates NOK 485 for a single per day incl. buffet bf. Restaurant famous for lunch buffet.

PRIVATE ACCOMODATION

Enjoy Bed & Breakfast (bf G H MA YG) 16:30-21:00h
☎ +49 (30) 215 1666 Fax: +49 (30) 217 52219
E-Mail: Info@ebab.com Homepage: www.ebab.com
Price 20 Euro. Accommodation sharing agency. All with shower & bf.

GENERAL GROUPS

Cabarosa (LLH-Oslo)
☎ 22 38 51 06 *Cabaret group.*
Den norske homofenien av 1990 (LLH)
☎ 22 35 49 95 *Choir.*
Drillarguri
☎ 22 33 70 15 *Twirling group.*
Fri Utblåsning (LLH)
☎ 22 44 90 91 *Music group.*

Homofile Og Barn
PO Box 68 38, St.Olavsplass, ✉0130 ☎ 22 55 55 65
Group for gays with children.
Homoversitas Osloensis
PO Box 87, Blindern, ✉0314
Student group.
Informationgroup for the School
☎ 22 67 57 77
LLH Sentralt• Landsforeningen for lesbisk og homofil frigjøring Mon-Fri 9-16 h
PO Box 68 38, St.Olavsplass ✉0130 *(Close to the National Art Gallery)* ☎ 22 36 19 48 Fax: 22 11 47 45 E-Mail: llh@czi.net
Homepage: www.llh.no
The gay/lesbian rights organization. Umbrella organization for various interest groups.

Mannegruppa i SMil Norge Tue 18-20.30 h
PO Box 34 56, Bjølsen, ✉0406 ☎ 22 30 27 38
S/M group for gay men.
Oslo Gay Naturists
☎ 22 37 84 98
Skeive Filmer
PO Box 68 38, St.Olavsplass, ✉0130 ☎ 22 20 19 60
Fax: 22 20 19 60 E-Mail: sfilmer@sn.no
Ungdomsgruppa (LLH-Oslo)
PO Box 6838, St.Olavsplass, ✉0130 ☎ 90 10 02 77
Homepage: http://www.login.eunet.no/~janda/ *Youth group.*

FETISH GROUPS

SLM Oslo
PO Box 703, Sentrum ✉0106 ☎ 22 17 40 90
E-Mail: slm@newmedia.no
Homepage: http://home.newmedia.no/slm/

HEALTH GROUPS

Aksept (Kirkens Bymisjon)
☎ 22 71 55 22 *Contact center for HIV-positive.*
Helseutvalget for homofile Mon-Fri 9-15 h
øvre Slottsgate 29 ✉0157 ☎ 22 33 70 15
Health organization for gays. Offices spread nationwide.
Helseutvalget for homofile Mon-Fri 10-16 h
øvre Slottsgate 29 ✉0157 ☎ 22 33 70 15
Homepage: www.helseutvalget.no
LMA • Landsforeningen mot aids
Universitetsgt 20 ✉0162 ☎ 22 42 37 90
Olafiaklinikken Mon 12-17, Tue-Fri 8-11 h
Olafiagangen 7 ☎ 22 08 29 50 *Center for preventative medicine. Counselling service for gays and lesbians.*
PLUSS
PO Box 835, Sentrum ✉0104 ☎ 22 33 01 60
Organization for HIV-positives.
Pluss (HIV-positive)
PO Box 835, ✉0130 ☎ 22 33 01 60

RELIGIOUS GROUPS

Åpen Kirkegruppe for homofile og lesbiske
PO Box 68 38, St.Olavplass, ✉0130 ☎ 22 11 59 79 *Christian group.*

SPORT GROUPS

Klatregruppe
c/o LLH ☎ 22 18 27 48 *Climbing group.*
Raballder
c/o LLH ☎ 22 35 71 05 ☎ 92 28 77 68 (Handball).

SWIMMING

-Langøyene (!,NU) Take the boat from Vippetangen to Langøyene, then go straight til you pass a kiosk. Take the small path to the gay nude area.
-Gay Beach (!,NU) Close to Paradisbukta. Take Bus 30 from downtown to the last stop (Bygdøy). Go along the small path on the right side of the parkinglot.

CRUISING

-Galgeberg (Jordalsgate, near Jordal Amfi. Take bus 37 from downtown. Best around midnight.)
-Sognsvann (Toilets and outdoors. Take the subway, 2nd car park from station, day and night)

Sandefjord - Vestfold

BARS

Bennigan Pub (B g)
Torggata 1 ☎ 33 46 68 50
Byefly (B g)
Torggata 1 ☎ 33 46 68 50
Sir James Pub (B g)
Søbergtorget ☎ 33 46 19 00
Speitet (B g MA)
Kvartal 19 ☎ 33 46 02 02

Skien - Telemark

GENERAL GROUPS

LLH Telemark lag Wed 20-22 h (Helpline and café)
PO Box 407, Kongensgate 10 ✉3701 ☎ 35 52 98 30
E-Mail: llh.telemark@go.to Homepage: http://go.to/llh.telemark

Stavanger - Rogaland

GAY INFO

LLH Rogaland Mon 18-20, Café Sat 13-15 h
Jelsagt 34, PO Box 1502, Kjelvene ✉4004 ☎ 51 53 14 46
Fax: 51 53 65 01
Homepage: http://www.powertech.no/~bjornto/llhrogaland.html

BARS

Gyldene Fontene. Den (B g)
St. Olaf ☎ 51 53 05 88
Sting (B glm MA)
Valbjerget 3 ✉ 4006 ☎ 51 53 24 40

CRUISING

-Skansekaien (from Victoria Hotel to Hurtigbåtterminalen)
-Bjergstedskaien (from Englansterminalen to the parking place by the grove, after dark)

Tønsberg - Vestfold

BARS

Kaptein Krok (B g)
Rådhusgt 30 ☎ 33 31 92 67
Lauritz (B g)
Nedre Langg 30 ☎ 33 31 23 20

CAFES

LLH Vestfold Wed 19-22 Sat 14-17 h
Halfdan Wilhelmsensallé 2B

GENERAL GROUPS

LLH Vestfold lag
PO Box 557 ✉3101 ☎ 33 31 06 10

Tromsø - Troms

BARS

Mirage. La (B G) 12-4 h
Storgata 42 ☎ 77 68 76 70
Prelaten (B g) 11-2 h
Sjøgate 12 ☎ 77 68 20 85

GENERAL GROUPS

Homopolaris
Hovedgården, Uitø, ✉ 9037 ☎ 77 64 64 53
Gay/lesbian/bi student group.
LLH-Troms lag (B D GLM)
Vestregt 2, ✉9008 *(1st floor)* ☎ 77 68 56 43

HEALTH GROUPS

Pluss Nord-Norge
Søndre Tollbug. 9 ✉9008 ☎ 77 62 04 85

Rådgivningstjenesten for homofile og lesbiske i Tromsø Mon 19-21 h
☎ 77 68 56 43
Tromsø komm. Helsekontor
☎ 77 62 04 85

Trondheim - Sør-Trøndelag

BARS

Café Remis (B CC D F GLM MA) Tue Wed 20-2, Fri 22-2.30, Sat 12-16 22-3 h
Kjøpmannsgate 12, PO Box 937 ✉7001 ☎ 73 52 05 52

GENERAL GROUPS

LLH Trondheim
Kjøpmannsgate 12, ✉7001 *(Entrance Erling Skakkes g)*
☎ 73 52 42 26 *Gay center, café, bookshop, various activities.*

HEALTH GROUPS

Helseutvalget for homofile
Olafv Trygvasons g 15 ✉7011 ☎ 73 52 45 57
E-Mail: hu-trd@sn.no
Infeksjonshelsetjenesten Miljøardelingen
Prinsensgate 61 ✉7011 ☎ 72 54 73 81 Fax: 72 54 61 67

RELIGIOUS GROUPS

Åpen Kirkegrupe (LLH) 1st Tue 19 h
PO Box 937 ✉7001

CRUISING

-BrattTrondheimra
-Jernbanestasjonen
-Sentralbadet

Vesterålen - Nordland

GENERAL GROUPS

LLH Nordland lag, avd Vesteråalen
PO Box 435, 8401 Sortland ☎ 76 12 27 80

Panama

Southern Central America

Initials: PA

Time: GMT -5

☎ Country Code / Access Code: 507 (no area codes) / 00

Language: Spanish; English

Area: 77,082 km² / 29,761 sq mi.

Currency: 1 Balboa (B/.) = 100 Centesimos

Population: 2,767,000

Capital: Panamá City

Religions: 92% Roman Catholic

Climate: Tropical climate that is hot, humid and cloudy. There's a prolonged rainy season from May to January and a short dry season that lasts from January to May.

● Homosexual acts are not mentioned in Panamanian law.

✸ Homosexuelle Handlungen werden in der panamaischen Gesetzgebung nicht erwähnt.

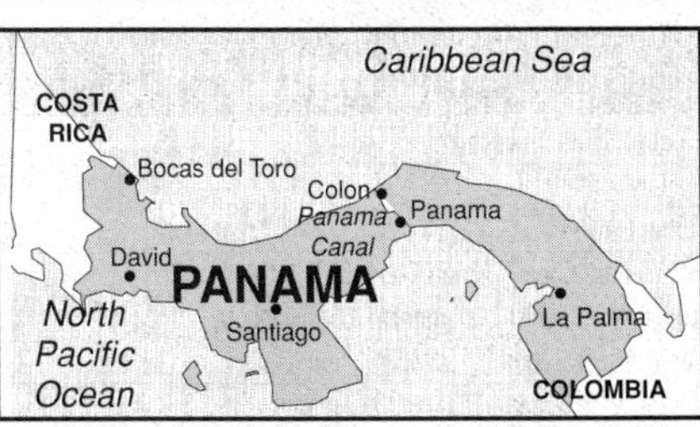

▲ Le code pénal panaméen ne fait pas état de l'homosexualité.

☆ La legislación panameña no contempla en ningún momento actos o actividades de carácter homosexual.

❖ Gli atti omosessuali non sono menzionati dal codice penale panamense.

Panamá City

BARS

Bar Discotequa (B D G MA)
Avenida J/Calle 9
Bar Tropical (ayor B G) -23 h
Calle 12 *(Old city)*
Boys Bar (Garage) (! B D GLM P MA TV WE) Fri-Sun 22.30-? h
Avenida Industrial, Esperanza, Tumba Muerto *(Edificio Sefame #2, Driveway beside the company „IHRE")*
Ecos Bar (ayor B D GLM WE) Sat 22-6 h
Avenida de los Martires *(Close to Parque Legislativo)*
La Deivi (B D G MA)
Via Tansistmica *(across from Sony)*
La Madrid (B G)
Calle 12
La Mami (B D G MA)
Calle 50 *(across from Mansion Dante)*
Michelle's (Hidalgo) (B D GLM P MA AC) Thu-Sun 21.30-4 h
Via Brasil *(across from Texaco gasstation, 2 blocks from Via España)*

CINEMAS

Cine El Dorado (g)
Avenida Central
Cine Tropical (g)
Calle Monteserrin/Calle I
Cine Variedades (g)
close to Cine El Dorado)

HOTELS

Residencial Turistico El Volcan
Calle 29 *(between Avenida 1 Sur &Avenida 2 Sur)*
Guests no problem

CRUISING

-Via Espana (from Via Argentina to El Panama Hotel)
-Avenida Central (near Hotel Intercontinental)
-Parque Legislativo (around the corner from Plaza 5 de Mayo)
-Avenida Cuba (R) (from Calle 29 to Calle 42).

Paraguay

Central South America

Initials: PY

Time: GMT -4

☎ Country Code / Access Code: 595 / 00

Language: Spanish, Guaraní (mostly bilingual)

Area: 406,752 km² / 157,047 sq mi.

Currency: 1 Guaraní (G) = 100 Céntimos

Population: 5,291,020

Capital: Asunción

Religions: 96% Roman Catholic

Climate: Varied climate from moderate in the east to quite dry in the far west.

● We have been told that homosexuality is not illegal as such in Paraguay. However, if a judge considers the accused to be „perverse" by reason of his homosexuality, this can be used to increase his punishment. Here, as in many macho countries, there are no signs of an emerging gay movement. Society's attitude toward gays ranges from indifferent to tolerant, providing their homosexuality is not made public.

✱ Wir erfuhren, daß in Paraguay Homosexualität an sich kein Straftatbestand ist. Allerdings könne ein Richter, wenn er das Schwulsein eines Täters als »pervers« erachte, diesen Umstand strafverschärfend berücksichtigen. Die Gesellschaft verhält sich gleichgültig bis tolerant, solange Schwule ihr Schwulsein nicht öffentlich machen.

▲ On nous a fait savoir qu'au Paraguay l'homosexualité en tant que telle n'est pas considérée comme un délit. Cependant, si un juge décide qu'un accusé est „pervers" en raison de son homosexualité, il pourra utiliser cet état de fait pour en rajouter et alourdir le verdict. Comme dans tous les pays machistes, pas le moindre signe d'émancipation homosexuelle. Les gens sont, en général, plutôt tolérants ou indifférents à l'homosexualité. On fiche la paix aux homosexuels, à condition qu'ils ne se fassent pas trop remarquer.

☆ Nos han informado que en Paraquay la homosexualidad no es un objeto penal. Sin embargo, si un juez considere la orientación homosexual de un acusado como algo pervertido, esto puede influir negativamente en la sentencia. Al igual que en otros países machistas, en Paraguay no existen los principios para el desarrollo de una organización homosexual. Siempre y cuando el comportamiento homosexual no sea muy evidente, la población paraguaya se comporta tolerantemente.

❖ Abbiamo saputo che in Paraguay l'omosessualità in sè non è un reato, benchè un giudice possa tenerne conto come aggravante se considera l'omosessualità dell'accusato una perversione. Come in molti altri paesi maschilisti, neanche in Paraguay esistono le premesse per la nascita di un movimento gay. La società resta indifferente o tollera fintanto che i gay non manifestano la loro omosessualità.

Asunción ☎ 21

BARS

Audace (B G MA)
Ayolas/Manduvirá

La Barca (B D GLM) Tue-Sat
Presidente Franco 564 *(Next to Hotel Embajador)*
Best on Sat.

Stop (B d G)
14 de Mayo, 477

DANCECLUBS

Spider (B D G MA)
Perú 568/ Azará

HOTELS

Guarani (AC B D E F H NG OS pi sa sb sol)
Oliva/Independencia Nacional *(ground floor)* ☎ 911 31
11 km to the airport. Centrally located. All rooms with telephone, bathroom and WC. Single US$ 114.

CRUISING

-Plaza de los Heroes (after dark)
-Streets near Hotel Guarani

Peru

Western Coast of South America

Initials: PE

Time: GMT -5

☎ Country Code / Access Code: 51 / 00

Language: Spanish, Quechua

Area: 1,285,216 km² / 496,222 sq mi.

Currency: 1 New Sol (S/.) = 100 Centimos

Population: 26,111,100

Capital: Lima

Religions: 92% Roman Catholic

Climate: Varied climate from tropical in the east to desert in the west.

● Homosexual acts among consenting adults are legal. An exception is made for military and police personnel, who can be punished with between 60 days to 20 years of imprisonment or discharge from the forces. Homosexuality can also be used as grounds for separation or divorce. Laws meant to protect »public morals« are often used against lesbians and gays. Society's attitude towards homosexuals is generally hostile and is heavily influenced by the Catholic Church. In the 1980's the founding of the organisation „Movimiento Homosexual de Lima" (MHOL) managed

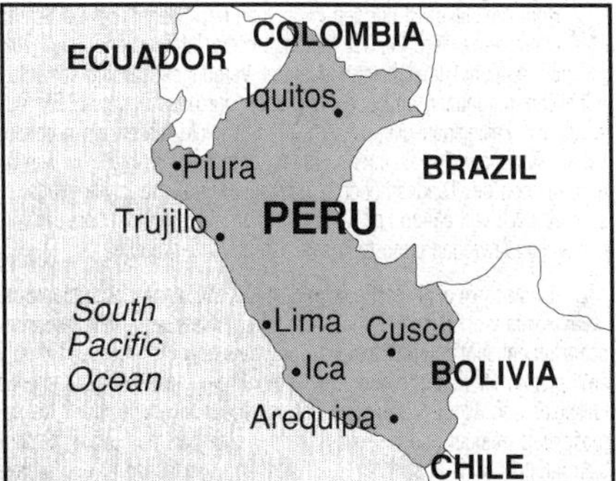

to bring about at least a slight change in the way the media treated homosexuality.

Homosexualität ist unter Einverständnis zwischen Erwachsenen legal. Eine Ausnahme besteht für Angehörige des Militärs und der Polizei, die bei homosexuellen Handlungen eine Strafe von 60 Tagen bis 20 Jahren Gefängnis erhalten oder aus dem Amt entlassen werden. Homosexualität wird als Trennungs- oder Scheidungsgrund anerkannt. Gesetze, die die »öffentliche Moral« betreffen, werden oft gegen Lesben und Schwule angewandt. Die allgemeine Einstellung der Bevölkerung gegenüber den Schwulen ist feindselig und wird zusätzlich von der katholischen Kirche beeinflußt. Die Gründung der Organisation »Movimiento Homosexual de Lima (MHOL)« hat in den 80er Jahren zumindest einen leichten Wandel in der Darstellung gleichgeschlechtlicher Lebensweisen in den Medien angeregt.

Au Pérou, les relations sexuelles entre adultes consentants ne sont pas un délit, sauf pour les membres de la police ou de l'armée qui, eux, risquent, selon les circonstances, 60 jours à 20 ans de prison, accompagnés d'un licenciement sec. L'homosexualité est une raison officielle de séparation ou de divorce. Les lois protégeant la «morale publique» sont fréquemment utilisées contre les gays et les lesbiennes.
Les Péruviens sont, dans l'ensemble, plutôt homophobes et l'Eglise catholique ne fait rien pour arranger les choses. Le MHDL, „Movimiento Homosexual de Lima" a été fondé au début des années 80. C'est grâce à lui que les choses ont pu bouger, surtout dans les média. Les récents changements politiques semblent cependant remettre tout ça en question.

Las relaciones homosexuales por acuerdo mutuo entre adultos son legales. Se excluyen a miembros de las fuerzas armadas y de la policía, que pueden ser condenados desde 60 días hasta 20 años de cárcel o pueden ser separados del cargo. La homosexualidad es reconocida como motivo de separación o divorcio. También se aplican leyes con respecto a la «moral pública» en contra de las lesbianas y los gays. La opinión pública es generalmente hostil e influenciada sobre todo por la iglesia católica. El «Movimiento Homosexual de Lima (MHOL)» inició en los años 80 por lo menos un cambio leve en la representación de formas de vida homosexuales en los medios de comunicación.

Gli atti omosessuali fra adulti consenzienti non sono illegali. Un'eccezione viene fatta per appartenenti alle forze militari e alpolizia, dove l'omosessualità può essere punita con la reclusione da 60 giorni fino a 20 anni o l'espulsione dal corpo. L'omosessualità può anche essere usata per le cause di separazione o di divorzio. Le leggi concernenti la „pubblica moralità" vengono spesso usate contro persone lesbiche e gay. Il comportamento generale della società verso gli omosessuali è ostile e pesantemente influenzato dalla presenza della Chiesa Cattolica. La costituzione del „Movimiento Homosexual de Lima (MHOL)" negli anni ottanta ha contribuito a cambiare l'opinione dei mass-media riguardo allo stile di vita di coppie dello stesso sesso.

Arequipa ☎ 054

SWIMMING

-Jaime Baños (pi) (Golfo 208, Miraflores. ☎ 213 06.)

Lima ☎ 01

BARS

Hedonismo (B G)
Av. Ignacio merino Cuadra 17

CAFES

Bohemia (F g YG)
Ovalo Gutiérrez *(San Isidro)*
Café Café (! F g YG)
Avenida Mártir Olaya *(At Parque de Miraflores)*

DANCECLUBS

Gitano (! B D G S)
Schell, 8th block *(Near Parque Kennedy. Miraflores)*
Imperio (B D G MA)
Calle Camaná/Plaza Francia *(Cercado)*
Perseo-Ice Palace (B D G MA) 17-5 h
Avenida Avicación 2514 *(San Borja)*
Thu/Sun free entrance, Fr- Sat $ 5,- admission
Splash (B D G YG)
Los Pinos 124 *(Miraflores)*
Voglia (B D G)
Avenida Ricardo Palma 336, Miraflor

RESTAURANTS

Haiti (B F g OS YG)
Avenida Diagonal/Primera Cuadra *(Miraflores)*
Opposite Parque Kennedy.

CINEMAS

Colmena (AYOR g MA)
Av. Comena cuadra 7, Avenida Nicolás de Piérola ☎ 428 45 25

SAUNAS/BATHS

Baños Turcos J. Pardo (AYOR B g OG sa sb wh WO)
Avenida José Pardo 192 *(Near Plaza Kennedy. Miraflores)*
Be discreet.
Baños Turcus Velvet (g NG sa sb)
Avenida Petit Thouars 4935 *(Miraflores)*
Be discreet.
Oupen S.A.C. Sauna (A AC B DR CC G MA msg sb sa)
Mon-Sat 14-23:00h, Sun 12-21:00h
Av 28 De Juno 171 , ✉Lima 18 *(Near Grand Hotel Miraflores, down town Miraflores)* ☎ 242 30 94

HOTELS

Hotel Residecial Roma (g H)
Ica 326

GENERAL GROUPS

Germinal
Barcelona 417, Pueblo Libre ☎ 462 47 13
Moviemento Homosexual de Lima (MHOL)
Mon-Fri 9-13, 16-20 h

Mariscal Miller 828 Jesús María ☎ 433 63 75 Fax: 33 55 19
Please write to: MHOL, PO Box 110289, Lima 11

HEALTH GROUPS

Via libre
☎ 433-0003
AIDS-hotline.

SWIMMING

-Beaches in the Miraflores area (near Restaurant »Costa Verde«)

CRUISING

-Avenida Nicolás de Piérola (also known as Colmena)
-Plaza San Martín (AYOR R)
-Parque de Miraflores/Parque Kennedy (between the church and the Municipal Hall, late on weekends, especially Sun)
-Parque Salazar (at the end of Av. Larco, Miraflores).

Philippines

Pilipinas

Southeastern Asia

Initials: RP

Time: GMT +8

☎ Country Code / Access Code: 63 / 00

Language: Pilipino. English, Cebuano, Tagalog, Iloco, Panay-Hiligayon,Bicol, Samar-Leyte

Area: 300,000 km² / 115,830 sq mi.

Currency: 1 Phillipine Peso (P) = 100 Centavos

Population: 77,725,862

Capital: Manila

Religions: 84% Roman Catholic

Climate: Tropical and marineclimate. The northeast monsoon lasts from November to April, the southwest monsoon from May to October.

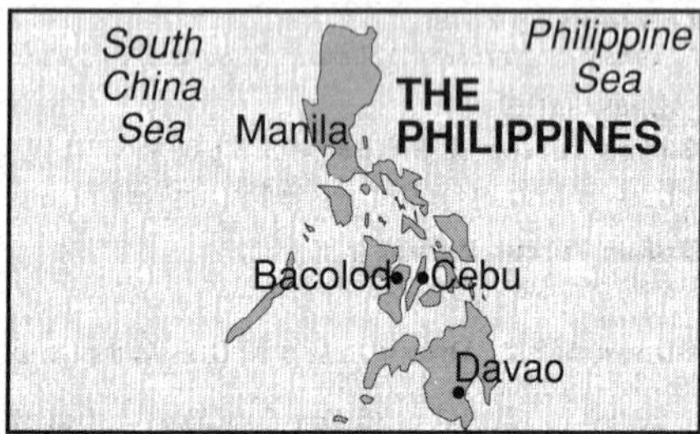

● Homosexuality is allowed in the Philippines, and the age of consent is 18. Our information is at present contradictory. The Philippines are known to have had anti-gay tendencies in the past, but their embassy in Bonn tells us a different story: »Gays lead a normal life, are accepted and even respected in their jobs. Gay organizations are of a purely social nature.« We have, however, heard of a case where a „Condom-café" (!) in Manila had to close due to protests by local residents that it was „immoral".

✱ Homosexualität ist auf den Philippinen nicht illegal und die Schutzaltersgrenze liegt bei 18 Jahren. Unsere Informationen sind zum jetzigen Zeitpunkt uneinheitlich. Aus der Vergangenheit sind schwulenfeindliche Tendenzen von den Philippinen durchaus bekannt. Die Botschaft der Philippinen allerdings meint: »Schwule führen ein normales Leben, sind akzeptiert, in ihren Berufen gar respektiert. Die schwulen Organisationen des Landes haben rein sozialen Charakter.« Allerdings haben wir auch von einem Fall gehört, in dem ein „Kondom-Café" in Manila wegen Anwohnerprotesten geschlossen werden mußte.

▲ L'homosexualité n'est pas un délit aux Philippines. La majorité sexuelle y est fixée à 18 ans. Les informations dont nous disposons actuellement sont contradictoires. Nous avons toujours entendu dire qu'il était plutôt mal vu d'être homosexuel aux Philippines. L'Ambassade des Philippines en Allemagne nous a fait savoir, en revanche, que „les homosexuels mènent une vie tout ce qu'il y a de plus normal, qu'ils sont bien intégrés dans la société et estimés et respectés au niveau professionnel". Les organisations gays aux Philippines auraient, en outre, avant tout une vocation sociale. Attention: on nous a, par ailleurs, rapporté qu'un café appelé „Condome" aurait été contraint de fermer suite aux plaintes des riverains, soucieux des bonnes moeurs.

☆ La homosexualidad en Filipinas no es ilegal, la edad de consentimiento es de 18 años. Nuestras informaciones son un poco contradietorias; del pasado sabemos de las tendencias hostiles contra los gays, a pesar de ello la embajada de las Filipinas nos ha informado que „los homosexuales llevan una vida normal, son aceptados por la sociedad, e incluso en sus trabajos son respetados. Las organizaciones homosexuales del país poseen un caracter puramente social". A pesar de ello hemos escuchado de un caso en el que un „Bar Condom" en Manila tuvo que ser cerrado debido a las protestas por parte de los vecinos.

❖ Le nostre informazioni sulla situazione attuale sono discordi. Mentre in passato ci era stato riferito che i gay nelle Filippine non conducono una buona vita e che i bar gay sono stati chiusi nel corso di una campagna contro il turismo di sesso e la prostituzione minorile, intrapresa dal governo, l'ambasciata delle Filippine a Bonn ci presenta un'altro quadro del paese: „i gay conducono una vita normale e vengono accettati e rispettati anche nel mondo del lavoro. Le organizzazioni gay sono apolitiche e hanno solo un carattere sociale. Solo l'accademia militare discrimina con il suo rifiuto i gay e le lesbiche, mentre dal 1993 accetta le donne". Comunque il caso della accademia militare è stato discusso nella stampa che ha espresso simpatia e solidarietà per i gay.

NATIONAL GAY INFO

Buy and Sell
PO Box 2181 MCPO, Makati, Metro Manila ☎ 35 35 35
☎ 35 35 31 Fax: 35 21 55
Classified Ads magazine. Penfriend service for men.

Bacolod - Negros ☎ 34

BARS

Spectrum Disco (B D F g H) 20-1 h
c/o Sea Breeze Hotel, San Juan Street ☎ 245 71

CRUISING

-City Plaza (mainly on the right side; gays often sit under „the gay tree" in the evening)

Baguio - Luzon ☎ 74

HOTELS

Venus Parkview Resort Hotel (g H NG)
19-A Kisad Road, Burnham Park ☎ 442 64 52 *or* ☎ *442 55 97.*
Good food.

BARS

Cafe Duo (B f G H MA) 18-? h
Manggayad, Malay Aklan ✉5608 *(near Lorenzo Beach Resort)* ☎ 634 26 39 ☎ 643 32 13 Fax: 922 97 50.

Coco Loco Bar (B F g OS) 10-24 h
Malay Aklan ✉5608 *(near Boracay Beach)* ☎ 288 30 28

HOTELS

Nigi Nigi Beach Resort (B CC F glm msg S)
Boracay Island, PO Box 4258, Manila ☎ 288 31 01
Fax: 288 31 12 E-Mail: niginigi@pworld.net.ph
Resort directly located at the beach. 20 rooms all with shower/WC, balcony/terrace and safe. Room service and own key available. Scuba diving and sailing possible.

CRUISING

-Southern part of the white beach where the rocks are (daytime).

Cebu ☎ 32

CINEMAS

Ultravistarama Theatre (G)
Legaspi Street ☎ 964 26

HOTELS

Cathay (AC B F H NG)
Colon Street/Pelaez Street ☎ 976 21
Central location, all rooms have AC, telephone, priv. bath.

CRUISING

-Around University of the Visayas, Colon Street
-South Expressway Bus Terminal (late at night)
-Pelaez/Colon interesection (day and evening; also arcade nearby) (tv)
-Public market
-Maroco Beach, Dumlob, Talisay (13 km from Cebu; rent a cottage; the swimming pool nearby can be fairly gay)
-Marigandon beach, Vanu Resort, Mactan
-Cebu Coliseum Roller Skating (afternoon and evening)
-Fuente Osmena (circular skating rink downtown, night)
-Boulevard Pub (22-? h)

Davao - Mindanao ☎ 82

HOTELS

Apo View Hotel (H NG)
J Camus Street, *(15 minutes from airport)* ☎ 748 61

Manila ☎ 2

TOURIST INFO

DOT Director for National Capital Region
Room 207, DOT Bldg., Rizal Park ☎ 587 902

BARS

Adam's & Adam's (AYOR B D f G r s tv)
Claro M. Recto/Evangelista, Santa Crus

Chico's (AC B D g S) 20-1 h
Timog Avenue, Quezon City ☎ 79 96 34
Beware of cheating, high prices.

Cine-Café (AC B f G MA)
Roces Avenue, Quezon City

Club 690 (AC B D glm MA OS S TV) 20-2 h
690 N.S. Amoranto Street, Quezon City ☎ 712 36 62
One of the most popular bars in Manila; rooms available upstairs. Sing-along bar managed by a wonderful host named Bunny.

Library. The (AC B F g MA S YG) 18-3 h
1779 Adriatico Street, Malate ☎ 522 24 84

Miss Piggy (B D G MA WE)
Adriatico Street, Malate *(near Library Bar)*

Stop Over (AYOR B D G YG) 21-4 h
1608 Mayhaligua/Rizal Avenues *Santa Cruz* ☎ 711 74 54

RESTAURANTS

Adriatico (AC B CC F G OS) 11-6 Sun 11-4 h
1790 M. Adriatico Street ☎ 58 40 59
Continental Spanish cuisine.

Igorot (B D F g MA R S) Gay Sat-Sun
West Avenue, Quezon City *(close to EDSA)*

CINEMAS

Alta Theater (G R)
Aurora Boulevard Cubao

Capitol Theater (G R)
Escolta Street

Ginto Theater (G R)
Quiapo Boulevard

Grace Theater (G R)
16th Avenue, Caloocan City

Joy Cinema (G R)
Libertad Street, Pasay City

Pearl Theater (G R)
Avenida Street

Times Theater (G R)
Quiapo Boulevard

MASSAGE

Datu (NY5) Therapy Massage (G MA msg R) 0-24 h
1823 FMSG Building, E. Rodriguez Street/New York Street *(white gate)* ☎ 721 10 32
Call for appointment.

HOTELS

Nigi Nigi Nu Noos 'e' Nu Nu Noos (B bf CC glm H msg)
PO Box 4258 ☎ 288 31 01 Fax: 288 31 12
E-Mail: niginigi@world.net.ph
Homepage: http://pworld.net.ph/user/niginigi

Palmas. Las (AC F g H pi wh)
1616 A. Mabini Street, Malate ☎ 50 66 61 Fax: 522 16 99
Very low prices and convenient situation.

Pension Kanumayan (b bf cc H pi)
2284 Taft Avenue, Malate *(Quirino LRT Station and Vito Cruz LRT Station)* ☎ 521-1161 to 66 E-Mail: Kanumayan@netasia.net
Rooms from US$ 26 to 64 per day.

Tropicana Apartment Hotel (AC B g H msg pi sa)
1630 L.M. Guerrero Street, Malate ☎ 59 00 81
Highly recommended by several readers.

HEALTH GROUPS

ClinicoMed
470 San Andres cor Del Pilar Street, ☎ 521 54 99 ☎ 536 08 40
Gay friendly.

Manila Doctor's Hospital
669 United Nations Avenue, Ermita ☎ 50 30 11
Initial consultation fee in the Emergency Section pesos 25, specialists start at 200.

CRUISING

-Harrison Plaza Shopping Center, 2nd floor (R YG) (14-20 h, students) -Amihan Gardens (Makati; in the evening)

Palavan ☎ 48

HOTELS

Kiao Sealodge (F glm) Dec-Jul
Uyunis Garden, Circulation Road, Puerto Princesa City, *5300*
☎ 433-3500
6 cottages with shower/WC, terrace. Hotel provides own key. Rates cottage US$ 25, full-board US$ 25. Lots of nature, trekking in rainforest possible.

Zamboanga del Sur - Mindanao

BARS

Rancho. El (B D F g S)
(in the city) Bar,disco & restaurant.

Poland

Polska

Eastern Europe

Initials: PL

Time: GMT +1

☎ Country Code / Access Code: 48 / 0 (wait for tone) 0

Language: Polish

Area: 312,683 km² / 120,727 sq mi.

Currency: 1 New Zloty (Zl) = 100 Groszy

Population: 38,664,000

Capital: Warszawa

Religions: 95% Roman Catholic

Climate: Moderate climate. Winters are cold, cloudy and moderately severe with frequent snow or rain. Summers are mild with with frequent showers and thundershowers.

Homosexuality is not mentioned in Polish legislation and the general age of consent is set at 18. Like in Czech republic and in Hungary, first debates about registered relationships are beginning to emerge. The influence of the catholic church is evidently receding, the society is becoming more open and tolerant. And so slowly, slowly, a gay scene is developing in the main cities.

Homosexualität findet im polnischen Strafgesetzbuch keine Erwähnung. Die allgemeine Schutzaltersgrenze liegt bei 18 Jahren. Die konservative Regierung unter Führung der Gewerkschaftsbewegung Solidarnoscz hat bis jetzt aber nicht erkennen lassen, daß sie an einer weiteren Liberalisierung der Gesetzgebung interessiert ist. Der Einfluß der katholischen Kirche geht nur langsam zurück. Allerdings läßt sich zumindest bei der städtischen Bevölkerung eine zunehmend Offenheit und Toleranz gegenüber Schwulen erkennen und so wundert es nicht, daß man auch nur in den Großstädten Ansätze einer sich entwickelnden Schwulenszene findet.

Le code pénal polonais ne fait pas état de l'homosexualité. En Pologne, la majorité sexuelle est fixée à 18 ans. En Pologne, comme en République Tchèque et en Hongrie, on commence à envisager l'éventualité du contrat d'union civile. Ici aussi, l'Eglise est en perte de vitesse: les mentalités évoluent dans le bons sens et les Polonais sont de plus en plus ouverts et tolérants. Les choses commencent à sérieusement bouger en Pologne particulièrement dans les grandes villes.

En el Código Penal polaco, la homosexualidad no es mencionada. La edad de consentimiento es de 18 años. Al igual que en la Rep. Checa y Hungría también en Polonia se están llevando a cabo los primeros debates sobre el registro de noviazgos. La influencia de la iglesia católica ha experimentado en los últimos años una disminución. La sociedad se ha vuelto más abierta y tolerante. Esta circunstancia ha permitido un cierto tipo de desarollo de un ambiente gay en las grandes ciudades.

La legge polacca non fa menzione dell'omosessualità. La maturità sessuale è per tutti di 18 anni. Come nella Repubblica Ceca ed in Ungheria anche in Polonia vengono cautamente aperti i primi dibattiti sulle relazioni registrate. L'influenza della chiesa cattolica sta retrocedendo palesemente e la società sta diventando sempre più aperta e tollerante. Così lentamente nelle grandi città polacche si stanno formando ambienti gay.

NATIONAL GAY INFO

Filo Gay & Les Magazyn
PO Box 733, 80-958 Gdansk 50 ☎ (058) 301 98 28

Inaczej 10-16 h
Softpress, PO Box 84, 60-971 Poznan 59 ☎ (061) 853 76 55

Nowy Men
PO Box 158, 00-975 Warszawa 12 *Ulica Warynskiego 6/89*
☎ (02) 25 08 40 Fax: 25 05 58

Stowarzyszenie Grup Lambda UW Universytet Warszawski
Krakowski Przedmiescie 24, 00-927 Warszawa 64 *(address for correspondence)*

NATIONAL COMPANIES

Pink Service
PO Box 158, 00-975 Warszawa 12, Ul. Warynskiego 6 m 89
☎ (022) 25 39 11

Augustów

HOTELS

Hotel Warszawa (B bf CC g H T W)
n/Jez. Hecko ✉16-300 *(located on sea side)* ☎ 643 28 05
Fax: 643 36 57 E-Mail: hotel_warszawa@hot.pl
Prices double Zl 190 per room, single Zl 110 per room.

Bielsko-Biala ☎ 030

CRUISING

-In front of railway station

Bydgoszcz

MEN'S CLUBS

Pracownia (B D DJR G MA, p)
Ul. Powst. WLKP 56 ☎ 345 22 78
Homepage: http://frik5.onet.pl/B//parara

Bytom ☎ 032

BARS

Country (B d G) Thu-Sun 18-4 h
Ul. Przemyslowa 1 ☎ 281 67 26
Fri, Sat Disco starts at 20 h.

Chalupy ☎ 058

SWIMMING

-Located on the Hel Peninsula. Drive to [P] C4 or C5. The nude beach is on the side towards the sea not towards the bay. Action in the bush near the beach. (AYOR)

Czestochowa

CAFÉS

Cafe Antyk (B GLM) Mon closed Tue-Fri 16-22 h, Sat, Sun 18-22 h
Kosciuszki 13

Debki ☎ 058

SWIMMING

-(AYOR) Nearly 65 km from Gdansk, has one of the most beautiful nude beaches on the Baltic Sea (The road ends in the village of Debki and from there walk west through the woods, over a covered wooden bridge and on for approx. 2 km along the beach. Most of the men on the nude beach are gay, mainly young people).

Gdansk ☎ 058

GAY INFO

Rózowy Puls
PO Box 34 ✉80-250 ☎ 48 72 53 Fax: 48 72 53
Informative & Cultural Bulletin of Inicjatywa Gdanska for Gays. Issued monthly and distributed by subscription and in some Polish gay bars free of charge.

BARS

Kogiel Mogel (B JD GLM) Mon-Thu 20-2, Fri-Sun 20-5 h
Ul. Lolobrzeska 39F

GENERAL GROUPS

Inicjatywa Gdanska Wed 17.30-19.30 h
PO Box 34 ✉80-250 *Ulica Waly Jagiellonskie 1, room 58 (2nd floor)* ☎ 31 31 03 ☎ 31 61 25 Fax: 48 72 53

HEALTH GROUPS

Wojewódzka Przychodnia Skórno-Wenerologiczna Mon-Thu-13 h Fri-12 h
Ulica Dluga 84/85 *(Old Town) HIV & STD tests. Room 5.*

SWIMMING

-Stogi (AYOR NU) (Tram Nr. 8 to the roundabout in Stogi. Walk along the beach about 1500 m to the right. Gay beach is right after the nude one.
-See also Chalupy/Debki

CRUISING

-Main railway station (Gdansk-Glowny)
-Railway Station Gdansk-Wrzeszcz
-Small park at the student's club »Zak« (corner of Waly Jagiellonskie/Hucisko-evenings and nights AYOR)

Gdynia

CRUISING

-Plac Kosciuszki (evenings; from the railway station straight ahead in direction of „White Fleet" harbor Skwer Kosciuszki)
-Station Gdynia-Orlowo (walk on main street in direction to Zoppot, there is a gas station and opposite to it a [P]; walk straight ahead about 200 m and you will find a forest and lawn area)
-Gdynia-Kolibki (NU) (take the City-train to Sopot / Kamienny Potok, walk approx. 300 m in the direction of Gdynia, past a camping ground to the gas station then take the path on the right to the sea.)
-All are AYOR
-Railway station Gdynia-Główna (City train section)
-Skwer Kosciuszki (near the cinema, in front the White Fleet Harbor
-Plac Kaszubski

Gorzów Wielkopolski

CRUISING

-Park Róz (AYOR)

Jelenia Góra ☎ 075

BARS

Galery (B D F g) Disco Fri-1 Sat-? h
(other days regular Restaurant hours)
Ulica Wroclawska 67 ☎ 216 94

CRUISING

-Park near railway station (AYOR) (evenings)

Katowice ☎ 032

BARS

Tropicana Club (B d DR F GLM) daily 12-24h, Disco Fri-Sat 21-4 h
Ul Mariacha 14 ☎ 206 94 10

CRUISING

-Andrzeja Place
-In front of Café Monopol (underground)
-New railway station

Kielce ☎ 041

CRUISING

-Railway station Dworzec PKP (evenings)

Koszalin ☎ 094

BARS

Oscar (B DR G) daily 17-? h. Parties on Sat.
Ul.Matejki 5 ☎ 346 24 45

CRUISING

-Main railway station (city underpass)

Kraków ☎ 012

BARS

Hades Nightclub (B D GLM MA YG) Mon-Thu 21-1, Fri-Sat 21-5 h
Ulica Starowislna 60 *(basement of house in front of Club Sindy)* ☎ 21 93 69 *Popular.*
Hali Gali (B d G) 18-? h
Ul. Karmelicka 10 *(Entrance form the gate) Sat disco and drag show.*

SAUNAS/BATHS

Sauna-Fitness Spartakus (AC b DR G MA sa sb WO) 11-23, Sun -21 h
Ulica Konopnickiej 20/Ulica Zamkowa ✉30-302 *(opposite Wawel Castle)* ☎ 666 022 *Entrance-fee zloty 22*

GENERAL GROUPS

Lambda Kraków Wed 19-20 h
PO Box 249 ✉30-960 ☎ 56 24 56

CRUISING

-Planty (Park around the old town)

Lódz ☎ 042

BARS

Ganimedes (B d GLM) daily 15-24 h
Ul. Piotrkowska 138/140 ☎ 637 29 33
Fri, Sat disco from 21h
Narraganset (B D DR GLM) Mon-Thu 16-24 h, Fri-Sat 20-5 h (disco)
Ul. Kosciuszki 93 ☎ (0)601 31 77 58 (mobil)

DANCECLUBS

Consul (B D GLM S SNU STV) Sun-Thu 19-24 h, Fri-Sat 19-? h
Al. Kosciuszki 39 ☎ 631 19 56 *Fri, Sat Disco from 20 h, new large danceclub with two halls.*

SEX SHOPS/BLUE MOVIES

Erotic Land (AC b CC DR G MA VS) Mon-Sat 10-21 h, Sun closed
Ulica Piotrkowska 48 ✉90-265 *(left doors)* ☎ 630 26 91

SAUNAS/BATHS

Parys (AC B CC d DR f G MA P s sol VS WE WO) Mon-Wed 13.30-23 h, Thu-Sat 13.30-1 h Sun 13.30-22 h
Ul. Piotrkowska 46 ✉90-265 *(near Fabryczna railway station)* ☎ 30 39 94

CRUISING

-Ulica Zielona 5-7 (near Cinema Mloda Gwardia)
-Ulica Narutowicza (especially in summer)
-Dworzec Kolejowy railway station
-Main railway station Lódz Fabryczna
-Park Zdrowie (Al. Unii)
-Railway station Lódz Kaliska
-Park Moniuszki (Ulica Nartowicza/Ulica Armi Ludowej)

Lublin

SWIMMING

-O.W.-Marina (AYOR) (Bus 8. Pass thru the nudist beach. Behind is the gay meeting point)

CRUISING

-Plac Litewski

Olsztyn ☎ 089

GENERAL GROUPS

Lambola-Olsztyn Thu 18-19 h
PO Box 377 ✉10-959 *Meetings: Ulica Kajki 3 (Monar Organization)* ☎ 27 22 09 *Please enclose an IRC.*

CRUISING

-Olsztyn Glowny (main railway station)

Opole

CRUISING

-Opole Gtowny/central station
-Ulica Krakowska, Rynek
-Opole Gtowny (walk straight into Ulica Krakowska)

Pabianice ☎ 042

SEX SHOPS/BLUE MOVIES

Sex-Shop Amor (g)
Ulica Sw. Jana 14

Piotrków Trybunalski ☎ 044

CRUISING

-Park (AYOR) (Ulica Kopernika, by night)
-Railway station/Dworzec PKP (evenings)

Poznan ☎ 061

GAY INFO

Gay Center & Help Line Fri 17-19 h
☎ 604-384 089 (mobile)
Inaczej Gay Monthly Magazine Mon-Fri 10-20 h
c/o Softpress, PO Box 47 ✉60-957 ☎ 061/847 89 18
Fax: 061/847 89 18 *Published by Softpress.*

BARS

Cafe 2000 (B D GLM)
Ul. Nowowieskiego 8
Fri and Sat disco.
Skorpio Pub - Danceclub (AC B D DR f GLM MA p s SNU stv VS) Mon-Wed 19-2 h, Thu Sat 21-? h
Ul. Garbary 62 ✉61-758 *(Entrance from Mostowastreet)*
Thu, Fri, Sat Disco,

SAUNAS/BATHS

Amigo (B DR F G p sa sb sol VS) Mon-Thu 16-22 h, Fri-Sat 16-24 h, Sun closed
Osiedle Lecha 120 ✉61-298 *(Back side of drugstore)*
☎ 601-941 700 (mobile)

SWIMMING

-Biskupice (g NU) (from Poznan go to Griesno to the lake of Kowalkie)

CRUISING

-Park K. Marcinkowskiego (AYOR) (by night)

Radom ☎ 026

CRUISING

-Park Ulica Zeromskiego
-Park Kosciuszki

Rzeszow ☎ 0457

GENERAL GROUPS

International-Gay-Friendship-Club
c/o T. Czeslaw, PO Box 258 ✉35-959

Sopot ☎ 058

GENERAL GROUPS

Lambda Sopot
PO Box 24 ✉81-806

Swinoujscie ☎ 0936

CRUISING

-Ferry Boat Pier and beach

Szczecin

BARS

Incognito (B d G) daily 21-? h
Ul Wojksa Polskiego 20 Homepage: www.gej.net/lokale/incognito
No Problem (B D GLM) 17-2 h
Ul Dworcowa 2

CRUISING

-Plac Brama Portowa & Planty (near Plac Zwyciestwa)

Torun ☎ 056

GENERAL GROUPS

Lambda Torun
PO Box 115 ✉87-116

CRUISING

-Plac Rapackiego
-Park near Club Wodnik (evenings)
-All are (AYOR)

Walbrzych ☎ 074

CRUISING

-Railway station Walbrzych Miasto (evenings)

Warszawa ☎ 022

GAY INFO

Men Magazyn
c/o Pink Service, Ulica Warynakiego 6 m. 89
Pink Service (G) Mon-Fri 11-16 h
Ulica Warynskiego 6 m. 89, ✉00-631 ☎ 25 39 11
Publishes Men Magazyn
Rainbow-Gay Centre Mon-Fri 10-17 h
Czerniakowska 178/16 ✉00-440 *(Entrance marked by rainbow)*
☎ 628 52 22 E-Mail: lambdawa@polbox.com
Support groups, helpline, sport groups, religious groups, etc.

BARS

Kozla Pub (B CC GLM p s YG) Sun-Thu 16-2 h, Fri-Sat 16-4 h
Ulica Kozla 10/12 ✉00-228 *(close to Nowy Rynek Square)*
☎ 831 84 03
Mykonos (B G MA)
Ulica Jana Pawla II 73 *(near Hotel Maria)*

DANCECLUBS

Delos (B D DR GLM S) Fri-Sat 22-? h
Ul. Jana Pawla II 71 ☎ 838 04 77

Paradise (B D Glm YG) Fri Sat 22-5 h
Wawelska 5 *(near stadium)*
Rudawka (B D F glm) Restaurant 10-24 h, Fri Gay Disco 23-5 h
Ulica Elblaska 53 *(Zolborz district)*

SAUNAS/BATHS

FanTOM (DR G p sa VS WO) 16-24, Fri Sat -? h
Ulica Bracka 20 A *(Entrance at 20, second courtyard, last door on right side)*
Sex shop, cinema, dark room, sauna and fitness centre. Cinema: 13-24, Fri -2, Sat -4 h. Popular. Sat parties 22-? h.
Galla (b DR G p sa sb MA YG) 14-23, Sat -1 h
Ulica Ptasia 2 *(Polish Travel Building)* ☎ 652 19 86

HEALTH GROUPS

Aids Help Line
Institute of Dermatology ☎ 29 79 77
Klinika AIDS
Ulica Wolska 37, ✉01-102
Hospital for HIV-positive, tests, health care.
Poradnia AIDS Ulica Leszno 17
Tests, health care.
Stowarzyszenie Woluntyriuszy Wobec AIDS
Phone Mon Thu 13-19 h
☎ 628 52 22
(Rainbow Gay Centre)

RELIGIOUS GROUPS

Christian Gay Group Phone Tue 18-21 h
☎ 628 52 22
(Rainbow Gay Centre)

CRUISING

-Park Skaryszewski-Praga
-Nudist beach Blota (20 km from Warszawa, walk from Blota 500 m in direction of Wista (nude area), then to your left)
-Central station (ground floor)
-Central railway station (WC)
-Bracka Street (near cinema shop)
-Plac Trzech kryzy (Park close to Ulica Ksiazeca, night)
-All are (AYOR)

Wroclaw ☎ 071

GAY INFO

Gay Forum 11-17 h
c/o Remick, PO Box 195 ✉50-900/2 ☎ 72 39 25

DANCECLUBS

Klub Scena (D glm OS p YG) Thu (g), Fri-Sat (G) 20-? h
Ulica Kazimierza Wielkiego 43 ✉50-077 *(Opera-Tram 3, 5, 10, 12, 23 Bus K, E, M)* ☎ 44 45 31
Entrance from the side street accross the backyard, look for the pink triangle, second floor.

SAUNAS/BATHS

Unigym (B DR G sa, VS) Sat 21 h until Sun 22 h
Ul. Zelwerowicza 16/18

GENERAL GROUPS

Dolnoslaska Grupa Gejów i Lesbijek
PO Box 879 ✉50-950/2

HELP WITH PROBLEMS

AIDS Telefon Zaufania Tue 17-21 h
☎ 21 05 52

SWIMMING

-Opatowicka Isle (behind zoological garden)

CRUISING

-Ulica Swidnicka (opposite of opera)
-Opposite Palaca of Justice
-Hanka Sawicka Park
-Wzgórze Polskie (near Panorama Raclawicka)

Zabrze

MEN'S CLUBS

Gay-Club „Contact"
PO Box 90, ✉41-800

Zakopane ☎ 032

CRUISING

-Kropowki Ulica

Portugal

Portogallo

Southwest Europe

Initials: P

Time: GMT

☎ Country Code / Access Code: 351 / 00

Language: Portuguese

Area: 92,389 km² / 35,671 sq mi.

Currency: Escudo (Esc). 1 EURO = 100 EURO Cents (The Euro can only be used in the clearance system)

Population: 9,927,556

Capital: Lisboa

Religions: 97% Roman Catholic

Climate: Maritime and moderate climate. The north is cool and rainy, the south warmer and drier.

The age of consent in Portugal is 16. Since its entrance into the E.C. in 1986, the situation for gays and lesbians has considerably improved. However the acceptance of homosexuality in the cities as well as in rural areas remains not as high as in other countries of Western Europe. The Catholic Church continues to play a significant role in the community. The past two years have been important for the gay movement in Portugal. On the 28th June 1997 the first time Gay Pride took place in Lisbon and in 1998 the organisation of the world exibition EXPO in Lisbon lead to a modernisation of Portugal . It is slowly developing into a paradise for gays, especially the classic holiday destinations: the Algarve, the Flower Island Madeira, the north metropole Porto or the capital city Lisbon.

Das Schutzalter liegt in Portugal generell bei 16 Jahren. Seit dem Beitritt zur EG im Jahre 1986 hat sich die Situation für Schwule und Lesben erheblich verbessert. Dennoch ist die Akzeptanz von Homosexualität sowohl in den Städten als auch auf dem Lande noch nicht so hoch wie in anderen Ländern Westeuropas. Die katholische Kirche spielt in der portugiesischen Gesellschaft nach wie vor eine große Rolle. Die letzten beiden Jahre jedoch waren für die Schwulenbewegung insbesondere in Lissabon von großer Bedeutung. Wie in vielen Metropolen schon längst üblich fand am 28. Juni 1997 zum ersten Mal ein Gay-Pride-Day statt. 1998 war Lissabon Ausrichtungsort der (Weltausstellung) EXPO, die für die Hauptstadt und nicht zuletzt für das ganze Land einen enormen Modernisierungsschub bedeutete. Als Paradies für Homosexuelle kann Portugal noch nicht gelten und dennoch scheinen Urlaubsklassiker wie die Algarve, die Blumeninsel Madeira, die Nordmetropole Porto oder die Hauptstadt Lissabon auf gutem Wege.

La majorité sexuelle au Portugal est fixée à 16 ans. Depuis l'adhésion du Portugal à la CE en 1986, la situation pour gays et lesbiennes s'est considérablement améliorée. Mais l'acceptance vis-à-vis de l'homosexualité n'est pas aussi grande que dans les autres pays d'Europe de l'Ouest, que ce soit à la ville ou à la campagne. L'église catholique joue encore un grand rôle dans la société portugaise. Mais les deux dernières années furent, surtout à Lisbonne, particulièrement importantes: pour la première fois, une journée de la Gay-Pride eut lieu le 28 juin 1997, comme dans beaucoup d'autres métropoles. En 1998, Lisbonne fût le lieu d'exposition d'EXPO (exposition universelle), ce qui a été symbole de modernisation pour la ville, mais aussi pour tout le pays.Le Portugal n'est pas un paradis pour homosexuels. Mais certains lieux de vacances classiques comme les Algraves, l'île des fleurs de Madère, la métropole du nord Porto ou même la capitale Lisbonne sont sur le bon chemin.

La edad de consentimiento está estipulada en 16 años, independientemente de la orientación sexual. Desde que Portugal entró en la Comunidad Europea en 1986, la situación para lesbianas y gays del país mejoró notablemente. Sin embargo, la aceptación de la homosexualidad en la sociedad no es muy alta, ni en las ciudades y naturalmente menos en zonas rurales. La situación es peor que en otros país de Europa Occidental, en parte debido a la fuerte influencia de la iglesia católica. Pero los dos últimos años han sido de mucha importancia para el movimiento gay: El 28 de junio de 1997 tuvo lugar por primera vez un Gay-Pride-Day en Lisboa y por supuesto la Expo en 1998 significó un gran impulso de modernización para el país entero y tuvo también una repercusión muy positiva para la comunidad gay. Aunque todavía Portugal está lejos de ser denominado un paraíso para homosexuales, parece ser que sitios como la zona de Algarve, la isla de flores Madeira, la metrópoli del norte Porto y la capital Lisboa están en buen camino.

L'età legale in Portogallo è di 16 anni ugualmente per etero e omosessuali. Dal 1986, l'anno dell'adesione del Portogallo alla CE, la situazione dei gay e delle lesbiche è migliorata notevolmente. Nonostante ciò né in città né in posti di campagna l'omosessualità viene accettata nella stessa misura come in altri paesi dell'Europa occidentale. La chiesa cattolica svolge ancora una notevole influenza. Gli ultimi due anni però hanno avuto una grande importanza per il movimento gay soprattutto a Lisbona. Mentre in molte metropoli il „Gay Pride Day" è già usanza comune, a Lisbona si è svolto per la prima volta il 28. luglio 1997. Nel 1998 a Lisbona è stata effettuata l'esposizione mondiale, l'EXPO, che ha portato con sè una spinta di modernizzazione non solo per la capitale, ma anche per tutto il paese. Il Portogallo non può essere detto un paradiso per omosessuali, ma sembra che i posti classici per il turismo come l'Algarve, l'isola di Madeira, la metropoli del Nord Porto o la capitale Lisbona siano in via di miglioramento.

NATIONAL GAY INFO

Gay International Rights 20.30.-24, Sun 15-18 h
PO Box 110 ✉4702 Brada Codex ☎ (0)253-27 92 96

ILGA Thu-Mon 21-24 h
☎ (0)21-887 61 16

Korpus
PO Box 22868 ✉1146 Lisboa Codex ☎ (0)21-357 15 20
The national gay magazine of Portugal.

Albergaria a Velha - Beira ☎ 0234

BARS

Café do Mercado (B g)
Casa 5, Mercado Municipal ✉3850

Albufeira - Algarve ☎ 0289

BARS

Dreams (AC B G MA) 21-3 h
Av. Sa. Carneiro, Centro Comercial Isamar Loje 13-14 ✉8200 *Montochoro* ☎ 58 74 41

Almancil ☎ 0289

RESTAURANTS

Memories Restaurante (F g)
EN. 125 ✉8135

Armaçao de Pêra - Algarve ☎ 0282

CRUISING

-Sand dunes (discreet nudity; action possible)

Aveiro - Beira ☎ 0234

BARS

Café Ria (B g)
Club Galitos 5/6 ✉3800

HEALTH GROUPS

Centro de Saude Tue Thu Sat 10-12 h
Avenida Dr. Lourenço Peixinho 138-140 ☎ 233 81

Hospital distrital de Aveiro (WE)
Avenida Artur Ravara ☎ 221 33

CRUISING

-Costa Nova beach (behind the camping)

Beja - Alentejo ☎ 0284

HEALTH GROUPS

Dispensario de Higiene Social Tue Wed Fri 14-16 h
Delegação de Saude, Rua Dr. Antonio José de Almeida 4 ✉7800 ☎ 230 81

Braga - Minho ☎ 0253

BARS

Copacabana (B G)
Avenida da Liberdade 4700 ✉4700

DANCECLUBS

Club 84 (b D g)
Galerias do Hotel Turismo, Praça João XXI ✉4700
Club 90 (B D g)
Centro Comercial Galecia, Praça de Maximinos ✉4700

RESTAURANTS

A Toca (b F g)
Rua do Souto ✉4700

HOTELS

Hotel Turismo (H NG)
Praça João XXI, Avenida de Liberdade ✉4700 ☎ 270 91
Centrally located.
Parque. Do (AC B g H)
Parque do Bom Jesus do Monte ✉4700 ☎ 220 48
Downtown neighbourhood location, hotel with garden. All rooms with telephone, priv. bath and WC. Single Esc 3.900-6.800, double 4.900-7.900 (bf incl.).

FETISH GROUPS

Club Marquis du Sade 21-24, WE 15-24 h
PO Box 110 ✉4702 ☎ 27 92 96

HEALTH GROUPS

Dispensario de Higiene Social Mon-Fri 9-12 h
Larrgo Poulo Osorio ☎ 270 41 *Ask for AIDS Help Group.*

CRUISING

-Bon Jesus do Monte (in the park)
-Centro Comercial GOLD-Center (especially when there are blue movies)
-Sta. Barbara Gardens
-Avenida des Combatentes

Bragança - Tras-os-Montes ☎ 0273

RESTAURANTS

Snack Bar Leal (b F G)
Avenida João Cruz 16 ✉5300

HEALTH GROUPS

Dispensario de Higiene Social Mon-Fri 10-12 h
Delegacão de Saude, Avenida João da Cruz 144 ✉5300 ☎ 103

CRUISING

-Railway station

Caminha ☎ 0258

SWIMMING

South of Caminha, even south of the camping site, nude beach in direction of Moleda do Minho.

Carvoeiro - Algarve ☎ 0282

HOTELS

Casa Marhaba (b bf G H MA OS pi)
Rua de Benagil, Alfanzina ✉8400 ☎ 35 87 20 Fax: 35 87 20 *Advance booking recommended. All rooms with own key. TV-/Video Lounge. Car rental available. Rates from £ 16.50/night, £ 95/week.*

Cascais - Extremadura-Lisboa ☎ 021

CRUISING

-Railway station (summer)
-Beaches at Poente
-Amusement Arcade (Rua Palmeira 4E)

Coimbra - Beira ☎ 0239

BARS

Mil Olhos (B D g p YG)
Santa Clara ✉3000

CAFES

Café International (b f g)
Avenida Navarro ✉3000 *(in front of railway station)*
Pigalle (B g r)
Avenida Sá da Bandeira 123/125 ✉3000
Santa Cruz (B g OS)
Praça Santa Cruz
Sing Sing (B F g OS YG)
Rua Castro Matoso ✉3000

DANCECLUBS

Via Latina (AC B D NG) 23-4, best after 1 h
Rua Almeida Garrett 1 ✉3000

CRUISING

-Jardim da Sereia (near kiosk, only at night)
-Railway station
-Shopping Center Sofia
-Praça da Republica

Espinho - Porto ☎ 022

SWIMMING

-Beach (between New Golf Hotel and town)

Estarreja - Beira ☎ 0234

HEALTH GROUPS

Santa Casa da Misericordia Thu only
✉3860 ☎ 421 63

CRUISING

-On the beach

Estoril - Extremadura-Lisboa ☎ 021

BARS

Café Yate (AYOR g MA OS pi YG)
Arcadas de Casino ✉2765 *(below casino)*
Jonh's Bar (B f g)
Rua Jeaquin ✉2765 *(near Aparthotel Nino Pilipe)*

CRUISING

-Estoril railway station
-Terrace near clock and above restaurant on promenade
-Behind railway station
-Piscina Tamariz, swimming pool (take train out of Lisboa; pool is opposite railway station Estbrol)

Faro, Ilha de - Algarve ☎ 0289

SWIMMING

-De Faco (NU) (on extreme right end)

CRUISING

-Jardim Manuel Bivar (ayor) (park at port)
-Café Allianca
-Near the „Miracoles"-gambling house

Figueira da Foz - Beira ☎ 0233

BARS

Brisma Mar (B G)
Praia de Leinos, Marinha das Ondas ✉3080
La Belle Epoque (AC B g MA OS p YG) 16-4 h, closed Tue
Rua Capitáo Argel de Melo 20, Alto do Forno - Buarcos ✉3080 *(near the camp site)* ☎ 43 48 88
Pôr do Sol (B g)
Rua dos Pescadores 60 ✉3080 *(Praia de Buarcos)*

CRUISING

-Around the casino and adjacent streets
-Buarcos Beach
-Praias a Sul

Funchal - Madeira ☎ 0291

BARS

Apolo Café and Funchal Café (B f g r)
Situated in the Largo da Sé on either side of a square where the Madeira youth gather most of the day. Something for everybody, but be discreet, because there are plenty of hustlers.
Beerhouseto Marina (B g MA) 10-4 h
Xarambinha, Largo Corpo Santo 29
Café do Theatro (B F glm MA OS) 15-24 h
Avenida Arriaga *(in Theatre building)*
Crazy Sailor (B F g)
Marina

CRUISING

-Santa Catarina Park (AYOR) (at Avenida do Infante)
-Avenida Arriaga (ayor) (stay in the lighted areas)

-Municipal Park
-Along the sea wall
-Beach Pocas do Governador

Ilhavo ☎ 0234

BARS

Opcåo (B G MA)
Av. Fernandes Lavrador 214 ✉3830 *(Barra)* ☎ 36 05 19

Lagoa ✉ 8400 ☎ 0282

HOTELS

Casa Marahaba (g H)
Rua de Benagil, Alfanzina ✉8400 ☎ 35 87 20

Lagos - Algarve ☎ 0282

GAY INFO

Gay News
PO Box 687,
Rua dos Carmachinhos 40 ✉8600 ☎ 76 49 07 Fax: 76 49 07
E-mail mop34115@mail.telepac.pt
Information service, room referral and car rental.

BARS

Eclipse Bar (A AC B f G MA p vs YG) 19-02:00h approx.
Rua Lançarote de Freitas 30A ✉8600 ☎ 76 82 19
Under new management.
Luisol (B G MA p) 19-2 h
Rua de S. José 21 ✉8600 ☎ 76 17 94

GUEST HOUSES

Ai que Bom (g H)
☎ (0931) 9221931 FAX 76 47 05.
Cottages and rooms.

Casa Pequena (bf b F GLM H MA NU pi wh) 24 h
PO BOX 133, Praia da Luz ✉8600 ☎ 78 90 68 Fax: 7890 68
Praia da Luz is a beach village 5 km west of Lagos. 2 double rooms with private bath, terrace, telephone, Sat-TV, radio and video. Rates Single Esc 7.000, double10.000, extra bed 2.000, incl.bf. Half-board from 2.000, Esc. per person. Minimum stay 3 nights.

Gay Guest House (B bf G H msg OS VS)
Rua dos Camachinhos 40 ✉8600 ☎ 76 49 07 Fax: 76 49 07
Centrally located. Rooms partly with bath. Rates single Esc 3000-3500, double 4500-5000, studio from 6000, appartment from 8000.

Oasis do Sul (bf g H MA NU OS pi W) Mar-Oct 0-24 h
Quatro Estradas, App. 689 ✉8601-908 ☎ 763 642 ☎ 761 914
4 double rooms with private bath, terrace, Sat-TV and video. Rates Single Esc 6.500-7.500, double 11.500-12.500, additional bed 5.000 (bf-buffet incl.).

Residencia Gil Vicente - In Korpus (b bf G H MA OS)
Rua Gil Vicente 26 ✉8600 ☎ 76 29 82
Rates single Esc 2500-3500, double 4000-5500 (depending on season).

Rubi-Mar. Residencial (bf CC g H) 24 h
Rua da Barrocia 70 ✉8600 (1st floor) ☎ 76 31 65
Fax: 76 77 49 Email rubimar01@hotmail.com
Rates single Esc 4000-6000 (winter/summer), with shower 5000-7000, double 5000-6000, with shower 6000-7500 (bf incl.) Most rooms have balconies. Centrally located, 2 minutes to the beach.

Terramar (glm MA OS)
Urb. Terramar, Lote 30, Torralthinha ✉8600 ☎ 78 27 16
Friendly atmosphere in a private house. Big roofterrace, close to nude beaches. 2 doubles with shared bathroom, 1 with balcony. Rates double ESC 6500-8500, single 4500 (Jun-Sep), 5000-6500 and 3500 (Jun-Sep).

CRUISING

-Promenade along the river
-Beach at the end of Meia Praia by the dunes (NU)

Leiria - Beira ☎ 0236

CRUISING

-Parque de Jardin central

Lisboa/Lissabon ☎ 021

● Lisbon with it's population of 680,000 is split between tradition and the modern age. The Portugese metropole is a mixture of old charm and modern living. With the world exibition EXPO, Portugal has succeeded to counteract it's reputation as the back yard of Europe. With this development the gay community has clearly gotten better. A year ago the first AIDS Solidarity Demo took place along side Gay Pride, as well as a Gay-Lesbian Film Festival. In Lisbon homosexuality still remains somewhat closed to general conversation. This might be due to the mentality of the Portugese, who are slow to accept change. Everyone can form his own opinion of Lisbon, whether it be a stroll through the Park Princip Real after a pub crawl, or a day spent on beach Nr. 17 (the Cost de Caprica) in the bushes behind the sand dunes. In 1999, besides the already successful AIDS March (May), Pride Festival (27 June) and Gay and Lesbian Film Festival (September), Lisbon will be the proud host of the 2nd World Conference on Homo Culture Lisbon 99 in the month of November.

✱ Lissabon mit seinen 680 000 Einwohnern meistert den Spagat zwischen Tradition und Moderne. Die portugiesische Metropole, der einst ein Weltreich zu Füßen lag, hat sich viel von seinem alten Charme bewahrt, der sich heute mit modernem Großstadtleben mischt. Mit der (Weltausstellung) EXPO ist es in der Stadt ganz am Rande des westlichen Europa gelungen, seinem Ruf als Hinterhof Europas entgegenzuwirken. Mit dieser Entwicklung hat sich auch die Situation für Homosexuelle deutlich verbessert. Schon ein Jahr zuvor fanden neben dem Gay-Pride-Day die erste Aids-Solidaritätsdemonstration sowie ein schwulesbisches Filmfestival statt. Über Homosexualität wird hier längst nicht so offen gesprochen wie in anderen europäischen Metropolen, was vielleicht auch an der Mentalität der Portugiesen liegt, die Dinge nicht allzu methodisch anzugehen. Für Lissabon jedoch gilt: Stille Wasser sind tief. Und davon kann sich jeder selbst ein Bild machen, sei es nach eienr nächtlichen Kneipentour im Park Principe Real oder am nächsten Morgen am Strand Nr. 17 der Costa de Caparica, dessen Gebüsche sich hinter den Dünen erstrecken. Im November 1999 wird -neben dem bereits erfolgreichen AIDS-March im Mai, dem Pride Festival am 27. Juni und dem Gay & Lesbian Film Festival im September- Lissabon Ausrichter der „2nd World Conference on Homo Culture: Lisbon 99" sein.

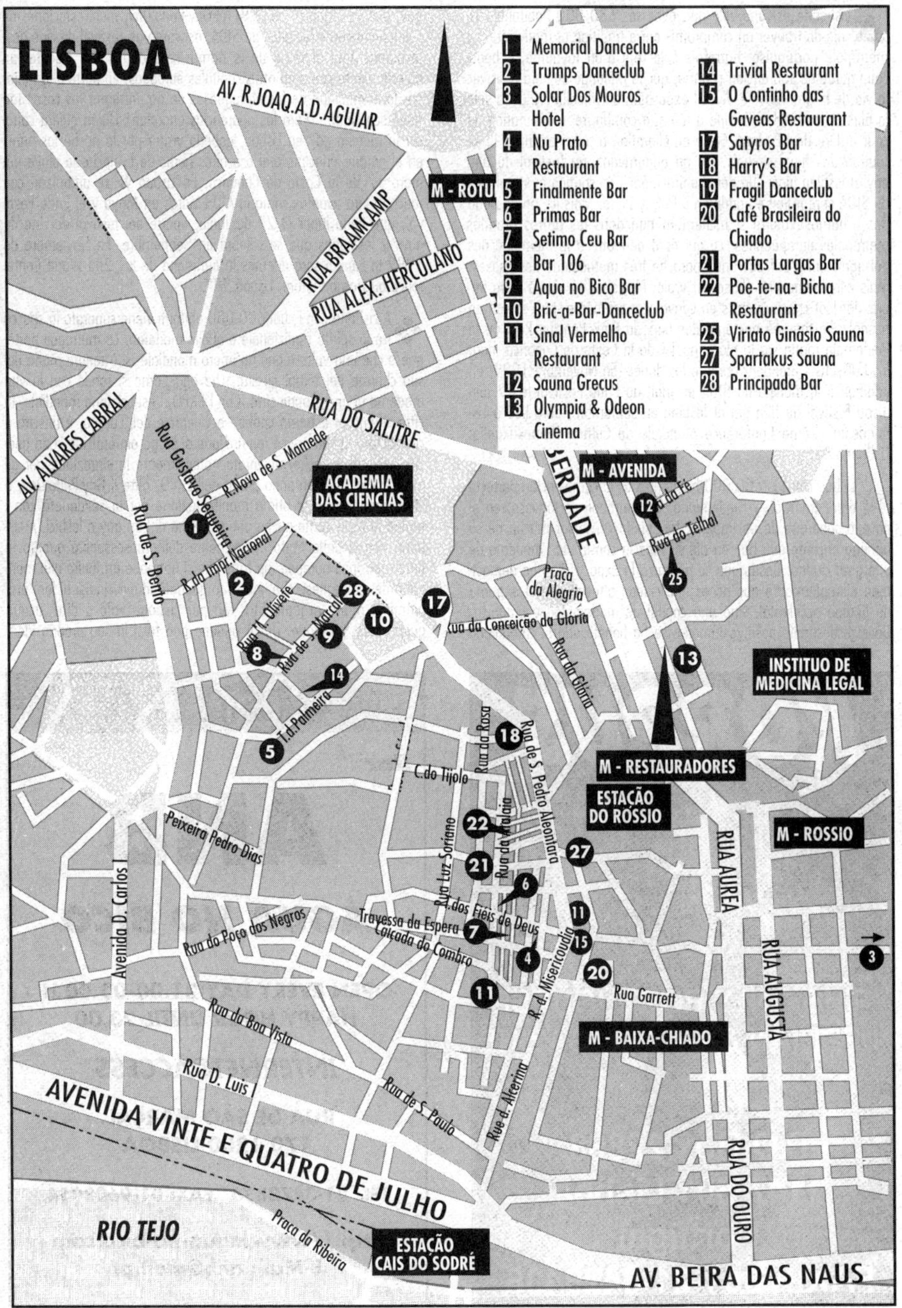
LISBOA
1 Memorial Danceclub
2 Trumps Danceclub
3 Solar Dos Mouros Hotel
4 Nu Prato Restaurant
5 Finalmente Bar
6 Primas Bar
7 Setimo Ceu Bar
8 Bar 106
9 Aqua no Bico Bar
10 Bric-a-Bar-Danceclub
11 Sinal Vermelho Restaurant
12 Sauna Grecus
13 Olympia & Odeon Cinema
14 Trivial Restaurant
15 O Continho das Gaveas Restaurant
17 Satyros Bar
18 Harry's Bar
19 Fragil Danceclub
20 Café Brasileira do Chiado
21 Portas Largas Bar
22 Poe-te-na- Bicha Restaurant
25 Viriato Ginásio Sauna
27 Spartakus Sauna
28 Principado Bar
AV. R.JOAQ.A.D.AGUIAR
RUA BRAAMCAMP
RUA ALEX. HERCULANO
M - ROTU
RUA DO SALITRE
AV. ALVARES CABRAL
R.Nova de S. Mamede
Rua Gustavo Sequeira
ACADEMIA DAS CIENCIAS
Rua de S. Bento
R.da Impr. Nacional
Rua M. Oliveira
Rua de S. Marçal
T.d.Palmeira
M - AVENIDA
Rua do Telhal
Praça da Alegria
Rua da Conceição da Glória
Rua da Glória
INSTITUO DE MEDICINA LEGAL
Rua da Rosa
Rua de S. Pedro Alcantara
C.do Tijolo
M - RESTAURADORES
ESTAÇÃO DO RÓSSIO
M - ROSSIO
Peixeira Pedro Dias
Rua Luz Soriano
Rua da Atalaia
RUA AUREA
Avenida D. Carlos I
Rua do Poço dos Negros
Travessa da Espera
Calcada do Combro
T.dos Fiéis de Deus
R. d. Misericordia
Rua Garrett
RUA AUGUSTA
M - BAIXA-CHIADO
Rua da Boa Vista
Rua D. Luis I
Rua de S. Paulo
Rue d. Alecrina
AVENIDA VINTE E QUATRO DE JULHO
RUA DO OURO
RIO TEJO
Praça da Ribeira
ESTAÇÃO CAIS DO SODRÉ
AV. BEIRA DAS NAUS

▲ Lisbonne est une ville qui, avec ses 680 000 habitants, essaie de trouver un compromis entre tradition et modernité. La métropole portugaise, autrefois à la tête d'un royaume, a beaucoup gardé de son ancien charme, qui se mélange aujourd'hui avec la vie de la grande ville. Avec l'exposition universelle EXPO, la ville la plus à l'ouest de l'Europe a réussi a combattre sa réputation de cour arrière de l'Europe. Cette amélioration a aussi profité à la situation des homosexuels. Un an auparavant, un festival du film gay et lesbien ainsi que des manifestations de soutien aux malades du SIDA eurent lieu en addition à la Gay Pride. Mais ici, on ne parle pas d'homosexualité si facilement que dans les autres grandes métropoles européennes, ce qui tient peut-être à la mentalité des portugais qui n'ont pas une approche très méthodique des choses. Mais à Lisbonne une chose est vraie: ne vous fiez pas à cette impression! et chacun peut s'en convaincre soi-même, que ce soit en faisant une tournée nocturne des bars du Park Principe Real ou le lendemain matin sur la plage no.17 de la Costa de Caparica, dont les buissons s'étendent derrière les dunes. En Novembre 1999, en addition à la marche du SIDA en mai, au Pride Festival le 27 juin et au festival du film gai et lesbien en septembre, aura lieu à Lisbonne la „2ème Conférence Mondiale de Culture Homosexuelle: Lisbonne 99".

☆ Lisboa con sus 680 000 habitantes es la combinación perfecta entre tradición y modernidad. La metrópoli portuguesa, en el pasado soberana de un imperio, ha sabido conservar mucho de su antiguo encanto que hoy en día se mezcla con la vida moderna de una gran ciudad. Desde que se organizó la Expo, Lisboa ha demostrado ejemplarmente que no es una ciudad atrasado en el extremo de Europa occidental, sino una capital de modernidad y progreso. De este desarollo positivo también se ha beneficiado la comunidad gay, que ya organizó en 1997 el Gay-Pride-Day, manifestaciones de solidaridad con infectados de SIDA, así como un festival de cine gay-lesbiana. Aquí el tema de la homosexualidad no se discute tan abiertamiente como en otras capitales europeas, en parte a lo mejor por la mentalidad de los portugueses de no enfrentar las cosas tan metódicamente. !Pero las aparencias engañan! Quien quiera conocer la marcha gay en Lisboa, debería visitar por la noche los bares en el parque Principe Real o a altas horas de la noche la playa número 17 de la Costa de Caparica. En Lisboa ya se organizan con mucho exito eventos como la AIDS-March en Mayo y el Pride Festival, que tiene lugar el 27 de Junio, aparte del festival de cine de gays y lesbianas que se celebra en Septiembre. En Noviembre de 1999 la capital será además la anfitriona de la „2nd World Conference on Homo Culture: Lisbon 99".

❖ A Lisbona con i suoi 680.000 abitanti viene superato lo spacco tra lo spirito tradizionale e quello moderno. La metropoli portoghese che una volta regnò un'imero mondiale, si è tenuta molto del suo charme dei tempi passati, che oggigiorno si fonde con la vita moderna di una grande città. Con l'EXPO, l'esposizione mondiale, la città situata al estremo confine occidentale dell'Europa, è riuscita a contrastare la sua antica reputazione di luogo dimenticato. Con questo sviluppo è anche migliorata notevolmente la situazione per gli omosessuali. Già un'anno prima dell'EXPO, oltre il Gay-Pride-Day, è stata organizzata la prima manifestazione per la solidarietà con i malati di AIDS come anche una rassegna di film gay e lesbici. A Lisbona non si parla tanto apertamente dell'omosessualità quanto in altre metropoli europee, un fatto che si potrebbe attribuire alla mentalità dei portoghesi, che non sono abituati ad avvicinarsi ai loro problemi in modo organizzato. Ma per Lisbona vale a dire: acque quiete sono profonde. Di ciò ognuno può farsi la sua propria idea,

sia nel parco Principe Real dopo un giro notturno nei bar o alla mattina susseguente nella spiaggia No. 17 della Costa de Caparica, dove, dietro le dune, sorgono i cespugli. A parte l'AIDS-March in maggio che ha già avuto qualche successo, il Pride Festival del 27 giugno e il Gay & Lesbian Film Festival in settembre, nel novembre 1999 a Lisbona avrà luogo la „2nd World Conference on Homo Culture: Lisbon 99".

TOURIST INFO

Camâra Municipal de Lisboa Departamento de Turismo
Pavilhão Carlos Lopes, Parque Eduardo VII ✉1070 ☎ 315 17 36

BARS

Água no Bico (AC B G MA YG) 21-2h
Rua de Sao Marçal 170 ✉1200 ☎ 379 60 95
Recommended.

Bar 106 (! AC B f GLM MA p W YG) 21.00-2:00 h. (Happy-hour until 23.30)
Rua de São Marçal 106 ✉1200-422 *(Bus 100 or 58)*
☎ 342 73 73
Also good for information.

Harry's Bar (B f G MA) 22-6, closed Sun. Best time 2-4 h
Rua S. Pedro de Alcântara 57/61 *(Bus 58/15)* ☎ 346 07 60

Keops (A B CC f g MA W) 19-4 h
Rua da Rosa 157-159 ✉1200 383 *(Bairro Alto)*

O Duche (AC B D G MA p S SNU STV YG) 22-4 h
Praça da Liberdade 33 D, Costa de Caparica ✉2825-355 *(outside of Lissabon)* ☎ 290 04 31

Portas Largas (B G MA YG) 20-4 h
Rua da Atalaia 105 ✉1200 *(Bairro Alto)* ☎ 346 63 79
Under the sign: Record. Very popular, ancient Bairro Alto-Bar, often fado-music.

Primas Bar (B f GLM MA W WE) Mo-Sa. 22:00-04:00h
Rua da Atalaia, 154 ✉1200-043 *Metro Baixa -Chiado, Bus 100 or 58*

Principado (B G MA) 21.30-2 h, closed Sun
Rua Cecílio de Sousa 94-A ✉1200

Satyros (B G MA p STV) 23-4 h, Show Thu-Sat 2.30 h.
Calçada da Patriarcal 6-8 ✉1200 *(Bus 58/15)* ☎ 342 15 25

Sétimo Céu (B glm s WE YG) 22-2 h
Travessa da Espera 54 ✉1200 *(Metro Chiado, Barrio Alto)*
☎ 346 64 71

Tejo Bar (A AC B g MA NG OS S WE) Closed Mon, Summer: 16-2 h, Winter: 21.30-2 h
Belo Do Vigário 1 A - Alfama ✉1100-613 *(Tram 28)*
☎ 886 88 78 *Also art gallery.*

CAFES

Brasileira do Chiado Café-Restaurante
(B bf F g MA OS YG) 8-2 h
Rua Garrett 120 *(Near Largo do Chiado. Metro Chiado)*
Old traditional café, nicely decorated.

Novo Passeio Publico (B F MA NG OS) 8-2 h
Avenida de Liberdade *(M° Restauradors)*
Between Travessa da Glória and Calcada de Glória.

Rosso Café (B CC F G MA OS) 9-2 h
Rua Ivens 53-61 (patio) *(Metro Chiado, entrance also from Rua Garrett 19 to patio)* ☎ 347 15 24

DANCECLUBS

Bric-A-Bar (AC B CC D G MA p s SNU) 21-4 h, closed Tue
Rua Cecílio de Sousa, 82-84 ✉1200 *(Bus100/58/15/ Tram20/24)* ☎ 342 89 71 ☎ 346 43 16 *Popular.*

Finalmente (AC B D GLM MA p r STV) 23-6. Show every night 2.30 h.
Rua da Palmeira 38 ✉1200 *(Bus 100)* ☎ 347 26 52
Daily very popular.

Frágil (AC CC D glm MA NG p W WE) 23-4 h
Rua da Atalaia, 128 ✉1200 *Metro to Chiado* ☎ 346 95 78

Memorial (AC B D gLm S) 23-4 h, Sun also 16-20 h, closed Mon
Rua Gustavo Matos Sequeira 42A ✉1200 ☎ 396 88 91
Show Thu, Fri, Sun 2.30 h

Trumps (AC B D f GLM MA p STV YG) 23-6 h, Show Wed Sun 2.30 h. Mon closed
Rua da Imprensa Nacional 104B ✉1200 ☎ 397 10 59

RESTAURANTS

Bota Alta (B CC F glm) 12-14.30, 19-24 h, closed Sat afternoon and Sun
Travessa da Queimada 35-37 ✉1200 *(Bairro Alto)* ☎ 342 79 59
Popular.

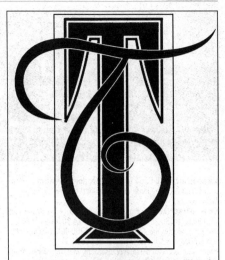

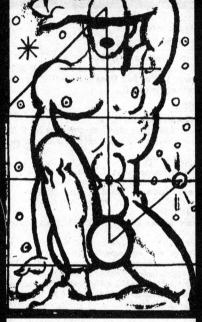

Casanostra (B CC e F glm) 12-24 h, closed Sat afternoon Mon
Travessa do Poço da Cidade 60 *(Bairro Alto)* ☎ 342 59 31
Italian cuisine.

Consenso (AC b CC F g MA) Lunch: 12.30-14.30 (Mon-Fri only), Dinner: 19.30-23.30 (Fr-Th.) and until 24.30 h weekends
Rua da Academia das Ciências 1-1 A ✉1200-003 (*Metro station Baixa-Chiado, Bus 58 - 100, Tram 28*) ☎ 346 86 11
Portuguese cuisine in a beautiful restaurant. Moderate prices. Reservations call 343 13 13.

Fidalgo (F g MA) 10-24 h, closed Sun
Rua da Barroca 27 ☎ 342 29 00 *Cheap food.*

Grémio (F g MA) 18-2 h
Rua do Grémio Lusitano 26 ☎ 346 88 68

Mama-Rosa (F g MA) Mon-Fri 12.30-15, 19.30-1, Sat 19.30-1, Sun 19.30-24 h
Rua do Grémio Lusitano 14 ✉1200 ☎ 346 53 50 *Italian food.*

Massima Culpa (F g)
Rua da Atalaia 35-37 ☎ 342 01 21 *Italian food.*

O Cantinho das Gáveas (F g MA) 12-15/19-24 h, closed Sat lunch
Rua das Gáveas 82-84 ☎ 342 64 60
Portuguese cuisine. The waiters speak many languages.

Os Balões (B CC F g yg) 9-0 h, closed Sat
Rua da Imprensa Nacional 116 ☎ 347 44 93
Cheap and good portuguese food.

Pap'Açorda (B F g) 12.30-14.30, 20-23 h, closed Sat afternoon and Sun
Rua da Atalaia 57-59 ✉1200 *(Bairro Alto)* ☎ 346 48 11
International food. Expensive.

Põe-te-na-Bicha (B CC F G MA) 19-24 h
Travessa da Água da Flor 36 ✉1200 *(Bairro Alto)* ☎ 342 59 24
Portuguese specialities.

Promotora Choop (AC B CC F g MA NG s WE) 11-2 h, closed Sun
Largo do Calvário 3 ✉1300 *(Tram 15, Bus 27, 56 or 38)*
☎ 362 31 02 Fax: 885 30 21

República (CC F g) 13-15/19-24 h, closed Sat
Rua Nova da Trindade 19 ☎ 347 25 80

Restaurante Nu Prato
Rua das Gáveas 15 ✉1200 ☎ 347-8069

Sinal Vermelho (CC F g MA) 12.15-15/19.15-23 h, closed Sat lunch and Sun
Rua das Gáveas 89 ☎ 346 12 52
Portuguese cuisine. The waiters speak different languages.

Trivial (CC F g Ma) 12-15, 19.30-23.30 h, closed Sun
Rua da Palmeira 44 A ☎ 347 35 52
Portuguese cuisine.

SEX SHOPS/BLUE MOVIES

Contra Natura Sex Shop (g) 10-1 h
Rua dos Correieros 163-169 *(near Rua Augusta)* ☎ 343 07 86

Espaço Lúdico Sex Shop (g) Mon-Sat 10-2, Sun 17-24 h
Rua do Conde Redonde 82

CINEMAS

Olympia Cinema (g r VS)
Rua dos Condes 13 *(near Avenida de Liberdade)* ☎ 342 53 09
Best time 16-18 h in this heterosexual porno cinemas with gay cruising.

SAUNAS/BATHS

Descan Sauna (b G og sa) Tue Thu Sat 9-21 h
Avenida da Republica 83-6 *(Metro Campo Pequeno)* ☎ 797 96 02

Grecus Sauna (b G MA og sa) 12-24 h, closed Sun
Rua do Telhal 77-4° ✉1150 *(4th floor/Metro Avenida)*
☎ 346 62 59

Oasis Sauna (b G MA sa sb VS) 12-23, Sun & public holidays -21 h
Rua do Salitre 85 *(Metro Avenida)* ☎ 352 46 26
Yellow sign. Many businessmen after work.

Spartacus Sauna (! AC B F G MA sa sb VS wh WO yg) 12-9 h
Largo Trindade Coelho 2 ✉1200 *(Bairro Alto)* ☎ 322 50 22
No sign! Best times 16-20 h, and later on WE. Very popular.

Viriato Ginásio Sauna (! B DR f G MA msg pi sa sb sol WO VS) 13-2, Fri Sat -6 h
Rua do Telhal 4-b ✉1150 *(Metro Avenida)* ☎ 342 94 36
With the biggest turkish bath in Portugal. Interior in art-deco style .

FITNESSTUDIOS

Ginásio Super Craque (AC g WO) Mon-Fri 7.30-22.30, Sat 10-18 h, Sun -14 h
Rua Capitão Ramires 17 A ✉1000 *Metro Campo Pequeño*
☎ 792 86 90

BOOK SHOPS

A Esquina cor de Rosa (A CC GLM MA W) 14:-24:00 h. Closed Sunday.
Travessa Montedo Carmo, 1 ✉1200-276 *Metro - Rato*
☎ 324 03 46 Fax: 324 03 47

CONDOMS SHOPS

Condómi Lisboa (CC glm MA) Wed-Mon 15-24 h
Casa das Camisinhas, Rua da Barroca 92 ✉1200-051
☎ 213 479 480
Condoms, lubricants, vibrators, books, gifts,... .

HOTELS

Pensão Alegria (G H)
Praça Alegria 12 esquerda ✉1250 ☎ 322 06 70 Fax: 347 80 70
All rooms with shower and phone.

Blue Angel Hotel (Anjo Azul) (H)
Rua Luz Soriano, 75 ✉1200-246 ☎ 347 80 69
E-Mail: Anjo.Azul@mail.Telepac.pt

Flor dos Cavaleiros Residencial (B bf CC g H)
Rua dos Cavaleiros 58, ✉1100 *(near Martim Moniz)* ☎ 887 22 86

Impala Hotel-Apartments (b CC g H MA)
Rua Filipe Folque 49 ☎ 314 38 53 ☎ 314 89 14 Fax: 357 53 62

Londres. Pensão (bf CC H NG)
Rua D. Pedro V. 53 ✉1250 ☎ 346 22 03 ☎ 346 87 39
Fax: 346 56 82 *Located near the gay bars. Rooms with phone.*

Sintra Auberge (B e f G H MA) 14-? h
Quinta da Capela ☎ 792 86 90
Rooming house with large garden 25 km outside of Lissabon.

Solar Dos Mouros (AC CC g H)
Rua Santo Antonio- ✉1100-351 ☎ 21-888 0155 Fax: 21-888 0155
NEW deluxe hotel.

GUEST HOUSES

Carlos Alberto Freire Cabaço Home Guest (bf G MG OG)
Rosa Damaceno N° 9 1°Andar ✉1900 ☎ 951 27 67

Monumental (g H)
Rua da Gloria 21 *(near Av. de Liberdade)* ☎ 346 98 07
Simple, basic pension. Rooms with shower or bath, WC, phone, TV.

PRIVATE ACCOMODATION

Enjoy Bed & Breakfast (bf G H MA YG)
16:30-21:00h
☎ +49 (30) 215 1666 Fax: +49 (30) 217 52219
E-Mail: Info@ebab.com Homepage: www.ebab.com
Price 22 Euro. Accommodation sharing agency. All with shower & bf.

GENERAL GROUPS

Associação Abraco Mon-Fri 10-13, 15-20 h
Rua da Rosa 243 - 1 *(Bairro Alto)* ☎ 342 59 29 ☎ 342 16 47
Fax: 343 24 19 *Help for people with HIV/AIDS.*

ILGA-Portugal 16:-20:00 h. Sun closed.
PO Box 212 81 ✉1131 ☎ 887 39 18 Fax: 887 39 22
Organizer of Gay Pride, Candle night and Gay Cinema Festival.
O Centro Comuniário Gay e Lésbico de Lisboa põe à sua disposição aconselhamento jurídico, médico e psicológico gratuito (com marcação), um centro de documentação, uma pequena livaria, acesso à internet, aconselhamento sobre VIH/SIDA e uma cafetaria. Todos são Bem Vindos!/The Lesbian and Gay Community Center has legal, medical and psychological counselling (appointment necessary) as well as a small bookstore, a document center, internet access, HIV/AIDS counselling and a small cafeteria. All are welcome!

Opus Gay Associacão
Rua Ilha Terceira 36, R/C ✉1000 ☎ 357 15 20
E-Mail: anser@esoterica.p Homepage: www.homepage.esoterica.pt

HEALTH GROUPS

Centro de Saude
Posto da Lapa ☎ 395 79 73 ☎ 395 79 78

Hospital Curry Cabral Consulta Dermato-Venereologia 8.30-13 h, Sun closed
Rua Beneficencia ✉1000 *No charge for medications or treatment.*

SWIMMING

-Aldeia do Meço (g NU) (30 km south of Lisboa in direction Lagoa de Albufeira. Then the road to Alfarim, right into the village. Follow the bad road to Aldeia do Meço.)
-Costa da Caparica (! AYOR G NU) (with the metro to Palhavâ, then Bus to Costa da Caparica. Small beach train to beach N° 17-19. Action is in the scrub forest)
-Praia dos Pescadores (g)
-Termas da piedade (g pi) (1.Jun-31.Oct, Alcobaça, 15 km from Lisboa. ☎ 420 65.)

CRUISING

All parks of Lisboa are dangerous!
-Avenida da Liberdade (R)
-Campo Grande (opposite the park)
-Shopping Centers:
-Libersil in Avenida da Liberdade (!)
-Amoreiras (20-? h)
-Imaviz
-Monumental
-Espaço Chiaob
-Guerin
-Castil
-Terminal (Rossio) (ayor R)
-Alvalade
-Park Eduardo VII (AYOR, very dangerous)
-Park Principe Real (Largo Principe Real)
-Universidad/Hospital Santa María (entrance from Av. Prof. Gama Pinto to Faculdade de Farmacia)
-Praça dos Restauradores (underground at Avenida de Liberdade. Also cruising)
-Praça do Comércio
-Bus station of Rodoviaria Nacional in Avenida Casal Ribeiro
-Rotunda (underground station in Praça Marques de Pombal)
-Picoas (= Imaviz)
-Praça do Império (AYOR)
-Campo Grande (at the end of Avenida da República)
-Railway stations: Rossio [2nd floor in the cafeteria (R)], Santa Apolonia, Cascais

Marco De Canaveses ☎ 0255

BARS

Piramide (b D F G pi)
✉4630

Monchique ☎ 0282

CAMPING

Foundation Desk (B F G) Olhos Negros, PO Box 8
✉8550-909 ☎ 911 912 Fax: 911 912
10 and 20 pax sleeping room. 6 camping sites. Also provides guest rooms. Provides laundry- and pick-up service, car park.Reservation is necessary.

Monte da Caparica ☎ 021

DANCECLUBS

Mister Gay (AC B CC D G MA p S SNU STV TV WE) Fri-Sat, before holidays 22-6 h
Quinta da Lilveira - Via Rápida ✉2825

Ovar - Beira ☎ 0256

SWIMMING

-Furedouro

Peniche ☎ 0262

SWIMMING

-Dunes between Peniche and Baleal 80 km north of Lisboa is the fishing town Peniche (Bus from Sol Expresso in Lisboa) with cheap accomodation and mixed discos. Best Jun-Sep.

Portimão - Algarve ☎ 0282

BARS

O Boémio (B D GLM MA) 22-? h
Rua de São José 28 ✉8500 *(Near the fish-market and old Portimão bridge)* ☎ 41 35 49

CRUISING

-Park and cafés near the Main Railway Station
-Round the „Café Inglesa" (evenings)
-Square of the Republic (R)

Porto - Douro ☎ 022

BARS

Moínho de Vento (B D G MA) 22-2, WE -4 h
Rua Sá de Noronha 78
Syndikato Club (B D G MA STV) Rua do Bonjardim 836 ☎ 208 43 83

CAFES

Brasileira (b f g MA)
Rua Sá Bandeira 61-91
Café na Praça
Centro Comercial Clérigos
Gente Gira (B D G STV)
Rua Barbosa de Castro 63
Petulia (b f g)
Rua Julio Dinis 775

DANCECLUBS

Swing (B D GLM YG) 22-4, Sat Sun -7 h
Rua Júlio Dinis, Parque Itália *(near Rotunda Boavista Shopping Center Brasilia)*

SAUNAS/BATHS

Oasis Sauna (B e G MA msg sa sb VS) 15-4 h
Rua Santa Catarina 763 ✉4000 ☎ 205 75 33
Tipo Sauna (g sa) Mon-Sat 15-22, Sun & public holidays -20 h
Rua da Conceicão 64 ✉4050 *(2nd floor)* ☎ 208 74 25

HEALTH GROUPS

Hospital J. Urbano Mon-Fri 9.30-12.30 h
Rua Camara Pestana ☎ 501 41

CRUISING

-Cliffs at the beach in front of Castelo do Queijo
-Praça da Liberdade
-Avenida dos Aliados
-Praça do Municipio
-Praça Mouzinho Alburquerque (Rotunda Boavista)
-Brasilia Shopping Center
-Railway station
-Castelo do Queito
-Praça D. João I
-Castelo do Queijo (cliffs at the beach and nearby streets)

Póvoa de Varzim - Póvoa de Varzim ☎ 0252

BARS

Diana Bar (B g OS)
Passeio Alegre ✉4490
Enseada (B g)
Passeio Alegre

SWIMMING

-Passeio Alegro Beach

Quarteira - Algarve ☎ 0289

BARS

Privilégio (B G MA) 22-2 h
Rua Gonçalo Velho 9 ✉8125 *(Neat the Lota)* ☎ 38 97 06

SWIMMING

-Park at end of Quarteira nearest to Vale do Lobo (NU r) (walk along the beach or cliff top in direction of Vale do Lobo; after the 2nd red sandstone cliff, you'll see dunes with bushes, within sight of Vale do Lobo; cruising and discreet action in the bushes)

S.B. Messines - Algarve ☎ 0282

HOTELS

Amigos. Casa (B bf F G H lj MA msg NU OS pi VS WO)
Larga Vista, Foral ✉8375 ☎ 565 97
10 minutes north of Albufeira and 10 minutes to the beach and the gay scene. All 4 double rooms with bathroom and satellite TV. Free pick up from Faro Airport. Rates £ 130 per person and week (bf incl.)

Setubal - Extremadura ☎ 0265

BARS

Iguana Bar (B GLM N) 21-2 h
Rua Pereira Cao 44 ✉2900 ☎ 210 83
Pátio das Cantigas (A AC B GLM OS r s) 21-3 h
Praca do Bocage 21 ✉2900 ☎ 290 57

CAFES

Bar Doca Nova
Rua da Saúde 28, R/C

DANCECLUBS

Chez Moi-Disco Bar (B D G)
A Almeida Garrett 67 ✉2900

SWIMMING

-Albarquel
-Arrabida camping
-Coelhos

-Figueirinha
-Galapagos
-Ilha de Troia/Troia Island (NU) (15 minutes from camping)

CRUISING

All cruising areas are AYOR
-Centro Comercial Bonfim
-Hotel Esperança
-Praça do Bocage (R YG)
-Avenida Luisa Tody (r)
-Rua dos Qurives
-Rua Antão Girão
-Estação Central de Camionetas

Tavira - Algarve ☎ 0281

BARS

Arco Bar (B G MA) 20-2, Fri Sat -3 h
Rua Almirante Candidos dos Reis 67 ✉8800 ☎ 235 37

CRUISING

-The small park along the river (Rua José Pires Padunha) or any sidewalk café (e.g. near the busstation).

Torres Novas - Alentejo ☎ 0249

DANCECLUBS

A Chamine (B D G r)
Rua dos Anjos 8 B.P. ✉2350
Galaxia (B D f g) 22.30-4 h
Casal-Saldanha, Vila Cidade ☎ 66 12 11

Torres Vedras - Extremadura ☎ 0261

BARS

Pastelaeria Imperio (B g r)
Paiva de Andrade 1 ✉2560

Viana do Castelo - Minho ☎ 0258

SWIMMING

-Cabedelo Praia/Town Beach (AYOR nu) (Take the ferry to town beach then walk to the dunes. Action in the wood behind the dunes.)

Vila do Conde - Douro ☎ 0252

CRUISING

-Beach (at night)
-Railway station

Vila Nova de Familicão ☎ 0252

BARS

Cafe Barão (B g)
Junto à Escola Secundaria 1 ✉4760
Cafe Pavilhão Municipal (B G r)
Avenida da França ✉4760
Cafe Primavera (B GLM)
Frente as Bombas da B.P. ✉4760
Confeitaria Elite (B g)
Avenida 25 Abril ✉4760

DANCECLUBS

MDS (B D G r)
Centro Comercial Aro ✉4760

RESTAURANTS

Pica Pau (b F g)
Parque de Maria II ✉4760

CRUISING

-Centro Comercial Aro
-Jardim Da Maria II
-Camara Municipal (WC)

Vila Nova de Milfontes ☎ 0283

HOTELS

Luis House (F G H)
Ap. 5 ✉7645 *(near Zambugeira/Lagos)*
Location near the cruising beach. For reservation write. Rates on request.

Vila Real de Sto. Antonio - Algarve

SWIMMING

-Monte Gordo beach (3 km from Vila Real de Santo Antonio)

CRUISING

-Avenue along the river by the garden
-Ponta Santo Antonio

Vilamoura - Algarve ☎ 0289

BARS

é Bar (AC B d f GLM MA OS) 21-04 h daily. Oct-Feb closed on Mo, Tu & We.
Rua da Botelha ✉8125 *Bus to Vilamoura center. Follow road to marina.* ☎ 314 553

DANCECLUBS

Kadoc (B D g NG s YG)
✉8125 *(on the road to Albufeira, 4km from Vilamoura)*

HOTELS

Quinta da Lua (b H glm pi) All year opening May 2000
Bernardinheiro 1662 ✉8800-513 *Nearest airport in Faro.*
☎ 96 10 70 Fax: 96 10 70
Opening May 2000. Rates in double room (incl. breakfast) May-Sep 7500,-9500, Esc. Oct-Apr '01 5000,-7500, Esc

Viseu ☎ 0232

BARS

Galeria 22 (B G)
Junto ao Adro da Sé ✉3500
Slot Machines (B G r)
Junto ao Hotel Avenida ✉3500

HEALTH GROUPS

Centro de Saude Distrital Mon Thu 14-16 h

CRUISING

-City park-Jardim da Cidade ou Parque

Réunion

Southeast Africa

Initials: REU

Time: GMT +4

☎ Country Code / Access Code: 262 (no area codes) / 00

Language: French

Area: 2,512 km² / 970 sq mi.

Currency: 1 French Franc (FF) = 100 Centimes

Population: 682,000

Capital: St. Denis

Religions: mostly Catholics

Climate: Tropical climate, that moderates with the elevation. It's cool and dry from May to November, hot and rainy from November to April.

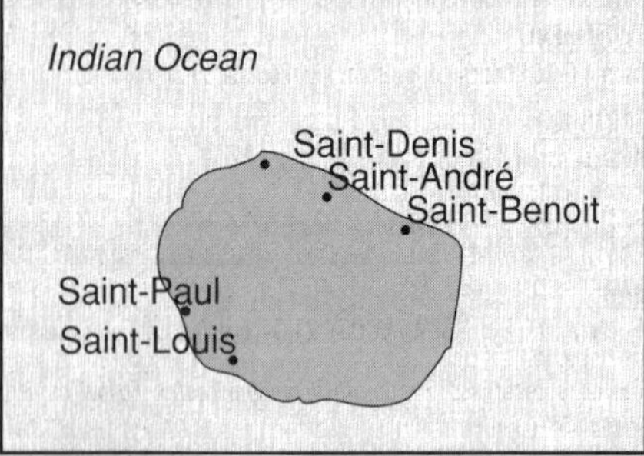

● The Réunion Islands are a French „Département d'Outre Mer". Legislation concerning homosexuality is the same as in ☛ France. The crossing from Mauritius to the Réunion Islands takes only about a half an hour. The landscape is so beautiful that the trip is certainly worth it.

✱ Réunion ist ein französisches »Département d'Outre-Mer«, die gesetzliche Situation entspricht der in ☛ Frankreich. Von Mauritius aus dauert die Überfahrt zu den Reunion Islands nur eine halbe Stunde, und die Landschaft ist so schön, daß sich ein Besuch allemal lohnt.

▲ La Réunion est un département français d'outre-mer. La législation y est donc la même qu'en ☛France métropolitaine. Depuis l'île Maurice, la traversée ne dure qu'une demi-heure. Le paysage est magnifique. A voir absolument!

☆ Reunión es un «Département d`Outre-Mer» francés, por lo tanto la situación legal corresponde a la de ☛ Francia. El viaje desde Mauritius hasta las Islas Reunión dura solamente media hora y el paisaje es tan bonito, que una visita merece sin duda la pena.

❖ Reunione è un „Département d'Outre Mer", la situazione legale corrisponde a quelle della ☛Francia. Il passaggio da Mauritius fino alle Isole Reunion dura solo mezz'ora, quindi vale la pena andarci.

Petite-Ile ✉ 97429

PRIVATE ACCOMODATION

Veremer B&B (AC bf E g H OS pi sol)
40 Ch. Sylvain Vitry ✉97429 *10 min. from St. Pierre, 1 km from the beach.* ☎ 31 65 10 Fax: 31 65 10
Gay owned B&B with spectacular view on the Indian Ocean.

Ravine de Cabris ✉ 97432

DANCECLUBS

Gay's Club (AC B D GLM MA S)
✉97432 ☎ 49 69 13

St. Denis ✉ 97400

BARS

Rallye. Le (B F g yg)
1 Rue de la Victoire ✉97400
Evenings on the terrace.
Ranger's. Le (B G VS)
240 Rue Maréchal Leclerc ✉97400 ☎ 94.12.10

SEX SHOPS/BLUE MOVIES

Adult' Video Show (CC DR glm MA msg s snu VS) 9-24 h
15 Rue Amiral Lacaze ✉97400 *(Barachois)* ☎ 41 15 05

HOTELS

Central (AC B F H NG OS)
37 Rue de la Compagnie ✉97400 ☎ 21 18 08
Central location, 15 min to the airport. All rooms with telephone, bathroom, WC, and balcony. Single FF 245-265, double FF 280-300.
Meridien (AC B F H NG OS pi sa)
2 Rue Doret ✉97400 ☎ 21 80 20
Central location, 15 min to the airport. All units with telephone, fridge, priv. bath, WC. Single FF 690, double FF 750, continental bf FF 52.

SWIMMING

-La Saline-les-Bas (about 60 km from St.-Denis, on the road to St. Pierre; when driving from St.-Denis, you cross St. Gilles, L'Hermitage and La Saline; about 600 metres after this last village, just after a small bridge, you will see the beach on the righthand side; cruising and nudism on the rocky shoreline; crowded on weekends, but there are always some young men around during the week, even when it is raining; although it is best to go by car, it is possible to take the bus to St. Pierre, and get out at La Saline)

CRUISING

-Le Barachois (r) (20-2 h, square in front of Hotel Meridien)
-Public Swimmingpool (at night)

St. Paul ✉ 97460

BARS

Annexe. L' (B G MA VS) Tue-Sun 13-1 h
378 Rue St. Louis Étang ✉97460 ☎ 45 50 31

St. Pierre ✉ 97250

GENERAL GROUPS

Homologue
✉97250 ☎ 25 32 68

Romania

Southeastern Europe

Initials: R

Time: GMT +2

☎ Country Code / Access Code: 40 / 00

Language: Romanian

Area: 237,500 km² / 91,699 sq mi.

Currency: 1 Leu (l) = 100 Bani

Population: 22,573,000

Capital: Bucuresti

Religions: 70% Romanian Orthodox, 6% Roman Catholic, 6% Protestant.

Climate: Moderate climate. Winters are cold and cloudy with frequent snow and fog. Summers are sunny with frequent showers and thunderstorms.

● In September 1996 the romanian parlament has decided, to return to the Ceaucescu-era: the article 200 of the penal code, the „homosexual paragraph", has been hardened. Homosexuality is punishable and disturbance of public order can be punished with imprisonment up to five years. In so doing, Romania has, in contrast to all expectations, not complied with the demands put to it by european and international organisations like the European Council, amnesty international and ILGA. Contrary to scrapping the legal persecution, it has augmented the penalty. Before this decision was made, the orthodox church of the country exerted massive public pressure. It has to be seen, whether the protests from Europe will help the gays and lesbians in Romania.

✱ Im September 1996 hat das rumänische Parlament die Rückkehr zu den Ceaucescu-Zeiten beschlossen: der Artikel 200 des Strafgesetzbuches, der „Homosexuellenparagraph", wurde verschärft. Homosexualität ist strafbar, bei „Erregung öffentlichen Ärgernisses" können Haftstrafen bis zu fünf Jahren verhängt werden.
Entgegen allen Erwartungen hat Rumänien damit den Forderungen europäischer und internationaler Organisationen wie Europarat, amnesty international und ILGA völlig entgegen gehandelt und die Strafandrohung nicht gestrichen, sondern erhöht.
Im Vorfeld dieser Entscheidung hat auch die orthodoxe Kirche des Landes massiven öffentlichen Druck ausgeübt.
Zuletzt wurde im Juni 1998 eine Gesetzesvorlage der Regierung, welche vorsah, den Artikel 200 aufzuheben, vom Abgeordnetenhaus abgelehnt.

▲ En septembre 1996, le Parlement roumain semble avoir décrêté le retour aux années Ceaucescu, tout du moins en ce qui concerne l'homosexualité. On a ressorti et „amélioré" l'article 200 du code pénal qui condamne les rapports entre personnes du même sexe. Toute personne portant „atteinte à la pudeur publique" risque une peine de prison pouvant aller jusqu'à 5 ans. On s'attendait à ce que la Roumanie supprime l'article 200, c'est le contraire qui s'est passé: on a renforcé les lois anti-pédés. La Roumanie va donc à l'encontre des revendications et recommandations des organisations européennes et internationales comme le Conseil de l'Europe, Amnesty International ou l'ILGA. L'Eglise orthodoxe a pesé de tout son poids pour renforcer la législation homophobe. Espérons que les gays et les lesbiennes des autres pays d'Europe vont se mobiliser pour accélérer le retour à la normalisation en Roumanie.

☆ En Septiembre de 1996 el parlamento rumano decidió regresar a los tiempos de Ceaucescu: el artículo 200 del código penal, el llamado párrafo homosexual, ha sido recrudecido. La homosexualidad es penada, y una transgresión a „la alteración de la moral pública" puede ser penada con hasta 5 años de prisión. Contra toda expectativa de organizaciones europeas e internacionales como el Consejo Europeo, Amnistía Internacional y el ILGA, Rumanía ha aumentado las penas en lugar de abolirlas. Lamentablemente la iglesia ortodoxa ha influido indirectamente en estas decisiones y ha presionado mucho en la opinón pública. La única esperanza es que las protestas masivas de toda Europa ayuden de una u otra forma a los gays y lesbianas rumanos.

❖ Nel settembre 1996 il parlamento rumeno ha deliberato il ritorno ai tempi di Ceaucescu: l'articolo 200 del codice penale, il paragrafo sugli omosessuali, è stato inasprito. L'omosessualità è punibile: per „oltraggio al pudore" la pena inflitta può raggiungere i 5 anni. A dispetto delle aspettative comuni la Romania ha ignorato le richieste di organizzazioni internazionali come il Consiglio d'Europa, Amnesty International e l'Ilga aumentando le proprie pene invece di abrogarle. Questa decisione è stata influenzata dalla forte pressione esercitata dalla chiesa ortodossa nazionale. Non si sa se le numerose proteste provenienti da tutta l'Europa potranno aiutare i gay e le lesbiche romeni.

Brasov

CRUISING

-Piata Sfatului
-Central Park (entrance opposite City Hall)
-Railway station

Bucuresti ✉ 78400 ☎ 01

BARS

Club R (B f g YG)
Calea Setbau Voda 70, Sector 4 ☎ 23 34 50

DANCECLUBS

Martin Disco (AC B CC D g p YG)
Ses. Stefan cel Mare/Calea Dorobantilor ☎ 321 49 45

RESTAURANTS

Pierrot (B F g) 19-24 h
Occidentului 44, Sector 1 *(200 m from casino)* ☎ 659 61 55

ESCORTS & STUDIOS

Andrei Escort Service (G)
PO Box 68-100 ✉78400 ☎ 92-48 86 43
E-Mail: razant@hotmail.com

SAUNAS/BATHS

Baia Grivita (g sa sb) Mon-Fri 10-18, Sat 9-14 h, closed Sun
Str. Sf. Voievozi nr. 1 *(near Gara de Nord, on Calea Grivitei)*

HEALTH GROUPS

Asociatia Româna Anti-Sida•ARAS
Str. Dr. Leonte nr. 1-3, sector 5 ☎ 311 20 78 Fax: 613 66 60
Centrul de Coordonare Dermato-Venerologic
Bulevardul Republici 133, Sect. 3 ☎ 642 53 70 Fax: 642 52 30
Spital de Urgenta
Ses. Stefan del Mare

SWIMMING

-Municipal Bath »Grivita« (g NG pi) (for men Wed Fri Sat 10-18, Sun 7-12 h, opposite Orthodox church)
-Hotel Turist (pi) (Bd. Poligrafiei nr. 1-5)
-Hotel Bucuresti (pi) (Calea Victoriei)
-Tei Toboc Beach
-Tei District

CRUISING

-Piata Universitatii (around International Hotel)
-Cismigiu Park
-All are (AYOR)!
-Calea Victoria 37 (near main post office, right from the entrance)
-Northern Railway Station
-Pedestrian underground Bulvardul Republici and Bulvardul Balcescu
-Park Cismigiu (entrance Bulvar, Magureanu)
-Park Cismigiu (entrance Brezo street)

Cluj ☎ 051

CRUISING

-Park opposite Maghiar Theatre
-Park behind National Theatre

Constanta ☎ 016

CAFES

Café de Vin (b f g) 10-23, Sat Sun -24 h
Bulvardul Republici 20 *(at Hotel Continental)*

CRUISING

-Bulvardul Tomis 79 (in the park opposite Railway Bureau CFR)
-Stefan cel Mare/Mihai Viteazul street (in pedestrian underground near the store »Tomis«)
-Bus station at sos. (Mangaliei/Teodor Burada 1 street)

Iasi ☎ 081

CRUISING

-Railway station
-Park near Culture Palace
-Copou Park

Sibiu ☎ 024

BARS

Bulevard (B g)
Nicolae-Balcescu-Street *(near Astra Park)*

SWIMMING

-Ocna Sibiului (10 km from Sibiu. Go by train from Sibiu Main Station to Ocna Sibiului. Get to the »La lacuri«, an area with natural salt seas)

CRUISING

-Astra Park
-Central Park

Timisoara ☎ 061

CRUISING

-Central Park
-Railway station
-Near Opera House

Russia

Rossija

East Europe and Northern Asia

Initials: RUS

Time: GMT +3...+12

☎ Country Code / Access Code: 7 / 8 (wait for tone) 10

Language: Russian

Area: 17,075,400 km^2 / 6,592,812 sq mi.

Currency: 1 Ruble (RUR)=100 Kopeks

Population: 146,861,022

Capital: Moskva (Moscow)

Religions: Russian Orthodox

Climate: The climate ranges from steppes in the south through humid continental in much of European Russia. Winters are cold, cloudy and sometimes severe with snow and rain. Summers are mild, although in Moscow may be very hot in July

Important gay cities: Moscow and St. Petersburg

● Homosexuality between consenting adults is legal. The age of consent is set at 14 years for both gays and straights.

✱ Einvernehmliche Homosexualität zwischen Erwachsenen ist legal. Das Schutzalter liegt für Hetero- wie Homosexuelle bei 14 Jahren.

▲ L'homosexualité entre adultes consentants n'est pas un délit. La majorité sexuelle est fixée à 14 ans pour tous (homos et hétéros).

☆ La homosexualidad por acuerdo entre adultos es legal. La edad de consentimiento es de 14 años, independientemente de la orientación sexual.

❖ L'omosessualità tra adulti consenzienti è legale. La maturità sessuale è di 14 anni per tutti.

NATIONAL GAY INFO

Gay.Ru
PO Box 1 ✉109457 Moskva Homepage: www.gay.ru/
Russian National Websit of Gays, Lesbians, Bi- and Transsexuals. The most comprehensive web-site covering all aspects of gay life in Russia and other republics of former USSR. Reliable, exhaustive and up -to-date information. English version available.

GenderDoc
PO Box 9 ✉125047 Moskva E-Mail: genderdoc@gay.ru
Gay and lesbian archives - the largest collection of books, magazines and clippings on gay, lesbians and transgendered issues. Founded in 1994.

NATIONAL PUBLISHERS

Argo-Risk
PO Box 12 ✉111402 Moskva E-Mail: argorisk@glasnet.ru
Homepage: www.gay.ru/english/argo/
Erotic magazine for gays. About 50 pages with photos, stories, letters etc.

Glagol Publishing House
Apt. 18, 20 Stary Arbat ulitsa Moskva *(Metro Arbatskaya)*
E-Mail: glagol@gay.ru Homepage: www.gay.ru/glagol
An well-established and renowned publisher of gay and lesbian books by both Russian and foreign authors.

Kolonna Publications
PO Box 24048 ✉170024 Tver E-Mail: kolonna69@mail.ru
Publishers of „Theme Series" - paperback books about gay life.

Mitin Zhournal (Mitya´s Magazine)
37-1-13 Nalichnaya ulitsa ✉199 406 St. Petersburg
☎ 352 47 54 E-Mail: olia@mj.spb.ru
Homepage: www.vavilon.ru/metatext/mitin.html
Published quarterly since 1985 by a group of amateurs. Not a gay editon, but many articles may be interesting for gays.

URANUS-Partner
c/o Mikhail Gladkikh ✉101 000 Gavpochtamt
Homepage: www.gay.ru/english/uranus/
Full-color literary almanac published annually.
All Russian gay magazines and books may be purchased from the gay online store „Lavka" (see below).

NATIONAL COMPANIES

Lavka - Gay Internet Store
PO Box 1 ✉109 457 E-Mail: lavka@gay.ru
Homepage: www.gay.ru/english/lavka/
Russian online store of gay items: Russian and international gay magazines, erotic CDs, videos, books and accessoires. Online and mail orders, credit cards accepted, shipping worldwide. Catalogue for free.

„Russian Version" Gay Video Internet Store
E-Mail: gayvideo@mail.ru Homepage: www.gay.video.da.ru
Wide range of Russian, American and European gay and lesbian videos and CDs. Orders via Internet, shipping worldwide.

TRAVEL & TRANSPORT

The Rainbow Tours
PO Box 1 ✉109 457 Moskva E-Mail: travel@gay.ru
Homepage: www.gay.ru/english/travel/
Gay travel agency. Tours to all destinations in Russia. Gay guides and interpreters. Information service for gay and lesbian travelers. Advice on accomodation and gay venues in Moscow and St. Petersburg.

Arkhangelsk - Arkhangelsk Region

GAY INFO

Arkhangelsk Gay Life Web Site
Homepage: www.rfsl.se/pitea/archangelsk.html *Personals and links.*

Astrakhan - Astrakhan Region ☎ 085100

CAFÉS

Prestige Café (Blue Oyster Cafeé) (B glm) Savushkina ulitsa *(next to old Detski Mir shop, Tram 1, A 2, Bus 4, 4k,25)*

DANCECLUBS

Aquarium Disco (B D glm NG) 19-? h
Sofil Perovskoi ulitsa *(Tram 3, Bus 15 and 18, two tops after Krasny most)*

GENERAL GROUPS

EGO
PO Box 264, ✉414000 *First gay association in the Volta Delta.*

Barnaul - Altaisky Krai ☎ 03852

GENERAL GROUPS

Siberian Initiative
PO Box 783 ✉656 054 ☎ 258 512

HEALTH GROUPS

Regional AIDS Center
62 Pyataya Zapadnaya ulitsa ☎ 20 335

Blagoveshchensk - Amurskaya ☎ 041622

HEALTH GROUPS

AIDS Center
149 Severnaya Street ✉675 000 ☎ 224 980

DANCECLUBS

Tri Popsenka (Three piglets) (B D f NG)
78A Lenina prospekt. *Mostley visited by gays thursdays.*

Irkutsk - Irkutsk Region ☎ 03952

GAY INFO

Association of Sexual Minorities „The League"
E-Mail: aegoroff@hotmail.com
Homepage: http://members.xoom.com/daboy2/

DANCECLUBS

Cage Night Club (B D g S WE)Fris-Sat 23-6 h
13-A Stanislavskogo ulitsa ☎ 532 654
Homepage: http://members.xoom.com/daboy2/cage.htm
Entrance fee US$ 3

CRUISING

- Central Park

Izhevsk - Udmurtia Republic ☎ 03412

HEALTH GROUPS

AIDS Center
17 Truda ultisa ✉426 067 ☎ 203 744

Kaliningrad - Kaliningrad Region

GAY INFO

Gay Kaliningrad Web Site
Homepage: www.gaylaliningrad.da.ru

BARS

Selena Café-Bar (B glm WE)
97 Moskovyky prospet
Mixed crowd before 23 h, mostly gay after 23 h.

Kaluga - Kaluga Region ☎ 08422

GENERAL GROUPS

Kaluga Area Union of Gays and Lesbians
PO Box 692 ✉248 030

Kirov - Vyatka ☎ 08332

DANCECLUBS

Green House Club (B D glm NG SNU WE) Thu-Sun 20-5 h
18 a Lomonossova Ulitsa

Kostroma - Kostroma Region ☎ 0942

GENERAL GROUPS

Goluboy Voskhod (Blue Sunrise)
PO Box 24 ✉156 010

Krasnoyarsk

SPECIAL INTEREST GROUPS

Siberian Friends/Sibirskiye druzya
PO Box 7678 ✉660092 Homepage: andrej@pcpostal.com
Siberian Pen Friends Club for correspondence all over the world.

Moskva ☎ 095

● Moscow, the capital of Russia, was founded in 1147 and now has more than 10 million of inhabitants. Moscow is not only the business center of Russia, but also a host of the most flamboyant Russian gay venues. Public attitudes towards homosexuality are very tolerant in Moscow, yet it is advisable to refrain from the public display of affection (such as holding hand in the street etc.) gay life is prospering in Moscow - every few month new clubs and saunas are opend. Please visit http://www.gay.ru for most up-to-date information on gay venues.

✷ Moskau, gegründet im Jahre 1147, ist mit seinen mehr als 8 Mio. Einwohnern sowohl das politische, als auch das kulturelle Zentrum Russlands. Die wichtigsten Impulse für die Schwulenbewegung gingen immer von der Hauptstadt aus. Die schwule Szene konzentriert sich um das berühmte Bolschoi Theater herum. Hier befinden sich die meisten Cruisings sowie viele Bars und Restaurants, die gerne von Schwulen und Lesben besucht werden.

▲ Fondée en 1147, Moscou a, avec ses 8 millions d'habitants, toujours été la capitale politique et culturelle de la Russie. Elle en a aussi toujours été la première ville gaye. Son influence à ce niveau a toujours été déterminante pour le reste du pays. Le quartier du Bolschoï est depuis toujours le bastion gay de la ville. C'est ici que l'on trouve la plupart des lieux de drague, bars et restaurants que fréquentent les gays et lesbiennes.

☆ Moscú, fundada en el año 1147, es con sus 8 millones de habitantes el centro político y cultural de Rusia. La capital ha sido siempre el epícentro de impulsos para la comunidad gay. El ambiente homosexual se concentra en los alrededores del famoso Teatro Bolschoi, donde se encuentra la mayoría de los sitios de cruising, a parte de bares y restaurantes muy frecuentados por gays y lesbianas.

❖ Mosca, fondata nel 1147, è con più di 8 milioni di abitanti la capitale politica e culturale della Russia. I maggiori impulsi per il movimento gay sono sempre partiti da qui. L'ambiente gay si concentra in maggior parte attorno al famoso teatro Bolschoi. Qui si trovano il più delle aree cruising e tanti bar e ristoranti frequentati volentieri da gay e lesbiche.

GAY INFO

Organicheskaya Ledi (Organic Lady)
PO Box 6 ✉123 181
Moscow lesbian publication.

BARS

Dary Moria (Sea Gift's) (B f G MA R) 10-3 h
Bldg. 6, 9 Maly Gnezdnikovky pereulok *(Metro Pushkinskaya, in the yard behint the Dary Morya supermarket, no sign on the door)* ☎ 229 77 09
Very cruisy, Crowded evenings.

ELF (AC B bf d F g lj MA p YG) Sun-Thu 11-24 h, Fri, Sat 11-3 h
Bldg. 1, 13 Zemlyanoi val *(Metro Kurskaya)* ☎ 917 20 14
Small and cozy café to chat with friends.

Gostinaya Chaikovskogo (B f G MA N R) 18-23.30 h
4 Triumfalnaya ploschad *(Metro Mayakovskaya, in the basement of Chaikovski Concert Hall)*
Cheap and cruisy.

Tri Obeziany (Three Monkeys) (AC B D F G MA p R SNU STV VS) 18-9 h
71 Sadovnicheskaya *(Metro Paveletskaya)* ☎ 953 09 09
☎ 951 15 63 Homepage: www.gay.ru/3monkeys
First private gay club in Moscow. Popular Mondays, Tuesdays and Wednesdays and Fri/Sat after 4 h. Also restaurant. Free entrance for men.

MEN'S CLUBS

Kazarma (AYOR B DR G MA R SNU VS WE) weekends 22-8 h
14 Presnensky val *(Metro Ulitsa 1905 Goda, in the basement of Khameleon Danceclub)* ☎ 255 63 43
Entrance fee about US $ 4, Men only, Darkrooms, videos, cruising.

DANCECLUBS

Central Station (B D G P SNU)
B.Tatarskaya 16/2, Str. 2 ☎ 959 4643
Most popular on WE. Entrance fee $3, incl. one free drink. Large beer $1+. Best drag show in Moscow. Male strip-dance after 02:00h. Young, stylish crowd. Busy but not over crowded.

Chance (! AC B D DR f G R S WE YG) 23-6 h
11/15 Volochaevskaya Ulitsa *(Metro Ploshchad Ilycha, DK Serp i Molot)* ☎ 298 62 47
The oldest gay club in Russia. Very popular. Entrance fee about US$ 5.

Cherny Lebed' (AC B D E GLM OG P S) 20-8 h
19 Novy Arbat Ulitsa *(Metro Arbatskaya, in the reataurant Angara, entrance from the courtyard)* ☎ 203 96 07
Very flashy and expensive.

Khameleon (Chameleon) (AYOR B D DR f g R S SNU WE YG) 22-8 h
14 Presnensky Val *(Metro Ulitsa 1905 Goda)* ☎ 253 63 43
Mixed danceclub, a lot of teenage straight boys and fag hags. Very crowded on weekends.

Nochnaya Sova (Night Owl) (AC B D DR F glm H N R S SNU sa WE YG) Tue-Sun 20-7 h
8 Golovinskoye chausee *(Metro Rechnoy Vokzal)* ☎ 452 71 75
Entrance fee about US$ 2. Sauna and hotel rooms are also available.

Pinocchio (AC B D F g MA p R S VS WE)
12 Ordzhonikidze Ulitsa *(Metro Leninsky Prospekt)* ☎ 955 21 86
No entrance fee for men, full of hustlers and sugar daddies.

Tsentralnaya Stantsia (Central Station) (! AC B D DR F G MA p S SNU STV WE) 19-7 h weekends
Bldg. 2, 16/2 Bolshaya Tatarskaya ulitsa *(Metro Novokuznetskaya)* ☎ 959 46 43 Homepage: www.gaycentral.ru
The best drag shows and male striptease in Moscow.

RESTAURANTS

Izba Rybaka (Fisherman´s Shelter) (AC B F NG) 11-24 h
48/13 Baumanskaya Ulitsa *(Metro Baumanskaya)* ☎ 267 63 08
Homepage: http://izba.rain.art.ru
Gay-owned restaurant. Good seafood cuisine.

SHOWS

Roman Victyuk´s Teater (G)
6 Stromynka Ulitsa *(Metro Sokolniki)* ☎ 268 06 69
Homepage: www.gay.ru/victyuk
The first openly gay theater in Russia.

SAUNAS/BATHS

Dolphin (B DR f G MA p pi R sa) Tue-Sun 18-23 h
20 Ivana Babushkina Ulitsa *(Metro Profsoyuznaya)* ☎ 129 22 47
Entrance fee US $ 10.

Nemo (B DR f G MA msg p pi R sa) 18-23 h
25 Novoalexeyevskaya Ulitsa *(Metro Alexeyevskaya, Vodopribor factory sport facilities building)*
Entrance fee US$ 4. Inexpensive, but not very clean.

VIP-Sauna (B DR f G OG msg p pi sa) 18-6 h
18 Sadovaya-Spasskaya Ulitsa *(Metro Turgenevksaya/chisty Prudy)* ☎ 207 00 41
Entrance fee US$ 5, Cozy and clean place with cute masseurs. Jacuzzi and flow in the pool.

BODY & BEAUTY SHOPS

Giorgio (B f g MA msg p sol)
17 Protochny pereulok *(Metro Smolenskaya)* ☎ 241 40 83

TRAVEL & TRANSPORT

Three Monkeys Travel Club (CC)
71/2 Sadovncheskaya ul. ✉113035 ☎ 953 09 09
☎ 951 15 63 Fax: 951 15 63 E-Mail: legion@centro.ru
English speaking staff. Assistance with gay guides, visas and accommodation.

GENERAL GROUPS

ARGO-Risk
PO Box 12 ✉111402 E-Mail: argorisk@glasnet.ru
Homepage: www.gay.ru/english/argo
☛Gay Publishers. ILGA member.

Charity Aid Foundation (CAF)
57 Sadovnicheskaya Ulitsa, 3rd floor, office 4 *(Metro Paveletskaya)* Fax: 792 59 29
American charity foundation extending support and offering legal assistance to NGOs, including gay and lesbian organizations.

Imena Foundation
Bldg. 1, 52/55 Bolshaya Pereyaslavskaya Ulitsa ✉129 110
☎ 933 42 33 E-Mail: names@aids.ru Homepage: www.aids.ru
Memorial project. Information for people with HIV & aids. AIDS testing center.

The Rainbow Sphere
PO Box 1 ✉104 457 E-Mail: shpere@gay.ru
Homepage: www.gay.ru/sphere
Voluntary Charity Non-profit Foundation Rainbow Sphere. Information on gay life in Moscow. Assistance to gays and lesbians. Support to professional associations of gays and lesbians. Publishing projects. For information on partnership opportunities please e-mail.

HEALTH GROUPS

Moscow AIDS Center
14/2, 8-ya Ulitsa Sokolinoy Gory ✉105 275 *(M° Semionovskaya)* ☎ 365 56 65

My i Vy (We and You)
Bldg. 2, 15 8-ya Ulitsa Sokolinoy Gory ✉105 275 ☎ 916 48 68
Fax: 916 48 68
Homepage: www.glasnet.ru/~weandyou/we_you.htm
Support and legal advice to HIV/Aids poeple.

SWIMMING

- Lebyazhka (G NU) (Metro Schukinskaya, then Tram 1, 21 or 28 direction Stroginsky most. Cross the bridge to the left spiral staircase down, to the end of the island, turn right and go again to the end.
- Serebriany Bor 1 (g NU) (Metro Polezhaevskaya, then Trolleybus 20, 21 65 or 86 and go to the nude beach it´s on the right side.

CRUISING

- Iliynsky Skver (Metro Kitai-Gorod, very popular in the evening).
- Teatralnaya Ploschad (Metro Okhotny Ryad, the square in front of the Bolshoi Theater)
- Pushkinskaya Ploschad (Metro Pushkinskaya/Tversaya, the square around the Pushkin monument)
- Park in front of the left wing of the Lomonossov University. (Metro universitet)
- Izmailovsky park (Metro Izmailovsky par, two paths which leading to the clearing).
- Paveletsky railway station. (Metro Belorusskaya), in the WC.
- Kursky railway station (Metro Kurskaya), in the WC

Murmansk - Murmansk Region ☎ 08150

GAY INFO

Murmansk Gays and Lesbians Web Sitze
Homepage: www.rfsl.se/pitea/murmanskrusski.html

GENERAL GROUPS

Murmansk Regional Public Association „Krug"
PO Box 70 33 ✉183 018 Homepage: www.ussr.to/All/krug/
Member of ILGA.

HEALTH GROUPS

AIDS Center
47 Tralovaya Ulitsa ✉183 038

CRUISING

- Zolotoy Lev Café (Samoylovoy Ulitsa)
- Logovo Bar

Nizhny Novgorod - Nizhegoroskaya ☎ 03435

GAY INFO

Nizhny Novgorod Gay Life Web Site
Homepage: www.lgg.ru/~gay-nn/
Personals, job offers, chat, gallery.

DANCECLUBS

Pyramida Club (B D f NG)
Rozhdestvenskaya Ulitsa *(at Irina Café, opposite Rechnoi Vokzal)*

GENERAL GROUPS

Public Association „Drugoi Bereg"/Human Rights Society
PO Box 233 ✉603 000 E-Mail: plas@osi.nnov.ru

CRUISING

- Ploschad Minina (the alley to the right from the Dmitievskaya tower of the Novgorod Kremlin)
- Kultury par (Metro Park Kultury), around the WC in the park.

Novokuznetsk - Kemerovo Region ☎ 08762

GENERAL GROUPS

Gay Information Center (GLM)
PO Box 220
✉654 032

Novosibirsk - Novosibirsk Region ☎ 03832

GAY INFO

Gay Novosibirsk Web Site
Homepage: www.gaynsk.da.ru
Guide to gay Novosibirsk.

CRUISING

- Square in front of the Opera Theatre.
- Beach on Obskoye More in Akademgorodok.

Omsk - Omsk Region ☎ 03812

GENERAL GROUPS

Omsk Center for Support of Sexual Minorities „Favorit"
Helpline on Tue 15-18 h (Moscow time)
PO Box 229 ✉644 046 ☎ 643 025 E-Mail: ocpsm@mail.ru
Sibirskaya Alternativa
PO Box 939 ✉644 046

CRUISING

- Square in front of the Drama Theater.

Petrozavodsk - Karelia ☎ 081400

GENERAL GROUPS

Christopher
E-Mail: christof@chat.ru Homepage:
www.geocities.com/WestHollywood/Stonewall/7525/index.htm
Karelian movement of gays, lesbians, bi and transsexuals.

Rostov-na-Donn - Rostov Region ☎ 08632

GENERAL GROUPS

Lyubov Sistem
PO Box 1143 ✉344 091 *LGB support group. Pen friend service.*

SKGK
PO Box 6161 ✉344 023 *North Caucasian Gay Club.*

Saratov - Saratov ☎ 08452

GENERAL GROUPS

Erotic Pen Friend Club
PO Box 3299 ✉410 054

CRUISING

-Lenin Park
-Shower Room on the beach of Hotel Zhemtshuzhina (late afternoon, when most people are leaving the beach)
-City Beach (between the harbor and Hotel Zhemtshuzhina)
-WC at the Circus
-At the Winter and Summer Theater
-»-Beach Teatralny (NU) (opposite Hotel Magnolie)
All are AYOR

St. Petersburg ☎ 812

GAY INFO

St. Petersburg´s Gay Web Site
Homepage: www.gay.spb.ru
Review of gay venues in St. Petersburg, news, info on the city.

BARS

Mono (AC B bf D G MA S) 22-6 h
4 Kolomenskaya ul. *(Metro Vladimirskaya/iJDostroevskaya)*
☎ 164 36 78 Homepage: www.monoc.ub.ru
Entrance fee US $ 2-4, Mondays men only. -Difficult for foreigners!
Club 69 (! AC B CC D DR F G MA S SNU STV VS YG) Tue-Thu, Sun 22-6 h. Fri, Sat 21-7 h
6 Vtoraya Krasnoarmeyskaya ul. ✉198005 *(Metro Tekhnologitchesky Institute)* ☎ 259 51 63 Homepage: www.club69.spb.ru
The oldest gay-club in St. Petersubrg, frequently visited by foreign tourists. Disco after 22, 2 bars, video hall, dark sex room. Entrance fee US$1-3. Special parties: Tue „Male Night", Thu, student pariy „Sexydance", Fri, Sat, „Crazy Male Strip".

CAFES

Michen (B GLM MA) Fri (gay parties) 18-22 h, Sat/Sun (lesbian parties) 18-22 h
62 Ol'ginskaya Allea *(Metro Udel'naya)* ☎ 554 02 93
Zsa-Lizu (A B F G s) 20-6 h
48 Shpalernaya ul. *(Metro Tchernishevskaya)* ☎ 110 09 28
Gay art cafe, erotic shows.

DANCECLUBS

Cabaret (B D DR f GLM MA S STV WE) Fri-Sat 23-6 h
5 Ploschad Truda *(The Sailor´s Club)* ☎ 312 09 34
Djungli (Jungle) (AC B D DR f GLM MA S WE) Fri-Sat 24-6 h
8 Blochina ul *(Metro Gorkowskaya/Sportivnaya)* ☎ 238 80 33
Entrance fee US $ 2, Shows begin at 1.30 h.
Kapris (B D gLm MA WE) Sunday evenings
3 Krzhizhanovskogo ul., korpus 1 *(Metro Ulitsa Dibenko)* ☎ 584 09 50
Lesbian cafe & disco.

SEX SHOPS/BLUE MOVIES

Intim (g)
2 Vosstania ul. *(Metro Ploschad Vosstaniya, 50 m from subway exit.)*
Russian gay magazines, etc.

SAUNAS/BATHS

Narciss (B DR f G MA msg P pi sa, VS YG) Tue-Sun 18-6 h
7/9 Krasnich Teckstil'tchikov ul. *(Near Smol'ninskie bani, 1st floor, left side, Metro Ploschad Vosstania))* ☎ 110 09 50
Entrance fee US $ 1 per hour.

Yamskie Bani (g sa sb) Wed-Sun 9-21 h
9 Pereulok Dostoevskogo *(Metro Vladimiskaya, Dostoevskaya, 3rd floor)* ☎ 312 58 36
At the showers area, popular place, especially interesting on Wed, Fri, Sat 18-21 h.

GENERAL GROUPS

Blue Sunrise Sistem 5-13
Ispolkomskaya ✉193167 ☎ 271 13 51 ☎ 305 04 88 Fax: 271 13 51 *ILGA Member.*

Krilijja
c/o Aleksander Kukharsky, a/b 108 ✉191186 ☎ 312 31 80 Fax: 312 31 80 E-Mail: krilija@ilga.org
ILGA-member.Gay and Lesbian Association, toursit agency, for for help, information and accommodation

HEALTH GROUPS

City Anti-AIDS Center
179-a Obvodnil Canal *(Metro Baltiskaya)* ☎ 259 94 05

SWIMMING

- Beach at old Finnish border. (Take train from Finland Railway Station (Finliandsky Vokzal). to Sestroretsky Kurort Station. From the station ca. 30 min. by foot along the sea side to the right up to the nudist beach.)

CRUISING

- Moskovyky Railway Station (Metro Vokzalnaya Ploschad, main hall, WC as well as WC at the other four city railway stations.).
- Small park near to the monument to Catherine the Great. (Metro Gostiny Dvor)
- Bolshoi Michailovsky Sad (Park behind the Russian Museum, Moika River embankment, Metro „Nevsky Prospekt), during daytime)
- WC at Sosnovsky Park (Metro „Tchernaya Retchka", bus 94/98 untill Svetlanovsky Prospekt.)
- WC at TSPKO (Kirov Recreation Park, Metro „Tchernaya Retchka.)

Twjer - Twjer Region ☎ 08222

GENERAL GROUPS

All Colors of the Rainbow
PO Box 2321 ✉170 023
Penfriends club for sexual minorities.

CRUISING

- Kazakov Square (on Sovetskaya ulitsa)
- Medical Academy Square (on Ploschad Revolutsii)

Vladivostok - Primorsky krai ☎ 04232

GAY INFO

Gay Vladivostok
Homepage: www.gay.ru/vladivostok
Info on gay life and venues in Vladivostok

BARS

Mandarin Club (B D f GLM) 18-3 h
51 a Krasnogo Znameni prospekt ☎ 25 56 09
Entrance fee US $ 2.

Voronezh - Voronezh Region ☎ 0732

HEALTH GROUPS

AIDS Center
109 Moskovsky Prospekt ✉39053 ☎ 145 440

Kirov - Vyatka ☎ 08332

DANCECLUBS

Green House Club (B D glm NG SNU WE) Thu-Sun 20-5 h
18 a Lomonossova Ulitsa

Senegal

Northwestern Coast of Africa
Initials: SN
Time: GMT
☎ Country Code / Access Code: 221 / 00
Language: Wolof and French
Area: 196,722 km² / 76,593 sq mi.
Currency: CFA Franc
Population: 9,723,150
Capital: Dakar
Religions: 92% Muslim
Climate: Hot and humid tropical climate. Rainy season (strong southeast winds) lasts from December to April, dry season from May to November.

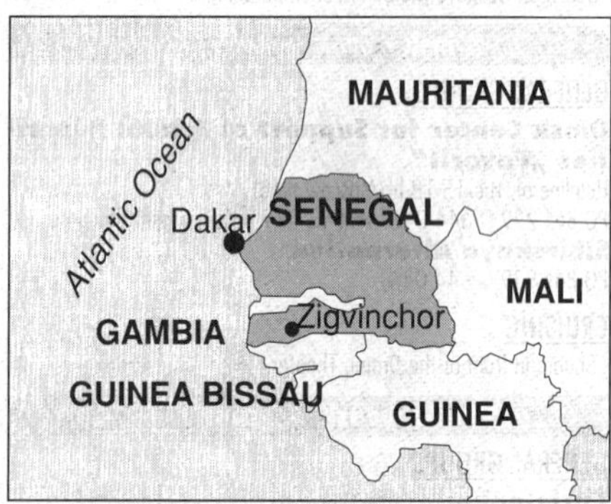

Thiaroye

BARS

Flamboyent. Le (B d F g T W) Tue-Sun 11-2 h
Route de Rufisque, km 21, Grand M'Bao *(20 km from Dakar)* ☎ 863 28 31
Bar & restaurant.

Singapore

Southeast Asia

Initials: SGP

Time: GMT +8

☎ Country Code / Access Code: 65 / 001

Language: Malay, Mandarin, Tamil and English

Area: 618 km^2 / 239 sq mi.

Currency: 1 Singapore Dollar (S$) = 100 Cents

Population: 3,491,000

Capital: Singapore

Religions: Buddhists and Taoists, Moslems and Christians.

Climate: Tropical climate, that is hot, humid and rainy. There are thunderstorms on 40% of all days, especially in April.

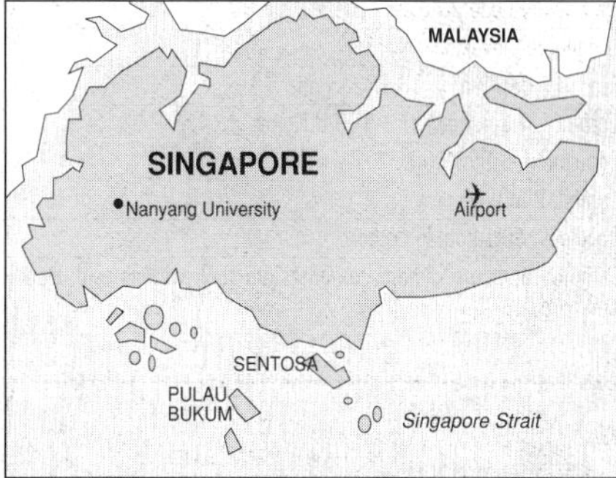

● Section 377 of the penal code punishes »offences against the order of nature« with 10 years to life imprisonment, and section 377a prohibits »gross indecency« between males, in public or private, with a maximum penalty of two years in prison. According to our information, the conduct of the police is prejudiced. Singapore's population is relatively young, as is the appearance of the city itself. It is characterized by high, modern buildings, as well as by streets and buildings which seem typically English. All the addresses listed below are straight-and-gay mixed. Favourite meeting places for Singaporean gays are Scotts Road and Orchard Road.

✱ Artikel 377 bestraft »Vergehen gegen die Natur« mit zehn Jahren bis zu lebenslanger Haft, und Abschnitt 377a sieht für öffentlich oder privat stattfindende »grobe Unzucht« zwischen Männern eine Gefängnisstrafe von bis zu zwei Jahren vor. Nach unseren Informationen verhält sich die Polizei diskriminierend. Die Bevölkerung von Singapur ist relativ jung. Ebenso jung ist das Stadtbild: Es wird geprägt durch moderne, hohe Bauten, aber auch durch Straßen und Gebäude, die sehr stark an England erinnern. Die unten angegebenen Adressen sind allesamt schwul-heterosexuell gemischt. Die singapurischen Schwulen treffen sich bevorzugt in der Scotts Road sowie der Orchard Road.

▲ A Singapour, l'homosexualité est un délit. Tout „crime contre nature" est puni de peines de prison allant de 10 ans à la perpétuité (article 377 du code pénal). On risque 2 ans de prison maximum pour „actes obscènes" entre hommes, en public comme en privé. D'après ce que nous savons, la police de Singapour fait tout pour rendre la vie impossible aux homosexuels et aux travestis.
Singapour est une ville jeune, aussi bien dans sa population que dans son architecture: gratte-ciels modernes, mais aussi quartiers rappelant étrangement l'Angleterre. Les adresses indiquées ci-dessous sont mixtes. Les gays de Singapour se retrouvent avant tout dans Scott Road et la Orchard Road.

☆ Artículo 377 del código penal castiga las «relaciones carnales contra la natura» con una pena desde 10 años de cárcel hasta cadena perpétua. El artículo 377 castiga «indecencias» entre hombres con una pena de hasta dos años de cárcel. Según nuestras informaciones, la polícia se comporta de manera discriminatória. La población de Singapur es relativamente joven. Igualmente joven es la imagen de la ciudad: está marcada por construcciones modernas y altas pero también por calles y edificios que recuerdan fuertemente a Inglaterra. Las direcciones citadas a continuación son de carácter mixto: frequentados por gays y heteros al mismo tiempo. Los gays de Singapur tienen su punto de reunión favorito tanto en las cercanías de la Scotts Road, como en la Orchard Road.

❖ La sezione 377 del codice penale punisce il „rapporto carnale contro natura" con la reclusione da 10 anni fino all'ergastolo, e la sezione 377a proibisce „l'indecenza volgare" fra uomini, in pubblico o in privato, con una pena massima di due anni di prigione. Secondo le nostre informazione la polizia discrimina i gay. La popolazione di Singapore è relativamente giovane. Anche il profilo architettonico della città è abbastanza giovane, connotato da palazzi alti e moderni, ma anche da strade ed edifici che ricordano molto alll'Inghilterra. Tutti gli indirizzi qui sotto indicati sono di locali a clientela mista. I gay di Singapore amano incontrarsi nell'area di Scotts Road come in quella di Orchard Road.

Singapore

BARS

Babylon Karaoke (B G VS) Sun-Thu 18-30-24 h, Fri,Sat 18.30-1 h
52 Tanjong Pagar Road ✉0208 *(Tanjong Pagar Metro Station)* ☎ 227 74 66

Boom Boom Boom. The (B g S) Tue-Thu 20.30-2 h, Fri, Sat -3 h
☎ 339 81 87
Call for location. Cover S$23 with 2 drinks. Male and female dancers. Comedy show.

Inner Circle Karaoke (B G VS) 78
Tanjong Pagar Road ✉0208 *(Tanjong Pagar Metro Station)*
☎ 222 84 62

Vincent's Lounge (B G)
304 Orchard Road, 06-05 Lucky Plaza ✉238863 ☎ 736 13 60

Vincent's Lounge II (B G) Sun-Thu 19-1 Fri/Sat -2 h
304 Orchard Road #06-01 Lucky Plaza ✉238863 *(Orchard Metro Station)* ☎ 732 06 69 *Karaoke.*

CAFÉS

Crossroads (B f g)
Scotts Road *(Marriot Hotel)*

Delifrance (B f g OS)
Scotts Road

Spinelli's (B f g)
Scotts Road (The Heren Building) *(opposite Mandarin Hotel)*

DANCECLUBS

Velvet Underground (B D F g OS YG) Thu-Sat
17, 19, 21 Jiak Kim Street ✉0316 ☎ 738 29 88

RESTAURANTS

El Felipe's Cantina Mexican Restaurant
(B AC F glm MA) Meals until 23 h
34 Jalan Mambong, Holland Village, 1027 ☎ 468 15 20
Reasonably priced mexican restaurant with excellent Margaritas and Enchiladas.

Pasta Italian Restaurant (AC B F glm MA)
23 Lorong Mambong, Holland Village, ✉1027 ☎ 467 09 17

HOTELS

Bencoolen (AC B F H OS)
47 Bencoolen Street ☎ 336 08 22
Downtown location, 20 min to the airport. Hotel with garden. All rooms (accessible without passing reception) are equipped with telephone, bathroom, and WC. Rates single from S$ 60.

Sea View Hotel (AC B D F g H pi sa sol)
Amber Close, Katong ☎ 345 22 22
Suburban location, 15 min from Gay Beach. There are no problems taking somebody into the rooms, which are equipped with telephone, kitchenette, priv. bath and balcony.

HEALTH GROUPS

Action for Aids 10-16.30 h
62b Raache Course Road ✉218568 ☎ 295 11 53
Fax: 295 55 67 E-Mail: bennijt@pacific.net.sg
Aids information & education. Anonymous HIV testing.

DSC STD Clinic Mon-Fri 9-17h, Sat 9-12 h, Sun closed
31 Kelantan Lane, Unit #02-16 ✉200 031 *(MRT-Bugis)*
☎ 293 96 48 Fax: 299 43 35 E-Mail: sg.aids@workmail.com
Anonymous HIV screening on saturdays 13-16 h. STD consultation Mon-Sat at office hours.

HELP WITH PROBLEMS

AIDS Helplines and Counselling Line Mon-Fri 8-17 h
☎ 254 16 11 (Helpline) ☎ 252 13 24

SWIMMING

-East Coast Parkway Beach (near »Big Splash« swimming pool, recommended; well known by Singaporean gays as »the Gay Beach«; particularly active with Singaporians on Sundays)
-Clark Hatch in Regent Hotel
-Westin-Stamford Hotel gym/sauna (Sat Sun 17-20 h. Be very discreet)

CRUISING

All cruisings are AYOR
-Lucky Plaza, Orchard Road (evenings)
-Orchard Road Pedestrain Mall (between Mandarin Hotel and Orchard Parade Hotel and between Marriot Hotel and The Paragon)

-Centrepoint, Orchard Road (cruisy Sat and Sun afternoon)
-Far East Plaza, Scotts Road
-Park Lane Shopping Mall, Selegie Road (Sun afternoon on all levels with a Singaporian crowd)
-River Valley Swimming Pool (opposite Liang Court Shopping Complex; be discreet!)
-Raffles City shopping lobby (near Westin Hotel)
-Raffles Place (called „The River, Chulia and Market Street, late)
-River Valley Swimming Pool (opposite Diamaru Shopping Centre)
-Takashimaya Shopping Centre (Orchard Road near the indoor waterfall area, Sat Sun afternoons)
-Orchard MRT station (evenings)

Slovakia

Slovensko

Central Europe

Initials: SK

Time: GMT +1

☎ Country Code / Access Code: 421 / 00

Language: Slovakian

Area: 49,035 km² / 18,932 sq mi.

Currency: 1 Koruna (Sk) = 100 Halierov

Population: 5,393,000

Capital: Bratislava

Religions: 60% Roman Catholic

Climate: Moderate climate. Summers are cool, winters cold, cloudy and humid.

● Homosexuality is not illegal, and the legal age of consent is fifteen. In the last few years, the public opinion of homosexuality has undergone considerable change. Following the establishment of gay and lesbian groups and organizations on the western model, more is heard of homosexuality in the media.

✱ Homosexualität ist nicht illegal. Die gesetzliche Schutzaltersgrenze liegt bei 15 Jahren. Die öffentliche Meinung hinsichtlich schwuler Themen hat sich in den letzten Jahren in positiv geändert. Nach der Gründung schwul-lesbischer Organisationen und Vereine nach westlichem Vorbild wird jetzt auch in den Massenmedien über Homosexualität mehr gesprochen und geschrieben. Die rechtliche Sitaution der Schwulen hat sich allerdings noch nicht verbessert.

▲ L'homosexualité n'est pas un délit en Slovaquie. La majorité sexuelle y est fixée à 15 ans. L'attitude de la population envers l'homosexualité a considérablement évolué ces derniers temps, car depuis qu'on a créé des associations et des groupes sur le modèle occidental, les médias abordent le sujet de plus en plus ouvertement.

☆ La homosexualidad es legal. La edad de consentimiento es de 15 años. La opinión pública en relación a la homosexualidad ha experimentado un cambio radical en los últimos años. Ahora, el tema de la homosexualidad se trata con más frecuencia en los medios de communicación, debido a la fundación de organizaciones gay y lesbianas, siguiendo modelos occidentales.

L'omosessualità non è illegale. L'età legale per avere dei rapporti sessuali è di 15 anni. Negli ultimi anni la gente ha cambiato di molto la propria opinione sugli omosessuali. Dopo la fondazioneà di organizzazioni gay e lesbiche secondo il modello occidentale, la stampa e la televisione trattano questo tema con crescente frequenza.

NATIONAL GAY INFO

Ganymedes
PO Box 4, Pošta 3 ✉83000 Bratislava ☎ (07) 25 38 88

Bratislava ☎ 07

BARS

Apollon G/L Klub (B d f glm p) Mon-Sun 18-2/? h
Panenská 24 ✉81000 ☎ 311 536
CD-Klub (B G MA) Mon-Sun 18-? h
Malé Pálenisko 44
D4 (Try Sudy) (AC B D DR F G VS) Mon-Sat 18-4 h
Jedlíkova ulica ☎ 310 913

SAUNAS/BATHS

Krytá Plaváren Pasiensky (g pi sa) Tue-Sun 10-20 h
Junácka ulica

HEALTH GROUPS

Ganymedes Helpline Mon Thu 17-20 h
☎ 25 38 88
Laboratory for AIDS-Institute of preventiv and clinical medicine
Limbova 14/Kramáre ☎ 37 35 60
Sexuologicke ambulancia N.P
Ružinovska 10
Dr. Castiglione.

SWIMMING

-Lake in Rusovce and in Rovinka near Bratislava

CRUISING

-Main railway station
-Hviezdoslavovo námestie
-Old Danube Bridge/university building/safarikovo námestie
-Jesenského Boulevard
-Park in front of Slovakian Philharmony „Reduta", near Slovak National Theatre (small park around, very busy)
-Park at State Hospital (Americké námestie) „Avion"

Handlová ☎ 0862

GENERAL GROUPS

Ganymedes SSL Pobočka
PO Box 47 ✉97251

Košice ☎ 095

GENERAL GROUPS

Ganymedes Košice
PO Box G 13 ✉043 43 01

Prievidza ☎ 0862

BARS

Expres Bar (g) 13-23 h
✉97101 *(near main railway station)*
G-Klub (g) 13-23 h
✉97101 *(near main railway and bus station)*

GENERAL GROUPS

Ganymedes Prievidza
PO Box 47, 97251 Handlová ✉97101

Trenčín ☎ 0831

GENERAL GROUPS

Ganymedes Trenčín
PO Box ✉91250

Trnava ☎ 0805

BARS

Bar Duha (B G MA) Mon-Sun 18-? h
Ulica Jana Milca 20 (24) ✉91701

Slovenia

Slovenija

Southeastern Europe

Initials: SLO

Time: GMT +1

☎ Country Code / Access Code: 386 / 00

Language: Slovenian

Area: 20,252 km² / 7,819 sq mi.

Currency: 1 Tolar (SIT) = 100 Stotin

Population: 1,972,000

Capital: Ljubljana

Religions: 70% Catholic

Climate: Mediterranean climate on the coast, continental climate with mild to hot summers and cold winters in the plateaus and valleys to the east.

● In Slovenia, the general age of consent is set at 14 years of age.

✱ In Slovenien liegt das Schutzalter allgemein bei 14 Jahren. Homosexualität wird von der Bevölkerung toleriert. Ein Gesetz, welches die Eintragung homosexueller Partnerschaften ermöglichen soll, ist in Vorbereitung.

▲ En Slovénie, la majorité sexuelle est en général à quatorze ans. L'homosexualité est tolérée. Une loi visant à permettre une inscription officielle des concubinages homosexuels est en préparation.

☆ En Eslovenia la edad de consentimiento es de 14 años.

❖ In Slovenia l'età legale per dei rapporti sessuali è di 14 anni.

NATIONAL GAY INFO

GALfon
☎ (0)61-132 40 89
Revolver
Kersnikova 4, ✉61000 Ljubljana ☎ (0)61-329 185
Fax: (0)61-329 185
Roza Klub
Kersnikova 4 ✉61000 Ljubljana ☎ (0)61-329 185
Fax: (0)61-329 185

Bled ☎ 064

CRUISING

-Beach between Toplice Hotel and the entrance to the bathing-place beneath Bled castle
-Beach on camping site Sobec

Celje ☎ 063

CRUISING

-Mestni Park (across the Savinja river)
-Railway station

Ljubljana ☎ 061

CAFES

Cafe Galerija (A B g) 10-24 h
Mestni trg 5 *(Old town)*
Magnus Café (A B GLM S) Fri Sat 20-? h, Wed, Thu, Sun - 24 h
Metelkova

DANCECLUBS

Klub K 4 (AC B D GLM MA S YG) Sun 22-4 h, Aug closed
Kersnikova 4 ☎ 132 40 89

GENERAL GROUPS

SKUC-Magnus
Kersnikova 4 ✉61000 ☎ 329 185

SWIMMING

-Beach on the Sava river (500m away from the Zagar Restaurant on the left bank. Popular in Jul/Aug)

CRUISING

-Park (AYOR) (by the railway behind the petrol station on the Tivolska cesta)
-Tivoli Park [P] (AYOR) (evenings)
-Railway station
-Old Town

Maribor ☎ 062

BARS

Stop (B glm MA) 18-23 h, Sun

CRUISING

-Park Ribnik (AYOR) (between the facility and the aquarium; 18-22 h)
-Railway station

Piran ☎ 066

SWIMMING

-Beach from Piran to Strunjan (nu)

CRUISING

-Coast walk (at night)
-Main street along coast in Portoroz (at night)

Ptuj ☎ 062

CRUISING

-City Park (epecially near Ribič)

South Africa

Suid-Afrika
Southern Africa
Initials: RSA
Time: GMT +2
☎ Country Code / Access Code: 27 / 09 or 091
Language: English, Afrikaans, Zulu, Xhosa, Tswana, Sotho, Swazi, Tsonga, Ndebele and Venda
Area: 1,221,037 km² /471,442 sq mi.
Currency: 1 Rand (ZAR) = 100 Cents
Population: 42,834,520
Capital: Cape Town (legislative capital) Pretoria (administrative capital)
Religions: 60% Christian
Climate: Mostly quite dry climate. Along the coast it's subtropical, days are sunny, nights are cool.

● South Africa is the only country of the world where it is a punishable offence to discriminate on grounds of sexual orientation. In contrast to other statesmen in the neighbouring states, such as Robert Mugabe from Zimbabwe who claims that „homosexuals are lower than pigs" and Sam Nujoma from Naibia who purports that homosexuals are „white perverts". Nelson Mandela has explicitly indicated in his vision of a „Rainbow Generation" that gays and lesbians have an equal standing in South Africa. It only remains a matter of time for the changes in South Africa to become legally recognisable. The A.N.C. supports equal rights and it will be even possible for gays and lesbians soon to get married. This positive development has lead naturally to a more visible gay scene and the emmergence of many new bars and clubs, particularly in the larger cities, such as Johannesburg, Pretoria, Cape Town and Durban.

Als bis jetzt einziges Land der Welt hat Südafrika in seiner Verfassung ausdrücklich auch die Diskriminierung aufgrund der sexuellen Orientierung unter Strafe gestellt. Im Gegensatz zu anderen Staatsmännern in den Nachbarstaaten wie z.B. Robert Mugabe (Zimbabwe), der behauptet hat „Homosexuelle seien niedriger als Schweine" und Sam Nujoma (Namibia), der Homosexuelle als „weiße Perverse" beschimpfte, hat Nelson Mandela die Schwulen und Lesben Südafrikas ausdrücklich als gleichberechtigte Bürger in seine Vision einer „Regenbogennation" mit eingeschlossen.
Noch müssen sich diese postiven Entwicklungen in Gesetzen niederschlagen, doch scheint es nur eine Frage der Zeit zu sein, bis dies geschieht. Der ANC will sich aktiv für die gesetzliche Gleichberechtigung von Homosexuellen einsetzen. Schwule und Lesben sollen sogar heiraten dürfen.
Dieses positive Umfeld hat natürlich dazu geführt, daß die schwule Szene immer sichtbarer wird, viele neue Bars und Clubs öffnen und sich Schwule und Lesben zunehmend in Gruppen organisieren, um ihre Interessen besser durchsetzen zu können. Diese Entwicklung ist aber momentan noch auf die größeren Städte wie Johannesburg, Pretoria, Kapstadt und Durban beschränkt.

L'Afrique du Sud est le seul pays au monde jusqu'à présent à inclure expréssement dans sa constitution un article visant la condamnation de la discrimination en raison des inclinations sexuelles. A l'inverse, d'autres chefs d'États de pays voisins comme Robert Mugabe (Zimbabwe), qui a déclaré que „les homosexuels sont plus bas que des porcs" et Sam Nujoma (Namibie) qui traite les homosexuels de „pervers blancs", Nelson Mandela a inclu les gays et lesbiennes d'Afrique du Sud dans sa vision d'une Nation „arc-en-ciel" en tant que citoyens égaux en droits. Ces décisions positives doivent encore être transformées en lois, mais cela ne semble être qu'une question de temps pour que cela se fasse. L'ANC veut s'engager activement pour l'égalité des droits des gays et lesbiennes. Ceux-çi devraient même avoir le droit de se marier. Tout cela mème au fait que la scène gay est devenue de plus en plus visible, que de nombreux bars et clubs ouvrent, et que les gays et lesbiennes s'organisent et se rassemblent en groupes pour mieux défendre leurs intêrets. Cette évolution ne concerne pour le moment que les villes de Johannesburg, Pretroria, Le Cap et Durban.

Sudáfrica es el único país en el mundo que prohibe en su legalización expresamente la discriminación de personas por causa de su orientación sexual. Mientras los presidentes de los estados vecinos rechazan los gays por completo, como por ejemplo Robert Mugabe (Zimbabue) quien dijó que los homosexuales „esten en un nivel más bajo que los cerdos" o Sam Nujoma (Namibia) que los insulta de ser „blancos pervertidos", su hómologo Nelson Mandela ha incluido los gays y lesbianas expresamente como ciudadanos con los mismos derechos en su concepto de la nación sudáfricana. Aunque todavía este desarollo positivo no se refleja en la legislación, parece ser solamente una cuestión de tiempo. El ANC afirmó su intención de luchar por los mismos derechos para gays y lebianas ante la ley, hasta se habló de la posibilidad de matrimonios homosexuales. Por esta base positiva el ambiente gay en las ciudades se hace notar cada vez más. Muchos bares y clubs han abierto últimamente y un gran número de gays y lesbianas se organizan ahora en grupos para hacer prevalecer mejor sus intereses. De momento este desarollo positivo se limita a grandes ciudades como Johanesburgo, Pretoria, Ciudad del Cabo o Durban.

Come unico paese al mondo la costituzione del Sudafrica contiene un paragrafo che condanna la discriminazione a seconda dell'orientamento sessuale. Al contrario degli uomini politici di altri stati africani, p.es. Robert Mugabe (Zimbabwe) che ha affermato che gli omosessuali siano inferiori ai maiali, e Sam Nujoma (Namibia) che ha insultato gli omosessuali chiamandoli „perversi bianchi"; Nelson Mandela ha incluso esplicitamente nella sua visione di una „nazione arcobaleno" i gay e le lesbiche sudafricani. Questi positivi sviluppi non trovano ancora riscrontro nelle leggi vigenti del paese, ma è solo questione di tempo fino a che questo avverrà. L'ANC si sta adoperando attivamente per l'equiparazione legale degli omosessuali. Secondo questo progetto, in futuro i gay e le lesbiche si potranno sposare. Quest'atmosfera positiva ha fatto sì che l'ambiente gay diventi sempre più visibile, che si aprono molti bar e club e che molti gay e lesbiche si uniscano sempre più numerevoli in gruppi per far valere i loro interessi. Al momento questo sviluppo si limita alle città più grandi come Johannesburg, Pretoria, Kapstadt e Durban.

NATIONAL GAY INFO

Exit Newspaper
PO Box 28827, Kensington ✉2101 ☎ (011) 622 2275
☎ & Fax: (011) 622 2275 E-mail exitnews@iafrica.com
Monthly gay and lesbian newspaper, published mainly in English. Information about events, venues, travel etc. Personal ads at US$ 10.

Gay SA
PO box 1910, Houghton ✉2041 ☎ (011) 648 9243
Fax: 487 1026 E-mail bek@icon.co.za
Homepage www.gaysa.co.za

National Coalition for Gay and Lesbian Equality (NCGLE)
PO Box 27811, Joubert Park ✉2044 ☎ (011) 487 3810
Fax: 339-7762 E-Mail: coalgr@iafrica.com

Outright
PO Box 3853, Halfway House ✉1685 2041 ☎ (011) 310 2633
Fax: 310 2643 E-Mail: outright@cis.co.za
Bimonthly glossy magazine, alternative lifestyles.

NATIONAL COMPANIES

Bare Wear
PO Box 1251, Scottburgh ✉4180
Men's underwear, swimwear, casualwear. Catalogue R 10.

CCCC
PO Box 1942, Cape Town ✉8000 ☎ & Fax: (021) 462 4019
Photographic books, calendars, magazines and novels. Catalogue for free.

Club International
Suite 251, P-Bag X31, Saxonwold ✉2132
Videos, magazines and books.

Barrydale - Western Cape ☎ 028

GUEST HOUSES

Greenman Cottage (bf G H lj msg NU pi)
1 Keerom Street ✉6750 ☎ 572 16 85

Tradouw Guest House (B bf glm H NU OS)
46 van Riebeeckstraat ✉6750 ☎ 572 14 34

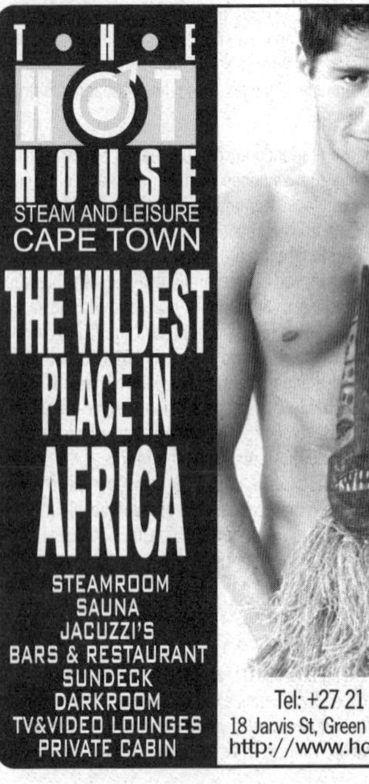

THE
HOT HOUSE
STEAM AND LEISURE
CAPE TOWN
THE WILDEST PLACE IN AFRICA
STEAMROOM
SAUNA
JACUZZI'S
BARS & RESTAURANT
SUNDECK
DARKROOM
TV&VIDEO LOUNGES
PRIVATE CABIN
Tel: +27 21 418 3888
18 Jarvis St, Green Point, Cape Town
http://www.hothouse.co.za

Benoni - Gauteng ☎ 011

BARS

Birdcage Club (B D G MA pi SNU STV)
50 Surprise Road, Brentwood Park ☎ 963 11 85

CRUISING

-Kleinfontein Dam (Warm Stream) (access can be gained via Swan Street; park car and walk through bushes and trees, very nice during late summer evenings)
-Benoni Plaza (WE evenings)
-Bus terminal

Bloemfontein - Free State ☎ 051

BARS

Club Buzerant Estate (B D G MA SNU)
Orange Grove Farm, Ferreira Road

HEALTH GROUPS

National Hospital 0-24 h
✉9301 ☎ 704 11

CRUISING

-FM Shopping Center (next to Bloemfontein Hotel)

Boksburg - Gauteng ☎ 011

CRUISING

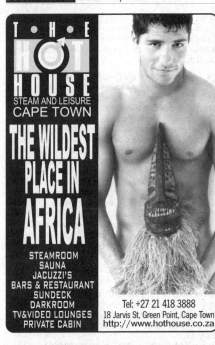

-Boksburg Lake (ayor) (close to Boksburg/Benoni Hospital. Very active. The whole Boksburg/Benoni side of the lake is used. From Johannesburg, follow Main Street out into R-23 Motorway. Leave the Motorway at the Boksburg Exit to the right, pass large „Pick & Pay" Hypermarket. Continue past „Pick & Pay" (now on your left) until you reach Cason Road at a T-junction. Turn left. Continue until next set of robots (traffic lights), where you turn right into Trichardweg. Pass the Cinderella Prison. 30 yards beyond the subway, turn right. Park the car in the car park and stroll along the dam wall or over the footbridge)
-Near Queens Hotel
-At „Pick & Pay", Hypermarket (9-17, Sat 9-13 h) (inside main entrance, turn right, 1st floor)

Brakpan - Gauteng ☎ 011

CRUISING

-Dam (opposite back entrance to Prince George Park sports ground)

Cape Town/Kaapstad - Western Cape ☎ 021

TOURIST INFO

„Friends" in Travel
5 Sommerset Road, Greenpoint *(Corner of Chiappini)*
☎ 421 13 33 ☎ (083) 444 85 55 (mobile) Fax: 421 13 28
Available 24 hrs 7 days a week. Members of IGLA
Gay Escape Travel (G)
105 Highlevel Road, Green Point ☎ 439 38 29 Fax: 439 38 61
GayNet Cape Town
☎ 422 19 25 ☎ 422 19 26 Fax: 422 19 95
E-Mail: info@gaynetcapetown.co.za
Homepage: www.gaynetcapetown.co.za
SAGALETI (Southern Africa´s Gay & Lesbian Travel Information Service
☎ (082) 693 41 06 (mobile) Fax: (011) 622 22 75
E-Mail: sagaleti@freemail.co.za
For all travel exquiries arround Southern Africa, including accommodation or special interests.

BARS

Blah Bar (B CC GLM) Mon-Sat 12-? h, Sun 17-? h
21 A Somerset Road, Green Point ☎ 419 55 99
Extravagance & Imagination sum up. Cape Town´s newest and trendiest cocktail bar.
Bronx Action Bar (B GLM MA) 20-? h, daily
Somerset Street, Green Point *(Corner of Sommerset & Napier Stree)* ☎ 419 85 47
Three bars, very popular.
Brunswick (B f Glm MA STV SNU) Mon-Sat 9-? h, Sun 10-? h
17 Bree Street *(Upstairs)* ☎ 25 27 39
Popular at evenings, solo cabaret artists and well known troupes, 2 bars, dance floor, restaurant.
Company. The (B DR G LJ MA OS VS) 21-? h
16 Hudson Street ☎ 21 53 05

CAFES

Domino's Café-Bistro-Bar (AC B bf CC F glm MA N WE) Mon-Sat 7.30-? h
100 Main Road, Sea Point ✉8001 ☎ 434 71 47
Obz Café (B bf F glm OS) Mon-Sat 9.30-23.30 h, Sun 18-22.30 h
115 Lower Main Road, Observatory ☎ 448 55 55

DANCECLUBS

Angel's (! AC B D DR glm YG) Fri-Sat22-? h
27 Somerset Road, Green Point ☎ 419 85 47

Detour (AC B D DR) Fri, Sat, public holidays 24-? h, in high season open every night.
Sommerset Road, Green Point
Cape Town´s top DJ´s playing international techno and uplifting house.

RESTAURANTS

Beehive (B CC F glm MA N OS s) Mon-Fri 12-2 h
56 Waterkant Street ✉8001 ☎ 419 75 74
Da Vinci (B CC F g)
Shop # 7, Glencairn Shopping Centre, Simon's Town ☎ 782 28 41
Firemansarms. The (AC B CC F g OS W) Mon-Sat 10.30-22.30 h
25 Mechau Street/Buitengracht ✉8001 ☎ 419 15 13
English pub & restaurant.

SEX SHOPS/BLUE MOVIES

Adult World (AC CC DR g MA VS) Mon-Sun 9-0 h
174 Main Road, Claremont ☎ 683 44 14
Adult World (AC CC DR g MA VS) Mon-Sat 9-? h, Sun 12-? h
36 Riebeek Street ✉8001 ☎ 418 74 55
Adult World (AC CC DR g MA VS) Mon-Sat 9-? h, Sun 12-? h
22 Spin Street, Parow Industria ☎ 933 20 29
Wet Warehouse (CC DR G SNU VS) Mon-Sat 9.30-19
1 Sea Street ☎ 419 04 58

ESCORTS & STUDIOS

Descreet (CC G msg R)
13 Glynnwill Terrace ☎ 465 17 30 ☎ (082) 705 1413 (mobile)
Elegant Victorian villa for a discreet rendezvous with highly qualified and talented masseurs. Decidedly upmarket and discreet.
Knights (G msg R) 0-24 h
Atlantic Seaboard ☎ 434 04 28
Their castle offers a nightly massage by hot, friendly, diverse knights.
Stallions (G msg R SNU) 11-2 h, daily
Beach Road, Sea Point ☎ 439 45 52
Good looking studs for massage and escorting. Strippers available, Upmarket, discreet, shower facilities, in/out and overnight service, secure paring.
The Barracks (G msg Vs SNU R) 24 h
20 Scott Street, Gardens ☎ 465 79 00
One of Cape Town´s newest upmarket massage studios. Easily accessible and discreet. One way viewing, videos, shower facilites, singles and couples.

SAUNAS/BATHS

Club Welgelegen (G H pi sa sb wh WO) 18-24 h
51 William Street, Mowbray ☎ 448 62 02
Entrance R 20 Also guest house, saltwater pool, WE restaurant.
The Hot House - Steam & Leisure (! AC B bf CC DR F G MA OS p sa sb VS wh YG) Mon-Thu 12-2 h, Fri 12-Mon 2 h
18 Jarvis Street, De Waterkant ☎ 418 38 88
Luxurious double volume lounge with 2 bars, restaurant, fireplace & satellite TV,. Steamroom, sauna, 2 spas, private cabins, video lounge, labyrinth & showers. Spectacular views from sundeck.
Steamers (AC B G MA pi sa sb sol VS wh WO) Mon-Thu 12-2, Fri 12-Mon 2 h
Wembly Road/Solar Road, Gardens ✉8000 ☎ 461 62 10

LEATHER & FETISH SHOPS

Sgt. Pepper`s (NG) 8.45-16.45 h, Sun closed
32 Shortmarket Street ☎ 23 20 01
Leather/Army clothing, boots, stickers, flags, jewelry.

TRAVEL & TRANSPORT

Africa Outing (CC GLM MA)
9 Allyone Road , Claremont ✉7708 ☎ 671 40 28 ☎ 683 7377E-Mail: afouting@iafrica.com
Gay Tour Operator.

BeauSéjour
☎ 788 27 10 Fax: 788 27 10 (John or Ken).
Custom tours of the Peninsula and Winelands.

GUEST HOUSES

Amsterdam (bf G H NU wh)
19 Forest Road ✉Oranjezicht 8001 ☎ 461 82 36
Fax: 461 55 75 E-Mail: ams@netactive.co.za
Homepage: www.amsterdam.co.za
Centrally located with stunning views. 9 double rooms, 3 single rooms. All rooms with bath/WC, TV, video, phone, own key. Fully equiped Gym. Fax, internet, laundry and airport shuttle awailable. Rates ZAR 150-350 pp sharing, ZAR 175-450 pp single.

Bayview Bed & Breakfast (bf g H OS)
12 Harrington Road, Simon's Town/Seaforth , Cape P. ✉7995
☎ 786 33 87 Fax: 786 33 87 E-Mail: bayview@yebo.co.za
Homepage: www.peninsulainfo.co.za/bayview
45 km south of Cape Town. 2 rooms, 1 with private bath/WC, 1 room with shared bath. Both rooms with TV and a terrace with bayview. Beaches in walking distance. Rates single ZAR 110-150 and double ZAR 160-240 (bf incl.). Weekly rates available.

Kinnert & Oliver Guest Houses (bf CC g H MA NU OS) 0-24 h
11 Arthurs Road, Sea Point *(Airport shuttle on request)*
☎ 439 92 37 Fax: 434 89 98.
Victorian style guest house. All rooms double. Close to Victoria & Alfred waterfront, olympic sized pool. Prices on request.

Lady Victoria (bf G H)
1 Kelvin Street, Upper Gardens ✉8001 ☎ 23 38 14
All rooms with en-suite bathrrom, TV, phone, radio.
Rates on request.

Liberty Lodge B & B (AC bf CC E F g H OS)
33 de Lorenth Street, Tamboerskloof ☎ 23 22 64 Fax: 23 22 74
E-Mail: liblodge@iafrica.com
Rates from ZAR 230-380, incl. bf.

Little Lemon. The (bf CC H G OS pi)
9 Antrim Road, Green Point ✉8001 ☎ 439 19 90
Fax: 434 42 09

Moorings (bf G H OS pi)
57 Belmont Avenue, Oranjezicht ✉8001 ☎ 461 00 81
Fax: 461 00 87

Quarters. The (G H)
76 Waterkant Street, De Waterkant ✉8001 ☎ 419 14 79
☎ (082) 557 08 24 (mobile) Fax: 21 59 14
Centrally located in the gay scene. Rooms with bath/WC, TV, phone and mini-bar.

Richborough Villa (AC b bf CC G H MA N OS) All year
5 Highworth Road, Sea Point ✉8001 *(Approx. 5 minutes to city center)* ☎ 443 465 50 Fax: 434 84 59
E-Mail: Tim@richborough.co.za
Homepage: www.Richborough.co.za
Central location. All rooms with bath/WC and TV and tea/coffee. 5 minutes walk to beach, clubs & nightbars close by. Own Keys. (See Richborough Villa Country Retreat)

Stanmar (B bf F G pi sa sb wh WO)
47 Williams Street, Observatory ☎ 448 20 14 Fax: 448 20 14

Twenty Nine (bf CC glm msg pi OS s sa wo)
29 Atholl Road, Camps Bay ✉8005 ☎ 438 3800 Fax: 438 3801
E-Mail: info@twentynine.net Homepage: www.twentynine.net
Within walking distance to the beach and downtown. 25 mins to airport. Pick up service available. 5 Double rooms

Verona Lodge (bf CC g H)
11 Richmond Road, Three Anchor Bay ✉8001 ☎ 434 94 77
Fax: 434 94 77
Five rooms with shower/WC, phone, fax, TV, video, minibar, own key.

PRIVATE ACCOMODATION

Abs-Fab (g H)
1 Albany Rd., Sea Point ☎ 439 40 67
Fax: 439 74 39 E-Mail: tdacpt@iafrica.com
Gay owned. 3 minutes walk from beach, and entral to shops and restaurants. Rates: from 130 ZAR per double room.

Le Freak
☎ +34-971-39 58 84 (international) *Private Guest House.*

Parker Cottage (bf G H)
3 Carstens Street, Tamboerskloof ✉8001 ☎ 424 64 45
Fax: 424 64 45 E-Mail: parkerco@mweb.co.za
Homepage: www.gaynetcapetown.co.za/parker_cottage.htm
Accommodation in gracious Victorian home. Four imaginatively decorated bedrooms. Continental/Health breakfast. Personal service, central location. Close to gay locations. Rates double from ZAR 195/single ZAR 280 per person and night.

Richborough Villa Country Retreat (AC B bf CC G MA N NU OS pi) All year
Hof Street, Riebeeck West ✉7306 *(90 km outside of Cape Town in the vinelands)* ☎ 022/461 2289 Fax: 022/461 2335
E-Mail: Tim@richborough.co.za
Homepage: www.Richborough.co.za
Self catering or B&B (meals on request). All rooms ensuite with bath/shower and WC, TV, AC. Secluded pool in olive grove. 90 km from central Cape Town in Riebeeck Valley winelands. Restaurants and pubs nearby. Wine tasting on surrounding wine farms possible.

HEALTH GROUPS

ATIC (Aids Training Information Counselling Centre)
☎ 400 34 00
Gay/Lesbian/Bisexual Helpline Mon-Fri 13-17 h, Sat-Sun 13-21 h
☎ 222 50
Triangle Project 9-17 h
Community House, 41 Salt River Road, Salt River ✉7925
☎ 448 38 12 Fax: 448 40 89 E-Mail: triangle@icon.co.za
Health information, couselling & support..

RELIGIOUS GROUPS

Gay Christian Community Sun 17.30 h at Quaker House, Hornsey Road/Rye Roda, Mowbray ✉7700
PO Box 36 137, Glosderry ✉7702 ☎ 61 27 50

SPORT GROUPS

Cape Organization for Gay Sports (COGS)
☎ 557 71 95

SWIMMING

-Graaff's Pool (NU g) (Sea Front Road, Sea Point. Opposite Winchester mansions Hotel, men only swimming area)
-Sandy Bay Beach (AYOR G NU) (Take M6 to Hout Bay and leave in Llangdudno)
-Clifton Beach (very nice beach)

CRUISING

all AYOR
-Sandy Bay, Llandudno (!)
-Beach and promenade along ocean in Sea Point (all night long, especially around Graaf's pool)
-Adelphi Centre, Main Rd., Sea Point

Durban - Kwazulu/Natal ☎ 031

BARS

Axis (B D Glm SNU)
4 Rutherford Street/Gillespie ☎ 32 26 03
Late Night Galleon (AC B bf d DR F G MA S) 9-4 h
Shop 5B, Nedbank Circle, 577 Point Road ☎ 32 46 89

CAFES

Garth`s Place (B f G MA) 10-24 h, Mon closed
Avonmore Centre, 9th Avenue/Clarence ☎ 23 73 28

DANCECLUBS

Pandora's (B D Glm YG) 21-? h
27 Hunter Street

SEX SHOPS/BLUE MOVIES

Fantasies (GLM)
320 West Street, Shop 113, 4001 *(1st floor)* ☎ 304 14 08
Sex toys and condoms. Ask for mail-order catalogue.

GENERAL GROUPS

Gayline Durban
PO Box 11744, Marine Parade ✉4056 ☎ 37 57 84
KwaZulu-Natal Provincial Coalition for Gay and Lesbian Equality
PO Box 30890, Mayville ✉4058 ☎ 260 11 49

HEALTH GROUPS

AIDS Foundation KwaZulz/Natal
☎ 21 33 03
Open Door
Room 1116, Colonial Towers, 332 West Street ☎ 304 67 01
HIV/Aids drop-in centre.

RELIGIOUS GROUPS

Grace MCC
☎ 23 04 05

SWIMMING

-Battery Beach (opposite Blue Waters Htl., especially WE)
-Beachwood (7 km north, turn off Northern Freeway at Beachwood sign, follow sign to Nature Reserve, turn left to dunes, very active)
-Rachael Finlayson Baths (g WE) (in the showers)

CRUISING

-Beach by Ocean Cinema (AYOR) (opposite Holiday Inn; night only)
-Battery Beach (opposite Blue Waters Hotel and down the beach to the Snake Park, 24 hrs, AYOR)
-City Square (AYOR) (opposite city hall)
-Toilets in Beach View Mall (opposite Killarney Hotel)
-Beachfront (from Addington to North Beach, esp. at night, AYOR)
-Toilets in „The Workshop" shopping centre (near City Hall)
-Beachwood (carpark, beach, toilets and dunes, NU, R, AYOR)
-AVN, 25 Woodford Grove, Stamford Hill

East London - Eastern Cape ☎ 082

BARS

Thumpers (B d g MA)
Recreation Road

GUEST HOUSES

The Castle Bed and Breakfast (b bf CC F H OS pi)
13 Acacia Drive, Beacon Bay ✉5241 ☎ 492 09 81 (mobile)
Fax: 47 38 66

HELP WITH PROBLEMS

St. Mary's Home for PWA's
☎ 43 75 17

CRUISING

-Eastern Beach (entire beachfront)

Franschhoek - Western Cape ☎ 021

HOTELS

Dieu Donné Guest Farm (g H)
PO Box 569 ✉7690 ☎ 876 21 31 Fax: 876 37 76
50 min. from Cape Town. 30 min. from Stellenbosch. 20 min. from Paarl.

Hermanus - Western Cape ☎ 028

GUEST HOUSES

Die Seemeeue (bf f GLM H)
60 Ghwarrieng Crescent, Vermont, Onrus River *(5 km from Hermanus, 110 km from Cape town.)* ☎ 316 24 79
☎ (0)83-763 65 72 (mobile) Fax: 316 24 79
3 double rooms and 1 apartment incl. WC/bath/shower. Rates from ZAR 100 per person and night.Close to beaches and nature reserves

Johannesburg - Gauteng ☎ 011

BARS

The Balcony Bar (B DR f G MA msg N OS SNU STV VS)
1st floor, 430 Commissioner Street, Fairview
Cactus Club (B D G MA SNU)
Tyrwhitt Avenue, Rosebank
Champions (B D F GLM MA OS s)
Wolmarans/Rissik Streets, Braamfontein *(Old Academy Theatre)*
☎ 725 26 97
Connections (B f g MA R) 11-2 h
1 Pretoria Street, Hillbrow *(in Hillbrow between Clarendon and Klein Street)* ☎ 642 85 11
Gotham City/58 (! B D DR G MA r S VS WE) 11-? h
58 Pretoria Street, Hillbrow
Jeb's Leather Bar (B DR lj MA)
2 Carnarvon Road, Bertrams
Minellis (B D glm OS YG)
Oxford Road, Rosebank
Trendy.
Skyline (B G MA R)
Harrison Reef Hotel, Pretoria Street, Hillbrow
Black scene.
Zoo (B DR lj MA SNU u VS)
Hopkins Street, Yeoville *Jack-off parties at weekend.*

RESTAURANTS

Caffe della Salute (B F g MA OS)
Sandton Square
La Contadina Restaurant (B CC F GLM MA OS) Mon-Thu 11-20, Fri Sat -23, Sun 9-17 h
12 Gleneagles Road, Greenside ☎ 486 26 26
Mea Culpa (B F g MA)
12 Keyes Avenue/Tyrwhitt, Rosebank ☎ 447 45 43
Thin Lyzzeez (B F g lj s)
Langermann Drive, Kensington
Pool table, bikers.

SHOWS

Market Theatre ☎ 834 20 46
Gay plays are sometimes featured. Call for information

SEX SHOPS/BLUE MOVIES

Garage Video Den (G VS) 12.30-19 h
54 Nottingham Road, Kensington ☎ 622 22 75
The Love Inn (G)
212 Lower Level, Carlton Centre, Commissioner Street
☎ 331 9531
Luv Land (g) Mon-Fri 8.30-18, Sat 9-15 h
Valley Centre, 396 Jan Smuts Avenue, Craighall Park *(Lower Level)*
☎ 789 81 03
Priapus (G VS) 11-20 h
Victory/Quinn, Parkhurst, Suite 251, P-Bag X31, *Saxonwold 2132*
☎ 880 83 16
Underground (CC DR G MA SNU VS) Mon-Thu Sat 9-19, Fri -23, Sun 11-19 h
10 Gleneagles Road, Greenside *(Entrance through Esteem books)*
☎ 880 8316
Video shows.

BOOK SHOPS

Esteem Books (CC G MA) Mon-Thu Sat 9-19, Fri -23, Sun 11-19 h
10 Gleneagles Road, Greenside ☎ 486 26 26

TRAVEL & TRANSPORT

Out in Africa Tours (CC GLM MA) 7-18 h
PO Box 2431, Cresta ✉2118 ☎ 852 78 07 Fax: 476 15 80
E-Mail: outin@iafrica.com

GUEST HOUSES

Graton (bf CC g H OS pi wh)
PO Box 92283, Norwood ✉2117 ☎ 728 23 40
☎ (082) 451 33 71 (mobile) Fax: 782 08 55

GENERAL GROUPS

National Caolition for Gay and Lesbian Equality
c Rockey Street, Yeoville ☎ 487 38 10

HEALTH GROUPS

AIDS Outreach
17 Esselen Street, Hillbrow ☎ 725 67 14 ☎ 725 67 24
AIDS information and support group.
Friends for life ☎ 922 40 00
Aids and HIV-positive support group.
Oasis Sat 15-19 h
Agstelaan 128, Mayfair ☎ 402 81 01
The Community Aids Info And Support Center
☎ 67 10 ☎ 61 11
The Living Sober Group Wed 19.30 h
c/o Yeoville Recreation Center ☎ 622 97 07
Branch of Alcoholics Anonymous for mainly gay people who have a drinking problem.

RELIGIOUS GROUPS

Gay Christian Community/Gay Christen Bond Sun at 17.30 h at Quaker House, 3 Gordon Terrace, Dornfontein
☎ 726 36 20

SPECIAL INTEREST GROUPS

JoBears
PO Box 5764 ✉2000 ☎ 616 56 20 Fax: 616 56 20
E-Mail: jobears@iafrica.com

SPORT GROUPS

The Organisation for Gay Sports (TOGS)
PO Box 462, Melville ✉2109 Fax: 802 55 89
E-Mail: tdal@sun.co.za
Homepage: www.icon.co.za/~stobbs/togs.htm
Offers hiking, running, tennis, squash, line dancing, volleyball, rugby.

CRUISING

-Rhodes Park, Kensington (AYOR) (below swimming bath)
-Zoo Lake, Saxonwold (AYOR)
-The Rose Garden, Emmarentia Dam (AYOR)

Kimberley - Northern Cape

BARS

Stallions (B D GLM)
c/o Queens Hotel, Stockdale.

Ohrigstad ☎ 013

GUEST HOUSES

Hannah Lodge (bf B CC glm H OS pi)
PO Box 98 ✉1122 ☎ 238 04 83 Fax: 238 03 34
Rates for double room ZAR 285-385, half-board.

Port Elizabeth - Eastern Cape ☎ 041

BARS

Rich`s (B GLM)
Cnr. Strand & Kemp Streets ☎ 992 16 64
Zips Club (B G MA) Wed Fri Sat 21-? h
Hancock/Drury Streets, North End ☎ 54 68 46

CRUISING

-Beach near Oceanarium
-Park in front of Edward Hotel (Donkin Memorial)
-Lighthouse Hill (at night)

Pretoria - Gauteng ☎ 012

GAY INFO

Ikhaya Lothingo („Home of the Rainbow")
(B GLM) Center Mon-Fri 10-22 h, Office Mon-Fri 10-15, Info Hotline Mon-Thu 19-22 h, Coffee Shop 10-22 h daily.
133 Verdoorn St., Sunnysidef ☎ 012/344 65 01/02
The Pretoriea gay and lesbian community center houses all GLO-P services. The Gay and Lesbian Organisation-Pretoria (GLO-P) was formed in 1993 and provides services aimed at promoting the well-being of lesbians, gays, bisexuals and transgender individuals. The center includes the office of a local gay and lesbian church as well as the Positive Women organisation and the Uthingo community coffe shop.

BARS

Cock's Eye (B F GLM MA OS STV VS) 12-? h
95 Gerard Moerdyk Street, Sunnyside ☎ 341 69 14
Bar and restaurant.
Pancake Palace (B f GLM) Mon & Thu 15.30-24 h, other days 10-24 h.
109 Gerard Moerdyk St., Sunnyside

DANCECLUBS

Jordan´s (B D GLM STV) 22-? h, daily
Hamilton Park Center, Arcadia *(Corner of Schoeman and Hamilton Street)* ☎ (083) 729 22 25 (mobile)
Cabere on Sundays, Wednesdays karaoke.
Stardust (B D GLM STV) 20-? h, daily
Pretorius Street ☎ 342 75 09
3000 square meters of gay clubbing. 3 dance floors, 10 bars. Drag shows are Sunday nights at 21.30 h.

RESTAURANTS

Blue Crane (B F glm OS)
Boshoff Street/Melk Street, Nieu Muckelneuk ☎ 346 28 48

SEX SHOPS/BLUE MOVIES

Adam (G VS)
179 Gordon Road, New Colbyn Center, Colbyn ☎ 342 43 95
Gay adult shop & mail order.
Adult World (G DR VS)
388 Pretoius St. Central

SAUNAS/BATHS

The Rec Room (DR G MA P sa sb VS wh) Fri-Sun 15-3, Mon-Thu 17-1 h
135 Church Street West ☎ 327 21 63

TRAVEL & TRANSPORT

Ulysses Tours & Safaris (g)
PO Box 13533 Hatfield ✉0028 ☎ 346 46 12
☎ (0)82 566 55 06 (mobile) Fax: 346 58 97
E-Mail: ulysses@lantic.co.za
Homepage: www.ulysses.co.za

GENERAL GROUPS

The Deaf Association for the Gays of Southern Africa (DAGSA)
60 Kantoor Avenue, Lynn East 0186 ☎ 800 38 85

HEALTH GROUPS

Embassy Drive Medical Centre Mon-Fri 8-17 h
1001 Pretorius Street, Hatfield ☎ 342 57 06 Fax: 342 57 81
HIV information and treatment. Assistance for medically callenged travellers. Call first.

CRUISING

- Springbok Park.(Corner of Hilda and Schoeman St., Hatfiled.)
- Burgerspark. (Opposite Hoiday Inn Garden Court, van der Walt st.)
- Central (AYOR, R)
- Austin Roberts Bird Sanctuary (behind the art gallery, New Muckleneuk.)

Randburg - Gauteng ☎ 011

GUEST HOUSES

Lala Kahle (b g H)
☎ 793 53 74

Robertson

GUEST HOUSES

Fraai Uitzicht 1798 - Historic Wine & Guestfarm (A b bf CC F glm MA N OS pi) 9-20 h, for hotel guests longer
Klas Voogles East (R60) *(Central located in Robertson Wine Valley, near Hofsprings, between Robertson and Aukton)* ☎ 626 61 56
E-Mail: fraai_uitzicht@lando.co.za
Homepage: www.lando.co.za/fraaiuitzicht
Rates: double ZAR 330, single ZAR 240 and Appartments ZAR 150 + ZAR 90 per person. All rooms are with WC/shower, TV.

Stellenbosch - Western Cape ☎ 021

GUEST HOUSES

Evergreen Lodge (bf CC glm H)
Cnr. Bosman & Murray Streets ✉7612 ☎ 886 68 32
Fax: 883 84 49.

Wilderness ☎ 0441

GUEST HOUSES

Palms Wilderness (B bf CC glm F H msg pi)
PO Box 372 ✉6560 ☎ 877 14 20 Fax: 877 14 22
E-Mail: Palms@pixie.co.za
Located in Wilderness National Park, 2 min. from the beach.

Spain

España - (Including Balearic and Canary Islands)

Southwest Europe

Initials: E

Time: GMT +1

☎ Country Code / Access Code: 34 / 07 (wait for tone)

Language: Castilian, Catalan, Basque, Galician (Gallego)

Area: 504,750 km² / 194,884 sq mi.

Currency: 1 Peseta (Pta). 1 EURO = 100 EURO Cents (The Euro can only be used in the clearance system)

Population: 39,754,000

Capital: Madrid

Religions: 99% Roman Catholic

Climate: Moderate climate. Summer in the interior is clear and hot, more moderate and cloudy along the coast. Winters are cloudy and cold in the interior, partly cloudy and cool along coast.

Important gay cities: Madrid, Barcelona, Ibiza, Sitges, Playa del Inglés (Gran Canaria), Torremolinos, Benidorm, Sevilla and Valencia

● The general age of consent is 16 years. However, to avoid any trouble with the law, you should steer clear of men under the age of 18 if you yourself are above it. Spain today lies right in the cultural center of Europe. To this, the autonomity of the Spanish provinces, as well as hosting major international events, has contributed much. Gay Spaniards have become very self-confident, and the gay scene is very communicative, open and interesting. Madrid and Barcelona are, of course, the centres of activity, but a number of beach resorts are also of importance: Sitges, Ibiza, Torremolinos, Palma de Mallorca, Benidorm and Lloret de Mar. In winter, a favourite meeting place for gays is Playa del Ingles on Gran Canaria. After all, Spain is Europe's number one holiday spot!

✱ Zwar liegt das allgemeine Schutzalter bei 16 Jahren; wer aber keinerlei rechtliche Gefahren eingehen möchte, sollte, wenn er über 18 Jahre ist, Männer unter 18 Jahren meiden. In Madrid gibt es ebenso wie in Katalonien eine Eingetragene Partnerschaft. Allerdings hat dies nur Auswirkungen auf Rechte, die in die Kompetenz der Provinz fallen wie z.B. Erbrecht, Mietrecht und Vertretungsrecht. Auf Landesebene ist ein ähnlicher Gesetzesentwurf am Widerstand der konservativen Regierung gescheitert.
Doch die schwulen Spanier sind sehr selbstbewußt geworden, und die Szene präsentiert sich interessant, kommunikativ und frei.
Barcelona und Madrid sind natürlich die Zentren. Bedeutend sind aber auch eine Reihe von Badeorten: Ibiza, Sitges, Torremolinos, Palma de Mallorca, Benidorm und Lloret de Mar. Im Winter trifft man sich in Playa del Ingles auf Gran Canaria. Schließlich ist Spanien Europas Reiseland Nr. 1!

▲ En Espagne, la majorité sexuelle est fixée à 16 ans. Soyez quand même prudents avec les mineurs de moins de 18 ans, si vous voulez éviter les ennuis. L'Espagne a retrouvé sa place au sein des grandes nations culturelles d'Europe, et ce grâce à la volonté et au tempérament de chacune de ses provinces et aux nombreuses manifestations culturelles ou sportives internationales. Les gays espagnols ont acquis une certaine assurance, les lieux gays sont intéressants, variés et animés. Madrid et Barcelone se disputent le titre de capitale gaye du pays. Mais n'oublions pas non plus les stations balnéaires gayes de Sitges, Ibiza, Torremolinos, Palma de Mallorca, Benidorm et Lloret de Mar. En hiver, on se retrouve à la Playa del Ingles sur Gran Canaria. L'Espagne est la destination touristique gay numéro 1 en Europe!

☆ Aunque la edad de consentimiento es de 16 años, para evitar problemas, se deberían evitar relaciones con jovenes menores de 18 años. En Madrid es posible el registro de parejas homosexuales. Estas „parejas de hecho", parecidas al matrimonio, no pueden ser comparadas con las de los paises del Norte de Europa, ya que tienen poco valor legal.
Los homosexuales españoles tienen hoy en día mucho más autoconfianza, y el ambiente es muy interesante, comunicativo y libre.
Madrid y Barcelona son los centros gay del país. Importantes son también los centro turísticos de Sitges, Ibiza, Torremolinos, Palma de Mallorca, Benidorm y Lloret del Mar. En invierno los gays se reunen en la Playa del Inglés en Gran Canaria. Yaque España se ha convertido en el país turístico número 1 de Europa.

❖ L'età legale per avere dei rapporti sessuali è di 16 anni, chi è già diciottenne però per evitare ogni pericolo dovrebbe scegliersi compagni maggiorenni. La Spagna si trova oggi nel centro culturale dell'Europa. A ciò hanno contribuito l'ostinatezza delle provincie spagnole per l'organizzazione di grandi avvenimenti internazionali. I gay spagnoli si sono emancipati e l'ambiente si presenta interessante, comunicativo e libero. Madrid e Barcellona sono naturalmente i centri più importanti, sono però di grande interesse anche alcuni centri balneari: Sitges, Ibiza, Torremolinos, Palma de Mallorca, Benidorm e Lloret de Mar. In inverno ci si incontra sulla playa del ingles alla Gran Canaria. In Europa la Spagna è la meta turistica numero uno.

NATIONAL GAY INFO

Atrevete
c/o Chavez, Quintana 20, 3 ✉28008 Madrid ☎ (91) 542 54 03
Fax: (91) 542 89 28
The spanish gay travel magazine. Published quarterly. For free in gay venues.

Mensual Guia Gay España. La
S.L., PO Box 20 28 ✉08080 Barcelona ☎ (93) 412 53 80
Fax: (93)412 33 57
Listings and maps from Spain, every year, about 60 pages, and a monthly magazine including photos, small ads, listings from Spain.

Shangay
PO Box 40 23 ✉28080 Madrid ☎ (91) 308 45 39
Biweekly gay newspaper. Distributed nationwide, special focus on Madrid and Valencia. Free at gay venues.

NATIONAL COMPANIES

Las Lagrimas de Eros
Apto. 3008 ✉46080 Valencia ☎ 382 49 38 Fax: 382 53 88
National mailorder company.

Odisea (g)
Espiritu Santo 33 ✉28004 Madrid ☎ 523 21 54
☎ 617/911676 Fax: 522 74 83 E-Mail: odisea@ctv.es
Homepage: www.revistaodisea.com *National gay magazine.*

Aguadulce ☎ 950

BARS

Milenium (B DR G MA VS) 21.30-3 h
Av Carlos III (Centro Commercial Neptuno)

Neptuno (B d DR G MG OG VS) 21-03 h, winter closed Mon
Avenida Carlos III *(Neptuno Centro)* ☎ 34 73 90

Sire. El (B d G MA p) 22-4.30 h, closed Mon
Nacional 340 *(1st floor, ca. 12 km from Almeria)* ☎ 34 14 02

Albacete ☎ 908

SEX SHOPS/BLUE MOVIES

Sex Shop (g)
Calle Pedro Coca 2

GENERAL GROUPS

Jovenes Gais Albacete JOGAL 18-21 h
PO Box 627 ✉02080 ☎ 96 65 62

Alicante ☎ 96

BARS

Boys (AC B DR G MA VS) 22-? h
Calle César Elguezábal 11

Desfici (AC B CC D GLM MA S STV WE) Wed-Sat 22-5 h
C/ Bazán 18 ✉03001
Monthly special events

Elefante Blanco (AC B d DR G MA r VS)
C/ Baron de Finestrat 3 ☎ 520 38 09

Enigma (! AC B DR G MA p VS YG) 21-3, Fri Sat 21-4, winter Sun 17-3 h
Calle Arquitecto Morelli 23

Horus-Pub (AC B d g MA STV) 21-h ?
C/ Cesar Elgvetabal 11 ✉03001 ☎ 939 629 999

Jardineto. El (AC B DR G MA r VS) 20-?
Calle Barón de Finestrat 5 ☎ 521 17 36

Missing (! AC B d DR G MA s VS YG) 22-3.30 h
Calle Gravina 4 ✉03002 ☎ 521 67 28

Montecristo (B G OG p vs) 22-3 h
Calle Ab-El-Hamet 1 ☎ 512 31 89

CAFES

Or y Ferro (A AC B f G MA s) 16-24 h, WE-2 h
C/ Belando 12 ✉03004

DANCECLUBS

Enigmas Disco (! AC B DR Glm MA OS s YG) Fri-Sun 1-?, summer daily 1-? h
Ctra. Villafranqueza → Tángel, km 5 ☎ 517 97 79
Very large, two floors.

Jardinetto Discoteca (AC B D DR G MA S SNU STV VS WE) 1-8 h, Summer: Mon closed, Winter: Mon-Wed closed
C/ Jorge Juan 18 ✉03002

SEX SHOPS/BLUE MOVIES

Cosmopolitan (g VS)
Calle Rafael Altamira 5 ☎ 514 48 22 *Popular.*

Portugal-3 (g VS)
Portugal,3

Quintana (g VS) 10-14 h, 17-21
Calle Poeta Quintana 41 ☎ 521 48 81

Sex Shop (g VS) 10-3 h
Calle Pintor Lorenzo Casanova

Sexyland (g VS)
Calle Segura 18 ☎ 520 08 26

SAUNAS/BATHS

Asia (B DR G MA sa sb VS) 15.30-21 h
C/. Cardenal Payá 17

Sauna 26 (B DR G MA sa sb vs) 15.30-21.30 h
Calle Poeta Quintana 26 ☎ 521 98 25

HOTELS

Casa Rural L'Almasera (A AC B bf CC g MG OS msg sa wh) Reception: 9-13.30 h, 17-21.30 h
Ciabadia 20 ✉03828 ☎ 551 42 32 Fax: 551 43 14

GUEST HOUSES

Residencia Mariola (g H)
C/ Hércules 9 bajo ✉03006 ☎ 510 16 88

GENERAL GROUPS

Lambda
Apto 1088 ✉03080

HEALTH GROUPS

Centro de'Informacia i Prevencio de la SIDA (CIPS)
Plaza España 6 ☎ 523 05 63

SWIMMING

-Cabo de Las Huertas (NU) (take bus S)
-Carabasi Beach (NU) (12 km south of Alicante, late afternoons and evenings)
-Marina o Camino del Rebello (NU) (Entrance at Camping Internacional de la Marina and Club Michel)
-Urbanova (NU) (Go to the direction of the airport. Entrance of the beach at Altet)
-Las Canas between Play de Altet and Urbanova (dunes between parking and beach)

CRUISING

-Coast (2 km) between Postiguet Beach and La Albufera (especially in summer)
-Calle de Isabel / Avenida de Elche / Calle del Doctor Just / Calle Quintiliano (this block and back, at night carcruising)

Almeria ☎ 950

DANCECLUBS

Abakos (B D Glm MA SNU STV W YG) 23-6 h, closed Mon
Calle Dr. Araez Pacheco 8
Dracena (B g) 16-14
Rafael Alberti, s/n (Oliveros)

SWIMMING

-Playa del Rio (g)
-Playa Serena, Urbanización Roquetas de Mar (g NU) (19 km from Almeria)
-Playa Nudista, Vera (g NU) (93 km from Almeria)

Avila ☎ 918

GENERAL GROUPS

Colectivo Gay de Avila
PO Box 105, 05080 Avila

Aviles ☎ 985

SEX SHOPS/BLUE MOVIES

Internacional Sex-Shop (g VS) 11-14, 16-21 h
Calle Periodista Pruneda 2 ☎ 556 77 96

SWIMMING

-Dunas de Espatal/Playa San Juan

Badajoz ☎ 924

BARS

Athos Club (B D DR G MA S) 22-? h
Calle Joaquín Sama 11 *(Plaza Chica)* ☎ 25 81 55

Balearic Islands

Islas Baleares

Climate: Mild winters, not colder than 10°C, and dry and hot summers with sometimes 45°C.

Important gay cities: Ibiza, Palma de Mallorca.

Formentera ☎ 971

BARS

Claro! En Cán Gavinu (B F GLM OS) 20-? h
Km 3,3 Ctre. San Francisco - La Mola ☎ 32 24 21

SWIMMING

-Platja de Llevant (G NU) (Take the boat from Ibiza to Formentera. Rent a bike and go towards Es Pujols around the saltwater lake Estany Pudent. 150 m after the »Tanga Bar« turn left and follow the path to the beach.)

Ibiza ☎ 971

● Ibiza belongs to the most important gay beach resorts of Europe. While the Canarian Playa del Ingles is visited mainly in winter, and Sitges has the near Barcelona to offer, Ibiza (ibizian: Eivissa) is the top summer destination for gays from May to mid-September. One of Ibizas strong sides is its intensive heterosexual club-nightlife, which is open and friendly towards gays. Moreover, the gay beach Es Cavallet and the extremely short distances of the gay scene, are a delight. Note, that the 'gay round' begins after supper at about 11-12 p.m. in C/. de la Virgen. After a stopover on the city walls (C/. Santa Lucia), you move up to Dalt Vila for dancing and cruising. If you stay outside Ibiza-town, hiring a car -which is however expensive- is rewarding. Nevertheless, the public bus transport is dense and includes the routes to the gay beach. A tip: If you crave for a quiet day on a really beautiful beach, go to Formentera with the ferry (60 minutes ride). Marvellous!

✱ Ibiza gehört zu den wichtigsten schwulen Badeorten Europas. Während das kanarische Playa del Inglés vor allem ein Winterziel ist und Sitges zusätzlich das nahe Barcelona bietet, ist Ibiza (ibizenkisch: Eivissa) ein absolutes Sommer-Topziel von Mai bis Mitte September.
Eine von Ibizas Stärken ist sein intensives Hetero-Disco-Nightlife, in dem auch Schwule getrost mitmischen können. Dazu kommt der schwule Traum-Strand Es Cavallet und die extrem kurzen Wege der schwulen Szene. Dabei ist zu beachten, daß die „schwule Runde" nach dem Essen gegen 23/24 h in der C/. de la Virgen beginnt. Über eine Zwischenstation an der Stadtmauer (C/. Santa Lucia) geht's dann hinauf nach Dalt Vila zum Tanzen und Cruisen.
Gerade wenn man außerhalb von Ibiza-Stadt wohnt lohnt ein -allerdings teures- Mietauto. Das Busnetz ist allerdings dicht und reicht bis an den schwulen Strand.
Zum Schluß noch ein Tip: bei Lust auf einen ruhigen und richtig schönen Strand-Tag fährt man in 60 Minuten mit der Fähre nach Formentera. Herrlich.

▲ Ibiza est l'île gaye numéro 1 d'Europe. Si Playa de Ingles, sur les Canaries, est avant tout une destination pour l'hiver et si Sitges offre l'avantage d'être à proximité de Barcelone, Ibiza (les autochtones disent „Eivissa") est, elle, le must touristique de la saison estivale. Une des principales attractions d'Ibiza sont les boîtes de nuit hétéros que fréquentent aussi les gays. A voir absolument: la plage gay „Es Cavallet". L'avantage d'Ibiza, c'est qu'on peut tout faire à pied. Le soir, ça commence à bouger aux environs de minuit, après le dîner, dans la C. de la Virgen. Passez par les remparts (C. Santa Lucia), puis montez à Dalt Vila pour aller danser et draguer. Ceux qui logent à l'extérieur d'Ibiza auront toujours intérêt, même si cela revient cher, à louer une voiture. La ville et ses environs sont bien déservis par les bus qui vous conduisent même jusqu'à la plage gaye. Ceux qui auront envie de passer une journée au calme et au soleil, prendront le bac pour Formentera (une heure de trajet) et passeront une journée inoubliable.

☆ Ibiza es uno de los balnearios gay más importantes de Europa. Mientras la Playa del Inglés de las Islas Canarias es sobre todo interesante en invierno y Sitges ofrece la cercanía a Barcelona, Ibiza es el destino veraniego ideal para gays entre los meses de Mayo hasta mediados de Septiembre. La isla se distingue por su fuerte y animada marcha nocturna heterosexual, donde los gays son siempre

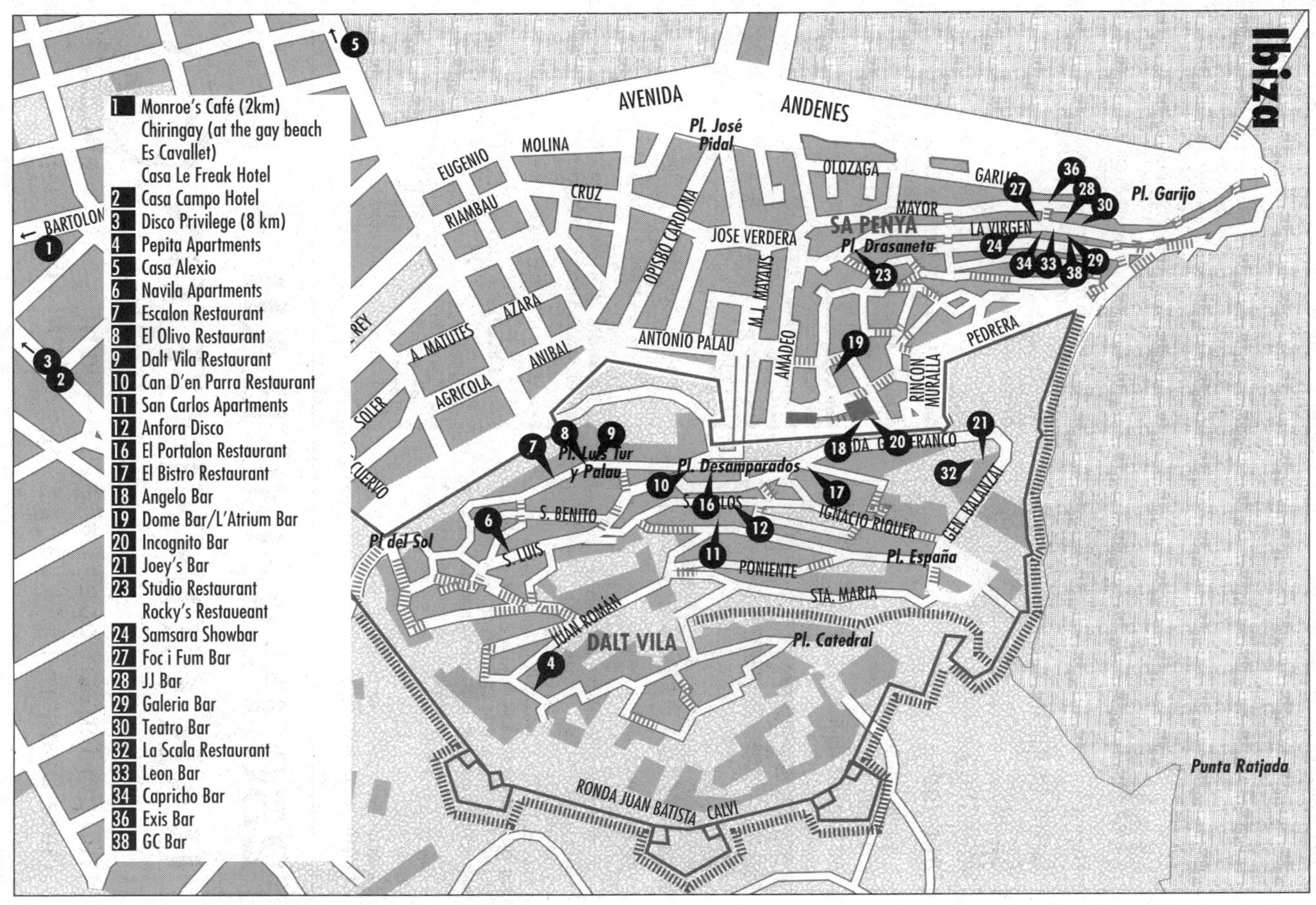
Ibiza
1 Monroe's Café (2km)
Chiringay (at the gay beach Es Cavallet)
Casa Le Freak Hotel
2 Casa Campo Hotel
3 Disco Privilege (8 km)
4 Pepita Apartments
5 Casa Alexio
6 Navila Apartments
7 Escalon Restaurant
8 El Olivo Restaurant
9 Dalt Vila Restaurant
10 Can D'en Parra Restaurant
11 San Carlos Apartments
12 Anfora Disco
16 El Portalon Restaurant
17 El Bistro Restaurant
18 Angelo Bar
19 Dome Bar/L'Atrium Bar
20 Incognito Bar
21 Joey's Bar
23 Studio Restaurant
Rocky's Restaueant
24 Samsara Showbar
27 Foc i Fum Bar
28 JJ Bar
29 Galeria Bar
30 Teatro Bar
32 La Scala Restaurant
33 Leon Bar
34 Capricho Bar
36 Exis Bar
38 GC Bar
AVENIDA
ANDENES
Pl. José Pidal
OLOZAGA
MAYOR
SA PENYA
Pl. Drasaneta
LA VIRGEN
Pl. Garijo
PEDRERA
RINCON MURALLA
GEN BALANZAT
Pl. España
IGNACIO RIQUER
STA. MARIA
Pl. Catedral
PONIENTE
Pl. Desamparados
AMADEO
M.J. MAYANS
JOSE VERDERA
OPISBO CARDONA
ANTONIO PALAU
Pl. Luis Tur y Palau
S. BENITO
S. LUIS
JUAN ROMÁN
DALT VILA
RONDA JUAN BATISTA CALVI
Pl del Sol
MOLINA
CRUZ
AZARA
ANIBAL
EUGENIO
RIAMBAU
A. MATUTES
AGRICOLA
SOLER
CUERVO
BARTOLON
Punta Ratjada

bienvenidos. No debe quedar sin mencionar la playa gay de ensueño „Es Cavallet", y la ventaja de la cercanía entre sí de todos los establecimientos gay. El llamado tour gay (ronda gay), empieza después de la cena entre las 23 y 24:00 horas en la calle de la Virgen. Despúes de una parada en la muralla de la ciudad en la calle Santa Lucia, se sube en dirección Dalt Vila para bailar e ir de cruising. Para los que residan fuera de la ciudad merece la pena alquilar un coche (aúnque es bastante caro). Sin embargo, la red de transporte público es densa y los autobuses llegan hasta las playas gay. Un consejo: Para disfrutar un día tranquilo en la playa, se recomienda una excursión a la encantadora isla de Formentor (approx. 1 hora en barco).

❖ Ibiza fa parte delle stazioni balneari più importanti d'Europa. Mentre la playa del inglés delle Canarie è una meta squisitamente invernale e Sitges, per la prossimità a Barcellona, rientra nel turismo urbano-culturale, Ibiza è in assoluto una meta estiva fiorente da maggio fino a metà settembre. Una carta vincente di Ibiza è la vita notturna nelle discoteche per eterosessuali, nelle quali anche i gay si mescolano armoniosamente. A ciò si aggiungono l'onirica spiaggia gay Es Cavallet e le viette della zona gay. Ricordatevi che il giro gay inizia dopo cena tra le 23 e le 24 nella c. de la Virgen. Dopo una pausa alla cinta muraria (c. Santa Lucia) si sale a Dalt Vila a ballare e a cercare compagnia. Se si vive fuori da Ibiza paese conviene, anche se è costoso, noleggiare un'auto. Il servizio degli autobus è efficiente e raggiunge la spiaggia gay. Infine ancora un consiglio: se avete voglia di trascorrere una giornata su una spiaggia bella e tranquilla Formentera è a solo un'ora di traghetto. Favoloso!

TOURIST INFO

Oficina de Turismo
Paseo Vara del Rey 13 ☎ 30 19 00

BARS

Angelo (! AC B G lj MA OS) 22-4 h, closed Mid Oct-Apr
C/. Via Alfonso XII - 11 ✉07800 ☎ 31 03 35
Atrium. L' (B g OS YG) 22.30-4 h, Winter only WE
C/. Via Alfonso XII 3 ✉07800 ☎ 908-43 24 43 (mobile)
Trendy and popular.
Bar Connection (B G) 22-04h
Plaza de Drassenta 1+2 ✉07800
Bronx (AC B DR G LJ MA OS s VS) 23-4 h
C/. Sa Carrossa 4 ✉07800
Capricho Bar (B G MA OS) 20-4 h
C/. de la Virgen 42 ✉07800 ☎ 19 24 71
Corazón Negro (B G MA OS) summer: 21-4 daily, winter: Wed-Sat 21-4 h
Calle de la Virgen 23 ☎ 619-18 40 67 (mobile)
Dome (B g OS YG) 22.30-4 h, closed Oct-Apr
C/. Via Alfonso XII 5 ✉07800 ☎ 31 14 56
Trendy and popular.
Es Passadis (AC B G MA OS) 22-4 h, in winter only WE
Carrer des Passadis 5, bajos ✉07800 ☎ 316 358
Carribean music and coctails.
Exis (B G MA OS) Apr-Oct 21-4 h
C/. de la Virgen 57 ✉07800
FABU ! VELVET (A B G MA OS s YG) 21-? h
Calle de la Virgen 72 ✉07800 ☎ 311 129 Fax: 311 129
Specialised in coctails
Foc i Fum (B G MA OS) 21-4 h, closed in winter
C/. de la Virgen 55 ✉07800 ☎ 31 33 80
Galeria (! A B G MA OS) 21.30-3 h, closed 20.Oct-Apr
C/. de la Virgen 64 ✉07800 *(opposite JJ Bar)*
Bar and art gallery.

GC Bar (AC B d DR G LJ MA s VS) 22.?h
C/ de la Virgen 32 ✉07800 *Leather bar.*
Incognito (! B G MA OS) 21.30-4 h
C/. Santa Lucia 23-21 ✉07800 ☎ 19 13 15
JJ Bar (! B G lj MA OS) 22-3 h, closed Mid Oct-Apr
C/. de la Virgen 79 ✉07800 ☎ 31 02 47
Terrace to observe the people, balcony overlooking the harbour. Macho and leather crowd.
Joey's (AC B DR G lj MA OS s) 23-4 h
Sa Carrosa 4, Dalt Vila ✉07800 ☎ 31 20 49
Open all year. From June to September Joey's Surprise Night at 0100.
Leon Bar (B G MA OS) 22-? h
C/. de la Virgen 62 ✉07800
Nada. La (AC f G MA OS) 20-4 h, closed Jan
C/ de la Virgin 10 ✉07800 ☎ 31 12 26
Teatro (! B G MA OS YG) 22-? h, closed Oct-Apr
C/. de la Virgen 83 ✉07800 ☎ 31 32 25
A very nice terrace to see and be seen.

CAFES

Central. Café (B bf f g MA) 8.30-20.30 h, closed Nov-Apr
C/. Galicia 6 ✉07800 *(Figueretas)* ☎ 30 17 26
Home-made German cakes and food.
Chiringay (! B F G MA) Apr-Oct 9.30-21 h
Playa Es Cavallet ☎ 18 74 29
Es Pas (B f g MA OS) 8-22 h, closed Sun and Jan/Feb
C/. Xeringa 7 ✉07800 *(Near market)* ☎ 31 18 57
Sandwiches, fruit juices; packed for lunch. Snacks all day.
Geminis (B bf F glm MA) 9.30-1 h, closed Oct-Apr
Paseo Maritimo *(Figueretas)*

Good morning...after!
...use them!
GIB AIDS
KEINE
CHANCE

Monroe's (AC B bf CC F glm MA) 9.30-3 h
C/. Ramón Muntaner 33 bajo ✉07800 *(Figueretas)*
☎ 39 25 41 Fax: 39 25 41
Drag shows Wed Fri sun 22.30 h. Home-made English food.

Palmeras. Las (B f g MA OS) 12-24 h
C/. Ramon Muntaner 38, Figueretes ✉07800 ☎ 39 16 81

DANCECLUBS

Anfora Discoteca (! AC B D DR G lj MA s VS YG) 0-6 h, Sun shows, closed 12.Oct-30.Apr
C/. San Carlos 7 ✉07800 *(Dalt Vila)* ☎ 30 28 93
2 floors. Shows.

Privilege (B D f g YG) 22.30-8 h, Fri one big gay part in the disco, closed Oct-May
(San Rafael) ☎ 30 40 81
Also on Mon many gays. Special party nights frequently advertised all over Ibiza. Admission Ptas 6.500. Best from 5, Fri from 3.30/4 h.

Space (B D g OS YG) 6.30-?, Fri Sat -18/? h
(Playa d'en Bossa, San José) ☎ 30 69 90
Techno. Popular.

RESTAURANTS

Bistro. El (F g MA OS) 20-1 h, closed Nov-Mar
Sa Carrossa 15 ✉07800 *(Dalt Vila)* ☎ 39 32 03
French cuisine. Also apartments available.

Brasa. La (b F g MA OS) 19-1 h, closed Sun
C/. Pere Sala 3 ✉07800 ☎ 30 12 02
International food. Beautiful garden.

beach bar and restaurant
open every day
Chiringay
PLAYA ES CAVALLET

Can D'en Parra (b CC F g MA OS) 20-01 h, closed in winter
C/. San Rafael 3 ✉07800 *(Dalt Vila)* ☎ 39 11 14
Has a nice terrace from which you can watch people going to and from the bars of Dalt Vila. Especialidad en carne a la brasa y pescado fresco.
Dalt Vila (B CC F g MA OS) Apr-Oct 20-1 h
Plaza de Vila 3-4 ✉07800 *(Dalt Vila)* ☎ 30 55 24
International cuisine.
Escalon (B F g MA OS) 20-1 h, closed 20.Oct-Apr
C/. Santa Cruz 6 ✉07800 *(Dalt Vila)* ☎ 30 32 79
German and international cuisine.
GULA GULA (B CC F G MG S T) 21-2 h, Nov-May closed
Estación Marítima, Puerta de Ibiza ✉07800 ☎ 311 121
☎ 609-894 810 (mobile) Fax: 311 121
Very beautiful view over the harbour
Nina's (AC B CC F glm MA OS W) 19-? h
Calle Isidoro Macabich 33 ✉07840 ☎ 33 22 43
El Olivo (b F g MA OS) 10-1 h
Placa de Vila 7 ✉07800 *(Dalt Vila)* ☎ 30 06 80
International cuisine; prices are surprisingly reasonable for the quality offered.
Plaza Santa Gertrudis. La (F g MA) 20-0.30 h closed Nov-Mar
Plaza Santa Gertrudis, 07800 Santa Gertrudis ☎ 19 70 75
Bus from Ibiza City to San Miguel ca. 20 minutes.
Portalón. El (B CC F g MA OS) 12-16/20-1 h
Plaza Desamparados 1-2 ✉07800 *(Dalt Vila)* ☎ 30 39 01
Fax: 30 08 52. *Local and international cuisine. Open all year.*
Rocky's. Restaurante (b F g MA OS) 19-2 h, Nov-Easter closed
C/. de la Virgen 6 ✉07800 ☎ 31 01 07
International food, specialist for Paellas.
Scala. La (B F G MA OS) 20-1 h, winter Mon Tue closed
Sa Carrossa 7 ✉07800 *(Dalt Vila)* ☎ 30 03 83
Swiss international cuisine.
Studio (b F g MA OS) 19.30-1.30 h
C/. de la Virgen 4 ✉07800 *(2nd entrance: Plaza de Sa Drassaneta 12)* ☎ 31 53 68
Fresh quality produce used for à la carte, set and vegetarian menus.

SHOWS

Samsara (B g MA OS STV) Mar-Sep 21-3. Show 0.30 h.
C/. de la Virgen 44 ✉07800 ☎ 619 631 634 (mobile)
International Show

SEX SHOPS/BLUE MOVIES

Stocki's Erotic World (AC CC glm MA VS) 10-4 h
C/. Carlos V 12 ✉07800 *(50 m to habour)* ☎ 31 20 05

PROPERTY SERVICES

Exclusive Ibiza Properties (G H pi) Mon-Fri 10-14, 17-20 h
PO Box 1133 ✉07800 ☎ 33 65 36 ☎ 670 83 80 06 (Mobile)
Fax: 30 35 84
Houses in the countryside of the island with swimming-pool and apartments on the sea front in Ibiza city. Special properties are rented in the absence of the owners.

All around the World...
GIB AIDS
KEINE
CHANCE
...use them!

HOTELS

Alexio. Casa (! AC B bf G H MA pi wh)
Barrio Ses Torres 16, Jesus ✉07819 *(Talamanca)*
☎ 31 42 49 ☎ (639) 63 25 22 Fax: 31 26 19
E-Mail: alexio@alexio.com Homepage: www.alexio.com
Beautiful and luxurious gay house, highly recommended. Rooms with bath, air conditioning and satelite-TV. Rental cars available for guests and with a car it's 5 minutes to the gay bars.

Can Romanica (bf glm H MA OS pi sol)
Carretera San Jose km 4, Puig Gros *(PO Box 49, St. Jorge)*
☎ (908) 63 81 28 (mobile) Fax: 34 71 30 25 66
Rates Double Ptas 10.500-14.500. Six spectaculary decorated rooms in mountainside villa. 10 minutes by car to Ibiza city and gay beach.

Casa Campo Guest House (bf Glm H MA OS pi)
Club San Rafael 18 ✉07816 *(San Rafael)* ☎ 19 82 01
Fax: 19 80 53
Location 5 min from Ibiza town near Disco „Ex Ku". Guest house in country style, beautifully furnished. Recommended. Rates single Ptas 10.000, double 13.000-19.000 (bf incl.).

Casa Le Freak (B bf G H MA msg pi) Open all year
Correos San Jorge, PO Box 80 ✉07800 ☎ 39 65 51
Near Es Cavalet beach. Rooms and bungalows with terraces.

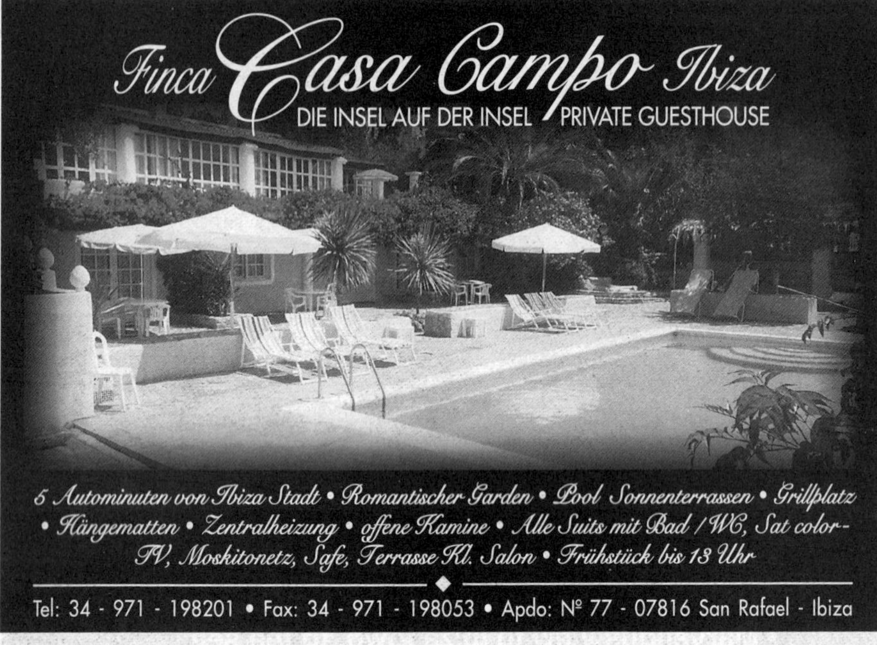

Finca Casa Campo Ibiza
DIE INSEL AUF DER INSEL PRIVATE GUESTHOUSE
5 Autominuten von Ibiza Stadt • Romantischer Garden • Pool Sonnenterrassen • Grillplatz • Hängematten • Zentralheizung • offene Kamine • Alle Suits mit Bad / WC, Sat color-TV, Moskitonetz, Safe, Terrasse Kl. Salon • Frühstück bis 13 Uhr
Tel: 34 - 971 - 198201 • Fax: 34 - 971 - 198053 • Apdo: Nº 77 - 07816 San Rafael - Ibiza

Don Quijote (b bf g H MA pi)
C/. Pais Basc 10 ✉07800 *(Figueretas)* ☎ 30 18 69 Fax: 34 13 58
Near the Beach. All rooms with bath, telephone and most with terrace. Summer: Single Ptas 5.815, double 9.485, triple 13.755. bf 830.

Finca Ibiza. La (AC B bf E f G H OS pi)
C/. del Cabussó 11, St Jordi ✉07817 *(3 km for Ibiza city center)* ☎ 30 10 04 Fax: 30 10 04
Double rooms & suites

Hotel Canonigo (B G H MA)
C/. Mayor 8 ✉07800 *(Dalt Vila)* ☎ 30 38 84 Fax: 30 70 43 E-Mail: hotelcanonigo@ctv.es
Elegant, renovated hotel in a 14th century building.

Navila Aparthotel (AC b g H MA OS pi) Open all year
C/. Luis 1 *(Dalt Vila)* ☎ 39 05 73 Fax: 30 08 52.
All rooms with bath, WC, phone, satellite TV, kitchen and big terraces with sea view. Single/double Ptas 16.000-25.000.

APARTMENTS

Casa Galería (GLM H) May-Sep
C./ Montblanc 2, St. Jorge ✉07817 *(On the bus-route Ibiza-Salinas, 200 m from the nearest bus stopj)* ☎ 39 64 64 ☎ 639-81 12 54 (mobile)
Two double rooms with Bath/WC, Sat-TV, radio, hair-dryer, own key, room service. With car park and garden.

Cenit Apartements (g H pi)
Los Molinos, Figueretas ✉07800 ☎ 30 14 04 Fax: 30 07 54
Rates Ptas 8.500 (high season).

Chiringay Casa (G H)
Playa Es Cavallet ☎ 18 74 29
For 3-6 persons. For reservation ask in Café Chiringay.

Delfin Verde Apartments (G H)
C/. Garigo 2 ✉07800 ☎ +31/20/421 00 00
Reservations through „De Gay Krant Reisservice".

Pepita Apartamentos (G H)
c/o El Portalón Restaurant, Plaza Desamparados 1-2 *(Dalt Vila & Figueretas)* ☎ 30 39 01 ☎ 30 08 52 Fax: 30 08 52
All with bath/shower, WC, some with balcony/terrace.

Ripoll. Apartments (g H)
C/. Vincente Cubruo 10/14 ✉07800 ☎ +31/20/421 00 00
Reservation through „De Gay Krant Reisservice", Amsterdam, NL.

SWIMMING

Nude bathing is permitted everywhere outside of town, where signs reading »Playa natural« show the way to the beach.
-Platja Es Cavallet (G NU) (from Ibiza-Town follow the signs to the airport, then to Platya Es Cavallet. [P] possible at the beach. Walk along the beach or the dunes to the far end with the bar Chiringay. Action is going on in the bushes behind the bar towards the other side of the peninsula).

CRUISING

-Southwest corner at top of old city walls (above La Muralla Bar on opposite side of the street
-Playa Figueretas (nights and early mornmings after barhopping)
-Rocas (entrada/entrance: Tunel frente al Ayuntamenta)

Mallorca - Palma de Mallorca ☎ 971

BARS

Abaco (B E g MA NG) 21-2 h
C/. San Juan 1 ✉07012 *(close to old stock market Lonja)* ☎ 72 49 39
Best from 22 h, nice patio in historic building, classic music.

Africa (B GLM MA N) 12-15, 18.30-24 h, closed Tue and Sun lunch
C/. Robert Graves 17, El Terreno ✉07015 *(100 m from Plaza Gomilla)* ☎ 731 548
Small but friendly.

Alibi (AJC DR G MA s VS) 22-4 h
C/. Terral 36 bajos, ✉07600 *(El Arenal)* ☎ 44 17 89

Aries Pub (B DR G MA VS) 23-8 h
C/. Porras 3 ✉07015 *(at Av. Joan Miró)* ☎ 73 78 99

Bruixeries (B GLM MA)
C/. Estanc *(Sa Llonja)*

Yuppi
Pub
Video Room • Joan Miro 106 • Palma de Mallorca

Flesh (AC B d G MA s VS) 22-4 h
Avenida Joan Miró 68 ✉07015 ☎ 455 146
GE (AC d DR G LJ MA VS) 24-4 h
Avenida Joan Miró 73 bajo ☎ 639 304 008 (mobile)
Marcus (AC B CC D DR G MA r s snu VS WE) summer: 23-4 h, winter: 22-3 h
Av. Juan Miró 54 ✉07015 ☎ 286 144
Miguel Cafeteria (B F g) 11-15, 18-23, winter 10.30-18.30 h
C/. Trasimeno 69, 07600 El Arenal *(Balneario 1, Bus 15)*
Querelle (AC B DR G MA OS SNU VS) 23-4 h, show 2 h
Avenida Joan Miró 52 ✉07015
Sa Bota (B d DR G lj MA VS) summer 22-4, winter 21-1 h
C/. de Trasime 73, 07600 El Arenal *(Near Balneario 1, 2nd line)*
☎ 44 44 29
Status Pub (AC B G MA) 22-4 h
Av. Joan Miró 38 ✉07015 ☎ 45 40 30
Popular & elegant with beautiful, fresh flowers.
Yedra. La (AC B glm MA YG) 23-? h, closed Sun
Av. Joan Miró 47 ✉07015
Popular late bar for all kind of people. Best from 6 h.
Yuppi Club (AC B DR G MA p VS YG) 22-6?, Fri Sat -8 h
Av. Joan Miró 106 ✉07015 ☎ 639 71 90 85 *Popular.*

CAFÉS

La Tasca (AC f GLM MA OS VS) 18-4 h, Mon closed
Av. Joan Miro 41 ✉07014 ☎ 45 04 68

DANCECLUBS

Black Cat (! AC B D DR G MA S VS YG) 24-7 h, best from 2

h, Show 3.30 h, winter: closed Mon
Av. Joan Miró 75 ✉07015
Good show, very popular.
G-Planet (AC B D DR GLM MA S YG) Sat 0.30-6 h
Mediterraneo ✉07004 ☎ 919 03 93 22 (mobile)
House music. Cover includes one free drink.

RESTAURANTS

El Jardin (B F GLM OS) Tue-Sat 19:30-?
Passatge C'an Fustera 10 ✉07184 *(20 min from Palma)*
☎ 971 670 840
A new restaurant bar in a wonderful setting. Outdoor terrace with classical music. Bar open til late.
Es Reco den Justin (A B CC F GLM MA N s W WE)
19-2 h, closed Wed
Avenida Joan Miro 80 ✉07015 ☎ 45 47 48
Fred's Bistro (g) 19-?
C/Virgilio, 21 (Ca'n Pastilla) ☎ 74 36 83

SEX SHOPS/BLUE MOVIES

Amsterdam (g VS) 11-22 h, Sun closed
Av. Argentina 34 ✉07011 ☎ 73 97 34
Erotic Toy Stories (CC G VS) 10-21 h
Pasaje Maneu 10 ✉07002 ☎ 72 78 65
Master's Sex Shop (g VS) 10.30-21 h, closed Sun
Gabriel LLabrés,11 *(near Plaza Saint Antonio)* ☎ 24 82 09
Non Stop (g VS) Mon-Sat 11.30-14, 16-22 h, closed Sun
Av. Joan Miró 38 ✉07015 *(Local 8)* ☎ 45 63 40
Sex Shop Amsterdam II (g VS) 11-14, 16-23
Avda Joan Miró, 15 (Gomila) ☎ 45 73 70
Video cabins, videos for sale, books and magazines

ESCORTS & STUDIOS

Tenorio (AC b CC G R VS) 16-3 h
Av. Joan Miro 54-A, 1st Floor ☎ 616 605 751 (mobile)
Callboys/Chicos de comania, all rooms with video

HOUSE OF BOYS

Casa Alfredo (B CC G pi R VS) 15-3 h
C/. Ramón Servera Moya 29 ✉07014 ☎ 45 44 77
Club Boys (A AC CC G MG msg p R VS) 0-24 h
C/ Antonio Ribas 42 ✉07006 ☎ 46 08 25

SAUNAS/BATHS

Aries (B G MA msg sa sb VS wh YG) 16-0 h
C/. Porras 3 ✉07015 ☎ 73 78 99
Admission Ptas 1.300 (incl. 1 free drink).
Spartacus (! B DR G MA pi r sa sb sol VS WO) 16-22 h
C/. Santo Espiritu 8, bajos *(near Plaza Mayor)* ☎ 72 50 07
Recently renovated, nicely decorated with art and sculptures. Admission Ptas 1.200.

HOTELS

Aries Hotel (B bf g H MA) Sauna 16-0, Pub 23-? h
C/. Porras 3 ✉07015 *(at Av. Joan Miró)*
☎ 73 78 99 Fax: 73 27 94
Rates single Ptas 3.500, double 4.000 (bf incl., with shower)
Casa Miramar (G H)
C/. Miramar 5 ✉07001 ☎ 72 59 98 Fax: 72 59 98
5 apartments, one maisonette and one luxury suite for four persons. Rates Ptas 10.000/day (2 small ap.) and 15.000 (3 big ap.).

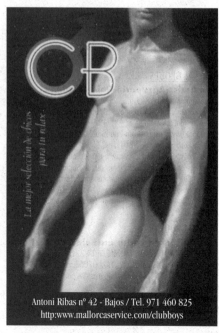

Hotel Rosamar (B bf G H OS) closed 6. Jan-20. Mar
Av. Joan Miró 74 ✉07015 ☎ 73 27 23 Fax: 28 38 28
E-Mail: rosamar@ocea.es
Homepage: www.illes.balears.net/rosamar
Rooms with bath, WC, phone and terrace.

GENERAL GROUPS

Ben Amics-Agrupació Gai i Lesbiana
Information Mon-Fri 19-21 h
C/. Imprenta 1, 1°, 1A (centro) ✉07001 ☎ 72 30 58
E-Mail: benamics@oem.es
Homepage: www.espanet.com/benamics
-Telèfon Rosa ☎ 900 601 601 18-22 h
-"Ben Amics" -bimonthly paper with articles, informations, gay scene listings of Mallorca, classified ads and photographies. Free in gay venues. Carnet GL for reduction in bars and shops available. Meetings all week. Mo: newspaper group, Tue: Aids prevention, Wed: Grupo de Amistad, Thu: Youth group, Fri: Lesbian group Beverages and snacks available.

HEALTH GROUPS

Ascociación de Lucha anti-sida de Mallorca ALAS Mon-Fri 10-13, 18-19, café Fri 19-22 h
C/. Cecilio Metelo 11, esc B, 2°,1A ✉07003 ☎ 71 55 66
☎ 71 44 88 Fax: 71 44 88 E-Mail: alas@espanet.com
Homepage: http://www.espanet.com/alas

Conselleria de Sanitat Mon-Fri 9-10.30 h
C/. Cecili Metel 18 ☎ 17 68 68
HIV testing anonymous and for free.

Escuela de Salud, Sida y Convivencia - FASE
Pza. Peixetería, 4, 2° ✉07001 ☎ 72 75 80 ☎ 900-111 000
E-Mail: fase@idecnet.com Homepage: http://www.idecnet.com/fase

SWIMMING

-Es Trenc (! g NU) (Take road to Campos del Puerto, then direction Colonia de Sant Jordi. Near restaurant El Ultimo Paraíso. Ca. 50 km from Palma)
-Playa de Illetas (g OG)) (gay at the end, bus 3)
-Playa del Mago (NU) (in Portas Vells at the rocks. Popular)
-Playa San Juan de Dios in Ca'n Pastilla (r NU)
-Playa Cala Aguua (NU) (rocky part north of the beach, cruisy in the forest)
-Ca'n Picafort (g) (Playa de Muro, action in the dunes between the two west side towers)
-Playa Cala Grand in Cala D'Or Centre (G)
-Playa San Carlos (g)
Playa y Dique del Oeste (Porto Pi), Bus EMT n°1 (directo), 3 y 21
Es Carnatge (Ca'n Pastilla), Bus EMT n°15
Cala Blava (Final S'Arenal), Bus EMT n°23
Playa de Muro (Ca'n Picafort) Inca, Autocares Bellver

CRUISING

-Promenade at city walls beneath Cathedral (AYOR) (steps and gardens)
-Placa de España (ayor) (R)
-Paseo del Borne
-Dique del Oeste (G) 24 h. Bus 3. At end of Paseo Maritimo, also cruising by car, no swimming)
-Camino de Jesus (R) (near river, by car)
-El Bosque (S'Arenal), Bus EMT n°15

Mallorca - Soller ☎ 971

HOTELS

Primavera Hotel (B CC F glm H OS)
Carretera Puerto de Soller 44 ☎ 63 46 76 Fax: 63 46 76
Rates single Ptas 2.000-4.000, double 3.500-6.000 with bath/WC.

Menorca ☎ 971

SWIMMING

-Son Bou (G NU) (15 km mainroad Mahon-Ciutadella; very cruisy in the dunes)

Barbate de Franco

SWIMMING

-Los Caños de Meca (you should go over the rocks)

Barcelona ☎ 93

Barcelona has been the secret capital of Spain for centuries, at least in economic and cultural terms, a fact shown by numerous sights, such as charming old city quarters, palaces, museums and churches. The administrative capital Madrid has only started catching up with Barcelona over the past few years. The urban renewal prompted by the 1992 Olympic Games helped give Barcelona a new face, but the old one has nonetheless been retained. Barcelonas »Modernismo« buildings, like Park Güell, Palais Güell, Casa Mila and the cathredal Sagrada Familia, are feasts for the eyes. »Modernismo« is the Catalonian version of art nouveau. The gay scene offers everything you might expect from a metropolis of over 2 million: two of the best gay discos in Europe, interesting saunas, bars, mixed restaurants; in short, everything your heart desires. You may find street signs and official notices confusing, especially if you have learned Spanish and are expecting it to be used here. In Barcelona, Catalan is spoken, and the language is considered an expression of their sovereignty. Even the flyers and leaflets of local gay groups are in Catalan; nevertheless everyone can speak and understand »Castillian«, which is what Spanish is called here.

✱ Zumindest in kultureller und wirtschaftlicher Hinsicht war Barcelona über Jahrhunderte hinweg die heimliche Hauptstadt Spaniens. Davon zeugen eindrucksvolle Altstadtviertel, Paläste, Museen und Kirchen. Erst seit einigen Jahren holt die Verwaltungshauptstadt Madrid wieder auf.
Die Olympischen Spiele von 1992 haben der Stadt ein neues Gesicht gegeben. Doch daneben gibt es auch Altes. Barcelonas Modernismo(i.e. Jugendstil)-Bauten sind absolute Augenweiden: Park Güell, Palais Güell, Casa Milá und die Kirche Sagrada Familia.
Die schwule Szene entspricht dem, was man von einer 2-Millionen-Metropole erwartet: Zwei der besten schwulen Discos Europas, interessante Saunen, Bars, gemischte Restaurants: alles, was das Herz begehrt.
Bitte wundern Sie sich jedoch nicht über die eigenartigen Schreibweisen von Straßenschildern und amtlichen Mitteilungen. Auch wer gerne sein Spanisch zur Anwendung bringen möchte, wird etwas enttäuscht sein: Die Barcelonesen sprechen Katalanisch und betrachten dies durchaus als Ausdruck ihrer Souveränität. So sind auch die örtlichen Mitteilungsblätter der Schwulengruppen auf katalanisch. Aber verstehen und sprechen können natürlich alle »Kastilisch«, wie man die spanische Sprache hier nennt.

▲ Depuis toujours, Barcelone est, au moins sur le plan culturel et commercial, la capitale secrète de l'Espagne. Les magnifiques quartiers de la vieille ville, les palais, les musées et les églises en sont la preuve incontestable. Ce n'est que depuis le retour de la démocratie que Madrid, capitale administrative, a retrouvé la position qu'elle occupait dans le passé. Les Jeux Olympiques de 1992 ont été l'occasion d'une vaste opération de construction et de rénovation. Modernisme et tradition donnent à Barcelone son visage d'aujourd'hui. Les bâtiments du «Modernismo» -la version catalane de l'art-déco- sont splendides: Park Güell, Casa Mila et l'église de la Sagrada Familia. Au niveau gay, Barcelone n'est pas en reste non plus: une des meilleures discothèques gays d'Europe, un des saunas les plus intéressants, des bars cuirs, des restaurants gays, bref tout ce qu'il faut pour être heureux! Ne vous laissez pas dérouter par l'orthographe particulière des panneaux de circulation et des inscriptions officielles. Ceux qui voudront mettre en pratique leurs connaissances en espagnol devront repasser, car tout Catalan qui se respecte parle avant tout sa langue. Les magazines gays sont donc tous en en catalan. Bien sûr, en Catalogne tout le monde comprend et parle le «castillan», comme on appelle ici l'espagnol.

☆ Al menos desde el punto de vista cultural y económico Barcelona fue durante siglos la capital española secreta. Impresionantes barrios antiguos, palacios, museos e iglesias testimonian ésto. Pero hace algunos años Madrid, la capital administrativa ha vuelto a recobrar terreno. Los juegos olímpicos de 1992 dieron una nueva cara a la ciudad que se conjuga a la perfección con las edificaciones antiguas ya existentes. Las construcciones modernistas de la ciudad son un deber: Parque Güell, Palacio Güell, Casa Milá y la iglesia de la Sagrada Familia. El ambiente gay responde a lo que se exige de una metrópoli de 2 millones de habitantes: dos de las mejores discotecas europeas, saunas muy interesantes, bares con clientela portadora de prendas de cuero, bares frecuentados por prostitutos, restaurantes gay, en fin, todo lo que a uno le apetece. El orgullo nacional de Catalunya también se refleja en el idioma: Aqui todos los letreros de las calles y las señalizaciones oficiales están escritas en catalán y los barceloneses usan poco el castellano. Por eso también los periódicos locales de las organizaciones gay están escritos en catalán. Pero por supuesto también se entiende y se habla el castellano.

❖ Per secoli, Barcellona è stata la capitale segreta della Spagna, almeno per ciò che riguarda la cultura e l'economia. Ci sono molte attrazioni che confermano ciò, per esempio gli affascinanti vecchi quartieri della città, i palazzi e i musei. Madrid è riuscita a raggiungere Barcellona solo da pochi anni. Le olimpiadi del 1992 hanno cambiato il volto della città, senza cancellare le tracce del passato. L'architettura modernista di Barcellona è un piacere per gli occhi, non perdetevi il parco Güell, palazzo Güell, la casa Milà e la chiesa della Sagrada Familia. L'ambiente gay corrisponde a ciò che ci si aspetta da una città di 2 milioni di abitanti: due delle migliori discoteche d'Europa, interessanti saune, bar, ristoranti misti, tutto ciò che il cuore può desiderare. Non meravigliatevi di fronte alle scritte dei cartelli stradali e alle insegne ufficiali. Chi desidera praticare un po' di castiglano („spagnolo" è un termine improprio) sarà un po' deluso: i catalani parlano catalano e considerano la loro lingua una espressione della loro sovranità. Così anche i volantini informativi del movimento gay sono scritti in catalano. Però non scoraggiatevi, il castigliano viene capito e parlato da tutti.

GAY INFO

Guía del Ocio Muntaner, 492, bajos ✉08022
☎ 418 50 05 ☎ 418 28 09 Fax: 417 94 71
E-Mail: guiaocio@idrup.ibernet.com
Homepage: http://www.guiadelociobcn.es
Weekly city guide in spanish.125 Pts Great source of information on what's going on in the city.

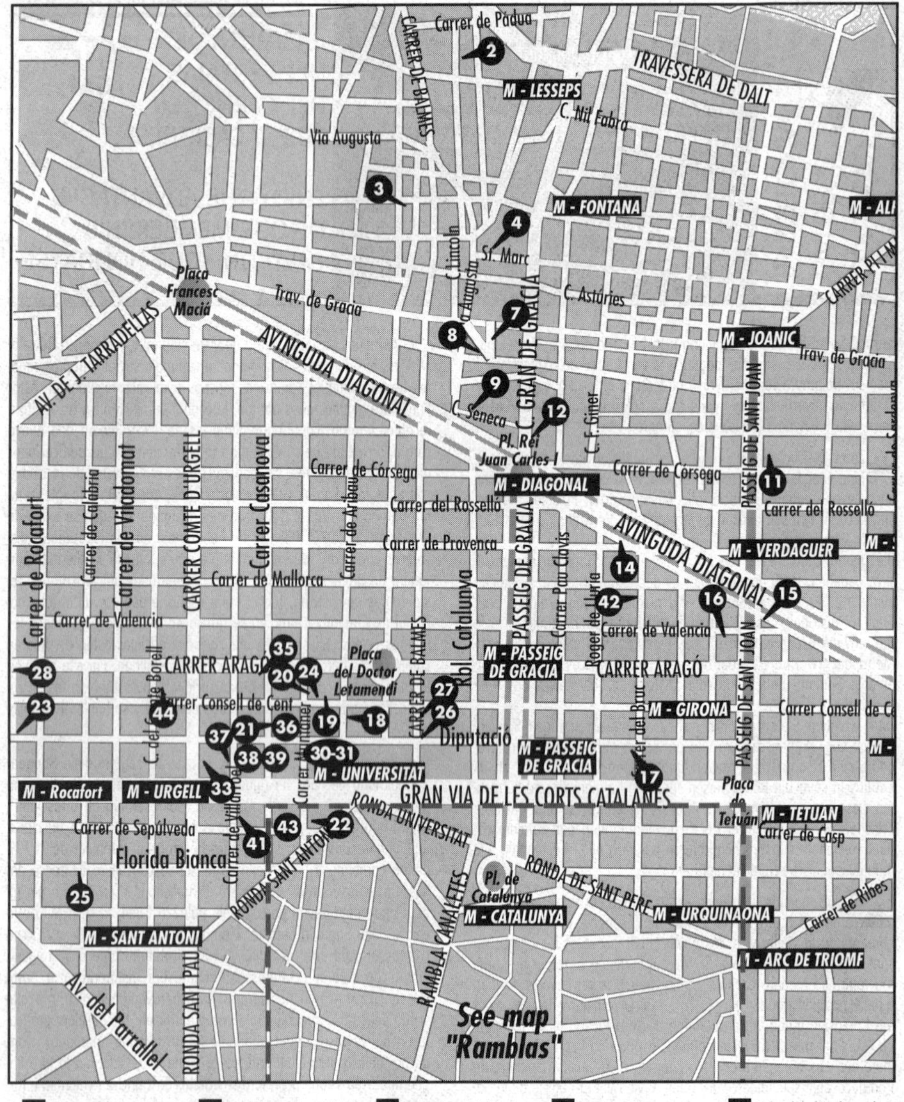

2 Sauna Padua
3 Roma Bar
4 Espai-Magic Bar
7 Café de la Calle Bar
8 Nois Quina Nit Bar
9 Bahia Bar
11 Eagle Bar
12 Martins Danceclub
14 New Chaps Bar
15 La Luna Danceclub
16 Topxi Bar
17 Sauna Bruch
18 Satanassa Danceclub
19 Este Bar
20 Punto BCN Bar
21 Sauna Casanova
22 Metro Danceclub
23 Thermas Sauna
24 Dietrich Bar
25 Sauna Galilea
26 Arena classic Danceclub
27 Arena Danceclub
28 Tatu Danceclub
30 Nostromo Sex Shop
31 Monaco Café
33 Ciber-Otic Bar
35 Castro Restaurant
36 Eterna Restaurant
37 La Diva Restaurant
38 Nois Gay Info
39 Absolutely Fabulous Fashion Shop
41 Guia Global Fashion Shop
42 Que Tal Guest Hostal
43 Café Miranda
44 Neron House of Boys

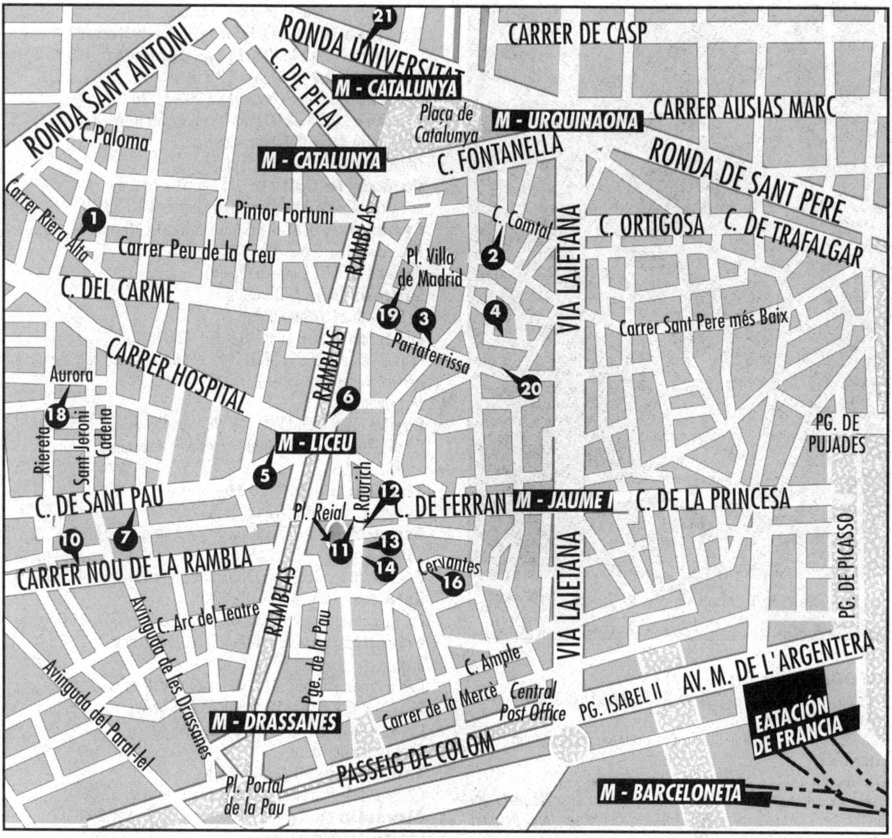

RONDA UNIVERSITAT
CARRER DE CASP
RONDA SANT ANTONI
C. DE PELAI
M - CATALUNYA
Plaça de Catalunya
M - URQUINAONA
CARRER AUSIAS MARC
C. Paloma
M - CATALUNYA
C. FONTANELLA
RONDA DE SANT PERE
Carrer Riera Alta
C. Pintor Fortuni
RAMBLAS
C. Comtal
C. ORTIGOSA
C. DE TRAFALGAR
Carrer Peu de la Creu
Pl. Villa de Madrid
VIA LAIETANA
C. DEL CARME
Carrer Sant Pere més Baix
Portaferrissa
CARRER HOSPITAL
Aurora
RAMBLAS
PG. DE PUJADES
Riereta
Sant Jeroni
Cadena
M - LICEU
C. Raurich
C. DE SANT PAU
Pl. Reial
C. DE FERRAN
M - JAUME I
C. DE LA PRINCESA
CARRER NOU DE LA RAMBLA
Cervantes
PG. DE PICASSO
Avinguda de les Drassanes
C. Arc del Teatre
RAMBLAS
Pge. de la Pau
VIA LAIETANA
C. Ample
AV. M. DE L'ARGENTERA
Avinguda del Paral-lel
Carrer de la Mercè
Central Post Office
PG. ISABEL II
M - DRASSANES
EATACIÓN DE FRANCIA
PASSEIG DE COLOM
Pl. Portal de la Pau
M - BARCELONETA

1 Zeus Gay Shop
2 Sauna Condal
3 Ovlas Fashion Shop
4 Regencia Colon Hotel
5 Morera Restaurant
6 Café de la Opera
7 Marsella Bar
10 London Bar
11 Hotel California
12 Padam Padam Bar
13 Sestienda Gay Shop
14 Dickens Bar / Bar EA3
16 Cómplices Bookshop
18 Aurora Bar
19 B.Free Fashion Shop
20 Polo Pelo Body &Beauty Shop
21 American Boys House of Boys

INFOGAI (G) Meeting: Fri 18-21 h
C/Paloma,12 baixos ✉08001 ☎ 318 16 66 Fax: 318 16 65
E-Mail: cgb@olemail.com
Free monthly gay paper issued by Col.lectiu GAi de Barcelona
Lambda
C/. Ample 5 ☎ 412 72 72
Free quarterly publication. News from the group Casal Lambda, the gay scene, cultural and political articles, addresses, and personal ads.
Línea G (G)
☎ 200 80 88 Fax: 200 02 08 E-Mail: edito@lineag.net
Free monthly gay paper with a personal ads section.
NOIS (! G)
Diputació, 174 entl. 1er A, Apdo. 94015 ✉08080 ☎ 454 38 05
☎ 454 38 05 Fax: 454 38 05 E-Mail: nois@alehop.com
Free monthly gay paper in spanish listing all the venues and attractions in gay Barcelona. Acurate city map. Available in every gay bar and stores.

TOURIST INFO

Oficina de Turismo
Gran Vía de las Cortes Catalanas 658 ☎ 301 74 43

BARS

Acido Oxido (AC B d DR G lj MA VS WE) 21-2.30 h, WE 3 h
C/ Joaquín Costa 61 ✉08001 *(Metro Universidad)* ☎ 412 09 39
Aire (A AC B G MA s) 22-3 h, Mon closed
C/. Enrique Granados 48 ✉08008 ☎ 451 84 62
Aurora (A AC B g p s W WE YG) 20-2.30, Fri-Sun & public holidays also 6-12 h
C/. Aurora 7 ✉08001 *(Metro Liceo/San Antonio)* ☎ 442 30 44
Bahia (A AC B d gLm MG WE) 22-3.30 h
C/. Séneca 12 *(Metro Diagonal/Fontana)*
Barbarella (AC B CC F G MA) 21-3 h, Mon closed
C/ Calabira 142-144 ✉08015 *(Metro Rocafort)* ☎ 423 18 78
Blended 04 (B G MA r) 19-3 h
Marià Cubí 55 *(Metro Fontana)* ☎ 200 71 26
Bunker (AC B DR G LJ MA VS) 21-2.30 h, WE-3.30 h
C/ Entenza 46 ✉08015 ☎ 426 93 92
Large darkroom with cabins and sling
Café de la Calle (AC B f Glm YG) 18-3 h
C/. Vich 11 ✉08000 *(Metro Fontana)* ☎ 218 38 63
Cyber Otic (A AC B d G MA S SNU STV WE YG) Wed-Mon 20-3 h, closed Tue, shows 1 h
Urgell 84 ✉08011 *(Metro Urgell)*
Dickens (B G MA N) 20-3 h
C/. Raurich 21 *(Metro Liceu)*
Dietrich (! AC B CC d F G S YG) 22-3 h
Consell de Cent 255 ✉08011 *(Metro Universidad, between Nuntaner and Aribau)* ☎ 451 77 07
Daily drag shows.
Eagle (AC B DR G LJ MA P S WE) Sun-Thu 20-2.30, Fri Sat -3 h
Passeig Sant Juan 152 ✉08037 *(Metro Verdaguer)*
☎ 207 58 56
EA3-Bar (B g MA R) 20-3 h
C/. Raurich 23 *(Metro Liceu)* ☎ 412 05 84
Espai-Magic (AC B d DR G lj MA msg r S SNU STV VS WE YG) 21-3 h
C/. San Marcos 18-20 ✉08006 *(Metro Fontana)* ☎ 415 36 10
Este Bar (A AC B Glm YG) 22-03 h
C/. Consell de cent 257 *(Metro Universidad)* ☎ 323 64 06
Frivolité (A AC B d G MA S) 20-3 h (winter), 22-3 h (summer)
C/ Casanova 71 ✉08011 *(Metro Gran Vía)* ☎ 323 10 00
Hot (A AC B D GLM MA S SNU STV VS W WE YG) 17-5 h
C/. Roger de Luria 40 ✉08009 ☎ 481 31 74
Cocktail bar and disco.
London Bar (B g MA) 19-5 h
C/. Nou de la Rambla 34 *(Metro Liceu)* ☎ 318 52 61
Marsella (AC B glm lj MA s) 21-2.30, Fri Sat -3.30 h
San Pau, 65 *(Metro Liceo)*
Medusa (A AC B d G MA s tv WE) 17-2.30 h
Casanova 75 ✉08011 *(Metro Gran Via/Urgell)* ☎ 454 53 63
Bar and cafeteria.
Monaco (A AC B CC d DR G MA s STV VS WE YG) Mon-Thu 20-2, Fri-Sat -3, Sun 18-2 h
C/. Diputación 210 ✉08011 *(Metro Universidad)*
New Chaps (AC B DR G LJ MA s VS WE) 21-3h
Avinguda Diagonal 365 *(Metro Diagonal)* ☎ 215 53 65
Leather bar
Nois Quina Nit (B G D S VS) 22-3 h
Riera de Sant Miguel, 59 ✉08006
Padam Padam (A AC B g MA) 19-3 h, closed Sun
C/. Raurich 9 ☎ 302 50 62
Classical music.
Punto BCN (! A AC B E G MA) 18-2, WE -3 h
C/. Muntaner 63-65 *(Metro Universidad)* ☎ 453 61 23
Remix (B d g) Mon-Sun 19-3 h
C/.Lleida, 23 *(Monjuïc-Pça. España)*
Roma (B f Glm MA) 19-2 h, Fri Sat -3 h
C/. Alfons XII 41 *(Metro Fontana)* ☎ 201 35 13
Popular.

Rosa. La (B gLM MA) Thu-Sun 20-3 h
Brusi 39 ✉08006 *(Entrance Augusta and San Elias)* ☎ 414 61 66
Theseo Bar (A B bf F g MA YG) 8.30-2.30, closed Sun; best evenings
C/. de Comte Borrell 119 ☎ 453 87 96
Topxi (AC B d DR G MA STV VS) 22-5, Show Mon-Thu 1.45, Fri-Sun 1.45, 4 h
C/. Valencia 358 ✉08000

CAFES

Antoniovs Libreria-Café (A b bf CC GLM s) Mon-Fri 10.30-14 h , 16.30-21 h, Sat 12-14 h, 16.30-21 h, Sun closed
Calle Josep Anselm Cavé 6 ✉08002 *(Metro Drassanes, between Ramblas and C/ Ample)* ☎ 301 90 70 Fax: 301 90 70
Bookshop and café.
Café de la Opera (B f NG OS) 10-2 h
C/. Ramblas 74 ✉08000 *(Metro Liceu)*
Gambistos (A AC B bf F G MA OS) 8-3 h, Sat, Sun 16.30-3 h
C/ Casanova 73 ✉08011 *(Metro Gran Vía/Urjell)* ☎ 323 10 00
G-Café (A AC B bf f G MA OS) 9-2 h, WE-3 h
C/ Muntaner 24 ✉08013 *(Metro Universidad)* ☎ 451 65 36
Oui Café (AC B f G MA OS VS) 17-2 h, WE-3 h
C/ Consell de Cent 247 ✉08011

DANCECLUBS

Arena Sala Classic (AC B D G MA VS YG) Fri Sat 24-6 h
C/. Diputació 233 ✉08007 *(Metro Universidad)* ☎ 487 83 42
Spanish music.
Arena Sala V.I.P. (! AC B D G MA VS YG) Fri Sat 24-6 h
C/.Gran Via de las Cortes Catalanas 593 ✉08007 *(Metro Universidad)*

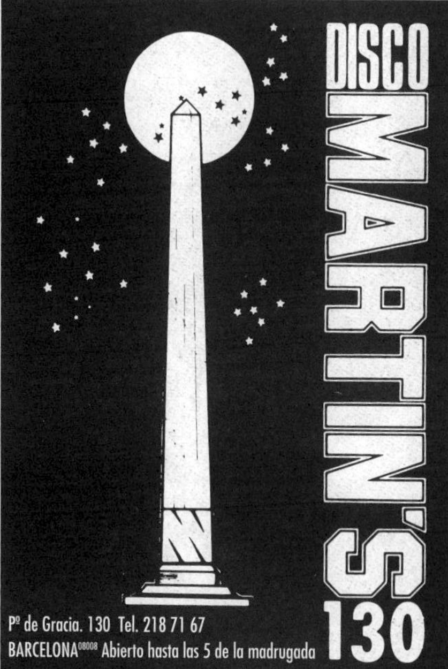

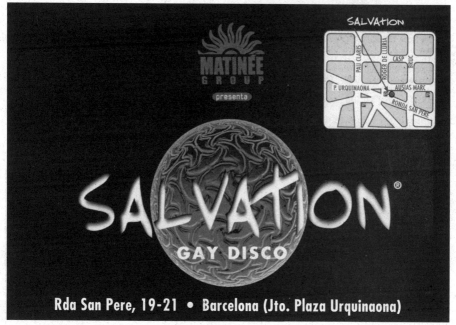

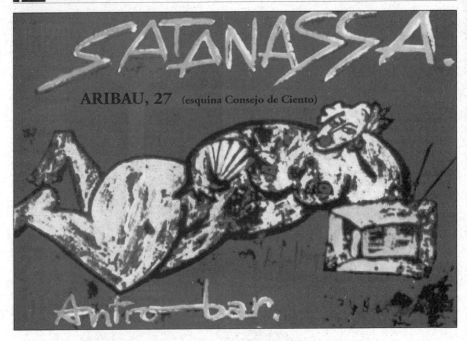

Luna. La (B D DR G MA snu VS) 21-3, WE -4, winter Show Sun 1 h
Avinguda Diagonal 323 ✉08000 *(Metro Verdaguer)*

Martin's (AC B D DR GLM lj MA R s VS) 0-5 h
Paseo de Gracia 130 ✉08008 *(Metro Diagonal)* ☎ 218 71 67

Metro (! AC B D DR G lj MA S STV SNU VS) 24-5, Sun also 19-22.30 h
C/. Sepúlveda 185 ✉08011 *(Metro Universidad)* ☎ 323 52 27

Salvation (AC B D DR G MA S SNU STV VS WE YG) Wed-Sat 24-6 h
Ronda San Pere 19-21 ✉08010 *(Metro Urquinaona)*
☎ 318 06 86

Satanassa (AC B D glm MA P s YG) 22.30-3 h
C/. Aribau 27/Conselo de Ciento ✉08011 *(Metro Universidad)*
☎ 453 61 41
Popular.

Tatu (AC B D DR MA S VS) 22-4.30, Sun 19-4.30. Show Sun-Fri 1.30, Sun also 21 h
C/. Cayo Celio 7 ☎ 425 33 50
Popular. Entry Ptas 500 incl. 1 drink.

RESTAURANTS

Café Miranda (! b F G MA) 21-1 h
C/. Casanova 30 ✉08011 *(near Gran Vía)* ☎ 453 52 49
Mediterranean cuisine in a nice ambiente.

Cafeti. El (F g MA) 13.30-15.30, 20.30-23.30 h, closed Mon & Sun evening
C/. Sant Rafael 18 ☎ 329 24 19
Spanish cuisine.

CAFÉ
miranda
gay restaurant
Casanova 30, 08011 Barcelona (entre Sepúlveda - Gran Via

gay teatro café
DIETRICH
Consell de Cent 255 (entre Muntaner y Aribau)

Castro Restaurant (AC B CC F G lj MA s WE) 13-16, 21-24 h, closed Sun
Calle Casanova 85 ✉08011 *(Metro Urgell)* ☎ 323 67 84
Menu at 1200 Pts (cocina mercado), menu à la carte at 3000 Pts

Diva. La (AC B CC F g MA STV) Tue-Sun 13-15.30 21-0.30 h, closed Mon
Diputacion 127 ✉08011 *(Metro Universidad/Urgell)*
☎ 454 63 98
Drag shows, cabaret.

Eterna (CC F g) 13-16 h, 21-24 h
C/ Casanova, 42 ☎ 453 17 86

La Veronica (AC CC F glm MA OS WE YG) Tue 20-1.30 h, Wed-Sun 13.30-1.30, Sat -2 h
C/ Avinyó, 30 ✉08002 ☎ 412 11 22

Little Italy (F g) 13.30-16/21-0, Fri-Sat -0.30 h
C/. del Rec 30 *(near P. del Born)* ☎ 319 79 73

Machin (g) 13.30-23 h
Passatje J. Llovera,11 ☎ 200 19 74

Mexico Lindo (B F g MA) 13-16, 20.30-1 h
C/. Regás 35/Laforja *(Metro: Fontana, Passeig de Gràcia)*
☎ 218 18 18
Mexican cuisine.

Morera. La (AC F glm lj MA W YG) 13-15.30, 20.30-23.45 h, closed Sun
Plaza San Agustín 1 ✉08001 ☎ 318 75 55 Fax: 302 65 11

Ovlas Cafe Restaurante (AC B bf CC F G MA s STV) 9.30-20.30, Sun closed
C/ Portaferissa 25 ✉08002 ☎ 412 38 36 Fax: 412 52 29
Italian food, menu del día, Sat 17-20 Show

La DIVA
gay restaurant
Diputación 127 / 08011 Barcelona
tel: 93 454 63 98

1 EURO =

40,3399	BEF	40,3399	LUF
1,95583	DEM	2,20371	NLG
166,386	ESP	13,7603	ATS
6,55957	FRF	200,482	PTE
0,787564	IEP	5,94573	FIM
1936,27	ITL		

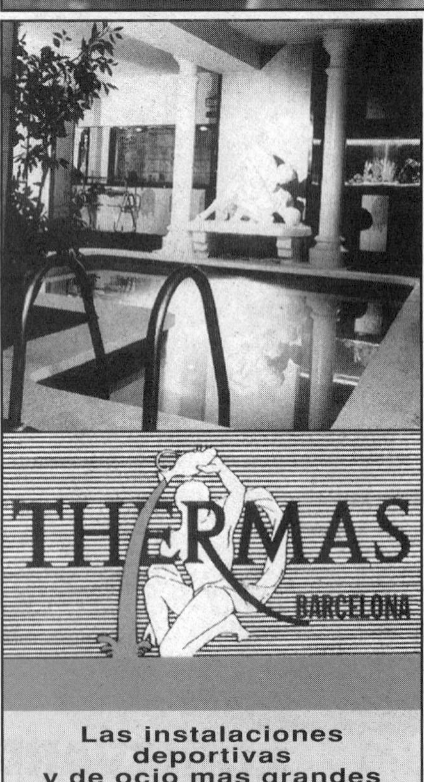

SEX SHOPS/BLUE MOVIES

Blue Box (g VS) 10-24 h
C/. Aragón 249
Blue Star (g VS) Mon-Fri 9-23 h, Sat-Sun 10-23 h
Avinguda de Roma 2-4 *(Edificio Torre Catalunya)* ☎ 426 32 16
Kitsch (g VS) 10-22, Sun 17-22 h
C/. Muntaner 17-19 *(At Gran Vía)* ☎ 451 20 48
Nostromo (AC CC G VS) 12-22
C/ Diputació 208 ✉08011 ☎ 323 31 94
Very cruisy cabins.
Nostromo (A DR GLM MA W YG) Mon-Sat 12-22, Sun and public holidays 17-22 h
C/. Diputación 208, Bajos ✉08007 *(Metro-Universidad)*
☎ 323 31 94
Sestienda Gay Shop (CC G MA VS) 10-21 h, closed Sun
C/. Raurich 11 ✉08002 *(Metro Liceu)* ☎ 318 86 76
Ask for information.
Sexgold (AC CC E g VS WE) 11-22, Sun & public holidays 16-22 h
C/. Balmes 180 ✉08006 ☎ 217 26 29 Fax: 200 70 45
Skorpius (g VS)
Gran Vía Corts Catalanes, 384-390
Zeus Gay Shop (AC CC G MA VS) 10-21 h, closed Sun
C/. Riera Alta 20 ✉08001 *(Metro Sant Antoni)* ☎ 442 97 95

CINEMAS

Arenas (b G OG) 15.30-23.30 h
C/. Cruz Cubierta 22 ✉08000 *(Metro España)*
Cine Diorama (AC DR G MA OG) 10.30-22 h
Plaza Buensuceso 5 ✉08000 *(Metro Cataluña)* ☎ 318 12 91
Walking down the Ramblas, 2nd street to the right. Popular in the evening. Entry Ptas 700.
Roma (g)
C/. Aragón 197 ✉08000 *(between Aribau and Muntaner)*

HOUSE OF BOYS

American Boys (CC G R VS) 24 h
Ronda Universidad 23, 3°, 2, B *(Metro Plaza Catalunya)*
☎ 412 75 33
Neron (CC G R tv VS) 0-24 h
Consejo de Ciento 185 3° 1-a ✉08006 *(Metro Urgel)*
☎ 451 10 28
Staus Chicos (AC G msg p R VS)
C/. Rosellon 328 ✉08025 *(Metro Sagada Familia)* ☎ 458 8578

AMERICAN BOYS

CHICOS DE COMPAÑIA
ALTO STANDING
*****

TEL.: 93 412 75 33

**- EXCLUSIVOS MODELOS MASCULINOS
(10 BOYS FROM 18 TO 28 YRS OF AGE
AWAIT YOU)
- INSTALACIONES DE LUSO HABITACIONOS
CON VIDEO, BAÑERA, JACUZZI, HILO MUSICAL,
AIRE CONDICIONADO.
LUXURY SUITES. STREAPTEASE. COPA GRATIS.
- COME AND SEE US.**

**PLAZA CATALUÑA
RONDA UNIVERSIDAD 23 III 2 B
SERVICIO PERMANENTE 24 H
SALIDAS HOTEL Y DOMICILIO
VISA - MASTERCARD**

**- WE SPEAK ENGLISH, FRANÇAIS, ITALIANO ...
HTTP://WWW.SEXOLE.COM/AMERICANBOYS.COM**

SAUNAS/BATHS

Bruch (B G MA msg sa sol wh wo VS) 11-23 h
C/. Bruch 65 ✉08000 *(Metro Girona)* ☎ 487 48 14
Admission Ptas 1150.

Casanova
C/. Casanova 57 ☎ 323 78 60

Condal (! B CC F msg sa sb VS wh) 12-6, Fri Sat 0-24 h
C/. Espolsasacs 1 ✉08002 *(Metro Cataluña)* ☎ 317 68 17
Entrance-fee Ptas 1300-1700.

Corinto (CCB F G MA r sa sb sol VS wh) 12-2 h We 0-24 h
C/. Pelayo 62 *(near Pl. Catalunya)* ☎ 318 64 22
Entrance-fee Ptas 1200-1600.

Galilea Sauna (! b CC F G MA MSG VS) 12-24, Fri-Sat 0-24 h
Calabria 59 ✉08015 *(Metro Rocafort)* ☎ 426 79 05
Admission Ptas 1400, Wed-Thu 1000Pts,- 23yrs 900.

Lesseps (B G MA msg sa sb VS) 10-22, Sun 15-22 h
C/. Mauricio Serrahima 9 ✉08012 *(Metro Lesseps)*
☎ 218 05 92

Padua (B CC f G msg sa sb sol VS wh WO) 14-22 h
C/. La Gleva 34 ✉08006 *(Metro Lesseps)* ☎ 212 16 54
Entrance-fee Ptas 1600.

Thermas (AC B bf CC DR F G MA msg pi R sa sb sol VS WE wh WO) 10-2, Fri Sun 0-24 h
C/. Diputación 46 ✉08000 *(Metro Rocafort L1)* ☎ 325 93 46
The largest gay sauna in Spain. Bar and restaurant offering spanish cuisine.

MASSAGE

Massajes E. Sorensen (g msg) 9-23 h
Corsega, 207 1er 2A ✉08036 ☎ 419 05 89 ☎ 908 444 596

BODY & BEAUTY SHOPS

Chaning Marsó (g) Mon-Sat 11-21 h, Sun closed
Diputació, 159 ☎ 454 24 10
Haircuts

Giovane Peluqueria (AC B g msg) 9-20, Sat -15 h, closed Sun
Avenida Mistral 28-30 ✉08015 *(Metro Rocafot)* ☎ 423 03 27
Beauty salon.

Polo-Pelo (g) Mon 15-20.30, Tue-Sat 10.30-23.30
Portaferrissa, 25 1er pis ☎ 412 38 42
Haircuts

BOOK SHOPS

Antinous (A B bf CC GLM) Mon-Fri 10.30-14, 16.30-21, Sat 12-21 h, closed Sun
C/. Josep Anselm Clave 6 ✉08002 *(Metro Drassanes)* ☎ 301 90 70
Books, magazines, videos, post cards, posters. Also mail-order.

Cómplices (GLM) Mon-Fri 10.30-20.30, Sat 12-20.30 h
Cervantes 2 ✉08002 *(Metro Liceu)* ☎ 412 72 83
Also very good for information about the gay scene.

CONDOM SHOPS

Condoneria Mon-Sat 10.30-14.00 16.30-20.30 h, closed Sun
Placa San Josep Oriol 7 *(Metro Liceu)* ☎ 302 77 21

FASHION SHOPS

Absolutely Fabulous (A AC CC G MA) Mon 17-20.30 h, Tue-Sat 10.30-14 h, 17-20.30 h
C/. Diputacion 163 ✉08011 ☎ 454 83 81

B.Free 10-14, 17-20 h
Plaza Vila de Madrid 5 *(Metro Catalunya)* ☎ 412 27 59
Clothes, accessoires, gay culture.

Guia Global (g)
Urgell 32 ✉08011

Ovlas 10.30-14, 16.30-20.30 h
C/. Portaferrissa 25, Tienda 34 ☎ 412 52 29
Clothes and accessories. Sell their own creations.

HOTELS

California Hotel (AC bf CC g H)
C/. Raurich 14 ✉08002 *(Fernando. Metro Liceu)* ☎ 317 77 66
Fax: 317 54 74 Homepage: www.seker.es/Hotel_California
Centrally located. Rooms with bath, air condition, phone and tv. Rates Ptas 6.000-10.000 (bf incl.)

Que tal (G H)
C/. Mallorca 290 ✉08008 ☎ 459 23 66 Fax: 459 23 66
10 double and 3 single rooms. Rooms partly with bath/WC.

Regencia Colon Hotel (AC B bf CC F g H)
C/. Sagristans 13/17 ✉08002 *(Metro Jaume I)* ☎ 318 98 58
Fax: 317 28 22 E-Mail: colon@ncsa.es
Homepage: www.hotelsearch.com
Three-star-hotel. Located in the Gothic quarter, only a few steps from the Ramblas, shopping and gay live. 55 rooms with bath, sat-TV, telephone, mini bar, AC, safe. Rates single Ptas 9.500, double 16.000, bf 1.200. Special discount for SPARTACUS-readers 10%.

GENERAL GROUPS

Casal Lambda Café Mon-Fri 17-21, Sa 17-23 h
C/. Ample 5, baixos ✉08002 (Metro Drassanes) ☎ 412 72 72
Fax: 412 74 76 Homepage: www.redestb.es/Lambda

Col.Lectiu Gai de Barcelona (C.G.B.)
Mon-Fri 19-21 h
C/. Paloma 12 baixos ✉08001 *(PO Box 32.016 08080; near Zeus Sexshop)* ☎ 318 16 66 Fax: *318 16 65*

HEALTH GROUPS

Actua! Mon-Fri 9-14 h, 16-19 h
C/. Gomis 38 bajo ✉08023 ☎ 418 50 00 Fax: 418 89 74
People living with AIDS.
Asociación Ciudadana Anti-Sida de Catalunya Mon-Fri 10-14, 16-21 h
Junta del Comerc 23 baja ✉08000
☎ 317 05 05 Fax: 301 41 82
Information and services concerning AIDS.
Departamento de Sanidad
Avenida Drassanes 17-21 ✉08000 *(Metro Universidad)*
☎ 441 29 97
HIV-testing.

HELP WITH PROBLEMS

Teléfono Rosa 18-22 h
☎ 900 601 601

RELIGIOUS GROUPS

Gays Cristianes de Cataluña Mon Sat 19.30-22 h
PO Box 854, ✉08080 ☎ 398 16 84
Meeting: Escudellers 53 1ã 2ã (Metro Drassanes).

SWIMMING

-Playa de Chernobil (g NU) (beside Barcelona near the Olympic City in S. Adrian de Besos. Metro Sant Roc. The beach is behind the TAGRA-factory. No bushes. Very popular. In winter car-cruising! This year a new nudist beach will open in Barcelona.)
-Playa Mar Bella (g NU) (Metro Ciudadela, then 2 km by foot)
-Playa de la Barceloneta (g)

CRUISING

All cruising areas are AYOR:
-Parque de Montjuic (especially between Avenida del Estadio and Avenida Rius y Taulet. Popular)
-Plaza de Catalunya (R)
-Station/Estación de Sants (very popular)
-San Andrés/Arenal Estación
-El Corte Ingles-Shopping Centre, Plaza de Catalunya, best opposite women clothing

Benidorm ☎ 96

● Benidorm is the jewel of the Costa Blanca, as it is famous for it's beautiful beach *Poniente*, which is considered to be one of the best seven beaches in the world by the U.N.O. The gay area is concentrated in the old village close to the beach. During the summer there is an interesting mixture of gay and straight discos.

✱ Benidorm ist das Juwel der Costa Blanca und berühmt für den wunderschönen Strand *Poniente*, den selbst die UNO als einen der sieben schönsten Strände der Welt bezeichnet. Die schwule Szene konzentriert sich in der Altstadt in der Nähe des Strandes. Während des Sommers gibt es hier eine interessante Mischung aus homo- und heterosexuellen Discos.

▲ Bénidorm est le bijou de la Costa-Blanca, et renommé pour la magnifique plage de *Poniente*, que même l'ONU considère comme l'une des sept plus belles plages du monde. Le milieu gay se concentre surtout dans la vieille ville, près de la plage. Pendant l'été, on y trouve un mélange interessant de clubs homo-et hétérosexuelles.

☆ Benidorm es la perla de la Costa Blanca y famosa por su encantadora playa *Poniente*, que fué hasta elegida por la ONU como una de las siete playas más bonitas del mundo. El ambiente gay se concentra en el casco antiguo de la ciudad cerca de la playa. Durante el verano, Benidorm ofrece una mezcla interesante entre discotecas homo- y heterosexuales.

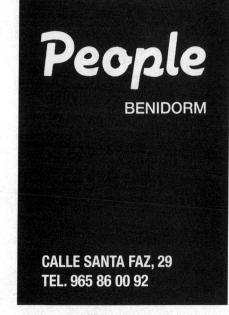

❖ Benidorm è la perla della Costa Blanca e famosa per la bellissima spiaggia *Poniente*, dichiarata perfino dall'Onu una delle sette spiagge più belle del mondo. La vita gay si concentra nel centro storico vicino alla spiaggia. Durante l'estate si trova un miscuglio interessante di discoteche per gay ed eterosessuali.

TOURIST INFO

Oficina de Turismo
Martínez Alejos 16 ☎ 585 32 24

BARS

Arcos Bar (AC B G MA) Summer: 19-3 h. Winter: 18-2 h, Mon closed
C/Sta Faz 31 ✉03500
Blue Moon.The (AC B bf F g MA VS) 11-1 h, Wed 20-1 h
C/ de la Palma 23 ✉03500
Englisch breakfast, lunch and dinner.
Chaplin (AC B G MA) 22.30-3 h
Calle San Vicente 16
Popular.
Company Bar (B G bf f LJ OS) 10-1 h
C/ San Miquel 16 ✉03500 ☎ 586 87 13
Desire (AC B G MA s VS) 20-? h
C/ San Lorenzo 1 ✉03500 ☎ 666 028 712 (mobile)
Diosa Bar. La (AC B G MA s) Summer 22-4 h, Winter 17-4 h
C/ San Vicente 17 ✉03500
Don Juan Bar (B f g H) 11-15, 18.30-2 h
C/. Santa Faz 28 ☎ 680 91 65

Eros (B DR G LJ MA VS) 0.30-6 h
Calle Santa Faz 24
Intimate English. The (B g MA S) 20.30-2 h
Calle La Palma 6 ☎ 680 38 76
Shows 23 h.
Kaffee Klee (B glm S) 17-3 Sat 21-3 h
Calle de Pal 9 ☎ 585 64 76
Look. The (B d DR G MA VS) 23-5.30 h
C/. Santa Faz 12 ☎ 680 16 89
Popular.
Meditereaneo (AC B G H MA VS) 22- h, closed Mon in winter
Calle Alicante 18 ✉03500 ☎ 585 67 60
Minerva Bar (AC B G MA) 22-4 h
Carretera San Vicente 22 ☎ 585 87 15
Popular.
New Siroco (B f g MA) 22-4 h
C/. Vivaldi 2, El Albir, 03580 Alfaz del Pi ☎ 686 70 17
Night. The (AC B d G MG S VS) 3-9 h
Calle Santa Faz 10 ☎ 680 82 85
Orpheo's (AC B d DR G MA VS) 22-4 h
Plaza Constitución 12
Popular late bar.
People (AC B d DR GLM lj MA VS YG) 22-4 h
Calle Santa Faz 29 ✉03500 ☎ 586 00 92
Popular, very friendly and good service.
Peppermint (B G MA) 22-3?, Mon Show 1 h
Calle San Vincente 11 ☎ 586 07 89
Popular.
Rich Bitch (AC B d G MA S STV TV) 21-? h, Shows daily 22-1 h
C/ de Pal 4 ✉03500 ☎ 666 055 906 (mobile)
Zanzibar (B DR G STV VS) 23-6 h
Calle Santa Faz 7 ☎ 586 78 07
Popular. STV at 1.30 h
42nd Street (AC B DR G MA r VS) 21-3 h
Avenida Uruguay *(under Hiper-Condor)*

CAFÉS

Café Bahia (b bf F g H MA OS) 9-24, winter 10-19 h
Calle Gijon 1 *(La Cala, near Hotel Bahia)* ☎ 586 55 25
Peter's Playa Bar (AC B GLM MA N) 10-22 h
Levante Beach, Edificio Iberia ☎ 681 24 78
Only day-time gay bar in Benidorm. Cozy and friendly atmosphere.
San Marcos (B bf F g MA OS) 10.30-3 h, closed winter Wed
Avenida de Alcoy 6/Avenida de Bilbao *(Playa de Levante, entrance at Iberia Apartment Building)* ☎ 585 65 56

DANCECLUBS

Terraza. La (AC B CC D DR GLM lj OS MA s SNU STV WE YG) 2-8 h, Sept-June only WE
Avor - Severu Ochor 31 ✉03500 *(In front of Benidorm Pallace)*

RESTAURANTS

Casa Abdul (B F g) 12-15, 19-24 h, Wed closed
Calle La Palma 13 ☎ 585 39 35
International cusine with a French/Marrocan touch.
Hierbas (F g MA) 19-23.30, winter also Sun 12-17 h
C/. Purisima 4 ☎ 586 86 32 Fax: 586 61 39
International - english cuisine.
O Sole Mio (B CC F g) 11-16, 19-24 h
Aud. Marina Baixa, Edificio Acanticados, Cala Finestrat
☎ 585 89 61

Secret Gardens. The (B F g MA) 19.30-? h
C/. Condestable Zaragozá 21 ☎ 680 69 18
French cuisine.

Tiffany's (AC b E F g MA) 19.30-24 h
Avenida Mediterráne 53, Edificio Casablanca 3 ☎ 585 44 68
Excellent international dishes. With life music.

Two Palms (F g MA) 19.30-23 h, Tue closed
C/. La Palma 30 ☎ 680 18 07
International - english cuisine.

Vagabund Restaurant. The (F g OS) Winter: 19.30-22.30 h, Summer 20-24 h
Calle Bon Retiro 4 ☎ 680 81 66
International cuisine.

SHOWS

Molino (B g MA STV) 22-?, Show 22.30 h
Avda. Beniardá 2 *(El Cruce)* ☎ 680 23 08

Sabrina (B g STV) 22-?, show 22.45 h
Av. Jaime I 9 *(under Hotel Sirena)* ☎ 585 36 06

SEX SHOPS/BLUE MOVIES

Sex Shop Benidorm (g MA VS) 10.30-13.30, 16-21.30 h, Sun closed
San Roque 6 ☎ 965/586 67 46

Show Center Sexyland (g VS) 10-24 h
Calle Marqués de Comillas 2 ☎ 680 64 00

SAUNAS/BATHS

Adonis Sauna (AC B G MA msg sa sb VS) 15,30-21.30 h
Calle Venezuela 4 *(Edificio Narcea, near Gasolinera Isleta, Avenida Jaime I)* ☎ 585 79 58

Sauna Scorpios (B G MA msg sa sb VS wh) 15.30-22 g
Calle Ruzafa *(Edificio Carrasco, next to bike shop)*

HOTELS

Casa Don Juan (B CC g H) 11-15 h, 19-2 h
C/. Santa Faz 28 ☎ 680 91 65 Fax: 680 48 86
6 double and 1 single room some with shower/WC and terrace.

GUEST HOUSES

Villa de los Sueños (bf CC f G H msg NU OS pi VS wh wo)
Carretera Finestrat 5 ✉03500 *(3 km above Benidom in a quit surrounding)* ☎ 586 88 24 ☎ 619 108 341 (mobile)
Fax: 586 21 06 E-Mail: willadelossuenos@ctv.es
8 double rooms and 2 suites incl. breakfast buffet. Rooms with Bath/WC, TV. Car rental, excursions, aiport service, half board available.

APARTMENTS

Front Line Apartments Benipark, Avda Armada Española 4, ✉03500 *Block 2, Apt. 6-7 c* ☎ 586 51 29
Swimming Pool, Tennis, Privat Parking Rates Jul-15 Sep Ptas 70.000/week, low season 45.000. 20 luxury apartments with a view of the cruising. Cruising areas around.

HEALTH GROUPS

Asociacion Civica a Afectados del HIV • SIDA, Amigos Benidorm, Marina Baixa
9-13, 17-21 h
Calle Gambo 6 - 2ã - 6 ☎ 680 44 44

SWIMMING

-La Cala (g NU MA) (Playa Poniente, by the rocks at the end of the beach. Popular, but dangerous.)

-Rincon de Loix (g) (at the end of the beach)
-Playa Levante, in front of „Peter´s Playa Bar(Popular)
-Playa Campomanes, ca. 10 km north of Benidorm (g NU)(near 03590 Altea, take road Altea-Calpe, before tunnel, under Pueblo Mascarat.
-Playa Racó Conill (g NU) bus to playa Finestrat, then walking in direction Alicante, up the hill and down to the beach and further on.

CRUISING

-Playa Poniente

Bilbao ☎ 94

BARS

Convento. El (B Glm d MA YG) 21-? h
Calle Esperanza 11
Heaven Club (B DR G MA VS) 22-3, WE -4.30 h
Calle Dos de Mayo 6 ☎ 416 17 10
High (B d DR G MA VS) 20.30-3.30, WE -4 h
Calle La Naja 5
Kasko (AC B CC d F G MA S) 123-2
C/ Santa Maria 16 ✉48005 *Casco Viejo)* ☎ 416 03 11
It´s also a reataurant, diners with piano music.
Mykonos (AC B DR G MA s SNU VS) 20-? h
C/General Castillo 4 ✉48003
Otxoa (B d g TV W) 20-3, WE -4 h
Calle Lersundi 10 *(Calle Heros)* ☎ 424 18 48
Santurio (B DR G MA R VS) 19-? h
Calle Lamana 5 ☎ 415 94 96
Sperma (B DR G MA r VS) 20-3, WE -4 h
Calle Dos de Mayo 6
Tabernville (B DR G MA) 21-3.30, WE -6 h
C/ Hernani 18 ✉48003 ☎ 415 35 76
Txoko Landa (B D GLM p s WE) Fri-Sat 23-2.30 h
Escalinatas de Solokoetxe 4 ✉48005 *(Metro Casco Viejo)*
☎ 415 07 19
Bilbao's gay movement bar.
28 (B gLM) 21-3 h
Calle Hernani 3

CAFÉS

Bizitza (B glm OS)
Calle la Torre/Casco Viejo
Bristol (B bf f G MA OS) 11-2 h, WE 19-4 h
Plaza Venezuela 1 ✉48001 *(Entrance via C/Principe)*
☎ 424 55 98
Ekklesía (B f glm MA) 10-15, 17-23, WE -2 h
Calle Hernani 3
Lamiak (B f GLM s W) 19-1, We -2. Winter 16.30-24, WE -2.30 h
Calle Pelota 8 ☎ 416 17 65
Nervion. El (B f G r W) 19-3 h
Calle Dos de Mayo 1
Sorgiñe (B f GLM OS) 19-1 h
Calle Pelota 4

DANCECLUBS

Bailongo (AC B D glm S STV) 20-3 h, WE -4.30 h
C/ Henao 6 ✉48001 ☎ 424 70 03
Gay only on Thu and Sun for show 22.30 an 1 h.
Congreso (B D g) 24-4 h
Calle Uribitarte 8
Conjunto Vacío (B d g) 22-4 h
Muelle de la Merced 3
Distrito 9 (! B D g WE) Fri Sat 1-? h
Calle Juan de Ajuariaguerra 17
Enigma (B D glm MA) 20-5 h, WE (G)
Calle Luis Iruarrizaga 7
Key (B D G STV) WE show 1 & 3 h Calle Cristo 3
La Cantora (AC B D glm MA S STV) 20-4 h, WE -6 h
C/ Henao 25 ✉48009 ☎ 423 77 18
Shows Wed and Sun 22.30 h and 1.30 h.

RESTAURANTS

Arrebato (A AC B CC D F glm MA S WE YG) 11-1.30 h
Muelle Marzana 4 ☎ 416 41 81
Deliciosa. La (B F g MA) 19-23 h
Calle Jardines 1 ☎ 416 35 90
Ruedo. El (B F G MA) 10-22 h, closed Sun
Calle García Salazar 6 ☎ 422 11 35
Good, cheap lunch.
Txiriboga (B F glm) 13-15, 19-23 h
Calle Santa María 11 *Bocadillos.*
Txomin Barullo (B F g W) 18.30-23.30 h
Calle Barrenkalle 40

SHOWS

Tiffany´s (AC B CC d e g MA S SNU STV TV) 23-6 h, Show 1.30-3.30 h
C/ Trancisco Macia 11 ✉48008 *(Near Museo Guggenheim)*

SEX SHOPS/BLUE MOVIES

American's (g VS) 10-3, Sun 10-14, 16-3 h
Calle Nicolás Alcorta 5 *(Galería Centro Zabalburo, 1st floor)*
Internacional (g VS) 10-2
Calle Nicolás Alcorta 7 *(Galería Centro Zabalburo; 1st floor)*
☎ 444 68 51
Sex Shop (g VS) 10-14, 15.30-22.30 h
Calle Ledesma 2 ☎ 424 40 23

SAUNAS/BATHS

Oasis (B DR f G sa sb sol VS W WO) Mon-Thu 17-22, Fri -8 h, Sat 17 h until Sun 22 h
Calle Atxuri 43 ☎ 433 66 30 *Entry Ptas 1.200, Thu 900.*
XQ 28 Sauna (B DR G f sa sb sol pi VS wh) 17-23, WE -8 h
Calle Nicolas Alcorta 5 ☎ 422 39 20
Entrance fee: Ptas. 1.300, Unter 25 and Thu Ptas. 1.000.

BOOK SHOPS

Libreria De Babel 10-14h, 17-21 h.
C/ de la Pelota 6 ✉48005 ☎ 416 85 83

GENERAL GROUPS

Aldarte Mon-Fri 10-13 h, Mon-Thu 17.30-20,30 h
Barroeta Aldawar 7 ✉48001 *(2nd Floor, Metro Albaudo)*
☎ 423 72 96 Fax: 423 72 96
Center for information, help with problem, archives.
EHGAM Mon-Fri 20-22
Escalinetas des Solokoetxe 4 ✉48005 ☎ 415 07 19
Gay library and archives. Publisher of »Gay Hotsa«. Friendly help with all sorts of problems.
T-4 Asoc. Ciud. lucha contra el sida
Alameda Gregorio de Revilla, 36 ✉48080 ☎ 422 12 40
Fax: 422 24 65 E-Mail: autopoyot4@mx3.redestb.es

HEALTH GROUPS

Comisión Ciudadana Anti Sida de Bizkaia
Mon-Fr 9-13, 16-20 h
Calle Bailén, 6 ✉48003 ☎ 416 00 55
Information and services concerning AIDS.

Gays por la Salud de Euskadi-T 4 10-23 h
Calle Autonomía 56 3., ✉48012 ☎ 422 12 40
Servicio Vasco de Salud (ETS) Mon-Fri 9-12 h
Calle Coctor Arcilza, planta baja ☎ 441 25 00
HIV-test.

SWIMMING

-Playa Larrabastera (La Salvaje)
-Playa Arrigunaga (Algorta)

CRUISING

-Azkorri
-Park Casilda Iturriza

Blanes ☎ 972

SWIMMING

-Playa los Pinos (NU) (cruising at the end of the beach.)

Burgos ☎ 947

BARS

Sebastian (AC B G MA OS S YG) 17-2.30, WE-4 h, Mon closed
C/ Trinidad 16 ✉09001 *(Near Palacio Capitanía)* ☎ 27 86 52
Sat shows or special events.
Trastienda. La (B glm) 20-2 h
Plaza de la Isla

CRUISING

-Pirazes de Cortez (day and evening)
-El Empecinado (park at the river, gardens of La Isla)

Cadiz ☎ 956

BARS

Café de Levante (B f glm YG) 20-1, Fri Sat -2 h
Calle Rosario
☛ also Puerto de Sta. Maria.

SEX SHOPS/BLUE MOVIES

Internacional (g VS) 10-22 h
Calle Pintor Murillo 2 ☎ 26 20 00

GUEST HOUSES

Pension „Torre Mar" (bf F H glm) 24 h
Calle Cordoba 30 ✉11550 *(50 m to the beach, 5 min. to the center)* ☎ 976 126 Fax: 976 126 E-Mail: ehlershd@aol.com
4 double rooms with WC/bath, Sat-TV

GENERAL GROUPS

FLHA
PO Box 64

SWIMMING

-Playa El Chato (NU) (on the way from Cadiz direction San Fernando)

CRUISING

-Playa de Cortadura (from the Edificio Alfa over the beach wall to the beginning of the beach; night and late night)
-Maritim Promenade (Victoria Beach; nights)
-Callejón del Blanco
-Bus station
-Train station
-Docks

Canary Islands

Islas Canarias

Time: GMT

Climate: subtropical sea climate, under the influence of the dry northeasterly winds which keep the temperatures at a pleasant level. Short winter rainy season.

Important gay cities: Playa del Ingles/Maspalomas (Gran Canaria), Las Palmas (Gran Canaria).

Fuerteventura ☎ 922

HEALTH GROUPS

Hospital Seguridad Social
Street to the Airport km 1 *(in Puerto del Rosario)*
☎ 85 04 99 ☎ 85 05 45

SWIMMING

-Dunas de Corralejo (g NU) (between Puerto del Rosario and Corralejo; sometimes)
-Playa Castillo, Caleta de Fuste (g MA NU)

Gran Canaria - Las Palmas ☎ 928

BARS

Bridge (B G MA SNU) 22-3 h, Show Thu
Calle Mariana Pineda 17
Recently renovated, new image.
Lady Pepa (B G MA) 21.30-3 h
Calle Sargenta Llagas 32

CAFES

Magic (B bf f GLM OS) 9-4 h
Plaza Feray 6 ✉35007 *(Zona Puerta)*
Nuevo Rio (! B F G MA OS r) 8-2 h
Parque Santa Catalina ☎ 20 30 48
Newly renovated, very popular.

DANCECLUBS

Faunos (AC B D G MA r VS WE) 23-? h
C/ Dr. Miguel Rosas 37 bajo ✉35007 ☎ 264 758
Flash (B D G STV VS WE YG) Tue-Sun 0-8, show Sun 2 h
Calle Bernardo de la Torre 86 *(near Parque Santa Catalina)*
Popular.

RESTAURANTS

Casa Pablo (B F g) Mon-Sat 13-16.30, 20-0.30 h
Calle Tomas Miller 73 ☎ 26 81 58
Menina (AC B jCC g MA S) 21-12 h, Mon closed
C/ Diderot 15 ✉35007 *(near by the port)* ☎ 269 546
Dinner Show
Rincón Vasco. El (A AC B CC F g MA) 13-16, 20-24 h, closed Sun evenings and Mon
Calle Hierro 4 ✉35009 *(near Playa Canteras)* ☎ 27 74 63

SEX SHOPS/BLUE MOVIES

Jomato'G (g VS) Mon-Sat 10-2, Sun 10-24 h
Calle Dr. Miguel Rosas 4 ☎ 22 15 02
Sala X (g VS) 11-0 h
C/ Tomás Miller 51 bajo ✉35007 *(Zona Puerto)*

SAUNAS/BATHS

Sauna Portugal (AC B DR G MA msg N P sa sb VS) 16-24 h
C/ Portugal 27 ✉35010 *(Near by La Playa de las Canteras)*
☎ 227 284

Trebol Sauna (B DR f G MA msg sa sb VS) 16-24 h
Calle Tomas Miller 55
Massage Ptas 2000.

HOTELS

Hotel Guacamayo (g H)
Calle Dr. Miguel Rosa 9

GENERAL GROUPS

Collectivo de Gays y Lesbianas de Las Palmas
Apto. 707, ✉35080

CRUISING

-Parque Santa Catalina/Calle Ripoche (r)
-Parque Romano
-Playa de las Canteras el Balneario
-Roques Muelle Deportivo
-Parque, Toilets San Telmo
-Estación de Guaguas

Gran Canaria - Playa del Inglés ☎ 928

● What can be said about some other gay holiday spots, can be said particularly about Playa del Ingles: It's on the edge. On the outer edge of Spain, of Europe. It could be said that its part of Africa. Playa lies in the utmost south of Gran Canaria, and the gay beach is found, naturally, in the utmost corner between Playa and Maspalomas. Gay nightlife offers the other extreme. Most but not all of the gay establishments like cafés, bars, discos, saunas and sex shops are in the *Yumbo Center*. This is very convenient. The venues range from dusky leather-bars to buzzling discos. The distances are no problem at all. The only reason you could need a car is if you want to make a trip round the island, which however can be also made by bus. And if you stay in one of the bungalows of Maspalomas, the nightly trips to and fro by taxi are easily affordable.

✱ Was für manchen anderen schwulen Urlaubsort gilt, gilt für Playa del Inglés ganz besonders: Es liegt am Ende. Am äußersten Ende Spaniens, ja Europas, eigentlich ein Teil Afrikas. Playa liegt im äußersten Süden, und der schwule Strand liegt natürlich in der äußersten Ecke zwischen Playa und Maspalomas.
Das schwule Nightlife bietet genau das andere Extrem. Im *Yumbo Centro* finden sich die meisten, wenn auch nicht alle, Cafés, Bars, Discos, Saunen, Sex Shops. Das ist sehr praktisch. Und dabei reicht die Palette wirklich von der schummrigen Lederbar bis zur heftigen Disco.
Die Wege sind in Playa kein Problem. Wer dort wohnt, benötigt einen Wagen höchstens für die Inselrundfahrt, die man aber auch per Bus unternehmen kann. Und selbst für die abendlichen und nächtlichen Fahrten von und nach Maspalomas -so man dort in einer Bungalowanlage wohnt- reichen die äußerst günstigen Taxen.

▲ Playa del Ingles est un vrai paradis gay. Cette station balnéaire est à l'extrême sud de l'Espagne, c.a.d de l'Europe, presque en Afrique. La plage gaye se trouve entre Playa et Maspalomas, au bout du monde pour ainsi dire. La vie nocturne gaye, c'est avant tout le „Yumbo Centro" où l'on trouve la plupart des cafés, bars, boîtes, saunas et sex shops, ce qui a l'avantage d'être pratique. Il y en a pour tout le monde: de la pénombre du bar cuir aux lasers des boîtes de nuit. Ici aussi, on peut tout faire à pied: pas besoin de voiture, sauf pour faire le tour de l'île, si une excursion en bus ne vous dit rien. Même pour les trajets de nuit entre Play et Maspalomas, vous n'aurez pas besoin de voiture, car les taxis sont bon marché.

☆ Lo que es valedero para otros centros túristicos gay, vale también para Playa del Inglés. Se encuentra geograficamente casi escondida y es el punto más alejado de España e incluso de Europa, en realidad es parte de Africa. La playa se localiza en el más extremo sur de la isla y los gays se reunen sobre todo en la parte de la playa más próxima a Maspalomas. La vida nocturna gay se concentra en el otro extremo de la isla. En *Yumbo Center* se encuentra la mayoría (no todos) de los cafes, bares, discos, saunas, sex shops etc.. La variedad de los sitios de ambiente es sorprendente: Aquí se encuentran desde oscuros bares de cuero hasta discotecas marchosas. Las distancias no suponen ningún problema. Un coche de alquiler se necesita solo para un recorrido de la isla, que se puede hacer hasta en autobus. A los turistas que vivan en Maspalomas recomendamos el taxi para sus salidas nocturnas, ya que es bastante económico.

❖ Ciò che vale per alcuni luoghi turistici gay vale particolarmente per la playa del Inglès: è il massimo. Il limite estremo della Spagna, dell'Europa, a dire il vero dell'Africa. Playa è situata all'estremo sud, e la spiaggia gay in un angolo estremo tra Playa e Maspalomas. La vita notturna gay offre naturalmente l'estremo opposto. Nel *Yumbo centro* si trovano, se non tutti, la maggior parte dei bar, delle discoteche,delle saune e dei sex shop. É molto comodo, e la gamma va dal più sordido bar sado-maso alla più vivace discoteca. A Playa le distanze non sono un problema, chi ci vive ha bisogno dell'auto solo per fare il giro dell'isola, che si può fare anche in autobus. Se vivete in un villaggio turistico ricordate che per le escursioni da e per Maspalomas i taxi sono particolarmente economici.

TOURIST INFO

Centro Insular de Turismo
Avenida España/Avenida Estados Unidos, PO Box 352 90
☎ 77 15 50

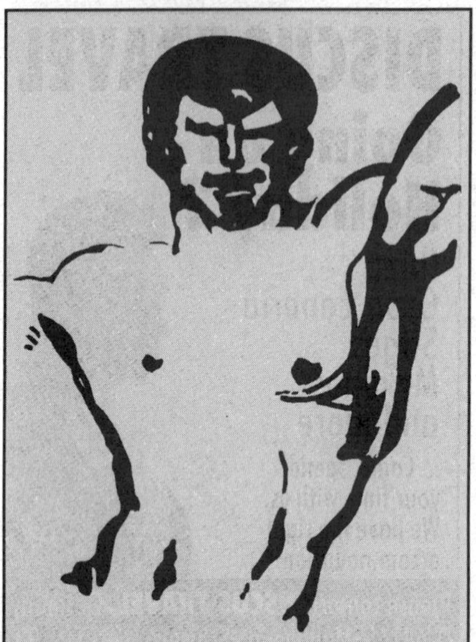

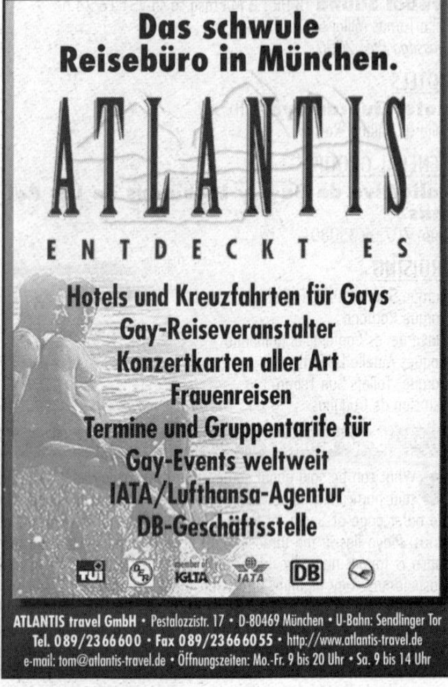

BARS

Adonis (B G MA OS) 19-?
Yumbo Centro, ✉35100 *(1st Floor)*
Popular.

Bärenhöhle (AC B DR G LJ MA OS VS) 20-3 h
Yumbo Centro ✉35100 *(1st Floor)* ☎ 769 692

Berlin Cafe Bar (B G MA OS) 19-3 h closed Sun
Yumbo Centro *(Planta 3a)*

The Block (B DR G LJ MA OS s VS) 21-3 h
Yumbo Centro ✉35100 *(Planta 1)*

Buddies (B f G MA OS s) 17-? h
Yumbo Centro *(Planta 1)*

Casablanca (B G MG OS S) 19-3h
Yumbo Centro, Local 111-113 ✉35100 *(1st Floor)*
Travestie show 4 x per week

Catwalk (AC B G MA OS S) 16-? h
Yumbo Centro ✉35100 *basement* ☎ 649-332 361 (mobile)
Tabledance

Centre Stage (! B G lj MA OS stv) 22-3, WE -3.30 h, Thu Leather & Feather Party
Yumbo Centro *(Planta 2)*

Construction (B DR G LJ MA OS SNU VS) 20-? h
Yumbo Centro ✉35100 *(basement)* ☎ 14 30 75
Leather Bar

Contact (B DR G LJ MA VS) 23-2 h
Yumbo Centro *(Planta 2)*

Cruise (! AC B DR G LJ MA VS) 23:30 - ?
Yumbo Centro *(Planta 2. Local 11-12)*

Diamonds (B G MA OS STV W) 21-? h
Yumbo Centro *(Planta 1)*

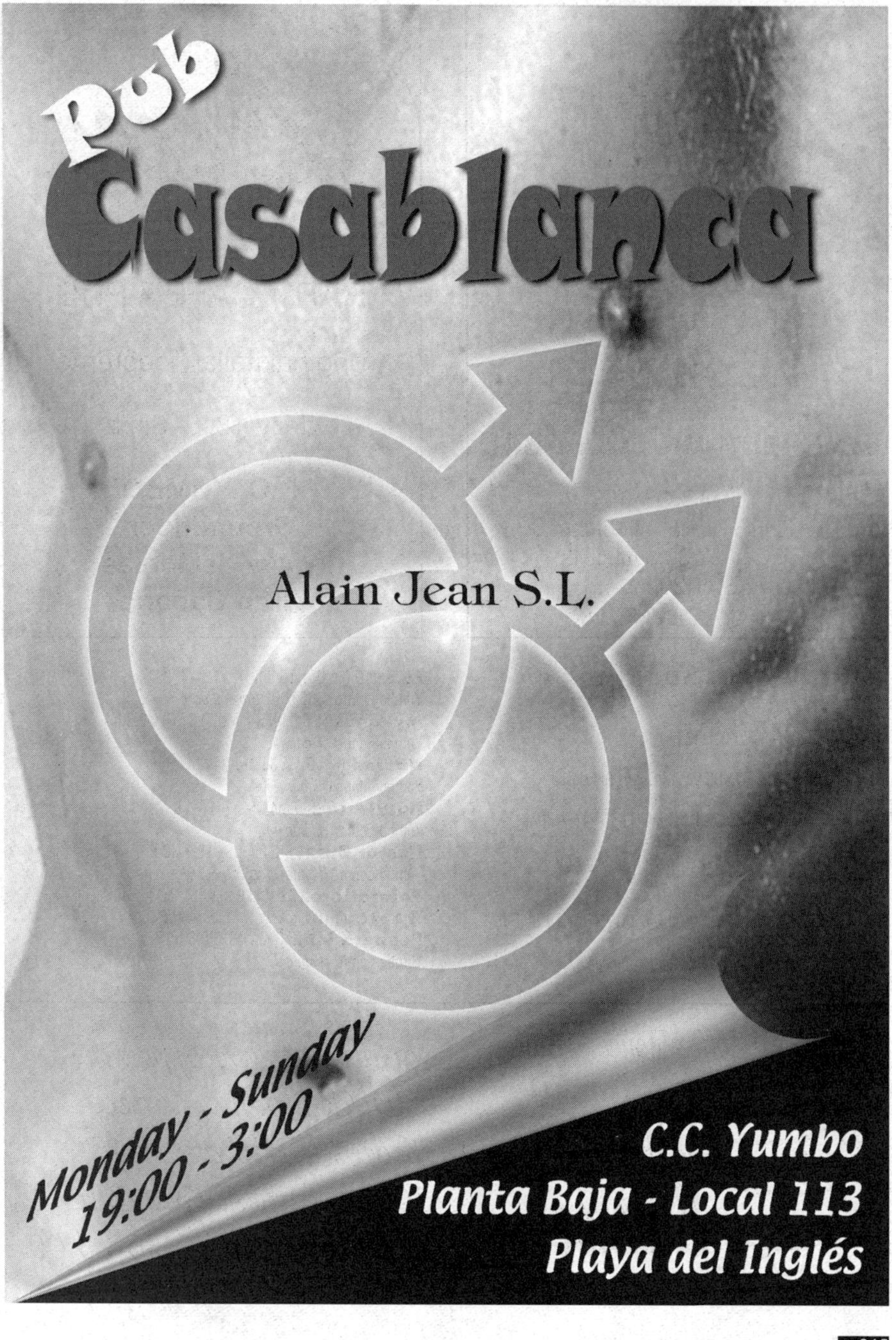

Pub
Casablanca

Alain Jean S.L.

Monday - Sunday
19:00 - 3:00

C.C. Yumbo
Planta Baja - Local 113
Playa del Inglés

Dicke Ei. Das (B G MA OS STV) 19-3, We -3.30 h, daily Show at 22 h
Yumbo Centro *(Planta 1)*
Du & Ich (B G MA OS) 19-3 h
Yumbo Centro *(Planta 1)*
First Lady (B D gLM OS s W) 20-3 h, Thu closed
Yumbo Centro ✉35109 ☎ 50 11 18
Gran Café Latino (! B f G MA OS YG) 16-2.30 h
Yumbo Centro *(Planta 1)* ☎ 76 12 69
Hollywood (B d G MA OS VS) 21-3 h, Sun closed
Yumbo Centro, Local 131-14 ✉35100
Music videos.
Hummel-Hummel (! B DR G MA OS S VS) 19.30-3 h
Yumbo Centro *(Planta 1)*
2 darkrooms, one for the young, one for the elderly.

Lux (B G MA OS) 18-3 h
Yumbo Centro ✉35100 *(Groundfloor)*
Mykonos (! B d DR G MA OS VS YG) 22-3 h
Yumbo Centro *(Planta 4)*
Na Und (B d G MA og OS) 21-3 h
Yumbo Centro *(Planta 1)*
Nachtcafé (B G MA OS stv) 21-4 h
Yumbo Centro *(Planta 1)*
Nestor Bar (! B G MA OS) 19-2:30 h
Yumbo Centro *(Planta 1)* ☎ 76 62 66
Pajaro Loco. El (B d G MA OS) 22-? h
Yumbo Centro *(Planta 2)*
Peppermint (B G MA OS) 20-3 h
Yumbo Centro *(Planta 1)*

Prison (B DR G LJ MA OS VS) Summer: 0-5 h, Winter: 23-5 h
Yumbo Centro *(Planta 2)* ☎ (609) 57 55 76 (mobile)

Spartacus (! B G MA OS) 20-2.30 h
Yumbo Centro *(Planta 1)*

Terry's Show (B G MA OS STV) 22-? h
Yumbo Centro *(Planta 2)*
Fri Sat show with frequent guest star Batusi Pérez Prado from Tropicana, Cuba.

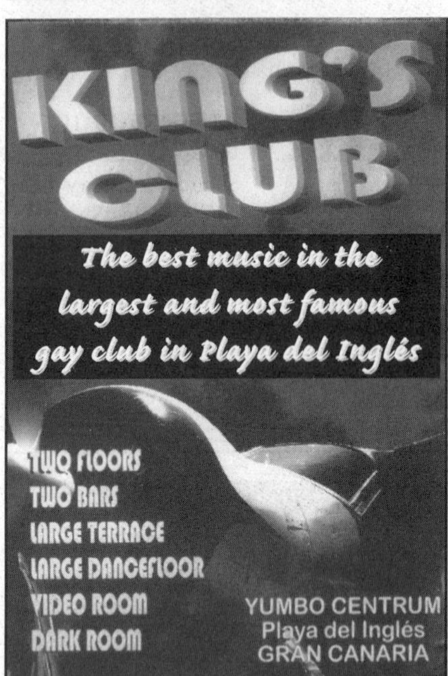

Toby's Bar (AC B glm MA s stv VS) 12-? h
Yumbo Centro
Twice a week Dragqueen-Show.
Tubos (! B G MA OS VS) 22-3, WE -3.30 h
Yumbo Centro *(Planta 4)*
Typisch Kölsch (AC B G MA r) 18-1 h
CC Metro, 2nd Floor ✉35100
Why Not (! AC B G MA VS) 22-? h
Yumbo Centro *(Planta 4)*
1. September (AC B G MG) 20.30-? h
Yumbo Centro, Local 131-01 *(1st Floor)*
English, German and Spanish spoken.

CAFES

Marlene (B CC G MA OS s) 10.30-1 h
CC Cita, Planta 2, ✉35 100 ☎ 768 514
Strand Apo-Theke (B F g) Mon-Fri 11-20, Sat Sun 15-? h
Oasis Centro Maspalomas ☎ 14 12 96
Follow the beach towards the fare, see the rainbow flag.
Café Wien (B f g OS) 9.30-23 h
Cita Centro *(Planta 2)* ☎ 76 03 80

DANCECLUBS

De Pinte (AC CC D E GLM MA OG OS) 22-5 h, Mon closed
Av. De Tirajana 1 ✉35100 ☎ 768 250
Kings Club (! B D DR G MA OS VS) 24-? h
Yumbo Centro, Planta 2 ✉35100
XL Men's Club (! B D G OS SNU STV YG) 22.30-5, WE -6 h, Show Tue Thu Sun 1.45 h
Yumbo Centro *(Planta 2; below mainroad)*

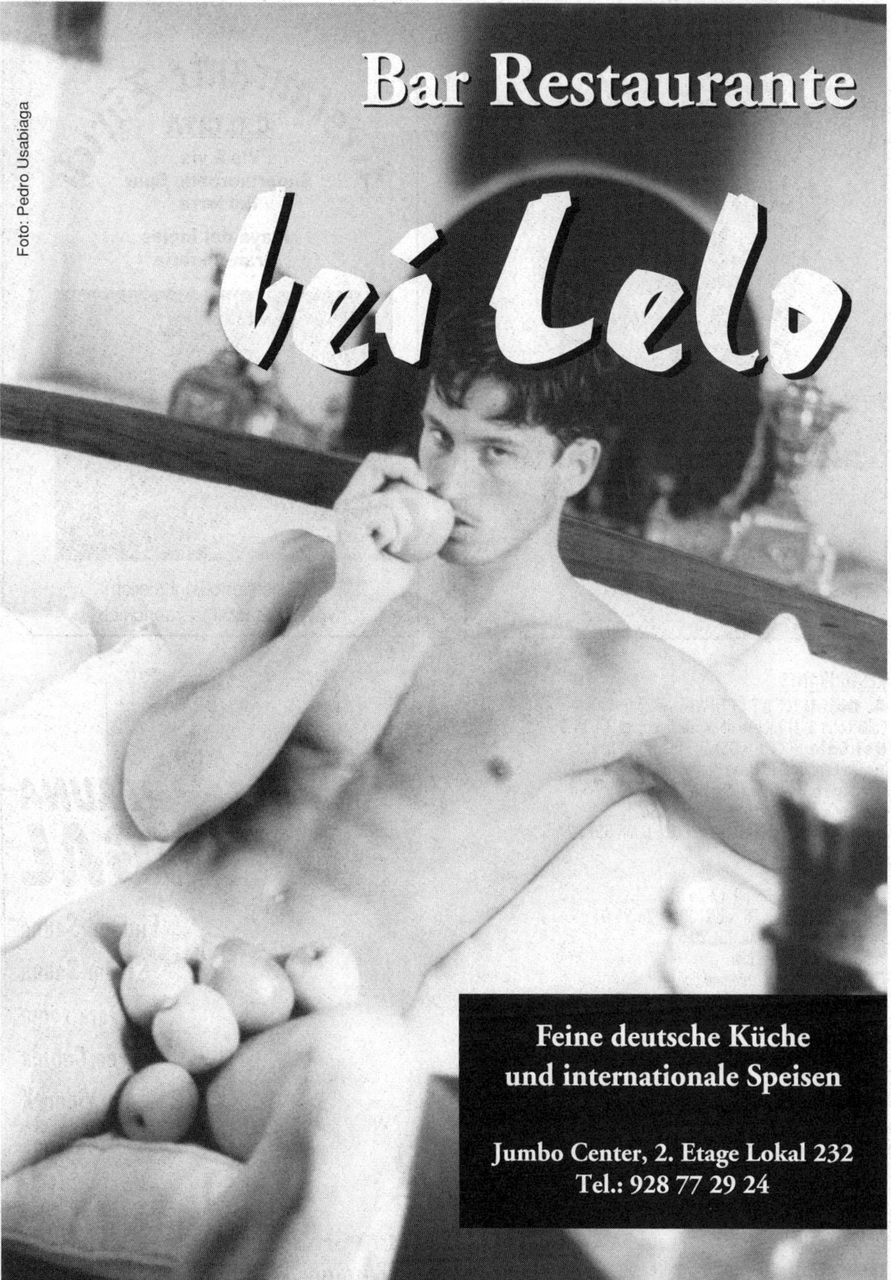
Foto: Pedro Usabiaga
Bar Restaurante
bei Lelo
Feine deutsche Küche
und internationale Speisen
Jumbo Center, 2. Etage Lokal 232
Tel.: 928 77 29 24

RESTAURANTS

A. Gaudí (CC B F G) Fri-Wed 18-24 h
Calle Cuba 3, El Tablero de Maspalomas ☎ 14 14 85
Bei Lelo (B CC F G OS) Thu-Tue 11-24 h
Yumbo Centro ✉35100 *(Planta 2a)* ☎ 77 29 24
Cockpit Burger Café (B F G OS) 19-5 h
Yumbo Centro *(Planta 2)* ☎ 77 20 56
Daniels Night-Bistro (B F G MA OS) 22-6 h
Yumbo Centro *(Planta 2)*
Snack-bar.
Merlin (B F G OS pi) 12-24 h
Avenida de Tirajana 18 ✉35100 ☎ 76 95 01
Monroe (B F G MA OS) 20-5 h
Yumbo Center, 2nd Floor
Fastfood restaurant, café and bar
Ola (B CC F g MA OS) 18-2 h, Thu closed
Yumbo Centro ✉35100 *(Planta 2)* ☎ 76 46 15
Valentine's (B F G OS) 19-23 h
Yumbo Centro *(Planta 2)* ☎ 77 06 48
International cuisine.
Zürich (AC B CC e F g OS) Winter: 17-23 h, daily. Summer: 18-24 h, Sun closed
CC Cita, Local 268 ✉35100 ☎ 774 697

SHOWS

Bille Travestie Show (g MG STV)
☎ 76 96 77
Dragshow artist.
Westphalia (B g OS STV) 9-1 h
Cita Centro *(Planta 1)* ☎ 76 13 51

WORLD OF GAY
MAN'S
PLAZA
Shop
Video
Movie
*DARKROOM
*CABINS
*AIRCONDITION
*GAY SHOP
WORLD OF GAY
WOG
FEEL THE HEAT
0034 28 764286
C.C. Yumbo 1ª Pl. Playa del Inglés

775 Ptas.
MAN'S
HOT HOUSE
WORLD OF GAY
*FINLAND SAUNA
*STEAM SAUNA
*DARKROOM
*VIDEO X
*FREE CABINS
*BAR - MASSAGE
WORLD OF GAY
WOG
FEEL THE HEAT
C.C. Yumbo Centrum 1ª Planta

MAN'S
GARAGE
WORLD OF GAY
GAY SHOP
VIDEO
CINEMA
CABIN
DARKROOM
WORLD OF GAY
WOG
FEEL THE HEAT
C.C. Yumbo Centrum 4ª Planta

SEXY
CONDOMERIE
EROTIC-SHOP
LAND
Cinema Cabins
Local 131-10
Tel.: (928) 76 42 86
Opening hours
16.30-0.30
every day

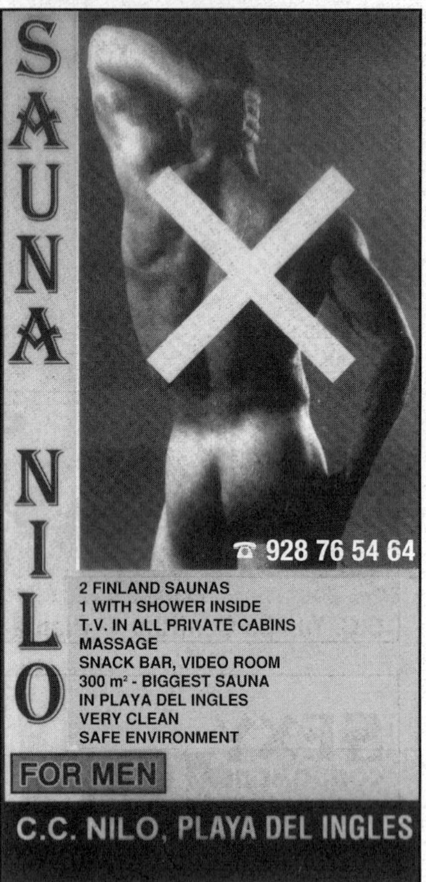

SEX SHOPS/BLUE MOVIES

Man's Garaje (AC CC G MA VS) 19.30-3.30 h
Yumbo Center *4th floor* ☎ 76 42 86
Darkroom with sling, all cabins with video.

Man's Plaza (AC CC DR G MA VS) 16.30-3.30 h
Yumbo Centro *(1st Floor)*

Sexyland (AC CC g MA VS) 16-8 h
Yumbo Center, planta Caja 131

SAUNAS/BATHS

Nilo Sauna (B f G MA msg p sa VS wo) 21-3 h
Nilo Centro ☎ 76 54 64
Easy to find: when entering the Nilo straight at the end of the aisle. 14 cabins with TV, 2 dry saunas. Special prize Wed Sat 2 for 1. Many canarios. Safe area, clean facilities.

Sauna Hot House (AC B CC DR G MA OS msg sa sb VS) 16.30-3.30 h
Yumbo Centro *(1st Floor)* ☎ 76 42 86

FITNESSTUDIOS

Enigma Victoria (b g sa sb wh WO) 9-21 h
Av. Gran Canaria 55 ✉35100 *(Hotel Engima Victoria)* ☎ 762 500

BODY & BEAUTY SHOPS

Salon 13 (g) Mon-Fri 9-13, 16-20, Sat 9-15 h
Sandia Centro *(Planta 1)* ☎ 76 16 60
Hair-cuts.

DECORATION

Pan Con Ajo - Arte & Decoravión (A g) 11-23 h
Yumbo Centro ✉35100 *(2nd Floor)*

FASHION SHOPS

Tassio (CC G) 17-23 h, Wed closed
Yumbo Centro ✉35100 *(Planta 2a)* ☎ 76 96 44
Men's clothing.

GALLERIES

Cumbreras (CC G)
Yumbo Centro, Local 111-08 ✉35100 ☎ 76 27 71

TRAVEL & TRANSPORT

Doris' Gay-Jeep-Safari (bf F G) Tour Wed Fri 9 h
☎ 751 902 Fax: 751 902
Jeep Safari: Ptas 6.500.

Sun Fun - Dieter´s Motorbike Rental (G) Mon-Fri 9-19 h, Sat 9-14 h, Sun 11-14 h
CC Gran Chaparral 161 ✉35100 ☎ 76 38 29 ☎ 619-18 50 66 (mobile) Fax: 76 38 29 Homepage: www.ci7.net/sun-fun
Also bikes available, Rates from Ptas. 2000 for a motor bike per day.

APARTMENTS

Pasion Tropical (bf B Glm H pi sol wh wo)
Calle las Adelfas 6, San Agustin ✉35100 ☎ 77 01 31
Satellite tv in all bungalows, seaview, open-air jacuzzi. Relaxed and exotic atmosphere. Rates per bungalow Pts 8.500 (low season), 10.000 (high season), bf. incl.

Robles. Los (B bf f G H MA NU OS pi VS)
Avenida de Finnmatkat 8 ☎ 76 38 71 ☎ +31/20/421 00 00 Fax: 76 38 71
Reservation through „De Gay Krant Reisservice", Amsterdam, Netherlands. Fully equipped apartments.

Tenesor (CC g H MA OS pi)
Av. Tirajana ☎ 770 122 Fax: 770 302
1 and 2 bedroom apartments in central Playa del Inglés near to Yombo Center.

Villa Mareu (CC G NU OS pi)
Raqueta 3 ☎ 770 122 Fax: 770 302
Luxury villa with two bedrooms, two bathrooms for individual rental close to dunes and beach.

Villas Blancas (B bf CC F G H NU OS pi S VS)
Av. T.O. Tjaereborg, Campo Internacional ✉35100 ☎ 168 169 Fax: 268 269 E-Mail: vb@boesweb.com
The bungalows, swimming pool and bar are surrounded by tropical gardens. Accomodation is self-contained and has twin bed rooms, bathrooms, living rooms are open to fitted kitchens. All bungalows are with terraces, satellite TV, VCR. The bistro restaruant serves breakfast, lunch and dinner. Also Bistro from 18-22h.

THE ONLY BEACH-FRONT GAY COMPLEX ON GRAN CANARIA
THE EXOTIC ATMOSPHERE YOU EXPECT FROM A TROPICAL ISLAN
Pasion Tropical
Sea view
20 meters from the ocean
Open air whirlpool
Buffet breakfast in the garden
Open air gym
Clothing optional
Swimming pool
Tropical gardens
Soft music in pool and gardens
Satelite Tv. In each room
Car, scooters and Mt. Bikes hire service
Quiet area
CALL US FOR ANY INFORMATION AND RESERVATIONS
Tel. 0034 - 928 770131
C/ Las Adelfas, 6 San Agustín 35130 Playa del Inglés GRAN CANARIA

Vista Bonita Villas (B bf CC f G H MA NU OS pi VS) 9-23 h
Calle Carmen Laforet, ✉35100 *(Urbanisación Sonnenland)*
☎ 142 969 Fax: 142 969
Good quality and economically priced accomodation. 20 fully equipped poolside villas and two penthouse apartments, all with private balconies, terraces, satellite TV, VCR, in house video channel.

HEALTH GROUPS

Amigos contra El Sida (A.C.S.) Mon-Tue, Thu-Fri 9-14, 17.30-19.30, Wed 9-14 h
Nilo Centro, Local 120 *(Planta Satano 1)* ☎ 76 48 49
Help and assistance for any question concerning AIDS in Spanish, English, French, German, Dutch.

SWIMMING

-Beach in front of Beach Bar No. 7 (! G NU)

CRUISING

-Cita Centro (toilet below Café Marlene)
-Yumbo Centro (from 0 h (ayor, r))
-Maspalomas Sand Dunes (AYOR) (in the small bushes, very popular)
-[P] Charco Maspalomas (Car-cruising 19-4 h)

GUEST HOUSES

Mar y Monte (bf glm H OS) Calle Pino de la Virgen 7 b ✉38789 ☎ 49 30 67 Fax: 49 30 67
Homepage: www.la-palma.de/marymonte
Rates from Ptas. 2.700,- per day & person.

La Palma - Santa Cruz de la Palma ☎ 922

APARTMENTS

Apartamentos La Fuente (g H MA OS sol) Mon-Fri 9-12, 17-20, Sat 9-12 h
Calle Perez de Brito 49 ✉38700 *(in the historic centre)*
☎ 415 636 Fax: 412 303 E-Mail: lafuente@infolapalma.com
Homepage: www.la-fuente.com
Fully equipped apartments. Price for two persons Ptas 4.600-7750, additional bed 1.200. 10 apartments and rental of further houses in the countryside and in the city as well as cars.

SWIMMING

-Playa Los Cancajos (g MA NU) (South of Santa Cruz. Walk along the beach from Los Cancajos to the south in direction of the airport, climb over the rocks. After about 30 minutes you reach the beach.)
-Playa Cuatro Monjas (g MA NU) (South of Playa Naos. Follow road to south just behind Puerta Naos. Leave car near banana plantations, follow path to the sea).

BARS

Tambo. El (B g MA) 20-2 h
Calle Luis Morote

HEALTH GROUPS

Hospital General 24 h
Carretera San Bartolomé s/n ☎ 80 16 36

CRUISING

-Castillo (from 23 h)

Lanzarote - Puerto del Carmen ☎ 928

BARS

Black & White (B d G MA) 21-4 h
Atántico Centro, Av. de la Playa 38
Free (B G MA stv) 21-3 h
Calle detrás del C.C. Atlántico
Show Fri & Sat

SEX SHOPS/BLUE MOVIES

JOMATO´G (g) 11-14 h, 16-20 h, Sun closed
CC Atlántico ✉35100 *(Downstairs)* ☎ 511 331

HEALTH GROUPS

British Scandinavian Clinic
C.C. Caletón Blanco ☎ 82 62 27

SWIMMING

-Playa Guasimeta (g nu) (behind the airport)
-Playa del Papagayo

Tenerife - La Laguna ☎ 922

BARS

Consulado (B g stv) Tue-Sun 20-2 h
Calle Antonio Torre Edward 45
Nashville Pub (B g) Sun-Thu 18.30-2, Fri Sat 18.30-4 h
Calle Dr. Antonio Glez 11

GENERAL GROUPS

Unapro
Calle Marqués de Celada 70, local 2 ☎ 25 96 54

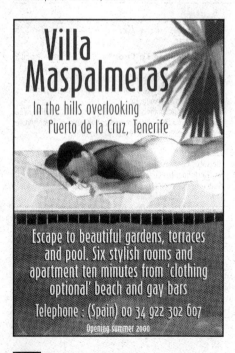

HIV/AIDS-Group.

CRUISING

-Estación de Guaguas

Tenerife - Playa de las Americas ☎ 922

BARS

Chaplin's Bar (AC B D DR G MA STV TV VS) 23-6/? h
C.C. Sayltien *(Souterrain)*

SWIMMING

-Los Christianos (NU) (reachable from Santa Cruz by bus)
-Playa de la Tejita (g NU) (very popular day and night; between El Medano and Los Abrigos)

CRUISING

-Playa de las Americas (after dark)

Tenerife - Puerto de la Cruz ☎ 922

BARS

Anderson Club (B d DR G MA OS) 22.30-6, Sat Sun 8-13 h
Avenida Generalisimo 24 *(Edificio Drago)*
D'Espanto (B d DR G MA OS vs) 23-4 h
Avenida Generalisimo 24 *(Edificio Drago)*
Incognito (B G MA) 21-5 h, closed Mon
Avenida Generalísimo *(Edificio Centro Avenida)*
Jim's (B G MA OS) 17-3, Fri Sat 17-5 h; summer 21-3, Fri Sat 21-5 h
Avenida Generalisimo 24, bajo *(Edificio Drago)*
Tabasco (B DR G MA vs) 21.30-8, summer 22.30-8 h
Avenida Generalisimo 15

DANCECLUBS

Anderson (B D G MA) 23-6 h
Avenida Generalísimo 24, bajo *(Edificio Drago)*
Despanto (B D G MA)
Avenida Generalísimo 24 *(Edificio Drago)*
Vampi's Discoteca (B D E G MA P S VS) Thu-Sun 24-8, Show 1.30 h
Avenida Generalisimo 24 *(Edificio Drago)*

RESTAURANTS

Casa Europa (B F g) Tue-Sun 18-24 h
Urbanisación Montalmar, 38250 Bajamar n8

GUEST HOUSES

Villa Maspalmeras (B bf CC f GLM H OS pi WO) Opening Summer 2000
Vista Panoramica 20 ✉38398 ☎ 302 607
Small and stylish guest house in beautiful gardens in hills overlooking Puerto De La Cruz.

SWIMMING

-Playa de los Patos (4 km east of town)

CRUISING

-Estación de guaguas
-Montañas del Amor
-Playa Martiánez
-Avenida de Colón (day and night)
-Plaza del Charco
-Playa Jardín/Castillo San Felipe

Tenerife - Santa Cruz ☎ 922

BARS

Blue Dreams Bar Suenos Azules (B G MA vs) 21-3 h
Calle San Miguel 14 ☎ 27 45 06

CAFES

Cloe Café-Restaurant (A B F g) Mon-Sat 12-2, Sun 18-2 h
Calle San Francisco Javier 36 ☎ 28 32 01

SEX SHOPS/BLUE MOVIES

Luna Sex Shop (AC CC g MA p VS) Mon-Sat 10-22, Sun 17.30-22 h
Calle Vincente Ferrer 75 bajos *(near Parque Garcia Sanabria)*

HEALTH GROUPS

Centro Dermatologico Fri-Wed 8.30-13 h
Calle San Sebastian 75 ☎ 27 93 97
Information and help concerning AIDS.

Unión para la Ayuda y Protección de los Afectados por el SIDA
Marqués de Celada 70, 38202 La Laguna ☎ 25 96 54
Fax: 63 32 23. E-mail unapro@redkbs.com.

SWIMMING

-Las Gaviotas (15 km from Santa Cruz, left side of the beach)
-Las Teresitas (take bus 914)
-Dársena Pescadora (Los Rusos)
-Benijos

CRUISING

-Estación de guaguas
-Plaza del Principe de Asturias
-Parque García Sanabria (r)
-Avenida Anaga (R)
-La Rambla del General Franco (between Parque Sanabria and Plaza de la Paz)

Canillas De Albaidas ☎ 95

HOTELS

Aparthotel Bar Los Chicos (B bf CC d F g H MA OS pi s W WO) 9-2 h
Cómpeta/Torrox ✉29755 *(behind Sayalonga-bus from Tore del Mar to Competa)* ☎ 255 35 95 Fax: 255 35 95
10 holiday apartments for 2-3 pers/4-6 pers.7500-16000 Pts. 3 singles/3 doubles 4400-8300 pts.

Cartagena ☎ 968

SEX SHOPS/BLUE MOVIES

Sexyland (g)
Calle Sagasta 55 ☎ 52 60 87

SWIMMING

-Playas de Calblanque (g NU) (between Cartagena and Cabo de Palos)

Ceuta ☎ 956

HOTELS

Puerta de Africa Hotel (g H)
Gran Vía 2 *(Near town hall)* ☎ 51 71 91 Fax: 51 04 30

Córdoba ☎ 957

BARS

Siena (B bf F g MA OS) 7-0.30/1 h
Plaza las Tendillas ☎ 47 30 05

DANCECLUBS

A 85 (B D GLM MA YG) 23-? h
Poligono Industrial Pedroches 85
Very popular.

Kiss (B d gLm OS YG) 21-?, Mon closed. Winter only Fri Sat 21-? h
Carretera de Almaden *(near Club Azland)*

Plató (B D g YG) Thu-Sun 23-6 h
Calle Gongora

GENERAL GROUPS

Liberación Gay de Córdoba (LGC) Tue 19-21 h
Calle San Fernando 68 ☎ 47 37 60 Fax: 48 44 59

CRUISING

-Parks Victoria (northern part) and Diego de Rivas (popular day and night) (MA)
-Park at Guadalquivir, Avenida del Alcazar (at San Rafael bridge; popular)
-Plaza de las Tendillas
-Ferial (near Calle Teresa de Córdoba y Hoces; at night carcruising)
-Los Naranjos (at Mesquita, some man, days only)
-Main railway station, Ronda de Cercadilla

Denia ☎ 96

SWIMMING

-Cala San Antonio (g NU) (Entrance Denia and Cabo de S. Antonio)

Estepona ☎ 939

BARS

Cheers (B GLM MA) 22-3 h
Caravaca, 32 ✉29680 *(Market-Old Town)* ☎ 80 41 05

Kiss (B glm MA) 19.30-4 h
Calle Victoria ☎ 56 82 16

RESTAURANTS

Robbies (B CC F glm)
Jubrique, 11 ✉29680
Gay owned, excellent food,

SWIMMING

-Costa Natura (NU,MA) (southern end gay, cruising in bushes) On N340 4km from Estepona, direction Algeciras. NudeCamp: Costa Natura.

Figueres ☎ 972

BARS

Natural Men Bar (B D DR GLM MA OS s VS WE) 22-6 h
Centre Aduana, Poligono Enporda, Vilamalla ✉17469
☎ 52 60 39

RESTAURANTS

Jalisco (B F glm) 12-0 h
C/. Tapis 21 ✉17600 ☎ 50 53 52
Mexican cuisine.

SAUNAS/BATHS

Sauna Sparta (AC B DR G MA sa VS WE) daily 16-22 h
C./ Sant Pau 82 ✉17600 *(Near the railway station)* ☎ 51 17 05

HOTELS

Hostal Androl y Camping Pous (AC B bf CC F g H) 7.30-24 h
Carretera Nacional II A, km 8.5 ✉17600 ☎ 67 54 96 ☎ 972/67 50 57
Also camping facilities.

Fuengirola ☎ 952

BARS

Stuart´s Bar (AC B D GLM MA OS) 21-? h
C/ Martinez Catena, Complejo Las Palmeras, Locales 38 & 39 ✉29640 *(in the backarea of Citröen Car Garaje & Hot Shot)* ☎ 610 827 549 (mobile)
Tontero (B GLM MA STV) 22-? h
Fuengirola Port
Very Very Boys (B G MA SNU) 22-? h
Puerto Deportivo

RESTAURANTS

Casa Vieja. La (CC F glm MA OS) 19-?, Sun also 12-16 h, closed Mon
Avenida de Los Boliches ✉29640 ☎ 266 44 07
Fax: 246 61 07. French cuisine.

HOTELS

Rio del Sol (B bf F G H pi)
Calle Cactus 14,
Torreblanca del Sol
Near Torremolinos and the nudist beaches Torrequebrado and Las Dunas in Cabo Pino. 3 rooms, one with bath. Private swimmingpool and Bar/Restaurante (NG)

CRUISING

-Paseo Marítimo (between Caracola Restaurant and London Pub, including new elevated promenade accross from London Pub; especially in summer)

Gandia ☎ 96

RESTAURANTS

San Roc i Ec Gos. Restaurante Aleman (A AC CC F glm WE) Tue-Sat 12-16, 21-0, Sun 12-16 h, closed Mon
C/. Hospital 10 ✉46700 ☎ 287 34 21 Fax: 287 34 21

Gerona

BARS

Big-Hit (B D g)
Avenida Ramón Folch 11

GENERAL GROUPS

FAGC
PO Box 681, 17080 Gerona

CRUISING

-Estación de Renfe
-Plaza de la Independeia
-La Rambla

Gijón ☎ 98

BARS

Escalera 7 (AC B DR G MA VS WE) 21-8 h
Calle Ezcurdia 40 bajo ✉33202 ☎ 534 21 80
Pipos (B DR G MA r VS) 20-8 h
Plaza San Augustín 2 ☎ 517 13 79

CAFES

Dindurra (B f NG) 8-24 h
Paseo de Begoña *(Teatro Jovellanes)*
Best 19-21 h.

DANCECLUBS

Eros (AC B D DR G MA S SNU) 0-7 h
Calle la Playa 17, ✉33202 ☎ 513 17 19

SEX SHOPS/BLUE MOVIES

Fantasías (g VS) Mon-Sat 10-3, Sun 10-14, 16-3 h
Calle Ezcurdia 49
Sex Shop (g VS) 10-14, 15.30-23 h
Avenida Pablo Iglesias 20 ☎ 536 28 85

HEALTH GROUPS

Comité Ciudadano Anti Sida de Asturias 9-14 h
Calle Ramon y Cajal 39, bajo ☎ 533 88 32
Information and services concerning AIDS.

SWIMMING

-Playa de Peñarrubia/La Providencia

CRUISING

–Statue La Madre de los Emigrantes
-Paseo de la Playa de San Lorenzo

Granada ☎ 958

BARS

Al Pie de la Vela (B G MA YG) 21.30-4, We -5 h
C/. del Darro 35, bajo *(near Alhambra)* ☎ 22 85 39
Fondo Reservado (B G MA YG) 22.30-4 h, closed Mon
Cuesta de Sta. Inés 4 *(Placeta de Santa Ines)*
Lolamento (A AC B d G MA s) 22-4 h, Mon Sun closed
Calle Buensuceso/Pontezuela ✉18002
Perfil (A AC B d f G MA stv) 17-5 h
Calle Rosario 10
Puerta del Vino (A AC B bf F glm MA OS WE) Summer: 18-2 h, Winter: 12-2 h
Paseo de los Tristes 5 ✉18010 ☎ 210 026
Ricon de San Pedro. El (B G MG YG) 21-4, Fri Sat -? h
Carrera del Darro 12
Bar de copas in the center of Granada.
Sal. La (B gLM MA) 22-5 h
C/. Santa Paula 11
Tic Tac (B DR G MA VS YG) 17-4.30, Fri Sat -5 h
C/. Horno de Haza 19
Versus (B e g MA) 21-4 h
Carrera del Darro 25, bajo *(just beside the Arabic bath from the XI Century)* ☎ 22 69 03
Beautiful interior. Spanisch cuisine. Recommended.
Viña II. La (B g MA og) 20-4, Fri Sat -5 h
C/. Concha 3
Very Andalusian in style and clientèle.

CAFES

Lisboa. Café (B bf f g MA) Mon-Thu 8-22 h, Fri-Sun -3 h
Calle Reyes Catalocicos/Plaza Nueva ✉18010 ☎ 21 05 79

DANCECLUBS

Angel Azul. El (B D DR G p S SNU STV VS YG) 22-6, Fri Sat -? h. Show Fri Sat 2 h
C/. Lavadero de las Tablas 15

SAUNAS/BATHS

Sauna Boabdil (B G sa MA VS) 17-23 h, Tue & Aug closed
Carretera de la Sierra 34 *(El Trevenque)* ☎ 22 10 73

GENERAL GROUPS

Asociación Andaluza de Gays y Lesbianas (NOS) Mon-Fri 1.30-13.30 h, 17.30-20.30 h, Sat 17-22 h
C/ Lavadero de las Tablas 15 ✉18002 ☎ 200 602 Fax: 200 602
„Triángulo" is the publication of the group. Every three months for free in gay venues with articles and a gay guide of Southspain.

HEALTH GROUPS

Bisagra. La Calle Chueca 8, 1b ✉18004 ☎ 52 13 52
Group for people with HIV/AIDS.

CRUISING

-Paseo de Basilios (at the border of the river Genil (popular car cruising at night)
-Los Jardines del Triunfo
-Estación de Renfe
-Estación de autobuses
-Camino de Purchil (car cruising or by bike, by day only)

Huesca

BARS

Candanchú (B f G)
Calle Coso alto
Papillón (B F G)
Calle San Lorenzo

DANCECLUBS

Tránsito (B D g)
Plaza de San Voto

CRUISING

-Estación de autobuses (Calle del Parque)
-Parque Municipal
-Zona del Hospital Provincial

Jaén ☎ 953

BARS

Noche. La (AC B D g GLM p S SNU STV WE) 22-6 h
Avenida de Andalucía 22 ✉23002 ☎ 27 30 34

SEX SHOPS/BLUE MOVIES

Amsterdam (g)
Calle Salido 23 *(near Calle San Clemente)*

GENERAL GROUPS

28 de Junio • Asociación Pro Derechos de los Homosex. Meeting Wed Sat 20-22
PO Box 443 ✉23080 ☎ 27 04 20

CRUISING

-Parque de la Victoria

Javea ☎ 96

SWIMMING

-Torre d'Ambolo (g NU) (C/. al cabo de la nau)
-Playa de la Cumbre del Sol (g NU)

La Coruña/A Coruña ☎ 981

BARS

Café Alfama (A AC B d GLM MA W WE) Tue-Fri 20-2, Sat Sun -3 h, closed Mon
Orzán 87, Bajo ✉15006 ☎ 20 46 21
Fibonacci (AC B glm MA YG)
R. Pasadizo do Orzán 2 *Very gay.*
Laberinto (AC B DR G MA p VS) R. Magistrado Manuel Artime 6
Very large place.
Marítimo (B G MA) 23.30-3.30 h
Av de la Marina s/n

SEX SHOPS/BLUE MOVIES

Fantasías (g VS) Mon-Sat 10.30-22.30, Sun 10.30-14, 16-22 h
Calle Rosalia de Castro 4

GENERAL GROUPS

Milhomes
PO Box 24 ✉15080

SWIMMING

-Playa de Bastiagueiro (on the rural road to the north, towards Ferreol, halfway between Santa Cristina and Santa Cruz.)

Leon ☎ 987

BARS

Capote (B G MA)
Lancia 3

CAFES

Gran Café (A AC d g lj MA N NG S WE) 15.30-3.30 h
C/ Cervantes 9 ✉24003 ☎ 27 23 01

DANCECLUBS

Chasis (AC D g YG)
Lancia 5

RESTAURANTS

Girola. La (A AC B CC d F glm lj MA OS W WE) 13.30-16, 21-23.30
Calle Ave Maria 2, esquina San Lorenzo 5 ✉24007 ☎ 27 05 69

SEX SHOPS/BLUE MOVIES

Internacional (g) 10-22 h
Calle General Sanjurjo 5 ☎ 24 85 72

CRUISING

-Jardines del Paseo de Papalaguinda
-Railway & bus station
Plaza del Ganado

Lérida/Lleida ☎ 973

DANCECLUBS

Big Ben (B D F g)
Carretera de Mollerussa
20 km from Lérida. Large entertainment center with bars, discos, gambling halls and restaurants. Not exclusively gay but very popular.

CINEMAS

Cine Xenon
Avenida Alcalde Rovira Rouve 3, Sala 1

CRUISING

-Campos Elíseos
-Campo Escolar
-Estación de Renfe
-Plaza Noguerola
-Parque La Mitjana
-Estacion Autobuses

Lloret de Mar ☎ 972

BARS

El David (AC B G YG) 23-3 h, in winter closed on Mon
C/. Migdia 53 ☎ 36 23 10
Incógnito (AC B G MA VS) 22-3 h, closed Oct-Mar
Calle Migdia 44 ☎ 36 71 89
Tortuga Bar (AC B G MA) 22-3 h, closed in winter Tue
C/. Santa Teresa 5 ☎ 37 05 69

CAFES

Manila (AC B G MA s) 12-3 h
C/. Venecia 60 ✉17310 ☎ 36 25 44

DANCECLUBS

Bubu. La (AC B D DR G MA) 23-3.30 h
C/. L'Areny 33 ☎ 36 71 89

RESTAURANTS

Restaurant Valls (F g) closed winter
C/. Santa Teresa 11 ☎ 36 43 89
Spanish and international cuisine.

SEX SHOPS/BLUE MOVIES

Lloret Sex Center (AC glm VS) Summer: 10-22, Rest of the year: Mon-Sat 10-13.30, 14-20.30 h
C/. San Tomàs 19 ✉17310 ☎ 37 04 43

HOTELS

Hostal Valls (F G H)
C/. Santa Teresa 11 *(near Bar Tortuga)* ☎ 36 43 89
Near to the gay scene. Single Ptas 2.000, double Ptas. 4.000. All room with bath/WC

APARTMENTS

Bubu Apartamentos (G H)
C/. L'Areny 33 *(near La Campaña)* ☎ 36 71 89
Large apartments. Rates Ptas 2.000-3.000, Jun Aug 4.000-5.000.
Tortuga Rooms (G OS)
C/. Santa Teresa 5 ☎ 37 05 69
25 km to the airport. Central location. A few steps to the local gay scene. Most units with kitchenette, priv. bath and access to balcony. Rates Ptas 2.500-3.500.

SWIMMING

-Boadella beach (g NU) (Busy and cruisy. There is a ferry from the town hall to this mixed beach. Gay part is on the left side of the docks. Mixed on the right side)
-Passeig Maritim/Trav. Venecia (Mixed beach in front of the bars)
-La Aguadilla (Take the boat to Blanes 1 station. No sand, but many cliffs and rocks. The cruising starts after the last ferry has left.)

CRUISING

-Around the castle

Madrid ☎ 91

● The majestic capital of Spain has impressive buildings, lots of sightseeing, and a truly wild gay scene. The gay scene is concentrated mainly in the area around the metro station Chueca, and if you look at the map, you will see that most of the gay bars are in walking distance from there. Expect a wild time in Madrid! You can do your sightseeing during the morning, perhaps spend the afternoon at a gay sauna, then move on to the cafés in the early evening, and at around 9 pm choose one of the many restaurants in the gay village for an inexpensive but delicious meal. The gay bars start getting lively around midnight, discos fill up around 3 and then stay packed all night.

✱ Die majestätische Hauptstadt Spaniens mit herrlichen Gebäuden, einer Menge Sehenswürdigkeiten und einer wirklich wilden schwulen Szene. Die schwule Szene konzentriert sich im Gebiet um die Metro Chueca. Betrachten Sie den Stadtplan und Sie werden sehen, daß die meisten der schwulen Bars zu Fuß erreichbar sind, wenn Sie in Chueca ankommen. Es erwartet Sie eine aufregende Zeit in Madrid! Besichtigen Sie die Sehenswürdigkeiten am Vormittag, verbringen Sie Ihre Nachmittage in den schwulen Saunen, gehen Sie am frühen Abend in die Cafés, und wählen Sie gegen 21 Uhr eines der vielen Restaurants in der schwulen Zone aus, um -nicht teuer, aber vorzüglich- zu Abend zu essen. Das Nachtleben beginnt gegen 24 Uhr in den Bars, ab 3 Uhr in den Discos. Das schwule Leben tobt dann bis zum frühen Morgen!

▲ Majestueuse capitale de l'Espagne: splendides édifices, innombrables sîtes touristiques et vie gaye trépidante. Le quartier autour de la station de métro Chueca est le bastion gay de la ville. Etudiez le plan et vous verrez que la plupart des bars gays sont accessibles à pied depuis cette station. A Madrid, vous passerez des vacances sauvages! Réservez vos matins pour le tourisme, passez vos après-midis au sauna, allez au café en début de soirée et, vers 21 h, choisissez l'un des nombreux restaurants du quartier gay pour un repas bon marché, mais délicieux! Les bars n'ouvrent qu'à partir de minuit, les danceclubs s'animent à 3 heures et ne désemplissent qu'aux aurores.

☆ Capital majestuosa de España con edificios bonitos, una cantidad de lugares interesantes para visitar y un ambiente gay verdaderamente loquísimo. Los locales gay se concentran en el area de la estación de Metro Chueca
. Fíjese en el mapa y verá Ud. que desde la paras Chueca, a la mayoría de los bares se puede llegar andando. Le espera una estancia turbulenta. Visite los lugares de interés durante las mañanas, pase las tardes en las saunas gay, en la temprana noche vaya a los cafés, y a eso de las 21 horas elija uno de los restaurantes de la zona gay, para tomar una cena no cara, pero deliciosa. La vida nocturna comienza a eso de las 24 horas y sigue toda la noche hasta la madrugada.

❖ La meravigliosa capitale della Spagna, con degli splendidi edifici, innumerevoli luoghi turistici e una vita gay molto attiva. La vita gay è concentrata soprattutto nell'area intorno a Metro Chueca. Osservate la cartina e capirete che tutti i bar gay possono essere raggiunti a piedi, una volta arrivati a Chueca. Potete aspettarvi un soggiorno selvaggio a Madrid. Visitate la città il mattino, passate i pomeriggi nelle saune gay, trasferitevi nei caffè la sera presto, circa alle 21, scegliete uno dei ristoranti gay della zona per una cena deliziosa e poco costosa. La vita gay nei bar comincia ad animarsi verso le 24 e prosegue praticamente per tutta la notte.

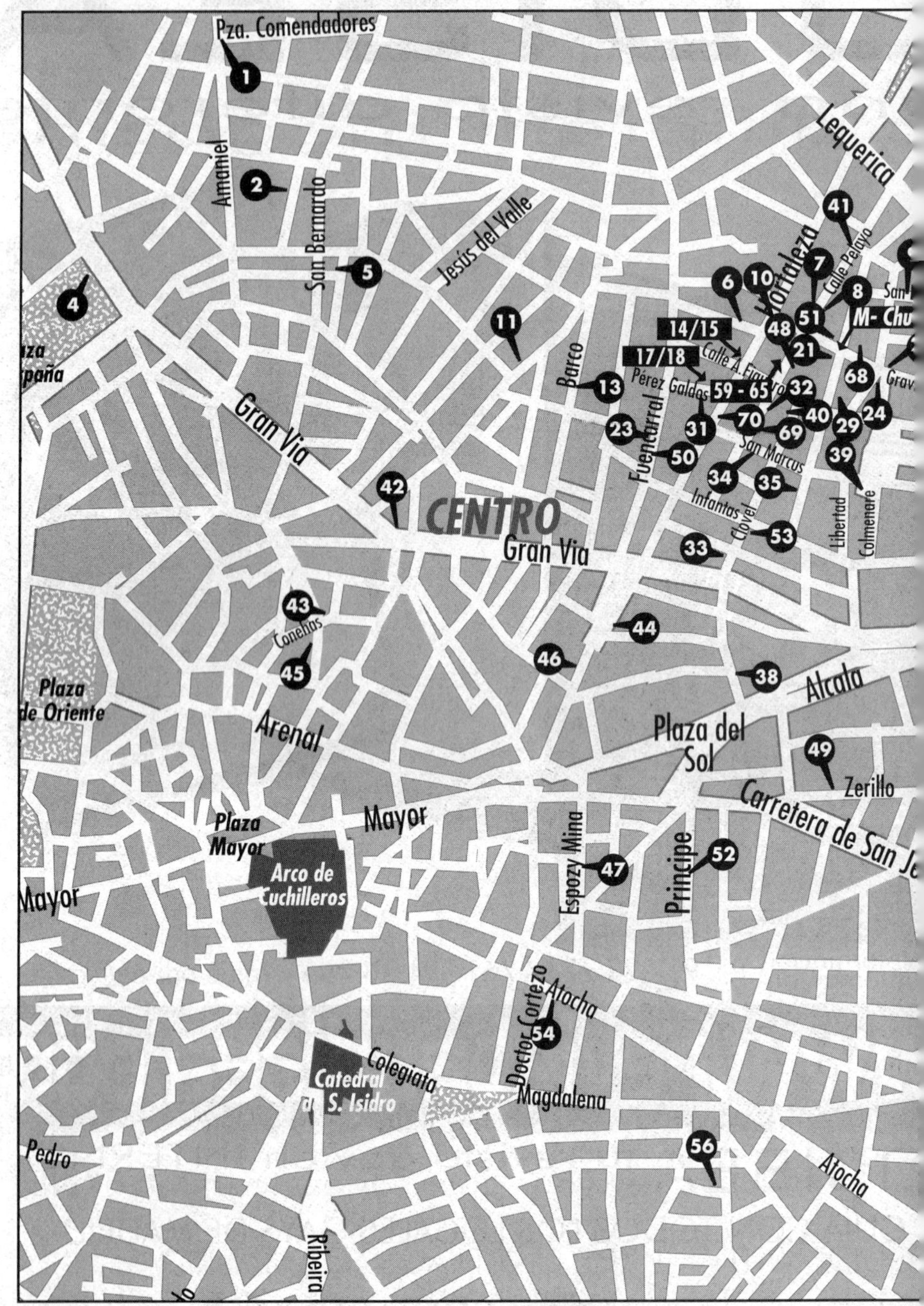

Pza. Comendadores
Amaniel
San Bernardo
Jesús del Valle
Lequerica
Hortaleza
Calle Pelayo
M- Chu
Barco
Calle A. Figueroa
Pérez Galdós
Fuencarral
San Marcus
Infantas
Clovel
Libertad
Colmenare
Gran Via
CENTRO
Gran Via
Conehas
Plaza de Oriente
Arenal
Alcala
Plaza del Sol
Zerillo
Carretera de San J
Plaza Mayor
Mayor
Arco de Cuchilleros
Mayor
Espozy Mina
Principe
Doctor Cortezo
Atocha
Colegiata
Magdalena
Catedral de S. Isidro
Pedro
Atocha
Ribeira

1 Sauna Comendadores
2 Sauna Paraiso
4 Sauna Plaza
5 Sauna Adan
6 El Candil Bar
7 El Sueño Eterno Bar
8 New Leather Bar
9 Lucas Bar
10 La Sastrería Café
11 Sala X Cinema
13 Video Show Bar Gay
14 Figueroa Café
15 Sauna Cristal
17 Cruising Bar
18 La Dame Noire Restaurant
21 Sachas Danceclub
22 Rimmel Bar
23 La Bubu Bar
24 Black & White Bar
26 Griffin's Danceclub
27 El 17 Bar
28 Lord Byron's Bar
29 Momo Restaurant
31 Bajo Cuerda Bar
32 Marsot Restaurant
33 XXX Café
34 XXX-Shop, Calle San Marcos
35 Ras Bar
38 Mad Café
39 Divina La Cocina Restaurant
40 El Armario Restaurant
41 A Brasileira Restaurant
42 Californiusa-Mundo Erotico Sexshop
43 Heaven Danceclub
44 Show Center Sexshop
45 Strong Center Danceclub
46 Californiusa American Sexshop
47 Hostal Valencia
48 La Bohemia Bar
49 Dumbarton Bar
50 Hostal Sonsoles
51 Clip Bar
52 Sauna Principe
53 Rick's Bar
54 Refugio Danceclub
56 La Lupe Bar
59 Madrid La Nuit Bar
60 Sauna Men
61 Happy Sex Shop
62 Eagle Madrid Bar
63 LL-Bar
64 El Rincón de Pelayo Restaurant
65 La Troje Café
68 Berkana Book Shop
69 Chez Pomme Restaurant
70 Hostal Odesa / Hostal Hispano Hotels

GAY INFO

Entiendes
COGAM, PO Box 18165 ✉ 28080
Bimonthly publication, about 64 pages. Cultural information and a gay guide of Spain. Ptas 500. At some newsstands and bars.

Gay Inform COGAM Mon-Fri 17-21 h
Fuencarral 37 *(Metro Tribunal/Gran Vía)* ☎ 523 00 70
Answers for nearly all questions concerning gay life.

Luna de Babilonia Mon 22-23.30 h,
Onda Verde FM 108 MHz
c/o COGAM, PO Box 18 165 ✉28080 ☎ 522 45 17

Mapa Gay de Madrid
c/o Berkana, Calle Gravina 11 ✉28004 ☎ 532 13 93
Fax: 532 13 93
Free gay city map of the gay bookshop „Berkana" in the gay scene.

Shangay
Apdo. de Correos 4.023 ✉28080 ☎ 308 11 03
☎ 308 66 23 Fax: 310 17 11 E-Mail: shangay@ctv.es
Free bimonthly gay paper listing all sites and venues in gay Madrid. Great information source on what's going on in the city.

TOURIST INFO

Información Turística
Plaza Mayor 3 ☎ 366 54 77

BARS

Adonis (AC B DR G MA VS) Tue, Wed, Sun 22-11 h, Thu-Sat 1-14 h
C/ Tres Cruces 8 ✉28004 *(Metro Gran Vía)* ☎ 522 82 65

Bajo Cuerda (AC B DR G MA SNU VS) 21-3/?, WE -?, SNU Fri Sat 1 h
Calle Perez Galdos 8 *(Metro Chueca)*

Black & White (AC B D G S SNU YG) 20-5, Fri Sat -6 h. Show Thu-Sun after 2 h.
Calle de la Libertad 34 *(Metro Chueca)* ☎ 531 11 41
Popular. Dance floor downstairs.

Bohemia. La (AC d E g MA OS P WE) Mon-Sun 20-? h
Plaza de Chueca 10 ✉28004 *(Metro Chueca)*

Candil. El (AC B g STV VS) 20-2, Fri Sat -2.30 h; TV-Show Fri Sat Wed 0.30 h
Calle Hernán Cortés 21 *(Metro Chueca)* ☎ 522 71 48

Clip (B G MA) 20-2 h
Calle Gravina 8 *(Metro Chueca)*

Cruising (! AC B D DR G lj MA VS YG) 19-3h, Fri Sat -3.30 h
Calle Pérez Galdós 5 *(Metro Chueca)* ☎ 521 51 43

Dumbarton (B G MA p) 19-2 h
Calle Zorilla 7 ✉28014 *(Metro: Sevilla)* ☎ 429 81 91

Eagle Madrid (B bf DR G LJ MA P VS) 11-2.30 h, Fri-Sat 11-3.30 h
Calle Pelayo 30 ✉28004 *(Metro Chueca)* ☎ 531 62 96

Fame. The (AC B bf d f G MA stv W) 9-2 h WE 9-3.30 h, Mon closed
C/ Pérez Galdós 1 and Fuencarral 36 ✉28004 *(Metro Cueca/Gran Via)* ☎ 532 12 86

Fragola (a AC B G MA) 21.30-3 h, Mon closed
Calle Buenavista 42 ✉28012 ☎ 903 97 12 *Cocktail-bar.*

Freedom (AC B d G MA s VS) 22.30-3.30, Mon closed
C/ Infantas 12 ✉28004 ☎ 523 45 38

Hot (AC B DR G lj MA p VS WE WO) 18-3, Fri Sat -4 h
Calle Infantas 9 ✉28004 *(Metro Chueca, Gran Via)*

Leather Bar (! B d DR G lj MA VS) 19-3, Sat -3.30 h
Calle Pelayo 42 *(Metro Chueca)* ☎ 308 14 62

Liquid (AC B CC d G MA VS WE) 21-3 h, WE -4 h
C/ Barquillo 8 ✉28004 ☎ 532 74 28 *Video bar*

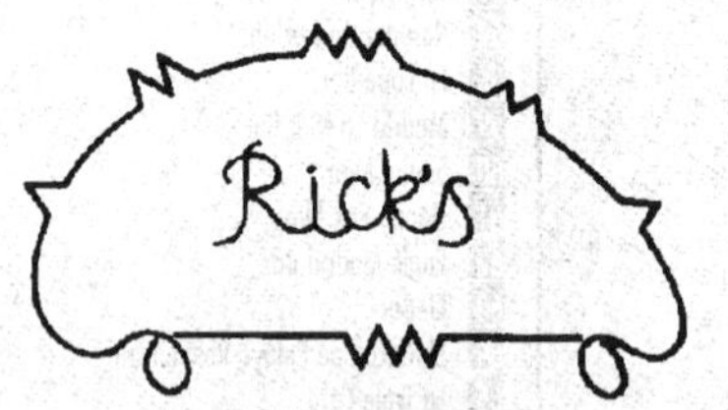

Tenemos la mejor clientela del mundo
The world's most exciting guests are here!

Antiguo, Moderno y el mas divertido
Old, modern and diverse

Todos los mediodías menú 1.100 pts.
Lunes a jueves noche menú 1.600 pts.
Domingo mediodía forfait 1.600 pts.

Pelayo, 19 • Telf.: 521 84 07
28004 - Madrid

LL Bar (B DR G MA S VS) 18-? h, Show Wed-Thu Sun 23.30, Fri Sat 1.30 h
Calle Pelayo 11 ✉28004 *(Metro Chueca)* ☎ 523 31 21
Popular. Two floors with two bars. Cabins.
Lord Byron's (B e G MA) 22-4, WE -5 h
Calle Recoletos 18 *(Metro Banco)* ☎ 575 00 00
During daytime cafeteria-restaurante.
Lucas Bar Mix (AC B d GLM MA s YG) 20.30-3.30 h
Calle San Lucas 11 *(Metro Chueca)*
Lupe. La (B f g s YG) 17-2, Fri Sat -3.30, Sun 13-2 h
Torrecilla del Leal 12 *(Metro Antón Martín)* ☎ 527 50 19
Mad. Café-Club (! A AC bf CC D F g MG OS S W) Mon-Wed 10-2, Thu -4, Fri Sat -5, Sun 13-0 h
Calle Virgen de los Peligros 4 ✉28013 ☎ 532 62 28
Madrid La Nuit (AC STV) 20-1 h
Calle Pelayo 31 ✉28004 *(Metro Chueca)* ☎ 522 99 78
Medium (AC B d G MA s STV) 17-2, Fri Sat -4 h
Calle Reina 17 ✉28004 *(Metro Chueca, Gran Via)* ☎ 523 02 25
Only esoteric bar in Spain, tarot lectures.
Mojito. El (A B Glm MA YG) 21-2.30, Fri Sat 21-3.30 h
Calle Olmo 6 *(Metro Antón Martín)*
Moskito Bar. The (AC B d GLM MA) 20-3 h
Calle Torrecilla del Leal 13 ✉28012 *(Metro Anton Martin)*
PK 2 (B d DR G MA VS) 20-? h
Libertad, 28 ☎ 531 86 77
Ras (AC B g s WE YG) 22-4, Fri Sat -4.30 h, Sun closed.
Calle Barbieri 7 ✉28004 *(Metro Chueca)* ☎ 522 43 17
Popular.
Regine's Terraza (B g YG) Summer only 21-? h
Paseo de la Castellana 56 *(near Emilio Castelar Square)*
Best time 0-3 h.
Rick's (B d g p YG) 22-5, Fri Sat -? h
Calle Infantas 26/Clavel *(Metro Chueca)* ☎ 531 91 86
Popular, gay late at night, good music.
Rimmel (! B DR G VS YG) 19-3 h
Calle Luis de Góngora 2 *(Metro Chueca)*
Sueño Eterno. El (B g MA) 20-3 h
Calle Pelayo 37 *(Metro Chueca)*
Tabata (B G YG) 22.30-5 h
Calle Vergara 12 *(Metro Opera)* ☎ 547 97 35
Troyans (AC B DR G LJ MA p VS) 21.30-3, Fri Sat 22.30-4 h, closed Mon
Calle Pelayo 4 *(Metro Chueca)*
3 bars. Very friendly and highly recommended. Headquarters of MSC Madrid.
Truck (B D G MA) Tue-Sun 22-5.30 h
Libertad, 28 ☎ 531 18 70
Video Show Bar Gay (AC B G MA S SNU VS) 16-24, SNU Sun 21.30 h
Calle Barco 32 ✉28004 *(Metro Gran Vía/Tribunal)*
☎ 639 20 87 16
Also video cabins.
Why not? (B g MA) 22-4 h
Calle San Bartolomé 7 *(Metro Gran Vía)*
17. El (B G MA) 21.30-3, WE -4 h
Calle de Recoletos 17 *(Metro Banco)* ☎ 577 75 12

CAFES

Acuarela Café (A B glm MA OS) 15-3 h, Sat, Sun 11-3 h
Calle Gravina 10
Color (AC B bf f G MA) 8-3 h
C/ Augusto Figueroa 11 ✉28004 *(Metro Chueca, Gran Vía)*
☎ 522 48 20
Breakfast, tapas, cakes
Figueroa. Café (! B f Glm MA) 12-1.30, Fri Sat -2.30 h

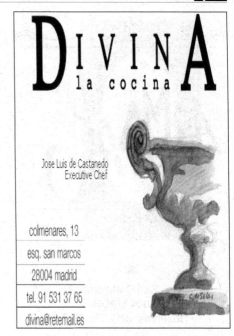

Calle Augusto Figueroa 17/Calle Hortaleza *(Metro Chueca)*
☎ 521 16 73
Jardin. El (AC B bf f G MA) 10-2, Fri Sat Sun -3 h
Calle Infantes 9 ✉28004 *(Metro Gran Via)* ☎ 521 90 45
Sastrería. La (AC B bf e F g MA WE YG) Mon-Thu 10-2 h, Fri-Sun 11-3 h
Calle Hortaleza 74 ✉28004 *(Metro Chueca)* ☎ 532 07 71
Popular designer cafe.
Star's Café-Dance (A AC B bf CC D F G snu YG) Mon-Thu 9-2, Fri -3, Sat 16-4 h ,Sun closed
Calle Marqués de Valdeiglesias 5/Calle Infanta ✉28004 *(Metro Banco)* ☎ 522 27 12
Trendy.
Troje. Café La (A B Glm MA) 16-2, WE -3 h
Calle Pelayo 26
Underwood (AC B CC f G YG) 15-1.30, Fri Sat -2.30 h
Calle Infanta 32 ✉28004 *(Metro Banco)* ☎ 532 82 67
International newspapers and magazines.
Urania's Café (A B GLM MA) Mon-Thu 17-0, Fri Sat -1, Sun 12-0 h
Calle Fuencarral 37 ✉28004 *(Metro Gran Via, Tribunal)*
XXX Café (AC B bf CC f G MA) Mon-Sat 9.30-2, Sun 16-2 h
Calle Clavel/Calle Reina *(Metro Gran Via)* ☎ 532 84 15

DANCECLUBS

Escape (AC B D GLM MA s) Thu 23-4.30, Fri Sat 1-7 h, Sun-Wed closed
Calle Gravina 13 ✉28004 *(Metro Chueca)*
Griffin's (AC D E G MG S) Sun-Thu 0-4.45, Fri -5.30, Sat -5.45 h
Calle Villalar 8 ✉28001 *(Metro Banco)* ☎ 576 07 25

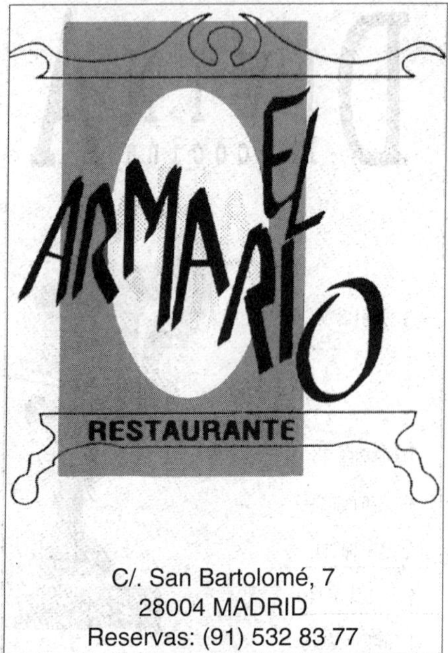

Heaven (AC B D dr G MA STV vs YG) 1.30-8, Fri Sat 2-10 h. Show Mon-Wed 3 h
Calle Veneras 2 *(Metro Santo Domingo)* ☎ 548 20 22
Popular WE early in the morning. Heaven-Techno-Gothic-Club Fri Sat 21-2 h
Ohm (B D G MA) Fri-Sat 0-6h
Plaza Callao, 4
Olimpo (AC B DR G MA S VS WE) Tue-Fri 23-6 h, Sat 23-7 h
C./ Advana 21 ✉28004 *(Metro Gran Via)* ☎ 531 16 95
Wednesday: underwear party, very popular
Priscilla (AC B CC D g MA) 19-3, Fri Sat -5 h
Calle San Bartolomé 6 ✉28004 *(Metro Gran Via)*
Refugio (AC B D DR G MA S VS WE) 0-? h, Mon, Tue closed
Calle Dr. Cortezo 1 ✉28012 *(Metro Sol, under Theatre Calderón)* ☎ 369 40 38
Sachas (AC B D GLM OS r STV) Disco Thu-Sun 20-5, Bar next door also Mon-Wed 20-3 h
Plaza Chueca 1 *(Metro Chueca)*
Shangay Tea Dance (B D Glm S YG) Sun 21-2 h
c/o Flamingo, Calle Mesonero Romanos 13/Gran Vía 34 *(Metro Gran Vía)* ☎ 531 48 27
Very popular.
Strong Center (! B D DR G lj MA SNU) 0.30-7, Fri Sat 0.30-9 h. Show Mon 3.30 h.
Calle Trujillos 7 *(Metro Santo Domingo)* ☎ 541 54 15

RESTAURANTS

Al Natural (F G)
C/ Zorilla, 11 ☎ 369 47 09
Health Food restaurant. Menu at 1.350 Pts
Armario. El (A AC CC F GLM MA stv W WE) 13.30-16, 21-24 h
Calle San Bartolomé 7 ✉28004 *(Metro Chueca)* ☎ 532 83 77
Just renovated.
Brasileira (F g MA) 13-16, 20-24 h
Calle Pelayo 49 *(Metro Chueca)* ☎ 308 36 25
Brasilian cuisine.
Cafe Miranda (AC CC F G MA S WE) 21-1 h
C/ Baravillo 29 Bajo ✉28004 ☎ 521 29 46
Chez Pomme (F g MA) 13.30-16, 20.30-23 h
Calle Pelayo 4 *(Metro Chueca)* ☎ 532 16 46
Vegetarian restaurant.
Cornucopia (AC CC F g MA) Tue-Sun 20.30-0, Tue-Fri 13.30-16, Sat Sun 17-20 h
Calle Flora 1 ✉28013 *(Metro Opera)* ☎ 547 64 65
Dame Noire. La (AC b CC F G) Tue-Thu 21-1, Fri, Sat 21-2, Sun -1 h
Calle Perez Galdós 3 ✉28004 *(Metro Gran Via)* ☎ 531 04 76
Divina, la cocina (AC CC F GLM MA W WE) Mon-Sat 13.30-16, Tue-Thu 21-0, Fri Sat 21-1 h
Calle Colmenares 13/San Marcos ✉28004 *(Metro Chueca, Gran Via)* ☎ 531 37 65
Dolce Vita. La (AC B CC F g MA) 13.30-16, 21-24 h
Calle Cardenal Cisneros 58 *(Metro Quevedo, Bus 16, 61, 149)* ☎ 445 04 36
Classic italian cuisine.
Gula Gula (AC CC F g MA s STV) 13-17, 21-3 h
Gran Vía 1 ✉28013 ☎ 522 87 64
Buffet-salad bar.
Hudson (AC b F G MA) 11.30-3 h, Mon closed
C./ Hortaleza 37 ✉28004 ☎ 532 33 46
Pizza & fast food
Marsot (b F g MA) 13-16, 20.30-24 h, closed Sun
Calle Pelayo 6 *(Metro Chueca)* ☎ 531 07 26
Good, cheap and very typical.
Momo (AC CC F glm MA W) 13-16, 21-24 h
Calle de Augusto Figueroa 41 ✉28004 *(Metro Chueca)* ☎ 532 71 62
Restaurante Vegetariano. El (AC b CC F MA NG) 13.30-16, 21-23.30 h, closed Mon & August
Calle Marqués de Santa Ana 34 *(Metro Noviciado/Tribunal)* ☎ 532 09 27
Non smoking vegetarian restaurant with salad bar.
Rincon de Pelayo. El (CC F G MA) 12.30-16.30, 20.30-1 h
Calle Pelayo 19 *(Metro Chueca)* ☎ 521 84 07
Sarrasin (A AC CC glm MA W WE YG) 13-16 h, 21-24 h
Calle Libertad 8 ✉28004 *(Metro Chueca)* ☎ 532 73 40

SEX SHOPS/BLUE MOVIES

B 43 Gay Shop (! CC G MA p) Mon-Sat 11-14, Sun 16-22, Summer 11-14, 17-21, Sun 17-22 h
Calle de Barco 43 *(Metro Gran Vía)* ☎ 531 49 88
Californiusa/American (g VS) 10-23 h
Montera 13 *(Metro Sol)* ☎ 531 35 05
Californiusa/Mundo Erotico (g VS) 10-2 h
Plaza de Callao 4 *(Metro Callao)* ☎ 522 81 56
Happy Sex (AC g VS) Mon-Thu 10-23 h, Fri-Sat 10-1 h, Sun 17-23 h
C/ Hortaleza 2 ✉28004 *(Metro Gran Via)* ☎ 532 4400
Libería Sexologica (g) 10.30-14.30, 17-21 h
Calle Hortaleza 38 ✉28004 *(Metro Gran Via)* ☎ 532 81 91
Books, magazines, comics, fotos, etc.
Sex Center Mundo Fantastico (g VS) 10-4 h
Calle Atocha 80 *(Metro Antón Martín)*

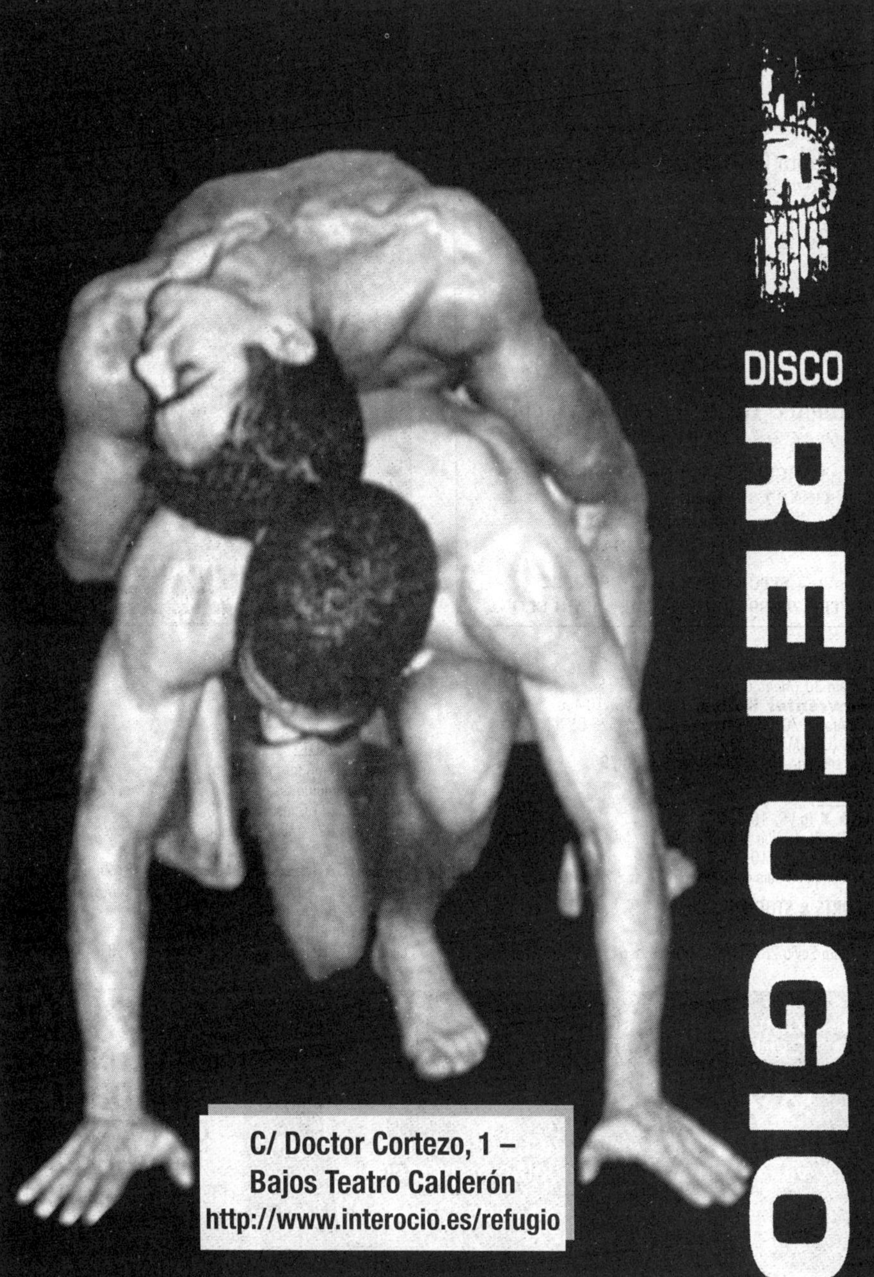
DISCO
REFUGIO
C/ Doctor Cortezo, 1 –
Bajos Teatro Calderón
http://www.interocio.es/refugio

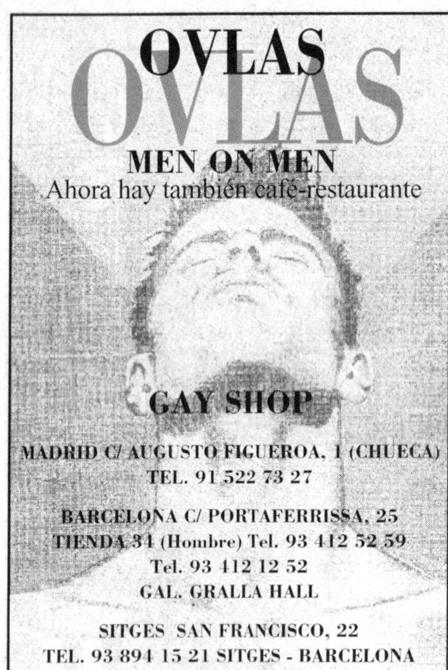

Show Center (g VS) 10-24 h
Montera 30 *(Metro Gran Vía)* ☎ 521 87 15
Showcenter Hollywood (g VS) 10-4 h
Calle Atocha 70 *(Metro Antón Martín)* ☎ 528 25 84
TVX (CC g MA VS) 10-22, Sun 12-21 h
Mejia Lequerica 16 ✉28004 ☎ 447 73 73

CINEMAS

Sala X (g VS) 10.30-24 h
Calle Duque de Alba 4 *(Metro Tirso de Molina)* ☎ 369 18 65
Sala X (g VS) 10.30-24 h
Calle Corredera Baja de San Pablo 37 ☎ 522 81 09

ESCORTS & STUDIOS

Antonio (CC msg) 24 h
C/ Arturo Sovia 267, 2°A ✉28033 ☎ 619 17 14 03 (mobile)

HOUSE OF BOYS

Skyphos
Triana 53 ✉28016 ☎ 350-48 12

SAUNAS/BATHS

Adan (B G MA msg pi R sa sb) 24 h
Calle San Bernardo 38 ✉28015 *(Metro Noviciado)* ☎ 532 91 38
Caldea (B f G msg sa sb sol) 24 h
C/ Valverde 32 ✉28004 *(Metro Gran Vía, Choece, Tribunal)*
☎ 522 99 56
Comendadoras (B G MA msg sa sb VS) 24 h
Plaza de las Comendadoras 9 ✉28015 *(Metro Noviciado)*
☎ 532 88 92
Cristal (b DR G MA msg og r sa sb VS) 24 h
Calle Augusto Figueroa 17 *(Metro Chueca)* ☎ 531 44 89

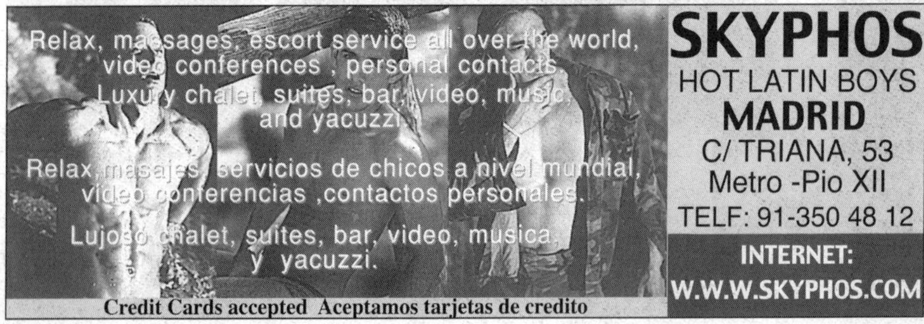

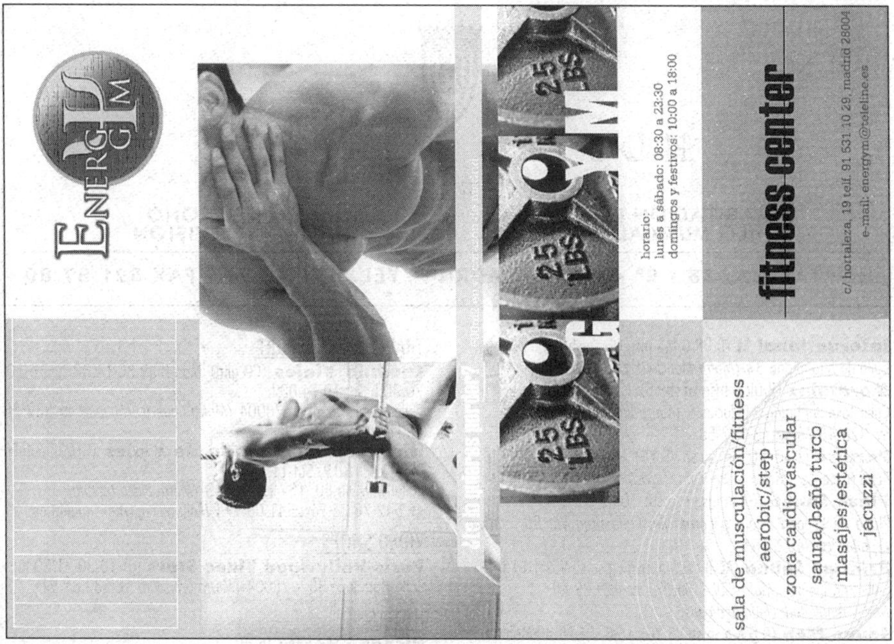
Energym
horario:
lunes a sábado: 08:30 a 23:30
domingos y festivos: 10:00 a 18:00
fitness center
c/ hortaleza, 19 telf. 91 531 10 29, madrid 28004
e-mail: energym@teleline.es
sala de musculación/fitness
aerobic/step
zona cardiovascular
sauna/baño turco
masajes/estética
jacuzzi

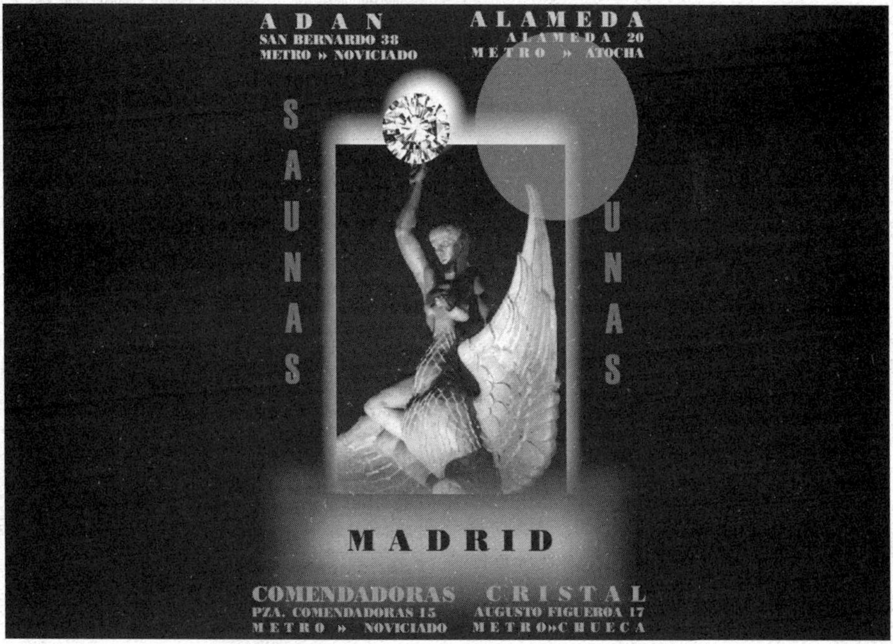
ADAN
SAN BERNARDO 38
METRO » NOVICIADO
ALAMEDA
ALAMEDA 20
METRO » ATOCHA
SAUNAS
SAUNAS
MADRID
COMENDADORAS
PZA. COMENDADORAS 15
METRO » NOVICIADO
CRISTAL
AUGUSTO FIGUEROA 17
METRO » CHUECA

International II (B DR G MA msg OG sa sb VS) 11-23 h
Calle de Altamirano 37 *(Metro Moncloa)* ☎ 541 81 98

Moratalaz (B DR G msg sa sb VS) 13-1, Fri Sat 0-24 h
Calle José del Prado y Palacios 5 *(Metro Vinatores)*
☎ 328 45 76 ☎ 437 77 56

Paraiso (! AC B G msg sa sb VS YG) 15-1 h
Calle Norte 15 *(Metro S. Bernado/Noviciado)* ☎ 522 42 32

Plaza Sauna (G MA msg r sa sb) 10-22 h
Plaza de España *(Galeria Comercial/Calle Gran Vía 88, Edificio España)* ☎ 548 37 41

Principe Sauna (AC B f G MA msg og sa sb VS) 10-1 h
Calle Príncipe 15 *(Metro Sol & Sevilla)* ☎ 429 39 49
Newly renovated, clean and cruisy.

Sauna Men (B G MA sa sb VS YG) 15-8, Fri 15.30-Mon 8 h
Calle Pelayo 25 *(Metro Chueca)* ☎ 531 25 83
Admission Ptas 1.000, -25 years 500.

FITNESSTUDIOS

Engergym (AC b CC glm msg sa sb WO) Mon-Sat 8.30-23.30, Sun 10-17 h
C/ Hortaleza 19 ✉28004 *(Metro Gran Vía)* ☎ 531 10 29
☎ 532 29 45

BODY & BEAUTY SHOPS

Hombre de Hoy 11-14, 17-21 h
C/ Infantas 10 ✉28004 *(Metro Chueca/Gran Via)*
☎ 522 30 73 Fax: 522 30 73

BOOK SHOPS

Berkana (CC GLM) Mon-Fri 10.30-14/17-20.30, Sat 12-14/17.30-20.30 h, closed Sun
Calle Gravina 11 *(Metro Chueca)* ☎ 532 13 93 Fax: 532 13 93
E-Mail: berkana@ctv.es Homepage: www.ctv.es/berkana/
Also very good for information point for the gay scene. Free gay map of Madrid. Catalogue on request.

FASHION SHOPS

Orlas 10.30-14, 16.30-22.30 h
Calle Augusto Figueroa 1 *(Metro Chueca)* ☎ 522 73 27

LEATHER & FETISH SHOPS

SR (CC G LJ W) Mon-Thu 11-14.30 17-21, Fri Sat 11-14.30 17-22 h, closed Sun
Calle Valgame Dios 6 ✉28004 *(Metro Chueca)* ☎ 531 59 26
Leather, rubber, uniform, piercing and tattoo.

TRAVEL & TRANSPORT

Lambda Viajes (CC glm) Mon-Thu9.30-14.30 h, 16.30-20.30 h Sat 10-14.00 h
Calle Fuencarral 43 ✉28004 *(Metro Chueca/Tribunal)* ☎ 532 78 33 Fax: 532 51 62

Navegaytour Agencia de Viajes (GLM) Mon-Fri 9.30-14, 16-19, Sat 11-14 h
Calle Gran Vía 80, 1° - 1 ✉28013 *(Metro Plaza Espana)*
☎ 542 78 35 Fax: 541 00 99 E-Mail: navegaytur@menet.es

VIDEO SHOPS

Paris-Hollywood Video Stars (g) 10.30-21.30 h
Calle Hortaleza 38 ✉28004 *(Metro Gran Via)* ☎ 532 81 91

HOTELS

Hispano Hostal (g H)
Calle Hortaleza 38, 2° ✉28004 *(Metro Chueca, Gran Vía; Bus 3,7,40)* ☎ 531 48 71 Fax: 521 87 80
Centrally located. Single Ptas 4.200, double 5.500. 21 rooms with bath/wc, telephone and TV.

Odesa. Hostal (G H MA)
Calle Hortaleza 38, 3°izq. ✉28004 *(Metro Chueca, Gran Vía; Bus 3,7,40)* ☎ 521 03 38 Fax: 521 03 38
E-Mail: m.g.d@mxs.redestb.es
Homepage: www.personal.redestb.es/m.g.d
Gay hotel. Centrally located. Rooms with shower/WC and TV, own key. Rates single Ptas 3.700, double 4.700 (tax incl.)

Puerta del Sol. Hostal (bf g H OS)
Puerta del Sol 14,4° ✉28013 *(4th floor)* ☎ 522 51 26
Fax: 552 98 15 E-Mail: puertadelsol@retemail.es
Homepage: www.212.49.141.42/webs/puerta_del_sol.htm

Sonsoles Hostal (CC glm H)
Fuencarral.18. 2° Derecha ✉28004 *(Metro Gran Via and Chueca)*
☎ 532 75 23 ☎ 532 75 22 Fax: 532 75 22
E-Mail: m.g.d@mx3.redestb.es
Homepage: www.personal.redestb.es/m.g.d
Rooms with bath, WC, balcony or terrace, telephone, fax, TV, radio and room service.

GUEST HOUSES

Valencia. Hostal
Espoy y Mina, 7 4° Derecha ✉28012 ☎ 521-18 45

APARTMENTS

Apartamentos Galdos (! GLM H OS)
Calle Perez Galdos 6 ✉28004 *(Metro Gran Via)*
☎ 531 28 98 Fax: 531 28 98
Apartment with double room Ptas 10.000, single 7.000.

O YOU KNOW THE TRUE PARTY
IF YOU HAVE NEVER BEEN IN MADRID, YOU
DON´T UNDERSTAND WHAT IS A TRUE NIGHT LIFE.
MADRID IS MOVE,
MADRID IS PARTY TWENTY FOUR HOURS A DAY

¡¡ LET´S GO!! LIVE IN THE CENTRE OF MADRID,
THE TOURISM AND THE SCENE ARE HERE.

HOSTAL PUERTA DEL SOL

IOSTAL PUERTA DEL SOL

OVERLOOKING THE SQUARE
BREAKFAST INCLUYED
FOR MORE OF TREE DAYS FULL BOARD

INGLE ROOM 6.000
OUBLE ROOM 8.000

Fax: (34) 91 552 98 15
Reservas: (34) 91 552 51 26

uerta del Sol 14, 4°
8013 MADRID

E-mail: puertadelsol@retemail.es
http://212.49.141.42/webs/puerta_del_sol.htm

PRIVATE ACCOMODATION

EG's City Apartments (glm H) all year
Conde de Ramanones 2 ✉28012 *(4th floor)* ☎ 619 44 02 32 Fax: 420 00 90
2 studios and 2 apartments in the city center with bath/WC or shower/WC, TV, Kitchenette, heating, Minibar and radio. Rates from Pts. 8.500 per night (max. 2 persons)

GENERAL GROUPS

Colectivo Gays y Lesbianas de Madrid (COGAM) Mon-Fri 17-21, Cafe 17-24 h
Calle Fuencarral 37 *(Metro Tribunal/Gran Vía)* ☎ 522 45 17 Fax: 524 02 00 E-Mail: cogam@ctv.es Homepage: www.cogam.org
Ask for their different groups.

FETISH GROUPS

MSC Madrid
Calle Pelayo 4 ✉28004 *Member of ECMC.*

HEALTH GROUPS

Centro de Promoción de la Salud Test Mon-Thu 9.30-10.30 h
Navas de Tolosa 10 *(Metro Callas-Sto. Domingo)* ☎ 532 23 67 ☎ 532 98 02
Free and anonymous HIV-testing.

Entender en Positivo (COGAM) Sun 17-21 h
Fuencarral 37 *(Metro Tribunal/Gran Vía)* ☎ 523 00 70
Confidential group.

RELIGIOUS GROUPS

Cohesión PO Box 510 57
Christian gays.

CRUISING

-Parque del Retiro (near sports zone; popular daytime; at night AYOR; Metro Atocha-Renfe)
-Plaza de la Lealtad (in front of Ritz Hotel, after 1h)
-Calle del Almirante (R)
-Calle del Prim (R)
-Plaza de Toros, Monumental, Parking (Metro Ventas, Carcruising from 22 h, very popular)
-Avenida de America (Calle de Cartagena, out of town, right side. Car-cruising from 22 h, popular)
-Parque Atenas (at night)
-Templo de Debod (at night)
-Casa de Campo (in the surrounding wood of Teleférico (cable railway) ground parking. 24 hours; at night: ayor)
-Estación de Chamartin (r)
-Estación sur de Autobuses, Metro Palos de la Frontera
-Estación de Atocha
-Cortes Ingles Shopping Center 1.Sol, 2.Goya, 3.Castellana
-Aeropuerto nacional (WE)
-La Vaguada Shopping Centre (downstairs, next to the Disney shop. Metro Barrio del Pilar. Popular)

Málaga ☎ 95

BARS

Konos (AC B G OS s W WE YG) 22-4 h
C/. Sagitario 3, Res. Bamonal, 1 - 1°6 ✉29631 *(Arroyo de la Miel)* ☎ 56 64 50

Noray (AC B g MA OS) 20-?
Puerto Marina, Pueblo Mrinero, Local G 9 ✉29620
Bar with meals.

El Porton (B f glm OS YG) 10-3 h
Plaza de la Merced 17 ☎ 260 18 50 *Popular.*

CAFES

Calle de Bruselas (AC B bf f g MA OS) 10-4 h
Plaza de la Merced 16 ✉29012 ☎ 260 39 48
Flor de Lis (A AC B bf f G MA OS) 9.30-4 h, Sun 12-4 h
Plaza de la Merced 18 ✉29008 ☎ 260 98 19

SEX SHOPS/BLUE MOVIES

Amsterdam (AC g VS)
Calle Duquesa de Parcent 1
Cosmopolitan (g VS) 10-24 h
Calle Muelle de Heredia 12 ☎ 222 15 83
Hamburgo (g VS)
Calle Casa de Campo 11
Sex Shop (g VS)
Plaza Bailén 2

SAUNAS/BATHS

Thermi Sauna (AC B bf CC DR f G lj MA msg P sa sb sol OS VS WE wh WO YG) 16-24h
Calle Pito 3 ✉29008 *(Centro)* ☎ 213 222 ☎ 217 012
Lesbian Day on Mon. Tattoo and Piercing studio.

BOOK SHOPS

Rainbow Liberia (A AC CC GLM) Winter: 10-14, 17-20.30 h, Sun closed, Summer: 10-14 h, 17.30-21 h, Sat afternoon & Sun closed
C/ Marín García 12 ✉29007 *(Near C/ Larios)* ☎ 260 88 07

GUEST HOUSES

Finca Leria Partido los Anéales ✉29500 *(40km northwest of Málaga)* ☎ 11 27 03 Fax: 11 27 03
E-Mail: fincaleria@maptel.es
Homepage: www.homestead.com/gayfinca/main.html
Rates from Ptas 3.375-5.000 for a single and 2.800-4.750 for a double room (without shower), 3.650-5.250 with shower, all include breakfast.

CRUISING

-Train station/Estación de Renfe (ayor, r)
-Paseo del Parque (AYOR) (nights)
-Jardines de Puerta Oscura (ayor r)
-Parabor de Golf beach (8 km from Málaga and Torremolinos, car cruising at night)

Marbella ☎ 95

BARS

Boccacio Inn (B G MA VS YG) 23.30-? h
Calle Puerto del Mar 7
Ojo (B G MA p S VS YG) 23.30-3, WE -? h, Show Sat
Calle Puerto del Mar 9 ☎ 277 16 79

RESTAURANTS

Dunas. Las (B f G MA)
At the Beach Cabo Pino; 5km from Marbella.
Finca Besaya (b F g s) 20-2 h
Rio Verde Alto ☎ 286 13 86
Telephone reservation only. 3-course menu Ptas 4.500.

La Comedia (B F g MA) Mon-Sat 19-?
C/ San Lazarro, 3 *(Plaza de la Victoria)* ☎ 277 64 78
Restaurant and Bar in the heart of the old town of Marbella.
Le Biarritz (CC F G MA OS) 13-16 h/20-24 h
Calle Ribera 122, Puerto Banus ✉29600 *(2nd line of seafront)* ☎ 281 12 48

HOUSE OF BOYS

Casa Bruno (AC G R) 14-22 h, Sun closed
☎ 282 57 80

SWIMMING

-Cabo Pino (Follow the coastal highway N-340 towards Torremolinos about 5 km to the km-marker 194, shortly after the Hotel Artola. Take the first right into the unmarked road, then the third left all the way to the end, then right down to the beach. Walk over the dunes, the beach bar »Las Dunas« is to your left and reach the most popular nudist beach on the Costa del Sol. The bus from Marbella to Fuengirola stops near Hotel Artola, from there by foot as above.)

CRUISING

-Paseo de Maritimo (at night some people)

Merida ☎ 924

BARS

Athos Club (AC B D DR GLM lj MA p s VS W WE) 21.30-? h
Calle Baños 23 bajo *(near Roman Theatre and Museum)* ☎ 33 05 74

Miami-Playa ☎ 977

HOTELS

Ferienpension Monty Mar (bf f glm H MA OS)
PO Box 113 ✉43892 ☎ 81 05 30
Nice villa with 8 rooms, all with bath/terrace. Full breakfast -11 h. Only 600 m from the beach. Rates for a double incl. bf DM 80-103 and DM 50-68 for a single. In May for women only. Guesthouse open from April to October. Miami-Playa is a tourist resort, located 80 km south of Sitges, well-known for its fine beaches.

SWIMMING

-Playa Nudista Torn (at L'Hospitalet de l'infant; also including pinewood for cruising)

Murcia ☎ 968

GAY INFO

No te Prives Meeting Fri 20 h
c/o Colectivo Gai de Murcia, PO Box 776, ✉30008 ☎ 29 54 84
10-page monthly newsletter. For free at gay venues.

BARS

Bacus (AC B DR G MA p STV VS) 19-2.30 h, Tue closed, Sun 21.30 show
Calle Isidoro de la Cierva 5B3 *(Galería Muñoz)*
Blaky Disco Pub (AC B DR G MA p s VS YG) 22.30-4.30 h Show Sun.
Calle San Antonio 1 *(Galería Muñoz)* ☎ 21 23 36
Popular, modern music bar/Bar músical moderno. Popular.
Odeon (B f GLM MA) 16-?, winter Sat Sun also 6-10 h (bf)
C/. Fuensanta 5 ☎ 22 16 41
Piscis Disco Bar (AC B D DR Glm MA p s VS) 22-4 h, Show Sun
Calle Enrique Villar 13/Trav. Santo Domingo 6 ☎ 23 89 62
Disco, video, surprise shows. Recommended and popular.
Vie en Rose. La (AC B DR G MA VS) 20-3 h
Rincón del Santo Domingo 7 *(Near Plaza Santo Domingo)*
☎ 600 416 253 (mobile)
5 Mentarios (AC B CC d G MA STV VS WE) 22-? h, Mon closed, Fri, Sat, Sun 6-? afterhour
C/ Torre de Romo 52 ✉30011 ☎ 346 122
Show Fri, Sat 1 h, Sun games and contests.

DANCECLUBS

Metropol (AC B D DR Glm MA S VS YG) Fri-Sun 2-6, Show Sun 3 h
Calle San Andrés 14 ☎ 28 39 23

SEX SHOPS/BLUE MOVIES

Internacional Sex-Shop (g VS) 10.00-22.00, Sun 10-14 h
Calle Enrique Villar 7 ☎ 24 82 15
Master's (g VS) 10-14, 16-22 h
Calle Mariano Ruiz Funes 5 ☎ 24 28 39
Sexyland (g VS) 10.30-1 h
Calle Los Bolos 1 ☎ 28 30 90

SAUNAS/BATHS

Nordik Sauna Masculina (B DR G MA sa sb VS) 15-22 h
Calle Cartagena 72 ☎ 25 91 20
Ulises Sauna (! B G MA msg STV sa sb sol VS WO YG) 15.30-14, Sat 15.30- 6 h
C/. Madre Elisea Oliver Molina s/n ✉30002 ☎ 25 43 12
Entrance-fee Ptas 1000-1400.

GENERAL GROUPS

Colecivo Gai de Murcia
PO Box 776, ✉30008

HEALTH GROUPS

Comité Ciudadano Antisida de la región Murcia (CASMU)
☎ 29 88 31 E-mail: casmu@lix.intercom.es
AIDS-information by phone.
Consejería de Sanidad Mon-Fri 9-14 h
Ronda de Levante 11 *(Main floor)* ☎ 23 51 41
Anonymous HIV-testing.

CRUISING

-El Corte Inglés - Shopping Centre, 3rd floor
-Paseo del Malecón (ayor) (and gardens; popular after sunset)
-Calle de Luis Fontes Pagan (car cruising)

Nerja ☎ 95

BARS

Blanco y Negro (B g MA)
Calle Pintada 35 ☎ 252 47 55

EDUCATION SERVICES

Giralda Center Languages Calle Jaen 7 ✉29780
☎ 52 33 98 Fax: 52 33 98 E-Mail: gircenternerja@arrakis.es
Homepage: www.giraldacenter.com
Language school.

SWIMMING

-Playa Catarijan (on the road from Malaga -N 340- to Nerja, between Nerja and Herradura. Turn of just before tunnel at the signs of Cerro)

Oviedo ☎ 98

BARS

Valentinos (B D DR G VS YG) 20-4 h
Calle Hermanos Pidal 28
Versace (AC B DR E G MA S SNU STV WE YG) Mon-Thu 21-4 h, Fri-Sun 21-7 h
Calle Campo Amor 24 Bj ✉33001 ☎ 521 83 11

CAFES

Santa Sede (B G MA) 20-1 h
Calle Altamirano 6
Tamara (B f glm YG) 11.30-15.30, 19-?; Aug only 19-? h
Calle Altamairano 6

SEX SHOPS/BLUE MOVIES

Internacional (g VS) 10-14, 16-22 h
Calle González del Valle 6 *(Galerías Pidal)* ☎ 525 24 99

SAUNAS/BATHS

Finalmente Sauna (B G msg pi sa sb sol VS) 17-23, Fri Sat 17-8 h
Calle Alvarez Lorenzana 22 ✉33006 *(Bajo; around the corner from El R)* ☎ 523 82 52

GENERAL GROUPS

Xente Gai Astur (XEGA)
PO Box 1397, Calle Gascona 12, 3° ✉33080 ☎ 522 40 29

HEALTH GROUPS

Centro de Orientación sobre el SIDA
Hospital Monte Naranco, Calle Vázquez de Mella s/n
☎ 523 07 50

CRUISING

-Calle Dr. Fleming/Calle Marqués de Mohías (after dark)

Pals

SWIMMING

-Bay of Pals (G NU) (10 minutes walk from Pals or the Gold Club, located near the installation of Radio Liberty)

Pamplona/Iruña ☎ 948

BARS

Alakarga (AC B GLM MA) 24-6 h
Plaza Monasterio de Azuelo 1 ☎ 26 60 05
M40 (AC B DR G MA VS) 23-4 h
Plaza San Juan de la Cadena 2

SEX SHOPS/BLUE MOVIES

Amsterdam Sex-Center (AC CC glm VS) 10-22 h
Calle Virgen del Puy 9 ✉31011 *(y Trasera)* ☎ 25 23 19
Haizegoa Amsterdam Sex Centre (g VS) 10-15, 17-22 h
Sancho Ramirez 35 *(Bus 7, near planetarium)* ☎ 17 72 99
Sex Mil 1 (AC CC glm VS) 10-22 h
C/ Virgon del Puy 9 ✉31011 *(near by Juzgado)* ☎ 25 23 19

HEALTH GROUPS

Comisión Ciudadana Anti Sida de Navarra
Calle Calderería 16, bajo ☎ 21 22 57
Comunidad Foral de Navarra
☎ 24 53 00 *HIV-testing.*

CRUISING

-Parque de la Taconera
-Plaza del Castillo
-Bus station (AYOR)

Pedreguer ☎ 96

BARS

Villa Romana Bar (AC B D Glm lj MA OS S) 23-? h
Partidá La Sella 23 *(Crta. de Ondara a Gata km. 194'5)*

SWIMMING

-Playa in Pedreguer (NU)

Platja d'Aro ☎ 972

BARS

Chapó (B G MA) 21-3 h, Mon closed
Victor Catalá s/n ☎ 82 52 50

SWIMMING

Cala del Pi (G NU) (from Platja d`Aro coming take the Camino de Ronda. After 15 min take the tunnel uphill.)

Ponferrada ☎ 987

DANCECLUBS

Temple (B D g r s)
Avenida de Portugal 1

Pontevedra ☎ 986

HEALTH GROUPS

Comité Ciudadano Anti Sida de Pontevedra
PO Box 603, ✉36080

CRUISING

-Jardines de la Alameda

Reus ☎ 977

BARS

Odeon (AC B D E GLM MA P s WE) 22-4 h, Sat -6 h
C/. Boule 7 bajos ✉43201 ☎ 619 800 380 (mobile)

Sabadell ☎ 93

BARS

Atic. L' (B DR GLM MA S VS) 20-3 h, closed Mon
C/. Mariá Aguiló 22
Laundry (B G MA) 20-3 h
C/. Can Viloca 62 *(La Creu de Barberá)* ☎ 909-7-88 40

Salamanca ☎ 923

GAY INFO

Radio Espacio Fri 21-22 h
89.5 FM

BARS

Boston (B g MA r)
Plaza de San Justo
Sarao (AC B DR G MA p S SNU STV VS) 23-4.30 h
Paseo de Carmelitas 11-21 ✉37002 ☎ 930 02 42 12

GENERAL GROUPS

Cogles Mon 19-21 h
PO Box 713, ✉37080 ☎ 24 64 71
Unión pro derechos de Gais y Lesbianas de Castille-León IGUALES
PO Box 4004 ✉37080
Publish their own bimonthly gay-lesbian magazine „Entre Iguales".

HEALTH GROUPS

Comité Ciudadano Anti Sida de Salamanca
PO Box 819, ✉37080 ☎ 21 15 77
Information and services concerning AIDS.

CRUISING

-Parque de Alamedilla (AYOR)
-Estación de Renfe
-Estación de autobuses

Salou ☎ 977

BARS

Pou. El (B G MA VS) 20-3 h
C/. Ramón Llull 4
Tres Coronas (B G MA S) 23-4 h; Show Fri Sat
C/. del Sol 72 *(near Plaza Venus)* ☎ 38 14 99

DANCECLUBS

New Chatelet (B G MA)
C/. Bruselas s/n

San Sebastian ☎ 943

BARS

Alboka (B glm yg) 14-3 h
Calle Easo 37 *(Urdaneta)*
Resaca. La (B e G MA og) 23-3 h
Paseo de Miraconcha 24
Trigono (AC B d G YG) 23-3 h
Calle del General Lersundi 6
Txirula Pub (AC B d G) 19-4 h
Calle San Martín 49

DANCECLUBS

Rontonda. La (B D g) 23-3 h
Paseo de la Concha s/n

BOOK SHOPS

Bilintx (NG) Mon-Sat 9-12, 16-20.00 h
Calle Esterlines 10 ☎ 42 02 24
Hontza (NG)
Calle Oquendo 4 ☎ 42 82 89

GENERAL GROUPS

EHGAM Tue 19.30-21.30 h
PO Box 16 32, ✉20080 *(Donostia)* ☎ 472 617 Fax: 473 789
E-Mail: ehgam@eusnet.org

SWIMMING

-Playa de la Concha (daytime)

CRUISING

-Paseo del Urumea
-Playa de la Concha (at night)
-Roques de Mompas

Santa Cristina D'Aro ☎ 972

DANCECLUBS

Mas Marco (A AC B CC D DR E GLM MA OS r s SNU STV VS YG) Summer: 22-5 h. Winter: 22-3 h, Sat, Sun -5 h
Ctra. Roca de Malvet Km. 1 *(1 km from Opel Garage at Costa Brava, 32 km north of Lloret de Mar)* ☎ 837 740
Free entrance.

Santander ☎ 942

BARS

Luna Pub. La (B g MA) -2 h
Calle Gran Mola

DANCECLUBS

Cuic (B D g WE) 1-6 h
Calle Panamá
Pacha Disco (B D g) Thu-Sun -3.30 h
Calle Gran Mola

HEALTH GROUPS

Consejería de Sanidad 9-14 h
Calle Marqués de la Hermida 8 ☎ 21 17 04

SWIMMING

-Playa del Puntal (Travel round the bay to Somo and walk the rest or take the ferry from Santander to Somo. The beach is a long isthmus with sand dunes along its length. Most gay activity is to be found approximately half the way along.)
-Playa de Valdearenas/Dunas de Liencres (10 km west of Santander, between Liencres and Boó, on the south side of the land spit in the dunes by the river Pas. You can reach it by bus from Santander)

CRUISING

-Paseo Pareda (after 24 h)
-Jardin Pareda (AYOR)
-Bus station/Estaciones del Autobuses
-Jardines de Piquío (nights)

Santiago de Compostela ☎ 981

GAY INFO

La hora Gay „Abrete de orellas" Fri 22-23 h
Radio Kalimero 108.0 FM

GENERAL GROUPS

Colectivo Gai de Compostela PO Box 191 ✉15780

HEALTH GROUPS

Comite Antisida de Santiago
Calle Fuente de San Miguel 2, bajo ☎ 57 34 01

Segovia ☎ 911

BARS

Amarote (B g MA YG)
Escuderos 5 ☎ 43 02 15

GENERAL GROUPS

Asociación Gay de Segovia (A.G.S.)
PO Box 285 ✉40080

CRUISING

-Train station
-bus station
-at the border of the river Eresma in the outskirts of the city

Sevilla ☎ 95

TOURIST INFO

Oficina de Turismo
Avenida de la Constitución 21 ☎ 422 14 04 Fax: 422 97 53

BARS

Arte (B G N OG) 22.30-3? h, closed Sun
Trastamara 19
Barón Rampante. El (A B G MA OS) 16-4 h
Calle Arias Montano 3 ✉41002
Bosque Animado. El (B f g MA OS S) Winter: Mon-Sat 16-?, Sun 12.30-? h, Summer: 20-? h
C/ Arias Moutano 5 ✉41002 *(Near Almeda de Hercules)*
Cafelito Muero Petri (A B F glm MA OS s) Summer: 20-? h, Winter: 17-? h
C/ Peral 1 ✉41002
Specialized in diffrent types of coffee
Frenessi (A AC B d G MA S STV VS W WE YG) 19? h
Pasaje Amor de Dios 2 ☎ 490 81 12
Galeria-Torneo (A AC B CC g MA S VS WE) 19-4.30 h
C/ Torneo 64 ✉41002
Designer bar.
Habanilla Café (A AC d F g GLM s TV W WE) 11-5 h
Calle Alameda de Hércules 63 ✉41002 ☎ 490 27 18
Old café from 1928.
Isbiliyya Café-Bar (B G MA OS YG) 20-5, winter 19-4 h
Paseo de Colon 2 ☎ 421 04 60
Popular.
Mirada. La (AC B DR G MA og r VS) 22-5 h, closed Sun
Calle Luis de Vargas s/n
Mundo. El (B D g MA S WE) 22.30-? h
C/ Siete Revueltas 5 ✉41004 *(Near by Plaza del Salvador/Zona Alfalfa)*
Disco-Bar
O. D. C. - Opción Delitto e Castigo (A AC B f G OS s) Winter: Mon-Sat 16-? h, Sun 14-?, Summer: 19-? h
Alameda de hercules 79 b ✉41003
Paseo Bar. El (B g MA OS YG) 20-22 h
Paseo Colon 2 ☎ 422 50 34
Best in the evenings.
Tocame (B G MA OS YG) 19-? h
Reyes Catolicos 25 ☎ 421 04 60
27 . El (AC B DR G MA R VS) 22-7 h, Mon closed
C/ Trastamara 27 ✉41001 ☎ 422 40 98
Rooms for rent.

CAFES

Cafe Hercules (B f G MA OS) 9.30-2 h
C/ Peris Mencheta 15 ✉41002 *(between Alameda de Hecules and C/ Felía)* ☎ 490 21 98
Central. Café (AC B F g MA OS) 11-4 h
Alameda de Hércules 64 ✉41002 ☎ 438 73 12

DANCECLUBS

Monnalisa (AC B D G s W WE YG) Thu-Sat and befor holidays 24-7 h
C/ Araona 15 ✉41001 *(Next to Estación de Cordoba)* ☎ 422 81 53

RESTAURANTS

Los Munditos (AC CC g MA W) Mon-Sat 13.30-16.30 h, Thu-Sat 21.30-23.30
Calle Carlos Canal 40 ✉41001 *(Near by Plaza Nueva)*
☎ 422 67 43
Sevillan cuisine.
Sopa Buba. La (AC F MA s) Mon- Sat 13.30-16 h, 21-23.30, Fri, Sat -24 h, closed Sun & Mon nights
Bailén 34 ✉41001 ☎ 456 48 84
Tel Aviv (F g) 14.30-16, 20-1, Fri Sat -2 h
Virgen de la Estrella 23 ☎ 445 76 33

SEX SHOPS/BLUE MOVIES

Internacional Sex-Shop (g VS) 10-22 h
Calle Sierpes 48 ☎ 456 45 97
Intimate (AC g VS) 11-1 h
C/ Monsalvez 5 ✉41001 *(at corner C/ Saucera)* ☎ 421 07 82
Video cabins for 2 or more.
Sex Shop Intimate (g) 10-14 h, 16-23 h, closed Sun
Calle Gravina 86
Sex Shop S.T. (g VS) 10.30-14.30 h, 17.30-22 h, Sun closed
Calle Trajano 29 *(near Alameda)*

SAUNAS/BATHS

Hispalis Sauna (AC B CC F G MA p pi sa sb sol VS WE wh) 11-24 h, Fri 11-7 h, Sat 14-7 h, Sun 14-24 h
Calle Céfiro 3 ✉41018 *(Bus 21, 24, 32: Corte Inglés Nervión)* ☎ 458 02 20
Admission Ptas 1.500, Tue Thu 1.200, under 26 years daily 1.000.
Nordik Sauna (AC B F G MA pi sa sb sol VS wh) Mon-Thu 11-23, Fri -7, Sat 15-7, Sun 13-23 h
Calle Resolana 38 ✉41009 *(Bus C 1-4, C 13, C 14)*
☎ 437 13 21

GUEST HOUSES

Casa Emililio (g H) ☎ 561 07 63
Rates single 2.000, double 4.000. Location 7 km from Sevilla.

HEALTH GROUPS

Comité Ciudadano Anti-Sida
Mo-Fri 10-14 h, 18-21 h
C/ San Luis 50 local ✉41003 ☎ 437 19 58
Information and services concerning AIDS. Free condoms.

CRUISING

-El Corte Ingles department store, Plaza del Duque (ayor) (best 4th floor)
-Santa Justa rail station (ayor)
-Vip shopping center (ayor) (Avenida Republica Argentina)
-Bus station (Calle Torneo)
-Parque de Maria Luisa (!) (evenings, also car-cruising)
-Jardines de Murillo
-Avenida de Tornea (near bus station)
-Plaza del Duque de la Victoria (r) (in front of El Corte Ingles)
-Parque del los Príncipes (until 21 h, than AYOR) (at the end of Avenida Rep. Argentina)
-Paseo de Colon (until 21 h, then AYOR)
-Parque del Alamillo

Sitges ☎ 93

●Despite its huge tourist industry, Sitges has managed to keep something of its old-world charm. Few places can boast such a high concentration of excellent gay hotels and apartments, so many busy gay bars, and a wide range of gay beaches. From May to the beginning of October, and again in February, the gay scene in Sitges is vibrant and colourful. Gay men flock here from all over Europe, and even from North America and Australia. It offers everything from small friendly bars and cafés to huge discotheques and first-class gay and mixed restaurants. And in any case, Barcelona, the Catalan capital, is more or less next door and can quickly be reached by train.

✱Trotz des Tourismus hat Sitges es geschafft, etwas von seinem alten Charme beizubehalten. Wenige Plätze haben eine solche Konzentration an ausgezeichneten schwulen Hotels und Apartmenthäusern, so viele betriebsame schwule Bars und eine Auswahl an schwulen Stränden.
Von Mai bis Anfang Oktober sowie während der Faschingszeit ist die schwule Szene von Sitges vibrierend und kunterbunt. Schwule aus ganz Europa und sogar aus Nordamerika und Australien strömen hierher. Es bietet alles: von kleinen, netten Bars und Cafés, riesigen Diskotheken bis hin zu schwulen und gemischten Restaurants erster Klasse.
Und für alle Fälle liegt ja Barcelona, die katalonische Metropole, fast vor der Haustür und ist in kürzester Zeit per S-Bahn erreicht.

▲Malgré le boom touristique des dernières années, Sitges a su préserver son charme d'autrefois. Rares sont les stations balnéaires où les hôtels, les locations, les bars et les plages où le rapport qualité/prix est si intéressant. De surcroît, Sitges est tout le temps fréquentée, surtout de mai à octobre et pendant le carnaval, où ça bouge beaucoup. Tous les gays d'Europe semblent s'y donner rendez-vous et on y vient même d'Amérique et d'Australie pour ces les petits bars sympas, les cafés intimes, les méga boîtes de nuit et les restaurants gays ou mixtes de première classe. Barcelone, la métropole catalane, est à deux pas d'ici. On y va en prenant les transports en commun.

☆A pesar de la gran cantidad de turistas, Sitges ha sabido conservar algo de su viejo encanto. Pocos lugares ofrecen tal concentración de excepcionales hoteles, apartamentos, bares y variedad de playas gay. Desde Mayo hasta Octubre, y otra vez durante el Carnaval, la comunidad gay de Sitges se muestra vibrante y alegre. De toda Europa y hasta desde Norteamérica y Australia vienen hombres gay a Sitges. Ofrece todo: desde pequeños y acogedores bares y cafés, hasta enormes discotecas y restaurantes gay y mixtos de primera categoría. A Barcelona, la capital catalana, se puede llegar en muy poco tiempo con la ayuda del tren regional.

❖Sebbene l'industria del turismo sia enormemente sviluppata, Sitges è riuscita a conservare il suo fascino di antica città. Poche località hanno una così alta concentrazione di ottimi hotel gay e appartamenti da affittare, un'enorme quantità di bar animati e una grande varietà di spiagge gay. Da maggio a ottobre e ancora durante il carnevale, la vita gay di Sitges è vibrante e variata; i gay vengono da tutta Europa, perfino dall'America e dall'Australia. C'è di tutto. Dai piccoli bar e caffè alle grandi discoteche e ai ristoranti gay e misti di prima categoria. In ogni caso la capitale catalana si trova a due passi ed raggiungibile in poco tempo con un treno metropolitano.

TOURIST INFO

Oficina de Turismo
Silvia Morena 1 ☎ 811 76 30 Fax: 894 43 05

BARS

Azul Bar (AC B G MA VS) 21-3h
C/. San Buenaventura 10 ✉08870 ☎ 894 76 34
Popular. Happy Hour 21-24h.

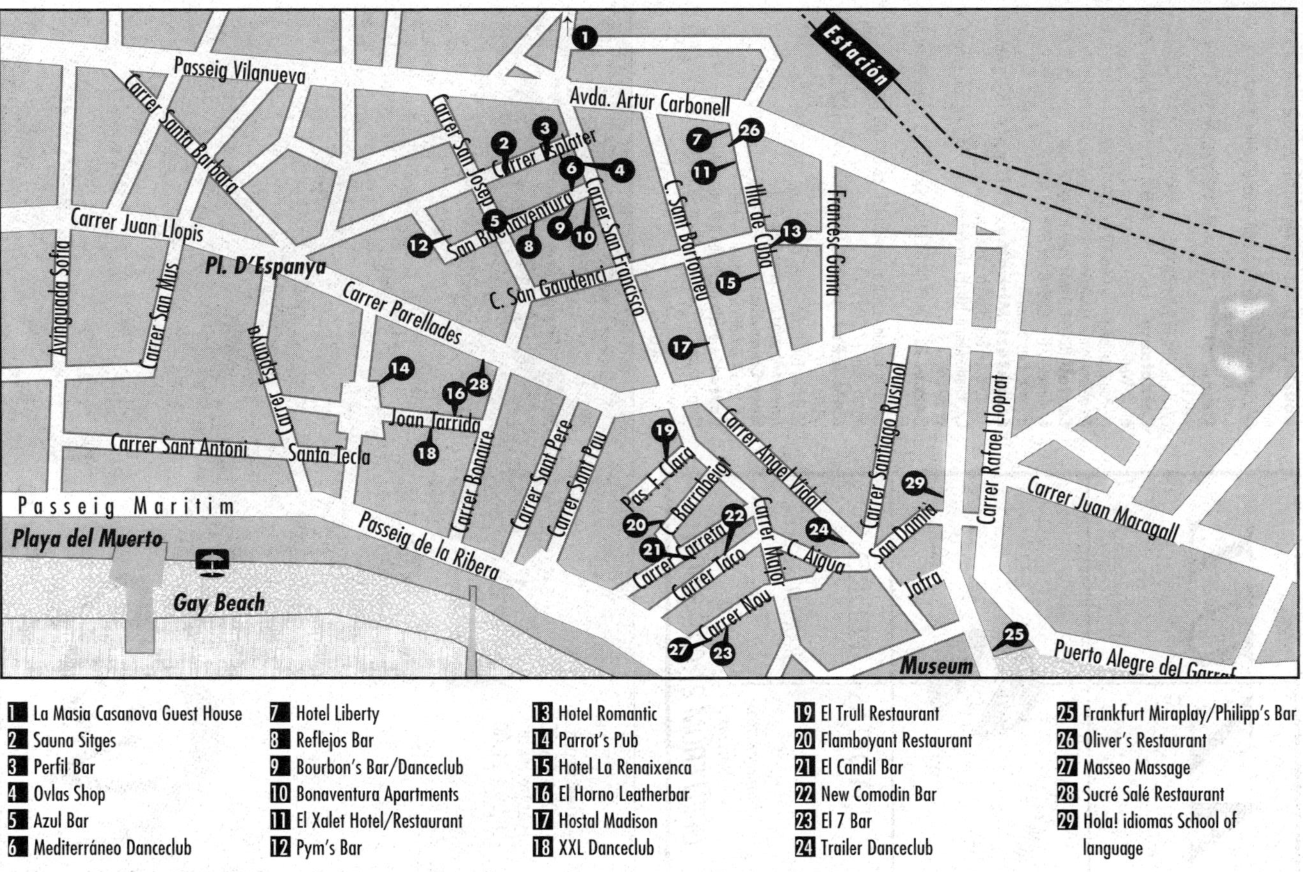

1 La Masia Casanova Guest House
2 Sauna Sitges
3 Perfil Bar
4 Ovlas Shop
5 Azul Bar
6 Mediterráneo Danceclub
7 Hotel Liberty
8 Reflejos Bar
9 Bourbon's Bar/Danceclub
10 Bonaventura Apartments
11 El Xalet Hotel/Restaurant
12 Pym's Bar
13 Hotel Romantic
14 Parrot's Pub
15 Hotel La Renaixenca
16 El Horno Leatherbar
17 Hostal Madison
18 XXL Danceclub
19 El Trull Restaurant
20 Flamboyant Restaurant
21 El Candil Bar
22 New Comodin Bar
23 El 7 Bar
24 Trailer Danceclub
25 Frankfurt Miraplay/Philipp's Bar
26 Oliver's Restaurant
27 Masseo Massage
28 Sucré Salé Restaurant
29 Hola! idiomas School of language

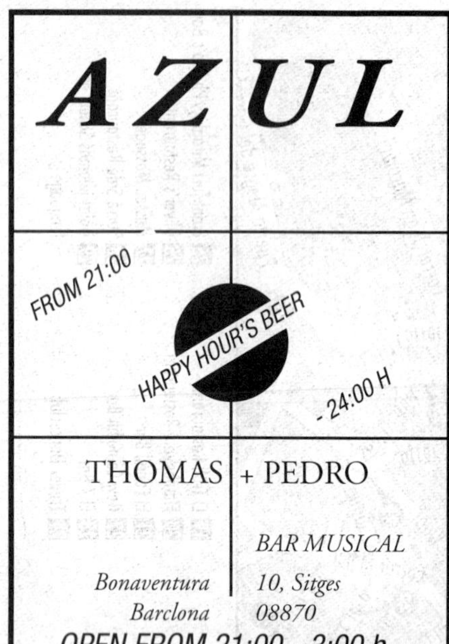

Bourbon's (! AC B D G MA VS YG) 22.30-3.30 h, in winter only Sat
C/. San Buenaventura 13 ✉08870 ☎ 03/894 33 47
Lively ambience. Very popular.

Candil. El (! AC B D DR G MA VS) 22-3, Fri Sat -3.30 h, closed Oct-Jan
C/. de la Carreta 9 ✉08870

Casablanca (A AC B Glm MA OG) 20.30-3 h, Winter: Closed Tue & Wed
C/ Pau Barrabeig 5 ✉08870 ☎ 894 70 82
Art gallery in the 1st floor

Castell (B CC F G MA) 20-2 h, Wed closed
C/ Carreta 21 ✉08870 ☎ 894 33 49
It´s also a restaurant

Frankfurt Miraplay/Philipp's (B f g MA OS) 10.30-3, Fri Sat -3.30 h, closed Nov-Feb
C/. Puerta Alegra 10 *(at the beginning of Playa de San Sebastian)* ☎ 894 97 43

Horno. El (! AC B DR G LJ MA VS) 17.30-3 h, Nov-Easter only Fri-Sun
C/. Juan Tarrida Ferratges 6 ✉08870 ☎ 894 09 09
Happy Hour 17.30-19 h.

Male à Bar. Le (AC D DR f G MA OS VS) 19-3 h, winter only WE
CC Oasis, Local 28 ✉08870
Terrace with salad bar, disco from 22 h.

New Comodín (AC B d G MA) 22-3, Fri Sat -3.30 h
C/. Tacó 4 ✉08870 ☎ 894 16 98

Parrot's Pub (AC B Glm lj MA OS s W) 17-3 h
Plaza Industria 2/Primero de Mayo ✉08870 ☎ 03/894 78 81

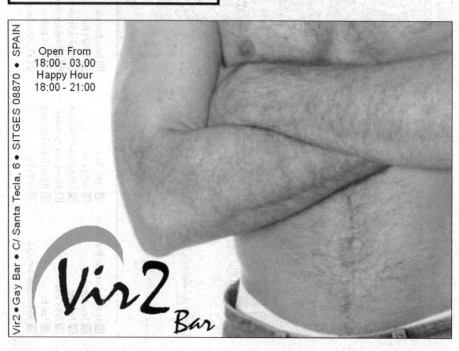

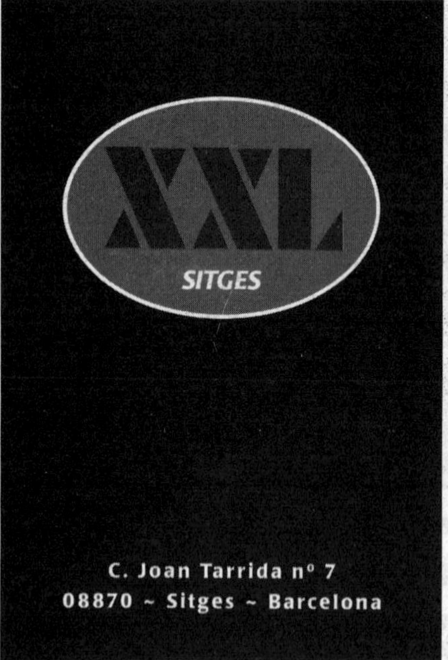

Perfil (B d DR G lj MA VS YG) 22.15-3 h
Espalter 7 ✉08870 ☎ 656 376 791 (mobile)
Pym's Bar (AC B d GLM MA s W WE) 20-3 h
C/. Sant Buenaventura 37 ✉08870
Reflejos (! AC B d G YG) 22.30-3, Fri Sat -3.30 h, closed in November
C/. San Buenaventura 19 ✉08870
VIR 2 (AC B CC d DR G lj MA r s VS YG) 18-3 h,
C./ Santa Tecla 6 ✉08870
XXL (! B d DR G MA VS YG) Easter-15. Oct 23-3.30 h, closed in winter
C/. Juan Tarrida Ferratges 7 ✉08870
7. El (AC B G MG s) 22-3, Fri Sat -3.30 h, in winter only Fri Sat
C/. Nueva 5

DANCECLUBS

Bourbon's (! AC B CC D G MA VS YG) 22.30-3.30 h, in winter only Sat
C/. San Buenaventura 13 ☎ 03/894 33 47
Mediterráneo (! AC B D G MA YG) 22-3.30 h, Easter-May only Fri Sat, closed Oct-Carneval
C/. San Buenaventura 6 ✉08870
Very large bar, popular.
The Organic Club (AC B D G MA S SNU STV) f24-6 h, winter only WE
C/ Bonaire 15 ✉08870 *Show WE 2 and 4 h.*
Trailer (! AC B D G MA YG) 24-5 h, closed Oct-Mar, but open Carneval, Apr/May & Easter week only WE
C/. Angel Vidal 36 ✉08870
Very popular.

RESTAURANTS

Chez Jeanette (AC F g MA) 13-16, 19.00-23.30 h, closed Nov & Dec.
C/. San Pablo 23 ✉08870 ☎ 894 00 48
Reasonable prices.

Flamboyant (B F G MA OS) 20-23.30 h, closed Oct-Mar
C/. Pablo Barrabeig 16 ✉08870 ☎ 894 58 11
International cuisine.

Ma Maison (B F G MA OS) 20.30-1, Sat Sun 13.30-15.30, 21-0.30 h, closed Nov
Bonaire 28 ☎ 894 60 54

Oliver's (AC CC E F MA NG) 20:30-23:30h, closed Mon.
Isla de Cuba 39 ✉08870 ☎ 894 35 16
Reasonable prices.

Racó de la Carreta. El (F G MA) 20.30-0.30 h
C/. de la Carreta 7

Sucré Salé (F g) 13.30-15.30, 20.30-0.30 h, closed winter: Tue and Nov
C/. San Pablo 39 ✉08870 ☎ 894 23 02
Crêps and salads.

Trull. El (! A AC CC E F G GLM MA MG) 19.30-?
C/. Mossén Félix Clará 3 ✉08870 ☎ 894 47 05
International meals.

SAUNAS/BATHS

Sauna Sitges (B G MA msg sa sol VS wh)
16 hours per day except Fri & Sat 17-22h
C/. Espalter 11 ✉08870 ☎ 894 28 63
Admission Ptas 1.200-1.500. Free condoms and lube on entering. Free solarium for SPARTACUS readers.

MASSAGE

Masseo (g msg)
C/ Nueva 11-13. Local 1 ☎ 894 71.35

EDUCATION SERVICES

Hola! Idiomas
Fransescu Gumà, 25 ✉08870 ☎ 894 13 33 Fax: 894 96 21
E-Mail: evila@holasitges.com Homepage: www.holasitges.com
Language school. Learn Spanish in Spain !

FASHION SHOPS

Dive Boutique 10-14, 17-22 h
C/. San Francisco 33
Men's clothier, underwear and accessoires.

Jazz Boutique 10.30-13.30, 17-21 h
C/. Bonaire 20 ☎ 894 99 63
Men's clothing.

JP Moda 10-14 h, 17-22 h
C/. Marqués de Montroig 2/Plaxa Industria ✉08870 ☎ 894 19 76

Mekzone 12-14h, 17-21 h
Calle Sant Pau 37 ✉08870
Underwear, beachwear, rainbow articles.

Ovlas 10.30-14 17-21.30 h
San Francisco 22 ☎ 894 15 21
Clothes and accessories, sell their own creations.

Ovlas 10.30-14 17-21.30 h
Paseo Vilafranca 3 ☎ 894 73 20
Clothes and accessories, sell their own creations.

PROPERTY SERVICES

Fincas Paradis Paseo de Vilanova, 10 ☎ 894 38 18 ☎ 607-300 896 Fax: 894 37 83
Homepage: www.fincasparadis.com

HOTELS

Hotel de la Renaixenca (B bf E G H MA) 21.3.-19.10.
C/. Isla de Cuba 13 ☎ 894 83 75 Fax: 894 81 67
Recommended mostly gay hotel. Bar also open to non-residents 19-23 h. High season is August.

Hotel Liberty (AC b bf CC G H OS)
C/. Isla de Cuba 45 ✉08870 ☎ 811 08 72 Fax: 894 16 62
E-Mail: hotelliberty_sitges@hotmail.com
Centrally located. Own key. Breakfast until 13 h. All rooms with satelite TV, telephone and mini-bar. Bar and garden. Rates single Ptas 7.500-12.000. Double 9.500-13.000.

Hotel Madison Bahia (AC b bf CC g H OS sol) 24 h
C/. de Parellades 31-33 ☎ 894 00 12 Fax: 894 00 12
25 double rooms with private bath/wc, 14 rooms with balcony or terrace, phone, satelite TV, heating. Rates (double as) single 4.500-8.000, double 5.500-9.500, additional bed 2.000.

Hostal Pension Madison (g H)
Sant Bartomeu 9 ✉08870 ☎ 894 61 47 Fax: 894 00 12.
Rates 2 single Ptas 4.500/8.000, 10 double 5.500/8.500 (low/and high season) with private shower/WC, van or heating, refrigerator, safe and balcony/terrace. Additional bed possible.

Hotel Romàntic (! B bf CC E g H MA sol)
C/. Sant Isidre 33 ✉08870 ☎ 894 83 75 Fax: 894 81 67
E-Mail: romantic@arrakis.es
Convenient location. Beautiful ancient mansion, romantic garden.

Recommended-mainly gay. Bar also open to non-residents 7-1 h. 18 Single Ptas 7.400-8.900, 40 double 10.400-13.000 (bf buffet 900). High season is August. Rooms with bath/WC or shower, (some with) balcony or terrace, telephone, safe and ventilators.
Xalet. El (F g H MA OS pi)
C/. Isla de Cuba 35 ✉08870 ☎ 894 55 79 Fax: 811 00 70
Recommended. Rooms with TV, phone, bath/WC, Minibar.

GUEST HOUSES

Antonio´s (CC Glm H)
Paseo Vilanova 58 ✉08870 ☎ 894 92 07 Fax: 894 64 43
5 double rooms with bath/WC, balcony, TV and rental of bikes.
Masia Casanova. La (CC G H NU OS pi VS)
Passaje Casa Nova, c/o Urbanizacion Vora-Sitges, ✉08870
☎ 818 80 58 Fax: 818 80 58
All suites with bath/WC, colour satellite TV.

APARTMENTS

Bonaventura Apartments (G H)
C/. Sant Bonaventura 7 ✉08870 ☎ 894 97 62 Fax: 894 97 62
6 fully equipped apartments. Rates Ptas 6.500-13.500/day.
Phillip´s Appartments (glm H)
C/ Port Alege 10 ✉08870 ☎ 894 97 43 Fax: 894 97 43
All apartments with Bath or Shower & WC, cocina, some with TV and balcony. Room service available. Rates from Ptas. 6.000 per day
Sitges Holiday Apartment
Pan Benazet 7, 3°, 1a ✉08870 ☎ 894 13 33
One apartment with bath/shower/WC, balcony or terrace, SAT-TV, radio, kitchen, room service. Weekly rates Oct-May Ptas 35.000, Jun-Sep 42.000, Jul Aug 49.000.

PRIVATE ACCOMODATION

Room Advice Service (g) 11-20h
Apartado de Correos 213 ✉08870 ☎ 6071 49 451
Fax: 8944 272 E-Mail: raservice@jahoo.es
Hotel and apartment reservations. German, English, French and Spanish spoken

SWIMMING

-Beach in front of Calipolis Hotel
-Playas del Muerto (G NU) (Two small beaches between Sitges and Vilanova i la Geltru. There is a shuttle bus from the Cathedral to Golf Terramar. Then take the road to the old Guardia Civil Headquarters and walk along the railway. First beach is mixed but the second is gay. At the side of the railway there is a forest with all kinds of possibilities)
-Playa El Espigón (ayor) (between Restaurant Picnic and Hotel Terramar, late at night and in the morning)

CRUISING

-C/. Primero de Mayo, C/. Marqués de Montroig (especially Café Mont Roig)

Tarifa ☎ 956

BARS

Las dos Columnas (A B GLM MA OS) 11-3 h
Silos 9 ✉11380 ☎ 68 47 33

CRUISING

-Bolonia Beach

Tarragona ☎ 977

BARS

Meson El Candil Café-Bar (B g YG)
Plaza de la Font 15 ✉43080

GENERAL GROUPS

Front d'Alliberament Gai de Catalunya
PO Box 11 17, 43080 ✉43080
Publishers of gay newsletter »Tarraco Gai«.

Torrelamata ☎ 96

DANCECLUBS

Boys (B D DR GLM MA VS) 21-3.30 h
San Antonio 50 *(near Cinema Segovia, Crta. Torrevieja)*

Torrelavega☎ 942

BARS

Don »D« (B d G)
Calle Marqués de Valdecilla y Pelayo 6

SWIMMING

-Dunas de Liencres

Torremolinos ☎ 95

TOURIST INFO

Oficina de Turismo
Bajos de la Nogalera, c/Guetaria local 517 ☎ 238 15 78
Oficina de Turismo
Avda. de la Constitución 21
☎ 422 14 04 Fax: 422 97 53

BARS

Abadia (B G MA OS VS) 23-4 h
La Nogalera 521
Ambiente. L' (B G h MA OS YG) 19-3, Fri Sat -4 h
Plaza Andalucia ☎ 205 08 36
Anfora (B GLM MA OS) 23-? h
La Nogalera 522
Arcos (B G p R) 22-? h
La Nogalera, Calle Danza Invisible 12 *(opposite Las Pampas Restaurant)*
2 Relaxrooms.
Bar Bacchus (AC B G LJ MA WE) 22-3 h
La Nogalera, Local 712
Bears meeting point.
Boys „R" Us (AC B DR G MA OS VS) Nov-May 17-?, Jun-Oct 20-? h
La Nagalera 19 ✉29620
Chessa (AC B G og OS) 22-3, WE -4 h
La Nogalera 408
Chicos Pub (B G MA YG) 10-3, Fri Sat -4 h
Plaza Andalucia *(Pasaje Pizarro bajo)* ☎ 237 22 43
Contacto (AC B DR G MA OS S VS) 22-4 h
La Nogalera 204
Popular.
Esquina (B G MA OS) 21-3, WE -4, winter only Fri-Sun
La Nogalera 203
In & Out Plaza (B glm MA OS WE) 20-? h
La Nogelera, Local 701 ☎ 939 95 34 68
Isadora (AC B d G MA OS S SNU STV) 22.30-6.30 h
La Nogalera, Loc. 207-208 ✉29620
Shows daily after 3 h.

JEl Candelero (B d G MA OS stv) 23-7 h
La Nogalera, Local 405 ✉29620
Fri & Sat show after 1.30 h.
Kaos (B d g MA OS YG) 22-3, WE -4 h
La Nogalera 107-110
Konos (AC B G S STV VS WE YG) 22-4 h
La Nogalera, Local 718 ☎ 954 50 28
Malú (B G MA OS) 20.30-3 h
La Nogalera 1103, Calle Danza Invisible *(opposite Los Pampas Restaurant)*
Men's Bar (B DR G lj MA VS) 22-5 h
La Nogalera 714 ☎ 238 42 05
Popular cruisy place. Offers also apartment rental service (ask for Frank).
Morbos (B G MA OS STV SNU) 23-6 h
La Nogalera 113 *Show 2 h*
Mousetrap. The (B bf F g MA) 10-16, 19-0 h, closed Mon
Calle Skal *(back of Pueblo Blanco)*
Okapi (AC B d DR GLM MA OS s VS WE) 21-? h
La Nogalera 504-505 *(next to station)*
English, French and Italian spoken.
Pempinel (B G MA p R) 18-3 h
Calle Skal 19
Pourquoi Pas? (B GLM OG) 21-3, Fri Sat -4 h
La Nogalera 703
Salsipuedes (B G MA OS s) 22-5 h, Mon closed
C/ Casablanca, Pueblo Blanco, Local 28 ✉29620
Soho (B d G YG) 22-6 h
La Nogalera 502 *Popular.*
Tensión (AC B DR G lj MA OS VS) 22-3 h
La Nogalera 524
Also Video- and Sex Shop. Popular.
The Black Rose - La Rosa Negra (AC B G MA R) 22.30-3.30 h
C/ Pasaje Rio Mundo 9 ✉29620 ☎ 237 57 61
Zatanazza (B G MA OS) 5-? h
La Nogalera 306

CAFES

Nogalera Café (B bf F g MA OS) 11-1.30? h
La Nogalera 519, Calle Danza Invisible
Poseidon (b bf CC F g MA OS W) 9.30-24, winter 9.30-18 h
Paseo Maritimo, Playa del Lido 3 *(at the gay beach)* ☎ 238 00 40
Popular.

DANCECLUBS

Diavolo (B D G YC) 24-? h
De la Cruz *(Edificio Centro Jardín)*
Bronx (AC D DR G LJ MA) Wed-Fri 3-8.30 h, Sat 5-17 h, Sun-Tue closed
Edificio Centro Jardin ✉29620
Parthenon (! B D DR G MA OS VS YG) 22-4?, WE -5 h
La Nogalera 716
Bar and disco. Very popular. Happy hour 22-24 h.
Passion (AC B D DR G MA S SNU STV WE) 3-8 h, winter only WE
C/ palma de Mallorca, Local 16 ✉29620

RESTAURANTS

Comedor. El (b F g MA OS) 20-24 h, closed Wed
Urb. Pueblo Blanco, Calle Casablanca ☎ 238 38 81
International Cuisine.
Crema. La (AC CC F g OS) 18-24 h, closed Thu
Calle Skal 19 ✉29620 ☎ 238 13 94
Spanish and international cuisine.
Escalera. La (CC F g) 19-? h
Calle Cuesta del Tajo 12 ✉29620 ☎ 205 80 24
Noray (b F g) 12-16, 20-24 h
Puerto Marina, 29620 Benalmadena Costa *(near Torremolinos)* ☎ (909) 14 76 14
Bar-Restaurant. Meeting point for local gays.
Poul's Steak House (B F g OS) 12-? h
Calle Skal 2 *(back of Pueblo Blanco)*
Zwei. Die (B F g MA OS) 19-?, Sun closed, winter also 12-14 h
Borio Antalus, La Nogalera 7 ☎ 237 88 11
International-german cuisine.

SEX SHOPS/BLUE MOVIES

Supersex (g VS) 11-1 h
Avenida Manantiales, Edificio Tres Torres
Venus (g) 11-23 h
Calle Hoyos, Edificio Congreso, bajos *(near bus terminal)*

SAUNAS/BATHS

Las Termas de San Miguel (AC B f G MA msg pi sa sb VS WE wh) 16-24 h
Avenida Carlota Alessandri 166 ☎ 238 87 40
Entry Ptas 1.500, cabin 2.250. 10 minutes by bus to the centre of town.

BOOK SHOPS

Codex (CC G) 11-14 h, 16-21.30 h (summer)
Pueblo Blanco, Local 14 ✉29620 ☎ 952/389 141

HOTELS

☛ Canillas de Albaidas
Guadelupe (B F G H) Restaurant: 12-16, 19-23 h, winter closed Tue
Calle Peligro 15 ✉29620 *(Bajondillo)* ☎ 238 19 37 Fax: 238 19 37
Rates single Ptas 2.500-5.000, double 3.500-7.000 (bath/WC in room). 10 double, 1 single.

Hostal Loreto (CC B bf G H)
Calle del Peligro 9, Playa Bajondillo ✉29620 ☎ 237 08 41
Fax: 205 23 98 E-Mail: loreto@raro.net.es
Rooms with bath/shower and WC, wash basin, balcony/terrace, apartments also with SAT-TV, radio, video, kitchen and waterbed on request.

GUEST HOUSES

Finca Leria (bf F G H msg)
Partido Los Anéales ✉29500 ☎ 211 27 03 Fax: 211 27 03
E-Mail: fincaleria@maptel.es
Homepage: http://homestead.com/gayfinca/main.html
45 minutes srom Torremolinos and the gy scene, B&B or half board available.

APARTMENTS

Apartamentos Buendia (H g) 24 h
Urb. Los Naranjos, Plaza Alpujarras 4 ☎ 238 65 17
Centrally located. Rates: Summer: single Ptas 4.500, double Ptas 6500. Winter: single Ptas 3.000, double Ptas 5.000

Estudios El Anexo (g H msg sa) 24 h
Avda. Carlota Alessandri 166 ✉29620 ☎ 238 87 40
Fax: 238 02 58
10 fully equipped apartments. Mainly gay. Rates summer Ptas 6.000/apartment, rest of the year 3.500/2 persons. 10 minutes by bus to the centre of town.

SWIMMING

-Playamar at Restaurant/Bar El Poseidon (G)
-Campo de Golfo, near Hotel Guadalmar (G) (between Torremolinos and Malaga -ca. 8 km from Torremolinos- daytime some cruising in the bushes; car cruising at night)
-Torrequebrado (g NU) (Beach after the casino between Torremolinos and Fuengirola in Benalmádena, first exit after casino and go back to the beach. There (G) at the right side)
-Las Dunas (G NU) (20 miles west of Torremolinos, just past Cabo Pino. Narrow stony beach, but busy dunes and wood at the end of the beach in direction Marbella. Parking at bar (F g) »Las Dunas«)

CRUISING

-Calle San Miguel (the shopping mall with the sidewalk cafes: „Heladería San Miguel" & „Bar El Toro")
-Plaza Andalucia (R)
-In front of the bus station (r)

Torrevieja ☎ 96

BARS

Coliseo (AC d DR G MA OS) 19-3 h
C/ San Pablo 12 ✉31800

SEX SHOPS/BLUE MOVIES

Eros (AC CC GLM VS) 10-1 h
Avenida Purisima 31, Playa del Cura ✉03180 ☎ 670 46 46

Valencia ☎ 96

GAY INFO

Paper Gai
c/o Colectivo Lambda de Valencia, PO Box 1197 ✉46080
Free bimontly publication. News from the gay scene, cultural and political articles on 24 pages.

Pols-Ter-Gai Wed 12.30-13 h
104.4 F.M. Radio

EROTIC-SHOP GAY
SPARTACUS

TOURIST INFO

Oficina de Turismo
C/ de la Paz 48 ☎ 352 40 00 Fax: 394 27 98

BARS

ADN (AC D GLM MA s W WE) 22.30-3.30 h
C/. Angel Custodi 10, Barri del Carme ✉46003 ☎ 391 79 88
Disco-Pub.
Contramano (B d G MA) 22-3 h
C/. Murillo 12
Guerra. La (AC B DR G MA VS) 20-3, Fri Sat-4 h, Sun -3.30 h
C/. Quart 47 ☎ 391 36 75
Five floors with different ambiance, large darkroom.
North Dakota Saloon (B G lj MA) 20-3 h
Plaza Margarita Valldaura 1 ☎ 357 52 50
OH! Valencia (B D DR OG STV VS WE) 22-4, Show Fri-Sun 1.30 h, Tue closed
C/. Murillo 26
Romeo (AC B DR G MA R SNU) 20-3 h
C/. del Mar 45/Calle de Bonaire ☎ 391 09 54
Also rooms for rent.
Studio 17 (AC B D G p YG) 19-1.30, Sun 18-2 h, closed Tue
C/. Cerrajeros 17/Plaza Redondo ☎ 391 82 03
Popular disco bar, best Fri-Sun.
Xandro's. Pub (AC B G MA p R VS) 18-2 h, closed Mon
C/. Derechos 30 ✉46001
Also rooms for rent.

CAFES

Café de la Seu (A AC B d f G MA OS s) 16-2 h, Tue closed
C/. Santo Cáliz 7 ✉46001 ☎ 391 57 15
Cafe de las Horas (A AC B f glm MA s) Winter: 16-?, Summer: 18-? h
C/ Conde de Almodóvas 1 ✉46003 *(Near Plaza Virgen)* ☎ 391 73 36
Cafe Infanta (A AC B d g MA OS) 19-3 h
Plaza Tossal 3 ✉46001 ☎ 392 16 23
Espai Obert (A B d f GLM MA OS s) Mon-Wed 17-22, Thu Sun -0, Fri Sat -2 h
C/. Salvador Griner 9 ✉46003 ☎ 391 20 84
Café Sant Miquel (AC B G MA OS) 19.30-3, Fri Sat -4.30 h, Mon closed
Plaza Sant Miquel 13 ✉46003 ☎ 392 45 96

DANCECLUBS

Goulue. La (AC B D G MA S YG) Wed-Sun 22-4 h
C/ Quart 32 ✉46003
Venial (! B D Glm S VS YG) 0-5, Fri Sat -6. Show Thu Sun 2.30 h
C/. Quart 26 ☎ 391 73 56
Victor's (B D DR Glm MA S) 1-5, Fri Sat -6. Summer daily -6 h. Show Fri Sat 3.30 h
C/. Doctor Monserrat 23 ☎ 391 70 81

RESTAURANTS

Amanida (AC b CC F g MA)
C/ Quart 17 ✉46001 ☎ 392 41 77
Salad bar & 2nd dish for Ptas. 1.700.
Boulevard Corinto (AC B bf CC F G H MA OS) 8.30-24 h
Urbanisacion Corinto 1 46529 Sagunto *(20 min. from Valencia on seaside)* ☎ 260 89 11 ☎ 267 19 12
De Pas (F g) 20-2 h, Tue closed.
C/. Sant Calze 7
Sandwiches.
Oficio de Boca (AC B bf CC F G OS) 12-16, 20-2 h, WE 20-2 h, Mon closed
C/. Corretgeria 33 ✉46001 ☎ 392 50 13
TasKeta (A B glm MA s) 19-? h
Plaza Santa Margarita 1 ✉46003 ☎ 392 35 91

SEX SHOPS/BLUE MOVIES

Afro (g) 9.30-22.30 h, closed Sun
Gran Vía Germanías 53/Calle Cuba ☎ 341 11 02
Blue Sex Factory (g VS) 9.30-22.30 h
C/. Bailen 28 ☎ 342 38 68
Erotik Planet King Video (g VS)
Av. Peres y Valero 48 ✉46006 ☎ 33 432 70
European Center (g VS) 11-14, 16.30-21.30 h
Avenida Constitución 26 ☎ 347 44 27
Evadán (g) 9.30-22.30 h
C/. Matías Parelló 14 ☎ 374 20 65
Moncho Internacional (g) 9.30-22.30 h
C/. Dr. Zamenhof 15 *(near »Nuevo Centro«)* ☎ 382 33 49
Sala X (g R VS) 11-20 h
Calle Alcoy 3 *(behind station and Plaza de toros)*
Nice men from the „barrio".
Sex Hollywood (g VS) 9.30-22.30 h
C/. Dr. Zamenhoff 5 ✉46008 ☎ 382 14 67
Spartacus (DR G VS) 9.30-22.30 h
C/. Flassaders 8 ✉46001 *(near Plaza Merced)* ☎ 352 56 62
Gay cabins upstairs.

SAUNAS/BATHS

Magnus Termas (! B DR f G msg sa sb sol VS wh WO) 10-24 h
Av. del Puerto 27 ✉46023 ☎ 337 48 92
One of the nicest sauna.
Olimpic
Vivons 17 ☎ 373 04 18

FASHION SHOPS

Genero Masculino (AC CC g MA YG) 10-13.30, 17-20.30 h
Avenida M. Cristina 3 ✉46001 ☎ 352 52 18
Men clothes.

APARTMENTS

Torre Corinto (AC B bf CC F g H N NG NU OS pi WO) Summer: 9-24 h, Winter: 9-20, Sat Sun -24 h
Urbanifacion Corinto 1 46529 Sagunto, Va *(20 min. from Valencia on seaside)* ☎ 260 89 11
Fax: 260 70 75. Email: conver@ehome.encis.es. Also restaurant.

HEALTH GROUPS

Asociació Valenciana Contra la SIDA (AVACOS) Mon-Fri 10-13, Wed Thu also 17-19 h
C/. Cuba 61 bajo,izq. ✉46006 ☎ 380 07 37
Centro d'Informario i Prevencio de la SIDS (CIPS) Calle Flora 7 ☎ 362 40 69
Comite Ciudadano Anti-Sida 10-14 h
C/. Flora 7 ☎ 361 88 11, ext 36

SWIMMING

-Playa del Saler (NU) (take bus from Plaza Porta del Mar to the end of the bus line, approximately 15 km south of Valencia. Walk south on beach for 1 to 2 km. It's very cruisy nearby the forest)
-Playa de la Casa Negra (NU) (On the same bus line at the golf course resort hotel)
-Playa de Malvarosa de Corinto (G NU) 20 mins. from Valencia to Sagunto, near Hotel Torre Corinto

CRUISING
-Billares Colon, Calle Lauria (R)
-Jardines del Turia (near Paseo de la Alameda)
-Paseo Alameda (also by car, at night)
-Calle Joaquín Ballester (r tv) (also by car, at night)
-Bus station/Estación de autobuses (near the »Ballkiss-Disco« in the park, best after 1 h, (r tv))
-Main train station/Estación de trenes central (ayor R)

Vall de Ebo / Alicante ☎ 96

HOTELS
Molino. El (A AC B F glm H OS) Wed-Sun 12.30-17-30, Sat 19.1 h
Carretera Pego, km. 8 ✉03789 ☎ 597 72 82
In Pego follow the sign „Cova del Rull-La Vall de Ebo". 15 minutes to the beach. Also camping. Laid in the hills.

Valladolid ☎ 983

BARS
Pub de Eddi 1900 (AC B D g MA snu VS WE) 20-4 h
Calle Alarcón 3 bajo ✉47001 *(Near Plaza Mayor)* ☎ 35 35 90

SEX SHOPS/BLUE MOVIES
International (g VS) 10-3 h
Calle San Blas 19 ☎ 26 18 37
Sex Shop (g VS) 10-22 h
Calle San Blas 17 ☎ 25 66 20

BARS
Roy Bleck (B D DR G MA VS) 24-4 h
Ruá Oporto 12 ☎ 22 30 46
Termas (B G MA) 22-6 h
Rúa Canceleiro 11 ☎ 22 55 37
7.4 (B g OS YG) Ruá Arenal 74 ☎ 22 78 05

SEX SHOPS/BLUE MOVIES
Cosmopolitan (g VS) 10.30-22.30, Sun 10.30-14, 16-22.30 h
Ruá Príncipe 22 *(Galerías)*

SAUNAS/BATHS
Azul (B G MA sa sb WO) 16-4 h
Rúa Roupeiro 67 ☎ 22 82 92
Termas (B f G MA pi sa sb) 16-6 h
Ruá Canceleiro 11 ☎ 22 55 37

SWIMMING
-Samil Beach (G nu) (at the rocks)
-Barra Beach (g NU)

CRUISING
-Garden at Club Náutico
-Gardens at Arenal (behind Comandancia de Marina)
-Estacion Renfe (railway station)
-Corte Inglés (WC)

Vitoria ☎ 945

BARS
Moët & Co (AC B GLM MA) Sun-Thu 19-3 Fri Sat -3.30 h
Calle Los Mantelli 1 *(junto a Calle Los Herrán 46)* ☎ 28 93 33

SEX SHOPS/BLUE MOVIES
Cosmopolitan Sex Shop (g)
Calle Manuel Iradier 42
Sex Shop (g)
Calle Tintoreria 51

GENERAL GROUPS
Gaytasuna Colectivo Gay de Alave Wed 20.30 h
Calle San Francisco 2 - 1° ✉01001 ☎ 25 77 66

HEALTH GROUPS
Comisión Ciudadana Anti-Sida de Alava
Mon-Fri 9-14, 16-20 h
Calle San Francisco 2 - 1° ✉01001 ☎ 25 78 66
Fax: 25 77 66.

Zaragoza ☎ 976

BARS
Mick Havanna (B DR G MA VS) 16-3, WE 16-5 h
Calle Ramón Pignatelli 7 */Avda. Cesaraugusto* ☎ 28 44 50
Sandor (B DR G MA VS) 21-4 h
Calle Loscos 13 ☎ 39 82 02
Urano (AC B G MA s VS) 18-? h
C/ Fita 8-14 ✉50005 ☎ 222 167

CAFES
Madalena. La (B F GLM MA OS)
C/ Mayor 48 ✉50001 ☎ 391 952
Recalada. La (A AC B G lj MA s)
C/ Madre Sacramento 20 ✉50004 ☎ 211 517

DANCECLUBS
Boy´s (AC B D G MA s VS) Thu-Sun 22-5 h
C/ Dato 18 ✉50005 ☎ 228 402
Boy´s (AC B D G MA s SNU STV WE) Thu-Sun 22-4 h
C/ Dr. Horno 25 ✉50004 ☎ 226 876
Oasis (AC B g MA S STV TV WE) 24-8 h
C/ Boggiero, 28 ✉50003
Show Fri & Sat from 1.30 h on, Special events for e.g. gay liberation day.
Sphinx (B D Glm MA) 22.30-6 h
Calle Madre Rafols 2 ✉50004 ☎ 44 10 11

RESTAURANTS
Flor Restaurante (AC B CC F G OS) 13.30-16, 20.30-24 Sun closed, Mon only evenings
C/ del Temple 1 ✉50003 ☎ 39 49 75

SEX SHOPS/BLUE MOVIES
Pignatelli (g VS) 10-22 h
Calle Ramón de Pignatelli 44 ✉50004 ☎ 43 71 99
Sexshop (G VS) 10-22 h
Jose Anselmo Clave *(opposite train station)*
Tubo. El (G VS) 10-22 h
Calle Cuarto de Agosto 15 *(Near Bar El Plata)*

SAUNAS/BATHS
Nordik Sauna (AC B G MA sa sb sol VS) 15-22 h
Calle Andrés Gurpide 4 ☎ 59 45 36
Very clean and highly recommended. Entry Ptas 1.400.

GENERAL GROUPS
Lesbianas y Gays de Aragón (LYGA) Mon 19-22 h, Fri 19-22 h (Youth group)
C/ Mayor 40 ☎ 39 55 77 Fax: 39 73 73

SWIMMING
-Rio Ebro (NU) (Between Avenida de Francia and Puente de la Almozara. In winter car-cruising at night.)

CRUISING
-Plaza de los Sitios (at night)
-Estación El Portillo (at night)

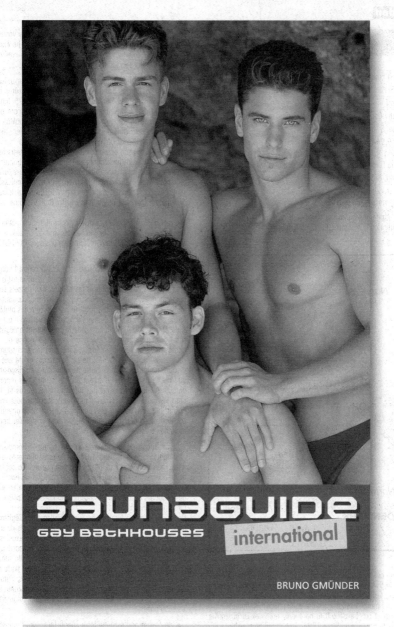

Sweden

Sverige

Northwest Europe

Initials: S

Time: GMT +1

☎ Country Code / Access Code: 46 / 009

Language: Swedish

Area: 449,964 km² / 173,731 sq mi.

Currency: 1 Swedish Crown (skr) = 100 Öre. 1 EURO = 100 Euro Cents; the Euro can only be used in the clearance system.

Population: 8,863,000

Capital: Stockholm

Religions: 89% Protestant

Climate: Moderate climate in south with cold, cloudy winters and cool, partly cloudy summers, the north is subarctic.

● There are no specific laws against male or female homosexuality in Sweden. The age of consent (15 years) is the same for both gays, lesbians and heterosexuals. Social opinion is markedly tolerant and many Swedish gays are open about their homosexuality. Even so, it can be difficult to be openly homosexual in smaller towns and in rural areas. Since 1994, »registered partnerships« are also recognized in Sweden: this is not the same as marriage, but it does give homosexual couples a similar legal status to that of heterosexual marriages. Anti-discrimination laws have been in force for some time, and each year public funds are made available for the financial support of gay organizations. Most of the gay venues are in the cities, but the scene is much smaller than might be expected in such a liberal country. It has become mandatory to notify officials of a positive HIV test result.

✸ Es gibt in Schweden keine speziellen Gesetze gegen männliche oder weibliche Homosexualität. Das Schutzalter liegt für Schwule/Lesben und Heteros bei gleichermassen 15 Jahren. Die Einstellung der Bevölkerung ist bemerkenswert tolerant und viele schwedische Schwule sind sehr offen mit ihrer Sexualität. Aber es gibt noch immer Schwierigkeiten, besonders in den Kleinstädten und auf dem Land. Hier ist Offenheit nicht immer möglich.
Seit 1994 gibt es in Schweden die „registrierte Partnerschaft", die zwar keine Ehe im herkömmlichen Sinne ist, aber homosexuellen Paaren eine rechtliche Stellung gibt, die der heterosexuellen Ehe sehr nahe kommt. Schon seit längerem gibt es ein Anti-Diskriminierungsgesetz. Außerdem stellt der schwedische Staat jährlich eine Summe zur Unterstützung homosexueller Organisationen zur Verfügung.
Die meisten der schwulen Einrichtungen sind in den größeren Städten, aber die Szene ist viel kleiner, als man in so einem liberalen Land erwarten mag. Man muß heute ein positives HIV-Test-Ergebnis den Behörden melden.

▲ En Suède, il n'existe aucune loi spéciale contre l'homosexualité masculine ou féminine. La majorité sexuelle est à 15 ans, pour les gays, les lesbiennes et les hétéros. Les suédois sont étonnemmment tolérants et de nombreux homos suédois sont très ouverts sur leur sexualité. Mais bien sûr il y a encore des problèmes, à la campagne et dans les petites villes. Là, l'ouverture n'est pas possible. Depuis 1994, il y a en Suède le „partenariat enregistré", qui n'est pas un mariage au sens propre, mais qui donne aux couples homosexuels une situation juridique très proche de la situation des couples hétérosexuels mariés. Depuis longtemps existe une loi anti-discrimination. De plus, le gouvernement met à la disposition chaque année une somme d'argent pour le soutien des organisations homosexuelles. La plupart des infrastructures gayes se trouvent dans les grandes villes, mais il faut remarquer que pour un pays si libéral, le milieu gay est plus petit que ce que nous attendions. En cas de test de dépistage VIH positif, il faut le signaler immédiatement aux autorités.

☆ En Suecia no hay leyes especiales contra la homosexualidad femenina o masculina. La edad de consentimiento es de 15 años, independientemente de la orientación sexual. La población sueca reacciona muy tolerantemente; gran cantidad de homosexuales viven su homosexualidad abiertamente. Sin embargo en las ciudades pequeñas así como en los pueblos del interior del país esta apertura sigue siendo dificil.
Desde 1994 existe también en Suecia el llamado „Registro de Parejas de Hecho" que aunque no es un matrimonio, les dá a los gay una base legal que se asemeja a la de los heterosexuales. Desde hace ya mucho tiempo existe una ley de antidiscriminación. El estado sueco pone a disposición cada año una determinada suma de dinero para el apoyo de organizaciones gay. La mayor parte de la infraestructura gay se encuentra en las grandes ciudades. Para un país tan liberal como este, el ambiente gay es sorprendentemente pequeño. En caso de ser HIV-positivo, es obligatorio comunicárselo a las autoridades.

❖ In Svezia non esistono leggi specifiche contro l'omosessualità maschile o femminile. L'età legale è di 15 anni ugualmente per etero e omosessuali.L'atteggiamento della popolazione è notevolmente tollerante, e molti gay svedesi si comportano molto apertamente per quanto riguarda la loro sessualità. Esistono ancora difficoltà nelle piccole città e nei paesi di campagna. Qui non è sempre possibile comportarsi apertamente. Dal 1994 in Svezia esiste la „registrazione ufficiale delle coppie di fatto", che non è l'equivalente del matrimonio, ma che garantisce alle coppie omosessuali una situazione legale molto vicina a quella delle coppie sposate eterosessuali. Già da molto tempo esiste una legge antidiscriminatoria. Inoltre lo stato svedese mette a disposizione ogni anno una certa somma alle organizzazioni omosessuali. La maggior parte dei centri gay si trova nelle città più grandi, ma l'ambiente è più ristretto di quanto si possa credere per un paese così liberale. Oggigiorno è d'obbligo mostrare il risultato positivo del test HIV alle autorità.

NATIONAL GAY INFO

Gay Radio Wed 21-22 h (FM 92,5 MHz)
Homosexuella Socialdemokrater
Saltmätargatan 18, 113 59 Stockholm
Homosexuella Socialister
PO Box 170, 101 23 Stockholm ☎ (08) 32 03 39
Kom Ut!
Box 350 101 26 Stockholm ☎ 08/736 02 17
E-mail: komut@rfsl.se Homepage: http://www.rfsl.se/komut/
Members magazine of the RFSL.
QX
PO Box 172 18 104 62 Stockholm ☎ (08) 720 30 01
or ☎ (070) 765 81 24 E-mail: qx@bahnhof.se
Free gay-lesbian magazine for Sweden. Featuring articles, dates, classified ads.

NATIONAL COMPANIES

AFD Show Productions
PO Box 873, 251 08 Helsingborg

NATIONAL GROUPS

DGN - Nät för gayföretagare
c/o Det Glada Nätet, Box 4053, 182 04 Enebyberg
E-mail: m8796@abc.se
Network for gayfriendly companies and managers.
Förenignen Homosexuella Läkare
c/o Sven Grützmeier, Venhälsan, Södersjukhuset, Stockholm
E-mail: sven.grutzmeier@mailbox.swipnet.se
Swedish Gay and Lesbian Physicians Association for gay and lesbian physicians, dentists and medical and dental students.
GALEJ Stockholm
PO Box 350, 101 26 Stockholm
Gaymoderaterna-Gay Conservatives Tue Sun 18-21 h
Saltmätargatan 18, 11359 Stockholm ☎ (08) 34 44 56
Regnbågen Stockholm
PO Box 350, 101 26 Stockholm ☎ 08/31 47 01
„The Rainbow" Group for deaf gay people.
RFTS Stockholm
PO Box 9083, 102 71 Stockholm E-mail: mail@rfs.a.se
Homepage: http://www.rfts.a.se/ National organisation for transsexuals.

Örebro - Närke ☎ 019

GAY INFO

Kanal Gay Wed 21-22, Sat 18-19 h (FM 95,3 MHz)

GENERAL GROUPS

RFSL-Örebro Café Mon-Fri 13-16, Tue 19-22, Disco Sat 21-2
c/o Orlando, Slottsgatan 19b, PO Box 447 ✉70148 ☎ 14 42 32

HELP WITH PROBLEMS

Gay Jouren Wed 20-23 h
☎ 12 25 50

SWIMMING

-Eyrabadet (g pi) (Eyragatan 1 B. Best Fri evenings)

CRUISING

-Stadsparken (in the garden and around the WC)
-Hamnplan (at the parking at night)
-Fallen (along the river, best in summer)

Öregrund - Uppland ☎ 0173

SWIMMING

-Talludden

Östersund - Jämtland ☎ 063

BARS

Lokalen (b f d GLM)
Gränsgatan 13 ☎ 100 668
Cafe Wed 19-20 h, party 1st Sat 21-2 h. Youth group Tue 19-22 h.

SAUNAS/BATHS

Storsjöbadet (f g NG sa sb sol wh WO) Mon-Fri 10-21 h, Sat-Sun 10-17
Krondikesvägen 94
Take Bus 2,6 or 9 from central bus station, southern direction to bus stop „Fritidsbyn". Behind Scandic Hotel. Interesting are 1st floor jacuzzi and men's side sauna/steam bath. Popular. Be discreet because it's a public bath.

GENERAL GROUPS

RFSL-Östersund Café Wed 19-22, Disco last Sat 21-2, women meet 3rd Tue 19-22 h
PO Box 516 ✉831 26 *(Entrance Gränsgatan)* ☎ 10 06 68
(Switchboard) Social group meets 2nd Sat. Call for info.

CRUISING

-Badhusparken (22-? h, from warehouse in the south to the motorway bridge in the north)

Borås - Västergötland ☎ 033

SEX SHOPS/BLUE MOVIES

Erocenter (g VS) 11-22 h
Sturegatan 29

GENERAL GROUPS

RFSL Thu 19-22 h, Pub Fri 21-1 h, Party last Sat 22-2.30 h
Magasinsgatan 1 ✉501 05 ☎ 10 69 70

Eskilstuna - Södermanland ☎ 016

GENERAL GROUPS

RFSL Café Wed 19-22, Disco occasionally, call for info
Noréusgatan 5, ✉63006 ☎ 51 00 69 E-Mail: eskilstuna@rfsl.se
Homepage: www.rfsl.se/eskilstuna

Falköping - Skaraborg ☎ 0515

CRUISING

-(P) McDonald's Drive through
-Main road E 20 ((P) Rabyhed, 10 km west of town)
-Klippberget (1 km north of McDonalds, direction Torshalla)

Falun - Dalarna ☎ 023

GENERAL GROUPS

RSFL Dalarna
PO Box 401 ✉79128

Gävle - Gästrikland ☎ 026

GENERAL GROUPS

RFSL Counselling Sun 19-21 h
Fjärde Tvärgatan 55 ✉80282 ☎ 18 09 67 Fax: 18 09 67

Göteborg - Bohuslän ☎ 031

GAY INFO

Gay Radio Sun-Mon 20-21 h (FM 103,1 MHz)
☎ 711 14 30 E-Mail: ggr@rfsl.se
Homepage: www.rfsl.se/gayradio/ggr/
RFSL-Centre-Göteborg Bookshop Thu 19-22 h
Esperantoplatsen 7 ✉40311 *(Bus 85)* ☎ 711 61 51
Fax: 711 32 57

BARS

Nemo (B F GLM) Thu 20-1, Fri-Sun -3 h
Bellmansgatan 7 ☎ 13 20 42
Park Lane (B g)
c/o Park Aveny Hotel, Aveny
Touch (B GLM) Wed 21-1 h
Esperantoplatsen 8 ☎ 11 14 20

CAFÉS

Café Hellmanns (b f GLM MA) Thu Sun 19-22 Sat 1-4 h
Esperantoplatsen 7 ☎ 711 61 51

DANCECLUBS

Sex (B D G S) Sun 21-3 h
Kungstorget 9 *(At Cue Club)*
Touch (B D F GLM MA SNU STV) Wed 21-1 Fri Sat 21.30-2 h
Esperantoplatsen 7-8 ☎ 711 14 20
Women disco 1st Fri of the month.

SEX SHOPS/BLUE MOVIES

Blue Video (G)
Andra Lnggatan 32
Nyhavn Sexshop (g VS) 11-22
Lilla Drottninggatan 3
Videolook (g) 24 hrs
Andra Långgatan 16 ☎ 12 55 71

BODY & BEAUTY SHOPS

Barbarella Piercing Tue-Fri 11-18, Sat -14 h, closed Mon, Sun
Fjärde Långgatan 6 ✉41305 ☎ 14 79 68 Fax: 14 76 18
Piercing. Free catalogue in Swedish available.

BOOK SHOPS

Rosa Rummet (GLM) Thu Sun 19-22 h
Esperantoplatsen 7 ☎ 11 61 51

LEATHER & FETISH SHOPS

Black Widow's Web
PO Box 11489 ✉404 30
S/M literature. Write for free catalogue.
S. Wollbrecht PO Box 52 36 ✉40224 ☎ 83 39 10

FETISH GROUPS

SLM Göteborg
PO Box 5220 ✉402 24
Homepage: www. geocities.com/WestHollywood/8483/
Member of ECMC.

HEALTH GROUPS

Gayhälsan Mon 17-19 h
Sahlgrenska Sjukhuset ☎ 60 34 42
PLUS
c/o Stadtsmissionen, Stigbergsliden 6 ✉414 63
Positiva Gruppen-Väst
Nordhemsgatan 50 ☎ 14 35 30
RFSL-Rådgivningen Mon-Fri 9-16 h
☎ 711 01 33

HELP WITH PROBLEMS

Gay Jouren
☎ 711 01 04

RELIGIOUS GROUPS

EKHO-Göteborg
c/o Studentprästerna, Föreningsgatan 32 ✉41127 ☎ 13 36 92

SWIMMING

-Saltholmen (g NU)
-Saltholmens kallbadhus (Nude coldbath house. Seperate departments for men and women)
-Smithska udden (G)
-Stora Amundön (Nudist beach, in summertime only)
-Valhallabadet (g)

CRUISING

-Slottskogen Park (only in the summer)

Götene - Skaraborgs län ☎ 0511

CRUISING

-Blomberg (outdoor bath)
-Kungsparken (at nighttime)
-Slottsskogen Park Cruising day and night

Halmstad - Halland ☎ 035

GAY INFO

Gay Radio Mon 20.30-21.30 h (FM 88,6 MHz)

SEX SHOPS/BLUE MOVIES

Erocenter (g VS) 11-22 h
Laholmsvägen 25

GENERAL GROUPS

RFSL-Halland Mon Wed 19-21 h
Lyckåkersgatan 7 ✉30004 ☎ 21 48 00 Fax: 21 48 00

HELP WITH PROBLEMS

Gay Jouren Mon Wed 19-22 h
☎ 12 07 22

SWIMMING

-Vilshärads Beach (NU)
-Heden, Hagön (NU)

CRUISING

-Norrekatts Park
-Heden, Hagön

Helsingborg - Skåne ☎ 042

BARS

Empire (B D f GLM MA S) Café 11-17 Sun Wed 19-22, Pub Fri 22-2, Disco 2nd/4th Sat 22-2.30 h
Pålsgatan 1 *(Near concert hall)* ☎ 12 35 32
Youth café Tue 19-22 h

SEX SHOPS/BLUE MOVIES

Erocenter (g VS) 11-22 h
Järnvägsgatan 27

Kosmos 11-21 h
Furutorpsgatan 73 ☎ 14 16 16

HOTELS

Hotell Kärnan (bf glm sa)
Järnvägsgatan 17 ✉25224 ☎ 12 08 20 Fax: 14 88 88
28 double rooms, 22 single rooms. All rooms with shower/WC, phone, satellite TV, radio, own key. Hotel provides car park amd TV room.

GENERAL GROUPS

RFSL
Pålsgatan 1, PO Box 21 18 ✉250 02 ☎ 12 35 32

CRUISING

-Rosenträdgården (in the evening around the old fortress Kärnan)
-Knutpunkten (innercity terminal on 2nd floor)

Hemavan - Lappland ☎ 0954

HOTELS

Sånninggårdens (AC B bf CC F glm H msg OS sb sol wh)
Klippen 2201 ✉920 66 *(Bus Lapplandspilen from Stockholm 0957-11915)* ☎ 330 00 Fax: 330 06
16 double rooms, all with Bath/WC on the corridor. Rooms with radio and safe. Hotel provide room service, car park, TV room, bycicle hire. Rates double skr 450-590, single 280-380 (bf incl.)

Jönköping - Småland ☎ 036

SEX SHOPS/BLUE MOVIES

Erocenter (g)
Vilhelm Thams gatan 24

GENERAL GROUPS

RFSL Jönköping (GLM)
PO Box 723 ✉55120 *(Västra Holmgatan 14)*

CRUISING

-Östra torget
-Idas park (Friardalen)

Karlskrona ☎ 0455

CAFÉS

Café Tre G (A bf g MA OS) Mon-Fri 9-20 h, Sat 9-18 h, Sun 10-18 h
Landbrogatan 9 ✉371 34 ☎ 251 65

Karlstad - Värmland ☎ 054

GENERAL GROUPS

RFSL Värmland
PO Box 634 ✉651 14 ☎ 054/15 20 90
Party once a month, café once a week, call for information.

HEALTH GROUPS

Noaks Ark
☎ (0570) 112 22

SWIMMING

-Skutberget (GLM OG) (westbound of the city)

Kristianstad - Skåne ☎ 044

GENERAL GROUPS

RFSL Kristianstad
PO Box 198 ✉291 22 ☎ 10 65 90
Help for young gays Fri 19-23 h.

SWIMMING

-Yngsjö Naturbad (in summer only)

CRUISING

-Tivoliparken (between theater and baths, northern section at night all year round)

Lidköping - Skaraborg ☎ 0510

CRUISING

-Nude beach (in summer only)
-Truve (outdoor bath)

Linköping - Östergötland ☎ 013

GAY INFO

RFSL Linköping (B D GLM) Café Tue 19-22 h, Disco odd weeks Sat 22-2 h, Pub even weeks Fri 21-23 h
c/o JOY, Nygatan 58 ✉58102 ☎ 13 20 22

HEALTH GROUPS

Noaks Ark
☎ 19 10 00

HELP WITH PROBLEMS

Gayjour Tue 19-22 h
☎ 31 03 33

CRUISING

-Simhallen
-Rydskogen (P behind Folkets Park)

Luleå - Norrbotten ☎ 0920

SEX SHOPS/BLUE MOVIES

Joker Video Shop (g VS) Mon-Fri 19-20 h
Stationsgatan 65

SAUNAS/BATHS

Badhuset (g)
Bastugatan 6-8

GENERAL GROUPS

RFSL-Luleå
PO Box 95 ✉971 04 ☎ 22 61 66 E-Mail: lulea@rfsl.se

HELP WITH PROBLEMS

Gayjouren Sun 19-22
☎ 170 55

SWIMMING

-Lulvikens Beach (gay to the right; you can pitch a tent in the forest)

Lund - Skåne ☎ 046

GAY INFO

Homo Sapiens
Gay Radio. Channel AF 99,1 MHz. Organized by gay student group.

BARS

Petri bar (B e F glm OS)
Petri Kyrkogata 7 ☎ 13 55 15
Smålands Pub (B glm)
Kastanjegatan 7

SEX SHOPS/BLUE MOVIES

Sexshopen (g)
Homepage: www.sexshopen.nu/
Online sale of sextoys and xxx-movies

FASHION SHOPS

Finunder (g)
Homepage: www.finunder.se/
Online sale of underwear.

GENERAL GROUPS

Lunds Gaystudenter 1st/3rd/5th Wed 20-24 h
c/o Akademiska föreningen, Sandgatan 2 ✉223 50 ☎ 15 71 34
E-Mail: gaystudenterna.lund@rfsl.se
Homepage: www.rfsl.se/lund/gaystudenterna/

HEALTH GROUPS

Venhälsan
☎ 10 11 65

RELIGIOUS GROUPS

EKHO-Syd
c/o Studentprästerna, Krafts Torg 12 ✉223 50
☎ 040/30 38 53

SWIMMING

-Lomma (nudist beach, 11 km west of Lund, north of Lomma; between a square artificial lake and the sea)

CRUISING

-Stadsparken (around the children's playground)

Malmö - Malmöhus län ☎ 040

GAY INFO

Gay Radio Sun 19.30-21 h (FM 89,2 MHz)
Gay/Lesbian Switchboard Fri 19-24 (adult) Thu 20-23 h (-age 23)
☎ 611 99 44 or 611 99 23.

BARS

Brogatan (B g)
Brogatan 12

CAFES

Dare (b f g) Mon-Fri 11-18 h, Sat 10-15 h
Fosievägen 27
S/M shop and café.
Hilda's café & catering (b f g) Mon-Fri 11-18 h, Sat 10-15 h
Kungsgatan 16 ☎ 28 01 37
Mais um Café (GLM MA) Sun 18-21 h
Monbijougatan 15 *(3rd floor)* ☎ 611 99 62

DANCECLUBS

Club Fyran (B G)
Snapperupsgatan 4 ☎ 23 03 11
Thu 21-0 h „Blue Boys Bar". 2nd, 4th Fri 23-3 h „The temple". 1st, 3rd Fri 23-03 (Swedish Leather Men)
Indigo (B D GLM LJ MA S) Wed 21-24, Pub/café Thu 21-24, Fri Sat 22-2 Sun 22.30-2 h even weeks.
Monbijougatan 15 ✉21153 *(3rd floor. Near Folkets Park)*
☎ 611 99 62
4:an (B D G MA) Fri-Sat 22-3 h, Pub Thu 20-24 h
Snapperupsgatan 4 ☎ 23 03 11

RESTAURANTS

Gustav Adolf (A AC B bf CC F glm MA OS W) 9-1 h
Gustav Adolf Torg 43 ☎ 611 22 72
Gay run and owned. Friendly staff
No Name Bar & Restaurant (CC F B glm) 11.30-0 Sun closed
S. Vallgatan 3 ✉21298 ☎ 121 298
Quality food at reasonable prices.
Restaurant G (B F g) 23-3 h
Gustav Adolfs torg ☎ 239 400 Fax: 977 777
E-Mail: lars.hector@malmo.mail.telia.com
Last Sunday of the month a 100% gay.

SEX SHOPS/BLUE MOVIES

Taboo (g)
Södra Förstadsgatan 81

HOTELS

Pallas. Hotel (bf GLM H MA)
Norra Vallgatan 74 *(in front of railway station)* ☎ 611 50 77
Fax: 97 77 77
Centrally located. Single skr 295, double 395.

GENERAL GROUPS

Benjamin-Syd Tue 19-21 h
☎ 611 99 23
Group for transsexuals.
Qpido
c/o RFSL Malmö, PO Box 2 ✉20120 ☎ 301 893
or ☎ 71 71 530 Youth group.
RFSL-Malmö
PO Box 2 ✉20120 ☎ 611 99 62

FETISH GROUPS

SLM Malmö
PO Box 112 ✉211 55 ☎ 30 18 93 E-Mail: streck@algonet.se
Member of ECMC.
ToE Secretariat
Slussgatan 21 ✉211 30 E-Mail: oerjan-schoenberg@ebox.tninet.se
ECMC's Nordic/Scandinavian Club's secretariat.

HEALTH GROUPS

Noaks Ark
Södergatan 13 ✉211 34 ☎ 611 52 15
Positiva Grupen Syd
Södergatan 13 ☎ 791 61
Group for HIV+.
RFSL Rådgivningen
Drottninggatan 36 ✉211 41 ☎ 611 99 50 Fax: 97 12 18
Counselling

RELIGIOUS GROUPS

EKHO-Syd
c/o Studentsprästerna, Kraftstorget 12 ✉223 50 ☎ 30 38 53

SWIMMING

-Ribersborg (on the west part of the beach, close to the harbor for small boats)
-Ribersborgs Kallbadhus (NU pi) (summer only, 9-19 h)
-Aq-va-kul (pi) (10-21 h. Regementsgatan, opposite Slottsparken. Ask for Turkish bath-sauna in 2nd floor.) Mon-Thu 9-21, Fri 9-20, Sat-Sun 10-18 h. ☎ 30 05 40

CRUISING

-Gustav-Aolfs-Torget
-P Stortorget
-Nobeltorge (WC)
-West part of Ribersborg beach-park (at the far end of the bycicle track towards Limnann, turn right into the woods after passing »Båskytteklubben«. Daytime in summer only.)
-East part of Ribersborg beach-park (in the bushes east of Ribersborgs Kallbadhus. Summer only from 22-? h)

-Slottsparken (by the tennis-courts. All year round at night)
-Södra/Östra promenaden
-Tivoliparken Kristianstad

Mariestad - Skaraborgs län ☎ 0501

CRUISING

-Ekudden (outdoor bath)

Motala - Östergötland ☎ 0141

CRUISING

-Hamnpiren
-Stadssparken
-Vätterpromenaden

Norrköping - Östergötland ☎ 011

GAY INFO

RFSL Café Wed 18-21
c/o Gamla Bro, Västgötegatan 15, ✉60202 ☎ 23 81 50

DANCECLUBS

Brittas (B D glm)
Drottninggatan 36 *Best Sat*
Club. Le (B D G) Disco 2nd/4th Sat 22-3, Pub 1st/3rd/5th Fri 22-2 h
Västgötegatan 15
Tango (B D glm) Every 2nd Fri
Tunnbindareggatan 34

VIDEO SHOPS

Röda Rosen (g) 12-24 h
Hospitalsgatan

CRUISING

-Karl Johansparken
-Järnvägsparken

Nyköping - Södermanland ☎ 0155

GENERAL GROUPS

RFSL (B d f GLM MA) Wed-Thu 19-21 h
Östra Kyrkogatan 15c ✉611 33 ☎ 21 02 29
Helpline during opening. Disco Sat (once a month) 21-1 h.

Piteå - Norrbotten ☎ 0911

GAY INFO

Gay Radio FM 95,3 MHz
☎ 144 40
Call for information.
RFSL-Piteå älvdal & norra Västerbotten
Polstjärnan (B d f GLM MA WE)
Polstjärnan, Aronsgatan 11 ✉941 24 *(In the yard)* ☎ 144 40
Gay switchboard Sun 19-21 h (0910) 222 22.

BARS

Polstjärnan (B D GLM MA WE)
Aronsgatan 11 *(in the yard)* ☎ 114 40
or ☎ *925 70*

RESTAURANTS

Pigalle (B CC d F glm MA)
Sundsgatan 36 ☎ 118 75

GENERAL GROUPS

RFSL Piteå Mon-Fri 9-16 h
Aronsgatan 11, „Polstjärnen" ✉941 24 ☎ 925 70 Fax: 925 70
E-Mail: polarstar@ilga.org

Skanör-Falsterbo - Skåne ☎ 040

SWIMMING

-Skanör Strand (NU)

Skellefteå - Västerbotten ☎ 0910

HELP WITH PROBLEMS

Gayjour Sun 19-21 h
☎ 222 22

Skövde - Skaraborg ☎ 0500

GAY INFO

RFSL Skaraborg Pub: 3rd Sat 20 h, Disco: 1st Sat 21 h
Storgatan 12 a ✉54126 ☎ 41 06 63

HELP WITH PROBLEMS

Jourtelefon
☎ 41 06 69

CRUISING

-Garpaparken
-[P] Lake Karstop
-Boulonger Wood

Skurup - Malmöhus län ☎ 0411

RESTAURANTS

Batsa (b F glm) 11-21, Wed-Sat -1 h
Stora torggatan 21 ☎ 439 01

Stockholm ☎ 08

● Stockholm is rightly called the „Venice of the North". That is for one part due to the many natural canals, that run through the old town, and for the other part to the beautiful historical buildings that so-am the canals. The whole swedish capital is a piece of art, formed by nature and architecture, that you'll remember for a long time. There aren't many major cities, that allow you to walk from the bustling city center into splendid forests in a quarter of an hour. We recommend especially a visit in the bright summer months, when the Swedes -usually a more reserved people- enjoy the long nights. A calm and relaxed rhythm then prevails in Stockholm and in the small gay scene.
Tips:
- Party on Sundays on the old boat „Patricia"
- A boats ride to the castle of *Drottningholm*
- A boats ride through the waters of the „Schären", the island group opposite to Stockholm, e.g. to Vaxholm.

✱ Stockholm wird zurecht das „Venedig des Nordens" genannt. Das liegt zum einen an den vielen natürlichen Kanälen, die die Altstadt durchziehen und zum anderen an den wunderschönen historischen Gebäuden am Wasser. Die schwedische Metropole ist ein Gesamtkunstwerk aus Natur und Architektur, das man so schnell nicht wieder vergißt. Es gibt wohl keine andere Großstadt, in der man innerhalb von 15 Minuten zu Fuß aus einer lebendigen Innenstadt in wunderschöne Wälder spazieren kann.
Wir empfehlen Ihnen besonders die hellen Sommermonate, wenn die sonst etwas reservierten Schweden die langen Nächte genießen. Stockholm ist dann geprägt von einem gelassenen und lockeren Rhythmus, der dann auch die kleine schwule Szene prägt.

STOCKHOLM - CENTRE

1 Stockholm Gay Centre
2 RFSL
3 Rosa Rummet Bookshop
4 BHus Bar
5 Tip Top Danceclub
7 Tip Top Restaurant
8 BHUS Ungdomscafé
9 Berlin Sex Shop
11 Element Café
12 US Video Blue Movies
13 Café Albert
14 Piccolino Café
15 Fatale-Hair Dressing Center Body & Beauty Shop
17 Nitty Gritty Fashion Shop
18 Manhattan Blue Movies
19 Hjärter Dam Bar
20 Kinks and Queens Bar
21 Spisa hos Helena Restaurant

STOCKHOLM - SÖDERMALM

1 Häcktet Danceclub
2 Patricia Danceclub
3 Side Track Bar
4 The Muscle Academy Fitness Club
5 Bottle and Glass Bar
6 SLM
7 Nils Emil Bakfickan Restaurant
8 The Basement Blue Movies
9 Revolt Sex Shop
11 Pensionat Oden Guest House

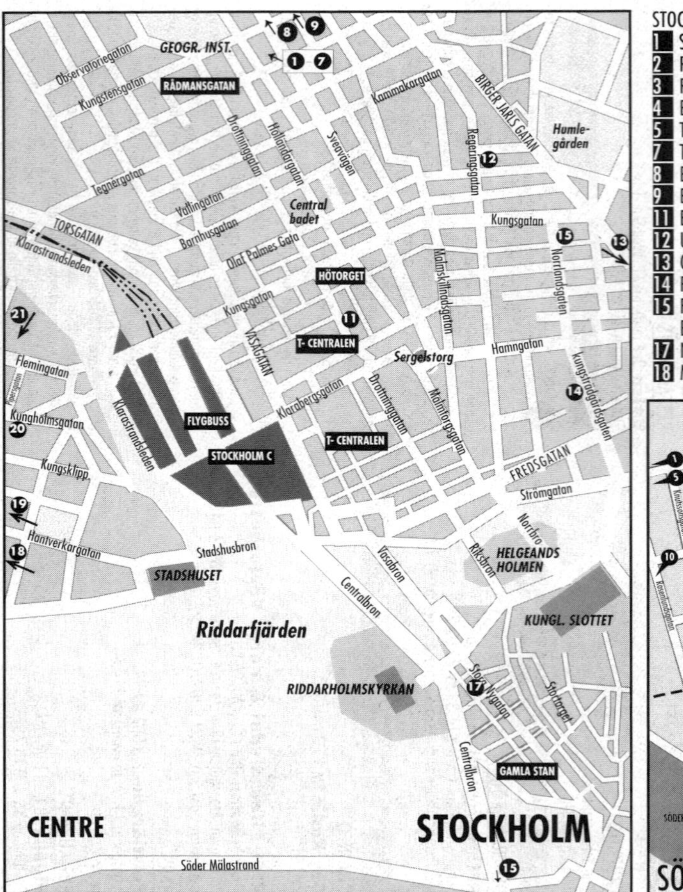

Tips:
-Sonntagsdisco auf dem alten Schiff „Patricia"
-Bootsfahrt zum Schloß Drottningholm
-Bootsfahrt durch die Schären (die Inseln vor Stockholm) z.B. nach Vaxholm

▲ Avec ses canaux, sa vieille ville et ses splendides monuments historiques, on dit que Stockholm est la Venise du Nord. La capitale suédoise est une oeuvre d'art à elle seule, l'union de la nature et de l'architecture. Un charme inoubliable! Dans aucune autre ville d'Europe, il n'est possible, en un quart d'heure de marche, de quitter le centre-ville pour se retrouver au beau milieu des forêts. Bien sûr, il est plus agréable de découvrir Stockholm en été, saison où les Suédois revivent littéralement. Les nuits y sont longues, l'atmosphère est sympathique et décontractée. C'est aussi valable pour lieux gays qui malgré leur petit nombre sont très accueillants et chaleureux. A faire absolument: la disco du dimanche sur l'ancien bâteau „Patricia", une excursion en bâteau au château de Drottiningholm ou encore dans les îles en face de Stockholm, p. ex. à Vaxholm.

☆ Debido a la gran cantidad de canales que la ciudad vieja posee y a los bellos edificios históricos junto al agua, Estocolmo es llamada la „Venecia del Norte". La capital sueca es una obra de arte compuesta tanto por su paisaje natural como y su arquitectura. No hay otra gran ciudad que ofrecen bellos parajes boscosos tan cercano del animado centro: allí se llega andando en solo 15 minutos. Recomendamos una visita en los meses de verano en que los suecos -generalmente un poco reservados- disfrutan al máximo de las noches. Estocolmo se caracteriza por su ritmo tranquilo y relajado que se refleja también el pequeño ambiente gay. Cosejos: -Domingos de disco en el viejo barco „Patricia". -Viaje en barco al castillo „Drottningholm". -Visita en barco de las islas frente a Estocolmo, p.ej. Vaxholm.

❖ Stoccolma viene chiamata con ragione la „Venezia del nord", ciò a causa dei numerosi canali naturali che attraversano il centro storico e dei meravigliosi edifici affacciati all'acqua. La metropoli svedese è un'opera d'arte difficilmente dimenticabile che fonde in sé architettura e natura. Non esiste nessun'altra grande città che permette di passeggiare in 15 minuti dal movimentato centro storico a boschi meravigliosi. Vi consigliamo i luminosi mesi estivi durante i quali gli svedesi, altrimenti piuttosto riservati, si godono la vita notturna. Il ritmo rilassato e lieve di Stoccolma coinvolge anche l'ambiente gay. Consigli:
- domenica in discoteca sulla vecchia nave „Patricia";
-giro in nave al palazzo Drottningholm;
-giro in nave alle Schären (le isole di Stoccolma) ad esempio a Vaxholm.

GAY INFO

Stockholm Gay Radio Thu Sun 19.30-20.30 h (FM 88 MHz)
☎ 736 02 16

TGT • The Gay Telegraph
☎ 32 32 32
Modem settings: 300, 1200, 2400 (8, N, 1).

TOURIST INFO

Stockholm Information Service
Kungsträdsgården ✉ 10393 ☎ 789 24 00 Fax: 789 24 50
E-Mail: stoinfo-se Homepage: www.stoinfo.se

BARS

BHus (! AC B CC D F GLM lj MA S YG) Mon 17-22, Tue-Thu Sun 15-20, Fri Sat -21
Sveavägen/Frejgatan *(T-Odenplan)* ☎ 34 11 05
Bar, disco, restaurant.

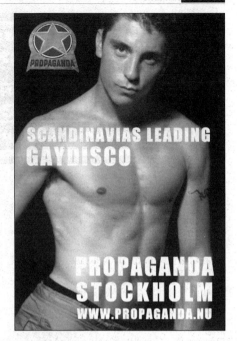

Bottle & Glass (B f g MA) Mon-Fri 16-1, Sat-Sun 14-1 h
Hornsgatan 136 *(T- Hornstull.)* ☎ 84 56 10
Thirty differtent kinds of beer. Pool-table, Black jack, Dart.

Hjärter Dam (B F g lj MA N OS tv) Wed-Sun 16.30-23.50, Kinky Bar Fri Sat 20.30-1 h
Polhemsgatan 23/Hantverkargatan *(T-Rådhuset)* ☎ 653 57 39
In the evenings: Privat club.

Incognito (B D G MA YG) 21-? h, closed Mon
Al. Wojska Polskiego 20 *(2nd floor)*

Junkyard Bar (B F g) Wed 21-1 h
Birkagatan 10 *(T- Eriksplan, Trainstation Karlberg)* ☎ 34 88 87
Bar and restaurant.

Kinks & Queens (B D glm LJ) Sat 20-3 h
Kungsholmsgatan 20 ☎ 653 41 46
Mixed S/M club.

Side Track (B CC F G MA) 18-24 h
Wollmar Yxhullsgatan 7 ✉118 48 *(T-Mariat Torget)*
☎ 641 16 88

SLM • Scandinavian Leather Men (B D G LJ MA P VS) Wed Fri Sat 22-2 h
Wollmar Yxkullsgatan 18, PO Box 17 241 ✉104 62 *(T-Maria Torget. Entrance at garage door)* ☎ 643 31 00

CAFÉS

BHUS-Ungdomscafé (a d f GLM S YG) Thu-Fri 15-19, Sat-Sun 13-18 h
BHUS-Baracken, Vanadislunden *(Located in a park, corner Sveavägen/Frejgatan, near HUS 1)*
☎ 34 11 05

Café Albert (b f g) Mon-Thu 7.45-1, Fri-Sat -5, Sun 9-1 h
Birger Jarlsgatan 5 ☎ 611 33 11
Mixed café in the city area. Perfect for checking out the city-crowds.

Dick Farmer (b f g) Mon-Fri 9-20, Sat 12-16 h
Drottningholmsvägen 9 ☎ 652 11 19

Element (A AC bf F GLM YG OS W) 8-22
Drottningsgåtan 73c *(T-Central), close to shopping area* ☎ 22 56 66
Spacious café with minimalistic, interesting architecture. Delicious meals.

Piccolino (! b f glm OS) Open till late
Kungsträdgården *(On the big square near the opera)*
The best place to see and be seen. In case of bad weather café may be closed.

DANCECLUBS

Häcktet (AC B CC D F GLM MA OS W) Wed Fri 19-1 h
Hornsgatan 82 ☎ 84 59 10
Popular mixed gay bar.

Patricia (! AC B D F G MA OS S STV W) Sun 18-5 h
Stadsgårdskajen 152 ✉116 45 *(On a ship. T-Slussen)*
☎ 743 05 70
Very popular. Good restaurant, all meals half price, free entrance in disco after restaurant visit.

Propaganda (! AC B CC D f G MA OS S TV VS W WE) Fri-Sat 22-3 h
Blekhomsterrassen 15, at Mike's ✉111 22 *(T- Centralen)*
☎ 15 17 01
Very popular. Changing locations. Check for time and location.

Tip Top (AC B bf CC D F G GLM MA OS STV W) 10-3 h
Sveaväsen 57 *(T- Rådmansgatan)* ☎ 30 73 37
Check local gay papers for up-to-date party-events and locations.

RESTAURANTS

Hermans Lilla Gröna (b F glm)
Katarina Bangatan 17 ☎ 640 30 10
Vegetarian dishes.

Nils Emil Bakfickan (B F g OS) Mon-Fri 11-22 h, Sat 13-22 h
Folkungatan 126 ✉116 30 *(Södermalm)* ☎ 641 33 87
Genuine Swedish restaurant. Outdoor seating.

Spisa hos Helena (B CC F g MA N WE) Mon-Thu 11-24, Fri -1, Sat 17-1 h, Sun closed
Scheelegatan 18 ✉112 28 *(T-Rådhuset)* ☎ 654 49 26
International cuisine. Main course skr 100-230. Also cocktail bar.

Svea Bar & Matsal (B F g)
Sveavägen 53 *(T- Rådmansgatan)* ☎ 31 59 50
or ☎ 31 12 25

SEX SHOPS/BLUE MOVIES

Basement. The (G MA VS) 12-6 h
Bondegatan 1 b ☎ 643 79 10
Popular.

Berlin (g VS)
Luntmakargatan 76 ☎ 612 09 76

Eros Video (DR G MA VS) 11-6 h
Hornsgatan 67 ✉118 49 *(T- Zinkensdamm), Söder*

Foxy (g) 10-22, Sun 12-22 h
Tomtebogatan 13 *(T-St. Eriksplan)*

Haga Video (G MA VS) Sun-Thu 11-4, Fri Sat -6 h
Hagagatan 56 *(T-Odenplan)* ☎ 33 55 44

Kino (g VS) 0-24 h
Döbelnsgatan 4 *(T-Rådmansgatan)* ☎ 24 41 41

Manhattan (G MA VS) Sun-Tue 12-24, Wed-Sat 12-6 h
Hantverkargatan 49 *(T-Radhuset)* ☎ 653 92 10
Very popular!

Red Light-Video
Roslagsgatan 32

Revolt Shop (G VS) Mon-Thu 11-22, Fri -20, Sat 12-18, Sun 14-19 h
Nytorgsgatan 21 A *(T-Medborgarplatsen)*
☎ 643 79 50
Renting of videos possible.

Roslags Video (g)
Roslagsgatan 43

US Video (AC b CC DR g MA VS W) 24 hrs
Regeringsgatan 76 ✉111 39 *(T- Hötorget)* ☎ 10 42 53
Popular darkroom.

Video Staden (g)
Roslagsgatan 25 ☎ 165 953

XS-Video
Tulegatan 39

SAUNAS/BATHS

You won't find any gay bath or sauna in Sweden. They all have been closed down. So we decided to list PUBLIC BATHS that are still interesting to the gay community in this section.
In Schweden gibt es keine schwulen Saunen oder Bäder. Sie wurden alle geschlossen. Wir haben uns entschieden, hier ÖFFENTLICHE SCHWIMMBÄDER zu listen, die für Schwule interessant sind.

Eriksdalsbadet (b F MA NG pi sa sol WO) 6-16, Sat Sun -13 h
Gräsgatan/Ringvägen *(T-Skanstull)*
Outdoor in summer.

Medis
Medborgarplatsen

Storkyrkobadet (NG MA pi sa) Tue Fri 17-20 h
(T-Gamla Stan) Small pool in medieval vaults.

FITNESSTUDIOS

Muscle Academy AB. The (b G sa sol WO) 13-22, Sat & Sun 16-20 h
Björngårdsgatan 1B ✉118 52 *(T-Maria Torget)* ☎ 642 63 06

BODY & BEAUTY SHOPS

Fatale - Hair Dressing Center (g) Mon 9-18, Tue-Fri 9-20, Sat 10-14 h
Norrlandsgatan 22 *(T- Hötorget, T- Östermalmstorg)* ☎ 611 54 54
Hair dresser in the city center.

BOOK SHOPS

Rosa Rummet Mon-Thu 15-20 h, Fri 15-18 h, Sat-Sun 13-16 h
PO Box 3444 ✉10369 *(Sveavägeen 57)* ☎ 736 02 15

FASHION SHOPS

Nitty Gritty (g) Mon-Fri 11-20, Sat 11-16 h
Stora Nygatan 7 *(old town)* ☎ 240 044
London style clothing.

LEATHER & FETISH SHOPS

Läderverkstan (G LJ) 12-18 h, Sat closed
Rosenlundsgatan 30 A ✉104 62 *(T-Mariatorget)* ☎ 668 58 69
Leather store, piercing etc.

MAIL ORDER

M&D Video
Kihlgrens Väg 3 ✉192 79 ☎ 594 702 10
Gayvideo mailorder

TRAVEL & TRANSPORT

Resebutik Noble Travel (CC glm MA) 10-18 h
Björngårdsgatan 1B ✉118 52 *(T-Bana Maria Torget)*
☎ 644 74 56 Fax: 644 24 23
E-Mail: noble@bahnhof.se

GUEST HOUSES

Pensionat Oden (g H)
Odengatan 38, 2 tr ✉11351 *(T Maria Torget)* ☎ 612 43 49
Fax: 612 45 01 E-Mail: info@kimab.se
Centrally located boarding house. 6 single, 18 double rooms with bath/WC on the corridor. All romms with satellite TV, minibar. Hotel provides won key, car park. Rates double skr 1095 (with bath), 595-895 (without bath), single skr 395- 695 (without bath) Try also: Pensionat Oden, Söder, Horsgatan 66B (T- Maria Torget)

PRIVATE ACCOMODATION

Enjoy Bed & Breakfast (bf G H MA YG) 16:30-21:00h
☎ +49 (30) 215 1666 Fax: +49 (30) 217 522 19
E-Mail: Info@ebab.com Homepage: www.ebab.com

GENERAL GROUPS

Benjamin Transexual Tue Thu 19-21 h
☎ 070/715 40 38
BHUS-Baracken
Baracken i Vanadislunden, PO Box 191 55 ✉10432 ☎ 34 11 05
Bi- and gay youth in Stockholm.
Bikupan
PO Box 3444 ✉10369
Föreningen BHUS Mon-Fri 19-22 h, Meeting Mon 19 h at Gay Center.
PO Box 19155 ✉104 32 ☎ (020) 78 33 66
Youth organisation for gays and lesbians.
Gay Studenterna
c/o Studentkårens Sociala Utskott, PO Box 50006 ✉104 05
☎ 16 55 03
University student group.
Gaytek
E-Mail: gaytek@ths.kth.se Homepage: www.gaytek.home.ml.org/
Student group at the Royal Institute of Technology.
GLIS-Grupo Latinoamericano por la Iqualidad Sexual Meeting Wed 18 h at Gay Center
Homosexuella Liberaler (GLM)
PO Box 3444 ✉10369
Homosexuella Pensionärer (OG)
PO Box 170 ✉101 23 ☎ 20 90 20
Stockholm Rubber Mens Club
c/o SLM, PO Box 17 241 ✉104 62 ☎ 643 31 00
Viking Bears
c/o Jan Lövbom, Industrigatan 6, 5tr ✉112 46
E-mail: vikingbears@geocities.com *For hairy and „Bear"-like men and their fans.*

FETISH GROUPS

SLM Stockholm
PO Box 172 41 ✉104 62 E-Mail: slm@slm.a.se
Homepage: www.slm.a.se *Member of ECMC.*

HEALTH GROUPS

AIDS-Jouren
☎ (020) 78 44 40
Noaks Ark-Röda Korset
Drottninggattan 61 ✉111 21 ☎ 23 50 60
Posithiva Gruppen (b F G MA P) Tue-Thu 15-23, Fri -2, Sat 20-2, Sun 15-19 h, Mon closed
Magnus Ladulåsgatan 8, ✉100 64 ☎ 720 19 60
Fax: 720 10 48
No alcoholic drinks on Sun.
RFSL Rådgivningen (G) Mon 9-21, Tue-Fri 9-16 h
☎ 736 02 10
Councelling service.
Riskförbundet för HIV-positiva (RFHP)
Gotlandsgatan 72 ✉11638 ☎ 714 54 10 Fax: 714 04 25
E-Mail: rfhp@mbox300.swipnet.se
Homepage: www.home2.swipnet.se
National organization for the hiv-positive.
Venhälsan Tue Thu 18-20.30
c/o Södersjukhuset Hospital, Ringvägen 52 ☎ 616 25 00
Anonymous hiv-testing & councelling free of charge.

HELP WITH PROBLEMS

Anonyma Alkoholister, Gay Group Tue 19, Sat 17 h
Sveavägen 57 *(1st floor, Gan Room)*
BHUS-Linjen (G YG) Mon Thu 19-22 h
☎ (020) 78 33 66
Youth Switchboard.
EKHO-Jouren
☎ (020) 78 77 76
Christian group.
Gay Jouren 20-23 h
☎ 24 74 65
PH-Center (W) Mon Wed-Fri 8.30-16, Tue 10-16 h
Wollmar Yxkullsgatan 25 ✉118 91 *(3rd floor)* ☎ 616 55 00
Fax: 616 55 11
Medical center, with a psychosocial approach, for gay and bisexual men. No charge.
P.L.U.S. Every other Sun.
c/o SLM, PO Box 172 41 ✉104 62 ☎ 643 31 06
Party for HIV-positives.
Positiva Gruppen
Magnus Ladulåsgatan 8 ✉10064 ☎ 720 19 60 Fax: 720 10 48
Youth-line ☎ 720 11 64. The Swedish organization for HIV-positive gay men. Editor of the magazine „T cellen".

RELIGIOUS GROUPS

EKHO every 2nd Fri 19-23 h
Katarinavägen 19, PO Box 19047 ✉104 32 *(T-Slussen)*
☎ 643 74 45
Ecumenical Christian gay group.
Galej-Homosexuella Judar
PO Box 350 ✉101 26 ☎ 736 02 11
Gay and Lesbian Jewish Organisation.

SWIMMING

-Frescati (G NU) (T-Universitetet, over the railway, left and through the woods)
-Långholmen (G NU) (T-Hornstull, west side, on the hill above the café)
-Solsidan (g NU) (T-Slussen, then Saltsjöbanan to Solsidan-Stop. Walk along Vårgärdsvägen until its end, then over the hill)
-North end of Kärsön Island (G NU) (bus from T-Brommaplan, get off at first stop after first bridge and walk around wheat field, then uphill through forest. Warm summer days until about 20 h. Plenty of action)

CRUISING

-Stadshusparken (small park by the water just north of the city hall)
-Skinnarviksparken (T-Zinkensdamm)
-Frescati (Near university, walk through tunnel under the motorway straight ahead through the park to the lake. One the left hand there is a rocky hill. Popular in summer!)

Sundsvall - Medelpad ☎ 060

BARS

RFSL Disco 2nd/last Sat 22-2, Wed 20-22 h café
Skolhusallén 23 ✉850 03 ☎ 17 13 30

GENERAL GROUPS

RFSL-Sundsvall 20-22 h
Skolhusallén 23 ✉85003 ☎ 17 13 30

CRUISING

-Badhusparken
-P Normalms

Trollhättan - Västergötland ☎ 0520

GAY INFO

RFSL last Wed 20-21 h on FM 90.6 MHz

GENERAL GROUPS

RFSL Trestad Café Wed 19-22, Thu 15-19 h, regular parties (D f GLM)
Stridsbergsgatan 8 ✉46121 ☎ 41 17 66

HELP WITH PROBLEMS

Gay Jouren
☎ 806 07

Umeå - Västerbotten ☎ 090

GENERAL GROUPS

RFSL-Umeå Café: Wed 19-22 h, Disco: 1st/3rd Sat
PO Box 38 ✉901 02 ☎ 77 47 10

Uppsala - Uppland ☎ 018

DANCECLUBS

Klub „68" (B D G) Wed Sat
Svartbäckgatan 68
RFSL Disco

GENERAL GROUPS

Foreningen Uppsala Gay Studenter (FUGS)
PO Box 30276 ✉75003
RFSL Uppsala Wed 19-23 Sat 22-2 h
PO Box 11 47 ✉751 41 ☎ 23 47 50

HELP WITH PROBLEMS

Gay jouren Mon 19-21 h
☎ 26 09 15

RELIGIOUS GROUPS

EKHO Uppsala
PO Box 1915 ✉751 49 ☎ 26 02 21

SWIMMING

-Fjällnora (summer beach to the left)
-Centralbadet (pi)
-Fyrishjon
-Kungshamn/Fredrikslund/Morga Hage/Turelund (not on WE)

CRUISING

-Storgatan (behind railway station, evenings and nights)
-Linnegatan (from the river up to Kingsgatan, late at night)

Varberg - Halland

SWIMMING

-Getterön (NU)
-Goda Hopp (NU)

CRUISING

-Strandpromenaden
-Kärleksparken

Värnamo - Småland ☎ 0370

SWIMMING

-Osudden (NU) (on the left side)

Västerås - Västmanlands län ☎ 021

GENERAL GROUPS

RFSL Västmanland (GLM)
PO Box 156 ✉72105 *(Emausgatan 41E)*

HELP WITH PROBLEMS

Telefonjour Wed 19-22 h
☎ 11 80 41

SWIMMING

-Kristiansborgsbadet
-Lögaränsbadet (in summer)

Växjö - Småland ☎ 0470

CAFES

Broquist konditori (f glm)
Stortorget

GENERAL GROUPS

RFSL Växjö (GLM) Café Wed 19-22, Sun 17-20, Party last Sat 21-2 h
Östregårdsgatan 8 ✉351 06 *(close to the cathedral)* ☎ 208 08
Helpline Wed 19-22 h

HEALTH GROUPS

Noaks Ark • Röda Korset
Kungsvägen 66 ✉35104 ☎ 193 81
Answering service Mon Wed Fri 10-12, 14-16 h ☎ 77 09 66.
Venhälsan
Hudkliniken Centrallasarettet ☎ 882 05
Ask for Anna-Greta.

SWIMMING

-Simhallen (best time Wed evenings. Open -22 h)
-Jägargap

CRUISING

-Linnéparken (evenings and nights in summer)

Visby - Gotland ☎ 0498

HEALTH GROUPS

Noaks Ark
☎ 21 68 50

SWIMMING

-Grynghällar (NU)
-Snäckgärdsbaden

CRUISING

-Almedalen Park
-Strandpromenaden

Ystad - Skåne ☎ 0411

SWIMMING

-Hagestad Natur-Reservat (NU) (beach 25 km east of Ystad)

CRUISING

-Market place/Stortorget

Switzerland

Schweiz • Suisse • Svizzera

Central Europe

Initials: CH

Time: GMT +1

☎ Country Code / Access Code: 41 / 00

Language: German, French, Italian, Rhaeto-Romanic

Area: 41,293 km^2 / 15,943 sq mi.

Currency: 1 Swiss Franc (sfr) = 100 Centimes or Rappen

Population: 7,325,000

Capital: Bern

Religions: 48% Roman Catholic, 44% Protestant

Climate: Moderate climate that varies with the altitude. Winters are cloudy and rainy or snowy. Summers cool to warm, cloudy and humid with occasional showers.

● In 1992, the age of consent in Switzerland was set at 16 years of age. Sexual relations between persons under 16 are not punishable by law. (Male) prostitution is permitted. The scene in Switzerland is concentrated around 3 cities: Basel, Geneva and Zurich.

✱ Das Schutzalter liegt in der Schweiz seit 1992 bei 16 Jahren. Kontakte zwischen unter 16jährigen bleiben straffrei. (Männliche) Prostitution ist erlaubt.
Die Szene der Schweiz konzentriert sich auf die drei Großstädte Basel, Genf und Zürich.

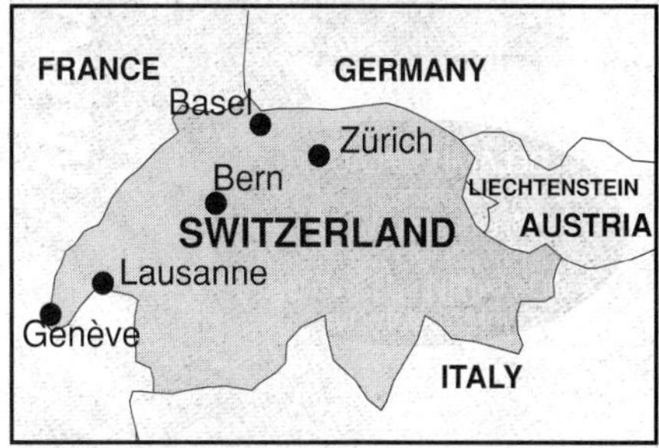

▲ L'homosexualité entre personnes adultes (plus de 16 ans) n'est pas un délit, en Suisse. Depuis 1992, la majorité sexuelle y est fixée à 16 ans. La prostitution masculine est tolérée. Bâle, Genève et Zurich sont les principales villes gays du pays.

☆ Desde 1992 la edad de consentimiento es de 16 años. Relaciones sexuales entre menores de 16 años permanecen libres de pena. La prostitución masculina está permitida. El ambiente gay en Suiza se concentra en las tres grandes ciudades del país: Basilea, Ginebra y Zurich.

❖ Dal 1992 in Svizzera i giovani sono sessualmente maggiorenni a 16 anni. I rapporti tra minori di 16 anni non vengono puniti. La prostituzione maschile è legale. L'ambiente gay in Svizzera è concentrato nelle 3 maggiori città: Zurigo, Ginevra e Basilea.

NATIONAL GAY INFO

A/K Anderschume/Kontiki - Das Schweizer Magazin für den schwulen Mann
Postfach 7979 ✉8023 Zürich ☎ 01/272 84 40
Fax: 01/272 84 40 Homepage: http://www.planetgay.ch
Swiss-german magazine for gays published quarterly. Interesting reports and comments about all topics regarding gay liberation and life style. Many book reviews, b/w art photographs. Commercial and classified ads. Text in German only. You can find additional English texts on the internet-homepage.

Coming In
C.P. 246 ✉1211 Genève ☎ 022/329 93 09
E-Mail: info@swissgay.com Homepage: http://www.swissgay.ch
Free booklet on the gay scene in Switzerland.

Cruiser/Cruiser KonAction
c/o Zbiro GmbH, Postfach 2363 ✉8031 Zürich
☎ 0878/88 18 88 Fax: 01/273 40 59 E-Mail: info@cruiser.ch
Homepage: http:///www.cruiser.ch
Bimonthly gay newspaper (50 pages) with information about the Swiss-German gay scene. Reports, Party guide and more. Free in gay establishments.

Dialogai Infos
C.P. 69 ✉1211 Genève
☎ 022/906 40 40 Fax: 022/906 40 44
Bimonthly gay publication for the gay French speaking community of Switzerland. Free at gay venues, else SFr 3.

Kontakt
c/o Belami Verlag AG, Postfach 8252 ✉8050 Zürich
☎ 01/313 15 05
Published every six weeks, approx. 100 pages, price Sfr 6, free in all gay establishments. Consists of classified and commercial ads, mostly from people offering friendship and/or sex.

Pink Elephant. The 1st Thu 21.20 h (UHF-Kanal 54)
c/o Dream Team Productions, Postfach 128 ✉8957 Spreitenbach
☎ 01/850 50 20
Videos can be ordered by mail.

Play Mec
Postfach 556 ✉3000 Bern
☎ 031/302 11 33 Fax: 031/302 11 33
Gay magazine with free personal ads and city-guide in German and French/Schwules Magazin mit kostenlosen Kontaktanzeigen und Stadtführer.

Schwulenarchiv Schweiz
Postfach 6311 ✉8023 Zürich Fax: 01/242 05 70
E-Mail: Schedler@pw.unizh.ch *Swiss gay archives.*

360°
C.P. 2217 ✉1211 Genève ☎ 022/789 18 62
Homepage: http://www.360.ch *The most important Swiss gay, lesbian and friends magazine in French. Good photos, interesting articles, entertaining and informative at the same time. Bimonthly. Available everywhere in Switzerland and at the border in France. Sfr 6.*

NATIONAL HELPLINES

Aids-Hilfe Schweiz (AHS)
Postfach 1118 ✉8031 Zürich ☎ 01/273 42 42
Prevention, information, and counseling for people with HIV/AIDS.

Rainbow Line 0-24, counselling Sun-Fri 19-21 h
☎ 0848/80 50 80
Information on homosexuality, bisexuality, coming-out, young gays, authorities, groups, meeting points, parties, safer sex,...

NATIONAL PUBLISHERS

Arcados Verlag
Rheingasse 69, Posfach 4433 ✉4002 Basel ☎ 061/681 31 32
Publishes books about Swiss gay history, literature, catalogues, etc.

Belami Verlag
Postfach 8252 ✉8050 Zürich ☎ 01/313 15 05
E-Mail: info@belami.ch Homepage: http://www.belami.ch
Publisher of »Kontakt«.

Kaos Editions
C.P. 246 ✉1211 Genève ☎ 022/329 93 09
Publisher of Swiss gay and lesbian guide „Coming in".

NATIONAL COMPANIES

ELC-Verlag
Postfach 493 ✉8280 Kreuzlingen
Gay video films.

Euro-Business Services Inc. (A CC G LJ) Mon-Fri 8-18 h
Schwaendi 63 ✉6170 Schupfheim *(Bahnhofstraße Bar Russia)*
☎ 041/485 70 87 Fax: 041/485 70 85
Immigration Services, consulting, leather/latex goods, travel guides, Gay Hospitality Exchange and more. For info send a self-addressed envelope with two international reply-coupons.

Gero-Schweiz Video Versand
Postfach 856 ✉8045 Zürich ☎ 01/451 26 16
Fax: 01/451 26 65 Homepage: http://www.gero.ch
Sale of videos, books and magazines.

Ikarus Entertainment
Postfach 115 ✉3054 Schupfen ☎ 061/713 11 72
Fax: 061/713 11 74 E-Mail: ikarus.ent@bluewin.ch
Homepage: http://www.ikarus-entertainment.ch
Gay porno videos production company active in Switzerland and Europe.

Kontiki Versand
Postfach 14 ✉8501 Frauenfeld
☎ 052/720 24 02 Homepage: http://www.access.ch/ak/
Sale of erotic male photo books, coming out books and videos. Catalogue on demand.

Librairie du Centaure
C.P. 44 ✉1211 Genève 19
☎ 022/733 98 33 Fax: 022/733 98 33
Mail order only gay bookshop.

NATIONAL GROUPS

Bartmänner Schweiz
Postfach 7560 ✉8023 Zürich
Group for hairy, bearded men and their admirers.

COSMA - Coordination Suisse des Ministères Sida et Aidspfarrämter
c/o Aids-Pfarramt beider Basel, Peterskirchplatz 8 ✉4051 Basel
☎ 061/262 06 66 Fax: 061/261 07 69
Swiss coordination of the Aids/HIV+ people assistance religious groups.

Lacets roses. Les (G MA)
c/o Heinz Rubin, Kirchgasse 2 ✉3700 Spiez
Swiss-German walking and hiking group.

Loge 70
Postfach 725 ✉8025 Zürich
E-Mail: loge70@gayleather.ch
Homepage: http://www.gayleather.ch/loge70
Swiss leather group. Member of ECMC. Publisher of a Info-magazine on the leather scene in Switzerland.
MediGay - Schwule und Lesben im Gesundheitswesen
Postfach 8107 ✉3001 Bern E-Mail: medigay@bboxbbs.ch
Homepage: http://www.bboxbbs.ch/home/medigay
Information network for gay- and lesbian-friendly doctors.
Network - Verein für Schwule Führungskräfte
Postfach 417 ✉8027 Zürich
Gay managers and CEOs/Schwule Führungskräfte.
Organisation suisse des enseignants et éducateurs/trices homosexuels (OSEHH)
C.P. 894 ✉1212 Grand-Lancy 1
Swiss gay teachers and educators organisation.
Pink Cross. Schwulenbüro Schweiz
Zinggstraße 16, Postfach 7512 ✉3001 Bern☎ 031/372 33 00 (office hours) Fax: 031/372 33 17 E-Mail: office@pinkcross
Homepage: http://www.pinkcross.ch
The Swiss national gay organization.
Stiftung „Stonewall"
Postfach 2115 ✉4001 Basel E-Mail: info@stonewall.ch
Homepage: http://www.stonewall.ch
Charity-group which supports gay-lesbian projects. Post-Account: PC 40-23202-2 Bank-Account: Basler Kantonalbank Konto: 59.785.90
Swiss Gay and Lesbian Sports
Postfach 2004 8051 Zürich
National coordination of gay sport groups. Member of Federation of Gay Games/EGLSF.
XLarge
Postfach 6018 ✉8023 Zürich ☎ 01/994 17 83
Club for bears, bulls, chubbies and those who like them. Offers power and combative sports.

HEALTH GROUPS

AIDS-Hilfe Schweiz 8.30-12 h, 14-17 h
Konradstrasse 20 ✉8005 Zürich ☎ 01-273 72 72
Fax 01-273 42 62.

COUNTRY CRUISING

A 1
-P Moosmüli (N 1-Stadtautobahn, zwischen/between Winkeln & Feldli Reitbahn)
-P Oberengstringen (N 1, Richtung/direction Baden-Zürich, vor/in front of Zürich)
A 20
-P Büsisee (Nordring Zürich, both sides/beidseitig)
A 1
-P between/zwischen »Morges« & »Aubonne«
A 12 (E27)
-P behind/nach »Matran«
A 2 (Chiasso ↔ Basel)
-P Lugano Sud/Nord (both sides)
-P Mendrisio (both sides)
-P Ceneri Sud/Nord (both sides)

Aarau ☎ 062

GAY INFO

Aargay
Postfach 11 ✉5616 ☎ 056/667 35 65 Fax: 056/667 35 65

HEALTH GROUPS

Aids-Hilfe Aarau Mon 8-12, Wed 15-19 h
Entfelder Straße 17 ✉5000 ☎ 062/824 44 50

CRUISING

-Schulpark am Ententeich/park of the school by the duck lake
-Bahnhofsunterführung/subway at the railway station

Arbon ☎ 071

BARS

Sternen Bar (B G)
St. Gallerstraße 32 ✉9320

Bad Schinznach ☎ 056

HOTELS

Rössli (B F glm)
Aarauerstraße 39 ☎ 443 11 23

Basel ☎ 061

GAY INFO

Pink Tube
c/o Arcados Verlag, Rheingasse 67 ✉4058 ☎ 681 31 32
Weekly leaflet with informations and dates.
Stuttgart & Zürich von hinten
c/o Bruno Gmünder Verlag, Postfach 610104 ✉10921 Berlin, Germany ☎ +49/30/6150030 Fax: +49-30-615 90 07
E-Mail: info@spartacus.de
The city guide book about Basle, Bern, Zurich and the German federal state of Baden-Wurttemberg. Useful general information and lots of addresses with extensive descriptions in English and German. Up-to-date maps. Erotic photos.

TOURIST INFO

Basel Tourismus Mon-Fri 8.30-18, Sat 10-16 h
Schifflände 5 ✉4001 ☎ 268 68 68 Fax: 268 68 70

BARS

Dupf (B f GLM MA OS YG) Sat-Thu 16-1, Fri -3 h
Rebgasse 43 ✉4058 *(Kleinbasel, right of river Rhine)*
☎ 692 00 11
Elle et Lui (B f Glm MA N OS W YG) Mon-Sat 19-3 h
Rebgasse 39 ✉4058 *(right of river Rhine)* ☎ 692 54 79
Zisch-Bar (B GLM OS) Tue 19-1 h
Klybeckstraße 1b ✉4057 *(im Foyer der Kulturwerkstatt-Kaserne)*

CAFES

Café Florian (B bf f glm MA) Mon-Fri 6-19 h, Sat-Sun 8-18 (brunch)
Totentanz 1 ✉4051 *(Tram11-Predigerkirche)* ☎ 261 57 54

DANCECLUBS

Isola Club (AC B D GLM MA s) Fri 21-1, Sat (G) 22-3 h
Gempenstraße 60 ✉4002 *(Gundeldingen, behind the cargo railway station)* ☎ 361 91 07

SEX SHOPS/BLUE MOVIES

Gerothek (CC G MA) Mon-Fri 11-20, Sat -18 h, closed Sun
Holeestraße 15 ✉4054 *(Tram 2-Zoo Dorenbach)* ☎ 421 00 41
Videos, toys and magazines
Partout l'amour (glm VS) 12.30-22 h
Dornacherstraße 63 ✉4053 *(Tram 16 bis/to Bahnhofunterführung)* ☎ 361 73 32

SAUNAS/BATHS

Mawi Club Sauna (B CC f G MA OS pi sa sb sol VS WE) 15-23 h
St. Alban-Vorstadt 76 ✉4052 *(near River Rhine left site, Wettsteinbrücke, Grossbasel)* ☎ 272 23 54
Popular.

Sauna Brunnenhof (f G msg sa sb OS) Mon-Sat 11-20.30, closed Sun
Brunngasse 8 ✉4052 ☎ 271 10 81

Sauna Sunnyday (AC B CC DR f G MA msg p s sa sb sol VS wh WO) 12-23 h, Fri -5 h, Sat Sun & public holidays 14-23 h
Grenzacherstraße 62 ✉4058 *(near River Rhine, right side, Wettsteinbrücke, in the basement of the building with the supermarket Migros)* ☎ 683 44 00
Beautiful sauna with nice equipment.

BOOK SHOPS

Arcados Buchladen (CC GLM) Sep-Apr: Mon-Fri 12.30-19, Sat 11-16 h, Mai-August closed Mon
Rheingasse 67 ✉4058 *(Tram6-Rheingasse/2-Wettsteinplatz)*
☎ 681 31 32 *Videos and books. Mail order service.*

CONDOM SHOPS

Condomeria Mon 11.15-14.30 15-18.30, Tue-Fri -18.30, Thu -20, Sat 10-17
Rheinsprung 4 ✉4000 ☎ 262 00 22

GIFT & PRIDE SHOPS

Sunnyday Shop (AC CC G MA p) Mon-Thu 12-23 h, Fri 12-5 h, Sat Sun 14-23 h
Grenzacherstraße 62 ✉4058 *(near Rheinpromenade)*
☎ 683 44 00
Books, postcards, calendars, pride articles, toys, videos, swim- and underwear.

HOTELS

White Horse (g H)
Webergasse 23 ✉4058 ☎ 691 57 57 Fax: 691 57 25

GENERAL GROUPS

Homosexuelle Arbeitsgruppen Basel-Stadt (HABS) Wed 20-22, Fri 17-20, Sat 14-18 h
Postfach 1519 ✉4001 ☎ 692 66 55

Rose - Bisexuelle und Schwule Jugendgruppe Basel Mon 19.30-? h at Fredy's Café-Bar
Postfach 4520 ✉4002 ☎ 692 66 55
Counselling/Beratung Wed 20-22 h (telephone). Meeting in SchleZ, Gärtnerstraße 55, 4057 Basel.

FETISH GROUPS

Brutus Basel
Lindenberg 23 ✉4058
Regular leather parties, visitors welcome.

HEALTH GROUPS

Aids-Beratungsstelle Kantonshopital Basel
Hebelstrasse 2 ✉4056 ☎ 265 24 31

Aids-Hilfe beider Basel
Clarastrasse 4 ✉4000 ☎ 692 21 22 Fax: 692 50 75

Aids-Pfarramt beider Basel
Peterskirchplatz 8 ✉4051 ☎ 262 06 66 Fax: 385 17 20
Offer pastoral and spiritual assistance to people with HIV/Aids and their relatives and friends.

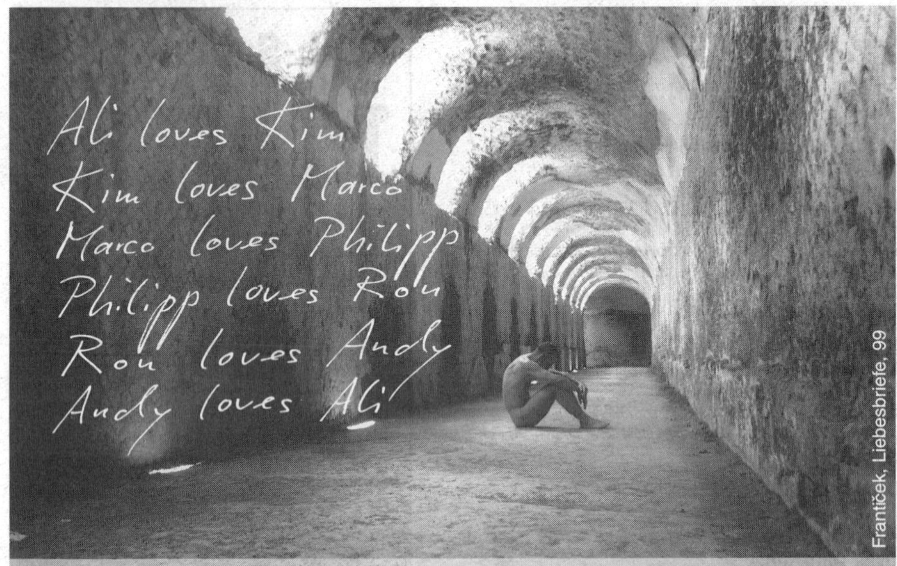
Ali loves Kim
Kim loves Marco
Marco loves Philipp
Philipp loves Ron
Ron loves Andy
Andy loves Ali
Frantiček, Liebesbriefe, 99
LOVELAND
XXX-STORE, MOVIE-RENT, MINI-CINEMAS
Gerechtigkeitsgasse 41, Parterre und Keller, Bern

Ökumenisches AIDS-Pfarramt beider Basel
Mon-Wed, Fri 9-12, Thu 14-17 h
Peterskirchplatz 8 ✉4051 ☎ 262 06 66 Fax: 261 07 69.
E-mail gyssler@swissonline.ch

HELP WITH PROBLEMS

HABS-Beratungstelefon Wed 20-21.30 h
Postfach 1519 ✉4001 ☎ 692 66 55

RELIGIOUS GROUPS

Homosexuelle und Kirche (HuK)
Postfach 215 ✉4006

SPECIAL INTEREST GROUPS

Schwul-lesbische Unigruppe (SLUG) 2nd Wed 19.30 h at Kaffi Schlappe, Klybeckstraße 1B
c/o Habs, Postfach 1519 ✉4001 ☎ 692 66 55 Fax: 692 66 55
E-Mail: SLUG@ubaclu.unibas.ch
Homepage: http://www.unibas.ch/uni/dienste/gruppierungen

SPORT GROUPS

Lesbian and Gay Sport Regio Basel
Postfach 467 ✉4021
Write for info on activities.

SWIMMING

-Northern shore of river Rhine (NU g) (between ferry station St. Alban and facility at the Solitude, Schaffhauserrheinweg)

CRUISING

-Barfüßerplatz (Underpass/Unterführung)
-Rheinweg (AYOR) (unter der mittleren Rheinbrücke an beiden Flußseiten an der Treppe/under the middle brigde on both sides of the river at the stairs)
-Wettsteinbrücke (AYOR r) (Nähe/near Park)
-SBB-station (near the French railways)
-Schützenmatt Park (AYOR) (Hinterseite des Bundesplatzes und Nähe der Straßenbahnhaltestelle/back part of Bundesplatz and near tram station)

Bern ☎ 031

GAY INFO

Hab-Info
HAB, Mühleplatz 11, Postfach 312 ✉3000
☎ 311 63 53
Social, political and news magazine published 6/year for the region Bern and Switzerland.

Homosexuelle Arbeitsgruppen Bern (HAB)
Mühleplatz 11, Postfach 312 ✉3000 *(centre)* ☎ 311 63 53 ☎ 031/311 11 97 Fax: 311 63 53 E-Mail: hab-anderland@bluewin.ch Homepage: http://www.gay-bern.ch
Call for information on activities. Publisher of „Hab Info".

Stuttgart & Zürich von hinten
c/o Bruno Gmünder Verlag, Postfach 610104 ✉10921 Berlin, Germany ☎ +49/30/6150030 Fax: +49/30/ 615 90 07
E-Mail: info@spartacus.de
The city guide book about Berne, Bale, Zurich and the German federal state of Baden-Wurttemberg. Useful general information and lots of addresses with extensive descriptions in English and German. Up-to-date maps. Erotic photos.

TOURIST INFO

Offizielles Verkehrs- und Kongreßbüro Bern
PO Box ✉3001 *(At Bahnhof)* ☎ 311 66 11 Fax: 312 12 33.

BARS

Different-Bar (A AC CC D G lj s WE) Wed 18-0.30, Thu-Sat -3.30 h
Gerechtigkeitsstraße 50 ✉3000 ☎ 077/53 89 64
In the Hotel Hospiz zur Heimat.
Samurai. The (B D GLM MA OS YG) 17-2.30, Fri-Sat -3.30 h
Aarbergergasse 35 ✉3011 ☎ 311 88 03

DANCECLUBS

ISC Club (B D glm) Thu 21-1, Fri Sat 22-0.30, Sun 21-? h
Neubrückstraße 10 ✉3012

RESTAURANTS

Amis. Les (B F g MA OS) Mon-Thu 11-0.30, Fri -3, Sat 9-3 h, closed Sun
Rathausgasse 63 ✉3011 ☎ 311 51 87
Beaujolais. Le (AC CC glm F OS) Mon-Fri 10-23.30, closed on WE
Aarberggasse 50/52 ✉3011 *(2 min from Samurai-Bar)*
☎ 311 48 86
French cuisine.

SEX SHOPS/BLUE MOVIES

Loveland Videos (CC g VS) 9-19, Thu -21, Sat -16, Sun closed
Gerechtigkeitsgasse 41 ✉3011 ☎ 311 45 33

SAUNAS/BATHS

Al Peter's Sundeck (! B CC F G MA OS sa sb sol VS wh WO) 12-23 h
Länggassstraße 65 ✉3012 *(Entrance/Eingang Schreinerweg 14)*
☎ 302 46 86
One of the biggest and best gay baths in Switzerland. Biosauna.
Studio 43 (B G lj MA OS sa sb sol VS WO) 14-23, last Sat-8 h
Monbijoustraße 123 ✉3007 *(Tram9-Wander)* ☎ 372 28 27
Bio-Soft-Sauna with Vital-Color-Sonne.

HOTELS

Belle Epoque (A B bf CC E f glm H OS)
Gerechtigkeitsgasse 18 ✉3011 *(20 min from the station)*
☎ 311 43 36 Fax: 311 39 36 E-Mail: info@belle-epoque.ch
Hotel and bar with precious Art Nouveau decoration.

GENERAL GROUPS

Jugendgruppe Coming Inn 1st, 3rd Mon 19.30 h at anderLand
c/o HAB, Postfach 312 ✉3000
Homepage: http://www.datacomm.ch/cominginn
Gay youth group.

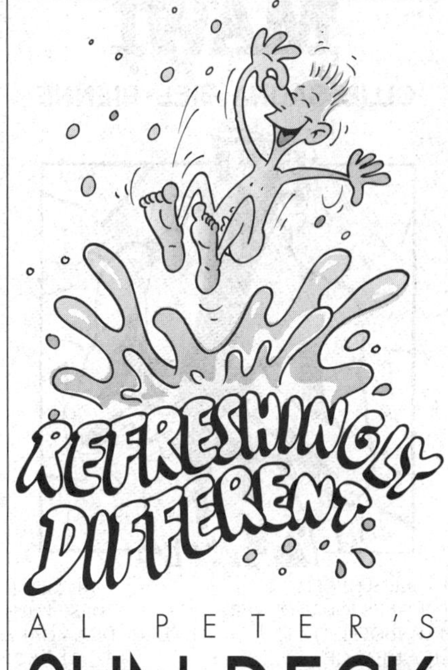

Schwul-Lesbisches Begegnungszentrum anderLand (A B d f GLM lj MA s W)
Mühlenplatz 11 ✉3011 *(5th floor)* ☎ 311 11 97
or ☎ & Fax: 311 63 53 E-Mail: hab-anderland@bluewin.ch

HEALTH GROUPS

AIDS-Hilfe Bern/Aide Sida Berne Mon Wed-Fri 9-12, 14-17 h, closed Tue
Monbijoustraße 32 ✉3001 ☎ 390 36 36 (German) ☎ 390 36 38 (French) Fax: 390 36 37 E-Mail: mail@aidshilfe-bern.ch
Prevention, information, and counseling for people with HIV/AIDS.

Oekumenisches Netzwerk Kirche und Aids
Postfach 5461 ✉3001 ☎ 385 17 17 Fax: 385 17 20
Offer pastoral and spiritual assistance to people with HIV/Aids and their relatives and friends.

RELIGIOUS GROUPS

HuK - Homosexuelle und Kirche Thu 19.30 at anderLand
Postfach 100 ✉3604

SPECIAL INTEREST GROUPS

Schwule Berner Sänger SCHWUBS Wed 19 h at Aula Seminar Marzili HMM, Brückenstraße 71
Gay choir.

Schwul-lesbische Unigruppe (SCHLUB) Brunch 3rd Sun 11 h at anderLand
c/o SUB, Lerchenweg 32 ✉3000

SPORT GROUPS

Gay and Lesbian Sport Bern (GLSBE)
Postfach 254 ✉3000 E-Mail: glsbe@rainbow.ch
Write for info on activities.

Rainbow Biker Bern/Gay Bikers 1st Wed 19.30 h at anderLand
☎ 971 89 31
Call for info on activities.

CRUISING

-Allmend
-Rosengarten
-Grosse Schanzen-Promenade (!) (vor der Universität, Eingang Schanzenstrasse/in front of university, entrance in Schanzenstreet)
-Casinoplatz (R) (underpass/Unterführung)
-Metro Parkhaus Waisenplatz
-Waisenhausplatz (R) (underpass/Unterführung)

Biel/Bienne ☎ 032

CAFÉS

Willi's Café (B g MA) Sun-Thu 6.30-22.30, Fri Sat 6.30-0.30 h
Neumarktstraße 14 ✉2500 ☎ 322 42 44

SAUNAS/BATHS

Mawi (AC B DR F G MA p sa sb VS W) 13.30-21 h
Bahnhofsplatz 11 ✉2502 *On the 4th floor.* ☎ 323 88 21

Sauna Sun Beach (CC DR f GLM MA msg NU p s sa sb sol VS WE) Wed Thu 14-22, Sat 15-6 (G), Tue Fri Sun 14-23 h (glm)
Dufourpassage 12 ✉2502 ☎ 323 23 63

CRUISING

-P SMH
-Centralplatz
-Marktplatz/market place

Boll-Sinneringen ☎ 031

RESTAURANTS

Rössli/Thai-in (CC F glm MA OS W) Tue-Thu 8.30-23.30, Fri -0.30, Sat 9-0.30, 17-22 h
Bernstraße 32 ✉3067 ☎ 839 24 28
Thai and Swiss specialties.

Brig ☎ 027

GENERAL GROUPS

Alpagai Oberwallis 2nd & last Wed 20-23 h at Restaurant Bellevue, Tunnelstraße 20
✉3900 ☎ 924 40 24

CRUISING

-WC, railway station, platform 1

Brunnen ☎ 041

HOTELS

Hôtel Bellevue au Lac (bf CC F g H) from Apr-Oct
Axenstrasse 2 ✉6440 *(direct at Vierwaldstättersee)* ☎ 820 13 18 Fax: 820 38 89

Bulle ☎ 029

SEX SHOPS/BLUE MOVIES

Planet X
67 Grand Rue ✉1630

Chur ☎ 081

BARS

Sonderbar (B glm)
Im Palace, Masanserstrasse 14 ✉7000 ☎ 253 33 56

CAFES

Café-Teria (b f glm)
Poststraße 6 ✉7000 ☎ 252 82 47

GENERAL GROUPS

Jugendgruppe Capricorn
PO Box 380 ✉7002
Homepage: http://www.spin.ch/homepages/Capricorn

HEALTH GROUPS

AIDS-Hilfe Graubünden
Loestraße 8a ✉7002 ☎ 252 49 00

HELP WITH PROBLEMS

Rosa Telefon Tue 19-21 h
☎ 253 67 66

Engelberg ☎ 041

GUEST HOUSES

Pension St. Jakob (bf f g H)
Engelbergstraße 66 ✉6390 ☎ 637 13 88 Fax: 637 13 88

Frauenfeld ☎ 054

GENERAL GROUPS

Homosexuelle Organisation Thurgau (HOT)
Postfach 355 ✉8501 ☎ 21 04 34
Meetings, sportgroup, choir. Call for more info.

Fribourg/Freiburg ☎ 026

SEX SHOPS/BLUE MOVIES

Exodus (g)
33 Rue Pierre Aeby ✉1700
Point X (g)
Rue des Bouchers

SAUNAS/BATHS

Maxim (b f G MA sa sb sol VS) Mon-Thu 14-21.30, Fri Sat 14-6, Sun 14-20 h
18 Grand-Places ✉1700 ☎ 322 72 25

GENERAL GROUPS

Sarigai - Association homosexuelle mixte
Tue Fri 20-? h
33 Route des Neiges ✉1709 ☎ 481 67 89 Fax: 481 67 89
E-mail sarigai@bluewin.ch

HEALTH GROUPS

Empreinte - Centre d'Information, d'animation et de soutien
57 Boulevard de Pérolles ✉1700 ☎ 424 24 84
Info SIDA Mon-Fri 9-20 h
✉1709 ☎ 426 02 99

CRUISING

-Grand-Place
-Place du Comptoir

Genève ☎ 022

GAY INFO

Dialogai - Association homosexuelle (AC B f G lj MA W) Mon Tue Fri 15-18, Wed -22, Thu 19-24, Fri 14-14, Sun (in winter) 11-15 h
11-13 Rue de la Navigation ✉1211 *(Bus 4-Zürich/Bus 4-Navigation)* ☎ 906 40 45 (information on activities) ☎ 906 40 40
Fax: 906 40 44 E-Mail: dialogai@hivnet.ch
Homepage: http://www.hivnet.ch/dialogai
Organises many activities on a range that goes from leather to

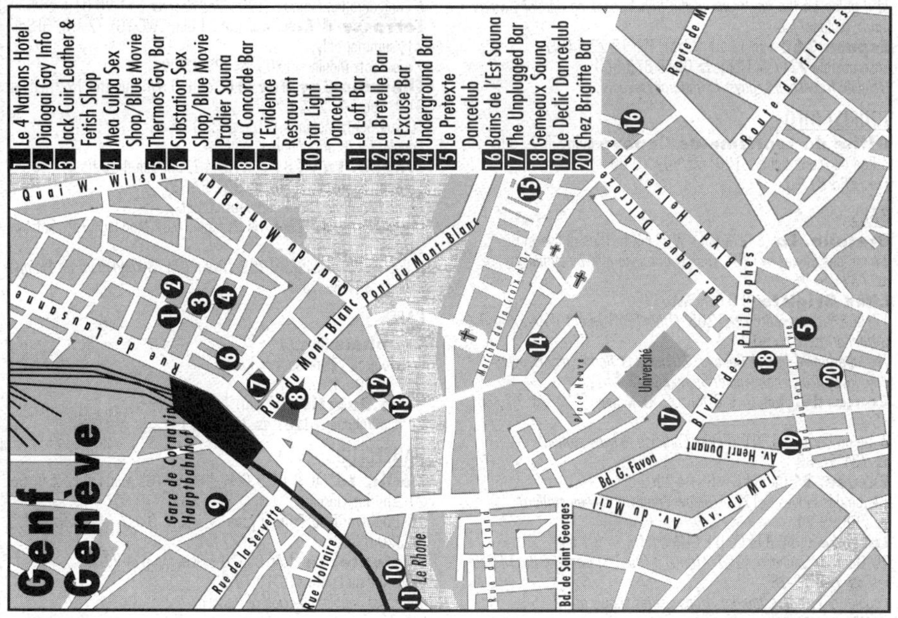

choir. Also health service. Parties every Sat (call for info). Publishers of a guide on the gay scene in the french-speaking part of Switzerland „Dialogai Infos".

Espace 360 Sun 16-21 (GLM), Thu 19-22 h (TV)
Case postale 2217 ✉1211 ☎ 0878 878 360
Helpline for lesbians, gays, bi and transsexuals.

TOURIST INFO

Office du tourisme de Genève Mon-Sat 9-18 h
3 Rue du Mont-Blanc ✉1201 ☎ 909 70 00
Fax: 788 81 70.

BARS

Bretelle. La (B GLM MA s W) 17-2 h, Thu-Sat live music
17 rue des Etuves ✉1201 *(Below Cornavin railway station)*
☎ 732 75 96

Chez Brigitte (B D GLM MA)
12 Rue Prévost-Martin ✉1205 *(Tram12/13-Pont d'Arve/Bus1/5-Hôpital)* ☎ 320 50 44
The alternative bar of Geneva. After hours Barbie nights every Friday, low prices, cool people. Starts late (3-4 h)

Concorde. La (B F G MA OS R) Mon-Fri 7-2, Sat 9-2, Sun 15-2 h
3 rue de Berne ✉1201 *(Below Cornavin railway station)*
☎ 731 96 80

Excuse. L' (AC B f G MG s) 4-2 h
11 rue des Etuves ✉1201 *(Below Cornavin railway station)*
☎ 738 99 24

Loft. Le (! AC B bf CC D F GLM MA OS S) 5-2 h
20 Quai du Seujet ✉1201 *(Tram13/Bus1-St.Gervais/Bus11-Seujet)* ☎ 738 28 28
Popular disco-bar-restaurant. Transvestites shows at 22.45 h.

Phénix Bar (B G) 16-2, Sun 18-2 h
6 Confédération Centre ✉1204 *2nd floor* ☎ 311 90 01

Terrasse d'Eté. La (B CC f Glm SWC YG) 17-1 h, Fri-Sat - 2 h, summer only
9 rue Goetz-Monin ✉1205 ☎ 329 93 09

Thermos Gay Bar (B CC d DR G MA) Tue-Thu 19-2, Fri-Sat 21-2, Sun 5-?, 21-2 h
10 Rue Goetz-Monin ✉1205 ☎ 320 72 65
Popular for its after hours.

Trappe. La (AC B F g MA p) 4-2, Sat Sun 4-10 h
13 Rue Sismondi ✉1201 ☎ 732 87 98
Best when discos close, night-restaurant.

Unplugged. The (AC B f glm MG) Mon-Fri 17-2, Sat Sun 21-2 h
3 Rue de l'Université ✉1205 *(Tram 12, 13-Rond-Point de Plainpalais)* ☎ 329 82 98

CAFES

C. Dubois (bf glm)
Carrefour de Villereuse 4 ✉1207
☎ 736 80 64

Yves Quartier (bf glm) Tue-Sun 7-19 h
24 Rue Voltaire ✉1201 ☎ 344 53 21

DANCECLUBS

Déclic. Le (AC B CC D GLM s VS W YG) Mon-Fri 17-2 h, Sat 21-2 h, Sun closed
28 Boulevard du Pont d'Arve ✉1205 *(Bus1/44-4/Tram12)*
☎ 320 59 14

Prétexte. Le (! AC B CC D E GLM MA p s) 22-5 h
9-11 Rue du Prince ☎ 310 14 28
The most popular gay club of Geneva.

Star Light (AC B CC D DR G MA SNU W) 22-5 h
20 Quai du Seujet ✉1201 ☎ 732 13 13
Une nuit par mois avec... Angie Becker (B D DR Glm tv vs) 1st Thu/month, 23-5 h
c/o Rêve d'O, Quai des Forces-Motrices ✉1205
Popular gay night with the best local DJs.

RESTAURANTS

Au Platane (F glm OS) Mon-Fri 8-24, Sat 18.30-24 h
91 Boulevard de la Cluse ✉1205 ☎ 329 71 98
Café Gallay (CC F glm)
Boulevard Saint-George 42 ✉1205 ☎ 321 00 35
Popular café restaurant with a mixed crowd. Reservation advised on WE.
Evidence. L' (B glm MA) 6-1, Sat-Sun 11-1 h
13 Rue des Grottes ✉1201
☎ 733 61 65

SEX SHOPS/BLUE MOVIES

Mea Culpa (G VS) 10-24 h
8 Rue Charles-Cusin ✉1201 ☎ 783 01 73
Substation (AC B CC DR G lj MA VS) Mon-Sat 11-24 h
14 Rue de Neuchâtel ✉1201 *(5 min from the station)*
☎ 900 14 69 or 900 14 67
250 m² on three floors, basement 100% gay with giant screen and labyrinth.

SAUNAS/BATHS

Avanchets. Les (AC B CC DR f G MA sa sb sol wh WO) 12-24, Fri -1, Sat -2 h, Tue Fri-Sat mixed
Avenue de Baptista/Avanchets-Parc ✉1220 *(5 min. from airport. Bus 10, 15, 23-Avanchets, near the shopping centre Balexert)*
☎ 796 90 66
Bains de l'Est (! B bf CC DR f G msg sa sb sol wh VS WO YG) 12-1, Fri-Sat -6, Sun 14-1 h, Tue Fri mixed
3 Rue de l'Est ✉1207 *(Tram12/Bus1/6/8-Terrassière)*
☎ 786 33 00
The most crowded sauna of Geneva.
Gémeaux (b f G OG sa sol) 11.30-22, Sat Sun 15-22 h
4bis Rue Prévost Martin ✉1205 *(Entry Rue des Sources)*
☎ 320 04 63
Sauna Pradier (b f G OG sa sol) 11.20-21 h, Sun 13.30-20 h
8 Rue Pradier ✉1201 *(Near Cornavin railway station)*
☎ 732 28 57

LEATHER & FETISH SHOPS

Jack Cuir (g LJ) 10-19, Sat -17 h, closed Sun
40 Rue de Monthoux ✉1201
☎ 731 89 15

NEWS STANDS

Chaboo (g) Mon-Fri 7.30-19, Sat 8-17 h
3 Rue des Pâquis ✉1201 ☎ 731 05 66
A good choice of gay magazines and cards.

TRAVEL & TRANSPORT

Cameleon Travel Mon-Fri 8-18 h
10b rue Emile Young ✉1205 *(near hospital)*
☎ 839 81 88 Fax: 839 81 90.
Email cameleontravel@hotmail.com

HOTELS

Hôtel les 4 Nations (H glm)
43 Rue de Zurich ✉1201 ☎ 732 02 24 Fax: 731 21 41

Hôtel Luserna (bf CC g H)
12 Avenue de Luserna ✉1203 *(between the station and the airport)* ☎ 345 46 76 ☎ 345 45 45 Fax: 344 49 36
E-Mail: info@hotel-luserna,ch
Homepage: httP://www.hotel-luserna.ch
Gays are welcome.

GENERAL GROUPS

Pink Cross. Secrétariat Romand
Case postale 49 ✉1211 ☎ 738 02 00 Fax: 738 02 00
French speaking office of the gay political association.

HEALTH GROUPS

Groupe Sida Genève (GSG) 9-17 h
17 Rue Pierre-Fatio ✉1204 ☎ 700 15 00
Support association for HIV/AIDS people, call for more information.
Hôpital Cantonal Mon Wed Fri 10-18, Sat 8-10 h
Policlinique de Médecine, 24 Rue Michel-du-Crest ✉1204 *(2nd floor)* ☎ 372 96 17 or 372 95 25
HIV testing.
Ministère SIDA
5 Place Jargonnant ✉1207 ☎ 736 24 26 Fax: 736 70 10
Offer pastoral and spiritual assistance to people with HIV/Aids and their relatives and friends.
PVA Genève
35 Rue des Pâquis ✉1201 ☎ 906 40 30
HIV+ people group.

SWIMMING

-Bains des Pâquis (Strand/beach very popular in summer)

CRUISING

-Parc des Bastions (ayor)
-Perle du Lac (parc)
-Parc Geisendorf
-Parc Bertrand
-Rue du Mont-Blanc (AYOR)
-St.Gervais (AYOR)

Hergiswil am See ☎ 041

HOTELS

Pilatusblick (AC bf CC F g H MA NU OS r)
Bergstraße ✉6052 *(Lake of Lucerne)* ☎ 630 11 61
Fax: 630 00 65 E-Mail: info@pilatusblick.ch
Homepage: http://www.pilatusblick.ch
Situated above the Lake of Lucerne, 20 minutes from the city of Lucerne with a spectacular view, this hotel offers quiet and comfortable rooms all with bath or shower/WC/radio/TV and minibar.

Hinwil ☎ 01

GENERAL GROUPS

Klick - Schwulengruppe Zürcher Oberland and Oberer Zürichsee 2nd/4th Wed at Kulturfabrik Wetzikon
Postfach 174 ✉8340 ☎ 938 04 08
Call or wirite for information on activities.

Interlaken ☎ 033

SAUNAS/BATHS

Club Sauna Horn (AC B G MA msg p VS) Mon 18-22, Sat 14-22 h (G)
Postfach 76, Harderstraße 35 ✉3800 ☎ 822 60 02

CRUISING

-Vor dem Hauptpostamt/in front of the main post office
-Bahnhof/railway station Interlaken West

Lausanne ☎ 021

GAY INFO

Chaps Club (G LJ)
Casde Postale 67 ✉1000 ☎ 078/619 69 69
News internet magazine for the army-leather-rubber scene in Europe: www.chaps.ch

BARS

Art Zoo (A AC B F glm MA OS W) Mon-Thu 17-1, Fri Sat -2, Sun 14-1 h
27 Rue du Petit-Chêne ✉1003 *In Les Galeries du Cinéma.*
☎ 340 05 12
Balcon. Le (B G MA) Fri Sat 23.30-? h
Place Centrale ✉1100 *(in D! Club, first floor)* ☎ 351 51 42
ML 16 (AC B CC DR G MA OS W) Mon-Thu 6.30-1, Fri -2, Sat 16-2, Sun -1 h
16 Avenue Mon Loisir ✉1006 ☎ 616 32 98
Bar-restaurant.
Saxo. Le (B E F g) Tue-Sun 18-2 h
3 Rue de la Grotte ✉1003 ☎ 323 46 83

MEN'S CLUBS

Cage Club - Sex Club for Uniform Men's (AC B DR f G LJ NU P p VS) Last Fri of the month 21-?
7 Avenie de Tivoli ✉1007 *(Entrance in the Pink Beach Sauna)*
☎ 311 06 05

DANCECLUBS

Jungle Gay Party (! A B CC D DR f GLM MA OS S) 22-5 h, only on public holidays, call for information
23 Rue de Genève ✉1003 *(in Le Mad)*
☎ 311 29 19
Very popular for ten years. A meeting point for all Swiss boys.
Trixx Gay Dance-Bar (! B CC D G P YG) Sun 23-4 h
23 rue de Genève ✉1003 *In the nightclub Le Mad.*
☎ 311 29 18
Best world DJ's playing. Happy hour 2for1 from 23-24 h.

RESTAURANTS

Ma Mère m'a dit... (A AC B bf CC F GLM MA OS s VS) Mon-Fri 6.30-2, Sat-Sun 5.30-2 h
8 Avenue de Tivoli ✉1007 *(in front of Pink Beach Sauna)*
☎ 311 06 70
Bar/restaurant in the gay street of Lausanne.

SEX SHOPS/BLUE MOVIES

Garage. Le (AC B CC DR G LJ MA NU VS) 11-23 h
22b Avenue de Tivoli ✉1007 *(in front of Sauna Pink Beach)*
☎ 320 69 69

SAUNAS/BATHS

New Relax Club (b f glm OG OS sa sb sol VS wh) Mon-Thu 12-24, Fri-Sun 12-5 h
Galerie St. François ✉1000 ☎ 312 66 78
Pink Beach (! AC B bf CC DR f G MA msg p sa sb sol VS wh WO) Sun-Thu 12-23, Fri -2, Sat -8 h
7 Avenue de Tivoli ✉1007 *(5 min from railway station)*
☎ 311 06 05
Two steam rooms, clean. Very popular sauna in centre of the town.
Top Club (! f G MA msg sa sb sol VS wh WO) 14-23 h
6 Rue Bellefontaine ✉1003 ☎ 312 23 66

LEATHER & FETISH SHOPS

Garage. Le (CC G lj MA VS) Mon-Sat 10-19
22a Avenue de Tivoli ✉1007 ☎ 320 69 69

GUEST HOUSES

Rainbow Inn (CC G H MA VS)
22 Avenue de Tivoli ✉1007 ☎ 312 92 98 Fax: 311 06 70
E-Mail: pinkinfo@cyberlab.ch

GENERAL GROUPS

Vogay (B GLM MA) 13 Avenue des Oiseaux ✉1000
☎ 646 25 35
Fax: 646 29 29. E-Mail vogay@freesurf.ch.

HEALTH GROUPS

Ministère SIDA
31 Rue de l'Ale ✉1003 ☎ 320 35 33 Fax: 320 35 35
Offers pastoral and spiritual assistance to people with HIV/Aids and their relatives and friends.

SWIMMING

-Beach (1 km from Morges reached through the forest)

CRUISING

-Parc du Denantou (Near/près Tour Haldimand)
-Promenade du Lac
-Parc de Montriond
-Passage souterrain Place St-François
-WC Theater Charles Monnard

Locarno ☎ 093

SWIMMING

-Delta della Maggia (G NU) (between Locarno and Ascona river Maggia, summer)

CRUISING

-Park near tennis court (Right and left side of the road along the Lago Maggiore)
-Ponte Brolla Grotten (summer AYOR g NU) (2km out of Locarno in direction Centovalli-Valle Maggia, at Ponte Brolla in front of Maggia bridge to the right, path to the grotten)
-Forest between stadium and city center (21-24 h)
-Railway station
-Small park around Casinotheatre

Lugano ☎ 091

GAY INFO

Centro informazione gay Ticino 10-24 h
Via Stazio 8 ✉6900 *(Massagno)* ☎ 968 17 17
E-Mail: spaziogay@ticino.com

MEN'S CLUBS

R-Axxion (B D DR G lj p s VS WE) Fri 22-2 h, Sat 23-4 h.
Via Cantonale ✉6915 ☎ 406 05 71
Tourists welcome

DANCECLUBS

Cocorico (B D f GLM MA OS S) 21-3 h
Via Riviera 7 ✉6900 *(Cassarate. Bus 2)* ☎ 51 30 66
Plaisir (B D f GLM MA S SNU) Sat only 23-5 h
Via Cantonale 10 ✉6916 *(Highway Gottardo exit Lugano-Sud direction Figino, 150 m after Ikea, Pallazzo Galbani)*

SAUNAS/BATHS

Gothic (B CC DR F G MA p sa sb sol VS YG) Sun-Thu 15-24, Fri-Sat and before holidays - 1 h
Vicolo Vecchio 3 ✉6900 *(Massagno. Near station)* ☎ 967 50 51
Very clean and popular.

GENERAL GROUPS

Comunità Gay Svizzera di Lingua Italiana (CGSI)
Fermoposta ✉6901 ☎ 53 35 00

HEALTH GROUPS

Progetto MSM di Aiuto AIDS Svizzero 10-24 h
Via Stazio 8 ✉6900 *(Massagno)* ☎ 23 17 17

CRUISING

-Piazza al Forte (P behind PTT central post office)
-Campo Marzio (Lugano-Cassarate close to the Lido)
-Parco Civico/Ciani (behind Mövenpick, closed 22.30 h)
-Parco Tassino (behind Main railway station, closed 22.30 h)
-Central station (platform 1)

Luzern ☎ 041

BARS

Capitol-Pub (B glm OS YG) Mon-Fri 16-0.30, Sat Sun 14-0.30 h
Zentralstrasse 45a ✉6003 ☎ 210 96 36

Heaven (AC B CC DR GLM MA) 17-? h
Burgerstrasse 21 ✉6002 *(in front of Parkhaus Kesselturm)* ☎ 210 41 43

Uferlos - Schwul-lesbisches Zentrum (AC B D GLM MA WE) Geissenseinring 14 ✉6005 ☎ 360 30 14
Organises many parties and events. Call for more info.

Widder (A AC B CC F GLM MA OS s W YG) Wed-Mon 11-0.30, Sun 14-0.30 h
Steinstrasse 2 ✉6004 ☎ 410 43 73
Bar-restaurant. Good Swiss and Austrian food. 2 bars on 2 floors.

SEX SHOPS/BLUE MOVIES

City-Shop (CC g VS)
Kramgasse 3 ✉6004 *(in front of Spengler)* ☎ 410 60 62

Erotic-Shop (CC g VS)
Bireggstrasse 20a ✉6003 ☎ 362 05 62

SAUNAS/BATHS

Discus Club Sauna (! AC B DR f G MA sa sb sol VS WO YG) Mon-Fri 13-23, Sat 13-2, Sun 13-22, 2nd Sat -6 h
Geissensteinring 26 ✉6002 *(Bus4/5-Tiefe)* ☎ 360 88 77

Tropica Sauna (DR f G MA p sa sb sol VS) 14-23, Fri/Sat -8 h
Neuweg 4 ✉6003 ☎ 210 11 50

GENERAL GROUPS

Homosexuelle Arbeitsgruppe Luzern (HALU) Helpline: Wed 20-22 h
Postfach 3112 ✉6002 ☎ 360 14 60
E-Mail: emil.schwyz@bluewin.ch.

Why Not
Postfach 2304 ✉6002
Gay youth group.

HEALTH GROUPS

AIDS-Hilfe Luzern Helpline: Mon 17-19 Wed 9.30-11.30 Thu 15-17 h
Wesemlinrain 20 ✉6006 ☎ 410 68 48

SPECIAL INTEREST GROUPS

Gemeinschaft Interesse für Theater (GifT)
Postfach 7304 ✉6007
Gay theater group.

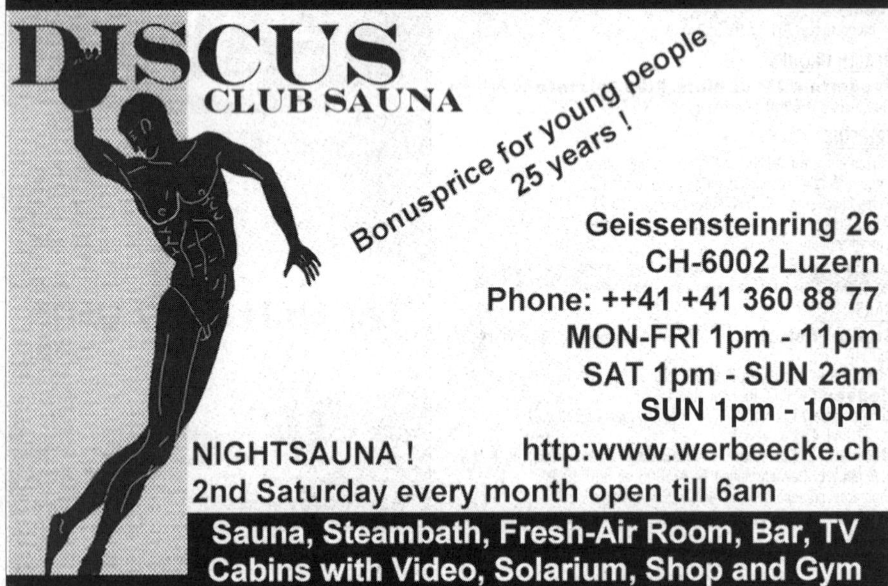

Zentralschweizer Schwulen-Motorrad-Club (ZSMC)
Postfach 2231 ✉6002
Please write for information.

SWIMMING
-Öffentliches Bad am See/public baths at the lake (Strandbad mit Sonnenbaden auf dem Sonnendach/bathing enclosure with sun bathing area on the sun decks, Nähe/near Hauptbahnhof/central station & Hotel Palace)

CRUISING
-Haldenstrasse (seitlich des/by the side of Grand Hotel National)
-Inseli Promenade, Park Aufschütte am See (Nähe Badeanstalt/close to bath)

Mendrisio ☎ 091

BARS
No Limits Asc. (B D DR G lj MA OS P VS WE) Sat 23-6 h, closed Sun-Fri
Via Zorzi 4 ✉6850 *(opposite Mercedes garage)*
☎ 630 03 85
Private club. Membership SFR 25.

Monthey ☎ 024

SEX SHOPS/BLUE MOVIES
Love-X-Video (AC CC g) Mon-Fri 13-18.30, Sat 10-17 h
3b Rue de Venise ✉1870 ☎ 472 16 49

Montreux ☎ 021

BARS
Il Baretto (B CC f g MA OS) Tue-Sun 17-1 h
34 Grand Rue ✉1820 ☎ 963 27 36

DANCECLUBS
Back Stage (B D glm) Tue-Sat 11-5 h
100 Grand Rue ✉1820

SWIMMING
-Villeneuve (NU) (at the end of the beach)

CRUISING
-Quai des fleurs (between Casino & Hotel Excelsior)
-P Bus stop »Bon-Port«
-Railway station (ticket office hall)

Morges ☎ 021

CAFES
Metropolis Café (B bf CC F glm MA) Mon-Thu 18.30-1, Fri Sat 6.30-2, Sun 21-1 h 20-22 Rue Louis-de-Savoie
✉1110 *(near Geneva Lake)*
☎ 803 23 33

Neuchâtel/Neuenburg ☎ 032

GENERAL GROUPS
Homologay 2nd and last Thu of the month 20-22 h
16 Rue Ph. Godet ✉2000 ☎ 721 10 42
Call for more information.

HEALTH GROUPS
Groupe Sida Neuchâtel Mon-Fri 8-11.30
6 Rue de Verger ✉2034 ☎ 737 73 37

CRUISING
-Jeunes Rives (path along the lake between university and harbour)
-Avenue de la Gare
-Place de la Poste (at harbour)

Olten ☎ 062

SEX SHOPS/BLUE MOVIES
Menzone (b G MA VS) Tue-Fri 16-21, Sat 10-12 h 13.30-16 h
Klarastraße 1 ✉4600 *(Bus 1-Bifang)* ☎ 296 56 53
Homepage: http://www.menzone.ch
Discount prices.

CRUISING
-Allee an der Aare/Alley at River Aare (Nähe der Dampfmaschine, abends/next to steam-engine, evenings)
-Zugunterführung an der Quelle der Aare/railway underpass near spring of River Aare

Schaffhausen ☎ 053

HEALTH GROUPS
AIDS-Hilfe Thurgau/Schaffhausen
Rathausbogen 15 ✉8200 ☎ 25 93 38
Les Homos
Postfach 3176 ✉8201 ☎ 052/624 68 60

CRUISING
-Bahnhof/Main Station
-Kiosk & Toiletten Bahnhofsunterführung/Toilets at the station

Sion ☎ 027

GENERAL GROUPS
Alpagai Thu 19-23, once a month Sat (B D G),
Counselling ☎ Wed 18-20 h
10 Grand-Pont ✉1950 *(2nd floor)* ☎ 322 10 11
Homosexual association (gay and lesbian). Information, counselling, bar, library.

HEALTH GROUPS
Antenne SIDA du Valais Romand
14 Rue de Condémines ✉1951 ☎ 322 81 85 Fax: 322.99.73
E-Mail: antenne.sida@vsnet.ch
Homepage: http://www.antenne.sida.vsnet.ch
Counselling, information for people with HIV/Aids and their families.

CRUISING
-Gardens near Banque Cantonale du Valais
-Near Église St. Guérin.
-WC in public garden (rue du Chanoine-Berchtold behind the bank, evenings)
-WC/in underground P of Planta (rue de Lausanne, afternoons)
-Tourist office (under the office)

Solothurn ☎ 065

BARS
Bigoudi (AC g MA) Tue-Thu Sun 8-23.30 Fri Sat 8-0.30 h closed Mon
Kronengasse 10 ✉4500 *(underneath/unterhalb Barockkirche)*
☎ 22 25 29

GENERAL GROUPS

Homosexuelle Arbeitsgruppe Solothurn (HASO) Meeting Mon 20 h at BZ Altes Spital
Postfach 508 ✉4502 ☎ 23 66 20

Sogay (b G MA p) Mon 20-? h
Oberer Winkel 2 ✉4502

HEALTH GROUPS

Aids-Hilfe Solothurn
Postfach 155 ✉4502 ☎ 622 94 11

St. Gallen ☎ 071

BARS

Hoppala Bar (AC B CC F G MA OS) Tue-Thu 17-?, Fri Sat 18-?, Sun 16-? h
Linsebühlstraße 96, Postfach 243 ✉9003 *(Stadtpark/Altstadt)* ☎ 222 72 22
Bus 1 Neudorf, Singenberg Busstop.

Peppermint-Bar (B CC d G MA) Mon-Fri 18-1 h
St. Jakobstraße 103 ✉9000 *(Bus 3-Olma)* ☎ 245 24 98

DANCECLUBS

Ozon (AC B CC D G W) Sun 21-3 h
Goliathgasse 28 ✉9000 ☎ 244 81 24
Gay Tea Dance on Sundays: Peppermint goes Ozon.

RESTAURANTS

Restaurant Gutenberg (F g) Tue closed
Hagenbuchstraße 28 ✉9000 ☎ 244 64 68

SAUNAS/BATHS

Olympic (B g sa) Mon-Sat 14-22 h, closed Sun
Torstraße 17 ✉9004 *(near Parkhaus Brühltor)* ☎ 245 44 24

FETISH GROUPS

Bären Club
Postfach 255 ✉9001 E-Mail: baerenclub@bluewin.ch
Write for info on activities.

HEALTH GROUPS

AIDS-Hilfe St. Gallen Tue 9-12, 19-21, Thu 19-21, Fri 9-12 h
Postfach 8, Tellstraße 4 ✉9001 ☎ 223 38 68

CRUISING

-Bahnhof/railway station
-municipal park/Stadtpark (Nähe/near Theater)

St. Moritz ☎ 081

BARS

Graffiti Bar (AC B CC f G MA p) 19-2 h
Plazza dal Mulin 2 ✉7500 ☎ 361 88
Open/Geöffnet Summer 01.07.-31.08. Winter 01.12.-15.04.

HOTELS

Hotel Löffler Garni (bf CC H N)
Via dal Bagn 6 ✉7500 ☎ 833 66 96 Fax: 833 88 48
E-Mail: loeffler@stmoritz.ch
Located right in the centre of St. Moritz-Bad with direct access to the ski pistes. All rooms wih bath/shower/wc/telephone/radio and TV. Rates from Sfr 180-320,-(double), 100-180,- (single).

Thun ☎ 033

RELIGIOUS GROUPS

Homosexuelle und Kirche Schweiz
PO Box 100 ✉3604
Publication/Vereinszeitung: Schildchrott.

CRUISING

-Bahnhof/railway station
-Aare Promenade
-Park Thunerhof

Uster ☎ 01

BARS

Uschteria 77 (B CC D g MA N) Tue -0.30 h
Zürichstraße 1 ✉8610 *(in shopping-centre/im Einkaufszentrum)* ☎ 940 70 44

CRUISING

-Municipal park/Stadtpark
-Quay/Schiffanlegestelle Niederuster
-Lido/Strandbad Uster am Greifensee

Vevey ☎ 021

CRUISING

-Place du Marché
-Bois d'Amour
-Passage souterrain Placette

Visp ☎ 027

HEALTH GROUPS

Aids-Hilfe Oberwallis
St. Martiniplatz 1 ✉3930 ☎ 346 46 68

Winterthur ☎ 052

GAY INFO

Derwisch (b f GLM) Sat 18-24 h
Badgasse 8 ✉8400 ☎ 213 81 88

SEX SHOPS/BLUE MOVIES

Satellit Winterthur Mon-Fri Sun 14-21, Sat 12-21 h
c/o Movie-House, Bollstraße 7 ✉8405 *(basement/im Untergeschoss)* ☎ 233 27 55
Videos, toys and magazines.

GENERAL GROUPS

WISCH - Winterthurer Schwule (G)
Postfach 294 ✉8401 ☎ 213 81 88
Call for info on activities.

HEALTH GROUPS

Aids Infostelle Winterthur 2nd floor
c/o Haus zur Einsamkeit, Lagerhausstraße 5 ✉8401 ☎ 212 81 41
Fax: 212 80 95

CRUISING

-Stadtpark/municipal park (19-22 h)

Yverdon ☎ 024

CRUISING

-P in front of railway station
-Plage d'Yvonnard (3 km direction Estavayer-le-Lac)

Zürich ☎ 01

● Zurich is the financial metropole of Europe. There has developed over the past few years in the older part of the city a small gay scene with bars, cafés and hotels reflecting the charm and comfort of Switzerland. Zurich has many gay saunas offering friendliness and warmth. The old proverb about Swiss cleanliness shows it's self from it's best side in the playful cruising areas of the saunas.

✱ Die etwas verträumte Bankenmetropole Europas hat auch dem schwulen Touristen Einiges zu bieten. In den letzten Jahren hat sich in der Altstadt eine kleine Szene entwickelt. Hier findet man Bars, Cafes und Hotels, die den Charme und die Gemütlichkeit der Schweiz wiederspiegeln.
Zürich hat zudem besonders viele Saunaclubs zu bieten. Ein Besuch lohnt immer, da neben besonderer Freundlichkeit auch angenehm große und freundlich gehaltene Naß- und Schwitzbereiche angeboten werden. Zum großen Teil bieten die Saunen verspielte Cruising- und Entspannungsmöglichkeiten, und die schon sprichwörtliche Schweizer Sauberkeit zeigt sich von der allerbesten Seite.

▲ Cette métropole banquière quelque peu rêveuse a aussi de quoi satisfaire le touriste gay. Au cours des dernières années, un petit quartier gay s'est crée au coeur de la vieille ville. On y trouve des bars, des cafés et des hôtels, qui reflètent le charme et le comfort de la Suisse Zürich a par ailleurs de nombreux saunas. Une visite vaut la peine, car en plus de la sympathie du personnel on trouve plusieurs grands espaces bien aménagés de saunas .La plupart des saunas offrent de nombreuses possibilités de cruising et de détente très agréable, et la renommée de la propreté suisse montre ici son côté le plus plaisant.

❖ Nella alquanto romantica metropoli bancaria di Zurigo, il turista gay vi trova abbastanza possibilità per divertirsi. Negli ultimi anni nel centro storico si è creato un piccolo ambiente gay. Qui si trovano dei bar, caffé ed alberghi, che danno una buona immagine dell'attrattività e dell'intimità della Svizzera. Vale la pena andare in una delle numerose saune, perché oltre alla gentilezza del personale offrono ampi e piacevoli spazi per impianti sanitari e saune. Molte saune dispongono di aree carine per il cruising e per il riposo, e la proverbiale pulizia degli Svizzeri mostra qui il meglio di sé.

GAY INFO

Pink Elephant. The Mon 22.20 & 1, Tue-Thu 23, 1 h on UHF 54

Stuttgart & Zürich von hinten
c/o Bruno Gmünder Verlag, PO Box 61 01 04, 10921 Berlin
☎ +49/30/6150030 Fax: +49/30/615 90 07.
E-mail: info@spartacus.de
The city guide book about Zurich, Bale, Berne and the German federal state of Baden-Wurttemberg. Useful general information and lots of addresses with extensive descriptions in English and German. Up-to-date maps. Erotic photos.

TOURIST INFO

Zürich Tourismus
Bahnhofbrücke 1 ✉8023 ☎ 215 40 00
Fax: 215 40 99.
Homepage http://www.zurichtourism.ch
E-mail zhtourismus@access.ch

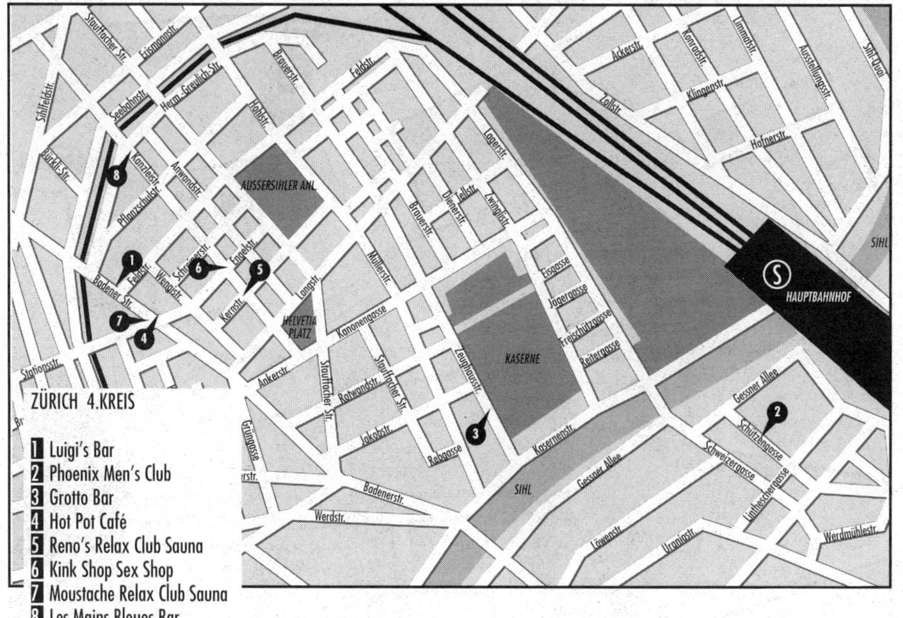

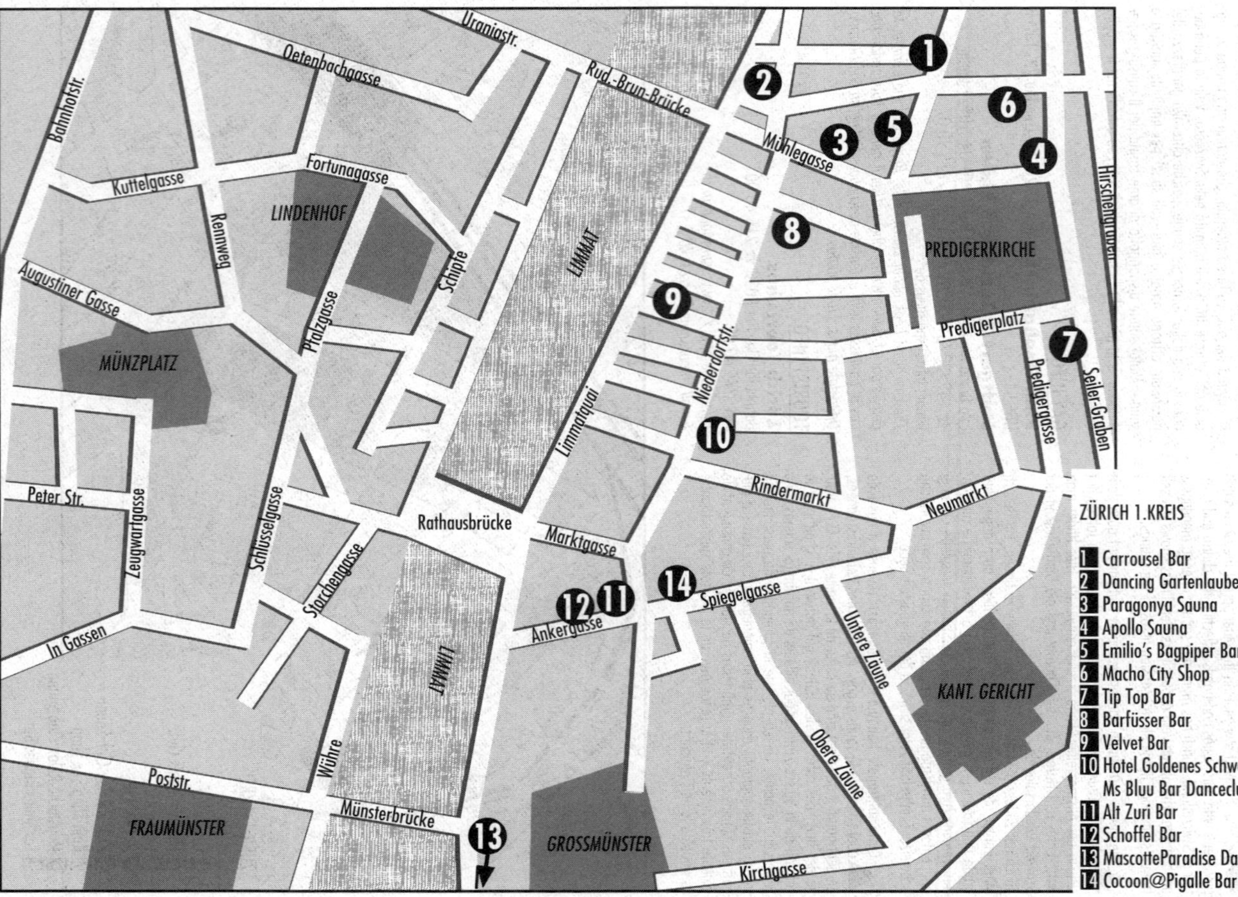
ZÜRICH 1.KREIS
1 Carrousel Bar
2 Dancing Gartenlaube Bar
3 Paragonya Sauna
4 Apollo Sauna
5 Emilio's Bagpiper Bar
6 Macho City Shop
7 Tip Top Bar
8 Barfüsser Bar
9 Velvet Bar
10 Hotel Goldenes Schwert/
Ms Bluu Bar Danceclub
11 Alt Zuri Bar
12 Schoffel Bar
13 MascotteParadise Danceclub
14 Cocoon@Pigalle Bar
Uraniastr.
Oetenbachgasse
Rud.-Brun-Brücke
Bahnhofstr.
Kuttelgasse
Fortunagasse
LINDENHOF
Rennweg
Schipfe
LIMMAT
Mühlegasse
PREDIGERKIRCHE
Predigerplatz
Predigergasse
Seiler-Graben
Augustiner Gasse
Pfalzgasse
MÜNZPLATZ
Niederdorfstr.
Limmatquai
Peter Str.
Zeugwartgasse
Schlüsselgasse
Rathausbrücke
Rindermarkt
Neumarkt
Marktgasse
Storchengasse
Spiegelgasse
Ankergasse
In Gassen
Untere Zäune
KANT. GERICHT
Obere Zäune
Wühre
Poststr.
Münsterbrücke
FRAUMÜNSTER
GROSSMÜNSTER
Kirchgasse

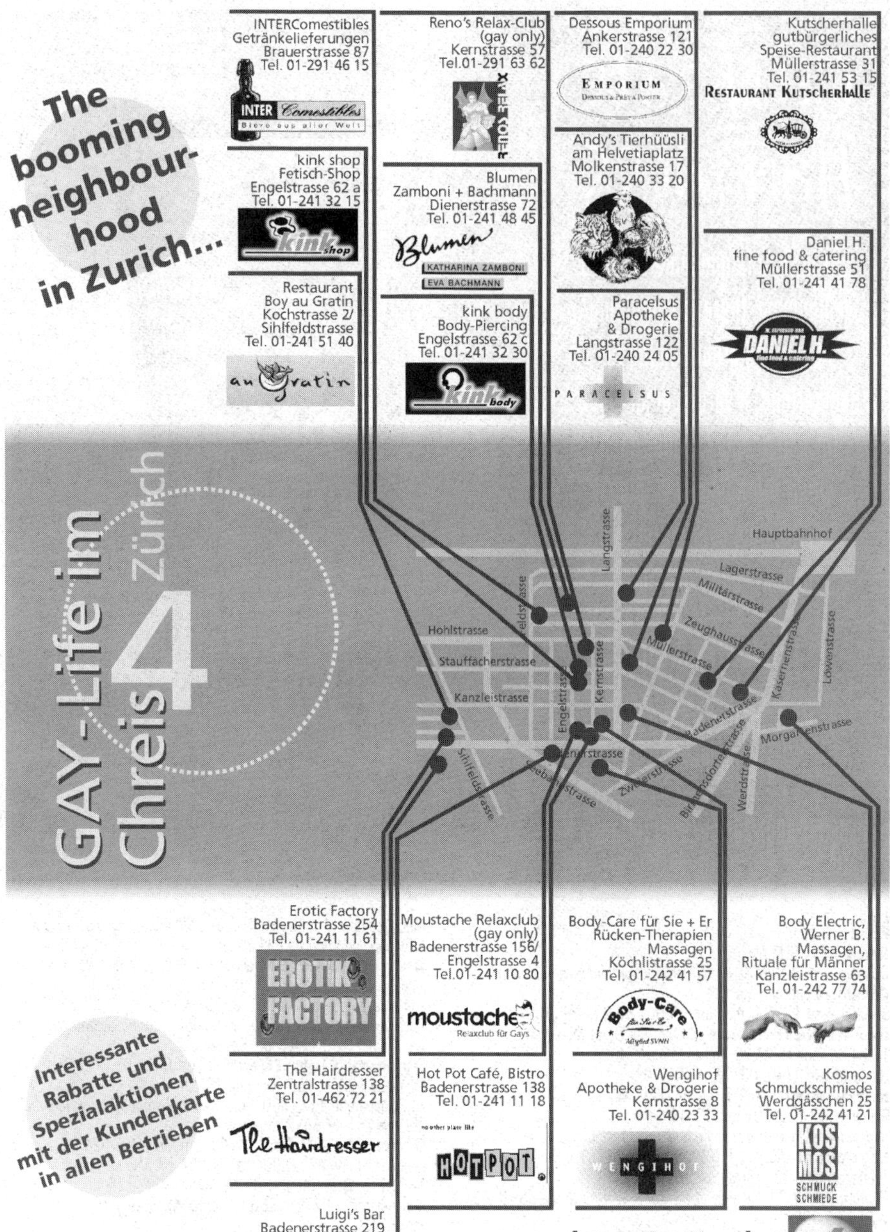
INTERComestibles
Getränkelieferungen
Brauerstrasse 87
Tel. 01-291 46 15
INTER Comestibles
Biere aus aller Welt
Reno's Relax-Club
(gay only)
Kernstrasse 57
Tel.01-291 63 62
Dessous Emporium
Ankerstrasse 121
Tel. 01-240 22 30
EMPORIUM
Kutscherhalle
gutbürgerliches
Speise-Restaurant
Müllerstrasse 31
Tel. 01-241 53 15
RESTAURANT KUTSCHERHALLE
The booming neighbourhood in Zurich...
kink shop
Fetisch-Shop
Engelstrasse 62 a
Tel. 01-241 32 15
kink shop
Blumen
Zamboni + Bachmann
Dienerstrasse 72
Tel. 01-241 48 45
Blumen
KATHARINA ZAMBONI
EVA BACHMANN
Andy's Tierhüüsli
am Helvetiaplatz
Molkenstrasse 17
Tel. 01-240 33 20
Daniel H.
fine food & catering
Müllerstrasse 51
Tel. 01-241 41 78
DANIEL H.
Restaurant
Boy au Gratin
Kochstrasse 2/
Sihlfeldstrasse
Tel. 01-241 51 40
au Gratin
kink body
Body-Piercing
Engelstrasse 62 c
Tel. 01-241 32 30
kink body
Paracelsus
Apotheke
& Drogerie
Langstrasse 122
Tel. 01-240 24 05
PARACELSUS
GAY - Life im Chreis 4 Zürich
Hauptbahnhof
Langstrasse
Lagerstrasse
Militärstrasse
Zeughausstrasse
Müllerstrasse
Hohlstrasse
Stauffacherstrasse
Kanzleistrasse
Engelstrasse
Kernstrasse
Kasernenstrasse
Löwenstrasse
Badenerstrasse
Morgartenstrasse
Sihlfeldstrasse
Zwerstrasse
Birmensdorferstrasse
Werdstrasse
Erotic Factory
Badenerstrasse 254
Tel. 01-241 11 61
EROTIK FACTORY
Moustache Relaxclub
(gay only)
Badenerstrasse 156/
Engelstrasse 4
Tel.01-241 10 80
moustache
Relaxclub für Gays
Body-Care für Sie + Er
Rücken-Therapien
Massagen
Köchlistrasse 25
Tel. 01-242 41 57
Body-Care
Body Electric,
Werner B.
Massagen,
Rituale für Männer
Kanzleistrasse 63
Tel. 01-242 77 74
Interessante Rabatte und Spezialaktionen mit der Kundenkarte in allen Betrieben
The Hairdresser
Zentralstrasse 138
Tel. 01-462 72 21
The Hairdresser
Hot Pot Café, Bistro
Badenerstrasse 138
Tel. 01-241 11 18
HOTPOT
Wengihof
Apotheke & Drogerie
Kernstrasse 8
Tel. 01-240 23 33
WENGIHOF
Kosmos
Schmuckschmiede
Werdgässchen 25
Tel. 01-242 41 21
KOSMOS
SCHMUCK SCHMIEDE
Luigi's Bar
Badenerstrasse 219
Tel. 01-462 51 51
LUIGI'S BAR
www.chreis4.ch
powered by: InternetService Tel. 01-310 26 26
InternetService

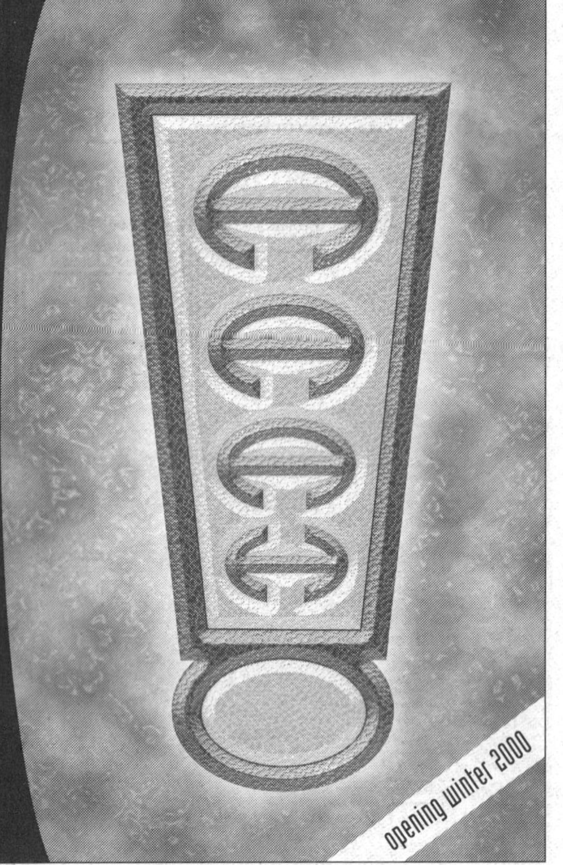

BARS

Aaah! (B f GLM MA)
Opening in winter 2000, further information under www.aaah.ch

Alt Züri (B f glm MA)
Schoffelgasse 11/Ankergasse 6 ✉8001 ☎ 251 24 38

Bar im Restaurant (B f glm MA OS s) Mon-Fri 17-24.30, Sat 18-24.30, closed Sun
Lägernstrasse 37 ✉8037 ☎ 367 07 07

Barfüsser (AC B CC F G lj MA OS r s W) 14-0.30 h
Spitalgasse 14 ✉8001 ☎ 251 40 64
Switzerlands' longest existing gay bar and restaurant.

Carrousel (AC B CC F G MA OS R) Sun-Thu 16-2, Fri Sat -4 h,
Zähringerstraße 33 ✉8001 ☎ 253 62 02
Warm meals til 02 and WE 'til 03:30h/ Warme Küche bis 02:00, WE bis 03:30h.

Cocoon @ Pigalle (AC B f GLM) 17.30-? h
Marktgasse 14 ✉8001 ☎ 266 18 77

Cranberry - the Juice & Booze Bar (AC B CC E G MA OS W) Sun-Wed 17-24.30, Thu -1, Fri Sat -2 h
Metzgerstraße 3 ✉8036 *(Tram 4/15-Rathaus)* ☎ 261 27 72
Very popular American cocktail bar.

Dancing Gartenlaube (AC B CC D F glm MA s W) Mon Tue Thu 20-2, Wed Sun 14.30-2, Fri 20-4, Sat 18-4 h
Zähringer Straße 33 ✉8001 ☎ 251 46 00
Kitchen open until around 30 min before closing/warme Küche bis ca. 30 min vor Schließung. Live music.

Dynasty Club. The (AC B CC f G MA OS r) Jul-Sept: Mon-Fri 17-2, Sat Sun 16-2, Oct-Jun: 15-2 h
Zähringerstraße 11 ✉8001 *(near central station/nähe Hauptbahnhof)* ☎ 251 47 56

Grotto Trübli Bar (B CC F glm MA OS) 14-24 h
Zeughausstraße 67 ✉8004 ☎ 242 87 97 *Also restaurant.*

Luigi's Bar (AC B CC f GLM MA OS s W) 17-2 h
Badenerstraßsse 219 ✉8003 *(Tram 2/3-Lochergut)*
☎ 462 51 51
New bar in the centre of Zürich with occasional shows.

Mains Bleues. Les (AC B CC F G MA) 17-24, meals -23 h
Kanzleistraße 15 ✉8004 *(near/nahe Stauffacher)* ☎ 241 73 78

© A MEMBER OF MEKDAENG'S
ZURICHS PLACES
gaycity.ch
the DYNASTY club
DYNASTY CLUB Zähringerstrasse 11, 8001 Zürich
CARROUSEL BAR-CLUB Zähringerstrasse 33, 8001 Zürich
A CLUB SAUNA DAMPFBAD APOLLO
MACHO
MACHO CITY SHOP Häringstrasse 16, 8001 Zürich
APOLLO SAUNA Seilergraben 41, 8001 Zürich
T&M The foremost gay place
PARAGONYA WELLNESS CLUB
MS BLUU AT THE T&M BAR DISCO Marktgasse 14, 8001 Zürich
HOTEL GOLDENES SCHWERT Marktgasse 14, Tel. 0041-01-266 18 18
PARAGONYA WELLNESS CLUB Mühlegasse 11, 8001 Zürich
schoffel
schoffel schoffelgasse 7, 8001 zürich, www.schoffel.ch
de Fuess
BARFÜSSER · SPITALGASSE 14 · ZÜRICH
SINCE 1956
BARFÜSSER BAR · RESTAURANT
The One and Only
Aschi's TIP TOP Cocktail Bar
BARFÜSSER BAR RESTAURANT Spitalgasse 14, 8001 Zürich
TIP TOP BAR Seilergraben 13, 8001 Zürich
Wirtschaft Bar Alt Züri
Cocoon PIGALLE
ALT ZÜRI Schoffelgasse 11 & Ankergasse 6, 8001 Zürich
STRICTLY GAY
STRAIGHT & GAY, GAYFRIENDLY
COCOON @ PIGALLE Marktgasse 14, 8001 Zürich
Haupt-bahnhof
Bahnhofbrücke
Central
Stampfenbachstr.
Zähringerstr.
Hirschengraben
Limmatquai
Mühlegasse
Rudolf-Brun-Brücke
Seilergraben
Neumarkt-Strasse
Rathausbrücke
Marktgasse
Münsterbrücke
Limmatquai
Rämistrasse
Bellevue
Theaterstr.
Quaibrücke
Bürkliplatz
Utoquai

Ms Bluu (AC CC D DR f G MA S STV VS) Tue-Thu 19-2 h, Fri Sat 19-4 h, Sun 19-4 h, Mon 19-2 h
c/o T&M, Marktgasse 14 ✉8001 *(near town hall)* ☎ 266 18 89
Disco, bar, show, snackbar, gogo dancers and more.

Predigerhof Bistro (B CC f G MG OS) 14-24 h
Mühlegasse 15 ✉8001 ☎ 251 29 85
Backyard garden.

Schoffel (B bf F glm MA OS) 9-24, Sun 10-18 h
Schoffelgasse 7 ✉8001 *(Tram 4/15-Rathaus)* ☎ 261 20 70
Fax: 261 20 70
Bar Restaurant.

Tip Top (B CC f G GLM r s YG) Sun-Thu 16-2, Fri Sat -4 h
Seilergraben 13 ✉8001 *(Tram 3/Bus 31-Neumarkt)* ☎ 251 78 22
Fax: 291 23 03.

Velvet Bar (B glm MA) Schneggengasse 8 ✉8001
☎ 252 27 37

MEN'S CLUBS

Phoenix Club (AC b d DR G LJ MA P VS WE) Wed 21-2, Fri 22.30-3, Sat 22.30-? h
Schützenstraße 33 ✉8902 *(located in the industrial area Bergermoos West at the end of the A4 highway)* ☎ 734 24 69 *Privat club for fetish friends (leather, latex, uniform). Strict dress code on Sat (call for info). ECMC Members welcome.*

CAFÉS

Café Marion (AC B bf CC F g MA r R W) Mon-Fri 6-23, Sat 8-23, Sun 9-23 h
Mühlegasse 22 ✉8001 ☎ 261 27 26

Hot Pot Café (A b bf F glm OS W) Mon-Fri 6.45-22.30, Sat 8-16 h, Sun closed
Badenerstraße 138 ✉8004 *(Tram2/3-Kalkbreite)* ☎ 241 11 18
Also restaurant.

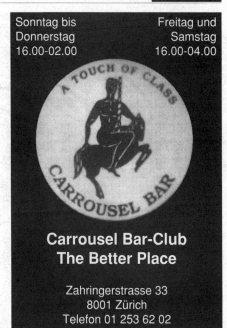

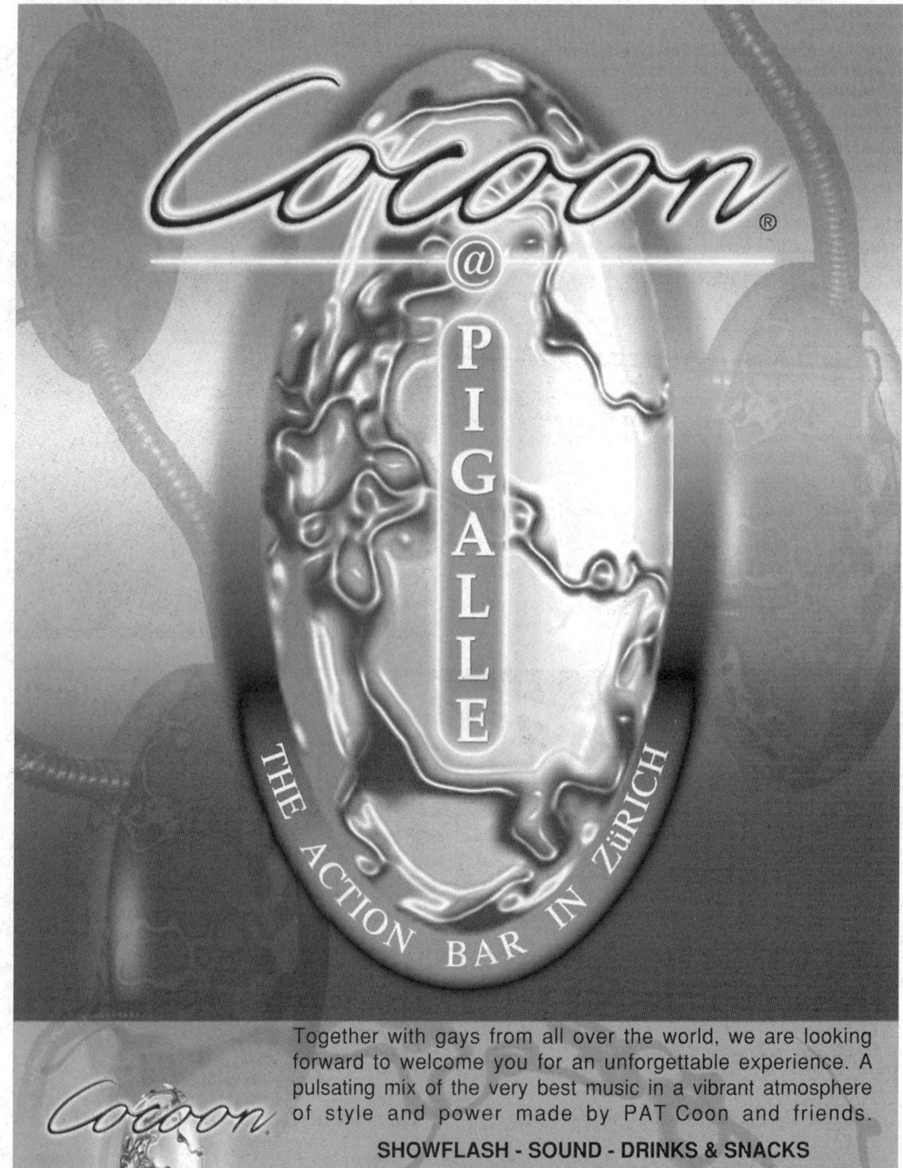
Cocoon®
@
PIGALLE
THE ACTION BAR IN ZüRICH
Cocoon
Together with gays from all over the world, we are looking forward to welcome you for an unforgettable experience. A pulsating mix of the very best music in a vibrant atmosphere of style and power made by PAT Coon and friends.
SHOWFLASH - SOUND - DRINKS & SNACKS
COCOON @ PIGALLE
MARKTGASSE 14 / 8001 ZüRICH / SWITZERLAND
PHONE: +41 1 266 18 77
WWW.GAYCITY.CH
OPEN 5:30 PM TILL LATE
KOSH

BOYS & MEN
Escortservice for Gentlemen
www.boys-men.com
Worldwide Escortservice with Top-Escorts from the heart of Europe (Vienna/Austria). All Creditcards.
Call (+43 1) 982 06 22

Odeon Café (B bf F g MA OS) Mon-Thu 7-2, Fri Sat -4, Sun 11-2 h
Limmatquai 2 ✉8001 *(near/Nähe Bellevue)* ☎ 251 16 50
The place where to be seen in Zurich.

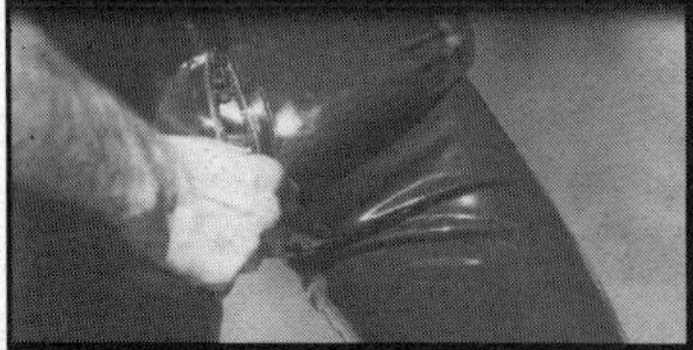

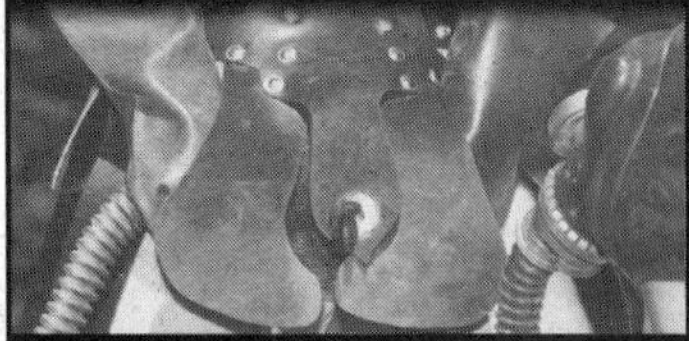

DANCECLUBS

Aera (! D DR G lj MA s WE) Sat 23-? h
Albulastraße 38/40 ✉8048 *(behind the shopping mall Letzipark, Tram 2-Kappeli/Tram 33-Luggwegstrasse)*
Underground club, house and techno music.
Bal. Le (B D L) Women only Sun 20-24
c/o Kongresshaus, Beethovenstrasse 8 ✉8001 ☎ 206 36 40
Labyrinth-Club (AC B D DR G lj MA P s SNU VS WE) Thu 23-6, Fri -8, Sat -12 h, closed Sun-Wed
Pfingstweidstraße 70 ✉8005 *(Tram-Escher-Wyss-Platz)*
☎ 440 59 80
Mascotte Paradise (B D G s) Sun 22-4 h
Theaterstraße 10 ✉8001 ☎ 252 44 81
Queer Dance (B D GLM W) Tue Sat 22-2 h
c/o Rage, Wagistrasse 13 ✉8952 *(In a suburb of Zurich, Bus 31-Wagonfabrik, Train-Schlieren)* ☎ 773 38 33
Hits of the 70's, 80's, 90's and more.
Sector C (B D DR G LJ MA VS W WE) Fri 22-4, Sat -5 (also open on Wed 21-2 h)
c/o Rage, Wagistraße 13 ✉8952 *(In a suburb of Zurich, Bus 31-Wagonfabrik, Train-Schlieren)* ☎ 773 38 33
Hardcore fetish club. Dresscode: leather, rubber, uniform etc.
Spidergalaxy (AC B D DR GLM MA P s) Fri-Sam 24-? h
Geroldstrasse 15 ✉8005 *(1 min from Bahnhof Hardbrücke)*

Zabi Disco Club (B D G MA) Fri 23-3 h
Leonhardstraße 19 ✉8001 *(Near main station, Tram 7/15-Haldenegg)* ☎ 271 22 50

RESTAURANTS

Barrique Weinrestaurant (B F glm)
Marktgasse 17 ✉8001 ☎ 252 59 41

Boy au Gratin (AC CC F glm OS W) Mon-Fri 11.30-14, 18-24, Sat 18-24 h, closed on Sun
Kochstrasse 2 ✉8004 *(Tram 2/3-Lochergut)*
☎ 241 51 40

Restaurant (A CC F glm MA OS VS) Mon-Fri 11.30-14, 19-24, Sat 18-24 h, closed Sun
Lägernstrasse 37 ✉8037 ☎ 361 07 07

Sunset Thai (CC F g OS W) 12-14, 18-0.30 h
Birmensdorferstraße 488 ✉8055 *(Tram9/14-Triemli)*
☎ 463 65 70 or 462 23 31

SEX SHOPS/BLUE MOVIES

BS-Laden (G) Mon-Fri 16-18.30, Sat 11-16 h, closed Sun
Anwandstraße 67/Pflanzschulstraße ✉8004 *(Tram8-Helvetiaplatz)*
☎ 241 04 41
Videos, books, magazines, leather, rubber.

Erotik Video Discount (AC CC G) 11-23 h
Sihlfeldstraße 58 ✉8003 *(Tram 2/3)* ☎ 451 21 01

Gerothek Mon-Sat 11-20 h
Giesshübelstraße 66 ✉8045 *(Tram13-Saalsporthalle)* ☎ 451 25 17
Videos, toys, magazines.

Kink Shop (CC DR G LJ s) Mon-Fri 12-20, Sat 10-16 h
Engelstraße 62 ✉8004 *(Tram 3-Kalkbreite)* ☎ 241 32 15
Leather, rubber, army, toys, videos, bodypiercing & -shaving.

Macho City Shop (CC GLM) 11-20, Sat 10-16 h, closed Sun
Häringstraße 16 ✉8001 *(Near Central Station/Nähe Hauptbahnhof)*
☎ 251 12 22
Books, magazines, CD's, videos.

HOUSE OF BOYS

Artist Service (CC msg P p s VS) Mon-Sat 12-23 h, closed on Sun and public holidays
Baslerstrasse 106 ✉8048 *(at Europabrücke)* ☎ 261 61 65
☎ 079/237 50 69

SAUNAS/BATHS

Adonis (b DR f G MG p sa VS) Mon-Fri 13-21, Sat -19 h, closed Sun
Mutschellenstraße 17 ✉8002 *(Tram 13-Waffenplatzstraße)*
☎ 201 64 16

Apollo (f G MG sa sb sol VS) Mon-Fri 12-22, Sat-Sun 15-21 h
Seilergraben 41 ✉8001 ☎ 261 49 52
Entrance-fee Sfr 24.

Moustache (! A AC B CC DR f G MA msg p sa sb sol VS YG) 12-23, Oct-May Sat -2 h
Badenerstraße 156b (IV) ✉8004 *(Entrance Engelstraße 4. Tram2/3/Bus32-Kalkbreite)* ☎ 241 10 80
Offers bio-sauna, plunge pool. Special youth and afternoon rates. The right spot for bears and the bearded. Admission sfr 29.

DOWNTOWN ZURICH

ZIMMER ZU VERMIETEN

An der Spitalgasse 3, möblierte Zimmer mit Dusche und Lavabo zu vermieten. WC und Küche auf dem Gang. Miete von 950.– bis 1400.– Fr. pro Monat. Kurzfristige Miete ab 10 Tagen möglich. Bitte ruf an für einen Besichtigungstermin.

ROOMS TO LET

In Zurich town centre, only 4 minutes from central station, at Spitalgasse 3, furnished rooms with shower and wash-basin to let between CHF 950.– and 1400.–. WC and kitchen in corridor. Short-term lettings from 10 days also available. Please call for a viewing.

CHAMBRE À LOUER

Dans le centre de Zurich, à 4 minutes seulement de la gare centrale, Spitalgasse 3, nous proposons des chambres meublées à louer de 950.–à 1400.– CHF. Douche et lavabo dans la chambre. WC et cuisine dans le couloir. La location est également possible pour de courtes périodes de 10 jours au moins. Vous pouvez nous appeler pour convenir d'une visite.

HABITACIONES PARA ARRENDAR

En el centro de Zurich, a cuatro minutos de la estación central de ferrocarriles, en la Spitalgasse 3, arrendamos habitaciones amuebladas con ducha y lavabo dentro de las mismas, a partir de CHF 950.– hasta 1400.–. WC y cocina en el corredor. También son posibles arrendamientos de corto tiempo a partir de 10 días. Por favor, llámenos para una visita.

QUARTOS PARA ALUGAR

No centro de Zurich, a 4 minutos da estação central do caminho de ferro, na Spitalgasse 31 alugamos quartos mobilados com ducha e lavatório dentro dos mesmos, a partir de CHF 950.– até 1400.– . WC e cozinha no corredor. Também são possíveis alugueres de curto tempo. Por favor, chame-nos para uma visita.

POKOJE DO WYNAJĘCIA

W centrum Zurychu, 4 minuty od Dworca Glównego, Spitalgasse 3, umeblowane pokoje do wynajęcia w cenie od 950.– do 1400.– franków szwajcarskich, wyposażone w prysznic i umywalkę. WC i kuchnia na korytarzu. Możliwosć wynajmu również na krótki okres - od 10 dni. Prosimy o telefoniczne umawianie się na ogladanie.

TELEFON 01 266 18 18

(HOTEL GOLDENES SCHWERT)

Bonus for young people: 16 – 25 years!

Steam bath
Bio-sauna with light spectrum
Finnish sauna
Cold plunge pool
Solarium
Relaxation room with cabins
Bar, TV/Video
Massage by appointment

moustache

Relaxclub for Gays

Badenerstrasse 156 b, CH-8004 Zürich
Entrance Engelstr. 4, Phone 01 241 10 80
http://www.moustache.ch
info@moustache.ch
Tram 2 and 3 or Bus 32 to Kalkbreite
Open daily from noon till 11 pm

vasistas graphique zurich

Mylord Sauna (f DR G msg OG P sa VS) Mon-Sat 14-22 h
Seebahnstraße 139 ✉8003 *(Tram2/3/10-Lochergut)* ☎ 462 44 66

Paragonya (! AC B CC DR f G p sa sb sol VS wh YG) 11.30-23 h
Mühlegasse 11 ✉8001 *(near main station/nahe Hauptbahnhof, near river Limmat, in the Post Office Building PTT)* ☎ 252 66 66
Biosauna

Reno's Relax (! AC b DR f G MA msg p r sa sb sol VS) Mon-Thu 12-23, Fri Sat -7, Sun 14-23 h
Kernstraße 57 ✉8004 *(Tram 8-Helvetiaplatz)* ☎ 291 63 62

BODY & BEAUTY SHOPS

Kink Body (CC GLM) Mon-Fri 12-20, Sat 10-16 h
Engelstrasse 62 ✉8004 *(Tram 3-Kalkbreite)* ☎ 241 32 30
Body manipulation, piercings shavings, tattoos.

BOOK SHOPS

EBS Erotic Book Store (glm) 11-18.30, Thu -21, Sat 10-16 h
Klingenstraße 33 ✉8005 ☎ 272 83 13
No admittance if you are under age of 16

Sec 52 Buchladen/Galerie (g) 10.30-18.30, Sat -16 h, closed Sun
Josefstraße 52 ✉8005 ☎ 271 18 18

CONDOM SHOPS

Condomeria Mon-Wed, Fri 11-18.30, Thu -21, Sat 10-16 h
Münstergasse 27 ☎ 261 45 49

HOTELS

Goldenes Schwert (bf CC f G H MA)
Marktgasse 14 ✉8004 *(central, in Zurich old town)*
☎ 266 18 18 Fax: 266 18 18 E-Mail: hotel@rainbow.ch
Located in the middle of the gay scene. All rooms with shower or bath/WC, TV, video, safe, phone.

Hotel Regina (B bf CC g H)
Hohlstraße 18 ✉8004 *(N°8 Helvetiaplatz/N°31 Kanonengasse)*
☎ 298 55 55 Fax: 298 56 00

Hotel Rothaus Zürich (CC g H) Reception 7-0.30 h
Sihlhallenstraße 1 ✉8004 *(Near Helvetiaplatz. Bus31-Militärstraße)* ☎ 241 24 51 Fax: 291 09 95
E-Mail: uhk@swissonline.ch
43 rooms with shower/WC, phone, TV and own key.
Price in double room from 98-120 SFR.

PRIVATE ACCOMODATION

Intakt Zimmervermittlung (G H)
Asylstraße 66 ✉8032 ☎ 079/441 33 03 ☎ 01/381 17 27
E-Mail: info@intakt.ch Homepage: http://www.intakt.ch
Gay private accomodation. Singles from CHF 42, doubles from 66. Fee per reservation 15.

GENERAL GROUPS

Homosexuelle Arbeitsgruppen Zürich (HAZ)
Mon-Fri 19.30-23 h
Sihlquai 67, Postfach 7088 ✉8005 *(near central station)*
☎ 271 22 50
Meeting point, library, counseling.

Spot 25 - Jugendgruppe Wed 19.30-22 h
Sihlquai 67, Posfach 4363 ✉8022 ☎ 273 11 77
E-Mail: info@spot25.ch
Youth gay and lesbian group.

THE REAL GAY-HOTEL
IN SWITZERLAND
Goldenes Schwert
© A MEMBER OF MEKDAENG'S
E-mail:
hotel@rainbow.ch
Internet Online:
http://www.gaybar.ch
Marktgasse 14
8001 Zürich/Switzerland
Phone 41.1.266 18 18
Fax 41.1.266 18 88

FETISH GROUPS

Leder- und Motorradclub Zürich (LMZ)
Postfach 2125 ✉8026 E-Mail: info@lmz.ch
Homepage: http://www.lmz.ch
Leather group.

HEALTH GROUPS

Oekumenisches Aidspfarramt
Universitätstrasse 48 ✉8006 ☎ 255 90 55 Fax: 255 44 10
Offers pastoral and spiritual assistance to people with HIV/Aids and their relatives and friends.

Zürcher AIDS-Hilfe Mon-Fri 9-13, 14-17 h, Helpline: Mon-Fri 14-17 h
Birmensdorferstraße 169 ✉8003 *(Tram 9/14-Schmiede Wiedikon)* ☎ 455 59 00 Fax: 455 59 19 E-Mail: mail@zah.ch

HELP WITH PROBLEMS

Act-HIV Tue Thu 9-13 h, Wed 19-22 h
Hallwylstraße 78 ✉8004 ☎ 291 37 20

Beratungsstelle für männliche Opfer sexueller Gewalt- Zürcher Sozialprojekte Mon-Fri 10-17, Wed-Thu -19 h
Hallwylstraße 78, Postfach 8155 ✉8036 ☎ 291 37 80
Fax: 291 23 88
Counseling in case of sexual violence.

RELIGIOUS GROUPS

HuK Zürich-Ökumenische Arbeitsgruppe Homosexuelle und Kirche
Postfach 7013 ✉8023 ☎ 311 73 12

SPECIAL INTEREST GROUPS

Zart und Heftig - Schwules Hochschulforum von Uni und ETH Zürich
Rämistraße 66 ✉8001 *(3rd floor)* ☎ 212 46 54
Homepage: http://www.zundh.unizh.ch
Gay and lesbian student group.

SPORT GROUPS

Euro Games 2000
Postfach ✉8023 E-Mail: info@eurogames.ch
Homepage: http://www.eurogames.ch
Organiser of the eurogames 2000 in Zurich.

Gay Bikers
Postfach 71 ✉5014
Homepage: http://www.datacomm.ch/gaybikers

Gay Sport Zürich Posfach 3312 ✉8021

SWIMMING

-Werdininseli (G NU) (Beach on a small island in the middle of River Limmat. Take tram 4 or Bus 80/89 to Tüffenwies. Go to the coloured wheel then to the end of the island)

CRUISING

-Bürkliplatz
-Beckenhofpark
-Einkaufszone/shopping mall »Shop Ville«
-Zeughausstraße (an den Barracken/at the barracks)
-Seepark Mythequai/Park Arboretum (! YG) (evenings)
-Waffenplatz
-Schaffhauserplatz
-Kreuzplatz
-Sihlpromenade (Sihlhölzli)
-Waffenplatzpark (AYOR LJ) (after midnight)
-Aussersihlanlage/Bäckeranlage (very AYOR)

Zug ☎ 042

HEALTH GROUPS

AIDS-Hilfe Zug Mon 14-17, Tue 9-13, Wed 12-16, 17-21, every 1st Sat 9-15 h
Zeughausgasse 9 ✉6300 ☎ 22 48 65

Taiwan

T`ai-wan

Off Mainland China

Initials: ROC

Time: GMT +8

☎ Country Code / Access Code: 886 / 002

Language: Chinese

Area: 36,981 km² / 14,275 sq mi.

Currency: 1 New Taiwan Dollar (NT$) = 100 Cents

Population: 21,908,100

Capital: Taipei

Religions: Confucianism, in the north (Mahajana) Buddhism, Taoism

Climate: Tropical and marine climate. The rainy season during southwest monsoon lasts from June to August. All year round cloudiness is persistent and extensive.

CHINA
East China Sea
Taipei
Taichung
TAIWAN
Kaohsiung
Philippine Sea

Neither the term „homosexuality" nor the concept of an age of consent exist in taiwanese legislation. Marriage is legal from the age of 18, and that too is the age people become fully accountable to the law. Yet, legally, people become of full age only when they're 20 years of age. Death penalty threatens when being seduced to homosexual acts while serving in the army.

Es gibt in den taiwanesischen Gesetzen weder den Begriff „Homosexualität", noch ein Konzept, das ein „Schutzalter" beinhaltet. Man darf zwar ab 18 heiraten und wird dann auch vollständig strafmündig, rechtlich volljährig wird man aber erst mit 20. Wer sich in der Armee zu homosexuellen Handlungen verführen lässt, wird mit der Todesstrafe bedroht.
Doch auch in Tawain läßt sich innerhalb der Bevölkerung langsam zunehmende Toleranz gegenüber Schwulen feststellen.

A Taïwan, la législation ne connaît pas le mot „homosexualité" et de restriction concernant la majorité sexuelle. Passé 18 ans, on peut se marier et on devient punissable par la loi. Ce n'est qu'à partir de 20 ans que l'on est considéré comme légalement majeur. A l'armée, les rapports entre personnes du même sexe sont passibles de la peine de mort.

En las leyes de Taiwan no aparec la palabra „homosexualidad", tampoco existe reglamentación alguna respecto a edades de consentimiento. El matrimonio esta permitido a patir de los 18 años, pero la mayoría de edad se alcanza a los 20. Quien mantenga relaciones homosexuales en el ejército está amenazado con la pena de muerte.

Le leggi di Taiwan non menzionano nè l'omosessualità nè la maggiore età sessuale. I cittadini di questo paese sono maggiorenni a 20 anni, a 18 però si possono sposare e sono maggiorenni penalmente. Chi nell'esercito si abbandona a rapporti omosessuali viene minacciato con la pena di morte.

Kaohsiung ☎ 07

BARS

Bolivia (B D YG)
10F. 80, Da jen Rd. ☎ 521-7032
Colour Plate (B G MA)
Tayou Street 5 *(2nd floor)* ☎ 551-3757
Encounter (B MA) 49, Wu Fu 4th Rd.
☎ 551-9090
Men's Talk (b d G) 20-5 h
B1 32, Ming Shing St. ☎ 211-7049
D on Sat.
Private Life (B g MA) 278,
Chi Hsien 3rd Rd. *(Basement)* ☎ 561-1100

SAUNAS/BATHS

Chen Tone (AC G msg sa)
☎ 215-1166
Han Chin (msg)
101, Hou Nan 2nd Rd. ☎ 216-7073
Michael Angelo (msg)
12F. 21, Gee Kuan St. ☎ 216-9052

CRUISING

-Kaohsiung Main railway station
-Lover River (near burned down shopping center)

Taichung ☎ 04

BARS

Ai Chiao (B g MA)
216, Chen Kung Rd. ☎ 221-1975
Celestial (B g MA)
3F 12, Tzi Yu Rd. Sec.2 ☎ 223-2348
Eternal Love (B g MA)
8F-3 12, Tzu Yu Rd. Sec.2 ☎ 222-4336
Hollywood (B g YG)
141, Chung San Rd. *(Basement)* ☎ 222-2863
King Fu Restaurant
Chi Kuang Street ☎ 223-2534
Molin Violet (B D g MA) 60,
Chung Shan Rd. *(Basement)* ☎ 220-2126
Sparrowlet (B g MA) 28,
Ming Tzu Rd. *(Basement)* ☎ 223-4467

CRUISING

-Main railway station
-Taichung park

Tainan ☎ 06

BARS

China Town (B D MA)
11F 72, Huan Ho South St. ☎ 06/220-8800

MASSAGE

Male Massage
PO Box 1350 ☎ 07/33 91 974
Pager 060732985.

CRUISING

-Main railway station facilities.

Taipei/Taipeh ☎ 02

BARS

Art (B g OG)
2F 147 Lin Sen North Rd. ☎ 571-3540
Buffalo Town (B D WE YG) 289
Linsen North Road *(12th floor)* ☎ 564-1172
Casablanca Pub (AC B D G MA)
N° 22, Lane 33, Section 1, Chung Shan North Road ☎ 563 78 95
Friendly staff. Karaoke.
Funky (! AC B D G YG)
B1, No.10, Sec.1,Han Chou Rd. S *(basement)* ☎ 394-2162
or ☎ 394-2290. Very popular on WE. Karaoke.
Jupiter (AC B G MA)
154 Po Ai Rd. *(basement)* ☎ 311-8585
President (AYOR B G R)
9 Teh Hwei Street ☎ 595-1251
Source. The (AC B d f G MA N W) 19-3 h
192 Nancheng Road, Sec. 2 *(near downtown)* ☎ 368 87 97
Fax: 368 87 95.
Traffic Fish (B g OG)
5 Chun Shan N. Rd., Sec.2 Lane 6 *(basement)* ☎ 562-7123
1/20 (B g YG)
137 Chon Hwa Rd. ☎ 382-0218

RESTAURANTS

Cupid Restaurant & Pub (AC B D F G MA) 20-4.30 h
154 Po Ai Rd. *(at new Garden Park) (Xin Gongyuan)* ☎ 311 85 85
Our Place (G F) 10-21 h
☎ 341-1057
Homestyle restaurant. Call for directions.

SAUNAS/BATHS

Da Fan (AC G MA msg sa VS wh) 0-24 h
5F, 195, Chung-Shiao West Road, Section 1 ☎ 381-1859
Very busy! Private rooms at no extra charge.
Hans Men's Sauna (AC G MA msg sa wh) 0-24 h
2F, 120 Hsi-Ning South Road ☎ 311-8681
Hilton Hotel Sauna (g msg sa sol wh WO) 10-20 h
(Basement)
Local and foreign gays.
Nong Lai (AC G MG msg sa VS) 0-24 h
5F, 155, Shih-Ning South Road ☎ 381-0891
Private rooms at no extra charge.
Royal Palace (Huang-Kong) (OG msg sa sb VS) 0-24 h
20, Hsi Ning South Rd. ☎ 381-5900

HOTELS

Brother (AC B F H NG)
255 Nanking East Road, Section 3 ☎ 712-3456
Downtown location, 40 min to the airport. All rooms with telephone, fridge, priv. bath, WC. Single NT$ 2.800-3.500, double 3.300.

CRUISING

-New Garden Park (Xin Gong Yuan) (best place is Pagoda Pond, 18-21 h)
-YMCA behind Hilton Hotel
-Little park in New Peitou (suburb of Taipei)
-Hung Lou Hsi Yuan (Red Building Theater Movie House)
-Yuan Huan Movie House (near Yuanhuan Road Circus, Chungking North Road)
-Kuang Hua Shang Chang (Basement of Kuang Hua Market on Hsinsheng South Road)

Thailand

Prathet Thai
Southeast Asia
Initials: THA
Time: GMT +7 (Summer +6)
☎ Country Code / Access Code: 66 / 001
Language: Thai. English
Area: 513,115 km² / 198,114 sq mi.
Currency: 1 Baht (B) = 100 Stangs
Population: 60,037,366
Capital: Bangkok (Krung Thep)
Religions: 95% Hinajana (Theravada) Buddhists
Climate: Tropical climate. The rainy, warm and cloudy southwest monsoon lasts from mid-May to September, the dry and cool northeast monsoon lasts from November to mid-March.
Important gay cities: Bangkok, Chiang Mai, Pattaya, Pukhet

● Homosexual acts have never been forbidden and the age of consent is 18. Threats of punishment for legal contravention have considerably increased in the past few years.
The blending of West European lifestyle and Buddhism reflects in the acceptance of gays by Thais. Astonishingly there is no stigma about prostitution in Thailand.
As in other neighbouring countries in South Asia there is a gay-lesbian movement, but in contrast to its neighbours there is no restrictiveness to the flourishing gay scene. Bangkok is the gay capital of the South and Pattaya is the only gay bathing resort of Asia.

✱ Es gab in Thailand nie ein gesetzliches Verbot homosexueller Handlungen. Das Schutzalter liegt bei 18 Jahren. Die Strafandrohungen für Zuwiderhandlungen, vor allem im Bereich der Prostitution, wurden in den vergangenen Jahren erheblich verschärft.
In Thailand vermischen sich westlich-europäische Einflüsse mit den buddhistischen Traditionen des Landes. Entsprechend liberal verhalten sich die Thais - zumindest in den großen Städten - Schwulen gegenüber. Ganz erstaunlich ist dabei, daß Prostitution absolut nicht stigmatisiert ist.
Wie in den Nachbarstaaten in Südostasien gibt es auch in Thailand ein schwul-lesbische Bewegung nur ansatzweise. Aber im Gegensatz zu den restriktiven Nachbarstaaten, hat sich in Thailand eine blühende schwule Szene entwickelt. Bangkok ist die schwule Hauptstadt Süd- und Südostasiens. Pattaya ist der einzige schwule Badeort Asiens.

▲En Thaïlande, l'homosexualité n'est pas interdite par la loi. La majorité sexuelle est fixée à 18 ans. Les condamnations pour non-respect de ces lois, surtout dans le domaine de la prostitution, se sont renforcées considérablement au cours des dernières années. En Thaïlande, les influences occidentales et européennes se mélangent à la tradition bouddiste du pays. Surtout dans les grandes villes, les thaïlandais se comportent de manière libérale à l'égard des homosexuels. Il est ainsi très surprenant de voir que la prostitution n'est pas du tout stigmatisée.
Tout comme dans les autres pays de l'Asie du Sud-Est, le mouvements gay et lesbien est encore embryonnaire. Mais contrairement à ses pays voisins plus restrictifs, la Thaïlande a développé un milieu gay florissant. Bangkok est la capitale gaye de l'Asie du Sud et du Sud-Est. Pattaya est la seule ville balnéaire gaye de l'Asie.

☆En Tailandia nunca han estado prohibidas las actividades homosexuales. La edad de consentimiento es de 18 años. Sobre todo en el campo de la prostitución y han sido intensificado las penas por contra vención.
En Tailandia se mezclan la influencia europea con las tradiciones budistas del país. De igual forma (liberal) se comportan los tailandeses homosexuales de las grandes ciudades. Es de admirar que la prostitución no es estigmatizada.
Al igual que los países vecinos del Asia menor, existen solamente los despuntes de un posible movimiento gay-lesbiano. A pesar de ello, en Tailandia se ha desarrolllado un colorido ambiente gay. Bangkok es la capital gay del Asia menor. Pattaya es el único balneario gay de Asia.

❖In Tailandia non è mai esistita una legge contro gli atti omosessuali. L'età legale è di 18 anni. Negli ultimi anni sono cresciuti gli avvisi di condanna per le trasgressioni in special modo nel campo della prostituzione minorile.
In Tailandia si fondono influssi culturali europei con le tradizioni buddiste del paese. Perciò l'atteggiamento della popolazione tai almeno nelle grandi città si mostra molto liberale verso i gay e è anche molto sorprendente che la prostituzione non venga additata dalla popolazione.
Come negli altri paesi del Sud-Est asiatico anche in Tailandia si ha solo un principio di un movimento politico gay e lesbico. Però al contrario dei più severi paesi confinanti, in Tailandia si è sviluppato un vivace ambiente gay. Bangkok è la capitale gay del Sud e Sud-Est asiatico. Pattaya è l'unica gay del paese.

NATIONAL GAY INFO

The saying »money makes the world go round« is applicable to many countries in the Far East.
Although one can make personal contacts with ease, caution is advised. Behind the facade there is frequently the desire to earn money for extra service

Grace, Male
P.O. Box 156, Dusit ✉10300 Bangkok
Magazines in Thai. But the pictures are internationally understood.
Internet addresses
-Dragon Castle: http://dragoncastle.net
-Dreaded Ned: http://www.dreadedned.com (Search Engine)
-GAMTH:
http://www.geocities.com/westhollywood/heights/2999/eindex.html (Gay Asian Men of Thailand)
-Gay Asian Links: http://members.aol.com/apxrds/gal.html
-Mens Club Publishing: http://www.chamon.com (Gay magazine in Thai and English)
-Pink Ink: http://www.khsnet.com/pinkink -
E-mail: pinkpage@hotmail.com (Monthly newsletter)
-Utopia (!): http://www.utopia-asia.com (Interesting and colourful site about gay Thailand and other Asian countries)

Men of Thailand. The
Floating Lotus/Bua Luang Books, PO Box 44, Ratcha Thewi ✉10408 Bangkok
Guide to gay Thailand. With listing, maps, and a lot of information about all aspects of gay life.
Midway
PO Box 599, Phra Kanong ✉10110 Bangkok
Bilingual gay magazine (English and Thai). Many beautiful pictures.
Mithuna Magazine
P.O. Box 586, Phra Khanong ✉10110 Bangkok
Gay Thai magazine.
Neon
P.O. Box 49, Dusit ✉10300 Bangkok
Magazine in Thai.
Thai Guys (!)
Fax: 02/6 74 27 51 E-Mail: thaiguys@loxinfo.co.th
New gay English magazine covering all Thailand. Featuring the main meeting points and information about the scene, contact and stories about gay life-style. Bimonthly.

NATIONAL PUBLISHERS

Gay Media Group
☎ 02/6 79 79 85 ☎ 01/6 10 95 81 Fax: 02/6 79 79 86
E-Mail: Info@gay-media.com
Homepage: http://ww.gay-media.com

Bangkok/Krung Thep ☎ 02

●For those who have never experienced before tropical cities with populations in the millions, will feel overwhelmed on landing in a city of tropical temperatures, enormous crowds in the streets, noise, and motorised conjestion in a city of over 6 million inhabitants. To over come this overwhelming experience it helps to relax, and to take in all sights and pleasures that this city has to offer. The city has a large number of palaces and temples, over crowded markets and the Chao Pyra River (the river of the King), which is the traditional transport artery and is still a rich pageant of life. Bangkok far surpasses other countries for it's turbulent colourfulnes. Shopping is a must! There is a varied selection of clothes, silk, jewellery and objects of art.
In Bangkok there are fundamentally three gay centres. Firstly, *Patpong* is regarded as the night life address for heteros and gays, especially two soi (or lanes) Patong I and Patong II that run between *Silom Road* and *Suriwong Road*. The gays concentrate themselves around soi 2, 4 and 6. It is suggested to avoid touts at the entrance to the gay soi. The second most important area is *Sukhumwit Road* and *Siam Square*. In contrast to Patong this area has the largest number of hotels and international restaurants. The third area is *Sapan Kwai*, which is further towards the airport. This is an area to meet Bangkokers or tourists looking for a break from the hustle and bustle of the inner city.

✱Wer tropische Millionenstädte nicht kennt, wird sich im Moment der Ankunft überwältigt fühlen: vom tropischen Klima, vom Menschengewirr in den Innenstadtgassen, vom dem enormen Verkehr, der mit kaum öffentlichem Nahverkehr und überlasteten Hauptstraßen in einer sich motorisierenden 6-Milionen-Metropole auskommen kann. Da hilft nur entspannen, noch mal hinsehen und genießen. Die Stadt bietet Paläste und Tempel in Hülle und Fülle. Die schwimmenden Märkte und der „Chao Pyra" (Fluß der Könige, die traditionelle Transportader der Stadt) sind an turbulenter Buntheit nicht zu übertreffen. Und Schoppen muß man! Bekleidung, Seide, Schmuck, Kunstobjekte lohnen jeder Besuch.
In Bangkok gibt es im wesentlichen drei schwule Zentren. Das *Patpong* ist ganz allgemein Die Nightlife-Adresse, auch für Schule. Benannt ist die Gegend nach den beiden Wegen (oder „Patpong") zwischen der *Silom Road* und der *Suriwong Road*. Dabei konzentrieren sich die schwulen Lokalitäten auf die soi Silom 2, 4 und 6. Von

den Schleppern am Eingang der schwulen soi sollte man sich tunlichst fernhalten. Da zweite wichtige schwule Areal ist die Gegend um die *Sukhumvit Road* und den *Siam Square*. Im Gegensatz zum Patpong ist dies eher das Viertel der großen Hotels und der internationalen Restaurants. Ein weiteres Gebiet ist *Sapan Kwai*, etwas außerhalb Richtung Flughafen gelegen. Hier trifft man eher Bangkoker an, oder Touristen, die sich einen Abend lang etwas Ruhe vom Volldampf der Innenstadt gönnen.

▲ Ceux qui ne connaissent pas les villes tropicales de plusieurs millions d'habitants seront très impressionnés en arrivant à Bangkok. Impressionnés par le climat, par la foule dans les rues étroites, par la circulation massive, marquée par la quasi inexistance de transports en commun et par des rues principales surchargées dans lesquelles les 6 millions d'habitants motorisés doivent circuler. Tout ce qui reste à faire est de se détendre, d'observer, et d'en profiter. La ville offre une quantité de palaces et de temples. Les marchés flottants et le Chao Pyra (fleuve des rois, l'artère du transport traditionnel de la ville), ne pourraient être plus colorés. Et le shopping est un must! On y trouve d'innombrables vêtements, de la soie, des bijoux, des objets d'arts.
A Bangkok il y a trois grands centres gays. Le *Patpong* est l'adresse nocturne par excellence, y compris pour les homosexuels. Ce quartier a été nommé d'après les deux grands chemins (ou „patpong") entre la *Silom Road* et la *Suriwong Road*. Les endroits gays sont concentrés sur les soi Silom 2, 4 et 6. Il vaut mieux rester à l'écart des ramasseurs à l'entrée des soi gays. Le second quartier gay est celui des *Sukhumvit Road* et de *Siam Square*. Au contraire du Patpong, c'est plutôt le coin des grands hotels et restaurants internationaux. Le troisième quartier est le *Sapan Kwai*, à l'ecart et situé dans la direction de l'aéroport. Ici, on rencontre surtout des thaïlandais, mais aussi des touristes qui veulent se reposer pour un soir des tumultes du centre ville.

☆ Quien no conozca ciudades tropicales con millones de habitantes, se sentirá en el momento de su llegada abrumado por el clima tropical, las masas de gente en las callejuelas del centro de la ciudad, el enorme tránsito vial que casi no posee red de servicio público y también por las abarrotadas calles principales de una metrópolí motorizada que cuenta con 6 millones de habitantes. Lo único que puede ayudar es relajarse, tratar de encontrarle diversión al asunto y gozarlo. La ciudad ofrece gran cantidad de palacios y templos para visitar. Los mercados flotantes de Chao Pyra („Río de los Reyes", vía de transporte tradicional de esta ciudad) son de un colorido turbulento que en ningún lugar del mundo encuentran un igual. Puedes ir de compras, adquirir prendas de vestir, seda, joyas y artículos de arte para hacer que una visita a esta ciudad se justifique.
En Bangkok hay tres centros homosexuales. El *Patpong* es considerado el centro nocturno homosexual. Esta región, es la loacalizada entre la *Silom Road* y la *Suriwong Road*. las localidades gay se concentran sobre todo en soi (callejuelas) Silom 2, 4 y 6. Es aconsejable no dejarse llevar al interior de ellas. La segunda región homosexual de importancia son los alrededores de la *Sukhumvit Road* y la *Siam Square*. En contraposición a Patpong este es un sector que se caracteriza por los grandes hoteles y restaurantes internacionales. El otro sector homosexual es *Sapan Kwai*, situado en las afueras de la ciudad de camino al aeropuerto. Este es visitado sobre todo por nativos y turistas que intentan escapar del alocado ritmo de la ciudad.

❖ Per chi non conosce ancora metropoli tropicali, verrà sopraffatto al momento dell'arrivo: dal clima tropicale, dalle affollatissime strade del centro, dall'enorme traffico stradale, carente di mezzi pubblici adeguati e dalle sovracariche strade principali in una sempre più motorizzata città di oltre 6 milioni di abitanti. In questo caso è consigliabile di prendere tutto con calma, guardarsi attorno e godere l'atmosfera eccezionale. La città offre tantissimi palazzi e templi. I mercati sull'acqua e il Chao Pyra („il fiume dei re", la tradizionale arteria principale di trasporto della città) sono insuperabili per la loro vivace turbulenza. E lo shopping! Ogni visita merita per l'abbigliamento, la seta, i gioielli e gli oggetti d'arte.
A Bangkok si trovano più che altro tre centri gay. La zona *Patpong* è generalmente conosciuta come il migliore indirizzo notturno, anche per clientela gay. La zona prende il nome dalle due strade (in tailandese „patpong") tra la *Silom Road* e la *Suriwong Road*. I locali gay si concentrano nelle soi Silom 2, 4 e 6. Si consiglia di tenersi a distanza dei cosiddetti accompagnatori all'inizio dei „soi" gay. La seconda area gay d'importanza è quella attorno alla *Sukhumvit Road* e alla *Siam Square*. Al contrario del Patpong, questa è la zona dei grandi alberghi e dei ristoranti internazionali. Un'altra zona è il *Sapan Kwai* situtata fuori città in direzione dell'areoporto. Qui è più facile incontrare nativi di Bangkok, o anche turisti che per una sera si vogliono riposare dalla frenesia della città.

GAY INFO

Bangkok Gay Festival
Homepage: http://www.khsnet.com/bgf
Info about the next Bangkok Gay Festival on November 5th, 2000.

Guide of Bangkok with Pink Page
19/32 Sukhumvit Road, Soi 65, Khlong Toey ✉10110
☎ 3900307 Fax: 3918006 E-Mail: pinkpage@hotmail.com
Homepage: http://www.geocities.com/westhollywood/5752
Monthly free newspaper with gay pages compiled by Trident. E-mail version available.

Look
Free weekly magazine with gay section.

This Week
Free weekly magazine. Its supplement „Afterdark" presents a gay guide.

TOURIST INFO

Tourism Authority of Thailand (TAT)
Le Concorde Office Building, 202 Ratchadapisek Road, Huay Khwang ✉10310 ☎ 6941222 Fax: 6941220 E-Mail: info1@tat.or.th

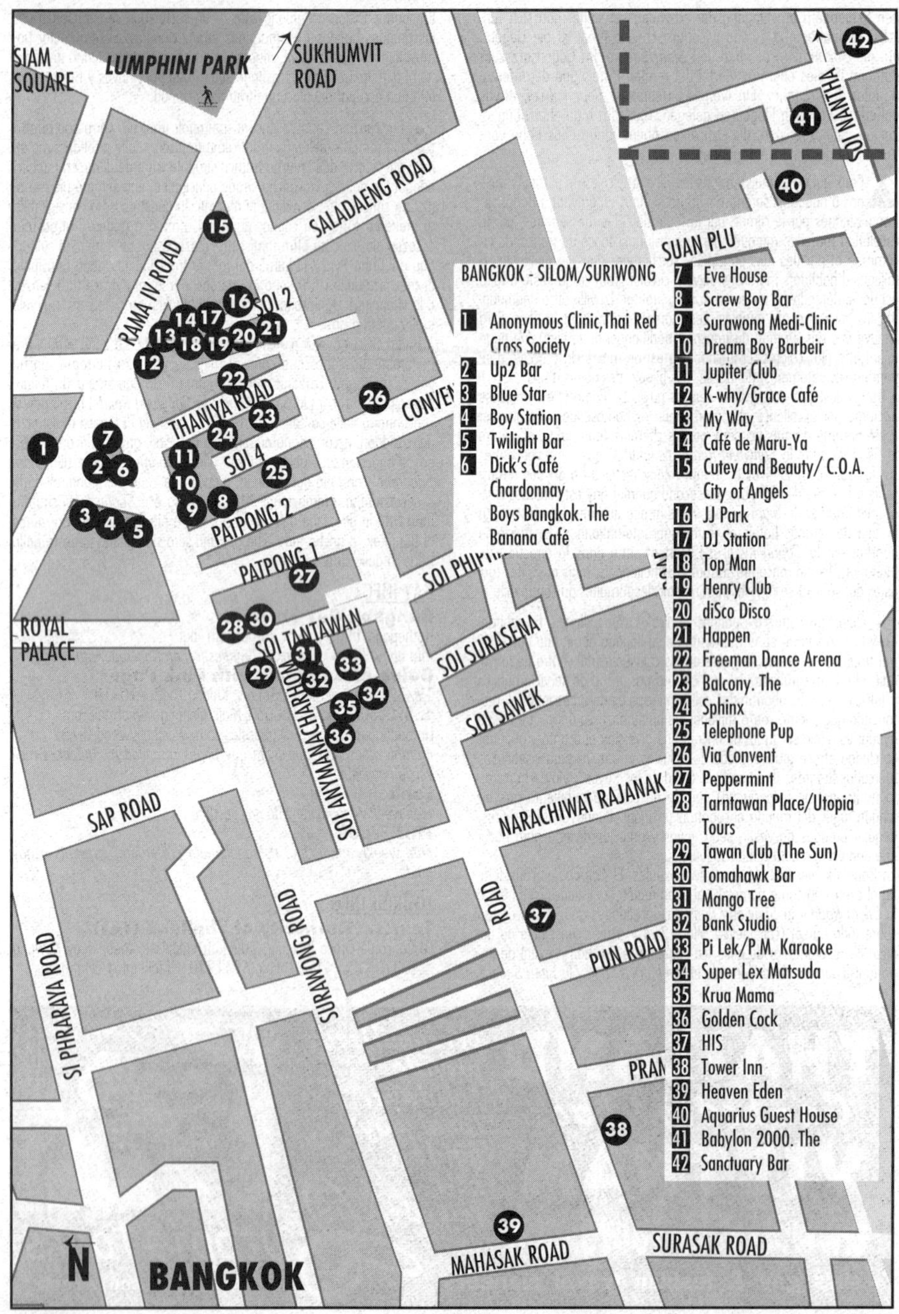
SIAM SQUARE
LUMPHINI PARK
SUKHUMVIT ROAD
SALADAENG ROAD
RAMA IV ROAD
SOI 2
THANIYA ROAD
SOI 4
PATPONG 2
PATPONG 1
CONVEN
SOI PHIPHI
SOI SURASENA
SOI SAWEK
SOI TANTAWAN
SOI ANYMANACHARHOM
ROYAL PALACE
SAP ROAD
SURAWONG ROAD
NARACHIWAT RAJANAK
ROAD
PUN ROAD
PRAM
SI PHRARAYA ROAD
MAHASAK ROAD
SURASAK ROAD
SUAN PLU
SOI NANTHA
N
BANGKOK
BANGKOK - SILOM/SURIWONG
1 Anonymous Clinic,Thai Red Cross Society
2 Up2 Bar
3 Blue Star
4 Boy Station
5 Twilight Bar
6 Dick's Café Chardonnay Boys Bangkok. The Banana Café
7 Eve House
8 Screw Boy Bar
9 Surawong Medi-Clinic
10 Dream Boy Barbeir
11 Jupiter Club
12 K-why/Grace Café
13 My Way
14 Café de Maru-Ya
15 Cutey and Beauty/ C.O.A. City of Angels
16 JJ Park
17 DJ Station
18 Top Man
19 Henry Club
20 diSco Disco
21 Happen
22 Freeman Dance Arena
23 Balcony. The
24 Sphinx
25 Telephone Pup
26 Via Convent
27 Peppermint
28 Tarntawan Place/Utopia Tours
29 Tawan Club (The Sun)
30 Tomahawk Bar
31 Mango Tree
32 Bank Studio
33 Pi Lek/P.M. Karaoke
34 Super Lex Matsuda
35 Krua Mama
36 Golden Cock
37 HIS
38 Tower Inn
39 Heaven Eden
40 Aquarius Guest House
41 Babylon 2000. The
42 Sanctuary Bar

THE BOYS BANGKOK

SHOW TIME EVERY NIGHT
10.30 P.M. 12 P.M. 1 A.M.

894/11-13 Soi Prathuchai
Suriwong Road, Bang Rak
Bangkok 10500 - Phone: 237 - 2006

DREAMBOY BARBEIR

Bangkok's most popular Go Go Boy Bar
Show time every night 22.30 and 0.30 h
100 sexy hosts on two stages!
With very special shows!

Don't miss the DREAMBOY experience
where your dreams come true.

35/3-4 Surawong Road, Bangkok 10500
next to Suriwongse Hotel ☎ 234-0830
for Taxi: DREAMBOY BARBEIR
35/3-4 ถ.สุริวงค์ หน้า โรงแรม สุริวงค์

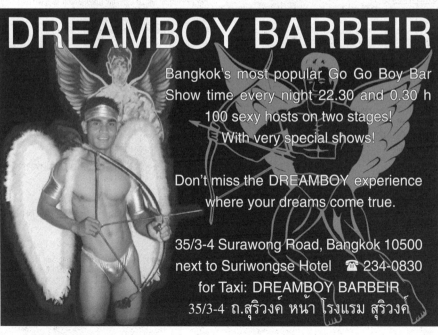

Bangkok/Krung Thep - Other Areas ☎ 02

BARS

Mon Copain (B G)
1091/74 Petchaburi Soi 33, Pathumwan ✉10330 ☎ 2552976
Sperm Entertainment (B G)
223/1 Soi 3, Pacharachbumpen Road, Huay Khwang ✉10320
☎ 6926025
New entertainment centre far outside the gay scene.

SAUNAS/BATHS

Abacus (B F pi sa WO) 15-23, Fri-Sat -1h
3141/2 Soi Ram, between Soi 81and 83, Ramkhamhaeng Road, Bang. api ✉10240 *(Opposite Ramkhamhang Hospital)*
☎ 01/9225656 (Mobile)
Sauna, gym, pool, restaurant, cyber corner.
David de Bangkok (G msg OS sa sb WO) 16-24 h
Ratakosin Mansion, 1 Chao Fa Road, Phra Pin Klao Bridge, Banglamphoo ✉10200 *(opposite National Theatre, close to Khao San Road)* ☎ 6290429
Sauna, steam, gym, roof garden and massage.
Orion Health Club. The (B F G pi sa sb VS WO)
210-212 Baromratchachonnee Road, Behind Merry King Department Store, Pin Klao, Arun Amarin, Bangkok Noi ✉10700
☎ 8846090
Sukhothai Health Club (G msg sa WO)
383 Sukhothai Road Soi 4, Dusit ✉10300 *(near corner of Soi 4)*
☎ 2413385
Sauna, gym, massage.
Uomo (G sa sb) Mon-Thu 16-23, Fri-Sun 16-24 h
549 Rama IX Road, Soi 49, Sounlong ✉10250 ☎ 7183666

FITNESSTUDIOS

Hercules Health Club (B F G sb WO) Mon-Thu 16-23, Fri-Sun 12-24 h
91/194 Siam Park City, Sukhapiban 2 Road, Siam Park Avenue, Bangapi ✉10230 *(near Fashon Island)* ☎ 9199609
Gym, sauna, steam, restaurant, escort.

TRAVEL & TRANSPORT

99 Travel
99/1 Moo 6, Srinakarin Road, Nongbon, Prawet ✉10260
☎ 7218160 ☎ 7218165 Fax: 7218169
E-Mail: info@99travel.com Homepage: http://www.99travel.com
Tour and travel management.

GENERAL GROUPS

Mituna Club
573/21 Samson Road, Dusit ✉10300
☎ 2824244

SWIMMING

The Mall, shopping centre in Thonburi (many gays come here to swim and cruise, afternoons)

CRUISING

-Sanam Luang (large open field between Wat Phra Keow, the Royal Palace, and Banglamphu)

Bangkok/Krung Thep - Sapan Kwai ☎ 02

BARS

Adam (AC B G S) 20-2 h
6/7-8 Pradipat Soi 20 (Soi Kaw Toey), Sapan Kwai ✉10400
☎ 2781191
One of the oldest go go bars in the area. Small but friendly.
Aladdin (B D G N S) 19.30-3 h
218/3 Pradiphat Soi 18 (Sahavaree 2), Sapan Kwai ✉10400 *(near Paradise)* ☎ 2712154
Small bar with go go dancing mainly for Thai customers.
Apache Boy (B G S) 20-2 h
1407/13-14 Soi Laleewan, Phahon Yothin Road, Sapan Kwai ✉10400 *(soi between Phahon Yothin Soi 13 and Pradiphat Road)*
☎ 2782756
Go go boys wearing tiny Indian costumes. Draws more and more foreigners.
Be High Boy (B G S)
11/1 Soi Laleewan, Phahon Yothin Road, Sapan Kwai ✉10400 *(soi between Phahon Yothin Soi 13 and Pradiphat Road)*
☎ 2796382
Small and quiet go go bar.
Belami (B E G N S) 19-2.30 h
971/29 Phahon Yothin Road, Samsennai, Phaya Thai ✉10400
☎ 2791434
Nice, elegant bar with hosts mainly for neighbourhood crowd.
Charming (AC B G)
2 Pradiphat Soi 17 (Soi Thawan Sak), Sapan Kwai ✉10400
☎ 2791437
Indeed a charming place.
Hippodrome (AC B CC G MA) 20-3 h
18 Pradiphat Soi 12 (Soi Santi Sewi), Sapan Kwai ✉10400 *(Behind Mido Hotel)* ☎ 2780413
Karaoke, pub and hosts. Where friends meet.
King's Heaven and Paradise Cocktail Lounge (B F G)
466/12 Phahon Yothin Road, Sapan Kwai ✉10400 *(soi beside Government Savings Bank, opposite Soi 13)* ☎ 2710602
Small bar and restaurant.
Oasis (B G S)
11/19 Pradipat Soi 20 (Soi Kaw Toey), Sapan Kwai ✉10400 *(soi Embassy Hotel, Pradiphat Road)* ☎ 2785058
Small go go bar and restaurant with karaoke.
Peak Point Entertainment '41 (B G) 1
019/4 Phahon Yothin Road, Phaya Thai ✉10400 *(in the alley beside Thai Farmer Bank)* ☎ 6170862
Hosts and karaoke in a small bar.
Seven Nights (B G S)
5/1-4 Pradiphat Soi 20 (Soi Kaw Toey), Sapan Kwai ✉10400
☎ 2799399
Small go go bar.
Stax Boy und Stax Karaoke Lounge (B G S STV) Fri-Sat ladyboy show at 1h
9 Pradipat Soi 20 (Soi Kaw Toey), Sapan Kwai ✉10400 *(soi Embassy Hotel)* ☎ 2784018
Two bars with drag shows and karaoke.
Street Boy (B G)
6/1 Soi Pradiphat 20, Sapan Kwai ✉10400 ☎ 2784739
Small new bar with go go boys and beer.

DANCECLUBS

M. C. Men Club (B D G)
169/25-26 Pradiphat Road, Sapan Kwai ✉10400 *(in front of Elisabeth Hotel)* ☎ 2781103
Karaoke and disco. No go go dancing.

SAUNAS/BATHS

Adonis II (G msg sa sb) Mon-Fri 16-23, Sat, Sun 13-23 h
169/44 Pradiphat Road (Soi Suthisarn), Sapan Kwai ✉10400 *(soi of Elizabeth Hotel)* ☎ 6184130
Small sauna mainly for Thais. 150 Baht.
V Club (F G msg wh WO)
52/1 Phahon Yothin Soi 7 (Soi Ari), Phaya Thai ✉10400 *(right side behind Soi Ari 4)* ☎ 2793322

One of the best saunas in Bangkok. Very friendly, nice location and well trained men for massage. They look like models because most of them also work as models. So do not close your eyes during your massage...

FITNESSTUDIOS

G.G. (Grey Gymnastics Men's Club) (AC B G MA msg WO) 16-23 h
1155/1 Ronachai Soi 2, Nakorn Chaisri, off Rama 6 Road, Phaya Thai ✉10400 ☎ 2793807
Sauna, gym, steam, massage, coffee-shop. Popular with local Thais and some foreigners only.

HOTELS

☛ also Si Lom/Suriwong for comment.
Elizabeth Hotel (glm H)
169/51 Pradiphat Road, Sapan Kwai ✉10400 *(between Soi 15 and 17)* ☎ 2710204 Fax: 2712539
Close to all gay venues in the area.
Liberty Garden (glm H)
215 Pradiphat Road, Sapan Kwai ✉10400 *(between Soi 19 and 21)* ☎ 2785018 ☎ 2799756
Close to all gay venues in the area.
Paradise 2 (bf B F G H S)
42/1 Phahon Yothin Soi 11, Sapan Kwai ✉10400 ☎ 2795609 ☎ 01/6357786 (Mobile)
Guest house, Titanic cocktail lounge with hosts, cabaret, weekend special shows. Also restaurant with Thai and Vietnamese food.
Pradiphat Hotel (AC B bf CC F g H MA)
173/1 Pradiphat Road, Sapan Kwai ✉10400 *(near Saphan-Kwai Center)* ☎ 2781470 ☎ 2781477 Fax: 2781478
Cheapest hotel in this area.

CRUISING

-JJ Park
-Chatuchak Park

Bangkok/Krung Thep - Si Lom Road/Suriwong Road ☎ 02

BARS

Balcony. The (! AC B F G MA N OS) Sun-Thu 19-2 h, Fri-Sat 19-3 h
86-88 Si Lom Road Soi 4 (Soi Jaruwan), Bang Rak ✉10500 ☎ 2355891
One of the very popular night spots for eating, drinking and meeting. For sure the most reasonable prices in the gay night life.
Blue Star (! AC B CC D F G MA S SNU VS) 21-2 h, show every hour
Duangthawee Plaza, 38/5-6 Soi Pratoochai, at 38 Surawong Road, Bang Rak ✉10500 ☎ 2332121
Sexy circus. Large go go bar with cute hosts and party every night. Lots of handsome dancers, colourful randy shows.
Boy Station (B G S)
Duangthawee Plaza, 38/5-6 Soi Pratoochai, at 38 Surawong Road, Bang Rak ✉10500 *(ground floor, below Blue Star)*
New go go bar.
Boys Bangkok. The (! AC B CC G MA S SNU STV) 20-2h, shows 22.30h, 24h, 1h
Duangthawee Plaza, 894/12-13 Soi Pratoochai, at 38 Surawong Road, Bang Rak ✉10500 ☎ 2372006
One of the best go go bars in town. Crowded every night. Lots of dancers and three special shows every night.
Café de Maru-Ya (B G)
944/18 Rama IV Road, Bang Rak ✉10500 *(Next to My Way)*
Karaoke bar mainly for Thais.
Chardonnay (AC B G S SNU) 20-2 h
Duangthawee Plaza, 894/9-10 Soi Pratoochai, at 38 Surawong Road, Bang Rak ✉10500 ☎ 2361198
Go go bar with very comfortable seatings and nice dancers.
Dream Boy Barbeir (! AC B G MA S SNU) 20-2 h
35/3-5 Surawong Road, Bang Rak ✉10500 *(opposite Duangthawee Plaza)* ☎ 2340830
Not only one of the largest, but for sure one of the best go go bars in Thailand. Dream Boy shows on two stages are usually packed crowded every night, colourful and exciting.
Eve House (B G)
18-18/1 Surawong Road, Bang Rak ✉10500 *(Opposite Soi Thaniya)* ☎ 2336506
Karaoke for Thais and their friends. Mainly interesting in the after hours.
Golden Cock (B G S SNU) 13-1h
39/27 Soi Rajanakarindra 1 (Soi Anuman Rajadhon) Surawong Road, Bang Rak ✉10500 *(Off Si Lom Soi 6, off Soi Than Thawan)* ☎ 2363859
Small but interesting go go bar. Opens in the afternoon.
Happen (B G)
8/14 Si Lom Soi 2, Bang Rak ✉10500 ☎ 2352552
A friendly bar to relax from the noise of the soi. Karaoke.
Henry Club (B G S SNU)
8/10-11 Si Lom Soi 2, Bang Rak ✉10500 ☎ 6327223
Go go bar with open window front to sneak in.
J.J. Park (AC B f g YG) 21-3 h
8/3 Si Lom Soi 2, Bang Rak ✉10500 ☎ 2351227
Jupiter (AC B G MA S) 20-2 h
31/1-33 Surawong Road (Soi Thaniya 2), Bang Rak ✉10500 *(Next to Suriwong Hotel)* ☎ 2374050
Big bar with shows.

Krua Mama (B F G)
39/16 Soi Rajanakarindra 1 (Soi Anuman Rajadhon) Surawong Road, Bang Rak ✉10500 *(Off Si Lom Soi 6, off Soi Than Thawan)*
Karaoke and restaurant mainly for Thais.

My Way (AC B G S VS) 16-1, Sat Sun 13-1 h
944/4 Rama IV Road, Bang Rak ✉10500 *(in small sub-soi off Rama IV Road between Si Lom Road and Suriwong Road)*
☎ 2339567
One of the oldest go go bars in Bangkok. Small and intimate place.

P.M. Karaoke (B F G)
39/19 Soi Rajanakarindra 1 (Soi Anuman Rajadhon) Surawong Road, Bang Rak ✉10500 *(Off Si Lom Soi 6, off Soi Than Thawan)*
Karaoke and restaurant mainly for Thais.

Sanctuary Bar (B G)
34/17 Soi Si Bumphen, Sathorn ✉10500 *(Near Malaysia Hotel)*
☎ 2871670
Nice little outside bar.

Screw Boy (AC B G S SNU W) 20-2 h
Patpong 2 Road, 37/3-17 Surawong Road, Bang Rak ✉10500 *(Next to Pink Panther, opposite KFC)* ☎ 01/6555055 (Mobile)
The only gay go go bar directly on Patpong among hundreds of straight places.

Sphinx (B F G) 18-2 h
100 Si Lom Soi 4 (Soi Jaruwan), Bang Rak ✉10500
☎ 2347249
Good food and friendly staff. The place for a dinner with your friend. Upstairs Pharaoh's Karaoke.

Super Lex Matsuda (AC B CC f G MA OS S SNU TV VS) 20-2 h
39/14-16 Soi Rajanakarinda 1 (Soi Anuman Rajadhon), Surawong Road, Bang Rak ✉10500 *(Off Si Lom 6, off Soi Than Thawan)*
☎ 2361633
Go-go bar with popular shows and outdoor seating.

Tawan Club (The Sun) (! AC B G lj msg NU S SNU VS WO) 20.30-2 h
2/2 Soi Than Thawan, Surawong Road, Bang Rak ✉10500 *(Corner of Surawong Road, Si Lom Soi 6)* ☎ 2345506
Muscles, muscles and more muscles. One of the oldest and best maintained bars in Bangkok. Exciting shows.

Telephone Pub (! AC B F G MA OS) 19-2 h
114/11-13 Si Lom Soi 4 (Soi Jaruwan), Bang Rak ✉10500
☎ 2343279
Wait for a call or call up a new friend from the telephone on your table. Excellent food (Thai and Western). Probably the most famous gay pub in Bangkok. Completely renovated.

Tomahawk Bar (AC B G S SNU)
7/3 Soi Than Thawan, Surawong Road, Bang Rak ✉10500 *(Corner of Surawong Road, Si Lom Soi 6)* ☎ 2362865
Go go bar in high-tech style and very cute and friendly staff.

Top Man Bar (AC B CC G MA S VS W) 20-2 h
8/9 Si Lom Soi 2, Bang Rak ✉10500 *(2nd floor)* ☎ 6328934
Go go bar.

Twilight Bar (AC B G S VS) 19.30-2 h
Duangthawee Plaza, 38/40 Soi Pratoochai, at 38 Surawong Road, Bang Rak ✉10500 ☎ 2361944
Go go bar with special shows every night.

Up2 Bar (B G OS S SNU) 20.30-2 h
928-930 Rama IV Road, Bang Rak ✉10500 ☎ 2353876
Go go bar in a backyard.
Most shows include muscle men, bodypainting, candle shows.

CAFÉS

Banana Café (B F G OS)
Duangthawee Plaza, 894/14-15 Soi Pratoochai, at 38 Surawong Road, Bang Rak ✉10500
Open air bar and restaurant.

Dick's Café (! B F G) 11-5 h
Duangthawee Plaza, 894/7-8 Soi Pratoochai, at 38 Surawong Road, Bang Rak ✉10500 ☎ 6370078
The pleasant coffee oasis directly in the heart of the gay scene. Excellent cappuccino and beautiful ambience. You will meet nice people all day, all night. They also have Thai food, sandwiches and cake.

Grace Café (B F G) 10.30-15, Dinner 17-2 h
942/51 A. Charn Isara Building 1, Rama IV Road, Bang Rak ✉10500 ☎ 2672099
Gay owned café and restaurant.

DANCECLUBS

Bank Studio (B D G) 20-? h
39-39/1 Soi Rajanakarindra 1 (Soi Anuman Rajadhon) Surawong Road, Bang Rak ✉10500 *(Off Si Lom Soi 6, off Soi Than Thawan)*
☎ 2366383
Everybody meets here afterhours.

diSco Disco (B D G)
8/12-13 Si Lom Soi 2, Bang Rak ✉10500 ☎ 2346151
Bar and disco. The Thai alternative to DJ Station.

D.J. Station (! AC B D G MA S VS) 22.30-3 h
8/6-8 Si Lom Road, Soi 2, Bang Rak ✉10500 ☎ 2664029
Best and most popular gay disco in Southeast Asia! Three floors packed crowded every night. Every night at midnight show with Puppet String and famous Miguel!

Freeman Dance Arena (! AC B CC D DR G MA OS S STV) 22-3 h
60/18-21 Si Lom Road, Bang Rak ✉10500 *(Small soi between Thanya Road and Si Lom Soi 2, opposite Si Lom complex. Sky train: Saladang)* ☎ 6328032
Bangkok's pleasant new gay disco with excellent shows and darkroom on the top floor. Cheerful crowd every night.

Peppermint (B D g TV)
Patpong 1 Road, Bang Rak ✉10500
After hour night spot that draws a very mixed crowd. More women than men, but not every woman is a woman! Go there after 3h.

RESTAURANTS

Mali (F glm)
43 South Sathorn Soi 1 (Soi Atthakan Prasit), Sathorn ✉10120 ☎ 6798693 ☎ 2867311 ext. 171
Thai and international cuisine.

Mango Tree (F glm OS)
37 Soi Rajanakarindra 1 (Soi Anuman Rajadhon) Surawong Road, Bang Rak ✉10500 *(Off Si Lom Soi 6, off Soi Than Thawan)* ☎ 2362820
Traditional Thai restaurant in a beautiful mango tree yard. Sometimes Thai live music.

Pi Lek (F glm OS)
39/13 Soi Rajanakarindra 1 (Soi Anuman Rajadhon) Surawong Road, Bang Rak ✉10500 *(Off Si Lom Soi 6, off Soi Than Thawan)* ☎ 2361636
Eat simple food outdoors and see the most colourful crowd.

Via Convent (F glm) 11.30-14, 18-23 h, Sat, Sun + Holiday dinner only
1 Convent Road, Bang Rak ✉10500 ☎ 2667162
One of the finest restaurants in the heart of Bangkok's night life. Italian and international food. And be sure, here they cook the spaghetti al dente, the steak rare or medium.

SAUNAS/BATHS

Babylon 2000. The (! AC b CC DR F G MA OS pi s sa sb wh WO) 12-24 h
34 Soi Nantha, South Sathorn Soi 1 (Soi Atthakan Prasit), Sathorn ✉10120 *(Moved 200 m down the soi)* ☎ 6797985
Bangkok's world famous and most popular sauna bath moves in the new millenium 200 meters down the soi to a new location with pool and hotel.

C.O.A. City of Angels (AC b CC DR F G MA sa sb VS WO) 15-23, Fri, Sat, Holiday 14-24 h
Si Lom Center Building, (Robinson Si Lom), Bang Rak ✉10500 *(17th floor, lift on the right side of Robinson Department Store)* ☎ 6328027
Sauna, gym, stream room, fitness room, restaurant and recreation centre for men only.

Heaven Sauna (AC B DR F G MA msg OS sa sb T VS WO) 15-23 h
Warner Building, 4th floor, 119 Soi Mahesak, Bang Rak ✉10500 *(Between Si Lom Soi 32 and 34)* ☎ 2669092
Gym, sauna, steam, roof garden, restaurant, massage, jacuzzi, video, darkroom.

K-Why (b CC DR F G MA S sa sb VS WO) Mon-Thu 16-23, Fri-Sun 16-24 h
942/51 A. Charn Isara Building 1, Rama IV Road, Bang Rak ✉10500 *(1st floor, behind Grace Café)* ☎ 2672098 ☎ 2672099

Sauna Asia (b G sa sb WO)
Tarntawan Place Hotel, 119/5-10 Surawong Road, Bang Rak ✉10500 *(between Patpong 1 and Soi Than Thawan)* ☎ 2362929
New sauna in the heart of the gay night life. Steam, sauna, gym, cabins, restaurant, bar.

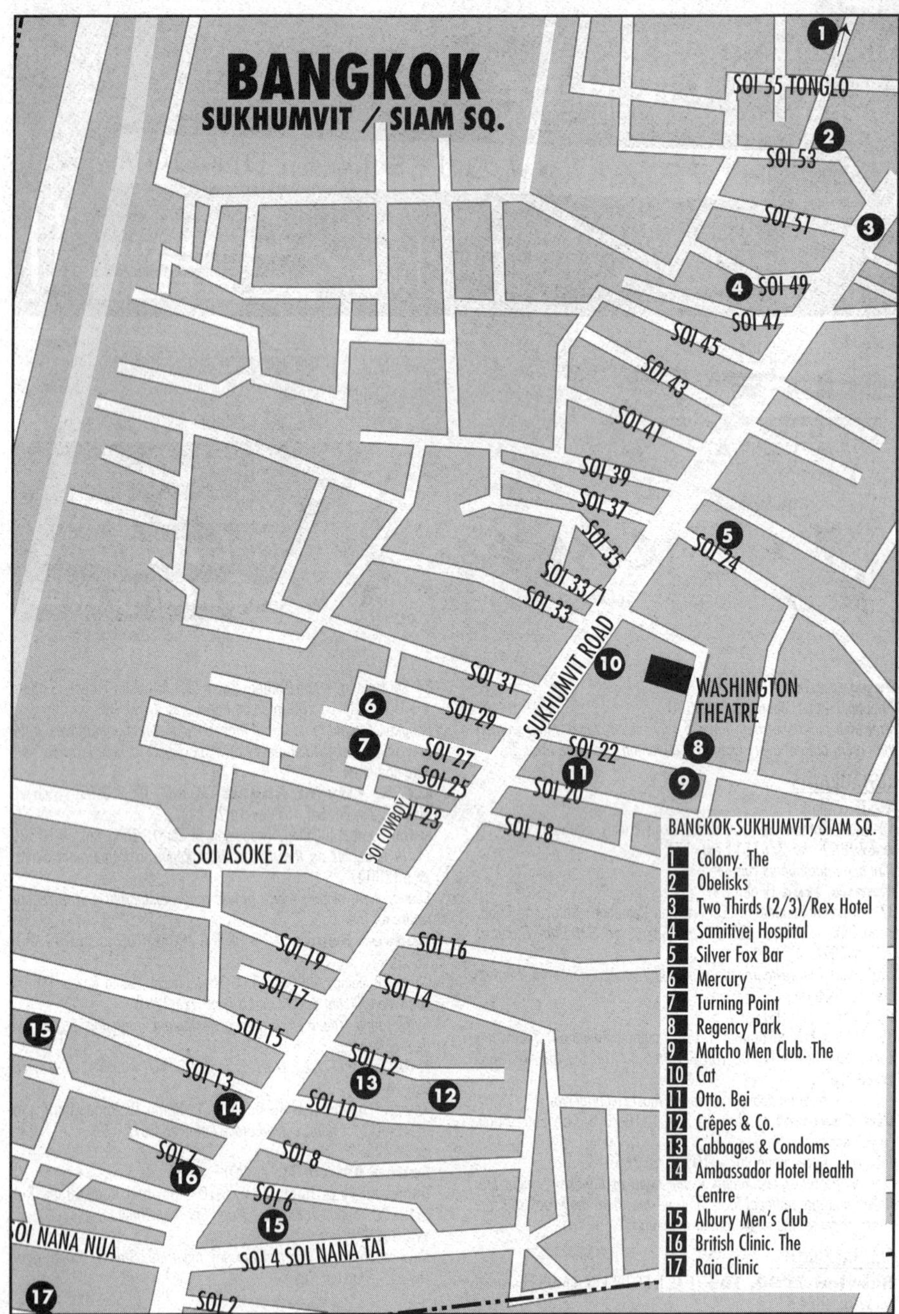
BANGKOK
SUKHUMVIT / SIAM SQ.
SOI 55 TONGLO
SOI 53
SOI 51
SOI 49
SOI 47
SOI 45
SOI 43
SOI 41
SOI 39
SOI 37
SOI 35
SOI 33/1
SOI 33
SOI 24
SUKHUMVIT ROAD
WASHINGTON THEATRE
SOI 31
SOI 29
SOI 27
SOI 25
SOI 23
SOI 22
SOI 20
SOI 18
SOI COWBOY
SOI ASOKE 21
SOI 19
SOI 17
SOI 16
SOI 14
SOI 15
SOI 13
SOI 12
SOI 10
SOI 8
SOI 7
SOI 6
SOI NANA NUA
SOI 4 SOI NANA TAI
SOI 2
BANGKOK-SUKHUMVIT/SIAM SQ.
1 Colony. The
2 Obelisks
3 Two Thirds (2/3)/Rex Hotel
4 Samitivej Hospital
5 Silver Fox Bar
6 Mercury
7 Turning Point
8 Regency Park
9 Matcho Men Club. The
10 Cat
11 Otto. Bei
12 Crêpes & Co.
13 Cabbages & Condoms
14 Ambassador Hotel Health Centre
15 Albury Men's Club
16 British Clinic. The
17 Raja Clinic

MASSAGE

Eden (G msg)
Warner Building, 4th floor, 119 Soi Mahesak, Between Si Lom Soi 32 and 34, Bang Rak ✉10500 ☎ 6359017
Homepage: http://www.heaven-eden.com
Oil and other special massages.

Eve House (glm msg)
18-18/1 Surawong Road, Bang Rak ✉10500 ☎ 2663846 ☎ 2663847
Traditional Thai Massage.

HIS (G msg) 12-24 h
Si Lom Plaza, 2nd floor, 491/10-11 Si Lom Soi 9, Bang Rak ✉10500 ☎ 2340063
Oil and cream massage, body scrub.

BODY & BEAUTY SHOPS

Cutey and Beauty (AC CC g) 11-20 h
Robinson Department Store, 5th floor, Si Lom Road, corner of Rama IV Road, Bang Rak ✉10500 ☎ 2358538
Hair designer. Speciality: Face Massage with oxygen. Staff trained with Vidal Sassoon and Toni + Guy in London. Gay owned and operated.

TRAVEL & TRANSPORT

Utopia Tours (GLM) 10-18 h
Tarntawan Place Hotel, 119/5-10 Surawong Road, Bang Rak ✉10500 *(between Patpong 1 and Soi Than Thawan)*
☎ 2383227 E-Mail: info@utopia-tours.com
Homepage: http://www.utopia-tours.com
Asia's gay travel pioneers. They will arrange your stay in Thailand and your tour to other Asian countries. Go there for information on the gay scenes.

HOTELS

Most of the hotels in Bangkok are gay friendly and there normally is no problem to bring your friend(s) upstairs. Many hotels are concerned for your security and will hold your visitor's ID Card during his stay. Only few luxury hotels have extra charge.

Babylon Barrack (AC b bf CC F G H MA pi)
34 Soi Nantha, South Sathorn Soi 1 (Soi Atthakan Prasit), Sathorn ✉10120 ☎ 6797985 Fax: 6797986
Homepage: http://www.babylonbangkok.com
New gay hotel. 40 rooms from 800 Baht/day. Same building as the new Babylon Sauna.

Malaysia Hotel (B F g H pi)
54 Soi Ngam Duphli, Rama IV Road, Sathorn ✉10120 *(Yannawa)* ☎ 6797127 ☎ 6797136 Fax: 2871457
E-Mail: malaysia@ksc15.th.com
Homepage: http://ksc15.co.th/malaysia
Located near the famous Babylon sauna and close to the gay nightlife, this budget friendly hotel is most popular among gay travellers.

Pinnacle Hotel Lumpine (bf H glm)
17 Soi Ngam Duphli, Rama IV Road, Sathorn ✉10120 ☎ 2870111 ☎ 2870131 Fax: 2873420 E-Mail: pinhl@loxinfo.co.th
Homepage: http://www.pinnaclehotels.com
Mixed hotel but gay friendly and close to the gay night life.

Rio Residence (AC b F g H MA sa sol wo)
88/2-3 Nanglinchi Road/Chan Road ✉10500 *(Tungmahamek Yannawa)* ☎ 2870041 Fax: 2873190
Comfortable hotel.

Tarntawan Place (! AC B bf CC F GLM H msg)
119/5-10 Surawong Road, Bang Rak ✉10500 ☎ 2382620 ☎ 2383228 E-Mail: tarntawan@tarntawan.com
Homepage: http://www.tarntawan.com
Bangkok's best gay hotel in the heart of the gay night life. Among many other services the Tarntawan offers 24 hour Business centre, lobby lounge and bar, safe deposit boxes, meeting rooms, karaoke, internet - e-mail access, tour desk and the gay travel agency Utopia Tours. Special discount rates for Spartacus Readers!

Tower Inn Hotel (g H pi sa wh WO)
533 Si Lom Road, Bang Rak ✉10500 ☎ 2378300 ☎ 2378304 Fax: 2378386
E-Mail: towerinn@bkk.a-net.net.th

GUEST HOUSES

Aquarius Guest-House (AC B bf CC F G H MA OS VS)
Bar open 19-1 h
243 Soi Hutayana, South Satorn Soi 3 (Soi Suanplu), Sathorn ✉10120 *(off South Satorn Road)* ☎ 2860217 ☎ 6793180
Fax: 2862174 E-Mail: aquarius@bangkok.com
Homepage: http://bangkok.com/mypage/aquarius
Gay guest house in residential area in a converted cosy house with garden. The nice owner speaks English.

Win's Guesthouse (AC B bf G H MA msg)
21/8501 Soi Ngam Dupli, Thanon Rama IV ✉10120 *(Sathorn)* ☎ 287-1435
14 double rooms , shared showers and WC. Good breakfasts not included in room rate. No hot meals.

GENERAL GROUPS

Long Yang Club Thailand (LYC)
P.O. Box 1077, Si Lom ✉10504 ☎ 867311 Ext. 125
E-Mail: thailand@longyangclub.org
Homepage: http://www.longyangclub.org/thailand

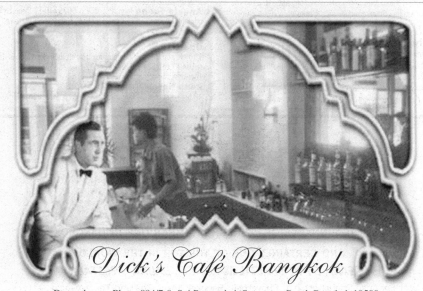

HEALTH GROUPS

Anonymous Clinic, Thai Red Cross Society
Mon-Fri 12-19, Sat 9-12 h
1871 Rama IV Road, Bang Rak ✉10500 *(At the Saowapha Institute, the Snake Farm)* ☎ 2564109
Anonymous HIV testing.

Surawong Medi-Clinic Mon-Fri 8.30-21, Sat 12-21 h
37/4-5 Surawong Road, Soi Surawong Plaza, Bang Rak ✉10500
HIV testing.

SWIMMING

-Malaysia Hotel (the hotel pool is open for public use for small fee and a favourite cruising place)

CRUISING

-Lumpini Park (6-20 h inside the Park, after dark around Rama IV monument. Corner of Rama IV/Si Lom Road. The most popular Bangkok cruising. Beware of hustlers)
-Robinson Department Store (Cruising around all entrances and toilets. Beware of hustlers)

Bangkok/Krung Thep - Siam

BARS

Planet Hollywood (B F glm) 11-2 h
Gaysorn Plaza, 999 Phloen Chit Road / Ratchadamri Road, Lumpini, Pathumwan ✉10330 ☎ 6561358
Mixed club and restaurant with excellent bands.

Saxophone (AC B CC F g MA) 18-3 h
3/8 Phayathai Road, Victory Monument, Phaya Thai ✉10400 *(at the Victory Monument, close to Mr. Donut and KFC)* ☎ 2465472
Beautiful pub with excellent life jazz & blues every night. Mixed.

SHOWS

Calypso Cabaret (B glm S STV) Shows at 20.15 and 21.45 h
Asia Hotel, 296 Phaya Thai Road, Pathumwan ✉10330 ☎ 2616355 (9-18 h) ☎ 2168937 (18-22 h)
Hundreds of tourists come with buses every night, only to find out, that the most beautiful women in Thailand are men.

SAUNAS/BATHS

Angelo Sauna (glm N sa sb VS) 1025/10-11 Ploenchit Road, Pathumwan ✉10330 ☎ 2529176 *Mainly for local crowd.*

HOTELS

Opera (glm H)
16 Petchburi 11 (Soi Somprasong 1) Petchburi Road, Phaya Thai ✉10400 ☎ 2524031 ☎ 2524032 Fax: 2535360
Popular within gays.

Reno Hotel (glm H)
40 Soi Kasem San 1, Rama 1, Pathumwan ✉10330 ☎ 2150026

OBELISKS SAUNA

Bangkok

Bangkok's most magnificent sauna in an 11 floor complex. Rich ornamental decorated in marble grand style. Super clean.

Nice restaurant, karaoke, well and modern equipped gym. Warm jacuzzi, steam bath, hot sauna, mysterious starry darkroom, video room and plenty of private rooms for your pleasure.

Roof top garden with refreshment bar, where you can enjoy the magnificent view over Bangkok, the roof jacuzzi and steam room in the midst of palm trees under the sky.

Imagine, how much you can enjoy! A place to meet hundreds of new friends in private and comfortable atmosphere.

Tel: (+66 2) 6 62 43 77, 6 62 43 78, Fax: 6 62 43 79

Open daily:	Mon – Fri 15.00 – 23.30 h
	Sat, Sun, Holiday 13.00 – 23.30 h
Admission:	Mon – Fri 200 Baht
	Sat, Sun, Holiday 220 Baht
Sky Train:	Thong Lor Station
For Taxi:	39/3-4 ถนน สุขุมวิท ซอย 53

Opening Hours
weekday 12.00-23.30 hrs
weekend 12.00-24.00 hrs

From mid 2000, **BABYLON** will move to an elegant new site.
More Facilities, Swimming Pool, & the **BABYLON** Barracks Hotel !

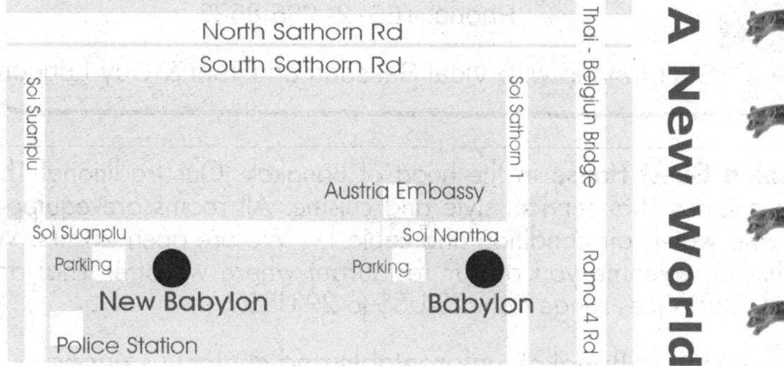

www.babylonbkk.com
info@babylonbkk.com

Tel : 213-2108, 679-8212
Office : 679-7985 Fax : 679-7986

CRUISING

National Stadium (P) (Rama 1 Road, Pathumwan)

Bangkok/Krung Thep - Sukhumvit Road ☎ 02

BARS

Mercury (B G MA msg)
116/1 Sukhumvit Soi 23 (Soi Prasan Mit), Khlong Toey ✉10110 *(2nd floor)* ☎ 6623021

Silver Fox (AC AYOR B G MA S TV VS) 12-1, happy hour 13-18.30 h
1/11 Sukhumvit Soi 24, Khlong Toey ✉10110 *(Behind Nimitr Restaurant)* ☎ 2585372

Turning Point (AC B CC d f G MA msg S sb STV) 20.30-2.30, show Fri Sat 23-23.30 h
120/19-20 Sukumvit Soi 23 (Soi Prasan Mit), Khlong Toey ✉10110 ☎ 6621103 ☎ 6621104
One of the finest host bars in town. Go there for karaoke and special entertainment. They have now steam bath and massage available.

Two Thirds (2/3) (B G H MA msg) 18-2 h
2/3 Sukhumvit Soi 34, Khlong Toey ✉10110 *(near Rex Hotel)* ☎ 2599619

RESTAURANTS

Bei Otto (AC B CC F glm) 12-1 h
1 Sukhumvit Soi 20, Khlong Toey ✉10110 *(Opposite Windsor Hotel)* ☎ 620892
Gay owned German restaurant, bakery and butcher.

Cabbages & Condoms (F glm MA) 11-22 h
10 Sukhumvit Soi 12, Khlong Toey ✉10110 *(Sky train: Asok. About 300 meters down the soi)* ☎ 2294610

Handycrafts & Thai restaurant. Eat and love safe: All the benefits from the restaurant will go to PDA (Population and Community Development Association).

Crêpes & Co (b F glm MA OS) 9-24 h
18/1 Sukhumvit Soi 12, Khlong Toey ✉10110 *(Sky train: Asok. About 400 meters down the soi)* ☎ 6533990
The only crêperie in Bangkok serving delicious brunch and dinner every day (more than 100 savoury & sweet different crêpes). Set up in an old Thai house and garden.

SAUNAS/BATHS

Cat (AC b F G MA msg sa sb) 15-24 h
450-452 Sukhumvit Road, Khlong Toey ✉10110 *(Between Soi 22 and 24, in the parkinglot of Washington Theatre)* ☎ 6634031
Small bar and sauna.

Colony. The (AC b DR F G MA msg OS pi sa sb wh WO VS) 15-? h
117 Soi Charoensuk, Soi Sukhumvit 55, Khlong Toey ✉10110 *(Off Sukhumvit Soi 55 (Soi Tonglor) and Sukhumvit 63 (Soi Ekamai))* ☎ 3914393
with restaurant in a cosy house with garden.

Obelisks. The (AC b CC DR F G MA OS sa sb VS wh WO) Mon-Fri 15-23.30, Sat, Sun, Holiday 13-23.30 h
39/3-4 Sukhumvit Soi 53, (Soi Bhai Dee Ma Dee), Khlong Toey ✉10110 *(Sky Train: Thong Lor)* ☎ 6624377
Eleven story luxury sauna with food, karaoke in a converted apartment building. Rich ornamental decorated marble style. Wonderful city view from the roof terrace

MASSAGE

Albury Men's Club (AC F G MA msg sb) 15-24 h
71/1 Sukhumvit Soi 11, Khlong Toey ✉10110 *(Close to the Ambassador Hotel. Sky train: Nana)* ☎ 2558920
Massage, gym, steam, restaurant, meeting place. One of the best and most famous places to relax your body.

Ambassador Hotel Health Centre (g msg) Mon-Fri 7-21, Sat Sun 9-21 h
171 Sukhumvit Road, Khlong Toey ✉10110 *(Near Soi 11)* ☎ 2540444
Massage with a bang. Ask for a man if you prefer.

Matcho Men Club. The (G msg) 15-24 h, 24 hour out service
316/18 Sukhumvit Soi 22, Soi Sainamthip, Khlong Toey ✉10110 ☎ 2597247
Oil massage for men by men.

BOOK SHOPS

Utopia 12-23 h
116/1 Sukhumvit 23, Khlong Toey ✉10110 ☎ 2599619
Gifts, books, magazines, gadgets, condoms etc.

HOTELS

☛ also Si Lom/Suriwong for comment.

Regency Park (AC g H pi)
12/3 Sukhumvit Soi 22, Soi Sainamthip, Khlong Toey ✉10110 ☎ 2597420 Fax: 2582862 E-Mail: utopia@best.com
Homepage: http://www.utopia-asia.com/acchotels.html
Utopia guest house. For discount booking send e-mail only.

Rex Hotel (bf g H)
762/1 Sukhumvit Road, Khlong Toey ✉10110 ☎ 2590106
All rooms have phone, fridge, bath, WC and balcony.

HEALTH GROUPS

British Clinic. The 8-12, 14-16, Sat 8-12 h
109 Sukhumvit Road, Khlong Toey ✉10110 *(between Soi 5 & 7)* ☎ 2528056 ☎ 2529179

Raja Clinic
6/20 Sukhumvit Soi 3/1, Khlong Toey ✉10110 *(North Nana)* ☎ 2535678

Samitivej Hospital
Sukhumvit Soi 49, Khlong Toey ✉10110 ☎ 3920911

Cha Am ☎ 032

HOTELS

Jolly & Jumper (glm H)
273/3 Ruamchit Road, Petchburi ✉76121 ☎ 433887
Fax: 433887
Country western guest house with steak house.

Novotel Gems (glm H)
251 Chao-Lai Road, Petchburi ✉76121 ☎ 434060 ☎ 434079
Fax: 434002 Homepage: http://www.hotelweb.fr

Regent Cha Am (glm H)
849/21 Petchkasem Road, Cha Am Beach, Petchburi ✉76120 ☎ 471480 ☎ 032/471486
Fax: 471491

Chiang Mai ☎ 053

This northern city was, for many centuries, the capital of an autonomous kingdom. Chiang Mai is very much smaller and quieter than the metropolis Bangkok. It is thus ideal for escaping the hectic life of the capital and the southern resorts. The old city walls are still intact in some places, and you will also find ancient temples, good shopping, beautiful scenery and excellent northern

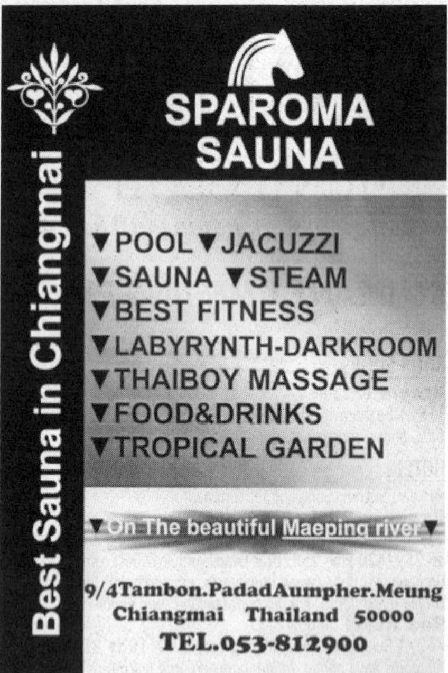

Thai cuisine. Despite an explosive increase in the number of gay bars two years ago, the gay scene in this city is still small. It reflects the culture and pace of the wider Chiang Mai community. Most bars look more like an extension of a living room: you sit on traditional cushions, enjoy a drink, talk, watch a show, all in an unhurried manner. All in all a unique experience, and well worth the journey.

Über viele Jahrhunderte war die nordthailändische Stadt die Hauptstadt eines autonomen Königreiches.
Chiang Mai ist sehr viel kleiner und stiller als die Metropole Bangkok. Es eignet sich hervorragend für's Ausspannen vom Trubel der Großstadt oder der südlichen Ferienorte.
Die Stadtmauern sind noch zum Teil intakt. Es gibt alte Tempel, eine schöne Landschaft, gute Einkaufsmöglicheiten und exzellente nordthailändische Küche.
Auch wenn es vor zwei Jahren eine regelrechte Explosion der Anzahl der schwulen Bars gab, ist die schwule Szene doch noch recht klein. Sie ist wie ein Spiegel der Stadt Stadt und ihrer Umgebung: Bars wirken eher wie eine Erweiterung des Wohnzimmers. Man sitzt auf traditionellen Kissen, geniesst einen Drink, unterhält sich, betrachtet die Show. Und das alles auf äußerst ruhige Weise. Alles in allem ein einzigartiges Erlebnis, das die Reise wert ist.

Située dans le nord du pays, Chiang Mai est l'ancienne capitale du royaume. Tout y est beaucoup plus calme qu'à Bangkok. C'est donc un endroit idéal pour souffler après le stress de la capitale ou l'agitation des stations balnéaires du sud.
Fortifications encore intactes, temples magnifiques, paradis du shopping, paysages splendides, cuisine excellente: tout y est! En revanche, encore peu de lieux gays, même après le boom des dernières années. Les bars gays sont souvent une sorte de prolongement de la salle de séjour du propriétaire. Assis sur des coussins, on sirote une boisson en papotant ou en regardant un show. Tout cela dans une ambiance bon enfant! Rien que pour ça, Chiang Mai vaut le détour!

Esta ciudad norteña fue durante muchos siglos la capital de un reinado autónomo. Chiang-Mai es mucho más pequeña y tranquila que Bangkok. Chiang Mai es una excelente alternativa a Bangkok o a los centros turisticos del Norte del país. La muralla de la ciudad se encuentra casi intacta. Hay templos, buenas posibilidades para ir de compras, un lindo paisaje y la excelencia de la cocina tailandesa norteña. A pesar de que hace dos años hubo una explosión de bares gay, el ambiente homosexual es pequeño, es el reflejo de la ciudad y sus alrededores. La mayoría de los bares son como una extensión de una sala de estar. Aquí te sentarás sobre almohadones, beberás algo, hablarás con alguien, observarás el ambiente y disfrutarás del show de una forma muy amena. Es una experiencia que vale la pena vivir.

Questa città del nord è stata per molti anni la capitale di un regno indipendente. Chiang Mai è molto più piccola e calma di Bangkok; è un ideale punto intermedio tra la frenetica Bangkok e le stazioni balneari del sud. Le mura della città si sono in parte conservute, vi sono vecchi templi da visitare, altrimenti si possono fare compere, visitare la campagna circostante o gustare l'eccellente cucina tailandese. L'ambiente gay è ancora ristretto, malgrado il boom di due anni fa che ora sta svanendo. L'ambiente gay riflette la cultura di tutti i giorni di questa regione: la maggior parte dei bar ha un aspetto casereccio, sembrano essere il soggiorno dell'abitazione del proprietario. Ci si siede su tradizionali cuscini, si beve qualcosa si chiacchera e si guarda uno spettacolo in tranquilla compagnia piacevole. Questa simpatica singolarità è per sè un buon motivo per fare il viaggio.

BARS

Adam's Apple (AC B F G MA msg S SNU STV VS) 22-1.30, show 23.30 h
1/21-22 Soi Viengbua, Chotana Road, Chang Peuak ✉50300 *(Opposite Lotus Hotel)* ☎ 220380
Go go bar.

Circle Pub (AC B G MA S) 20-2 h
161/7-8 Soi Erawan, Chang Phuek Road, Chang Peuak ✉50300 ☎ 214996

Coffee Boy. The (B G MA S) 20-2 h
248 Thung Hotel Road, Amphur Muang ✉50000 *(Soi to Chiang Mai Arcade)* ☎ 244458
Located in a beautiful ancient teak house.

Fan Club (B G) 19-1 h
161/108 Soi Chang Phuak 4, Amphur Muang ✉50000 *(opposite Bus Station 1)* ☎ 01/9567807 (Mobile)

Jungle Bar (B G) 20-1 h
Night Bazaar, Chang Klan Road, Chang Klan ✉50100

Macho (AC B G MA S) 20-2, Show at 22 h
8 Nantharam Soi 1, Hay-Ya, Amphur Muang ✉50000 *(opposite Wat Taht Kam)* ☎ 200904
Go go bar with cabaret show located in ancient teak home.

Man's Bar. A (B G) 20-24 h
Night Bazaar, Chang Klan Road, Chang Klan ✉50100 ☎ 01/6022551 (Mobile)

Marlboro Bar (B G) 18-1 h
Night Bazaar, Chang Klan Road, Chang Klan ✉50100 *(North side of Night Market)*

My Way (AC B G MA S) 20-1 h
3/5-6 Hatsadee Sewee Road, Chang Peuak ✉50300 ☎ 404361

New Lanterns' (B G MA OS S) 25/1 Rajchiangsaen Road Soi 2, Amphur Muang ✉50000 ☎ 271022
Go go bar and escort.

69 (B G) 20-1h
Night Bazaar, Chang Klan Road, Chang Klan ✉50100

DANCECLUBS

Bubble Disco (B D glm)
c/o Porn Ping Hotel, 46-48 Charoen Prathet Road, Chang Klan ✉50100 *(located near the river and the Night Bazaar)* ☎ 270099
Popular disco for gays and straights.

RESTAURANTS

Fascination (B F g S STV)
99 Suthep Road, Amphur Muang ✉50000 ☎ 810549
Has also cabaret shows.

Gallery. The (B F glm) 12-24 h
25-27 Jaremsrad Road, Amphur Muang ✉50000 *(On the River)* ☎ 248601 ☎ 248602

Garden Bar (B F g MA N OS W) 19h till late
2/25 Soi Viengbua, Chotana Road, Chang Peuak ✉50300 ☎ 215462 ☎ 215376

Gi-Gi (B F glm MA)
Lampoon Road, Amphur Muang ✉50000
Kruatek style, loud music, people tend to dance around the tables and Thai food can be ordered.

Grand Canyon (F glm)
Kad Sua Kaew Shopping Complex, 2nd floor, Huay Kaew Road, Amphur Muang ✉50000

J. J. Restaurant & Bakery. The (F glm OS) Shows at 23 h.
Montri Hotel, 2-6 Ragdammen Road, Chang Klan ✉50100 *(Opposite Tapae Gate)* ☎ 211069 ☎ 211070

Riverside (F glm)
9/11 Jaroenrat Road, at Nakhorn Ping Bridge, Amphur Muang ✉50000 ☎ 243239

Romantic Restaurant & Pub (AC B CC F G MA W) 19.30 h till late
1/21-22 Soi Viengbua, Chotana Road, Chang Peuak ✉50300 ☎ 220380 ☎ 220381

Swai Riang (F glm) Soi 8 Chiang Mai - Lampoon Road, Saraphi, Amphur Muang ✉50000 ☎ 322061
Gay owned and operated.

Tha-Nam (B F glm)
River Front, Amphur Muang ✉50000 ☎ 275125
Northern Thai cuisine. Mixed.

SAUNAS/BATHS

House of Male (B CC DR F G MA msg OS pi sb VS W WO) 12-24 h
19 Sirimangklajarn Road Soi 3, Tambol Suthep, Amphur Muang ✉50200 *(last house in the soi)* ☎ 894133

Sparoma Sauna. The (DR F G MA msg pi sa sb wh WO) 15-23 h
Silversand House, 100/25 Super Highway Road, Tambon, Fahum, Amphur Muang ✉50000 *(7th floor. Near Wat Padadd)* ☎ 812900
Sauna, steam, gym, restaurant, massage and nice balcony with view over Chiang Mai. Fun and friendly place.

HOTELS

Cherry House (AC b F G H MA msg sol)
21/7-8 Soi Ratchapruk, Huay Kaew Road, Amphur Muang ✉50000 ☎ 215207 Fax: 405244
E-Mail: servmind@chmai.loxinfo.co.th
Gay hotel. Rooms from 750 Baht, suites from 1,200 Baht. No charge for overnight guests. Massage possible. All rooms with shower/WC, balcony or terrace, telephone, Satellite TV, minibar, air-conditioning.

Coffee Boy Cottages (G H)
248 Toonghotel Road, Amphur Muang ✉50000 ☎ 247021
Fax: 247021

Lotus Hotel (AC B bf CC G H MA msg OS)
2/25 Soi Viengbua, Chotana Road, Chang Peuak ✉50300 ☎ 215376 Fax: 221340 E-Mail: mohamad@loxinfo.co.th
Homepage: http://www.angelfire.com/biz/lotushotel
One of the first gay hotel of Chiang Mai, located close to the bars in the north and part of the largest gay complex in the city. Rooms have bathroom, TV, fridge, mini bar. Rates about 800 Baht/night. The bar is the only streetside gay bar in Chiang Mai. Same management as Adam's Apple.

GUEST HOUSES

New Connection (AC B bf d F G H MA msg OS s) Restaurant 17-24, Pub 16-2 h
155 Rajmanraka Road, Phrasing Road, Amphur Muang ✉50200 *(Near Felix City Inn Hotel)* ☎ 276161 ☎ 814123
E-Mail: connection-cnx@gmx.net
Guest house, bar and restaurant. Room rates 150 - 490 Baht. Gay taxi service, pick up from airport or railway station.

CRUISING

-Taepae Gate (r, after 21 h)
-Narawat Bridge (evenings)
-Park opposite market near Post office
-Nong Buak Hat Park
-Huay Kaew Waterfall (daytime)
-Huay Kaew recreational park (Arboretum near zoo, Huay Kaew road opposite police station, evenings)
-Railway station (park in front)
-Bus station
-Fitness Park Chamgmai University International Centre (Nimmanhemmin Road, evenings)

Chiang Rai ☎ 053

BARS

Lobo Boy Boy (B g S)
528/25 Thaiwiwat-U-Thid Road, Amphur Muang ✉57000
☎ 752516

Hat Yai ☎ 074

BARS

Buddy Pub (B F G msg S) 11-2 h
37/2 Sriphuvanart Road, Song Khla ✉90110
☎ 420944
Go go boys, massage, food and drinks.
Jacks Pub. The (B G S)
Soi 16 Rath-U-Thit, Pracha-U-Thit Road, Song Khla ✉90110
☎ 425408

DANCECLUBS

Dance Zone (B D glm)
92/11 Petchakasem Road, Song Khla ✉90110
☎ 365876

HOTELS

Hansa Hotel and Café (B bf glm H)
361 Sutti Hansa Road, Song Khla ✉90110
☎ 359601 ☎ 359603

Hua Hin ☎ 032

BARS

Boys Red Indian. The (B G)
Hua Hin Bazar, Prachuapkhirikhan ✉77110 *(opposite Hotel Sofitel)*
☎ 01/8472673 (Mobile)
Doi Boy Cabaret (B G S)
53-54 Am Nuoi Sin Road, Soi Tana Vit Condo, Prachuapkhirikhan ✉77110 ☎ 515782
Guys Bar (B G)
58 Amnuay Sin Road, Prachuapkhirikhan ✉77110 *(opposite Supmitra Hotel)*
☎ 530170

DANCECLUBS

Doodle's Disco (B D g)
Melia Hotel, 33/3 Naretdamri Road, Prachuapkhirikhan ✉77110
Hua Hin Grand Disco (B D g)
Hua Hin Grand Hotel, 22272 Petchakasem Road, Prachuapkhirikhan ✉77110
Voice (B D g)
Hua Hin Grand Hotel, Prachuapkhirikhan ✉77110

RESTAURANTS

Muay Thai Gardens (F g)
Poonsak Road, Prachuapkhirikhan ✉77110

HOTELS

Mechai Hotel (H g)
57/2 Phetkasem Road, Prachuapkhirikhan ✉77110 *(Facing Chatchai Market)* ☎ 511035
Melia (g H)
33 Naresdamri Road, Prachuapkhirikhan ✉77110
☎ 511612 ☎ 511614 Fax: 511135
Sofitel Central (G H)
1 Damnernkasern Road, Prachuapkhirikhan ✉77110
☎ 512021 ☎ 512038 Fax: 511014

GUEST HOUSES

All Nations (B F glm H)
10/1 Deachanuchit Road, Prachuapkhirikhan ✉77110
☎ 512747 Fax: 530474
Ken Diamond Travel & Parichart Guesthouse (CC G H MA) Travel office: 9-22 h
162/6 Naresdamri Road, Prachuapkhirikhan ✉77110 *(150 m from the beach)* ☎ 513863 ☎ 513870 Fax: 513863
E-Mail: soe@prachuab.a-net.net.th
Rooms: Fan 150 Baht/night, 2000 Baht/month, AC: 300 Baht/night, 4500 Baht/month. Toilet and shower inside the rooms. Gay owned and operated.
Pattana (b bf F glm H MA OS W)
52 Naretdamri Road, Prachuapkhirikhan ✉77110 *(close to beach and centre)* ☎ 513393 Fax: 530081
Rates around 300 Baht.

CRUISING

-Monkey Temple

Koh Samui ☎ 077

BARS

Big Fun (B G)
Off Chaweng Beach Road, next to Oriental Gallery, Surat Thani ✉84320
Cage. La (B F f g MA N OS) 17-2.30 h
Chaweng Beach Road, next to Green Mango, Surat Thani ✉84320
Pub and restaurant. Mixed, but gay owned and operated. Music, buffet and couscous.
Christie's (B glm OS S STV)
Chaweng Beach Road, opposite Centre Point, Surat Thani ✉84320
(next to Roxy Bar)
Mixed outside bar with drag shows.
Free Way (B G)
Chaweng Beach Road, Centre Point, Surat Thani ✉84320 *(Next to Kelly's)*
Kelly's (B f lj MA N OS) 17-2 h
166/33 Chaweng Beach Road, Centre Point, Surat Thani ✉84320
(Behind Polmburger)
Friendly gay place. A good starting point to get information about the city's venues..
Palladium Boys Town (B G S)
166/21 Moo 2, Chaweng Beach Road, Centre Point, Surat Thani ✉84320 ☎ 413130
Roxy Bar (B G) Chaweng Beach Road, opposite Centre Point, Surat Thani ✉84320 *(besides Christie's)*

DANCECLUBS

Green Mango (B D glm)
Chaweng Beach Road, at the end of the Soi next to Centre Point, Surat Thani ✉84320

RESTAURANTS

Ban Thai Sea Food (F g)
Chaweng Beach Road, Surat Thani ✉84320
Chai Thalee Seafood (F g)
440/1 Thanon Maret, Surat Thani ✉84320 *(on the main road, after Lamai, before Hua Thanon)*
☎ 233267 ☎ 233350
Oriental Gallery/Upstairs (A B F g) 14-1 h
39/1 Moo 3, Bophut, Surat Thani ✉84320
☎ 422200☎ 230746
Asian arts, restaurant and music lounge.

TRAVEL & TRANSPORT

D. J. Paradise Tour (CC) Mon-Sat 12-20 h
Papillon Resort, 1&2 Chaweng Beach Road, Surat Thani ✉84320 *(at the very north end of Chaweng Beach)* ☎ 231169 ☎ 01/9826372 (Mobile) Fax: 231169 E-Mail: djparadi@samart.co.th
Homepage: http://www.djparadisetour.com
Gay owned and operated. Go there for information. Tours, hotel reservations, ticketing, diving excursions.

Saai Travel Service
124/1 Chaweng Beach Road, Surat Thani ✉84320
☎ 230477

HOTELS

Baan Samui Resort (E g H)
Chaweng Beach, Surat Thani ✉84320 ☎ 422415 Fax: 422412
Mixed and expensive.

Central Samui Hotel (g H)
38/2 Moo 3, Bor Phud, Chaweng Beach, Surat Thani ✉84320
☎ 230500

Long Island Resort (g H)
24/2 Moo 4, Lamai Beach, Surat Thani ✉84320 ☎ 424202

Montien House (g H)
5 Moo 2, Chaweng Beach, Surat Thani ✉84320 ☎ 422169
Fax: 422145

Papillon Resort (AC B bf CC F g H MA OS pi wh) 6-24 h
1 & 2 Chaweng Beach Road, Surat Thani ✉84320 *(at the very north end of Chaweng Beach)* ☎ 231169 Fax: 231169
E-Mail: djparadi@samart.co.th
Bungalow resort with new pool and French restaurant, bar, dive center, travel agency. Gay managed. No problem to bring your friend to your room. 20 bungalows with AC, mini bar, sat TV, video channel, shower, WC, phone. Rates: Low season from 1,490 Baht to 2,990 Baht, high season 2,000 Baht to 3,490 Baht.

SWIMMING

-Chaweng Beach
-Volley ball games (beach behind Christie's)

Lopburi ☎ 036

HOTELS

Lopburi Tai Pei Hotel (g H)
24/6-7 Surasangkram Road, Amphur Muang, ✉15000
☎ 411524

Nong Khai ☎ 042

GUEST HOUSES

Isan Orchid Guest Lodge (AC B bf G H MA msg)
87/9 Gaowarawud Road, Thabo ✉43110 *(the lodge is in a small soi difficult to locate. Take a Tuk-Tuk and ask for „Ban Farang Yai" (the big house of the western foreigner). Public buses to Thabo from Udon Thani (75 km) or Nongkhai (25 km). The guest house arranges your transport from the airport at Udon Thani or from the train at Nong Khai.)* ☎ 431665 ☎ 01/6474113 (Mobile)
Fax: 431665 E-Mail: isnorchd@nk.ksc.co.th
Bed 'n' Breakfast at „the gateway to Indo China" on the Mehkong River, across from Vientiane, Laos. Experience Thailand as it was before the tourist boom in a farming community. Prehistoric park, archaeological site. Rates: 1,200-1,300 Baht. English outside the hotel not spoken. Bar „Black & White".

Pattaya ☎ 038

● During the Vietnam War, this formerly sleepy fishing village (about two hours drive from Bangkok) was transformed into an American base providing GI's with rest and recreation before returning to combat. This past has somewhat tarnished its reputation somewhat but Pattaya has now developed into an international resort of considerable charm, particularly for gays. Foreign and local venue owners in Pattaya go to great lengths to augment the standards of gay entertainment and accommodation. The main gay section is concentrated in a small but lively area of South Pattaya which should not be left out. Pattaya is famous for its drag acts, which are particularly popular with straight tourists.

✱ Zwei Stunden von Bangkok entfernt befindet sich dieses ehemalige Fischerdorf, daß sich während des Vietnam-Krieges überraschend in ein Erholungszentrum der US-Amerikaner verwandelt sah. Die Vergangenheit hat den Ruf dieser Stadt etwas ramponiert (unter anderem auch, weil der vordere Strand wegen der Verschmutzung nicht benutzbar ist). Doch inzwischen ist Pattaya ein internationaler Urlaubsort von ganz beträchtlichem Charme, besonders für Schwule. Die ausländischen und heimatlichen Barbesitzer geben sich große Mühe, den Standard schwuler Unterhaltung und Unterbringung anzuheben.
In einem kleinem, aber lebhaften Gebiet Süd-Pattayas findet sich das Zentrum schwulen Lebens. Aber auch eine kleinere Zahl von guten Bars im Norden der Stadt sollte nicht ausgelassen werden. Pattaya wurden durch seine Travestie-Shows bekannte. Sie sind besonders bei Hetero-Touristen sehr beliebt.

▲ Pendant la guerre du Vietnam, cet ancien petit port de pêche (à environ deux heures de Bangkok) était une base américaine où se „reposaient" les GI's avant de retrouver au combat. La réputation de la ville en a beaucoup souffert. Après la guerre, la saleté de ses plages n'a pas aider à améliorer cette image. Aujourd'hui Pattaya est une station balnéaire de réputation internationale, particulièrement appréciée des gays. Les propriétaires d'établissements thaïlandais et étrangers ont particulièrement travaillé à améliorer la qualité en matière de divertissement et d'hébergement. Le quartier gay se trouve dans le sud de la ville, mais le nord a aussi quelques endroits intéressants à offrir. Pattaya est particulièrement réputée pour ses spectacles de transformisme dont raffolent les hétéros.

☆ Este antiguo pueblo pesquera se convirtió en un centro de descansa para Norteamericanos durante la guerra de Vietnam. Se encuentra a dos horas de viaje desde Bangkok. A pesar de que en su playa principal esta prohibido bañarse (debido a la contaminación) se ha desarrollado - y sobre todo para los homosexuales - una centro vaccacional internacional. Los dueños extranjeros y nativos de los bares gay de Pattaya han sabido mantener el grado del comfort y elegancia de sus locales. El ambiente gay está concentrado en una región pequeños bares gay en el Norte que no deberían dejar de ser vistados. Pattaya tiene fama por sus shows de trasvesties, muy frequentados por el público heterosexual.

❖ Durante la guerra del Vietnam questo villaggio de pescatori, distante due ore da Bangkok, è stato trasformato in centro di riposo per americani. La rinomatezza della città è stato prò compromessa del suo sporchissimo litorale. Negli ultimi anni però Pattaya è diventata un'amata meta turistica internazionale visitata anche da molti gay. I proprietari tailandesi e stranieri dei localistanno migliarando notevolmente lo standard, i confort e le infrastrutture alberghiere e di divertimento che Pattaya può offrire ai turisti. La parte più gay della città si trova in un piccolo ma vivace quartiere al sud di Pattaya. Tutavia non bisogna perdersi gli interessanti bar situati nella parte nord. Pattaya è famosa per i sui spettacoli di travestiti, molto amati dai turisti eterosessuali.

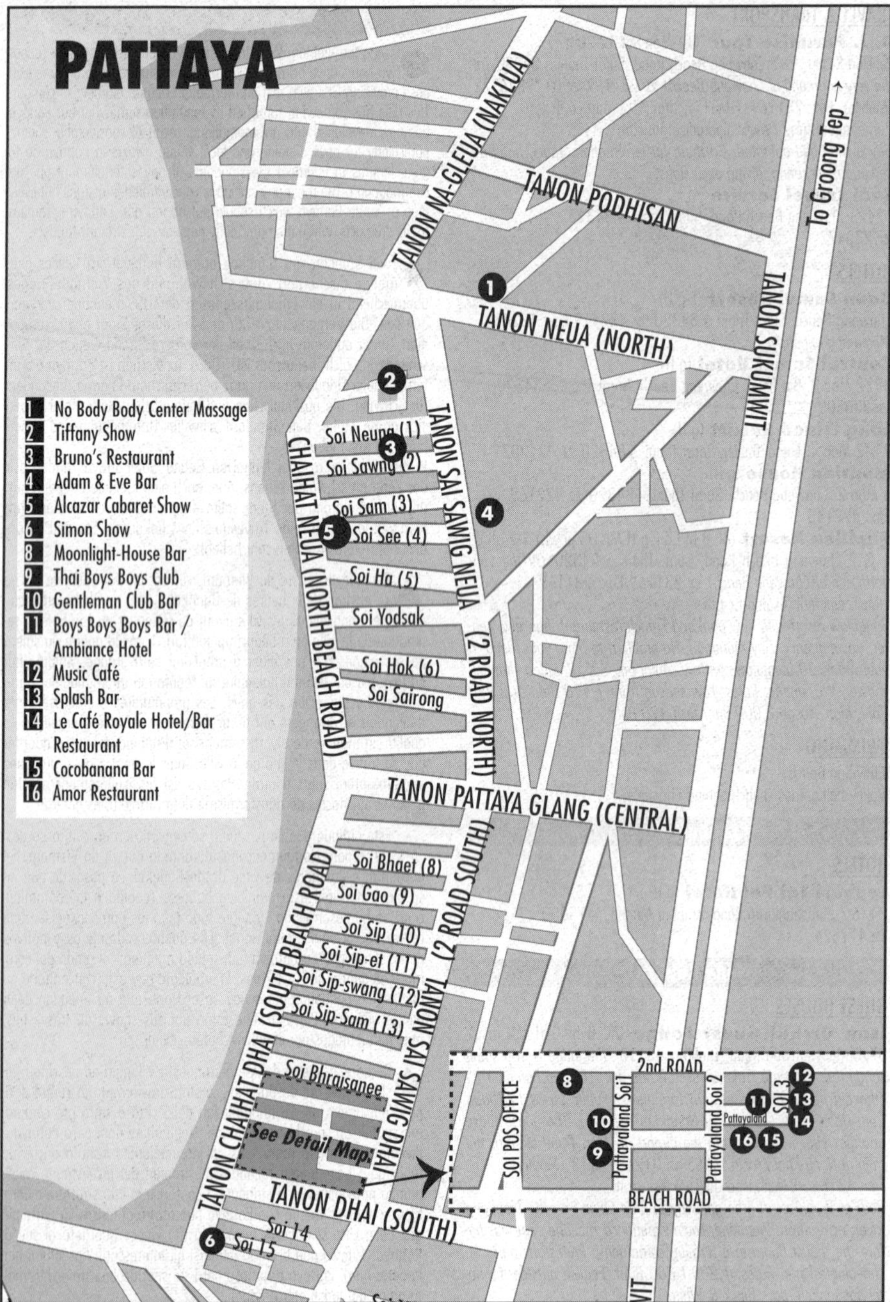
PATTAYA
1 No Body Body Center Massage
2 Tiffany Show
3 Bruno's Restaurant
4 Adam & Eve Bar
5 Alcazar Cabaret Show
6 Simon Show
8 Moonlight-House Bar
9 Thai Boys Boys Club
10 Gentleman Club Bar
11 Boys Boys Boys Bar / Ambiance Hotel
12 Music Café
13 Splash Bar
14 Le Café Royale Hotel/Bar Restaurant
15 Cocobanana Bar
16 Amor Restaurant
TANON NA-GLEUA (NAKLUA)
TANON PODHISAN
To Groong Tep →
TANON SUKUMWIT
TANON NEUA (NORTH)
TANON SAI SAWIG NEUA (2 ROAD NORTH)
CHAIHAT NEUA (NORTH BEACH ROAD)
Soi Neung (1)
Soi Sawng (2)
Soi Sam (3)
Soi See (4)
Soi Ha (5)
Soi Yodsak
Soi Hok (6)
Soi Sairong
TANON PATTAYA GLANG (CENTRAL)
Soi Bhaet (8)
Soi Gao (9)
Soi Sip (10)
Soi Sip-et (11)
Soi Sip-swang (12)
Soi Sip-Sam (13)
Soi Bhraisanee
See Detail Map
TANON CHAIHAT DHAI (SOUTH BEACH ROAD)
TANON SAI SAWIG DHAI (2 ROAD SOUTH)
TANON DHAI (SOUTH)
Soi 14
Soi 15
2nd ROAD
SOI POS OFFICE
Pattayaland Soi1
Pattayaland Soi 2
Pattayaland
SOI 3
BEACH ROAD

GAY INFO

Internet addresses
http://www.pattayagay.com

TOURIST INFO

Tourism Authority Of Thailand (TAT). Central Region Office 8.30-16.30 h
609 Moo 10, Pratamnak Road, Chon Buri ✉20260 *(up the hill, close to the sundial)* ☎ 427667 ☎ 428750 Fax: 429113
E-Mail: tatpty@chonburi.ksc.co.th Homepage: http://www.tat.or.th

Pattaya - Jomtien Beach ☎ 038

BARS

Bamboo's Bar (B G MA) 12-24 h
410/35 Thapaya Road (Jomtien Road), Chon Buri ✉20260
☎ 232315
Open host bar.

Nuttawut Café (B G MA OS)
410/37 Thapaya Road (Jomtien Road), Chon Buri ✉20260

GUEST HOUSES

Tui's Place (! AC B bf F G H MA OS) 8-21 h
318/77 Moo 12, Tambon Nongprue, Banglamung, Chon Buri ✉20260 ☎ 25 14 32, ☎ 23 10 45 Fax: 37 01 36
E-Mail: tui_69@hotmail.com
The only gay guest house, bar & restaurant right on Jomtiens beach, 20 meters to the gay seating. All rooms with AC, TV, phone, fridge, separate bath room. Very clean, so take off your shoes. Rooms 500 to 1,250 Baht/night. Take a shower here after swimming at the beach.

SWIMMING

-Jomtien Beach (Take the open taxi to Jomtien (10 Baht for foreigners), get off when you arrive at the beach, and use the brand new walkway to the right about 500 meters. You reach the gay area when you can see Tui's Place, the only gay hotel on Jomtien Beach. Rent a deckchair and wait for the things to happen)

Pattaya - Other Areas ☎ 038

RESTAURANTS

Balcony. The (B F g)
151/35 Moo 5, Soi Ananthakul, North Road, Chon Buri ✉20260 *(opposite city hall)* ☎ 411429

Bavaria House II (AC B CC F g)
Central Shopping Arcade, 216/62 Second Road, Chon Buri ✉20260 *(opposite Mike Shopping Mall)* ☎ 427790
German beer garden. Gay owned and operated.

Bruno's Restaurant & Wine Bar (AC CC E F glm MA N) 18-24 h, closed Mon
436/77 Sri Nakhon Centre, Chon Buri ✉20260 *(soi Regent Marina, corner of Second Road)* ☎ 361073 ☎ 424292
This gay owned restaurant has a great selection of international and Thai cuisine, an outstanding wine card. Bruno gives the place a personal touch of decent luxury.

Little Italy (AC B CC E F glm MA N) 16-24 h
215/68 Second Road, Chon Buri ✉20260 *(opposite Royal Garden Plaza)* ☎ 466252
Italian cuisine. Gay owned and operated.

PIC Kitchen (B F NG) 8-24 h
Soi 4 / Soi 5 Beach Road, Chon Buri ✉20260 ☎ 422774
Classical Thai cuisine in a beautiful Thai garden. Not gay but worth a visit.

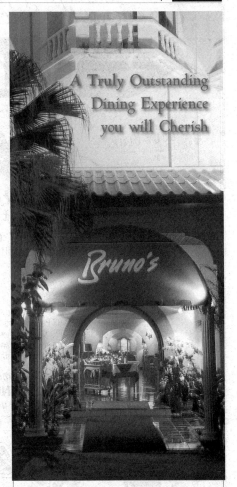

Samsara Lifestyle (AC B bf CC d E F glm MA OS s stv) 9-4 h
183/1 Beach Road, Moo 10 Nongprue, Banglamung, Chon Buri ✉20260 *(corner of Soi Post Office)* ☎ 710822
Mixed elegant, trendy pub and restaurant with life music and special gay parties. Look out for flyers.

SHOWS

Alcazar (! AC B glm S STV) 18.30, 20 and 21.30, Sat also 23 h
78/14 Second Road, Chon Buri ✉20260 *(opposite Soi 5)* ☎ 410505
The most famous show in Thailand. The Miss Alcazar Thailand contest every year in April always selects a man as the most beautiful woman.

Malibu (B g OS S STV)
Second Road, Chon Buri ✉20260 *(corner of Soi Post Office)*
Very popular (straight) cabaret with kathoey show.

Tiffany (B glm S STV)
464 Second Road, Chon Buri ✉20260 ☎ 421700
The biggest silicon breasts of Thailand.

SAUNAS/BATHS

Sport Man Studio Sauna (G sa sb WO)
151/ Moo 5, Soi Ananthakul, North Road, Chon Buri ✉20260 *(opposite city hall)* ☎ 410673

MASSAGE

No Body Body Center (msg) 13-23 h
151-151/1 Moo 5, Soi Ananthakul, North Road, Chon Buri ✉20260 *(opposite city hall)* ☎ 370170
Many different types of massage by men.

Pattaya - South Pattaya ☎ 038

BARS

Adam & Eve Home (AC B F G msg SNU tv) 11-22.30, club 20-2, show at 0.30 h
42/10 Sabajai Village, Sukhumvit Road, Chon Buri ✉20260
☎ 427413
This Thai restaurant, club and massage moved from Soi 2 to a more residential area.

DANCECLUBS

Marine Disco (AC B D glm)
Beach Road, Chon Buri ✉20260 *(Walking Street - The Strip)*
☎ 428583
Very mixed disco. Here everybody meets when the bars close.

SHOWS

ICON. The Club (! AC B CC D f G MA N S SNU) Wed-Sun and holiday Mondays 21-2 h
146/8 Thappaya Road (Jomtien Road), Chon Buri ✉20260 *(between South Pattaya and Jomtien)* ☎ 250300
One of the best shows in Thailand. Featuring their own dancing group „The ICONs". Live singer. Very popular.

Simon (AC B G MA S)
325/11 Beach Road, Chon Buri ✉20260 *(Walking Street - The Strip)* ☎ 429647
Kathoey shows. Same owner as Simon in Phuket.

TRAVEL & TRANSPORT

Taxi Services
In Front of Cerry Hotel, 270 Pratamnak Road, Chon Buri ✉20260
Ask at the reception for a limousine or take a taxi in front of the hotel. Pattaya-Bangkok about 1,000 Baht.

HOTELS

ICON Boutique Hotel (! AC B bf CC f G H OS pi) 146/8 Thappaya Road (Jomtien Road), Chon Buri ✉20260 *(between South Pattaya and Jomtien)* ☎ 250300 Fax: 250838
E-Mail: iconhotel@ine.inet.co.th
Homepage: http://www.iconhotel.com
Elegant and exclusive gay hotel between Pattaya City and Jomtien Beach. Beautiful rooms and pool.

Pattaya - South Pattaya/Boys Town ☎ 038

BARS

A-Bomb (AC B G msg)
325/75-76 Pattayaland Soi 2, Chon Buri ✉20260 *(corner of Pattaya 2nd Road)* ☎ 429043

Boys Club. The (AC B G S SNU STV) 20-3 h
325/28-30 Pattayaland Soi 1, Chon Buri ✉20260

Boyz, Boyz, Boyz (! AC B CC d f G MA S STV VS) 21-3 h
325/89-91 Pattayaland Soi 3, Chon Buri ✉20260 ☎ 421910
The No. 1 bar in Pattaya. Handsome boys, freelancers, local crowd, tourists, party and disco mix with sexy kathoey shows after midnight to a unique cocktail of fun and entertainment.

Charlie Boys (AC B G MA) 21-2 h
325/48-49 Pattayaland Soi 1, Chon Buri ✉20260

City Boys (AC B G MA)
325/52 Pattayaland Soi 1, Chon Buri ✉20260

Classic Boys Club (AC B G MA)
325/42 Pattayaland Soi 1, Chon Buri ✉20260
☎ 429868

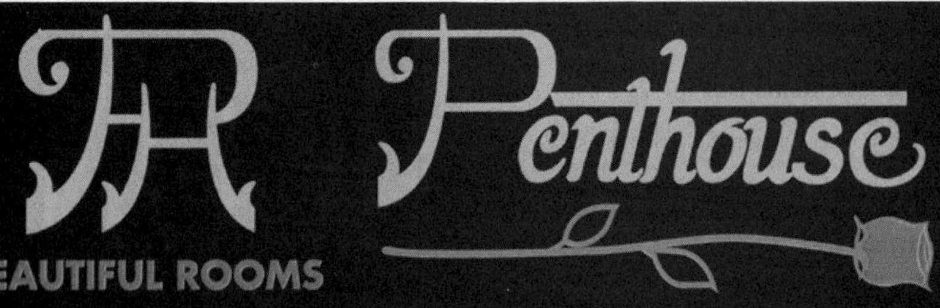

Cocobanana (AC B F G MA OS S) 12-3 h
244/10-11 Pattayaland Soi 3, Chon Buri ✉20260
☎ 710597
See and be seen. No go go boys.

Dream Boys (AC B G MA)
325/44-45 Pattayaland Soi 1, Chon Buri ✉20260

Gentleman Club (AC B G msg) 20-? h
325/27 Pattayaland Soi 1, Chon Buri ✉20260
☎ 429867

Moonlight House (AC B G MA S) 21-2 h
325/120-121 Second Road, Chon Buri ✉20260 *(north around the corner of Pattayaland Soi 1)* ☎ 423595

Music Café (B F G OS) 325/161
Pattayaland Soi 3, Chon Buri ✉20260 *(corner of Pattaya Second Road)* ☎ 426914
Open bar with German food. No go go.

Muttley's Bar (B G MA OS)
Sophon Court, Moo 10, 103/6-7 Soi 14, Chon Buri ✉20260
☎ 424846
Outside bar with very reasonable prices.

Nova Boy's Club (AC B G MA) 21-3 h
325/34-36 Pattayaland Soi 1, Chon Buri ✉20260 ☎ 429645

Od's Spot (B G MA OS)
Sophon Court, Moo 10, 103/14 Soi 15, Chon Buri ✉20260
☎ 710 321
Small outside bar.

Patta Patta (B D F MA)
Sophon Court, Moo 10, 103/9-10 Soi 14, Chon Buri ✉20260
☎ 422986
Music pub.

Splash (AC B CC f G MA msg pi VS) 21-3 h
325/107 Pattayaland Soi 3, Chon Buri ✉20260 ☎ 710578
Erotic swimming shows.

Star Boys Boys (AC B G MA)
194/23-24 Soi Welcome Plaza, Second Road (Soi Toyota Karaoke), Chon Buri ✉20260 *(opposite Pattayaland Soi 2)* ☎ 249852

Thai Boys Boys Club (AC B G MA S)
325/25-26 Pattayland Soi 1, Chon Buri ✉20260

Throb (! AC B d G MA S SNU) 21-3 h
325/108 Pattayaland Soi 3, Chon Buri ✉20260 ☎ 424099
Nightly male revue at 23.30 h.

CAFÉS

Ambiance Coffee Shop. The (AC B G MA) 0-24 h
325/89-91 Pattayaland Soi 3, Chon Buri ✉20260 ☎ 424099

RESTAURANTS

Amor Restaurant (B F G OS)
244/15 Pattayaland Soi 3, Chon Buri ✉20260
☎ 710680
Good food associated with the best overview of boyz town. Greatest selection of deserts.

Café Royale. Le (! AC B bf CC F G MA N OS S) 0-24 h
325/102-5 Pattayaland Soi 3, Chon Buri ✉20260
☎ 423515
The Piano Bar is the place to go for your dinner, to meet your friends and for sure the place to go after all other bars are closed. Have your breakfast in the sun or your dinner with candle light.
Ice Café Berlin (AC bf F g MA OS) 17-2 h
25/1-2 South Road, Chon Buri ✉20260
☎ 710188
Gay owned and operated.

SAUNAS/BATHS

Body Club. The (AC B CC f G MA msg sa sb wh WO) 10-22 h
325/106 Pattayaland Soi 3, Chon Buri ✉20260
☎ 424099
With fully equipped gym.

HOTELS

Most of the hotels in Pattaya are gay friendly and there normally is no problem to bring your friend(s) upstairs. Many hotels are concerned for your security and will hold your visitor's ID Card during his stay. Only few luxury hotels have extra charge.
Ambiance Hotel. The (AC B bf CC d F f G H MG msg OS sa sb) 325/89-91 Pattayaland Soi 3, Chon Buri ✉20260
☎ 424099 ☎ 425145 Fax: 422824
E-Mail: ambiance@loxinfo.co.th
Homepage: http://www.ambiance-pattaya.com
Exclusively high standard gay hotel and coffee shop in the centre of gay bars. Beautiful maintained rooms from 1,050 Baht/night, Suite 1,950 Baht/night, 2-bedroom suite: 3,000/night.
Café Royale Hotel. Le (! AC B bf CC F G H MA OS) 325/102-5 Pattayaland Soi 3, Chon Buri ✉20260 ☎ 428303 ☎ 423515 Fax: 424579
E-Mail: reservations@caferoyale-pattaya.com
Homepage: http://www.caferoyale-pattaya.com
Exclusively gay hotel in the heart of the gay centre. Well appointed quality accommodation. Room rates from 900 Baht, Suites from 1,950 Baht.
Penthouse Hotel (AC B bf CC D F f glm H MA msg OS VS W wh)
Pattayaland Soi 2, Chon Buri ✉20260 ☎ 429639
Fax: 421747 E-Mail: penthous@loxinfo.co.th
Homepage: http://www.penthousehotel.com
Mixed clientele, many gays and a unique place in the centre of the gay nights. Red lights, condoms and teddy supplied in the rooms. Showers, bath or jacuzzi, some with balcony. Restaurant, breakfast buffet. Rates: 20-50 US$.

CRUISING

-Beach Road (after dark underneath the trees along the beach close to Boyz Town)

Pattaya - Sunee Plaza/Day & Night Plaza ☎ 038

BARS

Bad Boy (AC B G MA)
273/62-64 Moo 10, Sunee Plaza, Chon Buri ✉20260 *(between Soi VC Hotel and Soi Yensabai)*
Black. The (AC B G MA)
273/93 Moo 10, Soi VC Hotel, Sunee Plaza, Chon Buri ✉20260
Beer bar.
Crazy Pub (! AC B G MA S SNU)
273/66-68 Moo 10, Sunee Plaza, Chon Buri ✉20260 *(between Soi VC Hotel and Soi Yensabai)* ☎ 713190
Realy a crazy pub. The oldest bar on Sunee Plaza. Randy shows on the central stage.
Forest House (AC B G MA)
273/94 Moo 10, Soi VC Hotel, Sunee Plaza, Chon Buri ✉20260
Corner bar to have a drink and meet a friend even when most of the other bars have closed.
Funny Boys (AC B G MA) 20/10-11
Moo 10, South Road, Day & Night Plaza Soi 1, Chon Buri ✉20260 ☎ 723055
Jack-In-The-Box (B G MA N OS) 15-2.30 h or later
273/56-57 Moo 10, Sunee Plaza, Chon Buri ✉20260 *(between Soi VC Hotel and Soi Yensabai)*
☎ 713 269
Open bar with hosts.
K. Boys (AC B CC d G MA OS s VS) 21-2 h
273/90-91 Moo 10, Soi VC Hotel, Sunee Plaza, Chon Buri ✉20260 ☎ 713479
New go go bar.
Lek's Beer Bar (AC B G MA)
273/58 Moo 10, Sunee Plaza, Chon Buri ✉20260 *(between Soi VC Hotel and Soi Yensabai)*
Leo Palace. The (AC B G MA)
273/73-76 Moo 10, Sunee Plaza, Chon Buri ✉20260 ☎ 713503
New go go bar.
Minou (AC B G MA OS)
273/43 Moo 10, Sunee Plaza, Chon Buri ✉20260 *(between Soi VC Hotel and Soi Yensabai)* ☎ 713471
Pineapple (AC B G MA)
273/46 Moo 10, Sunee Plaza, Chon Buri ✉20260 *(between Soi VC Hotel and Soi Yensabai)*
Playboy Bar (AC B G MA)
20/52-53 Moo 10, South Road, Day & Night Plaza Soi 2, Chon Buri ✉20260
Redgy's Place (AC B G MA OS)
273/44 Moo 10, Sunee Plaza, Chon Buri ✉20260 *(between Soi VC Hotel and Soi Yensabai)*
Super Boys (AC B G MA S SNU)
273/81-82 Moo 10, Sunee Plaza, Chon Buri ✉20260 *(between Soi VC Hotel and Soi Yensabai)*
Topman (AC B E G MA) 20-3 h
273/95-96 Moo 10, Soi VC Hotel, Sunee Plaza, Chon Buri ✉20260 ☎ 713228
White Night (AC B G MA OS)
273/97 Moo 10, Soi VC Hotel, Sunee Plaza, Chon Buri ✉20260

DANCECLUBS

Hollywood (B D glm MA)
32/64 Moo 10, South Road, Day & Night Hotel, Chon Buri ✉20260 ☎ 424975
Mixed Thai disco with live band. No cruising

RESTAURANTS

Butcher Hans Pub (AC B F g MA N OS) 18-? h
273/32-33 Moo 10, Sunee Plaza, Chon Buri ✉20260 *(between Soi VC Hotel and Soi Yensabai)* ☎ 01/8338139 (Mobile)
Good food and nice atmosphere.
Eldorado (AC B bf F G H MA OS W) Restaurant 9-24 h, Bar 16-3 h
273/84-85 Moo 10, Sunee Plaza, Chon Buri ✉20260 *(between Soi VC Hotel and Soi Yensabai)* ☎ 713259
Seven Bar (AC BF F G MA OS)
273/37-38 Moo 10, Sunee Plaza, Chon Buri ✉20260 *(between Soi VC Hotel and Soi Yensabai)*
Open restaurant, best overview of Sunee Plaza.

BODY & BEAUTY SHOPS

Boy Design (G)
257/11 Moo 10, Sunee Plaza, Chon Buri ✉20260 *(between Soi VC Hotel and Soi Yensabai, two Sois behind Sunee Plaza)*
☎ 01/9454764 (Mobile)
Diplom hair designer, trained in Paris and for sure very gay.

GUEST HOUSES

Tropy Guest House (AC B bf F G H OS)
273/84-86 Moo 10, Sunee Plaza, Chon Buri ✉20260
☎ 713480 Fax: 713481
Small guest house in the heart of Sunee Plaza. Rooms from 390 Baht/day to 5.500 Baht/month (low saison, 500 Baht/day, 7000 Baht/month high saison. Gay owned and operated.

Phitsanuloke ☎ 055

DANCECLUBS

Studio 54 (B D g)
38 Borom Trilokant Road, Amphur Muang ✉65000 *(in the basement of Pailyn Hotel)*

Phuket ☎ 076

● This large island (about the size of Singapore) is connected to the mainland by a causeway, and is located to the west of the narrow neck of land which connects Thailand to Malaysia. Formerly a series of unspoilt beaches with thatched hut cottages, it has now become a dependency of the international hotel chains. There are still enough of its beautiful beaches, however, to allow the tourist to find one to his liking. Patong is a good base from which to visit the beautiful islands of the Surin and Similan National Parks. The town of Phuket itself may be the commercial centre, but the main tourist and gay area is Patong Beach. Here you'll find superb watersports- and golfing facilities. The German and Italian influence is strong in Patong, so visitors from these countries will find their languages spoken and even their food available. Patong's gay scene is still searching for its identity: some bars copy the kind of place that you find in Pattaya or Bangkok, while others are trying to create something distinctly local and worthwile. The 'outdoor beer bars' are a typical feature of Patong, and the city is developing its own particular cabaret style.

✱ Diese große Insel (in etwa der Größe Singapurs) ist über einen Damm mit dem Festland verbunden und liegt auf der Westseite der Landenge, über die Thailand in Richtung Malaysia verläuft.
Aus einer unzerstörten Strandlandschaft mit Strohdachhütten ist ein Filialort internationaler Hotelketten geworden. Seinen Lieblingsstrand kann man sich natürlich trotzdem noch aussuchen. Und übrigens ist Phuket eine ideale Ausgangsbasis für Besuche auf den schönen Inseln der Nationalparks Surin und Similan.
Die Stadt Phuket selbst ist das kommerzielle Zentrum, aber das Hauptgebiet für Touristen und Schwule ist Patong Beach. Ein optimales Wassersport- und Golf-Revier. Deutscher und italienischer Einfluß sind stark in Patong, so daß Besucher aus diesen Ländern ihre Muttersprachen und sogar heimatliche Küche vorfinden.
Patongs schwule Szene ist noch auf der Suche nach ihrer Identität: einige Bars reflektieren nur Pattaya oder Bangkok, andere aber versuchen etwas eigenes und wertvolles zu schaffen. Dazu kommen die Patong-typischen »Outdoor beer bars« und die Entwicklung eines eigenen Kabaret-Stils.

▲ Pour aller à Phuket (île de la taille de Singapour), on passe par la digue qui la relie au continent. Phuket se trouve sur le côté ouest de l'isthme qui mène de la Thaïlande à la Malaisie. Il y a quelques années, on n'y trouvait encore que des plages et des huttes de paille. Aujourd'hui, les grands hôtels internationaux se suivent les uns les autres. Une consolation: les plages, elles, sont toujours aussi belles!
Phuket est le point de départ idéal pour aller découvrir les splendides îles Surin et Similan, parc naturel protégé. Phuket est le premier centre commercial de la région, mais les gays et les touristes préfèreront certainement Patong Beach, ses terrains de golf et ses sports nautiques. Patong fourmille d'Allemands et et d'Italiens, à tel point qu'on y parle la langue de Goethe et de Dante et qu'on y sert saucisses et pizzas. Les établissements gays de Patong n'ont pas encore de caractère propre. Certains bars se contentent de recréer l'atmosphère de Pattaya ou de Bangkok, d'autres essayent d'innover et de créer un style particulier, plus recherché. A ne pas manquer, les „Outdoor beer bars" et les boîtes style cabaret que vous ne trouverez nulle part ailleurs.

☆ Phuket, casi del mismo tamaño que Singapur, está unida a tierra firme por un dique. Phuket se encuentra al oeste del istmo que une Tailandia con Malasia. Esta gran isla, que se distinguió antes por sus playas tranquilas con los típicos chiringuitos de palma, se ha convertido hoy en día en uno de los lugares preferidos de las grandes cadenas hoteleras. De cualquier forma quedan todavía suficientes bellas playas, donde cada uno puede elegir su sitio preferido. Phuket es un buen punto de partida para visitar las lindas islas y a la vez parques nacionales de Surin y Similian.
El centro comercial de la isla es Phuket-Ciudad, sin embargo para los turistas gays la región Patong Beach es de mayor atracción. Esta región tailandesa es famosa por las posibilidades de la práctica de deportes acuáticos y los cursos avanzados de golf. En Patong hay una fuerte influencia alemana e italiana, por lo que turistas de estos países se podrán comunicar en su idioma materno y encontrarán también la comida típica de su país.
El ambiente gay de Patong busca aún su propia identidad. Algunos bares imitan Pattaya o Bangkok, otros intentan desarrollar sus propias ideas. Aquí encontramos los en Patong típicos «Outdoor beer bars», así como el desarrollo de un estilo propio de cabaret.

❖ Questa grande isola (grande quanto Singapore) è raggiungibile attraverso una diga che la collega al continente; è situata sul lato occidentale dell'istmo che conduce dalla Tailandia alla Malesia. Da un susseguirsi di spiagge incontaminate con capanne di paglia si è giunti a catene di filiali di hotel internazionali. Tuttavia le bellissime spiagge sono rimaste alla libera scelta del turista. Phuket è un punto di partenza ideale per un'escursione sulle splendide isole Surin e Similan, che sono un parco naturale protetto. Phuket è anche il primo centro commerciale della regione, ma la zona preferita dei gay è Patong Beach, dove vi sono campi da golf di importanza internazionale e la possibilità di fare sport acquatici. Patong è stata influenzata molto dagli italiani e dai tedeschi: i turisti di questi paesi dunque potranno parlare la propria lingua e gustare la propria cucina. L'ambiente gay di Patong è ancora alla ricerca della propria identità. Alcuni bar imitano l'ambiente di Pattaya e di Bangkok, altri invece cercano di creare un'atmosfera propria, più ricercata. Tipici di Patong sono gli „Outdoor beer bars" e i locali stile cabaret.

GAY INFO

Internet addresses
Gay Patong: http://www.beachpatong.com (site with many gay Phuket links. Up-to-date)
Gay Phuket: http://www.gayphuket.com

TOURIST INFO

Tourism Authority Of Thailand (TAT)
73/75 Phuket Road, Amphur Muang ✉83000 ☎ 211036
☎ 212213 Fax: 213582

BARS

Bicycle (B F G MA) 15-? h
5/16 Hat Patong Road, Aroomson Plaza, Patong Beach ✉83150 ☎ 342927
Thai and German food.

Black & White Music Factory (AC B D G S SNU) 20-2, show at 24 h
133/5-6 Rath-U-Thit Road, Paradise Complex, Patong Beach ✉83150 *(3rd soi, middle walkway)* ☎ 340758

David's Bar (B G MA OS S) 17-3 h
133/8 Rath-U-Thit Road, Paradise Complex, Patong Beach ✉83150 *(3rd soi, middle walkway)* ☎ 340312
Beer bar.

F1 (B G MA S)
123/2 Rath-U-Thit Road, Paradise Complex, Patong Beach ✉83150 *(1st soi, way in)*

Heaven (B G MA S)
127/6-7 Rath-U-Thit Road, Paradise Complex, Patong Beach ✉83150 *(2nd soi, north walkway)*

J & B (B G MA)
141/15 Rath-U-Thit Road, Paradise Complex, Patong Beach ✉83150 *(5th soi, way out)*

James Dean Bar (AC B CC G H MA OS) 15-3 h
125/10 Rath-U-Thit Road, Paradise Complex, Patong Beach ✉83150 *(1st soi, way in)* ☎ 344215
One of the oldest gay beer bars. Overnight stays possible.

My Way (! AC B G S) 14-2 h
125/15-17 Rath-U-Thit Road, Paradise Complex, Patong Beach ✉83150 *(1st soi, way in)* ☎ 342163
Without any doubt the best go go bar and show in town. Many beautiful hosts and special shows every night.

Passport (B G MA S) 14-2 h
125/3 Rath-U-Thit Road, Paradise Complex, Patong Beach ✉83150 *(1st soi, way in)* ☎ 344366

Patong A Go Go (B G MA S) 21-? h
123/6-7 Rath-U-Thit Road, Paradise Complex, Patong Beach ✉83150 *(1st soi, way in)* ☎ 341305

Pink Cadillac (B G MA OS S SNU) Show between 23-1 h
135/6 Rath-U-Thit Road, Paradise Complex, Patong Beach ✉83150 *(3rd soi, middle walkway)* ☎ 01/2701906 (Mobile)

Super Boy (AC B G)
38/100 Si Nam Yen Road

Tangmo (B G MA S)
141/24-26 Rath-U-Thit Road, Paradise Complex, Patong Beach ✉83150 *(opposite the 5th soi, way out)*

Uncle Charly's (AC B f G MA msg OS S STV VS) 20-3 h
77/64 Hat Patong Road, Aroomson Plaza, Patong Beach ✉83150 ☎ 342865

CAFÉS

Connect Bistro and Bar (AC B bf CC F GLM MA OS) 10-3 h
125/8-9 Rath-U-Thit Road, Paradise Complex, Patong Beach ✉83150 *(1st soi, way in)* ☎ 294195
Very friendly owners and staff, reliable internet service. Come here to get information on the gay life.

DANCECLUBS

Boat Bar. The (! AC B CC D DR GLM MA S STV) 21-? h
125/19-20 Rath-U-Thit Road, Paradise Complex, Patong Beach ✉83150 *(1st soi, way in)* ☎ 341237
The only gay disco in Phuket and a place where you have to go. Most friendly owner, great shows and many cute boys.

RESTAURANTS

Baan Rim Pa (AC B CC e F g MA) 12-24 h
223 Kalim Road, Group #1, Kathu, Patong Beach ✉83150 ☎ 340789 ☎ 341768 Fax: 342460
Spectacular dinners with view over Patong Bay. Piano bar. No chance to get a seat without reservation.

Bingo (B F G)
125/5 Rath-U-Thit Road, Paradise Complex, Patong Beach ✉83150 *(1st soi, way in)* ☎ 342176
Gay owned German restaurant and pub.

Sea Hag (! AC B CC F glm MA N) 11-24 h
78/5 Soi Permpong 3 (Soi Wattana Clinic), Thaveewong Road (Beach Road), Patong Beach ✉83150 *(50 meters inside the soi)* ☎ 341111
One of the best restaurants in town. Gay owned. A small place to really enjoy your dinner. Call for reservation. Price Range: 200-400 Baht/person.

Siam Restaurant (B F glm)
135/8 Rath-U-Thit Road, Paradise Complex, Patong Beach ✉83150 *(3rd soi, middle walkway)*

Thiphaluck (B F G)
125/7 Rath-U-Thit Road, Paradise Complex, Patong Beach ✉83150 *(1st soi, way in)*
Thai food and beer.

SHOWS

Queen Andaman Show (B g STV)
Middle Soi off Bangla Road, Amphur Muang ✉83000 *(middle Soi off Soi Bangla)*
Male drag shows every night in a very, very straight area.

Simon Cabaret (B D g S STV) Shows 19.30, 21.30 h
8 Sirirat Road, Katoo, Patong Beach ✉83150 *(2 km south of Patong)* ☎ 342011
One of the best female impersonator show in Thailand. Popular among foreign straight tourists but also gays.

MASSAGE

Alkazar Garden (b msg)
135/14-15 Rath-U-Thit Road, Paradise Complex, Patong Beach ✉83150 *(4th soi, south walkway)* ☎ 292588

TRAVEL & TRANSPORT

Sykinn Travel & Tours (AC CC glm MA)
62/012 Patong Condotel, Rath-U-Thit Road, Patong Beach ✉83150 ☎ 342476 ☎ 01/89347769 (mobile)
Fax: 342476
Very reliable service, friendly and well informed.

HOTELS

Beach Resortel. The (B CC F g H OS)
37 Moo 3, Thaveewong Road (Beach Road), Patong Beach ✉83150 *(behind the gay beach...)* ☎ 340544
Fax: 340848 E-Mail: beach@loxinfo.co.th
Friendly gay owned hotel right on the beach. Rooms 1,200 Baht low season, 1,800 Baht high season.

Club Bamboo (glm H msg sa WO)
247 Nanai Road ✉83150 ☎ 345 345 Fax: 345 345
E-Mail: Info@clubbamboo.com Homepage: clubbomboo.com
Gay owned and managed upscale hotel with 10 bungalows, 20 deluxe rooms, 4 suites, 3 penthouses. All rooms with cable tv, refrigerator, telephone.

Monte Carlo (AC B bf CC F G H MA OS)
135/9-11 Rath-U-Thit Road, Paradise Complex, Patong Beach ✉83150 *(3rd soi, middle walkway)* ☎ 340815 Fax: 340814
E-Mail: montecarlo@phuket.a-net.net.th
Nearly always booked out.

Phuket Cabana (AC B F g H MA pi)
41 Thaveewong Road (Beach Road), Patong Beach ✉83150
☎ 340138 ☎ 342100 Fax: 340178
E-Mail: cabana@samart.co.th
Homepage: http://www.impiana.com
Luxury hotel right on the beach. Rates between 3,200 Baht (May - October) and 6,800 Baht (November - April). Straight place but gay friendly.

Sky Inn (AC B F G H MA)
62 Patong Condotel, Rath-U-Thit Road, Patong Beach ✉83150 *(9th floor)* ☎ 342486 ☎ 340380 Fax: 340576
Very friendly staff. Close to night life area.

GUEST HOUSES

Connect (B bf CC F GLM H MA OS) 9-? h
125/8-9 Rath-U-Thit Road, Paradise Complex, Patong Beach ✉83150 *(1st soi, way in)* ☎ 294195 Fax: 294195 E-Mail: connectguesthouse@beachpatong.com
Homepage: http://www.beachpatong.com/connect
Nice and very friendly guest house in the heart of the gay night life. Come here and feel at home. Motorbike service (200 Baht). Laundry. 11 rooms with fan, AC or penthouse room from 400 to 900 Baht/night (low season) and 700 to 1450 Baht/night (high season).

Home Sweet Home (AC G H)
70/179-180 Rath-U-Thit Road, Paradise Complex, Patong Beach ✉83150 *(at the corner of 1st soi, way in)* ☎ 340756
☎ 340757 Fax: 340757
Lovely rooms with bath, phone, fridge and TV. Rates around 1,000 Baht. Enter through the Dow Wow Pub. Gay owned.

Rendez-vous Inn (AC B G g H)
143/14-15 Rath-U-Thit Road, Paradise Complex, Patong Beach ✉83150 *(5th soi, way out)* ☎ 342433
E-Mail: boonco@loxinfo.co.th
Homepage: http://www.boontarika.com
Newly renovated and new location. Beautiful rooms, well maintained. Rates from 500 Baht. Motorbike rental.

200 Years (G H MA)
141/8-9 Rath-U-Thit Road, Paradise Complex, Patong Beach ✉83150 *(5th soi, way out) New gay owned guest house.*

SWIMMING

-Freedom Beach (South part of Patong Beach)
-Patong Beach (The gay beach is right in front of the Beach Resortel. Beware of hustlers)

Sukhothai ☎ 055

HOTELS

Northern Palace Hotel (AC H) 43 Singhawat Road, Amphur Muang ✉64000 ☎ 611194
Rooms with phone and private bath.

HEALTH GROUPS

Medical Clinic 24 hour emergency
Phuket Hospitals, Soi Namyen, Amphur Muang ✉64000
English spoken.

CRUISING

-Bridge in centre of Sukhothai (17-24 h)
-Night market and open-air café (22-? h)

Trang ☎ 075

GUEST HOUSES

Chai's (bf G H MG NU OS)
22/3 Moo 3 T. Khuanpring, Amphur Muang ✉92000
☎ 01/6774031 (Mobile) Fax: 222909
Country-side location 20 min. from Trang. Beautiful garden and delicious fish cuisine. For nature lovers.

Udon Thani ☎ 042

DANCECLUBS

High Tech Music World (B D g)
2272 Chammusorn, Amphur Muang ✉41000 ☎ 241330

Yellow Bird (B D g)
Charoen Hotel, Pho-Sri Road, Amphur Muang ✉41000

Tunisia

Tunusija

North Africa

Initials: TN

Time: GMT +1

☎ Country Code / Access Code: 216 / 00

Language: Arabic, French

Area: 163,610 km / 63,170 sq mi.

Currency: 1 Tunesian Dinar = 1,000 Millimes

Population: 9.380.400

Capital: Tunis

Religions: 98% Muslim

Climate: In the north the climate is Mediterranean with hot, dry summers and rain in winter. In the south begins the Sahara desert.

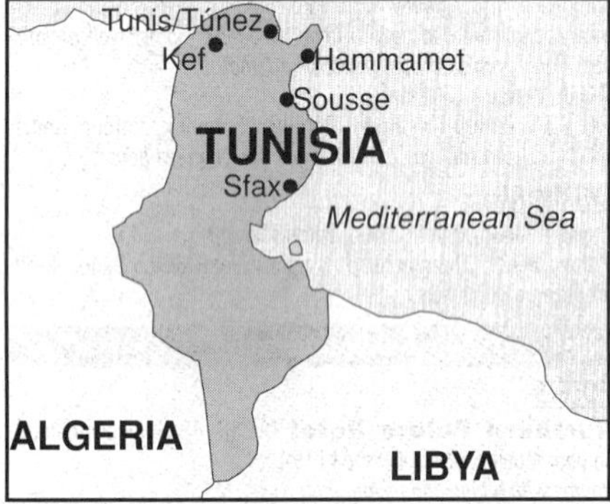

● Homosexuality is according to our latest knowledge illegal in Tunisia. The Tunisian society is still relatively intolerant towards homosexuals. This should be taken into consideration when visiting this country. Despite this a gay identity along with a gay infrastructure is developing even here, although at a very slow pace. Being too flamboyant can however lead to problems and should be avoided. For this reason we have decided this year (as was the case in the last edition of SPARTACUS) not to publish the few addresses we have for Tunisia.

✷ Homosexualität ist nach unserem Wissensstand in Tunesien illegal. Die tunesische Gesellschaft ist noch relativ unaufgeschlossen und ablehnend gegenüber Homosexuellen eingestellt. Dies sollte prinzipiell berücksichtigt werden, wenn man als schwuler Tourist dieses Land besucht. Zwar entwickelt sich auch hier, wenn auch nur sehr langsam, ein schwules Bewußtsein und eine schwule Infrastruktur, zu offensichtliches Gebärden kann jedoch zu erheblichen Problemen führen und sollte möglichst vermieden werden. Aus diesem Grund sehen wir auch dieses Jahr (wie auch in der vorangegangenen Ausgabe des SPARTACUS) davon ab, tunesische Adressen zu veröffentlichen.

▲ L'homosexualité est considérée comme un délit en Tunisie. La société tunisienne est relativement intolérante et fermée à ce sujet. Le touriste gay qui se rend en Tunisie doit donc être particulièrement vigilant. Même si une conscience et une infrastructure homosexuelles émergent peu à peu, un comportement trop ostentatoire peut créer de nombreux problèmes et est à éviter. C'est la raison pour laquelle nous avons décidé, comme d'ailleurs l'année précédente, de ne pas couvrir ce pays.

☆ Según nuestras informaciones, la homosexualidad es ilegal en Túnez. La sociedad de este país todavía tiene muchos prejuicios y rechaza los homosexuales. Hay que tener esto en mente, sin falta, al visitar el país como turista homosexual. Aunque muy lentamente, también en Túnez se están desarrollando una conciencia y una infraestructura gays. No obstante, puede acarrear problemas serios manifestar la homosexualidad en público, por lo que necesariamente debe evitarse por todos los medios. Por esta razón, este año (como también en la última edición de SPARTACUS) prescindimos de la publicación de direcciones o contactos en Túnez.

❖ Secondo quanto sappiamo, l'omosessualità in Tunisia è illegale. La società tunisina è relativamente ancora poco aperta e si mostra sfavorevole agli omosessuali. Chi visita la Tunisia come turista gay, dovrebbe tener presente questo fatto. Anche se si sta sviluppando - pur molto lentamente - una coscienza omosessuale e un'infrastruttura gay, comportamenti poco discreti potrebbero causare dei gravi problemi e sono quindi da evitare. Per questo motivo ci asteniamo pure quest'anno (così come nell'ultima edizione di SPARTACUS) dal pubblicare degli indirizzi in Tunisia.

SAUNAS/BATHS

Aquarium (b f G MA msg pi s sa wh) 0-24 h
Istiklal caddesi, Sadri Alisik Sodak 29 *(Taksim)* ☎ 251 89 26
Action allowed, free access rooms, but dirty. Entrance-fee US$ 10.
Çesme Hamami (G MA OG msg) 12.30-22 h
Voyvoda Cad./Persembe Pazari
Çukurcuma Hamami (b G MA msg sa pi) 9-18 h
57 Çukurcuma Caddesi, Siraselviler, Taksim
Gay action allowed.
Kösk Hamami (g MA msg) 13-22 h
Çatalçesme Sokak *(near Alayköskü) Sultanhahmet.*

FITNESSTUDIOS

Flash Gym (g WO)
Istiklal Cad. Aznavur Pasaji 4, Taksim. ☎ 249 53 47
Vakkorama (glm WO)
Vakkorama Center, Taksim. *(Basement of the Marmara Hotel)*
☎ 251 15 71
Expensive.

BOOK SHOPS

Mephisto (g NG)
Istiklal Cad. Taksim.
Kaos GL available.
Pandora (g NG)
Istiklal Cad. Büyük Parmakkapi Sok.3, Taksim. ☎ 45 16 67
Foreign books can be ordered.

FASHION SHOPS

Mod
Atlas Pasaji 2.Kat, Beyoglu.
Second-hand clothing in 60's and 70's style.
Seker Portakali Atlas Pasaji 2.Kat., Beyoglu.
Very trendy, flamboyant clothing from gay designer.

MAIL ORDER

EPAS (glm)
CC 33 80303, Mecidiyeköy. ☎ 533 33 34
Sex toys, condoms,etc.
Fantasia (glm tv)
PK 460 80224, Sisli ☎ 234 05 14
Pornograghic & erotic videos, each $20.
Royal Ltd. (glm) CC 58 80303, Mecidiyeköy. ☎ 418 65 32
☎ 418 65 33
Sex toys, condoms, etc.

TRAVEL & TRANSPORT

Dialogue
Divanyolu, Klodfarer Caddesi 2, Sultanahmet ☎ 517 99 06
Fax: 518 44 82
Hotel reservations, car rentals, exchange, airline reservation, general information.
Istamboul Insolite 9-21 h
c/o Galeri Türkis, Yerebatan Caddesi No. 15/A ✉34400
☎ 519 48 05
Gay city tours.

HOTELS

Hotel Eris (H NG)
Istasion Arkasi Sokagi No. 9, ✉34420 ☎ 511 36 70
☎ 527 89 51 Fax: 511 59 06
Friendly. Prices from US$ 30/single room.

HEALTH GROUPS

Aids Info Line-Association for Famila Planning
☎ 435 20 47 ☎ 435 20 48
Amerikan Hastanesi
Nisantasi ☎ 231 40 50
Private hospital. HIV tests.
Istanbul Çapa Tip Fakültesi
☎ 54 54 87
-Dermatology or Venerology Department. ☎ 524 54 87 HIV testing (Name required, but no ID's checked).
-Psychiatry Department, Psychotherapy and Psychoneurosis Unit. ☎ 534 00 00 Counselling on sexual identity problems.
Kadiköy Municipality
Saglik Isleri Müdürlügü (Health Services)
AIDS Info Center. HIV testing.
There is no anonymous test in Turkey yet, but in most of the private clinics and major hospitals, taking a HIV test is possible without showing an ID, giving a false name.

SWIMMING

-Florya Plajlari beach (three popular beaches within reasonable distances from the city; all quietly cruisy, especially Günes plaji)
-Küçük Cekmeçe Plaj/beach (NU) (Take subway from European Railway Station called Galata to Kanarya)
-Kilyos (beach at European part of the city, extending 3 km along Black Sea)
-Sile (beach at European part of city, extending 8km along the Black Sea, hidden bays in evening)

CRUISING

All are (AYOR) ***A lot of people will try to take your money introducing themselves as policemen during or after the relation. Homosexual acts are NOT a crime in Turkey. The best way is choosing your partner carefully. You can trust the people who accept themselves as gay openly.***

-Along Istiklâl Caddesi and around McDonalds in Taksim Square
-Sound and Light Show at the Blue Mosque (21 h every evening; great for cruising during and after the show)
-Park near Blue Mosque (AYOR) (under the trees day and night)
-Both sides of Galata Bridge (Galata Köprüsü) (Karaköy Square with »Efes Pilsen Bar« and in beer bar under the bridge next to Eminösü Square)
-Park Hamam
-Belgrad Forest (take bus from Besiktas, lovely place with various trees and Ottoman antiquities)
-Katiköy Park (on the coastal side, evenings and nights)
-Gallaria Shopping Mall (cafés and around the ice-skating rink, Bakirköy.)
-Ragetta (Bakirköy coast. The sidewalk cafés ant the cafés on the terrace.)
-Ortaköy (around the bars on the coast)
-Taksim Park (The Bosphorus side, day and night)
-Akmerkez Shopping Mall (Etiler)

Izmir ☎ 0232

BARS

Kapris (B g TV) 20-? h
Bozkurt Caddin/ 1264 Sokak *(Basmane)*
Rubem (B NG YG)
Attaturk Caddin 214a *(Alsancak)*
Samdan (B g) Fri-Sun 20-? h
1458 Aokak No. 28 *(Alsancak)*

GENERAL GROUPS

Association for Protecting Prostitutes and Homosexuals
6433. sok. 4-C, Yali Mah., Semikler ☎ 362 22 89

SWIMMING
-Çesme (touristic town (the biggest) 7 km from Izmir)
-Karaburun (Bus from Altay Meydane)
-Sigacek
-Pamucak

CRUISING
-Kültürparki (Fuar) (active around the pool near Mogamba Night Club)
-Kordon (waterfront boulevard, at night)
-Bornova (sidewalk-cafés)

Kayseri ☎ 0352

CRUISING
-Large park in the centre of town
-Favziçakma caddesi and Sivas caddesi

Kusadasi ☎ 0256

BARS
Z Bar (B g) 10-? h (in summer only)
17 Camikebir Mahallesi Tuna Sok. ☎ 614 81 72

HOTELS
Elit (B H NG)
Cifuk Yapi Koop, Dogan Sk. ☎ 15 128

CRUISING
-Tea Garden

Takirdag ☎ 0282

CRUISING
-Sea-front promenade

Ukraine

Ukraïna

East Europe

Initials: UKR

Time: GMT +2

☎ Country Code / Access Code: 38 / 8 (wait for tone) 10

Language: Ukrainian

Area: 603,700 km² / 233,089 sq mi.

Currency: 1 Hryvna (UAH) = 100 Kopeks

Population: 53, 100,000

Capital: Kiev (Kyiv)

Religions: Russian Orthodox, Roman Catholic

Climate: Moderate continental climate. Mediterranean only on the southern Crimean coast. The west and north are areas with the highest precipitation. Winters vary from cool along the Black Sea to cold farther inland. Summers are warm across the greater part of the country, hot in the south.

Homosexuality between consenting adults is legal. The general age of consent is set at 16 for both gays and straights.

Einvernehmliche Homosexualität zwischen Erwachsenen ist legal. Das Schutzalter liegt für Hetero- wie Homosexuelle bei 16 Jahren.

En Ukraine, l'homosexualité entre adultes consentants n'est pas un délit. La majorité sexuelle est fixée à 16 ans pour tous.

La homosexualidad por acuerdo entre adultos es legal. La edad de consentimiento es de 16 años, independientemente de la orientacion sexual.

L'omosessualità tra adulti consezienti e legale. La maturita sessuale e di 16 anni per tutti.

NATIONAL GAY INFO
Ganimed All Ukrainian Association
PO Box 76 ✉04211 Kyiv ☎ (044) 419 17 82
E-Mail: Lilia@ganimed.freenet.viaduk.net

Gay. Ru
Box 1 ✉109457 Moskva Homepage: www.gay.ru/
Russian National website for gays, lesbians, bi- and transsexuals. The most comprehensive web site covering all aspects of gay life in all Republics of the former USSR, including Ukraine. Reliable, exhaustive and up-to-date. English version available.

Gay Ukraine International
65-29 Mironositskaya vulitsa, Kharkov ☎ (0572) 65 02 85
Homepage: www.angelfire.vom/nt/oleg/
Gay guide to Ukraine in English on the net. Some of the information may be outdated.

NATIONAL PUBLISHERS
Moloko Entertainment
2 Pyatiletki vulitsa 31-54 ✉310007 Kharkov
Publisher of gay erotic sport video films and of „Soldat Lyubvi" (Soldier of Love), a magazine with erotic photo of Ukrainian athletic models.

Odyn Z Nas
30 Kominterna vulitsa ✉01001 Kyiv ☎ (044) 239 38 53
☎ (044) 239 38 52 Fax: (044) 239 38 52
Homepage: www.geocities.com/WestHollywwod/Cafe/7177/
Magazine of male aestetics.

Representative 1/10. Ukrainian Office
P.O. Box 2140, Donetsk Region ✉87500 Manupol
Homepage: www.gay.ru/english/1-10/
Bi-annual publication since 1991. Approximately 36 pages. Reports, essays, notes and articles on the gay scene.

NATIONAL COMPANIES
Asant Video P.O. Box 5357 ✉310125 Kharkov
Producer and distributor of gay erotic videos.

NATIONAL GROUPS
Nash Mir Center
P.O. Box 62 ✉91051 Lugansk ☎ (0642) 47 94 22
Homepage: www.geocities.com/Westhollywood/2118/

Gay and lesbian human rights organisation. (Nash Mir = Our World). Quarterly publication available.

GENERAL GROUPS

International Friendship Club (GLM) 12-22 h ask for Vladimir
PO Box B-451 ✉01001 Kyiv ☎ (044) 946 5709 International ☎ 294 657 709 Local calls
International contacts, penpals, exchange visits, work as photo models. Information, meetings, massage, entertainment. Please send us ICRs.

Cherkassy ☎ 0472

GENERAL GROUPS

Gay Club
P.O. Box 1821 ✉18015

CRUISING

-Square near the Theater of Music and Drama (234 Shevchenko ulitsa)
-Square near the railway station
-Square near the main bus station

Dnepropetrovsk ☎ 0562

BARS

Sterling Bar (B D F G) Wed 20 h
32 Petrovskogo ☎ 52 51 46 (private)

GENERAL GROUPS

Alter Ego
P.O. Box 141 ✉320069 E-Mail: club_int@hotmail.com

CRUISING

-Park Shevchenko

Donetsk ☎ 062

GENERAL GROUPS

Nash Mir
P.O. Box 1113 ✉83052 ☎ 335 20 80 (helpline)
Also health advise.

HEALTH GROUPS

Donetsk AIDS Center
1a Olimpieva vulitsa ☎ 266 71 47

CRUISING

-Square near the Krupskaya library
-Park near the Yuzhny (Southern) bus station

Kaniv ☎ 04736

GENERAL GROUPS

Kaniv Group (GLM MA msg) 18-22 h
PO Box 34, Post Office N2 ✉19000 *(next to Kyiv)* ☎ 272 49
A service of acquaintance for gays and lesbians.

Kharkov ☎ 0572

GAY INFO

Gay-Info Line 0-24 h, closed on Mon and Wed
☎ 45 06 50
Gay news and consultation in Russian, english or German.

Simona
25-6 Geroyev Truda vulitsa ✉310168
E-Mail: itl568@online.kharkov.ua
Quarterly bulletin of some interest for gays.

Zvezdy
20A-2 Geroyev Truda vulitsa ✉310168
(Zvezdy = the Stars) Weekly newspaper with news on the gay and bi scene, free contact ads.

BARS

Bozh'ya Korovka Cafe (golden Knop) (B glm) 11-22 h
37 Petrovsky vulitsa *(metro Universitet)*

Oscar Bar (B glm r)
31 Petrovsky vulitsa *(Metro Pushkinskaya)*
Luxurious „cowboy" saloon like in American westerns with an old piano. Expensive cocktails and light food served.

Sofi (B glm) 11-22 h
5 Lenin Prospekt *(Metro Nauchnaya)*
Small cafe for romantic atmosphere for gay couples.

Zolotoye Runo (b F G) 11-22 h
37 Sumskaye vulitsa *(Metro Universtitet)*
The oldest and most well-known gay cafe in Kharkov (since 1987), no alcoholic drinks (but visitors are allowed to bring some with if they eat), excellent Russian and Ukrainaian food for low budget. The gay meeting point in the evening.

DANCECLUBS

Contra (B D G STV) Fri 21-6 h
25 Mironositskaya vulitsa
Expensive gay disco with techno music, shows and male dancers.

Hobo (B D f G) Fri 21-6 h
120 Akademika Pavlova vulitsa *(Metro Akademika Pavlova)*
The most popular gay disco of the city.

Joy (B D G S SNU STV) Thu and Sun 21-6 h
26 Petrovsky vulitsa *(Metro Pushkinskaya) (no sign board outside, ask for the architect atelier „interior design")*
Most popular gay disco with pop music, transvestites shows and male stripers.

SAUNAS/BATHS

Banja 2 (glm sa sb)
140 Poltavsky Shlyakh vulitsa *(Metro Kholodna Gora)*
Mixed but popular within gay men Fri, Sat, and Sun after 18 h.

Zdorovye (glm pi sa sb)
7 Lermontovskaya vulitsa ☎ 47 65 65
Mixed but gay men meet there on Wed and Sat 17-21 h

TRAVEL & TRANSPORT

Gay Ukraine International
Fax: 380 572 65 02 85
Ukrainian visas and accomodations, city guide services and translations.

GENERAL GROUPS

World Connection
P.O. Box 8782 ✉310002
Gay match-makers.

CRUISING

-Svodoby ploschad (freedom Square) (YG) (near the Lenin Monument)
-Central Railway station (Metro Yuzhnyi Vokzal, platform 5 near toilets)
-Hydropark, Shevchenko vulitsa (Tram 15, 16, and 26) (WC near the entrance) and gay nude beach (cross two central bridges, turn right and walk at the end of the island, summer only)
-Kharkov State University, 4 Svobody ploschad' (WC on the 6th, 7th and 8th floor, cafe at the entrance of the library on the 7th floor)
-Gorky Park, Sumskaya vulitsa, (benches on the central alley and public faciltities near the tennis court)

Kyiv ☎ 044

GAY INFO

Kyiv Gay Telegraph
☎ pager 213 38 69 for #5002
Homepage: www.geocities.com/WestHollywood/Cafe/7177
Monthly gay information bulletin.

BARS

Stary Kyiv (B glm)
52 Kreschatik vulitsa *(across Bessarabsky market)*

DANCECLUBS

Big Boys Club (B D f G R) 19-6 h, closed Mon
26/2 Garmatna vulitsa *(Metro Shulyavskaya)* ☎ 435 06 13
Brodyachaya Sobaka (B D DR f G R WE)
10 Nesterovsky pereulok *(near Lvovskaya ploschad)* ☎ 441 44 32
(Brodyachaya Sobaka = Stray Dog).
Heaven (B D f R WE) Fri Sat 22-6 h
8/4 Zhelyabova vulitsa *(Metro Shulyavskaya)* ☎ 441 74 46
Kletka (AYOR B D DR f G R) 22-6 h, closed Mon
3 Kutuzova vulitsa ☎ 573 88 48

GENERAL GROUPS

Gay Wagon 19-23 h
P.O. Box 250 GW ✉252150 ☎ 491 27 43

HEALTH GROUPS

We Are With You
9-201 Georgievsky pereulok ✉252034 ☎ 228 73 85
AIDS support group.

CRUISING

-Khreshchatyk vulitsa (from the metro station to the Bessarabsky market)
-Park T.Shevschenko (across the main red building of the Kiev State University)
-Main railway station

Lutsk ☎ 03322

SWIMMING

-Beach on the island of Sty river

CRUISING

-Bistro on Peremogy prospekt (near the stadium)
-Neofit cafe on Lesyi Ukrainki vulitsa
-WC in the metro near Dom Byta on Leyi Ukrainiki vulitsa

Lviv ☎ 0322

CRUISING

-Pingvin cafe on Svodoby prospekt
-Kofeynaya on Armyanskaya vulitsa
-Alley in the front of the Opera House
-Bodrost' public bathhouse (35 Turgeneva vulitsa)

Nikolayev ☎ 0512

GENERAL GROUPS

LIGA
P.O. Box 66 ✉327002
Gay, lesbian and bisexual association of Nikolayev.

Odessa ☎ 048

DANCECLUBS

Hollywood (B D glm WE) Fri, Sat 22-6 h
Deribassovskaya vulitsa *(at the corner of Sadovaya vulitsa)*
☎ 24 61 91
Parnas (B D glm) 21-6 h, closed Mon
48 Grecheskaya vulitsa *(1st floor of the Russian Drama Theater)*
☎ 26 37 65
69 Night Club (B D GLM) Wed-Sun 22-6 h
32 Troitskaya vulitsa ☎ 21 40 00

SWIMMING

-Beach of Chkalov sanatorium

CRUISING

-Pushkin monument on Frantsuzsky boulevard
-City garden along Deribassovskaya vulitsa

Poltava ☎ 0532

CRUISING

Slavy Park (near the monument to Poltavskaya bitva)

Sevastopol' ☎ 0692

CRUISING

-Admirala Ushakova square (near Sailors' House)

Simeiz ☎ 0600

SWIMMING

-Beach under the Koshka mountain (30 km from Yalta by Bus 26 or 43, then direction Lenin Sanatorium, 50 meters ahead and down the sea, right after the rock overlooking the sea (Simeiz is a well-known gay resort in summer)

CRUISING

-Ezhiki (Hedghogs) Cafe

Simferopol' ☎ 0652

CRUISING

-Gurman cafe (11 Pushkina vulitsa)
-Square between the main post office and the Crimean Parliament
.Square near the new stage of Russian Groky Theater

Yalta ☎ 0692

CRUISING

-Near Yubileiny concert hall

Zaporizhzhe ☎ 0612

GENERAL GROUPS

Zaporizhzhe Center of Sexual Minorities
P.O. Box 3857 ✉330059 E-Mail: root@vilatex.zaporizhzhe.ua

CRUISING

-Velikoy Otechestvennoy Voiny ploschad' (across the City hall building)

Zhitomir ☎ 0412

GENERAL GROUPS

Gay Initiative Group
P.O. Box 32 ✉262012 Homepage: lgbt_zhitomir@yahoo.com

United Kingdom

Northwestern Europe

Initials: GB

Time: GMT

☎ Country Code / Access Code: 44 / 00

Language: English

Area: 242,100 km² / 93,451 sq mi.

Currency: 1 Pound Sterling (£) = 100 Pence. 1 EURO = 100 Euro Cents; the Euro can only be used in the clearance system.

Population: 58,970,000

Capital: London

Religions: 57% Anglicans, 15% other Protestants, 13% Catholics

Important gay cities: London, Manchester, Brighton, Edinburgh

● Since the new Labour government has taken power in the United Kingdom gay rights have been back on the UK political agenda. The age of sexual concent has been equalised, gays can serve in the military and sexuality education courses are now permissable in schools. There are 3 openly gay cabinet members and a few more openly gay members of parlament. Attitudes have been changing rapidly since Mrs Thatcher departed and though there is still some way to go, especially outside London, things have improved greatly. The scene in the UK is large and confident and is based mainly in London, Manchester, Edinburgh and Brighton, though wherever you go you will probably find some bar or club. There is an extensive local media and gay programs and characters on television are now common. However this is still Britain so sex in public places is frowned upon and too much public affection is not liked, gay or straight. British men are not generally into holding hands in the street or lots of public kissing and tend to be a little reserved at first, but get them back to your hotel room and you will find them as anyone else!

✱ Seitdem die Labour-Partei an der Regierung ist, hat sich die Rechtslage der Homosexuellen erheblich verbessert: Das Schutzalter liegt einheitlich bei 18 Jahren, Homosexuelle dürfen Militärdienst leisten und Sexualität darf seit neuem auch in den Schulen thematisiert werden. In der britischen Regierung sind gegenwärtig drei offen homosexuelle Kabinetsmitglieder, im Parlament sind einige weitere offen homosexuell lebende Mitglieder. Seit dem Ende der "Thatcher-Ära" hat sich vieles sehr schnell verändert, vor allem außerhalb von London sind große Fortschritte im Hinblick auf die Akzeptanz Homosexueller zu verzeichnen. Großbritannien verfügt über eine sehr große und selbstbewußte homosexuelle Szene. Ihre Zentren liegen vor allem in London, Manchester, Edinburgh und Brighton. Es gibt eine ausgeprägte schwule Presselandschaft und homosexuelle Themen oder Charaktere im Fernsehen sind schon fast selbstverständlich. Dennoch gibt man sich in Großbritannien in der Öffentlichkeit weiterhin eher prüde, gleich ob homo- oder heterosexuell. Nur selten wird man zwei Männer Hand-in-Hand oder sich innig küssend durch die Straßen gehen sehn. Aber auch wenn die Briten zunächst sehr reserviert wirken, hinter verschlossenen Türen entpuppen sie sich als ebenso zugänglich wie alle anderen Männer auf dieser Welt auch.

▲ Depuis que le gouvernement travailliste a pris le pouvoir au Royaume-Uni, les droits des homosexuels ont enfin repris une place dans le calendrier politique anglais. L'âge de la majorité sexuelle a été revue au même niveau pour tous, les gays peuvent servir dans l'armée et les cours d'éducation sexuelle sont maintenant autorisés dans les écoles. Trois membres du Cabinet ainsi que plusieurs parlementaires sont ouvertement gays. Les attitudes ont rapidement évoluées depuis le départ de Margaret Tatcher même s'il reste encore du chemin à faire, particulièrement en dehors de Londres. La scène du Royaume-Uni est grande et bien implantée et se concentre principalement dans les villes de Londres, Manchester, Edimbourg et Brighton, bien que l'on trouve aujourd'hui un peu partout des bars ou clubs gays. De nombreux journaux locaux, des programmes de radio, et une présence télévisuelle gays participent à la diversité de cette scène. Même si l'on reste en Angleterre, pays où les rapports sexuels dans les lieux publiques sont interdits et où une attitude trop affectée n'est que peu appréciée, que ce soit d'ailleurs de la part des hétéros ou des homos. Les Britanniques ne se tiennent que rarement par la main et ne s'embrassent que peu en public mais, une fois dans l'intimité, se révèlent tout aussi semblable que les autres hommes.

☆ Con la llegada del gobierno laborista al poder, los derechos de los homosexuales han vuelto a ser objeto de atención de la agenda política del Reino Unido. La edad de consentimiento sexual se ha igualado para todos, los homosexuales pueden servir en el ejército y la educación sexual está ahora permitida en las escuelas. Hay 3 miembros del gabinete ministerial y más miembros del Parlamento que son abiertamente gays. La actitud de la gente ha cambiado rápidamente desde que la señora Thatcher dejó el gobierno, sin embargo queda aún un buen camino por andar en este sentido. Especialmente fuera de Londres las cosas han mejorado enormemente. La escena en el Reino Unido es extensa y confiada y se centra principalmente en Londres, Manchester, Edimburgo y Brighton, sin embargo, donde quiera que vayáis encontraréis probablemente algún bar o club. Hay una gran red de medios de comunicación locales y los programas y personas gay se prodigan en televisión. De todas formas esto sigue siendo Gran Bretaña, de manera que el sexo o las pruebas de afecto en público están mal vistas, para gays o no. Los hombres ingleses no suelen ir cogidos de la mano o dándose besos por la calle y tienen la tendencia a ser algo reservados al principio, pero una vez en la habitación del hotel son tan agudos como cualquier otro.

❖ Con la llegada del gobierno laborista al poder, los derechos de los homosexuales han vuelto a ser objeto de atención de la agenda política del Reino Unido. La edad de consentimiento sexual se ha igualado para todos, los homosexuales pueden servir en el ejército y la educación sexual está ahora permitida en las escuelas. Hay 3 miembros del gabinete ministerial y más miembros del Parlamento que son abiertamente gays. La actitud de la gente ha cambiado rápidamente desde que la señora Thatcher dejó el gobierno, sin embargo queda aún un buen camino por andar en este sentido. Especialmente fuera de Londres las cosas han mejorado enormemente. La escena en el Reino Unido es extensa y confiada y se centra principalmente en Londres, Manchester, Edimburgo y Brighton, sin embargo, donde quiera que vayáis encontraréis probablemente algún bar o club. Hay una gran red de medios de comunicación locales y los programas y personas gay se prodigan en televisión. De todas formas esto sigue siendo Gran Bretaña, de manera que el sexo o las pruebas de afecto en público están mal vistas, para gays o no. Los hombres ingleses no suelen ir cogidos de la mano o dándose besos por la calle y tienen la tendencia a ser algo reservados al principio, pero una vez en la habitación del hotel son tan agudos como cualquier otro.

NATIONAL GAY INFO

Attitude
Northern & Shell Tower, City Harbour, London ✉E14 9GL
☎ (0207) 308 5090 Fax: (0207) 308 5075
Monthly colour magazine for £ 2.20. Over 100 pages of fashion, films, arts, nightlife and music. Glossy and light-hearted. Available at most good newsagents.

Bears Club UK
188 Main Road, Sidcup ✉DA14 6RL

BOYZ
Cedar House, 72 Holloway Road, London ✉N7 8NZ
☎ (0207) 296 6000 Fax: (0207) 296-0026
Free weekly scene guide with news, reviews (plus a hot pin-up). Two versions: London/Brighton and the national edition. Available at most gay venues in London and throughout the UK.

British Gay and Lesbian Sports Federation
c/o Central Station, 37 Wharfdale Road, London ✉N1 9SE
E-Mail: teamUK@gaygames.org

Campaign for Homosexual Equality (CHE)
PO Box 342 ✉WC1X 0DU London ☎ 0402/326 151

DNA Magazine
14a Newman Street, London ✉W1P 3HD ☎ (0207) 631 0955
Fax: (0207) 323 4253 E-Mail: dna.magazine@virgin.net.
Witty and funny magazine distributed nationwide.

EuroGuy
c/o Millivres Press, 3 Broadbent Close, London ✉N6 5GG
☎ (0208) 3489963 Fax: (0208) 348 002
Monthly pin-up magazine featuring young, cute models. Price £ 4.99, available in gay shops or by mail-order.

Gay and lesbian Penfriends 9-17 h
36, Edwalton Avenue, Peterborough ✉PE3 6ER
☎ (01733) 76 7242
E-Mail: penfriends@base2promotions.demon.co.uk

Gay Business Association (GBA)
Unit 10 Eurolink Centre, 49 Efra Rd, London ✉SW2 1BZ
☎ 07002 255 422 Fax: (0207) 737 3571

Gay Times (GLM)
Millivres Ltd., Ground Floor, 116-134 Bayham St., London ✉NW1 *(Worldwide House)* ☎ (0207) 482 2576
Homepage: www.gaytimes.co.uk
Monthly glossy full of news, reviews, interviews as well as comprehensive listings for Great Britain and Ireland. Availabe in all good newsagents in London and gay friendly outlets throughout the U.K.

Gay to Z
41 Cooks Road, London ✉SE17 3NG ☎ (0207) 793 7450
Fax: (0207) 820 1366
This phone directory of over 100 pages is bulging with telephone numbers of UK based gay and gay-friendly businesses and organisations.

Lesbian and Gay Switchboard
BM/Switchboard, London ✉WC1 3XX ☎ (0207) 837 7324

Pink Paper. The
Cedar House, 72 Holloway Rd., London ✉N7 8NZ
☎ (0207) 296-6210 Fax: (0207) 957-0046
Long running free weekly newspaper available throughout the UK at most gay venues and establishments. Covers all aspects of gay life from culture and entertainment to political issues and other news stories.

Pride Scotland
58a Broughton Street, London ✉EH1 3SA ☎ (0131) 556 8822

QX
Firststar, 24 Denmark Street, London ✉WC 2H 8NJ
☎ (0207) 379-7887 Fax: 379-7525
E-Mail: qxmag@dircon.co.uk Homepage: www.qxmag.co.uk
Club news, music, lifestyle, contacts.

Scots Gay (GLM)
Paperprint Ltd., PO Box 666, Edinburgh ✉EH7 5YW
☎ (0131) 539 0666 Fax: (0131) 539 299
Monthly magazine, covering all aspects of gay life in Scotland including comprehensive scene listings. Price £ 1.00, free in some gay venues.

Stonewall Lobby Group Mon-Fri 10-18 h (by appointment only)
16 Clerkenwell Close, London ✉EC1R 0AN ☎ (0207) 336 8860
The following free publications can be found in most gay bars/clubs etc.
-Boyz. (Free, weekly, colour newspaper with complete scene listings and reviews (plus weekly pin-up!))
-QX. (The scene and music magazine)
-DNA. (Monthly gay, satirical, sexy magazine)
See also National Publications.

NATIONAL PUBLISHERS

Gay Mens Press (GMP)
50 South Ealing Rd., London ✉W5 4QJ, PO Box 247, Swaffham PE37 8PA ☎ (01366) 328101 Fax: (01366) 32 81 02
E-Mail: david@gmppubs.demon.co.uk
One of the great gay publishers in the world. Publishes a range of best gay books, fiction and non-fiction. Retail trade is by mail-order. Ask for free catalogue.

NATIONAL COMPANIES

Clone Zone
37/39 Bloom Street, Manchester ✉M1 3LY
☎ (0161) 236 1398
Mail order company with shops in London, Manchester, Brighton and Blackpool. Jocks, clothes in leather and denim, swim wear, exotic wear, rubber, greeting cards, books etc. Catalogue for free.

Dangerous to know
17 A Newman Street, London ✉W1P 3HB ☎ (0207) 255 1955
Fax: (0171) 636 5717

Fantasy Erotique
PO Box 1019, Dersingham ✉PE31 6PJ ☎ (01485) 544 844
E-Mail: bubo@compuserve.co.uk
Mail order only. Catalogue for free by phone, E-mail or SAE. Leather, rubber and toys.
Gay Times Book Service
Camdem High Street, London ✉NW1 7BX ☎ 0207/267 0021
Worldwide mailorder of quality books
Honour (mo)
86 Lower Marsh, Waterloo, London ✉SE1 7AB
☎ (0207) 401 8219
Leather, rubber, toys. Catalogue for £ 5 (refunded on order).
RoB (G MG W) Mon-Sat 10.30-18.30 h
24 Wells Street, London ✉W1 3 FG ☎ (0207) 735 7893

NATIONAL GROUPS

Lesbian & Gay Christian Movement
Oxford House, Derbyshire Street, London ✉E2 6HG
☎ (0207) 739 8134 Fax: (0171) 739 1249
Terrence Higgins Trust Daily 12-22 h
London ✉WC1N 3XX ☎ (0207) 242 1010

Aberdeen - Grampian ☎ 01224

GAY INFO

Grampian Lesbian, Gay & Bisexual Switchboard Wed Fri 19-22 h
PO Box 174, Crown Street ✉AB9 1AA ☎ 63 35 00

DANCECLUBS

Lust at Deniros (B D GLM MA) 22-2 h
120 Union Street

HOTELS

Jasmine Guest House (glm H MA)
27 Jasmine Terrace ✉AB2 1LA ☎ 64 14 10 *Central and convenient. B&B rates single from £ 15, twin £ 12.00 per person*

HEALTH GROUPS

AIDS Helpline Tue Fri 19-21 h
☎ 57 40 00

Aberystwyth - Dyfed ☎ 01970

BARS

Boar's Head (AC B D f glm MA) 12-14 17.30-1 h, Sun closed, Fri-Sat (G)
Queens Road ☎ 62 61 06

DANCECLUBS

Treehouse (B f glm MA) (GLM) 2nd Tue/month 19-21.30 h
2 Pier Street ☎ 61 57 91

Aldershot - Surrey ☎ 01252

BARS

South Western Hotel (AC B D GLM MA N SNU STV YG)
11-23.30 h, 12-22 h
Station Road ✉9U11 1HT *(Opposite BR train station)* ☎ 31 80 91
Email: Robby@Tesco.Net

Ashford - Kent ☎ 01233

DANCECLUBS

Pink Cadillacs (B D f GLM lj MA OS SNU STV VS W WE YG)
Wed Fri-Sat 20.30-2 h
Canterbury Road, Charing ✉TN27 0EY *(A252) at the Woodland Country Club* ☎ 71 37 31

Ashton-Under-Lyne - Greater Manchester ☎ 0161

BARS

Blues Fun Bar (B D F glm MA S STV TV VS W)
Mon-Sat 22-2 h
211/215 mStamford Street, Stalybridge ✉OL6 7QB
☎ 330 32 12

Aviemore - Highland ☎ 01479

HOTELS

Auchendean Lodge Hotel (B bf CC F glm H MA T)
Dulnain Bridge ✉PH26 3LU ☎ 85 13 47
Located in a beautiful countryside. The 7 bedrooms are comfortably furnished, most with private toilets and bath or shower. All rooms have central heating, heated towel rails, tea / coffee making facilities, radio colour TV, handbasins and shaver sockets. Full Scottish breakfast and dinner served. Prices from £36-71 p/p.

Ayr - Strathclyde ☎ 01292

GUEST HOUSES

Daviot Guest House (H)
Queens Terrace ✉KA7 1DU
☎ 269678

Bangor - Gwynedd

SWIMMING

-Llanddwyn Beach (g). (Easiest access by car (parking fee £ 2). From Newsborough on W. coast of Anglesey follow signs for beach parking through forest. On the beach itself, turn left and walk for 15-20 minutes to where the dunes are highest.)

Barnsley - Yorkshire ☎ 01226

BARS

Baker Street (B g MA) (G) Tue 19-23, Thu 19-24 h
Sheffield Road ☎ 78 16 74

SAUNAS/BATHS

Greenhouse Health Club (B CC f G sa sb WE wh WO)
11-23:00h, Fri-Sat -02:00 h Sun 12-23:00h
56 Sheffield Road *(Junction 36. M1)* ☎ 73 13 05
Popular.

Barnstaple - Devon ☎ 01392

GAY INFO

Devon Gay & Lesbian Switchboard Mon 19:30-22:00h
☎ 422016 Homepage: www.egrorian.internetfci.com/~daved
Helpline and Switchboard.

Bath - Avon ☎ 01225

BARS

Bath Tap. The (B D GLM MA SNU STV) Mon-Sat 12-23, Sun -22.30 h
19 St. James Parade ✉BA1 1U2
☎ 40 43 44
Green Room in Garrick's Head (B f glm MA) 11-23, Sun 12-22.30 h
St. John's Place, Sawclose *(next to Theatre Royal)*

HOTELS

Kennard Hotel. The (bf CC glm)
11 Henrietta Street ✉BA2 6LL ☎ 31 04 72 Fax: 46 00 54
E-Mail: kennard@dircon.co.uk Homepage: www.kennard.co.uk
Each room has colour TV, direct-dial telephone, hairdryer and beverage facilities. Rates single £ 48, double 78-88. Full English or Continental bf incl.

GUEST HOUSES

Guesthouse (bf F G MA p)
10 Hawarden Terrace, Larkhall ✉BA1 6RE ☎ 31 01 18
Bed & Breakfast accommodation for gay men only. Naturists welcome.
Leigh House ☛ Bradford-upon-Avon

GENERAL GROUPS

Bath Gay Nudist Group
☎ 31 01 18 *(Colin and Ian)*
3M`s Gay men`s supper group
☎ 0177-968 66 72

HEALTH GROUPS

Gay Men's Health Project Bath & Western Wilshire
c/o St. Martins Hospital, Midford Road ✉BA2 2RP
☎ & Fax: 83 39 00
Information about HIV and AIDS.

HELP WITH PROBLEMS

Students Lesbian and Gay Line Tue 18-19.30 h
☎ 46 57 93

Bedford - Bedfordshire ☎ 01234

BARS

Barley Mow. The (B d GLM) Mon-Thu 12-15:00h, 19-23:00h, Fri & Sat 12-23:00h
72 St. Layes Street ☎ 35 93 55
Gay run pub. Disco Fri and Karaoke Sat.

DANCECLUBS

Clarence Hotel (B D GLM MA S SNU) 11-23:00 h
13 St. John Street ✉MK42 0AH ☎ 35 27 81

Belfast - Antrim ☎ 028

BARS

Crow's Nest. The (B F glm MA) Mon-Wed 11.30-23, Thu 11.30-24.30, Fri Sat 11.30-1 h
Skipper Street/High Street ☎ 90 32 54 91
Parliament Bar (AC B D F glm MA S) Mon-Sat 11.30-1.30, Sun 12-15, 19-23 h
2-6 Dunbar Street *(Next to Albert Clock)* ☎ 90 23 45 23

SEX SHOPS/BLUE MOVIES

Mystique (glm) Mon-Thu Sat 9.30-16, Sun 12-17 h, until late Thu-Fri
27 Gresham Street ✉BT1 4QN *(Back of Castle Court Shopping Centre)* ☎ 90 31 20 43
Videos, toys, cards and magazines

BOOK SHOPS

Soho Books
27 Gresham Street

HEALTH GROUPS

GUM Clinic (STD Clinic) Mon, Wed & Fri 8:30-12:00h, 13:30-15:30h Tue & Thu 08:30-11:00h
Royal Victoria Hospital, Infirmary Road. ☎ 90 894 777

Rainbow Project
33 Church Lane, ✉BT1 4QN ☎ 90 31 90 30
Fax: 90 31 90 31
Drop-in center

Bideford - Devon ☎ 01237

GUEST HOUSES

Bocombe Mill Cottage (bf G H NU OS)
Bocombe, Parkham ✉EX39 5PH *Will collect you from the station*
☎ 45 12 93 Fax: 45 12 93 E-Mail: info@bocombe.co.uk
Small B&B in beautiful setting close to the sea. All rooms with shower, TV and radio. Gourmet Dinner (five courses) from £ 27.50 p.p. served. Room rates single from £ 40 and 60 incl. English bf.

Birmingham - West Midlands ☎ 0121

GAY INFO

Lesbian & Gay Switchboard West Midlands
19-22 h
PO Box 3626 ✉B5 4LG ☎ 622 65 89
Helpline for lesbians and gays and everyone who needs it.

BARS

Fountain Inn. The (B bf CC G LJ MG OG) Mon-Fri 19-23:00 h, Sat & Sun 13-23:00h
102 Wrentham Street ✉BS 6QL ☎ 622 1452
Comfortable rooms with TV above this gay pub. Some rooms are en suite and the substantial full english breakfast is served downstairs in the bar area. Rates: Single from £ 25, Double £ 35.
Fox. The (B gLM MA OS W) Mon-Sat 19-23, Sun 19-22.30 h
17 Lower Essex Street ✉B5 6SN ☎ 622 1210
Jester. The (AC B G MA N) 12-23 h
Holloway Circus, Queensway ✉B1 1EG *(Opposite Dome Nightclub)*
☎ 643 0155
Missing (B d F G MA SNU STV W) Mon-Sat 12-23, Sun 16-22.30 h
48 Bromsgrove Street ✉B5 6NU ☎ 622 42 56
Partners Bar (AC B D GLM MA SNU STV) 13-23:00h
27-35 Hurst Street ✉B5 4BD *(Next to Hippodrome Theatre)*
☎ 622 4710
Route Two (AC B CC D F GLM S STV TV W YG) Mon-Sat 19-02:00, Sun 17-22.30 h
139-147 Hurst Street ✉B5 6JD ☎ 622 3366
Village Inn (B GLM H MA N OS s WE) Mon-Sat 13-23, Sun 12-22.30 h
152 Hurst Street ✉B5 6RY ☎ 622 4742

DANCECLUBS

Nightingale Club. The (AC B CC D F Glm lj MA OS SNU STV W WE YG) Mon-Thu 22-2, Fri Sat 21-3.30, Sun 21-1 h
Essex House, Kent Street ✉B5 6RD ☎ 622 1718
Fittings leather bar 18-22.30 h.
Subway City (AC B bf D F GLM lj MA P SNU STV TV W) Thu 22-3.30, Fri 22-4, Sat 22-4.30, Sun 21.30-2 h
Livery Street ✉B3 *(Under the archways by the Post Office Tower)*
☎ 233 0310

RESTAURANTS

Woodloft. The (A AC B bf CC E F GLM lj MA MG OS s W) 8-2 h, closed Mon
18 Kent Street ✉B5 6RO *(Next to Nightingales)* ☎ 622 6717

SAUNAS/BATHS

Greenhouse Health Club (B CC F G sa sb sol wh WO) 10-2, Fri -6, Sat 12-8, Sun 12-2 h
Willenhall Road ✉WS10 8JD *(Junction10, M 6)* ☎ 568 61 26

Looking Glass. The (CC f G MA sa sb sol WO) 12-23, Fri Sat 12-6 h
Kent House, Gooch Street North ✉B5 6QF *(Unit 5; Train Station-New Street)* ☎ 666 7529
Half price entrance Sun-Thu 18-20 h.

Spartan Health Club (F G MA P sa sol) 12-23, Sun 13-22:00 h
127 George Road, Erdington ☎ 382 3345

GIFT & PRIDE SHOPS

Clone Zone (GLM) Mon-Wed 10.30-19, Thu-Sat 10.30-21, Sun 12-18 h
84 Hurst Street ✉B5 4TD ☎ 666 6640
Extensive range of magazines, books, videos, clothing, leather, rubber, toys and more.

HOTELS

Monument Gardens (bf CC glm H lj msg p)
266 Monument Road, Edgbuston ✉B16 8XF ☎ 455 9459
Fax: 454 7307 E-Mail: sebshouse@aol.com
Each room has TV, video, direct dial telephone, refrigerator, tea/coffee facilities. Some en-suite rooms. Rates single from £ 26, double 35, en-suite 45.

Village Inn (B bf f GLM H MA OS W)
152 Hurst Street ✉B5 6RY ☎ 622 4742
Bright and spacious rooms available in this B&B. Ideally located above the very popular bar in the centre of the „Gay Village". Rates: Single £ 25, Double £ 38.50 incl. bf.

GENERAL GROUPS

Central Central Rainbow, Deaf Gays & Lesbians (GLM MA) 3rd Sat 20.30-23.00 h at „The Fox"
PO Box 4036 ✉B30 1AT ☎ 478 0562

FETISH GROUPS

Midland Link MSC meetings 1st 3rd Sun at The Fountain Inn, Wrentham St.
20 Mapperley Gardens, Moseley ✉B13 8RN
Member of ECMC.

RELIGIOUS GROUPS

Quest (L&G catholics) 20-22:00h
☎ 608 9153
(Malcolm)

SPORT GROUPS

Gay Outdoor Club 19.30-21.30 h
☎ 01902/757 624 ☎ 0958/403 931
Walking & swimming group

CRUISING

-Kennedy Gardens (AYOR) (Near Colmore Circus)
-Canal bank (AYOR) (Rear of Jug)
-Manzoni Gardens (AYOR) (Bull Ring)

Blackburn - Lancashire ☎ 01254

DANCECLUBS

C'est La Vie (B D GLM MA) Sun 20-24, Tue 21-2 h
11-15 Market Street ☎ 69 18 77

Blackpool - Lancashire ☎ 01253

● The weather in Blackpool is just too bad for it being a bath in the classical sense of the word. But fans of british trashy lifestyle will just love the fish and chips, the drag and karaoke shows. The main landmark of Blackpool is the 158 meter high „Tower". At its feet you'll find hustle and bustle: gambling halls on the piers, cinemas, fairs a.s.o. Just let yourself get carried away by it.

✱ Blackpool ist kein Seebad im klassischen Sinne. Das Wetter ist einfach nicht mild genug. Aber dafür kommen hier die Fans britischer Trashkultur bei Fish'n Chips, Travestie und Karaoke voll auf ihre Kosten.
Wahrzeichen der Stadt ist „The Tower" (158 m hoch). Zu seinen Füssen tobt das wahre Leben: Spielhallen auf den Piers, Kinos, Vergnügungsparks und so fort. Lassen Sie sich einfach vom Urlaubstrubel anstecken.

▲ Un temps clément vous permettra peut-être de vous baigner à Blackpool mais, même en cas d'intempéries, vous allez adorer les «fish and chips», les soirées karaoké et les spectacles de transformistes qu'offre cette ville. C'est au pied de la „Tower" (attraction principale de ville, une tour 158 m de harteur) que la fête bat son plein: les salles de jeux y côtoient cinémas et autres parcs d'attraction. Il ne vous restera qu'à vous laisser emporter et surtout à vous laisser charmer par la gentillesse des habitants de ce lieu.

☆ A veces el tiempo en Blackpool no es el mejor, pero de todas formas os encantarán el fish and chips y los karaokes. El punto principal de referencia de Blackpool es la "Tower", de 158 metros de altura. A sus pies tiene lugar el ajetreo de las salas de juego en el muelle, los cines y los bares. Dejaos llevar por el ambiente. La gente es amigable y os encantará.

❖ Blackpool non è una stazione balneare in senso tradizionale, poichè il tempo non è sufficientemente mite. Ciononostante gli appassionati della cultura trash britannica trovano il modo di spendere qui i loro soldi in fish'n chips, spettacoli di travestiti e karaoke. „The tower" (158 m.) è il simbolo della città. Ai suoi piedi vi è una vita spumeggiante: casin , cinema, luna park etc. Lasciatevi contagiare dall'euforia delle vacanze.

TOURIST INFO

Tourist Information Centre
1 Clifton Street ✉FY1 1LY ☎ 478 222 Fax: 263 68

BARS

Basil's on the Strand (! AC B D f GLM MA SNU STV VS) 12.30-0.30, Thu, Fri & Sat -02:00h, Sun 12-22.30 h
9 The Strand ✉FY1 2DW *(Walk towards North Pier)*
☎ 29 41 09

Flying Handbag. The (B d F GLM MA N S SNU STV VS W) Mon-Sat 11-23, Sun 12-22.30 h
170/172 Talbot Road ✉FY1 3AZ *(Next to Flamingo)*
☎ 255 22

Funny Girls (B glm STV) Mon-Sun 11-23 h
1-7 Queen Street ✉FY1 1NL ☎ 0125/29 11 44

Lucy's Bar (AC B D f GLM MA S SNU STV VS W YG) Mon-Sat 20-2, Sun 20-22.30 h
Talbot Square ✉FY1 1LB *(Below Rumours)* ☎ 29 32 04

Pepes Bar (B D f GLM MA SNU) Mon-Fri 12-1, Sat Sun 12-2 h
94 Talbot Street ✉FY1 1LR ☎ 266 91

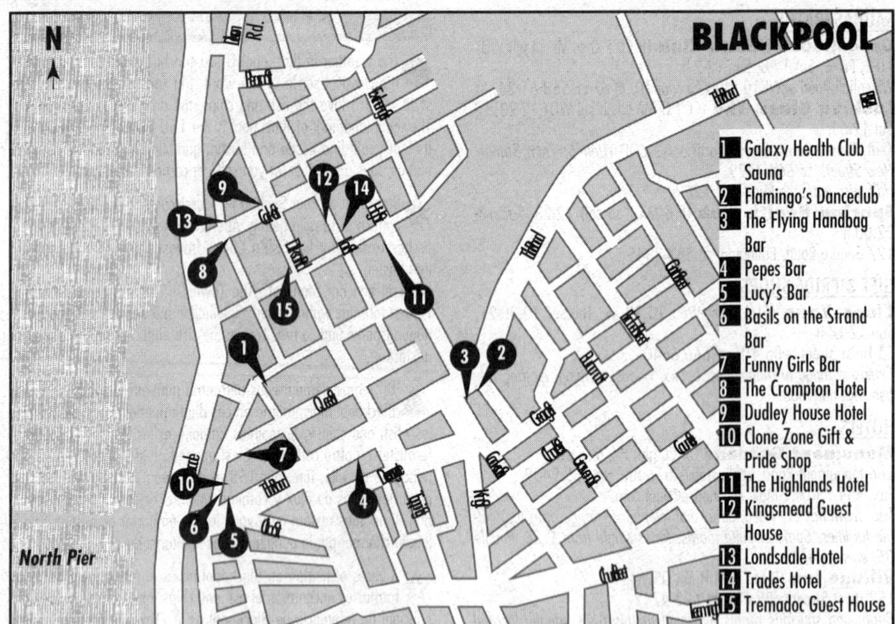

DANCECLUBS

Flamingo's (! B D f GLM MA S YG) Mon-Sat 22-2.00, Sun 21-24:00 h
170-176 Talbot Road ✉FY1 3AZ ☎ 6249 01

SAUNAS/BATHS

Galaxy Sauna & Steam Spa (AC b CC F G MA P sa sb sol VS wh) Sun-Fri 12-22, Sat 12-Sun 07:30h
25-27 Springfield Road ✉FY1 1QW *(near Metropole Hotel; Train Station-Blackpool North)* ☎ 29 46 10
Entrance-fee £ 9-12.

GIFT & PRIDE SHOPS

Clone Zone (GLM) Mon-Sat 11-18, Sun 12-17 h
3 The Strand, North Shore ✉FY1 1NX ☎ 29 48 50
Extensive range of magazines, books, videos, clothing, toys, leather, rubber and more.

TRAVEL & TRANSPORT

Progress Taxis Limited 24 h
158 Talbot Road ☎ 23 411
Gay friendly taxi service.

HOTELS

Abbeyville (GLM H LJ MA msg) closed Feb
39 High Street, ✉FY1 2BN *(6 doors from main station)* ☎ 75 20 72
Rates from £ 12-15 per person incl. bf.

Arendale Private Hotel (bf F glm H)
23 Gynn Avenue ✉FY1 2LD ☎ 35 10 44 Fax: 35 10 44
Small hotel with 7 rooms en-suite or with shared bath, all with radio. Rate from £ 19 incl. bf, dinner £ 4.50 extra. TV room.

Belvedere. The (B bf F glm H OS) Reception: Mon-Sun 8-24 h
77 Dickson Road, ✉FY1 2BX ☎ 247 33
Small hotel where the majority of the rooms are en suite, all have TV. Rates: from £ 16 p.p, incl. bf.

Brooklyn Hotel. The (b F glm H sa) Reception: Mon-Sun 7-23 h
7 Wilton Parade, ✉FY1 2HE ☎ 270 03 Fax: 246 22
En suite hotel, with sea view, serving evening meals where vegetarians are well catered for. The rooms have satellite TV. Rates: from £ 20 incl. bf.

Carlton House Hotel (B bf f glm H MA)
77 Abbington Street ✉7Y1 1PP ☎ 62 86 87
Rooms with TV, central heating, in this friendly guest-house. Rates from £ 11.50 incl. bf.

Colins Hotel (bf G H OS) 9-11
Cocker Street ✉FY1 1SF ☎ 205 41
Large guest house, some rooms en suite. Rates: £ 10-15, incl. bf.

Crompton Hotel. The (b bf glm H MA) closed Christmas
20 Cocker Street ✉F41 2BY *(Train Station-Blackpool North)* ☎ 29 15 83 Fax: 29 15 83
Gay owned hotel with 11 rooms with TV. Rates: from £ 15. incl. bf.

Dudley House Hotel (bf GLM)
27 Cocker Street ☎ 6209 88
13 rooms, some en suite rooms available. Rates: £ 15 p.p, incl. bf.

Hertford Hotel (B bf CC f glm H MA OS) All year
18 Lord Street ✉FY1 2BD ☎ 622 793
E-Mail: hertford@ceges.dircon.co.uk
Small gay owned hotel. Rooms en suite.

Highlands. The (b bf CC F glm H MA W) 46-54
High Street, ✉FY1 2BN ☎ 75 22 64
All rooms have satellite TV, and most are en suite. Bar with a pool table. Rates from £ 15, incl. bf.

Kingsmead Guest House (bf CC glm H MA msg OS) 8-24 h
58 Lord Street ✉FY1 2BJ ☎ 62 44 96
Fax: 0870-055 39 84. Email: kingsmead@hotel.demon.co.uk.
Lonsdale Hotel (b bf CC F glm H) 8-24 h
25 Cocker St. ✉FY1 2BZ ☎ 6216 28
Small hotel with private parking. All rooms en suite. Rates: from £ 16 incl. bf.
Mardi Gras. Hotel (B bf CC f G H MA)
41-43 Lord Street ✉FY1 2BD ☎ 75 10 87 ☎ 75 10 88
This hotel is also exclusively gay. All rooms are en suite with satellite TV. Bar is open until the early hours of the morning. Rates: Single from £ 14, Double from £ 28 incl. bf.
Nevada. Hotel (AC B bf f Glm H LJ MA N OS WE YG)
23 Lord Street ✉FY1 2BD ☎ 29 07 00
Centrally located guest-house, with a liscenced bar. All rooms with TV, and some en suite rooms are available. Full English bf served. Late licensed bar.
Sheron Hotel. The (bf CC F glm H MA OS)
21 Gynn Avenue ✉FY1 2LD ☎ 35 46 14
Small hotel with 9 rooms. Rates double with shared bath £ 25-32, en-suite £ 31-38, single £ 2 extra when available. English bf included. TV lounge.
Sunnyside Hotel. The (bf g H MA)
16 Charles Street ✉FY1 3HD ☎ 6229 83
Most rooms are en suite and all with TV.
Trades (B bf f G H lj MA sa sol)
51-55 Lord Street ✉FY1 2BJ ☎ 264 01 Fax: 6231 79
Exclusively gay hotel with 32 rooms, some of which are en suite. The bar is open until the early hours of the morning. All rooms with TV. The accomodation is basic.
Tremadoc Guest House (B bf F G H MA) 24h
127-129 Dickson Rd., North Sore ✉FY1 2EU ☎ 6240 01
All rooms with Satellite TV. Rates: £ 12-16, incl.bf.

GUEST HOUSES

Cosy Guest House (bf GLM H)
26 Milbourne Street ☎ 251 63
Very cosy with just 2 bedrooms! The friendly landlady makes you feel at home and she gives you free access to the kitchen and lounge. Rates: from £10 p.p incl. bf.
Sandolin Guesthouse (bf glm H MA OS) 8-? h
117 High Street ✉FY1 2DW *(Pink canopy over front door/Rosa Baldachin vorm Eingang)* ☎ 75 29 08
Gay-friendly guest house, all rooms with TV. Rates: from £ 12.50 p.p, incl. bf.
Sandylands Guest House (bf glm H lj)
47 Banks Street, North Shore ✉FY1 2BE ☎ 29 46 70
Fax: 29 46 70 E-Mail: sandylands@blackpool.net
Homepage: www.ndirect.co.uk/~sandylands/accom.htm
8 rooms with TV, tea/coffee, shower/WC on corridor. Rates from £ 12-15 incl. English bf.
Willowfield Guest House (bf CC glm MA N OS)
51 Banks Street ✉FY1 2BE ☎ 623406
Homepage: www.gayhotels.com/willowfield.html

PRIVATE ACCOMODATION

Chaucer House (bf G H MA) All year
59 High Street ✉FY1 2BN ☎ 29 90 99
Small B & B, some rooms are en suite. Rates: from £ 11 p.p incl. bf.

CRUISING

-Bethesda Square
-Lytham Road/station road opposite Grand Hotel
-Bond Street (back of the pleasure beach)
-North and Central Piers
-Silcocks amusement arcade (top of the building)
-Winter Gardens (AYOR) (downstairs, busy)
-Bust station Talbot Road
-Reuoe Park (summer only)
-Starr gate (Tram Terminus)
-Middle walk (AYOR RT) (busy)
-Middle walk (north of Metropole Hotel below the tram tracks. Busy in summer. Nights ayor)

Bolton - Greater Manchester ☎ 01204

BARS

Absolutely Fabulous (B GLM MA STV) 17-23 h
Clarence Street ☎ 39 37 05
Star. The (B d f GLM MA) Mon-Wed 17-23:00h, Thu, Fri & Sat 13-23:00h, Sun 12-22:30h
11 Bow Street ✉BL EQ *in town center*

DANCECLUBS

Church Hotel (B d GLM s) Mon-Tue -23, Wed-Sat -2, Sun -22.30 h. (L) Thu
174 Crook Street *(Opposite British Rail station)* ☎ 52 18 56

GENERAL GROUPS

LGB Friendship National Pen Pals
PO Box 2000, Horwich ✉BL6 7PG ☎ 66 77 47
Homepage: www.lgb.org.uk

Bournemouth - Dorset ☎ 01202

BARS

Bakers Arms (AC B D f GLM MA S W) Mon-Sat 11-23, Sun 12-22.30 h
77 Commercial Road ✉BH2 5RT *(Next to Triangle Club)* ☎ 55 55 06
Queens Hall. The (B D GLM MA N OS S SNU W) Mon-Sat 12-23, Sun -22.30 h
14 Queens Road ✉BH2 6BE ☎ 76 44 16
Triangle Club. The (B D GLM MA s SNU STV) Mon-Sat 21.30-2 h. Closed Sun
15 St. Albans Crescent ✉BH8 9EW *Town center* ☎ 29 76 07
Xchange Wine Bar (! AC B D F G MA S) Mon-Sun 12-1 h
4 The Triangle ✉BH2 5RY ☎ 29 43 21

CAFÉS

Legends Café Bar (B bf CC F glm MA N OS W) 10-23 h
53 Bourne Avenue ✉BH2 6DW ☎ 31 01 00

SEX SHOPS/BLUE MOVIES

Cerebus (CC g) Mon-Sat 9.30-17.30 h
25 The Triangle, ✉BH2 5SE ☎ 29 05 29

SAUNAS/BATHS

The Place
PO Box 3988 ✉BH8 0XH ☎ (0870) 24 11 274
Opening 2000 Call for more information.*
121 Gentlemen's Health Spa (b G MA sa sb) Mon-Sat 13-21, Sun 14-20 h
121 Poole Road, Westbourne, ✉BH4 9BG ☎ 75 75 91

HOTELS

Bondi Hotel (bf F G H MA OS)
43 St. Michael's Road ✉BH2 5DP ☎ 55 48 93 Fax: 55 48 93
E-Mail: colin+malcom@bondihotel.freeserve.co.uk
Small guest house, offering 7 bedrooms with TV and shared bathroom. Ask about the self-catering apartment. The local gay bars and clubs are just around the corner. Rates from £14 p.p, incl. bf.
Chine Beach Hotel. The (B bf CC d F GLM MA N OS p pi S sa sol STV WE) All year

14 Studland Road, Alum Chine ✉BH4 8JA *close to town & scene. 1 Min from beach.* ☎ 76 70 15 Fax: 76 12 18
E-Mail: thechinebeachhotel@btinternet.com
Large hotel, 25 comfortable rooms all of which are en suite and equipped with satellite TV. As well as the large pool there is direct access onto the Chine via the hotel garden. Rates: from £30 p.p. Lunch & dinner available. 24h drinks licence, 2 bars and 2 lounges. 3 crown award (tourist board recommemded).

Creffield Hotel. The (b bf G H MA OS)
7 Cambridge Road ✉BH2 6AE ☎ 31 79 00
All rooms are en-suite with TV and hair dryers. It is very centrally located and there is a large private car park.

Orchard Hotel. The (B bf CC f G H MA)
15 Alumdale Road, Alum Chine ✉BH4 8HX ☎ 76 77 67
E-Mail: orchard@orchard.co.uk
Homepage: www.orchardweb.co.uk/orchard
20 mins. walk to the town centre. Accomadation includes five en suite rooms and five rooms with shared facilities. Rates: from £ 15-20:50 per person

HEALTH GROUPS

Body Positive Mon 10-17, Tue Thu 13-17 h
c/o Drop in, 136 Commercial Road ☎ 29 73 86

HELP WITH PROBLEMS

Dorset L&G Helpline Mon-Fri 7.30-10.30 h
PO Box 316 ✉BHI 4HL ☎ 31 88 22

RELIGIOUS GROUPS

Metropolitan Community Church
Hannington Road, Pokesdown BM7 7J1 ☎ 43 08 88

SWIMMING

-Shell Beach.

CRUISING

-Alum Chine (Nights)
-Sea front (Busiest at night but may be worth taking a pleasant stroll during the day. 100-200 m either side of the pier)
-Park in centre of Bournemouth (Crusiest at night. Go to the quieter side of the square walking with the pier behind you in the direction of Westbourne until you reach the tennis courts.)
-Boscombe Gardens (Drive to Eastcliffe and walk down through the woody area to the gardens)

Bradford - West Yorkshire ☎ 01274

BARS

Bavaria Tavern (B D g) Mon-Thu 19-23, Fri-Sat 12-23, Sun 12-22.30 h. (L) Tue. Disco: Sat
Church Street, Heaton ☎ 48 76 81

Sun Hotel. The (AC B D f GLM H MA N OS STV WE YG) Thu-Sat 12-24:00h
124 Sunbridge Road ✉BD1 2ND ☎ 73 77 22
Accommodation available. All rooms with tea / coffee making facilities and TV.

CRUISING

-Manningham Park (by Lister Statue)
-Sunbridge Road
-Peel Park

Bradford-upon-Avon - Wiltshire ☎ 01225

GUEST HOUSES

Leigh House (bf f GLM H lj MA) all year
Leigh Road West ✉BA15 2RB *(near Bath)* ☎ 867835
E-Mail: leigh.house@virgin.net
Homepage: http://buisness.virgin.net/leigh.house

Bridgwater - Somerset ☎ 01278

BOOK SHOPS

Bookworm (CC glm)
25 St. John Street ☎ 42 35 12

HOTELS

Old Vicarage Hotel (B CC F glm H)
41-51 St. Mary's Street ☎ 45 88 91
Rates from £ 47.50

Brighton - East Sussex ☎ 01273

● Only 45 minutes from central London by train or car, Brighton is the biggest and most popular bathing area on the south coast. Its tranquility is a welcome change to the London bustle. You shouldn't miss seeing the Royal Pavillion, an indian-style palace built in 1823. Of course Brighton is at its best in summer but even in winter Brighton is well worth a visit. A very gay friendly atmosphere.

✱ Von London aus ist man in nur 45 min in Brighton, dem größten und beliebtesten Seebad an der Südküste. Die Szene hier ist eine willkommene Alternative zum Londoner Trubel. Am den Gay Pride Veranstaltungen nehmen im Mai jeden Jahres auch viele Londoner teil.

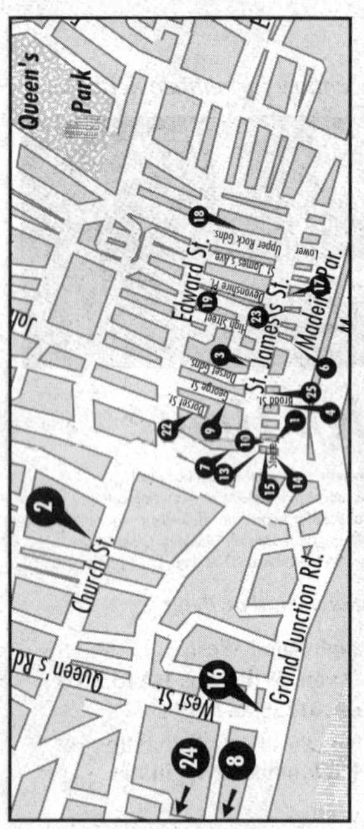

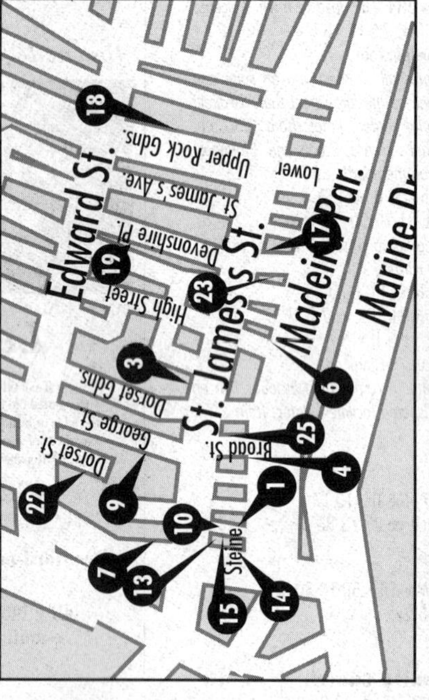

1 Aquarium Inn Bar
2 The Black Horse Bar
3 The Bulldog Tavern Bar
4 Amsterdam Hotel
Amsterdam Sauna
6 Legends Bar at
New Europe Hotel
Schwarz Bar
7 The Marlborough Bar
8 The Oriental Pub Bar
9 Queens Arms Bar
10 Queens Head Bar
13 Zanzibar
14 Club Revenge Danceclub
15 Secrets Club Danceclub
16 Wild Fruit At Paradox Party
17 Alpha Lodge Hotel
18 Cowards Guest House
19 Hudsons Hotel
22 Out Bookshop
23 Jesters Restaurant
24 Montpellier Hall Hotel
25 Shalimar Hotel

Wer allerdings Strandleben an sich sucht, wird erst außerhalb der Ortes fündig werden, in Brighton selber ist das Baden kein Vergnügen. Wenn man nicht gerade auf dem Palace Pier die Urlaubskasse verzockt, sollte man nicht den im indischen Stil erbauten Royal Pavillion von 1823 versäumen.

▲ A seulement 45 minutes du centre de Londres en train ou en voiture, se trouve Brighton, la station balnéaire la plus prisée de la côte sud britannique. Ici, vous trouverez un calme bienfaisant en comparaison de la vie tumultueuse de la capitale. La visite du «Royal Pavillion», un palace de style indien qui date de 1823, n'est à ne manquer sous aucun prétexte. Même si Brighton est évidemment mieux en été, une visite en hiver ne vous décevra cependant pas. Vous y trouverez toute l'année une ambiance très chaleureuse où les gays sont bienvenus.

☆ A sólo 45 minutos en tren o en coche de Londres, Brighton es la mayor y más popular zona de baño de la costa sur. Su tranquilidad puede suponer un buen cambio tras el ajetreo de Londres. No hay que perderse una visita al "Royal Pavillion", palacio en estilo indio que data de 1.823. Naturalmente, Brighton ofrece el máximo de sus posibilidades en verano, pero también merece la pena visitarse en invierno. Hay una atmósfera gay muy amigable.

❖ Da Londra si raggiunge Brighton in soli 45 minuti. Nella stazione balneare più grande e più amata della costa meridionale la vita gay è una benvenuta alternativa alla confusione londinese. Chi però cerca solo la vita da spiaggia in sè dovrebbe uscire dal paese visto che fare il bagno a Brighton non è piacevole. Se non avete già svuotato il portafoglio al Palace Pier non perdetevi il Royal Pavillion costruito in stile indiano nel 1823.

NATIONAL PUBLISHERS

G Scene
PO Box 2200 ✉BN3 3QS ☎ 749947 Fax: 726518
Magazine for Brigton and Hove

GAY INFO

Brighton Gay Switchboard Mon-Sat 18-22, Sun 20-22 h
☎ 69 08 25 ☎ 01273/204050
Write to: IB/Lambda, PO Box 449, Brighton, BN1 1UU.
Scene 22 (B G) 10-18:00h, Fri, Sat & Sun -19:30h
129 St. James Street ☎ 62 66 82
Brightons only gay shop & coffee bar.

TOURIST INFO

Tourist Information Centre (W)
10 Bartholomew Square ✉BN1 1JS ☎ 29 25 99

BARS

Aquarium Inn (AC B G MA s STV W YG) Mon-Sat 11-23, Sun 17-22.30 h
6 Steine Street ✉BN2 1TE *(Opposite Secrets)* ☎ 60 55 25
Black Horse. The (B F GLM MA OS S STV W) Mon-Sat 11-23, Sun 12-22:30h
112 Church Street ✉BN1 1UD *(Opposite Dome)* ☎ 60 68 64
Bulldog Tavern. The (AC B G MA VS) Mon-Sat 11-23, Sun 12-22.30 h
31 St. James Street ✉BN2 1RF ☎ 68 40 97
Happy Hour Mon-Fri 15-18 h.
Legends Bar at New Europe Hotel (B f GLM p) Mon-Sat 12-23:00h, Sun 12-22:30h.
31-32 Marine Parade ✉BN2 1TR ☎ 62 44 62

Marlborough. The (B f GLM MA MG s) Mon-Sat 12-23, Sun 12-16, 19-22.30 h
4 Princes Street *(Opposite Royal Pavilion)* ☎ 57 00 28
Oriental Pub. The (B GLM MA S STV) Mon-Thu 12-15, 19-23, Fri Sat 12-23, Sun 12-22.30 h
5/6 Montpelier Road ✉BN1 2LQ ☎ 72 88 08
Queens Arms (B d f GLM MA S STV W YG) 11.30-23, Sun 12-22:30h
7 George Street ✉BN2 1RH *(Off St. James Street)* ☎ 69 68 73
Queens Head (AC B bf D F GLM MA N STV W) Mon-Sat 12-23, Sun -22.30 h
10 Steine Street ☎ 60 29 39
Happy Hour 15-18 h.
Ruby's (B G)
43 Providence Street ☎ 570028
Schwarz Bar (AC B DR G LJ MA WE) Fri Sat 22-2 h
31/32 Marine Parade ✉BN2 1TR *(Basement of New Europe Hotel)* ☎ 62 44 62

DANCECLUBS

Gayte Club (D glm)
75-76 Grand Parade ☎ 242927
Revenge. Club (AC B D Glm MA SL SNU STV YG) Mon-Thu 22.30-2, Fri-Sat 22-2 h, closed Sun
32-34 Old Steine Street ✉BN1 1EL *(Opp. Palace Pier)* ☎ 60 60 64
Secrets Club (AC B D G MG N S) Mon-Sat 22-2 h
5 Steine Street ☎ 60 96 72
Wild Fruit at Paradox (! B D f GLM YG) 1st Mon/month 22-2 h
78 West Street ☎ 32 16 28
Zanzibar (AC B D GLM MA P S VS YG) Mon-Sat 14-2, Sun 16-22.30 h
129 St. James Street ✉BN2 1TH *(Just off the „Old Stein")*
☎ 62 21 00

RESTAURANTS

Capers (F)
27 Garden Street ☎ 675550
Fudges (AC CC F glm OS) 11-15:00 and 18-24:00h, Sun 11-15:00h
127 King's Road ✉BN1 2FA ☎ 20 58 52 Fax: 74 68 42
English seafront restaurant.
Jesters (AC B CC F glm MA TV W) Mon-Sun 12-23 h
87 St.James Street ✉BN2 1TP ☎ 62 42 33

SAUNAS/BATHS

Amsterdam Sauna
11-12 Marine Parade ☎ 689966
Bright'n Beautiful (f G sa sb sol) Mon-Sat 12-22, Sun 12-20 h
9 St. Margaret's Place *(Behind Hotel Metropol)* ☎ 32 83 30
Denmark Oasis Sauna (AC CC DR f G MA msg pi sa sb sol wh)
75/76 Grad Parade ✉BN2 2JA ☎ 689966
Unit One Sauna (AC f G MA msg pi sa sb WE) 11-23:00h
St. Margarets Flats, High Street, Rottingdean BN2 7HS *4 miles from the center of Brighton* ☎ 30 72 53

BOOK SHOPS

OUT! Brighton (CC GLM W) Mon-Thu 10-18, Fri Sat 10-19, Sun 11-17 h
4&7 Dorset Street ✉BN2 1WA *(opposite the Law Courts)*
☎ 62 33 56

TRAVEL & TRANSPORT

Cruising in Style (A AC B bf CC D d E f GLM LJ MA msg OS pi S sa sb sol W wh WO) 9-18 h

36 Marine Parade ✉BN2 1TJ ☎ 60 53 16 Fax: 60 53 16
Selling cruises on various deluxe ships or exclusive gay cruises.

HOTELS

Alpha Lodge Private Hotel (bf CC f GLM H MA sb) All year
19 New Steine ✉BN2 1PD ☎ 60 96 32 Fax: 69 02 64
Located close to the gay scene, this hotel caters well for the single traveller (many single rooms available). All rooms with radio and TV. Rates: single/shared bath £ from 21, en-suite up to 43 and double rooms £ 44-54. Steam room for free for guests on Wed, Fri and Sat. Full English bf served. Tv room. Open from Feb-Dec.
Amsterdam. The (AC b CC G MA OS sa sb YG) Bar: Mon-Sat 11-23:00h, Sun 12-22:30h Sauna : 18 - 06:00h
11-12 Marine Parade ✉BN2 1TL *In the heart of „gay village" Opposite Pier.* ☎ 688825 Fax: 688828 E-Mail: ams.htl@virgin.net
Hotel with bar and sauna. Large victorian seafront hotel. Large well appointed hotel. All rooms ensuite. Fabulous sea views. Prices include breakfast.Rooftop patio.Brightons largest cruise bar with a terrace. Sauna half price for residents. All usual facilities. Large 20 man steam & dry sauna areas.

Ashley Court Guest House (AC bf CC glm H) 0-24 h
33 Montpelier Road ✉BN1 2LQ ☎ 73 99 16
Small centrally located guest house, all rooms have TV and tea / coffee making facilities. Rates: Single £ 18, Double £ 32 incl. bf.

Court Craven Hotel (B bf f GLM H LJ MA u W)
2 Atlingworth Street ✉BN2 1PL *(Off St James's Street)* ☎ 60 77 10
Situated just off the main gay street this hotel offers rooms with showers, T.V, and tea / coffee making facilities. The hotel bar is popular with residents and their friends.

Cowards Guest House (bf CC G H OS)
12 Upper Rock Gardens ✉BN2 1QE ☎ 69 26 77
Centrally located guest house in which most rooms are en suite (2 have shower only). All rooms have tea / coffee making facilities and TV. Rates: Single £ 21-25, Double £ 42-55 bf. incl.

Hudsons Guest House (bf CC GLM H MA OS) all year 08-23:30h
22 Devonshire Place ✉BN2 1QA ☎ 68 36 42 Fax: 69 60 88
E-Mail: hudsons@brighton.co.uk
Homepage: www.brighton.co.uk/hotels/hudsons
Gay guest house. Friendly. All rooms have private showers, telephone and radio and hospitality tray . A full english or vegetarian breakfast is included. Rates double from £ 40-70, single £ 24-28, apartment available for £ 250-300 per week. English tourist board 3 diamond hotel.

Montpellier Hall (bf e F GLM H lj MA OS YG)
17 Montpelier Terrace ✉BN1 3DF ☎ 20 35 99 Fax: 70 60 30
Lovely Regency house with „grand" rooms and a beautiful walled garden. Private car park

New Europe Hotel (B bf CC GLM H MA p) 0-24 h
31-32 Marine Parade ✉BN2 1TR ☎ 62 44 62
This is the largest gay hotel in Brighton. Bars open until the early

hours of the morning. The rooms are en suite and have T.V and tea /coffee making facilities.

Shalimar Hotel (B bf CC E f GLM H MA) 08-23:00h
23 Broad Street ✉BN2 1TJ *Bus no.7 from station* ☎ 0 53 16
Fax: 0 53 16 E-Mail: shalimar@dircon.co.uk
Homepage: www.shalimar.dircon.co.uk
Each room has central heating, TV, telephone, clock/radio, hair-dryer, tea/coffee facilities, most have ensuite shower/bath/WC and are serviced all day. Full English or vegetarian bf. Closed over Christmas. Rates nightly per person £ 15-27. Discount for Spartacus readers.

GUEST HOUSES

Avalon Guesthouse (B bf CC GLM H MA)
7 Upper Rock Gardens ✉BN2 1QE ☎ 69 23 44 Fax: 69 23 44
E-Mail: avalongh@aol.com
All rooms with bath/shower, WC, radio. Rates double from £ 45 incl. bf. Bicycle hire, TV room and bar.

Catnaps Private Guest House (bf GLM H MA) 8.30-23 h
21 Atlingworth Street ✉BN2 1PL ☎ 68 51 93 Fax: 62 20 26
Centrally located guest house with a variety of rooms on offer, some with shower. Rates: up to single £ 18, double 36, twin 35 incl. bf.

APARTMENTS

Eastcliff House (G H MA OS) 09-22:00h
36 Marine Parade ✉BN2 1TR ☎ 623028 Fax: 605316
Self catering apartments. Weekly lets. Overlooking the beach.

HEALTH GROUPS

Body Positive 10-17, Sat 11-16 h, closed Sun
12 A Circus Street ✉BW2 2 QF ☎ 69 32 66
Fax: 62 20 06. Drop-In Centre, alternative therapies, information, support.

SWIMMING

-Telscombe Cliffs (G) (Take a bus to Saltdean. This is a very cruisy picnic venue at the weekends)
-Shoream Beach (g nu) (This is an unofficial nudist beach located opposite the old power station chimney)
-Angle Beach (G) (Located on the Brighton/Hove border this is the place to tan on a hot summer's day. It can also get quite cruisy when the clubs are closed)

CRUISING

-The Amsterdam Bar - Brightons only outside cruise terrace.
-Dukes Mound (Pathways through the bushes on the sand banks leading to the official nudist beach near the Marina at the end of Madeira Drive. Most interesting after clubs, but some action during the day too.)

Bristol - Avon ☎ 0117

GAY INFO

Bristol Lesbian & Gay Switchboard 20-22:00h
BLAGS, PO Box 49, Green Leaf Bookshop, 82 Colston *Street BS1 SBB* ☎ 942 08 42

BARS

Elephant. The (B GLM MA s STV YG) Mon-Fri 10.30-23, Sat 12-23, Sun 12-22.30, happy hour 12-18 h
20 St. Nicholas Street ✉BS1 1UB *(City centre)* ☎ 949 99 01

Griffin. The (B GLM lj MA) Mon-Sat 12-23, Sun 12-22.30 h
41 Colston Street, BS1 5AP *(just up from Colston Hall)*
☎ 927 24 21

Pineapple. The (B D F GLM MA S SNU STV YG) 12-23, Sun 12-22.50 h
37 St. Georges Road ✉BS1 5UU ☎ 907 1162
Friendly bar, sometimes Karaoke and Pop Quiz Night.

Queen Shilling. The (AC B D GLM MA S SNU YG) Mon 21-02:00h, Tue-Sat 20-02:00h, Sun 19-22:30h
9 Frogmore Street ✉BS1 5NA ☎ 9264342

Queens Shilling. The (B D F GLM MA SNU STV) Mon 19-23, Tue-Sat -2, Sun 17-22.30 h
9 Frogmore Street ✉BS1 5NA ☎ 926 43 42

DANCECLUBS

Castro's (B D GLM LJ MA) Mon-Thu 22-? Fri & Sat 22-06:00h, Sun 22-03:00h
72 Old Market ☎ 9220774

Lakota (AC B F glm P S W WE) Fri 22.30-5, Sat 21.30-4 h
6 Upper York Street ✉BS2 8QE *(Town Centre)* ☎ 942 62 08

RESTAURANTS

Michael's Restaurant (F glm) Tue-Sat 19-?. Lunch: Tue-Fri 12.30-15.30 h
129 Hotwell Road, Clifton BS8 4RU ☎ 927 61 90
International cuisine.

BOOK SHOPS

Green Leaf Bookshop (CC g) Mon-Fri 9.30-17.30, Sat 10-17 h
82 Colston Street ✉BS1 5BB ☎ 921 13 69

HOTELS

Abbotswould Bristol (bf f G H MA)
102 Abbotswood, Yate ✉BS17 4NE ☎ (01454) 324 324
Courtesy car from Rail Station. Discount for stays of more than 3 days.

GUEST HOUSES

Longreach (bf G H MA wh) 06-23:00h
1 Uplands Road, Saltford ✉BS18 3JQ *(between Bath & Bristol)*
☎ 01225/874724 E-Mail: lgreach@aol.com
Homepage: www.members.aol.com/lgreach
Elegant detatched house with great garden & views. Exclusively gay. All rooms with TV, tea trays, radio. Complimentary pick up from the station.

Woodstock (bf E glm H lj NU)
534 Bath Road, Brislington ✉BS4 3JZ ☎ & Fax: 987 1613
Small guesthouse in an 1800's Victorian home. Rates single GBP 30 and double 45 incl. full English bf.

GENERAL GROUPS

Black Lesbian & Gay Group (SAFAR)
PO Box 10, 82 Colston Street ✉BS1 5BB

Gay Men`s Chorus Meets: Wed
☎ 968 42 84

HEALTH GROUPS

Gay Men's Project of the Aled Richards Trust
8-10 West St., Old Market ✉BS2 0BH ☎ 955 10 00
Pride West meet Thu 20-22 h at Aled Richard Trust. The Trust is home of many HIV/AIDS groups. They offer information on HIV/Aids/sexual health and safer sex. Free condoms and lube. Info on gay scene and gay-friendly services available.

CRUISING

-The Promenade (Clifton; bushes and woodland, twilight)
-Sea Walls/Circular Road (AYOR) (Clifton; walk along Circular Road towards Sneyd Park; very busy at all times, police)
-Eastville Park (near Lake)
-Clifton Downs (AYOR) (near observatory, after dark, police)
-Berrow Sands (AYOR) (coast north of Burnham-on-Sea 20km from Bristol)
-Ashton Park (opposite Bristol City football ground)
-Stapleton Road (end of Fishponds Road)
-Redcross Street (near Old Market, Mon-Fri daytime only)

Burnham-on-Sea - Somerset ☎ 01278

SWIMMING

-Berrow Beach (NU) (Activity in the dunes)

Burnley - Lancashire ☎ 01282

BARS

Garden Bar. The (B d GLM) 11-23, Sun 12-22.30 h. (D) Fri-Sat
133 St.James Street ☎ 41 48 95

Bury St. Edmunds - Suffolk ☎ 01638

GUEST HOUSES

Pear Tree House (bf F GLM H N OS)
Chapel Road, West Row, Mildenhall ✉IP28 8PA ☎ 71 11 12
Fax: 71 11 12
Restored 240 year old house. All rooms with TV, tea / coffee making facilities and hairdryers. Reductions for longer stays. B&B from £ 17.50 p/p.

Cairnryan - Dumfries & Galloway ☎ 01581

HOTELS

Merchant's House. The (B bf CC F glm H MA WE) 9-1 h
Main Street, Cairnryan, Wigtownshire ✉DG9 8QX *(Near Stranraer)*
☎ 20 02 15
Gay owned guest house and restaurant. Short distance from P&O Ferry Terminal (Ferries to Northern Ireland). Most rooms with sea view. B&B £ 16p.p. (£ 14p.p. in winter).

Cambridge - Cambridgeshire ☎ 01223

BARS

Town & Gown Pub (B CC d F GLM MA W) 12-14:30h, 19-23:00h Sun 12-22.30 h
Northampton Street, Pound Hill ✉CB3 0AE ☎ 35 37 91

DANCECLUBS

Dot Cotton Club (D GLM YG) Last Sat/month 22-3 h
The Junction, Clifton Road ☎ 41 26 00

Tasty at Q Club (B D GLM MA TV) 2nd/4th Thu/month 22-1 h
Hills Road ☎ 51 59 57

GUEST HOUSES

Pear Tree House (bf CC F GLM MA OS) All year.
Chapel Road, West Row, Mildenhall ✉IP28 8PA *Rail-Cambridge.*
☎ 01638/711112 Fax: 01638/711112
E-Mail: peartree@hello.to Homepage: www.peartree.hello.to

GENERAL GROUPS

Cambridge Uni LGB Society Bar: Mon 21-23 h at University Centre
c/o CUSU, 11-12 Trumpington Street ☎ 740777

RELIGIOUS GROUPS

Lesbian and Gay Christian Movement
☎ 57 38 53 *(Richard)*

CRUISING

-Opposite Four Lamps (Victoria Avenue, near Midsummer's Green)

Canterbury - Kent ☎ 01227

GAY INFO

East Kent Friend and Switchboard Tue 19.30-22 h
PO Box 40 ✉CT1 2YE ☎ 01843
☎ *58 87 62*

Cardiff - South Glamorgan ☎ 029

GAY INFO

Cardiff & District
c/o 30 Glamorgan St., Canton ☎ 2064 02 87
(Mark) Self-Help-Group.

BARS

Exit Bar (B d GLM MA S STV T W YG) Wed-Sun 6-24, Mon Tue - 2 h
48 Charles Street, ✉CF1 4EF *(Opposite Club X)* ☎ 2064 57 21

King's Cross. The (! B F GLM MA W) Mon-Sun 11-23 h
Hayes Bridge Road/Caroline Street ☎ 20649 891

Minskys (B d F MA NG S STV W WE) Mon-Sun 11-23 h
42 Charles Street *(Entrance in Cathedral Walk)* ☎ 23 31 28

DANCECLUBS

Club X (AC B D f GLM lj MA s SNU W YG) Wed-Sat 22-2 h. WOW Club Wed-Sat.
39 Charles Street, ✉CF1 4EB *(Opposite Exit Bar, below Atlantica Café Bar)* ☎ 2064 57 21

SAUNAS/BATHS

Locker Room (b f G MA sa sb sol wh wo) 13-24, Sat-8 h
50 Charles Street ✉CF1 4EB ☎ 2022 03 88

HOTELS

Courtfield Hotel (B bf CC glm H MA N)
101 Cathedral Road ✉CF1 9PH ☎ 22 77 01
This renovated Victorian house has comfortable rooms with radio, TV, tea/coffee making facilities, some en-suite. Rates single (shared bath) £ 25 and double (en-suite) £ 55 incl. bf.

GENERAL GROUPS

Cardiff Students Lesbian, Gay & Bisexual Society
c/o University Union Cardiff, Park Place ✉CF1 3ON ☎ 2039 89 03

HEALTH GROUPS

AIDS Helpline Mon-Fri 10-22 h
PO Box 304, ✉CF1 9XA ☎ 0800 745 3445
☎0800 745 3445 (toll free)

CRUISING

-Bute Park (AYOR) (Day and night. Busiest at rear of music college.)

Carlisle - Cumbria ☎ 01228

HELP WITH PROBLEMS

Outreach Cumbria
☎ 60 30 75
Helpline for men.

Chelmsford - Essex ☎ 01245

BARS

Army & Navy (B g) (G) Wed 19-23, Sun 19-22.30 h only
Roundabout, Parkway ☎ 35 41 55

Cheltenham Spa - Gloucestershire ☎ 01242

BARS

Phoenix Inn (AC B CC d f GLM lj MA OS S SNU STV tv VS W YG) Mon-Fri 18-24, Sat 19-24, Sun 12-23.30 h
36 Andover Road ✉GL50 2TJ ☎ 52 94 17
Door closes Mon-Sat 23, Sun 22.30 h.
Pride of Leckhampton Inn (B F GLM MA s YG) 33 Shurdington Road ✉GLS3 OHY ☎ 52 77 63
Sherbets (AC B bf CC F glm MA OS W) Mon-Sat 11-14.30, 18-22.30, Sun 12-22.30 h
36 Andover Road ✉GL50 2TJ *(rear of Phoenix Inn)* ☎ 52 94 17
Sun Lunch from £ 2.75, Sat bf from £ 1.95.

DANCECLUBS

Racecourse Disco (B D g) Sat 21-2 h
Prestbury Race Cource ☎ 529417
Once a month „Handbag at the Racecourse" party on Sat. Free buffet. Theme nights.

HOTELS

B&B Heron Haye (bf glm H MA OS)
Petty Lane, Cleeve Hill ✉GL52 3PW ☎ & Fax: 67 25 16
4 miles out of Cheltenham, which is 20 miles from Stratford- upon-Avon. 2 doubles and 1 single room. Rates incl. bf £ 20 p.p..

PRIVATE ACCOMODATION

Heron Haye (bf GLM MA OS p WE) 08-22:00h
Petty Lane, Cleeve Hill ✉GL52 3PW ☎ 672516

CRUISING

-College Road
-Post Office Lane
-Old Bath Road (truckers)
-By town hall

Chester - Cheshire ☎ 01244

BARS

Liverpool Arms (AC B glm MA N YG) 11-23, Sun 12-22.30 h 79 Northgate Street ✉CH1 2HQ

GENERAL GROUPS

Clwyd and Cheshire Gay Group Meet alt Tue
☎ *(01978) 29 10 08 (Nigel)*

Chesterfield - Derbyshire ☎ 01246

BARS

Basement (B D GLM) Wed 20-23 h
Cavendish Street *(below Bluebell Inn)* ☎ 20 18 49
Manhattan Bar (B GLM s) (GLM): Sun-Wed 20-? h, (glm) Thu-Sat 50 Saltergate ☎ 23 20 42
Marsden`s (B d glm MA) Mon-Fri 13-15, 19-23, Sat 19-23, Sun -22.30 h
13 Marsden Street ✉S40 1JY *(Off Saltergate)* ☎ 23 26 18

Chichester - West Sussex ☎ 01243

BARS

Bell Inn. The (AC B CC F g MA OS W) 11.30-15 17-23, Sun 12-22.30 h
3 Broyle Road ☎ 78 33 88
Bar and restaurant.
Bush Inn. The (B CC d f GLM MA OS S) 10.30-23:00h, Sun 12-22:30h
16 The Hornet ✉PO19 4JG ☎ 782939

Colchester - Essex ☎ 01206

GAY INFO

Colchester Switchboard and AIDSline Mon-Fri 19-22. Drop in: Tue 18-20:00h
19 East Hill ✉CO1 2QX ☎ 86 91 91

BARS

Forbidden Gardens at the Minorios Café Bar (A B F GLM MA OS) Mon 19-23:00h
The Minorios Café Bar, East Hill ✉CO1 1VE *Next to bus station*
☎ 500169
Fox & Hounds (B D f GLM MA S SNU T W) Wed 19-24, Thu 20-24, Fri-Sat -2, Sun 12-15, 20-22.30 h, closed Mon-Thu
Bentley Road, Little Bromley ✉CO11 2PL *(Off A 120, 5 miles from Colchester)* ☎ 39 74 15

HEALTH GROUPS

HIV/Aids Helpline Mon-Fri 19-22 h
c/o Switchboard, ☎ 869191

Conwy ☎ 01492

HOTELS

Pennant Hall (B bf CC DR F G H MA N sa sb sol wh) Health Spa & Sauna: 12.30-22.30 h
Beach Road, Penmaenmawr ✉LL34 6AY *(Near railway station)*
☎ 62 28 78
Hotel & bar ideally situated for excursions to the coast and Snowdonia National Park. Most rooms en-suite.

Coventry - West Midlands ☎ 01203

HEALTH GROUPS

HIV Network
10 Manor Road ✉CU1 2LH ☎ 22 92 92 Fax: 63 42 48
Volunteer-led organisation to promote greater awareness HIV and AIDS and provide support for people living with HIV. Buddy service. Body Positive Grup.

MESMEN (Health project for men) Mon-Fri 10-17 h
c/o The HIV Network, 10 Manor Road ✉CV1 2LH ☎ 7622 92 92 ☎ 22 40 90 Fax: 63 42 48
HIV prevention and care

CRUISING

-Cathedral walls

Crewe - Cheshire ☎ 01270

GENERAL GROUPS

Crewe Gay Social Group Men Meets: 2nd Tue/month 19.30 h
☎ 21 14 55
(John)

Croydon - Greater London ☎ 020

GAY INFO

Croydon Friend Mon Fri 19.30-21.30 h
PO Box 464 ✉SE25 41T ☎ 8683 42 39

GENERAL GROUPS

Croydon Area Gay Society
PO Box 464 ✉SE25 4AT ☎ 8656 9802 *David*

Darlston - West Midlands ☎ 0121

SAUNAS/BATHS

Greenhouse Health Club (B CC F G sa sb sol wh WO)
10-2, Fri -6, Sat 12-8, Sun 12-2h
47 King Street (Junction 9 M 6)☎ 568 61 26

Derby - Derbyshire ☎ 01332

GAY INFO

Derby Friend Wed 19-22 h
☎ 34 93 33

BARS

Curzons Nightclub (B d F GLM MA N P S TV) Thu 20-2 (cabaret), Fri-Sat 20-2 (disco)
25 Curzon Street ✉DE1 1LH ☎ 36 37 39

Freddies Bar (AC B d f GLM MA s TV VS) Mon-Sat 19-23:30h Sun 19-22:30h
101 Curzon Street ✉DE1 1LH ☎ 20 42 90

Gallery. The (AC B F GLM MA N W) Mon-Thu 19-23, Fri-Sat 13-23, Sun 13-22.30 h
130 Green Lane ✉DE1 1RY *(Next to Little City car park)*
☎ 36 86 52

HEALTH GROUPS

Body Positive Meets weekly Mon-Fri 14-17:00h
PO Box 124 ✉DE1 9NZ ☎ 29 21 29 Fax: 29 21 29

CRUISING

-Fish Market (known to the trade as »Fish Cottage«)
-Bus station

Derrygonnelly - Fermanagh ☎ 01365

GUEST HOUSES

Pierce's Folly (bf glm H)
Dresternan ✉BT93 6FF ☎ 64 17 35

Doncaster - South Yorkshire ☎ 01302

BARS

Vine. The (B D GLM SNU STV) 19-23 h
2 Kelham Street, Balby ✉DN1 1RE

Douglas - Isle of Man ☎ 01624

GENERAL GROUPS

Ellan Vannin Gay Group
PO Box 195 ☎ 62 87 72
Information, Campagning, Social. Contact Alan after 18:00h

Dumfries - Dumfries & Galloway ☎ 01387

GAY INFO

Dumfries & Galloway Lesbian & Gay Phoneline Thu 19.30-21.30 h
c/o PO Box 1299 ✉DG1 2PD ☎ 26 91 61

GENERAL GROUPS

Dumfries and Galloway Lesbian & Gay Group
PO Box 1299, ✉DG1 2PD ☎ 26 18 18
Thu 19.30-21.30. Regular social meetings every Thu. Call for details.

Dundee - Tayside ☎ 01382

GAY INFO

Dundee LGB Switchboard Mon 19-22 h
PO Box 53 ✉DD1 3YG ☎ 20 26 20

BARS

Charlie's Bar (B D f glm MA) 75 Seagate
☎ 226840

DANCECLUBS

Liberty Nightclub (B D GLM S SL SNU VS YG) Wed-Sun 22.30-2.30 h
124 Seagate ✉ DD1 2HB ☎ 20 06 60

Durham ☎ 0191

GENERAL GROUPS

Durham University LGB Association Meets weekly
Durham Students Union, Dunelm House, New Elvet ✉DH1 3AN ☎ 374 3310 ☎ 374 3313 Fax: 374 3328
Homepage: www.dur.ac.uk/LGB

Eastbourne - East Sussex ☎ 01323

BARS

Hartington. The (B D f GLM MA S SNU STV) 11-23:00h
89 Cavendish Place ✉BN21 3RR ☎ 64 31 51
Various theme nights.

GUEST HOUSES

Freedom Guest House (bf GLM H MA) All year
105 Cavendish Place ✉BN21 3TY ☎ 41 10 01

Edinburgh ☎ 0131 - Scotland

● Edinburgh is the capital city of Scotland and one of the most beautifully situated cities in the world. The gay scene is mainly located in Newton and in Broughton Street, which depicts the tolerant atmosphere of the city and the relaxed lifestyle of the Edinburgh gays. Best month for sightseeing (the castle, old town center, museums) is in August, when the annual Arts Festival is celebrated.

✱ Edinburgh ist das Zentrum und die Hauptstadt Schottlands. Und es ist eine der am schönsten gelegenen Städte der Welt.
Die schwule Szene konzentriert sich in Newtown und in der Broughton Street. Dort spiegeln sich auch das tolerante Klima der Stadt und die relaxte Stimmung der Schwulen wider.
Ein optimale Gelegenheit, dieses Klima und die Sehenswürdigkeiten der Stadt (Schloß, Altstadt, Museen) kennenzulernen, bietet das jährlich im August stattfindende Festival.

▲ Edimbourg, centre et capitale de l'Ecosse, compte parmi les plus belles villes du monde. Les lieux gays sont concentrés dans le quartier de Newton, principalement dans la Broughton Street. Les gens ici sont calmes, détentus et il y règne un agréable climat de tolérance. Profitez de l'occasion qu'offre le Festival d'Edimbourg pour découvrir les curiosités touristiques de la vieille ville (château, vieux quartiers, musées) et goûter à l'atmosphère de cette agréable ville britannique.

☆ Edinburgo es centro y capital de Escocia y una ciudad privilegiada por su situación. Los locales gay se encuentran en Newtown y en la Broughton Street. Aquí se refleja el tolerante clima de la ciudad y el relajado ambiente gay. La fecha óptima para conocer este clima y los sitios de interés (castillo, ciudad antigua, museos etc.) es en Agosto, cuando se celebra anualmente el famoso festival de Edinburgo.

❖ Edimburgo, centro e capitale della Scozia, è una delle città meglio situate del mondo. La zona gay si concentra a Newtown e nella Broughton street dove si rispecchia il clima tollerante della città e l'atmosfera rilassante dell'ambiente gay. Il festival di Edimburgo, che ha luogo ogni anno in agosto, può essere un'occasione per visitare la città e le sue bellezze (il palazzo, il centro storico ed i musei).

GAY INFO

Edinburgh Lesbian, Gay & Bisexual Community Centre (b bf f GLM MA msg YG)
58-60 Broughton Street ✉EH1 3SA ☎ 557 1662
Fax: 558 1683.

Lothian Gay & Lesbian Switchboard Mon-Sun 19.30-22 h
PO Box 169, ✉EH1 3UU ☎ 556 4049

TOURIST INFO

Edinburgh & Scotland Information Centre
3 Princes Street ✉EH2 2QP ☎ 473 3800

BARS

CC Blooms (!AC B D GLM MA s SNU) Mon-Sat 18-3, Sun 16-3 h.
23 Greenside Place ✉EH1 3AA *(Next to Edinburgh Playhouse Theatre)* ☎ 556 9331
Disco every night from 22:30h.Thu-Sun Karaoke, Sun stipper.

French Connection (B f GLM MA N s STV) Mon-Sat 12-1, Sun 11-23:00h
87-89 Rose Street Lane North ✉EH2 3DT ☎ 225 7651

New Town Bar. The (AC B D f G lj MA N OS SNU) Mon-Sat 12-01:00h, Sun 12.30-01:00 h. Bar Intense (LJ) Thu-Sun 22-1 h

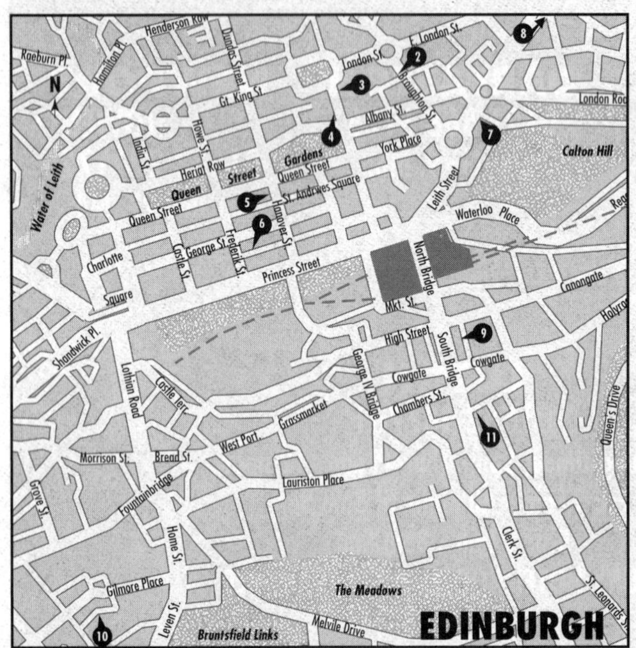

2 Blue Moon Café
3 Mansfield House Hotel
4 The New Town Bar
Intense at the Newtown Bar Party
5 Cyberia Café
6 French Connection Bar
7 CC Blooms Bar
8 No. 18 Sauna
9 Black Bo's Restaurant
10 Amaryllis Guest House
11 Fantasies Sex Shop

26b Dublin Street ✉EH3 6NN ☎ 538 7775
Basement leather & fettish bar open Thu-Sun.
Planet Out (AC B F GLM MA N S W YG) Mon-Fri 16-01:00h, Sat & Sun 12:30-01:00h
66 Baxter's Place ✉EH1 3AF ☎ 524 0061
Stag & Turret. The (B F GLM MA SNU STV) 12-02:00 h
1-7 Montrose Terrace ✉EH7 5DJ ☎ 478 7231

CAFÉS

Blue Moon Café (! A AC B bf F GLM MA) Bar: Mon-Thu 7-0.30, Sun 9-0.30 h. Café Sun-Thu 9-24, Fri-Sat -0.30 h.
1 Barony Street/36 Broughton Street ✉EH1 3SB ☎ 556 2788
Cyberia (b f glm) 10-22:00h, Sun 12-19:00h
88 Hanover Street ☎ 220 4403
Nexus Cafe Bar (A AC B bf F GLM MA N) 11-23 h
60 Broughton Street ✉EH1 3SA ☎ 478 7069
Nice cafe which is located in the LGB centre.
Web 13 (B f glm MA) Mon-Fri 9-22:00h, Sat -20:00h, Sun 11-20h
13 Bread Street ☎ 229 8883
Cybercafé

DANCECLUBS

Four BBBB's Club at Intense (B D G MA) 4th Fri 20-22 h
c/o New Town Bar, 26B Dublin Street ☎ 538 7775
Club for Big Beary Bulky Boys.
Joy (! AC B D GLM MA WE) Once a month Sat 22.30-03:00 h
Wilkie House, 207 Cowgate ✉EH1 1JD ☎ 467 2551

RESTAURANTS

Black Bo's (CC F glm MA) 18-22:00h, Fri & Sat 12-14:00h
57-61 Blackfriars Street, ✉EH1 1NB ☎ 557 6136
Charming vegetarian restaurant.
Claremont Bar & Restaurant. The (B F GLM lj MA N W) 11-1, Sun 12.30-1 h
133-135 East Claremont Street ✉EH7 45N ☎ 556 5662
Scotland:s only Science Fiction theme pub. Different groups meet here.

SEX SHOPS/BLUE MOVIES

Fantasies (glm) Mon-Sat 10-21, Sun 12-21 h
8b Drummond Street,EH8 9TU *(by the Festival Theatre)*
☎ 557 8336

SAUNAS/BATHS

No.18 (DR f G MA sa sb WE wh) Mon-Sat 12-22, Sun 14-22 h
18 Albert Place ✉EH7 5HN *(Leith Walk)* ☎ 553 3222
Sauna cabin, jacuzzi, steam room and rest room.

BOOK SHOPS

Bobbies Bookshop (g) Mon-Sat 10-17.30 h
220 Morrison Street ✉EH3 8EA *(near Haymarket)* ☎ 538 7069

GIFT & PRIDE SHOPS

Atomix (GLM) Mon-Sat 12-19, Sun 12-17 h
60 Broughton Street ✉EH1 3SA ☎ 558 8174
Videos, magazines, underwear etc.
Out of the blue (GLM) Sun-Wed 12-19:00h Thu-Sat 12-20:00h
1 Barony Street, Broughton ✉EH3 6PD *(basement)* ☎ 478 7048
Magazines, books, cards, videos, gifts, toys, body, swim & underwear.

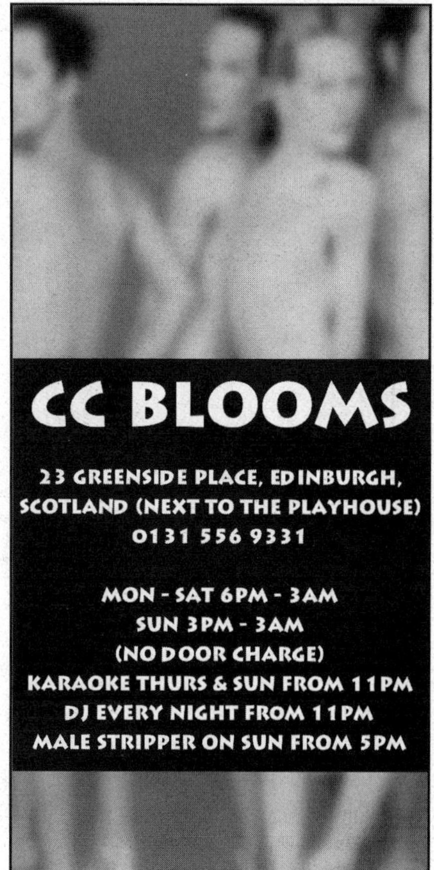

CC BLOOMS
23 GREENSIDE PLACE, EDINBURGH,
SCOTLAND (NEXT TO THE PLAYHOUSE)
0131 556 9331
MON - SAT 6PM - 3AM
SUN 3PM - 3AM
(NO DOOR CHARGE)
KARAOKE THURS & SUN FROM 11PM
DJ EVERY NIGHT FROM 11PM
MALE STRIPPER ON SUN FROM 5PM

HOTELS

Amaryllis Guest House (bf CC glm H MA)
21 Upper Gilmore Place ✉EH3 9NL ☎ 229 32 93 Fax: 229 32 93
Comfortable guest house furnished to a high standard. Easily accessible to the gay scene by public transport. All rooms have T.V and tea / coffee making facilities. Rates Vary seasonably from £ 20-30 incl. bf and p.p.
Mansfield House (AC bf CC GLM H MA)
57 Dublin Street ✉EH3 6NL ☎ 556 7980 Fax: 446 1315
E-Mail: mansfieldhouse@cableinet.co.uk
Gay guest house: All the rooms are spacious and elegantly decorated; one room is en suite and all have TV and tea / coffee making facilities. It is located within easy walking distance of the local gay pubs / clubs. Rates: single from £ 30 and twin (en suite) 70.
Thistle Court Hotel (H)
5 Hampton Terrace ✉EH12 5JD ☎ 3135500 Fax: 3135511
E-Mail: thistle@clansman.demon.co.uk

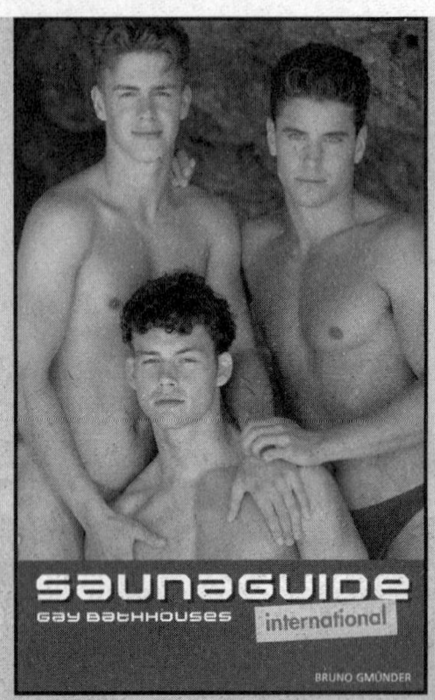

saunaguide
gay bathhouses
international
BRUNO GMÜNDER
▶ New in June 2000 ◀
▶ Worldwide Edition ◀
▶ Completely Updated ◀
BRUNO GMÜNDER VERLAG
P.O. BOX 61 01 04 • D - 10921 BERLIN

GUEST HOUSES

Admor House (bf glm H MA) All year 24h
74 Pilrig Street ✉EH6 5AS *10 minutes walk from city center*
☎ 554 4944 Fax: 554 4944
E-Mail: robin@admorhouse.freeserve.co.uk
Homepage: www.admorhouse.freeserve.co.uk
Stylish victorian town house decorated to a fine standard. En suite rooms available. All rooms have TV, tea/coffee making facilities. Gay owned.

Garlands Guest House (bf CC glm) all year
48 Pilric Street ✉EH6 5AL ☎ 554 4205 Fax: 554 4205
E-Mail: bill@garlands.demon.co.uk
Homepage: www.garlands.demon.co.uk

HEALTH GROUPS

Solas Café at SOLAS (A B F glm MA) Mon-Tue Thu-Fri 11-16, Wed 17-21 h
2/4 Abbeymount ✉EH8 8EJ ☎ 661 0982

CRUISING

-Calton Hill (Day or night AYOR)
-Regent Road (Night AYOR. Park car or yourself along side of the road.)
-Warrington cemetery (Night AYOR)

Elgin - Grampian ☎ 01340

GENERAL GROUPS

Moray Gay Group 2nd Wed of month 20.15 h
Lounge of the Cat's Whisker pub *(enter from car park)*
☎ 01343/(01463)
☎ *71 15 85 (Reach Out Highland)*

Exeter - Devon ☎ 01392

GAY INFO

Devon L&G Switchboard Mon 19.30-22 h
PO Box 178 ✉EX4 1TY ☎ 42 20 16

BARS

Loft at Bart`s Tavern. The (B D F Glm s) Mon-Thu 20-24, Fri-Sat 21-1, Sun 12-22.30 h
53 Bartholomew Street West ☎ 275 623

DANCECLUBS

Boxes on Tuesday (B D GLM MA YG) Tue 21-1 h
35/37 Commercial Road, The Quay

HEALTH GROUPS

AIDSline Helpline: Mon-Fri 19-22 h
Dean Clarke House, Southernhay East ✉EX1 1PQ ☎ 41 16 00
☎ 0800 328 5308
Office ☎ 515 04 AIDSline is a voluntary organisation which offers a wide range of services for people affected by HIV and AIDS.

HELP WITH PROBLEMS

L&G Counselling SW Mon 19.30-21.30 h
PO Box 178 ✉EX4 1TY ☎ 42 20 16

Farnham - Surrey ☎ 01252

DANCECLUBS

Ralph's Cellar (AC B D f G lj MA N OS P s) Fri 21.30-1.30, Last Sat/month 21-3 h
33 Shortheath Road ✉GU9 8SH ☎ 71 58 44
Private venue.

Folkestone - Kent ☎ 01303

BARS

Portland Hotel (B f glm MA) 11-23, Sun 12-22.30 h
2-4 Langhorne Gardens *(Opposite Leas Cliff Hall)* ☎ 251444

HEALTH GROUPS

South Kent Health Info for g&b men
Tue 16-19 h
☎ 22 88 13
(Richard)

SWIMMING

-Warren (NU) (45 minutes walk from East Cliff towards Dover. Small secluded unofficial bay. Popular)
-Sandwich (NU) (far end of the beach near the golf course)

CRUISING

-The Leas (AYOR)
-Warren

Galashiels - Scottish Borders ☎ 01896

CAFÉS

Green's Diner (A AC B CC f glm MA N WE) Tue-Sat 10-22:00h. Closed Sun & Mon.
4 Green Street ✉TD1 3AE *next to Tescos supermarket*
☎ 75 76 67

Gateshead ☎ 0191

HELP WITH PROBLEMS

Stag Project ☎ 490 1708
Confidential advice and information.

Glasgow - Strathclyde ☎ 0141

GAY INFO

Glasgow Gay and Lesbian Centre (B CC F GLM MA W) 10-24:00h
11 Dixon Street *(near to St. Enoch's Shopping Mall)* ☎ 221 7203
Fax: 221 7203 Email gglc@gglc.org.uk.
Homepage: http://www.gglc.org.uk/gglc/
Glasgow University LGB Society Meets weekly in QM Union
LGB Convener c/o John McIntyre Building ☎ 339 8541
Strathclyde Gay & Lesbian Switchboard 19-22 h
PO Box 38 ✉G2 2QF ☎ 332 8372

BARS

Austin's (B f GLM MA S STV) 12-24:00h. Food from 12-19:00h
16b Miller Street ✉G1 ☎ 221 0444
Court Bar. The (AC B bf glm MA N WE) Mon-Sat 8-24, Sun 12.30-24 h
69 Hutcheson Street *(Close to Bennets)* ☎ 552 2463
Straight until mid-evening
Delmonica's (AC B CC d GLM MA N s) 12-24 h
68 Virginia Street ✉G1 ☎ 552 4803
Victoria Bar (B glm MA) Mon-Sat 11-24
157-159 Bridgegait ☎ 552 6040
Real Ale bar
Waterloo. The (B f GLM MA STV W) 12-24 h
306 Argyle Street *(Central Station)* ☎ 229 5891

CAFÉS

Caffe Latte (AC B CC F glm MA) Mon-Sat 11-24:00h, Sun 12-24:00h
58 Virginia Street ✉G1 INU ☎ 553 2553
GLC Café/Bar (B CC F GLM MA W) 11-24:00h
11 Dixon Street *(Side entrance with gay flag)* ☎ 400 1008
Internet Café (B F glm) Mon-Fri 9-23, Sat 10-23, Sun 11-23 h
569 Sauchiehall Street ☎ 564 1052

DANCECLUBS

Bennets (AC B D f GLM MA S STV TV) Wed-Sun 23:30-03:30h
90 Glassford Street ✉G1 1UR *(near George Square)* ☎ 552 5761
Polo Lounge and Club. The (B CC D GLM MA) 12-1, Fri-Sun -3 h
84 Wilson Street, Merchant City ✉G1 1UZ ☎ 553 1221
Largest gay bar and club in Scotland. Very popular.

SAUNAS/BATHS

Centurion (CC f DR G sa sb sol wh WO) Sun-Fri 11-23:00h, Sat 11-07:00h
19 Dixon Street ✉G1 4AL *(St. Enoch Square Shopping Center)*
☎ 248 4485 *Entrance-fee £ 9.*

BOOK SHOPS

Centre Books at GLC (CC GLM) Mon 11-18, Tue-Sat 11-21, Sun 12-17 h
11 Dixon Street *(In the GLC)*

HOTELS

Berkely. The (bf glm H)
63 Berkely Street ✉G3 *(next to Mitchel Library)* ☎ 221 7880
Twins £ 23.50, dormitory 10.50.

GUEST HOUSES

Glasgow Guest House (bf glm MA)
56 Dumbreck Road ✉G41 5NP *(Near Burrell Collection)*
☎ 427 0129 Fax: 427 0129
Situated in a residential area, this guest house is not ideally central, however, it is easily reached by public transport. Two rooms are fully fitted for disabled guests and the rest have wash- basins and shared bathrooms. The common rooms are sociable and relaxed and the kitchen is completely at theguests disposal. Rates: from £ 17 p.p, incl. bf.

HEALTH GROUPS

Body Positive Mon-Thu 11-20:00h, Fri 11-17:00h
3 Park Quadrant ✉G3 6BS *(U-Kelvinbridge)* ☎ 332 5010
Fax: 332 4285
Support for those who are HIV+ or have AIDS.
PHACE West Mon-Fri 9-17 h
49 Bath Street, ✉G2 2DL *(Corner of Renfield Street)*
☎ 332 3838
HIV / AIDS charity offering services and information; free condoms and lubricant.
Steve Retson Project Tue 17.30-21.00h
Royal Infirmary, 16 Alexandra Parade ✉G31 2ER *(Dept. of GU Medicine, main outpatient building)* ☎ 211 4753
Free confidential advice and treatment for all sexual health issues concerning gay men; free condoms and lube.

SPORT GROUPS

Gay Outdoor Club (GOC)
PO Box 16124 ✉G12 9YT ☎ 334 0812

CRUISING

-Queens Park (Night AYOR; the most interesting area is the section closest to Victoria Road.)
-Kelvin Grove Park (Walk to the statue in the middle, but watch out for police.)

Gloucester - Gloucestershire ☎ 01452

DANCECLUBS

Hysteria at Crackers Night Club (B D G) Mon 21.30-2 h
Bruton Way ☎ 30 02 89

GUEST HOUSES

Yew Tree Cottage (bf GLM MA T) Bradley Hill, Soudley ✉GL14 2UQ *(In Forrest of Dean, 15 miles from Gloucester)*
☎ 01594/ 824 823 Fax: 82 43 17
Nice B&B in beautiful location. Rate from £ 17.50-20 p.p..

Grimsby - Humberside ☎ 01472

HELP WITH PROBLEMS

Gay Helpline Tue Thu 19-21 h
☎ 25 18 18

Guildford - Surrey ☎ 1483

GENERAL GROUPS

Guildford Area Gay Society Meets: Wed 20-22:00h
☎ 01403/(01252)
☎ *37 08 09 (Simon)*

Gunby - Lincolnshire ☎ 01754

BARS

Kings Head (B F D glm MA) 11-23:00h
Gunby Courner *(Near Spilsby and Skegness)* ☎ 89 06 38

Harlow - Essex ☎ 01279

GAY INFO

Lesbian and Gay Switchboard Mon-Fri 20-22:00h
☎ 63 96 37

Harrogate - North Yorkshire ☎ 01423

CRUISING

-Harlow Moor Road/Cornwall Road

Hastings - Sussex ☎ 01424

BARS

Club ID (AC B G lj MA N p S SNU STV) Thu-Sat 20-23, Sun 19:30-22.30 h, closed Mon-Wed
18-20 Prospect Place ✉TN34 1LN ☎ 72 22 40

HOTELS

Sherwood Hotel (B bf CC g MA NU)
15 Grosvenor Crescent, St.Leonards-on-Sea TN38 0AA ☎ 43 33 31
Five min driving from Hastings centre. All rooms with colour TV. Some rooms with private shower and toilet. Rates from £ 16.

Hebden Bridge - West Yorkshire ☎ 01422

BARS

Nelson's Wine Bar (A B d F glm MA) Mon 19-23:00h, Tue-Sun 16-23:00h
Crown Street ✉HX1 8AH ☎ 84 47 82

Hereford - Hereford and Worcester ☎ 01432

DANCECLUBS

Club Impulse at The Old Harp (B D G) Wed 21-1 h
54 Widemarsh Street *(Opp. multi-storey car park)* ☎ 27 73 30

Herne Bay - Kent ☎ 01227

GUEST HOUSES

Foxden Bed & Breakfast (bf glm H MA)
5 Landon Road ✉CT6 6HP ☎ 36 35 14
Gay owned, high quality B&B in quiet area close to sea and town centre. Rates single from £ 20 and double 40 incl. full English bf.

Hove - Sussex ☎ 01273

CAFES

Lizzie's Mon-Sat 08-16:00h
61 Blatchington Road ☎ 731193

RESTAURANTS

PJ's
117 Western Road ☎ 773586

SAUNAS/BATHS

Denmark Sauna (b f G MA msg sa sb wh) 12-22 h
84-86 Denmark Villas, Hove ✉BN3 3TJ *(near Hove station)*
☎ 72 37 33

Huddersfield - West Yorkshire ☎ 01484

GAY INFO

Lesbian and Gay Switchboard Sun 19-21, Tue 19-21 h
c/o KCVS, PO Box 293 ✉HD1 1WB ☎ 53 80 70

BARS

Greyhound Hotel. The (B D GLM H lj MA) Mon-Sat 19-23, Sun 12-22.30 h
16 Manchester Road ☎ 42 07 42
Disco on Wed & Sun.

Hull - Humberside ☎ 01482

GAY INFO

Humberside Friend Mon Thu 20-22, Sat 19-21 h
c/o CVS, 29 Anlaby Road ✉HU1 2PG ☎ 44 33 33
Men`s group (Sun 19-21) and Youth group (Sun 18.30-21). Call ☎ 58 97 42.

BARS

Polar Bear. The (B gLM WE)
229 Spring Bank *(Front bar only)* ☎ 32 39 59
Vauxhall Tavern. The (B D Glm S) 11-23, 12-22.30 h
1 Hessle Road *(Near Alexander Hotel)* ☎ 32 03 40

DANCECLUBS

Alexandra Palace Club Hotel (B D glm H s) 11-0.20, Sun -22.30 h. (D) Fr & Sa (G)
69 Hessle Road ☎ 32 74 55
Accomodation available. Only Gay on Fr & Sa.
Silhouette Club (B D glm)
Park St. ☎ 320 584

SAUNAS/BATHS

Blue Corner Health Club (F G MA P Sa Sb wh) Mo-Th 12:00-22:00 h, Su 13:00-22:00h. Fr & Sa 24h
High Street ☎ 620 775

BOOK SHOPS

Page One Books (GLM)
9 Princess Avenue ☎ 34 19 25

HEALTH GROUPS

Aids Action in Humberside Mo-Th 10-13:00h, We & Fr 19-21:00h, Sa 10-12:00h
Cornerhouse, 29 Percy St. ✉HU2 8HL ☎ 32 70 44 ☎ 32 70 60 Fax: 58 07 29
HIV & AIDS awareness, support, information and advice agency. Gay mens drop-in open Tue 19-21 h.

Inverness - Highland ☎ 01463

BARS

Nico's Bar/Bistro (B f glm MA N) Wed Fri 19-23 h
c/o Glen Mhor Hotel, Ness Bank ☎ 23 43 08

HOTELS

Station Hotel. The (B F H)
18 Academy Street ✉IV1 1LG
E-Mail: reservations@station-hotel.co.uk

GENERAL GROUPS

Gay Outdoor Club
☎ 751 258

CRUISING

-Bus station (AYOR)
-Railway station (AYOR)

Ipswich - Suffolk ☎ 01473

GENERAL GROUPS

Gay Group
PO Box 63IP4 2RB ☎ 01473/(01206)
☎ 57 81 65 (Brian)

HEALTH GROUPS

AIDS Helpline Tue Fri 19.30-22 h
☎ 01473/23 20 07

Isle of Mull - Strathclyde ☎ 01688

HOTELS

Ardbeg House Hotel (AC B bf d F g H msg s sa WE wh)
Dervaig, Isle of Mull ✉PA75 6QJ ☎ 40 02 54 Fax: 40 02 54
Picturesque village hotel.

Isle of Wight - Ryle ☎ 01983

BARS

Tin Tin's (B d f GLM MA) Mon-Sat 11-23:00h, Sun 12-22:30h
9 Anglesea Street, Ryde ✉PO33 2JJ ☎ 56 78 33

HOTELS

Dorset Hotel. The (B bf CC F glm H pi WE)
31 Dover Street ✉PO33 2BW ☎ 56 43 27 Fax: 56 43 27
All rooms en-suite. Rates £ 19.50 p.p., discount for SPARTACUS readers available.

Isle of Wight - Shanklin ☎ 01983

BARS

Plough & Barleycorn (B f GLM MA s) Fr 19-23:00h
4 North Road ☎ 86 28 82

Isleworth - Middlesex ☎ 0208

FETISH GROUPS

Leather Hands 2
2 Morton Avenue, Osterley ✉TW7 4NW
Member of ECMC.

Isleworth - Middlesex ☎ 0208

BARS

George. The (B d G MA OS s W) Mon-Sat 17-23, Sun 12-22.30 h, Cabaret Fri Sat
114 Twickenham Road ✉TW7 7DJ *(Opposite War Memorial/buses 37 and 267)* ☎ 8560 14 56

Jersey - St. Helier ☎ 01534

CAFÉS

Café des Artistes (A AC B CC d f glm MA) Tue-Fri 12-15:00h 17-01:30h , Sat 17-01:30h, Closed Mon
58-60 St. Saviour's Road ✉JE2 4AL ☎ 630811

GUEST HOUSES

Franklin Guest House (bf CC glm H OS) open Easter to end of September
65 St. Saviour's Road ✉JE2 4LA ☎ 30108 Fax: 610 575
Double rooms with bath/shower, WC and TV from £ 16-20 p.p. and single without bath/shower £ 14-18 full English bf included.

CRUISING

-Liberation Square
-Snow Hill
-Minden Place
-Broad Street
-The Weighbridge (ayor) (around the carpark, near the toilets, by night only)
-Portler Common (by day)
-The Rocks (an area of rocks near Green Street, looking to the sea, the rocks on your right reached by a short walk, watch the tide though, by day action)
-Portelet Beach (Summer months)
-Victoria Avenue (1st layby)
-Parade Gardens (after dark)

Kidderminster - Hereford and Worcester ☎ 01562

SPORT GROUPS

G.B.M.C.C.
☎ 01299 896177 *(Stuart) Gay bikers group*

King's Lynn - Norfolk ☎ 01553

BARS

Hob-in-the-Well. The (B glm) Th-Su 20:30-22:30h
Littleport Street ☎ 77 44 04

Kingston - Surrey ☎ 020

GENERAL GROUPS

Kingston University LGB Society Weekly (Term time)
Room 241, Pernhyn Road ☎ 8255 555

Kirkcaldy - Fife ☎ 01592

GAY INFO

Fife Friend Fri 19.30-22.30
PO Box 19 ✉KY1 3JF ☎ 26 66 88
Small voluntary phoneline offering support, advice and information. Monthly disco.

Lampeter - Dyfed ☎ 01570

GENERAL GROUPS

LG&B support group Meets weekly
c/o Students Union, Lampeter Uni ☎ 42 26 19
Social events/trips. Ask for welfare LGB officer.

Lancaster - Lancashire ☎ 01524

GAY INFO

L&G Switchboard Thu Fri 19-21 h
☎ 84 74 37
Gay Men's Social group meets 1st Fri. Lesbian & gay youth group for all under 21 meets Thu 18.30-21 h.

BARS

Dukes. Theatre/Cinema Bar (A B CC glm W) Mon-Sat 18-23, Sun 19-22.30 h
Moor Lane ✉LA1 1QE ☎ 674 61
Navigation (B F glm MA N OS) Summer 11-23:00h Winter 17-23:00h
Penny Street, Bridge Wharf ✉LA1 1XN *(Rear Thurnham Street car park)* ☎ 84 94 84
Draught German beers, Superb wine list, live music- evenings on this cruise ship.

CAFÉS

Single Step Co-Op (B f GLM)
78a Penny Street ✉LA1 1XN ☎ 630 21

GENERAL GROUPS

Lancaster University LGB Society Meets: Wed 17 h in Harrington Building (termtime only)
☎ 258 382

HEALTH GROUPS

Positive Action for HIV 10-16:00h 'til 18:00h on Th.
Unit 10, Lanc. Enterp. Workshops, White Cross ✉LA1 4XH
☎ 424 117 ☎ 419 597

Leeds - West Yorkshire ☎ 0113

GAY INFO

Leeds Switchboard 19-22 h, closed Tue
☎ 245 35 88

BARS

Bridge Inn. The (B F glm MA MG N s STV W WE) 11-23 h
1-5 Bridge End ✉LS1 7HG ☎ 244 47 34
New Penny. The (B glm MA s STV) Mon-Fri 13-23, Sat 12-16, 19-23, Sun 12-15, 19-22.30 h
57 Call Lane, ✉LS1 7BT
Old Red Lion (B f glm MA s W) Mon-Thu 11-15, 19-23, Fri, Sat 11-23, Sun 12-15, 19-22.30 h
2 Meadow Lane, ✉LS11 5BJ ☎ 242 67 79

DANCECLUBS

Nato (B D GLM MA YG) Red Raw: 1st Tue 21-2, Queer-doo: Sun 21-2 h
Walk 34, Middletown Road ☎ 238 0999
Popular venue
Queen's Court (AC B CC D F GLM MA S SNU STV T) Mon-Sun 11-23 (Cafe-Bar), Mon-Sat 22-2 h (Nightclub)
Queen's Court, Lower Briggate ✉LS1 6NA ☎ 245 94 49

RESTAURANTS

Metz (B CC F GLM MA) Mon-Thu 12-23, Fri-Sat -24, Sun-22.30 h
Baker House, Cavern Quarter ✉L2 6PT ☎ 0151/227-2282

SAUNAS/BATHS

Spartan Mantalk (f G MA sa sb wh) Mon-Sun 0-24 h
72 Bayswater Road, Harehills ☎ 248 77 57

HOTELS

Central Hotel (B bf CC H MA)
35-45 New Briggate, ✉LS2 8JD ☎ 294 1456 Fax: 294 1551
Hotel with a variety of rooms to suit all budgets, situated in the city centre. All rooms have T.V and tea / coffee making facliities and many are en suite. Rates from: Single £ 26-38, Double (en suite) £ 38-46 incl. continental breakfast.

RELIGIOUS GROUPS

Yorkshire MESMAC
PO Box 172 ✉LS7 3BZ ☎ 244 42 09

Leicester - Leicestershire ☎ 0116

GAY INFO

Leicester Lesbian Gay & Bisexual Centre (F GLM OS) Mon-Sat
45 King Street ✉LE1 6RN ☎ 254 74 12
Telephone Helpline Mon-Fri 09-17:00 h. Youth Group Thu 19.30-22 h.
Lesbian and Gayline Mo-Th 19.30-22 h
☎ 255 06 67

BARS

Bossa (B glm)
110 Granby St. ☎ 275 54 00
Dolly's (B CC D E GLM OS S VS YG) 11-15.30, 18.30-23 h. (D) Wed, Fri-Sun
34 Dover Street *(Off Granby Street)* ☎ 255 05 61
Leicester Place (B D g) 11-23, Sun 12-22.30, (D) Mon-Sat 22-24 (The Crown)
24 Dryden Street *(Off Lee Circle)* ☎ 251 07 85
Pineapple Inn. The (! B D f G H MA S) Sun-Thu 12-15, Fri-Sat 12-16, Mon-Wed 19-24, Thu-1, Fri Sat-2, Sun-22.30 h
27 Burleys Way ☎ 262 33 84
Cabaret Fri, stripper Sun, Sun lunch, accomodation available.

DANCECLUBS

Knight Life at The Pineapple Inn (! B D G MA S) Fri-Sat -2 h
27 Burleys Way ☎ 262 33 84
Rapture in the Asylum Fortnightly Fri 21-2 h
c/o Leicester University S.U., University Road ✉LE1 7RH
☎ 223 11 11
Shag (B D GLM) De Montefort Student Union Arena
☎ 255 55 76
Monthly Club. Call Uni LGB group for dates.

GENERAL GROUPS

Leicester Gay Group
☎ 251 58 10
(Neil) or ☎ (01509) 55 28 32 (Chris)
Leicester Lesbian and Gay Action
25 Walton St. ✉LE3 ODX ☎ 255 34 36
Campaign & lobbying grouzp

HEALTH GROUPS

AIDS Support Services Mo-Fr 09:30-16:30h
c/o Michael Wood Centre, 53 Regent Road ✉LE1 6YF
☎ 255 99 95
Men`s sexual health project 12-16 h
15 Wellington Street ✉LE1 6RN ☎ 254 17 47 Fax: 251 87 55

CRUISING

-Abbey Park (Abbey Lane near Canal Side, evenings)
-Tugby Picnic Area (AYOR MG) (A47 8 miles east of Leicester, daily)

Lincoln - Lincolnshire ☎ 01522

GAY INFO

Lincoln Switchboard Sun, Thu 19-22 h
PO Box 99 ✉LN4 2SD ☎ 53 55 53

HEALTH GROUPS

AIDS-Helpline Tue, Thu 9-17.30, Mon, Wed, Fri -19 h
☎ 51 39 99
Health Shop Mon-Fri 9-16.30 h
Portland House, 3 Portland Road ☎ 52 92 22
Drop-in center dealing with sexual health, alcohol and drug use.

Little Bromley - Essex ☎ 01206

BARS

Fox & Hounds (B D f GLM MA S) We &Th 19-24:00h, Fr & Sa 20-02:00h, Su 12-15 & 20-22:30h
Bentley Road ☎ 39 74 15

Liverpool - Merseyside ☎ 0151

GAY INFO

Merseyside Switchboard 19-22 h
☎ 708 95 52
Meryside Friend 19-22 h
36 Bolton St. ☎ 708 95 52

BARS

Baa Bar (B bf F glm OS s W YG) Mon-Sat 10-2, Sun 14-20 h
43-45 Fleet Street ☎ 708 6810
Brunswick Vaults. The (B glm MA) 11-23 h
69 Tithebarn Street ☎ 284 3258
Curzon Club (B D f GLM MA S SL SNU STV TV VS YG) Mo-Sa 12-02:00h, Su closed.
8 Temple Lane ✉L2 5RQ *(Off Victoria Street)* ☎ 236 5160
G-Bar (B GLM YG) Thu-Sat
Eberle Street *(Opposite Garlands)* ☎ 258 1230
Popular before and after Garlands
Lisbon. The (B glm MA YG) 11-23 h, best Sun
36 Victoria Street ✉L1 6BP ☎ 286 5466
Masquerade. The (B f GLM MA s) 12-23 h
10 Cumberland Street ✉L1 6BU ☎ 236 7786
Pacos (B G MA) Mo-Sa 12-23.00h. Su -22:30h
25 Stanley Street ✉L1 6AA ☎ 236 9737

CAFÉS

Café Tabac (A B F glm YG) Mon-Sat 9.30-23, Sun 10.30-17 h
126 Bold Street ☎ 709 3735

DANCECLUBS

Escape/E2. The (B D GLM MA S VS W YG) Tue Thu 22-4, Fri Sat 22-6 h
41-45 Paradise Street ✉L1 3BP
Garlands (B D GLM pi SNU TV YG) Thu-Sat 21-2 h
8-10 Eberle Street ✉L2 2AG ☎ 236 3307

RESTAURANTS

Greenbank (B F glm MA) Tue-Sun
332-338 Smithdown Rd. ☎ 734 4498
Wine bar / vegetarian restaurant.
Metz (B CC F GLM MA) Mon-Thu 12-23, Fri-Sat -24, Sun-22.30 h
New York Street *(Exchange Quarter)*

SAUNAS/BATHS

Dolphin Sauna (AC f G MA sa sb sol wh) 14-21.30 h
129 Mount Road, Wallasey ✉L45 9JS *(5 min from New Brighton Station)* ☎ 630 1516

HOTELS

Feathers Hotel (B bf CC F H MA)
119-125 Mount Pleasant ☎ 709 9655
Large, comfortable gay friendly hotel located in Liverpool city centre. All rooms have TV, telephone and tea / coffee making facilities. Rates: Single £ 44.95, Double £ 59.95 incl. full buffet breakfast.

GENERAL GROUPS

LGB Soc at Liverpool University Meets every Tue 20 h (termtime) at Lisbon Bar, Victoria St.
☎ 794 41 22 or ☎ *794 41 73*
Wirral Penninsulana Group Meets Wed 21-1 h at Queens Royal, Marine Promenade, New Brighton
☎ 630 6251 or ☎ 638 6371

HEALTH GROUPS

Healthwise Daily 10-22 h (free phone)
☎ (0800) 83 89 09
Health information/advice
Maryland Centre Mon-Tue Thu 9.30-17.30, Wed -21, Fri -18.30, Sat 11-17 h
8 Maryland St. *(off Hope St.)* ☎ 709 22 31
HIV testing, advice & info.

CRUISING

-Ainsdale Dunes (summer, nu)
-Otterspool Promenade (AYOR)
-Waterloo Marina, gardens and car parks in Crosby area (ayor)

Llandrindod Wells - Powys ☎ 01597

HEALTH GROUPS

Powys Aidsline Wed Sat 20-22.30 h
PO Box 24 ✉LD1 122 ☎ 82 42 00
or ☎ (0800) 45 43 91 (toll free)

Llandudno - Conwy ☎ 01492

DANCECLUBS

Broadway Boulevard (B D G S) every other Mon 20.30-0.30 h
Mostyn Brdwy ☎ 87 96 14

London ☎ 020

The capital city of the United Kingdom and without doubt the gay capital too. In the last ten years the gay scene has exploded with many new bars and clubs opening accross the city. The gay scene is centered around Old Compton Street in SoHo, right in the heart of the city, this is where you will find all the theatre shops, cafés, cinemas and many gay bars and clubs. However do not feel that this is the only area to see. Many of the interesting bars, clubs and saunas are to be found outside the centre. London is a very cosmopolitan city and you will find young gay people from all over the world who have come to settle here for a time to make use of the excellent club and bar scene that is unrivalled anywhere else in Europe. The underground system is extensive but be warned it does not operate after 22:30h. Alternatives such as night busses or taxis are available. Please remember the underground map bears very little relation to the geography of the city. Enjoy your time in vibrant London!

Die Hauptstadt Großbritanniens ist ohne Zweifel auch die bedeutendste Schwulen-Metropole des Landes. In den vergangenen zehn Jahren hat sich die Londoner Schwulen-Szene sehr stark vergrößert und so haben im gesamten Stadtgebiet viele neue Bars und Clubs eröffnet. Das Zentrum der Schwulen-Szene konzentriert sich um die Old Compton Street in Soho in der Londoner Innenstadt. Hier findet man verschiedene Theater, Shops, Cafes, Kinos und viele schwule Bars und Clubs. Man sollte aber nicht vergessen, daß dies nicht die einzige Möglichkeit ist in London schwul auszugehen: viele der weitaus interessanteren Bars, Clubs und Saunen liegen außerhalb des Zentrums. London ist eine sehr vielseitige und weltoffene Stadt. Man begegnet vielen jungen Homosexuellen aus aller Welt, die hierher gekommen sind, um einige Zeit das exzellente und für Europa einzigartige Nachtleben zu genießen. Das Londoner U-Bahn-System ist sehr gut ausgebaut, jedoch nur bis 23.30 Uhr in Betrieb. Anschließend ist man auf Nachtbusse (die meisten fahren vom Trafalgar Square) oder Taxis angewiesen ("mini cabs" sind günstiger und man kann über den Preis verhandeln, Vorsicht ist bei Taxis ohne Lizenz geboten). Ein schwules Taxi-Unternehmen, mit dem Namen "Freedom Cabs", befindet sich in der Old Compton Street direkt neben dem Balans. Bitte bedenken Sie, daß der U-Bahn-Plan nur einen geringen Einblick über die geographischen Ausmaße der Stadt ermöglicht.

La capitale du Royaume-Uni fait sans aucun doute également office de capitale gaye du pays. La scène homosexuelle a littéralement explosé ces dix dernières années et on a pu assister à l'ouverture, à travers toute la ville, d'une multitude de nouveaux bars et clubs. Plus particulièrement autour de Old Compton Street, dans le quartier de SoHo, vous trouverez une concentration de théâtres, de cafés, de cinémas, mais aussi de bars et clubs gays en plein coeur de la ville. Ce n'est cependant pas le seul quartier intéressant et beaucoup de saunas, bars et clubs se trouvent aussi en dehors du centre. Londres est une ville très cosmopolite et vous serez peut-être amenés à rencontrer un de ces nombreux jeune gay, venu récemment s'installer dans la capitale pour profiter pleinement d'une offre en sorties qui reste encore inégalée en Europe. Soyez attentifs au fait que les cartes de métro ne respectent pas forcément la géographie de la ville et que le réseau du métro, bien que très développé, ne dessert pas en delà de 22 heures 30. Des bus de nuits et taxis sont heureusement aussi disponibles partout. Il ne nous reste plus qu'à vous souhaiter un heureux séjour dans cette ville palpitante!

Es la capital del Reino Unido y sin duda la capital gay también. En los últimos 10 años la escena gay ha explotado con la apertura de muchos nuevos bares y clubes por toda la ciudad. La escena gay se centra alrededor de Old Compton Street en el SoHo, en pleno corazón de la ciudad; aquí es donde se encuentran todos los teatros, tiendas, cafeterías, cines y muchos bares y clubes gay. Pero no hay que pensar que ésta es la única zona a visitar. Muchos bares interesantes, clubes y saunas se encuentran fuera del centro. Londres es una ciudad muy cosmopolita donde se encuentra a mucha gente joven gay de todo el mundo que se ha establecido por un tiempo allí para poder disfrutar de la excelente escena de clubes y bares, sin comparación en toda Europa. La red de metro es muy extensa, pero tened en cuenta que no funciona después de las 11:30, por lo que tendréis que tomar un autobús nocturno (la mayoría salen de Trafalgar Square) o un taxi (los "mini cabs" son más baratos y se puede negociar el precio, pero cuidado con los que no tengan licencia). Hay una empresa gay de taxis en Old Compton Street, la puerta al lado de Balans, que se llama "Freedom Cabs. Recordad que el plano del metro guarda muy poca relación con la geografía de la ciudad, por lo que os recomendamos que utilicéis los mapas de la ciudad que os ofrece Spartacus para que no os paséis la mitad de las vacaciones por ahí perdidos.

La capitale della Gran Bretagna è senza dubbio anche la metropoli gay più importante del paese. Negli ultimi dieci anni la scena gay di Londra è molto cresciuta e quindi tanti nuovi pub e club hanno aperto in tutta la città. La scena gay è concentrata attorno alla Old Compton Street a Soho, al centro di Londra. Qui, si trovano diversi teatri, negozi, bar diurni, cinema e tanti pub e club gay. Però, non bisogna dimenticare che questa non sia la unica possibilità per uscire in locali gay: tanti bar, club e saune ancora più interessanti si trovano fuori del centro. Londra è una città molto eterogenea e cosmopolita. Si possono incontrare tanti giovani omosessuali da tutto il mondo che sono venuti a Londra per godere per un pò di tempo la vita notturna eccellente e unica nel suo genere in Europa. Il sistema della metropolitana è sviluppato molto bene, però è in funzione solo fino alle ore 23.30. Dopo quest'ora si deve ricorrere agli autobus notturni (la maggior parte dei quali parte dal Trafalgar Square) oppure ai tassì (cosidetti "mini cabs" costano di meno ed è possibile negoziare il prezzo, bisogna fare attenzione a tassì senza licenza). Una impresa gay di tassì si trova in Old Compton Street, proprio accanto al "Balans". Si deve prendere in considerazione che la mappa delle metropolitane non dia una precisa idea della dimensione geografica della città.

NATIONAL PUBLISHERS

Outcast
42 Birch Grove ✉W3 9SS London ☎ 0906/20 10 028
Homepage: www.outcast.co.uk
Queer current affairs magazine

GAY INFO

London Lesbian and Gay Switchboard (GLM p) 24 h
PO Box 7324 ✉N1 9QS London ☎ 7837 7324
E-Mail: admin@llgs.org.uk
Excellent, round-the-clock telephone helpline, providing support, advice and information for lesbians & gays.

Time Out
251 Tottenham Ct. Rd., ✉W1P 0AB London ☎ 7813 3000
This weekly city guide can be bought at all newsagents and newstands. It has a comprehensive gay section as well as news on all other aspects of life in the capital.

TOURIST INFO

London Tourist Board and Information Centre 08-18:00h
Victoria Station Forecourt ✉SW1V 1JU ☎ 7932 2000

BARS

Admiral Duncan. The (AC B CC f G GLM MA) Mon-Sat 11-23:00h, Sun 12-22:30h
54 Old Compton Street, SoHo ✉W1V 5PA *(U-Piccadilly)*
☎ 7437 5300
Refurbished after the SoHo bombing. Very busy bar especially evenings.

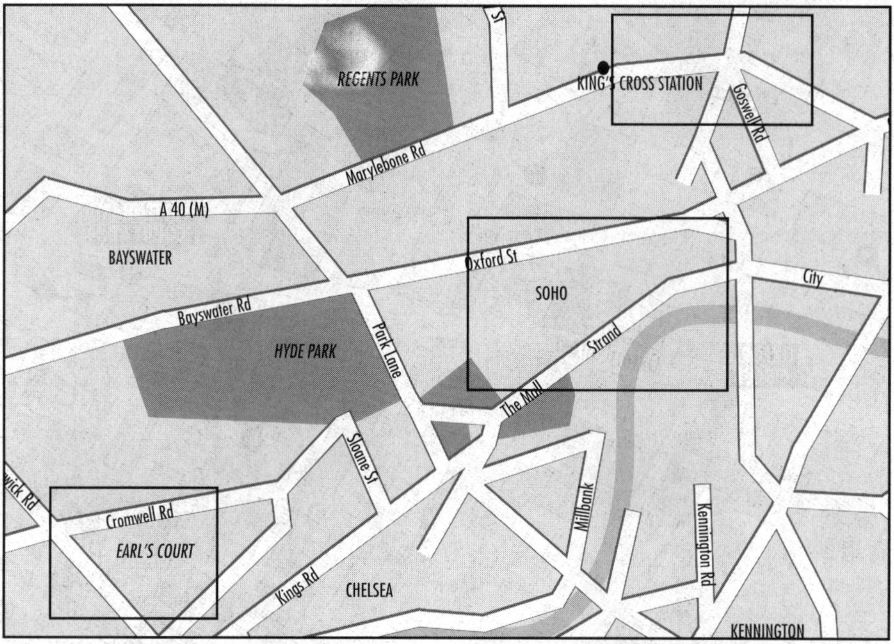
REGENTS PARK
KING'S CROSS STATION
Goswell Rd
Marylebone Rd
A 40 (M)
BAYSWATER
Oxford St
SOHO
City
Bayswater Rd
HYDE PARK
Park Lane
Strand
The Mall
Sloane St
Cromwell Rd
EARL'S COURT
Millbank
Kennington Rd
Kings Rd
CHELSEA
KENNINGTON

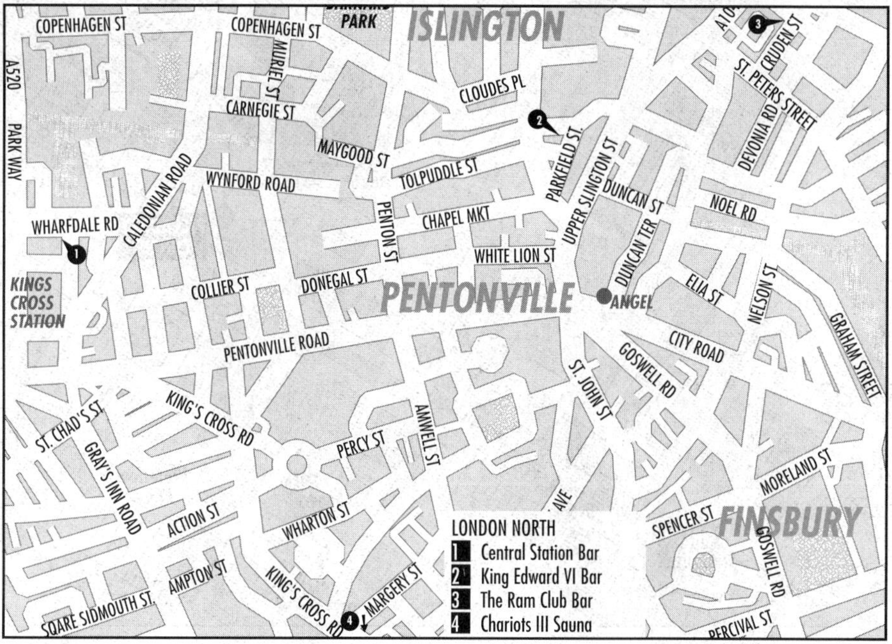
COPENHAGEN ST
COPENHAGEN ST
PARK
ISLINGTON
A520
PARK WAY
MURIEL ST
CARNEGIE ST
CLOUDES PL
CRUDEN ST
ST. PETERS STREET
DEVONIA RD
MAYGOOD ST
TOLPUDDLE ST
PARKFIELD ST.
UPPER SLINGTON ST
DUNCAN ST
NOEL RD
CALEDONIAN ROAD
WYNFORD ROAD
WHARFDALE RD
PENTON ST
CHAPEL MKT
WHITE LION ST
DUNCAN TER
KINGS CROSS STATION
COLLIER ST
DONEGAL ST
PENTONVILLE
ANGEL
ELIA ST
NELSON ST
PENTONVILLE ROAD
CITY ROAD
GOSWELL RD
ST. JOHN ST
GRAHAM STREET
ST. CHAD'S ST
KING'S CROSS RD
GRAY'S INN ROAD
AMWELL ST
PERCY ST
MORELAND ST
ACTION ST
WHARTON ST
SPENCER ST
FINSBURY
GOSWELL RD
AMPTON ST
KING'S CROSS RD
MARGERY ST
SQARE SIDMOUTH ST.
PERCIVAL ST
LONDON NORTH
1 Central Station Bar
2 King Edward VI Bar
3 The Ram Club Bar
4 Chariots III Sauna

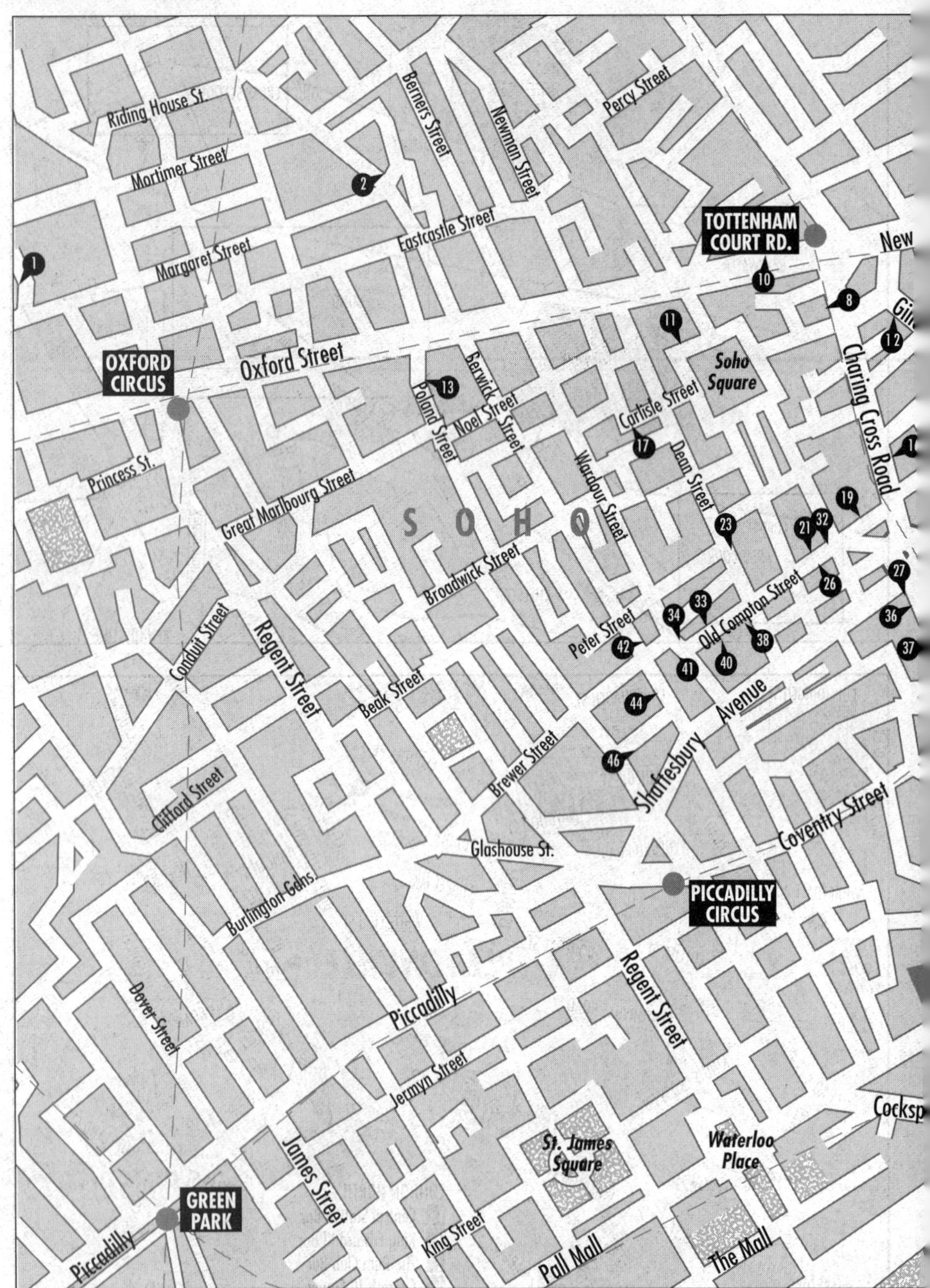

Riding House St.
Mortimer Street
Berners Street
Newman Street
Percy Street
Eastcastle Street
Margaret Street
TOTTENHAM COURT RD.
New
OXFORD CIRCUS
Oxford Street
Poland Street
Berwick Street
Noel Street
Carlisle Street
Soho Square
Charing Cross Road
Princess St.
Great Marlbourg Street
SOHO
Wardour Street
Dean Street
Broadwick Street
Old Compton Street
Peter Street
Conduit Street
Regent Street
Beak Street
Shaftesbury Avenue
Brewer Street
Clifford Street
Coventry Street
Glashouse St.
Burlington Gdns
PICCADILLY CIRCUS
Dover Street
Piccadilly
Regent Street
Jermyn Street
James Street
St. James Square
Waterloo Place
GREEN PARK
King Street
Pall Mall
The Mall
Piccadilly

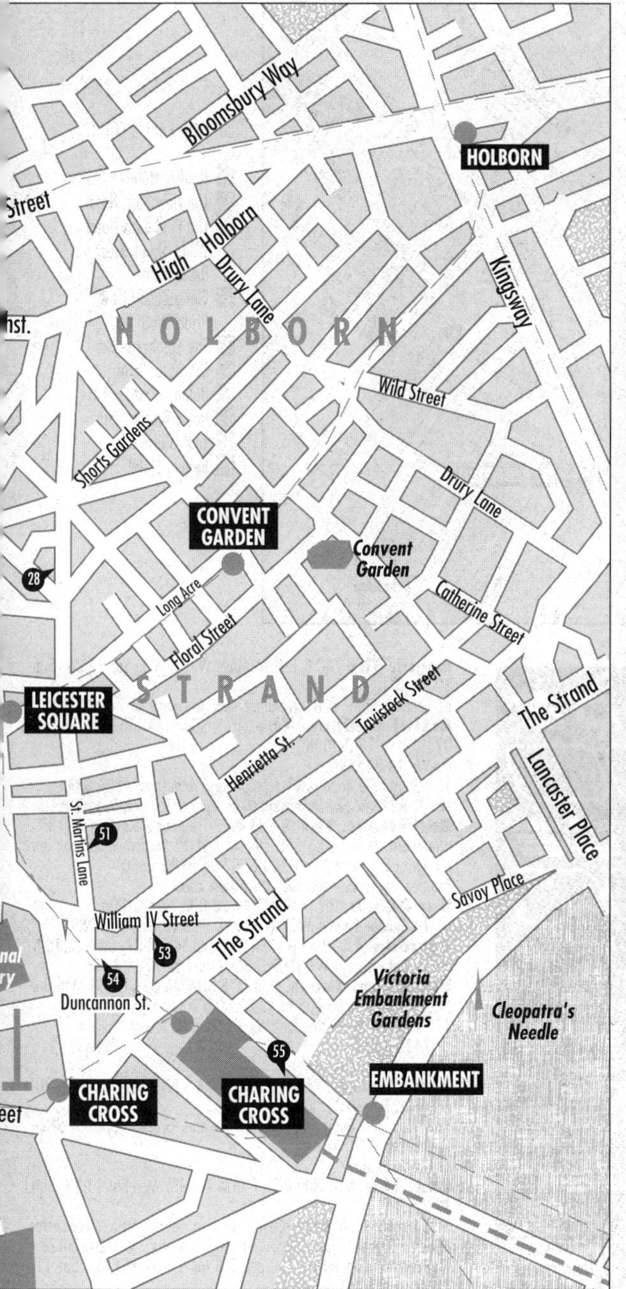

LONDON SOHO/HOLBORN

- **1** The Phoenix Danceclub
- **2** RoB Leather & Fetish Shop
- **8** G.A.Y. at the Astoria Party
- **10** Virgin Megastore
- **11** The Edge Bar
- **12** First Out Café
- **13** Kings' Arms Bar
- **16** Books etc. Bookshop
- **17** Candy Bar
- **19** The Stockpot Restaurant
- **21** Old Compton Cafe
- **23** Steph's Restaurant
- **26** American Retro Gift & Pride Shop
- **27** Gay T-Dance at the Limelight Party
- **28** The Box Bar
- **32** Outlet
- **32** Balans Café
- **32** Freedom Cars Travel & Transport
- **33** Clone Zone Gift & Pride Shop
- **34** Freedom Café
- **36** 79 CXR Bar
- **37** Ku Bar
- **38** Paradiso Bodyworks Sex Shop
- **40** Comptons of Soho Bar
- **41** Village Soho Bar
- **42** Escape Bar
- **44** The Yard Soho Bar/D-Tours
- **46** Bar Code Bar
- **51** Brief Encounter Bar
- **53** Kudos Bar
- **54** Halfway to Heaven Bar
- **55** Heaven Danceclub

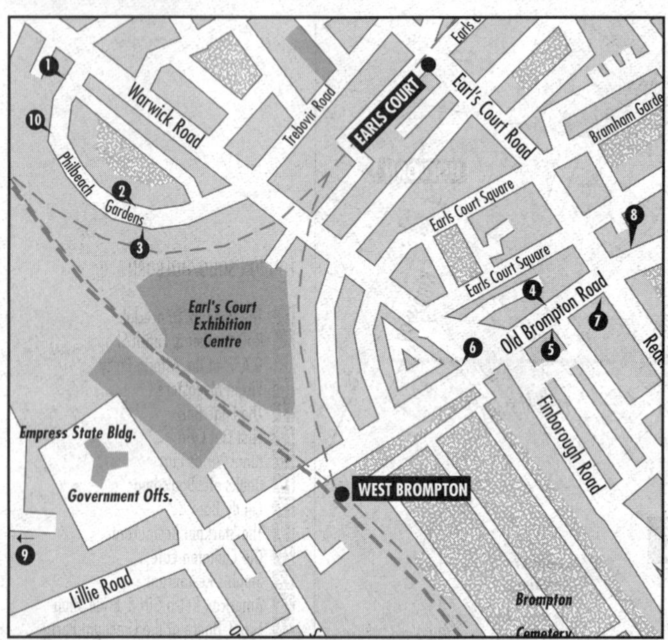

LONDON-EARL´S COURT

1 Halifax Hotel
2 The New York Hotel
3 The Philbeach Hotel Wilde About Oscar Restaurant
4 Clone Zone Gift & Pride Shop
5 The Colcherne Bar
6 Brompton's Bar
7 Balans West Café
8 Roy's Restaurant
9 Ted's Place Bar
10 Beaver Hotel

Angel. The (AC B F GLM MA s W YG) Mon-Sat 12-24, Sun 12-23.30 h
65 Graham Street ✉N1 *(U-Angel. Next to canal)* ☎ 7608 2656

Artful Dodger. The (B d f Glm MA) Th,Fr & Sa 14-02:00h, Su 13-24:00h
Mo-We 14-24:00h
139 Southgate Road ✉N1 *(U-Highbury/Angel)* ☎ 7226 0841
We- Towel Party. Su - Underwear Night. Gym & Sauna in Basement.

Backstreet. The (B G LJ MA P) Thu-Sat 22-3, Sun 21-1 h.
Wentworth Mews ✉E3 SAP *(U-Mile End.Off Burdett Road.Look out for light above entr.)* ☎ 8980 8557 ☎ 8980 7880
Leather and rubber club with strict dress code.

Bar Aquda (B F GLM MA) 12-23:00h, Su -22:30h
13-14 Maiden Lane ✉WC2 *(U-Covent Garden)* ☎ 7557 9891

Barcode (A AC B d f G lj MA VS) Mon-Sat 13-01, Sun -22.30 h
3-4 Archer Street ✉W1 *(U-Piccadilly Cicus)* ☎ 7734 3343

Black Cap. The (AC B bf CC F GLM MA OS STV TV) Mon-Thu 12-2 h, Fri Sat 12-3 h, Sun 12-22.30 h
171 Camden High Street ✉NW1 *(U-Camden Town)*
☎ 7428 2721
Drag/cabaret pub.

Black Horse. The (AC B d G MA S SNU STV) Mon-Sun 20-2 h, Fr & Sat 20-02:00h
168 Mile End Road ✉E1 4LJ *(U-Stepney Green. Opposite Globe Centre)* ☎ 7790 1684
Gay cabaret bar.

Box. The (A AC B bf CC d F GLM MA OS) Mon-Sat 11-23, Sun 12-22.30h
32-34 Monmouth Street, Covent Garden ✉WC2 9HA *(U-Leicester Square/Covent Garden. Opp. Cambridge Theatre.)* ☎ 7240 5828

Brief Encounter (AC B D G lj MA s SWC YG) Mon-Sat 11-23, Sun 12-22.30 h

41 St. Martin's Lane ✉WC2 4EA *(U-Leicester Square/Charing Cross. Next to London Coliseum)* ☎ 7240 2221

British Prince. The (AC B G S SNU VS W) Mon-Sat 12-23.30, Sun 12-22.30 h
49 Bromley Street, Stepney ✉E1 *(U-Limehouse)* ☎ 7790 1753

Bromptons (! AC B D G lj MA S) 18-2, Sun 20-24 h
294 Old Brompton Road ✉SW5 *(U-Earls Court, Exit Warwick Road)* ☎ 7370 1344
Very popular on weekends, cruisy atmosphere.

Cafe Au-Reole (B F GLM MA) 17-24, Sat-Sun 12-24 h
233 Earls Court Road ✉SW5 ☎ 7912 1409

Central Station (! A AC B D F G lj MA OS SNU STV VS YG) Mon-Wed 17-2, Thu -3, Fri -5, Sat 12-5, Sun 12-01:00h
37 Wharfdale Road ✉N1 *(U-King's Cross)* ☎ 7278 3294
Three floors. UK's only gay sports bar. Caberet bar, nightclub, and roof terrace.

Champion. The (AC B d G MA N OS s) 12-23, Sun 12-22.30 h
1 Wellington Terrace, Bayswater Road ✉W2 *(U-Notting Hill/Queensway)* ☎ 7229 5056

Coleherne. The (AC B G LJ MA W) 12-23, Sun 12-22.30; Detour Bar Fri-Sun 21.30-24 h
261 Old Brompton Road ✉SW5 *(U-Earl's Court)* ☎ 7244 5951

Comptons of Soho (! AC B CC F G LJ MA W) 12-23, Sun 19-22.30 h
53 Old Compton Street ✉W1 *(U-Picadilly)* ☎ 7437 4445

Due South (B G MA) Mon-Fri 16-?, Sat Sun 13-? h, Thu women only
35 Stoke Newington High Street ✉N16 ☎ 7249 7543

Duke of Wellington. The (B F glm MA N WE) 12-24, Sat 13-24, Sun 13-22.30 h
119 Balls Pond Road ✉N1 *(U-Highbury/Islington)* ☎ 7254 4338

Edge. The (! A B CC D F GLM MA W YG) 12-1, Sun 12-22.30 h. Evenings (G).
11 Soho Square ✉W1V 5DB *(U-Tottenham Court Road)* ☎ 7439 1313

Escape (B D F GLM MA) 16-3, Sun 16-22.30 h
8 Brewer Street ✉W1 *(U-Leicester Square)* ☎ 7734 2626

Gate Club. The (B CC G MA N) Mon-Sat 10-01:00h, Sun 22-24:00h 68 Notting Hill Gate ✉W11 3HT *(U-Notting Hill Gate)* ☎ 7229 0161

George. The (B F Glm MA STV OS) 17-23, Sun 12-22.30 h
114 Twickenham Road, Isleworth *(U-Hounslow East, plus a good walk)* ☎ 8560 1456 *Good Cabaret*

Gloucester. The (B CC F G MA N S W) 11-23, Sun 12-22.30 h
1 King William Walk ✉SE10 *(BR-Greenwich. Opposite Greenwich Park gates.)* ☎ 8293 6131

Halfway to Heaven (B d GLM MA S STV WE) 12-23 h, Sun 12-22.30 h
7 Duncannon Street ✉WC2 4JF *(U-Charing Cross. Next to Trafalger Square)* ☎ 7930 8312

Hoist. The (AC B G LJ MA) Fri-Sat 22-3 h
Railway Arch 47c, South Lambeth Road, ✉SW8 IRH *(opposite U-Vauxhall, Exit One, in arches)* ☎ 7735 9972

Jonathan's (B CC G MA N P) 15-23, Sun 13-15 19-22.30 h
16 Irving Street ✉WC2 *(U-Leicester Square. 1st Floor)* ☎ 7930 4770
Gay members club. Guests welcome.

King Edward VI (AC B bf F G MA N OS W WE) 12-24, Sun 12-22.30 h
25 Bromfield Street, Islington ✉N1 OPZ *(U-Angel.Corner of Parkfield St.)* ☎ 704 0745

King William IV (B F Glm lj MA N STV) 12-23, Sun 12-22.30 h
77 Hampstead High Street ✉NW3 1RE *(U-Hampstead)* ☎ 7435 5747
Not far from cruising area Hamstead Heath.

Kings' Arms (AC B CC F G MA s) 11-23, Sun 12-22.30 h
23 Poland Street ✉W1V 3DD *(U-Oxford Circus/Tottenham Court Road)* ☎ 7734 5907

Ku Bar (B GLM YG) 12-23, Sun 13-22.30 h
75 Charing Cross Road ✉WC2H ONE *(U-Leicester Square)* ☎ 7437 4303

Kudos (A B CC d F G MA s VS) Mon-Sat 11-23, Sun 12-22.30 h
10 Adelaide Street ✉WC2N 4HZ *(BR/U-Charing Cross)* ☎ 7379 4573.

Little Apple. The (AC B CC D F GLM MA OS s TV W) 12-24, Sun -23 h
98 Kennington Lane ✉SE11 4XD *(U-Kennington)* ☎ 7735 2039

LJ's (B D GLM STV) Tue-Sun 20-? h
140 London Road, Kingston-Upon-Thames, Surrey ☎ 8288 1448

Oak. The (B f D GLM MA) Mon-Thu 13-24, Fri-Sat -2, Sun 14-24 h
79 Green Lanes ✉N16 *(U-Manor House)* ☎ 7354 2791

Old Ship. The (B f GLM MA N S STV W) 18-23, Sat 19.30-23, Sun 13.30-22.30 h

Penny Farthing (AC B CC d F GLM MA N OS S STV W WE) 12-2, Sun 12-22.30 h
135 King Street ✉W6 9JG *(U-Hammersmith)* ☎ 8600 0941

Queen's Head (B F G MA OG OS) 12-23, Sat 11-23, Sun 12-22.30 h
27 Tryon Street ✉SW3 *(U-Sloane Square. Just off the King's Rd. opposite Safeways)* ☎ 7589 0262

Ram Club Bar. The (AC B CC f G MA T W) 15.30-24, Sat-Sun 11.30-24 h
39 Queen's Head Street ✉N1 8NQ *(U-Angel)* ☎ 7354 0576

Red Stiletto. The (B D F GLM MA N OS S SNU STV YG) 7-23, Sun 8-23 h
108 Wandsworth Road ✉SW8 *(U-Vauxhall. Near large Supermarket.)* ☎ 7771 21654

Retro Bar. The (B GLM MA s) 12-23, Sun 12-22.30 h
2 George Court ✉WC2 *(U-Charing Cross. Off the Strand)* ☎ 7321 2811

Rocket. The (B D GLM MA S) 11-23, Sun 12-22.30 h
10-13 Churchfield Road, Acton ✉W3 *(U-Acton)* ☎ 8992 1545
One bar with cabaret and one more cruisy one.

Royal Oak (AC B F GLM N s) 11-?, Sun 8-? (bf 8-12 h)
73 Columbia Road ✉E2 *(U-Old Street)* ☎ 7739 8204
Mexican restaurant upstairs

Royal Vauxhall Tavern (AC B D f GLM lj MA S SNU STV VS W) 20-24/1, Fri Sat 21-2 h, Sun 12-24 h
372 Kennington Lane ✉SE11 5QH *(U-Vauxhall. Near river and Vauxhall Viaduct.)* ☎ 7582 0833

Rupert Street (AC B CC F GLM MA W YG) 11-23, Sun 12-22.30 h
50 Rupert Street ✉W1V 7HR *(U-Picadilly Circus. Opposite The Yard)* ☎ 7734 5164
Stylish bar. Very popular in the evenings.

Shoot (B D G MA) 2nd Sun 18-24 h
Central Station, 37 Wharfdale Road ✉N1 ☎ 7278 3294
Strict dresscode : sportswear .

SubStation South (AC B D Glm lj MA YG) Mon 22-2, Tue Thu 21.30-2, Wed -3, Fri 22-5, Sat 22.30-5, Sun 21-3 h
9 Brighton Terrace, Brixton ✉SW9 *(U-Brixton)* ☎ 7737 2095
Different theme nights. Cruisy and popular.

Ted's Place (B D DR G MA P STV TV VS) Mon-Fri 19-late. Last Sun/ month 16-23:00h
305a Northend Road ✉W14 9NS *(U-West Kensington/U-West Brompton)* ☎ 7385 9359
Mon,Tue,Fri & Sun - men only.

Townhouse. The (AC B CC E F G MA P WE YG) Mon-Sat 18-23.30 (Bar), -1.30 (The Lounge), 19-1.30 h (Restaurant)
3 Green Street, Mayfair ✉W1Y 3RG *(U-Marble Arch and U-Bond Street)* ☎ 7499 4489
Private members club. 48 hours notice for membership. Restaurant, private dining room, bar and lounge. Reasonable prices.

Tube. The (B D GLM MA) 22-?, Fri-Sat -5 h
Falconberg Court ✉W1 *(U-Tottenham Court Road, behind Astoria)*

Two Brewers. The (AC B D GLM MA N S STV VS W WE) Mo-Th 12-02:00h, Fr & Sa -03:00h, Su -24:00h
114 Clapham High Street ✉SW4 7UJ *(U-Clapham Common)* ☎ 7498 4971

Underground (AC B CC D F G lj MA S SNU STV YG) 17-2, Thu-3, Fri-5, Sat 12-5, Sun 12-24 h
37 Wharfdale Road ✉N1 *(U-Kings Cross)* ☎ 7833 8925
See Central Station.

Village Soho (! AC B CC F G W YG) 12-23, Sun 12-22.30, meals 12-17 h

81 Wardour Street ✉W1V 3TG *(U-Piccadilly Circus. At the head of Old Compton Street)* ☎ 7434 2124
West Central (B GLM MA) 29-30 Lisle Street ✉WC2 *Underground station Leicester Sqaure (Chinatown)* ☎ 7479 7981
Large, Busy gay bar on three floors
White Hart. The (B f glm MA S W) 19-24, Sun 12-23.30 h
51 Station Road ✉N15 *(U-Tottenham Hale. In front of Blockbuster Video.)* ☎ 8808 5049
White Swan. The (AC B D G MA S SL SNU STV VS W) Mo 21-01:00h, Tu-Th 21-02:00h, Fr & Sa 21-03:00h, Su 17:30-24:00h
556 Commercial Road ✉E14 7JD *(U-Aldgate East / Limehouse Docklands Light Railway)* ☎ 7780 9870
Yard. The (! A B CC F GLM MA OS W YG) 12-23, meals 12-17, Sun 12-22.30 h
57 Rupert Street ✉W1V 7HN *(U-Piccadilly Circus / Tottenham Court Road)* ☎ 7437 2652
79CXR (AC B G MA) Mon-Thu 13-02:00h, Fri & Sat -03:00h Sun -22:30h
79 Charing Cross Road, SoHo ✉WC2H ONE *(U-Leicester Square. Cambridge Circus intersection)* ☎ 734 0769
Popular late bar. Happy hour daily and all day on Sun. DJ Thu to Sat.

CAFÉS

Balans West (AC B bf CC F GLM OS W YG) 8-1 h
239 Old Brompton Road ✉SW5 9HP *(U-Earl's Court)*
☎ 7244 8838
First Out Café Bar (A B bf F GLM MA) 10-23, Sun 11-22.30, Fri 20-23 h Women's night
52 St. Giles High Street ✉WC2 *(U-Tottenham Court Road. Next to Center Point.)* ☎ 7240 8042
Freedom (A B F glm MA S YG) 11-3, Sun -24 h
60-66 Wardour Street ✉W1
☎ 7734 0071
Old Compton Cafe (AC bf F GLM MA OS YG) 0-24 h
34 Old Compton Street ✉W1 *(U-Piccadilly Circus / Tottenham Court Road)* ☎ 7439 3309
Work in Progress at ICA (A B F g s) Mon 12-23, Tue-Sat 12-1, Sun 12-22.30 h
Nash House, The Mall ✉SW1 *(U-Green Park. Near Buckingham Palace)* ☎ 7930 3647

DANCECLUBS

Benjys 2000 (AC B D GLM s YG) Th-Sa 22-03:00h, Sun 21-1 h
562a Mile End Road ✉E3 *(U-Mile End)* ☎ 8980 6427
Carioca at Ruby's Dance Club (B D GLM MA) Sun 16.30-21 h
49 Carnaby Street ✉W1V 1PF *(U-Oxford Circus)* ☎ 8302 6651
16.30-17.30 Dance class Ballroom and Latin American
Club Travestie (AC B D GLM MA S STV TV W) 2nd/4th Sat 20.30-2:00 h
Stepney Nightclub, 373 Commercial Road ✉E1 *(U-Aldgate East. Entrance on Aylward St., off Jubilee St.)* ☎ 8788 4154
This TV/drag which has been running for the last nineteen years, attracts a mixed crowd. Every other Sat.
Club V (AC B D GLM s YG) 2nd Sat 21-03:00h
20-22 Highbury Corner ✉N1 *(U-Highbury and Islington. Upstairs at the Garage.)* ☎ 7607 1818
Coco Latté (D GLM) Fri 10:30-04:00h
59 Berkley Square ✉W1 *(U-Green Park)* ☎ 0956/198267
Duckie at the Vauxhall Tavern (AC B D GLM lj S VS W) Sat 21-2 h
372 Kennington Lane ✉SE11 *(U-Vauxhall)* ☎ 7582 0833
Fresca at The End (AC B D GLM YG) Sun 20-3.30 h
18 West Central Street ✉WC1 *(U-Tottenham Court Road)*
G.A.Y. at the Astoria (AC B D GLM MA s W) Mon Thu Pink Pounder 22.30-4, Fri Camp Attack 23-4, Sat G.A.Y. 22.30-5 h
157 Charing Cross Road ✉WC2 *(U-Tottenham Court Road)*
☎ 7734 6963
Mon Thu admission just GBP 1.
Gay Tea-Dance at The Limelight (! AC B D GLM MA YG) Sun 18-23 h
136 Shaftesbury Avenue ✉W1 *(U-Leicester Square)*
☎ 7437 0572
Heaven (AC B CC D f GLM MA S STV) Mon-Thu 22-3, Fri Sat -6, Sun 17-24 h
Under the Arches, Villiers Street ✉WC2N 6NG *(U-Charing Cross/Embankment)* ☎ 7930 2020
Events changing from night to night.
Love Muscle at The Fridge (! AC B bf D F GLM MA OS s WE YG) Sat 22-6 h, Sun - Fridge Bar 20-12:30h
Town Hall Parade, Brixton Hill ✉SW2 *(U-Brixton. Next to Brixton Town Hall)* ☎ 7326 5100
Mixed crowd with muscle boys and disco dykes. Fantastic lighting.
Phoenix. The (AC B D GLM MA STV YG) Fri Sat 22.30-3 h
37 Cavendish Square ✉W1 *(U-Oxford Circus)* ☎ 8551 1987
Reflex 2 (B D GLM MA) Fr & Sa 21-03:00h
184 London Road, Kingston-Upon-Thames, Surrey K2
☎ 8549 9911
Sundays at home (AC B D f glm MA s STV VS WE YG) (G) Sun 16:-0:00h
1 Leicester Square ✉WC2H *In SoHo U-Leicester Square.*
☎ 7964 2073 ☎ 7820 5606
7 floors, 5 bars, 3 clubs. The bst sound system. Exclusive members bar & restaurant with terrace.
Sundaze at the Duke of Edinburgh (D glm OS YG) Sun 14-22.30 h
204 Ferndale Road ✉SW9 *(U-Brixton)* ☎ 7498 7195
Trade (b D GLM P YG) Sun 4-13 h
Turnmills, 63b Clerkenwell Street ✉EC1 *(U-Farringdon)*
☎ 7250 3409 ☎7607 5700 (membership)
Call for membership before goint to the club
Tube. The (B D GLM MA) 22-4 h
Falconberg Court ✉W1 *(U-Tottenham Court Road, behind Astoria)*
☎ 7287 9608
Wayout at Charlies (AC B D f GLM MA S TV) Sat 21-4 h
9 Croswell Street ✉EC3 *(U-Aldgate)* ☎ 8363 0948
West Central (B D GLM MA) We-Sa 22:30-03:30h
29-30 Lisle Street ✉WC2 *(U-Leicester Square. Beneath the Polar Bear)* ☎ 7479 7981

RESTAURANTS

Amazonas (AC B CC F glm MA OS YG) 19-23, Sat Sun 12-15, 19-23 h
75 Westbourne Grove ✉W2 4UL *(U-Queensway/Bayswater. Behind Whiteley's Shopping Centre.)* ☎ 7243 0090
Mouth-watering Brazilian / South American food at reasonable prices
Atlantic Bar and Grill (AC B CC F glm) 12-2, Sun 19-23.30 h
20 Glasshouse Street ✉W1 *(U-Piccadilly Circus)* ☎ 7734 4888
Balans (! B bf CC F GLM MA OS S TV W WE YG) Mon-Thu 8-4, Fri-Sat -6, Sun -1 h
60 Old Compton Street ✉W1V 5PA *(U-Leicester Square/Piccadilly Circus)* ☎ 7437 5212

Balans West (B F glm MA) 8-1 h
239 Old Brompton Road ✉SW5 ☎ 7244 8838

Dome. The (b bf F glm) 9.30-? h
57-59 Old Compton Street ✉W1 *(U-Piccadilly)* ☎ 7287 0770

Drawing Room & Sofa Bar. The (AC B bf CC glm W) 12-24, Sat 11-24, Sun -18 h
103 Lavender Hill, Battersea ✉SW11 52L ☎ 7350 2564
Restaurant with seperate bar. Lunch and dinner served daily, brunch on weekends.

Ground Floor (B F glm MA)
186 Portobello Road ✉W11 *(U-Notting Hill Gate)* ☎ 7428 9931
Good food

Kavanagh's Restaurant (B F glm N) Tue-Fri 12.30-14.30, 19-22.30, Sat 19-22.30, Sun 12-15.30 h
26 Penton Street, Islington ✉N1 *(U-Kings Cross/U-Angel)* ☎ 7833 1380
Friendly restaurant. Good and reasonably priced cuisine.

Le Gourmet (AC CC F g MA) 18.30-23.30, Sun 13-15.30, 19-23 h
312 Kings Road ✉SW3 *(U-Sloane Square. 10 mins. walk down King's Road.)* ☎ 7352 4483

Roy's Restaurant (AC B CC F G MA s W) 18.30-23.30 h (last orders)
234 Old Brompton Road ✉SW5 ODE *(U-Earl's Court)* ☎ 7373 9995

Steph's (B CC E F GLM MA) Mon-Thu 12-15, 17.30-23.30, Fri Sat -24 h, cabaret brunch 1st Sun of month
39 Dean Street ✉W1V 5AP *(U-Tottenham Court Road/Leicester Square)* ☎ 7734 5976
Experience english cuisine at its best.

Stockpot. The (AC F MA NG) Mon-Tue 11.30-23.30, Wed-Sat 11.30-23.45, Sun 12-23 h
18 Old Compton Street ✉W1V 5PE *(U-Tottenham Court Road)* ☎ 7287 1066
Cheapest restaurant in central London.

Wilde about Oscar (b bf CC E F GLM MA OS p W) 19-22.30 h
30-31 Philbeach Gardens ✉SW5 *(U-Earl's Court; at Philbeach Hotel)* ☎ 7835 1858
Conservatory restaurant, serving french food. Newly renovated.

SHOWS

Madame Jo Jo's (AC B CC D E g MA STV) Mon-Sat 22-3 h
8 Brewer Street ✉W1R 3FP *(U-Piccadilly Circus)* ☎ 7734 2473

SEX SHOPS/BLUE MOVIES

Centaurus (A CC G) 10-18:30h. Sun closed
100 Old Street, Clerkenwell ✉EC1V 9AY *(Opposite St. Lukes Church. U-Old Street, exit 6)* ☎ 7251 3535 *Gay shop & video producers. B&B also available.*
Man to Man (G MA) Mon-Sat 10-19.30 h
57 Pembridge Road ✉W11 *(U-Notting Hill Gate)* ☎ 7727 1614
Paradiso Bodyworks (CC glm MA NG TV W) 11-21 h
41 Old Compton Street ✉W1V 5PN *(U-Piccadilly Circus / Tottenham Court Road)* ☎ 7287 2487 *T.V. friendly fetish boutique in the centre of Soho selling a wide selection of fetish clothing, S&M equipment, toys, lingerie, kinky boots (large sizes) & body jewellry.*
Pink Triangle (b CC G MA) 10-24, Sun 12-23 h
13 Brewer Street ✉W1 *(U-Piccadilly Circus)* ☎ 7734 0455
Zipperstore (AC CC G MA) 10.30-18.30 h
283 Camden High Street ✉NW1 7BX *(U-Camden Town. Next to Camden Lock Market)* ☎ 7284 0537
Wide selection of European and American gay magazines, books, cards, leather articles, rubber, toys, leisurewear and underwear.

ESCORTS & STUDIOS

Bill Glens & Adams (CC g msg) 10-2h
☎ 7706 2607 ☎ 09069 52 6969 (75p/minute)
Capital Services (CC G msg) Bookings -2 h
☎ 7630 7567
Portfolio service available by appointment.

VG
VILLA GIANNI
Why not visit our sumptuous and elegant new premises in Central London?
Alternatively, we can arrange for an attractive escort to visit you.
Absolute discretion assured.
We accept all major credit cards
www.villagianni.kirion.net
Call
020 72 44 9901
020 72 59 2529
Open daily 11.00am till late

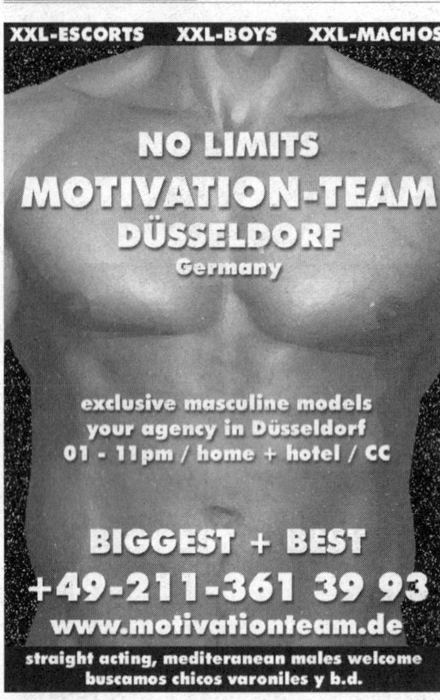

Club Burlingtons (G msg p R) Sun-Thu 12-3, Fri Sat -4 h
First Floor, 20 Queensberry Mews West ✉SW7 2DY *(U-South Kensington/U-Gloucester Road)* ☎ 584 6876

London Men Limited (CC G msg YG)
82 Louise Road ✉E15 4NW ☎ 8279 3956

Seduction (CC G msg) 24 h
☎ 8265 2000

Suited & Booted (CC G msg) 12:-01:00h
27 St. James Street ✉W1M 5HY *(U-Bond Street)* ☎ 7224 3312
Situated in the center of London in the busy Westend.

Thirty Plus (CC G msg)
☎ 8846 8593

Villa Gianni (AC b G msg p) 11-2 h
☎ 7244 9901 *or* ☎ *7259 2529.*
Call for details and address.

1st Class Guyz (CC G msg YG) please call for information
27 Old Glouchester Street ✉WC1N 3XX *(SoHo)*
E-Mail: info@guyz.co.uk Homepage: www.guyz.co.uk
For the best looking guys in London. Home/ hotel, worldwide visits. Please phone for an appointment.

HOUSE OF BOYS

Club Liberty (G)
☎ 7553 2114

SAUNAS/BATHS

Aquarius (b DR f G MA sa sb sol VS WE YG) 12-24, Fri 12-Sun 24 h
14 Gleneagle Road ✉SW16 6AB *(BR-Streatham)*
☎ 8769 6998

Chariots I (AC B F G MA msg pi sa sb sol VS wh WO) Mo-Sa 12-09:00h, Sun 12-24 h
Fairchild Street ✉EC2A 3NS *(U-Liverpool Street)* ☎ 7247 5333
*Large sauna in Roman style. Popular. **NEW***

Chariots II (AC B CC F G msg sa sb sol VS wh) Mon-Thu 12-24,Fri-12 to Sun -24 h (open all WE)
292 Streatham High Road ✉SW16 6HG *(BR-Streatham)*
☎ 8696 0929

Chariots III (AC B F G MA msg pi sa sb sol wh WO) Mon-Thu 11-23, Fri- 11 -Sun -23h (open all WE).
57-60 Cowcross Street ✉EC1 *(U-Farrington)*
☎ 7251 5553.

Health Club. The (DR f G MA sa sb TV wh) 13-0 h
800 Lea Bridge Road ✉E17 9DJ *(U-Leytonstone)* ☎ 8556 8082
£ 10 entrance fee, students £ 8.

H.P.S 156 (b f G MA sa sb sol wh WO YG) 11.30-23:30 h
16, The Broadway, Concord Center ✉W12 8PP *(U-Shepherds Bush. Shepherds Bush Green, opposite Boots.)* ☎ 8743 3264
2 saunas, steam room, cold plunge pool, jacuzzi, gymnasium, solarium, rest rooms and TV lounge.

Suited & booted

ESCORT AGENCY
0171 7224 3312

• Stunning, educated guys with great personalities and friendly attitude.
• One call to us and we makes all the arrangements.
• Portofolio and E- mail services available.
• London based agency with guys in many cities throught the world
• Or choose from our web site:
http.//www.suitedandbooted.com

CALL MARK OR PAUL ON
+44 (0) 20 7224-3312
FOR FURTHER DATAILS AND FRIENDLY ADVICE

Locker Room. The (f G MA msg sa sb sol VS YG) Sun-Thu 11-24:00h, Fri & Sat 11-04:00h
8 Cleaver Street, Kennington ✉SE11 *(Close to Kenninton Tube)*
☎ 7582 6288

Pacific 33 (AC f G MA P sa sb) Fr 11-Su 23:00h
33 Hornsey Road ✉N7 *(U-Holloway Road. Next to college)*
☎ 7609 8133

Pleasure Drome Central (b G MA sa sb sol WO) 0-24 h
125 Alaska Street ✉SE1 8XE *(U-Waterloo)*
☎ 7633 9194
Entrance £ 10/8.

Sailors Sauna (AC f G MA sa sb sol VS wh) Fri 12-Mon 00:00h, Tue 12-00:00h, Wed 12-Thu 06:00h, Thu 12:00-00:00h
574 Commercial Road ✉E14 7JD *near the „White Swan" U-Limehouse DLR-Line* ☎ 791 2808 *Entrance £10. Wed & Sun £5 (with flyer) weekends before 13:00h £7.00.*

Sauna Bar. The (B f G MA msg sa sb sol wh) Mon-Thu 12-24:00h, Fri-Sun 24h closes midnight Sun
29 Endell Street ✉WC2H 9BA *(U-Covent Garden)* ☎ 7836 2236
Beautifully decorated health spa in the heart of London, 5 minutes walk from Old Cromton St. with one of the biggest whirlpools in Europe. The only sauna in the UK licensed to sell alcoholic drinks. Rest rooms and friendly staff.

Star Steam (f G MA msg sa sb sol) 11-24:00h
38 Lavender Hill ✉SW11 5RL *(BR-Clapham Junction)*
☎ 7924 2269
Admission £ 11, £ 7.50 students.

Steaming at 309 (AC bf f G MA sa sb) Mon-Thu 11-23:00h, Fri-Sun 24hclose Sun 23:00h
309 New Cross Road ✉SE14 6AS *(U-New Cross)*
☎ 8694 0316

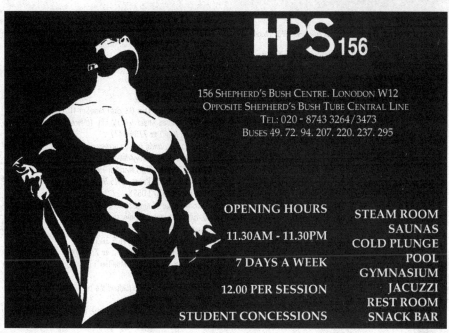

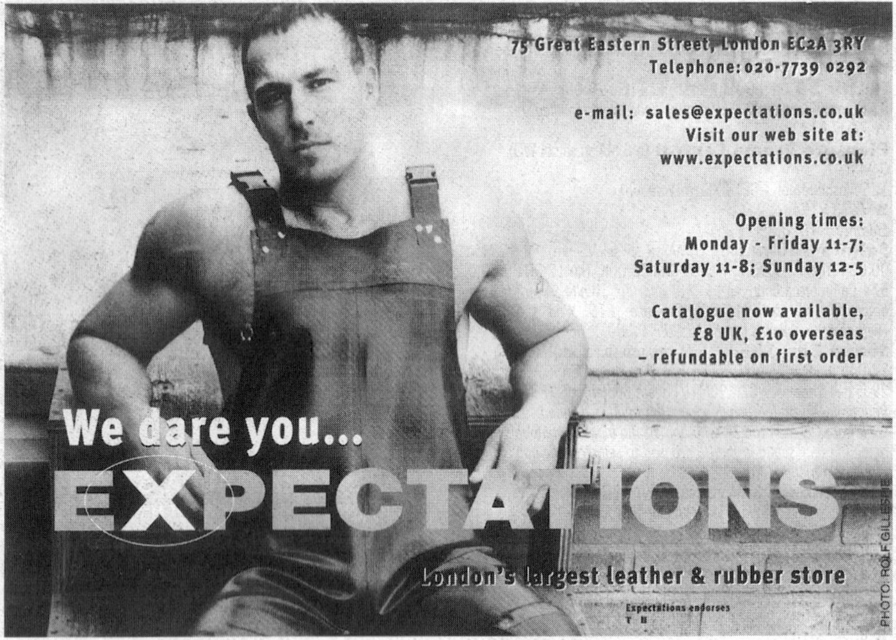

75 Great Eastern Street, London EC2A 3RY
Telephone: 020-7739 0292
e-mail: sales@expectations.co.uk
Visit our web site at:
www.expectations.co.uk
Opening times:
Monday - Friday 11-7;
Saturday 11-8; Sunday 12-5
Catalogue now available,
£8 UK, £10 overseas
– refundable on first order
We dare you...
EXPECTATIONS
London's largest leather & rubber store
PHOTO: ROLF GILLESPIE

FITNESSTUDIOS

Centre Point Gym (b f g MA sa sol wh WO) Mon-Fri 12-21:00h, Sat Sun 12-18:00 h
New Oxford Street ✉WC1 *(U-Tottenham Court Road. Under Centre Point.)* ☎ 7240 6880

Chelsea Sports Centre (glm MA NG pi sol WO)
Chelsea Manor Street ✉SW3 *(U-Sloane Square)* ☎ 7352 6985

London Central YMCA (b f glm MA pi sa) 07-22:30h, Sa & Su 10-21:00h
112 Great Russel Street ✉WC1 *(U-Tottenham Court Road)* ☎ 7637 8131

Paris Gym (AC CC G MA sa sol WO) Mo, We & Fr 14-22:00h, Te & Th 10-22:00h, Sa 10-20:00h, Su 15-20:00h
Arch 73, Goding Street ✉SE11 5AW *(U-Vauxhall. Behind Vauxhall Tavern)* ☎ 7735 8989

Soho Athletic Club (b bf CC f glm MA sol WO) Mon-Fri 7-22, Sat 10-22, Sun 12-18 h
10/14 Macklin Street ✉WC2B 5NF *(U-Holborn)* ☎ 7242 1290
Fax: (0171) 242 1099.

BOOK SHOPS

Books etc. (CC glm) 9.30-20, Tue 10-20, Sun 12-18 h
120 Charing Cross Road ✉WC2 *(U-Tottenham Court Road)* ☎ 7379 6838
Other centrally located branches include
-66 Victoria Street, SW1 ☎ 7931 0677
-16 Whiteley's of Bayswater W2 ☎ 7229 3865
-28 Broadway Shopping Centre, Hammersmith W6 ☎ 8746 3912
-Level 2, Royal Festival Hall, South Bank Centre SE1 ☎ 7620 0403

Gay's the Word (CC GLM) Mon-Sat 10-18:30h, Sun 14-18:00h
66 Marchmont Street ✉WC1N 1AB
☎ 7278 7654

GIFT & PRIDE SHOPS

American Retro (CC glm) Mon-Sat 10.15-19 h
35 Old Compton Street ✉W1V 5PL *(U-Piccadilly Circus / Tottenham Court Road)* ☎ 7734 3477
Clothes, books, cards, fashion accessories, and great gifts from Alessi and other contemporary designers.

Clone Zone (GLM) Mon-Sat 19-21, Sun 12-18 h
266 Old Brompton Road ✉SW5 9HR *(U-Earls Court. Opposite Colherne Pub)* ☎ 7373 0598
Extensive range of magazines, books, videos, clothing, toys, leather, rubber and more.Another store at 46 Old Crompton Street, W1.

Obsession (glm) Mon-Fri 9.30-18.30 h
18 Blomfield Street ✉EC2M 7AJ ☎ 7638 7491

Prowler Soho (CC) Mon-Thu 11-22.30, Fri-Sat 11-24, Sun 12-20 h
3-7 Brewer Street ✉W1 *(behind the bar Village and opposite The Yard)* ☎ 7734 4031
(0800) 45 45 66 (mail order service). Clothes, books, fashion and videos, big gift and music section.

LEATHER & FETISH SHOPS

Expectations (CC G MA) 11-19, Sat 11-20, Sun 12-17 h
75 Great Eastern Street ✉EC2A 3HU *(U-Old Street, Exit 3)*
☎ 7739 0292
Full made to measure and design service. Good selection of leather, rubber, and army surplus. Catalogue £5.

Honour (LJ) Mon-Fri 10.30-19, Sat 11.30-17 h, closed Sun
86 Lower Mash, Waterloo ✉SE1 7AB *(U-Waterloo)*
☎ 8450 6877 *Fetish wear, leather, rubber, toys.*

RoB London (CC LJ W) Mon-Sat 10.30-18.30 h
24 Wells Street ✉W1P 3FG *(U-Oxford Circus)*
☎ 7735 7893
Excellent selection of leather, rubber, toys and bondage gear for the serious fetish lovers.

TRAVEL & TRANSPORT

D Tours Ltd. (CC GLM) Mon-Fri 9.30-18:00 h, closed Sat Sun
59 Rupert Street ✉WIV 7HN *(U-Piccadilly Circus)*
☎ 494 4988 Fax: 494 4997 E-Mail: info@dtours.co.uk
Homepage : http:// www.dtours.co.uk Tour operator.

Freedom Cars (GLM) 24 h
2nf Floor, 52 Wardor Street ✉W1V 3HL ☎ 7734 1313
Fax: 74390399 E-Mail: freedom.cars@virgin.net
London's biggest Lesbian and Gay cab company. Also parcel service worldwide.

Man Around (CC GLM) Mon-Fri 9.30-18.00, Sat 10-14 h
89 Wembley Park Drive, Wembley ✉HA9 8EH *(U-North Wembley)*
☎ 8902 7177 Fax: 8903 7357

HOTELS

Beaver Hotel (b bf CC glm H NG p W) 7.30-24 h
57-59 Philbeach Gardens ✉SW5 9ED *(U-Earl's Court. Behind Earl's Ct. Exhibition Centre.)* ☎ 7373 4553 Fax: 7373 4553
Good value, basic rooms with direct-dial telephones. Private car-park with space for 20 cars. Rates: £ 39-90, inc.bf.

Halifax Hotel (bf CC G H MA) All hours
65 Philbeach Gardens, Earl's Court ✉SW5 9EE *(U-Earl's Court. Behind Earl's Ct. Exhibition Centre.)* ☎ 7373 4153
Just a few minutes walk to the local gay scene. All rooms with radio, intercom unit and TV. A few rooms have showers, but in any case there are showers and toilets on each floor. Rates single £ 30-45, double 50-60. Bf incl.
Please make reservations in advance

Montague on The Gardens (H)
15 Monatgue Street, Bloomsbury ✉WC1B 5BT *(U-Russell Square, U-Holborn, close to Euston & Kings Cross)* ☎ 7637 1001
Fax: (0171) 637 2516
Very comfortable and exclusive hotel. All rooms with bath/shower, WC, telephone/Fax, telephone, radio, hair-dryer, TV, suites have minibar, safe and air-condition.

New York Hotel. The (B bf CC F G H MA MG OS sa wh) 24 h
32 Philbeach Gardens ✉SW5 9EB *(U-Earls Court. Behind Earl's Ct. Exhibition Centre)* ☎ 7244 6884 Fax: 370 49 61
Luxurious gay hotel ideally located in the Earl's Ct. area. All rooms are en-suite and of a generous size, with cable T.V, direct dial telephone, tea / coffee making facilities, and a fridge. Rates from: Single £ 50, double 70, twin 70.

Outlêt (bf CC G H OS YG) Mon-Fri 10-7, Sat 12-5 h
60-62 Old Compton Street, Soho ✉W1V 5PA ☎ 7287 4244
Fax: 287 4247. Email: holidayaccommodation@outlet.co.uk. Homepage: http://www.outlet.co.uk. Brand new budget shared accommodation with lockers, kitchen, breakfast room with cable-TV, tea/coffee making facilities, bath/shower, patio area and telephone. Central to West End/"gay Soho". Rates £25 (1-6 nights), £17.85 (7 nights and more). Bf incl.

Philbeach Hotel. The (A B bf CC d F GLM H MA OS S TV) All year 24h
30-31 Philbeach Gardens, Earl's Court ✉SW5 9EB *(U-Earl's Court. Behind Earl's Ct. Exhibition Centre)* ☎ 7373 1244
Fax: 7244 0149 Homepage: ww.philbeachhotel.freeserve.co.uk
A well established gay hotel, with a late-opening bar and restaurant, Wilde about Oscar, which has just been refurbishedGarden, laundry, TV lounge, 24 hour room service, TV and telephone.

GUEST HOUSES

Jolly Good Place. A (bf GLM H)
31 Tremadoc Road ✉SW4 7NF *(U-Clapham North)* ☎ 7622 6018
E-Mail: jollygoodplace@compuserve.com
Homepage: www.geocities.com/WestHollywood/Village/9220
Small B&B in Victorian terraced house. Rooms with shared bath.

Noel Cowards Hotel (B CC GLM H MA msg) 07:30-23:00h
111 Ebury Street, Belgravia ✉SW1W 9QU *(U-Victoria)*
☎ 7730 2094 Fax: 0171/730 8697
E-Mail:sirncoward@aol.com
Homepage: www.members.aol.com/sirncoward/noel.htlm
Former home of Sir Noel Coward. Central gay guest house

Number Seven Guesthouse (AC bf CC GLM H MA p)
7 Josephine Avenue ✉SW2 2JU ☎ 86741880 Fax: 86716032
E-Mail: hotel@no7.com Homepage: www.no7.com

APARTMENTS

Central London Apartments (AC CC GLM) 9-22 h
(U-Tottenham Court Road) ☎ 0973/167 103 ☎ 797 7000
Superior 1 & 2 bedroom fully-furnished self catering flats with fully-aquipped kitchens, lounge/dining rooms and balconies. Spec incl fitted mirrored wardrobes, dimmer switches, tel/fax lines, video-entryphone and 2 lifts. Rates £ 100-225 per night (min 3 nights). Discounts for 1-3 month stays (TAC 5-20%).

Lesbian & Gay Accomodation Outlet (CC GLM H MA) Mon-Fri 10-19, Sat 12-17 h
60-62 Old Compton Street ✉W1V 5PA ☎ 7287 4244
Fax: 7287 4247 E-Mail: holidayaccomodation@outlet.co.uk.
Homepage: www.outlet.co.uk
Outlet's service offers one of the largest selection of shared & self-contained accommodation for holidays or long-term stays available to lesbians and gays in London.

PRIVATE ACCOMODATION

Geoffrey's Gaystay West One London (bf E GLM H msg) 09-22:00h
☎ 7636 5034 Fax: 323 9034 E-Mail: gaystay@yahoo.com
Homepage: www.gaystay.co.uk
A very central, downtown, private and exclusively gay B&B in the center of London with SoHo, the gay and theatre districts literally just down the street. Visit our website.

London Holiday Accommodation Mon-Fri 10-18:00h, Sat 12-16:00h, Sun - closed
34 Brunnel House, The Guinness Trust ✉N16 5TF ☎ 8809 1899
Fax: 8809 1899 E-Mail: sales@londonholiday.co.uk
Apartments from 65 per night/ 380 per week suitated in Covent Garden, Charing Cross Road, Bond Street,. Also gay holiday homes from 30 p/night. All guests met by host at the underground station and escorted to the property.

GENERAL GROUPS

Albany Trust
Balham High Rd. ✉SW17 7AL ☎ 8767-1827
Counselling service.

Croydon Area Gay Society
PO Box 464 ✉SE25 4AT
☎ 8771 1814 or ☎ 8651 0292.

Ealing Gay Group
PO Box 130 ✉W5 1DQ ☎ 8998 6708
(Peter or Neil)

Gay Nudist Group
PO Box 372, ✉WC1N 3XX ☎ 01752/50 00 31

Kingston and Richmond Area Gay Society (KRAGS)
PO Box 158 A, Surbiton ✉KT6 6RS ☎ 8397 4903
(David)

Notting Hill Lesbian & Gay Youth Group
Thu 19.30-22 h
☎ 7229 3266

Stonewall Lobby Group (GLM) Mo-Th 10-18:00 h, Fr 10-17:00h
16 Clerkenwell Close ✉EC1R OAN *(Farringdon tube station)*
☎ 7336 8860 Fax: 7336 8864
E-Mail: info@stonewall.org.uk Homepage: www.stonewall.org.uk
For details and a full list of publications, call or write to Stonewall..

West London Group for Homosexual Equality
☎ 7229 0481

FETISH GROUPS

London Blues. The (TLB) Meets Wed 20 h at STAG, 15 Bressenden Place SW1E 5DD
BM London Blues ✉WC1N 3XX ☎ 7607 8064
E-Mail: londonblues@geocities.com
Homepage: www.peterjd.demon.co.uk/tlb/index.html
Member of ECMC.

MSC London Meeting at „Jubilee Tavern, 79 York Road, Waterloo" Fri 21-22.30 h
BM Box MSCL ✉WC1N 3XX ☎ 7624 0305
E-Mail: john@fgrimshaw.freeserve.com

Rubber Man's Club Meets last Fri 21-2 at37 Wharfdale Road, Kings Cross
BCM RMC ✉WC1N 3XX
Member of ECMC.

SNC London Meets 2nd Fr 21:00h at Jubilee Tavern, 79 York Road, Waterloo.
BM SNC ✉WC1N 3XX E-Mail: sixtynineclub@btinternet
Member of ECMC.

HEALTH GROUPS

Aids Helpline Mon-Sun 15-22 h
☎ 7242 1010

Body Positive Gay Men's Group Mo 18-21:00h
14 Greek Street ✉W1 *(U-Picadilly Circus)* ☎ 7287 8010

Gay Men Fighting AIDS 10:30-16:30h
☎ 7738 6872

Regents Park Clinic Mo-Fr 09-18:00h, Sa 10-17:00h, Su 10-16:00h
184 Gloucester Place ✉NW1 6DS *(U-Baker Street)* ☎ 7402 2208
London's foremost private clinic for sexually transmitted diseases.

Terrence Higgins Trust Mon-Sun 12-22 h
☎ 7242 1010
Educational, fundrasing, referral service and support group. Advice and information on AIDS.

HELP WITH PROBLEMS

Alcoholics Support Group 19.30-22.30
c/o London Friend ☎ 7837 3337

Blenheim Project. The Mon-Fri 10-17 h
☎ 8960 5599
Advice & counselling for drug addiction.

Jewish Lesbian and Gay Helpline
Mon Thu 19-22 h
BM Jewish Helpline ✉WC1N 3XX ☎ 7706 3123
www.jglg.org.uk

London Friend 19.30-22 h
86 Caledonian Road ✉N1 9ON ☎ 7837 3337
An organization to help gays seeking an alternative to the scene and/or somebody to talk to. Has many social groups for different ages.

Turning point
☎ 7837 3337
For men who think they might be gay and want to meet others.

RELIGIOUS GROUPS

QUEST Group for Gay Catholics Fr 19-22 h
PO Box 25 85 ✉WC1N 3XX ☎ 7792 0234
E-Mail: quest@dircon.co.uk

SWIMMING

-Highgate Men's Pond (U-Hampstead Heath)
-Highbury Pool (U-Highbury and Islington)
-Oasis Pool (Endell St. WC2, ☎7831 1804; one indoor and one outdoor pool)

-Tooting Bec Lido (U-Tooting Bec)
-University of London Pool (Malet St.WC1 ☎ 7636 2818; host to „Out to Swim".

CRUISING

-Hampstead Heath (Activities 24 h, but most popular at WE and in evenings)
-Brompton Cemetry (Busy in the daytime (esp. lunchtime), near the back of cemetry near the crematorium)
-Holland Park Walk (ayor)(Busy after 23 h (esp. at WE). Start your walk the Holland Park Road junction, walk to the middle of the walk near the school, and jump the fence on the park side)
-Russel Square (ayor) (Anytime of night)
-Soho Square (summer)
-Public Toilets (attention should be taken due to police and camera surveillance. Notting Hill Gate / Tottenham Ct. Rd. are busy central favourites, especially at lunchtime and the afternoon rush-hour (17 h).)

Londonderry - Derry ☎ 01504

GAY INFO

Lesbian, Gay & Bisexual Line NW Thu 20-22 h
37c Clarendon Street *(Third floor)* ☎ 26 75 00

DANCECLUBS

Hennessey's Nightclub (B D GLM MA) Thu 22-1.30 h
64 Strand Road
Magee University (B D GLM MA) Alternate Fri
☎ 26 84 64
Contact Rainbow Project for further information.

BOOK SHOPS

Bookworm
16 Bishop Street ☎ 26 16 16

Loughborough - Leicestershire ☎ 01509

DANCECLUBS

Rickencampers at Rickenbackers American Bar (B d GLM MA STV W) Tue 19-23 h
Granby Street ☎ 21 62 20

Lowestoft - Suffolk ☎ 01502

HOTELS

Royal Court Hotel (B bf CC f g H MA NU W WE) All year
146 London Road South ✉NR33 0AZ ☎ & Fax: 56 89 01
Fully-licenced hotel and bar open to non-residents. B&B from £ 17.50 p.p.

Luton - Bedfordshire ☎ 01582

BARS

Shirley's Temple (B glm MA N s SNU STV) Mon-Wed 19-23, Thu 16-23, Fri-Sun 12-23 h
1 Liverpool Road ✉LU1 1RS ☎ 254 91
Popular.

SAUNAS/BATHS

Greenhouse Health Club. The (CC f DR G sa sb sol)
Mo-Th 11-02:00h, Fr 11-06:00h, Sa 11-08:00h, Su 12-24:00h
23 Crawley Road *(1/4 mile from railway station)* ☎ 48 77 01

Lynton - Devon ☎ 01598

BARS

Ye Olde Cottage Inne (B bf CC F glm H lj MA msg N OS) Mon-Sat 12-23, Sun -22.30 h
Lynbridge ✉EX35 6NR ☎ 75 35 70
Also room to let. Rates £ 20-25.

HOTELS

Mayfair Hotel. The (B bf CC glm)
Lynway ✉EX35 6AY ☎ 75 32 27
Ensuite rooms. Rates £20-25.

Maidenhead - Berkshire ☎ 01628

BARS

Custom House (B G MA) 11-23, Sun 12-22.30 h
90 Morrbridge Road ☎ 220 42

Maidstone - Kent ☎ 01622

BOOK SHOPS

Books & Mags Shop (glm)
46 Sandling Road ☎ 66 15 04

Manchester ☎ 0161

● For a long time Manchester was seen as a symbol for the rise and fall of the british industry. Today Manchester is back and going strong. Big business, banks, insurance agencies and high-tech industries show a strong presence. Most visible symbol of this process is the congress center G-Mex. Even sightseeing is possible in Manchester: the terribly terribly mancunian soap opera *Coronation Street* is produced in the Granada tv-studios; you can dine excellently in Chinatown and the industrial past can be studied in the *Museum of Science and Industry*. The *Gay Village* is located around *Canal Street*. Manchesters gay scene is the best and most diverse next to London. The colourful hustle and bustle in the summer months is quite astonishing.

✱ Lange galt Manchester als eines der Symbole für den Aufstieg und Fall der britischen Industrie. Heute ist Manchester wieder da und obenauf.
Die Industrie hat mit Banken und Versicherungen, mit Hi-Tech (z.B. Siemens oder IBM) wieder Tritt gefasst. Sichtbarstes Symbol ist das Kongreßzentrum G-Mex.
Selbst Sightseeing ist in Manchester möglich: In den Granada TV Studios wird die ur-britische Soap *Coronation Street* gedreht, in *Chinatown* lässt es sich bestens speisen und die industrielle Vergangenheit betrachtet man im *Museum of Science and Industry*.
Das *Gay Village* der Stadt hat sich rund um die *Canal Street* gebildet. Die Szene Manchesters ist nach der Londoner die beste und vielfältigste. Gerade in den Sommermonaten ist das bunte Treiben hier ganz erstaunlich.

▲ Manchester a longtemps symbolisé la grandeur et décadence de l'industrie britannique. Aujourd'hui, Manchester s'est refait une sacrée santé et ce, grâce aux banques, aux compagnies d'assurances et aux industries high-tech (Siemens ou IBM). Le bâtiment symbole de ce renouveau est le centre de congrès G-Mex. Côté tourisme, allez voir les studios de TV Granada où on tourne le sempiternel soap opera „Coronation Street". Allez aussi faire un tour à „Chinatown" et au „Museum of Science and Industry". Le quartier autour de „Canal Street" est aujourd'hui le bastion gay de Manchester qui est, après Londres, la deuxième ville gay du pays. Profitez des mois d'été pour visiter Manchester!

☆ Durante mucho tiempo Manchester fue el sibmolo del auge y de la caida de la industria britanica. Pero hoy en día la ciudad se ha recuperado y ocupa de nuevo un puesto líder en el país. Aquí se establecieron bancos, compañias de seguro y industrias de alta tecnología (como Siemens o IBM). El simbolo visible de este progreso es el centro de congresos G-Mex. Pero también desde el punto de vista turistico Manchester tiene mucho que ofrecer: En los estudios de televisión Granda se realiza el rodaje de la famosa telenovela in-

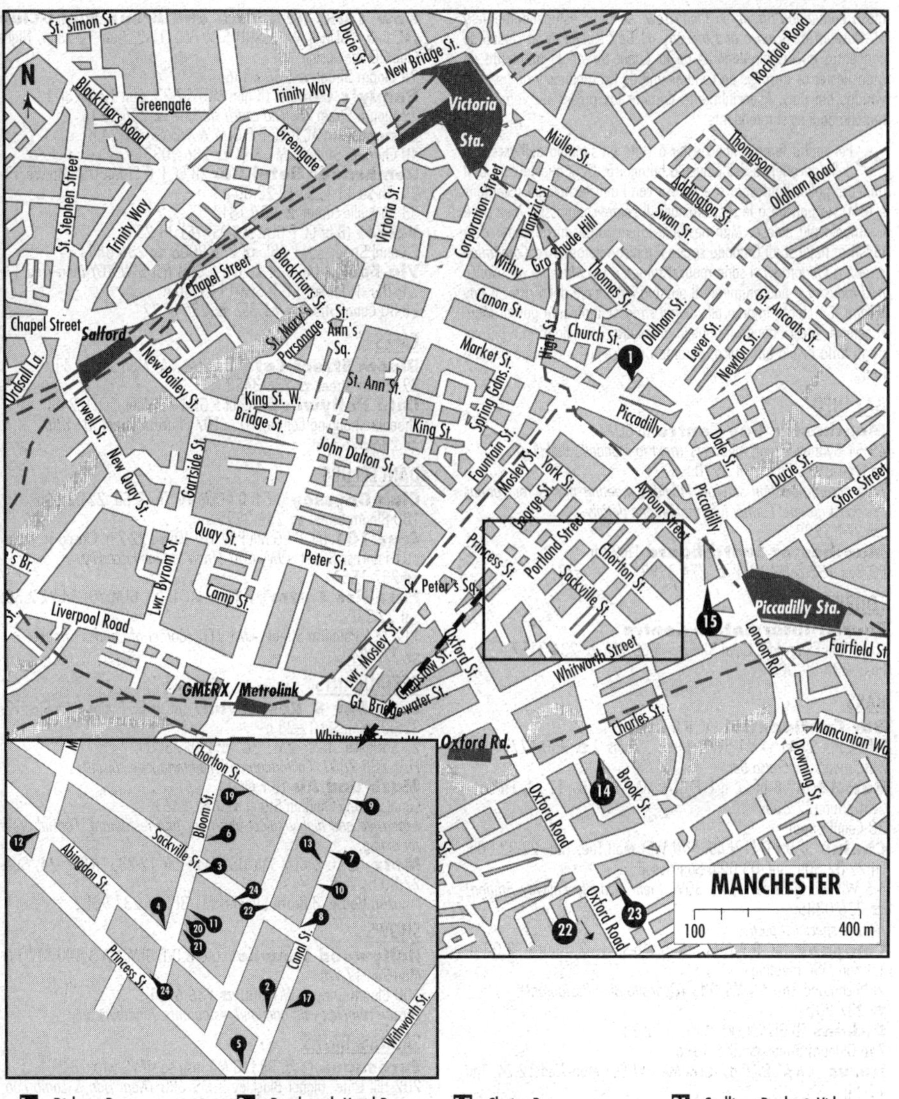

1	Dickens Bar	8	Rembrandt Hotel Bar	15	Chains Bar	21	Stallions Books & Videos Sex Shop
2	Manto Café Bar	9	Velvet Bar	16	Lush Bar & Restaurant	22	Carlton House Hotel
3	Napoleons Bar	10	Via Fossa Bar	17	Metz Restaurant	23	Manchester Gay Center
4	New York, New York and Bronx Night-Club Bar	11	Bloom Street Café	18	Clone Zone Gift & Pride Shop	24	Icarus Bar/Club Odyssey Danceclub
5	New Union Bar	12	Cruz 101 Danceclub	19	Mash and Air Restaurant		
6	Paddy's Goose Bar	13	Bar 38	20	Village Cars Travel & Transport		
7	Prague Bar	14	Paradise Factory Danceclub				

glesa *Coronation Street*; en *China Town* se come estupendamente y el *Museum of Science and Industry*. El *Gay Village* de la ciudad se concentra en los alrededoros de la *Canal Street*. El ambiente de Manchester es despúes de Londres uno de los mejores y de los más varidos del país. Especialmente durante los meses de verano, la marcha aquí es sorprendente.

Per molto tempo Manchester è stata un simbolo dell'ascesa e della decadenza dell'industria britannica. Oggi questa città è di nuovo a galla: l'industria si è ripresa con l'alta tecnologia (Siemens e IBM), le banche e le assicurazioni. Il centro-congressi G-Mex ne è il simbolo più palese. Manchester è interessante anche come città turistica: negli studi Granada si gira il mitico teleromanzo *Coronation street*, a *Chinatown* vi sono molti ristoranti e nel *Museum of Science and Industry* si può ammirare il passato industriale della città. Il *gay village* si è creato intorno alla *Canal street*. L'ambiente gay di Manchester è, prescindendo da quello di Londra, il migliore ed il più vario di tutta l'isola britannica; durante i mesi estivi è colorato più che mai.

GAY INFO

Manchester Gay Centre (b GLM)
49-51 Sydney Street, All Saints *(next to Mandella Building)*
☎ 274 3990 Fax: 274 3990
Free accommodation service. Provides meeting places for various specialist groups. Further information and details ☎ 274 3999.

Manchester Switchboard 16-22 h
PO Box 153 ✉M60 1LP ☎ 274 3999

TOURIST INFO

Tourist Information Centre
Town Hall Extension, Lloyd Street ✉M60 2LA ☎ 234 3157
Fax: 236 99 00

BARS

Bar Confidential (AC B G LJ MA)
Whitworth Street ✉M1 5WW *(near „Chains")* ☎ 950 5777
MSC meets Fr. Cruise Bar

Bar 38 (AC B bf CC d E F GLM MA S W YG) 11-24, Fri Sat -2.30, Sun -22.30 h
38 Canal Street

Chains (B D f G LJ N MA SNU WE) Mon,Tue, Thu 22-02:00h, Fri 22-02:30h, Sat -03:00h. Sun closed
4-6 Whitworth Street ✉M1 3QW *(near Picadilly Railway Station)*
☎ 236 0335
Host to specialist parties.

Company (AC B F G LJ MA P) Mo-Sa 16-2, Su 15-22.00 h. 1st Sun MSC meeting.
28 Richmond Street ✉M1 3NB *(Opposite Blue Restaurant)*
☎ 237 9329

Dickens (B GLM N TV) Mon-Sat 22-2 h
74a Oldham Street ☎ 236 4886

Icarus (! A AC B CC d F GLM MA s W YG) Mon-Wed 12-24, Thu 12-2 h
100 Bloom Street ☎ 236 39 95
Café and bar with live DJs.

Manto (! A AC B CC d F GLM MA s W YG) 12-23, Sun 11-22.30, Fri-Sat also 2.30-6 h (chill-out)
46 Canal Street ✉M1 3WD ☎ 236 2667

Napoleons (AC B D F G MA MG TV) 21-2 h, closed Sun
35 Bloom Street / Sackville Street ☎ 236 8800

New Union (AC B CC D f GLM MG OS SNU STV TV WE YG) Mon-Wed 11-1, Thu-Sat 11-2, Sun 12-22.30 h
111 Princess Street ☎ 228 1492

New York, New York and Bronx Night-Club (AC B D f GLM lj MA S SNU STV TV) 12-2, Sun 12-23 h, Night Club 20-bar closing.
98 Bloom Street ☎ 236 6556

Paddy's Goose (B glm MG) 12-23, Sun 12-22.30 h
29 Bloom Street *(Behind coach station)* ☎ 236 1246

Prague (A AC B CC D F GLM W WE YG) 11-24 h
40 Chorlton Street ✉M1 3HY ☎ 236 9033

Rembrandt Hotel Bar (B CC F G LJ MA OS) Mo-We 11-23, Th-Sa 11-1, Su 12-22.30 h
33 Sackville Street ☎ 236 1311

Velvet (B bf CC F GLM MA OS YG) 11-23 h
2 Canal Street ✉M1 3DE ☎ 236 9003 ☎ 236 6891

Via Fossa (AC B bf CC d E F GLM MA S W YG) Mon-Wed 11-24, Thu -1, Fri-Sat 11-2, Sun 11-22.30 h
28-30 Canal Street ✉M1 3EZ ☎ 236 8132

CAFÉS

Bloom Street Café (b f GLM MA) Mon-Sat 9-18 h
39 Bloom Street ☎ 236 3433

Café Hollywood (AC bf F GLM YG) Mon-Sun 0-24 h
Phoenix Shopping Centre, 105/107 Princess Street *M1 6DD*
☎ 236 5253

DANCECLUBS

Club Odyssey (AC B D f GLM YG) Tu & Sa 22-02:00h
100 Bloom Street ☎ 236 3995

Cruz 101 (AC D f G MA P W YG) Mo-Sa 22-2 h. Closed Tu & Su
101 Princess Street ✉M1 6DD *(Train Station-Piccadilly)*
☎ 237 1554

Paradise Factory. The (AC B D F GLM YG) Fri 22-2.30, Sat 22-3 h
112-116 Paradise Street ✉M1 7EN *(Corner of Charles Street)*
☎ 273 5422

RESTAURANTS

Lush Bar & Restaurant (AC B CC F glm MA) Sun 12-22.30, Mon-Sat 12-23 h
27 Sackville Street ✉M1 3LZ ☎ 288 7800
Fax: 288 7801. Californian and mediterranean cuisine.

Mash and Air (B F glm)
Canal Street/Chorlton Street ☎ 661 6161
Expensive and highly select plush bar and restaurant. Formal dress for dining.

Metz (B CC F GLM MA OS) Mon-Thu 12-23, Fri-Sat -24, Sun-22.30 h
Amazon House, 3 Brazil Street ✉M1 3PJ ☎ 237 9852

SHOWS

Hollywood Showbar (AC B D F GLM MA S SNU STV TV) Mon-Sun 17-2 h
100 Bloom Street ✉M1 6DD ☎ 236 6151
Leisure complex with bars and restaurants. Members only

SAUNAS/BATHS

Eurosauna (! AC DR f G MA msg sa sb VS wh) 13-21 h
202 Hill Lane, Higher Blackley ✉M9 6RG *(Near Lion & Lamb Pub, Victoria Avenue Bus Stop)* ☎ 740 5152

H2O Zone (f G sa sb sol wh) Mon-Thu 14-24, Fri Sat 14-7, Sun 14-19 h
36-38 Sackville Street ✉M1 3WA ☎ 236 3876

Nero's Roman Spa (b f G MA S sa sb sol wh) 12-24, Sat 12-3 h
Whitelegg Street, Bury, Greater Manchester ☎ 764 2576

BOOK SHOPS

Libertas (AC CC GLM) 11-19, Sat 12-18, Sun 12-16 h
105-107 Princess St.

GIFT & PRIDE SHOPS

Clone Zone (GLM) Mo-Th 11-22:00h Fr & Sa 11-23:00h, Su 13-19:00h
36-38 Sackville Street ✉M1 ☎ 236 1398
An extensive range of magazines, books, videos, clothing, leather, rubber, toys and more.

TRAVEL & TRANSPORT

Village Cars 24 h
Bloom Street ☎ 237 3383
Very gay friendly taxi service, licensed by Manchester City Council, offering a reliable and competitive service (no extra charge after midnight).

HOTELS

Carlton House Hotel (B bf CC GLM)
153 Upper Chorlton Road, Whalley Range ✉M16 7SH
☎ 881 4635
Comfortable hotel approximately 2 km south of the city centre. Rates: Single £ 25, Double £ 40 incl. bf. En suite rooms are also available for £ 45. Includes Stallions Sauna, discount for hotel guests.

Merchants (B bf g)
1 Back Piccadilly ☎ 236 2939
Rates: Single £ 15, Double £ 25.

Monroes (B bf F g H)
38 London Road *(opposite Main Station)* ☎ 236 0564
Hotel on top of a pub which also attracts a certain number of gay customers. Rates: Single £ 18, Double £ 30 incl. bf.

New Union Hotel. The (b bf CC f GLM H MA)
111 Princess Street ✉M1 6JB ☎ 228 1492
This hotelwith its popular bar, has been renovated and extended providing quality accommodation at a reasonable price. Rates: Single from £ 35, Double £ 45.

APARTMENTS

Clone Zone Apartments (GLM)
39 Bloom Street ✉M1 3LY ☎ 236 1398
Modern accomodation equipped with colour T.V, telephone, tea / coffee making facilities and a shared bathroom. Situated in the heart of the Gay Village. Rates frome £ 35.

GENERAL GROUPS

Gay Manchester Professionals 1st Thu
☎ 474 7585
Social/dining group for professional people in Manchester.

Long Yang Club (Gay Western & Oriental friends)
PO Box 153 ✉M60 1LP ☎ 366 7655
(David)

Manchester Deaf Gay Group „Triangle"
PO Box 153 ✉M60 1LP

FETISH GROUPS

Manchester Super Chain MSC Meet at Company Bar, Richmond Street - 1st Su 20:30h and 3rd Fr 22:00h
PO Box 104 ✉M60 1GY
Email: mscmsc@dircon.co.uk.
Homepage: http://www.users.dircon.co.uk/~mscmsc. Member of ECMC.

HEALTH GROUPS

Body Positive Group N W Tue/Thu 19-22 h
BP Center, 3rd Floor, Fairways House, 18 Tariff St. ✉M1 2EP
☎ 237 9717

Healthy Gay Manchester
Ducie House, 37 Ducie St. ✉M1 2JW ☎ 236 7600
Fax: 236 7611. Gay men's health project. Regular benefit parties at Chains.

Manchester Royal Infirmary
Oxford Road ☎ 276 5200
STD and HIV testing.

RELIGIOUS GROUPS

MCC Meets Sun 16.45, Tue 13.05 h at St. Peter's House, Oxford Road
PO Box 153 ✉M60 ILP ☎ 273 1567
E-Mail: revandy@easynet.uk
Homepage: www.easyweb.easynet.co.uk/~revandy
(Rev Andy Braunston)

Quest L&G Catholic Group
☎ 976 1210
(Ian)

CRUISING

-Piccadilly Gardens (Market Street side)
-Piccadilly Lock (Night AYOR. Go under the bridge at Rochdale Canal, entrance via Dale Street, a small stone doorway leading to a stairway)
-Rhodes Lodges (A 567 at Middleton)
Near Wilmslow:
-Styal Country Park (ayor) (bushes left and right of the river near the small bridge. Be discreet)
-Readsmear Lake (between Congleton and Alderney, after 350 m picnic area to the left, on the paths. Be discreet)
Near Handforth:
-Alderley Edge (Take a road off A34, turn right, Wizard Restaurant, woods on the right)

Mansfield - Nottinghamshire ☎ 01623

GENERAL GROUPS

Under 26 L&G Group Youth Line Mo 19-20:00h
The Folk House, Westfield Lane ☎ 428459

HEALTH GROUPS

MAPS (Mansfield & Ashfield Positive Support Group)
PO Box 3 ✉NG16 1QT ☎ 64 23 04
(Sarah) or ☎ 225 15 ext 4552 (Shaun)

Margate/Ramsgate - Kent ☎ 01843

BARS

New Inn (B d g s) Mon-Sat 17.30-23 h. Disco Wed Sat
New Street ☎ 22 37 99

SEX SHOPS/BLUE MOVIES

Pillow Talk (g) Mo-Sa 10:-18:00h
13 Marine Drive ☎ 29 40 69

Middlesbrough - Cleveland ☎ 01642

BARS

Cassidy's Club (B D f G) 11-23:00h Su 12.-22:30h
Grange Road ☎ 654411

DANCECLUBS

Strings (B D GLM) Th & Fr 22-02:00h, Sa 21-02:00h
47a Linthorpe Road ☎ 231 353

GENERAL GROUPS

Friend Meets Tue & Fri 19.30-21.30, drop-in 2nd Sat 15-17 h
St. Mary`s Centre, Corporation Road ☎ 24 88 88
(Minicom)

University of Teeside LGB Group
c/o Students Union, Borough Rd. ✉TS1 3BA ☎ 34 22 34
Fax: 34 22 41

HEALTH GROUPS

Cleveland AIDS Support (CAS)
☎ 25 45 98

RELIGIOUS GROUPS

Metropolitan Community Church Meets 1st Sun 15 h at St. Mary's Centre
PO Box 18, St. Mary's Centre, Corporation Road

Milton Keynes - Buckinghamshire ☎ 01908

GAY INFO

Milton Keynes Lesbian & Gay Switchboard
Th 19:30-21:30h
PO Box 153, Dawson Road ✉MK1 3AA ☎ 66 62 26

Newcastle-upon-Tyne - Tyne & Wear ☎ 0191

BARS

Barking Dog (B F glm MA S STV YG) Tue-Sat 11-23, Sun 12-22.30, Upstairs from 20 h
Marlborough Crescent ✉NE1 4EE *(Central Station)* ☎ 221 0775

Courtyard. The (B G MG MA N S STV) 17-23, Fri & Sat 12-23, Sun 12-22.30 h
78 Scotswood Road ✉NE4 7JB *(Central Station)*

Heavens Above (B GLM YG) Mon-Thu 20-23, Fri-Sat 21.30-23, Sun 20-22.30 h
2 Scotswood Road ✉NE4 7JH *(Above Courtyard)* ☎ 261 0488

Rockies (B d GLM MA OS S SNU STV) 19.30-23, Sun -22.30 h
78 Scotswood Road ✉NE4 7JH *(at Newcastle end of Redheugh Bridge)* ☎ 232 6536

Village. The (B D GLM)
Sunderland Street ☎ 261 8874

DANCECLUBS

Powerhouse. The (B D f GLM MA S) Mon-Sat 22-2, Tue-Wed -1 h
Waterloo Street ✉NE1 4DD *(Central Station)* ☎ 261 8874

Rock `N' Doris at Live Theatre (B D GLM s W YG)
C/O Pink Planet Promotions, P.O Box 58, Heaton *NE6 5YS*

Rockshots 2 (AC B D f glm MA N) Mon-Sat 22.30-2 h, Wed (GLM)
Alfred Wilson House, Waterloo Street ✉NE 1 4DE *(Central Station /Metro station)* ☎ 232 9648

SAUNAS/BATHS

Blue Corner Sauna (AC DR f G MA P sa sb sol VS YG) 11-22, Sun 13-20 h
164 B Heaton Park Road, Heaton ✉NE6 5170 *(near Heaton Library)* ☎ 240 01 22

HOTELS

Cheviot View (B bf CC GLM)
194 Station Road, Wallsend ✉E28 8RD ☎ 230 3662
☎ 07788 197011
Gay and lesbian guest-house. All rooms have TV and tea / coffee making facilities.

Hedgefield House (bf CC f GLM H MA msg OS) All year
Stella Road, Blaydon-upon-Tyne ✉NE21 4LR ☎ 413 73 73
Fax: 413 73 73
Beautiful country hotel in an old Georgian Residence close to Newcastle. All rooms are comfortably furnished. Rates standard room £ 42, kingsize room 50 and rooms with private bathroom or en-suite 60 incl. cont. bf.

GENERAL GROUPS

MESMAC North-East Mon-Fri 10-17 h
3rd floor, 11 Nelson Street ✉NE1 5AN ☎ 233 1333
Fax: 233 1551. Works with groups and individuals to increase positive choices arouund safer sex, and to offer general support to gay and bisexual men.

Newcastle University Lesbian, Gay, & Bisexual Soc.
c/o Porters Lodge, Union Building, Newcastle University
☎ 232 8402 *ext. 136 (ask for LGB Officer)*

Tyneside Young Gay & Bisexual Men's Group Tue 19.15-21 h
☎ 233 1333
(Lee/Chris)

University of Northumbria Globe Meets Thu 19.50 (term-time)
Porter's Lodge, Students' Union, Sandyford Road
☎ 227 4757

HEALTH GROUPS

BPNE
☎ 232 6411 ☎ 221 2277 (Helpline)
Confidential service offering information, advice and support on all aspects of HIV infection to people either infected or affected by HIV /AIDS.

CRUISING

-Copthorne Gardens (OG) (Close to Central Station; the cruisiest area is near the entrance on the same side as the Copthorne Hotel.).

Newport - Gwent ☎ 01633

BARS

Log Box. The (B glm)
Carpenter's Lane, High Street *(Side entrance to Hall of Fame)*
☎ 26 63 54
Back bar

DANCECLUBS

Cotton Club (B D G) 2nd Tue/month
Cumbrian Road ☎ 252 973
Gwent AIDS Support Group disco

SAUNAS/BATHS

Greenhouse Health Club (b CC F G MA sa sb sol WE wh WO) Mo-Th 11-23:00h, Fr & Sa 11-02:00h, Su 13-23:00h
24 Church Street ✉NP20 2BX *(Junction 27 on M4)* ☎ 22 11 72

HEALTH GROUPS

Gwent Aids Helpline Wed evening
☎ 223 456

Newton Abbot - Devon ☎ 01647

HOTELS

White Hart Hotel (B bf E F H MA NG) 7-0 h
The Square, Moretonhampstead ✉TQ13 8NF ☎ 44 04 06
Rates for a double £ 65 and for a single £ 43 incl. bf.

Northampton - Northhamptonshire ☎ 01604

GAY INFO

Gay Line c/o Northamptonshire Lesbian & Gay Alliance Tue 19-22:00 h

1st floor, Charles House, 61-69 Derngate ✉NN1 1UU ☎ 635 975
Call for details of LGB group meetings.

BARS

K2 (B D e GLM MA) Disco Fr & Sa, Karaoke on Su.
39 Sheep Street ✉NN1 2NE ☎ 228 22

Norwich - Norfolk ☎ 01603

GAY INFO

Norwich Gayline Mon 20-22 h (term time only)
☎ 59 25 05

BARS

Lord Raglan. The (AC B bf f G MA N OS s TV) 12-14, 19-23, Sun 12-15, 19-22.30 h
30 Bishop Bridge Road ✉NR1 3ET *(Close to Norwich Station)*
☎ 62 33 04
B&B available.

Lord Rosebery (B gLM S) Mon-Thu 19-23, Fri 12-14, 19-23, Sat 12-15, 19-23, Sun 12-22.30 h
94 Rosebery Road ☎ 48 61 61

Woolpack (B glm MA) 11-23, Sun 12-22.30 h
Muspole Street ☎ 61 11 39

DANCECLUBS

Jigsaw Club at The Talk (B D gLM MA) Fri 22-2 h
Oak Street ☎ 660 220

Loft Club (AC B D glm lj MA s STV) Mon-Sat 21-2 h (Thu+Sat gay)
80 Rose Lane ✉NR1 1PT ☎ 62 35 59

RESTAURANTS

Bailey's Bistro (B F glm) Mon-Sat 12-14.30, 17.30-?, Sun 19-? h
6 Pottergate *(City centre)* ☎ 62 67 63

BOOK SHOPS

Bookmark (CC) 9.30-17.30, Sat 9-17 h, cosed Sun
83 Unthank Road ✉NR2 2PE ☎ 76 28 55

Green City Central (glm) 42-46 Bethel Street ☎ 631007
Shop & information center inc. gay publications

GENERAL GROUPS

Act Up
PO Box 73 ✉NR3 1QD

HEALTH GROUPS

AIDS Helpline Tu & Th 20-22:00h, Sa 10-13:00h
☎ 61 58 16

Nottingham - Nottinghamshire ☎ 0115

GAY INFO

Nottingham L & G Switchboard Mon-Fri 19-22 h
7 Mansfield Road ✉NG1 3FB ☎ 934 8485

BARS

Admiral Duncan (AC B CC d f GLMMA S SNU STV W) Mon-Sat 21-24 h, closed Sun
74 Lower Parliament Street ✉NG1 1EH ☎ 950 2727

Forresters Inn (AC B d f GLM MA N OS W) 11-15:30h, 17:30-23:00h Su 11-23:00h
183 Huntingdon Street NG1 3NL ☎ 941 96 79

The Central (B f G) 11-15, 17.30-23, Sun 12-14, 19-22.30 h
Huntingdon Street ☎ 950 53 23

The Mill (B GLM MA) 11:30-16:00h, 19:-24:00h Su 12-22:30h
Woodpack Road ✉NG 1 1 GA ☎ 964 4941

DANCECLUBS

Revolution at Ocean (B D GLM) 1st Mon 21-2 h
Greyfriar Gate ☎ 958 05 55

BOOK SHOPS

Mushroom Bookshop (CC glm) 10-18 h, closed Sun
12 Heathcote Street ✉NG1 3AA ☎ 958 25 06

Soho Books (G)
147 Radford Road ☎ 978 35 67

GENERAL GROUPS

Eastern Rainbow (Deaf lesbian & gay group)
☎ 927 97 04
(Kevin-minicom).

GAI Project Mon-Fri 9-17 h
Health Shop, Broad Street ✉NG1 3AL ☎ 947 54 14
Fax: 955 4990. Sexual health drop-in which offers free & confidential sexual health services, including condoms, lubricant, HIV testing.

HELP WITH PROBLEMS

The Chameleon Group Thu 20-23 h
Wollaton Grange Community Centre, Tremayne Road ✉ NG8 4HQ
☎ 01159 /289479 (during group hours only)
Self help group for TV/TS.

RELIGIOUS GROUPS

Lesbian and Gay Christian Movement
☎ 925 55 14
(Paul)

Oldham - Greater Manchester ☎ 0161

GAY INFO

Oldham & Rochdale Switchboard Tue 17-19 h
☎ 678 94 48

BARS

Iguana (B glm) Mo-Sa 22-02:00h
171 Union Street, Rhodes Bank ☎ 652 56 62

SAUNAS/BATHS

Pennine Sauna. The (b g sa sb) GAY : Sa 13-19:00h , Su & Mo 13-21:00h & We 12-21:00h
96 Rochdale Road, Shaw *(Junction 21, 62)* ☎ 01706/ 84 20 00

Ormskirk - Lancashire ☎ 01772

HEALTH GROUPS

Heal
PO Box 26 ✉L39 2WE ☎ 55 55 25
Support service for people living with HIV/Aids.

Oxford - Oxfordshire ☎ 01865

GAY INFO

L&G Centre (G) Thu 20-23, (L) Fri 20-1 (D), Sat 12-16, 21-2 (B D GLM), Sun 19.30-22.30 h
North Gate Hall, St. Michale's Street ☎ 20 00 30

BARS

Jolly Farmers. The (B CC F GLM MA OS s) 12-23 h, Sun 12-22.30 h
20 Paradise Street ✉OX1 1LD *(Near Westgate Centre)*
☎ 79 37 59

Royal Blenheim (B CC f GLM MA N) 12-23:00h (-22:30h on Sun)
13 St. Ebbes ✉OX1 1PT ☎ 24 82 80

BOOK SHOPS

Inner Bookshop (glm) Mon-Sat 10-17.30 h
111 Magdalen Road ✉OX4 1RQ ☎ 24 53 01

GENERAL GROUPS

Gay Oxford
PO Box 144 ✉OX1 SX ☎ 01869/340 992
A group of gay men and women to provide social and personal assistance.

LGB Professionals Network
c/o Oxford Health Promotion ☎ 226042

HELP WITH PROBLEMS

Oxford Friend Tue Wed Fri 19-21 h
c/o Inner Bookshop, 111 Magdalen Street Road ✉OX4 1RQ
☎ 72 68 93

RELIGIOUS GROUPS

MCC Oxford
☎ 714 838

SPORT GROUPS

Swimout Meets: Mon 21 h at Marston Ferry Pool
☎ 24 33 89

CRUISING

-Angel Meadow (off St. Clements, Oxford, access via rear of car park, signposted)
-Hinksey Park (off Abingdon Road)

Paisley - Strathclyde ☎ 0141

GENERAL GROUPS

Paisley Forum 2nd & 4th Sun 20.30-22.30 h
Workshop Room, Paisley Arts Centre, New Street ☎ 887 26 49 *(Sandra)*

Penmaenmawr - Gwynedd ☎ 01492

HOTELS

Jack's Health Hydro/Pennant Hall (B bf F G H MA N OS p sa sb sol wh WO) 12.30-22.30 h
Beach Road ✉LL34 4AY *(Off A55/400m from Railway Station)*
☎ 59 61 39
10 bedrooms from £12.50 (incl. bf.) £4 sauna fee (6 visitor fee). Restaurant with full menu, bar open to non-residents. Coastal/Mountain area with many attractions.

Pennant Hall (B bf CC d F GLM H MA OS P S sa sb sol VS wh) Beach Road ✉LL34 6AY ☎ 622878 Fax: 622875
Homepage: www.gaypennanthall.co.uk
Exclusively gay country hotel.

Penzance - Cornwall ☎ 01736

HOTELS

Glencree Hotel (b bf glm H)
2 Mennage Road ✉TR18 4NG ☎ 362 026

Peterborough - Cambridgeshire ☎ 01733

BARS

Bridge. The (B d G MA) 19-23:00h Closed on Tu.
London Road ☎ 31 21 92

Plymouth - Devon ☎ 01752

BARS

Clarence (B glm) 11-23, Sun 12-22.30 h
31 Clarence Place, Stonehouse ☎ 60 38 27

Swallow. The (B f GLM MA N) 11-23, Sun 12-22.30 h
59 Breton Side ☎ 25 17 60

DANCECLUBS

Zeros Nightclub (B D f GLM MA) Mon-Sat 21-2, Sun 20-24 h, closed Tue
24 Lockyer Street
☎ 66 23 46

BOOK SHOPS

In Other Words Ltd. (CC glm W) 9-18, Sat 9-17.30 h, closed Sun
764 Mutley Plain ✉PL4 6LF ☎ 66 38 89
Large range of gay & lesbian books, magazines.

PRIVATE ACCOMODATION

Twoways Guest House (bf G H MA)
234 Saltash Road, Keyham ✉PL2 2BB ☎ 56 95 04
Two double rooms and one twin room in a Victorian house. Own key, TV and AC. Small and cosy.

GENERAL GROUPS

Allfellas Wed 19.30 h
☎ 556 192
Social group.

HEALTH GROUPS

Eddystone Group Mon Wed Fri 19-21, Tue Thu 10-1 h
☎ 25 16 66
Support group for people with HIV/AIDS.

HELP WITH PROBLEMS

AA L&G Group Meets: Wed 19.30 h
The Monastery, Scott Close, off Pike Road, Efford ☎ 55 14 10

Portsmouth - Hampshire ☎ 023

BARS

Martha`s (AC B CC D F GLM MA SNU STV) Bar 11-23, Sun 12-22.30, Disco Mon-Sat 22-2 h
227 Commercial Road ✉PO1 4BJ *(Town centre)* ☎ 9285 29 51

Old Vic (B F GLM MA) 11-23, Sun 12-22.30 h
104 St. Paul's Road, Southsea PO5 4AQ ☎ 92297013

SAUNAS/BATHS

Tropics Sauna & Solarium (b f G MA NU OS sa sb sol) Mon-Sat 12-22 h, closed Sunday
2 Market Way ✉PO1 4BX ☎ 9229 61 00

HEALTH GROUPS

Gay Men`s Health Project Mon-Fri 10-17:00h
☎ 9265 50 77

Preston - Lancashire ☎ 01772

BARS

Fruit Machine. The (B D f GLM) 28
Croft Street *(Off Marsh Lane)*

Oblivion (b GLM MA STV) 20-23:00h
12-14 Grimshaw Street

RESTAURANTS

Cannons Restaurant (B F glm) Tue-Sat 11-14, 19-23 h
37 Cannon Street ☎ 561 741

HEALTH GROUPS

Community AIDS Support Team
PO Box 17 ✉PR1 4UG

Reading - Berkshire ☎ 01734

BARS

Wynford Arms. The (B GLM) Mon-Fri 19.30-23, Sat 12-23, Sun -22.30 h
110 Kings Road ✉RG1 3BY ☎ 0118 958 9814

GENERAL GROUPS

Reach Out
PO Box 75 ✉RG1 7DU ☎ 0118 959 7276
Social group for gay youths.

HELP WITH PROBLEMS

Reading Helpline/Friend Tue Wed Fri 19.30-21.30 h
PO Box 75 ✉RG1 7DU ☎ (0118) 959 7269
A helpline for support, advice, places of interest in the local area, local events, general information, HIV/AIDS information, safer sex advice and much more.

RELIGIOUS GROUPS

Metropolitan Community Church (MCC)
☎ (01202) 763 609
(Rev. Stewart Harrison)

Redcar - Cleveland ☎ 01642

BOOK SHOPS

Books and Magazines (glm) Mon-Sat 9.30-17.15 h
5 Station Road ✉TS10 1AH ☎ 47 41 44

CRUISING

-Promenade from Granville Terrace towards Marske
-Sanddunes opposite blastfurnace at British Steel

Redhill/Reigate - Surrey ☎ 01737

HEALTH GROUPS

St. Peters House Project Mon-Fri 10-17:00h
☎ 24 10 44
Helpline for questions concerning HIV/AIDS. Home care support service provided.

Richmond - Greater London ☎ 020

BARS

Richmond Arms. The (AC B f G N S SWC W) Wed 11-23:00h, Thu 11-24:00h, Fri & Sat 11-01:00h, Sun 12-22:30h
20 The Square *(BR/U-Richmond, off Princes Street)*
☎ 8940 2118

Rochdale - Greater Manchester ☎ 01706

GAY INFO

Oldham & Rochdale Switchboard Tue 17-19 h
☎ *(0161) 678 94 48*

Rochester - Kent ☎ 01634

BARS

Ship Inn. The (AC B bf D F GLM lj MA N STV W YG) Mon-Sat 11-23, Sun 12-22.30 h
347 High Street ✉ME1 1DA *(Close to Chatham & Rochester railway station)* ☎ 84 42 64
Sun open for lunch, disco from Thu-Sun.

Runcorn/Halton - Cheshire ☎ 01928

BARS

Canalside (B F glm MA) Mon 16-23:00h, Tue & Wed 17-23:00h, Thu -Sun 12-23:00h
45 Canal Street ☎ 58 06 69

Ryde - Isle of Wight ☎ 01983

HOTELS

Dorset Hotel. The (B bf CC d f glm H pi) All year
31 Dover Street ✉PO33 2BW ☎ 564327 ☎ 01983/563892
Fax: 614635

Salisbury - Wiltshire ☎ 01722

CAFES

Shout! (b f G)
☎ 42 19 51

HEALTH GROUPS

Gay Men`s Health Project
Greencroft House, 42-46 Salt Lane ✉SP1 1EG ☎ 42 19 51
HIV information.

Sandbach - Cheshire ☎ 01270

BARS

Market Tavern (B d G MA) (G) only Thu evening
The Square ✉CW11 1AT ☎ 76 20 99

Scarborough - North Yorkshire ☎ 01723

HOTELS

Interludes Hotel (bf CC glm H)
32 Princess Street ✉YO11 1QR ☎ 36 05 13 Fax: 368597
E-Mail: interludes @mcmail.com
Homepage: www.interludes.mcmail.com
Nice Georgian building located in the heart of the Old Town. All rooms with hairdryer, colour TV, radio, central heating, most en-suite and with seaview. Non-smoking rooms only. No children. Dining room and bar for residents only. Elegant atmosphere.

CRUISING

-North Side Promenade (June-September)

Scunthorpe - Humberside ☎ 01724

HELP WITH PROBLEMS

Helpline Wed Fri 19-21 h
☎ 27 16 61

Shanklin - Isle of Wight ☎ 01983

CAFES

Hideaway. The (b F glm MA) Sun & Mon 10-16:30h, Wed-Sat 18:30-20:30h
St. Boniface Cliff Road ✉PO 37 6ET ☎ 86 41 45

Sheffield - South Yorkshire ☎ 0114

GAY INFO

Shout Centre Tue 16-19, Thu 18.30-21.30,
14-18 West Bar Green *(next to Fire Museum)* ☎ 267 0843
Gay/bi men's health & community centre. Ring for details.

BARS

Bar-celona (B GLM lj S STV T W) Mon-Thu 12-14, 19.30-23, Fri 12-23, Sat 19.30-23, Sun 20-22.30 h
387 Attercliffe Road ✉S9 3QU *(Opposite The Club. Bus 30, 52, 71)*
Cossack. The (B F G lj MA u W YG) Mon-Sat 12-23, Sun 12-22.30 h
45 Howard Street ✉S1 2LW *(Opposite railway station)*
Food daily from 12-18, happy hour Mon-Fri 17-19 h. Popular.
Norfolk Arm's (B D GLM MA SNU VS YG) 20-24, Fri-Sun 19.30-24, 2nd Fri X-loungers (glm) 20-? h
195 Carlisle Street ✉S4 7LT *(Near Meadow Hall/Bus 93 stops outside)* ☎ 275 24 69
Rutland Arms. The (B glm) 11-23, Sun 12-22.30 h
86 Brown Street ☎ 272 90 03

DANCECLUBS

Climax (B D GLM) 3rd Fri/month 22-2 h (term time only)
University of Sheffield Union, Park & Foundry ☎ 228 8777
Club Xes (B D f GLM lj MA OS S SNU TV WE) Mon-Thu 21:-01:00h, Fri & Sat 20-00:00h, Sun 20-22:30h
Carlisle Street ✉S4 7LJ ☎ 2752469
Planet (B D G) Wed-Sat 10-2, Sun 10-1 h
429 Effingham Road ☎ 244 01 10

GUEST HOUSES

Brockett House (bf F G H MA msg P VS) All year
1 Montgomery Road ✉S7 1LN *Bus no. 22 from city center*
☎ 258 8952 Fax: 211 2868
E-Mail: brockett_house@yahoo.com.
Homepage: www.brocketthouse.hypermart.net.
Non-smoking B&B with confortable guest rooms. Each room has tea/coffee facilities, TV, video, hairdryer. Rates with shared shower from £ 30-50, with private bath from £ 22. Gay owned and run.

GENERAL GROUPS

Bears Club Meets 1st Fri/month „The Norfolk Alms"
☎ 255 45 29

HEALTH GROUPS

Sheffield Centre for HIV and Sexual Health Mon-Fri 09-17:30h
☎ 267 8806
Ask for Rob or Anthony.

HELP WITH PROBLEMS

Gayphone Mon-Wed 19.30-21.30 h. Social groups meets Mon 20-22 h
☎ 258 81 99

Shepton Mallet - Somerset ☎ 01749

BARS

Waggon and Horses. The (A B CC E F MA NG s OS W) 11-15, 18-23.15, Sun 12-15, 19-23 h
Frome Road, Doulting Beacon ✉BA4 4LA ☎ 88 03 02

CRUISING

-Church car park

Shrewsbury - Shropshire ☎ 01743

CAFES

Fruit Bowl Coffee Shop. The (f GLM MA T W) Sat 12-16:00h, Tue 12-14´:00h, Thu 19-21:00h
The Wyle Cop Centre, Unit 3, 1a Wyle Cop ✉SY1 1UT *(Next to the Chinese Medicine Centre)* ☎ 34 41 79
Run by and for lesbian, gay & bisexuals.

RESTAURANTS

Peach Tree. The (b F glm)
21 Abbey Foregate ☎ 35 50 55

HEALTH GROUPS

Shropshire Gay & Bisexual Men`s Health Project. The Mon-Fri 12-16 h
Unit 4, 1a Wyle Cop ✉SY1 1UT ☎ 34 41 79 Fax: 34 42 69
Interaction L+G youth group meet Wed 16-20:00h

Sidmouth - Devon ☎ 01395

GENERAL GROUPS

EDGAR-East Devon Gay Advice & Recreation
☎ 03195/51 51 31
(John)

BARS

Greyhound. The (B D f GLM MA OS S SNU STV W YG) 12-15, 19-2, Sat 12-15, 19-3, Sun 19.30- 24 h
Colnbrook, Bypass A4 *(Junction 5 off M4)* ☎ 68 49 20

Southampton - Hampshire ☎ 01703

GAY INFO

Switchboard & AIDS Helpline Mon Tue Thu-Fri 19.30-22 h
PO Box 139 ✉SO14 0G2 ☎ 8063 73 63

BARS

Atlantic Queen (B f GLM MA STV) 11-23:00h
Bugle Street
Edge (B D G MA) 12-02:00h. Fri & Sat : The Box at Edge nightclub (D) -02:00h
St. Mary's Road ☎ 366 163
Magnum (AC B D f GLM lj SNU STV YG) Mon-Thu 21:30-02:00h, Fri & Sat 22-03:00h
113 St. Mary's Road ✉SO14 0AN
Victora. The (B GLM MA S) 17-23:00h, Sat 12-23:00h, Sun 12-22:30h
Northam Road, Northam ✉SO14 0PD *At end of Northam Road in cul-de-sac* ☎ 33 3963

BOOK SHOPS

October Books (glm) Mon-Sat 9-18 h, closed Sun
4 Onslow Road ✉SO14 0JB ☎ 8022 44 89

GENERAL GROUPS

Breakout Thu 19.30-21.30 h
☎ 22 33 44
Youth project for under 26's.
Southampton Gay Community Meets: Mon 20 h
☎ 8067 88 63
(Bob).

Southend-on-Sea - Essex ☎ 01702

BARS

Cliffs (B f g h STV) 11-23, Sun 12-22.30 h
48 Hamlet Road ☎ 34 44 66

DANCECLUBS

Eclipe at the Jack of Clubs (B D glm MA) 21:-02:00h
Lucky Road *(next to TOTS)* ☎ 467305
Eclipse disco - last Sat. every month and Bliss disco last Fri. every month.

FETISH GROUPS

Essex Leather MSC Meet 1st Sat 21:00h at Cliffs, 48 Hamlet Road.
PO Box 184 ✉SS2 6SD E-Mail: bill@tramline.demon.co.uk
Member of ECMC.

HEALTH GROUPS

Southend Aids Helpline Mon-Fri 18-22.00 h
☎ 0702/39 17 50

HELP WITH PROBLEMS

South Essex Switchboard
PO Box 5324 ✉SS2 1BF ☎ 344355

Southport - Merseyside ☎ 01704

DANCECLUBS

Hellbent at Underworld (B GLM) Sat 22-02:00h
4-6 Coronation Walk *(Off Lord Street)* ☎ 500 466

GENERAL GROUPS

Southport Gay Infoline Mon & Fri 11-18:00h
☎ 543 612

St. Albans/Hatfield - Hertfordshire ☎ 01727

BARS

Spritzers (B D f GLM LJ MA OS SNU STV) Mon-Wed 19-23, Thu & Fri -2 Sat-4, Sun12-16, 19-24h
Redbourn Road, Redburn ☎ 01582/794 053

FETISH GROUPS

Verulam MSC Meets: last Thu21 h at „ Load of Hay" - Watford
PO Box 158 ✉AL2 3UQ
Member of ECMC.

HEALTH GROUPS

Crescent Mon-Fri 10-16 h
c/o HIV Centre, 19 Russel Avenue ✉AL3 5ES ☎ 842 532
HIV testing.

St. Helens - Merseyside ☎ 01744

BARS

Flex 2 (B D glm MA STV) Wed 20-23:30, Sun 20-22.30 h
Tolver Street

HELP WITH PROBLEMS

L&G Helpline Mon Wed 19-21:00h
PO Box 135 ✉WA10 1JD ☎ 45 48 23

St. Ives - Cornwall ☎ 01736

HOTELS

Barkers (bf GLM MA p) All year exept Christmas time
11 Seaview Terrace ✉TR26 2DH ☎ 79 67 29
From £ 22/person. Lovely Edwardian house, overlooking harbour, near gay beach and town centre. Television lounge, full English breakfast. Tea / coffee making facilities. Closed for christmas.

GUEST HOUSES

Ryn Anneth Bed & Breakfast (bf GLM H MA) All year
Southfield Place ✉TR26 1RE ☎ 79 32 47
Quiet location. 4 minutes walk from town centre. Rates from £ 22.50 per person. Exclusively gay.

St. Leonards on Sea ☎ 01424

HOTELS

Sherwood Guest House (B bf CC f g NU)
15 Grosvenor Crescent ✉TN38 0AA *(BR-Mastings Station)*
☎ 43 33 31 Fax: 43 33 31
Hotel in seafront location. All rooms with TV, tea/coffe making facilities, some en-suite. Rates incl. bf from £ 16.50per person.

Stamford - Lincolnshire ☎ 01780

RESTAURANTS

Three Towers. The (B bf CC E F g MA N OS) Tue-Sat 19-23:00h, Sat 12-15:30h
39 Broad Street ✉PE9 1PX *(Opposite Brounes Hospital)*
☎ 755751
Gay owned restaurant with B&B in the center of town.

Stirling - Central Region ☎ 01786

BARS

Barnton Bistro (B f glm YG) Mon-Thu 10.30-23.45, Fri-Sat 10.30-0.45, Sun 12-23.45 h
3½ Barnton Street *(Near railway station)* ☎ 46 16 98

Stockport - Greater Manchester ☎ 0161

BARS

New Inn (AC B GLM MA N W) 19-23, Fri-Sat 12-15, 19-23, Sun 12-22.30 h
93 Wellington Road South ✉SK1 3SL *(Corner John Street/next to town hall)* ☎ 480 40 63
Wed is Quiz Night, Fri Karaoke.

Stoke-on-Trent - Staffordshire ☎ 01782

GAY INFO

North Staffs Switchboard Mon Wed Fri 20-22 h
PO Box 1, Advice House, Hanley ☎ 26 69 98

BARS

Club. The (B D G s) Mon-Sat 21-2 h
14 Hillcrest Street, Hanley ☎ 20 18 29
Queen and Crumpet. The (B GLM MA OS) Tue-Fri 12-16:00 & 19-23:00h, Sat 12-23:00h, Sun 13-22:30h
5 Hope Street, Hanley
☎ 28 99 25
Three Tuns. The (AC B D F GLM MA S STV W) 14-16, 19-23, Sun 13-22.30 h
9 Bucknall New Road, Hanley ✉ST1 2BA
☎ 21 34 08

DANCECLUBS

Ruby's (B D GLM MA) 19.30-2 h
14 Hillcrest Street, Hanley ☎ 20 18 29

SPORT GROUPS

Mustangs. The Tue 19.30 h
c/o The Club, 14 Hillcrest Street, Hanley ☎ 630 681
dancing group.

Stourbridge - West Midlands ☎ 01384

SAUNAS/BATHS

Heroes Health Club (B DR f G MA sa sb sol wh) Sun-thu 12-23, Fri Sat 12-2 h
4 Lower High Street ✉DY8 1TE ☎ 44 20 30

Stratford-Upon-Avon - Warwickshire ☎ 01789

BARS

The Monastery (B GLM STV S MA) Mo-We 20-02:00h, Th-Sa 20-02:00h & Su 19-22:30h
Watling Street, Fenny ☎ 373 018

Stroud - Gloucestershire ☎ 01452

GENERAL GROUPS

Gloucestershire Gay Community Mon-Fri 19.30-22 h (helpline)
☎ 30 68 00

Sunderland - Tyne & Wear ☎ 0191

GENERAL GROUPS

Liberal G&L Campaign
☎ 528 28 13
(Win)

HEALTH GROUPS

Wear Body Positive
☎ 548 3144

Stutton in Ashfield - Nottinghamshire ☎ 01623

HOTELS

Central Private Hotel (AC bf CC F g H MA msg W) Bar & Restaurant 18-21, Sun 12-14:00 h
1 Station Road ✉NG17 SFF *(Close to M1 J28)*
☎ 55 23 73 Fax: 44 31 06
B&B. Laundry service. Special meals for vegetarians available.

Swansea - West Glamorgan ☎ 01792

BARS

Champers (B GLM MA) 11-23, Sun 12-22.30 h
210 High Street ☎ 65 56 22
Station Inn (B GLM) 12-23:00h Sun -22:30h
63-64 High Street ☎ 457 977

HEALTH GROUPS

AIDS Helpline Thu 15-20 h
☎ 45 63 03

HELP WITH PROBLEMS

Advice Line Tue 18-21 h
☎ 45 63 03

Swindon - Wiltshire ☎ 01793

BARS

Cricketer's Arms. The (B G) 12-14.30, 19-23 h, Sun 12-22.30 h
14 Emlyn Square *(Near BR station)* ☎ 52 37 80
London Street (B D GLM YG) Mon-Wed 19-23:00h, Sun 19-22:30h
1 London Street ☎ 497 774
Red Lion (B f glm) 3 The City, Melksham
☎ (01225)70 29 60.

GENERAL GROUPS

Swindon Gay Community
c/o The Cricketers, Emlyn Square ☎ 523 033

HEALTH GROUPS

SPACE (Swindon Project for Aids Counselling & Education Mon-Thu 09-17:00h, Fri 09-16:30h
Frampton Villa, 9 Devizes Road ✉SN1 4BH ☎ 42 06 20
Fax: 48 48 79

Telford - Shropshire ☎ 01734

GAY INFO

Shropshire Switchboard Tue , Wed & Fri 20-22 h
PO Box 41, Wellington ✉TF1 1YG ☎ 232393

Torquay - Devon ☎ 01803

BARS

Ibiza (B D GLM MA) Mon-Sat 21-01:00h, Sun 20-22.30 h
3-4 Victoria Parade *(Under Queens Hotel)* ☎ 21 43 34
Meadfoot Inn. The (AC B f G MA N YG) 12-16, 19-23, Sun 12-15, 19-22.30 h
7 Meadfoot Lane ✉TQ1 2BW *(Near the harbour)* ☎ 29 71 12
Gay owned. A small intimate bar within walking distance of all gay hotels and clubs.
Rockies (B D f GLM MA N P) Sun-Thu 22-01:00h, Fri & Sat 22-02:00h
Rock Cottage, Rock Road ✉TQ2 5SP *(Town centre, next to main post office)* ☎ 29 22 79

HOTELS

Cliff House Hotel. The (B bf CC f G MA msg N NU OS s sb sol We wh WO YG) All year
St Marks Road, Meadfoot Beach ✉TQ1 2EH
☎ 294656 Fax: 211983
Exclusively Gay. Hotel with bar and gym area (steam room).
Ocean House Hotel. The (B bf CC F GLM H MA N OS pi sb sol WO)
Hunsdon Road ✉TQ1 1QB ☎ 29 65 38 Fax: 29 99 36
E-Mail: cshore@dircon.co.uk Homepage: www.oceanhouse.co.uk.
Very comfortable hotel situated in a beautiful garden. Rates from £ 29.50 p.p.
Oscars Restaurant & Hotel (B bf CC F GLM H MA)
56 Belgrave Road ✉TQ2 5HY ☎ 29 35 63 Fax: 29 66 85
E-Mail: oscarhtl@aol.com Homepage: www.oscars-hotel.com
Good food at reasonable prices. Quiet candlelight cellar restaurant. Vegetarians welcomed. 38 seats. in February. B&B accomodation. Comfortable rooms. Full English or vegetarian bf. Completely renovated.
Ravenswood Hotel (B bf CC glm MA OS)
535 Babbacombe Road ✉TQ1 1HQ ☎ & Fax: 29 29 00
Private car parking. Close to beaches and gay bars. Rates £ 14-18 in winter and £ 16-20 in summer p.p. incl. bf. 4 course dinner optional.

GUEST HOUSES

Rainbow Villa (bf CC f G H) All year
24 Bridge Road ✉TQ2 5BA ☎ 21 28 86 Fax: 21 28 86
E-Mail: rainbow@globalnet.co.uk
Three double rooms with shower & WC, TV, heating, own key. Rates double from £ 45-55, single 30-34.50 (bf incl.)

GENERAL GROUPS

Torbay Gay Community
☎ 29 20 55
(Ronnie).

SWIMMING

-Petittor Beach (7 km from the city in the suburb of St.Marychurch. Take bus from the beach to St. Marychurch or Modell Village. Then follow Petittor Road to the end.)

Truro - Cornwall ☎ 01726

HOTELS

Trewirgie House (bf F G H OS) March-November
Trewirgie Road, Redruth ✉TR15 2SX
☎ 01726/(01209) 212831
B&B located in fine period house and close to beaches. Beautiful garden. Rates £ 18-22.

Woodbine Villa (b bf DR F G H MA NU p sa VS) Men only sauna open to non-residents Wed Sun 18-22 h
Fore Street, Grampound ✉TR2 4QP *(Next to Guild Hall)*
☎ 01726/88 20 05
Friendly B&B in an old 18th century building, which is furnished with lots of antiques. Rates for a double from £ 21 p.p. and for a single from £ 23 p.p. incl. bf, shared bath. Three course evening mail with free wine £ 12 p.p. 5 miles to nude beach.

Tunbridge Wells - Kent ☎ 01892

GENERAL GROUPS

Turnbridge Wells Ind Gay Group (TWIGG)
Meets: Fri 20-24 h at Calverley Hotel, Crescent Rd. 8-12
☎ *(01580) 75 36 68 (Keith)*

Wakefield - West Yorkshire ☎ 01924

BARS

Dolphin Public House. The (B D GLM MA OS SNU STV) Mon-Sat 12-16, 19-24, Sun 19-24 h; Wed-Sun - cabaret
6 Lower Warrengate ✉WF1 1SA *(Near Cathederal)* ☎ 20 17 05

HEALTH GROUPS

HIV Centre
c/o Clayton Hospital ☎ 36 41 44

Wallasey - Merseyside ☎ 01051

SAUNAS/BATHS

Dolphin Sauna (AC f G MA sa sb sol wh) 14:-21:30h
129 Mount Road ✉CH45 9JS *(U-New Brighton Station)*
☎ 630 1516

Walsall - West Midlands ☎ 01922

BARS

Golden Lion. The (AC B d DR GLM MA p S VS W) Tue-Sat 19.30-2, Sun+Mon -24 h
41 Birchills Street ✉WS2 8NG ☎ 610977
Weekend lunch, disco.

Warrington - Cheshire ☎ 01925

HEALTH GROUPS

AIDS Helpline Mon Wed 19-22 h
☎ 41 71 34

HELP WITH PROBLEMS

Warrington LGB Helpline 2Tue 19-21:00h
☎ 24 19 94

Wells-Next-The-Sea - Norfolk ☎ 01328

BARS

Three Horseshoes. The (B bf F glm H MA N W) Pub: 11.30-15, 18-23 h
Bridge Street, Warham ✉NR23 1NL ☎ 71 05 47
Hotel with bar, located in rural area next to sea and gay beach.

Weymouth - Dorset ☎ 01305

HEALTH GROUPS

DASH Dorset Aids Support and Help Mon-Fri 9-17 h
5 Belle Vue ✉DT4 8DR ☎ 77 92 24

Whitby - North Yorkshire ☎ 01947

HOTELS

Sandbeck Hotel (bf CC H MA NG)
West Cliff ✉YO21 3EL ☎ 60 40 12
Small luxury hotel with 16 rooms, all en-suite. Hotel faces sea front. Rates incl. bf from £ 20 p.p. (low season) and £ 27.50 (high season).

Winchester - Hampshire ☎ 01962

GENERAL GROUPS

King Alfred's College LGB Society
c/o Students Unio, Sparkford Road ✉SO22 4NR ☎ 85 31 44

LGB Group Meets: Thu 19.30-22.30
☎ 85 26 91
(Ken) or ☎ *(01730) 26 29 17 (Paul)*

HEALTH GROUPS

Gay Men's Health Project
☎ 863511 ext 484

Windermere - Cumbria ☎ 015394

GUEST HOUSES

Lingmoor Guest House (bf F glm H MA WE YG) All year
7 High Street ✉LA23 1AF *(Very close to bus and train stations)*
☎ 449 47 Fax: 449 47

Windsor - Berkshire ☎ 01753

CRUISING

-Public toilets at Bachelor's Acre, central Windsor. Best time 13-16:00h weekends 14-17:00h.
- Public toilets in St Luke's Road, Old Windsor, times as above.

Woking - Surrey ☎ 01483

GENERAL GROUPS

LGB Support Group 1st/3rd Thu 19-21 h
Crescent Project, Heathside Crescent

HELP WITH PROBLEMS

Outline Tue 19.30-22 h
☎ 72 76 67

Wolverhampton - West Midlands ☎ 01902

BARS

White Hart. The (B f GLM lj MA S) Mon-Fri 11-16, 19-23.30, Sat -24, Sun 14-22.30 h
66 Worcester Street ✉WV2 4LQ ☎ 42 17 01

GENERAL GROUPS

Gay Men`s Group Meets alternate Sun
☎ 820 626

Gay Nudist Group Meet 20th of each month
☎ 84 41 85
(Neil).

HEALTH GROUPS

AIDSline Mon Tue Thu 9-17, Wed Fri 9-12 h
☎ 64 48 94
Reach-HIV and AIDS Support group Mon-Thu 18-20.45 h
Unit 20, BDC, 21 Temple Street ✉WV2 4AN ☎ 425 702

CRUISING

-West park, Chapel Ash (AYOR, police)

Worcester - Hereford & Worcester ☎ 01905

GAY INFO

Hereford & Worcester L&G Switchboard Tue, Wed & Thu 19.30-22 h
PO Box 156 ✉WR5 1BP ☎ 72 30 97
E-Mail: 101234.1637@compuserve.com.
Disco on every 1st Tue.

DANCECLUBS

Surrender (B D f GLM s) 1st Tue/month 21.30-2 h (G)
c/o Images Night Club, The Butts, PO Box 156 ✉WR5 1BP
☎ 72 30 97

GENERAL GROUPS

Gay Outdoor Club
☎ 278 42
(Louis)

York - North Yorkshire ☎ 01904

BARS

The Bay Horse
54 Gillygate ✉YO3 7EO ☎ 62 76 79
York Arms.The (B g MA) 11-23, Sun 12-22.30 h
26 High Petergate *(Near York Minster)*

RESTAURANTS

Churchill Hotel (B F glm)
Bootham ☎ 64 44 56

HOTELS

Astley House Hotel (AC bf CC glm H MA msg)
123 Clifton ✉YO3 6BL ☎ 63 47 45 Fax: 62 13 27
Small and friendly hotel close to the historic center of York. All rooms are en-suite with SAT-TV, radio alarm, tea / coffee making facilities, hair dryers and direct dial telephones. Free car park.

GUEST HOUSES

Bull Lodge (f glm H MA W)
37 Bull Lane, Lawrence Street ✉YO10 3EN *(1 km from city centre, on quiet side-street off A1079)* ☎ 41 55 22 Fax: 41 55 22
Rates £ 16-21 depending on season and length of stay. No credit cards.

GENERAL GROUPS

One in Ten Project Meets: Tue 19-21:00h
c/o Community House, 10 Priory Street ✉YO1 1EZ ☎ 61 26 29
Youth group under 21.
York Gay Group Mon 20-21:00 h
The Workshop, Marygate Lane ✉YO3 7BT ☎ 61 36 39

HEALTH GROUPS

Yorkshire M.E.S.M.A.C. Mon-Fri 10-13 h
c/o The Workshop, Marygate Lane ✉YO3 7BJ ☎ 62 04 00
Fax: 6620444
Service for gay men and bisexual men who have sex with men. Counselling service available. Free condoms.

CRUISING

-Riverbank adjacent to Museums Gardens to Clifton Ings.
-Lay by on A166 Bidlington Road (5 miles out of the city centre)
-Train station
-Bus station
-Wiggington Road (accross from hospital)
-Parking at Haxby Road (Gillygate Road)
-Museum Gardens (daytime)
-Toft Green (daytime)

40,3399	BEF	40,3399	LUF
1,95583	DEM	2,20371	NLG
166,386	ESP	13,7603	ATS
6,55957	FRF	200,482	PTE
0,787564	IEP	5,94573	FIM
1936,27	ITL		

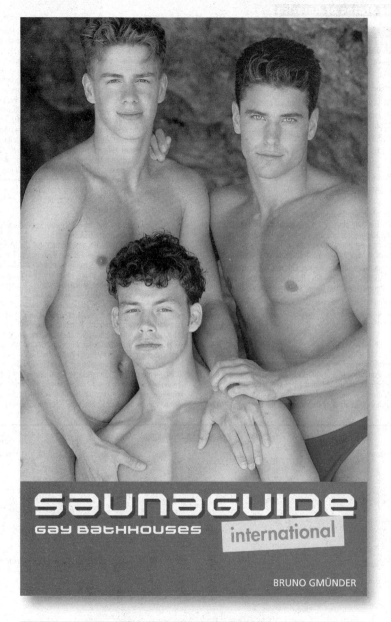

United States of America

North America

Initials: USA

Time: ☛ each state

☎ Country Code / Access Code: 1 / 011

Language: English;sporadically Spanish;20 million people do not speak English

Area: 9,363,123 km² / 3,615,102 sq mi.

Currency: 1 US Dollar (US$) = 100 Cents

Population: 270,311,756

Capital: Washington D.C.

Religions: 56% Protestant , 28% Catholic, 10% non, 2% Jewish, 4% other

Climate: Mostly moderate climate. Hawaii and Florida are tropical, Alaska is arctic. The great plains of the Mississippi are quite dry, the Great Basin of the southwest is very dry. The low winter temperatures in the northwest are ameliorated occasionally in January and February by warm chinook winds from the eastern slopes of the Rocky Mountains.

Important gay cities: Atlanta, Boston, Chicago, Dallas, Houston, Key West, Los Angeles, New York City, New Orleans, Palm Springs, Philadelphia, Provincetown, San Diego, San Francisco, Washington.

Further listingscan be found under:

- CARIBBEAN-Puerto Rico
- CARIBBEAN-Virgin Islands
- Guam

● Nowhere on the globe is there a gay scene bigger and more diverse than in the USA. It comprises the amazing gay communities in the big metropolises and small towns with a bar and a bookstore. Equally diverse is the legal situation. The US-constitution gives the right to each state to make its own laws. On the one hand there are several states in which oral and anal intercourse, be it hetero- or homosexual, is prohibited; on the other hand we find several states with anti-dicriminatory legislation. For details look unter the respective state. The age of consent is not laid down federally but does not exceed the age of 18 anywhere. In most of the states the penal code is based on a draft which the *American Law Institute* drew up in the sixties. This decriminalizes private sexual acts, to which the partners consent. The motto of the US-military seems to be: Don't ask, don't tell. Your sexual preference is not questioned, but it is also forbidden to express it publicly. The passing of the *Defense of Marriage Act* was a hard blow to the US gay-lesbian rights movement. Each state is still able to grant homosexual pairs legal partnerships, but other states need not accept them in their territory. From this edition onward, we will no longer list our US adresses solely under the city-headings. We now list them under both state and under city-name. It is nearly impossible to specifically declare anything „a must" for gay tourists. However, some of the american classics should not be missed by gays: metropolises like San Francisco, New York and Chicago; the gay resorts Provincetown, Miami Beach or Key West.

✸ Nirgendwo auf der Welt ist die schwule Szene dermassen groß und vielfältig wie in den USA.

Ebenso vielfältig zeigt sich die gesetzliche Lage. Die US-Verfassung erlaubt den Bundesstaaten das Erlassen eigener Gesetze. 19 Staaten haben Sodomiegesetze *Sodomy Laws* verabschiedet, die jegliche Art von Oral- und Analverkehr verbieten, gleichgültig ob er von Homo- oder Heterosexuellen praktiziert wird (13 Staaten). In 6 Staaten ist nur homosexueller Analverkehr verboten.

Auf der anderen Seite gibt es 10 Staaten, in denen Anti-Diskriminierungs-Bestimmungen *Anti-Discrimination-Law* gelten. 5 Staaten haben Partnerschaftsgesetze *Domestic Partnership Law* verabschiedet. Dies bedeutet, daß staatliche Arbeitgeber gewisse soziale Leistungen *domestic partner benefits* nicht nur verheirateten, sondern allen Arbeitnehmern gewähren, die in einer festen Partnerschaft leben. Das Schutzalter ist nicht bundeseinheitlich geregelt, liegt aber nicht über 18.

In 31 Staaten ist ein Strafgesetz in Kraft, das einem Entwurf des *American Law Institute* aus den 60er Jahren entspricht und einvernehmliche und private sexuelle Handlungen entkriminalisiert. Das Militär ist nach der Devise „Don't ask, don't tell" weiterhin sexual-

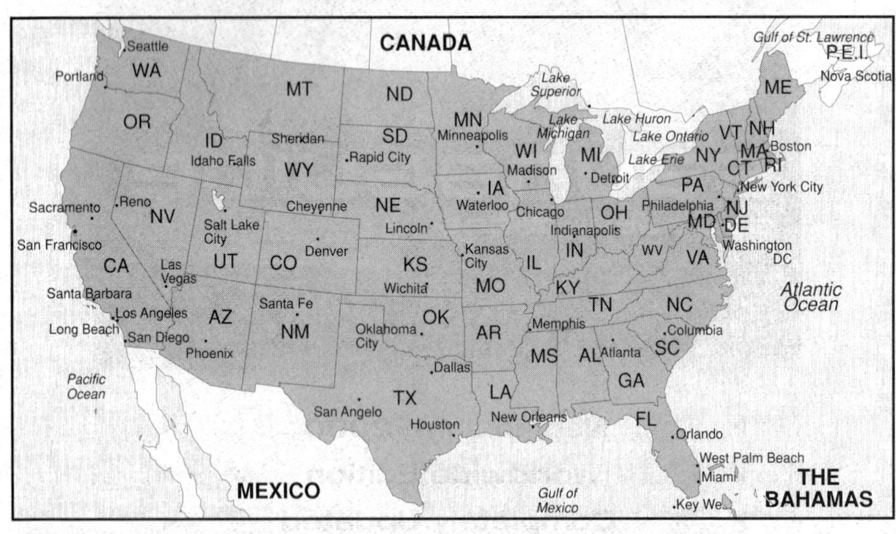

freier Raum, in dem sexuelle Präferenzen nicht erfragt, aber auch nicht ausgelebt werden dürfen.
Mit der Verabschiedung des *Defense of Marriage Act* mußte die US-amerikanische schwul-lesbische Bürgerrechtsbewegung eine Niederlage hinnehmen. Die meisten US-Bundesstaaten haben inzwischen auch auf landesebene die gesetzliche Anerkennung der homosexuellen ausgeschlossen *Anti-Marriage Bill.*
Wichtig zu vermerken ist jedoch, daß in zahlreichen Gemeinden und Städten weitgehende *Anti-Discrimination* und *Domestic Partnership Laws* existieren.
Um Ihnen die US-Adressen leichter zugänglich zu machen, haben wir sie nach Bundesstaaten, darin nach Städten geordnet. Abhängige Gebiete finden Sie am Ende des US-Teils. Dabei läßt sich kaum sagen, wohin ein schwuler Tourist reisen muß. Aber die amerikanischen Klassiker sollte jeder schwule Mann einmal gesehen haben. Dazu gehören Metropolen wie San Francisco, New York und Chicago ebenso wie die schwulen *resorts* Provincetown, Miami Beach oder Key West.

▲Les Etats-Unis sont le pays où l'infrastructure gaye est la plus variée et la mieux développée du monde. Des simples bars ou librairies de province aux puissantes et impressionnantes „gay communities" des grandes villes, il y en a pour tout le monde!
La situation des gays face à la loi varie d'un état à l'autre, car selon la constitution américaine, chaque état a le droit de promulguer ses propres lois. Dans de nombreux états, la fellation et la pénétration anale sont strictement interdites et ce, pour tous: homos et hétéros. Dans plusieurs autres états, il n'y a que les hétéros qui aient le droit de s'adonner aux joies de la sodomie. Ailleurs, en revanche, on a voté des lois antidiscriminatoires qui protègent les gays et les lesbiennes. Pour de plus amples informations, voyez pour chaque état séparément. La majorité sexuelle est fixée à 18 ans pour tous et dans tout le pays.
Dans la plupart des états, le code pénal en vigueur s'inspire d'un projet de loi de l'"American Law Institute" des années 60 qui décriminalise les relations homosexuelles entre personnes consentantes. L'Armée, elle, continue d'appliquer la devise „Don't ask, don't tell!" et se veut être un espace asexué où personne ne vous demandera vos préférences sexuelles et où personne, non plus, ne vous suggèrera ou encouragera à les vivre.
Les autorités ont fini par adopter le „Defense of Marriage Act". Le mouvement pour la défense des droits des gays et des lesbiennes américain a donc dû essuyer une sévère défaite. Chaque état a cependant la possibilité de proposer aux couples homos un contrat d'union sociale et aussi de le refuser ou l'annuler sur son territoire.
Nous ne classons pas les adresses ville par ville, mais état par état et pour chaque état, ville par ville. Cela permet d'y voir un peu plus clair, vu le nombre d'adresses américaines dont nous disposons! Aux Etats-Unis, le touriste gay ne sait où donner de la tête! Ne passez pas pas à côté de New York, San Francisco, Chicago et des stations balnéaires gays de Princetown, Miami Beach et Key West!

☆En ningún otro país del mundo existe un ambiente gay tan grande y variado como en los Estados Unidos. La gama va desde los fascinantes *gay communities* en las grandes ciudades, hasta los característicos bares y librerías en las ciudades pequeñas.
De igual forma se muestra también su situación legal. La constitución de los E.E.U.U. permite a los estados federales la promulgación de sus propias leyes. En muchos estados está prohibida la relación sexual oral o anal (tanto para homossexuales como para heterosexuales), en otros estados está prohibida solo para homosexuales. Por otra parte disponen muchos estados de leyes de antidiscriminación. Las particularidades de cada estado las encontrará en la rúbrica correspondiente. La edad de consentimiento no está regulada a nivel federal, pero esta no sobre pasa en ningún estado los 18 años.
En la mayoría de los estados vige el Código Penal de 1960 redactado por el *American Law Institute*. En ellas son descriminalizadas las relaciones sexuales privadas y por acuerdo mutuo. Los miembros de las fuerzas militares no son interrogados respecto a su dispoción sexual, pero tampoco se permite que la muestren abiertamente.
La aprobación del *Defense of Marriage Act* constituyó una pequeña derrota para el movimiento gay norteamericano. Aunque cada estado puede reconocer legalmente relaciones gay, algunos no las aceptan en su territorio.
Para su mejor orientación hemos ordenado las direcciones bajo el estado respectivo, territorios independientes los encontrará al final de la sección USA. Es muy difícil enumerar los lugares más interesantes para gays. La gama va desde el ambiente clásico de San Francisco, pasando por metrópolis como Nueva York y Chicago, hasta centros vacacionales como Provincetown, Miami Beach o Key West.

❖In nessun paese del mondo l'ambiente gay è così grande a vario come negli Stati Uniti. La gamma offre dalle travolgenti *gay communities* delle metropoli alle librerie e ai bar delle piccole città. Altrettanto varia è la legislazione. La costituzione statunitense permette ai singoli stati confederati di legiferare individualmente. Così in alcuni stati i rapporti orali ed anali sono vietati, indipendentemente dal fatto che vengano praticati da eterosessuali o da omosessuali, mentre in altri stati sono vietati solo i rapporti anali tra omosessuali. In altri stati invece esistono leggi contro la discriminazione dei gay. A riguardo forniamo precise informazioni nei paragrafi sui singoli stati. La maggiore età sessuale non è unica a livello federale, non supera però in nessun stato i 18 anni. Nella maggior parte degli stati è in vigore una legge, corrispondente ad un progetto degli anni 60 del *American Law Institute* che legalizza i rapporti sessuali tra consenzienti. In ambito militare regna il motto „don't ask, don't tell": nessuno indaga sulle preferenze sessuali dei colleghi, ma non è permesso mostrarle liberamente. Con l'approvazione del *Defense of marriage act* il movimento omosessuale dei diritti civili ha dovuto incassare una sconfitta. Tuttavia ogni stato può, in via teorica, permettere alle coppie omosessuali di registrarsi come nucleo famigliare. Tale legame, però, potrebbe non venire riconosciuto nel territorio di un altro stato. A partire dalla presente edizione di Spartacus non classifichiamo più gli indirizzi direttamente secondo la città, bensì, prima, secondo lo stato. Ciò rendera più accessibile la ricca lista degli USA; è persino difficile consigliare la meta più interessante per un gay. In ogni caso non perdetevi le classiche metropoli come San Francisco, New York e Chicago e neppure le località gay come Provincetown, Miami Beach o Key West.

NATIONAL GAY INFO

●Almost every large city of the U.S. offers free publications (available in bars or other gay venues) with calendar of events, personal and classified ads, and other features.

✸In fast jeder US-amerikanischen Großstadt gibt es in den Bars oder anderen schwulen Einrichtungen kostenlose Zeitschriften mit einem Terminkalender, wichtigen Adressen, Kleinanzeigen und anderen Inhalten.

▲Dans chaque grande ville des Etats-Unis, on trouve dans les bars et autres lieux gay des revues gratuites qui contiennent un agenda, des petites annonces, les adresses importantes, des petites annonces et autres.

☆En casi todas las ciudades importantes de los E.U. se distribuyen en los bares u otros establecimientos publicaciones gay que contienen informes sobre los acontecimientos mensuales, avisos personales, publicitarios y otras temáticas.

❖In quasi tutte le grandi città statunitensi si trovano nei bar o in altri locali gay le riviste gratuite con l'agenda, gli indirizzi importanti, annunci e altro.

Adonis BBS (G) 0-24 h
PO Box 10 72 West Palm Beach ⊠FL 33402
Fax: (561) 881-0358 Modem (561) 848-7681

Advocate. The
c/o Liberation Publication Inc., 6922 Hollywood Boulevard, Suite 1000 Los Angeles ⊠CA 90028-6148 ☎ (323) 871-1225
Fax: (323) 467-0173 E-Mail: info@advocate.com
Homepage: www.advocate.com
The national gay-lesbian news magazine. Featuring national and international news coverage from all areas that are of interest to the gay and lesbian community.

American Educational Gender Information Service (AEGIS)
PO Box 33724 Decatur ⊠GA 30033-0724 ☎ (770) 939-0244
Fax: (770) 939-1770 E-Mail: aegis@mindspring.com

Chiron Rising-CR
PO Box 2589 Victorville ⊠CA 92393
Published eight times a year. Publication for the mature seasoned man and his admirers.

Circuit Noize
PO Box 22656 Fort Lauderdale ⊠FL 33335 ☎ (954) 764-8210
Fax: (954) 764-6392 E-Mail: info@circuitnoize.com
Homepage: www.circuitnoize.com
Quarterly published containing all the latest news about the US party scene.

Damron Address Book
Damron Co., PO Box 42 24 58 San Francisco ⊠CA 94142
☎ (415) 255-0404 *USA, Canada, Caribbean, Mexico*

Damron Road Atlas
Damron Co., PO Box 42 24 58 San Francisco ⊠CA 94142
Features ca. 70 cities in the US and Canada with overview maps and extensive map material.

Drummer
PO Box 410390 San Francisco ⊠CA 94141-0390
☎ (415) 252-1195 *Monthly men's leather, S/M erotic magazine with related articles, fiction, comissioned art work, reviews, short stories, classified ads, and an abundance of photographs. 100 pages, published monthly by Desmodus Inc.*

Ferrari for Men
Ferrari International Publishing, Inc., PO Box 378 87 Phoenix ⊠AZ 85069 ☎ (602) 863-2408
Gay guide covering large areas of the world.

Fodor's Gay Guide to the USA
Fodor's Travel Publications, 201 E. 50th Street New York ⊠NY 10022 *Features ca. 30 cities and resorts in the US.*

Friction
Monumentum Publishing, 462 Broadway, Suite 4000 New York ⊠NY 10013 ☎ (212) 966-8400
Monthly gay erotic (novel) magazine, male nude drawings, some photos. Approximately 80 pages.

Gay and Lesbian Medical Association
211 Church Street, Suite C San Francisco ⊠CA 94114
☎ (415) 255-4547 E-Mail: AGLPNAT@aol.com
Homepage: members.aol.com/aglpnat/homepage.html

Gay USA
First Books, Inc., PO Box 57 81 47 Chicago ⊠IL 60657
☎ (312) 276-5911 *Features ca. 20 big cities and gay resorts.*

Gayellow Pages
Renaissance House, PO Box 533, Village Station New York ⊠NY 10014-0533 ☎ (212) 674-0120
One of the best and most complete gay guides of the USA. With accommodations, bars, businesses, churches, health care, lawyers, organizations, publications, switchboards etc.

Genre
7080 Hollywood Boulevard #1104, Hollywood, Los Angeles ⊠CA 90028 ☎ (323) 467-8300 Fax: (323) 467-8365
E-Mail: genre@aol.com *Monthly glossy lifestyle magazine.*

Guide. The
c/o Fidelity Publishing, PO Box 990593 Boston ⊠MA 02199-0593 ☎ (617) 266-8557 Fax: (617) 266-1125
E-Mail: theguide@guidemag.com Homepage: www.guidemag.com
Monthly magazine (US$ 3.50) featuring gay travel, entertainment, politics etc.

Heat
Heat Publications, 462 Broadway, Suite 4000 New York ⊠NY 10013 ☎ (212) 966-8400
Published 9 times a year, approximately 80 pages. US$ 4.95. Gay erotic magazine with colored photos and erotic stories.

Hero
8581 Santa Monica Boulevard #430 West Hollywood ⊠CA 90069 ☎ (310) 360-8022 Fax: (310) 360-8023 E-Mail: feedback@heromag.com Homepage: www.heromag.com
Glossy and stylish magazine for gay men.

Honcho
The Mavity Group, 462 Broadway #4000 New York ⊠NY 10013-2697 ☎ (212) 966-8400 Fax: (212) 966-9366
Monthly erotic gay magazine.

In Touch
13122 Saticoy Street North Hollywood ⊠CA 91605 ☎ (818) 764-2288 Fax: (818) 764-2307
Monthly men's erotic magazine, about 100 pages. Photos in color.

Inches
The Mavity Group, 462 Broadway #4000 New York ⊠NY 10013-2697 ☎ (212) 966-8400 Fax: (212) 966-9366
Monthly men's erotic magazine.

Inn Places
Ferrari Publications Inc., PO Box 378 87 Phoenix ⊠AZ 85069

☎ (602) 863-2408
International gay accommodation guide for men and women; approx 200pp.

Instinct Magazine
4235 Arch Drive, Suite 301 Studio City ✉CA 91604
☎ (818) 505-9205 Fax: (818) 505-9875
E-Mail: mail@instinctmag.com Homepage: www.instinctmag.com

International Directory of Gay & Lesbian Periodicals
The Oryx Press, 1250 West Grace, 1st floor, Chicago ✉IL 60611
Guide to Gay and Lesbian periodicals (international, which appears every two years.)

International Gay Rodeo Association (IGRA)
900 East Colfax Avenue, Denver ✉CO 80218 ☎ (303) 832-4472

Lambda Rising News
1625 Conneticut Avenue, Wahington ✉DC 20009-1013 ☎ (202) 462-7257 Fax: (202) 462-7257
Book reviews.

Mandate
The Mavity Group, 462 Broadway, 4th Floor, New York ✉NY 10013-2697 ☎ (212) 966-8400 Fax: (212) 966-9366
Monthly gay erotic magazine.

Men
c/o Liberation Publication Inc., 6922 Hollywood Boulevard, 10th Floor, Los Angeles ✉CA 90028 ☎ (213) 871-1225
Fax: (213) 467-0173 *Monthly publication. US$ 5.95. About 100 pages. Five nude pictorials per issue, plus erotic fiction and illustrations, video reviews, and letters from readers.*

MGW (Mom Guess What) 9-18 h
1725 L Street, Sacramento ✉CA 95814 ☎ (916) 441-6397
Monthly publication. Articles, ads and classifieds.

MI • Male Insider
Macho Publications, 462 Broadway Avenue, New York ✉NY 10013 ☎ (212) 966-8400
Distributed by Flynt Distributing Company, 9171 Wilshire Boulevard, Suite 300, Beverly Hills, CA 90210. Published quaterly, gay erotic magazine, approximately 80 pages, US$ 4.95.

National Gay & Lesbian Task Force Mon-Fri 9-19 h
1734 14th Street North West, Washington ✉DC 20009
☎ (202) 332-6483

Odysseus
PO Box 1548 Port Washington ✉NY 11050 ☎ (516) 944-5330
Fax: (516) 944-7540
Accomodation and travel guide with detailed and updated information about the USA and a few other countries.

Our World
c/o Our World Publishing, 1104 North Nova Road, Suite 251, Daytona ✉FL 32117 ☎ (904) 441-5367 Fax: (904) 441-5604
Gay and Lesbian Travel magazine, published monthly, US$ 4.95.

Places of Interest
c/o Ferrari Publications Inc., PO Box 378 87 Phoenix ✉AZ 85069
☎ (602) 863-2408 *USA, Canada, Caribbean, and Mexico; Gay travel guide with maps to gay locations for USA, Canada and the Caribbean. Also available, pocketsize, without maps.*

Playguy
The Mavity Group, 462 Broadway, 4th Floor, New York ✉NY 10013-2697 ☎ (212) 966-8400 Fax: (212) 966-9366
Monthly gay erotic magazine with emphasis on young males.

POZ
PO Box 1279, Old Chelsea Station, New York ✉NY 10113-1279
☎ (212) 242-2163 Fax: 212) 675-8505
E-Mail: pozmag@aol.com
For subcription service call toll-free (800) 883-2163. Magazine featuring information from, about and for people with HIV/AIDS.

Torso
The Mavity Group, 462 Broadway, 4th Floor, New York ✉NY 10013-2697 ☎ (212) 966-8400 Fax: (212) 966-9366
Monthly erotic magazine.

NATIONAL HELPLINES

CDC National AIDS Hotline
☎ (800) 342-2437

Gay & Lesbian National Hotline Mon-Fri 18-22, Sat 12-17 h (Eastern Standard times)
☎ 1-888-843-4564 Fax: 415/552 0649 E-Mail: glnh@glnh.org
Homepage: www.glnh.org

NATIONAL PUBLISHERS

Desmodus Inc.
2354 Market Street, San Francisco ✉CA 94114 *(top floor)*
☎ (415) 252 1195 Fax: (415) 252-8444 *Publisher of Drummer Magazine, Drummer Hardcore, Drummer Touch Customers.*

Gay and Lesbian Yellow Pages
4200 Montrose Boulevard, Ste. 480, Houston ✉TX 77006
Homepage: www.glyp.com *Publisher of annual telephone directories for the gay, lesbian, bisexual and trangender community.*

Liberation Publications Inc.
6922 Hollywood Boulevard, 10th floor, Los Angeles ✉CA 90028
☎ (213) 871-1225 Fax: (213) 467-0173
Publishers of The Advocate and Advocate Men magazines.

Persona Productions
PO Box 14022 San Francisco ✉CA 94114-0022
☎ (415) 775-6143 E-Mail: personapro@aol.com
Publisher of gay novels and nonpronographic videos.

Pridetime Productions
105 Charles Street, Suite 283, Boston ✉MA 02114
☎ (617) 723-5130 *Travel info on gay/lesbian life on video.*

Streetlife Video
PO Box 1872 New York ✉NY 10013 ☎ (212) 253-6034
Fax: (212) 477-7729 E-Mail: webmaster@streetlife.com
Black and latino videos.

Tom of Finland Company
PO Box 26716 Los Angeles ✉CA 90026 ☎ (800) 334-6526
Publisher of magazines, postcards, posters etc. with Tom's drawings. Catalogue available for US$ 10.

NATIONAL COMPANIES

A Different Light (GLM) 10-24 h
151 West 19th Street New York ✉NY 10011 *(at 7th Avenue)*
☎ (212) 989-4850 ☎ (800) 343-4002 (toll free)
Fax: (212) 989-2158 *Books. Ask for free catalogue.*

Bijou Video 0-24 h
1349 North Wells, Chicago ✉IL 60610 ☎ (312) 943-5397

Colt Studio
PO Box 16 08 Studio City ✉CA 91614 ☎ (818) 985-7751
Videos, magazines, calendars, posters, and more.

Different Drummer Tours
PO Box 528 Glen Ellyn ✉IL 60137 ☎ (708) 993-1716
International Tours.

Dragonfly (OUT-er Wear)
19 South West 2nd Street Gainsville ✉FL 32601 *(Upstairs)*
☎ (904) 375 2144
Mail order line of clothing geared to the gay/lesbian community.

Falcon Studios (G VS)
PO Box 880906 San Francisco ✉CA 94188-0906 ☎ 431-7722
☎ 1-800-227-3717 Homepage: www.falconstudios.com
Producers of porno films and magazines etc.

Gay Entertainment Television
7 East 17 Street, New York ✉NY 10003 ☎ (212) 255-8824
Three gay TV-shows: Party Talk, Inside/Out and Makostyle.

Hamburger Mary's ®International Office : Mon-Fri 09-16 h
PO Box 633 Corona Del Mar ✉CA 92625-0633
☎ 949/723 1230 E-Mail: HambrgMary@aol.com
Homepage: www.franchisemarys.com *Hamburger Mary's® International has trading registration in Australia, Europe and in the US. Franchise sales of Hamburger Mary's® restaurants.*

Jaybird's Toybox (LJ)
PO Box 74 66 Fort Lauderdale ✉FL 33338
Leather and erotica collection.

Jewelry by Poncé 1
417 S. Coast Highway, Laguna Beach, CA ☎ (800) 969-7464
Homepage: www.jewelrybyponce.com/1
Piercings, watches, earrings and pride rings.

Lambda Rising
Connecticut Avenue, Washington ✉DC 20009-1013
☎ (202) 462-6969 ☎ (800) 621-6969 Fax: (202) 462-7257
E-Mail: lambdarising@his.com

Malibu Sales 9-17 h
PO Box 4371 Los Angeles ✉CA 90078 ☎ (800) 533-8567
Mail order company of Advocate. Videos, magazines, etc.

Oscar Wilde Memorial Bookshop
15 Christopher Street, New York ✉NY 10014
☎ (212) 255-8097 *Ask for free catalogue.*

SVP
PO Box 1807 El Cajon ✉CA 92022 ☎ (619) 440-1020
Mail order for spanking videos.

NATIONAL GROUPS

Gay Airline & Travel Club
PO Box 69A04 West Hollywood ✉CA 90069 ☎ (213) 650-5112

Lesbian and Gay Immigration Rights Task Force
PO Box 7741 New York ✉NY 10116-7741 ☎ (212) 802-7264
Provides assistance to lesbian & guy immigrants including those seeking asylum through a national campaign of advocacy, support, education and outreach.

Lesbian, Gay & Bisexual People in Medicine
1890 Preston White Drive, Reston ✉VA 22091
☎ (703) 620-6600 *Over 400 members worldwide.*

Military & Police Uniform Association
PO Box 69A04 West Hollywood ✉CA 90069 ☎ (213) 650-5112

Military and Police Club, Int.
1286 University Avenue #142, San Diego ✉CA 92103-3392
E-Mail: mpcted@aol.com Homepage: www.mpcint.com

Names Project Foundation. The
310 Townsend Street, Suite 310, San Francisco ✉CA 94107
☎ (415) 882-5500 Fax: 882-6200 Homepage: www.aidsquilt.org

National Coalition of Black Lesbians & Gays
19641 West Seven Mile, Detroit ✉MI 48219

National Foot Network (NFN)
PO Box 150790 New York ✉NY 11215
A correspondence club for men into feet, footwear and related scenes.

National Leather Association
PO Box 541921 Houston ✉TX 77254 ☎ 713 527-9666
Mixed but mainly gay and lesbian leather group.

Seventh-Day Adventists Kinship Int., Inc.
PO Box 7320 Laguna Miguel ✉CA 92677 ☎ (714) 248-1299
E-Mail: sdkinship@aol.com Homepage: www.sdakinship.org

United at United
PO Box 88-1416 Los Angeles ✉CA 90009-1416
☎ (310) 285-8821 Fax: (310) 644-2563
Gay and lesbian employees of United Airlines.

USA-Alabama

Southeast USA

Initials: AL

Time: GMT -6

Area: 135.775 km^2 / 55,532 sq mi.

Population: 4,319,000

Capital: Montgomery

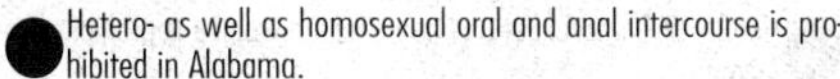

● Hetero- as well as homosexual oral and anal intercourse is prohibited in Alabama.

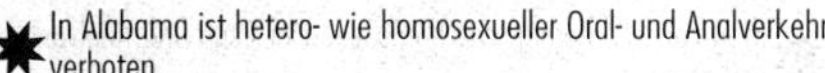

✱ In Alabama ist hetero- wie homosexueller Oral- und Analverkehr verboten.

▲ En Alabama, la fellation et la pénétration anale sont interdites pour tous, homos comme hétéros.

☆ Las relaciones sexules por vía oral o anal están en Alabama, tanto para heterosexuales como para homosexuales, prohibidas.

❖ In Alabama sono vietati i rapporti orali ed anali tra eterosessuali e tra omosessuali.

Birmingham ☎ 205

GAY INFO

Barnes Memorial Library
516 27th Street South ✉AL 35205 ☎ 326-8600
Largest gay/lesbian library in Alabama. Gay Center also here. Mon-Fri 18-22 h.

BARS

Club 21 (B D glm) Thu-Sat 22-4 h
117 1/2 21st Street North ✉AL 35203 ☎ 322-0469
Misconceptions Tavern (B F G VS)
600 32nd Street South ☎ 322-1210
Quest (B D GLM OS W) 24 hrs
416 24th Street South ✉AL 35233 ☎ 251-4313

BOOK SHOPS

Lodestar Books (GLM) 10-18, Sun 13-17 h
2020 11th Avenue South, ✉AL 35205 ☎ 939-3356

CRUISING

-Rushton Park (AYOR)

Huntsville ☎ 256

GAY INFO

Pink Triangle Alliance 9-21 h
☎ 539-4235

BOOK SHOPS

Rainbow's Ltd. (glm) Mon-Sat 11-21, Sun 13-18 h, closed Tue
522 Jordan Ln NW ✉AL 35805-2626

Mobile ☎ 334

BARS

B-Bob's (B D F GLM VS)
6157 Airport Boulevard No. 201 Plaza de Malaga ✉AL 36608 ☎ 341-0102
Exit (B D glm)
9 North Jackson Street ✉AL 36611 ☎ 694-0909
Gabriel's Downtown Bar (AC B CC d G MA) Mon-Thu 17-? h, Fri-Sat 19-? h, Sun 15-? h
55 South Joachim Street ✉AL 36602 *(Downtown)* ☎ 432-4900
Golden Rod (B f GLM)
13 South Joachim Street ✉AL 36602 ☎ 433-9175
Society Lounge (! B d GLM)
51 South Conception Street ✉AL 36602 ☎ 433-9141
Zippers (B d GLM)
215 Conti Street ✉AL 36602 ☎ 433-7436
Oldest gay bar in town

DANCECLUBS

Baton Rouge Dance Club (AC CC D GLM lj MA) Thu-Sun 21- ?
213 Conti Street ✉AL 36602 ☎ 433 2887

FITNESSTUDIOS

YMCA (bf g msg pi sa sb SWC YG)
101 N. Water Street ✉AL 36602 ☎ 438-1163
Gay on Sundays.

GIFT & PRIDE SHOPS

Rainbow Printing (glm)
1379 Smokerise Drive ✉AL 36695 ☎ 607-0041
Cards, envelopes, rubber stamps, announcements etc.

GENERAL GROUPS

Gay and Lesbian Student Alliance
University of South Alabama, University Center ✉AL 36688

HELP WITH PROBLEMS

Mobile AIDS Coalition
☎ 432-AIDS
Information and referral line.

RELIGIOUS GROUPS

Metropolitan Community Church
PO Box 6311 ✉AL 36660 ☎ 476-4621

CRUISING

-Downtown area
-Bel Air Mall (AYOR) (Sears restroom)
-Springdale Mall
-University of South Alabama (Restrooms in the University Center, Library and Humanities Bldg.)
-I-10 (P between Mobile and Pensacola, FL)
-Speedway gas station (Restrooms, truck drivers and adjacent streets, take I-65 North, exit at Moffet Rd., turn right, pass under the I-65, the first gas station on your right is Speedway)

Montgomery ☎ 334

BARS

Hojons (B D Glm S) 20-?, Sat -2 h, closed Sun-Mon
215 N. Court Street ☎ 269-9672
Jimmy Mac's (B D GLM P) 19-2 h
211 Lee Street ☎ 264-5933

USA-Alaska

Northern America

Initials: AK

Time: GMT -9

Area: 1,700,138 km² / 695,356 sq mi.

Population: 609,000

Capital: Juneau

Anchorage ☎ 907

GAY INFO

Anchorage Press
702 West 32nd Street, #203 ☎ & Fax: 561-7777

BARS

O'Grady's (B f glm MA)
6901 East Tudor Road ☎ 338-1080
Raven (B GLM lj MA OG) 11-?, Sun 12-? h
18 Gambell Avenue ☎ 276-9672
Wave. The (B glm D S VS W) 18-2.30 h, closed Sun-Tue
3103 Spenard Road ☎ 561-9283

SEX SHOPS/BLUE MOVIES

Cyrano's Bookstore & Café (b F glm S W) 10-22 h
413 D Street ☎ 274-2599

HOTELS

Aurora Winds Bed&Breakfst Resort (bf CC g wh wo)
7501 Upper O'Malley, AK 99516 ☎ 346-2533 Fax: 346-3192.
Rates from US$ 75 (single/winter) -125 (double/summer).

GUEST HOUSES

Aurora Winds Resort B&B (bf glm H) 7501 Upper O'Malley ☎ 346-2533
Cheney Lake B&B (bf glm H)
6333 Colgate Drive ☎ 337-4391
The Pink Whale (bf glm H)
3627 Randolph Street ☎ 561-9283

HELP WITH PROBLEMS

Gay/Lesbian Helpline
☎ 276-3909 *or* ☎ *258-4777*

Fairbanks ☎ 907

HOTELS

Fairbanks Hotel (CC glm H)
517 Third Avenue ✉AK 99701 ☎ 456-6411 Fax: 456-1792.
Email: fbxhotl@alaska.net *Located in the center of Downtown Fairbanks. Rates summer US$ 60-109, winter 35-49.*

Juneau ☎ 907

GUEST HOUSES

Pearson's Pond (AC bf CC f H MA msg OS wh)
4541 Sawa Circle ✉AK 99801-8723 ☎ 789-3772
Fax: 789-6722. Email: pearsons.pond@juneau.com
Homepage: http://www.juneau.com/pearsons.pond *Serene, private retreat on the banks of a peaceful pond. Rates US$ 99-229.*

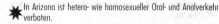

USA-Arizona

Southwest USA

Initials: AZ

Time: GMT -7

Area: 295,276 km² / 120,768 sq mi.

Population: 4,555,000

Capital: Phoenix

● Hetero- or homosexual oral and anal intercourse is prohibited in Arizona.

In Arizona ist hetero- wie homosexueller Oral- und Analverkehr verboten.

▲ Dans l'Arizona, la fellation et la pénétration anale sont interdites pour tous, homos comme hétéros.

☆ Las relaciones homosexuales o heterosexuales por via oral o anal están prohibidas.

❖ In Arizona sono vietati i rapporti orali ed anali tra eterosessuali e tra omosessuali.

Flagstaff ☎ 520

GAY INFO

Gay and Lesbian Info Line
☎ 525-1199

BARS

Charlie's (B glm)
23 North Leroux Street

BOOK SHOPS

Aradia Books 10.30-17.30 h, closed Sun
116 West Cottage Avenue, AZ 86001 ☎ 779-3817

CRUISING

-Thorp Park (AYOR) (sunset & on WE)

Glendale ☎ 602

HOTELS

Arrowzona Casitas (AC bf cc g H msg NU OS pi sa sb wh WO) Open all year
PO Box 11253 ✉AZ 85318-1234 *(located NW of Phoenix/Scottsdale)* ☎ & Fax: 561-1200
Located not far from downtown Phoenix. 17 condos with bath/shower/WC, balcony/terrace, phone, satellite TV, VCR, radio, minibar, full kitchen, safe, own key. Provides car park, bicycle hire, riding. Rates from US$ 99 per night per condo (bf incl.)

Phoenix ☎ 602

GAY INFO

The Community Center (GLM MA) 10-21 h
24 West Camelback Road, Suite C ✉AZ 85013 ☎ 265-7283
Fax: 234-0873 E-Mail: info@phxcenter.org
Gay, lesbian and bisexual community center.
Ferrari Publications
PO Box 355 75 ✉AZ 85069 ☎ (602) 863-2408
Publisher of different gay and lesbian travel publications.

Phoenix's Gay Community Yellow Pages
c/o Outwest Publications ☎ 277-0105 or ☎ (800) 849-0406 (toll-free). Fax: 277-1065 or (800) 231-3477 (toll-free).

TOURIST INFO

Phoenix & Valley of the Sun Convention & Visitor Bureau
400 E. Van Buren ✉AZ 85004 ☎ 254-6500 Fax: 253-4415

BARS

Apollo's (B d CC G lj) 8-1 h
5749 N. 7th Street ☎ 277-9373
Charlie's (B D F G) 12-1 h
727 W. Camelback Road ☎ 265-0224
Cruise bar.
Country Club Bar (B GLM MA N) Mon-Sat 11-1 h
4428 N. 7th Avenue ☎ 264-4553
Cruisin' Central (AYOR B G N R RT SNU) 6-1 h
1011 N. Central ☎ 253-3376
Downtown neighborhood pub. Thu night strip shows.
Harley`s 155 (B D GLM) 12-1 h
155 W. Camelback Street ☎ 274-8505
Also: back bar The Cell (B G LJ).
J.C.'s Fun One Lounge (B GLM) 11-1 h
5542 N. 43rd Avenue, Glendale ☎ 939-0528
Marly's (AC B d GLM MA N s) 15-1 h
15615 N. Cave Creek Road ✉AZ 85032 ☎ 867-2463
Nu Towne Saloon (B f G) 10-1 h
5002 E. Van Buren Street ☎ 267-9959
Wink's (! B bf f GLM S) 11-1
5707 N. 7th Street ☎ 265-9002
Popular.
307 Lounge (AC B G lj MA S STV W YG) Mon-Sat 6-1, Sun 10-1 h
222 E. Roosevelt Street ✉AZ 85004 ☎ 252-0001

SEX SHOPS/BLUE MOVIES

Castle Superstore (g VS) 0-24 h
300 East Camelback Road ✉AZ 85012 ☎ 266-3348
Leather, lingerie, magazines, books, DVD's, toys and more.
Castle Superstore (g VS) 0-24 h
5501 East Washington Street ✉AZ 85034 ☎ 231-9837
Leather, lingerie, magazines, books, DVD's, toys and more.
Castle Superstore (g VS) 0-24 h
8315 East Apache Trail ✉AZ 85207 ☎ 986-6114
Leather, lingerie, magazines, books, DVD's, toys and more.
Castle Superstore (g VS) 0-24 h
8802 North Black Canyon Highway ✉AZ 85051 ☎ 995-1641
Leather, lingerie, magazines, books, DVD's, toys and more.

SAUNAS/BATHS

Chute (AC b DR f G LJ NU P sb VS W WO) 0-24 h
1440 E. Indian School Road ✉AZ 85014 *(West Entrance)* ☎ 234-1654
Private club for bears and leathermen.
Flex Complex (B G msg P pi sa wh WO) 0-24 h
1517 S. Black Canyon Highway ☎ 271-9011

BOOK SHOPS

Obelisk The Bookstore (GLM W) Mon-Sat 10-22, Sun 12-20 h
24 W. Camelback, Suite A, AZ 85013 ☎ 266-2665
Fax: 266-8705 Books, cards, videos, music, magazines, t-shirts and more.

GIFT & PRIDE SHOPS

Unique on Central (GLM) 10-20 h
4700 N. Central, Suite 105 ✉AZ 85012 ☎ 279-9691
or ☎ (800) 269-4840. Pride shopping.

LEATHER & FETISH SHOPS

Tuff Stuff (LJ) 10-18, Sat -15 h, closed Sun Mon
1714 E. McDowell Road *(near 17th Street)* ☎ 254-9561

TRAVEL & TRANSPORT

First Travel MOn-Fri 8-18, closed Sat Sun
4700 North Central Avenue #205 ✉AZ 85012 ☎ 265-0666
Fax: 265-0135 *Full service travel agency serving the Gay Community since 1984.*

GUEST HOUSES

Arizona Sunburst Inn (AC bf CC G msg NU OS pi wh)
6245 N. 12th Place, AZ 85014 ☎ 274-1474
7 rooms with TV, partly with bath. Guest house provides TV room. Rates double US$ 79, single 69.
Larry's Bed & Breakfast (AC bf GLM H MA NU OS pi wh)
502 West Claremont Avenue ✉AZ 85013 ☎ 249-2974
E-Mail: kenezz@earthlink.net
RateRates: $50-70 per day. Rooms with private phone
Windsor Cottage (AC bf CC glm MA NU pi OS)
62 West Windsor ✉AZ 85003 ☎ 264-6309
Bath, cable-TV, refrigerator, microwave, laundry facilities. Rates single US$ 65-95, double 85-125. Addtional bed 15.

APARTMENTS

Arizona Royal Villa Resort (AC CC G H NU pi wh WO) 1110 East Turney Avenue #8 ✉AZ 85014 ☎ 266-6883
Fax: 279-7437 Toll Free ☎ (888) 266-6884
Email: azroyalvil@aol.com Homepage: http://www.royalvilla.com
7 double rooms and 8 apartments with bath/shower, telephone, TV, minibar, kitchenette, heating and own key. 15 minutes from the airport, convenient location, close to most valley bars. Rates US$ 50-100.

GENERAL GROUPS

Phoenix Gay Youth
☎ 938-3932

FETISH GROUPS

Arizona Rangers MC
PO Box 130 74, AZ 85002

HEALTH GROUPS

AIDS-Info Line
☎ 234-2752

RELIGIOUS GROUPS

MCC
1029 E. Turney Avenue/10th Street ☎ 268-5183

CRUISING

-Papago Park
-Camelview Plaza Mall
-Fiesta Mall
-Kiwanis Park

Sedona ☎ 520

GUEST HOUSES

Casa Tiigaua B & B (A AC bf CC GLM MA msg NU OS pi W wh)
PO Box 405, AZ 86339 (Uptown Sedona) ☎ 203-0102
or ☎ (888) 844-4282 (Toll free in USA) Fax: 204-1075
E-mail tiigaua@sedona.net. Homepage www.casatiigaua.com
6 suites . All rooms with jetted tub, fireplace, private decks/patios.

Tucson ☎ 520

GAY INFO

Observer Mon-Fri 9-16 h
PO Box 50733 ✉AZ 85703 ☎ 622-7176
Fax: 792-8382 E-mail: watcher@azstarnet.com
Homepage: http://bonzo.com/observer
Gay and lesbian newspaper for Tucson and Greater Arizona.
Wingspan Community Center
422 N. 4th Avenue ☎ 624-1779

BARS

IBT's (B D GLM OS S W) 12-1 h
616 N. 4th Avenue/5th Street ☎ 882-3053
Stonewall Eagle (AC B D f GLM MA N OS S SNU STV WE) 12-? h
2921 North 1st Avenue ✉AZ 85719 ☎ 624-8805
Monthly changing shows and events.
Venture-N (B f G lj T) 6-1, Sun 10-1 h
1239 N. 6th Avenue, AZ 85705 ☎ 882-8224

CAFÉS

Rainbow Planet Coffee House & Bistro (bf F GLM MA OS) Mon-Fri -23, Sat Sun -24 h
606 North 4th Avenue ✉AZ 85705 ☎ 620-1770
Tucson's only gay coffee house.

DANCECLUBS

Congress Hotel (A B bf CC D F g H MA OS s)
311 East Congress ✉AZ 85701 ☎ 622-8848
Rita's (B F GLM)
3455 East Grand Road ☎ 327-3390

SEX SHOPS/BLUE MOVIES

Bookstore Southwest. The 0-24 h
5754 E. Speedway Boulevard ☎ 790-1550
Speedway Books & Videos (g MA) 10-15, Fri Sat 10-17 h
3660 East Speedway Boulevard, AZ 85716 ☎ 795-7467
Tropicana Adult Bookstore (g) 0-24 h
617 West Miracle Mile, AZ 85705 ☎ 622-2289

HOTELS

Hacienda del Sol (G H pi)
5601 North Hacienda del Sol Road, AZ 85718 ☎ 299-1501
Sun Catcher (pi)
105 N. Avenida Javalina, AZ 85748 ☎ 885-0883
or ☎ (800) 835-8012 (Toll free.

GUEST HOUSES

Catalina Park Inn (AC CC glm MA OS)
309 East 1st Street ✉AZ 85705 ☎ 792-4541
Email: CPInn@flash.net Homepage: www.catalinaparkinn.com or www.bbonline.com/az/cpinn
6 rooms with private bath, phone, TV, some with fireplace. Rates US$ 95-125 plus tax. Gourmet bf.
Tortuga Roja B & B (AC bf CC GLM MA NU pi wh) 2800 E. River Road ✉AZ 85718 ☎ 577-6822 or ☎ (800) 467-6822
E-mail carl@arizona.edu
2 double rooms, 1 cottage with shower/bath/WC, phone, TV, radio, kitchenette, heating, own key. Hotel provides car park and TV room. Rates US$ 55-85, cottage 75-100 (bf incl.)

PRIVATE ACCOMODATION

Tortuga Roja Bed & Breakfast (bf CC G MA NU pi wh)
2800 East River Road ✉AZ 85718 ☎ 577 6822
E-Mail: redtrtl@goodnet.com

FETISH GROUPS

Desert Leathermen
PO Box 15 86, AZ 85702

HEALTH GROUPS

AIDS-Hotline 10-24 h
☎ 326-2437

RELIGIOUS GROUPS

Cornerstore Fellowship
2902 North Geronimo ☎ 622-4626

USA-Arkansas

Southern USA
Initials: AR
Time: GMT -6
Area: 137,742 km^2 / 56,337 sq mi.
Population: 2,553,000
Capital: Little Rock

● Homosexual oral or anal intercourse is prohibited in Arkansas.

✱ In Arkansas ist homosexueller Oral- und Analverkehr verboten.

▲ Dans l'Arkansas, la fellation et la pénétration anale sont interdites seulement pour les homosexuels.

☆ En Arkansas las relaciones homosexuales por vía oral o anal están prohibidas.

❖ In Arkansas sono vietati i rapporti orali ed anali tra omosessuali.

Eureka Springs ☎ 501

RESTAURANTS

Autumn Breeze (AC CC F glm MA) Mon-Sat 17-21, closed Sun and Jan Feb
190 Huntsville Road ✉72632 ☎ 253-7734
Award-winning restaurant. Wide-range of tastes, relaxing and uncluttered, selected wines. Every table has a view. Affordable price level.
Jim's & Brent's Bistro (AC CC F glm MA OS s W) 17-23 h, closed Wed Thu
173 South Main AR 72632 ✉72632 *(on Planer Hill)*
☎ 253-7457 Fax: 253-2370

GUEST HOUSES

The Woods Resort (AC CC GLM MA msg wh)
50 Wall Street ✉AR 72632 ☎ 253-8281
Homepage: http://www.eureka-usa.com/woods
One and two bedroom cottages. TV, VCR, full kitchen. Rates US$99-139 /night plus tax.

Fort Smith

CRUISING

-6th and Garrison Street (AYOR)

Little Rock ☎ 501

BARS

Backstreet (AC B D G MA P WE) 21-? h
1021 Jessie Road *(near Discovery III)* ☎ 664-2744
Private Club, but ask someone at the entrance to be their guest.

Discovery III (B D GLM S) Thu 21-2, Fri Sat 21-5 h, closed Sun-Wed
1021 Jessie Road ☎ 664-4784
Popular.

USA-California

Southwest USA

Initials: CA

Time: GMT -8

Area: 424,002 km^2 / 173,417 sq mi.

Population: 32,268,000

Capital: Sacramento

Important gay cities: Long Beach, Los Angeles, Palm Springs, Russian River, San Diego, San Francisco

● California is likely to be the most interesting of the US-states for gay men, which is not only due to the immense gay scene here, but also to the relaxed atmosphere in the *golden state* , the most populated of the US-states. There may be some politically conservative corners in California, but all consenting and non-aggressive sexual acts are legal and anti-discriminatory legislation can be found locally. San Francisco, although its scene has been diminished by AIDS, is a gay capital, a rainbow city, and provides a worthwhile stay. The gay holiday resort *Russian River* is situated in Guerneville, a short trip to the north. On the (car)ride to Los Angeles in the south, you'll pass the region of *Monterey* with its historical missions and scenic landscapes, which are popular tourist destinations. Onward to *Los Angeles,* or to be more precise, to *West Hollywood,* an embodiment of the american dream (or nightmare) of car fetishism, class distinction und body culture. A paradise for visitors delighting in body and bodies. *Disneyland* in Anaheim, Orange County and the seaside town *Laguna Beach,* well loved by artists and gays are situated to the south In *Palm Springs* visitors are presented with incomparably grandiose desert and mountain scenery. To the southwest, lying on the coast, is *San Diego,* a large city with a small reputation. But still the big military presence, boosts the local economy, and a lively gay scene.

✱ Kalifornien dürfte für schwule Männer der interessanteste US-amerikanische Staat sein. Das liegt nicht nur an der großen Szene des bevölkerungsreichsten US-Staates, sondern einfach auch an der relaxten Atmosphäre im *golden state.*
San Francisco ist, auch wenn AIDS die Szene zeitweise sehr schwächte, eine Rainbow-City und absolut sehenswert. Von dort ist es nur eine kurze Fahrt nordwärts nach Guerneville, dem Zentrum des schwulen Ferienreviers *Russian River.*
Auf dem (Auto-)Weg ins südlich gelegene Los Angeles liegt die bei allen Touristen als Zwischenstop beliebte Gegend von *Monterey* mit ihren historischen Missionen und Naturschönheiten.
Weiter also nach *Los Angeles,* oder genauer gesagt nach *West Hollywood,* dieser Verkörperung des amerikanischen (Alp-)Traums von Autowahn, Statusdenken und Körperkult. Für Körpersüchtige also ein himmlisches Paradies. Südlich davon liegen im Orange County *Disneyland* bei Anaheim und der ebenso bei Künstlern wie bei Schwulen beliebte Badeort *Laguna Beach.*
Mit Unmengen von Wasser, die Luft und Boden feucht halten, wird mitten in der Wüste das Ferienzentrum *Palm Springs* am Leben gehalten. Der Besucher wird hier mit einer unvergleichlich grandiosen Wüsten- und Bergszenerie verwöhnt. Südwestlich davon, an der Küste, liegt *San Diego.* Keine Stadt, die von sich reden macht. Aber eine der größten Städte der USA, mit dem Militär als wesentlichem Wirtschaftsfaktor und mit einer lebhaften schwulen Szene.

▲ La Californie est certainement l'état américain le plus intéressant pour le touriste gay de base, ce qui s'explique d'abord par la qualité de l'infrastructure gaye du plus peuplé des états américains et aussi et surtout par l'atmosphère particulière du „Golden State". En Californie aussi, on trouvera des coins et recoins plutôt conservateurs et rétrogrades, mais sachez bien que les relations sexuelles de tout genre, si elles sont placées sous le signe du consentement et de la non-violence, ne sont pas poursuivies par la loi. Certaines municipalités ont même pris des arrêtés antidiscriminatoires qui mettent homos et hétéros sur le même pied d'égalité.
San Francisco reste la „rainbow city" des Etats-Unis, même si le SIDA y a causé d'irréparables dégâts. Au nord de San Francisco, on trouve Guerneville et la station banéaire gaye par excellence „Russian River".
Sur la route de Los Angeles, au sud, on peut faire une pause dans la région de Monterey pour y visiter les missions catholiques historiques et jouir des merveilles de la nature.
En descendant encore plus dans le sud, sur Los Angeles, on arrive à West Hollywood, l'incarnation même du rêve/cauchemar américain: le paradis des body-builders, de l'argent et de la voiture. Plus au sud encore, on arrive à Orange County avec son Disney Land (près de Anaheim) et à la station balnéaire de Laguna Beach qui est très prisée par les gays.
En plein coeur du désert, Palm Springs, ville artificielle maintenue en vie par des hectolitres d'eau, offre aux touristes des paysages grandioses et inoubliables. Au sud-ouest de Palm Spring, il y a San Diego, une ville qui fait rarement parler d'elle, mais une des plus grandes du pays. L'Armée y est un des premiers employeurs. L'infrastructure gaye y est assez bien développée.

☆ California es el estado norteamericano más interesante para los homosexuales. Esto no se debe solo a la gran comunidad gay, sino también al relajado ambiente en el *Golden State.* Aunque California no esté libre de aspectos conservadores, aquí toda relación sexual por acuerdo mutuo y sin violencia está permitida. A nivel estatal existen incluso reglamentos de antidiscriminación. A pesar de que el SIDA la debilitó un poco, San Francisco continua teniendo un ambiente gay excepcional, su Rainbow-City tiene que ser visitada. Desde aquí y en dirección hacia el norte se llega al centro vacacional gay llamado *Russian River.* Si se viaja en coche hacia el sur en dirección Los Angeles se puede hacer una pausa en la región de *Monterey* que cuenta con mansiones coloniales de interés histórico así como bellezas naturales. Continuando se llega hasta *Los Angeles* o mejor dicho hasta el *West Hollywood,* ejemplo del típico sueño americano (o la pesadilla); el estatus social, el culto al cuerpo y el automovil como segunda vivienda. Si lo que te gusta es lucir tu cuerpo entrenado, estás aquí en tu paraíso. Más hacia el sur se encuentra en el Orange County *Disneyland* y en las cercanías de Anaheim se localiza el balneario *Laguna Beach* que es muy visitado por artístas y homosexuales. Con grandes cantidades de agua, se mantienen humedos el aire y los suelos de *Palm Spring.* Este centro vacacional en medio del desierto ofrece un paisaje de cadenas montañosas de especial belleza. Hacia el suroeste se encuentra *San Diego.* Esta ciudad a pesar de pasar un poco desapercibida, es una de las más grandes de los E.E.U.U., donde el ejercito ocupa un papel determinante en al ámbito económico y el ambiente gay se muestra bastante interesante.

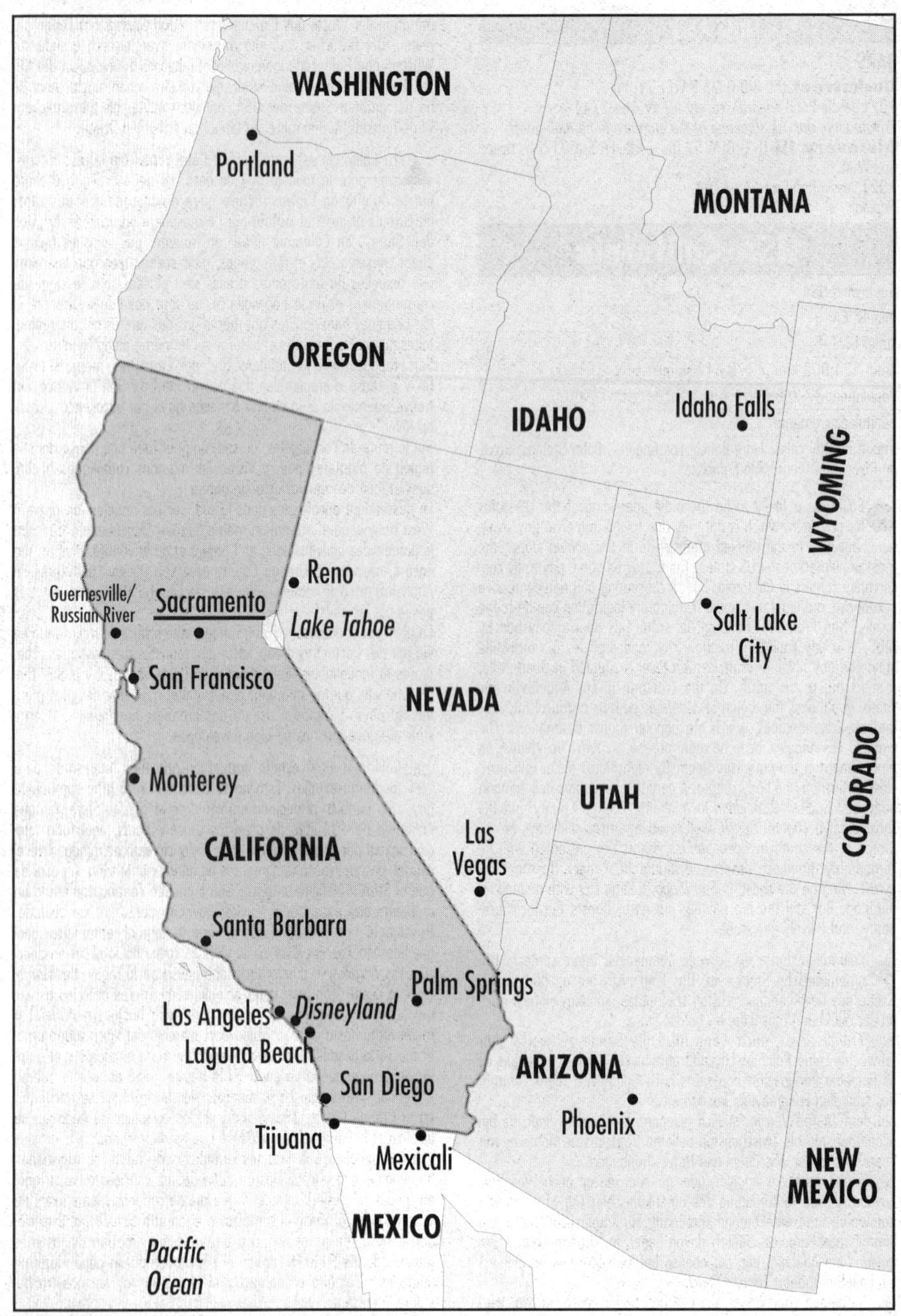
WASHINGTON
Portland
MONTANA
OREGON
IDAHO
Idaho Falls
WYOMING
Reno
Guernesville/
Russian River
Sacramento
Lake Tahoe
Salt Lake
City
San Francisco
NEVADA
COLORADO
Monterey
UTAH
Las
Vegas
CALIFORNIA
Santa Barbara
Palm Springs
Los Angeles
Disneyland
Laguna Beach
ARIZONA
San Diego
Phoenix
Tijuana
Mexicali
NEW
MEXICO
MEXICO
Pacific
Ocean

❖ La California dovrebbe essere lo stato più interessante per i gay. Ciò non dipende solo dal vasto ambiente gay dello stato più popolato della federazione, ma anche dall'atmosfera distesa del *golden state*. In raltà anche in California vi sono angoli conservatori, tuttavia in questo stato non sono punibili i rapporti sessuali non violenti praticati tra consenzienti e a livello locale esistono persino leggi contro la discriminazione. Anche se per un certo tempo l'AIDS ha indebolito l'ambiente gay, *San Francisco* è una città arcobaleno che merita di essere vista. Il viaggio verso Guerneville, al nord, è breve. In poco tempo potete raggiungere la zona di villeggiatura per gay Russian River. Sul tragitto per Los Angeles si trova la zona di *Monterey*, tappa amata da tutti i turisti per le sue missioni storiche e per le bellezze naturali. Si segue poi per *Los Angeles* o, più precisamente, per *West Hollywood*, la materializzazione del sogno americano, maniaco per le auto, lo status sociale e per il culto del corpo. Per chi dà molto valore all'aspetto fisico, dunque, è un vero paradiso. Più a sud nella contea di Orange si trovano *Disneyland* presso Anaheim e la stazione balneare di *Laguna Beach* amata da gay ed artisti. Con ingenti quantità d'acqua, che conferiscono umidità al suolo ed all'aria, viene mantenuto in vita, nel mezzo del deserto, la città turistica di Palm Springs. Qui il visitatore può godere un grandioso ed incomparabile paesaggio desertico e montano. A sud ovest sulla costa si trova San Diego, una delle più grandi città degli USA caratterizzata da basi militari (che costituiscono il fattore economico principale) e da un vivace ambiente gay.

Allegany ☎ 916

HOTELS

Kenton Mine Lodge (F GLM H)
PO Box 942 ✉CA 95910 ☎ 287-3212
Open durings season. Call for dates and room rates.

Anaheim ☎ 714

HOTELS

Anaheim A Penny Inn Motel (AC CC g H pi)
1800 West Lincoln Boulevard ✉CA 92801 ☎ 774-0950
Fax: 497-8598
County Comfort B&B (bf GLM H)
5104 East Valencia Drive ✉CA 92669 ☎ 532-2802

Auburn

CRUISING

-Nude Beach on American river (downstream)

Bakersfield ☎ 661

BARS

Casablanca Club (B D GLM) 18.30-2 h
1030 20th Street ✉CA 93301 ☎ 324-1384
The Cellar (B D GLM YG) 17-2 h
1927 K Street ✉CA 93301 ☎ 322-1229

GENERAL GROUPS

Friends 18.30-23 h
PO Box 304 ✉CA 93302 ☎ 323-7311
Support group & community outreach.
Gay AA Mon Wed 20 h
2421 Alta Vista Drive ✉CA 93305 ☎ 327-3724

CRUISING

-Beach Park (21st Street/Oak Street nights AYOR)

Boonville ☎ 707

RESTAURANTS

Boont Berry Farm Store (b F glm) 10-18 h, closed Sun
Highway 128, Santa Rosa-Ukiah ✉CA 95415 ☎ 895-3576

HOTELS

Toll House Bed and Breakfast (b bf F glm H wh) Thu-Tue
Highway 253, Santa Rosa-Ukiah ✉CA 95415 ☎ 895-3630
Fax: 895-3632

Buena Park ☎ 714

BARS

Ozz Restaurant (B D F GLM S)
6231 Manchester Boulevard ☎ 522-1542
Popular with Disneyland employees. Piano player & disco. Call for details.

Burbank

FETISH GROUPS

Iron Tigers MC
PO Box 70 91 ✉CA 91510
Harley-Davidson owners.

Castroville ☎ 408

BARS

Franco's Norma Jean Bar (B D F G S)
10639 Merritt Street ✉CA 95012 ☎ 633-2090

Cathedral City ☎ 760

HOTELS

The Villa Resort (CC GLM msg pi sa wh)
67-670 Carey Road ✉CA 92234 ☎ 328-72 11 Fax: 321 14 63
E-Mail: reservations@thevilla.com Homepage: www.thevilla.com
All rooms with bath/shower and WC, wash-basin, telephone, Satellite TV, radio, air-conditioning. Double and single room rates $49-130 incl. continental breakfast.

Cerritos ☎ 562

RESTAURANTS

Avenue 3 Cafe and Catering (AC CC F glm) 11-21 h
12612 South Street ✉CA 90703 ☎ 865-9215 Fax: 860-6575

Chico ☎ 530

GAY INFO

Gay Hotline
☎ 891-5718

GENERAL GROUPS

Chic State Student Group
☎ 898-4420

Clear Lake ☎ 707

HOTELS

Blue Fish Cove Resort (GLM pi)
10573 East Highway 20 ✉CA 95422 ☎ 998-1769
Sunset Point Resort (B F GLM sa)
12037 East Highway 20 ✉CA 95423-0455 ☎ 998-9475
Sunset Point Bar/Restaurant on premises.

CRUISING
-Austin Beach Park (Clear Lake Highlands
-Kneeling Park
-Library Park (Lakeport)

Cloverdale ☎ 707

HOTELS
Vintage Towers B&B (bf glm H)
302 North Main Street ✉CA 95425 ☎ 894-4535

Costa Mesa ☎ 714

BARS
Tin Lizzie Saloon (B G N) 12-2 h, WE 14-2 h
752 St. Clair Street ✉CA 92626 ☎ 966-2029

DANCECLUBS
Lion's Den (B D G MA)
719 W. 19th Street ✉CA 92627 ☎ 645-3830

Eureka ☎ 707

BARS
Club Triangle (B D glm) 21-2 h, Sun Gay
535 5th Street ✉CA 95501 ☎ 444-2582
Lost Coast Brewery Pub (AC B CC F glm MA N) 11-1h
617 4th Street ✉CA 95501 ☎ 445-4480
Lesbian brewpub.

BOOK SHOPS
Booklegger
402 2nd Street ✉CA 95501 ☎ 445-1344
Some Gay titles.

HOTELS
Carter House (bf H)
301 L Street ✉CA 95501 ☎ 444 8062

Fresno ☎ 209

GAY INFO
Community Link Inc.
1130 North Wishon ✉CA 93728 ☎ 264-6973
Call for drop-in hours.
G.U.S. Inc. Mon-Fri 8-17 h
1999 Tuolumne, Suite 625 ✉CA 93701 ☎ 268-3541
Counselling and referrals.

BARS
The Cave (B f G LJ MA) 16-02 h
4538 East Belmont ✉CA 93702 ☎ 251-5972
Express. The (B F D glm OS S VS) 17-2, Sun 15-2 h
708 North Blackstone ✉CA 93701 ☎ 233-1791
Palace (B glm S) 15-2 h
4030 East Belmont, ✉CA 93702 ☎ 264-8283
Red Lantern (B g N) 14-2 h
4618 East Belmont Street ✉CA 93702 ☎ 251-5898

SEX SHOPS/BLUE MOVIES
Only For You (glm) 12-22 h
1468 N. Van Ness Avenue ✉CA 93728 ☎ 498-0284
Video shop
Wildcat Book Store (g MA VS) 9-24, Sun 12-24 h
1535 Fresno Street ✉CA 93705 ☎ 237-4525
Erotica, magazines and videos.

BOOK SHOPS
Fig Garden Bookstore
5148 North Palm Avenue, ✉CA 93704
Gay/lesbian section.

FETISH GROUPS
Knights of Malta MC
Box 41 62, ✉CA 93744

RELIGIOUS GROUPS
MCC of Vineyard Sun 1.30 h
106 E. Shields Avenue ✉CA 93704 ☎ 224-3871

CRUISING
-Redeo Park (1st Street & Clinton Street)
-Roeding Park
-Tower District (Olive Street/Wishon Street)
-Woodward Park

Fullerton ☎ 714

SEX SHOPS/BLUE MOVIES
Errogeneous Zone
343 N. State College Boulevard ✉CA 92631 ☎ 879-3270

Garden Grove ☎ 714

GAY INFO
Orange County Gay and Lesbian Center 12-20 h, WE 18-22 h
12832 Garden Grove Boulevard ✉CA 92643 ☎ 534-0862

BARS
Happy Hour (B GLM)
12081 Garden Grove Boulevard ✉CA 92643 ☎ 537-9079
Nick's (B D G VS)
8284 Garden Grove Boulevard ✉CA 92644 ☎ 537-1361

DANCECLUBS
The Frat House (B D GLM VS) 21-2 h
8112 Garden Grove Boulevard ✉CA 92644 ☎ 897-3431
Popular.

Glenhaven ☎ 707

HOTELS
Lake Place Resort (AC glm H sa)
9515 Harbor Drive ✉CA 59443 ☎ 998-3331
Suburb location, 2 1/2 hours from San Francisco. All rooms with priv. bath/WC , kitchenette and balcony.

Hermost Beach ☎ 310

CAFÉS
Java Man Coffeehouse (A bf F GLM W WE) Mon-Fri 6-22 h, Sat+Sun 6-23 h
157 Pier Avenue ✉CA 90254 *(two blocks from beach)* ☎ 379 72 09
Oldest Coffeehouse in Hermost Beach in a Landmark beach house.

RESTAURANTS
Ocean Diner (AC bf CC F glm W WE) Mon-Fri 6-14 h, Sat+Sun 7-15 h
959 Aviation Blvd ✉CA 90254 *(next to Quality Inn Hotel)* ☎ 372 3739

Huntington Beach ☎ 714

TRAVEL & TRANSPORT

Golden Eagle Travel
7238 Heil Avenue ✉CA 92647 ☎ 848-9090

HOTELS

Colonial Inn Youth Hostel (glm H)
421 8th Street ✉CA 92648 ☎ 536-3315 Fax: 714-536-9485
Forty minutes south of Los Angeles International Airport. Dorms US$ 10 per person, double 12, weekly rates available.

Idyllwild ☎ 909

HOTELS

That Special Place (bf G H)
PO Box 21 81 ✉CA 92349 ☎ 659-5033
Bed & breakfast inn with individually decorated guest rooms with priv. baths and decks (some with fireplaces), and unsurpassed mountain views. Rates US$ 65-80, incl. bf.

Laguna Beach ☎ 714

BARS

Boom Boom Room (! B CC D G YG) 10-2 h
1401 Pacific Coast Highway ✉CA 92651 *(Mountain Road)* ☎ 494-7588
Hunky's Video Bar and Disco (AC B CC D glm VS YG) 10-2 h
1401 South Coast Highway ✉CA 92651 *(at Coast Inn)* ☎ 494-7588
Latest music videos and progressive house music.
Main Street (B GLM MA)
1460 South Coast Highway ✉CA 92651 ☎ 494-0056
Cozy piano bar.
Woody's (AC B CC F GLM MA) 17-01 h
1305 South Coast Highway ✉CA 92651 ☎ 376 8809

CAFÉS

Cafe Zinc Market
350 Ocean Avenue ✉CA 92651 ☎ 494-6302

RESTAURANTS

Cottage Restaurant (B bf F g MA OS WE) 7-15, 17-22 h
308 North Coast Highway ✉CA 92651 ☎ 494-3023
American cuisine.
Mark's (B F glm) 858 S.
Coast Highway ✉CA 92651 ☎ 494-6711

BOOK SHOPS

A Different Drummer Bookshoppe (CC GLM) 11-20 h
1027-A N. Coast Highway ✉CA 92651 ☎ 497-6699
Specialized in gay/lesbian literature, women's studies, spiritually & healing.

GIFT & PRIDE SHOPS

Gay Mart (! B CC G) 11-24 h
168 Mountain Road ✉CA 92651 *(across the street from Boom Boom Room)* ☎ 497-9108
Gifts, video rentals and club wear.

VIDEO SHOPS

Video Horizons (CC glm) Mon-Thu 11-21, Fri Sat -22, Sun 13-21 h
31678 South Coast Highway ✉CA 92677 ☎ 499-4519

HOTELS

By The Sea Inn (AC G H pi sa sb wh)
475 North Coast Highway ✉CA 92651 ☎ 497-6645
☎ (800) 297-0007 (toll free) Fax: 497-9499
Garden, downtown neighborhood location, 1,6 km from all gay bars, 20 min to the airport. All rooms with telephone, priv. bath, jacuzzi, some with kitchenette and balcony.
Carriage House (H G OS)
1322 Catalina Street, ✉CA 92677 ☎ 494-8945
Centrally located, 1 1/2 hours from L.A. airport. All rooms with kitchenette, priv. bath and balcony.
Coast Inn (B d f G H)
1401 South Coast Highway, ✉CA 92651 ☎ 494-7588
☎ (800) 653-2697 (toll free)
Also the „Boom Boom Room" and „Boom Café"
Hotel Firenze (H G)
1289 South Coast Highway ✉CA 92651 ☎ 497-2446
Tides Motor Inn (AC CC glm H OS pi)
460 North Coast Highway ✉CA 92651 ☎ 494-2494
Fax: 497-8598.

SWIMMING

-West Street Beach (at the south end of the laguna)

Lake Tahoe ☎ 619

HOTELS

Bavarian House B&B (bf GLM H)
PO Box 62 45 07 ✉CA 96154 ☎ 916/544-4411
☎ (800) 431-4411 (Toll free)

Lancaster ☎ 805

BARS

Back Door (B D GLM) 18-2 h
1255 West Avenue I ✉CA 93534 ☎ 945-2566

Long Beach ☎ 562

GAY INFO

Long Beach Gay & Lesbian Community Center (CC GLM MA S) 9-22, Sat 9-18 h
2017 East 4th Street ✉CA 90814 ☎ 434-4455 Fax: 433-6428
E-Mail: center@millenia.com, http://millenia.com/~center

BARS

Brit (B D G MA N) 10-2 h
1744 East Broadway Avenue ✉CA 90802 ☎ 432-9742
Happy hour 16-19 h
Broadway (B G MA N) 10-2 h
1100 East Broadway Avenue ✉CA 90802 ☎ 432-3646
Club Broadway (B D gLM MA N) 11-2 h
3348 East Broadway Avenue ✉CA 90803 ☎ 438-7700
Club 5211/Inspiration (AC B CC f GLM MA N S STV TV W WE) 8-2, Fri-Sat after hour club 2-4/? h
5211 North Atlantic Avenue ✉CA 90805 ☎ 423-9860
Happy hour daily 8-20 h
Crest. The (B G LJ MA OS) Wed-Mon 14-2, Tue 17-2 h
5935 Cherry Avenue ✉CA 90804 ☎ 423-6650
Executive Suite (B D GLM MA SNU) 20-2 h, Tue closed
3428 East Pacific Coast Highway ✉CA 90804 ☎ 597-3884

Falcon. The (AC B CC G MA N) 09-2 h
1435 East Broadway ✉CA 90802 ☎ 432-4146
Friendly cruise bar.
Fennel and Hops (B F glm)
1800 E. Broadway ✉CA 90802 ☎ 590-8773
Floyd's (B D G) 18-2, Sun 14-2 h, Mon closed
2913 East Anaheim Street ✉CA 90804 *(Entrance on Gladys Street)* ☎ 433-9251
Mineshaft. The (B G LJ MA) 10-2 h
1720 East Broadway Avenue ✉CA 90802 ☎ 436-2433
Happy hour 16-19 h. Popular.
Pistons
2020 Artesia Boulevard ✉CA 90805 ☎ 422-1928
Ripples (! AC CC D G MA S VS YG) 12-2 h
5101 East Ocean Boulevard ✉CA 90803 *(across street from beach)* ☎ 433-0357
Two levels, two bars, two dance floors, upstairs bar has a panaramic view of the Pacific Ocean, smoking patio in club.
Silver Fox (AC B G MA N VS) 12-22 h
411 Redondo Avenue ✉CA 90814 ☎ 439-6343
Happy hour is very popular.
Styx
5823 Atlantic Avenue ✉CA 90805 ☎ 422-5997
Sweetwater Saloon (B G MA N) 6-2 h
1201 East Broadway Avenue ✉CA 90802 ☎ 432-7044
Cruisy atmosphere

DANCECLUBS

Que Sera Sera (AC B D GLM MA S STV) Mon-Fri 17-2, Sat-Sun 14-2 h
1923 E. 7th Street ✉CA 90813 ☎ 599-6170

RESTAURANTS

Babouch Moroccan Restaurant (AC CC E F glm MA S W) Tue-Sun 17-24 h, closed Mon
810 S. Gaffey Street, San Pedro ✉CA 90731 ☎ 831-0246
Birds of Paradise (B F GLM MA S) 10-1 h
1800 E. Broadway ✉CA 90802 ☎ 590-8773
Happy hour 16-19 h
Madame JoJo (b F GLM) 17-22 h, Sun-Mon closed
2941 Broadway Avenue ✉CA 90803 ☎ 439-3672

SEX SHOPS/BLUE MOVIES

Hot Stuff (g)
2121 East Broadway ✉CA 90803 ☎ 433-0692

SAUNAS/BATHS

1350 Club (b CC G OS S sa sb VS) 0-24 h
510 West Anaheim Street ✉CA 90744 *(Los Angeles-Wilmington)* ☎ (310) 830-4784

RELIGIOUS GROUPS

Christ Chapel (GLM)
3935 East 10th Street ✉CA 90804 ☎ 438-5303

Los Angeles ☎ 213

● Nowhere in the US does the dream of stardom, wealth and luxury come more true than in Los Angeles. And nowhere else can the corresponding nightmare of highway congestions, brutal race riots and a gigantic city without urbanity be more vividly seen. Speaking of gay L.A. means in reality speaking of the autonomous city of *West Hollywood*, one of the gayest centers of north America. Santa Monica Boulevard could also be called Rainbow Boulevard. The gay center of Los Angeles is in *Silverlake* to the north of *Downtown*. Smaller centers of gay life are in the Valley to the north of Los Angeles conurbation, on the beaches to the west and in Long Beach to the south. A car is indispensible. With it you can reach the gay resort *Laguna Beach* in 90 minutes. A lot, which seems to be gay, is only a facade, but what can one expect in the city, where façades are produced for films. And looking behind the façade of Hollywood is nearly impossible; production halls are not that impressive. Small glimpses of the myth can be gotten on the *Walk of Fame* on Hollywood Boulevard or in the *Universal Studios* on Hollywood Freeway. But one product of Los Angeles is not just façade: the charity for AIDS-victims. Events like the *California AIDS Ride* (on bycicle) or the *AIDS Walk LA* bring large amounts of money for the AIDS-stricken, plus the opportunity to exhibit yourself and keep fit. An activity, which can also be done beautifully in *Venice* on the coast. More reasons for visiting L.A. are the pride-events or the gay days at *Disneyland*. For further activities have a look in one of four gay maganzines: *Edge, Frontiers, Nightlife* and *fab!*.

✸ Nirgendwo sonst kommen die USA dem Traum von Starruhm, Reichtum und Luxus näher. Und nirgendwo sonst ist der dazugehörige Alptraum eindrucksvoller zu erleben: Stundenlange Autobahnstaus, gewalttätige Rassenunruhen, eine Riesenstadt ohne jegliche Urbanität.
Spricht man in schwuler Hinsicht von L.A., dann meint man am ehesten die eigenständige Stadt *West Hollywood*, eine der schwulsten städtischen Gegenden Nordamerikas. Der Santa Monica Boulevard könnte ebensogut Rainbow Boulevard heißen. Los Angeles' schwules Zentrum findet sich in *Silverlake*, nördlich der *Downtown*.
Kleinere Ballungen schwuler Adressen finden sich auch im Valley (im Norden des Ballungsraumes), an den Beaches (im Westen) und in Long Beach (im Süden). Bei diesen Entfernungen ist ein Auto unerlässlich, mit dem man den recht schwulen Badeort *Laguna Beach* im Süden in etwa 90 Minuten erreicht.
Natürlich ist vieles, was so schwul erscheint, nur Fassade. Doch wie sollte es anders sein in der Stadt, in der sich die Fassade *Hollywood* befindet. Zu sehen ist von der allerdings nicht viel, Produktionshallen machen eben keinen Eindruck. Kleine Einblicke in den Mythos erlangt man dennoch am *Walk of Fame* am Hollywood Boulevard oder den *Universal Studios* am Hollywood Freeway. Ein Besuch des neuen Paul Getty Museums ist nicht nur für Kunstfreunde ein Muß.
Eines jedoch ist ganz sicherlich nicht aufgesetzt: Charity, Wohltätigkeit, für die Opfer von AIDS. Veranstaltungen wie der *California AIDS Ride* (per Rad) oder der *AIDS Walk LA* (per pedes) generieren Unsummen für die Betroffenen. Und damit ideale Gelegenheiten, sich sowohl zu zeigen, als auch fit zu halten. Eine Tätigkeit, die sich übrigens auch in *Venice* am Ozean vorzüglich betrachten lässt.
Weitere Gelegenheiten für einen Besuch LAs sind die Pride-Veranstaltungen oder die schwulen Thementage im *Disneyland* in Anaheim. Weitere Vorschläge entnimmt man einem der vier schwulen Blätter: *Edge, Frontiers, Nightlife* oder *fabs*.

▲ Nulle part ailleurs aux Etats-Unis, vous ne verrez ce que peut être le rêve américain: gloire, célébrité, luxe. Et aussi le cauchemar que ça peut être: embouteillages monstres, violentes émeutes raciales, ville énorme sans aucune urbanité et tutti quanti...
Quand on parle du Los Angeles gay, on pense plutôt à West Hollywood, un des bastions gays d'Amérique du Nord. Le Santa Monica Boulevard est aux mains des gays. Le centre gay de Los Angeles se trouve à Silverlake au nord de Downtown.
Les quartiers nord (Valley), ouest (Beaches) et sud (Long Beach) valent également le détour au niveau gay. Vu les distances, une voiture est nécessaire. Pour aller à Laguna Beach, par exemple, il faut environ une heure et demie. Attention: tout ce qui a l'air gay, ne l'est pas forcément! Comme beaucoup d'autres choses, tout est façade ici. Hollywood en premier lieu. D'Hollywood, on ne voit pas grand chose, si ce n'est que le „Walk of Fame" sur le Hollywood Boulevard ou les „Universal Studios" sur le Hollywood Freeway.

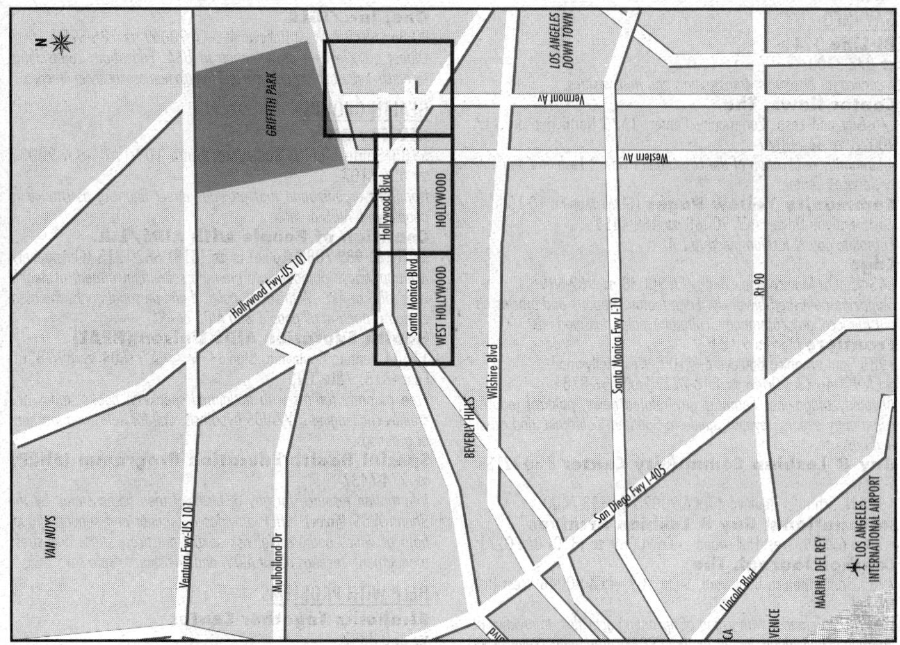

Une chose au moins n'est pas du cinéma: la „Charity" pour les victimes du SIDA. Le „California AIDS Ride" (course de bicyclette) et le „AIDS Walk LA" (course à pied) sont des manifestations qui rapportent d'importantes sommes d'argent que l'on distribue aux malades. Deux bonnes occasions de se montrer et de se maintenir en bonne santé. Les amateurs de culturisme se donnent rendez-vous à Venice Beach.
Profitez de la „Gay Pride" ou des journées gays de Disney Land (Anaheim) pour découvrir Los Angeles. Pour de plus amples informations, consultez les magasines gays „Edge", „Frontiers", „Nightlife" et „fab!".

☆ En ningún otro lugar de los E.E.U.U. se deja palpar el sueño de éxito, riqueza y lujo, pero tampoco en ningún otro lugar se pueden vivir en carne propia las pesadillas de los enormes congestionamientos viales, violentas disputas rasistas y la falta de sentido de urbanidad. Si se quiere hablar del ambiente gay de L.A. se debe hacer mención inmediata de la ciudad autónoma *West Hollywood.* El Santa Mónica Boulevard podría también llevar el nombre de Rainbow Boulevard. El centro gay de L.A. se encuentra en *Silverlake* al norte de *Downtown.* Pequeñas agrupaciones de direcciones gay se encuentran en Valley (al norte de la aglomeración urbana), en las playas (en el oeste) y en Long Beach (en el sur). Un coche es de vital importancia, debido a las grandes distancias que se deben recorrer. A *Laguna Beach* en el sur, se llega alcanzar en cuestión de 90 min.. Muchos sitios que parecen a primera vista ser gays, lo son solamente de fachada. Pero que se puede esperar de una ciudad que se dedica a la producción de ilusiones. No hay mucho que visitar de esta fábrica de suenos, ya que las salas de producción no provocan pasiones. Un pequeño vistazo en el mito que envuelve a esta ciudad se puede recibir en el *Walk of Fame* en el Hollywood Boulevard o en el *Universal Studios* en Hollywood Freeway. Las obras de caridad para los afectados de SIDA son de especial mención. La organización de eventos como *California AIDS Ride* (en bicicleta) o la *AIDS Walk L.A.* (a pie) generan grandes cantidades de dinero para los afectados así como la oportunidad ideal para mostrarse y mantenerse en forma. Otras oportunidades ideales para visitar L.A. son las fiestas de Pride Gay (orgullo gay) o los días de tematización de la cuestión homosexual en *Disneyland* en Anaheim. Las revistas *Edge, Frontiers, Nightlife* y *fab!* dan más informaciones detalladas.

❖ In nessun luogo gli Stati Uniti si avvicinano tanto al sogno di gloria, ricchezza e lusso come in questa città, e da nessuna parte è possibile vivere l'impressionante incubo concomitante il sogno: code stradali interminabili, violenti conflitti razziali e una città senza urbanità. Chi parla della vita gay di Los Angeles intende *West Hollywood,* la zona urbana più gay del Nordamerica. Il boulevard Santa Monica potrebbe chiamarsi bouleverd dell'arcobaleno. Il centro gay di Los Angeles si trova a *Silverlake* a nord di *Downtown.* Concentrazioni più piccole di indirizzi gay si trovano anche a Valley (a nord della zona densamente abitata), alle Beaches (ad ovest) e a Long Beach (a sud). Considerate le grandi distanze è indispensabile un'automobile: potrete raggiungere così in 90 minuti la stazione balneare di *Laguna Beach.* La vita gay è molto influenzata dalle apparenze, ma come potrebbe essere altrimenti ad Hollywood. Qui non vi è molto da vedere, considerato che i capannoni di produzione non sono un grande spettacolo. Potrete ottenere piccole impressione sul mito di Hollywood al *Walk of fame,* sull'Hollywood Boulevard o negli *Universal Studios* sull'Hollywood Freeway. Una cosa però non è artificiale: charity, la beneficenza per le vittime dell'AIDS. Manifestazioni come *California AIDS ride* (in bicicletta) o *AIDS Walk LA* (a piedi) raccolgono ingenti somme e creano occasioni per mostrarsi e per mantenersi in forma; è possibile fare sport anche a *Venice* sull'oceano. Altre occasioni per visitare L.A. sono le manifestazioni Pride e i giorni dei temi gay a *Disneyland* ad Anaheim. Potrete trovare altre informazioni nelle 4 pubblicazioni *Edge, Fontiers, Nightlife* o *fab!*.

GAY INFO

Bi-Line 0-24 h
☎ 873-3700
A service for bisexuals, transsexuals and transvestites.

Center News. The
c/o Gay and Lesb. Community Center, 1625 North Hudson ✉CA 90028 ☎ 464-0029
A bimonthly publication of the Los Angeles Gay & Lesbian Community Services Center.

Community Yellow Pages (GLM) Mon-Fri 10-18 h
2305 Canyon Drive, ✉CA 90068 ☎ 469-4454
Complete gay & lesbian guide to L.A.

Edge
6434 Santa Monica Boulevard ✉CA 90038 ☎ 962-6994
Magazine published biweekly. Edge features reports and articles about the local gay community, cultural events, classified ads.

Frontiers Mon-Fri 9-18 h
7985 Santa Monica Boulevard, #109, West Hollywood,
✉CA 90046 *CA 90046* ☎ 848-2222 Fax: 656-8784
Biweekly magazine. Features gay related news, political reports, community events, reviews, guide to Southern California, and classified ads.

Gay & Lesbian Community Center 8.30-22, Sat 9-22 h
1625 N. Schrader Boulevard ✉CA 90028 ☎ 993-7400

International Gay & Lesbian Archives
PO Box 69679, West Hollywood, ✉CA 90069 ☎ (310) 845-0271

Leather Journal. The
7985 Santa Monica Boulevard, Suite 109, ✉CA 90046 West Hollywood
Club News Calendar with listing of upcoming activities, Interviews of prominent individuals in the leather/S&M community, Reviews of major S&M/ leather communities in the U.S.A., classified ads.

Reactions
PO Box 12 70, Studio City, ✉CA 91614-0270
☎ (818) 877-1000 ☎ (818) 980-8800.

Tom of Finland Foundation
1421 Laveta Terrace, ✉ CA 90026 ☎ 250-1685
Fax: 213-481-2092
Non-profit archives established to collect, preserve, exhibit and publish Tom's drawings.

Update
1525 North Gardener Avenue, ✉CA 90046
Is a general newspaper published every Wed in Southern California. Features national and international news on the gay scene/reviews of movies, theater, art, music, books and sports; lots of classifieds.

TOURIST INFO

Los Angeles Convention & Visitor Bureau
633 West Fifth Street, Suite 6000 ✉CA 90071 ☎ 624-7300
Fax: 624-9746

RESTAURANTS

Marks Restaurant (AC B CC F G MA OS) Mon-Wed 18-22:30, Thu-Sat -01:30, Sun 11-14:30 & 17-22:30h
861 North LaCienega Blvb. ✉CA 90069 ☎ 310/652-5252

GENERAL GROUPS

Black & White Men Together
7985 Santa Monica Boulevard ✉CA 90046 ☎ (818) 250-0904

Gay and Lesbian Latinos Unidos
1625 Hudson Street ✉CA 90038 ☎ 780-9943

Golden State Gay Rodeo Association Greater Los Angeles Chapter
8033 Sunset Boulevard, Ste. 41, ✉CA 90046 ☎ (310) 498-1675

One, Inc./IGLA
PO Box 69679, West Hollywood ✉CA 90069 ☎ 735-5252
Oldest gay/lesbian organization in USA. Education, counselling, research, largest library on male and female homosexuality in America.

HEALTH GROUPS

AID for AIDS
6985 Santa Monica Boulevard, Suite 109-171 ✉CA 90038 ☎ 656-1107
Nonprofit organization that provides direct financial assistance to people with AIDS or ARC.

Coalition of People with AIDS/L.A.
☎ (818) 989-7085 (Louie) or ☎ (818) 662-1213 (Christopher)
A group whose purpose is to promote self-empowerment of people with AIDS or ARC. With social, political and personal goals, the association is open to all people with AIDS or ARC.

Health Education AIDS Liaison (HEAL)
11684 Ventura Boulevard, Studio City ✉ CA 91604 ☎ 896-8260
Fax: (818) 780-7093
Free monthly forums with acclaimed speakers; books, tapes and studies challenging HIV/AIDS hypothsis. Call for dates and locations of meetings.

Special Health Education Programm (SHEP)
☎ 274-7437
Information resource for gay or bisexual men administered by the Shanti AIDS Project. SHEP provides a seminar and support group, both of which address high-risk sexual practices, stress and stress managment, feelings about AIDS, and adjusting to safe sex.

HELP WITH PROBLEMS

Alcoholics Together Center
☎ 663-8882

Positive Living for US (PLUS)
☎ 885-0640 ☎ 852-1480
Support for HIV-positives.

Sex Information Helpline
☎ 653-1123

RELIGIOUS GROUPS

Beth Chayim Chadashim
6000 West Pico Boulevard ✉CA 90035 ☎ 931-7023
Jewish gays/lesbians. Services Fri 20.30 h.

Lutherans Concerned
☎ 660-6695
Worship, potluck held every 2nd Sun 17 h at St. Matthew's Lutheran Church, 11031 Camarillo Street, North Hollywood.

CRUISING

-Griffith Park (AYOR) (by golf course and Ferndale loop parking lot)
-Beverly Center
-De Longpre Park (AYOR)
-Santa Monica Boulevard (anywhere in West Hollywood)
-Main Street
-Area around block by Gauntlet II
-Sunset Drive (near Vista Theater)
-Encino Park (AYOR)
-Griffith Park (near Sonora and Victory)
-Sepulveda Dam Recreation Area (West end of parking lot)
-Valley Plaza Park

Los Angeles - Downtown ☎ 213

BARS

Red Head. The (B GLM MA N SNU) 14-2 h
2218 East 1st Street ✉CA 90033 ☎ 263-2995

Score (B D G N) 10-2 h
107 West 4th Street ✉CA 90013 ☎ 625-7382
Popular with Latinos.

DANCECLUBS

Catch One (B D GLM S W YG) 15-2, Fri-Sat -4, Thu-Sat from 21 h dancing
4067 West Pico Boulevard ✉CA 90019 ☎ 734-8849
Popular club which attracts a diverse crowd. Special theme nights.

SAUNAS/BATHS

Midtowne Spa (B G OS pi S sa sb VS wh) 0-24 h
615 South Kohler Street ✉CA 90021 ☎ 680-1838

Los Angeles - East L.A.

BARS

Plush Pony (D S)
5261 Alhambra Avenue ✉CA 90032 *(El Sereno)*
☎ (213) 224-9488
Mainly Latino clientele.

HOTELS

The Whittier House (AC F GLM MA OS) 1
2133 South Colima Road, Whittier ✉CA 90604
☎ (562) 941-7222
Near Disneyland. Early-California/Spanish style, antique furnishings, fireplace, TV. Two night minimum stay on weekends or holidays. Rates US$ 65-70, double $75-90 (bf incl.).

Los Angeles - Hollywood ☎ 213

BARS

Arena (B D GLM MA) Fri -4 h
6655 Santa Monica Boulevard ✉CA 90038 ☎ 462-1742

Blacklite. The (B GLM N) 6-2 h
1159 North Western Avenue ✉CA 90029 ☎ 469-0211

Faultline. The (! B G lj MA) Tue-Fri 16-2, Sat-Sun 14-2 h, closed Mon
4216 Melrose Avenue ✉CA 90029 ☎ 660-0889
Popular. Sun afternoon beer bust.

Ming's Dynasty (B G MA s) Tue-Sun 20-2 h
5221 Hollywood Boulevard ✉CA 90027 ☎ 462-2039

Rawhide (AC B CC f G LJ OS s VS) Tue-Thu & Sat 18-2 h, Fri 16-2 h, Sun 14-24 h
10937 Burbank Blvd ✉CA 91601 ☎ 818/760-9798

Spotlight (B G N R) 6-2 h
1601 North Cahuenga Boulevard ✉CA 90028 ☎ 467-2425

Study. The (! B G MA N) 10-2 h
1723 North Western Avenue ✉CA 90027 ☎ 464-9551
Friendly neighborhood cocktail lounge. Popular with Afro-Americans.

MEN'S CLUBS

M-B Club (CC DR G lj MA P VS) Mon-Thu 16-4, Fri -5, Sat 15-5, Sun -4 h
4550 Melrose Avenue ✉CA 90029 ☎ (323) 669-9899

DANCECLUBS

Circus Disco (! B D G MA) Tue 21-2, Fri 21-4 h
6655 Santa Monica Boulevard ✉CA 90038 ☎ 462-1291
Mainly Latino and African-American crowd

Probe (! AC B D G LJ P) Sat 21-10, Sun 21-2 h
836 North Highland Avenue ✉CA 90038 ☎ 461-8301
Best AC, best music and best bodies in LA. Please be prepared to show your bare chest. Membership US$ 20.

Tempo (! B D G s) 20-2, Fri-Sat -4 h
5520 Santa Monica Boulevard ✉CA 90038 ☎ 466-1094
Inexpensive and very friendly. GLM on Wed and Thu, L on Sun. Latino nights Tue.

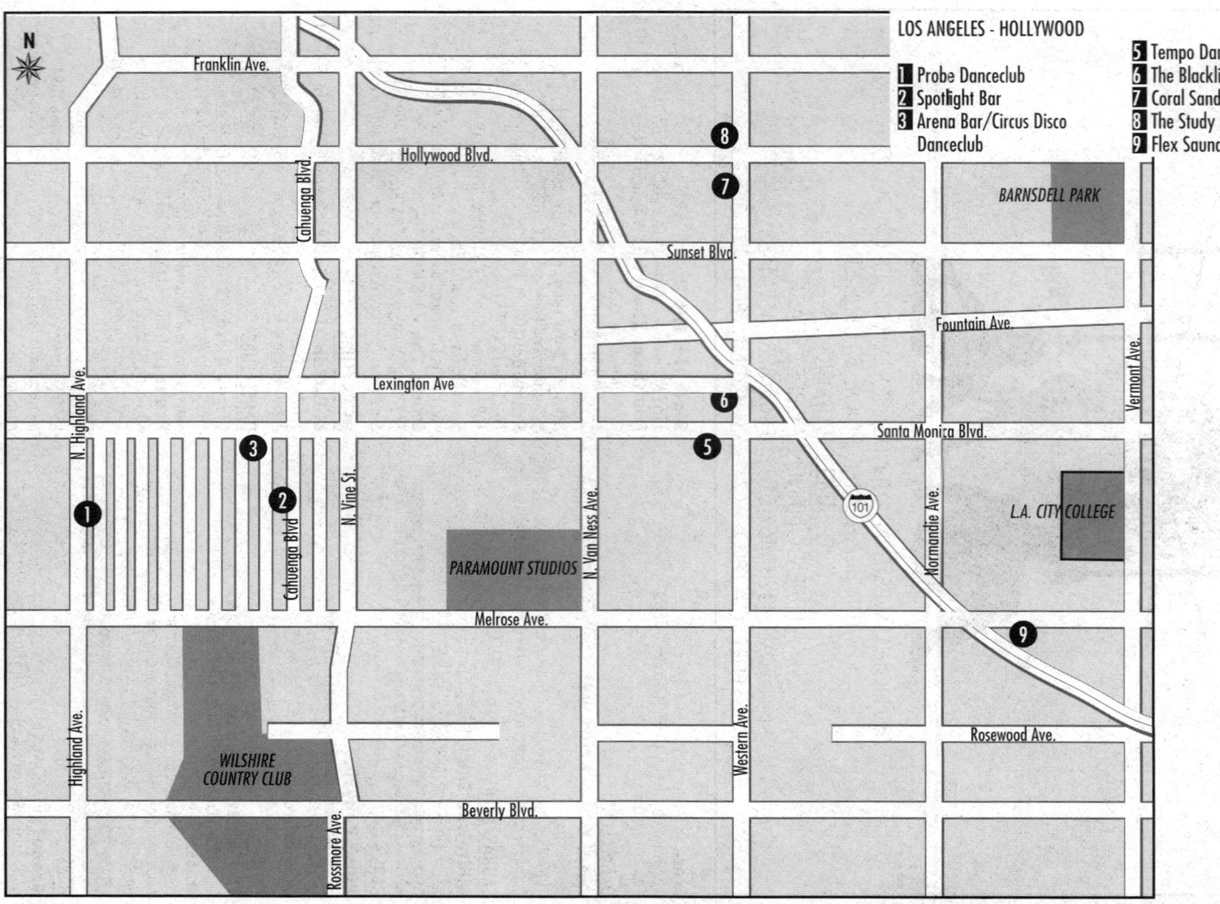
LOS ANGELES - HOLLYWOOD
1 Probe Danceclub
2 Spotlight Bar
3 Arena Bar/Circus Disco Danceclub
5 Tempo Danceclub
6 The Blacklite Bar
7 Coral Sands Hotel
8 The Study Bar
9 Flex Sauna
N
Franklin Ave.
Hollywood Blvd.
Cahuenga Blvd.
Sunset Blvd.
BARNSDELL PARK
Fountain Ave.
Vermont Ave.
Lexington Ave
Santa Monica Blvd.
N. Highland Ave.
N. Vine St.
Cahuenga Blvd
N. Van Ness Ave.
101
Normandie Ave.
L.A. CITY COLLEGE
PARAMOUNT STUDIOS
Melrose Ave.
Western Ave.
Rosewood Ave.
Highland Ave.
WILSHIRE COUNTRY CLUB
Beverly Blvd.
Rossmore Ave.

RESTAURANTS

La Poubelle (b F glm) Mon-Thu 17.30-23.15, Fri Sat 17.30-24 h
5907 Franklin Avenue ✉CA 90028 ☎ 462-9264 ☎ 465-0807
French cooking.

SHOWS

Cinegrill (AC B CC E f glm H MG S W) 2 shows each night
Roosevelt Hotel, 7000 Hollywood Boulevard ✉CA 90028 ☎ 466-7000
Cabaret.

SEX SHOPS/BLUE MOVIES

Casanova's East
1626 ½ Cahuenga Boulevard ✉CA 90028 ☎ 465-9435
Highland Books Inc. (g VS) 0-24 h
6775 Santa Monica Boulevard ✉CA 90028 ☎ 463-0295
Le Sex Shoppe 0-24
6315 1/2 Hollywood Boulevard ✉CA 90028 ☎ 464-9435
Pit Shop 14-2 h
1064 Myra Avenue ✉CA 90029 ☎ 660-0323

SAUNAS/BATHS

Flex (CC DR f G MA NU OS P pi sa sb VS wh WO) 0-24 h
4424 Melrose Avenue ✉CA 90029 ☎ 663-7786
Hollywood Spa (! AC G P sa sb VS wh WO) 0-24 h
1650 Ivar Avenue, Hollywood ✉CA 90028 ☎ 463-5169
ID required. Popular.

HOTELS

Chateau Marmont (AC b g H pi)
8221 Sunset Boulevard West ✉CA 90046 ☎ 656-1010
Very luxurious; 20 minutes from downtown Los Angeles, 30 min to the airport. All rooms with priv. bath/WC, telephone, kitchenette, balcony. US$ 90-400.
Coral Sands Hotel (AC bf G H lj pi sa wh) All year / 24h
1730 North Western Avenue ✉CA 90027 ☎ 323/467-5141 Fax: 323/467-4683
Located in the heart of Hollywood. All rooms with fridge, bath/WC, TV, telephone, safe, hair-dryer and room-service. Rates single from US$ 58, double 68 (+ tax) incl. bf.
Saharan Motor Hotel (AC CC f glm H MA N OS pi)
7212 Sunset Boulevard ✉CA 90046 ☎ 874-6700
E-Mail: Sahara-Jaco@worldnet.att.net
45 minutes to the airport. Hollywood location. All rooms with phone, kitchenette, bath/WC.

GUEST HOUSES

Hilltop House. The (AC bf G H pi wh)
3307 Bonnie Hill Drive ✉CA 90068 ☎ 883-0073 Fax: 969-0073
E-Mail: 81235@aol.com.

GENERAL GROUPS

International Gay Penpals
Ste. 320, PO Box 7304, ✉CA 91603

BARS

Bananas (B CC D G MA OS s SNU) 12-2 h
7026 Reseda Boulevard, Reseda ✉CA 91335 *(south of Sherman Way)* ☎ 996-2976
Special events every week, Good WE crowd. Cute young staff. Popular.
Bullet. The (B G LJ MA OS) 12-2 h, happy hour Mon-Sat 12-20 h
10522 Burbank Boulevard, North Hollywood ✉CA 91601 ☎ 760-9563
Escapades (! B D GLM MA N) 13-2 h
10437 W. Burbank Boulevard, North Hollywood ✉CA 92601 ☎ 508-7008
Pool tables. Popular.
Gold 9 (B D G MA N S) 11-2 h
13625 Moorpark Street, Sherman Oaks ✉CA 91423 ☎ 986-0285
Jox (B G N S) Mon-Fri 16-2, Sat-Sun 12-2 h
10721 Burbank Boulevard, North Hollywood ✉CA 91601 ☎ 760-9031
Lodge. The (! B d G N S) 12-2 h
4923 Lankershim Boulevard, North Hollywood ✉CA 91601 ☎ 769-7722
Neighborhood bar with fireplace. Popular.
Mag Lounge (B D G YG) 11-2 h
5248 Van Nuys Boulevard, Van Nuys ✉CA 91401 ☎ 981-6693
Popular dance bar.
Oasis (B G OS VS) 14-2 h
11916 Ventura Boulevard, Studio City ✉CA 91604 ☎ 980-4811
Cozy piano bar with a relaxed atmosphere.
Oxwood Inn (B D gLM) 15-2, Fri Sun 12-2 h
13713 Oxnard Street, Van Nuys ✉CA 91401 ☎ 997-9666
Queen Mary (! B G STV) Wed Sun 11-2 h
12449 Ventura Boulevard, Studio City ✉CA 91604 ☎ 506-5619
King's Den Bar on premises. Popular.
Rawhide (AC B CC D f G LJ MA N OS) Mon-Sat 18.30-2, Sun 14-24 h
10937 Burbank Boulevard, North Hollywood ✉CA 91601 ☎ 760-9798
Country western style.
Silver Rail (AC B G lj MA VS YG) Sep-May: Mon-Fri 16-2, Sat Sun 12-2 h, Jun-Aug: 10-2 h
11518 Barbork Boulevard, North Hollywood ☎ 980-8310

DANCECLUBS

Apache (B D G lj) Mon-Thu 20-2, Fri Sat 20-4, Sun 16-2 h
11608 Ventura Boulevard, Studio City ✉CA 91604 ☎ 506-0404
Popular.

RESTAURANTS

Venture Inn (B CC F GLM MA N WE YG) 11-2 h
11938 Ventura Boulevard, Studio City, ✉CA 91604 ☎ 769-5400

SEX SHOPS/BLUE MOVIES

Big Apple Video
10654 Magnolia Boulevard, North Hollywood ✉CA 91601 ☎ 769-0325
Le Sex Shoppe
4539 Van Nuys Boulevard, Sherman Oaks ✉CA 91403 ☎ 501-9609
Other stores : 21625 Sherman Way, Canoga Park and 12323 Ventura Boulevard, Studio City.

Twisted Video Rental & Sales
10530 Burbank Boulevard, North Hollywood ✉CA 91601 ☎ 508-0559

Video West
11376 W. Ventura Boulevard, Studio City ✉CA 91604 ☎ 760-0096

Video'n Stuff
11612 Ventura Boulevard, Studio City ✉CA 91604 ☎ 761-3162

SAUNAS/BATHS

North Hollywood Spa (G p S sa sb sol VS wh WO) 0-24 h
5636 Vineland Avenue, North Hollywood, ✉CA 91601 ☎ (800) 772-2582

Roman Holiday Health Club (B f G msg pi sa sb wh) 0-24 h
14435 Victory Boulevard, Van Nuys ✉CA 91401 ☎ 780-1320

HOTELS

L.A. Tura Motel (AC g H)
11745 Ventura Boulevard, North Hollywood ✉CA 91604 *(Studio City)* ☎ 762-2260
Gay bars within walking distance, downtown L.A. Rooms with color TV.

Los Angeles - Santa Monica & West L.A. ☎ 310

NATIONAL PUBLISHERS

Frountiers
8380 Santa Monica Boulevard #200 ✉CA 90069 ☎ 848 2222
E-Mail: sales@frountiersweb.com
LA leading gay and lesbian publication

BARS

Annex Club (B G N) 12-2 h
835 South La Brea, Inglewood ✉CA 90301 ☎ 671-7323

Caper Room (B G S) 11-2 h, Sun Mon 14-2 h
244 South Market Street, Inglewood ✉CA 90301 ☎ 677-0403

Connection (B D gLM) 14-2, Sat-Sun 12-2 h
4363 Sepulveda Boulevard, Culver City ✉CA 90230 ☎ 391-6817

The Friendship Bar (B G MA N OS) 12-2 h
112 West Channel Road, Santa Monica ✉CA 90402 ☎ 454-6024

Gauntlet II (AC B G LJ MA) Mon-Fri 16-2 h, Sat 14-2 h, Sun 15-2 h
4219 Santa Monica Boulevard ✉CA 90029 ☎ 323/669-9472
Leather bar.

Roosterfish (B G N OS) 11-2 h
1302 Abbot Kinney Boulevard ✉CA 90291 *(Venice)* ☎ 392-2123
Very popular with a diverse crowd.

RESTAURANTS

Golden Bull Restaurant (AC B CC F GLM MA OS) Mon-Sat 16.30-24, Sun 11-24 h
170 West Channel Road, Santa Monica ✉CA 90402 ☎ 230-0402

SAUNAS/BATHS

Roman Holyday Health Club (g msg sa wh) 0-24 h
12814 Venice Boulevard ✉CA 90066 *(Mar Vista)* ☎ 391-0200

SWIMMING

-Santa Monica Will Rogers State Beach (Entrada Drive/Pacific Coast Highway)
-Venice beach (Near Westminster Avenue/Ocean Front Walk. By lifeguard stand 15)

Los Angeles - Silverlake ☎ 213

BARS

Cuffs (! B G LJ MA) Mon-Fri 16-2/? h, Sat Sun 14-4/? h
1941 Hyperion Avenue ✉CA 90027 ☎ 660-2649
Popular.

Detour (B G lj MA N) 14-2 h
4100 Sunset Boulevard ✉CA 90029 *(near Sunset Boulevard)* ☎ 664-1189
Cruisy western bar.

The Faultline (B G LJ MA) Wed-Sat 18-2 h, Sun 14-24 h
4216 Melrose Avenue/Vermont ✉CA 90029 ☎ 660-0889
Popular with Latinos.

The Garage (B d G MA) 14-2 h
4519 Santa Monica Boulevard ✉CA 90029 ☎ 662-6802

Houston's Cabaret (B F G MA s) 11-2 h
2538 Hyperion Avenue ✉CA 90027 ☎ 661-4233
Food available, Sun brunch.

Hyperion Bar (! B D GLM N) 11.30-2, Sat -4 h
2810 Hyperion Avenue ✉CA 90027 ☎ 660-1503
Popular.

Le Bar (B D G SNU)
2375 Glendale Boulevard ✉CA 90039☎ 660-7595
Mainly Latino clientele.

Little Joy (B G N OG) 16-2 h, Sat-Sun 11-2 h
1477 Sunset Boulevard West ✉CA 90026 ☎ 250-3417
Neighborhood bar with pool tables and jukebox. Popular with Latinos.

Mr. Mike's Piano Bar (B G OG s) 11-2 h
3172 Los Feliz Boulevard ✉CA 90039 ☎ 669-9640

Silverlake Lounge (B d G N S) 10-2 h
2906 W. Sunset Boulevard ✉CA 90026 ☎ 663-9636
Mainly Latino crowd.

MEN'S CLUBS

Basic Plumbing (G P) Mon-Fri 20-4 h, Sat Sun 20-5 h
1924 Hyperion Avenue ✉CA 90027 ☎ 953-6731
Popular. ID required.

Prowl (B G lj VS) Wed-Sat 22-? h, Sun 18-? h
1064 Myra Avenue ✉CA 90029 ☎ 662-4726
Membership available. Admission US$ 6.

CAFÉS

Tsunami Coffee House (A AC f glm lj MA OS S) Tue-Sun 10.30-22 h
4019 Sunset Boulevard ✉CA 90029 ☎ 661-7771

RESTAURANTS

Casita del Campo (b F GLM) 11-23 h
1920 North Hyperion Avenue ✉CA 90027 ☎ 662-4255

Cha Cha Cha (b F glm) 11-23 h
656 North Virgil Avenue/Sunset ✉CA 90026 ☎ 953-9991
Delicious Carribean cuisine.

The Cobalt Cantina (A AC B CC F GLM N OS WE) Mon-Fri 12-23 h, Sat 11-23 h, Sun 10-23 h
4326 Sunset Boulevard ✉CA 90029 ☎ 953-9991
Very busy Fri evening, 2 for 1 prices until 19 h.

Crest Coffee Shop
3725 Sunset Boulevard ✉CA 90026 ☎ 660-3645

El Conquistador (AC B CC F GLM MA N OS s) 11-23.30 h
3701 Sunset Boulevard ✉CA 90026 ☎ 666-5136
Mexican restaurant.

Peloyan's (b F NG) closed Sun
1806 ½ Hillhurst Avenue ✉CA 90027 ☎ 663-0049
Armenian cuisine.

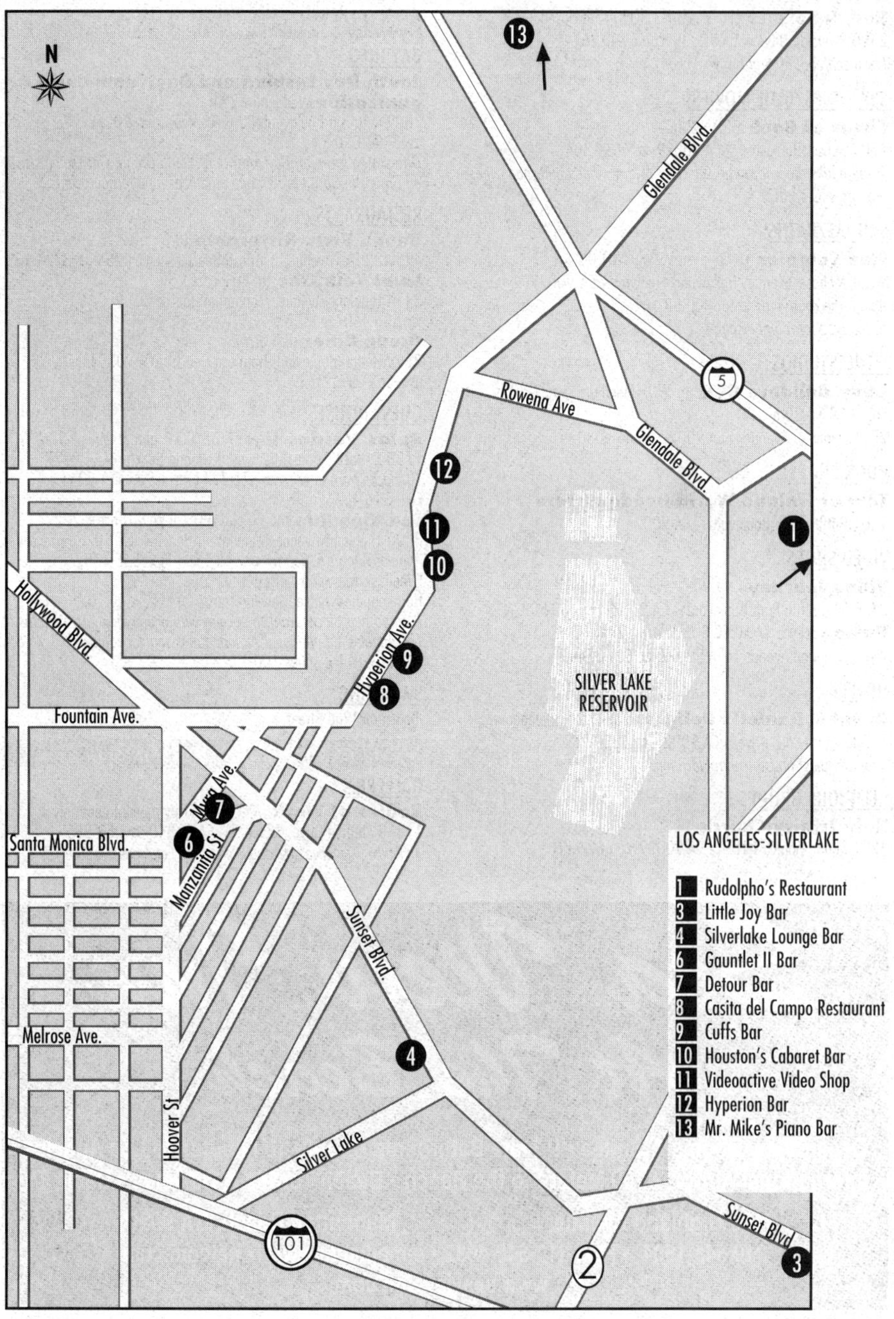
N
13
Glendale Blvd.
5
Rowena Ave
Glendale Blvd.
12
11
10
1
Hollywood Blvd.
Hyperion Ave.
9
8
SILVER LAKE
RESERVOIR
Fountain Ave.
Myra Ave.
7
6
Santa Monica Blvd.
Manzanita St
Sunset Blvd.
Melrose Ave.
4
Hoover St
Silver Lake
101
2
Sunset Blvd.
3
LOS ANGELES-SILVERLAKE
1 Rudolpho's Restaurant
3 Little Joy Bar
4 Silverlake Lounge Bar
6 Gauntlet II Bar
7 Detour Bar
8 Casita del Campo Restaurant
9 Cuffs Bar
10 Houston's Cabaret Bar
11 Videoactive Video Shop
12 Hyperion Bar
13 Mr. Mike's Piano Bar

Rudolpho's (b F glm S T) 11-3.30 h, Mon closed
2500 Riverside Drive ✉CA 90039 ☎ 669-1226
Fresh seafood, escargot & veal chops.

SEX SHOPS/BLUE MOVIES

Circus of Books (g) 6-2 h
4001 Sunset Boulevard ✉CA 90029 ☎ 666-1304
Retail bookstore with large selection of gay videos and magazines, aromas, lubes, toys.

SAUNAS/BATHS

Flex Complex (G OS pi sa VS wh WO) 0-24 h
4424 Melrose Avenue/Hollywood Freeway ✉CA 90029 *(entrance trough the courtyard)* ☎ 663-5858
ID required for membership.

FITNESSTUDIOS

Body Builders Gym (g WO) Mon-Fri 6.30-21.30 h, Sat Sun 9.30-17.30 h
2516 Hyperion Avenue ✉CA 90027 ☎ 668-0802

BOOK SHOPS

Tom of Finland World Headquarters
1601 Griffith Park Boulevard ✉CA 90026

VIDEO SHOPS

Video Journeys
2730 W. Griffith Park Boulevard ✉CA 90027 ☎ 663-5857
Videoactive (A AC CC GLM MA) 10-24 h
2522 Hyperion Avenue ✉CA 90027 ☎ 669-8544

HOTELS

David & Daniel's Delight (bf g H) 24 h telephone
1353 Elysian Park Drive ✉CA 90026 ☎ 250-5967
Intimate guest house, central location.

RELIGIOUS GROUPS

Holy Trinity Church
4209 Santa Monica #100 ✉CA 90029 ☎ 662-9118

Los Angeles - South Bay ☎ 310

GAY INFO

South Bay Lesbian and Gay Community Organization Wed Fri 19-22 h
2009-A Artesia Boulevard, PO Box 2777 ✉CA 90278
☎ 379-2850
Offers Men's Group, Gay AA Group, Youth Group, Out Dining, Lesbian Group, Bi Social Group, and organizes fund raising events.

RESTAURANTS

Buona Vista Ristorante (B F glm)
425-439 Pier Avenue, Hermosa Beach, ✉CA 90254 ☎ 372-2233
Local Yolk. The (bf CC F g YG)
3414 Highland Avenue, Manhattan Beach ✉CA 90266
☎ 546-4407
Ocean Diner (B F GLM)
959 Aviation Boulevard, Hermosa Beach ✉CA 90254
☎ (562) 372-3739

GUEST HOUSES

Palos Verdes Inn (AC B CC F glm H MA pi S W WO)
1700 S. Pacific Coast Highway, Redondo Beach ✉CA 90277
(3 blocks from beach) ☎ 316-4211 ☎ 1-800-421-9241
Fax: 316-4863
Sea View Inn (AC CC glm H OS pi WO) Office 8-22 h
3400 Highland Avenue, Manhattan Beach ✉CA 90266 *(near Los Angeles Airport & Beach)* ☎ 545-1504 Fax: 545-4052
E-Mail: seaview@ix.netcom.com
Homepage: www.seaview-inn.com
Located two blocks from the ocean with ocean view. 10 minutes to Los Angeles International Airport. Rates regular rooms US$ 70-85, deluxe 90-115, suites 100-135.

SWIMMING

-Beach at 32nd Street

Los Angeles - Sunland ☎ 818

GALLERIES

Bodies of Work (A CC GLM S) by appointment only
11350 Alethea Drive, Studio S ✉CA 91040 ☎ 352 0557
Art studio. Figurative classic nude paintings. Catalogue avalable US$ 5,-

Los Angeles - West Hollywood ☎ 213

GAY INFO

West Hollywood Convention and Visitors Bureau
☎ (800) 368-6020 *Toll Free information about the gay scene.*

BARS

Fire House (B D G YG) Sun T-dance 21-2 h
696 North Robertson Boulevard ✉CA 90096 ☎ (310) 289-1353

Gold Coast (! B D G MA N VS) 11-2 h, Sat Sun 10-2 h
8228 Santa Monica Boulevard ✉CA 90046 ☎ 656-4879
Popular video bar with cocktail hours. Cruisy atmosphere.

Hunters (B G N R) 19-2 h, Sat Sun 6-2 h
7511 Santa Monica Boulevard ✉CA 90046 ☎ 850-9428
Pool table.

Micky's (! AC B D F GLM OS SNU VS YG) 12-2 h
8857 Santa Monica Boulevard ✉CA 90069 ☎ (310) 657-1176
Popular. Various theme nights.

Mother Lode (! B G lj MA N VS YG) 12-2 h
8944 Santa Monica Boulevard ✉CA 90046 ☎ (310) 659-9700
Cocktail hours, pool table. Popular.

The Rafters (B G N VS) 12-2 h
7994 Santa Monica Boulevard ✉CA 90046 ☎ 654-0396

Rage (! A AC B CC D MA S VS W WE YG) 13-2 h
8911 Santa Monica Boulevard ✉CA 90069 ☎ (310) 652-7055
Very popular.

Revolver (! B G YG) 16-2 h, Fri-Sat -4 h, Sun 14-2 h
8851 Santa Monica Boulevard ✉CA 90069 *(corner San Vicente)*
☎ (310) 659-8851
Sun beer bust popular.

Spike (AC B G LJ MA rt s u VS) Mon-Wed 14-2, Thu-Sun -6 h
7746 Santa Monica Boulevard ✉CA 90046 ☎ 656-9343
Popular on weekends after 2 h when all the other bars are closed. Various theme nights.

Trunks (B G N VS) 13-2 h
8809 Santa Monica Boulevard ✉CA 90069 ☎ (310) 652-1015

7702 SM-Club (B D G LJ N YG) 6-2 h, Fri-Sat 0-24 h
7702 Santa Monica Boulevard ✉CA 90046 ☎ 654-3336
Popular after hour club after 6 h on weekends.

7969 (B D Glm S TV) 21-2 h
7969 Santa Monica Boulevard ✉90069 ☎ 654-0280
Various theme nights.

CAFÉS

Big Cup
7965 Beverly Boulevard ✉CA 90048 *(Los Angeles)* ☎ 653-5358

Buzz Coffeehouse (b glm)
8200 Santa Monica Boulevard ✉CA 90046 ☎ 876-4910
Popular

The Greenery Café (B f GLM YG)
8945 Santa Monica Boulevard ✉CA 90069 ☎ 275-9518

Mel n Rose's
8344 Melrose Avenue ✉CA 90046 *(Los Angeles)* ☎ 655-5557

Weho Lounge (f glm)
8861 Santa Monica Boulevard ✉CA 90069 ☎ (310) 360-0430

DANCECLUBS

Axis (! AC B CC D GLM SNU VS YG) 21-2.30 h, closed Mon-Tue. Wed Latino, Fri (L), Sat (G)
652 N. La Peer Drive North ✉CA 90069 ☎ (310) 659-0471
Largest Dancclub in West Hollywood.

Love Lounge (! AC B CC D G MA S VS) 21-2.30 h, closed Mon
657 N. Robertson Boulevard ✉CA 90069 *(behind Axis Nightclub)*
☎ (310) 659-0472
Theme events nightly.

RESTAURANTS

The Abbey (AC B bf CC F GLM MA N OS) 7-3 h
692 North Robertson Boulevard, ✉CA 90069 ☎ (310) 289-8410
Reservation advisable.

Caffe Luna (b F glm W) 8-3, Fri-Sat -5 h
7463 Melrose Avenue ✉CA 90046 ☎ 655-8647
Popular bistro cuisine.

Checca Restaurant & Niteclub (B d F GLM s) 11.30-2 h (meals Mon-Sat 18-23 h)
7321 Santa Monica Boulevard ✉CA 90046 ☎ 850-7471

Cobalt Cantina (A AC B CC F GLM N OS WE) Mon-Fri 12-23 h, Sat 11-23 h, Sun 10-23 h
616 N. Robertson Boulevard ✉CA 90069 ☎ (310) 659-8691
Mexican food.

Figs (b F glm)
7929 Santa Monica Boulevard ✉CA 90046 ☎ 654-0780
Home style, tasty and reasonably priced food.

French Quarter (! b bf CC F GLM OS) 7-2.30 h, Fri Sat 7-3.30 h
7985 Santa Monica Boulevard ✉CA 90046 ☎ 654-0898
Good food at reasonable prices. Popular Sun for brunch.

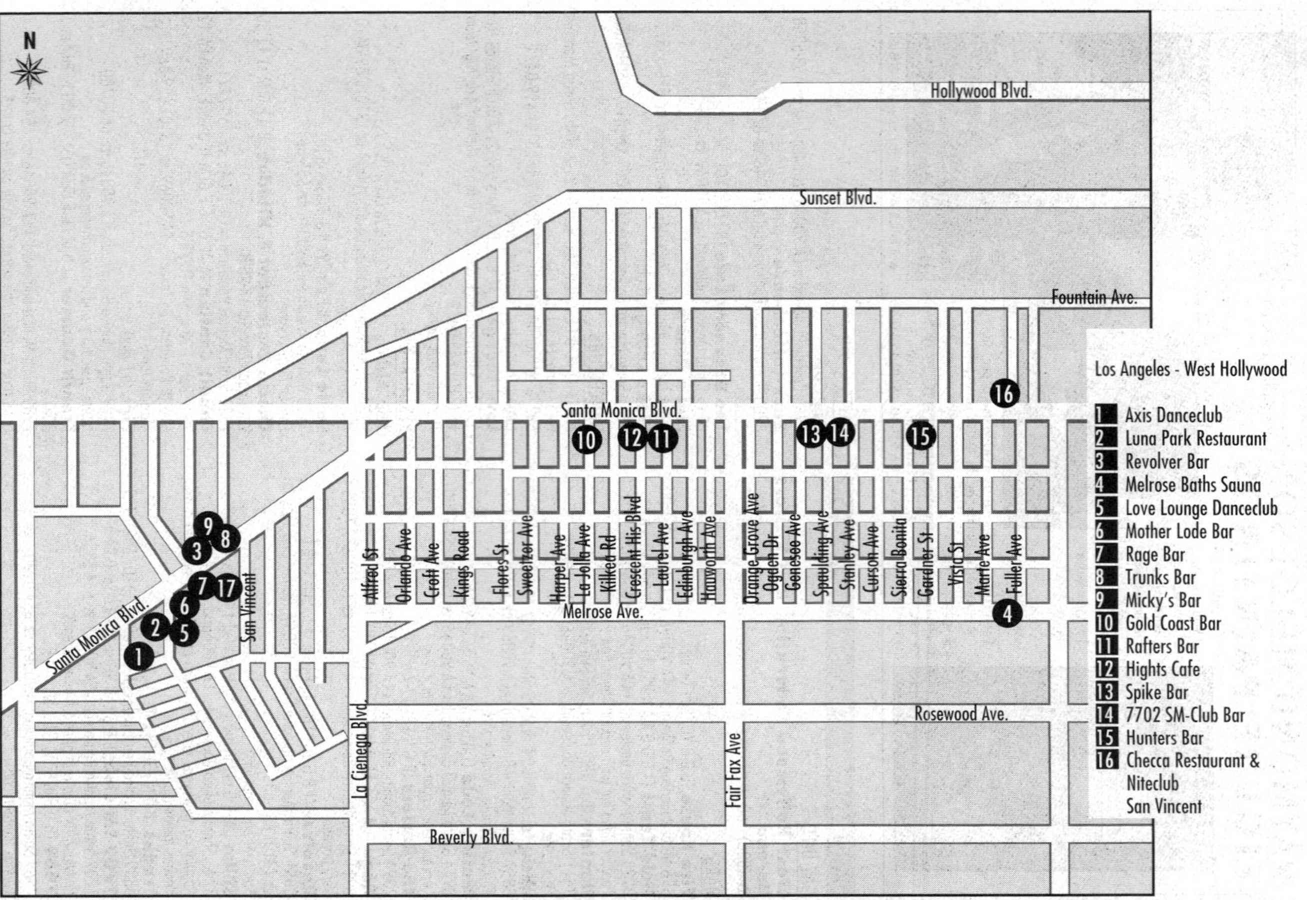

N
Hollywood Blvd.
Sunset Blvd.
Fountain Ave.
Santa Monica Blvd.
Santa Monica Blvd.
San Vincent
La Cienega Blvd.
Alfred St
Orlando Ave
Croft Ave
Kings Road
Flores St
Sweetzer Ave
Harper Ave
La Jolla Ave
Kilkea Rd
Crescent Hts Blvd
Laurel Ave
Edinburgh Ave
Hauworth Ave
Orange Grove Ave
Ogden Dr
Genesee Ave
Spaulding Ave
Stanley Ave
Curson Ave
Sierra Bonita
Gardner St
Vista St
Marie Ave
Fuller Ave
Melrose Ave.
Rosewood Ave.
Fair Fax Ave
Beverly Blvd.
Los Angeles - West Hollywood
1 Axis Danceclub
2 Luna Park Restaurant
3 Revolver Bar
4 Melrose Baths Sauna
5 Love Lounge Danceclub
6 Mother Lode Bar
7 Rage Bar
8 Trunks Bar
9 Micky's Bar
10 Gold Coast Bar
11 Rafters Bar
12 Hights Cafe
13 Spike Bar
14 7702 SM-Club Bar
15 Hunters Bar
16 Checca Restaurant & Niteclub
San Vincent

Hoy's Wok (b F glm W) 12-23 h, Sun 16-23 h
8163 Santa Monica Boulevard ✉CA 90069 ☎ 656-9002
Good chinese cuisine. Many vegetarian dishes.
Luna Park (AC B CC d E F glm MA OS S) 18-2 h
665 N. Robertson Boulevard ✉CA 90069 ☎ (310) 652-0611
Bar, restaurant, nightclub. Great shows.
Marix Tex-Mex (b F glm W) 11-24 h
1108 North Flores Street ✉CA 90048
Texas cuisine.
Mark's (B F glm)
861 N. La Cienega Boulevard ✉CA 90069 ☎ (310) 652-5252
Numbers Restaurant (B F G R) 17-2 h
8029 Sunset Boulevard ✉CA 90026 ☎ 656-6300
Yukon Mining Co. (AC F GLM OS) 0-24 h
7328 Santa Monica Boulevard ✉CA 90046 ☎ 851-8833
American steaks, seafood. Friendly staff.

SEX SHOPS/BLUE MOVIES

Casanova's West 10-1.45 h
7766 Santa Monica Boulevard ✉CA 90046 ☎ 650-9158
Circus of Books (g) 6-2 h
8230 Santa Monica Boulevard ✉CA 90029 ☎ 656-6533
Drake's Melrose (! AC CC G MA VS W) 0-24 h
7566 Melrose Avenue/Curson, ✉CA 90046 ☎ 651-5600
Originally designed, overwhelming selection of videos and magazines.
Drake's West Hollywood (AC CC G MA) 10-02.30 h
8932 Santa Monica Boulevard, ✉CA 90069 *(one block west of San Vicente Boulevard)* ☎ (310) 289-8932
Videos for sale/rent. Condoms, lube, magazines, guides on sale.
The Pleasure Chest (g LJ) 10-23 h
7733 Santa Monica Boulevard ✉CA 90046 ☎ 650-1022
☎ (800) 753-4536 (toll free, mail order) Fax: (213) 650-1176
Homepage: www.thepleasurechest.com
Erotic department store. Certainly one of the largest selections of leather goods and novelties.

ESCORTS & STUDIOS

Don-Bodybuilder & Escort (AC CC W WO)
☎ (310) 262-1000 ☎ (800) 792-7820

SAUNAS/BATHS

Melrose Baths (! B G OS S sa VS wh) 0-24 h
7269 Melrose Avenue ✉CA 90046 ☎ 937-2122
ID with photo required. Popular.

FITNESSTUDIOS

Athletic Club (AC bf CC F G MA msg OS pi sa sb wh WO)
Mon-Fri 5.30-23 h, Sat Sun 7-21 h
8560 Santa Monica Boulevard ✉CA 90069 ☎ (310) 659-6630
US$ 15.- day pass. Sun beds available. Very popular.

BOOK SHOPS

A Different Light (A AC CC GLM MA S) 10-24 h
8853 Santa Monica Boulevard, ✉CA 90069 ☎ (310) 854-6601
In the heart of West Hollywood's gay neibourhood. Thousands of titles, magazines, videos, gifts, cards etc
Circus of Books (g) 6-2 h
8230 Santa Monica Boulevard, West Hollywood, ✉CA 90047
☎ 656-6533
Retail bookstore with large selection of gay videos, magazines, books, aromas, lubes, toys.
Unicorn Bookstore (GLM) 10.30-22, Fri Sat 10-24 h
8940 Santa Monica Boulevard, ✉CA 90069 ☎ (310) 652-6253
A big choice of gay and lesbian books; newsstand.

Urban Inversion (CC W) 12-20 h
8246 Santa Monica Boulevard, ✉CA 90046 ☎ 654-8285
Books, gifts, cards.

EDUCATION SERVICES

New American Language Institute
PO Box 691153 ✉CA 90069 ☎ (310) 657-5440
Fax: (310) 854-6699

GIFT & PRIDE SHOPS

Dorothy's Surrender (CC G) 10-23.30 h
7985 Santa Monica Boulevard, ✉CA 90046 ☎ 650-4111
Gay gift shop.

LEATHER & FETISH SHOPS

Wayne's Leatherack
4216 Melrose Avenue ✉CA 90069 ☎ 913-3530

HOTELS

Le Parc Suite Hotel (AC B bf CC E F glm H msg N OS pi sa W WE wh) 24 h
733 North Knoll Drive ✉CA 90069 *(near Santa Monica Boulevard, shops, cafés and bars)* ☎ (310) 855-8888 Fax: (310) 659-8508

GUEST HOUSES

Le Montrose (AC bf f g H wh pi wo)
900 Hammond Street ✉CA 90069 ☎ (310) 855-1115
☎ (800) 776-0666 (toll-free) Homepage: www.travelweb.com
San Vincente Inn-Resort (! AC bf CC f G H MA msg NU pi sb sol wh WO YG) All year
845 North San Vincente Blvd ✉CA 90069 ☎ (310) 854-6915
Fax: (310) 289-5929 E-Mail: infodesk@sanvincenteinn.com
Homepage: www.sanvincenteinn.com
Friendly and only gay guesthouse in West-Hollywood. Excellent location. Most rooms have AC .Rates from US$ 59-US$ 199

RELIGIOUS GROUPS

West Hollywood Presbyterian Church
7350 Sunset Boulevard ✉CA 90069 ☎ 874-6646

Modesto ☎ 209

BARS

Brave Bull (B G LJ) 19-2 h, Sun 16-2 h
701 South 9th ✉CA 95354 ☎ 529-6712
Mustang Club (B D GLM S) Mon-Thu 16-2, Fri-Sun 14-2 h
413 North 7th Street ✉CA 95354 ☎ 577-9694

CAFÉS

Espresso Caffe (AC b bf CC F glm MA OS W) Mon-Thu 7-23, Fri -24, Sat 10-24, Sun -22 h
3025 McHenry Avenue ✉CA 95350 ☎ 571-3337
Also restaurant.

Monterey ☎ 831

BARS

After Dark (B D GLM OS VS) 20-2 h
214 Lighthouse Avenue ✉CA 93940 ☎ 373-7828

SWIMMING

-Garrapata Beach, Carmel (g NU WE)
-Carmel Park Beach (from dunes to North end)

CRUISING

-Veteran's Park (bushes & restroom, NG OG AYOR)

Oakland ☎ 510

RESTAURANTS

Bench and Bar (B D F GLM MA MG S SNU STV) 16-02 h
120-11th Street ✉CA 94607 ☎ 444 2266

PRIVATE ACCOMODATION

Mi Casa Su Casa (GLM)
PO Box 10327 ✉CA 94610 ☎ 531 4511 ☎ (800) 215 2272 (toll free) Fax: 531 4517 E-Mail: homeswap@aol.com
Homepage: www.well.com/user/homeswap
International home exchange and hospitality network.

Oceanside ☎ 619

BARS

Capri Lounge (B G N W) 10-2 h
207 North Tremont ✉CA 92054 ☎ 722-7284

SEX SHOPS/BLUE MOVIES

Midnight Books 0-24 h
316 3rd Street ✉CA 92054 ☎ 757-7832

Palm Springs ☎ 760

● Just imagine: You leave Los Angeles on the Interstate 10, driving through the desert. And suddenly, at the foot of its majestic mountain ranges, appears out of nothing a green oasis: Palm Springs. Palm Spring itself is only the biggest town of a whole string of towns, for who its name is a sort of trade mark. Here, gay live concentrates in Palm Springs, south of downtown, and in the six kilometres distant *Cathedral City* on Cathedral Canyon Drive. Following the boomyears of the eigthies, tourism slackened a bit. This baisse has, nevertheless, made Palm Springs more interesting for people with a smaller income. The peak times of Palm Springs are in March/April, when the *Dinah Shore golf tournament*, a popular sporting event attended by many lesbians takes place; in November with the popular *Gay Rodeo*; and at Easter, when the *White Party* with thousands of gay guests takes place. For further information look into one of the local magazines: *Bottom Line, MegaScene* or *Life Style*. Now, don't imagine Palm Springs to be a big city. There is no public transport, but you'll still need at least a bycicle, if not a car. Yet, too much sightseeing cannot be done as the variety of scenic attractions, which merit leaving the gay resorts, is limited. The dessert comes alive in the interesting *Living Desert Museum*, Indian culture and roots are found in the *Agua Caliente Cultural Museum* and *Mount San Jacinto* is visited by taking the *Palm Springs Aerial Tramway*. Palm Springs offers spectacular holidays for reasonable prices with relaxed recreation.

✸ Man stelle sich vor: von Los Angeles aus (in gleicher Entfernung auch von San Diego) fährt man auf der Interstate 10 durch die Wüste. Und inmitten dieser Ödnis mit ihren majestätischen Gebirgszügen taucht völlig unvermutet eine grüne Oase auf: Palm Springs.
Dies ist allerdings nur bedingt richtig, denn der größte Ort Palm Springs fungiert nur als „Markenname" für eine ganze Reihe von weiteren Orten. Das schwule Leben konzentriert sich zum einen in Palm Springs südlich der Downtown, zum anderen im etwa sechs Kilometer entfernten *Cathedral City* am Cathedral Canyon Drive.
Nach dem Boom der 80er Jahre hat sich das Tourismus-Geschäft etwas beruhigt. Diese Baisse macht Palm Springs allerdings auch wieder interessant für Leute mit schmalerem Geldbeutel. Weiterhin aber hat Palm Springs seine Spitzenzeiten: das *Dinah Shore Golfturnier* (Ende Mär/Anfang Apr) beschert der Stadt das größte lesbische Fest Amerikas, Ende November gibt es das *Gay Rodeo* (sehr beliebt) und zu Ostern die *White Party* mit Tausenden schwuler Partygäste. Weitere Informationen entnimmt man einem der schwulen Magazine vor Ort: *Bottom Line, MegaScene* oder *Life Style*.
Nun darf man sich diesen Ort nicht sonderlich groß vorstellen. Es gibt keinen öffentlichen Nahverkehr, so daß man zumindest ein Fahrrad benötigt, vielleicht aber auch ein Auto.
Allerdings wird man dieses nicht übermässig häufig für's Sightseeing einsetzen. Die Auswahl an Attraktionen, die den Weg aus dem schwulen Resort lohnen, ist begrenzt. Die Wüste lebt im interessanten *Living Desert Museum*, die indianischen Ursprünge finden sich im *Agua Caliente Cultural Museum* und per *Palm Springs Aerial Tramway* fährt man auf den Mt. San Jacinto. Hört sicht nicht spektakulär an? Natürlich nicht! Palm Springs heißt nicht spektakulär urlauben sondern günstig und ohne großen Szenestreß erholen.

▲ Imaginez un peu: vous venez de Los Angeles, vous traversez le désert sur la „Interstate 10" et au beau milieu du désert et des impressionantes chaînes montagneuses, vous apercevez tout d'un coup un mirage, une oasis. Vous êtes à Palm Spring!
Palm Spring, c'est plusieurs lieux regroupés sous le même nom. Les endroits gays intéressants sont à Palm Spring même (au sud de Downtown) et à Cathedral City (environ 6 km), au bord du Cathedral Canyon Drive.
Le boom touristique des années 80 est terminé. Palm Spring est aujourd'hui plus abordable, moins chère. Profitez des manifestations gayes et lesbiennes pour découvrir la région, par ex.: fin mars/début avril („Dinah Shore Golfturnier", la plus grande fête lesbienne du pays), à Pâques („White Party", fête gaye très courrue) et enfin, en novembre („Gay Rodeo", très populaire). Pour de plus amples informations, consultez les magasines gays locaux: „Bottom Line", „Mega Scene" ou „Life Style".
Palm Spring n'est pas très étendue. Les transports en commun sont inexistants. On a donc besoin d'un vélo ou d'une voiture.
Côté tourisme, il n'y a pas grand chose à faire, en dehors des lieux gays. A voir cependant: le „Living Desert Museum", le „Agua Caliente Cultural Museum" (Histoire indienne) et le Mont San Jacinto (prenez le „Palm Springs Aerial Tramway" pour y aller). Rien de bien excitant, somme toute! Palm Spring n'est pas le lieu où vous passerez de folles vacances, mais plutôt un endroit où vous pourrez vous remettre du stress et des fatigues des grandes métropoles californiennes.

☆ El oasis verde de Palm Springs se encuentra en medio del desierto aproximadamente a la misma distancia de L.A. que de San Diego. El nombre Palm Springs es tan solo la denominación de una gran cantidad de lugares. La vida gay se concentra por un lado en Palm Springs hacia el sur del downtown, por otro lado en la *Cathedral City* en Cathedral Canyon Drive, situada aprox. a 6 km. de Palm Springs. Después de la explosión turistica de los años 80 la actividad se ha apaciguado un poco, esto ha hecho que la ciudad se vuelva atractiva para turistas con poco dinero. Algunos de los acontecimientos anuales en los que la ciudad se llena son el *Dinah Shore Golfturnier* (finales de marzo y principios de abril) que brinda a la ciudad la fiesta lesbiana más grande de los Estados Unidos. A finales de noviembre se lleva acabo el *Gay Rodeo* y en la época de pascua *White Party* con miles de invitados gay. Las revistas *Bottom Time, MegaScene* o *Life Style* dan informaciónes más detalladas. Debido a que la ciudad no es muy grande no existen medios de transporte public, por ello se recomienda el uso de bicicletas o automoviles. La ciudad no ofrece muchos objetivos para visitar. El desierto se puede experimentar en el *Living Desert Museum*, los origenes y costumbres de la población indígena se aprecia en el *Agua Caliente Cultural Museum* y con el *Palm Springs Aerial Tranway* es posible trasladarse hasta el Monte San Jacinto. La ciudad ofrece un marco ideal para gays que se quieran recrear en un ambiente sin ningún estrés y a precios muy comodos.

PALM SPRINGS

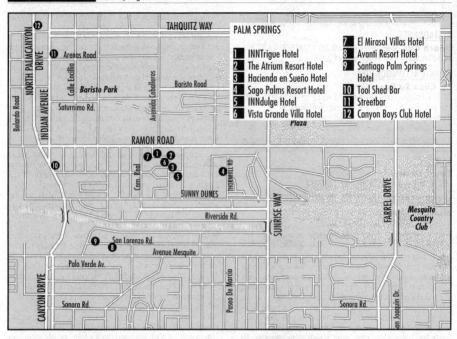

1 INNTrigue Hotel
2 The Atrium Resort Hotel
3 Hacienda en Sueño Hotel
4 Sago Palms Resort Hotel
5 INNdulge Hotel
6 Vista Grande Villa Hotel
7 El Mirasol Villas Hotel
8 Avanti Resort Hotel
9 Santiago Palm Springs Hotel
10 Tool Shed Bar
11 Streetbar
12 Canyon Boys Club Hotel

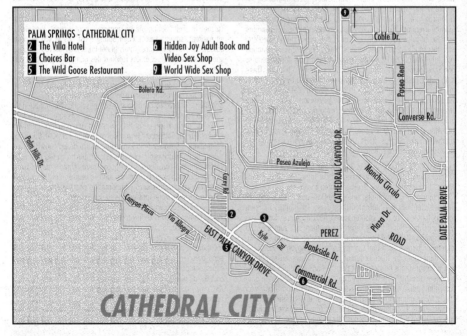

PALM SPRINGS - CATHEDRAL CITY

2 The Villa Hotel
3 Choices Bar
5 The Wild Goose Restaurant
6 Hidden Joy Adult Book and Video Sex Shop
9 World Wide Sex Shop

CATHEDRAL CITY

❖ Immaginatevi: da Los Angeles (a stessa distanza anche da San Diego) con la Interstate 10 si attraversa il deserto e, nel mezzo di questa solitudine dal maestoso profilo montano, appare l'oasi verde di Palm Springs. Questa località è la più grande e la più conosciuta tra i paesi dell'oasi. La vita gay si è concentrata a Palm Springs a sud del centro ed a sei chilometri di distanza a *Cathedral City* presso il Cathedral Canyon Drive. Dopo il boom degli anni 80 il settore del turismo si è calmato. Questa recessione ha reso Palm Springs interessante anche per coloro che hanno meno disponibilità economiche. Naturalmente anche Palm Springs ha i suoi periodi animati: il *Dinah Shore Golfturnier* (fine marzo/iniz. apr.) offre alla città la più grande festa per le lesbiche americane, a fine novembre ha luogo il *Gay Rodeo* (molto amato) ed a pasqua il *White Party* con migliaia di ospiti gay. Otterrete ulteriori informazioni nelle pubblicazioni locali *Bottom Line, Mega Scene* o *Life Style*. Non immaginatevi però questo luogo molto grande: poichè non vi è la metropolitana avrete bisogno di un'auto o di una bicicletta; ma non le userete per visitare la città visto che, salvo l'ambiente gay, le attrazioni sono limitate. Il deserto vive nell'interessante *Living Desert Museum* e nell'*Agua Caliente Cultural Museum* si trovano resti della civiltà indiana. Con la *Palm Springs aerial tramway* si raggiunge il Mt. San Jacinto. Non sembra spettacolare? Certo che no! Palm Springs non offre vacanze spettacolari, bensì vacanze economiche e senza stress.

GAY INFO

The Bottom Line
1243 Gene Autry Tr., Ste. K ✉CA 92263 ☎ 323-0552
The Bottom Line is published every second week with local news, scene articles and Guide with map to the desert area. About 52 pages. Free at gay venues.

TOURIST INFO

Palm Springs Tourism
401 South Pavillion Way ✉CA 92262 ☎ 778-8415
Fax: 323-8279

BARS

Blue Angel (A AC B CC GLM MA N OS S W YG) 17-2 h
777 East Tahquitz Canyon Way, ✉CA 92262-6784 *(The Courtyard, Suite 341)* ☎ 778-4343
CC Construction (AC B CC D DR GLM MA S VS W WE) Wed-Fri 19-2, Sat -4, Sun 16-2 h
1775 E. Palm Danyon Drive ✉CA 92264-1613 *(Smoketree Center, Suite G)* ☎ 778-1234
Popular.
Choices (B D G OS VS) Happy hour 17-21 Disco 21-2 WE -3 h.
68-352 Perez Road, Cathedral City ✉CA 92234 ☎ 321-1145
Dates Poolside Bar & Cafe (AC B bf CC F GLM MA OS pi VS) 8-22 h
67-670 Carey Road ✉CA 92234 *(Cathedral City)* ☎ 328-7211
Desert Palms Inn (AC B bf CC F G MA OS pi VS W wh) Cafe: 9-15, Wed-Sun 18-22, Bar: 10-24 h
67-580 Highway 111, Cathedral City ✉CA 92234 *(Cathedral City)* ☎ 324-300
Full service gay resort.
Streetbar (AC B GLM MA N s OS W) 14-2 h
224 E. Arenas Rd. ✉CA 92262 ☎ 320-1266
Happy hour daily 14-19 h. Popular.
Tool Shed (B G LJ) 10-? h
600 East Sunny Dunes Road ✉CA 92264 ☎ 320-3299

CAFÉS

Rainbow Cactus Cafe (AC B F GLM s) 11-2 h
212 S. Indian Canyon ✉CA 92262 *(at Arenas)* ☎ 325-3638

RESTAURANTS

Red Pepper (B CC F glm)
36-650 Sun Air Plaza ✉ CA 92262 ☎ 770-7007
Mexican cuisine.
Wild Goose. The (AC CC B F GLM s) 17.30-23.30 h
67-938 Highway 111 ✉CA 92234 *(Cathedral City)* ☎ 328-5775
Continental cuisine with entertainment.

SEX SHOPS/BLUE MOVIES

Hidden Joy Adult Book and Video (g)
68-424 Commercial Road ✉CA 92262 ☎ 328-1694
World Wide
68-300 Ramon Road ✉CA 92234 *Cathedral City* ☎ 321-1313

ESCORTS & STUDIOS

Boy Blue 0-24 h
☎ 322-7680

SAUNAS/BATHS

CBC Club Palm Springs (G MA N P sa sb sol VS wh WO) 0-24h
68-449 Perez Road/Cathedral Canyon Drive ✉CA 92234 *Cathedral City* ☎ 324-8588

LEATHER & FETISH SHOPS

Moonlighting Thu-Sun 18-6 h
614 East Sunny Dunes Road ✉CA 92264 *(at the Wood Shed)* ☎ 323-8830
Leather goods and novelties.

HOTELS

Alexander Resort (AC bf CC G H nu OS pi wh)
598 Grenfall Road ✉CA 92264 ☎ 327-6911
☎ (800) 448-6197 (toll free)
All rooms with priv. bath, TV, some with kitchenette. Rates US$ 79-99. downtown location, 10 minutes to gay bars.
The Atrium Resort (AC CC G H MA nu OS pi sol wh)
981 Camino Parocela ✉CA 92264 ☎ 322-2404
☎ (800) 669-1069 (toll free) Fax: 320-1667
Three km to the airport. Centrally located. One and two bedroom apartments with priv. bath and TV. Rates US$ 79-165. Check-in is at 574 Warm Sands Drive (Vista Grande).
Avanti Resort Hotel (AC bf CC G H NU OS pi wh) Office: 9-20 h
715 San Lorenzo Road ✉CA 92264 *(10 minute walk from downtown Palm Springs)* ☎ 325-9723 ☎ (800) 572-2779
Fax: 706/325-4357 E-Mail: psfun4U@aol.com
Bacchanal (AC bf CC G H NU OS pi wh) All year
589 Grenfall Road ✉CA 92264 ☎ 323-0760 ☎ (800) 806-9059
Fax: 416-4107 Homepage: www.bacchanal.net
Located in the Warm Sands enclave - within walking distance of restaurants and night clubs.
Canyon Boys Club Hotel (AC bf G H NU pi sa sb OS wh WO) Office: 9-23 h
960 North Palm Canyon Drive ✉CA 92262 ☎ 322-4367
☎ (800) 295-2582 Fax: 322-4024 E-Mail: info@CanyonClub.com
Homepage: www.CanyonClub.com
Rates US$ 59-119. On pool clothing is optional. All rooms with TV, video and refrigerator. 50ft pool and 16 man spa. See web site for more details.
Chestnutz (AC bf CC G MA msg NU OS pi VS wh)
641 San Lorenzo Road ✉CA 92264 ☎ 325-5269
☎ (800) 621-6973. Fax: 320-9535 E-Mail: chestnutz@aol.com.
Columns Resort (AC bf CC G MA NU pi sa wh) Office 8-22 h
537 Grenfall Road ✉CA 92264 ☎ 325-0655 Fax: 322-1436
E-Mail: rescolumns@aol.com

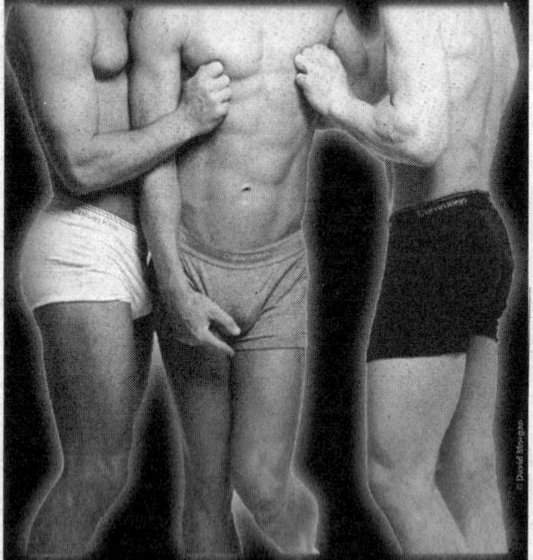

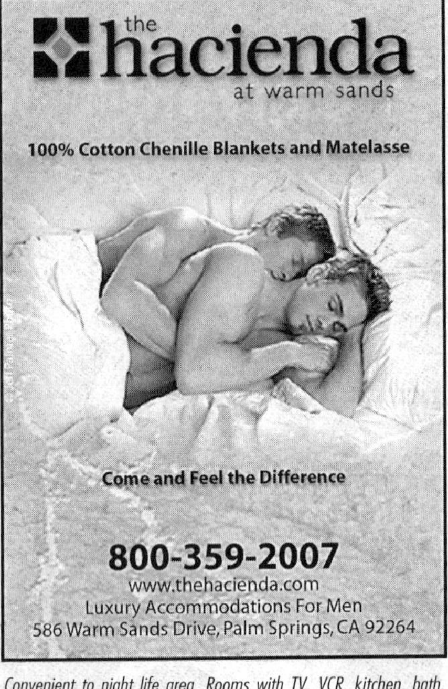

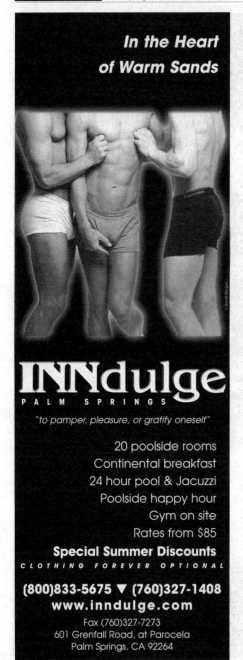

Convenient to night life area. Rooms with TV, VCR, kitchen, bath. Rates US$ 69-105.

Desert Knight (bf CC G H pi)
435 Avenida Olancha ✉CA 92264 ☎ 325-5456

Desert Palms Inn (AC B bf CC F G H MA OS pi S wh) Hotel lobby - 24h, Bar 09-2 h, Café 09-15, 18-22 h
67-580 Highway 111, Cathedral City ✉CA 92234 ☎ 324-3000 ☎ (800) 801-8696 (toll free) Fax: 770 5031
E-Mail: dpinn@desertpalmsinn.com
Homepage: www.desertpalmsinn.com
Special events held throughout the year, across the street from the largest gay disco in Palm Springs. 29 rooms overlooking beautifully landscaped gardens. Rates from US$ 49-149, See web site for more details.

Desert Paradise Hotel (bf G H NU pi wh) Office: 8-20 h
615 Warm Sands Drive ✉CA 92264 ☎ 320-5650
☎ (800) 342-7635 (toll-free)

Desert Stars Resort (bf G H)
1491 Via Soledad ✉CA 92264 ☎ 325-2686 Fax: 322-5054

El Mirasol Villas (AC bf CC f G H pi sb wh)
525 Warm Sands Drive ✉CA 92264 ☎ 327-5913
☎ (800) 327-2985 Fax: 325-8931 E-Mail: mirasolps@aol.com
Homepage: www.elmirasol.com
All rooms with phone, kitchenette, private bath/WC.

Hacienda at Warm Sands. The (AC bf CC G H MA NU pi wh)
586 Warm Sands Drive ✉CA 92264 ☎ 327-8111
☎ (800) 359-2007 Fax: 778-7890
Homepage: www.thehacienda.com
Located in a residential area only minutes away from most gay bars. One bedroom apartments. Luxuriously equipped. Rates please call or see our web site.

Inn Exile (AC b bf CC G H MA NU pi W wh WO)
545 Warm Sands Drive ✉CA 92264 ☎ 327-6413
☎ (800) 962-0186 Fax: 320-5745
E-Mail: innexile@earthlink.net Homepage: www.innexile.com
INNdulge (AC bf CC G H msg NU pi wh WO) All year / 24h
601 Grenfall Road ✉CA 92264 *(at Parocela)* ☎ 327-1408
☎ (800) 833-5675 Fax: 327-7273
E-Mail: inndulge@ix.netcom.com Homepage: www.inndulge.com
20 poolside rooms, clothing optional. Afternoon happy hour. 24 hour pool and jacuzzi. See website for more details
Inntimate (CC G H msg OS pi sol) Office: 8-20 h
556 Warm Sands Drive, CA 92264 ✉CA 92264 ☎ 778-8334
Toll free ☎ (800) 695-3846 Fax: 778-9937
Rates US$ 60-100 per room/night.
Mirage (CC G H NU pi wh) 555 Grenfall Road ✉CA 92264
☎ 322-2404 ☎ (800) 669-1069 Fax: 320-1667
Homepage: www.mirage4men.com
3 pools and 3 spas. See our web site for further details.
Posada. La (AC bf CC f G H NU pi)
120 West Vereda Street ✉CA 92262 ☎ 323-1402
☎ (888) 411-4949 Homepage: www.laposada.com
„Editors Choice Award '99" from „Out & About".
Racquet Club of Palm Springs (G H)
2743 N. Indian Canyon Drive ✉CA 92262 ☎ 325-1281
Fax: 325-3429. Homepage http://www.RCPS.com.
Sago Palms Resort (AC bf CC G H MA NU pi wh WO) Office 9-22 h
595 Thornhill Road ✉CA 92264 ☎ 323-0224
or Toll free ☎ (800) 626-7246 Email: sagopalmca@aol.com
Homepage: http://www.webworkps.com/sago/
Rates US$ 79-149. Suites with kitchen and fireplace.
Santiago Palm Springs (bf F G NU OS pi wh WO) 650 San Lorenzo Road ✉CA 92264 ☎ (800) 710-7729
Fax: 416-0347 E-Mail: santiagops@earthlink.net
Homepage: www.prinet.com/santiago
Triangle Inn (AC bf CC G H MG msg nu pi wh)
555 San Lorenzo Road ✉CA 92264 ☎ 322-7993
Toll free ☎ 800-732-7555 Fax: 322-0784 *Rates US$ 104-219.*
Versailles. Hotel (AC bf CC G H MA msg pi sol wh)
288 Camino Monte Vista/Indian Avenue ✉CA 92262 ☎ 320-2888
Ten min to the airport (free pick up). Centrally located. Gay bars within walking distance. All units with priv. bath, color TV, some with kitchenette. Rates US$ 75-150.
Villa. The (AC B bf CC d F GLM H lj MA msg N OS pi R S sa VS wh YG) All year / 24h
67-670 Carey Road, Cathedral City ✉CA 92234 ☎ 328-7211
☎ (877) PS VILLA (toll free) Fax: 321-1463
E-Mail: reservations@thevilla.com Homepage: www.TheVilla.com
Full service gay resort
Vista Grande Villa (CC G H NU pi wh WO)
574 Warm Sands Drive ✉CA 92264 ☎ 322-2404
Reservations Toll free ☎ (800) 669-1069.
E-mail: mirage4men@aol.com
All rooms with phone, TV/VCR, private baths. Rates US$ 69-165.
Warm Sands Villas (B CC G H NU pi VS wh) Office: 9-21 h
555 Warm Sands Drive ✉CA 92264 ☎ 323-3005
Fax: (760)323-4006. Toll free ☎ 1-800-357-5695
Exclusively gay resort, open all year. Bilingual (English/German) staff. Rates US$ 39.50-149.50 (WE bf incl.), 2 miles from airport, free parking. See advertisement on inside cover.
550. The (bf CC G H lj MA nu pi wh)
550 Warm Sands Drive ✉CA 92264 ☎ 320-7144
Toll free ☎ 1-800-669-0550 *Rates on request.*

GUEST HOUSES

InnTrigue (AC bf CC G H MA NU OS pi wh WO) All year
526 Warm Sands Drive ✉CA 92264 ☎ 323-7505
☎ (800) 798-8781 Fax: 323-1055
E-Mail: Inntrigue@Earthline.net
Homepage: www.gaytravelling.com/inntrigue *Rooms with microwave, coffe makers and fridge. See web site for more info.*

RELIGIOUS GROUPS

MCC Office Mon-Fri 10-17 h, service Sun 10.45 h at 610 Belardo PO Box 920, 653 Commercial Road, Suite 7 ✉CA 92262
☎ 322-9696

Pasadena ☎ 626

BARS

Boulevard. The (B D G VS) 11-2 h
3199 East Foothill Boulevard ✉CA 91107 ☎ 356-9304
Club 3772 (B D G S) 16-24, Fri 12-2, Sat Sun 14-2 h
3772 East Foothill Boulevard ✉CA 91107 ☎ 578-9359
Nardi's (AC B CC d f GLM MA OS S) Mon-Thu 15-02 h, Fri & Sat 13-02 h
162 N. North Sierra Madre Boulevard ✉CA 91732 ☎ 449-3152

CAFÉS

Equator Coffee House
22 Mills Place ✉CA 91105 ☎ 564-8656

SEX SHOPS/BLUE MOVIES

Le Sex Shoppe 0-24 h
45 E. Colorado Boulevard ✉CA 91105 ☎ 578-9260

HEALTH GROUPS

AIDS Service Center
126 W. Del Mar Boulevard ✉CA 91105 ☎ 796-5633

CRUISING

-Raymond Avenue Park (AYOR)

Pomona ☎ 909

GAY INFO

Gay/Lesbian Hotline 18.30-22 h
☎ 824-7618

BARS

Alibi East & Back Alley (B D GLM MA OS VS) 10-2, Fri Sat -4 h
225 South San Antonio Avenue ✉CA 91766 ☎ 623-9422
Mary's (AC B d F GLM MA N S STV) Mon-Thu 17-02 h, Fri, Sat & Sun 15-02 h
1047 East Second Street ✉CA 91766 ☎ 622-1971
Robbie's (B d F GLM S) Fri-Mon 17-2 h, Mon men only
390 2nd Street ✉CA 91766 ☎ 620-4371

CAFES

Haven Coffee House & Gallery
296 W. Second Street ✉CA 91766 ☎ 623-0538

SEX SHOPS/BLUE MOVIES

Mustang Adult Books (g) Mon-Thu 8-1, WE 0-24 h
959-961 North Central Avenue, Upland ✉CA 91786 ☎ 981-0227

SAUNAS/BATHS

Pleasure Spa (G P sa)
1284 South Garey Avenue ✉CA 91766 ☎ 622-0951

GENERAL GROUPS

K.S. Enterprises (G MA) Mon-Fri 9-17 h
PO Box 15 01, ✉CA 91769 ☎ 622-6312 Fax: 623-1810
E-Mail: Ken2world@aol.com.

Red Bluff

CRUISING

-Dog Island Park (days)
-Park along river (early evenings)

Redding ☎ 530

BARS

The Rex (B D F GLM YG) 19-2 h
1244 California Street *(enter at rear)* ☎ 243-7869

SEX SHOPS/BLUE MOVIES

Adult Bookstore 0-24 h
2131 Hilltop Drive ✉CA 96002 ☎ 222-9542

CRUISING

-Clear Creek Road (4 miles East of old 99, nude beach, summer)
-Lake Redding Park (near boad ramp, AYOR)

Redwood City ☎ 650

BARS

Shouts Bar and Grill (B D e GLM N W) 11-2 h
2034 Broadway ✉CA 94063 ☎ 369-9651
Safe and friendly place. Recommended.

SEX SHOPS/BLUE MOVIES

Golden Gate Books 0-24 h
739 El Camino Real ✉CA 94063 ☎ 364-6913

Reseda ☎ 818

BARS

Bananas ! (B CC D G MA OS s SNU) 15-2 h
7026 Reseda Boulevard ✉CA 91335 *(San Fernando Valley)* ☎ 996 2976

Riverside ☎ 909

DANCECLUBS

V.I.P. Club (B D F GLM W) Mon-Thu 16-2 h, Fri Sat -4 h, Sun 11-2 h
3673 Merril Avenue ✉CA 92506 ☎ 784-2370

SEX SHOPS/BLUE MOVIES

Le Sex Shoppe 0-24 h
3945 Market Street ✉CA 92501 ☎ 788-5194

Russian River ☎ 707

BARS

Rainbow Cattle Co. (B D GLM) 6-2 h
16220 Main Street, Guerneville ✉CA 95446 ☎ 869-0206
Popular

HOTELS

Camelot Resort (F GLM H OS pi)
PO Box 467 ✉CA 95446 *Guerneville* ☎ 869-2538
Conveniently located. Accomodations consist of attractive rooms, spacious cabins and deluxe 2 bedroom apartments.

Dew Drop Inn (B bf CC F g H MA N wh)
205 Main Street, Point Arena ✉CA 95468 *(29 miles north of Russian River)* ☎ 882-3027 ☎ (888) 338-9977
Located on the old Highway 1.

The Estate (B bf E F glm H pi)
13555 Highway 16 ✉CA 95446 *Guerneville* ☎ 869-9093
Elegant accommodation for people seeking comfort and luxury. All rooms with priv. bath, color TV, telephone. Distance to gay bars: 5 min drive. Rates US$ 75-150 (American bf incl.), meals available.

Ferngrove Resort (AC bf g H pi T)
16650 River Road ✉CA 95446 Guerneville ☎ 869-9992
Kitchens, fireplaces, barbecue area, TV, heated pool. Single US$ 50-100, double $80-150.

Fife's (a B bf CC d F glm H lj msg NU OS pi s W)
16467 River Road ✉CA 95446 *Guerneville*
☎ 869-0656 Fax: 869-0656
A classic country resort on the Russian River surrounded by redwood forests and meadows.

Highland Dell Inn (bf CC GLM H pi) Closed in Jan
PO Box 370 ✉CA 95462 *(Monte Rio)* ☎ 865-1759
☎ (800) 767-1759 (toll free) E-Mail: highland@netdex.com
Homepage: www.netdex.com/~highland
Located directly on Russian River.

Highlands Resort (bf GLM H MA msg NU pi wh)
14000 Woodland Drive ✉CA 95446 *(Guerneville)*
☎ 869-0333 Fax: 869-0370
Homepage: travel.org/HighlandResort
Convenient location, 20 min to the airport. All rooms with kitchenette, priv. bath. Other facilities: hot tub, campgrounds, TV lounge.

The Mountain Lodge (F glm H)
16350 First Street ✉CA 95446 Guerneville ☎ 868-3722

Paradise Cove Resort (bf GLM H pi)
14711 Armstrong Woods Road ✉CA 95446 Guerneville
☎ 869-2706
Suburb location, in the heart of local gay area. All rooms with kitchenette, priv. bath, WC, color TV and balcony.

Rio Villa Beach Resort (CC g H OS)
20292 Highway 116, Monte Rio ✉CA 95462 ☎ 565-1143
Fax: 865-0115 E-Mail: riovilla@sonic.net
Homepage: www.sonic.net/~riovilla

Russian River Resort (B bf CC F G H lj MA msg NU OS pi S VS W WE wh YG) Bar 9-2 h, restaurant 9-21 h
16390 4th Street, Guerneville ✉CA 95446
☎ 869-0691 ☎ (800) 417-3767 (toll free) Fax: 869-0698
E-Mail: tripleRRR@wclynx.com

TJ's Beach Resort (GLM H)
20292 Highway 116 ✉CA 95462 Monte Rio ☎ 865-1143
30 minutes to the airport. Suburb location, 5 min to local gay scene. Rooms with kitchenette, bathroom, WC and balcony.

Willows, The (bf GLM H OS)
15905 River Road ✉CA 95446 Guerneville ☎ 869-2824
Downtown neighborhood location, 5 min to local gay bars. All rooms with priv. bath and WC.

GUEST HOUSES

Jacques' Cottage (GLM H NU pi)
6471 Old Trenton Road, Forestville, ✉CA 95436 ☎ 575-1033
Fax: 573 8911 E-Mail: acques@wco.com

RELIGIOUS GROUPS

MCC Sun 12 h
at 14520 Armstrong Woods Road
PO Box 10 55, Guerneville ✉CA 95446 ☎ 869-0552

SWIMMING

-Guerneville (NU) (Beach on Russian River at Wohler Bridge)

Sacramento ☎ 916

GAY INFO

Being Gay Today (Cable Channel 17) Thu 22-23 h, repeat Fri 16-17 h, Sat 10-11 h
2659 LaVia Way ✉CA 95825 ☎ 456-8600
Sacramento's premier Gay & Lesbian Public Access Show.

BARS

Faces (AC B CC D GLM MA OS S VS W) 14-2 h
2000 K Street ✉CA 95814 ☎ 448-0706
Bar & disco.
Mercantile Saloon (B G OG r) 10-2 h
1928 L Street ✉CA 95814 ☎ 447-0792
The Mirage (B GLM N W) 11-2 h
601 15th Street ☎ 444-3238
Townhouse (B F G N W) 15-2, WE 10-2 h, Fri Sat dinner, Sun brunch.
1517 21st Street ☎ 441-5122
Western (B G lj) 6-2 h
2001 K Street ✉CA 95814 ☎ 443-9381

SEX SHOPS/BLUE MOVIES

Adult World (g)
5138 Auburn Boulevard ✉CA 95841 ☎ 344-9976

BOOK SHOPS

The Open Book (A AC CC f GLM MA) Sun-Thu 10-23 h, Fri Sat -24 h
910 21st Street ✉CA 95814 *(between I and J Streets)*
☎ 498-1004

GUEST HOUSES

Hartley House Bed + Breakfast Inn (AC bf CC glm MA msg OS wh) All year
700 22nd Street ✉CA 95816-4012 ☎ 431 78 55
☎ (800) 831-5806 (toll free) Fax: 431 7859
E-Mail: randy@hartleyhouse.com.
Homepage: www.hartleyhouse.com
Downtown location, 15 min. to airport. B&B inn with garden and deck are for sunbathing. Five rooms with bath/WC, phone, fax, TV, video, radio, own key. Rates single from US$ 115, double 129 (bf incl.).

GENERAL GROUPS

Lesbian & Gay Alliance
6000 J Street ✉CA 95819
☎ 451-5725

RELIGIOUS GROUPS

River City MCC Worship: Sun 9-11, 6h TV Minis try, Ch. 47: Mon 22. Tue 17 h Wed noon
3418 Broadway, ✉CA 95824 ☎ 454-4762
For youth: River City MCC Youth Group, same box, meetings MCC Sodal Hall Wed 19 h

San Bernardino ☎ 909

BARS

Prime Time Food & Spirits
127 W. 40th Street ✉CA 92407 ☎ 881-1286
Skylark (B D GLM) 9017
Inland Center Drive ✉CA 92408 ☎ 885-9151

SEX SHOPS/BLUE MOVIES

Bearfacts Adult Bookstore 0-24 h
1434 East Base Line ✉CA 92410 ☎ 885-9176

San Diego ☎ 619

GAY INFO

Lesbian & Gay Men's Community Center
3916 Normal Street, ✉CA 92103 ☎ 692-2077
The San Diego Gay Times
PO Box 346 24, ✉CA 92163
The Lesbian and Gay Historical Society of San Diego
PO Box 40389, ✉CA 92164 ☎ 260-1522
Update
PO Box 33148 ✉CA 92163-3148 ☎ 299-0500
E-Mail: updateEd@aol.com
Weekly newspaper for Southern California.

TOURIST INFO

San Diego Convention & Visitor Bureau
401 B Street ✉CA 92101 ☎ 232-3101 Fax: 696-9371

BARS

Bourbon Street (B G MA N OS S) Mon-Fri 12-2 h, Sat 11-2 h, Sun 9-2 h
4612 Park Boulevard ✉CA 92116 *(University Heights)*
☎ 291-0173
Entertainment every night. Happy hour Mon-Fri 12-19 h.
Brass Rail (B D G S tv VS) 10-2 h, Thu Latino night
3796 5th Avenue, Hillcrest ✉CA 92103 ☎ 298-2233
The Caliph (B g S) 11.30-2 h
3100 5th Avenue ✉CA 92103 ☎ 298-9495
Capri Lounge (B G MA)
207 North Tremont ✉CA 92054 *(Oceanside)* ☎ 722-7284
Chee Chee Club (B G MA N r) 6-2 h
929 Broadway ✉CA 92101 ☎ 234-4404
Cheers (B G MA) 10-2 h
1839 Adams Avenue ✉CA 92116 *(University Heights)*
☎ 298-3269
Club San Francisco (b G MA) 10-2 h
3412 University Avenue ✉CA 92104 *(North Park)* ☎ 563-9614
Beer & wine only.
The Flame (B D gLM s)
3780 Park Boulevard, ✉CA 92103
Lesbian bar. Boys Tue.
Flicks (B G VS YG) 14-2 h
1017 University Avenue ✉CA 92103 ☎ 297-2056
Popular.
The Hole (B F G) ?-4 h
2820 Lytton Street ✉CA 92110 *(Point Loma)* ☎ 226-9019
Mainly military clientele.
Kickers (B D F G LJ S)
308 University Avenue ✉CA 92103 *(Hillcrest)* ☎ 491-0400
The Loft (! AC B CC G MA N) 10-2 h
3610 5th Avenue ✉CA 92103 ☎ 296-6407
The Matador (B D g) 12-2 h
4633 Mission Boulevard ✉CA 92109 *(Pacific Beach)*
☎ 483-6943
Beach bar.
Moby Dick's (AC B G MA N OS s VS) 12-22 h
642 West Hawthorn Street ✉CA 92101 *(Harbour area)*
☎ 338-9966
North Park Country Club (AC B GLM MA N W) 13-2 h
4046 30th Street ✉CA 92104 *(North Park)* ☎ 563-9051
Popular beer bar
Number One Fifth Avenue (AC B G) 12-2 h
3845 5th Avenue ✉CA 92103 *(no sign)* ☎ 299-1911
Smoke-friendly patio.

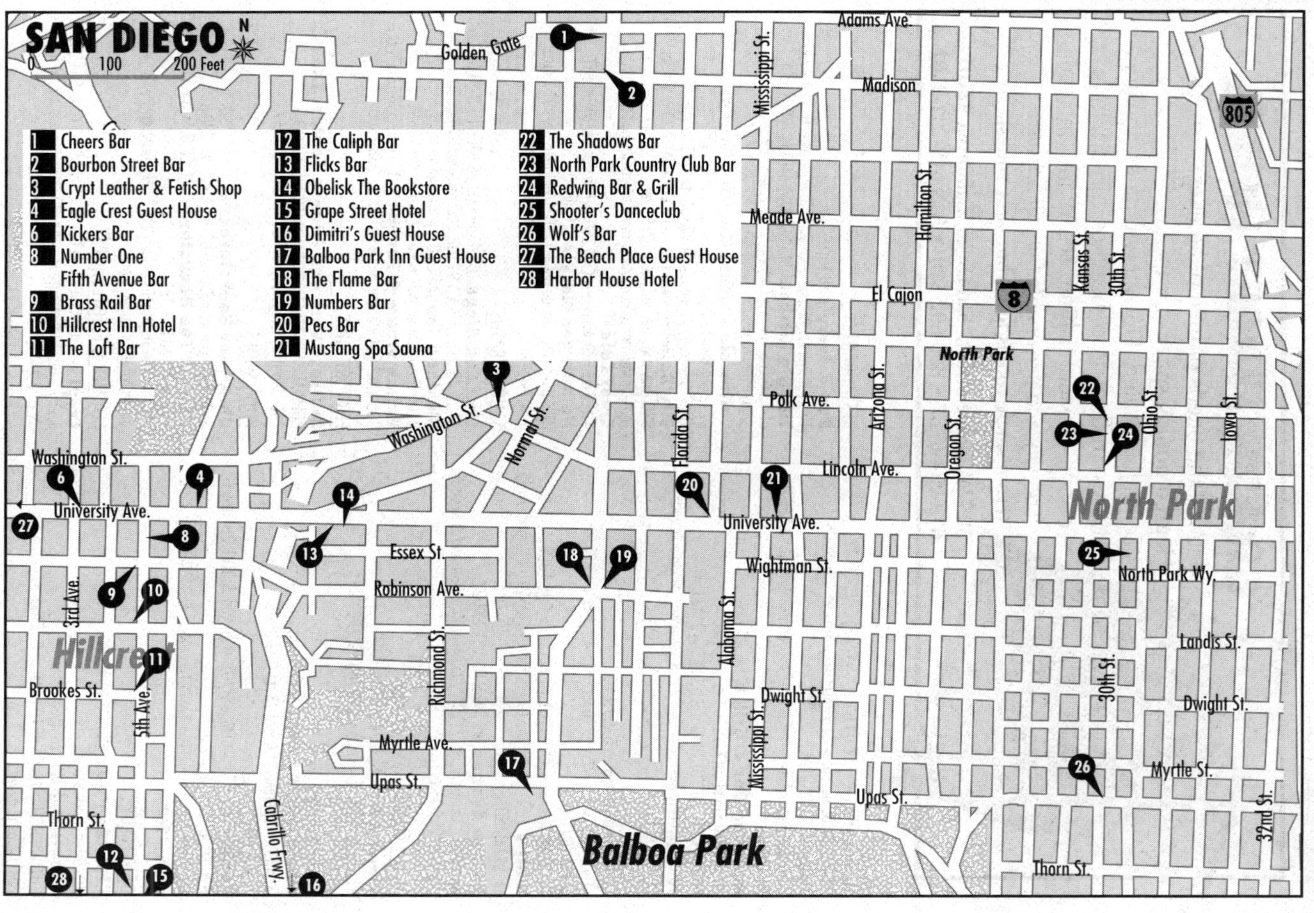
SAN DIEGO
N
0 100 200 Feet
1 Cheers Bar
2 Bourbon Street Bar
3 Crypt Leather & Fetish Shop
4 Eagle Crest Guest House
6 Kickers Bar
8 Number One
Fifth Avenue Bar
9 Brass Rail Bar
10 Hillcrest Inn Hotel
11 The Loft Bar
12 The Caliph Bar
13 Flicks Bar
14 Obelisk The Bookstore
15 Grape Street Hotel
16 Dimitri's Guest House
17 Balboa Park Inn Guest House
18 The Flame Bar
19 Numbers Bar
20 Pecs Bar
21 Mustang Spa Sauna
22 The Shadows Bar
23 North Park Country Club Bar
24 Redwing Bar & Grill
25 Shooter's Danceclub
26 Wolf's Bar
27 The Beach Place Guest House
28 Harbor House Hotel
Golden Gate
Adams Ave.
Madison
Mississippi St.
805
Meade Ave.
Hamilton St.
Kansas St.
30th St.
El Cajon
8
North Park
Polk Ave.
Arizona St.
Oregon St.
Ohio St.
Iowa St.
Washington St.
Normal St.
Florida St.
Lincoln Ave.
Washington St.
University Ave.
University Ave.
North Park
Essex St.
Wightman St.
North Park Wy.
Robinson Ave.
3rd Ave.
Hillcrest
Richmond St.
Alabama St.
Landis St.
Brookes St.
5th Ave.
Dwight St.
30th St.
Dwight St.
Mississippi St.
Myrtle Ave.
Myrtle St.
Upas St.
Upas St.
32nd St.
Thorn St.
Cabrillo Frwy.
Balboa Park
Thorn St.

Numbers (AC B CC D f G lj MA N OS P r S VS W) 12-2 h
3811 Park Boulevard ✉CA 92103 *(Hillcrest)* ☎ 294-9005
Pecs (B G lj MA) ?-4 h
2046 University Avenue ✉CA 92104 *(North Park)* ☎ 296-0889
Popular.
Redwing Bar & Grill (B F G MA N WE) 10-2 h
4012 30th Street ✉CA 92104 ☎ 281-8700
Rich's (B D G YG) Thu-Sat 21-2 h, Sun 19-2 h
1051 University Avenue ✉CA 92103 *(Opposite shopping-mall)* ☎ 497-4588
Popular.
The Shadows (b G VS) 14-2 h
4046 30th Street ✉CA 92104 *(North Park)* ☎ 563-9051
SRO (B CC GLM MA N) 10-2 h
1807 5th Avenue ✉CA 92101 *(Uptown)* ☎ 232-1886
Wolf's (B G LJ) 3404 30th Street ✉CA 92104 *(North Park)* ☎ 291-3730
#1 5th Avenue (AC B G N OS VS) 12-02 h
3845 5th Avenue ✉CA 92103 *(Between Robinson and University Ave.)* ☎ 299-1911

MEN'S CLUBS

Cinema F (G VS) 0-24 h
1202 University Avenue ✉CA 92103 ☎ 298-0854

CAFÉS

David`s (f GLM MA OS) Mon-Thu 7-24, Fri-Sun 0-24 h
3766 Fifth Avenue ✉CA 92103 ☎ 294-8908
Nice and friendly place.
Euphoria (A bf f GLM OS YG) Mon-Wed 6.30-1.30, Thu-Fri 6.30-2.30, Sat-Sun 7-2 h
1045 University Avenue, ✉CA 92103 *(near Rich's Rainbow Block)* ☎ 295-1769

DANCECLUBS

Club Montage (B D F G OS VS YG)
2028 Handcock Street
Shooters (B D G VS) 12-2 h
3815 30th Street ✉CA 92104 *(North Park)* ☎ 574-0744
Pool tables and darts.

RESTAURANTS

Ben & Jerry's (B F g)
1254 University Avenue ✉CA 92103 *(Hillcrest)* ☎ 294-4212
The Big Kitchen (bf f GLM OS) 6-14 h, WE 7-15 h
3003 Grape Street ✉CA 92102 ☎ 234-5789
Snacks and bf from US$ 3-5.50.
California Cuisine (A AC CC F g MA OS WE) Tue-Fri 11-22 h, Sat Sun 17-22 h
1027 University Avenue ✉CA 92103 ☎ 543-0790
City Delicatessen (! AC B CC F GLM) 7-24 h, Fri Sat 7-2 h
535 University Avenue ✉CA 92103 ☎ 295-2747
Large restaurant offering American and jewish specialties.
Crest Café (B F g)
425 Robinson Avenue ✉CA 92103 *(Hillcrest)* ☎ 295-2510
Hamburger Mary`s (b F glm OS)
308 University Avenue ✉CA 92103 *(Hillcrest)* ☎ 491-0400
Very popular

SAUNAS/BATHS

Club San Diego (B D f sa sb sol VS wh WO) 0-24 h
3955 4th Avenue ✉CA 92103 *(Hillcrest)* ☎ 295-0850
Mustang Spa (AC CC G P pi r sa sol wh)
2200 University Avenue, ✉CA 92104 ☎ 297-1661
Vulcan Steam & Sauna (AC B f G sa sb wh) 0-24 h
805 West Cedar Street, ✉CA 92101 ☎ 238-1980

FITNESSTUDIOS

Hillcrest Gym and Fitness Center. The (AC CC f GLM MA WO) Mon-Fri 6-22, Sat 8-20, Sun 8-18 h
142 University Avenue, ✉CA 92103 ☎ 299-7867

BOOK SHOPS

Blue Door Bookstore (glm)
3823 5th Avenue, ✉CA 92103 *(Hillcrest)* ☎ 298-8610
Obelisk-The Bookstore (! AC CC GLM W) Mon-Sat 10-23 Sun 12-20 h
1029 University Avenue ✉CA 92103 *(Hillcrest)* ☎ 297-4171
Books, cards, music & more.

LEATHER & FETISH SHOPS

Crypt (! CC GLM WE) Mon-Thu 11-23, Fri Sat 11-24, Sun 2-22 h
1515 Washington Street ✉CA 92103 *(across from Topsy's)* ☎ 692-9499
Leather & novelties.

HOTELS

Grape Street Hotel (AC bf CC DR G H LJ MA NU pi W wh YG) 24 hours
505 West Grape Street ✉CA 92101 *(Three blocks from Grape Street Pier)* ☎ 234-6787 ☎ (800) 692 51 01 Fax: 231-3501
Centrally located. From single rooms to harbor view suites.

Harbor House Resort (AC bf CC G H nu p wh WO YG)
642 West Hawthorn ✉CA 92101 ☎ 338-9966
☎ 888-338-9966 (toll-free) Fax: 338-9977
E-Mail: Harbrhouse@aol.com
Homepage: www.gaywired.com/Harborhouse.html
Open all year long. Walking distance to all venues

Hillcrest Inn (CC G H lj wh) 8-24 h
3754 5th Avenue ✉CA 92103 ☎ 293-7078
☎ (800) 258-2280 Fax: 293-3861 E-Mail: hillcrestinn@juno.com
In the heart of Hillcrest gay area. Rooms with phone, TV, fridge, priv. bath. Rates US$ 55-59.

GUEST HOUSES

Balboa Park Inn (AC bf CC GLM H MA OS wh)
3402 Park Boulevard ✉CA 92103 *(next to San Diego Zoo)* ☎ 298-0823 ☎ 800-938-8181 (toll free) Fax: 294-8070.
Complex of four Spanish colonial buildings, centrally located. Each suite with queen-sized bed, fridge, phone, some also with kitchen and jacuzzi.

Beach Place. The (AC CC G H NU VS wh)
2158 Sunset Cliffs Boulevard ✉CA 92107 *(4 blocks to beach)* ☎ 225-0746 E-Mail: beachplace@webtv.net.
Homepage: www.sony.inergy.com/beachplace.
Fully equipped small apartments.

Dimitri's Guesthouse (bf G lj MA msg NU pi sa W wh)
931 21st Street ✉CA 92102 ☎ 238-5547
Central location, airport pick-up. Priv. bath. Rates from $45-75/room/night

Downtown Inn. The (AC CC GLM H LJ H)
660 G Street ✉CA 92101 ☎ 238-4100 Fax: 238-5310
In the Gaslamp Quarter. All rooms with bath/shower, microwave, fridge. Call for rates, you get special rates if you mention the Spartacus.

Eagle Crest (bf G H)
3942 8th Avenue ✉CA 92103 ☎ 298-0350
A small, intimate Bohemian hotel in the heart of the gay Hillcrest district.

Harbor Lights Inn (AC bf CC f G H MA msg p pi W wh)
505 West Grape Street ✉CA 92101 ☎ 234-6787
☎ (800) 692-5101 (toll free) Fax: 231-3501
E-Mail: HarbrHouse@aol.com
Great view over San Diego. Rates US$ 33-125. Heated pool.

Keating House. The (AC bf F glm H)
2331 2nd Avenue ✉CA 92101 ☎ 239-8585 Fax: 239-5774
Conveniently located Victorian residence. 3 km to the airport and to gay bars. Shared baths. Rates US$ 65-90 incl. full-board.

Point Loma (bf GLM H)
3350 Rosecrans Street, ✉CA 92110 ☎ 224-9800
☎ 800-828-8111 (toll free) Fax: 224-0928

PRIVATE ACCOMODATION

Kasa Korbett (bf F GLM msg OS W wh) All year
1526 Van Buren Avenue ✉CA 92103-2419 ☎ 291-3962
E-Mail: kasakorbett@hotmail.com
Free transport to aiport/train station. Bed and breakfast with kitchen use.Rates for double rooms US$ 79, studios 99, incl. bf.

GENERAL GROUPS

Aztec Bowl
4356 30th Street ✉CA 92104 *North Park* ☎ 283-3135

HEALTH GROUPS

Beach Area Community Health Center
3705 Mission Boulevard ✉CA 92109 ☎ 488-0644
Offers gay male screening programm, STD clinic, general medicine.

Park Center for Health
4067 Park Boulevard ☎ 296-0224 or 296-7310
Internal medicine with comprehensive immunity, HIV, ARC and AIDS evaluations. Psychological Counseling.

HELP WITH PROBLEMS

Hot-Line 0-24 h
☎ 236-3339
Crisis team emergency counseling.

RELIGIOUS GROUPS

MCC Sun 9.45, 18.45, Wed 19 h
4333 30th Street *(North Park)* ☎ 280-4333
or ☎ 297-0875

SWIMMING

-Black's Beach (G NU) (In the north of San Diego take direction of La Jolla and University of California San Diego then follow route to Torrey Pines Hang Gilder Park. P in front of the beach. Gay section is at the north side. Action in the dunes.) AYOR police.

CRUISING

-Balboa Park (along 6th Ave., south of Quince Street, best afternoons)

San Francisco ☎ 415

● „San Francisco punished!" was the heading of a Los Angeles newspaper after the big earthquake of 1906. It seems that the more conservative south of California was able to see a positive side to the disastrous events. This is not too astonishing. San Franciso is the perfect example of what the Americans call *liberal*, what can best be transcribed as open-minded. Without this open-mindedness an ethnically diverse city like this could not operate smoothly. And without it San Francisco would never have become the capital of the gay community. In the seventies *Castro Street* became a refined, very 'upmarket' looking center of gay-lesbian America. Also of importance are the areas around *Polk Street* with a grand view from nearlying Nob Hill and *SoMa*, South of Market, a very fashionable part of the city with nice clubs and cultivated shopping facilities. It is presumed, that the foundation of San Francisos gay tradition was laid in the licentious era of the gold rush. In the fifties the first gay and lesbian groups and organisations were founded. But the gay boom came in the sixties, when the police warned the public of the 70.000 gays and lesbians in the city. This warning sounded, for many, more like an invitation and the run on S.F. began. With success came crises. Harvey Milk, an openly gay member of the city council was shot by another of its members. Following the mild sentence of the murderer, riots spread, which showed, how brittle the ghetto-paradise Castro Street really was. The eighties were the era of AIDS, which plunged the *gay community* of the city into one of its deepest crisis. Even today, every second gay is presumed to be hiv-positive. The AIDS-crisis has led to a profound change in the gay scene. Lesbians have often filled the posts left behind by stricken gays, and have engaged themselves in service groups for HIV-positives and AIDS-sufferers. Today lesbians are present everywhere, more than in most other cities. A car is not needed in S.F. You can reach every corner with the subway (BART), daylight trains (MUNI) and bus, however it can take time, as public transport is not very well coordinated. San Francisco is larger than it may seem. If you want to get to know the gay side of S.F., take a *Cruisin' the Castro* tour, a roundtrip through the city and its gay history. More information can be obtained by looking into the very recommendable *Bay Area Reporter* and *Oblivian Magazine*. San Francisco is worth a visit, but don't expect warm weather in summer and the typical San Francisco fog means it can get quite cold in the mornings and evenings.

✱ „San Francisco bestraft!", so lautete nach dem großen Erdbeben von 1906 die Schlagzeile einer Zeitung in Los Angeles. Offensichtlich gewann man der Tragödie im konservativen Süden Kaliforniens durchaus eine positive Seite ab.
Erstaunen muß daß nicht, denn San Francisco ist wirklich ein Musterbeispiel für das, was US-Amerikaner *liberal* nennen. Etwas, das man am ehesten mit tolerant übersetzen könnte. Ohne Toleranz könnte eine ethnisch dermaßen vielfältige Stadt sicher nicht reibungslos funktionieren. Und ohne sie wäre San Francisco wohl nie eine der Hauptstädte der schwulen Welt geworden.
In den 70er Jahren hat sich die *Castro Street* zu einem heute sehr gepflegt, sehr *upmarket* wirkenden Zentrum des schwul-lesbischen Amerika entwickelt. Ebenfalls von Bedeutung sind zum einen die Gegend um die *Polk Street* (tolle Aussicht vom nahen Nob Hill) und *SoMa*, South of Market, eine sehr angesagte Ecke mit tollen Clubs und anspruchsvollem Shopping.
Es wird vermutet, daß die ersten Grundsteine für San Franciscos schwule Traditionen bereits in der als zügellos geltenden Goldgräberzeit gelegt wurden. In den 50er Jahren unseres Jahrhunderts wurden die ersten schwulen und lesbischen Gruppen und Organisationen gegründet. Zu einem regelrechten Run auf die Stadt kam es in den 60er Jahren, als die Polizei vor den 70.000 Schwulen und Lesben in der Stadt warnte(!); eine Warnung, die auf viele Schwule auf dem Land wie eine Einladung wirkte.
Mit den Erfolgen kamen die Krisen. Harvey Milk, offen schwuler Stadtrat in den 70ern, wurde von einem Stadtratsmitglied erschossen. Auf das milde Urteil folgten Unruhen, die offenbarten, wie zerbrechlich das Ghetto-Paradies Castro war.
Die 80er Jahre wurden zum Zeitalter von AIDS und haben die *gay community* der Stadt in eine ihrer tiefsten Krisen gestürzt. Noch heute gilt jeder zweite Schwule als HIV-positiv. Doch gerade die AIDS-Krise hat zu einer tiefgreifenden Wandlung der Szene geführt: oftmals haben Lesben die Funktionen erkrankter Schwuler eingenommen, haben sich in Hilfsgruppen für Positive und an AIDS Erkrankte eingesetzt. Heute sind Lesben in San Francisco so sichtbar wie an kaum einem anderen Ort.
Wer in diese Stadt kommt, benötigt kein Auto. Mit BART (U-Bahn), MUNI (S-Bahn) und Bus kommt man gut durch die Stadt, auch wenn es wegen mangelnder Abstimmung lange dauern kann. Übrigens ist San Francisco nicht so klein, wie es den Anschein hat.
Die schwule Seite der Stadt lernt man am besten bei einer *Cruisin' the Castro* Tour kennen, einem Rundgang durch die Stadt und ihre schwule Geschichte. Weitere und aktuelle Infos stehen im empfehlenswerten *Bay Area Reporter* oder im *Oblivian Magazine*.
San Francisco ist immer eine Reise wert, einen warmen Sommer

aber sollte man nicht erwarten, denn im sommerlichen Nebel morgens und abends kann es recht kühl werden.

▲ „San Francisco punie!" titrait un quotidien de Los Angeles le lendemain du grand tremblement de terre de 1906. Le sud conservateur de la Californie s'est réjoui de cette terrible catastrophe et cela ne surprend personne, car San Francisco est, et a toujours été, une ville progressiste et tolérante. „Liberal" disent les Américains, ce qu'on pourrait traduire par „large d'esprit". Et c'est bien cette tolérance et cette ouverture d'esprit qui permet à la ville de fonctionner comme elle fonctionne: mélange des races et des cultures et, en plus, capitale mondiale des gays.
Depuis les années 70, Castro Street est le bastion gay/lesbien des Etats-Unis. C'est aujourd'hui un quartier très soigné, très „upmarket". A voir également: autour de Polk Street (vue magnifique depuis la Nob Hill toute proche) et South Market („SoMA"), très mode, avec de nombreux clubs et de jolies boutiques.
On dit qu'à l'époque des chercheurs d'or, San Francisco avait déjà acquis ses lettres de noblesse gayes. Dans les années 50, on y a fondé les premières associations gayes et lesbiennes du pays. Ce n'est que dans les années 60 qu'a eu lieu le „rush" gay sur la ville. La police n'a rien trouvé de mieux que d'affoler les touristes en criant haut et fort que 70.000 gays et lesbiennes vivaient à San Francisco. Inutile de dire que, dans le reste du pays, certaines personnes ont eu vite fait de prendre cette mise en garde pour une invitation!
Toute médaille a ses revers et les problèmes ont vite surgi. Dans les années 70, Harvey Milk, conseiller municipal qui vivait ouvertement son homosexualité, a été assassiné par un autre membre du conseil municipal. Le jugement indulgent prononcé par la Justice a déclenché une vague d'émeutes à Castro. Le paradis gay de Castro Street a su se montrer rebelle et combatif.
Avec l'épidémie de SIDA dans les années 80, la ville a plongé dans une des plus profondes crises de son histoire. Aujourd'hui encore, on dit qu'un gay sur deux est séropositif. La crise déclenchée par la maladie a permis aux gays de se retrouver et de se restructurer. Dans de nombreux cas, ce sont les lesbiennes qui ont pris la relève des gays malades ou morts pour les remplacer dans leurs fonctions. Elles se battent aujourd'hui pour les groupes d'aide et de soutien aux malades du SIDA. A San Francisco, les lesbiennes font aujourd'hui partie du décor, comme nulle part ailleurs aux Etats-Unis.
Pas besoin de voiture pour visiter San Francisco. Le métro, le RER et le bus sont les moyens de transport les plus pratiques, même si les changements de lignes sont souvent peu pratiques et mal coordonnés. Notez bien que San Francisco n'est pas si petite qu'elle en a l'air!
Pour faire connaissance du San Francisco gay, faites donc une visite guidée „Cruisin' the Castro". Vous découvrirez la ville et ses traditions gayes. Pour de plus amples informations, consultez le très bon „Bay Aera Reporter" et „Oblivian Magazine".
San Francisco est intéressante toute l'année. Attention, l'été y est relativement frais. Le matin et le soir, il ne fait pas chaud, surtout les jours de brume.

☆ „¡San Francisco castigado!" ese fue el titular de un periodico de Los Angeles despúes del gran terremoto de 1906. Por lo visto el sur más conservador de California era capaz de ver hasta un lado positivo de esta tragedia. Y no es de extrañar, ya que San Francisco representa todo, lo que llaman los norteamericanos *liberal,* que se traduce mejor como tolerante. Y la tolerancia es imperscindible para hacer funcionar la conviviencia en una ciudad que dispone de una multiplicidad étnica como San Francisco. Sin ella San Francisco no se habría convertido en una de las capitales mun-

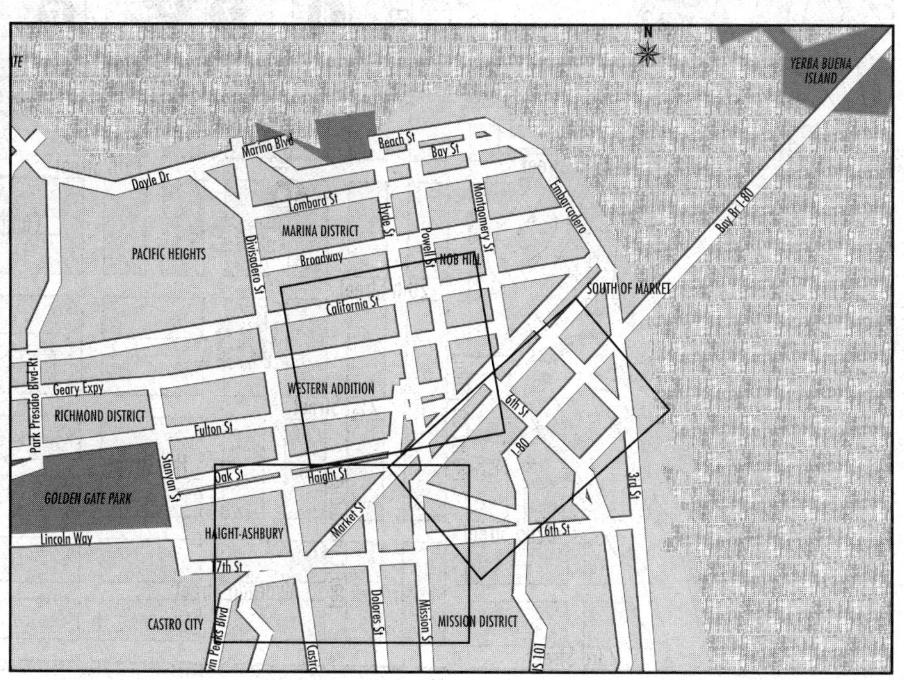

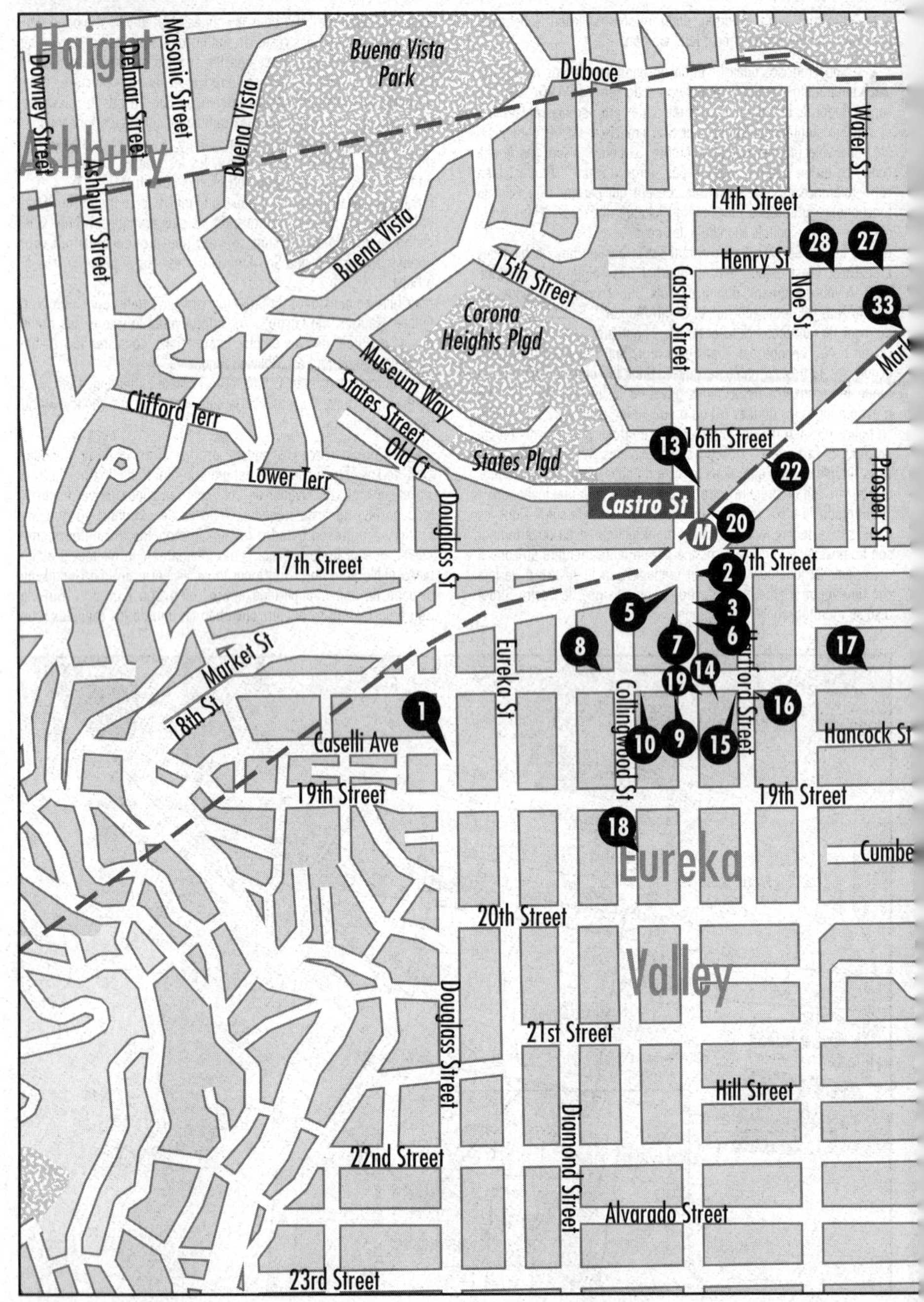
Haight Ashbury
Downey Street
Delmar Street
Masonic Street
Ashbury Street
Buena Vista
Buena Vista Park
Buena Vista
Duboce
Water St
14th Street
Henry St
Castro Street
Noe St.
15th Street
Corona Heights Plgd
Museum Way
States Street
Old Ct
Clifford Terr
Lower Terr
States Plgd
16th Street
Castro St
Prosper St
17th Street
17th Street
Douglass St
Market St
18th St
Eureka St
Collingwood St
Hartford Street
Caselli Ave
Hancock St
19th Street
19th Street
Eureka Valley
20th Street
21st Street
Douglass Street
Diamond Street
Hill Street
22nd Street
Alvarado Street
23rd Street
1
2
3
5
6
7
8
9
10
13
14
15
16
17
18
19
20
22
27
28
33
M

SAN FRANCISCO
Castro Area/Mission District

- **1** Belvedere House Guest House
- **2** Twin Peaks Bar
- **5** Daddy's Bar
- **6** A Different Light Bookstore
- **7** Phoenix Bar
- **8** The Pendulum Bar
- **9** Badlands Bar
- **10** The Edge Bar
- **13** Inn on Castro Guest Houses
- **14** Midnight Sun Bar
- **15** Castro Country Club Bar
- **16** Moby Dick Bar
- **17** Men's Room Bar
- **18** The Villa/San Francisco Views Guest House
- **19** Uncle Bert's Place Bar
- **20** The Café Bar
- **22** Pasta pomodoro Restaurant
- **24** Pilsner Inn Bar
- **25** Transfer Bar
- **26** Willows B&B Inn Guest House
- **27** 24 Henry Guesthouse
- **28** Castillo Inn Guest House
- **29** Dolores Park Inn Guest House
- **30** Inn San Francisco Guest House
- **31** Esta Noche Bar
- **32** Baby Judy's/Leisure Lodge at the Casanova Danceclub
- **33** Thai House Bar & Café Restaurant
- **34** Eros Men's Club
- **35** The Mint Bar
- **36** La India Bonita Bar
- **37** Andora Inn Guest House
- **38** The Parker House Guest House

ton Street
2
reet
Lafayette
Park
Buchanan Street
Clay Street
Sacramento Street
19
18
Polk Street
Larkin Street
17
California Street
Laguna Street
Octavia Street
California Street
Van Ness Avenue
14 - 16
Street
Austin St
32
13
Bush Street
Franklin Street
12
31
Fern St
Webster Street
Sutter Street
Gough Street
1
20
Hemlock St
9
10
Post Street
Cedar St
Geary Boulevard
8
Myrtle St
O'Farrell St
7
22
Olive St
Ellis Street
Willow St
Tenderloin
Eddie Street
Larch St
29
Turk Street
Elm St
Golden Gate Avenue
McAllister Street
Fulton Street
Civic
Grove Street
Octavia Street
Ivy St
Center
reet
Linden St
3
9th Street
reet

SAN FRANCISCO
Hayes Valley/Polk Street Area/Downtown

- **1** The Majestic Hotel
- **2** Alta Plaza Bar
- **3** Marlena's Bar
- **4** Steamworks Bathhouse Berkeley Sauna
- **5** The Chateau Tivoli Hotel
- **7** The Gangway Bar
- **8** Old Rick's Gold Room Bar
- **9** Polk Gulch Saloon Bar
- **12** Reflections Bar
- **13** Leland Hotel
- **14** Polk Rendevouz Bar
- **16** The Kimo's Bar
- **17** N'Touch Bar
- **18** The Cinch Bar
- **19** The Swallow Bar
- **20** Motherlode Bar
- **21** Pensione International Guest House
- **22** Atherton Hotel
- **24** The Hob Nob Bar
- **26** Aunt Charlie's Lounge Bar
- **29** Wooden Horse Bar
- **30** Dottie's True Blue Café
- **31** Quetzal Café
- **32** Grubstake Restaurant
- **33** Renoir Hotel
- **34** Allison Hotel

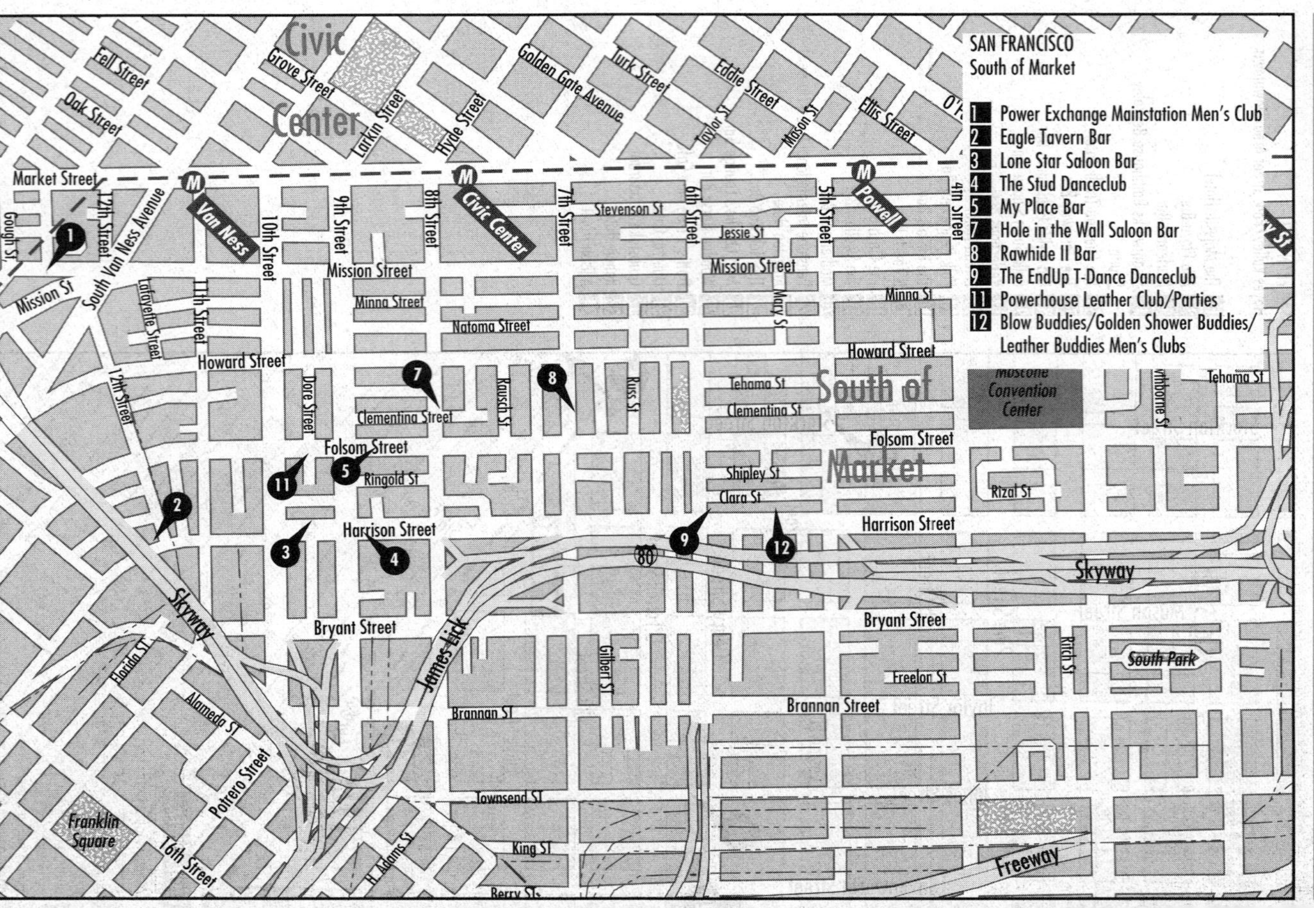
SAN FRANCISCO
South of Market
1 Power Exchange Mainstation Men's Club
2 Eagle Tavern Bar
3 Lone Star Saloon Bar
4 The Stud Danceclub
5 My Place Bar
7 Hole in the Wall Saloon Bar
8 Rawhide II Bar
9 The EndUp T-Dance Danceclub
11 Powerhouse Leather Club/Parties
12 Blow Buddies/Golden Shower Buddies/
Leather Buddies Men's Clubs
Civic Center
Fell Street
Oak Street
Grove Street
Larkin Street
Hyde Street
Golden Gate Avenue
Turk Street
Eddie Street
Taylor St
Mason St
Ellis Street
Market Street
Gough St.
12th Street
South Van Ness Avenue
Van Ness
10th Street
9th Street
8th Street
Civic Center
7th Street
Stevenson St
6th Street
Jessie St
5th Street
Powell
4th Street
Mission St
Mission Street
Mission Street
Lafayette Street
11th Street
Minna Street
Natoma Street
Mary St
Minna St
Howard Street
Howard Street
12th Street
Dore Street
Clementina Street
Rausch St
Russ St
Tehama St
Clementina St
South of Market
Moscone Convention Center
Tehama St
Folsom Street
Folsom Street
Ringold St
Shipley St
Clara St
Rizal St
Harrison Street
Harrison Street
80
Skyway
Skyway
Bryant Street
Bryant Street
James Lick
Florida St
Alameda St
Gilbert St
Ritch St
South Park
Freelon St
Brannan St
Brannan Street
Potrero Street
Townsend St
Franklin Square
16th Street
H. Adams St
King St
Berry St
Freeway

diales gay. En la década de los '70 la *Castro Street* se convirtió en el centro gay-lésbico de E.E.U.U., hoy en día se ha convertido en el centro elegante y *upmarket* de la cultura homosexual. De mucha importancia lo son los alrededores de la *Polk Street* y *SoMa* South of Market, lugar en el que se encuentran atractivos clubs y tiendas de compra de gran estilo. Se cree que la base de la tradición gay de San Francisco fue cimentada en los desenfrenados tiempos de la busqueda de oro. En los años '50 se formaron los primeros grupos gay y lesbianos de la ciudad. En los años '60 la ciudad comenzó a tomar auge cuando la policia advertía sobre los más de 70.000 gays y lesbianas de la ciudad. Esta advertencia fungió como una invitación para gran cantidad de homosexuales de las zonas rurales. Junto con los éxitos llegaban también las crisis. Harvey Milk miembro del ayuntamiento de la ciudad, fue asesinado por uno de sus colegas debido a su orientación sexual. A la suave pena jurídica siguieron grandes desordenes que dejaron ver que delicado era el Paraíso-Ghetto Castro. La década de los '80 se convertieron en los tiempos del SIDA y condujeron a la *Gay Community* de la ciudad a una de las crisis más grandes de su historia. Aún hoy en día uno de cada dos homosexuales está infectado con el virus del SIDA. Pero la crisis del SIDA condujo a un cambio radical en el ambiente gay de la ciudad. Con frecuencia fueron lesbianas que pasaron a ocupar los puestos de los gays enfermos. En pocos sitios se encuentra una presencia tan masiva de lesbianas como en San Francisco. La ciudad se puede visitar sin la necesidad de tener que alquilar un coche. El transporte publico con el BART (metro), el MUNI (tren) y buses ofrecen un buen servicio. La parte gay de la ciudad se conoce de lo mejor tomando el tour llamado *Cruisin' The Castro* que ofrece una vuelta por la ciudad y su historia homosexual. Informaciones actuales y de otro tipo se reciben también de el *Bay Area Reporter* o el *Oblivian Magazine*. San Francisco vale la pena, sin embargo no se debe esperar que el verano sea caliente.

❖ „San Francisco punita", questo fu il titolo di un quotidiano di Los Angeles dopo il grande terremoto del 1906. Ovviamente il sud della California, molto conservatore, scoprì nella tragedia un lato positivo. Non c'è da sorprendersi poichè San Francisco è veramente un'esempio di ciò che gli americani chiamano *liberal*. Ma senza tale atteggiamento liberale una città così varia etnicamente avrebbe molto più conflitti e non sarebbe mai divenuta una delle capitali gay mondiali. Negli anni '70 la *Castro street*, oggi molto curata, molto *up market*, è divenuta il centro dell'America omosessuale. Altrettanto importanti sono le zone intorno alla *Polk Street* (con vista spettacolare dalla vicina Nob Hill) e a *SoMa*, South of Market, un angolo molto alla moda con ottime discoteche e negozi di lusso. Si presume che le fondamenta della tradizione gay siano state gettate durante la disinibita epoca dei cercatori d'oro. Negli anni '50 del nostro secolo sono stati fondati i primi gruppi e le prime organizzazioni di gay e lesbiche. Ma il grande afflusso di omosessuali è avvenuto negli anni '60, quando la polizia, con un avviso d'allarme, ha reso nota la presenza di 70.000 gay e lesbiche nella città. Per i gay americani questo avviso è stato piuttosto un invito. Ma dopo il successo venne la crisi: Harvey Milk, assessore gay, negli anni '70 venne assassinato da un membro del consiglio comunale. In seguito ad una condanna troppo leggera vi furono dei disordini che rivelarono la fragilità di Castro, il ghetto paradisiaco. Negli anni '80 si aprì l'epoca dell'AIDS che trascinò la *gay community* in una profonda crisi. Malgrado la profilassi si suppone tutt'oggi che un gay su due sia positivo. L'AIDS ha introdotto radicali cambiamenti: spesso donne omosessuali hanno rimpiazzato gay ammalati, si sono formati gruppi di positivi e gruppi di assistenza per i malati. In nessun luogo come a San Francisco le lesbiche sono così emancipate. Chi visita la città non ha bisogno di un'auto, si può spostarsi con il BART (metrò), il MUNI (tram) e gli autobus, anche se spesso perderà tempo a causa di una imprecisa coordinazione delle linee. Il modo migliore per conoscere la parte gay della città è un *Cruisin' the Castro*, un giro attraverso la città e la sua storia gay. Troverete altre informazioni nel giornale *Bay Area Reporter*.

GAY INFO

Bay Area Reporter (BAR)
395 9th Street, ✉CA 94103 ☎ 861-5019 Fax: 861-7230.
Weekly newspaper for the greater Bay area, about 48 pages, free at delivery points in Bay Area. News, sports & entertainment of interest to the gay community.

Bear
2215R Market Street, Suite 148, ✉CA 94114 ☎ 552-1506 Fax: 552-3244
Bimonthly publication

Gay Area Youth Switchboard
PO Box 846, ✉CA 94101 ☎ 386-GAYS
For sexual minority youth (13-25 years). Information/referral, peer counseling, community/survival rescources, updates on activities/events.

Odyssey Magazine
584 Castro Street, # 302, ✉CA 94114-2500 ☎ 431-7911 Fax: 431-7911 E-Mail: odysseysf@aol.com.
Free magazine availasble at gay venues.

San Francisco Frontiers Mon-Fri 9-18 h
2370 Market Street ✉CA 94114 *(2nd floor)* ☎ 487-6000

TOURIST INFO

San Francisco Visitor & Convention Bureau
201 Third Street, Suite 900 ✉CA 94103 ☎ 974-6900 Fax: 227-2602.

BARS

Alta Plaza (B e F GLM MA S) 16-2, restaurant open Mon-Thu 17.30-22, Fri-Sat -23, Sun 10-15 h
2301 Fillmore Street/Clay ✉CA 94115 *(Pacific Heights)*
☎ 922-1444

Aunt Charlie's Lounge (B G N OG tv) Sun-Thu 6-24, Fri-Sat -2 h
133 Turk Street ✉CA 94102 *(Between Taylor and Jones Streets)*
☎ 441-2922

Badlands (! AC B G LJ MA VS) 11.30-2 h
4121 18th Street ✉CA 94114 *(Between Castro and Collingwood)*
☎ 626-9320
Cruisy atmosphere.

Bench and Bar (B D F G S) Mon-Fri 15-2, Sat 17-2, Sun 11-2 h
120 11th Street, Oakland, ✉CA 94607 ☎ 444-2266
Every Fri „Latin Explosion"

Cable Reef (B d GLM MA SNU) 12-2 h
2272 Telegraph Ave, Oakland ✉CA 94612 *(Near Grand Avenue)*
☎ 451-3777
Different theme nights.

Cafe Mars (B d glm YG) Mon-Sat 17-2 h
798 Brannan Street/7th Street ✉CA 94103 *(SOMA)*
☎ 621-MARS
Formerly frequented mostly by gays, now straight guys and girls party here too.

Café. The (B D GLM) 12-2 h
2367 Market Street ✉CA 94114 *(Between 16th and 17th Streets)*
☎ 861-3846
Popular

Castro Country Club (b Glm MA OS) Mon 14-24, Fri -1, Sat 10-1, Sun -24 h
4058 18th Street ✉CA 94114 *(Between Hartford and Castro Streets)* ☎ 552-6102 *No alcohol served.*

Cinch Saloon. The (B G MA N OS) 6-2 h
1723 Polk Street ✉CA 94109 *(Between Washington and Clay Streets)* ☎ 776-4162
Club Rendez-vous (A AC B D GLM MA S SNU) -2 h
1312 Polk Street ✉CA 94109 *(At Bush Street)* ☎ 673-7934
Newly opened in Nov.'99. Male strippers
Club 18 (B G) 120
11th Street Oakland, ✉CA 94607 *(BART-Lake Merritt)* ☎ 444-2266
Comfort Zone (B GLM YG) 21-2 h
581 5th Street, Oakland ✉CA 94607 ☎ 510/ 869-4847
Predominately afro-american crowd and their friends.
Daddy's (B G LJ MA N) 6-2 h
440 Castro Street ✉CA 94114 *(Between Market and 18th Streets)* ☎ 621-8732
Popular
Eagle Tavern. The (AC B CC f G LJ MA N OS S) 12-02 h
398 12th Street ✉CA 94103 *(Corner of 12th and Harrison streets)* ☎ 626-0880
Heated outdoor patio.
Edge. The (B G LJ MA N) 12-2 h
4149 18th Street ✉CA 94114 *(Muni)* ☎ 863-4027
El Rio (B D f GLM MA S OS) 15-2, Mon -24 h
3158 Mission Street/Precita ✉CA 94110 ☎ 282-3325
Live entertainment. Nice backyard with lots of plants. Popular. Mixed white and Latino crowd.
Esta Noche (B D GLM MA STV YG) 14-2 h
3079 16th Street ✉CA 94103 ☎ 861-5757
Wed popular drag shows. Mostly Latino crowd.
Expansion Bar (B GLM MA N) 10-1 h
2124 Market Street ✉CA 94114 *(Between 14th and 15th Streets)* ☎ 863-4041
The Gangway (B G N OG) 6-2 h
841 Larkin Street ✉CA 94109 *(Between O'Farrell and Geary Streets)* ☎ 885-4441
Ginger's Too (B G N OG) 10-2 h
43 6th Street ✉CA 94103 *(Between Market Street and Mission Streets)* ☎ 543-3622
Ginger's Trois (B f G N) Mon-Fri 10-22 h, closed Sat-Sun
246 Kearny ✉CA 94108 *(In Financial District, between Sutter and Bush Streets)* ☎ 989-0282
The Giraffe (B D Glm MA) 8-2 h
1131 Polk Street ✉CA 94109 *(Between Post and Sutter Streets)* ☎ 474-1702
Popular
Hob Nob. The (B G N OG) 6-2 h
700 Geary Street/Leavenworth ✉CA 94109 ☎ 771-9866
Hole in the Wall Saloon (B G LJ MA) Tue-Thu 12-2, Fri-Mon 6-2 h
289 8th Street ✉CA 94103 *(Between Folsom and Howard Streets)* ☎ 431-4695
Very popular bar. Friendly predominantly biker and leather crowd.
La India Bonita (B G MA N STV) 13-2 h
3089 16th Street ✉CA 94103 *(Between Mission and Valencia Street)* ☎ 621-9294
Popular drag shows in Spanish every Sat and Sun at 23 h. Friendly staff and relaxed atmosphere. Mixed white and Latino crowd.
Kimo's (AC B CC d Glm MA N STV W) 8-2 h
1351 Polk Street/Pine Street ✉CA 94109 ☎ 885-4535
The Lion Pub (AC B e G MA) 15-2 h
2062 Divisadero Street/Sacramento Street ✉CA 94115 ☎ 567-6565
Lone Star Saloon (! B G LJ N OG OS) 12-2, Sat-Sun 6-2 h
1354 Harrison Street ✉CA 94103 *(Between 9th and Folsom Streets)* ☎ 863-9999
Popular. Lots of bears. Nice patio.
Marlena's (B GLM MA N STV) 12-2, Sat-Sun 10-2 h
488 Hayes Street ✉CA 94102 *(Between Octavia and Gough Streets, Hayes Valley)* ☎ 864-6672
Fri at 24 h drag show.
Men's Room (B G MA N) 12-2 h. Cocktail hour 16-19 h Mon, Thu & Fri.
3988 18th Street ✉CA 94114 *(Between Noe and Sanchez Streets)* ☎ 861-1310
Friendly atmosphere.
The Metro (B F GLM OS YG) 14-1 h, restaurant 17.30-23 h
3600 16th Street ✉CA 94114 *(Between Noe and Market Streets)* ☎ 703-9750
Tue karaoke night. Popular on weekends. Nice terrace overlooking Market Street.
The Midnight Sun (! B G VS YG) 12-2 h
4067 18th Street ✉CA 94114 *(Between Castro and Noe Streets)* ☎ 861-4186
Oldest video bar in town. Cruisy atmosphere.
Mint. The (B F GLM MA OS S) 11-2 h
1942 Market Street ✉CA 94102 *(Between Haight and Duboce Streets)* ☎ 626-4726
Best karaoke bar in SF. Karaoke hours Mon-Thu 21-2, Fri 20-2, Sat Sun 16-2 h. Also restaurant.
Moby Dick (B Glm N YG) 12-2 h
4049 18th Street/Hartford ✉CA 94114
Friendly and relaxed atmosphere
Motherlode (B glm S TV) 6-2 h
1085 Post Street ✉CA 94109 ☎ 928-6006
The place to go for transvestites and transsexuals and their fans.
My Place (B G LJ MA) 12-2 h
1225 Folsom Street ✉CA 94103 *(Between 8th and 9th Streets)* ☎ 863-2329
Most diverse crowd in the city.
N'Touch Bar (B D G S SNU STV YG) 15-2 h
1548 Polk Street ✉CA 94109 ☎ 441-8413
For those who fancy Asian men. Very popular on weekends. Cruisy atmosphere.
Old Rick's Gold Room (B G N OG) 6-2 h
939 Geary Boulevard ✉CA 94109 *(Between Polk and Larkin Streets)* ☎ 441-9211
Small neighbourhood bar.
The Pendulum (! B G MA) 6-2 h
4146 18th Street ✉CA 94114 *(Between Collingwood and Castro Streets)* ☎ 863-4441
Where black and white men meet. Very popular. Good R&B music.
Phoenix (AC B D G lj VS WE YG) 12.30-2 h
482 Castro Street ✉CA 94114 ☎ 552-6827
Popular with a mixed crowd. Cruisy atmosphere.
Pilsner Inn (B Glm N OS) 9-2, Sat-Sun 7-2 h
225 Church Street ✉CA 94114 *(Between Market and 15th Streets)* ☎ 621-7058
Polk Gulch Saloon (B G r tv) 8-2 h
1100 Polk Street/Post Street ✉CA 94109 ☎ 771-2022
Mixed crowd
Polk Rendevouz (B G MG N) 8-2 h
1303 Polk Street ✉CA 94109 *(Between Bush and Pine Streets)* ☎ 673-7934
Powerhouse (! B G LJ) 16-2, Sat-Sun 12-2 h
1347 Folsom Street/Dore Alley ✉CA 94103 *(Between 9th and 10th Streets)* ☎ 552-8689
Definitely a must for all leather men. Thu they host the Sissy Bar. Lots of tattoed and pierced guys enjoy the relaxed atmosphere. Go-go boys.

Stripper Nights
Premium Well
Always a Party
1312 POLK St. @ Bush
415.673.7934
www.clubrendez-vous.com

Rawhide II (B D Glm MA) 16-2, Fri-Sun 12-2 h
280 7th Street ✉CA 94103 *(Between Folsom and Howard Streets)* ☎ 621-1197
Country/Western music, popular.
Reflections (B f G OG R) 6-2 h
1160 Polk Street ✉CA 94109 *(Between Post and Sutter Streets)* ☎ 771-6262
Good snacks
The Swallow (B e G N OG) 10-2 h
1750 Polk Street ✉CA 94109 *(Between Clay and Washington Streets)* ☎ 775-4152
Transfer (B Glm MA N WE) 11-2, Sat-Sun 6-2 h
198 Church Street/14th Street ✉CA 94114 ☎ 861-7499
Trax (B GLM MA N) 12-2 h
1437 Haight Street ✉CA 94117 *(Between Masonic and Ashbury Streets)* ☎ 864-4213
Popular and only gay bar in the Haight/Ashbury district.
Twin Peaks (B GLM MA N OS) 6-2 h
401 Castro Street/Market Street ✉CA 94114 ☎ 864-9470
No bottled beer available. Always busy, it has a nice interior terrace from where you can overlook what's going on on Market Street.
Uncle Bert's Place (B GLM MA N OS) 6-2 h
4086 18th Street ✉CA 94114 *(Between Castro and Noe Streets)* ☎ 431-8616
Relaxed atmosphere
White Horse (B CC D GLM lj MA N W) Mon-Tue 15-2, Wed-Sun 13-2 h
6551 Telegraph Avenue Oakland ✉CA 94609 ☎ (510) 652-3820
Oldest gay bar west of the Mississippi. Popular.
Wooden Horse. The (B G lj MA S STV) 6-2 h
622 Polk Street ✉CA 94102 *(Muni)* ☎ 771-8063

MEN'S CLUBS

Blow Buddies (! DR G MA NU P) Thu 19:30-3 h, Fri & Sat 21-04 h, Sun 18-0:30 h
933 Harrison Street ✉CA 94017 *(Between 5th and 6th Streets)* ☎ 863-4323
Other clubs at the same location: -Golden Shower Buddies (2nd Wed / month) -Underwear Buddies (3rd Wed / month) -Leather Buddies (4th Wed/ month). Call for info.
Eros (CC G MA msg sa sb YG) Sun-Thu 16-0 h, Fri-Sat -4 h
2051 Market Street ✉CA 94114 *(at Church Street)* ☎ 864-3767
Power Exchange Mainstation (DR G MA VS)
74 Otis ✉CA 94103 *(Between S. Van Ness and Gough Street)* ☎ 487-9944 *Admission fee.*
Rubber Corps (G LJ) 1st Sat/month 21-2 h
(call for location) ☎ 552-7979
Steam Works (! AC DR G MA msg P sa sb VS wh WO YG) 0-24 h
2107 4th Street/Addison, Berkeley ✉CA 94710 *(Near University Avenue in Berkeley)* ☎ (510) 845-8992
Take the Bay-Bridge direction Oakland, than exit University Avenue from Interstate N° 80. ID with photo required. Popular gay bath.

CAFÉS

Dottie's True Blue Cafe (b bf f GLM) 7.30-14 h
522 Jones Street ✉CA 94102 *(Between Geary and O'Farrell Streets)* ☎ 885-2767
The perfect place to enjoy a delicious breakfast. Very popular on weekends for brunch.

Flore. Cafe (F G OS) Mon-Sat 8.30-22.30 h, Sun 9-20.30 h
2298 Market Street/Noe Street ✉CA 94114 ☎ 621-8579
Popular. Rather mixed in the evenings.

Harvey's (B bf F GLM MA S) 9-2 h
500 Castro Street/18th Street ✉CA 94114 ☎ 431-4278
Cute and friendly staff.

Jumpin' Java (b f glm YG) 7-22 h
139 Noe St./14th St. ✉CA 94114 ☎ 431-5282

Quetzal (AC b bf F GLM MA OS s VS W) 6-23, Sat, Sun 7-23 h
1234 Polk Street ✉CA 94109 ☎ 673-4181

DANCECLUBS

Asia at the King Street Garage (AC B D G MA s WE) 2nd/4th Fri 22-3 h
174 King Street ✉CA 94107 *(Between 2nd and 3rd Streets)* ☎ 974-1156
Lots of cute young Asian girls and boys who enjoy themselves. Very cute go-go dancers.

Baby Judy's Discotheque and Leisure Lodge at the Casanova (B D GLM YG) Wed 22-2 h
527 Valencia Street ✉CA 94110 *(Between 16th and 17th Streets)*
Popular dance club which attracts a young and very mixed non-mainstream crowd.

The Box (AC B D Glm YG) Thu 21-2.30 h
715 Harrison Street ✉CA 94107 *(Between 3rd and 4th Streets)* ☎ 647-8258
Two bars, very popular dance club.

Divas (AC b D G MA S STV TV YG) 06-02 h. Dancefloor Wed-Sat 22-02 h
1081 Post Street ✉CA 94109 ☎ 474-3482

EndUp T-Dance (B f GLM MA s TV W YG) Fri 20-Sat 16 h, Sat 20-2.30 h, Sun 5.30-2 h
401 6th Street ✉CA 94103-4706 ☎ 896-1095
This place gets packed on Sun mornings. For all non-stop party-goers this is the place to be.

Fag Fridays at the Endup (! B D Glm OS YG) Fri 22-5.30 h
401 6th Street/Harrison ✉CA 94108 ☎ 263-4850
Popular alternative dance club. Very relaxed atmosphere. Nice patio.

Futura at the King St. Garage (AC B D G LJ MA s WE) 2nd and 4th Sat 21-3 h
174 King Street ✉CA 94107 *(Between 2nd and 3rd Streets)* ☎ 974-1156
Popular gay Latino dance club, which attracts some Black and White boys too. Not every Sat, check dates.

King Street Garage (AC B D glm lj MA s WE) 1st/3rd Fri/month 0-6 h
174 King Street ✉CA 94107 *(Between 2nd and 3rd Streets)* ☎ 947-1156

Pleasuredome at Club Townsend (AC B D G LJ MA s W WE) Sun 21-6 h
177 Townsend Street ✉CA 94107 *(Between 2nd and 3rd Streets)* ☎ 974-1156
Lots of a hungry guys dance to the latest tunes. This is a must !

Sissy Bar at Powerhouse (B D GLM SNU YG) Thu 21-2 h
1347 Folsom Street/Dore Alley ✉CA 94103 *(Between 9th and 10th Streets)* ☎ 552-8689
Rather a hang out than dance atmosphere. Nevertheless recommended, if you want to enjoy the company of a diverse crowd, that is somewhat different than the usual house queens.

The Stud (! B D G STV YG) 17-2 h, Thu dykes only
399 9th Street/Harrison Street ✉CA 94103 ☎ 863-6623
Mon popular Funk Night which attracts a mixed black and white crowd (21-3 h). Every Tue The Stud hosts the popular Trannyshack club for Trannies and their admirers. The drag show at 24 h is a must (22-3 h). Wed Midweek beer-bust. Highly recommended. Sun 80 Something alternative club attracts a very relaxed crowd (21-2 h).

Sundance Saloon at The King Street Garage (AC B D GLM LJ MA WE) Sun 18-23 h
177 Townsend Street ✉CA 94107 ☎ 974-1156
Two-stepping and line dancing.

Universe at Club Townsend (AC B D GLM LJ MA s W WE) Sat 21.30-7 h
177 Townsend Street ✉CA 94107 *(Between 2nd and 3rd Streets)*

☎ 974-1156
The place to be on a late Sat night. Very busy after 2 h when a mixed crowd, among them lots of hunky bare chested guys, enjoy themselves and the cute go-go dancers dance to the hottest House and Techno music. Cruisy atmosphere.
Vertigo at the Endup (B D GLM OS YG) Sat 23-4 h
401 6th Street/Harrison ✉CA 94103 ☎ 703-7172
Popular dance club. Nice outdoor patio.

RESTAURANTS

Baghdad Café (bf F GLM MA OS) 0-24 h
2295 Market Street/16th Street ✉CA 94114 ☎ 621-4434
Inexpensive and good food. Busy late at night. They serve vegetarian dishes too.
Café Akimbo (b CC F glm MA) Mon-Thu 11.30-15, 17.30-21, Fri-Sat 11.30-15, 17.30-22 h, closed Sun
116 Maiden Lane ✉CA 94108 *(near Grant, Union Square)* ☎ 433-2288
Elegant but casual restaurant serving Californian cuisine.
Café do Brasil (b bf F glm MA s) 07.30-21.30 h
1106 Market Street ✉CA 94102 *(at 7th Street)* ☎ 626 6432
Exotic bruch at WE. Thu-Sun Churrasco (Brazilian barbecue). Specialities from Bahia, seafood, Feijoada and vegetarian dishes.
Grubstake (AC bf F GLM MA) Mon-Fri 17-4, Sat-Sun 10-4 h
1525 Pine Street ✉CA 94109 *(Between Polk and Van Ness Avenue)* ☎ 673-8268
Hamburgers, chili, steaks and breakfast. Highly recommended, friendly service. Meeting place after the bars are closed. Popular Portuguese dinner Sat night.
Hot'n Hunky (B f G) 11-24 h
4039 18th Street near Hartford ✉CA 94132 ☎ 621-6365
Hamburger restaurant.
La Mediterranée (F glm) closed Mon
288 Noe ✉CA 94114 *(near Market)* ☎ 431-7210
Good and inexpensive food, nice staff
Millennium (b CC F GLM MA W WE) Tue-Fri 11-30-14.30 h (lunch), Tue-Sun 17-21.30 h (dinner)
246 McAllister Street ✉CA 94102 ☎ 487-9800
Award winning vegetarian cuisine in a fine dining and romantic atmosphere.
Pasta pomodoro (! b F GLM) ?-24 h
2304 Market Street ✉CA 94114 *(Castro)* ☎ 558-8123
This popular and always busy restaurant offers great inexpensive Italian food. It attracts a very gay crowd which doesn't mind to wait to get a table.
Taqueria San Jose #1 (b F glm) Mon-Thu 7-1 h, Fri-Sat -4 h, Sun -3 h
2830 Mission Street ✉CA 94110 *(Between 24th and 25th Streets)* ☎ 282-0203
Very cheap and delicious Mexican food.
Thai House Bar & Café (F glm)
2200 Market Street/Sanchez ✉CA 94114 ☎ 864-5006
Inexpensive and delicious Thai food.
Valentine's Café (! b CC F GLM) Wed-Thu 11-14.30 h, 17.30-21.30 h, Fri -22 h, Sat-Sun 8-15.30, 18-22 h
1793 Church Street ✉CA 94131 *(Between 29th and 30th Streets)* ☎ 285-2257
Great vegetarian food at reasonable prices.
Without Reservation (b bf F glm) 7.30-2.30 h
2451 Harrison Street ✉CA 94114 *(Between Market and 18th Streets)* ☎ 861-9510
Breakfast, lunch and burgers.
Zuni Café (B F glm)
1658 Market Street ✉CA 94102 ☎ 552-2522
Very trendy place, nice staff, reservation advisable.

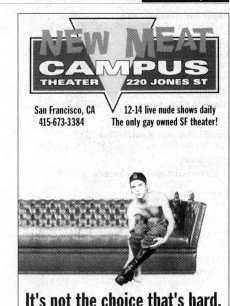

SHOWS

New Meat Campus Theater (A AC DR G MA S SNU VS YG) Sun-Thu 11-24 h, Fri & Sat -2 h
220 Jones Street ✉CA 94107 *(off Market street at 6th street)* ☎ 673 3384 ☎ 346 9165
Male strip club, Multi xxx screen cinema, Video arcade. 12-14 live nude shows daily. All day pass only US$ 10.
Theatre Rhinoceros Performances Wed-Sun
2926 16th Street, ✉CA 94103 *(Mission District)* ☎ 861-5079
America's oldest and foremost theatre devoted only to gay and lesbian issues.

SEX SHOPS/BLUE MOVIES

Campus Cinema (G SNU VS)
220 Jones/Turk Street ✉CA 94102
Circle J Cinema (G S VS) 10-24 h
369 Ellis Street ✉CA 94102 ☎ 474-6995
Admission fee.
City Entertainment
960 Folsom Street ✉CA 94107 ☎ 543-2124
Folsom Gulch
947 Folsom Street ✉CA 94107 ☎ 495-6402
Frenchy's
1020 Geary Street ✉CA 94109 ☎ 776-5940
Good Vibrations (GLM) Sun-Thu 11-19, Fri Sat -20 h
1210 Valencia Street ✉CA 94103 ☎ 550-7399
Popular, well-equipped sex toy store, also mail-order.
Jaguar Sun-Thu 10-23, Fri Sat -24 h
4057 18th Street ✉CA 94114 ☎ 863-4777
Nob Hill Cinema (G R S VS) 11.45-1.30 h
729 Bush Street/Powell, ✉CA 94108-3402 ☎ 781-9468

Tearoom Theater. The (G S VS) 9-2 h, closed Fri Sat
145 Eddy Street ✉CA 94102 ☎ 885-9887

SAUNAS/BATHS

Steamworks Bathhouse Berkeley (AC DR f G MA msg NU P sa sb VS WE WO) 24 hours daily
2107 Fourth Street, Berkeley ✉CA 94710 ☎ 510/845 89 92

FITNESSTUDIOS

Market Street Gym (GLM wh WO YG) Mon-Fri 6-22, Sat Sun 9-20 h
2301 Market Street, ✉CA 94114 ☎ 626-4488

Pacific Heights Health Club (GLM)
2358 Pine Street/Fillmore Street ✉CA 94115 ☎ 563-6694

BOOK SHOPS

A Different Light Bookstore (! CC GLM) 10-24 h
489 Castro Street, ✉CA 94114 ☎ 431-0891

Cody's Books (glm)
2454 Telegraph Avenue ✉CA 94704 *Berkeley* ☎ 845-7852

GIFT & PRIDE SHOPS

Does your Mother know... (CC GLM W) 9.30-22 h
4079 18th Street, ✉CA 94114 *(Castro Street)* ☎ 864-3160

LEATHER & FETISH SHOPS

A Taste of Leather 12-20 h
317-A 10th Street/Folsom Street ✉CA 94103 ☎ 252-9166
Also catalogue available for US$ 3.

Stormy Leather Tue-Sun 12-18 h, Fri 12-19 h
1158 Howard Street, CA 94103 ✉CA 94103 *(between 7th and 8th)* ☎ 626-1672

TRAVEL & TRANSPORT

Joie de Vivre Hotels, Inc. (GLM)
246 McAllister Street ✉CA 94102 ☎ 1-800-738-7477
Fax: 861-0954
Hotel reservation service for gays & lesbians.

Now, Voyager Travel
4406 18th Street, ✉CA 94114 ☎ 626-1169 ☎ 800-255-6951 (toll free) Fax: 626-8626

SFGayTours.com (CC G MA MG)
173 Elsie Street ✉CA 94110 ☎ 648 7758
Homepage: www.sfgaytours.com
Gay tours of San Fransisco and bay area (gay clubbing, dining, theatre, shopping and gay weddings).

VIDEO SHOPS

Captain Video (g)
2358 Market Street ✉CA 94114 ☎ 552-0501
Home delivery service for videos.

Captain Video (g)
2398 Lombard Street ✉CA 94123 ☎ 921-2839

HOTELS

Allison Hotel (bf CC glm H MA)
417 Stockton Street ✉CA 94108 ☎ 986-8737 ☎ (800) 628-6456 (toll free)
All rooms with color cable TV, some with private baths. Continental bf incl. in price.

Amsterdam Hotel. The (G H) 749 Taylor Street ✉CA 94108 ☎ 673-3277
20 minutes to the airport. Central location. 12 minutes walk from gay bars. All rooms with phone, some with bath/WC. Single US$ 38-52, double 42-56, incl. bf.

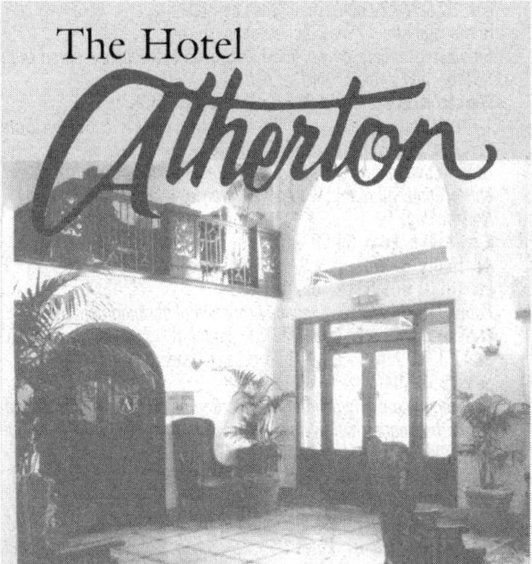

Atherton Hotel (B CC F GLM H MA)
685 Ellis Street/Larkin Street ✉CA 94109 ☎ 474-5720 ☎ (800) 474-5720 (toll-free) Fax: 474-8256
E-Mail: reservations@hotelatherton.com
Homepage: www.hotelatherton.com
Nineteen km to the airport. Centrally located in the Civic Center district. 21 double rooms, 54 single rooms with priv. bath/WC, phone, satellite TV, radio, safe, heating.

Chateau Tivoli. The (bf CC glm H MA) Office: 8-22 h
1057 Steiner Street ✉CA 94117 ☎ 776-5462 Fax: 776-0505
E-Mail: mail@chateautivoli.com
Rates US$ 110-250 per night incl. bf. Champagne brunch at WE. Cheese & wine evenings. Victorian townhouse from 1892 with very elegant interior.

Civic Center Hotel (G H)
20 12th Street/Market and Van Ness Streets ✉CA 94103 ☎ 861-2373
Daily US$ 20 and up, weekly US$ 70 and up.

Ivy Hotel (G H) 539
Octavia Street ✉CA 94102 ☎ 863-6388

Leland Hotel (bf G H)
1315 Polk Street/Bush Street ✉CA 94109 ☎ 441-5141 ☎ (800) 258-4458 (toll free).
All rooms with telephone, some with kitchenette or frigidaire, many with bathroom and WC. Very reasonable prices.

Majestic. The (AC B bf F g H)
1500 Sutter Street ✉CA 94109 ☎ 441-1100 Fax: 673-7331.

Mosser Victorian Hotel (B F GLM)
54 Fourth Street ✉CA 94103 *(South of Market area)* ☎ 986-4400 ☎ (800) 227-3804 Fax: 495-7653
All rooms with TV.

National Hotel (GLM H)
1139 Market Street ✉CA 94103 ☎ 864-9343
Convenient location. Rates US$ 20-30.

Renoir Hotel (B bf F glm H MA) all year/24h
45 McAllister at Market Street ✉CA 94102 *(Downtown, only three blocks north of Folsom Street)* ☎ 626-5200 ☎ (800) 576-3388 (toll free) Fax: 626-0916 E-Mail: sales@renoirhotel.com
Homepage: www.renoirhotel.com
Friendly, cosmoplitan boutique hotel. Close to all gay neibourhoods. 135 rooms and 2 suites all with private bath/ telephone, TV with cable TV. See website or call fro special rates.

Union Square Hotel (B bf GLM H)
114 Powell Street ✉CA 94102 ☎ 397-3000
Downtown location. 10 min by subway to Castro Disctrict. All rooms with telephone, TV, bathroom, WC. Rates US$ 68-70.

GUEST HOUSES

Andora Inn (b bf f GLM H OS)
2438 Mission Street ✉CA 94110 ☎ 282-0337 ☎ (800) 967-9219 (toll-free) Fax: 282-2608 E-Mail: AndoraSF@aol.com
Homepage: www.andorainn.citysearch.com
B&B in a restored Victorian home located in the thriving Mission District just a few blocks from the Castro. All rooms with TV, video and radio. Rates double/shared bath USD79-119 and double/suites with private bath 199-249 incl. expanded continental bf. Elysium Café & Bar located on the first floor.

Baby Bear's House (bf CC GLM H) All year
1424 Page Street ✉CA 94117 ☎ 255-9777
E-Mail: babybear@babybearshouse.com
Homepage: www.babybearshouse.com
2 rooms and a studio with bath/WC, telephone/fax, TV, VCR, own key. See web site or call for more information

Belvedere House (bf e GLM H wh) 598 Belvedere Street ✉CA 94117 *(near the Castro, the Haight-Ashbury and Golden Gate Park)* ☎ 731-6654
Fax: 476-9672 Email rstern@itsa.ucsf.edu
Homepage http://www.belvederehouse.com.
Small, reasonably priced guest house. Rates double/shared bath USD 65 and single 55 incl. bf buffet.

Bock's Bed and Breakfast (bf gLM MA OS)
1448 Willard Street, ✉CA 94117 *(two blocks to Golden Gate Park)* ☎ 664-6842 Fax: 664-1109
Lovely Edwardian residence in the Parnassus Heights area. Convenient location. All rooms with priv. entrance, telephone, bath and TV. No smoking.

Castillo Inn (bf CC G H)
48 Henry Street ✉CA 94114 *(Castro District)* ☎ 864-5111 ☎ (800) 865-5112 Fax: 641-1321
Rates US$ 55-75 incl. expanded continental bf. Apartment available.

Dolores Park Inn (bf CC E glm MA N OS wh) Office 14-22 h
3641 17th Street ✉CA 94114 (Castro District) ☎ 621-0482 or ☎ 553-6040
Gay venues are in walking distance. Rooms are individually decorated with antiques, some have kitchens and priv. bath. All have balcony and tv. Rates single US$ 89-179, double 109-189.

Inn On Castro. The (! bf GLM H MA) Office: 7.30-22.30 h
321 Castro Street/Market Street ✉CA 94114 ☎ 861-0321
20 minutes to the airport. Located in the heart of Castro gay area. No smoking indoors. Rates US$ 75-145 incl. bf. Restored Edwardian building.

Inn San Francisco. The (bf g H MA wh) Office: 7-23 h
943 South Van Ness Avenue ✉CA 94110 ☎ 641-0188
☎ 800-359-0913 (toll free) Fax: 641-1701
Restored 1872 Victorian Mansion in Mission neighborhood location. All rooms with phone, fridge, priv. bath (4 rooms with shared bath), color TV and radio. All rooms very nicely furnished. Rates US$ 75-175. Healthy bf buffet. Hot tub in the beautiful garden. Hosts Marty and Fred make sure you enjoy your stay.

Parker House. The (bf CC G H MA sb OS) All year
520 Church Street ✉CA 94114 *(Castro District)* ☎ 621-3222
Fax: 621-4139 E-Mail: parkerhse@aol.com
Homepage: www.parkerguesthouse.com
Rates from US$109-199. Rooms with private bath, cable TV, telephone/modem. Very comfortable. Library and large gardens. See web site for more information.

Pension San Francisco (CC F GLM H MA YG)
1668 Market Street ✉CA 94102 ☎ 864-1271
☎ (888) 864-8070 (toll free) Fax: 861-8116
Rooms with bath. Rates on request.

Pensione International (AC bf CC glm H MA N)
875 Post Street ✉CA 94109 ☎ 775-3344 Fax: 441-2157
A Victorian styled bed & breakfast hotel in the Polk Street and Union Square area. Rates upon request

Phoenix Inn. The (A AC B bf F g H MA msg N OS pi)
601 Eddy Street ✉CA 94109 ☎ 776-1380
☎ (800) 2489-466 (toll free) Fax: 885-3109
25 minutes to the airport. Located half a block from Polk Street. All rooms with phone, priv. bath, WC, and balcony.

San Francisco Views-The Villa (bf G H pi OS wh)
379 Collingwood Street ✉CA 94114-2818 *(parallel to Castro Street)* ☎ 282-1367 ☎ (800) 358-0123 (toll free) Fax: 821-3995
E-Mail: sfviews@aol.com
Homepage: www.gaysf.com/hotels/villa/villa.htm
Centrally located. Nice view. Rates US$ 90-170. Small heated pool.

Willows. The (bf CC GLM H MA) Daily 9-21 h
710 14th Street ✉CA 94114-1106 ☎ 431-4770 Fax: 431 5295
E-Mail: Vacation@WillowsSF.com Homepage: www.WillowsSF.com
Located in the Castro district, 25 min. to the airport. All non-smoking rooms with voice mail phones. Rates from US$ 82-120 (bf incl.) Please call or send e-mail for tourist info. package.

24 Henry Guesthouse (bf CC GLM H MA)
24 Henry Street ✉CA 94114 ☎ 864-5686 ☎ (800) 900-5686 (toll free) Fax: 864-0406 E-Mail: HenrySt24@aol.com.
In the Castro district. All rooms are non-smoking.

PRIVATE ACCOMODATION

Friends (bf GLM H msg)
PO Box 460795 ✉CA 94146 ☎ 826 5972 Fax: 642 3700
Homepage: staywithfriends@pacball.net
Prive bed and breakfast accommodation. In-house masseur. Please call or see web site for details.

GENERAL GROUPS

Affiliated Bigmen's Club
584 Castro Street, Suite 139J ✉CA 94114 ☎ (800) 501-3090
E-Mail: abc@chubnet.com
Meeting once a year on Labor Day.
Alice B. Toklas Lesbian/Gay Democratic Club
PO Box 113 16, ✉CA 94101
Committee to Preserve our Sexual & Civil Liberties
PO Box 42 23 85, ✉CA 94142-2385

FETISH GROUPS

California Eagles MC
PO Box 146 65 ✉CA 94114-0665 ☎ 267-0560
Cheaters MC
130 Hancock Street, ✉CA 94114
The Society of Janus
PO Box 67 94, ✉CA 94101
Non-profit educational and social organization for adults with S/M interests.

HEALTH GROUPS

Body Electric School of Sexual Healing
6527A Telegraph Avenue, ✉CA 94609 *(Oakland)* ☎ 653-1594
San Francisco City Clinic Mon Thu 9.30-18, Tue Wed Fri 8-16 h
356 7th Street ☎ 864-8100

HELP WITH PROBLEMS

Bashing Hotline
☎ 1800 347-HATE
Gay Legal Referral
☎ 621-3900
Gay Rescue Mission
☎ 863-4882
Helpline
☎ 772-4357

RELIGIOUS GROUPS

Congregation Sha'ar Zahav Mon-Fri 9-15 h
220 Danvers Street, ✉CA 94114 *(in upper Castro district)*
☎ 861-6932 E-Mail: shaarzahav@igc.apc.com
Jewish gays & lesbians.
MCC Services Sun 9, 11, 19 h
150 Eureka Street, ✉ CA 94114 ☎ 863-4434

SWIMMING

-Seal Rock Beach (Enter El Camino del Mar at the west end of Geary street and go from P downhills)

CRUISING

-Ocean beach (between Dutch windmill on Fulton street and Murphy windmill on Lincoln Way)
-Lafayette Park (nights, around the tennis courts)
-Buena Vista Park

San Jose ☎ 408

BARS

A Tinkers Damn (B d G)
46 North Saratoga Avenue, Santa Clara ✉CA 95051 ☎ 243-4595
Hamburger Mary's (! AC B D F GLM MA OS s) 11-2 h
170 W. St. John ✉CA 95110 ☎ 947-1667
This restaurant and club attracts a diverse queer crowd with relaxed atmosphere. Very popular.
Mac's Club (B G N tv)
349 South 1st Street ✉CA 95113 *(Near San Carlos)*
☎ 998-9535
Oldest bar in San Jose.
Renegades (B G LJ MA OS) 11-2 h
393 Stockton Avenue/Cinnabar ✉CA 95126 ☎ 275-9902
Cruise bar.
Stockade at Bucks Saloon (B G LJ) 12-2 h, WE 0-24 h
301 Stockton Street/Julian Street ✉CA 25126 ☎ 286-1176
641 Club (B d G OS) 14-2 h, WE 11-2 h
641 Stockton Avenue ✉CA 95216 *(Between Villa and Schiele Ave)*
☎ 998-1144

SAUNAS/BATHS

Watergarden (G H MA P OS sa sb sol VS wh WO) 0-24 h
1010 The Alameda/Atlas Street ✉CA 95120 ☎ 275-1215
Very nice garden with a big jacuzzi. Relaxed atmosphere.

LEATHER & FETISH SHOPS

Leather Masters
969 Park Avenue ✉CA 95126 ☎ 293-7660

San Luis Obispo ☎ 805

GIFT & PRIDE SHOPS

Twisted Orbits (GLM YG) Mon-Sat 11-19 h
778 Marsh Street ✉CA 93401 ☎ 782 02 78 Fax: 545 94 79

San Pedro ☎ 310

RESTAURANTS

Babouch Moroccan Restaurant (AC CC E F g lj MA S W) Tue-Sun 17-22 h
810 South Gaffey Street ✉90731 ☎ 831-0246

Santa Barbara ☎ 805

GAY INFO

Pacific Pride Foundation Mon-Fri 9-17 h
126 East Haley Street, #A-11 ✉CA 93101 ☎ 963-3636
Fax: 963-9086
Social Service Agency with community center. Gay and Lesbian Ressource Center.

BARS

Fathom (B CC D GLM OS S VS) Wed - Sat 18-2 h, Sun 16-02 h
423 State Street ✉CA 93030 *(Downtown Santa Barbara between Guiterrez and Haley Street)* ☎ 730-0022

RESTAURANTS

Chameleon Restaurant And Bar (A B CC d F GLM STV VS) Seasonal: Summer 7 days a week, Winter closed Mon-Tue
421 East Cota Street ✉CA 93101 ☎ 965-9536 Fax: 565-5645
Drag-shows on Saturday.

SEX SHOPS/BLUE MOVIES

For Adults Only (glm) 0-24 h
223 Anacapa ✉CA 93101 ☎ 963-9922

SWIMMING

-Cabrillo Beach (East of wharf)
-East Beach (NU)
-Padero Lane Beach (Summers AYOR)

Santa Cruz ☎ 831

GAY INFO

Lesbian/Gay/Bisexual Center Call for hours
1328 Commerce Lane ✉CA 95060 ☎ 425-5422

BARS

Blue Lagoon (B D GLM S VS W) 16-2 h
923 Pacific Avenue ✉CA 95060 ☎ 423-7117

CRUISING

-Beer Can Beach (AYOR)
-Bonney Doon Beach (8 miles North on Highway 1)

Santa Rosa ☎ 707

GAY INFO

We The People
453 Stoney Point Road ✉CA 95401 ☎ 573-8896

BARS

Santa Rosa Inn (B D GLM) 12-2 h
4302 Santa Rosa Avenue ✉CA 95407 ☎ 584-0345
Piano Bar Fri 17-20 h.

CAFÉS

Aroma Roasters (GLM) 7-24 h
95 5th Street ✉CA 95401 ☎ 576-7765

SEX SHOPS/BLUE MOVIES

Santa Rosa Adult Books
3301 Santa Rosa Avenue ✉CA 95407 ☎ 542-8248

BOOK SHOPS

Sawywer's News Sun-Thu 7-21 h, Fri Sat 7-22 h
733 4th Street ✉CA 95404 ☎ 542-1311

TRAVEL & TRANSPORT

Holidays at Sea/Sunquest Travel Club (CC) 9-17 h
1208 Fourth Street ☎ 573-8300 ☎ Toll free (800) 444-8300
Fax: 573-9992
Santa Rosa Travel
542 Farmers Lane ✉CA 95405 ☎ 542-0943
☎ (800) 227-1445 (Toll free)
Sun Quest
1208 4th Street ✉CA 95404 ☎ 573-8300
☎ (800) 444-8300 (toll free)

Sausalito

CRUISING

-Black Sand Beach (off Lookout Road)

Sherman Oaks ☎ 818

BARS

Gold 9 (AC B d G MA) 11-2 h
13625 Moorpark Street ✉CA 91423-3722 ☎ 986-0285

Sonoma ☎ 707

GUEST HOUSES

Sonoma Chalet Bed & Breakfast (AC bf CC)
18935 Fifth Street West ✉CA 95476 ☎ 938-3129
Fax: 996-0190
Swiss-style farmhouse and country cottages in the wine country north of San Fransisco.

Stanford ☎ 415

GAY INFO

Lesbian, Gay and Bisexual Community Center (LGBCC)
Firetruck House *(across from Tresidder Union, 2nd floor)* ☎ 725-4222

Stockton ☎ 559

BARS

Paradise (B D GLM S YG W) 18-2, WE 16-2 h
10100 North Lower Sacramento Road ☎ 477-4724

BOOK SHOPS

Adult Books
332 North California ✉CA 95202 ☎ 941-8607

Tahoe Paradise ☎ 530

HOTELS

Driftwood Cafe (b F glm H) 8-15, winter 7-15 h, closed Wed
4115 Laurel Avenue ✉CA 95708 ☎ 544-6545
Ridgewood Inn (GLM H)
1341 Emerald Bay Road ✉CA 95708 ☎ 541-8589
Silver Shadows Lodge (GLM H pi wh)
1251 Emerald Bay Road ✉CA 95708 ☎ 541-3575

GUEST HOUSES

Black Bear Inn (bf CC glm)
1202 Ski Run Boulevard ✉CA 96150 ☎ 544-4411
Fax: 544-7315 E-Mail: info@TahoeBlackBear.com
Homepage: www.TahoeBlackBear.com
A luxuary lodge with 5 guest rooms plus three cabins. All rooms with private bath, fireplace, kingsize beds TV and full breakfast.
Sierrawood Guest House (AC bf F GLM H MA N NU VS wh) 0-24 h
3374 Grass Lake Road, ✉CA 96155-0194 *(near South Lake Tahoe)* ☎ 577-6073 Fax: 527-4739 E-Mail: swooddave@aol.com
Homepage: www.q-net.com/sierrawood
Rates from single/night US$ 90, double 125-150. Bf and dinner incl.

Upland ☎ 909

SEX SHOPS/BLUE MOVIES

Mustang Adult Books & Videos
959-961 N. Central Avenue ✉CA 91786 ☎ 981-0227

Vacaville ☎ 707

GAY INFO

Solano County Gay/Lesbian Info Line
☎ 448-1010

Vallejo ☎ 707

BARS

Nobody's Place (AC B CC d f GLM OS W) 12-2 h
437 Virginia Street CA 94590 ✉94590 ☎ 645-7298

Ventura ☎ 805

BARS

Club Alternatives (B D GLM W) 14-2 h, WE 12- h
1644 East Thompson Boulevard ✉CA 93001 ☎ 653-6511

SEX SHOPS/BLUE MOVIES

Three Star Adult News 0-24 h
359 East Main Street ✉CA 93001 ☎ 653-9068

CRUISING

-Bates Beach (between Ventura & Santa Barbara, AYOR)
-Emma Wood Street Beach

Victorville ☎ 619

BARS

West Side 15 (b GLM) 12-2 h
16868 Stoddard Wells Road ✉CA 92394 ☎ 243-9600

SEX SHOPS/BLUE MOVIES

Oasis Adult Department Store
14949 Palmdale Road ☎ 241-0788

CRUISING

-Pebble Beach Park (AYOR)

Walnut Creek ☎ 925

BARS

Club 1220 (B d GLM W) 16-2 h
1220 Pine Street ✉CA 94596 ☎ 938-4550
JR's (B D GLM W) Sun-Thu 17-2 h, Fri-Sat -4 h
2520 Camino Diablo ✉CA 94596 ☎ 256-1200
Lesbian night every Sat. Popular.

West Sacramento ☎ 916

HOTELS

Continental Hotel (F glm H pi)
1432 West Capital Avenue, ✉CA 95691 ☎ 371-3660

USA-Colorado

Western USA

Initials: CO

Time: GMT -7

Area: 269,618 km^2 / 110,274 sq mi.

Population: 3,893,000

Capital: Denver

Aspen ☎ 970

GENERAL GROUPS

Aspen Gay and Lesbian Community Fund
9-17 h
520 East Cooper, Suite 16 81611 ✉CO 81612 ☎ 925-4123
☎ 925-9249 (24 h hotline) Fax: 925-4146
E-Mail: aspengay@rof.net
Call for more informations about events such as Aspen G&L Ski Week and Summerfest.

CRUISING

-Hyman Street Mall

Boulder ☎ 303

BARS

The Yard (AC B d GLM MA N s W) Mon-Fri 16-2 h, Sat-Sun 14-2 h
2690 28th Street, Unit C ✉CO 80301 ☎ 443-1987
Friendly atmosphere.

SEX SHOPS/BLUE MOVIES

The News Stand 9-1 h, Sun 10-12 h
1720 15th Street ✉CO 80302 ☎ 442-9515

CRUISING

-Chataquea Park
-Pearl Street Mall
-University of Colorado (men's locker room at recreation center)

Breckenridge ☎ 970

HOTELS

The Bunkhouse Lodge (b bf CC G H MA sa VS wh)
13203 Hwy 9 ✉CO 80424 ☎ 453-6475 Fax: 453-3977
E-Mail: bhlodge@colorado.net.
Homepage: www.bunkhouselodge.com
Rates single US$ 40-60, double $60-120 (bf incl.).
Mountain House (GLM H pi sa)
PO Box 6 ✉CO 80424 ☎ 453-6475
Priv. & shared bath, all rooms with telephone, TV. Kitchenette.

Colorado Springs ☎ 719

BARS

David's (B D F GLM MA S)
2125 East Fountain Boulevard ☎ 444-0400
The Hide & Seek Complex (AC B CC D F GLM lj MA OS S SNU STV) 10.30-? h
512West Colorado Avenue ✉CO 80905 ☎ 634-9303
5 bars & restaurant

HOTELS

Pike's Peak Paradise (bf GLM H)
PO Box 57 60, Woodland Park, CO 80866 ☎ 697-6656
In the outskirts of Colorado Springs.

CRUISING

-Palmer Park (Sections called «Lazy Lane» and «South Canyon»)

Denver ☎ 303

GAY INFO

Gay and Lesbian Community Center of Colorado 10-22 h
1245 East Colfax ✉CO 80218 ☎ 831-6268
Data Call/Colorado Athletic Exchange/Library Information/referral/support groups/meeting space/peer counselling/outreach speaker's bureau /women's committee.
Gay, Lesbian and Bisexual Community Center of Colorado Mon-Fri 10-19 h
☎ 837-0166
Out Front
244 Washington Street ✉CO 80203 ☎ 778-7900
Fax: 778-7978 E-Mail: outfrontc@aol.com
Published every other Fri, Colorado's No.1 gay publication. Features national news, reports and articles about the gay community, calendar of events, bar specials and classifieds.

Quest Magazine Mon-Fri 8-16 h
430 South Broadway ✉CO 80209 ☎ 722-5965
Monthly publication. Features articles on movies, book reviews, gay events, lots of ads and places of interest for gays. Approximately 40 pages.

TOURIST INFO

Denver Metro Convention & Visitors Bureau 8-17 h
1555 California, Suite 300 ✉CO 80202 ☎ 892-1112
☎ (800) 645-3446 Fax: 892-1636 Homepage: www.denver.org

BARS

BJ's Carousel (AC B CC F G lj MA N S STV) Mon-Fri 12-2 h, Sat-Sun 10-2 h
1380 S. Broadway ✉CO 80210 ☎ 777-9880
Sun bf
Bricks (B f G N)
1600 East 17th Avenue ✉CO 80218 ☎ 377-5400
Brig (B f GLM N)
1600 East 17th Avenue ☎ 377-5400
Charlie's (B CC d F G LJ MA OS S) 10-2 h
900 East Colfax Avenue ✉CO 80218 ☎ 839-8890
Country/western style dance bar.
Club Stud (B G LJ MA)
255 South Broadway ✉CO 80209 ☎ 733-9398
C's (B D GLM MA) 16-24 h, Fri Sat 16-2 h, Sun 14-2 h
7900 East Colfax Avenue/Trenton ✉CO 80220 ☎ 322-4436
Happy hour 7 days a week 16-19 h.
The Den (B F GLM N OS) 10-2 h
5110 West Colfax Avenue ✉CO 80219 ☎ 534-9526
Restaurant: Mon-Thu 11.30-14 h, 17.30-22 h, Fri Sat 17.30-22.30 h, Sun brunch 10-15 h.
Detour (B F gLM N) Tue Men's night.
551 East Colfax Avenue ✉CO 80203 ☎ 861-1497
The Elle (B d f GLM MA S) 15-? h Happy hour 16-19 h
716 West Colfax Avenue ✉CO 80204 *(Civic Center/Cherry Creek)* ☎ 572-1710
Grand Bar (B CC E GLM MA OS VS) 11-2 h
538 East 17th Avenue ✉CO 80203 ☎ 839-5390
Mostly business clientele.
Highland Bar (B GLM N)
2532 15th Street ✉CO 80211 ☎ 455-9978
Mike's (AC B d GLM LJ MA N S STV VS W) 11-2 h
60 South Broadway ✉CO 80209 ☎ 777-0193
R&R Denver (AC B f GLM MA N s WE) Mon-Fri 11-2, Sat-Sun 9-2 h
4958 East Colfax Avenue ✉CO 80220 ☎ 320-9337
Happy hour Mon-Fri 11-13 h, Sat-Sun 9-12 h
Snake Pit (! B D f Glm S W) 17-2 h
614 E 13th Avenue ☎ 831-1234
Triangle Denver (AC B CC d f G LJ MA s) Mon-Sat 15-2 h, Sun 11-2 h
2036 Broadway ✉CO 80220 ☎ 293-9009
Wrangler (B G LJ MA)
1700 Logan ✉CO 80203 ☎ 837-1075
Cruise bar.
Zippz (AC B f G MA N SNU STV) 10-2 h
3014 East Colfax Avenue ✉CO 80206 ☎ 321-6627

CAFES

Dad's (b f GLM N)
282 South Pennsylvania Street ✉CO 80209 ☎ 744-1258

DANCECLUBS

Club Proteus (B D GLM)
1669 Clarkson Street *(at 17th)* ☎ 869-4637
Compound. The (AC B D G LJ MA N YG) Mon-Sat 7-2, Sun 8-2 h. Dancing 21-2 h
145 Broadway ✉CO 80203 ☎ 722-7977
Foxhole at Centerfield Sports Bar (AC B CC d f GLM MA N OS YG) Sun 15-2 h
2936 Fox Street ✉CO 80216 ☎ 298-7378
Every Sunday on the patio all summer.
Maximilian's (B D f glm OS) Fri Sat after hour
2151 Lawrence Street ✉CO 80205 ☎ 297-0015
Tracks 2000 (AC B CC D f GLM MA N OS S STV TV VS WE YG) Thu 20-1.45 h, Fri 21-1.45 h, Sat, Sun 21-? h
2975 Fox Street ✉Co 80216 ☎ 292-6600
Large gay nightclub, on Wed sometimes special events, Thu & Sun until 23 h 16+, Fri ladies night, Sat Circuit.

RESTAURANTS

Club 404 (B F glm)
404 Broadway ☎ 778-9605
Restaurant and bar
Nobody's Business (B F glm N)
800 Decatur Street *(I-25 and 8th Avenue)* ☎ 825-4521

SEX SHOPS/BLUE MOVIES

Heaven Sent Me (AC CC MA WE) 10-22 h
482 South Broadway ✉CO 80206 ☎ 331-8000
Gay gift items and rainbow merchandise.

SAUNAS/BATHS

CCC-Community County Club (AC CC G MG P sa sb wh WO YG) 0-24 h
2151 Lawrence Street ✉CO 80205 ☎ 257-2610
Denver Swim Club (AC CC f G MA NU P pi sb VS wh WO) 0-24 h
6923 East Colfax ✉CO 80220 ☎ 321-9399
Midtowne Spa (b CC G OS S sa sb VS wh) 0-24 h
2935 Zuni Street ✉CO 80211 ☎ 458-8902
Various theme rooms.

FITNESSTUDIOS

Broadway Bodyworks (glm WO)
160 South Broadway ✉CO 80209 ☎ 722-4342

BOOK SHOPS

Category Six Books (AC G W WE) Mon-Sat 10-18, Sun 11-17 h
42 South Broadway ✉CO 80209 ☎ 777-0766 Fax: 777-0782
Gay bookshop
Isis Bookstore (glm) 5701
East Colfax Avenue ✉CO 80220 *(at Ivanhoe)* ☎ 321-0867

GUEST HOUSES

Elyria's Western Guest House (AC bf CC GLM H NU wh) 4700 Baldwin Court ✉CO 80216 ☎ 291-0915
Fax: 296-9892 E-Mail: JamesE.Klismet@usa.net
Homepage: www.bestinns.net/usa/co/rdewgh.html
Small B&B. Rooms with shared bath, radio and TV. Rates single US$40 and double $50 incl. cont. bf.

Twin Maples B&B (AC CC G H msg) Open all year
1401 Madison Street ✉CO 80206 ☎ (888) 835-5738
Fax: 394-4776 E-Mail: twinmaples@boytoy.com
Homepage: boytoy.com/twinmaples.htm
Located in the heart of historical Denver. 3 double rooms with facilities on the corridor, all rooms with balcony, phone, TV, radio, heating. Hotel provides TV room. Rates double US$ 160, single $85 (bf incl.)

Victoria Oaks Inn (AC bf E CC F glm)
1575 Race Street ✉CO 80206 ☎ 355-1818 Fax: 331-1095
E-Mail: Vicoaksinn@aol.com
Rates US$ 60-95 (cont. bf included). 9 rooms with private and shared baths. All with minibar, cable TV and VCR, some with kitchenette. No pets, no kids.

GENERAL GROUPS

Auraria Lesbian & Gay Alliance
1006 11th Street ✉CO 80204 ☎ 556-3317

Coming Out/Being Out Group
☎ 831-6268

Girth & Mirth of the Rockies
PO Box 2351 ✉CO 80201 ☎ 420-0102 ext 46
E-Mail: girthmirthotr@usa.net
Meeting 1st Sat at Capital Hill Community Center, 13th Williams at 19.30 h

Parents and Friends of Lesbians & Gays
☎ 333-0286

FETISH GROUPS

City Bikers MC
PO Box 98 16, ✉CO 80209 ☎ 733-1231

Knights of Malta
PO Box 98 36 ✉CO 80209 ☎ 744-6400

HEALTH GROUPS

Colorado AIDS Project (CAP)
☎ 837-0166

RELIGIOUS GROUPS

Congregation Tikvat Shalom
PO Box 66 94 ✉CO 80206 ☎ 331-2706
Jewish gays. and lesbians.

Evangelicals Reconciled
PO Box 20 01 11 ✉CO 80220 ☎ 331-2839
Gay and lesbian Evangelican Christians.

MCC of the Rockies
980 Clarkson Street ✉CO 80218 ☎ 860-1819

CRUISING

-Berkley Park
-Chessman Park
-Danish World (R) (upper level arcades, Grant & Sherman between 13th and 14th Street)
-May D.& F. Store (AYOR) (downtown and Aurora Mall)
-16th Street Mall
-Royal Host Motel (area around)
-Stapleton International Airport (AYOR) (mezzanine level & change rooms, behind mosaic)
-»The Point« (AYOR) (north west of I-70 and Sheridan Road)
-UCD (East Classroom Building, 3rd floor)
-U of D (Boettcher Hall, downstairs & library)

Durango ☎ 970

HOTELS

Leland House / Rochester Hotel (AC bf CC f glm H MA OS)
721 E. Second Avenue ✉CO 81301 *(located in the historic downtown)* ☎ 385-1920 ☎ (800) 664-1920 (toll free)
Fax: 385-1967 E-Mail: leland@rochesterhotel.com
Homepage: www.rochesterhotel.com
All rooms with private bath, radio and TV, studios with kitchenette. Rates studio US$75-109, single $95-159, double $105-199 incl. bf buffet.

Woodland Park ☎ 719

HOTELS

Pikes Peak Paradise (bf GLM H MA wh) 8-22 h
PO Box 57 60 ✉CO 80866 ☎ 728-8282
Northwest of Colorado Springs. Bed & Breakfast in comfortable rooms. A full `all-you-can-eat' breakfast buffet is offered as well as light snacks and beverages. Rates US$ 55-65.

USA-Connecticut

Northeast USA
Initials: CT
Time: GMT -5
Area: 14,358 km^2 / 5,872 sq mi.
Population: 3,270,000
Capital: Hartford

Hartford ☎ 860

BARS

Chez Est (B D G OS) 15-1 h, Sun 12-1 h
458 Wethersfield Avenue ✉CT 06114 ☎ 525-3243
Popular.

Nicks (B G)
1943 Broad Street ✉CT 06114 ☎ 522-1573

RESTAURANTS

Summit Hill Cafe (B F GLM)
Zion Street/Summit Street ✉CT 06106 ☎ 547-1921

BOOK SHOPS

Reader's Feast Bookstore & Cafe (b GLM)
529 Farmington Avenue, CT 06105 ✉CT 06105 ☎ 232-3710

New Haven ☎ 203

GAY INFO

Gay Switchboard Mon-Thu 20-23 h
☎ 624-6869

BARS

Partners (B D GLM MA p s VS YG)
365 Crown Street
☎ 776-1014

168 York Street Café (B GLM W) 14-1 h
168 York Street ☎ 789-1915

SEX SHOPS/BLUE MOVIES

Video Expo and Magazine Center (glm)
754 Chapel Street ☎ 562-5867

CRUISING

-Chapel Street (from York to park)
-East Rock Park
-Yale University (Woolsey Hall and library)
-New Haven Information Pavillion
-Parking areas between Route 95 and shore line-night car cruising.

USA-Delaware

Northeast USA

Initials: DE

Time: GMT -5

Area: 6,448 km² / 2,637 sq mi.

Population: 732,000

Capital: Dover

Rehoboth Beach ☎ 302

GAY INFO

-Letters from Camp Rehoboth (Gay owned and gay-friendly businesses)
-The Underground (entertainment)

TOURIST INFO

Camp Rehoboth (CC GLM MA OS) 10-19 h
39 Baltimore Avenue ✉DE 19971 ☎ 227-5620 Fax: 227-5604
E-Mail: info@camprehoboth.com
Homepage: www.camprehoboth.com
Community center publishing a bi-weekly magazine.

BARS

Blue Moon (B F GLM) Thu-Mon 18-22, Sat -23, Sun brunch 11-15 h
35 Baltimore Avenue ✉DE 19971 ☎ 227-6515
Popular.

DANCECLUBS

Renegade (B F GLM) Sun-Tue 11-2 h, Wed-Fri 16-2 h, Sat 11-3 h
4274 Highway One ✉DE 19971 ☎ 227-1222

RESTAURANTS

Adriatico Ristorante (b F g)
North 1st Street ✉DE 19971 ☎ 227-9255
Italian food.
Black Porch Cafe (B F GLM)
21 Rehoboth Avenue ✉DE 19971 ☎ 227-3676
Cloud Nine (B F G) 234
Rehoboth Avenue ✉DE 19971
Creative menu.
The Deli (b F g)
50 Wilmington Avenue ✉DE 19971 ☎ 226-2088
La La Land (b F g)
221/2 Wilmington Avenue ✉DE 19971 ☎ 227-7244
Palms Restaurant (B F GLM) Thu-Sun 15-2 h, dinner 18-22 h, Sun brunch 10-15 h
234 Rehoboth Avenue ✉DE 19971 ☎ 227-0800
Sydney Sidestreet (b F g)
25 Christian Street ✉DE 19771 ☎ 227-1339
Tijuana Taxi (b F GLM)
207 Rehoboth Avenue ✉DE 19771 ☎ 227-1986
Mexican cuisine.

BOOK SHOPS

Lambda Rising (AC CC GLM MA VS W) Summer 10-24 h, winter -20 h
39 Baltimore Avenue ✉DE 19971 ☎ 227-6969
Gay, lesbian, bisexual and transgender books, videos, magazines and gifts. Free local guides.

HOTELS

Beach House (g H pi) 15 Hickman Street ✉DE 19971 ☎ 227-7074
Heated pool with private sundeck, color cable TV in each room.
Guest Rooms at Rehoboth (G H)
45 Baltimore Avenue ✉DE 19771 ☎ 227-8355
Downtown, reasonable rates.
Paper Nautilus (GLM H)
42 1/2 Baltimore Avenue ✉DE 19971 ☎ 227-1603
The Rams Head Inn (bf G H MA NU pi sa wh WO)
Road 2, PO Box 509 ✉DE 19971 ☎ 226-9171
Rates US$ 35-110. Call ahead for reservations.
Rehoboth Guest House (AC bf CC GLM) 8.30-21 h
40 Maryland Avenue ✉DE 19971 ☎ 227-4117
☎ (800) 564-0493 E-Mail: reho@guesthse.com
12 double rooms, 1 apartment, parly en-suite in 100 years old renovated Victorian Beach house. All rooms with balcony/terrace, bath/shower/WC, heating, own key. Rates on season US$ 65-185, off season 50-85.
Renegade Resort (AC B F G H pi s) 4274
Highway One ✉DE 19971 ☎ 227-1222
Private bath, TV. Very cruisy.
Southside Suites (G H)
45 Deleware Avenue ✉DE 19771 ☎ 227-8355
Downtown, reasonable rates.
Valhalla Resort (AC bf CC H MA msg OS pi W WO)
8 Anna B Street, ✉DE 19971 ☎ 226-1408 Fax: 226-0134
Completely enclosed complex with total privacy and parking. Resort offers courtesy transportation to beach, restaurants and bars.

GUEST HOUSES

The Shore Inn (AC bf CC G MA pi wh) closed Jan
703 Rehoboth Avenue ✉DE 19971 ☎ 227-8487
☎ (800) 597-8899 E-Mail: horeinn@ce.net
Homepage: beach-net.com/shoreinn.html
14 rooms with private bath, refrigerator, tea/coffee facilities, TV and telephone in centrally located house. Rates on season single US$ 120, double $140, mini suite $160, off season single $50, double $65, suite $75. Bf incl.
Silver Lake Guest House (AC bf CC GLM H MA)
133 Silver Lake Drive ✉DE 19971 ☎ 226-2115 ☎ (800) 842-2115 Fax: 226-2732 Homepage: www.silverlakeguesthose.com
Beautifully located at the Silver Lake. 13 double rooms, 2 appartments with shower/bath/WC. All rooms with balcony/terrace, phone, TV, heating, own key. Guest house provides car park. Rates from $75 to $300 according to season and room/apartment.

SWIMMING

-Poodle Beach (at the end of Queen Street
-Cape Henlopen State Park (North Shores)

Wilmington ☎ 302

BARS

Roam (A AC B CC D F GLM MA N S STV WE) Fri 17-2 h, Sat-Thu 18-2 h
913 Shipley Street ✉DE 19801 ☎ 658-7626

RESTAURANTS

The Shipley Grill (A AC B E F g N W WE) Sun 17-21 h, Mon-Thu -22 h, Fri Sat -23 h
913 Shipley Street ✉DE 19801 ☎ 652-7797 Fax: 652-5064
Upscale restaurant.

814 Club (B F G)
814 Shipley Street ✉DE 19801 ☎ 657-5730

USA-District of Columbia

East USA

Initials: DC

Time: GMT -5

Area: 177 km^2 / 72 sq mi.

Population: 529,000

Washington D.C. ☎ 202

● Leonard Matlovich's tombstone reads: 'They gave me a medal for killing a man, and discharged me for loving one'. This symbolizes very well the ambivalent face of Washington, a face which makes it a first class travel destination. The *District of Columbia* (D.C.) comprises only the city of Washington. Containing only 600.000 inhabitants in a conurbation of a population of 4 million, it is surprisingly small. This shows Washington being no buzzing *business town*; Washington is the federal government and politics is business here. Seen under this perspective, the business center of Washington is the *Mall*, which is lined by many political institutions and US symbols like the *White House* or the *Vietnam Memorial*, or by museums like the *Holocaust Museum*. The Mall is most beautiful in March and April when the cherry trees blossom. The gays have learned to live with the presence of the federal institutions. Accordingly there is lobbying for gay interests, with which not only the gay scene is preoccupied, but also the gay town newspaper, the *Washington Blade*. When going out, the Washingtonians favour the area around the *Dupont Circle*, northwest of the White House. No car is needed for expeditions here or to other city quarters. The subway is fast und will transport you savely to (nearly) any destination. Nevertheless: Where gay nightlife is not in the vicinity of Dupont Circle, always take a taxi. Two attractions must be mentioned: the impressive *Union Station*, the giant railway station, now a shopping and restaurant center, and *Mount Vernon*, the pittoresque dwelling of George Washington. The gay resort *Rehoboth Beach*, situated two hours distant in Delaware, is worth the trip.

✱ Es existieren keine einschränkenden Gesetze einvernehmlichen Sex betreffend. 1977 wurde ein *Anti-Discrimination Law* verabschiedet. Seit 1992 gilt im D.C. ein *Domestic Partnership Law*. Es wurde bis jetzt noch keine *Anti-Marriage Bill* eingebracht.
Der *District of Columbia* (D.C.) besteht nur aus der Stadt Washington. Mit ca. 600.000 Einwohnern in einem 4-Millionen-Ballungsraum ist er erstaunlich klein. Das zeigt, daß Washington selbst keine quirlige *business town* ist. Washington ist die Bundesregierung. Politik ist das Geschäft dieser Stadt.
So gesehen ist das „Geschäftszentrum" die *Mall*, an der entlang sich viele politische Institutionen und US-amerikanische Symbole wie *Weißes Haus* oder *Vietnam Memorial* finden. Dazu gehören auch zahlreiche Museen wie das *Holocaust Museum*. Die schönste Zeit ist übrigens, wenn entlang der Mall im März/April die Kirschbäume blühen.
Die Schwulen Washingtons haben sich mit der massiven Präsenz des Bundes eingerichtet. Es wird entsprechender Lobbyismus für schwule Interessen betrieben. Womit sich, neben der Szene auch die schwule Zeitung der Stadt, die *Washington Blade*, beschäftigt. Und wenn sie denn ausgehen, die Washingtonians, dann tun sie das bevorzugt in der Gegend um den *Dupont Circle*, nordwestlich des Weißen Hauses. Um diese und andere Gegenden innerhalb der Stadt zu erkunden, benötigen Sie kein Auto. Die Washingtoner U-Bahn bringt Sie schnell und sicher (fast) überall hin. Trotzdem: dort, wo schwules Nightlife abseits des Dupont Circle liegt, nachts ein Taxi benutzen.
Zwei Attraktionen sollen noch erwähnt werden: die beeindruckende *Union Station*, der zum Shopping- und Restaurantkomplex umgestaltete, gewaltige Bahnhof der Stadt und *Mt. Vernon*, der pittoreske Wohnsitz George Washingtons. Als Ausflugsziel empfiehlt sich schließlich der schwule Badeort *Rehoboth Beach*, zwei Stunden entfernt in Delaware gelegen.

▲ Sur la pierre tombale de Leonard Matlovich, on peut lire: „L'Armée m'a décerné une médaille pour avoit tué un homme. L'Armée m'a viré pour en avoir aimé un autre". Washington est la ville des contradictions. C'est donc une ville qu'il faut absolument avoir vue!
Le District of Columbia („D.C."), c'est la ville de Washington. Elle ne compte que 600.000 hàbitants, mais se trouve au coeur d'une agglomération de 4 millions d'habitants. Washington n'est pas une „business town", Washington, c'est le gouvernement fédéral. Le business, ici, c'est la politique.
L'artère vitale de Washington, c'est le Mall, le long duquel on trouve les symboles et les institutions des Etats-Unis: la Maison Blanche, le Mémorial de la Guerre du Vietnam, le Musée de l'Holocauste... En mars et avril, les cerisiers qui bordent le Mall sont en fleur. C'est le moment idéal pour visiter Washington!
Les gays de Washington ont pris leur parti de la présence des institutions politiques et s'attachent à défendre leurs intérêts, ce que fait „Washington Blade", le magazine gay de la ville. Quand les gays de la capitale sortent, c'est dans le quartier autour de Dupont Circle, au nord-ouest de la Maison Blanche. Pas besoin de voiture pour découvrir Washington: prenez le métro! Il est rapide et sûr. Enfin, presque partout. Si vous sortez le soir, en dehors du Dupont Circle, il est plus prudent de prendre un taxi.
Ne passez pas à côté de Union Station (ancienne gare transformée en un méga centre commercial) et de Mont Vernon (pittoresque résidence de George Washington). Pour une excursion hors de la capitale, allez à Rehobotho Beach. Cette station balnéaire gay se trouve dans l'Etat du Delaware, à deux heures de voiture de Washington.

☆ La lápida de Leonard Matlovich tine la siguiente inscripción: „Me concedieron una medalla por matar a un hombre y me despidieron por amar a uno". Washington posee muchos de esos conceptos disonantes y precisamente eso es lo que la hace valiosa como destino turístico de primer clase. El *District of Columbia* (D. C.) y la ciudad de Washington son la mismacasa y con aprox. 600.000 habitantes y con 4 mill. si se incluyen los habitantes de sus alrededores es sorprendentemente pequeña. Washington es el *business town* de la nación. Washington es el gobierno federal y el pan diario de esta ciudad es la política. Visto desde este punto de vista, el centro de negocios lo es el *Mall* en el que se situan muchas de sus instituciones políticas y símbolos norteamericanos como *La Casa Blanca* o el *Vietnam Memorial*. También se encuentran gran cantidad de museos como el *Holocaust Museum*. Una visita al Mall en los meses en los que sus cerezos florecen (marzo y abril) es muy recomendable. Los gays de Washington han aprendido de vivir con la presencia masiva federal. Dentro del ayuntamiento hay representantes de los gays que velan por sus intereses. El periódico *Washington Blade* apoya también estos intereses. El centro gay de la ciudad se encuentra sobre todo en los alrededores de *Dupont Circle* al lado noroeste de la Casa Blanca. Para visitar estos sitios y otros den-

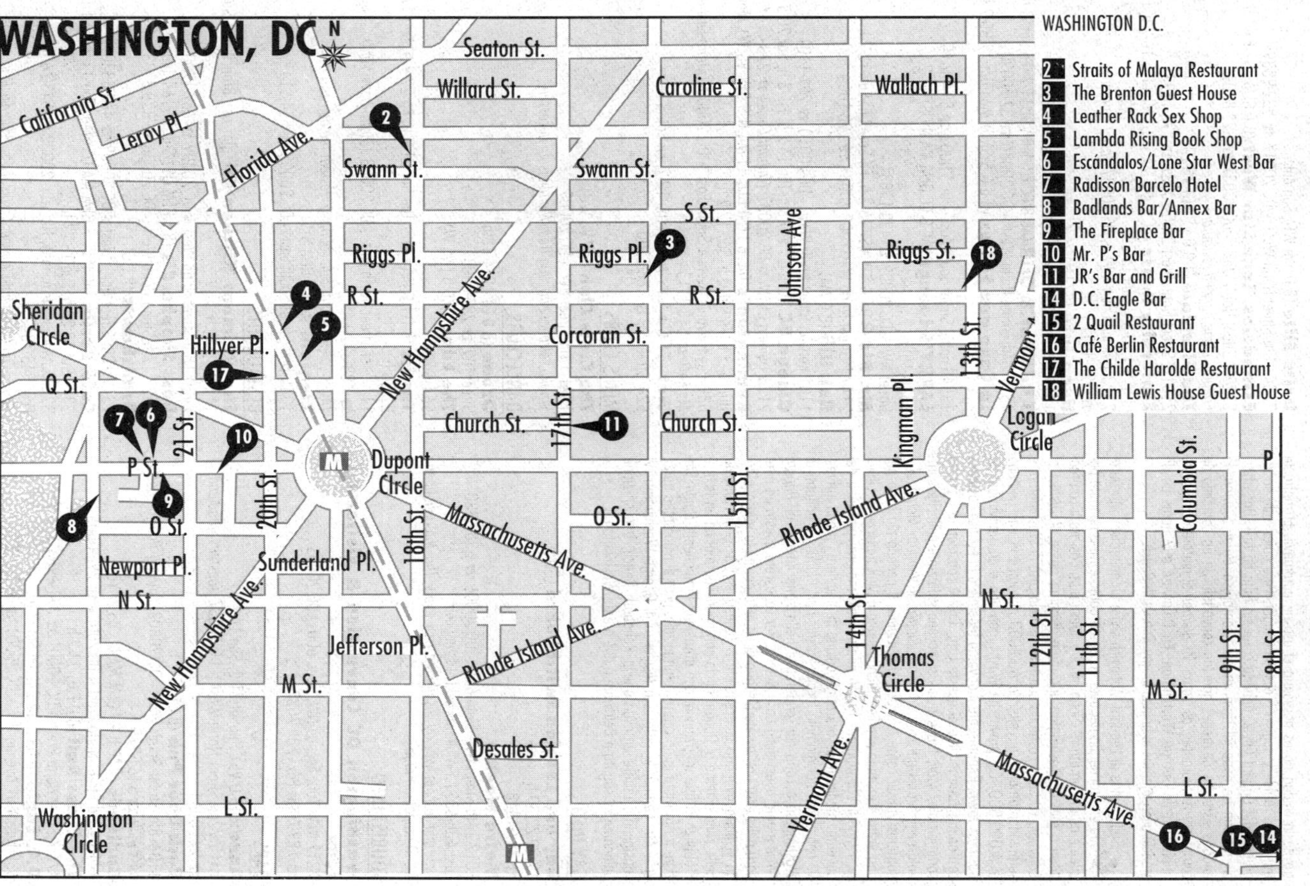
WASHINGTON, DC
N
WASHINGTON D.C.
2 Straits of Malaya Restaurant
3 The Brenton Guest House
4 Leather Rack Sex Shop
5 Lambda Rising Book Shop
6 Escándalos/Lone Star West Bar
7 Radisson Barcelo Hotel
8 Badlands Bar/Annex Bar
9 The Fireplace Bar
10 Mr. P's Bar
11 JR's Bar and Grill
14 D.C. Eagle Bar
15 2 Quail Restaurant
16 Café Berlin Restaurant
17 The Childe Harolde Restaurant
18 William Lewis House Guest House
Seaton St.
Willard St.
Caroline St.
Wallach Pl.
California St.
Leroy Pl.
Florida Ave.
Swann St.
Swann St.
S St.
Riggs Pl.
Riggs Pl.
Riggs St.
Johnson Ave
R St.
R St.
Sheridan Circle
Hillyer Pl.
Corcoran St.
New Hampshire Ave.
13th St.
Vermont
Q St.
Church St.
17th St.
Church St.
Kingman Pl.
Logan Circle
21 St.
P St.
Dupont Circle
P
O St.
20th St.
18th St.
Massachusetts Ave.
O St.
15th St.
Rhode Island Ave.
Columbia St.
Newport Pl.
Sunderland Pl.
N St.
New Hampshire Ave.
N St.
14th St.
12th St.
11th St.
9th St.
8th St.
Jefferson Pl.
Rhode Island Ave.
Thomas Circle
M St.
M St.
Desales St.
Vermont Ave.
Massachusetts Ave.
L St.
L St.
Washington Circle

tro de la ciudad no es necesario el uso de automovil. El metro te transporta rápido y seguro a casi todo lugar. Pero quien sale en las afueras del Dupont Circle, deberta coser sin falta un taxi. Dos atracciones son de especial mención. El asombroso *Union Station*, la enorme estación de trenes que fue convertida en un complejo de compras y restaurantes, asi como *Mt. Vernon* el pintoresco lugar de habitación de George Washington. En Delaware a 2 horas de distancia aconsejamos el balneario gay *Rehoboth Beach*.

Sulla lapide di Leonard Matlovich's vi è un epitaffio: „Mi conferite una medaglia per aver ucciso un uomo e mi congedate per averne amato un altro." Sono proprio questi numerosi tratti contraddittori a fare di Washington una meta di prima classe. Il *District of Columbia* (D.C.) è costituito unicamente dalla città di Washington; è sorprendentemente piccolo: ha 600.000 abitanti con una periferia di 4.000.000. Ciò prova che Washington non è una movimentata *business town*. Rappresenta il governo federale e la politica costituisce l'anima commerciale di questa città. Così è considerato il centro commerciale, *Mall*, lungo quale si trovano istituzioni politiche, simbolo degli Stati Uniti, come la *Casa Bianca*, il *Vietnam Memorial* e numerosi musei come l'*Holocaust Museum*. Il periodo più bello per una visita è in marzo-aprile, quando lungo il Mall fioriscono i ciliegi. I gay di Washington si sono adattati alla massiva presenza del governo: mediante associazioni cercano di difendere i propri interessi, appoggiati dal giornale locale *Washington Blade*. Gli abitanti di Washington escono con preferenza nella zona intorno al *Dupont Circle* a nord ovest della Casa Bianca. Per conoscere questa ed altre parti della città non avrete bisogno di un'auto poichè la metropolitana vi porta ovunque velocemente e (quasi) senza rischi. Tuttavia nelle zone esterne al Dupont Circle non rinunciate mai ad un taxi; é d'obbligo in fine menzionare due attrazioni: l'imponente *Union Station*, trasformata in un centro commerciale, ricca di ristoranti e negozi e *Mt. Vernon*, la pittoresca residenza di George Washington. Vi consigliamo inoltre un'esursione a Rehoboth Beach, una stazione balneare gay situata a Delaware a due ore da Washington.

GAY INFO

Gay and Lesbian Switchboard (GLM)
19.30-22.30 h
☎ 387-4348

Metro Weekly
1012 14th Street NW, Suite 615 ✉DC 20005 ☎ 638-6830
Fax: 638-6831 E-Mail: mweekly1@aol.com
Gay and lesbian weekly distributed free every Thu throughout the DC Metropolitan area.

TOURIST INFO

Washington DC Convention & Visitor Bureau
1212 New York Avenue NW, Suite 600 ✉DC 20005
☎ 789-7000 Fax: 789-7037

BARS

Annex (B G VS) Thu-Sat 21-2, Sun 16-? h
1415 22nd Street North West ✉DC 20037 *(upstairs „Badlands")*
☎ 293-0064

Back Door Pub (B G) 17-? h
1104 8th Street South East ✉DC 20003 *(second floor at Bachelor's Mill)* ☎ 546-5979

Badlands (! AC B D f GLM MA N s VS W YG)
1415 22nd Street North West ✉DC 20037 ☎ 296-0505

The Brass Rail (B D F G) 11-2 h
476 K Street North West ✉DC 20001 ☎ 371-6983

D.C. Eagle (B G LJ) 12-2 h, Fri Sat -3 h
639 New York Avenue NW ✉DC 20001 ☎ 347-6025

Delta Elite (B D glm WE) Sun only
3734 10th Street North West ✉DC 20017 ☎ 832-9839

Escándalos/Lone Star West (B F GLM r S) 16-? h
2122 P Street North West ✉DC 20037 ☎ 822-8909
Friendly piano bar and restaurant.

The Fireplace (! B G VS YG) 13-2 h
2161 P Street North West ✉DC 20037 ☎ 293-1293

Fraternity House (AC B d G MA s VS) Mon-Thu 16-2 h, Fri -3 h, Sat 20-3 h, Sun 15-2 h
2123 Twining Court N.W. ✉DC 20037 *(alley entrance)*
☎ 223-4917

Hung Jury (B GLM)
1819 H Street North West ✉DC 20006 ☎ 785-8181

J.R.'s Bar & Grill (AC B CC F G lj R VS) 11-2, Fri Sat -3 h
1519 17th Street North West ✉DC 20036 ☎ 328-0090

La Cage aux Follies (B d G S SNU) Mon-Thu 19.30-2 h, Fri Sat -3 h
1354 Cupitol Street South East ✉DC 20003 ☎ 554-3615

LARRY'S Lounge (AC B CC GLM MA N OS) 17-2 h
1840 18th
Street NW ✉DC 20009 ☎ 483-1483

Mr. P's (B D f G STV VS) 15-2 h, Fri Sat -3 h, Sun 12-2 h
2147 P Street North West ✉DC 20037 ☎ 293-1064

Nob Hill (B G MA)
1101 Kenyon Street North West ✉DC 20010 ☎ 797-1101

Omega DC (AC B G s VS) Sun-Thu 16-2 h, Fri -3 h, Sat 20-3 h
2123 Twining CT NW ✉DC 20037 *(Dupont Circle)* ☎ 223-4917

Remington's (AC B CC d GLM LJ MA N S STV VS W) Mon-Thu 16-2 h, Fri Sat -3 h, Sun 12-2 h
639 Pennsylvania Avenue South East ✉DC 20003 *(Metro-Eastern Market)* ☎ 543-3113

Wet (B F Glm S VS W) Sun-Thu 19-2, Fri Sat -3 h
52 L Street SE ☎ 488-1200

MEN'S CLUBS

The Crew Club (G P VS WO)
1321 14th Street NW ✉DC 20009
Smoke, alcohol and drug free. Membership necessary.

DANCECLUBS

Ozone (B D G) 1214 18th
Street NW ☎ 293-0303

The Edge (B D G f VS W)
56 L Street

Tracks (B D f G MA s WE) Thu Sat 21-? h, Fri 22-? h, Sun 17-22.30 h
1111 1st Street South East ✉DC 20003 *(Metro-Navy Yard)*
☎ 488-3320
Thu is college night, Sun country/western tea dance.

Ziegfeld's (B D GLM STV)
1345 Half Street South East ✉DC 20003 ☎ 554-5141

RESTAURANTS

The Belmont Kitchen (B F glm os) Brunch Sat Sun 11.30-15.30 h
2400 18th Street North West ✉DC 20009 ☎ 667-1200

Boss Shepherd's (B F GLM OS) Sun 11-16 h brunch
1527 17th Street North West ✉DC 20036 ☎ 328-8193

Bradshaw's (B F G)
2319 18th Street North West ✉DC 20009 ☎ 462-8330

Café Berlin (AC B CC F GLM MA OS) Mon-Thu 11-22 h, Fri -23 h, Sat 12-23 h, Sun 16-22 h
322 Massachusetts Avenue, NE ✉DC 20002 ☎ 543-7656
Fax: 543-7863
German and continental cuisine. Casual dress. Patio dining in season.

Café Japon (B F G)
2032 P Street North West ✉DC 20036 ☎ 223-1573
Cafe Luna (A B bf F glm OS YG) 11-2 h
1633 P St., NW ✉DC 20036 ☎ 387-4005
Italian cuisine.
Childe Harolde Restaurant and Saloon
(! AC B CC F glm MA N OS) Sun-Thu 11.30-2 h, Fri Sat 10.30-3 h
1610 20th Street North West ✉DC 20009 *(metro Dupont Circle-Q Street exit)* ☎ 483-6700 ☎ 485-6701
One of the oldest restaurants in Washington, full menue, great seafood and steaks, lots of sandwiches, best burger in DC.
Fasika's Ethiopean Restaurant (b F g) ?-1 h
2447 18th Street North West ✉DC 20009 ☎ 797-7673
La Fourchette (B F GLM)
2429 18th Street North West ✉DC 20009 ☎ 332-3077
Lauriol Plaza (b F g) 12-24 h, Sun 11-24 h
1801 18th Street North West ✉DC 20009 ☎ 387-0035
Louis (B F G lj)
476 K Street North West ✉DC 20001 ☎ 371-2223
Lucy's and Fred's (B F GLM YG) 18-22 h
56 L Street South East ✉DC 20003 *(at Lost & Found)*
☎ 488-1200
Mr. Henry's (AC B CC F GLM MA N OS W) Mon-Sat 11.30-2, Sun 10-2 h
601 Pennsylvania Avenue S.E. ✉DC 20003 ☎ 546-8412
Pan Asian Restaurant (B F g)
2020 P Street North West ✉DC 20036 ☎ 872-8889
Paramount Steak House (AC b CC F glm OS) 10.30-24 h, Fri Sat -? h
1609 17th Street North West ✉DC 20009 ☎ 232-0395
Steaks and seafood.
Perry's (AC B F glm OS YG)
1811 Columbia Road NW ✉DC 20009 ☎ 234-6218
Japanese and nouvelle cuisine.
Red Sea (b F g)
2463 18th Street North West ✉DC 20009 ☎ 483-5000
Ethiopean food.
Ribs and More (AC b F G)
2122 P Street North West ✉DC 20037 ☎ 822-8909
Sala Thai Restaurant (B F g)
2016 P Street North West ✉DC 20037 ☎ 872-1144
Skewers (b F g)
1633 P Street North West ✉DC 20036 ☎ 387-7400
Straits of Malaya (AC B CC F glm MA N OS W) Mon-Fri 12-14 h, 17.30-2 h
1836 18th Street North West ✉DC 20017 *(Dupont Circle)*
☎ 483-1483
Malaysian cuisine.
Trio (AC b F GLM OS)
1537 17th Street/Q Street ✉DC 20002
Zapata's (B F g) 601 Pennsylvania Avenue South East ✉DC 20003 ☎ 546-6886
Mexican food.
2 Quail (AC CC E F glm MA NG) 11.30-14.30 h, 17-23 h
320 Massachusetts Avenue NE ✉DC 20002 *(M-Union Station)*
☎ 543-8030

SEX SHOPS/BLUE MOVIES

Follies Theater 0-24 h
24 O Street South East/Half Street ✉DC 20003 ☎ 484-0323
Pornos, male burlesque and Sun buffet. Videos also for sale.
Pleasure Place (AC GLM MA) Mon Tue 10-22, Wed-Sat -24, Sun 12-19 h
1063 Wisconsin Avenue North West ✉DC 20007 *(Georgetown-bus & subway Foggybottom)* ☎ 333-8570 or ☎ (800) 386-2386
Erotic boutique, leather, fetish wear, toys, condoms, etc.
Pleasure Place (AC GLM MA) Mon-Tue 10-22, Wed-Sat -24, Sun 12-19 h
1710 Connecticut Avenue NW ✉DC 20009 *(Dupont Circle-bus & subway)* ☎ 483-3297

SAUNAS/BATHS

Club Washington (G P sa) 0-24 h
20 O Street South East ✉DC 20003 ☎ 488-7315

FITNESSTUDIOS

GHC The Gloryhole (G VS) 11-3 h, Fri Sat 0-24 h
24 O Street SE ✉DC 20001 ☎ 863-2770

BOOK SHOPS

Lambda Rising (AC CC GLM MA VS W) 9-24 h
1625 Connecticut Avenue North West ✉DC 20009 *(Metro-Dupont Circle, Q Street exit)* ☎ 462-6969
Gay, lesbian, bisexual and transgender books, videos, magazines and gifts. Free local guides.

GIFT & PRIDE SHOPS

The Outpost
1706 Connecticut Avenue NW ✉DC 20009
Cards T-shirts, jewelry and accessories for gay guys.

LEATHER & FETISH SHOPS

The Leather Rack (G LJ)
1723 Connecticut Avenue NW ✉DC 20009 ☎ 797-7401
Leather accessories, cards, and T-shirts designed exclusively for gay men.
The Pleasure Chest (GLM) 10-22, Wed-Sat -24, Sun 12-17 h
1710 Connercut Avenue North West ✉DC 20009 *(Durpont Circle)*
☎ 483-3297
Leather, erotica, toys, retail.
S&M Leathers 16-24 h
628 New York Avenue North West ✉DC 20001 ☎ 682-1160

TRAVEL & TRANSPORT

Tande Reservations
☎ 800-209-9408
Can assist you to find accommodation from Bed and Breakfast to guesthouses to motels to apartments in Washington and a number of other US cities. No fee.

HOTELS

The Carlyle Suites Hotel (AC B bf CC glm H N) 1731 New Hampshire Avenue ✉DC 20335 ☎ 234-3200
Lovely Art deco hotel welcoming gay visitors. Rates from US$ 89.
Radisson Barceló Hotel (AC B bf CC F H OS pi W WO)
2121 P Street, ✉DC 20037 *(1 block from subway Dupont Circle)*
☎ 293-3100 ☎ (800) 333-3333 (Toll Free) Fax: 857-0134
4 star European hotel (Spanish owned) in the heart of the gay community.
Savoy Suites Hotel (AC B bf F glm H NG pi wh) 2505 Wisconsin Avenue North West ✉DC 20007-4575 ☎ 337-9700
☎ (800) 944-5377 Fax: 337-3644
Many rooms with kitchen and jacuzzi. Rates US$ 65.

GUEST HOUSES

The Brenton (AC bf CC G MA) Office 13-21 h
1708 16th Street North West ✉DC 20009 *(4 blocks from Dupont Circle)* ☎ 332-5550 ☎ (800) 673-9042 (toll free)
Fax: 462-5872
Victorian townhouse near Dupont Circle. 8 doubles all with shared bath/WC, phone, radio, heating, own key. Hotel provides bar and TV room. Rates US$ 79 per room, suite $99 (en-suite, kitchen, TV/VCR), bf incl.

Capitol Hill Guest House (AC bf CC glm H) Open all year
101 5th Street N.E. ✉DC 20002 ☎ 547-1050 Fax: 547-1050
Located in the historic district of Capitol Hill. 6 doubles, 2 singles, 1 apartment. Rooms partly with bath/WC. Rates double US$ 55-100, single $45, apartment $115-125 (bf incl.)

Hotel Montecello (AC B F H NG)
1075 Thomas Jefferson Street North West ✉DC 20007
☎ 337-0900 Fax: 333-6526 E-Mail: gdidc@aol.com
Each suite with kitchen and separate bedroom. Rates from US$ 185.

Kalorama Guest House at Woodley Park (AC bf glm MA OS) 9-21 h
2700 Cathedral Avenue North West ✉DC 20008 ☎ 328-0860
Fax: 328-3827

The William Lewis House (AC bf CC G H wh)
1309 R Street N.W. ✉DC 20009 ☎ 462-7574 Fax: 462-1608
Email: wlewishous@aol.com Homepage: www.wlewishous.com
Located near gay bars. 5 rooms with shared bath, rooms with phone, heating, own key. Guest house provides safe and TV room. Rates single US$ 75, double $85 (+ tax, bf incl.)

GENERAL GROUPS

Gay People's Alliance (GLM)
George Washington University ✉DC 20006 *800 21st Street North West, Room 420, DC 20006* ☎ 676-7590

FETISH GROUPS

Centaur Motorcycle Club
PO Box 341 93, Martin Luther King Station ✉DC 20043-4193

FFA, Washington DC
PO Box 461 ✉DC 20044

Highwaymen TNT
PO Box 545 ✉DC 20044-0545

Lost Angels
901 5th Street NE ✉DC 20002

HEALTH GROUPS

AIDS Action Council
☎ 547-3101

AIDS Information Line
☎ 332-2437

Whitman Walker Clinic
1407 S Street North West ✉DC 20009 ☎ 797-3500
☎ 833-3234 (Hotline 19-23 h)

HELP WITH PROBLEMS

Gay Hotline 19-23 h
☎ 833-3234
General information, referral, peer counselling, crisis intervention.

RELIGIOUS GROUPS

Bet Mishpachah
☎ 833-1638 *Jewish gays. Shabbat Service Fri 20.30 h; Cultural, social & educational programs.*

Dignity Sun 19.30 h
☎ 332-2424 *Gay Catholics.*

Metropolitan Community Church (GLM) Worship Sun 10.45 & 19 h
415 M Street North West ✉DC 20001 ☎ 638-7373

USA-Florida

Southeast USA

Initials: FL

Time: GMT -5

Area: 170.314 km² / 69.658 sq mi.

Population: 14,654,000

Capital: Tallahassee

Important gay cities: Fort Lauderdale, Key West, Miami, Miami Beach, Orlando, St. Petersburg, Tampa

● Laws don't seem to be everything in life. Hetero- and homosexual oral and anal sex is prohibited in Florida, and yet it is today the prime state for gay holidaymakers. Of course, this development did not appear out of nothing. The sinking prices for interstate and oversea flights, the presence of Florida in the media or the everlasting popularity of gay classics like Fort Lauderdale or Key West have contributed to it. By the way: when on a (south) Florida trip, don't miss a ride in a convertible along the Florida Keys to Key West. In inner Florida the Walt Disney Corporations gay-friendly stance is impressively shown by their favours granted to gay employees and the *Gay Day at Disneyworld.* This fun-park and the others around Orlando are only a few hours drive to the fun-and-thrill-park where everything is for real, the *John F. Kennedy Space*

Center at Cape Canaveral. The most important center, around which the gay part of Floridas tourism industry revolves, is *South Beach*, the southern tip of Miami Beach. Its Art-Deco buildings with their pastel shade façades, the palm trees, the beautiful people-all of this blends to create *the* trendy holiday destination of the nineties.

In Florida ist sowohl hetero- wie homosexueller Oral- und Analverkehr verboten. Es gibt kein *Anti-Discrimination Law*, jedoch haben einige Gemeinden ein solches verabschiedet, darunter Key West, Miami Beach, Palm Beach und Tampa. Landesweit gibt es ebenfalls kein Gesetz zur *Domestic Partnership*, doch gilt dies in einigen Städten (z.B. Miami Beach und Key West). Die *Anti-Marriage Bill* wurde ratifiziert.

Trotz dieser restriktiven Gesetzgebung ist Florida das Reiseziel Nr. 1 in den USA. Die große Präsenz in den schwulen Medien oder auch die traditionelle Popularität schwuler Klassiker wie Fort Lauderdale oder Key West. Überhaupt: wenn möglich sollte in einem (Süd-)Florida-Urlaub nie die Cabrio-Fahrt entlang der Florida Keys nach Key West fehlen.

In Mittelflorida setzt die Walt Disney Corporation schwulenfreundliche Firmenpolitik eindrucksvoll in Vergünstigungen für die schwulen Mitarbeiter und den *Gay Day at Disneyworld* um. Dieser Vergnügungspark und die übrigen um Orlando sind nur einige Stunden Fahrt vom realen „Theme Park" *John F. Kennedy Space Center* am Cape Canaveral entfernt.

Wichtigster Dreh- und Angelpunkt für den schwulen Teil von Floridas Tourimusindustrie ist derzeit *South Beach*, die Südspitze von Miami Beach. Die pastellfarbenen Art-Deco-Gebäude, die Palmen, die schönen Menschen- all das vermengt sich zum trendgemäßen Urlaubsziel der 90er Jahre.

Apparemment, en Floride, on n'a pas l'air de prendre la loi très au sérieux. La fellation et la pénétration anale entre couples homos ou hétéros sont, en principe, interdites. Malgré tout, la Floride est aujourd'hui la destination vacances numéro 1 des gays américains, ce qui n'est pas le fruit du hasard. Les vols nationaux et internationaux bon marché, la présence de la Floride dans les média et le cinéma, la popularité des stations balnéaires de Fort Lauderdale et Key West ont fait de cet état fédéral un des hauts-lieux touristiques des Etats-Unis. A faire absolument: descendre la côte en direction de Key West en décapotable!

La Walt Disney Corporation met en pratique une politique plutôt homophile: avantages pour les employés gays et „Gay Day at Disneyworld" pour les visiteurs. Ce parc d'attractions est, comme les autres autour d'Orlando, à quelques heures de voiture d'un autre parc bien plus réel: Cape Canaveral.

South Beach, la pointe sud de Miami Beach, est le haut-lieu du tourisme gay en Floride. Les bâtiments art-déco dans les couleurs pastel, les palmiers, la beauté et la jeunesse des gens: voilà pourquoi la Floride est la destination touristique „in" des années 90.

Por lo visto las leyes no lo son todo en la vida. En Florida las relaciones homosexuales y heterosexuales por vía oral y anal estan prohibidas, y sin embargo Florida es hoy en día uno de los destinos turisticos gay número 1 de los E.E.U.U.. A este hecho han contribuido los baratos costos de vuelo (dentro de los E.E. U.U. y a través del Atlántico), la presencia de Florida en muchos medios de comunicación o bien la tradicional popularidad de los lugares clásicos gay (Fort Lauderdale y Key West). En Florida central el *Gay Day at Disneyworld* se ha convertido en una atracción, en el que la Corporación Walt Disney afirma su política gay en la medida en la que los trabajadores gay de la empresa obtienen descuentos. Este parque de diversiones y los restantes en los alrededores de Orlando

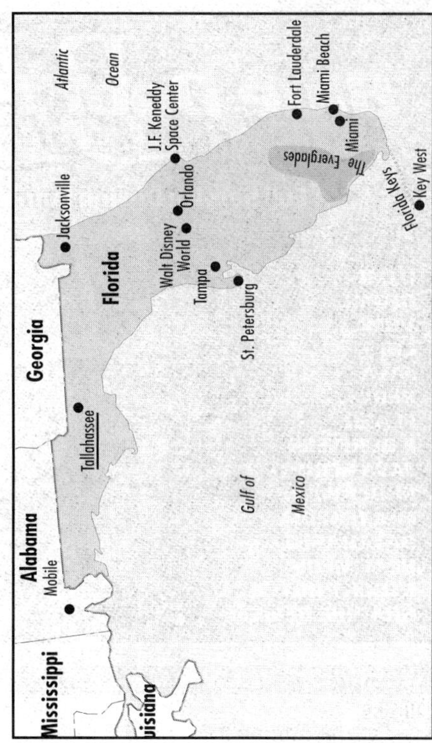

estan tan solo a unas cuantas horas del „Theme Park", *John F. Kennedy Space Center* en Cabo Cañaveral. El sitio clave para el turismo gay de Florida es por el momento *South Beach* en el más extremo sur de Miami Beach. Los colores pasteles de las edificaciones Art-Deco, las palmeras y la gente guapa hacen de este lugar el destino turístico de moda de los años '90. A próposito: turistas el (en sur) de Florida deberían aprovechar para hacer una excursión en un descapotable por los Florida Keys hacía Key West.

Evidentemente le leggi non sono tutto nella vita: in Florida i rapporti orali e anali praticati sia da eterosessuali che da omosessuali sono vietati. Nonostante ci , per i gay, la Florida, in USA, è la meta turistica numero uno; ciò non è casuale, bensì dipende dalla diminuzione del prezzo dei voli (interni e d'oltre Atlantico), dalla presenza della Florida nei mass media e dalla fama di luoghi gay come Fort Landerdale o Key West. Se siete in vacanza nel sud della Florida non perdetevi in nessun caso un giro in decappottabile a Key West lungo la Florida Keys. Nella Florida centrale la Walt Disney Corporation attua una politica aziendale a favore dei gay, con agevolazioni per i dipendenti gay e con il *Gay Day at Disneyworld*. Questo parco divertimenti ed altri presso Orlando distano poche ore d'-auto dal „Theme Park" *John F. Kennedy Space Center* presso Cape Canaveral. Attualmente il punto centrale del turismo gay della Florida è *South Beach*, all'estremità meridionale di Miami Beach. Gli edifici art decò color pastello, le palme e la bella gente si mescolano e creano la meta turistica più alla moda degli anni '90.

Boca Raton

CRUISING

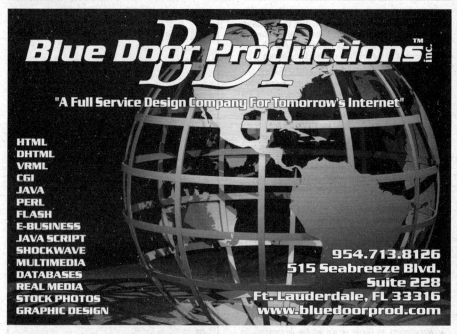

-Spanish River Park (AYOR)

Bradenton ☎ 941

SEX SHOPS/BLUE MOVIES

C&J Adult Center
4949 14th Street West ✉FL 34207 ☎ 755-9076

CRUISING

-Coquina Beach

Clearwater ☎ 813

BARS

Lost & Found (B GLM)
5858 Roosevelt Boulevard ✉FL 34620 ☎ 539-8903
Pro Shop (AC B CC f G MA N OS WE) Mon-Sat 11:30-02 h, Sun 13-02 h
840 Cleveland Street ✉FL 33755 ☎ 447-4259

DANCECLUBS

Triangles (AC B D E G OS S SNU VS YG)
5858 Roosevelt Boulevard ✉FL 34620 ☎ 539-8903

HEALTH GROUPS

VD-Clinic (glm)
10 North Myrtle ✉FL 34615 ☎ 461-2727

RELIGIOUS GROUPS

MCC (GLM) dinner Wed 19.30, service Sun 19.30 h
2470 Nursery Road ✉FL 34624 ☎ 546-8619

Cocoa Beach ☎ 407

BARS

Mango Tree (b F GLM) Dinner. Closed Mon.
118 North Atlantic Avenue ✉FL 32921 ☎ 799-0513
Fine dining.

Dade City ☎ 352

PRIVATE ACCOMODATION

Sawmill Campground (AC cc G H lj msg NU OS pi)
21710 US Highway 98 ✉FL 33523 *(45 min north of Tampa, 1 hour west of Orlando)* ☎ 584-0664 Fax: 583-0896
E-Mail: flsawmill@aol.com Homepage: www.flsawmill.com
Entertainment on WE. US$ 49 (2 people) 59 (4 people).

Daytona Beach ☎ 904

BARS

Barndoor (B F G N) 11-3 h
615 Main Street ✉FL 32118 ☎ 252-3776
Barracks (B D Glm lj) Mon-Sat 17-3, Sun 16-3 h
952 Orange Avenue ✉FL 32114 ☎ 254-3464
Beach Side Club (B D G S) 12-3 h
415 Main Street ✉FL 32118 ☎ 252-5465
Hollywood Complex (B D GLM S) 11-3h, Dancing Fri Sat.
615 Main Street ✉FL 32118 ☎ 252-3776

HOTELS

Oasis Beach Motel (glm H)
3169 South Atlantic Avenue ✉FL 32118 ☎ 967-8862
Rates on request

GUEST HOUSES

Villa. The (AC bf CC E f glm H MA msg OS p pi VS wh WO) 8-22 h
801 North Peninsula Drive ✉FL 32118 ☎ 248-2020
Fax: 248-2020
All rooms with color TV-VCR, tub/shower Tile Baths, A/C + Heat in an historical Spanish mansion. Continental breakfast, newspaper, T.V. Lounge, Game Room, complimentary coffee & soft drinks, non-smoking. Prices from US$ 50-140.

GENERAL GROUPS

Live & Let Live AA
1130-B Ridgewood Avenue ✉FL 32114 ☎ 258-9407

CRUISING

Boardwalk & beach (AYOR) (in front of sightseeing tower)

Fort Lauderdale ☎ 954

GAY INFO

Gay Lesbian Community Center (AC GLM MA) Mon-Fri 10-22, Sat 13-22 h, closed Sun
1164 East Oakland Park Boulevard, Suite 300 ✉FL 33334 *(3rd floor)* ☎ 563-9500 Fax: 563-9007. E-mail glccftl@aol.com

Hot Spots
5100 North East 12th Avenue, ✉FL 33334
☎ 928-1862 Fax: 772-0142
Homepage: www.hotspotsmagazine.com
»Florida's most entertaining gay publication« with ads and calendar of events. Weekly publication.

Rainbow Carpet. The
☎ 983-4668 Homepage: www.sunny.org
Accommodation service for Fort Lauderdale.

Scoop Florida
2219 Wilton Drive ✉FL 33305 ☎ 561-9707 Fax: 561-5970
E-Mail: scoop@scoopmag.com Homepage: www.scoopmag.com
Weekly gay news and entertainment magazine covering Florida.

TOURIST INFO

Greater Fort Lauderdale Convention & Visitor Bureau
200 East Las Olas ✉FL 33301 ☎ 765-4466 Fax: 765-4467

BARS

Adventures (B G MA)
303 SW 6th Street, Pompano Beach ✉FL 33060 ☎ 792-9577

Bill & Jerry's Filling Station (AC B G MA N)
1243 North East 11th Avenue ☎ 525-9403

Boots (B G LJ MA N OS) 12-2, Sat 8-3 h
901 South-West 27th Avenue, ✉FL 33312 ☎ 792-9177

Bushes. The (AC B CC G MA N S) 9-2 h
3038 North Federal Highway, ✉FL 33306 ☎ 561-1724

Cathode Ray (B GLM N OS VS YG) Sun-Fri 14-2, Sat 14-3 h
1105 East Las Olas Boulevard ✉FL 33301 ☎ 462-8611

Chainz (AC B D DR G LJ MA N) Sun-Thu 13-2, Fri Sat -3 h
1931 South Federal Highway ✉FL 33316 ☎ 462-9165

Chaps (AC B G LJ MA) 14-? h
1727 North Andrews Extension ☎ 767-0027

Eagle. The (AC B d G LJ MA VS) Sun-Thu 15-2, Fri Sat -3 h
1951 North West 9th Avenue ✉FL 33311 ☎ 462-7224
Popular. Leather bar

End Up Lounge (B d G) Mon-Fri 16-4, Sat-Sun 22-4 h
3521 W. Broward Boulevard ✉FL 33312 ☎ 584-9301

Everglades in Chainz (AC B d G LJ MA N) Sun-Thu 15-2 h, Fri-Sat 15-3 h, in Winter open from 13 h
1931 S. Federal Highway ✉FL 33316 ☎ 462-9165

Georgies Alibi (AC B glm MA) Sun-Fri 11-2, Sat -3 h
2266 Wilton Drive ✉FL 33305 ☎ 565-2526

Hideaway. The (AC B G MA N S OS VS) Mon-Thu 14-02, Fri & Sat -03, Sun 15-02 h
2022 North East 18th Avenue, ✉FL 33304 ☎ 566-8622
Cozy, friendly, pool table.

Johnny's (B D G R SNU) 12-2, Sat 12-3 h
1116 West Broward Boulevard ✉FL 33312 ☎ 522-5931

Monas (AC B glm MA)
502 East Sunrise Boulevard ☎ 525-6662

Omni (AC B CC D E GLM MA S W) Mon Thu 15-21, Tue Wed Fri Sun -2, Sat -3
1421 East Oakland Park Boulevard ✉FL 33334 ☎ 565-5151

Ramrod (AC B d G LJ MG OS SNU VS) 3-14 h
1508 North East 4th Avenue ✉FL 33304 ☎ 763-8219
Dresscode (levi, leather and uniform) after dark. Happy hour daily 15-21 h. Very popular.

DANCECLUBS

Copa. The (B D GLM MA OS S TV) 21-4 h
2800 S. Federal Highway ✉FL 33316 ☎ 463-1507

Pier. The (AC B CC D f G MA OS S VS WE) Wed, Fri & Sat 21 - ?
3333 North East 32nd Avenue ☎ 630-8990

Saint (B D G lj MA) 16-2, Sat -3 h
1000 West State Road 84 ✉FL 33315 ☎ 525-7883

RESTAURANTS

Chardees Dinner Club (B CC F g)
2209 Wilton Drive, ✉FL 33305 ☎ 563-1800

Mustards Bar - Grill (AC B CC F G MA) 11-?
2256-60 Wilton Drive ☎ 564-5116

Sukhothai (B F glm)
1930 East Sunrise Boulevard ✉FL 33304 ☎ 764-0148
Thai food. Popular with gays.

Tropics (B F GLM S)
2004 Wilton Drive ✉FL 33305 *(NE 4th Avenue)* ☎ 537-6000
Restaurant, Biano Bar, Cabaret

Victoria Park Restaurant (B F GLM)
900 NE 20th Avenue ✉FL 33304 ☎ 764-6868
Popular.

SEX SHOPS/BLUE MOVIES

Catalog X (AC GLM) Mon-Fri 9-22, Sat 10-21, Sun 10-19 h
850 NE 13th Street ✉FL 33304 ☎ 524-5050
The largest gay and lesbian emporium in the U.S.

SAUNAS/BATHS

Apollo Gym and Sauna Club (AC b DR G MA N p sb wh WO YG) 24h
2449 Wilton Drive ✉FL 33305 *(off NE 4th Ave)* ☎ 523-3993
Opening autumn 2000 Over 10.000sq f of relaxing area.*

Club. The (! AC CC f G MA NU p pi sa sb wh WO) 0-24 h
400 West Broward Boulevard ✉FL 33312 ☎ 525-3344

FASHION SHOPS

Audace (g) Mon-Thu 10-22, Fri-Sat 10-24, Sun 12-22 h
813 East Las Olas Boulevard, ✉FL 3330

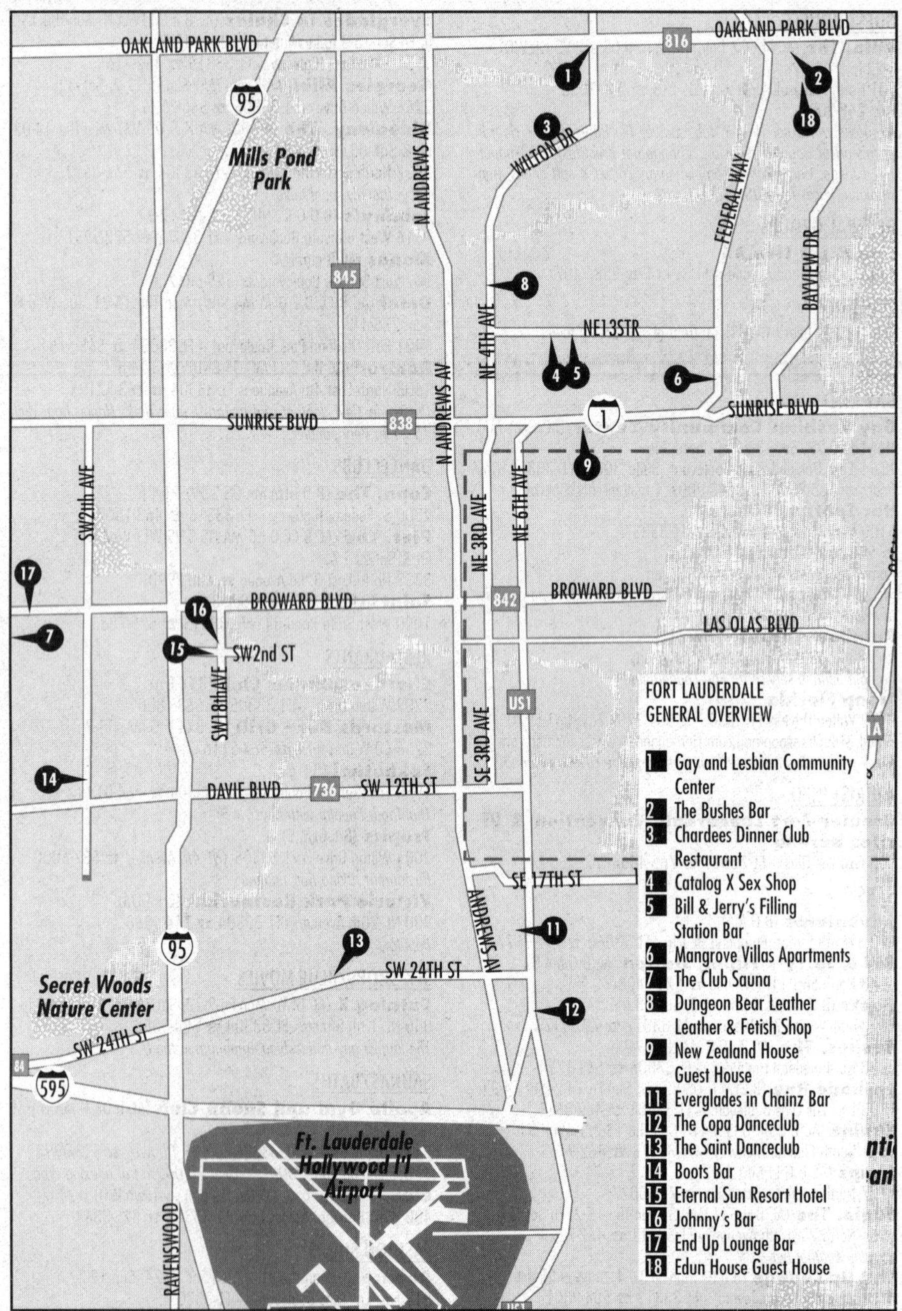
OAKLAND PARK BLVD
816
OAKLAND PARK BLVD
95
Mills Pond Park
N ANDREWS AV
WILTON DR
FEDERAL WAY
BAYVIEW DR
845
NE 4TH AVE
NE13STR
N ANDREWS AV
SUNRISE BLVD
838
1
SUNRISE BLVD
SW2th AVE
NE 3RD AVE
NE 6TH AVE
BROWARD BLVD
842
BROWARD BLVD
LAS OLAS BLVD
SW2nd ST
SW18thAVE
US1
SE 3RD AVE
DAVIE BLVD
736
SW 12TH ST
SE 17TH ST
ANDREWS AV
95
SW 24TH ST
Secret Woods Nature Center
SW 24TH ST
84
595
Ft. Lauderdale Hollywood I'l Airport
RAVENSWOOD
FORT LAUDERDALE GENERAL OVERVIEW
1 Gay and Lesbian Community Center
2 The Bushes Bar
3 Chardees Dinner Club Restaurant
4 Catalog X Sex Shop
5 Bill & Jerry's Filling Station Bar
6 Mangrove Villas Apartments
7 The Club Sauna
8 Dungeon Bear Leather Leather & Fetish Shop
9 New Zealand House Guest House
11 Everglades in Chainz Bar
12 The Copa Danceclub
13 The Saint Danceclub
14 Boots Bar
15 Eternal Sun Resort Hotel
16 Johnny's Bar
17 End Up Lounge Bar
18 Edun House Guest House

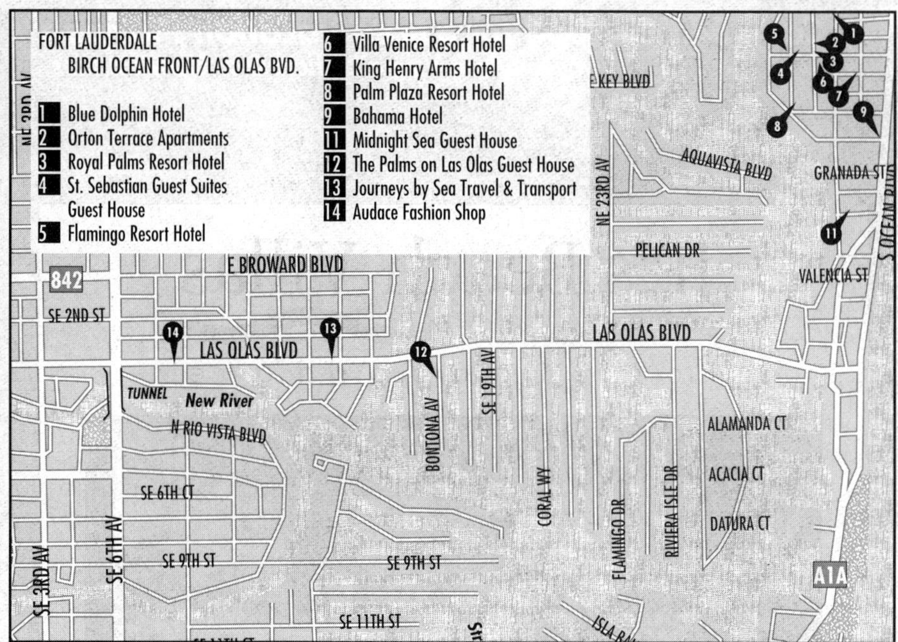

Clothes Encounters (AC CC GLM MA)
1952 East Sunrise Boulevard ✉FL 33304 *(Gateway Shopping Centre)* ☎ 522-2228
T-shirts.

GIFT & PRIDE SHOPS

Catalog X Retail & Clothing Outlet
850 NE 13th Street ✉FL 33304 ☎ 524-5050
Huge selection of clothing, swimwear, magazines, dance CD's, adult toys, lubes, pipes & papers, greeting cards, pride products, custom leather shop, and videos for rent or sale.

LEATHER & FETISH SHOPS

Dungeon Bear Leather (LJ) Mon-Thu 20-2, Fri Sat 18-3, Sun -2 h
1508 NE 4th Avenue ✉FL 33339 ☎ 523-1035

Wicked Leather (CC G MA)
2422 Wilton Drive ✉FL 33305 ☎ 564-PLAY
Selection of leather, rubber, toys and bondage. Full made to measure and design service.

PR & PHOTOGRAPHY SERVICES

Blue Door Productions Inc
515 Seabreeze Boulevard, Suite 228 ✉FL 33316 ☎ 713-8126
Fax: 713-8165 Homepage: www.bluedoorprod.com
Web site design, gay stock photography, graphic design and photography services.

TRAVEL & TRANSPORT

Journeys by Sea Inc. (AC B bf F GLM MA NU)
1402 East Las Olas Boulevard, Suite 122 ✉FL 33301
☎ 522-5865
Fax: 522-5836 or ☎ (800) 825-3632, Fax: (800) 8255956 (Toll free). E-Mail: info@journeysbysea.com.
Homepage http://www.journeysbysea.com.
Gay yacht vacations in the Caribbean are all-inclusive. All meals, bar and port taxes are included for a daily rate of US$ 150.

HOTELS

Bahama Hotel (AC bf B CC F G H msg OS pi wh WO)
401 North Atlantic Boulevard (A-1-A) ✉FL 33304 ☎ 467-7315
☎ (800) 622-9995 Fax: 467-7319
E-Mail: bahama@bahamahotel.com
Homepage: wwww.bahamahotel.com
Hotel with patio bar at poolside, parking palce, large tanning deck, heated swimming pool. Rates rooms: US$ 85-153, efficiency 115-179.

Blue Dolphin Hotel (AC bf CC G H MA msg pi)
725 North Birch Road ✉FL 33304 ☎ 565-8437
☎ (800) 893-2583 (toll free) Fax: 565-6015
E-Mail: 75372.1737@compuserve.com
Homepage: www.gaywired.com/unity/bluedolp.htm
Heated pool. Close to gay clubs, bars and restaurants.

Brigantine. The (AC bf b CC G H OS pi) Office: 8-20 h
2831 Vistamar Street ✉FL 33304 ☎ 565-6911
☎ (877) 565-6911 (toll-free) Fax: 565-8911
E-Mail: info@brigantinehotel.com
Homepage: www.brigantinehotel.com
All rooms with fridge, microwave, coffee maker, phone. A fully equipped kitchen is in addition available for apartments and efficiencies. Heated pool and guest laundry room. Rates: rooms US$ 65-115, efficiencies 85-145, apartments 105-175.

GREATER FORT LAUDERDALE *Immerse yourself.*

New Zealand House

Join us for a New Zealand style tropical getaway at a moderately priced, cozy 8-room guest house. Clothing optional pool Cenvenient to all gay bars and restaurants. Contact Ric & Warren 888-234-5494 Web: www.newzealandhouse.com

908 N.E. 15th Avenue
Ft. Lauderdale, FL 33304
954-523-7829 Fax: 954-523-7051

Proud member of IGLTA

Orton Terrace

• Guest Rooms •
• 1 & 2 Bedroom Apartments •
All with Refrigerators, Microwave
Cable TV/Videos/VCR

Call About Our Affordable Rates

800-323-1142
US, Carib, CAN

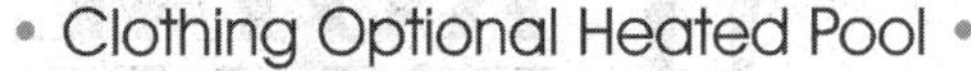

• Clothing Optional Heated Pool •
• Barbeque Grill •
• Continental Breakfast •
• Steps to the Beach •

Community Room with Computer Includes Internet Access

e-mail: orton@ortonterrace.com
Web: www.ortonterrace.com

IGLTA 954-566-5068 • FAX 954-564-8646
606-Orton Ave., Ft. Lauderdale, FL 33304

GREATER FORT LAUDERDALE
Immerse yourself.

THE
BLUE
DOLPHIN
A PREMIER FT. LAUDERDALE BEACH MEN'S RESORT
Private Enclosed Sundeck · Heated Pool
Superior Accommodations · Steps to Beach
Continental Breakfast · Off-street Parking
725 North Birch Road, Ft. Lauderdale
Toll Free (UK): 0800 89 001-800 893 2583
Free Call (D): 0800 225 5288-800 893 2583
954-565-8437 FAX 954-565-6015
E-Mail: 75372.1737@compuserve.com
http://www.gaywired.com/unity/bluedolp.htm
IGLTA

The
Grand
Resort

Fort Lauderdale Rolls Out The Rainbow Carpet.

Feel the warmth and excitement of Fort Lauderdale's gay-friendly accommodations. Fort Lauderdale was voted 1999 "Destination of the Year" by Out & About.

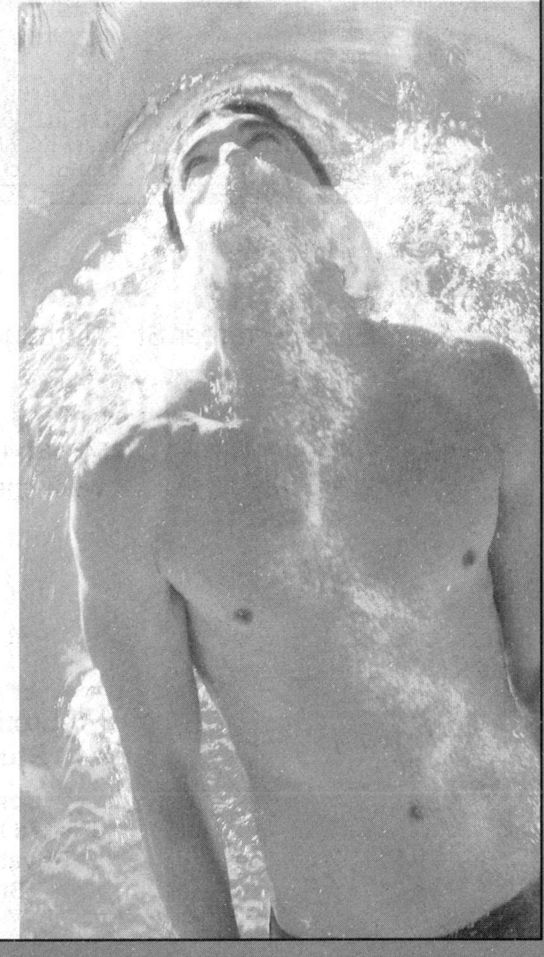

www.sunny.org
954-983-4668

IGLTA

GREATER FORT LAUDERDALE
Immerse yourself.

Ft. Lauderdale's Newest Boutique Hotel
Venice Beach
Guest Quarters
Spacious Suites
Close To Everything
Guest Lounge
Steps To The Beach
(954) 564-9601 • (Toll Free) 800-533-4744
Fax: (954) 564-5618
552 N. Birch Rd (at Terramar) Fort Lauderdale, FL 33304
www.veniceqtrs.com

Eternal Sun Resort (AC CC G H MA NU OS pi wh) 1909 South West 2nd Street ✉FL 33312 ☎ 462-6035 Fax: 522-2764
E-Mail: MrIbiza@aol.com Homepage: www.EternalSun.Org
Formerly Kelly's Guesthouse. All rooms have cable TV, phones, refrigerator and microwave. Tropical garden with pool.

Fazenda. La (bf f G H pi wh)
835 West Las Olas Boulevard, ✉FL 33312 ☎ 832-9014
Centrally located. Rooms with priv. bath. Rates on request.

Grand Resort. The (AC CC G H OS pi wh WO)
539 North Birch Road ✉FL 33304 ☎ 630-3000
☎ (800) 818-1211 (toll-free) Fax: 630-3003
Homepage: www.grandresort.net
Rooms, suites or villas with cable TV, VCR, voice-mail, fridge, coffee maker. Call for rates.

King Henry Arms (AC bf CC GLM H OS pi)
543 Breakers Avenue ✉FL 33304-4129 ☎ 561-0039
☎ (800) 205-5464 (toll free) Fax: 563-1246
Single rooms US$ 49-81, double 64-96, studio 76-107, apartment 81-119, all with private bath, refrigerators and some with kitchens. Continental bf included.

Palm Plaza Resort (bf G H OS pi)
2801 Riomar Street ✉FL 33304 ☎ 254-1985
☎ (888) 954-7300 (toll free) Fax: 954-566-1105.
Homepage: www.palmplazaresort.com
Comfortable rooms and apartments.

Royal Palms Resort (AC bf CC GLM H MA msg NU OS pi)
2901 Terramar Street ✉FL 33304 ☎ 564-6444
☎ (800) 237-7256 (toll free) Fax: 564-6443
E-Mail: ryalpalms@aol.com Homepage: www.royalpalms.com
Double rooms and appartments with bath, WC, phone, fridge, cable TV, cd-players. Rates for 2 people US$ 125-269 incl. bf.

Sun n' Spalsh (AC bf CC G H NU OS pi WO)
1129-35 North Victoria Park Road ✉FL 33304 ☎ 467-2669
☎ (888) 842-9352 (toll-free) Fax: 467-1385
Homepage: www.GAY-FLA.com
Home of „Fort Lauderdale's Gay Men's Nude Swim Club". All rooms with TV and VCR and free telephone with unlimited computer connection. Call for rates.

Venice Beach Guest Quarters (AC bf CC glm H OS pi VS wh)
552 North Birch Road ✉FL 33304 ☎ 564-9601
☎ (800) 533-4744 (toll-free) Fax: 564-5618
Homepage: www.veniceqtrs.com
Studios and suites with bath, full kitchen, phone, cable TV, radio, AC. Stereo, VCR in addition for suites. Guest computer station available, guest laundry, sundeck, heated pool. Rates rooms: US$ 65-85, studios 75-120, suites 85-150, extra person 15.

Villa Venice Resort (AC CC G LJ MA msg OS pi VS) 8-22 h
2900 Terramar Street ✉FL 33304 ☎ 564-7855 Fax: 564-7859
Homepage: www.samemaster.com/villa
Double room US$ 69, studio 89, apartment 110-250. Heated pool.

GUEST HOUSES

Coral Reef (A AC bf CC G pi wh WO) Office: 8-20 h
2609 North East 13th Court ✉FL 33304-1505 ☎ 568-0292
☎ (888) 365-6948 (toll-free) Fax: 568-1992
E-Mail: Coralref@aol.com Homepage: members.aol.com/coralref/
Rates in-season US$ 79-119, off-season 81-105.

Drifting Sands (glm H)
524 Bayshore Drive ✉FL 33304

Edun House (bf G H NU OS pi) 2733 Middle River Drive ✉FL 33306 ☎ 565-7775 Fax: 565-7912
E-Mail: Edun2733@aol.com
Homepage: members.aol.com/edunhouse
Guest house with swimming pool, fitness room, massage possible,

nude sunbathing/nude bathing possibility, clothing always optional. All rooms with bath/WC, telephone, Satellite TV, radio, air-conditioning. Rates from US$ 79-139 incl. Continental breakfast.

Gemini House (AC bf G H msg NU OS pi wh WO)
☎ 568-9791 Fax: 568-0617 E-Mail: GeminiHse@aol.com
Homepage: www.geminihse.com
Gay Male Naturist Vacation in Bed and Breakfast tradition. Rooms with bath, cable TV and VCR. Heated pool, hot tub, outdoor shower, gym, free local calls. Call for info on exact location.

Midnight Sea Guesthouse (AC bf Glm H NU OS VS wh)
3005 Alhambra Street ✉FL 33304 ☎ 463-4827
☎ (800) 910-2357 (toll free) Fax: 522-7604
E-Mail: midnightse@aol.com Homepage: www.midnightses.com
All rooms with priv. bath, AC, cable TV, refrigerator, some with kitchen and telephone. From US$ 49 to US$ 199/night. Nude sunbathing & jacuzzi in tropical garden. Special discount for students and -25 years.

New Zealand House (AC CC G H msg nu OS pi)
908 North East 15th Avenue ✉FL 33304 *(1,5 miles from the beach)* ☎ 523-7829 Fax: 523-7051
Homepage: www.newzealandhouse.com
Rooms from US$ 65-95 (single) and 75-110 (double).

Palms on Las Olas. The (AC bf CC G H MA pi) 9-21 h
1760 East Las Olas Boulevard ✉FL 33301 ☎ 462-4178
☎ (800) 550-7656 (Toll-free) Fax: 463-8544
E-Mail: info@palmsonlasolas.com
Homepage: www.palmsonlasolas.com
Heated pool. Rates without tax US$ 70-140 /night.

Paradiso Tropical Guest Cottages (AC b bf CC G MA msg NU OS pi wh)
1115 Tequesta Street ✉FL 33312 ☎ 462-0066
☎ (800) 644-7977 (toll free) Fax: 462-0066

Saint Sebastian Guest Suites (AC bf CC G H msg pi) Office: 8-20 h
2835 Terramar Street ✉FL 33304 ☎ 568-6161 ☎ (800) 425-8105 (toll free) Fax: 568-6209
Rooms with private bath, refrigerator, TV, telephone, some with kitchen. Rates US$ 59-119.

Sea Eagle (AC bf CC G LJ NU pi wh WO)
2609 North East 13 th Court ✉FL 33304 ☎ 568-0292
Fax: 390-0904

Sea Grape House (AC B bf CC G H NU OS pi VS wh)
1109 North East 16th Place ✉FL 33305 *(minutes walk for gay epicentre and beach)* ☎ 525-6586
☎ (800) 447-3074 code 44 (toll-free) Fax: 525-0586
E-Mail: CGrapeHse@aol.com Homepage: www.seagrape.com
All rooms with TV, VCR and phone. Call for rates.

APARTMENTS

Flamingo Resort (bf CC G MA msg NU OS p pi)
2727 Terramar Street ✉FL 33304 ☎ 561-4658
☎ (800) 283-4786 Fax: 568-2688
E-Mail: flamingors@aol.com
Homepage: www.theflamingoresort.com
Heated pool. Call for rates. Apartments with fully equipped kitchens.

JP's Beach Villas (AC CC GLM H OS pi) 4621 North Ocean Drive (A-1-A) ✉FL 33308 ☎ 772-3672
☎ (888) 992-3224 (toll-free) Fax: 776-0889
E-Mail: info@jpsbeachvillas.com
Homepage: www.jpsbeachvillas.com
All apartments and efficiencies with cable TV and phone and fully equipped kitchens. Heated pool. Near shopping, clubs and restaurant. Rates from US$ 100-175.

Mangrove Villas (AC CC G H NU pi)
1100 North Victoria Park Road ✉FL 33304 ☎ 527-5250
☎ (800) 238-3538 (toll free) Fax: 764-1968
E-Mail: villasftl@aol.com. Homepage: www.mangrovevillas.com.
Each villa is a small house with bedroom, bath, living, dining and fully equipped kitchen. Daily houseman service. Rates US$ 89-169 (high season), 60-95 (low season).
Orton Terrace (AC bf CC f G H MA NU OS pi VS)
606 Orton Avenue ✉FL 33304 ☎ 566-5068
☎ (800) 323-1142 (toll free) Fax: 564-8646
E-Mail: orton@ortonterrace.com Homepage: www.ortonterrace.com
One and two bedroom apartments with fridge, microwave, cable TV, VCR, continental bf included. Community room with computer including internet access.
Villa Torino (AC CC glm H)
3017 Alhambra Street ✉FL 3304 ☎ 527-5272
Homepage: www.VillaTorino.com
Apartments for rent daily, weekly or monthly. Call for info and rates.

GENERAL GROUPS

South Florida Gay Pride Committee
PO Box 2048 ✉FL 33303 ☎ 523-3737

HEALTH GROUPS

Health Link
3213 N. Ocean Boulevard, Suite 6 ✉FL 33308 ☎ 565-8284

RELIGIOUS GROUPS

MCC Services Sun 9, 10.30 & 19, Wed 19.30 h
330 South West 27th Street ✉FL 33315 ☎ 462-2004

SWIMMING

-Fort Lauderdale beach (g) (In front of the Candy Store, and between Terramar Street and Las Olas)
-Beach opposite of North-East 18th Street (One mile north of Sunrise Boulevard)
-Lloyd Beach State Recreation Area (Take U.S. 1 to Dania Beach Boulevard, east to A1A. Follow signs to park entrance. First parking lot on right. Admission charge. Caution: Undercover police in T-rooms)

CRUISING

-Holiday Park (South side of Sunrise Boulevardat North-East 12th Avenue. Check out parking area)

Fort Myers ☎ 941

GAY INFO

Gay Switchboard 0-24 h
PO Box 546 ✉FL 33902 ☎ 275-1400

BARS

Bottom Line. The (AC B CC D f GLM MA OS S VS W) 15-2 h
3090 Evans Avenue ✉FL 33901 ☎ 337-7292
☎ (800) 839-6823 (Toll-free)

RESTAURANTS

Oasis. The (B F glm)
2222 McGregor Boulevard ✉FL 33901 ☎ 334-1566

GENERAL GROUPS

Queer Nation/SW Florida Chapter
c/o Support Inc. ☎ 275-1400
Ask to be transferred to Queer Nation Representative.

HELP WITH PROBLEMS

AIDS-Hotline
☎ 337-AIDS

SWIMMING

-Bunch Beach (John Morris Parkway. South end of beach AYOR)

Fort Walton Beach ☎ 904

BARS

Choo Choo's Pub (AC B GLM LJ S) 16-4 h
223 Highway 98 East ✉FL 32548 *(adjacent to Frankly Scarlet)*
☎ 664-2966
Frankly Scarlett (AC B D GLM LJ MA S STV) Sun-Wed 19-2, Thu-Sat -4 h
217 Highway 98 East ✉FL 32548 *(adjacent to Choo Choo's Pub)*
☎ 664-2966

Gainesville ☎ 904

GAY INFO

Gay Switchboard (GLM) 18-23 h, computer system 23-8 h
PO Box 12002 ✉FL 32604-0002 ☎ 332-0700

BARS

Ambush. The (B G LJ) 16-? h
4130 North-West 6th Street ✉FL 32609 ☎ 376-3772
Melody Club. The (! B D GLM OS SNU STV W) 20-2 h
4130 North-West 6th Street ✉FL 32609 ☎ 376-3772
Oz (B G)
7118 West University Avenue/Tower Road ✉FL 32609 *(I-75)*
Phil's Bar and Resort (B GLM)
County Road 316, Reddick, Ocala ✉FL 32686 *(1.5 miles west of State Road 25 A)* ☎ 591-9924
Call about membership.
Quake. The (AC B D F GLM MA OS S WE YG) 16-2 h
7118 West University Avenue ✉FL 32607 ☎ 332-2553
University Club (B GLM STV)
18 East University Avenue ✉FL 32601 ☎ 378-6814

HEALTH GROUPS

Alachua County Public Health Unit
730 North-East Waldo Road ✉FL 32601 ☎ 336-2356 ext.153 or 154

HELP WITH PROBLEMS

AA Gay New Life (glm) 20 h Sun.
☎ 332-0700 ☎ 372-8091

CRUISING

-Newman's Lake (AYOR)
-Park at North East 16th Avenue/Main Street (days)
-Bivens Arm Park
-Lake Alice (at the University)

Gulfport ☎ 727

BARS

Sharp A's Lounge (AC B CC d f GLM MA N S SNU STV) 16-2 h
4918 Gulfport Boulevard South ✉FL 33707-4940 ☎ 327-4897
Gay bar with liquor store.

Hallandale ☎ 305

BARS

Underpass (B D G S) Tue-Sun
100 Ansin Boulevard ✉FL 33009 ☎ 547-8800

Holiday ☎ 727

BARS

Lovey's Pub (AC B d f GLM MA s W) Mon-Sat 10-2, Sun 13-2 h
3338 U.S. Highway 19 ✉FL 34691 ☎ 849-2960

Hollywood ☎ 323

SEX SHOPS/BLUE MOVIES

Hollywood Book & Video (g VS) 0-24 h
1235 South State Road 7 ✉FL 33023 ☎ 305/981-2164

CRUISING

-Young Circle (AYOR)

Jacksonville ☎ 904

BARS

Boot Rack Saloon (B G lj OS) 14-2 h
4751 Lenox Avenue ✉FL 32205 ☎ 384-7090
Bo's Coral Reef (B D G)
201 North 5th Avenue ✉FL 32250 *(Jacksonville Beach)*
Club Carousel (B D F glm S) Sat (G) 19-2 h
8550 Arlington Expressway ✉FL 32211 ☎ 725-8282
In Touch Tavern (b GLM N W) Mon-Sat 12-2, Sun 15-2 h
10957 Atlantic Boulevard ✉FL 32225 ☎ 642-7506
Junction Tavern. The (A AC b f GLM MA N OS S W) 14-2 h
1261 King Street ✉FL 32204 ☎ 388-3434
Metro (AC B CC D f GLM LJ MA N S SNU STV W WE YG) Mon-Fri 16-2, Sat 18-3, Sun -24 h
2929 Plum Street ✉FL 32205 ☎ 388-8719
Park Place Lounge (B G N W)
931 King Street ✉FL 32204 ☎ 389-6616
Third Dimension 3D (AC B CC D f G MA S SNU STV TV VS W) Mon-Fri 15-3, Sat 16-3, Sun 17-3 h
711 Edison Avenue ✉FL 32204-2904 ☎ 353-6316
18-21 years old allowed after 21 h.
616 (AC B CC d f GLM lj MA OS S SNU) 16-2 h
616 Park Street ✉FL 32204 ☎ 358-6969

SAUNAS/BATHS

Club Jacksonville (G pi sa sb vs wh WO) 0-24 h
1939 Hendricks Avenue ✉FL 32207 ☎ 398-7451
The cost of membership for six month $ 12.

SWIMMING

-Beach in the Jacksonville area (G) (25 miles south of Jacksonville on A1A at the end of South Ponte Vedra Beach. The entrance can be found at the Guano River Boat Ramp. Once across the sand dune, go to the right about 200 yards. There is some dune activity but can be rather risky as the police regularly patrol the beach)

CRUISING

-Boone Park
-Friendship Park (AYOR)

Jasper ☎ 850

HOTELS

Mystic Lake Manor (AC bf F G MA pi wh WO) 8-24 h
PO Box 1623 ✉FL 32052 *(8.4 miles off 1-10 in Northern Florida)* ☎ 973-8435
Located on a 30 acre lake. Boating and fishing. Private rooms with private baths, private rooms with shared baths and dormitory.
Swan Lake B&B
238 Route 129, PO Box 1623 ✉ FL 32052 ☎ 904/792-2771

Key West ☎ 305

● Key West is at the most southern point of the U.S.A. The best way to get there is by hire car from Miami or to take the shuttle bus from Miami International Airport. The scenic trip across the US 1 to Key West takes roughly three hours and offers the best impression of the island. For those who are not able to wait - take a direct flight from Miami. In Key West you will find a very open minded crowd. Gays are so intigrated in the community that they are almost not noticeable in every day life. Duval Street, known as the „longest street of the world" connecting the Atlantic with the Gulf of Mexico, is the main shopping district. But watch out for the shops bearing the rainbow flag, many of these are tourist traps. The „Fantasy Fest" takes place every year in October, which is the largest attraction of Key West. At this time of year this small island seems to almost bursts with gays and lesbians gathering here from all corners of the globe. After indulging in the sight seeing trip, including the Ernest Hemingway Home, there is not much for the gay tourist to do, apart from relaxing by the pool in his guest house. The early evening starts with a cocktail (normally complimentary in all good guest houses). Most action takes place in the early hours of the morning in the hot tub ! The best time to travel to Key West is in the winter when there are still tropical temperatures. For all actual events it's a good idea to refer to the free gay magazines „Celebrate!", „Gay West" or „Southern Exposure Guide", which are nearly always available from every guest house reception.

✱ Key West ist der südlichste Punkt der Vereinigten Staaten. Die letzte Insel der Florida Keys besucht man am besten, indem man sich auf dem Festland einen Wagen mietet oder am Miami International Airport den Bus-Shuttle nimmt. Über die US 1 gelangt man -ohne es zu verpassen- innerhalb von drei Stunden nach Key West. Somit erhält man gleich die besten Eindrücke dieses Eilands. Diejenigen, die es kaum erwarten können, nach Key West zu gelangen, sollten direkt von Miami ein Flugzeug nehmen. In Key West erwartet einen das aufgeschlossenste Völckchen, das man sich vorstellen kann. Homosexuelle werden so offenherzig in die Gemeinde aufgenommen, daß sie im Alltag kaum auffallen. *Duval Street*, die liebevoll »die längste Straße der Welt« genannt wird, da sie den Atlantik mit dem Golf von Mexico verbindet, stellt die Einkaufsmeile Key Wests dar. Man hüte sich aber vor den Geschäften, die zwar mit der Regenbogen-Flagge getarnt sind, sich jedoch als reine Schwulen-Fallen herausstellen. Im Oktober findet jährlich die größte Attraktion Key Wests statt: das *Fantasy Fest.* Zu diesem Zeitpunkt scheint die kleine Insel aus allen Nähten zu platzen, pilgern doch aus aller Welt Schwule und Lesben hierhin. Da es neben Attraktionen, wie das *Ernest Hemingway Home*, kein wirklich touristisches Muß gibt, kann man in seinem *guest house* gnadenlos am Schwimmingpool entspannen. Abends beginnt das alles mit einem Cocktail (in guten Gästehäusern normalerweise im Preis inbegriffen). Das interessante findet früh morgens im Hot Tub statt ! Ideale Reisezeit für Key West ist der Winter, denn dann herrschen hier noch tropische Temperaturen. Aktuelle Veranstaltungen entnimmt man am besten den kostenlosen Schwulenmagazinen *Celebrate!, Gay West* oder *Southern Exposure Guide.* Diese sind an fast allen Rezeptionen erhältlich.

▲ Key West est le point situé le plus au sud des États-Unis. La meilleure façon de visiter cette île, la dernière des keys de Floride, est de louer une voiture ou de prendre une navette de l'aéroport. En environ trois heures, en passant par la US 1, vous arriverez à Key West avec en prime une vue imprenable d'ensemble. Les plus impatients d'entre vous peuvent cependant s'y rendre en avion depuis Miami. A Key West, vous trouverez la population la plus ouverte qui soit. Les homosexuels sont si bien intégrés à la communauté que l'on ne les remarque presque pas. La *Duval Street*, surnommée „la plus longue rue du monde", car elle relie l'Atlantique au Golf du Mexique, est la rue marchande de la ville. Mais méfiez-vous des magasins qui arborent les couleurs de l'arc-en-ciel! Ce sont des véritables attrape-nigauds. Chaque année, en octobre, a lieu à Key West le plus grand événement de l'année: la *Fantasy Fest.* Pendant cette péride, l'île est véritablement surpeuplée de gays et lesbiennes venus en pèlerinage des quatre coins du globe. A l'exception de cet événement, l'île n'offre pas beaucoup d'activités, hormis peut-être la visite de la maison d'*Ernest Hemingway.* Il vous restera donc à vous prélasser au bord de la piscine de votre *guest house.* Le début de soirée commence avec un cockail (normalement gracieusement offert par tout *guest house*de ce nom). Le moment le plus palpitant de la journée se situera aux premières heures du matin lorsque que vous vous plongerez dans votre jacuzzi. L'hiver est la saison idéale pour se rendre à Key West, car les températures y sont encore tropicales. Les journaux gratuits comme *Celebrate!, Gay West* ou le *Southern Exposure Guide*, disponibles dans toutes les réceptions, vous indiquerons où sortir.

☆ Key West está situado en el más extremo sur de los Estados Unidos. La mejor manera de visitar la última isla de los Florida Keys es alquilando un coche en tierra firme o cogiendo el autobus que parte del aeropuerto de Miami. Por la autopista US 1 se llega en tres horas a Key West. De esta manera se puede apreciar la belleza natural de esta isla. Si se tiene prisa, se debe coger el avión directamente en Miami. Los habitantes de Key West son abiertos y afables. Los homosexuales están tan integrados en la comunidad, que en la vida cotidiana pasan casi desapercibidos. La *Duval Street*, que se llama también cariñosamente la „calle más larga del mundo", ya que une el Atlantico con el Golfo de México, es la calle comercial de Key West. Un consejo: Cuidado con las tiendas que intentan atraer clientela con la bandera de arcoiris, ¡no son más que trampas para homosexuales! En Octubre se celebra anualmente la mayor atración de Key West: El „Fantasy Festival". En estas fechas la isla se llena de gays y lesbianas, que vienen de todas las partes del mundo para participar en estas festividades. Aparte del *Hemingway Home*, no hay muchos sitios de visitar y por ello uno puede dedicar sus vacaciones completamente al relax en los *guest houses.* El invierno es la fecha óptima para visitar Key West, ya que en esta temporada se pueden disfrutar aquí todavía temperatures tropicales. Para informarse sobre actividades y fiestas del momento recomendamos las revistas gay gratuitas *Celebrate!, Gay West* o *Southern Exposure Guide*, que se puedan obtener en casi todas las recepciones.

❖ Key West è il punto più al sud degli USA. L'ultima isola del Florida Keys è da visitare alla meglio con una macchina a noleggio che ci si può procurare sulla terraferma o con il servizio navetta dell'aeroporto di Miami (International Airport Bus Shuttle). Dalla US 1 si arriva senza sbagliarsi nel giro di tre ore a Key West. Così si raggolgono già le prime impressioni di quest'isola. Per coloro che non vedono l'ora di arrivare a Key West è consigliabile prendere un volo diretto da Miami. A Key West ci aspetta la popolazione più aperta che si possa immaginare. Gli omosessuali vengono accolti così apertamente nella società del posto che non danno più nell'occhio nella vita quotidiana. La *Duval Street* viene chiamata amorevolmente la strada più lunga del mondo, perché congiunge l'Atlantico con il Golfo del Messico e rappresenta anche la zona shopping di Key West. Si avverte però di fare attenzione ai quei negozi che mettono in mostra la bandiera dell'arcobaleno, ma che poi risultano una truffa per la clientela gay. Ogni anno in ottobre ha luogo l'avvenimento più importante per Key West: il *Fantasy Fest.* In questo periodo la piccola isola sembra scoppiare dalla moltitudine di „pellegrini" gay e lesbiche provenienti da tutto il mondo. Siccome oltre a certi punti d'attrazione come la *Ernest Hemmingway Home* non esistono mete propriamente turistiche è possibile oziare perennemente nel suo *guest house.* Il periodo ideale per un viaggio a Key West è l'inverno, perché si ha un clima tropico. Informazioni attuali sui singoli avvenimenti si trovano nei giornali gay *Celebrate!, Gay West* o *Southern Exposure Guide* che vengono distribuiti gratuitamente in quasi tutte le reception degli alberghi.

GAY INFO

Celebrate !

1315 Whitehead Street ✉FL 33041 ☎ 296-1566
Fax: 296-0458 E-Mail: editor@celebrate-kw.com
Weekly magazine.

Gay Guide to Key West

☎ 294-4603 E-Mail: keywestgay@aol.com
Colour guide and map to Key West.

KEY WEST

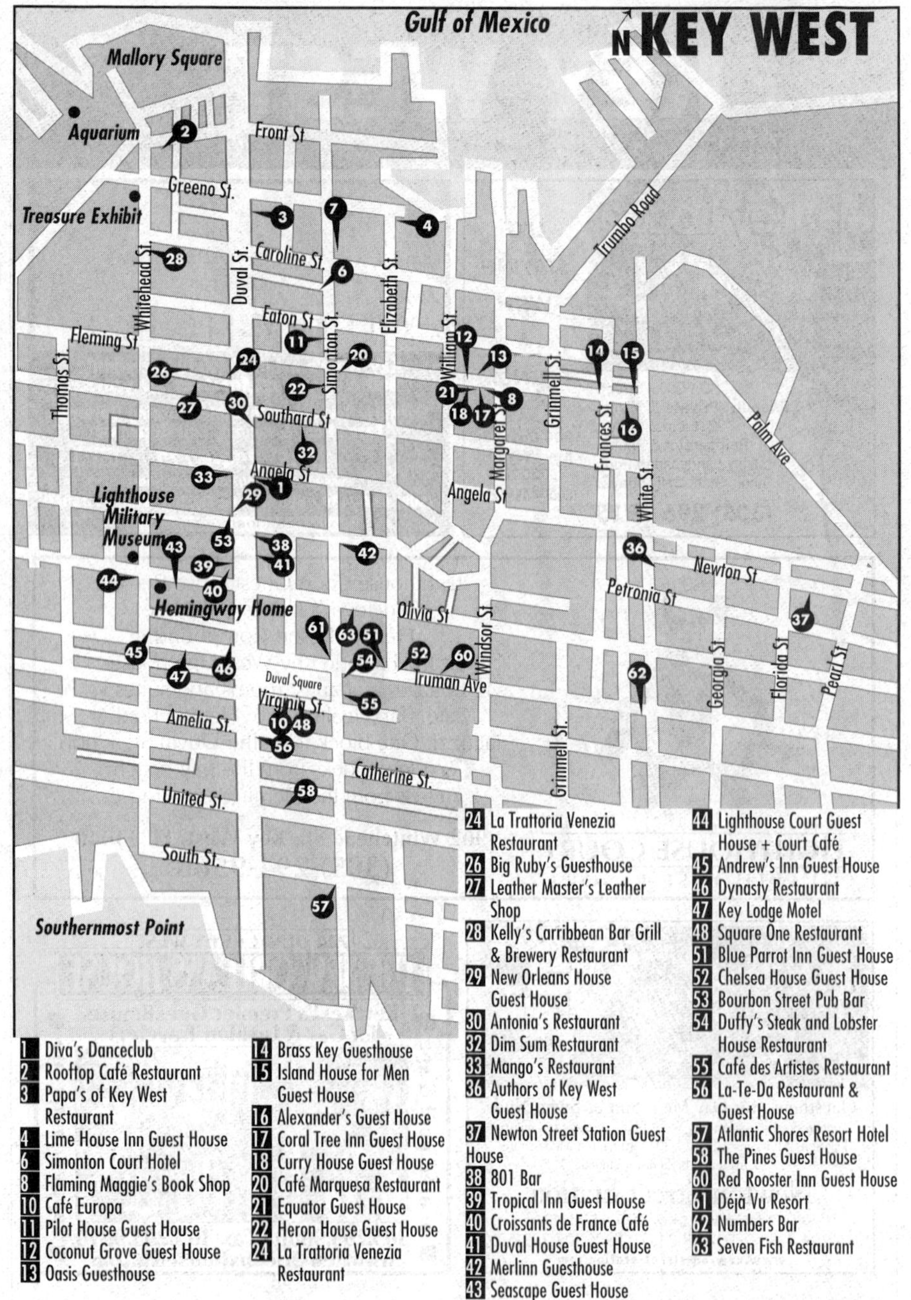

1 Diva's Danceclub
2 Rooftop Café Restaurant
3 Papa's of Key West Restaurant
4 Lime House Inn Guest House
6 Simonton Court Hotel
8 Flaming Maggie's Book Shop
10 Café Europa
11 Pilot House Guest House
12 Coconut Grove Guest House
13 Oasis Guesthouse
14 Brass Key Guesthouse
15 Island House for Men Guest House
16 Alexander's Guest House
17 Coral Tree Inn Guest House
18 Curry House Guest House
20 Café Marquesa Restaurant
21 Equator Guest House
22 Heron House Guest House
24 La Trattoria Venezia Restaurant
24 La Trattoria Venezia Restaurant
26 Big Ruby's Guesthouse
27 Leather Master's Leather Shop
28 Kelly's Carribbean Bar Grill & Brewery Restaurant
29 New Orleans House Guest House
30 Antonia's Restaurant
32 Dim Sum Restaurant
33 Mango's Restaurant
36 Authors of Key West Guest House
37 Newton Street Station Guest House
38 801 Bar
39 Tropical Inn Guest House
40 Croissants de France Café
41 Duval House Guest House
42 Merlinn Guesthouse
43 Seascape Guest House
44 Lighthouse Court Guest House + Court Café
45 Andrew's Inn Guest House
46 Dynasty Restaurant
47 Key Lodge Motel
48 Square One Restaurant
51 Blue Parrot Inn Guest House
52 Chelsea House Guest House
53 Bourbon Street Pub Bar
54 Duffy's Steak and Lobster House Restaurant
55 Café des Artistes Restaurant
56 La-Te-Da Restaurant & Guest House
57 Atlantic Shores Resort Hotel
58 The Pines Guest House
60 Red Rooster Inn Guest House
61 Déjà Vu Resort
62 Numbers Bar
63 Seven Fish Restaurant

Gay West
PO Box 1471 FL 33041 ☎ 292-1183 Fax: 292-9357
E-Mail: gaywest@conch.net
Gay West is published twice a month.

Southern Exposure Guide
819 Peacock Plaza, Suite 575 FL 33041 ☎ 294-6303 Fax: 295-9597 E-Mail: exposure@bridge.net
Homepage: www.bridge.net/~exposure
Monthly guide to Key West area. Complete map of Old Town, calendar of events and local information.

TOURIST INFO

Florida Keys/Key West Tourist Board
3406 N Roosevelt FL 33040 ☎ 296-1552 Fax: 296-0788

BARS

Bourbon Street Pub (B GLM MA) 12-4 h
730 Duval Street FL 33040 ☎ 296-1992

Numbers (B D G N S) 16 4 h
1029 Truman FL 33040 ☎ 296-0333

801 Bar (B GLM N OS) 11-4 h
801 Duval Street FL 33040 ☎ 294-4737
Hosts Dan's bar every day after 21 h.

CAFES

Café Europa (B bf F GLM OS W) 8-22 h
1075 Duval Street C-13 (Duval Square) FL 33040 ☎ 294-3443
Bistro Café. Authentic European Pastries & Breads baked daily fresh on the premises.

Court Cafe at Lighthouse Court (b bf CC F glm) 9-16 h
902 Whitehead Street FL 33040 ☎ 294-9588

Croissants de France (b CC F glm) ?-23 h, closed Wed
816 Duval Street FL 33040 ☎ 294-2624

DANCECLUBS

Diva's (B D glm STV) Mon-Sun 22-? h
711 Duval Street ☎ 292-8500

La Te De at La Terraza (B CC D GLM MA pi) Sun 16.30-20.30 h
1125 Duavl St. FL 33040 ☎ 296-6706
Very popular.

RESTAURANTS

Al Fresco's (B F glm OS)
419 Appelrouth Lane FL 33040 ☎ 296-3770
Italian with a twist. Casual outdoor dining (indoor also available).

Alice's on Duval (B CC F glm OS)
1114 Duval Street FL 33040 ☎ 292-4888
Tropical atmosphere with open air (but indoor) dining.

Antonia's (AC B CC F glm W) 18-23 h
615 Duval Street FL 33040 ☎ 294-6565
Regional Italian cuisine.

Blue Heaven (B CC F glm)
729 Thomas Street FL 33040 ☎ 296-8666
Specializing in island dishes.

Cafe Blue (B CC F glm)
1202 Simonton Street FL 33040 ☎ 296-7500
Mediterranean cuisine.

Café des Artistes (B CC F glm) 18-23 h
1007 Simonton Street FL 33040 ☎ 294-7100

Café Europa (B bf F GLM OS W) 8-22 h
1075 Duval Street C-13 (Duval Square) ✉FL 33040 ☎ 296-0266
European Bistro/Restaurant. European & Island Cuisine. German Beer & Wine.

Camille's (bf CC F G MA)
703 ½ Duval Street, ✉FL 33040 ☎ 296-4811
Sunday brunch.

Caribe Soul (CC F glm) 11-15 h & 18-21 h
320 Petronia Street ✉FL 33040 ☎ 296-0094
Gay owned and operated. Homestyle American and Caribbean Food.

Dim Sum (b CC F glm) 18-23 h, closed Tue
613 ½ Duval Street ✉FL 33040 ☎ 294-6230
Asian cuisine.

Duffy's Steak and Lobster House (B CC F glm) 11-23 h
1007 Simonton Street ✉FL 33040 ☎ 296-4900
American cuisine.

Dynasty Restaurant (b CC F glm) 17.30-22.30 h
918 Duval Street ✉FL 33040 ☎ 294-2943

El Siboney (B CC F glm) 900 Catherine Street ✉FL 33040
Best Cuban food in Key West.

Kelly's Carribbean Bar Grill & Brewery (B CC F glm)
301 Whitehead Street ✉FL 33040 ☎ 293-8484
American and Carribean cuisine. The establishment is owned by actress Kelly McGillis.

Mango's (B CC F glm) 7-24 h
700 Duval Street ✉FL 33040 ☎ 292-4606
International cuisine.

Marquesa. Cafe (B CC F glm) 18-24 h
600 Fleming Street ✉FL 33040 ☎ 292-1244

Michael's (B CC F glm)
532 Margaret Street ✉FL 33040 ☎ 295-1300
Chicago Style Steak House, very expensive.

Papa's of Key West (b CC F glm) 11-24 h
217 Duval Street ✉FL 33040 ☎ 293-7880
American and Italian cuisine.

Pepe's (B CC F glm) 6.30-23 h
806 Caroline Street ✉FL 33040 ☎ 294-7192

Rooftop Café (B CC F glm) 9-1 h
310 Front Street ✉FL 33040 ☎ 294-2042

Seven Fish (B CC F glm)
632 Olivia Street ✉FL 33040 ☎ 296-2777
A favorite with the gay community.

Square One (B CC F glm)
1075 Duval Street ✉FL 33040 *(Duval Square)* ☎ 296-4300
American cuisine.

Trattoria Venezia. La (B CC F glm) 18.30-23 h
524 Duval Street ✉FL 33040 *(Old Town)* ☎ 296-1075
Italian cuisine; seafood.

Yo Sake (b CC F glm) 18-23.30 h
722 Duval Street ✉FL 33040 ☎ 294-2288
Japanese cuisine.

FITNESSTUDIOS

Club Island for Men (B G NU pi VS sa sb wh WO)
1129 Fleming Street *(entrance on White Street)* ☎ 294 6204

BOOK SHOPS

Flaming Maggie's Books, Art & Coffee (GLM)
Mon-Sun 10-18 h
830 Fleming Street (at Margaret) ✉FL 33040 ☎ 294-3931

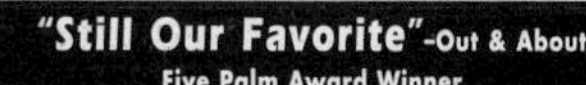

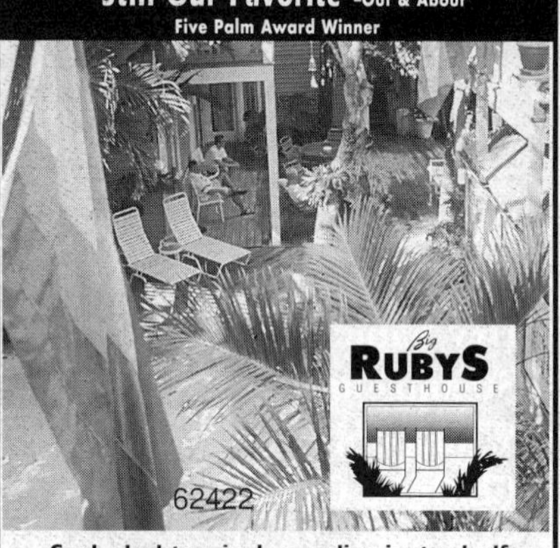

LEATHER & FETISH SHOPS

Leather Masters (CC LJ) 12-0, Sun 12-18 h
418-A Appelrouth Lane ✉FL 33040 ☎ 292-5051

PR & PHOTOGRAPHY SERVICES

Key West Business Guild
PO Box 1208 ✉FL 33041 ☎ 294-4603
☎ (800) 535-7797 (Toll-free)
Local information, maps etc.

TRAVEL & TRANSPORT

Hanns Ebensten Travel, Inc. (G) Mon-Fri 9-17 h, closed Sat Sun
513 Fleming Street, ✉FL 33040 ☎ 294-8174 Fax: 292-9665
Operator of Tours, cruises and expeditions for men.

HOTELS

Atlantic Shores Resort (AC B bf CC d F GLM H lj MA NU OS pi s)
510 South Street ✉FL 33040-3118 ☎ 296-2491
☎ (888) 414-4102 (toll free) Fax: (305) 294-2753
E-Mail: atlshores@aol.com
Homepage: www.atlanticshoresresort.com
Rates US$ 110-150 (high-season), US$ 80-100 (off-season).

Blue Parrot Inn (AC bf CC g H nu OS pi)
916 Elizabeth Street ✉FL 33040 ☎ 296-0033
☎ (800) 231-BIRD (Toll-free)
Ten minutes to the airport. Two blocks from gay scene. All rooms

Chelsea House (AC bf CC glm H pi)
707 Truman Street ✉FL 33040 ☎ 296-2211
☎ (800)-845-8859 (toll free) Fax: 296-4822
Rooms with priv. bath. Rates US$ 75-159.

Douglas House (AC bf CC g H MA OS pi wh) 8-23 h
419 Amelia Street ✉FL 33040 ☎ 294-5269
☎ (800)833-0372 (toll free) Fax: 292-7665
Rates US$ 88-205, incl. bf.

Eaton Lodge Historic Inn and Gardens (bf g H OS pi wh) Office: 8-21 h
511 Eaton Street ✉FL 33040 ☎ 292-2170
☎ 800 294-2170 (toll free)
Pool, lush landscaping, bf incl. Full bar during hospitality hour.

Habitation. L' (AC bf CC GLM H OS)
408 Eaton Street ✉FL 33040 ☎ 293-9203 Fax: 296-1313
Double rooms US$ 52-109, studio 72-109, incl. breakfast.

Heron House (AC bf CC g H MA OS pi) 24 hours
512 Simonton Street, ✉FL 33040 ☎ 294-9227
☎ 1-800-294-1644 (Toll Free) Fax: 294-5692
Downtown location. All rooms with priv. bath/WC, balcony. Rates US$ 85-220.

Key Lodge Motel (AC CC glm H OS pi) 8-22 h
1004 Duval Street ✉FL 33040 ☎ 296-9915
☎ (800) 458-1296 (toll free)
Rooms with phone, private bath/WC, some with kitchenette. Rates US$ 70-163.

La-Te-Da (AC B bf CC d F GLM H lj MA msg N OS pi S STV wh)
1125 Duval Street ✉FL 33040 ☎ 296-6706 ☎ 296-0438
E-Mail: latedakw@aol.com
Hosts the popular Tea Dance. Good restaurant and barbecue outdoors.

ATLANTIC
SHORES
RESORT • KEY WEST

Lighthouse Court (AC B CC F G H pi wh WO)
902 Whitehead Street ✉FL 33040 ☎ 294-9588 Fax: 294-6861
All rooms with fridge and priv. bath, some have kitchenette and balcony. Health club, video bar and café on the premises. Rates US$60-235.
Rose Lane Vacation Rentals (CC glm H pi)
524 Rose Lane ✉FL 33040 ☎ 292-6637
☎ (800)654-2781 (toll free) Fax: 294-6500
Rates US$ 96-107.
Sea Isle Resort (AC bf CC G H NU pi wh WO)
915 Windsor Lane ✉FL 33040 ☎ 294-5188
☎ (800) 995-4786 (toll free) Fax: 296-7143
Homepage: www.seaisleresort.com
All rooms with fridge, private bath, cable TV and telephone. Rates US$ 75-250 incl. bf.
Seascape (AC bf CC g H OS pi wh)
420 Olivia Street ✉FL 33040 *(located in old town)* ☎ 296-7776
☎ (800) 765-6438 (Toll-free) Fax: 296-7776
E-Mail: seascapokw@aol.com
All rooms with private bath, queen size beds and color TV.
Simonton Court (AC B bf CC glm H OS pi wh) 8.30-18 h
320 Simonton Street ✉FL 33040 ☎ 294-6386
☎ (800) 944-2687 (toll free) Fax: 293-8446
Downtown location. All rooms with kitchentte, priv. bath, TV. Rates US$ 100-350.
Tropical Inn (CC glm H)
812 Duval Street ✉FL 33040 ☎ 294-9977
Rooms with priv. bath, sundecks, some with TV, kitchenette, spa. Rates US$ 70-140.

GUEST HOUSES

Alexander Palms Court (AC CC glm OS pi wh)
715 South Street ✉FL 33040 ☎ 296-6413
☎ (800) 858-1943 (toll free) Fax: 292-3975
Alexander's Guest House (AC bf CC GLM OS pi wh)
1118 Fleming Street ✉FL 33040 ☎ 294-9919 Fax: 295-0357 E-Mail: alexcghouse@aol.com Homepage: www.alexghouse.com
Centrally located. All rooms with private bath/WC, fridge, some with balcony. Rates US$ 79-180.
Andrew's Inn (AC B bf CC g H MA OS pi) 8-22 h
Zero Whalton Lane ✉FL 33040 *(900 Block of Duval Street)*
☎ 294-7730 Fax: 294-0021
Oldtown location. All gay bars within three blocks. All rooms with private baths, private entrances. Rates US$ 98-158, incl. bf.
Authors of Key West (A AC bf CC glm H lj MA OS pi) Office: 9-19 h
725 White Street ✉FL 33040 *(central)* ☎ 294-7381
☎ (800) 898-6909 (Toll-free) Fax: 294-0920
E-Mail: lionxsx@aol.com Homepage: www.authors-keywest.com
Convenient location, 10 min to gay bars. All rooms with cable, priv. bath/WC, kitchenette. Summer rates US$ 109-165, winter rates 135-245. Home of the Alexander Project, international male-oriented art organisation (www.alexanderproject.com).
Big Ruby's Guesthouse (AC bf CC GLM H MA OS pi wh)
409 Applerouth Lane ✉FL 33040 *(1/2 block off Duval Street)*
☎ 296-2323 ☎ (800) 477-7829 (toll free)
E-Mail: keywest@bigrubys.com Homepage: www.bigrubys.com
Full breakfast included, complimentary wine + beer, heated swimming pool, gay/lesbian clientele. All rooms with shower/WC, washbasin, air-conditioning, TV.
Brass Key Guesthouse. The (AC bf CC GLM H OS pi W wh)
412 Frances Street ✉FL 33040-6950 ☎ 296-4719
☎ (800) 932-9119 (toll free) Fax: 296-1994
Homepage: www.brasskey.com
All rooms with fridge, private bath/WC, balcony. Rates US$ 150-280 (high-season) and US$ 70-160 (off-season), bf. incl.
Coconut Grove Guest House (AC bf CC G OS pi wh WO) 817
Fleming Street ✉FL 33040 ☎ 296-5107 ☎ (800) 262-6055
Fax: 296-1584 E-Mail: cocgro@ibm.net
Homepage: www.coconutgrovekeywest.com
All rooms with kitchenette, priv. bath/WC, and balcony. Rates US$ 55-220.
Coral Tree Inn (B CC G H MA nu OS pi wh) Office: 8-22 h
822 Fleming Street ✉FL 33040 ☎ 296-2131
☎ (800) 362-7477 (toll free) Fax: 296-9171
E-Mail: oasisct@aol.com Homepage: www.coraltree.com
Rooms with priv. bath, AC, coffee makers, fridge, TV, VCR, and phone. Rates US$ 105-185 (high-season), US$ 80-125 (off-season). Out & About Editor's Award.
Curry House (AC bf CC E G H MA nu OS pi wh) 8-20 h
806 Fleming Street ✉FL 33040 ☎ 294-6777
☎ (800) 633-7439 (toll free)
Homepage: www.gaytraveling.com/curryhouse
All rooms with fridge, balcony, bath/WC. Rates US$ 75-150.
Cypress House (AC bf CC g H pi) 8-20 h
601 Caroline Street ✉FL 33040 ☎ 294-6969
☎ (800) 525-2488 (toll free) Fax: 296-1174
E-Mail: CypressKW@aol.com
Downtown location. Two block from gay bars. Some rooms with kitchenette, priv. bath/WC. Rates US$ 65-190
Déjà Vu Resort (bf G H NU pi wh)
611 Truman Ave. ✉FL 33040 ☎ 292-9339
Duval House (AC bf CC glm H pi) 8.30-22.30 h
815 Duval Street ✉FL 33040 ☎ 292-9491
Rates US$ 75-250 (high-season), US$ 75-150 (off-season).
Equator Resort (! AC CC bf G H MA NU OS pi wh) 818 Fleming Street ✉FL 33040 ☎ 294-7775 ☎ (800) 278-4552 (toll free) Homepage: www.equatorresort.com
Very welcoming staff in a very attractive setting. Breakfasts are a treat. Watch out for the action in the hot tub in the early hours of the morning !
Island House for Men (AC B bf CC G NU pi sa wh WO)
1129 Fleming Street ✉FL 33040 ☎ 294-6284
☎ (800) 890-6284 (toll free) Fax: 292-0051
Homepage: www.islandhousekeywest.com
Under new management. Located in Old Town. All rooms with AC, some with kitchenette, priv. bath/WC, fridge.
Knowles House (AC bf CC glm H pi)
1004 Eaton Street ✉FL 33040-6925 ☎ 296-8132
☎ (800) 352-4414 (toll free) Fax: 296-2093
E-Mail: knowleshse@aol.com.
Homepage: www.members.aol.com/knowleshse
8 double rooms with bath or shower, SAT-TV, radio, own-key. Rates US$ 70-125 (off season), 109-165 (on season). Bf incl.
Lime House Inn (bf CC G H MA NU pi wh) 9-18 h
219 Elizabeth Street ✉FL 33040 ☎ 296-2978
☎ (800) 374-4242 (toll free) Fax: 294-5858
All rooms with kitchenette, priv. bath/WC, and balcony. Rates US$ 40-130.
Mangrove House (bf CC G H NU OS pi wh)
623 Southard Street ✉FL 33040 ☎ 294-1866
☎ (800) 294-1866 (toll free) Fax: 294-8757
E-Mail: mangrove@conch.net.
Homepage: www.conch.net/~mangrove

Marrero's Guest Mansion (AC bf CC GLM H OS pi wh) Office: 8-21 h
410 Fleming Street ✉FL 33040 ☎ 294-6977
Fax: 292-9030 E-Mail: Marrero's@aol.com
Homepage: www.gaytraveling.com/marrero's
Bicycle hire possible. Rates US$ 115-190 (high-season), US$ 85-160 (off-season), incl. Continental breakfast.
Merlinn Guesthouse (AC bf CC F glm H pi s)
811 Simonton Street ✉FL 33040 ☎ 296-3336 Fax: 296-3524
Centrally located. All rooms with priv. bath. Rates US$ 65-150.
Nassau House B&B (AC b bf CC glm H pi W) 9-21 h
1016 Fleming Street ✉FL 33040 ☎ 296-8513
☎ (800) 296-8513 (toll free) Fax: 293-8423
E-Mail: nassau@conch.net. Homepage: www.nassauhouse.com
New Orleans House (AC B bf CC G H NU pi wh)
724 Duval Street ✉FL 33040 ☎ 293-9800 Fax: 293-9870
E-Mail: NOHouseKW@aol.com
Homepage: www.NewOrleansHouseKW.com
Rates for double rooms US$ 70-150, cottages 125-275.
Newton Street Station (AC bf CC G H NU OS pi WO)
1414 Newton Street ✉FL 33040 ☎ 294-4288
☎ (800) 248-2457 (toll free) Fax: 292-5062
E-Mail: JohnNss@aol.com
Homepage: www.newton-street-station.com
Quiet location, private and shared baths, free bycicles. All rooms have AC, TV and refrigerator. Rates double USD 60-100 and studios 80/150 incl. continental bf.
Oasis Guest House (AC B bf CC G H NU pi wh) Reservation 8-22 h.
823 Fleming Street ✉FL 33040 ☎ 296-2131
☎ (800) 362-7477 (toll free) Fax: 296-9171
E-Mail: oasisct@aol.com Homepage: www.oasiskeywest.com
All rooms with fridge, priv. bath, balcony, TV. Rates US$ 105-185 (high-season), US$ 80-125 (off-season). Out & About Editor's Award.
Pilot House (AC CC glm H pi wh)
414 Simonton Street ✉FL 33040 ☎ 293-6600
Toll free ☎ 800-648-3780. Fax: 294-9298.
E-Mail: KeyWestLodging@sprynet
Homepage: http://www.KeyWestLodging.com
Rates high season US$ 175-300, summer 100-200.
Pines Guesthouse. The (AC CC G H OS pi wh) 521 United Street ✉FL 33040 ☎ 296-7467 ☎ (800) 282-7463 (toll free) Fax: 296-3928
Centrally located. Rooms with phone, priv. bath. Rates US$ 65-130.
Red Rooster Inn (bf G H nu OS pi)
709 Truman Avenue ✉FL 33040 ☎ 296-6558 Fax: 296-4822
E-Mail: chelseahse@aol.com
Homepage: www.chelseahse@aol.com
Rates winter US$ 105-160, mid-season 79-119, summer 59-89.
Terraza. La (B bf CC F glm MA NU OS pi)
1125 Duval Street ✉FL 33040 ☎ 296-6706
☎ (800) 528-3320 (Toll-free) Fax: 296-0438

APARTMENTS

Southern Most Hospitality (AC glm H msg NU pi wh) 524 Eaton Street, Suite 150 ✉FL 33040 ☎ 294-3800
☎ (888) 294-3800 (Toll-free) Fax: 294-9298
E-Mail: KeyWestLodging@Sprynet
Homepage: www.KeyWestLodging.com
Rates for 2-3 room suites 225-500, cottages 150-225, apartments 100-175.

HEALTH GROUPS

AIDS Help, Inc.
Truman Annex, PO Box 4374 ✉FL 33040 ☎ 296-6196
☎ (800) 640-3867 (Toll-free)
Counselling, information and support for Monroe County's HIV+ population.
Helpline, Inc. 24 hours
PO Box 2186 ✉FL 33045 ☎ 296-HELP ☎ 294-LINE
Immuncare
520 Southard Street ✉FL 33040 ☎ 296-8593
Medical, nutritional, pharmaceutical, financial and social services to treat HIV.
Old Town Medical Center Mon-Fri 9-11.30 h
520 Southard Street ✉FL 33040 ☎ 296-8593 ☎ 296-4990
Fax: 296-4868
General medical care, office and hospital.

RELIGIOUS GROUPS

Metropolitan Community Church Key West
Wed 19, Sun 9.30, 11, Sun feellowship 10.30 h
1215 Petronia Street ✉FL 33040 ☎ 294-8912

CRUISING

-Duval Street
-Fleming Street
-Mallory Square (at sunset)
-Monroe Country Beach (Reynolds Street, Pier)

Lake Worth ☎ 407

BARS

Palm Beaches Inn Exile (B G MA S VS YG) Mon-Sat 15-2, Sun-24 h
6 South J Street ✉FL 33460 *(West Palm Area)* ☎ 582-4144
Video nightclub.

VIDEO SHOPS

Harold Video (g VS)
4266 Lake Worth Road ☎ 964-2470

Lakeland ☎ 813

BARS

Dockside (B D F GLM S W) 16-2 h
3770 Highway 92 ✉FL 33804 ☎ 665-6021
Roy's Green Parrot (b D G S) Mon-Sat 16-2, Sun-24 h
1030 East Main Street ✉FL 33801 ☎ 683-6021

Madeira Beach ☎ 813

BARS

CockTail Club (B G MA) 14601
Gulf Boulevard ✉FL 33108 ☎ 391-2680
Entrance in the rear of the building. Beach access.

Melbourne ☎ 407

BARS

Saturdays Lounge (B D GLM OS S) Tue-Sun 14-2 h
4060 West New Haven Avenue ✉FL 32904 ☎ 724-1510

SWIMMING

-Beach at the end of the Eau Gallie Causeway
-Canova Beach (AYOR) (nights)
-Melbourne Harbor Marina (AYOR)

Miami ☎ 305

GAY INFO

Contax Guide Tue-Fri 10-16 h
901 North East 79th Street ✉FL 33138 ☎ 757-6333
Fax: 756-6488

Switchboard of Miami Inc. 0-24 h
444 Brickell Avenue, Suite 450 ✉FL 33131 ☎ 358-1640
☎ 358-4357 (helpline) Fax: 377-2269
Homepage: www.switchboardmiami.org
Crisis counseling, referrals and information.

Weekly News. The Tue-Fri 10-17 h
901 North East 79th Street ✉FL 33138 ☎ 757-6333
Fax: 756-6488 E-Mail: info@twnmag.com
Florida's weekly gay newspaper featuring places of interest throughout the state, as well as reports and reviews. Free at gay venues.

TOURIST INFO

Greater Miami Convention & Visitor Bureau
701 Brickell Avenue, Suite 2700 ✉FL 33131 ☎ 539-3000
Fax: 539-3113

BARS

Cactus Bar + Grill (AC B CC F G S SNU OS VS YG) Mon-Sat 15-3 h, Sun 12-3 h
2041 Biscayne Boulevard, Dade County ✉FL 33137 ☎ 438-0662

Cactus Saloon (B F G VS)
2041 Biscayne Boulevard ✉FL 33137 ☎ 573-6025

Eagle Miami (B G P) 20-3 h
1252 Coral Way ☎ 860-0056
Cruise Bar.

El Carol (B g MA N) 11-3 h
930 South West Le Jeune Road/42nd Avenue ✉FL 33134
☎ 448-9148

Southpaw Saloon (B G lj)
7005 Biscayne Boulevard/70th Street North East ✉FL 33138
☎ 758-9362

Splash (AC B D GLM OS VS) 16-2 h, closed Mon
5922 South Dixie Highway ✉FL 33143 ☎ 662-8779

Stables (B G LJ) 9-3 h
1641 South West 32nd Avenue ✉FL 33145 *(Coral Gables)*
☎ 446-9137

Waterfront. On the (B D GLM S)
3615 N W South River Drive ✉FL 33142 *(near airport)* ☎ 635-5500
The best Latin gay bar in town.

DANCECLUBS

O'Zone (! B D G MA) 21-5 h
6626 S Red Road/S W 57th Avenue ✉FL 33143 ☎ 667-2888

RESTAURANTS

Balans (B bf F glm OS)
1022 Lincoln Road ✉FL 33139

Terrasse. La (b F g)
429 Espanola Way, Coral Gables ✉FL 33139 ☎ 538-2212

SEX SHOPS/BLUE MOVIES

Bird Road Book & Video (g VS) 0-24 h
6833 Bird Road ✉FL 33155 ☎ 661-9103

Biscayne Book & Video 0-24 h
11711 Biscayne Boulevard ✉FL 33181 ☎ 895-9009

Cutler Ridge 0-24 h
2316 South West 57th Avenue ✉FL 33155 ☎ 266-5877

Happy Adult Books (g VS) 0-24 h
9514 South Dixie Highway ✉FL 33156 ☎ 661-9349

J+R Book And Video 0-24 h
7455 South West 40th Street ✉FL 33155 ☎ 262-6570

Palace Videos 0-24 h
190 North East 167th Street ✉FL 33162 ☎ 949-8855

Pleasure Chest at Club Body Center (G LJ VS)
2991 Coral Way ✉FL 33129 ☎ 448-2214
Erotica, leather, etc.

Prime Time (DR G VS) 0-24 h
14750 North East 16th Avenue ✉FL 33161 ☎ 948-6745
Glory holes, very active.

Red Road Books & Videos (G VS) 0-24 h
2316 S Red Road ✉FL 33155 ☎ 266-5877

167 Street XXX (g VS) 0-24 h
14 North East 167th Street ✉FL 33162 ☎ 949-3828
Very active.

BOOK SHOPS

Lambda Passages (CC GLM) Sun 12-18, Mon-Sat 11-21 h
7545 Biscayne Boulevard ✉FL 33138 ☎ 754-6900
Gay and lesbian video rental club and bookstore.

HOTELS

Cactus Bed & Breakfast (AC B CC F H MA pi S SNU wh)
2041 Biscayne Boulevard, Dade County ✉FL 33137 ☎ 438-0662
Fax: 438-9576.

Miami River Inn (bf CC GLM H OS pi wh)
118 South West South River Drive ✉FL 33130 *(S.W. 2nd Street and S.W. 4th Avenue)* ☎ 325-0045 ☎ (800) HOTEL 89 (toll free) Fax: 325-9227 E-Mail: miami100@ix.netcom.com
Miami's only gay Bed & Breakfast. 40 rooms individually decorated. Historic buildings from 1906-1913. Centrally located across the Miami river. The only historic Inn in Miami.

GUEST HOUSES

Brigham Garden's Guesthouse (AC glm H)
1411 Collins Avenue ✉FL 33139 ☎ 531-1331
Fax: 538 9898. Email: brigham@interpoint.net
Homepage: http://www.brighamgardens-mbch.com
7 double rooms, 20 studios and 2 apartments with bath or shower, WC, cable TV, telephone, kitchenette. Rates double rooms US$ 60-85. Studios 75-110. Apartments 100-130. Additional bad US$ 5.

HELP WITH PROBLEMS

Gay Lesbian Bisexual Hotline of Greater Miami
7545 Biscayne Boulevard ☎ 759-3661

RELIGIOUS GROUPS

Dignity
☎ 443-9509
Catholic gays.

CRUISING

-Bayside Market (lots of Latin and Brasilian tourists)

Miami Beach ☎ 305

●Miami Beach (or *SoBe*, South Beach) is a very trendy place. It's interesting to take a look at the reasons for this: The most obvious reason is the *National Historic District*, consisting of 800 renovated Art-Deco-houses. A kitsch dream in pastel shades. Another reason is the clever way that the city government has used the media and dreamlike beach and palm scenery, to promote the city. The *Ocean Drive* is the boulevard next to the beach, where the beautiful

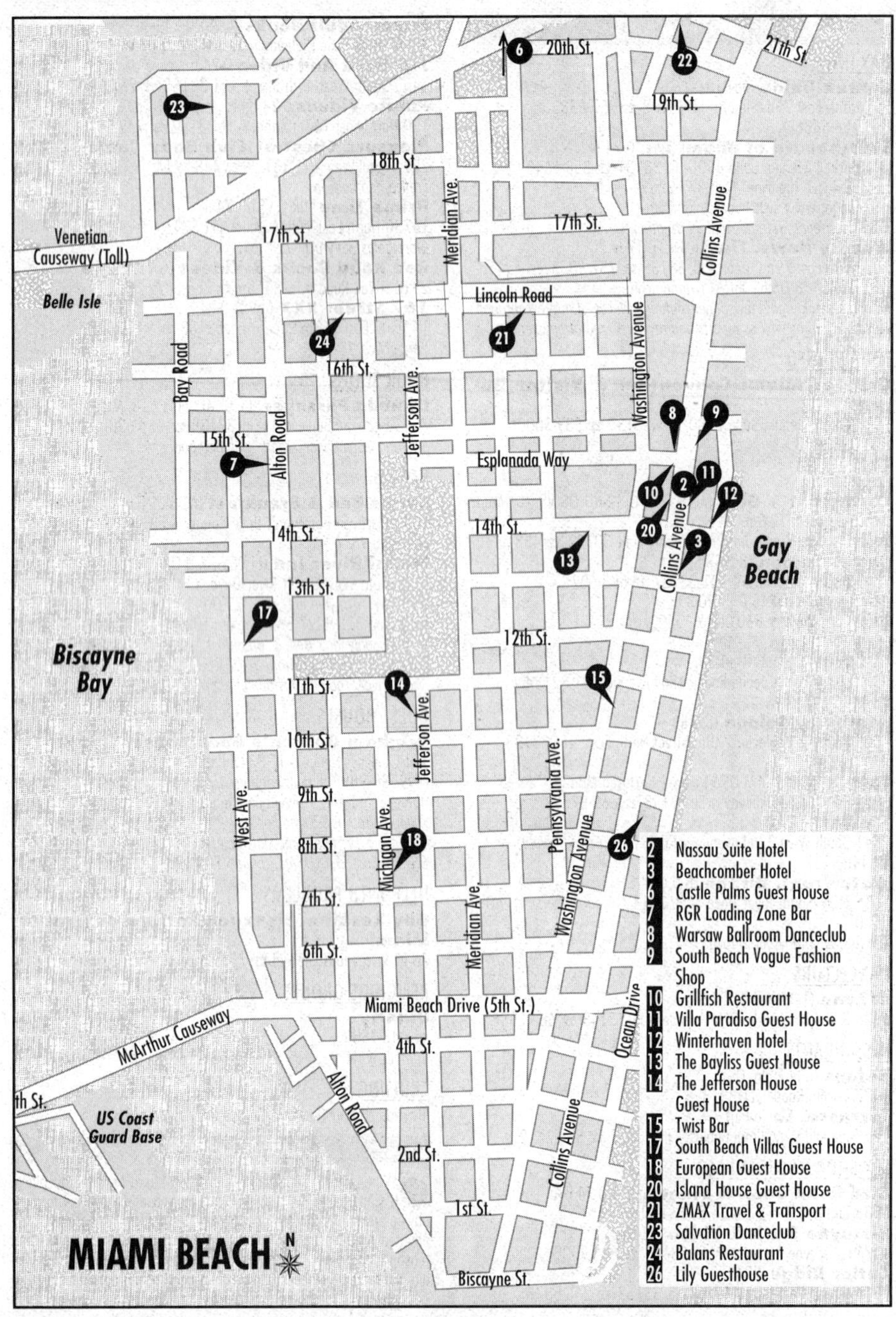
20th St.
21th St.
19th St.
18th St.
Meridian Ave.
17th St.
17th St.
Collins Avenue
Venetian
Causeway (Toll)
Belle Isle
Lincoln Road
Washington Avenue
16th St.
Bay Road
Jefferson Ave.
15th St.
Alton Road
Esplanada Way
14th St.
14th St.
Collins Avenue
Gay
Beach
13th St.
12th St.
Biscayne
Bay
11th St.
Jefferson Ave.
10th St.
Pennsylvania Ave.
9th St.
West Ave.
Michigan Ave.
Washington Avenue
8th St.
Meridian Ave.
7th St.
6th St.
Ocean Drive
Miami Beach Drive (5th St.)
McArthur Causeway
4th St.
Alton Road
US Coast
Guard Base
Collins Avenue
2nd St.
1st St.
MIAMI BEACH
N
Biscayne St.
2 Nassau Suite Hotel
3 Beachcomber Hotel
6 Castle Palms Guest House
7 RGR Loading Zone Bar
8 Warsaw Ballroom Danceclub
9 South Beach Vogue Fashion Shop
10 Grillfish Restaurant
11 Villa Paradiso Guest House
12 Winterhaven Hotel
13 The Bayliss Guest House
14 The Jefferson House Guest House
15 Twist Bar
17 South Beach Villas Guest House
18 European Guest House
20 Island House Guest House
21 ZMAX Travel & Transport
23 Salvation Danceclub
24 Balans Restaurant
26 Lily Guesthouse

and the wanna-be-beautiful saunter along. Parallel to it run Collins and Washington Avenue, which form one side of the gay right angle. The other side is the *Lincoln Road Mall*, a real pedestrian zone (!), in the US (!). Along one of these axes you'll find all gay establishements of the town in walkable distances. It is best to find accomodation in this area and save yourself renting a car. The best time to visit is between October and April, peak season around christmas right into January. Important event are the parties, which begin with *thanksgiving day* (last Thu in November). The climax of this party season is the Winter Party in February. Information about this, and more, can be obtained from the gay magazines *Circuit Noize, Hotspots, TWN* and *Wire*. One thing is exceptionable. SoBe is situated right next to a major city, Miami. And this city has many things to offer: Little Havanna (SW 8th Street/SW 11th Avenue), where the cuban immigrants have settled, Showtime in Seaquarium, or shopping and strolling around Bayside Marketplace, Coral Gables or Coconut Grove.

Miami Beach (oder modisch *SoBe* für South Beach) ist trendy. Es lohnt sich, den Gründen dafür nachzuspüren.
Der offensichtlichste Grund ist der *National Historic District*, 800 renovierte Art-Deco-Häuser. Ein Kitschtraum in Pastell. Ein weiterer Grund sind die Medien: die Stadtverwaltung hat -auch mit Hilfe der Strand-und-Palmen-Traumkulisse- in den letzten Jahren für verstärkte Medienpräsenz der Stadt gesorgt und sie damit noch bekannter gemacht. Und noch interessanter für die Medien.
Der *Ocean Drive* ist die Flaniermeile der Schönen und Schön-Sein-Wollenden direkt am Strand, parallel dazu verlaufen Collins und Washington Avenue und bilden damit die eine Seite des schwulen rechten Winkels. Die andere Seite bildet die *Lincoln Road Mall*, eine richtige Fußgängerzone(!), und das in Amerika. Entlang dieser beiden Achsen finden sich alle schwulen Etablissements des Ortes innerhalb überschaubarer Distanzen. In dieser Gegend sollte man auch übernachten, so daß man kein Auto benötigt.
Die beste Zeit liegt zwischen Oktober und April, die Hochsaison um Weihnachten bis in den Januar. Wichtige Events sind die Parties, mit denen es nach *Thanksgiving* (letzter Do im Nov) los geht. Höhepunkt ist die Winter Party im Februar. Alles darüber hinaus entnimmt man den schwulen Blättern *Circuit Noize, Hotspots, TWN* und *Wire*.
Eines ist allerdings ungewöhnlich: SoBe liegt in direkter Nachbarschaft zu einer Großstadt, Miami nämlich. Und diese Stadt hat einiges zu bieten: Little Havanna (SW 8th Street/SW 11th Avenue), in dem sich die kubanischen Einwanderer niedergelassen haben, Showtime im Seaquarium und Shoppen und Bummeln im Bayside Marketplace, Coral Gables oder Coconut Grove.

Miami Beach (ou „SoBe" pour South Beach, comme disent les initiés) est l'endroit „in" de Floride. Voyons donc pourquoi! C'est d'abord grâce à ses 800 maisons art-déco soigneusement rénovées qui forment ce qu'on appelle le „National Historic District". Un vrai rêve dans les couleurs pastel! Les médias y sont également pour beaucoup. La municipalité a joué la carte de la presse et du cinéma et les investisseurs n'ont eu aucun mal à s'installer dans ce décor de rêve, sous les palmiers de Floride. SoBe y a gagné sur tous les plans: toujours plus célèbre, elle attiré encore plus d'investisseurs et d'entreprises.
Ocean Drive, immédiatement au bord de la plage, est la promenade où l'on vient pour voir et être vu. Les dieux et les déesses du littoral s'y bousculent. Les simples mortels aussi. Les artères parallèles sont Collins et Washington Avenue. Elles délimitent le quartier gay avec, de l'autre côté, Lincoln Road Mall, une vraie zone piétonne, chose assez rare en Amérique. C'est le long de ces deux axes que l'on trouve tous les lieux gays de la ville. On peut tout faire à pied, donc pas besoin de voiture, si vous habitez dans le quartier.
Le meilleur moment pour visiter Miami Beach, c'est entre octobre et avril. La fête bat son plein entre mi-décembre et mi-janvier. Les fêtes commencent après „Thanksgiving", le dernier jeudi de novembre. On atteint le summun en février avec la „Winter Party". Pour de plus amples informations sur le calendrier des manifestations, consultez les magasines gays locaux „Circuit Noize", „Hotspots", „TWN" et „Wire".
Une des curiosités de SoBe, c'est sa proximité de Miami qui est, elle-même, n'est pas inintéressante: Little Havanna (SW 8th Street/SW 11th Avenue), son aquarium maritime (Seaquarium), ses boutiques et ses boulevards commerçants de Bayside Market, Coral Gables ou Coconut Grove.

Miami Beach (o como se suele decir hoy en día *SoBe* South Beach) está de moda. Una de las razónes es el *National Historic District* que cuenta con 800 edificaciones recientemente reformados en el estilo Art-Deco, un cursi sueño en color pastel. Otra razón son los medios de comunicación que con ayuda de la municipalidad y la belleza de las playas y palmeras se han encargado de dar a conocer más la ciudad. El *Ocean Drive*, la pasarella de la gente guapa y de aquellos que desean serlo, se encuentra directamente junto a la playa, paralela a ella se localizan también las avenidas Collins y Washington. Estas forman uno de los centros gay de la ciudad. La *Lincoln Road Mall* es una zona peatonal (¡Y esto en Estados Unidos!) que también se distingue por su afluencia gay. A lo largo de estas calles y avenidas se encuentran los establecimientos gay del lugar. Es aconsejable pernoctar en esta zona, asi no se necesitará un automovil. Los mejores meses de visita son Octubre y Abril, el tiempo de mayor apogeo es la navidad. Los eventos más importantes son las fiestas que inician después del *Thanksgiving* (día de gracias) (último jueves de Noviembre). El punto culminante es la fiesta de invierno, que se celebra en Febrero. Las revistas *Circut Noize, Hotspots, TWN* y *Wire* informan sobre los acontecimientos importantes. SoBe se localiza directamente en la vecindad de una gran ciudad: Miami, y esta ciudad tiene muchas cosas que ofrecer: Little Havanna (SW 8th. Street/SW 11th Avenue) en la que los emigrantes cubanos se han asentado.Recomendamos la visita al Seaquarium, asi como ir de compras en Bayside Marketplace, Coral Gables o Coconut Grove.

Miami Beach (o *SoBe*, South Beach) è molto alla moda per diversi motivi. Uno è il *National Historic District*, composto da 800 case ristrutturate, in stile art decò: un sogno kitsch dai colori pastello. Un altro motivo è dato dai mass media: l'amministrazione comunale, aiutata dagli scenari favolosi della spiaggia e delle palme, ha incentivato la presenza della città nei film e nelle riprese televisive rendendo Miami ancora più famosa e sempre più interessante come scenario cinetelevisivo. Direttamente sulla spiaggia, l'Ocean Drive è il passeggio dei belli e di coloro che desiderano esserlo; parallelamente corrono la Collins e la Washington Avenue che insieme formano una parte della zona gay. L'altra parte è costituita dalla *Lincoln Road Mall*, una zona pedonale (molto rara in America). Lungo queste due vie, a piccola distanza, si trovano tutti i locali gay del luogo. Conviene alloggiare in questa zona per fare a meno dell'auto. Il periodo migliore per una visita è tra ottobre ed aprile mentre l'alta stagione va da Natale a gennaio. I *parties* sono eventi molto importanti: il primo è il *Thanksgiving* (l'ultimo giovedì di novembre) ed il culmine il *Winter Party* in febbraio. Otterrete maggiori informazioni nei giornali *Circuit Noize, Hotspots TWN* e *Wire*. SoBe si trova in prossimità di Miami che offre a sua volta molti svaghi: Little Havanna (SW 8th Street/SW 11th Av.) dove giungevano gli immigrati cubani, Showtime nel Seaquarium o una passeggiata in Bayside Marketplace, Coral Gables e Coconut grove.

GAY INFO

Miamigo
1234 Washington Avenue, Suite 200-202 ✉ FL 33139
☎ 532-5051 Fax: 532-5498
E-Mail: miamigomag@aol.com Homepage: www.miamigo.com
Good quality monthly magazine featuring reports and listing on the gay scene in Florida.

Wire
927 Lincoln Road ✉FL 33139 ☎ 538-3111 Fax: 538-9666

BARS

Boardwalk (B G r SNU VS) 15-5 h
17008 Collins Avenue/Sunny Isles Causeway ✉FL 33160 *(North Miami Beach)* ☎ 949-4119 *Stripper Bar.*
Friends (B G MA r S VS) 15-6 h
17032 Collins Avenue ☎ 949-4112
Lucky`s (B G)
1969 71st Street ✉FL 33141 ☎ 868-0901
RGR's Loading Zone (B G LJ) 18-5 h
1426 A Alton Road ✉FL 33139 ☎ 531-5623
Behind Dominos & Subway. Rear entrance in alley behind Starish of 14Ct. Check out the Leather Zone for the hottest Leather accessories.
Ted's Hideaway South (B F g N OG)
124 Second Street ✉FL 33139
Twist (! AC B CC D G lj MA N OS s SNU STV VS) 13-5 h
1057 Washington Avenue ✉FL 33139 ☎ 538-9498
Westend (B GLM) 12-5 h
942 Lincoln Road ✉FL 33139 ☎ 538-9378
Pool tables.
821 (B glm) 12-3 h, Thu Ladies night
821 Lincoln Road ✉FL 33139 ☎ 531-1158
Piano Bar

DANCECLUBS

Groove Jet (B D gLM) Fri & Sat 21-5 h
323 23nd Street ✉FL 33139 ☎ 532-2002
Liquid (B D G YG) Sun 22-6 h
1439 Washington Aveune ☎ 532-9154
Pump (B D G YG) Fri, Sat 4-?
841 Washington Avenue ☎ 538 PUMP
Salvation (B D GLM) Sat 22-5 h
1771 West Avenue ☎ 673-6508
Score (! B D G MA YG) Thu, Fri & Sat 22-? , Sun 20- ?
727 Lincoln Road ☎ 535-1111
T-Dance on Sun.
Uncle Charlie's (B D G)
5922 South Dixie Highway ✉FL 33143
Warsaw Ballroom. The (! B D GLM S SNU YG) Wed-Sun 22-? h
1450 Collins Avenue, South Miami Beach ✉FL 33139
☎ 531-4555
Gay Megadisco. Very popular on Wed. - Amateur strip show.

RESTAURANTS

Balans (AC B bf CC F GLM MA N OS W WE YG) Sun-Thu 8-24 h, Fri-Sat 8-1 h
1022 Lincoln Road ✉FL 33139 *(next to Colony Theatre and to new cinema complex)* ☎ 534-9191
Caffe Torino (B D F G S TV)
1437 Washington Avenue ✉FL 33139 ☎ 351-5722
Good reasonably-priced Italian cuisine.
Front Page Cafe (bf CC F GLM OS) 8-2 h
607 Lincoln Road ✉FL 33139 ☎ 538-3734
Grillfish Restaurant (F glm MA N) 18-? h
1444 Collins Avenue, ✉FL 33139 *(Corner Esponala Way/Collins Avenue)* ☎ 538 99 08
Seafood restaurant. Price range US$ 7.95-14.95. Specializing in fresh grilled fish and diliciously sauced seafood pasta dishes.
Norma's on the Beach (F glm)
646 Lincoln Road ✉FL 33139 ☎ 532-2809

Palace Bar & Grill (B F glm OS YG) 9-2 h
1200 Ocean Drive/12th ✉FL 33139 ☎ 531-9077
Popular on Sun after beach.

FITNESSTUDIOS

Club Body Tech (CC glm msg WO) 6-22, Sat 8-21, Sun 9-19 h
1253 Washington Avenue, ✉FL 33139 ☎ 674-8222
Gridiron (g WO)
1676 Alton Road ✉FL 33139
Gay friendly.
Idols Gym (g WO)
1000 Lincoln Road ✉FL 33139

FASHION SHOPS

Beach Safari (CC GLM W) 9-19 h
205 Eleventh Street ✉FL 33139 ☎ 673-4510
Swimwear, pridewear, sunglasses and beach items.
South Beach Vogue (CC GLM W) 9-19 h
1461 Collins Avenue ✉FL 33139 ☎ 673-8840
Swimwear, pridewear, beach items and more.

GIFT & PRIDE SHOPS

Catalog X Retail & Clothing Outlet (AC GLM)
1510 Alton Road, South Beach ✉FL 33139 ☎ 534-1029
Huge selection of clothing, swimwear, magazines, dance CD's, adult toys, lubes, pipes & papers, greeting cards, pride products, custom leather shop, and videos for rent or sale.

Gaydar (CC GLM W) 11-22 h
718 Lincoln Road ✉FL 33139 ☎ 673-1690
Gay and lesbian department store.

PROPERTY SERVICES

Bret Taylor-Real Estate
420 Lincoln Road, Suite 260 ✉FL 33139 ☎ 1-800-438-2783
Fax: 674-8980.

TRAVEL & TRANSPORT

ZMAX Travel and Tours, Inc. (G) 10-18 h
420 Lincoln Road, Suite 239, ✉FL 33139 ☎ 532-0111
Mail: PO Box 398179, Miami Beach, FL 33239.
Fax: 532-1222. Toll free numbers: USA:800-864 6429, Australia:800-124-012, France:05.90.17.53, Germany:0130/81 72 95, Italy:1678-73182, Spain:900-94-1162, Switzerland:155 0078, United Kingdom:0800-96-0827.

HOTELS

Abbey Hotel (AC bf CC E F g H OS sol NU)
300 21st Street ✉FL 33139 ☎ 531-0031 Fax: 672-1663
E-Mail: reservations@abbeyhotel.com
Homepage: www.abbey.com
Art Deco elegant designed hotel-restaurant. Rooms with all facilities. Parking place available. Prices from US$ 99-195.

Beachcomber (AC CC glm E H)
1340 Collins Avenue ✉FL 33139 ☎ 531-3755 Fax: 673-8609
E-Mail: southbcomber@worldnet.att.net
All rooms with Bath/shower/WC, wash basin, telephone, Cable TV, air conditioning. Rates from US$ 89-135.

Castle Palms (AC bf CC E f G MA msg NU pi sa OS wh WO)
2300 Prairie Avenue ✉FL 33140 *(10 minutes to Lincoln Road)*
☎ 672-2080 ☎ (888) 327-9118 (toll free) Fax: 672-0804
E-Mail: Info@castlepalms.com Homepage: www.castlepalms.com
Wholly renovated luxury resort with 8 King Suites. All suites with private bath, telephone, voice-mail, fax, computer connection, air-conditioning, TV, VCR, refrigerator, microwave, fan and alarm. Heated pool, tropical garden and patio, work-out room, parking place. Rates from US$ 135-235. Bf incl.

Decowalk Hotel (AC bf CC f g H) 9-18 h
928 Ocean Drive ✉FL 33139 ☎ 531-5511
Located next to the gay beach in the very most busy part of Miami Beach.

Kenmore Hotel (B f glm OS pi) 0-24 h
1050 Washington Avenue ✉FL 33139 *(South Beach)*
☎ 674-1930 Fax: 534-6591
Large outdoor pool, bar, cafe. Call for rates.

Nassau Suite Hotel (AC CC glm E H)
1414 Collins Avenue ✉FL 33139 ☎ 534-0043 Fax: 534-3133
Homepage: www.nassansuites.com
All rooms with bath/shower/WC, wash-basin, telephone, kitchenette, air-conditioning. Rates from US$ 99-170. Additional bed US$ 10.

Penguin & President Hotel (CC glm H)
1418 Ocean Drive ✉FL 33139 ☎ 534-9334 Fax: 674-7809
E-Mail: penguin_hotel@sprynet.com
Homepage: www.home.sprynet.com/sprynet/penguin_hotel
Rooms with bath or shower, WC, telephone, SAT-TV, safe, own key, room service. Rates single US$83-118 double 98-128. Additional bed 15. US$.

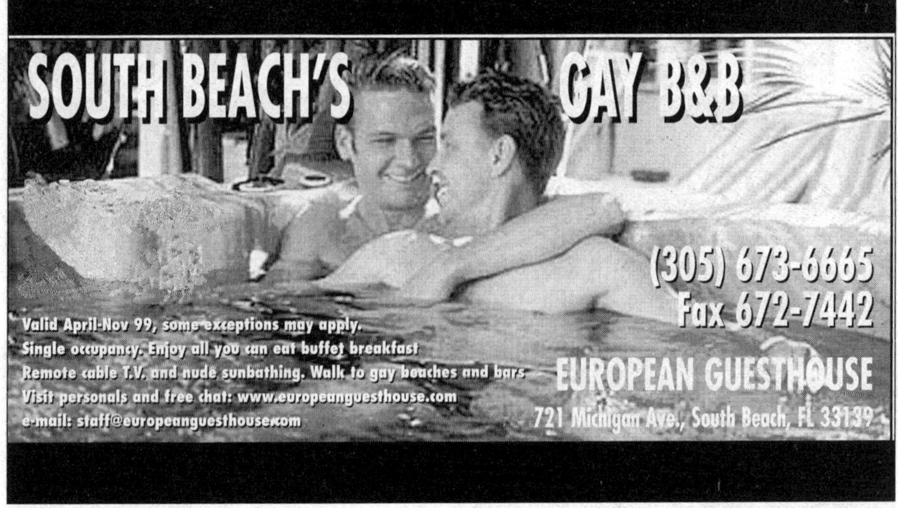
SOUTH BEACH'S GAY B&B
(305) 673-6665
Fax 672-7442
Valid April-Nov 99, some exceptions may apply.
Single occupancy. Enjoy all you can eat buffet breakfast
Remote cable T.V. and nude sunbathing. Walk to gay beaches and bars
Visit personals and free chat: www.europeanguesthouse.com
e-mail: staff@europeanguesthouse.com
EUROPEAN GUESTHOUSE
721 Michigan Ave., South Beach, FL 33139

Shelborne Beach Resort. The (B F glm H OS pi wh WO)
1801 Collins Avenue ✉FL 33139 ☎ 531-1271
☎ 800-327-8757 (toll free) Fax: 531-2206

Shore Club Resort (B F glm H pi)
1901 Collins Avenue, ✉FL 33139 ☎ 538-7811
☎ (800) 327-8330 (toll free)

Surfcomber. The (B bf glm H pi)
1717 Collins Avenue, ✉FL 33139 ☎ 532-7715
☎ 0130-815 526 (toll free from Germany) Fax: 532-2780

Winterhaven Hotel (AC B CC f glm MA N OS)
1400 Ocean Drive ✉FL 33139 *(South Beach)* ☎ 531-5571
☎ 800-395-2322 (toll free) Fax: 538-3337
Direktly opposite beach and close to gay night life. Art Deco style hotel. All rooms with TV, telephone and safes and most rooms offer an ocean view. Rates from US$ 50-100.

GUEST HOUSES

Bayliss Guest House (AC CC glm E H)
504 14th Street ✉FL 33139 ☎ 531-3755
All rooms with bath or shower/WC, wash-basin, telephone, Satellite TV.

Colours Destinations (Hotel reservations)
255 W. 24th Street, ✉FL 33140 ☎ 531-3601 Fax: 534-0362
E-Mail: newcolours@aol.com

European Guesthouse (AC bf CC Glm H MA NU OS p wh) 8-24 h
721 Michigan Avenue ✉FL 33139 *(in the center of the art deco district in South Beach)* ☎ 673-6665 Fax: 672-7442
E-Mail: staff@europeanguesthouse.com
Homepage: www.europeanguesthouse.com
Walking distance to the beach and gay bars. 12 double rooms, 1 studio, all rooms with bath or shower and WC, balcony or terrace, telephone, Satellite TV, radio, air-conditioning.

Island House (AC bf CC Glm H msg NU wh) 9-23 h
715 82nd Street ✉FL 33141 ☎ 864-2422 ☎ (800) 382-2422 (toll free) Fax: 865-2220 E-Mail: ihsobe@bellsouth.net.
Rates summer US$ 49-89, winter 69-129, bf. incl. All rooms have color cable TV, room phones, complimentary continental breakfast each morning, & complimentary weekend welcome cocktails.

Island House (AC bf CC G H) 9-23 h
1428 Collins Avenue ✉FL 33139 ☎ 864-2422
☎ (0800) 382-2422 (toll free) Fax: 865-2220
E-Mail: ihsobe@bellsouth.net
Homepage: www.islandhousesouthbeach.com
Largest guest house in South Beach. Rates US$ 69-129 (winter) and 49-99 (summer) inc. continental bf buffet.

Jefferson House. The (AC bf CC E GLM H MA OSA pi)
1018 Jefferson Avenue ✉FL 33139 *(South Beach)* ☎ 534-5247
Fax: 534-5953 E-Mail: sobejhouse@aol.com
Homepage: www.thejeffersonhouse.com
Located near Flamingo park. All rooms with private entrance bath, color TV and telephone. Rates single from US$ 109, double from 140. Heated pool.

Key Guesthouse (AC CC GLM H MA N OS) 0-24 h
835 Collins Avenue, ✉FL 33139 ☎ 535-9900 Fax: 535-0077
Rates on request.

Lily Guesthouse (bf glm H)
835 Collins Avenue ✉FL 33139 ☎ 535-9900 ☎ 800-535-9959 (toll free) Fax: 535-0077
In the heart of South beach, luxurious rooms with cable TV, answering machine, telephone and refrigators.

Normandy South (AC bf CC G H msg NU pi wh WO)
Oct-May
☎ 674-1197 Fax: 532-9771 E-Mail: normandyso@aol.com
All rooms with marble bath, AC, cable TV, fridge, VCR on request. Rates high season US$ 120-175, low season 80-120. bf. incl.

South Beach Villas (AC bf CC G H MA pi wh) Office: 9-24 h
1201 West Avenue #4 ✉FL 33139 *(Between Alton and West Avenue)* ☎ 673-9600 ☎ (888) 429-7623 (toll free)
Fax: 532-6200 E-Mail: gaysobe@aol.com
Homepage: www.southbeachvillas.com
Renovated 16-unit nArt Deco building with private courtyard, dazzling heated pool, jacuzzi and deluxe continental breakfasts. A lush and tropical oasis within walking distance of all the magic that makes South Beach the „American Riviera".

APARTMENTS

Villa Paradiso (AC CC glm H OS)
1415 Collins Avenue ✉FL 33139 ☎ 532-0616 Fax: 673-5874
E-Mail: villap@gate.net
Rates from US$ 69-145. All apartments with color TV, ceiling fan, phone, kitchenette, fridge, maid service, private bath.

SWIMMING

-12th Street beach (off Ocean Drive)
-Haulover Beach (Collins Ave. (A1A), north of Bal Harbour)

CRUISING

-Ocean Drive (particulary at 12th Street)
-Around the Flamingo Park (particulary at Meridian Avenue at 13th Street, the park closes from 24 to 5 h)
-Bathhouses at Ocean Drive (10th and 14th Street)

Naples ☎ 941

BARS

Galley. The (AC B bf F GLM MA) 16-?, Sat Sun 11-? h
300 5th Avenue South #121 ✉FL 33940 ☎ 262-2509

CAFES

Cafe Flamingo (B g) 8-2, WE-1 h
947 3rd Avenue North ✉FL 33940 ☎ 262-8181

GENERAL GROUPS

Gay People of Naples
☎ 353-3326

HEALTH GROUPS

AIDS-Hotline
☎ 263-CARE

Ocala ☎ 904

BARS

Connection (B GLM N S W) 15-2 h
3331 S. Pine Avenue (US 441) ☎ 620-2511

Orlando ☎ 407

GAY INFO

AID/Orlando (GLM) 0-24 h
☎ 648-9161
Gay Community Services (GLM)
714 East Colonial Drive ✉FL 32803 ☎ 425-4527
Counseling, rap groups, speakers bureau, library, social events.
Gay Lesbian & Bisexual Community Center of Central Florida (GLBCC) (A AC CC d f GLM s) Mon-Thu 11-21, Fri -18, Sat 12-19, Sun 13-18 h
934 N. Mills Avenue ✉FL 32803 ☎ 425-4527
☎ 843-4297 (24 h hotline) Fax: 228-8230
E-Mail: info@glbcc.org Homepage: www.glbcc.org
Social support community center.

BARS

Cactus Club (B F GLM OS) 14-2 h
1300 North Mills Avenue ✉FL 32803 ☎ 894-3041
Club. The (B D Glm SNU STV)
578 N. Orange Avenue ✉FL 32809 ☎ 426-0005
Especially busy Wed & Sat.
Crews (B G MA N) 15-2 h
4716 S. Orange Avenue *(at Holden in the Kwik Stop Plaza)*
☎ 850-6033

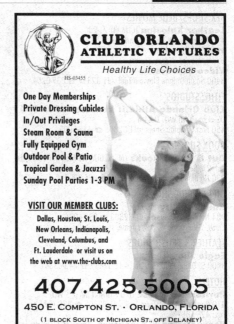

Full Moon Saloon (AC B d f G LJ MA OS VS) 12-2 h
500 North Orange Blossom Trail ✉FL 32805 ☎ 648-8725
Cruise bar. Monthly full moon parties.
Hank's (AC B d G lj) 12-2 h
5026 Edgewater Drive ✉FL 32810 ☎ 291-2399
Orlando Eagle (B D G LJ) 12-2 h
3400 South Orange Blossom Trail ✉FL 32805 *(at the Complex)*
☎ 843-6334
Parliament House (B G LJ S)
410 North Orange Blossom Trail ✉FL 32805 ☎ 425-7571
Southern Nights (AC B D f GLM MA OS S tv) 16-2 h
375 South Bumby Avenue ✉FL 32803 ☎ 898-0424

DANCECLUBS

Power House Disco (B D G S YG) 20-2 h
410 North Orange Blossom Trail ✉FL 32805 *(at Parliament House)* ☎ 425-5771

RESTAURANTS

Dog Out (B F GLM) 0-24 h
410 North Orange Blossom Trail ✉FL 32805 *(at Parliament House Hotel)* ☎ 305/425-7571
Uncle Walt's Backstage (! AC B CC d e F G MA S) 16-2 h
5454 International Drive ✉FL 32819 *(5 min from Disney, Universal, MGM)* ☎ 351-4866
Cabaret shows Wed Fri Sat, 2 shows nightly, cover US$2-3. Piano Bar Thu Fri Happy hour. Appetizer menu, pizza, pasta.
Union Deli (bf CC F glm MA)
337 North Shine Avenue ☎ 894-5778

SEX SHOPS/BLUE MOVIES

Leather Xplosion (GLM LJ) 21-2 h
410 North Orange Blossom Trail ✉FL 32805
☎ 425-7571 ext139
Books, movies, videos, leather.

Video Express (VS)
3400 South Orange Blossom Trail ✉FL 32839 ☎ 839-0204

FITNESSTUDIOS

Club Orlando Athletic Ventures (AC CC f G MA P OS pi sa sb wh WO) 0-24 h
450 East Compton Street ✉FL 32806 ☎ 425-5005

BOOK SHOPS

Out & About Books (AC CC GLM W) Mon-Thu 10-20, Fri-Sat -21, Sun 12-19 h
930 North Mills Avenue ✉FL 32803 ☎ 896-0204

GIFT & PRIDE SHOPS

Rainbow City (CC GLM)
934 North Mills Avenue ✉FL 32803 ☎ 898-6096
Cards, T-shirts, magazines, bumper stickers, gifts.

LEATHER & FETISH SHOPS

Eagle Shop (LJ)
3400 S. Orange Blossom Trail ✉FL 32839 ☎ 843-6334

HOTELS

Parliament House (B D F GLM H MA pi S WO)
410 North Orange Blossom Trail ✉FL 32805 ☎ 425-7571
Fax: 425-5881

Veranda Bed & Breakfast. The (AC CC bf glm msg OS pi wh WO)
115 North Summerlin Avenue ✉FL 32801
☎ 849-0321 ☎ (800) 420-6822 (toll free)
Historic building. Rates US$79-159. Colour dable TV, VS library, telephone, kitchen, fridge, coffee/tea facilities.

GENERAL GROUPS

Bears of Central Florida
PO Box 647 ✉FL 32802-0647

FETISH GROUPS

Black Star MC
c/o Loading Dock, 3400 South Orange Blossom Tr. ✉FL 32839

HEALTH GROUPS

AIDS-Hotline
☎ (800) 342-2437 (toll free)

VD Clinic
832 West Central ✉FL 32805 ☎ 420-3600

RELIGIOUS GROUPS

Joy MCC
2351 S. Ferncreek Avenue ✉FL 32806 ☎ 894-1081

CRUISING

-Colonial Plaza Shopping Mall
-Eola Park & Drive (AYOR)
-Fashion Square Shopping Mall

Panama City Beach ☎ 904

BARS

Fiesta Room (AC B D GLM lj MA r S STV) 20-3, Fri-Sat -4 h
110 Harrison Avenue ✉FL 32401 ☎ 784-9285

Royale Lounge. La (AC B d GLM lj MA r) 15-3, Fri-Sat 16-4 h
100 Harrison Avenue ✉FL 32401 ☎ 784-9311

SWIMMING

-Seagrove Beach (NU) (west of Panama City Beach)
-Phillip's Inlet County Beach (1/2 mile West of Ramsgate Harbor)

Pensacola ☎ 850

BARS

Emerald City (AC B D GLM MA OS P s STV W WE) Wed-Sun 15-3 h
406 East Wright Street ✉FL 32501 ☎ 433-9491

Red Carpet (B D GLM OS S) 15-2.30 h
937 Warrington Road ✉FL 32507 ☎ 453-9918

Red Garter (B D GLM S YG) 20-2h, closed Mon Tue
1 West Main Street ✉FL 32501 ☎ 432-9188

Roundup (B G VS YG) Mon-Fri 15-2, Sat 13-2, Sun 13-1 h
706 East Gregory Street ✉FL 32501 ☎ 438-8482

SWIMMING

-Beach on Santa Rosa Island (Fort Picken's „BA" Beach)
-Gay Dunes Beach (Dunes and Trails 7 miles West of Navarre Beach)
-Penscola Beach

CRUISING

-Old Chimney (near bluff on scenic highway)

Port Richey ☎ 813

BARS

BT's (B CC G MA S) 18-2 h
7737 Grand Boulevard ☎ 841-7900

Riviera Beach ☎ 407

BARS

Dakota Lounge (B G) 3051
Broadway ✉FL 33404 ☎ 863-5863

Sarasota ☎ 941

BARS

Club Rowdy's (AC B CC d DR G lj MA OS S VS) 12-2 h
1330 27th Street ✉FL 34243 ☎ 953-5945

H.G. Rooster's (AC B d G MA OS s SNU VS) 15-2 h
1256 Old Stickney Point Road ✉FL 34242 ☎ 346-3000

HOTELS

Normandy Inn (bf g H OS)
400 North Tamiami Trail ✉FL 34236-4822 ☎ 366-8979
☎ (800) 282-8050 (Toll-free)
With own tropical outdoor cafe called „Billa Bowlegs Banana Patch".

GUEST HOUSES

Vera's Place Bed & Breakfast (AC bf G p pi)
3913 Chapel Drive ✉FL 34234 ☎ 351-3171
Private bath, heated pool, full breakfast.

CRUISING

-Gulfstream Avenue (P) (Ringling Boulevard and Gulfstream)
-North Lido Beach
-Palm Avenue (AYOR R)

Satellite Beach ☎ 407

SEX SHOPS/BLUE MOVIES

Space Age Books & Temptations
63 Ocean Boulevard ✉FL 32937 ☎ 773-7660

St. Petersburg ☎ 813

BARS

D.T.'s (B G S) 14-2 h
2612 Central Avenue ✉FL 33712 ☎ 327-8204
Golden Arrow (B G) 13-2 h
10604 Gandy Boulevard ✉FL 33702 ☎ 577-7774
Haymarket Pub (B G MA W) 16-2 h
8308 4th Street No. ☎ 577-9621
New Connection (B D GLM W) 13-2 h
3100 3rd Avenue North ☎ 321-2112

RESTAURANTS

Keystone Club Restaurant (B F g) Mon-Fri 11.30-14.30 17-22 h
320 4th Street North ✉FL 33701 ☎ 822-6600
Fresh seafood, French and domestic wines. Specialty: Prime Angus Beef Filets.

SEX SHOPS/BLUE MOVIES

4th Street Books & Videos (g VS)
1427 4th Street/14th Avenue ✉FL 33706 ☎ 821-8824

HOTELS

Suncoast Resort Hotel (A AC B bf CC D F GLM H LJ MA OS pi S SNU STV W WO)
3000 34th Street, South ✉FL 33711 *(only minutes from the Gulf of Mexico beaches)* ☎ 727/867-1111 Fax: 727/867-7068
Homepage: www.suncoastresort.com
120 hotel rooms & suites, 6 bars, 3 restaurants, 30,000 Sq. Ft. shopping mall, 15,000 Sq. Ft. convention area, 9 tennis courts, 2 volleyball courts, swimming pool, 8000 Sq. Ft. gym.

FETISH GROUPS

Adventurers-Suncoast MC
PO BOX 8043 ✉FL 33738

HEALTH GROUPS

VD-Clinic
500 7th Avenue ✉FL 33706 ☎ 894-1184

SWIMMING

-Pass-a-Grille Beach (southern end)
-Treasure Island/Beach in front of Bedrox

CRUISING

-Bayshore Drive (from 2nd Street to Vinoy Park)
-Maximo Park
-Pass-a-Grille Beach (below 8th Street)
-Skyway Bridge Park

Tallahassee ☎ 850

BARS

Brothers (AC B CC D GLM OS S WE YG) 16-2 h
926 West Thorpe Street ✉FL 32303 ☎ 386-2399
Club Park Avenue (B G S VS YG) 21-2 h
115 East Park Avenue ✉FL 32301 ☎ 599-9143

CRUISING

-Rest Area US 319 North
-Florida State University (library)
-Last Lake (southwest on Route 373)
-Park by post office (opposite Club Park Avenue)

Tampa ☎ 813

GAY INFO

Gazette. The
☎ 689-7566
Hotline 19-23 h
1222 South Dale Mabry Street ✉FL 33611 ☎ 229-8839
Stonewall
3225 S. MacDill Avd. S-220 ✉FL 33629 ☎ 832-2878
Fax: 887-3544

BARS

Angel's (B G MA SNU) Mon-Sun 11-?
4502 South Dale Mabry ✉FL 33611 ☎ 831-9980
Annex. The (B G) 11-? h
2408 West Kennedy Boulevard ✉FL 33609 ☎ 254-4188
City Side (B G OS S)
3810 Neptune Street ✉FL 33629 ☎ 254-6466
Howard Avenue Station (B D G snu)
3003 North Howard Avenue ✉FL 33607 ☎ 254-7194
Jungle (AC B CC D GLM MA N OS VS) 15-3 h
3703 Henderson Boulevard ✉FL 33609 ☎ 877-3290
Keith's Lounge (B Glm N) 13-3 h
14905 North Nebraska Avenue ☎ 971-3576
Metropolis (B G MA S)
3447 West Kennedy Boulevard ☎ 871-2410
Rascal's (B D F GLM W) 16-3, Thu-Sat -4.30, Sun 12-3 h
105 W. Martin Luther King Boulevard ☎ 237-8883
Tampa Brigg. The (AC B G LJ MA N OS SNU VS) 15-03 h
9002 North Florida Avenue ✉FL 33604 *(south of Busch Boulevard)* ☎ 931-3396
Tampa's oldest gay owned and run bar. Male strippers Fri & Sat.
Tampa Eagle (AC B CC DR G LJ MA OS) Mon-Sat 19-3, Sun 17-3 h
302 South Nebraska Avenue ✉FL 33602 ☎ 223-2780
2606 Club (AC B G lj MA) 20-3 h
2606 North Armenia Avenue ✉FL 33607 ☎ 875-6993
Cruising western style bar.

DANCECLUBS

Pleasuredome (! B D GLM STV)
1430 East 7th Avenue/15th Street ✉FL 33605 *(Ybor City)*
☎ 247-2006

SEX SHOPS/BLUE MOVIES

Buddies Video (G VS)
4322 W. Crest Avenue ✉FL 33614 ☎ 876-8083
XTC (glm VS)
4829 Lois Avenue ✉FL 33614 ☎ 871-6900

SAUNAS/BATHS

Club Tampa Baths (B f G NU P sa wh) 0-24 h
215 North 11th Street ✉FL 33602 ☎ 223-5181

FITNESSTUDIOS

Metro Flex (G WO)
2511 Swann Avenue ✉FL 33609

GUEST HOUSES

Gram's Place (AC b bf CC F glm H lj MA N NU OS wh)
3109 North Ola Avenue ✉FL 33603 ☎ 221-0596
E-Mail: GramsPl@aol.com
Homepage: http://members.aol.com/GramsPl/index.html

FETISH GROUPS

FFA, Tampa Bay
1230 East Mohawk Avenue ✉FL 33610

CRUISING

-Picnic Island Park
-Ben T. Davis Beach (AYOR) (Campbell Causeway)

West Palm Beach ☎ 561

BARS

H.G. Rooster's (AC B G MA OS s SNU VS) 15-3, Fri Sat -4
823 Belvedere Road ✉FL 33405 ☎ 833-4045
Kozlow's (B F glm OS) 12-2, Fri Sat-4 h
6205 Georgia Avenue ✉FL 33405 ☎ 533-5355
5101 Bar (B G N W) Mon-Thu 7-3, Fri Sat-4, Sun 12-3 h
5101 South Dixie Highway ✉FL 33405 ☎ 585-2379

HOTELS

Hibiscus House (AC B bf CC glm MA OS pi)
501 30th Street ✉FL 33407 ☎ 863-5633 ☎ (800) 203-4927 (Toll-free) Fax: 863-5633 Homepage: www.hibiscushouse.com
Rates US$ 65-150 (low season), 95-230 (high season).

GUEST HOUSES

Casa Piña (AC bf G H pi)
PO Box 17 602 ✉FL 33416 ☎ 820-8872
E-Mail: lambskul@ix.netcom.com
Rates US$ 45-110.

CRUISING

-Curry Park (AYOR)
-Dixie Highway (from Belvedere Boulevard to Forrest Hill)
-MacArthur Park Beach
-Seawall (summers)

Wilton Manors ☎ 954

CAFES

Chardees Courtyard Cafe (bf F GLM MA) 7-15 h
2211 Wilton Drive ✉FL 33305 ☎ 563-2499

RESTAURANTS

Chardees Dinner Club (AC B d F G MA S) 16.30-1 h, Sun Brunch 11-15 h
2209 Wilton Drive ✉FL 33305 ☎ 563-1800
Piano Bar. Traditional American cuisine.

Good morning...after!
...use them!
GIB AIDS
KEINE
CHANCE

USA-Georgia

Southeast USA
Initials: GA
Time: GMT -5
Area: 153.952 km² / 62,966 sq mi.
Population: 7,486,000
Capital: Atlanta

● The highest court of the land in Georgia has repealed the Sodomy Laws.

✷ In Georgia sind 1998 die Sodomie-Gesetze durch den Höchsten Gerichtshof außer Kraft gesetzt worden.

▲ En Georgia, la loi sur la sodomie a été retirée par la Haute Cour de Justice en 1998.

☆ El tribunal supremo de Georgia abolió en 1998 los leyes de sodomia.

❖ In Giorgia nel 1998 sono state abolite dalla Corte maggiore tutte le leggi contro la sodomia.

Athens ☎ 706

DANCECLUBS

Boneshakers (B D GLM) closed Sun
433 East Hancock Avenue ✉GA 30601 ☎ 543-1555
Special events.

Atlanta ☎ 404

GAY INFO

Atlanta Gay Center
63 12th Street ✉GA 30309 ☎ 876-5372
Help Line 18-23 h
☎ 892-0661
The News
67 12th Street ✉GA 30309 ☎ 876-5372
A publication of the Atlanta Gay Center.

TOURIST INFO

Atlanta Convention & Visitor Bureau
233 Peachtree Street NE, Ste. 2000 ✉GA 30303 ☎ 521-6600

BARS

Atlanta Eagle (B D G LJ) 19-? h, Sun 17-? h
308 Ponce De Leon Avenue ✉GA 30308 ☎ 873-2453
Blake's on the Park (B Glm MA N OS S vs) 15-4 h, Sun Brunch 12-15 h
227 10th Street ✉GA 30309 ☎ 892-5786
Buddies (B G)
2345 Cheshire Bridge Road ✉GA 30324 ☎ 634-5895
Buddies Midtown (B G)
239 Ponce de Leon ✉GA 30324 ☎ 872-2655
Bulldogs & Co. (B G lj OS) Mon-Sat 10-4 h, Sun 14-4 h
893 Peachtree Street ✉GA 30308 ☎ 872-3025
Cruisy. Popular Sun pm.
Burkhart's Pub (AC B CC G MA N OS s) 14-3 h
1492-F Piedmont Avenue ✉GA 30309 *(Near Ansley Square)*
☎ 872-4403
Coronet Club (G SNU)
5275 Roswell Road ✉GA 30350 ☎ 250-1534
Male strippers. Bring your own alcohol. (BYOB)

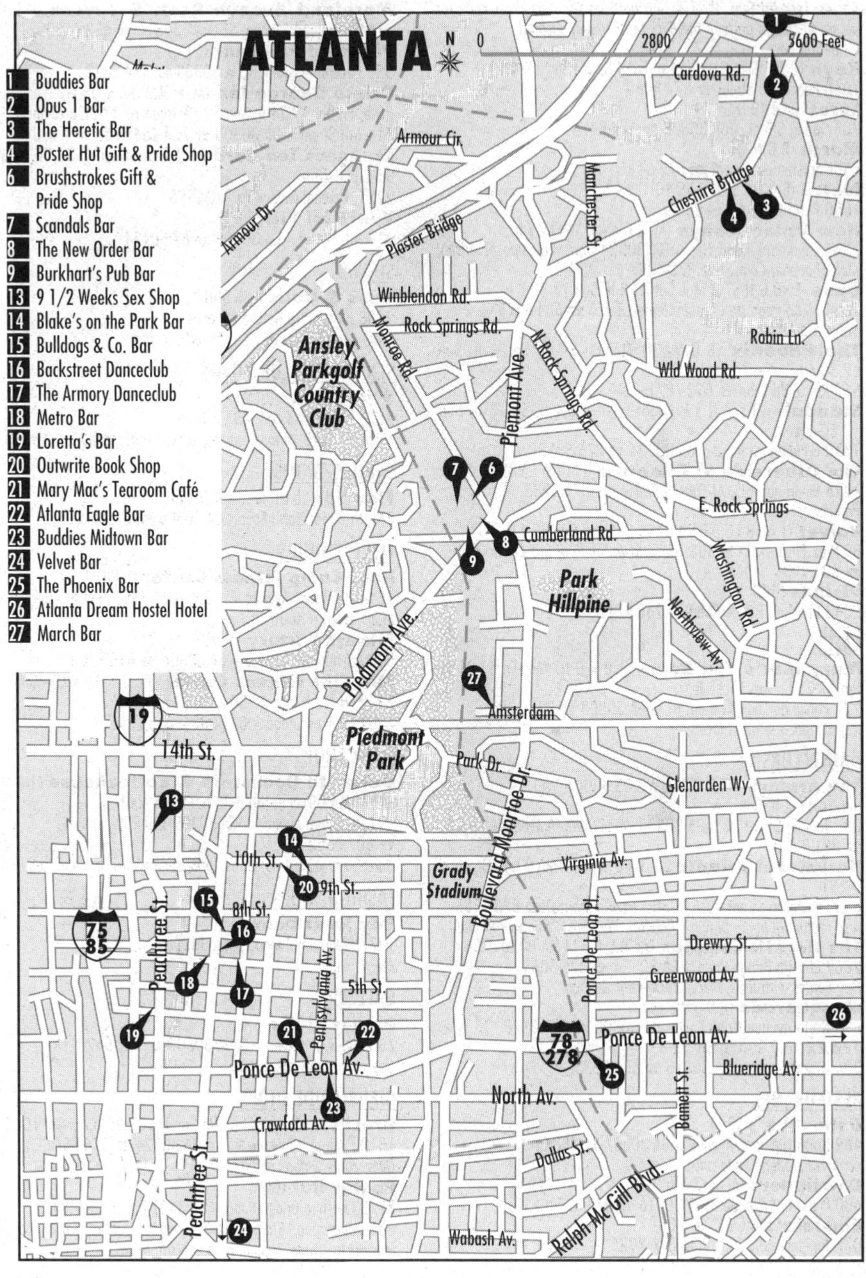
ATLANTA
N
0
2800
5600 Feet
1 Buddies Bar
2 Opus 1 Bar
3 The Heretic Bar
4 Poster Hut Gift & Pride Shop
6 Brushstrokes Gift & Pride Shop
7 Scandals Bar
8 The New Order Bar
9 Burkhart's Pub Bar
13 9 1/2 Weeks Sex Shop
14 Blake's on the Park Bar
15 Bulldogs & Co. Bar
16 Backstreet Danceclub
17 The Armory Danceclub
18 Metro Bar
19 Loretta's Bar
20 Outwrite Book Shop
21 Mary Mac's Tearoom Café
22 Atlanta Eagle Bar
23 Buddies Midtown Bar
24 Velvet Bar
25 The Phoenix Bar
26 Atlanta Dream Hostel Hotel
27 March Bar
Cardova Rd.
Armour Cir.
Manchester St.
Cheshire Bridge
Armour Dr.
Plaster Bridge
Winblendon Rd.
Monroe Rd.
Rock Springs Rd.
Ansley Parkgolf Country Club
Piemont Ave.
N.Rock Springs Rd.
Rabin Ln.
Wld Wood Rd.
E. Rock Springs
Cumberland Rd.
Washington Rd.
Park Hillpine
Northview Av.
Piedmont Ave.
Amsterdam
19
14th St.
Piedmont Park
Park Dr.
Boulevard Monroe Dr.
Glenarden Wy
10th St.
9th St.
Grady Stadium
Virginia Av.
8th St.
75
85
Peachtree St.
Ponce De Leon Pl.
Drewry St.
Greenwood Av.
Pennsylvania Av.
5th St.
78
278
Ponce De Leon Av.
Blueridge Av.
Ponce De Leon Av.
North Av.
Barnett St.
Crawford Av.
Dallas St.
Peachtree St.
Ralph Mc Gill Blvd.
Wabash Av.

The Heretic (AC B D F G lj MA s u VS W) 12-4 h
2069 Cheshire Bridge Road ✉GA 30324 ☎ 325-3061
Shows 1st/3rd Sun. Wed & Sun parties with strict dress code for access to certain parts of the bar! Leather shop located inside the bar.
Kaya (B D F GLM S) 12-24 h, Fri -4 h, Sat Sun 17-4 h
1068 Peachtree Street ☎ 874-4460
Loretta's (B D G)
708 Spring Street ✉GA 30308 ☎ 874-8125
March (B G MA)
550c Amsterdam Street ☎ 872-6411
Metro (B G MA S SNU VS YG) 15-4 h
1080 Peachtree ☎ 874-9869
New Order Lounge (AC B G MA N W) 14-2 h
1544 Piedmont Road NE, ✉GA 30324 *(on back side of Ansley Mall Shopping Centre)* ☎ 873-4059
Opus 1 (B G N STV) Mon-Sat 21-? h, Sun 12.30-? h
1086 Alco Street *(at Cheshire Bridge Road)* ☎ 634-6478
Show Sun.
The Phoenix (B G MA N) Mon-Fri 9-4 h, Sat -3 h, Sun 12.30-4 h
567 Ponce de Leon ☎ 892-7871
Scandals (B f G N s W) Mon-Fri 11.30-4 h, Sat -3 h, Sun 12.30-4 h
1510 G-Piedmont Road ✉GA 30324 ☎ 875-5957
The Otherside of Atlanta (B D f GLM S VS) 17-4 h
1924 Piedmont Rd. *(At Chesire Bridge)* ☎ 875-5238
Popular
Velvet (! AC B CC D g S VS YG) Sat-Mon Gay 22-4 h.
89 Park Place ✉GA 30303 *(downtown South of Ritz-Cartlton)* ☎ 681-9936
Visions (B G)
2043 Cheshire Bridge Road ☎ 248-9712

CAFES

Mary Mac's Tea Room (! B F G N) Mon-Fri 11-21 h, Sat 17-21 h, Sun 11-15 h
224 Ponce de Leon Avenue, NE ✉GA 30308 ☎ 876-1800
A good place to meet locals.

DANCECLUBS

The Armory (AC B D GLM MA OS S VS W WE)
Sun-Fri 16-4 h, Sat -3 h
836 Juniper Street NE ✉GA 30308 *(MARTA-North Avenue)* ☎ 881-9280
Backstreet Atlanta (AC B CC D f GLM MA S tv we) 0-24 h
845 Peachtree Street ✉GA 30308 *(rear entrance)* ☎ 873-1986
Also featuringCharlie Brown's Cabaret. Very busy. Shows Thur-Sun.
The Heretic Complex (AC B D F G LJ MA N VS) 10-4 h
2069 Chesire Bridge Road ✉GA 30324 ☎ 325-3061
Gay Center with Bars, Disco, Restaurant & Shop.
Masquerade (B D g WE YG)
695 North Avenue North East ✉GA 30308 ☎ 577-8178
Traxx (B D G s OS) Sat 22-4 h
306 Luckie Street ✉GA 30313 ☎ 681-5033

RESTAURANTS

Babushka's (F g)
469 North Highland Avenue ✉GA 30307 ☎ 688-0836
Eastern European style cuisine.
Cowtippers (AC B CC F g OS)
600 Piedmont Avenue ✉GA 30316 ☎ 874-3751
Einstein's (AC B CC F g OS)
077 Juniper ✉GA 30309 ☎ 876-7925
Mambo Restaurante Cubano (F G)
1402 North Highland Avenue ✉GA 30306 ☎ 876-2626
Moreland Avenue Rest. & Tavern (B F GLM)
1196 Moreland Avenue, SE ✉GA 30316 ☎ 622-4650
Pleasant Pleasant (E F g)
555 Peachtree Street ✉GA 30303 ☎ 874-3223
Prince George Inn (AC F GLM MA N OS W) Wed Thu 17-23 h, Fri Sat 17-24 h, Sun 12-15 (brunch) 17-22 h (dinner)
114 6th Street ✉GA 30308 ☎ 724-4669 Fax: 872-9934
St. Agnes Tea Garden (B F glm) Mon-Fri 8-14 h, 18-22 h, Sat Sun 8-23 h
222 E. Howard Avenue ☎ 370-1995
Veni Vidi Vici (E F g)
41 14th Street ✉GA 30309 ☎ 875-8424

SHOWS

Guys & Dolls (glm SNU)
2788 East Ponce de Leon Avenue
Male and female strippers. Mixed crowd.

SEX SHOPS/BLUE MOVIES

9 ½ Weeks (GLM)
2628 Piedmont Road ✉GA 30324
Lingerie, Cards, lotions, games, gifts, leather, adult toys, videos.

SAUNAS/BATHS

Flex Spa (b f G pi sa sb) 0-24 h
76 4th Street North East ✉GA 30308 ☎ 815-0456

FITNESSTUDIOS

Boot Camp Fitness Center (g WO)
1544 Piedmont Avenue #105 *(Ansley Mall, next to Ansley Square Mall)* ☎ 876-8686
Fitness Factory (g WO)
500 Amsterdam Avenue ✉GA 30306 ☎ 815-7900
Mid-City Fitness Center (AC G sa sb WO) Mon-Thu 6-23 h, Fri -22 h, Sat 10-20 h, Sun 11-17 h
2201 Faulkner Road ✉GA 30324 ☎ 321-6507

BOOK SHOPS

Outwrite Bookstore & Coffeehouse (! A AC CC F GLM MA OS) Sun-Thu 8-23 h, Fri Sat -24 h
991 Piedmont Avenue ✉GA 30309 *(MARTA-Midtown)* ☎ 607-0082
Books, music, videos, cards, gifts, sandwiches, hot and iced drinks.

FASHION SHOPS

Boy Next Door
1477 Piedmont Avenue ✉GA 30308
Men´s wear

GALLERIES

Planet Claire
753 Edgewood Avenue ✉GA 30307 ☎ 522-5620
Gay community arts center.

GIFT & PRIDE SHOPS

Brushstrokes (CC GLM) Sun-Thu 10-22 h, Fri Sat 10-23 h
1510 Piedmont Avenue N.E. ✉GA 30324 ☎ 876-6567
Gifts, cards, videos and more.
Poster Hut (GLM)
2175 Cheshire Bridge Road ✉GA 30324 ☎ 633-7491
Gay Department Store. Clothing, leather, rubber, fetish, housewares, clocks, cards, stationery, posters, artwork.

LEATHER & FETISH SHOPS

Gryphon Leathers
2069 Cheshire Bridge Road ✉GA 30324 ☎ 325-3061

Mohawk Leather
306 Ponce de Leon ✉GA 30308 ☎ 873-2453

TRAVEL & TRANSPORT

Midtown Travel 9-17 h, Sat 10-15 h
1830 Piedmont Road, #F ✉GA 30324 ☎ 872-8308
Travel agency.

HOTELS

Atlanta Dream Hostel (AC b CC glm H)
115 Church Street ✉GA 30030 *(MARTA-Decatur)*
☎ 370-0380 Fax: 370-1966 E-Mail: dram96@mindspring.com
Homepage: www.mindspring.com/~dream96
7 double rooms partly with shared facilities. All rooms with heating and own key. Hotel provides TV room, restaurant. Rates double US$ 36-42, single 25-32.

Midtown Manor (GLM H)
811 Piedmont Avenue, N.E., ✉GA 30308 ☎ 872-5846
☎ (800) 724-4381

GUEST HOUSES

Abbett Inn (AC bf CC GLM)
1746 Virginia Ave, College Park ✉GA 30337 *(Close to hartsfield Intern. Airport)* ☎ 767-3708 Fax: 767-1626
E-Mail: abbettinn@bellsouth.net Homepage: www.abbettinn.com

GENERAL GROUPS

ACLU-Lesbian/Gay Rights
233 Mitchell Street, Suite 200 ✉GA 30303 ☎ 523-6201

Atlanta Fairie Circle
☎ 622-4112
Monthly potlucks & discussion groups for gay men interested in personal liberation & social change.

Black & White Men Together
☎ 794-2968

Gay Atheist League
☎ 875-8877

HEALTH GROUPS

AIDS Information Line
☎ 876-9944

HELP WITH PROBLEMS

Gay Helpline 18-23 h
☎ 892-0661

RELIGIOUS GROUPS

Congregation Beth Haverim
☎ 642-3467
Jewish gays.

Integrity (Episcopal)
All Saints Church ☎ 875-2720

CRUISING

-Cabbage Town (AYOR) (Grant Park)
-Chattahoochee Park (AYOR) (nature trails)
-Cypress Street/»The Strip« (AYOR) (alley between Peachtree & West Peachtree from 6th to 8th Streets)
-Lenox Square Mall
-Peachtree Center Shopping Gallery (800 Peachtree N.E.)
-Piedmont Park (AYOR) (nature trails & botanical gardens)

Augusta ☎ 706

BARS

Walton Way Station (B D GLM MA S) 21-3 h, closed Sun
1632 Walton Way ☎ 733-2603

Savannah ☎ 912

BARS

Club One (B D glm s) Mon-Sat 21-3 h
1 Jefferson Street ✉GA 31401 ☎ 232-0200

Faces II (B f G lj MA)
Lincoln Street 17 ✉GA 31401 ☎ 233-3520

Loading Dock. The (AC B g MA s) Mon-Sat 17-3 h
641 Indian Street ✉GA 31401 ☎ 232-0130

Sonic Sound Lab at Felicia's (AC B CC D F GLM LJ MA S STV VS WE) Mon-Sat 16-3 h, Sun 16-2 h
416 West Old Liberty Street ✉GA 31401 *(Next to Bank of America)* ☎ 238-4788
Also a restaurant.

GUEST HOUSES

912 Barnard Bed & Breakfast (AC bf f GLM MA)
912 Barnard Street ✉GA 31401 ☎ 234-9121 Fax: 944-0996
2 single rooms with bath, shower, WC, balcony, TV, VCR, own key and room service. Casual, home-like atmosphere. Rates US$ 89 plus 12 % tax per room, per night, bf incl.

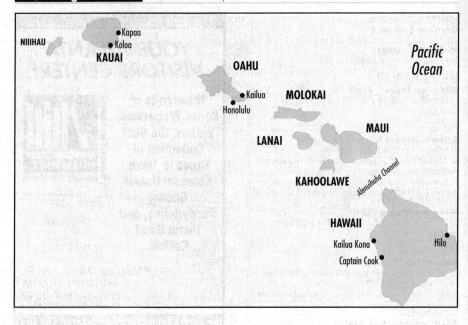

NIIHAU
Kapaa
Koloa
KAUAI
OAHU
Pacific Ocean
Kailua
Honolulu
MOLOKAI
MAUI
LANAI
KAHOOLAWE
Alenuihaha Channel
HAWAII
Kailua Kona
Hilo
Captain Cook

PRIVATE ACCOMODATION

Green Palm Inn (AC bf cc glm H)
546 East President Street GA 31401 *(historic district)*
☎ 447-8901 ☎ (888) 606-6668 Fax: 447-6668
E-Mail: greepalminn@aol.com
Rooms with AC, bath, phone, radio, TV. Own key and car place. One studio with kitchen. Rates from US$ 79-139.

USA-Hawaii

Pacific region USA

Initials: HI

Time: GMT -10

Area: 28.313 km² / 11,580 sq mi.

Population: 1,187.000

Capital: Honolulu

Important gay cities: Honolulu and Waikiki

● The highest court in Hawaii has not decided yet whether homosexual couples will be able to get married in the future.

✷ Zur Zeit liegt noch keine Entscheidung des obersten hawaiianischen Gerichts darüber vor, ob in disem Bundesstaat homosexuelle Paare künftig heiraten können.

▲ Le Haut Tribunal de l'état de Hawaï n'a pas encore décidé si les couples homosexuels pouvaient se marier.

☆ La Corte Suprema Hawaiana aún no ha decidido si en un futuro cercano será posible el matrimonio entre parejas homosexuales.

Il tribunale superiore hawiiano non ha ancora deliberato se prossimamente le coppie gay si potranno sposare.

NATIONAL COMPANIES

Douglas Simonson Fine Arts (A CC)
By appointment only
4614 Kilauea Avenue HI 96816 ☎ 737-6275 Fax: 737-6275
E-Mail: simonson@pixi.com
Homepage: www.douglassimonson.com
Male posters, prints, notecards and original art. Ask for catalogue.

Hawaii ☎ 808

GAY INFO

Gay Hawaii
☎ 923-2400 Homepage: gayhawaii.com

TRAVEL & TRANSPORT

Hawaiian Gay Excursions
☎ 667-7466 ☎ (800) 311-4460 (toll free) Fax: 667-5401

Hawaii-Captain Cook ☎ 808

HOTELS

Samurai House (g H)
RR 1 PO Box 359 HI 96704 ☎ 328-9210
A traditional Japanese inn. Rates from US$ 40.

GUEST HOUSES

Hale Aloha Guest Ranch (AC bf GLM MA msg NU OS wh) 8-20 h
84-4780 Mamalahoa Highway ✉HI 96704 ☎ 328-3188
☎ (800) 897-3188 (toll free) Fax: 328-8955
E-Mail: vacation@halealoha.com Homepage: www.halealoha.com
Luxurious house located on the mountain side of Mauna Loa Volcano overlooking Kona coast of the Big Island of Hawaii. 3 guest rooms with shared bath and kitchen. Mastersuite with private jacuzzi tub. Rates: room US$ 70-80, suite $140. Bf incl.

RBR-Farms Bed and Breakfast (bf cc G H NU pi wh)
PO Box 930 ✉HI 96704 ☎ 328-9212
☎ (800) 328-9212 (Toll-free) Fax: 328-9212
E-Mail: rbrfarms@gte.net Homepage: www.konaweb.com/rbr
Rates double US$ 75-85, single $60-70.

Hawaii-Hawi ☎ 808

HOTELS

Hale Anuenue (Rainbow House) (bf GLM H pi WO)
PO Box 371 ✉HI 96719 ☎ 889-6187
Ten minutes from Kamehameha Park with large pool, tennis courts and gym. Shared bath single US$ 55, double 65, Cottage with bath 75 plus 9% state tax. Deposit one nights rate.

Hawaii-Honaunau ☎ 808

GAY INFO

Matt's Rainbow Tours/Rainbow Handbook Hawaii (GLM)
PO Box 100 ✉HI 96726 ☎ 328-8654
Gay Tour Company & Gay Travel Guide book of Hawaii.

Hawaii-Kailua Kona ☎ 808

BARS

Mask Bar & Grill (B D F G STV) 18-2 h, disco Fri Sat 22.30-? h
75-5660 Kopiko Street ✉HI 96740 *(at Cathedral Plaza)*
☎ 329-8558

The Other Side (AC CC g MA N WE) Mon-Thu 12-24 h, Fri Sat -2 h
74-5484 A-120 Kaiwi Street ✉HI 96740 *(In old industrial area)*
☎ 329-7226

HOTELS

Big Island Guest House (bf g H msg NU)
77-344 Nohealani Street ✉HI 96740-9785 ☎ 324-6712

Hale Kipa 'O Pele (bf cc G H msg wh)
75-5852 Alii Drive ✉HI 96745 ☎ 329-8676 ☎ (800) 528-2456 (toll-free) E-Mail: halekipa@gte.ne
Rates US$ 65-85.

Plumeria House (g H)
77-6546 Naniloa Drive ✉HI 96740 ☎ 322-8164
Rates US$ 45 per day, 250 per week. Six miles south of Kailua, located between two beaches. Vacation rental with private bath, kitchenette, TV and phone.

Royal Kona Resort (bf CC g H msg pi S)
75-5852 Alii Drive ✉HI 96740 ☎ 329-3111
☎ (800) 774-KONA (USA & Canada) Fax: 329-7230
E-Mail: hhr@hawaiihotels.com Homepage: www.royalkona.com
Large, comfortable resort hotel. Rates US$ 99-250, bf $10.

SWIMMING

-Honokohau Beach (G NU) (On highway 19 between Kailua-Kona and Kona airport turn onto the road to Honokohau Boat Harbor. Take the first road to the right then follow the trail that leads north then to the left through the bushes. At the ocean the right end of the beach is the gayest.)

CRUISING

-Kahaluu Beach Park (near 5-mile-marker)

HOTELS

Vacation Rental (g H)
PO Box 717 ✉HI 96754 ☎ 828-1626
Two bedroom rental.

GUEST HOUSES

Pali Kai Bed and Breakfast (bf glm H pi wh)
PO Box 450 ✉HI 96754 ☎ 828-6691 ☎ (888) 828-6691 (toll-free) Fax: 828-1271 E-Mail: Palikai@aloha.net
Homepage: www.palikai.com
Hilltop with 360° views on ocean, mountains, waterfalls. Rates US$ 90 (+tax), cottage $125 (+tax).

APARTMENTS

Kalihiwai Jungle Home (AC G msg NU)
PO Box 717 ✉HI 96754 ☎ 828-1626
E-Mail: thomasw@aloha.net
Homepage: www.hshawaii.com/kvp/jungle/
One luxury bedroom with full kitchen, Hawaiian art and furnishing, bath, fireplace and a large deck and hammock overlooking the waterfall, jungle and mountain landscape. Daily rates US$ 100-150.

CRUISING

-Donkey Beach (at Dirt Road, south of 12 mile marker, walk toward beach)

Hawaii-Pahoa ☎ 808

RESTAURANTS

The Godmother (B bf CC d F glm MA OS W) 8-15 h, 16-? h
PO Box 1163 ✉HI 96778 *(On the main street in historic Pahoa)*
☎ 965-0055
Restaurant and bar. Italian cuisine.

HOTELS

Huliaule'a Bed and Breakfast
PO Box 10 30 ✉HI 96778 ☎ 965-9175
Rates US$ 65-80 per night.

Kalani Resort (A AC bf CC F glm H MA msg NU OS pi s sa W wh WO)
RR2, Box 4500, Pahoa Beach Road ✉HI 96778-9724 *(Located at the Pahoa Beach Rd.)* ☎ 965-7828 ☎ (800) 800-6886 (toll-free) E-Mail: kalani@kalani.com Homepage: www.kalani.com
Oceanside getaway on a non-commercial coast. Also a healing & culture center offering various workshops and a yearly Pacific Men's gathering. Camping available.

The Volcano Ranch (G H)
13-3775 Kalapana Highway ✉HI 96778 ☎ 965-8800
Homepage: haleakala.aloha-net/v-ranch
Rates US$ 15-120.

GUEST HOUSES

Pamalu Guest House (AC GLM MA msg NU pi sb)
RR2, Box 4023 ✉HI 96778 *(8 km from Pahoa)* ☎ 965-0830
Fax: 965-6198
Guest ranch with bath/shower/WC, terrace, TV/Video room in the

Volcano Nationl Park. Work-out in nearby facilities. Rates single US$ 60, double $80-100 incl bf. Additional bed US$30. Diffrent swimming possiblities: pool, ocean, fresch water lake.

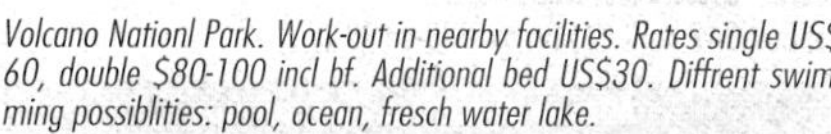

Hawaii-Volcano Village ☎ 808

GUEST HOUSES

Hale Ohia Cottages (bf CC glm OS W wh) 8-17 h
11-3968 Hale Ohia Boulevard, PO Box 758 ✉HI 96785 *(1 mile from Hawaii Volcanoes National Park)* ☎ 967-7986
☎ (800) 455-3803 (toll free) Fax: 967-8610
E-Mail: haleohia@bigisland.com Homepage: www.haleohia.com
Rates US$ 75-135.

Kauai-Anahola ☎ 808

GUEST HOUSES

Mahina Kai B&B Beach Villa (bf F glm H msg N OS pi wh)
4933 Aliomanu Road ✉HI 96703 ☎ 822-9451

Kauai-Kapaa ☎ 808

BARS

Sideout Bar and Grill (B CC F GLM MA N s) Mon-Sun 12-2 h
4-1330 Kuhio Highway ✉HI 96746 ☎ 822-7330

RESTAURANTS

Buzz's Steak & Lobster (B CC F g) lunch 11-15 h, happy hour 15-17 h, dinner 17-22.30 h
484 Kuhio Highway ✉HI 96746 ☎ 822-7491
Located in the Coconut Plantation Market Place. Seafood, steaks, lobster. Tahitian interior design.

HOTELS

Mala Lani (G H wh)
5711 Lokelani Road ✉HI 96746 ☎ 823-0422

GUEST HOUSES

Aloha Kauai B&B (bf GLM H MA OS pi W)
156 Lihau Street ✉HI 96746 ☎ 822-6966
☎ (800) 262-4652 (toll free)
Rooms with shared bath, TV, ceiling fan. Breakfast and sunset refreshments included. Rates US$ 60-90.

Hale Kahawai Bed & Breakfast (G H)
185 Kahawai Place ✉HI 96746 ☎ 822-1031 Fax: 823-8220

Royal Drive Cottages (G H msg)
147 Royal Drive ✉HI 96746 ☎ 822-2321 Fax: 822-7537
E-Mail: sand@aloha.ne
Homepage: www.planet-hawaii.com/~royal/
Rates US$ 80-130.

SWIMMING

-Little Beach (g NU) (in Makena to the right of »Big Beach«. Do not leave things in your car because of thiefs.)

Maui-Haiku ☎ 808

APARTMENTS

Kailua Maui Gardens (g H pi wh)
SR Box 9 ✉HI 96708 ☎ 572-9726 ☎ (800) 258-8588 (Toll-free) *Different apartments and cottages in a beautiful garden.*

Maui-Hana ☎ 808

APARTMENTS

Hana Plantation Houses of Maui (CC g H msg NU OS wh WO)
PO Box 489, ✉HI 96713 ☎ 923-0772 ☎ (800)228-4262 (toll free) Fax: 922-6008 Homepage: www.hana-maui.com

Maui-Kahului ☎ 808

GAY INFO

Both Sides Now
PO Box 50 42 ✉HI 96732 ☎ 244-4566 Fax: 573-1156
Maui monthly newsletter, also information line about social events.

Maui-Kihei ☎ 808

APARTMENTS

Luana Kai Resort (cc g H pi sa wh)
940 South Kihei Road ✉HI 96753 *(15minutes from airport, at the beach)* ☎ (800) 699-1127 (Toll-free) ☎ 879-1268
Fax: 879-1455 E-Mail: luanakai@mauigateway.com
Homepage: www.gpsolutions.com/lunakai
All condominiums with kitchen, bath, radio, satellite TV, phone. The resort is fronting 6 miles of sand beach. Prices from US$ 79-169.

Makena Surf (AC cc g H pi wh)
940 South Kihei Road ✉HI 96753 *(30 minutes from airport, 2 minutes from the beach)* ☎ 875-7737
E-Mail: luanakai@mauigateway.com
All condominiums with AC, bath, phone, kitchen, TV, radio. Sport facilities.

Wailana Beach House (AC G H)
14 Wailana Pl. ✉HI 96753 ☎ 874-3131 ☎ (800) 399-3885 (toll free) Fax: 874-0454 Homepage: www.wailanabeach.com
10 studios with kitchenette, air conditioning, phone and cable TV. Private sun deck with whirl pool. Barbecue grill.

Maui-Kula ☎ 808

GUEST HOUSES

Camp Kula-Bed & Breakfast (AC bf CC G H MA NU OS) open year round
PO Box 111 ✉HI 96790 ☎ 878-0000
☎ 800-367-7546 (toll free) Fax: 878-2529
Centrally located on the lush slopes of the Haleakala Crater, near Haleakala National Park. No public transportation. Rental cars on Maui only.

Maui-Lahaina ☎ 808

HOTELS

Royal Lahaina Resort (AC B F bf CC g H msg pi wh)
2780 Kekaa Drive ✉HI 96761 ☎ 661-3611 ☎ (800) 44-ROYAL (toll free) Fax: 661-3538 E-Mail: hhr@hawaiihotels.com
Homepage: www.2maui.com
All rooms with shower/bath/WC, phone, TV, radio, safe. Rates US$ 215-750 per night. Bf buffet 11.50.

Wailuku Grand Hotel (B F GLM H OS) Open all year.
2080 Vineyard Street ✉HI 96793 ☎ 242-8191
In the center of Old Wailuku Town, 10 minutes from the beach. Shared bath, TV in room. Rates US$ 22.50-30.50.

Maui-Makawao ☎ 808

TRAVEL & TRANSPORT

Gay Tour Guide
☎ 572-1589 *A gay tour guide who provides tours by private car.*

APARTMENTS

Maui Network
PO Box 10 77 ✉HI 96768 ☎ 572-9555
Condominium vacation rentals.

Maui-Paia ☎ 808

HOTELS

Huleo Point Flower Farm (AC glm H pi wh)
PO Box 11 95 ✉HI 96779 ☎ 572-1850
E-Mail: huelopt@maui.net
Half an hour to the airport on the road to Hana. Close to natural pools and waterfalls. Rates from US$ 135/night (2 people). Gay owned farm with beautiful views and luxurious apartments/flats.

Maui-Puunene ☎ 808

TRAVEL & TRANSPORT

Royal Hawaiian Weddings (GLM) Mon-Fri 9-18 h
PO Box 424 ✉HI 96784 ☎ 659-1866
☎ (800) 659-1866 (toll free) Fax: 875-0623
Weddings for gays and lesbians from US$ 359,- up to 1.949,-.

GUEST HOUSES

Andrea`s Maui Condos (GLM H msg pi sa wh)
POBox 1411 ✉HI 96784 ☎ (800) 289-1522 Fax: 879-6430
E-Mail: andrea@maui.net Homepage: www.maui.net/~andrea
2 double rooms, 2 single rooms with bath/shower/WC, phone, TV, VCR, radio, own key.

RELIGIOUS GROUPS

New Liberation MCC
PO Box 347 ✉HI 96784 ☎ 879-6193

Molokai-Kalua Koi ☎ 808

HOTELS

Hana Plantation Houses (H)
PO Box 249 ✉96713 ☎ 248-7868 ☎ (800) 228-4262 (Toll free)

Oahu-Aiea ☎ 808

SEX SHOPS/BLUE MOVIES

C'n'C
Aiea Shopping Center ✉HI 96701 ☎ 487-2944

Susie's 0-24 h
Aiea Shopping Center ✉HI 96701 ☎ 486-3103

Oahu-Honolulu ☎ 808

TOURIST INFO

Hawaii National Tourist Office 2270 Kalakaua Avenue, Suite 801 ✉HI 96815 ☎ 923-1811 Fax: 923-8991

BARS

Hula`s Bar & Lei Stand (AC B D GLM MA S W) 10-2 h
134 KapahuluAve., Waikiki ✉HI 96815 *(at Waikiki Grand Hotel, 2nd Floor)* ☎ 923-0669
Weekly events. Also Internet Cafe.

In-Between (B G N) 15-2 h
2155 Lau'ula St., Waikiki *(Across Planet Hollywood in the walkway)* ☎ 926-7060

MEN'S CLUBS

Max's Gym (AC b CC DR f G sa sb OS VS WO YG) Mon-Sun 0-24 h
444 Hobron Lane, Eaton Square, 4th Floor *(in the shopping mal)*
☎ 951-8233
A private club for men, featuring a full bodybuilders gym with sports trainer equipment, free weights, steam room, sauna, showers, lockers, private video rooms and the outdoor Café Max.

DANCECLUBS

Angles Waikiki (AC B D G S) 10-2 h
2256 Kuhio Avenue ☎ 923-1130 *Popular.*
Fusion (AC B D G) 18-4 h
2260 Kuhio Avenue, Seaside (3rd floor) ✉HI 96815
☎ 924-2422 *Popular.*
Venus (B D glm S) 21-4 h
1349 Kapiolani Blvd. *(Below the China Hosue)* ☎ 951-8671
Live entertainment 6 nights a week, including male revues and femal impersonator shows. Gay Night every Sunday. Specials every night and many special surprise events.

RESTAURANTS

Cafe Sistina (B F glm)
1314 S. King Street ✉HI 96814 *(Interstate Building)*
☎ 526-0071
JM Restaurant (B F glm)
1040 Richards Street ✉HI 96813 *(downtown)* ☎ 524-8789
Pieces of Eight (B F g) Dinner 17-23 h, Bar -2 h
250 Lewers Street, Waikiki ✉HI 96815 ☎ 923-6646
Waikiki's original steak and seafood restaurant. Dinners served 17-23 daily; Piano-bar 19-24 h.
Sunset Grill (B F glm)
500 Ala Moana Boulevard ✉HI 96813 ☎ 521-4409

FASHION SHOPS

80% Straight Inc.
1917 Kalakaua Ave., Waikiki ☎ 941-9996
Fashion, gifts, books, accesories and more.

GALLERIES

Simonson (CC G)
4614 Kilauea Avenue, #100-330 ✉HI 96816 ☎ 737-6275
Fax: 737-6275 E-Mail: simonson@pixi.com
Homepage: www.douglassimonson.com
Paintings, drawings, prints of the male nude by Douglas Simonson. Mail and E-Mail order. Over 700 works on the web site.

TRAVEL & TRANSPORT

Pacific Ocean Holidays (GLM) 9-17 h, closed Sat Sun
PO Box 882 45, ✉HI 96830-6245 ☎ 923-2400 ☎ (800) 735-6600 (toll free) Fax: 923-2499 E-Mail: poh@gayhawaii.com
Gay Huwaii Vacation Packages.

VIDEO SHOPS

Diamond Head Video (AC CC g VS W) 9-24 h
870 Kapahulu Avenue ✉HI 96816 ☎ 735-6066

HOTELS

Coconut Plaza Hotel (glm H)
450 Lewers St. Waikiki ✉HI 96815 ☎ 923-8828
☎ (800) 882-9696 Fax: 923-3473
Homepage: www.coconutplaza.com *Complementary daily breakfast buffet, in-room kitchenette and outdoor pool.*
Honolulu Hotel (AC CC GLM H MA msg) 0-24 h
376 Kaiolu Street, Waikiki ✉HI 96815 ☎ 922-2824

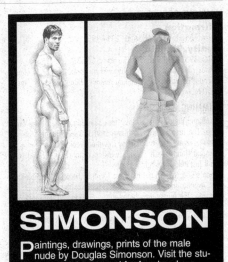

☎ (877) 922-3824 Fax: 922-5514 E-Mail: hulagirl@hula.net
Parking available, 2 blocks from the beach. Theme rooms with complete kitchen, Rates from $49 per night to $105 per night.
Waikiki Joy Hotel (glm H pi wh)
320 Lewer St. Waikiki ✉HI 96815 ☎ 923-2300
☎ (800) 733-5569 (toll free) Fax: 924-4010
All rooms and suites with private jacuzzi tubs, stereo system and air conditioning. Complimentary continental breakfast. Swimming pool, sauna, parking.

GUEST HOUSES

Cabana at Waikiki (bf G H wh OS)
2551 Cartwright Rd., Waikiki ✉HI 96815 ☎ 926-5555
☎ (877) 902-2121 (toll free) Fax: 926-5566
E-Mail: reservations@cabana-waikiki.com
Homepage: www.cabana-waikiki.com
15 charming single bedroom suites with kitchen. 8-man whirl pool.
Queen's Surf Vacation Rentals (GLM H)
C/O Waikiki Grand Hotel, 2nd Floor *(Waikiki)* ☎ 732-4368
☎ (888) 336-4368 (toll free) Homepage: www.ndhi.com/qs/
Gay owned and operated vacation rentals in the Waikiki Grand Hotel. newly renovated designer units, some with kitchenette, Take the elevator to Hula's Bar.

GENERAL GROUPS

Life Foundation (GLM)
233 Keawe St. Suite 226 ✉HI 96813-5405 ☎ 521-2437
☎ 521-1552 Homepage: www.lifefoundation.org
Provides free confidential services with HIV/AIDS, and HIV prevention program for the community.

RELIGIOUS GROUPS

Affirmation
PO Box 75131 ✉HI 96836 ☎ 239-4995

Dignity/Honolulu
PO Box 3956 ✉HI 96812-3956 ☎ 536-5536
Catholic communion lithurgy followed by social hour at St.Mark's Episcopal Church, 539 Kapahulu Avenue, Honolulu every Sun at 17.30 h.

SWIMMING

-Ala Moana Beach Park (Across from shopping center of the same name. The area where the beach start to curve at the Diamond Head end usually has a small gay crowd on weekdays.)
-Diamond Head Beach (Within walking distance of Waikiki. Gay area is just below the lighthouse.)
-Queen's Surf (G) (To get there, go towards Diamond Head on Kalakaua Avenue into Kapiolani Park and look for the pavilion on the right side. The grassy area between the pavilion and the snack bar: voilà! THE gay beach.)
-Waikiki Beach (Extremely long beach. The gay section is on the oceanside of the park, almost adjacent to Queen's Surf, approximately ½ of a mile east of the middle of the straight scene.)

Oahu-Kailua ☎ 808

CRUISING

-Kailua Beach Park (AYOR)
-Kona Market Place

Oahu-Kaneohe Bay ☎ 808

GUEST HOUSES

Ali'i Bluffs Windward Bed & Breakfast (bf glm H OS pi)
46-251 Ikiiki Street ✉HI 96744 ☎ 235-1124
☎ (800) 235-1151 (toll free) Fax: 235-1124
E-Mail: donm@lava.net
Rates from $60-75 according to season. Luxurious home with pool and large breakfast.

USA-Idaho

Northwest USA
Initials: ID
Time: GMT -7
Area: 216.456 km² / 88,530 sq mi.
Population: 1,210,000
Capital: Boise City

●Hetero- as well as homosexual oral and anal intercourse is prohibited in Idaho.

✷In Idaho ist hetero- wie homosexueller Oral- und Analverkehr verboten.

▲Dans l'Idaho, la fellation et la pénétration anale sont interdites, pour tous, homos et hétéros.

☆En Idaho las relaciones homosexuales y heterosexuales por vía oral o anal está prohibidas.

❖In Idaho sono vietati i rapporti orali ed anali tra eterosessuali e tra omosessuali.

Boise ☎ 208

BARS

Emerald City (B D GLM) 10-2 h
415 S. 9th Street ✉ID 83702 ☎ 342-5446

Partners (B gLM)
2210 Main Street ☎ 331-3551

8th Street Balcony Pub (B glm) 14-2 h
150 North 8th Street #224 ☎ 336-1313

CRUISING

-Ann Morrison Park (near archery range)
-Front Street

USA-Illinois

Great Lakes region USA
Initials: IL
Time: GMT -6
Area: 150.007 km² / 61,352 sq mi.
Population: 11,896,000
Capital: Springfield

Chicago ☎ 312

●Winter can be quite hard in Chicago. The climate is severe, but it fits the tough, blue collar image of this city, which makes its money with steel, meatpacking and transportation. Could that be the reason why the competition for *International Mr. Leather* is held in Chicago each year on the Memorial Day weekend? The city has been known as the slaughter house of the nation, earning the nickname „Porkopolis". Of course, Chicago also has more sophisticated sides, eg. Shop 'til you drop in Water Tower Place. By taking a boat tour called the Architecture River Cruise, you can get a good look at the architectural designs of Sullivan, van der Rohe, Jahn or Wright. The great fire of 1871 destroyed much of downtown; the city has been rebuilt in a sleek, functional, modern style. The gay scene is concentrated around New Town, which is also known as Boys Town. A name that suits us just fine. Most of the gay bars and businesses are situated along North Halsted Street, between Barry Avenue and Grace Street. One highlight of the summer festival season is Nort-Halsted Market Days, a street festival held in late July or early August. The gay scene is quite diverse but not as glamorous as New York or LA. Although gay nightlife may not be very spectacular, there is also less attitude and snobbery than in some other cities. People in the Midwest tend to be friendly and outgoing. The easiest way to get around town is on the rapid transit trains, but you will need a car to visit the gay resorts of *Douglas* and *Saugatuck*, which are located on the eastern shore of Lake Michigan.

✷Nun gut: die Winter in Chicago können recht hart sein. Aber als odentlicher Chicagoer verläßt man seine Stadt dann selbstverständlich nicht. Das Wetter ist eben rauh, doch das paßt zum Arbeiter-Image dieser Stadt, die ihr Geld mit Stahl, Fleisch und Transporten verdient. Ist das vielleicht der Grund dafür, daß hier alljährlich am Memorial-Day-Wochenende die Wahlen zum *International Mr. Leather* stattfinden?
Genausogut könnte es daran liegen, daß Chicago das Schlachthaus der Nation war und gerne „Porkopolis" (pork, engl. = Schweinefleisch) genannt wurde. Und aus den Häuten Tausender toter Tiere muß man doch was machen können, oder?
Aber selbstverständlich hat Chicago auch milde Seiten: z.B. „Shop 'til you drop" im *Water Tower Place*. Vom Boot des *Architecture River Cruise* aus kann man die Werke von Sullivan, van der Rohe,

Jahn oder Wright betrachten. Kein Wunder also, daß sich diese Stadt unschrill und schnörkellos präsentiert, verbrannte doch die Historie im großen Feuer von 1871.
Die Chicagoer Szene konzentriert sich in *New Town* oder netter formuliert *Boystown*. Entlang der North Halsted Street findet sich hier zwischen Barry Avenue und Grace Street der größte Teil der schwulen Einrichtungen. Spektakuläre Auftritte sollte man von der Chicagoer Szene aber nicht erwarten. Der Outdoor-Höhepunkt ist z.B. das Straßenfest *NortHalsted Market Days* Ende Juli/Anfang August.
So unspektakulär die Szene bei aller Reichhaltigkeit auch ist, so warmherzig sind doch die Menschen *in Middle-West*. Was auf den Aussenstehenden rauh wirken mag, entpuppt sich bei näherem Hinsehen als Empfang mit offenen Armen.
In der Stadt kommt man mit der Hochbahn gut zu recht. Ein Auto benötigt man höchstens für einen Besuch der schwulen Badeorte *Douglas* und *Saugatuck*, die auf der anderen Seite des Lake Michigan liegen.

▲ D'accord, à Chicago, les hivers sont plutôt durs, mais tout habitant de Chicago qui se respecte ne met pas la clé sous le paillasson pour autant! Le climat est rude, ce qui correspond bien à l'image de cette ville industrielle qui a fait fortune dans les aciers, la viande et les transports. Rude et dure: voilà Chicago! Rien d'étonnant, donc, à ce qu'on organise ici tous les ans pour le week-end du Memorial Day les élections de M. Cuir International. Chicago, c'est aussi les abattoirs de la nation, ce qui lui vaut le nom de „Porkopolis". Et que fait-on des peaux des milliers de cochons égorgés chaque année? Des blousons et des pantalons de cuir! La boucle est bouclée.
Mais Chicago a aussi de bons côtés, comme p. ex. le „Shop 'til you drop" dans le Water Tower Place. Depuis le bâteau de l'"Architecture River Cruise", on peut admirer les réalisations de Sullivan, van der Rohe, Jahn ou Wright. Le grand incendie de 1871 a entièrement détruit le centre-ville. Le nouveau Chicago est donc fonctionnel, lisse et sans fioriture.
Les quartiers gays sont dans le district de Newton qu'on appelle aussi „Boystown", non sans un sourire entendu. C'est le long de Halsted Street (entre Grace Street et Barry Avenue) que l'on trouve la plupart des établissements gays. N'attendez rien de spectaculaire de la vie gay de Chicago! La plus belle fête en plein air a lieu fin juillet/début août: les „NortHalsted Market Days".
Si le Chicago gay n'a rien d'extravagant, les gays, eux, sont en revanche très gentils et ouverts, à l'image des gens du Middle West. Même si, au premier abord, on peut avoir l'impression d'avoir affaire à des rustres.
Le métro aérien est le meilleur moyen de se déplacer en ville. Une voiture n'est indispensable que pour aller voir Douglas et Saugatuck qui sont les stations balnéaires gays sur l'autre rive du Michigan.

☆ Hay que reconocer que los inviernos en Chicago pueden ser muy duros. Pero para sus habitantes no es ningúna razón de dejar su ciudad. El clima es duro, al igual que la imagen de la ciudad con sus obreros que ganan sus sueldos con acero, carne y transportes. La industria de carne de cerdo y el apodo „Porcopolis" (porc=en inglés carne de cerdo) no han sido una coincidencia. Quiza sea por ello que anualmente en el Menorial-Day-Weekend se lleva a cabo la elección del *International Mr. Gay Leather*. Pero Chicago tiene mucho más ofrecer, p. ej. „Shop'til you drop" en el *Water Tower Place*. Los trabajos artísticos de Sullivan, van der Rohe, Jahn o Wright, pueden ser observados desde el barco de *Architecture River Cruise*. El ambiente gay se concentra en el *New Town* que se conoce también como „Boystown". A largo de la North Halsted Street se encuentran la major parte de los establecimientos gay. El ambiente de la ciudad no es nada espectacular. Uno de los puntos

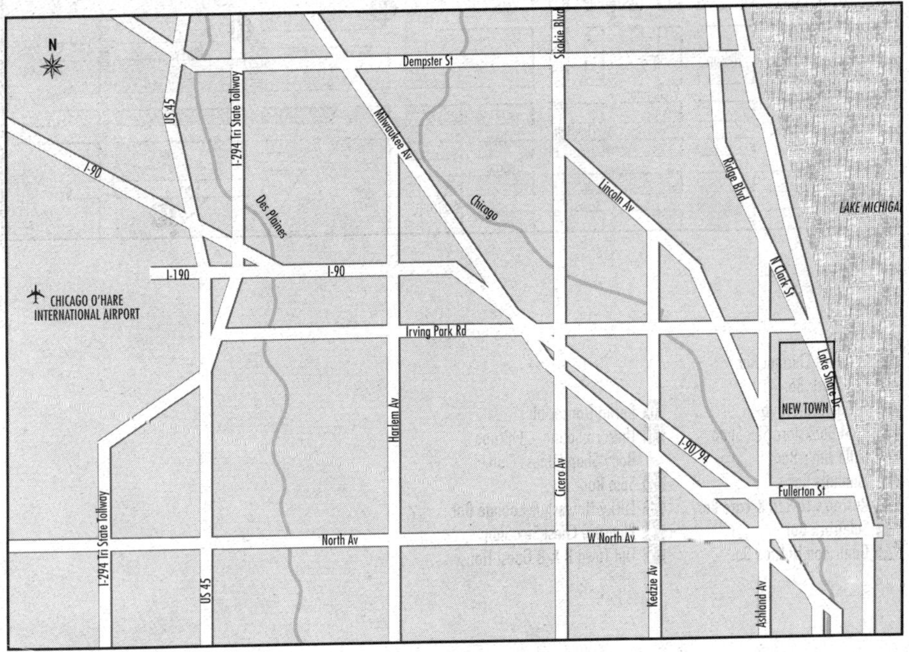

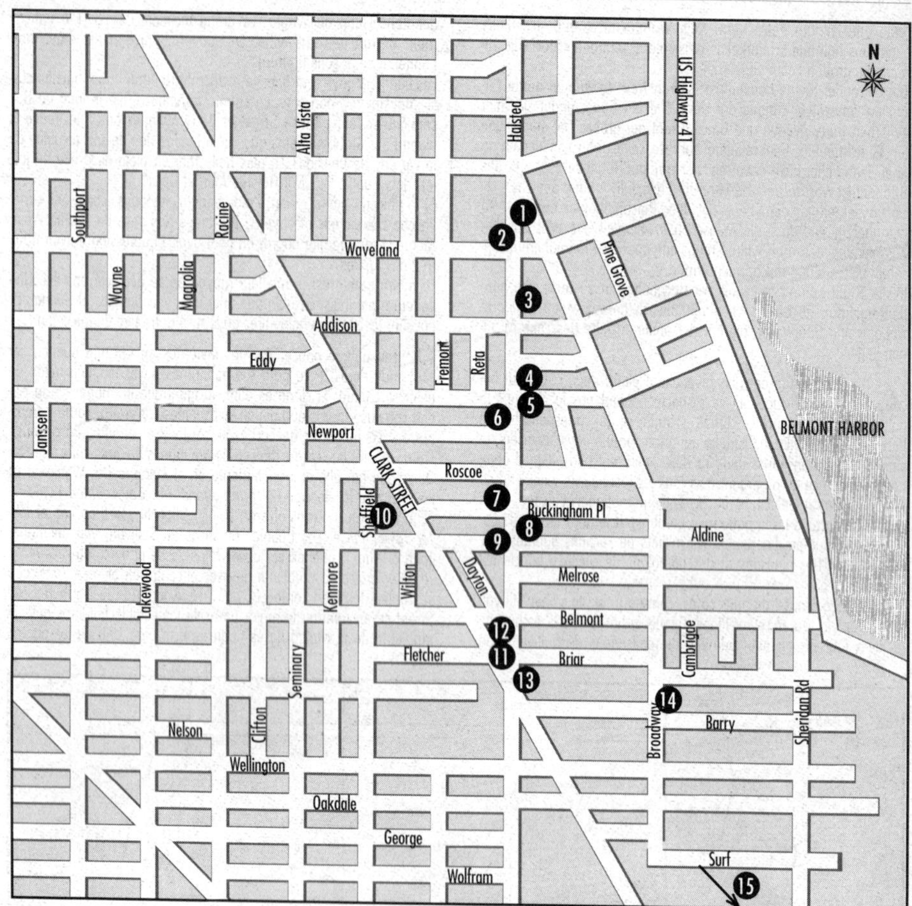

CHICAGO
NEW TOWN

1 Charlie's Chicago Bar
2 Cell Block Bar
3 Fusion Danceclub
4 RAM Bookstore Sex Shop
5 Little Jim's Bar
6 Manhole Bar
7 Roscoe's Tavern & Café Bar
8 Sidetrack Bar
9 Gentry on Halsted Bar
10 Berlin Danceclub
11 Unicorn Sauna + Chicago Body Shop Fitness Club
12 Spin Bar
13 Lucky Horseshoe Lounge Bar
14 Pleasure Chest Sex Shop
15 Old Town B & B Guest House

festivos culminantes es la fiesta callejera *North Halsted Market Days* a finales de Julio e inicios de Agosto. La actitud agradable y amistosa de las personas en *Middle West* se refleja en la tranquilidad del ambiente gay. Dentro de la ciudad, el medio de transporte más utilizado lo es el metro. Un auto sería de gran ayuda si se desean visitar los balnearios *Douglas* y *Saugatuck* que se encuentran al otro lado del lago Michigan. En general la ciudad presenta hoy en día una imagen moderna y funcional, ya que en el gran fuego de 1871 se destruyó la gran parte de sus edifícios históricos.

❖ L'inverno a Chicago può essere veramente freddo, ma un verace abitante di Chicago naturalmente non lascia la città per questa ragione. Il tempo rigido è consono all'immagine operaia di questa città che guadagna i propri soldi con l'acciaio, la carne ed i trasporti; è forse questa la ragione per la quale proprio qui ha luogo durante il Memorial-Day-Weekend l'elezione dell'*International Mr Leather*? Chicago era in passato il macello del paese, e per questo veniva chiamata „Porkopolis". E con le pelli delle migliaia di animali uccisi bisognava pur far qualcosa, non è vero? Naturalmente Chicago ha anche lati più moderati: ad esempio „Shop 'til you drop" nella *Water Tower Place*. Dalla nave dell'*Architecture River Cruise* è possibile osservare le opere di Sullivan, van der Rohe, Jahn o Wright. Dal punto di vista architettonico Chicago si presenta monotona, senza fronzoli, perché nel 1871 fu vittima di un grave incendio. L'ambiente gay si concentra nella *New Town* o, meglio detto, nella *boystown*. La maggior parte dei locali gay si trova tra la Barry Avenue e la Grace street lungo la North Halsted street. Tuttavia non aspettatevi niente di spettacolare. Il culmine è la festa all'aperto di *North Halsted Market Days* alla fine di luglio, inizio di agosto. Se nel Middle West l'ambiente non è spettacolare le persone sono in compenso calde ed affettuose: all'inizio sono un po' riservate ma poi vi accoglieranno a braccia aperte. Per girare la città sono sufficienti i mezzi pubblici; vi servirà un'auto solo se visiterete le stazioni balneari di *Douglas* e *Saugatuck* situate sulla sponda opposta del lago Michigan.

GAY INFO

Gay Chicago Magazine
3121 North Broadway ✉IL 60657 ☎ (773) 327-7271 Fax: (773) 327-0112 E-Mail: gaychimag@aol.com
Entertainment guide for the gay community, containing calendar of events, photos, columns and personal ads. Published weekly, 80-96 pages, US$ 2. Subscriptions available (80 annually, 40 semiannually).

Lambda Publications Inc.
1115 West Belmont, Suite 2-D ✉IL 60657 ☎ (773) 871-7610 Fax: 871-7609 E-Mail: outlines@suba.com
Homepage: www.suba.com/~outlines
The Voice of the Gay & Lesbian Community: Outlines Weekly, Nightlines, En La Vida, OUT! Resource Guide, Clout! Business Report and Blacklines.

Leather Archives and Museum (GLM LJ) Sat 14-24 h (and by appointment)
5007 North Clark Street ✉IL 60640 *(2 blocks East of Ashland at Devon)* ☎ (773) 275-1570 Fax: 545-6753
One of the largest collection in the world open to serious research by appointment only.

Positively Aware
c/o Test Positive Aware, 1317 West Belmont ✉IL 60657
☎ (773) 404-8726

TOURIST INFO

Chicago Convention & Visitor Bureau
2301 South Lake Shore Drive ✉IL 60616 ☎ 567-8500
Fax: 567-8533

Concierge Exclusif (CC GLM) Mon-Fri 9-17 h
75 East Wacker Drive, Suite 3600 ✉IL 60601 ☎ 849-3604
Fax: 857-0805 E-Mail: kylecaskey@aol.com.
Homepage: http://members.aol.com/kylecaskey/index.html
Assistance with obtaining theatre/concert/sport tickets, limousine transportation, hotel accomodations, restaurant reservations, massage services, tours, car rentals and more.

BARS

Annex 3 (AC B CC G MA N s W) 12-2 h
3160 North Clark Street ✉IL 60657 ☎ (773)327-5969
Very nice and comfortable.

Baton Show Lounge (! AC B GLM MA STV) 20-4, Sat -5 h, closed Mon
436 North Clark Street/Hubbard Street ✉IL 60610 ☎ 644-5269
Great shows!

Big Chicks (B glm s tv) 12-2 h
5024 North Sheridan Road ✉IL 60640 ☎ (773) 728-5511

Buck's Saloon (B G OS) 10-2, Sat 9-2, Sun 12-? h
3439 North Halsted Street ✉IL 60657 ☎ 525-1125

Buddies' Bar & Restaurant (A AC B bf F GLM lj) 7-2 h, Sun 12-2 h, dining room closed Mon
3301 North Clark/Aldine ✉IL 60657 ☎ 477-4066

Cell Block (B d DR G LJ MA VS W) Mon-Fri 16-2 h, Sat 14-? h, Sun -20 h
3702 North Halsted ✉IL 60614 ☎ (773) 665-8064

Charlies Chicago (B d G) Sun Wed-Fri 15-4, Sat -5 h
3726 N. Broadway ✉IL 60613 ☎ (773) 871-8887

Charmer's (AC B GLM MA N) Mon-Fri 16-2, Sat 16-3, Sun 12-2 h
1502 West Jarvis Avenue ✉IL 60626 ☎ 465-2811
Neighbourhood bar with friendly atmosphere.

Chicago Eagle (AC B DR G LJ MA) 20-4, Sat -5 h
5015 North Clark Street ✉IL 60640 *(next door to Man's Country Baths)* ☎ (773) 728-0050
Home of International Mr. Leather. Inc.

Clark's on Clark (B GLM MA) 16-4, Sat 16-5, Sun 20-4 h
5001 North Clark Street ✉IL 60640 ☎ (773) 728-2373

Closet (AC B D GLM VS) 14-4, Sat Sun 12-4 h
3325 North Broadway ✉IL 60657 ☎ 477-8533

Cocktail (AC B GLM MA N VS W) 16-2, WE 14-2 h
3359 North Halsted Street ✉IL 60657 ☎ (773) 871-8123
Popular.

Dandy's (B GLM S) 12-? h
3729 N. Halsted Street ✉IL 60613 ☎ 525-1200
Piano bar.

Different Strokes (AC B GLM MA N OS) Sun-Fri 12-2 h, Sat -3 h
4923 North Clark Street ✉IL 60640 ☎ (773) 989-1958
Pleasant neighborhood bar. Comfortable setting with very friendly staff.

Escapades (B D GLM VS) 20-4, Sat -5, Sun 14-4 h
6301 South Harlem ✉IL 60638 ☎ 229-0886

Flash! (B D GLM S) 19-2 h
1450 E. Algonquin, Schaumburg *(adjacent to 1450 East)*
☎ (708) 925-9696

Gentry (AC B CC G MA S VS W) Sun-Fri 16-2 h, Sat -3 h
440 North State Street ✉IL 60610

Gentry on Halsted (AC B CC G MA S VS W) Sun-Fri 16-2 h, Sat -3 h
3320 North Halsted Street ✉IL 60657

Hideaway II (B D G S VS WE YG) 16-2 h
7301 West Roosevelt Road, Forest Park ✉IL 60130 *(near Harlem Avenue)* ☎ (708) 771-4459
Chicago's most popular bar on Mon night.

Inn Exile (A AC B d G MA N s VS W) Sun-Fri 20-2 h, Sat -3 h
5758 West 65th Street ✉IL 60638-5504 *(near Midway Airport)*
☎ (773) 582-3510

Jeffery Pub (AC B D GLM MA N VS) Mon-Sat 10.30-4 h
7041 South Jeffrey Boulevard *(Jackson Park in Chicago's south shore neighborhood)* ☎ 363-8555
African American Bar.

Legacy 21 (AC B D GLM MA N S VS WE) 20-4 h, Fri Sat piano player
3042 West Irving Park Road ✉IL 60618 ☎ 588-9405

Little Jim's (AC B G LJ MA N r VS) 9-4, Sun 12- h
3501 North Halsted Street ✉IL 60657 *(at Cornelia Street)*
☎ (773) 871-6116
Very popular neighborhood bar. Large afternoon crowds daily.

Lucky Horseshoe Lounge. The (! AC B G MA S SNU sol T) 14-2, Sat 12-3, Sun -2 h, nightly dancers
3169 North Halsted Street ✉IL 60657 ☎ (773) 404-3169

Manhandler (AC B G MA OS) 12-4, Sat -5 h
1948 North Halsted Street ✉IL 60614 ☎ 871-3339
Friendly staff. Warm atmosphere.

Manhole (B D G LJ S VS) Mon 19.30-?, Tue-Sun 20-? h (best 1.30-4 h)
3458 North Halsted Street ✉IL 60657 *(opposite Little Jim's)*
☎ (773) 975-9244
Front bar, at the back bar & disco Fri Sat dress code leather, rubber or shirtless.

Marigold Bowling Arcade (B G)
828 West Grace ✉IL 60613 ☎ 935-8183

Mr. B's (AC B d G MA N) Wed-Sat 13-2 h, Sun-Thu 14-2 h
606 State Line Road, Calumet City *(On Illinois/Indiana state line)*
☎ (708) 862-1221

North End. The (AC B G MA N S VS WE) Mon-Fri 15-? h, Sat Sun 14-? h
3733 North Halsted Street ✉IL 60613 *(near Bradley Pl.)*
☎ (773) 477-7999
Pool tables. Male dancers occasionally.

Nutbush (AC B d GLM MA N S VS WE) Mon-Fri 15-2 h, Sat-Sun 13-2 h
7201 Franklin, Forest Park ✉L 60606 *(at Harlem Avenue)*
☎ (708) 366-5117
Located near suburb of Oak Park.

Off The Line (B gLM VS) Mon-Fri 17-2 h, Sat 12-2 h, Sun 12-2 h
1829 W. Montrose ✉IL 60613 ☎ 528-3253

Pour House (AC B D GLM MA N WE) 20-4 h, closed Mon
103 155th Place, Calumet City ✉IL 60409 ☎ (708) 891-3980

Roscoe's Tavern & Café (! A AC B D F GLM S OS VS YG) Mon-Fri 14-2 h, Sat-Sun 12-2 h
3356 North Halsted Street ✉IL 60657 ☎ (773) 281-3355
One of the most popular bars and dance clubs in Chicago. A must.

Second Story Bar (B G)
157 East Ohio Street ✉IL 60611 ☎ 923-9536
Sidetrack (! AC B GLM OS S VS WE YG) Mon-Fri 15-2 h, Sat Sun 14-2 h
3349 North Halsted Street ✉IL 60657 *(two doors south of Roscoe's)* ☎ (773) 477-9189
This video-bar always attracts a very good and attractive crowd, especially after 21 h, and Sun late afternoons.
Spin (B Glm D VS) 16-2 h
800 West Belmont ✉IL 60657 ☎ (773) 327-7711
Temptations (B D GLM S) 16-4 h
10235 W. Grand, Franklin Park ✉IL 60131 ☎ (708) 455-0008
Touché (B G LJ) Mon-Fri 17-2 h, Sat Sun 15-? h
6412 North Clark Street ✉IL 60626 ☎ 465-7400
Traveler's Rest (B G) Mon-Sat 10-? h, Sun 12-? h
1138 W. Granville ✉IL 60660 ☎ 262-4225
1450 East (B D GLM VS) 17-2 h
1450 E. Algonquin, Schaumburg ✉IL 60173 *(adjacent to Flash!)* ☎ (708) 925-9696
2nd Story Bar (AC B G) Mon-Fri 12-2 h, Sat-Sun 15-2 h
157 East Ohio Street ✉IL 60611 ☎ 923-9536

DANCECLUBS

Berlin (AC B D GLM SNU STV VS W YG) Sun 18-4, Mon 20-4, Tue-Fri 17-4, Sat 20-5 h
954 West Belmont Avenue ✉IL 60657 ☎ (773) 348-4975
Unique and worth stopping by. Always packed late in the evening. Best Thu after 22 h.
Clubhouse (B D G) Fri-Sat/Mon 23-? h
440 North Halsted Street ✉IL 60622 ☎ 421-3588
Fusion (AC B CC D GLM MA S SNU STV W WE) Fri 22-4, Sat 22-5 h
3631 North Halsted Street ✉IL 60613 *(gangway entrance)* ☎ 975-6622
Generator (B D GLM) 21-2 h
306 N. Halsted ✉IL 60661 ☎ 243-8889
Neo (AC B D glm S VS WE YG) 21-4 h
2350 North Clark Street/Fullerton ✉IL 60614 ☎ 528-2622
Progressive music.
Numbers (B D G OS vs) 16-4 h
6406 Clark Street ✉IL 60626 ☎ 743-5772
Vortex (B D Glm S VS YG) Wed-Sun 21-4 h
3631 North Halsted Street ✉IL 60613 ☎ 975-6622
WE adm.US$ 6 after 22 h.

RESTAURANTS

Big Daddies (F G) 11-? h
2914 North Broadway ✉IL 60657 ☎ (773) 929-0922
Chicago Diner (B F g) 3411 North Halsted Street ✉IL 60657 ☎ (773) 935-6696
Vegetarian cuisine.
Cornelia (B F GLM)
748 West Cornelia Avenue ✉IL 60657 ☎ (773) 935-7793
Fireplace Inn (B F g)
1448 North Wells Street ✉IL 60610 ☎ 664-5264
Mama Mimi (B F g)
111 West Hubbard Street ✉IL 60610 ☎ 321-0776
Rhumba (B F glm)
3631 N. Halsted ☎ (773) 975-2345
Sottosantos (B F g)
5025 North Clark Street ✉IL 60640 ☎ (773) 878-6360

SHOWS

Bailiwick's Pride Series (AC CC GLM S) Performances Thu-Sun
1229 West Belmont ✉IL 60657 ☎ (773) 883-1090
Greenhouse for gay and lesbian theater and performance.

Zebra Crossing Theater (GLM S)
4223 North Lincoln ✉IL 60618 ☎ (773) 248-6401
Year-round gay-lesbian theater.

SEX SHOPS/BLUE MOVIES

Banana Video 4923 N. Clark ✉IL 60640 *(2nd floor)*
☎ (773) 561-8322

Bijou Theatre (AC DR G OG SNU VS) 0-24 h
1349 North Wells Street/Schiller Street ✉IL 60610
☎ 337-3404 *$ 13 admission, $ 1 membership.*

Cupid`s Treasures (CC glm MA TV W WE) Mon-Thu 11-2 h, Fri Sat 11-1 h
3519 North Halstead Street ✉IL 60657 ☎ (773) 348-3884

Pleasure Chest (g) 12-24 h
3143 North Broadway ✉IL 60657 ☎ (773) 525-7151

RAM Bookstore (AC CC DR G MA VS)
3511 North Halsted Street ✉IL 60657 ☎ (773) 525-9528

SAUNAS/BATHS

Man's Country (AC f G MA NU S sb SNU VS wh) 0-24 h
5015 North Clark Street ✉IL 60640 *(next to Chicago Eagle)*
☎ (773) 878-2069
Bath house and entertainment complex. Nude strip shows on Fri and Sat.

Steamworks. The (AC CC DR f G MA P sa sb VS wh WO) 0-24 h
3246 North Halsted Street ✉IL 60657 ☎ (773) 929-6080

Unicorn Club (AC CC f G MA P sa sb VS wh WO YG) 0-24 h
3246 North Halsted Street ✉IL 60657 ☎ (773) 929-6081
Membership required, but travellers welcome. Perhaps one of the best saunas in Chicago. Friendly staff. Attracts good-looking crowd. Two floors. Condoms provided.

FITNESSTUDIOS

Chicago Body Shop Fitness Center (AC CC f G MA P sa sb VS wh WO YG) 5-22, Sat Sun -20 h
3246 North Halsted ✉IL 60657 ☎ (773) 248-7717

BOOK SHOPS

Leslie's (G) 10-1 h
738 N. Clark ☎ 751-9672
Videos and books.

RAM Bookstore & Video (GLM)
3511 North Halsted Street ☎ (773) 525-9528
Gay bookstore and video shop.

Unabridged Bookstore (GLM) Mon-Fri 11-21 h, Sat 10-19 h, Sun 11-18 h
3251 North Broadway Street ✉IL 60657 ☎ (773) 883-9119
Mixed bookstore with large gay/lesbian section.

GIFT & PRIDE SHOPS

Gay Mart
3457 N. Halsted ✉IL 60657 ☎ (773) 929-4272
Gifts and cards.

LEATHER & FETISH SHOPS

Eagle Leathers and Piercing (g) 16-24 h, closed on Mon
5005 North Clark Street ✉IL 60640 *(next door to Chicago Eagle)*

Male Hide Leathers, Inc (GLM) Tue-Thu 12-20, Fri Sat 12-24 h
2816 North Lincoln Avenue ✉IL 60657 ☎ (773) 929-0069

VIDEO SHOPS

R.J's Videos
3452 N. Halsted ✉IL 60657 ☎ (773) 871-1810

Specialty Video Films (G VS)
3221 North Broadway ✉IL 60657 ☎ (773) 248-3434

HOTELS

Abbott Hotel (AC glm H)
721 West Belmont, ✉IL 60657 ☎ (773) 248-2700

Cass Hotel (H)
640 North Wabash Avenue ✉IL 60611 ☎ 787-4030 ☎ (800) 2277-850 Fax: 787-8544
Central location. Rates from US$ 49.

City Suites Hotel Chicago (g H MA) 0-24 h
933 West Belmont Street ✉IL 60657 ☎ (773) 404-3400 Fax: (773) 404-3405
Close to gay bars.

Diplomat Hotel (AC glm H vs)
3208 North Sheffield ✉IL 60657 ☎ (773) 549-6800

Park Brompton Hotel (g H MA) 7.30-23.30 h
528 West Brompton Place ✉IL 60657 *(close to gay bars)*
☎ (773) 404-3499 Fax: 404-3495
Rates from US$ 79. Recommended.

Surf Hotel (g H MA) 555 West Surf Street ✉IL 60657
☎ (773) 528-8400 Fax: (773) 528-8483

GUEST HOUSES

Deeks Den (AC CC G wh) Office: 9-23 h
1919 West Greenleaf Avenue ✉IL 60626-2305 ☎ (773) 381-1118 Fax: (773) 381-1116 E-Mail: Deeksden@hotmail.com
Rates US$ 80-95.

Old Town Bed & Breakfast (AC bf CC F G H lj MA msg NU OS sol wh WO)
1442 North North Park Avenue ✉IL 60610-1227
☎ 440-9268 Fax: 440-2378
Luxurious Art Deco mansion with only four guest suites. Large common rooms, restaurant kitchen, small gym, private roof decks, office and penthouse sitting room.

Villa Toscana Guest House (AC bf CC GLM H MA OS)
3447 North Halsted Street ✉IL 60657-2414 ☎ (773) 404-2643
Fax: (773) 404-3488 E-Mail: rochus1@ibm.net
7 rooms with TV, telephone, some with shared bath. Continental bf. Garden.

PRIVATE ACCOMODATION

The Caritas Network
75 East Wacker Drive, Suite 3600 ✉IL 60601 ☎ 857-0801
Fax: 857-0805 E-Mail: Gaycaritas@aol.com
Homepage: www.freedomweb.com/caritas/
Caritas offers bed & breakfast accommodations in private gay homes throughout America . Each host is carefully screened and inspected by Caritas, reasonable prices,

GENERAL GROUPS

Bear Naked Chicago
O Box 3506 ✉IL 60532

Black & White Men Together
☎ (773) 334-2012

Chicago Area G&L Chamber of Commerce
3712 North Broadway ✉IL 60613-4198 ☎ (888) 452-4262
Homepage: www.glchamber.org
Business owner association.

Chicago Area Republican Gay Organization
☎ (773) 271-1777

Chicago Professional Networking Association Meets at Ann Sather's Restaurant,
929 W. Belmont990 W. Fullerton Avenue ✉IL 60614
☎ (773) 296-2767
Non-profit business and social networking. Call for more information.

Committee of Black Gay Men
☎ (773) 973-5851

GREAT (G) 18-24 h
☎ (773) 248-5188

Illinois Gay and Lesbian Task Force (IGLTF)
☎ (708) 445-1164

FETISH GROUPS

Chicago Cossacks
PO Box 25 12 ✉IL 60690

Chicago Hellfire Club
PO Box 54 26 ✉IL 60680

International Mr. Leather, Inc. (LJ)
5015 North Clark Street ✉IL 60640 ☎ (773) 878-3844
☎ (800) 545-6753 Fax: (773) 878-5184 E-Mail: info@imrl.com
Homepage: www.imrl.com
Now in its 22nd year, May 26-29, 2000.

HEALTH GROUPS

AIDS Foundation of Chicago
411 South Wells, Ste. 300 ✉IL 60607 ☎ 922-2322
Fax: 922-2916

AIDS Hotline 10-22 h
☎ (800) 243-2437

AIDS Pastoral Care Network 9-17 h or by appointment
☎ (773) 975-5180

Cook County Hospital AIDS Project
☎ 633-7810 ☎ 633-5182 (Appointments)

Stop AIDS Chicago
909 West Belmont ✉IL 60657 *(2nd floor)* ☎ (773) 871-3300
Fax: (773) 871-3300 *Discussion group.*

Test Positive Aware
1317 West Belmont ✉IL 60657 ☎ (773) 404-8726
HIV and fellowship & information network.

CRUISING

-Montrose Harbor (between Montrose Street and Foster Street. Cruisy from dusk-11 h.)
-Belmont Street „rocks" at the lakefront (WE afternoons during summer)
-Halsted and Broadway Streets (between Belmont and Addison. Many gay shops and restaurants)

Peoria ☎ 309

BARS

Quench Room (B GLM) 17-1 h
631 West Main Street ✉IL 61606 ☎ 676-1079

SEX SHOPS/BLUE MOVIES

Swingers World
335 Adams Street ☎ 676-9275

CRUISING

-Bradley Park
-Detweiller Park (days)
-West Main Street (between 600 and 1600 blocks, by foot or car)

Springfield ☎ 217

BARS

New Dimensions (B D GLM VS) 21-? h
3036 Peoria Road ✉IL 62702 ☎ 544-3861
Smokey's Den (B D GLM) Sun-Thu 16-1, Fri Sat 16-3 h
411 East Washington Street ✉IL 62701 ☎ 522-0301

SEX SHOPS/BLUE MOVIES

Expo One Books
300 North 5th Street ✉IL 62701 ☎ 544-5145

CRUISING

-Douglas Park (on I-94 North near Zion)
-Lake Springfield

USA-Indiana

Central Northeast USA
Initials: IN
Time: GMT -5
Area: 94.328 km² / 38,580 sq mi.
Population: 5,864,000
Capital: Indianapolis

Bloomington ☎ 812

GAY INFO

The Bloomington Beacon 20-24 h
PO Box 3307 ✉IN 47402 ☎ 336-4299

BARS

Bullwinkle's (B D GLM S) 17-3 h, closed Sun
201 South College ✉IN 47404 ☎ 334-3232
The Other Bar (B GLM) 16-2 h, closed Sun
414 South Walnut Street ✉IN 47401 ☎ 332-0033

SEX SHOPS/BLUE MOVIES

College Avenue Adult Bookstore (glm) 0-24 h
1013 North College Street ✉IN 47401 ☎ 332-4160
Large gay section, very cruisy.

Fort Wayne ☎ 219

GAY INFO

Ga Out-Reach 24 h
☎ 456-6560
Gay/Lesbian Helpline Mon-Thu 19-22, Fri Sat 19-24, Sun 18.30-21 h
☎ 744-1199

BARS

After Dark (B GLM MA N S VS) Mon-Sat 18-3.30 h, closed Sun
231 Pearl Street ✉IN 46802 ☎ 424-6130
Riff Raff's (B F Glm N W) Mon-Sat 16-3 h, closed Sun
2809 W Main Street ☎ 436-4166

Indianapolis ☎ 317

GAY INFO

Out & About Indiana
133 West Market Street #105 ✉IN 46204-2801 ☎ 923-8550
Fax: 923-8505 *Info service and social club for gays and lesbians.*
Outlines
133 West Market Street, #105 ✉IN 46204 ☎ 923-8550
Fax: 923-8505
Weekly publication
The Word
501 Madison Avenue, Suite 307 ☎ 725-8840 Fax: 687-8840
Monthly publication

BARS

Brothers Bar & Grill (B F GLM)
822 North Illinois ✉IN 46204 ☎ 636-1020
Illusions (B G MA N S)
1446 East Washington ☎ 266-0535
Our Place (B G MA OS) 16-3 h, closed Sun
231 East 16th Street ✉IN 46202 ☎ 638-8138
The Ten (B gLM N STV)
1218 North Pennsylvania
☎ 638-5802
Best drag shows in town
Utopia (B d F gLM WE) 17-2, Fri Sat -3 h
924 North Pennsylvania ✉IN 46204 ☎ 638-0215
The Varsity Lounge (AC B bf CC F GLM MA WE) Mon-Sat 10-3, Sun 12-0.30 h
1517 North Pennsylvania Street ✉IN 46202 ☎ 635-9998
Also restaurant.
501 Tavern (B G LJ MA) 17.30-3 h, closed Sun
501 North College ☎ 632-2100

CAFES

The Abbey (b bf f glm)
771 North Massachusetts Avenue ☎ 269-8426

DANCECLUBS

Metro & Colours (B D F GLM OS)
707 Massachusetts Avenue ✉IN 46204 ☎ 639-6022
The Unicorn Club (B D G p SNU YG)
122 West 13th Street ✉IN 46202 ☎ 262-9195
The Vogue (B D glm MA) Sun (G)
6259 North College Avenue ✉IN 46220 ☎ 259-7029

RESTAURANTS

Aesop's Tables (B F glm)
600 North Massachusetts Avenue ☎ 631-0055
Good Mediterranean food
Canary Café (b F glm)
621 Ft. Wayne Avenue ✉IN 46204 ☎ 635-6168

SEX SHOPS/BLUE MOVIES

Bookland (glm)
137 West Market ☎ 639-9864
Adult books
115 New Jersey (G)
115 New Jersey
Magazines and videos

SAUNAS/BATHS

Club Indianapolis (AC CC G MA P pi sa sb sol wh WO) 0-24 h
620 North Capitol Avenue ✉IN 46204 ☎ 635-5796
The Works (B G H MA OS P sa sb sol VS wh) 4
120 North Keystone Avenue ✉IN 46205 ☎ 547-9210

BOOK SHOPS

Borders Books (glm)
5612 Castleton Corner Lane ✉IN 46250 ☎ 849-8660

Out Word Bound ...books with pride Mon-Thu 11.30-21 h, Fri 11.30-23 h, Sat 10-23 h, Sun 12-18 h
625 N. East Street *(Downtown)* ☎ 951-9100
Specialized in lesbian & gay books plus cards, magazines, pride items, gifts, mainstream books etc.

GENERAL GROUPS

Country Club (GLM)
PO Box 44469 ✉IN 46204
☎ 579-9171 *Country and western dancing group*
Fellowship
PO Box 2331 ✉IN 46206 ☎ 921-9713
Support group for lesbians and gay men
Indianapolis Men's Chorus
c/o Crossroads Performing Arts ☎ 931-9464
PFLAG-Parents and Friends of Lesbians and Gays
☎ 545-7034

FETISH GROUPS

Circle City Leather
PO Box 1632 ✉IN 46206

HEALTH GROUPS

Circle City AIDS Coalition
3951 North Meridian Street, Suite 200 ✉IN 46208 ☎ 632-0123
Damien Center 8.30-20.30 h
1350 North Pennsylvania Street ✉IN 46202 ☎ 632-0123
Fax: 632-4362 Homepage: www.damien.org
AIDS care center

HELP WITH PROBLEMS

Indianapolis Youth Group
☎ 541-8726

RELIGIOUS GROUPS

Dignity Indiana
PO Box 431 ✉IN 46206 ☎ 767-4273
E-Mail: dignityindy@rocketmail.com
Homepage: www.gayindy.org/dignity
Gay and lesbian catholic group. Meetings at St.Thomas Azuines Church every 2nd Sun at 18 h.
Gay and Lesbian Jewish Group
5413 Graceland Avenue ✉IN 46208 ☎ 633-9285
Presbyterians for Lesbian and Gay Concerns
28 North Dearborn ✉IN 46201 ☎ 236-1170

SPORT GROUPS

Frontrunners (GLM)
PO Box 88765 ✉IN 46208-0765 ☎ 767-5034

CRUISING

-all AYOR
-Glendale Shopping Center (Sun only)
-Holiday Park
-American Legion Park

Lake Station ☎ 219

BARS

Axcis Nightclub & Lounge (AC B D F GLM MA S SNU STV VS) Mon-Sat 19-3 h, Sun 17-0.30 h
2415 Rush Street ✉IN 46405 *(next to water tower)*
☎ 962-1017
Piano Lounge open Thu, Fri, Sat 22-1 h. Latin night on Mon. Popular on Fri.

New Albany ☎ 812

GUEST HOUSES

Beharrell House (AC bf CC GLM H OS WO)
343 Beharrell Avenue ✉IN 47150 *(near Louisville/Kentucky)* ☎ 944-0289
Small B&B in a restored 100 year old home with a big deck and yard. All rooms have ceiling fans, clock/radio and cable TV. Rates double/private bath US$ 95 and double/shared bath US$ 65 incl. continental bf.

South Bend ☎ 219

SHOWS

Seahorse II Cabaret (AC B CC D GLM MA S STV) Mon-Thu 20-3.30, Fri Sat 19-3.30 h
1902 Western ✉IN 46619 ☎ 231-9139 Fax: 233-5903
Shows on Wed-Sat at 22 and 1 h.

USA-Iowa

Middlewest USA
Initials: IA
Time: GMT -6
Area: 145.754 km² / 59,613 sq mi.
Population: 2,852,000
Capital: Des Moines

Cedar Rapids ☎ 319

BARS

Warehouse Saloon (B D G MA S) 17-2 h, Sun 17-24 h
525 H Street South West ✉IA 52404 ☎ 365-9044

CRUISING

-Ellis Park (AYOR)
-Linndale Mall

Des Moines ☎ 515

GAY INFO

Gay Info Line 0-24 h
☎ 279-2110

BARS

Blazing Saddles (B G LJ) 11-2 h, Sun 16-24 h
416 East 5th Street ✉IA 50309 ☎ 246-1299
Brass Garden (B D GLM S YG) 18-2, Sun 18-24 h
112 East 4th Street ✉IA 50309 ☎ 243-3965

SEX SHOPS/BLUE MOVIES

Gallery Book Store 0-24 h
1114 Walnut Street ✉IA 50309 ☎ 244-2916

HOTELS

Kingman House (bf glm H)
2920 Kingman Boulevard ✉IA 50311 ☎ 279-7312

CRUISING

-Gay Loop (AYOR) (Keo Park between 4th and 5th Streets)
-Birdland Park (AYOR)
-Greenwood Park
-Margo Frankel Woods (AYOR)
-Valley West Mall (upper level)

Sioux City ☎ 712

DANCECLUBS

3 Cheers (AC B D GLM MA N S TV) 21-2 h
414 20th Street ✉IA 51104 ☎ 255-8005

USA-Kansas

Middlewest USA

Initials: KS

Time: GMT -6

Area: 213.111 km² / 87,162 sq mi.

Population: 2,595,000

Capital: Topeka

● Homosexual oral and anal intercourse is prohibited in Kansas.

✸ In Kansas ist homosexueller Oral- und Analverkehr verboten.

▲ Au Kansas, la fellation et la pénétration anale sont interdites seulement pour les homosexuels.

☆ En Kansas están las relaciones homosexuales por vía oral o anal prohibidas.

❖ In Kansas sono vietati i rapporti orali ed anali tra omosessuali.

Kansas City ☎ 502

RELIGIOUS GROUPS

Metropolitan Community Church Services Sun 10.30, Wed 19.30 h
12510 West 62nd Terrace #106, Shawnee Mission ✉KS 66216 ☎ (913) 631-1184

Topeka ☎ 785

CRUISING

-Gage Park (AYOR)
-Kansas Avenue (downtown by car)

Wichita ☎ 316

BARS

Our Fantasy (B D GLM OS YG) 16-2 h closed Mon-Tue
3201 South Hillside ✉KS 67216 ☎ 682-5494
T-Room (B GLM lj N) 12-2 h
1507 South Pawnee ✉KS 67211 ☎ 262-9327

RESTAURANTS

The Harbour Restaurant (F GLM)
3201 South Hillside ✉KS 67216 ☎ 681-2746

GENERAL GROUPS

The Center-Berdache Archives (A AC f GLM s W)
Mon-Fri 18-22 h, Sat 12-24 h, Sun 12-18 h
111 N. Spruce ✉KS 67208 ☎ 262-3991
Community Center, library, archive.

RELIGIOUS GROUPS

MCC
1704 Santa Fé ✉KS 67211 ☎ 267-1852

USA-Kentucky

Central East USA

Initials: KY

Time: GMT -5

Area: 104.665 km² / 42,807 sq mi.

Population: 3,908,000

Capital: Frankfort

Lexington ☎ 606

GAY INFO

Lexington Gay and Lesbian Services Wed-Fri 20-23 h
PO Box 114 71 ✉KY 40575 ☎ 231-0335
Info and referrals; social events, newsletter.

BARS

Bar, Inc. The (A AC B CC D GLM lj MA N S STV) Mon-Fri16-1 h Sat-3.30 h
224 East Main Street ✉KY 40507 ☎ 255-1551
Crossings (AC B G LJ OS S W) 16-1 h, closed Sun
117 North Limestone Street ✉KY 40507 ☎ 233-7266

RESTAURANTS

Montparnasse Café (F GLM)
224 East Main Street ✉KY 40507 *(at The Bar Complex)*
☎ 255-1551

SEX SHOPS/BLUE MOVIES

Bookstore. The
942 Winchester Road ✉KY 40505 ☎ 252-2093

CRUISING

-Jacobson Park (AYOR)
-University of Kentucky (Fine Arts Building)
-Woodland Park

Louisville ☎ 502

GAY INFO

Gay and Lesbian Hotline 18-1 h
☎ 897-2475
Letter. The
PO Box 3882 ✉KY 40201 ☎ 636-0935

BOOK SHOPS

Carmichael's (glm) 1
295 Bardstown Road ✉KY 40204 ☎ 456-6950

GENERAL GROUPS

Bluegrass Bears Kentucky
PO Box 370 01 ✉KY 40233-7001

CRUISING

-The Falls (across Ohio River in Jeffersonville, Indiana)
-Central Park (4th and Magnolia)
-Fourth Street (between St. Catherine and Hill)
-Iroquois Park
-Cherokee Park (at the fountain)

Paducah ☎ 270

RESTAURANTS

Tribeca Mexican Cuisine (AC B CC F glm S W) Mon-Sat 11-24 h, closed Mon
127 Market House Square ✉KY 42001 ☎ 444-3960
Authentic Mexican food restaurant.

PRIVATE ACCOMODATION

1857 Bed & Breakfast (AC bf CC GLM LJ wh)
127 Market House Square ✉KY 42001 *(heart of downtown)*
☎ 444-3960 ☎ (800) 264-5607
Rooms with bath, phone, cable TV. Rates US$ 65-85. Completely renovated.

USA-Louisiana

South USA

Initials: LA

Time: GMT -6

Area: 134.275 km² / 54,918 sq mi.

Population: 4,352,000

Capital: Baton Rouge

● Hetero- as well as homosexual oral and anal intercourse is prohibited in Louisiana.

✷ In Louisiana ist hetero- wie homosexueller Oral- und Analverkehr verboten.

▲ En Lousiane, la fellation et la pénétration anale sont interdites pour tous, homos et hétéros.

☆ En Louisiana las relaciones homosexuales y heterosexuales por vía oral o anal están prohibidas.

❖ In Lousiana sono vietati i rapporti orali ed anali sia tra omosessuali che tra eterosessuali.

Baton Rouge ☎ 225

BARS

Argon (B g)
2160 Highland Road ✉LA 70802 ☎ 336-9400
Buddies (B g)
450 Oklahoma ✉LA 70802 ☎ 346-1191
George's (B G MA)
860 St. Louis Street ✉LA 70802 ☎ 387-9798
Hide-A-Way Club (B G MA)
7367 Exchange Place ✉LA 70806 ☎ 923-3632
Mac's (B G MA) 20-2 h
668 Main Street ✉LA 70801 ☎ 387-9963
Mirror Lounge (B D GLM S) 14-2 h, closed Sun
111 Third Street ✉LA 70801 ☎ 387-9797

BOOK SHOPS

Hibiscus Bookstore Mon-Fri 10-15, Sat Sun 12-18 h
116 Main Street ✉LA 70801 ☎ 387-4264

PRIVATE ACCOMODATION

Brentwood House (AC bf F G NU VS wh wo)
PO Box 40872 ✉LA 70835-0872 ☎ 924-4989 Fax: 924-1738
E-Mail: tomsin@ix.hetcom.com
Home stays in residential area. Shared bath/wc. Rates for 1-2 guests US$ 69-75. Weekly rates available.

CRUISING

-Capitol Lakes (AYOR) (and adjacent area)
-Cortana Mall
-Highland Road Park (AYOR)
-Louisiana State University (AYOR) (Allen Hall)

Hammond ☎ 504

BARS

Chances (B D GLM MA) Fri Sat 21-2 h
42357 Veterans *(right off exit #40, I-12)* ☎ 542-9350

Harvey ☎ 504

BARS

The Full Moon (B G MA)
424 Destrehan ✉LA 70058 ☎ 341-4396

Lafayette ☎ 318

BARS

Images (B G MA)
524 West Jefferson ✉LA 70501 ☎ 233-0070
Ole Blue Note (B g)
115 Spring Street ✉LA 70501 ☎ 234-9232
Whispers (B D GLM YG) 20-? h, closed Mon Tue
408 Maurice Street ✉LA 70506 ☎ 234-7054

CRUISING

-Garrard Park (AYOR)
-Northeast Louisiana University (library)
-U.S.L. Library and Wharton Hall (2nd and 3rd floor)

Lake Charles ☎ 318

BARS

Billy B's (B G MA)
704 Ryan ✉LA 70601 ☎ 433-5457
Crystal's (B F glm YG) 20-3 h, closed Sun-Tue, Fri (G), Sat (L)
112 West Broad Street ✉LA 70601 ☎ 433-5457

Metairie ☎ 504

BARS

4-Seasons/The Out Back (B G MA)
3229 North Causeway Boulevard ✉LA 70002 ☎ 832-0659

New Orleans ☎ 504

● Feel like Scarlett O'Hara once in a lifetime? The more than decadent south state mansion *Nottoway* boasts enough rooms for living your romantic dreams and *Cajun country* in the west of New Orleans beautiful outing opportunities. But don't take your outing in summer; then the city is far too hot and humid. But while the heat recedes during the other seasons, the humidity stays, New Orleans being situated between *Lake Pontchartrain* and the gulf of Mexico. In between is rather little space, so that you can get along without a car in this not too big city. Be as it may, as a tourist you are likely to hang out in *Vieux Carré*, the enchanting old city center and tourist magnet. The more gay part of this quarter, which is also THE gay quarter of the city, is the area to the northeast of St. Ann Street. Newest events and locations can be drawn from tho magazines *Ambush* or *Impact*. the most lively event in town is the *Mardi Gras*, THE (gay) festival in New Orleans. No other event shows more distinctly, what New Orleans is all about: a real multicultural feeling in this city, where Africans, Choctaw-Indians, French, Irish, Caribeans, Spa-

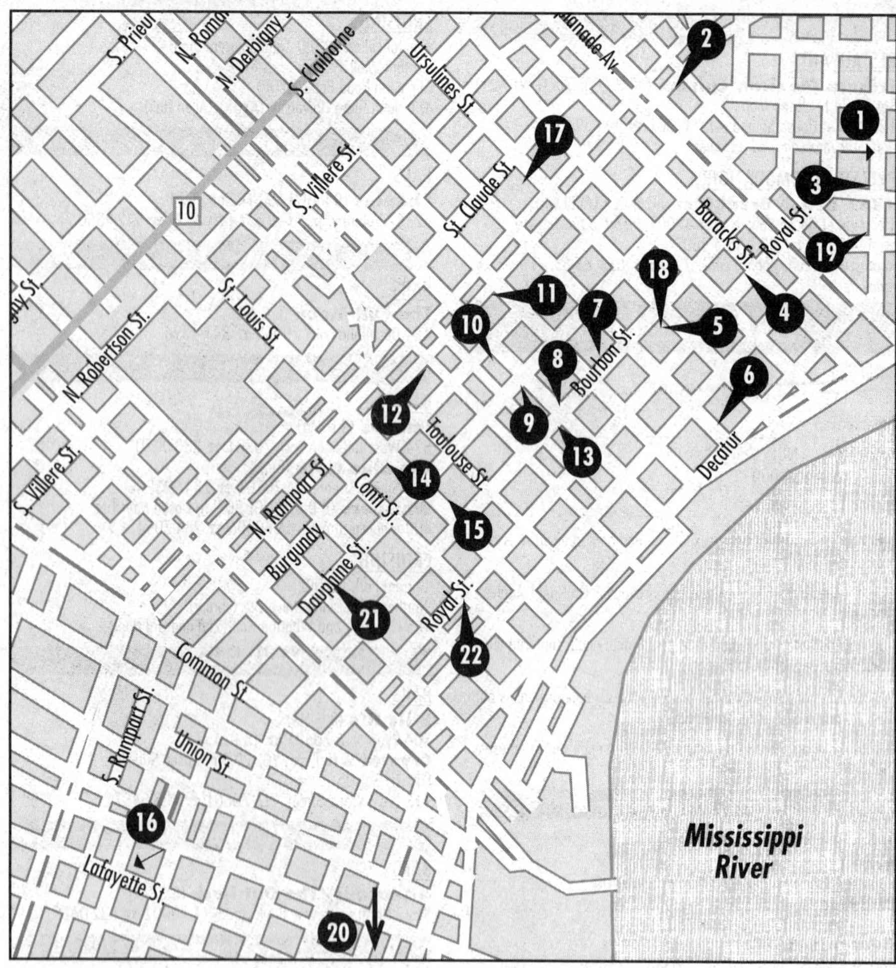

NEW ORLEANS

1 Big Easy Guest House
Macarty Park Guest House
Copper Top Bar
La Dauphine Guest House
2 Deja Vu Guest House
3 Rubyfruit Jungle Bar
4 Golden Lantern Bar
5 Ursulines Guest House
6 MRB Bar
7 Café Lafitte in Exile Bar
8 Bourbon Pub Bar
9 Good Friends Bar
10 Rawhide Bar
11 Wolfendale's Bar
12 Footloose Bar
13 Oz Danceclub
14 Corner Pocket Bar
15 The Roundup Bar
16 The Greenhouse
Guest House
17 French Quarter B&B
Guest House
18 Rober House Condos
Apartments
19 Faubourg Marginy Bookshop
20 The Club Sauna
21 La Dauphine Guest House
22 Royal Street Courtyard
Guest House

nish and many more have left their marks. And, naturally, the gays, which are one of the many, colourful *communities* of the city. The Mardi Gras is in a very special way the „southern" art of celebrating, of music (jazz!), of good food and „laissez-faire", an art of living which can only prosper here. By the way: for the right morsel of romanticism take the river ferry from the aquarium to Audubon zoo, and ride the St. Charles Avenue Streetcar back into town.

✸ Einmal im Leben fühlen wie Scarlett O'Hara? Das ultra-dekadente Südstaaten-Herrenhaus *Nottoway* hat genügend Zimmer für romantische Träume, und das *Cajun country* westlich von New Orleans bietet einige dieser Ausflugs-Perlen.
Ausflüge, für die man sich nicht den Sommer vormerken sollte. Die Stadt ist dann viel zu heiß und viel zu feucht. Obwohl die Hitze während des restlichen Jahres weicht, bleibt die Feuchtigkeit denn auf der einen Seite New Orleans' liegt der *Lake Pontchartrain*, auf der anderen der Golf von Mexiko.
Und dazwischen ist eher weniger Platz, so daß man in der nicht übermässig großen Stadt gut ohne Auto auskommt. Es ist so oder so sehr wahrscheinlich, daß man als Tourist meist im *Vieux Carré*, dem bezaubernden Altstadt-Touristenmagnet, unterwegs ist. Die schwulere Hälfte dieses Viertels, das auch DAS Homo-Viertel der Stadt ist, ist die Gegend nordöstlich der St. Ann Street. Was gerade genau angesagt ist, entnimmt man den Zeitungen *Ambush* oder *Impact*.
Die bunteste Seite der Stadt ist *Mardi Gras* (☛ Events), DAS (schwule) Fest der Stadt. Keine andere Feier veranschaulicht besser, was New Orleans ausmacht: echtes Multi-Kulti-Feeling in einer Stadt, in der Afrikaner, Choctaw-Indianer, Franzosen, Iren, Kariben, Spanier und viele andere ihre Spuren hinterlassen haben. Und natürlich auch die Schwulen, die eben eine der vielen, bunten *communities* der Stadt sind. Mardi Gras, das ist in besonderem Maße die „südliche" Kunst des Feierns, der Musik (Jazz!), des guten Essens und des „Laissez-Faire", eine Kunst, die nur hier gedeihen kann.
Übrigens: für die richtige Prise Romantik zum Schluß nimmt man die Flußfähre vom Aquarium zum Audubon Zoo und fährt mit der St. Charles Avenue Streetcar zurück in die Stadt.

▲ Jouer Scarlett O'Hara au moins une fois dans sa vie? Oui, c'est possible! La demeure de Nottoway, symbole de la décadence du Sud, a suffisamment de chambres pour réaliser le plus romantique de vos rêves! Et le Pays Cajun, à l'ouest de la Nouvelle Orléans, regorge de curiosités touristiques.
Tant d'excursions qu'on ferait mieux de faire en automne ou en hiver, car, l'été, la chaleur est tellement étouffante en Louisiane qu'on en reste collé au pavé. Si les températures deviennent supportables l'hiver, l'humidité, elle, reste pesante toute l'année, car sachez que la ville est coincée entre le Lac Pontchartrain et le Golfe du Mexique. La superficie de la ville est donc assez restreinte, ce qui offre l'avantage de pouvoir quasiment tout faire à pied: pas besoin de voiture! D'autant plus que quand on visite La Nouvelle Orléans, on a du mal de s'extraire du „Vieux Carré", le pôle d'attraction numéro 1 de la ville. Attention: c'est aussi le bastion gay de la Louisiane. 50% de sa superficie est entre les mains des gays, Commencez à St Ann Street et remontez vers le nord. Pour savoir que faire, quand et où aller, consultez les magasines gays locaux „Ambush" ou „Impact".
La Nouvelle Orléans, c'est le carnaval, c'est „Mardi Gras". Aucune autre manifestation ne montre mieux le caractère multiculturel de la ville. Africains, Indiens Choctaw, Français, Irlandais, Espagnols et Antillais ont marqué la ville de leur empreinte. Les gays, eux aussi, forment une communauté qui, aujourd'hui, fait définitivement partie du décor et qui a aussi son mot à dire. Jazz, cuisine excellente, art de vivre et de faire la fête, ambiance laisser-faire décontractée: tout ça, c'est la Nouvelle Orléans!
Au fait: Traversez le fleuve en bac pour aller de l'aquarium au zoo Audubon et revenez en ville avec le St Charles Avenue Street Car: un souvenir inoubliable!

☆ ¿Sentir como Escarlata O'Hara una vez en la vida? La ultra decadente mansión del estado sureño *Nottoway* tiene suficientes dormitorios para sueños románticos, y el *Cajun Country* al oeste de Nueva Orleans ofrece algunos sitios encantadores. Aunque so se deberían visitar precisamente en verano, ya que en estas fechas la ciudad es muy calurosa y humeda. Mientras que en el resto del año el calor cede, la humedad persiste, porque Nueva Orleans está situada entre el *Lake Pontchartrain* y el Golfo de México. La ciudad es pequeña, así que los trayectos se pueden hacer a pie. El centro turístico de la ciudad es el magnífico *Vieux Carré*. El sector gay de la ciudad esta en la región moroeste de la St. Ann Street. Las revistas *Ambush* o *Impact* informan sobre los sitios gay de moda. El acontecimiento gay anual de mayor relevancia es el *Mardi Gras*. Ninguna otra fiesta manifiesta de igual forma la especialidad de Nueva Orleans: un sentimiento multicultural en una ciudad en la que africanos, indios Chovtaw, franceses, irlandeses, caribeños, españoles y muchos otros, han dejado sus huellas. Y por supuesto los homosexuales que constituyen uno de los variopintos grupos de la ciudad. Mardi Gras es sobre todo la manifestación del arte sureño de celebrar fiestas, de la música (jazz), la buena comida y del dejar hacer „Laissez-Faire", un arte que solo aqui puede florecer. Consejo: Tome el barco del Aquarium en dirección Audubon Zoo y viaje con el St. Charles Avenue Streetcar de regreso a la ciudad.

❖ E sentirsi per una volta come Scarlett O'Hara? L'ultra decadente casa padronale del sud *Nottoway* ha abbastanza stanze per sogni romantici e la *Cajun Country* ad ovest di New Orleans offre alcune di queste perle. Queste escursioni non sono consigliabili in estate, poichè la città è troppo calda ed umida. Mentre il caldo diminuisce durante il resto dell'anno l'umidità resta. New Orleans infatti è situata tra *Lake Pontchartrain* e il golfo del Messico. A causa di queste frontiere naturali la città non è molto grande pertanto non è necessaria un'auto per girarla. I turisti si muovono di solito nel *Vieux Carrè*, l'incantevole centro storico della città. Il quartiere gay occupa la metà del centro, nella zona a nord est dalla St. Ann Street. Otterrete ulteriori informazioni sui giornali *Ambush* o *Impact*. Il momento più colorato della città è il *Mardi Gras*, la festa gay per eccellenza. Nessun altro festeggiamento mostra meglio l'essenza di New Orleans: un vero spirito multiculturale in una città in cui africani, indiani Choctaw, francesi, irlandesi, centroamericani, spagnoli ed altri hanno lasciato le proprie tracce; naturalmente anche i gay formano una delle variopinte comunità della città. Mardi Gras rappresenta il modo di far festa tipico del sud, con musica (jazz), buona cucina ed il „laissez faire" che esiste solo qui. A proposito: se volete un po' di romanticismo prendete il battello da Aquarium a Audubon Zoo. Potrete poi rientrare in città con la St.Charles Avenue Streetcar.

GAY INFO

AMbush
PO Box 712 91 ✉LA 70172-1291 ☎ 522-8049 Fax: 522-0907
Bi-weekly newspaper with reports, calendar of events, guides and ads. Subscription US$ 45/year.

The Amistad Research Center
Tulane University, 6823 St. Charles Avenue ✉LA 70118
☎ 866-5535

Exit
PO Box 19328 ✉LA 70179-0328 ☎ 482-1743

Impact Gay News Mon-Fri 10-18 h
PO Box 52079 ✉LA 70152 ☎ 944-6722 Fax: 944-6794
E-Mail: mail@impactnews.com
Twice-monthly newspaper for Gulf South. Free at gay venues.

Lesbian & Gay Community Center (A GLM S) 12-19 h
2114 Decatur Street ✉LA 70116 ☎ 522-1103
Refferals for lodging, meals, counseling, support group.

TOURIST INFO

New Orleans Metropolitan Convention & Visitors Bureau
1520 Sugar Bowl Drive ✉LA 70112 ☎ 566-5011
Fax: 566-5046 Homepage: www.nawlins.com

BARS

Angles (B GLM) 15-4 h, Sat Sun 17-4 h
2301 N Causeway Boulevard ✉LA 70001 *(Metairie)*
☎ 834-7979

Big Daddy's (B f GLM)
2513 Royal Street ✉LA 70117
☎ 948-6288

Boots (B glm) Wed-Sat 18-0, Sun 16-0 h
2601 Royal Street ✉LA 70117 ☎ 945-7006
Cruise/bear bar.

Bourbon Pub & Parade (AC B G MA VS) 0-24 h
801 Bourbon Street ✉LA 70116 ☎ 529-2107
Cruise bar.

Cafe Lafitte in Exile (AC B G lj MA VS) 0-24 h
901 Bourbon Street/Dumaine Street ✉LA 70116 ☎ 522-8397
Oldest gay bar in the US. Very popular. 24 hours of D.J. music.

Copper Top Bar (AC B CC f G MA N W) 0-24 h
706 Franklin Avenue ✉LA 70117 ☎ 948-2300
Neighborhood bar

The Corner Pocket (B g SNU YG) 24 hours.
940 St. Louis Street/Burgundy Street ✉LA 70112 ☎ 568-9829
Male strippers Thu-Sun 20-? h

The Country Club (B G NU P pi WO) 10-6 h (closed in winter)
634 Louisa Street ✉LA 70117 *(near Royal Street)* ☎ 945-0742
Two bars, hot tub. US$ 5 cover.

Footloose (AC B f G MA N s STV) Mon Tue 14-2, Wed 16-2, Thu 14-2, Fri-Sun 0-24 h
700 North Rampart Street ✉LA 70116 ☎ 524-7654

Four Seasons (B D G) Mon-Fri 11-? h, Sat 16-? h, Sun 13-? h.
3229 North Causeway/17th Street ✉LA 70002 *(Metairie)*
☎ 832-0659

Friendly Bar. The (B GLM MA)
2301 Chartres Street
☎ 943-8929

The Full Moon (B g) Wed-Sun 21-? h
424 Destrehan Avenue, Harvey ✉LA 70058 *(West Bank)*
☎ 341-4396
Suburban.

Golden Lantern (B G MA N) 0-24 h
1239 Royal Street ✉LA 70116 *(at Barracks9* ☎ 529-2860
Second-oldest gay bar in the French quarter. Friendly neighborhood bar.

Good Friends Bar (AC B GLM MA) 0-24 h
740 Dauphine Street ✉LA 70116 ☎ 566-7191

The Men's Room (B G LJ P) 21-5 h
941 Elysian Fields Avenue/Rampart Street ✉LA 70117 *(above Phoenix Bar)* ☎ 945-9264
Dress code.

The Mint (B GLM S P W) 12-3 h
504 Esplanade ☎ 525-2000
Popular.

MRB (B G S) 0-24 h
515 St. Phillip ✉LA 70116 ☎ 523-7764

The Phoenix (B G LJ S) 0-24 h
941 Elysian Fields Avenue/Rampart Street ✉LA 70117
☎ 945-9264

Rawhide (AC B G lj MA) 0-24 h
740 Burgundy Street/St. Ann Street ✉LA 70117 ☎ 525-8106
Popular

The Roundup 24 hours
819 Saint Louis Street ✉LA 70112 ☎ 561-8340

Rubyfruit Jungle (B D glm) 16-?, WE 13-? h
640 Frenchmen ✉LA 70116 ☎ 947-4000

TT's (B GLM S) 12-? h
820 North Rampart Street ✉LA 70116 *(near Dumaine Street)*
☎ 523-9521

Wolfendale's (B D G VS) 16-5 h. Thu-Sun (D) 22-? h.
834 North Rampart Street ✉LA 70116 ☎ 523-7764

DANCECLUBS

Oz (B D GLM SNU vs YG) 0-24 h
800 Bourbon Street ✉LA 70116 ☎ 593-9491

RESTAURANTS

Buffa's (B F GLM) 22-2 h
1001 Esplanade Avenue ✉LA 70116 ☎ 945-9373
Home cooking!

Cafe Sbisa (AC CC F glm OS) 17.30-22.30 h
1011 Decatur Street ✉LA 70116na ☎ 522-5565

Clover Grill (AC bf CC F glm MA) 0-24 h
900 Bourbon Street ✉LA 70116 *(at Dumaine Street)*
☎ 523-0904

Feelings Cafe (AC B CC F glm MA N OS W) Sun-Thu 18-21, Fri-Sat 18-23, Fri Sun 11-14 h
2600 Chartres ✉LA 70117 *(near French Quarter)*
☎ 945-2222

Lucky Cheng's (F GLM TV)
720 Saint Louis Street ✉LA 70112 ☎ 529-2045

Mama Rosa's (B CC F glm) Tue-Sun 10.30-23.30 h
616 North Rampart Street ✉LA 70112 ☎ 523-5546
Italian food and sandwiches.

Mona Lisa (B CC F GLM) Tue-Fri 17-23 h, Sat Sun 21-2 h
1212 Royal Street ✉LA 70116 ☎ 522-6746
Pizza and salads.

La Peniche (B F g) 0-24 h
1940 Dauphine Street ✉LA 70116 ☎ 943-1460

Petunia's (CC F g)
817 St. Louis Street ✉LA 70112 ☎ 522-6440

The Quarter Scene (AC bf CC F glm) 7-24 h (closed tue)
900 Dumaine Street ✉LA 70116 ☎ 522-6533
Good and inexpensive lunch meals. No alcoholic drinks.

Vera Cruz (B CC F glm)
1141 Decatur ✉LA 70116 ☎ 561-8081
Mexican cuisine.

SAUNAS/BATHS

The Club (b f G sa sb sol VS wh) 0-24 h
515 Toulouse Street ✉LA 70130 ☎ 581-2402

FITNESSTUDIOS

Gay Bowling League
Mid-City Lanes ☎ 482-3133

New Orleans Gay and Lesbian Tennis Association
☎ 482-2192

Team New Orleans
☎ 947-6643

Volleyball New Orleans
☎ 899-1538 ☎ 945-4634.

BOOK SHOPS

Bookstar (g)
414 North Peters Street ✉LA 70130 ☎ 523-6411
Faubourg Marigny Books (CC GLM W) Mon-Fri 10-20, Sat-Sun 10-18 h
600 Frenchmen Street ✉LA 70116 ☎ 943-9875

LEATHER & FETISH SHOPS

Gargoyles Leather
1205 Decatur Street ✉LA 70116 ☎ 529-4387
Mail order available.
Gay Mart
808 North Rampart Street ✉LA 70116 ☎ 523-5876
Second Skin Leather Company (GLM) 12-22 h, Sun 12-18 h
521 Rue Saint Philip ✉LA 70116 ☎ 561-8167
Mail order available.

PROPERTY SERVICES

New Orleans Real Estate Service
2316 rue Dauphine, ✉LA 70117 ☎ 948-2217 Fax: 948-3420.

TRAVEL & TRANSPORT

French Quarter Reservation Service (GLM lj pi) Mon-Fri 9-17 h, Sat 10-14 h
940 Royal Street, Suite 263 ✉LA 70116 ☎ 523-1246
Fax: 527-6327 E-Mail: fqrsinc@linknet.net.
Homepage: www.neworleansreservations.com

HOTELS

The Frenchmen Hotel (AC bf F glm H pi)
417 Frenchmen Street, ✉LA 70116 ☎ 948-2166 Fax: 943-2328
Rooms with bath, phone and TV.
Garden District. The (AC bf glm H OS)
2418 Magazine Street ✉LA 70130 ☎ 895 43 02
Beautifully furnished Victorian town house built in 1890. All rooms with private bath, balconies, ceiling fans, open fire places and cable TV. Suites with full kitchens available. Call for detailed information and rates.
Rathbone Inn (AC bf g H wh) 8-19 h
1227 Esplanade Avenue ✉LA 70116 ☎ 947-2100
☎ (800) 947-2101 Fax: 947-7454
Rooms with priv. bath, kitchenette. Rates US$ 90-145.
Rue Royal Inn (AC CC g H) Office 8-19 h
1006 Royal Street ✉LA 70116 ☎ 524-3900
☎ (800) 776-3901 Fax: 558-0566
All rooms with priv. bath, fridge. Rates US$ 85-165.

GUEST HOUSES

Big Easy Guest House (AC bf CC f GLM)
2633 Dauphine Street ✉LA 70117 ☎ 943-3717
☎ (800) 679-0640 (toll-free) E-Mail: BigEasyGH@aol.com
Located near the French Quarter. in a private home dated circa 1850. All rooms with private bath/WC, telephone, TV and private entrance. Rates double US$ 60 and up, incl. continental bf. Lush, semi-tropical patio. Rooms furnished with lots of antiques. German spoken.
Bon Maison Guest House (AC CC glm H MA OS)
835 Bourbon Street ✉LA 70116-3106 ☎ 561-8498
Fax: 561-8498 E-Mail: bmgh@acadiacom.net
Homepage: www.bonmaison.com
Small guest house in a restored townhouse (built in 1833). Hotel with garden and lovely planted patio with tables, chairs and outdoor grill. All rooms with private shower baths, kitchenette (refrigerator, microwave, toaster and coffee maker), air-condition, private phone and color cable TV. Rooms in the slave (!) quarter units US$ 75 and suites $125 (tax included).
Bourgoyne Guest House (AC CC glm H MA)
839 Bourbon Street ✉LA 70116 *(in French Quarter)* ☎ 524-3621
☎ 525-3983
Located on bustling Bourbon Street the Guesthouse is located in an 1830s Creole mansion with balconies, galleries, winding staircases and a lush, green courtyard. The two suites are furnished with antiques and have private bathrooms (one with solarium), TV and fully equipped kitchen. Rates US$ 70-160. Studio apartments available with double bed, dining area, private bath and kitchen. Rates US$ 80-170.
Deja Vu Guest House (AC CC G H MA)
1835-37 rue des Rampart, North ✉LA 70116 *(close to French Quarter & Marigny bars)* ☎ 945-5912 Fax: 948-6396
1830's style creole cottages with living room, kitchen, priv. bath, WC, TV. Rates single US$69 plus 12 for each extra person. Cottages 100. Limousine available.
Faubourg Guest House (AC GLM MA msg OS)
1703 Second Street ✉LA 70113-1631 ☎ 891-1994
French Quarter B&B. The (AC CC GLM H MA msg pi)
1132 Ursulines Street ✉LA 70116 *(French Quarter)* ☎ 525-3390
Fax: 593-9859
Full kitchen, 2 bedrooms, bath, living room, swimming pool. Rates Jun-Aug US$ 60-75, Sep-May 75-89.
The Greenhouse Inn (bf E GLM H msg OS pi wh WO)
1212 Magazine Street ✉LA 70130 ☎ 525-1333
☎ (800) 966-1303 Fax: 525-1306 E-Mail: GreenInn@aol.com
Comfortable guesthouse built in 1840. Swimmingpool and spa

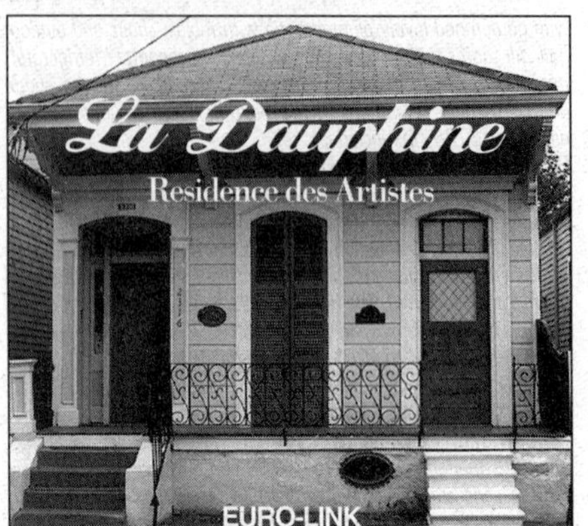

(open year round). All rooms with private bath/WC, color TV, video, minibar and telephone (with modem jacks).

La Dauphine Résidence des Artistes (AC CC G H MA OS)
2316 Rue Dauphine ✉LA 70117 ☎ 948-2217 Fax: 948-3420
E-Mail: LaDauphine@aol.com Homepage: www.ladauphine.com
Renovated Victorian, 100-year-old house. Relaxed atmosphere. All rooms with private bath/WC, telephone, Sat-TV, video, hair-dryer, some with balcony. Rates single US$ 65-85 and double 85-110. Weekly discounts available. Non-smoking. Continental bf included. Two dogs on premises. Bicycles provided. Free Airport pick up for weekly stays.

Lafitte Guest House (AC bf g H OS)
1003 Bourbon Street ✉LA 70116 ☎ 581-2678 Fax: 581-2678
Convenient location. All rooms with priv. bath, WC, telephone and some with balcony.

Lion's Inn B&B (AC bf CC G H MA pi wh)
2517 Chartres ✉LA 70117 ☎ 945-2339 ☎ (800)485-6846
Fax: 949-7321 E-Mail: lions@gs.net
Homepage: www.lionsinn.com
Small B&B in renovated 140 year old Edwardian house. Beautiful garden with jacuzzi. All rooms with telephone, cable TV, radio and hair-dryer. Rates single/shared bath $45-70, double/shared bath $65-110, double/private bath $75-130, loft $100-150 depending on season. Continental bf incl.

Macarty Park Guest House (AC bf CC glm H pi wh) 8.30-22 h
3820 Burgundy Street ✉LA 70117-5708 ☎ 943-4994
☎ 521-2790 Fax: 943-4999 E-Mail: faxmehard@aol.com
Homepage: www.macartypark.com
8 double rooms, 2 studios and 6 apartments in a cottage-style home all with bath/shower/WC, balcony, phone, fax, TV, radio, kitchenette (studios) and kitchen (apartments). Rates single/double $ 59-115, studios $99-115 and apartments $95-160, continental bf included.

Maison Dauphine (AC bf glm H wh)
2460 Dauphine Street ✉LA 70117 *(located in Foubourg Marigny, near the French Quarter (Vieux Carré)* ☎ 943-0861
Fax: 943-0861
All suites feature living area, bedroom, private bath, direct-dial telephone, answering machine, refrigerator, microwave oven, TV, air condition and heating controls.

Mazant Guesthouse (AC bf glm H OS)
906 Mazant Street, LA 70116 ✉LA 70116 ☎ 944-2662
30 min to the airport. Downtown neighborhood. Hotel with garden. All rooms with kitchenette.

New Orleans Guest House (AC b bf CC glm N) closed 20-25 Dec.
1118 Ursulines Street ✉LA 70116 *(French Quarter)*
☎ 566-1177 ☎ 566-1179
Built in 1848. The Slave Quarters have been renovated into guest units. All 14 rooms with private bath, TV, air-condition, radio and telephone. Rates US$ 79-99 incl. continental breakfast. All taxes extra.

Olde Town Inn (AC CC glm H)
1001 Marigny Street ✉LA 70117 ☎ 949-5815
Homepage: www.fqaccommodations.com

Pauger Guest Suites (AC glm H MA OS pi) Office: 8-24 h
1750 North Rampart Street ✉LA 70116 *(near French Quarter)* ☎ 944-2601
Rooms with private bath, telephone, cable-TV, refrigerator, microwave oven. Pool, car park, at walking distance to Gay venues. Rates single from US$ 50, double from $60. Weekly discount.

Royal Barracks Guesthouse (AC CC G MA N NU OS p VS wh WO) Reservations: 9-21 h
717 Barracks Street ✉LA 70116 *(between Royal and Bourbon Street)* ☎ 529-7269 ☎ (888)-255-7269 Fax: 529-7298 E-Mail: rbgn@acadiacom.net
B&B in restored Victorian building in the historic French Quarter. Quiet location. All rooms with cable TV, radio, ceiling fan, private bath. Private patio with hot tub. Rates Sep-May US$ 95-150, Jun-Aug $65-110.
Royal Street Courtyard (AC bf CC GLM H wh)
2446 Royal Street ✉LA 70117 *(near French Quarter)* ☎ 943-6818 E-Mail: royalctyd@aol.com.
Studios and apartments with bath/shower/WC, balcony or terrace, TV, telephone, video, kitchenette, heating, own key. Rates US$ 75-95 incl bf.
Ursuline Guesthouse (AC GLM H LJ MA OS wh) Office 9-21 h
708 Rue des Ursulines ✉LA 70116 *French Quarter* ☎ 525-8509 ☎ (800) 654-2351 Fax: 525-8408
20 minutes to the airport Centrally located. In the heart of local gay scene. All rooms with phone, bath/WC and balcony.

APARTMENTS
Rober House Condos (AC glm H OS pi)
822 Ursulines ✉LA 70116 *(French Quarter)* ☎ 529-4663
Fax: 527-6327

GENERAL GROUPS
Act up Meeting Wed 20 h at 504 Frenchmen
☎ 944-4546
Gay Nudist
☎ 899-2549
LAGPAC (GLM)
PO Box 530 75 ✉LA 70153 ☎ 527-0050
New Orleans Gay Men's Chorus
☎ 245-8884
P-FLAG
PO Box 15515 ✉LA 70175 ☎ 895-3936
TwentySomething
☎ 836-9242

FETISH GROUPS
Knights D'Orleans
PO Box 508 12 ✉LA 70150
Lords of Leather
PO Box 72105 ✉LA 70172

HEALTH GROUPS
New Orleans AIDS Task Force
1407 Decatur ✉LA 70116 ☎ 944-AIDS
PWA Coalition
☎ 944-3663
RAIN Regional AIDS Interfaith Network
☎ 523-3755
United Services for AIDS
☎ 522-5239

RELIGIOUS GROUPS
Grace Fellowship in Christ Jesus
3151 Dauphine Street ✉LA 70117 ☎ 944-9836
Integrity
☎ 899-2549
Jewish Gay and Lesbian Alliance
☎ 525-8286
Metropolitan Community Church Services Sun 10.30 h
1128 St. Roch Avenue ✉LA 70117 ☎ 945-5390

SPORT GROUPS
Frontrunners Running Club
☎ 523-3834

CRUISING
-Audubon Park (AYOR)
-Belle Promenade (West Bank)
-City Park (AYOR)
-Oakwood Shopping Center (AYOR)
-Riverwalk
-Tulane University (AYOR) (cafeteria, library & student union)
-U.N.O. (business administration building & library)
-Vieux Carre (especially Bourbon Street between Toulouse & Ursulines Streets)
-Woldenberg Park

Slidell ☎ 504

BARS
Billy's (B GLM MA) Tue-Sat 19-2, Sun 17-1 h
2600 Highway 190 West ☎ 847-1921

St. Joseph ☎ 318

HOTELS
Garrett Drake Guest House (AC bf B G H pi)
PO Box 316, LA 71366 ✉LA 71366 ☎ 766-4229
Priv. and shared baths.

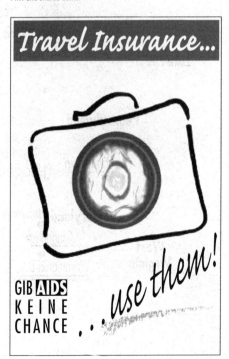

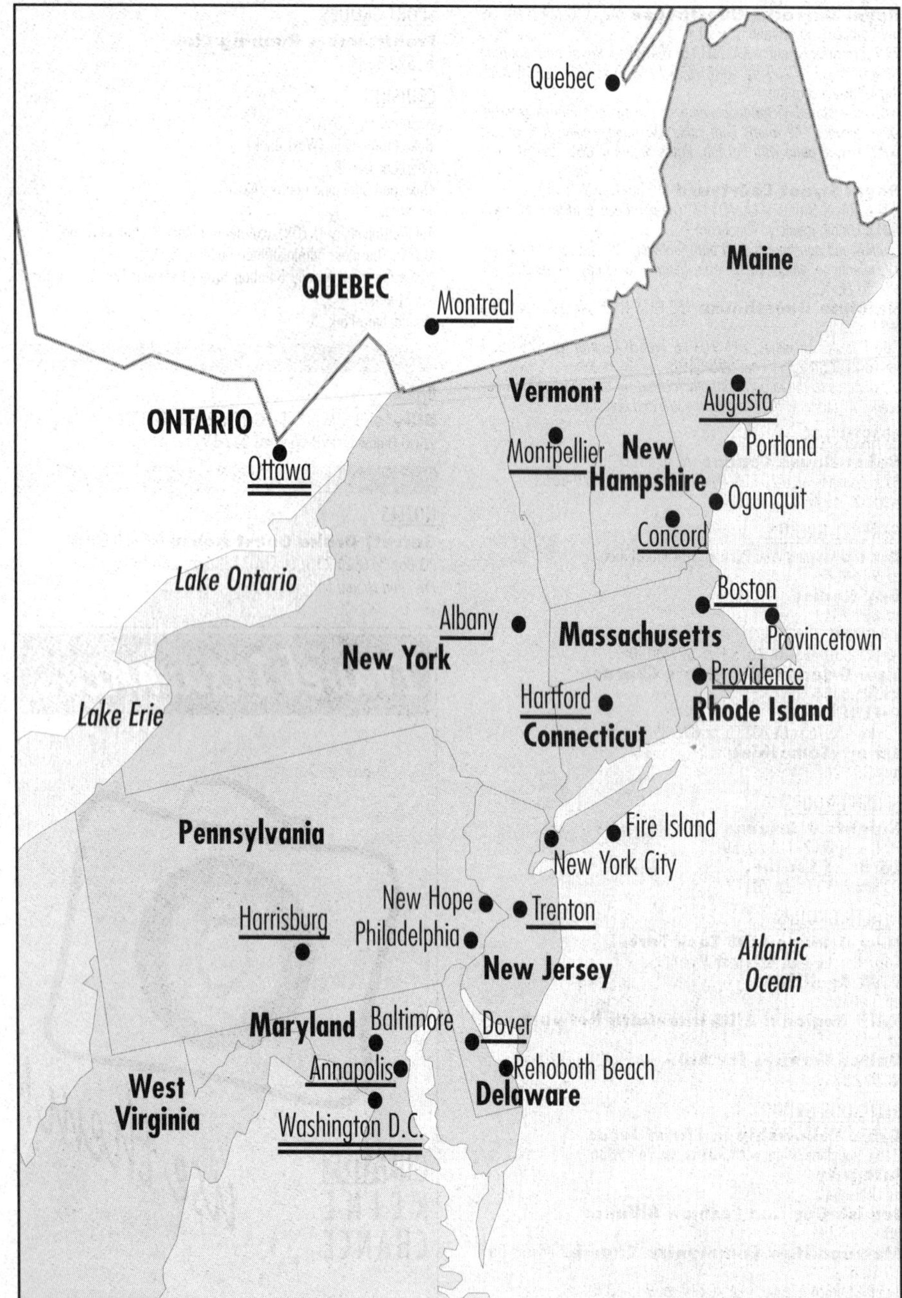
Quebec
Maine
QUEBEC
Montreal
Vermont
Augusta
ONTARIO
Portland
Ottawa
Montpellier
New Hampshire
Ogunquit
Concord
Lake Ontario
Boston
Albany
Provincetown
Massachusetts
New York
Providence
Hartford
Rhode Island
Lake Erie
Connecticut
Pennsylvania
Fire Island
New York City
New Hope
Trenton
Harrisburg
Philadelphia
Atlantic Ocean
New Jersey
Maryland
Baltimore
Dover
Annapolis
Rehoboth Beach
West Virginia
Delaware
Washington D.C.

USA-Maine

Northeast USA

Initials: ME

Time: GMT -5

Area: 91.653 km² / 37,486 sq mi.

Population: 1,242,000

Capital: Augusta

Caribou ☎ 207

GENERAL GROUPS

Northern Lambda 19-21 h
PO Box 990 ✉ME 04736 ☎ 498-2088
Operates in northeastern Maine and northwestern New Brunswick (Canada). It publishes a newsletter ten times yearly. Holds regular meetings and operates a library.

Hallowell

GENERAL GROUPS

MLGPA Maine Lesbian/Gay Political Alliance
PO Box 232, ✉ME 04347

Lincolnville Beach ☎ 207

HOTELS

Sign of the Owl (bf G H)
RR2 Box 85, ✉ME 04457 ☎ 338-4669
9 miles north of Camden, near beach and restaurants.

CAMPING

Old Massachusetts Homestead Campground (pi) 8.30-22.30 h
US Route 1 ✉ME 04849-0005 ☎ 789-5135
E-Mail: campme@mint.net Homepage: www.masscamp.com
Cozy cabins with private bath and decks. Rates USD 55-69. Ocean view nature trails and beaches nearby.

Naples ☎ 207

GUEST HOUSES

Lamb's Mill Inn (AC bf CC f GLM OS sb wh)
Lamb's Mill Road, ✉ME 04055 *(Country Road 0.5 mile outside the town, Western Mountains, Lake Region of Maine).* ☎ 693-6253
E-Mail: lambsmitl@pirot.net
6 rooms with private baths, TV, refrigerator, air condition. Rates US$ 90-120 in season (May-Nov) rest of the year US$ 70-100.

Ogunquit ☎ 207

● Located just 70 miles north of Boston, Ogunquit is the quieter and smaller alternative to Provincetown. The village itself is pretty and the beach is white and many miles long. Oqunquit is busy in the summer months and really peaceful for the rest of the year. There are a few gay bars but don't expect a party scene here. This is the perfect place to recover from the daily hassle, walk along the beach, visit the art galleries and have a romatic dinner in one of the good restaurants. There are several gay guest houses who offer good quality accomodation at very reasonable prices. To get to Ogunquit you need a car which is recommended anyway to explore the beautiful scenery. Many guest houses close after the Columbus Day Weekend in the middle of October.

✱ 120 Kilometer nördlich von Boston gelegen ist Ogunquit die kleinere und ruhigere Alternative zu Provincetown. Der hübsche Ort verfügt über lange, weiße Dünenstrände. Saison ist in Ogunquit im Sommer. Den Rest des Jahres geht es hier sehr beschaulich zu. Es gibt einige schwule Bars, doch sollte man an das Nachtleben keine zu große Erwartungen stellen. Dies ist der perfekte Ort um sich bei ausgiebigen Strandspaziergängen, einem Besuch in einer der zahlreichen Galerien oder bei einem gemütlichen Abendessen bei Kerzenschein, vom Streß des Alltags zu erholen. Die schwulen Pensionen bieten alle komfortable Unterkünfte zu sehr zivilen Preisen. Nach Ogunquit reist man am besten mit dem eigenen Auto, denn nur so läßt sich die schöne Umgebung bequem erkunden. Viele Pensionen schließen nach dem Columbus Day Wochenende Mitte Oktober.

▲ Située à 120 km au nord de Boston, Ogunquit offre une alternative plus calme et plus petite à la ville de province. Cette jolie ville possède de longues plages de dunes blanches. La saison la plus intéressante à Ogunquit, c'est l'été. Le reste de l'année, Ogunquit est assez calme. Il y a quelques bars gays, mais il ne faut pas s'attendre à trouver une vie nocturne particulièrement animée. Mais c'est l'endroit rêvé pour de longues promenades sur la plage, des visites dans quelques-unes des nombreuses galeries, ou pour un dîner comfortable aux chandelles pour se reposer du stress quotidien. Les pensions gay offrent toutes un hébergement comfortable à des prix raisonnables. Il est préférable de se rendre à Ogunquit en voiture pour pouvoir visiter les alentours. Noter que de nombreuses pensions ferment leurs portes après le week-end de Colombus Day, fin Octobre.

☆ Situada a 120 km. al norte de Boston es una pequeña y tranquila alternativa a Provincetown. Ogunquit posee una linda y larga playa de arena blanca. La temporada alta es en verano, durante el resto del año la ciudad es bastante tranquila. Hay algunos bares gay, sin embargo no se debe esperar mucho de la marcha nocturna. Este es el lugar perfecto para hacer largo paseos por la playa, para visitar alguna de las numerosas galerías o para librarse del estrés cotidiano a la luz de las velas de una agradable cena en uno de sus restaurantes. Las pensiones gay ofrecen una confortable estancia a precios relativamente comodos. Para llegar a Ogunquit se debe utilizar preferentemente un coche, solo así se puede apreciar lo hermoso de su paisaje. Muchas pensiones cierran sus puertas a mediados de octubre después del fin de semana de Columbus Day.

❖ Situato a 120 km a nord di Boston, Ogunquit è la variante più piccola e tranquilla rispetto a Provincetown. Il posto carino è dotato di spiagge bianche. L'alta stagione è in estate. Ci sono varie bar gay, però è meglio di non aspettarsi troppo di una vita notturna. E il posto ideale per fare delle passeggiate, visitare una delle numerose gallerie d'arte o cenare in un dei piacevoli ristauranti al lume di candela. Le pensioni gay offrono alloggi a prezzi moderati. Conviene andare ad Ogunquit con la propria macchina, perché solo così si è in grado di conoscere i dintorni con facilità. Molte pensioni chiudono a metà ottobre dopo la fine settimana del Columbus Day.

TOURIST INFO

Chamber of Commerce
☎ 646-2939
Call for free information package

BARS

The Club (AC B D G MA VS) 21-1 h, Sun 17-1 h
13 Main Street ✉ME 03907 ☎ 646-6655
Dance and video bar.

Front Porch (AC B F GLM MA) May-15th Oct 16-1 h
PO Box 796 ✉ME 03907 ☎ 646-3976
Small piano bar. Open on some WE in winter (special holidays).

CAFES

Poor Richard's Tavern (B f glm) 17.30-21.30 h
Perkins Cove at Shore Road/Pine Hill ☎ 646-4722
Open May-October

RESTAURANTS

Arrows (b F glm) Tue-Sun 18-21 h
Berwick Road ✉ME 03907 *(2.5 km north of center)* ☎ 361-1111
Open June-November

Jonathan's (A AC B CC F glm S W) 17-21 h
2 Bourne Lane ✉ME 03907 ☎ 646-4777
Continental food

The Lobster Shack (b F glm)
Perkins Cove ☎ 646-2941

GUEST HOUSES

Admiral's Inn (bf glm H pi)
70 South Main Street ✉ME 03907 ☎ 646-7093
Open year-round

Beauport Inn (AC bf CC f g MA OS W WE)
102 Shore Road ✉ME 03907 ☎ 646-8680
E-Mail: lobster@cybertours.com
Homepage: ogun-online.com/beauport
4 rooms with private baths. Rates US$ 70-115 incl. cont. bf. No pets, no kids.

Clipper Ship (AC bf CC glm H) 1st May-15th Oct.
170 U.S. Route 1 ✉ME 03907 ☎ 646-9735
B&B in two restored buidlings (dated 1820 & 1890) in central location. Short walk to the beach. All rooms with TV, some with private bath, own decks and kitchens. Rates US$ 40-85 (off season), US$ 55-130 (on season) incl. bf. Kids and pets welcome.

Gazebo Inn (AC bf glm H pi)
PO Box 668 ✉ME 03907 ☎ 646-3733
Rates double/private bath US$ 65 (Oct-May) and $95 (June-Sep) incl. full gourmet bf. Close to the beach. On trolley line.

The Heritage of Ogunquit (bf gLM H OS wh)
Marginal Avenue ✉ME 03907 ☎ 646-7787
Homepage: wwwone-on-onepc.com/heritage
5 rooms with private and shared bath. Rates USD 70-80 incl. cont. bf. Non-smoking rooms available. Kids welcome, no pets.

The Inn at Tall Chimneys (AC bf CC GLM H wh)
94 U.S. Route 1, ✉ME 03907 ☎ 646-8974
Centrally located B&B. Rooms with Sat-TV, radio, hair-dryer. Single/shared bath US$ 40 (spring/fall) and $50 (June-Sep), double/shared bath $45/65 and double/private bath$48/89 (full bed) or $55/95 (queen bed) incl. continental bf. Some rooms with balcony. Two large decks. Open Apr-Nov.

The Inn at Two Village Square (AC bf CC G MA pi sol wh WO) Mid-May-Mid Oct, Office: 7-22 h
135 U.S. Route 1 ✉ME 03907-0864 *(hillside overlooking the village square)* ☎ 646-5779 Fax: 646-6797
E-Mail: Theinntvs@aol.com Homepage: www.q-net.com/theinntvs
Comfortable Victorian guesthouse with view over the village and ocean. Large decks, heated pool and hot tub. TV room, cozy fire-place. Bicycle hire and gy faciltities. All rooms with radio and TV. Rates US$ 50-125.

Leisure Inn (AC bf G H OS) May 15-Oct 15
6 School Street ✉ME 03907-2113 ☎ 646-2737
E-Mail: ysaint@aol.com Homepage: members.aol.com/reysaint
B&B in a restored building built in 1915. All rooms with TV, most with air-condition. Rates double/private bath US$ 65-95 and double/shared bath $55-75 incl. cont. bf. On-site parking. Walking distance to bars and beach. No kids, no pets.

Moon over Maine (AC bf CC G H OS wh)
6 Berwick Road ✉ME 03907 ☎ 646-6666 ☎ (800) 851-6837
E-Mail: moonmaine@aol.com
Homepage: www.members.aol.com/moonmaine
All rooms with private bath, balcony, radio and SAT-TV. Rates USD 49-119 depending on season incl. cont. bf. Kids welcome, no pets.

Ogunquit Beach Inn (A AC B bf CC f GLM H MA)
Check-in: 14-19 h
8 School Street, ✉ME 03907 *(Village center)* ☎ 646-1112
☎ 888-976-2463 Fax: 646-8858 E-Mail: ogtbeach@aol.com
Just 5 minutes from the beautiful beach. All rooms with telephone, Sat-TV, radio, video, apartments with kitchenette, most with private baths. Rates US$ 50-125 depending on season. Apartment US$ 900 per week (summer rates). Expanded continental bf served.

The Ogunquit House (AC bf CC GLM H MA OS) 15 Mar-2 Jan, 8-22 h
3 Glen Avenue, ✉ME 03907 ☎ 646-2967
E-Mail: ogunquitHS@aol.com
In walking distance to the beach. All rooms with balcony. Rates. off season US$ 45-85, in season US$ 65-135 incl. continental breakfast.

Old Village Inn (bf glm H)
30 Main Street ✉ME 03907 ☎ 646-7088

Rockmere Lodge B&B (bf CC E glm H msg)
40 Stearns Road ✉ME 03907 ☎ 646-2985 Fax: 646-6947 E-Mail: rockmere@cybertours.com
Homepage: www.chickadee.com/rockmere
Eight rooms with private bath and TV. Rates double US$ 100-165 incl. cont. bf. Ocean views.

The Seasons Hotel (bf glm H)
178 U.S. Route 1 ✉ME 03907 ☎ 646-6041

White Rose Inn (AC bf glm H)
64 South Main Street ✉ME 03907 ☎ 646-3432
Rooms with private bath, TV, some with refrigerator and microwave. Rates US$ 85-109 (July-August), $39-60 (Sep-Apr) and $45-95 (May-June). Rooms with shared bath available (not from Sep-Apr) for $65-75 (July-Aug) and $45-65 (May-June). Breakfast buffet incl. in price. TV room.

Yellow Monkey Guest House (AC bf GLM H)
168 Main Street ✉ME 03907 ☎ 646-9056
Close to beach, shops and restaurants. Rooms with private and shared bath, TV in every room. Rates on request.

Portland ☎ 207

BARS

Blackstone's (B GLM OG) 16-1, Sun 12-1 h
6 Pine Street ✉ME 04102 ☎ 775-2885

Somewhere (AC B CC f GLM MA N S VS) 16-1 h
117 Spring Street ✉ME 04101 ☎ 871-9169
Piano on Friday and Saturday, Karaoke on Tuesday and Thursday.

RESTAURANTS

Katahdin (b F glm) 17-22 h, closed Sun
106 Spring Street ☎ 774-1740

CRUISING

-Deering Oaks Park (AYOR) (off Park Avenue)
-Maine Mall (not very active)

Tenants Harbor ☎ 207

HOTELS

East Wind Inn (F glm H)
PO Box 149, ✉ME 04860 ☎ 372-6366
Priv. and shared baths, telephone.

USA-Maryland

East USA

Initials: MD

Time: GMT -5

Area: 32.134 km² / 13,142 sq mi.

Population: 5,094,000

Capital: Annapolis

● Homosexual oral and anal intercourse is prohibited in Maryland.

✸ In Maryland ist homosexueller Oral- und Analverkehr verboten.

▲ Dans le Maryland, la fellation et la pénétration anale sont interdites seulement pour les homosexuels.

☆ En Maryland las relaciones homosexuales por vía oral o anal están prohibidas.

❖ In Maryland sono vietati i rapporti orali ed anali tra omosessuali.

Baltimore ☎ 410

GAY INFO

Baltimore Alternative. The
PO Box 23 51 ✉MD 21203 ☎ 235-3401 Fax: 889-5665
E-Mail: BaltAlt@aol.com Homepage: www.baltalt.com
Free monthly newspaper.

Baltimore Gaypaper
241 West Chase Street ✉MD 21201 ☎ 837-7748
Fax: 837-8512 E-Mail: editor@bgp.org
Biweekly newspaper. Features local and international news, reviews, cultural events and classifed ads. 32 pages.

Gay & Lesbian Switchboard 19.30-22.30 h
☎ 837-8888

BARS

Allégro (B d GLM VS YG) 16-4 h, Tue men's night
1101 Cathedral Street ✉MD 21201 ☎ 837-3906

Baltimore Eagle (B G LJ MA) 16-2 h
2022 North Charles Street ✉MD 21218 *(Entrance on 21st Street)*
☎ 823-2453

Club Atlantis (AC B CC G SNU)
615 Fallsway ✉MD 21202 ☎ 727-9099

Club Bunns (B G)
606 West Lexington Street ☎ 727-6064

Club 1722 (B G) 1722
North Charles Street ☎ 727-7431

Hippo (B D G MA s TV) 1
West Eager Street ☎ 547-0069

Leon's (B F G MA) 11-2, lunch available 11-15 h
870 Park Avenue ✉MD 21201 ☎ 301/539-4993

Stagecoach (B D GLM W) 16-2 h
1003 N. Charles Street ☎ 547-0107

Unicorn (B D G MG N) Mon Fri 19-2 h, Sat Sun 15-2 h
2218 Boston Street ✉MD 21231 ☎ 342-8344

CAFES

Coconuts Cafe (B gLM)
331 West Madison Street ☎ 383-6064
Mainly women.

DANCECLUBS

1722 (D glm YG)
1722 North Charles Street ☎ 727-7431
Very popular after-hour club. Bring your own bottle.

RESTAURANTS

Central Station (B F Glm MA N VS) 11.30-2 h
1001 N. Charles Street ☎ 752-7133
American cuisine. Also a popular gay bar.

Gampy's (b F glm) 11.30-2, Fri Sat 11.30-3 h
904 North Charles Street ✉MD 21201 ☎ 837-9797
Typical American food from the different regions at reasonable prices. Recommended!

Louie's Book Store Café (b F g)
518 North Charles Street ☎ 962-1224
American cuisine. Also a bookstore.

Mount Vernon Stable (b F glm)
909 North Charles Street ☎ 685-7427

SEX SHOPS/BLUE MOVIES

Big Top (g) 0-24 h
429 East Baltimore Street ✉MD 21202 ☎ 547-2495

Center News
205 West Lafayette Street ✉MD 21201 *(near park)*
☎ 301/727-9544

BOOK SHOPS

Lambda Rising (AC CC GLM MA VS W) 10-22 h
241 West Chase Street ✉MD 21201 *(In Gay Community Center)* ☎ 234-0069
Gay, lesbian, bisexual and transgender books, videos, magazines and gifts. Free local guides.

TRAVEL & TRANSPORT

Adventures in Travel
3900 North Charles Street ✉MD 21218 ☎ 467-1161

HOTELS

Mount Vernon Hotel (AC B bf CC F glm H MA)
24 West Franklin St. ✉MD 21201-5090 ☎ 727-2000 ☎ (800) 537-8483 Fax: 576-9300
Friendly hotel located in the Mount Vernon neighborhood, the area containing most of the gay bars. Rates from US$ 69 to US$ 109 per night.

GUEST HOUSES

Chez Claire Bed & Breakfast (AC bf CC glm H MA p) 8-22 h
17 West Chase Street ✉MD 21201-5404 *(in historic Mt. Vernan area)* ☎ 685-4666 Fax: 837-0996
All rooms with telephone and TV. Rates single US$ 60-75, double 65-80 (bf incl.).

Mr. Mole (AC bf glm H)
1601 Bolton Street ✉MD 21217 ☎ 728-1179
B&B in old town house. 5 suites with private and shared baths. Rates incl. bf US$ 80-145. Kids over 10 ok, no pets.

William Page Inn (AC bf CC glm H MA wh)
8 Martin Street, Annapolis ✉MD 21401-1716 ☎ 626-1506
Located in the Historic District of Annapolis.

GENERAL GROUPS

Black and White Men/People of All Colors Together 3rd Fri 19.30 h at 241 West Chase Street
PO Box 33186 ✉MD 21218 ☎ 583-3938 Fax: 235-3191
E-Mail: bpbalt@aol.com

HEALTH GROUPS

Chase Brexton Health Services
1001 Cathedral Street ☎ 837-2050
Also provides mental health services.

RELIGIOUS GROUPS

Dignity
PO Box 12 43 ✉MD 21203 ☎ 325-1519
Gay & lesbian catholics.

Integrity
c/o Emmanuel Church, 800 Cathedral Street ✉MD 21201 ☎ 732-0718
Lesbian and gay Episcopalians

MCC Sun 15, Wed 19 h
3401 Old York Road ✉MD 21218 ☎ 889-6363

Hagerstown ☎ 301

DANCECLUBS

Headquarters (B D F GLM S) 17-? h
41 North Potomac Street ✉MD 21740 ☎ 797-1553

Silver Spring ☎ 301

HOTELS

Northwood Inn (g H)
10304 Eastwood Avenue ✉MD 20901 ☎ 593-7027

USA-Massachusetts

Northeast USA
Initials: MA
Time: GMT -5
Area: 27.337 km^2 / 11.180 sq mi.
Population: 6,118,000
Capital: Boston
Important gay cities: Boston and Provincetown

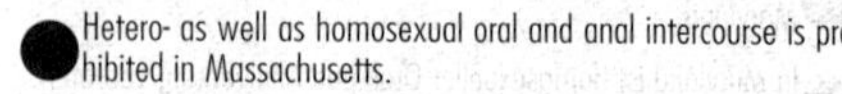

● Hetero- as well as homosexual oral and anal intercourse is prohibited in Massachusetts.

✱ In Massachusetts ist hetero- wie homosexueller Oral- und Analverkehr verboten.

▲ Dans le Massachusetts, la fellation et la pénétration anale sont interdites pour tous, homos et hétéros.

☆ En Massachusetts las relaciones homosexuales y heterosexuales por vía oral o anal están prohibidas.

❖ In Massachusetts sono vietati i rapporti orali ed anali sia tra eterosessuali che tra omosessuali.

Amherst ☎ 413

GUEST HOUSES

Ivy House B&B (bf glm H)
1 Sunset Court ✉MA 01002
☎ 549-7554 E-Mail: ivyhouse@shaysnet.com
Small B&B in restored colonial home. All rooms with private bath. Rates US$ 40-90 incl. bf. 100 miles west from Boston.

SWIMMING

-Cummington gay beach (Park car at Swift River Rest Stop on Route 9 and walk 1 mile through woods.)

Boston ☎ 617

GAY INFO

Bay Windows
1523 Washington Street ✉MA 02118 ☎ 266-6670
Weekly publication, about 25 pages. US$ 0.50. Features news, arts & entertainment, interviews, media watch column.

TOURIST INFO

Greater Boston Convention & Visitor Bureau
Prudential Tower, Suite 400 ✉MA 02199 ☎ 536-4100

BARS

Boston Eagle (B G lj) 15-2 h
520 Tremont Street ✉MA 02116 ☎ 542-4494
Cruise bar.

Fritz (B F GLM N) 12-2 h
26 Chandler Street ✉MA 02116 *(at Berkeley)* ☎ 482-4428
Brunch Sat Sun 11-15.30 h.

Geoffrey's Cafe - Bar (AC b bf CC F GLM MA) 9-23 h
578 Tremont Street, South End ✉MA 02118 ☎ 266-1122
Casual dining with wine bar.

Jacque's (B D G S TV)
79 Broadway/Piedmont Street ✉MA 02116 *(behind Howard Johnson's)* ☎ 426-8902

Luxor (AC B G VS YG)
69 Church Street/Stuart Street ✉MA 02116 ☎ 423-6969
Comfortable video bar. Also: Mario's (restaurant) and Jox (sports bar).
Paradise (B D F G lj SNU) Mon-Wed 17-1 h, Thu-Sun -2 h
180 Massachussetts Avenue, Cambridge ✉MA 02139
☎ 864-4130
Cruisy bar.
Ramrod (AC B DR G LJ) 12-2 h
1254 Boylston Street ✉MA 02215 ☎ 266-2986
Spike (B G LJ) Wed-Sun
965 Massachusetts Avenue ☎ 427-7807
119 Merrimac (AC B G LJ N) 10.30-2, Sun 12-2 h
119 Merrimac Street/Stanford Street ✉MA 02114 ☎ 367-0713

MEN'S CLUBS

Safari Club (DR G P sol VS WO) 0-24 h
90 Wareham Street ✉MA 02118 *(second floor between Albany & Harris)* ☎ 292-0011 *ID required.*

CAFES

Centre Street Café (b f G)
597 Centre Street, Jamaica Plain ✉MA 02130 ☎ 524-9217
Everyday Cafe (bf CC f g MA OS) Mon-Fri 7-21 h, Sat 9-21 h, Sun -17 h
517 Columbus Avenue ✉MA 02118-3003 ☎ 536-2119
Tremont Ice Cream (b f G)
584 Tremont Street ✉MA 02116 ☎ 247-8414

DANCECLUBS

Avalon/Axis (A AC B D G MA S tv YG)
13 Lansdowne Street ✉MA 02215 *(in the Fenway)* ☎ 262-2424
Only Sun 9-2 h, straight all other days.
Buzz (B D GLM YG) Sat 22-? h
67 Stuart Street ☎ 267-8969
Popular.
Manray (B D glm) Gay Thu „Campus" 21-1 h, Sat „Liquid" 22-? h
21A Brookline Street/Central Square, Cambridge ✉MA 02139
☎ 864-0400

RESTAURANTS

Club Café (! AC B CC D e F GLM S VS) 11-2, dinner 18-22 h
209 Columbus Avenue ✉MA 02116 *(at Berkeley)* ☎ 536-0966
Features some of Boston's best jazz musicians and exquisite American and continental cuisine. Highly reccommended.
Icarus (B F g) Sun brunch
3 Appleton Street ✉MA 02116 ☎ 426-1790
Mario's (B F GLM MA) 17.30-2 h
69 Church Street ✉MA 02116 ☎ 542-3776
Italian cuisine.
On the Park (A AC b bf CC F glm MA) Tue-Thu 7-30-22.30 h, Fri-Sat 17-30-23 h, Sat-Sun 9-15 h brunch.
1 Union Park ✉MA 02118 ☎ 426-0862

SEX SHOPS/BLUE MOVIES

Art Cinema I+II (G)
204 Tremont Street ✉MA 02116 ☎ 482-4661

BOOK SHOPS

Downtown Books
697 Washington Street ✉MA 02111 ☎ 426-7644
Glad Day Bookstore (GLM) Mon-Thu 9.30-22 h, Fri Sat -23 h, Sun & holidays 12-21 h
673 Boylston Street ✉MA 02116 ☎ 267-3010 Fax: 267-5474

We think the World of you
540 Tremont Street ✉MA 02116 ☎ 423-1965

FASHION SHOPS

Vernon's Specialties
386 Moody Street ✉MA 02154 *(Waltham)* ☎ 894-1744
All your needs for cross dressing, including on site beauty salon. Mailorder catalogue available.

VIDEO SHOPS

The Movie Place (CC G VS) 10-22, Sun 12-22 h
526 Tremont Street ✉MA 02116 ☎ 482-9008

HOTELS

Chandler Inn (AC B bf GLM H lj MA)
26 Chandler Street ✉MA 02116 *(at Berkely)* ☎ (800) 842-3450
B&B hotel located near Back Bay train station. Gay owned. Brunch Sat and Sun 11-15.30h. All rooms with priv. bath, WC and phone.
463 Beacon Street Guest House (glm H)
463 Beacon Street ✉MA 02115 ☎ 536-1302
Single/double US$ 50-95, also special weekly rates available.

GUEST HOUSES

Amsterdammertje (bf GLM H MA OS)
PO Box 1731 ✉MA 02205-1731 *(Near ocean)* ☎ 471-8454
Fax: 471-8454 Homepage: www.bbonline.com/ma/am
Small B&B, 15 minutes from Downtown in a quiet neighborhood at the ocean. Rooms with shared bath, telephone, radio, TV, video and hair-dryer. Rates single US$ 69, double 99. Non-smoking.

Oasis Guest House (AC bf CC glm H OS) Office: 8-24 h
22 Edgerly Road ✉MA 02115 *(Green Line-Convention Center)*
☎ 267-2262 Fax: 267-1920 E-Mail: oasisgh@tiac.net
Homepage: www.oasisgh.com
15 minutes from the airport. Located in the heart of Boston, close to the gay scene. All rooms with phone, color TV, some with private bath and balcony. Rates from US$ 72-119.

GENERAL GROUPS

Babson Gay & Lesbian Alliance
PO Box 631, Babson Park ✉MA 02157 *Wellesley*
Boston College Gay/Lesbian Support Group
Haley House, 314 Hammond Street, Chestnut Hill ✉MA 02167
Boston Lesbian & Gay Political Alliance
PO Box 65, Back Bay Annex ✉MA 02117 ☎ 265-0348
Boston University Lesbian/Gay Law Association
775 Commonwealth Avenue ✉MA 02215 ☎ 353-9804
c/o Program, Resource Office, George Sherman Union
Gays at MIT (GAMIT)
☎ 253-5440
Greater Boston Gay Men's Association
PO Box 10 09 ✉MA 02205
Monthly meetings with guest speakers & informal social hour.
University of Massachusetts/Boston Lesbian & Gay Center
c/o Students Activities Center, Harbor Campus, ✉MA 02125 *Dorchester* ☎ 929-8276

FETISH GROUPS

Leather Knights 1st Thu
c/o Ramrod, 1254 Boylston Street ✉MA 02215

HEALTH GROUPS

AIDS Action Committee Mon-Fri 12-20 h, Sat -18 h
131 Clarendon ✉MA 02116 ☎ 437-6200
Direct services to people with AIDS; councelling for all concerned; education and advocacy.
Fenway Community Health Center
16 Haviland Street ✉MA 02115 ☎ 267-0900 ☎ 267-9001 (Helpline).
Second location: 93 Mass Avenue. Sexually transmitted disease treatment; HIV education and testing program; general medicine; gay and lesbian victim recovery program.

RELIGIOUS GROUPS

Dignity (GLM) Sun 17.30 h
355 Boylston Street at Arlington Street Church ✉MA 02116
☎ 536-6518
MCC Sun 19 h
131 Cambridge Street at Old West Church ✉MA 02114 ☎ 437-0420

CRUISING

-Revere Beach (G NU) (2 miles north of Boston downtown, on the boulevard between Band Sand and Kelly's. Take the blue line to Revere Beach or Wonderland Station.)
-The Fens at Victoria Gardens (in the high reeds along the river, near Boylston Street)

Edgartown ☎ 508

HOTELS

Captain Dexter House (AC bf glm H MA OS)
35 Pease's Point Way, ✉MA 02539 *(PO Box 27 98)* ☎ 627-7289

Ipswich

SWIMMING

-Crane's Beach (NU) (from sunrise to sunset. Off old Route 1. Fee varies from US$ 3 to 10 per car depending on season and day. Cape Cod style beach, the sand dunes at the southern end become very cruisy.)

Martha's Vineyard ☎ 508

HOTELS

Captain Dexter House (AC bf glm MA OS)
100 Main Street, Vineyard Haven ✉MA 02568 ☎ 693-6564
Rates US $65-160.

GUEST HOUSES

Martha's Place Inn (AC bf CC GLM H MA OS) 9-21 h
114 Main Street, Vineyard Haven ✉MA 02537 ☎ 693-0253
E-Mail: info@marthasplace.com
Homepage: www.marthasplace.com
Rates US$ 175-275 (in-season) and $125-225 (value season).

Northampton ☎ 413

GAY INFO

Community Prideline
☎ 584-4848

DANCECLUBS

The Grotto (B D F GLM S) 17-1 h
25 West Street ☎ 586-6900

GENERAL GROUPS

Venture Out (glm)
☎ 584-3145
Outdoor adventure group. Weekly events.

CRUISING

-Route I-91 Springfield →Northampton, Ⓟ behind Exit 17B
-Route I-91 Northampton →Springfield, Ⓟ behind Exit 18 (near Easthampton and Holyoke)

Provincetown ☎ 508

● This is how *the gay resort par excellence* should be: Far from major cities (Boston being 150 km away) and situated at the end of a longstretched peninsula. It takes two and a half hours by car to reach Provincetown from Boston, taking Highway 6, which circulates *Cape Cod Bay*. Be prepared that crossing the bridge to the peninsula can take quite some time. Provincetown owes its development to artists, who moved and settled there at the beginning of the century. In the sixties the town became very popular for all those not conforming politically or sexually to the conservative norm. Best time to visit is between Memorial Day (May 30) and Labour Day (1st Monday in September). As there is no gay magazine in Provincetown it is best to obtain information at the *Provincetown Business Guild*, the gay „chamber of commerce", which also organizes the special event *Carnival Week* in mid August.

✱ So gehört es sich für *den schwulen Badeort par excellence*: abseits einer Großstadt (Boston ist 150 km entfernt) und am Ende einer -in diesem Fall- Landzunge.
Zweieinhalb Stunden benötigt man per Auto nach Provincetown von Boston aus, wenn man die *Cape Cod Bay* auf dem Highway 6 umrundet. Es kann übrigens sehr lange dauern, bis man die Brücke auf die Landzunge überquert hat.
Provincetown verdankt seine Entwicklung Künstlern, die seit Anfang

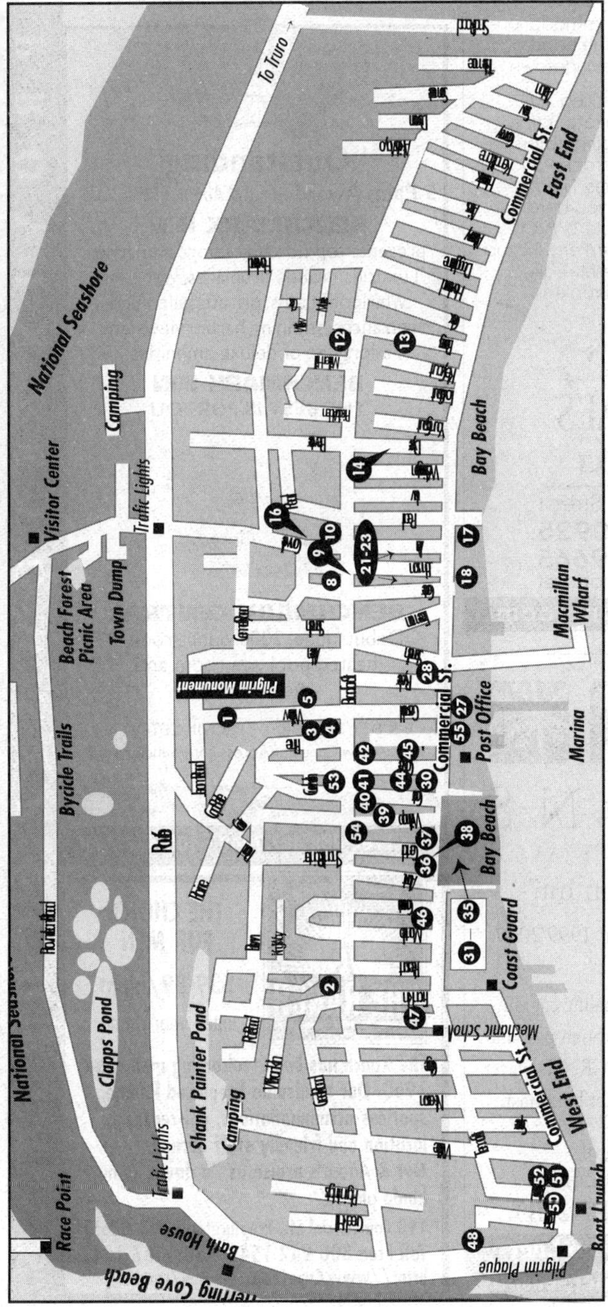

1 The Chicago Guest House
2 The Lamplighter Inn Guest House
3 Six Webster Place Guest House
4 Fairbanks Inn Guest House
5 Howard's End Guest House
8 Chancellor Inn Guest House
9 Sunset Inn Guest House
10 Admiral's Landing Guest House
12 Normandy Guest House
13 Mayflower Apartments
14 Benchmark Inn
16 Dexter's Inn Guest House
17 Angel's Landing Guest House
18 Captain's Guest House
21 Coat of Arms Guest House
22 Elephant Walk Inn Guest House
23 Prince Albert House Guest House
27 Lobster Pot Restaurant
28 Moffett Guest House
30 The Ranch Guest House
31 Pied Piper Bar
32 Anchor Inn Guest House
34 The Sandpiper Beach House Guest House
35 Boatslip Beach Club Hotel
36 Rose & Crown Guest House
37 White Wind Inn Guest House
38 Harborside Realty Apartments
39 Watership Inn Guest House
40 Revere Guest House
41 Brass Key Guest House
42 Backstreet Bar
44 Roomers Guest House
45 Atlantic House Guest House
46 Grand View Inn Guest House
47 Shire Max Inn Guest House
48 Land's End Inn Guest House
50 The West End Inn Guest House
51 Eighteen O Seven Guest House
52 Renaissance Apartments
53 Carl's Guest House
54 Beaconlight Guesthouse
55 Crown and Anchor Hotel

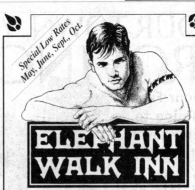

des Jahrhunderts dorthin zogen und sich niederliessen. Wirklich beliebt wurde der Ort dann in den 60er Jahren als Zuflucht für all jene, die politisch oder sexuell von der konservativen Norm abwichen.
Die beste Zeit für einen Besuch liegt zwischen Memorial Day (30. Mai) und Labour Day (1. Montag im September). Es gibt keine schwule Zeitung in Provincetown, am besten besorgt man sich Infos bei der *Provincetown Business Guild*, der schwulen „Handelskammer", die übrigens auch Mitte August das special event *Carnival Week* veranstaltet.

▲ Provincetown est une station balnéaire idéale: loin de tout, au bout d'une presqu'île. Boston est à 150 km.
Il faut deux heures et demie pour aller de Boston à Provincetown en voiture, par la „Highway 6" qui contourne Cape Code Bay. Provincetown doit sa renommée aux nombreux artistes qui, dès le début du siècle, y sont venus en villégiature, mais ce n'est que dans les années 60 qu'elle a définitivement acquis ses lettres de noblesse en offrant asyle à tous ceux qui, victimes de persécutions politiques ou sexuelles, ont fui le conservatisme et l'étroitesse d'esprit de la société américaine.
Le meilleur moment pour découvrir Provincetown, c'est fin mai (Memorial day, 30 mai) et début septembre (Labour Day, 1er lundi du mois). Il n'y a pas de magasines gays locaux à Provincetown. Pour savoir que faire, où sortir, comment et avec qui, consultez le „Provincetown Business Guild" ou à la „Chambre de Commerce" gay. Elle organise chaque année mi-août la „Carnival Week".

☆ Provincetown se encuentra cerca de la gran ciudad Boston (a 150 km. de distancia) y al final de una pequeña península. Se puede decir que cuenta geograficamente con las condiciones ideales para ser denominada balneario gay. Con coche se tarda aproximadamente 2,5 horas desde Boston, si ve va por la autopista 6 pasando por Cape Cod Boy. El traspaso del puente para llegar a la península suele tardar bastante. El desarrollo de Provincetown es de agradecer a los artistas que al inicio de este siglo se mudaron a vivir en este lugar. Este sitio tomó auge en la década de los '60 cuando muchos gays encontraron en él, el lugar de escape a la política sexual y las normas conservativas de la sociedad. La época ideal para visitar Provincetown es entre el Memorial Day (30 de Mayo) y el Labour Day (1er. lunes de Septiembre). No hay publicaciones gay. Informaciones sobre los acontecimientos del momento se obtienen del *Provincetown Business Guild*, la Camara de Comercio Gay. Que organiza también a mediados de agosto la *Carnival Week*.

❖ Al margine di una grande città (Boston è a soli 150 km) e alla fine di una appendice di terra: ciò si addice alla stazione balneare gay per eccellenza. Provincetown dista due ore e mezza d'auto da Boston, percorrendo la Highway 6 lungo *Cape Cod Bay*. Provincetown deve il proprio sviluppo agli artisti che vi si trasferirono all'inizio del secolo. Anche se solo durante gli anni '60 è divenuta realmente ambita da tutti coloro che si distanziavano politicamente e sessualmente dalla norma. Il periodo migliore per una visita è tra Memorial day (30 maggio) e Labour day (primo lunedì di sett.). Provincetown non ha un proprio giornale gay. Potrete ottenere informazioni presso il *Provincetown Business Guild*, la „camera di commercio gay" che organizza a metà agosto la manifestazione *Carnival Week*.

GAY INFO

Provincetown Business Guild (GLM)
PO Box 421-94 SP ✉MA 02657 ☎ 487-2313
Homepage: www.ptown.org
Call for a free gay guide to Provincetown.

BARS

Atlantic House (B D G LJ OS S) 11-1 h
8 Masonic Place ✉MA 02657 ☎ 487-3821
Backstreet Bar (B CC G MA OS S SNU YG)
9-11 Carver Street/Bradford Street ✉MA 02657 ☎ 487-0688
Boatslip Beach Club (! B D GLM MA pi OS s) Apr-Oct
161 Commercial Street ✉MA 02657 ☎ 487-1669
Very popular, especially the daily tea dance.
Bubala's by the Bay
183 Commercial ✉MA 02657
☎ 487-0773
Crown and Anchor Motor Inn (B D F G H s) 10-1 h
247 Commercial Street ✉MA 02657 ☎ 487-1430
Pied Piper (B D G)
193 A Commercial Street ✉MA 02657 ☎ 487-1527

CAFES

Café Blase (b F g)
326 Commercial Street ✉MA 02657 ☎ 487-9465
Fat Jack's Café (F g)
335 Commercial Street ✉MA 02657 ☎ 487-4822

RESTAURANTS

Euro Island Grill (B F glm OS) -1 h
258 Commercial Street ✉MA 02657 ☎ 487-2505
Grand Central
5 Masconic Place ✉MA 02657
Lobster Pot (b F g)
321 Commercial Street ✉MA 02657 ☎ 487-0842
Mews Waterfront Dinning (AC B CC F glm MA s)
Summer: 18-1 h daily, 11-1 weekends, Winter: 18-24 h daily, expect Wed.
429 Commercial Street ✉MA 02657 *(East End)* ☎ 487-1500
International specialties. restaurant & café.
Post Office Café Cabaret (B F G MA S)
303 Commercial Street ✉MA 02657 ☎ 487-3892
Upper Deck (g F T)
247 Commercial Street ✉MA 02657 ☎ 487-1430
Seafood with the best view over the bay.

FITNESSTUDIOS

Mussel Beach Health Club (AC CC sol sa WO) 6-21 h
35 Bradford Street ✉MA 02657 ☎ 487-0001
Provincetown Gym & Fitness Center Inc.
(AC CC GLM MA msg WO) 6-21 h (season) 7-20 h (off season)
81 Shank Painter Road ✉MA 02657 ☎ 487-2776

BOOK SHOPS

Now Yoyager (GLM) 10-23 h
357 Commercial Street ✉MA 02657 ☎ 487-0848
Mysteries gay and lesbian books. Selected fiction and non-fiction.
Provincetown Bookshop (GLM) 10-23 h
246 Commercial Street ✉MA 02657 ☎ 487-0964

GALLERIES

Charles Batliuik Gallery (A)
432 Commercial Street ✉MA 02657 ☎ 487-3611

TRAVEL & TRANSPORT

In Town Reservations & Travel Service Summer: 8-20 h, Off-season: 9-17 h, closed Sun.
4 Standish Street ✉MA 02657 ☎ 487-1883 Fax: 487-6140
Homepage: intownres@aol.com
Free service: locate and reverse Gay & Lesbian inns, hotels, cottages and houses for visitors to Provincetown. Also travel agency.
Provincetown Reservation System 10-18 h
293 Commercial Street ✉MA 02657 ☎ 487-2400
Fax: 487-6517 E-Mail: ptownres@ptownres.com
Room reservations, travel agency, tickets.

HOTELS

Boatslip Beach Club (B bf CC D F GLM H MA pi s T) Apr-Oct
161 Commercial Street, PO Box 393 ✉MA 02657 ☎ 487-1669
Fax: 587-6021. Call toll-free within the U.S. (800) 451-SLIP.
E-Mail: boatslip@provincetown.com.
Homepage: www.provincetown.com/boatslip
Beach location, queen or double bed, private bath, TV and sea view. Rates US$ 65-160.
The Commons Guesthous & Bistro (B CC F GLM H MA N OS) Jun-Sep: 8-24 h, Oct-May 16-24 h (closed Tue Wed)
386 Commercial Street ✉MA 02657 ☎ 487-7800
Fax: 487 6114 E-Mail: commons@capecod.net
Hotel with restaurant & bar.
Crown and Anchor (B CC D F glm H MA pi s) 11-1 h
247 Commercial Street, PO Box 111 ✉MA 02657
☎ & Fax: 487-1430
All rooms with private bath, some have TV. Rates USD 59-102.
Gifford House Inn (B bf CC D GLM H N OS STV) Office: 9-23 h
9-11 Carver Street ✉MA 02657 ☎ 487-0688
☎ (800) 434-0130 (Toll-free) Fax: 487-4918
Rooms with private bath. Rates USD 45-158. extra bed 20 incl. continental bf. More than 140 years old restored home situated on a hill overlooking the bay. Also danceclub and bar.

LAND'S END INN
22 COMMERCIAL STREET
PROVINCENTOWN
MA 02657
Telephone (508) 487-0706
800-276-7088
Unique rooms
with spectacular views at the
very tip of Cape Cod

Provincetown Inn (glm H)
1 Commercial Street ☎ 487-9500 Fax: 487-2911
The rooms have private bath, color TV, telephone. Call for rates.

GUEST HOUSES

Admiral's Landing (AC bf CC G H MA OS VS) office: 8-22 h
158 Bradford Street ✉MA 02657 ☎ 487-9665
☎ (800) 934-0925 (Toll-free) Fax: 487-4437
E-Mail: admiral@capecod.net
Homepage: www.admiralslanding.com
Cottages with kitchenette. All rooms with bath, TV, VCR, phone, fridge and fireplaces. Non-smoking. Rates double with shared bath US$ 55-125, studio 74-119.

Ampersand Guest House (AC bf CC GLM H MA)
6 Cottage Street ✉MA 02657 ☎ 487-0959
E-Mail: ampersand@capecod.net
Homepage: www.capecod.net/ampersand
Nicely furnished with lots of restored antiques. Rates double/shared bath US$ 55-80, double/private bath $65-110, studio (with view over the yard and water) $75-130. Bf incl. Fireplace and sun deck. TV room.

Anchor Inn (CC g H) 9-21 h
175 Commercial Street ✉MA 02657 ☎ 487-0432
Private bath, balcony. Off season US$ 75-95; season 95-135.

Angel's Landing (F glm H)
353 Commercial Street ✉MA 02657 ☎ 487-1600
Kitchenette, private bath, balcony. Rates US$ 45-75.

Atlantic House (B D G H MA LJ S)
4-6 Masonic Place ✉MA 02657 ☎ 487-3821

Beaconlight Guest House (AC bf CC E Glm H MA wh)
12 Winthrop Street ✉MA 02657 ☎ & Fax: 487-9603
Toll-free ☎ (0800) 696 9603. E-mail: beaconlite@capcod.net
Homepage: http://www.capecod.net/beaconlight/
Very comfortable and awarded B&B. All rooms with private bath, refrigerator, telephone, cable TV, video and hair-dryer. Rates double USD 40-85 (Dec-Apr 7), 55-125 (Sep 23-Nov), 85-150 (high season), suite USD 80-200 depending on season incl. continental bf. Reservation recommended. Lovely garden and private decks.

Benchmark Inn (AC bf CC E G H msg OS pi wh)
6-8 Dyer Street ✉MA 02657 *(central)* ☎ 487-1542
☎ (800) 942-1542 (Toll-free) Fax: 487-3446
E-Mail: parkhd@aol.com
Homepage: www.CapeCodAccess.com/benchmark/
Rooms with telephone, TV, video, radio, minibar, safe, hair-dryer, some with balcony and kitchenette.Heated pool and spa room. Rates double/shared bath US$ 59-89, single room/shared bath 39-75 incl. bf. Additional bed US$ 30.

Bradford-Carver House. The (AC bf CC GLM H MA OS) Office: 9-21 h
70 Bradford Street ✉MA 02657-1363 ☎ 487-4966
or Toll-free ☎ (0800) 826-9083. Fax: ☎ 487-7213
Small Guesthouse in a historic home. All rooms have private bath, heating, cable TV, video and refrigerator. Rates USD 39-59 (winter), 49-79 (spring/fall) and 80-150 (summer) incl. continental bf. Video library and TV room.

Brass Key Guesthouse. The (AC bf CC GLM H OS pi W wh)
12 Carver Street ✉MA 02657 ☎ 487-9005 Fax: 487-9020
Toll-free ☎ (800) 842-9858.
Historic sea captain's house built 1830's. All rooms with priv. bath, TV, VCR, phone, fridge. Rates US$ 120-200 (season) to 60-145 (off-season), bf incl.

Burch House (B F glm H OS)
116 Bradford Street ✉MA 02657 ☎ 487-9170
Private bath, balcony, some rooms with kitchenette. Rates US$ 40-67 (season) and 27-40 (off season), bf incl.

The Captain and His Ship (AC bf CC E glm H MA OS) 8-23 h
164 Commercial Street ✉MA 02657 ☎ 487-1850
☎ (800) 400-2278
Guesthouse in a restored captain's home built in the last century. All rooms with color TV, video, telephone and refrigerator, most with private bath, some with lovely water view. Rates room/private bath US$ 65-150 and with shared bath $ 55-75 depending on season. Continental bf incl. Smoke free establishment.

Captain's House. The (bf G H lj MA OS)
350A Commercial Street ✉MA 02657 ☎ 487-9353
Toll free (800) 457-8885
Private and shared baths. All rooms with TV, some with refrigerator. Rates USD 75-95. Open all year round.

Carl's Guest House (AC CC G H MA NU OS sol wh)
68 Bradford Street ✉MA 02657 ☎ 487-1650
☎ (800)-348-CARL E-Mail: info@CarlsGuestHouse.com
Homepage: www.CarlsGuestHouse.com
Excellent location, clean, comfortable, friendly and affordable. Own private sundeck. TV room. Rates single US$ 29-69, double without shower/bath 39-99, with shower/bath 59-129. Men only.

Carpe Diem Guesthouse (AC bf CC GLM H)
12 Johnson Street ✉MA 02657 *(Center of town; half a block from Harbor Beach)* ☎ 487-4242 ☎ (800) 487-0132 Fax: 487-4242
E-Mail: carpediem@capecod.net
Homepage: www.capecod.net/carpediem
13 double rooms with shower/WC, balcony or terrace, telephone, hairdryer, air-conditioning, own key, room service, fax, video, heating and TV. Breakfast buffet incl. Car park. Rates double $65-225 .

Chancellor Inn (G H)
17 Center Street ✉MA 02657 ☎ 487-9423
Chicago House. The (bf CC G H MA OS)
6 Winslow Street ✉MA 02657 *(2 minutes from centre)*
☎ 487-0537 ☎ (800) 733-7869 (toll-free)
E-Mail: chicagohse@aol.com Homepage: www.chicagohse.com
9 private bath, 2 shared bath, 2 apartments and a town house (up to 6 persons). All rooms with TV, some with radio. Rates US§ 40-135. Nice decks.
Coat of Arms (AC B bf CC G H MA OS) Office: 7-21 h
7 Johnson Street ✉MA 02657 ☎ 487-0816
Old Mid Victorian House in the centre of town. Rates US$ 50-75 (off season), 60-95 (on season). No private bath.
Dexter's Inn (bf GLM H OS)
6 Conwell Street ✉MA 02657 ☎ 487-1911
or Toll free ☎ (888) 521-1999 All rooms with private bath, TV and refrigerator. Continental bf included in price. Call for rates. Open year round.
The Dunes (CC GLM H) 9-21 h
125 Bradford Street Ext. ✉MA 02657 ☎ 487-1956
☎ (800)-475-1833 (toll free) Fax: 487-2436
E-Mail: jeff@thedunesprovincetown.com
Homepage: www.thedunesprovincetrown.com
Rates from $39 to $69, Apartments from $69 to $109.
Eighteen O Seven House (AC bf CC G H MG)
54 Commercial Street ✉MA 02657 ☎ 487-2173
E-Mail: ptown1807@aol.com
Open year round. Private & shared bath, kitchenette.
Elephant Walk Inn (AC bf CC GLM H OS VS) April 20-November 10
156 Bradford Street ✉MA 02657 ☎ 487-2543
☎ (800) 889-9255 E-Mail: elephant@capecod.net
Homepage: www.elephantwalkinn.com
Rooms with shower/WC, phone, fax, TV, video, minibar, AC, heating and own key. Car park. Continental bf incl. Rates: double US$ 52-132, single 52-132, additional bed 25.
Elm House (AC bf G lj H)
9 Johnson Street ✉MA 02657 ☎ 487-0793 Fax: 487-7549
Close to the beach. Rates from US$ 50-85.
Fairbanks Inn (bf GLM H OS)
90 Bradford Street ✉MA 02657 ☎ 487-0386
Call for rates
Gabriel's Apartments and Guestrooms (AC bf CC E GLM H msg NU sa WO)
104 Bradford Street ✉MA 02657-1441 ☎ 487-3232
Fax: 487-1605. Email: gabriels@provincetown.com.
Homepage: http://www.provincetown.com/gabriels
All rooms and apartments with bath, balcony, cable-TV, refrigerator. Apartments with fully equipped kitchen. Rates double US$ 55-110, apartment 80-185.
Grand View Inn (bf CC GLM MA OS)
4 Conant Street ✉MA 02657 ☎ 487-9193
Fax: 487-2894. Email: vanbelle@capecod.net
Located in picturesque West End of town with outside deck with a view on the bay. Rates US$ 45-100 (off season), 65-125 (on season) incl. continental bf.
Heritage House. The (bf glm H)
7 Center Street ✉MA 02657 ☎ 487-3692
Airport pick-up, close to beach. Parking. Rooms with shared bath. Call for rates.

Howard's End (bf G H)
5 Winslow Street ✉MA 02657 ☎ 487-0456
Call for more information
The John Randall House (AC bf CC GLM H) 9-21 h
140 Bradford Street ✉MA 02657-1435 ☎ 487-3533
☎ (800)573-6700 (toll free) Fax: 487-3533
E-Mail: jrhouse@capecod.net
Homepage: www.capecod.net/johnrandall/
Free parking, priv. bath, cable TV, VCR
Lamplighter Inn. The (AC bf CC G H MA NU OS)
26 Bradford Street ✉MA 02657 ☎ 487-2529
☎ (800) 263-6574 (toll-free) Fax: 487-0079
E-Mail: lamplite@lamplite.com
Homepage: www.capecodaccess.com/lamplighter
All rooms with TV, video, telephone, balcony, some with private bath. Rates USD 39-99 (without bath) and 59-179 (with bath) incl. continental bf depending on season. The B&B is located on top of a hill in a restored house built in the 1800s with a beautiful view.
Land's End Inn (AC CC bf CC H OS wh)
22 Commercial Street ✉MA 02657 ☎ 487-0706
☎ (800) 276-7088 (toll-free)
Nicely furnished rooms and fully equipped apartments. Rates US$ 87-165 (off season) and 120-190 (high season). Suites with balcony and jacuzzi available (USD 185-285). Continental bf included. TV room.
Lotus Guest House (CC Glm H)
296 Commercial Street ✉MA 02657 ☎ 487-4644
Rates from US$ 55 (single) -170 (suite).
Moffett House (CC G H LJ MA)
296 A Commercial Street ✉MA 02657 ☎ 487-6615
☎ (800) 990-8865
Rates off season US$ 45-75, on season $55-105.
Normandy House (AC bf CC G MA NU OS wh WO)
184 Bradford Street ✉MA 02657 ☎ 487-1197
Rates US$ 50-115.
Pilgrim Colony Inn (bf CC GLM H) May-Oct
670 Shore Road, North Truro ✉MA 02652 ☎ 487-1100
All rooms with private bath. Rates US$ 69-89. Free coffee and newspaper each morning.
Prince Albert House (AC G MA OS) 8-22 h
166 Commercial Street ✉MA 02657 ☎ 487-0859
or Toll-Free ☎ (800) 992-0859. Email: palbert@capecod.net
Homepage: http://www.capecod.net/princealbert
No smoking, 8 rooms with private baths, 2 with shared rooms. All rooms with color TV, video and small refrigerator. Rates on season US$ 75-160.
Ranch Guestlodge (B bf G lj H MA OS VS)
198 Commercial Street, PO Box 26 ✉MA 02657 *(central)*
☎ 487-1542 ☎ (800) 942-1542 (Toll-free) Fax: 487-3446
E-Mail: parkhd@aol.com
Homepage: www.CapeCodAccess.com/ranch
Sundeck and streetside patio. TV room and private bar. All rooms with shared bath. Sport activities nearby. Rates single US$ 39-75 and double US$ 59-89 coffee/tea included. Additional town $US 30.
Revere Guest House (bf CC GLM H) 9.30-21 h
14 Court Street ✉MA 02657 ☎ 487-2292
E-Mail: reveregh@tiac.net
Homepage: www.provincetown.com/revere
Small B&B in a restored Captain's home (dated 1830). All rooms with TV, telephone, studio with kitchenette. Rates: $40-85 (off season): $65-145 (in season)

"This house on the quiet west end has undergone thorough renovation and emerged a winner. A large and comfortable common room, tasteful, yet understated guest rooms and friendly management make this a great choice"
Highly recommended
OUT&ABOUT
W
WEST END INN
44 Commercial St.
Provincetown, MA 02657
508-487-9555
www.westendinn.com

Romeo's Holiday (AC bf GLM NU wh)
97 Bradford Street ✉MA 02657 ☎ 487-6636
☎ (877)- MY-ROMEO Fax: 487-3082
E-Mail: freenite@romeosholiday.com
Homepage: www.romeosholiday.com
9 double rooms with shower/WC, TV, radio, hair-dryer, own key. Rates US$ 39-129. Continental bf incl.

Roomers (bf CC GLM H)
8 Carver Street ✉MA 02657 ☎ 487-3532
Rooms with private bath, cable TV, doubles with water view. Rates USD 110-150 (summer). Lower rates during off-season. Quiet and elegant house.

Rose & Crown Guesthouse (b bf GLM H OS)
158 Commercial Street ✉MA 02657 ☎ 487-3332
Priv. bath, kitchenette. US$ 40-100 (bf incl.).

Sandpiper Beach House. The (AC CC GLM H MA OS pi)
165 Commercial Street, PO Box 646 ✉MA 02657 ☎ 487-1928
Fax: 487-6021 Toll free ☎ (800) 354-8628.
Waterfront Victorian guest house. All rooms with private bath and TV. Rates USD 105-195 (summer) incl. bf. Lower rates in off-season.

Shamrock Motel (AC CC G H pi wh)
49 Bradford Street ✉MA 02657 ☎ 487-1133
Fax: (617) 963-2727 E-Mail: shamrock@gis.net
Motel, cottages & apartments. Rooms with private bath, cable-TV, refrigerator. Rates USD from 130 (in season), 80 (mid season) and 65 (low season) incl. full continental bf.

Shire Max Inn (bf CC G H)
5 Tremont Street ✉MA 02657 ☎ 487-1233
Call for rates

Six Webster Place (AC bf CC Glm H OS sol W wh)
6 Webster Place ✉MA 02657 ☎ 487-2266
Fax: 487-9242, E-Mail: sixwebster@capecod.net
Homepage: http://www.sixwebster.com
Rooms with shower/WC, TV, video, telephone, fax, radio, own-key. Rates off season US$ 70-135, on season 100-185.

Sunset Inn (bf CC GLM H NU OS) April 15-November 1
142 Bradford Street ✉MA 02657 *(one block to centre)*
☎ 487-9810 ☎ (800) 965-1801 (toll-free) Fax: 487-9810
E-Mail: sunset1@capecod.net
Homepage: www.sunsetinnptown.com
Rooms with shower/WC, telephone, TV. radio, own key. Non-smoking in the rooms. Homemade bf. Free parking. Rates US$ 49-125.

Watership Inn (CC G H MA OS)
7 Winthrop Street ✉MA 02657 ☎ 487-0094 *Built in about 1820. Rooms mostly with private bath, color cable TV. Rates US$ 36-90 (winter) and $61-200 (summer) plus taxes, incl. continental bf.*

West End Inn (bf CC GLM H MA)
44 Commercial Street ✉MA 02657 ☎ 487-9555
☎ (800) 559-1220 Fax: 487-8779
E-Mail: warren@westendinn.com
Homepage: www.westendinn.com
All rooms with private bath/WC, TV, video, fax, radio, minibar, kitchenette, hair-dryer, own key. Own car park. Rates US$ 69-150.

White Horse Inn (AC glm H MA)
500 Commercial Street ✉MA 02657 ☎ 487-1790
Rates from $40 to 70/room + taxes. Lots of antique furnishing and many paintings. Very close to the beach. German spoken.

White Wind Inn (AC bf CC GLM H)
174 Commercial Street ✉MA 02657 ☎ 487-1526
☎ (888) 449-WIND Fax: 457-4792
E-Mail: wwinn@capecod.net. Homepage: www.whidewindinn.com
Single rooms with bath/shower/WC, balcony, TV, video, radio, refrigerator. Rates US$ 75-2000 (incl. bf) depenting on season.

Windsor Court (AC bf CC G H MA pi wh)
15 Cottage Street ✉MA 02657 ☎ 487-2620
E-Mail: windsorct@capecod.net
Key West style luxury guesthouse. Rooms with private bath, TV, some with kitchen. Own entrance. Rates US$ 55-125. Weekly rates .

APARTMENTS

Harborside Realty (H)
162 Commercial Street ✉MA 02657 ☎ (800) 838-4005
Rental of apartments and houses

Hargood House Apartments (GLM H OS)
493 G Commercial Street ✉MA 02657 ☎ 487-9133
Complete kitchens. Off season US$ 62-116/night, in season 570-1020/week.

Mayflower Apartements (F GLM H)
6 Bang Street, MA 02657 ☎ 487-1916

Renaissance Apartments (GLM H MA) May-Oct
46-48 Commercial Street ✉MA 02657 ☎ 487-4600
Comfortable and completely furnished apartments with private bath and deck. Own parking space. Weekly rentals (Sat-Sat) only. Rates US$ 770-910 studio (on 3rd fllor) 735. Cable TV and telephone in each apartment. No pets.

PRIVATE ACCOMODATION

Seasons (AC cc bf E F GLM H VS)
160 Bradford Street ✉MA 02657 *(central)* ☎ 487-2283
☎ (800) 563-0113 (Toll-free) Fax: 487-2283
E-Mail: seasons@capecool.net
Homepage: www.capecool.net/seasons
Bed and Breakfast with 5 double rooms with bath, satellite TV, VCR, radio. Car park and own key. Rates US$ 80-125.

HEALTH GROUPS

Provincetown AIDS Support Group
PO Box 15 22 ✉MA 02667 ☎ 487-9445 Fax: 487-0565

GROUPS

Provincetown Business Guild (GLM) Mon-Fri 9-14 h
115 Bradford Street ✉MA 02657 ☎ 487-2313 Fax: 487-1252
E-Mail: pbguild@capecod.net Homepage: www.ptown.org
Promotion of Gay & Lesbian tourism in Provincetown.

Randolph ☎ 781

BARS

Randolph Country Club (B D F GLM pi P YG)
44 Mazzeo Drive, Route 139 ✉MA 02368 ☎ 961-2414

Sheffield ☎ 413

GUEST HOUSES

Howden Farm (AC bf CC glm MA)
303 Rannapo Road ✉MA 01257-9619 ☎ 229-8481

Springfield ☎ 413

BARS

Jam's (B GLM)
632 Page Boulevard ✉MA 01104 ☎ 736-9734
Just Friends (B D G LJ) 11-2 h
23 Hampden Street ✉MA 01103 *(three floors)* ☎ 781-5878
The Quarry (B G LJ) 21-2 h, closed Wed
382 Dwight Street ✉MA 01103 ☎ 736-9384
The Pub (B D GLM S) Mon-Sat 21-2, Sun 16-2 h
382 Dwight Street ✉MA 01103 ☎ 734-8123
Dance bar downstairs.

RESTAURANTS

Rosie's Place (b F glm) Wed-Sun 17-22 h
382 Dwight Street ✉MA 01103 *(at the Pub Bar)* ☎ 734-8123

CRUISING

-Downtown Mall
-Forest Park (picnic area near Recreation Department)
-Liberty Street (AYOR) -Springfield Bus Terminal (AYOR)

Ware ☎ 413

HOTELS

The Wildwood Inn (AC bf cc glm H MA OS)
121 Church Street ✉MA 01082 ☎ 967-7798 ☎ (800) 860-8098
1.5 hours drive west from Boston. Rooms with shared and private bath. Rates US$ 50-95 incl. full bf.

Worcester ☎ 508

BARS

Club 241 (B D F G YG) 14-2 h
241 Southbridge Street ✉MA 01608 ☎ 755-9311
Mailbox Lounge (B G lj) 14-2 h
40 Grafton Street ✉MA 01608 ☎ 799-4521
Leather night last Sat/month.

CRUISING

-Rest Stop (on 140, Upton)
-Block around Portland & Salem Streets

USA-Michigan

Great Lakes region USA
Initials: MI
Time: GMT -5
Area: 250.465 km² / 102,440 sq mi.
Population: 9,774,000
Capital: Lansing
Important gay cities: Detroit and Saugatuck

● Hetero- as well as homosexual oral and anal intercourse is prohibited in Michigan.

✱ In Michigan ist hetero- wie homosexueller Oral- und Analverkehr verboten.

▲ Dans le Michigan, la fellation et la pénétration anale sont interdites pour tous, homos et hétéros.

☆ En Michigan las relaciones homosexuales y heterosexuales por vía oral o anal están prohibidas.

❖ In Michigan sono vietati i rapporti orali ed anali sia tra omosessuali che tra eterosessuali.

Ann Arbor ☎ 734

GAY INFO

Gay Hotline Mon-Fri
☎ 662-1977

BARS

\'aút\Bar (AC B bf CC F GLM MA N OS W) 16-2 h
315 Braun Court ✉MI 48104 ☎ 994-3677
Kitchen hours: Sun-Thu 16-23, Fri Sat -1, Sun -15 h.

DANCECLUBS

Nectarine Ballroom (B D GLM VS YG) Tue and Fri 21-2 h
510 East Liberty Street ✉MI 48104 ☎ 994-5835

BOOK SHOPS

Borders Book Shop 10-18 h
303 South State Street ✉MI 48104 ☎ 668-7652

CRUISING

-Rest Stop (AYOR) (north on US 23 at 31 mile marker)
-Dexter Rest Stop (south side of I-94 West)

Atwood ☎ 616

GUEST HOUSES

Wunderschönes B&B (bf F GLM H lj MA WO)
12410 Antrim Drive, Ellsworth ✉MI 49729 *(near Grand Traverse Bay and Lake Michigan beaches)* ☎ 599-2847
Extended self-catering stays possible.

Detroit ☎ 313

GAY INFO

Cruise Mon-Fri 11-17 h
660 Livernois, Ferndale ✉MI 48220 ☎ 248/545-9040
Fax: 248/545-1073 E-Mail: cruisedet@aol.com
Weekly news and entertainment publication serving Michigan, Ohio and Indiana gay/lesbian communitiy.

BARS

Adam's Apple (AC B f G MA N) 15-2 h
18931 West Warren Avenue ✉MI 48228 ☎ 240-8482
Clean, friendly atmosphere.

Back Pocket (B F G MA) 17-2 h
8832 Greenfield Road ✉MI 48228 *(near Joy Road)* ☎ 272-8374

Gigi's (AC B CC D f GLM MA p r S SNU STV TV) Mon-Fri 12-2, Sat Sun 14-2 h
16920 West Warren Avenue ✉MI 48228 *(near South Field freeway)* ☎ 584-6525
Two bars on different levels, dancing every night, shows on Mon, thu, Fri and Sat.

Gold Coast. Club (B G SNU) Mon-Sat 19-?, Sun 15-? h.
2971 East Seven Mile Road/Mitchell Street ✉MI 48234
☎ 366-6135
Male dancers Mon-Sat 21 h, Sun 20 h. Draft beer $1.

Hayloft Saloon (B G MA) Mon-Sun
8070 Greenfield Avenue ✉MI 48228 *(near Tireman)*
☎ 581-8913

Karma (B D glmM TV)
22901 Woodward Avenue, Ferndale ✉MI 48203
☎ 248/541-1600

Male Box. The (B D G stv) Mon-Fri 14-2, Sat Sun 12-2 h
3537 East Seven Mile Road ✉MI 48234 *(3 blocks East of the Gold Coast)* ☎ 892-5420

Mirage (B D GLM)
31 North Walnut, Mt. Clemens ✉MI 48043 ☎ 810/913-1921

Number's (D F G VS) 20-4 h.
17518 Woodward ✉MI 48203 ☎ 868-9145
After hours with grilled chicken, hamburgers, etc. Dancing downstairs and quieter lounge upstairs.

Off Broadway (B D GLM)
12215 Harper Avenue ✉MI 48213 ☎ 521-0920

Other Side. The (B F G) after hours
16801 Plymouth Road ✉MI 48227 *(near Southfield Freeway)*
☎ 836-2324

Pronto Video Bar (B f GLM)
608 Washington, Royal Oak ✉MI 48067 ☎ 248/544-7900

Rainbow Room (B D GLM S STV) Wed-Sun 19-2, shows at 22.30 and 24 h
6640 East 8 Mile ✉Mi 48234 ☎ 891-1020

Regines (B D GLM)
11 East McNichols ✉MI 48203 ☎ 865-4747

R&R Saloon (B D DR G LJ)
7330 Michigan Avenue ✉MI 48210 ☎ 849-2751

Sam's Tiffany's on the Park (B D G LJ OS)
17436 Woodward Avenue ✉MI 48203 *(near Parkhurst)*
☎ 883-7162
Popular on Thu and Sun.

Stiletto's (B GLM S snu) Wed-Sun 10-2 h
1641 Middlebelt Road *(between Michigan and Cherry Hill)*
☎ 734/729-8980

Stingers (B D F GLM VS) Mon Fri 18-2, Sat Sun 20-2 h
19404 Sherwood Street ✉MI 48234 *(side entrance)*
☎ 892-1765

Woodward (B d F G) DJ on WE
6426 Woodward Avenue ✉MI 48202 *(near Milwaukee)*
☎ 872-0166

DANCECLUBS

Backstreet (B D G W YG) Wed Sat 20-2 h
15606 Joy Road ✉MI 48228 ☎ 272-8959
Popular.

Menjo's (B D G OS S) Mon-Wed 12-20, Thu Fri 12-2, Sat Sun 13-2 h
928 West McNichols Road/Hamilton Street ✉MI 48203
☎ 863-3934

Zippers (B D G STV VS) Wed-Mon 21-? h
6221 East Davidson ✉MI 48212 ☎ 892-8120

RESTAURANTS

Como's Restaurant (B F glm)
22812 Woodward Avenue, Ferndale ✉MI 48220 *(at 9 Mile Roade)* ☎ 248/548-5005

Dolce Vita. La (A B d F GLM) Dancing Tue night. Dinner Wed-Sat
17546 Woodward ✉MI 48220 *(Ferndale)* ☎ 856-0331
Very good Italian food, light jazz.

Pronto (B F glm)
608 South Washington, Royal Oak ✉MI 48067
☎ 248/544-7900

Rhinoceros (B F d GLM)
265 Riopelle ✉MI 48207 ☎ 313/259-6937

SEX SHOPS/BLUE MOVIES

Escape Book Store 10-23 h, closed Sun
18728 West Warren Avenue ✉MI 48228 ☎ 336-6558

Fifth Wheel (g) 10-24 h
9320 Michigan Avenue ✉MI 48210 ☎ 846-8613

SAUNAS/BATHS

TNT Complex (G pi sa sb sol VS WO) 0-24 h
13333 West Eight Road ✉MI 48235 ☎ 341-5322

BOOK SHOPS

Chosen Books (GLM)
120 West 4th Street ✉MI 48064 *(Royal Oak)* ☎ 543-5758
Literature, games, cards, posters, gifts.

GENERAL GROUPS

Affirmations Community Center (GLM)
195 West Mile, Ferndale ✉MI 48220 ☎ 248/298-7105

Triangle Foundation (GLM)
19641 West 7 Mile ✉MI 48219 ☎ 537-3323

RELIGIOUS GROUPS

Dignity
1050 Porter Street ✉MI 48226 *(at 6th Street)* ☎ 278-4786
Catholic gays; church services Sun 18 h at Marygrove College.

Douglas ☎ 616

DANCECLUBS

Douglas Disco (AC B CC D GLM MA SNU STV)
c/o Douglas Dunes Resort, 333 Blue Star Highway ✉MI 49406
☎ 857-1401

HOTELS

Douglas Dunes Resort (AC B CC GLM H MA pi)
PO Box 369 ✉MI 49406 ☎ 857-1401 Fax: 857-4052
Big gay and lesbian resort near Lake Michigan. Rooms en-suite or with shared bath/WC, balcony, telephone, radio, some with kitchenette.

Lighthouse Motel (AC bf glm H pi)
130th & Blue Star Highway ✉MI 49406 ☎ 857-2271
Rooms with private and shared bath, all with kitchenette, fridge and TV.

GUEST HOUSES

Douglas House B&B (AC bf CC glm H OS) May-Oct
41 Spring Street ✉MI 49406-140 ☎ 857-1119
Small B&B in private home. 4 rooms with private bath.

Kirby House. The (A AC bf CC glm MA NU OS pi wh)
294 West Center Bx 1124 ✉MI 49406 ☎ 857-2904
Fax: 857-2904 Homepage: www.bbonline.com/mi/grandescape
B&B in Victorian manorhouse.

Ellsworth ☎ 231

PRIVATE ACCOMODATION

Wunderschönes Bed & Breakfast (bf F f GLM H lj MA msg OS WO)
12410 Antrim Drive ✉MI 49729-9741 ☎ 599-2847
Rates US$ 80-90. Discounts for 3 days and longer stays. Private beach. Surrounded by golf course and nature preserve.

Flint ☎ 810

BARS

State Bar (B D GLM)
2512 South Dort ✉MI 48507 ☎ 767-7050

DANCECLUBS

Club Triangle (B D GLM)
2101 South Dort ✉MI 48507 ☎ 767-7552

Grand Rapids ☎ 616

GAY INFO

Network (Gay/Lesbian Network of Western Michigan) Mon-Fri 18-22 h
909 Cherry Street South East ✉MI 49503 ☎ 458-3511
Fax: 458-4294
Information and referral. Monthly publication.

BARS

Cell. The (B D G LJ VS)
76 South Division Avenue ☎ 454-5800
City Limits (B D GLM)
67 South Division Avenue ☎ 454-8003

DANCECLUBS

Diversions (B D F GLM YG)
10 Fpountain Street NW ✉MI 49503 ☎ 451-3800

SEX SHOPS/BLUE MOVIES

Cini-Mini (g) 11-2 h
415 Bridge Street NW ✉MI 49501 ☎ 454-7531

SAUNAS/BATHS

Diplomat Health Club (G sa)
2125 South Division Avenue ✉MI 49501 ☎ 452-3754

BOOK SHOPS

Sons & Daughters (glm)
962 Cherry SE ✉MI 49506
☎ 459-8877

CRUISING

-Rest Stop (US 131 North)
-Rest Stop (I-96 West)
-Ann Street Park (AYOR)
-City Centre (downtown shopping mall)

Kalamazoo ☎ 616

BARS

Brothers (B D GLM)
209 Stockbridge ✉MI 49001
☎ 345-1960

Missias (B D glm)
62 Portage Street ✉MI 49001
☎ 381-4140

DANCECLUBS

Zoo. The (B D GLM)
906 Portage Street ✉MI 49001
☎ 385-9191

BOOK SHOPS

Triangle World (GLM)
551 Portage Street ✉MI 49007
☎ 373-4005

Lansing ☎ 517

GAY INFO

Gay/Lesbian Hotline Mon-Fri 19-22, Sun 14-17 h
PO Box 65 65, East Lansing ✉MI 48826-6565 ☎ 332-3200

BARS

Club 505 (B D GLM)
505 East Shiawassee ✉MI 48912
☎ 374-6312
Esquire (B F Glm N OG W) 12-2 h
1250 Turner ☎ 487-5338
Spiral (B D GLM)
1247 Center Street ✉MI 48906 ☎ 371-3221

GENERAL GROUPS

Lansing Association for Human Rights
PO Box 6565, East Lansing ✉MI 48826 ☎ 332-3200
E-Mail: lahr1@geocities.com Homepage: come.to/lahr

CRUISING

-Rest stop (AYOR) (on I-96, Okemos)
-Rest stop (AYOR) (on Highway 27, 1 mile north of 127)

Saugatuck ☎ 616

BOOK SHOPS

Mother Moon (glm)
127 Hoffman ☎ 857-4407

GUEST HOUSES

Grandma Arlene's House B&B (bf CC GLM H OS WE wh) open Fri-Mon only
2135 Blue Star Highway, Fennville ✉MI 49408 ☎ 543-4706
Small B&B with 4 single rooms with private baths, hair-dryer and color cable TV.
Kirky House. The (A AC bf CC glm H MA N NU OS pi wh) close for Christmas
294 West Center Street, PO Box 1174 ✉MI 49453 ☎ 857-2904
☎ (800) 521-6473 (Toll-free) E-Mail: kirbyinn@aol.com
8 double rooms with shower/WC, heating, own key. Free bikes, good off street parking.
Moore's Creek Inn (bf CC glm H) 820 Holland Street ✉MI 49453 ☎ 857-2411
☎ (800) 838-5864 (Toll-free)
Small B&B in 1900s townhouse. All rooms with private bath. No kids, no pets.

CAMPING

Camp It (GLM)
Route 6635, 118th Avenue, Fennville ✉MI 49408 ☎ 543-4335
Big campsight under gay management. TV lounge. Laundry facilities. Store and supermarket nearby. No kids.

USA-Minnesota

Great Lakes region USA

Initials: MN

Time: GMT -6

Area: 225.182 km² / 92,099 sq mi.

Population: 4,686,000

Capital: Saint Paul

Important gay cities: Minneapolis/Saint Paul

● Hetero- as well as homosexual oral and anal intercourse is prohibited in Minnesota.

✸ In Minnesota ist hetero- wie homosexueller Oral- und Analverkehr verboten.

▲ Dans le Minnesota, la fellation et la pénétration anale sont interdites pour tous, homos comme hétéros.

☆ En Minnesota las relaciones homosexuales y heterosexuales por vía oral o anal están prohibidas.

❖ In Minnesota sono vietati i rapporti orali ed anali praticati sia tra eterosessuali che tra omosessuali.

Minneapolis/St. Paul ☎ 612

GAY INFO

Focus Point
401 North 3rd Street, #230, Minneapolis ✉MN 55401
☎ 288-9008
Weekly newspaper.

Gay and Lesbian Community Action Council
310 East 38th Street, Minneapolis ✉MN 55409 ☎ 822-0127
☎ (800) 800-0350 (Toll-free)

Lavender Magazine (CC GLM)
2344 Nicollet Avenue, Suite 300, Minneapolis ✉MN 55404
☎ 871-2237 E-Mail: info@lavendermagazine.com
Homepage: www.lavendermagazine.com
Biweekly newspaper. On-line version available.

TOURIST INFO

Greater Minneapolis Convention & Visitor Bureau 8-17 h
33 S 6th Street, Minneapolis ✉MN 55402 *(4000 Multifoods Tower)* ☎ 348-7000 Fax: 335-5841 Homepage: http://www.minneapolis.org

BARS

Body Shop (B G LJ)
1415 University Avenue West, St. Paul ✉MN 55104 *(in the back of the Town House)* ☎ 646-7087

Brass Rail (B G N s) 10-1 h
422 Hennepin Avenue, Minneapolis ✉MN 55401 ☎ 333-3016

Club Metro (AC B CC D F GLM MA OS S STV YG) Mon-Thu 16-1, Fri-Sat 15-1, Sun 14-1 h
733 Pierce Butler Rte, St. Paul ✉MN 55104 ☎ 489-0002

Gay 90's (! B D F GLM lj MA S SNU STV VS)
408 Hennepin Avenue, Minneapolis ✉MN 55401 ☎ 333-7755
Upper Midwest's largest gay entertainment complex: 7 bars, 2 dance floors.

Over the Rainbow (B GLM) 249
West 7th Street *(St. Paul)* ☎ 228-7180

Richie's (B GLM) 2211
Lowry Avenue North, Minneapolis ☎ 588-8145

Saloon (B D F G)
830 Hennepin Avenue, Minneapolis ✉MN 55401 *(at 9th Street)*
☎ 332-0835
High energy dance music.

Town House (AC B GLM MA) Mon-Fri 14-1, Sat Sun 12-1 h
1415 West University Avenue West, St. Paul ✉MN 55104
☎ 646-7087
Western style bar.

Trikkx (B D F GLM MA s W)
Mon-Thu 16-1, Fri -3, Sat 12-3, Sun -1 h
490 North Robert Street ✉MN 55101 ☎ 651/224-0703
German spoken. Man spricht Deutsch.

19 Bar (AC B CC f GLM MA N OS) Mon-Fri 15-1, Sat-Sun 13-1 h
19 West 15th Street, Minneapolis ✉MN 55403 ☎ 871-5553
Low prices, pool tables, voted best neighborhood bar 1999.

CAFES

Cafe Wyrd (b bf GLM) 7-1 h
1600 West Lake Street, Minneapolis ☎ 827-5710

Cafe Zev (b bf f glm) 7-1, Fri Sat -2 h
1362 LaSalle Avenue, Minneapolis ☎ 874-8477
Popular.

DANCECLUBS

Ground Zero (B D GLM MA) Thu (LJ)
15 Northeast 4th Street ☎ 378-5115

RESTAURANTS

Black Forest Inn (F glm)
1 East 26th Street, Minneapolis ✉MN 55404 ☎ 872-0812
German food.

BOOK SHOPS

A Brother's Touch (AC CC GLM MA W) Mon-Fri 10-21, Sat 11-20, Sun 12-17 h
2327 Hennepin Avenue South ✉MN 55405 ☎ 377-6279
Books, cards, gifts, music, T-shirts, jewelry.

GIFT & PRIDE SHOPS

Rainbow Road (GLM) 10-22 h
109 West Grant Street, Minneapolis ✉MN 55403 ☎ 313/872-8448 *Bookstore/Variety Store.*

HOTELS

Hotel Amsterdam (AC bf CC f G H p)
828 Hennepin Avenue, Minneapolis ✉MN 55403 ☎ 288-0459
Fax: 288-0461 E-Mail: hotel@scc.net
Homepage: http//www.gaympls.com
European-style hotel. Gay bar and restaurant on-site. Rates for single rooms with shared bath USD 30-50.

GUEST HOUSES

BeYourself Executive Inn (bf glm H NU)
1093 Snelling Avenue South, St. Paul ✉MN 55116 ☎ 698-3571
All rooms with TV/video and private bath.

Como Villa B&B (AC bf GLM H)
1371 West Nebraska Avenue, St. Paul ✉MN 55108 ☎ 647-0471
Non-smoking establishment. No pets, no kids. Rooms with private and shared bath. Central location.

GENERAL GROUPS

Bisexual Connection
PO Box 13158, Minneapolis ✉MN 55414

PFLAG
PO Box 19290, Minneapolis ✉MN 55419 ☎ 825-1660

FETISH GROUPS

ATONS of Minneapolis
PO Box 2311, Minneapolis ✉MN 55402 ☎ 738-7343
Leather group for gay men.

Knights of Leather
PO Box 582601, Minneapolis ✉MN 55458-2601 ☎ 870-7473

HEALTH GROUPS

AIDS Information Mon-Fri 9-22, Sat 12-17 h
☎ 373-2437

Aliveness Project
730 East 38th Street, Minneapolis ✉MN 55409 ☎ 822-7946
Support and services for people with AIDS, ARC and who are HIV positive.

Minnesota AIDS Project Mon-Fri 8.30-17.30 h
1400 Park Avenue ✉MN 55404 ☎ 341-2060

HELP WITH PROBLEMS

Gay & Lesbian Hotline 12-24 h
☎ 822-8661 *or toll-free* ☎ *(0800) 800-0907*

RELIGIOUS GROUPS

Affirmation/United Methodists for LGB Concerns
101 East Grant Street, Minneapolis ✉MN 55403 ☎ 874-6613

Integrity/Twin Cities c/o University Episcopal Center 1st/3rd Fri 19.30 h
317 17th Avenue Southeast, Minneapolis ✉MN 55414
☎ 825-2301
Gay and lesbian Episcopalians.

Lutherans Concerned/Twin Cities Mon-Fri 8.30-17 h, worship every 3rd Fri
100 North Oxford Street, St. Paul ✉MN 55104 *(St. Paul Reformation Lutheran Church)* ☎ 224-3971 E-Mail: jolwhalen@aol.com

SPECIAL INTEREST GROUPS

Girth & Mirth/Twin Cities
PO Box 4288, Hopkins ✉MN 55343 ☎ 934-4332

SWIMMING

-32nd Street Beach (32nd Street & West Calhoun, gay beach)

CRUISING

-Hennepin Avenue (AYOR) (downtown)
-IDS Tower (indoor mall, „Crystal Court")
-Loring Park & Oak Grove (AYOR)
-Mississippi River Flats (AYOR) (East River Road, opposite Shriners Hospital)
-University of Minnesota (Minneapolis Campus, Gay Community Center, Coffman Memorial Union at 2nd floor, Northrop Auditorium at 3rd floor)

USA-Mississippi

South USA
Initials: MS
Time: GMT -6
Area: 125.443 km² / 51,306 sq mi.
Population: 2,731,000
Capital: Jackson

● Hetero- as well as homosexual oral and anal intercourse is prohibited in Mississippi.

✷ In Mississippi ist hetero- wie homosexueller Oral- und Analverkehr verboten.

▲ Dans le Mississipi, la fellation et la pénétration anale sont interdites pour tous, homos comme hétéros.

☆ En Missisippi las relaciones homosexuales y heterosexuales por vía oral o anal están prohibidas.

❖ In Mississipi sono vietati i rapporti anali ed orali praticati sia tra omosessuali che tra eterosessuali.

Biloxi ☎ 601

BARS

Joey's on the Beach
878 Ravenwood Court ✉MS 39532 ☎ 435-5639

CRUISING

-Beach Highway (between Biloxi and Gulfport)
-Edgewater Shopping Center (AYOR)
-Gulf Coast Beach (between Holiday Inn and Coliseum)

Hattiesburg ☎ 601

BARS

Courtyard. The (B D F GLM S)
107 E. Front Street ☎ 545-2714

Jackson ☎ 601

GAY INFO

Gay & Lesbian Community Switchboard
PO Box 7737 ✉MS 39284 ☎ 373-8610 *or* ☎ *435-2398.*

Gay & Lesbian Hotline
☎ 435-2398
Action Line 24 hrs. for the Gulf Coast Area.

Kudzu Konnection
☎ 957-1259

Mississippi Voice
PO Box 7737 ✉MS 39284 ☎ 924-3333 Fax: 354-2251
Published monthly.

BARS

Club City Lights (b D GLM) Wed Fri-Sun 22-? h
200 North Mill Street ✉MS 39201 *(Mill & Amite)* ☎ 353-0059

Jack and Jill's (AC B D f GLM lj MA s STV WE) Fri, Sat 21-? h
3911 Northview Drive ✉MS 39206 ☎ 982-5225
Beer only bar.

Jack's Construction Site (AC B d f GLM lj MA N OS S) 17-? h
425 North Mart Plaza ✉MS 39206 ☎ 362-3108
Beer only bar.

Star. The (AC B bf CC F GLM MA S W) Mon-Sat 17-1, Sun 12-22 h
400 E. South Street, Hinds County ✉MS 39201 *(across from main post office)* ☎ 352-5111
Piano bar. Also restaurant. Live music.

SEX SHOPS/BLUE MOVIES

Heritage Video
1515 Terry Road ✉MS 39204 ☎ 354-5555

Terry Road Bookstore
1449 Terry Road ✉MS 39204 ☎ 353-9156
Adult books and videos.

GENERAL GROUPS

American Civil Liberties Union (ACLU) of Mississippi
PO Box 2242 ✉MS 39225 ☎ 355-6464

Aurora Transgender Support for Central Mississippi
PO Box 1306, Florence ✉MS 39073 ☎ 845-1328

Mississippi Gay & Lesbian Task Force
PO Box 7737 ✉MS 39284 ☎ 924-3333
Host of Lambda AA, Mississippi Phoenix Coalition, Mothers of AIDS Patients, Prime Timers and Overeaters Anonymous for Gays and Lesbians.

HEALTH GROUPS

Adopt-A-Friend Project
PO Box 2055 ✉MS 39225 ☎ 924-3333

HIV-PWA Project of Mississipi
Drawer 8342 ✉MS 39294 ☎ 371-3019

Southern AIDS Commission - Jackson Office
PO Box 8457 ✉MS 39284 ☎ 371-3019 Fax: 371-3156 E-Mail: gvvs78a@prodigy.com

Support Group for those Living with HIV/AIDS
☎ 922-9687

RELIGIOUS GROUPS

Integrity (Episcopal)
St. Phillip's Episcopal Church ☎ 853-4978

CRUISING

-Jackson State Library
-Smith Park (AYOR)

USA-Missouri

Middlewest USA
Initials: MO
Time: GMT -6
Area: 180.546 km² / 73,843 sq mi.
Population: 5,402,000
Capital: Jefferson City
Important gay cities: Kansas City and St. Louis

● Homosexual oral and anal intercourse is prohibited in Missouri.

✱ In Missouri ist homosexueller Oral- und Analverkehr verboten.

▲ Dans le Missouri, la fellation et la pénétration anale sont interdites seulement pour les homosexuels.

☆ En Missouri las relaciones homosexuales por vía oral o anal están prohibidas.

❖ In Missouri sono vietati i rapporti anali ed orali tra omosessuali.

Kansas City ☎ 816

GAY INFO

News Telegraph
PO Box 100 85 ✉MO 64171 ☎ 561-6266 Fax: 561-2623
Biweekly newspaper

TOURIST INFO

Greater Kansas City Convention & Visitor Bureau
100 Main Street ✉MO 64105 ☎ 221-5242 Fax: 691-3805

BARS

Buddies Lounge (B G MA N r) 6-3 h
3715 Main Street ✉MO 64111 ☎ 561-2600 *Popular*

Fox (B G MA N)
7520 Shawnee Mission Parkway, Overland Park
☎ (913) 384-0369

Mari's Saloon & Grill (B F GLM N S)
1809 Grand Boulevard ✉MO 64116 ☎ 283-0511

Missy B's (B G STV) Mon-Sat ?-3 h
805 West 39th Street ✉MO 64111 ☎ 561-0625
Mon/Wed Drag shows, Fri/Sat live music & vocals

Other Side (B G VS) closed Sun
3611 Broadway ✉MO 64111 ☎ 931-0501
Video bar.

Sidekicks Saloon (AC B CC d G MA r s) Mon-Sat 14-3 h, closed Sun
3707 Main Street ✉MO 64111 ☎ 931-1430

Tootsie's New Place (B gLM MA N)
1822 Main Street ☎ 474-4638

Vineyard (B G MA S)
1108 Grand Avenue ☎ 421-1082

DANCECLUBS

Cabaret Club (B D G S SNU STV VS YG) ?-3 h
5025 Main Street ✉MO 64112 *(near 50th St.)* ☎ 753-6504
Wed-Sun drag and strip shows.

Dixie Belle Saloon (B D F G LJ OS)
1922 Main Street ✉MO 64108 ☎ 471-2424
Café, patio bar, cruise bar and leather shop.

RESTAURANTS

Metropolis (B F GLM)
303 Westport Road ☎ 753-1550

SEX SHOPS/BLUE MOVIES

Erotic City (glm) 0-24 h
8401 East Truman Road ☎ 252-3370
Ray's Playpen (glm) 0-24 h
3235 Main Street ☎ 753-7692

SAUNAS/BATHS

1823 Club (b G LJ MA OS P sa sol VS) 0-24 h
1823 Wyandotte ✉MO 64108

BOOK SHOPS

Borders (glm)
9108 Metcalf, Overland Park ☎ (913) 642-3642
Larry's Gifts and Cards Inc. (GLM) Mon-Fri 10-7, Sat 10-18.30, Sun 10-17 h
205 Westport Road ✉MO 64111 ☎ 753-4757

LEATHER & FETISH SHOPS

Spike's Leather
1922 Main ✉MO 64108 *(Downstairs at Dixie Belle)*

HOTELS

Inn the Park (bf glm H pi)
3610 Gilham Road ✉MO 64111 ☎ 931-0797
B&B in private home. All rooms with private bath, color cable TV and VCR.

GUEST HOUSES

Doanleigh Inn. The (AC bf CC E glm msg T)
217 East 37th Street ✉MO 64111 *(Hyde Park area)*
☎ 753-2667 Fax: 531-5185. E-mail: doanleigh@aol.com
Homepage: http://www.doanleigh.com
Luxury B&B in an old Georgian mansion with fireplaces and antique furnishings. All rooms with bath/WC, hair-dryer, balcony, telephone, Sat-TV, video and radio. Rates USD 85-150 incl. bf buffet. No pets, kids on request.

HEALTH GROUPS

Kansas City Health Department
1423 East Linwood ✉MO 64109 ☎ 923-2600
KC Free Health Clinic Midtown
2 East 39th Street ✉MO 64111 ☎ 753-5144
HIV-testing.

HELP WITH PROBLEMS

Gay and Lesbian Alcoholics Anonymous
☎ 531-9668
Gay Talk Line 18-24 h
☎ 931-4470

RELIGIOUS GROUPS

Affirmation
5709 Virginia Avenue ✉MO 64110 ☎ 363-6892
United Methodists gay and lesbian group.
Metropolitan Community Church
3801 Wyandotte ✉MO 64171 ☎ 931-0750
Trinity United Methodist Church
620 East Armour Boulevard ✉MO 64109-2247 ☎ 931-1100
Fax: 831-1101 E-Mail: TUMCkcmo@aol.com
Homepage: http://www.gbgm-umc.org/trinitymi01

CRUISING

-Rest Stop (on I-29 near airport)
-Country Club Plaza
-Liberty Memorial Mall (AYOR)
-Loose Park
-McGee (AYOR R) (between 10th and 11th Street)

Springfield ☎ 417

SEX SHOPS/BLUE MOVIES

Sunshine News and Arcade
3537 West Sunshine Street ✉MO 65807 ☎ 831-2298

CRUISING

-Phelps Grove Park (AYOR)

St. Louis ☎ 314

GAY INFO

Access Line
☎ 533-6155
Infoline about gay life in St. Louis. Recorded message.
Gay and Lesbian Community Center
☎ 997-9897
Lesbian and Gay News Telegraph. The
c/o Piasa Publishing Co., PO Box 142 29A ✉MO 63178
☎ 664-6411 Fax: 664-6303
SLAM
☎ 771-7739 E-Mail: slam edit@aol.com
Bar guide.
St. Louis Gay & Lesbian Community Services
Gay/Lesbian Hotline 18-22 h daily
PO Box 232 27 ✉MO 63156 ☎ 367-0084

TOURIST INFO

St. Louis Convention & Visitors Commission
One Metropolitan Square ✉MO 63102 ☎ 421-1023
Fax: 421-0394

BARS

Alibi's (B D F G S SNU STV)
3016 Arsenal ☎ 772-8989
Clementine's (AC B CC F G LJ MA N OS) Mon-Fri 10-1.30, Sat 8-1.30, Sun 11-24 h
2001 Menard Avenue ✉MO 63104 *(at Allen Avenue)*
☎ 664-7869
Gay cruising bar & sidewalk restaurant for guys into leather, levis and western clothing.
Drake Bar. The (B G N OS) 16.45-1.30 h, closed Sun
3502 Papin Street ✉MO 63110 ☎ 685-1400
Piano nightly. Fri/Sat 21 h Jazz
Grey Fox Pub (B G MA N)
3503 South Spring ☎ 772-2150
Loading Zone (B GLM VS YG) closed Sun
16 South Euclid Avenue ✉MO 63108 ☎ 361-4119
Magnolia's (B D F G lj S) 16-3, Sun 11-3 h
5-9 South Vandeventer ✉MO 63108 ☎ 652-6500
Very popular restaurant, café, bar and disco.
Mags (B D F G LJ S VS) ß-
5 South Vandeventer ✉MO 63108 ☎ 652-6500
Nero Bianco (B G MA N)
6 South Sarah ☎ 531-4123
The name „Black and White" in italian says it all.
St. Louis Eagle. The (B G LJ MA W) Mon-Fri 15.30-1.30, Sat 12-1.30 h, closed Sun
17 South Vandeventer ✉MO 63108 ☎ 535-4100

DANCECLUBS

Complex Nightclub. The (AC B CC D F G lj MA OS STV) 18-3 h. Food served Wed-Sun 18-22.30 h.
3515 Chouteau Avenue ✉MO 63103 ☎ 772-2645
Dance club and restaurant.

Faces (B D DR G LJ S SNU STV VS)
130 4th Street

RESTAURANTS

Angels (B F GLM LJ W) 11-3 h
3511 Chouteau Avenue ✉MO 63103 ☎ 772-2645
American cuisine

Duff's (B F glm MA)
92 North Euclid Avenue ☎ 361-0522
American cuisine. Full bar.

Niner Diner (b F GLM)
9 South Vandeventer ☎ 652-0171
American cuisine.

Ninth Street Abbey (b F glm)
1808 South 9th Street
☎ 621-9598
International cuisine.

South City Diner (b F glm) 0-24 h
3141 South Grand ☎ 772-6100
American cuisine.

SAUNAS/BATHS

Club St. Louis (f G pi sa sb sol VS wh WO) 0-24 h
2625 Samuel Shepard Drive ✉MO 63103 *(near Jefferson)*
☎ 533-3666

BOOK SHOPS

Left Bank Books (A AC glm W) 10-22, Sun 11-18 h
399 N. Euclid Avenue ✉MO 63108 *(at McPherson)* ☎ 367-6731
General bookstore with large lesbi-gay section.

Our World Too (AC CC GLM MA W) 10-21.30, Sun 12-20 h
11 South Vandeventer ✉MO 63108-3221 ☎ 533-5322
Bookshop and mail order service.

LEATHER & FETISH SHOPS

Ngamson Leather & Lace
2822 Cherokee ☎ 772-5818

GUEST HOUSES

A St. Louis Guesthouse (AC CC GLM msg OS wh)
1032-38 Allen Avenue ✉MO 63104 *(in historic Soulard)*
☎ 773-1016 E-Mail: garryhawk@aol.com
Homepage: http://www.q-net.com
Two suites with private bath, cable TV, VCR, fridge, small kitchen and phone. Rates US$ 75-110 per night.

Brewer's House Bed & Breakfast (AC bf CC GLM H lj MA NU wh) reception 7-24 h
1829 Lami Street ✉MO 63104 *(south of downtown near brewery)*
☎ 771-1542
Small B&B in historic home. Rooms with private bath, telephone, TV, video, radio, kitchen and hair-dryer. Rates USD 70-75 incl. continental bf.

Napoleon's Retreat Bed & Breakfast (AC bf CC glm H MA) reception 7-22 h
1815 Lafayette Avenue ✉MO 63104 *(1 mile from downtown in historical district)* ☎ 772-6979 ☎ (800) 700-9980
Fax: 772-7675
Homepage: http://www.bbonline.com/mo/napoleons
4 rooms and 1 apartment in 1880s townhouse. Bath or shower, WC, telephone, TV, own key and room service. Rates single US$ 70-95, double 80-125. Full-board.

GENERAL GROUPS

People of All Colors Together
PO Box 8052 ✉MO 63108 ☎ 231-6931

FETISH GROUPS

Blue Max Cycle Club
PO Box 233, Main Station ✉MO 63166

Gateway MC
PO Box 140 55 ✉MO 63178

HEALTH GROUPS

VD Control
634 North Grand Avenue ✉MO 63103 ☎ 658-1025
Venereal diseases.

HELP WITH PROBLEMS

Gay and Lesbian Alcoholics Anonymous
☎ 436-1858

St. Louis Gender Foundation (TV)
☎ 997-9897 *Support group for transgendered people.*

RELIGIOUS GROUPS

Dignity Meets Sun 19.30 h
at Trinity Episcopal Church, 600 North Euclid Avenue
PO Box 771794 ✉MO 63177 ☎ 995-4612
Gay and lesbian catholics.

SPECIAL INTEREST GROUPS

GAMMA Support Group
☎ 567-2076
Support group for gay men who are married, separated or divorced.

USA-Montana

North USA

Initials: MT

Time: GMT -7

Area: 380.850 km² / 155,767 sq mi.

Population: 879,000

Capital: Helena

Billings ☎ 406

BOOK SHOPS

Barjon's (g) Mon-Sat 9.30-17.30 h
2718 3rd Avenue North ✉MT 59101 ☎ 252-4398
Alternative books with gay/lesbian titles.

Missoula ☎ 406

BARS

AmVets (B D f G MA S tv) ?-1.30 h
225 Ryman ✉MT 59801 ☎ 728-3137
Popular after 22.30 h

CAFES

Catalyst Espresso (b glm MA)
111 N. Higgins Avenue ✉MT 59801 ☎ 542-1337

Ronan ☎ 406

GUEST HOUSES

North Crow Ranch (bf GLM MA msg NU OS wh) May-Oct
2360 North Crow Road ✉MT 59864 *(5 miles north-east of Ronan)*
☎ 676-5169 E-Mail: gamine@ronan.net

Homepage: http://www.ronan.net/~gamine
The ranch features a tasteful balance of comfort and outdoor activity in a natural setting of forest, field and stream. Spend the night in a tent, tipi or a cabin.

West Yellowstone ☎ 406

GUEST HOUSES

Campobello Lodge at Bar N Ranch (F GLM MA S wh) 3111 Targhee Pass Highway ✉MT 89758 ☎ 646-9682
E-Mail: barnranch@wyellowstone.com

USA-Nebraska

Middlewest USA

Initials: NE

Time: GMT -6

Area: 200.358 km² / 81,946 sq mi.

Population: 1,657,000

Capital: Lincoln

Lincoln ☎ 402

GAY INFO

Gay-Lesbian Youth Talkline
☎ 473-7932

BARS

Panic. The (B D GLM lj) Mon-Fri 16-1, Sat 13-1, Sun 13-23 h
200 South 18th Street ✉NE 68508 ☎ 435-8764
Q (AC B D DR GLM lj MA S SNU STV W) Tue-Sun 20-1 h
226 South 9th Street ✉NE 68508 ☎ 475-2269
Small cruise bar within the bar open on Fri Sat 22-1 h.

GIFT & PRIDE SHOPS

Avant Card (g) Mon-Wed 10-19, Thu 10-20, Fri/Sat 10-17.30, Sun 13-17 h
1323 O Street ✉NE 58510 ☎ 476-1918
Wide range of greeting cards with gay lesbian themes.
Christie's Toy Box Mon-Thu 9-23, Fri/Sat 9-24, Sun 12-21 h
2029 O Street ✉NE 68510 ☎ 477-6566
Wide range of cards, movies toys and accessories.
Euphoria (g) Mon-Sat 10-18.30, Sun 12-17 h
4139 O Street ✉NE 68510 ☎ 488-8853
Wide range of greeting cards with gay and lesbian themes.

LEATHER & FETISH SHOPS

Boog's Rockand Roll Boutique Mon-Fri 12-19 Sat 12-6 h
122 South 52nd Street/O Street ✉NE 68501 ☎ 483-2263
Leather goods, costumes and undergarments.

GENERAL GROUPS

Parents and Friends of Lesbians and Gays
☎ 467-4599
UNL Gay/Lesbian Student Association
Union, Room 234 ☎ 472-5644

HEALTH GROUPS

Nebraska AIDS Project
3818 Sheridan Boulevard ✉NE 68506 ☎ 484-8100 ☎ (800) 782-AIDS (Toll-free)

CRUISING

-Antelope, Pioneer, Wilderness and Van Dorn Parks (AYOR/police)
-I-80 Westbound (west of 56th Street exit AYOR)
-Gateway Mall
-University of Nebraska City Union (restrooms on 2nd floor)
-University of Nebraska Love Library (old building, 2nd floor)
-Route 77 (AYOR) (15 miles north, near Ceresco)
-15th Street (between D & H, „Fruit Loop", very popular)

Omaha ☎ 402

BARS

Diamond Bar (B G lj N) Mon-Sat 21-1, Sun 12-1 h
712 South 16th Street ✉NE 68102 ☎ 342-9595
Max. The (B D GLM S VS YG) 21-1 h
1417 Jackson Street ✉NE 68102 ☎ 346-4110
Popular.
Run. The (B D G LJ) Sun-Thu 14-1, Sat 14-4 h
1715 Leavenworth Street ✉NE 68102 *(near 18th)* ☎ 449-8703

CRUISING

-Milks Run (R) (Howard & Jackson Streets between 16th and 18th, nights)
-Benson Park
-Carter Lake
-Hanscom Park
-Towl Park (AYOR) (wooded area & jogging path)
-Westroads Shopping Center Mall

USA-Nevada

West USA

Initials: NV

Time: GMT -8

Area: 286.367 km² / 117,124 sq mi.

Population: 1,677,000

Capital: Carson City

Important gay cities: Las Vegas and Reno

Lake Tahoe ☎ 702

GUEST HOUSES

Lakeside Bed & Breakfast - Tahoe (bf GLM H MA NU OS P sb VS wh) PO Box 8, Crystal Bay ✉NV 89402
☎ 831-8281 Fax: 831-7329 E-Mail: tahoeBnB@aol.com
2 double room and 1 suite with bath/shower/WC, telephone, fax, TV, video, radio, hair-dryer. Skiing in winter, swimming and boating in summer.

Las Vegas ☎ 702

GAY INFO

Gay & Lesbian Community Center 10-17 h
PO Box 70481 ✉NV 89170 ☎ 733-9800
E-Mail: tashahill@aol.com

BARS

Angles/Club Lace (B GLM N VS YG) 0-24 h
4633 Paradise Road ✉NV 89109 *(at Tropicana)* ☎ 733-9677
Angels is more popular with gay men while women prefer Club Lace.
Back Door Lounge (B G MA N) 0-24 h
1415 East Charleston ✉NV 89104 *(downtown)* ☎ 385-2018

Backstreet (B d GLM N) 0-24 h
5012 South Arville Road ✉NV 89118 *(off West Tropicana)*
☎ 876-1844
Western-style, country dancing on Fri and Sat.
Bamboleos (B G MA)
713 East Ogden Street ☎ 474-9060
Latino bar.
Buffalo. The (B G LJ MA VS) 0-24 h
4640 Paradise Road ✉NV 89109 ☎ 733-8355
Popular. Home of the Satyricon Motorcycle Club.
Choices (B G N) 0-24 h
1729 East Charleston Boulevard ✉NV 89104 ☎ 382-4791
Eagle (B d G lj MA S STV W)
3430 East Tropicana/Pecos ✉NV 89121 *(at Pecos)* ☎ 458-8662
Poker machines.
Flex (B d GLM MA N snu) 0-24 h
4371 West Charleston Street ☎ 385-3539
Gipsy (B D GLM S YG)
4605 Paradise Road ✉NV 89109 ☎ 733-9677
Good Times (AC B D f GLM MA N s) 0-24 h
1775 East Tropicana Avenue #1 ✉NV 89119 *(at Liberace Plaza)*
☎ 736-9494
Snick's Place (B G MG)
1402 South 4th Street ☎ 385-9298

CAFES

Mariposa Cafe (A AC F GLM MA OS s tv W YG) 18-6 h
4643 Paradise Road ✉NV 89119 ☎ 650-9009

DANCECLUBS

Badlands (B D GLM MA OS) 0-24 h
953 East Sahara Avenue, No. 22-B ✉NV 89104 ☎ 792-9262
Country western bar.

RESTAURANTS

Freezone (B F GLm) 610
East Naples ✉NV 89109 *(across from the Buffalo)* ☎ 794-2300

SAUNAS/BATHS

Apollo Spa & Health Club (AC CC DR G MA N p pi sb SNU wh WO) 0-24 h
953 E. Sahara Avenue A-19 ✉NV 80104 *(in Commercial Center)*
☎ 650-9191

BOOK SHOPS

Get Booked (GLM)
4643 Paradise Rd. ✉NV 89109 *(opposite Angles/Club Lace)*
☎ 737-7780 Homepage: http://www.getbooked.com

GUEST HOUSES

Lucky You B&B (AC bf G MA p pi sa sb)
☎ 384-1129 Fax: 384-1129
Rooms with shower or shared bath, telephone, fax, TV, video, radio, hair-dryer, own key and room service. Full American bf incl. Call for more info on location.

FETISH GROUPS

Desert Brotherhood MC
PO Box 71145 ✉NV 89170

HEALTH GROUPS

AIDS Information
☎ 474-2437

RELIGIOUS GROUPS

MCC
PO Box 3488 ✉NV 89036 ☎ 384-2325

SPECIAL INTEREST GROUPS

Las Vegas Bears
PO Box 34263 ✉NV 89133 ☎ 658-7548
Neon Squares
PO Box 46161 ✉NV 89114 ☎ 253-9435
GLB country and western dance group.

SWIMMING

Lake Mead (North on Las Vegas Blvd., past Hollywood Blvd. through the desert to the stop sign. Turn left and go on for exactly 4.8 miles, turn right on the gravel road at highway marker 8.0. Go left at every fork in the road. Park your car in the lot overlooking the lake. Hike north for 5 min. into a little ravine and over a hill along a narrow trail.

Reno ☎ 702

GAY INFO

Reno Informer
PO Box 33337 ✉NV 89523 ☎ 747-8833

BARS

Bad Dollys (B d f gLM) 15-3 h, WE 0-24 h
535 East 4th Street ✉NV 89512 ☎ 348-1983
Western style bar.
Five Star Saloon (B d f Glm s) 0-24 h
132 West Street ☎ 329-2878
Quest (B Glm MA) 12-5, WE 0-24 h
210 West Commercial Road ☎ 333-2808
1099 Club (B d f Glm lj MA S VS) 0-24 h
1099 South Virginia ✉NV 89502 ☎ 329-1099
Popular western style bar.

DANCECLUBS

Visions (B D Glm YG) Mon-Thu 12-4, Fri 12-Mon 4 h
340 Kietzke Lane ✉NV 89502 *(one block south of East Second Street)* ☎ 786-5455 *Popular.*

SEX SHOPS/BLUE MOVIES

Suzie's Adult Video (glm) 0-24 h
195 Kietzke Lane ✉NV 89502 ☎ 786-8557
Wide selection of gay videos, magazines, cards etc.

FITNESSTUDIOS

Steve's Gym (G WO) 0-24 h
1030 West 2nd Street ☎ 323-8770

BOOK SHOPS

Grapevine Books (GLM)
1450 South Wells Avenue ✉NV 89502 ☎ 786-4869
Wide selection of gay & lesbian books, magazines, cards etc.

LEATHER & FETISH SHOPS

Fantasy Fire
1298 South Virginia ☎ 323-6969

GENERAL GROUPS

Comstock Grizzlies
PO Box 12102 ✉NV 89510
Social group for gay men.

FETISH GROUPS

Knights of Malta MC
PO Box 7726 ✉NV 89510

RELIGIOUS GROUPS

MCC Sun 17 h
☎ 826-3177

USA-New Hampshire

Northeast USA
Initials: NH
Time: GMT -5
Area: 24.219 km² / 9,905 sq mi.
Population: 1,173,000
Capital: Concord

Bethlehem ☎ 603

GUEST HOUSES

Highlands Inn (bf CC d f H L MA msg OS pi S W wh)
PO Box 118, Valley View Lane ✉NH 03574 *(Route 302, 2 miles east of I93 exit 40)* ☎ 869-3978 ☎ 1-877-537-2466 (Toll-free)
Fax: 537-2466 E-Mail: vacation@highlandsinn-nh.com
Homepage: http://www.highlandsinn-nh.com
Located in a beautiful setting in the White Mountains this comfortable Inn is the perfect place to relax. Lovely views from most rooms. Heated swimmingpool (in summer). Alpine skiing (in winter). All rooms are non-smoking but a smoking area is available. Nearest airports Portland, Montreal and Boston (2-3 hours drive). Lesbians only!

Centre Harbor ☎ 603

HOTELS

Red Hill Inn (AC B bf CC F glm OS pi W wh) Office: 8-22 h
Route 25B/College Road, RFD 1, PO Box 99 M ✉NH 03226
☎ 279-7001 Fax: Email: info@redhillinn.com
Homepage: http://www.redhillinn.com
Countryside location. All rooms with priv. bath, WC and balcony.

Manchester ☎ 603

BARS

Merrimac Club (B D GLM P) Mon-Fri 11-1.30, Sat Sun 12-1.30 h
201 Merrimack Street ✉NH 13103 ☎ 623-9362

Portsmouth ☎ 603

SEX SHOPS/BLUE MOVIES

Peter's Palace 9-23 h
Route 1 Bypass North ✉NH 03801 *(near Myrtle and Rockingham)* ☎ 436-9622

CRUISING

-Hilton Part - Dover Point Road
-Pierce Island (dock area)

USA-New Jersey

Northeast USA
Initials: NJ
Time: GMT -5
Area: 22.590 km² / 9,239 sq mi.
Population: 8,053,000
Capital: Trenton

Asbury Park ☎ 908

BARS

Bond Street Bar (B G)
208 Bond Street ✉NJ 07712 ☎ 776-9766
Down the Street (B D F G S VS YG) 12-2 h
230 Cookman Avenue ✉NJ 07712 ☎ 988-2163
Beergarden, beach crowd. Very popular.
Phoenix. Club (B D G S) 14.30-2.30 h
427 Cookman Avenue ☎ 775-9849

Atlantic City ☎ 609

BARS

Brass Rail. The (AC B f GLM MA N S SNU) 0-24 h
10 South Mt. Vernon Avenue ✉NJ 08401-7003 ☎ 348-0192
Popular local bar, friendly atmosphere. Dinner and late snacks served.
Rendezvous (B d f G)
137 South New York Avenue ✉NJ 08401 ☎ 347-8539
Studio Six Video Dance Club (AC B D G MA OS P SNU VS) 22-8 h
12 St. Mount Vernon Avenue ✉NJ 08401 ☎ 348-3310
Hot dance club.

DANCECLUBS

Reflections (B D G)
South Carolina/Boardwalk ✉NJ 08401

RESTAURANTS

Mama Mott's (f F G)
151 South New York Avenue ✉NJ 08401 ☎ 345-8218

HOTELS

Fraternity House. The (AC G H)
18 South Mt. Vernon Avenue ✉NJ 08401 ☎ 347-0808
All rooms with priv. baths.

GUEST HOUSES

Ocean House (AC bf CC G MG NU VS) Office 10-22 h
127 South Ocean Avenue ✉NJ 08401-7202 *(central, 100 yards form the beach)* ☎ 345-8203
Gay men only. Offers a comfortable place for men in a clothing optional and intimate atmosphere, where there is a possibility of meeting others with similar interests. Call for rates.
Surfside Resort Hotel (AC B CC D F GLM H MG OS P pi S sb wh) Bar 0-24, Disco 22-8 h
18 South Mt. Vernon Avenue ✉08401-7003 ☎ 347-7873
☎ (800) 888-277-SURF (Toll-free) Fax: 347-6668
Homepage: http://www.studiosix.com
All rooms with private bath-rooms with hair-dryer, color-TV, refrigerator, suites available. Large private sundeck. The Brass Rail Tavern and Studio Six Video Dance Club are part of the hotel complex.

Boonton ☎ 201

DANCECLUBS

Connexions (B D G MA)
202 Myrtle Avenue ✉NJ 07005 ☎ 263-4000

Cherry Hill ☎ 609

DANCECLUBS

Gatsbys (B D G YG)
760 Cuthbert Boulevard ✉NJ 08002 ☎ 663-8744

CRUISING

-Cooper River Park

Hoboken ☎ 201

DANCECLUBS

Excalibur 2001 (B D GLM S SNU STV)
1000 Jefferson Street ✉NJ 07230 *(less than one hour drive from Manhattan)* ☎ 795-1023
Multi-level nightclub with 6 bars.

Jefferson Township ☎ 201

BARS

Yacht Club. The (B CC D f GLM MA s SNU) Mon-Sat 19-3, Sun 14-3 h
5190 Berkshire Valley Road ✉NJ 07438 *(North Jersey)* ☎ 697-9780

Jersey City ☎ 201

BARS

Uncle Joe's (B G MA)
154 1st Street ✉NJ 07302 *(North Jersey)* ☎ 653-9173

Morristown ☎ 973

GENERAL GROUPS

Gay Activist (GAAMC) Mon 20.45 h
at Morristown Unitarian Fellowship, 21 Normandy Heights Road
Gay and Lesbian Youth in New Jersey (GA-LY-NJ)
PO Box 137, Convent Sn. ✉NJ 07961 ☎ 285-1595

HELP WITH PROBLEMS

Helpline 19.30-22.30 h
☎ 285-1595

Plainfield ☎ 908

PRIVATE ACCOMODATION

Pillars of Plainfield Bed & Breakfast. The (AC bf CC glm H MA OS)
922 Central Avenue ✉NJ 07060-2311 ☎ 753-0922
☎ 888-PILLARS E-Mail: pillars2@Juno.com
B&B in a Victorian-Georgian mansion in the historic district. All suites have private bath, phone/voice mail, and cable-TV. Non-smoking. Dog on premises. Big garden. Rates US$99-139.

River Edge ☎ 201

BARS

Feathers (B G) 21-2, Sat -3 h
77 Kinderkamack Road ✉NJ 07661 *(North Jersey)* ☎ 342-6410

Somerset ☎ 908

BARS

Den. The (AC B CC DR f GLM lj MA N s VS W) 20-2, Sun 17-2 h
700 Hamilton Street ✉NJ 08873 ☎ 545-7354

Trenton ☎ 609

BARS

Buddies Pub (B GLM) 17-2, WE 18-2 h
677 South Broad Street ☎ 989-8566
Center House Pub (B glm) 16-2, WE 19-2 h
499 Center Street ☎ 599-9558

Wallington ☎ 201

BARS

Topaz Meadowlands (B D G MA VS) 21-? h, closed Mon
225 Paterson Avenue ☎ 916-0472

USA-New Mexico

Southwest USA
Initials: NM
Time: GMT -7
Area: 314.939 km² / 128,810 sq mi.
Population: 1,730,000
Capital: Santa Fé

Albuquerque ☎ 505

GAY INFO

Common Bond Community Center 19-22 h
4013 Silver Avenue South East, PO Box 268 36 ✉NM 87125 ☎ 266-8041
New Mexico Rainbow
PO Box 4326 ✉NM 87196 ☎ 255-1634
Monthly gay and lesbian newspaper which caters primarily for the northern parts of new Mexico.
OUT! Magazine
PO Box 27237 ✉NM 87125 ☎ 253-2540
Monthly gay and lesbian magazine for all of New Mexico

BARS

Albuquerque Social Club (B GLM LJ MA P)
4021 Central Avenue North East ✉NM 87198 ☎ 255-0887
Foxes Lounge (B G D MA W) 10-2, Sun 12-24 h
8521 Central North East Avenue ☎ 255-3060
Ranch. The (B D G LJ) 11-2, Sun 12-24 h
8900 Central South East ✉NM 87123 ☎ 275-1616

DANCECLUBS

Albuquerque Mining (B D G MA OS VS) 9-2 h
7209 Central Avenue North East ✉NM 87108 ☎ 255-0925
Pulse Nightclub (AC B CC D GLM lj MA N OS SNU STV VS WE) Tue-Sat 19.30-2 h, Sun-Mon special events
4100 Central Avenue South East ✉NM 87108 *(in Nob Hill, on RT. 66)* ☎ 255-3334
Popular bar and nightclub.

SEX SHOPS/BLUE MOVIES

Castle Superstore (g VS) 0-24 h
5110 East Central Avenue S.E. ✉NM 87108 ☎ 262-2266
Leather, lingerie, magazines, books, DVD's, toys and more.

FITNESSTUDIOS

Pride Gym (AC b CC f G MA msg OS P sb W wh WO) Mon-Fri 7-22 h, Sat 10-18 h, Sun 12-17 h
1803 3rd Street N.W. ✉NM 87102-1411 *(North of Downtown, 4 blocks south of Interstate 40 at Exit 159A)* ☎ 242-7810

DECORATION

In Crowd (A AC CC W) Mon-Sat 10-18, Sun 11-16 h
3106 Central South East ✉NM 87106 ☎ 268-3750
Gift shop and gallery.

GUEST HOUSES

Brittania & W.E. Mauger Estate (AC bf CC f glm H MA)
701 Roma Avenue N.W. ✉NM 87102 ☎ 242-8755
☎ (800) 719 9189 E-Mail: maugerbb@aol.com
Homepage: http://maugerbb.com
Each room has private bath, phone, TV, refrigerator. Rates US$ 79-179 incl bf. Evening wine and cheese.

HEALTH GROUPS

New Mexico AIDS Services Tue 17.30-19.39 h
4200 Silver South Eeast #D ✉NM 87108 *(near Community Center)* ☎ 266-0911 Fax: 266-5104
Information, HIV-testing, counselling, assistance.

Pecos ☎ 505

HOTELS

Wilderness Inn (G H)
PO Box 11 77 ✉NM 87552 ☎ 757-6694
15 miles from Santa Fé.

Radium Springs ☎ 505

HOTELS

Radium Hot Springs Resort (B F GLM H pi)
PO Box 40 ✉NM 88054 ☎ 525-1983

Santa Fe ☎ 505

TOURIST INFO

Convention & Visitor's Bureau
☎ 984-6760 ☎ (800) 984-9984 (Toll-free)

CAFES

Telecote Cafe (bf f glm)
1203 Cerrillos Road ☎ 988-1362

DANCECLUBS

Drama Club (B D GLM STV)
126 North Guadelupe Street ☎ 988-4374
This is the only location im town that is really gay.

RESTAURANTS

Blue Corn Cafe (b F glm)
133 Water Street ☎ 984-1800
Good Mexican food.

Geronimo (AC B CC E F glm MA N OS) 11.30-14.30, 18-22 h
724 Canyon Road ✉NM 87501 ☎ 982-1500
Very good Mediterranean cuisine.

Santacafe (b F glm OS) Mon- 11.30-14/18-22 h
231 Washington Avenue ✉NM 87501 ☎ 984-1788
Very good Asian and Southwestern cuisine.

Vanessie (B F Glm)
434 West San Francisco Street ✉NM 87501 ☎ 982-9966
Mixed restaurant, the bar is rather gay.

GUEST HOUSES

Four Kachinas Inn (bf glm H OS)
512 Webber Street ✉NM 87501 ☎ 982-2550 Fax: 989-1323
E-Mail: 4kachina@swcp.com
Homepage: http://www.southwesterninns.com/fourkach.htm
Small B&B with comfortable rooms all with private baths, color cable TV and private patios. Rates USD 75-130 incl. cont. bf. No pets.

Hummingbird Ranch (bf glm H)
Route 10, PO Box 111 ✉NM 87501 ☎ 471-2921
Small guest house 7 miles from the city centre. Rooms with shared baths, kitchens, fridge, fireplace amd cable TV.

Inn of the Turquoise Bear (bf CC GLM H lj MA msg OS VS) Office: 7-20 h
342 East Buena Vista Street ✉NM 87501-4423 ☎ 983-0798
☎ (800) 396-4104 Fax: 988-4225
E-Mail: bluebear@roadrunner.com
Homepage: www.turquoisebear.com
Historical ambiance, walking distance to downtown attractions. All rooms with bath/shower/WC, balcony/patio, telephone, cable-TV,

video and hair-dryer. Rates double US$ 95-195 incl. bf buffet. Afternoon wine & cheese hour. IGLTA member. Out & About Editor's Choice Award 1999, Preservation Award, City of Santa Fe 1999.

Open Sky B&B (bf CC E GLM H msg OS wh)
134 Turqoise Trail ✉NM 87505 ☎ (800) 244-2475
E-Mail: SkyMiller@aol.com
Homepage: http://www.bestinns.net/USA/NM/opensky.html
Small B&B in ranch house. All rooms with private baths, fridge and color TV.

Triangle Inn. The (AC bf CC f GLM MA OS W wh)
PO Box 32 35 ✉NM 87501 ☎ 455-3375 Fax: 455-3375
E-Mail: triangleSF@aol.com
Homepage: http://www.roadrunner.com/~triangle/
Studios with shower/WC, balcony, TV/video, telephone, radio, kitchenette/kitchen and hair-dryer.

Water Street Inn (bf glm H)
427 West Water Street
☎ 984-1193
Comfortable rooms all with private bath.

CRUISING
-Rest Stop (on I-25 15 miles south of Santa Fe)
-DeVargas Mall

Silver City ☎ 505

GALLERIES

Long Road Gallery
06 North Bullard ✉NM 88061 ☎ 388-5088

Thoreau ☎ 505

PRIVATE ACCOMODATION

Zuni Mountain Lodge & Tour (AC bf F g lj MA os s)
PO Box 5114 ✉NM 87323 ☎ 862-7769 Fax: 862-7616
Private accommodation in remote location surrounded by pine forest overlooking high-mountain landscape.

Valdez ☎ 505

HOTELS

Taos Stone House (! A g H MA msg sb)
PO Box DD, Valdez ✉NM 87580 ☎ 776-2146
☎ 1-800-771-2189 (Toll-free)
Beautiful rustic location.

USA-New York

Northeast USA
Initials: NY
Time: GMT -5
Area: 141.080 km² / 57,701 sq mi.
Population: 18,137,000
Capital: Albany
Important gay cities: Fire Island and New York City

Albany ☎ 518

GAY INFO

Capital District Lesbian/Gay Community Center 19-23, Sat Sun 15-23 h
332 Hudson Avenue ✉NY 12210 ☎ 462-6138

BARS

☛ also Lake George, NY

JD's Playhouse (B D G N)
519 Central Avenue ✉NY 12206 ☎ 482-9546

Longhorn's (B G lj N) 23-6 h
90 Central Avenue ✉NY 12206 ☎ 462-4862

Oh-Bar (AC B G MA N) 14-4 h
304 Lark Street ✉NY 12210 ☎ 463-9004

One Flight Up (B D G WE) Wed-Sun 21-4 h
76 Central Avenue ✉NY 12206 *(above Waterworks)*
☎ 465-6400

CRUISING
-Empire State Plaza (AYOR)
-Washington Park (AYOR)

Binghamton ☎ 607

BARS

Numbers (B D GLM lj S) Sun-Thu 21-1, Fri Sat 21-3 h
Upper Court Street ✉NY 13904 *(in Rocket Center)* ☎ 775-3300

Risky Business (B D GLM MA VS) Sun-Thu 17-1, Fri Sat 20-3 h
201-203 State Street ✉NY 13901 ☎ 723-1507

Squiggy's (B D GLM MA) Sun-Wed 20-1, Thu 17-1, Fri-Sat 17-3 h
34 Chenango Street ☎ 722-2299

CAFES

Tom's Coffee Cards & Gifts
176 1/2 Main Street ✉NY 13905 ☎ 733-8500

CAMPING

Hillside Campgrounds (D G pi)
PO Box 726 ✉NY 13902 ☎ 756-2833

GENERAL GROUPS

B/C Bears
PO Box 1642 ✉NY 13902

Lesbian & Gay Studies Coalition
#621, GSO, Box 514 SUNY-Binghamton ✉NY 13902
☎ 617/729-7250

PFLAG (Parents and Friends of Lesbians & Gays)
PO Box 728, WVS ✉NY 13905 ☎ 729-5616

HEALTH GROUPS

AIDS Hotline
☎ 723-6520

Anonymous HIV Testing
☎ 800-562-9423

Broome County Health Department STD Clinic
☎ 778-2839

Southern Tier AIDS Program Office
☎ 798-1706

SPECIAL INTEREST GROUPS

LGBU University Union
SUNY Binghamton ✉NY 13902

CRUISING
-Rest Stop (on Route 81 North, lollipop heaven)
-Cole Park
-Greyhound Bus Depot (AYOR)

Brentwood ☎ 516

SEX SHOPS/BLUE MOVIES

Heaven Sent Me (DR g VS)
108 Cain Street ✉NY 11717 ☎ 434-4777
Private video viewing booths.

Buffalo ☎ 716

BARS

Buddies (AC B CC D f G lj MA OS s SNU STV W) 13-4, Sat Sun 12-4 h
31 Johnson Park ✉NY 14201-2348 ☎ 885-1313
Popular.
Cathode Ray (B G VS YG) 13-4 h
26 Allen Road ✉NY 14202 ☎ 884-3615
Club 153 (B GLM MA OS YG) Fri-Sat 22-4 h
153 Delaware Avenue ✉NY 14213 ☎ 842-6825
Compton's (B G MA) 1239
Niagara Street ✉NY 14213 ☎ 881-6799
Stagedoor. The (B G MG OS S) 17-4 h
20 Allen Street ✉NY 14202
Underground (B D Glm MA) 16-4, Sat-Sun 12-4 h
274 Delaware Avenue ✉NY 14202 ☎ 855-1040

CAFES

Java Temple. The (b bf f glm) WE -2 h
57 Allen Street

DANCECLUBS

Club Marcella c/o Theater Place (B D f glm SNU STV) 622 Main Street *(at Shea's)*
Fuel (B D G LJ MA)
884 Main Street

RESTAURANTS

Mothers (b F glm) WE -3 h
33 Virginia Place

SAUNAS/BATHS

Sauna 655 (b f G P sa sb) 0-24 h
655 Main Street ✉NY 14203 ☎ 852-2153

BOOK SHOPS

Book & News (glm)
3102 Delaware Avenue ✉NY 14217 ☎ 877-5027
Talking Leaves (glm) Mon-Sat 10-18 h
3144 Main Street ✉NY 14214 ☎ 837-8554

TRAVEL & TRANSPORT

Destinations Unlimited
130 Theaterplace

GENERAL GROUPS

Gay and Lesbian Youth Services (GLYS) Mon, Tue, Thu, Fri 18-21 h
c/o YWCA, 190 Franklin Street ✉NY 14202 *(lower level)*
☎ 855-0221 Fax: 855-0661 E-Mail: glyswny@juno.com

HEALTH GROUPS

AIDS Community Services
☎ 847-2441
AIDS Family Services
320 Porter ✉NY 14201 ☎ 881-7655
Benedict House
24 Plymouth Avenue ✉NY 14201 ☎ 834-4940

Catskill Mountains ☎ 518

GUEST HOUSES

Palenville House B&B (bf CC GLM H MA wh)
JCT RTS 23A & 32A, POBox 465, Palenville ✉NY 12463 *(10 miles from Woodstock-New York)* ☎ 678-5649
☎ (877) 689-5101 (Toll-free)
Fax: 678-9038 E-Mail: Palenville@aol.com
Homepage: members.aol.com/palenville
Turn-of-the-century Victorian home. 5 double rooms with bath/shower/WC, TV, VCR, radio. Suites with fireplace and jacuzzi. Rates US$ 75-145. Outdoor activities.
Red Bear Inn (A B bf CC F g H lj OS p WE) HCI
Box 40, Route 42, West Kill ✉NY 12492 ☎ 989-6000
☎ 888-BEAR INN
Located 2 hours drive north of New York City close to the Hudson Valley. Private bath. Also bar and restaurant. Outdoor activities.

East Hampton ☎ 516

HOTELS

123 North Main (AC CC glm H MA pi)
Memorial Day-Mid September
132 North Main Street ✉NY 11937 ☎ 324-2246
Some rooms with AC and priv. bath. Rates US$ 110-250.

Fire Island ☎ 516

Not that a misunderstanding emerges: Fire Island is no New York Provincetown and no Key West. It just doesn't have the size. New Yorkers own a house here, or know somebody who owns a house. Tourists must see where they find an accomodation. Both towns, which are of interest to gays, *Cherry Grove* and *Fire Island Pines* are, after all, more or less small villages. The tranquile and remote Fire Island can only be reached by ferry. The distance from New York to Sayville is approximately 70 km. This town is connected with The Pines by ferry (going regularly from May to October). The Pines is rather stylishly orientated, body conscious and very gay. Cherry Grove is prefered by middle-class gays and lesbians and occasionally by heterosexuals. Both lie quite near to one another. The one mile inbetween, also called the *Meat Rack*, is a highly frequented dune landscape. Nightlife does not exist in abundance; private parties prevail. A very well known and rewarding highlight of the year exists: The *Gay Men's Health Crisis Morning Party* in August.

Nicht das jetzt ein Mißverständnis entsteht: Fire Island ist kein New Yorker Provincetown oder Key West. Dafür reicht die Größe einfach nicht. Als New Yorker hat man hier ein Haus oder kennt jemanden mit Haus. Als Tourist muß man sehen, wo man unterkommt. Schließlich sind die beiden für Schwule interessanten Orte, *Cherry Grove* und *Fire Island Pines* eher kleine Dörfer.
Das ruhige und abgeschiedene Fire Island erreicht man nur per Fähre. Von New York City sind es etwa 70 km bis Sayville. Von dort gehen Fähren (Mai-Okt regelmässig) nach The Pines, das eher stylingorientiert, sehr körperbewußt und sehr schwul ist, und Cherry Grove, das von Lesben, Schwulen aus der Mittelschicht und gelegentlichen Heteros bevorzugt wird.
Beide Orte liegen nicht sonderlich weit auseinander: Auf der einen Meile dazwischen befindet sich eine hochfrequentierte Dünenlandschaft, auch *Meat Rack* genannt
Das Nightlife ist nicht gerade üppig, denn vieles läuft eher auf privater Party-Ebene. Einen weithin bekannten und äußerst lohnenden Jahres-Höhepunkt gibt es trotzdem: Die *Gay Men's Health Crisis Morning Party* im August.

▲ Que les choses soient claires: Fire Island n'est pas le Provincetown ou le Key West des New Yorkais! Fire Island est bien trop petite! Les New Yorkais y ont soit une maison, soit un ami qui y possède une maison. Les touristes, eux, doivent se débrouiller eux-mêmes. Seuls Cherry Grove et Fire Island Pines sont intéressants pour les gays. Attention: ce ne sont que de petits villages!
Pour jouir du calme de Fire Island, il faut d'abord prendre le bac. Il y a environ 70 km entre New York City et Sayville d'où on prend le bac (circule régulièrement de mai à octobre) jusqu'à The Pines et Cherry Grove. Cherry Grove est plutôt fréquentée par les gays et les lesbiennes middle-class et quelques hétéros qui se sont égarés par là, alors que The Pines est presque exclusivement homo stylé, body-buildé. Entre les deux, il y a une dune assez fréquentée où l'on peut faire des rencontres. On l'appelle „Meat Rack".
La vie nocturne est loin d'être trépidante. Les gens se retrouvent plutôt en privé. A Fire Island, l'évènement de l'année, c'est le „Gay Men's Health Crisis Morning Party" en août.

☆ Hay que tener claro que Fire Island no es el Provincetown o el Key West de Nueva York, para ello es simple mente demasiado pequeña. Fire Island es una popular zona residencial para gente de Nueva York. De especial intéres para turistas gay son *Cherry Grove* y *Fire Island Pines* que en realidad no son más que pequeños pueblos. A la tranquila y retirada Fire Island se llega solo ferry. Desde Nueva York son aprox. 70 km. hasta Sayville. Desde este lugar parten los ferrys (entre mayo y octubre regularmente) hacia The Pines y Cherry Grove. The Pines es un sitio gay muy elegante, donde se da mucha importancia a la aparencia y los cuerpos entrenados; Cherry Grove es preferida y visitada por lesbianas y gays de la clase media incluso de vez en cuando por heterosexuales. Ambos sitios se encuentran tan solo separados por las muy frecuentadas dunas *Meat Roack*. La vida nocturna no es muy extensa, la mayor parte de ella se lleva a cabo en fiesta privadas. En agosto se vive el punto culminante anual gay, el *Gay Men's Health Crisis Mornig Party*.

❖ Che non nascano malintesi: Fire Island non è nè una Provincetown nè una Key West di New York, non è abbastanza grande. Molti abitanti di New York hanno qui la seconda casa o conoscono qualcuno che ce l'ha. Per i turisti invece è più difficile trovare alloggio, poichè sia *Cherry Grove* che *Fire Island*, benchè siano luoghi interessanti per i gay, sono dei piccoli paesi; è possibile raggiungere la piccola ed isolata Fire Island per traghetto. Da New York City a Sayville vi sono solo 70 km. Da qui partono regolarmente dei traghetti per The Pines, località frequentata da gay dove regna il culto del corpo e della moda, e per Cherry Grove, frequentata da gay e lesbiche di classe media e da eterosessuali. Queste località non sono distanti tra loro: sono separate da un paesaggio di dune molto frequentato che viene chiamato *meat rack*. La vita notturna è piuttosto tranquilla poichè si svolge principalmente attraverso feste private. Tuttavia in agosto ha luogo l'avvenimento dell'anno che merita di essere conosciuto:il *Gay Men's Health Crisis Morning Party*.

BARS

Blue Whale Bar (B D g)
Picketty Ruff ✉NY 11782 *(near Fire Island Boulevard)*
☎ 597-6131
Ice Palace (B D F G pi S) Sun-Fri 12-4, Sat -8 h
Cherry Grove ✉NY 11782 *(at Beach Hotel)* ☎ 597-6600
Monster. The (B D F GLM YG) 16-4, dinner 19-23.30 h
Ocean Walk, Cherry Grove ✉NY 11782 *(near Dock Walk)*
☎ 597-6888
Pines Pavillon (B F D g) 16-18 h tea dance
Picketty Ruff at Fire Island Boulevard ✉NY 11782
☎ 597-6677

RESTAURANTS

Cultured Elephant (B F glm OS)
Picketty Ruff ✉NY 11782 *(near Fire Island Boulevard)*
☎ 597-6060
Top of the Bay (B F G OG)
Dock Walk/Bay Walk, Cherry Grove ✉NY 11782 ☎ 597-6699

HOTELS

Cherry Grove Beach Hotel (A AC B CC D GLM H lj MA msg NU OS pi S STV TV W WE) May 1-Oct 1
PO Box 537, Cherry Grove ✉NY 11782 ☎ 597-6600
Fax: 597-6651 E-Mail: grovehotel@aol.com
Homepage: http://www.grovehotel.com
Holly House (bf G H) May 15th-Sep 30th
Holly Walk, Box 96, Cherry Grove ✉NY 11782-4097
☎ 597-6911
Sea Crest (b glm H)
Lewis Walk at Main Walk, Cherry Grove ✉NY 11782
☎ 597-6849

GUEST HOUSES

Belvedere Guest House (bf CC G H MA NU OS pi wh WO) May-Oct
33 Bay View Walk, Cherry Grove ✉NY 11782 ☎ 597-6448
Old mansion with garden, fountain and water views. Bf on WE only. 38 en suite rooms with balcony/terrace, TV, VCR, radio, own key.
Carousel Guest House (bf G H OS) May-Oct
PO Box 4001, Cherry Grove ✉NY 11782-0998 ☎ 597-6612
Suburb location, 1 hour to the airport.
Dune Point (F GLM H)
PO Box 78, Sayville ✉NY 11782 ☎ 597-6261 Fax: 597-7048
Shared and private room facilities.
Pines Place (bf G H MA pi) May-Oct, closed in winter
PO Box 5309, Fire Island Pines ✉NY 11782 *(Sayville Ferry Service to Fire Island Pines)* ☎ 597-6162 Fax: 597-6162
E-Mail: PinesPlace@aol.com Homepage: www.pinesplace.com
All rooms with phone, TV, ocean-view with balcony, partly with own bath/WC. Rates on request.

CRUISING

-Anywhere and everywhere from the time you get on the ferry, but especially the west end of the boardwalk at The Pines and the »Meat Rack« and bushes between Cherry Grove & The Pines.

Ithaca ☎ 607

DANCECLUBS

Common Ground (B D F GLM MA OS S W) Thu-Sun 16-1 h
1230 Danby Road (Route 96B) ✉NY 14850 *(across American Legion)* ☎ 273-1505
Nightclub & restaurant.
Tilt a Whirl (B D G MA) Thu night
The Haunt, 114 West Green Street ✉NY 14850 ☎ 273-1505

RESTAURANTS

Cabbage Town Cafe (F g)
404 Eddy Street ✉NY 14850 ☎ 273-2847

GENERAL GROUPS

Cornell Lesbian Gay Bisexual Coalition
207 Willard Strait Hall, Cornell University ✉NY 14853
☎ 255-6482
Ithaca Lesbian Gay & Bisexual Task Force
PO Box 283 ✉NY 14581

HEALTH GROUPS

AIDS Hotline
☎ 800-333-0892

AIDS Work
De Witt Office Complex, 215 North Cayuga Street ✉NY 14850
☎ 272-4098

SPECIAL INTEREST GROUPS

Ithaca College Gay & Lesbian Association
Campus Union Building ✉NY 14580 ☎ 274-3011

Lake George ☎ 518

HOTELS

King Hendrick Motel (AC F GLM H OS pi)
Route 9, Box 623 ✉NY 12845 ☎ 792-0418 *Centrally located, all units with kitchenette, priv. bath, balcony, color cable TV.*

Long Island ☎ 516

HEALTH GROUPS

Long Island AIDS Care Mon-Fri 9-17, recorded messages -21 h, Sat-Sun 9-21 h
☎ 385-2437 *Information, support services.*

SWIMMING

-Jones Beach (G NU) (from South End Station left down the beach)

Long Island / Nassau County ☎ 516

BARS

Blanche (AC B GLM N OS S) 20-4 h
47-2 Boundary Avenue, South Farmingdale ✉NY 11735
☎ 694-6906

Pal Joey's (B G) Mon-Thu 16-4, Fri-Sun 20-4 h
2457 Jerusalem Avenue, North Bellmore ✉NY 11710
☎ 785-9301

Porsche Club. The (B D GLM)
1317 Broadway, Hewlett ✉NY 11557 ☎ 374-5671

Long Island / Suffolk County ☎ 516

GAY INFO

Gay Spirit (G) Tue 18-19 h WUSB, 90.1 FM
c/o WUSB, SUNY, Stony Brook ✉NY 11790 ☎ 246-7900

BARS

Bunk House. The (B D G LJ stv) 20-4 h
192 Montauk Highway, Sayville ✉NY 11782 ☎ 567-2865

Forever Green (B d GLM) 20-? h
841 North Boom Avenue, Lindenhurst ✉NY 11757 ☎ 226-9357

Long Island Eagle (AC B G LJ MA OS) Mon-Sat 21-4, Sun 16-4 h
94 N. Clinton Avenue, Bay Shore ✉NY 11706 ☎ 968-2250
Home of L.I. Ravens M.C.

Mr's (B G)
608 Sunrise Highway, West Babylon ✉NY 11702 ☎ 661-9580

SEX SHOPS/BLUE MOVIES

Adult Shop (g)
6083 Sunrise Highway, Holbrook ✉NY 11741 ☎ 472-9519

HOTELS

Cozy Cabins (GLM H) 1st Apr-30th Nov
PO Box 848, Wainscott ✉NY 11101 ☎ 537-1160

132 North Main (AC bf CC GLM H NU OS pi W)
Memorial Day-Labor Day Weekend (Summer only)
132 North Main Street, East Hampton ✉NY 11937 ☎ 324-2246
Centrally located, two hours from JFK-Airport. Hotel with garden. All rooms with refrigerator, some with priv. bath.

New York ☎ 212

● The centre of gay life is *Christopher Street*, where, on 28th June 1969, gays forcefully resisted the ongoing and arbitrary police raids. This historical site is an absolute must for every gay tourist.

It's best to visit New York in spring or autumn; Winter and summer in this extreme city can include extreme temperatures. The best way to get around town is the subway (and for going from the main airport JFK to city center). For going home after a night out in the gay scene we recommend taking a taxi. Information about gay cultural events and nightlife can be obtained through the party-magazines *Next* and *HomoExtra (HX)*. In addition to these, the *N.Y. Gay and Lesbian Community Center* is a help for orientating yourself. The biggest and most important gay-lesbian event in New York is the *Gay Pride Parade* in June.

As is often the case: People talk about New York but in reality mean only one of the five *boroughs*, namely Manhattan. The other four (Bronx, Brooklyn, Queens and Staten Island) are not so interesting for gays. Gay life is concentrated in Manhatten.

But there are changes emerging. *The Village* (i.e. Greenwich Village), situated around *Sheridon Square*, is indeed still very colourful, but an equivalent and very trendy center of gay life has evolved in *Chelsea*, corner of 8th Avenue and West 17th Street, with a tendency of moving to the north above the 23rd Street.

The skyline of Manhattan is truly spectacular, especially when viewed at night from the Staten Island ferry. New York is the home of several world class museums with rich, extensive collections, e.g. the Metropolitan Museum of Art and the Modern Museum of Art. The section of Fifth Avenue on the eastern border of Central Park is known as Museum Mile. Central Park itself is reasonably safe during the day. The architectural treasures range from the imported *The Cloisters* on 190th Street to the *World Trade Center* in downtown. The most beautiful treasures can be found while shopping along 5th Avenue between 50th and 59th Street in the weeks before Christmas.

Gay nightlife in New York has a decidedly long tradition. Areas like Times Square or The Village were already trendy places in the twenties. Nightclubbing in New York can sometimes be rather straining (starts late into the night; lively bustle often not before 1.00 a.m.), but it's also exceptionally easy going (no taboos concerning stimulants and dark rooms) and communicative (inquisitve tourists and lonely business men).

The gay public around Christopher Street may be a bit older, a bit rougher than elsewhere, but that doesn't diminish its popularity. But: *East Village* is slowly but surely overtaking its western neighbour as an artists center and quarter. *Chelsea* has evolved from a middle class residential area for whites and latinos to a new and modern gay Mecca of NY. This is for instance shown by the traditional gay bookshop *A Different Light* having moved to 7th Avenue. The redevelopment of the Chelsea Piers contributed to this. We'll have to wait and see, whether the plans to redevelop the area around *Times Square* will really displace the strip-shows and porn cinemas residing there.

A tip at the end: If time and travelplans allow, you should at least take a daytrip to *Fire Island*, the gay bathing mecca of the metropolis (look undor *Firo Island*).

The listing is divided into 8 parts. We divided Manhatten into *Downtown, Village & Chelsea* (with city map), *Midtown* (with city map) and *Uptown*. There is an extra chapter for each of the 4 boroughs Bronx, Brooklyn, Queens and Staten Island. Addresses on Long Is-

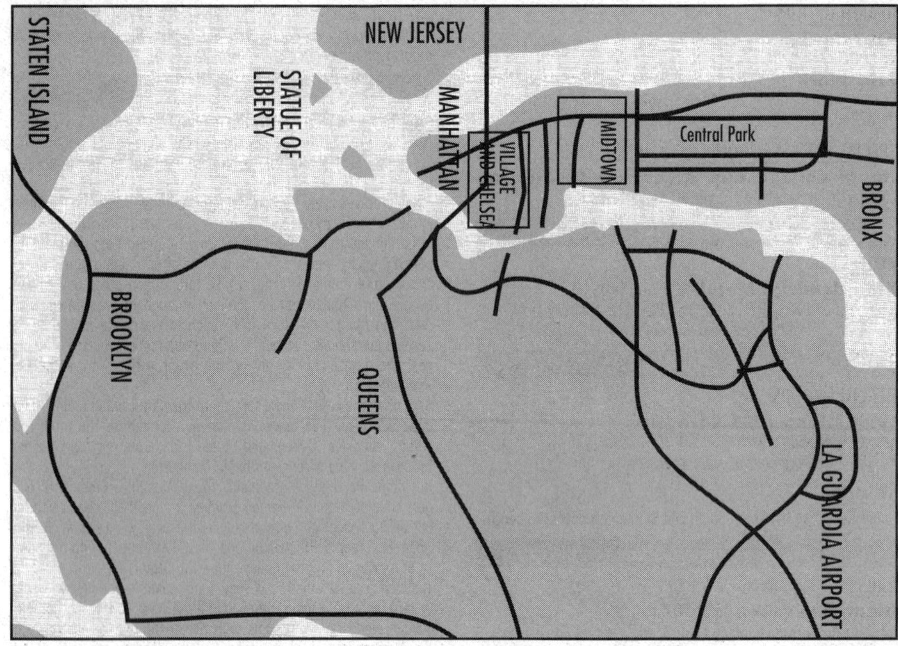

land (look under *Long Island*) have been divided into *Nassau County* (west) and *Suffolk County* (east).

✱ Der Mittelpunkt der schwulen Welt liegt in der *Christopher Street*, dort, wo sich am 28. Juni 1969 Schwule zum erstenmal massiv und handgreiflich gegen fortwährende willkürliche Polizeirazzien wehrten. Dieser historische Ort ist ein absolutes Muß für jeden homosexuellen Touristen.

Am besten sieht man sich New York im Frühjahr oder Herbst an, denn Winter und Sommer halten extreme Temperaturen für diese extreme Stadt bereit. Für die Wege in der Stadt (und vom Flughafen JFK in die Stadt) empfiehlt sich auf jeden Fall die *subway*. Taxis sind eher das optimale Verkehrsmittel für nächtliche Heimfahrten nach einer Szene-Tour. Informationen über schwule Kulturereignisse und zum schwulen Ausgehen lassen sich am besten den Party-Blättern *HomoExtra (HX)* und *Next* entnehmen. Darüberhinaus bietet sich das *N.Y. Gay and Lesbian Community Center* als Orientierungshilfe an. Das wichtigste und größte schwul-lesbische Ereignis der Stadt ist die *Gay Pride Parade* im Jun.

Wie das so oft der Fall ist: Man spricht von New York, meint aber doch nur einen der fünf *boroughs*, Manhattan nämlich. Die anderen vier (Bronx, Brooklyn, Queens und Staten Island) sind für Schwule uninteressant. In Manhattan konzentriert sich New Yorks schwules Leben.

Und dies ist in Bewegung geraten: zwar ist *The Village* (i.e. Greenwich Village) um den *Sheridan Square* immer noch sehr bunt, aber ein gleichwertiger und angesagter Schwerpunkt schwulen Lebens hat sich in *Chelsea*, an der Ecke 8th Avenue und West 17th Street gebildet. Mit der Tendenz, sich Richtung Norden über die 23rd Street hinaus weiterzubewegen.

Für Touristen ist New York City eine schier unerschöpfliche Schatzkiste: Kunstschätze entlang der *Museumsmeile* östlich und südlich des -tagsüber nicht übermässig gefährlichen- *Central Parks*. Die Architekturschätze reichen vom importierten *The Cloisters* an der 190th Street bis zum *World Trade Center* in Downtown. Auch wenn die Straßen dann voll sind: Shopping ist am schönsten in den Wochen vor Weihnachten entlang der 5th Avenue, zwischen 50th und 59th Street.

Schwules Nightlife hat in New York eine ausgesprochen lange Tradition und schon in den 20er Jahren waren Gegenden wie der Times Square oder das Village angesagt. Ausgehen in New York ist manchmal anstrengend, denn es geht spät los, Trubel kommt oft nicht vor 1 Uhr auf. Die Szene befindet sich zur Zeit im Umbruch, was auch an den Säuberungsaktionen des republikanischen Bürgermeisters Guiliani liegt. So wurden zahlreiche Darkrooms geschlossen. Geplant ist auch die Schließung von Sexshops, die sich näher als 1000 m an einer Kirche oder Schule befinden. Immer beliebter werden bei vielen Schwulen gepflegte Cocktail-Bars. Das *East Village* läuft seinem West-Pendant rund um die Christopher Street langsam den Rang als Künstlerviertel ab. *Chelsea* hat sich von einer Mittelklasse-Wohngegend für Weiße und Latinos zum neuen und modernen schwulen Mekka New Yorks entwickelt. Beitragen wird zu dieser Entwicklung sicherlich auch die Sanierung der Chelsea Piers. Die Sanierung der Gegend um den *Times Square* zeigt tatsächlich Wirkung: Disney-Millionen und Familienfreundlichkeit verdrängen den rauhen Charme der Schmuddel-Sex-Shops und Pornokinos.

Ein Tip zum Schluß: Bei genügend Zeit im Reiseplan sollte ein zumindest eintägiger Besuch auf *Fire Island*, dem schwulen Bademekka der Metropole, eingeplant werden (siehe dort).

Das Listing ist in acht Teile untergliedert: Manhattan haben wir in *Downtown, Village & Chelsea* (mit Stadtplan), *Midtown* (mit Stadtplan) und *Uptown* gegliedert. Für jedes der vier Boroughs Bronx, Brooklyn, Queens und Staten Island gibt es ein kleines Extra-Kapitel.

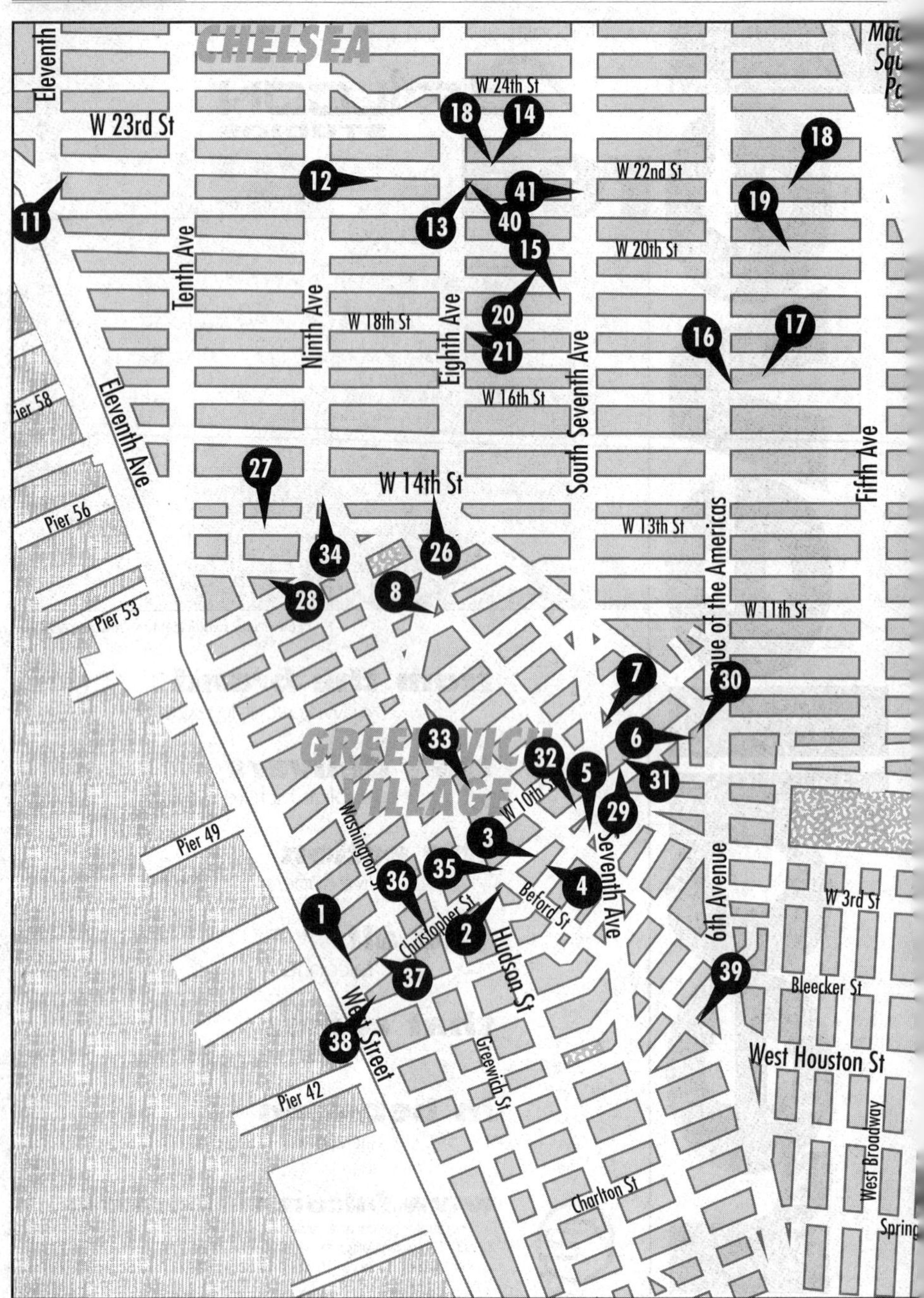
CHELSEA
GREENWICH VILLAGE
Eleventh
W 23rd St
W 24th St
W 22nd St
W 20th St
W 18th St
W 16th St
W 14th St
W 13th St
W 11th St
Tenth Ave
Ninth Ave
Eighth Ave
South Seventh Ave
Avenue of the Americas
Fifth Ave
Eleventh Ave
Pier 58
Pier 56
Pier 53
Pier 49
Pier 42
Washington St
W 10th St
Christopher St
Beford St
Hudson St
Seventh Ave
6th Avenue
W 3rd St
Bleecker St
West Houston St
West Street
Greewich St
Charlton St
West Broadway
Spring
Madison Square Park

NEW YORK CITY
Manhattan/Village & Chelsea

1 Sneakers Bar
2 Christopher Street Bookshop Sex Shop/Blue Movie
3 Ty's Bar
4 Marie's Crisis Bar
5 The Monster Bar & Danceclub
6 Oscar Wilde Bookshop
7 Julius Bar
8 Incentra Village House Guest House
11 Eagle Bar
12 Colonial House Inn Guest House
13 The Break Bar
14 Unicorn Sex Shop/Blue Movie
15 A Different Light Bookshop
16 King Danceclub
17 Splash Bar
18 Barracuda Bar
19 West Side Club Men's Club
20 G Lounge Bar
21 Viceroy Restaurant
22 Dick's Bar
23 Wonderbar
24 Boiler Room Bar
25 The Bar
26 Chelsea Pines Inn Guest House
27 The Lure Bar
28 Hell Bar
29 Stonewall Bar
30 Pieces Bar
31 New York Bodyworks Shop
32 Boots & Saddle Bar
33 Gay Pleasures/Creative Visions Bookshops
34 J's Hangout Men's Club
35 The Hangar Bar
36 Two Potato Bar
37 The Dugout Bar
38 Keller's Bar
39 Bar d'O
40 Rawhide Bar
41 B.M.W. Bar

Adressen auf Long Island (siehe dort) haben wir nach *Nassau County* (westlicher Teil) und *Suffolk County* (östlicher Teil) sortiert.

▲ Si une rue sur terre peut se targuer d'être LA première rue gay du monde, c'est bien la Christopher Street! Là où, pour la toute première fois, le 28 juin 1969, les gays se sont violemment rebellés contre les contrôles intempestifs et permanents de la police. La Christopher Street, c'est un lieu historique! Un must pour le touriste gay!
Le meilleur moment pour visiter New York, c'est au printemps ou en automne, car on y étouffe en été et on y gèle en hiver. Pour aller de Kennedy Airport en ville, comme pour les trajets quotidiens, il n'y a rien de mieux que le métro. Pour les trajets nocturnes d'une boîte à l'autre, le taxi est plus sûr et plus pratique. Pour savoir où aller, que faire, avec qui et comment, jetez un oeil dans les magasines gays locaux „Next" et „Homo Extra". Pour commencer, allez donc faire un tour au „New York Gay and Lesbian Community Center". Vous y trouverez tous les renseignements et les tuyaux que vous cherchez. L'évènement numéro 1 au calendrier gay, c'est la „Gay Pride Parade" qui a lieu tous les ans en juin.
Quand on parle de New York, on ne pense généralement qu'à celui des généralement qu'à celui des 5 „boroughs" qui porte le nom de Manhattan. Les 4 arrondissements restants (Bronx, Brooklyn, Queens et Staten Island) ne sont pas d'un intérêt majeur pour le touriste gay de base. C'est, en effet, à Manhattan que bat le coeur homo de New York.
Le bastion gay est -et a toujours été- Greenwich Village, surtout autour de Sheridan Square, même si, depuis quelque temps, c'est à Chelsea que ça bouge le plus, à la hauteur de la 8th Avenue et de West 17th Street en remontant jusqu'à la 23th Street.
Le paysage urbain de New York est tout bonnement époustouflant. Les musées regorgent de trésors. Ils se trouvent au sud et à l'est de Central Pak qui, lui, est devenu bien plus sûr que dans le passé. Au niveau architecture, il y en a pour tous les goûts: des „Cloisters" (pur produit d'importation) au World Trade Center. Pour faire du shopping, rien de tel que le quartier entre la 50th et la 59th Street avant les fêtes de fin!
La vie nocturne de New York, c'est quelque chose! Times Square et Greenwich Village sont les quartiers qui bougent la nuit et ce, depuis les années 20. Sortir à New York, ce n'est pas une sinécure: ça commence tard, les gens ne se montrent qu'après une heure du matin. Fatiguant, mais assez cool: les darkrooms, les stimulants et excitants de toute sorte ne choquent plus personne. Fatiguant, cool et aussi communicatif: les touristes et les gens de passage contribuent à rendre l'atmosphère conviviale et décontractée.
Dans la plupart des bars de Christopher Street, les gens ont passé la quarantaine et peuvent paraître un tantinet rudes. Ils n'en sont pas pour autant des brutes! Dans l'East Village (qui commence à faire concurrence au West Village), le public est plus jeune. Ce quartier plutôt middle-class est en train de devenir le quartier des artistes, la Mecque des jeunes gays blancs ou latinos. Un signe qui ne trompe pas: la librairie gay „A Different Light" a récemment déménagé pour s'installer dans la 7th Street. L'aménagement des quais de Chelsea va certainement accélérer cette métamorphose qu'est en train de connaître le quartier. Verra-t-on enfin disparaître les ciné porno et les peep shows de Times Square? Cela semble moins sûr!
Un tuyau pour finir: s'il vous reste du temps, allez donc faire un tour à Fire Island, la station balnéaire gay de New York (Cf. rubrique Fire Island).
Nous avons divisé New York en 8 parties: Manhattan avec Downtown, Village et Chelsea (plan), Midtown (plan) et Uptown. Pour chacun des autres arrondissements (Bronx, Brooklyn, Queens et Staten Island), vous avez un chapitre particulier. Les adresses de Long Island sont classées sous „Nassau County" (partie ouest) et „Suffolk

County" (partie est).

☆ El punto central del mundo gay se encuentra en la *Christopher Street*, donde que el día 28 de junio de 1969 los homosexuales por primera vez protestaban masivamente, incluso haciendo uso de los puños, contra las redadas policiales arbitrarias al azar. Este sitio es un lugar de importante valor histórico para todo visitante gay. Nueva York ofrece su mejor cara en la primavera o en otoño, mientras en verano y invierno las temperaturas son extremas. Para transladarse dentro de la ciudad (y desde el aeropuerto) se recomienda el uso del *subway* (metro). Los taxis son el medio transporte óptimo a altas horas de la noche. Informaciones sobre los acontecimientos gay más importantes se encuentran en las revistas *Next* y *HomoExtra (HX)*. El *N.Y. Gay and Lesbian Community Center* ofrece también ayuda para orientarse dentro de la ciudad. El evento gay-lesbiano más grande es la *Gay Pride Parade* en junio de cada año. Aunque Nueva York se compone de cinco *bouroughs* (Manhattan, Bronx, Queens y Staten Island), la mayoria de la gente piensa en Manhattan cuando se habla de ella. Los otros cuatro, no son, desde el punto de vista gay, muy interesantes. En Manhattan se concentra la vida gay de Nueva York. Los barrios *The Village* (Greenwich Village) y el *Sheridan Square* son homosexuales por excelencia y tradición, pero también el igualmente importante y nuevo centro gay *Chelsea* en la esquina 8th. Avenue y West 17th. Street, con la tendencia de expansión hacia el norte sobre la 23rd Street se ha puesto de moda. Nueva York ofrece innumerables puntos de atracción turísticos y posee una enorme cantidad de tesoros. La *Milla de Museos* al este y sur del *Central Park* ofrece a todo lo largo increibles obras artísticas. Dentro de los tesoros arquitectónicos encontramos desde *The Cloisters* en la 190th. Street, hasta el *World Trade Center* en downtown. Los tesoros a la venta se obtienen sobre todo en las semanas antes de la navidad en la 5 th. Avenue entre la 50th. y la 59th. Street. La vida nocturna gay en Nueva York tiene una larga tradición, incluso en los años '20 los alrededores del Time Square o las Village eran ya muy prometedoras. Vivir el ambiente de Nueva York puede ser muy cansado (las actividades inician no antes de la 1 de la madrugada), pero también muy agradable (estimulantes y cuartos oscuros no son tabú) y comunicativo (debido a los turistas curiosos y a los hombres de negocios solitarios). En los alrededores de la Christopher Street el público es un poco mayor y brusco. El *East Village* ha adquirido la fama de barrio artístico con el público correspondiente. *Chelsea* ha pasado de ser un barrio residencial de clase media para blancos y latinos, al nuevo centro moderno de la vida gay en Nuva York. Esto ha sido subrayado por la mudanza de la famosa librería *A Different Light* en la 7th. Avenue. La remodelación de Chelsea Piers contribuirá con seguridad a este desarrollo. Es de esperar que la nueva igagen que se está dando al sector cercano al *Times Square* no relege los muchos Strip-Shows y cines porno de los alrededores. Consejo: una vista a la Fire Island, esta es el balneario gay por excelencia de Nueva York. El listado esta dividido en 8 partes: Manhattan la hemos dividido en *Downtown, Village & Chelsea* (con mapa), *Midtown* (con mapa) y *Uptown*. Para cada uno de los otros cuatro boroughs (Bronx, Brooklyn, Queens y Staten Island) hay un capítulo extra. Las direcciones de Long Island las hemos acomodado bajo los nombres *Nassau County* (parte este) y *Suffolk County* (parte oeste).

❖ La *Christopher Street* è il centro del mondo gay, dove il 28 giugno 1969 per la prima volta i gay si sono difesi in massa, ed in modo aggressivo, contro le ripetute ed arbitrarie repressioni della polizia. Visitare questo luogo storico è un obbligo per ogni turista. Le stagioni migliori per visitare New York sono la primavera e l'autunno considerato che in estate ed in inverno si registrano sempre temperature estreme. Per gli spostamenti urbani (anche dall'aereoporto JFK al centro) vi consigliamo di usare la *subway*. I taxi sono consigliabili per il rientro in albergo dopo una nottata nell'ambiente gay. Troverete informazioni sugli avvenimenti culturali gay e sugli appuntamenti rilevanti nelle pubblicazioni *Next* e *Homo Extra*. Inoltre, come punto di orientamento, esiste il *New York Gay and Lesbian Community Center*. L'evento gay più importante della città è la *Gay Pride Parade* in giugno. Spesso accade che quando si parla di New York si intende solo uno dei cinque *boroughs*, ossia Manhattan. Gli altri quattro (Bronx, Brooklyn, Queens e Staten Island) non sono molto interessanti per i gay. La vita gay di New York infatti si concentra soprattutto a Manhattan: le zone calde sono *The Village* (i.e. Greenwich Village), intorno a *Sheridan Square*, tuttora vivace e frizzante, e da poco *Chelsea*, all'angolo tra la 8th avenue e la West 17th street, che tende a svilupparsi verso la 23rd street. New York offre attrazioni di prima classe ed enormi tesori: opere d'arte, nel viale dei musei a sud est del Central Park (che di giorno non è eccessivamente pericoloso), tesori architettonici che variano da *The Cloisters*, importato e ricostruito nella 190th street, al *World Trade Center* nel centro. I tesori più belli li troverete durante le settimane prenatalizie lungo la 5th avenue tra la 50th e la 59th street. La vita notturna gay di New York ha una lunga tradizione: già negli anni '20 zone come il Village o Times Square erano conosciute. Uscire di sera è spesso faticoso (il movimento inizia tardi, spesso non prima dell'una), ma l'ambiente è disinibito (vibratori e darkroom non sono un tabù) e comunicativo (i turisti e gli uomini d'affari in viaggio sono molto disponibili). Intorno alla Chirstopher street la gente è un po' ruvida e non più molto giovane. L'*East Village* sta cedendo il suo ruolo di quartiere artistico alla sua parte occidentale. Chelsea è divenuto, da quartiere residenziale della classe, media bianca e sudamericana, la mecca dei gay. Ciò è confermato anche dal trasferimento della tradizionale libreria *A different light* nella 7th avenue. A questo cambiamento contribuirà sicuramente anche la ristrutturazione del Chelsea Piers, anche se non è ancora sicuro se i piani di rinnovo di questa zona respingeranno i cinema a luce rossa e i locali di spogliarelli qui situati. In fine un consiglio: se avete tempo a sufficienza dedicate almeno un giorno a *Fire Island*, il lido gay della metropoli. Gli indirizzi sono stati classificati in 8 gruppi: abbiamo diviso Manhattan in *Downtown, Village e Chelsea* (con piantina), *Midtown* (con piantina) e *Uptown*. Per ognuno dei quattro quartieri Bronx, Brooklyn, Queens e Staten Island presentiamo un piccolo capitolo a parte. Abbiamo diviso gli indirizzi di Long Island (vedi elenco) in Nassau County (parte occidentale) e Suffolk County (parte orientale).

GAY INFO

Gay and Lesbian Switchboard
332 Bleecker Street, Suite F-18 ✉NY 10014 ☎ 989-0999

Gay Televison Groups-CCTV
c/o Rick X, PO Box 790 ✉NY 10108

Gayellow Pages 12-17.30 h
PO Box 533, Village Station ✉NY 10014 ☎ 674-0120
Fax: (212) 420-1126 E-Mail: gayellow_pages@juno.com
Annual regional guide, 96 pages. US$ 3.95.

HX Magazine
c/o Two Queens, 230 West 17th Street ✉NY 10011 *(8th floor)*
☎ 352-3535 Fax: 352-3596 Homepage: www.hx.com
Good weekly gay nightlife and entertainment magazine available for free at gay venues. Lesbian version also available (HX for her).

Lesbian and Gay Community Services Center (A AC CC d GLM MA S TV VS W) 9-23 h
One Little West 12th Street ✉NY 10014 *(West Village)*
☎ 620-7810 Fax: 924-2657 E-Mail: info@gaycenter.org
Homepage: http://www.gaycenter.org
THE NYC Community center providing help and support in case of any problem, archival collection, library, museum, over 300 groups, social events, legal advice, and more. Bimonthly newsletter „Centervoice".

Metrosource
180 Varick Street ✉NY 10014 *(5th floor)* ☎ 691-5127
Gay and lesbian guide to New York. Excellent articles about certain aspects of gay and lesbian lifestyle in the city, community and business directories. Published four times a year.

National Museum of Lesbian and Gay History
c/o Lesbian and Gay Gay Community Services Center, 208 West 13th Street ✉NY 10011 *(West Village)*
New founded in 1989. Including library and archives.

New York Blade News Mon-Fri 9-17 h
242 West 30th Street ✉NY 10001 *(4th floor)* ☎ 268-2701
Fax: 268-2069 Homepage: jlamont@nyblade.com
Newspaper covering national and local, arts and entertainment news, contains classifieds and some events listings.

New York Gay and Lesbian Yellow Pages
4200 Montrose Boulevard, Ste 480 ✉TX 77006 ☎ 691-8960
Homepage: www.glyp.com

Next
121 Varick Street ✉NY 10013 *(6th floor)* ☎ 627-0165 Fax: 627-0633
Weekly publication. Bar/Club guide. Info on New York's scene.

Parlee Plus/Equal Time the News
13 South Carl Avenue, Babylon ✉NY 11702 ☎ 516/587-8669
Monthly magazine with bar guide.

Pat Parker/Vito Russo Center Library Mon-Thu 18-21, Sat 13-16 h
208 West 13th Street ✉NY 10011 ☎ 620-7310 ext. 302 Homepage: www.gaycenter.org
Over 10,00 books, 300 videos and 55 periodicals.

Twist
PO Box 7908 Rego Park ✉NY 11347 ☎ 718/381-8776 Fax: 718/366-8636
Little monthly magazine with info on the scene and bars listing available for free at gay venues.

Vice
c/o VICE Publishing Inc., PO Box 20281 ✉NY 10011-0003
☎ 727-2787 Fax: 727-3190 E-Mail: vice@nycnet.com
Arts and entertainment magazine.

TOURIST INFO

New York Convention & Visitor Bureau
2 Columbus Circle ✉NY 10019 ☎ 484-1200 Fax: 246-6310

ESCORTS & STUDIOS

Agency N.Y. Escort Agency (CC G)
☎ 481-4000 Fax: 481-2549 E-Mail: theagencyny@aol.com

Chelsea Guys ☎ 533-5600
Homepage: www.chelseaguys.com
From college men to porn stars.

TRAVEL & TRANSPORT

Sailing Affairs (F GLM MA OS)
404 East 11th Street ✉NY 10009-4541 ☎ 228-5755
Fax: 228-8512 E-Mail: sailingaff@aol.com
Captained sailboat charters for individuals or small groups. Day trips, sunset sails, weekends on 38 foot yacht. Gay owned and operated.

PRIVATE ACCOMODATION

Enjoy Bed & Breakfast (bf G H MA) 16.30-21 h (central European time)
☎ +49 (30) 215 1666 Fax: +49 (30) 217 52219
E-Mail: Info@ebab.com Homepage: www.ebab.com
Price US$ 55. Accommodation sharing agency. All with shower & bf.

New York Bed & Breakfast Reservation Center. The (GLM)
☎ 977-3512
Wide range of Bed & Breakfast accomodations in private homes in New York City.

Pride NYC B&B Service (H)
☎ 807-9857 Fax: 807-9857 E-Mail: cadkm@aol.com
Homepage: http://www.prideaccommodations.com
Rooms with bath/WC, TV, telephone, balcony or terrace, kitchen, heating and own key.

Rainbow Roommates (AC CC GLM MA W) Mon-Fri 11-19, Sat 12-18 h
268 West 22nd Street ✉NY 10011 *(corner of 8th Street)*
☎ 627-8612 Fax: (800) 421-9833
E-Mail: rainbowroommate@nycnet.com
Homepage: nycnet.com/rainbowroommates/
Gay roommate and real estate service.

GENERAL GROUPS

ACLU Lesbian and Gay Rights Project
132 West 43rd Street ✉NY 10036 ☎ 944-9800

ACT UP New York Mon 19.30 h
at LGCSC, 208 West 13th Street
☎ 642-5499 Fax: 966-4873 Homepage: www.actupny.org

Asian and Friends New York
☎ (718) 488-0630

Center For Lesbian And Gay Studies. The (CLAGS)
Graduate Center, City University of New York, 33 West 42nd Street ✉NY 10036

Coalition for Lesbian and Gay Rights
☎ 627-1398

Gay and Lesbian Anti-Violence Project 0-24 h
☎ 807-0197
Counselling and referral.
154 Christopher Street ✉NY 10014 *(West Village)* ☎ 807-7433
Organises the annual Pride Week.

Senior Action in a Gay Environment (SAGE)
305 7th Avenue ✉NY 10001 *(16th floor. Chelsea)* ☎ 741-2247
Organisation for senior lesbians and gays.

Twenty-Something
c/o The Center, One Little West 12th Street ✉NY 10014
☎ 439-8051
Youth group.

FETISH GROUPS

Eulenspiegel Society/TES
PO Box 2783, Grand Central Station ✉NY 10163 ☎ 388-7022
Pansexual S/M group.

Excelsior Motorcycle Club
PO Box 1386, Bowling Green Station ✉NY 10274-1130

Gay Male S/M Activists (GMSMA) (B f G p sa)
332 Bleecker Street, Suite D23 ✉NY 10014 ☎ 727-9878
For safe and responsible S/M.

Golden Shower Association (GSA)
332 Bleecker, # K-95 ✉NY 10014
Its name says it all. Write for info on activities.

Hot Ash
PO Box 20147, London Terrace Station ✉NY 10011
For cigar fetishists of every sexual orientation.

Iron Guard NYC
PO Box 291 Village Station ✉NY 10014

New York Bondage Club (NYBC)
PO Box 20064 ✉NY 10014 ☎ 620-7673
Men only. Meets on Fri at 8 pm at J's Hangout.

HEALTH GROUPS

Aids Hotline 9-21 h
☎ 447-8200
NYC Department of Health.

aidsinfonyc.org
E-Mail: webman@aidsinfonyc.org Homepage: www.aidsinfonyc.org
Extensive site with page providing information on Aids and related services in NYC.

American Indian Community House HIV/AIDS Project (AICH)
404 Lafayette Street ✉NY 10003 *(2nd floor)* ☎ 598-0100
E-Mail: thomasaich@aol.com

Body Positive. The Mon-Fri 9-18 h
19 Fulton Street, Suite 308 B ✉NY 10038 ☎ 566-7333
Fax: 566-4539
Education, medical info and support groups. Publisher of a magazine about HIV and AIDS. Published monthly, about 48 pages. Free at gay venues. Also available in Spanish language edition.

Central New York AIDS Hotline
☎ (315) 475-AIDS

Community Health Project Tue Thu 18-21 h
208 West 13th Street ✉NY 10011 *(West Village) (2nd floor)*
☎ 675-3559
Walk in clinic for VD, AIDS.

Gay Men's Health Crisis
Tisch Building, 129 West 20th Street ✉NY 10011-1913
☎ 367-1000 Fax: 367-1220
A not-for-profit, volunteer-supported and community-based organization comitted to national leadership on the fight against Aids.

H.E.L.P./Project Samaritan Wed 20 h
at the Center Residential Health Care Facility, 1401 University Avenue ✉NY 10452 ☎ 718/681-8700 Fax: 718/681-8700
E-Mail: psiadm@aol.com Homepage: www.aidsnyc.org/help-psi
66-bed nursing home for people with Aids/HIV who are recovering substance abusers.

People with AIDS. Coalition of New York
50 West 17th Street ✉NY 10011 *(8th floor)* ☎ 647-1415
☎ (800) 828-3280 (Hotline) Fax: 647-1419
Organisation dedicated to the self-empowerment of people living with Aids/HIV.

HELP WITH PROBLEMS

Alcoholics Anonymous
☎ 683-3900

Gay Men's Therapy Group
420 West 24th Street, Suite 1B ☎ 243-8798

Psychology Discussion Group
Ninth Street Center, 151 First Avenue, Suite 25 ✉NY 10003
☎ 228-5153
Discussion group dealing with homosexuality and creativity, gender and identity, masculinity and feminity.

RELIGIOUS GROUPS

Congregation Beth Simchat Torah Service Fri 8.30 h
57 Bethune Street ✉NY 10014 *(West Village)* ☎ 929-9498
New York's Gay and Lesbian Jewish Synagogue.

Dignity New York (GLM) Service Sun
at St. John's in Greenwich Village
☎ 866-8047 Fax: 866-8047
Lesbian and gay catholics.

Metropolitan Community Church Services Sun 10 h at the Center, Sun 19 h at 135 West 4th Street
446 West 36th Street ✉NY 10018 ☎ 629-7440 Fax: 629-7441

SPECIAL INTEREST GROUPS

Bears International
332 Bleecker Street, Suite F4 ✉NY 10014

Girth and Mirth Club of New York
PO Box 10, Dept. G, Pelham ✉NY 10803 ☎ 914/699-7735

M.A.N. ☎ 535-3914
Gay Male Social Nudists.

MetroBears New York
PO Box 1802 ✉NY 10185-1802 ☎ 978-5080
Social organisation for bears and their admirers.

SPORT GROUPS

Team New York
PO Box 26 ✉NY 10011 ☎ 439-8179
Homepage: members.aol.com/teamny1998
Umbrella organisation for athletes, sport teams and cultural festival participants who participates in the Gay Games.

New York - Bronx ☎ 718

BARS

Up & Down Bar (B GLM D S)
1306 Unionport Road ☎ 822-9585
Go-go girls and boys in the Bronx.

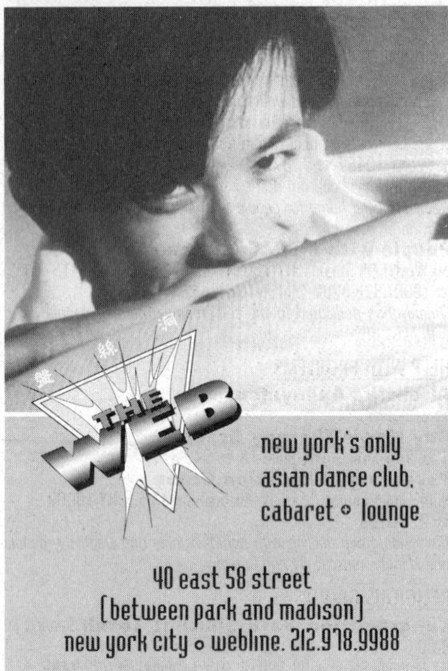

THE WEB
new york's only
asian dance club.
cabaret ◦ lounge
40 east 58 street
(between park and madison)
new york city ◦ webline. 212.978.9988

ANN STREET
ENTERTAINMENT CENTER
YOUR STOP IN THE FINANCIAL DISTRICT FOR QUALITY INTIMATE ENTERTAINMENT PRODUCTS
21 ANN STREET
BETWEEN BROADWAY/NASSAU
212-267-9760
MON-FRI 7AM-11PM
SAT 10AM-11PM
SUN 10 AM-7PM

HEALTH GROUPS

Gay Men's HIV+ Support Group Mon 18-20 h
c/o Bronx AIDS Services, One Fordham Plaza No.903, ✉NY 10458 ☎ 295-5605

New York - Brooklyn ☎ 718

BARS

Sanctuary Lounge (B GLM)
444 7th Avenue ☎ 832-9800
Gay and lesbian mixed crowd.

DANCECLUBS

Spectrum (AC B D GLM MA OS SNU STV) Wed-Sat 21.30-4 h
802 64th Street ✉NY 11220 ☎ 238-8213
The movie „Saturday Night Fever" was filmed here.

HEALTH GROUPS

Brooklyn AIDS Task Force, Inc.
☎ 212/783-0883

Touch AIDS Community Dinners Mon 17.30 h
Friends Meeting House, 110 Schermerhorn Street ☎ 518-2806
Free dinners for PWA's.

New York - Manhattan/Downtown ☎ 212

SEX SHOPS/BLUE MOVIES

Ann Street Entertainment Center (CC G VS)
Mon-Fri 7-23, Sat 10-23, Sun 10-19 h
21 Ann Street ✉NY 10038-2405 *(between Broadway and Nassau Streets)* ☎ 267-9760

SAUNAS/BATHS

Wall Street Sauna (B F G sa) Mon-Fri 11-20 h
1 Maiden Lane ✉NY 10038 *(11th floor)* ☎ 233-890

GALLERIES

Wessel and O'Connor Gallery (G) 242 West 26th Street ✉NY 10013 *(Chelsea, between 7th and 8th Avenues)*
☎ 242-8811

New York - Manhattan/Midtown ☎212

BARS

Chase (B G YG) 255
West 55th Street ✉NY 10019 *(between broadway and 8th avenue)* ☎ 333-3400
70s-style coffee bar and cocktail lounge.

Cleo's 9th Avenue Saloon (B G MA N) 8-4 h
656 9th Avenue/46th Street ✉NY 10036 *(Lower West Side)*
☎ 307-1503

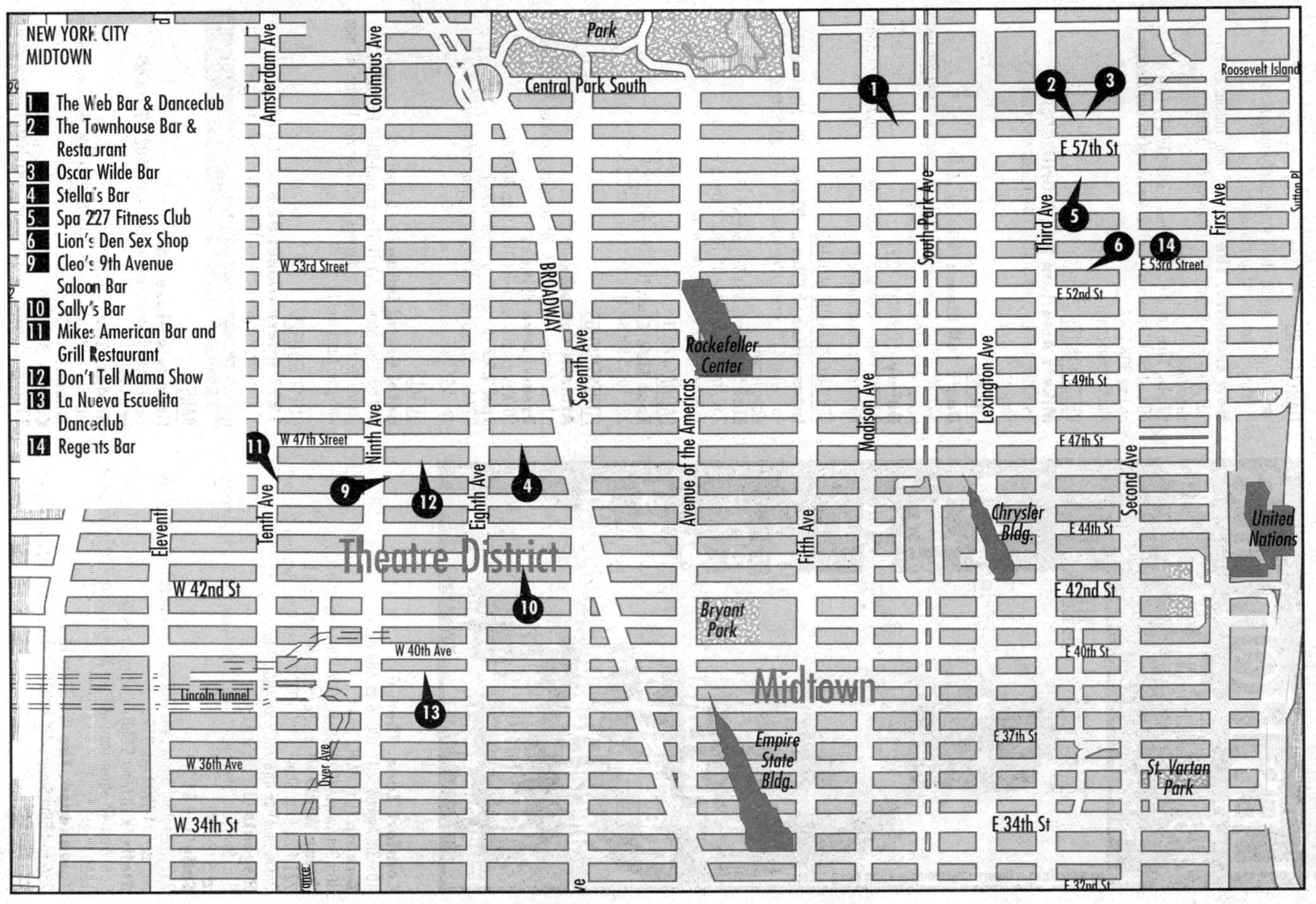
NEW YORK CITY
MIDTOWN
1 The Web Bar & Danceclub
2 The Townhouse Bar & Restaurant
3 Oscar Wilde Bar
4 Stella's Bar
5 Spa 227 Fitness Club
6 Lion's Den Sex Shop
9 Cleo's 9th Avenue Saloon Bar
10 Sally's Bar
11 Mikes American Bar and Grill Restaurant
12 Don't Tell Mama Show
13 La Nueva Escuelita Danceclub
14 Regents Bar
Park
Central Park South
Amsterdam Ave
Columbus Ave
BROADWAY
Seventh Ave
Avenue of the Americas
Madison Ave
South Park Ave
Lexington Ave
Third Ave
Second Ave
First Ave
Roosevelt Island
Sutton Pl
E 57th St
E 53rd Street
E 52nd St
E 49th St
E 47th St
E 44th St
E 42nd St
E 40th St
E 37th St
E 34th St
E 32nd St
W 53rd Street
W 47th Street
Ninth Ave
Tenth Ave
Eighth Ave
Eleventh
Fifth Ave
W 42nd St
W 40th Ave
W 36th Ave
W 34th St
Dyer Ave
Lincoln Tunnel
Theatre District
Midtown
Rockefeller Center
Chrysler Bldg.
United Nations
Bryant Park
Empire State Bldg.
St. Vartan Park

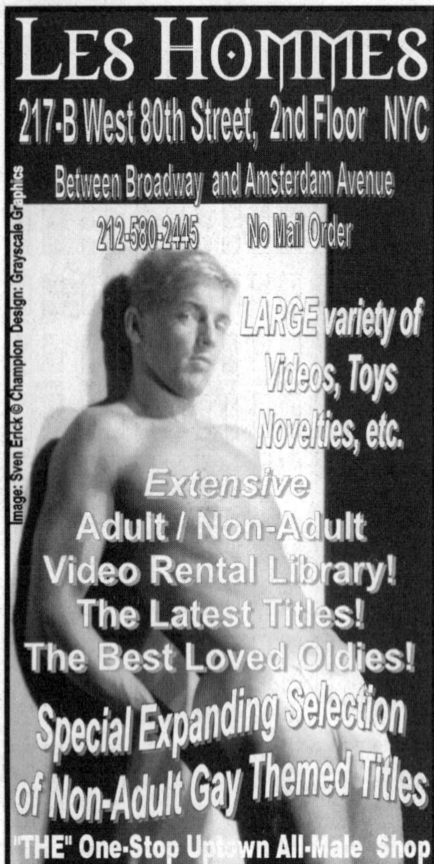

Comfort Zone. The (B G VS)
405 3rd Avenue ✉NY 10016 ☎ 684-8376
Dakota (B G MA N) 14-4 h
405 3rd Avenue/29th Street ✉NY 10016 ☎ 684-8376
Oscar Wilde (AC B CC E f GLM MA N s) 16-4 h
221 East 58th Street ✉NY 10022 *(East Side. Between 2nd and 3rd Avenue)* ☎ 486-7309 ☎ 486-0905
Regents (B G E F S) 12-4 h
317 East 53rd Street ✉NY 10022 *(between 1st & 2nd Avneues)* ☎ 593-3091
Sally's (B G S TV)
252 West 43rd Street ✉NY 10036 *(Downstairs at the Hotel Carter)* ☎ 944-6000 ext. 212
Stella's (B Glm r S SNU) 12-4 h, shows WE
266 West 47 Street (east of Eight Avenue) ✉NY 10036 ☎ 575-1680
Townhouse. The (B E G MA) 16-3 h
236 East 58th Street ✉NY 10022 *(between 2nd and 3rd Avenue)* ☎ 754-4649

DANCECLUBS

☛ You should always check the local gay magazines for up-to-date listings of parties and special events.

New Escuelita. The (B D glm) Mon, Thu-Sat 22-? h
301 West 39th Street ✉NY 10018 ☎ 631-0588
Very latino.
Web. The (AC B CC D G LJ MA S SNU STV VS) 16-4 h
40 East 58th Street ✉NY 10022 *(between Park and Madison Streets)* ☎ 308-1546
Mostly Asian crowd.

RESTAURANTS

Mike's American Bar & Grill (B F g)
650 10th Avenue ✉NY 10036 *(West Side)* ☎ 246-4115
Popular.

SHOWS

Don't Tell Mama (B GLM S) 16-4 h
343 West 46th Street ✉NY 10036 *(between 8th and 9th Avenues)* ☎ 757-0788 *Two cabaret rooms.*
Gaiety (f G R SNU) 12-?
201 West 46th Street ✉NY 10036 *(at Broadway)* ☎ 221-8868
New York's oldest male burlesque.

SEX SHOPS/BLUE MOVIES

International Film & Video (g VS) Mon-Fri 9-17 h
453 West 47th Street ✉NY 10036 ☎ 245-8039 ☎ 245-8027
Video rental.
Lion's Den (G VS) 9-1, Sat-Sun -2 h
230 East 53rd Street ✉NY 10022 ☎ 753-7800
Videos, magazines, toys, and more.

SAUNAS/BATHS

East Side Club (B f G sa sb VS WO)
227 East 56th Street ✉NY 10022 ☎ 753-2222

FITNESSTUDIOS

Athletic Complex (g)
3 Park Avenue ✉NY 10016 *(at southeast corner of 34th Street)*
Prescriptive Fitness (g)
50 West 54th Street ✉NY 10019 ☎ 307-7760
Spa 227 (B f G msg p sa sol) 0-24 h
227 East 56th Street ✉NY 10022 *(Near 3rd Avenue)* ☎ 754-0227

HOTELS

Hotel Grand Union (AC CC F g H MA)
34 East 32nd Street ✉NY 10016 ☎ 683-5890 Fax: 689-7397
Central location close to theatres and Greenwich Village. All rooms with priv. baths and TV.

GUEST HOUSES

1291 International B&B (AC CC g H MA)
1596 Lexington Avenue ✉NY 10021 ☎ 465-7333

New York - Manhattan/Uptown ☎ 212

BARS

Brandy's Piano Bar (B glm S)
235 East 84th Street/2nd Avenue ✉NY 10028 *(East Side)* ☎ 650-1944
Bridge. The (B G MA) 16-4 h
309 East 60th Street ✉NY 10028 *(East-Side, between 2nd and 1st Avenue)* ☎ 223-9104
Candle Bar (B G lj N MA) 14-4 h
309 Amsterdam Avenue/74th Street ✉NY 10023 *(Upper West Si-*

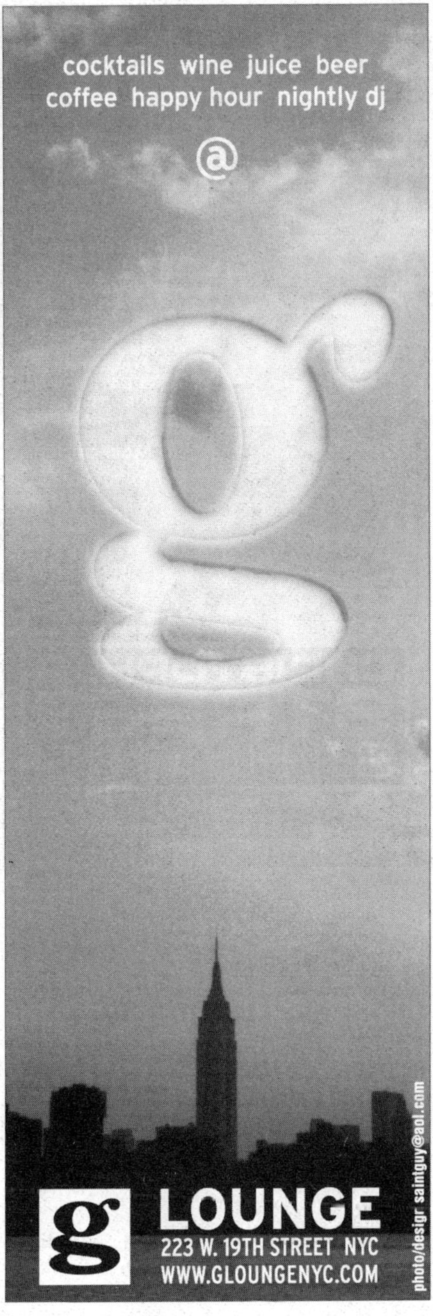
cocktails wine juice beer
coffee happy hour nightly dj
@
g
g LOUNGE
223 W. 19TH STREET NYC
WWW.GLOUNGENYC.COM
photo/design saintguy@aol.com

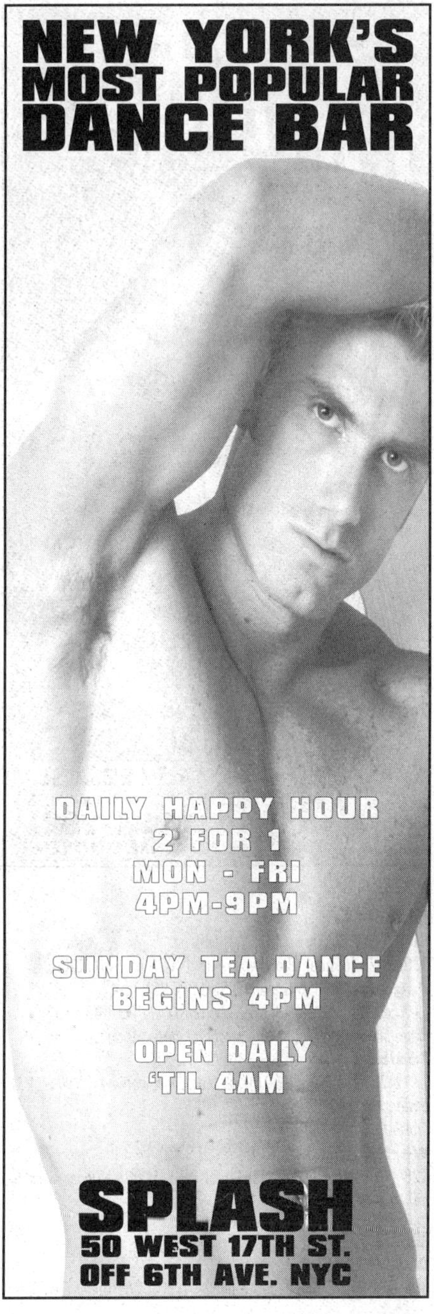
NEW YORK'S
MOST POPULAR
DANCE BAR
DAILY HAPPY HOUR
2 FOR 1
MON - FRI
4PM-9PM
SUNDAY TEA DANCE
BEGINS 4PM
OPEN DAILY
'TIL 4AM
SPLASH
50 WEST 17TH ST.
OFF 6TH AVE. NYC

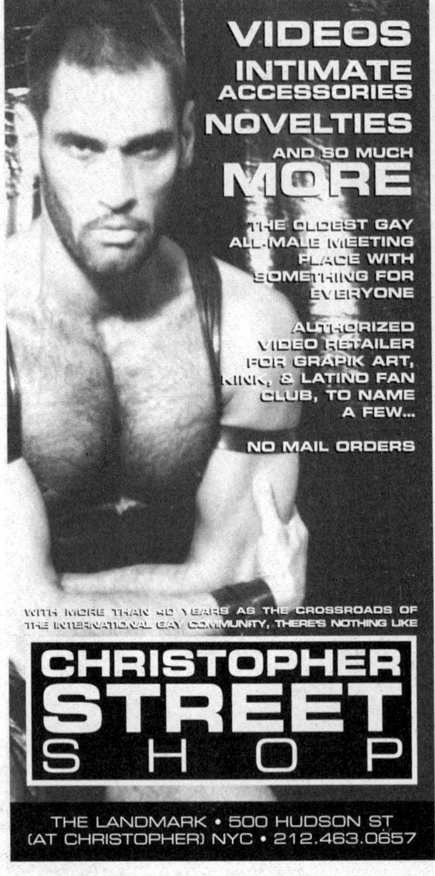

de) ☎ 874-9155

Eight of Clubs (B G MA N OS)
230 W. 75th Street/Broadway ✉NY 10023 ☎ 580-7389

Pegasus (A AC B G MA N S SNU STV VS) 16-4 h
119 East 60th Street ✉NY 10022 *(East Side)* ☎ 888-4702
Piano bar and club room with a cabaret stage. Asian crowd on WE.

Toolbox. The (B G S SNU VS) 12-2 h
1742 2nd Avenue ✉NY 10022 *(East-Side, between 90th & 91st Streets)* ☎ 348-1288
Cruise Bar.

Works. The (AC B E GLM MG N S VS) 14-4 h
428 Columbus Avenue/81st Street ✉NY 10024 *(Upper West Side)* ☎ 799-7365

SHOWS

Diva (B F glm S)
306 East 81st Street/2nd Avenue ✉NY 10028 *(Upper East Side)* ☎ 650-1928
Piano bar.

SEX SHOPS/BLUE MOVIES

Les Hommes (AC CC G MA VS) Sun-Thu 10-2, Fri, Sat 10-4 h
217-B West 80th Street ✉NY 10024-7002 *(2nd floor)* ☎ 580-2445

HOTELS

Sugar Hill • International House (B f g H)
722 Saint Nicholas Avenue ✉NY 10031 *(Harlem)* ☎ 926-7030
Fax: 283-0108 E-Mail: infohostel@aol.com
Homepage: www.hostels.com/sugar/

CRUISING

-Central Park (enter from 72nd Street entrance. Near the lake on the west side you'll find „The Ramble")

New York - Manhattan/Village & Chelsea ☎ 21

☛ **This part includes Greenwich Village, the East Village and Chelsea.**

Androgyny (B d TV YG) Tue-Thu 18-2, Fri 18-4, Sat 20-4 h
35 Crosby Street ✉NY 10014 ☎ 613-0977

B Bar (! AC B D G YG) Tue 23-? h
40 East 4th Street ✉NY 10003 ☎ 475-2220
The weekly party „Beige" on Tue attracts the trendiest gay fashion crowd of New York. Beautiful place, live DJs and handsome men. Not gay the rest of the week.

Bar. The (B G N) 13-4 h
68 2nd Avenue/4th Street ✉NY 10003 *(East Village)*
☎ 674-9714 *Very friendly atmosphere, good jukebox.*

Barracuda (! AC B G MA S STV VS) 16-4 h
275 West 22nd Street ✉NY 10011 *(Chelsea, between 7th and 8th Avenue)* ☎ 645-8613
DJs and drag shows nightly.

Blu Bar (B G MA VS)
161 West 23rd Street ✉NY 10011 *(Chelsea)* ☎ 633-6113
New cruise bar with cyberstations.

B.M.W. Bar (A AC B bf CC F GLM lj MA N) Mon-Son 0-24 h
199 7th Avenue ✉NY 10011 *(Chelsea, between 21st and 22nd Street)* ☎ 229-1807
Every day live music: Jazz, guitar. Cigar bar.

Boiler Room. The (B GLM YG) 16-4 h
86 East 4th Street ✉NY 10003 *(East Village)*
☎ 254-7536
Large bar with an eclectic crowd of young men.

Boots & Saddle (B G lj) 8-4, Sun 12-4 h
76 Christopher Street ✉NY 10014 *(West Village)*
☎ 929-9684

Break. The (AC B G N OS VS YG) 14-4 h
232 8th Avenue/22nd Street ✉NY 10011 *(Chelsea)*
☎ 627-0072
Friendly cruising neighborhood bar with an outdoor patio.

Cock. The (B GLM MA S STV) 21.30-4 h
188 Avenue A ✉NY 10009 ☎ 946-1871
Cabaret shows on Wed, Fri and Sat. Popular.

Crazy Nannie's (B D gLm MA)
21 South 7th Avenue ✉NY 10011 ☎ 366-6312
Can be fun depending on the night. Check lovcal paper for events. „DQNY" parties on Mon.

Dick's Bar (B G N)
192 2nd Avenue/12th Street ✉NY 10003 *(East Village)*
☎ 475-2071

Dugout. The (B d G MG N)
185 Christopher Street ✉NY 10014 *(West Village)* ☎ 242-9113

Dusk Lounge (B Glm MA) Mon-Wed 18-2, Thu-Sat 18-4 h
147 west 24th Street ✉NY 10011 ☎ 924-4490
New upscale lounge with a Florida atmosphere.

Eagle (AC B G LJ MA VS) 22-4 h
142 11th Avenue/21st Street ✉NY 10011 *(Chelsea)*
☎ 691-8451
Very popular on weekends.

G Lounge (AC B CC GLM MA N W YG) 16-4 h
223 West 19th Street ✉NY 10011 *(Chelsea between 7th & 8th Avenue)* ☎ 929-1085
Very popular modern bar.

Hangar. The (AC B G LJ MA N s SNU STV VS WO) Mon-Fri 15-4, Sat 14-4, Sun 13-4 h
115 Christopher Street ✉NY 10014 *(West Village)* ☎ 627-2044
Popular hangout for locals and gay tourists.

Hell (AC B G MA) Sun-Thu 19-4, Fri Sat 17-4 h
59 Gansevoort Street/Washington Street ✉NY 10014 *(West Village)* ☎ 727-1666
Bar and lounge with DJs in the meat-packing district.
H2O (AC B G MA S SNU)
443 East 6th Street ✉NY 10009 *(East Village) (off Avenue A)*
☎ 979-9291
I.C. Guys (B G S SNU)
443 East 6th Street ✉NY 10003 ☎ 979-9291
Swimsuited bar hunks dance every hour...
Julius (B f GLM) 11-2 h
159 West 10th Street ✉NY 10014 *(West Village)* ☎ 929-9672
One of the oldest gay bars in NYC. Great hamburgers.
Keller's Bar (B D G lj N)
384 West Street/Christopher Street ✉NY 10014 *(West Village)*
☎ 243-1907 *African-American crowd.*
Liquids (B glm YG) 18-4 h
226 East 10th Street ✉NY 10014 *(East Village)* ☎ 677-1717
Friendly mixed bar.
Lure. The (AC B G LJ MA VS W) 20-4 h
409 West 13th Street/9th Avenue ✉NY 10011 *(West Village)*
☎ 741-3919 *For serious leather crowd.*
Marie's Crisis (B glm MA S) 14-4 h
59 Grove Street/7th Avenue ✉NY 10014 *(West Village)*
☎ 243-9323 *Piano bar.*
Meow Mix (B D GLM S YG) Sat-Wed 17-4 h
269 East Houston Street ✉NY 10009 ☎ 254-0688
Cute boys and girls.
Mother (AC B D glm TV YG) 22-6 h
432 West 14th Street ✉NY 10014 ☎ 366-5680
Two floors bar with dance floor. Check in local papers for special events. Jackie 60 nights (cyber-fetish) last Tue of the month.
Oaks. The (B F GLM) Tue-Sun 18-4 h
49 Grove Street ✉NY 10014 *(West Village)* ☎ 367-9390
Pieces (B G S SNU VS) 14-4 h
8 Christopher Street ✉NY 10014 *(West Village)* ☎ 929-9291
Tue karaoke and Thu go-go boys.
Rawhide (AC B G LJ MA N) Mon-Sat 8-4, Sun 12-4 h
212 8th Avenue ✉NY 10016 *(Chelsea, at 21st Street)*
☎ 242-9332
Popular neighborhood bar for leather and western fans.
Sneakers (B G N) 12-4 h
392 West Street ✉NY 10014 *(West Village. Between Christopher & 10th Street)* ☎ 242-9830
Spike. The (! B d F G lj) 21-4 h
120 11th Avenue/20th Street ✉NY 10011 *(Chelsea)*
☎ 243-9688 *Mixed during the week, LJ on weekends! Attracts leather fans from all the State.*
Splash (AC B D G lj S SNU VS YG) 16-4 h
50 West 17th Street/6th Avenue ✉NY 10011 *(Chelsea)*
☎ 691-0073 *Popular with a mixed crowd.*
Starlight Bar and Lounge (AC B E GLM MA N) Wed, Thu, Sun 21-3, Fri, Sat -4 h
165 Avenue A ✉NY 10009 *(between 10th and 11th Street)*
☎ 475-2172
The new lounge in the East Village. Same owners as Wonder Bar. Gay and Lesbian fashion and entertainment crowd.
Stonewall (B G s) 16-4 h
53 Christopher Street ✉NY 10014 ☎ 463-0950
Where it all started. Now with a new look.
Two Potato (B F G S STV)
145 Christopher Street ✉NY 10014 *(West Village)* ☎ 255-0286
African-American crowd. Great atmosphere.
Ty's (AC B G lj MG N) Mon-Fri 14-4, Sat Sun 13-4 h
114 Christopher Street ✉NY 10014 *(West Village)* ☎ 741-9641
Wonder Bar (AC B E GLM MA N) 18-4 h
505 East 6th Street/Avenue A ✉NY 10003 *(East Village, between Avenues A & B)* ☎ 777-9105
Nice upscale gays and lesbians bar, entertainment crowd, live DJ nightly.

MEN'S CLUBS

J's Hangout (B DR G) 24-8 h
675 Hudson Street/14th Street ✉NY 10014 ☎ 242-9292
After-hour sex club.

CAFES

Espresso Bar (b f glm)
82 Christopher Street ✉NY 10014 *(West Village)* ☎ 627-3870
One of the best sandwiches in town.

DANCECLUBS

☛ You should always check the local gay magazines for up-to-date listings of parties and special events.
King (! AC B D DR G P S WS YG) 17-4 h
579 6th Avenue ✉NY 10011 *(Chelsea. Between 16th & 17th Streets)* ☎ 366-5464
Life (AC B D glm YG) Sun (G) 23-4 h
158 Blecker Street ✉NY 10014 *(at Thompson Street)*
☎ 420-1999
„Boy's Life" parties on Sundays. Mixed on Thu.
Monster (B D G) 16-4, Sat Sun 14-4 h
80 Grove Street/Sheridan Square ✉NY 10014 *(West Village)*
☎ 924-3558
Popular West Village bar and disco. Lots of latin boys.
Twirl (AC B D Glm s VS YG) Sun-Thu 17-2, Fri Sat 17-4 h
208 West 23rd Street ✉NY 10011 ☎ 691-7685
High-tech two level dance/video bar with live Djs.

RESTAURANTS

Brunetta's (B F g OS)
90 1st Avenue ✉NY 10009 *(East Village, between 11th & 12th Streets)* ☎ 228-4030
Very good Italian food, nice garden.
Caffe Torino (B F G)
39 West 10th Street ✉NY 10014 *(West Village, between 6th and 7th Avenues)* ☎ 675-5554
Italian cuisine.
Candy Bar and Grill (B F GLM) 16.30-4 h
131 8th Avenue ✉NY 10014 *(At 16th Street, Chelsea)*
☎ 229-9702
Chelsea Bistro and Bar (AC B CC F glm MA) Mon-Thu 17.30-23, Fri 17.30-24, Sat 17-24, Sun 17-22.30 h
358 West 23rd Street ✉NY 10100 *(Chelsea)*
☎ 727-2026 Fax: 727-2180
One of the best French restaurant of Manhattan.
Chez Ma Tante (b F g OS)
198 West 10th Street ✉NY 10014 *(West Village)* ☎ 620-0223
Circa (B CC F glm lj OS YG) 11-16 h (lunch), Sun-Thu 18-0, Fri Sat -1 h
103 Second Avenue/6th Street ✉NY 10003 *(East Village)*
Restaurant-bar.
Cola's (B F glm)
148 8th Avenue ✉NY 10011 *(Chelsea)*
☎ 633-8020
Popular
Community Bar & Grill (AC B CC F GLM MA OS W) 12-15.30, 18-23 h
216 7th Avenue ✉NY 10011 *(Chelsea)* ☎ 242-7900

Empire Diner (B F G) 0-24 h
210 10th Avenue/22nd Street ✉NY 10011 *(Chelsea)*
☎ 243-2736

Flamingo East (A AC B CC F glm YG) 18-4 h
219 2nd Avenue/13th Street ✉NY 10003 *(East Village)*
☎ 533-2860

Florent (AC B bf F glm MA W) Mon-Fri 9-5, Sat Sun 0-24 h
69 Gansevoort Street ✉NY 10014 *(West Village)* ☎ 989-5779
Great French baguettes.

Garage (B F glm)
99 7th Avenue South ✉NY 10014
☎ 645-0600 Fax: 627-3889
American cuisine.

Mary Ann's (B F g)
116 8th Avenue/16th Street ✉NY 10011 *(Chelsea)*
☎ 633-0877
Mexican food.

Meriken (B F g)
189 7th Avenue/21st Street ✉NY 10011 *(Chelsea)*
☎ 620-9684
Japanese cuisine.

Paris Commune. The (AC B CC F glm MA) 11-15, 18-24, Sat Sun 10-15.30 18-24 h
411 Bleecker Street ✉NY 10014 *(West Village)* ☎ 929-0509
Reservation advisable. French cuisine.

Restivo (B F GLM MA N OS) 12-24 h
209 7th Avenue ✉NY 10022 *(Chelsea, at 22nd Street)*
☎ 346-4133
Bar and restaurant. Italian cuisine.

Roettele A.G. (B F g OS)
126 East 7th Street ✉NY 10009 *(East Village)* ☎ 674-4140
European cuisine. Nice garden.

Salon de Sade (B F glm LJ)
206 West 23rd Street ✉NY 10010 ☎ 727-8642
Gastonomical house of pain where you can meet the local leather crowd and have your friend spanked for the desert. Funny.
Stingy Lulu's (B F glm)
129 Saint Mark's Place/Avenue A ✉NY 10009 *(East Village)* ☎ 674-3545 *American cuisine.*
Tiffany's Diner (B F G)
222 West 4th Street ✉NY 10014 *(West Village)* ☎ 242-1480
Universal Grill (B F glm)
44 Bedford Street ✉NY 10011 *(West Village)* ☎ 989-5621
Good brunch.
Viceroy Restaurant (B g MA W) Sun-Wed 11.30-24, Thu-Sat -1 h
160 8th Avenue/18th Street ✉NY 10011 *(Chelsea)*
☎ 633-8484

SHOWS

Bar d'O (! B Glm MA S STV)
29 Bedford Street
✉NY 10014 ☎ 627-1580
One of the most famous drag cabaret show of the world. Live singing by Joey Arias, Raven-O, Sherry Vine and the others.
Duplex. The (B d GLM MA S STV) 16-4 h
61 Christopher Street ✉NY 10011 ☎ 255-5438
Cabaret/piano bar with singing staff and comics.
Eighty Eight's (B GLM S STV) 16-4 h
228 West 10th Street ✉NY 10014 *(Chelsea)* ☎ 924-0088
Piano bar/cabaret with a mixed crowd.
Lips (B F GLM S STV) 21.30-? h
2 Bank Street ✉NY 10014 *(at Greenwich Avenue)* ☎ 675-7710
Restaurant with drag show during and after the dinner.
Lucky Cheng's (B F G S STV)
24 1st Avenue ✉NY 10013 *(East Village) (at 2nd Street)*
☎ 473-0516
Original New York pan-Asian drag theme restaurant. Drag show in the basement.

SEX SHOPS/BLUE MOVIES

Christopher Street Shop (AC CC G MA VS) Sun, Thu 12-4, Fri, Sat 12-6 h
500 Hudson Street ✉NY 10014-2818 *(at Christopher Street, West Village)* ☎ 463-0657
Harmony Video (G VS) 0-24 h
139 Christopher Street ✉NY 10014 *(West Village)* ☎ 366-9059
Videos, magazines and cabins.
Unicorn (AC CC G MA VS) Sun-Thu 12-4, Fri Sat -6 h
277c West 22nd Street ✉NY 10011-2702 *(Chelsea, between 7th and 8th)* ☎ 924-2921

CINEMAS

All Male Jewel Theatre (B DR VS) Sun-Thu 10-3, Fri Sat 10-5 h
100 3rd Avenue ✉NY 10003 *(East Village)* ☎ 505-7320

SAUNAS/BATHS

West Side Club (B f G sa sb VS WO) 0-24 h
27 West 20th Street ✉NY 10011 *(2nd floor)* ☎ 691-2700

FITNESSTUDIOS

Chelsea Gym (G) 267
West 17th Street/8th Avenue ✉NY 10011 *(Chelsea)*
☎ 255-1150
David Barton Gym (G)
552 6th Avenue/15th Street ✉NY 10011 *(Chelsea)*
☎ 772-0004

BODY & BEAUTY SHOPS

R.J. White Jewelry, Inc. (AC CC GLM) Wed-Sat 13-19, Jul Aug: Tue-Fri 13-19 h
107 Christopher Street ✉NY 10014 *(Between Hudson and Bleecker)* ☎ 242-0540

BOOK SHOPS

Creative Visions (AC CC GLM MA) 11-23 h
548 Hudson Street ✉NY 10014 *(2 blocks north of Christopher Street, West Village)* ☎ 645-7573
Magazines, periodicals, travel guides, paperback framed art.
Different Light. A Sun-Thu 11-21, Fri Sat 11-23 h
151 West 19th Street ✉NY 10011 *(Chelsea)* ☎ 989-4850
Over 7000 gay and lesbian books, tapes, records, and videos. Café now open, serving coffee and light food.
Oscar Wilde Bookshop (AC CC GLM) Sun-Fri 12-20, Sat -21 h
15 Christopher Street ✉NY 10014 *(West Village)* ☎ 255-8097
Fax: 255-8195 E-Mail: WildeBooks@aol.com
Homepage: www.OscarWildeBooks.com
World's oldest gay and lesbian bookshop. Large collection of rare & out of print books.

CONDOM SHOPS

Condomania Mon-Thu 11-23, Fri Sat 11-24 h, closed Sun
351 Bleeker Street ✉NY 10014 *(West Village)* ☎ 691-9442

FASHION SHOPS

New York Bodyworks (CC) 11.30-22 h
45 Christopher Street ✉NY 10014 ☎ 645-0301
Clothing store for bodyworkers.

GALLERIES

Ganymede Gallery (g)
220 West Houston Street ✉NY 10014 *(Between 6th Avenue and Varrick Street)* ☎ 255-6755

LEATHER & FETISH SHOPS

DeMask N.Y. (CC glm)
135 West 22nd Street ✉NY 10011 *(Chelsea)(between 6th and 7th Avenue)* ☎ 352-2850
Ranging from street wear to heavy leather and rubber. NYC branch of the famous European fetish house.
Leather Man (LJ)
11 Christopher Street ✉NY 10014 ☎ 243-5339
Noose. The
261 West 19th Street ✉NY 10011 *(Chelsea)* ☎ 807-1789
Pleasure Chest. The l
56 7th Avenue South ✉NY 10014 *(West Village)* ☎ 242-2158

TRAVEL & TRANSPORT

Acquarian Travel and Entertainment Service 8-17 h
292 8th Avenue Suite 1 ✉NY 10001 *(Chelsea)* ☎ 741-0708
Travel and accomodations agent.

VIDEO SHOPS

Gay Pleasures (AC CC GLM MA VS) 11-23 h
548 Hudson Street ✉NY 10013 *(2 blocks north of Christopher Street, West Village)* ☎ 255-5756
8 mm film, slides, photos, gay videos.

HOTELS

Greenwich Village Lodging (AC bf H) Office 9-22 h
36 Commerce Street ✉NY 10014-3755 *(near Christopher Street)* ☎ 741-0126 Fax: 741-6399 E-Mail: GVlgLodging@aol.com
Wholly renovated 1841 landmark located in a sleepy, tree-lined hideaway located near the Bedford-Barrow-Commerce Hictoric District. All rooms with private bath, fireplace, cable-TV, telephone and answering machine, refrigerator.
Hotel 17 (glm H)
225 East 17th Street ✉NY 10003 *(Union Square Subway)* ☎ 475-2845 Fax: 677-8178
Beautiful hotel with kitsch/original decoration. Madonna was photographed here. Popular with drag queens. Guests not allowed at night.

GUEST HOUSES

Chelsea Mews Guest House (AC G H MA)
344 West 15th Street ✉NY 10011 *(Chelsea)* ☎ 255-9174
3 doubles, 5 singles. All rooms with phone and own key. Rates US$ 85-165 with/without bath. Parking garage available.
Chelsea Pines Inn (AC bf CC GLM H OS)
317 West 14th Street ✉NY 10014 *(Chelsea)* ☎ 929-1023
Fax: 620-5646 E-Mail: cpiny@aol.com
Homepage: www.q-net.com/chelseapines
In the Greenwich Village/Chelsea area, 30-45 minutes to airports. Rates US$ 89-139. Private and shared bath. All rooms with telephone, cable TV and refrigerator. Own key.
Colonial House Inn (A AC bf GLM H MA msg sol)
318 West 22nd Street ✉NY 10011 *(Chelsea. Between 8th and 9th Avenue)* ☎ 243-9669 Fax: 633-1612
E-Mail: houseinn@aol.com Homepage: www.colonialhouseinn.com
Located in Chelsea, 45 mins. to airport. 20 rooms, partly with private bath.
Incentra Village House (! AC CC GLM H) Tel only 9-21 h
32 8th Avenue ✉NY 10014 *(West Village)* ☎ 206-0007
Fax: 604-0625
Historic Inn, downtown location, 12 km to the airport. All 12 rooms with TV, phone, kitchenette, priv. bath and WC. Nicely furnished, recommended! Rates: suites US$ 130-179, double 149-179, single 99-129 (+ tax).

New York - Queens ☎ 718

BARS

Amnesia (B d GLM MA) 12-4 h
32-03 Broadway, Astoria ☎ 204-7010
Atlantis 2010 (B GLM D S STV SNU) 21-4 h
76-19 Roosevelt Avenue, Jackson Heights ✉NY 11372 ☎ 457-3939
BS East/Breadstix (AC B G MA S SNU VS W) Sun-Fri 17-?, Sat 19-? h
113-24 Queens Boulevard, Forest Hills ✉NY 11375 *(Next to P.C. Richards)* ☎ 263-0300
Video bar withamateur strip show on Fri and live go-go boys on Sat.
Friends Tavern (B G) 16-4 h
78-11 Roosevelt Avenue, Jackson Heights ✉NY 11372 ☎ 397-7256
Magic Touch (B D GLM S SNU) 16-4 h
73-13th 37th Road, Jackson Heights ✉NY 11372 *(Jackson Heights)* ☎ 429-8605
Music Box (B G N S)
40-08 74th Street, Jackson Heights ✉NY 11372 ☎ 457-5306

DANCECLUBS

Krash (AC B CC D f GLM MA P r S SNU STV) Mon Thu-Sat & Holidays 22-5 h
34-48 Steinway Street, Astoria ✉NY 11101 ☎ 937-2400
Very latino.

SAUNAS/BATHS

Northern Men's Sauna (G sa sb) 12-? h
3365 Farrington Street ✉NY 11372 *(Flushing)* ☎ 359-9817

HEALTH GROUPS

AIDS Center of Queens County
☎ 896-2500 or ☎ 275-2094 *Direct services for people with AIDS.*

CRUISING

-Forest Park (the footpath parallel to Park Lane South beginning at Metropolitan Avenue, best at night)
-Roosevelt Avenue (woodside, between 69th and 79th Street)

Niagara Falls ☎ 716

HOTELS

Rainbow House(bf F glm H)
423 Rainbow Boulevard ✉NY 14303 ☎ 282-1135
25 minutes to the airport. Centrally located. All rooms with priv. bath and balcony.

Rochester ☎ 716

GAY INFO

Empty Closed
179 Atlantic Avenue ✉NY 14607

BARS

Anthony's (B d GLM MA N) 12-2 h
522 East Main Street ✉NY 14604 ☎ 325-2060

Avenue Pub (B GLM N)
522 Monroe Avenue ✉NY 14607 ☎ 244-4960
Bachelor Forum (B D G LJ N)
670 University Avenue ✉NY 14607 ☎ 325-6930
Common Grounds (B G MA N)
139 State Street
Muthers (B G N)
40 South Union Street
Tara Cocktail Lounge (B GLM MA) 12-2 h
153 Liberty Pole Way ✉NY 14604 ☎ 232-4719
Popular piano bar.

DANCECLUBS

Club Marcella (B D GLM MA SNU STV) Thu-Sun
123 Liberty Pole Way *Very popular dance club. Drag on Sun.*

SAUNAS/BATHS

Rochester Spa and Body Club. The (b G sa sb sol OS WO) 0-24 h
153 Liberty Pole Way ✉NY 14604

TRAVEL & TRANSPORT

Great Expectations Travel
2349 Monroe Avenue ✉NY 14618 ☎ 244-8430 Fax: 244-8749

GENERAL GROUPS

Gay Alliance of Genesee Valley Mon-Thu 13-21.30, Fri 13-18 h
713 C Monroe Avenue ✉NY 14607 ☎ 316/244-8640

Sayville ☎ 516

BARS

Bunkhouse (AC B D G MA N s YG) 19-4, Sun -3/4 h
192 North Main Street ✉NY 11782 ☎ 567-2865

Schenectady ☎ 518

BARS

Blythewood. The (B F G) 21-4.30 h
50 North Jay Street ✉NY 12305 ☎ 382-9755
Clinton Street Pub (B glm) 12-4 h
159 Clinton Street ✉NY 12305 ☎ 382-9173

Seaford ☎ 516

BARS

Auntie M's (AC B f GLM MA S SNU STV) 17-4 h
3547 Merrick Road ✉NY 11783

Syracuse ☎ 315

GAY INFO

Gay Telephone Line 19-23 h
☎ 423-3599

BARS

Armory Pub (B G LJ r) 8-2 h
400 South Clinton Street ✉NY 13202 ☎ 471-6618
Ryan's Someplace Else (B D G VS YG) Thu-Sat 20-2, Sun 12-2 h
408-410 Pearl Street ✉NY 13203 ☎ 471-9499
Trexx (B D Glm S W YG) Thu, Sun 20-2, Fri, Sat -4 h
319 N. Clinton Street ☎ 474-6408

SEX SHOPS/BLUE MOVIES

Boulevard Books (g VS) 24 hrs
2576 Erie Boulevard ✉NY 13214 ☎ 446-1595

FETISH GROUPS

Ledermeister. Der
1172 West Onondaga Street ✉NY 13204

CRUISING

-Thunder Park

Utica ☎ 315

BARS

Options (B D GLM) 17-2 h, closed Mon-Tue
1724 Oriskany Boulevard, Yorkville ✉NY 13502 ☎ 724-9231
That Place (B D G LJ MA OS P s) 20-2, Fri 16-2 h
216 Bleecker Street ✉NY 13501 ☎ 724-1446

BOOK SHOPS

Adult World
319 Oriskany Boulevard, Yorkville ✉NY 13495
Playtime Boutique
26 Orinsky Boulevard, Yorkville ✉NY 14395

GENERAL GROUPS

Greater Utica Lambda Fellowship (GULF)
2nd & 4th Mon 19 h
at Plymouth Bethesda Church, 500 Plant Street, Oneida Square
PO Box 122 ✉NY 13503-0122 ☎ 894-3565
E-Mail: gaycny@aol.com
Lesbian and Gay Concerns Network
c/o UU Church, 12 Ford Avenue, Oneonta, NY 13820

FETISH GROUPS

Utica Tri s, M.C., Gay Men's Leather & Levi Club (G LJ)
PO Box 425 ✉NY 13503-0425

White Plains ☎ 914

GAY INFO

Gayzette
156 South Broadway ✉NY 10605 ☎ 328-6463 Fax: 771-9663
E-Mail: Gayzette1@aol.com
Monthly newspaper for New York, Bergen county, Westchester, Rockland, Fairfield (CT), Bergen (NJ), New York City and Long Island. Free at gay venues.

BARS

Stutz (B D G S VS) Mon-Fri 17-4, Sat Sun 20-4 h
202 Westchester Avenue ✉NY 10601 ☎ 761-3100

CRUISING

-Rest Stop (15 miles north on I-684)

USA-North Carolina

East USA

Initials: NCA

Time: GMT -5

Area: 139.397 km² / 57.013 sq mi.

Population: 7,425,000

Capital: Raleigh

Hetero- as well as homosexual oral and anal intercourse is prohibited in North Carolina.

In North Carolina sind hetero- und homosexueller Oral- und Analverkehr verboten.

En Caroline du Nord, la fellation et la pénétration anale sont interdites pour tous, homos et hétéros.

En Carolina del Norte las relaciones homosexuales y heterosexuales por vía oral o anal están prohibidas.

In North Carolina sono vietati i rapporti anali ed orali tra omosessuali e tra eterosessuali.

Asheville ☎ 828

BARS

Club Metro (B G lj S) HC: 19-2.30, Barbershop: Tue-Sun 21-2.30, CM: Thu Fri 22-3, Sat 22-6 h
38 North French Broad Avenue ✉NC 28801 ☎ 258-2027

O'Henry's (AC B d GLM lj MA N P S SNU STV) 12-2 h
59 Haywood Street ✉NC 28801 ☎ 254-1891

DANCECLUBS

Scandals (B CC D f GLM MA P S STV VS WE) Fri, Sat 22-3 h
11 Grove Street ✉NC 28801 ☎ 252-2838

BOOK SHOPS

Malaprop's Bookstore Mon-Sat 10-20 h
61 Haywood Street ✉NC 28801 ☎ 254-6734

HEALTH GROUPS

Western NC AIDS Project
PO Box 2411 ✉NC 28802 ☎ 252-7489

CRUISING

-»The Cage« (block around Federal Building)

Blowing Rock ☎ 704

GUEST HOUSES

Stone Pillar Bed & Breakfast (A bf CC glm H)
PO Box 1881, 144 Pine Street ✉NC 28605 ☎ 295-4141
E-Mail: tonepillar@blowingrock.com
Homepage: www.blowingrock.com/northcarolina/stonepillar
Rates US$ 55-60 (single), 65-95 (double).

Charlotte ☎ 704

GAY INFO

Q Notes
PO Box 221841 ✉NC 28222 ☎ 531-9988 Fax: 531-1361
E-Mail: pridtype@vnet.net

BARS

Central Station (B G MG)
2131 Central Avenue ☎ 377-0906

Chasers (B d GLM P SNU VS W) 17-2, Sun 16-2 h
3217 The Plaza ✉NC ☎ 339-0500

Hartigan's Pub (B GLM F N)
601 S. Cedar Street ☎ 347-1841

Liaisons (B D GLM S VS) 16-1 h
316 Resselaer Avenue ✉NC 28203 ☎ 376-1617
Popular

Masquerade (B d G SNU YG)
3018 The Plaza ☎ 344-1770

Oleen's (AC B D G MG N P STV S TV)
1831 South Blv. ☎ 373-9604

CAFES

Tic Toc Coffee Shop (A f g OS)
512 N. Tyron Street ☎ 375-5750

DANCECLUBS

Club Myxx (B D glm P)
3110 N. Tyron Street ☎ 525-5001

Mythos (AC B CC D g P STV YG) Wed-Thu 22-3 h, Fri 22-6 h, Sat 22-4 h, Sun var. special events.
300 North College Street ✉NC 28202 *(City center)* ☎ 375-8765

Scorpio's Lounge (B D GLM S VS) 21-2 h
2301 Freedom Drive ✉NC 28208 ☎ 373-9604

300 East Stonewall (B D GLM MA OS) WE -4 h
300 East Stonewall ☎ 347-4200
Very popular

RESTAURANTS

Cosmos Café (B F NG)
6th Street & N. College Street ☎ 372-3553

Fat City (B F NG)
3127 N. Davidson Street ☎ 343-0240

300 East (B F NG) 300
East Boulevard ☎ 332-6507

SEX SHOPS/BLUE MOVIES

Highway 74 Video & News (g MA VS)
3514 Barry Drive ☎ 399-7907

Independence News (G MA VS)
3205 The Plaza ☎ 332-8430

Queen City Video & News (g MA VS)
2320 Wilkinson Boulevard ☎ 344-9435

BOOK SHOPS

White Rabbit Books
834 Central Avenue ☎ 377-4067
Good selection of magazines, videos and guides.

GIFT & PRIDE SHOPS

Paper Skyscraper
330 East Boulevard ☎ 333-7130

Urban Evolution
1329 East Boulevard ☎ 332-8644

HEALTH GROUPS

AIDS Hotline Mon-Fri 8.30-17 h
☎ 333-AIDS (2437)

CRUISING

-Freedom Park (AYOR)
-Plaza Road (AYOR R)
-South Park Shopping Mall

Durham ☎ 919

BARS

Boxer's (AC B D G S YG) Tue-Sat 20.30-3 h Sun 18-? h
5504 Chapel Hill Boulevard ✉NC 27707 *(at Straw Valley, Route 15-501 at I-40)* ☎ 489-7678
Boxer´s Ringside (B D G)
308 West Main St.

SEX SHOPS/BLUE MOVIES

Atlantis Video News (G VS) Mon-Thu 11-2, Fri Sat 11-17, Sun 13-2 h
522 East Main Street ✉NC 27701 ☎ 682-7469
Gay magazines, video rentals, sex goods, peep shows.

Fayetteville ☎ 910

BARS

Call ahead for easy entry to Private Clubs.

DANCECLUBS

Spektrum (B D G SNU STV) 17-3 h
107 Swain Street ☎ 868-4279
Studio 315 (B D G MA SNU STV) 315 Hay Street

Greensboro ☎ 336

BARS

The Palms (B d GLM N S) 21-1.30 h
413 North Eugene Street ✉NC 27401 ☎ 272-6307

DANCECLUBS

Warehouse 29 (AC B D Glm OS P SNU VS WE) Fri-Sat 21.30-4, Sun 15-3.30 h. closed Mon-Thu
1011 Arnold Street ✉NC 27405 ☎ 333-9333

GIFT & PRIDE SHOPS

White Rabbit Books & Things (GLM) Mon-Fri 10-21, Sat 10-19, Sun 13-18 h
1833 Spring Garden Street ✉NC 27403 ☎ 272-7604

HEALTH GROUPS

TRIAD Health Project
PO Box 5716 ✉NC 27435 ☎ 275-1654

Hickory ☎ 828

DANCECLUBS

Club Cabaret (B D GLM MA)
101 North Center Street ☎ 322-8103

Raleigh ☎ 919

GAY INFO

The Front Page
PO Box 279 28 ✉NC 27611 ☎ 829-0181 Fax: 829-0830
E-Mail: frntpage@aol.com.
Bimonthly publication with local and international features, classifieds. Serving North and South Carolina.

BARS

Flex (B D G LJ) 17-?, Sun 14-? h
2 South West Street ☎ 832-8855
Special theme nights
Legends (AC B D Glm P S YG) Mon-Sat 20-1, Sun 17-1 h, Thu women only
330 West Hargett Street ✉NC 27601 ☎ 831-8888
Very popular. Cruisy atmosphere.

DANCECLUBS

Capital Corral (AC B D G MA P VS WE) 20-? h, Sun 14-? h
313 West Hargett ✉NC 27601 ☎ 755-9599

SEX SHOPS/BLUE MOVIES

Bachelor's Video Mon-Thu 10-2, Fri-Sun 10-3 h
3411 South Wilmington Street ✉NC 27603 *(next to Pizza Hut, no sign)* ☎ 779-0995
Gay books, magazines, video rental, peep shows.
Our Place (AC CC G MA VS) 24 h
327 West Hargett Street ✉NC 27609 ☎ 833-8968
Video booths, video tapes, tape rentals.

BOOK SHOPS

Adult Books (g VS) 0-24 h
1433 South Wilmington Street ✉NC 27603
Books, porno magazines, video rental, peep shows, sex goods.

GIFT & PRIDE SHOPS

White Rabbit Books & Things (GLM) Mon-Fri 11-21, Sat 11-19, Sun 13-18 h
309 West Martin Street ✉NC 27601 ☎ 856-1429
Gay and lesbian articles from books to videos.

CRUISING

-West Hargett Street (around gay bars and bookstore)
-Unstead State Park (Glenwood Avenue, near Brownleigh Drive. In cars and around Lake Area. Take steps down to Lake-follow path to the left. Daytime only. Be discreet.)

Rocky Mount ☎ 919

CRUISING

-Battle Park (parking lots and forested areas).

Spruce Pine ☎ 704

HOTELS

Lemon Tree Inn (AC bf CC f glm H MA wh) 872 Greenwood Road ✉NC 28777 ☎ 765-6161

Wilmington ☎ 910

BARS

Mickey Ratz (AC B D GLM MA OS P S SNU STV W) 17-2.30 h, closed Mon
115 South Front Street ✉NC 28401 ☎ 251-1289

DANCECLUBS

Nocturna (AC D DR GLM OS S YG) 21-4 h
121 Grace Street ☎ 815-8583

GUEST HOUSES

Inn on Orange. The (CC glm H pi)
410 Orange Street ✉NC 28401 ☎ 815-0035
☎ (800) 381-4666.

CRUISING

-Wrightsville Beach (north end)
-Hugh Macrae Park (Orange + 2nd Street, car cruising 20-0 h)

Wilson ☎ 919

CRUISING

-Parkwood Mall (mens restroom)
-Lake Wilson (parking lot near mens restroom)

USA-North Dakota

North USA

Initials: ND

Time: GMT -6

Area: 183.123 km^2 / 74,897 sq mi.

Population: 641,000

Capital: Bismarck

Fargo ☎ 701

RESTAURANTS

Fargo Fryn's Pan (glm) 0-24 h
300 Main St ✉ND 58103 ☎ 293-9952

BOOK SHOPS

Adult Books and Cinema X
417 NP Avenue, ✉ND 58102 ☎ 232-9768

CRUISING

-Broadway (nights)
-Bus depot

USA-Ohio

Great Lakes region USA

Initials: OH

Time: GMT -5

Area: 116.103 km^2 / 47,486 sq mi.

Population: 11,186,000

Capital: Columbus

Important gay cities: Cincinnati, Cleveland and Columbus

Akron ☎ 330

BARS

Adams Street Bar (AC B D f G MA S SNU STV) Mon-Fri 16.30-2.30, Sat 15-2.30, Sun 21-2.30 h
77 North Adams Street ✉OH 44304 ☎ 434-9794
Roseto Club (B D F GLM) 18-1 h, closed Sun
627 South Arlington Street ✉OH 44306 ☎ 724-4228
Tear-ez (B GLM MA) 11-2.30, Sun 23.30-2.30 h
360 South Main Street ☎ 376-0011
Popular

DANCECLUBS

Interbelt Nite Club (B D GLM VS YG WE) Mon, Wed, Fri-Sun 20-? h
70 North Howard Street ✉OH 44308 ☎ 253-5700
The only all-gay disco in Akron. Patio bar in summer. Very popular.

SAUNAS/BATHS

Akron Steam/Sauna (G sb wh)
41 South Case
Club Akron Inc. (G sa wh)
1339 East Market Street ✉OH 44305 ☎ 784-0309

CRUISING

-Main Street near the Tear EZ and Club 358. (AYOR) (Also the side streets close by.)
-Main Street/Mill Street (in front of public library)
-Metropolitan Park in Goodyear Heights on Eastwood Avenue (in the parking lot by the baseball field)

Canton ☎ 330

BARS

La Casa's Golden Door (B G MA N) 13-2.30 h
508 Cleveland Avenue N.W. ☎ 453-7432
540 Club / Eagle (AC B f G LJ N) Mon-Sat 21-2.30, Sun 18-2.30 h
540 Walnut Avenue North East ✉OH 44702 *(next to Y.M.C.A.)*
☎ 456-8622

CAFES

Sidestreet Cafe (b bf f glm T) 15-1 h
2360 Mahoning ☎ 453-8055

DANCECLUBS

Boardwalk (B D GLM MA S) 16-2.30 h, closed Sun
1227 West Tuscarawas Street ☎ 453-8000

Cincinnati ☎ 513

GAY INFO

Alternating Currents (GLM) Sat 15-17 h
on WAIF 88.3 FM
PO Box 6126 ✉OH 45206
Gay and Lesbian Community Center Mon-Fri 19-23 h
☎ 651-0070
Greater Cincinnati GLBT News
PO Box 14971 ✉OH 45250-0971 ☎ 665-6809
E-Mail: liquata@hotmail.com

BARS

Colors (B GLM MA N VS)
4042 Hamilton Avenue ✉OH 45223 ☎ 681-6969
Golden Lions (B d G MG N S) 19-2.30 h
340 Ludlow Avenue ✉OH 45202 ☎ 281-4179
Milton's Tavern (B glm N)
301 Milton Street
Plum Street Pipeline (! AC B D f GLM lj MA S SNU STV OS YG) Sun-Thu 16-21.30, Fri Sat -3 h
241 West Court Street ✉OH 45202 ☎ 241-5678
4 bars on 4 floors.
Shirley's (B D gLM W) 20-2.30, Sun 16-2.30 h, closed Mon
2401 Vine Street ✉OH 45219 ☎ 721-8483
Shooters (B d G s W) 16-2.30 h
927 Race Street ✉OH 45219 ☎ 381-9900
Simon Says (B G N W) 11-2.30, Sun 13-2.30 h
428 Walnut Street ✉OH 45202 ☎ 381-8196
Spurs (B d G LJ s W) 16-2.30 h
326 East 8th Street ☎ 621-2668
Subway (B D G N S) 17.30-2.30 h
609 Walnut Street ✉OH 45202 ☎ 421-1294
Vertigo (B GLM MA N)
1 West Corry Street ☎ 684-9313

DANCECLUBS

Dock (B D GLM OS S VS) 20-2.30, Fri Sat 20-4 h
603 West Pete Rose Way ✉OH 45202 ☎ 241-5623

RESTAURANTS

Carol's Corner Café (! B bf F GLM) Sun-Fri 11-2.30, Sat 16-2.30, meals -1 h
825 Main Street ✉OH 45202 ☎ 651-2667

Mullane's Parkside Cafe (B F GLM MA)
723 Race Street ✉OH 45202 ☎ 381-1331

LEATHER & FETISH SHOPS

ACME Leather & Toy Co. (G LJ) 16-2.30 h
326 East Eight Street ✉OH 45202 *(at Spurs)* ☎ 241-6874

GUEST HOUSES

Prospect Hill B&B (AC bf CC e glm H wh)
408 Boal Street ✉OH 45210 ☎ 421-4408 Fax: 421-4408
Homepage: www.bbonline.com/oh/prospect/
Old Victorian townhouse located on a hill overlooking the city. All rooms with Sat-TV, radio, fax, fireplaces and a sitting area. Rates double/shared bath USD-99-129 and double/private bath 109-129. A full bf buffet is incl. in the price. Non-smoking establishment.

RELIGIOUS GROUPS

Dignity
PO Box 983 ✉OH 45202 ☎ 557-2111
Catholic lesbians and gays
Integrity
4905 Chalet Drive, #11 ✉OH 45217 ☎ 242-7297
Lesbian and gay Episcopalians
New Spirit MCC
5501 Hamilton Avenue ✉OH 45224 *(at Belmont)* ☎ 681-9090
Sunday Worhip Services 19 h. (All Services and Events meet at the church unless otherwise announced.)

SPORT GROUPS

Frontrunners (and Walkers)
☎ 651-0070

CRUISING

-Burnett Woods (AYOR)
-Mt. Airy Forest (AYOR)
-Mc Farland Street (between 3rd and 4th Street, after the bars close)

Cleveland ☎ 216

GAY INFO

Gay People's Chronicle
PO Box 5426 ✉OH 44101 ☎ 631-8646 Fax: 631-1082
Grid Radio 16-3 h on 96.9 FM
Live music directly from The Grid Dance Club
Lesbian & Gay Community Center Mon-Fri 12-17 h
1418 West 29th Street ✉OH 44113 ☎ 522-1999
Fax: 522-0025
Lesbian & Gay Hotline 15-23, Sat 10-18, Sun 15-22 h
☎ 781-6736

BARS

Code Blue (A AC B CC d GLM MA s SNU STV) closed Mon
1946 St. Clair Avenue ✉OH 44114 ☎ 241-4663
Five Cent Decision (AC B D f GLM MA W) 18-2.30 h
4365 State Road ✉OH 44109 ☎ 661-1314
Leather Stallion Saloon (AC D G LJ MA OS s SNU) 15-2.30 h
2205 St. Clair Avenue ✉OH 44114-4046 *(downtown)*
☎ 589-8588
Oldest gay bar in Cleveland, since 1970. Very popular Sun afternoon.
MJ's Place (B d G MA S) 16-2.30 h, closed Sun
11633 Lorain Ave. ✉OH 44111 ☎ 476-1970
Numbers (B D G S VS W YG) 22-3 h, closed Mon Thu
620 Frankfort Avenue ✉OH 44113 ☎ 621-6900
Popular Wed/Sun
Rockies (AC B CC D G lj MA OS SNU VS) 16-2.3 h
9208 Detroit Avenue ✉OH 44102 ☎ 961-3115
Sexx (B D G MA OS S) 10-2.30, Sun 12-2.30 h
11213 Detroit Avenue ✉OH 44102 ☎ 221-8576
Cruise bar
The Hawk (B f G LJ s) 10-2.30 h, closed Sun
11217 Detroit Avenue ✉OH 44102 *(near 112th Street)*
☎ 521-5443

DANCECLUBS

Grid. The (! AC B CC D G MA SNU VS YG) Mon-Thus 17-2.30 h, Fri-Sat 17-3 h, Sun 16-4.30 h
1281 West 9th Street ✉OH 44113 *(Warehouse district, downtown)* ☎ 623-0113
High tech dance floor, tow levels, wideo, poo.l table, video games, pinball.
U4ia Nite Club (! B D Glm OS S tv WE) Fri-Sun 21.30-3 h
10630 Berea Road ✉OH 44102 ☎ 631-7111
Cleveland's largest gay dance club.

RESTAURANTS

Billy's Cafe (B F glm) 11-21 h, closed Mon
11100 Clifton Boulevard ✉OH 44102 ☎ 281-7722
My Friends (B F glm MA)
11616 Detroit Avenue *Popular late-night restaurant*

SEX SHOPS/BLUE MOVIES

West Nine Street Video and News
1273 West Ninth
Magazines, newspapers and wide selection of video titles

SAUNAS/BATHS

Club Cleveland (B G sa sb sol OS VS WO) 0-24 h
1448 West 32nd Street ☎ 961-2727
Flex (B f G lj sa sb VS wh WO) 0-24 h
1293 West 9th Street ☎ 696-0595

BOOK SHOPS

Body Language (CC GLM W) Mon-Sat 11-22 h, Sun -18 h
11424 Lorain Avenue/West 115th Street ✉OH 44111 *(at Lorain)*
☎ 251-3330
Books, cards, clothing, magazines and erotic videos.
Books & Magazines Mon-Sat 9.30-17.15 h
5 Tation Road

GENERAL GROUPS

Foot Fraternity (G MA)
POBox 24102 ✉OH 44124
☎ +1-440-449-4114 Fax: +1-440-449-0114
International group for friends of feed, etc.

HEALTH GROUPS

Ohio Dept of Health AIDS Hotline 13-23 h
PO Box 61 77 ✉OH 44101 ☎ (800) 322-2437

RELIGIOUS GROUPS

Chevrei Tikva 1st/3rd Fri
PO Box 181 20 ✉OH 44118 ☎ 932-5551
Jewish gays & lesbians.

CRUISING

-Ambassador Bowling Lanes (Sun 13 h)
–Metropolitan Park (AYOR) (Memphis & Tiedman Street)
-N. Chagrin Reservation Park (AYOR)

Columbus ☎ 614

GAY INFO

Outlook Newspaper
Outlook Publishing, PO Box 242824 ✉OH 43224 ☎ 268-8525 Fax: 268-0762 E-Mail: outlookpub@aol.com
Biweekly GLB newspaper
Stonewall Columbus (AC GLM MA W) Mon-Thu 10-19, Fri -17 h
1160 North High Street, ✉OH 43201-2411 ☎ 299-7764 Fax: 299-4408 E-Mail: stnwall@ix.netcom.com
Organization fighting for gay and lesbian rights in Ohio.

BARS

Club Diversity (AC B CC GLM MA N s) Tue-Thu 16-1 h, Fri 16-2.30, Sat 18-2.30 closed Sun, Mon
124 East Main Street ✉OH 43215 *(Downtown Columbus)* ☎ 224 40 50
Club 20 (B G N S) 13-2.30, Sat 11-2.30 h
20 East Duncan Street ✉OH 43202 ☎ 261-9111
Downtown Connection (B G MA)
1156 North High Street ✉OH 43201 ☎ 299-4880
Gay sports bar
Eagle in Exile (AC B G LJ MA N U WE) Wed-Sat 21-2.30 h
893 North 4rth Street ✉OH 43201 ☎ 294-0069
Strict dress code
Grapevine Café (AC B bf F GLM MA S W) Tue-Sat 17-1, Sun 12-23 h
73 East Gay Street ✉OH 43215 *(Downtown)* ☎ 221-8463
Sun Brunch.
Havana Video Lounge (AC B CC G MA s VS) 17-2.30 h
862 North High Street ✉OH 43215 *(in the heart of the Short North at First Avenue)* ☎ 421-9697
Bar with videos and cigar lounge.
Remo's (AC B CC d F G lj MA N s SNU STV W WE) Mon-Sat 9-2.30 h
1409 South High Street ✉OH 43207 ☎ 443-4224
Slammers (B F GLM OS W) 11-1, WE 15-1 h
202 East Long Street ✉OH 43215 ☎ 224-8880
Summit Station (B gLM MA S)
2210 Summit Street ✉OH 43201 ☎ 261-9634
Tradewinds II (B d G LJ) Tue-Sun 16-2.30 h, Disco Fri Sun 20-2.30 h, Sat 22-2.30 h
117 East Chestnut Street ✉OH 43215 ☎ 461-4110
3rd Fri Club Centurion (GLM LJ)
Tremont (B G MG N S) 10-2.30, Sun 13-23 h
708 South High Street ✉OH 43206 ☎ 445-9365
Trends (B G MA) 17-2.30 h
40 East Long Street ✉OH 43215-2911 *(in front of Garage, near High Street)* ☎ 461-0076

CAFES

Coffee Table (A AC bf f GLM MA N OS WE) Mon-Thu 7-24, Fri -1, Sat 8-1, Sun 9-22 h
731 North High Street ✉OH 43215 ☎ 297-1177
Hollywood & High (AC bf CC f GLM OS) Mon-Thu 7-23, Fri -24, Sat 8-24, Sun 9-22 h
850 North High Street ✉OH 43215 ☎ 294-2233

DANCECLUBS

Axis (B D G MA) Thu-Sun 22-2.30 h
630 North High Street ✉OH 43215 ☎ 291-4008
Club Alive! (b f D GLM MA)
203 King Avenue ✉OH 43201 ☎ 297-8990
Columbus Eagle (D G MA VS) 20-2.30 h
232 North 3rd Street ✉OH 43215 *(at Hickory)* ☎ 228-2804
Garage (B D G STV OS) 17-2.30 h
40 East Long Street ✉43215-2911 *(behind Trends, near High Street)* ☎ 461-0076
Large dancefloor, especially popular with students on Sat
Wall Street (D GLM MA s STV VS) Tue-Sun 20-2.30 h, closed Mon
144 North Wall Street ✉OH 43215 ☎ 464-2800

RESTAURANTS

Antibes. L' (AC B CC F glm) Tue-Thu 17-21, Fri Sat -22 h, closed Sun-Mon
772 North High Street, Suite 106 ✉OH 43215-1456 *(Near the convention center, side entrance)* ☎ 291-1666
King Avenue Coffeehouse (A AC CC F glm MA) Mon 17-22, Tue-Thu 11-22, Fri-Sat -23 h, Sun brunch: 10-15, bistro 17-22 h
247 King Avenue ✉OH 43201 *(near the corner of King and Neil Avenues)* ☎ 294-8287
Vegetarian cuisine. Lunch, dinner, juice bar, catering.
Out On Main (AC B CC F GLM MA s WE) Mon-Thu 16-22 h, Fri,Sat 5-23 h, Sun Brunch 11-14.30 h, 17-21 h
122 East Main Street ✉OH 43215 ☎ 224-9510 ☎ 224-9520
Popular restaurant and bar. Delicious food.
Union Station Video Café (AC B CC F G MA VS) 11-2.30 h
630 North High Street ✉OH 43201 *(one block north of the convention center in Short North)* ☎ 228-3546
Restaurant and video bar.

SAUNAS/BATHS

Club Columbus (AC CC G MA P pi sa sb sol wh WO YG) 0-24 h
795 West 5th Avenue ✉OH 43212 ☎ 291-0049

BOOK SHOPS

An Open Book 10-22, Sun 10-20 h
761 North High Street ✉OH 43215 ☎ 291-0080

VIDEO SHOPS

Metro Video (AC CC GLM) Mon-Sat 11-24, Sun 12-24 h
848 North High Street ✉OH 43215 ☎ 291-7962

HOTELS

Five Forty-Two (AC bf GLM H OS)
542 Mohawk Street ☎ 621-1741
Small B&B. Room with private bath, color cable TV and VCR. Rates US$ 75-95. No kids or pets.

GUEST HOUSES

The Brewmaster´s House (AC bf G H) 24 h
1083 S. High Street ✉OH 43206 *(Exit US Route 7f1 at Greenlown to High, located lext to BP service station at corner of High and Greenlawn.* ☎ 449-8298 Fax: 449-8663

GENERAL GROUPS

Black & White Men Together
☎ 267-1610
Capital LGB Association
☎ 236-6269
Social group for LGB students at Capital University.
Columbus Asians and Friends (GLM)
PO Box 10814 ✉OH 43201 ☎ 488-4297

The Columbus Gay Men's Chorus
177 Naghten Street ✉OH 43215-2613 ☎ 228-2462
Columbus Ursine Brotherhood
PO Box 16822 ✉OH 43216
Group for hairy men and their fans
GLB Student Services
OSU, Ohio Union, 1739 North High Street ✉OH 43210
☎ 292-6200
Men of All Colors together 1
160 North High Street ✉OH 43201-2411 ☎ 267-1610
PFLAG-Parents, Families & Friends of Lesbians and Gays Meets 4th Sun 14-16 h
at Unitarian Universalist Church, 93 West Weisheimer
PO Box 340101 ✉OH 43234 ☎ 227-9355

FETISH GROUPS

Dragon Leather Club
PO Box 06417 ✉OH 43206 ☎ 258-7100

HELP WITH PROBLEMS

AA Gay and Lesbian
☎ 253-8501
Coming Out Support Group for Men 2nd/4th Mon 19 h
☎ 299-7764 Fax: 299-4408

RELIGIOUS GROUPS

Christ United Support Group (GLM)
Northminster Presbyterian Church, 203 King Avenue ✉OH 43201-2774 ☎ 297-6317
Congregation Beth Tikvah Fri 20 h
6121 Olentangy River Road, Worthington ☎ 885-6286
Dignity
203 King Avenue ☎ 451-6528
Catholic lesbians and gays.
New Creation MCC
787 East Broad ✉OH 43205 ☎ 237-2844

CRUISING

-O.S.U. Botany and Zoology Building (Basement, Sep-Jun 9-21 h, Jul-Aug 9-17 h, closed Sat Sun)
-Larkins Hall (Gymnasium, 4th floor, 7-22 h)
-Ohio Union (AYOR) (Basement)
-The Beach (Whittier Street, west of High and Front Streets)
-Big Walnut Park (on Livingston Avenue east of Hamilton Street)
-Park of Roses (on North High, just north of Clintonville, next to public library)
-Bull Run Park (AYOR OG) (on Clime Road, west of Georgesville Road, before 23 h)
-Lou Berliner Park (AYOR) (on Greenlawn Avenue, between High Street and I-71, before 23 h, busy all year)

Dayton ☎ 937

GAY INFO

Dayton GLB Hotline
☎ 274-1776

BARS

The Asylum (B G MA N)
605 East Patterson Boulevard
City Cafe (B bf f Glm MA r stv snu)
121 North Ludlow *(Talbot Towers Building)* ☎ 223-1417
Busy every night of the week. Various nightly entertainment, karaoke, strippers, drag shows, etc., mainly for gay men of all ages, very cruisy, pool table.
D.J.'s Saloon (AC B CC f G LJ MG OS SNU VS W) Mon-Fri 12-2.30, Sat-Sun 15-2.30 h
237 North Main Street ✉OH 45402 ☎ 223-7340
Jessie's Celebrity Club (AC B D E GLM lj MA SNU STV VS W YG) Sun-Thu 20-2.30, Fri-Sat -4 h
850 North Main Street ✉OH 45405 ☎ 461-2582
The Right Corner (AC B CC GLM MA N) Mon-Sat 12-2.30 h, Sun 13-2.30 h
105 East Third St. ✉OH 45402 ☎ 228-1285
Stage Door (B G lj) 12-2.30 h
44 North Jefferson Street ✉OH 45402 ☎ 223-7418
1470 West (B D G MA SNU STV) 34 North Jefferson
☎ 293-0066

FETISH GROUPS

Great Lakes Leather Coalition
PO Box 24426 ✉OH 45424 ☎ 233-9162

CRUISING

-DeWeese Park
-Wright State University WSU (Library, Millet Hall on 2nd floor)

Lima ☎ 419

BARS

Somewhere (AC B D f GLM MA s SNU STV) Sun-Thu 19-?, Fri Sat 20-? h
804 West North Street ✉OH 45801 ☎ 227-7288

Logan ☎ 740

HOTELS

Summit Lodge Resort (bf CC F GLM H pi sa wh WO)
26500 Wildcat Road ✉OH 43149 ☎ 385-3521
E-Mail: Sumlodge@aol.com
Homepage: http://cimarron.net/usa/oh/summit.html
A rustic country lodge just 45 miles south-east of Columbus. Rates from US$ 50 to 110 for lodge rooms, camping $25 (bf incl.)
Summit Lodge Resort (bf glm H pi sa wh)
PO Box 951-Code A ✉OH 43138 ☎ 385-6822

GUEST HOUSES

Spring Wood Hocking Hills Cabins (b GLM H wh)
28560 Blackjack Road ✉OH 43138 ☎ 385-2042
Cabins for 4 or 8 people with private baths, kitchenettes, refridgerators and fireplace. Kids ok. rates US$ 85-90.

Lorain ☎ 216

BARS

The Serpent (B d GLM MA OS)
2223 Broadway ☎ 246-9009

Monroe ☎ 513

BARS

Old Street Saloon (B GLM MA N) 1
3 Old Street ✉OH 45050 ☎ 539-9183

Newark ☎ 614

BARS

Bulldog Lounge (B G MA N)
35 North Third Street ✉OH 43055 ☎ 345-9729

Sandusky ☎ 419

DANCECLUBS

Rainbow Bay (B D GLM MA) Wed-Sun 16-2.30 h, closed Mon Tue
306 West Water Street ☎ 624-8118
Popular

Springfield ☎ 937

BARS

Chances (B GLM MA OS P S) 20.30-2.30 h, Tue closed
1912-1914 Edwards Avenue ✉OH 45503 ☎ 324-0383

Toledo ☎ 419

BARS

Blue Jeans (B F GLM)
3606 Sylvania Avenue ✉OH 43623 ☎ 474-0690
Bretz (B D G VS) Mon-Thu 14-2.30, Fri Sat 14-4 h
2012 Adams Street ✉OH 43624 ☎ 243-1900
Caesar's Show Bar (B D glm) Wed-Sun 19-2.30 h
133 North Erie Street ✉OH 43624 ☎ 241-5140
Hooterville Station (B D LJ) 17.30-2.30 h
119 North Erie Street ✉OH 43624 ☎ 241-5140
Rustler Saloon (B G LJ) 14-2.30 h
4023 Monroe Street ✉OH 43606 *(rear entrance)* ☎ 472-8278

CRUISING

-Franklin Park Mall
-Ontario Street (between Washington Street and Jefferson Street)
-Southwick Mall

Warren ☎ 330

BARS

The Queen of Hearts (AC B d f GLM lj MA OS r s SNU YG) 14-2.30 h, Happy Hour 14-21 h
132-134 Pine Avenue S.E. ✉OH 44481 ☎ 395-1100

DANCECLUBS

The Alley (B D GLM MA) 14-2.30 h
441 East Market Street ☎ 394-6991
Crazy Duck (B D GLM MA S) 17-2.30, Sat 20-2.30 h
121 Pine Avenue ☎ 394-3825

Youngstown ☎ 330

BARS

Sophie's Lounge (B D f GLM lj MA r S SNU STV TV VS WE) Mon-Fri 17-2.30, Sat 21-2.30, Sun 22-2.30 h
2 East LaClede Avenue ✉OH 44507 ☎ 782-8080

USA-Oklahoma

Middlewest USA
Initials: OK
Time: GMT -6
Area: 181.048 km² / 74,048 sq mi.
Population: 3,317,000
Capital: Oklahoma City

Homosexual oral and anal intercourse is prohibited in Oklahoma.

In Oklahoma ist homosexueller Oral- und Analverkehr verboten.

Dans l'Oklahoma, la fellation et la pénétration anale sont interdites seulement pour les homosexuels.

En Oklahoma las relaciones homosexuales por vía oral o anal están prohibidas.

In Oklahoma sono vietati i rapporti orali ed anali tra omosessuali.

Oklahoma City ☎ 405

GAY INFO

Gay and Lesbian Community Services Center 19-22, Fri Sat -24 h
☎ 525-2437
Gayly Oklahoman
PO Box 609 30 ✉OK 73146 ☎ 528-0800
Monthly newspaper with events calendar, guide to Oklahoma, book review, classified ads.

BARS

The Copa (B D GLM YG)
2200 North-West 39th Expressway ✉OK 73112 *(at the Habana Inn)* ☎ 528-2221
Finishline. The (B D GLM) 12-? h
2200 North-West 39th Expressway ✉OK 73112 *(at the Habana Inn)* ☎ 528-2221
The Park (A B d G OS SNU VS) 17-2 h, Sun 15-2 h
2125 North West 39th Street ✉OK 73112 ☎ 528-4690
Tramps (AC B d f G lj MA OS P r STV VS) 12-2 h
2201 North West 39th Street ✉OK 73112 ☎ 521-9888

DANCECLUBS

Angles (B D GLM s VS YG) Wed-Sun 21-2 h, Tea dance Sun
2117 North West 39th Street ✉OK 73112 ☎ 528-0050
Modern gay disco, video etc.
The Wreck Room (D f YG) Fri Sat 21-? h
2127 North West 39th Street ☎ 525-7610 *No alcohol.*

HOTELS

Habana Inn Gay Hotel Complex (AC B bf CC D EF GLM H MA N pi STV)
2200 North West 39th Expressway ✉OK 73112 ☎ 528-2221
☎ 800-988-22 21 (Reservation only) Fax: 528 04 96
Homepage: www.habanainn.com *30 double rooms, 145 single rooms. All rooms with shower/bath & WC, wash-basin, telephone, Satellite TV, Air-conditioning, heating. This huge gay complex has 2 swimming pols, 3 gay clubs, a restaurant, an adult gift shop and is located in the heart of the gay strip. Rates: Single from US$ 42-56, Double from US$ 54-70, Suites from US$ 70 per day. Weekley rates available.*

CRUISING
-Lake Heffner (AYOR)
-Shepperd Mall
-Trosper Park

Tulsa ☎ 918

BARS
Lola's (B G STV) 2630 East 15th Street ✉OK 74104
☎ 749-1563
Silver Star Saloon (B D G) Wed-Sun 19-2 h
1565 South Sheridan ✉OK 74112 ☎ 834-4234
Tool Box (B D G LJ) 12-2 h
1338 East 3rd Street ✉OK 74120 ☎ 584-1308

CRUISING
-Boulder and Boston (between 5th and 10th Streets)
-River Parks (at 21st Street)
-Turkey Mountain Park (61st and South Elwood Streets)
-Woodward Park

USA-Oregon

Northwest USA
Initials: OR
Time: GMT -8
Area: 254.819 km² / 104,221 sq mi.
Population: 3,244,000
Capital: Salem

Eugene ☎ 541

BARS
Club Arena (AC B D GLM s VS) 21-2.30 h
959 Pearl Street ✉OR 97401 ☎ 683-2360
E-Mail: clubarena@aol.com.

GENERAL GROUPS
MPowerment Project Thu Fri 15-18, Sat 15-22 h
1414 Kincaid Street ✉OR 97403 ☎ 683-4303

Medford

GIFT & PRIDE SHOPS
Castle Superstore Adult Retail
113 Progress Drive ✉OR 97504
Videos, leather, lingerie, magazines, toys, novelties, books, DVD's.

Portland ☎ 503

BARS
Boxx's (B GLM VS YG) 12-2.30 h
1035 South West Stark Street ✉OR 97205 ☎ 226-4171
Very popular gay night on Thu
The Brigg (B D glm VS WE YG) 15-4 Sun-Thu, Thu (G), Fri-Sat (glm)
1035 South West Stark Street ✉OR 97205 *(connected to Boxx's)*
☎ 226-4171
More straight.
The Eagle (B DR G LJ MG U VS)
1300 West Burnside Street ✉OR 97209 ☎ 241-0105
Popular. Darkroom upstairs.
The Embers (B D f GLM MA STV WE YG)
110 North West Broadway ✉OR 97209 ☎ 222-3082
Very popular bar/disco, good nightly Drag shows.
Scandals (AC B F G MA) 11.30-2.30 h
1038 South West Stark Street ✉OR 97205 ☎ 227 58 87
Silverado (B d F G MA SNU VS) 9-2.30 h
1217 South West Stark Street ✉OR 97205 ☎ 224-4493
Wed-Sun 20-2h male strippers. Cruisy atmosphere. Very popular.
Three Sisters Tavern (B D F GLM) 12.30-2.30 h, Sat Sun 12.30-3 h
1125 South West Stark Street ☎ 228-0486
Latino crowd and latino dance music.

DANCECLUBS
LaLuna (B D GLM MA) Mon
215 South East 9th Street ☎ 241-5862
Panorama (b CC D g lj MA W WE YG) Fri 21-4 h, Sat -4.30 h
341 SW 10th Street ✉OR 97205 *(next to Boxx's and the Brigg)*
☎ 221-7262

RESTAURANTS
Chameleon (B F glm MA) 17-21.30 h
2000 North East 40th ☎ 460-0084
Good food. Popular with gays and lesbians.
Hobo's (b F glm S) 16-2 h
120 North West 3rd Avenue ✉OR 97209 *(Old Town)*
☎ 224-3285
Popular for drinks and dinner after work.
JOQ's (B G MA)
2512 North East Broadway ☎ 287-4210
Saucebox (AC B CC D F f glm MA OS) Tue-Thu 11.30-24, Fri -2, Sat 17-2 h
214 South West Broadway ✉OR 97205 ☎ 241-3393
Pan-Asian restaurant for dining and dancing.
Starky's (AC B CC F GLM MA OS) Mon-Sat 11-2 h, Sun 9.30-2 h
2913 SE Stark Street ✉OR 97214 ☎ 230-7980

SHOWS
Darcelle XV (B CC F glm S STV) Wed-Sat 13-2 h
208 North West 3rd Avenue ✉OR 97209 *(in Chinatown)*
☎ 222-5338 Fax: 248-6771

SAUNAS/BATHS
Club Portland (g sa)
03 South West 12th Avenue ✉OR 97205 ☎ 227-9992
Continental Club (G sa)
303 SW 12th Ave. ✉OR 97205 ☎ 227-9992

GUEST HOUSES
Sullivan's Gulch B&B (bf CC GLM H)
1744 North East Clackamas Street ✉OR 97232 ☎ 331-1104
Fax: 331-1575 E-Mail: bbskip@teleport.com
Homepage: www.teleport.com/~thegulch/
Small B&B in a restored Portland home built in 1907. Smoke free establishment. All rooms with telephone, TV and radio, two with balcony. Rates room/private bath US$ 85 and with shared bath $ 70 and incl. an expanded continental bf.

GENERAL GROUPS
Cascade Bears
25 South West 10th Avenue #125 ✉OR 97205
F.I.T.S. Gay and Lesbian Bowling League
3031 South East Powell ✉OR 97207 ☎ 581-1804
Fax: 581-1804
Gentle Giants of Oregon
PO Box 1844 ✉OR 97207 ☎ 241-4535
E-Mail: chubstuf@teleport.com.

LGBA-Lesbian, Gay, Bisexual Alliance
PO Box 751 ✉OR 97201 ☎ 725-5681
E-Mail: lgba@sg.ess.pdx.edu.
Parents and Friends of Lesbians and Gays (PFLAG)
PO Box 8944 ✉OR 97207 ☎ 232-7676
Phoenix Rising Foundation Youth Programs
620 South West 5th Avenue, Suite 710 ✉OR 97204
☎ 223-8299
Portland Bisexual Alliance
PO Box 412 ✉OR 97207 ☎ 232-9275
Portland Gay Men's Chorus
PO Box 3223 ✉OR 97208 ☎ 460-3689
Sexual Minority Youth Recreation Center - SMYRC Fri-Sat 16-24 h
424 East Burnside ✉OR 97214 ☎ 872-9664
The Alliance c/o Portland Community College Tue-Fri 13-19 h. Meets Wed 11.30-12.30 h
Sylvania Campus, 12000 South West 48th Street ✉OR 97219
☎ 977-4131 E-Mail: mfiorent@pcc.edu

HEALTH GROUPS

Cascade AIDS Project - Speak to your Brother 9-17 h
620 South West 5th Avenue, Suite 300 ✉OR 97204
☎ 223-5907
Service and information for HIV positive people and people living with Aids. Discussion groups, social activities, HIV-testing.
HIV Center
3835 South West Kelly Street ☎ 223-3444
HIV Testing for Gay & Bisexual Men c/o Cascade AIDS Project
620 South West 5th Avenue, Suite 300
Names Project Portland Chapter
PO Box 5423 ✉OR 97228 ☎ 650-7032

RELIGIOUS GROUPS

Dignity
PO Box 6708 ✉OR 97228 ☎ 295-4868
Roman Catholic Lesbians and Gays
Trinity Episcopal Church
147 North West 19th Avenue ☎ 222-9811

CRUISING

-Rest Stop (I-5, both sides)
-Columbia Park (AYOR)
-East Delta Park (showers)
-Rooster Rock State Park (East end of beach, 30 miles East of Portland)
-Sauvie's Island (West end of beach near parking lot)
-Washington Park (by Lewis and Clark Mounument, Burnside & 25th)

Salem ☎ 503

GAY INFO

Community News
PO Box 663 ✉OR 97308 ☎ 363-0006
Oregon's oldest monthly gay & lesbian newspaper, 16 to 32 pages.

Tigard ☎ 503

TRAVEL & TRANSPORT

The Travel Shop l
0115 SW Nimbus Ave., Suite 600 ✉OR 97223 ☎ 648-8533

Tiller ☎ 514

CAMPING

Kalles Family Ranch (GLM MA)
233 Jackson Creek Road ✉OR 97484 ☎ 825-3271
Fax: 825-3299 E-Mail: rkalles@pioneer-net.com
Homepage: www.coguide.com/out/kalles.htm
Large outdoor kitchen, wash house with bath and shower. Rates US$ 16 per night + US$ 2 for electric and water hookup. Only Gay and Lesbian campground in Oregon.

USA-Pennsylvania

Northeast USA
Initials: PA
Time: GMT -5
Area: 119.291 km² / 48,790 sq mi.
Population: 12,020,000
Capital: Harrisburg
Important gay cities: Philadelphia, Pittsburgh

Allentown ☎ 610

BARS

Candida's (B D F GLM) 14-2 h
247 North 12th Street ✉PA 18102 ☎ 434-3071
Stonewall (B D F GLM VS YG) 21-2 h, closed Sun
28-30 North 10th Street ✉PA 18101 ☎ 432-0706

CRUISING

-Leigh Park (near Keck's Bridge)
-Turner Street (AYOR R) (between 9th and 10th)

Bethlehem ☎ 610

DANCECLUBS

Diamonz (AC B CC D F GLM MA OS S SNU STV) 16-2 h
1913 West Brond Street ✉PA 18018 *(5 minutes off Route 22)*
☎ 865-1028
Restaurant with 3 separate bars: sport bar, lounge and danceclub on two levels.

Erie ☎ 814

BARS

The Zone (AC B D f GLM MA s)
1711 State Street ✉PA 16501 ☎ 459-1711
Call for opening hours.

CRUISING

-Erie Mall (downtown)
-Preque Isle Park Beach

Harrisburg ☎ 570

GAY INFO

Gay & Lesbian Switchboard Mon-Fri 18-22 h
☎ 234-0328

BARS

Neptune (B D F G)
268 North Street ✉PA 17101 ☎ 233-0581
Strawberry Cafe (B f G) closed Sun
704 North 3rd Street ✉PA 17113 ☎ 234-4228

RESTAURANTS

Paper Moon (B F GLM) Mon-Fri lunch 11.30-14.30 h, Tue-Sat dinner 16-22 h, Sun brunch 11.30-14.30 h
268 North Street ✉PA 17101

Kutztown ☎ 610

BOOK SHOPS

Action Center Adult Bookstore
Route 222 & Kempville Road ✉PA 19530 ☎ 683-9393
Especially busy daytimes and early evenings.

Lancaster ☎ 717

BARS

Tally Ho (B D GLM MA) 18-2 h, Sun 20-2 h
201 W. Orange Street *(Ground floor)* ☎ 299-0661

RESTAURANTS

The Loft (B F glm)
201 W. Orange Street ✉PA17603 *(1st floor)* ☎ 299-0661
International cuisine.

GUEST HOUSES

Maison Rouge B&B (bf CC glm H OS)
2236 Marietta Avenue ✉PA 17607 ☎ 399-3033
☎ (800) 309-3033
Small B&B in a beautifully restored Victorian home. All rooms with shower/WC. Rates US$ 85-125 incl. a full bf.

Levittown ☎ 717

BARS

The Attic (B CC F gLM MA)
168 South Main Street ✉PA 17545 *(located above The Cellar)*
☎ 665-6211

The Cellar (B CC D F GLM MA S)
168 South Main Street ✉PA 17545 *(located in the basement)*
☎ 665-1960

BOOK SHOPS

Variety Adult Bookstore 0-24 h
6909 Bristol Pike ✉PA 19057 *(US 13 South, north of Airport Road exit, southbound side)* ☎ 547-2373
Mixed crowd, lots of action.

Manheim ☎ 717

BARS

The Cellar (AC B CC d f GLM MA S) Mon-Wed 17-24, Thu-Sat -2 h, closed Sun
168 South Main Street ✉PA 17545 ☎ 665-1960

New Hope ☎ 215

BARS

The Cartwheel. (AC B CC D F GLM lj MA OS SNU STV VS) 11.30-2 h
437 Olde York Road ✉PA 18938 *(at junction highway 202)*
☎ 862-0880
Popular bar and restaurant.

CAFÉS

Cafe Galleria (A bf f gLM)
93A Main Street ☎ 862-6860

RESTAURANTS

Raven (B F Glm H MA T)
385 West Bridge Street ☎ 862-2081
Good quality.

Rosemont Cafe (b bf F glm)
88 Kingwood-Stockton Road, Rosemont, NJ ☎ (609) 397-4097
20 minute drive from New Hope. Delicious food served all day. Reservation recommended. Try the desserts. No credit cards. Bring your own bottle.

BOOK SHOPS

The Book Gallery (GLM)
19 West Mechanic Street
☎ 862-5110

GUEST HOUSES

The Fox & Hound Bed & Breakfast of New Hope (AC bf CC f GLM OS wh)
246 West Bridge Street ✉PA 18938 ☎ 862-5082
E-Mail: foxhound@beenet.com Homepage: www.foxhoundinn.com
Romms with bath/WC, some with fireplaces, tub jacuzzis and first floor outside entrance. Rates from USD 70-170.

Logan Inn (bf g H)
10 West Ferry Street ✉PA 18938 ☎ 862-2300
Rates US$ 85-95.

Victorian Peacock B&B (bf gLM H pi wh)
309 East Dark Hollow Road, Pipersville ☎ 766-1356
Comfortable B&B in a large Victorian estate. All rooms furnished with antiques. Rates US$ 65-165.

Philadelphia ☎ 215

● When talking about Philadelphia, you'll have to talk about Washington D.C. and New York City first. This may seem funny, but in the 18th century Philadelphia was on its way to become the most important city in the US. After all, here the 13 states of the union declared their independence from Great Britain on 4th July 1776 and here the US-constitution was developed in 1788. But soon New York took over the economical leadership of the country; Washington D.C. the political. Accordingly enormous gay scenes have evolved in both cities in the 20th century. Seen from hindsight: what a piece of luck for Philadelphia. No other Convention & Visitors Bureau in the US will provide you with such an allround gay information package (including gay-pertinent travelling news and a small gay guide in city-map format) about its city like the one in Philadelphia. Being gay or lesbian is a very normal thing here in Philly, where the freedom of the US made its start. More gay infos about the city can be found in the *Philadelphia Gay News* or in its smaller rival, the *Au Courant*. The best time of the year for a visit here (and its greater neighbours) are spring and autumn. The biggest festivity of the local 'community' takes place in the middle of May: the *PrideFest*. So if you want to party, party, party, Philadelphia isn't quite the right place for you. But the mainstream-gay will find everything he needs, moreover on weekends, in the gay quarter between *Juniper* and *Quince Street* (east to west direction) and *Walnut* and *Pine Street* (north to south direction). Anyway: Most people come here to see the *Independence National Historic Park* with *Independence Hall* and *Liberty Bell*. They flock to *Walt Whitman House* in Camden, New Jersey, or take a cartrip to the country, to New Hope, Pennsylvania, which has become a popular gay outing destination.

✸ Will man etwas über Philadelphia erfahren, muß man zuerst über Washington, D.C. und New York City reden. Warum? Nun: Philadelphia war im 18. Jahrhundert auf dem Weg zur wichtigsten Stadt der USA. Schließlich erklärten sich hier am 4. Juli 1776

die 13 ersten Staaten der Union von Großbritannien unabhängig, und hier wurde 1788 die Verfassung der USA entwickelt.
Bald aber übernahm New York die wirtschaftliche Führung des Landes, Washington D.C. die politische. Entsprechend haben sich dann im 20. Jahrhundert in beiden Städten überwältigende schwule Szenen entwickelt. Heute muß man sagen: was für ein Glücksfall für diese Stadt.
Von keinem anderen Convention & Visitors Bureau der USA bekommt man auf Anfrage ein derart umfassendes schwule Info-Paket (inkl. einschlägiger Reise-News und einem kleinen Gay Guide im Stadtplanformat) wie von dem Philadelphias. Schwul oder lesbisch sein, das ist in Philly, wo die Freiheit der USA ihren Anfang nahm, eine recht normale Sache.
Weitere schwule Infos über die Stadt findet man in den *Philadelphia Gay News* oder im *Au Courant*, dem kleineren Konkurrenten. Die besten Jahreszeiten für diese Stadt sind, wie für die großen Nachbarn, Herbst und Frühjahr. Mitte Mai findet auch das größte Fest der örtlichen „community" statt: *PrideFest*.
Wer also Party, Party, Party will, ist nicht unbedingt richtig hier. Der Durchschnitts-Homosexuelle aber findet alles Notwendige, zumal am Wochenende und im schwulen Viertel zwischen (in Ost-West-Richtung) *Juniper* und *Quince Street* und (in Nord-Süd-Richtung) *Walnut* und *Pine Street*.
Und sowieso: Man kommt doch hierher, um sich im *Independence National Historic Park* mit *Independence Hall* und *Liberty Bell* umzusehen. Man pilgert zum *Walt Whitman House* in Camden, New Jersey. Oder man macht per Auto einen Ausflug auf's Land, nach New Hope, Pennsylvania, das sich zu einem beliebten schwulen Ausflugsort gemausert hat.

▲ Pour parler de Philadelphie, il faut d'abord parler de Washinton D.C. et de New York City. Cela vous étonne? Sachez qu'au 18ème siècle, Philadelphie était la plus importante ville d'Amérique, car c'est ici que les 13 états de l'Union ont proclamé leur indépendance de la couronne britannique le 4 juillet 1776. C'est aussi ici que l'on a élaboré la Constitution américaine en 1788.
Philadelphie a donc failli devenir capitale, mais c'était sans compter New York et Washington D.C. qui ont se sont respectivement partagé le pouvoir économique et le pouvoir politique.
Dans aucune autre ville des Etats-Unis, le Convention & Visitors Bureau ne met à votre disposition autant de brochures et d'informations purement homos. Cela va même jusqu'au petit plan gay de la ville! A „Philly", là où est née l'idée américaine de la Liberté, être gay ou lesbienne est la chose la plus naturelle du monde!
Pour de plus amples informations, jetez un oeil dans les „Philadelphia Gay News" ou dans „Au courant". Comme pour New York et Washington, le printemps et l'automne sont les meilleurs saisons pour visiter la ville. Mi-mai a lieu la „Pride Fest", la manifestation gay de la „community".
Si vous venez au Etats-Unis pour faire la fête, encore la fête et toujours la fête, vous serez déçu par Philadelphie. Notez bien que l'homo de base trouve quand même tout ce dont il a besoin. Donc: pas de pénurie à Philadelphie! Les week-ends, ça bouge pas mal dans le quartier gay entre Juniper et Quince Street et Walnut et Pine Street.
De toute façon, on vient à Philadelphie pour voir le „Independence National Historic Park", le „Independence Hall" et la „Liberty Bell". On fait son pélerinage à la „Withman House" à Camden, dans le New Jersey. On peut aussi aller à New Hope (Pensylvanie) en voiture ou en avion. C'est le lieu de villégiature des gays de la région.

☆ Si se quiere saber algo sobre Filadelfia se debe hablar primeramente de Washington D.C. y de la ciudad de Nueva York. En el siglo XVIII Filadelfia se encontraba en el mejor camino para convertirse en la ciudad más importante de los Estados Unidos. El 4 de julio de 1776 se declararon independientes de la Gran Bretaña los primeros 13 estados norteamericanos y aqui se desarrolló también en 1778 la constitución de los E.E.U.U.. Muy pronto sería Nueva York la ciudad que tomaría el poder económico del país y Washington el político. En el siglo XX. se desarrollaron en ambas ciudades grandes centros gay. Hoy en día esto se puede considerar como una gran suerte para Filadelfia. En ningúna otra oficina para turistas („Convention & Visitors Bureau") se obtienen informaciones tan detalladas para gays. Ser homosexual en Philly es una cosa bastante normal, que no es de extrañar, ya que esta ciudad es la cuna y el orgullo de la libertad estadounidense. Más informaciones gay se encuentran en el *Philadelphia Gay News* o en el *Au Courant*. La mejor época para visitar la ciudad son el otoño y la primavera. A mediados de mayo se lleva a cabo la *Pride Fest*, la celebración anual más importante. Aunque Filadelfia no es la ciudad adecuada para los que busquen solamente marcha y fiestas, homosexuales encuentran aqui todo lo que necesitan para satisfacer sus necesidades sobre todo los fines de semana. El sector gay de la ciudad se encuentra en dirección este-oeste en *Jupiter* y *Quince Street* y en dirección norte-sur *Walnut* y *Pine Street*). Puntos turísticos de atracción son el *Independence National Park* con *Independence Hall* y *Liberty Bell* o se puede vistar *Walt Whitman House* en Camden, Nueva Yersey. Recomendamos también una excursión en coche a el New Hope, Pennsylvania que se ha convertido ultimamente en un destino turístico homosexual de moda.

❖ E impossibile conoscere Philadelphia senza conoscere prima Washington D.C. e New York; è sorprendente, nel XVIII secolo Philadelphia stava per diventare la città più importante degli Stati Uniti: qui il 4 luglio 1776 tredici stati dell'Unione si dichiararono indipendenti dalla Gran Bretagna e sempre a Philadelphia, nel 1788, fu scritta la costituzione. Poco dopo però New York divenne il centro

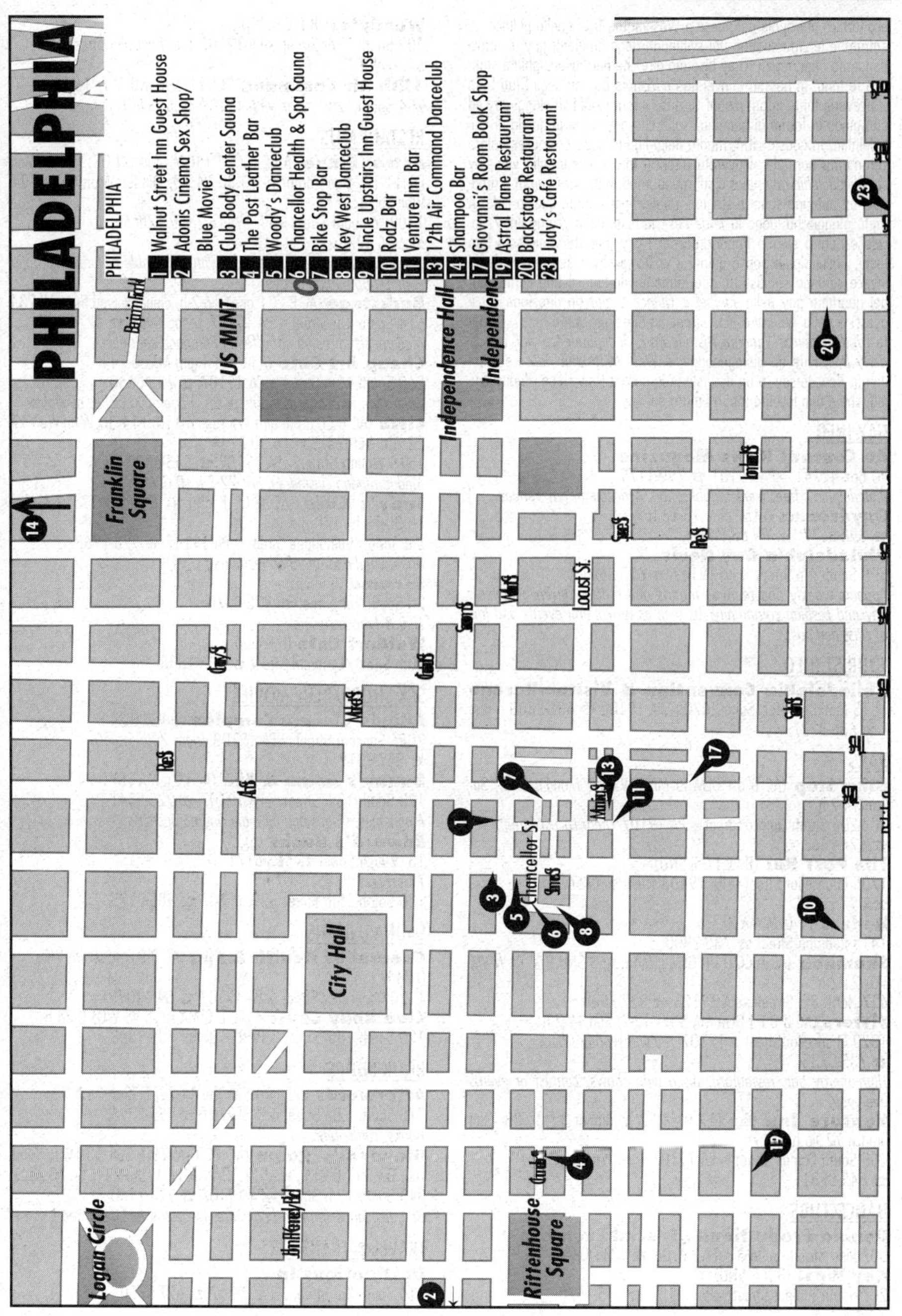
PHILADELPHIA
PHILADELPHIA
1 Walnut Street Inn Guest House
2 Adonis Cinema Sex Shop/ Blue Movie
3 Club Body Center Sauna
4 The Post Leather Bar
5 Woody's Danceclub
6 Chancellor Health & Spa Sauna
7 Bike Stop Bar
8 Key West Danceclub
9 Uncle Upstairs Inn Guest House
10 Rodz Bar
11 Venture Inn Bar
13 12th Air Command Danceclub
14 Shampoo Bar
17 Giovanni's Room Book Shop
19 Astral Plane Restaurant
20 Backstage Restaurant
23 Judy's Café Restaurant
US MINT
Independence Hall
Franklin Square
Locust St.
Chancellor St.
City Hall
Logan Circle
Rittenhouse Square

economico principale del paese e Washington D.C. quello politico. In entrambe le città si sono poi sviluppati degli ambienti gay di corrispondente importanza. Oggi bisogna dire che per Philadelphia è stata una fortuna. In nessun Convention e Visitors Bureau degli Stati Uniti si ricevono tante informazioni (incluse informazioni su viaggi gay ed una guida in forma di piantina) sulla vita gay come in quello di Philadelphia. In questa città, madre della libertà, essere omosessuale è veramente normale. Troverete ulteriori informazioni sulla vita gay sul *Philadelphia gay news* o sul meno importante *Au Courant*. Primavera ed autunno sono le stagioni migliori per visitare questa città. A metà maggio ha luogo la *Pride Fest*, la festa della „community" locale è l'unico evento importante per i gay. Per chi vuole solo fare festa, Philadelphia non è quindi il posto giusto. I gay più moderati invece saranno soddisfatti, specialmente durante il fine settimana, nel quartiere gay nella *Juniper* e *Quince Street* (in direzione est e ovest) e nella *Walnut* e *Pine street* (in direzione sud e nord). Visitate l'*Indipendence National Historic Park, Independence Hall* e il *Liberty Bell*. Fate un pellegrinaggio a *Walt Whitmann House* a Camden in New Jersey, o un'escursione in auto a New Hope, Pennsylvania, che è una località molto amata dai gay.

GAY INFO

Au Courant News Magazine
PO Box 42741 ✉PA 19101 ☎ 790-1179
Philadelphia's free, weekly publication. Available at gay venues.
Gaydreams (GLM) Sun 15-16 h
☎ 898-6677 *WXPN 88,9 FM*
Philadelphia Gay News
505 South 4th Street ✉PA 19147 ☎ 625-8501
Appears weekly and features reports and articles on Philadelphia's gay and Lesbian community, as well as on cultural events and lots of classified ads.

TOURIST INFO

Philadelphia Convention & Visitor Bureau
1515 Market Street, Suite 2020 ✉PA 19102 ☎ 636-3300
Fax: 636-3327.

BARS

Bike Stop (AC B d f GLM LJ MA N VS W) Mon-Fri 16-2, Sat Sun 14-2 h
204-206 South Quince Street ✉PA 19107 *(near Locust Street)*
☎ 627-1662
The Post Bar (B CC f G lj SNU)
1705 Chancellor Street ✉PA 19103 *(near 17th Street)*
☎ 597 23 38
Rodz (B d F GLM MA N)
1418 Rodman Street ☎ 735-2900
Shampoo (AC B CC D DR GLM lj MA msg S SNU STV TV W WE YG) 21-2 h
417 North 8th Street ✉PA 19123 ☎ 922-7500
Sisters (AC B D F f GLM MA S W) 15-2, Sun 12-2 h
1320 Chancellor Street ✉19107 *(behind Woody's bar)*
☎ 735-0735
High-energy bar, restaurant, disco with shows, contest or events everyday.
Venture Inn (B F MG N) 12-2 h, dinner 17.30-23, Sun brunch 12-16 h
255 South Camac Street ✉PA 19107 *(near Spruce Street)*
☎ 545-8731

DANCECLUBS

Dennio Productions „Special Events"
507 Pine Street, Suite 3 ✉PA 19106 ☎ 931-0060
Key West (B D G SNU)
207 South Juniper Street ✉PA 19107 ☎ 545-1578
Woody's (! B D Glm YG)
202 South 13th Street ✉PA 19107 *(at Chancellor Street)*
545-1893
12th Air Command (B D f G MA SNU STV) 16-2 h
254 South 12th Street ✉PA 19107 ☎ 545-8088

RESTAURANTS

Astral Plane (A AC B CC F f GLM LJ MA N OS) Lunch: Mon-Fri 11-14, Sun (brunch) 10.30-14.30, Dinner: Mon-Tue 17-24, Wed-Sun 15-2 h
1708 Lombard Street ✉PA 19416 *(near 17th Street)*
☎ 546-6230
Romantic atmosphere restaurant with collectable pictures and objects and a Bohemian alcove.
Backstage (AC B CC F glm) 16-2 h, dinner served from 18-23 h
614 South 4th Street ✉PA 19147 *(near Kater)* ☎ 627-9887
Medium sized restaurant offering European specialties.
Cheap Art Café (A AC bf F f glm MA) 0-24 h
260 South 12th Street ✉PA 19107 ☎ 735-6650
Diner-style food at reasonable prices. Vegetarian dishes available.
Circa (AC B CC d E F glm W) Tue-Fri 11.30-14.30, Mon-Wed 17-22, Thu-Sat -23, Sun 16.30-21 h
1518 Walnut Street ✉PA 19102 ☎ 545-6800
Mediterranean cuisine. Fri-Sat 22-? h (D GLM).
Judy's Cafe (AC B CC F glm N) Mon-Sat 17.30-?, Sun 10.30-15 h
3rd Street/Bainbridge Street ✉PA 19147 ☎ 928-1968
Gay owned and operated restaurant.
Serrano (b F glm)
20 South 2nd Street ☎ 928-0770
Thai & French cuisine
Waldorf Cafe (b F glm)
20th Street/Lombard Street ☎ 985-1836

SEX SHOPS/BLUE MOVIES

Adonis Cinema Complex (G VS) 0-24 h
2026 Sansom Street ✉PA 19103 *(near 20th Street)*
☎ 557-9319
Danny's Adam & Eve (AC CC g MA VS) 0-24 h
133 South 13th Street ✉PA 19107 ☎ 925-5041
Magazines, videos and all male cinema upstair's.
Edward's Books (g)
1319 Arch Street ☎ 563-6171
Tomcat (G VS) 11-2 h
120 South 13th Street ✉PA 19107 ☎ 985-9725

SAUNAS/BATHS

Chancellor Health & Spa (AC B F G sa sb wh WO) 0-24 h
1220 Chancellor Street ✉PA 19107 ☎ 545-4098
Club Body Center (AC B G MA sa sb VS WO) 0-24 h
120 South 13th Street ✉PA 19107 ☎ 735-9568

BOOK SHOPS

Afterwords (CC glm) Sun-Thu 11-22, Fri-Sat -24 h
218 South 12th Street ✉PA 19107 ☎ 735-2393
Books, cards, gifts.
Giovanni's Room (AC CC GLM MA) Sun 13-19 h, Mon, Tue, Thu 11.30-21 h, Wed 11.30-19 h. Fri 11.30-22 h, Sa 10-22 h
345 South 12th Street ✉PA 19107 ☎ 923-2960
Gay, lesbian & feminist bookstore. Largest of its kind in the US.

TRAVEL & TRANSPORT

Destinations Inc.
616 South 3rd Street ✉PA 19147 ☎ 627-0300

HOTELS

Alexander Inn (bf CC E GLM H WO)
304 South 12th Street ✉PA 19107 *(central, adjacent to gay bars)* ☎ 923 3535 ☎ (877) ALE-INN (toll-free) Fax: 923 1004
E-Mail: info@alexanderinn.com Homepage: www.alexanderinn.com
Old Phildalphia hotel with designer rooms and art-deco furnishing. B&B atmosphere. Rooms with bath, phone, TV from US$ 89 incl. breakfast buffet. 24 hours fitness center.

GUEST HOUSES

Gaskill House Bed & Breakfast (H)
312 Gaskill Street ✉PA 19147 ☎ 413-0669 Fax: 413-0669
Glen Isle Farm (CC g H)
130 S. LLoyd Avenue, Downington ✉PA 19335 *(30 miles west of Philadelphia)* ☎ (610) 269-9100 Fax: (610) 269-9191
Rates US$ 69-89.
Uncles Upstairs Inn (AC B bf CC Glm H)
1220 Locust Street ✉PA 19107 ☎ 546-6660 Fax: 546-1653
All rooms with color TV, ceiling fan, fridge and private baths. Pets ok. Rates USD 75-95 incl. cont. bf.
Walnut Street Inn (AC bf CC GLM H)
1208 Walnut Street ✉PA 19107 ☎ 546-7000 Fax: 546-7573
All rooms with private bath, radio, TV and hair-dryer. Rates USD 95 incl. cont. bf.

GENERAL GROUPS

Bi-Unity
PO Box 41905 ✉PA 19101 ☎ 724-3663
Men of All Colors Together Meets 3rd Fri 19.30-22 h at William Way Community Centre
PO Box 42257 ✉PA 19101-2257 ☎ (610) 277-6595
Fax: 277-6595 E-Mail: MactPhilly@geocities.com
Homepage: www.Geocities.com/WestHollywood/Village/6571

HEALTH GROUPS

Community AIDS Hotline
☎ 985-2437
toll-free ☎ (800) 985-2437

HELP WITH PROBLEMS

Gay & Lesbian Counseling Services Mon-Fri 18-21 h
☎ 732-8255

RELIGIOUS GROUPS

Beth Ahavah
☎ 923-2003
Integrity 1st Wed 19 h
c/o Holy Trinity Church, 1904 Walnut Street ✉PA 19103
☎ 382-0794
Gay and lesbian Episcopalians
MCC Sun 19 h
PO Box 8174 ✉PA 19101 ☎ 563-6601

SPORT GROUPS

GO! Philadelphia
PO Box 15784 ✉PA 19103 ☎ 969-8948
Outdoors club for guys and lesbians

Pittsburgh ☎ 412

GAY INFO

Gay and Lesbian Community Center Phoneline Mon-Fri 18.30-21.30, Sat 15-18 h, closed Sun
☎ 422-0114
Out/Out Publishing Co. Inc. Mon-Fri 10-17 h
1000 Ross Avenue ✉PA 15221 *(2nd floor)* ☎ 243-3350
Fax: 243-7889 E-Mail: publisher@outpub.com
Monthly publication serving Pennsylvania, Ohio, West Virginia. News, entertainment, calendar of events, classified ads.
Planet Q
PO Box 81246 ✉PA 15217 ☎ 683-9741 Fax: 683-7910
E-Mail: PlanetQ@aol.com
Monthly publication

BARS

Brewer's Hotel (B G LJ MA) 10-2 h
3315 Liberty Avenue ✉PA 15201 ☎ 681-7991
Cruisy atmosphere
Holiday Bar (B G OS YG) Mon-Sat 14-2 h
4620 Forbes Avenue ✉PA 15213 ☎ 682-8598
Cruisy atmosphere
Images (B GLM VS) Mon-Sat 16-2 h
965 Liberty Avenue ✉PA 15222 ☎ 391-9990
Karaoke
Jazi's (B D G MG lj OS r) Mon-Sat 19-2 h
1241 Western Avenue ✉PA 15233 ☎ 323-2721
Cruisy atmosphere
Pittsburgh Eagle (AC B f G LJ MA VS W) Tue-Sat 20-2 h, closed Sun-Mon
1740 Eckert Street ✉PA 15212 ☎ 766-7222
Real Luck Cafe „Luckys" (AC B D F GLM MA N OS s SNU) 15-2 h
1519 Penn Avenue ✉PA 15222 ☎ 566-8988
2 floors.

DANCECLUBS

C.J. Deighnan's (B D F GLM MA) 19-? h
2506 West Liberty Avenue ☎ 561-4044
Donnie's Place (B D GLM lj) 17-? h
1226 Herron Avenue ✉PA 15219 ☎ 682-9869
3 floors.
House of Tilden (B D GLM P) 20-3 h
941 Liberty Avenue ✉PA 15222 ☎ 391-0804
After-hours club
Metropol (B D glm S YG) 20-?h
1600 Smallman Street ✉PA 15222 ☎ 261-2221
Popular Thu.
Pegasus Lounge (AC B D G lj MA s STV VS) Tue-Sat 21-2 h, closed Sun Mon
818 Liberty Avenue ✉PA 15222 ☎ 281-2131
Most popular gay disco in town.

RESTAURANTS

New York, New York (B F GLM S OS) Mon-Fri 16-2, Sat 14-2, Sun 11-2 h
5801 Ellsworth Avenue ✉PA 15232 ☎ 661-5600
American cuisine, brunch on Sun.

SEX SHOPS/BLUE MOVIES

Golden Triangle News (CC g) 0-24 h
816 Liberty Avenue ✉PA 15222 ☎ 765-3790

SAUNAS/BATHS

Arena Health Club (B G sa) 0-24 h
2025 Forbes Avenue ✉PA 15219 ☎ 471-8548

BOOK SHOPS

Bookstall closed Sun
3604 5th Avenue ✉PA 15213 *(near Meyran)* ☎ 683-3030

Head's Togerther/Bookworm
1914 Murray Avenue ☎ 421-7104
Large lesbigay selection
St. Elmo's (glm) ?-21 h, Sun -16 h
2208 East Carson Street ✉PA 15203 *(Southside)* ☎ 431-9100
Large selection of gay and lesbian books

HOTELS

Brewer's Hotel (G H OS)
3315 Liberty Avenue ✉PA 15201 *(above bar)* ☎ 681-7991
Inexpensive accomodation in boarding house. Rooms with shared baths.

GUEST HOUSES

The Inn on the Mexican War Street (AC bf CC F GLM H)
604 West North Avenue ✉PA 15212 ☎ 231 65 64
Located in the historic district. All rooms with bath/shower/WC, hair-dryer, baclony, telephone, TV, video, radio, apartments with kitchenette/kitchen. Rates US$ 75-300 (incl. bf).
Walnut Street Inn (bf glm H)
1208 Walnut Street ✉PA 19107 ☎ 546-7000
☎ (800) 887-1776 Fax: 546-7573

GENERAL GROUPS

Asians & Friends (G MA)
PO Box 99191 ✉PA 15233-4191 ☎ 521-1368
Fax: 521-1368 E-Mail: afpgh@hotmail.com
Meetings every 2nd Sat (Potluck Dinner) and last Sat (Business/Movie night) at 20 h. Publishers of the bi-monthly newsletter „Ring of Fire".
Black and White Men Together
PO Box 8772 ✉PA 15221 ☎ 242-7361
Burgh Bears
PO Box 1451 ✉PA 15230 ☎ 521-2327
Renaissance City Choir Men´s rehearsal meets Mon 19.30-22 h at East Liberty Presbyterian Church
PO Box 10282 ✉PA 15232-0282 ☎ 362-9484
Gay and lesbian choir

FETISH GROUPS

Three Rivers Leather Club
PO Box 8485 ✉PA 15206

HEALTH GROUPS

AIDS Task Force
☎ 242-2500
Persad Center
☎ 441-9786

RELIGIOUS GROUPS

Affirmation
PO Box 10104 ✉PA 15232 ☎ 683-5526
GLB United Methodists
Bet Tikvah
c/o Persad Center, 5150 Penn Avenue ✉PA 15224
☎ 441-9786 *GLB Jews*
Dignity
PO Box 362 ✉PA 15230 ☎ 362-4334
GLB Catholics
Integrity
PO Box 3, Verona ✉PA 15147 ☎ 734-8409
GLB Epsicopalians
MCC
4836 Ellsworth Avenue ☎ 683-2994

SPORT GROUPS

Frontrunners
☎ 681-6055
Iron City Squares
☎ 381-1625
GLB square dance group

Reading ☎ 610

BARS

Red Star (B D G LJ OG) Winter Mon-Sat 17-2, summer Mon-Sat 20-2 h
11 South 10th Street ✉PA 19602 ☎ 375-4116
Scarab (B D G YG) Tue-Sat 20-2 h, Sun Mon closed
724 Franklin Street ✉PA 19611 ☎ 375-7878

CRUISING

-Mount Penn (above Reading, daytime along main drag starting at Pagoda. MA especially after 17 h.)

State College ☎ 814

GAY INFO

Gay and Lesbian Switchboard 18-21 h, closed Sun
☎ 237-1950

BARS

Chumley's (B GLM) 18-2 Sun, 16-2 h
108 West College ✉PA 16801 ☎ 238-4446
Mr. C's (B D glm YG) Mon evenings
112 West College Street ✉PA 16801 ☎ 234-1031

CRUISING

-The Wall (100 block of College Avenue)
-Penn State (Hertzel Union Building, Recreation Hall and men's locker rooms)

Valley Forge

CRUISING

-Valley Forge National Historical Park (AYOR) (Routes 23 & 422, ?-22 h, parking area near Betzwood Bridge, park car and follow trails into woods. Also most parking areas, especially off Route 23, even late into the night.)

Wycombe ☎ 215

HOTELS

Wycombe Inn (AC F GLM H T)
1073 Mill Creek Road ✉PA 05777 *Bucks Country* ☎ 598-7000
Suburb location, 70 min to the airport, 13km to gay scene of New Hope. All rooms with telephone, kitchenette, priv. bath and WC.

York ☎ 717

BARS

Fourteen Karat (B D F G VS) Mon-Sat 19-2 h, closed Sun
659 West Market Street ✉PA 17406 ☎ 846-5029

CRUISING

-100 block of Duke and Queen Streets
-Saint George Street Square

USA-Rhode Island

Northeast USA

Initials: RI

Time: GMT -5

Area: 4.002 km^2 / 1,636 sq mi.

Population: 987,000

Capital: Providence

Hetero- as well as homosexual oral and anal intercourse is not anymore prohibited on Rhode Island.

Im Juni 1998 wurde das 102 Jahre alte Gesetz, welches sowohl homo- wie heterosexuellen Analverkehr verboten hatte, zurückgenommen. Es existieren keine einschränkenden Gesetze einvernehmlichen Sex betreffend mehr. 1995 wurde ein *Anti-Discrimination Law* verabschiedet. Obwohl es kein Gesetz zur *Domestic Partnership* gibt, zählt Rhode Island damit zu den fortschrittlicheren Staaten, zumal 1998 auch eine *Pro-Marriage Bill* eingebracht wurde. Diese sieht vor, die rechtliche Benachteilung von gleichgeschlechtlichen Paaren, die heiraten wollen, zu beenden. Eine Entscheidung darüber steht noch aus.

En juin 1998, la loi vieille de 102 ans qui interdisait les relations anales, qu'elles soient homo-ou hétérosexuelles, a été annulée. Il n'existe donc plus aucunes lois restrictives concernant les relations sexuelles basées sur un commun accord.En 1995, une *Anti-Discrimination Law* a été votée. Même si il n'y a pas de loi concernant le concubinage des homosexuels (*Domestic Partnership*), Rhode Island compte parmi les États les plus progressifs, surtout depuis 1998, où un projet de loi *Pro-Marriage Bill* a été déposé. Cette loi prévoit d'éliminer les inconvénients juridiques pour les couples de même sexe qui veulent se marier. La décision concernant ce projet de loi n'a pas encore été prise.

Despúes de 102 años, se abolido en 1998 la ley que prohibía relaciones sexuales por via anal tanto por homo-como por heterosexuales. Hoy en día la ley permite las relaciones sexuales por acuerdo mutuo. En 1995 se aprobó una *Anti-Discrimination Law* y aunque no exista ningúna posibilidad de registrar parejas de hecho, Rhode Island puede ser considerado como uno de los estados más progresivos. En 1998 se presentó una moción para igualar las condiciones legislativas para parejas homosexuales que desean contraer el matrimonio. Todavía no se tomó una decisión definitiva al respecto.

Nel giugno 1998 è stata abrogata la legge del 1896, che vietava il rapporto anale sia tra omosessuali sia quello tra eterosessuali. Non esistono più leggi che limitano il sesso consensuale. Nel 1995 è stata approvata l'*Anti-discrimination Law*. Anche se non esiste una legge sul *Domestic Partnership*, Rhode Island è uno dei paesi più progressivo, tanto più che nel 1998 è stata presentata una *Pro-Marriage Bill*, che prevede l'abolizione di svantaggi riguardanti la posizione legale delle coppie omosessuali che intendono sposarsi. La rispettiva decisione non è stata ancora presa.

Newport ☎ 401

HOTELS

The Brinley Victorian Inn (bf f glm H)
23 Brinley Street ✉RI 02840 ☎ 849-7645
20 km to the airport. Convenient location. All rooms with priv. bath, WC, and a few with fridge.

GUEST HOUSES

The Hydrangea House (A AC bf CC glm msg)
16 Bellevue Avenue ✉RI 02840 ☎ 846-4435
☎ (800) 945-4667 Fax: 846-6602
Homepage: www.hydrangeahouse.com
6 elegant non-smoking rooms with bath, incl. bf. Rates US$ 100-280. Special winter rates.

Prospect Hill Guest House (AC b bf CC GLM H MA OS) Bar: 13-1 h
32 Prospect Hill Street, ✉RI 02840 ☎ 847-7405
E-Mail: prospectgh@aol.com.
Homepage: www.impulz.net/buzzardsbay/newport
Small, nicely furnished, non-smoking guest house. All rooms with bath/WC, telephone, TV, radio, minibar and kitchenette (microwave, coffee maker, full sink and refrigerator). Extended continental bf (incl.) served in your room. Rates on request.

CRUISING

-First Beach(Eastons Beach)(in front of the concession stands)

Providence ☎ 401

BARS

Blinky`s (AC B d GLM MA W) Sun-Thu 12-1, Fri Sat 12-2 h
125 Washington Street ✉RI 02903 ☎ 272-6950

Changes (B g)
525 Eddy Street ✉RI 02903 ☎ 861-8025

Club In-Town (B G)
95 Eddy Street ✉RI 02903 ☎ 621-8739

Mirabar (B D G S W) 15-1 h
35 Richmond Street ✉RI 02905 ☎ 331-6761

Wheels (AC B d f GLM lj MA N r s YG)
125 Washington Street ✉RI 02903

Yukon Trading Co. (AC B D G LJ MA N) Sun-Thu 16-1 h, Fri Sat -2 h
124 Snow Street ✉RI 02903 ☎ 274-6620

DANCECLUBS

Galaxy (B D G S) Sun Thu 12-1, Fri Sat 12-2 h
123 Empire Street ✉RI 02903 ☎ 831-9206
Thu country & western night. Fri strip contest.

Gerardo's (B D F G S) Thu strip contest
1 Franklin Square ✉RI 02903 ☎ 274-5560

69 Union Street Station (B D GLM s)
69 Union Street ✉RI 02903 ☎ 331-2291

RESTAURANTS

Gerardo's Supper Club (B F GLM)
1 Franklin Square ✉RI 02903 ☎ 274-5560

SEX SHOPS/BLUE MOVIES

Upstairs Bookshop (g)
255 Allans Avenue ✉RI 02903 ☎ 785-1324

SAUNAS/BATHS

Club Body Center (B G P sb) 0-24 h
257 Weybosset Street ✉RI 02903 ☎ 274-0298
Membership $15, locker 9.

HEALTH GROUPS

Rhode Island Project AIDS Hotline 9.30-20 h
☎ 277-6502

HELP WITH PROBLEMS

Gay Helpline 19-23 h
PO Box 56 71, Weybossett Hill Station ✉RI 02903 ☎ 751-3322

RELIGIOUS GROUPS

MCC Sun 19 h
134 Matthewson Street ✉RI 02903 *(near Washington Street)*
☎ 272-9247

USA-South Carolina

Southeast USA
Initials: SC
Time: GMT -5
Area: 82.902 km^2 / 33.906 sq mi.
Population: 3,760,000
Capital: Columbia

Hetero- as well as homosexual oral and anal intercourse is prohibited in South Carolina.

In South Carolina sind hetero- und homosexueller Oral- und Analverkehr verboten.

En Caroline du Nord, la fellation et la pénétration anale sont interdites pour tous, homos et hétéros.

En Carolina del Sur las relaciones homosexuales y heterosexuales por vía oral y anal están prohibidas.

Nel South Carolina sono vietati i rapporti anali ed orali tra eterosessuali e tra omosessuali.

Charleston ☎ 843

BARS

Dudley's (B D G N P) 16-?, Sun 14-? h
346 King Street ✉SC 29401 ☎ 723-2784

RESTAURANTS

Fannie's Diner (B F glm) open all day
137 Market Street ✉SC 29401 ☎ 723-7121
Magnolias (F g)
185 East Bay Street ✉SC 29401 ☎ 577-7771
Papillon (F g)
1 Market Street ✉SC 29401 ☎ 723-6510
Italian cuisine.
82 Queen (F g OS)
82 Queen Street ✉SC 29401 ☎ 723-7591

HOTELS

Charleston Beach B&B (AC b bf GLM H nu OS pi wh)
118 West Arctic Avenue ✉SC 29439 *(Folly Beach)* ☎ 588-9443
Close to Charleston, SC. Rate $75.
Fifty Folly Place (AC bf glm H OS)
50 Folly Road ✉SC 29407 ☎ 571-4171
Hotel with garden, 25 min from downtown. All rooms with priv. bath and WC. US$ 50-90 (bf incl.).
Mills House Hotel (g H)
Meeting Street/Queen Street ✉SC 29401 ☎ (800) 874-9600

GENERAL GROUPS

Low Country Gay and Lesbian Alliance
PO Box 98 ✉SC 29401 ☎ 577-5139

RELIGIOUS GROUPS

MCC Sun 19, Wed 20, Fri 19.30 h
4583 F Durant Avenue ✉SC 29406 ☎ 747-6736

Columbia ☎ 803

GAY INFO

In Unison
PO Box 80 24 ✉SC 29202 ☎ 771-0804
E-Mail: NUnison@aol.com

South Carolina Coalition of Lesbians and Gay Men Tue-Fri 18-22 h, Sat 14-22 h, closed Sun Mon
1108 Woodrow Street ☎ 771-7713

BARS

Art Bar (a B d glm ng)
Lady Street *(one block north of Gervais)*
Candy Shop (B D GLM) Thu-Sun 23-? h
1903 Two Notch Road ✉SC 29204
Capital Club (B GLM P)
1002 Gervais Street ✉SC 29201 ☎ 256-6464
Private gentleman's club.
Downtown (B d G MA p r S)
1109 Assembly *(previously Ikon; across from State House)*
Gay strip bar.
Tracks (B d GLM p) Lincoln Street *(between Whaley and Blossom)*
Mostly lesbian bar.

CAFES

Goatfeathers (b F glm) 17-? h
2017 Divine

DANCECLUBS

Metropolis (! B D MA P S OS YG) 22-?, Fri-Sun 21-? h, closed Mon
1800 Blanding Street ✉SC 29202 ☎ 799-8727
Large disco with three separate bars and terrace.

SEX SHOPS/BLUE MOVIES

Big Ex-Citing Emporium
4333 Fort Jackson Blvd.
☎ 738-3707
Book Exchange
39 Broad River Road ☎ 772-6728
Nicki's X-Citing Novelties
311 Broad River Road ☎ 798-1010
Video Magic & Mags
5445 Two Notch Road ☎ 786-8125

BOOK SHOPS

Moxie
631-C Hardon Street
Small gay section.

NEWS STANDS

Intermezzo Newsstand, Bookstore and Tobacconist
2015 Divine *(next to Goatfeathers)*
Small gay section.

GENERAL GROUPS

PFLAG Columbia
PO Box 1838 ✉SC 29202-1838
SC Pride Center
1108 Woodrow Street, PO Box 12648 ✉SC 29211 ☎ 771-7713
South Caralina Gay and Lesbian Business Guild
PO Box 7913 ✉SC 29202-7913
Univ. of SC Bisexual, Gay and Lesbian Association
PO Box 80098 ✉SC 29225 ☎ 777-7716

Youth Out Loud
☎ 771-7713
Help hotline.

RELIGIOUS GROUPS

Lutherans MCC Columbia
PO Box 8828 ✉SC 29202-8828
MCC Columbia
1111 Belleview Avenue ✉SC 29201
Unitarian Universalist Fellowship of Columbia
2701 Heyward Street ✉SC 29205-2523 ☎ 799-0845

CRUISING

-Rest Stop (on I-26 South)
-Lake Murray Dam
-Univ of South Carolina (Russel House, Blatte PE Center lockers, pool and Thomas Cooper Library)
-Senate Street from Capitol to Gregg Street (ayor. Very busy at night)
-Main Street

Ehrhardt ☎ 803

HOTELS

Ehrhardt Hall (B H)
PO Box 246 ✉SC 29801 ☎ 267-2020

Greenville ☎ 803

GAY INFO

Gay Switchboard
☎ 271-4207

BARS

New Attitude (B D GLM) Wed-Sun 21-2 h
706 West Washington Street ✉SC 29601 ☎ 233-1387
Stone Castle (B D GLM S VS YG) 20-4, Sat Sun 20-2 h
8 Legrande Boulevard ☎ 235-9949

Johns Island ☎ 843

RESTAURANTS

St. Johns Island Cafe (AC b bf CC F glm OS W) Mon-Sat 7-21, Sun 9.30-14 h
3140 Maybank Highway ✉SC 29455 *(between downtown Charleston and Kiawah Island)* ☎ 559-9090

Myrtle Beach ☎ 843

BARS

Underground (B G) 821
Main Street ☎ 448-5844

CRUISING

-Beach at 82nd Avenue
-Hurlock Park

Spartanburg ☎ 864

BARS

Cheyenne's Cattlemen's Club (AC B D G P S YG)
995 Ashville Highway, SC ✉SC 29303 *(Exit 72-C off I-85 towards Spartanburg)* ☎ 573-7304
Guests should call ahead for entrance arrangements.

USA-South Dakota

North USA
Initials: SD
Time: GMT -6
Area: 199.744 km² / 81,695 sq mi.
Population: 738,000
Capital: Pierre

Rapid City ☎ 605

GUEST HOUSES

Camp Michael Guesthouse (AC bf F GLM MA wh)
13051 Bogus Jim Road ✉SD 57702 ☎ 342-5590
E-Mail: michael@campmike.com
Homepage: www.campmike.com
Secluded and quiet, located in the Black Hills, 12 miles from Rapid City. Rates single: US$ 59, couple US$ 69, discounts for 3 days or longer.

Sioux Falls ☎ 605

GAY INFO

Gay Hotline and Lesbian Alliance Coalition
24 hrs
☎ 332-4599
The Office
2404 West Madison Street ✉SD 57104 ☎ 335-9546
At the Metropolitan Community Church; coffeehouse and community center.

BARS

Touche`z (AC B D f GLM lj MA s W) 20-2 h
323 South Phillips Avenue ✉SD 57102 *(entrance in rear of alley)* ☎ 335-9874

SEX SHOPS/BLUE MOVIES

Studio One Book Store
309 North Dakota Avenue ✉SD 57102 ☎ 332-9316

CRUISING

-Faywick Park 2nd Avenue & 11th Street

USA-Tennessee

Central East
Initials: TN
Time: GMT -6
Area: 109.158 km² / 44,645 sq mi.
Population: 5,368,000
Capital: Nashville
Important gay cities: Memphis, Nashville

Chatta ☎ 423

BARS

Chuck's Bar (AC B d DR f GLM LJ MA N OS S W WE) Sun-Thu 18-1 h, Fri-Sat 18-3 h
27 W. Main Street ✉TN 37408 *(Downtown)* ☎ 265-5405

GIFT & PRIDE SHOPS

Condoms etc. Rainbow Merchandise (AC CC) Sun-Thu 18-1 h, Fri-Sat 18-3 h
27 W. Main Street ✉TN 37408 ☎ 266-3668 Fax: 267-7990

Greeneville ☎ 423

HOTELS

Timberfell Lodge (AC B bf F G LJ msg NU OS pi sa wh)
Route 11, PO Box 94 A ✉TN 37743 ☎ (423) 234-0833
☎ (800) 437-0118
Located 400 km from Atlanta in the Smokey Mountains. All rooms with TV and telephone. Rates US$ 84-144. Rooms with shared and private bath.

Knoxville ☎ 423

GAY INFO

Gay/Lesbian Helpline 19-23 h
☎ 521-6546

BARS

Carousel II (B D GLM S) 21-3 h
1501 White Avenue South ✉TN 37920 ☎ 522-6966
The Electric Ball Room (AC B CC D f GLM lj MA S SNU STV YG) Wed-Sun 20-3 h
1213 Western Avenue ✉TN 37921 ☎ 525-6724 Fax: 689-2577

CRUISING

-Cumberland Avenue (around St. John's Church)
-Downtown between post office and Public Library
-Tyson Park (AYOR)

Memphis ☎ 901

BARS

Another Bar (B D G)
1351 Autumn ✉TN 38104
☎ 272-0903
Fancy's (B g)
887 South Highland ✉TN 38111 ☎ 452-9286
Jackie's (B G) 1
74 Madison Avenue ✉TN 38104
☎ 272-1104
J-Wag's Lounge (AC B CC d f GLM MA N OS r S SNU STV W) 24 hours
1268 Madison Avenue ✉TN 38104 ☎ 725-1909
Pipeline (B G LJ MA)
1382 Poplar Avenue ✉TN 38104
☎ 726-5263

SEX SHOPS/BLUE MOVIES

Airport Bookmart
2214 Brooks Road East ✉TN 38132 ☎ 345-0657
Paris Adult Theater (g)
2432 Summer ✉TN 38112
☎ 323-2665

BOOK SHOPS

Fantasy World (g)
1814 Winchester Road ✉TN 38116
☎ 346-2086

LEATHER & FETISH SHOPS

Men of Leather at J-Wag's Mon-Thu 12-23, Fri Sat 13-1 h
1268 Madison Avenue ✉TN 38104

HEALTH GROUPS

Memphis Center for Reproductive Health
1462 Poplar Avenue ✉TN 38104 ☎ 274-3550

RELIGIOUS GROUPS

MCC Memphis
PO Box 24 15 92 ✉TN 38124
☎ 324-1769

Nashville ☎ 615

GAY INFO

Nashville Gay and Lesbian Community Center 18-21 h, Infoline daily 17-22 h.
703 Berry Road ✉TN 37204 ☎ 297-0008
Homepage: www.nashcenter.org
The Center is the place to go for information regarding the Nashville gay community. The Center Library has more than 500 books.
Nashville GayWeb
Homepage: www.nashvillegayweb.com
Query
c/o Pyramid Publishing ✉TN 37202-4241 ☎ 259-4135
Published weekly.

BARS

The Chute Complex (B D F G MA)
2535 Franklin Road ✉TN 37204 *(attached to The Nashville Eagle)*
☎ 297-4571
The Gas Lite Lounge (AC B CC f GLM MA N s) 16.30-3 h
167 1/2 8th Avenue North ✉TN 37203 ☎ 254-1278
Piano bar.
The Jungle (AC B CC d F glm MA r SNU STV VS W) 11-3 h
306 4th Avenue South ✉TN 37201 ☎ 256-9411
Cruisy atmosphere
The Nashville Eagle (B G LJ MA)
2535 Franklin Road *(attached to The Chute)* ☎ 297-4571
Your Way Cafe and Bar (B G N)
515 2nd Avenue South ✉TN 37210 ☎ 256-9411

DANCECLUBS

The Connection (! B D GLM MA)
901 Cowan Street ☎ 742-1166
Nashville's largest bar and danceclub.

RESTAURANTS

Julian's Eatery (B F GLM MA) Wed-Sun 20-24 h
901 Cowan Street *(at Connections)* ☎ 742-1166
Nouvelle American cuisine
Town House Restaurant (AC B bf CC F glm) Mon-Fri 8-14.30 h
165 8th Avenue North ✉TN 37203 *(at Savage House Inn)*
☎ 254-1277
Southern-style cuisine

World's End (B F glm YG) 16-2 h
1713 Church Street ✉TN 37203 *(near Vanderbilt University)*
☎ 329-3480
American cuisine

SEX SHOPS/BLUE MOVIES

Metro News 0-24 h
822 5th Avenue South ☎ 256-1310
Calls itself „the worlds largest adult bookstore".

BOOK SHOPS

OUTLOUD! Books & Gifts (CC GLM) Mon-Thu 10-22h, Fri-Sat -23 h, Sun 11-22 h
1709 Church Street ✉TN 37203 *(Between 17th & 18th street)*
☎ 340-0034 Fax: 320-3285

GUEST HOUSES

The Savage House Inn (AC bf CC glm H)
165 8th Avenue North ✉TN 37203 ☎ 244-2229
Small B&B located in the oldest house in downtown Nashville. All rooms are furnished with antiques. Rooms have telephone, TV and some have private baths. Rates US$ 65-75, special rates for extended stays available. Conference facilities.

GENERAL GROUPS

Girth and Mirth
PO Box 121886 ✉TN 37212
Southeastern Gay Rodeo Association Meets 2nd Sun 17 h at The Chute
☎ 226-7124
Tennessee Vals Meets 2nd Sat 19 h
PO Box 92335 ✉TN 37209 ☎ 664-6883
Homepage: www.transgender.org
Group for crossdressers, transvestites and transgendered people.

FETISH GROUPS

Conductors L/L (G)
PO Box 40261 ✉TN 37204-0261
onthly meetings at The Eagle, The Chute Complex, Nashville every 2nd Fri at 22.30 h.

HEALTH GROUPS

Nashville CARES
209 Tenth Avenue South, Suite 160 ☎ 845-4266
AIDS information and support.

HELP WITH PROBLEMS

Gay and Lesbian AA Wed 6.30-7.30 h
St. Ann's Episcopal, 5th and Woodland ☎ 298-1050

RELIGIOUS GROUPS

Affirmation
☎ 254-7628 *Gay and lesbian United Methodists*
Integrity
☎ 333-7509 *Gay and lesbian Episcopalians*
MCC
PO Box 121172 ✉TN 37212 ☎ 874-9636

Rogersville ☎ 423

HOTELS

Lee Valley Farm (CC F GLM MA NU pi wh)
142 Drinnon Lane ✉TN 37857 ☎ 272-4068
E-Mail: eesfarm@usit.net
Cabins and campgrounds. Rates from US$ 50 (single) to 125 (couple). Sports activities incl. riding, hiking, fishing, etc.

USA-Texas

South USA
Initials: TX
Time: GMT -6
Area: 695.676 km² / 284,531 sq mi.
Population: 19,439,000
Capital: Austin
Important gay cities: Austin, Dallas, Houston, San Antonio

Amarillo

CRUISING

-Rest Stop (on I-40, 20 miles east)
-Amarillo College (biology building and business building)
-Elwood Park
-The bushes (Eakle Park, Polk and 29th Street)

Austin ☎ 512

GAY INFO

Fag Rag
PO Box 10 34 ✉TX 78767 ☎ 416-0100 Fax: 416-6981
E-Mail: PhagRag@aol.com
Gay Hotline 0-24 h
☎ 472-4357

BARS

Bout Time (B G MA) 7-2 h
9601 Interstate 35 North
☎ 832-5339
Cedar Street (B GLM MA OS) 16-2 h
208 West 4th Street ☎ 708-8811
Outdoor jazz club.
Chain Drive (B G LJ MA) 14-2 h
504 Willow Street ✉TX 78701 ☎ 480-9017
Edge. The (B GLM MA N) -2 h
213 West 4th Street *(next to Oilcan Harry's)* ☎ 480-8686
Forum. The (AC B CC D G MA OS SNU STV VS W WE YG) Sun-Thu 14-2, Fri-Sat -4 h
408 Congress Avenue ✉TX 78701 ☎ 476-2900
Naked Grape. The (B d GLM OS YG) 10-2 h
611 Red River Street ✉TX 78701 ☎ 476-3611
Very cruisy.
Splash (B G OS S SNU VS)
406 Barzos ☎ 477-6969

CAFES

Carrusso's Cafe (b bf f glm MA)
307 West 5th Street ☎ 457-0722

DANCECLUBS

Charlie's (AC B CC D G MA OS S SNU STV W) 14-2 h
1301 Lavaca Avenue/13th Street ✉TX 78701 ☎ 474-6481
Oil Can Harry's (AC B D G MA S OS VS YG) 14-2, Fri-Sat -4 h
211 West 4th Street ✉TX 78701 *(near Guy Town)* ☎ 320-8823
Popular especially after 23 h.
Rainbow Cattle Company (B D GLM MA) 14-2 h
305 West 5th Street ☎ 474-9800
Western bar.

RESTAURANTS

Eastside Cafe (B f glm) 11-22 h
2113 Manor Road ✉TX 78722 ☎ 476-5858
Manuel's (A AC B CC F glm MA WE) 11-22.30, Sun brunch 12-15 h
310 Congress Avenue ✉TX 78701 ☎ 472-7555/4442
Mexican cuisine

SHOWS

Esther's Follies (b D GLM S STV) Shows Thu 20, Fri-Sat 20 22 h
525 East 6th Street ☎ 320-0553

SEX SHOPS/BLUE MOVIES

Pleasure Shop (g VS) 0-24 h
603 West Oltorf/South 1st Street ✉TX 78704 ☎ 447-1101
Adult videos
Tapelenders (GLM VS) 9-24, Sun 11-24 h
1114 West 5th Street #201 ✉TX 78703

SAUNAS/BATHS

Midtowne Spa (b CC DR G MA sa sb VS wh WO) 0-24 h
2509 Pacific Avenue ☎ 302-9696

FITNESSTUDIOS

World Gym (G WO)
115 East 6th Street ☎ 479-0044 *Cruisy atmosphere.*

BOOK SHOPS

BookPeople (glm)
6th Street at Lamar Street ☎ 441-9757
Large selection of gay and lesbian books.

GUEST HOUSES

Carrington's Bluff (AC bf CC E glm H MA)
1900 David Street ✉TX 78705 ☎ 479-0638 Fax: 476-4769
E-Mail: governorsinn@earthlink.net
Homepage: http://www.citysearch.co,/aus/carringtonbluff
B&B in central location. All rooms with private bath, TV, radio and hair-dryer.
Citiview B&B and Spa (bf glm H OS pi wh) 1
405 East Riverside Drive ✉TX 78741 ☎ 441-2606
☎ (800) 278-8439 (Toll-free) Fax: 441-2949
Homepage: http://www.hyperweb.com/cityview
Small B&B in a Frank Lloyd Wright-style home. All rooms with TV, stereo and private bath.
Governor's Inn (AC bf CC E glm H) 611
West 22nd Street ✉TX 78705 ☎ 871-8908 Fax: 476-4769
E-Mail: governorsinn@earthlink.net
Homepage: http://www.citysearch.com/aus/carringtonbluff
B&B in nice old mansion. All rooms with private bath, TV, phone, radio and hair-dryer.
Summit House B&B. The (AC bf F GLM H LJ MA msg OS)
1204 Summit Street ✉TX 78741-1158 ☎ 445-5304
E-Mail: summit@texas.net
Homepage: http://www.summit.home.texas.net
Small B&B located on an old Indian campground just two blocks from the Colorado river. Rooms with private and shared baths, one studio with kitchenette.

HEALTH GROUPS

AIDS Services of Austin
☎ 451-2273

RELIGIOUS GROUPS

Affirmation
7403 Shoal Creek Boulevard ✉TX 78757
☎ 451-2329
GLB Methodists.
MCC Austin
5 Woodward Street ✉TX 78704 ☎ 416-1170
Mishpachat Am Echad
PO Box 9591 ✉TX 78766
☎ 451-7018
Jewish gays and lesbians.

SPECIAL INTEREST GROUPS

Gay & Lesbian Student Association
PO Box 275 ✉TX 78713 ☎ 471-4387

SWIMMING

-Hippie Hollow (AYOR G NU) (Highway 2222 west to #620, turn left to the Mansfield Dam and follow the signs. You reach the gay area over the rocks east of the parking lot)

CRUISING

-Pease Park (along Lamar Boulevard near West 15th from 22 h)

Bryan ☎ 409

BARS

Club. The (B CC D GLM MA N STV) Tue-Sat 21-2 h
308 North Bryan Avenue ✉TX 77803 *(in Bryan/College Station)*
☎ 823-6767

Corpus Christi ☎ 512

BARS

Hidden Door (B G lj) 11-2, Sun 12-2 h
802 South Staples Street ✉TX 78404 ☎ 882-0183

CRUISING

-Seawall (AYOR)

Dallas ☎ 214

GAY INFO

Dallas Voice
3000 Carlisle, Suite 200 ✉TX 75204 ☎ 754-8710
Weekly publication.
Gay and Lesbian Community Center Mon-Fri 10-18, Sat 12-18 h
2701 Reagan Street ✉TX 75219 ☎ 528-9254
This Week in Texas
3300 Regan Street ✉TX 75219
☎ 521-0622 Fax: 520-8948
Contents news, health, calendar, classified ads, guide. Published weekly.

TOURIST INFO

Dallas Convention & Visitor Bureau
1201 Elm Street, Suite 2000 ✉TX 75270 ☎ 746-6677
Fax: 746-6688

BARS

Anchor Inn (B G MA R S SNU VS YG) 18-? h
4024 Cedar Springs Road ✉TX 75219 ☎ 528-4098
Big Daddy's (B G MA S VS) Wed-Sat 18-? h
4024 Cedar Springs Road ✉TX 75219 ☎ 528-4098
Brick. The (AC B CC D LJ MA N W) 12-2, Fri-Sat -4 h
4117 Maple Street ✉TX 75219 ☎ 521-3154
Dallas Eagle (B G LJ) 16-2 h, Sat after hours
2515 Inwood Street, #107 ✉TX 75235 *(rear entrance)*
☎ 357-4375

Fraternity House. The (B D G MA S SNU)
2525 Wycliff #120 ☎ 520-1415
Theme nights.
JR's Bar and Grill (AC B f GLM MA s YG) 11-2 h
3923 Cedar Springs Road ✉TX 75219 *(at Throckmorton)*
☎ 528-1004
Moby Dicks (AC B CC GLM OS VS YG) 12-2 h
4011 Cedar Springs Road ✉TX 75219 ☎ 520-6629
Numbers (B G S) 12-? h
4024 Cedar Springs Road ✉TX 75219 ☎ 526-4098
Pub Pegasus (B G N W) Mon-Fri 10-2, Sat 8-2, Sun 12-2 h
3326 North Fitzhugh Road ✉TX 75204 ☎ 559-4663
Side 2 Bar (B GLM N W) 10-2 h
2615 Oaklawn Avenue ✉TX 75219 ☎ 528-2026
Throckmorton Mining Company (AC B G LJ MA) 13-2 h
3014 Throckmorton Street ✉TX 75219 *(near Cedar Springs Road)*
☎ 521-4205
Western style bar.
Zippers (B G lj N S SNU) 12-2 h
3333 North Fitzhugh Road ✉TX 75204 ☎ 526-9519

DANCECLUBS

Boxx Office/La Mariposa (B D G MA SNU)
2515 North Fitzhugh ☎ 828-2665
Crews Inn (B D G lj OS S W YG) 12-2 h
3215 North Fitzhugh Avenue ✉TX 75204 ☎ 524-9510
Round-Up Saloon (B D G LJ W) 13-2 h
3912-14 Cedar Springs Road ✉TX 75219 ☎ 522-9611
Western style bar and danceclub.
Village Station (B D G lj MA OS SNU VS W YG) 21-3, Sun 20-3 h
3911 Cedar Springs Road ✉TX 75219 ☎ 215/526-7171

RESTAURANTS

Hunky's (B F glm)
4000 Cedar Springs Road ✉TX 75219 ☎ 522-1212

SEX SHOPS/BLUE MOVIES

Alternatives (G VS)
1720 W. Mockingbird Lane ☎ 630-7071
Tapelenders (GLM VS) 9-24, Sun 11-24 h
3926 Cedar Springs Road ✉TX 78219 ☎ 528-6344

SAUNAS/BATHS

Club Body Center Dallas (b G sa sb VS wh WO) 0-24 h
2616 Swiss Avenue ✉TX 75204 ☎ 821-1990
Midtowne Spa (AC CC DR f G MA NU P S sa sb VS wh WO) 0-24 h
2509 Pacific Avenue ✉TX 75226 ☎ 821-8989

BOOK SHOPS

Crossroads Market Bookstore & Cafe (AC CC f GLM MA SWC W) 7-24 h
3930 Cedar Springs Road ✉TX 75219 ☎ 521-8919

LEATHER & FETISH SHOPS

Shades of Grey Leather (CC W) Mon-Thu 11-20, Fri Sat -22, Sun 12-18 h
3930-A Cedar Springs Road ✉TX 75219-3518 ☎ 521-4739
Leather/Fetish/SM-shop. Men and women.

GUEST HOUSES

Courtyard on the Trail (AC bf glm H NU OS pi)
8045 Forest Trail ✉TX 75238 ☎ 553-9700
Comfortable small B&B 6 miles from the city centre. Rooms with private baths, modem line, color cable TV and VCR. Private garden and sundeck. No kids and no pets.
Inn on Fairmont (bf CC GLM H OS W wh)
3701 Fairmount ✉TX 75219 ☎ 522-2800 Fax: 522-2898
Nicely furnished Bed & Breakfast in the heart of the Oak Lawn/Turtle Creek area close to clubs and bars. Seven bedrooms with private baths, and TV.
Symphony House (CC G H pi wh)
6327 Symphony Lane ✉TX 75227 ☎ 388-9134
E-Mail: SymphonyHouse@webtv.net
Room for up to ten people in four bedrooms; 2 bathrooms; 2 living areas, kitchen.

GENERAL GROUPS

Couples-Metro-Dallas
PO Box 803156 ✉TX 75380 ☎ 504-6775
Support group for gay and lesbian couples.
Men of All Colors Together
PO Box 190611 ✉TX 75219 ☎ 521-4765

HEALTH GROUPS

AIDS Information Line 9-21 h
☎ 559-2437

RELIGIOUS GROUPS

Beth El Binah
PO Box 191188 ✉TX 75219 ☎ 497-1591
GLB Jews.
Cathedral of Hope MCC Sun 9, 11, 18.30, Wed Sat 18.30 h
5910 Cedar Springs Road ☎ 351-1901 Fax: 351-6099
E-Mail: CoHNews@aol.com
Dignity
PO Box 190133 ✉TX 75219 ☎ 521-5342 ext. 832
GLB Catholics
Integrity
PO Box 190351 ✉TX 75219 ☎ 520-0912
GLB Episcopalians.

CRUISING

-Bachman Lake
-Cedar Springs Road (between Oaklawn & Dallas North Toll Road)
-Eastfield College (at night)
-Film World & Kit Kat Book Sore (Industrial Boulevard)
-Greyhound Bus Depot
-"Homo Heights" (Oakland and Lemmon Avenues)
-Kiest Park (best on Sun)
-Lee Park (AYOR)
-Mid Continent Truck Stop (on Big Town Boulevard off I-20,east of I-30)
-News Stand Adult Book Store on Cedar Springs Road
-Paris Book I & II (AYOR) (Harry Hines Boulevard)
-Red Lottor Nows (AYOR) (Harry Hincs Boulevard)
-Reverchon Park (AYOR) (trails and trees)
-S.M.U. Main Library (1st & 2nd floor)
-Tower Bay Park (Lake Lewisville)
-Town East Mall (Sears)
-White Rock Lake (AYOR)
-Cedar Springs Road (AYOR) (south of to Maple Street, between Regan and Knight Streets)

El Paso ☎ 915

BARS

Apartment (B G)
804 Myrtle Avenue ✉TX 79901 *(near Virginia Avenue)*
San Antonio Mining Co. (B GLM OS) 15-2 h
800 East San Antonio Avenue ✉TX 79901 ☎ 533-9516
Whatever Lounge. The (B G MA R) 14-2 h
701 E. Paisano Drive ✉TX 79901 ☎ 533-0215

DANCECLUBS

New Old Plantation (B D GLM MA S VS YG) 21-2, Fri Sat 21-4 h, closed Mon Tue
301 South Ochoa Street ✉TX 79901 ☎ 533-6055

HEALTH GROUPS

Southwest AIDS Committe Mon-Fri 8.30-17 h
1505 Mescalero Drive ✉TX 79925-2048 ☎ 772-3366
Fax: 772-3494
Tillman Health Centre
222 South Campell ✉TX 79901 ☎ 543-3560

HELP WITH PROBLEMS

AIDS Information Line
☎ 543-3574 (English)
☎ 543-3575 (Spanish)

CRUISING

-Rest stop-20 miles on I-10 (AYOR) (tourists and truckers)
-Dyer Street (AYOR R) (after dark, weekends)
-McKelligon Canyon (off Alabama, near Beaumont Hospital)

Fort Worth ☎ 817

BARS

Across the Street (B D G) 20-2 h
659 South Jennings Avenue ✉TX 76104 ☎ 332-0192
Magnolia Station (B G MA S) Wed-Sun 20-? h
600 West Magnolia Avenue ✉TX 76104 ☎ 332-0415
651 (B D G lj W) 12-2 h
651 South Jennings Avenue ✉TX 76104 ☎ 332-0745
Western style bar.

CRUISING

-Rest Stop (on I-35 South)
-Benbrook Lake (AYOR) (off US 377, southwest of town)
-Forest Park (picnic area)
-Rockwood Park (days)
-T.C.U. (Burnett Library)

Galveston ☎ 409

BARS

Cocktail Lounge (AC B d f Glm lj MA N OS R S STV) 8-2, Sun 12-2 h
2501 Rosenburg ✉TX 77550 ☎ 765-9092
Drag shows on week-ends.
Evolution (B D glm)
2214 Ships Mechanic Road ✉TX 77550 ☎ 763-4212
Kon Tiki (B D glm SNU VS) 16-2 h
315 23rd Street ✉TX 77550 ☎ 763-6264
Robert's Lafitte (AC B d f GLM lj MA N OS r s STV) 22-2, Sun 12-2 h
2501 Avenue Q ✉TX 77550 ☎ 765-9092

SWIMMING

-Stewart Beach

Gun Barrel City ☎ 903

BARS

Friends (AC B CC d f GLM MA N OS P S STV W) Mon-Fri 16-24, Sat 15-1, Sun 15-24 h
602 South Gun Barrel Lane ✉TX 75147 *(on highway 198, next to the Wagon Wheel Reastaurant)* ☎ 887-2061

Houston ☎ 713

GAY INFO

Gay & Lesbian Switchboard 15-24 h
☎ 529-3211
Houston Voice. The Mon-Fri 9-18 h, closed Sat Sun
500 Lovett Boulevard, Suite 500 ✉TX 77006 ☎ 529-8490
Fax: 529-9531
Weekly gay and lesbian newspaper.
Houston's Gay and Lesbian Yellow Pages
PO Box 660 45 ✉TX 77266 ☎ 942-0084
This Week in Texas-Twit
811 Westheimer Road, #111 ✉TX 77006 ☎ 527-9111
Fax: 527-8948
Weekly free gay and lesbian news magazine. Available at most gay venues.

TOURIST INFO

Greater Houston Convention & Visitor Bureau
801 Congress ✉TX 77002 ☎ 227-3100 Fax: 227-1408

BARS

Briar Patch (B G N) 14-2 h
2294 W. Holcombe ✉TX 77030 ☎ 665-9678
Chances (B GLM MA N)
1100 Westheimer ☎ 523-7217
Cousins (B G S) Fri Sat shows
817 Fairview/Converse Street ✉TX 77006 ☎ 528-9204
E.J.'s (AC B d f GLM lj MA N OS SNU STV W) 7-2 h
2517 Ralph Street ✉TX 77006 ☎ 527-9071
JR's Bar & Grill (A AC B CC GLM MA N S SNU VS WO) 12-2 h
808 Pacific Avenue ✉TX 77006 *(near downtown)* ☎ 521-2519
Very popular and cruisy.
Lazy J (B G MA)
312 East Tuam Street ✉TX 77006 ☎ 528-9343
Lola's (B glm N YG)
2327 Grant Street ✉TX 77006 ☎ 528-8342
Mary's (B G LJ MA OS) Fri Sat -2 h
1022 Westheimer Road ✉TX 77006 ☎ 527-9669
Cruisy atmosphere.
Montrose Mining Co. (AC B CC G LJ MA N OS S SNU WO) Mon-Fri 16-2, Sat Sun 13-2 h
805 Pacific Avenue ✉TX 77006 *(near downtown)* ☎ 529-7488
Very popular.
Pacific Street (AC B D G LJ MA) 21-2 h
710 Pacific Street ✉TX 77006 ☎ 523-0213
Q.T.'s (B G N YG) Mon-Sat 8-2, Sun 12-2 h
608 Westheimer Street ✉TX 77006 ☎ 529-8813
Ripcord (B G LJ MG OS r T) Sun-Thu 13-2, Fri-Sat -4 h
715 Fairview ✉TX 77006 ☎ 521-2792
Sante Fe Bar and Patio (A AC B CC GLM MA N S SNU VS WO) 12-2 h
804 Pacific Avenue ✉TX 77006 *(near downtown)* ☎ 521-2519
Video and party bar.

Venture-N (AC B CC d DR G LJ MG N OS R S SNU STV W) 12-2 h
2923 South Main Street ✉TX 77002 *(neat downtown)*
☎ 522-0000
611 Hyde Park Pub (AC B CC f G lj MA N OS r SNU W) Mon-Sat 7-2, Sun 12-2 h
611 Hyde Park Boulevard/Stanford Street ✉TX 77006
☎ 526-7070

CAFES

Barnaby's Cafe (B F glm) 11-22, Fri Sat -23 h
604 Fairview/Standford ☎ 522-0106
Charlie's (B F glm MA)
1102 Westheimer ✉TX 77006 ☎ 522-3332

DANCECLUBS

Brazo's River Bottom (B D Glm lj)
2400 Brazos Street ✉TX 77706
Numbers (B D glm YG)
300 Westheimer *(between Montrose and downtown)*
☎ 526-6551
Picasso (B D GLM MA S SNU VS) closed Mon
2151 Richmond Avenue *(in Shepherd Plaza)* ☎ 520-8636
Rich's (B D G YG)
2401 San Jacinto Street ✉TX 77002 ☎ 759-9606
South Beach (AC B CC D E GLM MA S SNU STV VS WO YG) Wed-Sat 21-3, Sun 20-3 h
810 Pacific Avenue ✉TX 77006 ☎ 521-9123
Most popular disco in town.

RESTAURANTS

Baba Yega's (B CC F glm MA) 10-22 h
2607 Grant Street ✉TX 77006 ☎ 522-0042
Chapultepec (B F glm)
813 Richmond Avenue ✉TX 77006 ☎ 522-2365
Mexican food.
Magnolia Bar & Grill (b F glm)
6000 Richmond Avenue ☎ 781-6207
Cajun food.
Sierra (B F glm MA)
4704 Montrose ☎ 942-7757
Trendy restaurant serving delicious food.

SEX SHOPS/BLUE MOVIES

French Quarter (G P VS)
3201 Louisiana Street ✉TX 77006 ☎ 527-0782

SAUNAS/BATHS

Club Houston (b G sa sb P pi VS wh) 0-24 h
2205 Fannin Street ✉TX 77002 ☎ 659-4998
Midtowne Spa (b G sa sb P pi wh) 0-24 h
3100 Fannin Street ✉TX 77004 ☎ 522-2379

BOOK SHOPS

Crossroads Market Bookstore & Cafe (AC CC f GLM MA W) 7-24 h
1111 Westheimer Road ✉TX 77006 ☎ 942-0147
Inklings-an alternative bookshop (AC CC GLM MA) Tue-Sat 10.30-18.30, Sun 12-17 h, closed Mon
1846 Richmond Avenue ✉TX 77098 ☎ 521-3369
Books, music and information.

LEATHER & FETISH SHOPS

Leather by Boots (G LJ) 12-20 h
711 Fairview ✉TX 77006 ☎ 526-6940
at the Ripcord Sat Sun 15-2 h ☎ 526-0444.

GUEST HOUSES

Lovett Inn. The (AC bf CC GLM H MA pi W wh) Office: 10-20 h
501 Lovett Boulevard ✉TX 77006 *(near downtown)*
☎ 522-5224 Fax: 528-6708 E-Mail: lovettinn@aol.co
Homepage: www.lovettinn.com
Rooms with private bath, TV, radio, balcony and coffee/tea, some rooms with bar, jacuzzi and VCR. Located in a 1920s Southern home. Prices range US$ 75-200.
Montrose Inn (AC bf CC G H) Office 9-22 h
408 Avondale ✉TX 77006 *(close to gay bars)* ☎ 520-0206
☎ (800) 357-1228 (Toll-free)
Centrally located in the gay bar district. 7 double rooms, partly with shared bath.

GENERAL GROUPS

Houston Gay and Lesbian Political Caucus
Meeting 1st Wed 19 h at Houston Lesbian and Gay Community Center
PO Box 666 64 ✉TX 77266-6664 ☎ 521-1000 Fax: 861-8208
E-Mail: hglpc@neosoft.com

HEALTH GROUPS

Aid for AIDS
PO Box 664 14 ✉TX 77266 ☎ 526-6077
AIDS Hotline 9-21 h
☎ 524-2437

RELIGIOUS GROUPS

Dignity Sat 19.30, Sun 17.30 h
PO Box 66821 ✉TX 77266-6821 ☎ 880-2872
Catholic gays and lesbians.
Lutherans Concerned
2515 Waugh Drive ☎ 528-3269
Unitarian/Universalists for Lesbian and Gay Concerns
5200 Fannin Street ✉TX 77004 ☎ 526-5200

SPECIAL INTEREST GROUPS

Lone Star Nudists (G)
PO Box 66621 ✉TX 77266
☎ 866-8847 (24 h) E-Mail: Biearthguy@hotmail.com

SPORT GROUPS

Houston Outdoor Group (GLM)
PO Box 980893 ✉TX 77098 ☎ 526-7688

CRUISING

-Bayland Park (on Bissonet)
-Corner of Michigan and Yupon „Club Luscene"
-Galleria Mall/Skating Rink (AYOR)
-Golden Star Theatre (r) (912 Prairie Street, 24 hours)
-Memorial Park and adjacent pathway (AYOR)
-Rest Stop (15 E. on I-10)
-Rest Stop (on I-10 / Columbia)
-Rice U (Memorial Center & Library)
-University of Houston (library, 2nd floor & all A.A. Hall)
-Vicinity of both bus depots
-Westheimer (Montrose)
-Y.M.C.A.

Lubbock ☎ 806

DANCECLUBS

Metro (B D GLM) 19-2 h
1806 Clovis Road ☎ 740-0006

GENERAL GROUPS

Lubbock Lesbian/Gay Alliance 2nd Wed 19.30 h
PO Box 64746 ✉TX 79464 ☎ 766-7184

San Antonio ☎ 210

BARS

Annex (B G LJ MA OS)
330 San Pedro Avenue ✉TX 78212 ☎ 223-6957
Eagle Mountain Saloon (B GLM MA OS)
1902 McCullough Avenue ☎ 733-1516
Mick's Hideaway (B GLM MA N) 15-2 h
5307 Mc Cullough Avenue ✉TX 78212 ☎ 828-4222
Pegasus (B D G MA OS SNU)
1402 North Main Avenue at Laurel ☎ 299-4222
Cruisy atmosphere.
Rebar (B G LJ MA u)
826 San Pedro at Laurel *(upstairs at Woody's)* ☎ 271 9633
Cruising bar.
Silver Dollar Saloon (AC B G MA s OS VS) 14-2 h
1418 North Main Avenue ✉TX 78212 ☎ 227-2623
Sparks (AC B D G MA SNU VS) 12-2 h
8011 Webbels ✉TX 75218 ☎ 653-9941
Woody's (B G LJ MA)
826 San Pedro at Laurel ☎ 271-9633
2015 (B D G N SNU)
2015 San Pedro Avenue ✉TX 78212 ☎ 733-3365

DANCECLUBS

Bonham Exchange (AC B CC D GLM MA SNU) Mon-Tue Thu 16-2, Wed -3, Fri -4, Sat 20-4, closed Sun
411 Bonham Street ✉TX 78205 ☎ 271-3811
Multi-level dance club hosting up to 2000 people.
Saint (B D GLM STV YG) Sun-Thu 22-2, Fri Sat -4 h
1430 North Main Avenue ✉TX 78212 ☎ 225-7330

SEX SHOPS/BLUE MOVIES

Apollo News (glm)
2376 Austin Highway ☎ 653-3538
Adult bookshop.
Encore Video (glm VS)
1031 North East Loop 410 ☎ 821-5345

SAUNAS/BATHS

Executive Spa (b G MA sa WO) 0-24 h
1121 Basse Road ✉TX 78215 ☎ 732-4433

DECORATION

San Angel Folk Art Gallery (A AC CC GLM W YG) 11-18 h
110 Blue Star ✉TX 78204 *(Blue Star Art Compley)* ☎ 226-6688
Mexican and latin folk art gallery. Owner & staff very friendly, helpful & informative. Good place to tap into gay community.

GUEST HOUSES

Adam House B&B (bf glm H)
231 Adams Street ☎ 224-4791
Small B&B in 1900s home. All rooms with cable TV and private bath. No smoking.
Painted Lady Inn on Broadway. The (AC bf CC E GLM H MA msg OS wh)
620 Broadway ✉TX 78215 *(downtown close to convention center Alamo)* ☎ 220-1092 Fax: 299-4185
E-Mail: travel2sa@earthlink.net
Homepage: http://www.bestinns.net/usa/tx/paintedlady.html
All rooms and suites with private bath, TV/VCR, radio, some with kitchenette.
San Antonio Bed & Breakfast (bf GLM H wh)
510 East Guenther ✉TX 78210 ☎ 222-1828
Small B&B in a 1980s home. Rooms with private bath. Rates USD 89-100 incl. bf.

HELP WITH PROBLEMS

Crisis Hotline 0-24 h
☎ 227-4357

RELIGIOUS GROUPS

Dignity Sun 17.30 h
St. Anne's Street and Ashby Place *(at St. Anne's Convent)*
☎ 558-3287
Gay and lesbian christian group.

South Padre Island ☎ 956

HOTELS

New Upper Deck. The (AC bf CC GLM H MA NU P pi VS wh WO)
120 East Atol Street, PO Box 2309 ✉TX 78597 *(1/2 block to gay beach)* ☎ 761-5953 Fax: 761-4288
E-Mail: spiup@aol.com Homepage: www.NewUpperDeck.com
Hotel in resort area with nude beach, kitchen and laundry facilities, TV lounges. All rooms with priv. bath, TV, VCR and balcony. Nautical locker room. Pirices range US$ 55-120 (without tax)

USA-Utah

West USA
Initials: UT
Time: GMT -7
Area: 219.902 km² / 89,940 sq mi.
Population: 2,059,000
Capital: Salt Lake City

● Hetero- as well as homosexual oral and anal intercourse is prohibited in Utah.

✱ In Utah ist hetero- und homosexueller Oral- und Analverkehr verboten.

▲ Dans l'Utha, la fellation et la pénétration anale sont interdites pour tous, homos et hétéros.

☆ En Utah las relaciones homosexuales y heterosexuales por vía oral y anal están prohibidas.

❖ Nell'Utah sono vietati i rapporti anali ed orali tra eterosessuali e tra omosessuali.

Escalante ☎ 435

GUEST HOUSES

Rainbow Country B&B and Tours (AC bf CC glm H wh)
586 E. 300 Street, PO Box 333 ✉UT 84726
☎ 826-4567 or ☎ (800) 252-8824 (toll-free).
Email rainbow@color-country.net *Rates on request.*

Ogden ☎ 801

BARS

Brass Rail (B G MA) 15-1 h
103 27th Street ✉UT 84401 ☎ 399-1374

Salt Lake City ☎ 801

GAY INFO

Concerning Gays and Lesbian - Radio (GLM) Wed 12.30-13 h
208 West 800 South ✉UT 84101 *KRCL 91.1 FM* ☎ 363-1818
Gay Helpline 24 hrs
☎ 533-0927

BARS

Bricks (AC B D g MA OS P S STV VS YG) Tue-Sat 21.30-2 h
579 West 200 South ✉UT 84101 ☎ 328-0255
Private club.
Inbetween (B D G OS)
579 West 200 South Street ✉UT 84101 ☎ 328-3392
Sun. The (B D f glm P S OS YG) 12-? h
702 West 200 South Street ✉UT 81104 ☎ 531-0833
Private members club.
Trapp. The (AC B CC D f GLM LJ MA OS P s VS W YG)
102 South 600 West ✉UT 84101 ☎ 531-8727
Country/Western music & dancing.

CAFES

Coffee Garden. The 7-22 h
898 East 900 Street ✉UT 84104 *(northwest corner of 9th & 9th)* ☎ 355-3425

DANCECLUBS

Club Vortex (B D glm P)
#32 Exchange Place ✉UT 84111 *(downtown)* ☎ 521-9292
Gay owned and operated. Salt Lake's hottest dance club. Private club.

SEX SHOPS/BLUE MOVIES

Hyatt's Magazine Store (AC CC glm MA VS) Mon-Sat 8-24, Sun 8-23 h
1350 South State ✉UT 84115 ☎ 486-9925
Gay and lesbian magazines and videos.
Video One (GLM)
484 South 900 West ✉UT 84101 ☎ 539-0300

GENERAL GROUPS

Gay & Lesbian Community Council of Utah
Utah Stonewall Center ✉UT 84101 ☎ 363-3002
Outreach 3rd Mon every month
☎ 978-2690 *(Cathy). Education and community relations.*
Utah Stonewall Center Mon-Fri 8-22 h
361 North 300 West ✉UT 84101-2603 ☎ 539-8800
Includes library with over 3,000 circulating items. Many different organizations meet here. Call for details. Also includes a coffee-shop.

HEALTH GROUPS

People With AIDS Coalition of Utah
1390 South 1100 East # 107 ✉UT 84105 ☎ 484-2205
Utah AIDS Foundation
1408 South 1100 East ✉UT 84105 ☎ 487-2100 (Information hotline) ☎ 1-800-FON-AIDS

SPECIAL INTEREST GROUPS

Lesbian & Gay Chorus of Salt Lake City
☎ 536-6040

SPORT GROUPS

Out Outdoors Club 2nd & 4th Tue 19-20 h
Utah Stonewall Center ✉UT 84101 ☎ 487-9348 *(Karen)*
Planned outdoor activities for Lesbians and Gays.

CRUISING

-Liberty Park
-Memory Grove Park
-South Main (and surrounding area, evenings)
-Vicinity of Greyhound Bus Depot

USA-Vermont

Northeast USA
Initials: VT
Time: GMT -5
Area: 24.903 km^2 / 10,185 sq mi.
Population: 589,000
Capital: Montpelier

Brattleboro ☎ 802

BARS

Rainbow Cattle Co. (AC B D GLM MA N) Wed-Sun 20-1 h
Route 5, East Dummerston ✉VT 05301 ☎ 254-9830

HOTELS

Mapleton Farms (bf G H)
RD 2, PO Box 510, Putney ✉VT 05346 ☎ 257-5252
Convenient to gay swimming area, skiing. Restored 1803 farmhouse with spacious rooms, priv. and shared baths. Full country bf.

Burlington ☎ 802

BARS

135 Pearl (AC B D GLM lj MA N s) 19.30-2, Fri Sun 17-2, Sat 17-1, dancing Thu-Sat 22-3 h
135 Pearl Street ✉VT 05401 *(at the north end of Church Street)* ☎ 863-2343

HOTELS

Black Bear Inn (b bf CC F glm H OS)
4010 Bolton Access Road ✉VT 05477 *(half an hour from Burlington)* ☎ 434-2126 Fax: 434-5161
Mountaintop country inn nestled in the heart of Vermont's Green Mountains. For nature and sport lovers.
Howden Cottage (bf f glm H)
32 North Champlain Street ✉VT 05401 ☎ 864-7198
Convenient location. Non-smoking resort.

CRUISING

-Battery Park (North Public Beach)
-Main Square (opposite Bus Terminal)
-Univ of Vermont (Baily Howe Library, 3rd and 4rth floor)

Dorset ☎ 802

HOTELS

Marble West Inn (bf G H OS)
West Road ✉VT 05251 ☎ 867-4155
Elegant country hospitality. priv. bath.

Grafton ☎ 802

HOTELS

Wayfarer (glm H)
PO Box 147 ✉VT 05146 ☎ 843-2332

Shaftsbury ☎ 802

HOTELS

Country Cousin B&B (AC bf CC GLM H OS wh)
Old Depot Road ✉VT 05262 ☎ 375-6985 Fax: 375-6985
A farmhouse with hot tub and swimming pond.

Stowe ☎ 802

HOTELS

Buccaneer Country Lodge (F glm H pi)
1390 Mountain Road ✉VT 05672 ☎ 253-4772
Priv. and shared baths, cable TV in room, hot tub.

Waterbury ☎ 802

GUEST HOUSES

Grünberg Haus (bf CC glm H MA OS sa wh)
Route 100 South, RR 2, Box 1595 SP ✉VT 05676-9621 *(3 miles south of the village)* ☎ 244-7726 ☎ (800) 800-7760 (Toll-free) Fax: 244-1283 E-Mail: grunhaus@aol.com
Homepage: www.waterbury.org/grunberg *Handbuilt chalet.*

USA-Virginia

East USA
Initials: VA
Time: GMT -5
Area: 110.792 km^2 / 45,313 sq mi.
Population: 6,734,000
Capital: Richmond

● Hetero- as well as homosexual oral and anal intercourse is prohibited in Virginia.

✱ In Virginia ist hetero- und homosexueller Oral- und Analverkehr verboten.

▲ En Virginie, la fellation et la pénétration anale sont interdites pour tous, homos et hétéros.

☆ En Virginia las relaciones homosexuales y heterosexuales por vía oral o anal están prohibidas.

❖ In Virginia sono vietati i rapporti orali ed anali tra omosessuali ed tra eterosessuali.

Cape Charles ☎ 757

GUEST HOUSES

Sea Gate Bed & Breakfast (AC bf g H MA)
9 Tazewell Avenue ✉VA 23310-3127
☎ 331-2206 Fax: 331-2206 E-Mail: seagate@pilot.infi.net
4 rooms with bath, balcony, phone, tv, radio. Rates US$ 80-90, add. bed $15.

Charlottesville ☎ 804

GAY INFO

Gay and Lesbian Helpline Sun-Wed 20-23, Thu 19-21 h
☎ 971-4942

BARS

Club 216 (B D G MA P S W) Thu 21-2, Fri Sat -4 h, closed Mon-Wed
216 W. Water Street *(rear entrance)* ☎ 296-8783

HEALTH GROUPS

Men to Men C-ville AIDS/HIV Services Group
☎ 979-7714

CRUISING

-Rest Stop (Route 64, west of Ivy)
-Lee Park (AYOR)

Norfolk ☎ 757

GAY INFO

Gay Info Line 19-22 h
☎ 423-0933

BARS

Charlotte's Web (B D F GLM S)
6425 Tidewater Drive ☎ 853-5021
Garage. The (B F G lj) Mon-Fri 20-2, Sat 18-2, Sun 13-2 h
731 Granby Street ✉VA 23510 ☎ 623-0303
Nutty Buddys (B g)
143 East Little Creek Road ✉VA 23505 ☎ 588-6474

CAFES

Charlies (B F glm) 7-15 h
1800 Granby Street ☎ 625-0824

BOOK SHOPS

Lambda Rising (AC CC GLM MA VS W) 10-22 h
9229 Granby Street ✉VA 23503 ☎ 480-6969
Gay, lesbian, bisexual and transgender books, videos, magazines and gifts. Free local guides.
Phoenix Rising (GLM)
619 Colonial Avenue ✉VA 23507 *(2nd floor)* ☎ 622-3701

CRUISING

-Ghent Gay Ghetto (around Colley and Princess Anne Road)
-Ocean View Public Park (AYOR)
-Watside Park (South Military Highway, days)

Richmond ☎ 804

GAY INFO

Gay Information Line
☎ 353-3626

BARS

Babes (B g)
Auburn Street/West Cary Street ✉VA 23221 ☎ 355-9330
Broadway Café (B D F G) Mon-Fri 17-2 h
1624 West Broad Street ✉VA 23220 ☎ 355-9931
Fielden's (B D G P YG) Wed-Sat 24-6 h
2033 West Broad Street ✉VA 23220 ☎ 359-1963

BOOK SHOPS

Biff's Carytown Bookstore (glm) 10-18, Sun 10-15 h
2930 West Cary Street ✉VA 23221 ☎ 359-4831

FETISH GROUPS

Teddy Bear Leather Club
PO Box 255 45 ✉VA 23260-5545

CRUISING

-The Block (Grace and Franklin between Adams and 3rd)
-The Rocks (James River Park, North Bank near South end of Meadow St)
-Belle Isle (James River Park)
-Bryant Park (summer)
-Byrd Park (AYOR)
-Monroe Park
-Pumphouse Drive (summer)
-The Battle Abby (behind the VA museum)

Roanoke ☎ 540

BARS

Backstreet Café (B F GLM MA)
356 Salem Avenue ☎ 345-1542

GIFT & PRIDE SHOPS

Out Word Connection (GLM)
114-A Kirk Avenue, SW ☎ 985-6886
Gay pride shopping.

Virginia Beach ☎ 757

HOTELS

Coral Sand Motel (AC Glm H)
PO Box 1125, 2307 Pacific Avenue ✉VA 23451-0125
☎ 425-0872 ☎ (800) 828-0872 (Toll-free)
One Block from ocean.

USA-Washington

Northwest USA
Initials: WA
Time: GMT -8
Area: 184.672 km² / 75,530 sq mi.
Population: 5,610,000
Capital: Olympia

Kennewick ☎ 509

SEX SHOPS/BLUE MOVIES

Castle Superstore Adult Retail
24 hours
522 N. Columbia Center Boulevard ✉WA 99336 ☎ 374-8276
Videos, leather, lingerie, magazines, toys, novelties, books, DVD's.

Kent ☎ 253

BARS

Trax Bar & Grill (B D F GLM)
226 1st Avenue South ✉WA 98032 ☎ 854-8729
New gay bar and night club.

Lake Quinault ☎ 206

HOTELS

Rain Forest Resort Village (B F GLM H s)
Route 1, PO Box 40 ✉WA 98575 ☎ 288-2535
Suburb location. All rooms with kitchenette and priv. bath.

Port Angeles ☎ 360

GUEST HOUSES

Maple Rose Inn (bf CC g H wh WO)
112 Reservoir Road ✉WA 98363 ☎ 457-7673
E-Mail: maplerose@tenforward.com
Homepage: http://www.northolympic.com/maplerose
Most rooms with kitchenette, cable-TV, VCR, telephone, private bath.

Seattle ☎ 206

GAY INFO

G.S.B.A. Guide & Directory
2033 Sixth Avenue, #804 ✉WA 98121 ☎ 443-4722
Yearly directory to gay or gay friendly businesses.
Seattle Gay News
1605 12th Avenue #31 ✉WA 98122 ☎ 324-4297
Fax: 322-7188 E-Mail: sgnl@sgn.org
Homepage: http://www.gayseattle.com
Local weekly news & entertainment newspaper.

BARS

C.C. Attle's (B F G MA VS)
1501 E. Madison ✉WA 98122 ☎ 726-0565
Changes (B G N)
2103 North 45th Street, Wallingford ✉WA 98103 ☎ 545-8363
Crescent. The (b G OG)
1413 East Olive Way ☎ 720-8023
Cuff Complex. The (! AC B CC D F G lj MA VS) The Cuff: everyday 11-2, back bar, dance and patio: Thu, Fri Sat 21-2, Sun 18-2 h
1533 13th Avenue ✉WA 98122 *(on Capitol Hill)* ☎ 323-1525
One of the most popular men's bar in Seattle.
Double Header (b d G OG RT s)
407 2nd Avenue South *(near Washington)* ☎ 464-9918
Oldest gay bar on West Coast.
Eagle (B G LJ) 14-2 h
314 East Pike Street ✉WA 98122 ☎ 621-7591
A man's rock-n-roll club.
Elite II (b G MA N)
1658 East Olive Way ☎ 322-7334
Elite. The (b G N)
622 Broadway East/Roy ☎ 324-4470
Madison Pub (b G N OG)
1315 East Madison ✉WA 98122 ☎ 325-6537
R Place (b G MA VS) 14-2 h
619 East Pine Street ✉WA 98122 ☎ 322-8828
Games.
Re-bar (B D glm S YG)
1114 Howell Street ✉WA 98101 ☎ 233-9873
Sea Wolf Saloon (B d F G) 14-2 h
1413 14th Avenue ✉WA 98122 ☎ 323-2158
Timberline Tavern (b GLM lj OS MA) 18-2 h
2015 Boren Avenue ✉WA 98121 ☎ 622-6220
Largest country dance bar on West Coast with lessons Tue-Fri. 19.30-21 h

CAFES

Glo's (b bf glm) Wed-Fri 7-14, Sat-Sun 7.30-14.30 h
1621 E. Olive Way ✉WA 98102 ☎ 324-2577

DANCECLUBS

Neighbours (B D F G YG)
1509 Broadway East/Pike Street ✉WA 98122 *(entrance rear alley)* ☎ 324-5358
Also restaurant.
Spintron (B D GLM)
916 East Pike Street ✉WA 98122 ☎ 568-6190

RESTAURANTS

Broadway New American Grill. The (F glm) Mon-Fri 10-2, Sat-Sun 9-2 h
314 Broadway East ✉WA 98102 ☎ 328-7000
Coastal Kitchen (bf F glm)
429 15th Avenue East ✉WA 98112 ☎ 322-1145
Flora. Cafe (F g)
2901 E. Madison ✉WA 98112 ☎ 325-9100
Hamburger Mary's (B F g)
1526 East Olive Way ✉WA 98122 *(upstairs)* ☎ 324-8112
Hana's Lounge (B F g)
1914 8th Avenue ✉WA 98101 ☎ 340-1591 ☎ 340-1536
Jack's Bistro (B F G OS s)
405 15th Avenue East ✉WA 98122 ☎ 324-9625
Jade Pagoda (B F g)
606 Broadway East ✉WA 98102 ☎ 322-5900
Mae's Cafe (bf f glm) 7-15 h
6412 Phinney Avenue N. ✉WA 98103 ☎ 782-1222
Thumper's (AC B CC F GLM MA OS S VS W) 10-2 h
1500 East Madison ✉WA 98122 ☎ 328-3800

SAUNAS/BATHS

Club Seattle (G sa P VS) 0-24 h
1520 Summit Avenue ✉WA 98122 ☎ 329-2334
Club Z (DR f G LJ MA P sa VS) Mon-Thu 16-9, Fri 16-Mon 9 h
1117 Pike Street ✉WA 98101 ☎ 622-9958
Three floors, 54 rooms, video lounge...

BOOK SHOPS

Bailey-Coy Books (CC glm) Mon-Thu, Sun 10-22, Fri, Sat 10-23 h
414 Broadway Avenue East ✉WA 98102 *(Bus 7/43)*
☎ 322-8842
Large selection of gay/lesbian books.
Beyond the Closet Bookstore (GLM) Sun-Thu 10-23, Fri Sat -24 h
518 East Pike Street ✉WA 98122-3618 ☎ 322-4609 ☎ (800) 238-8518 (Toll-free)
Exclusively gay & lesbian bookshop, carrying gay fiction, non-fiction, magazines and erotica.
Fremont Place Book Co. (gLM)
621 N. 35th ✉WA 98103 ☎ 547-5970

GIFT & PRIDE SHOPS

Pink World (GLM)
Broadway Market, 400 Broadway Avenue East ✉WA 98102

LEATHER & FETISH SHOPS

Pink Zone. The (AC CC GLM MA) Mon-Sat 10-22, Sun 11-21 h
211 Broadway Avenue E ✉WA 98112 *(on Capitol Hill)*
☎ 325-0050
Outrageous and fun fashion, tattoos and body piercing.

TRAVEL & TRANSPORT

Council Travel (g)
219 Broadway Avenue East ✉WA 98102 ☎ 329-4567
It's Your World (g)
1411 East Olive Way ✉WA 98122 ☎ 328-0616

HOTELS

Country Inn (bf glm H)
685 Juniper, Issaquah ✉WA 98027 ☎ 392-1010
Country living.
Gaslight Inn (CC GLM H OS pi)
1727 15th Avenue ✉WA 98122 ☎ 325-3654
Landes House (bf g H OS wh)
712 11th Avenue East ✉WA 98102 ☎ 329-8781
Shafer Baillie Mansion (G H sol)
907 14th Avenue East ✉WA 98112 ☎ 329-4628
Suburb location, 5 blocks to gay bars. All rooms with telephone, priv. bath, WC and balcony.

GUEST HOUSES

Bacon Mansion. The (bf CC glm H) Office: 8-20 h
959 Broadway East ✉WA 98102 ☎ 329-1864
☎ (800)) 240-1864 (Toll-free) Fax: 860-9025
E-Mail: baconbandb@aol.com
Homepage: http://www.site-works.com/bacon
Rooms with phone, private voice-mail, TV, data. Rates US$ 79-159 incl. bf.
Hill House B & B (bf CC glm H)
1113 East John Street ✉WA 98102 ☎ 720-7161
☎ (800) 720-7161 (Toll-free) Fax: 323-0772
Scandia House B & B (bf GLM H MA)
2028 34th Avenue South ✉WA 98144-4923 ☎ 725-7825
Fax: 721-3348 E-Mail: scandia@nwlink.com
Near Capitol Hill and downtown.

FETISH GROUPS

Generic Leather Productions
1122East Pike Street #800 ✉WA 98122
Knights of Malta MC
PO Box 210 52 ✉WA 98111
Seattle Men in Leather
1122 East Pike Street ✉WA 98122 ☎ 781-4461
E-Mail: info@seattlemeninleather.org
Homepage: www.seattlemeninleather.org
A gay men's social group promoting the Seattle men's leather community. Call or write for info on activities.

RELIGIOUS GROUPS

Tikvah Chadasha Service 2nd Fri
1919 East Prospect ✉WA 98112 ☎ 329-2590
Jewish gays and lesbians.

Silverdale ☎ 360

SEX SHOPS/BLUE MOVIES

Castle Superstore Adult Retail 24 hours
2789 NW Randall Way ✉WA 98383 ☎ 308-0779
Videos, leather, lingerie, magazines, toys, novelties, books, DVD's.

Spokane ☎ 509

GAY INFO

Gay and Lesbian Community Services 24 hrs
☎ 489-2266
Stonewall News Northwest
PO Box 3994 ✉WA 99220-3994 ☎ 536-5635 Fax: 534-2246

BARS

Hour Place (B D F G S) 17-2 h
415 West Sprague ✉WA 99204 ☎ 838-6947

SEX SHOPS/BLUE MOVIES

Castle Superstore Adult Retail 24 hours
11324 E. Sprague ✉WA 99206
Videos, leather, lingerie, magazines, toys, novelties, books, DVD's.
Spokane Arcade 0-24 h
1125 West 1st Avenue ✉WA 99204 ☎ 747-1621

CRUISING

-High Bridge (NU) (People's Park)
-Manito Park -Mission Park

Tacoma ☎ 253

BARS

Airport Tavern (B G LJ)
5406 South Tacoma Way ✉WA 98405 ☎ 475-9730
Casey's Tavern (B G LJ) 6-2 h
2810 6th Avenue ✉WA 98406 ☎ 572-7961
Twenty-fourth Street Tavern (B D GLM S) 12-2 h
2405 Pacific Avenue ✉WA 98402 ☎ 572-3748

RESTAURANTS

Gold Ball Grill & Spirits (B d F GLM MA OS W)
14-2 h
2708 6th Avenue ✉WA 98406 ☎ 627-0430

SEX SHOPS/BLUE MOVIES

Castle Superstore Adult Retail 24 hours
6015 Tacoma Mall Boulevard ✉WA 98409 ☎ 471-0391
Videos, leather, lingerie, magazines, toys, novelties, books, DVD's.

CRUISING

-Nude beach (follow railroad track 1 mile north of Chambers Creek)
-Pacific Avenue (between 13th & 15th)

USA-West Virginia

East USA

Initials: WV

Time: GMT -5

Area: 62.759 km² / 25,668 sq mi.

Population: 1,816,000

Capital: Charleston

Charleston ☎ 304

BARS

Grand Palace (B D F GLM S VS) 17-3.30 h
617 Brooks Street ✉WV 25301 *(near Smith Street)* ☎ 342-9532

SEX SHOPS/BLUE MOVIES

Arcade News and Books
230 Capitol Street ✉WV 25301 ☎ 344-2281

CRUISING

-The Block (AYOR) (Summers, Donnally, Capitol & Christopher Street)

Huntington ☎ 304

BARS

Driftwood Lounge (AC B D f GLM LJ MA P p r S SNU STV VS) Mon, Thu, Fri 17-3.30, Sat, Sun 14-? h
1121 7th Avenue ✉WV 25701 *(near Marshall University Campus)*
☎ 696-9858

SEX SHOPS/BLUE MOVIES

Fourth Avenue News
1119 4th Avenue ✉WV 25701 ☎ 525-6861

CRUISING

-5th and 7th Avenues (between 11th and 12th Streets)

USA-Wisconsin

Great Lakes region USA

Initials: WI

Time: GMT -6

Area: 169.643 km^2 / 69,383 sq mi.

Population: 5,170,000

Capital: Madison

Appleton ☎ 920

BARS

Rascals Bar & Grill (B F GLM OS)
702 East Wisconsin ✉WI 54911 ☎ 954-9262

Green Bay ☎ 920

BARS

Brandy's II (B G LJ)
1126 Main Street ✉WI 54301 ☎ 437-3917
Java's (B GLM VS)
1106 Main Street ✉WI 54301 ☎ 435-5476
Napalese Lounge (B D GLM) Sun-Thu 16-2, Fri Sat 16-2.30 h
515 South Broadway ✉WI 54303 ☎ 432-9646
Sass (AC B d GLM MA N S) Tue-Thu 18-2, Fri-Sun 17-2.30 h
840 South Broadway ✉WI 54304 ☎ 437-7277
Za's (AC bf CC D f G OS S YG)
1106 Main Street ✉WI 54301 ☎ 435-5476

CRUISING

-Rest Stop (AYOR) (on US 41, South of DePere)
-Rest Stop (Wisconsin 141, eastside near city limits)

Lodi ☎ 608

GUEST HOUSES

Prairie Garden Bed & Breakfast (AC b bf CC GLM MA msg NU OS VS wh)
West 13172 Highway 188 ✉WI 53555 *(half an hour north of Madison)* ☎ 592-5187 ☎ 800-380-8427
E-Mail: prairiegarden@bigfoot.com
Homepage: http://www.prairiegarden.com
Located near Lake Wisconsin. Rates start at US$ 55 (bf incl.)

Madison ☎ 608

GAY INFO

Gay Center Mon-Fri 9-17, 19-22 h
1127 University Avenue ✉WI 53715 ☎ 255-4297
Nothing to Hide, Cable Channel 4, GAY TV Wed 21.30 h

BARS

Barracks. The - Club 5 - Foxhole. The - Planet Q (AC B bf CC D GLM LJ MA OS S SNU STV TV VS) Restaurant: Tue-Sun 17-22, Sun brunch 10.30 14 h, Bars and club: Mon-Thu 16-2, Fri Sat -2.30, Sun 15-2 h
5 Applegate ✉WI 53713 ☎ 277-9700 ☎ 277-8700
Gay and Lesbian restaurant, 3 bars, nightclub.
Geraldine's (B D GLM) 16-2 h
3052 East Washington Street ✉WI 53704 ☎ 241-9335
Greenbush (B F glm) 16-2 h
914 Regent Street ✉WI 53715 ☎ 257-2874
Rod's (AC B CC D DR f G H LJ MA S VS W) 16-2.30 h
636 West Washington Avenue ✉WI 53703 ☎ 255-0609
Shamrock Tavern (B D F glm) 11-2 h
117 West Main Street ✉WI 53703 ☎ 255-5029

SWIMMING

-Mazomanie Beach (Nude beach-30 miles Northwest on Highway Y, 4 miles north to Laws Road, then turn onto gravel road, at the end. One of the best in the Midwest. Camping, swimming, campfires, fun, owls, fishing, trees, cameraderie, tolerance, beauty!)
-Lake Mendota

CRUISING

-Burrows Park
-Fairchild Street (opposite library near square)
-James Madison Park

Menomonee Falls ☎ 414

TRAVEL & TRANSPORT

Horizon Travel Mon-Fri 9-17.30, Sat 11-14 h
N81 W15028 Appelton Avenue ✉WI 53051 ☎ 255-0704
Fax: 255-0708

Milwaukee ☎ 414

GAY INFO

In Step
1661 North Water Street, Suite 411 ✉WI 53202
☎ 278-7480 Fax: 278-5868 E-Mail: instepnews@aol.com
Winsconsin's LesBiGay community newspaper.
Q Voice
PO Box 923 85 ✉WI 53202 ☎ 278-7524 Fax: 272-7438
E-Mail: qvoice@aol.com
Wisconsin Light
1843 North Palmer Street ✉WI 53212 ☎ 372-2773
Articles on local events and news.

BARS

B Bar (B D GLM MA)
1579 South 2nd Street ☎ 672-5580
Dance bar
Ballgame. The (B F D G S VS) 12-2 h
196 South 2nd Street ✉WI 53204 ☎ 273-7474
Barbie's Playhouse (B GLM)
700 East Meinecke ✉WI 53212 ☎ 374-7441
Boot Camp Saloon (AC B G LJ OS) Sun-Thu 16-2, Fri Sat - 2.30 h
209 East National Avenue ✉WI 53204 ☎ 643-6900
Leather bar with parking and patio.
C'est La Vie (B D G N SNU YG) 12-2, Fri Sat 12-2.30 h, Fri Sat shows
231 South 2nd Street ✉WI 53204 ☎ 291-9600
Dish (AC B D gLm) 17.30-22 h, closed Tue
235 South 2nd Street ✉WI 53202 ☎ 273-3474
Popular lesbian bar, gays welcome.
Fannies (B D gLm)
200 East Washington ✉WI 53204 ☎ 649-9003
Fluid (AC B CC G) 17-? h
819 South 2nd Street ✉WI 53204 ☎ 645-8330
Cocktail lounge specializing in Martini's. Warm atmosphere with no attitude and friendly staff. Crowded on week-ends.

In Between (AC B f glm YG) Mon-Thu 17-2, Fri -2.30, Sat-Sun 15-2 h
625 South 2nd Street ✉WI 53204 ☎ 273-2693
Popular music bar.
Kathy's Nut Hut (B F GLM S)
1500 West Scott ✉WI 53201 ☎ 647-2673
Milwaukee Eagle (! B DR G LJ MA) 20-2 h
300 West Juneau Avenue *(at corner of North 3rd Street)*
☎ 273-6900
Dresscode for backroom only. Very popular.
M&M Club (AC B CC F GLM MA OS S) 11-2 (meals -23 h)
124 North Water Street ✉WI 53202 ☎ 347-1962
Piano bar and restaurant.
South Water Street Docks (AC B G lj MA N s W)
354 East National Avenue ✉WI 53204 ☎ 225-9676
Station 2 (B gLM N)
1534 West Grant Street ✉WI 53215
☎ 383-5755
This is it (AC B Glm MA N) 15-? h
418 East Wells Street ✉WI 53202 ☎ 278-9192
Very diverse crowd. Friendly atmosphere.
Triangle (A B G MA N) Mon-Fri 17-?, Sat Sun 15-?
135 East National Avenue ✉WI 53204 ☎ 383-9412
Woody's (B G MA N)
1579 South 2nd Street ✉WI 53204 ☎ 672-0806
1100 Club (AC B bf d F Glm LJ MA S W WE) Mon-Wed 7-2, Fri-Sat -2.30 h
1100 South 1st Street ✉WI 53204 ☎ 647-9950
Western style Bar & Restaurant. Steaks and seafood.

CAFES

Annex Cafe (AC bf F GLM LJ MA W YG) 10-4 h
1106 South 1st Street ✉WI 53204 ☎ 672-1217
Pier 221 (b bf f glm)
221 North Water Street ☎ 272-0555

DANCECLUBS

Club 219 (B D GLM S VS) Mon-Thu 16-2, Fri Sat 15-2.30, Sun 15-2 h
219 South 2nd Street ✉WI 53204 ☎ 276-2711
Eagle (B D G LJ)
300 West Juneau ✉WI 53203 ☎ 273-6900
La Cage (! B F Glm S VS WE YG) 21-2, Sun 16-2 h
801 South 2nd Street ✉WI 53204 ☎ 383-8330

RESTAURANTS

Glass Menagerie at M&M Bar (F GLM) Lunch, dinner & Sun brunch.
124 North Water Street ✉WI 53202 ☎ 347-1962
La Perla (AC B CC F glm)
734 South 5th Street ✉WI 53204 ☎ 645-9888
Mexican food.
Mama Roux (b F glm)
1875 North Humboldt ☎ 347-0344
Cajun food.

SEX SHOPS/BLUE MOVIES

J.R. News (G) 0-24 h
831 North 27th Street ☎ 344-9686

BOOK SHOPS

After Words Bookstore Mon-Thu 11-22, Fri -23, Sat 10-23, Sun 12-18 h
2710 North Murray Avenue ✉WI 53211 ☎ 963-9089

HOTELS

Park East Hotel (bf F glm H)
916 East State Street ✉WI 53202 ☎ 276-8800
Gay friendly hotel overlooking the lake. Rooms with telephone, minibar, cable TV, video, and private bath, non smoking rooms available.

GENERAL GROUPS

Gay & Lesbian Community Center (GLM)
PO Box 1686 ✉WI 53201 ☎ 643-1652
Milwaukee LGBT Community Center
170 South 2nd Street ✉WI 53204 ☎ 271 2656 Fax: 271 2161
E-Mail: execdirector@mkelgbt.org Homepage: www.mkelgbt.org
Social and educational programs provided

FETISH GROUPS

Beer Town Badgers
PO Box 840 ✉WI 53201

HEALTH GROUPS

AIDS Resource Center Of Wisconsin Mon-Thu 8-21, Fri 8-17 h, closed Sat Sun
PO Box 92487 ✉Wi 53202-0487 *(820 North Plankinton Avenue)*
☎ 273-2729 ☎ (800) 359-9272 (Toll-free) Fax: 273-2357
Homepage: www.arcw.org *HIV counseling & testing, men's and women's support groups. Call for detailed information.*

HELP WITH PROBLEMS

Galano Club (AA) 18-22 h
☎ 2796-6936
Gay Hotline 0-24 h
☎ 444-7331
Gay People's Union Hotline 19-21 h
☎ 562-7010

RELIGIOUS GROUPS

Dignity
PO Box 597 ✉WI 53201 ☎ 444-7177
Lesbian and gay Roman Catholics.
Metropolitan Community Church
PO Box 1421 ✉WI 53201 ☎ 332-9995

SPECIAL INTEREST GROUPS

Girth & Mirth
PO Box 862 ✉WI 53201

CRUISING

-Astor Street (between Juneau and Kilbourn)
-Wisconsin Avenue (between 10th and 17th)

Superior ☎ 715

BARS

JT's Bar & Grill (AC B F GLM MA S SNU STV) Mon-Fri 15-?, Sat Sun 13-? h
1506 North 3rd ✉WI 54880 ☎ 394-2580
Trio Bar (B gLM MA N) ?-2, Fri-Sun -2.30 h
802 Tower Avenue ✉WI 54880 ☎ 392-5373

Wausau ☎ 715

BARS

Oz (B D GLM MA s) Mon-Sat 19-? h, Sun 17-? h, Wed and Sun Beer Bust
320 Washington Street ✉WI 54403 *(next to the mall)*
☎ 842-3225

USA-Wyoming

West USA
Initials: WY
Time: GMT -7
Area: 253.349 km² / 103,620 sq mi.
Population: 480,000
Capital: Cheyenne

Thermopolis ☎ 307

GUEST HOUSES

Out West B+B (CC glm H)
1344 Broadway ✉WY 82443 ☎ 864-2700
Rates US$ 40-50.

Uruguay

South America
Initials: U
Time: GMT -3
☎ Country Code / Access Code: 598 / 00
Language: Spanish
Area: 177,414 km² / 68,500 sq mi.
Currency: 1 Uruguayan Peso (urug$) = 100 Centésimos
Population: 3,239,000
Capital: Montevideo
Religions: 57% Roman Catholic
Climate: Warm moderate climate. Freezing temperatures are almost unknown.

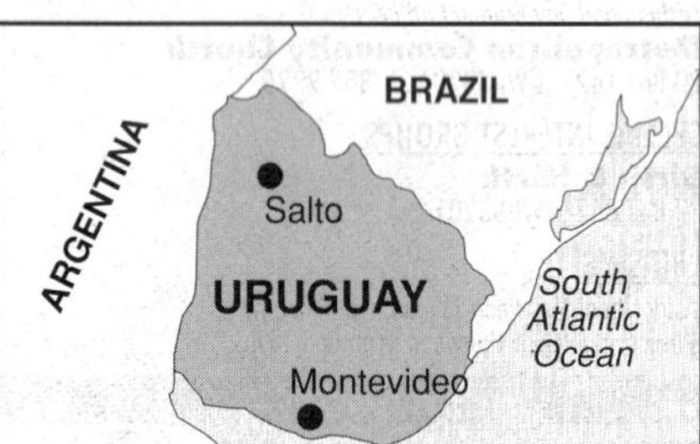

● Homosexuality is not illegal here. We have no exact information on the legal situation at present. The gay scene is in any case growing rapidly.

✱ Homosexualität ist in Uruguay nicht illegal. Genauere juristische Informationen liegen uns nicht vor. Die Szene hat sich in den letzten Jahren beachtlich vergrößert.

▲ En Uruguay, l'homosexualité n'est pas un délit. C'est tout ce que nous pouvons dire à ce sujet. Ces derniers temps, on a ouvert de nombreux bars et boîtes de nuit.

☆ La homosexualdad en Uruguay no es ilegal. Lastimosamente no poseemos informaciones legales más exactas. El ambiente gay ha crecido enormemente en los últimos años.

❖ L'omosessualità in Uruguay non è illegale. Non abbiamo a disposizione informazioni legali più precise. Negli ultimi anni l'ambiente gay si è esteso notevolmente.

Montevideo ☎ 2

GAY INFO

Guía Triángulo Amatista
PO Box 6346, C.P. 11000
Comprehensive Guide to Uruguay.

BARS

Avanti (B D f GLM MA) 21-6 h
Avenida Dr. Fernández Crespo/Lima

DANCECLUBS

Cain (B D GLM)
Cerro Largo y Fernández Crespo
Casta (AC B CC D E G MG s WE) Wed 22-2 h, Fri, Sat 24-5 h
Gonzalo Ramiriz 2121 ☎ 400 65 39
Espejismo (AC B D GLM MA P S) Thu-Sun 23-5 h
Jackson 872/Rambla ☎ 408 4736 E-Mail: Espejismo86@hotmail.com.
Ibiza (AC B D DR GLM MA r SNU VS) Thu-Sun 1-7 h
Yaquarón 1795 & Pozo del Rey ☎ 924 80 83
Thu strip show.

RESTAURANTS

Doña Flor Restaurant (CC E F NG) Mon-Fri 12.30-15 20.30-24, Sat 20.30-24 h
Boulevard Artigas 1034 ☎ 78 57 51

SEX SHOPS/BLUE MOVIES

Complement (glm MA) Mon-Fri 10-20 h, Sat Sun closed
Rio Nego 1320, 3rd floor, Ě 308 ☎ 98 17 16
Etasy (glm MA) Mon-Fri 10-19, Sat -14 h
Avenida 18 de Julia 1268, 9th floor, #904 ☎ 98 6154

CINEMAS

Atlas II (G MA) 12.30-23 h
Uruguay 1167 ☎ 90 64 77
Cine Private (G)
Convención 1290/San José
Cine Tres Cruces De Luxe (G)
Salvador F. Serra 2349
Cinema Yi (G MA) 14-23 h
Carlos Quijano 1275/Soriano ☎ 91 33 68

HOTELS

Continental (AC bf H sb WO)
Paraguay 1373/Avenida 18 de Julio ☎ 92 20 62 Fax: 90 27 37
Embajador (AC bf H)
San José 1212 ☎ 92 17 21 Fax: 92 00 09

GENERAL GROUPS

Homosexuales Unidos Thu Sun 20-22 h
Venezuela 1491/Magallanes
Political activities, advise, general information/Actividades políticas, asistencia, información general.

SWIMMING

-Playa Miramar (G MA) (Rambla Tomás Berreta, Bus 104/105 from downtown)
-Playa Turisferia (take bus from Avenida Italia direction Lagomar or Solymar till bus-stop Avenida Ing. Luis Giannattasio/Avenida de la Playa)

CRUISING
-Facultad de Derecho (g MA) (19-23 h. Avenida 18 de Julio, 2nd floor)
-Avenida 18 de Julio (MA) (23-? h. Entre/between Plaza Independencia y/and Avenida Dr. Fernández Crespo)
-Rambla República del Perú (Entre/between la Plaza Daniel Muñoz y/and la Plaza W. Churchill)
-Avenida General Flores (YG) (21-? h. Entre/between Bulevar Jose Batlle and/y Ordoñez y Camino Corrales)
-Plaza de Ejército (YG) (21-? h)

Paysandú ☎ 722

BARS
Malikibu II (B glm MA R) 23-5 h
Proyectada Segunda/Enrique Chaplin

CAFÉS
Horse Power (! B f glm MA YG) 20-5 h, closed Mon
Uruguay N° 699/Dr. J. Silvan Fernández

DANCECLUBS
Brujas Internacional (AYOR b D glm P S TV VS YG) 23-5 h
Luis Batlle Berres/25 de Mayo
Far West (B D GLM) L.
Gómez y Gran Bretaña
O'Clock (B D GLM)
Rioja 111

CRUISING
-Avenida 18 de Julio (Entre/between Baltazar Brum y/and Cerrito)
-Avenida España (Entre/between Bulevar Artigas y/and Cerrito)

Piriapolis ✉ 20200 ☎ 432

DANCECLUBS
Vértigo (B D glm YG) Fri Sat 0-5 h
Rambla de los Argentinos s/n° ✉20200 *(at the city limits)*

HOTELS
Argentino (AC bf B F H OS WO)
Rambla de los Argentinos & Armenia ☎ 30 54
Miramar (AC H)
Rambla de los Argentinos No. 1082 ☎ 25 44

Punta del Este ☎ 42

CAFÉS
Petit Cafe' (f glm)
Av. Gorlero esq. El Estrecho

DANCECLUBS
Red Bay (B D glm MA S)
Calle 10 No. 825 esq. Calle 9
Space (AC B D glm OG P S YG) Thu-Sat 0-6 h
Rincon del Indio, Ramba Lorenzo Pacheco, Parada 31

LEATHER & FETISH SHOPS
Black Gama (NG)
Calle 27/Avenida Gorlero ☎ 456 57
Leather Corner (glm)
Calle 31/Avenida Gorlero ☎ 419 01

HOTELS
Americana (AC bf H)
Calle 32 No. 638 ☎ 807 94
Playa (B H NG)
Avenida Gorlero/Risso ☎ 822 31 Fax: 872 72
Rooms with air conditioning, fridge, phone and private bath.

Vanuatu

Oceania
Initials: VU
Time: GMT +11
☎ Country Code / Access Code: 678 (no area codes) / 00
Language: English and French; Bichelamar
Area: 12,189 km² / 4,706 sq mi.
Currency: 1 Vatu (VT)
Population: 183,000
Capital: Port-Vila (on Efate)
Religions: 80% Christian
Climate: Tropical climate that is moderated by southeast trade winds.

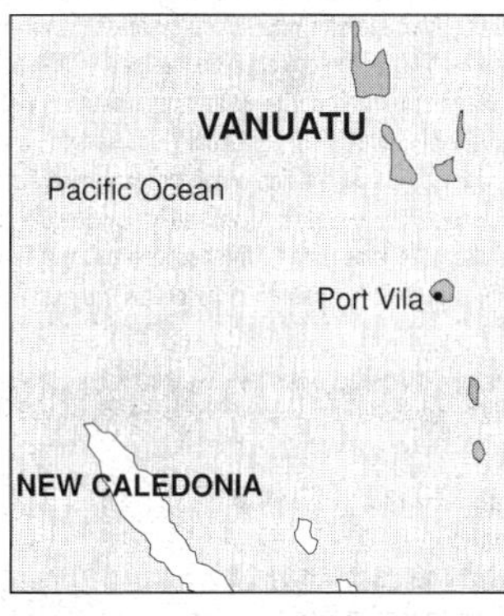

● Vanuatu, »the land that rises from the ocean«, has seen the development of a modest gay scene. The capital, Port-Vila, is a small town of 16,000 inhabitants, mostly Melanesians, but also Polynesians, Europeans, Vietnamese, and Chinese. Melanesians traditionally have little difficulty dealing with the concept of homosexual desires. We have no exact information on the legal situation here, but it is supposedly more liberal in Vanuatu than on neighbouring islands. This is the perfect place for spending beautiful, quiet and relaxed holidays.

✱ »Das Land, das sich aus dem Meer erhebt«. Hier hat sich eine eher zurückhaltende schwule Szene entwickelt. Die Hauptstadt Port-Vila ist eine Kleinstadt mit knapp 16.000 Einwohnern, meist Melanesier, daneben Polynesier, Europäer, Vietnamesen und Chinesen. Den Melanesiern bereitet schwule Lust traditionell wenig Bauchschmerzen. Die zur Zeit gültigen Gesetze, sie liegen uns leider nicht im einzelnen vor, sollen im Vergleich zu denen benachbarter Inseln im südlichen Pazifik eher liberal sein. Hier kann man einen schönen, ruhigen, entspannten Urlaub verbringen.

▲ Le «Pays qui sort de la mer» (indépendant depuis le 30.7.1980) est un archipel de plus de 70 îles. Pas grand chose encore, au niveau gay. Port-Vila, la capitale de l'archipel, est une petite ville de 16.000 habitants, en majorité des Mélanésiens.

Pour le reste, ce sont des Polynésiens, des Européens, des Vietnamiens et des Chinois. L'homosexualité ne semble pas être un sujet tabou. La législation actuelle (nous ne disposons, hélas, d'aucune information concrète) semble être plutôt tolérante, si on compare avec les autres pays du Pacifique Sud. Calme et détente assurés à Vanuatu!

☆ «El país que sumerge del mar». Aquí se ha desarrollado un ambiente gay más bien discreto. La capital Port-Vila es una pequeña ciudad con apenas 16,000 habitantes, la mayoría melanesios, aparte de polinesios, europeos, vietnamitas y chinos. Tradicionalmente el deseo gay no ha sido cosa que les haya dado dolores de cabeza a los melanesios. Las leyes actualmente vigentes, desgraciadamente no las tenemos en detalle, parecen ser, en comparación con las de los demás vecinos de Pacífico Sur, más bien liberales. Aquí se pueden disfrutar unas vacaciones preciosas, tranquilas y relajadas.

❖ „La terra che sorge dall'oceano" è costituita da più di 70 isole. Si è sviluppata una vita gay di dimensioni alquanto modeste. La capitale, Port-Vila, è una piccola cittadina di 16,000 abitanti, in gran parte Melanesiani ma anche Polinesiani, Europei, Vietnamiti e Cinesi. Tradizionalmente, ai Melanesiani l'omosessualità non crea soverchi problemi. Non lo sappiamo con assoluta sicurezza, ma le notizie che ci sono giunte parlano di una situazione legale senz'altro più liberale che nelle isole vicine. Una vacanza bella, quieta e rilassante, quindi, che aspetta soltanto di essere assaporata fino in fondo.

Port Vila

BARS

Bar Cascade (B F g) *(south of town)*
Late night cabaret.
Houstalet. L' (B D F g) 18-3 h
(south of town on road to Wharf)
Prive (B D P g YG) 21.30-3 h
(south of town on road to Wharf)

RESTAURANTS

Pandanus Restaurant (B F g) closed Mon
(on main road east of town)

CRUISING

-Around Cinema Hickson (south of town)

Venezuela

South America
Initials: YV
Time: GMT -4
☎ Country Code / Access Code: 58 / 00
Language: Spanish, in some areas Indian languages
Area: 912,050 km² / 352,143 sq mi.
Currency: 1 Bolivar (vB) = 100 Céntimos
Population: 23,242,000
Captial: Caracas
Religions: 95% Roman Catholic
Climate: Tropical climate that is hot and humid. It's more moderate in the highland.

● There are no legal restrictions on homosexuality in this Latin American country, but a number of administrative barriers can make life difficult. Gay rights are openly discussed, though, thanks to the gay organization „Entendido".

✱ Es gibt in diesem lateinamerikanischen Land keine gesetzlichen Beschränkungen des Rechts auf Homosexualität, aber eine Reihe behördlicher Diskriminierungen. Immerhin wird öffentlich über das Recht auf Homosexualität debattiert, was auch der Schwulenorganisation »Entendido« zu verdanken ist.

▲ Au Vénézuéla, l'homosexualité n'est pas un délit. Ce qui ne veut pas dire que les autorités fichent automatiquement la paix aux gays! La question du droit à l'homosexualité est abordée dans les médias et ce, surtout grâce à l'action de l'association gay «Entenido».

☆ En este país sudamericano no existe ningún tipo de restricción legal del Derecho a la Homosexualidad, pero sí que existe una serie de discriminaciones por parte de las autoridades. Con todo, el debate entorno al derecho a la homosexualidad tiene lugar a puerta abierta, lo que también se debe a las actividades de la organización gay «Entendido».

❖ In questo paese latino-americano non esistono restrizioni contro l'omosessualità, ma la discriminazione operata dal governo è notevole. Nonostante gli ostacoli, ora si discute apertamente dei diritti dei gay, questo soprattutto grazie all'organizzazione gay „Entendido".

Barquisimeto - Estado Lara ☎ 051

BARS

Albert (B glm MA)
Calle 38 *(between Carreras 23 & 24)*
Bar Banana (B glm MA) Calle 14 *(between Carreras 30 & 31)*
Dulce Pimienta (B glm MA)
Calle 19 *(between carreras 20 & 21)*
Johny´s (B glm MA)
Calle 18 *(between carreras 29 & 30)*
El Tizón (B f G MA r)
Carrera 16 *(between Calle 29 and Calle 30)*

DANCECLUBS

Shonkry's (! B D GLM)
Carrera 18/Calle 42

CRUISING

-Museo de Barquisimeto
-Ateneo de Barquisimeto
-Hotel Barquisimeto Hilton (Bar)

Caracas - Distrito Federal ☎ 02

TOURIST INFO

Corpo Turismo
Plaza Venezuela, Centro Capriles 7°

BARS

Copa´s Dancing Bar (B D glm MA) 21-? h
Calle Guaicaipuro, Torre Taeca, El Rosal
La Cotorra (B F G MA) Centro Comercial, Paseo Las Mercedes *(near Tamaro Hotel Inter-Continantal)* ☎ 992 06 08
Dos Barras (! B F G MA)
Pasaje Ascunción (between Av. Abraham Lincoln/Casanova *(near Plaza Venezuela/Sabana Grande Metro)* ☎ 729 406
El Rincón del Gabán (! B G YG) 17-2 h, Fri Sat -5 h
Avenida San Antonio 38, Sabana Grande *(beteween Av. Abraham Lincoln/Casanova, Pl. Venezuela Metro)* ☎ 762 78 07
Greenfields (B D GLM MA)
Centro Commercial Las Mercedes
Tasca Pullman (B G MA) 18-5 h
Av. Francisco Solano Lopez *(1st floor of Ovidio Building)*
☎ 761 11 12
Popular
The Same Side (B GLM MA SNU)
Av. Casanova/Calle El Colegio, Sabana Grande ☎ 76 60 54
Fri & Sat strip show,
The West Side (B d G LJ SNU)
Calle Chacaíto, Chacaíto ☎ 952 75 15
Tortilla (B G MA) Mon-Sat 19-? h
Avenida San Antonio *(between Av. Abraham Lincoln/Casanova, Pl. Venezuela Metro)*

CAFÉS

Cafe Con Leche (B glm MA)
Av. Libertador, Edf. Libertador, Local 1-A, El BosQue ☎ 731 16 83

DANCECLUBS

Tiffany´s Club (! B D e glm P VS YG) 23-5 h, Sun closed
(Av. San Juan Bosco) *(in the basement of the Cinte Altamira building)* ☎ 266 63 71
Zig Zag (B D G LJ YG) 15-7 h, Mon closed
Av. Libertador *(between Av. Las Acacias/Las Palmas, Metro Plaza Venezuela)*
Popular on Sun. Only recommended if you speak Spanish.

SAUNAS/BATHS

Baños Turcos Suecos (G MA msg sa sb) 7-21 h
Calle el Mango, Urb. San Antonio *(Metro Pl. Venezuela, near corner with Avenida Las Acacias)* ☎ 793 77 66
Sauna Arcoiris (G MA sa sb VS) 14 21 h
Av. Andrés Bello/Calle La Colina *(near Teatro Alberto Paz, Sateveca)* ☎ 793 71 81 *Show on Sunday.*

TRAVEL & TRANSPORT

Take A Break Tours Mon-Fri 8.30-17.30 h, closed Sat Sun
Torre Britanica, Mezzanina 1, Sector A, Local 4, *(U-Altamira)*
☎ 263 49 42 Fax: 263 39 30 *Travelagency.*

HOTELS

Gran Melia Caracas Hotel (B F H NG)
Av. Casanova & Recreo. Sabana Grande ☎ 762 81 11
New hotel with 432 rooms within walking distance to the gay nightlife. Rates from US$ 275.
Tampa Hotel (B bf CC F H NG OS)
Av. Fco.Solano Lopez No.9, Sabana Grande *(U-Sabana Grande)*
☎ 762 37 71 Fax: 762 01 12
Recommended. Rates starting at US$ 51/Single.

HEALTH GROUPS

ACCI - Acción Ciudadana Contra el SIDA
☎ 232 79 38 Fax: 235 92 15
E-Mail: accsi@ccs.internet,ve Homepage: internet.ve/accsi
Hospital Universitario de Caracas Mon-Fri 13-18 h
Piso 8 *(8th floor)* ☎ 662 88 05
Free diagnosis and treatment, contact tracing, health education activities on the subject of VD Prevention through conferences, interviews, television programmes, leaflets, etc..
Unidad Sanitaria del Sur Mon-Thu 12-15 h
Final de la Avenida Roosevelt ☎ 61 41 47

SWIMMING

-Playa Bahia de Cata (Maracay, about 3 hours from Caracas)
-Playa Camuri Chico (La Guayra & Pantaletu, very gay)
-Playa Camuri Grande (Naiguata)
-Playa Chuspa (La Sabana)
-Playa de los Angeles (AYOR)
-Playa Macuto Sheraton (next to the Hotel) (popular)
-Playa Marina Grande

CRUISING

-Centro Comercial Paseo Las Mercedes, Urb. Las Mercedes (AYOR)
-Centro Comercial Chacaito
-Centro Simon Bolivar, El Silencio
-Calle Real de Sabana Grande
-Centro Plaza (in front of United States Embassy, evenings)
-Plaza Candelaria (AYOR) (after 18 h)
-Avenida Casanova (r)
-Hotel Tamamaco (r)
-Cafés along Boulevard de Sabana Grande
-Centro Comercial Ciudad Tamanaco
-Avenida Abraham Lincoln (AYOR)
-Paseo Los Ilustres (AYOR)
-Plaza Caracas (AYOR)
-Plaza Diego de Lozada (AYOR)
-Ateneo de Caracas (WE) (Plaza Morelos)
-"El Circuito" (Car-cruising on Avenida Francisco Solano between Avenida Negrín and Avenida Los Jabillos)
-Parque Los Caobos (AYOR WE) (by Teresa Careños Theatre)
-Parque Central (AYOR WE) (by Hilton Hotel and including Contemporary Museum

SWIMMING

-Playa San Luis (Along the beach, near the »Vivero« and Hotel Los Bordones. Cruising activity. Let People ask for a cigarette. Sometimes R but not dangerous or expensive.)

Isla Margarita - Estado Nueva Esparta ☎ 095

BARS

Hilton Hotel (B H NG)
Calle los Uveros-Porlamar ☎ 62 33 33

DANCECLUBS

Mosquito Coast (AC B D F g MA R T WE) 18-6 h
(behind Bella Vista Hotel) ☎ 61 35 24
Village (AC B D g WE YG)
Avenida Santiago Mariño

RESTAURANTS

Moise's Restaurant (B F NG r T)
Playa El Aqua
Gay owner, mostly straight crowd,

TRAVEL & TRANSPORT

New Life Tours (g)
Avenida Joaquin Maneiro 53 - Pampatar ☎ 62 50 46
Travel Agency (IGTA-Member, accomodation, yacht charters)

CRUISING

-Avenida 4 de Mayo
-Avenida Santiago Mariño
–Playa Bella Vista (AYOR)(behind Mosquito Coast, best in the afternoon)
-Playa el Morro (AYOR)(in front of Sol y Mar, best in the afternoon)
-Beach between Playa Moreno and Playa Caracola (from the Hilton hotel 500m past the new harbour)

La Guaira - Distrito Federal ☎ 031

HOTELS

Macuto Sheraton (AC B D E F H NG pi sol)
Urbanización Caraballeda, Avenida La Costanera ☎ 94 43 00
Separated from beach, where local beautiful, often bisexual young men do crowd. Bar extremely cruisy (20-1 h), some staff members are also gay. In the nearby village of Caraballeda, several bars and cafés open until 2 or 3 h (YG). All rooms are with telephone, priv. bath and balcony. Rates US$ 70-95.

Maracaibo - Estado Zulia ☎ 061

BARS

Bosque.El (B G MA) Fri-Sun 21-4 h
Avenida 9 *(between Calles 76 and 77)*
Diamond White (B D E G MA p YG)
Calle 77 *(Near Calle 3 D)*
Mara Bar (B E g MA WE) 11-1 h
Avenida 2 *Hotel del Lago, Milagro*
Meson de Chimitas (B D G MA YG) Thu-Sun 21-4 h
Avenida 13A/Calle 76
Stu Ricardo (B G MA)
Avenida 3G/Calle 77 *Bohemian atmosphere.*
Union (B G MA) Avenida Bella Vista *(between Calle 83 & 84)*

CAFES

Kabuki (B f G MA) 8-22 h
Boulevard 5 de Julio *(Calle 77 between Avenidas 12 and 13)*

HOTELS

Roma (H NG MA)
Avenue Bella Vista/Calle 86 ☎ 22 08 68/77
You may rent a simple room by the hour or for the whole night. Single Bs 2.000/night.

CRUISING

-Centro Comercial Costa Verde (shopping mall)
-Avenue Bella Vista (off Avenue Cecilio Acosta)
-Boulevard 5 de Julio (Calle 77)
-Paseo Ciencias (ayor) (afternoons and nights)

Mérida - Cord de Mérida ☎ 074

CRUISING

-Plaza Bolivar
-Teleferico
-Parco Los Chorros de Milla

Puerto La Cruz - Estado Anzoátegui ☎ 081

BARS

Guatacarazo. El (B NG r)
Paseo Colon Boulevard
Parranda (B g)
Paseo Colon Boulevard
Studio (B d e NG YG)
Avenue Americo Vepucio *(Morro resort area)*

DANCECLUBS

Con Sabor Latino (AC B D GLM S) 20-4 h
Calle Bolivar *(Edificio Alsyru, 2nd floor)*
Hato. El (B D G MA S) 24-5 h
Calle Democracia N° 6

HOTELS

Doral Beach (B H NG pi)
Avenue Americo Vespucio, PO Box 42 75 ☎ 879 11
Melia Puerto La Cruz (B bf F H NG pi T) *(at the end of Paseo Colon)* ☎ 69 13 11
Fax 69 12 41.

SWIMMING

-Doral Beach
-Cangrjo Beach
-El Morro
-Silver Island
-Guanta Harbor
-Caracas Islands (within the Mochima National Park)
-Arapito Beach
-Colorada Beach

CRUISING

-Paseo Colon
-Plaza Bolivar
-Hotel Melia Beach
-Doral Beach
-Silver Island

San Cristóbal - Estado Táchira ☎ 076

HOTELS

Bella Vista (B H NG)
Calle 9/Carrera 9
Tama (B F H pi) Avenida 19 de Abril *(Urb. Pirineos)* ☎ 55 44 77
Convenient location, 1 hour to the airport. All rooms with priv. bath, WC and telephone. Single Bs 375, double 430.

Valencia - Estado Carabobo ☎ 041

BARS

Cuevas de Louis Candela. Las (B g)
Avenida Bolivar
Posada.La (B G)
Los Sauces/Avenue Bolivar

CAFÉS

Cafeteria Atrium (B F g)
Centro Prof. Avenue Bolivar

DANCECLUBS

Rose & Flower (B D G VS YG)
Urb. Las Rosas, Lincoln Ave.
Very popular, two floors.

CRUISING

-Plaza Bolivar (in and around Hotel Intercontinental)

SWIMMING

-Morrocoy beach (NU)

Vietnam

Viet-nam

South East Asia

Initials: VN

Time: GMT +7

☎ Country Code / Access Code: 84 / 00

Language: Vietnamese; partly French and English (in the south)

Area: 331,689 km^2 / 128,065 sq mi.

Currency: 1 Dong (D) = 10 hào = 100 xu

Population: 77,896,000

Capital: Hanoi (Ha-noi)

Religions: mostly Mahajana-Buddhist

Climate: Tropical climate in the south, monsoonal climate in the north with hot, rainy season that lasts from mid-May to mid-September and warm, dry season between mid-October and mid-March.

● Vietnam has no laws prohibiting homosexuality, although there are strong penalties for prostitution. Homosexuality has strong roots in Vietnamese culture, although open public behaviour and Western gay lifestyles are not tolerated by Vietnamese society. Vietnam so far has no strictly-gay venues.
English is widely spoken everywhere in Vietnam. Very few people speak French, which is no longer politically correct.

✸ In Vietnam gibt es keine Gesetze, die sich gegen Homosexualität richten, jedoch ist Prostitution illegal und wird streng bestraft. Homosexualität ist in der vietnamesischen Kultur stark verwurzelt, auch wenn auffällige öffentliche Verhaltensweisen, wie der westliche schwule „lifestyle", von der vietnamesischen Gesellschaft nicht toleriert werden. Bisher hat sich in Vietnam keine organisierte homosexuelle Szene etablieren können.
Englisch ist weitverbreitet und wird von den meisten Menschen in Vietnam gesprochen. Wenige sprechen Französisch, jedoch gilt diese Sprache als politisch nicht korrekt.

▲ Le Vietnam n'a pas de lois condamnant l'homosexualité. De sévères peines sanctionnent par contre la prostitution. L'homosexualité a de profondes racines dans la culture vietnamienne mais un comportement ouvert similaire à celui des occidentaux ne serait pas toléré ici. Le Vietnam n'a pas encore une scène gaye bien établie.
L'anglais est couramment parlé dans tout le pays. Certaines personnes pratiquent encore le français bien que cette langue ne soit plus considérée comme politiquement correcte.

☆ SPANISH UEBERSETZUNG REIN. In Vietnam non esistono leggi contro l'omosessualità, però la prostituzione è illegale e viene punita severamente. L'omosessualità ha forti radici nella cultura vietnamita pur non tolerando comportamenti poco discreti come anche lo stile di vita gay occidentale. Fin'ora non si trovano né locali per sesso né locali esclusivamente omosessuali.
La lingua inglese è molto diffusa e la maggior parte dei vietnamiti la parla. Pochi parlano anche il francese il che non è molto popolare per la storia coloniale del Vietnam.

❖ In Vietnam non esistono leggi contro l'omosessualità, però la prostituzione è illegale e viene punita severamente. L'omosessualità ha forti radici nella cultura vietnamita pur non tolerando comportamenti poco discreti come anche lo stile di vita gay occidentale. Fin'ora non si trovano né locali per sesso né locali esclusivamente omosessuali.
La lingua inglese è molto diffusa e la maggior parte dei vietnamiti la parla. Pochi parlano anche il francese il che non è molto popolare per la storia coloniale del Vietnam.

NATIONAL COMPANIES

Utopia Tours (!)
Homepage: www.utopia-tours.com

NATIONAL GROUPS

Nguyen Friendship Society
Homepage: www.GoVietnam.com/NFS
Underground AIDS prevention program for gay/bi men.

Ha Noi

BARS

Café Lieu (G N)
20 Quang Trung Street/Ha Hoi Street
GC (AC B G)
Bao Khanh Street
Sparks Bar (AC B g)
88 Lo Duc Street

DANCECLUBS

Apocalypse Now (B g D)
338 Ba Trieu Street
Metal Disco (B g D)
Cua Nam Street

HOTELS

Camellia Hotel (H)
Thuoc Bac Street

Trang An Hotel (H)
51 Hang Gai Street

GUEST HOUSES

Real Darling Café and Guesthouse (H)
33 Hang Quat

CRUISING

-Ba Dinh Square (AYOR R) (here you meet soldiers after dark)
-Hoan Kiem Lake (R) (particularly in the park around the bridge to Ngoc Son Pagoda after dark)
-Outdoor cafés at the bend in Bao Khanh Street
-Thien Quang Lake (R) (opposite Lenin Park after dark)
-Tran Hung Dao Street (AYOR)
-Quan Phong Lan (AYOR) (Near Hai Phong City Theatre and garden. Many sailors)

Hô Chi Minh City (Sai Gon)

BARS

Quan 241 (B g F) Best after 19.30 h
Nguyen Thi Minh Khai *(on the roundabout where Nguyen Thi Minh Khai, Ly Thai To and Nguyen Van Cu meet)*

CAFÉS

Bich Lien Coffee (b bf g)
26 Dien Bien Phu Street, District 10

Hao Thi Quán (b bf g)
636 Le Hong Phong, District 10
Coffee house.

Phong Cat Café (b bf g) Sun mornings
Nguyen Van Troi Street *(next to Saigon Lodge)*

343 Café (b bf g)
343 Nguyen Trai Street, District 1

373 Café (b bf g)
373/44 Cach Mang Thang Tam, Tan Binh District

DANCECLUBS

Apocaplypse Now (B D g OS R) 23-? h
29 Mac Thi Buoi Street, District 1 *(at the end of Thi Sach Street)*

Long Van Cultural Entertainment Center (B D g) On Mon
Dien Bien Phu Street, District 3

Zouk (B g D R)
191 Nguyen Hue, District 1 *(Opposite Oscar Hotel)*

RESTAURANTS

Tu My 2 (! g F S)
53 Nguyen Thi Minh Khai, District 1

FITNESSTUDIOS

Workers Club (g sa sb pi WO)
55 Nguyen Thi Minh Khai Street
Cruisy especially in the showers and locker rooms below the pool in the late afternoon.

HOTELS

Evergreen Hotel (H)
261 Hai Ba Trung Street

Hong Kong Mini Hotel (H)
22 Bui Vien

Thai Thien 1 Hotel (g H) 31
Le Anh Xuan Street

Thai Thien 2 Hotel (g H) 142
Bui Thi Xuan Street

CRUISING

-Nguyen Binh Khiem Street, Nguyen Du Street and Nguyen Trung Ngan Street (AYOR) (after dark near the zoo)
-Sai Gon Superbowl (near the airport)
-Tu Xuong Street (AYOR) (Near the Cach Mang Thang Tam Roundaybout and Café Cay Dua. After dark)
-Turtle Fountain (look for "Con Rùa" on street maps. After dark)
-Waterfront area at the end of Nguyen Hue Boulevard (AYOR) (After dark)

Hoi An

CRUISING

-Along the quay after sunset. Beware of hustlers.
-Main beach (especially at dawn and late afternoon)

Nha Trang

HOTELS

Khatoco Hotel (g H)
9 Biet Tru

Vien Dong Hotel (g H)
1 Tran Hung Dao

CRUISING

-Boulevard along the beach (At the sunset especially with motorbike)
-Palm groves along the beach (AYOR) Beware of huslers (after 23 h)

Yugoslavia

Jugoslavija

Southern central Europe

Initials: YU

Time: GMT +1

☎ Country Code / Access Code: 381 / 99

Language: Serbian. Albanian, Montenegrinian, Hungarian

Area: 102.173 km²/39,449 sq mi.

Currency: 1 Yugoslavian Dinar (Din)

Population: 10,410,000

Capital: Beograd

Religions: 65% orthodox, 19% Muslim, 4% Roman Catholic

Climate: Continental climate in the north with cold winters and hot an. The central portion has continental and Mediterranean climate. The South is Adriatic along the coast with hot and dry summers and autumns and relatively cold winters with heavy snowfall inland.

● In all remaining parts of the former Yugoslavia, homosexuality is now legal. The only age of consent we have on record is that of Montenegro, set at 14 years.

✱ In allen Teilen Rest-Jugoslawiens ist Homosexualität heute legal. Wir kennen nur die montenegrinische Schutzaltersgrenze von 14 Jahren.

▲ L'homosexualité n'est plus en délit, dans ce qui reste de la Yougoslavie. Dans le Monténégro, la majorité sexuelle est fixée à 14 ans.

☆ La homosexualidad ya no es ilegal en todos los territorios del resto de Yugoslavia. La única edad de consentimiento de nuestro conocimiento es la de Montenegro: 14 años.

❖ In Serbia l'omosessualità è completamente proibita, mentre nel Montenegro si possono avere rapporti a partire dai 14 anni

NATIONAL PUBLISHERS

Agencija Nikolof Design
Kralja Petra Prvog 15 ✉21000 Novi Sad ☎ (021) 33 43 64

Gay Revija
c/o Nikolof Design, Kralja Petra Prvog 15 ✉21000 Novi Sad ☎ (021) 33 4
Copy for DM 5 (Eurocheque).

Beograd/Belgrado - Serbia ✉ 11000 ☎ 011

BARS

Academia (B D g S YG) 23-6 h
Raiceva/Knez Mihajlova ✉11000 *(Basement of Art & Design Academy)*

Platoj Cafe Club (B glm MA)
Vasina ulica ✉11000

Prostor Club differing days 23-4 h
Sarajevska 26 ✉11000 *(Near train station)*

Saga Club (B G MA) Sun 21-6 h
Marsala Tolbuhina/14 Decembra street ✉11000 *(Bus 19/21/22)*

CAFÉS

Moskva Hotel (B g OG)
Terazije Place ✉11000 *(At Sweet-Coffee-Shop)*

SAUNAS/BATHS

Javno Kupatilo (g NG)
Dusanova street ✉11000
Only on man's days.

HEALTH GROUPS

Infektivna Klinika
Klinicki center Srbije ✉11000 ☎ 68 33 66
HIV-screening. Ask for Dr. Jevtovic.

CRUISING

-Usce Park (ayor) (around Museum of Modern Art, at nights)
-Karadjordjev park (ayor) (JNA street, close to Slavija Place, opposite Sveti Sava Cathedral, at night)
-Ada Giganlija Lake
-Cvetni Trg to Srpskih Vladara street (opposite Yugoslovensko Dramsko Pozoriste)
-Zemunski gradski Park (in Zemun)
-Main Train/Main Bus station
-Sremska street/Terazije place (underground passage)

Novi Sad - Serbia ✉ 21000

BARS

Queen (B G P) Fri Sat 24-7 h
c/o Novi Sad Hotel ✉21000 *(Opposite Main train station)*

CAFES

Atrium (B glm) 24-? h
Pasiceva street ✉21000

Royal (g)
c/o Putnik Hotel, Ilije Ognjanovica street ✉21000 *(1st floor)*

DANCECLUBS

Contrast (B D G) Sun
Kisacka street ✉21000

CINEMAS

Arena (g NG) 10/17 h
Bul. Mihajla Pupina ✉21000 *(Behind Hotel Park)*
Only during porno-projection.

EALTH GROUPS

Higijenski Institut
Bul. Revolucije ✉21000
Aids testing and information. Contact Dr. Borisa Vukovic.

CRUISING

-Garden in front of the rail way station (ayor) (at night)

-Futoski Park (Futoska street, behind Hotel Park, evenings)
-Becar Strand
-Kamenjar Beach
-SPENS shopping center (ground floor)

Podgorica - Montenegro ✉ 81000

CRUISING
-Park opposite Hotel Crna Gora (AYOR)
-Train and bus station

Subotica - Serbia ✉ 24000 ☎ 024

CRUISING
-Railway station
-Park opposite Main train station (only evenings)
-Park opposite City Sport center
-Palicko Jezero (NU) (very popular)

Ulcinj - Montenegro

SWIMMING
-Along the beach (12 km!)
-Camping area of »Ada« (NU)

Velika Plana ☎ 026

GENERAL GROUPS
Gay Yugoslav SM Initiative (GYSM) Mon Tue 16-20 h
c/o Miodrag, Massukina 9 ✉11320 ☎ 52 26 74

Zambia

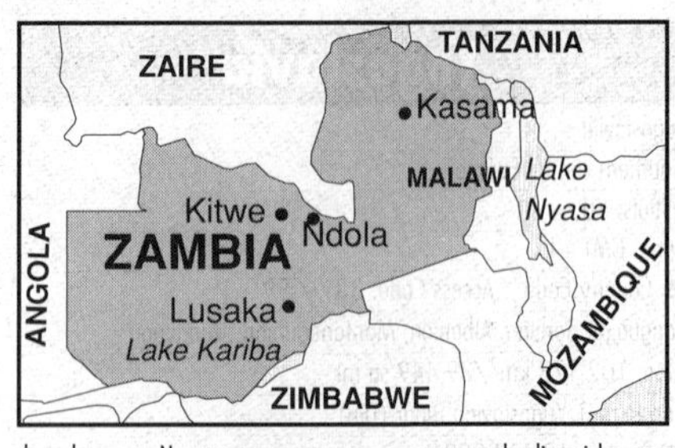

Southern central Africa
Initials: Z
Time: GMT +2
☎ Country Code / Access Code: 260 / 00
Language: English (official)
Area: 752,618 km^2 / 290,586 sq mi.
Currency: 1 Kwacha (K) = 100 Ngwee (N)
Population: 9,461,000
Capital: Lusaka
Religions: 75% Christian
Climate: Tropicalclimate that is modified by altitude. The rainy season lasts from October to April.

● Homosexual relations between men of any age are illegal according to Articles 155-158 of the penal code. The maximum penalty is fourteen years imprisonment. In spite of this legislation, the administration occasionally insists that there are no homosexuals in Zambia, and that there is therefore nothing to punish. We have no information on the general attitude of society towards gays.

✱ Homosexuelle Beziehungen zwischen Männern jeden Alters sind gemäß den Artikeln 155-158 des Strafgesetzbuches illegal. Die Höchststrafe liegt bei 14 Jahren Gefängnis. Jedoch vertreten die Behörden des Landes gelegentlich die Meinung, in ihrem Staat gebe es gar keine Homosexuellen und somit auch nichts zu bestrafen. Über die Einstellung der Bevölkerung gegenüber Schwulen ist uns nichts bekannt.

▲ En Zambie, l'homosexualité masculine est un délit, même entre adultes consentants (articles 155 à 158 du code pénal). On risque un maximum de 14 ans de prison, même si, bizarrement, les autorités du pays affirment que l'homosexualité n'existe pas dans le pays. Nous ne sommes pas en mesure de dire si les gens, là-bas, sont plutôt homophobes ou homophiles.

☆ Las relaciones homosexuales entre hombres, sean de la edad que sean, constan como ilegales de acuerdo con los párrafos 155-158 del Código Penal. La pena máxima comprende 14 años de cárcel. Así y todo, las autoridades de este país sostienen a veces la opinión de que en Zambia no existen homosexuales-y asi tampoco hay nada que castigar. Sobre la actitud de la población hacia los gays sabemos casi nada.

❖ I paragrafi 155-158 del codice penale considerano illegali le relazioni omosessuali fra maschi di qualsiasi età. Quattordici anni di prigione rappresentano il massimo della pena comminabile. Nonostante tutto, però, il governo s'è dato gran pena per sottolineare che in Zambia il problema non esista. Non abbiamo informazioni sull'atteggiamento generale nei confronti dei gay.

Kitwe ☎ 2

BARS
Cobalt Room Bar (B d F H NG YG)
c/o Hotel Edingurgh, PO Box 218 00 *(city centre)* ☎ 21 68 63

CRUISING
-In front of the „Zamby"
-Squash Club (after business hours; also restaurant at Squash Club which is the only place where you may safely eat meat in Zambia; not far from city center)

Lusaka ☎ 1

BARS
Lusaka Hotel (ayor B D F g H NG WE)
Katondo Road, PO Box 300 44 ☎ 21 73 70
Mukumbi Bar (B H NG)
c/o Hotel Intercontinental, Haile Selassie Avenue *(top floor)* ☎ 21 23 66
Hotel rates upon request.

DANCECLUBS
Moon City (B D g NG) 22-5 h
(off Cairo Road, next to Bank of Zambia)
Although not gay, it is possible to meet gays in this huge disco.

Ndola City ☎ 2

BARS
Copper Smith Arms Hotel (B E F g H NG YG)
PO Box 710 63 *(opposite railway station)* ☎ 23 95
Top Hat Bar (B f g LJ YG) *(opposite Zambian Airways, St. Patrick's)*

HOTELS
Intercontinental Cuisine Hotel (b d F H NG YG)
PO Box 715 38 *(in city center)* ☎ 47 75
New Savoy Hotel (b d F H NG YG)
2446 Buteko Avenue, PO Box 718 00 *(in city center)* ☎ 39 33

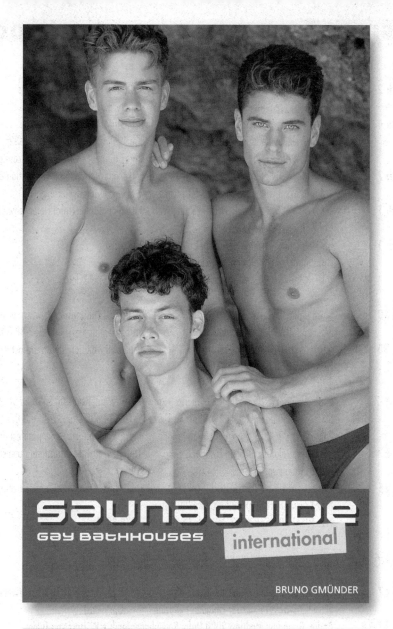

SPARTACUS Events Calendar 2000

March 2-6 Miami Beach, Southbeach, FL, USA: Winterparty 2000 (Info: Dade Human Rights Foundation; Tel. +1-305-538 27 12; http://www.winterparty.com)

March 4 Sydney, NSW, Australia: Gay and Lesbian Mardi Gras (Info: Sydney Mardi Gras, 21-23 Erskineville Road, Erskineville 2042, NSW, Australia;TEL. +61-2-9557-4332; Fax +61-2-9516-4446; Email: mardigras@mardigras.com.au; www.mardigras.com.au)

March 7 New Orleans, LA, USA: Mardi Gras Day (Info: New Orleans Metropolitan Convention & Visitor Bureau, Tel. +1-504-5665 50 11, http://www.neworleanscvb.com)

March 11-18 Lenzerheide, Switzerland: SWING (Skiing With International Gays (Info: Hotel Schweizer Hof, Tel. +41-81-384 01 11)

March 18-25 Les Deux Alpes, France: European Gay Ski Week (Info: http://www.alternativeholidays.com, Tel. +33-4-76 79 75 00, Fax +33-4 76 79 20 37, Email: info@deuxalpes.com)

April 30 Washington, DC, USA: MILLENIUM MARCH ON WASHINTON (Info: http://www.mmow.org, Email: MMOW2000@aol.com, TEL. +1-818-893-4075, (within USA) 800-253-88 00)

April 30 Amsterdam, Netherlands: Queensday (Info: For further information please contact local switchboards.)

May 1-7 Philadelphia, PA, USA: PrideFest America (Info: PrideFest America, 200 S. Broad Street, Suite 600, Philadelphia, PA 19102, USA; TEL. +1-215-732 33 78 or +1-800-990 33 78; Fax +1-215-790 97 51; Email: info@pridefestamerica.com; http://www.pridefest.org)

May 6 Bruxelles, Belgium: Belgien Lesbian & Gay Pride (Info: For further information please contact local switchboards.)

May 25-29 Chicago, IL, USA: INTERNATIONAL MR. LEATHER 2000 (Info: email: imrl@mindx.com, http://www.imrl.com/iml2000/iml2000.htm, TEL. (USA) 800-545-6753, (outside USA) +1-773-878-3844)

June 1-4 Zürich, Switzerland: EuroGames 2000 (Mulitsports Festival. Info: http://www.eurogames.ch)

June 17 Vienna, Austria: CSD Wien (Info: CSD Wien, Wasagasse 12/3/5, A-1090 Wien/Vienna; TEL +43-1-319 44 72/33; Email: info@pride.at; www.pride.at)

June 17-18 Berlin, Germany: Stadtfest 2000 (Info: Regenbogenfonds e.V., Herr van Tulden, Fuggerstr. 7, 10777 Berlin, Germany; TEL +49-30-214 735 86; Fax +49-30-214 735 88)

June 18-25 New York City, NY, USA: Pride Week 2000 (Info: www.nycpride.org, Email: hopout@aol.com, TEL. +1-212-807-7433)

SPARTACUS Events Calendar 2000

June 24-25 San Francisco, CA, USA: 2000 san francisco pride (Info: SFLGBTPPC Inc., 1230 Market Strieet PMB 241, San Francisco, CA 94102-4801, USA; TEL. +1-415-864-3733; Fax +1-415-864-5889; Email: sfpride@aol.com; www.sf-pride.org)

June 24 Berlin, Germany: CSD Berlin (Info: Berliner CSD e.V., Stadtbahnbogen 530, 10623 Berlin, Germany; TEL. +49-30-787 036 30; Fax +49-30-787 036 31; Email: juergen-bieniek@gmx.de; www.berlin-csd.de)

June 30-July 2 Cologne, Germany: CSD Köln (Info: CSD Veranstalungs-GmbH, Rubensstr. 8-10, 50676 Köln/Cologne, Germany; TEL. +49-221-47 47 898; Fax +49-221-47 47 897; Email: info@csd-cologne.de; www.csd-cologne.de)

July 1 London, Great Britain: London Mardi Gras 2000 (Info: Mardi Gras 2000, 3P Leroy House, 436 Essex Road, London, N1 3QP, UK; TEL. +44-20-7688 0110; Fax +44-20-7688 0111; Email: info@londonmardigras.com; www.londonmardigras.com)

July 1-9 Roma, Italy: World Pride Roma 2000 (Info: TEL.+39-06 54 13 985, http://www.worldpride2000.com)

October 12-15 Atlanta, Georgia, USA: InterPride World Conference 2000 (Info: InterPride -IP2000- Atlanta Pride Committee, Inc., 828 West Peachtree Street, Suite 212, Atlanta, GA 30308 USA; Email: IP2000@mindspring.com; http://www.interpride.org; TEL. +1-404-876-3700; Fax +1-404-876-3702)

November 3-4 Amsterdam, Netherlands: Leather Pride Amsterdam (Info: Leather Pride Netherlands BV, PO Box 2674, 1000 CR Amsterdam, The Netherlands; http://www.leatherpride.nl; Email: info@leatherpride.nl; TEL. +31-20-422 37 37)

November 13 Sydney, NSW, Australia: Sleazeball (Info: Sydney Gay and Lesbian Mardi Gras Association, TEL. +61-2-9557-4332, Fax +61-2-9516-4446)

December 1 World Aids Day

Index

This index contains all countries, the states, territories and provinces of Australia, Canada and the US and all cities and islands that are listed in SPARTACUS.

A

C

H

I

M

O

Ö

P

U

Ü

V

T

Yes please, send your current rate card and advertising information!
Ja, bitte schicken Sie mir Ihre aktuellen Mediadaten!
Oui, envoyez-moi votre liste de prix concernant les annonces publicitaires.
Si, mandatemi, per favore, il vostro listino prezzi relativo agli spazi publicitari.

Name of our establishment:

Our postal address: 

Further Information

Sonstiger Hinweis / Informations complémentaires

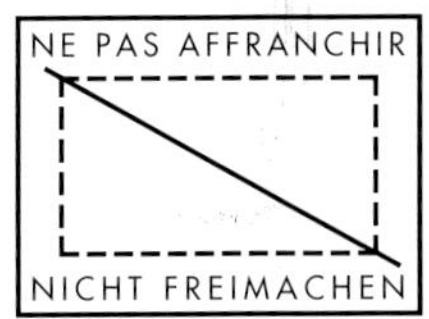

RÉSPONSE PAYÉE / WERBEANTWORT
ALLEMAGNE

SPARTACUS
INTERNATIONAL GAY GUIDE
BRUNO GMÜNDER VERLAG
PO Box 61 01 04
D-10921 Berlin
GERMANY

Sonstiger Hinweis / Informations complémentaires

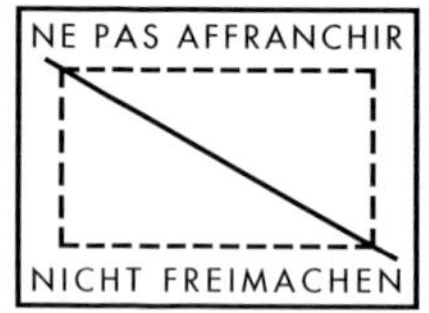

RÉSPONSE PAYÉE / WERBEANTWORT
ALLEMAGNE

SPARTACUS

INTERNATIONAL GAY GUIDE

BRUNO GMÜNDER VERLAG
PO Box 61 01 04
D-10921 Berlin
GERMANY

User's Info

☐ NEW ☐ CLOSED

Name of Establishment

Owner

Address

City

Country

Near

Phone

Fax

E-mail

SPARTACUS-Codes

Opening Hours

CODES

ENGLISH

!	A must for the international tourist
A	Art exhibits
AC	Air conditioning
AYOR	At your own risk. Dangerous place with risk of personal attack or police activity
B	Bar
bf	breakfast
CC	Major credit cards are accepted
D	Discotheque
DR	Darkroom
E	Elegant. Appropriate dress advisable
F	Food. Full meals available.
G	Gay. Exclusively or mostly male homosexuals
GLM	Gay and lesbian mixed crowd
H	Hotel or pension welcoming gay guests
LJ	Leather and jeans
MA	Mixed ages
MG	Middle-aged gays
msg	Massage offered
N	Mostly of local interest and with local patrons
NG	Not exclusively gay, but interesting for gays
NU	Nudist area
OG	Mostly older gays
OS	Terrace or garden
P	Private club or strict door control
p	You must ring to enter.
pi	Swimming pool
R	Frequented by hustlers
S	Shows or other special events
SNU	Strip shows
STV	Dragshow
sa	sauna
sb	steam bath
sol	Solarium
TV	Transvestite and / or transsexual clientele
VS	Video shows
WE	More popular on weekends
wh	Whirlpool / jacuzzi
WO	Work-out equipment available
YG	Younger gays (18-28)

Codes in lower-case letters can mean a limitation.

DEUTSCH

!	Ein Muß für den internationalen Touristen
A	Kunstausstellungen
AC	Klimaanlage
AYOR	Auf eigenes Risiko, möglicherweise gefährlich
B	Bar
bf	Frühstück
CC	Wichtigste Kreditkarten akzeptiert
D	Disco
DR	Darkroom
E	Elegantes Publikum
F	Restaurant
G	Ausschließlich schwule Männer
GLM	Ausschließlich schwul-lesbisches Publikum
H	Unterkunft
LJ	Fetisch-Publikum
MA	Gemischte Altersklassen
MG	Schwule mittleren Alters
msg	Massage möglich
N	Nachbarschaftsbar; Gäste vom Ort
NG	Nicht schwul, aber interessant
NU	FKK/Nacktbademöglichkeit
OG	Eher ältere Schwule
OS	Aussenplätze; Straßencafé, Terrasse, Garten
P	Privatclub/Strenge Kontrollen
p	Sie müssen klingeln
pi	Swimmingpool
R	Stricher im Publikum
S	Shows/Veranstaltungen
SNU	Stripshows
STV	Travestieshows
sa	Finnische Sauna
sb	Dampfsauna
sol	Solarium
TV	Transvestiten im Publikum
VS	Videovorführungen
WE	Betrieb vor allem am Wochenende
wh	Whirlpool/Jacuzzi
WO	Bodybuilding möglich
YG	Junge Schwule (18-28 J.)

Codes in Kleinbuchstaben bedeuten im allgemeinen eine Einschränkung.

CODES

FRANÇAIS

!	un must pour le touriste international
A	exposition d'art
AC	climatisation
AYOR	à vos risques et périls!
B	bar avec boissons alcoolisées
bf	petit déjeuner
CC	cartes de crédits courantes acceptées
D	boite de nuit
DR	dark room
E	tenue correcte exigée
F	restaurant
G	clientèle exclusivement gay
GLM	fréquenté uniquement par les gay et lesbiennes
H	hôtel ou pension où les gay sont volontiersreçus
LJ	cuir et jeans
MA	tous âges
MG	homosexuels d'âge moyen
msg	possibilité de massage
N	bar de quartier, clientèle du coin
NG	pas forcément gay, mais intéressant
NU	possibilité de nudisme
OG	homosexuels plutôt âgés
OS	plein air: cafés, terrasses, jardins
P	club privé ou contrôle strict à l'entrée
p	il faut sonner
pi	piscine
R	fréquenté aussi par des gigolos
S	spectacle ou autre manifestation
SNU	strip-shows
STV	spectacle de travestis
sa	sauna finlandais
sb	bains turcs
sol	solarium
TV	fréquenté aussi par travestis et transexuels
VS	présentation de vidéos
WE	ouvert plutôt le week-end
wh	whirlpool, jacuzzi
WO	possibilité de faire de la musculation
YG	jeunes homosexuels (18 à 28 ans)

Un code en minuscule implique en général une restriction

ITALIANO

!	un dovere per il visitatore internazionale
A	esposizione d'arte
AC	aria condizionata
AYOR	a vostro rischio e pericolo
B	bar
bf	colazione
CC	vengono accettate le principali carte di credito
D	discoteca
DR	darkroom
E	pubblico elegante
F	ristorante
G	esclusivamente gay
GLM	exclusivamente gay e lesbiche
H	alloggio
LJ	per amanti del feticcio
MA	tutte le età
MG	gay di media età
msg	possibilità di massaggi
N	località con gente del quartiere
NG	non per forza gay, ma interessante
NU	possibilità di nudismo
OG	gay piuttosto anziani
OS	posti all'aperto; caffé lungo la strada, terrazza, giardino
P	club privato / controlli severi
p	bisogna suonare
pi	piscina
R	frequentato anche da gigolò
S	shows/spettacoli
SNU	stripshows
STV	travestie show
sa	sauna finlandese
sb	bagni a vapore
sol	solario
TV	frequentato anche da travestiti
VS	video
W	accessibile per persone in sedia a rotelle con accompagnamento
WE	aperto soprattutto a fine settimana
wh	whirlpool/jacuzzi
WO	possibilità di fare body-building
YG	gay giovani (18-28)

Codici in lettere minuscole significano in generale una limitazione.

君もやろう*

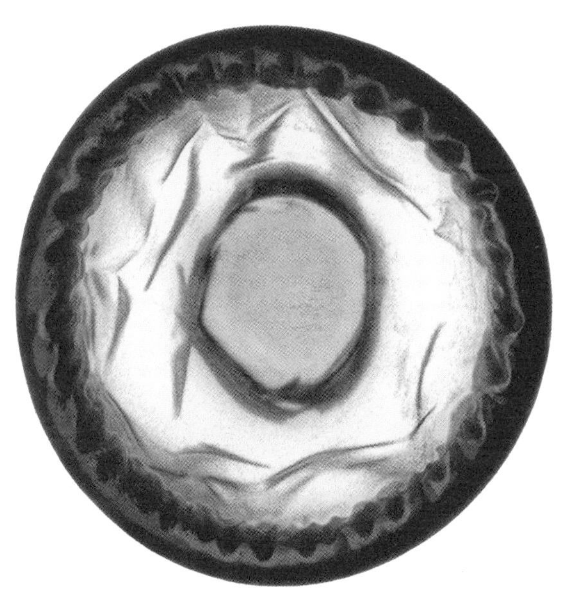

GIB AIDS KEINE CHANCE

***mach's mit.**

Telefonberatung: 0221-89 20 31 (www.aidsberatung.de). Kostenloses Informationsmaterial erhalten Sie bei der Bundeszentrale für gesundheitliche Aufklärung, 51101 Köln. Internet: www.bzga.de